The
CHELSEA HOUSE LIBRARY
of LITERARY CRITICISM

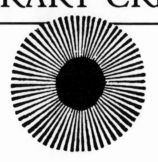

The CHELSEA HOUSE LIBRARY of LITERARY CRITICISM

TWENTIETH-CENTURY AMERICAN LITERATURE

Volume 6

General Editor

HAROLD BLOOM

1987
CHELSEA HOUSE PUBLISHERS
NEW YORK
NEW HAVEN   PHILADELPHIA

MANAGING EDITOR
S. T. Joshi

ASSOCIATE EDITORS
Janet Benton
Peter Cannon
Beth Heinsohn
Patrick Nielsen Hayden
Teresa Nielsen Hayden

EDITORIAL COORDINATOR
Karyn Gullen Browne

COPY CHIEF
Richard Fumosa

EDITORIAL STAFF
Marie Claire Cebrian
Anthony Guyda
Stephen L. Mudd

RESEARCH
Ann Bartunek
Tom Weber

PICTURE RESEARCH
Susan B. Hamburger
Elie Porter

DESIGN
Susan Lusk

Printed and bound in the United States of
America.

Library of Congress Cataloging in Publication
Data

Twentieth-century American literature.
  (The Chelsea House library of literary criticism)
  Bibliography: v. 1, p.
  1. American literature—20th century—History and criticism—Collected works.
2. Authors, American—20th century—Biography—Dictionaries. I. Bloom, Harold. II. Series.
PS221.T834 1985 810'.9'005 84-27430
ISBN 0-87754-802-1 (v.1)
      0-87754-806-4 (v.6)

Acknowledgments for selections used in this
volume commence on page 3872.

CONTENTS

The Index to this series, *Twentieth-Century American Literature*, appears in Volume 8.

ILLUSTRATIONS

ABBREVIATIONS

Am	America	*MPS*	Modern Poetry Studies
AnR	Antioch Review	*NAmR*	North American Review
AS	American Scholar	*NR*	New Republic
At	Atlantic Monthly	*NY*	New Yorker
BB	Books at Brown	*NYEP*	New York Evening Post
Bkm	Bookman (New York)	*NYHT*	New York Herald Tribune Books
BMCN	Book-of-the-Month Club News	*NYRB*	New York Review of Books
CE	College English	*NYTBR*	New York Times Book Review
CL	Canadian Literature	*ObjN*	The Objectivist Newsletter
CLAJ	CLA Journal	*PR*	Partisan Review
CLQ	Colby Library Quarterly	*Prog*	Progressive
CnR	Contemporary Review	*PSch*	Prairie Schooner
Com	Commonweal	*RCF*	Review of Contemporary Fiction
CR	Chicago Review	*SAQ*	South Atlantic Quarterly
Critn	Criterion	*Shen*	Shenandoah
Dal	Dalhousie Review	*SoR*	Southern Review
DrR	Drama Review	*Spec*	Spectator
EJ	English Journal	*SR*	Saturday Review
Esq	Esquire	*SwR*	Sewanee Review
HdR	Hudson Review	*TLS*	Times Literary Supplement
JP	Journal of Philosophy	*VQR*	Virginia Quarterly Review
JPop	Journal of Popular Culture	*YR*	Yale Review
Lon	London Magazine		

E. J. PRATT

1882–1964

Edwin John Pratt was born in Western Bay, Newfoundland, on February 4, 1882, to the Rev. John Pratt and Fanny Pitts Knight. He was educated at Methodist College, St. John's, Newfoundland, and Victoria College, University of Toronto (B.A. 1911, M.A. 1912, B.D. 1913, Ph.D. 1917), studying philosophy and writing theses on demonology and Pauline eschatology. He was ordained into the Methodist ministry in 1913, but experienced a crisis of faith in the aftermath of World War I. Ontological concerns became a primary factor in his poetry, causing critics to label him everything from a Christian humanist to an atheist. His first book of poetry, *Rachel: A Sea Story of Newfoundland in Verse*, was privately printed in 1917; the next year he married Viola Whitney, with whom he had one daughter in 1921. He taught English at Victoria College from 1920 to 1953, and edited *Canadian Poetry* magazine from 1936 to 1942.

Pratt published his first major collection, *Newfoundland Verse*, in 1923. Its contents were typical of the short poetry he would write throughout his career (including *Many Moods*, 1932; *The Fable of the Goats and Other Poems*, 1937; *Still Life and Other Verse*, 1943, and others; the definitive volume is *The Collected Poems of E. J. Pratt*, edited by Northrop Frye, 1958). They primarily concerned single incidents, directly described, and were written in tightly controlled traditional forms, frequently achieving impressive effects through their starkness of subject and tone.

Pratt is primarily known for his experiments in longer verse forms, particularly narrative verse. *The Witches' Brew* (1925) set the tone for most of his later long poetry, particularly in its use of straight narrative combined with a lively running commentary by the author. Pratt also gives freer rein to his language in his longer works, which are more colorful and evocative than his shorter poems.

The Witches' Brew is, however, unusual among Pratt's work in that it is farcical; he returned to more serious concerns with *Titans* (1926) and *The Iron Door* (1927). *The Iron Door* represents Pratt's attempt to rationalize belief in God following the death of his mother. *Titans* was the first of Pratt's works to attract significant attention; it concerned evolution and battle as metaphors for the tenuousness of human existence, themes that would continue to pervade his later work.

Later significant long poems include his sea epics *The Roosevelt and the Antinoe* (1930), *The Titanic* (1935), and *Behind the Log* (1947); *Brébeuf and His Brethren* (1940) is the culmination of a career of theological speculation and is usually considered the best of Pratt's narrative works. *Towards the Last Spike* (1952), his last long poem, presents the construction of the Canadian transcontinental railway as a metaphor for human evolution and the triumph of man over his environment through technology.

E. J. Pratt is generally considered Canada's most important narrative poet, and indeed one of the most significant poets in Canada's literary history. He was awarded various literary prizes and honorary degrees, including the Governor-General's Award three times, and was created a Companion of the Order of St. Michael and St. George in the King's Honours List in 1946. He died in Toronto on April 26, 1964.

SANDRA DJWA
From "The Problem Hero: *Brébeuf and His Brethren*"
E. J. Pratt: The Evolutionary Vision
1974, pp. 92–110

The Roman Church . . . when the Reformation began, was roused by that fierce trumpet-blast to purge and brace herself anew. Unable to advance, she drew back to the fresher and comparatively purer life of the past; and the fervors of mediaeval Christianity were renewed in the sixteenth century. (Francis Parkman, *The Jesuits in North America*)

If *The Titanic* explores the problematical nature of human progress and suggests that regression is an inevitable part of this process, *Brébeuf and His Brethren* (1940) asserts man's capacity to transcend the impulse for self-preservation, to move forward along the evolutionary road through a determined "will" that is channelled into the sternly disciplined way of the cross. Yet even so, Pratt does not change his ironic perspective on the human condition, nor does his account of the Jesuit saint depart from that heroic and muscular Christianity which Pratt admires and which has affinities with that of Kipling and Henley. In his martyrdom, Brébeuf reverts to the fighting blood of his ancestors "known to chivalry— / In the Crusades; at Hastings." A lion at bay rather than the expected Christian lamb, he answers his captors, "roar for roar."[1] His endurance through torture becomes the primary exemplar of Christian heroism, and his death, the "martyr's seed" which flowers with the establishment of Christianity in New France.

There has been little agreement among critics discussing the poem beyond the acknowledgement that *Brébeuf and His Brethren* is Pratt's finest narrative poem and the most significant interpretation of Canada's historical past. John Sutherland and Northrop Frye describe it as Christian epic but E. K. Brown, Carl F. Klinck and Henry G. Wells are content with the term "heroic epic." The view of the poem as an expression of Christian humanism is undercut by Vincent

Sharman's recent assertion of Pratt's "atheism" and by the "reverent agnosticism" ascribed to Pratt by Peter Buitenhuis in his Introduction to the *Selected Poems*. We might suspect that such opposite views of the same poem can only arise from an essential dichotomy within the work, a dichotomy perhaps linked to the distinction between the "heroic" and the "Christian." But the real problem of the work seems to go far deeper. In essence, it appears to be the dichotomy between the transcendent seventeenth-century Christianity of Brébeuf, the poem's subject, and the human-centered, turn-of-the-century, new theology of Pratt, the poet. In other terms, the poem may dramatize a certain conflict in Pratt's own mind regarding the nature of the religious life and its motivations.

Pratt originally trained as a minister in the United Church but he did not take up a pastorate when ordained; instead, he lectured at the University of Toronto, at first in psychology and then in English literature. Scattered comments from those who knew him and the evidence of the unpublished *Clay*, written just as he was concluding his doctorate (on Pauline eschatology) suggest that Pratt suffered a crisis in faith and came to the conclusion that he was not suited to the religious life. We might speculate that part of the appeal of the Brébeuf narrative may have been that it was the account of a man who did continue in the religious life; in Pratt's *Brébeuf* the focus is very often upon motivation. Furthermore, the poem is dedicated to Pratt's father who was for many years a Methodist minister in Newfoundland. In this context, the poem may be seen not only as an exploration of the religious experience but also, perhaps, as Pratt's own apologia to the father whose example he could not follow.

As previously suggested, the dichotomy in the poem seems to arise from Pratt's attitude to his subject. An essentially religious man, at least in the sense that he accepts the mystic experience, he is in full sympathy with Brébeuf, seventeenth-century mystic and Catholic saint; yet concurrently, as a former divinity student, experimental psychologist, and a student of Freud's disciple, Ernest Jones, Pratt is also impelled to present the great Jesuit from the twentieth-century perspective. This modern perspective includes the historical Jesus of the United Church divinity school at Toronto in 1910 (hence a tendency to explain miracle in terms of human psychology), a working knowledge of Frazer's *The Golden Bough*, and that vision of human personality which accepts Freudian sublimation. It also stresses those mixed motives which are a part of every man, even the saint; hence the emphasis on Brébeuf's "will" and the implications that the Jesuits may pervert Christianity in the process of conversion. Despite these underlying implications, the surface narrative and the triumphant conclusion of the poem assert that Brébeuf's final sacrifice of self—regardless of motivation—is ultimately and magnificently justified by the establishment of Christianity in New France. The question to be answered is whether these implications seriously undercut the central religious narrative.

Our first impression of *Brébeuf and His Brethren* is that it is a magnificently structured Christian epic; the character of Brébeuf is effectively developed, the symbolic construction powerful and the narrative extremely well paced. The action is cyclic, beginning and ending with a cross, an altar and the renaissance of religious faith. Book I establishes the historical background of the Counter-Reformation and religious revival. "The story of the frontier like a saga / Sang through the cells and cloisters of the nation" calling Fathers Brébeuf, Massé and Charles Lalemant to the Jesuit mission of New France. In 1624, famine and the English blockade of Quebec force the Jesuits back to France; the interval of Book II is used to stress the spiritual zeal of the missionaries and to foreshadow Brébeuf's sacrifice on the altars of Huronia. In 1663, New France is restored and Book III establishes the initial confrontation of Christian "civilization" with Indian "savagery." Ironically, the Jesuits teach and the Hurons accept Christianity as a new and superior demonology. Developing excerpts from Brébeuf's famous letter to France ("You must sincerely love the savages / As brothers ransomed by the blood of Christ"), Book III concludes with Brébeuf's vision of "*the royal way of the Holy Cross.*"

The pivotal chapter of Pratt's epic is Book VI. Describing the fore-doomed mission to the Petuns and the Neutrals, "a labour which for faith / And triumph of the spirit over failure / Was unsurpassed in record of the mission," it establishes the almost unbridgeable polarities of Indian and priest. The Jesuits, fired by religious zeal and symbolically the incarnation of the holy spirit, are viewed by the Indians as "demons" or "incarnated plague" whose baptizing ritual brings death. The inevitable conflict between the two is dramatized by Brébeuf's climactic vision of a "moving cross" advancing from the country of the Iroquois, "*and huge enough to crucify us all.*"

The narrative steadily gains momentum in Book VII with the capture and torture of Father Jogues, and the martyrdoms of his French and Indian brethren. In a highly effective change of pace in Book IX, there is a brief moment of pastoral respite as the Fathers experience a "pipe-dream" of hope:

> . . . Strawberries in July,
> October beechnuts, pepper roots for spice,
> And at the bottom of a spring that flowed
> Into a pond shaded by silver birches
> And ringed by marigolds was water-cress
> In chilled abundance. So, was this the West?
> The Wilderness? . . . [2]

But the narrative accelerates implacably in Book XI with the capture of Forts St. Ignace and St. Louis, and with them Fathers Brébeuf and Lalemant. Led back to St. Ignace and the stake, Brébeuf recalls the celebration of his last Mass and his final dedication to Christ; "*Take ye and drink—the chalice of my blood.*" Book XII chronicles the martyrdoms of Brébeuf and Lalemant. The poem concludes full circle with the return to the altar—to the twentieth-century celebration of Mass at the Martyr's Shrine at Huronia.

The symbols of the Catholic mass (the altar with its candles and cross, host and wine) are adapted as the controlling symbols of the poem. The central concepts underlying these symbols are those of incarnation, the spirit of God in man, and transubstantiation, the religious symbolism of the mass in which the host and the wine are transmuted to the body and blood of Christ through the sacrifice of the priest. In the first few lines of the poem the metaphor of incarnation is developed; the winds of God as manifested in the "bugles" of the Counter-Reformation engender again the saints "incarnate." The vision of the frontier mission

> . . . brought to earth the prophets and apostles
> Out of their static shrines in the stained glass.
> It caught the ear of Christ, reveined his hands
> And feet, bidding his marble saints to leave
> Their pedestals for chartless seas and coasts
> And the vast blunders of the forest glooms.
> (CP, 245)

In this second metaphor, Christ's hands and feet are reveined with new blood by the Jesuit missionaries. Brébeuf, Jesuit soldier of God, is the incarnation of religious zeal ("Lion of limb and heart, he had entrenched the faith, / Was like a triple palisade himself "). Through the vows of his order and in his office as priest he is identified with the sacrificial bread and wine of the mass: "I shall be broken before I break them." His identification with the way of the cross and the crucified Christ is made explicit in his first vision of Christ on the Via Dolorosa in Book I and elaborated in Book II at Rennes where Brébeuf recognizes that if he returns to New France there will be "broken altars / And broken bodies of both Host and Priest." His vow to sacrifice body and blood "As willingly as now I give this drop" indicates his choice, a choice which is confirmed by a revelation of *"the royal way of the Holy Cross."* His subsequent vow *"never to fail Thee in the grace / Of martyrdom, if by Thy mercy, Thou / Dost offer it to me"*[3] is a further step along the way of the cross which culminates in his final mass where, as priest officiating at the sacrifice, Brébeuf sacrifices his body and blood for that of Christ.

In the mass, the altar candles symbolize Christ, "the victim of the flames," and this association is also developed in Pratt's poem where Jesuit "fires" of zeal impel the Fathers toward their ultimate sacrifice.[4] These fires of zeal are, in turn, contrasted with the barbaric torture fires of Huron and Iroquois; in effect, through each successive martyrdom, the priests transmute torture fire into sacrificial holocaust. This concept of sacrifice is dominant; almost every book of this epic centers on either a cross or a sanctuary, beginning with Brébeuf's initial vision at Bayeux of the crucified Christ and pivoting with his vision of the huge cross advancing towards Huronia. The poem reaches a climax with Brébeuf's martyrdom and a reference to the source of his faith: "the sound of invisible trumpets blowing / Around two slabs of board, right-angled."

This emphasis upon the way of the cross was central to Pratt's initial vision of the poem. He first wrote the conclusion, the section describing the death of Brébeuf (which he confessed moved him more than anything else he ever wrote) and only then did he turn to the preceding chain of events which led Brébeuf to the stake. Pratt told E.K. Brown that the whole poem began with a search for "a simile for the Cross which would express alike shame and glory, something strongly vernacular set over against cultivated imagery and language. Two slabs of board—nails—Jewish hill, and so forth, contrasted with lilies, robes and so forth." As Brown aptly observes, this method of composition implies "the way of a poet for whom character is a symbol rather than a dramatic complex."[5] As a character, Brébeuf is clearly the embodiment of muscular Christianity and part of the 'sport' of the poem is the extent of his endurance. Furthermore, the focus of the poem, centering as it does upon steadfast "will" enabling him to endure and ultimately give up his life for his belief, is not without some ambiguity in Pratt's presentation.

On one hand, "will" is seen as a desirable trait; channelled into "a life and a redemptive Death", it is that quality which ensures the transplanting of Christianity to New France. Prevented in their first attempt to reach Huronia and deserted in the wilderness by their Huron guides, the Fathers still reach their goal, "tattered, wasted, with feet / Bleeding—broken though not in will." Once in Huronia, there are the minor martyrdoms of stifling smoke in the lodges, cold, lack of sleep, hunger or inedible food, and continual harassment: "uncovenanted fleas / That fastened on the priestly flesh like hornets, / Carving the curves of favour on the lips, / Tailoring the man into the Jesuit coat." The narrative speculates if there could be a limit to the endurance, obedience, and self-control required by "the iron code of good Ignatius":

> How often did the hand go up to lower
> The flag? How often by some ringing order
> Was it arrested at the halliard touch?
> How often did Brébeuf seal up his ears
> When blows and insults woke ancestral fifes
> Within his brain, blood-cells, and viscera,
> Is not explicit in the written story.
>
> (CP, 254)

On the other hand, Jesuit will can carry implications of spiritual pride; Brébeuf's vow, "I shall be broken before I break them," can suggest *hubris*. In the larger context of the poem, the statement becomes an ironic *double entendre* in which "them" can refer not only to his immediate vows but also to the Indians. Brébeuf's body is, in fact, broken before he "breaks" the Iroquois. In immediate context, his vows refer to his vocation as priest:

> This is the end of man—*Deum laudet*,
> To seek and find the will of God, to act
> Upon it for the ordering of life,
> And for the soul's beatitude.
>
> (CP, 246)

But in contrast to Pratt's documentation of the spiritual humility of Jogues and Chaumont, Brébeuf is never presented as questioning his spiritual state. His initial vow of dedication to the way of the cross is not dependent upon the commands of his superiors (as is Chaumont's vow) nor does he ever appear to question (as does Jogues) the distinction between a martyrdom ordered by God's will and one which is the culmination of man's own desire. Captured by the Iroquois and expecting death, Jogues is offered a providential ransom but delays "that he might seek / Counsel of God and satisfy his conscience" for "How close to suicide / Would be refusal?" Brébeuf, in contrast, celebrates his last mass without question although "he had known it was to be the last." The fact that Pratt does develop these contrasts in the narrative suggests that he means his readers to consider them. Then too, Pratt's literal description of Brébeuf's last mass, although convincing and magnificently placed in the narrative, is not without a faint tinge of irony:

> *Graciously receive*
> *My life for His life as he gave His life*
> *For mine . . .*
> *This is my body.*
> *In like manner . . .*
> *Take ye and drink—the chalice of my blood.*
>
> (CP, 293)

The tone of this passage is reverent, Brébeuf's words have the sanction of the litany of the mass; nonetheless, on second reading we do feel somewhat uncomfortable with this passage. Perhaps, in the context of the poem's controlling metaphor of incarnation, it suggests too explicitly (almost in terms of fertility myth) that Brébeuf has taken on the Godhead.

Furthermore, a tone verging on the satiric compels us to look closely at the manner in which Jesuit will is channelled into conversion. Although the mission to the Hurons is initially not successful, the Indians are captivated by the marvels of a corn mill, a magnet, a magnifying glass, and writing:

> . . . marvels on which the Fathers built
> A basis of persuasion, recognizing
> The potency of awe for natures nurtured
> On charms and spells, invoking kindly spirits
> And exorcising demons. . . .
>
> (CP, 256)

The Hurons soon convert the white men's God into Indian spirits and demons: an *"oki"* dwells in the clock and Jesuit magic can bring light from the darkness of the universe (the moon's eclipse). The Fathers pray for a release from drought "and the Bird of Thunder came with heavy rain, / Released by the nine masses at Saint Joseph." Because the Fathers encourage these "marvels," they take on the role of Arendiwans or sorcerers to the Indians.

The ethics of Christianity prove most difficult to teach, but Father Garnier recognizes and manipulates the power of primitive fear by sending to France for religious pictures:

> . . . one
> *Only* of souls in bliss: of *âmes damnées*
> Many and various—the horned Satan,
> His mastiff jaws champing the head of Judas;
> The plummet fall of the unbaptized pursued
> By demons with their fiery forks; the lick
> Of flames upon a naked Saracen;
>
> (CP, 266)

In this substitution of the fear of the devil for the Christian God of love, the Fathers not only take advantage of the superstitious "racial past" of the Indians, they enter into it themselves and lay themselves open to charges of black magic by the Indians as Brébeuf himself admits in his famous letter to France.

Pratt's many references to the documentary facts of *The Jesuit Relations*[6] (the letter, the moon's eclipse, the religious pictures) may lead us to speculate that any supposed ambivalence in his characterization of the Jesuits and especially Brébeuf, may be inherent in his source material. This is partially the case but at the same time we must acknowledge that Pratt consciously chose and developed the material of his narrative. There are very few references to religious humility on the part of Brébeuf in the *Relations*; furthermore, in the several additional sources from which Pratt developed his poem we do find a somewhat ironic perspective upon the Jesuit saint. Pelham Edgar first suggested to Pratt that the story of Brébeuf, previously treated only in prose, might be a likely subject for a great Canadian epic. Edgar would have been familiar with prose accounts of the Jesuit mission because his own book, *The Romance of Canadian History* (1902), was edited from Francis Parkman's *The Jesuits in North America* (1867), in turn based upon *The Jesuit Relations*.[7] Edgar in particular notes "the Titanic effort of will with which Brébeuf repressed all show of suffering," and he also captures Parkman's ironic perspective on the Jesuit saint: "Extravagant as were the chimeras which fed the fires of his zeal, they were consistent with the soberest good sense on matters of practical bearing."[8]

In the composition of *Brébeuf and His Brethren*, Pratt seems to have moved from Parkman to the *Relations* and Brébeuf's spiritual journal. He combined visits to the Martyrs' Shrine at Huronia (Midland, Ontario) with a study of Catholic liturgy and doctrine.[9] His perspective on the character of Brébeuf would appear to be an amalgam of Parkman's account with that of the *Relations* but both are contained within his own ironic vision of the human condition. Pratt presents the Jesuit martyr as a man of immense courage, stature, and religious zeal, the major heroic figure of Canadian history. Yet, because Pratt's subject in the larger sense is also man and not only St. Jean de Brébeuf, this view is tempered by implications of human weaknesses. In particular, there are slight suggestions that Pratt sees Brébeuf's temptations, like that of Eliot's Becket, as the temptation "to do the right deed for the wrong reason."[10] There are suggestions of psychological causation for the first vision and there are slight implica-

tions that *hubris* may enter into his desire for martyrdom. Yet, paradoxically, under all this, as Parkman firmly asserts, there lies the "solid nucleus of saint and hero."[11]

Francis Parkman, an eminent Victorian, brought the function of a Lytton Strachey to *The Jesuit Relations*. His books, especially *The Jesuits in North America*, are consistently informed by the ironic perspective which refuses to establish the expected paradigm of unenlightened savage and spiritual father; instead he moves towards a recognition of the real kinship between Brébeuf and his Indian brethren. In the following passage he turns from a discussion of Indian magic (dream feasts and food rituals for the purpose of exorcising demons) to the baptismal rites of the Jesuits:

> Turning from the eccentricities of the "noble savage"
> to the zealots who were toiling, according to their
> light, to snatch him from the clutch of Satan, we see
> the irrepressible Jesuits roaming from town to town
> in restless quest of subjects for baptism.[12]

The parallel between Jesuit "vision" and Indian "dream," between Jesuit "baptism" and Indian "exorcism," is too striking to be ignored. Parkman's contemporary, the Canadian Abbé Casgrain, sharply criticizes this perspective: "The work of Mr. Parkman is a denial of religious belief. The author rejects the Protestant as well as the Catholic dogma: he is purely rationalistic."[13] Parkman is indeed a rationalist, but it can be argued that he does affirm the validity of the faith to its Jesuit practitioners even while suggesting they were misguided. This attitude is explicit in his description of Brébeuf's vision of the great cross moving across Huronia:

> To explain such phenomena is the province of
> psychology, and not of history. Their occurrence is
> no matter of surprise, and it would be superfluous to
> doubt that they were recounted in good faith, and
> with a full belief in their reality.
>
> In these enthusiasts we shall find striking exam-
> ples of one of the morbid forces of human nature; yet
> in candor let us do honor to what was genuine in
> them,—that principle of self-abnegation which is the
> life of true religion, and which is vital no less to the
> highest forms of heroism.[14]

On the whole, Pratt adapts from Parkman's account the equivocal play on the word "brethren" referring to Indian and Jesuit alike and to the ironic relation between the two. He follows Parkman's chronology quite consistently and the slight changes in historic event which he does make are clearly intended to tighten the narrative structure. However, Pratt does add to the poem particular details and oblique narrative comment which would seem to relate to his own view of Brébeuf's character. Brébeuf's first vision at Bayeux is one such detail:[15]

> And in Bayeux a neophyte while rapt
> In contemplation saw a bleeding form
> Falling beneath the instrument of death,
> Rising under the quickening of the thongs,
> Stumbling along the Via Dolorosa.
> No play upon the fancy was this scene,
> But the Real Presence to the naked sense.
> The fingers of Brébeuf were at his breast,
> Closing and tightening on a crucifix,
> While voices spoke aloud unto his ear
> And to his heart—*per ignem et per aquam.*
> Forests and streams and trails thronged through his
>   mind,
> The painted faces of the Iroquois.
>
> (CP, 245)

In this description, Pratt provides both the religious sanction for miracle ("the Real Presence to the naked sense") and slight implications of Freudian projection ("The fingers of Brébeuf were at his breast, / Closing and tightening on a crucifix"). It might be objected that the meditation on the cross is an essential part of the Ignation exercises and need not be taken to imply psychological projection. But there is additional evidence in the poem that Pratt was aware of the significance of gesture as projection. [16] Furthermore, there is no reference to a Bayeux vision in the spiritual journals of Brébeuf or in *The Jesuit Relations* as there is for later vows. Consequently we must conclude that in this introductory scene, Pratt subtly prepares the reader for the unfolding of Brébeuf's character. This opening scene appears to be a merging of Brébeuf's several visions of the cross (all in New France) with the continental locale and ironic perspective of Francis Parkman's description of the Paris vision of the young priest, Olier:

> He was praying in the ancient church of St. Germain des Prés, when . . . he thought he heard a voice from Heaven, saying that he was destined to be a light to the Gentiles. It is recorded as a mystic coincidence attending this miracle, that the choir was at that very time chanting the words, *Lumen ad revelationem Gentium:* and it seems to have occurred neither to Olier nor to his biographer, that, falling on the ear of the rapt worshipper, they might have unconciously suggested the supposed revelation. [17]

In a much gentler manner than Parkman, Pratt seems to suggest that the realm of psychology might also be invoked in relation to Brébeuf's vision. This concern with psychological factors is not surprising when we consider that both "Demonology" and *Pauline Eschatology* emphasize the essential humanity of the historical Christ and stress the psychological rationale for miracle. Further, it does not deny to Brébeuf the sincerity of his belief, although it does, of course, emphasize, as does William James in his *Varieties of Religious Experience*, the significance of the human impulse in religious experience.

Pratt's use of his historical sources also suggests a stress on the human. Brébeuf, at prayer, is described as hearing a voice command:

> "*Rise, Read!*"—Opening the *Imitatio Christi*,
> His eyes "*Without design*" fell on the chapter,
> *Concerning the royal way of the Holy Cross,*
> Which placed upon his spirit "*a great peace*".
> And then, day having come, he wrote his vow—
> "*My God, my Saviour, I take from thy hand*
> *The cup of thy sufferings. I invoke thy name:*
> *I vow never to fail thee in the grace*
> *Of martyrdom, if by thy mercy, Thou*
> *Dost offer it to me. I bind myself,*
> *And when I have received the stroke of death,*
> *I will accept it from thy gracious hand*
> *With all pleasure and with joy in my heart:*
> *To thee my blood, my body and my life.*" [18]
> (CP, 265)

The vow cited in *The Jesuit Relations* also contains a qualifying clause in which Brébeuf states that he will remain faithful to the vow of martyrdom "save only that . . . it might be to the interests of your glory to behave otherwise in the matter." [19] However, as Pratt omits this and as he does emphasize "without design," the passage is slightly slanted. Here, as in the earlier italicized reference to one picture "*only* of souls in bliss" as contrasted to many pictures of hell and *âmes damnées*, Pratt's irrepressible sense of irony is holding up the precise words of the text for our closer inspection and drawing our attention to the incongru-

ities. This same irrepressible irony takes pleasure in the catalogue of the picturesque which accompanies the baptism of Peter (Tsiouendaentaha) and, passing over into the satiric, points out that some of the Hurons, proceeding from their religious primers (pictures of Hell), are confusing the ceremony of Baptism with that of the Last Judgement and hell-fires.

Despite this alternation of tone, an alternation less noticeable in the narrative flow than it is in retrospect, there is no denial of the faith or mystic experience which motivates the Jesuits:

> And often, when the body strength was sapped
> By the day's toil and there were streaks of blood
> Inside the moccasins, when the last lodge
> Rejected them as lepers and the welts
> Hung on their shoulders, then the Fathers sought
> The balm that never failed. Under the stars,
> Along an incandescent avenue
> The visions trembled, tender, placid, pure.
> (CP, 272)

Pratt's sensitivity to the mystic experience is revealed in this cadence from Book VI. Through the device of placing two sets of alliterative consonants together, and by the progression and modulation of vowel sounds within the even beat of the iambic pentameter, the line pulses and shimmers like the hallucinatory visions it describes.

Paradoxically, this acceptance of the mystic experience coincides in the narrative with the ironic perspective and with the habit of mind which always views the spiritual in relation to its human embodiment. The paradigm for the latter is perhaps a combination of the historical Jesus ("O Son of Man" as Pratt writes in "The Highway") with the Jesuit practice of vivifying or realizing the passion of Christ. Consequently, the Christianity of the historical Jesus and the Christianity of the transcendent Jesus seem to co-exist in the poem. Furthermore, because Pratt always displays the spiritual ideal in its human or incarnate form, it must also coincide with human weakness. Jesuit will is a case in point. On one hand, it ensures the dissemination of the faith; on the other hand, it can be perverted. The Indian warrior code has this same potential. Brébeuf's letter to France recruiting priests for the mission had argued that the "savages" were "brothers ransomed by the blood of Christ." Ironically, as the narrative indicates, there is very little difference between Indian and priest. The Indian converts more than equal the chivalric ideal of the Jesuits (as is evidenced by the sacrifices of Eustache and Onnonhoaraton) while Brébeuf's martyrdom is more than equal to the Iroquois warrior code. However, when watching the Hurons torture an Iroquois captive, Brébeuf recognizes that there is a distinction between animal and savage nature—the "reason" of the civilizing process which can be so easily perverted.

> . . . He knew that when
> A winter pack of wolves brought down a stag
> There was no waste of time between the leap
> And the business click upon the jugular.
> Such was the forthright honesty in death
> Among the brutes. They had not learned the sport
> Of dallying around the nerves to halt
> A quick despatch. A human art was torture,
> Where Reason crept into the veins, mixed tar
> With blood and brewed its own intoxicant.
> (CP, 261)

As in the lyric "Autopsy on a Sadist (After Lidice)" published shortly after *Brébeuf and His Brethren*, Pratt sees man's movement towards torture and murder as the civilized perversion of reason, a taint or "toxin" in the blood. In this sense, the moral heart of *Brébeuf and His Brethren* is to be found in the struggle between the "zeal," or spirit of God, in the blood of Brébeuf and his Jesuit and Indian brethren and the amoral "toxin" or "adulterate" of savage nature, whether this savage nature is manifested in the occasional primitive impulses of the Fathers or the torture fires of Huron and Iroquois. *Brébeuf*, like much of Pratt's earlier work, is an exposition of the evolution of human ethics.

In a schemata where Christ's sacrifice represents the apogee of man's ethical evolution, the passion is of supreme importance. And, as Fred Cogswell and Peter Buitenhuis have recently remarked, much of the impact of Pratt's *Brébeuf* is to be found in the torture scenes.[20] For Pratt, the torture fires seem to represent the "trial" at which the strength of the spiritual ideal is tested against the strength of its adversary — savage nature. The emotional impact of the final scene arises not only from our recognition of the tooth and claw ferocity with which the Iroquois rend Brébeuf's body but also from the progression of Pratt's argument which records the monstrous "reason" of cruelty: "Where was the source / Of his strength . . . ? In the bunch of his shoulders . . . ? In the thews of his thighs . . . ?

> Was it the blood?
> They would draw it fresh from its fountain. Was it
>   the heart?
> They dug for it, fought for the scraps in the way of
>   the wolves.
>
>   (CP, 296)

The sheer power of rhetoric and argument carries us along even as we are appalled by the action described. Ultimately, the poem maintains, the source of Brébeuf's strength is not to be found in its physical incarnation—the body and blood—but in the historic sacrifice of which they are symbols:

> . . . in the sound of invisible trumpets blowing
> Around two slabs of board, right-angled, hammered
> By Roman nails and hung on a Jewish hill.
>
>   (CP, 296)

Brébeuf's passion, in context, becomes a final transsubstantiation. In anthropological terms, the sacrifice of the mass is a civilized transformation or sublimation of human sacrifice, a connection which Pratt would have known from his early readings of Frazer's *The Golden Bough*.[21] Brébeuf's death struggles, presented by Pratt as a reversion to man's primal past (a "lion at bay" he answers his tormentors "roar for roar") is received by the Iroquois in much the same fashion as primitive man might have participated in the ritual death and dismemberment of the fertility god. Furthermore, Brébeuf's ritualized death (in terms of the Iroquois code) is described as having the same effect as the burial of Frazer's Hanged Man;

> Near to the ground where the cross broke under the
>   hatchet,
> And went with it into the soil to come back at the
>   turn
> Of the spade with the carbon and calcium char of the
>   bodies,
> The shrines and altars are built anew; the *Aves*
> And prayers ascend, and the Holy Bread is broken.[22]
>
>   (CP, 298)

In effect, his blood fertilizes the soil for the rebirth of Christianity in New France. Yet the undercurrents of fertility myth are ultimately subsumed, as they are historically, into the matrix of Christian belief; Brébeuf's sacrifice is in imitation of Christ's death and supports the Christian ideal. Ragueneau observes after the martyrdoms of Brébeuf and Lalemant: "all

that torture / And death could do to the body was done. The Will / And the Cause in their triumph survived."

As the stoicism of these last lines indicates, Pratt had found in Brébeuf, soldier of God, a subject and action ideally suited to the heroic vision and dominantly martial energy of his poetry. In the simplest sense, Brébeuf is an amalgam of two of Pratt's earlier protagonists —the powerful giant creature equipped with an unlimited capacity to endure and the Christ-like hero whose actions are governed by the ethical ideal. In this poem, as in Pratt's earlier work, the movement towards ethical action is associated with physiology (the impulse of the nerves translated into the human "will" which follows Christ's example); and the moral imperative becomes part of the inner world, "invisible trumpets" sounding within the moral consciousness of the Jesuit martyr. As ethical man, Brébeuf moves out from the particularity of his Catholic martyrdom to become the embodiment of the ethical ideal as it struggles against amoral nature. In a still larger sense, the poem written against the background of the emerging World War II is a parable of what Pratt saw as the struggle of the ethical sense against the cosmic immorality which he identified with the Nazi movement.

Our aesthetic response to the poem is a problem still to be explored. If, in fact, there are ironic undercurrents to the narrative, why is it that *Brébeuf and His Brethren* still impresses us as a convincing religious poem? For some readers, notably Buitenhuis and Sharman, this has not been the case; but for the great majority, it is. My own impression is that Pratt is true to the religious heart of the poem—the mystic experience—which is genuinely and finely presented. Because of this, because Brébeuf is universally known as a Christian martyr, and because of the dominantly reverent tone of the poem, the poet has considerable latitude to be ironic and even satiric without upsetting the aesthetic mean. Small human foibles (or so they seem in passing), related in an ironic or satiric tone, are welcomed by the reader as amusing interludes breaking the tension and the urgency of the poem's movement toward the passion. In fact, we tend to underestimate the significance of many of these elements at first reading, muted as they are by the sweep of the poem. Yet, when we do perceive that Pratt is pointing out similarities between will and *hubris*, between priest and Indian, and between religious sacrifice and fertility myth, we are at the same time conscious that the religious justification is dominant.

In *Brébeuf*, as in the short lyric "From Stone to Steel" (1932), Pratt is working within an historical and ethical evolutionary framework which establishes the primitive cave, fertility myth, and human savagery as one pole of human experience and the temple, Christianity, and self-sacrifice as the other. This framework is emphasized by Brébeuf's passion which is received by the Iroquois according to their primitive code of human sacrifice and by the Jesuits according to their Christian code. For both, the sacrifice embodies the ideal. In general, Pratt's Brébeuf, like the historical Jesus, is humanized and as such he is subject to the ironies of the human condition—including spiritual pride and regression—which inform Pratt's own view of man. The poem does provide a specifically Christian framework for Brébeuf's heroism, but as this framework is contained within Pratt's own vision of evolutionary ethics (in which the Christian ethic represents the pinnacle of human evolution), he is able to hold in suspension both the human focus and the Christian imperative.

The purpose of this focus upon the human and upon the evolution of man, of society, and of religion is perhaps to unify and generalize the epic: to move it out from its religious particularity of one man (or more accurately, one group of men) at one time to a paradigm of all ethical men at all times of crisis. Like T.S. Eliot in *Murder in the Cathedral* (1935), Pratt has invoked a hero from the national past whose actions are an example to the troubled present. The symbolism of Brébeuf as a figure of strength and virtue assaulted by savage hordes but courageously enduring to ultimate moral victory was not missed by Canada, then at war. To present Becket as a man for the times, Eliot had supplemented an essentially religious narrative with the psychology of Becket's martyrdom. Less overtly, Pratt added to the Brébeuf narrative suggestions of the psychological perspective and of a human-centered ethic.

As I mentioned earlier, Pratt began to write the poem with the ringing lines of the climax, the image of the cross to which the omniscient narrator ascribes Brébeuf's strength. The cross, described bluntly and placed within the context of human history ("Roman nails," "Jewish hill"), although it can be taken as an example of the Jesuit practice of vivifying, strongly emphasizes the crucifixion as an historical event. If the model for the crucifixion was initially that of the historical Jesus, a dichotomy between the climax of the poem and the series of religious events which led Brébeuf towards it, might be indicated.

On the other hand, Pratt's selections from and additions to the original Brébeuf narrative were quite in accord with his own unified vision of evolutionary theology. Given this, it is reasonable to suppose that when he provides both a religious and a psychological motive for the same action, the reader is meant to accept both as parallel and not necessarily contradictory motivations. But not all readers can appreciate Pratt's unified vision; for some, the very fact there is an alternative divides the emotional response, opening up within the poem a serious dichotomy between Pratt's human-centered evolutionary ethics and the trancendent Christianity of his seventeenth-century subject. Because of this, *Brébeuf and His Brethren*, so convincing a religious epic when experienced as a whole, does exhibit some ambiguity when we focus on individual scenes. As an expression of Pratt's admiration for the religious struggle, it is appropriate that he dedicated the poem to his father. At the same time, Pratt's humanist but somewhat unorthodox new theology provides at least one indication that he would have found the conventional United Church pulpit of 1917 rather confining.

Notes

1. Pratt's conception of Brébeuf as "a lion at bay, not a lamb on the altar" seems to have been a fusion of Father Ragueneau's remarks regarding Lalemant, the "lamb" who died as a "lion," with the phrase, "roar for roar," applied to Brébeuf in a school text and recalled by Mrs. Pratt to her husband.
2. E. J. Pratt. *Collected Poems*, second edition (Toronto: Macmillan, 1962), p. 285. Hereafter cited as CP.
3. In the first edition of *Brébeuf and His Brethren*, the lines read "never to fail you in the grace/Of martyrdom, if by your infinite mercy/You offer it to me." The effect of the change is that of religious distancing: a shift in tone from the colloquial to the formal address of ritual.
4. Sister St. Dorothy Marie, "The Epic Note in the Poetry of E.J. Pratt," Master's thesis, University of Ottawa, 1956.
5. E. K. Brown, *On Canadian Poetry* (Toronto: Ryerson, 1944), pp. 155–56.
6. Reuben Gold Thwaites, ed., *The Jesuit Relations and Allied Documents: Travels and Explorations of the Jesuit Missions in New France, 1610–1791*, vol. 34 (Cleveland: Burroughs Bros., 1898).
7. Alixe Catherine Paisley, "Epic Features of *Brébeuf and His Brethren* by E. J. Pratt," Master's thesis, Assumption University of Windsor, 1960.
8. Pelham Edgar, *The Romance of Canadian History*, ed. from the writings of Francis Parkman (Toronto: Morang, 1902), p. 87.
9. Paisley, "Epic Features of *Brébeuf and His Brethren*," p. ii.
10. T. S. Eliot, *Murder in the Cathedral* (London: Faber and Faber, 1935), p. 44.
11. Francis Parkman, *The Jesuits in North America* (See Boston: Little, Brown & Co., 1963), p. 495.
12. Ibid., pp. 184–185.
13. Ibid., pp. iii–iv.
14. Ibid., pp. 198–199.
15. There are no records of Brébeuf's spiritual life at Bayeux.
16. As a Demonstrator in Psychology in the Department of Philosophy at Victoria College, the University of Toronto, Pratt would have been familiar with experiments in stimulus response, particularly in relation to Wilhelm Wundt's psychology. Wundt, like Freud, interpreted gesture as an indication of a will to action and Pratt was aware of the Freudian implications of gesture as suppressed desire. The desire of the young braves of the Neutral Nation to kill the Jesuits is evidenced by gesture: "Convulsive hands were clutching/At hatchet helves."
17. Parkman, *The Jesuits in North America*, p. 283.
18. These lines differ from the version in the first edition of the poem, as noted in Note 2.
19. *The Jesuit Relations*, 34: 167.
20. Fred Cogswell, "E. J. Pratt's Literary Reputation," *Canadian Literature* 19 (Winter 1964); Peter Buitenhuis, Introduction to *Selected Poems of E. J. Pratt* (Toronto: Macmillan, 1968).
21. Pratt cites Frazer and fertility myth in "Demonology" and several verses from *Clay*, later published in *Newfoundland Verse* (1923), contain a section, "The Seed Must Die," patterned on the fertility myth structure.
22. In the first edition of *Brébeuf and His Brethren*, these lines are preceded by the following:

> Three hundred years have gone, but the voices that led
> The martyrs through death unto life are heard again
> In the pines and elms by the great Fresh Water Sea.
> The Mission sites have returned to the fold of the Order.

PETER BUITENHUIS
From "E. J. Pratt"
The Canadian Imagination, ed. David Staines
1977, pp. 49–68

It was at Victoria College, as a fledgling assistant professor of English, that I first met Ned Pratt. Although he had retired from the college some years before, as long as he could make it down from his Rosedale home he kept up the habit of lunching twice a week at the Senior Common Room. He had a great fund of anecdote and a precious gift of friendship, even for someone so much younger than himself. Along with the other lunchers at that austere but good table, I basked in the glow of his stories and the warmth of his benevolence. Later on, after I had read a good deal of his work, I was to recall Henry James's short story "The Private Life," which was based on his observations of Robert Browning. James frequently encountered the dining-out Browning, smooth, debonair, eminently social, and then turned to the poetry to find the image of a complex, difficult, even lonely individual. He could reconcile the two Brownings only by inventing an alter ego, a serious shade who sat upstairs at the writing table while the social mask went down to dinner. Something of this doppelgänger quality was to be found, I think, in Pratt. Many of the studies of the man stress his sociability, and they repeat, sometimes ad nauseam, the anecdotes, particularly those of his

Newfoundland days, that attached themselves like limpets to the poet. The alter ego has consequently often suffered isolation, as the commentators have caroused with the smiling public man downstairs. The poet George Johnston was probably closer to the truth of the man when he wrote in an obituary notice, "For all his friendliness and good fellowship there was something awesome and aloof about him, so that for my part, although I always felt at home in his company, I could not imagine being intimate with him." He found the same to be true of Pratt's poetry: "It is grand, moving, serious; one feels at home with it but not intimate."

There is also in Pratt's intellectual tradition a high seriousness that is part of what seems to us the aloofness of the nineteenth-century man of letters. He was profoundly influenced early in his life by the evolutionary theory. Whereas the ideas of Darwin, Spencer, and Huxley had their strongest effect in Britain in the late nineteenth century, they were still current enough in Canada in the early twentieth to be issues of controversy, as they were in the southern parts of the United States. In the still-primitive conditions of the Canadian Far West and the Eastern seaboard, where Pratt grew up, the wilderness of plain, sea, and rock gave a meaningful setting to the clash of forces taking place within society. Pratt's work is filled with images of primitive nature and evolutionary history. It seemed natural to him to write of molluscs, of cetacean and cephalopod, of the Pliocene epoch, of Java and Piltdown man. The evolutionary process early became and always remained the central metaphor of his work. It gave him the themes of his best lyrics and provided him with the solid framework within which he could achieve an epic style. The evolutionary metaphor persisted in Pratt's work long after it had ceased to have much force for the twentieth-century poetic and philosophic mind.

The evolutionary theory came into conflict, of course, with the Christian belief in which Pratt had been brought up, and it probably had a good deal to do with his decision to leave the ministry. What he later came to believe has been the subject of continuing debate in Pratt criticism. Commentators have called him a Christian humanist, an agnostic, and an atheist.

In a close examination of the question in *E. J. Pratt: The Evolutionary Vision* (1974), Sandra Djwa concluded that Pratt's synthesis of evolutionary thought brought him to a belief that was "both Christian and humanistic." On reflection, I have come to believe that Pratt, like many poets, could not commit himself finally to any dogma, but was interested in dramatizing the problem of belief in a variety of contexts. Such a dramatization is found in the poem "The Iron Door," written after the death of his mother. The door closes after the dead, but Pratt in a vision catches

> the sense
> Of life with high auroras and the flow
> Of wide majestic spaces;
> Of light abundant; and of keen impassioned faces,
> Transfigured underneath its vivid glow.

The vision fades, but not even the "blindness falling with terrestrial day" can "cancel half the meaning of that hour . . ." Pratt does not commit himself to either a denial or an affirmation of an afterlife, but he does show that belief itself is a reality that can transform life and give even the skeptical earthbound mind a vision of beauty and meaning.

The question of belief is central to Pratt's most successful poem, *Brébeuf and His Brethren* (1940). On the one hand, Vincent Sharman can claim that the poem is a kind of ironic put-down of the achievement of the seventeenth-century Jesuits in their attempt to convert the Indians to Catholicism. He believes the conclusion of the poem "The Martyrs' Shrine" to be a bitter indictment of twentieth-century Canadians. And on the other, I heard a paper presented at a 1976 conference on E. J. Pratt in Ottawa in which the writer claimed that the poem was a sustained and deliberate apologia for what the Jesuits did, full of high praise for their bravery and belief.

However, Pratt, as both a writer of epic and an historian, has an all-encompassing view of the events and can include both the irony and the achievement. He made a close reading of both the *Jesuit Relations* and Parkman's version of the events in *The Jesuits in North America in the Seventeenth Century*. Unlike Parkman, Pratt was able to escape quite successfully from his Protestant upbringing to write a remarkably sympathetic account of the mission. Yet he was too much aware of the larger forces at work on the continent to subscribe entirely to the orthodox church view. *Brébeuf* is about the whole French imperial effort in New France. That effort had a secular as well as a sacred mission. The duality of the theme is mirrored in the character of the warrior-priest, Brébeuf, himself. References to Richelieu, Mazarin, and the lilies of France demonstrate Pratt's concern with both forces and serve to show that, to some extent at least, the Jesuits were being used by the French ministers of the crown to further their dreams of empire. A converted native population would be a friendly one, and the importance of Indian alliances in the struggle among the French, Dutch, and British for control of North America can hardly be overstated. In the French and Indian wars of the eighteenth century, the combination of French soldiers and Iroquois warriors was to bring France as close to winning the continent as it ever came, before Wolfe put an end to those ambitions with the capture of Quebec in 1759.

Brébeuf and His Brethren abounds in ironies. The priests have the task of converting the natives to a sophisticated and quite abstract system of belief. But the Indians are seen as far down on the evolutionary scale. Behind the Frenchmen are centuries of culture and learning, the achievements of the French cathedral-builders, the traditions of chivalric warfare, the splendors of Renaissance cuisine and viniculture. This civilization is juxtaposed with the filthy primitivism of the Indians, with their smoke-filled lodges, revolting food, and savage warfare. Pratt's descriptions not only stress the enormous difficulty of the Jesuits' task, but also underline the virtual certainty of its failure.

The narrative demonstrates how closely a tribe's or a nation's religion is a product of a culture and its needs, and it establishes a real sympathy for the bewildered natives. Obviously, a religion that promises a heaven without hunting, war, feasts, and tobacco was about as useful to the Indians as a tomahawk without a head. Only the Jesuits' resort to the primitive symbolism of the Christian hell could make much impression on the imagination of the Indians. Again and again, the Jesuits are forced to oversimplify and substitute to convey even the crudest notions of their religion. What happens, in effect, is that they have to go backward many centuries along the path of evolution to make any contact with the savages. The ultimate meeting of minds of Jesuit and Indian comes not on the question of belief but on the common ground of physical endurance. One after another, the priests go to their excruciating deaths, torn and racked by tortures that surpass in refinement even those devised by the Medici. Some of the most effective parts of the poem deal with details of torture.

Pratt stresses that it was no mean achievement of Christian belief and culture to arm men more effectively against torment than could the most stoic capacity for endurance demanded by the Iroquois code. The final magnificent set piece of Brébeuf's torture—which Goya commemorated in a horrifying painting—shows how the priest reverts to his warrior heritage, becomes a lion at bay, and gives his foes "roar for roar" until he conquers this secular source of defiance to come to rely at last on the vision of that earlier crucifixion.

The design of the poem finely echoes its central conflict—the Old World against the New, Catholicism versus savagery. It is put together in mosaic form, usually under yearly dates, charting the triumphs and the heartbreaks of the missionaries. It is carefully built, piece by piece, so that an overwhelming sense of the myriad problems facing the Jesuits is conveyed. From the 1635 section on, the tension slowly mounts as the reader is made increasingly aware of the terrible and inevitable destruction facing the priests. The succession of captures, tortures, and murders works toward its climax in the martyrdom of Brébeuf. The priests scarcely emerge as individuals, as is fitting. Theirs is a joint venture, and the successes and sufferings are shared. At the same time, they become representatives of historical forces, as do the Indians, so that the conflict between the two groups is both elemental and unavoidable. Yet the poem is saved from impersonality by the innumerable details of ceremonials, meals, vegetation, lodge construction, language, and gesture. It is moved forward by a tremendous narrative energy that Pratt, almost alone among twentieth-century poets, possesses. The blank verse is heavily alliterative, but not oppressively so. The rhythms are varied by many run-on lines, and the harmony is established by a sure control of assonance and contrast. Close analysis will reveal the skill with which Pratt adapted the rich variety of syntactical patterns inherent in English to the demands of his metrics.

In *Brébeuf*, *contra* Winfield Townley Scott, there are innumerable gems of phrasing, such as "the subtle savagery of art," "the rosary against the amulet," "hermit thrushes rivalled the rapture of the nightingales," "gardens and pastures rolling like a sea / From Lisieux to Le Havre." In each of these phrases, the broad themes and conflicts of the poem are suggested, just as in the least metaphor or image, reverberations are sounded that echo through the poem, enrich its texture, and strengthen its form. Verbal sketches abound:

> At the equinoxes
> Under the gold and green of the auroras
> Wild geese drove wedges through the zodiac.
>   They suffered smoke
> That billowed from the back-draughts at the roof,
> Smothered the cabin, seared the eyes; the fire
> That broiled the face, while frost congealed the
>   spine.

Themes, metaphor, and vision come to a climax in the death of Brébeuf, as the Indians search for the source of that enormous vitality and endurance:

> Was it the blood?
> They would draw it fresh from its fountain. Was it
>   the heart?
> They dug for it, fought for the scraps in the way of
>   the wolves.
> But not in these was the valour of stamina lodged;
> Nor in the symbol of Richelieu's robes or the seals
> Of Mazarin's charters, nor in the stir of the *lilies*
> Upon the Imperial folds; nor yet in the words
> Loyola wrote on a table of lava-stone
> In the cave of Manresa—not in these the source—
> But in the sound of invisible trumpets blowing

> Around two slabs of board, right-angled, hammered
> By Roman nails and hung on a Jewish hill.

Most of Pratt's other notable epic pieces are set on or by the sea, which remained throughout his career the source of his most deeply felt emotions and his most effective imagery. His earliest published essay in the epic form was *The Witches' Brew* (1925), an octosyllabic mock-epic in which a drunken tomcat leads an attack on behalf of the fishes on the warm-blooded creatures of the earth. The humor seems now heavy-handed and the satire too drawn out, but the poem was for Pratt a useful experiment in the form of the long poem and in the possibilities of great power struggles—an essential element in his epic vision from then on.

It was a short step from there to *The Cachalot* (1926), an account of a sperm whale's attack first on a kraken and then on a whaling ship. Comic elements are still there, as in the description of the whale's anatomy:

> And so large
> The lymph-flow of his active liver,
> One might believe a fair-sized barge
> Could navigate along the river.

In *The Cachalot*, however, Pratt, like Melville, marries a comic to a serious theme and gives an exciting picture of epic conflicts under and on the sea. Pratt had undoubtedly read *Moby-Dick*, but brought to the conflict his own sense of pace and drama. Both men loved the sea, and both were fascinated by the forces of the universe and found an appropriate symbol for that force in the sperm whale. The major difference between the narratives of *Moby-Dick* and *The Cachalot*—aside from length—is that Melville's whale survives the encounter with the whaling ship. Pratt's whale is merely that; unlike Moby-Dick he does not carry the weight of symbolic ambiguity, the profound mystery at the heart of things, an enormous and perhaps inextinguishable life-energy. Pratt's cachalot can be weighed and measured. He is tremendously powerful but finite; a creature of the sea, but warm-blooded. Caught, sleeping and unaware, by the whaling ship, he gives epic battle to the combined forces of man and technology ranged against him. It is a battle to the death, sustained with courage on both sides, and completed by a magnificent charge:

> All the tonnage, all the speed,
> All the courage of his breed,
> The pride and anger of his breath,
> The battling legions of his blood
> Met in that unresisted thud,
> Smote in that double stroke of death.

Epically, Pratt progressed from this titan to *The Titanic* (1935). The sinking of the great ship was a subject exactly fitted to Pratt's talents, requiring technical and historical knowledge, a sense of epic dimension, and, above all, an awareness of the ways of the sea and sailors. Sailors are notoriously superstitious. Centures of experience have shown that when things can go wrong, through carelessness, indifference, or chance, they invariably do. It is a wise sailor who reads the signs of the skies or the pattern of events which may point to disaster. To heed them hurts nothing; to disregard them invites the fates. The omens on the maiden trip of the *Titanic* down the Solent are ignored as part of the pattern of pride which causes the captain to proceed at full speed through the ice field, when every other ship has slowed to a crawl.

Underlining and appearing to justify the captain's pride is the apparently foolproof construction of the ship, so brilliantly described by Pratt. The *Titanic* appears to be far more than a ship—it is a luxury hotel whose appearance and services seem to deny the limitations of any sea-borne vessel. The ship's luxury helps create the illusion of complete security which cocoons the first-class passengers. Only the gambling scene, rich in irony, indicates the peril toward which the ship is proceeding.

Meanwhile the iceberg, reduced from its cathedral-like shape to what Pratt calls the "brute / And palaeolithic outline of a face," drifts toward its rendezvous, its long claw stretched out underwater at precisely the depth at which it can rip through the double hull of the ship. The *Titanic* moves at top speed toward its destiny, ignoring the many radio signals from all around warning of the danger. The collision itself is barely felt by those on board, another irony underscoring the still apparent security of a ship doomed to rapid destruction.

The only thing which redeems the occasion is the heroism of a few men and women—the stokers and engineers who stay at the job down below, the officers, crew members, and passengers who stay calm, the wife and the small boy who give up their places in the lifeboats,

> In those high moments when the gambler tossed
> Upon the chance and uncomplaining lost.

All that power and luxury slide beneath the waves and leave behind them the iceberg, "the master of the longitudes." As Pratt wrote in his notes to the poem, "There was never an event outside the realm of technical drama where so many factors combined to close all the gates of escape, as if some power with intelligence and resource had organized and directed a conspiracy." The brilliant structure of the poem, with its matched opposites, all the way from the great ship and enormous iceberg down to rhymed decasyllabic couplet, emphasizes the form of this august event. Destruction is virtually certain to come to anyone who neglects the iron rules of the sea.

A maritime disaster is also the theme of another epic poem, *The Roosevelt and the Antinoe* (1930), which recounts how the captain and crew of the American liner *Roosevelt* rescue many of the crew of the sinking British freighter *Antinoe*. Even when things are done in the proper seamanlike manner, as they were in this incident, there is no guarantee of safety, as men are lost in spite of efficiency and heroism. In this poem, as in earlier work, the sea seems to be the ally of prehistoric forces. As a lifeboat is lowered into the water from the davits of the *Roosevelt*,

> Below, like creatures of a fabled past,
> From their deep hidings in unlighted caves,
> The long processions of great-bellied waves
> Cast forth their monstrous births which with grey fang
> Appeared upon the leeward side, ran fast
> Along the broken crests, then coiled and sprang
> For the boat impatient of its slow descent
> Into their own inviolate element.

Later in Pratt's career, when he came to write epics in celebration of the battle against Nazi tyranny, the image of the sea changed. For the sailors coming to the aid of the trapped soldiers in Pratt's poem *Dunkirk* (1941),

> Their souls had come to birth out of their racial myths.
> The sea was their school; the storm their friend.

Pratt's patriotism carried him at times into strident propaganda in *Dunkirk*, but in *Behind the Log*, written after the war in 1947, the language is freed from this flatulence and renders, in strikingly idiomatic blank verse, the reality lying behind the traditional laconic form of the logbook

> That rams the grammar down a layman's throat,
> Where words unreel in paragraphs, and lines
> In chapters. Volumes lie in graphs and codes,
> Recording with an algebraic care
> The idiom of storms, their lairs and paths;
> Or, in the self-same bloodless manner, sorting
> The mongrel litters of a battle signal
> In victories or defeats or bare survivals.

Here it is the centuries of tradition and duty as well as the boring, tiring, demanding, and occasionally heroic facts of convoy duty concealed in the log which Pratt seeks to transmute into poetry.

Ranged against the miscellaneous collection of freighters and the four escort vessels which constitute the convoy is the sea power of Nazism, the U-boat. In *Behind the Log* submarines are personified into

> Grey predatory fish [that] had pedigreed
> With tiger sharks and brought a speed and power
> The sharks had never known, for they had been
> Committed to the sea under a charter
> Born of a mania of mind and will
> And nurtured by a Messianic slogan.

The slogan is, I suppose, "Heil Hitler," and it represents for Pratt that abstract rhetoric and demonic lust for power and destruction which for him typified fascism. Against the rhetorical demonism is ranged the laconic language of the log: the complex web of signals, technologies, duties, observations, and rituals that make up the discipline of convoy duty.

Here again, as in *Dunkirk*, the sea becomes an ally. To exploit the alliance of the sea, the convoy turns north, to leave the beaten sea lanes

> And in the ambiguity of the wastes
> To seek the harsh alliance of the ice
> And fog, where Arctic currents were more friendly,
> And long nights blanketed the periscopes.

This alliance partly breaks down in clear weather and moonlight, and the U-boat wolf pack does get through to wreak a terrible havoc among the freighters. Men drown, are fried by burning oil, or blown to pieces in explosions. The escorts strike back. Hunting by sonar, they seek out their prey and destroy them by depth charges.

Suffering terrible losses, the convoy struggles on. In the end it is the work of disciplined men, their knowledge of the sea and navigation, their skill in handling ships and weapons, and the alliance with the waters that brings the convoy through. Pratt makes the point, perhaps the central point of modern war, that the ultimate victory is achieved not by the Nelson touch but by the combined, unrelenting tasks of many men. And he skillfully draws together the themes of *Behind the Log* in a complex web of imagery of writing, type, blood, body, and machinery. The whole is given a sacramental power by the pun on the word "mass" at the beginning of this excerpt:

> No one would mould the linotype for such
> A mass that might survive or not survive
> Their tedium of watches in the holds—
> The men with surnames blotted by their jobs
> Into a scrawl of anonymity.
> A body blow at the boilers would untype
> All differentiations in the blood
> Of pumpmen, wipers, messmen, galley boys
> Who had become incorporate with the cogs
> On ships that carried pulp and scrap to Europe.

The sacramental vision is given a further intensity by a later passage describing the blowing up of the tanker *Stargard*:

Where find the straws to grasp at in this sea?
Where was the cause which once had made a man
Disclaim the sting of death? What ecstasy
Could neutralize this salt and quench this heat
Or open up in victory this grave?
But oil and blood were prices paid for blood
And oil. However variable the time,
The commerce ever was in barter. Oil
Propelled the ships. It blew them up. The men
Died oil-anointed as it choked the *"Christ!"*
That stuttered on their lips before the sea
Paraded them as crisps upon her salver.

The insistent biblical imagery of baptism, anointing, communion, crucifixion, and resurrection transform the anonymity of the men behind the log into an identity with the individual who made the supreme sacrifice by dying on the cross. The point is subtly made that the deaths of these almost anonymous individuals cumulatively had an effect similar to the sacrifice of the Lord in bringing ultimate victory over the powers of evil.

In his last epic, Pratt forsook the sea to record the conquest of the land by the builders of the continental railroad. In *Towards the Last Spike* (1952) it is the perilous "sea of mountains" that the railroad men have to cross rather than the ocean seas, and it is a task requiring as much nerve and sinew as the other journeys. As in *Brébeuf and His Brethren*, Pratt employs a mosaic technique to organize his disparate materials, but since *Towards the Last Spike* contains a good deal of political material, it is looser in form than his other epics. The gigantic nature of the theme tends to give an air of impersonality to the poem, and Pratt often resorts to personification in efforts to overcome this. He makes a monster out of the Laurentian shield and a lady out of British Columbia, just as Frank Norris personified the wheat and the railroad in *his* rail epic, *The Octopus*. Fortunately for Pratt, the giganticism of his geographical forces is almost matched by the human heroes, William Van Horne, the American railroad builder, and Sir John A. Macdonald, prime minister of Canada. The two men are complementary in the poem: Sir John, the rhetorician and skilled parliamentarian, supplies the dream of continental union; Van Horne, engineer and administrator, supplies the force and skill that make the dream come true. *Towards the Last Spike* is not narrative history—Ned Pratt was ironically asked by one of his critics where his coolies were—but it is the stuff of myth, a vigorous, trenchant, swiftly moving narrative in which a nation's ideals and aspirations are given expression and form. Pierre Berton's history of the building of the railroad, *The National Dream*, gives the full story, but does not have the mythical dimension of *Towards the Last Spike*.

A. J. M. Smith has called Pratt "the only Canadian poet who has mastered the long poem." My agreement with this dictum is one reason why I have not left myself much space in which to discuss his shorter poems. Some of them are fine achievements of precision and perception, but it is significant that the most fruitful source of lyric poetry—love—seemed close to him. One of the few love poems in his canon, "Like Mother, Like Daughter" (1937), clearly shows Pratt's ambivalence about the ruling passion:

You caught the *male* for good or ill,
And locked him in a golden cage.

There are references to Keats's forlorn knight-at-arms in the first stanza, while the catalog of women heroines in the poem, "Helen, Deirdre, Héloïse / Laura, Cleopatra, Eve!" seems more catastrophic than celebratory. For Pratt the domain of women seemed to represent temptation and imprisonment, while that of men represented adventure, liberation, and the possibility of heroic action. In "The Deed," for example, Pratt wonders what has happened to the beauty which inspired lovers to sing serenades, minstrels to praise cavalcades, and the poets to write of fruits, flowers, and birds. His own answer is that beauty for him lies not in these things, but in the act of heroism—the almost hopeless dive for the boy's body by an unnamed swimmer:

This was an arch beyond the salmon's lunge,
There was a rainbow in the rising mists:
Sea-lapidaries started at the plunge
To cut the facets of their amethysts.

So it can be claimed that Pratt's lyric impulse expressed itself not in the conventional themes, but in versions of the heroic. These can be tragic in tone, as in "The Deed," or comic, as in "Carlo," a poem about a Newfoundland dog who rescues more than ninety people from a wreck. At the end of the poem Pratt promises to intercede with St. Peter at the heavenly gates in the attempt to get the dog into heaven where he belongs. Pratt wrote several comic poems about animals, but one of them, "The Prize Cat," ends in savagery when the cat goes after a bird:

Behind the leap so furtive-wild
Was such ignition in the gleam,
I thought an Abyssinian child
Had cried out in the whitethroat's scream.

The tension between high breeding on the one hand and savagery on the other in fact supplies the subject for many of the shorter poems. Pratt was always concerned with the evolutionary process, but insisted, too, that the distance between caveman and civilized man is often as short in spirit as it is long in time. Ironically, some of man's greatest technological achievements tend to shorten the distance, as is shown in Pratt's most successful, and most typical, lyric, "From Stone to Steel":

From stone to bronze, from bronze to steel
Along the road-dust of the sun,
Two revolutions of the wheel
From Java to Geneva run.

The snarl Neanderthal is worn
Close to the smiling Aryan lips,
The civil polish of the horn
Gleams from our praying finger tips.

The evolution of desire
Has but matured a toxic wine,
Drunk long before its heady fire
Reddened Euphrates or the Rhine.

Between the temple and the cave
The boundary lies tissue-thin:
The yearlings still the altars crave
As satisfaction for a sin.

The road goes up, the road goes down—
Let Java or Geneva be—
But whether to the cross or crown,
The path lies through Gethsemane.

Here the journey of man is more like a circle than a straight line, but in a good many other poems the journey is terminated by death—usually death by water. Here again thematic concerns are similar to those in the epics. In the ironic little poem "The Drag-Irons," the dead captain comes up from Davey Jones's locker "with livid silence and with glassy look," a parody of his long years of command. Another poem on the same subject, but with a completely different tone, is "Come Not the Seasons Here," one of Pratt's quietest and most effective works. Probably the poem's model is Shakespeare's song "Come Away Death," although the imagery does not concern itself with death directly, but with the seasons. However, the traditional sense of growth associated with spring, summer, and autumn is undercut by the imagery: cuckoo, poppy, shed bloom, sere leaf, brown pasture. The kingdom of death takes over imperiously in the last stanza, in frozen air and glacial stone. This Canadian pastoral is, I take it, about the power of sorrow to destroy the perception of vitality in nature.

The Canadian environment presses in relentlessly on the subject matter of the short poems, as the titles themselves reveal: "The Toll of the Bells," "The Ground Swell," "The Fog," "The Shark," "A Dirge," "The Ice-Floes,"—all in Pratt's first collection, *Newfoundland Verse* (1923). "The Way of Cape Race," "A Prairie Sunset," "Putting Winter to Bed," "Frost," and "The Lee-Shore" appear in the second collection, *Many Moods* (1932). "The Unromantic Moon," "A November Landscape," "Myth and Fact," and "Newfoundland Seamen" are among his later poems. Canada does not offer a climate or a culture hospitable to the tender and lyrical impulses of man.

Canadian life has, on the other hand, been conducive to the development of man's ingenuity, toughness, and resistance. Margaret Atwood has made this the theme of her book about Canadian literature, *Survival*. There is a good deal of the survivor instinct in Pratt's work, but it is not often the grim and desperate affair that Atwood makes it out to be. In one of Pratt's most typical poems, "The Truant," survival becomes a joyful as well as a defiant necessity. The poem's purpose is to show the undying spirit of man when confronted by the ultimate tyrant, the Panjandrum, who represents himself as God, but is merely, as Northrop Frye has noted, "the mechanical power of the universe." Man refuses the Panjandrum's order to join the cosmic ballet and so is condemned by the god to endure palsy, deafness, blindness, old age, and other humiliations. Man merely laughs in the god's face, asserts that he himself created the god, discovered the organization of his universe, and

> Lassoed your comets when they ran astray,
> Yoked Leo, Taurus, and your team of Bears
> To pull our kiddy cars of inverse squares.

Condemned to death, he rings out his defiance, basing his case on the long history of man's resistance to force and tyranny. He ends, "No! by the Rood, we will not join your ballet." It is in this poem that Pratt's poetic personality of wit, humor, toughness, pride, and technical skill most clearly emerge.

Frye has concisely captured the particular quality of Pratt's individualism in his introduction to the second edition of *The Collected Poems* (1958):

> When everybody was writing subtle and complex lyrics, Pratt developed a technique of straightforward narrative; when everybody was experimenting with free verse, Pratt was finding new possibilities in blank verse and octosyllabic couplets. He had the typical mark of originality: the power to make something poetic out of what everybody had just decided could no longer be poetic material. He worked unperturbed while the bright young men of the twenties, the scolding young men of the thirties, the funky young men of the forties, and the angry young men of the fifties were, like Leacock's famous hero, riding off rapidly in all directions.

Twentieth-century poets in general either have tended to be ahistorical or have used history as a kind of rubbish dump from which to pluck bits and pieces to titillate their imaginations. Winfield Townley Scott reflects the antihistorical attitude in his condemnation of Pratt's use of events. But artists, even poets, cannot continue to evade or to play with history with impunity. Pratt's intellectual training and inclination enabled him to regard history as a great unfolding process from which he could select at will stories and incidents that could serve his large poetic purposes. He could consequently write epics of the Canadian experience, such as *Brébeuf* and *Towards the Last Spike*, that no other contemporary poet could have tackled. Most poets seem to have felt that there was nothing much worth saying about the Canadian past. Earle Birney's "Can. Lit." is an example:

> we French&English never lost
> our civil war
> endure it still
> a bloody civil bore
> the wounded sirened off
> no Whitman wanted
> it's only by our lack of ghosts
> we're haunted

Pratt suffered from no lack of ghosts, and he was able over the years to create a usable past for the contemporary Canadian imagination.

Pratt's roots in older poetic traditions also enabled him to write descriptively and lyrically about the Canadian landscape. In this endeavor he was, of course, preceded by many poets such as Marjorie Pickthall, Bliss Carman, and Archibald Lampman, but Pratt's scientific bent brought a new precision to his depiction of the Canadian scene, particularly in its severity and grandeur, that previously only the painters of the Group of Seven had adequately captured. Although Pratt remained preeminently a poet of the sea, and particularly of the rock-bound, storm-lashed, Newfoundland coast that provided him with his earliest images, he emerged from regionalism to discover the inland plains and mountains and to record them with love and fidelity.

Canada did not find an adequate myth- and image-maker in poetry until E. J. Pratt appeared. It was fortunate that the individualistic and slightly anachronistic form of his imagination enable him to fulfill this role so late in the national day, in an age when mythmakers had all but disappeared.

REYNOLDS PRICE

1933–

Edward Reynolds Price was born on February 1, 1933, in Macon, North Carolina, to William Solomon and Elizabeth Rodwell Price. He was educated at Duke University (B.A., *summa cum laude* and Phi Beta Kappa, 1955) and Merton College, Oxford (Rhodes Scholar, B.Litt., 1958). He edited the *Archive* in 1954 and 1955. He was a Writer-in-Residence at the University of North Carolina and the University of Kansas and has taught at Duke University since 1958. He is a devout Christian and views his faith as a central factor in his work: "That tragicomic vision of history as creation-fall-redemption-judgement-justice seems to me . . . quite simply, true to observable fact; above all to the facts of my own life." This tragicomic structure pervades Price's fiction.

Price's first novel, *A Long and Happy Life*, was published in its entirety in *Harper's* in 1962, and later that year issued as a book. It was well received by the critics, as were his next two books, the short-story collection *The Names and Faces of Heroes* (1963) and the novel *A Generous Man* (1966). Price's next novel, *Love and Work* (1968), was more controversial; some critics preferred his comic treatments of naive adolescents in rural North Carolina and his likeable if absurd Mustian family stories to the more mature, sophisticated protagonists and personal, abstract concerns of his later fiction. The short-story collection *Permanent Errors* (1970) continued in this new direction and received similarly mixed notices.

The Surface of Earth (1975) chronicles the history of a family through the first half of the twentieth century; it is Price's most ambitious work, presenting its story through several disparate narrative devices. *The Source of Light* (1981) is a sequel. Like all Price's later work, the saga received mixed reviews, although many of Price's supporters felt that he was clearly at the height of his powers.

Price's other works include several books of verse, a play (*Early Dark*, 1977) based on *A Long and Happy Life*, and much nonfiction, including several religious books. He is unmarried and lives alone in rural North Carolina.

General

I think the South as *we* knew it essentially ceased to exist about the time I started paying full fare at the movies, which was 1945. That is to say there are still an enormous number of the symptoms and the traditions and the tones and feelings of the South—those which are valuable and those which are execrable—very much in evidence. But it seems to me that they are quite arguably hangovers, remnants, and that the young Southerners whom one meets now—certainly the ones who get to universities—are arriving with assumptions which are utterly different from those that, say, I arrived at Duke with in 1951, age eighteen, having grown up in small North Carolina towns, gone to high school in Raleigh, the son of a Southern family—a Southern Depression family. I do feel very Southern. I feel it more than ever when I go away from the South; and I always sigh with relief when I see that, you know, cardinal on a sign near South Hill, Virginia, which says "Welcome to North Carolina." I say, and sort of sigh, "I'm back." Everyone is just a little nicer than they are anywhere north of there. That, basically, is the reason I keep coming back to the South, I think; why I live there. But I don't know; it may indeed be vanishing fast. I think there'll certainly go on being Southern writers, but what they'll be writing about I don't know because one doesn't know what's going to be affecting any individual Southerner, age eighteen, who's alive this minute, perhaps in this room. I feel that your obsessions, if you are eighteen to twenty-five now, are very different from what, say, mine were. My great fear as a child was destitution because of the Depression. My father lost the only house he ever built because he couldn't borrow fifty dollars. I mean, are you ready for that? I go out and buy a, you know, a brief case any day that costs fifty dollars; and he couldn't borrow it to buy the house with—make the next payment. And the sort of people who are likely to write, it seems to me, are not having the sorts of problems now that I had as a boy—not seeing their parents humiliated, say, in the way that I did or that, sixty years before, a generation of Southern writers saw their parents humiliated by Reconstruction. ⟨. . .⟩

One of the things I find—in a way I think one of the things we are talking about and haven't yet mentioned—is of course the vanishing of the countryside, even in the South. It's seldom discussed in connection with the novel or poetry. You know the kind of question one is asked all the time: what about the famous "death of the novel"? what about the new freedom to use sex in fiction? But something considerably more interesting, I think, is: what about the fact that it's getting harder and harder not to live in the heart of some ghastly metropolitan monster? Just endless, you know, Burger King stands—"Home of the Whopper." I mean, where do you go from there, except into nightmare? We tend to think of the novel as an urban form; but, in fact, it's very difficult to think of any great novel before, say, Kafka which occurs *entirely* in a city. Think of the great novelists of the nineteenth—the eighteenth and nineteenth century. Most of the plots, in fact, hinge on a pendulum swing of visits to the city, visits to the country. The earliest novels are about people traveling around the countryside, with occasional visits to London or Berlin or Madrid. What's going to happen when it's all Burger Kings? Is it possible to write an urban novel now which is about anything except nightmare? The novels of Kafka are nightmare novels. Some of the more successful all-urban American novels like *Invisible Man* are essentially novels about nightmare. Is it really possible—anymore—to write a novel set entirely in New York City which is really about anything else? I mean, I tried to live in New York for a while and, you know, it was nightmare. There are lots of people who claim to love it and to be unable to breathe anywhere else; but they are not going to be able to breathe *there* much longer.

⟨. . .⟩ I think we talk about the South as though it's something about the size of this room; and everyone does. The South is about—it's a country about the size of France, if you look at it on your map. I once was writing a book review and I wondered, "How big is the South?" I thought, you know, it was about the size of Arizona or something; and I started trying to figure up how many square . . . and it was roughly the size of France. It's a good big *country*; and it has had these internal regions—these internal slight shiftings and shades of intensity of feeling, language, dress, dialect, speech, and so forth. How much of this is still preserved and how much is likely to last another five years is interesting and problematic. I think, for instance, that my mother and father's generation, born at the turn of the century—my father was born in 1900—that they and their brothers and sisters could have sat down in a room with their resurrected great-great-grandparents and conducted a perfectly understandable conversation. They would have known exactly what one another was talking about, with maybe just a few updatings of idiom and so forth. But it's all that my nieces and nephews, age eighteen, can do to sit down in a room with their parents today, much less conduct a conversation. The generation gap—and it certainly exists—is occurring with a rapidity perhaps greater than ever before in history. I've tried to think if there's ever been a time when one's students—who are not much more than ten years younger than one—are another *creature*. It's happened now, it seems to me, in a large way; and I don't know any way to stop it, short of turning the whole South into some kind of Williamsburg, which would be indeed to destroy it in perhaps a more unnatural way than it's being destroyed now. ⟨. . .⟩

I think the oldest kind of poetry, the oldest kind of *art*, is celebration, magic and celebration of some sort—to celebrate what's mysterious, what you don't understand, with your fingers crossed in the hope that somehow you will get to understand it or with the hope that you'll be able to start pulling the strings a little bit better. I mean, if you paint a bison on the wall of your cave, somehow you are hoping that you can catch a better bison tomorrow, or that you can stop the bison that's sort of stampeding in your direction. Or if you make a psalm to God, you are celebrating the fact that the world seems mysterious and seems organized, seems somehow to be all one thought. I think the problem that any artist has now is that the number of things to celebrate is diminishing daily—and I mean that quite seriously—that it's very difficult now to celebrate nature. You've got to get in a car and go and hunt the nature to celebrate, you know, unless you happen to live in Yosemite National Park; and that somehow is unnatural because it had to be declared off-limits to Burger Kings—I hope the manager of Burger King isn't offended if he is here today.

In a way, you know, if you drive from Raleigh, North Carolina, to Richmond, Virginia, and then, God help you, on to New York, you begin to think that the only thing to celebrate is a sort of Robinson Jeffers vision of nuclear disaster—and I'm quite serious. One gets in a frame of mind in which one thinks that the only hope would be to blot it out and start over. And then if you read a book of popular science like, say, Fred Hoyle's *The Nature of the Universe* and you read about that beautiful galaxy in Andromeda out there that looks like a toy—just suspended out there, you know, you find that it's only 2,500,000 light-years away; it's 30,000,000 light-years in diameter. Then you can't get all that upset about Burger

Kings, and you wouldn't at all mind having, somehow, the whole thing go up in a kind of lovely reach toward that.
—REYNOLDS PRICE, "The Writer and His Tradition," *The Writer and His Tradition: Festival Proceedings*, ed. Robert Drake, 1969, pp. 12–27

The fingers of Reynolds Price creep steadily, evenly, over people, things, and properties of existence, seen and unseen. They are like the fingers of the blind, ruthlessly gentle, respectfully demanding. They seem to enjoy inspection as an end in itself. Maybe that is why some say that Price is all manner. But if they do, they take the endings of his stories too much for granted; they consider them to be more of the same. Not so. *There* the fingers stop feeling. They go over into a recognizable sign language. They are now the fingers of the dumb, and they talk. His way is as simple and as tensile as that.

Read the first part of his story in *Permanent Errors*, "The Happiness of Others," and see how this process works its way along. Price feels, through Charles Templin, the seeming failure of a love affair. Alienation is come at through surface, muted comprehension of objects by Charles and Sara in an English church: of a long-since desecrated Lady Chapel; of an over-smooth, unworthy neoclassical bust of a poet; of long-dead merchants' graves in the churchyard. The agreement is too complete, too unrumpled, for the vexatious ways of love. But that is being examined. The time for proof has not yet come.

The shepherd lad, warm from sleep, is ominously examined. The examining fingers are Charles's: ". . . he [the shepherd] might have been awakened that instant by warmth, drawn from sleep under leaves by sun, the melted snow." But the hands also feel the back of Sara's head—her face toward the shepherd constantly, as long as their passing car allows her to see him.

The hands have almost made the transition to talk.

They do, as this second-to-last paragraph moves on. They summarize (often a typical ending of a Price story—A *Q.E.D.*—fine threads, an elongation of the alphabet and floating numbers, drawn to a point) what they have felt. They signal conclusion.

The one-sentence final paragraph announces the ultimate transition of examination: "But Blenheim now, dinner, sleepless night, their final day."

The *essentialness* of the shepherd has brought, seemingly, finality and irrevocably emphasized apartness. The last paragraph is kindly—not glib or rude. It informs the simple and confirms the subtle.

The four-part story winds its way through analogy and circumstance; it paradoxically brings home the eventual blunt blows of indirection. In particular, the section called "Dachau" is mighty in inversion: it reminds us of the double-talk of our tenderest relationship, the recoil upon us of actions misinterpreted and the brutally, tartly happy recognition of the truth that has lurked slyly within them. Sara's imagined poem says, "Parallels meet. It is how the world is made." The story ends with firm, disarming tenderness: "Sara, come back."

I have spent time on this story, for I think it is the finest in the collection. Price is not kind to his readers. He puts them to work—which is not polite, particularly in the United States where everybody has a compulsion to be simple-mindedly clear, especially in literature dealing with sex. The multitude is had compassion on, and all is more explicit than the way of birds and bees, which often cannot be observed but have to be read about—in books. Price, in this respect as in others, is not considerate. He is not basic, for that expression is meaningless.

He is; and his being is worth the trouble. That is unpardonable of him.

His first story definitely stands out. (It is only fair to say that this is not an orthodox collection of short stories: the book also contains beautifully written elegies, memories, and impressions.) The long narrative "Walking Lessons" is weaker: it shows the defects of Price's qualities; there is too much shifting of gears. He is seen at times working too hard at what he is trying to get at. The worst part is the gruffly man-to-man approach at the opening: it won't do. But another reviewer said something like this, disastrously—for himself. The concluding pages are the best: there Price polishes the bright metal ball of his story until you can hold it in your hand, feel symmetry, and see, in all directions, light. It didn't need the early awkward attempts at polish, or any spit.

Reynolds Price's versatility lies also in his ability to be indignant, gently and yet angrily, as in the elegy on a mother. In quite another situation it brings to mind D. H. Lawrence's anger over the ruthless intrusion of death into the life of Paul Morel's mother, the near-laying of the fault at her own door, the intrusion of death, through her, into himself. The situations are billions of miles from each other. So is the technique. But the essential factor is there: an aghastness, not fear, and an aggressive wonder at what death can crudely do to our bodies and through them, to the allness of our selves. Only, Price is tenderly normal with the mother.

Reynolds Price, they say, writes well, very well. I wonder if "they" realize all that they are saying. Just good writing? Excellent writing? It bears thinking over.—JOHN HAZARD WILDMAN, "Beyond Classification: Some Notes on Distinction," *SoR*, Jan. 1973, pp. 233–35

Works

Reynolds Price's first novel, *A Long and Happy Life* (1962), was an unusually distinguished performance, as impressive in the lyricism of its style as it was in the renewed vitality he brought there to his time-worn theme (the fearful and immense complexities of human love). Amidst a spate of pornographic and programmatic novels, it stood out like a beacon of life and light or, at the least, a breath of fresh country air. Price was not afraid to *narrate* (something many of our fiction writers have either forgotten how to do or now disdain to do), nor was he afraid to retell one of the oldest stories in the world.

Such, however, is not the verdict one must finally render on his second novel, *A Generous Man*. The *story* here is essentially the coming of age, both sexually and intellectually, of Milo Mustian, older brother of Rosacoke Mustian, the heroine of Price's first novel. And the action is centered in and around Milo and the community's joint efforts to find his younger brother, Rato, Rato's dog, Phillip, suspected of being rabid, and a twenty-foot python named Death, which has escaped from a carnival side show, all of whom have disappeared into the woods.

In certain ways, the narrative line may remind readers of Eudora Welty's "The Wide Net," where a whole community is united to find a missing wife (or her drowned body) and emerges from its quest more solidly joined, despite its diversity, than ever. (Both Price's novel and Miss Welty's story end on a somewhat comic note: though "Death" is killed, both Rato and Phillip return safe and sound, as does the missing Hazel in "The Wide Net.") Price's style is also reminiscent of Miss Welty's, especially in her later works, as is also what seems his predilection here for the mythical or perhaps allegorical.

But here all resemblance both to Miss Welty and to

himself ends because Price seems to have gone off now in quest of strange gods. His theme in *A Generous Man* seems much the same as that of his first novel; but it often appears confused because, in speaking of love, he frequently seems to be dealing mainly with sex. And there are enough bedroom gymnastics and phallus-worship, described in graphic if "poetic" detail, to satisfy the most ardent disciple of D. H. Lawrence. And at times it's all just plain silly, as when the sheriff, Rooster Pomeroy, impotent to satisfy his young wife, more or less thanks Milo for having spent the afternoon with Kate in bed and presumably begotten the son he so desperately wants. In fact, Price seems to imply, more than once, that there are very few human ailments which a good trip to the bedroom or, in a pinch, the woodshed cannot straighten out. And it's all mixed up with some sort of "meaningful" chase after "Death," and daughters and mothers and sons and lovers all being reunited and understanding each other. What to make of it all remains finally, at least for this reviewer, something of a mystery.

Furthermore, Price's style, which seemed so powerful and moving in his first novel—shot through as it was with perceptions of natural beauty of the freshest intensity—seems to have degenerated here into a *manner*. His prose has become more modish, as his theme has become more muddled. A case in point is his fondness for the simple sentence with a simple subject but endlessly compound predicate, which has a certain hypnotic power but eventually becomes tedious and finally no substitute for a legitimate *style* which supports and reinforces the theme at every step.

This novel is supposed to present, apparently, a dramatic rendering of an elemental human experience, one fraught with pain and peril, which all men must finally undergo. Its possibilities for beauty and drama are certainly endless; but Price appears content to give us a fifteen-year-old North Carolina boy, wise both in speech and in thought far beyond his years—more a suburbanite Ivy Leaguer than a country boy whose folks raise tobacco. When he lets North Carolina speak and act for itself, Price is on home territory and safe. When he tries to impose a false intellectual and stylistic sophistication on his native material, it will simply not support this factitious superstructure, with a resulting loss of clarity and power. For all his implications about the necessity of both give and take in human love, Price's treatment involves largely the give and take of sex: his metaphysics becomes largely acrobatics. Finally, as Rosacoke remarks when Milo is discoursing on the dramatic events of "Death's" escape, "Just call it a snake. I'll know who you mean." Price might have done better if he had followed this advice more closely himself. His talent is a very fine one. Let us hope that he will not further abuse it. —ROBERT DRAKE, "Coming of Age in North Carolina," *SoR*, Winter 1967, pp. 248–50

> Thanne shewe I forth my longe cristal stones,
> Ycrammed ful of cloutes and of bones,—
> Relikes been they, as wenen they echoon.

If an author can be puckish enough to say in his note to the reader that his book is "in various ways, a set of variations," a reviewer and admirer ought to be able to get away with choosing a couple of the book's preoccupations to talk about without knowing whether they are ways, variations, or neither. I choose time and names.

Two women in the collection (*Permanent Errors*) attempt suicide; one lives, the other dies (success or failure at suicide seem to press the language of achievement beyond meaning). Of the former's life, the author says, "the circular past—she its willing victim." The same could be said for most of the characters in these stories. They believe their lives have already happened, and they wish to be left alone to study the remains. They are reliquarians, rapt in their desire to give whole attention (whole lives!) to the event that so clearly shaped their lives, only to find their gaze interrupted by the teeming eventful present. A rich emblem of this troublesome present is the state of Charles Tamplin in "Scars": he and Sara have separated, their love a bust, she home to America, he to a room, his thought, his art, iconography. His afternoon rest is shattered by his landlady and her lascivious pal, who, as he stands in the middle of the floor clutching only a towel around his nakedness, run at him and try to pull it away. They are after his vitals—just a look see, of course, but his protection is flimsy, his need great: he strikes the girl friend in the face. The game ends. But the lesson is clear enough: need does not bar the door, most men can live without meaning. Reflection is purchased; the price is other's needs, other's lives.

The truth that these stories vaunts is, things happen in the past. It's not easy to remember. For these characters, action is past, the present is for thinking, the future hypothetical, chancey. The past is also lethal, threatening to take vengeance on the present for not being included: errors take place, like everything else, in the past, their permanence demands continuance. The pressure of the past on the present, its tyranny, ends a few of the stories in simple cries for help, for what is not possible: reversal—Gatsby's desire that Daisy annihilate those five years with Tom Buchanan.

The relation of present thinking (writing) to past event is the axis these writings turn on, though the energy of the thinking, the massive attempt at meaning, often overwhelms the really spectacular actions that surround the thinking. Let me emphasize that these stories do not *take place* in the past; they are lived out in a furious, tumultuous present. But it is strange how completely the thought swallows, say, the dinner at the cafe in "Waiting at Dachau," or the shooting in "Walking Lessons." Meaning is in the mind. Again, the present is for making sense of the past, outliving it.

The exclusion of the characters also issues from the shadow of the past on their lives; each seems not to fit in, somehow—each has blood on his hands. Parts of four of the stories take place inside cars or trucks, windows presumably rolled up. It is almost as if the world were dying around them, and, Struldbruggs, they were condemned to immortality.

One last suggestion about time in *Permanent Errors*: the characters are no lovers of the past. They respect and fear the past as Emerson and Hawthorne and, nearer in time but no closer to home, John Berryman do; that is, they do not live on easy terms with the past. They do not snuggle up to history, they honor it by flight. True regard.

And names. "Name us, name us," the speaker calls to the reader in "Walking Lessons," and proceeds with the job himself. Indeed, "Walking Lessons," a long story which takes perhaps two-fifths of the entire collection, is an exercise in naming; the speaker finds the title that suffices at the end of his story—then makes us a gift of his wife's name. The supernatural significance of names for the Navajo is played on throughout "Walking Lessons" and, pointedly, the speaker's name is never given.

The volume is awash with titles: each of the four sections has a title, each story has a title, and parts of two stories have titles. Many of them seem interchangeable, or, if not detachable, surely supplemental—"Walking Lessons" are what all the characters need, for example.

But more important, the way the characters understand is

by naming (the other old Adam in us), as if to tame chaos around them in the oldest way. In an important sense, the *meaning* of "Walking Lessons" is the name Beth. The gift is not analysis, but words—yea, art.

And may I name the author not alchemist (or not *only* alchemist), but haruspex, who predicts the future by staring at entrails—who could look at what so many others avoid without learning? Or, *and*, Chaucer's Portrait of the Artist, The Pardoner (absurd? name another), who by art names his world as it must be, then holds forth the least of it for worship: his work. And last to touch on Reynolds Price's candor.

He uses language for the rarest (oldest?) of reasons, to say the truth. In the presence of this writing, the reader may think of Carraway's discomfort at the disclosure of confidences, but, another name, I believe he would be better to sit still, albeit painfully, with The Wedding Guest. The tales may turn your head, but the voice is worth attending to. Nobody I know of writes better prose.—HENRY SLOSS, "Price's Reliques," *Shen*, Spring 1971, pp. 94–96

When a work of fiction as compelling and original as Reynolds Price's latest novel ⟨The Surface of Earth⟩ comes along, it deserves evaluation in its own terms. Why should the reader worry if, in its relatively straightforward narrative, its rich, rhythmical and rather formal language and its brooding obsession with family as a kind of fate which a child must come to terms with before he can be free "to walk clean away into his own life," it seems to be out of step with the march of most contemporary fiction?

More important is the fact that it meets what seems to me the supreme test of a novel: it manages to recreate a world and people it with characters as complex and stubbornly mysterious as those in life, and it draws the reader into that world—sensually, emotionally and intellectually—to the point that he experiences those lives and earns whatever insights may be gained from them.

In this, his longest and most ambitious novel, which took ten years of planning and three years of writing, Reynolds Price focuses on the harm that parents do, through the flawed choices, emotional failures and unsatisfied hungers they pass on to their children unto the third and fourth generation. Indeed, the biblical estimate seems conservative here when one considers that although the action begins in 1903 on the evening of 16-year-old Eva Kendall's elopement with her Latin teacher, Forrest Mayfield, the book opens with a conversation in which the Kendall children are drawing from their father details of their maternal grandfather's suicide. ("What's shameful, sir, in wanting the truth?" Eva asks "We're all nearly grown. . . . It's our own story.") And the novel ends, 491 pages later, with that suicide's great-great-grandson, Hutch Mayfield, struggling to put his heavy inheritance behind him.

A narrow focus? Perhaps. But unquestionably an important one which takes the reader beneath the surface of events into the interior world, even the unconscious world, of the principal characters.

Only after I had closed the book and separated myself from the Mayfields and the Kendalls did I begin to think about what the book lacked in variety of pitch, the leavening effects of humor and attention to immense social forces, the two World Wars and the Depression, for example, which must have touched even families as remote and self-absorbed as these in rural North Carolina and Virginia.

This curious deafness to the din of the world outside the family may be partially explained by the fact that Mr. Price presents his characters to us during periods of emotional crisis when they are forced to make, in minutes, choices that they and their children will spend decades, even lifetimes, living out.

The technical decision to present the family epic in three sections, representing episodes in 1903–5, the 1920's and 1944, was a happy one, I think. It gives the narrative the energy that comes from compression and forces the reader to become actively involved in piecing together what has happened during the intervening decades from random scraps of conversation and recollection, just as one must do, for example, at a family reunion.

Despite the book's length and what begins to seem toward the end a plethora of explanations and confessions from the characters themselves, the narrative remains, on the whole, surprisingly succinct, displaying Mr. Price's gift for catching whole landscapes in a few images, whole characters in a few telling gestures or fragments of talk. And what a luxury it is to be immersed in his majestic prose.

There is, however, a static quality to the novel as fragments of human experience are seized and held for microscopic observation, then analyzed at length from shifting points of view in dreams, in letters and in endless talk. This quality is suggested in the Blake-like image which the author has designed for the jacket of the book—a fixed sun face gazing with an intensity that threatens to burn through surfaces to the mysteries beneath them.

Admittedly, only a small patch of the surface of earth is under scrutiny here, a geographic area bounded on the south by Raleigh and Fontaine, North Carolina; on the north by Richmond and Washington; on the west by Goshen and the Shenandoah Valley; and on the east by the Atlantic at Virginia Beach. But this small area is evoked with such authority and examined so relentlessly that the reader feels, at times, perilously close to penetrating to that core which one character defines as "the heart of the world . . . the precious meaning of life and pain."

When one of the most talented novelists of our day sets this kind of revelation as his goal, it is cause for celebration by all of us who, like Forrest Mayfield, still hope to find in fiction some "wisdom" that "will prove more useful and slightly less wearing than the raw fray of life."

The fact that his Promethean effort is only partially successful should not diminish our respect for its daring and its high seriousness. Reynolds Price, himself, seems to be acknowledging the limits of the individual artist in several key passages near the end of the novel which I would like to quote here.

The thoughts are those of Hutch Mayfield, Eva and Forrest's only grandson, the youngest of the ten lives "bent crooked" by the reckless elopement with which the novel begins. The scene is a hillside near a delapidated resort hotel in Goshen where the 14-year-old boy has come to rest away from his father, Rob, and where he is considering beginning his own life as an artist:

> By noon Hutch was thinking he'd finished his picture. It was clear lines drawn with his best hard pencil, no smearing, no shadows. . . .
> It was the one thing he *had* made this morning, unaided, from what the earth offered of its visible skin—the surface it flaunted in dazzling stillness, in the glaze of rest, to beg us to watch; then grope for its heart. . . .

Hutch realizes that he has drawn the leaves "badly" but appreciates the fact that "the opposite rocks, the back of the mountain, the line of Alice's back and head, her farmer's hat—

they were right and true, his own gift offered to the world in return." He reaches for an eraser to strip the leaves from his trees, then remembers his great-aunt Rena's warning when he began to modify the clear lines of an earlier drawing:

> May I tell you? The whole world is waiting to see what you are ruining." He had stopped and said, "Ma'm? I'm not that good"; and Rena said, "Not you—the secrets of God. The whole world is waiting in expectation for the revelation of the secrets of God. You've just now drawn their excellent likeness and are ruining it." . . .

So he spared the trees now. He trusted to wait till the secret of leaves, if nothing more, came into his power. First the power to watch one green leaf in stillness; then the dark banked branches in all their intricate shifting concealment—concealed good news (that under the face of the earth lay care, a loving heart, though maybe asleep: a giant in a cave who was dreaming the world, a tale for his long night) or concealed news of hatred embellished with green (that a sight like this or a shape like Rob's was only the jeering mask of a demon who knew men's souls and guided their steps). It seemed, now at least, that any such power would come here if anywhere. This place was an entrance. He'd need to wait here.

Beyond the description of artistic failure, as well as success, I read here a commitment to keep on working "at the entrance" which I hope comes, through Hutch, from Reynolds Price himself.

Although this powerful novel seems in the end to be overweighted with wordy explanations of the emotional demands, debts and failures that constrict the Mayfields' and the Kendalls' lives, it represents a leap forward by a gifted novelist into visionary territory which few of his contemporaries have the courage to explore, territory which, if conquered, can yield the hard-won wisdom of the human heart.—ANNE HOBSON FREEMAN, "Penetrating a Small Patch of the Surface of the Earth," *VQR*, Autumn 1975, pp. 637–41

What happens in America—and other places too—to novelists who get off to stunning starts, who, in their early work, display great talents and interesting minds, and then, before they reach full middle age, disappoint us? Does the academy ruin them, as the old argument runs? Is our world unfit for the creation of art as some of us have insisted?

⟨. . .⟩ Price's book has already generated disagreement in distinguished quarters, and I am pained to have to enter the fray, as it were, on the side of the enemy. But the truth will out, has indeed emerged, I suspect, in the ranks of Price's most ardent admirers; and the truth is that *The Surface of the Earth* is a very bad book, pretentious and dull and utterly wrongheaded. The novel is a forty-year chronicle of two families, the Mayfields and the Kendals; and its ponderous story-line need not be recapitulated. Things get under way when Eva Kendal elopes with Forrest Mayfield; this marriage ends as a result of the hard birth of Rob Mayfield, who in turn grows up, marries, and loses his wife in childbirth, which is the continuation of an old family habit since we learn on the first page that Eva's grandmother died while giving birth. I do not mean to make light of what Price has tried to do or to deny the dangers of child-bearing in the days before penicillin. And I am aware of the way in which some novelists—D. H. Lawrence, for example—can tie generations together in fiction by the repetition of gestures and ceremonies and events. But Price works with a heavy hand. In almost every word he insists on his seriousness, the significance of the events as they unfold; and as if to underline the images that he wishes us to grasp, he repeats himself again and again through the course of the novel.

Miscegenation is rampant. Children of mixed blood are born, one of whom, the son of a Mayfield, becomes a major character in the novel. Older generations interfere in the lives of the young; misunderstandings accrue; marriages are disrupted. Forrest recognizes his kinship to the mulatto Grainger, as does Rob in his turn; both attempt to expiate the old sin; both fail. Forrest allows himself to be deprived of his wife with hardly a protesting word, then takes up with another woman who treats him better than he deserves. Eva survives quite well by herself. The men are weak, unreliable; the women are strong. Events, characters, gestures—males lying down on top of other males, not in sexual irregularity, but in mystic farewell—lead finally to a similarity of voice, a stylistic monotony that for a quarter of a million words is unrelieved. All the characters think in the same phrases, write the same letters, use the same diction when they speak.

I would suggest two things that have gone wrong in this novel. First, it appears to be a totally cerebral performance. One never gets the feeling that Price turned a corner and found a surprise, that events ever moved in a way he had not expected, or that the characters ever took over the dialogue and found their own words. Whatever the actual case may have been, the action has all the earmarks of having been given its final dimensions according to a procrustean plan. Second, I think Price has been injured by his determination to be Southern above all else. I want to linger over this point only long enough to say that the Southernness is studied and therefore stilted. The South Price writes about is not the South of his experience but the South he has learned about in books. Even in his rendition of the society he has drawn from a literary blueprint; he does not quite play straight. One of the reasons we do not believe in Grainger and Forrest and Rob and the others is that they are not really Southerners of the first half of this century. Instead they are anachronisms, people enlightened by the later views and opinions of Reynolds Price. He has made them as he wishes they might have been, their morals reconstructed to suit the prejudices of the present, their social consciousness sharpened to fit a later time. This is romanticism in its destructive manifestation.—WALTER SULLIVAN, "Gifts, Prophecies, and Prestidigitations: Fictional Frameworks, Fictional Modes," *SwR*, Winter 1977, pp. 116–19

ALAN SHEPHERD
"Notes on Nature in the Fiction of Reynolds Price"

Critique, Volume 15, Number 2 (1973), pp. 83–94

It's very difficult now to celebrate nature. [1]

R eynolds Price is not a writer in whose work nature and the relation of man and nature seem of the first importance, as they do, in different senses, in the fiction of Faulkner, Warren, Wolfe, O'Connor, or Dickey. Whatever the difficulties, though not because of them, Price is not given to celebrating nature. Beyond the dark pastoral of *A Long and Happy Life* (1962) and the jokes-in-character turned rather grim romance of *A Generous Man* (1966), an engagement with nature is consistently evident in Price's fiction through which characters receive or miss messengers, signs, emblems from the world of nature, whole lives changed in the process. "It was a messenger, sign" [2] registers the protagonist's perception that a dying bat he has discovered on the lawn, lice-covered, weak, frightening, subsequently killed and buried, intimates his wife's approaching suicide. She does kill herself: the sign is true. So

indeed are they all, though some are inconsequential and many are misapprehended. Where do these signs originate? "The world of nature" is an answer, true as far as it goes but incomplete. More comprehensively, one says the Great World, the supernatural, whose existence, presence, and force are intimated, even affirmed, most clearly in Price's recent work. One might indeed consider the stories collected in *Permanent Errors* (1970) or *Love and Work* (1968), the author's best novel, as religious statements, though not of a conventional variety.

When to the dying bat of Price's story one adds certain prominent deer, dogs, snakes, hawks, herons, and blood suckers, one may begin to visualize a company out of Thornton W. Burgess. Such is not to be found, of course; nor are any gigantic, ageless bears or enormous heroic marlin in residence. Price is not ecological nor allegorical nor consistently symbolical. Since *A Long and Happy Life* and *A Generous Man* offer the clearest, most obvious examples of the juxtaposition of men and beasts, of natural phenomena as emblems to the perceptive or wary human observer, and thereby aid in the articulation of central concerns, we shall consider these two novels first, reserving other possibilities for other works.

Far in the woods, past Mr. Isaac's spring, Rosacoke Mustian, protagonist of *A Long and Happy Life*, walks with a friend, Mildred Sutton, walking "till we come to an open field where somebody is growing something." [3] They find, instead, a deer which looks at them, then vanishes. Years later, with Mildred dead at twenty-one in childbirth and Rosacoke herself deserted—for the time—by her boy friend, Wesley Beavers, Rosacoke returns to the spring, wondering, hoping that:

> Surely the deer was there and even if she failed to see him, wouldn't he still see her?—peeping through the cluttered woods with his black eyes, watching every step she took, twitching his tail in fright, and not remembering that other summer day, not connecting this changed tall girl with the other one he had seen, not wondering where the black girl was, not caring, not needing—only water, grass, the moss to lie in and the strength of his four legs to save his life. (32)

As a preface to any commentary on this extended and central quotation, Price's observation may be sufficient caveat:

> Python [*A Generous Man*] and deer were, for me, first—and indeed finally—python and deer, *things* grander in their own mysterious life than I or my characters could ever make them by meditation. [4]

Not to make of the passage something it is not, and honoring Price's expressed intention, one can see that the images of the deer and the spring recur throughout the novel; that they represent one aspect of nature, an abiding, self-regulating beauty, the deer or his kind surviving, the spring clearing after being muddied; and that natural phenomena display no care, comprehension, much less compassion. Further, one might conclude that Rosacoke feels a certain attraction, not envy, as she imagines the simplicity and enforced self-sufficiency of the animals' existence, particularly since her own life has become unprecedentedly complicated and since she feels strongly the need to give, with little expectation of return from Wesley.

When, finally, Rosacoke gives herself to Wesley, they are in the woods, looking, as they say, for a buck and two does which they had earlier seen crossing the road. Not surprisingly, after giving Wesley all she has left and receiving in return "I thank you, Mae" (104), not even her name, Rosacoke muses that "Him [Wesley] and that deer are something similar" (99). And so they are, though Price develops another image that perhaps more fully illuminates Wesley's nature and Rosacoke's relation to him. When first she set eyes on Wesley, he was sitting in the top of a pecan tree surveying the countryside, oblivious of her below. On several subsequent occasions, as when she is—almost hopelessly—going to ask Mrs. Beavers what she can do, has done wrong, Wesley assumes for Rosa the form of a hawk:

> his tan wings locked to ride the air for hours (if the air would hold and the ground offer things to hunt) and his black eyes surely on her. . . . Rosacoke wondered if they wouldn't touch *her*—his wings—and her lips fell open to greet him, but he was leaving, taking the music with him and the wind. (91)

One notes similarities with the deer passage, cited previously: the animal or bird attractive, free, self-sustaining, and—as she hopes—looking. Yet Rosacoke now casts herself in a Leda-like role, to be brushed, struck, uplifted, by a fierce killing bird. The point, then, is not simply that the characters are delineated and deepened through the development of such natural images, though they are, and skilfully; or that Rosacoke perceives, discovers herself and others, notably Wesley, in such figures, though—again—she does, and credibly; but that such images, experiences, are emblems of their lives and fates. To conclude the deer and hawk matter, as the novel itself concludes, Rosacoke is the (pregnant) Madonna in the Christmas pageant, whose lips fall open "as if she would greet some killing bird" (189), and who a moment later finds "her mind roaming empty and freer than it had been since the first time she saw the deer in broad daylight at the edge of the broomstraw ring" (191).

One further example may more directly establish the function of such images as messengers, signs, particularly since it is offered by the author and is not associated with any of the characters' perceptions. Rosacoke, numb, desolate, has just announced her pregnancy to Wesley, and he has asked the inevitable question: "Understand what I say—you don't know nobody but me, do you Rosa?" (168):

> So both of them failed to notice the one thing that might have helped—rare as lightning in late December, a high white heron in the pond shallows, down for the night on its late way south, neck for a moment curved lovely as an axe handle to follow their passing, then thrust in water for the food it had lacked since morning. (169)

How might the heron have helped? By offering, being, an image of sustaining natural beauty, a sign, by being received as messenger. Price is right and careful not to lift the bird from its place in nature: it is rare, beautiful; moving on, it looks at them, but it is hungry. And they miss it.

A Generous Man, perhaps better termed a romance than a novel, has suffered considerable indignities from reviewers and critics who have set it down as a playful allegorical quest for the great snake Death. That a part of the author's intention slipped past undetected is not surprising: Price's observation that he let the name Death "become one more nail in the coffin I was building for the great Southern hunt"[5] might well come as news even to the attentive reader. Nature, the importance of man's relationship to nature, or, put another way, man's being a natural creature, shows not in the guying of such mythicized solemnities as the hunt but rather in a sense of place radically altered from the one communicated in *A Long and Happy Life*. Theodore Solotaroff speaks of this

contrast: "Much of Rosacoke's world, though no less coarse, had been composed as a kind of vibrant emptiness of woods, fields, and lonely roads. Milo's was filled in by a community of misfits and clowns."[6]

One natural image may serve as a kind of *exemplum* or signal, one which reaches Milo Mustian, the book's protagonist. He is one of a sheriff's posse searching the woods for an escaped carnival snake, an enormous python, which eventually comes to a fairly bad end, shot but insured. However, the search party uncovers, almost every yard of the way, "something worthless and beautiful;" one such discovery is "the wolfish skull of a murdered weasel which Milo paused and lifted to study."[7]

> Its globed brain case was cleanly drilled by a perfect hole—bullet or tooth?—and though every uneaten muscle and nerve had been leeched away by months of rain, it was still so fierce in its rigid symmetry of fissures, foramina, nerve-paths, arches that it seemed to burn, to radiate, and Milo held it at full arm's length to ease its threat, to focus and calm his blurring eyes (the liquor had struck). . . . The stench of its secret clinging life scalded his nostrils, and he said to himself in his new man's voice but silently, "I am drunk like my Daddy the night he was killed . . . and God will punish me surer than sunrise." (132)

After further dark reflection and threatening tears, Milo "drew back the skull and flung it so hard that, striking a tree, it exploded" (132). Milo's punishment is nothing more dramatic or less inevitable than living past the end of *his* day, past the point of almost unalloyed possibility, his gifts intact and sought after, to become the charred, embittered figure who appears ten years later in *A Long and Happy Life*. One notes the weasel's terrible ferocity, unspent even in death, pointed up by the technical terminology, an aspect of and a response to nature far removed from deer, heron, or even hawk. And Milo reacts with fear, revulsion, anger, and violence.

A Generous Man does not reside in a single image; contrasting images might be cited. The drilled skull, a miniature *memento mori*, intimates something of Milo's world, discoveries and prospects. In death the weasel serves as signal or messenger of his human fate, finitude, to which Milo clearly though not presciently responds, and the tone of the passage accords well with Price's highlighted depiction of Milo's hour of splendor against the panoramic dark.

Price's two volumes of short stories, *The Names and Faces of Heroes* (1963) and *Permanent Errors*, illustrate several strategies in the delineation of man's relation to nature, man's heightened perception of his own identity in that relation. With the exception of "A Chain of Love" and the title story, *The Names and Faces of Heroes* seems an effort, largely successful, at the revivification of cliches, Price undertaking to make the worn and familiar new and his own. In "The Anniversary" Miss Lillian Belle decorates the grave of one William (Pretty Billy) Williams, who died, under not so mysterious circumstances, on the day before their wedding, years before. To receive her narrative and to offer increasingly broad hints of Billy's regular destination in his unaccompanied, all-day horseback rides in the week preceding the wedding, a young Negro boy, Wash, is introduced. Although Miss Lillian Belle, by her own assertion, is "a mighty good forgetter,"[8] Nettie Pitchford, in whose house he expired, was clearly on Pretty Billy's mind. As the story closes, Miss Lillian Belle returns home

> towards what she could see—the light, that was all, the sun on the spilled paint, the sudden flashing

reaching out to her even down here, shining like Christmas all those years ago or like her own old eyes as bright now in remembering as some proud mountain yielding the sun its flanks of snow or some white bird settling its slender wings with the softest cry into dying light. (91-2)

The two similes at the end (eyes/proud mountain/white bird) serve largely to decorate, seem an ill-considered grace note. We do not require to be told who or what Miss Lillian Belle is or resembles; the passage is cited, then, not so much because it fails to do what was done elsewhere—Rosacoke and the hawk, Milo and the weasel skull—but because it represents another strategy, considerably less successful.

Permanent Errors, as Price notes in a foreword, represents "the attempt to isolate in a number of lives the central error of act, will, understanding which, once made, has been permanent, incurable, but whose diagnosis and palliation are the hopes of continuance" (vii). By and large the stories are fine, intense, complex, sterner stuff than those in *The Names and Faces of Heroes*. Two of them will display different yet complementary perspectives on man and nature. In "Good and Bad Dreams," a six-part sequence, the first, "A Sign of Blood," introduces a husband and wife, well into the worst of times, the wife ultimately to commit suicide, the husband to survive. The wife departs the house in the first sentence yet neither escapes the other in what follows. He, feigning sleep until she is safely away, anticipates with narcissistic pleasure a free, solitary day, nine hours alone, reading, drawing, listening to music. Standing before the mirror, "an archaic Apollo," he communes with his image: "*You must change your life*" (136). Not in the mirror but out in the yard his eye catches something, unidentifiable at a distance, to be—potentially—an agent of change, and "he felt the day begin to leak from his grip" (137).

It is a bat, broken, nearly—or as he thinks at first, wholly—dead, lice-infested, the first he has ever seen up close. "He felt instantly stripped again and vulnerable, precisely in his eyes and throat" (137). Once prodded, it stretches its wings, bares pink gums and needle teeth, "and—surely—screamed."

> He knew it would rush at his face—his eyes—and he dropped the shovel to run; ran three steps. Then he stopped to see, remembering her—as though she were there in the window above him, his panic slamming at her. (138)

Here the complex and central structure of association which directs the story is identified. Without exercising excessive ingenuity, one may say that the bat, near death, intimates the wife, approaching suicide; that the husband's instinctive fear for his eyes and throat, the image in the mirror, relates to his need to protect himself from his wife, from her pain; and that in dispatching the bat, as he shortly does, he is, in his panic, "slamming at her."

Not yet a "permanent error," the husband's extant errors are, possibly, still correctable. Restoring himself through reflection on why the bat so frightens him—"Childhood icons? Halloween, vampires? Or older even, archetypal?" (139)—the husband concludes that the bat must be removed before his wife returns, because, as he is pleased to think with perhaps some self-serving justice, the sight would be too much for her. But why, he asks, ought he have to protect her? "Let her grow her own rind or shrink from sight. God knew he'd grown *his*" (139).

He kills the bat, easily, buries it, and shortly discovers why, as he thinks, it would change his life: "It was messenger,

sign." "She will kill herself." Messenger perhaps, and reflecting, again perhaps, "the celestial joker's usual taste" (140). To read the bat's advent thus is both legitimate in the story and validated by the author's practice elsewhere. The reader is also at liberty, even compelled, to consider this climactic revelation in light of the husband's known fears and desires, in terms of the association previously developed, and with respect for his insulated self-regard. That things *will* happen, that his wife is to die, may obviate certain problems for a man likely to be in attendance, even as the awareness creates others.

"A Sign of Blood" is not only amenable to comprehensible summary and fairly close analysis but represents a kind of *locus classicus*. The setting is not notably rural, as might be observed by way of objection to my remarks on Price's first two novels (deer, hawks, weasels, and herons *live* near Rosacoke and Milo). The story illuminates, complexly but clearly, one point of connection between man and nature. We see both how and why the husband interprets the sign and are left not with ultimate truth but with complementary possibilities.

The last story, of some ninety-five pages, to be considered is "Walking Lessons," which treats a young man, much resembling the protagonist of "A Sign of Blood," whose wife has recently committed suicide. To outdistance his grief he goes to visit a friend, a lapsed medical student, Blix Cunningham, now a VISTA worker among the Navajo, who has taken up with Dora Badonie, a young Navajo girl suffering through the early stages of multiple sclerosis. Understanding among the three is marginal, discontinuous; their futures bleak; the Arizona setting beautiful, awesome, ultimately desolate, terrible. The Indians are, by the VISTA man's testimony, "weirder than snakes" (162) and survive, barely and miserably, on Coke, Roma Tokay, Skoal Wintergreen Flavored Chewing Tobacco and other unknown resources. To the Indians the writer-protagonist is simply another affliction, husband of a suicide whose ghost, according to their belief, will follow him by night. He is a witch, dangerous. To Cunningham, he is an unfeeling monster, fatal.

The crisis and climax of the story evolve from the attempt of Blix, the narrator, Dora, and a few drunken hangers-on to recover Dora's grandmother's pickup truck, stuck in the mud somewhere far up the Zuñi road. After failing and losing their own truck, the original three walk out, while the narrator has cause to wonder whether he will be able to make it, be deserted, or simply be killed. The long march across country, through an alien and hostile environment, is important not as it represents a struggle of man with nature but as it affects mental processes, psychological displacement. Through the first hour of walking the cloud cover holds, the cold is bearable, even exhilarating, and keeps the snow frozen. "I had won, would win. Won what?—freedom, competence" (230). Another hour brings more penetrating cold, a new rhythm, "the coded message any fool could read: *It is possible to die. Here. Soon*" (231). Such awareness brings closer to acceptance ties that have not previously bound the narrator to his wife, dead; to Dora, knowing of her death, though she ascribes her illness to touching a snake; to Blix and Dora and their doomed union, recalling and chastising his own marriage. But the end is not yet: during a break Cunningham asks what he must do, not about getting out, but about Dora and the rest of his life; the narrator can only say that he had made *his* way out because he wanted to.

The sky opens "like a gullet, black and bottomless," the "fierce stars" by the tens of thousands stream their "titanic ray-therapy" (235), the power line, inviolate, hums overhead, the airport beacon at Gallup lifts away. The saving truth offers itself, but not as a means of escape: the narrator wanted his wife dead, but he cannot, as he is invited to do by his would-be victim, kill Dora. Finally, he asks forgiveness of his dead wife's surrogate, and—as someone begins to shoot at them from a house nearby—he steps in front of Blix. He is happy, "if being past fear and with all debts paid is a brand of happiness" (250). There remains only the last confession: "She is dead and dumb. Hammer-dead. Her name was Beth" (253).

The end, when it comes, is as radical a conversion and nearly as mystical: a new man emerges and departs for the motel. Such communication as has occurred is a triumph, framed, drawn out, properly diminished and almost cut off by miles and miles of the Zuñi road up to 7,000 feet, mud, snow, freezing cold, moonlight, cliffs. All of nature is more than backdrop, other than animate force, more concrete than influence: it is *there*, to be known, contended with, powerful, alien, instinct with life, with that of the narrator's wife among them, and clearly it is not—for a man like the narrator—to be lived with too long.

Price's more recent novel, *Love and Work*, offers variations on and apparent contradictions to the thesis that the point of contact of man and nature, as of man and the supernatural, is important and may be crucial—that its informed perception could and does change whole lives. Nature is scarcely allowed entrance in the life of Thomas Eborn, another teacher-writer, another lost soul hugging his cherished freedom, and the protagonist of the novel. To be sure, he has by heart "Tintern Abbey," which he recites while shaving, another mirror gazer, and he reads to his class "To Autumn," but neither goes well with his sophomores, and he acknowledges failure, theirs not his:

Lines like

> . . . *Nature never did betray*
> *The heart that loved her* . . .

would get at most a sneer; at least, a shrug. ("But what he means by love," Eborn thought, "they miss entirely, having wrecked the word.")[9]

Eborn himself, as shortly develops, understands love little better than he does nature, experiencing both at one or two removes, and his errors are indeed permanent. Clearing the house of his mother, recently dead, he

> saw a green shoot beneath a small table. He went there and squatted—four inches of ivy had entered the room from the wall outside, threading mortar and boards till it found a crack in the white baseboard and hung there in dimness. He reached to pull it; then stopped, exultant, his throat free from all the hands that had held it. "I am free," he thought. "This has all surrendered." (55)

Perfectly in character, he interprets the sign, messenger, happily concluding that it intimates his freedom *from* all distractions, rather as he believes his work has freed him. The self-deluding falsity of such a perspective is the burden of the novel.

Nature of any description is little in evidence in *Love and Work*, the focus turned inward, the protagonist self-absorbed, living life at second hand or attempting to recreate it in charming vignettes of his parents' meeting and courtship, which his wife, who knows him, sets down as "easy lies" (108). The message that ultimately reaches and desolates him comes directly, inescapably, without intermediary, in the presence of his mother and father, and "he sees that, always, from the first, they have faced one another only, static in ecstasy, sealed in their needlessness, one another's goal—won at last and for good." "He knows he must stand in it [the roar of light] all his life—and, worse, beyond—in full sight of them, their atrocious joy; but separate, lidless, scalding in their trail" (143).

The three novels and three stories discussed should support a few general conclusions regarding Price's sense and fictive use of nature. Price clearly espouses no program after the manner of the Agrarians. In his fiction the naturalistic perspective receives no adherence; the pastoral mode, in so far as the term describes his first novel, was a point of departure. Speaking once in an interview, Price adverted to a home truth:

> The countryside, however, has at least the advantage for the artist of permanence. It can provide for him the objects of meditation, in the presence of which the literally human qualities of his life can be understood, calmed, controlled and shaped. The profoundest examination of this dilemma is Wordsworth's preface to the *Lyrical Ballads*.[10]

His saying this does not make Price a Romantic, for he has already shown that the "literally human qualities" of life are best grasped, interpreted, and communicated in and through a place where man's status as created and creating being, where his amphibian nature and the more constant spectacle of his fall from grace, irresistibly present themselves.

Notes

1. Robert Drake, ed., *The Writer and His Tradition* (Knoxville: Univ. of Tennessee Press, 1969), p. 27. The speaker is Reynolds Price.
2. Reynolds Price, *Permanent Errors* (New York: Atheneum, 1970), p. 140. Subsequent references are to this edition.
3. Reynolds Price, *A Long and Happy Life* (New York: Atheneum, 1962), p. 6. Subsequent references are to this edition.
4. Wallace Kaufman, "A Conversation with Reynolds Price," *Shenandoah*, 17 (Spring 1966), 12–3.
5. Reynolds Price, "News for the Mineshaft," *Virginia Quarterly Review*, 44 (Autumn 1968), 658.
6. Theodore Solotaroff, "The Reynolds Price Who Outgrew the Southern Pastoral," *Saturday Review*, 26 Sept. 1970. p. 28.
7. Reynolds Price, *A Generous Man* (New York: Atheneum, 1966), p. 132. Subsequent references are to this edition.
8. Reynolds Price, *The Names and Faces of Heroes* (New York: Atheneum, 1963). p. 90. Subsequent references are to this edition.
9. Reynolds Price, *Love and Work* (New York: Atheneum, 1968), p. 17. Subsequent references are to this edition.
10. Kaufman, p. 19.

FREDERIC PROKOSCH

1908–

Frederic Prokosch was born on May 17, 1908, in Madison, Wisconsin, the son of a distinguished linguistics scholar, Edouard Prokosch, and Mathilde Dapprich, a well-known concert pianist. He was educated in this country and abroad before receiving his B.A. from Haverford College in 1926. Prokosch did graduate work in literature at the University of Pennsylvania (M.A. 1928) and Yale (Ph.D. 1933), and studied at Cambridge University on a Guggenheim Fellowship in 1937–38.

Prokosch's first published work was a novel, *The Asiatics*, which appeared in 1935. A critical and popular success, it was praised by Thomas Mann and André Gide, and was translated into seventeen languages. His second work of fiction, *The Seven Who Fled*, received the Harper Prize in 1937. Prokosch was also praised for his poetry, beginning with the publication of *The Assassin* in 1936, and in 1941 he was awarded the Harriet Monroe Lyric Prize from *Poetry* magazine; he published three more volumes of poetry, the last, *Chosen Poems*, in 1947.

In addition to his writing Prokosch was a champion squash player in France and Sweden in the late 1930s, and served with the Office of War Information during World War II in Stockholm. After the war he moved to Rome; he held a Fulbright Fellowship at the University of Rome in 1951–52, and returned to the United States the following year.

Although Prokosch produced a steady output of fiction over the years—his sixteenth volume, *America, My Wilderness*, appeared in 1972—critical interest in him steadily declined following his initial celebrity in the late 1930s. He once more drew praise, however, with the publication in 1968 of *The Missolonghi Manuscript*, a fictionalized revision of a diary believed to have been written by Byron during the last four months of his life. Prokosch's autobiographical *Voices: A Memoir* was published in 1983. Prokosch currently makes his home in the Maritime Alps region of southeastern France.

Works

POETRY

To read these poems ⟨in *The Assassins*⟩ is to encounter a new creative energy of a high order, expressing itself with a sure dominance of its medium. From his recently published first novel, *The Asiatics*, it was evident that Frederic Prokosch had the sensitiveness to word and image which constitutes poetic receptivity; this volume shows that he can bring to the materials of poetry the formal discipline needed to make a complete poem. The images are brilliantly, even bizarrely colored, and at times unexpected to the point of violence. A less skilful and less serious poet would use them merely to disturb. Here, however, through their power of evocation, their canalization into stately music, and their organization into a unified mood, they not only excite but exalt.

The mood which recurs throughout the book is a reptilian watchfulness and tension, the hushed breathing of a world between two wars. It is conveyed by images of cutting, of fever, of nocturnal fears and sudden whirring wings. The poet's theme is the search, over the exotic places of the earth, for "the concerted will and the quiet heart, and the sure and sharpened spirit." The assassins are "the dead, and the dead of spirit"; they are preparing to strike, and they elicit visions of falling cities:

> This is the final dreading
> Of history ending, an end to living and terror
>   spreading,
> The dead destroying, the living dying, the dream
>   fulfilling,
> The long night falling and knowledge failing and
>   memory fading.

These lines have analogies with the poetry of T. S. Eliot, yet Prokosch's world, one feels, has recuperative powers that are not present in Eliot's except by hocus-pocus: it is alive with a vital force that is damned, warped, tortured, but full of subtle potencies still. The realm of nature has, for transient moments, generated the realm of grace, and may do so again, after the destruction. Such is, perhaps, the framework of doctrine behind the poems; yet it is not allowed to obtrude. The realization is so consistently in sensuous terms that one must read it several times before perceiving that this is not sheer poetry of feeling.

Frederic Prokosch is an American cosmopolite not yet thirty. If there is immaturity in these poems, it is not to be found in a mechanical echoing of his masters. He appears to have learned from Valéry, Auden, and above all St.-Jean Perse, as well as from Eliot. But he has put what he has learned to his own uses, and his adaptations of Greek metrical and stanzaic patterns have a rigor of form latterly desired but not achieved by many other poets. His shortcomings, such as they are, consist in a tendency to lushness, a reliance upon exotic imagery in some places where quotidian would be more effective, and a substitution of décor for drama.—PHILIP BLAIR RICE, "A World between Two Wars," *Nation*, Oct. 3, 1936, p. 398

In the ordinary, limited sense of the word, Frederic Prokosch cannot be called a prophetic poet, yet the constantly recurring theme of imminent disaster, of darkness, of the disintegration of society, which leads, in the end, to chaos, gives his poetry ⟨in *The Carnival*⟩ the dominant tone of something very much like prophecy. Again and again, underneath the flowing music of individual poems, one encounters the horror of aimless destruction, the final flooding-over of decay; but this horror, made clear in *The Assassins*, seems to have forced the poet to give way to an "immense despair." In other words, the ruined castle, the broken column, the "Mantuan farm" have assumed a disproportionate importance.

And the dilemma is not to be hastily brushed aside. If one

insists that Prokosch is trying to escape the difficulties of affirmation, then one needs a definition of "escape" that will include Henry James, Hawthorne, Eliot, and Conrad Aiken, as well as the more obvious victims of this carelessly handled word. For, one might say, Prokosch has discovered the ruins of Angkor Thom, and like many others, he is bewitched; decay can fascinate as well as repel. Like James, Prokosch acknowledges the artistry and the flaw of the golden bowl; unlike James, he will not have it broken. Neither does Prokosch seem to have any Maggie Verver to resist and foil the rottenness; or at least his resistance has not as yet been called into vigorous play. Love, as a combative force, fails because (as John Peale Bishop wrote, reviewing the earlier book of poems) it only sharpens the poet's awareness of the general doom. The only other indications of a possible solution lie either in the acceptance of night, or in the scattered statements which appear in "Ode," a kind of spiritual autobiography:

> The javelin and the discus
> Shone in my palms and plans for a clean and living
> America. Those were the symbols of power.
> . . .
> There is a demand and a life. And the moving shapes
> Of the forsaken shall now be my forest, my legend.

What I have called a "solution" for Prokosch's dilemma lies most obviously, perhaps, in his future treatment of the proposal stated in the last lines quoted above. Any further indication of a way out comes only by remote implication; "New Year's Eve" and "Journeys" are two poems which suggest, almost exclusively by implication, another solution. But one cannot help speculating a little whether this way out can be found by holding so tenaciously to this single thread, even though the thread gives Prokosch tremendous consistency. For in spite of the insistence that it is better to "be blindly in love Than gloat on the lyric *was* or the lustrous *will be*," the actual images and examples of splendor follow a course that leads back into the past, a one-way street that has all the appearances of eventually revealing itself as a blind-alley. Yet, there is some proof that Prokosch can find affirmation in the present, and that he can see the details of experience very clearly. Now and again, however, one has the curious feeling that something has been left out, not by accident, but deliberately, as if Prokosch were unwilling to risk a temporary misunderstanding for the sake of an immediate response.

When he is writing at his best, these difficulties dwindle into insignificance. The best poems in *The Assassins* are equally as fine as the best of *The Carnival*. Yet there is a great variety within the sphere of reference which Prokosch has drawn for himself, and he manages to use a number of images and symbols over and over with a surprising freshness. Snow, flame, golden fruit, the stars, dark forests, names of places, are all woven into the texture of the writing with great skill. The sense of time is acute. The craftsmanship is obviously the result of more than a little discipline, in spite of some loose joints. The opening stanzas of "Hesperides" may well serve as an illustration:

> The two Americas are the realms of the eagle
> Where the fleet-winged shadow falls on the dance
>   and the kiss:
> Wild horses race through the storm on the skirting
>   islands and the fever of flight
> And the power forever to change and assume new
>   passions
> Is our dangerous modern talent: which, when I sailed

> Furthest away, so suddenly I remembered, so sud-
>   denly understood!
> For here too the blazing orchards and the release
> Of streams, and the fifty jubilant scents of a valley
> And the hood of snow on the roof, and the rushing
>   torrent, monstrous, eternal,
> Delight, and are long recalled, though recalled in
>   silence . . .

It is romantic poetry; the Americas envisioned by Prokosch are distant from the Americas of the other poets of his generation; distant, too, from the ordinary romantic vision. At the same time, it contains a warning not unlike the warning in the work of other younger poets, the threat of a second Middle Ages.

But the calm assurance with which the horror is expected, taken for granted, almost, may well be responsible, in part, for not only the virtues but the vices of this poetry. It may account for the lapse which produces a figure like "our little violins Again will touch our loneliness," for seas which "Enormously dispel Each hour." Inversely, it may be responsible for the haunting "Hesperides," "New Year's Eve," and "The Castle."—SAMUEL FRENCH MORSE, "Spectre over Europe," *Poetry*, Nov. 1938, pp. 89–92

An unsympathetic reader will find Mr. Prokosch a sort of decerebrate Auden, an Auden popularized for mass-consumption; and since Auden himself has been, lately, so successful in the attempt to provide one, it is hard to see in Mr. Prokosch much more than a work of supererogation. But this is a shallow view; Mr. Prokosch's success in the romantic and superficial exploitation of Auden's materials and methods is really incomparable—a triumph unmitigated by the odd intelligence and sensibility that adulterate obstinately even the laxest and most mechanical of Auden's pages. (A person who knows Auden's poetry well will notice his influence in *Death at Sea* many hundreds of times, in tone, form, images, rhetoric and content. Mr. Prokosch's earlier poetry is less singularly derivative.) Mr. Prokosch has sublimated Auden's worst vices and Auden's easiest virtues into a method; it is the mechanical operation of this method that produces the mass of *Death at Sea*—the poems pour out like sausages, automatic, voluptuous, and essentially indistinguishable. The "Love" that is the *deus ex machina* of Auden's worst lapses is the tutelary deity of Mr. Prokosch's poetry: his world-view is too sentimental and palely irresponsible—too *fashionable*—to be valued as much more than an effective romantic pose. He replaces Auden's Freudianism with a psychology that amounts to—*To know anything is to forgive anything*; and for Auden's demi-Marxism he substitutes the *Weltanschauung* of "Manfred" or a Sunday-supplement Spengler. (He has a Shelleyan fondness for the atlas as a bedside book; the argument of many of his poems is virtually, Death and darkness fall over Samarkand, Bokhara, Timbuctoo—fall, in fact, over the great big world.) The list or panorama, a tangle of picturesque details resolved by the blankest of generalizations, is his favorite structural device: *the consumptive cries on the dear Danubian banks, the Senegalese sheds his scalding tears beside the Niger, the Eskimo weeps icicles into Hudson Bay—why, they're all crying*: and you have your poem. (You're wrong if you think the *dear Danubian banks* is mine.)

But do not let me give the impression that Mr. Prokosch's poems are failures; the effects are second-hand and second-rate—but oh, so effective! The surface of the poetry has the immediate appeal the able and sensational popularization of a new technique always has; and under that surface bubbles the same old romanticism that infected us all in our cradles. How many ladies' clubs yet unorganized will prickle to the raptures of this verse! Naturally, not everyone will be pleased with such easy and florid romanticism; I read the poems with annoyance and mild pleasure, and thought Mr. Prokosch's obvious gifts childishly misused. But so much glitter and flow and scope have turned better heads than mine. On the dust-jacket of *Death at Sea* are testimonials by Stephen Spender, Robinson Jeffers, Michael Roberts, Edwin Muir and *The Manchester Guardian*—and others by Yeats and Eliot are referred to; I mention these to bear out my last statement, and to show that my opinion is a dissenting one which the reader should be properly cautious about accepting.—RANDALL JARRELL, "Poets Old, New and Aging," NR, Dec. 9, 1940, p. 800

NOVELS

The Asiatics is not a novel, if by a novel one means a narrative wherein characters are not only presented but also portrayed and developed. There is here only brilliant presentation in rapid succession of a series of disconnected although fundamentally similar persons. The slight and only unifying external thread is the "I" of the author. There is, however, a unity deeper than this; it is the unity of a continuing and exclusive point of view which sees only that which it is prepared to see, only the persons within this chosen scope of vision, and of those persons only the aspects it prefers.

This scope, this aspect, is best expressed in the author's own words:

> Take away our clothes, our food, our liquor, our quaint sexual pleasures, our fatiguing little conversations, and our loathsome excitements about this and that; what's left? . . . Nothing's left, because we never really believed anything, we never rose above the world of objects, we never deep down within us were alive. It's the age of inversion, the negative age.

But within these limits—and one must accept the author's right to act upon his own point of view, and I have no quarrel with this one more than another, except that people who hold it do not seem able to get much fun out of being alive—this is an extraordinarily clever book. That is, Frederic Prokosch describes the world of objects—and in this world are to be included his people—with a physical closeness which fills our nostrils with reek and scent, which sets alive din and music in our ears, and sometimes makes the stomach sick with its reality. The section on India, particularly, portrays with terrifying accuracy a certain part of Indian human nature.

But I am interested in this book especially for what it symbolizes. It is a fine example of a type of novel now being written by certain young writers, wherein is to be found extraordinarily accurate and vivid portrayal of physical sensation without any further penetration into or understanding of life. Sense leads to nothing, means nothing, beyond itself. Characters are conceived as bodies only, moving blindly in the dark. We do not know what they think and feel. About them is always the smell of death and corruption. I am reminded of an old Chinese superstition which teaches that when death comes, the three souls leave the body first, and only gradually and reluctantly do the seven earthy spirits depart, so that there is an interval when the souls—that is, the seat of intelligence and moral sense—are gone, and the body is given over to the earthy spirits. Then even though he were a good man in life the corpse does the most blindly evil deeds, and he must be bound with ropes lest he harm even those whom he once loved. So in a sort of phosphorescent native evil the characters of this book stir blindly upon its pages.

It is not fair, I think, to call this book *The Asiatics*, not only because, physically, so little of Asia is included—Japan and China and Russia are omitted—but because the whole of the robust, active, humorous, everyday aggressive life in all Asia is omitted, and this is to omit most of Asia, after all.

But it is, of course, an author's right to omit all he likes. And within the small circle this author has chosen, it must be fully granted that he gives us a brilliant, though glancing, and glittering array of pictures. To read it is to have the experience, with the author, of moving through strange and alien crowds, to see for a moment the turn of an unknown head, the curve of foreign lips, the sound of melancholy, unfamiliar singing, the touch of a stranger's hat and too caressing hand, and then to pass on.—PEARL S. BUCK, "People and Scenes of Modern Asia," SR, Nov. 16, 1935, p. 6

In *The Seven Who Fled*, Frederic Prokosch's Harper prize novel, we find *The Asiatics* elaborated into frozen symmetry. The subject matter, though more rationalized in the second novel, is essentially the same. Asia is Mr. Prokosch's Magic Mountain. To Asia Mr. Prokosch's contemporary Europeans come, not, as one might think, to escape from reality but, as he thinks, to live cheek by jowl with it. On the hot, barren plains and the terrible mountains of Asia life achieves a super-real incandescence; burning as in a tubercular fever it transforms itself more rapidly than in Europe to its ultimate ashes. Decomposition of the flesh and degeneration of the character are in Asia accelerated; yet flesh and character, in their brief lifetime, are more intensely, extremely themselves than in the padded world of the West. For Mr. Prokosch's characters a trip through the interior of Asia automatically becomes a voyage of self-exploration, an excursion into self-consciousness. In *The Asiatics* one introspective globe-trotter, a young American, shoulders the burden of discovery and definition; in *The Seven Who Fled* the weight is distributed among seven Europeans—an Englishman, a Belgian, a Russian, a German, an Austrian, a Spanish lady, and a Frenchman.

To warrant this division of responsibility one would expect a rather sharp and meaningful differentiation of experience. Yet one finds the reverse. The outlines of personality, feeling, and behavior are blurred until the characters seem to dissolve into one another. Even the physical adventures do not differ notably from one character to the next—cold, privation, disease, and compulsive sexual erraticism are the common lot; while on the spiritual plane each person finds in Asia but one thing—heightened sensibility, which is reached via physical hardship, death or its contemplation, and memory. Searching out the meaning of life Mr. Prokosch's people come upon it in the very molecules of existence, in the assaults of natural objects and forces upon the nervous system, or, at secondhand, in the memory of former assaults made in childhood and adolescence, when the receiving apparatus was most highly tuned. Since Mr. Prokosch's characters are mere borderline cases, minor decorative personalities from the fringes of Western society, not actors but sufferers on the Western stage, they have no validity as symbols of either Europe or its respective states; and the novel breaks down into a simple catalogue of sensations, a confession of the meaninglessness of meaning. The characters, indeed, have so little personal identity, so little individual clearness of tone, that the novel in the end reduces itself to a catalogue of the author's sensations, the author's private confession.

The range of the author's sensations is narrow, and for all his admiration of intensity the sensations themselves are not very vigorous. His book is full of "little spasms," "little plans," "little gardens," "little moments." He is a connoisseur of the gentle, the tender, the delicate, the pure, the simple, the sweet, the hesitant; and an academician of the tremor. "Touching" is his favorite designation for the people he likes and the situations he relishes; and the "viciousness" and "corruption" which so much enchant him must always coexist with the gentler qualities. Thus in Mr. Prokosch's novel, for all its cosmic aspirations, its League of Nations personnel, its dedication to violence and the doctrine of extremes, the Magic Mountain becomes a dwarf flower garden, and the terror of the super-real expresses itself in an elegant *frisson*.—MARY MC-CARTHY, "The Latest Shudder," *Nation*, Sept. 18, 1937, p. 296

The author of *The Asiatics* carries his own Asia with him, and his publishers do wrong to suggest that in his new novel "he has forsaken Asia for America and has written a far more realistic story." His Asia is not the kind you can easily dispense with—sliding another scene behind the characters: it is a heavy rich romantic mood which has nothing to do with geography, the mood of Mr. de la Mare's *Arabia*, and it absorbs quite blatantly anything which may be of use to it—*Hindoo Holiday* supplied the material for one of the best chapters in *The Asiatics*, just as the commentator of *The River* has helped to write some pages in *Night of the Poor*. One cannot call this plagiarism: some writers use and adapt other men's lives; Mr. Prokosch seems to use and adapt the books he has read. He has immense gusto for literature—there is something very young, very innocent and very greedy about his novels; he doesn't discriminate well between flavours so long as they are spiced enough, and he thrusts in the ruthless gunman out of the films and the motherly prostitute out of how many young men's novels just as they stand, leaving them to be digested by the overpowering juices of the romantic mood. They glimmer oddly and thinly up at us out of his maw, the skeletons of other people's people.

Night of the Poor is the story of a boy, Tom, who was meant to catch a train at Prairie du Sac in Wisconsin for his family home in Texas; his uncle with whom he had lived was dead, and he was leaving one secure way of life for another. But it didn't turn out that way. The old car kept breaking down on the road to the station until it was hopeless to expect to catch the train, so off he went suddenly, like the character in a fairy story, with Pete, a hired man, leaving the other two of his uncle's men fiddling with the car. "To the other two clung the scents of the farmyard; farmyard motions, farmyard calm. But all over Pete hung the sunny, yawning, prowling fragrance of the land itself." So the Odyssey begins, the dangerous tramp through Illinois, Indiana, Kentucky, Louisiana. Pete kills a man over a black girl and they are hunted by the police: Tom loses Pete and picks up other companions—a girl he loves who goes off with a New Mexican and whom he finds again at his journey's end, stray people who are supposed to represent the unemployed migrants of America, but who are curiously undifferentiated. They all have ideas about life, death, "all that immortality crap," philosophy, "that old geezer Aristotle": the background is orientally rich with birds and wild flowers and coca-cola signs; he sees a lynching. . . . The writing is often admirable—the killing of a snake: "It wriggled a moment, then lay still, and began to exude its acid scent of death"; sometimes tiring—because all the people Tom meets (they can be distinguished no other way) are physically monstrous with goitres or sores or just fat. We get a little weary of reading: "She was the fattest woman he'd ever seen. She bulged, she billowed, she cascaded. Each moment seemed as if it must be

her last before bursting . . ." and so on for a paragraph. Nevertheless, this book does not belong to the great fictional morass. It is a genuine imaginative achievement to have made a kind of opium dream out of the burst sandwich-bag, the empty cider bottle, the Cameo cinema and the co-ed girl. —GRAHAM GREENE, *Spec*, Oct. 20, 1939, p. 556

Since Frederic Prokosch's original success in the Nineteen Thirties with *The Asiatics* and *The Seven Who Fled*, he has continued to fashion in the manner of Petronius and Apuleius a series of picaresque novels, highly imaginative works which owe little or nothing to those novels of manners and of character which have dominated Western literature for over a century.

In his latest book, *Nine Days to Mukalla*, he has produced yet another variation on his central legend, disaster and flight, anticipation and arrival. The plot's construction will be familiar to his readers. Four people en route from India to Europe, crash in an airplane on an island near the coast of Arabia. They are forced to travel overland and by sea to Mukalla, a town from which they will be able to rejoin their civilization. Before the journey's end, however, two have perished; those who survive die, too, in another sense, since they are changed, demoralized by suffering, by disaster, by encounters with fantastic strangers and unfamiliar powers.

Yet despite a great deal of superficial excitement, the drama of their flight is essentially unhuman. They are not men and women, but archetypes whose relationships lack immediacy. They are shadows engaged in ritual, their deeds possessing meaning only in relation to the sensuous world, to the natural world at its most implacable—a glittering, heightened place of symbol where shadow-figures cross shining deserts yet leave no single mark of passage upon the sand. As in Prokosch's other books, it is not the people but the design which matters: a vision of human beings shipwrecked and forced to flee through hostile country, harried by a nameless enemy, by that "antique horror prowling across the face of the world . . . half chaos, half intention, half elemental and half human; something which civilized man must battle forever, must be killed by or kill."

And this horror? This enemy? In context, Prokosch means it to be that will to destruction so remarkable in our race. But, in a larger sense, the amorphous evil which provides the tension in all his works is, finally, the fact of death itself, the grim reward of many journeys, the cold truth beyond Mukalla. His voyagers combat their enemy with the only weapon they possess: they live and, living, like Kafka's creatures, they attempt the castle because they must.

Prokosch's gifts, specifically, are lyric not psychological—unusual equipment for a twentieth century novelist. In the one book where he tried for a novel of relationship, *The Idols of the Cave*, he failed because he could not manage the psychological counterpoint which has been the main concern of the post-Jamesian novel. Yet, at his best, as in this work, he writes a rich evocative line with which he creates sensuous worlds he has never seen except with the eye of a superlative imagination. Here, once again, he renders that vision which is obsessively his own: the traveler in strange country, the sunburned Ulysses of his poems, the alien who moves across time, anticipating with a melancholy fascination his last arrival, a private death in some ironically gleaming land.—GORE VIDAL, "Disaster and Flight," *NYTBR*, March 22, 1953, p. 6

Perhaps, at this moment, someone in Tacoma or Birmingham is working away at a book as bad as Frederic Prokosch's fourth published novel 〈*A Ballad of Love*〉. This is doubtful, because a novel as bad as this one requires a sensibility almost as specialized as a good writer's—one which has a tremendous flair for literary debris.

"The meaning? The message? That is for you to decide," says the narrator of this non-book. But who can indicate even a plot-line, let alone a message? Henni, "born in the woods of Carinthia one summer morning in 1914—on the very day, as luck would have it, when a shot was fired in Sarajevo," goes to America, wanders into almost-people on three continents, quiveringly loves some of them, and ends up alone in Paris after World War II.

The jacket blurb invites us to remember Camus' claim that Frederic Prokosch is the inventor of the "geographical novel, in which he mingles sensuality with irony, lucidity with mystery." The Prokosch of this book is not up to captions for postcards. Here is an absolutely typical passage of his "geographical" prose:

> Finally spring began to crawl over that great lonely territory. Fragrant streams came trickling from the hills and foaming waterfalls poured into the gullies. The deep of the forest was filled with infinitesimal bubbling noises. Under the fresh new sunlight the pebbles in the river shone like topaz. Puffy clouds moved luxuriantly over the empty black fields and the cows wandered forth through their soggy pastures.

Such beauties are pieced out with lists of books, dishes, place-names, and with conversations like the following:

> "Look," said Paolo, "at the stars. I've never seen them so brilliant."
> "Millions and millions," said Stella. "It's rather terrifying, isn't it?"
> "Just think, dear," said Paolo. "We're nothing but grains of dust in the universe."
> "It makes life seem desperately short. And utterly pointless," said Stella.
> "Come," said Paolo, somewhat nervously. "Let's change the subject. Let's talk about Art."

If it is claimed that this passage burlesques vapidity, then the whole novel is burlesque, for its vapidity is unflawed. Nor can its emptiness be disguised by what the blurb calls its subject, "the multifarious forms of human yearning." A novel organized as variations on a theme must be subsidized by narrative and style. There is no such subsidy here, not meat enough for a shadow.—RICHARD G. STERN, "Lost in Geography," *NYTBR*, Oct. 30, 1960, p. 49

Mr. Prokosch's first novel, *The Asiatics*, was published in 1935. It was a romantic story of faraway places and it was a great popular and critical success in Depression America, as was also his second novel, *The Seven Who Fled*, another story of adventure in mysterious lands. Prokosch gathered rather more than his share of impressive dust-jacket quotes from figures as august as Yeats and Thomas Mann. He published several volumes of poetry which came in for similar praise. Young Dylan Thomas was to acknowledge his influence. Prokosch's novels were widely translated and he became a literary figure of international stature, being especially admired in France and Germany. He was young and famous—and handsome—and the world was his home.

And then it all gradually slipped away. He continued to publish novels. The current one is his fifteenth and his twenty-second book. But by the end of World War II the public was looking for a new crop of involved writers and Prokosch's romantic note was *passé*. He attempted, in more than one book, a more "realistic" approach to his material but these efforts were not entirely successful and he has always returned, with better luck, to a world of romance and adventure and mystery and a touch of the supernatural.

The Missolonghi Manuscript affords Prokosch an opportunity to work within his natural bent but with the helpful form and restraint of fictionalized biography. The novel purports to be the last notebooks of Byron, written as he approaches his end as a dilettante revolutionary in Greece. Life, to be sure, provides incidents rather than plots but Byron's vivid, peripatetic existence is a natural for Prokosch's talents and Byron's melancholy summing-up provides us with an emotional unity if not a factual truth about the poet's life. There is the difficulty of putting words into the mouths of great writers that will do at least fictional justice to their real talents, but, while Prokosch's "poetic" style is hardly what we would expect of Byron, it is not implausible.

It is, however, still a little difficult to believe that we are listening to the real Byron talk. The attempts at verisimilitude are superficial so far as any psychological probabilities are concerned. For one thing, the fictional Byron's death-bed "frankness" about his sexual adventures would, I suspect, shock the original Byron considerably—though the novel is not notably shocking in contemporary terms. It has, in fact, the note one so often encounters in current novels of working very hard at being outrageous without quite making the grade. The whole "frankness" situation must be quite enraging to the novelist now in his 60s, say, who wanted to be naughty 30 years ago but did not dare and who is now forced into a slightly embarrassed exploitation of the new freedom. It seems to me that some of the innuendoes in the novels of Prokosch's early years were considerably more ear-reddening than the current bluntness, but then of course my ears don't redden as easily now.

It may well be that Byron's life was even more irregular than is popularly supposed. Indeed, the putative incest in his career is sloughed over rather quickly in order to afford him time for a shot at everything this side of necrophilia. I only found it difficult to believe that the real Lord Byron could have been so obsessed with the excremental functions, however "natural" he may have regarded them.

But these are not major cavils. More seriously, if we are to judge the book with any stringency as a biography, *The Missolonghi Manuscript* is flawed by Mr. Prokosch's reading himself into Byron's emotional and intellectual life. Some external parallels do suggest themselves. Byron, as Prokosch, came to early fame and material success only to watch it drain away with the years. Criticism and neglect followed the early acclaim. Like Byron, Prokosch has been a wanderer in the earth, the embodiment of his own picaresque heroes, an "internationalist" before his time.

As to whether at 36 Byron looked back upon his life with quite this melancholy languishing, that is quite another matter. Of course the figure we have before us in the novel may not be Prokosch any more than it is Byron. It may well be the same sad and handsome young man who wandered through the pages of *The Asiatics*, the young man whose pleasures were the poetry and mystery of existence and whose melancholy and wonder were a response not to any actual circumstances of his own existence or specific concern with the problems of Greece, say, or Vietnam, but a generalized, almost glandular, response to life itself. But to life in faraway corners of the world, where violence can explode as in real life, and the grit of life is as abrasive—but always with an ambience of the "poetic." It is life in soft focus, the camera angles are artful and the technicolor is always tasteful.

Prokosch is reported, curiously, as feeling an affinity with Nabokov, and the suggestion is instructive. They are both "realistic" within a poetic context. In many ways Nabokov is far less a realist than Prokosch but Nabokov's realism attains a magic quality which Prokosch aims at in his way but does not achieve because of some technical inadequacy or failure of larger artistic vision—or both. Nabokov's Lolita becomes a real person but Prokosch's Lord Byron becomes a fictional one.
—WILLIAM JAMES SMITH, *Com*, April 12, 1968, pp. 111–14

AL PURDY

1918–

Alfred Wellington Purdy was born on December 30, 1918, in Wooler, Ontario, the son of a farmer and his wife. He attended Trenton Collegiate Institute and Albert College, and served with the Royal Canadian Air Force for six years during World War II. While establishing his career as a poet he worked in various factories for fifteen years after the war. He has taught at Simon Fraser University, in British Columbia; at Loyola University in Montreal; at the University of Manitoba; and at the University of Western Ontario.

Purdy's first book of poetry, *The Enchanted Echo*, was published in 1944, and was followed by more than two dozen additional volumes. A collection of his verse, *Being Alive: Poems 1958–78*, appeared in 1978. He was the recipient of the Governor-General's Literary Award in 1966 for *The Cariboo Horses*, and the following year received the Canadian government's Centennial Medal. His additional honors include the Canada Council's Senior Literary Award (1973), the A. J. M. Smith Award (1974), and the Jubilee Medal (1978). Purdy was elected to the Academy of Canadian Writers in 1977.

Purdy married in 1941 and is the father of a son. He lives in Ameliasburgh, Ontario.

DENNIS LEE
"Running and Dwelling: Homage to Al Purdy"
Saturday Night, July 1972, pp. 14–16

"The Runners" is a touchstone in Al Purdy's poetry. Two Gaelic prisoners, brother and sister, are put ashore by Norsemen to explore a minute part of what is now Canada. They are not at home in the strange land and cannot begin to dwell in it; so they run. Yet they are also not at home with their European masters, to whom they choose not to return; so they go on running. Yet they are still not at home in the land, so they continue to run . . .

Donald Creighton undertook to order the history of our running and dwelling. George Grant has thought its coherence. And Al Purdy explores that history as presence by making poems.

Many of Purdy's poems are themselves acts of running and dwelling. For three and a half decades he has hauled his receiving apparatus east and west, north and south through Canada. He has discovered, feature by feature, the thing we knew beforehand, but which we cannot believe until its particulars are made real in words: that we are half spooked and half at home here; that we cannot master the space we have been thrown in, yet are claimed by it and will be at home nowhere else; that we cannot return in time to Europe, yet have learned from it the vocabulary of being human and can at most speak partial sentences of our own in that language.

Purdy runs through Canada—or, as he often insists, he limps, shambles, crashes and staggers through Canada—in search of dwelling places in the space and time we inhabit. The places he has found—pre-eminently Roblin Lake, but with real temporary way-stations in Newfoundland, Baffin Island, Vancouver and the rest—he marks with poems. And around those poems lies the vast eerie space of our half continent.

Similarly, the times he has found authentic—U.E.L. time, as it drifts like wispy snake-fences into the ground of the present, the enduring time of prehistoric artisans, the personal time of his own loves and hates, his parents' and grandparents'—are tenuous moments in a field that loops back to Stone Age men and out through intergalactic light years.

The full complexion of our dwelling, in Purdy's poetry, will come clear later. But we can note as fact one, that for him our ancestors were those runners who did not dwell naturally on the continent; and that any dwelling is therefore an achievement—as in "My Grandfather's Country"—which is fragile in the great reaches of the country, and in the greater reaches of space-time. He speaks those reaches, and we meet again on the page the fragility we already knew.

Purdy locates our dwelling in time and space; he *places* us. That is a job for a lifetime, and it is what he has lived for. He has pursued the job with the obsessive sense of vocation of a David Thompson or Etienne Brûlé. That sense is sheer folly to balanced men, and by some freak accident it has led once again to the achievement of history.

Comparison with the great explorers is not an idle figure. Purdy has replicated, on the human plane we inhabit, the essential acts of the explorers: travelling, charting, naming, the tenuous beginnings of dwelling. If world (as Heidegger has it) is earth dwelt in and known by men, he has moved in world, where the explorers travelled over earth. But to explore our part of world and report what is there—what is actually there, not what maps from abroad say should be there—is as difficult and heroic an achievement as the great feats of four and three centuries ago.

To report on world as we live it is not just to recite the inventory of our places, times and acts. It is to embody, in words, our historic modes of dwelling here. Then the words are consonant with the world from which they arise; they *are* world, for they embody our ways of being on earth with a first clarity. Others have done part of our inventory, as has Purdy; but he is the first to embody our ways of being world.

Purdy's grand peer on this continent, of course, is Walt Whitman. The breadth of Whitman's catalogues, like the breadth of Purdy's travelogues, ensures the coverage of Significant National Data. But while that has its own importance, it is not germane. For Whitman was the first to achieve, in poetry, the gestures of being an American human being. He cast his discovery of the Americans' presence in North America in terms that were consonant with that presence: megalomania, celebration of progress and naïve victory over place, and the triumphs of energetic willing of countless atomized individuals, each named Walt Whitman.

During the last fifteen years Purdy has achieved the same thing above the 49th parallel, defining the gestures of being an English-Canadian human being by enacting them in poems. He casts his discovery of the northern dwelling in the new world in terms equally consonant with *our* way of being here: elegiac manic-depression, celebration of the silencing victory of place, and the bare endurance of men and women whose names and faces blur, but whose lust and whose moments of authentic making do not crumble wholly. Between them, Whitman and Purdy accomplish the first native mapping of North America. There is a century between their projects, but there have also been centuries between the exploration of neighbouring geographies.

I am not sure whether the question is even valid, which is the better poet; certainly I cannot answer it, as I am so much at home in the one and so little in the other. What counts is that each did what was called for: he discovered what was actually there in his half of the continent—because he could *see* it outside him, by some miracle of vision, and because it was already inside him teeming for its language. Purdy is our Whitman, as Whitman was America's Purdy. But to be Canada's Whitman is to write, by definition, unlike Walt Whitman. After we note the generic kinship of two continental explorers, each is defined by what he grew out of and set down on paper. (The same thing applies in Quebec; if a poet there has discovered his country in this way it is probably Gaston Miron, and he writes like Gaston Miron.)

This places Whitman and Purdy as new world poets; it does not rank them among other poets in the history of English literature. For what it matters, both seem to me in that context middling poets of the second rank.

What I mean by seeing Purdy as the major explorer of the Canadian experience of being-here has only marginally to do with the junkets recorded in his poetry, and almost nothing to do with any attempts he has made to define a Canadian essence. Even though Purdy's compulsion to see the country again and again is a necessary part of his exploration, it is not the essential part; and even though an identity crisis is near the centre of Canadian dwelling, it does not produce poetry when it is being resolved by verbal formulations of identity.

Purdy's reflexes are native, and it is in this that his essential exploring consists. He has responded to things that go on here as a man who is at home here; that is, he has responded with that stubborn, half-at-home, half-alien ambivalence of the runners—even though by now it has necessarily grown more complex.

Purdy cannot be European, and will not be American; yet he endures here, not knowing what he is to be. In *that baffled enduring*, he lives the paradox of this half of the continent. For we have been in North America but not whole-heartedly of it; and somehow we have also been of North America, but not whole-heartedly in it; and as we have lived those contradic-

tions—consistently, though in confusion—our primal necessity has been to survive. Incredibly, for two hundred years, Canadians have chosen—despite our friends abroad, and despite the business community and the financial institutions and the Liberal Party at home—to survive, and to endure our contradictions. For Quebec, that survival has had a positive goal: the perpetuation of the French fact, with all that implies for language, church and culture. For English Canada, it has been a different kind of survival: that of enough autonomous space that we could go on, in confusion, seeking a way of being here which would recognize we were not in Europe, and yet would recognize the American way as a dead end. In Purdy's best poetry that lucid confusion and that choice are present, not as a formulation of identity but right in the grain of the poem, issuing from the ontology of our dwelling here.

When he contemplates the country north of Belleville, Purdy sings and stammers instinctively that we belong to the land—it does not belong to us, we are not American. Yet he is unable to see a way for men to live here in cities under the sensed dominion of earth and sky—we are not pre-technological Europeans. Yet he goes on enduring, and trying confusedly to find a way to be here—he is Canadian. The confusion, of course, is not mere scatter-headedness; it is lucidity about what is impossible in our fate.

As he bends elbows with the drunks in the Quinte Hotel he celebrates the sodden levelling energies of the American "common man," because he is one; and he is still gripped by the traditional and aristocratic demands of "great art," because he makes it; and he will go on, ruefully and bawdily out the other end of the poem, enduring that contradiction, which can in principle not be resolved and which to live is an astonishment.

Purdy's Canada is Upper Canadian, of course. One would no more try to disguise this than think of apologizing for it. But I cannot see that anyone's experience of the country has ever been rooted in all the real estate contained by our geographical boundaries—and see nothing in the exhortation that it should be but the plea for an unnatural and crackpot virtuosity, like playing five musical instruments at once. A poet who merely wrote from sea to sea would merely be a bore in motion. The locale of Purdy's roots does not limit the quality of his exploration, and in fact the enduring contradiction that we are can be approached only through one's own roots and region.

It is in getting the instinctive knowledge of how things are for us down on paper—not in the words but behind them, and beneath them and through them—that Purdy has mapped Canadian world, instance by instance, with an ampleness and a beery precision that Lampman, Pratt and Layton, good poets though they often are, scarcely embark on. To this extent, that he has embodied the tensions of our dwelling here in the musculature and movement of his poems, Purdy has himself opened room for us to dwell. We can comment at length, some day, on the quality of the workmanship and the suitability to our climate of what he has built. But what we need to notice at the beginning is that we did not have poetry before that opened our dwelling here; and now we do.

To carry this approach to Purdy where it wants to go, one would have to think in detail about the structure of his sense of our time and our space; about the gaps in his exploration; about the characteristic points at which his imagination kindles and his words go incandescent; and about his insistence on bad taste, self-consciousness and mawkishness as elements in his own speaking voice. I have not attempted these things here, nor have I looked at the private poems which have been Purdy's other vocation. It is unfortunate that there is still no single volume through which to approach his life work satisfactorily. His recent *Selected Poems* is so misleadingly titled as to be almost a con job, though by pairing it with *Love in a Burning Building* you can get most of the essential Purdy.

There are writers who should get the Nobel Prize before Al Purdy—Ezra Pound, for instance, Pablo Neruda, Jorge Luis Borges, Jean Genet, Elias Canetti. And there are some who should get it after him who will undoubtedly get it first, for the assumptions scarcely exist—even in his own country—within which Purdy's achievement can be discerned, much less assessed with finality. Meanwhile, though: homage to a poet of surpassing excellence.

OFELIA COHN-SFECTU
"The Privilege of Finding an Opening in the Past: Al Purdy and the Tree of Experience"
Queen's Quarterly, Summer 1976, pp. 262–69

One of the most famous moments in contemporary literature is that in Sartre's *La Nausée*, when Antoine Roquentin contemplates a tree in the public gardens of a small French town. The experience the young historian undergoes at the sight of the dark mass of roots brutally plunging through the ground is the celebrated existentialist sickness—the revulsion and horror caused by the realization that under the veneer of individual manifestations, there is only one ultimate reality: matter, infinite and viscous—man himself being not the center of any creation, but merely another form of physical substance.[1] There is in contemporary Canadian literature an equally interesting moment: Al Purdy in the Baffin Islands (*North of Summer*) looking at some dwarf Arctic trees and noticing, full of contempt, their desperate struggle to survive for a short time in a hostile environment. Yet suddenly aware that their roots "must touch permafrost/ice that remains ice for ever," that they "use death to remain alive," and therefore turn to movement something which by definition is a halt, the poet is impressed by "the dignity of any living thing," no matter how humble a form of life it represents.[2]

In both cases, the reader is presented with moments of perfect identification of thought and actual existence, moments which jolt the individual and oblige him to break with previously formed patterns of thought. Ambivalent in nature, such acts of consciousness can maim the human being with the knowledge of his impermanence and insignificance, or on the contrary, can become the basis for man's transcendence of his own earthly life, without ceasing to embrace it. In Purdy's case, moments of self-awareness represent at once burdens that put his spirit in peril, and points of departure towards a mode of existence more authentic than the merely biological one. In this context, the tree, with its roots penetrating deeply into the soil and branches forking toward the sky, becomes the most appropriate symbol for his attempt to order his consciousness of human reality, and put himself in harmony with the patterns he discerns in the universe.

Indeed, the image of the tree crystallizes the basic postulate of a philosophy in terms of which the most characteristic mode of human experience is not the concept of time as formulated by science, but the psychological time of the individual. This psychological time is conceived by the Canadian poet not as a smooth, horizontal continuum flowing away from a past into a future, but symbolically as a vertical axis representing the subjective, dynamic relation between events which have happened, are happening and will happen. It is the existence of this inner axis that explains the transcendental unifications of experience felt by the human being, which make past and future appear intensely real and quivering with potency. Purdy, therefore, attempts to achieve release from a solely physical existence by descending subjectively to the level of mythical roots, in order to emerge better equipped into the ever-distending scope of experience. He does not dismiss as unimportant man's horizontal movement in time according to clocks and calendars, yet he advocates an incessant exercise in spiritual athletics with a view to transcending the limitations which the human condition imposes upon the individual, and thus, giving dignity to an existence which might otherwise be regarded as a purely biological accident. Purdy considers the possibility of engaging mentally in a vertical temporal motion rather than simply following a horizontal sequence of moments as the major point of difference between man and other species on earth. This human uniqueness he singles out for literary analysis, and if his particular interest lies with the past spiritual roots of man, it is because he believes that at the level of roots, the integration between the individual and the general is achieved, and death is conquered by life in vital and mental form.

In *Wild Grape Wine*, Purdy refers to "lost children of the time"—a descriptive phrase which is most fundamental to his discussion of the human condition. Man's life is not only insignificant within the general cosmic framework, but also subject to crucial spatial and temporal limitations. Hence the poet states that the living of a life is similar to the crossing of a field—not a hospitable one, but a "dark landscape" where the hostility of the natural environment is augmented by man's behaviour towards his fellow men. With this spatial index attached to it, the crossing is not a pleasant walk, but, as we see in the *Selected Poems*, a precarious sequence of "backbreaking days / in the sun and the rain." Given a temporal index too, human life is also fugitive and tragically short. One need only breathe or sigh, and everything changes from "is" to "was," taking man closer and closer to his final destination. And when that moment comes, somebody knocks on the door of a man's life, and though he would like to answer: "I am not at home / I am not at home," he has to step out and meet the caller. The transitoriness and unique direction of human life are irreducible. And when Purdy raises his eyes in search of an answer, it is a sky empty of everything that he sees: only death as an absolute and infinite nothingness.

Confronted with the question of his destiny in a world which surrounds him with unintelligible and uncontrollable elements, the individual feels at once lost and trapped. Trapped not only into existence, for he is not able to decide his own birth, but once born, trapped within a unique frame of motion: passage from childhood, when he rides, as in *Cariboo Horses*, "naked with the summer in his mouth," to old age, when he waits in stupefaction for life "to jerk to a halt." The entire world appears to him inhabited by huge black flies reigning supreme over foxes, which at night remove their teeth for safekeeping, and old women who stuff their dentures up their rectums. At the same time, forced by reality to admit that he is only a "protein formula" able by accident to contemplate its own destiny, and watch all its aspirations end up in damp ground, man sees his own existence as grotesque, superfluous and possessed by a nightmarish quality. Indeed, under the pressure of the blend of agony and screaming which is life, no positive orientation seems to be able to relieve the despair which causes Purdy's cry in *Poems for All the Annettes*: "if that's being human it's best done with."

Yet, fully aware of the distinction which exists between time in nature and time in human experience, Purdy resists the temptation of nihilistic despair. If any life is to cross a field, he reasons, then human life is "to cross many fields," for the scientific time is only partially the time of the human being. There are aspects of time which, though not meaningful within the framework of objective time, are significant in the context of human experience. Hence time can be ransomed once man achieves the essential step of disengaging himself from the restrictive matrix of the objective. "All hours the day begins," says the poet, proclaiming the independence of the time defined as psychological from the one called scientific. With human specificity as the tightrope that conscious man walks, Purdy feels free to explore the complex world of the mind.

What he discovers is that the concomitant existence of the objective and the subjective makes each present moment more meaningful, that an experiential depth denied to the merely sensory perception can be achieved by the imposition on each "now" of an additional dimension which, though not objective, is no less authentic. This point is made in a number of poems, but in "House Guest" *(Poems for All the Annettes)* or "The Beavers of Renfrew"[3] the possibility of integrating experience is elaborated and articulated more clearly. Here, Purdy argues that during one morning, for instance, one may mentally cover man's entire journey from snarling ape to *Homo sapiens;* indeed, that one single instant is enough for the mind to link events separated by millennia and experience the whole of creation. Objectively, therefore, man's life is given limits; subjectively, though, it is practically limitless. Fully convinced of this idea, in his latest volume of poems, *In Search of Owen Roblin* (1974), Purdy relegates the objective meaning of time to a second place: "Time that tick-tocks always in my body / its deadly rhythm is only a toy of the mind."

With the realization that part of the biological equipment of man is the ability to superpose two different temporal movements, comes the recognition of the dignity of being a conscious man, who, aware of the ultimate absurdity of all existence, is capable of experiencing "something basically satisfying real and valid" even in the simple fact of being a husband. Thus because in the absence of an outside agency to supply him with a reason for existing, he has been able to find an inner principle to sustain him in life. Indeed, he derives the strength necessary to live from reaching a state of acquiescence where a man accepts the fact that as an individual he possesses neither permanence, nor stability, but as part of a continuum, is timeless. This is why "the sense of the mystery of time by which things happen and are lost, happen and endure" becomes, as David Helwig has duly remarked, the central theme of Purdy's creation.[4]

In the face of reality, "The youth-burning faith in a unique self / dies just damn well dies," and the poet accepts the fact that he, his ancestors and his descendants are but manifestations of the same principle assuming different forms whether below or above the surface of the earth, whether manifested or manifesting. A mere particle in the continual flow of humanity, the human being is born into individual identity; he dies, but the race continues; he ceases to exist, but mankind does not, and present throughout Purdy's work is his endeavour to achieve a conceptual integration of mankind as a huge "joint account," while preserving the individual integrity of each man.

Purdy knows that men have in common both an identity of person and of nature. "A lump" in the throat of a person alive, says the poet, corresponds to an "Adam's apple" in that

of his predecessors; and in the voices of the people around, he distinguishes a certain quality "relayed there from the beginning of human time," representing the enduring, superimposed upon continuous change. At this point, it should be noted that without denying the significance of the horizontal chain of generations, it is the spiritual continuance, not the genetic one, that is the focus of Purdy's attention. Therefore he does not conceive of his ancestors as part of an existence already accomplished, and hence, deprived of significance. On the contrary, he believes that predecessors long gone back to the earth come to life again through the present-day people; that like trees, they sprout through their descendants, not in flesh, but in spirit. This is why when he mentally talks to his grandfather, the discussion does not take place between grandfather and grandson, but between "old man" and "younger self." For the same reason, he considers that the description of any individual, that of John Way of Roblin's Mill, for instance, is inadequate "unless you include what came after / all of us from all of him / as we have our shadowy children." Genealogy, therefore, is not read, but lived; descendants partake of their ancestors' weaknesses; but they also share their strengths, for what they ultimately have in common is human weakness and human strength. Purdy himself feels "all dead men / chanting hymns" tunnelling towards him underground and addressing themselves to his "hearing blood." Each individual, being a repository of a heavy load of ancestral messages, the essential difference between individual moments is effaced, and, as the poet pretends in "News Reports" *(Poems for All the Annettes)*, it becomes perfectly possible for Hannibal to drive his elephants into Toronto, or for Alexander the Great to bulldoze the Kremlin; names only are different, essences are the same. "What happened still happens," Purdy concludes, placing the open-ended structure of many of his poems in the service of a strong belief in the existence of a universal continuity which includes all humans.[5]

In truth, a time structure based on dynamic movement, always the same, yet perpetually diversified in form, gives a special perspective to Purdy's poems: patterns are always discernible behind small particulars. When he describes cowboys riding horses at 100 Mile House *(Cariboo Horses)*, he actually dramatizes the coming into momentary existence of a particle of timeless history. Similarly, in *Wild Grape Wine*, the terms of the discovery of the new land by the two Gaelic runners, brother and sister, is a significant situation enduring outside place and time, though expressed through the details of individual characteristics at a definite place and time. The words of the woman: "I am afraid of this dark land," are equally applicable within a geographical or psychological context.

As the objective realm stretches away towards that remoteness which is both far away in space and long past in time, there comes a point where details cease to be important, and the subjective swallows the objective. This is the time told about in legends and myths, and can be known only mentally. Symbolically, therefore, it can be reached not by a horizontal movement backwards, but by plunging vertically below the surface of the present. At the level where the dead Marthas and Josephs of Roblin's Mill meet and mingle with the Mycenaen warriors and the Dorset giants, the ultimate unity of human experience reveals itself, and in order to know it, Purdy urges his readers to dive through time, to go back "down the long stairway/we all came up when we were born." In this respect, it has been correctly noted that while walking through the "Ruins of an Indian Village" *(Wild Grape Wine)*, or while contemplating "The Archeology of Snow" *(Love in a Burning Building)*, Purdy does not mentally converse with a certain group of people, but "actually encounters the entire race of man."[6] And significantly enough, in his most recent work, he is not so much in search of his grandfather as he is of Owen Roblin, the founder of the village. For of ultimate importance to him is not establishing the history of his own family, but tapping a spiritual heritage. Believing that "whatever is underneath a village / and a one-time pioneer settlement goes deeper / rooted inside human character / contemporary as well as ancient," Purdy wants to pierce imaginatively the town pavement built there where the village was before, to enter the past and make its spirit available to himself, and through his poetry, to others.

But why is this mental communion with ancestors important to man? What does the sense of human unity underlying individual multiplicity gain for him? Self-knowledge and love for his fellow men, comes Purdy's unequivocal answer. Indeed, through mental communion with the past, man recognizes equivalence in the gestures of his predecessors, and is able to explore his own self, unafraid of darkness and failure. This idea is present throughout his work; but again, in his latest volume, is brought to mature expression. "After being them I become myself again / rooted in Year One of all the directions I am travelling," Purdy admits, following his spiritual search at Roblin's Mill. Having recovered a better sense of himself and, simultaneously, having taken in the input that comes from accepting the reality of human continuity, man finds it easier to reconcile himself to the knowledge of his own transiency. As an individual he lacks permanence, but he contains his ancestors as his descendants contain him, and this knowledge helps him conquer his own solitude. The world stops being simply plural. Instead, it opens towards man and receives him as member of the same community, abolishing thus the age-old conflict between the whole and its parts. With strong roots in the past and branching towards the future, man no longer feels bordered by waste and helplessness, but discovers himself part of a universe where chronological time is no longer important. "Wandering through Roblin's grist mill / I began to stop feeling sorry for myself / taking strength from them," the poet reports, setting up spiritual communion with the past as a powerful energizing source for the present.

Linda Sandler has noted the monotony, yet striking beauty, of the illustrations to *In Search of Owen Roblin*.[7] Indeed, loyal to Purdy's desire to express through his poems a fundamental conception rather than to capture the looks of things, Bob Waller has used extensively images of trees—standing trees, rooted in the soil where Purdy's ancestors are not buried, but "planted"; trees which represent at once the dead "sprouting buds," and the people alive "stemmed" in the graveyard. The illustrator's choice of images complements and sustains the poet's choice of words in an attempt to affirm not only that death is a contributor to life, but also that the quest for roots helps man to overcome self-centeredness and be able to participate emotionally in the world. And with this, one comes to the crux of Purdy's thinking.

Having as its object to descend as low as possible and immerse man in the spiritual experience of other generations of people, the search for roots is one means which man can use in order to rid his spirit of the burden of individuality. Freed from the prison of his own self, and with his soul rendered supple and flexible, the individual can merge himself in love with other beings and give life the profundity which it lacks otherwise. "Love is as absolute as death is," the poet states, locating and assessing the spark of existence. The hockey game which is life can be played only by a team, "breast to breast," each member depending and relying on all others. Suffering

and even death can be mitigated if men assume responsibility for one another as do the two runners in the poem with the same name, referred to earlier. And the fact that Purdy chooses them to be brother and sister underlines the idea of universal brotherhood, which should be the regulating concept of an individual's life. Ideally, of course, one should be able to be emotionally involved with the lives of others to the point of self-effacement. Ideally, one should be able to lose one's life as an individual and gain one back simply as an "hombre" who "gave himself away free to those who wanted him / his total self and didn't keep any." Undoubtedly, to detach oneself spiritually from the world is far easier an option than to take on the travail of sharing love for the world and participating in the work of transfiguring it. But if the supreme end of men is to be able "to rehearse the earth music together," love is the sovereign and sole means to do it.

> Stay with me in the same world
> or I am lost and desolate
> . . .
> that you are here at all
> delays my own death
> an instant longer,

sings the idiot boy of *Love in a Burning Building*, calling attention to the ultimate and universal spiritual reality accessible to mankind.

This is not to say that Purdy conditions man's capability to extend love to others on having first communed spiritually with past generations. To find an opening in the past by using the subjective dimension of time was one of the human privileges which he himself used. His poems are of that essentially humanistic inspiration concerned to communicate the experience of living through the tragic paradox of the human condition, not bent on prescribing rules. And while it is undeniable that there are other ways to reach the same goal, it is also undeniable that on the pathway which his argument opens, the mind can move with confidence. The pessimism pervading the intellectual climate of our age has taken its toll in relation to the poet. He sees the beauty of "the blue folded hills / of the hawk's surveillance and the sun's dominion," but concludes that, ultimately, "there is no choice for man except the grave." Yet he is not exhausted by the knowledge of man's transiency, but is able to conceive a vision of mature reflection, of scrupulous severity against facile despair or facile optimism. Indeed, fully aware that in this century no beliefs can be built that are not based on "the recognition of the uniqueness of man, and a pride in his gifts and works,"[8] Purdy grounds his message in the plasticity of human behaviour, in man's capacity to engage mentally in a vertical temporal movement, rather than following a merely horizontal sequence of moments.

Recognizing that man's reason for existence is not supplied by an external agency, but that it is consubstantial with the individual who thinks, Purdy urges man to abandon thoughtless living and conformism, to stop indulging in that "carrot-like behaviour" which erodes the difference between man and other species on earth. What he proposes is a life during which man transcends his objective existence while still embracing it fully, a life during which man renders himself able "to hear the accents of Jacob's voice, while feeling the hands of Essau."[9] And though he knows that victory is never completely achieved, and that therefore the effort should be unremitting, Purdy believes that it is in the power of the human being to transform life from the "noble struggle / of being a fool," into the noble struggle of being a man. For this

Canadian poet, life is not the ultimate four letter word. Purdy loves life, and wants to live. To say "Include me out of it all," as does one of the voices in *Wild Grape Wine*, would be to express an option that is incomprehensible to him.

Notes

1. For a perceptive analysis of the nature of the existentialist sickness, see Georges Poulet, *Le Point de départ* (Paris: Plon, 1964), pp. 216–36.
2. *15 Canadian Poets*, ed. by Gary Geddes and Phyllis Bruce (Toronto: Oxford University Press, 1970), p. 42.
3. Ibid., pp. 40–42.
4. David Helwig, "Four Poets" (review article), *Queen's Quarterly*, 79, No. 3 (Autumn 1972), 405.
5. Purdy's use of the continuous form of verbs, as well as the open-endedness of some of his poems have been the subjects of Mike Doyle's attention in "Proteus at Roblin Lake," *Canadian Literature*, 61 (Summer 1974), 7–23.
6. See George Bowering, *Al Purdy* (Toronto: Copp Clark, 1970), p. 64.
7. Linda Sandler, "Purdy on Owen Roblin," *Tamarack Review*, 65 (March 1975), 98–100.
8. Jacob Bronowski, *The Ascent of Man* (Boston: Little, Brown, 1973), p. 432.
9. Arnold Toynbee, *A Study of History* (London: Oxford University Press, 1972), p. 469.

JAMES PURDY

1923–

James Purdy was born on July 17, 1923, in Ohio. He claims that the exact location of his birthplace is unknown, but he appears to have spent a period of his youth in the northeastern Ohio town of Bowling Green, identified as the setting of his novel, *The Nephew* (1960). Purdy attended the University of Chicago and the University of Puebla, Mexico, and taught at Lawrence College in Wisconsin from 1949 until 1953. After working briefly as an interpreter in Latin America, France, and Spain, he began to write full time in 1953.

Purdy's early works of fiction, *63: Dream Palace* (a novella) and *Don't Call Me by My Right Name* (short stories), were printed privately by him in 1956 after being rejected by commercial publishers. Later that year William-Fredericks brought out a censored version of *Don't Call Me by My Right Name*, and in 1957 *63: Dream Palace* was published with additional stories as *Color of Darkness* by New Directions; it was reissued in 1961 by Lippincott with an introduction by Edith Sitwell. Purdy received critical acclaim for his first full-length novel, *Malcolm*, published in 1959 and subsequently made into a successful play, and for his collection of short stories, *Children Is All* (1962).

Purdy has published nearly two dozen volumes of fiction and poetry, some of them self-illustrated, and his short stories have been widely anthologized. Purdy's recent fiction includes the novels *Mourners Below*, published in 1981, and *In the Hollow of His Hand* (1986). He has received grants from the National Institute of Arts and Letters, the Guggenheim Foundation, and the Ford Foundation.

Purdy makes his home on Henry Street, in Brooklyn, where he has lived for many years.

The opening sentence (of *Malcolm*) won me over at once. It has the beautifully matter-of-fact clarity of a fairy tale (complete with the reference to gold), the stark realism of the documentary, and the provocative deadpan of the satire. "In front of one of the most palatial hotels in the world, a very young man was accustomed to sit on a bench which, when the light fell in a certain way, shone like gold." It is as devastating in its confident completeness as the famous opening of Jane Austen's *Pride and Prejudice*: "It is a truth universally acknowledged, that a single man in possession of a good fortune must be in want of a wife." Yet what worlds apart these two openings are! Jane Austen is talking to an audience she knows about a society she knows, in the confident assurance that the patterns of that society, treated with the proper kind of irony, yield valuable public truths about the relationship between private impulse and public convention. James Purdy is looking at an aspect of familiar American society with a gaze of such disturbing steadiness that the familiar becomes bizarre under his (and our) eyes and the real turns into the fantastic. At first one is tempted to call *Malcolm* a symbolic fantasy, but—though I dare say some critics will find little difficulty in explaining the symbols to us—the more we read the book the more we come to realize that the characters and events are not symbolic of something or of some things: they are *themselves*, and their haunting comic mystery derives from their being so very much themselves. We do not look through them to find a satire on America: or rather, we can and do look through them and find that satire, but that is not what the book is finally seen as leading us to do. The quiet precision of Purdy's style deploys the characters and events before us with such steady conviction that in the end we do not look beyond them but *at* them, and watch the real become the fantastic and the fantastic become the real until this beautifully engineered confusion of categories distills its own kind of satiric humor.

The hotel is not the most palatial in the world, but *one of the most palatial*; the man is not just a conventional "young man" but a *very young man*, and the suggestion is that the author knows exactly who he is (though we don't); and the bench only "shone like gold" *when the light fell in a certain way*. Qualifications imply truth, suggest accuracy. The impression is that the author is not writing a novel, but writing what he knows. The wealth of invention is deliberately disguised as what happens to have occurred. We are never allowed to see the author in control of his materials (and this, of course, is proof of his supreme control); the cool inconsequence of the narrative—the inconsequence of real life with the impression of fantasy and the suggestion of vast but always escaping meanings—is achieved by the total suppression of the narrator. Here indeed is Joyce's ideal: "The artist, like the God of creation, remains within or behind or beyond his handiwork, refined out of existence, indifferent, paring his fingernails." Yet Purdy's method is no more Joyce's than it is Jane Austen's: Joyce achieves a level of fantasy in *Ulysses* through exploiting reverie and periodically dissolving the surface realism of the action into the dream world of one of the characters, while Purdy is the deadpan reporter throughout. When he does have to record a character's impression, he objectifies that impression by such a device as the use of "one" (rather than "I" or "he"): "Malcolm was not only astonished to see that Kermit Raphaelson was a midget but that he looked quite handsome and clever, and differed from any other young man only in the matter of size: one merely felt one was looking at him with the wrong end of the eye-piece." Note what is happening here. A simple truth is being told—for is it not a simple truth that midgets differ from other people only in size?—yet it is made to seem odd, because of the hero's matter-of-factly recorded astonishment at his observation. This is one of the uses to which Purdy puts Malcolm's youth and dumbness and inexperience: he observes everything freshly, is quite incapable of distinguishing between the routine and the extraordinary, so that by the end the reader is persuaded that the routine and the extraordinary are indeed but different aspects of the same thing. The reader is persuaded of even more than that: he comes to feel that the two categories "routine" and "extraordinary" are meaningless. Why shouldn't a young man whose father has disappeared sit on a bench outside a palatial hotel until he is accosted by an astrologer who gives him the address of a Negro undertaker named Estel Blanc? It is amazing how quickly we are trapped into taking Malcolm's view of everything: "But what would I have done . . . if you had given me up?" Malcolm wondered almost to himself. "I mean, what would I have done about addresses!" Malcolm, and the reader too by this time, takes it for granted that getting more addresses from a casually met astrologer is important; indeed, he cannot now imagine how he could have managed without them. It is all absurd, but by now we cannot tell why, and so the whole category of absurdity has to disappear. It is most artfully done. ⟨. . .⟩

It is difficult to sum up the comic qualities of *Malcolm*. The novel creates its own kind of comedy as it moves, partly through the confronting of the uncomprehendingly polite Malcolm with a crazy sequence of characters and situations, partly by the elements of parody and irony in those characters and situations themselves, partly by deliberate shifts in style, and always by the shifting vitality of the dialogue. The more one reads the novel, the more one discovers new ironies and absurdities in the dialogue. "But when all is said and done, Malcolm, kiddy, you are not in our class. O.K.? I hope I do not offend." The words of Eloisa Brace the portrait painter to Malcolm as she sends him away to Girard Girard, with their modulation of five different kinds of clichés—popular argument, affectionate diminutive, pseudo-sociological metaphor, ordinary colloquial slang, tried pomposity—provide a microcosm of the range of stylistic ironies in the book. It is a very funny book, and whatever else the careful reader will find in it, he will find the delight of truly original comedy.—DAVID DAICHES, "A Preface to James Purdy's *Malcolm*," *AnR*, Spring 1962, pp. 122–30

One reviewer of James Purdy's remarkable novel, *Malcolm*,

last year, while admitting that Mr. Purdy "has a strong talent, even a genius" (a claim with which this reporter entirely agrees), doubted that he might ever "come to terms with the familiar, the vulgar, the everyday." In his second novel and third volume of fiction, Mr. Purdy has done just that. *The Nephew* introduces us to a dozen thoroughly familiar characters, even type-characters, in the relentlessly everyday world of small-town Rainbow Center; and it follows their stunted successes and casual disasters around the year, from one Memorial Day to the next.

"Memorial" is, indeed, a key word and the motivating piety of the story. For what happens and what we find out about the residents of Rainbow Center result from the effort of an elderly, retired schoolteacher Alma Mason, to collect from her neighbors enough information about her nephew Cliff (missing and believed dead, in Korea) to write a memorial of him. From such willfully outdated and unpromising material, James Purdy has fashioned a small work of authentic fictional art. And he has demonstrated a range and variety in his steadily strengthening talent—one of the most decisive literary talents to have appeared since the last war—to which one happily sees no obvious bounds.

It is, in the present case, as though some of the stories in *Winesburg, Ohio* had been rewritten by Eugene Ionesco. These apparently typical characters—from the imperial nonagenarian, Mrs. Barrington, through Faye Laird's senile and bloodthirsty mother (in portraying whom, Mr. Purdy releases his old, wild hilarity) to Alma Mason's deaf older brother Boyd—are all, in fact, oddly disjointed. They seem to utter their ritualistic banalities through partly frozen lips. About one of them, a nervous German professor named Mannheim, Mr. Purdy remarks at a certain moment: "His jaw sagged like that of a man who has suffered recently a mild stroke." But nearly everyone in *The Nephew* shows signs of having suffered a mild stroke.

Mr. Purdy, in short, is artfully suggesting a slight paralysis in the contemporary psyche, whereby we have gotten somewhat unstuck from reality, and unstuck from one another. If, as a consequence, the world of *The Nephew* is our world but our world seen weirdly (though lovingly), it is because—Mr. Purdy implies—only the weird perspective can catch at the truth. So he gives us the familiar, almost the folksy, cut across by strange gusts of what turns out, surprisingly, to be reality. This interaction is conveyed in the very sentence structures of the book, in such antic, disturbing juxtapositions as: "The night of the day of Faye's talk with Alma and Boyd's with Mrs. B.. was humid and hot, pervaded by the smell of ketchup." For reality continues to announce itself: vulgarly, at first, like a suppressed hiccup or the smell of ketchup. The movement of the story is from detachment to reality, from vulgarity to beauty, from a faint, ominous timelessness and placelessness to a known "here" and a settled "now."

A quiet but absolute compassion colors the final sentences which conclude that movement, as Alma and her brother, old and tired, sit close together, their white hair shining in the darkness; while "through the open windows there came the faint delicious perfume of azaleas. The courthouse clock struck ten." We experience, in those sentences, the rare and exhilarating sense of an artistic purpose perfectly fulfilled. —R. W. B. LEWIS, "Our Jaws Are Sagging after Our Bout with Existence," *NYTBR*, Oct. 9, 1960, p. 5

There is a double edge to the quite remarkable talent of James Purdy. The simplest view of this may be taken by looking at the two novels he has so far published. *Malcolm* is a wildly fantastic narrative in symbols, but *The Nephew*, if not lacking in interior meanings, is first of all a straightforward Midwestern neighborhood story. Yet the simple view of Purdy is not easily maintained, for he is more likely to blend what I think we may call the realistic and the surrealistic visions. He is rather complex and special. This was evident in the arresting short stories, eventually collected as *Color of Darkness*, which brought him such high praise several years ago; we have it again in this new collection of nine stories and two brief plays (*Children Is All*).

Playwriting is a new departure for Purdy, so let us look first for a moment at these.

The shorter of the two, *Cracks*, presents a very old lady, her nurse-companion, and a small child. It consists largely of the musings of the old lady on life and death. Then when we have the old lady solo in darkness a Figure appears and they converse also of life and death. But the Figure, close-wrapped and half-shadowed in darkness, identifies himself as the Creator and says the world has come to an end. Nevertheless the vision concludes—or the old lady wakens from a dream?—and we are back with nurse, child, morning and an affirmation of ever-continuing creation.

Children Is All, the longer play, is one of those "waiting for" situations which we have had at least from *Lefty* to *Godot*. Here the regional atmospherics compare to *The Nephew*. We await with a middle-aged, middle-class woman the return after fifteen years in the Pen of her son who, perhaps unfairly, had been jailed for stealing bank funds. We are asked to believe (1) that in all those years she has never visited Billy and (2) that when he arrives in the night, wounded, and quickly dies in her arms she does not recognize him—though her house companion and a neighboring child know perfectly well it is Billy. Thus the play moves into symbols of human dissociation, of human estrangement or nonrecognition, and thus we have another dimension.

That James Purdy can—almost always—blend these strata of real and surreal effectively there is no doubt. It is this that gives so much of his writing an air of strangeness. For one thing, he never assumes the role of omniscient author: his characters enact the episode; and we are teased—not told—into some knowledge beyond what they know. Also, to the extent I can put my finger on the main trick (and I use the word with no pejorative intent) it is this: Purdy, line for line, is a master of living speech, but with utterly real speech he more often than not creates a bizarre situation.

Almost any story in *Children Is All* illustrates what I mean. A girl has an undefined but tension-building encounter with a swimming instructor. Two young men are rooming together, and one asserts terrifying, utter power over the other. A naked and aging school teacher, after being raped, wanders across town to the home of a former student, now a pathetic teacher of music who has just lost his mother, and he takes her into his house with trepidation but finally, impotently, beside him into his bed. A man, also aging, wants to possess his daughter-in-law.

And so on. Always the vigor of creative talk (it is not surprising, from the stories, that Purdy is attracted to plays) building, to put it mildly, the special drama.

All this would add up really to tricks only, if it were not conceived in such penetrating compassion. In the second play the child reads from a book, "I felt the zephyrs of death blowing from the cracks in my surroundings." Such zephyrs blow chilly through these stories. The basic themes are loneliness and separateness. Where lives touch, or almost touch, there is terror. The author, as I say, is never on stage. But we know him

by what attracts him and by the brooding wonder with which he probes it. So Purdy continues to be the exciting writer he has been from the very first.—WINFIELD TOWNLEY SCOTT, "The Zephyrs of Death," *NR*, Nov. 17, 1962, pp. 25–26

James Purdy's third novel, *Cabot Wright Begins*, is more like his first, *Malcolm*, than his second, *The Nephew*. That is, it's a fantastic and ironic tale, told with great plainness and wit. As in *Malcolm*, the theme is both funny and bitter: the travails of innocence. *Malcolm*, which is more strictly picaresque in form relates the encounters, with various worldly and decadent types, of a very young man, innocent to the point of uproarious numbness. In *Cabot Wright Begins*, the figure of innocence is more complex. Indeed, it is split in two.

One innocent is Cabot Wright, recently released from prison after serving a sentence for raping more than 300 women. He is from a good family and was a model husband and rising young man on the Stock Exchange; now he is hiding out in a disreputable boarding house in Brooklyn Heights.

The other innocent is Bernie Gladhart, also young but already a professional *schlemiel*, most recently a used car salesman from Chicago, who has been dispatched by his middle-aged wife to Brooklyn Heights to find Cabot Wright and write the Great American Novel about him.

In the earlier novel, the young Malcolm dies, literally exhausted to death by his experience of the world, but in *Cabot Wright Begins* both of the innocents survive and even achieve a kind of wry triumph. Bernie returns to Chicago and selling cars, disabused of both man-eating wife and dreams of literary glory. And Cabot Wright, after running the gauntlet of a number of wacky mentors, soul-healers and prophets, finally purges himself in a paroxysm of laughter.

Cabot Wright Begins is, in many ways, the most ambitious of Purdy's novels. It might be loosely described as a bravura work of satire—a satire on pornographic fantasy, a satire on New York literary life, a satire on affluent eccentric mid-century America. Except that satire is perhaps too narrow a term to convey the kind of comedy that Purdy writes, comedy in the tradition that includes both *Candide* and "The Goon Show." Purdy shares comedy's traditional preoccupation with states of emotional anesthesia (the "dead pan") and with emotional deformity; his characters are "humors," parodies; and the particularities of social satire are not so particular as they may seem, but rather the vehicle for a universal comic vision. It is a bitter comic vision, in which the flesh is a source of endless grotesqueness, in which happiness and disaster are equally arbitrary, and equally unfelt.

Not all of Purdy's fiction is like *Cabot Wright Begins*. Within the substantial body of work which he has published in the last decade—three novels, a novella, two books of stories and two short plays—one can discern at least three Purdys. There is Purdy the satirist and fantasist; Purdy the gentle naturalist of American, particularly small-town American, life; and Purdy the writer of vignettes or sketches, which give us a horrifying snapshot image of helpless people destroying each other. In other words: a Purdy that can be compared, respectively, with Nathanael West, with Wright Morris, with Carson McCullers. (I'm speaking of possible companions, not influences.)

I must admit that I prefer the Purdy represented in *Cabot Wright Begins* and *Malcolm*—the side of Purdy that can be compared with Nathanael West—to the others. Purdy's most impressive gift seems to me to be for dark comedy, that is, for the rhetoric of exaggeration. This is not to slight his other gifts. He has a marvelous ear, especially for a certain kind of crankish earnest American speech, Midwestern or Middle Southern, that is beautifully used in his stories. But it doesn't seem to me that Purdy has the gift for great realistic writing; his work lacks the body, the vigor, the unselfconsciousness that realistic writing requires. Realistic fiction would also demand that he transcend his rather limited vocabulary of character, in which such types as innocent young men, predatory middle-aged women, and saintly half-cracked old people recur with insistent regularity. *Cabot Wright Begins* is not then, a realistic novel, though it is, surely, a powerful vision of a very real America. And it is a very American book, too; at least since Hawthorne, the "romance" or "tale" has often prospered in our fiction at the expense of the novel.

Anything Purdy writes is a literary event of importance. He is, to my mind, indisputably one of the half dozen or so living American writers worth taking seriously. Any reservations about his work I have suggested should be understood to assume the deservedly high place he now holds in contemporary letters. Yet the question remains as to whether Purdy, a brilliant writer, will become something even more. *Cabot Wright Begins* does nothing to indicate that this will happen.

Purdy's new novel is a looser, freer, gayer book than *Malcolm*. But it lacks *Malcolm*'s formal perfection and hardness. Its targets seem more gross, its argument more diffuse, its construction uneven. There are moments in *Cabot Wright Begins* when the joke (of a man *toujours prêt*, of the sexual compliance of all women, of a literary scene of unending corruption and fatuity) seems to go on too long. But there are also admirable passages—especially, in the later part of the book, the excerpts from Mr. Warburton's "sermons"—where Purdy pulls out all the stops and writes at the top of his form. Purdy's dangerous tendencies to sentimentality and to flatness, exhibited most of all in *The Nephew*, seem wholly conquered when he gives vent to the inspiration of fantasy, and to his marvelously inventive gift for parody.

Cabot Wright Begins may not be Purdy's best book, but it is one of his best. It is a fluent, immensely readable, personal and strong work by a writer from whom everyone who cares about literature has expected and will continue to expect, a great deal.—SUSAN SONTAG, "Laughter in the Dark," *NYTBR*, Oct. 25, 1964, p. 5

"Millions of us live where all streets are ugly and the streets go on and on forever," Sherwood Anderson lamented of the Chicago of the twenties. A decade after Windy McPherson's son came to town, Eustace (Ace) Chisholm finds the same streets to be just as long and even uglier. For while Success, to Sam McPherson, meant becoming a tycoon; to Ace it means sleeping with one. *Eustace Chisholm and the Works* is a rephrasing of the Horatio Alger legend within a homosexual frame.

Daniel Haws, a twenty-five-year-old ex-soldier, and landlord of a tenement he has named The 1887 Building, is in love with his seventeen-year-old tenant, Amos Ratliffe; but doesn't speak his love because he isn't conscious of it. He runs The 1887 like a barracks from breakfast to bedcheck, with no locks on the doors; then comes sleepwalking to Amos' bed, talks endearingly and returns to his own sack. Amos loves Daniel sleeping or awake. How either earns a living we aren't informed.

Ace Chisholm, Penniless Poet, is a better pimp than he is a poet. And if he appears less concerned about having contracted syphilis and infecting his wife, Carla, than he is about the future of Amos Ratliffe, it figures.

After a fling at adultery, Carla returns home—more penitent for having deserted her husband than for having infected her lover—to find hubby sleeping with a retarded bear named Clayton Harms. Will the two men accept Carla? No. But they'll tolerate her so long as she has steady work. For Carla knows that a woman's happiness depends upon having more and more taken from her by a man whom she has married without knowing why. This is the same magic formula for Total Misery adopted by Bella Cratty, of Mr. Purdy's 63: *Dream Palace*, while Parkhearst Cratty pursued Fenton Riddleway.

Meanwhile, back in The 1887, Maureen O'Dell, who loves everybody, has become pregnant by Daniel Haws. Amos accompanies her to Beaufort Vance, Negro Abortionist, where both Amos and the reader are overwhelmed by nausea.

"Why are we dead anyhow?" Parkhearst Cratty wanted to know—a question that might have been asked by one of those two-headed chickens that Anderson's father preserved in small glass jars. Because Mr. Purdy's barnyard grotesques are sidestreet solitaries pursued by bad marriages; they wander without purpose away from the light in Jackson Park instead of Winesburg. Both outposts are peopled by the stillborn and the aborted.

But Anderson's people were aborted by life, and would have lived if only they could have; while Mr. Purdy's people choose not to live: "*If everything could be a garden with the ones you always want and with drinking forever and ever*" the greatwoman of *Dream Palace* grieves—twenty years before anyone on Dorchester Avenue heard of a Playboy Club. One can care about someone whom life has cornered, but what can one feel for the person who *arranges* to be cornered in an empty lot?

Meanwhile, back in Ace's flat, The Bear has hauled home the homosexual alcoholic forty-year-old darling of the Fast Department-Store Set, Reuben Masterson. Ace and Maureen conspire to peddle Amos to Masterson in order to get themselves expensive clothes at a fantastic discount. Masterson must now make a cruel decision: Should he marry Maureen or Amos? Grandmother Masterson, the moneybags matriarch of the Masterson millions, prefers that her grandson marry Maureen because she senses that the chances of the Masterson dynasty getting an heir would be larger if Reuben married a woman instead of a boy.

Meanwhile, back in the army, Daniel Haws heroically sacrifices his love for Amos by rejoining the army—where he promptly shows up naked beside his commanding officer's bed. So much for Man's inhumanity to Man.

Meanwhile, back in the Masterson mansion and under the eye of the matriarch, Amos finds comfort in the hutch of Sven The Swedish Gardener. Enter Masterson. Seeing his gardener in the bathrobe he has given his fiancé, he sobers up long enough to fly into a rage. Master whups slave. Slave fights back. Both men fall to their knees in a reconciliation that flames into love without either standing up, while Amos watches enviously. Enter Grandma, catching all three clowns; and thereupon takes a running fit that culminates in a stroke. Amos hitchhikes home.

Meanwhile, back in the army, Daniel Haws is being savaged by Captain Stadger. Meanwhile, back in Southern Illinois, we learn that the reason Amos ran away from home was because he was having an affair with his mother. If you haven't had enough of this fifth-rate *avant-garde* soap opera by now, switch to Maggie Daly.

Readers familiar with Mr. Purdy's previous work will have the uneasy feeling here that they've ridden this carrousel before. Fenton Riddleway has become Amos Ratliffe; Parkhearst Cratty is now Ace Chisholm; Bella Cratty is Carla Chisholm; and Grainger the greatwoman is now Grandma Masterson. The difference in this carrousel, however, is that this one goes off the ground and never comes down.

What makes the book such a deadly bore, what makes the

reader's mind boggle, is that the author is unaware of anything preposterous about men who believe so firmly in both prayer and faggotry that they can go from sex to penitence without getting off their knees.

Cartoon-characters are not necessarily fatal. In Terry Southern's *Candy* they broke us up. But the difference in Mr. Purdy's and those of *Candy* is the difference between Little Orphan Annie and the illustrations of Edward Gorey. Indeed, had this book had Mr. Gorey's hand, it would have been a riot. As it is, it is simply a book whose most striking aspect is its unimportance.—NELSON ALGREN, "It's a Gay and Dreary Life," *Critic*, Aug.–Sept. 1967, pp. 67–68

It is not unusual in James Purdy's works for the dead to command the living. The absent nephew is the main presence in *The Nephew*; the vanished Summerlad family obsesses the memory and imagination of the storyteller in *Jeremy's Version*. For Purdy, life and death are mutually penetrable. The living, shorn of laughter and tears, may wander, ghostlike, through pallid existences, while the passion of—and for—the dead survives the grave.

In *Mourners Below*, Purdy's latest demonstration that "terrible events are the order of the universe," a dead brother dictates the destiny of his grieving family. The novel focuses on Duane Bledsoe, 17, whose two older half-brothers, Douglas and Justin, have been killed in war. Duane's parents are divorced, and in his father, Eugene, with whom he lives, Duane encounters only "deep wells of silence" and a refusal to mourn their common loss. Alone in his grief, Duane welcomes the company of his brothers' ghosts, particularly that of his beloved Justin.

The first third of *Mourners Below* is Purdy's account of the costs of repression—a skillful psychological portrait of a father whose profound emotional inhibitions cripple those around him. But this psychological realism explodes into something wilder and more comic—and finally more terrible—once Duane receives an invitation to a costume ball from the luscious Estelle Dumont.

Estelle is another of Purdy's irresistible, devouring women, kin to Elvira Summerlad in *Jeremy's Version* and Madame Girard in *Malcolm*. Once Justin's mistress, she will not be content until she recaptures Justin in Duane. The costume ball is wonderfully metaphorical; before it begins, each of the novel's characters, from the Bledsoes' housekeeper, Mrs. Newsom, to Duane's tutor, Duke La Roche, to Estelle herself, is comically intent on finding the pliable Duane just the right costume to cloak his identity.

The rites of passage for a Purdy adolescent are never easy. They entail the twinned savagery of sex and violence, neither executed without blood. Before Duane can come into his own, he must survive an all-night orgy with Estelle and a brutal rape by two ruffians who—like just about everyone else in the book—confuse him with Justin.

The narrative pace quickens and the improbability of events mounts as *Mourners Below* speeds to a conclusion. Plot revelations are few; revealed instead are the passionate depths to which these characters, at first so vacant and bloodless, can descend.

Mourners Below recapitulates many of Purdy's concerns—with small-town families in crisis, the explosiveness of contained emotion, the marriage between the dead and the living. Purdy sees to the heart of relations between the sexes, mourning the dreadful chasm between them. He celebrates the bonds between brothers, between father and son, even as he underlines the near impossibility of intimacy. Creating a

world where the supernatural merges with the real, he illuminates a reality whose core, if not its contours, matches our own.—JULIA M. KLEIN, *NR*, July 18, 1981, p. 39

GERALD WEALES
From "No Face and No Exit:
The Fiction of James Purdy and J. P. Donleavy"
Contemporary American Novelists
ed. Harry T. Moore
1964, pp. 143–49

In "Mrs. Benson," one of the stories in James Purdy's *Children Is All*, the titular heroine and her daughter sit in an English tearoom in Paris talking casually "about people they had both known in Philadelphia twenty-odd years ago," an activity as impersonal as the yearly meeting that has brought them together. The name of Mrs. Carlin comes into the conversation, and Mrs. Benson, who "had always been loath to 'tell,' to reminisce," recalls something that once happened (or almost happened) between her and the older woman. "But, Mrs. Carlin had already begun to entertain her guests in one part of the house . . . and to *live* herself in another! She had begun dividing up her life in that way!" Mrs. Carlin, who must have thought she saw something familiar in Mrs. Benson (having just been deserted by her husband, Mrs. Benson assumed that "*she* had never been too happy in her marriage, either"), asked the younger woman to "the 'real' part of the house" and later invited her to live there if she wanted to. Since in Purdy's world, it is impossible for a person ever to get beyond that part of the house where one receives guests, Mrs. Benson had to refuse. Still, she did have a glimpse into the living room, and it stays with her: "I don't know *why* I treasure what Mrs. Carlin said to me . . . But it is one of the few things that any other human being ever said to me that I do hold on to." The story told, she lapses again into the impersonality that keeps her and her daughter in one another's guest room, and the two women go out into Paris together and alone. Midway through her story, almost breaking it off, Mrs. Benson cries out, "Oh, it's all so *nothing!*" It is not only *something*; it is a *something* that pervades all of James Purdy's work.

The assumption is that all of us, in so far as Purdy really has the word on all of us, live in a house divided. For the most part the interior room, the "real" one, the one where we *live*, is sealed off from the ones in which we meet other people, talk to them, desire them, marry them, kill them, construct them in our own image. Once in a while we open the door ever so slightly and let someone look in, but what he sees there is a reflection. "*Mon semblable, mon frère*," he cries and we say "Who, me?" and slam the door in his face. The need to open the door ("This here is an emergency phone call, Operator," shouts the desperate man in "Daddy Wolf") and the impossibility of being recognized is the subject of most of Purdy's work—the early short stories in *Color of Darkness* and the later ones in *Children Is All*, the novella *63: Dream Palace*, the play *Children Is All* and the two novels *Malcolm* and *The Nephew*.

Since the man in the interior room is so hard to get to, since he can be seen infrequently and then only obliquely, the suspicion begins to grow that he is not there at all. He becomes a kind of silly putty that assumes the shape of whatever it lies against. He becomes whatever another person, in a scramble to escape his own facelessness, wants him to be. Girard Girard in *Malcolm*, about to marry Laureen, explains that he is "entirely,

entirely alone" and that he wants Malcolm "For my own—for Laureen's and my own." Since there is no chance of Laureen and Girard having the same "own," Girard is demanding that Malcolm be two things at once. Or rather, that he be the raw material out of which each of them can construct his own consolation. Most of us are failures as raw material since our acts—we are busy on our own consolation construction projects—make us break out of the neat and defining lines others have drawn around us. "I cannot go on being Mrs. Klein," the woman insists in "Don't Call Me by My Right Name," although she is willing to go on being married to Mr. Klein; she cannot understand that, so far as he is concerned, that makes her Mrs. Klein. In many of the short stories and in *Children Is All* (in which Edna Cartwright's convict son comes home to be recognized and in which she can give him recognition only in act not in word), Purdy treats the struggle between conflicting needs. In the longer fiction, he provides leading characters who are little more than what others make of them. Malcolm describes himself, "I am, well, as they say, a cypher and a blank." Fenton Riddleway in *63: Dream Palace* may not be quite the *tabula rasa* that Malcolm is—he has a brother Claire to remind him of his West Virginia origins—but the other characters in the story use him as though he were Malcolm.

It is Cliff Mason in *The Nephew* who is the perfect Purdy hero. He never exists at all. We are introduced to him in the first chapter through a quarrel over the content of his letters between his Uncle Boyd and his Aunt Alma (brother and sister who live together and with whom Cliff lived before he went into the army); they cannot even agree on his handwriting:

> "He writes a good clear hand," Alma said, reading.
> "Just a bit childish," Boyd said, low . . .

In the second chapter a telegram (with "several misspellings") informs them that Cliff is missing in action. When, near the end of the novel, his death is confirmed, Alma explains: "There wasn't even enough left of him to ship home in his casket. There was nothing of our Cliff left." In this he is like Malcolm, who is buried in an elaborate ceremony, flawed only by the insistent rumor—spread by the coroner and the undertaker—that there is no corpse at all. Although the problem of whether Cliff is alive or dead nags at Alma through much of the book, his existence (or lack of it) is not altered by substituting the specific *dead* for the ambiguous *missing*. In describing Mrs. Barrington, "the old monarch," who through age (she is almost 90) and position has become a combination goddess, arbiter, sage and meddler to the neighborhood, Purdy says of her long-dead husband: "His actual death came like a mere corroboration to the public of the old suspicion that he had never existed at all."

The Nephew is the story of Alma's attempt to write a memorial of Cliff. "I'm writing down everything I can remember about him, you see," she tells a friend, who opens the record book and is confronted with blank pages. Insisting that she does have memories but that she cannot get Cliff clearly in mind, Alma sets out to discover him through people and through things. There are not many things and they are not much help. There is the formal photograph of Cliff, which "seemed almost retouched," which "made him look almost pretty in that pose," and there are the photographs that Vernon Miller took of him, which burn up before Alma and Boyd can do more than glance at them. There are Cliff's old clothes which Alma, "holding them as carefully as if she wished not to lose all the folds and creases Cliff had left behind in them," locks away in a chest; one is reminded of the "shrine" that Grainger makes of Russell's room in *63: Dream Palace*.

There are the papers and the *curriculum vitae* that Professor Mannheim has saved from Cliff's college days. There are his letters, but, as Alma says, "Cliff *doesn't* say too much in a letter." His uncommunicative letters are reminiscent of the record that the dying Malcolm makes of his "conversations," which is read only by Madame Girard, who no longer has occasion to mention Malcolm or his manuscript; and of the writings of Fenton Riddleway, who puts things down on paper so that he can understand them. Whether from lack of audience or lack of content, what these three young men write fails to declare them.

The people whom Alma consults are even less helpful than the things Cliff leaves behind him. She starts out imagining that she knew Cliff and discovers that everyone has a different Cliff. Boyd thinks he knew Cliff because of the night he found the young man, drunk, with four thousand dollars stuffed in his pockets and unable to explain where the money came from. It came from Vernon Miller, who thinks he knew Cliff, too. "Cliff was the loneliest boy I think I ever knew, outside of maybe me," says Vernon, and later, "Cliff maybe was unhappiness." Unable to break out of his own trap, as friend and servant and perhaps lover to Willard Baker, even after Mrs. Barrington has given him money to run away, Vernon passes the money on to Cliff, his way of making a vicarious escape. "He didn't know him from Adam," according to Willard. Professor Mannheim, it turns out, had confided in Cliff, told him about an affair he was having with a student (now his second wife) and had listened to Cliff's own troubles, which, of course, he dismissed; Mannheim thinks of him in terms of "how much he was expecting," but a foreigner and a radical, never accepted by the town he has lived in for years, Mannheim may have made of Cliff a reverse image of his own disappointment. "I don't think Cliff and he saw one another *at all*," says Boyd.

Alma never gets more than a few "sentence fragments" into her record book. In fact, she is in danger of losing rather than gaining from her research. Her Cliff, the young man who loved his old aunt and uncle and liked being with them, disappears, until Mrs. Barrington restores him. She does so, first, by giving Alma the memorial she wrote of her dead husband (also blank pages). She offers Alma the conventional comfort in the idea that it is her love for Cliff, not Cliff's for her that is important, but she goes beyond that to assure Alma that Cliff did really love her and Boyd. "You needn't believe me, of course. But I think you do, or will." The fine ambiguity of that last line (for in the end Alma and Boyd do accept that Cliff loved them) accounts for the presence of Clara Himbaugh in the novel. A Christian Scientist who wanders in and out of the action, making a conversion here, a suggestion there (the memorial is her idea), Clara represents fairly directly the need of everyone in the novel to find something which will confirm his own existence. "I guess Vernon is my Christian Science maybe," says Willard. I guess Cliff is Alma's Christian Science maybe ("Cliff meant not just everything now but perhaps all there had ever been"), and to serve that purpose he needs only the existence that Alma gives him.

The Nephew, then, becomes the aunt's book. Alma learns a little about the way we invent the people around us (Mrs. Barrington's superiority, for instance, comes as much from Alma as from Mrs. Barrington), but fortunately not enough to keep her from finding her Cliff again. Boyd says, "We none of us, I'm afraid, know anybody or know one another." His words could be an epigraph not only for *The Nephew*, but for all of Purdy's work. In *Malcolm*, the hero sits on a golden bench in front of a luxury hotel (trailing clouds of glory, do we come), waiting for his father who has died and/or disappeared. Toward the end of the novel, Malcolm says, "Maybe my father never existed." Enticed into the world by Professor Cox (cocks launch us all into the world), Malcolm passes from character to character, each of whom lives in his own fantasy world and wants to acquire Malcolm the malleable as comfort and confirmation. "What did I buy you for, kiddy?" asks Melba, shortly before Malcolm dies. In *63: Dream Palace*, Fenton Riddleway wanders through a city in which lost souls seem to be trying to make contact with and trying to avoid one another. Grainger's mansion is specifically compared to the ALL NIGHT THEATER Fenton visits and implicitly to the park where Parkhearst picks him up. Parkhearst, Grainger, Bruno—all want to acquire him. "Why are we dead anyhow?" asks Parkhearst. "Is it because of our losing the people we loved or because the people we found were damned?" The short stories deal mostly with a moment in which someone recognizes a friend, a lover, a child as a stranger ("Color of Darkness," "Why Can't They Tell You Why?") or with a moment in which such close strangers indulge each other's masquerade ("Encore," "Goodnight Sweetheart").

For all of its persistence of theme, Purdy's work is not so much of a piece as this discussion suggests. He ranges from the dusty macabre of *63: Dream Palace* to the grotesque and sometimes funny comedy of *Malcolm* to the deceptive matter-of-factness of *The Nephew*. There is great range, too, in quality. His stories often appear to be slices, slabs cut out of something not quite perceivable. Ordinarily, he arrests his characters at a moment when drunkenness, uncontrollable garrulity, fear, some strong emotion brings a revelation which is, usually, oblique, suggestive, amorphous. The longer fiction—except for *The Nephew*—seems like a string of such moments. "Texture is all," Madame Girard says in *Malcolm*, "substance nothing." Her sentence might be a description of most of Purdy's work. At his weakest, his texture is only mannerism and his revelations become banal or vaguely "poetic" in the ugly sense of the word. When he is more effective, his arrested moments become vivid enough to suggest substance or to hide its absence. When he is better still—when Malcolm, running from the dead Gus, drops and breaks the testimonial shaving mug that Madame Rosita has awarded him for his sexual performance—the moment becomes a vehicle that carries us directly into some kind of truth. At his best, texture and substance become one. So far, that has happened only in *The Nephew*.

THOMAS PYNCHON

1937–

Thomas Ruggles Pynchon, Jr., was born on May 8, 1937, in Glen Cove, New York. He attended Cornell University, where he majored in English literature, studying under Vladimir Nabokov; he also studied engineering and modern physics, subjects that have had a profound influence upon his work. After a stint in the U.S. Navy in the late 1950s he returned to Cornell and received his B.A. in 1958.

During the early 1960s Pynchon worked as an editorial writer for Boeing Aircraft in Seattle, Washington. His first short story, "Mortality and Mercy in Vienna," was published in *Epoch* in 1959; over the next five years he published several more short stories, most of which were collected in *Slow Learner* (1984).

Although Pynchon has published only three novels, each of them has made a considerable impact. *V.* (1963) received the William Faulkner First Novel Award, *The Crying of Lot 49* (1966) received the Rosenthal Foundation Award, and *Gravity's Rainbow* (1973) won the National Book Award. *Gravity's Rainbow* was also unanimously recommended for the Pulitzer Prize by the 1974 Pulitzer Prize Committee, but the decision was rejected by the Pulitzer Prize Board, who found the novel "obscene" and "unreadable" and chose to give no award that year.

Thomas Pynchon is an extremely private man; very little is known about his life since the publication of *V.* in 1963. Nonetheless, his relatively small output has received a volume of critical attention matched by few living American writers; certainly, he is the leading figure of the post-1960 black humor/fabulist school of fiction that also includes such writers as John Barth, Robert Coover, and Donald Barthelme. He has published no new fiction since 1973.

General

EARL SHORRIS
"The Worldly Palimpsest of Thomas Pynchon"
Harper's, June 1973, pp. 78–83

The debaters—Heraclitus, Parmenides, and Pythagoras—are seated on the altar of the church of Saint Germain-des-Près. Behind them, a great mural depicts Christ, Aphrodite, and Orpheus in an endless odyssey. Noam Chomsky, Claude Lèvi-Strauss, and R. D. Laing sit in the audience, each in his separate pew. Overhead, V-2 rockets and B25 bombers pass each other en route to their respective targets, and across the street at the Deux Magots, Yankee sailors, fascists, physicists, paranoiacs, highwaymen, and Maltese nationalists practice alchemy by stealing each other's mail. The synapse that connects them all is misshapen, horrifying, apocalyptic, clumsy, and, above all, ambitious.

The synapse functions as a great tent, the unifying element of a circus that floats up and back across centuries, transcending its audiences, amusing them to death before it moves on, always featuring the same acts, changing only the costumes. The performance is an orgy, and every performer is a god-philosopher-clown. A garrulous and omniscient ringmaster provides the direction and commentary, speaking through a post horn, assuring the audience that the grotesque wonders within the tent prove the existence of the world outside.

There are some jokes under the tent, many of them in the form of comic names: Genghis Cohen, Benny Profane, Geli, Slothrop, Scheissvogel, Roger Mexico, Stencil, Mafia, Winsome, Charisma, Oedipa, and a rock group called the Volkswagens. Almost all of the names are also clues, for the form of the show is a search, a mystery in which everyone wears a mask that must be removed to reveal the object of the search. As the show progresses, the ringmaster provides clues to the clues, increasing the tension with the stripping away of each new mask. Because the performers wear masks, the circus can have no other structure; the masks rather than the performers interact, the ringmaster presides over everything, omnipotent, capricious, possessed of a seemingly preternatural intelligence.

To make the show more interesting, the ringmaster, who is also an artisan of diabolical capability, sometimes repaints the masks during the intermission, implying that beyond metempsychosis, which Chomsky, Lèvi-Strauss, and Descartes might explain through the existence of structures in the mind, there is a kind of schizophrenia of sanity, the territory of Laing.

The show belongs to Thomas Pynchon, master of fact, cataloguer of mythology, genius of the arcane history of man. In his new novel, *Gravity's Rainbow*, Mr. Pynchon has found an ending for the show, one that has no earthly sequel.

Perhaps the readers of his earlier novels should have expected such an ending, knowing that he views the human situation as a grand and terrible subject, as deep as myth and as broad as dreaming. His novels ridicule the concept of invention; they toy with our perception of what he calls preterition, the holes of memory that disable the present; they cast doubt on every human act. It is the work of the cruelest of metaphysicians, the art of disappointment, religious and therefore despairing of this world. With each novel he darkens and enlarges the cloud he casts. One wonders why he bothers to speak at all. It is the same question that must be asked of any Jeremiah. What is the force that impels them to the lonely act?

We live, we speak, Beckett might answer; what other choice is available to us? We also read, and Mr. Pynchon makes that pleasure into a task. The man is nearly deaf, he has some sort of vendetta against the simple stage direction of dialogue "he said," and he writes in spasms. It is a brave effort, this seeking of one's own pulse and daring to hew to it, but the pulse Mr. Pynchon has found is not a rhythm that sweeps us up into it; he writes in the most bruising, hobbling prose style this side of a German philosopher. A Calvinist doggedness is required to read all 760 pages of *Gravity's Rainbow*.

"Are you blokes *aware*," they're trying to teach him English English too, heaven knows why, and it keeps coming out like Cary Grant "that Jerry—old Jerry, you know—has been *in* that The Hague there, shooting his bloody rockets at that London, a-and *using*, the . . . Royal Dutch Shell headquarters *building*, at the Joseph Israel-plein if I remember correctly, for a radio *guidance* transmitter?"

The pity is that Mr. Pynchon's stylistic goals are admirable; he is searching for the same complex imitations of complexity that Joyce, Proust, Faulkner, and now William Gass use so beautifully. There is no reason to think that he will

not soon succeed. The man is only thirty-five years old, and the language of each of his novels is more interesting than the last.

In a writer of less intelligence, the stylistic flaws would be fatal—imagine John Kenneth Galbraith's ideas in Marx's style. There is no danger of that with Mr. Pynchon. The structure of V., published when he was only twenty-six years old, is a brilliant idea for a novel. The puzzle of the title is Venus, but not merely Venus as she was known in one place and time. V. is Venus moving westward and forward in time, Venus in all of her incarnations: Asherah, Asteroth, Astarte, Isis, Urania, and Aphrodite. V. is the Venus of love and desire, the goddess of rape, incest, adultery, ritual prostitution, bearded here, armed there, protectress of sailors, the Phoenician creature the Hebrews called Shame.

Venus and her variations are the structure of the novel; the search for her is the plot. But Pynchon is a wily satirist; the question of the identity of V., the revealing of variation after variation on his palimpsest, takes place during two generations, wanders the world, and picks apart much of the foolishness of modern America.

The fascination of the novel, like the fascination of Venus herself, is irresistible. One arrives at the Louvre at the first time, knowing that she is there, ready to scoff, to be greater than temptation. The long and narrow exhibition rooms are preparation, the marble is cool and the light is gray. There is an urge to touch the features of the philosophers, to have that connection with the Golden Age. The guards are there, those fifty-centime crusts in black wrappings, born to interfere. The Golden Age passes into a final room. It is crowded with tourists and children stamping their passports with the sight of her on a pedestal. Evanescent styles, lacquered hair, aesthetic blindness, the dampness of stupidity fill the room. She is turned today to catch the light along her right side. Stumps, cracks, chips, a stone, that's all she is. And then there is a fantasy of touching one's lips to the elegance of her back, a certainty that her breasts are not stone, the desire to feel her breath, to experience the smoothness of her promise. She wills her worshippers into love. It is the Venus that Thomas Pynchon knows so well. It is the population around her he despises so thoroughly.

For the love of Venus one forgives her flaws. So it is with the novel; the idea overcomes the lack of character, the callow jokes, the Procrustean shoes that pinch at every other step, the unsteady tone. Venus saves the novel. She is the only truly realized character, and she was there in our minds before she took up with Benny Profane the sailor, or Benny went hunting alligators in the sewers of New York, or Stencil went to Malta, or Ayn Rand or materialism or phony Bohemianism or war or politics were ridiculed.

As V. is in one sense a novel of East Coast lunacy in the 1950s, Pynchon's second novel, *The Crying of Lot 49*, is an exploration of West Coast lunacy in the 1960s. It is a brief work, more direct than either of the others, and it has a character, Oedipa Maas, who is drawn with sufficient life to give the novel a line of progress in its own time. There are some carry-overs from V.: The Kazoo Concerto, the name Chiclitz, and the Yo-Yo image, though we are spared Mr. Pynchon's borrowing from the Greek in connection with the Yo-Yo-apocheir (a combination of away and hand, used in V. as a pun on aphelion).

The one important aspect of *The Crying of Lot 49* that does not appear in either of the other novels is that we care not only about Oedipa's search for the paranoid post-horn gang, we care about Oedipa herself. She is human, an eviscerated Californian falling into the cavity of herself, finding in the floating debris around her nothing solid enough to hold her up.

The success of the novel resides in the possibility of the reader experiencing a parallel to Oedipa; seeking the unknowable as she does, tinkering with the dark places of the mind that lie in wait for one in a state of islands, technology, paranoia, drugs, cash culture, and the fearful inability to admit the existence of the resolutions of responsibility, age, or death.

It is a terrifying novel. There are few other places in literature where the idea of the void is more certain. Even Beckett is overshadowed here, for he lacks California as a prop. Even Beckett cannot give us the anguish of a woman married to a former used-car salesman who has become in his middle years a Top Forty disc jockey and an eater of hallucinogens. There is no better guidebook to the society that has grown up in California, no more fierce admonition against getting lost in its mores.

Gravity's Rainbow, the gigantic resolution of his circus *sub specie aeternitatis*, proceeds, like all of Mr. Pynchon's novels, on several levels and is superficially organized around a search, this time for a German rocket. The novel begins in England during the last days of World War II. Buzz bombs have been replaced by the terrifying V-2 rockets that fly faster than sound, announcing themselves by their explosions. The book follows a group of English, American, German, African, and Russian scientists, soldiers, mystics, fools, crooks, perverts, victims, and children through the search for the secret German rocket that may or may not have been launched or even completed before the German surrender. The incidents that move the plot are unrelievedly horrible; simple deceit is the kindest act in the novel, the ugliest depravity is its routine; a Hebrew prophet could not paint a worse or more didactic picture. *Gravity's Rainbow* is as ambitious as *The Divine Comedy*, but it unfortunately lacks the grace, clarity, and loving commitment to true imagination that makes art of Dante's work. Perhaps the world is too old and too complex for great works of imagination to be made. Perhaps a modern Dante would find the naming of Purgatory and Hell an infringement on the copyright of history and be limited to satire and senseless mysticism. Mr. Pynchon would seem to say so; he has become a philosopher of the worn-out world, an implier of entropy, a pitchman for the comedy of death.

At the core of his work is the notion of a layered culture—the palimpsest is his metaphor—in which each new variation is written over the last. He seeks always for the original writing, then passes through the variations, adding his own work as the latest, perhaps the last, layer. The result is not a wholeness achieved through continuity, but a line of shards, the last of which contains the apocalyptic atom.

Heraclitus wrote the original parchment on which *Gravity's Rainbow* is superimposed. The novel is made of strife, seeming to agree with Heraclitus that everything lives by the death of something else and that the end of strife is also the end of the world. But it is a novel based mainly on the Orpheus myth. Parmenides' answer to Heraclitus, the solid sphere of "it is," provides the philosophical tension. The resolution is perhaps a victory for Heraclitus or the promise that the Pythagorean harmony of opposites will follow in a messianic future.

Man, as conceived in *Gravity's Rainbow*, is the creature known to Orphism; he has eaten the ashes of the Titans, punishment awaits him in the Netherworld of a universe born of Night. One may only wait for the release of the soul from the body, the end of the terrible transmigrations in the freedom that comes after purification.

The Orpheus of the novel finds the Underworld by descending through a toilet. He chases the secret rocket from England to France to Germany. As Orpheus belongs to Apollo and Dionysus, the hero of Mr. Pynchon's novel is a mathematician and mouth-organ player and a lover of drunkenness and sex. In his journeys up and back from the Netherworld he not only encounters most of the Greek Pantheon but ranges across Babylonian astrology and Hebrew myth, sails on a ship called the *Anubis* for an Egyptian weighing of the hearts of the dead, meets himself in Rilke's version of the Orpheus myth, gives us reason to think of the twins of Mani's vision, and manages to find entrance to Christianity through the ravages of science gone berserk. The characters range from Hansel and Gretel to Hades, from the Titans to the Erinyes, from General Electric and I. G. Farben to Athena. Incarnations mix and fade; the palimpsest is fluid, no erasure is complete; the myths of Western civilization evolve, for we are the society of history and accumulation, an idea that Mr. Pynchon has caught exactly.

In arriving at that exposition of Western civilization, the author demonstrates his astonishing erudition and ability to integrate ideas, but in so doing he sacrifices the novel. What is left is a comic tour of the history of Western thought, a history that finally overwhelms even Mr. Pynchon and leads his novel to a soggy end. It could not be otherwise; the time is too late for cosmogonies. Men have walked on the moon, teaching us that it is not the silver egg of Night from which Eros was hatched; mysticism is a hideout for fools.

Mr. Pynchon thinks otherwise. In his search for the mysterious rocket, Tyrone Slothrop moves from Poisson distributions in London and crackpot science at a former mental hospital outside the city to orgiastic sex on the French Riviera. THEY seem always to be menacing him, menacing all of us. Everything is suspicion—spies and counterspies and counter-counterspies. The hero goes AWOL, travels to Germany, trades with black marketeers, contests the Russians to see who will discover the secret of the rocket.

Meanwhile, we learn about the rocket, piece by piece, one agonizing clue at a time, as the evil nature of man is revealed: the monstrous Blicero, torturer of sweet Gottfried; Tchtcherine, the Russian brother of the black African Enzian who leads Germany's black rocket corps; Greta, the film star and mother of little erotic Bianca, who is revealed in the dream of a Japanese officer; and Katje, the inconsistent Eurydice-Gretel. Pavlovian theory, plastics technology, rocket science, and a vision of motion picture film as world metaphor are presented to us along with racial, political, and economic theory. There are comic moments, funny names. The plotting is marvelously intricate, but there are no characters to give us an experience of the novel; we follow shadows to their conclusion.

After 760 ingenious pages, the rocket is explained. Then we are told that we are in a theater, and that apocalypse is imminent. But we shall not endure apocalypse alone. Coming with us is the gentle one, he who has been scourged by incarnate evil. It is Gott (God) fried (peace). That is the revelation and the resolution of *Gravity's Rainbow*, the culmination of the brilliantly intricate enormity of the construction, the final coruscation of the grotesque synapse.

The world is ended, a thought of considerable magnitude but not of any great immediacy. Other problems, duties press: dinner or Vietnam, a child refusing neglect, Nixonian compassion, evening's breath entering through an open window, an unsettled tooth. The novel is a disappointment; circus is not really drama; and the clowns of Mr. Pynchon's circus are not truly funny. It can only be concluded that the form of his humor is a deceit, a pose, yet another of the masks he manufactures.

Of course we laugh, but it is dire comedy; we laugh from uneasiness, hoping to save ourselves, to avoid his sneer by staying out of the circus. Satire has its failings as art, but Mr. Pynchon's work fails beyond that, for it allows us the luxury of cruelty and it lures us into smugness by being a puzzle, a game of Botticelli at which only the most literate can play.

The novel skates along the macrocosm but fails to touch the limits of the universe; they are perhaps more easily reached through the inspection of a single point from which lines may emanate that touch infinity's curve. Even if it is dreamed, the world must be made of things, beginning at some point. So novels are made of chapters, paragraphs, sentences, words. It is there, in the words, that Mr. Pynchon's novels falter: the earlier novels lack things, the new novel has its things in lists. In neither case do the things have flesh, and without flesh there cannot be character.

Perhaps it is the genre that fails, perhaps hopeless and haughty satire can be no more than Mr. Pynchon has made of it. Great art comes upon us like an unexpected scent of new flowers; we are resurrected by it. Satire leaves us the less for having read it. We laugh and inflate ourselves, rising like eighteenth-century balloonists on a bubble of superheated air, adoring the view from the heavens. Nothing has been made; the most brilliant satire is still an assertion of the world as it is, for it is dependent upon the masks we have already assigned, a confirmation of our prejudices. Satire holds no promise; it is to the world as criticism is to art. Both satire and criticism have their functions, but only art and the world can stand by themselves, facing each other in profound opposition. The novel of satire is no more than a road map, full of symbols, an accurate guide to the explored world, a Baedeker, an amusing preachment, even a commandment.

For all of its inventions, Mr. Pynchon's work lacks imagination; it is never more than an argument with the world. The art of fiction demands more. Whether the writer proposes comedy or tragedy is of little matter; the heart has its requirements.

NEIL SCHMITZ
"Describing the Demon:
The Appeal of Thomas Pynchon"

Partisan Review, 1975, pp. 112–25

When we look at this display of passions, and the consequences of their violence; the Unreason which is associated not only with them, but even (rather we might say *especially*) with *good* designs and righteous aims; when we see the evil, the vice, the ruin that has befallen the most flourishing kingdom which the mind of man ever created, we can scarce avoid being filled with sorrow at this universal taint of corruption: and, since this decay is not the work of mere Nature, but of the Human Will—a moral embitterment—a revolt of the Good Spirit (if it have a place within us) may well be the result of our reflections. (Hegel, *The Introduction to The Philosophy of History*)

Given all the evil, the vice and the ruin that has befallen the world set forth in John Hawkes' *The Cannibal* (1949) and William Burroughs' *Naked Lunch* (1959), and again in Saul Bellow's *Mr. Sammler's Planet* (1969), Hegel's remark seems an apt introduction to contemporary American fiction.

Certainly *this* kingdom, the "last, best hope of earth," has stopped flourishing and its writers, confronted decade by decade with the spectacle, show all the signs of moral and philosophical exasperation. The "Good Spirit" rarely speaks in their fiction and its tone is ironic when it does speak. It has lost an eye in wartime Poland and since then taken the Apomorphine Treatment. It whistles a thin tune in the dark of postwar history. As Hawkes explained in 1962, his moral stance is to have no stance. Only the writer who "maintains most successfully a consistent cold detachment toward physical violence . . . is likely to generate the deepest novelistic sympathy of all," he wrote in *The Massachusetts Review*, "a sympathy which is a humbling before the terrible and a quickening in the presence of degradation." What animates Hawkes in this essay is his admiration for Djuna Barnes' comic treatment of violence in *Nightwood*, her stylistic equipoise in the face of Unreason, and finally he elevates the cool elegance of her writing to the status of an existential leap. He too believes in fiction, "hard, ruthless, comic" fiction that finds "a language appropriate to the delicate malicious knowledge of us all as poor, forked, corruptible, the feeling of pleasure and pain that comes when something pure and contemptible lodges in the imagination—I believe in the 'singular and terrible attraction' of all this." History in such fiction no longer exists as a coherent formation of events. Neither Hegelian nor Marxist, it has no destination, no implicit meaning—it is only a place, an environment, a theater in which everything happens and where, before flats that signify 1918ness or 1930ness or 1945ness, this "poor, forked, corruptible" Everyman enacts our common and immutable fate. Yet how often can these horrors be rehearsed before the terrible becomes merely the exotic, before the writer himself begins to participate in the alienation of the humane? It is a question Alfred Kazin asked in examining Jerzy Kosinski's *The Painted Bird* and one that Susan Sontag recently rephrased in contemplating the photographs of Diane Arbus. For the artist, however, whether Hawkes or Arbus, hardness is not so much a mode as an ethic, the ethic of the survivor who uses ironic detachment as a shield against the overwhelming data of his own immediate history. When Hawkes humorously knocks off the sole good man in *The Cannibal,* an inept schoolteacher named Stintz, braining him with his own tuba, he expresses the truth that after Paschendale and Verdun, after Dresden and Hiroshima, there is no rebirth, and at the same time he refuses the burden of hope. "To have humanism," Fausto Maijstral reminds us in Thomas Pynchon's first novel, *V.* (1963), "we must first be convinced of our humanity. As we move further into decadence, this becomes more difficult." The question in that modern art which strives to represent this mangled world is not, then, historical, Hegel's question: "to what principle, to what final end these enormous sacrifices have been offered," but rather the question so relentlessly stated by Burroughs in *Naked Lunch:* what *is* human?

In Pynchon's fiction the obscene so finely wrought in *Nightwood* and sparingly told in *The Cannibal* is epically extended and retold. Like Hawkes, Pynchon writes novels that are "hard, ruthless, comic," fiction that reveals exactly what is done when the hook is surgically removed from a Jewish nose or how in castration the scrotum is clenched and the testes spilled. But the most intense suffering that occurs in his fiction is intellectual, not physical, and in this regard Pynchon is the most violent of our modern writers, typically amassing great volumes of knowledge in specific detail only to mystify and confound the obstinate knowers who search in his texts for the right reading, for the true interpretation. He is interested not in those who operated the ovens at Dachau but in those who devised them, in those systems and technologies that enabled the Eichmanns, gave them timetables and switches to pull. All the enigmas painstakingly left unresolved in *V.* and *The Crying of Lot 49* (1966) are resumed and massively rephrased in his most recent novel, *Gravity's Rainbow*. Characters recur (notably Mondaugen and Weissman from *V.*), themes and motifs recur, anarchic parties begun in the short story, "Entropy" (1960), reconvene, there are historical and geographical intersections, Henry Adams and James Clerk Maxwell are once more recited, and Tyrone Slothrop, recognizably doomed, undertakes in this novel the same quest that harried and frustrated Herbert Stencil in *V.* and Oedipa Maas in *Lot 49*. But to conclude from all this evident continuity that Pynchon still coolly inhabits the world projected in the earlier fiction is to misread the significance of *Gravity's Rainbow*.

The first two novels are essentially Melvillean masquerades in which Pynchon himself operates as the confidence man. They are, in effect, positionless, centered only by the movement of the questions asked. In *Gravity's Rainbow* Pynchon moves from poised inquiry to statement. "Jamf was only a fiction," Slothrop finally realizes, "to help him explain what he felt so terribly, so immediately in his genitals for those rockets each time exploding in the sky . . . to help him deny what he could not possibly admit: that he might be in love, in sexual love, with his, and his race's death." Slothrop is finally abandoned, thrown away as the protagonist, and in his place Captain Blicero (Weissmann transmogrified) speaks with a compelling directness. When we first meet Weissmann in *V.*, he is a German officer stationed in Southwest Africa during the twenties, a Nazi sympathizer spiritually in transit from Roehm's SA to Himmler's SS—simply another version of Hawkes' cannibal, Zizendorf. Magnified as Blicero in *Gravity's Rainbow*, he is a protean figure, the keeper of the Rocket's secret, the secret Slothrop finally in fear and trembling apprehends. It is Blicero who supervises the creation of the Rocket, who launches it to rise and struggle with the gravitational pull of the mundane. "I want to break out—to leave this cycle of infection and death," he asserts at the end of the novel. "I want to be taken in love: so taken that you and I, and death, and life, will be gathered, inseparable, into the radiance of what we would become. . . . " As we shall see, this rhapsody of transcendence does not celebrate the profuse richness of the world, its teeming *thereness*, nor does it propose, as one reviewer suggests, a "defense against suicide." Blicero is not a Pierre Bezukhov yielding at last to the round wholeness of the compossible. He sings instead a very old Cathar song, the "white" song sung by the "wolf of Pontus," Marcion, by his disciples Tatian and Apelles, and most importantly by Manes.

From the start Pynchon has played knowledgeably with the Manichean perspective in his writing, spelling it out on numerous occasions, but always stating it as the probable, as a thesis, the curious strain that runs through Calvinism and which becomes curiouser and curiouser as history leans on its New Jerusalem. In *Lot 49* Oedipa is told of an obscure band of seventeenth-century flesh-despising Puritans, the Scurvhamites, who were ultimately all seduced by the Demiurge and brought over into darkness. In *V.* there is a "Bad Priest" who teaches the young girls in Malta "to become nuns, avoid the sensual extremes—pleasure of intercourse, pain of childbirth," who similarly advises the boys "to find strength in—and be like—the rock of their island," telling them that the "object of male existence was to be like a crystal: beautiful and soulless." Children are readily drawn to a Manichean conception of the world, it is noted in *V.*, particularly children who must deal

with the inexplicable cruelties of war. The allure of Gnostic and Manichean thought in Pynchon's writing is obvious. For the Manichean stands outside history, free, not at all surprised by the evil he discerns in this sublunary world. In *V.*, while the revolt of the Bondelswaartz swirls around him in Southwest Africa, Kurt Mondaugen steadfastly pursues his scientific experiment with sferics (atmospheric radio disturbances), quixotically trying to decode a message from the random crackling. The time is 1922, but this revolt has occurred before, at the beginning of the century, and it will recur all over Africa, Asia and Latin America. Bombing the poorly equipped Bondels, the Germans rehearse for Guernica and Rotterdam. Inside Foppl's farm, where a continuous orgiastic party is maintained for the duration of the conflict, the colonials frolic like decadent Berliners. Outside their walls an entire race is exterminated. Is there a suprahuman language spoken in the ether, an utterance that, once transcribed, will either judge or justify this barbarous spectacle? Weissmann steals Mondaugen's logbooks and graphs, playfully interpolating his own interpretation into Mondaugen's disguised theological quest. In creating this world, the horror that surrounds Mondaugen, what did God mean? Weissmann's decoded text breaks down into two readings: GODMEANTNUURK and DIEWELTISTALLESWASDERFALLIST. Placed in this specific historical context, Wittgenstein's statement: "The world is all that the case is," becomes a chilling oracular response, at once a confession of the circularity of language and a relegation of the human to the natural. In Weissmann, who is portrayed as a transvestite, the heresiarch makes his traditional appearance. Like his predecessors who interpolated and excised the Gospels (Marcion cut from Luke all reference to the physical generation of Christ and Manes simply took what he needed from the Scriptures and synthesized it with Zoroastrian texts), Weissmann is a deft exegete, the exemplary shape-shifter. And in *V.* he already belongs to the great heresy of our era, Fascism, a movement that begins conspiratorially—not unlike the Trystero System that beguiles Oedipa in *Lot 49*.

Not all the confusion in this important novel is contrived. In the Trystero symbol of the muted post horn Pynchon ambivalently renders at once the notion of resourceful and healthy subversion (the breaking of a postal monopoly) and the silencing of the phallus, the silence of inversion and death. For if the enigma of the Trystero System compels Oedipa to recognize a world larger and more significant than her own, demands that she realize otherness, its sign, the muted post horn, is also the chosen emblem of the Inamorati Anonymous, an odd fellowship of solipsistic exlovers who have forsworn passion, who deny the value of the other. Oedipa's Sphinx is a mysterious and aptly named American industrialist, Pierce Inverarity, whose riddle, a puzzling will, requires that she enter history to resolve it. Thus she sets out to discover the nature of her inheritance, but where is the correct entrance, whose theory of the past truly explains what happened and what is happening? She encounters a series of couriers, a series of texts and messages (most notably a cryptic Jacobean play, *The Courier's Tragedy*) whose diverse meanings are at once indefinite and equivalent, reducible only to the Wittgensteinian proposition in *V.* The text of that ambiguous play, strewn with double meanings and strange allusions, will say whatever she wants it to say, so she is told at one point, but this is not what Oedipa wishes to learn. Like Melville's Pierre Glendinning, she desires to be embraced by the truth, whether dark or radiant, and in that embrace escape the isolation of private and relative meaning.

It is system-making, the thinking and writing of history,

that concerns Pynchon in *Lot 49*. Like the Abbé Breuil in the caves at Altamira or Alexander Marshack in those at Pech Merle, Oedipa tries to read the writing on the wall, but in her case the writing is on the wall of a john in southern California or spray-scrawled on traffic signs. It is, seemingly, a futile quest. All the clues and signals given her do not lead to her demystification. The plot of *Lot 49* does not unravel. Like an old Hollywood serial, the novel merely breaks off at a climactic moment, suspends itself in the midst of mystery. The tragedy of the courier is compounded by a double deceit. We cannot trust the veracity of his information nor can we trust ourselves. That play and this fiction finally constitute the same text, the text rewritten as it is read: Kinbote's *Pale Fire*, Menard's *Quixote*. Interpreting Oedipa's interpretation, the reader is drawn into her enchantment. But how is this maze constituted? Using as his paradigm the postal system devised by Francis von Taxis in the sixteenth century, a system that soon cast its network across the Netherlands, Germany, Austria, Italy and Spain, Pynchon invents an antagonistic system, the Trystero, a synoptic heretical and revolutionary underground that intercepts and subverts the official system of communication. Discourse in the form of the document is thus fatally compromised at its source (both historically and artistically) since its intentionality is always questionable. Who speaks in this letter, a fat and prosperous Tirolese burgher or a frantic concealed member of the Trystero? Because it determines the transmission of language, the sending and receiving of information, the postal franchise is clearly the most important in human society. The Postmaster (like the Roman Catholic Church imposing Latin on the Swabians, the Danes and the Franks) has the ability to define and structure consciousness itself. But the mails are always blackmailed. Following the advice of Burroughs to cut up and fold in, the phone phreak insinuates himself into the Bell System and speaks to a puzzled bonze in Cambodia. Pynchon knows the fate of Latin in southern California. Yet there is no solace to be found in the proliferation of idioms or cults since each idiom inevitably aspires to become Latin, to monopolize discourse. In *State and Revolution* Lenin declares: "To organize the *whole* national economy on the lines of the postal service, so that the technicians, foremen, bookkeepers, as well as *all* officials, shall receive salaries no higher than a 'workman's wage,' all under the control and leadership of the armed proletariat—this is our immediate aim." And *this*, Pynchon seems to suggest, is what constitutes the unholy dialectic of history—a struggle for the post office, the right to be the godlike Postmaster who impersonally operates in society like Maxwell's Demon sorting molecules in its closed, two-chambered box. Each would-be Postmaster dreams the death of history, the stasis of an even temperature eternally balanced by a perfected social system intelligently regulating its energies without losses, without decadence.

In *Lot 49* Oedipa is finally directed to John Nefastis, the inventor of an experimental Maxwellian box. "Communication is the key," he informs her. "The Demon passes his data on to the sensitive, and the sensitive must reply in kind. There are untold billions of molecules in that box. The Demon collects data on each and every one . . . the sensitive must receive that staggering set of energies, and feed back something like the same quantity of information. To keep it all cycling." Since the work of the Demon parallels Oedipa's in the novel, it is often argued that the Demon metaphorically describes the function of the imagination which strives to create order in the world. Yet as Anne Mangel points out in her useful essay, "Maxwell's Demon, Entropy, Information: *The Crying of Lot 49*" (*TriQuarterly*, 20, Winter, 1971), the Demon is a part of the problem, not its resolution. Maxwell had imagined a vessel divided into two portions, the temperatures of which would be raised and lowered without an entropic expenditure of energy by an ingenious exchange of swift and slow molecules, a theory later challenged by Leo Szilard and Leon Brillouin who argued that the Demon would require visual illumination to make its selection of molecules and thus necessarily increase the rate of entropy. And indeed the more Oedipa sorts and selects in her attempt to bring Inverarity's estate "into pulsing stelliferous Meaning," the more diffuse and disparate grows the evidence. In effect Nefastis has created a microcosm of the world, an idea of history. Oedipa makes the mistake of identifying with the Demon, she wants to be the "dark machine in the center of the planetarium" projecting the universe, whereas in fact she is inside Nefastis' figurative box and a part of its flux, a sensitive Oedipa sorted rather than sorting, sent rather than sending.

As all his critics have noted, Pynchon's application of the second law of thermodynamics to the modern world generally follows the thesis advanced by Henry Adams in *The Rule of Phase Applied to History* (1909). History is subject to the rule of entropy, Adams argues, and is therefore intensifying its processes as it approaches its apocalyptic close, piling event upon event in the last wild thrashing of human time. In Pynchon's interpretation, however, this thesis is subtly turned. As it appears in *V.* and *Lot 49*, history is, if anything, a vile invention specifically designed to interfere with the random exhaustion of human energy. By constantly devising (through its lesser demons) totalitarian systems of mediation, institutionalized versions of the Demon, it seeks to keep the social world of men going. History is *not* natural, but an imposition of human will, a rebellion. The Hegelian Idea of Freedom that ostensibly answers our questioning gaze when we turn from the "slaughter-bench" of history reveals itself in *V.* (and most powerfully in *Gravity's Rainbow*) as the perverse Adversary, the Idea that impels Europeans into Africa to hound the ahistorical Hottentots up out of their holes into consciousness, into awareness of the master/slave relationship. What obsesses Pynchon is not the entropic end of history, but the spectacle of historical repetition. And in rendering this vision he refers us to John Adams, not Henry Adams, the John Adams who diligently studied the political science of Machiavelli. How does a state escape the turning historical wheel that generates aristocracies out of monarchies and democracies out of aristocracies, turning again and again, toppling innumerable Romes? The constitution Adams envisioned stabilizes that endless and bloody round, serves as a perpetual motion machine demonically checking and balancing political exchanges of power. It is the essence of the American Dream, the perfect social contract, an agreement based on synchronic principles and yet open to diachrony. And through the operative intelligence of that text, a constitution fashioned to sense political disequilibrium, America brings history to its poised culmination—the wheel turns no more. James Clerk Maxwell is not only an important physicist, but also, in the contrivance of that theoretical box, an American poet.

Yet the constitution fails, yielding to the corporate bylaws of GM, the governance of Yoyodyne, an aerospace firm whose original business was the construction of gyroscopes for children. As Christianity hardens into orthodoxy, it engenders heresies; as the Taxis postal system begins to monopolize discourse in the post-Renaissance, the Trystero System emerges as its counterforce; so, too, does Pierce Inverarity's technological, IBM-controlled America constantly create its conspiratorial other. In its presence as an abstraction, the Demon broods like the Gnostic Demiurge over all this cyclical, circular, and ultimately absurd molecular behavior, this Sisyphean labor of the secondary demons, the incessant rut of their desire. The Idea of History is the Idea of the Demon. Thus Oedipa sits passively inside the box of American history at the end of *Lot 49*, waiting to be acted upon, waiting for the Demon to come and cry her fate. She is also inside the box of her body still looking at the world through "dark green bubble shades," still a captive maiden in the tower of her being looking for the "knight of deliverance." How, then, is she to be released? In *Lot 49* Oedipa's knights are all self-effacing, suicidal, men with muted horns. They have nothing to tell her. Driblette, the enigmatic director of *The Courier's Tragedy*, vanishes into the steam of a shower stall like the Cheshire Cat and is seen no more. Her husband, Mucho, is maddened by the omnipresent sign of the National Automobile Dealers' Association, a sign that "said nada, nada, against the blue sky." And nothing is the utterance of the cryer in this fiction which breaks off before the cry is heard.

In *Gravity's Rainbow* the "knight of deliverance" appears: Blicero, the suprasexual fashioner of the Schwarz-gerät, the black apparatus that will enable the V-2 rocket to break free of gravity and enter the realm of radiance. Yo-yoing like Benny Profane in *V.*, Slothrop wanders through the novel, an escaped pawn in the technological chess game of the Second World War. In his search for the meaning of his fate, as he tries to find an elusive and mysterious rocket, a particular rocket cryptically noted in captured SS manifests, he becomes increasingly irrelevant, increasingly ludicrous, finally a cartooned figure—Rocketman in a pig mask. Pynchon turns savagely on him, this typically American Ishmael, because in effect it is the typically American Ahab, Blicero, who now commands his attention. This disconcerting shift in narrative focus has confused many of the novel's readers, turning them into amazed and nervous Starbucks. Walter Clemons advises in *Newsweek*: "Pause, try to understand, and when you fail, move on, trusting in Pynchon who is a visionary artist in superlative control. . . ." The ruined landscape Slothrop traverses in this narrative is the same landscape, more or less, that appears in *Nightwood* and again in *The Cannibal*, the landscape of nightmare awake and realized in the world. He encounters the same chaotic mingling of disordered social classes, swims through the same thick sea of sexual perversion. But *Nightwood* is profoundly elegiac. If its cruelties and horrors are minutely rendered, the novel presents at the same time a mythopoeic sense of life as the life corrupted, the life lost. It mourns the loss of our Edenic animality, the original body through which we come polymorphously into the tragic alienation of self-consciousness:

> Sometimes one meets a woman who is beast turning human. Such a person's every movement will reduce to an image of a forgotten experience; a mirage of an eternal wedding cast on the racial memory: as insupportable a joy as would be the vision of an eland coming down an aisle of trees, chapleted with orange blossoms and bridal veil, a hoof raised in the economy of fear, stepping in the trepidation of flesh that will become myth; as the unicorn is neither man nor beast deprived, but human hunger pressing its beast to its prey.

And while it is true that *Nightwood* concludes with Robin Vote, the eland-woman, on all fours, debased, imitating a rabid dog, the force of this conclusion depends on the measure we have been given, that luminous creation myth.

There are passages in *Gravity's Rainbow* where Pynchon writes with a similar grace and lyrical precision. The long meditation that occurs when Roger Mexico and Jessica visit a small church in Kent on Christmas Eve is simply a *tour de force*, superb prose, a discourse that figures the conjunction of an incoming V-2 and the twinkle of the Christmas star:

> Lower in the sky the flying bombs are out too, roaring like the Adversary, seeking whom they may devour. It's a long walk home tonight. Listen to this mock-angel singing, let your communion be at least in listening, even if they are not spokesmen for your exact hopes, your exact, darkest terror, listen. There must have been evensong here long before the news of Christ. Surely for as long as there have been nights bad as this one—something to raise the possibility of another night that could actually, with love and cockcrows, light the path home, banish the Adversary, destroy the boundaries between our lands, our bodies, our stories, all false, about who we are: for the one night, leaving only the clear way home and the memory of the infant you saw, almost too frail, there's too much shit in these streets, camels and other beasts stir heavily outside, each hoof a chance to wipe him out, make him only another Messiah . . . while here in this town the Jewish collaborators are selling useful gossip to Imperial Intelligence.

But the measure in this passage is not really given, the interpolated phrase, "all false," undercuts Roger's longing, and what fills the meditation, what impels it forward, is Pynchon's loathing for the continuity of the obscene in history, the overwhelming sense that it has always been thus, always as dire. The only stars that speak in this firmament are those that come crashing down to explode in our faces. So wicked is the world depicted in *Gravity's Rainbow*, so burdened with lunacy and despair, that indeed it deserves to be ended. In this regard, the novel's final section, "Counterforce," deserves close scrutiny. For it is here that Slothrop sinks, an unredeemed Ishmael, that Blicero fires his last significant rocket, the 00000, and Pynchon clarifies his primary metaphors.

Although the plot of *Gravity's Rainbow* is not easily summarized, its general outline can be sketched. One crowded narrative line traces Slothrop's peregrination through the last years of the war into the beginning of the postwar period, a journey that takes him from London (where the rockets are falling) to Peenemunde (where the rockets are built and launched). This particular arc of the plot mordantly describes in its multitudinous events and sub-plots, its tales within tales, the chaotic, conspiratorial, strife-torn world of the historical, the world of the preterite. An esoteric branch of British Intelligence dominated by an obsessed Pavlovian scientist, Edward Pointsman, detects a correlation between V-2 strikes in London and the random scores of an American officer (Slothrop) who has placed stars on a map in his office to indicate the places where his seductions prospered. He is sent to France (without understanding the nature of his mission) to be used as a human dowser, set loose and then followed as he erotically senses and tracks down a mysterious rocket the Germans have assembled, possibly the rocket whose mysterious Schwarz-gerät is a rudimentary nuclear device. A maniacal behaviorist who resembles Dr. Benway in *Naked Lunch*, Pointsman is an exemplary would-be Demon, the omnipotent transmitter sorting, sending and controlling human (and historical) behavior. Like his SS counterparts in Dachau and Buchenwald, Pointsman has no scruples in experimenting with human subjects. At "The White Visitation," formerly an insane asylum, he has assembled a research team that combines psychics and psychologists, white and black magic, whose single-minded purpose is the pursuit of control. Pointsman looks beyond their immediate task, the knowledge and prediction of the unknown, that inexplicable rain of flying bombs, and envisions a world that looks very much like B. F. Skinner's _Walden Two_, the earthly paradise of a benevolent concentration camp. In this account Pynchon retrieves all the punning and word play he had exercised in _V._ on the concept and institution of Intelligence. The bureaucratic conflict and the career-making that embroils Pointsman's establishment in constant turbulence mirrors the actual struggle that went on between Duncan Sandys and Lord Cherwell as British Intelligence sought to comprehend the threat of the V-2 rocket in the last days of the war. Similarly it reflects the struggle that involved the Germans on their side of the Channel as the Wehrmacht and the Luftwaffe contended for the privilege of launching the rocket. All the demons in _Gravity's Rainbow_, the knowers and spies, are doubled—Germans and British, Americans and Russians. And what they all seek to know is _the_ Demon, the secret of the rocket that will enable whoever finds it to rule the world, control its destiny, impose the peace. Thus the second half of the novel ironically follows the well-known race toward Peenemunde and the capture of its mysteries, the capture of Wernher von Braun. Yet all this plotting, both historical and narrative, this expense of intelligence, divulges only a brutal joke. The true mystery is not there: it is under Soldiers' Field in Chicago. Late in the novel, as Slothrop sits listlessly in Berlin, a scrap of newspaper informs him: MB DRO ROSHI.

In escaping Pointsman's surveillance in southern France, Slothrop becomes the equivalent of a randomly bouncing molecule slowly and inexorably wearing down. He escapes only Pointsman's plot, not the box of history or the box of his nature. Nor do any of the lovers, rogues, artists and swindlers whose fortunes either coincide or collide with his. Those few who esteem tenderness in the novel, notably Leni Pökler, a young German Marxist, and Roger Mexico, are inevitably deprived, betrayed by their lovers, betrayed by their idealism. Slothrop's search for the rocket leads him into the bowels of the earth, the Mittelwerke at Peenemunde, and into the darkness of the body itself where he circles, a guideless Dante, all the terraces of sexual depravity. Episode by episode, borrowing from de Sade, Havelock Ellis, and undoubtedly Burroughs, Pynchon catalogues the various positions and possibilities. This is the furiously coupling and uncoupling world that Pointsman strives to master demonically, whose exchanges he attempts to systematize. It eludes him. When first met in the narrative, he is trying to seize a stray dog for his laboratory and comically fails, getting his foot caught instead in a loose toilet bowl. Near the end of the novel he castrates the wrong man and is thoroughly disgraced. But his disgrace is not necessarily a good sign in _Gravity's Rainbow_, an indication that tyranny is as finite as tyrants. It proposes rather the hopelessness of history and the ignorance of knowledge.

The contraposed emergence of Weissmann/Blicero in _Gravity's Rainbow_ inscribes the novel's other narrative, its other discourse. For where Slothrop's plot-line is fouled with numerous plots, comically entangled with questions, false identities, doppelgangers, lost lovers, vindictive enemies, strewn with surreal episodes, Blicero moves steadily and surely toward his appointed goal. He is the Bad Priest, the heresiarch whose doctrine is Gnostic transcendence, Manichean purification, whose science exists only for the uses of magic, whose disciples understand from the start that what he pursues in his cruelty is the clarity of the absolute. Unlike Pointsman who serves the Demon, Blicero is the master of whiteness. His African pupil and former lover, Enzian, discovers in Europe the meaning of that whiteness: "love, among these men, once past the simple feel and orgasming of it, had to do with masculine technologies, with contracts, with winning and losing. Demanded, in his own case, that he enter the service of the rocket. . . . Beyond simple steel erection, the Rocket was an entire system _won_, away from the feminine darkness, held against the entropies of lovable but scatterbrained Mother Nature: that was the first thing he was obliged by Weissmann to learn, his first step toward citizenship in the Zone." To Blicero also belong Katje Borgesius and Gottfried, blonde and blond, a matched pair of selfless 0's whom Blicero instructs in the chastisement of the flesh, the negation of its will. It is the ecstatically sodomized Gottfried, a bleached and neutered boy sheathed in Impolex, a plastic skin, whom Blicero sends up in the 00000 rocket as his cerebral seed. That orgasm strains against the pull of the physical world, the pull of history, the pull of human desire, strains to reach the whiteness beyond space and time, Poe's whiteness, Melville's whiteness, the "colorless all-color" from which, Ishmael confides in _Moby Dick_, we all shrink. But Brennschluss inevitably comes too soon for the 00000, it burns out like the novel itself striving at this far reach, falls back toward Los Angeles into our time even as the novel itself spirals back into literature, into self-reflexive fiction, its own specific gravity.

Where are we, then, at the conclusion of _Gravity's Rainbow_? Looking at the moon. "Is the cycle over now," Blicero speculates, "and a new one ready to begin? Will our new Deathkingdom be the Moon?" Govinda Lal's fugitive manuscript in _Mr. Sammler's Planet_ begins with much the same question: "How long will this earth remain the only home of Man?" In Bellow's novel, however, we are on familiar ground since both Dr. Lal and Mr. Sammler are ironic humanists whose moon-talk is comfortably situated in the civility of philosophical discourse, but in Pynchon's fiction the ground is far from defined, far from safe. For one thing, this admirable Ahab wears the uniform of a Schutzhäftlingsführer. _Gravity's Rainbow_ begins with an epigraph citing Wernher von Braun's belief in a spiritual existence after death, and of course von Braun was one of the principal engineers who designed the V-2. Like the fictive Blicero who stands apart from the concerns of the preterite, the muddle of politics, von Braun has always insisted that his work on the rocket was dedicated to a higher vision. Unlike Hitler and Goebbels who saw in it the instrument of revenge, Wagnerian tympani, and unlike Gerhard Degenkolb, Walter Dornberger and Albert Speer who were fascinated by the technological aspects of the rocket, von Braun's eyes were presumably lifted upward, beyond good and evil, toward the purity of space. Pynchon appropriates that version of von Braun and transforms it, turning von Braun's convenient piety into the knowledge of the Manichean who knows, above all, that liberation is attained only against nature, against the pull of gravity. The thrust of von Braun's rocket is thus the same act as the thrust of Blicero's cock up Gottfried's ass, a denial of the woman's belly, earth's womb.

Through the mock-historicity of _V._ and _Lot 49_, as we have seen, Pynchon himself elusively plays Stencil's game of "approach and avoid," beguiling his readers with mazes of information that lead nowhere. In their dark, Stencil, Oedipa and Slothrop feel their way along the walls of the womb-world that confines them, looking for an opening, looking (to use an apt phrase) for the light at the end of the tunnel. No such light is ever shed. Yet Pynchon's Manichean view of their dilemma is itself constrained, not wholly realized or believed. There are two rockets fired at the end of *Gravity's Rainbow*, the 00000 and the 00001, the first containing Gottfried and the second Enzian, "a good Rocket to take us to the stars, an evil Rocket for the World's suicide, the two perpetually in struggle." Both rockets are nonetheless on death trips, both seek the only bright and splendid way out, the way of the Elect, leaving Slothrop alive beneath them, earthbound and mediocre. The true struggle in *Gravity's Rainbow* is thus between Pointsman and Blicero, Demon and Demon, between modes of death. And here Pynchon's fiction reenters the sphere of history. For these two eminent figures are allegorical representatives not of Light and Dark, Good and Evil, Spirit and Matter, but of the Bourgeois and the Heroic.

In his "hard, ruthless, comic" approach to the history of the Second World War, Pynchon refuses one by one the liberal pieties and moral postures that typically inform such histories. He writes instead a comic novel whose locus is V-bombed London, the concentration camp, destroyed Berlin, throwing in at the end, off-stage, the dull bang at Hiroshima. Yet out of all the burlesque and parody, the caricature and comic routines, he strives to retrieve, or at least reinvent, the value of evil. For what threatens Slothrop's humanity is not the violence of war, but the blankness of peace. He is most alive when the London air is taut with the screaming imminence of his death. Life is lived best amid those tight chances, lived most intensely when there is no complacent middle securing it, only sharp perilous extremes. The ethic Pynchon finally renders in *Gravity's Rainbow* is the ethic of the desperado, not the ethic of the survivor inclosing himself in cool ironies. So the novel is extravagant in style, conception, technique, an extravagance that often overspills into self-indulgence, but which neverthe-less constitutes the core of the book. It is through this extravagance that Pynchon insists on his otherness, his anar-chic criminality. The meaningless world described in *V.* and *Lot 49* frames this fiction. It is the outlying horrific space that surrounds the Götterdämmerung of 1945. What menaces Stencil and Oedipa in their constant search for the plot is the nausea of the sufficient sameness of everyday life, the common plotless course of bourgeois existence that wears down without significance to an inconspicuous death in a Home for the Aged. Blicero struggles to explode this "cooperative structure of lies," this rationalized world where everything and everyone is named and known.

> The Oedipal situation in the Zone these days is terrible. There is no dignity. The mothers have been masculinized to old worn moneybags of no sexual interest to anyone, and yet here are their sons, still trapped inside inertias of lust that are 40 years out of date. The fathers have no power today and never did, but because 40 years ago we could not kill them, we are condemned now to the same passivity, the same masochist fantasies *they* cherished in secret, and worse, we are condemned in our weakness to imper-sonate men of power our own infant children must hate . . . So generation after generation of men in love with pain and passivity serve out their time in the Zone, silent, redolent of faded sperm, terrified of dying, desperately addicted to the comforts others sell them, however useless, ugly or shallow, willing to have life defined for them by men whose only talent is for death.

Thus Pynchon restores Ahab to us, Captain Blicero of the SS, the evil father whose malice is our only hope of heroism, whose metaphysical ass-fucking promises us a glamorous

death, death with our boots on. But seemingly to no avail. "The petit-bourgeois is a man unable to imagine the Other," Roland Barthes writes in *Mythologies*. "If he comes face to face with him, he blinds himself, ignores and denies him, or else transforms him into himself. In the petit-bourgeois universe, all the experiences of confrontation are reverberating, any otherness is reduced to sameness." This has been Pynchon's fate, the smarmy embrace of toleration. He shares the National Book Award this year with Isaac Bashevis Singer.

ALFRED MacADAM
"Pynchon as Satirist: To Write, to Mean"
Yale Review, June 1978, pp. 555–66

Since 1963, Thomas Pynchon has published three texts: *V.* (1963), *The Crying of Lot 49* (1966), and *Gravity's Rain-bow* (1973); all of them have been called novels. There is nothing shocking in this, but we may wonder just what it means, since the word "novel" seems devoid of meaning. What such an appellation might suggest outside a literary context and where it might locate the text in the various semiotic systems of our society would be interesting areas to explore: we might find that the word novel has much more meaning as a commercial term than it does as an esthetic term; we might find, further, that novels are used mainly as psychological mirrors by their readers, having a function analogous to the astrological chart or the do-it-yourself psy-chotherapy manual. For literary criticism, however, the term has become an embarrassment. To preserve the term novel, then, it may be necessary to rob it of many of its important authors, especially those, like Pynchon, who are actually satirists.

When we read a Pynchon text we may be disconcerted by it, but we usually find ourselves comfortable with at least one of its elements: setting. In fact, Pynchon's *mise en scène* may be the only reason for calling his books novels. He is as archeologically precise about places and things as Flaubert, although he should probably be compared to the Flaubert of *Salammbô*. In that text, Flaubert transports Emma Bovary's problems back to Carthage, rendering both Emma and the setting abstract. Pynchon, on the other hand, creates a false familiarity in the mind of the reader which makes him forget that what he is reading is not a study of people in a historical setting but the clash of personified ideas surrounded by the things of the twentieth century. Flaubert and Pynchon are opposites that converge: Flaubert makes the alien familiar by recreating the problems of the nineteenth-century bourgeoisie in Carthage and Pynchon makes the familiar strange by having his personifications collide in a setting we know only too well.

This disjunction between character and setting is the first indication that Pynchon is a satirist, that he is reworking satire as a modern-day disciple of Petronius, Apuleius, or Voltaire might. In addition to this use of a pasteboard, *trompe-l'oeil* setting, there are three other aspects of his work that support a reading of them as satires: his characters are associated with ideas or *idées fixes*, his scenes take precedence over his plots, and his characters' psychological development is reduced to a minimum. The difference between satire and, for example, novel may be seen in two areas: character and plot. Novelistic plots, as Fielding suggests in *Tom Jones*, both echoing and modifying Cervantes, tend toward history writing, and it would not be unreasonable to suggest that the particular form of history used as the model for novelistic plots is the develop-

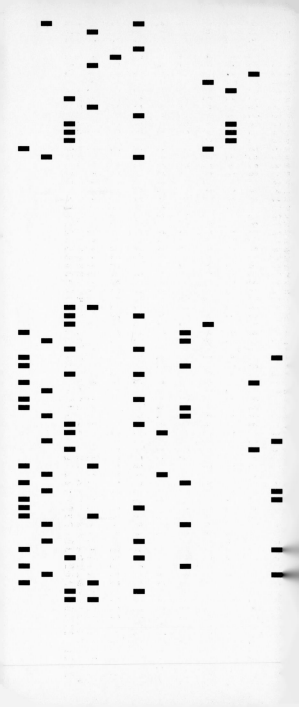

mental sort we associate with Hegel. At least this is the kind used in the most orthodox novels, Scott's *Waverley*, Balzac's entire *Comédie Humaine*, and Faulkner's *Sartoris*. In all of these texts, character is fully exploited in order to create figures as human as possible, even as those same characters are associated with one or another antagonistic side in the battleground of dialectical history.

We cannot become "intimate" with characters in either satire or romance because they never acquire psychological depth. In both genres, character is subordinated to some greater concept, either ideas, in the case of satire, or archetypes, especially those associated with fertility, death, regeneration, or sterility in the case of romance. In both genres, characters are impenetrable, not human, and this alien quality is only mitigated by occasional outpourings of sentiment and flashes of wit. The relationship between satire and romance, with regard to character, is interesting because of the antithetical nature of the two genres: romance tends toward the noble, the heroic, and the superhuman, while satire tends toward the roguish or ordinary. The blending of the two, in *Don Quijote* for example, generates an irony which has become a constant in Western literature.

The juxtaposition of romance and satire is also important for understanding Pynchon's esthetic enterprise because he appropriates one of romance's principal plots, the quest, and uses it for satiric purposes. This recalls the development of the picaresque satire in Spain after *Lazarillo de Tormes* (1554): the paratactic rogue's life takes on the unity of the saint's life by being told from a postconversion perspective. The *pícaro's* quest for survival is translated into a quest for moral salvation. This transformation is particularly important for Pynchon's satires because it infuses the search or quest with irony, returning the reader by a circuitous route to the irony of the *Lazarillo*, where Lazarillo's search for a place in the world is resolved when he exchanges his human dignity for a full stomach.

All three of Pynchon's texts are ironic quests, but *V.*, his first, is the most mysterious. It is a search for something or someone, V., but what V. is is never made clear. The search ends in mystery and death, and all the reader knows at the end is that the enigma concerns the existence or nonexistence of something "out there," something that either possesses meaning or not. But whatever it is must be at all costs ascertained, and this idea of a mystery-to-be-resolved is what defines the reader's situation in all three of Pynchon's satires. *V.* is arranged in such a way that, as a totality, it seems to be defying the reader to find a system of meaning. This dare, this either/or crux, is in fact the result of yet another juxtaposition, that of faith and paranoia, and it is through this juxtaposition that Pynchon makes his readers participate in his texts as though they were characters. Faith may be understood as belief in the existence of things unseen, God understood as the primary factor in religious belief. Taken out of a theological context, the same definition may be used to define paranoia, the belief in the existence of things unseen, things that are dangerous and threatening. The difference rests on the malignant nature of the unseen reality for the paranoiac and the beneficent nature of the unseen reality for the faithful. Pynchon never resolves that enigma, leaving an important decision up to the reader.

The reader of *V.*, or so it would seem, cannot help but create meaning as he reads. Despite what may be warnings to the contrary, the reader will inevitably forge both meaning and unity, a plot that signifies, out of a series of chapters from disparate but related stories. The fact that the text is bound as a volume virtually guarantees this creation of meaning, although this very act is one of the pitfalls the author is preparing for his meaning-bound readers. The book begins in 1955 and ends in 1919, a reversal which suggests that time in the text

does not have the same relationship to space and meaning it has in romance, where plots are often, as in *Parzifal*, linked to the changes of the seasons. If there is any meaning in that sense in *V.* it is not one the reader will arrive at after a meandering but basically linear journey. Meaning will come, if it does, in a flash, like some sort of grace.

There are, naturally, other texts that resemble *V.*, other texts in which episodes are heaped together in such a way that it is the decision of the reader to determine the presence or absence of meaning. Huxley's *Eyeless in Gaza*, Marc Saporta's *Composition Number 1*, Julio Cortázar's *Hopscotch*, or Guillermo Cabrera Infante's *Three Trapped Tigers* might be examples. In all of these books, as in *V.*, the reader is the most important character, whose principal problem is the invention or discovery of meaning in the text. Whether he will exist in doubt and disregard the problem of meaning completely, or whether he will postulate a meaning for the text, is his dilemma. What one does with the text, in the last analysis, is determined by one's esthetics: If literature is taken to be a form of communication in which actual information is passed on to the reader, finding a meaning in the text may be a way of justifying both the text and the reading. If, however, literature is taken to be the esthetic or decorative use of language, in which nothing but the pleasure of the text itself is communicated, then the problem of meaning will be no more a problem than the morality of a crime in a detective fiction: it is merely a part of the text, not something to be taken in isolation.

The clash of faith and paranoia, grace and fulmination is the subject of *The Crying of Lot 49*. *Gravity's Rainbow* takes an element present in both *V.* and *The Crying of Lot 49*, the international corporation, and identifies it as the occult, meaningful system "out there," although while the system is supposed to possess meaning, it is never made clear just what its meaning is, as if meaning could be divorced from intentionality. All we learn in the three books is that the corporation, the Yoyodyne corporation which appears first in *V.* and reappears in the other two texts, stands on both sides of all political, social, and ethical fences. In *Gravity's Rainbow*, the protagonist discovers he is actually the "product" of the company, and in *The Crying of Lot 49* we learn that Pierce Inverarity, the dead man who may be the invisible force behind Oedipa Maas's quest, is an owner of Yoyodyne Inc. This manifestation of an order in the world may suggest a religious element in the books, since recognition and fear of the Deity are central to religious experience, or it may be that to discover the existence of such systems and such omnipotent though mortal beings as Pierce Inverarity may be horrifying.

The Crying of Lot 49 reveals both Pynchon's sense of literary genres and his attitude toward meaning in literature. This slim volume mediates between two very large-scale enterprises, *V.* and *Gravity's Rainbow*, and may be taken as the ironic rewriting of the romance plot of enlightenment (a parody of either *The Golden Ass* or perhaps *La Nausée*) or as a detective fiction in which the detective, like Oedipus, is both the investigator and the object of investigation. Whether by chance or design, *The Crying of Lot 49* stands as a pivotal text in Pynchon's oeuvre: it restates the central issue of *V.*, to make order of confusion or remain in doubt, in the shape of a classical satire, a narrative interspersed with verse interludes, here in the form of songs. This model provides the structure for *Gravity's Rainbow*, the spectacular difference being that of scale. By getting to the heart of *The Crying of Lot 49*, by examining both its intellectual preoccupations and its use of the structure of classical satire, it is possible to isolate all the distinctive features of Pynchon's fiction.

The most typical of all the devices in Pynchon's repertoire is his use of trick names: how are readers supposed to react to a woman named Oedipa? The Sophoclean or Freudian association is inevitable, and baffling, but an understanding of the device as a device and not as the knot which, once unraveled, opens the way to some deeper meaning, may make Pynchon's esthetics more comprehensible. Our task is to understand the device, not to decipher it. Pynchon's onomastic punning produces a kind of Brechtian "alienation effect," reminding the reader that what he is reading is a fiction, that the words here are only words. And words point, as inevitably as Oedipa points to Oedipus, to other words: it is the act of postulating an interpretation for those words, the act of conferring a particular meaning on them that, once again, defines the reader's dilemma with regard to the text. The interpretation will, of course, tell more about the reader than it will about the text.

Pynchon seems to have modeled his text on a short story by Jorge Luis Borges, "The Approach to Al-Mu'tasim" (1935), from the *Ficciones* (1944) collection. (It might be noted in passing that Pynchon's interest in Borges is strong, to the point that he presents a theory of Argentine literature and of Borges himself in *Gravity's Rainbow*, p. 264.) Borges's story is a bogus book review in which Borges, or his narrator, pretends to be writing about *The Approach to Al-Mu'tasim*, by one Mir Bahadur Alí, "the first detective novel written by a native of Bombay City," a text damned (apocryphally) by the English essayist Philip Guedalla as "a rather uncomfortable combination of those allegorical poems of Islam which rarely fail to interest their translators and those crime fictions which inevitably baffle John H. Watson and refine the horror of human life in the most irreproachable hotels of Brighton" (translations mine). The copy Borges reviews also bears a spurious prologue by yet another English literary figure, Dorothy Sayers, just to make its credentials all the more "irreproachable."

The plot is simple: an Islamic Indian kills a Hindu in a riot. He flees and while hiding finds a horrible man who mentions in passing a few mysterious names. The next day the unnamed protagonist sets out to investigate those names. The search, the quest for whatever lies behind those names, which would seem to be the "good," leads the protagonist, like Kim, over all of India, to all levels of life. In the last scene he approaches the final name, Al-Mu'tasim, an encounter Borges does not describe. He does note that in the second, revised edition, the one he reviews, the text is rendered allegorical: Al-Mu'tasim becomes a symbol of God, the search a search for Him. Pynchon appropriates this story or plot summary and fleshes it out, although it seems he prefers the earlier, less obviously allegorical version, where Al-Mu'tasim's identity is still ambiguous.

Borges's two editions represent the fate of the text once the writer finishes writing it: the primitive version is the unread text or the text as it is being read, while the second is the text interpreted, where ambiguities are accounted for and meaning postulated. Borges goes so far as to make the author just one more reader, one more interpreter whose alterations disfigure the text. Unless we revise *The Crying of Lot 49* and make it too into an allegorical quest for God, we must be content with uncertainty. We can never, if we eschew allegorization, know if Tristero and the W.A.S.T.E. system are good or evil, and we accept the fact that we will never know who is bidding for lot 49 at the end of the narrative. We agree that there is nothing more to the story than unresolved mystery.

Borges resolves the "lady or the tiger" crux Pynchon leaves undecided because he wants to maintain the pose of the book reviewer and because he wants to show the *disponibilité* of any literary plot, its susceptibility to interpretation. Both Pynchon and Borges deploy their material in their own way, but both are rewriting the same plot, the quest. Borges lets his protagonist remain nameless because he knows it is not the fate of the characters which is at stake but the repetition of a plot, while, paradoxically, Pynchon's use of overtly symbolic names is an inversion of the same device: the names have so many potential meanings they can have no single meaning. Both texts tend toward abstraction and embody an esthetic that views literature as the orchestration of known structures, the reassembly of elements which may be recombined infinitely. Literature in these texts is a gloss on literature, a metaphor about metaphor, words about words, utterances devoid of meaning but willing to accept whatever the reader offers.

One way, then, of approaching *The Crying of Lot 49* is to dismiss the reader's quest for meaning from the inquiry. Instead of dispelling ambiguity for the sake of coherence or intellectual security, the reader would focus his attention on how the text deploys its devices and how it translates the satiric tradition. We might begin with character: Mucho Maas, Metzger, Hilarius, and the others stand as foils for Oedipa Maas; she is chosen to be Pierce Inverarity's executrix, they are not. None of them is meant to be the *pharmakos*, the propitiatory victim figure Northrop Frye, René Girard, and Jacques Derrida have studied in such detail in *Anatomy of Criticism*, *La Violence et le sacré*, and *La Dissémination*. These characters are only updated types. For the Panglossian pedant of traditional satire, Pynchon substitutes the mad psychoanalyst. The rest of Oedipa's male companions embody one or another profession, from lawyer to disc jockey, each in his way caricaturing all members of his profession. The rock groups and the Yoyodyne chorus stand as ironic commentators on the action, their traditional role in satire.

Another fixture of satire reworked here is the relentless outpouring of information. Pynchon includes an inordinate amount of scientific knowledge about such matters as entropy and the calculus theorem abbreviated as "dt" or "delta-t." Entropy, divorced from both physics and communication theory and translated into literary speculation, defines the relationship between a text and a tradition. A text may simply reiterate the given patterns of a literature as long as there is enough energy in the system, the complex relationship between readers and writers, to sustain it. But somewhere in the business of literary production the system begins to lose energy—epics, for example, are today only sporadically written and even more rarely read. In order to revitalize the process, some agency recombines elements present in the tradition so that work may go on. This would seem to be the role of the individual author: he cannot contribute new elements to the process, but he certainly can recombine them in a new way, or, more importantly, infuse new power into the system by means of irony. Pynchon's irony, like Borges's, is that of the "re-writer," the author who insinuates his work into the tradition by writing a text which seems to be something else: Borges is nominally a reviewer, Pynchon a mystery writer.

The importance of irony in this revitalization cannot be overemphasized. And Pynchon's irony is derived primarily from juxtaposition: he wants romance and satire to clash and to create a situation in which the reader will realize that both genres are nothing more than fictions, not mirrors of the age or imitations of life. Irony is the energy of the re-creating writer because he creates that space where incongruities may flourish, where meaning as an objective of the text is made totally literary instead of extratextual.

In this sense, Oedipa Maas is a metaphor for the reader, just as Pierce Inverarity may be understood to represent the artist. His name, as suggestive as hers, renders both roles sexual, the artist being the masculine, the reader feminine. His given name, Pierce, complements this sexual division of labor by evoking the phallic stylus violating the white purity of the page, while his last name, Inverarity, hints at such concepts as inveracity and inversion, the illusory or lying aspect of writing. The text constitutes the communion of these two archetypes, the writer who leaves of himself only the misleading traces of his will (the pun transforming a mental act into a printed text), and the reader who executes it, seeing it in an extraordinarily dark glass. Oedipa follows Pierce's map, and it is through this act that the calculus concept becomes a literary metaphor: she charts his course as if it were the trajectory of a projectile instead of a literary plot (another pun, perhaps even more suggestive than the first). She sacrifices her life in order to carry out his ambiguous will, but without her sacrifice, entropy would once again threaten the system. Without the participation of the reader, the text would cease to exist. Oedipa's role in the text might also, therefore, be regarded as that of novice, analogous to Lucian's in *The Golden Ass*, a passing through (in this case) of an esthetic rite of passage. A further irony, the reversal of the sexual roles of reader and writer, takes place when the reader re-creates the text in interpretation; the text becomes then the reader's, itself subject to reinterpretation.

Oedipa's role as reader and interpreter is alluded to throughout *The Crying of Lot 49*, but perhaps the most significant instance occurs at the beginning of chapter 2, when she first comes to San Narciso, Pierce Inverarity's city in southern California. She associates Pierce's realm, as she observes it from above, with a printed circuit: "there were to both [San Narciso and the printed circuit] outward patterns a hieroglyphic sense of concealed meaning, of an intent to communicate" (p. 13). What the actual message is, what the meaning is of the circuit or city, which both stand as signs in an unknown script, is the plot she sees spread out before her. Just as in one version of Borges's story the search is its own justification and not the outcome of the search, the searcher, in this case, the reader, would seem to be the real object of the quest. Oedipa, in the same passage, senses the adumbration, the shadow of Pierce (who once disguised his voice as that of Lamont Cranston, the Shadow), and the narrator calls it "an odd, religious instant," vaguely horrifying yet wonderful. Suddenly the geometry of the scene changes: instead of looking down on San Narciso, Oedipa is in the middle of things, the eye of a hurricane. Outside the eye, she thinks, words are being pronounced, but whatever they may express is beyond her comprehension. Here Pynchon inverts ironically both the idea of the sublime and all traditional literary uses of mountain ascents as approaches to enlightenment. Oedipa is variously looking down at a man-made landscape, an artifact as artificial as a literary plot, or standing at the center of a silent whirl, excluded from communication, divorced from the Word, yet tantalized by the possibility both may exist. Fixtures taken from a literary tradition concerned with producing awe through language are here made grotesque: if there is a divinity in this text, it is Pierce Inverarity, Proteus, wearing one more disguise.

Another romance device revitalized through irony here is the interpolated tale. Here it is Richard Wharfinger's Jacobean drama *The Courier's Tragedy*, a bogus text worthy of comparison with Mir Bahadur Ali's *The Approach to Al-mu'tasim*. We notice that the play constitutes a gathering point for two of *The Crying of Lot 49*'s principle themes, the Echo and Narcissus relationship between Oedipa and Pierce (which is a motif: San Narciso, the Saint Narcissus of Wharfinger's play, and Echo Courts, the motel in San Narciso where Oedipa stays), and the concept of language as a failed system of communication, one which has only a shadow existence, an "intent to communicate" (just as road systems, printed circuits, urban design all seem to be attempts to say something, although what that may be is unknown), while true communication can only take place between those linked by bonds other than language, those who have been initiated into secret societies. Of course, what is communicated among the initiates is not a message but the fact of communality, which would make them like circuits through which an electric current would flow. Wharfinger, much sicker than his namesake "Sick Dick," member of yet another rock group, wrote, according to Driblette, his twentieth-century director, another "re-worker" analogous to Borges and Pynchon, only to entertain. What Oedipa, as well as Pynchon's unsuspecting reader, may wonder is why a public would want to be entertained in such a way, but we see in the sadomasochistic relationship between text and reader another image of Pierce and Oedipa, the reader submitting to the will of the text. The interpolated play, like its traditional counterparts, reflects and comments on the major action: *The Crying of Lot 49* is entertainment and it entertains, like Gothic romance, by posing mysteries, enigmas not to be resolved but to be enjoyed for their own sake.

It is perhaps as entertainment that all satires should be read instead of being defined, as they have been, as literature's commentary on society's foibles. Satire may use its didacticism as an *apologia pro vita sua*, but to reduce Swift, Pope, and Peacock to the level of censor is to trivialize their texts as esthetic enterprises. What Pynchon attempts to do in his writings is to create a literature that destroys the concept that art must mirror life. His texts constantly point out their own artificiality, their identity as literature, and consistent with this mockery of the dictates of literary realism is a turn toward intellect, to the mind as creator of unreal systems, especially philosophy and theology.

Pynchon would probably never deny the legitimacy of either discipline as a discipline, but he uses those fields of speculation as elements in a fiction, a game played for its own sake. The ideology of satire, as Pynchon writes it, is not to reform the reader, who would then, presumably, reform the world, but to reclaim for literature one of the purposes essential to all rhetorical exercises: to delight.

WILLIAM M. PLATER
From "In Which Various Things Come Together"
The Grim Phoenix: Reconstructing Thomas Pynchon

1978, pp. 187–98

The theory claims the role of a great scientific theory. Its synthetic power allows us to apprehend many disparate facts. In its development, it rediscovers some banal facts as landmarks; others, unexpected (for example, the uncertainty principles), justify it as a method of presentation. (Abraham Moles in *Information Theory and Esthetic Perception*)

If criticism offers any theory of Pynchon's fiction, its synthetic power may be only a socially acceptable form of paranoia, in which the critic voluntarily becomes the center of an elaborate plot hatched by some remote author. An exhausting array of facts seduces admirer and skeptic alike into the comfortable fantasy of their own ordered labyrinths, coaxing them with numbing certainty and indifferent guile. By remaining personally and aesthetically remote Pynchon feeds a contemporary mania for the very idea of paranoia. In a world that has seen this particular psychosis become a principle of international politics in such forms as the cold war, of international economics in giant oil, chemical, and communications cartels, or of religions in the hundred or so holy wars that have occurred in the past three decades, the question of who is paranoid and who is not is vital and relevant, and perhaps always has been. Pynchon forces his readers—and most acutely, his critics—to resolve this question before reaching any conclusion and thus forces them to demystify or naturalize his texts. ⟨. . .⟩ the reader is put in precisely the same situation as Oedipa Maas: either there is a coherent structure to Pynchon's fiction or the reader imagines it; or Pynchon has deliberately launched a plot aimed at the reader to make him or her sense a structure; or the reader fantasizes such a plot. A meta-solution is possible, but it requires ignoring the evidence of the novels.

The critical concern about structure is real since it is, finally, the center of Pynchon's fiction—the minotaur of his particular labyrinth. Although originally one of the Hippocratic categories of mental illness referring to deterioration, paranoia was given its modern connotation primarily by Emil Kraepelin at the end of the last century. It now generally refers to a form of psychosis based on a logical structure of relationships that interprets reality in terms of evidence of persecution. The paranoid believes that someone or some group is out to get him and sustains this belief with evidence that to his mind is irrefutable. Two characteristics of paranoia are particularly noteworthy: it is a psychosis of interpretation and it depends on a careful ordering of unconnected evidence to prove the existence of persecution. Paranoia is a highly rigorous, integrative, self-preserving mode of behavior amid assumed or real cultural chaos. It is often mistaken for normalcy and not infrequently is a formula for political and economic success precisely because its methods are those most highly regarded by the sane portion of humanity. When put in terms of control or power, paranoia's imaginary premises of persecution are indistinguishable from facts and certainly have to be considered within the realm of reality. Pynchon was prophetic, but not the least bit ironic, in beginning the fourth section of *Gravity's Rainbow*, "The Counterforce," with a quotation from Richard M. Nixon: "What?"[1] Thus paranoia retains its usefulness as a clinical classification, but its application goes far beyond any psychological condition. Paranoia, in one sense, is no more of a disorder than guilt and the term, at least, is used with an easy familiarity that raises hardly anyone's eyebrows.

Paranoia serves Pynchon well as a model, or extended metaphor, for a number of reasons, not the least of which is its decontaminated, socially acceptable use as description of real, imagined, and unconfirmed conspiracies. Its logical structure—the process of relating evidence—implies a structure for his own fiction, not unlike a great scientific theory. Although the clinical paranoid would organize uncertainties out of existence, Pynchon bases his use of the paranoia metaphor precisely on uncertainties, because both ambiguity and the more specific implications of uncertainty relations nourish paranoia and make any psychosis difficult to establish clinically. The question of whether a conspiracy is real or not remains an open one, a matter of interpretation. Paranoia also offers the advantage of allowing him to work with a dialectic of

good and evil, the persecuted victim and the enemy conspiracy, without obligation to substantiate, defend, or even explain. Again, it is a matter of interpretation, of designing a logical structure that will accommodate all the evidence. It is for this reason that paranoia may be the closest we can come to naming any theory that explains Pynchon's fictional world. From this perspective it is not difficult to see why so many themes, ideas, characters, evidences . . . are related. In the paranoid interpretation of Pynchon's stories and novels, the isolated system, the manipulation of reality and illusion, and the movement toward death transfigured are all logically related. They are evidence of some cosmic-scale, elitist conspiracy determined to use most of humanity and all of the earth's resources for its own ends, to derive its life from the death of everyone else. It is at this point that the reader, like Tchitcherine after taking Oneirine, is overwhelmed by the possibility that there really is a connection: "Like other sorts of paranoia, it is nothing less than the onset, the leading edge, of the discovery that *everything is connected*, everything in the Creation . . ." (703).

A conspiracy or plot is a defining characteristic of all Pynchon's novels. Although the uncovering of each conspiracy supplies the momentum for all the novels, and although the conspiracies each show all the characteristics of paranoia, the device is not simply repeated. In fact, the most paranoid among us might suspect that there is only one conspiracy and that the more we read the more evidence we uncover that points to some grand design we cannot quite see. After all, Kurt Mondaugen and young Weissmann were together with V. in the Südwest; Mondaugen went to work for the same Bloody Chiclitz who hired Benny Profane, who was a business partner of Pierce Inverarity, and who had been involved in the postwar scramble for the German technology—which Weissmann/Blicero and Mondaugen had developed; and, of course, a seemingly unaging Pig Bodine appears in a variety of places. How much coincidence can be tolerated before being organized into a system varies with the paranoid, but there is certainly evidence of something. Beyond these superficial relations, however, lies a connection that reflects Pynchon's serious concerns and his maturity as an artist. Any reader must be impressed with the fact that Pynchon not only returns to the idea of conspiracy for each novel, but he also increases the complexity of its function and of his own vision. It would be tempting merely to ascribe his preoccupation with paranoia to the disorder and suspicion of the decades since World War One, and the development of his vision to cynicism and experience. Surely these factors are involved, but more significant is the possibility that Pynchon views paranoia as a social and aesthetic form rather than as metaphor or psychosis—a form for relating the individual to community, to some external truth (or system of belief), for counteracting what appears as an increasingly entropic world. Delusion, illusion, fantasy, or hallucination is no longer a defining characteristic of paranoia as a form. Given the reality that is considered sane, paranoia may be regarded as a form of life amid so much waste, so much death.

The quests of Stencil, Oedipa, and Slothrop ⟨. . .⟩ demonstrate, on reflection, that these searches for evidence of conspiracy may all be classified as paranoid. ⟨. . .⟩ That Stencil, Oedipa, and Slothrop can simultaneously be engaged in a traditional quest, a Dashiell Hammett–like pursuit of clues, a stylized recapitulation of life, a movement through time, a tour, and an enactment of paranoid suspicions is testimony to the vibrancy of the form and to Pynchon's skill, but it may be that the only important feature is the form's capacity as a relational process. The object of the paranoid search is confirmation of some controlling group or force, which, once discovered, would be a confirmation of death; the process of searching, however, is life-sustaining and at the same time a form for relating the individual to death. The paranoid search also creates a functional community in the absence of any community at all and is thus a form for relating the individual to society. The paranoid search creates a framework for structuring facts and thereby provides a mechanism for accommodating accident or fortune even if it cannot be reconciled. And the paranoid search, by relating facts, creates its own history, one that is a function of the present.

Herbert Stencil's search for V. and the facts he carefully incorporates into a V-structure are a paranoia that turns him into "clownish Stencil . . . bells ajingle, waving a wooden, toy oxgoad."[2] Nonetheless the pursuit is all there is to Stencil's life. It keeps him animate and therefore he must take it seriously; it is a necessary delusion, whose goal is "to affirm that his quarry fitted in with The Big One, the century's master cabal. . . . If she was a historical fact then she continued active today and at the moment, because the ultimate Plot Which Has No Name was as yet unrealized . . ." (210). Though he feels himself V.'s victim, Stencil recognizes that a successful search will mean that the Plot will be realized. In effect, the search aims toward his own victimization and is an individual mode of relating to death. The V-structure reorganizes and recreates a personal history. Stencil's father had been engaged in "real" intrigues and conspiracies and his theory of the Situation that has no objective reality had been a mechanism for accommodating paranoid delusions. The younger Stencil inverts history and his father's model to make suspicions actual. Although in his hands the senior Stencil's tools of spying are comic—"cloak for a laundry sack, dagger to peel potatoes" (51)—they are the same tools. The search for V. also provides Herbert Stencil with a community. His father's only legacy had been "good will in nearly every city in the western world among those of his own generation" (43) so that he was able to survive in a "population coming more and more to comprise sons and friends of the originals" (44). Stencil's inquiries also provide a reason for relating to others outside his father's descended community, people who might be useful. Without this mode of relation, "it would then be he and V. all alone, in a world that somehow had lost sight of them both" (44). Having gleaned his father's journals and contacts for facts, Stencil must rely on accident, "waiting for a coincidence" (45), to provide additional information that he can incorporate. Paranoia thus supplies the mechanism for relating chance and willful human agency in a simple form. When on Malta Stencil finds that his facts fit too well, that "events seem to be ordered into an ominous logic" (423), he confronts his paranoia for what it is. Though Fausto mocks Stencil gently with his playful comment that "thirteen of us rule the world in secret" (425), he acknowledges that such delusions are necessary.

Stencil's paranoia is echoed in a number of minor characters: Godolphin has his Vheissu; Fairing has his parish of rats; Foppl has his 1904 uprising; and the senior Stencil has his Situation. While none of these visions rival Herbert Stencil's in complexity or pursuit, they do constitute the milieu of the novel and, like so many stencilized versions of the one paranoid preoccupation, allow Pynchon to comment on paranoia as social structure. Though Pynchon relies heavily on parody and satire in V., the forms of paranoia are too important merely to be ridiculed. Even if Stencil bears the brunt of an elaborate joke played on Henry Adams and scholars of like mind, he is saved from burlesque and the novel from trumpery by Pynchon's own seriousness. The author brings his readers continually to the brink of laughter only to remind them that we all do search for structures, that there are conspiracies that have killed 60,000 Hereros and stacked Jewish corpses like rusted car bodies, that a novel can be a "mirror," and that life does go on despite the odds against it. V. is a self-consciously funny novel whose humor is sustained by the way in which everything in its creation seems to be related. While much of the novel's artistic success may be due to such authorial self-consciousness, its significance for Pynchon's subsequent works lies in its development of a relational form.

The efficacy of paranoia is fully established in *The Crying of Lot 49*. Pynchon no longer needs the crutch of parody or the external existence of Henry Adams's systematized thought to carry the burden of meaning. Summoned from the lethargy of Tupperware parties, suburban herb gardens, and the organized tower of her own ego by Pierce Inverarity's will, Oedipa Maas suspects that her inheritance is America but that she is an exile. The novel unfolds with her discovering the way in which facts "fitted, logically, together,"[3] the way in which revelations "seemed to come crowding in exponentially, as if the more she collected the more would come to her, until everything she saw, smelled, dreamed, remembered, would somehow come to be woven into The Tristero" (58). The course of her quest parallels Stencil's in that she perceives another order of existence behind the world of appearances: "It was not an act of treason, nor possibly even of defiance. But it was a calculated withdrawal, from the life of the Republic, from its machinery. Whatever else was being denied them out of hate, indifference to the power of their vote, loopholes, simple ignorance, this withdrawal was their own, unpublicized, private. Since they could not have withdrawn into a vacuum (could they?), there had to exist the separate, silent, unsuspected world" (92). This, of course, is the world of the Tristero—its "constant theme, disinheritance" (120). Oedipa finds herself between two worlds, between inheritance and disinheritance. The clues she pieces together into the structure she comes to know as the Tristero—her paranoia— also begin to define by contrast the suspected world of appearances. Oedipa's search is not the simple construction of a conspiracy aimed at her, though that is a possibility; rather, it is evidence of the void that she must structure in the relations she establishes among facts, people, history, and her own impending death. As her former community of normal relations breaks down with the disintegration of her husband, her psychoanalyst, and her lover, she discovers a new, though hardly more stable, community of people in her clues. The difference is important because it shows her an isolation redeemable not by people but only by a form. The object of Oedipa's search is, finally, paranoia itself:

> Change your name to Miles, Dean, Serge, and/or Leonard, baby, she advised her reflection in the half-light of that afternoon's vanity mirror. Either way, they'll call it paranoia. They. Either you have stumbled indeed, without the aid of LSD or other indole alkaloids, onto a secret richness and concealed density of dream; onto a network by which X number of Americans are truly communicating whilst reserving their lies, recitations of routine, arid betrayals of spiritual poverty, for the official government delivery system; maybe even onto a real alternative to the exitlessness, to the absence of surprise to life, that harrows the head of everybody American you know, and you too, sweetie. Or you are hallucinating it. Or a plot has been mounted against you, so expensive and elaborate, involving items like the forging of stamps and ancient books, constant sur-

veillance of your movements, planting of post horn images all over San Francisco, bribing of librarians, hiring of professional actors and Pierce Inverarity only knows what-all besides, all financed out of the estate in a way either too secret or too involved for your non-legal mind to know about even though you are co-executor, so labyrinthine that it must have meaning beyond just a practical joke. Or you are fantasying some such plot, in which case you are a nut, Oedipa, out of your skull. (128)

Though there is humor in her discoveries and though Oedipa herself is capable of Stencil's style of caricature, the humor that persists is the result of irony, that which preserves in the face of incalculable odds, that which holds a mirror up to anyone who takes herself too seriously. Even as Oedipa awaits the crying of lot 49 in a room she knows to be filled with men who have pale, cruel faces, she can say to Genghis Cohen, "Your fly is open," and wonder what "she'd do when the bidder revealed himself" (137). It is perhaps this ironic self-awareness of the character (rather than of the narrator) that distances Oedipa from Stencil most, but it is also her form of paranoia. The dimensions of the conspiracy and the structure of proof have grown beyond the personal to the social in Pynchon's second novel. Stencil needs his V-structure to keep him animate; it is a singular possibility. Oedipa, however, finds herself trapped between alternatives, both of which are paranoid: "Either Oedipa in the orbiting ecstasy of a true paranoia, or a real Tristero. For there was either some Tristero beyond the appearance of the legacy America, or there was just America and if there was just America then it seemed the only way she could continue, and manage to be at all relevant to it, was as an alien, unfurrowed, assumed full circle into some paranoia" (137). With *The Crying of Lot 49* Pynchon seems to be taking the form of paranoia as far as it can go, since in Oedipa it appears to hold within its embrace all the alternatives: America, the Tristero, and Oedipa's alien existence.

If Pynchon's second novel represents an experimental perfection of the form, it is the function of *Gravity's Rainbow* to permit the form its own existence, to see what happens when paranoia is not limited by the consciousness of a single character. ⟨. . .⟩ a working definition of paranoia in *Gravity's Rainbow* is the discovery that everything in the creation is connected. This principle seems to hold true for Pynchon's creation itself. Ostensibly Tyrone Slothrop is the primary paranoid and the successor to Stencil and Oedipa. While Slothrop early in the novel promises to be a worthy heir—he even offers several proverbs for paranoids—he allows his carefully constructed structure of evidence to disintegrate as he has the final pieces of his puzzle within grasp. It may be only his name that betrays him since "sloth" has at its root both the meaning of "sleuth," the dogged tracker, and "sloth," the lazy dawdler. Slothrop is alternately both until he begins to disintegrate and his family's past catches up with him: "There is in his history . . . a peculiar sensitivity to what is revealed in the sky" (26). In his ancestor's case it had been the hand of God "pointing out of the secular clouds, pointing directly at him" (27). Tyrone had always thought the rocket was the hand pointing at him and he sought the special Rocket 00000 with all the reluctant fascination he could muster. The hand comes for him at a crossroad in the form of a rainbow and a remembrance of "days when in superstition and fright he could *make it all fit*, seeing clearly in each an entry in a record, a history: his own, his winter's, his country's . . . " (626). It is not possible to say what the end of Slothrop's own paranoid search may mean, but the rainbow, the crossroad, the disintegration, and the lines quoted from the last

of Rilke's *Sonnets to Orpheus* suggest that Slothrop has undergone a Rilkean transformation. He and his paranoia have become one in death transfigured, a continuity of nature rather than man. With Slothrop Pynchon takes paranoia as a form to its limit; victim and conspiracy, search and discovery, isolation and community, life and death may not finally be merged, but they are brought into an ultimate relation. As he looks at the rainbow, "he stands crying, not a thing in his head, just feeling natural . . . " (626). Stencil refuses any confirmation of his paranoia. We are not permitted to see Oedipa's confirmation, if she has one. And Slothrop's end is noticeably unclimactic, despite its suggesting a sexual climax. Although Slothrop escapes conclusive classification, he does become the focus of another paranoia, the creative paranoia of the counterforce.

Slothrop's paranoia is only one of many included in *Gravity's Rainbow*. ⟨. . .⟩ Pynchon is simply allowing the form unrestricted play. Among the more notable paranoids and paranoias are Tantivy Mucker-Maffick, who, in a variety of "operational paranoia" (25), thinks every German rocket has his name painted on it; Edward Pointsman, whose belief in Pavlovian paranoia leads him on his Slothropian experiment; Roger Mexico's paranoid vision of the White Visitation as some sort of "psychic-unity-with-the-Controlling-Agency" (124); Thomas Gwenhidwy's idea of the "City Paranoiac" (172); Pökler's multiple paranoias concerning the Rocket and his daughter, "his dream of the perfectly victimized" (426), his "love something like the persistence of vision, for They have used it to create for him the moving image of a daughter" (422), and his vision of the Perfect Rocket that "is still up there, still descending" (426) on him; Slothrop's own feeling of "anti-paranoia, where nothing is connected to anything" (434); Greta Erdmann's paranoia about Jewish children; Närrish and von Göll's analysis of the Zone's rampant paranoias and their own respective rocket and film versions; Otto Gnahb's views on "the Mother Conspiracy" (505); Lyle Bland's involvement with "the Great Pinball Difficulty" (581); Byron The Bulb's knowledge of the "international light-bulb cartel" (649); and the other paranoias of Säure Bummer, Wimpe, Tchitcherine, Enzian, the collective crowd aboard the *Anubis*, and all the others already implied in earlier discussions. There is not a single character in *Gravity's Rainbow* who is not implicated in some paranoid fantasy, including inanimate characters such as films, rockets, drugs, trains. . . .

Paranoia itself is a character of such magnitude that it dominates the novel; finally, paranoia is all that holds *Gravity's Rainbow* together, forcing the reader to establish his own sense of plot. Of course the conspiracy is of such complexity that no one can hold all the pieces, establish relations among all the possible interlocks. It would take a computer to correlate all the facts "before we'd have a paranoid structure worthy of the name" and, as the narrator informs us just about the plot involving Lyle Bland, even the computer would not be above suspicion: "Alas, the state of the art by 1945 was nowhere near adequate to that kind of data retrieval. Even if it had been, Bland, or his successors and assigns, could've bought programmers by the truckload to come in and make sure all the information fed out was harmless" (582).

Such is Pynchon's fascination with his subject that he offers his readers a structure, a technique for interpretation, in the form of "Proverbs for Paranoids." As Kenneth Burke and others such as Weber and Freud have noted, proverbs are stylized or strategic responses to the very situation that posed the need for them and, in a sense, function as names for shared attitudes. Although amusing, Pynchon's proverbs serve as a mechanism for reducing hysteria by naming it. They are collected here without reference to the particular Slothropian situation that called for each of them; they are provided by the narrator because "everyone has agreed to *call them other names* when Slothrop is listening . . ." (241).

> Proverbs for Paranoids, 1: You may never get to touch the Master, but you can tickle his creatures. (237)

> Proverbs for Paranoids, 2: The innocence of the creatures is in inverse proportion to the immortality of the Master. (241)

> Proverbs for Paranoids, 3: If they can get you asking the wrong questions, they don't have to worry about answers. (251)

> Proverbs for Paranoids, 4: *You* hide, they seek. (262)

> Paranoids are not paranoids (Proverb 5) because they're paranoid, but because they keep putting themselves, fucking idiots, deliberately into paranoid situations. (292)

As names for Slothrop's particular terror, the Proverbs imply a structure. If situations can be recognized and named, they can be organized. Thus Slothrop's private fantasy is made public and his personal system is generalized into a principle that will take the name "counterforce." It is a principle that incidentally invites the reader both to create a plot for the novel and, more directly, to participate. Pökler's "Victim in a Vacuum!" song is addressed to the reader as well.

> (All together now, all you masochists out there, specially those of you don't have a partner tonight, alone with those fantasies that don't look like they'll ever come true—want you just to join in here with your brothers and sisters, let each other know you're alive and sincere, try to break through the silences, try to reach through and connect. . . .) (415)

Notes

1. Thomas Pynchon, *Gravity's Rainbow* (New York: Viking Press, 1973), p. 617. All subsequent references are noted in the text within parentheses.
2. Thomas Pynchon, V. (New York: Bantam Books, 1968), p. 50. All subsequent references are noted in the text within parentheses.
3. Thomas Pynchon, *The Crying of Lot 49* (New York: Bantam Books, 1967), p. 28. All subsequent references are noted in the text within parentheses.

DOUGLAS FOWLER
From "Pynchon as Gothicist"
A Reader's Guide to Gravity's Rainbow
1980, pp. 28–43

An artist to whom Pynchon alludes very frequently is T.S. Eliot, and the affinity between Pynchon and Eliot is important and yet far more subtle and complex than it may seem at first glance. Conrad's *Heart of Darkness* is the single most helpful analogue in understanding Pynchon's narrative procedures. And Pynchon's ethical and political sensibility, his uneasiness with organized power and his feeling for the helpless victim he sets up to be destroyed might best be compared to some contemporary writers who share this aspect of his concerns—they might be called the School of Cold War Gothic, and I include in it Norman Mailer, Tom Stoppard, J. D. Salinger (especially the Salinger of "Teddy"), and the late Richard Fariña, to whom *Gravity's Rainbow* is dedicated. But then these are all *literary* references, and if we should read

much of *Gravity's Rainbow* with Eliot's dark lyricism in mind, we also need to acknowledge that Plasticman comics, Abbott & Costello movies, and the kind of self-consciously smutty horseplay that used to be the staple of undergraduate humor magazines are also indispensable references in understanding Pynchon's created worlds. It is in fact his jarring oscillation between morose poetic eloquence and the scruffiest PopCult, his unwillingness to oblige himself to any sense of decorum or even a consistent tone that have created some of the most troublesome problems we have in reading him.

First, the Eliot connection.

In the lyric "Journey of the Magi," an old king recalls for us with harrowed dismay the miraculous experience he cannot even now put into words (nothing outside of nature can be put into words) and it is the predilection for creating a speaking consciousness that has glimpsed a world beyond this world that subtly unites Pynchon with Eliot. The speaker in Eliot's poem tells us haltingly about his pilgrimage to the terrible miracle in Bethlehem, and that he would now "be glad of another death," would now find his own death a release, for he has foresuffered along with the newborn Christ Christ's own destruction: "were we led all that war for / Birth or Death?" A Birth intended for Death, then. The agony of human consciousness chained into nature and yet aware of something beyond it is always at the core of Eliot's verse, and the Christian myth within that verse—in "The Journey of the Magi," *The Waste Land*, "Marina," as well as in *Four Quartets* and *Ash-Wednesday*—is not really a celebration of the Nativity or of the Resurrection, but a poetic rendering of Gethsemane and Golgotha and of the waterless agony on the cross, of the days *between* Crucifixion and Easter, of death-in-life waiting on life, meaning, life-beyond-death. For Eliot, the human situation is an agonized imprisonment within this time, this place, these insignificant events and the meaningless ignominy of our appetites, the very air we find about us now so "thoroughly small and dry."

Since all of Pynchon's fiction is the story of nature penetrated by supernature, he has found Eliot an important model. Both artists must find some way of making the language of this world convey the sense of a world beyond, and both use reticence and a subtle allusiveness to convey this effect. Eliot's old king has found in Bethlehem not only "evidence and no doubt" of a birth, but also "hands . . . dicing for pieces of silver" and "three trees on a low sky," obviously prefigurations of Christ's betrayal, agony and death. This sort of imagery tells us almost overtly how to read the poem into which it has been set like a focusing lens; the poem demands that we apprehend Christ's mortal destruction *within* His birth, and we have little trouble deciphering Eliot's intention in this instance. Two moments are to be collapsed into one moment, Birth and Death into Birth-Death, and the poet indicates this via fragments of the Christ story absolutely familiar to us: three wise men and Bethlehem and a stable (compare the passage from Pynchon), but also three crosses and the dicing beneath one cross for the garments of a dead man not yet quite dead. "I had seen birth and death, / But had thought they were different." Here, miraculously and terribly, birth and death are fused into one and are not different at all. And as always, Eliot evokes the supernatural by a cautious deployment of familiar symbolism, with the logically impossible intersection of the timeless with the time-bound that always obsessed him as a metaphysical subject made available to us by means of the juxtaposition.

Pynchon introduces the supernatural into all of his created worlds in something of the same manner when, for example, he indicates to us what will finally happen to Oedipa Maas in *The Crying of Lot 49* by his use of the Rapunzel fairytale: "what keeps [the captive maiden] where she is is magic, anonymous and malignant, visited on her from the outside and for no reason at all."[2] But here the captive maiden is confined like Rapunzel in what Pynchon only *compares* to a tower, because the literality of the original fairytale tower has been transmuted into an unnameable field of force; and yet Pynchon's maiden is no less literally confined than is Rapunzel (just as an electromagnetic field is no less real than an iron cage, or a tower, even though you can't see it), it is simply that the means of her confinement is nothing he cares to put into visible, nameable particulars. "As things developed," Pynchon goes on to tell us, Oedipa "was to have all manner of revelations" (9). Ominous revelations, of course, and finally perhaps even fatal ones. But these revelations will not include the discovery of either the means of or reasons for her confinement—every piece of fiction Pynchon has published could well begin with *Once upon a time*—and he is careful to deflect our expectations away from the *merely* human, the *merely* psychological, forewarning us that Oedipa's revelations will not "be about Pierce Inverarity, or herself; but about what remained yet had somehow, before this, stayed away." (9–10).

Eliot's supernatural is benign. In his work, human consciousness is that which witnesses, suffers, and desires to escape, but it is purposefully tormented inside a "time-ridden" world constructed expressly for that torment. *God* and *Love* are proper nouns Eliot uses to indicate the vivisectionist who remains *outside* of time, beyond desire, indifferent even to our simple wish that He reveal Himself. But the torment is at least intentional, and although we cannot guess its purpose, our tormentor has arranged our agony for valid ends:

> Love is the unfamiliar Name
> Behind the hands that wove
> The intolerable shirt of flame
> Which human power cannot remove
>   ("Little Gidding")[3]

And if the suffering of Hercules in the shirt of Nessus is one of the most terrifying images from classical mythology—a magic tale is always at the heart of Eliot's major verse just as it is always at the core of Pynchon's fiction—so the image of a surgical operation is perhaps one of the most frightening correlatives from the contemporary world that a writer might use to evoke terror, and Eliot casts human torment as the inescapable consequence of surgery in "East Coker." As we shall see, Pynchon also uses surgery to create spectacular terror.

If Pynchon does not call his tormentors Love or God, they, or They, are still as powerful and deliberate as Eliot's surgeon plying his "steel" torment: "Who would that be, watching so civil and mild over the modeltop?"[4] It is of course the same otherworldly presence Tyrone Slothrop feels *inside* himself, an incursion from some other dimension "known to Slothrop though not by name, a deformation of space that lurks inside his life, latent as a hereditary disease" (374/435). Finally the forces that Pynchon will only call "They" will be done with Slothrop and leave him "scattered" all over the German occupied Zone; of course no one knows why or how "the hit will come," but every morning, "before the markets open, out before the milkmen, They make Their new update, and decide on what's going to be sufficient unto the day" (544/634). We can only guess as to Their motives, but we realize in each of Pynchon's stories that there is a vast and sinister scheme working itself out, and its torments are *intended*: the Inanimate in *V.*, the Tristero in *The Crying of Lot 49*, "They" in *Gravity's Rainbow* are all *conscious* malignancies, *directed* invasions.

Both Eliot and Pynchon then take the same situation for the heart of their work: humanity imprisoned within a cage designed for an experiment upon it. That Eliot's poetic speakers enunciate an attitude toward this designed torment we reflexively call "religious" perhaps muffles with conventionality our awareness that he is depicting supernatural forces, and the connecting feature of the comparison between Eliot and Pynchon is their depiction of supernatural intentions directed toward our world from a world beyond it. Eliot always writes of the "point of intersection of the timeless / With time"—the lines here are from "The Dry Salvages," but the same concern underlines all of Eliot's verse. In the same manner, we begin to see Pynchon's work more clearly if we recognize that he is always writing about a "succession of encounters between groups of the living and a congruent world,"[5] and that he is fascinated by the idea that one portion of the created universe derives its motive power not from the "will of God," but from "some opposite Principle, something blind, soulless; a brute automatism" that conducts solely to "eternal death" (*The Crying of Lot 49*, p. 116).

It should come as no surprise to notice that Pynchon is in debt to Eliot for important patterns of imagery; for example, both artists use the image of a Shadow to express the irreducible mortal difference between our world and the world behind it. "Falls the Shadow," repeated to close three straight stanzas, is the most crucial element in the incantation of "The Hollow Men," and of course Eliot has himself gone back to the Twenty-third Psalm and perhaps to "The Charge of the Light Brigade" to find his correlative suggesting the cosmic finality of a world whimpering to its end; his Shadow is nothing less that the Shadow of Death, and it falls across our world from "death's twilight kingdom." Similarly, when Pynchon comes to write the climactic sequence of his colossal rocket-novel, Gottfried's mind is filled with his lover and destroyer Blicero's last whisperings to him: first star and twilight, and the "true moment of shadow" when you can see the first needle-stroke of starlight in the sky—"the single point, and the Shadow that has just gathered you in its sweep . . ." (760/887).

Eliot and Pynchon also share a taste for the gothic, for exquisite modulations of horror, blasphemy, and shock for its own sake, and there is in their work that sense of excited self-indulgence in the loathsome that our libertarian inhibitions might usually prevent us from acknowledging. But as the most brilliant and tough-minded of our contemporary critics, Leslie Fiedler, points out, our national literature has always been "essentially and at its best nonrealistic, even antirealistic . . . bewilderingly and embarrassingly a gothic fiction, nonrealistic and negative, sadist and melodramatic."[6] Such a large and inky generalization may seem heretical and stagey, especially when it's couched in the sort of vocabulary it has always been Fiedler's pleasure to use against the cautious gray gentility of academic discourse. And yet doesn't this claim really answer to our own unofficial impressions? It seems to me that it is as gothic sensationalists that both Eliot and Pynchon should be read, even if we must keep in mind that they are of course a great deal more than that, too. Both Eliot and Pynchon are *radical* artists, and we can never afford to ignore the degree to which they have departed from the usual (and therefore, usually ignored) premises of literary creation. Place this caption from Fiedler under almost any extended passage in Pynchon and see how well it fits: there has been, he claims, a consistent and "disturbing relationship between our highest art and such lowbrow forms of horror pornography as the detective story, the pulp thriller, and the Superman comic book, all of which are . . . the heirs of the gothic."[7]

The freakish and sensational content of Eliot's verse has

never been sufficiently emphasized, and for half a century we have been too quick to accept that verse as a morally constructive sermon with edifying fright as its central mechanism—art for the soul's sake. Eliot's moral intentions and sympathies are real enough (so are Pynchon's, for that matter) but if we return to the immediate impressions created in us by, say, *The Waste Land* and try to discard or at least diminish our preconceptions about what we think we *ought* to be finding in it, I think we discover a poem in which uplift and improvement and inner peace have been replaced by stroboscopic flashes of lurid tableaux; we find a gothic and sensational poem, the stage-properties of which include a drowned sailor and an impotent king, "hooded hordes"[8] from out of the sources of our deepest nightmare; bats with baby faces descending walls head-downward (significantly enough, Eliot borrowed this famous bit from Bram Stoker's thriller *Dracula* and Pynchon uses it, too). There are "dirty" modern ears and more bones than English poetry has seen since John Webster. There are an abundance of rats, spiders, and there are the silent dead flowing maggotlike over London Bridge, an image Pynchon will in turn borrow almost intact for *Gravity's Rainbow* (537/625). One of Eliot's repeated classical allusions in *The Waste Land* is to the rape of Philomela, and the line "withered stumps of time" calls up with shocking clarity a paraplegic survivor of the explosives used with such catastrophic abandon on the Western Front. Eliot has provided his poem with a central consciousness, the aged androgyne Tiresias, who is not only blind but neither dead nor alive, male or female (and evoked for us as a loathsome freak with "wrinkled female breasts . . . wrinkled dugs"). Harridans in a pub discuss self-induced abortion, the listless fornication of soiled clerks is Eliot's central image of sexual union, and our spiritual condition is suggested by the evocation of "broken fingernails and dirty hands." Almost every line in the most famous poem of our century is saturated with an exquisite Jacobean loathsomeness, or with images from classical mythology fraught with perverse horror, and the modern world itself is given to us solely in terms of a soiled and dull-witted animality. "Are you alive, or not?" one of the voices in *The Waste Land* asks, and that terrible question sends out concentrics of disquiet into every line of poetry Eliot ever wrote. All his poems are attempts to answer the riddle of consciousness chained into nature, the horror of watching with "lidless" eyes the destruction of the "infinitely gentle / infinitely suffering" riches of consciousness by a brutal "time-ridden" world without visible meaning. The central consciousness in Eliot's poetry is a witness to its own exquisite torturing, sometimes a witness to its own extinction. It cannot act.

Gothic effects, especially gothic effects as perceived by witnesses whose sensibilities are too delicate or perverse to deal with them, are fundamental in Pynchon, too, and in story after story his favorite characters helplessly witness and suffer bizarre and bloody events. Here again the sensational and lurid nature of a writer's work has been reflexively diminished by our fixation with regarding serious art as being intrinsically beyond violence and grotesquery for its own sake. But just as the simple act of counting the corpses that pile up in the course of *Hamlet* verges on an embarrassing revelation as to the bloodthirsty sensationalism that was obviously part of its intention—James Agee said that the accumulation of onstage dead in the last scene reminded him of a "hold full of herring"—so too a glance at the astonishing amount of sensationalism in Pynchon's fiction tells us a good deal about his sensibility and leads us toward conclusions very difficult to explain within the humanistic clichés and unconvincing pieties of contemporary criticism. Pynchon's first published story, "Mortality and

Mercy in Vienna," is an account of events leading up to the mass slaughter of the guests at a Washington, D.C. cocktail party by a hallucinating Ojibwa Indian armed with an automatic rifle, and it is significant that the massacre might have been prevented by the story's progatonist, Cleanth Siegel (not all of Pynchon's characters have such wonderful names), if Siegel had listened to the soft-hearted *mensch* within himself rather than to the "nimble little Machiavel" inside who of course opts for the spatter of blood. In "Entropy," the central consciousness is a recluse named Callisto who discovers with sure horror that the final thermodynamic whimper of our world is at hand and numbly watches his mistress break out the windows of their apartment so that they will freeze to death together. The protagonist in "Under the Rose," a British spy called Porpentine, allows himself to be destroyed by a half-human antagonist with an electric switch sewn into its arm. Esther Harvitz's nosejob in V. is not only performed on her by her surgeon-lover, but his other patients—a "rogues' gallery of malformed" (V., 90)—are described for us with loving squeamishness and accumulate into a sort of prose pantheon of Dick Tracy monstrosities: "a bald and earless woman"; a young girl with a skull fissured with three "paraboloid" peaks and a disastrous acne condition running down her face "like a skipper's beard"; a man with three nostrils and no upper lip; a "sexless being" whose hereditary syphilis has caused its face to collapse, "nose hanging down like a loose flap of skin," and the "chin depressed at the side by a large sunken crater containing radial skin-wrinkles" (90). The plastic surgeon himself, Schoenmaker, had in his youth watched Army surgeons restore "the worst possible travesty of a human face" (86) belonging to a WWI pilot by implanting in it inanimate materials that they know will soon be rejected by the pilot's natural antibodies, leaving the man a clinical monster. Pynchon's sensational gothicism combined with his refusal to judge "the various horrors [he] coldly narrates"[9] are taken to task by one puzzled and disappointed critic, who finds the grisly five-page account of Esther's nose operation, detailed by Pynchon right down to the last snip of scissors and snap of bone, "completely uncomfortable . . . so much so that it requires, from me at least, an act of will to keep reading through it." And Pynchon has an even headier brew of blasphemy, sex, and death to round out the climax of the episode in V. he calls "V. in Love": Victoria's young lover, a danseuse called Melanie l'Heuremaudit, dies impaled through the vagina by a spear held aloft by the corps de ballet, the girl having left out of her costume "the one inanimate object that would have saved her" (389).

A colonist in Southwest Africa loses his mistress to suicide and the strand wolves eat her breasts, and a simple summary of the "disassembly" of Victoria Wren during the aerial siege of Malta in 1945 sounds like the climax of a gothic playlet as parodied by the Monty Python comedy troupe: disguised as a cleric the Maltese urchins call The Bad Priest, Victoria, who has *literally* given herself over to the seductive incursions of the inanimate kingdom into our world (and into her body, bit by surgical bit), becomes trapped by bomb debris; finding the Bad Priest helpless, the children ghoulishly examine her only to discover that she is composed of *objects*—an artificial foot, a wig that conceals a "scalp tatoo of a two-colour Crucifixion," a star sapphire sewn into the naval that the children pry out with a bayonet; false teeth; a glass eye "with the iris in the shape of the clock" (322) that the children cut out of the skull. The passage reaches its gothic climax when the helpless witness to these events, Fausto Maijestral, performs the rites of Extreme Unction for the dying creature, using for the chrism ointment "her own blood, dipping it from the naval as from a chalice"—

and one need hardly point out that blasphemy against the Church has always been a staple of gothic sensationalism.

The bones of dead American infantrymen are sold for cigarette-filter charcoal in *The Crying of Lot 49*, and Pynchon takes fiendish delight in making a blood-spattered cartoon out of his parody of a Jacobean revenge play, *The Courier's Tragedy*. *Gravity's Rainbow* contains what is perhaps the most shocking scene in recent American literature, Brigadier Ernest Pudding atoning for the catastrophe of the Passchendael trenches by submitting himself to humiliation and physical pain at the feet of Katje Borgesius; not only does Katje, in her role of Domina Nocturna and incarnation of Death, apply physical chastisement to Pudding's scarred flesh, "his withered ass elevated for the cane" (243/273), but the old man is also obliged to eat the shit out of her body: "he leans forward to surround the hot turd with his lips, sucking on it tenderly, licking along its lower side . . . he is thinking, he's sorry, he can't help it, of a Negro's penis, yes he knows it abrogates part of the conditions set, but it will not be denied, the image of a brute African who will make him behave" (235/274). Later on in the book we will witness a surgical castration.

The importance of our own cruelty and destructive impulses in the experience of literature has never been given anything like the attention it deserves, and the very vocabulary with which we would have to begin discussing the subject—*sadism, masochism, suicide*—is still contaminated with hospital odors and those connotations of criminal deviation we are unlikely to casually assign ourselves. And yet, like it or not, terror, violence, irrevocable loss and catastrophic suffering are some of the most obvious properties of our literature, and it seems long past the time when a smack of dainty parlor radicalism should still cling to the claim that art is sometimes a dream-state wherein we can act out fantasies of destruction and self-immolation we cannot allow ourselves to act out in the real world. An artist's business is not to salvage souls or mend the world, but to create in any way he can a world of intensity in which for a privileged moment we can forget our boredom. The great omission of all fantastic fiction is almost by definition the reality we are reading it to escape. And it is also too easily forgotten that this moment must be *virtually* inconsequential—without consequence. *Inside* the artistic experience we participate and yet we must not be made to pay. Literary theorists have too quickly turned away from the large and obvious dissimilarity between the fantastic world and the real one—fantastic art offers a moment of acetylene intensity which makes use of commonplace realities solely as a disguise; nothing could be less suitable as a design for living or as a vehicle for comment on life.

The claim that Pynchon is in large measure a *gothic* artist needs some amplification. M. H. Abrams gives us a shorthand definition of the mode of gothicism centering on its creator's attempt to "evoke chilling terror by exploiting mystery, cruelty, and a variety of horrors,"[10] and he points out that of course the term is now usefully applied not simply to the ugly mysteries of an Ann Radcliffe monastery or the bizarre decay of a great and ancient family in a story of Poe's, but also to a type of terror-intending fiction which may do without medieval trappings as long as its events are "uncanny, or macabre, or melodramatically violent"; and Abrams also notes that the source of gothic terror is now frequently an "aberrant psychological state," not just a supernatural evil. One element that also must be interwoven into any complete definition is the presence within the form, shaping its structures and energies, of the world of nightmare; as Joe David Bellamy points out, "nightmares antedate and are the true prototype of all gothic forms."[11] So although the definition can only be approximate, we use the term "goth-

icism" to indicate the importation of nightmare into art: Leslie Fiedler remarks this crucial importation, and points out that the essential burden of the gothic tale is to take us "out of the known world into a dark region of make-believe . . . which is to say, [into] a world of ancestral and infantile fears projected in dreams."[12] Dream-forms are the key.

Where then does the contemporary artist find the materials for his gothic terror, for the dream become art? Given that problem, we consider and then immediately turn away from our century's most prodigious catastrophes—Verdun, Auschwitz, Hiroshima—and this in itself tells us a good deal about the aesthetics of terror, the pleasurable beauty of terror that lies at the heart of gothicism. The fact that trench warfare, extermination camps, and the experimental destruction of large civilian populations by means of atomic weapons were *real* perhaps has something to do with our revulsion with their use as merely aesthetic properties and materials, but then Truman Capote creates a gothic masterpiece out of real murders no less hideous for his "non-fiction novel" *In Cold Blood*. What is the difference? Perhaps this: at Verdun, Auschwitz, and Hiroshima, human life counted for nothing at all, and the pleasurable terrors of gothicism depend upon the assumption that human life counts for everything. The gothic is not an absurd or existential mode, it is a romantic one—and the difference between these terms is nothing less than the difference between no-meaning and meaning. Speaking about the extermination camps in his excellent study *Violence in the Arts*, John Fraser remarks that the essential horror of the camps was the fact that "the actual intensity of the suffering . . . [the] heightened sense of the consciousness of other people"[13] was utterly benumbed, for the famous horrors of the Final Solution all center on the perfect *indifference* of administrator, guard, and functionary to the human life it was their duty to destroy. It is this indifference that disqualifies Auschwitz from gothic possibilities. Pynchon can parody *The White Devil* in *The Crying of Lot 49* by having his wicked usurper Niccolo grind and dye the bones of his enemies for writing ink—the grisly joke is still then a matter of *passion*, the intense emotion of hatred, the intense satisfaction of having that hatred revenged. But the technological fact that the human body can actually be rendered down into soap loses its *artistic* usefulness when we realize that at the destruction complexes of the Third Reich this rendering was not a matter of passionate revenge, or of any sort of passionate feeling at all, but simply a matter of bureaucratic momentum, a scrupulous attention to duty, orders, and the task at hand.

The real terrors of the Final Solution are not in its fantastic excesses of cruelty and sadism, and Fraser points out the falsity of what he calls the "most common cliché image" from the camps, that of "the shaven-headed prisoner being whipped to work by the glossy-booted S.S. man."[14] The history of our species is fraught with savage murder, burnings, ritual sacrifices, exterminations, to say nothing of slave labor. But what these modern camps made appallingly obvious was the complicity its victims could be induced to take *in their own destruction*, the degree to which sheer attention to the routines and processes of destruction, even to the routines and processes that conduct to one's own destruction, can be the supreme motive force in human affairs. Fraser points out that the camps can best be understood as "complex bureaucracies operated to a large extent by the prisoners themselves, with all the struggles for power, prestige, and privilege which one finds inside any bureaucracy."[15] The moral conscience of the Twentieth Century has been writhing in impalement on the terrible fact that such things as Auschwitz were even possible, but I think that the aesthetic unsuitability of the camps gives us the real insight into the core of their unique horror. It is a horror which seems only at first to derive from the sheer magnitude of the numbers killed, but I think that finally the horror of Auschwitz lies in the terrifying recognition that the energies of a great many people were engaged in operating as efficiently as possible the most astonishing social machinery in all history: a vast and intricate killing device the function of which was genocide and the operation of which was left to indifferent bureaucrats and complicit victims. A sure litmus test for gothic material is simply to ask if it can be parodied, for parody in the comic exaggeration of excess and demands overinflation in its subject. Auschwitz cannot be parodied because there is no emotion there to be exaggerated. The importance of this fact is central to my understanding of Pynchon, for the degree to which Pynchon is a gothic artist and the degree to which he is a gothic parodist tell us a good deal about what kind of a writer he is and how to go about setting him into a context of like concerns and techniques. Literary people have in every instance been astonished by Pynchon's erudition and by his capabilities as a researcher and reporter and encyclopedist, but it has been little noticed that in a 760–page novel recreating the historical cataclysm of the Second World War (and Michael Wood speaks for all of us when he remarks that "even if Pynchon were in London getting bombed in 1944, I can't see how he could remember so much . . . I have no idea how [he] does this"[16]) the forced labor camps are given part of a single paragraph, nothing more (see the Pökler episode, 433/505). Nor do we find in this war novel a direct representation of almost any of the famous phenomena of the war—the Normandy landings or the manned bombing of German industry or, say, Vonnegut's fire-bombed Dresden; we hear nothing of Patton's armored campaigns toward the Rhine, the French resistance, the war in North Africa, the Italian campaigns, the Coral Sea, the colossal death-struggle on the Eastern front, nor does Pynchon even picture again the aerial seige of Malta that he worked up so effectively in V. Just to compare Pynchon's book with the hair-raising physicality of infantry combat in *The Naked and the Dead* or with Salinger's allusive use of the death-camps to unhinge his sensitive young survivor in "For Esmé, with Love and Squalor" makes apparent the enormous difference in atmosphere.

Pynchon is not interested in the merely historical, physical or factual, nor is he even interested in presenting the merely psychological. He is interested in Mystery, and his war is the Rocket. Passing beyond sight and sound on its mission of catastrophe, its path a great rainbow bent taut by gravity, its assembly and deadly uses calling forth from its attendant priesthood all the atavistic terrors and delights that surround flight, fall, birth, fire, and death, the Rocket is that weapon of all weapons most highly charged with gothic mystery—excepting of course the atomic bomb, a weapon Pynchon specifically links to the supernatural in the sequence on pages 693/808. Leslie Fiedler points out that science fiction is "the gothicism of the future,"[17] and that just beneath its moral pretensions and pseudo-scientific hocus-pocus, it is essentially terror fiction dressed in the trappings of imagined technology. No advice can be more helpful to the reader of Pynchon than to remind him that he is putting himself into the hands of an artist whose deepest concern is with a highly specialized terror. Even the comic and cartoonlike sequences of *Gravity's Rainbow* are touched with the adumbrations of terror: Slothrop costumed as a trenchcoated correspondent or as Rocketman or as a heroic pig-hero pratfalling his way through half a dozen adventures in the Zone is not an image Pynchon intends for us to mistake for the existential solemnities of *The Spy Who Came In from the*

Cold, but the reader also feels that parody here is more of an acknowledgement of an overextended genre's overtaxed clichés than it is that sort of parodic excess which explodes a plot-vehicle set in motion simply to be disintegrated. True parody is anticlimactic, but Pynchon's stories are always romantic art, even though they are sometimes romantic art disguised as a cartoon; the anticlimaxes of true lampoon are not what we find in them.

It is no accident that both Eliot and Pynchon are drawn to, and draw from, Joseph Conrad, especially *Heart of Darkness*, for Conrad's tale may well be the purest form of gothicism in our century. One of the epigraphs of "The Hollow Men" is "Mister Kurtz—he dead!", and Pynchon's story "Mortality and Mercy in Vienna" not only includes that line too, but borrows for its rhetorical climax Conrad's image of the strange and terrible and ultimately indescribable mysteries that Kurtz took part in at the Inner Station; Cleanth Siegel finds himself playing the role not only of host but of father-confessor at the party, and when he realizes that his departed doppelgänger, David Lepescu, had anticipated tonight's events he comes to perceive that a mystery hovers in this place, a possessing spirit, malign and implacable:

> . . . the heart of a darkness in which no ivory was ever sent out from the interior, but instead hoarded jealously by each of its gatherers to build painfully, fragment by fragment, temples to the glory of some imago or obsession, and decorated inside with the artwork of dream and nightmare, and locked finally against a hostile forest, each "agent" in his own ivory tower, having no windows to look out of, turning further and further inward and cherishing a small flame behind the altar (200).

In the next two paragraphs, Siegel walks away from the private "imago or obsession" bodied forth as mass murder— "He shrugged. What the hell, stranger things had happened in Washington. It was not until he reached the street that he heard the first burst of the BAR fire" (201).

To say that *Heart of Darkness* is a study of what one critic calls "the mortifying diseases of nineteenth-century imperialism"[18] is to be at once correct and ridiculous—like describing *Gravity's Rainbow* as a book about V-2 Rockets. Making extravagant use of purple inks on loan from Poe, Conrad has created a sort of prose Rorschach blot, and the impossibility of our reducing its convolution, shading, and haunting symmetries to any sort of adequate paraphrase is one proof of the tale's success. Notice how little *happens* in the story—a man named Marlow tells at length (at incredibly length!) of a European ivory-agent named Kurtz whose methods of getting treasure from the native cannibals were both utterly unsavory and wonderfully successful. Evidently this Kurtz chap went native in some fashion or other, and then he died—and died of no simple medical affliction, we are given to understand. He left a fiancée this side of death, and his personal magnetism and singular genius were such that we expect she'll never get over him. Period.

Little enough action for a tale of such length, one would assume, but then an extraordinary proportion of those 30,000 words are really not words at all, but fragments of magic incantation, the verbal cinders of otherworldly energies, a language that can only point in the direction of an experience no language can describe. *Uncontrollable, unspeakable, ineffable, inscrutable, impenetrable, intolerable* (to thought), at once *exalted and incredible* (degradation), *inconceivable, indefinable, unearthly, inappreciable, impossible, invincible, inexplicable, implacable, unfathomable, insoluble, unapproachable, irresistible*: perhaps no story in our heritage surrenders itself to a vocabulary more difficult to paraphrase or more fraught with menacing abstractions that words can neither define nor picture. Conrad's tale takes the evils of the white man's burden for its starting-point, but these human evils are only "mere incidents of the surface," and Marlow assures us that the "inner truth is hidden—luckily, luckily." He himself has *almost* seen it, but he tells us (more than a dozen times) that he cannot convey in words the smallest fraction of those unholy terrors. And nothing we can say about the story will pull its central mystery into the light—for with Conrad, just as with Eliot and Pynchon, one must remember that the artist has recognized as the first principle of aesthetic terror that an ogre's approaching footsteps are immeasurably more frightening than any portrait of the ogre himself, fangs and all. One of the most brilliant and useful insights from Tom Stoppard's *Rosencrantz and Guildenstern Are Dead* is on the diminishment of the wonderful by the ordinary—for the ordinary is simply the wonderful seen too often. One man sees a unicorn, and the vision may be either real or a hallucination; then a second man sees the unicorn, too:

> "My God," says [the] second man, "I must be dreaming, I thought I saw a unicorn." At which point, a dimension is added that makes the experience as alarming as it will ever be. A third witness, you understand, adds no further dimension but only spreads it thinner, and a fourth thinner still, and the more witnesses there are the thinner it gets and the more reasonable it becomes until it is as thin as reality, the name we give to common experience. . . . [19]

Like Conrad, Pynchon knows that to give a local habitation and a name to the wonderful is inevitably to trivialize it, to dissolve the magic terrors of the glimpsed and the guessed in the universal solvent of everyday reality. As Fiedler puts it, "for the abominable, to be truly effective, must remain literally unspeakable." [20] Part of the charm of Pynchon's fiction lies for me in his contempt for the good gray banalities of the creative writing industry (a subdivision of the mega-institution J. D. Salinger calls America's "United English Department"), especially in regard to all those clichés about "writing from one's own experience" that have become part of the collective unconscious of America's literary community. In *Gravity's Rainbow*, Pynchon does not bother to confine himself to his own experience, or indeed to a single set of interacting characters, a single locale, or even a single century. The invasion of our world by a mysterious force called "They" is depicted in various stages of what will be, we are assured, a successful siege. Pynchon's 73 scenes show us in flashes the struggle between kingdoms, not the consequences of psychological event, and the reader must understand that Pynchon is always writing out of *this* tension, not out of the humanistic givens of the Jamesian tradition.

The expectation that a novel introduces us to a single set of characters and then tells us what happens to them is one of the common denominators we unconsciously use when we make bedfellows of, say, *Roxana*, Lilliput, tilting at windmills, symbolic sea mammals, Bloomsday, a West Egg bootlegger, *The Grapes of Wrath*, and the love affair of a middle-aged Frenchman with an American nymphet. We have grown used to the idea that, in important literature, action is character; which is to say, character is everything. This convention is so rooted and over-familiar in our expectations that it has become almost invisible to us, but we will misread Pynchon's fiction if we expect its action to signify something important about its actors. They are witnesses or victims in the War of the Worlds, not personalities who create their own destinies.

Critics and literary theorists trying to "place" Pynchon would be wise to borrow the first precept of an even older profession: *First, do no harm.* I suspect that this investigation of Pynchon's achievement, contribution, significance, and legacy will turn out to be a more difficult task than simply demonstrating his resemblance to, say, Joyce or Dante or Melville, although of course those resemblances are real enough in many ways. ⟨. . .⟩

Most of the people who have written about him have emphasized Pynchon's humanistic concerns, and his use of technological expertise to show us the dangers of science violating nature; to be sure, *Gravity's Rainbow* is loaded with that message. But I see such a message as in large part only the lip-service a gothicist *always* pays to virtue and right thinking. Never forget that in *all* gothic melodrama, the virtuous victims get the good lines but the ogres, wolves, witches, giant apes, and apocalyptic Rockets really provide the fun. I think Kingsley Amis is right when he points out that a readerly taste for pretended horror is "no more connected with an appetite for real horror, real blood, than [it is with] an interest in the Theatre of Cruelty or the bullfight." [21] Why keep on denying that we like those destructive thrills, *as long as they're only make-believe?* Many who have written on Pynchon seem much too anxious to present him as a humanistic novelist with redeeming social concerns, although they allow that he sometimes stoops to horseplay, despairing parody, or a few edifying chills in order to share his vision with us. But it seems to me more revealing to view Pynchon as a vastly capable writer of science fiction (Fiedler's "the gothicism of the future") than it is to insist that he is a humanistic novelist, or a satirist bent on mending the world. The impulses that created *Gravity's Rainbow* seem to me to have been largely gothic, and the novel makes extensive use of the only gothic locale that retains any mystery and terror for us in a thoroughly secular, disenchanted age: the laboratory. It is no accident that Pynchon's novel has a *mise en scène* of operating tables, caged experimental animals, chloroform, surgical masks and gleaming scalpels, sodium amytal injections, graph paper, wind tunnels and aerodynamic equations, Mach numbers and chi squares, ballistic experiments conducted in the field, electromagnetic and chemical theory, synthetic gasoline factories and factories that once created plastics, atomic explosions photographed or implied or prophesied, even an entire underground rocket works—and finally, triumphantly, the interior of the Rocket itself (and one can add that, like almost any list of the phenomena in *Gravity's Rainbow*, this one is far from exhaustive). In a study of the history of terror literature that he calls *The Gothic Flame*, Devendra P. Varma points out the "gentle and unconscious revulsion" such artists feel toward the spirit of an enllightened, rationalistic age, the collective impression they give of being "tired of too much light." [22] For whatever it's worth, I think I sense this sort of impulse in Pynchon. He is creating a magic world more interesting than ours and he frequently goes to science and technology for his vocabulary, metaphysics, costumes, and props. Isn't this a description of science fiction? I emphasize this point because it has been so obvious as to have been ignored. Science fiction is a sub-genre that has (rightfully) been denied much serious attention up to now by the literary establishment; but Pynchon is a gothic writer of the science fiction persuasion, nevertheless. As G. M. Hopkins once said, common sense is never out of place anywhere.

Gravity's Rainbow is saturated with references to Rilke and lines from his poetry, and it seems important in understanding Pynchon's magic world to point out that, of all poems of any worth, Rilke's are the most difficult to either describe or paraphrase, but that we can at least be certain they imply everywhere the overwhelming desire to drive beyond *this* life, *these* realities, *this* contemptible moment. The *Duino Elegies* or the *Sonnets to Orpheus* begin several inches off the ground then and immediately fly off toward that same Transforming, Transcending Kingdom of Beyond that Eliot or Conrad couldn't describe, either: Rilke is the consummation of that tendency of German thought that Jean-Paul Richter encapsulated once and for all in the last century with his claim that, if the French ruled the empire of the land and British that of the sea, the Germans were sovereign in the empire of the air. In fact, *Wagner, Nietzsche,* and *Rilke* are three captions under a dotted-line trajectory out toward the fiery blue of the Other Kingdom—or, to change the metaphor, three stages in the distillation of that mystical-intellectual nitroglycerine with which Hitler blew history off its rational iron rails. Pynchon loves Rilke because of this anti-rationalism, and if we subtract Pynchon's sense of humor and horseplay and his love of the animated cartoon, I think he can be most revealingly placed in the context of what we might call German Expressionism, circa 1910–1930. Here we find the affirmation of instinct, Dionysus, female and anti-paternal values, and a corresponding disgust with Wilhelmine Germany, with stern, paunchy Bismarck, with any and every emblem of the tyrant-father. Here Franz Jung writes an essay called "Morenga," its subject the tragic collision of German Imperialism with the Hereros in Sudwestafrika; *Metropolis* and *The Cabinet of Dr. Caligari* bring fantastic gothic dream-forms from out of the child's mind onto the screen, and Leopold Jessner produces an Expressionist *Wilhelm Tell* for the stage; Stravinsky, Schoenberg, Anton Webern and Alban Berg experiment with the genetic structure of music and the little magazines bear titles like *Aktion, Revolution,* and *Kain*. The surreal, the fantastic, and the exaltedly criminal are celebrated, and there is suddenly a cult of suicide. Bourgeois life is furiously reviled, of course, but perhaps an even more subtle and explosive contempt begins to be expressed for the average moment and its unimpressive possibilities. Young people from respectable families are at war with the police. Max Weber comes to represent the oppression of rationality.

A line can be drawn from every term enumerated here straight into *Gravity's Rainbow*, and it seems like a promising place to start in assessing Pynchon's relationship to the previous. But what any age chooses to make of its great fantasists constitutes nothing less than its intellectual essence, and one can only say with confidence that people will continue to be fascinated and alarmed with Pynchon for a long time to come. He is at the least a gifted prose stylist who has added magic to an age badly in need of it. Yeats, in his own struggle to create a magic for himself and his times, pointed toward an imaginative reality that anticipates even a book as strange and singular as *Gravity's Rainbow*: "it is as though

myth and fact, united until the exhaustion of the Renaissance, have now fallen so far apart that man understands for the first time the rigidity of fact, and calls up, by that very recognition, myth."[23]

Notes

1. T. S. Eliot, *Collected Poems, 1909–1962* (New York: Harcourt Brace Jovanovich, 1963), p. 100.
2. Thomas Pynchon, *The Crying of Lot 49* (New York: Bantam Books, 1967), p. 11. Subsequent references appear parenthetically in the text.
3. Eliot, *Collected Poems,* p. 207.
4. Thomas Pynchon, *Gravity's Rainbow* (New York: Viking, 1973/New York: Bantam Books, 1974), pp. 501/584.
5. Thomas Pynchon, *V.* (New York: Bantam Books, 1964), p. 271.
6. Leslie Fiedler, *Love and Death in the American Novel* (New York: Dell, 1966), p. 9.
7. Ibid., 144.
8. Eliot and Pynchon both adapt the Grail quest for their work. In his famous notes for *The Waste Land* Eliot cited formal anthropological sources like Jessie L. Weston's *From Ritual to Romance* and Sir James Frazer's *The Golden Bough* as his access to the myth; I would guess Pynchon's access to the same myth might be via Wagner, or at least originated with his interest in Wagner. But the real difference seems to me to lie in the fact that Eliot uses the myth as a serious descriptive metaphor (our age *as* a Waste Land awaiting God), whereas Pynchon uses the myth largely for its exciting magic: after all, *Paradise Lost* and *Dracula* are very different works of art, even if they *are* both magic tales about winged insurgencies against our world by dark eminences from another.
9. George Levine, "Risking the Moment," in George Levine and David Leverenz (eds.), *Mindful Pleasures: Essays on Thomas Pynchon* (Boston: Little, Brown, 1976), p. 119.
10. M. H. Abrams, *A Glossary of Literary Terms* (New York: Holt, Rinehart & Winston, 1971), p. 69.
11. Joe David Bellamy (ed.), *Superfiction: or the American Story Transformed* (New York: Random House, 1975), p. 11.
12. Fiedler, p. 114.
13. John Fraser, *Violence in the Arts* (Cambridge: Cambridge University Press, 1974), p. 98.
14. Ibid., 100.
15. Ibid.
16. Michael Wood, "Rocketing to Apocalypse," *New York Review of Books* (March 22, 1973), p. 22.
17. Fiedler, p. 508.
18. William M. Chace, *The Political Identities of Ezra Pound and T. S. Eliot* (Stanford: Stanford University Press, 1973), p. 119.
19. Tom Stoppard, *Rosencrantz and Guildenstern Are Dead* (New York: Grove Press, 1967), p. 21.
20. Fiedler, p. 121.
21. Kingsley Amis, *What Became of Jane Austen? and Other Questions* (London: Jonathan Cape, 1970), p. 127.
22. Devendra P. Varma, *The Gothic Flame* (London: Russell and Russell, 1966), p. 209.
23. W. B. Yeats, *A Vision* (New York: Macmillan, 1956), pp. 211–12.

Short Stories

TONY TANNER
From "Early Short Fiction"
Thomas Pynchon
1982, pp. 23–39

Pynchon's first published story was 'The Small Rain' (*The Cornell Writer*, 6 (March 1959)). There are already clearly discernible types, themes, even atmospheres, which he will develop in subsequent work. The main figure is Nathan Levine, who has deliberately enlisted in the army. He is stationed at some desolate piece of nowhere in Louisiana which he actually likes. He likes the inertia, the inaction, the repetition, the not having to think (he is a graduate from CCNY), and the not having to feel. This cherished immunity from feeling is to be a dominant and recurring phenomenon in Pynchon's work. He is also, paradoxically enough, a communications expert. However, his unit is suddenly ordered into action when a hurricane devastates the bayou country of southern Louisiana. Although Levine likes most of all to 'sleep' or drift off into pornographic novels—notably, one called *Swamp Wench*—the disaster stirs him into some kind of action and change. 'He was also starting to worry: to anticipate some radical change, perhaps, after three years of sand, concrete and sun.' This emergence into a degree of wakefulness and activity is provoked by two things: the disaster, and the hundreds of hideous corpses that have to be dragged from the water; and the college kids on the campus where they have been stationed. There is not only perpetual rain but the air is full of the smell of death. Levine begins to see the horror and the reality of it. He also sees how cut-off from it all the college kids are, 'each trying to look at it as something unusual and nothing they had ever been or would ever want ever to be part of.' Levine has a vision of a kind of life—or death-in-life—which is

> something like a closed circuit. Everybody on the same frequency. And after a while you forget about the rest of the spectrum and start believing that this is the only frequency that counts or is real. While outside, all up and down the land, there are these wonderful colors and x-rays and ultraviolets going on.

Too many people in Pynchon's world try to prolong life as 'a closed circuit' in some way or another, so that they can 'forget about the rest'. On impulse—it is not his official job—Levine joins the men on one of the tugs who are picking up the dead bodies. It is a wasteland indeed—'gray sun on gray swamp'—the rain not bringing fertility and new life, but death. The point is that Levine at least makes the gesture of doing something. 'Levine worked in silence like the others . . . realizing somehow that the situation did not require thought or rationalization. He was picking up stiffs. That was what he was doing.' It is as though the actual vision of—and contact with—death has brought him out of his anaesthetized and paralysed state. Not, of course, that he can do much about the situation, nor does he experience any miraculous transformation. But he acted, and it seems to indicate that he cannot go back into his old state. Instead, he sees himself living the life of a wanderer.

> He had a momentary, ludicrous vision of himself, Lardass Levine the Wandering Jew, debating on weekday evenings in strange and nameless towns with other Wandering Jews the essential problems of identity—not of the self so much as an identity of place and what right you really had to be anyplace.

We do not see his future, but just such displaced wanderers will roam through Pynchon's later fiction.

Near the end Levine picks up a coed who calls herself "little Buttercup". For a night in a cabin in a nearby swamp she is, indeed, his 'swamp wench'. Partly because his attitude towards women appears to be basically pornographic, and partly because of the girl's 'incapacity to give', there is no love, no human contact at all, in the coupling. Afterwards, Levine says 'In the midst of great death, the little death.' Doubtless he intends a pun (death as sexual climax), but it points to a larger truth: that what should be the act of love has been turned into an act of death. This deformation of sex into death—or the substitution of death for love—is one of the modern malaises to which Pynchon returns and which he analyses in his longer fiction. When Levine leaves the area, it is still raining, and he says to a friend, 'Jesus Christ I hate rain.' His friend answers, 'You and Hemingway. Funny, ain't it. T. S. Eliot likes rain.' This may be seen as a rejection of Eliot's values or poetic stance, though Levine is no Hemingway. Still, he has been shaken out of his nonchalance, that cultivated non-identity or emotional anonymity of the 'enlisted man'; he has lost some of his immunity from feeling. Although we last see him asleep (again), he cannot, we feel, ever go 'back' to the inert condition he was in at the start, living like a 'closed circuit', and forgetting all the rest.

Pynchon's next story was 'Mortality and Mercy in Vienna' (published in *Epoch*, 9 (Spring 1959)). Summarized very reductively, it can be described as an account of a party in Washington (the first of many such parties in Pynchon's work which invariably degenerated into violence and chaos), at the end of which, we infer, a strange Indian from Ontario (Irving Loon) starts to massacre all the guests prior, again we infer, to eating them. Stated thus baldly, the idea of the story might seem to be just a piece of sick—very sick—humour. But into this remarkable story Pynchon has packed a number of very suggestive notions which are important in relation to his later work. We can start with the title, which comes from *Measure for Measure*. When the Duke, Vincentio, effectively 'abdicates' in the first scene, he hands over all his ducal power to Angelo:

> In our remove be thou at full ourself;
> Mortality and mercy in Vienna
> Live in thy tongue and heart.

The theme of self-removal and substitution of authority is central to Pynchon's story, in which Washington is depicted as being as degenerate and corrupt as the Vienna in Shakespeare's play, and in which a hugely disproportionate 'justice' is meted out to the errant and debauched guests, just as the death penalty imposed upon Claudio is quite incommensurable with his sin or crime of making Julietta ('fast my wife') pregnant. The problem, in both works, is how do you—can you, can anyone?—cure or heal a degenerate and, as it were, 'damned' society? In Shakespeare's play, Escalus offers a kind of pragmatic doctoring, Angelo a would-be Messianic healing which is both hypocritical and inhuman, and the Duke a type of apocalyptic judgement which is truly just, therapeutic—and merciful.

Pynchon's story also starts with an abdication and a substitution. The main figure, Cleanth Siegel, a junior diplomat, arrives at a party only to find that his original host, Rachel, will not be there. Instead he finds a somewhat crazed man, David Lupescu, whom Siegel half recognizes as a *Doppelgänger* and who instantly siezes on Siegel as 'Mon semblable . . . mon frère' and also 'a sign, a deliverance'. He hands over responsibility for the party to Siegel with words that are loaded with religious resonance. 'It's all yours. You are now the host. As host you are a trinity: (a) receiver of guests . . . (b) an enemy and (c) an outward manifestation, for *them*, of the divine body and blood.' As he leaves, Siegel asks him where he is going, and Lupescu answers in words that deliberately invoke Conrad's *Heart of Darkness*. 'The outside . . . out of the jungle . . . Mistah Kurtz—he dead.' So by a use of literary reference or intertextuality, a device that Pynchon makes more use of than any other living writer—mixing writings, in Barthes's words—the Washington party is not only Shakespeare's Vienna but also Conrad's jungle (with a trace of Baudelaire's particular Paris). One question will be: how will Siegel act as the designated and chosen substitute 'host'? Like the Duke, or Angelo; like Marlow or Kurtz? Will he be a true host—or go crazy?

The question is quite central to Pynchon's work, so I shall go into it in a little more detail. Siegel is a mixed figure. His mother is a Catholic and he grows up religious, until he gives up his faith (at college he is known as Stephen—a nod at Joyce). But he retains inside him 'the still small Jesuit voice'. On the other hand there is a 'nimble little Machiavel' inside him who not only enjoys 'scheming and counterscheming' and 'manipulating campus opinion' but is also—as Machiavelli advised—capable of delegating cruel actions to others. (Machiavelli is an important figure in Pynchon's work.) He is, then, as one of his college friends murmurs, a 'House divided against itself', the reference here, of course, being to Christ's words in Mark 3:24–6:

> How can Satan drive out Satan? If a kingdom is divided against itself, that kingdom cannot stand; if a household is divided against itself, that house will never stand: and if Satan is in rebellion against himself, he is divided and cannot stand: and that is the end of him.

As we discover, Siegel, finally, 'cannot stand'. When he was younger he had regarded himself as 'a kind of healer . . . a prophet actually, because if you cared about it at all you had to be both', though he was worried that one could easily become 'something less—a doctor, or a fortune-teller'. The possibility of any real healing and prophecy recurs throughout Pynchon. More generally, the problem becomes nothing less than how to be in the contemporary world, particularly if it is as infernal as the Washington party implies. One way is to cultivate disengagement, emotional immunity: keeping 'cool', to use a term deployed by Pynchon. But that, of course, can lead to paralysis and inhumanity. The other extreme is to want to be a great healer and prophet, but that can lead to a different kind of inhumanity—and madness (Kurtz). Pynchon's work is constantly seeking to discover something in between these two extremes.

In Siegel's case at the party he goes through different phases. He acts as a 'father-confessor' to a number of 'the whole host of trodden-on and disaffected': he looks 'compassionate' and listens while people expose to him 'synapses and convolutions which should never have been exposed . . . the bad lands of the heart'. In his way he gives them 'absolution or penance, but no practical advice'. (Kurtz's eloquence contained no 'practical hints'; Marlow is more pragmatic.) But for a time he does attempt positive, practical, restorative work: 'This little Jesuit thing, this poltergeist, would start kicking around inside his head . . . and call him back to the real country where there were drinks to be mixed and *bon mots* to be tossed out carelessly and maybe a drunk or two to take care of.' This proto-religious instinct to 'take care' of people is supplemented by his 'true British staff-officer style to bite the jolly old bullet and make the best of a bad job'. But then he gets 'fed up' with the role he feels has been imposed upon him: 'It was a slow process and dangerous because in the course of things it was very possible to destroy not only yourself but your flock as well.' He starts to disengage himself.

The crisis is precipitated by the Indian, Loon (lunatic). Siegel remembers hearing about his tribe, the Ojibwa Indians, in an anthropology course. Because of their bleak and austere way of life, living always on the brink of starvation, this tribe is prone to 'psychopathy' and 'saturated with anxiety'. The Ojibwa hunter characteristically experiences a 'vision' after which

> he feels he has acquired a supernatural companion, and there is a tendency to identify . . . [for] the Ojibwa hunter, feeling as he does at bay, feeling a concentration of obscure cosmic forces against him and him alone, cynical terrorists, savage and amoral deities which are bent on his destruction, the identification may become complete.

This feeling or state of mind is one experienced by many subsequent figures in Pynchon's work. And, most importantly perhaps, these Indians have strong 'paranoid tendencies'—the

first time the word 'paranoid' appears in Pynchon, but 'paranoia' is to become one of his central concerns. In the case of the Ojibwa their paranoia can lead to the 'Windigo psychosis', which, briefly, leads them to identify with a supernatural figure—the Windigo—who eats people, thus turning them into 'frenzied cannibals' who first 'gorge' themselves on their 'immediate family' and then start to devour people at random. From certain signs Siegel realizes that Irving Loon is very close to the 'Windigo psychosis' and is thus about to erupt into devastating violence and cannibalism. This does indeed bring the 'Moment of truth' for Siegel.

If he has read the signs correctly, 'Siegel has the power to work for these parishioners a kind of miracle, to bring them a very tangible salvation. A miracle involving a host, true, but like no holy eucharist.' He has it in his power to 'save' the whole group; but he has lost his concern with them, thinking he 'should tell all these people to go to hell'. In effect he sends them there. He suddenly sees Irving Loon starting to load a rifle and realizes that the massacre is about to start. Siegel is 'paralyzed'. Then, realizing he has 'about sixty seconds to make a decision', the different parts of the house divided against itself—the Machiavel, the Jesuit, the gentle part, the 'John Buchan hero' part—agree that there is really only one course to take; 'it was just unfortunate that Irving Loon would be the only one partaking of any body and blood, divine or otherwise'. He issues no saving warnings but simply walks away, encased in a chilling indifference. As he hears the first screams and shots, 'He shrugged. What the hell, stranger things had happened in Washington.' Such insouciant callousness is a terrible sign of man's ability to dehumanize himself. Siegel has indeed allowed his 'flock' to be 'destroyed', and in the process he has destroyed himself—as a human being—as well. Satan cannot drive out Satan; and that is the end of him. Irving Siegel is not just an example of a failed healer, a false prophet. He is both a product and a representative of a society that has accepted—indeed, eagerly embraced—'mortality' on an ever-increasing scale, and has forgotten the 'mercy'.

'Low Lands' followed in 1960 (*New World Writing*, 16). In strict narrative terms it is about a lawyer named Dennis Flange who one day decides not to go to work so that he can drink with the garbage man, Rocco Squarcione. They are joined by an old navy friend of Flange, a gross figure named Pig Bodine (who recurs in later work). This is too much for Flange's wife Cindy and she orders them all out of the house. Rocco takes the others in his truck to a large garbage dump—vividly evoked by Pynchon, as we might expect—and introduces them to Bolingbroke, the watchman and 'king' of the dump. He puts them up for the night in his shack after they have told sea stories. Flange is awakened by a call from a girl who turns out to be a midget gypsy named Nerissa, who is convinced she will marry an 'Anglo'. She leads him by secret tunnels to her underground room. The story concludes with his agreeing to stay with her—at least for a while. The story takes place on three different levels: Flange's house above the sea; the dump at sea level; the subterranean complex of secret tunnels. Each has a different kind of residence: Flange's house was a minister's house from the 1920s; then there is the watchman's shack; finally Nerissa's room underground. There are connections: the house is full of secret tunnels associated with the smuggling that went on in the twenties, in which the minister was involved and to which he took a 'romantic attitude'; these are echoed by the network of underground tunnels beneath the dump, constructed in the thirties by a terrorist group called 'the Sons of the Red Apocalypse', and in the present time of the story occupied by gypsies.

As the story progresses, Flange moves further away from his wife, and further away from established society, first to the company of nonconformists and social derelicts, then yet further away to the gypsies—socially completely ostracized, 'rubbish' in social terms, and only able to 'live' by night. For 'further away' we could read 'deeper away', since for Flange the action is a continual descent. The house is up, the dump is down ('It seemed to Flange that they must be heading for the centre of the spiral, the low point') and the gypsy's room yet further down ('He had not realized that the junk pile ran to such a depth'). In every case, going from room to room Flange is going from womb to womb—as he knows—and perhaps prior to some regeneration and redemption (the ending leaves it deliberately equivocal; it might also be a descent into fantasy or even insanity). But a descent it is (Flange's 'Molemanship' is referred to), through varying strata of society's 'rubbish' (starting with the established society itself), and Flange is indeed burrowing. He is also drawn to the sea: 'he had read or heard somewhere in his pre-adolescence that the sea was a woman and the metaphor had enslaved him and largely determined what he became from that moment.' At times he also sees the sea as a 'waste land which stretches away to the horizon'. Nerissa the midget is a kind of mermaid of the dump. Flange's 'drowning' in the dump may make possible a sea change in his life, in his conception of the world. Just before he is summoned by Nerissa he falls asleep misquoting *The Tempest* and wondering whether he has perhaps 'suffered a sea change into something not so rare or strange'.

This leads us to another aspect of the whole story: among other things it is a tissue of references, allusions, quotations and misquotations, ironic echoes and parodies—mixed writings. Writers and works thus evoked in some way include T. S. Eliot (with a light travesty of the Waste Land myth), Shakespeare's *The Tempest*, *Henry IV* (Bolingbroke, of course), *The Merchant of Venice* (Nerissa is Portia's maid), *Alice's Adventures in Wonderland*, Keats's *Endymion*. More distinctly the story is a clear echo, and rewriting, of Washington Irving's story—so crucial for American literature—'Rip Van Winkle'. In all this mixing of writings and rewritings, Pynchon is not simply amusing himself or winking at learned readers. We should see this activity—which continues throughout his major works—more as a sifting (or 'burrowing' back) through not exactly the 'rubbish' and 'waste' of our literary past but through its accumulations to see what can be re-used (recycled, perhaps) for depicting his particular fictional world. We do not have to identify the other texts, but we do have to be alert for clues. Alert on all sides—noting, for example, that the 1920s are associated with the irresponsible 'romanticism' of the minister's house, while the 1930s saw the founding of 'the terrorist group called the Sons of the Red Apocalypse' when the whole social and political climate had changed. Pynchon is, among other things, a notable historical novelist, as *Gravity's Rainbow* was supremely to reveal. And again he can see that neither of the two suggested ways of being in—or against—society, worked or can work: the delusions of romanticism are matched by the delusions of apocalyptic revolutionary politics (they both used 'tunnels', but society still stood).

The story concludes with the beginning of the emergence of a new attitude in Flange, whether it is 'dream' or genuine transformation. Earlier we had read that he had a recurring dread of shrinkage—of himself, and of the world:

What he worried about was any eventual convexity, a shrinking, it might be, of the planet itself to some palpable curvature of whatever he would be standing

on, so that he would be left sticking out like a projected radius, unsheltered and reeling across the empty lunes of his tiny sphere.

At the end, in Nerissa's room, he has a different attitude. And it is important to note that to Flange she looks like a child (just as her pet rat looks like her child): children are always a source of value in Pynchon and attitudes to them always indicative of something positive or negative in an adult. The story ends:

And then: I wonder why Cindy and I never had a child.

And: a child makes it all right. Let the world shrink to a *boccie* ball.

So of course he knew.

'Sure' he said. 'All right. I'll stay.' For a while, at least, he thought. She looked up gravely. Whitecaps danced across her eyes; sea creatures, he knew, would be cruising about in the submarine green of her heart.

So of course *we* do *not* know—except that something is happening to Flange, and that Pynchon has produced a text that is rare and strange, ranging through many moods and tones, dense with resonances and implications, and ending at an equivocal suspended moment which has a haunting beauty all its own.

'Entropy' was published in 1960 (*Kenyon Review*, 22). It is composed like a fugue, and relevant words like 'stretto', 'counterpoint' and 'fugue' occur in the text. The 'counterpoint' is mainly between two floors of a Washington apartment building. Downstairs one Meatball Mulligan is having a 'lease-breaking party' which seems to be degenerating into chaos. Upstairs a figure named Callisto and his girlfriend Aubade live in a curious fantasy room: a 'hothouse jungle it had taken him seven years to weave together. Hermetically sealed, it was a tiny enclave of regularity in the city's chaos, alien to the vagaries of the weather, of national politics, of any civil disorder.' 'They did not go out.' Outside there is rain and it is the season of the 'false spring'. Two notable conversations take place in the growing din of the party. One concerns communication theory.

Tell a girl: 'I love you'. No trouble with two-thirds of that, it's a closed circuit. Just you and she. But that nasty four-letter word in the middle *that's* the one you have to look out for. Ambiguity. Redundance. Irrelevance, even. Leakage. All this is noise. Noise screws up your signal, makes for disorganization in the circuit.

Upstairs Callisto and Aubade have indeed created a 'closed circuit', just he and she. But such hermetically maintained order is a form of death. Noise indeed 'screws up your signal', but this might have a potential value if you want to cause 'disorganization in the circuit'. This, I think, can apply to Pynchon's work, which does indeed make for 'disorganization' in the customary circuits. So we must be prepared for 'Ambiguity. Redundance. Irrelevance, even. Leakage.' They may be the condition for the emergence of new kinds of signal. On the other hand, as Pynchon's story indicates, total noise—total chaos—would mean just no communication at all.

This problem is made clear in another form in the other conversation I wish to mention. There is a jazz quartet at the party and after pushing experimentation to the limit—there are distinct echoes of Gerry Mulligan and Ornette Coleman—they finally 'play' a completely silent piece, using no instruments. As the group's leader, the Duke, admits, the next logical extension 'is to think everything'. And thus to pass beyond music—and communication—altogether. The Duke says that they still have some problems, and Meatball says

'Back to the old drawing board.' '"No, man," Duke said, "back to the airless void."' Again this reflects on Pynchon's own position as a writer seeking some radically new form of fictional 'music'. He does not want to go back to 'the old drawing board'; but he knows that the 'airless void' is a place where no messages—no music—can take place at all.

An 'airless void' is something like what Callisto and Aubade have created in their 'hothouse' refuge. It is a deliberate retreat from the world. Drawing on Henry Adams and Gibbs, Callisto outlines his preoccupation with 'entropy' (an idea used not only in thermodynamics but in information theory); like Adams, Callisto speaks of himself in the third person:

> he found in entropy or the measure of disorganiza-
> tion for a closed system an adequate metaphor to
> apply to certain phenomena in his own world . . . in
> American 'consumerism' discovered a similar ten-
> dency from the least to the most probable, from
> differentiation to sameness, from ordered individu-
> ality to a kind of chaos. He found himself, in short,
> restating Gibbs' prediction in social terms, and
> envisioned a heat-death for his culture in which
> ideas, like heat-energy, would no longer be trans-
> ferred since each point in it would ultimately have
> the same quantity of energy; and intellectual motion
> would, accordingly, cease.

As he talks, he is trying to save the life of a young bird by warming it in his hands—transferring heat—but he finally fails, since he has indeed brought about an entropic state in his 'closed system'. What frightens him is that the temperature outside has remained at 37 degrees Fahrenheit for some days, and he takes this as an 'omen of apocalypse'. But while the idea of entropy is very important in Pynchon's work we should note that it is metaphor embraced, not by the author, but by the self-isolated Callisto. (It is worth noting that at one point he is looking for 'correspondences' and he thinks of Sade, and what happens to Temple Drake in *Sanctuary*, and *Nightwood*—all works or authors alluding to acts of sexual perversion.)

While it might seem that there is a simple opposition between the accelerating chaos downstairs and the calm upstairs ('arabesques of order competing fugally with the improvised discords of the party downstairs'), it is not, of course, so simple—as the conclusion intimates. Mulligan finds himself confronting a somewhat similar choice to that which confronted Siegel and confronts many other figures in Pynchon: give up, or try to do something?

> The way he figured, there were only two ways he
> could cope: (a) lock himself in the closet and maybe
> eventually they would all go away, or (b) try to calm
> everybody down, one by one. (a) was certainly the
> more attractive alternative. But then he started think-
> ing about that closet. It was dark and stuffy and he
> would be alone. . . . The other way was more a pain
> in the neck, but probably better in the long run. So
> he decided to try and keep his lease-breaking party
> from deteriorating into total chaos . . .

It might not be a radical solution, but it is a gesture against chaos, a neg-entropic act; while upstairs the girl Aubade finally breaks the window of their hothouse with her bare hands

> and turned to face the man on the bed and wait with
> him until the moment of equilibrium was reached,
> when 37 degrees Fahrenheit should prevail both
> outside and inside, and forever, and the hovering,
> curious dominant of their separate lives should re-
> solve into a tonic of darkness and the final absence of
> all motion.

There is a kind of perfect music which acts like a 'closed system' and finally resolves all into a terminal sameness: there is a noise which might indeed lead to chaos (a terminal sameness of another kind) but which might also permit new signals and provoke some counterforce against chaos, against terminal sameness—against entropy. The attractions of 'the closet' in the madness of the modern world are clear enough in Pynchon, but so is the need to resist those attractions in some way. The 'closed circuit', the sealed-off refuge, the hothouse world of fantasy, the dangerous seductiveness of metaphors of doom (like entropy): these can all lead to inhumanity and death. Pynchon, the writer, moves and manœuvres between the 'old drawing board' and the 'airless void'.

'Under the Rose' (*Noble Savage*, 3 (1961)) was later reworked as chapter 3 in *V.*, but a few points should be noted about the story, since it revealed for the first time another dimension of Pynchon's imagination: his ability to reconstruct history for his own purposes (the astonishing range of this reconstructive gift was only to emerge fully in *Gravity's Rainbow*). It is set at the time of the Fashoda Crisis of 1898. This was the climax of a series of conflicts between Great Britain and France, and although it resulted in the *entente* of 1904 it revealed the possible dangers of the international conflicts always latent in the period of late imperialism, and it could be seen, retrospectively, as an omen of the First World War. Fashoda was the strategic centre of the Egyptian Sudan, land of the Upper Nile, and both the British (under Kitchener) and the French (under Marchand) engaged in a race to capture it—forces converging on a single point (as they will on Malta in *V.*). National feelings ran so high that it did indeed bring the countries to the brink of war.

Pynchon's story is concerned with the spying that went on in the background—'spying's Free Masonry'—and the sense of the approach of some 'sure apocalypse'. One German spy longs for a big, final war, an Armageddon. The English spy, Porpentine, has 'conceived the private mission of keeping off Armageddon'. But they are both 'comrade Machiavellians, still playing the games of the Renaissance'. All the spies operate 'in no conceivable Europe but rather in a zone forsaken by God, between the tropics of diplomacy, lines they were forbidden forever to cross'. A similar 'zone' is to reappear in *Gravity's Rainbow*. One spy looks forward to the possible great war as effecting a great 'cleaning': 'Armageddon would sweep the house of Europe so. Did that make Porpentine champion only of cobwebs, rubbish, offscourings?' And Pynchon, too? Porpentine is another of those Pynchon figures concerned with the problems of being a 'saviour'.

> Porpentine found it necessary to believe if one
> appointed oneself saviour of humanity that perhaps
> one must love that humanity only in the abstract.
> For any descent to the personal level can make a
> purpose less pure. Whereas a disgust at individual
> human perversity might as easily avalanche into a
> rage for apocalypse.

There are references to an increasing inclination to turn to the 'inanimate' (a girl 'daft for rocks', a man who has himself wired up so that he can operate like a machine), a dominant motif in *V.* Porpentine, old-fashioned, crosses a 'threshold' into 'humanity': it is fatal, and the story ends up with his death. The larger question posed—if there is a larger question than the problem of being 'human' in the modern world—is one that hangs over all Pynchon's subsequent work.

> It was no longer single combat. Had it ever been? . . .
> They were all in it; all had a stake, acted as a unit.

Under orders. Whose orders? Anything human? He doubted . . . excused himself, silent, for wanting so to believe in a fight according to the duello, even in this period of history. But they—no, it—had not been playing those rules. Only statistical odds. When had he stopped facing an adversary and taken on a Force, a Quantity?

All the 'rules' of an earlier world have gone. There is now only a 'they'. Or, rather, an 'it'. We are entering the modern world.

Two more short pieces by Pynchon may conveniently be mentioned here, although they were written after the publication of V. 'The Secret Integration' (*Saturday Evening Post*, 237 (19 December 1964)) concerns a group of boys led by Grover Snodd who indulge in various attempts at sabotaging the local paper mill or the school—an undertaking named Operation Spartacus (after the film). Most of them are childish adventure games, and as 'plots' they fail when it comes to the lines of authority laid down by the adult world, though there is some anarchic resentment against 'the sealed-up world adults made, remade and lived in without him'. The title refers to the events that follow the moving of a black family, the Barringtons, into the town of Mingeborough: the white adults are all bigots and behave hysterically at the presence of the black family in their community. Among other things, they cover the front lawn of the Barrington house with garbage. When the gang of boys discover this—and the gang includes the black boy Carl Barrington—they 'begin kicking through it looking for clues'. (Looking for clues in garbage is a recurrent activity in Pynchon!) The clues they find reveal that a good deal of the garbage comes from their own homes. Through shame or feelings of helplessness they effectively abandon Carl, and he drifts away into the darkness, off to the old derelict mansion which is their secret hideout. Carl is in every sense a reject, and constructed out of rejections—indeed, we finally discover that he is an 'imaginary playmate'.

> Carl has been put together out of phrases, images, possibilities that grownups had somehow turned away from, repudiated, left out at the edges of the town, as if they were auto parts in Etienne's father's junkyard—things they could or did not want to live with but which the kids, on the other hand, could spend endless hours with, piecing together, rearranging, feeding, programming, refining. He was entirely theirs, their friend and robot, to cherish, buy undrunk sodas for, or send into danger or even, as now, at last, to banish from their sight.

So they leave their fantasy friend Carl and return 'each to his own house, hot shower, dry towel, before-bed television, good night kiss, and dreams that could never again be entirely safe.'

Another incident involves another black, a vagrant and a drifter named Mr McAfee. The children go to the hotel to try to help him (he is an alcoholic, and one of the children is already a member of Alcoholics Anonymous!). At one point the children try to telephone a girl the man once knew. This gives Tim an intimation of just what kind of terrifying loneliness is possible: 'Tim's foot felt at the edge of a certain abyss which he had been walking close to—for who knew how long—without knowing'; he sees 'how hard it would be, how hopeless, to really find a person you needed suddenly, unless you lived all your life in a house like he did, with a mother and father'. The white adults drive McAfee out of town next morning. Again, the children are really helpless. The town has certainly not accepted 'integration'. Tim asks his friend Grover, a maths prodigy, what the word 'integration' means:

> 'The opposite of differentiation,' Grover said, drawing an x-axis, y-axis and curve on his greenboard. 'Call this function of x. Consider values of the curve at any point little increments of x'—drawing straight vertical lines from the curve down to the x-axis, like the bars of a jail cell—'you can have as many of these as you want, see, as close together as you want.'
>
> 'Till it's all solid,' said Tim.
>
> 'No, it never gets solid. If this was a jail cell, and those lines were bars, and whoever was behind it could make himself any size he wanted to be, he could always make himself skinny enough to get free. No matter how close together the bars were.'

Grover knows that the lines are artificial, but in fact in the adult world they do operate as cell bars, and instead of integration plus differentiation this white society will try to maintain a rigid and exclusive sameness, as solid as it can make it. The ultimate emptiness and deadness of such a society is manifest in the new housing estate as perceived by the children:

> But there was nothing about the little, low-rambling, more or less identical homes of Northumberland Estates to interest or to haunt . . . no small immunities, no possibilities for hidden life or other worldly presence: no trees, secret routes, shortcuts, culverts, thickets that could be made hollow in the middle—everything in the place was out in the open, everything could be seen at a glance; and behind it, under it, around the corners of its houses and down the safe, gentle curves of its streets, you came back you kept coming back, to nothing: nothing but the cheerless earth.

The end of the story sees the end of fantasy, of rebellion and perhaps of innocence, for the children have encountered the nasty realities of adult prejudice inside their own comfortable homes. But this kind of man-made landscape of 'nothing' becomes an increasing source of dread in Pynchon's work. Elsewhere and in different ways the rebellion against the 'sealed-up world adults made' goes on—and must go on.

Pynchon's one piece of journalism, 'A Journey into the Mind of Watts' (*New York Times Magazine*, 12 June 1966), was a study of the Los Angeles slums where the riots took place. Perhaps predictably, Pynchon is drawn to the Watts Towers, some towers made literally out of garbage by an Italian immigrant, Simon Rodia, who devoted his life to these weird constructions—'his own dream of how things should have been: a fantasy of fountains, boats, tall openwork spires, encrusted with a dazzling mosaic of Watts debris.' Pynchon describes Los Angeles as 'a little unreal' because, 'more than any other city, [it] belongs to the mass media'. And Watts lies 'impacted at the heart of this white fantasy'. Pynchon describes how violence is inevitable in the circumstances. The people who live in Watts are among those disinherited for whom Pynchon has such a particular sympathy. He notes not only their actual poverty but the emptiness of their lives: 'Watts is full of street corners where people stand, as they have been, some of them, for 20 or 30 years, without Surprise One ever coming along.' Life without 'surprise'—the unpredictable, the random, 'difference'—is no life at all. It is also in keeping with Pynchon's imagination that he should end the piece on a proto-apocalyptic note. He describes an example of Watts art: 'it is a broken TV set, inside the cavity that once held the picture tube there is a human skull'. It is called: 'The Late, Late, Late Show'. And Pynchon knows what they meant by that.

V.

JOHN A. MEIXNER
From "The All-Purpose Quest"
Kenyon Review, Autumn 1963, pp. 729–32

As I started to write about Thomas Pynchon's novel, I suddenly grew drowsy and began to hear voices in a dream. They were faint at first, but in time they singled themselves out into those of a young man and a professor of indeterminate—or perhaps variable—age:

"And I had this thought," the young man was saying. "You know those pieces I wrote for the Writer's Workshop? Well, I'm planning to put them together. You know, make them into a novel."

"Yes?"

"It's going to be a real big novel. I'm going to put everything in it. It'll be like life itself—which is insane, really. It'll express the vast confusion of the century we live in."

"I see, but how do you plan to fit all these pieces together?"

"There's always The Quest."

"Yes, I might have expected it. But for what? Love? Salvation? Success? An Advanced Degree? Death? One's True Father? One's True Mother? The Meaning of Meaning?"

"Oh, all of them, all of them."

"To be sure. Well, now that you've got this sorted out so clearly, how do you propose to embody this quest? Kafka's used The Castle. That's out. Wolfe, the Hills Beyond. Melville, the White Whale. Forster, the Marabar Caves. Henry James, Europe. Kerouac (I believe), Denver."

"Yes, I puzzled about that for some time. Everything I thought of limited me so. I wanted an *expanding symbol*, you see. Like a nebula. One with nearly endless reference. After all, I thought, the quest is upward to the light. That's Paradise. That's Perfection. That's Permanence. That's Plato. It's also phallic, I'll bet. And pantheism, and passion, and putrescence (according to one school), and Pericles, and penance."

"And Pavlov."

"Yes. And pustules, and piss, and profit."

"And platitudes."

"Yes. And Pankhurst and paparezzi and Papen and Pius XII and Prometheus and Pershing. And—how could I have forgotten it—Past and Present. And there's more!

"Now doesn't it make you wonder that there's something very curious about all this? A compelling, pregnant affinity of names? And I said to myself what do all these have in common? Along with prince, prostitute, peasant, and priest? What brings order out of all this welter and chaos of associations and subtle explosions of meaning?"

"My nose is slightly itching."

"It's *P!*"

"Yes. I thought it might be."

"*P* is the secret."

"Now that *is* interesting. . . . But, tell me, what will be the setting of your novel?"

"Everywhere!—naturally. London, Nice, Geneva, Rome, East and West Berlin, Athens, Dublin, Dar-es-Salaam, Luanda, Delhi, LA, Butte, Houston. In bars, on buses, in cathouses, in the White House, the Orangerie, lots of different pads, the Yangtze, the Congo, underneath the Pennsylvania Turnpike."

"But aren't you rather inexperienced to write convincingly about so many different places?"

"Why *do* old people always try to put down the young?"

"Well, I'm not sure that we do. Anyway, I don't think we succeed."

"I've *traveled*, you know. Two summers ago I was in Europe. And I prowled around with Michelins and Muirheads and phrase books. And I've always been fascinated by the travel section of *The New York Times*."

"Still—I hope you won't think me tedious—if your quest is so grand and, as you say, takes in everything, won't it be necessary for you to have a very great deal of knowledge to draw on for your book?"

"Well, of course. But, you see, I do know an immense amount, really. That's the advantage of a university and a liberal education. Take physics. I've learned about inertia and torque and the second law of thermodynamics. And matter and anti-matter. They're all symbolic of the human condition, I think. For a time I was going to be an engineer. And there's piles and piles of stuff from anthropology and political science and abnormal psychology. And almanacs—they're wonderful. You can just copy out a list, say, of track records broken in one nine-month period. Plenty of meaning in that, if you know how to find it. And I can put in a lot of jokes from bull-sessions with the fellows, and from bashing around the country on Greyhounds."

"And your hero? Or I suppose he'll be an anti-hero? He'll quest for this *P*, is that it?"

"Probably. Or maybe his doppelgänger will, and he'll be looking on from the other side of the mercury, denying himself, among other things, to the feminine principle; except maybe for Alice. Things hurt too much."

"That was a little compressed, but I think I follow you. Well now. Tell me. Are you just perhaps by chance acquainted with the work of a young writer, a few years older than you, by the name of Pynchon?"

(Brief silence.) "You mean V., don't you? *Mine* will be different. It'll be lower case! And instead of a period, which is terribly terminal, you know, I'll have a dash, like this: *p*—, continuing on into the future. Pynchon's you see, been raped by Henry Adams. I'm a William James–Archibald MacLeish man. Besides, I have this deep, deep, intuition that P is just a more significant *letter* than V."

"Oh, I daresay it is. Still, despite that, won't people remark that you've merely aped Pynchon?"

"Oh, people! They'll say anything. *My* book will be original. I'll introduce other continents. I'll use the Pacific. Different kinds of scenes. Pynchon has this gang plot to steal Botticelli's *Birth of Venus* from the Uffizi. Well, I saw that painting too, and was so impressed with it—only I would have used the *Primavera*—that I wanted to do something with it myself. I could see that the Uffizi was universal. Obviously, I can't use that now. But I've already blocked out another episode, really much better, more central to the issues, in Rome. It's this gang who break into the Vatican Museum and by morning remove all the fig leaves that were fitted on to those Greco-Roman statues back in the Counter-Reformation. It goes on for three chapters. Isn't that imaginative?"

"Oh, wildly. But, tell me, Pynchon's book, you were impressed by it, I take it? And you agree, I assume, that 'neither the reader nor the American novel will remain unchallenged or unchanged by it'—as I remember seeing somewhere."

"Oh, yes! It's a book that makes all sorts of things possible.

"I mean, here's a fellow with an incredible, an astonishing vision. We're all becoming inanimate, and the world is running down. I may not agree, as I said. But it *is* a tremendous theme, isn't it? And it's very amazingly worked out, so that you almost *feel* the vital connection between his historical and his contemporary plots. It almost *does* explain things."

"I was bored."

"Well, I was too, I guess. But I found the way he put it together terribly interesting, as a writer, you know. And the daring of it too."

"Oh, I don't fault him on daring. It's original in its way: this all-purpose quest for V. What bothers me is that it's been wasted. The book was published at least two years before it should have been. So we have an idea, we have a method. But it's been spoiled. These things, on such scale, take maturing, of the book and of the writer. To weed out the junk, to re-do the vital parts, to decide what one's voice is (to *have* one, even). Now the idea's been ruined, permanently for Pynchon, and of course for every other writer."

"You don't think he's a good writer?"

"I think he's ambitious. This won't be the last we'll hear from him. But, no, I don't see the signs of a *good* writer, not so far. He has a certain vaunting feeling for abstractions. But his sensibility strikes me as dull and locked-in. The quality of his mind isn't interesting. It drones. And the amount of sheer bad writing in the book is staggering. Take this passage, for example:

> For that moment at least they seemed to give up external plans, theories and codes, even the inescapable romantic curiosity about one another, to indulge in being simply and purely young, to share that sense of the world's affliction, that outgoing sorrow at the spectacle of Our Human Condition which anyone this age regards as reward or gratuity for having survived adolescence. For them the music was sweet and painful, the strolling chains of tourists like a Dance of Death. They stood on the curb, gazing at one another, jostled against by hawkers and sightseers, lost as much perhaps in that bond of youth as in the depths of the eyes each contemplated.
>
> He broke it first. "You haven't told me your name."

"But isn't that parody. Isn't the book full of parody?"

"I wish I could be so sure it *was* parody. In the sense of intentional, meaningful, mocking. Near as I can make out, the bulk of it is simply writing in the manner of other authors (chiefly melodramatic ones), the way that most young writers do it. (And that hundreds of young writers around the country could do more skillfully, as a matter of fact.) But even if it were intentional parody, what would be the point? How does it *work*—artistically, expressively, in the book? Most of this so-called parody is in the historical sections. But is the manner of E. Phillips Oppenheim to be taken *seriously* as a rendering of the force of history? The whole thing is sophomoric. It's not a matter of his choosing. I don't think he could have written it differently, simply because he doesn't command any other knowledge or equipment to write about it with."

"He does better, doesn't he, with the contemporary scenes."

"Yes, naturally. Certainly they're more interesting. I rather liked his nose-operation chapter and the one in which Profane hunts alligators in the sewers, and some other things. And the historical episode in Southwest Africa caught my imagination, particularly the closing pages, which are very powerful. But just consider what the book would be if one took out all that phony ballast of the past. Merely a string of not very

interesting, very much the same, episodes of bumming around, in which every time Pynchon's invention flags he introduces a new set of characters, names actually, none realer or deeper than the last. The usual refuge for the novice writer. In fact, there isn't one convincingly-explored character in the whole book. Which is, I suppose, another way of saying there's little sense of aliveness, of reality on any meaningful level, in the work."

RAYMOND M. OLDERMAN
From "The Illusion and the Possibility of Conspiracy"
Beyond the Waste Land: A Study of the American Novel in the Nineteen-Sixties
1972, pp. 123–44

Understanding Thomas Pynchon's mysterious novel V. is like understanding the twentieth century. Pursue V. and you are like Herbert Stencil, the "century's child," born in 1901, buried in the outrageous facts of contemporary experience, and convinced that "events seem to be ordered in an ominous logic." V. is everything that happens in the twentieth century and everything that might happen—as if you could clutch a handful of the times from our atmosphere and tack a letter on it, making it palpable so it can be poked around and examined, if not known. Pynchon has attempted to show us the essential qualities of our time. Like a prose version of Eliot's *The Waste Land*, V. pictures a world where love and mythology have failed, and it points out the path we follow: "The street of the 20th Century, at whose far end or turning— we hope—is some sense of home or safety. But no guarantees. A street we are put at the wrong end of, for reasons best known to the agents who put us there. If there are agents. But a street we must walk."[1]

In a sense, Pynchon is creating the mystery of Fate itself. For, ultimately, understanding V. is understanding the compulsive direction we take in our headlong plunge down the street of our century. As always with Fate, V. leads us to wonder if we take that plunge because of mysterious forces guiding us, or if the plunge as well as Fate, V., and everything else is the way it is because we are the way we are. For Herbert Stencil, V.'s "emissaries haunt the century's streets." For the more reliable Fausto Maijstral, "There is more accident to it than a man can ever admit to in a lifetime and stay sane." Thus, we have the two poles of Fate, and the essential mystery of V.—either there is some ominous logic to the direction of man's life or life is a series of random accidents defined only by the impulses of the living. In either case, however, the direction of our plunge is clear to Pynchon. Insofar as Fate is knowable, insofar as V. is identifiable, and insofar as our future is predictable, it all points to a "dream of annihilation." V. as woman, V. as war, V. as conspiracy—it all adds up to what old Godolphin discovers about Vheissu in 1898 or what Von Trotha puts into effect in 1904—"Vernichtungs Befehl" (Annihilation Orders.) Annihilation is the nightmare of the twentieth century, and it is perhaps our Fate—a possibility brought to our attention in 1945 when young Herbert Stencil begins his quest and the United States drops the Atomic Bomb. The mystery of V. is the mystery of why we pursue our destruction; it is the mystery of fact in the twentieth century, which points repeatedly to the madness of annihilation—not to the hope of love, but to the waste land after the holocaust, to "the desert, or a row of false shop fronts; a slag pile, a forge where the fires are banked, these and the street and the dreamer, only an inconsequential shadow himself in the landscape, partaking of the soullessness of these other masses and shadows; this is the 20th Century nightmare" (p. 324).

V. encompasses three realms, interrelated in a process which attempts to make us understand the essential qualities of our century and the extensiveness of our nightmare. "The process is a part of daily news," Richard Poirier tells us, "and no other novelist predicts and records it with Pynchon's imaginative and stylistic grasp of contemporary materials."[2] The three realms of the novel are the private, the public-political, and what might be called the metaphysical. The private realm evolves from the stories of Benny Profane, Rachel Owlglass, the Whole Sick Crew, and Fausto Maijstral's confessions. The action takes place between December 1955 and September 1956. It ends with Benny Profane running down a Malta street in sudden blackness toward the sea. Abandoned and teamed with Brenda Wigglesworth, the "inviolable Puritan," Benny seems finally at the end of his Street, on the edge of his own "Day of Doom."

The public, political, and international realm includes all the stories that relate to the Lady V. and the events of twentieth century upheaval:

1898—Egypt; Fashoda; Victoria Wren

1899—Florence; Venezuelan uprising; Plot to steal the *Birth of Venus*; Intimations of World War I; The Vheissu Plot involving Vesuvius, M. Vogt, his spy school, and Victoria Wren

1901—Herbert Stencil's birth: Queen Victoria's death

1904—Von Trotha's Vernichtungs Befehl, putting down Black uprising in South West Africa by introducing brutalities surpassed only in World War II

1913—Paris; Intimations of Russian Revolution; Stirrings of World War I; The Lady V. nameless and in love with Melanie l'Heuremaudit; Russia and the Orient linked in a suspected "movement to overthrow Western Civilization"

1918—Evan Godolphin's face ruined; World War I; Inspiration of young Schoenmaker

1919—Death of Sydney Stencil; Malta's June Disturbances; Intimations of World War II and Mussolini; Veronica Manganese

1922—Uprising in South West Africa; Foppl's decadent seige party; Intimations of Hitler; Vera Meroving; Hedwig Vogelsang

1934—Fairing's Parish in New York sewers, with Veronica the rat; Intimations of World War II and possible apocalypse; American Depression

1943—Bombing of Malta in World War II; In Valleta, Malta, the death and dismantling of the Lady V. disguised as the transvestite "Bad Priest"

1945—Beginning of Herbert Stencil's quest; Atomic Bomb

1956—Stencil's abandonment of Malta in pursuit of Mme Viola, an oneiromancer, a diviner of dreams, who might finally reveal the dream of annihilation that Stencil pursues

Other public events are scattered throughout the book as Pynchon keeps us aware of world news, current fashions, and wide-scale catastrophes, natural and otherwise. Herbert Stencil moves in both the private and public realms on his mysterious quest, but Stencil is a third-person object himself, with no real private being. He may be a quester, but he is no Grail Knight—he is as much a schlemiel and a human yo-yo as Benny Profane. He is indeed the century's child, functioning

only to help us understand the century, but not as a redeemer. He is not even a seeker of identity, for Pynchon, like other novelists of the sixties, mocks the whole tired idea of an identity search by putting the jargon we have evolved to describe that search into the mouths of the *Time*-Magazine–reading, fashionable decadents called the Whole Sick Crew. Pynchon is not interested in failed redeemers; he is interested in the waste land itself, in the landscape of the twentieth century, the Street which has become, according to Fausto Maijstral, "the Kingdom of Death."

The third realm in the novel deals with the metaphysical, or perhaps ontological, question of whether V. exists as an actual force or only as the fictional heading under which we list the random facts of twentieth-century life. Do the facts of our century's private and public life add up to an actually existing force that has seized control over man's life, or are we constructing a demon to explain why man has lost the power of significant individual action and become a little less human? What better explains the fabulous direction contemporary fact has taken, the mystery of absurdity, and the threat of annihilation—what better explains the loss of man's coveted *virtù* than the existence of some usurping power symbolized, aptly, by the letter V. and meaning not individual excellence, but wide-scale, untouchable, metaphysical Conspiracy. Pynchon's V. deals with that same mystery we have seen to be the compelling preoccupation of the novel in the sixties—to requote Benjamin DeMott's words: given the nature of contemporary experience, our worst nightmare is "that events and individuals are unreal, and that power to alter the course of the age, of my life and your life, is actually vested nowhere."[3] V. presents a series of visible manifestations in public and private life that hint at a mystery behind everyday fact. As we are told, the Lady V. as well as every other V.-word from the V-Note Bar to Via dei Vecchietti are only "symptoms" of what makes our world a waste land. The symptoms and the V.'s are everywhere (even the color of the hardbound V. is violet). The question is: do the symptoms reveal a master cabal still in the making, a universal paranoia, or a world deluded by its need for mystery and meaning, its need to replace a lost mythology? (Even Herbert Stencil admits he may only be driven by something "buried" in him "that needed a mystery.")

As I have mentioned and as I hope to demonstrate, V. is the essential nature of our century, pointing always toward our haunting communal "dream of annihilation"; however, only after we have examined the symptoms and manifestations of that dream, all the public and private appearances of V., can we say in what sense Pynchon feels V. to be an actually existing entity. It is the same question we have seen before—is it possible that deep in the soul of our century we will discover not the American Dream but a dream which proves we ourselves are the source of a waste land world gone mad; or is there really an unknown Master Conspiracy, a Big Bad Wolf? The question itself may sound like ripe material for a joke, and so it is at times, but that only makes it one more example of black humor, of the comic becoming nightmare; the fear of conspiracy is a real fact in contemporary life—it is perhaps the stuff that V.'s are made on.

By using a series of repetitions, verbal echoes, and baffling coincidences, Pynchon interrelates the private, the public, and the metaphysical realms of his book, and gives us the sense that V. is omnipresent. Any thing we learn in any realm contributes toward an overall understanding of V. What is true about Victoria Wren is true of Vheissu and helps us understand V., the essential nature of the twentieth century. The implied sexuality of Esther's nose operation recalls the sexual nature of Lady V., who is often a seducer and a saint combined (like Victoria Wren and Veronica the rat), and that in turn relates to Fina Mendoza who is the spiritual leader and gang bang for a New York street gang. The private and public realms join to point out that abuse of sexuality is one pervasive symptom of V. and of our century; therefore abuse of sexuality is one of the things that leads us by steps toward fulfilling our dream of annihilation. For example: the sexuality of Esther's nose job is a comic inversion of the usual joke about men and the length of their noses, demonstrating a vaguely unhealthy reversal of role playing; the next step, a little less funny, is Mafia Winsome's tyrranical theory of "Heroic Love," where the woman is the aggressor; one step further and the reversal of roles becomes an undeniable inversion when the Lady V. appears as the Bad Priest, a transvestite, who in that role is finally annihilated. Picking up the events of the book at any point can lead to what Pynchon repeatedly calls a "daisy chain" of events, interrelating the private and the public realms and centering around some one quality of twentieth-century life.

Pynchon, we come to see, sets up his own version of correspondences; that is, the private individual does in microcosm what the public governments do in macrocosm, thereby raising an individual foible to a public, and perhaps universal, metaphysical principle. Benny Profane cannot love just as governments cannot get along, and Rachel tells him, "You've taken your own flabby, clumsy soul and amplified it into a Universal Principle (p. 383). In the same way, Plots come into being. Just as the individual assigns causes to situations he does not understand, the government assigns causes on a grand scale—Presto! we have Causes, Plots, Conspiracies. "People read what news they want to and each accordingly builds his own rathouse of history's rags and straws. . . . God knows what is going on in the minds of cabinet ministers, heads of state and civil servants in the capitals of the world. Doubtless their private versions of history show up in action" (p. 225). While old Godolphin fumbles with his doubtful stories of Vheissu, perhaps a fictional place, old Stencil theorizes that Vheissu is a code name for Venezuela which indicates a plot to take over the world by invading a subterranean network of tunnels through volcanoes starting first with Vesuvius. The plot is revealed by Madame Vogt as she plays her viola da gamba, and as some real Venezuelans plot the theft of Botticelli's *Birth of Venus*. Not only have we moved from the realm of private idiosyncrasy to that of public affairs (resulting in a riot), but the mysterious V. has multiplied itself into a metaphysical principle of Plot. We know it is untrue, as we do of other plots in the novel, but the point here is that comprehension of private failures leads by analogy to an understanding of public dilemmas; V., the dream of the century, can be approached on any level. Thus, as we come to understand the characteristics of V. we recognize the widespread mystery of its existence. When old Godolphin tells us Vheissu with its rainbow of colors is a "dream of annihilation," we are prepared to register this as the essential truth about the colorful Lady V. and V. in general.

The intertwinings of plot and the parallels between different realms in the world of V. not only instruct us in the step-by-step metaphysics of conspiracy, but also make us wonder if in Pynchon's world conspiracies might not sometimes be true. Could all these connections be accident? German names and German characters constantly appear in connection with ominous intimations. Plotters in Egypt 1898 meet in a German beer hall, and so do plotters in 1899 in Florence; Germans are behind the scenes in Paris 1913; Foppl's German castle is the scene of strange machinations in

1922 and Von Trotha's cruelty in 1904 foreshadows World War II. The suggestions are numerous, and every manifestation of V. occurs in connection with some possibility of influence on a real and historical war.

Pynchon also uses coincidence in his fictional plot; not only does Stencil cross the lines from one part of the story to the next, but so do Hugh and Evan Godolphin, Father Fairing, and Fausto Maijstral. The coincidences built into the fictional plot of V. reinforce the thematic question of whether things happen by chance or by malicious design. Other kinds of parallels in the book make us aware that Pynchon is focusing on the waste land of the twentieth century rather than trying to characterize certain people: Benny Profane has a theory of Streets and so does Fausto Maijstral; Rachel Owlglass and Rooney Winsome talk of decadence, so do Mondaugen and the director of ballet, M. Itague—the Street and twentieth-century decadence are emphasized, not the characters, whose theories and discussions are almost interchangeable. The traditional device of foreshadowing is used as another kind of parallel between the different realms of the novel: Benny's old dream-joke about the boy with the golden screw in his navel, who removes the screw and loses his ass and all his other parts, warns us of the fate of Lady V., who has a sapphire removed from her navel and is literally disassembled by children on the island of Malta; and it is also another dream of annihilation. There are even verbal echoes that occur periodically in different voices: "the balloon's gone up," "the dance of death," "the world is all that the case is," and "keep cool, but care." Songs appear throughout the book no matter what the setting or who the characters involved. All this complex echoing and interrelating of the private, public, and metaphysical realms, similar to Eliot's method in *The Waste Land*, contributes to the mystery of the book and makes it clear that V. is everything symptomatic of our century and that all the symptoms point toward a communal dream of annihilation.

The two major symptoms of the twentieth century, as both Pynchon and Eliot have described them, are the inversion of love and the inversion of religion. Thus, every public and private appearance of V.—as woman, place, or concept—is connected to these two characteristics. The inversion of love is demonstrated in the abuse of sex and in the continued appearance of war. The inversion of religion appears not only through the distorted beliefs of Father Fairing and Victoria Wren but through the substitution of belief in conspiracy for faith in a supreme Being. If, for example, we were to follow the progressive appearances of the Lady V.—Victoria Wren in 1898 and 1899; V., the lover of Melanie l'Heuremaudit in Paris 1913; Veronica Manganese on Malta in 1919; Vera Meroving and her accomplice Hedwig Vogelsang in South West Africa in 1922; and the Bad Priest in Valletta, Malta 1943—if we were to scrutinize these appearances of one kind of V., we would find in each case the inversion of love in transvestitism, fetishism, lesbianism, or simple exploitation; we would find the intimation of one of our wars; and we would find religion transposed into a private extreme and into a mystical suspicion of some controlling malicious Force that connects the Lady V. with all the master cabals of the century.

Mondaugen's story of South West Africa not only demonstrates how humanity is perverted by war and is led to mass annihilation performed with relish, but it includes the perversions of Hedwig Vogelsang whose purpose is to "tantalize and send raving the race of man," and who has sex with Mondaugen only when he is ravaged by scurvy. Veronica the rat is not just the product of Father Fairing's inversion of religious principles; she is also his hope for a postwar society and she is an ambiguous mixture of saint and seducer. Yoyodyne is not simply an unscrupulous producer of weapons; it is another manifestation of V. since it manufactures "Vergeltungswaffe" (destructive reprisal weapons). Anywhere we find the letter V. in Pynchon's book it is connected to sex, war, or conspiracy. History itself, it is suggested, may be nothing more than the "jitterings and squeaks of a metaphysical bedspring."

Each manifestation of V. also shows how the inversion of love and the inversion of religion are controlled by our communal dream of annihilation. Pynchon supplies a definite three-stage pattern for each manifestation: decadence, decline to the inanimate, and then annihilation. The pattern is illustrated by the Lady V. who begins as eighteen-year-old Victoria Wren, believing in her own *virtù,* her power to control the movements of fortune. But later we learn "Victoria was being gradually replaced by V.; something entirely different, for which the young century had as yet no name" (p. 410). As we follow her transformations she becomes progressively more decadent and progressively more inanimate. In the end her hair is false, her feet are artificial, her eye is glass, and in place of a belly button she owns a star sapphire. She has become a Bad Priest, perverting the Word and spirit of religion. More inanimate than animate, she is annihilated by children, taken apart as if she were an object to be dismantled. Thus, the Lady V. is not V. itself but an illustration, a prediction of what V. can be, a symptom of the direction of the twentieth century which is still at the decadent stage but is moving toward the inanimate.

The final image of the book presages an extraordinarily gloomy end to the road of the century and to the mystery of V. Old Stencil is annihilated at sea, quickly, quietly, and totally by accident. While young Stencil pursues his illusion of an "ultimate Plot Which Has No Name," and thinks he is in pursuit of V., we learn that V. does not even provide the paradoxical comfort of a planned conspiracy—our annihilation will have no more meaning than Stencil's accidental death or assassination by the bullet of a random psychotic.

Since Pynchon feels we are still in the decadent stage and have only begun the movement toward the inert and the inanimate, he devotes a good deal of his book to documenting the modes of this century's decadence. "'A decadence,'" we are told, "'is a falling-away from what is human, and the further we fall the less human we become. Because we are less human, we foist off the humanity we have lost on inanimate objects and abstract theories'" (p.405). Decadence makes everyone a sexual object, or a statistic in war, or the object of Conspiracy. Pynchon uses the Whole Sick Crew to illustrate decadence in the stylish set and in modern art—in the users of allusions and painters of cheese danish, in effete sophisticates and "Catatonic Expressionists." The Crew are wastelanders right down to the bar they frequent, where "Time, gentlemen, please" echoes from Eliot's waste land. Aimless and bored, they yo-yo from one stale party to the next. They convert themselves to objects; take the case of Fergus Mixolydian, who, to watch TV, "devised an ingenious sleep-switch, receiving its signal from two electrodes placed on the inner skin of his forearm. When Fergus dropped below a certain level of awareness, the skin resistance increased over a preset value to operate the switch. Fergus thus became an extension of the TV set" (p. 56). Even Rachel Owlglass has her moments of "MG love" when she croons love words to her car and strokes the gear shift. Benny the schlemiel, who cannot live in peace with inanimate objects, becomes himself as inanimate as a yo-yo. Fausto Maijstral has a period when he becomes one with the landscape of the waste land, having "taken on much of the non-humanity of the debris, crushed stone, broken masonry, destroyed churches and auberges of his city" (p. 307).

Pynchon is continually concerned with contemporary indications of the inert and the inanimate and is at least semiserious when he calls the twentieth century a "Neo-Jacobean" age of decadence. His concern is best illustrated by Benny Profane's confrontation with SHROUD (synthetic human, radiation output determined), and SHOCK (synthetic human object, casualty kinematics). SHROUD, a research instrument for Yoyodyne Munitions, measures the effect of radiation fallout, and SHOCK measures the effect of automobile accidents. For Pynchon, they measure two more approaches to twentieth-century annihilation. SHROUD, somehow given the power to make prophetic statements for Benny Profane only, warns him that man is already on his way to nonbeing. Pointing out the similarity between an automobile graveyard and Auschwitz, SHROUD describes for Benny "thousands of Jewish corpses, stacked up like those poor car-bodies. Schlemihl: It's already started" (p. 295). The decadence of the century goes beyond the fitful inanities of the Whole Sick Crew; Pynchon's weaving of fact and fiction, his play upon actual history, and his almanac statistics turn the book from a game with mysteries to a genuine presentation of the mystery of contemporary fact. Locked behind the mystery of V. is not a fantasy for keen readers and would-be secret agents, but the shockingly recognizable facts of our experience.

With the realization that Pynchon means V. to represent a plunge toward annihilation, brought about by our decadence and growing "non-humanity" and based on the facts of twentieth-century inversion of love and religion, we can return to the question that haunts this book and so many others written in the sixties. What Force has gained control over our lives and led us to pursue V., to pursue our own annihilation? Pynchon is very aware that in recent years the fear of conspiracy has become more and more a part of daily news, that "we have men like Stencil, who must go about grouping the world's random caries into cabals" (p. 153). (We might note the present-time action of V. begins shortly after the McCarthy Hearings closed.) In lucid moments we may find it hard to believe someone could truly postulate the existence of a real metaphysical force, or a real organization, that with its own logic and malicious purpose is controlling the extremes of modern experience. Without some such logic, however, we may be forced to admit that the intricate fate of our century hangs on nothing purposeful, malicious or otherwise.

By allowing the reader to see more of what goes on than any of the characters do, Pynchon makes it clear that the appearances of V. are not manifestations of a Plot but simple chance events. One of the most effective tensions of the book comes from the reader's desire to make V. into a universal principle of conspiracy even though he has enough contrary information to know that what happened in Florence was a tissue of accidents, that Vheissu is no stronghold for world conspirators, and that old Stencil was not killed by agents of a master cabal who felt he knew too much. We are trapped by the outrageous coincidences of modern fact into wanting to believe that some Force "continues active today and at the moment, because the ultimate Plot Which Has No Name is as yet unrealized." But that desire is exactly what Pynchon means to point out—we seek the logical causes and we construct the fictions that create our problems and result in wars. There is no mysterious force behind V., but there is our misplaced impulse to uncover some Power external to man which is the source of our insane dream of annihilation—the spiritual yearning of wastelanders who live without mythology and feel compelled to construct one from the outrageous but stony materials of modern fact. The period after the V in Pynchon's title leads us to believe there is a word behind the mystery and leads us to turn random symptoms into an unholy kind of Word become flesh. We prove Pynchon's point even as we read: we can accept no God, but we can invent and pursue His inversion. Like all good black humor, Pynchon's comedy about plot and paranoia combines the funny with the horrible and traps our conscience in the combination. Our own fiction of conspiracies and our own half-wish–half-fear that some force controls our lives is only one more symptom of our dream of annihilation. The actual way in which Conspiracy helps us pursue that dream lies not in its real existence, but in our paranoid reactions; we respond to the world as if Conspiracy were true and our response makes its effect as real as if it did exist—as real, at least, as the Russo-Americans arms race.

Plots and conspiracies, then, are illusions. When Pynchon confronts us with the intertwining facts of experience, he wants us to recognize, as Fausto Maijstral does, that the intertwining is pure accident. We are to tell ourselves what old Stencil tells himself: "Don't act as if it were a conscious plot against you. Who knows how many thousand accidents— a variation in the weather, the availability of a ship, the failure of a crop—brought all these people, with their separate dreams and worries, here to this island and arranged them in this alignment?" (p. 483). Further, when we look for meanings and purposes in life itself, we must, Pynchon tells us, cease to be "Tourists" and begin to see beneath the "gaudy skin" to the heart of human life. Like old Godolphin, standing alone in the vast waste land at the South Pole, we must eventually strike through the surface spectacle of things and discover the essential truth—that there is "Nothing." This is the discovery of the void, the recognition that we live in a meaningless waste land with no hope of a Grail Knight to deliver us, though, still, we live. "There could have been no more entirely lifeless and empty place anywhere on earth" (p. 205).

But Pynchon does not leave us entirely in so desolate a place; there are some characters in the book who strike through to this discovery of the void *and recover*, as if from the lifeless, to make the same simple affirmation we have seen to be characteristic of the sixties—"life is the most precious possession you have." Rachel Owlglass, McClintic Sphere, and Fausto Maijstral—each, having faced the waste land and an inanimate rocklike existence, makes some discovery about the nature of love that turns his rock to shelter, just as Eliot's "red rock" becomes a shelter in his waste land. For Fausto the rock is Malta; for redheaded Rachel and for McClintic Sphere, it is the strength they gain from understanding what it means to give, sympathize, and control. Both Rachel and McClintic lose in their attempt to communicate love and both recognize the limitations love has in making life meaningful, but both go on giving and caring. McClintic's recognition is one of the most positive and tender moments of the book: he tells Paola, who is leaving him and whom he loves, that he has not understood things until that moment.

> "Lazy and taking for granted some wonder drug someplace to cure that town, to cure me. Now there isn't and never will be. Nobody is going to step down from heaven and square away Roony and his woman, or Alabama, or South Africa or us and Russia. There's no magic words. Not even I love you is magic enough. Can you see Eisenhower telling Malenkov or Khrushchev that? Ho-ho. Keep cool but care." [p. 366]

Pynchon gives us little else as a counterbalance to our communal dream of annihilation—only the small though decidedly positive communal hope that we can all keep cool but care. And yet, even as McClintic informs Paola of these simple but affirmative sentiments, Pynchon informs us that "somebody had run over a skunk a ways back. The smell had followed him for miles."

Fausto's affirmative stance is undoubtedly meant to be Pynchon's major alternative to a waste land world running out of alternatives. Although Fausto goes no further than McClintic, giving us nothing more firm than keep cool but care, his regeneration on Malta, "a cradle of life," is decidedly meant to illustrate the possibility of reversing the trend toward annihilation, of coming back from the inanimate and recovering from the scars of war and the sight of V. Having lived through the war and having seen the Lady V. meet her death, Fausto has gained the essential knowledge of life, death, and the twentieth century. He understands V. but has no illusions about conspiracy, for he tells us, "Only one thing matters: it's the bomb that wins" (p. 332). Until his regeneration Fausto's progress from youth to war-weary cynic—from Fausto I to Fausto III—is a model of what Pynchon means by decadence and the movement toward the inanimate. "'Decadence, decadence,'" Fausto writes, labeling the war-caused split in his personality Fausto II and Fausto III, "'What is it? Only a clear movement toward death or, preferably, non-humanity. As Fausto II and III, like their island, became more inanimate, they moved closer to the time when like any dead leaf or fragment of metal they'd be finally subject to the laws of physics'" (p. 321).

Fausto hits his lowest point as he inertly watches the children dismantle the Bad Priest, the final avatar of the Lady V. It is then that he becomes "inanimate" and "rocklike," a thing one step from the dead—Fausto III, debris and a ravaged soul, waiting with Malta for his annihilation by bomb. But Fausto recovers; he becomes Fausto IV, who has "inherited a physically and spiritually broken world," a true waste land, and yet somehow finds reason to endure as a living human being. Pynchon never tells us exactly what it is that regenerates Fausto; he himself admits: "Of Fausto III's return to life, little can be said. It happened. What inner resources were there to give it nourishment are still unknown to the present Fausto. This is a confession and in that return from the rock was nothing to confess" (p. 345). Perhaps while kneeling and administering last rites to the dying Lady V., half woman and half inert object, Fausto saw in her the image and the symptom we are all supposed to see. Perhaps with the rubble of a bombed waste land stacked around him he saw the future of the century, the cryptograph V. as a whole, revealing the terror of everyone's annihilation, the terror that all of us could be dismantled by our own future as the children dismantled Lady V. Perhaps Fausto was just not ready to administer last rites to all of human life.

Ultimately, Pynchon wants us to recognize that Malta itself, "the womb of rock," has something to do with Fausto's regeneration. There is much about Pynchon's Malta that could provide an inspiration to survive: it has a mythology, not just the old Knights of Malta, but myths like the history of Mara, teacher of love, told to us by Mehemet the sea captain; it is a place curiously untouched by time, whose people "don't feel the fingers of years jittering age, blindness into face, heart and eyes" (p. 321)—they are not forced into the patterns of history and so perhaps can avoid the decadence that usually accompanies the progress of time. Malta is an island of rock, but instead of being the kind of rock that indicates a waste land of the inanimate, Malta is a rock that sustains its people. Because it is a rock, it is able to withstand the daily bombing it receives in World War II—and because it endures, its people endure. "Malta, and her inhabitants, stood like an immovable rock in the river Fortune, now at war's flood" (p. 325). The Maltese people assign human qualities to their island— "invincibility," "tenacity," "perseverance"—and instead of being themselves led toward decadence, the inanimate, and final annihilation, they emulate their beloved island and learn human endurance from a rock. What Pynchon finds most important is that Fausto and the Maltese people develop a sense of community based on the indestructibility of their rock. Malta teaches them to give, sympathize, and control, or, in McClintic Sphere's more accessible, reduced, war-torn form, to keep cool but care. It is the caring and the giving that makes the Maltese survive and teaches Fausto enough control so that he can return from his vision of annihilation to a simple affirmation of life. Pynchon uses the principle of correspondence mentioned earlier—paralleling the private microcosm with the public or metaphysical macrocosm—to intimate Fausto is reborn because he discovers he can be like Malta and so endure. "As the Ark was to Noah so is the inviolable womb of our Maltese rock to her children" (p. 318).

Nonetheless, to assign any real value to Malta is a "delusion." Pynchon is not suggesting that we see Malta as an ideal place, or even that we see it as a symbol of genuine sanity, like Joseph Heller's use of Sweden at the end of *Catch-22*. Instead, we must admit that it "has no value apart from its function; that it is a device, an artifice" (p. 326). As we have already learned, when you strike beneath the skin of any twentieth-century value, you will find Nothing. Scrutiny of what happened on Malta would show that the communion it supported was as much a result of accident as old Stencil's death was. Any elevation of Malta to a universal principle is an illusion, as V. the conspiracy is an illusion, as a tourist's view of the skin of life is an illusion. What Pynchon has made clear is that in the face of the waste land of this century some kind of illusion is necessary for man to remain human—and that some illusions are better than others. The pursuit of V. is a bad illusion because it leads toward annihilation rather than toward an affirmation of life. By speaking of Malta as a woman and by describing it as a place with a certain absence of color, in contrast to the gaudy colors associated with V., Pynchon makes us compare the illusion of V. with the illusion surrounding Malta. Belief in Malta is a good illusion because it produces a sense of communion and a feeling that man can endure. It is a fruitful illusion, important not because it offers the hope of a new set of absolute values, but because it provides an image of something human in the midst of the inhumanity of war and helps reverse Fausto's movement toward death. Thus, it convinces Fausto of the possibility of his own humanity. "To have humanism," he tells us, "we must first be convinced of our humanity. As we move further into decadence this becomes more difficult" (p. 322).

As we have seen repeatedly in the novel of the sixties, there is only one important quest—to affirm life no matter how negative the facts of experience may be. To do so we may have to create our own illusion, we may have to build our own fable and play the role of the poet, for as Fausto tells us, "It is the 'role' of the poet, this 20th Century. To lie." Our century has gone as far as it can go in destroying old illusions; to regain value one must discover new illusions; the writer, accordingly, may have to become once again the illusion-maker, the fabulist. Fausto's poet friend makes it clear that lies and illusions are necessary even for the tourists of the world who have never yet recognized the void.

> If I told the truth
> You would not believe me.
> If I said: no fellow soul
> Drops death from the air, no conscious plot
> Drove us underground, you would laugh
> As if I had twitched the wax mouth
> Of my magic mask into a smile—
>
> (p. 326)

Since we must have illusions, Pynchon cautions us, let them be like Malta and not like Herbert Stencil's V.—pick a good dream, not the one about annihilation.

Notes

1. V. (Philadelphia: Lippincott, 1963), pp. 323–24. Page numbers for all further citations will be included parenthetically in the text.
2. *New York Times*, 1 May 1966, p. 5.
3. "Looking for Intelligence in Washington," *Hells and Benefits* (New York: Basic Books, 1962), p. 96. These words were italicized in the original.

The Crying of Lot 49

ROBERT MURRAY DAVIS
"Parody, Paranoia, and the Dead End of Language
in *The Crying of Lot 49*"
Genre, December 1972, pp. 367–77

If, as George Jean Nathan said, satire is what closes on Saturday night, most critics of the novel have tried to prevent allegory from appearing at all. In the thirties, Philip Rahv huffs, we all *knew* that allegory was an inferior mode.[1] More recently, however, critics and, far more important, novelists have begun to question the adequacy of a "naive ontology" which accepts reality as given, even obvious, and judges the characters in terms of their adjustment to a reality defined largely in terms of socio-psychological norms, and to construct, if not allegories, fictional vehicles in quest of a tenor. Some, of course, take refuge in a series of sight-gags, like Terry Southern; or in rather sophomoric philosophizing, like Kurt Vonnegut; or in a desperate and foredoomed quest for pooh-bear innocence, like Richard Fariña. Judged at its best, however, this body of work raises questions not only about our moral but—closer to home for most of us—our literary values. Thomas Pynchon's *The Crying of Lot 49*, his second and so far his last novel, published in 1966, is a particularly good example of the post-realistic novel not merely because it uses many of what have become stock black comic devices but because it uses them to embody a deeper and ultimately very serious theme, the possible death of the American dream or, in broader terms, the death of wonder and the total entropy of energy and of communication.[2]

On the simplest level, the novel deals with the efforts of Mrs. Oedipa Maas to execute the will of Pierce Inverarity, her former lover, one-man lateral monopoly, and founding father of San Narciso, California. Inverarity's estate is hopelessly involved, and Oedipa is soon diverted into and then obsessed by her discovery of coincidences and patterns that seem to indicate a gigantic, intricate, and perhaps ominous underground postal organization named Tristero, whose symbol is a muted post horn (circle, triangle, trapezoid) and whose clientele are the dispossessed, the mad, and the rebellious of right and left, all the way from the Peter Pinguid society (whom the Birchers think paranoid) to the C.I.A.—Conjuración de los Insurgentes Anarchistas. In the end, convinced that she is either paranoid or that a conspiracy exists, and that she prefers either eventuality to the world she has always known, Oedipa prepares to confront the representatives of Tristero at the auction of their stamps, the "lot 49" which gives the novel its title.

On one level, Pynchon's novel is a very funny book. Some critics, including John Barth, have objected to the character names as too obviously comic, but they *are* comic and, as we shall see, many of them have a concealed significance. Besides Oedipa Maas, there are Dr. Hilarius, her psychiatrist, who makes Fu Manchu faces and dispenses LSD to his patients to help them find the bridge inward; Emory Bortz, a specialist in the plays of Richard Wharfinger, among them *The Courier's Tragedy*; Genghis Cohen; Mike Fallopian; Manny Di Presso; Stanley Koteks; and many others including John Nefastis, inventor of the Nefastis Machine, whose name is an anagram of isn't safe, and also, in the form *Nefasti*, refers to "days of ill omen," during the Athenian festival which on the surface honors Dionysus and at its heart "is a great ritual for appeasing the dead." [3]

Many of the situations in the novel are also extremely funny. There is a game of Strip Botticelli which culminates (the climax is later) in a drunken couple trying to evade a can of hair-spray run amok and impressing even the teenage rock group who have recently participated in "a surfer orgy . . . involving a five-gallon can of kidney suet, a small automobile with a sun roof, and a trained seal" (24). John Nefastis likes to make love to the accompaniment of television reports on Viet Nam or, even better, China: "You think about all those Chinese. Teeming. That profusion of life. It makes it sexier . . ." (79).

Even better are Pynchon's parodies: of rock lyrics; of a 30's musical Crimean War movie featuring Baby Igor, his father, and a St. Bernard in a submarine, with songs like "My doggie, my daddy, and me"; and, the *pièce de résistance*, the Jacobean revenge play, *The Courier's Tragedy*, which deserves a comparison with Max Beerbohm's "Savonarola." The play features a goat shot from a cannon; a traitor's tongue ripped out and set afire to the accompaniment of the lines "Thy pitiless unmanning is most meet / Thinks Ercole the zany Paraclete. / Descended this malign, Unholy Ghost, / Let us begin thy frightful Pentecost" (47); a Cardinal forced to consecrate to Satan a chalice of his own blood and to elevate his own big toe and say, "This is my body"—the first time, a spectator comments, that he has told the truth in fifty years; "a refreshingly simple mass stabbing" (51) to vary the pace; and miscellaneous orgies, mass murders, and mutilations. As one member of the audience observes, "It plays . . . like a Road Runner cartoon in blank verse" (53).

Despite the comic surface, *The Crying of Lot 49* is fundamentally serious. Parody and paranoia, two concepts important to any reading of the novel, have in common their prefix, which means, among other things, "beside, alongside of, beyond." Moreover the early pages of the novel abound in such words as "hieroglyphic," "hierophany," and "hieratic," all of which have associations with the sacred or holy. Both prefixes denote a level of existence beside or above the literal and observable; both assume that no statement, from the word to the longest discourse, contains its own meaning, rather that it points to something else, all the way from the paranoid's "I wonder what he meant by *that*" to the sacred writings which conceal from the uninitiated as much as they reveal about the doings of the gods.

Pynchon deals with these ideas not in terms of statement or solution but of paradox and dichotomy. Art can be mere distraction, like the Porky Pig cartoon that the nonagenarian Mr. Thoth gets mixed with his grandfather's tales of killing Tristero agents disguised as Indians. Or it can be self-enclosed and solipsistic, as in the Remedios Varo painting, which portrays "a number of frail girls with heart-shaped faces, huge eyes, spun-gold hair, prisoners in the top room of a circular tower, embroidering a kind of tapestry which spilled out the slit windows and into a void, seeking hopelessly to fill the void: for all the other buildings and creatures, all the waves, ships and forests of the earth were contained in this tapestry, and the tapestry was the world" (10). Or, according to the director of *The Courier's Tragedy*, Randolph Driblette, dramatic art is not the words but the reality within the director's mind: "I'm the projector of the planetarium, all the closed little universe visible in the circle of that stage is coming out of my mouth, eyes, sometimes other orifices also" (56). Struck by this view and by the recurrence of the muted post horn and other evidence which seems to point to Tristero, Oedipa queries herself, "*Shall I project a world?*" (59) and almost immediately begins to succumb to a "growing obsession, with 'bringing something of herself'—even if that something was just her presence—to the scatter of business interests that had survived Inverarity. She would give them order, she would create constellations . . . " (65).

As this quotation indicates, all the means of encountering and structuring reality are closely related, and images of self-contained and enclosed systems recur throughout the novel. The streets of San Narciso and the waterways of Fangoso Lagoons are disturbingly like printed circuits in transistor radios; Pierce's will and San Narciso itself—both expressions of Pierce's personality—are likewise self-sufficient. As the novel progresses, the systems become larger. California itself becomes a unit with highways as a circulatory system, Oedipa a particle within that system. In the end, stumbling along a railroad track, Oedipa thinks of the tracks and the telephone lines as a vast network, San Narciso assumed into the larger whole, America. Perhaps, as the religious fanatics who produced a pornographic version of *The Courier's Tragedy* believed, "Creation was a vast, intricate machine. But one part of it, the Scurvhamite part, ran off the will of God, its prime mover. The rest ran off some opposite Principle, something blind, soulless; a brute automatism that led to eternal death . . . But somehow those few saved Scurvhamites found themselves looking out into the gaudy clockwork of the doomed with a certain sick and fascinated horror. . . . One by one the glamorous prospect of annihilation coaxed them over, until there was no one left in the sect . . ." (116).

With expansion, of course, comes a shift in perspective: the artist can remain above and behind his handiwork, like the God of creation; the solipsist can retreat within the watertight structure he has created; Mucho Maas, Oedipa's husband, permanently tripped out on LSD, "perhaps having had his vision of consensus as others do orgasms, face now smooth, amiable, at peace," envisions a universe in which "Everybody who says the same words is the same person if the spectra are the same only they happen differently in time, you dig? But the time is arbitrary. You pick your zero point anywhere you want, that way you can shuffle each person's time line sideways till they coincide. Then you'd have this big, God, maybe a couple hundred million chorus saying 'rich, chocolaty goodness' together, and it would all be the same voice." The vision has enabled him to believe in his job—he is a disc jockey for station KCUF—and to bear it, as he could not bear the world of N.A.D.A. (for National Automobile Dealers' Association) and the used car lot from which he fled, for, "When those kids sing about 'She loves you,' yeah well, you know, she does, she's any number of people, all over the world, back through time . . . but she loves. And the 'you' is everybody. And herself" (106). Inside or outside, the creater or observer of a closed structure is safe. Oedipa can do textual study of *The Courier's Tragedy*, and the evil Duke Angelo and his minions cannot harm her; she can attempt to explicate (or execute, or prove) Inverarity's will, yet retain for a time her northern Californian's superiority to all that it names; the Nefastis machine does not move when she attempts to contact Maxwell's Demon, who is supposed to reside within it.

Yet enclosure can become a cosy trap, in terms of both psychology and physics. Pynchon's earlier short story "Entropy"[4] is like a thematic model for *Lot 49*. One of the characters, Callisto, finds "in entropy or the measure of disorganization for a closed system an adequate metaphor to apply to certain phenomena in his own world . . . a tendency from the least to the most probable, from differentiation to sameness, from ordered individuality to a kind of chaos. He envisioned a heat-death for his culture in which ideas, like heat-energy, would no longer be transferred, since each point in it would ultimately have the same quantity of energy; and intellectual motion would, accordingly, cease" (283–284). In a scene counterpointing Callisto's meditations, an expert in communication theory has quarreled with his wife because he has said that you can "talk about human behavior like a program fed into an IBM machine," an analogy crucial to communication and to information theory. He maintains that language is *not* a barrier but "a kind of leakage" in which words like "love" cause "Ambiguity. Redundance. Irrelevance, even. Leakage. All this is noise. Noise screws up your signal, makes for disorganization in the circuit" (285). Meanwhile, Callisto's friend Aubade strives desperately to balance meaning and the noise which threatens "The architectonic purity of her world" and "which she had continually to readjust [by a process called feedback] lest the whole structure shiver into disarray of discrete and meaningless signals" (283). In "Entropy," the process of balance fails, the temperature settles irretrievably at 37 degrees Fahrenheit.

The characters in this short story regard the analogy between physics and communication as cause for despair; John Nefastis in *Lot 49* constructs his machine by using the coincidental resemblance of the equations for entropy in heat-engines and for entropy in communication. It is, he says, a metaphor which "connects the world of thermodynamics to the world of information flow." Maxwell's Demon connects the two fields: he sits in a box, sorting molecules into hot and cold, and the temperature differential can be used to drive a heat-engine—thus violating the Second Law of Thermodynamics, producing perpetual motion, and giving you something for nothing. Nefastis adds to Clerk Maxwell's theory the notion that "Communication is the key": the Demon has to pass on the data he accumulates on the molecules, and "At some deep psychic level he must get through. The sensitive must receive that staggering set of energies, and feed back something like the same quantity of information. To keep it all cycling" (77). As the various metaphors of enclosure in the novel imply, escape from entropy cannot occur on what Nefastis explicitly calls "the secular level"; renewing energy must come from the psychic or even the spiritual level. Jesús Arrabal, the anarchist, gives Oedipa another term for those energies—miracle—which he defines as "another world's intrusion into this one. Most of the time we coexist peacefully,

but when we do touch there's cataclysm. Like the church we hate, anarchists also believe in another world. Where revolutions break out spontaneous and leaderless, and the soul's talent for consensus allows the masses to work together without effort, automatic as the body itself. And yet, señá [sign, token, password], if any of it should ever really happen that perfectly, I would also have to cry miracle. An anarchist miracle" (88–89).

A miracle, of course, is a mystery, and a mystery is by definition different from anything we know—and possibly less pleasant. Most important, it *is* different, representing a realm which humanly created structures can feebly and partially reflect but cannot enclose and control and which may be immune to physical and spiritual entropy. Such a realm is both attractive and dreadful. Metzger, Baby Igor of the movie grown up, asserts that the film is a closed system, though the order of reels may be changed, yet refers with alternating triumph and uneasiness to parts of the action which the movie does and cannot show. Tristero, it becomes increasingly clear, is not merely an invention of Wharfinger's parodists but, within the world of the novel, a real organization with a long history of desperate, even murderous opposition to official postal systems, especially to the Thurn and Taxis system, which existed in *our* world. The American Tristero—the name implies both sadness and malignity in Italian, an intimate meeting by mutual consent in English—serves as a communications network for clients who are odd and probably destructive, such as AC-DC, the Alameda County Death Cult, whose members "Once a month . . . choose some victim from among the innocent, the virtuous, the socially integrated and well-adjusted, using him sexually, then sacrificing him" (90). Oedipa begins to realize that she is being led through various clues to a final revelation which she both desires and fears, for in the process she is stripped of her defenses, of her security, and of her men—Driblette walks into the Pacific; Mucho retreats into himself; Metzger elopes with a nymphet—just as she is stripped of her clothing and penetrated by Metzger in the game of Strip Botticelli, in which every answer costs you something as your opponent reveals himself. At last she must confront the knowledge that either there is a deeper reality or that she has created the whole structure and is therefore mad.

Although ultimately Pynchon refuses to decide whether Oedipa is mad or sane, he clearly hopes that she *is* sane—and wants his readers to hope so as well. One of the ways in which he fosters this attitude is by the multiple allusiveness of the names. Oedipa Maas, of course, is both the classical seeker after self-knowledge, whatever the cost, and everywoman. At least as important is the literal meaning of her last name in Dutch: loophole. She comes from Kinneret-by-the Sea—the modern name for Galilee—and she travels to San Narciso. Mythologically and historically, there are at least four Narcissuses: 1) the self-entranced figure of Greek myth who depended upon an echo, just as Inverarity may have constructed the whole plot in order to have Oedipa-Echo reflect and in some sense insure his continued existence; 2) the freedman who was secretary to the Emperor Claudius, grew very rich, and, according to the *Britannica*, betokens the development of a centralized bureaucracy; 3) Saint Narcissus, Bishop of Jerusalem who helped to determine the "method of keeping the Paschal festival" and to whom Pynchon alludes as "changing well-water to oil for Jerusalem's Easter lamps" (94); and 4) the martyr bishop of Genoa who was waylaid and assassinated.[5] When Oedipa visits Hilarius, her psychiatrist, in order to have him tell her that she is imagining Tristero, she discovers him firing wildly at invisible Israeli agents. He advises her to cherish her fantasy: "What else do any of you have? Hold it tightly by its little tentacle, don't let the Freudians coax it away or the pharmacists poison it out of you. Whatever it is, hold it dear, for when you lose it you go over by that much to the others. You begin to cease to be" (103). Since he has obviously gone round the bend, his advice might seem suspect. On the other hand, his name can be traced to three saints: one thought that he was being persecuted and engaged, according to S. Baring-Gould, in "actions of more than questionable canonicity,"[6] and though Dr. Hilarius tries to be a good Freudian, he cannot help but believe in and obey the urgings of the dark, irreconcilable elements in man's nature. The other two St. Hilariuses combatted the Eutychians and the Arians, heretics who, from different directions, denied the mystery of Christ's dual nature—denied that, in fact, the Word could be made flesh.[7]

Whatever she learns or fears, Oedipa never abandons her allegiance to the word. As she holds an old wino with DT's, she thinks of the symbol in calculus, dt, "a time differential, a vanishingly small instant in which change had to be confronted at last for what it was, where it could no longer disguise itself as something innocuous like an average rate; where velocity dwelled in the projectile though the projectile be frozen in midflight, where death dwelled in the cell though the cell be looked in on at its most quick" (95–96). Like the saint, the clairvoyant, the paranoid, the dreamer—and the artist—all of whom "act in the same special relevance to the word, or whatever it is the word is there, buffering, to protect us from," the old man has a special knowledge because "there is high magic to low puns." "The act of metaphor," she thinks, "was a thrust at truth or a lie, depending where you were: inside, safe, or outside, lost" (95). Madness, dreams, sanctity, clairvoyance: all are attempts to escape the gray world of nada, of entropy, of the round tower from which Oedipa waits to be delivered. Oedipa finally acknowledges, in her meditations on the railroad tracks, that either there is a transcendent meaning—or only the earth; either a moral universe or an aimless one; either a reality to a "Tristero beyond the appearance of the legacy America, or . . . just America, and if there was just America then it seemed the only way she could continue, and manage to be at all relevant to it, was as an alien, unfurrowed, assumed full circle [another enclosure] into some paranoia" (137). Finally she goes to the auction to confront the representatives of Tristero, and the novel ends as the auctioneer spreads "his arms in a gesture that seemed to belong to the priesthood of some remote culture; perhaps to a descending angel" (138), a reluctant but finally obedient handmaiden, willing to put on, if she can, the knowledge with the power, embody the word herself, and realize the metaphors of pregnancy which Pynchon establishes in the final pages of the novel.

Perceptive critics like Richard Poirier[8] and Robert Sklar have discussed the novel as a nearly definitive statement about the American dream at the end of the road and as "a radical political novel."[9] "Journey into the Mind of Watts," Pynchon's article of 1966 that as far as I can determine is his latest publication, lends support to these views with its scorn of the white world's "well-behaved unreality" and avoidance of basic realities "like disease, like failure, violence and death" and of the "enormous priest caste of shrinks who counsel moderation and compromise as the answer to all forms of hassle."[10] But Pynchon is demanding more than a sense of social reality: he speaks in the article and in his novel of the need for possibility, for miracle, for "transcendent meaning." Callisto in "Entropy," like his predecessor Henry Adams and

like his creator, realizes "that the Virgin and the dynamo stand as much for love as for power; that the two are indeed identical; and that love therefore not only makes the world go 'round but also makes the boccie ball spin, the nebula precess" (288). If love disappears or is subject to entropy, if we cannot communicate with Maxwell's Demon, if Pierce Inverarity has not succeeded in beating death by only a little, then there is at the end of human and cosmic history only the loss of individuality, only physical and spiritual heat-death. This is a religious vision, fundamentally; and though it is dangerous to chart a living author's course, I think that this fact accounts for Pynchon's five-year silence. In *Lot 49* he reaches the verge of statement, of a leap of faith, confronting dichotomies symbolized with twinned ones and zeroes, as in a gigantic computer. My students tell me that a zero with a one through it is a symbol for philosophy—and also for "no information available." In *Lot 49*, philosophy is no longer adequate, and Pynchon cannot accept no information. If Pynchon is not able to make the leap of faith, he can only retreat and thus repeat himself—a kind of literary entropy. If he attempts to go forward, he is facing thematic and technical problems of learning the Word and then giving flesh to it that would daunt all but the hack or the major artist.[11]

Notes

1. Philip Rahv, "Fiction and the Criticism of Fiction," *Kenyon Review*, 18 (Spring 1956), 281.
2. *The Crying of Lot 49* (New York: Bantam Books, 1967). Further references are given parenthetically in the text.
3. Gilbert Murray, *Five Stages of Greek Religion* (Garden City, N.Y.: Doubleday Anchor Books, 1955), pp. 15–16. The book was published in successive versions in 1915, 1925, and 1951.
4. "Entropy," *Kenyon Review*, 22 (Summer 1960), 277–292. Subsequent references are given parenthetically.
5. S. Baring-Gould, *Lives of the Saints* (Edinburgh: John Grant, 1914), XII, 702; III, 313.
6. Ibid., V, 75–78. For the other saints of the same name, see I, 182 and X, 157–158.
7. Billy M. Harrall, a student in my course in Popular Narrative Forms, sees a sexual pattern in the names Pierce and Fallopian, with Stanley Koteks, a frustrated inventor, representing menstrual flow or frustrated conception.
8. Richard Poirier, "Embattled Underground," *New York Times Book Review*, 1 May 1966, pp. 5, 42–43.
9. Robert Sklar, "The New Novel, USA: Thomas Pynchon," *Nation*, 205 (25 September 1967), 280.
10. "Journey into the Mind of Watts," *New York Times Magazine*, 12 June 1966, p. 34ff.
11. According to Russell Bates' report of a conversation with Harlan Ellison, Pynchon refused permission to reprint his story, "Secret Integration," in *Dangerous Visions*, edited by Ellison, and tried to withdraw from publication *The Crying of Lot 49* on the grounds that it was not good enough to publish.

FRANK KERMODE
From "The Use of the Codes"
Approaches to Poetics, ed. Seymour Chatman
1973, pp. 68–74

In *The Crying of Lot 49*, Pynchon's Oedipa, as her name implies, is ⟨. . .⟩ confronted with riddles and with the obligation to discover an order. The origin of these riddles is in doubt; it may be the nature of the human world, viewable as waste or as system; it may be a man called Inverarity, who in turn may be either untruth or *dans le vrai*. The book is crammed with disappointed promises of significance, with ambiguous invitations to paradigmatic construction, and this is precisely Oedipa's problem. Is there a structure *au fond*, or only deceptive galaxies of signifiers? Like California itself, the text offers a choice: plenitude or vacuity. Is there a hidden plot concerning an almost Manichaean conflict, which makes sense, whether evil or benign, of the randomness of the world?

Consider the opening: we find Oedipa returning from a Tupperware party; I understand that on these occasions goods are sold outside the normal commercial system. She stands in her living-room before a blank television set (communication system without message) and considers the randomness she projects on the world: thoughts about God, a Mexican hotel, dawn at Cornell, a tune from Bartok, a Vivaldi concerto for kazoo. Soon we hear about the coded voices of Inverarity, the culinary jumble of a Southern Californian supermarket, her husband's life as a used-car salesman, systematizing, giving meaning to, the trash in old cars. Now he works on a pop radio station, the communication system—without content—of another culture. Later he will start *listening* to Muzak, another type of the empty system. In a world where the psychiatrists provide material for paranoid fantasies, and lawyers are locked in imaginary rivalries with Perry Mason, everybody is tending toward his own dissident universe of meaning; Oedipa is Rapunzel, her own reality let down like hair from her head. Minority cultures, bricolaged from pop, old movies, astrology, coexist in a world whose significances, if any, relate to no conceivable armature.

But Oedipa has "all manner of revelations," and a shadowy armature seems to be taking shape. Is she still in her head, or is the great plot real? If so, is it malign? To discover it may be the same thing as inventing it. What Peter Berger and Thomas Luckmann call "the social construction of reality" proceeds because there are phenomena we cannot simply wish away; death is one, but there are others. The construction is what our social situation permits—say, the national limits, the limits of California, ultimately the limits of dissident groups and our protestant selves. As we plot against reality we comply with or deviate from the institutionalized plots; a great deviation is called a sect if shared, paranoia if not. There is always a way of coding the material, even that which on other views is simply waste. Having instituted a system one keeps it intact either by legitimating extraneous material or, if that is too difficult, or the threat too great, by nihilating it.

Making sense of other somewhat arbitrary symbolic universes, understanding their construction, is an activity familiar to all critics. Certainly it involves choices, a limitation of pluralities. The activity of the critic, thus understood, is nomic. It seeks order, and is analogous to the social construction of reality. What Oedipa is doing is very like reading a book. Of course books can be read in very strange ways—a man once undertook to demonstrate infallibly to me that *Wuthering Heights* was an interlinear gloss on Genesis. How could this be disproved? He had hit on a code, and legitimated all the signs. Oedipa is afraid she may be like that man, or that she is drifting into paranoia, the normal hermeneutic activity in disease, and Pynchon's great subject.

She has contact with many sects: in advanced societies, such as Southern California, "socially segregated subuniverses of meaning," as Berger and Luckmann observe,[1] tend to multiply. When she sees a way of linking them together Oedipa is conscious of other terrors than paranoia. She dreads the anomic, the world collapsed into filth and randomness; but she also dreads an evil order. Pynchon invents the Scurvhamite sect, who abandoned a very mechanical double predestinari-

anism ("nothing ever happens by accident") for the consolations of single predestination to damnation. Yet even on her wild San Francisco night Oedipa doesn't unambiguously believe in the patterns to which the evidence is apparently pointing. For instance, she dismisses the evidence of the children's rhymes. The entire structure is *à la fois posé et décu*. We do not learn whether the dove, harmonizer of tongues, which would make all these meaning-systems mutually intelligible, descended with the auctioneer's hammer; *au fond*, the plot remains suspended.

What concerns us is precisely the existence of what seem to be systems that could transmit meanings, as in the account of San Narciso, the town which looks like a printed circuit, "an intent to communicate. There'd seemed no limit to what the printed circuit could have told her (if she had tried to find out); so, in her first minute of San Narciso, a revelation trembled, just past the threshold of meaning." The revelation would be of the kind that explains the whole of history, the present condition of America, Inverarity, Wharfinger's play, and so on; it woul explain how waste has meaning, just as, couched as an acronym, WASTE forms a sentence ("We await sad Tristero's empire"). But Oedipa is poised on the slash between meaning and unmeaning, as she is between smog and sun; interminably confronted with meaningless binary choices—artificial light in sunlight, the statue of the hooker/nymph, which is both still and windblown—and by repetitions of the San Narciso situation: windows and bottles emptily reflecting the sun, messageless. The need of a revelation, the sense that such systems exist to transmit sense, drives us to find meaning in them, for we feel "as if, on some other frequency . . . words were being spoken." This is the sense in which Professor Mendelson is right in emphasizing the pentecostal themes in the book; fifty may follow forty-nine, and if it were called we should all become competently polyglot, able to hear the words we think are being spoken but cannot quite hear.

This is why Oedipa continues her game of strip-Botticelli with the world. Her trial run with Metzger—merely on the plot of an old movie—sensitized her for a revelation; just as the flight of the rogue aerosol foreshadows a world which, though unpredictable, is determinate. And so she continues to spot the clues, though never sure where they are, in her head or out there. The text only says it is "as if . . . there were a revelation in progress all round her." Options remain naggingly open, as when the naval action of Peter Pinguid, that ancestor of Inverarity, is described: "off the coast of what is now Carmel-by-the-Sea, or what is now Pismo Beach, around noon or possibly towards dusk, the two ships sighted each other. One of them may have fired; if it did the other responded." This niggling dubiety is Oedipa's, and the text's.

The messages sent by the illicit system are normally without content; this could be true of the novel. The clues pile up. *The Courier's Tragedy* (played in a theater located between a traffic-analysis firm and a wildcat transistor outfit, circulation and communication) relates not only to the supposed history of Tristero but to incest, tongueless attempts to pray, an anti-Paraclete. The bones of the dead are turned into ink, a means of empty communication (or into wine and cigarettes, which belong to other systems). Ralph Driblette has heard a message in the system of the play; so could Oedipa, if she gave herself to it. Everything can be legitimated, systematized. But there are only clues, "never," we are told, "the central truth itself, for if that should blaze out it would destroy its own message irreversibly." If the systems are to work, and the book to work as a system, it will be because the reader can do what Oedipa could not when confronted with Maxwell's demon:

make the piston move, reverse the entropy of communication as that device reverses physical entropy. But if you make the eyes of this novel move, or if you believe in the original plot on which it depends, you risk a kind of madness, which is the ultimate human cost of holding everything together in a single design. The systems are there to be filled: children's rhymes, the "coded years of uselessness" in the mattresses of the poor, the societies of queers and failed suicides, all to be handled if you want a central truth, a word to reconcile your time with eternity. Nobody helps; Oedipa's friends drop away. The more she encodes the trash of America the more critical her isolation becomes. She is like the poor of whom she has heard, camping among telephone wires; she walks as if inside a digital computer, among either-ors, waiting for the systems to contain a message. Either there is a Tristero, or she is "orbiting in the ecstasy of a true paranoia."

We can't, of course, be told which, and we question the novel as Oedipa does the Tristero plot. That plot is pointed to as the object of some possible annunciation; but the power is in the pointing, not in any guarantee. One could talk for hours about this remarkable work, but at the bottom of all one said would be the truth that it imitates the texts of the world, and also imitates their problematical quality. If one coded *Lot 49*, its radical equivocations would be instantly evident—the cultural code, for example, is as little the inert congeries proposed by Barthes as the hermeneutic code is a progress to *dévoilement*. Its separation from its exterior and its totality are precisely what it is *about*. It is an invitation to the speaking animal to consider what he makes of the world into which he introduces his communication systems; and it asks him to read a text, to reread it, to produce it if that is a better word. In its totality it posses the choice: *plein/vide*, as it so often does in its texture. To seek an answer is to be disappointed, *déçu*. Deception is the discovery of the novel, not of its critics.

Notes

1. Peter L. Berger and Thomas Luckmann, *The Social Construction of Reality* (New York, 1967), p. 85.

Gravity's Rainbow

ROBER NADEAU
"Thomas Pynchon"
Readings from the New Book of Nature
1981, pp. 135–48

At Cornell University, where Thomas Pynchon first won a scholarship to study engineering physics and later took a degree in English, one of his professors "wonderingly remembers his apparently voracious appetite for the complexities of elementary particle theory."[1] Although many critics, some of whom have written articles with titles that would seem to belong in the pages of *Scientific American*, have speculated upon the manner in which concepts from physics function as aspects of Pynchon's bizarre fictional landscape, we have yet to appreciate how pervasive such concepts are in the determination of both design and meaning in all his novels. The implications of discoveries made in the new physics are not merely the source of new ideas which Pynchon incorporates into a traditional novelistic framework; they are rather the basis for a radically new conception of the nature of human identity and societal organization, which Pynchon has chosen to express in a highly appropriate but nevertheless extremely problematic narrative mode.

Known to devour complicated treatises in math and physics at one sitting for "fun," Pynchon's acquaintance with ideas from the new physics is formidable, and he is also, as I shall try to demonstrate, quite sensitive to their implications in human terms. It is now a well-established convention in Pynchon criticism to comment that every particular in his narratives interrelates and interconnects with every other particular, but it is not frequently observed that out of that vast interplay of dynamic particulars we do not arrive at that sense of "meaning" we expect to be a consequence of reading highly structured narratives. The patterns or designs that emerge in a careful study of Pynchon's novels tend toward closure, toward that final point of logical connection that would allow us to fix relationships and draw conclusions, but he almost invariably refuses to make those final connections. The analytically trained critic ferrets out a network of antinomies, polar oppositions, either-or configurations in the hope of discovering deep structure and hidden meaning, but the fictions will simply not be contained by such coordinate systems.

Pynchon's acute awareness that the forms resident in our subjective realities are ill-equipped to describe or contain reality itself is probably best illustrated in the title of his first novel. Critics still continue to catalog the repetitions of v's in *V*. in what is obviously a very frustrating attempt to uncover a closed system of relation. Pynchon's confidence trick on the literary critic, a species of humanity he clearly has very little use for,[2] was to select from the alphabet—that system of characters we use to represent or configure our written transcriptions of the real—the letter which is nicely illustrative of what Pynchon considers to be one of our more invidious habits of mind. V. (note the period) as figure is a beautiful parody of either-or categorical thinking in that the seeming oppositions in the trajectory of the lines can be traced to and in some sense exist in the point of connection which is their base. It is no accident, of course, that the one character in the novel who most assiduously seeks to impose either-or configurations on the tissue of events, Sidney Stencil (note the play on mimesis in the last name), drowns in a whirlpool in the closing paragraph of the novel.

A more accessible statement on the delimiting effects of the either-or is found in *The Crying of Lot 49*. Oedipa Maas recalls viewing a painting in Mexico City which is described in the following manner:

> . . . in the central painting of a triptych, titled "Bordando el Manto Terrestre" [Embroidering the Cloak of Earth] were a number of frail girls with heart-shaped faces, huge eyes, spun-gold hair, prisoners in the top room of a circular tower, embroidering a kind of tapestry which spilled out the slip windows into a void, seeking hopelessly to fill the void: for all the other buildings and creatures, all the waves, ships and forests of the earth were contained in this tapestry, and the tapestry was the world.[3]

On one level the passage is a nice metaphoric description of Oedipa's plight in the novel as she traces the seeming connections in Inverarity's vast business empire and struggles to believe that her perceptions of its design are actual and not merely symptomatic of growing paranoia. Pynchon offers, however, an additional comment on the following page which makes his motive for metaphor a good deal more obvious: "Having no apparatus except gut fear and female cunning to examine this formless magic, to understand how it works, how to measure its field strength, count its lines of force, she may fall back on superstition, or take up a useful hobby like embroidery, or go mad, or marry a disk jockey. If the tower is everything, and the knight of deliverance is no proof against its magic, what else?" (11).

To understand all lines of force within a force field is, in the view of contemporary physics, an impossibility because to do that would require a knowledge of all events occurring simultaneously in the cosmos. More important, the tower, or the world-constructing mind of the individual, is not "everything," and an acceptance of its limitations, which Oedipa in part at least acquires, is entirely necessary in order to negotiate the world of experience as Pynchon sees it. Paranoia in Pynchon's fiction is not, as some critics have claimed, a viable mode of self-protection in the face of societal breakdown and the demise of controlling symbolics—it is simply the last tower retreat of the individual whose mental tapestry has displaced all sense of relatedness to the human community.

Any critic who chooses to tackle all *Gravity's Rainbow* in one chapter is either terribly ambitious or very foolish or both. The novel is encyclopedic in scope, not unlike Joyce's *Ulysses*, and will doubtless preoccupy critics of the modern novel for many years to come. What I will do here is suggest that the key to an improved understanding of this massive fiction may well be concepts from the new physics, and to indicate some of the directions in which we might move to explore their applications.

The preface—taken from the writings of one of those architects of the rocket technology which could serve to obliterate us all at any moment—is not to be taken without some sense of irony, but it also provides some useful insights into the design and meaning of *Gravity's Rainbow*: "Nature does not know extinction; all it knows is transformation. Everything science has taught me, and continues to teach me, strengthens my belief in the continuity of spiritual existence after death (Werner von Braun)."[4] If von Braun is reading from the new book on nature, and I presume he is, he is quite right in saying that nature undergoes unceasing transformations, and, if the big-bang theorists are correct, will continue to evolve out of itself new modes of being. Further, if mass is a form of energy, and if all particles function in terms of and in some sense are all other particles, there is a continuity in all natural process which includes us even if a particular configuration of molecular activity (*self*) ceases to be. If von Braun's deity is like that of Whitehead, the never-finished becoming of nature's process,[5] there is continuity in our spiritual existence after death as well. Pynchon, whose sense of deity definitely resembles that of Whitehead, provides in the novel seemingly endless demonstrations of the fact that Western man has great difficulty accepting this new metaphysic because his tendency to impose either-or categorical systems on the fluid process of life mitigates against that acceptance.

The following is a description contained in the novel of the structure of *Gravity's Rainbow*:

No, this is not a disentanglement from, but a progressive *knotting into*—they go under archways, secret entrances of rotten concrete that only looked like loops of underpass . . . certain trestles of blackened wood have moved slowly by overhead, and the smells of coal from days far to the past, smells of naphtha winters, of Sundays when no traffic came through, of the coral-like and mysteriously vital growth, around the blind curves and out the lonely spurs, a sour smelling of rolling-stock absence, of maturing rust, developing through those emptying

days brilliant and deep, especially at dawn, with blue shadows to seal its passage, to try to bring events to Absolute Zero. (3–4).

As any anthropologist knows, the human environment in large part is a creation of the human intellect and reflects the forms resident in man's mind. The world that is not ourselves is the mystery, the void, which we seek to fill up and contain with mental constructs. The characters in *Gravity's Rainbow* move through man-made constructions, the archways and underpasses that are extensions of the forms in their minds, but they inevitably encounter the "mysteriously vital growth," the unknown and unknowable in natural process. The major characters, with the exception of Slothrop at one crucial point, weave lines of linear connection between people, events, and circumstances in an effort to obviate the framing process itself by encompassing and transcending its most basic principle of organization—the either-or. The knotting process, the novel, becomes a kind of Gordian knot which must be cut through by intuition because it cannot be untied by logical analysis alone. The tangled web of the various narrative lines becomes finally Pynchon's way of demonstrating that all systems of analysis, or all closed symbolics, predicated on absolutes lead ultimately to a state of confusion and chaos within which the alienation of the individual is an inevitability. The frequent references in the novel to Goedel's Theorem, which states that we cannot prove any logical system does not contain contradictions in its basic precepts because to prove the system correct we must get outside of it, are also indicative of Pynchon's bias against the Western mode of valuation and truth seeking.

Events in the novel would arrive at absolute zero in a metaphoric sense if the rocket at the close of the narrative had exploded over the Orpheus movie house in Los Angeles, but the rocket does not explode. It reaches, says the narrator, the "last immeasurable gap about the roof of this old theater, the last ΔT" (887). In order to understand what Pynchon means by absolute zero we must comprehend the use of the Δt in the logistics of rocket technology. The Greek letter Δ represents in calculus infinitesimals, and the Δt is a mathematical notation for units of time used to plot the range and trajectory of a rocket in flight. The following is Joseph Slade's admirable attempt to explain the function of the Δt in lay terms:

Here the parabola is sliced up by integrals from a base line stretched between the rocket's point of firing and its point of impact. Those lines are artificial and arbitrary. Along the parabola itself an infinite number of lines can be drawn, and each two of them—as double integrals—bound a moment in time, relative to course of distance. As the rocket moves along its path, and as it passes these artificial divisions, it has passed through a change in time—designated by the Δt. Theoretically, precisely because the number of divisions can be extended infinitely, the rocket can be said to be poised in the sky ("The Perfect Rocket is still up there, still descending" [426], approaching final zero in an asymptotic—approaching but never reaching infinity—curve, like Zeno's famous arrow).[6]

Another aspect of the parabolic shape of the rocket's flight which serves to explain the notion of absolute zero is that if we bisect a parabola each side perfectly mirrors the other. The rocket becomes a kind of universal icon for several characters and groups in the novel because it appears in flight to reconcile polarities or to unify oppositions in approaching absolute zero. Absolute zero is, then, for the rocket worshippers the point of transcendence which takes up into itself all discrepant particulars—it symbolizes the alpha and omega of all being.

What Pynchon has done here with dreadful mastery is to give us a graphic illustration, in terms of our most advanced and lethal technology, of a mode of constructing reality which in his view mitigates against our proper sense of relation to the whole. Since the rocket worshippers frame out experience in closed systems and symbolics, they arbitrarily fragment (put into time frames) their vision of themselves and others. In the effort to arrive at closure of the system or symbolic, the ultimate Δt which is absolute zero, they must deal with all particulars in terms of oppositions, either-or categories, in the hope that all such antinomies will resolve themselves into unity at the final point of transcendence. In physics, as Pynchon knows very well, entropy, a quantity related to the number of accessible quantum states available to a system, will tend toward the greatest number of states when the system is isolated. This results in a decrease in the amount of energy available for work as well as more disorder among the atoms in the system. Since characters in a Pynchon novel function, as many critics have noted, in terms of their interrelatedness or interconnectedness to other characters, we can safely conclude that he feels that individuals do not in actuality live in isolated systems. The concept of entropy is rather Pynchon's metaphor for our compulsion to construct and maintain closed, isolated systems which induces a sense of dislocation and fragmentation in relation to the whole.

What the rocket worshippers in the novel fail to understand is the nature of the force of gravity. If the resistance of any object to acceleration is a measure of its interaction with the rest of the cosmos, then the rocket at rest in its gravitational field is just as close to absolute zero as the rocket at its highest point of trajectory in flight. What Pynchon implies here in his treatment of the rocket worshippers is that irreconcilable polarities and oppositions are fictions of the mind which have no real existence in nature. Our effort to transcend them to reach the absolute is simply a product of our failure to realize we are at absolute zero without making any effort at all in the sense that our participation in the life of the entire cosmos is a given.

The most pervasive presence in *Gravity's Rainbow* is not a character but an organization or system. The "Firm," controlled by "They," is a vast network of corporations and cartels, like General Electric, Shell, Siemens, I. G. Farben, and Standard Oil. It appears not only to be more powerful than any national government but to manipulate all of them in its own interests. The Firm's authority, as Slade notes, "stems from classical physics, which does rest on cause and effect relationships between forces and objects."[7] The system controlled by They apparently originated after one Kekule von Stradonitz dreamed of an uroborus, saw some uses that could be made of that conceptual form in researching new chemical properties, and gave up his architectural profession to pursue them. In a crucial passage in the novel Pynchon's narrator describes the results in this way:

> The Serpent that announces, "The World is a closed thing, cyclical, resonant, eternally returning," is to be delivered into a system whose aim is to violate the cycle. Taking and not giving back, demanding that "productivity" and "earnings" keep on increasing with time, the System removing from the rest of the World those vast quantities of energy to keep its own tiny desperate fraction showing a profit: and not only most of humanity—most of the World, animal, vegetable and mineral, is laid waste in the process.

> The System may or may not understand that *it's* only buying time. And that time is an artificial resource to begin with, of no value to anyone or anything but the System, which sooner or later must crash to its death, when its addiction to energy has become more than the rest of the World can supply, dragging along with it innocent souls all along the chain of life. (480–81)

The Firm's desire to maintain and extend control over other systems leads to more research into the life of nature in the hope of discovering principles that would allow them to produce more salable technologies and consumer goods—the most important of which are Imipolex G and the rocket. In doing such research, however, the Firm discovers that there are principles in the life of nature which call into question the efficacy of simple causality, hierarchical organization, and closed systems. The inventor of Imipolex G, the mysterious Jamf who did the operant conditioning research on the infant Slothrop, recognizes, for example, that relativity theory has moral implications. In a lecture attended by Pokler, Jamf counsels his students to stay in touch with their lion, his term for their aggressive, territorial instincts: "The lion does not know subtleties and half-solutions. He does not accept sharing as a basis for anything! He takes, he holds! He is not a Bolshevik or a Jew. You will never hear relativity from the lion. He wants the absolute. Life and Death. Win and lose" (673).

As long as individuals continue to see themselves as discrete and separate entities who must dominate or submit to the domination of others in the ruthless struggle for power, the Firm will maintain its control. At the close of another lecture, Jamf encourages his students to "'move beyond life, toward the inorganic. Here is no frailty, no mortality—here is Strength and the Timeless.' Then his well-known finale, as he whipped the scrawled C-H on his chalkboard and wrote, in enormous letters, Si-N" (676). A commitment to things, to rampant materialism with the concomitant concern with systems of exchange and distribution, is, Jamf gleefully proclaims, an immoral act. Max Weber, whom Pynchon quotes in the narrative, explains why this is the case. The rationalization of our efforts to impose design and pattern on all transactions within the human community easily develops into an irreversible process which depersonalizes and objectifies individuals.[8]

Enzian, who is probably the best spokesman in the novel for Pynchon's view on materialism and technocracy, perceives that the real crises during the war "were crises of allocation and priority, not among firms—it was only staged to look that way—but among the different Technologies, Plastics, Electronics, Aircraft, and their needs which are understood by the ruling elite" (607). If you deify technology, Enzian continues, "it'll make you feel less responsible, but it puts you in the neutered, brother, in with the eunuchs keeping the harem of our stolen Earth for the numb and joyless hardons of human sultans, human elites with no right at all to be where they are" (607). The enemy in *Gravity's Rainbow* is not the ruthless romantic individualism of totalitarian and/or fascist dictators, but rather the ruthless romantic individualism of all leaders, including the Marxists, who dominate through closed systems and symbolics in the name of material well-being. All the other forms of romantic idealism, Pynchon implies, simply serve the interests of such leaders.

The two most ardent devotees to romantic individualism in the novel are Weissman-Blicero and the Hereros Enzian, both of whom are utterly taken with the concept of absolute zero and see the rocket as symbol, or icon, for transcendence of polarities. Virtually all Blicero's thoughts and actions are motivated by his passion to attain the absolute through transcendence of opposites. His imaginatively perverse sexual encounters with Katje, Gottfried (God's peace), and Enzian, his love of Rilke's "Tenth Elegy" (an intensely romantic poem celebrating the impossible union of the actual and ideal) are all manifestations of the desire, as he tells Gottfried, "to leave the cycle of infection and death. I want to be taken in love: so taken that you and I, and death, and life, will be gathered inseparably, into the radiance of what we would become" (844).

Enzian, whose passion to transcend polarities features a curious form of redemption for the Hereros, wants to create a condition in which the "people will find the Center again, the Center without time, the journey without hysteresis, where every departure is a return to the same place, the only place" (370). Since the rocket, says the scientifically minded Enzian, "embraces all deviations in one single act" (271), it symbolizes, like the mandalic form of the Herero village, the union of all seeming oppositions, the ultimate congruence of all either-ors. One might speculate here that Enzian's native mysticism should allow him to accept more readily the implication of the new physics, but, as Pynchon makes clear, Europe came to Africa and "established its order of Analysis and Death" (842). Mandalas in mystical traditions, generally used as meditation devices, are not considered to be transcriptions of nature but rather constructs of the mind. Infected by the Western analytical tradition, Enzian thinks in terms of irreconcilable oppositions that can only be annihilated through a physical event—death. He is, in other words, a thoroughly Western thinker like Blicero.

Pokler is another character manipulated by the Firm in the production of Rocket 00000, but he is more representative of the manner in which the majority of us deal with systems we cannot ultimately affect or understand. Pokler is particularly useful to the Firm because he has technical knowledge of advanced scientific concepts, but continues to construct his subjective reality in essentially Newtonian terms. He is the "cause-and-effect man" (186) who presumes that there is a certain inevitability in a chain of events which precludes radical decision making. As he sits at the very center of the target area during a rocket test, which was the safest place to be because the chances are "astronomically against a perfect hit," Pokler cannot help thinking of "all tolerances of the guidance cooperating toward a perfect shot" (496). In an attempt to convince his wife Leni that astrological predictions have no merit Pokler asserts that no one system can produce a change in any other. To this Leni replies, "Not Produce . . . not cause. It all goes along together. Parallel, not series. Metaphor. Signs and Symptoms. Mapping on to different coordinate systems, I don't know" (186). Since Pokler as a rationalist is incapable of intuiting that all human activity is interconnected and also that much of that activity is irrationally motivated, the designs of the Firm make no sense to him. Even though he has cause to wonder that the Ilse whom Blicero allows him to see two weeks a year in payment for his work on the rocket might not be the same person from one year to the next, Pokler insists, finally, upon a causal connection between the images of a daughter passing before him and assumes they make up a single identity.

One of the more interesting of the Firm's innovations is the White Visitation and its related intelligence-gathering agencies. Aware of the implications of the new physics, and, consequently, of the limits of rationality, the Firm maintains at "a disused hospital for the mad, a few token lunatics, an enormous pack of stolen dogs, cliques of spiritualists, vaudeville entertainers, wireless technicians. Couéists, Ouspensk-

ians, Skinnerites, lobotomy enthusiasts, Dale Carnegie zealots, all exiled by the outbreak of war from pet schemes and manias damned" (89). The Firm studies such people in an incredible variety of ways in an apparent attempt to discover heretofore unknown processes in nature that will allow them to extend their control over individuals.

The Firm's first director of the White Visitation, General Pudding, believed in "a literal Chain of Command, as clergymen of earlier centuries believed in the Chain of Being" (88). The second, who assumes control covertly, is another either-or thinker with a Newtonian world view. The determinist Dr. Pointsman (whose name means switchman on the railroad in British slang) selects as his sacred text Pavlov's *Letters to Pierre Janet*, and his principal object of study is Tyrone Slothrop. Pavlov was, says the narrator, "fascinated with 'ideas of the opposite.' Call it a cluster of cells, somewhere in the cortex of the brain. Helping to distinguish pleasure from pain, light from dark, dominance over submission" (55). When the idea of the opposite is weakened, Pavlov speculated, the individual enters an "ultraparadoxical phase" which is the condition of mental illness in all its manifestations. Since Slothrop's chance sexual encounters in London, the last location of which he "symbolizes" on a map, coincide with the location of the next German rocket strike after a "mean lag" of "about 4½ days" (99), Slothrop appears to be able to effect a reversal of cause and effect. Pointsman's hypothesis is that Slothrop is capable of a "transmarginal leap" in which "ideas of the opposite have come together, and lost their oppositeness" (57).

The irony is that Pointsman is correct in asserting that Slothrop is capable of such transmarginal leaps, but his capacity to do so does not account for his seeming ability to predict target areas nor is it in any sense a sign of mental disturbance. Another character, Roger Mexico, also predicts the location of strikes, but his method is scientific. Roger uses a Poisson distribution equation, a mathematical system dealing in probabilities of occurrence in the "domain of zero to one" (63), which discloses the overall pattern of strikes but not the precise location of any one strike. As Roger explains to the dismayed determinist Pointsman: "Every square is just as likely to get hit again. The mean hits aren't clustering. Mean density is constant" (63).

Although the odds against Slothrop predicting the precise location of even one strike are astronomical, anyone familiar with the new physics should know that Slothrop's chance sexual encounters are no more predictive of precise target locations than Mexico's probability equations. We could assume that the Firm has arranged for the correspondence by following Slothrop's movements and arranging a strike at the location of his last sexual liaison, but that does not seem likely since the chances of engineering a direct hit are, as we saw in our discussion of Pokler, miniscule. What was overlooked by all the researchers who attempt to explain the correspondence is that Slothrop's behavior does not allow prediction of the precise "time" of the rocket strike. If space and time are one dimension, then we must conclude, no matter how incredible the circumstance, that it is only chance or hazard that makes the patterns on the maps of Slothrop and Mexico identical.

Critics in growing numbers have driven themselves to distraction looking for logical connections which would allow for a rational explanation for this "ambiguity" in the novel. (It is probably the most sardonic trick Pynchon has played on his analytically minded readers to date.) The clues are everywhere, but there is again that gap in logical, linear connections which precludes closure. Slothrop has early connections with the Firm through his Uncle Bland, and his education at Harvard was paid for by the Firm in return for allowing the infant Slothrop to be experimented upon by Jamf. The "Conditioned stimulus = X" (97) which Jamf used to evoke the hardon response could be, it is suggested at various points, sound, light, German technical language, and the smell of Imipolex G. There is even some suggestion that the penis which Slothrop thought to be his own is made of Imipolex G, a substance which has "erectile" properties. Perhaps telepathic communication exists between Slothrop and Katje who tells him in lowered voice, "you were in London . . . while they were coming down. I was in Gravenhage . . . while they were going up" (243). Or, ignoring the clues and opting for the simplest explanation, we might conclude that Slothrop is capable of precognition.

What Pynchon has done here, with a vengeance some may fail to appreciate, is to provide another of his demonstrations that the Newtonian world view, which features along with the Western mind itself either-or categorical thinking, simple causality, immutable law, determinism, and discrete immutable substance, is not a viable mode of dealing with experience. The Firm in *Gravity's Rainbow* is Pynchon's way of advertising the dangers on the social, political, and economic levels of continuing to frame out experience in this fashion. The consequence on the level of subjective experience are the usual afflictions of Pynchon's characters— alienation and paranoia.

The way in which to counter this seemingly inexorable movement toward the abyss is, Pynchon suggests, a radical change in our sense of relation to the external environment. The key to understanding how such an assertion is made in *Gravity's Rainbow* is much the same as the key to understanding Pynchon's intentions in his first novel—it is a letter, or in the case of his last novel a scientific notation as well, read as figure. The X as it is used in the description of Jamf's experiment on Slothrop is the unknown stimulus, but it is also an intersection of lines. Slothrop is clearly the nexus through which the knotting-into process of narrative lines cross or connect, but there is another sense of connectedness at work in the novel of much greater importance. The effect of gravity on light traveling unimpeded through the cosmos is to bend it into a trajectory, which we now recognize as the symbol of eternity, until it travels back to precisely its point of departure—the X, if you will, as the place of launch and target area become one. When we last see Slothrop in the novel he is looking up at gravity's rainbow: "and now, in the zone, later in the day he became a crossroad, after a heavy rain he doesn't recall, Slothrop sees a very thick rainbow here, a stout rainbow cock driven down out of pubic clouds into Earth, green valleyed Earth, and his chest fills and he stands crying, not a thing in his head, just feeling natural . . . " (729). The sense of communion which is only hinted at here in Slothrop's vision of the lovemaking of earth and sky is made more explicit at the close of the novel. Having placed his reader in a movie theater about to be annihilated by nuclear energy, Pynchon instructs us all to sing a hymn written by Tyrone's ancestor William:

> There is a hand to turn the time,
> Though thy Glass today be run,
> Till the Light that hath brought the Towers low
> Find the last poor pret'rite one . . .
> Till the Riders sleep by ev'ry road,
> And through our crippl'd Zone,
> With a face on ev'ry mountainside,
> And a Soul in ev'ry stone. . . .
>   (887)

If we take the hymn out of an eighteenth-century context and read it as another of those interconnected fragments of this fiction, we arrive at some fruitful speculations. If *Hand* is a reference to the God of Whitehead, whom I have already identified as the God of Pynchon as well, then time is quite literally turned in the space-time continuum by the Being which is identical with the process of all nature's becoming. The *Light*, or energy, that can in nuclear explosion bring down a world constructed in terms of closed symbolics (*Towers*) is the same light, or energy, which could allow the *preterite*, Pynchon's term for one controlled by the elect or the system's managers, to sense his oneness with the cosmos. If that were the case the *Riders*, the carriers of information which allows the system to perpetuate itself, would sleep, and a zone, like that in the novel, would emerge in which the possibility of free election exists because the controlling symbolics or systems are not in force. It is then that a holistic vision is possible—a sense of relation which breaks down the barriers between self and world ("a face on ev'ry mountainside"), and reveals all that which seemed inanimate (*stone*) as alive with a force and spirit that is also ourselves. "Now everybody—" sing (887).

Notes

1. Frank D. McConnell, "Thomas Pynchon," in *Contemporary Novelists*, ed. James Vinson (New York: St. Martin's Press, 1972), p. 1034.
2. Pynchon has an agreement with his publisher that stipulates that no critical studies of his own work can be published by them if they wish to maintain their contract with him.
3. Thomas Pynchon, *Crying of Lot 49* (New York: Viking Press, 1967), p. 10.
4. Thomas Pynchon, *Gravity's Rainbow* (New York: Viking Press, 1974), p. 1.
5. Alfred North Whitehead, *Process and Reality* (New York: Free Press, 1960), p. 254.
6. Joseph W. Slade, *Thomas Pynchon* (New York: Warner Paperback Library, 1974), p. 219. Also see Lance W. Ozier, "The Calculus of Transformation: More Mathematical Imagery in *Gravity's Rainbow*," *Twentieth Century Literature* 21, no. 2 (May 1975): 193–210.
7. Slade, p. 215.
8. See Max Weber, *The Protestant Ethic and the Spirit of Capitalism*, trans. Talcott Parsons (New York: Scribner's, 1958).

ROGER B. HENKLE
"The Morning and the Evening Funnies: Comedy in *Gravity's Rainbow*"
Approaches to Gravity's Rainbow, ed. Charles Clerc
1983, pp. 273–90

There is nothing humorous about death in the morning. Especially when one is hung over and filthy, as Pirate Prentice is on the morning that opens *Gravity's Rainbow*. Just before waking, Pirate had dreamed of a darkened railway carriage full of "drunks, old veterans still in shock . . . hustlers in city clothes, derelicts, exhausted women with more children than it seems could belong to anyone."[1] He comes to in an apartment draped with the drinking companions of the night before: snoring, hacking, smelling of booze, sweat, and semen. "How awful. How bloody awful." Pirate climbs out onto his roof garden and looks East, and there, a white vapor trail on the horizon, is Death on its way to London, possibly to Pirate. Another German rocket arches along its silent, nearly invisible ballistic path.

But almost immediately, Pynchon's comic powers go to work on morning death. Pirate Prentice whips up his outrageous banana breakfast: banana omlets, mashed bananas molded in the shape of a British lion rampant, banana croissants and banana mead and banana flambé. "Now there grows among all the rooms, replacing the night's old smoke, alcohol and sweat, the fragile, musaceous odor of Breakfast: flowery, permeating, surprising, more than the color of winter sunlight. . . . It is not often Death is told so clearly to fuck off" (V10/B11).

The banana, itself a parody of the rocket. The banana, arching as if in its own parabolic flight away from its branch, ending in its own *Brennschluss*. The banana, another classic phallic symbol as is the German rocket in all its imagery in *Gravity's Rainbow*. A rich and natural thing, however; nutritious, fragrant, contributing to man's health and not his destruction. Therein lies the working of Pynchon's comedy—the metaphorical reduction of the fearful into the playful. Control of the ominous by converting it imaginatively into a subject for ludicrous parody of all its elements. Metaphorical transformation has been Pynchon's chief comic method since V.; it is not only the source of some of his most brilliant set pieces, but is, as Fausto Maijstral observed in V., the poet's chief way of keeping alive humane illusions in the face of depersonalization.

The metaphorical process of comic imitation and variation preserves the balance between Pynchon's seriousness about paranoia and the control mechanisms of modern corporate existence, and the objectivity he must have, as an artist, in order not to be victimized by his own material. Seriousness is deadly in Pynchon's universe; only those like Roger Mexico and Tyrone Slothrop who can maintain the capacity to laugh at themselves escape the obsessional. Take the case of the humorless, arch-conspirator Pointsman, for instance, who callously manipulates people in the service of dehumanization, and who is incapable of acquiring a humorous perspective—thus unable to see how ludicrous is the ultimate nightmare of the Pavlovian experimenter with dogs: a confrontation with the

> stalking Reichssieger von Thanatz Alpdrucken, that most elusive of Nazi hounds, champion Weimaraner for 1941 . . . his liver-gray shape receding, loping at twilit canalsides strewn with debris of war, rocket blasts each time missing . . . [until at last] the gray dog can turn and the amber eyes gaze into Ned Pointsman's own. . . . (V142–43/B166–67)

Pointsman is doomed to live within his obsessions until they grow surrealistically supernatural and devour him. Pynchon, however, maintains a constant poise through the comic involution of his own most cherished and worked ideas—as in, for instance, the comic scene in which Slothrop is obliged to go through the Disgusting English Candy Drill, by sampling Mrs. Quoad's hoarded English candy "delights": pepsin-flavored nougats with chewy camphor gum centers, hard sour gooseberries with powdered cloves inside, eucalyptus-flavored fondants with grape gum arabic cores. More than a take-off on the notoriously eccentric English sweet tooth, it is also a metaphoric reduction of the joined Pynchon images of war and sex. One particularly debilitating English bonbon is shaped after a six-ton earthquake bomb, and it (or another in Mrs. Quoad's arsenal) detonates in Slothrop's mouth like an explosive charge, deadening the nerves, sending "freezing, frosty-grape alveolar clusters" into his lungs, and giving him a momentary floating feeling (V116–19/B135–38). The sensation is not unlike that of sexual climax, also, and in the next paragraph we encounter Slothrop, limp and exhausted from intercourse.

The connection between the transformative powers of art and the workings of comedy have been made by several of the major theoreticians of comedy. Freud describes it as a process of "wit-work" by which a joke-teller or comic writer must rework the animosity in any comic attack into a manner of presentation that is socially acceptable and, in some cases, aesthetically pleasing. Arthur Koestler also notes the tendency of comic invention to shade into the creative—to move beyond pure attack or reductiveness into new combinations or elaborations. [2] Ernst Kris, a follower of Freud's, advances an analysis that is particularly relevant to comedy in modern Western societies, where, as in *Gravity's Rainbow*, the humor must deal not so much with a specific comic target, such as an authority figure, but with the vaguer paranoias and neuroses that characterize our existence in a world whose operations of evil are diffused and impersonal. Kris suggests that the comic probes along the edge of the comic writer's submerged anxieties. It parries our fears, and constantly advances to what Pynchon might call the "interface" with psychic disequilibrium. [3]

In the comedy of *Gravity's Rainbow*, that darker edge is never far removed. When Pynchon charges up for sustained comic narrative, he is snappy, brusque, and a bit nervous.

> [Pirate] will then actually *skip* to and fro, with his knees high and twirling a walking stick with W. C. Fields' head, nose, top hat, and all, for its knob, and surely capable of magic, while the band plays a second chorus. Accompanying will be a phantasmagoria, a real one, rushing toward the screen, in over the heads of the audiences, on little tracks of an elegant Victorian cross section resembling the profile of a chess knight conceived fancifully but not vulgarly so— . . .
>
> In 1935 he had his first episode *outside* any condition of known sleep—it was during his Kipling Period, beastly Fuzzy-Wuzzies far as eye could see, dracunculiasis and Oriental sore rampant among the troops, no beer for a month, wireless being jammed by other Powers who would be masters of these horrid blacks, God knows why, and all folklore broken down, no Cary Grant larking in and out slipping elephant medicine in the punchbowls out here. . . . (V12–13/B14–15)

A dazzling performance of tripping fast talk, of the quick allusion, the sketchy detail, the exotic reference. An ornate patina of near-vaudevillian mannerism, old bits, fill and patter develops into a kind of routine. Comedy saves us through such rituals of language and quick change; we pass off the horrors by distracting ourselves from them. It is fixation, after all, that stultifies; it is the devotion of time and attention to a thing that imbues it with intolerable significance. Yet we sense at times an uneasiness in such frenetic comic virtuosity. Too much quick change, hinting, as comedy often does, that it is a dangerously thin cover, and, sure enough, the tricks do not turn fast enough on the narrative surface of *Gravity's Rainbow* to keep the book itself from being obsessive. The Rocket, and death, and conspiracy-theory lurk behind all the comedy. Pynchon undoubtedly wants a certain amount of such tension—it is a darkly comic vision—but he betrays also the perilousness of his enterprise, the difficulty in keeping the comic method from being a quirky, troubled, almost reflexive operation.

The metaphoric character of his writing harbors similar perils. For the repetition in another form, even if in a ludicrously reductive one, of the motifs of the novel tends to keep those motifs constantly in mind. No matter how many times one transmogrifies the image of explosion—into orgasm, into eating, into defecation—it lingers in our consciousness, constantly receding, perhaps, but still wavering into view, a red image on the mind's fatigued retina. For, as I have argued elsewhere,[4] Pynchon's commitment to a metaphoric reconstitution may signify an inability to achieve a total imaginative transmutation of his material. The "ghost of Walter Rathenau" defines the problem in a cynical way: "'But this is all the impersonation of life. The real movement is not from death to any rebirth. It is from death to death-transfigured. The best you can do is to polymerize a few dead molecules. But polymerizing is not resurrection'" (V166/B194). On the imaginative level, the book struggles with the same difficulties, of getting beyond what is largely reconversion and into a different creative frame, in which the old lines of connection, the familiar realizations of desires and anxieties, are replaced with a new vision.

Pynchon's use of comedy suggests, in fact, that Western man finds himself more and more caught up in the analogies of his own discoveries in physics and his technology. The episode of Byron the Bulb involutes the problems of the human characters in the novel. Byron represents the human tendency to anthropomorphize inanimate objects and give them a mock human consciousness. Byron yearns for immortality; he tries to organize an insurrection among light bulbs to break away from the "grid." The humor in this episode recalls Charles Dickens's comic responses to the onset of the dehumanization of modern urban life: his tendency to play with the idea of an interchange of psychic forces between the animate and the inanimate. In Dickens, chimney stacks grinned and peered maliciously, walls ominously creaked, clothes and furniture mimicked human beings. Conversely, the victimized little people and the fanatic villains of the London underworld took on queerly inanimate qualities, often becoming projections of their function in a bureaucratic, technical world. Dickens's crucial observation was that the last desperate act of men and women who find themselves becoming dehumanized is to entertain the idea that a common energy permeates all things; in this manner, they can project into inert objects some of the vitality and "personality" that is being denied or stifled in *them*. The people in *Gravity's Rainbow* constantly engage in the same practice: Blicero's imprisonment of Gottfried in the final German rocket is his ultimate, insane attempt to fuse together the two things into which he had projected his own unsatisfying love: the boy and the machine. Similarly, we are told that Franz Pökler became an "extension" of the Rocket long before it was ever built because Leni had denied him love. Technology becomes the Great Substitution for what is missing on the human level; the laws of physics replace what used to be mysteries of human behavior.

As Joseph Slade and Edward Mendelson have pointed out,[5] Pynchon's ideas in *Gravity's Rainbow* have been influenced by the writings of Max Weber. Part of Weber's thesis holds that post-Reformation man has cultivated the notion of "objectivity" as a means of establishing his individuality and freedom. Gradually, however, this has produced alienation, and then forms of nearly mechanistic dehumanization. In what is described as "more Ouspenskian nonsense," a medium working for the White Visitation describes the process: "'Putting the control inside was ratifying what de facto had happened—that you had dispensed with God. But you had taken on a greater, and more harmful, illusion. The illusion of control. That A could do B. But that was false. Completely. No one can *do*. Things only happen . . .'" (V30/B34). The

first illusion, following on the progress that Weber describes, is that human will can effect changes—the illusion (which we will discuss later) of cause and effect. As the society becomes less responsive to individual will, and as man's confidence in rational control over his destiny wanes, essentially toward the end of the nineteenth century, then one loses the conviction that individual intention will achieve its goals. One becomes increasingly a "victim" of circumstances; the twentieth-century comedy of the victim, the "little man," the non-hero in the absurd universe, gathers imaginative force. A theory of comedy—Henri Bergson's[6]—emerges in 1900 that adequately captures this impression, arguing that comedy is a response to our awareness that we often behave mechanistically. We laugh at what has become automaton-like in the presumably human; comedy, with its transmogrifying powers, attempts to reassert human flexibility and self-control. In part this progression explains why comedy has become such a prevalent mode in twentieth-century literary expression; it explains, perhaps, why Pynchon writes comic novels about the present condition. For comedy is the most appropriate means of registering our internalized disquiet over the uneasy relationship that we have toward our increasingly mechanized existence, and our futile projections in response to it.

It is interesting to note also that the avant garde artistic movements at the turn of the century were, in a large sense, a variation on the process that Weber describes. The tendency toward objectification, in a movement like cubism, and the abstractions of surrealism were both prompted by the determination of a generation of artists to assert their *individuality* in the face of bourgeois conformity. But the expression of that individuality often took the form of conscious dehumanization; in an effort to avoid the sentimentalist, conformably rationalistic, and habitual qualities of bourgeois "realism," a major group of artists developed an agonistic vein of expression that had the effect of continuing the comic interplay of the human and the inanimate. Much of Pynchon's writing toward the end of *Gravity's Rainbow* is consciously surrealistic—an involuted configuration of the pattern that seeks to "control" dehumanization through comic play with some of the forms that dehumanization has taken.

A corollary to this problem emerges in the dilemma that Pökler faces. Each year the German government grants him a brief furlough, which he spends with his daughter Ilse, who has become a prisoner of the state and implicitly a hostage for Pökler's loyalty. Seeing his daughter so rarely, Pökler harbors the uneasy notion that perhaps he is not being given the same child each time (and, indeed, that may be the case). "So it has gone for the six years since. A daughter a year, each one about a year older, each time taking up nearly from scratch. The only continuity has been her name . . . and Pökler's love—love something like the persistence of vision, for They have used it to create for him the moving image of a daughter, flashing him only these summertime frames of her, leaving it to him to build the illusion of a single child . . ." (V422/B492). Here, metamorphosis itself is in question; perhaps it is not a real change, but the illusion of transformation. The issue penetrates to the very nature of the comic power itself: is that too simply a series of temporary displacements, and not really a transforming continuity? Can art exceed the limitations of its material if it must necessarily build on fractions of time and situation? Are we condemned to a series of quick projections of essentially formulaic reworkings of mundane material?

The issue of the powers of comedy to transform its subject matter is further complicated by an essential paradox in comedy itself. We have been speaking of comedy as if it were an expression of the human instinct for freedom and flexibility. We have noted its reliance upon the transformative powers of art. We are familiar with its changeableness, its irreverence. When George Santayana or Suzanne Langer or Henri Bergson or Northrop Frye[7] speak of comedy, they all emphasize its vitalistic spirit; it is organic, transformative, free-wheeling. And that surely is how it works in much of *Gravity's Rainbow*, when Pynchon's metaphors compare rockets and bananas, when his narrative language takes off on one of its buck-and-wings. But comedy has also been associated with stasis. It has been a means of escaping time as well as of riding the crest of time's flux. Indeed, comedy in the last two hundred years has enjoyed a kind of double status; it has been both a means, an approach or point of view (as when we speak of a comic rendering of reality, or a comic play with it), and it has also been, for many artists, a separate plane of existence. Northrop Frye describes comedic expression in terms of a mythos, and postulates various phases of the mythos in which the characteristic actions occur and a characteristic mood prevails.[8] In some of these phases, the world is enchanted and still, a "green world" in which the vicissitudes of normal existence are suspended and an aura of innocence, freedom, and delight envelops everything. Dickens was intrigued with such an alternative mode of human existence, and he associated it, in the writings of his *David Copperfield* period, with the fairy tale. It was a respite from the hard demands of the competitive adult world of modern life, a marvelously frozen imaginative realm in which nothing aged or corrupted or disintegrated. This curiously inconsistent yet enduring attitude toward the comic lies at the heart of Pynchon's vision of the Zone in part three of *Gravity's Rainbow*. For the Zone belongs neither to the Germans nor the Allies; it has no government, no body of conspiratorial forces governing it. Slothrop thinks that "maybe that anarchist he met in Zürich was right, maybe for a little while all the fences are down, one road as good as another, the whole space of the Zone cleared, depolarized . . . without even nationality to fuck it up. . . ." (V556/B648). Comedy and change thrive in the Zone, and part three of the book represents an extended series of metamorphosizing, anarchic episodes. And it offers the illusion of being temporarily outside of time—that is, outside of the "official" measurements of time, for it is at the end of one war and before the corporate forces can get the program organized for another.

For romantic appeal of the comic paradox of vitality and stasis enriches what is surely one of the comic high points of *Gravity's Rainbow*: the aerial battle between Slothrop and Major Marvy's men. In a wild Katzenjammer chase, Marvy and his besotted troops have pursued Slothrop through the labyrinths of the Mittelwerke, and now are bearing down upon Slothrop as he tries to escape in Herr Schnorp's balloon. Singing "another verse that's worse than the other verse" of the German version of an old fraternity drinking song, "In Prussia they never eat pussy," Marvy's men buzz Slothrop's balloon with their plane. Slothrop and Schnorp hurl custard pies, the ultimate comic prop: "He flings it, perfect shot, the plane peeling slowly past and *blop* gets Marvy right in the face. Yeah. Gloved hands paw at the mess. The Major's pink tongue appears. Custard drips into the wind, yellow droplets fall in long arcs toward earth" (V334/B389). Suddenly the balloon drifts into a gigantic cloud, and the anarchic, uproarious action of the comic chase is muffled, suspended. A scream of "Oh, fuck!" signifies that a well-aimed custard pie has hit the engine cowling; there are a few frantic shots from Marvy's crew, a sputtering of the plane's engine, and one vein of comedy has been superseded by another. In a memorable piece of description, the triumphant Slothrop and Schnorp float above the green of German fields, the clouds pink and broken up with the setting sun, and they watch the shadow of the earth race across Germany at 650 miles an hour. For a moment they are in the ecstasy of removal, sailing miles above time's darkening, speeding effects.

But as the image of a suspended interlude suggests, the green world in which comedy's imagination resides is a temporary respite. It is an illusion, just as is the false sense of freedom in the German Zone. History, politics—the "normal" measures of time—will reassume their sway and force men back into their mechanistic roles. Indeed, what we came in the 1960s to call the "military-industrial complex" had always been bent toward the spoliation of the comic vision. The horrible little triangle of Blicero and Gottfried and Katja enacting Hansel and Gretel had been Blicero's parodic debasement of the charm of enchantment. The mock fairy-tale kingdom of Zwölfkinder, with its Glass Mountain twinkling rose and white, its elf king and queen, its soda water fountains, was a cynical German charade. The legacy of World War II was the despoiling of the children.

And beyond that, Western culture, in its orientation toward time and function, has never been able to integrate its dream of a comic-imaginative green world into its mode of consciousness. In English Victorian culture, where the idea thrived, it followed a steady decline into puerility. From the vitalistic, energetic embodiment of it in Dickens's Mr. Pickwick, it evolved into the passive retreats of Dickens's own fairy tale vision, then into Carroll's Wonderland of talking creatures, and then into the heavily sentimental Peter Pan. From its essentially pastoral origins, in which it offered a critique of, and a commentary on, the "real" world of adults, the green world, heavily charged with post-Romantic childhood worship, declined into anti-adult retreat. The American version of it, which was ostensibly more activist and rebellious, nonetheless has proved to be an equally inadequate alternative. One of the chief distinctions between American and European versions has been the anti-intellectualism, and there is no denying that it has had a certain appeal for him. From the very first scenes of *V.*, Pynchon has taken a particular fancy to the boyish high jinks of fraternity parties and sailors' shore leaves. Pig Bodine appears as a comic "hero" in both novels, and his particular brand of humor is the gross-out. At times, indeed, "comic" life in the Zone can best be described by the single word "raunchy." In addition, Pynchon favors a comic-strip humor. Major Marvy's bloated face can almost be envisioned leering out of a Sunday funnies frame, colored florid red, and in the next panel his gang of baddies lurching out of the cockpit and side windows of his little plane, waving their arms. It is "Pirate" Prentice, and it is Rocketman; Slothrop in his green cape and dehorned helmet, legs spread, fists on hips, straddling the body-strewn scene yelling, "Fickt nicht mit der Raketemensch!" *Gravity's Rainbow* seems at times like an old "Terry and the Pirates"—or more likely, "Steve Canyon," who was very big in the fifties. And the version of human life—and more important, the version of history—is distressingly like that of those funny-paper staples. For it is a Daddy Warbucks romanticization of the military-industrial complex. It looks upon modern human affairs with much the same simplistic point of view that characterizes the non-intellectualism of aspects of American popular culture. And it, as much as Peter Pan, refuses to take a complexly "adult" outlook on human events.

To be fair, we must acknowledge that Pynchon is conscious of the orientation of this material. For instance, the various images of idealized golden girlhood that constitute an ingredient of the American popular culture's formula gather together in the nymphet Bianca, late in part three. She is, explicitly, an embodiment of all the despoiled children—the Ilses and Katjes—of the novel; and when Slothrop witnesses the grotesque spontaneous orgy that erupts as she is spanked by Margherita (shortly after Bianca did her Shirley Temple imitation), and when Slothrop himself makes love to her, Slothrop realizes that he is participating in the debauching of a cultural icon. Specifically, she is the American golden-haired girl, whom you saw out of the windows of the passing Greyhound bus, whom you watched Lindy Hop, whom the comic strips glorified, and he is not sure that she was ever real—"she must be more than an image, a product, a promise to pay . . ." (V472/B551). Pynchon is aware that this version of The Girl Next Door, The Girl Back Home, The Girl That I Marry, is a nostalgically blurred concept, fraught with the urge to return to preadult innocence of vision. Yet we perceive that a part of that worship of the golden girl was the desire to despoil her. Even the supposedly simplistic formulas of the comic-strip culture do not come clean; they are confused with lust and a nostalgia for innocence. And yet this should be no surprise; for, just as the green world of the imagination has been a repository for all the desires and feelings that hard-paced everyday life cannot seem to accommodate, it has also harbored that other dimension of human life for which the open and dominant cultural expression has had no mode of presentation: sex. In so much of English and American culture, sex has been an outlawed or tabooed subject; thus it has been driven into other, oblique forms of expression—forms that were often either highly sanitized and romanticized in a fairy-tale manner, or were pornographic. In *Gravity's Rainbow*, we are frequently conscious of an uneasy slippage into perverse forms of sexuality, as if the characters were incapable of defining love in any other way. But that slippage had always been a thinly disguised background to "green world" idealizations of love and innocence; we all know about Lewis Carroll's supposedly illicit feelings toward little girls; we all understand what Shirley Temple's fetching little dance steps aroused.

Slippage—signifying the instability of values and attitudes—is what ultimately proves the bane of the comically "free" existence. The age-old charge against comedy—particularly favored in the Puritan ethos that Max Weber chronicles—centered upon its potentiality for chaos. Comedy's origins lay in the saturnalia, interludes of celebrative disarray that vented the anxieties and tensions of the normally ordered and hierarchical cultures. The belief lingered well into the nineteenth century that if the spirit of comedy, with its irreverence, its amorphousness, its changeableness, were allowed to prevail in a society, or a pocket of society, the consequence would be anarchy, immorality, and finally disintegration. Comedy (especially in its imaginary green worlds) was a nice place to visit, but nobody wanted to live there long. And this proves to be the case with the comically oriented Zone in *Gravity's Rainbow*. Because life in the Zone is by its very nature ad hoc—"Temporary alliances, knit and undone"—and because the previous American and British cultural visions of comic interludes have been so elusive and ingenuous in their orientations, existence in the Zone proves to be dangerously unstable. In a bewildering series of episodes, the "plot" lines ravel and unravel, characters wander the countryside and the rubble of the cities, meet and part, connect and miss connections. Underneath it all lurks the danger of psychic breakdown. For with no values to sanctify, with disillusionment the legacy of war, and with cultural

heritage discredited, an individual has precious few concepts on which to reconstruct himself.

An early metaphoric excursion illustrates the potential hazards of giving way completely to subjective flux. Slothrop, in a drug-induced fantasy, yields to all the anti-social, comically free-wheeling impulses that he suppresses in ordinary contexts. He imagines that he has fallen into a toilet bowl and is floating through the sewer system. His is the "excremental vision" familiar to Western satire and comedy, the vision of Jonathan Swift, or of Samuel Beckett when he says that "the way down is the way out." Slothrop serves as a manic commentator on the waste of a gorged society because he is able, for a moment, to indulge himself in all his perverse fascinations. Slothrop releases himself from the inhibitions that constrict him. But the content that emerges from the unconscious is unsettling. It exposes not only the normal human inclination toward the scatalogical, to befoul oneself, but it also reveals unexpectedly strong animosities toward blacks, in particular. Fear of being buggered by a black triggers the fantasy. It is almost as if tolerance toward blacks and other minorities were something that is maintained in Slothrop only under the constraints of the superego. Once these constraints vanish, a disturbing discharge of race-hatred, violence, perversion—random fecal matter of hate and fear and self-loathing—tumbles out. And it warns the reader that once all the socially dictated conformities are broken down, even if in the comic flux, we are vulnerable to irrational tendencies that we could not imagine that we harbored.

Thus, in the Zone, Slothrop discovers himself frequently on the verge of self-disintegrating indulgence. In order to love Margherita, he must torture her, and in a vivid instant he realizes that sadism contains a perverse fascination for him. "Whatever it is with her, he's catching it. Out in the ruins he sees darkness now at the edges of all the broken shapes, *showing from behind them*. . . . Across the facade of the Titaniapalast, in red neon through a mist one night he saw DIE, SLOTHROP. One Sunday . . . a crowd of little kids in soldier hats folded from old army maps plotted to drown and sacrifice him" (V446/B520). He is on the edge of psychic death.

Too often comedy breaks out in mayhem, and too often there are willing victims to every random bit of violence, every sadism, every perversion. Pynchon has long been intrigued by the mentality of subject peoples. The Hereros, a doomed race, fulfill a confusing role in Nazi Germany; like lemmings they have streamed into the homeland of their torturers to attend upon the German's casual whims of sadism. "They calculate no cycles, no returns, they are in love with the glamour of a whole people's suicide—the pose, the stoicism, and the bravery. . . . The Empty Ones can guarantee a day when the last Zone-Herero will die, a final zero to a collective history full lived. It has appeal" (V318/B369–70). As the name of the people suggests, they are hero-zero, the anti-heroes of the twentieth century, symbolic carriers of the widespread disease of passivity, of impotence. The society that Pynchon depicts is under the control of no man; its institutions seem to be entropic in their self-sustaining quality. Hence the modern sense of powerlessness, of the inability to control events, to work one's will.

The comic literature of the last fifty years has placed particular emphasis upon this perspective; we have a rich tradition of the comic victim, the Chaplinesque clown, the little man who is buffeted by the whims of Fortune, abused by venal "authority figures" and who yet preserves the essential human decencies. Such a little man has been the staple of our situation comedies. He is Buster Keaton, Red Skelton, Laurel and Hardy, and even, in his cheeky way, W.C. Fields. He is Kingsley Amis's Lucky Jim, John Hawkes's Skipper, James Joyce's Leopold Bloom. The rise and survival of such a cultural figure suggests that comic expression has seized upon a felt quality of modern life. Since comedy is the "open" mode, since it is, as Suzanne Langer says, the mode of Fortune, and tragedy is the mode of Fate, it has been the natural vehicle for this feeling. And, intriguingly enough, the advent of this particular comic vision—of the little man victim rolling with the punches—has corresponded with the critique of the notions of human intentionality and its workings, and of cause and effect, at the end of the nineteenth century. In particular, Henri Bergson, in *Time and Free Will*, and Friedrich Nietzsche, in *The Will to Power* (and, in a different way, Arthur Schopenhauer in several writings), raised the first questions about Western man's long-hallowed way of looking at human intention and human activity. They both argue that the notion of causality is an illusion; we *surmise* cause and intention from the "schema of the effects." As so often happens, a social observation begins to correlate with philosophical theorizing to form the background for a perspective on life that literature begins to express in more and more explicit terms.

There can be little doubt that Pynchon is probing, in *Gravity's Rainbow*, the implications of this possible change in our way of thinking about human behavior. The vast majority of characters in the novel do, of course, cling to the idea that human will can operate in the way that we have been accustomed to believe that it does—that one makes choices, forms intentions, and acts from those intentions, and that what happens politically and socially in the world is a result of individuals engaged in this process. But there are some individuals, notably Roger Mexico, who argue that we must "'junk cause-and-effect entirely, and strike off at some other angle'" (V89/B103). Leni argues the same thing against Franz Pökler, although she is not quite sure how to articulate it: "He was the cause-and-effect man. . . . 'There is no way for changes out there to produce changes here.' 'Not produce,' she tried, 'not cause. It all goes along together. Parallel, not series. Metaphor. Signs and symptoms. Mapping on to different coordinate systems. I don't know . . .' She didn't know, all she was trying to do was reach" (V159/B186). Mexico is more specific; it is a principle of randomness that governs our existence. And little does he know, but he has an unlikely coconspirator, the German film-maker von Göll, busily at work, producing "under the carpet" motion pictures that ridicule cause and effect: "a reverse world whose agents run around with guns which are like vacuum cleaners operating in the direction of life—pull the trigger and bullets are sucked back out of the recently dead into the barrel, and the Great Irreversible is actually reversed as the corpse comes to life to the accompaniment of a backwards gunshot . . ." (V745/B870).

I am indebted to Joseph Slade's book *Thomas Pynchon* for an insight into the significance of this idea for Pynchon. Slade suggests that it comes from exploratory work by the psychologist C. G. Jung and the physicist Wolfgang Pauli on the notion of coincidence and noncausal phenomena.[9] Jung and Pauli raise the possibility that we deceive ourselves in assuming that the operative pattern in many incidents and happenings is causality, and that we must open ourselves up to other ways of looking at physical behavior. We must entertain the idea of randomness and chance as an operative principle in the unfolding of human events. I touch upon this subject in writing about comedy in Pynchon because it seems to me that Pynchon is toying with a world view that has been essential to

the comic in the last fifty years. Opposed in *Gravity's Rainbow* is, on the one hand, the noncomic orientation that has governed Western thought for hundreds of years—an orientation that attaches *consequences* to things, that suggests we are responsible for the shape of our societies and our lives, that all action has meaning, and derives from some form of intentionality—and, on the other hand, the comic orientation, which suggests that we trust to luck, ride the crest, develop an anarchic, free-wheeling attitude toward life. If the latter is truer to the physical and psychic actualities of our condition, then the comic literature that portrays man as essentially a victim of circumstances is the genuinely prophetic mode—or at least the apter mode.

Pynchon probes the frontiers of this concept in *Gravity's Rainbow*, but goes no further because it is a heady realm nearly impossible to navigate in the narrative prose of a cause-and-effect tradition. Arthur Koestler points out that Jung found it difficult to proceed on the terms he had suggested, and ended up postulating a concept of synchronicity that showed "the apparently insurmountable difficulties of breaking away from our ingrained habits of thinking in terms of cause and effect."[10] Koestler says that whenever earlier Western philosophers developed a similar line of thought, they almost invariably attempted to reconcile randomness with cause and effect by returning to the idea of an omniscient, God-like intelligence that unified everything. Lyle Bland in *Gravity's Rainbow* appears to have been pursuing such a course. In his advanced stages of Masonic mysticism, Bland claimed to be journeying (while lying on his back on the couch in his study) "underneath history: [he imagines] that history is Earth's mind, and that there are layers, set very deep, layers of history analogous to layers of coal and oil in Earth's body" (V589/B687). Bland, as comic a voyager into philosophical netherlands as one could conceive, does finally, after settling his affairs ("One night he called his whole family together around the davenport in the study. Lyle, Jr. came in from Houston. . . . Clara drove down from Bennington and Buddy rode the MTA in from Cambridge" [V590–91/B688]), depart his physical chains altogether. He abandons all contexts, even the couch, for his ultimate trip into Randomness.

Few others are able to abandon their human contexts so completely. And, in fact, the "charm" of world war had been the total context that it supplied for those involved in it. We are told of a

> long-time schiz . . . who believes that *he* is World War II. He gets no newspapers, refuses to listen to the wireless, but still, the day of the Normandy invasion somehow his temperature shot up to 104°. Now, as the pincers east and west continue their slow reflex contraction, he speaks of darkness invading his mind, of an attrition of self. . . . The Rundstedt offensive perked him up though, gave him a new lease on life. . . . (V131/B152)

More people than the long-time schiz relied on the war for focus and direction. Slothrop disappears from the coordinates of other people's concern, and thus, in a way, from existence, because of the end of the German campaign. Mexico's love for Jessica is only a creature of the War. Hence it is problematic that a noncausal world view could ever gain acceptance for Western peoples, who are so reliant upon historicity and upon control theories for the contexts of their lives.

Indeed, Pynchon suggests that everything we do and think about is programmed in some way by our social and cultural contexts, and that ultimately all we will be able to do, even in a comically open world view, is rehearse a wider variety of programs. This plight comes to the surface at the time of what is presumably Slothrop's first disorientation. At the beginning of part two, we see him at the rest and recreation spa, Casino Hermann Goering. His first time out on the beach, he espies a gigantic octopus grasping a lovely blonde in its tentacles, about to pull her out to sea. Slothrop rushes to her rescue, not yet aware of what a fanciful parody it is on the themes of his situation: the octopus a fitting analogue to the many-tentacled corporate conspiracy; the blonde a symbol for all the cultural values the Allies are fighting for (including both purity and sexuality); and Slothrop's action a splendid, comic-book illustration of heroism, taking control of one's situation, and so on. Unfortunately, the octopus is Grigori, the Fabulous Octopus of the Pointsman lab's Pavlovian experiments, the girl is Katje Borgesius in the employ of the White Visitation, and the entire episode has been staged. Slothrop recognizes all this in short order—"What th' fuck's going on?" (V187/B218)—and immediately contracts paranoia. Subliminally, we as readers make the connection between the state of paranoia and staged effects, and we are haunted with the implication that every mental state, even so devastating as the pattern of this one, is a schema. As we progress through the novel, we perceive more and more that the historical and psychohistorical aspects of Pynchon's version of the world are highly theatrical. Constantly the text shifts us from "actual events" to cinematic, comic-strip, or fictional analogues to them. The interpenetration is so intense in *Gravity's Rainbow* that one must conclude that there is *nothing* that people do or think about that is not fit somehow into a scheme. Fatality and suffering, love—everything—has its repertoire of scenarios that we unconsciously apply to every situation. We cannot act without our texts, even in a contingent, random world (for comedy has supplied us with many texts for chaos, and pornography and psychological literature with many texts for psychic disorientation).

If anything, Pynchon seems to emphasize this fact more and more. The reminders are interlaced in narrative description: "The story here tonight is a typical WW II intrigue . . ." (V247/B287) or "It's a Sunday-funnies dawn, very blue sky with gaudy pink clouds in it" (V295/B343). Human life in the Zone is a patchwork of scenarios and frantic roles. The Argentine gaucho-anarchist Squalidozzi turns to the German movie-maker Gerhardt von Göll in the hope that von Göll will be able to script an appropriate actuality for him and his men. Von Göll is heady with the recent success of his "invention" of the Schwarzkommando, whom he had conjured up as a devious Allied trick and then found out later that they existed. "'It is my mission,' he announces to Squalidozzi, with the profound humility that only a German movie director can summon, 'to sow in the Zone seeds of reality. The historical moment demands this, and I can only be its servant. My images, somehow, have been chosen for incarnation. What I can do for the Schwarzkommando I can do for your dream of pampas and sky . . .'" (V388/B451). A new scenario is needed for the Argentines, since they do not seem to be able to get their act together:

> The crew that hijacked the U-boat are here out of all kinds of Argentine manias. El Ñato goes around talking in 19th-century gaucho slang—cigarettes are "pitos," butts are "puchos," it isn't caña he drinks but "la tacuara," and when he's drunk he's "mamao." Sometimes Felipe has to translate for him. Felipe is a difficult young poet with any number of unpleasant enthusiasms, among them romantic and unreal notions about the gauchos. He is always sucking up to El Ñato. . . . Luz is currently

with Felipe, though she's supposed to be Squalidozzi's girl—after Squalidozzi disappeared on his trip to Zürich she took up with the poet on the basis of a poignant recitation of Lugones's "Pavos Reales," one balmy night lying off Matosinhos. For this crew, nostalgia is like seasickness: only the hope of dying from it is keeping them alive. (V383–84/B446)

Everyone in the Zone, and in the wake of the War, is having trouble keeping his act together. The characters, and the narrative vision itself, rely more frequently on comic-strip, literary formulas and on cinematic schemes for organizing and interpreting the episodes of their lives. When Von Göll (in the role of Springer) abandons his faithful companion Närrisch, surrounded by trigger-happy Russian troops and apparently doomed, Slothrop criticizes him for the treachery. Von Göll is unconcerned; Närrisch, like the Asp or Punjab or any number of characters from the comic strips, has been last seen on many occasions in apparently hopeless circumstances, only to reappear again. "'But what if they *did* shoot him?'" Slothrop asks. "'No. They weren't supposed to,'" von Göll answers. "'Springer, this ain't the fuckin' *movies* now, come on.'" "'Not yet. Maybe not quite yet'" (V527/B614). By the end of the novel, it *is* the movies. Major Marvy is arrested, mistaken for Slothrop, and castrated—a poetic revenge that will bring the entire theater audience to delighted applause. Roger Mexico wreaks his vengeance on Pointsman and the Corporate Conspiracy by breaking into their board meeting, jumping on the board table, whipping out his cock, and pissing on the shiny table, the papers, the ashtrays. As security police dash into the room, Mexico dives under the table, the men colliding and butting heads as they grapple for him, and then begins the escape: ". . . Aficionados of the chase scene, those who cannot look at the Taj Mahal, the Uffizi, the Statue of Liberty without thinking chase scene, chase scene, wow yeah Douglas Fairbanks scampering across that moon minaret there—these enthusiasts may find interest in the following . . ." (V637/B742).

As such a passage suggests, the narrative of *Gravity's Rainbow* becomes more and more self-conscious as the contexts of the War and the plots that circulated within it break down and randomness prevails. The comic narrative method of the last phases of the novel is not that of the earlier phases, in which metaphor was used to discharge the tensions of a rigid, inhumane world order. Rather, we have now *improvisation* in the face of manic disorder. Part four is largely made up of spliced stories, comic routines, skits, film clips, vignettes. One senses the strain in a narrative mode that had its origins and its greatest successes in approaching its materials from the point of view of cause and effect, now struggling to dominate a fragmented, random world view. That "conventional" novelistic mode can only summon up its old schemata, but even these are briefer, less cohesive and gradually more remote, as in the final pages, Pynchon deals out his material through tarot cards—signifiers of the mysteries of the random. *Gravity's Rainbow* charts some sort of ritual passage in the uses and the outlook of comedy. Initially the comedy serves to vent the anxieties and pressures of a hardened world. Then, in the long section dealing with life in the Zone, the comedy is an excursion into flux and freedom, a working through of its own "green world" and pop culture manifestations, and a penetration deep into its own perverse shadows—across that dark "interface" that Ernst Kris speaks of. Finally comedy engages in a kind of frenetic improvisation, an exhibition of virtuosity, as it flashes rapidly through scenarios and quasi-cultural schemata in an attempt to cope with the challenges of randomness. And at the end of *Gravity's Rainbow*, we are invited to follow the bouncing ball—an almost parodic analogue of the novelistic mode's dogged struggle to master an emerging new comic vision.

Notes

1. Thomas Pynchon, *Gravity's Rainbow* (New York: Viking Press, 1973; New York: Bantam Books, 1974), p. 3 (Viking), p. 3 (Bantam). Subsequent references will be to both editions.
2. Sigmund Freud, *Jokes and Their Relation to the Unconscious*, trans. James Strachey (1905; rpt. New York: Atheneum 1966); Arthur Koestler, *The Act of Creation* (New York: Macmillan, 1964).
3. Ernst Kris, *Psychoanalytic Explorations in Art* (1952; rpt. New York: Schocken Books, 1964), pp. 173–216.
4. Roger B. Henkle, "Pynchon's Tapestries on the Western Wall," *Modern Fiction Studies* 17 (1971): 207–20.
5. Joseph Slade, *Thomas Pynchon* (New York: Warner Books, 1974); Edward Mendelson, "Gravity's Encyclopedia," in George Levine and David Leverenz, eds., *Mindful Pleasures: Essays on Thomas Pynchon* (Boston: Little, Brown, 1976), pp. 161–96.
6. Henri Bergson, "Laughter" (1900), reprinted in *Comedy* (Garden City, N.Y.: Doubleday, 1956).
7. George Santayana, "Carnival," in *Soliloquies in England and Later Soliloquies* (New York: Charles Scribner's Sons, 1922); Suzanne Langer, *Feeling and Form* (New York: Charles Scribner's Sons, 1953); Bergson, "Laughter"; Northrop Frye, *Anatomy of Criticism* (Princeton: Princeton University Press, 1957).
8. Frye, pp. 163–86.
9. Slade, pp. 214, 215, 236. The essays by Pauli and Jung appear in *Naturerklärung und Psyche*, Studien aus dem C. G. Jung-Institut, No. 4 (1952).
10. Arthur Koestler, *The Roots of Coincidence* (New York: Random House, 1972), pp. 97–98.

AYN RAND

1905–1982

Ayn Rand, originally Alice Rosenbaum, was born on February 2, 1905, in St. Petersburg (now Leningrad), Russia, to Fronz and Anna Rosenbaum, a prosperous Jewish couple. She graduated from the University of Leningrad in 1924 and two years later emigrated to Chicago, where relatives of her mother were living at the time. After Chicago she moved on to settle in Hollywood, where she worked as a movie extra, wardrobe stock clerk, and junior scriptwriter; in her spare time she brushed up on her English and wrote fiction. She also met Frank O'Connor, who was also working as a movie extra, and they were married in 1929.

In 1937 Rand took an unpaid job as a typist with architect Eli Jacques Kahn in order to research her novel, *The Fountainhead*, which was published in 1943 and became a best-seller. She continued to hold a variety of jobs in the motion picture industry throughout the 1930s and 1940s, and wrote the screenplay for *The Fountainhead*, which was filmed in 1949. After 1951 she devoted herself full time to writing and lecturing. Following the publication of her novel *Atlas Shrugged* in 1957 she ceased writing fiction in order to devote herself to the exposition of Objectivism, a system of thought encompassing aesthetics, economics, and philosophy, which stressed pro-capitalist lassez-faire economics, radical individualism, and a romantic-idealist approach to art. Among her works from this period are *For the New Intellectual: The Philosophy of Ayn Rand* (1961), *The Virtue of Selfishness* (1964), and *The Romantic Manifesto* (1969).

Ayn Rand died in New York City on March 6, 1982.

Personal

It was during the summer of 1914 that she read a story which she recognized, then and later, as marking a crucial turning point.

One quiet afternoon, Alice turned, as she often did, to her stacks of French magazines. Leafing through a boys' magazine of adventure stories, she stopped at one entitled "The Mysterious Valley," and began to read. Time stood still. Her life stood still, as if waiting for its purpose. Many years later, she talked about the story and her feeling for it.

"It was a love affair for me from the first installment. It was about English officers in India, kidnapped by an evil rajah, a monstrous old villain who is plotting to overthrow British rule. Two officers set out to avenge their friends, who they think are dead; then there follow a number of exciting adventures, until the men find the mysterious valley where the hero and the other men are imprisoned in a cage in a temple; the rajah is going to kill them. But the hero, Cyrus—the kind of feeling I had for him, it still exists, it's in essence everything that I've ever felt for Roark, Galt, Nathan, Frank, or all my values. There's nothing that I can add in quality to any important love later on that wasn't contained in that. Except that being the first, the intensity was almost unbearable. I was a woman in love in a serious sense. The whole reality around me lost all meaning. If, before, I felt that I was imprisoned among dull people, now it was: They don't know, but *I* do— *this* is what's possible.

"One illustration that particularly impressed me was a picture of Cyrus standing with a sword. He was a perfect drawing of my present hero: tall, long-legged, with leggings but no jacket, just an open collar, his shirt torn in front, open very low, sleeves rolled to the elbows, and hair falling down over one eye. The appearance of my heroes, and what is *my* type of man, was completely taken from that illustration."

As Ayn Rand, in middle age, talked about Cyrus, the excitement of youth was in her voice and face, like a woman remembering her first love, never to be challenged, never again to be matched.

"Cyrus was a man of enormous audaciousness, defiant independence. All the other officers in the prison were afraid of the rajah and broken in spirit—except Cyrus. He stood holding on to the bars of the cage, hurling insults at the rajah. He was threatened with torture, with whipping, but he was completely defiant—he laughed!

"One of the rescuers climbed on the shoulders of an enormous idol in the temple, put two flashlights into the eyes of the idol and flashed their beams over the assemblage. The Indians were terror-stricken by the lights, and fled, abandoning the cages. Then began the difficulty of escaping the valley—all kinds of adventures, with secret corridors and a pool filled with crocodiles. At the last moment, they found that the rajah was holding a beautiful blond English girl prisoner; they rescued her, and escaped with her.

"In the last installment, they are climbing a steep ladder of metal rungs up the side of a cliff. Cyrus is carrying the girl on his shoulders. They had planted dynamite to go off just as the Indians were pursuing them—a dam broke, water covered the valley, and all the villains perished—and the hero married the girl." ⟨. . .⟩

"Cyrus was a *personal* inspiration," she explained, "a concrete of what one should be like, and what a man should be like. He was a man of action who was totally self-confident, and no one could stand in his way. No matter what the circumstances, he'd always find a solution. He helped me to concretize what I called 'my kind of man'—that expression, which I carried thereafter, began with that story. Intelligence, independence, courage. The heroic man."

In the child who was Alice Rosenbaum, Ayn Rand was being born. One can observe in her novels that the spirit of Cyrus became the spirit of all the fictional heroes she would create. Howard Roark in *The Fountainhead* was Cyrus, John Galt and Hank Rearden and Francisco d'Anconia in *Atlas Shrugged* were Cyrus. The name "Kira," which she chose for the heroine of *We the Living*, is the Russian feminine version of "Cyrus." As an adult, she would translate Cyrus's courage and daring into intellectual terms; but the basic nature of "the heroic man" was never to alter. Alice Rosenbaum, age nine, was on fire with the human possibility she had seen; Ayn Rand was to hold that fire throughout her life, as the source of a literary career that burned into the consciousness of generations of men and women. It was not the stories in her novels, it was not the literary style, it was not the events that most accounted for the fame she was to achieve; it was the portrayal of the human potential: it was Cyrus.

Talking about her childhood discovery, Alice said: "Thereafter, for the next three years, Cyrus was my exclusive love. I felt totally out of the concerns or reality of anybody. What they were interested in didn't matter at all to me, because I knew something much higher. The story made the reality around me more bearable, because it made concrete the reality of what I valued. My feeling was 'This is what *I* want out of life.'"—BARBARA BRANDEN, "Prologue," *The Passion of Ayn Rand*, 1986, pp. 12–14

General

Ayn Rand is a rhetorician who writes novels I have never been able to read. She has just published a book, *For the New Intellectual*, subtitled *The Philosophy of Ayn Rand*; it is a collection of *pensées* and arias from her novels and it must be read to be believed. Herewith, a few excerpts from the Rand collection.

> It was the morality of altruism that undercut America and is now destroying her.
>
> Capitalism and altruism are incompatible; they are philosophical opposites; they cannot co-exist in

the same man or in the same society. Today, the conflict has reached its ultimate climax; the choice is clear-cut: either a new morality of rational self-interest, with its consequence of freedom . . . or the primordial morality of altruism with its consequences of slavery, etc.

Then from one of her arias for *heldentenor*:

> I am done with the monster of "We," the word of serfdom, of plunder, of misery, falsehood and shame. And now I see the face of god, and I raise this god over the earth, this god whom men have sought since men came into being, this god who will grant them joy and peace and pride. This god, this one word: "I."
>
> The first right on earth is the right of the ego. Man's first duty is to himself.
>
> To love money is to know and love the fact that money is the creation of the best power within you, and your passkey to trade your effort for the effort of the best among men.
>
> The creed of sacrifice is a morality for the immoral . . .

This odd little woman is attempting to give a moral sanction to greed and self interest, and to pull it off she must at times indulge in purest Orwellian newspeak of the "freedom is slavery" sort. What interests me most about her is not the absurdity of her "philosophy," but the size of her audience (in my campaign for the House she was the one writer people knew and talked about). She has a great attraction for simple people who are puzzled by organized society, who object to paying taxes, who dislike the "welfare" state, who feel guilt at the thought of the suffering of others but who would like to harden their hearts. For them, she has an enticing prescription: altruism is the root of all evil, self-interest is the only good, and if you're dumb or incompetent that's your lookout.

She is fighting two battles: the first, against the idea of the State being anything more than a police force and a judiciary to restrain people from stealing each other's money openly. She is in legitimate company here. There is a reactionary position which has many valid attractions, among them lean, sinewy, regular-guy Barry Goldwater. But it is Miss Rand's second battle that is the moral one. She has declared war not only on Marx but on Christ. Now, although my own enthusiasm for the various systems evolved in the names of those two figures is limited, I doubt if even the most anti-Christian free-thinker would want to deny the ethical value of Christ in the Gospels. To reject that Christ is to embark on dangerous waters indeed. For to justify and extol human greed and egotism is to my mind not only immoral, but evil. For one thing, it is gratuitous to advise any human being to look out for himself. You can be sure that he will. It is far more difficult to persuade him to help his neighbor to build a dam or to defend a town or to give food he has accumulated to the victims of a famine. But since we must live together, dependent upon one another for many things and services, altruism is necessary to survival. To get people to do needed things is the perennial hard task of government, not to mention of religion and philosophy. That it is right to help someone less fortunate is an idea which has figured in most systems of conduct since the beginning of the race. We often fail. That predatory demon "I" is difficult to contain but until now we have all agreed that to help others is a right action. Now the dictionary definition of "moral" is: "concerned with the distinction between right and wrong" as in "moral law, the requirements to which right action must conform." Though Miss Rand's grasp of logic is uncertain, she does realize that to make even a modicum of sense she must change all the terms. Both Marx and Christ agree that in this life a right action is consideration for the welfare of others. In the one case, through a state which was to wither away, in the other through the private exercise of the moral sense. Miss Rand now tells us that what we have thought was right is really wrong. The lesson should have read: One for one and none for all.—GORE VIDAL, "Two Immoralists," *Esq*, July 1961, pp. 113–14

Just as men of ambition for material values do not rummage through city dumps, but venture out into lonely mountains in search of gold—so men of ambition for intellectual values do not sit in their backyards, but venture out in quest of the noblest, the purest, the costliest elements. I would not enjoy the spectacle of Benvenuto Cellini making mud-pies.

It is the selectivity in regard to subject—the most severely, rigorously, ruthlessly exercised selectivity—that I hold as the primary, the essential, the cardinal aspect of art. In literature, this means: *the story*—which means: the plot and the characters—which means: the kind of men and events that a writer chooses to portray.

The subject is not the only attribute of art, but it is the fundamental one, it is the end to which all the others are the means. In most esthetic theories, however, the end—the subject—is omitted from consideration, and only the means are regarded as esthetically relevant. Such theories set up a false dichotomy and claim that a slob portrayed by the technical means of a genius is preferable to a goddess portrayed by the technique of an amateur. I hold that *both* are esthetically offensive; but while the second is merely esthetic incompetence, the first is an esthetic crime.

There is no dichotomy, no necessary conflict between ends and means. The end does *not* justify the means—neither in ethics nor in esthetics. And neither do the means justify the end: there is no esthetic justification for the spectacle of Rembrandt's great artistic skill employed to portray a side of beef.

That particular painting may be taken as a symbol of everything I am opposed to in art and in literature. At the age of seven, I could not understand why anyone should wish to paint or to admire pictures of dead fish, garbage cans or fat peasant women with triple chins. Today, I understand the psychological causes of such esthetic phenomena—and the more I understand, the more I oppose them.

In art, and in literature, the end and the means, or the subject and the style, must be worthy of each other.

That which is not worth contemplating in life, is not worth re-creating in art.

Misery, disease, disaster, evil, all the negatives of human existence, are proper subjects of *study* in life, for the purpose of understanding and correcting them—but are not proper subjects of *contemplation* for contemplation's sake. In art, and in literature, these negatives are worth re-creating only in relation to some positive, as a foil, as a contrast, as a means of stressing the positive—but *not* as an end in themselves.

The "compassionate" studies of depravity—of dipsomaniacs, drug addicts, murderers, psychotics—which pass for literature today are the dead end and the tombstone of Naturalism. If their perpetrators still claim the justification that these things are "true" (most of them aren't)—the answer is that this sort of truth belongs in psychological case histories, not in literature. The picture of an infected ruptured appendix may be of great value in a medical textbook—but it does not belong in an art

gallery. And an infected soul is a much more repulsive spectacle.

That one should wish to enjoy the contemplation of *values*, of the *good*—of man's greatness, intelligence, ability, virtue, heroism—is self-explanatory. It is the contemplation of the *evil* that requires explanation and justification; and the same goes for the contemplation of the mediocre, the undistinguished, the commonplace, the meaningless, the mindless.

At the age of seven, I refused to read the children's equivalent of Naturalistic literature—the stories about the children of the folks next door. They bored me to death. I was not interested in such people in real life; I saw no reason to find them interesting in fiction.

This is still my position today; the only difference is that today I know its full philosophical justification.

As far as literary schools are concerned, I would call myself a Romantic Realist.

Consider the significance of the fact that the Naturalists call Romantic art an "escape." Ask yourself what sort of metaphysics—what view of life—that designation confesses. An escape—from what? If the projection of value-goals—the projection of an improvement on the given, the known, the immediately available—is an "escape," then medicine is an "escape" from disease, agriculture is an "escape" from hunger, knowledge is an "escape" from ignorance, ambition is an "escape" from sloth, and life is an "escape" from death. If so, then a hardcore realist is a vermin-eaten brute who sits motionless in a mud puddle, contemplates a pigsty and whines that "such is life." If *that* is realism, then I am an escapist. So was Aristotle. So was Christopher Columbus.—AYN RAND, "The Goal of My Writing," *ObjN*, Oct. 1963, p. 38

Rand's use of "integrity" is surely based on the second definition in the *Oxford English Dictionary*: unimpaired or uncorrupted state, original perfect condition; and perhaps even the obsolete usage meaning sinlessness. No wonder the boundaries must be fenced, reinforced, and patrolled. If the behemoth's condition is threatened by the corrupt "hordes of envious mediocrities"—then Rand condones any protective action, whatever the cost. When his own housing project is about to be completed with some modifications he does not approve, Roark destroys his creation—better purity in others' homelessness than corruption of his aesthetics.

Violence, as *strong* action, finds ample rationalization. Never mind that a basic principle of Rand's Objectivist philosophy is the prohibition of the initial use of physical force against others: to the ideal man, any attempt to thwart his will justifies any response. True, Roark's violence might not be with a gun or his fists; nevertheless his actions are distinctly violent and perhaps unexpected from the heroic figure Rand calls "the portrait of an ideal man." Ignore for the moment the "violence" of his drawings and his "violent" signature; it is in the expression of love, the most human of feelings—one would suppose even for a rational prototype—that Roark's violence becomes intense. To begin with, his first physical contact with the woman he loves, Dominique, is qualifiedly, rape.

> It could be the act of a lover or the act of a soldier violating an enemy woman. He did it as an act of scorn. Not as love, but as defilement. And this made her lie still and submit.

Making love is an act of slavery. "When she felt him shaking with agony of pleasure unbearable even to him, she knew that she had given that to him, that it came from her, from her body, and she bit his lips and she knew what she wanted her to know." How appropriate that it is *Playboy Magazine*, which has its own ambivalent "philosophy" regarding male-female attitudes, in which Rand reveals her distinct sexism:

> Man is born with certain physical and psychological needs, but he can neither discover them nor satisfy them without the use of his mind. Man has to discover what is right or wrong for him as a rational being. His so-called urges will not tell him what to do. . . . [However], a man is equipped with a certain physical *mechanism* and certain needs . . . (my emphasis).

Her analysis leaves us with the alternative interpretation that Roark's behavior—his forceful exploitation of another's body/ energy for his own masturbation—is *rational*. Thus, it is not stretching Rand's terms of reference or her philosophy to conclude that she *rationally* supports this kind of brutal domination.

If, as Rand further claims, "sex must not be anything other than a response to the [highest] values," what are we to make of the encounters of Roark and Dominique? "[I]t was— as it had to be, as the nature of the act demanded—an act of violence." Forcible, contemptuous possession does not offend Rand. Whereas the Victorian vernacular for orgasm was "spending," and now we speak of "coming" (and Reich suggested that the concept should be "giving"), for Roark it is "taking." Naturally, the values of a writer's philosophy need not be held by any of her characters, and normally such a critique would be inappropriate; but Rand invites this kind of comparison once she makes it clear, as she has, that Howard Roark is an "ideal man." That man must take from woman is only natural, according to Rand; after all, "the essence of feminity is hero-worship—the desire to look up to a man. . . ." In "An Answer to Readers about a Woman President" (1968), Rand confirms the male exclusive on responsibility and leadership: being President "would be an unbearable situation for a truly rational woman. To act as the superior, the leader, virtually the *ruler* of all men she deals with, would be an excruciating psychological torture."

Apparently, other forms of torture are bearable. Would it be unfair to suggest that for Rand it is precisely on the edge of bearability that pleasure awaits?

> [Roark] wanted her [but] it amused him to wait, because he knew that the waiting was unbearable to her. He knew that his absence bound her to him in a manner more complete and humiliating than his presence could enforce. He was giving her time to attempt an escape, in order to let her know her own helplessness when he chose to see her again. . . . Then she would be ready either to kill him or to come to him of her own will. The two acts would be equal in her mind.

While Roark tortures his property, Dominique dedicates her life to minimizing her hero's pain. In fact—perversely?—she prevents architectural commissions being granted to Roark in a noble attempt to protect him from what she assumes will be much agony when the inevitable compromises are forced on this great, unbending individualist. After convincing a prospective client not to hire Roark, Dominique goes to his room.

> I want to sleep with you. Now, tonight, and at any time you may care to call me. . . . I want you like an animal . . . or a whore. . . . I hate you for what you are; for wanting you, for having to want you. I'm going to fight you . . . I'm going to pray that you can't be destroyed. . . . But I will fight to block every step you take. . . . I have done it to you today—and that

is why I shall sleep with you tonight. . . . I want to be owned, not by a lover, but by an adversary who will destroy my victory over him . . . with the touch of his body on mine.

Pandering to the popular love-as-aggression mentality, Rand describes their embrace ending with "a surrender more violent than her struggle had been."—PHILIP GORDON, "The Extroflective Hero: A Look at Ayn Rand," *JPop*, Spring 1977, pp. 704–6

EDWARD CAIN
From "Ayn Rand as Theorist"
They'd Rather Be Right:
Youth and the Conservative Movement
1963, pp. 37–50

"I decided to become a writer," says Ayn Rand, "not in order to save the world nor to serve my fellow men, but for the simple, personal, selfish, egotistical happiness of creating the kind of men and events I could like, respect, and admire . . . I did not start by trying to describe the folks next door—but by inventing people who did things the folks next door would never do."[1]

Among the writers of the far Right, none has proposed a more earnest philosophical defense in depth than Ayn Rand. She has extended gratuitously an intellectual umbrella over political positions most ultraconservatives have not yet dared to occupy. In a paean to self-interest that would make any arch-Rotarian blush, Miss Rand announces through her architect hero in *The Fountainhead*: "I came here to say that I do not recognize anybody's right to one minute of my life. Nor to any part of my energy. Nor to any achievement of mine. No matter who makes the claim, how large their number or how great their need. . . . I wish to come here to say that I am a man who does not exist for others."[2]

How does she carry this off? It's done in stages through her four novels and a philosophical essay. First came *We the Living* (1936), a story about the evils of totalitarian society in the U.S.S.R. Kira speaks to Andrei, a commissar whom she has used but who is not her true love (only her comrade): "You came as a solemn army to bring a new life to me. You tore that life you knew nothing about out of their guts—and you told them what it had to be. . . . You came and you forbade life to the living."[3]

Anthem (1938) projects a totalitarian society of the future. Collectivism has poisoned society to its roots; everything is reduced to primitivism. The local science institute has just invented candles. The word "I" has vanished; only the plural is used, "we" and "they." It's very confusing during love scenes. People are identified by serial numbers, as in the telephone directory. Listen to the exchanges: Liberty, Solidarity, Equality, Collective, International, Similarity—and all the other political pejoratives. The collective spirit is grotesquely portrayed when "We," hoping for the job in science, gets a "Life Mandate" as a street sweeper. We reply: "The will of our brothers be done," and sing a "Hymn of Equality," or you could render the "Hymn of the Collective Spirit."

The drama concerns the frustrated street sweeper who escapes into the great uncharted forest and becomes an "I." The three holy words of the new life become "I will it!" Reflecting on his bondage, the hero decides that "to be free, a man must be free of his brothers. That is freedom. That and nothing else."[4] The fable closes with a new man cutting a new word over his portal: "EGO," a new anthem.

With *The Fountainhead* (1943) we return to the contemporary scene and turn to a more intellectual theme. In fact, twelve publishers thought the novel was too intellectual, and refused to publish it. A half-million sales proved that this was an error. Here among the skyscrapers, executives, and literati of New York City, Miss Rand probes at what she considers to be the ideological cancer leading us to the mindless society in *Anthem*.

Spokesman for this villainy is Ellsworth Toohey, liberal critic, architectural journalist, and general "do-gooder." (He's short and dumpy. You wouldn't like him.) Here is Ellsworth's trouble: "I don't believe in individualism, Peter. I don't believe that any one man is any one thing which everybody else can't be. I believe we are all equal and interchangeable."[5]

Preach selflessness, continues Ellsworth. Since the supreme ideal is beyond man's grasp, he will eventually give up all ideals and take comforts in effortless drifting. "Enshrine mediocrity—and all the shrines are razed." The quickest way to induce stagnation is to reassure men that they can't really go any higher. One of the quickest ways to breed mediocrity is to urge all men to sacrifice, and allow none to profit. Deny incentive to aspiration. Declare a moratorium on reason. Then if there is anything left standing, kill by laughter. Tell people that a sense of humor is an unlimited virtue. If you can kill reverence, you can kill the hero in man.

This giggling, unheroic mediocrity is the enemy, and the enemy is seen on all sides. Why so omnipresent? Because, Ellsworth confesses, "everything I have said is contained in a single word—collectivism." The new opiate, the "Great Bromide," the seductive siren of the hour is *collectivism*. The word is made to cover any cooperative venture.

Miss Rand's antipathy to collectivism approaches phobia. "I don't work with collectives," says hero Roark, "I don't consult. I don't cooperate." This was when he was asked to collaborate with several other architects in planning a world's fair. Enlightened self-interest is the only antidote, and "enlightenment" refers to the self, not to others. Independence is felt to be the sole measure of value: "What a man is and makes of himself; not what he has or hasn't done for others." Architect Roark makes it quite clear where others should stand and what they are after. "When the first creator invented the wheel, the first second-hander responded. He invented altruism. . . . The only good which man can do to one another and the only statement of their proper relationship is—'Hands Off!'"

Roark prefers reason and ideas to emotions and people. He is moralistic, and "internalizes" authority. Listen to him lay into the second-handers, the noncreators who are unreflective parasites. "They have no concern for facts, ideas, work. They're concerned only with people. They don't ask: 'Is this true?' They ask: 'Is this what others think is true?' Not to judge but to repeat. Not to do, but to give the impression of doing. Not creation but show. Not ability but friendship. Not merit but pull."[6]

Here is Ayn Rand's central theme: The splendid isolation of the individual. It's not misanthropy, but classical cynicism. *Cynos* is the Greek word for dog. Members of the school of Cynics were thought to be doglike in their boorish captiousness and indifference to the proprieties of life. Manners, customs, and the niceties of social intercourse, as well as the larger problems of political relationships, were thought to be without value, and therefore could be ignored.

The Fountainhead finally erupts in a climactic courtroom speech of Roark's in which he defends his action of dynamiting (without loss of life) a public housing project he had designed because some lesser bureaucrats altered his plans without his knowledge. And since you can't sue the government, what else could any self-respecting architect do? "I agreed to design Cortland for the purpose of seeing it constructed as I designed it and for no other reason." Furthermore, he couldn't find out which second-hander among the dozens in authority could be held to account. It is difficult to know which should infuriate us more: knowing that someone had presumed to alter Roark's design, or not being able to determine guilt in the bureaucratic maze. Anyway, this victory of the collective spirit over the creative will prove to be both short-lived and Pyrrhic. The architectural sacrilege is expiated by dynamite, and the jury acquits on the basis of justifiable immolation.

For those who didn't get the point of *The Fountainhead*, Miss Rand wrote *Atlas Shrugged* (1957). Here she wasn't taking any chances. The plot is very definitely subordinated to the ideological line. Characters have little more substance than the symbols she used in *Anthem*. This is avowedly a philosophical novel. The forces of Good and Evil are clearly arranged on a simplified checkerboard. All battles are fought in the full light of day. Readers might be appalled or pleased, but they could never be confused, by the issues.

The setting is the near present. The slow poison of the welfare state is just taking hold. The initiative and drive of entrepreneurship have been systematically bred out of society and a strange lethargy bred in. The economy is gradually unwinding, but most people do not know why. A few key businessmen and other creative spirits do know. One of them speaks, giving us the title situation: If you saw Atlas, the giant who holds the world on his shoulders, standing with buckling knees and trembling arms but still trying to hold the world aloft with the last of his strength, and the greater his effort the heavier the world bore down on his shoulders—what would you tell him to do? The answer: To shrug.

So, led by the most resolute of individualists, John Galt, a few of the most select creative spirits decide to withdraw into a mountain retreat and go on strike against society. Let's see them make a go of it now! In a sixty-page justification of his move, Galt announces: "We are on strike, we the men of the mind. We are on strike against the creed of unearned rewards and unrewarded duties. . . . We are evil according to your morality. We have chosen not to harm you any longer. We are useless according to your economics. We have chosen not to exploit you any longer. . . . It's your moral code that's through this time."[7] The only redemption for those behind is not to return to morality—they have never known any—but to discover it.

The story concerns the attempt of Galt and his followers to persuade the creative souls remaining behind to give up the hapless fight against the second-handers and looters and join his strike. To give you an idea of what he is up against, the heroine, Dagny Taggart, of flawlessly tailored mind, body, and raiment, is doing a bang-up job of running her family's railroad in spite of incompetent help. She is John's prime target, in more ways than one. But she won't budge for over nine hundred pages. This is undoubtedly a reflection of Grandfather Taggart's steadfast independence. When this founder of the line was desperate for funds for his railroad, he threw down three flights of stairs a gentleman who offered him a government loan. Instead he pledged his wife against a loan for one million dollars. You can see John's problems.

As an index of how sick society had become, Miss Rand describes a prosperous automobile factory that falls into the hands of hapless idealistic heirs. Not content with implementing a fair-shares plan, they organize the plant on the basis of the Marxian formula "From each according to his ability, to each according to his need." Of course, everything and everybody goes to pot.

The remedy for the moral and economic malaise of the world is to admit bankruptcy and go into receivership under John Galt's New Morality: Face the fact that pride is man's highest value and that it must be earned. There will be no conflict among men who reject the unearned. These are the men who neither make sacrifices nor accept them. The symbol of respect for human beings is the Trader. Miss Rand insists that a trader earns what he gets, and does not give or take the undeserved. He never asks to be paid for his failures. And he never gives his love or esteem except in trade for his own pleasure, which he can receive only from men he can trust and respect.

Here is a Benthamite calculus of pleasures with a vengeance, minus, of course, the part about "the greatest happiness of the greatest number." Miss Rand does go on to say that man's one moral obligation to others is his rationality. What does this tell us? Let's turn to her latest work, *For the New Intellectual* (1961), to examine the larger context of her theory of egotism.

America, proclaims Miss Rand, is culturally bankrupt. We have been betrayed by our intellectual bodyguards, most of whom are frightened zombies preaching the impotence of reason and contributing to the atmosphere of self-righteous depravity, guilt, panic, despair, boredom, and evasion. They present a "grotesque spectacle of militant uncertainty." Depravity is a result of not sufficiently exalting man. Guilt comes from either an irrational belief in original sin or the refusal to reject altruism. Despair is the product of the uncertainty of all norms and values. This refusal to accept absolute standards leads to evasion and ends in boredom.

After this warm-up, we are introduced to a new psycho-epistemology—a psychology of knowledge (or "the New Rand Atlas," as Donald Malcolm of the *New Yorker* has it). Intellectual history is portrayed as an endless contest between Attila (brute force), the Witch Doctor (faith and superstition), and the Thinker (creative reason). With the gusto of Spengler and the glibness of his *Decline and Fall of the West*, Miss Rand demonstrates that the intellectual climate of an age depends on how these three forces are in combination. Usually it is a case of a distrustful alliance of Attila and the Witch Doctor against the Thinker.

Things weren't too bad by the time of the Renaissance. The firm hold of the mystics had been broken. Then Descartes had to come along and start talking about "the prior certainty of consciousness" and innate ideas. This let the Witch Doctor in through the back door. Philosophers who chose to abandon reality joined the mystics and became known as Rationalists. Those who clung stubbornly to reality by abandoning their mind became Empiricists. The man who finally closed the door to reason and made possible an alliance of force and faith was Kant. He did this by turning the world over to Attila, but reserving the realm of morality to the Witch Doctor. *And* it was a morality of self-sacrifice, of altruism. Furthermore, Kant insisted that reality as seen by man's mind is a distortion; men can never really see things as they are. Unfortunately, laments Miss Rand, Kant is still the dominant intellectual influence today. Hence we believe that reality is mere appearance, that rational certainty is impossible, and that morality is altruism.

Pragmatism—"whatever one wishes to be true *is* true . . . provided it works or makes you feel better"—sold a bill of goods

to science and left us without any absolute principles or standards. When you combine Kant's subjectivism with pragmatism, whatever the majority says is true. All of the post-Kantian idealists are dismissed. Hegel is pure Witch Doctory and Marx pure Attila-ism. What's left?

Apparently we left the track back with Aristotle. He is the sole survivor of Miss Rand's critique. It is his logic that is so highly esteemed. Aristotle's logic has two features: the Law of Identity insists that whatever you are talking about you must mean, and not something else; and the Law of Contradiction holds that a thing cannot both be and not be at the same time.

This gives us a method of logic, but how is reason related to reality? Ayn Rand suggests a new philosophy: objectivism. Things exist independently of our consciousness of them. No sort of perceiving consciousness is required to establish their validity. Form (the way we have of recognizing things; for example, "squareness" or "dryness") exists only *in* matter, not outside or apart from it. This, says Miss Rand, is Aristotle's metaphysical realism. But Aristotle went on to say that form has a universal substance to embody it. Such a substance is the unmoved mover, God. All change and motion depend upon this Mover. Even matter is ultimately merely potentiality or possibility. (Later Idealists say matter is the energy of God's mind.)

Since Miss Rand rejects God and all theistic explanations, she cannot base much of a metaphysical case on Aristotle. She is so nimbly eclectic, it is impossible to assign her to any of the recognized philosophical schools. Borrowing Aristotle's logic and the bottom half of his theory of knowledge (that is, the real exists), Miss Rand rejects the top half (God), his ethics and his political philosophy. Without admitting any debt, she seems to borrow Hegel's concept of the "concrete-universal," which asserts that thought and reality are identical and there are no things-in-themselves beyond experience. But she cannot bear the idealistic consequences. God is waiting around the corner there, too.

Does Miss Rand mean that everything is object? This would bring her into the materialist camp, where she appears to be more at home. Professor Ralph B. Perry has suggested the term "panobjectivism" for those believing that all reality is to be found in objects. This also would make her a monist, which means that she has given up the attempt to distinguish between idea and object. If idea and object are not two but one, which is the one? If you answer, object, what happens to the subject? Miss Rand's vaunted individualism would be sold short.

Perhaps what Miss Rand is really playing is axiology, the theory of value. Rather than giving us a new theory of knowledge in any terms we can recognize, isn't she really trying to give us a justification for a new standard of values? The primary question in such an inquiry is whether values are subjective or objective. Subjective value is wholly related to the private feelings of the individual, and social subjectivism means that environment and human conditions determine all value. The objectivist claims that there is more to the meaning of value than just the individual experience of it. He insists that a value judgment (the aurora borealis is beautiful) is just as objective a fact as our sense perception (I have seen the aurora borealis). Objectivism goes on to see that the aurora borealis is beautiful for the universe whether you saw it or not. Furthermore, the values of science cannot be subjective, or it would be meaningless. Reason itself demands objective norms.

In her campaign against subjectivism, Miss Rand is limited by her repudiation[8] of the coherence theory of truth. Hegel has a good statement of this: "The true is the whole." Your theory must not only be consistent; it must also be coherently connected with your whole picture of experience. The more connections, the better, and you are morally obligated to explore as many aspects of experience as you can.

For example, when Howard Roark decides to blow up the public housing project because of its bastardized architecture, he is being relentlessly consistent with all of his personal philosophy of egoist self-interest, but the coherence of his action is another matter. When you start balancing the aesthetic satisfaction of one man against the needs, interests, and rights of others, you are engaging in coherence theory. You may well decide that Roark's truth is not *as* true as that of others. You also must appraise his actions in terms of objective norms.

Miss Rand's objectivism seems to unravel at this point. The one major defense offered for the architect's action is that his sensibilities as a creator-producer were being outraged. The dynamiting was the product of individual subjectivism. If not the hedonistic "I enjoy it," then the egoistic voluntarism of "I desire it." Without any higher or truly objective reference, you are apt to end up in the anarchy of subjectivism where value is determined by dynamite caps. The difficulties of attempting to bind together egotistical self-interest with a theory of objectivism are endless.

The comparison with Nietzsche is obvious and tempting. All of the Rand heroes tell the truth and shoot straight. These, says Nietzsche, are the great Persian virtues. They are "the great despisers of things as they are" and the "great adorers and arrows of longing for the other shore," says Zarathustra. Certainly Roark and John Galt are Nietzsche's "free spirits," the bridges to the superman. Resentment of the noncreative looters is explicit in one of his apothegms: "It is not enough to possess a talent: one must also have your permission to possess it—eh, my friend." This supreme confidence in talent is matched by near eloquence in describing the untalented masses. Where Nietzsche speaks of "the superfluous ones," "the many too many," and (a real gem) "cobweb spinners of the spirit," Miss Rand replies with "human ballast" and those in a state of "unfocused stupor." Neither can abide the weak or the meek.

Yet Nietzsche is criticized in *For the New Intellectual* because he sacrifices others to the self. This violates John Galt's sacred oath: "I swear—by my life and my love of it—that I will never live for the sake of another man, nor ask another man to live for mine."

How does a heroic free spirit manage this? Above all, one must be a free trader: "A free mind and a free market are corollaries." Miss Rand insists that the intellectual's rebellion against "commercialism" is really a rebellion against "the open market of ideas . . . where no protector exists but objective reality." The finest expression of this free trade in ideas is capitalism, which "demands the best of every man—his rationality—and rewards him accordingly." While the intellectual is bankrupt, the businessman (who applies the science of the laboratory) has done "a superlative job."

Now Miss Rand has to prove that capitalism has not involved the sacrifice of men and their interests. To do this she would have to answer more than Marxist critics. The neat trick is to prevent free traders from treading on each other in a society where altruism has been eradicated. The Communist utopia appears simple by comparison. You can't even distill a social utilitarianism out of this, because the individual creator-thinker is the sole judge of utility.

We are almost reduced to Nietzsche's answer: anarchy. Zarathustra spoke of the state, that new idol, as "the coldest of all cold monsters." Miss Rand is willing to take us along as far

as Adam Smith. We are allowed a police force, law courts, and the military—provided we accept implicitly Smith's story about an "Unseen Hand" that guides entrepreneurs down their separate paths of economic virtue. But since all transcendent referents are taboo, we are to be denied even this comfort.

A chaotic political theory results. The concept of equality has been caricatured beyond recognition in all four novels. Any attempt at government regulation is immediately Rousseau forcing people to be free. The suggestion that private power might have to be tamed is never seriously considered. Human nature is defined in hopelessly naïve terms. Property rights are to be absolute (to be guaranteed by a constitutional amendment). A mythical golden age of free trade is presumed to exist. Minority interests may be exerted over political consensus. And political parties seem to be in an absolute limbo. Not much democratic theory is left.

What is Ayn Rand's appeal? People we used to describe as economic royalists might take indiscriminate comfort in her unlimited defense of free enterprise. The general public ("human ballast"?) likes her absorbing storytelling. And she has a message that might well impress certain inquiring minds. Her philosophy, *For the New Intellectual*, has a beguiling plausibility about it at first glance. Young intellectuals who are looking for an earnest but nonreligious (Miss Rand's system is a triumph of her justice over love) defense of our capitalism with forceful, humorless, unashamed bravado might be quite willing to listen—especially if they shared her blind spots in the social sciences. She is standing up to the Communists, sounding the call for absolute standards, and willing to give unlimited recognition to merit.

Certainly Miss Rand has a bold, energetic, and alert mind. She boasts that she sold her first novel (*We the Living*), first movie (*The Red Pawn* to Universal), and first play (*The Night of January 16th*, 285 Broadway runs). Her books have now sold over two million copies. The "Class of '43" commemorates publication of *The Fountainhead*. It is a group of young people interested in her ideas who meet for weekly discussions. Nathaniel Branden, New York City psychologist, has organized the Nathaniel Branden Institute, and gives a series of lectures on Miss Rand's philosophy. These are given twice a year in New York City and Philadelphia and by means of tape recordings in a dozen other United States and Canadian cities. Los Angeles, for example, draws about a hundred at one of these taped sessions. Most of those attending are college students. ⟨. . .⟩

The type of student to whom Miss Rand would appeal is very limited but qualitatively very important. He is very likely to picture himself as someone whom John Galt might call to his mountain retreat. Bright, alert, and conscious of his capacity, he would admire the boldness of heroic action. Having something to offer, he feels there should be appropriate reward for a job well done, and has probably long despised the "second-handers," or drones, who have had to crib from his chemistry reports or term papers.

Miss Rand does not appeal to those whom she labels "militantly uncertain." Her primary appeal is to those confident of their talent, especially those who feel that the talented, "the producers," are not being adequately recognized or rewarded. The young man who has no wealth except talent is suceptible, especially if he has avoided what he might refer to as sentimental egalitarianism.

No one has ever launched a more horrendous attack against the egalitarian implications of the welfare state than Ayn Rand. Young people bred in an era of prosperity who believe that their talents or times will never make them dependent upon the benevolences of a welfare state are apt to stress the malevolent consequences inferred by its critics. Moral autonomy must not disintegrate into obsequious dependence, and excellence must never give way to mediocrity.

Self-reliant young men going into the nonacademic professions and business careers are more likely to resent the drone implications of a welfare society. Miss Rand provides an ethical depth defense of this resentment.

Capitalism itself has enhanced its reputation since World War II. The remarkable success of the German free economy demonstrated what could be done with more verve. Prosperity and the greater participation of Americans in investments such as mutual funds identified more people with capitalism and helped wash away some of the old prejudices. Furthermore, capitalism was no longer identified with the enemy fascism. In being anti-Communist, one tried harder to be even more sympathetic with capitalism.

Young people don't joke about capitalism as they once did. For those young men whose families always took capitalism seriously and/or successfully, this new sympathetic mood allowed them to remain sophisticated and pretty much à la mode while they searched even further for rationalizations of their status or predispositions. Ayn Rand is an intoxicating discovery to such young people.

The only force that could definitively undermine Randian egotism is the Christian exposé of pride. But the species of religious "revival" experienced after World War II did not feature a prominent reaffirmation of original sin, with the exception of a few neo-orthodox intellectuals. The inevitable self-righteousness incident to prosperity and anti-Communism remained unmolested.

The religious defense of young people was not reinforced on this front. If anything, self-satisfaction has been heightened by a sense of economic security and crusading anti-Communism. This makes for a weak spiritual defense on the part of heroically disposed young men of capacity whose ethical guard has given in to Miss Rand's blandishments.

I think Ayn Rand will become an increasing favorite of those discomfited by democratic liberalism and looking for a new world view. In a new preface to her first novel, she says someone must restore a view of the forest to people who have been too busy looking at the trees. The new forest view is presented in contrasts made more absolute by constant recourse to the *non sequitur*. For example, the police state is always inferred from democratic socialism. (Actually, no democratic socialist state has ever gone Communist.) The momentum of the *non sequitur* allows one to affirm that a new proposal is just a "first step" toward something more disastrous—with a minimum of discussion about the nature of the proposed step.

For the conspiracy-conscious, for those who above all want to feel that they are not being "duped" by the next step, Ayn Rand's militant arguments are indeed persuasive. Foremost among her supporters will be those who have never accepted the counsel of James Harrington who wrote in the seventeenth century: "The wisdom of the few may be the light of mankind, but the interest of the few is not the profit of mankind."

Notes

1. *Twentieth Century Authors*, First Supplement, Wilson, 1955.
2. *The Fountainhead*, Bobbs-Merrill, 1943, p. 678.
3. *We the Living*, Macmillan, 1936, p. 388.
4. *Anthem*, Pamphleteers, Inc., 1946, p. 118.
5. *The Fountainhead*, p. 562.
6. Ibid., p. 599.
7. *Atlas Shrugged*, Random House, 1957, p. 937.
8. "Objectivism rejects in its entirety the coherence theory of truth, with the corollary idea of 'degrees of truth,'" says her disciple Nathaniel Branden.

JOHN CROWE RANSOM

1888–1974

John Crowe Ransom was born on April 30, 1888, in Pulaski, Tennessee, to John James Ransom and Ella (née Crowe) Ransom. He was educated at Vanderbilt University (B.A. and Phi Beta Kappa, 1909) and Christ Church College, Oxford (Rhodes Scholar, B.A. 1913). He accepted a position with the English department at Vanderbilt in 1914, where he taught until 1937; from 1937 to 1958 he taught at Kenyon College. During this time he was also a guest lecturer at various colleges throughout the South and West of the United States. He served with the U.S. Army from 1917 to 1919, achieving the rank of first lieutenant. In 1920 he married Robb Reavill; they had three children and remained married until Ransom's death.

Ransom published his first book of poetry, *Poems about God*, in 1919, but first attracted a significant amount of attention with his third book, *Chills and Fever* (1924). By this time he and fellow poet Allen Tate had founded the *Fugitive*—which they edited from 1922 to 1925—and the Agrarian school of poetry, celebrating the rural South and advocating an agrarian economy over the currently developing industrialism. Ransom's other well-known book of verse from this period is *Two Gentlemen in Bonds* (1927), after which he largely stopped writing poetry, confining his efforts to criticism and revision.

In 1939 Ransom founded the *Kenyon Review*, which he edited until 1959. The *Kenyon Review* was the vanguard of the New Criticism movement, of which Ransom was a central figure. The New Critics advocated the study of a work of art as an object in itself, independent of such concerns as the circumstances of its writing, the reaction of the audience, and the author's intentions. Ransom quickly became one of the most influential critics of his generation; among his major critical works

James Purdy

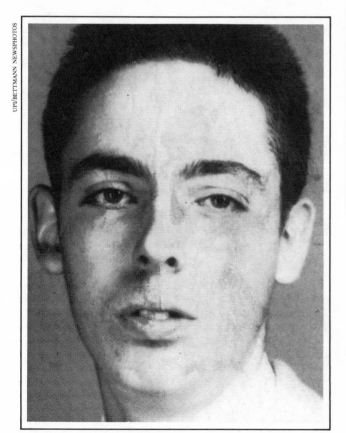

Thomas Pynchon

Reynolds Price

JOHN CROWE RANSOM

MARJORIE KINNAN RAWLINGS

JOHN RECHY

AYN RAND

are *The World's Body* (1938) and *The New Criticism* (1941). He also edited a *Kenyon Review* retrospective called *The Kenyon Critics* (1951). Shorter pieces by Ransom were published in *Beating the Bushes: Selected Essays 1941–1970* (1972).

As a poet, critic, teacher, and editor, John Crowe Ransom exerted a considerable influence on the theory and writing of contemporary poetry. He was awarded the Bollingen Prize for Poetry in 1951, and received the National Book Award in 1964 for his revised *Selected Poems* (1963). He died on July 3, 1974.

DELMORE SCHWARTZ
"Instructed of Much Morality:
A Note on the Poetry of John Crowe Ransom"
Sewanee Review. Summer 1946, pp. 439–48

The appearance of Ransom's *Selected Poems* suggest reflections, full of a modest joy, about the modest triumphs of virtue, both in poetry itself and in the weird, vague, treacherous amphitheatre of poetic reputation. When most of the poems in this book appeared, American poetry was dominated by such trumpeters and maestri as Carl Sandburg, Vachel Lindsey, Edgar Lee Masters, and Edwin Arlington Robinson. It is unfair to join Robinson with the other poets, except in terms of the functioning of poetic reputation. Reputation is the point; the poets who seemed significant and big and what I believe is known as major have suffered the fate of huge balloons. Meanwhile such poets as Marianne Moore, Wallace Stevens, and William Carlos Williams have emerged through the strength of a genuineness which was perhaps the reason for their not being recognized at their true worth immediately. Ransom is another such author, and there is a moral for publishers in the persistence of his reputation. Some authors, good as well as bad, appear to think that they must publish a book every year, if the great beast which is the pubic is to remember and read them. Ransom has published perhaps six new poems, some of them his best ones, in the past twenty years. Meanwhile, despite the absence of renewal, his poems have remained important in the one truly indubitable way that poetry can remain important: namely, they have been read again and again by other poets and—purest of all laurels—they have been read by those who are beginning to write poetry, those who want to write poetry, and those who are trying to learn how to write poetry. This may seem a somewhat meager existence; but it is the only alternative, given literary curiosity in America, to not being read at all.

A strange instance of this modest triumph of genuiness occurred when, in 1935 in England, Geoffrey Grigson suddenly published a brief essay in praise of Ransom's poetry. The instance is strange in several ways. No new volume by Ransom had appeared, for one thing; and then, it has been clear in general that, were it not for the existence of T. S. Eliot, America to British literati would be virtually indistinguishable from Australia; and strange most of all because Grigson had labored in vain to make head or tail of modern American poetry, finding only that Frost was provincial, James Agee wrote as if he had no roof to his mouth, William Carlos Williams was bogus, and Wallace Stevens was a "stuffed goldfinch," "a Klee without rhythm"! Yet Grigson's comments on Ransom, however inconsistent with his other judgments, were very perceptive. He guessed that Ransom had studied Hardy, he said that "there was not much else in American poetry like Ransom," and that Ransom "defended himself by irony against an inclination to the pathetic," and that, in fine, Ransom's two books, *Chills and Fever*, and *Two Gentlemen in Bonds*, were "two of the most delightful collections published since the War." Not too much ought to be made of this praise, though it is always cheering

when American literature is not identified abroad with such authors as Steinbeck, Saroyan, Robinson Jeffers, and Carl Sandburg. For Grigson's remark that there was not much else in American poetry like Ransom is both true and false. It is true that the total effect of his poems is unlike that of any other poet. But nonetheless there is a significant resemblance to other poets so far as language and style are concerned, and the sum of this significant resemblance can perhaps best be stated by citing Wallace Stevens. Both poets make a like use of dandyism of surface, of irony, and of a mock-grand style. Here are samples which, so far as the texture of the style goes, might have been written by either poet:

When this yokel comes maundering,
Whetting his hacker,
I shall run before him,
Diffusing civilest odors
Out of geraniums and unsmelled flowers.
It will check him.
. . .
I placed a jar in Tennessee
And round it was, upon a hill.
It made the slovenly wilderness
Surround that hill.
. . .
If the lady hath any loveliness, let it die.
For being drunken with the steam of Cuban cigars,
I find no pungence in the odour of stars,
And all my music goes out of me on a sigh.
. . .
But now, by our perverse supposal,
There is a drift of fog on your mornings;
You in your peignoir, dainty at your orange cup,
Feel poising round the sunny room
Invisible evil, deprived and bold.
All day the clock will metronome
Your gallant fear; the needles clicking,
The heels detonating the stair's cavern.

The first two are excerpts from Stevens, and the second two are passages in Ransom. I have deliberately chosen samples in which there is a likeness of subject-matter to some of Stevens's best known poems. It is not, however, such a likeness which is important, but the way language is used and the attitude *toward* language. Both poets use the grand style with mockery and playfulness, and both poets correct the excess inherent in this mock grandiloquence by that use of the colloquial and the concrete which may seem to the future to be the most marked aspect of modern poetry. Of the two poets, Stevens has followed out the possibilities of this idiom with much greater intensity and consistency. But the irony in Stevens is defensive; he seems at times to be discounting or trimming the serious emotions with which he is concerned, as if he were suspicious of them. In Random, however, the irony is most often an expression of the very painfulness of the emotion:

The little cousin is dead, by foul subtraction,
A green bough from Virginia's aged tree,
And none of the country kin like the transaction,
Nor some of the world of outer dark, like me.

Here the wryness of tone accomplished by rhyming *subtraction* and *transaction* should serve as an instance of how the irony is part of the emotion, and not, as in Stevens, a kind of guard which surrounds it.

It is natural to speculate about this likeness in style, in attitude toward language, of the two poets. There can be no question of the influence of one poet upon the other, although, insofar as a period style may be said to be the source of the resemblance, it is true that there may be some common influence upon both. If one went through the files of *Poetry: A Magazine of Verse, The Smart Set,* and *The Dial,* one would come upon many poems—by such very different authors as Conrad Aiken, Maxwell Bodenheim, Donald Evans, and even Edna St. Vincent Millay!—in which the convention of the high poetic is used with irony. And there is even, I think, a resemblance to the exotic, foreign and bravura quality of the prose styles of H. L. Mencken and James Branch Cabell. But these resemblances, far from being a matter of literary influence, suggest a common situation which involves the whole human being, namely, the relationship of the author to the age. The way that the language is used would thus have as its fundamental cause the attitude of society to poetry and the consequent attitude of the poet to his art. When the poet is regarded as a strange, rare and abnormal being, it is natural that he should mock at the same time as he enjoys the language of the grand manner. Perhaps there is further illumination, in literary history which has not yet been written: the overstuffed upholstery which is the rhetoric of late Victorian poetry was rejected by the poets who began to write between 1910 and 1920. One has only to cite the concern with speech, direct statement, and concreteness which were the declared aims of the founders of the *vers libre* movement. Now if we suppose that poets like Stevens and Ransom were caught, so to speak, in the midst of this shift from rhetoric in the grand manner to the direct concreteness of (what was then) the new poetry, we have perhaps placed the kind of literary energy which is the source of their ironic styles and their resemblance to each other. The irony of their language can thus be attributed to the tension and conflict they felt with regard to the two conceptions of what poetry ought to be.

In "Philomela," a poem which has had the misfortune to be much anthologized so that, like a famous symphony, repetition has imposed a transient triteness upon it, Ransom deals directly with the fate of poetry in our time:

> Procne, Philomela, and Itylus,
> Your names are liquid, your improbable tale
> Is recited in the classic numbers of the nightingale.
> Ah, but our numbers are not felicitous,
> It goes not liquidly for us.
>
> . . .
>
> Up from the darkest wood where Philomela sat,
> Her fairy numbers issued. What then ailed me?
> My ears are called capacious but they failed me,
> Her classics registered a little flat!
> I rose and venomously spat.
>
> Philomela, Philomela, lover of song.
> I am in despair if we may make us worthy,
> A bantering breed sophistical and swarthy;
> Unto more beautiful, persistently more young,
> Thy fabulous provinces belong.

It is probably needless to suggest that to compare this poem with Keat's "Ode to The Nightingale" is to see the distance between the romantic and the modern poet. But since I have not quoted the entire poem, perhaps it is necessary to emphasize the fact that the poet's doubt of the nature of modern poetry—he has said in an unquoted stanza that he felt "sick of my dissonance"—is a mixed one. He is not entirely displeased that he belongs to "a bantering breed sophistical and swarthy," and if he feels that "our numbers are not felicitous" nor liquid, he also finds Philomela's classics "a little flat." Indeed there is a pleasure in the use of the language throughout which suggests that far from preferring felicitous and liquid numbers, the poet prefers to be able to write verses in which he can say that he "venomously spat," an instance of the kind of diction which the Romantic poet would be incapable of using, and which the Elizabethan dramatic poet found more and more necessary as he moved from the liquid and empty felicity of Spenser to the choppy and perception-burdened versification of Donne and Webster.

To return to the comparison between Ransom and Stevens, they are alike in their attitude toward language and their themes are often alike. But the ultimate direction is quite different. Stevens moves toward a contemplation of symbols and ideas abstracted from any time and place; and when in his recent poems he returns to the time and the place of the present, the present also becomes some kind of abstraction. Ransom on the other hand returns always to the relationship of human beings to each other and to the immediacy and particularity of existence. The human beings are present chiefly for the sake of declaring an attitude toward existence. Robert Penn Warren has pointed out that Ransom's characteristic form is "the little objective fable, with a kernel of drama." *Kernel* is exact, for it is hardly more than a kernel of drama. Neither the characters nor the drama are important for their own sake, as in many of the lyrics of Robinson and Eliot. It is the meaning of the fable which determines the place or rôle of all the other properties of the poem. And this meaning comes through so much by way of the tone of the poem,—a tone which is by turns playful, charming, gay, offhand, and sardonic—that the seriousness of the meaning and of the whole poem may easily be missed. Consider, for example, a poem such as "Conrad In Twilight":

> Conrad, Conrad, aren't you old
> To sit so late in your mouldy garden?
> And I think Conrad knows it well,
> Nursing his knees, too rheumy and cold
> To warm the wraith of a Forest of Arden.
>
> Neuralgia in the back of his neck,
> His lungs filling with such miasma,
> His feet dipping in leafage and muck:
> Conrad! you've forgotten asthma.
>
> Conrad's house has thick red walls
> And chips on Conrad's hearth are blazing,
> Slippers and pipe and tea are served,
> Butter and toast, Conrad, are pleasing!
> Still Conrad's back is not uncurved
> And here's an autumn on him, teasing.
>
> Autumn days in our section
> Are the most used-up thing on earth
> (Or in the waters under the earth)
> Having no more color nor predilection
> Than cornstalks too wet for the fire,
> A ribbon rotting on the byre,
> A man's face as weathered as straw
> By the summer's flare and winter's flaw.

Butter and toast, Conrad, are pleasing! How readily the careless reader may be put off by the seeming triviality of such a line, so that he misses its essential connection with the extraordinary last stanza and the theme of the body's decay and death over which this poem, like so many others by Ransom, agonizes. The prose quality of the last stanza, the shift in rhythm from the jingling with which the poem begins to the flat, direct statement of the last stanza, the significance of the image of "a ribbon rotting on the byre," the conclusiveness and the beauty of the last line (which is secured by means of assonance as well as by the visual and emotional connotations of "the summer's flare")—all of these qualities may be disregarded if the reader does not grasp the easy tone and jingling rhythm as a *preparation* for the last stanza.

As this poem is concerned with death, so the hard fact of death is the most frequent subject, and the reader encounters an astonishing number of funerals and corpses. (In one of his essays, Ransom remarks in passing that a man may go out of his mind if he thinks too much about death.) And where the conclusion is not as radical as that, there is frustration, disappointment, and despair. When the subject is not a dead boy or a dying lady, it is the impassable distress that lovers feel at the thought of death, as in "Vaunting Oak," where a lady "*instructed of much mortality*" cites a great oak as an instance of permanence and then, when the oak is struck, hears in the reverberance "like a funeral, a hollow tone." A mind instructed in mortality has a natural love of the body, and it is without sympathy for any denial of the body's beauty or actuality, a denial to which the mind is often tempted. Thus, in "The Equilibrists," two lovers who are separated by honor forever, are told that "great lovers lie in Hell," "they rend each other when they kiss," and "the pieces kiss again," while in Heaven there is not only no marriage, but the soul is bodiless; and the implication is that in this way Hell is preferable to Heaven. So, in another poem, the head is accused of seeking decapitation, of seeking "to play truant from the body bush," of traducing the flesh, but "Beauty is of body," the body's love is necessary to the head, and without the body's love the living world is colorless and empty. So too, in "Address to the Scholars of New England," we hear that

> There used to be debate of soul and body,
> The soul storming incontinent with shrew's tongue
> Against what natural brilliance body had loved

In the psychomachia of this poet, the character of the debate has reversed itself, the soul storms against itself for being in the least faithless to the body. Furthermore, to be faithful to the body and to love the body is to be aware of its degradation, its decay, and its death. Here again a detailed comparison with Stevens would be fruitful. I have in mind particularly Stevens's "Sunday Morning," and "The Emperor of Ice Cream": "Let be be finale of seem/The only Emperor is the Emperor of ice cream." And Ransom's best poem must be quoted as a whole, if one is to see how this concern with death can mount to a vision of life in which everything (from children and "the pretty kings of France" to a dressing-gown, buckberries in blue bowls, the "warning sibilance of pines" and "the heels detonating the stair's cavern") is seen in the cold, cloudy light of the fact of mortality:

PRELUDE TO AN EVENING

Do not enforce the tired wolf
Dragging his infected wound homeward
To sit tonight with the warm children
Naming the pretty kings of France.

The images of the invaded mind
Being as the monsters in the dreams
Of your most brief enchanted headful,
Suppose a miracle of confusion:

That dreamed and undreamt become each other
And mix the night and day of your mind;

And it does not matter your twice crying
From mouth unbeautied against the pillow

To avert the gun of the same old soldier;
For cry, cock-crow, or the iron bell
Can crack the sleep-sense of outrage,
Annihilate phantoms who were nothing.

But now, by our perverse supposal,
There is a drift of fog on your mornings;
You in your peignoir, dainty at your orange cup,
Feel poising round the sunny room

Invisible evil, deprived and bold.
All day the clock will metronome
Your gallant fear; the needles clicking,
The heels detonating the stair's cavern.

Freshening the water in the blue bowls
For the buckberries, with not all your love,
You shall be listening for the low wind,
The warning sibilance of pines.

You like a waning moon, and I accusing
Our too banded Eumenides,
While you pronounce Noes wanderingly
And smooth the heads of the hungry children.

CLEANTH BROOKS
"The Doric Delicacy"

Sewanee Review, July–September 1948, pp. 402–15

Modernist poetry is characterized by a complete revulsion against poetic diction. It has banished the *e'ens*, and *thou's*, the *pleasant leas*, and *soft gales*, and with them archaic diction in general. But the poetry of John Crowe Ransom, though its modernity is patent, makes constant use of archaic diction, some of it as quaintly antique as that of Spenser, whom Ben Jonson chided for having "writ no language." For example, in Ransom's verse the enemy "up clomb . . . in no airy towers"; "the rooster" is seen "footing the mould"; a melancholy young friar becomes a "lugubrious wight"; the poet can even frame such a salutation as "Sweet ladies, long may ye bloom, and toughly I hope ye may thole."

Ransom's use of the archaic, it scarcely need be said, is not Spenserian, either in method or effect: the ancient words are not chosen to poetize the matter; they are not amiably decorative; as Ransom employs them, they are absorbed into a special idiom of distinct character whose very principle is a kind of tough-minded modernity. Yet it is startling that the archaic occurs at all; and among the modern poets, the fact is almost unique. It is worth pondering, for it may indicate a way in which to engage the special quality of Ransom's work. And though this use of the archaic does not point back to the poetry of Spenser, there is one elder poet to whom it does point unmistakably: John Milton.

For Milton too devised an idiom which was at once highly personal and yet for his time distinctively modern; and in it he too incorporated elements of archaic diction such as one hardly finds in contemporaries like Donne or Denham or Marvell. We can, to be sure, isolate out of Milton's verse, Chaucerian forms arrived at perhaps *via* Spenser, but the total impact of the verse is not Spenserian. It is sharply contemporary. Most of all, it is distinctively Miltonic.

But I should hesitate to suggest this parallelism between Milton and Ransom if I did not feel that it was simply one item in a larger parallelism; and, in any case, I hesitate to raise the question of parallels without some rather precise qualifications.

The use of literary parallels is nowadays a somewhat discredited critical device, and justly so; for the matching of "parallels," like source hunting, has too often been pursued as a mechanical exercise. The statistics which it yields are usually quite barren. Yet, a comparison of the work of one poet with another can, on occasion, be illuminating—most of all perhaps when we have put away any preoccupation with borrowings and influences, and are content to use the one case merely to provide a perspective from which to view the other.

The minor poems of Milton seem to me to stand in some such relation to Ransom's poetry. Ransom's poetry enables one better to discern the Miltonic strategy, and the poems which Milton published in the 1645 volume can throw a good deal of light on *Chills and Fever* and *Two Gentlemen in Bonds.*

But having claimed so much for this relationship, I want to make doubly clear what I do *not* maintain: that there is any conscious imitation on Ransom's part. I have collected no specific "borrowings." So far as I know they do not exist. In any case, they are not to my purpose here.

Even the more general parallels between the two men are scarcely to my purpose, though I think that it may be interesting to mention a few of the more striking ones: their common "Protestantism," their learning, their sense of tradition and their insistence on maintaining the continuity of the tradition. The poetry of both men shows the deep impress of classical letters. (Ransom read "Greats" at Oxford.) Yet there is in both men something which at a first glance seems at variance with the suavity which we associate with a predominant training in humane letters: there is a kind of logical rigor, something of a penchant for positivism. It is not quite fair to say with Saurat that Milton is unhappy with all mysteries including the great Christian mysteries, and demands that everything be plain as a pikestaff. But there is in Milton what amounts to an inveterate rationalism; and there is a comparable quality in Ransom, as his interest in positivism, particularly as displayed in his critical volumes, indicates.

One is tempted to go on and name an even more curious parallel: Milton wrote, and Ransom has written, on theology. Ransom has wryly called his *God without Thunder* "home-brew theology," but it is a descriptive term which somewhat scandalously applies to *De Doctrina Christiana.* For Milton's book is a brilliant personal reordering of his own position rather than an ecumenical document, and, whatever Milton's intention, was scarcely calculated to win any more converts, had it been published, than the publication of *God without Thunder* actually did win.

But this parallel is probably too special and accidental to be significant. Better to return to the common trait of a highly personal idiom, a striking trait which has already been mentioned. In this quality Ransom certainly matches Milton. Someone has remarked that, if he found any three consecutive lines of Ransom scribbled on a scrap of paper on a desert island, he would have no difficulty in pronouncing them to be Ransom's. Milton's individual quality is almost as indelible; yet, as we know, it is won from a mélange of borrowings. Any one of Milton's poems is a tissue of allusions, semi-quotations, and echoes from the classic writers and the Elizabethans; but the borrowed matter is always digested and absorbed. The Miltonic poem is not a mosaic; it is an articulated whole; the tone is unified, individual, almost unique.

I have already forsworn source hunting in this examination of Ransom's poetry. But the nature of his characteristic fusion of the archaic and the contemporary, of the Latinized diction and the native idiom—the terms on which the fusion

is made, the tensions involved, the tone thereby established—an examination of such matters as these can tell us a good deal about the essential poetry of both Milton and Ransom.

In the case of Ransom, of course, the prevailing tone is ironic, and Ransom's consistent role as an ironist was brilliantly treated some years ago by Robert Penn Warren. With Ransom, one of the obvious functions of the Latinity and the hint of the archaic is to parody the grand manner and to establish the ironic tone which is the consistent tone of Ransom's verse. There is no need here to repeat Warren's discussion. In what follows I have something a little more special in mind: the examination of further qualities which are related to irony, but which transcend irony, being indeed common to Milton's minor poetry as well as to Ransom's.

It scarcely needs to be observed that Milton too is a witty poet, and nowhere more so than in his diction. Milton early gave up the metaphysical conceit, at least in the form in which we associate it with Donne. But, even in his latest poetry, he continued to make use of what I should call a submerged wit, and his more verbal wit (corresponding to the puns in Donne) is characteristically achieved by playing the Latin meaning of a word off against its developed English meaning. The earth, for example, becomes "this punctual spot" (Latin *punctum*, a dot); or "Hell saw / Heav'n ruining from Heav'n," i.e., Heaven sloughing off from Heaven as a ruin and Heaven falling (Latin *ruina*, a falling down). The witty quality is easily obscured by the academic habit of regarding these instances as merely the result of Milton's scholarship or pedantry. But when Milton has Heav'n ruin from Heav'n, or writes, of the fallen angels' rebellion, that God "tempted [their] attempt," there can be no question of the wit.

Much of Ransom's more verbal wit takes precisely this form; one can find half a dozen examples in a single poem. Consider, for example, his "Vaunting Oak." The anecdote around which the poem is built is slight. The girl walking with her lover, in her happiness, points to a great oak tree as a proper symbol of the endurance of their love. But her lover, with sorrowful irony, is forced to point out that the aged tree is hollow, already prepared to fall.

It is the Latinized diction (along with archaic diction and a rather formal patterning of sentence structure) which the poet uses to invest the anecdote with its special quality. The great tree, imagined as fallen, is described as "concumbent." Its massive bole (symbol of the eternal) rears up against the sky: "Only his *temporal* twigs are unsure of seat. . . ." The leaves flutter in the wind "in panic round the stem on which they are captive"—literally *held* (*captivus*) though the poet is glad to retain the English sense of *captive* also. That is, the leaves would flee in their panic if they were not held prisoners.

Thus far in the poem, the Latinisms have been used primarily for a kind of conscious grandiloquence, a kind of parody of the grand manner. But the instances that follow play meaning against meaning for witty ironical effects. The heart of the young girl has been "too young and mortally / Linked with an unbeliever of bitter blood." *Mortally* is darkly, ominously, but the word is presumably used also because the two are linked by marriage, irrevocably, "till death do them part." The girl finds in the great tree an "eminent witness of life"; *eminent*, of course, in the general sense of "signal" or "remarkable," but the specific Latin sense of *eminent* becomes a normal extension of the metaphor of the tree—Latin *eminens*, projecting, lofty. The great tree projects above the humbler "populace/Of daisies and yellow kinds," which are too ephemeral to serve as symbols for the perdurability of love.

Suddenly the poem shifts into the colloquial (though the

Latinized diction and formalized phrasing intermittently occur for ironic effect):

> And what but she fetch me up to the steep place
> Where the oak vaunted?

As they run up the steep hill the girl knows better than to make her boast among the ephemeral flowers of a season. But once arrived beneath the great tree, she murmurs

> "Established, you see him there! forever."

But the "unbeliever of bitter blood" cannot allow her to remain in her "pitiful error." He tests the tree:

> I knocked on his house loudly, a sorrowing lover . . .

At the hollow reverberation,

> "The old gentleman," I grieved, "holds gallantly,
> But before our joy shall have lapsed, even, will be
>   gone."

Up to this point the poem is a half playful, half wistful commentary on the frailty of human love. But the opening measures of the poem, even if we regard them at a first reading as an almost wicked parody on the grand style, have done something to universalize the experience. The little anecdote has been told against a background. The lover's original mockery of himself as an "unbeliever of bitter blood" now becomes more than playful. His challenging the oak is not trivial and special: it is typical. The highly personal little anecdote has thus been taken out of a merely personal context. When, therefore, he proceeds to knock more sternly, the tone of the poem modulates into a deeper and more serious note in which the grand manner, earlier parodied, is reasserted this time with full seriousness, so that the answering reverberation from the hollow tree can be justly called a "dolorous cry."

> I knocked more sternly, and his dolorous cry
> Boomed till its loud reverberance outsounded
> The singing of bees; or the coward birds that fly
>
> Otherwhere with their song when summer is sped,
> And if they stayed would perish miserably;
> Or the tears of a girl remembering her dread.

The poem achieves a proper climax and a powerful one as the boom from the hollow oak is made to swell into a great cry of lament which smothers every sound in the spring scene—the singing of bees, the calls of the birds and the sobbing of the girl. But if we are to express the poet's strategy in terms of diction, we have to say that the ironic use of the formal and pompous diction of the earlier lines of the poem has guaranteed and made possible the powerful and utterly serious use of "dolorous" and "reverberance" in the closing lines of the poem.

But the most important special characteristic which Ransom shares with Milton is what must be called, for want of a better term, aesthetic distance. Indeed, the poem just discussed provides an instance: it employs a considerable measure of aesthetic distance. The scene is given an almost formal quality; the reader is kept well back from the scene; characteristically, the "unbeliever" is not revealed as the "me" of the poem—the speaker—until the poem is half over.

With Milton, the measure of aesthetic distance is nearly always great. This aesthetic distance is not aloofness: the prim young puritan keeping his distance from the common world that lies about him. It is not to be characterized merely as a sense of form: Donne's "Canonization" is as firmly and as exquisitely "formed" as anything in Milton. (Both Donne and Milton at their best give us poetry in which form and content cannot be separated.) The quality to which I refer is not even to be defined as a high degree of formality, for whereas Milton

is rarely casual, he can be surely "informal" enough. He does not stand on his dignity in "L'Allegro" and "Il Penseroso."

Yet there is in all of Milton's work a large measure of aesthetic distance. The scene is framed, the stance of the observer is carefully implied, a sense of perspective is definitely, if quietly, indicated. Even in "L'Allegro" and "Il Penseroso" a certain detachment is always indicated, and it is this detachment as much as anything else that gives these poems their special flavor of coolness. Indeed, an inspection of Milton's earliest show piece, the "Nativity Hymn," will reveal that Milton's sense of aesthetic distance is already fully developed. The scene is panoramic—the whole world, quieted and stilled, is laid out beneath our gaze. We see the dove of peace descending through the successive spheres; and later, from a comparable vantage point, we are allowed to view the slinking away of pagan gods in Greece, in Syria, in Lybia, as the divine influence flows over the whole known world. Even at the end of the poem, we are not brought up to the manger to kneel with the poet. It is evidently from a distance that we see the whole scene, for it is a tableau conceived amply enough to include "Heaven's youngest teemed star" shining above the stable, "and all about the Courtly Stable, bright harnessed angels . . . in order serviceable."

I would not make too much of what may be thought an accidental quality of Milton's poetry, but I am convinced that it is not accidental. As a device it is closely related to the characteristic tone which is set and sustained in one after another of the minor poems. It is closely related to Milton's particular vision of reality—his characteristic way of "seeing" his world.

The measure of aesthetic distance in Ransom's poetry is thoroughly comparable to Milton's. It is controlled by the poet for his own effects, to be sure. But it is quite as pervasive as in Milton and as fundamental to Ransom's variations of tone. "Necrological" will furnish a nice and apposite example. The youthful friar who views the battlefield is quite removed from the issues. The battle is over, "the living all were gone," and the young friar himself as observer is withdrawn, at the end of the poem, lost in a "vast surmise," as still as the dead men themselves.

But this last example is rather special. The very theme of the poem is the remove at which the young friar stands from the issues of a torn and violent world. "Spectral Lovers" will provide a less specially weighted and therefore more cogent illustration of Ransom's charactersitic use of aesthetic distance.

> By night they haunted a thicket of April mist,
> Out of that black ground suddenly come to birth,
> Else angels lost in each other and fallen on earth.
> Lovers they knew they were, but why unclasped,
>   unkissed?
> Why should two lovers go frozen apart in fear?
> And yet they were, they were.

The lovers are spectral indeed: they are, as it were, made to materialize out of the mist. They "haunt" a thicket of April mist; it is as if they had suddenly come to birth out of that black ground; or else they are angels "fallen on earth," and perhaps fallen in that they are lost in each other. But they are spectral also in the sense that is to provide the torment described in the poem: their lack of grossness, the restrictions which they impose upon the flesh, their ideal quality.

A less tough-minded poet, a less ambitious and brilliant poet, would scarcely have dared to humanize and agonize these creatures of the mist. He would have left them a shade too ethereal, glimmering "white in the season's moon-gold

and amethyst." It is typical of Ransom that he should be able
to present them realistically.

Ransom presents the man even wittily:

And gesturing largely to the moon of Easter,
Mincing his steps and swishing the jubilant grass,
Beheading some field-flowers that had come to pass,
He had reduced his tributaries faster
Had not considerations pinched his heart
Unfitly for his art.

But if the realistic and witty description jars with the
spectral quality of the lovers, it would seem to jar also with the
uncolloquial and "literary" language that the lovers are made
to speak.

This for the woman:

Should the walls of her prison undefended yield
And open her treasure to the first clamorous knight?
"This is the mad moon, and shall I surrender all?
If he but ask it I shall."

This for the man:

"Blessed is he that taketh this richest of cities:
But it is so stainless the sack were a thousand pities.
This is that marble fortress not to be conquered,
Lest its white peace in the black flame turn to tinder
And an unutterable cinder."

The power of the contrasts and of the tensions which are
thus set up is obvious. The interesting question will be how, in
view of the violence of these tensions, the poem holds together
at all. The answer surely lies in the last stanza and the
perspective which it establishes.

The first line of this last stanza, "They passed me once in
April in the mist," pushes the whole scene back into a past
time. It does something more. This is the first time that the
"me" of the poem, the observer who speaks the poem, has been
mentioned. The speaker, then, is not one of the lovers. The
lovers have been described actually from the outside. The
calculated language which the lovers have spoken has been
imagined for them, since the words are not audible even to
each other. The formalized, almost ritual-like quality of their
action is thus accounted for. For the spectral lovers prove to be,
now that the vantage point of the speaker is established for us,
a construction evoked with pity, with understanding, with
irony, by the "me" of the last stanza, out of himself and out of
the two forms which have silently passed him in the mist.

It is much the same kind of effect that one gets at the end
of Milton's "Lycidas" when the "I" of the poem, he who has
spoken the passionate though formalized lament, suddenly is
reduced to a figure mentioned in the third person, the uncouth
swain whose thought is "eager," but who, in spite of his
confident declaration that Lycidas, like the day star, has risen
and now "flames in the forehead of the morning sky," himself
inhabits a workaday world in which suns rise and set and in
which now, at the end of his song, the actual sun has dropped
again "into the western bay."

I have said that the effect is much the same. Perhaps I
should say rather that the effect is comparable, for the device
as Milton uses it just reverses Ransom's: we conclude with a
figure in the third person rather than, as with Ransom, with a
first person, a "me" whom the spectral lovers have passed. But
the effect gained by the sudden establishment of a controlling
perspective is much the same.

I should like, however, to conclude these notes with a
later poem and a finer poem than those I have discussed. For
the large measure of aesthetic distance is a constant in
Ransom's poetry and can be illustrated from his later work as

easily as from his earliest. The poem I have in mind is the
beautiful "Prelude to an Evening." On the surface it is an
intensely personal poem with a husband speaking to a troubled
wife and addressing her directly as "you." The directness
suggested by the "you" is further enforced by his imagining her
in the domestic scene "dainty at [her] orange-cup," her "heels
detonating the stair's cavern," "freshening the water in the blue
bowls," "smoothing the heads of the hungry children," etc.

But the poem must not be allowed to work itself out as an
intensely personal poem, for managed so it would violate its
theme. If there were real closeness between the speaker and the
"you" to whom ostensibly he speaks the poem, the "drift of fog
on your mornings" would be dispelled. For her there would be
no "warning sibilance of pines."

The speaker of the "Prelude" apologizes wryly for himself
as the "tired wolf/Dragging his infected wound homeward."
But he has succeeded in infecting his mate, and for her the
"images of the invaded mind," because only hinted at, become
more monstrous than for him. This he knows, and the poem
is a delicate and tender account of her day as he imagines it
from his vantage point of guilt and tender concern. He can see
the "too banded Eumenides"; she cannot see them, but can
only sense them through their troubling effect upon him.

But the tenderness must not be permitted to cloud the
picture. Each detail must be registered with clean detachment
and with full realism if the experience presented is not to be
robbed of its significance. The details in their realism and in
their domesticity are faithfully rendered: her "mouth
unbeautied against the pillow" as she cries out in her sleep
from some nightmare; the "needles clicking" as she knits; her
abstracted air as she makes her "Noes but wanderingly" to the
questioning children.

All of this means, however, that the imagined scene must
be patterned, ordered in a particular perspective, "seen" by the
tired husband from his stance outside the room and outside the
context of a special day. He has said that it is by "our perverse
supposal" that the drift of fog has come upon her mornings; but
the re-created scene too is a "supposal," his supposal, his
imagined recreation of the scene, and it gains its intimacy and
its tenderness because it is "supposed" with clarity and detachment.

You in your peignoir, dainty at your orange-cup,
Feel poising round the sunny room
Invisible evil, deprived and bold.
All day the clock will metronome
Your gallant fear; the needles clicking,
The heels detonating the stair's cavern.

Freshening the water in the blue bowls
For the buckberries with not all your love,
You shall be listening for the low wind,
The warning sibilance of pines.

You like a waning moon, and I accusing
Our too banded Eumenides,
You shall make Noes but wanderingly,
Smoothing the heads of the hungry children.

Like so many of Ransom's finest poems, this poem is a
triumph of tone; and aesthetic distance is, of course, an aspect
of tone, a special ordering of the poet's attitude toward his
material, a liberation of the elected poem from the particular
and accidental emotions of the poet as man rather than as
artist.

Ransom's poems, I have suggested, are always ordered
very carefully in this fashion, just as Milton's are so ordered,
and it is this control of perspective that constitutes Ransom's

special claim to a kind of classical decorum. It is a claim well worth pressing. It is a quality which is rare enough in modern poetry and for the want of which the modern poets have suffered, and, one predicts, are likely to suffer more.

Be that as it may, there is in modern poetry nothing else quite like this quality of Ransom's. Wallace Stevens, our other special master of perspective and of tone, is perhaps a comparable figure, but his general method is quite other than Ransom's and perhaps much more special and limited than Ransom's. In any case, our age has produced nowhere else a poetry so fine grained, so agate hard, so tough minded as that contained in *Chills and Fever* and *Two Gentlemen in Bonds*. It wears well. After some twenty-odd years, it has worn very well indeed, outlasting verse that once appeared a great deal more exciting or profound. It belongs to that small body of verse which, one predicts, will increasingly come to be regarded as the truly distinguished poetry of the Twentieth Century.

ROBERT PENN WARREN
From "Notes on the Poetry of John Crowe Ransom at His Eightieth Birthday"
Kenyon Review, 1968, pp. 319–23

Notes: That is all I am prepared to give, and the fact is strange. Strange, because since the first issue of the *Fugitive* magazine I have read, I think, every poem of John Crowe Ransom as it appeared, sometimes even in manuscript, and have memorized many of them. Once, some thirty-five years ago, I wrote an essay about them, which, after two or three years, was published. Between that time and this, I have looked back over it only once, and with distaste. Looking back at it again, I am confirmed in an old feeling that the piece did not really indicate the deeper reality I had sensed in the poems. Now that I am invited, for a happy occasion, to write something on John Crowe Ransom, I find that, even today, I do not have the right topic, the name of the *thing*, whatever the thing may be, that has held me year after year.

There was, however, a period—when I was nineteen to twenty-five years old—when I rebelled against that power exercised by the poems—and exercised, so unwittingly I may add, by their author, It was not merely that I, overwhelmed by the new poetry of Eliot, was puzzled and confused by the coldness of Ransom toward it: puzzled, confused, and at moments outraged, chiefly because of my passion for Ransom's poetry. Nor was it merely that as I blundered into my own poetry I had to fight off, not always successfully, what William Yandell Elliott, one of the Fugitives, had called "Johnny's bag of tricks," as well as T. S. Eliot's. Nor merely that the very coherence, intellectual and emotional, of Ransom's poetry was a painful reproach to my own attempts at poetry, which fact I blindly resented. My rebelliousness stemmed, I now suppose, from a resentment against the cast of the author's mind, a mind which made such graceful gestures, enunciated such deep truths, and exercised such fascinating authority for me, even as I knew, in despair, that I could never emulate that grace, live by those truths, nor accept such authority. My own nature was too volatile, awkward, and angry, and all the harmony and control embodied in the poetry and the man seemed to undercut life-possibility for me and deny life-need.

But the rebellion was imperfect. Even then I was still immersed in the poetry, and was gradually coming to under-

stand that what continued to move me was not "Johnny's bag of tricks," and to understand, however dimly, that the pervasive theme of the poetry, even the very existence of the poetry, involved, in all its harmony, the disharmonies of life, mastering them without denying them. The writing of that old essay signified, I should now hazard, the end of the imperfect, and loving, rebellion against the poetry, as well as of the other more unconscious rebellion. By that time no longer a student, but a colleague, even if a very junior one, and a friend, if a very overawed one, I discovered in that house a characteristic gaiety, and easy gallantry against the difficulties of life, a spirit of play which pervaded even the most serious concerns, and which merged, I am tempted to say, with a sense of ritual. All this was a revelation to me, who had lived by the excitements and violences of life, rather than by acceptances; and was, no doubt, behind that fumbling little essay.

Now, looking again at the old essay, it occurs to me that what was wrong with it was a mechanical quality. I was so concerned to define a focal origin for the poetry that I sometimes confused the idea of such a focal origin with that of a formula. I was trying to find a mere pattern of ideas when I should rather have been trying to find a characteristic movement of mind— of being. My desire to fix on such a focal origin for Ransom's poetry sprang not merely from the youthful notion that there is a master-key for everything, a magic word, but also from a need to place Ransom's poetry, which I had found indispensable to me, in relation to the Pound-Eliot strain, which dominated the age into which I had been born. And the need to do this may have had its roots in the fact that I myself, in trying to write poetry, and in thinking about poetry, was torn between the Pound-Eliot strain and another possibility, shadowy to me and undefined, which, though not like Ransom's poetry, then seemed nearer to it, in some way, than to anything else.

I do not now want to rewrite that old essay, but what I then thought I had found was that the irony of Ransom's—his parables of men without sense of direction, of men who, incomplete, could not fathom nor perform their natures—was derived from the same fragmented world as were *The Waste Land*, the *Cantos*, and *The Sound and the Fury*. In other words, if Ransom did not, like Pound, Eliot, and Faulkner, dramatize a world suffering from the then famous "dissociation of sensibility," and devise an allusive, fragmented style to illustrate the malaise, he at least offered, in his sequential narratives and orderly style, a diagnosis of that malaise as his subject, and found in the malaise the grounding of his characteristic irony of "chills and fever."

When I showed him the essay, he read it with attention, and then, with charming but (I thought) irrelevant friendliness, asked if he couldn't have his middle name back. The title, by some slip, was "The Irony of John Ransom"—and so "Crowe" got put back where it belonged. After some thought, he made a remark about hoping that his poems were worthy of the attention lavished upon them. Then he got up, strolled over to a window of his office, looked out for an instant, and as a kind of afterthought added that, as far as "dissociation of sensibility" in the modern world went, he was rather inclined to think that man was, naturally, born as a kind of "oscillating mechanism." That was all.

The subject of my essay was, it seemed, politely declining to be saved for modernity. That much must have penetrated my density as I walked away with the manuscript in my pocket. He was saying, it occurred to me years later, that he was not writing about modern man, but about man. If modern man came in as a case in point (as modern man most surely did), it was under that rubric.

But, meanwhile, I kept remembering the phrase "oscillating mechanism." So that was what he saw as the underlying fact of his poems, the source of his style! With that in mind, I reread—and now reread—that first strange little volume, *Poems about God*, which appeared in 1919 by a "1st Lieut. Field Artillery, AEF." There are, in fact, several strange things about it.

The earliest piece in the book, "Sunset," was written in May 1916, and one strange thing here is that the author, who was twenty-eight, had never written a poem before. Another strange thing is that the poem is, in its own awkward way, concerned with the theme that was to prove central to Ransom's poetry: the haunting dualism in man's experience. Most bookish young men try their hand early at poetry. Why hadn't this one? Most poets have to work from poem to poem over a considerable length of time toward their central concern, have to discover it through their poetry. Why could this tardy poet hit so soon on his? There are, of course, no final answers to such questions, but we must risk some.

Here we must first hazard an answer to the second question, and that would be that Ransom had been living, consciously and unconsciously, with that central concern, in one form or another, for a long time and with great intensity. In other words, the underly theme did not need to be discovered; it must have been there, and urgently.

To come to the first question, we may surmise that Ransom turned to poetry, even so tardily, because there was more than intellectual urgency involved. And here, as an aside, he had never written any prose either, beyond that required by the routines of his life. If the theme of the poetry had been, we can argue, of merely intellectual urgency, it would seem logical, in the light of his special philosophical training and interest, to suppose that he would have approached the issue by way of prose speculation. In any case, the issue was not only there, it was not of merely intellectual and professional concern; it had been, and was being, lived into. It was, in fact, life, and, as life, not ever to be totally defined intellectually, a polarity of life having many manifestations, constantly changing its terms, a split in the human possibility, a tension among desires, among obligations, among pieties. From this the poetry would spring, because poetry gave the only way to deal with the issue.

Not that the first poem, or any poem ever to come, could resolve the issue. It could not even, in the end, name it. It could merely give one dramatic manifestation of the unnamed—or even unnamable—root-issue, just as subsequent poems could merely multiply and refine new manifestations. As Ransom once remarked, there is always something "inconclusive" about the endings of his poems—and how could it be otherwise if the very theme is one of ambiguities, of "oscillation," of a split in the self as well as in the world? If, however, the poetry could afford no conclusions, it could afford a release and a mastery through objectification; and afford, through the mounting variety of instances, the sense that the issue was not special to the self but built into the human condition, and could therefore more readily, in its commonness and inevitability, be confronted.

MILLER WILLIAMS
"What Grey Man Is This? Irony"
The Poetry of John Crowe Ransom
1972, pp. 29–38

A sense of irony is the abiding realization that every human statement contains its own contradiction and that every human act contains the seeds of its own defeat. From this comes the realization that there are no pure truths and that there are no pure men or pure women or pure causes or pure motives. There is neither the simply holy nor the simply unholy. John Calvin and Camus alike understood that man's very lot is one of awful irony, as he finds his rational self facing a nonrational universe, his hungering and homesick soul facing an incomprehensible and indifferent God. This is the terrible wisdom which moves perceptibly through Ransom's poems.

He gives irony its most dramatic expression in the polarity of statement. In "Armageddon" it is Christ who is bloodthirsty, while Satan tells us that he is weary of war and prefers the fellowship of good talk: the "Old Man Playing with Children" finds that he and the child are "equally boy and boy"; "The Equilibrists" are beautiful in their eternally unconsummated and undenied love; the Friar in "Necrological" becomes as one with the slain soldiers.

The several forms of irony are working all at once in Ransom's poems. What we have called simple irony, the tension between things as they seem to be or ought to be and things as they are, or between what is expected and what comes to be, is built into the structure of the last poem mentioned, as it is present also when we sense that "Judith of Bethulia" has a strange and permanent interest in the severed head of the enemy chieftain and might not have gone reluctant to the orgy.

It is present in "Vaunting Oak," when the tree—the "symbol of love"—responds to a knocking with a hollow and funerallike tone and in another way when we realize that the poem "Dead Boy" is not about the boy dead, the "first-fruits," but the tree's "sapless limbs, the shorn and shaken."

It is present, spelling out still something of Camus' absurdity, in the confrontation of Ransom's people and the real world they can neither ignore nor live in. This duality is everywhere in the poems, as are the conventionally treated ironic situations, the death of the young, the inefficacy of innocence, the self-destroying essence of sexual love.

All this is structural, but its effectiveness—as in the case of equilibrium-tension—depends on the texture, on the sense of irony which is woven into it.

Socratic irony, by which we come painfully to knowledge through ignorance, works through a number of the poems, notably "Necrological," where the good Friar stumbles his way through platitudes and stock responses for the questions implicit in the carnage he sees around him and comes thereby to a recognition of the inadequacy of his ready answers and then to a final identification with the dead, who, in the most terrible irony, are "solicited" with "sweet cries" by the "kites of Heaven." And working through all of the poems is what Wasserman[1] has called Schlegelian irony, the revelation of the poet's subjective self through the objectivity of his work.

This is no more true of Ransom's poetry than it is of any serious work, poetry or fiction, except that Ransom contrives (and the term here is not pejorative)—to invest his poems with an objectivity in such a way that we are able to see the contrivance function more clearly—perhaps the word is more dramatically—than we can with most writers. We can see him when he decides to step back from his subject, and we can watch him move in again; we know when, and he intends for us to see by what means, he becomes disengaged or disengages us the readers. We know at once when he wants to move himself into the poem; we sense his personal feelings in the closing of "Janet Waking" as strongly as they are spelled out in the closing lines of "The Equilibrists." But these feelings are betrayed as well in the cooler passages of all three poems by the very objectivity which the poet builds to keep the passions out of the picture.

Through all this there still operates the pervasive irony of tone, the tension between sentiment inherent in the situation and the apparent inappropriateness of the language, whether it is the Latinate language of objectivity or the language of wit. He "combines an amusing texture," as George Williamson puts it, "with serious emotion."[2] He treats the potentially maudlin with a classical language, a classical detachment. Louis Rubin sees "The underlying mood of Ransom's poetry" as "terror and savagery masked by urbanity; the tension of a violent content described in bloodless language."[3] In the use of wit—in "Captain Carpenter," for instance, or even "Piazza Piece"—the amusing, almost comical pose balances the tendency of the subject to be overintent, to take itself too seriously, to be puffed up, pretentious.

This is the peril of many of the themes to which Ransom is drawn. Few poets would approach, with much hope of success, stories about a little girl whose pet chicken has died; about a woman whose lovely flowers have been cut down by a storm; about a little dead boy; about a dead girl whose geese miss her when she has gone. The poetry of Ransom is—more so even than the poetry of his companions in the New Criticism—informed by the attitude evident here, a strongly and consistently ironic view of the world. It invests the best of his work with credibility and with that strange quality of disengaged compassion which we have come to recognize as a part of his signature. There is love, naked but sufficiently distant, and there is grandeur and majesty, real and full of honor but crowned by wit: the detachment which Bradbury has called "the enabling act of poetry."[4] In the two poems which follow, perhaps as well as in any of Ransom's work, we can see the act of detachment as the enabling act by which the poet reveals his subjective self in the carefully objective line.

JANET WAKING

Beautifully Janet slept
Till it was deeply morning. She woke then
And thought about her dainty-feathered hen,
To see how it had kept.

One kiss she gave her mother.
Only a small one gave she to her daddy
Who would have kissed each curl of his shining baby;
No kiss at all for her brother.

"Old Chucky, old Chucky!" she cried,
Running across the world upon the grass
To Chucky's house, and listening. But alas,
Her Chucky had died.

It was a transmogrifying bee
Came droning down on Chucky's old bald head
And sat and put the poison. It scarcely bled,
But how exceedingly

And purply did the knot
Swell with the venom and communicate
Its rigor! Now the poor comb stood up straight
But Chucky did not.

So there was Janet
Kneeling on the wet grass, crying her brown hen
(Translated far beyond the daughters of men)
To rise and walk upon it.

And weeping fast as she had breath
Janet implored us, "Wake her from her sleep!"
And would not be instructed in how deep
Was the forgetful kingdom of death.

DEAD BOY

The little cousin is dead, by foul subtraction,
A green bough from Virginia's aged tree,
And none of the country kin like the transaction,
Nor some of the world of outer dark, like me.

A boy not beautiful, nor good, nor clever,
A black cloud full of storms too hot for keeping,
A sword beneath his mother's heart—yet never
Woman bewept her babe as this is weeping.

A pig with a pasty face, so I had said,
Squealing for cookies, kinned by poor pretense
With a noble house. But the little man quite dead,
I see the forbears' antique lineaments.

The elder men have strode by the box of death
To the wide flag porch, and muttering low send
  round
The bruit of the day, O friendly waste of breath!
Their hearts are hurt with a deep dynastic wound.

He was pale and little, the foolish neighbors say;
The first-fruits, saith the Preacher, the Lord hath
  taken;
But this was the old tree's late branch wrenched
  away,
Grieving the sapless limbs, the shorn and shaken.

The "little cousin," as dangerous an opening as the "little body" of John Whiteside's daughter, is removed to the right distance by the introduction of an apparently out-of-place term with connotations far from the *ambiente* of the poem. "Foul subtraction" suggests a transaction and carries the sense that such dying, albeit unpleasant, is not outside the realm of the day-to-day business of this world. It is a world, after all, which cares little for the concerns of man. This is one of Ransom's most effective uses of Latinate terms with deliberate reference to the root meaning, a practice which allows him to speak with a precision not possible in the modern sense of the words and at the same time with a remarkable ambiguity.

He takes us to the deeper meaning, the almost lost meaning, of the word, which now to our ears acts as a connotation of the word, so that technical and objective as the terms are, they become in Ransom's line three-dimensional. "Subraction" is a drawing from under; "transaction" is a carrying across. This last, especially since it is followed by the "world of outer dark," puts us in mind of the River Styx, and we are in a context at once more classical, more distant, and more noble than we were before.

The irony of the poem is not found primarily in the tension between the family's status and the observation that the boy was "a pig with a pasty face" nor in the pull between the seriousness of the subject and the tone of the language. It is at least half in the realization we must be drawn to that, if the boy had lived, the dynasty would probably not have survived with him. Antique, indeed, are the forbears' lineaments.

More often than not, the ironic view Ransom takes of the world, which gives rise to the equilibrium-forces in the poems, is itself born of Ransom's concern with the "dissociation of sensibility," Eliot's term applied by Warren to the poetry of Ransom a generation ago. [5]

Ransom tells us that very early in his life he had come to distrust abstraction. From this continuing and finally rationalized distrust has come much of the concreteness of his images, the reluctance to philosophize in the poems, and his advocacy of the ontological approach to criticism. We know that in Ransom's view abstraction brings man to nothing, addressing itself as it must to the mean, the typical. As the idea of a chair must include all chairs, it can describe no chair in particular. Ransom is interested in *particular* chairs, for it is the particular and concrete to which we react with feeling, that insinuates itself into our memories as part of an experience past, or that we see, touch, fall out of or bump into as part of an experience. For the senses the abstract chair does not exist. It is not a part of those particularities with which God has built the world, but instead is a part of man's attempt to dominate that world. It is useless to the poet.

Furthermore, it is dangerous to employ abstractions. We can learn so effectively to abstract, to generalize, to intellectualize, that we are no longer able to respond intuitively to the first experience; we give it over to the head, which makes fact always subject to abstract consideration and disintegrates the concrete and immediate thing there before us. Experience as contact with the world, through the senses, becomes impossible.

The mind which lives on abstraction and the mind which hunts out the concrete are working at cross-purposes; if they ever meet, it is in collision. Summing up Ransom's thinking, Louise Cowan puts it this way: "The inner content of his poetry derives . . . from the very core of human existence, which . . . is shaken by the two antithetical attitudes: the scientific and philosophic desire to possess and control and the religious and aesthetic urge to contemplate and love." [6] It has not been put better.

But however the conflict is seen, the body has—as Ransom might say—capitulated. Science, or the scientific myth, has given force and direction to abstraction as a way of life, and man has learned—has been urged—to intellectualize his passions.

If Ransom would have had it otherwise, he does not tell us that the head should not function but that it should not function as a thing unto itself, apart from the sensate flesh and dominant over it. It is the dissociation which Ransom abhors; ironically, that separation of parts which requires the balance we would not need if our parts were not apart. It is this which turns his mind to equilibria, to polarities.

In "Painted Head" he mourns the decapitation of man, who can no longer think and feel as one thing, can no longer hold a fact and its idea together, cannot decide whether he wants to exult in the world or manipulate it; man who is forever tripping over his own head:

> By dark severance the apparition head
> Smiles from the air a capital on no
> Column or a Platonic perhaps head
> On a canvas sky depending from nothing;
>
> Stirs up an old illusion of grandeur
> By tickling the instinct of heads to be
> Absolute and to try decapitation
> And to play truant from the body bush;
>
> But too happy and beautiful for those sorts
> Of head (homekeeping heads are happiest)
> Discovers maybe thirty unwidowed years
> Of not dishonoring the faithful stem;

> Is nameless and has authored for the evil
> Historian headhunters neither book
> Nor state and is therefore distinct from tart
> Heads with crowns and guilty gallery heads;
>
> Wherefore the extravagant device of art
> Unhousing by abstraction this once head
> Was capital irony by a loving hand
> That knew the no treason of a head like this;
>
> Makes repentance in an unlovely head
> For having vinegarly traduced the flesh
> Till, the hurt flesh recusing, the hard egg
> Is shrunken to its own deathlike surface;
>
> And an image thus. The body bears the head
> (So hardly one they terribly are two)
> Feeds and obeys and unto please what end?
> Not to the glory of tyrant head but to
>
> The estate of body. Beauty is of body.
> The flesh contouring shallowly on a head
> Is a rock-garden needing body's love
> And best bodiness to colorify
>
> The big blue birds sitting and sea-shell flats
> And caves, and on the iron acropolis
> To spread the hyacinthine hair and rear
> The olive garden for the nightingales.

Science is handmaiden to the arts, or better be, he says, then shifts the metaphor to suggest a deeper relationship: the humanities give science its soul, without which science is a monster.

As large as Ransom's concern for the dehumanizing effect of abstraction, growing partly out of that and manifesting itself in every poem, woven through every texture, is the ironic view. It is as natural to Ransom's mind, surely, as any fury. It is the voice of the stoic, the quality of the poet, And he says so in a statement which comes close to being a personal *ars poetica*.

AGITATO MA NON TROPPO

> This is what the man said,
> Insisting, standing on his head.
>
> Yes, I have come to grief,
> It was not furtive like a thief,
> And must not be blown up beyond belief.
>
> They know I have no bittern by the lake
> To cry it up and down the brake,
> And nothing since has been like Dante's fury
> For Beatrice who was not his to bury,
> Except, if the younger heart faltered, they may know
> How Shelley's throbbing reed sang tremolo.
>
> They say, "He puts a fix upon his mind
> And hears at bedside or in the moaning wind
> The rumor of Death; yet he can't mount one tear
> But stalks with holy calm beside the terrible bier."
>
> Lest we wreck upon a reef,
> I go according to another brief,
> Against their killing blasts of grief.
>
> My head, outposted promontoried chief,
> Frowned, and elected me to the common grief,
> By whose poor pities I'm shaken, but not as a leaf.

Here is grief understated; something on the poet's mind, told but muted, a story played out across a field at dusk, or woven into a tapestry. He is shaken, but not much. In the poem as in the man, in the rational humanist who dislikes equally the extreme show of pleasure or the blatant display of grief, this is the way it has to be. It is the world as Ransom would have it, and it is the world his characters dwell in.

Notes

1. G. R. Wasserman, "The Irony of John Crowe Ransom" *The University of Kansas City Review*, XXIII, No. 2 (Dec. 1956), 151–160.
2. George Williamson, "Donne and the Poetry of Today," *A Garland for John Donne*, ed. by Theodore Spencer (Cambridge, Mass., 1931).
3. Louis D. Rubin, Jr., "John Ransom's Cruel Battle," *Shenandoah*, IX (Winter 1958), pp. 23–25.
4. John M. Bradbury, "Ransom as Poet," *Accent*, XI (Winter 1951) 45–47.
5. Robert Penn Warren, "John Crowe Ransom: A Study in Irony," *The Virginia Quarterly Review*, XI, No. 1 (Jan., 1935), 93–112.
6. *The Fugitive Group: A Literary History*, Louisiana State University (Baton Rouge, 1959), p. 235.

MARJORIE KINNAN RAWLINGS

1896–1953

Marjorie Kinnan Rawlings was born August 8, 1896, in Washington, D.C., to Arthur Frank Kinnan and Ida May (née Traphagen) Kinnan. She showed interest in writing as a six-year-old, and her parents encouraged her; at eleven she won a two-dollar prize for a story published in the *Washington Post*. Her father, to whom Rawlings was close, died when she was seventeen.

Rawlings attended the University of Wisconsin, where she studied under the poet William Ellery Leonard, receiving her B.A. in 1918. She married fellow writer Charles A. Rawlings in 1919, and for the next several years the couple supported themselves through newspaper writing in New York while attempting unsuccessfully to sell fiction.

In 1928 Rawlings and her husband took a vacation to Florida, and were so taken with the climate and countryside that they sold everything they had and bought a seventy-two-acre farm and orange grove at Cross Creek, Florida. Rawlings lived there for the next several years, giving all of her time to fiction. She sold her first story, "Cracker Chidlings," to *Scribner's Magazine* in 1930, and "Jacob's Ladder" later the same year; the latter story attracted the attention of Maxwell Perkins, who became her friend and editor.

Charles and Majorie Rawlings were divorced in 1933, and Marjorie stayed on alone at Cross Creek. Her story "Gal Young Un" won first prize in the O. Henry Memorial Award in 1932, and her first novel, *South Moon Under*, was published the same year to moderate critical acclaim. Her second novel, *Golden Apples* (1935), was less well received; but her third, *The Yearling*, with its simple and painful story of a twelve-year-old boy on the threshold of maturity, caught between an idyllic childhood and the necessity to face unpleasant reality, struck a powerful chord with the readership of the time. It won the Pulitzer Prize for fiction in 1939 and established her reputation. It remains a classic of children's literature, and, despite the excellence of many of Rawlings's short stories, *The Yearling* is almost wholly responsible for her place in American literature today.

In 1940 Rawlings published her short-story collection *When the Whippoorwill*; the next year she married restaurant owner Norton Sanford Baskin. She published *Cross Creek*, a series of autobiographical essays, in 1942. Though not fiction, the book contains some of her best descriptions of places and characters.

Rawlings's last novel, *The Sojourner*, was published in 1953; she died later that year of a cerebral hemorrhage at the age of fifty-seven. A posthumous book written for children, *The Secret River*, was published in 1955.

Writing fiction for adults about a child in a child's world is a delicately difficult literary undertaking. Too many writers attempt it. Most of them fail. Perhaps a major reason for the failures is that most such stories either are frankly autobiographical or become so despite the author's desperate struggles. Leaning wistfully back into the mind and person of the child he thinks he was, the writer produces a character made up of his own hurts and nostalgias, of impossibly mature and knowing afterthoughts, of his sad desire to think that, had not life so strangely buffeted him, he would have been all the great and beautiful things his infant self must surely have contained. The results are usually garbled amateur psychiatric tracts, and very rarely literature.

Majorie Kinnan Rawlings has succeeded where so many have failed, and *The Yearling* is a distinguished book. Her Jody Baxter lives, a person in himself, within the boundaries of his own years and his own world. One-third intuition, one-third knowledge, one-third perception, the boy moves through the Florida river country, and the chronicle of his year is unforgettably written. The Baxters scratch subsistence from an 'island' clearing in the swamps. Jody sees those swamps, the animals that live in them, the dry weather and the flood weeks, the flicker in the grass which is a snake and the rustle in the woods which is a bear, without self-consciousness, naked of legend.

Even a Thoreau cannot report on the world outdoors as a child might. The naturalist sees only those things which concern his informed eye. To a child the barn and the woodshed are as much a part of the natural workable landscape as the lizard under the log. Mrs. Rawlings has done a small miracle in that she knows this, never stops to interpret, never once steps outside Jody's perceptions, never mars her great skill by pausing to explain. She has captured a child's time sense, in which everything lasts forever and the change of season takes him always unawares.

The year of Jody's life which *The Yearling* gives us is the one during which the boy passes from childhood to adolescence. One spring, when the book opens, he builds himself a fluttermill, which is a wonder and a secret delight. The next spring, when the book closes, he builds himself a fluttermill, and sees it only as a foolish 'play-dolly' from which he can draw no comfort for his growing pains. During that year he has owned the pet his loneliness craved for, has adored and sheltered it, and seen it killed by the just and inexorable law of the poor, who dare not harbor any luxury which threatens their slender food supply. The boy's feeling for his fawn is as superbly understood a piece of writing as any animal-human relationship in literature.

The Yearling is never sentimental, never mawkish. Set in a period shortly after the Civil War, in a little-known part of the United States, it gets its effects without documentation or quaintness. The sort of Americans with whom the book deals would be as easy in the presence of Boone, Lincoln, or Mark Twain as they would be abashed by William Faulkner's tortured characters. Jody's parents and their neighbors are realists. Food is where you grow and hunt it, water where you dig it, God in individual behavior. The book smells of sweat and wind, rain and parching corn, wood fires and herb brews, courage and clean despair. It is as American as the Mississippi. And it is emphatically not this month's 'great American novel.' It is a fine and quiet book, to be read and read again, standing for unhysterical judgment on its own earth-planted feet. —FRANCES WOODWARD, *At*, June 1938

I've been a straight fan for Marjorie Rawlings ever since I read "Benny and the Bird Dogs," the second story in ⟨When the Whippoorwill⟩. It is one of the most wide-open and gusty things you ever read, and funny as hell. Benny had made some money selling gopher holes to Yankees during the boom, bought him a Model-T and seven pied bird dogs to sit in the back seat as he tore up the roads, cutting the fool. He taught them to sit in seven rocking-chairs on the front porch too, and rock. "Bird dogs is natural to have around," his wife complained. "I was raised to bird dogs. But it ain't natural for 'em to rock in rocking-chairs. There's so terrible many of them, and when they put in the night on the porch laying in the rocking-chairs and rocking, I don't close my eyes for the fuss." It took his wife the length of the story and almost a lifetime to find that men were like varmints and you should pay them no mind—and that, as much as anything else, is what the story is about, though like all Mrs. Rawlings' stories it also manages to be about everything.

"Varmints" is another story to put with the bird dogs, and there is some amusing and fascinating lore in "Alligators," and "A Plumb Clare Conscience." I like Mrs. Rawlings' more easy and robust moods better than what you might call her prize moods—more pathetic, more monotonous, as in *The Yearling*, for example, and "Gal Young 'Un," which is included here. And in a piece like *Jacob's Ladder*, which runs almost eighty pages of one defeat after another, the disadvantages in fiction of a restricted region and restricted simple minds show fairly: after too short a while there is nothing for the characters to do but the same things over.

But Mrs. Rawlings needn't be typed as a humorist, as you will see from her short direct pieces: "The Enemy," "A Crop of Beans," "The Pardon." Her stories from inland-Florida life are written out of a full heart and understanding of her people;

however odd and vanishing as types, their trouble is universal and they are both vivid and easily knowable. The writing has fine dialogue and pictures, and the story-teller's way. Taking one with another, this collection places Marjorie Rawlings among the first ten American story writers today.—OTIS FERGUSON, "They Still Tell Stories," *NR*, May 20, 1940, pp. 679–80

The earth will survive bankers and any system of government, capitalistic, fascist or bolshevist. The earth will even survive anarchy." Now that's fine, just the kind of shot in the arm we all need today. And barring some rude cosmic shakeup it is a forecast to bet on, perhaps to live by—if you can live by the kind of earthy mysticism that muddies the five senses and good sense too. The quotation is from Majorie Kinnan Rawlings' *Cross Creek*, a book I've read twice within a week and both times with a mixture of pleasure and irritation. The pleasure may be derived from nearly every page, because Miss Rawlings as a writer is above all a fine workman and careful writing comes high these days. But the irritation is what finally sticks and it comes, as it so often does with Steinbeck, from the realization that Miss Rawlings is getting by on talent rather than stature.

Cross Creek is her informal, first-person account of the tiny Florida community where she lives, writes and works a combination subsistence farm and orange grove. If you know *The Yearling*, the locale will be home. If not, you will have your bearings soon enough. For Miss Rawlings is at her very best in creating a sense of place. She is primarily an observer and along with her fine eye and sound ear she has the patience to hunt for the perfect recording word or phrase. This book is best when Miss Rawlings is describing the lush Florida countryside, the local vegetation and wild life. She can, to be sure, find more beauty that stabs the heart than exists in nature for most readers; but these descriptive passages are clearly superior to anything of the sort written by an American in many years.

What is disturbing in *Cross Creek* is Miss Rawlings' placid acceptance of things as they come, a readiness to accept the status quo in life which, given her streak of mysticism, brings her pretty close to the ivory-tower girls. If Miss Rawlings were just a nice lady nature-writer, the point wouldn't be worth bringing up. But her interest in people and in the twenty-four hours a day business of living is enormous; at least half of her book is about her neighbors, Negroes and whites, and there are certain conclusions implicit in her judgments. One is that character and dignity are somehow aristocratic heirlooms. And once blessed with these, a man or woman may get urbanely through life without being nicked too much. Miss Rawlings is gracious enough to concede that even a Negro might thus get by, even though, at Cross Creek, his relationship to white men is definitely that of servant to master. That too has come to seem as it should be and one of the most annoying things in the book is the complacent but persistent emergence of a G⟨one⟩ W⟨ith⟩ T⟨he⟩ W⟨ind⟩ attitude toward the Negro.

But in the end, of course, such matters are forgotten in the final mystical shakedown. For surely, says Miss Rawlings, Cross Creek belongs to no one, no more to her than to the aged, dignified Negress who still does for white folks. It may belong to the red-birds. Yes, that's it. And "to the wind and the rain, to the sun and the seasons, to the cosmic secrecy of seed, and beyond all, to time." Take it away.—MAX GISSEN, "Back to Earth," *NR*, April 6, 1942, p. 469

LLOYD MORRIS
"A New Classicist"

North American Review, Autumn 1938, pp. 179–84

Among the rising generation of American novelists, none has given more valuable pledges to the future than Marjorie Kinnan Rawlings. She has been publishing for only six years. She has produced only three books and a very few short stories. But these—each in its way almost flawless— attest the possession of superior gifts and a genuine vocation. That her work received immediate praise from the critics is not surprising. It is strong, subtle, and exquisitely fashioned. In no way spectacular or topical, it might easily have missed widespread popular success. The intervention of a book club determined otherwise. By distributing to its members her first and, more recently, her latest, books, it served a useful purpose. Few recent novels have so well merited wide circulation, or the subsequent rewards of the best-seller lists and purchase by Hollywood.

Because Mrs. Rawlings locates her stories in the hammock country of Florida—a district unfamiliar to prosperous tourists, and never before exploited in our fiction—most critics have reported her as a "regional" novelist, relating her work to that intensive study of local environment and folkways which today preoccupies many American writers. There is, of course, an obvious justice in this interpretation. But it is also misleading, and tends to obscure the major import of this author's work.

It was not a critic of this generation who asserted that only three subjects exist for literature: man's relation to the world of nature, to his fellows, and to his God. But, although temporarily out of fashion, the formula has seldom been improved, and from time to time writers emerge whose perception of life brings their work within its terms. Of these, Mrs. Rawlings is clearly an example. Few other contemporary American novelists exhibit so marked a detachment from the problems, the currents of opinion, the pressures and tensions which characterize American life today. So complete is her detachment from the specifically contemporary and the transient as, occasionally, to perplex her readers. It would be easy, for instance, to accept *The Yearling* as a story of today; nothing in the first half of the book contradicts this assumption; only one passage of dialogue, revealing that two middle-aged characters are Civil war veterans, identifies the period of the story as the past. In the case of so intelligent and meticulous a craftsman as Mrs. Rawlings, it is absurd to suppose that this detachment, and the rigorous exclusions which it imposes, are purely accidental. They are obviously dictated by a personal perception of life, by a concern for ultimate rather than relative values, and by an intention to present experience in its most simple and enduring forms.

To make this point is merely to suggest that Mrs. Rawlings is essentially a classicist, writing at a moment when the dominant accent of our fiction is romantic. Her work more closely resembles Miss Cather's *My Ántonia*, or Mrs. Wharton's *Ethan Frome*, than it does the novels of Ernest Hemingway or Erskine Caldwell. But, although a classicist in her perception of life, she is a romantic in her literary endowment. Sensibility is its most impressive element, and imparts to Mrs. Rawlings's writing certain qualities more familiar in poetry than prose fiction. The sheer expressiveness of her prose will be noted by every reader. In passage after passage of her novels, a casual gesture or fleeting look is charged with meanings which her characters—by turns so eloquent and so reticent—cannot utter. Or a mood, a motive, a subtle complex of feelings and impulses, may be communicated by a minute modulation of light or color that transforms the landscape. And only a sensibility more than normally acute could register, with the astonishing rightness of Mrs. Rawlings's dialogue, the cadences and inflections of an idiom which sometimes rises to primitive poetry, and sometimes sinks to an inarticulate growl. This sensibility and this expressiveness are, in short, a kind of medium or instrument. For with them Mrs. Rawlings makes comprehensible and convincing a world that might otherwise seem part illusion, and part nostalgic memory.

The world which Mrs. Rawlings has chosen to portray has its topographical counterpart in reality. It is the wild jungle of inland Florida, sparsely populated by the Crackers, and bordered by the groves of those who grow oranges for northern markets. But although *South Moon Under* and, in less measure, *Golden Apples* may have justified a belief that she was primarily concerned with its local peculiarities, her use of it in *The Yearling* proves that this is not the case. For, in this latest and certainly finest of her three novels, she has written a universal parable. And in it, the world of Florida's hammock country is merely an archetype of all worlds in which man's spirit can emerge victorious or vanquished from the incessant conflict which is his life.

In choosing a subject at once so significant and so simple, Mrs. Rawlings reveals herself the mature artist, disciplined to complete awareness of her limitations and her resources. The minor blemishes which appeared in her two earlier novels, and which occurred only when she forced her talents to uncongenial tasks, are entirely absent from *The Yearling*. Within the terms of its intention, this is as nearly a perfect work of art as American fiction can display.

The story portrays the life of the Baxters, a family inhabiting an "island" or clearing in the depths of a forest which isolates them from their nearest neighbors, as well as from the world at large. All the action of the book passes within the clearing, the surrounding forest, the Forrester clearing, and the tiny river settlement where infrequent trading takes place. Penny Baxter, a little man though a mighty hunter, his stout wife Ory, and their twelve-year-old boy, Jody, are the protagonists. Their lives touch those of the Forresters, a wild and roistering family living on a distant "island," and those of the Huttos, and Boyles the storekeeper, who dwell in the river settlement. But, for the most part, they live to and for themselves, in a world quite literally of their own making which, but for their unremitting vigilance, would succumb to the encroachments of the jungle and the depredations of wild animals. They are proud, self-reliant, hard-working, and their life is an unending struggle with the conflicting purposes of nature.

One year of their experience is crystallized in the story, and its meaning made explicit at the end. Into that year Mrs. Rawlings has compressed the irreducible events which collectively furnish a common denominator for all human existence. Childhood and adolescence, the stern business of getting a livelihood, courtship and mating, the rearing of the young, the incidence of age, the passing of the torch, and finally death: all these are encompassed within four seasons of the Baxters' life. During that year, Jody passes from adolescence into manhood, Penny from vigorous maturity into age and decay. During it, likewise, the fortunes of the Baxters prosper and wane, flood devastates the hammock country, old Slewfoot the wily bear is pursued and finally slain in a passage that vividly recalls Ahab's pursuit of Moby Dick. And during it, we have been admitted to what is probably the most tender and beautiful love story recorded by American fiction: the love of Jody for Flag, the pet fawn which he captured in the forest, brought home and tamed because Penny overruled Ory's objections, and was finally condemned to slaughter because Flag, true to his natural instincts, twice ate the Baxter crops.

The meaning, the true import of this novel is incarnated by the story of Jody and Flag. Oddly enough, the equivalent symbols have been recently employed, and to much the same effect, by another American novelist. They were used by John Steinbeck in *Of Mice and Men*, as admirable a novel in its way as *The Yearling*. In it, the companionship of Lennie, the idiot, assuaged the intolerable loneliness of George; and that of his ailing dog, the misery of Candy's old age: Lennie dies by George's hand, and old Candy is compelled to connive in the slaughter of his pet. Mr. Steinbeck's purpose was not Mrs. Rawlings's, yet the symbols by virtue of their universal relevance made his story a reading of all life. Mrs. Rawlings's intention was to offer precisely this reading of life, and she therefore makes its significance explicit in the closing pages of her novel. Flag has been slaughtered, Jody has deserted his home and returned to it. Penny, broken now and bedridden, sums it all up.

> I'm goin' to talk to you, man to man. You figgered I went back on you. Now there's a thing ever' man has got to know. Mebbe you know it a'ready. 'Twa'n't only me. 'Twa'n't only your yearlin' deer havin' to be destroyed. Boy, life goes back on you. . . . You've seed how things goes in the world o' men. You've knowed men to be low-down and mean. You've seed ol' Death at his tricks. You've messed around with ol' Starvation. Ever' man wants life to be a fine thing, and a easy. 'Tis fine, boy, powerful fine, but 'taint easy. Life knocks a man down and he gits up and it knocks him down agin. I've been uneasy all my life. . . . I wanted you to frolic with your yearlin'. I knowed the lonesomeness he eased for you. But ever' man's lonesome. What's he to do then? What's he to do when he gits knocked down? Why, take it for his share and go on.

So much for the parable that lies at the heart of *The Yearling*. It is conceived strictly within the terms of a Puritan ethics, and represents a characteristically American attempt to reconcile the beauty, the pathos, and the indiscriminate cruelty of man's existence and nature's. To some readers, other aspects of Mrs. Rawlings's novel will seem more important. Docility, which is perhaps the end of all philosophy, may be only the beginning of wisdom: Mrs. Rawlings's intelligence makes no effort to carry us further. Her sensibility does. It plunges us deeply into the hearts and the perceptions of a child, a wise man, and a brave woman. It recreates for us those fundamental attitudes of the human spirit which make life endurable, and those inalienable experiences of love and beauty which enable us to live it without shame. With *The Yearling*, Mrs. Rawlings rightfully takes her place among our most accomplished writers of fiction.

LAMAR YORK
From "Marjorie Kinnan Rawlings's Rivers"
Southern Literary Journal, Spring 1977, pp. 91–99

"Sense of place" is the most descriptive phrase to emerge from the relatively small amount of criticism on the works of Marjorie Kinnan Rawlings. The phrase appeared first in a review of *The Yearling* in the *Times Literary Supplement* on December 24, 1938, and has been used since by her critics, whether directly or indirectly, in placing her in the categories of regionalist, local colorist, Southern gothicist, and twentieth-century realist. One of the two full-length books on Rawlings, Gordon Bigelow's *Frontier Eden*, epitomizes in its imaginative and provocative title her preoccupation with creating a locale.

Rawlings herself best expressed the meaning and importance of a "sense of place" when she said in her autobiographical *Cross Creek*, "the matter of adjustment to physical environment is as fascinating as the adjustment of man to man, and as many-sided. The place that is right for one is wrong for another, and I think that much human unhappiness comes from ignoring the primordial relation of man to his background."[1] Among the memorable elements of her stories, probably the "sense of place" and her "cracker" characters have been most admired by her readers, but "place" has been interpreted largely as preoocupation with the pictorial description of setting. The phrase "sense of place" may be used, however, in a broader critical evaluation of the artistic merit of her stories. Place, or setting, is used in her Florida stories as the chief architectonic element for showing her essential theme that in order to be happy, man must know or discover a realtionship to a suitable physical setting.

Rawlings uses rivers in her writings as the chief aspect of place and as the chief thematic element of setting. In all her stories in which man seeks to identify with his natural environment, there is a consciousness of the river either as the outside limits of the setting or as the connecting link between her setting and the rest of the world.

She came to love the rivers in North Central Florida which outline the scrub, known today as the Ocala National Forest; the two which appear prominently in her fiction are the St. Johns and the Ocklawaha. She described this river-bordered world: "The Florida scrub was unique. . . . There was perhaps no similar region anywhere. It was a vast dry rectangular plateau, bounded on three sides by two rivers. The Ocklawaha, flowing towards the north, bounded it on the west. At the northwest corner of the rectangle the Ocklawaha turned sharply at right angles and flowed due east, joining, at the north-east corner, the St. Johns river which formed the eastern demarcation. . . . Within these deep watery lines the scrub stood aloof, uninhabited through its wider reaches."[2] This is from *South Moon Under*, her first novel, and is thus her earliest description of the river borders which were to become in succeeding works the framework of her sense of place for Cross Creek and the scrub.

Though not a symbolist, despite her emergence as a writer during the fluent years of deliberate symbolists, she is indeed a strongly conscious literary artist. Dismissed lightly at times as merely descriptive, Rawlings's novels are carefully knit together through the use of description itself as a structural element in her plot, rather than as simply an elaboration of the real story. But of all the geographical entities focused on in her writing—clearings, landings, hammocks, pine islands, homesteads—the description of rivers is the most significant to the course of her story-telling art as well as to her own life. Rivers were for her the perfect conceptualization of order because they offered structure without excessive orderliness. She protested another form of boundary, the elegance of a new fence at her Cross Creek home, because it would bring "a wanton orderliness that is out of place" (CC, p. 9).

Her own career shows the need for such boundaries as rivers, which give a sense of place. Her fullest treatments of the river as a meaningful structure in human life are in *South*

Moon Under and *Cross Creek*, her first and last long works, respectively, of central Florida life, and thus the boundaries of the most successful part of her writing life. In *South Moon Under*, the river as a means of expressing order receives more attention than in any of her other books. Her use of rivers declines gradually through each succeeding novel until its final appearance in a closing chapter of *Cross Creek*. It is as though her use of rivers were like a trip up-river. Her use of rivers continually diminishes from one book to the next, as the width and depth of a river continue to diminish as one proceeds up it, till finally the source is reached. Finally, at the end of her career, trying to break out of the mold of the world within the river boundaries, she wrote *The Sojourner*, a novel whose setting is far removed from the scrub world within the river borders she had used so successfully; it was critically deemed her least artistic book, probably because its artistry is obvious rather than natural; the rivers of the Florida books were artistic boundaries because they were natural boundaries.

Mrs. Rawlings saw the enormous significance of river traffic in human history when in 1928 she settled in Cross Creek, a place where that traffic was still a vital economic force. When she arrived in Florida the Ocklawaha and the St. Johns were still relatively important to interior commerce from the port at Jacksonville, but Cross Creek was not caught up in the industrial flurry between the two world wars, and even Florida's tourism boom in the 1920's moved down the east coast of the state and missed the town. Since 1928, however, freight has been shipped into the interior by railroad and, at the present, by truck.

It is probably because of these circumstances that she attempted to use rivers and river lore as an economic factor as early as her second published story, *Jacob's Ladder*. The main characters, Mart and Florry, a young cracker couple, go from job to job, but always in some relationship to the river. Mart's first job, fishing on a large interior lake, presumably Orange Lake, is reached by way of the creek which leads into it. When Mart and Florry must find new work, they go to the maze of channel islands which make up the mouth of the Withlacoochee River, where he takes up salt water fishing in the open Gulf of Mexico. Learning their way about the seemingly endless inlets and creeks which make up the river mouth is difficult, but "At a certain point it could be said, 'Here, now, the river is alive.'"[3] This is the first of the passages in which rivers take on symbolic properties. The idea for Mart and Florry seems to be that if they can distinguish the actual river from the many inlets which look like the river, then they can never be lost again. It is meant to be meaningful both literally and figuratively. Similarly, when Mart and Florry are driven by bad weather to abandon life on the Gulf, they go with Eph Harper into the scrub to make moonshine. They build their still in a palmetto thicket above the Ocklawaha, where "They were . . . safe from the river side" (*JL*, p. 81).

Another natural element, the weather, is a main structural element in this story, which begins and ends with great storms; each of Mart's jobs is terminated or made intolerable in some way by weather conditions. But it is already obvious in this early story that Marjorie Kinnan Rawlings was describing natural phenomena and setting not because she was unable to create character or story, but because she was putting to work in her stories the theory that men must find a harmonious relationship with their surroundings, "that happiness and fulfillment are functions of place."[4]

South Moon Under is her fullest exploration of a river as an architectonic element. The novel is about many of the basic forces operating on human life, all of which are summarized in the elemental pull of the moon on the scrub hunters and the animals they hunt, just as the moon manipulates the tides that rise and fall in the St. Johns River. The river is represented for the most part as beneficent, as it is for the character Lant, who turns to the river for its cypress logs to sell for food when money runs low before trapping season, or for the men who, sustained by river water during the day-long toil, build Lant's cabin to "put the mark of civilization on the clearing" (*SMU*, p. 16). When his grandchild is born, Lant must send the new father for the doctor by way of the river in order to save time. It is the same river from which the new father had taken his betrothal gift earlier in the story. When revenue agents fail to find the rascal Zeke's still, they know "The river was safe, after all; intruders came, but they went away; and swamp and hammock and scrub was safer" (*SMU*, 99). The river even makes a great secret of the corpse of Cleve, to secure the peace for Lant and Kezzy, who have had to kill Cleve in unprovable self-defense. But the river is also the same force that the sea is in Stephen Crane's "The Open Boat"; while it can be benevolent or malevolent, it leans toward neither. At times in the novel the river's role is uncertain; Lantry, who has killed a revenuer in North Carolina, tells his daughter Piety, "I gits a dream, sometimes . . . I gits taken by surprise from the river" (*SMU*, 44).

At other times the river seems to play a malevolent part, as when the simple-minded Ramrod Simpson is "afflicted" at his baptism in the river; the preacher falls in a hole and hits Ramrod's head on a rock getting him out of the river, leaving him "afflicted." The river is a carrier of disease: "Early in March the influenza struck along the river. There were a dozen deaths on the piney-woods side. Then it crossed the river into the scrub" (*SMU*, 111). Willy Jacklin meets his death on the river because he is unequal to its danger-filled challenge. Finally, when the novel's main conflict, that between Lant and Cleve, comes finally to a climax, "Neither river nor swamp nor hammock nor impenetrable scrub could save a man from the ultimate interference. There was no safety. There was no retreat. Forces beyond [Lant's] control, beyond his sight and hearing, took him in their vast senseless hands when they were ready. The whole earth must move as the sun and moon and an obscure law directed—even the earth, planet-ridden and tormented" (*SMU*, 327).

Helping at times, hurting at others, the river takes on its own personality. The character it acquires suggests the very fundamental role it plays in the lives of those who live on it. When Kezzy originally contemplates marrying Cleve, which means leaving the scrub, she is comforted that "Anyways, if I marry Cleve and leave the scrub, I still got the river" (*SMU*, 202). At times dependable, at times treacherous, it is always a living presence in their lives. When Lant is moonshining on the river, he strains to hear sounds of intruders coming by way of the river, but only hears "the murmur of the river current. It breathed sometimes like a live thing" (*SMU*, 225). Though alive, it does not have the changing personality of another human, but "flowed interminably but as though without advance. The boy [Lant] thought that he had been always in this still, liquid place. There was no change. There was no memory and no imagining. . . . Nothing existed but the brown, clear water, flowing in one spot forever" (*SMU*, 164).

Although a passive character, seldom made to seem deliberately benevolent or malevolent, the river nevertheless operates as a deciding factor in the lives of those who live on or near its banks. In *South Moon Under* it is a line of demarcation outlining the edges of the scrub sanctuary. Lantry's life commences properly only when he "crosses the river" (*SMU*,

2) into the safety and anonymity of the scrub: "They had moved in actual distance no more than twenty-five miles. But they had crossed the river into the scrub. The clear dark stream divided one world from another" (*SMU*, 5). Because Willy Jacklin has been disliked as a son-in-law, Lantry insists that he be carried back across the river, out of the scrub, for burial. That same day Lantry himself dies, so that "In the afternoon Willy Jacklin was buried on the west side of the river and Lantry was buried on the east" (*SMU*, 79). Again, the river is clearly a line of demarcation between two versions of the life of men in that the young boy Lant must cross the river to go to school. One side of the river holds for him the possibility of formal education; the other side, the scrub, makes possible a real education for the real world. The end of his formal schooling is signified when he recrosses the river from school for the last time after two years (*SMU*, 70). The reader suspects that Lantry's side of the river and the education it offers is the side which by this time has become most attractive to Marjorie Kinnan Rawlings herself, despite her Phi Beta Kappa key.

Having determined that the scrub gave her a "sense of place," Marjorie Rawlings went on in *South Moon Under* to describe not only the way its rivers give it boundary, but also how they meet its elemental need for water itself, a larger abstraction of her theory. The scrub can be a hot, dry area in the long Florida summer:

> Dog days came in and lay like hot lead on scrub and river. The August sun blazed on the pine trees and scorched the corn in the field. Chickens went with wings lifted to cool themselves and hounds panted in the shadows underneath the houses. Folk went to bed exhausted and awakened at daybreak in an invisible blanket. The mocking-birds stopped singing and the snakes began to shed. Every one stepped warily, for the rattlesnakes had become blind and vicious. Sand gnats swarmed in clouds and passed the sore-eyes from one baby to another. Women who had saved May-water from the rains in May doled it out to cure the affliction. Children whimpered and fretted in the heat. The old folks grew irritable. Even soft-cooked grits did not feel smooth and good against the palate. Chills and fever went the rounds. Tempers were short. (*SMU*, 297–98)

Florida is a place of natural extremes, as winter visitors still discover. And despite its natural dryness, the scrub can be flooded, as Rawlings was to describe in a future novel, *The Yearling*. But in *South Moon Under* Rawlings develops in a large sense her feeling of the necessity for water. At one point in the story trouble is precipitated by a cattle fence which blocks everyone and their stock from the river, their life supply, a theme further developed in the short story "The Enemy." Similarly, rain is a necessary element, not only to fill the obvious needs of plant and animal life, but also because people need the rain's benediction. Early in the novel, for example, rain falls the morning after the almost simultaneous burial of Piety's husband, Willy Jacklin, and her father, Lantry; Piety says to her son: "Hit's always so. You take notice, son, hit'll always rain after a buryin'. Hit's planned so o' purpose. The rain washes out the tracks o' the dead along with the tracks o' the livin'. Hit wouldn't do to have the earth all yopped up with the tracks o' the dead" (*SMU*, 82). Again, later, rain washes away tell-tale tracks after another killing. Lant has killed Cleve, the ne'er-do-well, who had been jealous of Lant's success. The river, too, comes to Lant's aid as a burial site of which there can be no future discovery. But the unpredictable rain only occasionally falls in the scrub. So Rawlings's characters must cling to the scrub's edge, as the scrub itself "was uninhabited. Where there was true scrub, there would never be human habitation. . . . With humankind, which must have water, it [the scrub] had no concern" (*SMU*, 125). The big scrub, then, gives her a "sense of place" only through its rivers, which mean life for her characters, as for herself; she had found her own abiding place on Cross Creek, the lovely stream connecting two of Florida's largest inland lakes, themselves linked by way of rivers to the Atlantic.

Notes

1. Marjorie Kinnan Rawlings, *Cross Creek* (New York: Charles Scribner's Sons, 1942), p. 31. Further citations are given in the text, identified as (*CC*).
2. Marjorie Kinnan Rawlings, *South Moon Under* (New York: Charles Scribner's Sons, 1933), p. 2. (*SMU*)
3. Marjorie Kinnan Rawlings, *Jacob's Ladder* (Coral Gables, Fla.: Univ. of Miami Press, 1950), p. 70. (*JL*)
4. Gordon E. Bigelow, *Frontier Eden: The Literary Career of Marjorie Kinnan Rawlings* (Gainesville: Univ. of Florida Press, 1966), p. 47.

JOHN RECHY

1934–

John Rechy was born in El Paso, Texas, in 1934 of Mexican-American parents. He received a B.A. from Texas Western College and served during the 1950s with the U.S. Army in Germany. He received further education at the New School for Social Research in New York City while embarking on his writing career.

Rechy's first novel, *City of Night*, appeared in 1963 and attracted wide attention for its vivid portrayal of homosexuality and male prostitution; it remains his best-known work. Rechy's other novels include *Numbers* (1967), *This Day's Death* (1970), *The Vampires* (1971), *The Fourth Angel* (1972), and *Rushes* (1979). A work of nonfiction, *The Sexual Outlaw*, appeared in 1977. Rechy has also written a screenplay for *City of Night* and has adapted *Rushes* for the stage. He has contributed original fiction and nonfiction, as well as translations from the Spanish, to literary periodicals and has been widely anthologized.

Rechy, who has taught writing at Occidental College and the University of California, maintains residence in Los Angeles and New York City.

The failure of *City of Night* seems to me to lie in the unconvincing manner in which Rechy attempts to use a metaphor and to create a metaphorical level in his novel. Here there is the paradoxical situation of a failure to make the metaphor work coupled with an overconsciousness that it should be there working. Thus, in *City of Night* there exists a confused and inadequate literal level and an overabundance of reminders (other metaphors—such as the city of night, and the Inferno; the excesses of a style where buildings rise in supplication, where buildings are "knife-pointed," and parks are "lonesome") that the novel is to have a metaphorical level. In this last respect, the novel's Chicago section seems especially crude.

The novel's literal level involves the encounter of the individual male prostitute and the world of male prostitution, meant to represent the encounter between the individual and the American reality in terms of the possibility of or destruction of love. That for the most part the novel's hero seems present implicitly—almost as if the self were obliterated in its encounter—might seem to represent the relationship between the individual and the reality which surrounds him and envelopes him. But in three places, Rechy makes his hero exist explicitly. And what Rechy does in these three places only confuses the relationship between the individual homosexual and the hustling world and seems to contradict what sections like the novel's Chicago section appear to assert. The relationship is never clear.

City of Night begins with a chapter of childhood remembrance. But one soon discovers there is no real character created here, despite the emphasis on an "I" which rarely appears elsewhere in the novel. This chapter is a chapter created around five or six incidents and images which will occasionally appear in various forms elsewhere, and which are too patently symbolic, and yet as symbols too fragile for the weight of the experiences and incidents of the novel. The past of the "I" seems too heavily manipulated, too artificial. Incidents such as the young boy's sitting on his father's lap, receiving money and affection, are inadequate in two respects. They force upon us the various identifications we are to make; and they obscure the literal relationship of the "I" to the hustling world.

But throughout the novel one does not know what this "I" really is. In the Jeremy section (in bed with a youngish man who has picked him up, and with a Mardi Gras outside which brings together the homosexual world and the "straight" world, and thus works something like Pershing Square and the novel's Chicago section, Rechy's hero engages in a dialectic on love), Rechy's hero discovers that his desire to be loved and his refusal to give love in return is really a form of love. This, in part, is meant to explain his existence in the literal hustler's world. But this has little relationship to what is presented elsewhere of the encounter of the individual and the American reality—or what is presented elsewhere of Rechy's hero. It, in fact, is gratuitous, and does not seem at all meaningful. And in the very last section of his novel, at the end of Mardi Gras, on Ash Wednesday, and in New Orleans (where a church broods over the city), after an orgy of anonymous sex, and where Rechy's "I" encounters more and more voices which reveal the "ice age of the heart"; a resolution for the "I" is imposed upon the novel, as if the conclusion to a carefully created development of character. Rechy's hero undergoes a personal anguish, penitence, and desire for redemption. We are given then an image of the "I" hardly in keeping with any other image we have been given of the "I." The "I" is removed from the context of the other elements of the novel, and the novel's literal level is further confused.

This divorcing of elements can be seen in the way in which Rechy presents his hustler's world, despite the hint of a vague scheme controlling the materials of this world. The manner in which this world is presented seems to overwhelm its own metaphorical function, and thus to be separate from such parts of the novel as the Chicago section, the description of the Mardi Gras in the New Orleans section, and the description of Pershing Square, as well as being separate from the chapters which attempt to create a character out of the novel's narrator. For the multitude of details, the immensity of details concerning the hustler's world and the "gay world" are ultimately a part of a journalistic impulse, their justification no longer lying in an attempt to create a metaphor for an American reality and to present and cope with that reality, seeing it in terms of specific characteristics, describing and judging it. The real relationship between the "I" and the hustler's world is that of a tour guide to his homosexual travelogue.

What exists on this novel's literal level has little to do with what should exist on its literal level, if the terms of that literal level are to represent the terms of the novel's real theme—the individual confronting an American reality, and the individual unable to love in this reality. Yet, in sections like the Chicago section, and in a prose reminiscent of "America has a thousand lights," Rechy urges upon us his real theme and his literal level as metaphor. *City of Night* is filled with a style which, Henry Heifitz has noted in his review in a recent issue of *Studies on the Left*, "drools," and in which Rechy "sprays images everywhere." And it is filled with obvious devices to remind us that a world of hustlers and "scores" is like a world of pensioners in a park, or ruined people in a run down bar, or married people at a Mardi Gras. In James Baldwin's *Giovanni's Room* the realization that a "gay" bar and the "gay world" are to represent the America from which David comes and the America that is within him is subtly suggested. In (Gore Vidal's *The City and the Pillar*) it is in one place stated. And in Rechy's novel, it is stated again and again.—STANTON HOFFMAN, "The Cities of Night: John Rechy's *City of Night* and the American Literature of Homosexuality," *CR*, Vol. 17, Nos. 2–3 (1964), pp. 202–4

RICHARD GILMAN
"John Rechy"
The Confusion of Realms
1963, pp. 53–61

The temptation is almost irresistible—and I don't suppose I shall be able to withstand it entirely—to try to score off John Rechy's *City of Night*, to set up against its grotesque and graceless exhibition a scintillating road show of your own. This fictionalized account of a homosexual *Wanderjahr* is so pervasively bad, so ludicrous a performance at all but one or two points, yet so strenuously intended to be big and revelatory and dangerous, that putting it down seems like the clearest of cultural duties. Well, cultural duties have a way of turning into opportunities for a display of the self, and indeed a good deal of what I have read or heard about the book since it came out has been characterized by just this public honing of wit and invective at the expense of the issues which Rechy's painful and symptomatic creation, and the painful and symptomatic popular response to it, have raised.

As I say, I sympathize with critics like Alfred Chester. It is so satisfying to play the game and so easy: for example, the line I would love to pursue is a theory of how Grove Press, dismayed by the failure of the age to produce enough ugly, outrageous, know-nothing yet *vital* and *talented* writers on its own, has finally been compelled to fashion one in the office. And it is even easier and more pleasurable to score off Rechy psychologically, by establishing—or at any rate asserting—how much more complex and mature are your own ideas about sex and love than his. We all like to think the mantle they took off D.H. Lawrence when he died fits, don't we?

Yet I can't see what all this has to do with criticism. I don't know how it can take account of the dreadful earnestness—which could never have been faked or formulated—of *City of Night*; or of the reasons why it should be so widely regarded, by even such a substantial and putatively reliable witness as James Baldwin, as a sort of furious masterpiece of new statement; or, most central of all, of the really dramatic way it illustrates the present widespread confusion of art and life. There exists these days a naïve and cave-dwelling commitment to extreme situations and modes of behavior, a hang-up on perversity and perversion as sources of aesthetic truth, and John Rechy's lugubrious book is *its* masterpiece.

Not that there is anything at all extreme about the pressure, temperature and effect of *City of Night*, which is exactly what makes the whistles and the eyebrows that have been going up so truly disheartening. Surely the most ferocious of the many ironies that surround the book is the fact that it should promise so much shock and perturbation and turn out to be so flat, cowed and inhibited. From one end to the other Rechy's work smells of repression, both psychological and imaginative, and of narcissism of an especially depleting and devitalizing kind. Perhaps the most unpleasant aspect of the response to the book is that among many of its admirers this enervation and onanistic self-embrace is seen as strength, or, on a subtler level, as exemplary and sacrificial: *our* story, told for us by a new culture hero.

It is a case, evidently, of the wish being father to the thought. The particular activities that are chronicled in *City of Night*—male prostitution, camping, erotic degradation of various kinds—are real, sanguinary and extreme enough in themselves, but what happens to them in Rechy's unwizardly and weakness-diffusing hands is another matter. Whatever this blue-jeaned *voyage à la bout de la nuit* may have been in actuality, it has not survived its metamorphosis into literature, it has no status in the imagination nor any cautionary, redemptive or insurrectionary power. And since bad writing corrupts by recoil the life it is drawn from, the last sad effect of Rechy's book is to lay under a heavier onus than before the events and feelings which he presumably wished with such desperation to understand and to redeem.

I have been calling his work a "book" and the reason for this is that I am unable to find a way to call it a novel. This may seem to be an academic matter, but it is actually at the center of what I think is wrong with *City of Night*. The novel is the most open of genres in our time, but we can still give it a basic definition as a long piece of imaginative prose in which a transformation takes place—experience, from whatever realm, being converted into form. This form is then the justification and truth of the experience, instead of—as in Rechy's attempt and in certain works of Mailer and Kerouac, most outraged poetry, a large part of Baldwin's *Another Country* and all of James Jones—the experience trying to justify the form or its deficiencies. What all these works have in common, though they are of course of greatly uneven value, is that, in Yeats's phrase, they exibit the will doing the work of the imagination, and that they rest to one degree or another—Rechy's most completely—on a belief in the direct convertibility of experi-

ence into art, indeed on the identity of certain kinds of experience with art.

If what I have been saying is true, then *City of Night* isn't a string of short stories either, as most reviewers have described it, since none of its parts, with the dubious exception of the well-known *Miss Destiny* episode, is developed, seized from the chaos and interchangeability of raw material and given an ineluctable shape, none is released from the melancholy of potential being through the actuality of style.

The account of a homosexual *Wanderjahr*, I called it, and this seems to me accurate on several grounds. In the first place the book simply sets down, with autobiographical fidelity we may assume, the sexual things (there are no others) that happened to its author, and the thoughts—treated like things—that occurred to him in a number of cities over a period that feels like a year. (And if it should turn out that nothing of all this really happened to Rechy, that he wrote it from someone's else's story, it wouldn't disturb the description or indictment, since the book would then be another person's biography, but that person still blind, rigid, untalented and hence unable to tell us anything interesting or convincing about himself.) Beyond that there is at its back the pressure of a vague search for *meaning*, a decision to go picaresquely around an established circuit of warranted possibilities and a belief that the wandering will in itself supply the reasons for having undertaken it.

The narrative proper begins in New York, where Rechy, or his fictional "I," enters upon his life as a male prostitute. First, however, there is a segment of early history, a flashback to an El Paso boyhood, in which an attempt is made to uncover the psychic and emotional origins of the malady (instructively enough, it is never referred to as one, being described instead as a "restlessness," a "hunger," an "inner anarchy" and so on). The whole section, which sets the tone for endless self-confabulation to follow, is extraordinarily embarrassing, the quintessence of derivative Freudianism and adolescent substitution of grandiose categories and hypostatized states of being for concrete acts and sensations. Any page you turn to will yield lines like these:

> "I hate you—you're a failure—as a man—as a father!"
> From my father's inexplicable hatred of me and my mother's blind carnivorous love, I fled to the Mirror.
> I would stand before it thinking: I have only Me!

It is not a digression but the essence of any consideration of *City of Night* if a few more remarks are made right here about Rechy's lamentable style. One calls it that for want of a better word, but it is in fact nothing but an infinitely derivative literary manner, its elements appropriated by Rechy from among whatever has seemed to him to have been sanctioned and frozen as "important" writing about quests and young men's fevers. He is able occasionally to capture the speech of queens and hustlers, that is to say when he is reporting and not composing, but if there is anything that undercuts the book's pretensions to rebellion and savage new light-bringing, it is the nearly unbroken conformism of its preponderant style.

From his ugly compound words ("darkcities," "angry-faces," "somefarwhere") to his sonorously clichéd renderings of encounters and self-encounters ("we cling to each other in a kind of franticness"; "the restlessness welled insatiable inside me"; "I get the feeling . . . that silence is a person listening to me, watching . . .") and dismally arty evocations of place (Chicago has "wounded streets," New York is a "heaven-piercing" city), it is possible to see influences as diverse as

Thomas Wolfe, Nelson Algren, Kerouac, James T. Farrell and, as Mr. Chester pointed out, Truman Capote and Djuna Barnes, but there may be a hundred others lurking behind these.

The point is that Rechy is endlessly susceptible to influence because he can bring none of his own to bear. Kierkegaard said that if a man has true ideas he has style immediately, and Rechy has no ideas, true or otherwise; he only possesses what *happened* to him. The result is that it has to come out sounding as though it happened to someone else, or rather—much worse—as though it never happened at all but was always marooned in "literature."

Between these two parodoxical and reciprocal fates—to be nothing but an accumulation of atrocious and unmediated facts and at the same time to be nothing but a deposit of gelid literary borrowings—*City of Night* spends almost all of its existence. When Rechy's narrator has had enough of hustling in Times Square, he moves on to the next scene, to Los Angeles, the center of the outdoor cult and legendary slave market, then to San Francisco, then Chicago, and finally New Orleans, for Mardi Gras and the ultimate Revelation. "And I think: Beyond all this—beyond that window and the churning world, out of all, all this, something to be found: some undiscovered country within the heart itself. . . ."

This is the rhythm and the vocabulary we have been dealing with all along: the portentous music, the repetitions, the windy nonsense about "something else," a Truth still to be discovered, while what does exist—the sexual transactions and sexual prowling—are entirely deprived of their weight and specificity and anguish by Rechy's refusal to really look at them, to call them by their names or to see them in any perspective except their own. When a writer continually employs indefinite nouns like "something," "somewhere," "someone," it is a sure sign that he is still mired in adolescence, in the age of Titles instead of names, Feeling instead of emotions, Desire instead of wants.

There are times when the lacerating actuality of what is happening to him and his inability to understand it or even to confront it bring Rechy to a frustration that is close to paroxysm, and bring us to a degree of pity:

> . . . this was the moment when I could crush symbolically (as in a dream once in which I had stamped out all the hatred in the world) whatever of innocence still remained in me (crush that and something else—something else surely lurking—but what—what!!).

He never finds out of course; it is in the nature of such writing that one doesn't find out. But the passage I have just quoted does reveal one motive about which Rechy is perfectly straightforward, if irretrievably dishonest with himself. He wishes, he says, to stamp out innocence in himself, and the events of the book in fact derive what continuity they have from this process, which, however, like Rechy's search for an equivalent to Love, is much more a matter of gaining in brutality, ignorance and self-deception than of losing anything at all. Why he should wish to rid himself of an innocence he has never established he had, he is unable to say, but there are enough clues, and two explicit scenes, to allow us to come to our own conclusions.

In the first scene he has the chance to rob a customer but cannot bring himself to do it. "Somehow," he characteristically reflects, "I knew—in that room just now—I had failed the world I sought." A few months later, with a similar opportunity, he doesn't fail. And so it turns out that the biggest influence of all, not stylistically or imaginatively, God knows, but what with all proper sorrow for the corruption of the word we shall have to call metaphysically, is Jean Genet. Rechy has read Genet or heard about him, learned of his choice to *be* a thief and a prostitute since society had decided that he was, and has tried to put his own illness in the service of some such moral revolution as Genet's. It is very much as if some ordinary, untalented gambler and epileptic had decided to pretend he was Dostoevsky.

The urge may be perennial but we are in an especially unchastened period of such pretension. What Rechy lacks, what all our writers *manqué* lack who wish to *be* Genet or Rimbaud or Lautréamont or Lawrence, is of course everything that the latter possess: a true dream of violence as cure, profundity, lateral vision, a language, a demon. What they lack most radically of all is the knowledge that the rebellion has to be carried out within language and form themselves, that the material is a guarantee of nothing and may be a gross impediment. Even Genet could not do justice in fiction to the extreme violence and perversity of his life; when he found the proper form, it was the drama, and drama, moreover, which broke the old patterns after having passed beyond the specificities and autobiographical *culs-de-sac* of his own existence.

But if you do not know that art has its own life and laws, you will never understand why grave, passionate, anguished or terrible events in the world cannot simply be transferred or transliterated so as to make comparable events in literature. There are no good novels about earthquakes, prairie fires, strikes, tidal waves or orgies, and the reason is that these things are too much themselves; there is no getting a purchase on them or a way into human reality. By the same token the great novels about war or murder or erotic disaster are precisely triumphant because they modulate these devastations through the perspectives, or memory, of peace, reverence and love.

The Marquis de Sade, who wished to pursue perversion to its furthest limit, was a bad novelist, but he was a responsible phenomenon and a valuable witness. John Rechy is neither. More a victim perhaps than an originator, riding the latest wave of irresponsibility in the name of action and of being true to one's calamity, he would not be worth talking about if what he represented were not worth talking about. And what he represents is the distance we have come from an understanding of realms of being, of the dialectic between body and soul and between heaven and hell, and from a knowledge that art is perfect authenticity or it is nothing.

If, as it seems, we are in a period when we can scarcely even believe in love and peace, let alone exist in them, let us by all means strike out for them with all the violence we possess, but let us remember that the end is a restoration, not a perpetual rebelliousness, and let it be our own violence, not another's. If we find ourselves homosexual, or impotent, or cursed, or a hustler, or a Negro in a white world, or a white man in a Negro world, or in jail, or in *Esquire*, or on horse, or on the road—it doesn't mean that we are artists, and may mean, if we celebrate ourselves and cultivate our pain, that we can never be. We are equal to our own lives, but our imaginations have to make a leap. The deepest shame of a book like *City of Night* is that it cradles its furies and impotencies without understanding or being affected by them, and so without understanding or affecting anything else.

BEN SATTERFIELD
"John Rechy's Tormented World"
Southwest Review, Winter 1982, pp. 78–85

In addition to his nonfiction opus, *The Sexual Outlaw*, John Rechy has written five novels that vividly describe the physical and emotional terrain of the misfit, novels that explore with varying degrees of success the terrifying landscape of the taunted and tortured, of the desperate and deviant, of those who suffer the pain of "lost" life—in short, the damned. What makes Rechy's characters different from the "outsider" figure popular in American literature is that Rechy's people are alienated from themselves and nature as well as society; and what makes Rechy's world crueler than, for instance, Dreiser's is its unrelenting hostility. Rechy evokes not just the indifference of society to pain and suffering, but the outright malignancy of the world at large, a world in which death is final, religion is false, and love is seldom found. Whether we confirm it or not, that world is recognizable, and Rechy's presentation of it is worth examining—in moral terms, if no other.

City of Night, Rechy's first novel—and the only one to receive much critical attention—is a homosexual odyssey or *Wanderjahr* that begins in El Paso, moves to New York City, Los Angeles, San Francisco, Chicago, and New Orleans, then ends "American style," as Leslie Fiedler has casually noted, "with a return to Mom and Texas." Containing one of the most lugubrious collections of grotesques in modern literature, this book unveils the subculture of male prostitutes, clients, queens, and hustlers who do not love but cling "to each other in a kind of franticness" that is characteristic of Rechy's world, a jungle of fear, emptiness, and anxiety where there is no salvation. (I use "grotesque" in essentially the same sense that Flannery O'Connor used it in her essay, "The Grotesque in Southern Fiction." It applies to characters and experiences the writer makes alive "which we are not accustomed to observe every day, or which the ordinary man may never experience in his ordinary life.") Because of its subject matter and the sexual explicitness of the prose, this book is often referred to as an "underground classic."

But Rechy is a moralist, not merely a countercultural revolutionary, and his use of "sensational" material is not for the easy purpose of sensation, as those critics who belabor the superficial suggest. Underneath all the ugliness and perversion of his novels is a childlike innocence and remarkable sensitivity. Rechy shows us the world as he sees it, without coating the stark reality with lies that will obscure and make it palatable to a culture so steeped in duplicity and dissimulation that it seldom sees the truth, to a nation so anxious that it voraciously consumes books of sexual content simply because it refuses to face the truth of sexuality or to deal honestly with it. Rechy is outraged at the world, and I contend that he writes "outrageous" books in an effort to jolt society in the groin of its hypocrisy. Like the guileless child in "The Emperor's New Clothes," he sees the truth, but he does not state it quietly; he screams, "Look! See!"

And what we see is the pain and loneliness of people without love; what we see is the terrible consequence of the failure to love; and what I hope we can see as a result is the absolute necessity of love in a world without redemption, a world of franticness and death.

Franticness, a familiar word in Rechy novels, describes the ambience of his characters; also, the word *savage* and some form of *ferocious* appear as often as *implacable* does in

Faulkner, helping to reflect the feeling of menace that Rechy draws from society. Not only is the world hostile, Rechy declares, but the nature of existence is horrifyingly brutal:

> Years, years, years ago, I had stared at my dead dog, buried under the littered ground of our barren backyard and dug out again, and I had seen in revulsion the decaying face. Now, as if I had dug beneath the surface of the world, I saw that world's face.
>
> And it was just as hideous.

In Rechy, civilization is a mask on the face of wildness, and wildness is mere animal existence without tenderness and love. Without love, Rechy seems to avouch, we are savages, and his novels manifest this belief. He makes his vision apparent by shock, like Flannery O'Connor, who said: "To the hard of hearing you shout, and for the almost-blind you draw large and startling figures."

Most of Rechy's characters are homosexuals, which means they are not only deviants but outcasts from society, and all are deeply troubled. They are in conflict with society and in opposition to nature itself, as evinced in their homosexuality and "perversions." (I am going to view sexual deviation as both a symbol and a symptom, because I believe Rechy perceives it this way.) Most of the protagonists are fatherless in the literal sense, but all are orphans in the emotional sense, just as they all are lost and homeless in the large sense. They do not belong—to anybody or anything—and they agonize, wanting love and getting only sex (and it sometimes an expression of hate); wanting acceptance and getting only tolerance or exploitation; wanting life, but feeling death. They live in a state of ferity disguised by the thin veneer (mask) of civilization, which is easily stripped away to lay bare a savage reality.

But that reality exists, and Rechy implies it exists because we do not meet our full potential as human beings, because we do not care enough, love enough, feel enough for ourselves and our fellow human beings. We make ourselves animals by failing to be human. Recurrent words and phrases connected with the wild and primitive convey this impression unmistakably. In all Rechy's novels the use of animal terms to describe human behavior is consistent, and is especially used in conjunction with the sexual acts. I believe these acts are associated with brutality, savagery, and wildness not just because sex is an animal drive, but because the acts are dehumanized. Without love the participants are groping savages, inchoate creatures longing for the affection that will temper and humanize their lives. (The animal imagery identifies sexual behavior as negative and debased without the author's having to make overt statements. I conclude that the lack of real love, in Rechy's eyes, reduces his characters to the low level of brutes and savages whose behavior is described in animal terms to indicate its debased quality.)

The milieu of the homosexual is vicious and frightening. This "gay world," as Stanton Hoffman calls it, "functions as a metaphor for a destructive and despair ridden American reality." A perceptive reader, Hoffman sees the same kind of structure in the gay world that exists in the society as a whole, and therefore believes that Rechy reflects America in his underworld creations.

City of Night reflects, in exclamatory prose, a "grubby world" that is "gasping" and horrible, a world made up of malicious anthropomorphic cities filled with "allnight moviehouses" in whose balconies and back rows homosexuals gather "like dark vultures" searching for prey. The city of night is, of course, a metaphor, and an accurate one for what is being described, but Rechy is not meticulous in his descriptions of real cities. On page 26 he refers to New York City as "a Cage," and a mere thirteen pages later this "Cage" becomes an "islandcity" which is "like an electric, magnetic animal"—and fifty pages later it's a "jungle." Making a consistent image out of the tropes is impossible, but it is easy to perceive the feeling, which is unmistakably negative, as is most of the animal imagery. Here, for example, is a scene of sexual behavior: "Like a dog retrieving a stick and bringing it back to its master, with his teeth clutching the buckle, he slid the belt out of the pants straps—and he crouched on all fours brandishing the belt before me, dangling it from his mouth extended beggingly toward me."

This sounds enough like an excerpt from Krafft-Ebing's *Psychopathia Sexualis* so that I am certain no one of sound mind is likely to argue that it does not portray a human being in a degraded manner. Pathology, not love, is Rechy's province, and the anguished habitants of this pitiable domain at times hardly seem human. There is no substitute for salvation, Rechy says in all his writing, and love is our salvation; without it, we are brutes, not truly human, and doomed to painful failure with any surrogate.

City of Night was followed by *Numbers*, a dreary homosexual scorecard in which the protagonist, Johnny Rio, sets himself the goal of achieving thirty sexual "scores" within a period of ten days. (Rechy heroes, lacking love and fearfully craving it, like to feel desired, and the greater the number of poeple who desire them, the more successful they feel in their substitution.) Griffith Park in Los Angeles is the setting for much of the activity—graphically described—but dark movie balconies are also used for fleeting and frantic trysts that are meaningless except as "numbers" to add to the scorecard. It is significant that the movie house is used as a place of rendezvous, since it is the home of unreality, of illusion, of dreams projected in images larger than life—a place where the disappointed can meet in the dark and try to capture for a moment the illusion of love.

Johnny is a truly pathetic character, driven by a kind of franticness that is exacerbated by nerve-ripping panic and terror in his furtive encounters, and at the same time dulled by an enveloping ennui that is absolutely deadening. The best feeling he experiences is a sense of being alive, and he tries to use sex as a life stimulant. It fails: "And what does he feel? A screaming need still unfulfilled." There is no love in the book, and at the novel's end, the protagonist, lacking the human touch of warmth and caring, continues his futile but compulsive attempt to fill the void with numbers: the last line of the book is "Thirty-seven!"

In *This Day's Death*, the protagonist Jim Girard faces trial in Los Angeles Superior Court on a charge of homosexuality. As we might expect, the law is powerful, threatening, and anything but just, a symbolic distillation of the social structure that rejects Jim and forces him into the helpless role of victim. The recurrent image of tyranny is concentrated in the mechanical process of the law:

> It was a hostile world, that world of criminal proceedings: Too often a defendant was reduced to a mere entity caught in opposing crosscurrents of court proceedings, as impersonal as a ball in a competitive game. What was won or lost had little to do with the instrument of the game. And as the ponderous abstract machinery of court proceedings moved inexorably, that machinery began to attain a definite threatening identity while a defendant felt his reduced, fading; finally—possibly—invisible?

Jim is from El Paso, but he goes back and forth to the city of lost angels and "lost defendant angels," where he sees the "same haunted, hunting, lost breed of faces he had been among on the insomniac streets of exile America." We are indeed in Rechy country, among the forlorn and afflicted who are both predator and prey, victim and victimizer in frenzied loveless encounters.

The only love Jim expresses is a kind of guilt-induced obligatory love for his mother, but even the mother-son relationship provides another form of trap, and his feelings are ambivalent and vacillatory. His mother is dying, her body wracked by unknown malevolent invaders of a nameless illness, "*la cosa*," an unseen terrible force from the pathogenic world that constitutes a different kind of "invisible trap" from the one Jim is caught in.

Again in this novel, sex is so identified with brutality, savagery, and wildness that Jim sees the sexual act as "symbolic slaughter," a manifestation of rage and anger, a way of ventilating his resentment through human violation—or of passing on to others the pain and suffering the world has heaped upon him.

The Vampires is an incredible novel, hastily written, about a group of bizarre people who gather on a Caribbean island to indulge in sadistic games that tear away the lies sustaining them. The island, being itself cut off, is an appropriate setting for these isolated people who suffer a kind of death in life. One of the characters is so numbed that he feels dead, and seeks pain just to feel alive. Another, a male prostitute plagued by impotence, previously enjoyed the desire others felt for him (while he felt contempt for them) because he wanted to feel loved—but the sex was never enough to overcome the feeling of emptiness. "Nothing was enough," he says, underscoring a thematic complaint.

What these people seek is deliverance, escape with a capital E. "It's not possible to Escape," one of them proclaims. "Life attacks. It comes roaring at you." And life, as Euripides said long ago, is a misery. Rechy's characters agree, for they are victims all, wretched, driven, tormented, lost. And in their misery they prey on each other, seemingly helpless to do otherwise but to pass on what they get from the world, oftentimes in the form of "sexual slaughter," which is a parody of love, a travesty of the only thing that could save them.

In *The Fourth Angel*, Rechy presents four El Paso adolescents who, in an attempt to find themselves, experiment with sex, alcohol, various drugs, and even people. Jerry, a fairly sensitive youth whose mother has recently died, joins a tough girl, Shell, and two boys, Cob and Manny, who call themselves the angels. Hoping to fill the void in his life, Jerry becomes the fourth angel and participates in the explorative escapades of the group. One of the things these juveniles like to do is catch people giving expression to their vices. They claim to want to "get into" other people's heads, but what they seem to enjoy is the vulnerability of those who are exposed—especially those whose sexual proclivities are exposed—and the concomitant superiority of their own position. For example, in an abandoned house by a bar, these "angels" catch two men engaged in sodomy and terrorize them. They try to force the couple to complete the act under their gaze, but the men are too frightened to perform and are released:

> The two stumble past them.
> "Like animals," Cob's words shoot out in accusation.
> "Man, we really freaked them out," Manny says.
> "Animals!" Cob yells after the two.

"Animals!" Shell seizes the word, laughing harshly. *"Animals!"*

"Animals!" Manny joins them.

"Animals" Jerry echoes softly.

It is grindingly obvious that the youths are hurling an epithet, a disparaging label of shame and disgrace. That homosexual behavior is vastly more common to humans than to so-called lower animals is immaterial. The men, in giving vent to the sex drive without the favor of love, admit a connection with the animal world, confess that they share a need which is purely animalistic, and therefore, in the view of the gang members, they are base and low.

Later, these four "angels," under the influence of LSD, enter a supermarket and enrage a woman customer:

The woman turns fiercely from them, driving the cart like a tank. But in those moments, Jerry saw her mean face crumbling before him, folding over into a hideous, tortured rubber mask, melting. The curlers transformed into rolled horns pasted on her head, her pores opening ferociously, she had become a violent, irrational—yet strangely frightened—animal.

Whatever is ugly or irrational is usually presented in animal terms, despite the fact that irrational violence is far more characteristic of human beings than of animals.

Near the end of the novel, Cob and Shell fight for some kind of emotional supremacy, and Cob enlists Manny's aid in a sexual attack upon Shell as Jerry observes: "Swiftly, circling her like a cunning animal, Cob pulls her dress down. Naked in tatters, she looks savagely beautiful."

Savage and *animal* are terms Rechy uses to relate to sexual activity, of both heterosexual and homosexual variety. As we have seen, however, there is no evidence of real love displayed between any of the sexual partners, and the sex acts appear to be acts of lust that are distorted, warped, or perverted in terms of what is normally defined as acceptable behavior by community standards. Rechy writes of the reduced, "the tarnished fugitives of America," as he said in *City of Night;* and his characters are loveless creatures who, driven by lust and frustration, seek any form of "love" they can find, however aberrant, however ersatz. But they are also symbols, and they function to demonstrate the disastrous result of the failure to love, and hence define the necessity of love. All Rechy's books are, in this sense, negative demonstrations of a very positive and moral appeal.

In the broadest sense, I believe Rechy makes a tacit plea that civilization be made the face of man (not just a mask), the human being be transformed into an honestly humane creature who would not need a mask, whose own face would be truly civilized, and whose world would not be wretched. Love is the alembic, the only hope, the only salvation. There is absolutely no substitute. If Rechy screams "Look!" and if he seems at times to be writing at the top of his voice, it is because his message is desperately important, and his audience is decidedly hard of hearing.

ISHMAEL REED

1938–

Ishmael Reed was born on February 22, 1938, in Chattanooga, Tennessee, the son of an autoworker and his wife, and was educated at the State University of New York at Buffalo. In 1965 he co-founded the *East Village Other* and *Advance*, a community newspaper in Newark. His first novel, *The Free-Lance Pallbearers*, was published in 1967, and *Conjure*, his first collection of poetry, appeared in 1972. Other works of fiction by Reed include *Yellow-Back Radio Broke-Down* (1969), *19 Necromancers from Now* (1970), *Mumbo Jumbo* (1972), *The Last Days of Louisiana Red* (1974), and *Flight to Canada* (1976). Reed's poetry has been widely anthologized and collected in two additional volumes, *Chattanooga* (1973) and *Secretary to the Spirits* (1975).

Reed has contributed articles and reviews to a variety of periodicals, including *The New York Times*, *Ramparts*, and *Liberator*. He was nominated for the Pulitzer Prize in poetry in 1973, and has received awards from the National Institute of Arts and Letters, the National Endowment for the Arts, and the Guggenheim Foundation.

Reed is really a historical novelist. It's just that he doesn't write historical novels the way they used to. And for him the 1920s is a critical and symbolic period in the history of the confrontation between American blacks and whites. In *Mumbo Jumbo* he attempts to interpret—or rather reinterpret—that period through fiction, though *fiction* is not really the word to describe this work. Unlike fiction, it contains graphics, some twenty-two pictures—photographs, drawings, symbols, signs—that function not to illustrate scenes from the plot, as in the romantic novels of years ago, but to reinforce visually a point or a feeling conveyed by the words in the text. It also contains a pseudo-academic system of quotes and footnotes, even a bibliography at the end. Sometimes Reed himself intrudes parenthetically. The graphics are nearly always successful, adding a humorous pungency to the ridicule or invective. The quotes and footnotes are seldom successful. They often seem gratuitous and pretentious. Yet, both techniques serve Reed's purpose. *Mumbo Jumbo* has the texture of a weird history book.—JERRY H. BRYANT, "Who? Jes Grew? Like Topsy? No, Not Like Topsy," *Nation*, Sept. 25, 1972, p. 245

Reed's significance as a poet and novelist has always resided in the questions constantly posed in his texts, his attempt to write his way parodically out of the fictional forms and poetic modes imposed on him. The motive of Neo-HooDooism, he argues in *Conjure*, is to create a uniquely Black mode of writing, a form of artistic discourse flooded with African and West-Indian values that will liberate the writer from the constraint of Anglo-American modes and return him to his creative sources.

Yet this desire to regain lost origins, a pure language, is obviously an American obsession, and the farther out Reed swung in his eclectic mythologizing the closer he came to the central texts of literary modernism, the point from which he had started. In *Chattanooga* the African reference is muted. Loup Garou, the mythopoeic hero of *Yellow-Back Radio Broke-Down*, now appears as an inner and restless self, a psychological entity:

> If Loup Garou means change into
> When will I banish mine?
> I say, if Loup Garou means change
> Into when will I shed mine?
> This eager Beast inside of me
> Seems never satisfied

American culture remains a "poison light," a force that distorts and falsifies the consciousness of Black people, but the struggle against it is stated in the modesty of the subjunctive mood. If *Conjure* is in every sense of the word a manifesto, *Chattanooga* is a testimony that reveals at times a certain tedious garrulity in Reed's voice. When the problem of what and how to write no longer is the topic of one's writing, then what and how to write with freshness and power becomes a problem.—NEIL SCHMITZ, "Down Home with Ishmael Reed: *Chattanooga*," *MPS*, Autumn 1974, p. 206

⟨. . . Black⟩ Marxist and/or Muslim and/or Christian uptightness is all part of what Reed calls the Atonist Order, an impulse towards regimentation and uniformity epitomized by the ancient Egyptian pharaoh Ikhnaton, whose monotheistic worship of the Sungod Aton its name recalls. Neo-HooDooism, while rooted in Egypt, traces its descent not from Ikhnaton but from Osiris, as Reed makes clear in *Mumbo Jumbo* as well as in the poem "Why I Often Allude to Osiris":

> ikhnaton brought re
> ligious fascism to egypt.
> where once man animals
> plants & stars freely
> roamed thru each other's
> rooms, ikhnaton came up
> with the door.
> (a lot of people in new york
> go for him—museum curators
> politicians & tragic mulattoes)
> i'll take osiris any
> time.
> prefiguring JB he
> funky chickened into
> ethiopia & everybody had
> a good time. osiris in
> vented the popcorn, the
> slow drag & the lindy hop.
> he'd rather dance than rule.
> *(Conjure, 43)*

One of the necessary corollaries of Neo-HooDooism's encouragement of individual creativity and artistic freedom is a commitment to pluralism. (This commitment is what leads Reed to work with people of various racial and cultural backgrounds in undertakings like the Before Columbus Foundation.) The *Vodun* religion of Haiti, from which neo-Hoo-Dooism in large measure derives, is accordingly a pluralistic, which is to say a pantheistic or polytheistic one. The *Vodun* "pantheon," moreover, is always open to *new* loas. Zora Neale Hurston, in the book *Tell My Horse*, to which Reed often refers, points out that *Vodun* worshippers not only tolerate but actually seek out new loas, allowing even occurrences as

unmiraculous as, say, being protected against a sudden rainstorm by a tree's foliage to provide the occasion for the revelation of a previously unknown spirit (in this case the beneficent spirit which resides in the tree). Reed uses this openness to new loas as a symbol of artistic innovation, referring to the cornmeal and water drawings called *veves*, which are used in *Vodun* to invoke the loas, as "markings which were invitations to new loas for New Art." (*Mumbo Jumbo*, 49)

The difference between Atonism and Neo-HooDooism is brought out even by such incidental detail as the fact that LaBas burns several different aromas of incense in his office: "Incense is burning. Sandalwood, myrrh and many other formulas which survived the ban when the Catholic Church decreed that only frankincense be used in ceremonies" (*Mumbo Jumbo*, 50). The difference, again, is that which separates the monistic from the pluralistic, the rigid from the flexible, the enforcement of uniformity from the acceptance of diversity. The Neo-HooDoo openness to variety is also indicated by the recurrence throughout Reed's work of references to gumbo, a dish which not only requires a variety of ingredients but can also be prepared in a variety of ways. (Hence the exclamation "we have *many varieties!*" in the passage from *The Picayune Creole Cook Book*, which serves as the epigraph to *The Last Days of Louisiana Red*.) When Reed counsels Houston Baker to "be 'real Black people' . . . by learning how to make gumbo" he could be addressing the entire Black Aesthetic movement, telling it not to confuse unity with uniformity, not to prescribe formulas which are in the end "as painful as a spiked collar." In the poem "Jacket Notes," he says that "Being a colored poet / Is like going over / Niagara Falls in a / Barrel" and that "what really hurts is / You're bigger than the / Barrel" (*Chattanooga*, 55). Black Aesthetic theorizing, in its more prescriptive, pontifical moments (e.g., Ron Karenga), represents a further tightening of the barrel's girth. In the face of this as well as other perceived threats, Reed's work has become an increasingly self-reflexive campaign for artistic freedom. Thus of Quickskill in *Flight to Canada*:

> He preferred Canada to slavery, whether Canada was exile, death, art, liberation, or a woman. Each man to his own Canada. . . . They often disagreed about it, Leechfield, 40s. But it was his writing that got him to Canada. "Flight to Canada" was responsible for getting him to Canada. And so for him, freedom was his writing. His writing was his HooDoo. Others had their way of HooDoo, but his was his writing. It fascinated him, it possessed him; his typewriter was his drum he danced to. (Pp. 88–89)
> —NATHANIEL MACKEY, "Ishmael Reed and the Black Aesthetic," *CLAJ*, March 1978, pp. 364–66

JEROME KLINKOWITZ
"Ishmael Reed's Multicultural Aesthetic"
Literary Subversions:
New American Fiction and the Practice of Criticism
1985, pp. 18–33

Those dour guardians of official culture Ishmael Reed calls "high-ass Anglo critics" have alway had trouble with his work, especially when they try to segregate facts from fiction. Even his partisans have rough going from time to time as they try to pigeonhole this writer who's built much of his career on the flamboyant eclipsing of stereotypes. Take a friend who's been wondering if he should zap poor Ishmael for being a "grant-hoarder" (the term is Reed's and he isn't one). This investigator's crowning argument is that among the contributors' notes to *Yardbird Lives!* (coedited with Al Young for Grove Press in 1978), Reed simply lists himself as "a businessman," as if admitting he's in league with the folks who run America's acronymic corporations and grants establishments.

"Hey wait," I beg my friend and cite Reed's disclaimer from the first page of his funniest novel, *The Last Days of Louisiana Red* (Random House, 1974), a note which warns that "in order to avoid detection by powerful enemies and industrial spies, nineteenth-century HooDoo people referred to their Work as 'The Business.'" The insipid grant-getting hustle my friend rightly condemns is hardly The Business our novelist describes, for if you read into *Louisiana Red* you'll find the HooDoo Businessmen have their own name for such shenanigans every decent person would deplore: Moochism, as in Cab Calloway's "Minnie the Moocher." But for the victims of a monocultural education, artists like Calloway don't exist.

Businessman, HooDoo, Mama's Boy, High-Ass Anglo Critic—these are just a few of the words Ismael Reed uses in both his essays and his fiction to articulate that odd confusion of history and imagination which so uniquely characterizes our times. Seeing how well his novel, *The Terrible Twos* (New York: St. Martin's, 1982), and essays collected in *God Made Alaska for the Indians* (New York: Garland, 1982) work together will help straighten out my grant-busting colleague, but it's worth remembering that Reed has been doing this for over two decades while the rest of us have been slowly catching up. Take this description of "Dualism" from his *Catechism of d Neoamerican Hoodoo Church* (London: Paul Breman, 1970), a carefully articulated program of aesthetics masquerading as a book of poems:

> i am outside of
> history. i wish
> i had some peanuts, it
> looks hungry there in
> its cage
> i am inside of
> history. its
> hungrier than i
> thot
>
> (p. 17)

In *The Terrible Twos*, Reed is supposedly outside of history; he sets his story in 1990, when the President is a former male model, the economy is worse than ever, and all that's left to trickle down is Christmas, which a bunch of power-hungry goons who run the country successfully buy and sell. *God Made Alaska for the Indians*, on the other hand, assembles eight essays and an afterword on environmentalists. Native Americans, literary politicians, prize fight promotions, male sexuality, race relations, the troubles in Ulster as seen by Irish-Americans, and the problems of multicultural artists—all of which deal directly with the demoralizing state of events since 1976 when Reed's last collection was assembled. But with an author like Reed in control, there's no real difference in subject or in method, and the result is a penetrating vision which by now surely ranks as the new decade's most insightful literary critique of American morals and manners.

It's at this intersection that the battle over Reed's work is fought: can the identity of history and imagination, just because our age apparently confuses them, be a valid method

for the critique itself? For years, Reed has been complaining about the intellectual colonialism which judges American literature by nineteenth-century English and European standards—"all those books in rusty trunks," as he puts it, which by contrast make his own writing seem "muddled, crazy, and incoherent." In his attack on these old-order standards, Reed does disrupt some emotionally held ideals, but his genius is to base his method solidly within the multicultural American lower-middle class, which he claims is more ready to allow "the techniques and forms painters, dancers, film makers, and musicians in the West have taken for granted for at least fifty years, and the artists of other cultures for thousands of years." Hence, you'll find Reed talking about (and writing like) Cab Calloway, who since 1928 has never lacked a low-brow audience, black or white, rather than the intellectually uptown musicians more conventionally taken as models. You can also find him listening to Native Americans describing their two-century battle against Russian and American white men, where he quickly notes their method:

> On the bombing of Angoon, another Tradition Bearer, George Davis, told me that in 1880 an American ship tried out a cannon-like gun and hit a whale. The whale leaped out of the ocean and "screamed like a wolf," he said as he told me a story part fiction, part autobiographical, part nonfiction (the new fiction is at least 20,000 years old). (P. 32)

Syncretism is one of the few formally abstract words in Reed's critical vocabulary, and he feels it is the key to a true national American literature reflecting the uniquely multicultural art which has evolved here. "Anglo" culture, as he calls it, then becomes one element among many, and the only loss is that of a dominant intellectual academy sworn to upholding the beliefs of a long-dead order. Gabriel García Marquez says much the same about his own multicultural, coastal Caribbean background where, as opposed to the rigidly colonial Spanish culture of the highlands capital in Bogotá, history and fiction were allowed to blend, making truth "one more illusion, just one more version of many possible vantage points" where "people change their reality by changing their perception of it." Within this aesthetic, fact and imagination become one. And as our present age has been shaped by this union, so Reed creates a common method for writing novels and essays by using the best of it while warning of its dangers when abused.

Both *The Terrible Twos* and *God Made Alaska for the Indians* are filled with Reed's customary mischief and fun. In the novel, President Dean Clift does things like helping sell merchandising rights to Santa Claus and declaring Adolf Hitler a posthumous American citizen, but balks when his advisors plan nuclear war with Nigeria as a way of wiping out the economically "surplus people" on both sides. Meanwhile, back in the quotidian reality of *God Made Alaska*, Reed's research uncovers a "late nineteenth century American movement called Teutonism" in which a serious politician "proposed a way of ridding the land of both the unwelcome black and Irish: 'Let an Irishman kill a Negro and get hanged for it'" (p. 81). Both books are hilarious in their accounts of people being swallowed by their own cultural signs, but things get serious when Reed shows how dangerous a dead semiotics—a code of social behavior deriving from discredited cultural authority, such as monocultural white male dominance—can be. Mama's boys, Daddy's girls: both the real and fictional worlds suffer from them, and the biases of hot-sell TV and high-powered establishment educations only make things worse. There's a "scolding missionary tone" (p. 9) in the Sierra Club's attack on the Shee Atika tribes, and also a peculiar rhetoric to the presidential advice offered by *The Terrible Twos'* wealthy Colorado brewer who boasts that "my family has been making beer since they came through the Cumberland Pass with Dan Boone. They shot Injuns alongside Mordecai Lincoln and joined old Andy Jackson in his war against the Seminoles" (p. 102). Why should this self-styled King of Beer worry about the Native Americans his commercial development, Christmas Land, will drive from their Alaska homes? "Injuns come and Injuns go," he blathers, "but Regal Beer is here for eternity" (p. 102). Is monocultural America really this bad? Every paragraph in *God Made Alaska* makes it seem worse, because Reed shows how it happens:

> Native-American historians accuse Arthur Schlesinger, Jr., of omitting any reference to the Trail of Tears of the Cherokee Nation in his Pulitzer Prize-winning *The Age of Jackson*. Schlesinger, and others, prepare for leadership people like Reverend Billy Moyers, a former advisor to a President, who only recently found out that slavery wasn't merely the practice of some ignorant white trash overseers, but was endorsed by the judicial and legislative bodies of the time. His guest, A. Leon Higgenbottom, author of *In the Matter of Color*, was polite. He could have mentioned how American churches sold slaves to raise money to support their missionaries abroad, and how The American Government Sold Slaves to Raise Revenue!! (Pp. 6–7)

In our time, history and imagination are confused because there's been a king-hell conflict going on between two rival sign-making authorities, one authentic (the multicultural and nativistically American lower-middle class, which has invented jazz, blues, rock and roll, country swing, comic books, detective novels, fast food, and other items native to our shores) and the other a carry-over from a long-dead power (the European colonization, with its monocultural rhetoric and monological dictates). What can Reed do in these circumstances: write a counter-history of the Western world, as Khachig Tölölyan says Thomas Pynchon has done, exposing "the patriarchal and technological white West" while rallying for "the imposed-upon" who've been "inscribed with other peoples' meanings"? That's the negative side of his program, but our man Reed takes such positive joy in the real American culture which now and then wins a fight that Pynchon's solution seems fully unsatisfactory—there's too much joy to miss, both in exposing the phonies and giving credit for the good stuff.

God Made Alaska for the Indians is a commentary about being a necessary outsider to the monocultural elite. "Ismael Reed?" some people will ask; "If he's not on the inside of our academic and publishing establishments, who is?" As if to answer, these eight essays range across contemporary America to indicate how one-sided and exclusionary its standards of cultural authority still are. And not just for black Americans. Reed's adversary vision is important because there is an entire national culture being systematically outlawed by an educational and media organization pledged to a set of ideals blind to what "nativistic" (meaning Afro-American, Hispanic-American, Oriental-American, even lower-middle-class Polish-American) literature is. "Here so long / We got spirit," Reed quotes the Alaskan-American poet Andy Hope, who like Reed has to keep laying down the challenge for attention: "Look me in the eye when I talk and you'll remember what I say" (p. 34).

Despite the great social turnabout in the 1960s which helped get Reed and other necessary outsiders rolling, official American culture is still very much a closed code. Roland Barthes would call it petit-bourgeois thinking, a dullish inability to image anything other than itself, but the crying shame is that here in America it is not even our own petit-bourgeois standard which is pulling down the blinds and locking the windows: it's a monocultural, monological, male-dominant and classically white European set of values which even as it died abroad took on an artifically new colonial life here. And despite all the radical social changes and curricular revisions, that attitude remains so strong as to be incessantly stifling, making contemporary studies a nuisance-ridden affair of having to continually struggle out from beneath the wet blanket of old, implacable cultural attitudes.

That's why Reed, whose "continuing autobiography of the mind" this collection is (following straight upon *Shrovetide in Old New Orleans* which was prefaced from the Alaska village where the new book's first essay begins), feels obliged to range from Sierra Club-Native American battles through the Ali-Spinks heavyweight championship bout and various linguistic, sexual, racial, and revolutionary topics to the book's most impressive essay on the crazy spectacle of some displaced New York poets pumping a Buddhist revival in woolly Colorado's Boulderado Hotel. Something, folks, is very wrong out there, and Ismael Reed is the practicing artist and cultural theorist who can tell us why.

My interest in Reed's work is personal, a concern absolutely central to his arguments in *God Made Alaska*. Anyone working on innovative American literature will inevitably confront the same problems he outlines here, and Reed's essays are helpful because they explain so much of what has been going haywire in our culture—for black writers, non-elitists, Native Americans, and whoever else can't fit the establishment's Aristotelian and colonial standards. And we're not talking about the trials of some foggy avant-garde. Closed attitudes precede nativistically American work like bad news moving in advance of a known troublemaker. In 1981, the editor of an ongoing literary encyclopedia wrote me in desperation for a piece on Walter Abish, the novelist who'd caught academia off guard by winning the first PEN/Faulker prize—it turned out this editor couldn't find a single scholar able "to comprehend Abish's work, let alone write about it." In 1982, the publisher of a supposedly on-the-ball San Francisco quarterly returned my essay on Richard Kostelanetz unread, saying he found it "impossible to deal with a writer whose values and methods" he couldn't understand. The pity is that this stuff has been going on, it seems, forever; way back in 1976, Reed's *Yardbird 5* reprinted my even earlier report of walking into what I'd hoped would be a wide-ranging and open-minded literary gathering at San Francisco State University and being accosted by an old-style Americanist who answered my friendly "Hello, I'm Jerry Klinkowitz" with a rather hysterical and fully unprovoked diatribe: "Ronald Sukenick! Ronald Sukenick! I can't read him! I just can't read him!" Close behind was the department's top graduate student, pledged to a thesis on the academically acceptable Thomas Pynchon (a fine Aristotelian decked out in classically European values), chattering "Monkeys at typewriters! Monkeys at typewriters!" In this climate of self-professed illiteracy which characterizes so many English departments and publishing houses, there is not much one can answer back. Too often my own response has been to cash in my hand and call for pizza and beer. Reed, however, sticks around and fights, armed with a finely articulated brief against this claustrophobic set of cultural rules.

Reed's stature is, in part, measured by the greatness of his enemies, and in *God Made Alaska* he finds himself aligned against the entire Anglo establishment which disparages anything outside colonial culture, from the blues to cowboy novels (just two of the notable art forms unique to our shores). There is a very definite anti-American mindset to these constrictive attitudes; in one of the very first critical histories of our country's writing, *The Spirit of American Literature* (New York: Dodd, Mead and Co., 1911), Bostonian John Macy postulated that "in literature nationality is determined by language rather than by blood or geography" as a way of justifying his claim that "American literature is a branch of English literature, as truly as are English books written in Scotland or South Africa" (p. 3). Nobody would be so outrageous as to go on record with that specific claim today, but the spirit behind it sets the rules by which culture gets funded, published, and taught. Lower-middle-class Americans of all ethnic backgrounds are taxed to support a European-culture-oriented tradition of grand opera, symphony, and ballet they will never see or hear, even if they wanted to. When the environmentalists of the Sierra Club present their claims to Native American land, Reed notes that "they often used arguments which sounded similar to the Romanov's appeal to divine rights. The rest of us lacked 'qualifications.' We didn't meet their 'standards'" (p. 4). The methods of "colonizing" Alaskan tribes in the nineteenth century, "naturalizing" them at the century's turn, or locking up their assets for "the national interest" now, Reed shows, are all based on the same monocultural arrogance that proclaims white male standards as the only ones with value.

By these same terms, a black heavyweight champion of the world becomes the unimaginable Other, the role Ken Norton was obliged to play in *Mandingo* and *Drum*: "The women want to ball him, and the men want to do battle with him; some people want to do both" (p. 39). So much for official cultural standards, which an innovative champ like Muhammad Ali can subvert by going directly to the people whom the establishment has counted out more subtly but no less effectively: "He is more effective because he speaks to Americans in American images, images mostly derived from comic books, television, and folklore. To be a good black poet in the 60s meant capturing the rhythms of Ali and Malcolm X on the page. . . . His prose is derived from the trickster world of Bugs Bunny and *Mad* Comics" (pp. 43–44). Reed identifies a further split between official and authentic culture in his challenge to Dick Cavett and John Simon on the issue of "Black English." How can it be "eradicated," Cavett asks and Simon implores. "You'd have to eradicate the black people" is the obvious linguistic answer, which Reed finds a "chilling thought, considering that there are historical precedents for people being exterminated because they didn't speak and write the way others thought they should" (p. 67). But more practically, Reed adds, there is a crucial difference between the received language of official culture (which is by definition drained of personal imagination for the purposes of "doing business" smoothly) and the way people within the culture actually think, speak, and feel:

> You not gone make me give up Black English. When you ask me to give up my Black English you askin me to give up my soul. But for everyday reasons of commerce, transportation-hassleless mobility in everyday life, I will talk to 411 in a language both the operator and I can understand. I will answer the highway patrolman who stops me, for having a broken rear light, in words he and I both know. The highway patrolman, who grew up on Elvis Presley,

> might speak Black English at home, because Black English has influenced not only blacks but whites too. (P. 68)

Right there is the issue: for mundane points of information, free of characterizing value, official language will have to do. But in terms of artistic expression and communication, where culture's lasting business takes place, there is another, nativistically American language which gets systematically discounted by the "King's English" crowd which insists that the discourse of novels, plays, and poems be conducted in the same tongue, now so stiffly formal because it represents a culture which died one hundred years ago on a land mass three thousand miles away. And because the real American culture is kept at home behind closed doors, the marketplace language is itself never transformed, and so through no free choice of their own white cops find themselves speaking to black citizens in an outmoded language formed by structures of colonial authority bearing small relation to the lives they personally lead. Richard Ohmann's *English in America* made this point nearly ten years ago, but Freshman Writing standards remain those of nineteenth century England because that's from where our official culture derives its values.

Stale images, such as the black-male-as-rapist, come from stale thinking, and Reed shows how there is easy money to be made from traffic in such worthless symbols. Meanwhile the real issue is deliberately ignored, for "the most lethal macho is white macho, since white men have the extravagant means with which to express it. If the nuclear button is pushed, it will, no doubt, be pushed by a finger belonging to a white male. While black macho might be annoying, white male macho could be the death of us" (p. 73). But the official culture "reads white," having "more regard for whites in Europe than for nonwhites in America" (p. 77) simply because the old standards of judgment point in that direction. When a culture is so isolated from its everyday personal language and values, it atrophies. Hence, Reed's well-meaning desire to "stir up some mischief" which at least shakes open a few minds and closes a few mouths: "Ethnic purity. White superiority. The Nazis were doing in the streets what some white Liberal Arts departments preach elsewhere." Or even more tellingly, he suggests to an MLA meeting "that certain characteristics of blacks in novels written by white liberal intellectuals reminded me of the Nazi caricatures of their victims. A commotion ensued. I thought I was going to have to slug my way out of the hall" (p. 79). But as he learns from the Irish Republicans speaking at their own cultural center, "the victors will not be those who inflict most, but those who endure the most" (p. 99).

At times in the past Reed's stridency has cost him part of his audience, but the gentler fun of *Twos* and *Alaska* is calculated to open some minds even as it closes some mouths. The egoless self-apparency of his method, based as it is on the common language and sentiment of most Americans far away from the intellectual centers, virtually guarantees this; for when Reed simply "sits back and takes it all in" as the monocultural aristocrats hang themselves with their own devoluted chatter, how can you help but take his side? The emotional two-year-olds of his novel are their own worst enemies; there's no need for the author to turn the knife in them as he's been tempted to do in earlier novels. In *Alaska*'s most conclusive essay, "American Poetry: Is There a Center?", watch Reed stare in disbelief as Michael Brownstein pumps him with the information that "the hottest scene in the country was taking place in Boulder," which thanks to the Naropa Institute's presence in the Colorado hills has made the place an "energy center." A few months before, the smart boys had been telling Reed that all the action was just north of San Francisco Bay, but his checking revealed that their idea of the source, Bolinas, "was a mere watering hole for international artists, intellectuals, and people who grew up in households with five maids" (p. 105). So now he sits listening to this academic enthusiast "who sometimes looks like a guy who wore a prep school cap and shorts at one time" claiming that Boulder's where it's at. Whose side are you on through all of this? Where do you think "the center for American poetry" might really be? At the essay's end, far from the circus in Colorado (described with merciless accuracy), Reed finds his answer: "In every poet's heart."

Monology works in curious ways, and Reed can speak his mind without slandering Brownstein, who he quickly admits is a good and thoughtful poet. It's the system, Reed advises, which makes this transplanted Tennessean sound so bad: "People in centers see themselves as the center because they can't see the whole scene with an eye for detail" (p. 120). Reed's ideal, which is a lot closer to the American reality which lies beyond the suffocating pale of Manhattan, Boulder, and Bolinas, is one of multicultural syncretism—of a truly national literature which can absorb radically different contributions and come out stronger for it. But the old system of "pledged allegiance to Anglo culture" still dominates the news media, publishing, and education. Idi Amin is everyone's favorite black ruler; alternatives to white culture in America are discussed by CBS on the level of "tacos and watermelons", plus "there was that sad issue of *Partisan Review* (44, no. 2 [1977]) called 'New York and National Culture: An Exchange,' in which a panel of New York intellectuals claimed to represent National Culture when in reality they sounded like village people whispering about haunted houses" (p. 114). Like the Romanovs, those who've assumed they hold divine rights do not change roles easily.

What Reed calls the Anglo establishment thrives on dead signs, cliches of a once-living culture which now misdirect and deplete our country's imaginative energy. Therefore, his first job is to expose this state of affairs and then to bring our language and its signs back to life as self-apparent realities. *God Made Alaska for the Indians* does this for the history we've shared since 1976, and *The Terrible Twos* takes further license to push the argument through fiction. All systems are fictions, our times have taught us, and fictions in turn create functional realities. Reed likes to deomonstrate how the folks in control manipulate us—that's the wickedly funny part. Ishmael Reed triumphs as an American writer when he seizes the oppressor's tools and forges his own reality: a perception of disparate forces brought together in a single complex vision which is clearly superior, based as it is on a broader range of seeing and expressing. Consider what the media and the police made of Patty Hearst's kidnapping by the Symbionese Liberation Army, and how Reed's method pulls it all together:

The security problem. From the early revolts there had always been the security problem. Even Gullah Jack couldn't protect Vesey from it. The American Secret Police has caused conflict between the Black Panthers and the United States; bugged Huey Newton's apartment; but the SLA brought out the Keystone in them. They flaunted their presence before the authorities, creating an arabesque American myth involving Patty Hearst and Cinque. Arabian nights of California, the rich white girl and her genie; the Dragon has come. Visionary hostage-takers, Artaud's mad actors, burning up on television. Now the psychodramatic politician was on the scene. One man, no leaks, unless he's schizoid and rats on himself. The first time rebellion could achieve a force equal to the opponents of rebellion. Eight thousand tons of plutonium were missing. Who had them? Enough to make 80 A-bombs. (P. 90)

What a way to live, but that's what much of our culture has turned out to be, as rival sign-making systems fight it out in books and films and on records and TV. Like *God Made Alaska for the Indians*, *The Terrible Twos* is much more than a simple counter-history: quoting a penitent Nelson Rockefeller from the lowest circle of Hell and playing with some off-the-record apocrypha about his death from a group of corporate scoundrels, Reed can pull together the many different and contradictory levels of our contemporary American "truth" and give us a persuasive account of how we live today. Reed the novelist and essayist is a careful semiotic researcher who, once he's done the hard work of running up and down the stairs for facts, gives language free play to project itself into previously unexplored corners of public experience, lighting up some truths which those afflicted with cultural tunnel vision might otherwise never see.

Yet official standards remain belligerently exclusive and reductively stereotypical: "It's too bad that the different cultures which go to make up American civilization are communicating only on the tacos and watermelons level" (p. 125). Such proscriptions only weaken the parties who make them; for, as Reed argues, "the drive against integrating schools being waged by some oily politicians is regrettable since it's the white students who really need it if they are to survive in a complicated, multicultural world" (pp. 125–26). Who suffers most? "It is the white students who are being culturally suffocated because even black C students have it over them; they're bicultural, and the hispanic students are tricultural." But the ugliness and viciousness of an official culture, Aristotelian in its aesthetic and colonialistic in its ethic, for the most part prevails. "At this time in American history," Reed concludes, "we are like ghosts talking gibberish through different dimensions, and stupid men do not make good mediums" (p. 126).

KENNETH REXROTH

1905–1982

Kenneth Rexroth enjoys a well-deserved reputation as one of his generation's most eclectic and wide-ranging poets. His career spans six decades (from the twenties through the seventies), and both as painter and as poet he was associated with many of the most influential movements of his time, including Objectivism, Imagism, Cubism, and the Beats.

Rexroth was born on December 22, 1905, in South Bend, Indiana, to Charles Marion and Delia (née Reed) Rexroth. Both his parents died by the time he was thirteen years old, his mother of gangrene and his father of alcoholism. During the three years following his father's death Rexroth lived with an aunt in Chicago, where he attended Englewood High School and the Chicago Art Institute. He was by this time already active as a painter, poet, actor, director, journalist, and political radical.

At the age of sixteen Rexroth worked his way to the West Coast and back, beginning a series of travels that over the next several years would take him to Mexico and to Europe twice, the first time (in 1926) by working his way over on a ship and the second time (in 1948) via a Guggenheim fellowship. Rexroth's earliest poetry was written during this period. In 1922, at the age of seventeen, he wrote a long philosophical poem *The Homestead Called Damascus*, published in 1957 in the *Quarterly Review of Literature*. He married his first wife, Andrée Dutcher, in 1927, and finished his second long poem, "Prolegomena to a Theodicy" (published in Louis Zukofsky's *Objectivist Anthology*, 1932) that same year. Throughout the twenties and thirties Rexroth was also active as a painter, primarily as a Cubist.

Rexroth became involved with American leftist politics during the Depression, and was a conscientious objector in World War II; his poems of the period, largely collected in his first book, *In What Hour* (1940), reflect this concern. The book received mixed reviews but won the California Literature Silver Medal Award. Unfortunately, the publication of his first book and subsequent award were offset by the death of Andrée in 1940. Rexroth married Marie Kass, a nurse, later that year, but the marriage ended in divorce in 1948; Rexroth married his third wife, Marthe Larsen, the following year, and they had two children.

Rexroth's second book, *The Phoenix and the Turtle* (1944), was more personal in tone and better received. His next several books, particularly *The Signature of All Things* (1950) and *The Dragon and the Unicorn* (1952), solidified his reputation as a poet of considerable range and clarity. During the mid-1950s Rexroth helped inspire the San Francisco Rennaissance and became a mentor to the Beat Generation, earning the title "Godfather of the Beats" through his organizing of poetry readings in San Francisco and propagandizing for the movement in the pages of such journals as the *Nation*. Though he later renounced the Beats in disillusionment, his poems of the time (collected in *In Defense of the Earth*, 1956) were enthusiastically received as excellent examples of the form. Rexroth was also active as a critic and prolific translator (translating poems from Japanese, French, Spanish, and Chinese) during the fifties.

In 1961, Kenneth and Marthe Rexroth were divorced; Rexroth married his fourth wife, Carol Tinker, in 1974. His output did not diminish during his last two decades: the sixties saw publication of *An Autobiographical Novel* (1966) and several more books of verse, most significantly *The Collected Shorter Poems* (1966) and *The Collected Longer Poems* (1968), which brought the majority of his verse into print. His last book of poetry, *New Poems*, was published in 1974, but he continued to be active as a translator and critic throughout the seventies, publishing five books of essays and five books of translations during the decade, as well as editing two volumes of translations of single authors (*The Selected Poems of Czeslav Milosz*, 1973, and *Seasons of Sacred Lust* by Kazuko Shiraishi, 1978).

Kenneth Rexroth died on June 6, 1982, of heart disease in Montecito, California.

Examples of Kenneth Rexroth's verse are by now familiar to readers of the literary and poetry journals (who may or may not confuse him with the two other Kenneths—Fearing and Patchen); ⟨*In What Hour*⟩, however, is his first book. As an integrated performance it is less than notable; in many of the poems, the time-honored sources—Eliot, Pound, Stevens, Crane, Auden—fairly crackle from the page. Rexroth makes little effort to harmonize these loyalties; the result is a book hag-ridden by antecessors, of whom none contradict the critical truism: that their strength lies in their defiance of successful imitation.

Liberal citation from *In What Hour* might substantiate these remarks, but more significant is the case of Rexroth himself. He is, I believe, an "objectivist" (which is to say, a streamlined "imagist"—Pound has on occasion given his name and capacious blessing to both cliques); but the tag implies little that the verse itself cannot better demonstrate. The logomachic style, by any other name, would be as apparent; here articulation is further impeded by the ambiguity of the unarticulated idea. Rexroth's countenancing of a purgation and a correction (presumably Marxian) of modern society is obliquely expressed. The symptoms of his dissatisfaction are those common to all of his generation—all, that is, but the misanthropic few. The poet, eating, remembers the starving Spaniard; a transport plane reminds him of bombed civilians, and so on, until the swollen guilt-sense intoxicates his being with neural bewilderment. What is he to do? Like another Californian, he might forswear all communal sympathies and marry the hawk; but again, like Nicola Sacco, he might fight and fall "for the conquest of the joy of freedom for . . . the poor workers." Of this dilemma, and its consequences to the poetic sensibility, Philip Henderson has written intuitively and at length in his book, *The Poet and Society.*

Rexroth's fulminations lack the pyrotechnics that make Auden exciting reading, but they are no less incoherent than the worst of Auden for being more cryptically conceived. Yeats's remark that "We make out of the quarrel with others rhetoric, but of the quarrel with ourselves, poetry," requires an addendum to validate the propagandizing function of rhetoric—a function, no doubt, to which Rexroth, like Auden, subscribes *ex animo.* But if Auden's career has incited a plethora of rhetoric, Eliot's has not; it remains to Rexroth to harness the pair together in such lines as:

> Before the inevitable act,
> The necessity of decision,
> The pauper broken in the ditch,
> The politician embarrassed in the council,
> Before the secret connivance,
> Before the plausible public appearance,
> What are the consequences of this adultery?

Elsewhere, Stevens is respectfully saluted:

> The avid eyes of gravid mice entice
> Each icy nostrum of the zodiac, *etc.,*

and there are "letters" to Auden and to Yvor Winters, a repudiation of Santayana, and an exercise in Whiteheadian objectivity called "Organum." Pervasive throughout the non-political items (they are few) is the predilection for "daring" metaphors and word-combinations suggestive of that disconsolate incantator, Hart Crane.

I am not unaware of the dangers of this "I've seen *you* before" indictment; Rexroth might conceivably have the stuff of a superior poet despite any number of derivations, but the hint of inadequate assimilation carried by the present book is too constant for easy dismissal. The poet has little that is new to say, and his devices for speech are fully as familiar as the polemic itself. In the poem, "August 22, 1939," he describes his literary career thus far as "twenty years at hard labor." If that is so, we could scarcely expect his poems to be greatly unlike those articles fashioned by prison inmates for a stipend. I dislike stressing the parallel, but the Rexroth of *In What Hour* sorely needs either a change of occupation or a parole. —WILLIAM FITZGERALD, "Twenty Years at Hard Labor," *Poetry*, Nov. 1940, pp. 158–60

If you call Shakespeare's *Pericles* a poem, it has to stand up against a certain set of values; if you call it a play, that's something else again. It might be a good play but a bad poem or the reverse. I shall not try to evaluate these four plays (collectively titled *Beyond the Mountains*) of Kenneth Rexroth other than as verse, for they are destined, I feel sure, to be read rather than acted. What a pity! They and other plays in modern verse should be acted out before they can be judged as drama. There is no stage for it. There is NO stage in America suitable for it.

At the start I plead that the problem of writing dramatic verse for the contemporary stage is complicated for me almost beyond solution. When the scene is cast in a day the intimacies of whose speech is unknowable to us, the difficulties are increased though the practice is reputable and so we must accept it. Then place the action in ancient Greece where at a remote period the theatre reached a zenith never since equaled for sustained tragic effect and where are you? You're up against Racine and the dignity of the French twelve-syllable line. There is Shakespeare, of course, but that's something else again: an Elizabethan robustness of language and metaphor cannot today be imitated without a condescension on the part of the hearer, which is fatal.

The four plays, *Phaedra, Iphegenia, Hermaios,* and *Berenike* are grouped under a general heading, *Beyond the Mountains.* Based on classical Greek myths, they have the theatrical form of the folk dance, with dialogue as verse. This dialogue offers a solution to the problem I presented above— read as verse, it is superb. Rexroth, happily, has eschewed the iambic pentameter throughout. What can be done with our speech in the situations he chooses to present is excellently done; his Phaedra, for instance, is no Frenchwoman. The line is savage and brief.

For Rexroth is one of the leading craftsmen of the day. There is in him no compromise with the decayed line of past experience. His work is cleanly straightforward. The reek of polluted Shakespeare just isn't in it, or him. I don't know any Greek, but I can imagine that a Greek, if he knew our language as we ought to but don't, would like the athletic freshness of these words; he'd like their elementary candor, the complete absence here of the sexual lamb chop, French fries and petit pois (frozen from a can).

As verse, reading them through, the plays are a delight to me for the very flow of the words themselves. The pith is there, don't mistake me, and there with a jolt to it (in the very line, I want to make it clear) that goes well below the surface. But the way of the writing itself is the primary attraction. It palls, at times, I acknowledge it, but that is the defect of the method. It does not falsify. It is a feat of no mean proportions to raise the colloquial tone to lines of tragic significance.

There are bound to be errors from an excess of devotion to a necessary method, we can't know everything at once; even after the ten years of work Rexroth has given these plays there are spots I do not admire (as if that were always necessary).

I have a curious feeling about the work as a whole that, though it is not acknowledged in the text, we have been given a sort of Essay on Man: spring, summer, fall and winter. Rexroth might smile at this, but near the beginning Iphegenia and Achilles surely swim in warm waters while, in the *Berenike* ice is creeping in from all sides. The tale, as it stands, is of the final blotting out of the Hellenic remnants. And so for all of us soon perhaps.

Sex? It is all sex. I once knew a metal worker who would pick up a red-hot horseshoe between his bare thumb and fingers without injury. But you've got to know how, to do that. An elementary passion, such as that which moves these characters, if it is integral in the play of the words, which it brilliantly is, affects these words violently; it doesn't lie over them like slime. Why else do you suppose men read the sports pages?

I add to that that I have never been so moved by a play in verse in my time.—WILLIAM CARLOS WILLIAMS, "Verse with a Jolt to It," *NYTBR*, Jan. 28, 1951, p. 5

Kenneth Rexroth's autobiography, like those of Granville Hicks and Alfred Kazin, points to the special difficulties this genre offers any writer. Although it is not a true autobiography, Fitzgerald's *The Crack-Up* has always seemed to me a book which the writer of an autobiography should seek to emulate. It has the consciousness of its own truth, and while it takes a good look at the skeleton in the closet, it does so with a minimum of sentimentality and self-consciousness. It was no longer the most handsome skeleton around when he wrote this book, but it was Fitzgerald's own—and *The Crack-Up* remains an example of that kind of honesty which prevented him from becoming "a punch-drunk pug fighting himself in the movies," as he once said of Hemingway. A rare honesty—neither nasty nor sentimental—it is the quality which every writer of an autobiography must strive to acquire.

Perhaps this is not a very good way to begin a review of *An Autobiographical Novel.* Life is difficult enough for a writer without subjecting him to comparison with genius. Nor do I mean that Kenneth Rexroth is dishonest. But *An Autobiographical Novel* is portentous in its very simplicity, and the kind of equilibrium it lays claim to simply does not exist in this world. I am sorry about this, for Kenneth Rexroth is not only a talented poet and translator; he also seems to have survived in pretty good shape a brittle and self-seeking world. But in re-creating his first 21 years, he is "playing simple"—and to play simple is a peculiarly immodest modesty. An assessment of self, after all, demands the consciousness of what one measures that self against. Perhaps this is what makes *The Education of Henry Adams* the best of all American autobiographies. Adams might have been no more than a querulous patrician, but he had to measure himself against all those Adamses who stood, like a row of Roman statues, in a long line behind him. The model for Kenneth Rexroth's "picaresque adventure" is Kenneth Rexroth. Bohemians should not speak into tape recorders; not, at least, until they know who made the choices as limited as they were.

The first two chapters of *An Autobiographical Novel* are devoted to the genealogy of the Rexroth family, both here and in Germany. It is not until Chapter 3 that Rexroth himself appears, born in South Bend, Ind., on December 22, 1905. Prior to the First World War, northern Indiana seems to have been a children's paradise. We can accept Kenneth Rexroth's word for that, since there are stranger things in American history. After all, historians tell us that in 1912 more than 16 per cent of Oklahomans opted for Eugene Debs for President. And so we can accept an Indiana which has been "animated by the spirit of a won revolution." But it is not until Rexroth goes to live in Chicago at the age of 12, following the death of his mother and father, that the world he is writing about takes on greater credibility. It is probably not Mr. Rexroth's fault, but his Midwest seems far less real to me than those "Freudianized Deweyites" he is so intent on needling. Rexroth is as keen on the Midwest as he is down on Freud, and while I am willing to follow Bohemia a long way down the road I am afraid that I cannot follow it that far.

Once he has arrived in Chicago, Rexroth is most intent on his precociousness, and he seems to have set about being precocious in an amazingly analytical fashion. The reader would like to hear more about the Irish Catholics and Jews of Studs Lonigan's Fifty-Fifth and the El. At this point, however, Rexroth insists on the pre-eminence of Rexroth. His "closest friend" is "the Jewish boy who married Studs Lonigan's sister," but all we learn about that boy is that he was "always dressed in the latest thing out of *Vanity Fair*" and that he "was at least as precocious" as Rexroth himself. With that, he disappears from the narrative, as do so many other figures of note. On page 130, for instance, the reader is introduced to a veritable creative *Who's Who*, all of whom Rexroth met as a 15-year-old boy in the salons of Chicago. But they exist as a mere gallery

of names, a kind of batting order of the famous. It is one of the problems that Rexroth seems to have had in writing this book. He must mention those he knew, like Clarence Darrow and Sherwood Anderson, but he must also pretend that knowing them was of no special significance. Perhaps it wasn't, but then why drop the names?

It may have been Chicago that fostered Rexroth's tough-guy sentimentality; he is capable of writing; "No virgin saying her rosary in a convent is as innocent as an elderly debauched whore and pick-pocket." And he feels compelled to hold the world in judgment and to feed us those judgments in the glibbest of manners: "American fiction, even Hawthorne, even Melville . . . seems to me to be absolute trash"; his idea of the academic world is vintage 1920; his whores, gangsters and drifters all seem descended from the Hollywood of the 1930s; his succession of legacies inherited from unknown relatives at just the right time is terribly contrived (even if they actually happened); his memory is selective in an unselective way; the idyllic bliss of his sexual encounters, along with the baiting of Freud and psychoanalysis, is tedious and contrived, the groaning belly sounding off in the hungry head; even his religion and his radicalism, the two most appealing aspects of his life, are essentially self-conscious and idealized.

And yet, after one has said all this, the fact remains that *An Autobiographical Novel* has a strange appeal, the appeal of a world that, even if it never existed, should have existed. Rexroth can be truly moving, especially when he permits the development of his own receptivity to experience, when he stops showing off the hair on his chest and concentrates on the real job of the writer of autobiography—to feed us the experience of a life that, whatever its peculiarities, has been lived with appetite and zeal.

But for too much of this book he is so self-conscious about his emergence as the young artist and Bohemian that he becomes the victim of his life. It was lived, we feel, to be written about later, or at least to be told to the listeners of Pacifica Radio. In his preface, Kenneth Rexroth wrote: ". . . possible out of the narrative a self can be deduced." For this reviewer, at least, that self remains hidden.—LEONARD KRIEGEL, "Rexroth: Citizen of Bohemia," *Nation,* June 6, 1966, pp. 688–89

ALFRED KAZIN
"Father Rexroth and the Beats"
Reporter, March 3, 1960, pp. 54–56

When the young beatniks or literary hipsters became news in San Francisco a few years ago, an older poet and critic, Kenneth Rexroth, seemed to appear everywhere at their side like the shade of Virgil guiding Dante through the underworld. Rexroth, who had lived in San Francisco since the 1920's and had from early youth been connected with almost every "advanced" literary-radical-Bohemian movement, from the Wobblies and the John Reed Clubs to the objectivist movement in poetry and abstractionism in painting, suddenly became a public figure. He was an originator of the jazz-poetry readings and an extremely effective reader and teacher of poetry on the San Francisco radio. The enthusiasm of the hipsters for orphic art and poetry unfortunately went hand in hand with a professionally exploited ignorance. Rexroth, who had grown up in bitterest poverty and had never completed his high-school course, had the fanatical learning of the self-educated. He published translations from Chinese,

Japanese, Greek, Latin, Spanish, French; he spoke as an authority on jazz and painting as well as on poetry. There was no subject within the range of interest of the new writers on which he disclaimed being an authority, yet by temperament he was a firebrand, a come-outer, a hundred per cent radical-anarchist—no compromiser with what he always called "the social lie."

In an essay for the now defunct *New World Writing* called "Disengagement: The Art of the Beat Generation," Rexroth made out an extremely interesting case for Jack Kerouac before *On the Road* was published, and attributed the recent deaths of Dylan Thomas and Charlie "Bird" Parker, the great Negro saxophonist, to a social order so murderous and corrupt that the only possible recourse for the new writers had now to be "disaffiliation," absolute refusal to work "within the context of this society." This essay, though written in a loud and showy style that did not inspire the reader's trust, nevertheless seemed to me the valuable testament on the Eisenhower years of a veteran American radical who identified himself with all the old robust traditions of native protest. Although there was something about Rexroth's essay that suggested a man looking for a weapon, I recognized in his mordant comments on professor-writers and the decadence of big-city intellectuals a real old-fashioned American sorehead of the type of the old Populists screaming against the moneyed East. And I welcomed this not only because I prefer radicals—people who want to transform society—to the beatniks playing at poverty and drugs and looking for a "thrill," but also because Rexroth's smoldering violence against every surface of the American Establishment, his choked-up bitterness, made him, by the sheer momentum of his tendency to exaggeration, a humorist. Rexroth's unforgettable elegy on the death of Dylan Thomas ("You killed him, Oppenheimer the Million-Killer,/ You killed him, Einstein the Gray Eminence. . . .") is in its sheer uncontrol one of the funniest as well as one of the angriest poems of our time. It takes a really unusual writer today to say a good word for science, but the usual romantic clap-trap about science as the enemy reached in Rexroth's poem the positive pinnacle of outrage. Groucho Marx screaming "I'd horsewhip you if I had a horse!" is really not much funnier than Kenneth Rexroth screaming in one poem against Henry Luce, *Mademoiselle*, T. S. Eliot, the Statue of Liberty, the liberal weeklies, the cocktail habit, Brooks Brothers, and the university quarterlies—"the vaticides/Crawled off with his bowels to their classrooms and quarterlies." Those two clever night-club mimics, Mike Nichols and Elaine May, were right to parody Rexroth's poem as fashionable apocalyptic radicalism, and before long Rexroth was himself appearing in new Bohemian joints like the Five Spot Café in New York's Cooper Square.

Alas, "Disengagement: The Art of the Beat Generation" is not in this new book of Rexroth's essays ⟨*Bird in the Bush: Obvious Essays*⟩. The reason, it seems, is that the beatniks, whom Rexroth seemed to be introducing and explaining to the American public, have became too ridiculous and disgusting to take seriously. "I will not take those would-be allies which Madison Avenue has carefully manufactured and is now trying to foist on me. . . . The Beat Generation may once have been human beings—today they are simply comical bogies conjured up by the Luce Publications . . . the trained monkeys, the clowning helots of the Enemy. They came to us late, from the slums of Greenwich Village, and they departed early, for the salons of millionairesses." (This is a fair specimen of Rexroth's usual moderateness of tone; I forget which Frenchman it was who wrote "*La vérité est dans la nuance*," but he couldn't have discovered this from reading Rexroth. Rexroth writes even critical prose in the style of *New Masses* covers of the 1930's: slashing black-and-white, drawn with a knife. Down with the enemy! Down with "corn-fed metaphysicals" and "country gentlemen"! Down with "subway Neanderthals"! Down and down and damn and damn!)

It is a fact, however, that the beat writers whom Rexroth once heralded have now become rather famous in their own right, and it is striking that his appreciations in this book are devoted largely to established figures like D. H. Lawrence and Samuel Beckett, Henry Miller and Martin Buber and Yeats—plus the painters Morris Graves and Mark Tobey and J. M. W. Turner. But the bitter phrase in Rexroth's preface, "They came to us late," reveals the deep prejudice of a writer over fifty that there is an old radical-avant garde tradition that the beatniks do not represent. This affirmation of "us"—what Rexroth and so many other ex-radicals fondly used to call "the movement"—is curious. Rexroth is a writer who will never make his peace with "the system," with what he unchangeably calls "the social lie." He is so natural a romantic anarchist that a literary historian in the future could decipher all the secondary characteristics of today's romanticism from Rexroth's writings alone. He has the ingrained bitterness of those who have grown up in poverty, who have had to educate themselves in public libraries, who are constantly enraged by the attempt of university "new critics" to divorce literature from life, by the attempt of our leading statesmen, with their pseudomoral imbecilities, to evade the unsettling future. The best of his poems breathe an insatiable nostalgia for the insurgency of American literature before the First World War, for the moral freedom of the 1920's, for the early 1930's, when many an honest writer still thought that he could work with the Communists. His book is in part the intellectual autobiography of a whole generation of American writers born around 1905—and more particularly of Western writers, writers attached to the Wobblies and the ideal of the free "working stiff," writers who to their own minds incarnate the manly democratic West against the wealthy decadent East.

However, Rexroth's belief that his experience constitutes the norm of American insurgency and literary radicalism, and that younger writers are to be regarded as "the trained monkeys, the clowning helots of the Enemy," is as trying as anybody else's nostalgia for the good old days. This country no longer attaches any spiritual value to poverty, and Rexroth's dear old "innocent Jewish mechanics and Italian peasants" are as bourgeois as the rest of us. When Rexroth proudly insists that unlike those who have sold out, "Life with us goes on just the same," he is talking through his hat. His book, though full of nostalgia for the radical past, has no radical content whatever. Rexroth is no longer interested in society, just in obtaining the largest possible freedom from it. He has nothing interesting to say about contemporary society, he merely denounces it: "The contemporary situation is like a longstanding, fatal disease. It is impossible to recall what life was like without it. We seem always to have had cancer of the heart. . . . The first twenty-five years of the century were the years of revolutionary hope . . . Now the darkness is absolute . . . We have come to the generation of revolutionary hopelessness. Men throw themselves under the wheels of the monsters, Russia and America, out of despair, for identical reasons. . . . Writing this, sitting at my typewriter, looking out the window, I find it hard to comprehend why every human being doesn't run screaming into the streets of all the cities of the world this instant."

None of this is very enlightening about anything, and I suspect that what bothers Rexroth is not the despair but the gluttony and selfish ease, which cannot but enrage the man who has had to fight his way up with laborious suffering. One of Rexroth's very best insights in this book is into the capitalist psychology of Rimbaud—so often cited by Rexroth's friend Henry Miller as the rebel incarnate, but as Rexroth says, the very type of the entrepreneur, and never so happy as when he openly played the part. One can discount Rexroth's inverse snobbery about American neuroses being "actually, by and large, palpitations of behavior due to unsatisfied bourgeois appetites and lack of life aim." But he is in the path of truth when he says: "It is possible to mistake a demoralized craving for Cadillacs for 'revolt.' . . . Genuine revolt goes with an all-too-definite life aim—hardly with the lack of it." However, it must be admitted that while Rexroth as a critic always tries to stir up the Philistines, to agitate and to unsettle, he is actually not very interesting. He is a terrible show-off of his own learning, and though he calls himself a literary journalist in the tradition of Huneker, Mencken, and Wilson, he seeks to impress rather than to persuade. He is an impressionist of art, of all the arts, rather than a critic, and there is a certain solemn rapture about his attempts to put jazz and painting into words. But it is typical of Rexroth's lack of objective concern with ideas that although he profoundly admires Martin Buber, he thinks Buber sadly amiss in sticking to Judaism. "It is pitiful to watch a man of Buber's intelligence and goodness struggling in the toils of an outworn and abandoned social paranoia. . . . Why do people bother? If they must have a religion, the basic texts of Taoism, Buddhism, Confucianism need no such reworking."

A dilettante is someone who thinks that he can pick and choose from the world's arts and religions as if they were a department store. Again and again Rexroth betrays his fatherly place in the beat movement by his glibness of cultural allusion, by his admiration for sensation and violence, by his belief, so typical of all the culturally frivolous, that the Orient has transcended the intellectual torment of the West. A dilettante is a man who uses his anger to entertain society, not to change it. "I began to realize I was back in America, a place I try to keep away from." A dilettante is a man who writes that all the scientists in the universities are "genocidists," that "the practice of literature today is the practice of acquiescence," and that religion, any religion, may serve to stimulate the writer's imagination but should not involve tiresome considerations about God.

Mr. Rexroth is a dilettante. Mr. Rexroth, when all is said and done, is a beatnik himself. Let who will write the nation's laws, he says, so long as *he* continues to scorn them.

RICHARD FOSTER
"The Voice of a Poet: Kenneth Rexroth"
Minnesota Review, Spring 1962, pp. 377–84

When a couple of years ago my pleasure in reading through Kenneth Rexroth's first collection of essays, *Bird in the Bush*, led me to take an attentive look at his poetry, I was struck by the anomaly that so good a poet had been so ostentatiously ignored by the ruling literary culture of his time.[1] Until I looked into *Bird in the Bush* I had known Rexroth only as a name connoting a poetry that had never grown up to Auden, a poetry of rabid convictions and shapeless outcries, a poetry skewered in the labor programs of the thirties and yelling ever since. I found that the essays were not only fierce, but also funny and literate. And when I went on from there to the poems I heard a voice all right, but it was a voice

that said and sang far more variously than I had ever guessed it could.

The only poet of major importance with a voice since Yeats—though exceptions might be made for Robert Graves and the later work of Wallace Stevens, and I take it the case of Dylan Thomas is at least uncertain—is William Carlos Williams. And though he has been universally respected and admired, he has been outside the mainstream of twentieth-century Anglo-American poetry. The perpetual extinction of personality has not been a foundation principle of Williams' artistic or spiritual credo as it has been of Eliot's, and his antipathy to Eliot's influence is well known. Rexroth, who has also been outside the mainstream, and as an early admirer of Williams expressed much the same set of antipathies, looks rather like the antiphon of Auden in the way that Williams is the antiphon of Eliot. The kind of poetry Auden wrote was "iconic"—a fancy name for what Rexroth has dubbed "construction"—rather than expressive and personal. To Eliot and Auden and the influential critics of the forties, the poet is conceived of primarily as a "craftsman" of language. But to Rexroth and Williams the poet is much more than a craftsman. It is the difference between "Popinjay" and "Vates," to use two of Rexroth's own favorite characters. The poet is conceived by Rexroth as a kind of prophet or bard. Thus the singleness one feels in all Rexroth's work. Not poems, but poetry—discreet local moments in a single continuum of utterance. A voice. And it is a voice that seems especially worth listening to at this moment when so many poets with voices are beginning to be heard, and so many established voiceless poets are trying to find their voices by exploring the very traditions which Rexroth has been nourishing on now for years.

Rexroth's poetry is in a much older tradition than that of American individualist ecstasy, which he shares in to some extent with Whitman, Hart Crane, and William Carlos Williams. His main tradition is a less provincial one than that, a less strident and ambitious one than that, and one much less prone to artificial supercharging of the sort given it recently by the so-called "Beat" poets. I don't know quite how to name it, except to call it the *personal* or *humane* tradition of lyric poetry—from the tragedy and passion and humor of the late Roman and Medieval lyric poets to the pathos and sweetness and dignity of the classic Japanese. Perhaps I am only saying that Rexroth is a fine universal lyric poet whose work has affinities with much of the best lyric poetry of the past. He is no barbaric yawper, as I had always believed. Oh sometimes, as in his barbaric elegy for Dylan Thomas, he gets mad ("You murdered him, you sons of bitches/In your God damn Brooks Brothers suits!"), but it is sincere anger, and it has that power. And he knows well enough, as he tells us in his fine introduction to Lawrence's poems, that sometimes when you care enough you have to become longwinded and that's that. His worst fault is his own version of official philosophical talk—the same kind of thing that blemishes some of his prose, and that many times blemished Lawrence's. In his long poems, such as *The Dragon and the Unicorn*, a one hundred and seventy-pager published in 1952, where he has lots of Occidental room to verbalize his abstract thinking, there are fistfuls of passages like "Unless we can find somewhere/In the course of rebirth the/Realization of all/Persons through transcendence/Of the self, what I have called/Extra-personalization. . . ." Sappho and Tu Fu must have burned up thousands of infinitely better passages. And Rexroth himself ought, by every right instinct of his good human nature, to abhor such dull blather. But of course even this is part of the voice—the honest voice succumbing to its childish weakness for pedantry. It is no violation of the person, only of sanity, and it is an infrequent kind of badness to boot. Rexroth is really bad, however, *false* to the person that is his theme and to the voice that gives it being, when he falls back slackly, as he occasionally does on the ready-made rhetoric of salon wit ("History's stockholder's private disasters/Are amortized in catastrophe"), or of soapbox incendiarism ("Far/Away in distant cities/Fat-hearted men are planning/To murder you while you sleep"), or of gift book love-schmaltz (". . . I still catch fish with flies/Made from your blonde pubic hair"), which is only silly Lawrence prose.

I am cataloguing the weaknesses so I can clear the decks for the strengths and beauties of Rexroth's poetry, which are considerable and numerous. To date Rexroth has published six books of his own poetry, in addition to a volume of verse drama and several volumes of translations. His earliest work is collected in *The Art of Worldly Wisdom*, first published in 1949. Most of it is work from the late twenties and early thirties, and it is what he seems willing to call "cubist" in nature. It is arid, obscure, not much fun. Though it is stylistically one with the latter work—the language is basically the excerpting of the most of the syntactical arrangements that make simple—it suffers *in extremis* from the philosophical afflatus and communication possible. Its special obscurity is roughly like a long series of grunts, mumblings, and blurtings heard muffled through a motel wall. Except for a few very oriental and very clear love poems, most of the book is dead artifact. Things pick up mightily in his first published book, *In What Hour* (1941), where there are some memorable and deeply felt articulations of the special ideological traumata of the thirties. It is refreshing to encounter, in this day of poetry's stylish inconsequence, a poem as passionately "about" something as Rexroth's "Requiem for the Spanish Dead," or the chillingly prophetic "The Motto on the Sundial," a kind of "Second Coming," which ends,

> It is later than you think, there is a voice
> Preparing to speak, there are whisperings now
> And murmuring and noises made with the teeth.
> This voice will grow louder and learn a language.
> They shall sit trembling while its will is made
>   known,
> In gongs struck, bonfires, and shadows on sundials.
> Once it has spoken it shall never be silenced.

Social apocalypse is the abiding context of Rexroth's poetry—the semi-farcical slaughter of bodies and souls in peace and war, out of which rises phoenix-like the living flames of persons, shaped in love, anger, visionary ecstasy, and holy dying. Self, loved ones, lovers, in moments of fulfillment or recognition, and through and over all the beauty and power of Nature, which, though it is the ultimate extinguisher of persons, is also the natural enemy of society, which is the enemy of persons. These are the themes and occasions of Rexroth's best and most characteristic poems, the best of which are in three books, *The Phoenix and the Tortoise* (1944), *The Signature of All Things* (1949), and *In Defense of the Earth* (1956).

Some of the most memorable are elegiac poems, ranging in mood from the beautiful personal elegies for the poet's mother and for his first wife, Andrée, to the superb classical assaults—some of them are adaptations or actual translations—upon the pretensions and pomposities of man in his physicality and mortality. I must quote just one of the latter, from *The Phoenix and the Tortoise*, to demonstrate their ferocious humanity:

> I know your moral sources, prig.
> Last night you plunged awake screaming.

> You dreamed you'd grown extremely old,
> Lay dying, and to your deathbed,
> All the girls you'd ever slept with
> Came, as old as you, to watch you die.
> Comatose, your blotched residues
> Shrivelled and froze between stiff sheets;
> And the faces, dim as under
> Dirty water, incurious,
> Silent, of a room full of old,
> Old women, waited, patiently.

Perhaps the truly essential Rexroth is found in the love poems. Almost all of his good poems could be said to be love poems. From the sweetly reserved translations of Chinese and Japanese poems, to Rexroth's own intense, free-flowing poems, the theme is love. Love—the recognition of mortality, the turning of the seasons and the great, silently commentative drift of the constellations overhead, and the stepping forth into full, intense, imaginative reality of mortal persons, lover, wife, child, and friend. There are so many good and true Rexroth poems of this kind that selection and discrimination is difficult. They crowd to be heard. One of the most moving of them is "'. . . About the cool water,'" from *The Phoenix and the Tortoise*, in which the words of Sappho, the effulgence of midsummer, the deep, still lateness of afternoon, and the slow, full passion of lovers lying together in the orchard of a ruined New England farm fuse, as in the momentum of a complexly counterpointed piece of music, into a love poem of astonishing immediacy. There is nothing between: the poem is intensely the act. Another love poem, a different love, but with the same beautiful immediacy, is "A Letter to William Carlos Williams," in *The Signature of All Things*. It is like Burns' love for Lapraik, and like his verse letters. It begins, "Dear Bill." Williams is like St. Francis, Brother Juniper, and "the Fool in Yeats," and he has the mystic's gift of "wonderful quiet" ("Each year a sheaf of stillness,/Poems that have nothing to say," like "the archetype, the silence/Of Christ, when he paused a long time and then said, 'Thou sayest It'"). The letter concludes, after citing Williams' line, "I who am about to die," (which "sends/A shudder over me. Where/do you get that stuff, Williams?"), with a charming and touching personal tribute: Rexroth imagines a distant day when the passaic will be called the Williams River, and a young woman, walking beside it, will explain to her children that

> He was a great man. He knew
> It was beautiful then, although
> Nobody else did, back there
> In the Dark Ages. And the
> Beautiful river he saw
> Still flows in his veins, as it
> Does in ours, and flows in our eyes,
> And flows in time, and makes us
> Part of it, and part of him.

This is a delicate and deeply felt personal tribute—an intimation of the poet's immortality, a definition of his power and role in the human community. The letter concludes, "With love and admiration,/Kenneth Rexroth."

Rexroth's love poetry is the poetry of small things; of the everydayness of being alive with the whole mind and heart; of the casual, perfect, personal silences; of fulfillment and peace; and sometimes of intense, glowing, vision. The vision poems—the poems in which the values of being human and alive are not merely taken hold of and realized, but are translated, exalted to the intensity of holy vision—are perhaps the best of all. "Gic to Har," in *In What Hour*, finds the poet leafing in arid listlessness through the encyclopedia; he comes upon "Grosbeak," and suddenly a blinding memory of boyhood and the first rapt hearing of the bird's song comes upon him, the memory renewing him and refreshing him in the way of a mystical experience. "Climbing Alone All Day," in *The Phoenix and the Tortoise*, describes the poet's descent at sunset from a day in the mountains, his glimpse of the home campfire's smoke rising in the canyon, "A human thing in the empty mountains," and the whirling vision of the loved one dancing and singing with beautiful life in the welcoming flame and smoke: "This moment of fact and vision/Seizes immortality,/Becomes the person of this place."

There is no inconsistency between such moments of vision and the moments of rage and contempt. They are all part of a singleness, the single voice and the single integrity. As Rexroth writes in his essay on Kenneth Patchen, "If the conscience remains awake, there comes a time when the practice of literature is an intolerable dishonesty, the artist is overridden by the human being and is drafted into the role of Jeremiah." The human beauty and value realized in the poem "Climbing Alone All Day" is what is fought for, defended by the Jeremiad "Thou Shalt Not Kill." In the scale of values ecstasy and vision precede moral earnestness. But in the rough, knotty medium of actual life Jeremiah precedes Vates—walking a little ahead, toughly clearing the way, quieting the hubbub by shouts. Clearing the way for such a lyric moment as this, from *The Phoenix and the Tortoise*—one of the fullest and most delicate moments I have found in any poet:

> Now, on this day of the first hundred flowers,
> Fate pauses for us in imagination,
> As it shall not ever in reality—
> As these swifts that link endless parabolas
> Change guard unseen in their secret crevices.
> Other anniversaries that we have walked
> Along this hillcrest through the black fir forest,
> Past the abandoned farm, have been just the same—
> Even the fog necklaces on the fencewires
> Seem to have gained or lost hardly a jewel;
> The annual and diurnal patterns hold.
> Even the attrition of the cypress grove
> Is slow and orderly, each year one more tree
> Breaks ranks and lies down, decrepit in the wind.
> Each year on summer's first luminous morning,
> The swallows come back, whispering and weaving
> Figure eights round the sharp curves of the swifts,
> Plaiting together the summer air all day,
> That the bats and owls unravel in the nights.
> And we come back, the signs of time upon us,
> In the pause of fate, the threading of the year.

"There is a lot of bullshit in Lawrence, Miller, or Patchen," Rexroth writes in the introduction to *Bird in the Bush*. And I think he would be among the first to see why you might also say something like that of him. As a matter of fact he has written a poem about his weakness for abstraction—the weakness of commitment. It is called "Precession of the Equinoxes":

> Time was, I walked in February rain,
> My head full of its own rhythms like a shell,
> And came home at night to write of love and death,
> High philosophy and the brotherhood of man.
> After intimate acquaintance with these things,
> I contemplate the changes of the weather,
> Flowers, birds, rabbits, mice and other small deer
> Fulfilling the year's periodicity.
> And the reassurances of my own pulse.

Rexroth gets angry and goes abstract himself because he cares with an intensity that goes sometimes beyond "art." But an angry man can still be a good poet, even one of the best. Here are some lines of poetry—Jeremiah leaning towards Vates, perhaps softening:

> And in even such stew and stink as Tacitus
> Once wrote of, his generals, gourmets, pimps, pol-
> troons,
> He found persons of private virtue, the old-fashioned
> stout ones
> Who would bow the head to no blast; and we know
> that such are yet with us.

Who wrote this? Robert Penn Warren, one of our most "official" men of letters. And how alike his and Rexroth's humanism can be, in spite of the Original Sin technicality! And how alike also their poetry, often—in sensibility, even in movement. They love the same things. Read Warren's beautiful book of poems called *Promises* and you know you have found one of the best American lyric poets. Read *The Phoenix and the Tortoise*, *The Signature of All Things*, and *In Defense of the Earth* and you'll know you've found another.

Notes

1. This state of affairs is somewhat rectified, perhaps, by the fact that Rexroth is given three pages of consideration in M. L. Rosenthal's *The Modern Poets* (Oxford University Press, 1960), while John Crowe Ransom receives hardly three words. But in Roy Harvey Pearce's rather more considerable, and on the whole more spokesmanly, *The Continuity of American Poetry* (Princeton University Press, 1961), Rexroth is not even mentioned.

ERIC MOTTRAM
From "Introduction"
The Rexroth Reader
1972, pp. 9–13

Kenneth Rexroth's memoirs *An Autobiographical Novel* are the result of a tape-recorded account of his childhood, adolescence and young manhood, made in 1959 for his young daughters. The fifty-four-year-old writer does not compose some maudlin 'even tenor of his days' but looks back in happiness, and a happiness defined as activity, a variety of exposure to other people and fresh situations and an unusually wide range of self-expression. Rexroth calls his opportunities luck, but in fact he offered himself to America in his youth as few men could. He has always enjoyed being both contemporary and scholarly, and this was partly due to the training of his childhood, which prepared him for a range of pleasures from unpuritan sexuality to the incipient monasticism of the Holy Cross Monastery on the Hudson River. *An Autobiographical Novel* is the book of a youth on which Rexroth built everything he has been able to enjoy—to study, make love well, paint, cook cowboy style, write poetry, dance, act, translate from the Greek and Chinese and write anthropology and essays on every matter except literary criticism. But the pleasure is penetrated by commonsense rationalism. The irrational sticks in his throat and the art and music he likes tend to be intellectually patterned rather than sensuous. On the other hand, he is an old-fashioned landscape-romantic, whose visionary moments take place in natural space—like this experience, during one of his spells as cookee and wrangler, of dawn on the west side of the Rockies.

Sitting on a horse in the midst of illimitable miles of sagebrush and rock under the paling stars is an experience like those described by the mystics—the smell of greasewood and juniper smoke, the strong smell of horses as you come on them in the chill air, the stringent smells of the land itself, the sound of thrashers and wrens waking up the country, the sharp aseptic smell of mountain streams in the night.

It says everything for the empirical richness of the man that his Catholicism is mainly a love of the rituals of a semi-pagan order, the liturgy, the backlog of scholars and the sacraments which 'transfigure the rites of passage, the physical acts of the human condition.' This oscillation between restless experiencing and stablizing reading, painting, writing and study is the structure of a long worked-out freedom. The Absurd and the Mystery he recognizes but leaves to those who can really use them. What he hedges at is clear from the bohemian sexuality of his memoirs—the sexual morality of Catholicism and, by implication, Christianity itself.

Rexroth is a man of temperament and passion but not of violence, either sought or given. He is no bodily pugilist, whatever the aggressiveness of some of his opinions:

> The most offensive element in Catholicism, for me, is its sexual morality, and I believe that the hysterical frustration which it has engendered is the root of the incredible violence and dishonesty of the history of Western man since Constantine. I don't think puritanism is especially Protestant. The modern Church is unfairly criticized for its neopuritanism. The permissive morality of the Renaissance and eighteenth century which survived until recent times in the Latin countries was really an episode; the puritanism of the great medieval Scholastics and the Fathers of the Church is much more rigorous than that of Calvin, Luther, and John Knox. Mary Stuart would have had a far rougher time than she did had she fallen into the hands of St. Augustine.

Rexroth is an artist and a radical—an American artist and an American radical; that is, he is conscious of the European inheritance of injustice and intolerance when he attacks American capitalist exploitation and the American history of intolerance against Indians and Negroes. The early experience he lived out between 1905 and 1930 between art, bohemianism and politics gives him a right to take a radical stance:

> Protestantism, at least in its orthodox form, has always filled me with loathing. Its basic spiritual dilemma is simply incomprehensible to me. I have never found anything in my experience, internal or external, to justify a vision of the world suspended from two metaphysical poles, one utterly contingent and one absolute in every conceivable sense, and both lost in the night of nonbeing. For this reason not only is the whole Augustinian tradition meaningless to me—Kierkegaard has always seemed to me to be a miserable and silly man, badly in need of what the psychiatrists call 'help'—but the existentialist dilemma which has haunted French philosophy since Descartes is likewise meaningless to me. Not only that, but what is after all only a subtle modification of it, the epistemological worry of the English, is at least as meaningless.
> What I have gained from Christianity as such is a belief in ethical activism.

That belief takes the form of 'the binding force of a community of love,' the evolution of society out of 'what Marx calls human self-alienation in modern life—the lack of significant work, the lack of mechanism in society to give meaning to the most important events and situations in life, the lack of organic

community.' Beliefs are not in themselves radical activism but 'unstable things at best and an intelligent man holds millions of them in his life, almost all of them fugitive and contradictory. Furthermore, belief is easily come by . . . Facts, happenings, experiences are different. We are not asked if we accept them; we discover ourselves living them.' This is Rexroth's action—pragmatic opinion following living and personal discovery. And after his packed life, he can make later life statements without being laughably naive, boring or full of fake wisdom or cracker-barrel advice. His visionary experience is not slotted rapidly back into dogma or guruism. Throughout his life he has been influenced by too many men and women—freely acknowledged—to expect any one to sit at his feet, like the ideological disciples of the 'thirties and 'forties or the Movement of the 'sixties. The conclusion of his autobiography does not sum up in the manner of an aged TV performer dispensing philosophical clichés, but there is a glamour which, curiously, is not preserved in the characteristic dryness of his poems.

Where the life and the poems meet is in their mutual concern for that radical inheritance from Marx and anarchistic leftism of the inter-war period, excellently presented in one of his best poems, 'Noretorp—Noretsyh':

> Rainy, smoky Fall, clouds tower
> In the brilliant Pacific sky.
> In Golden Gate Park, the peacocks
> Scream, wandering through falling leaves.
> In clotting night, in smoking dark,
> The Kronstadt sailors are marching
> Through the streets of Budapest. The stones
> Of the barricades rise up and shiver
> Into form. They take the shapes
> Of the peasant armies of Makhno.
> The streets are lit with torches.
> The gasoline drenched bodies
> Of the Solovetsky anarchists
> Burn at every street corner.
> Kropotkin's starved corpse is borne
> In state past the offices
> Of the cowering bureaucrats.
> In all the Politisolators
> Of Siberia the partisan dead are enlisting.
> Berneri, Andreas Nin,
> Are coming from Spain with a legion.
> Carlo Tresca is crossing
> The Atlantic with the Berkman Brigade.
> Burharin has joined the Emergency
> Economic Council. Twenty million
> Dead Ukrainian peasants are sending wheat.
> Julia Poyntz is organizing American nurses.
> Gorky has written a manifesto
> 'To the Intellectuals of the World!'
> Mayakofsky and Essenin
> Have collaborated on an ode,
> 'Let *Them* Commit Suicide.'
> In the Hungarian night
> All the dead are speaking with one voice,
> As we bicycle through the green
> And sunspotted Californian
> November. I can hear that voice
> Clearer than the cry of the peacocks,
> In the falling afternoon.
> Like painted wings, the color
> Of all the leaves of Autumn,
> The circular tie-dyed skirt
> I made for you flares out in the wind,
> Over your incomparable thighs.
> Oh splendid butterfly of my imagination,

Flying into reality more real
Than all imagination, the evil
Of the world covets your living flesh.

The poet in San Francisco, looking towards the Pacific and Asia, and through Asia to Russia and Europe, and imagining the living present of revolutionary writers as he moves within his own community of love: it is the Rexroth ideal. Here is the beginning of a possible recovery from old error in the human order. Catholicism may still attract him, as it did Henry Adams, and like Williams James, he is concerned with experience of the 'timeless, spaceless, total bliss.' But he has no confidence in yoga or drugs: 'Vision which is so conditioned is self-defeating because it must always be exceptional.' Again, like Adams, he is attracted to Buddhism in so far as its visionary capacity is 'developed by a kind of life rather than by manipulation.' But in the main his pragmatic empiricism relieves him of the burden of joining a dogma and frees him to enjoy what he can understand and make over into a minimal, non-systematic synthesis of his experience, gathered year by year. His long poems, 'The Phoenix and the Tortoise' and 'The Dragon and the Unicorn,' are part of that process, and like the autobiography are a steadying, recollecting action by the artist in the man. They make no conclusions:

> Each of us is a specific individual . . . each of us draws his own mystery with a knowing which precedes the origins of all knowledge. None of us ever gives it away. No one can.

DANIELA M. CIANI
"Kenneth Rexroth: Poet of Nature and Culture"
For Rexroth, ed. Geoffrey Gardner
1980, pp. 14–22

Virginity—if it ever were possible for any nation—has not been one of America's characteristic traits for quite some time, and a harsh feeling of deception now grips her intellectuals. It is all too well known that the rise to empire of a nation exacts a high cost in diminishing respect for the individual. Kenneth Rexroth is one of the outstanding personalities in contemporary American culture. He has always openly fought any threat to intellectual freedom and basic human needs. He is a man of action, a scholar, a poet and a master.

Still, strong links subsist between Rexroth and a traditional sense of what it is to be American. His work is rooted in it. This is not to say that America is his sole or particular focal point, nor that his language and rhythms are merely experiments in the peculiarities or innovations of American English. Rexroth actually deals with the broadest and most diverse human and cultural issues, but in so doing he uses images and references that strongly recall American landscapes and all phases of American life. He anchors his thought to them. He constantly returns to them and they, in turn, have become part of him. His very passion for freedom, equality and independence is reminiscent of the original American vision. Such feeling of rootedness in America stands out all the stronger when held in relation to Rexroth's profound knowledge of other civilizations, always confronting them to abolish limits to understanding. Not being an academic writer, he does not move backwards from his reading of Classical, Oriental, or Continental literatures to the comprehension of his own reality, and he never appears to be involved in a self-conscious effort to recover American culture and identity. On the contrary, he seems to live and breathe them, while endeavoring to broaden and deepen them. In this sense, Rexroth, with scholarly discipline and his eyes open to the needs of our immediate days, continues a tradition already established by earlier American writers and artists.

There are two outstanding features of Rexroth's poetry: nature and culture. His attitude towards both springs from the same need to be an active participant in all that surrounds him. Rexroth's relationship to nature is an intimate one. He has derived his knowledge of it from direct experience, which he has always widely and deeply cultivated. His *An Autobiographical Novel* confirms this. It is evident there how a loving curiosity about rivers, lakes, mountains, prairies, animals, sciences are one with the understanding of life itself—they stand in an organic relationship. It is from this that Rexroth's whole philosophy springs. In contrast to those of the English Romantic poets who developed principles of "organic poetry", and in contrast to Walt Whitman himself, who, in his fusion with nature, almost becomes a human metaphor for it, Kenneth Rexroth has believed it best to discover a role of his own—as a unique human being—within the realm of nature and in concert with it. From this follows his philosophy of love—or, rather, the lack of competition. Hence his recognition of and respect for the reciprocals; hence, in the most immediate and concrete terms, his faith in and devotion to freedom. His whole poetry is substantiated by this faith and devotion. Nature is the scene of his reflections, particularly when they are freest and convey, with the greatest lyricism and vigor, the image of the human being who is the poet. As in "No Word":

> The trees hang silent
> In the heat . . .
>
> > Undo your heart
> > Tell me your thoughts
> > What you were
> > And what you are . . .
> >
> > > Like bells no one
> > > Has ever rung.

—an intimate moment of person to person communication, private, unique, precious, delicate. In the background are the trees which, in the rigor of the short poem, must have their role: to the eyes and heart of the poet, their presence, no matter how far removed or scant, is a co-presence with that of the woman. They belong there. The poet is seen here in a serene and inclusive embrace of both woman and setting; it is an embrace since he intimately understands and holds them, serene because of the devotion, generosity and confidence implied. Rexroth never separates the natural world from the self; it is a part of him and is portrayed as such in his poetry.

In "On What Planet", practicing rock climbing with a group of mountaineers, Rexroth absorbs the joys of nature, observing and tenderly interpreting its moments:

> The warm air flows imperceptibly seaward
> The autumn haze drifts in deep bands
> Over the pale water . . .
> We look over fifty miles of sinuous
> Interpenetration of mountains and sea . . .

He indicates the place and the animals—the egrets and the owls—which he observes with exquisite finesse and great care for detail. The image we have, then, is not that of an idyllic stroll in search of rest or of some emotion "to recollect", rather it is an image of strenuous climbing, after which the mind is relaxed and refreshed and the body newly strengthened. The human dimension is deepened by the introduction of a young girl:

> A young girl with ash blond hair
> And gentle confident eyes.
> She climbs slowly, precisely,
> With unwasted grace . . .
> She turns to me and says, quietly,
> "It must be very beautiful, the sunset,
> On Saturn, with the rings and all the moons."

This is a vivid portrait of a man who actively partakes of his surroundings and depicts for his reader moments of passive pleasures, when immersed in nature, and moments of active pleasures when he traverses nature in order to discover and assimilate its wealth. In the eyes of this lover of nature, the girl becomes part of that complement to his own self which all the outer universe is.

In Rexroth's poetry love is a form of communication, both physical and spiritual, which occurs spontaneously between the poet and his beloved. The frame is always provided by the natural milieu, the setting for present moments or the reminder of past moments. If such association is indicative of the close relationship between Rexroth and nature, it is also one further indication of his philosophical standpoint: just as he feels attraction for and dedication to nature, so he also observes its laws, including those of love relationship. The result is his particular spontaneity and freedom in living and expressing love and a poetry that catches its fleeting but imperishable nuances. This is evident in "When We with Sappho". The lovers plunge into summer, are permeated by it and transfer its brightness and life into their own bodies:

> We lie here in the beefilled, ruinous
> Orchard of a decayed New England farm,
> Summer in our hair, and the smell
> Of summer in our twined bodies,
> Summer in our mouths . . .
> All about us the old farm subsides
> Into the honey bearing chaos of high summer.

Notwithstanding the intensity and instinctive force of their transport, there is no lack of tenderness: there are similitudes that link the woman to the suavity of sleep—"your grace is as beautiful as sleep"—and to the glister of the sky—"And it is as though I held / In my arms the bird filled / Evening sky of summer." Time in this celebration of love, loses its sequential dimension so that, simultaneously, it may feed on the past (the reading of Sappho) and be projected into the future: "We have grown old in the afternoon. / Here in the orchard we are as old / As she (Sappho) is now." Silence emphasizes their private emotions: "Do not talk any more. Do not speak. / Do not break the silence until / We are weary of each other." Evening takes over the afternoon, and repose embraces both nature and the lovers: "Your body moves in my arms / On the verge of sleep." All this conveys a flavor of intimate peace and physical content, savored by both sentiment and intellect.

Nature's omnipresence, in Rexroth's poetry, is not solely a means by which to enrich both momentary joys and lasting treasures; still more, it is the mindful testimony of what in life once was and now is gone forever. In "Andrée Rexroth", a poem for his late wife, Rexroth writes:

> Now once more gray mottled buckeye branches
> Explode their emerald stars . . .
> I know that spring again is splendid
> As ever . . .
> But these are the forest trails we walked together,
> These paths, ten years together.
> We thought the years would last forever,

> They are all gone now, the days
> We thought would not come for us are here.
> Bright trout poised in the current—
> The raccoon's track at the water's edge—
> A bittern booming in the distance—
> Your ashes scattered on this mountain—
> Moving seaward on this stream.

And in a poem dedicated to his mother, "Delia Rexroth", he remembers her this way:

> Under your illkempt yellow roses,
> Delia, today you are younger
> Than your son . . .
> Near the willows by the slow river,
> Deep in the earth, the white ribs retain
> The curve of your fervent, careful breast;
> The fine skull, the ardor of your brain . . .

Rexroth maintains a position in relation to culture that is identical to his position in relation to nature. Just as he understands and lives nature as a complement to his unique human dimensions, so culture—reading, art and all cultural experimentation—is for him a means to better understand and interpret reality. It broadens and deepens both consciousness and conscience. The physical world and the call to an organic collocation are not sufficient for a poet whose intelligence requires not only a direct and immediate sort of knowledge but also a kind of knowledge that can help him find his place within both social life and the history of humanity in its relationship to reality. From this derives, for Rexroth, an attitude that leads to dynamism and conflict. Knowledge of the past and of what is remote extends the horizons of one's own culture: from contigency and individuality to community and universality. So we find in Rexroth's poetry not only cultural references and the record of his personal and inner acquisition of them, but also constant attention to whatever has been innovative and of enduring value. There is always rebellion against whatever is static or prejudicial to liberty and responsible growth, against obscurantism and dogma.

A consequence of these basic needs is Rexroth's adherence to those cultural phenomena which, in their aim toward new forms of communication and new viewpoints, break through old structures, making their way to new interpretations of reality. His literary career has grown from this "existential" standpoint. For example, in "Fundamental Disagreement with Two Contemporaries", written in 1932, we can sense the disagreement, but the overall impression is that it comes as the consequence of an underlying and basically different attitude. That is, while the Dadaists and Surrealists had developed a sense of wrath and, particularly, of cynicism, Rexroth was sustained by the fundamental optimism of Cubism.

Control over form and care for content are found in all those poems in which Rexroth—inspired by poets like Reverdy—seizes the manifold aspects of reality and decomposes them in a structure which is screened from appearances: they are clean and "cubist". By this method, both Rexroth's perceptions and his interpretation of reality can find their place. Such poems are a source of confrontation for the reader, who, once he has reshaped the mosaic, becomes the free interpreter of what he has been offered. Of course, the reading of Rexroth's poetry is never passive or easy.

Even when he is very personal and confines himself to autobiographical moments, Rexroth proposes to share his memories and experiences with his reader, indicating insight's particular relevance in discerning inner pleasures and allurements:

My head and shoulders, and my book
In the cool shade, and my body
Stretched bathing in the sun, I lie
Reading beside the waterfall—
Boehme's "Signature of All Things".
. . . The long hours go by.
I think of those who have loved me,
Of all the mountains I have climbed,
Of all the seas I have swum in.
The evil of the world sinks.
My own sin and trouble fall away
Like Christian's bundle, and I watch
My forty summers fall like falling
Leaves and falling water held
Eternally in summer air.
                              ("The Signature of All Things")

By stimulating a conscious response towards a particular reality, both through his use of abstract concepts and cultural references in the poem above, Rexroth encourages not only a dialectic attitude towards what he says, but also arouses his reader's desire to be similarly intimate with the materials of the culture to which we all belong. Clear evidence of this is provided by those works Rexroth has specifically composed for broader diffusion and more direct communication: social, political and factual poems, which are meant primarily for public readings. Their provocative tone—as well as their familiar language, cadences and rhythms—is combined with accurate references to specific episodes and facts which the auditor must know, or want to know, in order to get the message and be capable of personal judgment. Examples are "Thou Shalt Not Kill" [1955] and "Noretorp—Noretsyn" (*Hysteron-Proteron*) [1957]. Since it often happens that facts and ideas are not openly divulged, Rexroth challenges his audience by offering them all the information, his opinions about it all and his reactions. Thus he accomplishes the function of poet as "seer" and *vates* in just the way the records of our tradition say poets are to be defined.

All this may, at times, be costly for Rexroth in terms of speculative or stylistic refinement. But the same is true of the work of others, where it often is the result of an artist's isolation from the world, either imposed on him or chosen as a secure refuge. Kenneth Rexroth withdraws from such games—and does not hesitate to denounce them—in order to keep faith with his principles and continue as an acute perceiver of man's surrounding reality and inner vitality.

Particular mention should be made of Rexroth's activity as a translator, especially from Far Eastern languages. In fact, together with the poetry, Rexroth has translated the very terms of deep and sophisticated cultures where nature appears to have been abstracted from matter and has then come to be reshaped within a philosophy of life combining both the sensual and the ethereal. His own more recent poetry has undergone the influence of Far Eastern traditions: pure, clear-cut images conveying a world of meanings:

Cold before dawn,
Off in the misty night,
Under the gibbous moon,
The peacocks cry to each other,
As if in pain.

Notwithstanding the tortuous distance between the ideal state hoped for in nineteenth-century America and the actuality to which the course of history has led, Kenneth Rexroth's love for the American soil, his belief in freedom, his attraction to nature and dedication to culture, his devotion to teaching and his interest in the Far East have all allowed him to persist as a master poet deep in the American grain.

ELMER RICE

Elmer Reizenstein

1892–1967

Elmer Rice was born Elmer Reizenstein in New York City on September 28, 1892. At the age of fourteen he left school to support his family, working first as an office boy and then as a law office clerk. He studied law at night and received an LL.B. *cum laude* from New York Law School in 1912, but instead of going into practice he announced his intention to write. Simplifying his name to Rice, he wrote a play, *On Trial*, and naïvely mailed it to a producer. Surprisingly, it was accepted and produced successfully in 1914; it is remembered today because it employed for the first time on the American stage the technique of the flashback.

For the next nine years Rice eschewed the commerical stage, devoting his time to amateur theatrical organizations in New York City, primarily the Morningside Players and the University Settlement Dramatic Society. Four early plays were produced during this period: *Iron Cross, Home of the Free, For the Defense,* and *Wake Up, Jonathan.* In 1923 the Theatre Guild produced his play *The Adding Machine,* which depicted the unbearable monotony of office drudgery. It was a success both in America and England, and led to Rice's collaboration with Dorothy Parker on *Close Harmony* (1924) and with Philip Barry on *Cock Robin* (1928).

Because of Rice's increasingly radical political and economic views and his sharp criticism of commercial theatre, he became an unpopular figure among conventional producers and had difficulty in getting his new play, *Street Scene*, staged. A tragedy featuring characters who live in a New York tenement, it was finally produced in 1929, was a critical and popular success, ran for more than a year, won the Pulitzer Prize, and was made into an acclaimed motion picture. A well-received musical version of *Street Scene* was produced in 1947 with music by Kurt Weill and lyrics by Langston Hughes.

Rice wrote more than two dozen plays in the years following *Street Scene*, most notably *We, the People* (1933) and *Dream Girl* (1945), but none of his subsequent works enjoyed the critical and popular success of the earlier production. During the 1930s Rice served briefly as New York Regional Director of the Federal Theatre Project, but resigned in protest against censorship from Washington. Throughout his life Rice spoke out on behalf of a variety of liberal causes and was closely associated with the American Civil Liberties Union.

Rice married twice and was the father of five children. He died in Southampton, England, on May 8, 1967.

In a dry season, when so many theatres are closed and not a few managers have given up the game for the nonce and gone off to sunny beaches and Hollywood, Mr. Elmer Rice's *Street Scene* has come to many people as a treat, an excellent play, a worthy entertainment; and there is no need to throw any blight over the flower of their enthusiasm. In the realm of the blind, following the Spanish proverb, let the one-eyed be king; we may cheer *Street Scene* and wish it well.

In a setting by Mr. Jo Mielziner, cleverly realistic without being foolishly so, and photographic without idle intrusions of dusty neighborhood detail from Ninth Avenue, where the play is laid, we see the story unwind itself entertainingly, with an amiable pace and plenty of time for the talk of the apartment house people as they go in and out, with engaging colors drawn from the contact of diverse nationalities—Jews, Germans, Irish, Italians and 100 percent Americans—and with a due complaisance and tidy willingness to please. There is a genuinely expert economy in the way in which the life of the Maurrant family is conveyed to us, and an economy of means that is even more expert in the portrait of the wife's career, this doomed Anna Maurrant, whose husband is brutal and indifferent in his treatment of her, is given to drink, is full of principles and ideas as to what a family should be and what his own has got to be, he'll see to that!

The inmates of the apartment house, then, go in and out, linger about the doorstep in the stifling summer heat, sit at their windows, gossip of their children and each other, of the little husband on the third floor who acts as if he were having the baby instead of his thin bit of a wife, of the Hildebrand family whose head has disappeared and who are about to be dispossessed. And through the whole texture of conversation they weave the thread of this pale woman's tragedy on the second floor, the visits of the milk collector that they have all observed, the spreading scandal about Mrs. Maurrant. Idly and emptily they are doing her to death, but it is all part of the day's chatter and the neighborhood news. We see Rose, her daughter, and the married suitor, who wants to take her from the job in his office and set her up in an apartment and a place on the stage; we see Maurrant himself, a member of the stagehands' union, a drinker, sullen and bullying. Meanwhile, Mrs. Jones has something to say about everything, takes her husband, George, to task, and her dog, Queenie, to walk, and professes complete ease of mind about her children, one of whom is a hulking thug and the other almost a tart.

From that on, the play runs its course, clearly foreseen. The baby is born upstairs, Mrs. Maurrant tends the mother all night, she is even more brutally treated by her suspicious husband; he says he is going out of town with a show, her daughter is at the funeral of a member of the firm she works for, and Mrs. Maurrant asks the milk collector—cleverly portrayed by the author as by no means attractive and thus the more indicative of the woman's despair—to come up to her rooms. The husband returns, kills the lover, and mortally wounds the wife, and after a long search is caught by the police. Rose, his daughter, refuses the attentions of the married suitor, and at the last does not accept the love of the Jewish student; she goes away for her own life, with her own ideas about one's dependence on something within oneself and reflections on the history of her father and mother in the light of that theory, not without some smear of egotism—with its attendant confusion—on her own part.

All this time, as a kind of matrix for the story, people have been passing, an ingenious assemblage of types and interests, curiosities of the town, vignettes of Manhattan, incidents of a day, and so on and so on, rendered with an amiable and accurate diversity that carries matters pleasantly along. And in the apartment house itself the well-edited sayings of the different persons and races accompany this drab pageantry and street genre.

Mr. Rice's directing is good. Among the many players necessary for this *monde* of the West Side, Miss Mary Servoss, as the tragic central figure of the woman who is killed, gives a performance that is always convincing, and that, while she is on the stage, lifts the scenes to something like pathos and point. Miss Erin O'Brien Moore, as her daughter, Rose, has to surmount many platitudinous approaches to the character, and speeches that are without imagination or reality, but plays well; she presents a young image that our eyes easily believe in, and a sincere and simple rendering of the character so far as is possible with the lines written for her to speak. Miss Beulah Bondi's Mrs. Jones is excellent playing.

So much for *Street Scene*, then, which on one plane of consideration is pleasantly entertaining. On another plane, where you take the play seriously and where you ask yourself whether for an instant you have believed in any single bit of it, either as art, with its sting of surprise and creation, or as life, with its reality, *Street Scene* is only rubbish, or very close to rubbish. For me, who was not bored with it as an evening's theatre, it is something less than rubbish; it is theatrical rubbish, in that curious, baffling, embodied and persuasive way that the stage provides. The presence of living beings in the rôles engages us, and gives a certain plausibility to whatever takes place and a certain actuality to any character whatever. But is it possible that anyone who could understand the values in the first act of *Anna Christie*, for example, or a play of Chekhov's, could fail to see that the last act in *Street Scene*—to take the most conspicuous let-down in the play—is empty and made up? The girl has found her mother shot, has seen blood, at the hospital she has seen her mother die without speaking, she has seen her father caught and torn and bleeding; the Jewish boy, who loves her so much, offers to leave everything and go away with her, and she stands there making a sent01tious little speech about dependence on oneself and so on and so on, while nurses with perambulators appear and various persons come prowling around the scene of a murder, and the obvious life goes on, with amusing remarks from odd characters, and the rest of it—obliging journalism in sum. It must be a very elementary principle that the essential idea of a work of art goes through it, and that the themes and conceptions to be expressed must lie inherently in the substance of it, and that they are to be expressed in creation, not in superimposed sentiments. And so it follows that this pseudo-significant patter that the playwright has put into the mouth of his heroine at this point is a bad omen for the play's significance.

Must we gloomily conclude that what most human beings like in the theatre is a farrago of living matter with the sting taken out of it? If this Anna Maurrant's life and death really bit into us, cost us something, instead of providing a mere thrill and the comfort of pseudo-thought afterward, would we not wreck the stage for rage when we see how little this matter has stung the dramatist? One of the ways we know a work of art is by what its unity in kind has cost, precisely in the same way that the soul within him, determining his form as he comes into the world, prevents a man's having the bulk, strength and peace of an elephant. One of the ways we can tell an artist is by the extent to which reality puts the fear of God into him. A painter, for example, of no worth will paint you anything from Napoleon crossing the Alps to an old mill in Vermont, but a real painter trembles before the mere character of human hands and the problem of their conversion into the unity that is his style.

On a milder level of discourse, we may say that the acting in *Street Scene* furnishes a good instance of one of the problems in the art. For the most part the company at the Playhouse is made up of people who fit the characters ready-made. An Italian plays an Italian, a Jewess a Jewess, and so on. In the hurry and pressure of things there is little time to discover or train actors, perhaps, and perhaps the need for actuality in this particular piece led the casting toward these ready-made types. The result is that in *Street Scene* there is a good deal of entertainment that comes from watching these actual people as we might see them on Ninth Avenue, but very little interest in watching them as actors. They are mostly neither bad nor good. Their resemblances are better than their acting, and they themselves seem more convincing than what they say. As a minor by-product of the perplexity induced by such a situation, I have no idea whether the player written down as Mrs. James M. Qualen, whose janitor, Olsen, seems to me the best performance of the evening, is only a Nordic of that ilk, chosen for his type, or is a capital actor.—STARK YOUNG, "Street Scene" (1929), *Immortal Shadows*, 1948, pp. 106–9

Elmer Rice clings to the contemporary theatre by providing a new play with increasing irregularity. His most recent work, *Cue for Passion* in 1958, was written forty-four years after *On Trial*. Unlike Behrman, Rice did have a cue for passion. He was always a man committed to causes, a fighter for drastic social reform. He wrote anti-Nazi plays (*Judgment Day*), plays about labor and censorship (*We, the People*), and calls for responsible liberalism in government leadership (*American Landscape*). *Cue for Passion* is a far cry from his earlier work. It is a modern retelling of the Hamlet story. Not only the title but the characters and plot are based on the Shakespearean play, and audience interest lies in making the correlations. Everyone from Polonius to Horatio is present in a tricky parallel, reaching to a hallucinatory reappearance of a dead father.

Tony Burgess comes home from two years in Asia, sulky, perverse, intractable, a melancholy suburbanite. He believes his stepfather, Carl Nicholson, had been his mother's lover and was the murderer of his father. On a palatial California estate he sets out to avenge his father's death, but Tony has a mother fixation and a reverse Oedipus complex. He identifies himself with the lover's role and is unable to kill his stepfather, for that would be to destroy himself. His anger is not directed at the evil represented by Carl, but at his own guilt. Carl did what Tony had only dreamed of doing. Tony does not kill his "uncle" because he himself had wanted to kill his father. *Hamlet's* richness, its multiple overtones, its relationship to basic problems of good and evil, give way to Tony's multiple neuroses. This Hamlet story with a Freudian twist still retains Rice's strong dialogue and shows a keen mind commenting on modern living, but it bogs down in the present-day obsession with psychiatry. With too many playwrights—and Elmer Rice falls victim to his own warning—drama becomes a case study. Rice, like Behrman, is aware of the contraction in the contemporary theatre; he said recently, "Too many playwrights today seem to be beating their breasts and feeling sorry for themselves."

Rice's recent miscue should not obscure the contribution he has made to the American theatre. Any playwright who has written as much as he has is entitled to an occasional lapse. In the early twenties he was courageous enough to experiment in his finest and most enduring work, *The Adding Machine*. Four decades later, the tale of Mr. Zero has continuing relevance. A machine-dominated world that reduces individuality to numbers and makes soulless manipulators of its servants has never been more dramatically represented. Zero is capable of one moment of passion—he murders his boss and goes to the Elysian Fields. Here, where he is relieved of all mundane problems, he can be happy, but Zero has become unalterable. He remains an adding machine. He is compelled to go back to earth for his reincarnation, but the heavenly agents know that Zero is beyond redemption. Even in Heaven, he remains a Puritan. Not only is he tied to the machine; he has become a machine himself in his response to love, life, and beauty. The Theatre Guild production, with Zero running back and forth in a forest of man-sized adding-machine keys, was a triumph of the theatre of fantasy and a powerful social commentary.

Street Scene (1929), Rice's Pulitzer Prize-winning play, was a radical departure from drawing-room intrigue and middle-class drama, with its depiction of the swirling life in the slums of New York. The story has the melodramatic ingredients of a drunken father, an unfaithful mother, young lovers, revolver shots, and police arrests, but employs the arts of the theatre in kaleidoscopic scenes, to make the protagonist an entire community rather than specific individuals—an American *Lower Depths*. The people cluttered in the vast loneliness of New York tenements are depicted as the helpless victims of social forces. Poverty destroys beauty, compassion gives way to cruelty, and neighbors derive pleasure from the downfall of others. Public charity and social work are shown in their scheming inadequacy. On a large canvas, a cross-section of urban depression was given dramatic form. *Street Scene* was a forerunner of the Living Newspaper and one of the early demonstrations of the power of theatre as historical documentation. With a score by Kurt Weill and lyrics by Langston Hughes, the musical version has become a popular favorite.

After World War II, Rice wrote less frequently. His association with the Playwrights Company gave him a continuing outlet for his plays, even though they were of dubious merit. *The Grand Tour* (1951) was a sentimental romance about a schoolteacher on a European trip; *The Winner* (1954) was a last stab at legal evidence as drama. *Dream Girl* (1945) and *Cue for Passion* (1958) are further evidence of the change in Rice's outlook. He no longer is fighting for social causes, but has, like so many others, retreated to personal psychological studies. At heart, despite his plays of social protest, Rice is an incurable romanticist.

A skillful performer in varying styles, Rice was able to learn from European developments. *The Adding Machine* is reminiscent of expressionistic plays by Ernst Toller and Georg Kaiser. *Street Scene*, in sharp contrast, moves from abstract concepts and anonymity of the individual to the detailed realism of Emile Zola combined with the reportage devices of Epic theatre. *On Trial* initiated the flashback technique, now so widely used in motion pictures and on the stage. His many plays of courtroom evidence, derived from his training as a lawyer, are close to Bertolt Brecht's plea for the theatre as tribunal, even though Rice imposes a suspense-crisis thriller structure.

He retained enough vitality to depart from all his previous styles in the ebullient and witty fantasy *Dream Girl*, an engaging comedy of a daydreaming young girl who fancies herself in love with three different men. As her agile imagination pictures events, they unfold on stage. The technique is again cinematic, although, on stage, revolving platforms and blackouts replace the dissolve to effect rapid changes from reality to fantasy. Georgina Allerton, the young lady, is a delightfully incurable romantic; her scenes have become audition exercises for aspiring actresses, and the play is assured of endless revivals as summer stock fare. The plot is weak, but clever dialogue and ingenious staging have made the play a perennial favorite. Under its innocuous boy-gets-girl triviality lies the maxim that dreams should be balanced by at least a minimum of practicality and that too acute a preoccupation with dull reality should burst into flights of fancy, lest it degenerate into cynicism and apathy.

For Elmer Rice, champion of the underprivileged, to have written a Freudian *Hamlet* and a teen-age love story is no cause for condemnation. The finest writers will turn out a potboiler now and then. George Bernard Shaw offered his "pleasant" comedies to a reluctant Victorian audience, but an acute wit and an undeviating social commitment give meaning to his most contrived action-melodramas. Rice was not a profound or an original thinker, but a talented adaptor of current ideas, even those that were unpopular. His courage was admirable, but the McCarthy era, which quieted rebellious minorities, gave him no inspiring causes to defend. A skilled veteran of his craft, he could always turn out a well-constructed play sprinkled with brilliant comments on contemporary life, but the fire was gone. A generation without a cause left him without the "cue for passion" that had raised a rich talent above mediocrity. The one movement that has now inspired the young and aroused their willingness to sacrifice for others came too late in his life. He would have written, otherwise, a stirring tribute to the fighters for civil rights.

Elmer Rice is in the unique position of being both a playwright and an active worker in behalf of other playwrights. Like Edward Sheldon, that great human being who, though practically blind and suffering from his own anxieties, never failed to help other writers, and whom Rice knew in his youth, he has never failed to come to the assistance of others. His own life may be his most enduring monument. Always a man of principle, he did not hesitate to act when moral issues were at stake. When he was New York area director of the Federal Theatre Project, he resigned in protest when the State Department refused to permit the opening of *Ethiopia*, the first of the Living Newspaper presentations. In 1951, he left the Playwrights Television Theatre when the networks and agencies intensified the use of a blacklist of actors. In an open letter he declared,

I have repeatedly denounced the men who sit in the Kremlin judging artists by political standards. I do not intend to acquiesce to the same procedures as followed by police commissars who sit in the offices of advertising agencies or business corporations.

As the dean of American playwrights, Rice has been a member of the board of directors of the Dramatists Guild and of the American National Theatre and Academy, and retains his chairmanship of the National Council on Freedom from Censorship. More directly connected with the theatre was his active participation in the formation of the Playwrights Company, an effort to eliminate the commercial producer. His force as a personality has been felt, and his love of the theatre is indestructible. He commented a few years ago on the dearth of good plays, "Fantasy is too deeply rooted to be eradicated. So long as people continue to dream and to dramatize themselves there will be theatre." Here, perhaps, lies the motivation for *Dream Girl* and *Cue for Passion*.—ALLAN LEWIS, "The Tired Deans—Elmer Rice and S. N. Behrman," *American Plays and Playwrights of the Contemporary Theatre*, 1965, pp. 136–40

JOSEPH WOOD KRUTCH
From "The Drama of Social Criticism"
The American Drama since 1918
1939, pp. 230–39

Mr. Rice's first produced play was *On Trial* (1914), a courtroom melodrama, novel chiefly because it called for a revolving stage which made possible the "flash back" technique borrowed from the moving picture. It earned him a modest fortune and the next few years were devoted to another melodrama, to the dramatization of a short story, and to a collaboration with Hatcher Hughes on the comedy *Wake Up, Jonathan* (1921). None of these efforts was conspicuously successful and none except the last of any particular interest. Then, in 1923, the Theatre Guild produced *The Adding Machine* and Mr. Rice became the Guild's first American "discovery."

Mr. Zero, the hero of this play, is an aging nonentity employed as an office worker, and also, as his name suggests, a symbol of all the despersonalized helots who perform the routine tasks of a commercial civilization. When he is discharged from his job because an adding machine has made him unnecessary, he rebels for once in his life, stabs his boss to death, is executed for murder and ascends to a heaven in which he is put to work at a machine of the very sort responsible for his downfall. But even heaven cannot use him as he is, and when the curtain falls he is on his way back to earth to try again.

Mr. Rice may or may not have remembered the button maker in *Peer Gynt* but *The Adding Machine* is not so much an imitation of anything—not even of the German expressionistic drama from which the technique was doubtless borrowed—as it is an original synthesis of half a dozen elements all of which were characteristic of current rebellion in the arts. In the first place there is, of course, the concern with human nature at its nadir, with the cipher not the great man as hero. What one gets is accordingly not tragedy but anti-tragedy and the story of a man without even the brute strength which had given *The Hairy Ape* at least one distinction. But, as in the case of *The Hairy Ape*, the dream world is called upon to contribute irrational elements capable of intensifying the atmosphere of a play which would otherwise fall as flat as a day in the life of Mr. Zero himself, and the whole becomes, not a series of rational events, but a nightmare.

It begins with a long soliloquy in which the wife of the hero reveals her soul in the course of some meditations on marital fidelity and the movies. Like the meditations in James Joyce's *Ulysses* it is ostensibly the stenographic report of a "stream of consciousness" but actually so intensified and formalized that it becomes a fitting introduction to the Walpurgis night which follows. The very monotonous insistence of its vulgarity hypnotizes the imagination and one passes easily into the world of half-insane fantasy where the main action takes place. Moreover, the formal unity and hence the artistic success of the piece depends upon the fact that the spell of the nightmare is never broken and no attempt is made to interpret it in fully rational terms. Ten years later Mr. Rice, like many of his fellows, would have been unable to write the play because he would by then have been too sure that he knew precisely what it meant, and the nightmare which has here all of a nightmare's not quite definable logic would have become a mere allegory with all of an allegory's childishly mechanical symbolism. In *The Adding Machine* the author was describing a vision in which he saw a typical human cipher rendered contemptible by his own spiritual nullity and then destroyed by a machine capable of performing his absurd little function better than he could perform it himself. Ten years later Mr. Rice would have been capable only of explaining a theory which made spiritual nullity the product of a society which misused its mechanical tools. And the fact remains—however lamentable it may be—that visions still make better plays than theories ever have.

Mr. Rice devoted the next few years to adaptations and collaborations which added little to his reputation. Then in *Street Scene* (1929) he returned again to the life of the urban proletariat for a theme to be treated in a very different manner and in a very different mood. In *The Adding Machine* he had made his central character not an individual but a symbol because the story of a cipher can be made to seem even dubiously important only if one is made to feel that the story of one is the story of thousands. But Mr. Rice is not by temperament a man given to either abstraction or despair and he turned in *Street Scene* (instinctively, no doubt) to the opposite but more familiar method of dignifying the story of humble folk. He sought, that is to say, to discover even in the squalor of the slums men and women with character enough and passion enough to make them respected as individuals, and he wrote in consequence a melodrama with genuinely tragic implications. In one sense it is, therefore, the antithesis of *The Adding Machine*.

The method is the method of that realism which strives for the typical and yet stops just short of the point where all sense of particularity is lost. The entire action takes place in front of a typical New York tenement. The intent is to present a cross-section of the life in such a metropolitan microcosm, and the curtain rises upon a neighborly group on the front steps exchanging platitudes about the heat. Presently the janitor deposits the ashcan upon the sidewalk, a boy on roller-skates shouts to his mother on the third floor for a nickel to buy an ice-cream cone, and by a dozen such trivial incidents the rhythm of tenement existence is established. For a time we admire the accuracy with which these routine events are mimicked, but as the play proceeds the stress is laid more and more upon the lives and characters of certain individuals. Before mere recognition has palled as a source of pleasure, various little domestic dramas begin to emerge; then the

attention is gradually focused more and more upon one of them; and the play reaches its climax in a melodramatic scene of unusual intensity—a scene of violence which made even the hardened playgoer grip his seat and stifle the involuntary and agonized "Dont', don't!" which he was about to shriek across the footlights. The events which lead up to it are artfully managed, the tension grows tighter and tighter as the moment approaches, and the scene itself is as vivid as such a scene can possibly be.

Obviously, a part of the interest which the play holds is the result of this mere melodramatic tension which the author has managed to generate by the use of devices as old as melodrama itself. Equally obviously he intended that it should take on an additional importance by virtue of the fact that the scene presented and the manners delineated are typical enough to constitute a commentary upon a portion of our civilization—even indeed to suggest a criticism of a society which generates slums and compels human beings to live in them. But this is not all, for the central story of the oppressed wife and of the pathetic little love affair which precipitates the catastrophe also suggest the irrepressible aspiration of human nature toward some sort of self-fulfillment. She is not a mere Zero. She is capable of resolution, of courage, and of choice. She is therefore capable also of dignity and the story of her fate is the possible subject of a genuine tragedy.

Mr. Rice never wrote again so good a play because he never again showed himself capable of being equally serious without sacrificing his interest in character to his interest in a theory and a lesson. *Street Scene* is a "proletarian" play in the simple sense that it is a play whose dramatis personae are all members of the proletariat. It is also a "proletarian play" in the sense that the form taken by the conflict and by the catastrophe is determined in part by the physical environment amidst which the characters live and the economic conditions against which they struggle. But the attention is centered upon the interplay of passions, and the personages are interesting chiefly, not because they are oppressed, but because, despite oppression, they have remained human beings.

After *Street Scene* Mr. Rice produced in rapid succession three plays lighter in tone and rather obviously intended primarily as contributions to the popular theater. Of these, *See Naples and Die* (1929) was a failure; *The Left Bank* and *Counsellor-at-Law* (both produced in 1931) conspicuously successful. Both the latter are narrowly topical in a way that neither *The Adding Machine* nor *Street Scene* had been since both deal with what used to be called "the humors" of a specific milieu—in one case that of the tourist's Paris; in the other a New York lawyer's office. But both are also characteristic of Mr. Rice because they exhibit his great skill as a practical playwright and, what is more important for the present discussion, because they spring out of that eager concern with the phenomena of contemporary life which, in the case of these two plays, renders even its trivia interesting to him.

No contemporary dramatist has (or rather had) a keener ear or a shrewder eye. No matter what milieu he chose to present in a play, one might be sure that its salient features would be recorded with an exactitude which both the camera and the phonograph might envy. What most of us have only seen or heard he has noticed; and the result is a spectacle at once novel and familiar—familiar because we have met every one of its elements before, amusingly novel because we have never previously realized just how characteristic these familiar things were. The titter of recognition is the response which he is surest to win, and realism of a kind could hardly be carried further. In *The Left Bank* his room in a cheap Parisian hotel is perfect in its verisimilitude and so too are all the things that go on in it. The bathroom two flights up and the telephone three flights down are nature herself; so too are the obsequious but incompetent male chambermaid, the light which goes on over the bed when it is turned off in the room, and the hideous wallpaper which is convincingly declared to be worse in the next room than in this. Whoever has taken his course at the Dôme—and what American under fifty has not?—will smile with malicious pleasure and feel, besides, a certain pride in the realization that he too is in a position to appreciate the jest. For a time the Left Bank was, hardly less than Kansas, a part of the American scene. "Et in Arcadia ego," murmured the spectator. He too knew whereof Mr. Rice was speaking. He too had tried to forget a damnably inadequate bath by reflecting on the superiorities of European civilization, and he too had babbled of the graciousness of Parisian life while munching stale *croissants* beside a bed of incomparable hideousness. But none of these reflections quite last the evening out, and as the minutes rolled by, one became more and more acutely aware that Mr. Rice had nothing new to say concerning the problem of the expatriates.

Obviously these latter are running away from themselves and obviously that is something which no one can do successfully. Their roots are in American soil and can draw their sustenance from nowhere else—even though, perhaps, it is just as well that every rebel should find out that fact from himself. If they want a different civilization they will have to build it for themselves since, as the *raisonneur* of the play remarks, "It seems to me that we have got to go where the world is going, not where it came from." All this and more along the same sensible line is said well in *The Left Bank*; but something less familiar would be necessary to make the play more than the rather amusing comedy it is. If the scene is to be familiar and the characters are to be typical, then there is a crying need for novelty somewhere, for the pleasure of recognition, genuine though it be, is not by itself enough for a great or really stirring play.

All that has just been said of *The Left Bank* might be applied with very little change to *Counsellor-at-Law*. The latter play, to be sure, professes to be serious in its undertone since it is concerned with the personal tragedy of a self-made lawyer who is compelled by force of circumstances to wander through certain not too attractive back-alleys of practice; but the effect is primarily the effect of comedy, and there is an entire gallery of characters so justly drawn that one recognizes them immediately as exquisitely lifelike. Certain sections of the play—notably the first scene of the first act which establishes the atmosphere—succeed so admirably that they might stand by themselves as complete sketches. Time and time again the spectator is moved irresistibly to laughter by the perfect rightness of some remark made by an office boy, a telephone operator, or a dowager from the East Side. Few will remember the plot; many probably remember the youth in whose possession was always to be found the volume from the law library which dealt with rape.

ANTHONY F. R. PALMIERI
"Conclusion"
Elmer Rice: A Playwright's Vision
1980, pp. 192–98

The drama was the last of the literary genres to come of age in America. In fact, not until the advent of the First World War did it show signs of developing into a serious art, worthy of comparison with its counterparts in Europe. As late as the middle of the second decade of the twentieth century, American drama was in such a static condition and lagged so far behind the modernist movement that one historian of letters, Alan Downer, has remarked: "Half a century after Ibsen and Strindberg, and several decades after Chekhov and Hauptmann and the reformers of the Continental theatres and their repertories, theatre in the United States was still tied to the dramatic forms and conventional attitudes of the past. A wholly commercial operation, it insisted that its function was to entertain, and it defined entertainment as escapism."[1] In sum, American commercialism plus the cultural lag—in the arts and sciences we were still going to school to Europe—made a discouraging equation.

The coming-of-age of the American theater begins with the emergence of Eugene O'Neill as a playwright of consequence. He was the first to win critical acclaim in the world theater.[2] But no theater achieves world stature by the exploits of one man alone. The heights that O'Neill was scaling were soon to be attempted by other gifted American dramatists. And if none of these was surpassing the master himself, they were at least staking out new and promising territory. Perhaps the most underrated of this group of playwrights, which along with O'Neill was responsible for the sudden maturation of our drama, is Elmer Rice. Though in prolificness and durability as a playwright Rice outdoes his fellows, and though his impact on our theater, aside from the mere writing of plays, probably surpasses that of any of the others, he has been the subject of only two books and of one doctoral dissertation. Such are the vagaries of critical and academic fashions. Clearly, Rice deserves more attention.

Of O'Neill's contribution to the American theater, Alan Downer has argued that it was three-fold: "He wrote plays that were highly original in form, indebted to but not imitative of the whole repertory of world theatre; he devised or assisted in devising unique methods of staging, carefully adjusted to the demands of each new play; he reflected in subject matter and theme not the contrived world of the theatre, or some conventional world of the past, but the life and thinking of his own time."[3] With few apologies one could easily substitute Rice's name here for O'Neill's.

About the time when O'Neill was sitting in on Professor Baker's Drama 47 class at Harvard and some years away from his first Broadway production, Rice was already on the boards with a hit that broke with tradition by introducing the flashback technique to the American theater. In itself, this might have been no startling innovation, for very likely Rice borrowed the technique from the movies. But certainly his effort to break new ground must have encouraged other playwrights, perhaps even O'Neill himself. Besides, Rice's introduction of this novel device forced another innovation on the American theater, the jacknife stage: the gain here was in removing a major restriction in dramaturgic art by making it possible to change scenes with an Elizabethan-stagelike rapidity.

Indeed, it might be argued that as Rice's best only O'Neill

is his superior. In prolificness and versatility he is unmatched by anyone but that giant of our theater. Compare him with his fellows recalling that he is productive from 1914 through four decades—Rice at least stands along with his contemporaries: Sidney Howard, Paul Green, Marc Connelly, George S. Kaufman, George Kelly, Maxwell Anderson, Sidney Kingsley, S. N. Behrman, Philip Barry, Lillian Hellman, Clifford Odets, Robert Sherwood, Thornton Wilder, and William Saroyan. His list of credits cannot be denied. Moreover, throughout his career Rice remained an innovator.

For example, in 1923 he gave the world *The Adding Machine*. Granted that in such expressionism O'Neill had preceded him—with *The Emperor Jones* in 1920 and *The Hairy Ape* in 1922—still Rice's play was very different from these. It was the first important American drama to focus on the dehumanization of the American middle class as victim of a mechanized and quantified society. Furthermore, Rice uses the aside in *The Adding Machine* as a means of revealing the inner and secret thoughts of his characters, a technique that O'Neill did not attempt until *Welded*, produced a year later, in 1924, and one that he did not fully exploit until *Strange Interlude* in 1928.[4] Some sense of Rice's achievement in this regard may be gained from, for instance, W. David Siever's observation that *The Adding Machine* and John Howard Lawson's *Roger Bloomer* (1923) together represent "the high water mark of expressionism in America."[5] Then in 1929 came the naturalistic *Street Scene*, a play so radical in its departure from accepted formulas for the American theater, and so demanding in its stage devices and in casting, that it very nearly failed, for practical reasons, to get on the boards. Today *Street Scene* is recognized as one of Rice's masterpieces. Then, with *We, the People* in 1933, Rice experimented with something like audience participation. In this departure he might have encouraged Odets to try something similar in, for example, *Waiting for Lefty* (1934) and possibly Wilder in *Our Town* (1938). *A New Life* (1943) brought yet another innovation: Rice's was the first drama to feature a childbirth scene in full view of the audience. Even in his declining years Rice remained *avant garde*. In his 1954 drama, *The Winner*, he cast a Negro in a role in which the racial problem was not a factor. And that was another "first" in the American theater.

Nor does the tally end here. No American playwright was more abreast of the times than Elmer Rice. For example, when the work of Freud, Jung, Adler, and company made psychoanalysis important to an understanding of individual persons and of the human condition, and when many native playwrights began to reflect at least something of this new psychology, Rice was one of the first in the field. Admittedly, O'Neill beat Rice to the draw in *Diff'rent*, a 1920 study of sexual frustration, and again in *The Emperor Jones*, a dramatizing of Jung's "collective unconscious" that reached the boards in the same year. Still, in *Wake Up, Jonathan* (1921) Rice and his collaborator, Hatcher Hughes, treated changing concepts of child psychology. In both *The Adding Machine* (1923) and *The Subway* (1929) Rice handled repressed sexuality, and he employed the oedipal motif in *Black Sheep* (1923). For perspective on Rice's response to the new psychology it might be noted that neither George Kelly's *Craig's Wife* (a study of a neurotically domineering woman) nor Sidney Howard's *Silver Cord* (a study in mother-fixation) reached the boards until 1925 and 1926 respectively; Philip Barry's treatment of regression in his comedy *In a Garden* came in 1925, and two years later came S. N. Behrman's *The Second Man*, which deals with the alter ego.

Clearly, in his subject matter and themes Rice was often

enough ahead of his fellow playwrights. For instance it is curious that, though the pacifist attitude and the disillusionment with war and the growing realization that war is not the romantic adventure traditionalists would lead us to believe appear so frequently in the poetry and fiction of the 1920s, no major dramatist of that decade dealt with these matters. Maxwell Anderson and Laurence Stallings did, to be sure, combine their talents to produce a fine war play in *What Price Glory* (1923); but that work is in many respects romanticized, with an aura of high-spirited adventure common to earlier war literature. In this respect it differs radically from Rice's *The Iron Cross*, which was produced as far back as 1917.

With the coming of the Great Depression, Rice turned his attention, as did many other playwrights then, to the sickness of his country, to the two major concerns of the period: social and economic injustice. He had, however, as far back as 1916, in *The House in Blind Alley*, attacked the indifference of society to the evils of child labor; and in *Street Scene* he had counted up the human costs of the lower-middle-class environment. Now, once again, Rice comes to grips with the social and political ills of an era. In plays like *We, the People, Judgment Day, Between Two Worlds*, and *American Landscape*—these four done between 1933 and 1938—he used the stage in behalf of social and political reform. In these ventures Rice surely holds his own among contemporaries like Maxwell Anderson (*Both Your Houses* [1933] and *Winterset* [1935]), Lillian Hellman (*Days to Come* [1936]), Clifford Odets (*Waiting for Lefty* [1934] and *Awake and Sing* [1935]), and Sidney Kingsley (*Dead End* [1935]). Moreover, Rice is the first American playwright to recognize and reveal the menace of Nazism, which he does in *Judgment Day*; Clifford Odets's one-acter, *Till the Day I Die*, was not staged until one year later, in 1935. And in *American Landscape* he is the first to deal with the Nazi threat emanating from within our own society, for Lillian Hellman's somewhat comparable *Watch on the Rhine* follows Rice three years later, in 1941.

Though he made no fetish of novelty or innovation for their own sakes, throughout his career Elmer Rice was regularly in the vanguard. Sometimes—one thinks of *The Iron Cross, The House in Blind Alley, Street Scene*, and *Judgment Day*—he was so far ahead of the crowd that he appeared to be alone. Even as his career approached its end, his keenness of insight and the breadth of his social interests did not diminish. He saw quite early that a major problem in the postwar world would be one of living in a loveless universe grown accustomed to brutality and violence and lawlessness, a world where "as on a darkling plain . . . ignorant armies clash by night." Rice's statement of this problem and his answer to it appear in his 1951 drama, *Love Among the Ruins*.

None of this is meant to argue that, next to O'Neill, Elmer Rice is the greatest figure in American drama. Granted, the quality of his work is uneven. Sometimes Rice falls so far below classics like *The Adding Machine* and *Street Scene* as to tempt one to apply to him the old nursery rhyme: When he was good, he was very very good; / And when he was bad, he was horrid. Nevertheless, Rice should not be denied his rightful place among those few who in the first half of the present century brought the American drama to worldwide recognition.

One paradox is that perhaps Rice's greatest strength is related to his chief failing. That is, like Shaw, he would use the theater as a platform for discussing the ills and self-deceptions of society. His impulse was that of the reformer, not merely in the art of dramaturgy, but also in the actuality of the real world. Sometimes he slid too easily into the didactic or the propagandistic. For all that, his better plays are very little dated.

One aspect of his struggle was to maintain his integrity as a serious artist and yet somehow make his way on commercialistic Broadway. Few other dramatists of Rice's stature hit this double-edged problem so head-on. For everyone he fought the good fight against conditions that at best are uncongenial to and at worst destructive of genuine creativity in playwriting. His directorship of the New York Federal Theatre Project and his helping to found the Playwrights' Company are only two passing episodes in a long and strenuous career. Because he took his own art seriously, he strove to improve the quality of the theater, to widen its appeal, and to improve the working conditions of all those involved in it. Always something of a crusader, Rice has had an impact on American drama and on American life that goes beyond the mere writing of plays and extends to the very heart of that theater and that life. To borrow from the title of one of his last published plays, Rice himself had many cues for passion. In speeches, articles, interviews, books, and in his dramas, he attacked the status quo of

Broadway; he struggled against censorship in all the arts; he was always the enemy of bigotry, intolerance, social and political injustice; he championed freedom and dignity for the individual. In his vision of America, Rice was committed to the tradition of liberalism, in the best sense of that problematic term. The American theater indubitably has been a little healthier and American society a little better because a youngster named Elmer Leopold Reizenstein one day decided to give up the practice of law and make the stage his career.

Notes

1. Alan Downer, "The Revolt from Broadway," in A *Time of Harvest: American Literature 1910–1960*, ed. Robert E. Spiller (New York: Hill and Wang, 1962), p. 42.
2. Ibid., p. 43.
3. Ibid., p. 46.
4. W. David Sievers, *Freud on Broadway: A History of Psychoanalysis and the American Drama* (New York: Hermitage House, 1955), p. 104.
5. Ibid., p. 140.

ADRIENNE RICH

1929–

Adrienne Cecile Rich was born on May 16, 1929, in Baltimore, Maryland, to Arnold Rice and Helen Jones Rich. She was educated at Radcliffe College, receiving a B.A. in 1951. In 1953 she married Alfred Conrad, a Harvard economist; they had three children before Conrad's death in 1970. Rich has taught at a number of colleges and universities, including Swarthmore College, Columbia University, City College of New York, Brandeis University, and Douglass College; since 1981 she has been a Professor-at-Large at Cornell University. She has lived with historian-writer Michelle Cliff since 1976.

Rich received support for her writing from an early age, publishing two books of juvenilia as a young child (*Ariadne, a Play in Three Acts and Poems*, 1939, and *Not I, But Death, a Play in One Act*, 1941). Her first two books of poetry as an adult, *A Change of World* (1951) and *The Diamond Cutters and Other Poems* (1955), were traditional in form and largely concerned with the themes prevalent at the time. "I know that my style was formed first by male poets: . . . Frost, Dylan Thomas, Donne, Auden, MacNiece, Stevens, Yeats," she has said. "What I learned chiefly from them was craft." Though derivative, her early poems were executed wtih skill and control, and received praise from W. H. Auden and others.

With *Snapshots of a Daughter-in-Law* (1963) Rich found her own voice: angry, personal, and direct. She began to experiment with looser, open forms, and resorted less often to personae and borrowed voices to communicate her message. *Necessities of Life* (1966) continued this development, focusing on solitude and sexuality in particular. Both books were hailed as evidence of Rich's maturity and individuality as a poet.

Leaflets (1969) was, if anything, more individual than either of the two previous volumes, but the reception was decidedly more mixed. This volume dealt much more explicitly with political issues of the day, and some critics saw this as an unfortunate distancing mechanism between Rich and the reader. Others regarded it as a welcome advance in Rich's vision of herself and her position in the world. Her direct, unadorned style developed further with *The Will to Change* (1971), as did her commitment to poetry as a polemical instrument for social change.

Diving into the Wreck (1973), though maintaining Rich's overtly political stance, returned to the level of purely personal experience to develop her themes of sexual, social, and political conflict. The results were troubling and powerful, and the critical consensus held this to be her best book yet, a successful fusion of her mature personal and political concerns. It was a co-winner of the 1974 National Book Award for Poetry.

The Dream of a Common Language marked another advance in Rich's poetry; the air of frustration and anger that pervades much of her mature poetry was replaced by a quiet determination for change and a celebration of herself as she is now.

Rich remains a political poet, but she is as concerned with the aesthetics of communicating a message as with the message itself. In addition to her poetry Rich has written sociological-feminist studies such as *Of Woman Born* (1976) and *Compulsory Heterosexuality and Lesbian Existence* (1981). Her selected poetry is contained in *The Fact of a Doorframe: Poems Selected and New 1950–1984* (1984).

ADRIENNE RICH
From "When We Dead Awaken: Writing as Re-Vision"

College English, October 1972, pp. 21–25

My own luck was being born white and middle-class into a house full of books, with a father who encouraged me to read and write. So for about twenty years I wrote for a particular man, who criticized and praised me and made me feel I was indeed "special." The obverse side of this, of course, was that I tried for a long time to please him, or rather, not to displease him. And then of course there were other men—writers, teachers—the Man, who was not a terror or a dream but a literary master and a master in other ways less easy to acknowledge. And there were all those poems about women, written by men: it seemed to be a given that men wrote poems and women frequently inhabited them. These women were almost always beautiful, but threatened with the loss of beauty, the loss of youth—the fate worse than death. Or, they were beautiful and died young, like Lucy and Lenore. Or, the woman was like Maud Gonne, cruel and disastrously mistaken, and the poem reproached her because she had refused to become a luxury for the poet.

A lot is being said today about the influence that the myths and images of women have on all of us who are products of culture. I think it has been a peculiar confusion to the girl or woman who tries to write because she is peculiarly susceptible to language. She goes to poetry or fiction looking for *her* way of being in the world, since she too has been putting words and images together; she is looking eagerly for guides, maps, possibilities; and over and over in the "words' masculine, persuasive force" of literature she comes up against something that negates everything she is about: she meets the image of Woman in books written by men. She finds a terror and a dream, she finds a beautiful pale face, she finds La Belle Dame Sans Merci, she finds Juliet or Tess or Salomé, but precisely what she does not find is that absorbed, drudging, puzzled, sometimes inspired creature, herself, who sits at a desk trying to put words together.

So what does she do? What did I do? I read the older women poets with their peculiar keenness and ambivalence: Sappho, Christina Rossetti, Emily Dickinson, Elinor Wylie, Edna Millay, H.D. I discovered that the woman poet most admired at the time (by men) was Marianne Moore, who was maidenly, elegant, intellectual, discreet. But even in reading these women I was looking in them for the same things I had found in the poetry of men, because I wanted women poets to be the equals of men, and to be equal was still confused with sounding the same.

I know that my style was formed first by male poets: by the men I was reading as an undergraduate—Frost, Dylan Thomas, Donne, Auden, MacNiece, Stevens, Yeats. What I chiefly learned from them was craft. But poets are like dreams: in them you put what you don't know you know. Looking back at poems I wrote before I was 21, I'm startled because beneath the conscious craft are glimpses of the split I even then experienced between the girl who wrote poems, who defined herself in writing poems, and the girl who was to define herself

by her relationships with men. "Aunt Jennifer's Tigers," written while I was a student, looks with deliberate detachment at this split.

> Aunt Jennifer's tigers stride across a screen,
> Bright topaz denizens of a world of green.
> They do not fear the men beneath the tree;
> They pace in sleek chivalric certainty.

> Aunt Jennifer's fingers fluttering through her wool
> Find even the ivory needle hard to pull.
> The massive weight of Uncle's wedding band
> Sits heavily upon Aunt Jennifer's hand.

> When Aunt is dead, her terrified hands will lie
> Still ringed with ordeals she was mastered by.
> The tigers in the panel that she made
> Will go on striding, proud and unafraid. [1]

In writing this poem, composed and apparently cool as it is, I thought I was creating a portrait of an imaginary woman. But this woman suffers from the opposition of her imagination, worked out in tapestry, and her life-style, "ringed with ordeals she was mastered by." It was important to me that Aunt Jennifer was a person as distinct from myself as possible—distanced by the formalism of the poem, by its objective, observant tone—even by putting the woman in a different generation.

In those years formalism was part of the strategy—like asbestos gloves, it allowed me to handle materials I couldn't pick up barehanded. (A later strategy was to use the persona of a man, as I did in "The Loser.") I finished college, published my first book by a fluke, as it seemed to me, and broke off a love affair. I took a job, lived alone, went on writing, fell in love. I was young, full of energy, and the book seemed to mean that others agreed I was a poet. Because I was also determined to have a "full" woman's life, I plunged in my early twenties into marriage and had three children before I was thirty. There was nothing overt in the environment to warn me: these were the '50's, and in reaction to the earlier wave of feminism, middle-class women were making careers of domestic perfection, working to send their husbands through professional schools, then retiring to raise large families. People were moving out to the suburbs, technology was going to be the answer to everything, even sex; the family was in its glory. Life was extremely private; women were isolated from each other by the loyalties of marriage. I have a sense that women didn't talk to each other much in the fifties—not about their secret emptinesses, their frustrations. I went on trying to write; my second book and first child appeared in the same month. But by the time that book came out I was already dissatisfied with those poems, which seemed to me mere exercises for poems I hadn't written. The book was praised, however, for its "gracefulness"; I had a marriage and a child. If there were doubts, if there were periods of null depression or active despairing, these could only mean that I was ungrateful, insatiable, perhaps a monster.

About the time my third child was born, I felt that I had either to consider myself a failed woman and a failed poet, or to try to find some synthesis by which to understand what was happening to me. What frightened me most was the sense of drift, of being pulled along on a current which called itself my destiny, but in which I seemed to be losing touch with whoever

I had been, with the girl who had experienced her own will and energy almost ecstatically at times, walking around a city or riding a train at night or typing in a student room. In a poem about my grandmother I wrote (of myself): "A young girl, thought sleeping, is certified dead." [2] I was writing very little, partly from fatigue, that female fatigue of suppressed anger and the loss of contact with her own being; partly from the discontinuity of female life with its attention to small chores, errands, work that others constantly undo, small children's constant needs. What I did write was unconvincing to me; my anger and frustration were hard to acknowledge in or out of poems because in fact I cared a great deal about my husband and my children. Trying to look back and understand that time I have tried to analyze the real nature of the conflict. Most, if not all, human lives are full of fantasy—passive day-dreaming which need not be acted on. But to write poetry or fiction, or even to think well, is not to fantasize, or to put fantasies on paper. For a poem to coalesce, for a character or an action to take shape, there has to be an imaginative transformation of reality which is in no way passive. And a certain freedom of the mind is needed—freedom to press on, to enter the currents of your thought like a glider pilot, knowing that your motion can be sustained, that the buoyancy of your attention will not be suddenly snatched away. Moreover, if the imagination is to transcend and transform experience it has to question, to challenge, to conceive of alternatives, perhaps to the very life you are living at that moment. You have to be free to play around with the notion that day might be night, love might be hate; nothing can be too sacred for the imagination to turn into its opposite or to call experimentally by another name. For writing is re-naming. Now, to be maternally with small children all day in the old way, to be with a man in the old way of marriage, requires a holding-back, a putting-aside of that imaginative activity, and seems to demand instead a kind of conservatism. I want to make it clear that I am *not* saying that in order to write well, or think well, it is necessary to become unavailable to others, or to become a devouring ego. This has been the myth of the masculine artist and thinker; and I repeat, I do not accept it. But to be a female human being trying to fulfill traditional female functions in a traditional way *is* in direct conflict with the subversive function of the imagination. The word traditional is important here. There must be ways, and we will be finding out more and more about them, in which the energy of creation and the energy of relation can be united. But in those earlier years I always felt the conflict as a failure of love in myself. I had thought I was choosing a full life: the life available to most men, in which sexuality, work, and parenthood could coexist. But I felt, at 29, guilt toward the people closest to me, and guilty toward my own being.

I wanted, then, more than anything, the one thing of which there was never enough: time to think, time to write. The fifties and early sixties were years of rapid revelations: the sit-ins and marches in the South, the Bay of Pigs, the early anti-war movement, raised large questions—questions for which the masculine world of the academy around me seemed to have expert and fluent answers. But I needed desperately to think for myself—about pacifism and dissent and violence, about poetry and society and about my own relationship to all these things. For about ten years I was reading in fierce snatches, scribbling in notebooks, writing poetry in fragments; I was looking desperately for clues, because if there were no clues than I thought I might be insane. I wrote in a notebook about this time:

Paralyzed by the sense that there exists a mesh of relationships—e.g. between my anger at the chil-

dren, my sensual life, pacifism, sex, (I mean sex in its broadest significance, not merely sexual desire)—an interconnectedness which, if I could see it, make it valid, would give me back myself, make it possible to function lucidly and passionately. Yet I grope in and out among these dark webs.

I think I began at this point to feel that politics was not something "out there" but something "in here" and of the essence of my condition.

In the late '50's I was able to write, for the first time, directly about experiencing myself as a woman. The poem was jotted in fragments during children's naps, brief hours in a library, or at 3 a.m. after rising with a wakeful child. I despaired of doing any continuous work at this time. Yet I began to feel that my fragments and scraps had a common consciousness and a common theme, one which I would have been very unwilling to put on paper at an earlier time because I had been taught that poetry should be "universal," which meant, of course, non-female. Until then I had tried very much *not* to identify myself as a female poet. Over two years I wrote a 10-part poem called "Snapshots of a Daughter-in-Law," in a longer, looser mode than I'd ever trusted myself with before. It was an extraordinary relief to write that poem. It strikes me now as too literary, too dependent on allusion; I hadn't found the courage yet to do without authorities, or even to use the pronoun "I"—the woman in the poem is always "she." One section of it, No. 2, concerns a woman who thinks she is going mad; she is haunted by voices telling her to resist and rebel, voices which she can hear but not obey.

The poem "Orion," written five years later, is a poem of reconnection with a part of myself I had felt I was losing—the active principle, the energetic imagination, the "half-brother" whom I projected, as I had for many years, into the constellation Orion. It's no accident that the words "cold and egotistical" appear in this poem, and are applied to myself. The choice still seemed to be between "love"—womanly, maternal love, altruistic love—a love defined and ruled by the weight of an entire culture; and egotism—a force directed by men into creation, achievement, ambition, often at the expense of others, but justifiably so. For weren't they men, and wasn't that their destiny as womanly love was ours? I know now that the alternatives are false ones—that the word "love" is itself in need of re-vision.

There is a companion poem to "Orion," written three years later, in which at last the woman in the poem and the woman writing the poem become the same person. It is called "Planetarium," and it was written after a visit to a real planetarium, where I read an account of the work of Caroline Herschel, the astronomer, who worked with her brother William, but whose name remained obscure, as his did not.

In closing I want to tell you about a dream I had last summer. I dreamed I was asked to read my poetry at a mass women's meeting, but when I began to read, what came out were the lyrics of a blues song. I share this dream with you because it seemed to me to say a lot about the problems and the future of the woman writer, and probably of women in general. The awakening of consciousness is not like the crossing of a frontier—one step, and you are in another country. Much of woman's poetry has been of the nature of the blues song: a cry of pain, of victimization, or a lyric of seduction. And today, much poetry by women—and prose for that matter—is charged with anger. I think we need to go through that anger, and we will betray our own reality if we try, as Virginia Woolf was trying, for an objectivity, a detachment, that would make us sound more like Jane Austen or Shakespeare. We know more than Jane Austen or Shakespeare knew: more than Jane Austen because our lives are more complex, more than Shakespeare because we know more about the lives of women, Jane Austen and Virginia Woolf included.

Both the victimization and the anger experienced by women are real, and have real sources, everywhere in the environment, built into society. They must go on being tapped and explored by poets, among others. We can neither deny them, nor can we rest there. They are our birth-pains, and we are bearing ourselves. We would be failing each other as writers and as women, if we neglected or denied what is negative, regressive, or Sisyphean in our inwardness.

We all know that there is another story to be told. I am curious and expectant about the future of the masculine consciousness. I feel in the work of the men whose poetry I read today a deep pessimism and fatalistic grief; and I wonder if it isn't the masculine side of what women have experienced, the price of masculine dominance. One thing I am sure of: just as woman is becoming her own midwife, creating herself anew, so man will have to learn to gestate and give birth to his own subjectivity—something he has frequently wanted woman to do for him. We can go on trying to talk to each other, we can sometimes help each other, poetry and fiction can show us what the other is going through; but women can no longer be primarily mothers and muses for men: we have our own work cut out for us.

Notes

1. Adrienne Rich, *A Change of World* (Yale University Press, 1951). Quoted by permission of the author.
2. "Halfway," in *Necessities of Life* (W. W. Norton and Company, 1966), p. 34.

ALICIA OSTRIKER

From "Her Cargo: Adrienne Rich and the Common Language"

American Poetry Review, July–August 1979, pp. 6–10

I

Adrienne Rich is a poet of ideas.

In most poetic circles, it is unfashionable to espouse ideas—except, of course, for ideas about technique. There exists in America a national poetry industry owned and operated by skilled poetic technicians, hundreds, perhaps thousands of whom write flawlessly, and they all agree that form is an extension of content. Yet to discuss the nature and implications of the philosophical and moral positions in most American poems would be like discussing the tastiness of *papier-mâché* apples and oranges. The pieces resemble fruit marvellously to the eye. Other cardboard fruit makers examine and enjoy and rank them. Young disciple fruit makers come to schools to learn the craft. There is considerable complaining that the public does not want to buy, which is understood to be the defect of the public. On a vastly expanded scale, we have an equivalent to Pope's "mob of gentlemen who wrote with ease." For minor critics as well as minor poets, the identification of poetry with craftsmanship is comforting.

A difference between major and minor poetry is that the former announces ideas, the latter fills in the blanks.

> I celebrate myself and sing myself,
> And what I assume you shall assume,
> For every atom belonging to me as good belongs to
>   you.

That is an idea.

> Hypocrite lecteur, mon semblable, mon frère!

That is another.

> Your mother dead and you unborn,
> your two hands grasping your head,
> drawing it down against the blade of life,
> your nerves the nerves of a midwife
> learning her trade.

That is another, of a comparable magnitude. It manifests a serious and therefore arguable set of assertions about the actual world outside its art, and demands, as ideas in poetry so often demand: you must change your life. The lines come from Rich's "The Mirror in Which Two Are Seen as One." Like Whitman's and Baudelaire's, these lines depend on the assumption that the writer's mind exists to embody the implicit meaning of a culture at a moment in time, the place history has marched to, intelligence at its keenest pitch; and to bring the reader there. They declare a state of awakened consciousness—the poet's—and claim that the present actual consciousness of the writer, and the latent consciousness of the reader, are identical.

Whitman asks us to think that we are innocent and great. Baudelaire asks us to think that we are guilty and wearily disgusted. Rich asks us to think that we need to give birth to ourselves.

Thought in poetry lives by its metaphors. There is an echo here of Matthew Arnold's Victorian lament that he lived between "two worlds, one dead, the other powerless to be born," an idea with which Rich agrees so forcefully and angrily that she transforms the figure to its opposite.[1] By "worlds," Arnold meant civilizations. Rich refuses to see present and potential civilizations as "worlds" in some cosmic void remote from each other and from us, distinct from the individual will. As a woman, she reexamines the birth metaphor in a way that would astonish Arnold. A healthy civilization might give birth to another as a live mother gives birth to a live child. A healthy individual mother might have living powers engaged in the maturation of her young. But as things are, Rich says, we must be born again by our own agency. We can and must give birth to ourselves, create ourselves. Moreover, to give birth is naturally a feminine activity. (An implication is that if *men* want to struggle into life and not die stillborn in the womb of that old bitch gone in the teeth, that botched civilization, they will have to feminize themselves.) It requires not Christlike wounded surgeons plying the steel, not Confucian philosopher-kings, but midwives. The midwife is an important figure in Rich because she lacks social status, lacks patriarchal apparatus, and comes from a buried, barely surviving tradition of powerful working females. By rediscovering this tradition, women will grow strong.

Does the reader agree with the poet? The reader cannot think: oh, it is only *poetry*. One grapples with Rich, one wrestles and hugs, one agrees and disagrees intensely. ⟨. . .⟩

III

Why, in Rich's writing, does one find so little joy, so little sense of the power of joy? Why does the work come from a sense of unrelieved crisis in which nothing can be celebrated, nothing savored? Rich is not, one feels, a poet to whom love—untheoretical, undoctrinal love—comes easily, either toward herself or toward others. She does not employ memories of childhood wholeness. She does not construct desirable fantasies. There is suffering, and then there is more suffering, with "no imagination to forestall woe," almost as if suffering itself were a value. In this respect Rich differs from feminists like

Marge Piercy and Robin Morgan, Alta and Judy Grahn, whose work suggests that women's sense of their own wholeness, and the gladness that accompanies wholeness, is indispensable for a feminist revolution. To journey with Rich is to travel painfully in the wilderness, to be warned against the fleshpots of Egypt and the golden calf, to feel the backward drag of slavery, and to struggle with all one's might against it. But the struggle requires a vision. Rich's readers need to know about the female equivalent of the burning bush, the voice of the covenant, the promised land. They need to know about the goddess. Lacking the imagination's projection of a world without victims, a self unvictimized, unmastered, complete—and it is for the poets to give us this, to articulate the delight that is *there*, latently, as much as women's despair is *there*—lacking this, the will to change is helplessly fettered.

A more dismaying aspect of Rich's work to me is her partisanship. Explicitly or implicitly, since *Snapshots*, Rich's position has depended on the idea of an enemy. Her "I" affirms by excluding, her communal "we" implies a hostile "they." Of course "we" know who "they" are. For a period after *Snapshots* the poet uses male figures sympathetically; there are poems of kindness and hopefulness addressed to her husband; there is Orion, her brother-double; there are friend/lover figures in *Leaflets*, and the male artists Chekhov, Ghalib, Rodin, Berrigan, Artaud, Godard in *Leaflets* and *The Will to Change*. In *Diving* the poet defines herself as the androgyne, the being who is at once female and male. But men in this volume are depicted universally and exclusively as parasitic on women, emotionally threatened by them, brutal—the cop is identified with the rapist—and undeserving of pity. "His" mind is a nightmare of possessiveness, conquest, and mysogyny. The poet dreams of killing this man, but killing is

> Not enough. When I dream of meeting
> the enemy, this is my dream:
>
> white acetylene
> ripples from my body
> effortlessly released
> perfectly trained
> on the true enemy
>
> raking his body down to the thread
> of existence
> burning away his lie
> leaving him in a new
> world; a changed
> man

I hope not to oversimplify this issue. Women's anger is real, and it is legitimate. We see it surfacing everywhere in women's writing, the best and the worst (I suppose it is missing only from the mediocre), like a scream from a mouth that has just been un-gagged. This anger needs acknowledgment. Unacknowledged, it poisons and cripples. But when an angry woman implies that she fantasizes punishing her enemy purely for his own good, she begins to resemble the officer who said he burned the village to save it. It is pleasant and self-deceptive to feel that "I" or "we" are violent only in response to "their" violence. It is pleasant to believe that agressiveness, competitiveness, selfishness, egotism, violence, are "their" characteristics, not mine. The unfortunate truth is that they are human characteristics. The liberated will find these impulses newly released within themselves, and may want to take responsibility for them. ⟨. . .⟩

IV

The Dream of a Common Language at last gives us Rich as visionary. *Dream* implies this. *Language* means not only words, poetry—several of the poems are about "a whole new poetry"—but any form of communication, including the touch of bodies, and including silence. It means the ability "to name the world" essential for gaining strength in the world; and "the drive to connect," through symbols and in actuality, with each other, the world, and ourselves. *Common* language means a faith that attempts to communicate can succeed, that we can connect, not as privileged persons or under special circumstances, but in ordinary dailiness.

The core of the book is its exploration of loving woman-to-woman relationships. Rich speaks of mothers and daughters, literal and figurative sisters, cohorts in poetry, lovers, ancestresses. She sees all women as actually or potentially conjoined by a common love-memory of a mother's body:

> our faces dreaming hour on hour
> in the salt smell of her lap . . .
> how she floated great and tender in our dark . . .
> and how we thought she loved
> the strange male body first
> that took, that took, whose taking seemed a law . . .
>   And how beneath
> the strange male bodies
> we sank in terror or in resignation . . .

"Sibling Mysteries," from which this passage comes, traces Rich's eroticism:

> the daughters never were
> true brides of the father
> the daughters were to begin with
> brides of the mother
> then brides of each other
> under a different law
> let me hold you and tell you

As a flute song of personal meditation, "Sibling Mysteries" is hauntingly lovely. As a myth of female sexuality, it is too narrow. Yes, women's initial erotic experiences are maternal-infantile. So are men's. Yes, perhaps mature sexuality attempts to recover and replay the blissful mother-child union. Perhaps all adult tenderness, all affection, finds its source and models itself on those memories. This idea could explain a great deal about human romance—not confined to love between women.[2] For some women, the stereotypic dominant-father subordinate-mother family pattern does not apply. For some, the physicality of our mothers never stopped being available. And for some, heterosexual experience has never meant terror or resignation; on the contrary. William Blake's *Notebook* contains a short poem entitled "The Question Answered":

> What is it men in women do require?
> The lineaments of Gratified Desire.
> What is it women do in men require?
> The lineaments of Gratified Desire.

Age twenty, I became a Blakean when I read this. I find the Lesbian Imperative offensively totalitarian, and would prefer to defend human diversity as well as human liberty.

Three other poems in *Dream* excite my skepticism. The opening pieces on Marie Curie and Elvira Shatayev appear to romanticize feminine martyrdom; the latter is an all-female *liebestod*. Where is the portrait of a woman whose power kills neither others nor herself? "Hunger" seems marred by a naive belief that women's love, "hosed" on the world, would eliminate its literal and figurative famines. Those who believe in infallible feminine virtue may recall the comparable virtue of the American Worker in the 1930s.

These are comparatively tangential matters, not vitiating this volume's courageous spirit, its transformations, the beauty of its poetry. The force of love, negligible in her earlier books, here brings Rich a resolution to trust, to move from victimization toward responsibility and choice, and to reject (notwithstanding the aura of the first two poems) martyrdom:

> I believe I am choosing something new
> not to suffer uselessly

she says in one poem; and in another,

> the woman who cherished
> her suffering is dead. I am her descendant.
> I love the scar tissue she handed on to me
> but I want to go on from here with you
> fighting the temptation to make a career of pain.

Rich's fear lest she "use" those she loves in the old way of sexual (or literary) exploitation is scarcely a traditional theme in love poetry; it might well become so. Both in the book's central section of twenty-one love poems, and in the framing poems around them, one senses not simply the will to change but the accomplishment.

The most important poems break new ground metaphorically. "Origins and History of Consciousness," opening in the poet's crisis-haunted room, moves to a dream of walking into water:

> My bare feet are numbed already by the snow
> but the water
> is mild, I sink and float
> like a warm, amphibious animal
> that has broken the net, has run
> through fields of snow leaving no print;
> this water washes off the scent
> *you are clear now*
> *of the hunger, the trapper*
> *the wardens of the mind—*

This of course recalls "Diving into the Wreck," but the speaker of "Diving" needed props—rubber suit, knife, camera, book of myths, schooner, ladder—which this speaker, entering her animal nature, can discard. As she does something natural, not unnatural, sea shrinks to the intimacy of a pond in woods. Cold transforms itself magically to warmth. She who had to do everything "alone" in "Diving" is rewarded in her dream by a companion, "another animal/swimming under the snow-flecked surface of the pool." Moreover, where "Diving" closes under water, "Origins and History of Consciousness" resurfaces. It returns from dream to reality. The pond in woods becomes the city of muggers. But the poet recapitulates her decision of risked love as a descent "in a darkness/ which I remember as drenched with light," and resolves to move outward. The poem ends with a sense of introducing Eros into Civilization.

"Natural Resources," another poem of transformations, revives and synthesizes two metaphors from *Snapshots:* the aerial cargo of the new woman, and the "abandoned mineshaft of doubt" in "Double Monologue." The latter poem had grieved that "our need mocks our gear." Now the mine is filled with certitude. A rainbow arches toward the core of a hill, the hill holds treasure yearning to be discovered. While "the routine of life" goes on aboveground, the woman miner descends to hard labor in a kind of inverse astral projection. There she discerns images of the lives of past women, their precious domestic artifacts, the work they did and handed down from one generation to the next, the work that she must continue. Although "the women who first knew themselves/ miners, are dead," the whole import of the poem is a celebration of a subterranean tradition of women's strength.

The technique employed in these two poems is a kind of

overlay of transparencies. Present and past, reality and imagination, the life of the self and the lives of other selves, the spatially enclosed and the spatially unenclosed, are held in a tenuous, luminous balance. In the penultimate poem of *The Dream of a Common Language*, Rich depicts the synthesizing and liberating imagination in action. The place of "Toward the Solstice" is a country house, presumably the same one as in "From an Old House in America," and again there is feminine space: a room, the earth. Its time is "the thirtieth of November . . . the thirtieth of May," a first snowstorm and a spring torrent are falling outside, simultaneously, beautifully described in detail. The poet is "trying to hold in one steady glance / all the parts of my life," and is meditating on her need to perform a rite of separation between herself and the past. She realizes that the required ritual may be simply that she listen to her own pulse, which contains the falling snow and the rainstorm, and she both longs and fears to do this. The poem reminds me of Frost's "Directive" and of Blake's moment of "Time less than a pulsation of the artery," which is equal to six thousand years because in this moment the poet's work is done. Rich is more tentative than either Blake or Frost. But she is being visionary. She is being metaphysical. The tyranny of Time, which is as real in our mental lives as any social or political tyranny, is mentally suspended here in a way I have not seen before. A philosophically developed feminism may mean an alterantive idea of time and change, neither linear as in Hebrew tradition, cyclic as in Classical philosophy, or juxtaposed against Eternity as in Christianity. There is a flexing of the mind here, and no sense of an enemy. I am filled with curiosity to see more of what Rich can do along these lines, confident that whatever comes next will be an advance. What does not change is the pressure of Adrienne Rich's intelligence, as constant as the daylight in a love poem, "Nights and Days":

> I walk to an eastern window, pull up the blinds:
> the city around us is still
> on a clear October morning
> wrapped in her indestructible light.

Notes

1. The figure in Arnold is impersonal and non-biological. In Rich it is personal and biological. Rich's "you" is an unspecified woman who may be the poet or may be Everywoman. Although "The Mirror in which Two Are Seen as One" does not concern itself explicitly with collective as against individual experience, its implications are (and this is typical for Rich) social and historical. "The Mirror" appears in *Poems Selected and New, 1950–1974*, NY: W. W. Norton, 1974, p. 193.

2. This is a central and well-argued idea in Dorothy Dinerstein's recent *The Mermaid and the Minotaur*, a study of the effects of the mother-infant bond, and the fact that there is no comparable father-infant bond, on adult psychic and social life. Dinerstein feels that heterosexual romance is an attempt to recreate the emotional intensities of infancy.

CAROL P. CHRIST

From "Homesick for a Woman, for Ourselves:
Adrienne Rich"
Diving Deep and Surfacing:
Women Writers on Spiritual Quest
1980, pp. 75–81

According to two of her most important critics, "from the beginning [Adrienne] Rich's theme, personal and collective, has been woman in the patriarchy: her own identity, the identity of woman on man's established terms; and, more and more urgently, the possibility of identity on her own, on woman's own terms."[1] While much of Rich's poetry has centered on the subjective realm of personal relationships, she has recognized the connection between the personal and the political: "there is no private life which is not determined by a wider public life," reads the epigram to *Diving into the Wreck* (*DW*, 2).[2]

Women's relationships take place within a world that has been defined for centuries by men and that only recently is beginning to be defined by women. In Rich's vision, women's relationships with men become symbolic of the energy that can transform a culture of power valued so much as power, while women's relationships with women become symbolic of the power that can transform a culture of power and death into a culture of life and rebirth. That Rich's recent poetry has a political dimension has been obvious to serious readers of her poems—both to those who have found Rich's politics annoying and distracting and to those who have found this element enlightening and exhilarating.[3] That Rich's poems also have a spiritual dimension has been less clearly recognized.

Adrienne Rich's understanding of woman in the patriarchy and woman's quest for identity on her own terms has followed parallel courses with that of Mary Daly, her close personal friend. According to Daly, feminism is not simply a political and social movement (though it most certainly is that), it is also a spiritual journey that begins in an *experience of nothingness*, a shattering of the conventional pieties that had supported the self, comparable to the mystic's dark night of the soul. When supported by the *courage to see*, the clear-sighted facing of the emptiness at the heart of conventional views of the self, it leads to an ontological insight, a *new seeing* or revelation of "what is," which then requires a *new naming* of self and world.

The experience of nothingness and the courage to see are at the heart of the poems in *Diving into the Wreck*. The "wreck" into which the poet dives is the dark underside of marriage and politics in the patriarchal world. Beneath the myths of civility, love, and power wielded to protect, Rich discovers a landscape of terror. Emotional distance and control turn to violence in men; self-effacement smolders into consuming rage in women. For Rich, "personal problems" with men become emblematic of a destructive lack of concern for life and growth characteristic of the world men have shaped.

To describe the wreck she finds, Rich uses extreme language. No *conservateur* of present reality,[4] Rich imagines apocalyptic destruction that will bring purification: she speaks of "testing bombs" (*DW*, 3), of fire "feeding on everything" (*DW*, 47), of "ice . . . forming over the earth" (*DW*, 11). While sharing the apocalyptist's penchant for purifying fire and ice, Rich's vision is particularly feminist. The fire she imagines is fueled by the anger of women who have suppressed themselves for too long. The apocalypse that she envisions may be the inner transformation of women whose anger consumes their ties to the patriarchal world rather than an external destruction.

In order to face the nothingness at the heart of patriarchal marriage and politics, Rich had to give up many of the myths that had shaped the lives of women of her generation—"whole LP collections, films we starred in / playing in the neighborhoods . . . the langauge of love-letters, of suicide notes" (*DW*, 3)—a whole romantic fantasy in which women's lives were defined entirely by their relationships (or lack thereof) to men. Giving up these fantasies required the courage to see. In Rich's poetry, revelation is expressed in imagery of visionary seeing. She speaks of lying "awake under scarred plaster" (*DW*, 11), of "another eye" that opens "underneath my lids" (*DW*, 17), of "waking first" "in a house wrapped in sleep" (*DW*, 20). The poet's acute vision enables her not only to see the wreck, but also to imagine ways to transcend it. Rich thus begins to speak of "diving down" beneath the culture and its values and of going back into history in search of a healing vision.

In the first poem in *Diving into the Wreck*, "Trying to Talk with a Man," Rich writes of nothingness in a relationship with a man. Trying to talk with him is like "testing bombs," the landscape they inhabit is a "desert" with "deformed cliffs" filled with "dull green succulents," images of destruction and ugliness (*DW*, 3). Though they are "surrounded by a silence" (*DW*, 3), the man does not even realize that there is a problem in communication. To him the desert is no metaphor, and he talks idly of the adventures of people who are stranded in such locales. Though unable to touch the poet emotionally, he nonetheless communicates a will to dominate, a "dry heat" that "feels like power" (*DW*, 4), his emotionless conversation filling the space in which she might venture to speak. Recognizing the futility of trying to talk with him, the poet feels "more helpless with you than without you" (*DW*, 3), realizing, perhaps for the first time, that the feared state of being a woman without a man might be easier than the frustration of living with one whose life runs on a different course from her own. Though helpless with the man, the poet begins to value herself, in particular the sensitivity he lacks. Her own "acute angle of understanding" appears to her as "an underground river" and a "locus of the sun," the only signs of life and renewal in an otherwise desolate place (*DW*, 3).

In "When We Dead Awaken," Rich continues to explore the wreck. Images of failed relationships, "stones . . . souvenirs of what I once described / as happiness" (*DW*, 5) are juxtaposed with images of senseless destruction in war, "guerillas are advancing / through minefields" and urban decay, "trash / burning endlessly in the dump" (*DW*, 5). The poet now begins to connect the personal and the political: the emotional insensitivity men display in relationships is also reflected in their insensitivity to human suffering in foreign wars and in city ghettos. Like Doris Lessing, Rich suggests that women's intense focus on the personal life provides them with insights into the forces that operate in public life.

As in the previous poem, Rich places hope in the creative vision of women, choosing an image from women's traditional work. She imagines women "working with me to remake / this trailing knitted thing, this cloth of darkness, / this woman's garment, trying to save the skein" (*DW*, 5). Though the image recalls women's traditional role of knitting clothes for her family, Rich transforms it. The image suggests that women can disentangle themselves from the darkness of patriarchal culture and create a new culture out of the threads they hold. ⟨. . .⟩

The tremendous power that is unleashed when women have the courage to see the nothingness of male-defined culture and relationships is further explored in other poems in *Diving into the Wreck*. As her vision enables her to see the wreck more and more clearly, Rich turns increasingly to apocalyptic imagery. In "The Phenomenology of Anger," she meditates on things that are about to burst into flames—"a pile of rags the machinist wiped his hands on" (*DW*, 27), the mowed hay during a heat wave (*DW*, 27). The poet imagines herself egging the fire on, "huddled fugitive / in the warm sweet simmer of the hay / muttering: *Come.*" Rich imagines women's anger as a purifying fire that will consume the faceless unrestrained male violence that gunned down babies in My

Lai and that visits itself on women in more restrained form in the bedroom. In another poem, "The Ninth Symphony of Beethoven Understood at Last as a Sexual Message," Rich meditates on the masculine nature of violence, which filled the newspapers during the Vietnam war. In that poem Rich suggests that male power when disconnected from the day-to-day involvement in home and family life egotistically asserts itself without regard for others. Beethoven's "isolated soul / yelling at Joy from the tunnel of the ego" (*DW*, 43) is not unrelated to corporate executives in America "masturbating / in the factory / of facts" (*DW*, 28) in "Phenomenology." In the latter poem Rich in a horrifying image juxtaposes men's inability to express feelings in relationships with women to men's apparent lack of feelings for the lives they destroy in war. "I suddenly see the world / as no longer viable: / you are out there burning the crops / with some new sublimate / This morning you left the bed / we still share" (*DW*, 29). Even more graphically, "Last night, in this same room, weeping / I asked you: *what are you feeling? / do you feel anything?* / Now in the torsion of your body / as you defoliate the fields we lived from / I have your answer" (*DW*, 29). For Rich the man in her bed whose feelings are locked inside himself, whose body lies rigid and contorted as she weeps, is emblematic of that kind of male emotional distance and control that can tolerate the violence of the Vietnam war, the defoliation of crops, and the killing of the babies of women.

As she explores the anatomy of her relationships with men, Rich comes to a conclusion that is shared by many women who have lived all their lives with men: "'The only real love I have ever felt was for children and other women. / Everything else was lust, pity, / self-hatred, pity, lust'" (*DW*, 30). Mary Daly's term "the courage to see" seems especially appropriate here. Women's lives have been so shaped by the expectations expressed in the stories of men that women have often not even experienced their own experience. As the woman in "Dialogue" says, "*I do not know / who I was when I did those things / or who I said I was / or whether I willed to feel / what I read about*" (*DW*, 21). Because the experience of nothingness is so deep for women within a culture defined by men, Rich imagines an apocalyptic solution as her escape. "Night after night / awake in prison, my mind / licked at the mattress like a flame / till the cellblock went roaring" (*DW*, 31). This image of fiery destruction is repeated in other poems in *Diving*. The poet views herself as "wood, with a gift for burning" (*DW*, 20), in one poem, and in another describes her mind "burning as if it could go on / burning itself, burning down / feeding on everything / till there is nothing in life / that has not fed that fire" (*DW*, 47).

While images of liberation through fiery destruction are frequent elsewhere in the volume in "Diving into the Wreck" Rich imagines herself as an undersea diver exploring a wrecked ship in order to "see the damage that was done / and the treasures that prevail" (*DW*, 23). As other images in the poem make clear, the poet's undersea exploration is metaphor for an interior journey to the source of her inner power, "I have to learn alone / to turn my body without force / in the deep element" (*DW*, 23), and for a quest to find a mythic prehistory when women were revered. Though having read "the book of myths" (*DW*, 22), the poet is keenly aware that even stories of ancient times are told from a male perspective: the book of myths that she carries is one "in which / our names do not appear" (*DW*, 24). She is seeking the primal source, "the wreck and not the story of the wreck / the thing itself and not the myth" (*DW*, 23). The revelation that arrests her in this poem is the androgyne.

This is the place.
And I am here, the mermaid whose dark hair
streams black, the merman in his armored body
We circle silently
about the wreck
we dive into the hold
I am she: I am he.

                                           (*DW*, 24)

That she is speaking of a revelation is clearly indicated in her words and imagery. The undersea exploration is a pilgrimage; the diver enters the waters of transformation and rebirth, and her stark announcement "This is the place" indicates that she has reached the sacred center. For Rich the androgyne represents a buried treasure, a centering vision of wholeness that might enable women and men to move beyond the deformed symbiosis of male power and female submission. [5]

Notes

1. Barbara Charlesworth Gelpi and Albert Gelpi, "Introduction," *Adrienne Rich's Poetry: Texts of the Poems, the Poet on Her Work, Reviews and Criticism* (New York: Norton, 1975), p. xi.
2. Adrienne Rich, *Diving into the Wreck* (New York: Norton, 1973). Page references to poems from *Diving into the Wreck* appear in parentheses in the text preceded by *DW*.
3. See, for example, Albert Gelpi, "On Adrienne Rich: The Poetics of Change," pp. 130–48, and Robert Boyers, "On Adrienne Rich: Intelligence and Will," pp. 148–60, in *Adrienne Rich's Poetry*, for negative views of Rich's politics.
      See Erica Jong, "Visionary Anger," pp. 171–75; and Wendy Martin, "From Patriarchy to the Female Principle: A Chronological Reading of Adrienne Rich's Poems," pp. 175–89, *Adrienne Rich's Poetry*, for positive views.
4. Boyers finds this tendency of hers upsetting.
5. The revelation of the androgyne in *Diving into the Wreck* (1972) parallels Rich's friend Mary Daly's vision of androgyny as the new being in *Beyond God the Father*. In "The Stranger," Rich describes herself as the "androgyne," "the living mind you fail to describe / in your dead language / the lost noun, the verb surviving / only in the infinitive" (19). Mary Daly expresses precisely the same ideas in similar language, suggesting mutual influence.

ADELAIDE MORRIS
From "Imitations and Identities:
Adrienne Rich's A *Change of World*"
Modern Poetry Studies, 1981, pp. 136–59

When W. H. Auden selected Adrienne Rich's A *Change of World* for the Yale Younger Poets Award in 1951, he took the occasion to stress a quality he would later see as poetry's ulterior purpose: "by telling the truth, to disenchant and disintoxicate."[1] His foreword to the volume pauses on Rich's command of craft but lingers over her clear-eyed sobriety. She does not, he rejoices, thrust herself into the center of her work, exhibit a private fantasy system, make a virtue of confession, or value her subjectivity simply because it belongs to her. Her poems are nimble, crisp, and clear, their merits, as Auden describes them, resembling those of well-trained school children: they are "neatly and modestly dressed, speak quietly but do not mumble, respect their elders but are not cowed by them, and do not tell fibs."[2]

Auden's assessment of A *Change of World*, avuncular as it is, remains one of the most acute. If, as his foreword asserts, "reading a poem is an experience analogous to that of encountering a person" (7), the person he describes is exactly the one Rich meant him to meet. The volume, however, includes another person, one who seems to exist behind the poems. This person bears somewhat the same relation to the constructed public self Auden discerned as the young Yeats bore to his muscular, urbane speakers: the assertive mask, for Rich as for Yeats, covers a hesitant face.

Describing A *Change of World* some twenty years later as "a book of very well-tooled poems,"[3] Rich located its craft in the act of covering. Because its language functioned less to discover than to display, the words worked, in her image, "more as a kind of facade than as either self-revelation or as a probe into one's own consciousness."[4] The facade is an excellent image for these architecturally intricate and static poems, poems whose elegantly undisrupted exposition seems to conceal as much as it reveals. To modify Auden's terms, these may be poems which speak quietly in order to hold down a yell and which, though they may not fib, do not quite tell the whole truth. They are, Rich summarizes, "poems in which the unconscious things never got to the surface."[5]

How, then, are we to read them? Where are we to locate their meaning: how much lies in the facade, which we can describe in detail? How much resides in the rooms behind, interiors we must infer from the exterior? Reading the poems for the first rewards attention to their intricate and accomplished formal structures, to the interplay of paradox and irony, to the decorous and often witty language; reading for the second demands consideration of such things as the frequent gap between poet and persona and the occasional incongruity between stated and embedded themes. Each of these methods applies with ease to some of the poems, with difficulty to others, but usually they form excellent supplements for each other.

There is a third way to read, however, one which complements the first two and which Rich herself suggests in her discussion of the apprentice poems of D. H. Lawrence. This is to stress not so much the pattern in each poem as its unfolding across poems, to search not so much for statements as for struggles between statements. In this view, apprentice poems are strategies toward the making of a self and the reader's task is to attend as much to this process as to its products. What Rich, therefore, reaches to discern in the early poetry of D. H. Lawrence is "the process, the struggle, of choice, the wrestling out of other identities into his own, the growing knowledge that [the poets who influenced him], though natural affinities, can provide no final solutions: he must create his own forms."[6]

This description of Lawrence's early work fits Rich's own apprenticeship, her long struggle, stretching through *The Diamond Cutters* and into *Snapshots of a Daughter-in-Law*, to wrestle out of other identities into her own. The four parts of this essay describe four aspects of the process: the imitation of the style and substance of preceding poets, the development of a series of defenses against a menacing world, the constructing of formulas to account for that world, and, finally, the tentative voicing of an identity which, years later, she would recognize as her own. Looking back on her first volume, Rich described the author as "the girl who wrote poems, who defined herself in writing poems."[7] In the interaction between this vulnerable and largely unseen being and the prim, rather proud persona Auden encountered lies much of the interest, tension, and movement of A *Change of World.*

Some of the composure in the volume's persona is borrowed from the generation of poets who established the characteristic tones and topics of modern poetry and from the generation who succeeded to this tradition. "My style was formed," Rich summarizes, "first by male poets: by the men I was reading as an undergraduate—Frost, Dylan Thomas, Donne, Auden, MacNiece, Stevens, Yeats."[8] What she learned from them was

both a style and a stance: a metrical skill so flexible that each line seems to meet its formal requirements with conversational ease and a posture of mature disillusionment, an austerely anti-Romantic emphasis on the limitations of human nature.

The technical brilliance of A *Change of World* is almost casual. The poems move easily in blank verse paragraphs. English sonnets, and heroic couplets, trimeter, tetrameter, and pentameter, triplets, quatrains, and stanzaic patterns of all varieties. They demonstrate not only a mastery of versification but also, as Auden testifies, "an ear and an intuitive grasp of much subtler and more difficult matters like proportion, consistency of diction and tone, and the matching of these with the subject at hand" (10).

Technical competence, Rich told an interviewer, "was something I learned the way people learn arithmetic or to play scales."[9] While her mother kept her at piano practice so relentlessly that she developed a series of facial tics,[10] her father, selecting two poets from his largely Victorian, pre-Raphaelite library, taught her to write verse by copying every day from Blake and Keats.[11] The picture of the student poet Rich draws in "Juvenalia," a poem from *Snapshots of a Daughter-in-Law*, recalls the dutiful schoolgirl Auden sketches in his foreword, except that Rich emphasizes the underside of her performances, the anger and restlessness of an entrapped apprentice:

> Again I sit, under duress, hands washed,
> at your inkstained oaken desk,
> by the goose-neck lamp in the tropic of your books,
> stabbing the blotting-pad, doodling loop upon
>   loop . . .
> as I dip the pen and for aunts, for admiring friends,
> for you above all to read,
> copy my praised and sedulous lines.[12]

By moving from Blake and Keats to the modern masters, Rich developed the style of A *Change of World*, a style which could incorporate doodling loops and stabbed blots, but she does not yet abandon the habit of imitation, of skilled but sedulous copying.

The voice in A *Change of World* is so versatile as to seem at times almost ventriloquistic. Poems with the garrulousness of the neurotic-violent Frost rub against poems with the sweet decorative archaism of early Yeats, the aphoristic intensity of Emily Dickinson, or the quick, caustic wit of W. H. Auden. From each of these poets, as to a lesser extent from Eliot, Stevens, and MacNiece, Rich picked up characteristic tricks and tones of language, elements she seemed to need to master before she could fully possess her own individual dialect. ⟨. . .⟩

When asked what holds the poems within a collection together, Rich answered with an interesting metaphor: they are often, she replied, "ways of taking hold of the wild animal at different points, or trying different strategies to seize the animal, some of them succeeding better than others maybe . . . toward the zeroing in on the experience."[13] The experience confronted again and again in A *Change of World* is vulnerability—on the one hand there is a menacing world, a world of storms, mobs, wars, and death, of deceptions, disputes, disasters, and imminent doom; on the other is a small stoical self, a self which did not make this world, does not especially understand it, and seems to have little or no effect upon its workings. Each poem in the volume can be read as a strategy for containing this experience.

Given a threatening world and a vulnerable self, one reasonable response is to take on the voice of someone who seems to have mastered or at least understood the situation, and from this perspective Rich's poems of imitation might also be described as gestures of defense. But there is a series of poems whose plot is more directly defensive. The strategy in these poems is not to seize experience so much as to achieve a necessary and saving distance from it. Some of the most effective poems in *A Change of World*, these offer four plans of evasion: moving inwards, stepping backwards, moving upwards, or stepping sideways.

A persistent spatial pattern in *A Change of World* is the retreat to a room from whose window the self peers cautiously out upon chaos. This pattern structures the volume's first poem, "Storm Warnings" (17–18), setting a tone of anxious alertness which never recedes. The poem's plot is the withdrawal of the self before forces symbolized by winds "walking overhead . . . moving across the land," rising, whining, and, perhaps most threateningly, insisting. The poem suggests and then rejects a series of escapes: the book is put down, the pillowed chair abandoned, and the predicting instruments— barometer, thermometer, and clock—set aside as fragile and inconsequential. The "sole defense" affirmed is defense by enclosure. The candles are sheathed in glass and the windows are closed, then shuttered, then curtained.

The solution, though boldly stated, seems uneasy, for the poem's imagery suggests that the protagonist has locked the door with the threat inside. Rich's personification of the weather is not simply poetic embellishment: as the winds walk overhead, her persona paces underneath driven by "weather in the heart" which "alike come[s] on / Regardless of prediction" and, as we infer, despite precaution. Alertness does not avert change; measurement cannot master the elements; and retreat from outer forces only leaves her fronting the currents of an inner realm.

The defense of turning inwards is, then, both passive and solipsistic. The most disturbing hint of its danger, however, is a strange periphrasis Rich uses in the final stanza. Though the windows are shuttered, she says, wind whines through the keyhole's "unsealed aperture." After emphasis on shutting, sheathing, and closing, the urge of the poem is now to seal. Because the word "aperture," however, usually denotes the opening in a lens which admits light and, by extension, the part of the eye which receives images of the outer world, the implication is that sealing the keyhole would result in blindness as well as imprisonment, a retreat so thorough as to suggest entombment.

A less drastic defense, and certainly a less introverted one, is named in the title of one of the volume's longest poems— "Stepping Backward" (56–59). Stepping backward, like the next defense, moving upward, occurs for the purpose of seeing more clearly. Two interlinked hypotheses are at work here: first, that the poet observes and names but does not act, and second, that detachment, the withholding of action, is a precondition of knowledge. A predictable consequence of these ideas is that Rich's early poems are largely abstract. There is not much hearing, little smelling, less tasting, and no touching in them. They are, as Margaret Morrison stresses, mainly visual: "In nearly every one of the poems in *A Change of World* and *The Diamond Cutters*, she sees, observes, watches, views, looks at, glances at, gazes at, perceives, spies or inspects objects, people, or events in the world around her or in the world of the people she describes at a second remove."[14]

"Stepping Backward" seizes the theory of perception-by-detachment as a defense against love's disorderly intrusiveness. It is, in Richard Howard's fine description, a "lonely, tart, gallant (poem) . . . with an almost desperate stiffening in the lines' insistence on 'ceremony.'"[15] As other poems in the volume present barely controlled terror, this offers a barely curbed urge to flee, but we are fortunate here, as we aren't

elsewhere, in knowing the source of the experience, the personal instigation behind the universal statements. This "very guarded, carefully-wrought poem," Rich told Elly Bulkin, "deals with a relationship with a woman . . . whom I was close to in my late 'teens, and whom I really fled from— I fled from my feelings about her."[16] ⟨. . .⟩

In stepping backward compassion and intellect balance and the poet is distant but respectful. When perspective is achieved by moving upward, however, the stance is less attractive. Its result is not compassion but a mastery achieved largely through condescension. Again the poet retreats to her room, but this time, as in "A View of the Terrace" (29–30) and "The Uncle Speaks in the Drawing Room" (44–45), the window looks down. The emotion in both poems is hostile: in the first poem the subject is "the porcelain people," painted and precious, whom the speaker wishes to shatter by throwing pebbles; in the second the subject is a sullen mob of "missile-throwers" who would shiver the uncle's chandelier. The distastefulness of both poems comes partly because the speaker, whether aggressor or target, peeps out from a privileged hiding place. The defense is executed with an easy-hearted snideness which tends to vanish when the speaker abandons detachment and descends into the world. ⟨. . .⟩

Because it has no virtue beyond self-preservation, side-stepping is an extreme example of the defensive strategy which is so much a part of the struggle in Rich's first volume. In its extremity it critiques the others, putting into question withdrawal from life as a method of living. Withdrawal from life as a method of writing, however, remains an important part of Rich's aesthetic into her third volume, for as long, that is, as she is comfortable with the distinction between living and writing, acting and articulating. It is preserved because of the privilege Rich accords to clarity, precision, and intellectual patterning.

Moving inward, stepping backward, moving upward, and sidestepping—this series of strategies offers access to strains we can identify in *A Change of World* as Rich's own: a pattern of needs, a habit of experience, a project of perception. These defenses have many functions, but one of the most important is by separating the self from experience to prevent movement, contact, interchange, alteration—everything Rich will later define as growth. It is ironic that the push of a volume entitled *A Change of World* would be to hold off change, and yet an obsession of the volume is the menace of change. This is the "wild animal" the poems again and again attempt to subdue. ⟨. . .⟩

"Aunt Jennifer's Tigers" (19) follows "Storm Warnings," the poem which closed window, curtain, and shutter between interior and exterior worlds. Like "Storm Warnings" it concerns fear, a private and a public realm, and a mode of living which limits as it protects the protagonist, but this is a much brisker, bolder poem:

> Aunt Jennifer's tigers prance across a screen,
> Bright topaz denizens of a world of green.
> They do not fear the men beneath the tree;
> They pace in sleek chivalric certainty.
>
> Aunt Jennifer's fingers fluttering through her wool
> Find even the ivory needle hard to pull.
> The massive weight of Uncle's wedding band
> Sits heavily upon Aunt Jennifer's hand.
>
> When Aunt is dead, her terrified hands will lie
> Still ringed with ordeals she was mastered by.
> The tigers in the panel that she made
> Will go on prancing, proud and unafraid.

The strategy here—both Aunt Jennifer's and Rich's own—is

not so much to hide from experience as to transform it, and there is a new spaciousness in the frankness with which fear is admitted and the fierceness with which it is, if only momentarily, transcended.

Everything in the versification reinforces the thought. Whereas the tigers prance with occasional anapestic rambunctiousness, "the massive weight of Uncle's wedding band" is properly and ponderously iambic (until it "sits heavily," in a sedate spondee, upon Aunt Jennifer's hand). The alliterative *p* as the proud tigers prance and pace becomes a voiceless fricative *f* as, driven by fear, Aunt Jennifer's fingers flutter and find. The assonance of the long *e* sound links words from both camps: the green and tree and certainty of the tigers and the fear and screen (and perhaps even a suppressed scream) of Aunt Jennifer. The closed couplets arranged in quatrains give the poem balance without stasis, and the rhymes function wonderfully to reinforce the reason: the ring on her hand is indeed a constricting band, as the tigers that she made are her effort to be proud and unafraid.

The needlework imagery which binds this poem as well as "Mathilde in Normandy" and "Design in Living Colors" may be a glance at one art form which is sanctioned for women; whether or not this is the case, however, "Aunt Jennifer's Tigers" is a poem about a woman artist by a woman artist. The theory both inside and behind the poem is Yeats's theory of the mask, the idea that the self generates its opposite in art. If Aunt Jennifer is as meek as her tigers are sleek, as dull as they are glossy, as baffled as they are bold, then perhaps we might infer by extension that the poet is in turn her opposite. "It was important to me," Rich has written, "that Aunt Jennifer was a person as distinct from myself as possible—distanced by the formalism of the poem, by its objective, observant tone—even by putting the woman in a different generation." [17] This simple screen between author and readers, transparent as it later became to both, permitted Rich to drop her defenses, restrain her formulas, and thereby liberate the energy, humor, and directness which characterize her finest work.

In this poem Uncle's massive wedding band encompasses Aunt's life so completely that even after death her hands will remain "ringed with ordeals she was mastered by." Because this poem focuses on effect rather than cause, we have little to amplify through what ordeals she was mastered or even, so efficacious is the passive construction, the exact active agent: Uncle? marriage itself? Aunt's own internalized reflexes? Three things suggest, however, that the culprit was less a person than a rite: the emphasis on the ring, a metonymy which in stressing the institution makes the nameless Uncle seem only its temporary representative; the word "ordeal," whose connotation of extreme suffering is particularized in its denotation of a social ritual used to determine guilt or innocence by submitting the accused to painful tests; and, finally, the later poem "An Unsaid Word," which in developing the theme of the painful test locates it in the restrictions of a woman's role.

"An Unsaid Word" (51) is one of only three poems in *A Change of World* where the subject is immediately and unequivocally a woman. [18] Its seven iambic tetrameter lines divide into two three-line units and a comment:

> She who has power to call her man
> From that estranged intensity
> Where his mind forages alone,
> Yet keeps her peace and leaves him free,
> And when his thoughts to her return
> Stands where he left her, still his own.
> Knows this the hardest thing to learn.

Part of the tension in the poem is the apparent pull of the rhyme scheme against the thought pattern, for in this the first four lines, which rhyme abcb, seem to divide from the last three, which cluster dcd. The two divisions, however, reinforce and enrich each other, for while the 3/3/1 structure sustains the subject of the woman's power, its abnegation, and a comment, the 4/3 structure splits the predominant focus on the man from the subordinate focus on the woman.

As in "Aunt Jennifer's Tigers" the rhymes augment the thought. The first line-ending, "man," is the poem's only unrhymed word, replicating the privilege of solitary status automatically accorded the male by his culture. The following rhymes—"intensity" and "free"—particularize his autonomy which the next pair, by juxtaposing he who is "alone" with she who is "his own," sets against her contingency. The final rhyme, "return" and "learn," seems to summarize his choice and her necessity, for she must, so the woman's part is written, train herself to be constantly present for his inconstant desire.

This poem makes it quite clear that responsibility lies with Aunts as well as Uncles, that the woman "has the power to call her man"; yet it is also clear that the social command is to relinquish her power, to "keep her peace and leave him free." The title implies both thoughts: she has the world but has chosen the negative not-to-say rather than the active call. The man, on the other hand, is characterized by unquestioned, unchecked power, power which need neither force itself to "stand . . . still" nor channel itself to tasks but instead wanders at will. "Forage" is an excellent verb for this: not only does it imply a sweeping, unsubdued search for supplies but it also assumes an aggressive right to raid someone else's supply. This connotation is reinforced by an overtone of the phrase "estranged intensity," a phrase which implies that the intensity is gained by turning away feeling and maintained by staying at a distance. The suggestion is that at least part of his energy is diverted from its original use or possessor, from the women who must give up her freedom and intensity to supply him with his.

If the directness of "Aunt Jennifer's Tigers" was released by an obvious persona, the force of this poem seems to have been liberated by an extremely ambiguous last line. This self-abnegation would indeed be "the hardest thing to learn," but is the hardest the best? or is it the hardest because it is the most alienating and self-destructive? or because it is not yet learned, cannot in fact be learned without relinquishing much of the fierceness embedded within the lines and behind the words? The poet's point is freely made from behind what may have seemed a safe screen of indeterminacy.

When reprinting her poems in the selected edition of 1975, Rich did not revise or "remake the woman of twenty, or thirty, in the light of the woman of forty-five," [19] but she did remove one of the screens, the male pronoun in the poem "Afterward." Originally selecting the masculine pronoun because a "notion of 'universality' prevailed which made the feminine pronoun suspect, 'personal'" (and also, perhaps, because it masked a painfully private moment), she changed it in 1975 "not simply as a matter of fact but because [it altered], for me, the dimensions of the poem." [20] The change places "Afterward" (43) in a cluster with "Aunt Jennifer's Tigers" and "An Unsaid Word" and permits us to see it as a poem aboutsomeone who has relinquished the discipline, severity, and pride Rich deemed necessary to the artist for something less fine and aloof, perhaps the compassion, tenderness, and humility pressed upon women:

> Now that your hopes are shamed, you stand
> At last believing and resigned,

And none of us who touch your hand
Know how to give you back in kind
The words you flung when hopes were proud:
Being born to happiness
Above the asking of the crowd,
You would not take a finger less.
We who know limits now give room
To one who grows to fit her doom.

The last couplet is a slight surprise after two preceding quatrains; it snaps the poem shut with the click of a door, the clank of a tomb.

The speaker of this volume is very much one who, like Auden, knows limits and, like Frost, delights in such paradoxes as growth into doom, but she is also, unlike her models, a woman with a particular set of woman's pressures and woman's privileges. The more she comes to admit her identity into her poem the less she is comfortable with knowing limits, giving room, and, least of all, accommodating herself to doom. The more she senses her own strength, the less her protagonists close themselves behind shutters and her poems draw about themselves the protective strategies which characterize her first volume. In looking back at *A Change of World* she told David Kalstone, "I'm amazed at the number of images of glass breaking—as if you're the one on the inside and the glass is being broken from without." It had taken almost twenty years to turn the image inside out, so that "now," she can add, "I guess I think of it in reverse. I think of the whole necessity of smashing panes if you're going to save yourself from a burning building."[21]

Notes

1. "Writing," in *The Dyer's Hand and Other Essays* (New York: Random, 1962), p. 27.
2. *A Change of World* (New Haven: Yale Univ. Press, 1951) p. 11. All further references to this volume will appear in parentheses after the citation.
3. Stanley Plumly, Wayne Dodd, and Walter Tevis, "Talking with Adrienne Rich," *Ohio Review*, 13, No. 1 (1971), 31.
4. Plumly interview, 30.
5. Plumly interview, 31.
6. "Reflections on Lawrence," rev. of *The Complete Poems of D. H. Lawrence, Poetry*, 106 (1965), 218.
7. David Kalstone, "Talking with Adrienne Rich," *Saturday Review*, 22 April 1972, p. 57.
8. "When We Dead Awaken: Writing as Re-Vision," in *On Lies, Secrets, and Silence: Selected Prose 1966–1978* (New York: Norton, 1979), p. 39. This essay first appeared in *College English*, 34, No. 1 (1972), 18–25, but for ease of reference citations will be to the reprinting.
9. Robert Shaw and John Plotz, "An Interview with Adrienne Rich." *The Island*, 1, No. 3 (1966), 2.
10. *Of Woman Born: Motherhood as Experience and Institution* (New York: Norton, 1976), p. 224.
11. Plotz/Shaw interview, 2.
12. *Snapshots of a Daughter-in-Law* (New York: Norton, 1963), p. 32.
13. Plumly interview, 33.
14. "Adrienne Rich: Poetry of 'Re-Vision,'" Diss. George Washington Univ. 1977, p. 19.
15. "Adrienne Rich: 'What Lends Us Anchor But the Mutable?'" in *Alone with America: Essays on the Art of Poetry in the United States since 1950*, (New York: Atheneum, 1969), p. 427.
16. "An interview with Adrienne Rich: Part I," *Conditions*, No. 1 (1977), 64.
17. "When We Dead Awaken," in *On Lies, Secrets, and Silence*, p. 40. For a similar comment, see Plumly interview, 31.
18. The others are, of course, "Aunt Jennifer's Tigers" and "Mathilde in Normandy." Though implied by lines like "You will perhaps make love to me this evening" (24), the protagonist of "Kursaal" is never identified as a woman, nor, interestingly, is either the speaker or the subject in "Stepping Backward" so identified.
19. *Poems Selected and New, 1950–1974* (New York: Norton, 1975), p. xv.
20. *Poems Selected and New*, p. 247.
21. Kalstone interview, p. 57.

MORDECAI RICHLER

1931–

Mordecai Richler was born on January 27, 1931, in Montreal, and grew up in the Jewish section of the city, St. Urbain Street. He attended Sir George Williams University. In 1951 he left Canada and became a freelance writer in Paris (1952–53) and London (1954–72). He returned to Quebec in 1972.

Richler's first novel, *The Acrobats*, was published in 1954. This was followed by *Son of a Smaller Hero* (1955), *A Choice of Enemies* (1957), *The Apprenticeship of Duddy Kravitz* (1959), *The Incomparable Atuk (Stick Your Neck Out)* (1963), *Cocksure* (1968), and *St. Urbain's Horseman* (1971), which won the Governor-General's Award. *The Street: Stories* appeared in 1969. In addition to fiction for adults, Richler has written several collections of essays and reviews and a children's book, and has edited several anthologies, including *Canadian Writing Today* (1970) and *The Best of Modern Humor* (1983). Richler has also written for film, including the screenplays for *Duddy Kravitz* (1974) and *Joshua Then and Now* (1985).

Richler is married and the father of five children, and lives in Westmont, Quebec.

Much of *Cocksure* recalls the flickering two-dimensional satire of the Twenties. The central villainous character, the Star Maker, reminds one of middle-period Aldous Huxley—in say, *After Many a Summer*; he is a Hollywood film mogul with absolute power of life and death over all his minions, which surely makes him at least twenty years out of date, though the details of how he works are genuinely funny-horrible and ingenious. However, the best thing in the book, for my money, is Polly Morgan, a girl whose mind has been entirely formed on films, to the extent that she has no real experiences at all; e.g., she will invite her lover to a feast, gastronomic or amatory and suddenly cut from the gleaming preliminaries to the happily sated afterglow, leaving out the main business alto-gether as films do. The cardboard hero finally meets his death because of this tendency on her part, in a grotesquely neat twist of plot.

Cocksure certainly keeps one reading, and often laughing, and perhaps I sound dyspeptic and square, but, six weeks from today, I doubt whether I'll be able to remember what it was all about. As Mr. Richler is far too sharp not to know, this is the fate of all satire that lashes out without having a definite place to lash out _from_—all these modern absurdities are ridiculed, but in the name of what? Only breakneck inventiveness can keep the reader from noticing that the whole thing is an Indian rope-trick.—JOHN WAIN,"Puppeteers," _NYRB_, Aug. 22, 1968, p. 34

⟨_St. Urbain's Horseman_⟩ is one of those current extravagent performances with a raconteur for a narrator. Canadian (this time) and Jewish jokes and pain, lore about stages of life and recent history. If you don't like the manner you can't like the book:

> Back in Montreal Jake made straight for the bar in Central Station, ordered a double whisky, and paid for it with American money.
> "Montreal is the Paris of North America," the waiter said. "I trust you will enjoy your stay, sir."
> Jake stared at his change. "What's this," he asked, "Monopoly money?"
> "It's Canadian."
> Jake laughed, pleased.
> "Canada's no joke. We're the world's leading producer of uranium. Walter Pidgeon was born in this country."

or:

> In the afternoons they studied for their bar mitzvahs at the Young Israel synagogue and at night they locked the door to Arty's room, dropped their trou-sers to their ankles, and studied themselves for bush growth. Pathetic miserable little hairs, wouldn't they ever proliferate? Duddy Kravitz taught them how to encourage hair growth by shaving, a sometimes stinging process. "One slip of the razor, you schmock, and you'll grow up a hairdresser. Like Gordie Shapiro." Duddy also told them how Japa-nese girls were able to diddle themselves in ham-mocks. Of course Duddy was the bushiest, with the longest, most menacingly veined, thickest cock of all. He won so regularly when they masturbated against the clock, first to come picks up all the quarters, that before long they would not compete unless he accepted a sixty-second handicap.

Well, that is the most familiar tone now in fashion; you can quote it easily, like it or not like it equally easily, feel superior to it at whim or peril.

The question is not, Is it art? but, Can you make a novel out of it? To which the theoretical answer is a forceful yes while the answer in practice is usually a qualified no. Malamud's self-pity shrinks to nothing beside the self-regard of Richler's narrator. There is nothing he will not try to package with humor and anguish: the Fifties, Jews on Germans, assimilation, mod-ern London, Toronto, the sexual and hygenic trials of the middle-aged rich, the sexual revenges of the down-trodden, the tendency of lives to approach tabloid journalism. Richler's aim is almost encyclopedic, and he knows full well he has left himself wide open to the charge that he offers nothing new:

> Years and years ago, he recalled, another Jake, ponderously searching for a better way than St.

Urbain's had started out on his intellectual trek immensely heartened to discover, through the books that shaped him, that he wasn't a freak. There were others who thought and felt as he did. Now the same liberated bunch dissatisfied, even bored him. The novels he devoured so hopefully, conned by overexcited reviews, were sometimes diverting, but told him nothing he had not already known. On the contrary, they only served to reaffirm, albeit on occasion with style, his own feelings. In a word, they were self-regarding.

> To read of meanness in others, promiscuity well observed or greed understood, to discover his own inadequacies shared no longer licensed him, any more than all the deaths that had come before could begin to make his own endurable.

A nice point.

For any novelist, the way out of the box that Richler so cleverly constructs around himself here is not to go on trying to convince others that they are not freaks, which is the usual praise of his kind of book. It is to test his style and his anecdotes and his autobiography by means of a real story. Richler senses this, and he tries to keep his narrator from being only another instance of charming and arrested adolescence. At the begin-ning of the novel Jake Hersh, a wealthy television director in London, is going on trial for participation in some wild sexual shenanigans. As we go along we gradually learn what the shenanigans allegedly were, near the end we come pretty close to knowing Jake's complicity in them. And that is all carefully connected with Jake's boredom with the present, his fear of death, his search for his tawdry but heroic lost cousin, the first St. Urbain's horseman, and with his co-defendant, a really funny and grubby pervert from the East End.

But "connected with" is all we can say here. Richler wrote, before this, three rather ordinary raconteur novels, and he saw he needed a story. But the one he comes up with, neat and "connecting" thought it may be, is a raconteur's story, shaggy and timed, incapable of testing anything. And the test of _that_ is the narrative voice. If the story were really a story, the voice would alter as it encounters the changes the plot forces it to recognize; consult _Catch-22_, that very good novel, on this point. As yet Richler sees the need for testing with his story more than he knows how to do it. He simply is too attracted by his own gaudy attractiveness, and the only limits he allows for are those he defines for himself, not those discovered in a fiction. The voice in _Catch-22_ changes each time it retells its story, which means we do not end up where we began; the voice in _St. Urbain's Horseman_ is by comparison static completing itself, encountering nothing anew. I like Richler's voice, but wish it would give itself sterner tasks to do.—ROGER SALE, "What Went Wrong," _NYRB_, Oct. 21, 1971, pp. 3–4

Swift, Yeats says,

> . . . has sailed into his rest;
> Savage indignation there
> Cannot lacerate his breast.
> Imitate him if you dare.

It will be to Richler's everlasting credit, since works of art endure, that he does dare to imitate Swift, in more than a few ways. _Gulliver's Travels_ was the first English novel to take advantage of symphonic form, inadvertently since the form itself was only just coming into being. In _Gulliver_ there are the four lively movements, liveliest of all being the third, a swirling prose scherzo, all over the geographical and thematic place. And the fourth movement, in Houyhnhnmland, recapitulates and resolves the themes woven into the first three. Which is a way of saying that *St. Urbain's Horseman* is *Gulliver* come round again. Most of the writing devices Richler uses have sanction, in that Swift also used them. Just as Swift laces burlesque passages through *Gulliver*, Richler laces them through *Horseman*. Just as Richler intrudes expository asides into his narrative, Swift intrudes even more of them into his: passages concerning law, education, family life, written in over Lemuel's shoulder. And both writers hold to the crucial rule that, as their scepticism cuts the ground from beneath their protagonists' feet, redemption will occur not in pronouncements but in the act, the art of writing. If the human spirit is to prevail over the grimness of things, it will prevail in the interstices of the words themselves: "there is a music at the heart of things."

And there is another decisive similarity, though it leads to an even more decisive difference. Both novelists choose as protagonist a fool whom they then trap into experiences which will reveal and, they hope, cure the foolishness. Gulliver doesn't seem exactly cured at the last, since he's mad enough to believe that he's almost a horse and likes it that way— farewell mankind! Yet he's an awfully human horse. If you met him trotting down the street, you'd be less likely to weep for mankind lost than to smile. Jake isn't exactly cured either, since he does leave the question of Joey's death open, implying that he might some day climb back on to the nightmare desire that vengeance shall be Joey's, Harry's and his. But the similarity that leads to difference is a deeper one. Both Lemuel and Jake are atheists; Jake by direct acknowledgement of the fact that throughout his ordeals he never once calls on God's help, as his creator did every evening of his adult life. Which means that both fools must call on their human resourcefulness to outface or outfox the surrounding grimness. But Swift takes Lemuel's atheism as the basic foolishness that branches out into all his other idiocies, driving him finally outside human boundaries, to Horseville. Richler takes Jake's atheism as a source for his tenacious humanity, the stubbornness with which he clings to fair play for such sorry specimens as Joey and Harry Stein. Swift, then, is on God's side, laughing, while Richler is on man's side, needing to laugh, trying.

Because this is so, Swift would see Richler playing the fool to his fool by imposing on him an untenable proposition that mankind can go it alone. Yet were he to sail on out of his rest and re-appear on a sudden London to tell Richler so—fool Mordecai!—it would surely be a double sign. Sign of his belief that God forgotten is man abandoned. But sign also that the Horseman from Canadhnhnmland has written his way into the kind of company he, Swift, always did prefer. Which is a long way for a spiky boy from St. Urbain's Street to have travelled. Even Duddy, swindled out of his role as major figure, would be impressed. And one see's Horse Lemuel trotting briskly along, but turning solicitously to Horseman Jake, flat on his back again: You see Jacob, we Houyhnhnms have been doing this longer than you Canadhnhnms.—WARREN TALLMAN, "Need for Laughter," *CL*, Spring 1973, pp. 82–83

As its title might lead you to expect ⟨*Joshua Then and Now*⟩, Mordecai Richler's new novel, his first for nine years, is the story of the hero's life from childhood to the present, but in form it is far from chronological. Joshua Shapiro, we learn, was born and brought up in the Jewish community of Montreal, his father a prize-fighter and petty criminal, his mother a suburban beauty with aspirations to be a burlesque dancer. As a young man ambitious to be a writer, Joshua went to Europe in the 1950s, acquiring Experience in Paris, Ibiza and Lon-

don, where at the height of the Suez crisis he stole Pauline, golden daughter of a WASP Canadian Senator, from her wet husband, and married her himself. Then back to his roots in Montreal, where he raised a family, made a reputation as a sports writer and, less successfully, tried to resist being drawn into the Montreal Smart Set, personified by Jack Trimble,— the pseudo-English tycoon and his predatory, promiscuous wife Jane. Pauline's ne'er-do-well brother, Kevin, returning to his old haunts, exploits and is exploited by the Trimbles, and upsets the equilibrium of Joshua's marriage.

The novel begins at this end of the story, with Joshua recovering from a serious accident and suffering several other crises and setbacks, including the disappearance of his wife. The narrative skips backwards, forwards, and back again, as erratically as it zig-zags in space, and we piece together the chronicle of Joshua's life from scattered fragments. The technique is not new, but I have seldom seen it used more skilfully. It has the great advantage of opening many questions at the outset of the novel, the answers to which are delayed till almost the end. What was the nature and cause of Joshua's accident? Why was his wife having a nervous breakdown at the time she disappeared? Why is Joshua suddenly hitting the headlines as a notorious homosexual, and how come he was wearing black silk panties when Officer McMaster called to return his car? And who is the freak burglar in the Westmount area who does not steal anything, but plays practical jokes on *nouveaux riches* Jews, such as washing all the labels off Pinsky's collection of vintage wines, or erasing the signature from Dr Jonathan Cale's (*né* Kugelman) authentic A. Y. Johnson landscape?

By juggling with chronology, Mordecai Richler superimposes a "plot" on a "story" in E. M. Forster's sense of those terms (of a story, we ask, "and then?", of a plot, "why?") and thus has the best of both narrative worlds. The method also justifies leaving considerable gaps in the story, without which it would stretch to unmanageable proportions.

For *Joshua Then and Now* is a book brimming with characters and intrigues, comic and serious, glamorous and grotesque, that a more parsimonious novelist might have spread over several novels. There is, for instance, Joshua's father Reuben, who has an inimitable way of retelling the Old Testament stories:

> "But Job, he's a tough nut, and he continues to
> believe in God, though he does come round to
> contending with him, as they say, Quote, Wherefore
> do the wicked live, become old, yea, and mighty in
> power? unquote. Which is really sticking it to God,
> who naturally loses his temper. 'Hey there', God
> says, 'hey you little prick, where were you when I
> made the world? Can you make thunder? Or rain?
> Or the rest of it?'"

There is Joshua's uncle Oscar, who is always phoning him with ideas for profitable inventions like instant spray-on sunglasses or motorized suitcases. There is his friend Seymour, a tireless philanderer whose characteristic toast is "Here's to the kisses we snatched and vice versa", and Seymour's wife, Bessie, who has decided that her mission in life is to counsel the dying but is unfortunately prone to mix up the patients in the hospital; and Issy who has to try and outwit his own electronic burglar alarm system when he wants to raid the refrigerator in the middle of the night—one of several superb comic set pieces in the novel. There is a lot of local colour—Ibiza before and after the tourist boom, London before and after it began to Swing, Montreal's freezing winter streets and idyllic summer lakes. There are fascinating historical digressions about Canadian politics and the Spanish Civil War; wry cultural footnotes on changing *tempora et mores* ("Rabbis, who once gave you a clap on the ear if you sat down to eat without pronouncing the prescribed blessing, now wrote books telling you everything you wanted to know about cunnilingus"); and brilliant verbal snapshots like "sour septuagenarians shuffling down a hospital corridor to file a good bowel movement, as if that were proof against a carcinoma."

Joshua Then and Now is so good a novel—so entertaining, so cleverly constructed and tautly written—that it seems churlish to wonder why it isn't a great one; or, if that is asking too much, an indispensable one. Yet even as one chuckles and nods and turns the pages thoroughly enjoying the tale, a niggling doubt makes itself felt: what exactly is the *point* of this novel? What, in sum, is it saying?

According to Roland Barthes, all any literary text ever says in abstract terms is: there is love, there is death; and there is certainly plenty of both in *Joshua Then and Now*. The text must, however, defamiliarize these commonplaces so that we apprehend them, as it were, for the first time. The trouble with *Joshua Then and Now* is that much of it seems vaguely familiar—not in detail, but in general style. Offered as an account of the modern world, it strikes us rather as an account of that world as already represented in a hundred modern novels—most of them, paradoxically, less vivid, intelligent and witty than this one. Too often we feel that this or that episode is introduced for the sake of an effect to which we can instantly give a literary label: the Zany, the Rabelaisian, the Bitter-Disillusioned, the Lump-in-the-throat-Sincere.

Too many of its characters seem to have come from some Central Casting of the modern novel—especially the modern American novel, and most especially of all the modern American Jewish novel. The reason why this should be so is perhaps explained by a passage in which Joshua (whose attitude to writing seems more like a novelist's than a journalist's) muses on the impossibility of integrating his Jewish identity with his Canadian nationality:

> Canadian-born, he sometimes felt as if he were condemned to lope slant-shouldered through this world that confused him. One shoulder sloping downwards, groaning under the weight of his Jewish heritage (burnings on the market square, crazed Cossacks on the rampage, gas chambers, as well as Moses, Rabbi Akiba, and Maimonides); the other thrust heavenwards, yearning for an inheritance, any inheritance, weightier than the construction of a transcontinental railway, a reputation for honest trading, good skiing conditions.

It would not be surprising if Mordecai Richler, whose background has much in common with his hero's, having failed to find a native cultural tradition to which he could belong, should have been drawn into the powerful gravitational field of the American novel of Bellow, Roth, Heller and the rest. He can certainly hold his own there, but does not shine with the distinctive, originality that one might hope for from a writer so richly endowed with literary skills. Of those skills, *Joshua Then and Now* gives ample evidence. It remains, when all one's reservations have been entered against it, a thoroughly enjoyable, exhilarating read.—DAVID LODGE, "To-ing and Fro-ing," *TLS*, Sept. 26, 1980, p. 1056

What is Mr. Richler's secret? How has he contrived to defeat the universal (in New York, anyway) belief that all news from above the 49th parallel is cataleptically boring? Well, yes, to tell the truth, he contrived it partly by getting out. During the 1950's and 60's he based himself in London, competing on equal terms with the best of his Commonwealth generation—V.S. Naipaul, Brian Moore, Dan Jacobson, Doris Lessing—and more than holding his own. But in 1971, homesick for blizzards, he returned to his town in the bush, Montreal, *hors concours*, and from there has achieved his extraordinary eminence as the one Canadian able to conjure foreigners into reading about the Great Blank North. How is it done?

⟨In *Home Sweet Home*⟩ he does it, first, by unkilting the Tartan Peril. Canadians like to see themselves as the Scots of North America—canny, sober, frugal folk of superior education who by quietly terrible Calvinist virtue will inherit the 21st century. Canadian children learn in their pine cradles to revere the names of John Kenneth Galbraith, Louis B. Mayer, Saul Bellow, Teresa Stratas, Donald Sutherland and the other Canadian-born who, with demure cunning, have sliced like knives through butter into the fat, flighty culture below the border, usurping its seats of might. Mr. Richler, jeering, cuts through this complacent myth like—well, a razor through oatmeal. What it's about, he demonstrates derisively, is hunger: Inside each decorous three-piece Canadian suit is a Californian lotus-eater lusting to get out. Those shadows slipping ominously from the trees in your backyard aren't about to take over the house. They're coming to press covetous noses to the 3,000-mile picture window that stretches from the Bay of Fundy to Juan de Fuca Strait, licking lips at the goodies within and gawping at your television.

He jeers, but affectionately, seeing that it's not only comic. If you get your image of the world, as Canadians do, from someone else's television and journals that never mention your existence, you begin to doubt your reality. *Home Sweet Home* offers several lamentably funny studies of Canadian desperation to prove we're somebodies in someone else's terms. Mr. Richler visits the home of Karsh of Ottawa—the only home outside the United States, he's informed, ever visited by Edward R. Murrow on *Person to Person*—and watches an acolyte tape-record the *pensées* of the photographer who built a career making executives look like Churchill and Schweitzer. He attends a Mr. Universe contest in Montreal whose short, bulging contestants all receive medals as consolation for watching the title go to Mr. America. He even turns his satire on himself. Lured to the Academy Awards ceremony by an Oscar nomination for *The Apprenticeship of Duddy Kravitz*, he's ignored by its distributors, loses to Mario Puzo and brings away only a Writer's Guild award for "the best American comedy adapted from another medium."

The same hunger for recognition, he suggests, underlies Canada's recent fits of nationalism, French and Anglophone. Perhaps if we stopped being sober, virtuous good neighbors, someone to the south might notice. At a press conference to launch something called the Committee for an Independent Canada, the first question is "What does, um, Washington think of your plans?" When Prime Minister Trudeau calls a national emergency because fear of an armed coup has emptied Montreal's streets, Mr. Richler has another explanation. "The streets, I felt, has been abandoned not because Montrealers were afraid, but because they were all gathered gleefully round their TV sets waiting for Walter Cronkite to pronounce. Look, look, there we are. Real at last. On CBS, NBC, ABC."

In some ways' he's Canada's Sinclair Lewis, guffawing with despairing scorn at the Babbittry and boosterism of a new, uncertain society. That may be part of his secret; though Canada admits to no Middle West, the nerve he touches runs all the way down Middle North America. But he's a truer writer than Lewis; he manages to produce caricature that is truthful. Lewis achieved laughter by exaggeration. Mr. Richler's specialty is the exaggerations people have perpetrated on themselves, whose absurdity betrays the truth they wished to hide. His two best pieces are almost pure pathos. One is a memoir of his father, a lifelong loser whose one tragicomic gesture against anonymity was spotting errors in the movies he drowned his Sundays watching. ("Franchot Tone's in this tank in the desert, and he says 'O.K., men, let's go. Attack!' . . . But if you look closely, the fuel gauge is indicating EMPTY.") The other is a requiem for the greatness of the Montreal Canadiens, lost in the rush to sell one of Canada's rare glories, ice hockey, as a commercial sport to the Sunbelt.

He has a Canadian love of the underdog who seizes his day—small boys who cheerfully disrupt parades, jokers who put out tongues at the camera, the man in Arctic Yellowknife who, asked what social institution would most improve the town's quality of life, replied "A whorehouse." Ultimately, his humor is absurd with a capital, philosophic A—cartoons of small figures asserting themselves ludicrously in a huge, cold space too vast for names or postures to carry across it. Perhaps that's his real secret. His Canada looks not unlike the universe.—RONALD BRYDEN, "Northern Light," *NYTBR*, June 3, 1984, pp. 32–33

Blessed with a sharp eye, a keen sense of irony and a gift for characterization, Mordecai Richler has written four or five excellent novels. Such books as *The Apprenticeship of Duddy Kravitz* and *St. Urbain's Horseman* are among the few Canadian works of fiction to have found a large audience outside the country. Because of this, perhaps, Richler stands in a privileged position. Although he produces fiction less and less frequently, he continues to be the prime interpreter of his native country to bored, bemused or baffled foreigners. The editors of *Life* and the *New York Times*, *Esquire* and *Harper's*—even *Encounter* and *The Spectator*—can be relied upon to trot him out whenever his inoffensive homeland happens to impinge on their consciousness.

Richler lived for nearly twenty years in London, where he performed a role similar to that which Salman Rushdie, Clive James and Conor Cruise O'Brien assume for other nations. Unfortunately, he did not perform it well. The publication of *Home Sweet Home* affords sour proof of Richler's sheer inadequateness as an interpreter of Canada to the English-speaking world. A collection of nineteen articles written over the past quarter-century, the book includes essays on such disparate topics as broadcasting and body-building, the trials of life as a script-writer and the tribulations of Montreal's professional baseball team. The only unity comes from Richler's awkward, acerbic style and from his passionate denunciations of Quebec nationalism.

Born and brought up in a Jewish, working-class district of central Montreal, he spares little love for the Anglophile captains of industry and culture who flourished in the city he knew as a child forty years ago. But he reserves his scorn for the new masters of Quebec, the *indépendantistes* of the Parti Québecois who seek political sovereignty for the province, along with some form of economic association with English-speaking Canada. Richler describes the PQ as "an abomination" and compares one of its ex-ministers to Torquemada. The party's leader, René Lévesque, is characterized in these ungainly terms: "The chain-smoking Lévesque seemed obviously, even dangerously, weary, high-strung and romantically wrong politically. Richler offers little evidence to support his adverbs.

His zeal to discredit the PQ leads him to play fast and loose with the facts. Discussing the government's language legislation, for example, he states "Bill 101 ruled that wherever a child came from—abroad, or even from another Canadian province—it had to be educated in French, unless one of its parents had been to an English school in Quebec." In fact, the law allows a child who was receiving English-language education in the province in 1977 to finish his schooling in English, and it grants the same right to any younger brothers or sisters. Furthermore, a man or woman who lived in Quebec in 1977, and who had been educated in English anywhere in the world, continues to enjoy the right to send children to English-language schools. Nor does the law prevent any resident of the province, no matter what his citizenship or mother tongue, from attending one of the junior colleges or the three universities that function in English. The supposedly repressive and intolerant provisions of Bill 101 are for the most part more generous to Quebec's English-speaking population than are the laws anywhere else in Canada towards French-speaking minorities. Yet Richler describes the PQ's language law as a "vengeful and mean-minded . . . enormity". He fails to grasp that in the 1960s and 70s the assimilation of tens of thousands of immigrants (Greek, Italian, Portuguese and so on) into English-language culture had begun to menace the survival of Quebec as a distinct, Francophone society. The real irony is that Bill 101, by providing Quebeckers with a large measure of linguistic and cultural security, has deprived the *indépendantiste* movement of its strongest weapon.

Richler knows next to nothing about western Canada or the Maritime provinces, and his travel articles in *Home Sweet Home* can be disconcertingly inept: "The mountains are a spectacular sight and their initial effect is totally exhilarating." But more important than mere clumsiness is his recurrent inability to carry on an argument for more than two paragraphs without resorting to snide digressions or witty irrelevance. "Canada is enduring bad times", he announces portentously; but the evidence moves swiftly from unemployment statistics to a discontented American who pitches baseballs in Toronto, and to the failure of Canada's best ice-hockey players to defeat the national team of the USSR. Richler's attempts at sarcasm often founder on his political innocence: "an especially deep P.Q. constituency group, taking the long view, resolved that the new country of Quebec should adopt a pacifist foreign policy, which is to say, Americans could relax, we were not about to reclaim Louisiana." Instead of considering the hazards or merits of a withdrawal from NATO, he makes a gratuitous sneer at Quebec nationalism. An ill-judged effort to compare President Kennedy's statement "Ich bin ein Berliner" with President Carter's neglect to announce "Moi aussi, je suis Montréalais" only points out the world of difference that exists between a linguistically divided Montreal and a physically divided Berlin.

The subject of Canadian nationalism provokes in Richler a telling unease. He dedicates *Home Sweet Home* to his publisher Jack McClelland, who served as co-chairman of the Committee for an Independent Canada—which Richler prefers to dismiss as "a hard-line nationalist faction". ("Hard-line" and "faction" are both, of course, terms that convey an unearned derision.) Rather than facing up to the issues which the CIC addressed, especially the economic domination of Canada by American business, Richler tries to blacken the nationalist movement by focussing on a few of its wilder and sillier offshoots. His rhetorical position resembles that of worried North American men who still seek to disparage feminism by mocking the women who once burned bras. For all its jauntiness and buoyancy, his own prose sometimes betrays the insecurity of the colonized. In an essay on the National Ballet of Canada, he can find no better way to describe its quality than by quoting the critics of the *New Statesman*, the *Guardian*, the *Observer* and the *New York Times*, as if the only proof of artistic excellence were international esteem.

Like Canada's National Ballet, *Home Sweet Home* has met with approval in the USA and Britain. But it is still an annoying and unreliable book, every page of which needs to be approached with a sceptical, alert intelligence. Its most rewarding essays are two personal memoirs, "My Father's Life" and "St. Urbain Street Then and Now", which have a warmth, a freshness, and a depth of understanding absent from Richler's political and social commentary. If he would stick to what he comprehends, his name would appear in print less often. But the rest of the world might have a clearer vision of Canada.
—MARK ABLEY, "Oh God, oh Montreal," *TLS*, Dec. 21, 1984, p. 1470

VICTOR J. RAMRAJ
From "Diminishing Satire: A Study of V. S. Naipaul
and Mordecai Richler"
Awakened Conscience:
Studies in Commonwealth Literature
ed. C. D. Narasimhaiah
1978, pp. 264–68

Richler, ⟨. . .⟩ though he does not deny satirical pieces in his novels, protests against an interviewer categorising him as satirist pure and simple. This, Richler observes, ignores his larger concern with the novel of character and with being the loser's advocate rather than his castigator, which he sees to be the novelist's primary moral responsibility.[1] This preference is reiterated in Richler's essays and interviews. Significantly, he stated of the early writings of himself and his coterie (which included Terry Southern and David Burnett), that satire (which does not require knowledge of the psyche and inner complexity of the individual or society but only of the moment of folly and vice) was shrewdly settled upon because it did not "betray knowledge gaps of day to day experience."[2] Satire, then, can be used by Richler as a stylistic device rather than a straight expression of attitude.

The satirical vision springs from firm convictions of what is right and wrong, unimbued with any hesitancy, vacillation, or ambivalence. The satirist in the published form of his work does not weigh, balance, and sift evidence, resolve queries, wrestle with doubts like a member of the judicial bench; he more closely approximates the prosecutor, who having convinced himself of the accused's guilt sets about to convict him relentlessly. As Basil Willey says: the satirist "must, whether deliberately or not, miss precisely these aspects of the ignoble thing which in fact make it endurable to the non-satiric eye: that is to say, he must ignore the explanation of the thing satirised."[3] It is interesting to note in relation to their political stance that Richler and ⟨V. S.⟩ Naipaul are unhesitantly convinced of the rightness of only two or three causes: Naipaul said to Derek Walcott: "You cannot commit yourself unless your cause is absolutely pure. I think there have really been only two good causes within recent times: against Hitler and possibly in South Africa."[4] And Richler says: "We've lived through two great horrors, in our time, the murder of the Jews

and Hiroshima, and the rest disappears. . . . One must . . . figure out where he stands in relation to [them]. . . ."[5]

What informs Richler's tone from his very first novel is less a satiric and more an ambivalent vision. Though satire appears sporadically but sharply, and though he has written (in *Cocksure*) the most serious Canadian satirical novel and therein has employed one of the most grotesque satirical images (of Star Maker) in contemporary literature at large, nevertheless his ambivalent, vacillating, conflicting vision does restrictively affect any sustained, cogent satire in his novels. All Richler's protagonists from Andre Bennett of *The Acrobats* to Jake Hersh of *St Urbain's Horseman* are questing, troubled souls searching for values in a world where absolutes have disappeared. And it becomes difficult to chastise satirically when yardsticks of judgment have not been decided upon.

In *The Acrobats* and *A Choice of Enemies* Richler's protagonists, Andre Bennett and Norman Price, conduct their search in post-war Europe where causes and ideologies are seen by the young Richler to inform and govern human relationships. Satire plays a very minor role in these novels for the protagonists are not sure of what is evil and what is good, what should be censured and what should be sanctioned. The title of *A Choice of Enemies* reflects their predicament. Richler is concerned with the pain, the frustration, the disillusionment, the bewilderment, and the ennui of his seekers, one of whom does not live long enough to realise that truth is not to be found in ideologies and political causes. In *The Acrobats*, Andre does make one emotional outburst against Canadian culture, but Richler focuses on the impassioned anger and resentment of his troubled protagonist, intending no controlled satiric distancing. Perhaps the only piece of cogent satire is a brief dig at four dignitaries at a Spanish fiesta who sit aloofly from the ubiquitous misery around them, and whose mechanical, orchestrated behaviour is satirically set against the passion and spontaneity of the street dancers. But this is a digressive piece, not wholly digested within the novel. *A Choice of Enemies* has a measured, unruffled, contemplative tone. Sometimes it rises to mild sardonicism through the character of the protagonist (the main consciousness of narration), but it is his very character which prevents this mild sardonic attitude from becoming satirical. An aloof, contemplative man, Norman Price reprimands himself for not being more generous and tolerant; and to avoid being considered cold and detached, he makes every effort to be pleasant. The one cogent satiric passage is again digressive and undigested here: Richler briefly satirises cultural programmes on Canadian television through Charlie Lawson, a character viewed with sympathetic concern by the author and protagonist in the rest of the novel.

Son of a Smaller Hero and *The Apprenticeship of Duddy Kravitz* are Richler's two novels wherein the Jewish society of Montreal features prominently. Some aspects of this society annoy and dismay Richler, but others appeal to him. He does not sweepingly or indiscretely poke fun at the inhabitants. He observes the members of this richly complex society in all their guises and forms, sympathising with their predicament at times and censuring them when they deserve it. The censured in his novels are the materialistic, the pompous, the dullards, and the bigoted. In *Son of a Smaller Hero*, Richler, however, is less concerned with satirising these shortcomings than with the struggles of Noah Adler, another unanchored, questing soul who embodies the contradictions and ambivalences of someone seeking himself. Noah does reject several aspects of his Montreal Jewish society, but his criticism is never sharp or vicious, for in fact he does not know what to believe in. It is not until the end of the novel that he has found something to adhere to (and even then what he has found is vague). Throughout the rest of the novel he experiences an emotional bind in his relationship with the Jewish community, rejecting it and accepting it, seeking to escape from it yet returning to it for assurance. In this quandary, Noah is unable to administer firm chastisement; and, instead of becoming a persecutor of his people, he reveals himself to be a troubled, tormented young idealist in this *Bildungsroman*.

Certain readers of Richler's other Montreal Jewish novel, *The Apprenticeship of Duddy Kravitz*, believe that Richler mocks and censures the young Jewish protagonist, presenting him as a money-grabbing *pusherke* from the Montreal ghetto. But Richler has said otherwise: "A character like Duddy Kravitz possibly has enormous strength in that he's not, in that book, sufficiently perceptive or sensitive to believe in his own death, and that does give acquisitive money-making people a lot of strength and energy and vitality, which I both *admire and despise*."[6] And elsewhere he candidly states of Duddy: "I don't think of him as fundamentally unsympathetic."[7] An examination of the novel bears out Richler's response to his protagonist. He is portrayed almost simultaneously as a waif of circumstances and environment (no morality is imparted him; he has no mother, of whom he asks for with pathetic recurrence; he is ignored by members of his family who favour his brother, Lennie, the designated doctor of the family; he is considered a cipher socially and academically), and as a man of free will who chooses the wrong way of life (Uncle Benjy's letter, read posthumously by Duddy, underscores this). Richler shows that Duddy, in order to escape the harsh and oppressive realities of his environment—a business jungle, where survival of the fittest is the law—must play according to the questionable values of that environment, and then ironically become himself a victim of those values. Unnecessary and unaccommodated, overlooked and ignored, Duddy seeks to lose his status as a nonentity in the eyes of his unheeding family and environment. The only way he knows how is by taking his grandfather's platitudinous advice literally: a man without land is a nobody. Towards the end of the novel, Uncle Benjy on is deathbed is Richler's voice, and he realises that Duddy's obsession with land is not that of a money-grabbing *pusherke* for Duddy has just refused his financial offer; Duddy's tooth-and-nail struggle for land is only an expression of his need to be wanted and heeded. Though Richler doesn't sanction Duddy's unscrupulous efforts to acquire Lac St Pierre, he does suggest what would have happened to him had he not fought the business jungle by its rules: the manqué comedian Cuckoo Kaplan, the gullible Lennie, and the disillusioned Mac-Pherson (with whom the novel significantly opens) all succumb to the jungle. Duddy himself in fact almost did; at one point he suffers what appears to be a nervous breakdown, and is overwhelmed by *ennui*.

In his study of Duddy Kravitz it is a remarkable achievement on Richler's part that he succeeds in never making Duddy satirically repellent when he shows his vices and in never making him a romanticised, sentimental figure when he presents him as a poor creature who cannot help but be moulded by his social environment. Richler is aware both of the worst and of the possibility for good in his protagonist, and he is neither his castigator nor his advocate. He does not intend that the reader should make a simple sympathetic identifica-

tion with, or an easy rejection of, the young protagonist. Such responses would be a gross simplification of Richler's achievement and energising ironic vision. Were Duddy a real-life acquaintance of the reader it is true that he would be on his guard against Duddy; however, with Duddy contained between the covers of the novel, Richler invites us to shed our biases and to look objectively at him, though like the author we may not be able to make up our minds about whether we should admire or despise him. There are the inevitable Richlerian certain set pieces of satire on social pretensions and hypocrisies; and two characters with some thematic and structural functions—Cohen and the Boy Wonder—are satirised. The predominant tone of the novel, however, is characterised by an energising ambivalence.

In *The Incomparable Atuk*, Richler leaves the Montreal Jewish world for Toronto's cultural scene. He shows here that the Canadian society is walled in by a narrow nationalism which encourages the fabrication of national heroes and heroines of pedestrian proportions, creates an insularity that seeks to exclude all outside influence (particularly that of America), and fosters the parochial cultural man. This is a work, however, which though it is not equated with his journalistic articles, is dismissed by Richler as a light novel, a holiday piece, "more of a spoof."[8] It is not satire primarily but farce, wherein laughter is used for laughter's sake rather than to mock or ridicule. Richler is certainly caricaturing attitudes and manners, drawing creatively from the pseudo-cultural type, but often his characters cease to represent something and they just are. They are not so much satirical caricatures as originals, however unreal they may be. Often, too, Richler becomes so absorbed with his zany plots and zestful situations that he is distracted from whatever censuring intentions he may have had. One obvious illustration is the situation in which Sergeant Jock Wilson of the Royal Canadian Mounted Police finds himself towards the end of the novel. Initially, Richler appears to be using him as a means of satirising the ineptitude of this police force and the fastidiousness and officiousness with which it undertakes to entrap communist students. But any potential satire gives way to farce in the scenes of mistaken identity where Jock and Jean-Paul McEwen, both masquerading as their opposite sex, fall in love. In the final hilarious farcical scene of this sub-plot, whatever satirical butt there was disappears completely as Richler, following this episode to its most unlikely extreme, tells of Sergeant Jock, disguised as a woman winning the Miss Canada crown, and preparing, on orders from his superiors, for the Miss Universe contest.

Notes

1. Taped interview with Earle Toppings, *Ontario Institute for Studies in Education*, Toronto, 1970.
2. *Shovelling Trouble*, Toronto, McClelland & Stewart, 1972, p. 36.
3. *The Eighteenth-Century Background: Studies on the Idea of Nature in the Thought of the Period*, London, Chatto & Windus 1940, p. 107.
4. Interview with Derek Walcott, p. 5.
5. Interview with Donald Cameron, in *Conversations with Canadian Novelists II*, Toronto, Macmillan, 1973, p. 117.
6. Graeme Gibson, Interview with Mordecai Richler, *Eleven Canadian Novelists*, Toronto, McClelland & Stewart, 1973, p. 290. (italics mine).
7. Ibid., p. 270.
8. Interview with John Metcalf, *Journal of Canadian Fiction*, Winter 1974, p. 74.

ISHMAEL REED

ELMER RICE

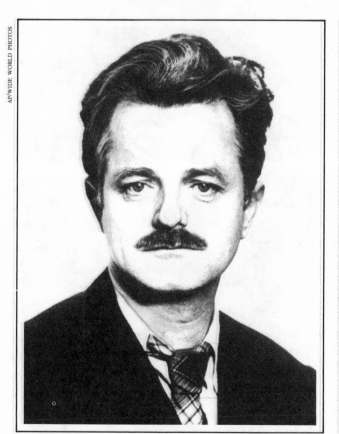

KENNETH REXROTH

ADRIENNE RICH

THEODORE ROETHKE

EDWIN ARLINGTON ROBINSON

CONRAD RICHTER

MORDECAI RICHLER

CONRAD RICHTER

1890–1968

Conrad Richter was born on October 13, 1890, in Pine Grove, Pennsylvania, the son and grandson of ministers who were themselves the descendants of tradesmen, soldiers, blacksmiths, and farmers similar to the characters who later appear in his historical fiction. After finishing high school at the age of fifteen, Richter went to work at a variety of jobs while he read widely, trying to educate himself. A series of articles in the *Bookman* about newspaper writers prompted him to become a journalist, and while still in his teens he began a long career as a reporter for and editor of small-town newspapers.

Richter moved to Cleveland around 1910 and began writing and selling stories to periodicals, receiving wide attention with the publication of "Brothers of No Kin" in *Forum* in 1914. It was included in the *Best Short Stories of 1915* and later became the title piece of Richter's first story collection, published in 1924.

Because of his wife's failing health—Richter had married in 1915 and had one daughter—the family moved to Albuquerque in 1928. Richter continued to write in his spare time, turning out popular stories to supplement his income as a journalist and businessman. But in 1933 he decided to devote his attention full time to serious fiction. A second volume of stories, *Early Americana*, was published in 1936; his first novel, *The Sea of Grass*, appeared in 1937 and was widely acclaimed. Both deal with Western and Southwestern themes, an area in which Richter grounded himself by doing intensive research in newspaper files and libraries and by interviewing surviving pioneers. In recognition of *The Sea of Grass* and his next novel, *The Trees* (1940), Richter received the gold medal for literature in 1942 from the Society of Libraries of New York University. *The Trees* was the first volume of Richter's acclaimed trilogy about the Pennsylvania-Ohio frontier in the late eighteenth and early nineteenth centuries; the second volume, *The Fields*, appeared in 1946, and the third, *The Town*, in 1950. The trilogy was republished as *The Awakening Land* in 1966 and was later dramatized on television.

Richter continued to write short stories and a number of other novels. Late in life, following his return to Pennsylvania from New Mexico in the 1950s, he produced two more major, critically praised works: *The Waters of Kronos* (1960), which won the National Book Award; and its sequel, *A Simple Honorable Man* (1962), the first two volumes in a projected trilogy about rural Pennsylvania left uncompleted at his death on October 31, 1968.

During his lifetime Richter published fourteen novels, four volumes of short stories, and three book-length essays on his personal philosophy, which attempted to explain human behavior in terms of a theory of physical and psychical energy: *Human Vibration* (1925), *Principles in Bio-Physics* (1927), and *The Mountain on the Desert* (1955). A fifth volume of short stories, *The Rawhide Knot*, was published posthumously in 1978.

General

Conrad Richter has a great fund of information of the precise sort that a historical novelist must have. He knows what his people looked like and the clothes they wore, how they built and furnished their cabins, how they married and buried their dead, what happened after an Indian raid, how they farmed their crops, what their jokes were and the songs they sang. This knowledge, however, is never more than the underpinning of his story. There is no surface decoration here—merely the facts of pioneer existence springing from a background of simple necessity. ⟨. . .⟩

Conrad Richter's novels give the impression of definite achievement within a limited field. Alfred Kazin, however, has recently pointed out the importance of the minor writer in an age of crisis like our own. It is more difficult today to do what the novelist has done in the past, to create a real human scene whose meanings are revealed in terms of character and story, than it is to imitate the great novelists who have struggled with language, fable, and symbolism to find new forms for the novel and a new concept of man and history. The imitative form of much modern fiction, the concern for world values, are symptoms of a new provincialism which uses the loose struc-

ture of the novel to write political doctrine, battle reports, biography, private mysticism. Richter works within a recognizable and authentic folk tradition. He is an example of Kazin's minor novelist, the traditional story-teller. In *The Trees* and *The Fields* people and story are sufficient to support the structure and meaning of these novels, without need for a larger framework of topical reference. The simple and sometimes lyric effects of Richter's work are the results of a discipline that shows itself in several ways.

Form is always appropriate to the themes and substance of his books. Perhaps it is significant that he began as a writer of short stories, for he seems to have little talent for the loose-gaited novel as it has usually been written in America. His method at best is episodic rather than chronological. Externally *The Sea of Grass* consists of only three episodes which span a generation in time. Several of the chapters in *The Trees* and *The Fields* exist as short stories complete in themselves. These books derive from the earlier *novella*, a determinable form of single effect. In the short novel, time and space are relative. The writer must cut sharply across a day-to-day unfolding of events to find the revealing situation or crisis in the lives of his people. An illuminating episode can compress the experience of a lifetime. Character must be deftly drawn to satisfy the needs of each situation. And the short novel is easily adapted to the story as reminiscence, for a narrator can move backward and forward in time to balance what has already happened with the immediate scene. Richter has mastered the unity of effect which the short novel demands.

In the process he has tuned a simple, colloquial style rich in elemental feeling and precise in narrative effect. It is the pioneer speech assimilated from old letters and records and regional imagery, just remote enough from our own speech to be convincing but never archaic. One example will serve. In one section of *The Fields* Sayward has been left with her children during a period of frontier famine. She goes out to find game with a rifle she has never used, and she shoots at a wild turkey in the woods:

> When she opened her eyes from the thunderclap, nothing but the frozen woods lay in sight. The snow among the butts stretched from here to yonder, empty of bird or beast. She couldn't mind when she felt so spited and downhearted. She felt like she couldn't get up from her knees. Then from behind the granddaddy log, a bronze and gold feathered wing heaved up and fell out of sight. Hardly could she believe her good fortune when she got there, and hardly could she get her hands on it quick enough so it couldn't get away. She told herself she could go back to her hungry young ones now. Wouldn't their mouths gape and their eyes pop when they saw their mam come across the clearing with a whole slew of turkey cock, its blood-red wattles a dragging on the snow! Tomorrow she would take some white meat, a drumstick and a second joint over for Mrs. Covenhoven, Genny and Guerdon. Her own young ones would have plenty to eat till Portius got back.

This prose, written with occasional incorrectness of folk speech, is capable of sharp and evocative effects. There is first of all the appearance of the scene itself—"frozen woods lay in sight," "a bronze and gold feathered wing heaved up," "blood-red wattles a dragging on the snow." On another level there is the expression of the primitive instinct for survival, a physical joy in the prospect of rich food. The closing sentences of the passage indicate something quite different, a sense of social responsibility on Sayward's part not only to her family but also to her frontier neighbors in like distress.

Conrad Richter's novels are regionalism as art. Although criticism cannot grow too solemn over them, they deserve attention because they have added much to our understanding of the regional scene. As a writer he is still in mid-career. A new short novel, *Always Young and Fair*, has been announced for early publication. This is a story of life in a Pennsylvania town from the Spanish war on, and it is drawn from Richter's own background and experience. Later *The Town* will continue his story of the forest conquered and a town settled on the Ohio frontier. Clearly *The Fields* is not a stopping place in his survey of the American past.—DAYTON KOHLER, "Conrad Richter: Early Americana," *CE*, Feb. 1947, pp. 225–27

During the last two decades Conrad Richter has published a series of stories and novels recalling to vivid life the adventures and feelings of the American pioneers. *The Sea of Grass* told of the disintegration of a cattleman's kingdom in the early Southwest, and it achieved fame: it was chosen as the first of an anthology of *Great Short Novels* (edited by Edward Weeks) and was made into an excellent moving picture. In 1940 *The Trees* described even more vividly the lives of a family of the earliest settlers of the Ohio Valley. In 1946 *The Fields* and in 1950 *The Town* carried this story to its conclusion in the Civil War and

the end of the pioneering era. Between these four novels other successful stories of other pioneers appeared; but these are the best, and *The Town* completes a cycle. Since its publication also marks the author's sixtieth birthday, it is time to take stock of his achievement.

The only novelist with whom Conrad Richter can well be compared is Willa Cather, whose pioneer heroes and heroines, like his, came from both Middle West and Southwest and whose tales, like his, were told with a kind of classic restraint. But Richter belongs to a later generation, which both sees the pioneers from a longer perspective and (paradoxically) enters into their lives with a greater emotional immediacy. Between the generations of Willa Cather and of Conrad Richter a myth has begun to form, and this myth has worked to deepen and (in some ways) to distort the tales of the contemporary writer. Between the direct clarity of *O Pioneers* and the plotted complexity of *The Town* the generation of Freud and Sherwood Anderson has intervened, with its rediscovery of Melville and the symbolic method.

But Richter has usually been called a simple realist, and all his tales have genuinely been characterized by a careful artistry, a classical condensation, and an emotional restraint. *The Sea of Grass* was a perfect short novel, with hardly a word wasted, and *The Trees* ran but little longer. All these pioneer novels have been packed with homely, realistic detail resulting from the author's lifelong absorption in the folk tales, newspaper accounts, diaries, and historical records of an earlier age. Not only external details but the very language and style of his writing have been authentically and consciously early American. By contrast, his symbols have never been explicit and his myth may perhaps be subconscious. But in his last book this myth has become increasingly dominant, and it distinguishes all his best novels from the more purely realistic pioneer tales of Willa Cather and (more recently) of A. B. Guthrie, Jr. —FREDERIC I. CARPENTER, "Conrad Richter's Pioneers: Reality and Myth," *CE*, Oct. 1950, pp. 77–78

Works

This year's Pulitzer award in fiction is particularly welcome because it calls attention to a truly major achievement in the American novel. I refer not merely to Conrad Richter's *The Town*, for which the prize was given, but to the trilogy of which it forms the concluding part. These three novels, *The Trees*, *The Fields* and *The Town*, taken together, form, in my opinion, the finest creative achievement we have had on the theme of the westward movement in American life. It would be a pity if those readers unfamiliar with Mr. Richter's work turn only to the book named in the award; for while it is true that each volume of the trilogy can be read for itself, much is lost if *The Town* is not approached as a part of the whole.

Some time ago, in this column, I expressed the opinion that the West had only recently been receiving the kind of treatment it deserves from our novelists, and that Mr. Richter, in company with A. B. Guthrie and Walter Van Tilburg Clark, had been pointing the way. But Mr. Clark, though he has written of the West from a fresh approach, has not concerned himself with the westward movement, and Mr. Guthrie has not dealt with the complete cycle of the pioneer experience.

That cycle in its entirety, from wilderness life to town life, forms the framework for Mr. Richter's trilogy. Through each of its phases—the nomadic life of the hunter, the turning to the soil, the building of a settled community, we follow the fortunes of a family up to the coming of the fourth generation. Wisely, I think, Mr. Richter chose as the central figure of his story, not a man but a woman, because it is the woman who stands, so to speak, at the center of life, and when you are dealing with successive generations, what happens is most fully observed through her eyes. The world that Mr. Richter recreates for us is viewed chiefly as it was looked upon by Sayward Luckett, a child in the opening chapters of *The Trees*, an old woman on her death-bed at the end of *The Town*.

Sayward is, to my mind, the fullest and most living portrait of the pioneer woman that has ever been drawn. The picture is not in the slightest degree sentimentalized. At its core is the quality of enduring strength, and if that quality had not been multiplied thousands of times over in women like Sayward Luckett, the history of this country would have run a different course. Their story is one of the greatest in the world's history, and it is one that has never been told in the factual detail that it merits. No women ever lived a harder life; none ever met it more bravely. And it has never been imaginatively projected as convincingly as in Mr. Richter's trilogy.

These books are an extraordinary achievement in bringing the past close. One hesitates to call them historical novels. They have nothing of the synthetic quality that ordinarily is found in that form. From the time you enter the forest with the Luckett family you live in the world they knew. You see it with their eyes. Why do these books achieve such complete reality? The answer does not lie entirely in Mr. Richter's craftsmanship, skilled as it is. It lies also in the intensity of his identification with his material, about which he is explicit in the "Acknowledgments" which preface *The Town*:

"Finally," he writes, "the author wants again to set down his obligation to those men and women of pioneer stock among whom he lived both in the East and West, whose lives and whose tales of older days gave him a passionate love for the early American way of thought and speech, and a great respect for many whose names never figured in the history books but whose influence on their own times and country was incalculable."

And what was the meaning of the pioneer experience? Sayward's youngest son sits by her bedside as she dies, and reflects: "Hardship and work, that's what his mother always harped on. Once when at home he had refused to work on the lot, she had said, 'You're going to live longer than I do, Chancey. Watch for all kinds of newfangled notions to take away folks' troubles without their having to work. That's what folks today want and that's what will ruin them more than anything else.' Could there be something after all in this hardship-and-work business, he pondered. He had thought hardship and work the symptoms of a pioneer era, things of the past. He believed that his generation had outlived and outlawed them, was creating a new life of comfort, ease, and peace. And yet war, the cruelest hardship of all, war between brothers, was on them today like a madness. Did it mean that the need for strength and toughness was to be always with them, that the farther they advanced, the more brilliant and intelligent they became, the more terrible would be the hardship that descended upon them, and the more crying the need of hardihood to be saved?"

That was a century ago. And now?—J. DONALD ADAMS, *NYTBR*, May 20, 1951, p. 2

The Light in the Forest (1953) is now Conrad Richter's best-selling novel, surpassing his Pulitzer Prize winning *The Town* (1950), and the National Book Award winner, *The Waters of Kronos* (1960). That it should sell so well is not surprising. Writing it after long and painstaking research into Indian-white relations in Pennsylvania and Ohio during the

middle of the eighteenth century, Richter skillfully recreates an era in a short novel that is both good fiction and good history.

Conrad Richter's abiding interest in early America has produced outstanding results. His trilogy, *The Trees* (1940), *The Fields* (1946), and *The Town*, is a classic treatment of the subjugation and settlement of the Ohio forests by pioneers whose plucky, intrepid foray into the wilderness awed him. These pioneers whom he admired and loved are made of the stuff of greatness: that "early American quality" of courageous hardiness that helped tame a continent and create a nation. But Richter is a fair, objective, and high-minded researcher and author. Although some of the hardships encountered by these pioneer whites stemmed from the Indians' natural reluctance to give up their land, he always tried to see the Indians' side too, something that has not been done very often in American writing. The result of this double vision is the picture of the Indian that emerges from the pages of *The Light in the Forest*. Richter's Delaware (Leni Lenape) is neither the overidealized noble savage of some authors nor the equally distorted treacherous pagan of so many others. He is an objective rendering in fiction of the Delaware Indian that Richter found in all of the sources, both oral and written, that were available to him. The Leni Lenape live again in these pages, as undistorted as in historical writing at its best, but with the vividness that only a great novel can give. The author's stated aim was "not to write historical novels but to give an authentic sensation of life in early America." All those who have read *The Light in the Forest* know how admirably he succeeded in accomplishing this aim.

A fact Richter considered remarkable moved him to write this novel. In the "Acknowledgments" he writes: "In records of the Eastern border, the author was struck by the numbers of returned white captives who tried desperately to run away from their flesh-and-blood families and return to their Indian foster homes and the Indian way of life." To anyone who had read the conventional accounts of the Indian mode of life this would seem surprising. Richter felt that it was a facet of early America worth exploring. His research led him to two works in particular: the Reverend John Heckewelder's *Indian Nations*, and David Zeisberger's *History of North American Indians*. Another valuable source of information was the "Narrative of John Brickell's Captivity Among the Delawares," which appeared in the *American Pioneer* in 1842. From these and many other sources Richter garnered the information needed to transform the accounts of many unhappy returned white captives into a single story. It also gave him an opportunity to deal with some of the problems of the settlers of his native state, Pennsylvania, during the years immediately preceding their fight for independence. More than careful research is needed to make a good novel, however; a believable, engaging story is essential. True Son's search for identity is just such a story.

The boy's final statement, "Then who is my father?" is the central question of the novel. John Butler-True Son is a boy growing to manhood with divided loyalties. Born a white and raised by white parents until four, he is then stolen by Indians with whom he lives until he is 15. His white father is replaced by Cuyloga, an honorable and heroic Delaware leader. But two fathers mean two allegiances, even though the boy feels allegiance only to the Indian throughout most of the novel. A faint, vague stirring in his blood, a vestigial remnant of his white heritage, causes him in the end to alienate irrevocably his Indian father. It is this tension created by the two distinct claims to the boy's loyalty and affection that makes the story exciting. These claims are the basis for the exploration of the Indian and white cultures that claim him, and keep the description of the two ways of life at the very center of the novel. The danger is a prejudiced view for or against either of these cultures. Richter assiduously avoids this pitfall. ⟨. . .⟩

The Light in the Forest is a finely wrought novel of a boy's tragic predicament. True Son is accidentally caught between two worlds; losing the one of his choice, he is forced back to the other. There will be no fond welcome for him in Paxton where his partially scalped uncle and rejected parents wait. After living so long in an Indian culture he learned to cherish, he will never be able to adjust fully to the white culture of Paxton. When he is shackled, as the old Negro predicted, he will know it—the worst thing that can happen to a man. Even Richter's restraint and understatement have not dulled the attractiveness of the Indian way of life. This slim volume stands as a corrective to the Indian distorted beyond recognition in hundreds of novels, motion pictures, television plays, and articles. Its honest picture of Delaware life restores to the Indian some of the dignity and integrity stolen from him by his detractors. In language and manner the Delaware emerges as a man of faith and honor. And yet the novel does not give the impression that every Indian acted like every other. There is a wide range of behavior, from the primitively violent Thitpan to the wise and courageous Cuyloga. True Son, at least, had found a Shangri-La with them. One wonders at the end if he will ever find it again.—MARVIN J. LaHOOD, *"The Light in the Forest: History as Fiction," EJ,* March 1966, pp. 298–304

Richter's criticism of the cult of comfort, which emerges as themes of protest in *Early Americana, The Sea of Grass,* and the Ohio trilogy, is one of his major reasons for reacquainting us through historical fiction with our early American heritage. Richter's respect for pioneer values as a check to the moral bankruptcy which has attended the cult of comfort accounts for his lifelong preoccupation with the frontier experience as a source of literary materials. His study of the past provided him with an historic image: a change in the human condition attended by a cultural loss. He locates the beginning of this change in the historic transition from the rugged living conditions of the frontier community to the high living standards, but crass materialism, of the mid-nineteenth century industrial community.

The Ohio trilogy records this historic change in the human condition and points up the essence of the cultural loss by means of a thematic structure of affirmation and protest. *The Trees* and *The Fields* affirm pioneer values. The steady conflict with natural adversity on the wilderness frontier—apotheosized by the hard work of clearing a virgin forest to make way for homes, fields, and a reasonable security—causes the pioneers in the community of Moonshine Church constantly to summon and build up their energies for survival. In the process, Sayward, her family, and her neighbors develop a unique quality of mind and spirit, a quality of hardihood and ethical courage.

The Town, on the other hand, protests those social forces of economic materialism and collectivism which bring about the destruction of these values. The radical shift in attitude toward suffering and pain, which is reflected in the hypersensitivity, physical weakness, and moral confusion of Chancey Wheeler, the child of the industrial revolution, is in explicit contrast to the attitude shared by Sayward and her contemporaries. The pioneers, in their common sense philosophy, intuitively accepted the need for hardship and discipline in their lives. Tutored only by experience, they came to consider life's misfortunes and adversities to be providential, the wise dispensation and discipline of the gods. Furthermore, they

came to that painful self-knowledge that the issues of life must be embraced personally. The great lesson experience teaches Sayward is that she cannot be strong for others without destroying their own strength.

The surface narrative of the Ohio trilogy is thus connected with a background meaning: the cosmic role of hardship and discipline as a means of grace. The theme of cosmic order and individual destiny gives unity to the three novels by providing a principle for selecting those details and episodes which enable Richter to coordinate structure and meaning. There is a consistent correlation between the artistic pattern of the Ohio trilogy and the philosophical structure of Richter's perception of the reality beneath the appearances.

The pervasive sense of cosmic order and the consistent conception of character and human behavior explain in large part the structural unity and coherence of the Ohio trilogy; however, the emotional power of the three novels owes much to another dimension of Richter's art—its tragic vision.

Although the enormous sense of loss reflected in the past-present polarity of the tales in *Early Americana* hint at a growing tragic awareness in Richter's art, it is not until *The Sea of Grass* and the Ohio trilogy that his tragic vision receives an impressive and symbolic expression, and that the relationship of this tragic sense to his psychological theories is made clear. In the action of both *The Sea of Grass* and the Ohio trilogy, Richter confronts the irreducible facts of suffering and death; and in his characterization of Brock Chamberlain and Chancey Wheeler, he suggests the immutable limitations imposed upon human personality by the tyranny of blood consciousness and the irresistible flux of time. Richter's later appeal to the Cronos myth to explain the hostility between father and son in *The Waters of Kronos* illuminates his earlier sense of loss at the tragic erosion of time, which has been the subject of all of his fiction. The mechanistic determinism of time-as-emasculator, the sense of mortality that grows heavier in the Ohio trilogy, and the apparent helplessness of each succeeding generation to be reconciled to the one that went before it contribute to an essentially tragic insight into the modern loss of identity and sense of spiritual alienation characteristic of contemporary man.

The present, in repudiating the past, suffers a tragic paralysis of the spirit, and contemporary man thus stands alone, unaccommodated, condemned to search out the meaning of existence without any revelation save that of his own experience.

Richter's tragic vision empowers all of his art, but much of the enduring appeal of the Ohio trilogy derives from its organic relationship to the traditions of primitivism and transcendentalism; its thematic structure of affirmation and protest, which helps to order the realistic historical narrative, relates it to the regionalist tradition of the novel of the soil, a tradition which embraces the stoic values of primitivism, the tenacious confirmation of the land, and the spiritual values which inhere in a transcendent conception of the cosmos.

Although it is not all of the truth to say that Richter has devoted the major portion of his literary life to the meticulous reconstruction of an earlier world he might have loved and to the analysis of a contemporary one he hated, there can be no question of his love affair with pioneer America and of his disaffection with contemporary civilization. His commitment to primitive ideals is heightened by his personal sense of loss and nostalgia which threatens at times to carry him to an uncritical preference for the past. "His nostalgia, however, does not lead him to sentimentality", writes Granville Hicks, "and he is incapable of the sensationalism that spoils so much of the fiction written about the pioneers." Moreover, Richter's philosophical convictions show that his preference for the past transcends mere sentiment and becomes a serious indictment of the modern preoccupation with economic materialism as the means to progress in the human condition.

It is not difficult to understand why Richter's temperament, so remarkably akin to that of the mid-nineteenth century transcendentalists, with their revolt against materialism, their distrust of the machine in the garden, and their symbolic interpretation of the frontier, prompted him to fasten his mind on the West, not only as a place in space and time, but as an image of the spiritual frontier all men must face in their encounter with cosmic order. His fictional recovery of the West in *Early Americana, The Sea of Grass,* and especially in the Ohio trilogy is not simply an attempt to recreate authentically the atmosphere of a unique experience in our national history; it is also an attempt to evoke the symbolic power of the West as metaphor and to make this power accessible to contemporary man.

In recreating the historical West in a prose style so rich in emotional immediacy and so happily lacking in that preterit quality which characterizes most frontier fiction, and in suggesting the intimate and mysterious continuity of past and present in the cultural consciousness of Americans, Richter has reacquainted us with a dynamic native metaphor, a metaphor which has played a significant role in shaping the American mind itself. That "early American quality" of mind—resolute, courageous, self-reliant, and willing to confront the hard realities of existence with determination and with confidence in future possibilities—is given apt metaphoric expression in the image of the Western frontier. Richter has long grasped the significance of what Archibald MacLeish has recently declared regarding the strength of America as a country of extremes, of many opposites made one: "The American dream has been a dream of the west, of the world farther on. . . . West is a country in the mind, and so eternal."—CLIFFORD D. EDWARDS, "Conclusion," *Conrad Richter's Ohio Trilogy,* 1970, pp. 189–92

MARVIN J. LaHOOD
From "Richter's Pennsylvania Trilogy"

Susquehanna University Studies, June 1968, pp. 5–13

The first two volumes of Conrad Richter's second trilogy are a remarkable achievement. Seldom has a man written more candidly of himself and his relatives than has Richter in *The Waters of Kronos* (1960) and *A Simple Honorable Man* (1962). Mr. Richter has not yet begun the third book, which will be about his own life as an artist.

In this second trilogy (the first: *The Trees,* 1940; *The Fields,* 1946; *The Town,* 1950) Mr. Richter honestly attempts to portray his struggles with life's most teasing intellectual and spiritual problems: man's existence before and after this life, the differences in character from person to person, the father-son relationship, and the old problem of fate versus free will. He also exhibits in these two novels a great pride in various ancestors from whom he received what he considers a priceless legacy. *The Waters of Kronos* and *A Simple Honorable Man,* published after Mr. Richter reached seventy, offer an invaluable insight into the mind and works of one of America's ablest authors.

The writing of *The Waters of Kronos* was a labor of love. In it the protagonist, John Donner, is very much like Richter

himself, and Unionville, the scene of the novel, is Richter's beloved birthplace and present home, Pine Grove, Pennsylvania. The novel opens as John Donner, a noted writer, now seventy, comes back to the place of his birth to visit his ancestors' graves. The town itself is now covered by the dammed-up waters of the Kronos River. At dusk John Donner walks to the old Unionville road which borders the cemetery where an old man on a wagon pulled by three horses agrees to take him into Unionville. Incredulous, John Donner goes down the steep hill with his guide and finds the town as it was sixty years earlier. He spends the rest of the novel re-examining the scenes of his childhood and his several relatives as they were at the turn of the century. He meets everyone of importance in his childhood except his mother; at novel's end he waits for her in the house next door to hers. 〈. . .〉

The Waters of Kronos has a much greater impact when its autobiographical implications are understood, yet few of its reviewers suggested that it might be essentially factual. Naturally they were puzzled by John Donner's journey back through time; and they are correct in feeling that what he learns doesn't seem to be important enough to justify the suspense generated throughout the novel. When the novel is read in connection with Richter's life and his other works, however, its meaning becomes clear.

The Waters of Kronos ends with an attack on the Oedipus complex:

> Now, why should the knowledge that he was after all his father's son give him . . . relief and freedom? Was it his earlier discovery that the son-father-hate legend was fiction, after which it had no more power over him; that he and not his father was the monster?[1]

In *The Mountain on the Desert* (1955), his only long nonfiction work, Richter attacks Freud and his followers in a long chapter. What is also significant is that throughout his fiction the mother is the heroine, the father neither clearly drawn nor clearly understood. At seventy, Richter was able to look back on his relationship with his father, who had been dead twenty years, and see more clearly what both he and his father were like.

Both biographical and autobiographical accounts of Conrad Richter's life have been published over the years. The details given in *The Waters of Kronos* describing Unionville, John Donner, and his relatives fit many of these facts. The Kronos River and Kronos Street in Unionville are Swatara Creek and Swatara Street in Pine Grove. He had, in his previous novel about Pine Grove, *Always Young and Fair* (1947), kept the name Swatara for the main street. In that novel appeared the Markle Mansion on Methodist Church hill. It appears on the same hill in *The Waters of Kronos.*

Conrad Richter is disguised only by name. Donner, like Richter, is a writer who published his first novel when he was in Albuquerque, New Mexico. His father, Harry, was first a storekeeper and then a minister. He likes bird watching and walking, Richter's two hobbies. His uncle, great-uncles, grandfather, and great-grandfather are ministers, as were Richter's. He has an Aunt Jess who told him stories and encouraged him as a writer. His great-grandfather, Squire Morgan, fits exactly Richter's description of his great-grandfather Squire Conrad. Both Richter and Donner have a maternal grandmother who dies at an early age from injuries sustained in a fall at a picnic.

Identifying Conrad Richter with John Donner makes it possible to examine the main problems of the novel in connection with Richter the writer, and with his works.

Richter, it seems to me, intended this identification to be made. The novel opens:

> For seven days the man who lived by the Western Sea had driven eastward toward the place where he was born, and every day he asked himself the same question. Why had he come?[2]

He comes because he has an illness he has never been able to name or cure. This illness is due to an unresolved fear which he has suffered from childhood. He carries a photograph showing his parents and his two younger brothers in "the old sitting room." Behind them are two doors, one to the stairs and one to the kitchen. White light streams from under the door to the kitchen; all through his mature years he has had a desire to open that door.

> He was a fairly able man who had reached honors envied by some other men, but never was he able again to get through that closed door. This, he suspected, was part of the source of the pain that sometimes came to his head.[3]

Why must this successful author get back to the world of his youth? What unsolved problem of his childhood has worried him all his life?

> His father, he felt, had always sung at home in riddles, saying in music what he could never bring himself to reveal in speech. As a boy he had thought these particular words a warning to him to give up his youthful, dissenting ways, his shying from church and people, and enter into his father's hearty way of life and religion.[4]

The shy and diffident John Donner found it hard to communicate with his father. ⟨. . .⟩

⟨. . .⟩ At his great-grandfather's funeral he sees his family at the church. His father sits on the aisle, "vigorous and alert as if to protect them from the contagion of death and all its malignancies."[5] It is this concept of death as contagious and malignant that is the first clear clue we are given concerning the horror which has dogged John Donner throughout his life.

Near the novel's end he faints in front of a neighbor's home and she takes him in and gives him a bed. His family's home is next door. He asks for his mother, and the boy Johnny comes to tell him that Mrs. Donner will come the next day to see him. This is a chance the old man must take advantage of: he asks the boy if his mother still keeps his light lit for him at night. The boy reluctantly answers "yes." Then he asks him about his nightmares—the boy is surprised that he knows. Then the old man asks the crucial question: "'. . . did you ever hear voices—after you're awake? I mean—that remind you of something, perhaps somebody in your nightmare?'"[6] The boy answers "yes," but he will not, perhaps cannot, tell the old John Donner whose voice it is that terrorizes him.

Then John Donner calls the neighbor. She doesn't answer, and he realizes with horror that the voice he has just heard is the voice he has feared all his life. He looks in the mirror and sees a decaying old man. Now he knows why Johnny didn't answer him when he asked whose voice it was that frightened him.

> So that was why he wouldn't reply! It was the great deception practiced by man on himself and his

fellows, the legend of hate against the father so the son need not face the real and ultimate abomination, might conceal the actual nature of the monster who haunted the shadows of childhood, whose name only the soul knew and who never revealed himself before the end when it was found that all those disturbing things seen and felt in the father, which as a boy had given him an uncomprehending sense of dread and hostility, were only intimations of his older self to come, a self marked with the inescapable dissolution and decay of his youth.[7]

The death of the body can be a terrifying thing. Richter is not as certain of immortality as his preacher-father was, and these doubts are what make death terrible. If Portius Wheeler is correct when he tells his son Chancey that there is no life after death, then death is indeed a formidable foe. But Chancey doesn't believe Portius the agnostic, and I don't think that Richter does either, finally.

What gives him hope and joy at the end of *The Waters of Kronos* is not just that he no longer identifies his fear with his father, but also that he can now draw strength from a source hitherto unavailable to him. He realizes that he is, despite his old age, "still the real and true son of his powerful, ever-living father, the participant of his parent's blood and patrimony."[8] He realizes now that his father is "ever-living" in his son, with the immortality that breed insures. He also realizes the meaning of his father's favorite song, a song also sung in "New Home" (1934):

> I'm a pilgrim
> And I'm a stranger.
> I can tarry, I can tarry
> But a night.[9]

His father had known all along that he was immortal, that this earth was not his permanent home but only a place of trial. And with this realization Richter becomes aware of why his father prayed, prayers that as a boy he found painful and embarrassing. His father was fighting, with prayer, the forces of evil and death.

> Now he could see that the cloud came from else-where, from uncontrollable sources, that his father had fought that cloud all his life with what forces at his command, and they were more powerful forces than the boy had realized, born of the strong fiber and convictions of his time.[10]

With this realization of the truth about his father and their relationship, Richter was ready to write his father's fictional biography, *A Simple Honorable Man*.

Notes

1. Conrad Richter, *The Waters of Kronos* (New York, 1960), p. 169.
2. Richter, *Waters*, p. 3.
3. Richter, *Waters*, p. 28.
4. Richter, *Waters*, p. 45.
5. Richter, *Waters*, p. 116.
6. Richter, *Waters*, p. 152.
7. Richter, *Waters*, p. 161.
8. Richter, *Waters*, p. 169.
9. Richter, *Waters*, p. 173.
10. Richter, *Waters*, p. 175.

LAURA RIDING

1901–

Laura Riding was born Laura Reichenthal in New York City on January 16, 1901; she adopted the surname Riding in 1926. She was educated at Girls' High School, Brooklyn, and attended Cornell University. She married Louis Gottschalk in 1920; they were divorced in 1925. In 1941 she married Schuyler B. Jackson; they remained married until Jackson's death in 1968. She and Robert Graves founded the Seizen Press in 1928, and *Epilogue* magazine in 1935. She and Graves also collaborated on a novel (*No Decency Left*, 1932), two books of criticism (*A Survey of Modernist Poetry*, 1927, and *A Pamphlet against Anthologies*, 1928), and a translation of Georg Schwarz's *Almost Forgotten Germany* (1936).

Although Riding published several novels and collections of short stories (notably *Progress of Stories*, 1936, revised 1982), she is primarily known for her poetry. She first received attention when the Fugitive poets awarded her a prize of $100 and made her an honorary Fugitive in 1924. Her first book of verse, *The Close Chaplet*, was published in 1926; over the next dozen years she published eleven more volumes of original poetry (*Voltaire: A Biographical Fantasy*, 1927; *Love as Love, Death as Death*, 1928; *Poems: A Joking Word*, 1930; *Twenty Poems Less*, 1930; *Though Gently*, 1930; *Laura and Francisca*, 1931; *The Life of the Dead*, 1933; *The First Leaf*, 1933; *Poet: A Lying Word*, 1933; *Americans*, 1934; *The Second Leaf*, 1935) before abruptly abandoning poetry with the publication of her *Collected Poems* in 1938, citing "reasons of principle." She has published no original poetry since then, devoting her life to the study of linguistics.

Laura Riding's poetry was particularly noted for its strong personal voice and use of concrete imagery, combined with an abstract tone that created a powerful but sometimes distancing effect. Her poetry is collected in *Selected Poetry: In Five Sets* (1970) and *The Poems of Laura Riding* (1980).

Works

One can make several statements about Miss Riding's poems (in *Collected Poems*). They contain a high proportion of monosyllables; the lines and sentences are short; human beings are depersonalized, abstractions are often personified; the words are unevocative and colourless, stripped of all but one meaning, though most of the personal names—Druida, Lucrece, Amalthea, Chloe—evoke myths or legends; many of the poems start with a singing rhythm which is soon discarded; and Miss Riding has coined several abstract words, such as manyness, neitherhood, whoness, bodement, skyhood and nextness. But one cannot discuss the subjects of the poems, or indeed say what the subjects are, except in the words of the poems themselves:

> What is to be?
> It is to bear a name.
> What is to die?
> It is to be name only.
> And what is to be born?
> It is to choose the enemy self
> To learn impossibility from.

By cutting out colour, music and metaphor, Miss Riding achieves lines as pregnant as a proverb:

> To each is given what defeat he will.

But proverbs and maxims are unreadable in bulk—see the works of Tupper; we can stand only a limited amount of abstraction (though Miss Riding can stand a great deal more than most of us), and we ask that abstraction should be distilled from fulness of experience. And for most people that means experience of the senses as well as experience of the intellect. But Miss Riding will have very little to do with the senses:

> We can make love miraculous
> As joining thought with thought and a next,

> Which is done not by crossing over
> But by knowing the words for what we mean.

Miss Riding's way of uncovering reality is to find a name for it (hence her coined words); she gives these names—beauty, truth, love, otherness, unlove, unplainness—an independent existence of their own in her poems, and she seems to be trying to make us apprehend universals as vividly as we usually apprehend particulars. But if this process is carried too far for the reader, he may feel that the poems end by losing reference to anything outside the mesh of language. Taken separately the poems are never meaningless—in every one we can relate the abstract universals to particulars of our own experience; but if we read the 475 pages of Miss Riding's collected works consecutively, words like 'beauty' and 'love' begin to lose their bodily associations, and the poems become as bleak as books of aesthetics that never mention a picture or a poem. In terms of Miss Riding's own canons of criticism, this effect is due to a failure in the reader; but many of her poems appeal to readers who feel that both in her criticism and her poetry Miss Riding over-emphasises the need for a particular kind of austerity. The reasons that such a reader would give for liking 'Nothing so far but moonlight', or 'All the Way Back', might well seem irrelevant to Miss Riding.

> Bill Bubble in a bowler hat
> Walking by picked Lida up.
> Lida said 'I feel like dead'.
> Bubble said
> 'Not dead but wed'.
> No more trouble, no more trouble,
> Safe in the arms of Husband Bubble.

By her practice and influence, Miss Riding has helped several poets to write simply about abstractions, to avoid trivial decoration and irrelevant music, and to preserve the integrity

of their words. Her peculiar use of Old Testament parallelism
in place of simile—

> The wind suffers of blowing,
> The sea suffers of water,
> And fire suffers of burning,
> And I of a living name—

and her use of a verbal music that is directly related to her
meaning, has enabled Miss Riding to write a kind of philosophical poetry of unusual precision (which in her Preface she
denies doing), but there are moments when the austerity that
has enabled her to achieve so much becomes a stumbling-
block in the way of the reader.—JANET ADAM SMITH, "Books of
the Quarter," *Critn*, Oct. 1938, pp. 113–15

Miss Riding prefaces her book of collected poems with an
address to the reader which is remarkable for its pretentiousness. In it she answers the charge of obscurity by saying that
those who find her work difficult are reading poetry for the
wrong reasons. Her poems can only be read for the right
reasons and are therefore written for the right reasons.

After the clarity and shrewdness of *A Pamphlet against
Anthologies*, this kind of mystic simplism is disturbing. After
looking through the whole volume the total effect is also
disturbing. Miss Riding's technical maturity is not to be
questioned; there is felicity of phrase and originality in
abundance, yet the bulk of the work seems to be a substitute for
life rather than the product of integrated experience. There is
such a barren rejection of all sensuality, (even word-color),
such an imprisoning self-consciousness, such a dry dissection
of the last cerebral quiver, that one is driven to psycho-
analytical conjecture to find excuses for many of the poems.

It is true that the position of the woman artist in society is
a difficult one. Traditionally, bourgeois society has allowed
women "accomplishments" such as needlework, piano playing
of a mild sort, or "water color drawings". Women attempting
to establish independence as artists have been handicapped by
inherited feelings of inferiority, by restricted social activity
because of economic position, and by superimposed masculine
notions of "the gentler sex". As a result we have large numbers
of highly sentimental women writers who wallow in their own
emotions and wave their sex like a flag. Artists of real stature,
like Miss Riding, are undoubtedly affected by this situation and
react strongly in the opposite direction. In her poems she is
apparently trying to capture certain enduring formal qualities.
In so doing, however, she depends far too much on abstraction, she is too much afraid of letting direct experience creep
in. She is indifferent to the salutary housecleanings of the
imagists. Instead of honestly aiming at the target, she insists on
looking into an arrangement of mirrors and firing over her
shoulder.

In some ways her work is characteristic of the post-war era
of expatriates, the era when most artists were completely
dissociated from society, for there is no echo in her poems of
anything that is going on in the world today, there is not even
the general sense of revolt, which is present in surrealism,
against an order of ideas. All her revolts take place internally.
What is worse, only too many of them result in mere negation:

> Where a wind over empty ground went blowing
> And a large dwarf picked and picked up nothing.
>
> . . .
>
> Holes in maps look through to nowhere.

Or a sense of sterility:

> If now seems little known
> Of joys, of origins,
> It is that there were none.

> . . .
>
> As a stone suffers from stoniness . . .
> So I of my whoness.
>
> . . .
>
> The tympanum is worn thin,
> The iris is become transparent,
> The sense has overlasted.
>
> . . .
>
> Our doomsday is a rabbit age
> Lost in the sleeve of expectation.

The mood of the *Waste Land* hardly seems valid for a
contemporary artist.

All this does not mean that Miss Riding does not attain
certain very fine effects. Her earlier poems especially achieve a
kind of nursery-rhyme magic. They are the simplest poems in
the book and the most direct.

> Home, thieves, home.
> Mother Damnable waits at her counting table.
> Thieves do the thieving,
> But she does the counting.
> Home, thieves, home.

When she permits herself to use an image it is often memorable.

> Druida followed,
> Not to bless him, not to curse him,
> Not to bring back the bridegroom,
> But to pass him like a blind bird
> Seeing all heaven ahead.

It is unfortunate so much of the book is made up of arid and
pretentious writing which reveals Miss Riding as strangely
uncritical of her own work:

> Where is now?
> Now is where I am.
> Where am I?
> I am what I say.
> What do I say?
> I say myself.

And so on—grammatical repetition, similar to Stein, but
lacking the charm of Stein's non-sequiturs.

It is to the poets of Miss Riding's generation that we must
turn for maturity and technical finish, for elegant detail and firm
use of language. But these qualities are not enough. It seems
more and more certain that English and American poetry must
discover new sources of vitality. Since the war, serious verse has
been written by and for a small group of individualists. Their
experiments in form, their defiance of poetic platitude are important and valuable contributions which must not be disregarded. Today, however, the crisis in ideologies, the sharpening
of social conflict throws a searchlight on the arts. They can no
longer remain the consolation of a few aesthetes. The people
have need of art—and art must come to its own defense in the
battle to preserve culture and civilization.

How can Miss Riding with her magnificent sensitivity and
her keenly analytical mind still feel that the dissection of her
personal malaise, her expatriate consciousness, is an adequate
and satisfying task for her fine poetic equipment?—H. R.
HAYS, "The Expatriate Consciousness," *Poetry*, May 1939,
pp. 101–4

"All men are deceived by the appearances of things,"
Heraclitus wrote, "even Homer, himself, the wisest man in
Greece, who was deceived by boys catching lice: they said to
him, 'what we have caught and killed we have left behind us,
but what escapes us we bring with us.'" In 1933, Laura Riding

renounced poetry and left her poems behind her. They were dead for her in that Heraclitean sense. She felt, at that time, she had reached "poetry's limit" as a "humanly perfect word use"—that even with the great agility she admits to have possessed, it was impossible, in her "poet-role," to catch truth.

It is interesting that the scale of the poems is a lifetime and not a half-life, despite the fact that the poet was 37 when she stopped writing and is now in her 70s. It is almost as if she had been able to gauge, from the start, her own trajectory, the capacity of lung and wing, and had compressed her work in that proportion.

She is an anomaly among modern poets, especially those who try to surprise the "truth" in their own functioning— whose intricate inner works come in transparent cases. Their poetry resembles those wonderful telephones whose circuitry is exposed behind Lucite: all the confessions, emergencies, mistakes, trivia, impulses, obscenities, secrets, static—the dailiness of speech—visible. But Laura Riding carefully reformalizes her inner life to conceal the intimate correspondences. The voice is aloof, even from itself—as deliberate as that of a religious utterance. Miss Riding finds contemporary poetry "suffused with a light of drab poetic secularity"; it lacks moral beauty for her. It is not surprising, then, that her own poems seem to have been written to outlast all familiarity.

In intent, they have a kinship with the conscientiousness of the 17th century, the struggle for grace revealed in the poetry of the Puritans, or of Herbert. Laura Riding wrestles with imperfection, with her own humanness, with the "corrupt oxygen of time." She aspires and despairs; she courts the absolute in language and in feeling, and her poems are the score of her assaults upon and lapses from this tidemark.

Such an insatiable mistrust of the subjective is, I think, rather alien to most modern readers—a trial, a complicity more strenuous than they are used to. In a way, I was reminded of Gertrude Stein's distinction between human nature and the human mind. Human nature was weather, sorrow, politics, identity, sex. The human mind was land seen from the air, and it wrote "what any human mind years after or years before can read, thousands of years or no years." Laura Riding's poems invite us to read them in that way—their form is a finality.

At its best, her language is desert language, dry and oracular. Its great resources take great effort to extract:

This is the account of peace,
Why the rugged black of anger
Has an uncertain smile-border
Why crashing glass does not announce
The monstrous petal-advance of flowers,
Why singleness of heart endures
The mind coupled with other creatures.
Room for no more than love in such dim passages
Where between kinds lie only
Their own uncertain edges.

At less than its best, it is tightly coiled, almost impacted, and we don't enjoy the full resilience of its intelligence. Sometimes this extreme difficulty, as in the desert, can become monotonous and even sterile. She has in her zeal parched it beyond rot, but beyond the capacity to bear life. The head swims, one begins to feel silly, to lose one's place.

The "five sets" of the title work like gears, of different power and size, which engage our sense of her ideas, their movement, their development in sequence. We begin with the process of self-definition, the learning of our "littleness"; this separation is honed, refined. A sense of "whoness" and of "otherness" emerges, and conflict. For this "whoness" interferes constantly with the awareness that is beyond it and greater

than it—a peace, a balance, a fusion, Oriental in its rejection of identity, that has been cultivated, traditionally, through denial. Her self-suspicion is almost a refrain: "base lust and tenderness of self" . . . "self-choked falsity" . . . "self-forgery."

In the late poems, the poet has failed to abstract herself. She has been unable to manipulate language to its perfection, to extricate herself from it. Being alive has meant being imperfect, and it is failure, misunderstanding, that make these poems the great ones. The easy, and sometimes pretentious remoteness of the early work is gone—it has been compromised by experience:

None dances whom no hate stirs:
Who has not lost and loathed the loss,
Who does not feel deprived.
Slyest rebellion of the feet,
The chaste and tremulous disport
Of children, limbs in passionless wave—
None dances whom no hate stirs,
Or shall not stir.

Laura Riding's work has received, from a special public, the respect it deserves. Her notion of the "spiritual best in language" has influenced a special following. But her work has a radical aspect which has not, I think, been fully recognized. She has written some of the finest feminist poems I know: "I Am"; "The Divestment of Beauty"; and especially, "The Auspice of Jewels," which is a classic by any standard. Before any of her contemporaries, she understood how women had been:

Kept safe from flagrant realness
The forgeries of ourselves we were—
When to be alive as love feigned us
We must steal death and its wan splendours
From the women of their sighs we were.

Her feminism seems to develop late in the poems—and has a direct bearing on her decision to abandon poetry. When she asks women to "forego the imbecile/Theology of loveliness," she is also addressing herself as a poet. Men and literature have always "connived" against her truth, preferred her beauty; have always lied to her—and now both have reached what she calls in *The Telling*, "the half-point, the finality of divided being."

Leaving poetry behind is, I think, the gesture not only of the artist who felt it was impossible to achieve wholeness through poetic language, but also of a woman whose self had been an "enemy" because it had never truly been her own. The artist deceived by appearances was the woman frustrated by her self-forgery. The poet-role and the sexual role oppressed her in the same way: they both "postponed human beginning," as she says in *The Telling*.

Her poems have another sense when they are read with the caution she attaches to them: they "excite a sense of wherein the failure of poetry lies." This failure, this finality, excites hope of an afterlife. "If, in writing, the truth is the quality of what is said, told, this is not a literary achievement: it is a simple human achievement."—Judith Thurman, "Forgeries of Ourselves," *Nation*, Nov. 30, 1974, pp. 570–71

MICHAEL KIRKHAM
From "Laura Riding's Poems"

Cambridge Quarterly, Spring 1971, pp. 303–8

While the linguistic ideals which have since led her to demote poetry in the ranks of verbal expression deserve, I believe, careful consideration, this need not obscure for us the fineness of the poems. Readers have found her 'difficult', and very little of what there is of commentary on her work shows even elementary comprehension. But the 'difficulty' is not of that sort common in twentieth century poetry—an obscurity caused by excessive dependence on implicit meaning in word-use. Each poem is a fully presented process of thought: the logic is stage by stage complete, cutting no semantic corners, the whole is as explicit as can be. The challenge to the reader's understanding comes from the originality and therefore unfamiliarity of the view displayed in her poems of human existence.

For this reason some introduction to her 'thought', however brief and simplified, is in order. The view taken is essentially moral—in the sense that she is primarily concerned with distinguishing between good and bad existence. The conviction motivating all her writing is that goodness can be achieved fully only in the good use of words, which consists in 'perfect fidelity to oneself (in a single management of intonation and thought) in their use'. In one of her poems, 'Disclaimer of Person', she anticipates for language a condition in which 'I my words am'. But this is not all: for her, goodness ultimately is truth to something larger than, though including, the separate self, and she considers language to be uniquely the medium through which such goodness might be realised because it can express the humanity of not one self but all selves. In language alone an individual finds the full extent of his humanity—a humanity exceeding the limits of the individual self. She distinguishes, that is, between the selfhood of individuality and the selfhood of our full humanity, 'a representative selfhood'—and words can transmute the first into the second only 'if self be truly subjected to the conditions of language' as she conceives them. This equation of language with the moral existence makes for a poetry in which the use of words, while they are being used, is also on occasions the theme of the poem. Thus, to represent the self that is at the same time more than self, she writes of 'a voiceless language'—thought not cramped by the personality of the speaker—with full human selfhood 'the story hushed in it'.

In many of her poems is heralded the attainment of this fullness of being which is also a 'human fullness of utterance'. Names and descriptions of this condition vary—among them are 'truth', 'eternity', 'finality'—but it is necessary to grasp the relationship to this of another condition termed 'death', a keyword in Laura Riding's vocabulary. 'Known death is truth sighted at the halt'; it is not truth itself, but the ending of falsity preliminary to truth. If life is a continuous experience of incompleteness, a vessel filling but never full, then death is life's potentiality at last fully known—'When death-whole is the seed/And no new harvest to fraction sowing'—and the prelude to what in her later work she has called everlasting life.

Laura Riding the poet is the maker of her own thoughts—and the style of speech to express them. As the trend of her thinking is away from categories and towards a conception of being as 'an indivisible experience'—'Thought not divided, thinking/A single whole of seeing'—so the most striking quality of her poems is their treatment of reality in its general rather than its particular forms. There are no objects for their own

sake in her poetry, no specific occasions not raised to a general status. She looks for 'the common denominator' of experiences. (I am indebted to a perceptive essay in *Chelsea* 12 by Sonia Raiziss for this phrase and an observation referred to later; I also find my description coinciding with hers at one or two other points.)

For specific comment we need a poem to look at. Here is a conveniently short poem, 'Afternoon'.

> The fever of afternoon
> Is called afternoon,
> Old sleep uptorn,
> Not yet time for night-time,
> No other name, for no names
> In the afternoon but afternoon.
>
> Love tries to speak but sounds
> So close in its own ear.
> The clock-ticks hear
> The clock-ticks ticking back.
> The fever fills where throats show,
> But nothing in these horrors moves to swallow
> While thirst trails afternoon
> To husky sunset.
>
> Evening appears with mouths
> When afternoon can talk.
> Supper and bed open and close
> And love makes thinking dark.
> More afternoons divide the night,
> New sleep uptorn,
> Wakeful suspension between dream and dream—
> We never knew how long.
> The sun is late by hours of soon and soon—
> Then comes the quick fever, called day.
> But the slow fever is called afternoon.

One way of understanding this is to set it in the context of 'thought' already outlined. So, this is a characterisation of living by implicit contrast with what it fails to be: time ('day') is seen in implicit relation to timelessness, its blankness and anguish and lack of meaning in relation to 'love' which is a desire for fullness of being, its ceaseless ongoing ('more afternoons') in relation to finality, the tyranny of sleep and the darkened mind and the wakefulness that is merely empty restlessness in relation to an entire waking desperately anticipated and forever withdrawing itself from reach. Within the verbal pattern of the poem 'afternoon' is time as most intensely and exclusively itself. The concern with the possibilities of naming, speaking and thinking is central to the poem. The framing of a language expressive of life brought to finality would signify the speakers' presence to goodness; living within the fever of time, however, impedes speaking with such conclusiveness—'no names/In the afternoon but afternoon'. A distinction is drawn between speaking and talking. 'Love tries to speak' the single speech of general truth, but cannot because its words' meanings in their range of reference do not break the boundaries of self. To 'talk'—in the sense it has in the poem placed immediately after this one, 'The Talking World'—is to 'speak mingled', to speak in the separateness of individuality, and not with the singleness of truth; thus, here, it is the plurality of 'mouths' that converts speech into talk and renders talking powerless to prevent the recurrence of time's fever.

What I shall say of this poem is characteristic of many of her poems. Its plot has three parts: first a cryptic statement of the thought, using the basic elements of the poem's imagery—like a closed bud; then a gradual unfolding of the thought's intricacies; finally, in the last three lines, a rounding-back to the original general statement, further reduced to its essentials and set in a life-context of the widest coverage. The imagery is not really metaphorical: it provides, rather, particular instances of a general reality, and word and thought are more nearly identical. It is as though the poet has set out to convince us that one word, 'afternoon', contains the central experience of the poem, seen within a certain order of meanings and values: preliminary statements are made with the word; there follow demonstrations of its sense-range; and, finally, the word is used in a logical formulation that makes it—packed now with all it *can* say—identical with that experience. The imagery *is* the poem, the poem's thought. Its introduction is direct not oblique; correspondences are laid out plainly if concisely. It startles by all it manages to say, and by the subtlety with which it exposes the internal relations of the whole thought. Lineation and verbal patterns (original and expressive of the thought) are designed to spell out with fastidious exactitude these thought-relations. One way of exposing the inter-connections of a thought is worth noticing. Statements or phrases are paralleled—by being given successive lines, or by similarity of grammatical or syntactical form, or by both, as in the case of the three lines beginning 'More afternoons . . .'—in such a way that, while the shape of the thought stays the same, the thought grows rapidly in inclusiveness.

This procedure is one notable consequence and expression of the unitary nature of Laura Riding's thought. It is manifested also in another quality of metaphor in her poetry: that it focuses not an accident of likeness but real, essential correspondence. One of her finest poems, 'Auspice of Jewels', may illustrate this. In the unfolding of one image, the adornment of women with the 'given glitter' of jewels, she explores ramifications of the thought that men's idealising conception of women has been, in fact, a 'passionate neglect' of their inner reality. In the middle of this comes a comparison:

> We are studded with wide brilliance
> As the world with towns and cities—
> The travelling look builds capitals
> Where the evasive eye may rest
> Safe from the too immediate lodgement.

The distraction afforded by jewels (the 'given glitter') and built cities is not merely a comparable, but the same, phenomenon: the eye-of-the-mind's evasion—dazed by the multiple 'fascinations' of the extrinsic—of the single, intrinsic reality. The two parts of the comparison have a common relation to the parent thought.

Laura Riding has made little use in her poems of the idioms and tones of casual, everyday speech. Current fashions are against her, but this should not distract us from the liveness of her language: expressing—one poem alone cannot illustrate the range—gravity, urgency, irony, wit. She eschews the accidental qualities of words; they are rather respected, and applied to, for all they can say outright, attention being paid equally to the fullness, and to the natural boundaries, of meaning: they have an air of 'thus far and no further' in their demarcation of meanings. In a number of poems, sparsely represented here, prepositional and adverbial forms take on substantive functions—an example is 'The sun is late by hours of soon and soon'—the purpose of which is to give these forms their proper semantic values. Though thought is concentrated, diction is always plain. Her language—a point made by Sonia Raiziss—is centred on nouns and verbs, both with a clean thrust to them, and richness as well as precision of meaning is achieved without adjectival pageantry.

All commentators have had something to say about intellectual strictness in Laura Riding's poems. True, her mind is vigilant, incisive, unsentimental—but is not, as they have also said, dry or cool. 'Thought', in this poetry, includes in its voice-utterance and the concentrated intensity of the thought-process an unusual degree of personal engagement with the thought. There is no attempt to enact feeling, but feeling is the accompaniment of her drive to extract the essence of experiences: order is an integral necessity, not an elegance, in her. In 'Afternoon', the tight line, tight in rhythm and logic, the words circling back on themselves, in the *process* of clarifying the internal relations of the thought give us the choking, claustral quality of the experience—and the need to break its spell.

This poet's thinking is, then, scrupulous, thorough, concentrated and, yes, passionate; above all, it is integrative. Her concern with experience is, in the sense indicated in my third paragraph, moral, and in its scope, and largeness of caring, religious. Whether evaluation is central or incidental to a poem's intention—it is never absent—no private motives are allowed to weigh in the scales of judgement. The presence of a sharply critical consciousness is notable, sometimes expressing itself in a mode of grotesque comedy while nevertheless avoiding the dangers of personal excess. Wit everywhere in her poetry is the extra-shine of lucidity as thought is brought to a fine point of definition, as in the phrase 'passionate neglect', quoted earlier from 'Auspice of Jewels'. And the critical note, present in many of her poems, has no monopoly in the full intonation of her poetry. Tones range from the taut painfulness of 'Death as Death' or the held anguish of 'Afternoon' to the grandly pacing cadences—grandeur without posturing—of 'By Crude Rotation' and the smooth, lightly accented movement and tender plainness of 'The Forgiven Past'. But in all the varieties of tone can be heard the voices of responsibility to, and companionship with, our humanity in its erratic journeying towards fullness of being.

Faber has done well to win this selection from Laura Riding. It would be good to have also available the *Collected Poems* . . . and what else she will allow to be reprinted . . . and *The Telling* in book form.

JOYCE PIELL WEXLER
"Poems of Passionate Intelligence"
Laura Riding's Pursuit of Truth
1979, pp. 40–48

Thought is often considered abstract, but Laura Riding considered thought the most intense aspect of life. For her, thought was the total experience of consciousness that distinguished human beings from the natural world, and she made her poetry a record of her mind becoming aware of itself. Convinced she was accomplishing something new, she avoided using common poetic devices such as analogy, allusion, or sensory imagery. Her response to her awareness of her thoughts was neither vague nor general, and there is nothing abstract about her poems. They treat a range of subjects that extends beyond those usually considered intellectual. Even poems about love and lust express the speaker's mental response to her feelings.

The poems of *Love as Love, Death as Death* (1928) implement the critical principles Riding elucidated in her essays of that year. The title emphasizes the literalness of her purpose: she wanted to know love as love, death as death, each thing as itself. She tried to understand the immutable realities these familiar but ineffable words signified. As she said in her essays, her poems are variations on a single theme to isolate the essence or "self" of the subject. The integrity of the poem required that all aspects of form serve the theme. She used metaphor sparingly to show that things cannot be known by their resemblance to other things, and she controlled diction and syntax strictly in order to suit her theme rather than to suit conventional usage. As a result, in the terminology of *A Survey of Modernist Poetry*, these poems are "difficult" because they are "accurate."

"Death as Death" illustrates her method of taking a theme frequently subjected to metaphorical explanations and defining it literally. Acknowledging that it is harder to know things as they are than to know what they are like, the poem concedes the difficulty of understanding death:

> To conceive death as death
> Is difficulty come by easily,
> A dullness fallen among
> Images of understanding,
> Death like a quick cold hand
> On the hot slow head of suicide.
> So it is come by easily
> For one instant. Then furnaces
> Roar in the ears. Then hell is live.
> Then the elastic eyes hold paradise
> At visible length from the invisible mind.
> Then hollowly the body echoes
> "Like this, like this, like nothing else."

The proximity of the opposite ideas of "difficulty" and "easily" initiates a series of contrasts (dullness/understanding, quick cold hand/hot slow head, hell/paradise, visible/invisible) similarly patterned to force the reader to dwell on the meaning of each word to comprehend the phrase fully. The juxtaposition of opposite terms brings together the obviousness of the problem and the elusiveness of an answer. It also delineates the boundaries that fail to encompass the meaning of death.

The potential suicide may expect to learn what death is the moment before he or she dies, but that instant is filled with the terror of facing the unknown, not with knowledge of death. Images of what death has been compared to rush into mind—furnaces, hell, paradise—but they do not satisfy the need to know. Although one can imagine extremes of sensation, knowledge does not fall within their range.

The second stanza withdraws from the frenzy of the suicide. His or her case has illustrated a desperate attempt to understand death, and the poem proceeds to offer calmer reflections on death and knowledge:

> Like nothing, a similarity
> Without resemblance. The vivid eye,
> Closing upon difficulty
> Opens upon comparison,
> Postpones acceptance of the premonition
> As a gift too plain, for which
> Gratitude has no language,
> Foresight no vision.

In contrast to the vivid imagery of the first stanza, the analytical terms of the second assert that comparison will never produce knowledge of the thing itself. The simile of dissimilarity denies the value of analogy and warns that comparison interferes with direct knowledge. The poem suggests that direct premonition of death is our only source of knowledge, though we recoil from the difficulty of accepting this "gift." Lacking "language" and "vision," the true poet must wait in silence until they are provided by intuition.

Riding understood premonition as the mind's gradual, spontaneous discovery of itself—an innate capacity she believed society taught us to distrust. She had complete confidence in the power of intuition to retrieve humanity's inherent knowledge of itself. Articulating her understanding of death in this poem with scrupulous honesty, she refused to pretend that she knew more than she did. Death remains the ultimate unknown. In addition to the truthfulness of her statement, however, the aural effect of the poem's precisely balanced polarities and the corresponding balance of parallel syntax and cadence confer an aesthetic finality to her idea. The harmony between thought and form makes the poem precise, immediate, and intense.

Attempting to understand other complex states of consciousness in *Love as Love, Death as Death*, Riding also found that it was easier to describe what they were not than what they were. "Footfalling" undertakes the problem of defining modulation—the indefinite period of movement between distinct poles. The poem describes modulation in several cases: walking, speaking, and thinking. All three have periods of suspended activity that share distinguishing characteristics. The connection among these actions in the poem is not metaphorical but parallel. Although it occurs in various actions, modulation is considered a distinct process.

Taking advantage of the parallel relationships in modulation, the poem makes terms that are appropriate to each action interchangeable:

> A modulation is that footfalling.
> It says and does not say.
> When not walking it is not saying.
> When saying it is not walking.
> When walking it is not saying.

Modulation is neither an action nor the cessation of an action but the period between action and rest:

> Between the step and alternation
> Breathes the hush and modulation
> Which tars all roads
> With confiding heels and soles and tiptoes.
> Deep from the rostrum of the promenade
> The echo-toothed mouth of motion
> Rolls its voice
> And the large lips are heard to tremble
> While the footfalls shuffle.

The parallel between walking and speaking provides a vocabulary to describe the transitional state that otherwise resists description. The rhythm imitates the back-and-forth motion of a pendulum, and the repetition of diction and syntax fosters a mood of uneasiness supported by indications of trembling and shuffling, as if someone anxiously were pacing back and forth.

The second stanza adds the third case, thinking. Riding perceived the visible characteristics of walking and speaking in thinking. Using physical instances to illuminate the parallel case of thought, she benefits from analogy without losing sight of the literal reality of any of the three:

> It says and does not say.
> When the going is gone
> There is no memory.
> Every thought sounds like a footfall
> And a boot like a thought kicks down the wall.

The force of these final lines suggests that the poet's interest in analyzing modulation in walking and speaking was to understand the way it functioned in thinking more fully. Instead of regarding thought as a "stream of consciousness" as many of her contemporaries did, Riding spoke of "a thought" as a distinct occurrence. In the poem, "thought" is not a continuous register of conscious and unconscious impressions but is as distinct as a step or a word.

Riding focused on a state of suspension again in "All Nothing, Nothing."[1] She used another series of polarities to describe a range of experience that failed to encompass her subject. The poem conveys the queasiness of occupying an uncertain, indefinite area between definable positions. Using short lines and an iambic rhythm, the form reinforces the idea of teetering between poles:

> The standing-stillness,
> The from foot-to-foot,
> Is no real illness,
> Is no true fever,
> Is no true shiver;
> The slow impatience
> Is no bad conscience; . . .
> All nothing, nothing.

The vague malaise of being outside a nameable condition is like no known malady. The list of complaints that do not describe the "standing-stillness" provides boundaries that establish the scope of the condition without actually defining it. As in "Death as Death," the denial of similarities clarifies the subject without resorting to the simpler method of comparison.

Finally, "standing-stillness" is reduced to "nothing." Nothing definite causes these ominous symptoms, or rather being conscious of nothingness causes them. The meaning is clearest in the last lines of the poem, which form a funnel of narrowing polarities. "Standing-stillness" is:

> Without significance
> Of further sense
> Than going and returning
> Within one inch,
> Than rising and falling
> Within one breath,
> Than chattering and shivering
> Between one minute and the next
> Like a will without will quivering
> Between life and life, death and death,
> Life and death.

The poles are separated by an inch, a breath, a minute, a lifetime. Depending on direction, the movement between these poles is going or returning, rising or falling, chattering or shivering, living or dying. In all these cases, the poles are distinct, but the period of suspension between them is ineffable. The last two lines condense the poem to its essence. The span of a lifetime is a "standing-stillness" between this life and the next, or this death and the next, again depending on point of view, certainly between life and death.

The expression of nothingness in this poem contrasts sharply with Riding's special use after 1929 of "nothing" to signify the ultimate value of the "unreal." But before 1929, "nothing" usually had negative connotations, and love still meant a union between a man and a woman. Knowing love as love was the theme of many poems in 1928, but of these "Love as Love"[2] is the most complete guide to her feelings because it portrays a spectrum of moods as love changes. In a series of nine sections, the poem sketches a range of experiences that together dramatize the course of love from its hopeful beginning to its disillusioned ending.

In Part I the difficulty of man and woman achieving harmony is related to language. Aware of the wit in associating love with language and in the vocabulary for courtship that this connection provides, the speaker analyzes the division between man and woman:

> Woman, the greeting term
> Of Man unto the female germ,
> And Man, the cry of Woman
> In this colloquy,
> Have grown so contrary
> That to uncross them
> We must combine samely next
> Among the languages,
> Where calling is obscene
> And words no more than mean.

Combining "among the languages" and using words meaningfully, individuals could overcome their isolation. When "words no more than mean," when they are not used deceptively, man and woman will be able to achieve a true union based on spiritual intimacy.

Part II illustrates how strong the bond of love can be. These lovers defy death:

> "Yes!" to you is in the same breath
> "No! No!" to Death.
> And your "Yes! Yes!" to me
> Is "No!" to Death once firmly.
> The Universe, leaning from a balcony,
> Says: "Death comes home to me
> Covered with glory, when with such love."
> But such love turns into another stair.
> Death and the Universe are another pair.

Affirmation of their love pledges them to life and shelters them from the apparent temptation of Death and the Universe. The poet imagines that the Universe, that cosmic order indifferent to personal wishes, would relish Death glorified by "such love." But turning into "another stair," the lovers leave Death and the Universe behind. As in "Death as Death," suicide attracts Riding, but in both poems she sees its promise of knowledge as false. Rather than please Death by bringing such love to it, she chooses to live.

Part III distinguishes love from "gross needs," or the necessities of nature:

> Gross need in gross satisfaction
> Self-breeds and self-flatters.
> Simple need in simple need confides,
> Which breeds love, the kind pain.
> Life wants, and has.
> We want, but have not.
> We have not life, that us has.
> Life has us, but we each other have.

The lovers' concern for each other, born of confided spiritual needs, protects them from the base exigencies of life, just as it protected the lovers in Part II from Death and the Universe. Love's generosity and harmony permit the lovers to transcend their natural selves. Life may include the lovers, but it does not confine them.

The relationship between love and sex, one "gross need" that "self-breeds and self-flatters," was expressed from a feminist point of view in many of Riding's early poems. It was most fully examined in "The Tiger," a long poem included in *Love as Love, Death as Death*, and in "The Damned Thing," a segment of *Anarchism Is Not Enough*. In the latter she wrote:

> The intelligent major part of their intimacy incorporates sex without sentimental enlargement: it is an effect rather than a cause.[3]

Regarding sex as a secondary element of love, Riding believed that when it became primary, love was doomed.

Of the nine sections of the poem, Part IV portrays the fullness of love with the greatest emotional intensity. A rapid succession of images suggests the happy difficulty of trying to tell a man how much he is loved:

> Dear image of my mind,
> Shadow of my heart,
> Second footfall and third
> Partner of my doubleness
> And fourth of this—
> Love stops me short of counting to the end,
> Where numbers fail and fall to two,
> Then one, then nothing, then you.

She begins an almost traditional list of counting the degrees of their intimacy, but, unlike Elizabeth Browning, Riding terminates her list of metaphors rather than reach an end that would circumscribe her love. Instead, she counts backward, expressing a concentration and intensification of love. She proceeds from the two of them to the one they have become, to the "nothing" of an "unreal" intensity, and climactically to the beloved himself.

The following sections portray the descent of love from the pinnacle of intimacy expressed in Part IV to the point where lust supplants love. Part V notes how time dulls mere passion:

> Our months astonish, as meals come round.
> So late! So soon!
> We cry waterily like a pair of pigeons
> Exclaiming whenever nothing happens
> But commotion inwardly
> Irises their bosoms.
> Little more we know than birdlikeness,
> Our mouths open wide, our breath comes quick,
> We gape like the first ancestors
> And look to magic.

As months go by, the lovers become birdlike in their involvement with time, meals, and diversions. Regressing from a spiritual plane, they lose their human understanding, becoming primitive believers in magic, and worse, animal-like.

Lust is associated with death in Part VI. Unlike the lovers who circumvent Death in Part II, the woman of Part VI fears that her lover's lust bodes death:

> Your face is death asleep
> And my praise wakeful on it.
> But wake not, death,
> And wake not, guarded face.
> So you are womanly and I can kiss
> All manliness away
> That might awaken harshly
> And seize me without praise
> In eyes lusting but to bury me
> In eternal blindness, and deeply.

The capacity for lust separate from love is related to manliness, the cause of the division between them. If he were "womanly," his selfish passion would not disregard her sensibilities or her response. When her inner self is ignored, when she is taken "without praise," she feels dead.

The failure of lovers to sustain their spiritual intimacy is more desperate in Part VIII. The lovers attempt to pretend their love is still strong by playing their old roles:

> You bring me messages
> From days and years
> In your time-open eyes
> And I reply to these
> And we see nothing of each other
> But a language, and this is ancient.
> How we approach is hidden in a dream.
> We close our eyes, we clutch at bodies,

> We wake at dream's length from each other
> And love shamefully and coldly
> Strangers we seem to know by memory.

The history of their love, and of all love, is contained in the messages they exchange. But when the messages are not infused with immediate feelings, they are empty phrases of an ancient language. Words lose their meaning when they no longer represent spiritual realities. According to *A Survey of Modernist Poetry*, a poet should remind people what language means and keep language faithful to reality, as lovers must. The poetic expression of the idea, however, is incontrovertible.

The final section of "Love as Love" presents a still bleaker picture of the emptiness of unfelt phrases:

> We know which jingling spells
> Which understanding, but jingling
> Is all our understanding.
> Like dunces we still shall kiss
> When graduated from music-making.

Words that once conveyed love have become meaningless jingles. The lovers remember what the words used to mean, but the love born of confided needs has degenerated into empty embraces and "music-making." The vignettes that form the poem portray various episodes, but a single definition of love emerges. Love is an emotion born of confiding, of sharing spiritual intimacies with another, and it is killed by spiritual withdrawal.

As deeply experienced as "Love as Love" seems, it exemplifies Riding's effort to understand the essence of a subject. Although everyone learns the course of love in unique circumstances, the poem expresses what she considered constant. While her essays stress the need for the poet to articulate a universal experience, her poems focus on the personal immediacy of the experience. Love was as suitable a subject as death or modulation because Riding did not divorce thought from feeling. Poets were privileged to unite all aspects of consciousness in their work and leave the problems of generalizing and categorizing to philosophers and scientists. For her, thought included the full range of consciousness, which encompassed emotion and intuition, and excluded unmediated sensory impressions—the instincts and the unconscious.

Notes

1. The similarity of this poem, which appeared in *Love as Love, Death as Death* (1928), to W. H. Auden's "Between attention and attention . . . " is comparable to other similarities between her work and his that prompted her to comment on his borrowings in "Some Autobiographical Corrections of Literary History," *The Denver Quarterly*, Winter, 1974, pp. 21–24. Robert Graves also impugned Auden for borrowing from Riding in "These Be Your Gods, O Israel!" *The Crowning Privilege* (London: Cassell, 1955), p. 130.
2. "Love as Love" is quoted as it appears in *Love as Love, Death as Death* (1928). It was included in revised form as "Rhythms of Love" in *Collected Poems* (1938).
3. Laura Riding, *Anarchism Is Not Enough* (London: Jonathan Cape, 1928), p. 188.

BARBARA ADAMS
From "Laura Riding's Autobiographical Poetry: 'My Muse Is I'"

Concerning Poetry, Fall 1982, pp. 71–87

Riding's idealism, along with a sure linguistic sense and a deep autobiographical drive, had provided her poetry with its power and its purpose. She demanded that poetry serve truth, just as she demanded that it serve the real self. For all intents and purposes, Riding's view of poetry, up to 1940, was religious. She expressed its moral purpose in the original preface to *Collected Poems*: "To live in, by, for the reasons of, poems is to habituate oneself to the good existence."[1] Forty years after giving poetry up, she makes her former position even more explicit in the new introduction to the 1980 re-issuing of the same collection: "I was religious in my devotion to poetry."[2] Whatever other psychological reasons there may have been, the attempt to live up to such a high moral standard in her life and art probably had much to do with Riding's extreme actions: the suicide attempt in 1929, and the leaving off of writing poetry after 1938. Her moral aesthetics could not settle for almost-perfect.

Riding's *Collected Poems*, re-issued as *The Poems of Laura Riding* in 1980, records the quest for perfection as it is closely bound to her life and thought. Each poem tells us something about the real woman, but each one also makes a bid for something more, a higher state of being. As she announced with such conviction in the 1938 preface, "existence in poetry becomes more real than existence in time—more real because more good, more good because more true."[3] The good, the true, and the poetic self are Riding's trinity of faith, the creed upon which she founded her craft. We have only to look at the preface to the 1970 *Selected Poems* to understand how consistent is this faith, even to the renunciation of poetry because Riding became aware of "the discrepancy between the creed and the craft of poetry . . . its religious and its ritualistic aspects."[4]

Riding believes literally in the perfectability of language and of the self. In theory, the perfect self can be embodied in perfect language; the relationship between self and language is therefore crucial to her work. In one of her early books of criticism, she had said plainly, that "a poem is an advanced degree of self" and that poetry was "the tongue of the Self."[5] This creed required the language of revelation, and, for a time, poetry was that language. After 1940, Riding came to believe that poetry was too elitist, too much a "crafted" medium to serve the democracy of revelation. Similarly, she found that the individual self could not be perfected except as part of the One perfect self. This later doctrine has been fully expressed in Riding's 1972 evangel, *The Telling*. Today, she believes that perfection lies in the "rational meaning" of words, in the apprehension of ultimate being in Oneness through language. The high moral purpose remains consistent in Riding's thought, but the instrument of its working out has changed from poetry to language as a whole, from a particular poetic self to an all-inclusive one self.

Nevertheless, out of her desire to achieve perfection in poetry, and out of the tension between the ideal self of the poems and the imperfect actual self, Riding created more than two hundred poems. She incorporated one hundred eighty-one of them in the *Collected Poems* to tell the "story" of her struggle to develop her real or poetic self. This book represents one of the earliest, perhaps the first in the modernist tradition, consciously autobiographical poetic sequences. Its arrangement is a narrative one, according to the Preface, the poems being ordered to correspond chronologically with phases in the protagonist's life. The "heroine" is Riding's self, and the "plot" tells of her experiences in America, England and Spain. These locations help the reader correlate the fictional world of the poems to actual events in the poet's life.

The autobiographical arrangement follows a simple thematic development divided into five parts. The first four parts record events in sequence in the persona's life from childhood to Christmas 1937, the title of one of the last poems in the fourth section. The focus is on interior developments in her thinking, rather than on external happenings. The word "occasion" signifies the nature of the first three phases of thought, while "continual" suggests the final phase that is reached in part four. "Poems of Mythical Occasion," the first section, covers the years 1910 to 1926 approximately, corresponding to Riding's childhood and young womanhood. The chief motifs concern questions of identity against a background of an unhappy family and an alien environment, and sexual anxiety. The first poem in the book sets the theme:

> The stove was grey, the coal was gone.
> In and out of the same room
> One went, one came.
> One turned into nothing.
> One turned into whatever
> Turns into children.[6]

Later stanzas in this early sequence prefigure the long debate Riding was to have with herself concerning the pleasures, pains and tyranny of sexuality:

> Love's the only thing
> That deceives enjoyably.
> Mother Mary and her Magdalenes,
> We don't care a curse how much we're deceived
> Or deceive.
>   . . .
> Bill Bubble in a bowler hat
> Walking by picked Lida up.
> Lida said 'I feel like dead.'
> Bubble said
> 'Not dead but wed.'
> No more trouble, no more trouble,
> Safe in the arms of Husband Bubble.

The fictitious name "Lida" further underscores Riding's identification with heroines at the heart of our sexual mythologies which impale woman on phallic fantasies.

"Poems of Immediate Occasion," the second part of *Collected Poems*, covers the brief period Riding spent in England, 1926–1929. A time of intense conflict and productivity, these years saw the resolution of the conflict with Graves and his wife, the beginning of Riding's international reputation as poet and critic, and the near-death of Riding in a fall from a high window. While identity remains the central concern, the doubts of a woman in love and a growing obsession with death dominate this section. These themes merge in a five-part poem which ostensibly describes the false gaiety of the year 1927, but which actually reveals the poet's mounting and terrible inner conflict. These lines from "In Nineteen Twenty-Seven" even expose her suicidal thoughts some two years before obeying that impulse:

> Then, where was I, of this time and my own
> A double ripeness and perplexity?
> Fresh year of time, desire,
> Late year of my age, renunciation—
> Ill-mated pair, debating if the window
> Is worth leaping out of, and by whom.

"Poems of Final Occasion," the third section, covers the years 1930–1935, including crisis and recovery and the shift from England to Majorca. Besides the usual existential questions of identity, these poems begin to come to terms with life and death in a matter-of-fact way, and to find peace of mind in the very act of writing the poem. At last, the poet can say, "At last we can make sense, you and I,/You lone survivors on paper." At the same time, she still wars with herself and the eternal questions of identity:

What is to be?
It is to bear a name.
What is to die?
It is to be name only.
And what is to be born?
It is to choose the enemy self
To learn impossibility from.
And what is to have hope?
Is it to choose a god weaker than self,
And pray for compliments?

The bitter truths of this catechism leave the poet alone, with no resource and no other god, none but "the enemy self." As despairing as is this faith in the self, Riding salvages some faith in a more traditional God, "meeting" him in death and discovering that His callous creation of her is little different from her creation of poems. According to this progression of thought, the poet bears a quasi-godlike status because of his "mouth":

Because of being by name a poet,
A creature neither man nor God.
Yes, such a creature by name,
But featured like both man and God—
Like God a creature of mind,
Like man, a creature of mouth.

"Poems Continual," the fourth and last of the chronological sections, contain the last poems Riding wrote while living on Majorca with Robert Graves, ending late in 1936 when the Spanish Civil War forced their evacuation. This move also effectively ended their relationship, though it dragged on for a few more years while they roamed about Europe and England and eventually came back to the United States. There, Riding and Graves parted for good, and Riding met and married Schuyler S. Jackson, her second husband (Riding had been married briefly in her early twenties to a history professor she met while a student at Cornell). These last poems reveal some of the turmoil of world events in the Thirties, but their main emphasis is on the persona's maturation into a self-possessed woman able to cope more easily with questions of identity through her poetry. They also show a decided cooling of love's sexual urgency and an ability to sublimate even that in poetry, especially in the self-explanatory poem "When Love Becomes Words":

And I shall say to you, 'There is needed now
A poem upon love, to forget the kiss by
And be more love than kiss to the lips.'
     . . .
The writing of 'I love you'
Contains the love if not entirely
At least with lovingness enough
To make the rest a shadow around us. . . .

Another notable achievement of this final stage of self is the sequence *Memories of Mortalities*, a four hundred fifty four line autobiography of the poet's inner life which recapitulates the major theme of the entire *Collected Poems*. It begins with her birth, assuming the burdens of the human condition through her "snake" mother and "fox" father, shows her futile rebellion against mortality and schooling, and leads to the poet's break-through in achieving an independent identity by "writing her story herself."

"Histories," the fifth and last part of *Collected Poems*, stands slightly to one side of the developing poet's story but parallels its main themes. It consists of three long sequences which represent important experiments in the longer poem and mixed media. "Voltaire," written in 1921 when Riding was a student at Cornell, is a biography of the philosopher's beliefs

and doubts, recounted in twelve parts, each part introduced by a prose paragraph and followed by clever, slyly neo-classical verse. In this choice of subject, Riding shows at the age of twenty a decided taste for rational thought. In form, the poem shows a precocity that dazzles critics and fellow poets alike. Roy Fuller notes, for instance, "Voltaire's" "varied and original poetic texture and its individual solution of the problem of the long poem in our age."[7]

"Laura and Francisca," the second of the Histories, combines vivid autobiographical details of Riding and Graves's life on Majorca. A fey little girl called Francisca symbolizes the ideal inner being of the poem's chief character "Laura." Written soon after their arrival on Majorca and not long after the traumatic events of Riding's near-death and Graves's divorce from Nancy Nicholson, the poem records the surface details of everyday life in simple, sensuous language. Visitors, meals, mail, domestic trifles and the hard work of operating the hand-press take up the time while "Laura" and "Robert" heal their wounds. But Francisca represents the other Laura, the "anti-narcissus of me," the poet's Muse: "My muse is I," says the poem's Laura. Thus, in 1930, Riding reaffirmed her poetic philosophy—a poetics of the self that made explicit use of any autobiographical data, the real and the imagined.

"The Life of the Dead" written in 1933 is the last of the Histories and by far the most idiosyncratic of Riding's poems. A surreal allegory of the modern world, this poem of more than a thousand lines depicts vanity fair in ten tableaux. Each of the ten poem-pictures is written first in French and then in English, and is accompanied by an illustration. The illustrations were conceived by Riding and executed by John Aldrich in a deChirico manner. Of all the poems, "The Life of the Dead" is the most directly involved with social and moral concerns in the immediate world. A virtuoso satire constructed with dazzling skill, it reveals Riding's Swiftian side—the self turned towards the real world, seeking its perfection along with her own. All three Histories, though widely different in outward form and subject, share the same concern for the integrity of the self and the necessity for cherishing it in an historically, geographically and morally unstable world.

The careful structure and inner consistency of Riding's *Collected Poems* are no less remarkable than the authoritative quality of the poet's voice. That voice is obviously dominated by intelligence but contains as well a strong element of intuition that emerges from the center of being. Riding's voice derives from a similar combination of intellect and intuition found in Emerson—an interior monologue that scrutinizes self with puritan fervor. It also resembles Dickinson's, whose voice, said Henry James, "maps the landscape of the soul." This tradition in American poetry leads its poets deeper and deeper into the self, into an endless ontological quest. It is what gives it its characteristic religious flavor, redolent of Biblical rhythms, imagery and syntax as in Riding's early poem "Incarnations":

Do not deny,
Do not deny, thing out of thing.
Do not deny in the new vanity
The old, original dust.

From what grave, what past of flesh and bone
Dreaming, dreaming I lie
Under the fortunate curse,
Bewitched, alive, forgetting the first stuff . . .
Death does not give a moment to remember in

Lest, like a statue's too transmuted stone,
I grain by grain recall the original dust
And looking down a stair of memory, keep saying:
This was never I.

The thrust of this kind of poetry is always towards the solution of the problems of identity. If "this was never I," then what *is* I becomes the task of the poem. The chief solution for Riding, found frequently in the later poems, is to enter a "unitary somewhere" in poetry. Here, the self exists in pure perfection, rescued from time and the transitory pleasures and pains of living. In Riding's aesthetic, she makes a "last covenant" with truth—the truth in poetry: "'I have arrived here/And will discover to myself what *is* here.'" That this solution was only hoped for but never fully achieved in her poems led to the abrupt cessation of Riding's morally-demanding poetry. The autobiography of the self, its interior monologue, fell silent after the publication of the *Collected Poems*.

Riding's poetry has elements common to much recent American poetry—the search for a unified identity, an obsession with death and the hope of transcendence through art. It is a self-conscious and tension-ridden poetry, but more detached and abstract than that of her contemporaries. Where Hart Crane invented a mythology from a fusion of self, word and world, Riding created an aesthetic from self and word only. Where Eliot found his voice in the past, Riding found hers in an eternal inner self. Where Wallace Stevens rejoiced in the supreme fiction created by his imagination, Riding insisted that the word-created self was more real than reality. The self, to Riding, is the supreme reality. And where Edwin Arlington Robinson—reported by Riding to be one of her first influences—created a variety of neurotics to express alienation, Riding invented (or inhabited) only a single persona whose inner dialectic allowed a full expression of her thoughts and feelings. What is special about Riding's poetry is that it is a continuous interior monologue, telling the story of her inner being. This is the rationale of the *Collected Poems*, establishing a self in poetry, "more real, because more true." ⟨. . .⟩

Notes

1. Laura Riding, "Preface," *Collected Poems* (New York: Random House, 1938), p. xxvii.
2. Introduction, *The Poems of Laura Riding* (London: Carcanet, 1980), p. 2.
3. "Preface," *Collected Poems*, p. xxvi.
4. *Selected Poems: In Five Sets* (New York: Norton, 1972), p. 11.
5. *Anarchism Is Not Enough* (New York: Doubleday, 1928), p. 119.
6. *Collected Poems*, p. 3. This, and all subsequent quotations from Riding's poems are taken from this edition.
7. Roy Fuller, "The White Goddess," *the Review*, No. 23, Sept.–Nov. 1970, p. 5.

ELIZABETH MADOX ROBERTS

1886–1941

Elizabeth Madox Roberts was born in Perrysville, near Springfield, Kentucky, in 1886, the daughter of descendants of Kentucky pioneers. She was sickly as a child and spent part of her youth in the Colorado mountains. Roberts was unable to attend college for many years because of ill health but finally received a bachelor's degree from the University of Chicago in 1921. In that year she won the Fiske Prize awarded by the university for a volume of poems that later became her first published work (*Under the Tree*, 1922). Roberts continued writing poetry, winning the John Reed Memorial Prize of *Poetry* magazine in 1928 and the Poetry Society of South Carolina Prize in 1931. Her first novel, *The Time of Man* (1926), a moving account of Kentucky hill-dwellers, won her national recognition as a first-rate story-teller and remains her best-known work.

Roberts published a collection of short stories (*The Haunted Mirror*, 1932) and another volume of poetry (*Song in the Meadow*, 1940), in addition to seven more novels, the last, *Not by Strange Gods*, in 1941. She died in Orlando, Florida, on March 13 of that year, the victim of anemia.

A recent school of criticism has made much of the fact that American literature has so rarely sprung directly from the American soil, has contained so meagerly the elements of folk culture: love of the land that sweetens the labor upon it; love of the life it brings forth, plant and animal; love of tools and material things fashioned by the hand of man for his work upon the earth; instinctive affection for fellow-men who born of the same mother, share the same inheritance. Pioneering has played a great part in American fiction, but the theme of the pioneer has been the conquest, not the growth of the soil. It has been our boast that we have never had a peasantry—social change and promotion have been too rapid to permit human life to sink its roots deeply into the earth. American treatment of the land has tended toward exploitation, not cultivation; and it is exploitation which is recorded in our literature. A sense of this poverty in the native sources of culture has shown itself in an attempt to claim for ourselves the civilization of the Indians of the Southwest and find in it the basis of a truly American art. Again, the racial inheritance of foreign peasant stocks has been laid under contribution, notably in Miss Cather's fine novel *My Ántonia*. The recognition of the richness of Negro life in the primary sources of art is a sign of the same awakening. It is Miss Roberts's distinction that in her first novel she has followed a strain of American life which contains the elements in which American fiction has been so often lacking, seen them with the eyes of a poet, and entered into them with an instinctive knowledge and feeling which are the gifts of a true imagination.

The Time of Man is the story of Ellen Chesser, daughter of Henry and Nellie Chesser, poor whites, wanderers upon the Kentucky roads, sojourners here and there by chance on the land by which and for which they live. An instinct for permanence leads them in each new tarrying place to make a home of the two-roomed cabin which is allotted to them, to gather tools and utensils and household gear, a little stock—a cow, a few hens—to plant flowers. Then the sense of failure in permanent adjustment, the lack of ownership of the soil which they till, vaguely working, drives them forth. This is the pathos of their poor lives—the instinct for home constantly defeated yet constantly renewed.

Ellen at ten is a social being. When the wagon breaks down and the family is thrown on the land of Hep Bodine her first thought is to rehearse her story to tell to a woman, another wagon dweller, whom she has met on the road and lost again. For a long time she has no companions but the turkeys she tends and the heifer which she saved at birth. She cries out against her loneliness.

All at once she lifted her body and flung up her head to the great sky that reached over the hills and shouted:

"Here I am!"

She waited, listening:

"I'm Ellen Chesser! I'm here!"

Her voice went up in the wind out of the plowed land. For a moment she searched the air with her senses and then she turned back to the stones again.

"You didn't hear e'er a thing," she said under breath. "Did you think you heard something a-callen?"

Gradually at each settlement she makes friends, first the boys and girls of neighboring farms, then the men and women whose labor and sorrow she shares. Love comes to her, and desertion, and again love and children and betrayal and new hope. But always there is the call of the land. Ellen and the man she has taken are talking in the sweet, rhythmical speech of the country that falls on the ear like verse.

"By spring," says Jasper Kent, "I aim to find some fields worth a man's strength. I'm plumb tired trafficken about good land and bad as it comes. I aim to go a long piece from here."

"Once when I was a youngone Pappy went to Tennessee and I saw cotton in bloom. We saw cotton grow."

"I'm plumb tired trafficken about."

"Saw cotton a-growen. The people gathered it after a while in big baskets, piled up white."

"We'll go to some pretty country where the fields lay out fair and smooth. A little clump of woodland. Just enough to shade the cows at noon."

"Smooth pasture is a pretty sight in a country, rollen up and cows dotted here and yon over it, red shorthorns and white and dun."

"And you won't say 'I know a prettier country in Adair or in Shelby or Tennessee.' Mountains or not."

"Smooth pastures, we'll have."

"Whatever I can do to pleasure you, Ellie. The house like the way you want."

"And the house fixed up, the shutters mended and the porch don't leak. To sit on a Saturday when the work is done. A vine up over the chimney. Once I saw a far piece from here. . . . "

And always there is the answer of the road, beckoning away from the land which they do not own, inviting them with new promise, forbidding them to stay. Ellen's deepest, unconscious memories are bound up with it.

Going about the rough barnlot of the farm above Rock Creek, calling in the hens, breaking them corn, Ellen would merge with Nellie in the long memory she had of her from the time when she had called from the fence with so much prettiness, through the numberless places she had lived or stayed and the pain she had known, until her mother's life merged into her own and she could

scarcely divide the one from the other, both flowing continuously and mounting. . . . It had seemed forever that she had traveled up and down roads, having no claim upon the fields but that which was snatched as she passed. Back of that somewhere in a dim, darkened dream like a prenatal vision, she saw a house under some nut trees, a place where she lived, but as clearly seen as this she could see her brother Davie and the others, the more shadowy forms of the older children, although all of them were dead before she was born. So that this house with the odor about it of nut shells was all imbedded now in the one dream that extended bedimmed into some region where it merged with Nellie's memories. Life began somewhere on the roads, traveling after the wagons where she had claim upon all the land and no claim, all at once, and where what she knew of the world and what she wanted of it sparkled and glittered and ran forward quickly as if it would always find something better.

At the end of her story as at the beginning she is in flight, her goods piled about her on the wagon, her children beside her, seeking the new fair land which is the goal of her pilgrimage.

It is needless to mark further the fine literary quality of Miss Roberts's novel. It will be said, indeed, that the book is written to theme, the great pervading theme of man's seeking; but so abundant and so real is the material in which the experience is rendered, so homely and intimate the background, so vivid the picturing of nature through its succession of seasons, so deep the sense of humanity in the characters, especially in the epic figure of Ellen, above all so perfect is the unity of tone, marred by no note of falseness or exaggeration that one feels in this book an almost perfect blending of idea and substance, of soul and body. It is life, not fiction, or rather it is the higher fiction which is the meaning of life.—ROBERT MORSS LOVETT, *NR*, Sept. 8, 1926, pp. 74–75

In her new novel, *My Heart and My Flesh*, Miss Roberts takes the most interesting, and the most dangerous, step that a contemporary novelist can take—she takes a step into the unconscious. Where Mr. Joyce has gone (notably in the famous "Walpurgisnacht" section of *Ulysses*) and to some extent Mr. Lawrence and Mr. Anderson, Miss Roberts also makes bold to fare; and as one of the first novels in which a woman author has made this attempt *My Heart and My Flesh* cannot fail to be interesting.

To say that on the whole it is more interesting than successful is to do Miss Roberts no dishonor. This business of sinking oneself in the perilous underworld of affects, or of alternating these explorations with more superficial swimmings in the chaotic welter of conscious and semi-conscious feelings, the minute-by-minute feelings that mark a human awareness, is fraught with technical dangers which the more conservative novelist never faces. How, if one is thus going behind and into a personality, giving the whole maelstrom of identity, is one to give a shape and a design to the novel which embodies it?

The answer to this question is not an easy one. In fact, there is a sense in which there is no answer, no *formulated* answer, at all. All that the novelist can do is to meet his particular problem empirically: given the particular chaos with which his hero or heroine provides him, he must allow, as far as he can, the material to evolve a living and dynamic design of its own. It is more than likely that in the accepted meaning there will be no "shape" at all—little or nothing of the kind of roundness in complexity which we can enjoy in the novels of

Henry James, for example; little or nothing of the obvious dramatic completeness which we find, without effort, in *Jude the Obscure* or *The Return of the Native*.

The most easily recognizable sense in which this method can take a "form"—this Proustian microscopy of the soul—is in a strict and manifest working-out of the psychological determinism. We note, as we proceed with our outpouring of a mind's contents, that there are certain major preoccupations, not to say obsessions. These are indeed the features which set apart this mind as individual. We watch these and analyze them; we observe how they come into conflict, as the narrative unfolds, with other preoccupations or with the necessities of the external world; and our sense of completion will arise, and with it a sense as of accomplished design, when out of these flowers an inevitable action or decision or an inevitable "change of mind."

It is toward this sort of climax that Miss Roberts works. Her heroine—whose "mind" is the stage and action of the story—is seen to be in a process of emotional adjustment to a psychological problem, or group of problems, which is too much for her. And in the stating of the problem, the setting of the stage, Miss Roberts has given us some brilliant work. Theodosia becomes extremely real to us—we believe in her. We feel her world with an extraordinary richness. We are there with her, in the midst of a decaying Southern family; we share with her the peculiar horror she feels for her father, the pity and understanding she feels for her grandfather, the singular mixture of loathing and fascination with which she is alternately drawn and repelled by her negro half-sisters and her negro half-brother. We experience also, admirably, the erotic confusion into which she is thus brought with regard to her own love affairs. And in the course of this exposition Miss Roberts gives us a few very powerful scenes—notably that in which Stiggins, as counterpoint to the quarrel between Lethe, the negress, and Theodosia, recounts, in singsong ritualistic narrative, the story of the killing of a rat. This is admirable. And almost as good (though now and then with evidences of strain and unreality) is the dialogue passage in which, during acute stress, Theodosia's personality is dissociated. The splitting of the unconscious, at this point, into a group of quarreling voices, each pursuing its own theme regardless of the others, is excellent: so very good, in fact, that one wishes that it had been just a shade better and a little more completely and deeply "worked." At this point in the story one wants exactly this kind of drastic and dramatic explosion in the unconscious—everything in the *donnée* indicates it as necessary: but Miss Roberts has unfortunately understated it, with the result that her real psychological climax, and with it the final "shaping" of her novel, is unsatisfactory.

More superficially, one might object to Miss Roberts's method that she gives us too much, and too continuously, a consciousness in which there is too little conceptual *definiteness*. The affective stream is rich—and all the more necessary, therefore, if the reader is not to drown in a sort of world of plush, is an occasional oasis of concrete and conscious analysis—analysis, that is, performed on her environment, or on herself, by the heroine. This is especially true as concerns Theodosia's love affairs. Here it is almost as if Miss Roberts had funked her problem: almost as if she weren't *quite* sure of her ground. Conway and Albert and Caleb are a little vague; and vague, too, in the crises of her relations with them, are Theodosia's reactions. And, inasmuch as Theodosia is permitted by the author to "see" her relations with these men only in a blurred and unconceptual manner, and to see also, in as blurred a manner, the more critical of her scenes with them,

the reader is all too often left completely in the dark. What *did* happen, one wonders, between Theodosia and Frank? One simply doesn't know. And one is uncomfortable, in much the same fashion, as regards Theodosia's music.

Miss Roberts was on thin ground here—she hasn't entirely escaped sentimentality in her treatment of this somewhat threadbare theme. When Theodosia goes out with her fiddle to play to the fields and trees one edges toward the door. And one is a little unconvinced by the emotional mysticism into which Theodosia wanders when her music comes uppermost. One almost regrets that this element—surely needless—had to come into the story at all.

Perhaps these are trifling objections. In the main, one is grateful to Miss Roberts for a deeply moving story—and a story excellently written. Miss Roberts has a lot of the poet in her. Her prose is fine and sensitive. There are blemishes in it—an overfullness now and then, a conscious lushness carried too far, and a trick of reiteration which she may have borrowed from Mr. Anderson.

Of somewhat more importance, if we must speak of blemishes, is the prologue. This is misleading: it strikes one as a complete mistake. It is too long, too detailed, too much developed as through another pair of eyes. The reader expects Luce Jarvis (who is a charming young person) to reappear: and she never does. It is with a sense of deep frustration that, with chapter one, one finds that one must begin all over again, all over again submit to the author's initial exploration of a mind.—CONRAD AIKEN, *NYEP*, Nov. 12, 1927, p. 10

Miss Roberts died four days before this volume of short stories (*Not by Strange Gods*) was published. She was fifty-five, and her first book, *Under the Tree*, a volume of short poems about childhood, came out nineteen years ago. In those nineteen years she published two volumes of verse, two of short stories, and seven novels, or more than a book a year. She must have been writing steadily, and it is easy to believe that she did little else. She never married, she was painfully shy, she stayed close to Kentucky, where she was born and where she died. Her life was uneventful in a superficial sense, probably, but in the world she had made she must have lived intensely and passionately.

This world is, by the map, Kentucky. But it is a Kentucky that lived solely in Miss Roberts's mind and heart. Her first and best novel, *The Time of Man*, introduces a Kentucky Tobacco Road. The food is bacon and pone, the houses are cabins, nobody has enough to wear or to eat, nobody goes anywhere or does anything except be born and grow up and marry and die. But this world is as different from Mr. Caldwell's world as day from night. Out of his shiftless poor whites Mr. Caldwell wrings irony, wit, tragic squalor. Miss Roberts is without humor and she is never squalid. Nobody was ever less of a tractarian than she. A good illustration of this is the first story in *Not by Strange Gods*, "The Haunted Palace." In it a fine manor house, deserted by the gentry that had once lived in it, tumbling down, set in a tangled park, is taken over by a share-cropper and his family. In the great parlors, with their carved white woodwork and their polished floors, the share-cropper and his wife bring their sheep at lambing time. The house is filled with ghosts—of the music that had been made on the grand piano, of blue and gold wall hangings, of stables full of blooded horses, and a lovingly tended garden. But the polished floors are slippery and wet, and two dead lambs have been thrown in the great fireplace out of the way. In about thirty pages Miss Roberts presents two completely different modes of living, two educations, two cultures. But she is not concerned with whether one is "better" than the other, or whether one is the result of the other. Here they are, sharply drawn, and moral judgments are complicated things. If you must have one, you will have to make it yourself.

In this world she has made there is a great deal of poetry. It is in the songs the people sing, the thoughts the young girls—and even the old men—have, most of all in their common speech: "I want to be like you are, but you want to be like some other kind you can't name or say." "There's always fault on both sides, though, and it's never all one person's blame, I always say." "Then I recollect spring. Yes I recall. Then come fall and warm politics on. I recollect the barbecue on the creek and old man Hardin on the stump for office." "I feel like I could pick up a hill or I could break open a mountain with my fist, and what call have I got to be afeared of a lonesome sound tonight?" These quotations, chosen at random from several books, are indicative of the poetically unreal, strange, and yet winning speech of Miss Roberts's characters. They are dialect, full of old saws and folk wisdom. Paradoxically, they sound like the authentic speech of these particular people, although these people never lived, in Kentucky or anywhere else.

Miss Roberts's world is never seen quite clearly. There is always the illusion of distance, of muffled sound, of indistinct edges, of a veil between the persons in the book and the reader. Even in *My Heart and My Flesh*, when the social stratum is different, and the characters are urbane and cultivated, there is still this feeling of distance, of persons not quite human, although—another paradox—not unreal.

Finally, if in some sense this Kentucky is unreal, it is nevertheless continually fresh and interesting, the language is sweet and strange, the people are warm, passionate, complicated. Although probably Miss Roberts reached her peak in her first book, all the qualities that made it original and appealing are in the last one. American literature would be inestimably poorer if Kentucky had never known her; and if she had never known her own peculiar Kentucky.—DOROTHY VAN DOREN, *Nation*, June 28, 1941, pp. 758–59

Although her first novel was not published until she was forty-five years old, Elizabeth Madox Roberts was by no means a "primitive" artist. Indeed, she was almost completely the reverse—a highly self-conscious aesthetician and craftsman. Scattered throughout her journals and letters are persistent efforts to discover what her own personal limitations as an artist were, and how best to bend these limitations to the production of fine art. In her journal she notes: "Two ways seemed always open to me as one having such environmental influences as mine, and such physical and mental equipment. One the way of satire, the other the way of symbolism working through poetic realism." The way of satire is illustrated only in her fantasy, *Jingling in the Wind*; in all her other novels, as well as in the most successful sections of *Jingling in the Wind*, the sustained note of composition is "symbolism working through poetic realism." What she meant by this is clarified in the following:

> I will tell you why we continually go back to realism in art. Somewhere there is a connection between the world of the mind and the outer order—It is the secret of the contact that we are after, the point, the moment of union. We faintly sense the one and we know as faintly the other, but there is a point at which they come together, and we can never know the whole of reality until we know these two completely. And so we pursue first the one and then the other. We probe deeper and deeper

into the world of sense and experience and we say "Now I have it, it is thus" . . . and presently it is seen that we haven't it yet and we make another try with a newer realism or some of us try for it the other way around.

Elsewhere she succinctly summarizes her characteristic mode of approach, saying: "I have tried for great precision in rendering sensuous contacts—the points where poetry touches life."

Miss Roberts was early nurtured on the idealistic philosophy of Bishop Berkeley, her father's favorite philosopher, and this influence is a pervasive tincture in her thinking. The sovereignty of mind, or spirit, over unformed matter is basic to her understanding of life and distinctively colors her concept of the artistic process. "Life is from within, and thus the noise outside is a wind blowing in a mirror." Until the life "outside" becomes comprehended within—until sensation is transformed into idea, or poetry—the outside life is as meaningless as "a wind blowing in a mirror." Such a philosophic idealism could easily lead to abortive ends. It could constrict itself into an imprisoning solipsism which denies validity to anything outside one's own fantasy projections. It can distort the meaning of life into anything the egotistical assigner of meanings wants it to mean, and by denying a reality principle, end in insanity or fatal frustration. By cutting the deep roots between experience and values, it can cause moral paralysis, perversion, and intellectual suicide. If there is no connection between the world of the mind and the outer order, the mind has only itself to feed upon and growth is impossible. But Miss Roberts was aware of the dangers of unqualified idealism to the artist and to the human being, and she sought assiduously to avoid those dangers.

Her aim, both personal and artistic, was to focus on those points "where poetry touches life"—where mind and matter, idea and sensation, vision and fact, intermingle, shape and are shaped, and produce conjointly a flood of identity within the perceiving spirit, wherein the outer order is creatively absorbed and the world of the mind comprises a new universe. This, she believed, was the area where her art could operate most effectively—where the artistic symbol, itself a fusion of idea and thing, could communicate that which could not be communicated by any other means.

She was dedicated to her art because she saw it as a handmaiden to a greater energy—for her, the elemental energy in life—love. For though she writes that "life is from within" and the noise outside negligible, she qualifies this world-denying isolation by adding: "But love is a royal visitor which that proud ghost, the human spirit, settles in elegant chambers and serves with the best." And, as will become clear in the examination of her specific novels, "love" for Miss Roberts is not only the outgoing desire which moves man to accept from, and share with, other men the unique selfness which one has; but, even more basically, the force itself which brings man to the points where poetry touches life, where one's very selfness is created. The moments of union—the vital experiences of truth, of virtue, of beauty—which mark the successive spirals of growth for the individual spirit, are themselves love-created. The absence of love is for Miss Roberts, in a many-layered sense, always synonymous with death.

Her novels, then, served a twofold purpose. For her, personally, they were metaphors of experience—love creations through which her own inner spirit could expand, absorb the materials of itself, and integrate itself into a new and more vital level of growth. But because she also possessed a deep sense of responsibility to the body of mankind of which she was a part, they are also love offerings to mankind—symbols of her experience which she contributed in the hope that other men might use them for their own growth. Both purposes are eloquently pointed to in her statement: "It is the function of art to enlarge one's experience, to add to man more tolerance, more forgiveness, to increase one's hold on all the out-lying spaces which are little realized in the come and go of every day."—EARL H. ROVIT, "Introduction" to *Herald to Chaos*, 1960, pp. 5–8

ROBERT PENN WARREN
From "Life Is from Within"

Saturday Review, March 2, 1963, pp. 20–21, 38

Stories grow out of place and time, but they also grow, if they are any good, out of the inner struggle of the writer; as Elizabeth Madox Roberts puts it: "Life Is from Within." So we think of the girl growing up isolated by poverty, dreams, and persistent bad health, trying to find a way for herself, but gradually learning, in what travail of spirit we cannot know except by inference, that hers would not be the ordinary, full-blooded way of the world. And how often in the novels do we find some vital, strong person, usually a man, described as "rich with blood"—and how much ambivalence may we detect behind the phrase?

Over and over again, the heroine of a novel is a young woman who must find a way. There is Ellen Chesser of *The Time of Man*, who struggles in the dire poverty of the poor white, in ignorance, in rejection by the world and by her first lover, toward her spiritual fulfilment. There is Theodosia Bell of *My Heart and My Flesh*, who suffers in the ruin of her genteel family, in the discovery of the father's licentiousness and of her mulatto sisters and brother, in rejection in love, in frustrated ambition as a musician in a physical and nervous collapse that draws her to the verge of suicide, but who finds a way back. There is Jocelle, of *He Sent Forth a Raven*, who is trapped in a house of death (as Theodosia was trapped in the house of her aunt), is deprived of her lover, is shocked and fouled by a random rape, but who finds a way. ⟨. . .⟩

As she put it in her journal, Elizabeth Madox Roberts had originally thought of "the wandering tenant farmer of our region as offering a symbol for an Odyssy [*sic*] of man as a wanderer, buffetted about by the fates and weathers." But by the time she began to write, the main character was Ellen Chesser, the daughter of such a man, and we see her, in the opening sentence of the novel, age fourteen, sitting in the broken-down wagon of their wanderings, writing her name in the empty air with her finger. This "Odyssy" is, essentially, a spiritual journey, the journey of the self toward the deep awareness of identity, which means peace. As for the stages of the journey, again we may turn to the journal:

> I. A Genesis. She comes into the land. But the land rejects her. She remembers Eden (Tessie).
> II. She grows into the land, takes soil or root. Life tries her, lapses into loveliness—in the not-lover Trent.
> III. Expands with all the land.
> IV. The first blooming.
> V. Withdrawal—and sinking back into the earth.
> VI. Flowering out of stone.[1]

The numbering here does not refer to chapters, but to the basic movements of the story, which the author took to be, to adapt

the phrasing of one of the reviewers, an emblem of the common lot, a symbol of the time of man.

The abstract pattern given in the journal is, in the novel itself, fleshed out in the story of Ellen Chesser. In this life of shiftless wandering she yearns for a red wagon that won't break down. Later, as she passes by the solid farmhouses set amid maples and sees the farmers on sleek horses or encounters their wives with suspicion in their glance, and learns that she is outcast and alienated, she yearns for things by which to identify herself. "If I only had things to put in drawers and drawers to put things in," she says, remembering herself begging old clothes at the door of a rich house. And later still, when she has found her man, she dreams of "Good land lying out smooth, a little clump of woodland, just enough to shade the cows at noon, a house fixed, the roof mended, a porch to sit on when the labor was done"—all this a dream never to come quite true.

What does come true in the end—after the betrayal by her first love, after the struggle against the impulse to violence and suicide, after love and childbearing, after unremitting work and the sight of reward tantalizingly just out of reach, after betrayal by the husband and reconciliation over the body of a dead child, after the whipping of her husband, by night riders, as a suspected barnburner—is the discovery of the strength to deal with life. "I'll go somewhere far out of hearen of this place," her husband says, nursing his stripes. "I've done little that's amiss here, but still I'd have to go." And she says: "I'd go where you go and live where you live, all my enduren life." So they take to the road again: "They went a long way while the moon was still high above the trees, stopping only at some creek to water the beasts."

Thus the abstract pattern is fleshed out with the story of Ellen, but the story itself is fleshed out by her consciousness. What lies at the center of the consciousness is a sense of wonder. It is, in the beginning, the wonder of youth and unlettered ignorance, simple wonder at the objects of the world, at the strange thing to be seen at the next turn of the road or over the next hill, at the wideness of the world, sometimes an "awe of all places," and a "fear of trees and stones," sometimes a wonder at the secret processes of the world, as when her father tells her that rocks "grow," that some have "shells printed on the side and some have little snails worked on their edges," and that once he "found a spider with a dragon beast in a picture on its back." But all the wonder at the wideness and age and ways of the world passes over into wonder at the fact of self set in the midst of the world, as when in a lonely field Ellen cries out against the wind, "I'm Ellen Chesser! I'm here!"

Beyond naïve wonder and the deeper wonder at the growth of selfhood, there is a sense of life as ritual even in the common duties, as an enactment that numenously embodies the relation of the self to its setting in nature, in the human community, and in time. Take, for example, the scene where Ellen is engaged in the daily task of feeding the flock of turkeys—turkeys, by the way, not her own:

> She would take the turkey bread in her hand and go, bonnetless, up the gentle hill across the pasture in the light of sundown, calling the hens as she went. She was keenly aware of the ceremony and aware of her figure rising out of the fluttering birds, of all moving together about her. She would hear the mules crunching their fodder as she went past the first barn, and she would hear the swish of the falling hay, the thud of a mule hoof on a board, a man's voice ordering or whistling a tune. . . . She would

crumble down the bread for each brood near its coop and she would make the count and see to the drinking pans. Then she would go back through the gate, only a wire fence dividing her from the milking group, and walk down the pasture in the dusk. That was all; the office would be done.

This sense of ritual, here explicit for the only time but suffusing the book, is related to the notion of "telling." Ritual makes for the understanding of experience in relation to the community of the living and the dead; so does "telling." Ellen, when the family first drops aside from the life of the road, yearns to see her friend Tessie, one of the wanderers, for in "telling" Tessie of the new life she would truly grasp it. Or the father sits by the fire and tells his life: "That's the story of my life, and you wanted to know it." Or Jonas, the lover who is later to jilt Ellen, makes his courtship by a "telling" of his sin. And later on, Jasper "would come that night and tell her the story of his life and then, if she was of a mind to have him, they would get married."

The novel is not Ellen's own "telling," but it is a shadow of her telling. The language, that is, is an index of her consciousness, and as such is the primary exposition of her character and sensibility. But it is also the language of her people, of her place and class, with all the weight of history and experience in it. We can isolate turns and phrases that belong to this world: ". . . if he comes again and takes off the property he'll maybe have trouble and a lavish of it too." Or: "I got no call to be a-carryen water for big healthy trollops. Have you had bad luck with your sweethearten?" But it is not the color of the isolated turn that counts most. It is, rather, the rhythm and tone of the whole; and not merely in dialogue, but in the subtle way the language of the outer world is absorbed into the shadowy paraphrase of Ellen's awareness, and discreetly informs the general style. For instance, as she sits late by the fire with her first love, Jonas, with her father snoring away in the bed across the room:

> The mouse came back and ate crumbs near the chairs. Ellen's eyes fell on the little oblong gray ball as it rolled nearer and nearer. Jonas was sitting with her, tarrying. It was a token. She looked at his hand where it lay over her hand in her lap, the same gaze holding the quiet of the mouse and the quiet of his hand that moved, when it stirred, with the sudden soft motions of the little beast. The roosters crowed from farm to farm in token of midnight and Henry turned in his sleep once again.

It is, all in all a dangerous game to play. In a hundred novels for a hundred years we have seen it go sour, either by condescension or by the strain to exhibit quaint and colorful locutions—which is, in fact, a symptom of condescension. But in *The Time of Man* it is different. For one thing, the writer's ear is true, as true as, for example, that of Eudora Welty, Caroline Gordon, Andrew Lytle, Erskine Caldwell (at times), William Faulkner, or George W. Harris, the creator of Sut Lovingood. Like all these writers, who differ so much among themselves, Elizabeth Madox Roberts is able to relate, selectively, the special language to her own special vision. For another thing, the language is not a facade over nothingness, like the false front of a nonexistent second story of the general store on the main street of a country town. It is, rather, the language of a person, and a society, which is realized in the novel with a sober actuality.

If *The Time of Man*—or *My Heart and My Flesh* for that matter—is as good as I think it is, how did it happen to disappear so soon, almost without a bubble to mark the spot?

We may remember, however, that this is not the first good book, or writer, to go underground. There is, for one thing, what we may call the natural history of literary reputation. When a writer dies we find, immediately after the respectful obsequies, the ritual of "reassessment"—which is another word for "cutting-down-to-size." In the case of Elizabeth Madox Roberts the ordinary situation was aggravated by the fact that her later work had declined in critical and popular esteem. The firm grip on social and individual actualities which undergirded the poetry of sensibility in the first two novels had, in the later work, been progressively relaxed. More and more we find a dependence on allegory and arbitrary symbolism; and with the natural base cut away the poetry moves over into prettification and preciosity.

Furthermore, this situation—which, we may hazard, had some relation to her gradual withdrawal into illness—was in a setting which would, in any case, have made for the rejection of even her earlier work. It was the period when a critic as informed as David Daiches could reject Conrad because, at least as Daiches believed, he "does not concern himself at all with the economic and social background underlying human relationships." Or when Herbert Muller could reject Flaubert as irrelevant to the age. Or when Maxwell Geismar could reject Faulkner as a "dissipated talent" and the victim of a "cultural psychosis," explaining that in him "the heritage of American negation reaches its final emphasis." So we can see why *The Time of Man* fell out of fashion: the novel presents Ellen Chesser, not in active protest against the deprivation and alienation of the life of the sharecropper, but in the process of coming to terms, in a personal sense, with the tragic aspect of life.

The agenda of the 1930s carried many items bearing on the urgent need to change the social and economic environment but none bearing on the need to explore the soul's relation to fate. Any literary work that was concerned with an inward victory was, in certain influential quarters, taken as subtle propaganda against any effort directed toward outward victory. It was as though one had to choose between the "inner" and the "outer."

What was true in the world of literature was even more vindictively true in the world of actuality. There, even when the awareness of the desperate need for changing the economic and social arrangements was coupled with an awareness of the worth of the individual who was a victim of the existing order, the tendency was to accept the graph, the statistic, the report of a commission, the mystique of "collectivism," as the final reality. The result was that, in that then fashionable form of either-or thinking, the inner world of individual experience was as brutally ignored as by an overseer on a Delta cotton farm.

It is now possible that we are growing out of this vicious either-or thinking. We may now see that we do not need to choose, and that if we do choose, in anything more than a provisional, limited sense, we are denying reality and are quite literally verging toward lunacy. And verging, in fact, toward a repetition of the bloodiest crimes of this century.

Elizabeth Madox Roberts says that "Life is from within," and her typical story is, to repeat, the story of an inner victory. In dealing with the dispossessed of the South she has, like Eudora Welty or Faulkner or Katherine Anne Porter or James Agee (to refer to a document of the 1930s, *Let Us Now Praise Famous Men*), recognized the dignity of the lowliest creature. But she knew that to recognize fully the dignity of any creature demands that we recognize the anguish of the collision with actuality. So in the story of Ellen Chesser we find no scanting of the grimness of fact, of the pinch of hunger, of the contempt in the eyes met on the road, of the pain of the lash laid on the bare back.

She was aiming, she wrote in her journal, at a fusion of the inner and the outer, at what she called "poetic realism":

> Somewhere there is a connection between the world of the mind and the outer order—it is the secret of the contact that we are after, the point, the moment of union. We faintly sense the one and we know as faintly the other, but there is a point where they come together, and we can never know the whole of reality until we have these two completely.

This is as good a description as any of what *The Time of Man* was trying to make of Ellen Chesser's relation to herself and to the world. The novel is, in a sense, a pastoral, but only a false reading would attribute to it the condescension, the ambiguous humility on the part of writer and reader, and the sentimentally melancholy acceptance of the status quo which often characterize the pastoral. No, it is the inner reality of Ellen and of her people that, in the end, makes social protest significant, makes social justice "just."

Perhaps now, after the distortions of the 1930s and the sicknesses of the 1940 and 1950s, we can recover *The Time of Man*. Perhaps we can even find in it some small medicine against the special sickness and dehumanizing distortions of the 1960s. Perhaps we can profit from the fact that Elizabeth Madox Roberts came, to adapt the lines by Yeats on John Synge,

> Towards nightfall upon a race
> Passionate and simple like *her* heart.

Notes

1. The references are drawn from *Herald to Chaos*, by Earl H. Rovit (Louisville: University of Kentucky Press, 1960.)

EDWIN ARLINGTON ROBINSON

1869–1935

Edwin Arlington Robinson was born on December 22, 1869, in Head Tide, Maine, to Edward and Mary Palmer Robinson. He studied at Harvard University from 1891 to 1893, and worked as the secretary to the president of Harvard in 1897. He published his first book of poetry, *The Torrent and the Night Before* (1896), at his own expense. A revised version was published as *The Children of the Night* in 1897, which was praised by President Theodore Roosevelt. Roosevelt appointed Robinson to a position in the New York office of the Collector of Customs, where Robinson worked from 1905 to 1909. During this period Robinson unsuccessfully attempted to write plays for the New York stage (published as *Van Zorn*, 1914, and *The Porcupine*, 1915) in addition to his poetry.

Robinson spent most of his life doing very little but writing poetry. He was not widely known or appreciated for many years; when he eventually received some attention from British critics, many Americans assumed he was British himself. His poetry was very traditional for the time, to the point (some felt) of conservatism; however, his themes were universal and powerfully dealt with, and he struck a strong chord with a large audience when his poems finally achieved wide distribution. After many years of anonymity, he was for the last several years of his life perhaps America's best-known poet, along with Robert Frost. He was awarded the Pulitzer Prize for Poetry three times. He published more than two dozen books of poetry during his lifetime; among the best-known are *The Man against the Sky* (1916); *Merlin* (1917); *Lancelot* (1920); *The Three Taverns* (1920); *Avon's Harvest* (1921); *Roman Bartholow* (1923); *The Man Who Died Twice* (1924); *Tristram* (1927), considered by many to be his greatest work; *Cavender's House* (1929); *The Glory of the Nightingales* (1930); *Nicodemus* (1932); *Amaranth* (1934); and *King Jasper* (1935). His collected poetry was issued in 1937, and various editions of selected poetry have been published subsequently.

Robinson was a private man who was uncomfortable with people. He never married. He spent much of the last twenty-four years of his life at the McDowell Colony in Peterborough, New Hampshire, with frequent visits to New York and Boston. He died on April 6, 1935.

Personal

It all comes back to me; those lines of pain
On the fine forehead, just above the eyes;
And then the sudden hesitating strain
Of hands which strove to hide those lines again,
With infinite slow patience; then, the cheeks,
Motionless, just a little too drawn in,
As one who chews upon the word he speaks:
And hesitates in shuddering surmise
Before he will begin
To show what thing is hidden
Under his lowered eyes.

And then the slow dumb wheel
Of a face like a fine-chiselled mask;
Till suddenly they opened upon you, in desperate appeal,
Eyes like a hurt dog's, wishing you to feel
The unanswerable questions they could ask:
Then lowering again, they made as if to shift
Apart in irritable pride,
As if they feared you might have caught their drift;
The look of a king disqualified
By some mad blunder of a fool
From rule.
Now this man was a life-long pioneer;
Where other men saw art as false and stale,

He saw it only hard and clear,
A fountain of icy strength in the far sunlight:
He strode out through the gale,
And through the trackless night
Of cold contempt towards his goal;
While in his soul
Rose nothing but the need to speak and die.
All the proud glory, the fine ecstasy
Of song had been to him a lonely doom
Making more stark his sense of loss and gloom,
Dogging the noble and the beautiful.
He had not dared to pause and snatch a kiss
From the hot lips of life, as other men,
Then go on with a heart more full
Towards his goal, in manhood's might again:
He strode on fearful only he might miss
The light that lured him, far, 'mid peak and fen.
And so I saw him sitting there,
In his wicker chair,
Mournfully patient, waiting, hoping,
That at the last, for all his groping,
And floundering through the formless dark
Without a single brother spark,
There yet might come reward at last
For all the sacrifices of the past.
But, as I watched him carefully,
With that close mouth half awry
Under the neatly clipped mustache,
That mouth over which there hovered,
Like a spark amid the ash,
Sometimes for a little while
The faint shy echo of a smile;
I felt that there would be no goal at all for him:—
Nothing but the dull dim
Slow aching of regrets to fret away
Their worn-out clay:
Nothing but that long track which he had trod,
And shaped and battered to a hard high-road:
Which many more lucky than he might travel yet
Before the red sunset;
For which few men might thank him, but most would soon
     forget.
              —JOHN GOULD FLETCHER, "Portrait of Edwin
                Arlington Robinson," *NAmR*, Autumn 1937,
                pp. 24–26

When I think of Edwin Arlington Robinson, I see a tall, stooped man in a grey suit and a little white tennis hat, carrying a cane, as he walked across the fields to his studio at the MacDowell Colony, in Peterborough, New Hampshire. Or I see a rather sad-looking man gazing down into his plate at breakfast or dinner, looking up suddenly with a bleak expression when a remark was addressed to him, a twinkle coming into his eyes just before he answered. His dry wit was usually offered with an appearance of solemnity, except for the expression in his eyes.

My first notion of Mr. Robinson was wrong; I thought he was cold and more than a little haughty, and that he particularly disliked women. It took about a month to begin to know him, seeing him at least twice every day, and sometimes oftener, in the informal companionship of the Colony, and often eating at the same table with him. If I had met him in New York, or in any ordinary social way, it would probably have taken ten years. I found that he was shy and reserved, but far from haughty.

Mr. Robinson did not like to be treated as a celebrity. He knew, of course, that he was famous, but he disliked autograph-hunters and persons who stared at him. He preferred to be treated as just another human being. Once he showed me a clipping that read: "Mr. Robinson is the most self-effacing of authors. He is known by hardly twenty people." He smiled and said, "If you don't go with a brass band in front of you, they say you're a recluse." He almost never talked about himself or his poetry. Whenever I could, I used to draw him out on literary subjects, for it seemed a waste of opportunity to talk to him about spinach, or cigarettes, or beer. I remember once being the fourth at the table with Edwin Arlington Robinson, William Rose Benét, and Padraic Colum—and the talk turned to *Little Lord Fauntleroy!*

I never asked Mr. Robinson definitely about his own poetry; I felt it would be presumptuous. I wanted to ask him about Richard Corey, and kept hoping the subject might come up by accident, but it never did. We used to talk about what I was doing, and Mr. Robinson used to ask me about the different persons in my book, *William Wordsworth of Rydal Mount*, about why De Quincey turned against Wordsworth, about Sara and Hartley Coleridge, and about Frederick W. Faber, whose sonnets he liked. I remember being much excited one day when he said to me, "I shall be interested to see your book."

He liked Wordsworth and Keats, he wrote sonnets to such minor poets as George Crabbe and Thomas Hood; but his great idol was Shakespeare. Before I began to know him, I was eager to see his studio—that little stone house among the pines, with the porch out back facing Monadnock. It was understood at the Colony that no one ever went to another person's studio unless definitely invited. Especially did one not go to Mr. Robinson's studio. But I used to stroll down that way sometimes—by chance—and happen to look up as I passed his window. He seemed always to be sitting in a rocking-chair, reading; and later, I found that his desk was full of Shakespeare—Sidney Lee's *Life*, numerous volumes of Shakespeare's works, nothing but Shakespeare. ⟨. . .⟩

In one way, Mr. Robinson was like many other intellectuals—he devoured mystery stories. He got them from the lending library in the village and was delighted to find a new one. Sometimes former members of the Colony would send him two or three, and he read them and passed them on. He was a poor sleeper, and used detective stories as a sedative, often reading far into the night. He liked only a certain kind—as most connoisseurs do.

He enjoyed music, too—good music. Some of the composers would give us concerts in the evening, sometimes their own compositions and sometimes the classics. The young man who called himself Scotch often played the violin, and Mr. Robinson sat quietly enjoying the music. Occasionally, he made special requests, and his selections showed his knowledge and appreciation of music. The composers seemed honored by the audition he gave them.

Every evening after dinner Mr. Robinson played a modified form of billiards, or pool. He was apparently not very skilful in the game, but stuck to it year after year. One of his sonnets is called "Doctor of Billiards," and an etcher and painter with whom he often played said that Mr. Robinson autographed a volume of poems for him, "To my Pool Partner,"—making the "P" look strangely like an "F." ⟨. . .⟩

Two summers I knew Mr. Robinson, ten weeks each time. The second summer, that of 1934, I arrived at the Colony on Sunday night. I was already seated at breakfast on Monday morning when Mr. Robinson came downstairs. I had purposely sat at another table in case he should not quite remember me. When he came in, he walked across the dining room, greeted me by name, and said that he was glad I was back. All summer I was easy and natural with him, for I felt that I was accepted.

The last morning of my stay at the Colony, in September, when I was returning to New York, I went over to tell Mr. Robinson good-by. Again it was breakfast, and I sat a while with him. I told him that I was really no writer, that I had come to the Colony to finish a particular book, and that it was almost done. Then I told him that I might have to develop into a writer after all, for I hated not to come back to the Colony.

"You write another book," he said slowly, "and come back."

Those were the last words he ever said to me, for he died the following April.

Everyone knows something of the poet, Edwin Arlington Robinson, but I feel that I had a special privilege in knowing—even slightly—the genuine, kindly man, Mr. Robinson.—FREDERIKA BEATTY, "Edwin Arlington Robinson as I Knew Him," SAQ, April 1944, pp. 375–81

General

Even with his early poems Edwin Arlington Robinson was "interested in using an idiom unfamiliar as poetry". He said that it took him twenty years to accustom people to his method. This poetic idiom was to preserve the rhythms of ordinary speech within the traditional forms; it finally resulted in the flowing blank verse that is peculiarly his own. There was a forecast of maturity in *Captain Craig* and great understanding in "Ben Jonson Entertains a Man from Stratford", but not until he wrote *Merlin* in 1916 did Mr. Robinson reach his full power; he believes that his best poetry is "somewhere" in the Arthurian poems because, he explained, "The romantic framework enabled me to use my idiom more freely".

Unlike so many twentieth-century poets he maintains that "there is room for sufficient variation within the conventional forms of poetry". "Poetry must be music", he said, "not that it must jingle, but it *must be music*. And that is the defect of free verse. Maybe it's possible to write musical free verse, but I've never read any. And it's not memorable either. I cannot recall a single poem written in free verse, can you?" Only second to his demand that poetry be music, Mr. Robinson believes that "poetry must *bite*". It is in making the traditional poetic forms serve his own ends that Mr. Robinson offers a clear proof of his greatness—here once again one discovers that to the man of genius there is no freedom so useful as restraint. "There is no such thing as the sonnet," he said, "there are only individual sonnets."

The people in Mr. Robinson's poems are so real that even Amy Lowell supposed that the men from Tilbury were portraits. Surely Richard Cory and John Evereldown were living men! At least the poet must have known their models in his native Gardiner, in the State of Maine? But he assured me that only one of all his characters was done from life; that one was Captain Craig, who was suggested by an elderly Jew. The others came to him much as did Flammonde, who appeared one night when Mr. Robinson was sitting in a movie-theatre: "Suddenly", he told me, "I saw Flammonde and I could hear the poem quite clearly. All the lines were there and I only had to write them down".

This gift for creating men led naturally to the dramatic dialogues, which have caused Mr. Robinson's name to be linked with Browning's, and to the narrative poems which are also dramas. When we talked about *Tristram*, he said, "I like to be familiar with my characters and their development before I start a poem. *Tristram* took two entire summers to write and I worked out its structure somewhat as a playwright would work out a play". This did not surprise me, but I was uncertain what he would say when I asked him whether the Arthurian poems were allegories, whether they were intended to parallel the great War. He said that they tell of "the breaking-up of the old order", and when I mentioned the objections of certain of his critics to this interpretation (Ben Ray Redman said "The people in *Lancelot* are more alive than symbols have a right to be"), he answered, "It is all there—it is all quite clear".

I asked him about his two plays, *Van Zorn* and *The Porcupine*, which were written about 1915, being curious to hear what he would tell me. He agreed that his friendship with William Vaughan Moody might have had something to do with his writing them and then he explained, "But I'm not a playwright. A play must be *direct*—there is no chance for a movement of light and shade".

It seems to me that no truer description can be made of Edwin Arlington Robinson's blank verse than that phrase, a movement of light and shade. It perfectly expresses the delicacy of effect, the subtle play, which makes his poetry so lovely. And it explains the flexibility which can portray the inward workings of men even to the shadows of thought.

Though he has been called the poet of the submerged self, he says that the psychological observation in his poetry is accidental. Nor is he interested in the exploration of pathological extremes; it is true that Fernando Nash, *The Man Who Died Twice*, may seem a sort of case-history, but it is a poetic case-history and the method is always the poet's method. In talking about his men Mr. Robinson said, "Well, for that matter, I suppose anyone who leaves the middle of the road is abnormal in one way or another".

He finds it "more interesting to write about failure than success", and so most of his poems are about people who fail in one way or another. Sometimes, like Timberlake in *Matthias at the Door*, they are rich in the gold that is "not negotiable", sometimes they fail as Merlin did when he left Camelot for Vivian, sometimes they are afraid, and again, as with Matthias, they are not yet born—

> . . . There's a nativity
> That waits for some of us who are not born.
> Before you build a tower that will remain
> Where it is built and will not crumble down
> To another poor ruin of self, you must be born.

There are many reasons for defeat in these lives, but always they discover, as did Lancelot, that

> The Vision shattered, a man's love of living
> Becomes at last a trap and a sad habit,
> More like an ailing dotard's love of liquor
> That ails him, than a man's right love of woman
> Or his God.

This Vision is not only the cosmic vision; it is the personal vision, the inner truth of his own nature which is the persuasion by which a man lives. This gone, through mistake or accident, and like Hamlet he will say, "I have lost all my mirth". "Hamlet", Mr. Robinson commented to me, "was a failure."

Which is fate and which is folly? Or are they the same? These are the questions that perplex Mr. Robinson's people. But whatever else is uncertain, the wisest know, as Timberlake told Natalie, that

> There is no cure for self;
> There's only an occasional revelation,
> Arriving not infrequently too late.

There is a choice, yes, but the choice is circumscribed, and man is, more surely than he likes to admit, the storehouse of his own destiny. "I think man's pattern is there before him," Mr. Robinson said. And then he added, "but it's difficult to discuss these ideas, we're getting metaphysical and our terminology may mean such different things".

Though Edwin Arlington Robinson's conception of self is the poet's vision, it does present much the same conclusion taught us by psychology, and this, I think, helps us to read his poetry with an understanding ear. We, too, have learned that our fate is in the tissue of our bodies and we know that we can create our own havoc. This knowledge is inspiring or disillusioning according to the results achieved; the World War made us feel fated to disaster, disaster which grew out of our own nature as men, and we dropped into the "bleak and arid despair" which Joseph Wood Krutch analyzed in *The Modern Temper*. Edwin Arlington Robinson experienced the War, and he experienced it with the deeper sensitivity of the poet, but his vision of man was the poet's vision, and he is still able to say "I think man is more than he seems".

The idea of fate lying within man is present in all great tragedy—in Shakespeare when he wrote *Hamlet*, for example. Aristotle said in the *Poetics* that tragedy is brought about "not by vice or depravity, but by some error of judgement". We know that though the devil tempted Marlowe's Dr. Faustus, he would not have fallen but for his vanity and his lust for power.

The psychology of sex is an explanation of one part of that self about which Mr. Robinson writes, and it has furnished the generation since the War with a sort of gospel of fate. Eugene O'Neill depended on this fate-consciousness when he wrote *Mourning Becomes Electra* in answer to his own question of whether it was possible "to get a modern psychological approximation of fate" into a play for a modern audience.

Unlike O'Neill, Edwin Arlington Robinson has not tried to achieve his tragic effects by revealing the workings of sexual pathology. Instead, he has written about the conflicts of people trying to live with their ideals and their mistakes. No words are more often on our lips than success and failure, and no modern writer—poet, dramatist, or novelist—has examined their meaning more closely.—NANCY EVANS, "Edwin Arlington Robinson," *Bkm*, Nov. 1932, pp. 676–78

It is one of the anomalies of contemporary literature that Mr. Robinson, who has given us a score of great lyrics, should continue to produce ⟨. . .⟩ long narrative poems, one after another, until the reader can scarcely tell them apart. We may only guess the reason for this. Our age provides for the poet no epos or myth, no pattern of well-understood behavior, which the poet may examine in the strong light of his own experience. For it is chiefly those times that prefer one kind of conduct to another, times that offer to the poet a seasoned code, which have produced the greatest dramatic literature. Drama depends for clarity and form upon the existence of such a code. It matters little whether it is a code for the realization of good, like Antigone's; or a code for evil like Macbeth's. The important thing is that it shall tell the poet how people try to behave, and that it shall be too perfect, whether in good or in evil, for human nature. The poet seizes one set of terms within the code—for example, feudal ambition in Macbeth—and shows that the hero's faulty application of the perfect code to his own conduct is doomed to failure. By adhering strictly to the code, the poet exhibits a typical action. The tension between the code and the hero makes the action also specific, unique; the code is at once broken up and affirmed, the hero's resistance at once clarified and defined by the limits thus set to his conduct.

Macbeth asserts his ego in terms of the code before him, not in terms of courtly love or of the idealism of the age of Werther: he has no choice of code. The modern character has the liberty of indefinite choice, but not the good fortune to be chosen, as Macbeth and Antigone had.

Mr. Robinson has no epos, myth, or code, no suprahuman truth, to tell him what the terminal points of human conduct are, in this age; so he goes over the same ground, again and again, writing a poem that will not be written.

It has been said by T. S. Eliot that the best lyric poetry of our time is dramatic, that it is good because it is dramatic. It is at least a tenable notion that the dramatic instinct, after the Restoration and down to our own time, survived best in the lyric poets. With the disappearance of general patterns of conduct, the power to depict action that is both single and complete also disappears. The dramatic genius of the poet is held to short flights, and the dramatic lyric is a fragment of a total action which the poet lacks the means to delineate.

It is to be hoped that Mr. Robinson will again exercise his dramatic genius where it has a chance for success: in lyrics. Meanwhile it would be no less disastrous to Mr. Robinson's later fame than to our critical standards, should we admire him too abjectly to examine him. Let him then escape the indignity of Hardy's later years when such a piece of bad verse as "Any Little Old Song" won egregious applause all over the British Isles. That Mr. Robinson is unable to write badly will not excuse us to posterity.—ALLEN TATE, "Edwin Arlington Robinson" (1932), *Reactionary Essays on Poetry and Ideas*, 1936, pp. 199–201

In 1933 Edwin Arlington Robinson was the "most famous of living American poets." Today his good gray name is attached to a handful of short poems that are exhibited in the respectable anthologies. But he is no longer an audible voice in poetry except to those sturdy readers who take time to wonder why the long poems are not as good as they should be, or to a few rigorous and lonely poets who find Robinson, for one reason or another, indispensable. But if one poet is indispensable to another, the reason is likely to be interesting. To come upon Robert Lowell reading Crabbe's tales, for instance, is to witness a strange and exhilarating encounter. And if such authority issues from a poet as relentlessly unfashionable as Robinson, we are almost obliged to attend to it. Our text is the *Collected Poems*, a daunting book of almost 1,500 pages.

In offering Robinson as a poet of continuing relevance we shall find it necessary to make some concessions, and it is well to make them sooner rather than later. And it may even be useful to give the largest concession immediately. If we think of T. S. Eliot as perhaps in the highest degree a characteristic poet of this century, then we must concede at once that Robinson either did not know or was indifferent to the movements of feeling that lead to Eliot's revolutionary poems. And we know that such ignorance, such indifference, are hard sins to forgive. We think, for a nearer comparison, of Yeats, almost an exact contemporary, only four years older than Robinson. Genius apart, Yeats clearly ploughs a deeper furrow. We have only to compare Yeats's "Upon a Dying Lady" with Robinson's "For a Dead Lady" to see that Yeats took far greater risks of sensibility and that he seized the advantage of a much deeper personal and social context in which to work. Robinson's lady dies and proves what the poets have always told us, that time is a vicious reaper, going far beyond the duties of his post. Yeats's lady dies not to make a point or to show herself a tragic heroine. A certain kind of death fittingly concludes a certain kind of life, thereby endorsing both; to embody this is her task. Yeats exposed himself to the contingency of other people and knew that the image of his work would have to fit the squirming facts. Robinson at an early age came to know certain things, and he thought that there was nothing else to know. These things became his property, and we have them in the poems in that capacity. Many of the later poems are attempts to protect his property in an age of subversion and falling prices. The things he knew were, for the most part, the old terms, old categories, and he thought that they would serve every occasion. And perhaps in the long run they will. But Robinson underestimated the pressure they would have to bear. A term like "sincerity" is a case in point. Now, after Gide and Mann and D. H. Lawrence, we may still be ignorant of its meaning, but at least we know that the meaning is elusive. Robinson uses the word as if it were his property, impregnable. In *Captain Craig*, for instance, he says:

> Take on yourself
> But your sincerity, and you take on
> Good promise for all-climbing.

Again, Robinson pushed his property very hard. He put great stock in the idea of vision and action, and indeed a major theme is the disproportion between the two, the gap between what one can see and what one can realize in action. But it is not endless in its resource. Robinson keeps nudging us to witness his theme and to acknowledge that it is his very own. In *Merlin*, for instance, Vivian says:

> Like you, I saw too much; and unlike you
> I made no kingdom out of what I saw—

But if this is Vivian it might equally be any one of twenty speakers in Robinson's poems. People in these poems see too much, or else they see it too late. Either way they are frustrated, and like Seneca Sprague they visit some of their frustration upon the reader, who has heard it all from Robinson before. Too much or too late; we are born at a bad time; vision and action do not synchronize. After a while, in Robinson's poems, this note begins to sound like a list of rules for membership in a gloom club. Robert Frost, irritated by one of George Russell's platitudes in the same key, wrote a splendid poem to say that the times are neither wrong nor right. Robinson never confronted this fantastic possibility, though he could have found it easily by consulting Emily Dickinson. In Book IX of *Tristram* Mark walks the battlements, groaning, "Had I known early/All that I knew too late . . . " We hear this again in *Amaranth* and in many other poems. In *King Jasper* it isn't even a matter of vision—everything that happens comes, like Zoë, too late. Robinson's trains are scheduled never to arrive on time; we are all men against the sky. To use the terms of "The Wandering Jew," "the figure and the scene/Were never to be reconciled." Robinson became more and more lugubrious about this in his later poems. Indeed, "Miniver Cheevy" is the only poem in which he treats it lightly, and it is one of his finest poems for that very reason:

> Miniver Cheevy, born too late,
> Scratched his head and kept on thinking:
> Miniver coughed, and called it fate,
> And kept on drinking.

Robinson came to lose this note, and it passed to other hands, notably to John Crowe Ransom in "Captain Carpenter." And in his later years Robinson felt that life consisted entirely of ironies great and little, and he became their devoted chronicler. Indeed, this was true to such an extent that when a phrase from a Robinson poem lodges in the mind or comes up unbidden, it is invariably a gray generalization like "the sunlit labyrinth of pain," "time's malicious mercy," "time's offend-ing benefits," "the patient ardor of the unpursued," or "a dry gasp of affable despair." And the fretful note increased, especially after *The Man against the Sky*. Robinson's favorite color was gray, while most readers have now been schooled to prefer, if anything in that line, downright black. Hence we feel that poems like *Cavender's House* have everything that a good poem needs except variety, so that even the well-made sounds become dull, like the "sequestered murmuring" of *Captain Craig*. (There is a letter of Hopkins to Baillie in 1864 in which he offers terms for a discrimination of styles, and one of these he calls "Parnassian." This is a kind of style that is all too characteristic of its author. And Hopkins says that when a poet palls on us it is because of his Parnassian: we "seem to have found out his secret." (Robinson has a great deal of Parnassian in those 1,500 pages.)

If we need a phrase to stand for these concessions, Robinson gives one in *The Glory of the Nightingales* when he speaks of "the embellished rhetoric of regret." This is the signature tune of his work, or much of it, apart from its greatest occasions. In *Amaranth* the stranger says:

> I am one Evensong, a resident
> For life in the wrong world, where I made music,
> And make it still. It is not necessary,
> But habit that has outlived revelation
> May pipe on to the end.

And so, alas, it does.—DENIS DONOGHUE, "Edwin Arlington Robinson, J. V. Cunningham, Robert Lowell," *Connoisseurs of Chaos: Ideas of Order in Modern American Poetry*, 1962, pp. 129–33

Rereading Robinson it occurs to you that something came into American poetry—American literature—with E.A.R.: something not easy to define. It wasn't his characteristic form, the dialogue or monologue or dramatic scene, the narrative condensed to its essential crystal. Browning had already polished that device and Browning had been read in the United States. Neither was it Robinson's peculiar attitude toward style, his mastery of syntax—the taut, deliberate purposefulness of the sense of the words riding the sound of them like a skillful surfer on his changing wave. Others had practised the syntactical arts also: that long, intricate sentence at the start of *Avon's Harvest* tastes, if you break the meter, like Henry James.

What is it then that strikes you as new, as first seen, in Robinson's work—new, I mean, as of the time when it was written? Not a new world, certainly: Robinson was no explorer of the undiscovered, though he had a curiosity about the dark. Not a new music: Robinson's tunes are simple and familiar—often too familiar. Not a new way of seeing. There are fewer visible images in Robinson than in most: Dante's eternal squinting tailors never got to Tilbury Town. No, what strikes you as you read Robinson now—what catches your ear first and then your half attention and after that your speculating mind is not so much the shape or sound or even substance of what is being said as the manner of the saying.

What is new is the speaker. And I mean the *speaker*, not what is meant or implied by such terms of the contemporary critical vocabulary as "Mask" or "Persona." Robinson's mask was his face, his own for all purposes—business-like glasses, trim moustache—but his way of speaking in his poems was his way of speaking in his poems, for otherwise he rarely spoke. He had—he developed in his work—a Voice in the sense in which Villon had a Voice which gave humanness a different timbre, and Sappho had a Voice which sharpened the taste of life, and Li Po had a Voice which made a place for laughter—a place which all the sententious solemnity of Chairman Mao and all the ranting of his mechanized adolescents have not been able quite to drown.

I am not comparing E.A.R. with Villon and Sappho and Li Po: I respect his integrity too much. I am saying only that he made for himself a Voice in the same sense they did. His poems were new poems under the sun not because form or theme or style was new but because the speaker was: new as a man and new too as a man of his time and country. We say, when we do not think what we are saying, that Whitman's was the American voice, but clearly it wasn't. Whitman celebrated America—what it was and what it might have been—but the voice in which his America was celebrated was no more American than the rhythms. Delete the place names and the geographical evocations and you are out at large on the timeless, placeless tone of the lyric self. Or we say, more carefully, that Thoreau's voice was American, as indeed in many ways it was, but not in the essential way. Thoreau's was the voice of the American idea, alive and talking back to the universe, but it did not *sound* in the native tone: it sounded of Thoreau.

With Robinson it was the other way around by both measures. He did not speak for the American idea. When he mentioned America there was a glint in his voice like the glint of his glasses.

> You laugh and answer, 'We are young;
> O leave us now and let us grow'—
> Not asking how much more of this
> Will Time endure or Fate bestow.

And certainly he never celebrated the blond young continent and its innocent dream. But when it comes to the Voice itself, to the speaker spoken in the Voice, Robinson was more American than either and therefore—the world having moved in the direction it has—more modern, for if Crèvecoeur were to ask his famous question now he would have to reply that his American is well on his way to becoming modern man. (Perhaps he would add, Hélas!)

Fifty years ago readers took the tone of Robinson's for "downeast" and thought of Head Tide and Gardiner when they heard his voice. Fifty years ago Richard Cory who "was always human when he talked" and persuaded us that he "was everything / To make us wish that we were in his place" but who, one summer night, "Went home and put a bullet through his head" was an introverted Yankee. But those fifty years have passed and few would make the provincial application now. The irony is applicable on too broad a stage.

And of course it is the irony that makes Robinson so particularly our own. He speaks for us in our inexplicably aborted time as no one else, even among the very great, quite does. His tone knows truths about us we don't know ourselves—but recognize. We don't despair—not quite—and neither does Robinson. But we don't hope either as we used to and Robinson, with no bitterness, has put hope by as well. His is the after voice, the evening voice, and we neither accept it nor reject it but we know the thing it means.

It is all in that extraordinary poem he put into the mouth of Ben Jonson entertaining a Stratford Alderman and explaining Shakespeare's "old age"—his forties.

> The coming on of his old monster Time
> Has made him a still man; and he has dreams
> Were fair to think on once and all found hollow.
> He knows how much of what men paint themselves
> Would blister in the light of what they are;
> He sees how much of what was great now shares
> An eminence transformed and ordinary;

> He knows too much of what the world has hushed
> In others, to be loud now for himself. . . .
> But what not even such as he may know
> Bedevils him the worst: his lark may sing
> At heaven's gate how he will, and for as long
> As joy may listen but *he* sees no gate
> Save one whereat the spent clay waits a little
> Before the churchyard has it and the worm.
> —ARCHIBALD   MACLEISH,   "On   Rereading
> Robinson," *CLQ*, March 1969, pp. 217–19

YVOR WINTERS
"Conclusion"
Edwin Arlington Robinson
1946, pp. 143–49

I have expressed my belief that Robinson's long poems are mostly unsuccessful and represent a waste of effort; that the best of them is *Lancelot*, an impressive poem in spite of many imperfections, and that *Merlin*, though it is hardly a great poem, contains great poetry; that Robinson's most successful work is to be found among his shorter poems and poems of medium length, of which we may cite for the moment such examples as "Hillcrest," "Eros Turannos," "The Wandering Jew," "Many Are Called," "The Three Taverns" and "Rembrandt to Rembrandt." Of Robinson's more obvious faults I have already said enough. There remain certain questions of more or less interest: What kind of relationship does Robinson have to the poets who precede and who follow him? To what extent do any of his weaknesses affect his great poetry? How does he compare to the other great poets, American or British, who have written in English?

In the second decade of the present century, when the so-called poetic Renaissance was at the height of its reputation and when Robinson was beginning to attract attention, it was common to see Robinson mentioned as a forerunner of such poets as Masters, Lindsay and Sandburg, and there is still a tendency to refer to him as a kind of ancestor of much or all of that which has come since. The origin of this idea is apparently to be found in the directness and honesty of his style, as if, in the first place, such a quality were new, and as if, in the second place, it were characteristic of the poetry in question. Nothing, I think, could be less judicious. Masters, Lindsay and Sandburg are sentimental poets with no gift for thought and no command of their craft; the first two are forgotten except as they survive in high school curricula, and the third will soon follow them; they belong to a generation which mistook the inept outburst of the amateur for the direct statement of honesty. The more talented poets of the same period, such as Pound and Eliot, represent a conscious effort to dissolve thought and structure in feeling and in sensory perception, and the poetry which has proceeded from them, the bulk of the poetry of the past two decades, exhibits the same tendency in talents which are, for the most part, less impressive than the talents of Lindsay and Sandburg. Stevens is similar to Pound and Eliot in this respect, except for a few of his earlier poems, such as "Sunday Morning"; but Stevens in his thought is committed to the process of dissolution which in the main he follows, and his best poetry resembles Robinson only in its exhibition of a great native gift and a traditional method. Louise Bogan writes in a style as purely classical as that of Robinson, but her sources, so far as they appear, are in the sixteenth and seventeenth centuries; and although she is one of the best poets of our time, she is hardly characteristic of our time or at least of what passes for it among our poets and critics. Frost resembles Robinson more closely than does any other, but the resemblance is stronger upon first glance than upon second and tends to disappear with re-examination. The resemblance is strongest between such poems as "Isaac and Archibald" and some of Frost's narratives in blank verse; but the resemblance depends mainly upon the brute and impersonal fact that both poets come from much the same part of the country and sometimes write about it. The resemblance is in part due to the fact that Robinson is more nearly colloquial in a few such minor poems as this than he is in his greater and that Frost has tended to make a discreet mannerism of colloquial speech (which is not quite the same thing as the plain speech of the man of letters, such as one finds in Robinson's greatest work). The resemblance is due in part also to the fact that this poem by Robinson is minor: Frost is an Emersonian Romantic who celebrates the minor incident, the eccentric attitude and the fleeting perception; he frequently does it with extraordinary beauty, and I trust will long remain an ornament to our literature, but to compare him to the author of "The Wandering Jew" and of "Rembrandt to Rembrandt," on the grounds either of resemblance or of greatness, is pointless.

I have already mentioned the poets who seem to me to have influenced Robinson; the two most considerable influences, I believe, are Browning and Praed. But of these, Browning is an influence only on a small portion of Robinson's work, and not on a very important portion, and Praed at most is merely a point of departure. If one tries to compare Robinson to practitioners of the other forms of literature, one runs the risk of being superficial and perhaps inaccurate, but the effort, if not taken too seriously, may have a little value; and it has long appeared to me that his closest spiritual relatives, at least in America, are to be found in the writers of fiction and of history in his generation and the two or three generations preceding. I have called attention to his having certain more or less Jamesian vices as a narrator, but I am thinking now of his virtues: of the plain style, the rational statement, the psychological insight, the subdued irony, the high seriousness and the stubborn persistence. In respect to one or another of these qualities, one may find him related to such a mind as that of Henry James, but perhaps more obviously to Edith Wharton and Motley and Francis Parkman, and perhaps even at times to Henry Adams. He is, it seems to me, the last great American writer of their tradition and not the first of a later one; and the fact that he writes verse is incidental. There was little verse of major importance produced in this country in the nineteenth century and in the early twentieth; there was a good deal of major prose; and Robinson is more closely comparable to the great masters of prose than to the minor poets.

In reading Robinson's verse during a period of approximately twenty-five years, I have always felt a certain deficiency, even in some of the best of it, and I have heard the same deficiency mentioned by other readers: the deficiency is easy to indicate—it is a certain dryness, a lack of richness in the language—but it is not so easy to define with any precision. One may read such a poem as "Hillcrest," admire it and recognize its greatness, and yet feel, however fallaciously, that one has more or less exhausted its interest after a few readings; whereas one is likely to return repeatedly to such poems as George Herbert's "Church Monuments" or Robert Bridges' "Dejection." It is hard to lay one's finger on the precise reason. I have chosen these two poems by Herbert and Bridges because

they forestall what might seem the most obvious explanation: the intellectuality of Robinson and his relative freedom from sensory imagery. These poems are at least equally intellectual and are quite as free from sensory imagery, and one could easily add other poems to the list: "Down in the depths of mine iniquity," by Greville; "If Beauty be the mark of praise," by Jonson; and "Thou hast made me," by Donne; and these are only a few. I think the explanation may lie in two causes, which are perhaps related, and which I have already discussed: a certain deficiency in Robinson's ear, which results at times in a somewhat mechanical and imperceptive rhythm—I am referring not to his meters or his stanzas, but to the way he uses them—and a distrust of the suggestive power of language in favor of an unnecessary fullness of expository statement, a fullness which sometimes degenerates into simple cleverness. In regard to the second point, I am not objecting either to the rational structure of his poems or to their rational content, for of those the reader must by now be aware that I approve; but to a slightly unnecessary subdivision and restatement of matter, a slight lack of concentration. These defects are the defects of Praed and Holmes and poets of their type, of poets who may be skillful, ingenious, civilized and amusing, but who are not quite serious about their subjects and not quite masters of their language. In Robinson's weaker poems, especially in his narratives, the defects are deadly. In his secondary successes, such as "Two Gardens in Linndale," they are very obvious; and one feels them in some of his greater poems, slightly in "Hillcrest" and "Eros Turannos" and plainly in "For a Dead Lady." On the other hand these defects are diminished to the point of being negligible in such poems as "Veteran Sirens," "The Wandering Jew," "Many Are Called," "The Three Taverns" and "Rembrandt to Rembrandt." If the tide ever sets against Robinson's reputation—and if it does not, sooner or later, his reputation will be an exceptional one—I think that these defects will be the reason. But it seems to me that the defects are merely defects, like any others, and should be given no more importance than the defects of many another great poet. The vatic pomposity of Wordsworth is ruinous to most of his work and can be detected in his best; the grammatical machinery of Milton's sonnets is almost always a little too great for the occasion and sometimes endeavors to enforce unity upon unrelated matter; and there is the excessive ingenuity of the Metaphysical School. It is unfortunate that Robinson published so voluminously, for one becomes irritated in reading him through, just as one becomes irritated in reading Wordsworth or Tennyson, and one becomes nervously aware of his faults and is inclined to see them even where they do not appear. No poet can publish in this manner with impunity, and as time goes by the risk will become progressively greater: even a genius as great as Wordsworth, a hundred or two hundred years hence, might succeed in burying his worth under the mountains of his mediocrity.

These defects are the initial defects of a manner and a temperament, defects which Robinson held under reasonable control in a great many poems, and eliminated, or all but eliminated, from seven or eight. In the diminution of these faults and in the more or less comparable process of universalizing his New England mind, he became on certain occasions one of the most remarkable poets in our language. His style at its best is as free from the provincialism of time and of place as the best writing of Jonson or Herbert. This impersonal greatness of style has been seldom achieved in the twentieth century; one finds it in some of the greatest work of the nineteenth century poets: in the "Ode to Duty," by Wordsworth; in "Tiresias," by Tennyson; in parts of "The Pope," from *The Ring and the Book*; in a number of lyrics by Hardy, such as "In the Time of the Breaking of Nations"; and above all, perhaps, in a few poems by Bridges: for example, in "Dejection," "Eros," "Low Barometer" and "The Affliction of Richard." It is among these British poets of the last century and of the turn of the century that Robinson seems at moments to find his closest relatives and quite possibly his closest rivals on this side of Milton and Dryden; and his position in relation to these poets is not that of the lowest.

LAWRANCE THOMPSON
"Introduction"
Tilbury Town:
Selected Poems of Edwin Arlington Robinson
1953, pp. ix–xvi

One high tribute which we pay quite unconsciously to the poetic art of Edwin Arlington Robinson is that many of us know some of these Tilbury Town poems by heart without ever having tried to memorize them. Hitherto isolated and scattered through some fourteen hundred pages of Robinson's *Collected Poems*, these familiar faces have always seemed to lean toward each other, talk to each other, explain each other, even gossip about each other. They belong together, and this critical act of bringing the best of them together is intended as a further tribute to Robinson's various artistic skills.

We naturally remember these Tilbury Town poems as many-sided. If we start by calling them stories-in-verse we are never far wrong because each contains some qualities of narrative, mixed with subtle qualities of song. If we go on to say that their flavor recalls the bittersweet tang of a firm Down East apple we do no injustice to the universality of their appeal. If we take them as terse and elliptical probings into obscure psychological motivations we again include most of them. If we remember some of them as miniature poetic scenes in the larger Tilbury Town drama, we honor an essentially dramatic element in them all. But first and last our pleasure is to enjoy them for the peculiar felicity of Robinson's utterance, for the ironically witty turns of word and phrase, for the apt rhythms and cadences of the lines, and for the cunningly varied structures which give new vitality to old verse forms.

As soon as we notice that most of these poems are explicitly or implicitly integrated by the gathering metaphor of the Tilbury Town backdrop or setting, we quickly discover that three different tensions of interest are evoked, poetically and dramatically; that at least three different kinds of conflict are interwoven. At first glance we are aware of the obvious conflicts within or between these imagined characters whom Robinson has brought to life in or on the edge of Tilbury Town. A second glance makes us feel that most of these characters are represented as being in conflict with the prudent and conventional morality of Tilbury Town, where the group tends to pass relentless judgment on all misfits and failures who find themselves at odds with the money-conscious worship of material success. A third glance is not necessary to make us realize that the poet-as-observer, standing apart from the Tilbury Town group, on the one hand, and from the isolated individuals, on the other hand, shows an open hostility toward the Tilbury Town group and shows sympathetic compassion for the misfits, the failures, the disappointed. Because any single one of these conflicts would be adequate for purposes of poetic and dramatic narrative, we enjoy this rich interplay of conflicts as sheer poetic luxury.

Yet our pleasures are increased when we notice the consistency with which Robinson makes use of sly wit and wry humour to keep his double-edged response under artistic control and balance. The majority of the human predicaments here described are essentially tragic or at least pathetic, and the danger was that Robinson's deep compassion might have gotten out of hand. It never does, I think, and one kind of pleasure available to us is to notice the variety of ways in which he avoids this pitfall. Detachment is implicit in the essentially dramatic role of the poet-as-observer; but the beauty of that detachment, artistically considered, becomes most apparent only after we have let the poet sensitize our ears to those extraordinary modulations of tone which he somehow manages to catch and imprison through his skillful and cunning arrangements of words. His most oblique comments on either the misfits or the ostracizing group are conveyed through mere nuances of tone which range through ironic wit, playfulness, teasing, smiling, indulgence, tenderness, pity, sarcasm, bitterness, scorn, together with all the possible permutations and combinations. Yet always, beneath or through the usually gentle spirit of his human comedy (which for Robinson is one type of tragedy), the poet invites us to join him in refusing to pass quick judgments against the actions of his isolated characters in or on the edge of Tilbury Town.

All the technical factors which I have mentioned, so far, are utilized concurrently by Robinson as a complex means to the end of illuminating his own scale of values and his ulterior conceptual concerns. Indirectly and variously, he concentrates our attention on dramatized evidence that no human errors, disappointments, failures, need be viewed as destroying the wellsprings of human dignity or crippling the potentials of spiritual self-realization. Again and again he finds symbolic ways for suggesting that many of his isolated individuals have learned how to translate different forms of hurt and loss into perceptions which somehow compensate for hurt and loss.

Yet he goes even deeper to hint that his most persistent probings beneath the surface of either the tragic or the pathetic are performed to intensify his and our awareness of that which remains unknown and unknowable in the human predicament. His kind of poetic hesitation, on the verge of discovery and revelation, seems offered repeatedly as an implicit corrective for the cocksure faultfinding of the Tilbury Town group, which is always inclined to insist that there is no mystery about human action; that the individual who fails is somehow to blame for whatever happens.

As soon as we are aware of the extensions of meaning made available to us through the poet's double-edged attitude toward the town and the isolated individuals, we can advance one step further in our enjoyment of certain symbolic meanings implicit in the structures of these poems. Robinson has frequently been criticized for achieving surface effects of obscurity, uncertainty, vagueness; but this would seem to be a risk he deliberately took. If the modes and structures of these separate pieces occasionally perplex those who insist that poetry should begin and end with vivid concrete imagery; if Robinson's brooding manner may seem to involve too often the blurred, the puzzling, the elliptical, perhaps we may find that this aspect of his art is justified because it helps him dramatize and illuminate a recurrent theme. Repeatedly he invites the reader to linger over baffling actions or situations which suggest several possibilities of explanation, but which admit no certainties of explanation. Perhaps it could be said that Robinson uses his compressed idiom to require such deliberate and thoughtful progression that we have no choice: we must read closely, slowly, hesitatingly, cautiously, wonderingly, if we are to comprehend even the specific details of the surface meaning. As we perform that necessary process of close reading and contemplation and reconsideration, perhaps it dawns on us that we ourselves are thus acting out an important aspect of the poet's meaning.

An illustration may be in order here. Consider what happens to us when we confront and are confronted by that cryptically inferential fragment of a story entitled "The Whip." If we could remember our first reading of it, probably all of us would confess that we reached the end of those five tight octaves with a disturbed sense of bafflement as to whether even a surface meaning had been adequately realized by the poet. Although our understanding of "The Whip" may have increased with each successive reading, we admit that we have not yet resolved and removed our initial sense of perplexity. Isn't it possible that the poet had a particular purpose in mind, when he created that effect? In retrospect, we remember a few specifics which can be summarized briefly. The immediate situation represents the poet-observer as musing over an open casket which contains the body of an acquaintance who has recently drowned himself. Meditatively, and yet with the slightest hint of irony in his voice, the poet conducts a necessarily one-sided conversation with the dead man in an attempt to find an answer to the obvious question: why did he do it? But the circumstantial evidence, stated or guessed, in the poet's soliloquy merely heightens his (and our) sense of perplexity. From the evidence poetically given us, we tell ourselves cautiously that this dead man's troubles seem to have stemmed from an inner conflict involving his doubts as to whether his wife had always been faithful to him. But the poem starts with something more than a hint at this inner conflict:

> "The doubt you fought so long,
> The cynic net you cast . . ."

In the total context provided by the poem, there are several hints that the dead man had seemed anxious to prove the truth of his suspicion, cynically, and almost as though he would have been somehow disappointed if his suspicion had not been true. In this sense, the title seems to pick up a first metaphorical extension: the husband may have used his doubt as a whip. Whether or not he ever caught any proofs in his "cynic net," we are not told; but late in the poem we gather that on the last day of his life he became involved in an absurd horseback chase after the wife and the man suspected as lover, riding together in full view of the pursuer; that as the husband overtook them, the wife turned and struck him across the face with her crop or whip. This little symbolic action the poet half guesses because of a curious welt he notices on the face of the dead man. Poetically considered, the images of the welt and the whip would seem to invite the reader beneath the surface of appearances and actions to speculate concerning the motives of both husband and wife. "Doubt" is obliquely represented as having caused certain blind spots in the husband's vision. But if blind to love, the poet wonders, would wounded pride be an adequate motive for suicide? Or is it possible that his own perception of some analogy between his doubting, and her striking with the whip, may have cured one of his blind spots and restored one kind of vision? Perhaps, at the end, he was not so blind as his neighbors thought. Is it possible that his suicide might be considered as a kind of recognition-scene? All these questions are suggested by the poet's brooding speculation, and although he is not certain as to motives, his questionings have evoked in him (and in us) enough compassion to restrain fault-finding judgments against either the husband or the wife who struck with a whip.

This is only one possible interpretation of the poem, and I give it merely to suggest Robinson's way of using poetic structure, and of requiring close reading of us, to let us act out an important aspect of his sub-surface meaning. Whenever we do follow him below appearances into the darkly mysterious realm of complex psychological mystery, those of us who seek clarified and simplified meanings are likely to find ourselves in company with the disappointed guest who visited Old King Cole:

> And once a man was there all night,
> Expecting something every minute.

In reading any of these tantalizing poems, perhaps our greatest surprise and pleasure is evoked by our ultimate discovery that Robinson manages to pass enough whole light of psychological consciousness through the immediate prism of his poetry to refract a few colors with sharpness and brilliancy. Notice also that the immediate prism is ingeniously created through the pertinently intricate interplay of words, phrases, rhythms, verse forms, all of which contribute something to the total effect. After we have recognized the peculiar nature of the prosodic difficulties which Robinson boldly set for himself, in some of his poems, and then so gracefully overcame, we return to this aspect of his artistry with heightened admiration.

Robinson's extraordinary technical cunning was earned during long years of painstaking practice and experiment, while he waited for recognition. He was forced to develop patience of at least two kinds because, during those apprentice years spent in his home town of Gardiner, Maine, he suffered constantly from what he felt to be the hostility of many hard-headed Yankee townspeople toward such a seemingly shiftless occupation. Gardiner, a thriving river-town on the Kennebec, bustled so earnestly with enterprise and money-making that most of its citizens were impatient with anything that could not be translated into dollars and cents. Hence there is no difficulty in understanding why Robinson chose to embody in his imagined Tilbury Town some of those tensions and conflicts which he felt in his mingled love and hate for his down-Maine New England heritage.

While still trying to discover his own idiom, poetically and spiritually, he watched three other members of his family achieve material success. His father crowned a prosperous business career by becoming a director in two Gardiner banks. His older brother Herman made himself locally famous as a shrewd financial investor and then courted and married the loveliest girl in town. His still older brother Dean carried out medical training at Bowdoin and then began practice as a promising physician. On the streets of Gardiner, neighbors stopped this mere poet and observer to ask reprovingly, "And what are you going to do with yourself, Win?" It would have sounded silly if he had told them the truth. After having spent only two years at Harvard he had returned to Gardiner and had settled down at home to do nothing but write, write, write. Gradually his neighbors stopped enquiring, and merely implied the question in reproachful side-glances.

"Life's Little Ironies" was the wry title of a Hardy story which Robinson discovered and enjoyed reading, during these days. All too soon he endowed the phrase with personal and first-hand meanings. Just when he feared that he himself might prove to be a failure even in his own eyes, the health of his vigorous and prosperous father collapsed so frighteningly that he became a burdensome invalid in the home. A little later, his two brothers returned home as different kinds of failure. His brother Dean subsequently killed himself. Further biographical details are unnecessary, here. Enough for us to know that under his own roof in Gardiner, Maine, Robinson found abundant cause for brooding over questions as to how one should define and evaluate the ulterior meanings of disappointments, disgrace, failure. His desire to defend his brothers and himself against criticism heightened his impatience with the smugly Puritanical conventionalism of his non-artistic model for Tilbury Town, and his bitterness found vent of the sort reflected in the following letter to a former Harvard classmate, written three years before the appearance of Robinson's first (privately printed) book of poems:

"Gardiner is a small place, relatively, but it contains a good deal of weather at certain seasons of the year. In the past week—ever since my return from Cambridge—the place has been a frozen hell to me. Here I am, shut in by myself with only one or two people in town that I care two snaps of my fingers for (and who, in turn, care about as much for me) with no prospects except of the most shadowy nature, and hardly enough interest in the general political scheme of things to work out interest at six percent without cudgelling my brain more than I should over a proposition in Bokardo. I do not mean to say that I consider myself totally an ass (though they may) but merely that I lack a general interest in the practical side of things that may play the devil with my progress in this little journey to God knows where, which we are all making just now. I am afflicted with a kind of foolish pride that stands in my way every day of my life and which I am continually making heroic efforts to kick out. But it is 'no go.' I keep as much as I began with and if I end up a penniless *gent* full of golden theories of fame and riches I shall not lay all the blame, if there be blame in the matter, to myself; I shall not feel that it all might have been different, had I changed my opinions and actions a little when my mind was young and flexible. My philosophy does not swallow this teaching of our good old grandfathers who worked sixteen hours and sang psalms and praised heaven that a life is what we make it. And let me beg here that you may not permit any of your ambitious pupils to write essays on 'Every man the architect of his own fortune.'"

Deeply hurt, during those early years in Gardiner, Robinson gradually completed his self-assigned task of self-discovery and went on to use his poetry in part for purposes of self-defense and in part for purposes of self-justification. His wound, like Mercutio's, might seem trivial to others; but it would do. Sardonically he phrased another aspect of his discovery to one of his friends thus: "There's a good deal to live for, but a man has to go through hell really to find it out." What he found out, painfully, gave sharpness of color and phrasing and feeling and thought to the happy-sad music of all his poetry, particularly to his Tilbury Town poems.

The autobiographical aspects of the Tilbury Town poems are obviously of least importance. All we need remember, here, is that Robinson, while making continued use of the raw materials provided by his own experience, gradually learned more and more about the values of dramatically projecting his own personal perceptions through objective characterizations and portrayals of the human heart in conflict with itself. His own deeply cultivated sense of New England reticence and decorum must have helped him transmute his particular and private viewpoint into a genuinely classic and universal quality of poetic statement, which pictures afresh the old-new truths concerning inseparably tangled joys and sorrows, inextricably meshed good and evil, as viewed against the contrasted background of those Tilbury Town prejudices and assumptions which sort out all values in terms of either black or white. These poems represent his highest artistic achievement: they have earned him a well-deserved and distinguished position among our best American authors.

WILLIAM H. PRITCHARD
From "Edwin Arlington Robinson: The Prince of Heartachers"
American Scholar, Winter 1978–79, pp. 95–100

The volume on which Robinson's achievement can be judged to have deepened and extended itself is *The Man against the Sky* (1916). After it he published very few short poems ("they just ceased to come") and few readers today are tempted to make an argument that the long poems—whether Arthurian or domestic-psychological—form a solid basis for appreciation. Occasional purple patches, fine lines here and there, but on the whole prolix, fussy, and somehow terribly misguided—the long poems are stone-dead. Winters has a lovely paragraph on Robinson as a "belated and somewhat attenuated example" of a certain sort of New Englander (Winters is viewing this from the Pacific hills) "in which ingenuity has become a form of eccentricity; when you encounter a gentleman of this breed, you cannot avoid feeling that he may at any moment sit down on the rug and begin inventing a watch or a conundrum." This characterization fits the humorous Robinson, but also the contriver of long poems, ingeniously spun out of whole cloth and really about nothing in particular.

There is a habit of comparing Robinson with Henry James, and indeed (remembering H. G. Wells's description from *Boon*, as well as other descriptions) it is superficially plausible if one considers late James generally, say the stories in *The Finer Grain*. But there is an important difference: much energy appears to have gone into the techniques of cultivated attenuation and reader-subversion James was intent on practicing. His narrative renditions of appearances and places are done with sweep and boldness, and there is much comedy in the dialogues among characters, for all their murkiness. Robinson's overall "flat" tone, the monotonous narrative presence at the center of his tales, keeps the cap on everything, allowing no voice to break free of it even momentarily; thus the poems drag their slow lengths along and feel extremely wearied.

In arguing that Robinson's reputation as a significant modern poet depends mainly on a group of lyrics and lyrical narratives from *The Man against the Sky*, rather than on the later longer narratives, I should also add that the title poem of the 1916 volume appears to me virtually unreadable, not "one of the most fitly eloquent of modern poems," as it has been called. Flatulence seems instead the quality characterizing the endless maundering which the problem we are supposed to care about (Where was the Man against the Sky going? What does it all mean anyhow?) is subjected to:

> Shall we, because Eternity records
> Too vast an answer for the time-born words
> We spell, whereof so many are dead that once
> In our capricious lexicons
> Were so alive and final, hear no more
> The Word itself, the living word no man
> Has ever spelt.
>
> . . .
>
> If after all that we have lived and thought,
> All comes to Nought,—
> If there be nothing after Now,
> And we be nothing anyhow,
> And we know that,—why live?

One feels that Groucho Marx is the only appropriate person to respond to these questions. At any rate such "eloquence" should have had its neck wrung, the way Robinson was wringing it in shorter poems written at the same time.

My own list of the poems for which Robinson will be most remembered and the nature of which needs to be defined more clearly in order to locate his peculiar kind of genius includes "For a Dead Lady," from *The Town Down the River*; and the following ones from *The Man against the Sky*: "The Gift of God," "Eros Turannos," "The Unforgiven," "Veteran Sirens," "The Poor Relation," and "Hillcrest." After 1916 only one poem, "The Sheaves," seems clearly in their class. This is roughly Yvor Winters's list of "great" poems, with "The Gift of God" added (which I am certain should be there) and "The Unforgiven" (about which I have more doubts). But Winters was unable or did not attempt to give a satisfactory account of why they were to be taken as great poems; he tells us that in general the writing is "distinguished" and that the moral vision (particularly in "Hillcrest," with its criticism of romantic escape into nature) is disenchanted and gravely sane. On the basis of these poems and a few other selected ones, Winters found Robinson to be a much finer poet than Frost, insisting that although they bore a superficial resemblance—mostly on the grounds of their shared interest in colloquial speech and New England material—any comparison in terms of "greatness" was pointless, since Frost was so clearly minor and Robinson so clearly not.

The judgment might not be worth dwelling on, had it not been made again by two extremely intelligent critics of Robinson's work. Warner Berthoff, for example, finds Robinson's command of tone more consistently "major" than Frost's; while Irving Howe finds his dramatic poems superior to Frost's in their fullness of experience, tragic awareness, command of the "middle range" of life. These critics emphasize and share a sense of Robinson's "weight," as opposed to surface brilliances or the sudden felicities of which Frost is master; Robinson's preeminence is signaled by his larger and deeper authority.

I myself find Frost both more interesting and "weightier" than Robinson, but am less concerned with arguing that case than with suggesting that three of Robinson's very best poems—"For a Dead Lady," "Eros Turannos," and "The Gift of God"—are remarkable for something other than weight or fullness of experience or complexity of moral feeling. In each of them I am struck by the simplicity of their "content" or subject, by contrast with the charming elaborations of their form, the attractiveness they show as tuneful fables about all-too-human situations. With each poem one wonders, just briefly, whether there wasn't a trick in it somewhere, whether the narrating presence is really as calm, as wise, as understanding of life as it appears to be over the compass of the poem.

"For a Dead Lady" presents in its first stanza the special Robinson gambit that words, langue, are inadequate to express the soul, the essence of a person—are inadequate to take the measure of any human being:

> No more shall quiver down the days
> The flowing wonder of her ways,
> Whereof no language may requite
> The shifting and the many-shaded.

Yet it must be said that the poet isn't interested in trying to express much about what this lady (supposedly "based" on his mother, Mary Robinson) was like. He tells us only that nobody else's eyes will "fringe with night/Their woman-hidden world" the way hers did; that her laugh is now silent; that her forehead and (a curious detail) her "little ears" have gone away; and that her breast has ceased to rise and fall. But the way in which the

above-quoted lines work as poetry is for themselves to act as a flowing wonder of words, artfully creating the dead lady's specialness by employing striking phrases which somehow seem just right, precisely the way to describe "it," but which also can't be expatiated on and which don't abide our questions about what exactly they mean. Just *how* were her "ways" a "flowing wonder"? Or how did this wonder "quiver," or what were the shifting, many-shaded tones she manifested? One does not pursue these questions but they might need to be answered if we were to praise Robinson as a poet of moral depth and complexity of human presentation. Instead he gives us the splendid third stanza:

> The beauty, shattered by the laws
> That have creation in their keeping,
> No longer trembles at applause,
> Or over children that are sleeping;
> And we who delve in beauty's lore
> Know all that we have known before
> Of what inexorable cause
> Makes Time so vicious in his reaping.

It is extremely satisfying to participate in a confession of our common ignorance when confronted by death the reaper. The perfect positioning of "shattered," "inexorable," and "vicious," the nice shift in the sense of ways in which the lady no longer "trembles," the weary certainty in the repetition of "Know all that we have known before"—above all, the seeming inevitability of the rhymes, the strength and simplicity of the rhythm—it is these essentially verbal, rather than moral or psychological, effects which make us respond with grave assent.

The single most acute statement ever made about Robinson's lyrics was Conrad Aiken's in his 1921 review of *Avon's Harvest* where he identified the central characteristic of Robinson's verbal technique. Speaking of the poetry up through 1910, Aiken noted its "technical neatness" and also confessed to suspecting it of speciousness: ". . . what we suspect is that a poet of immense technical dexterity, dexterity of a dry, laconic kind, is altering and directing his theme, even inviting it, to suit his convictions in regard to style." Aiken is tempted to call it "padding" but decides against so harsh a word. At any rate it "took shape at the outset as the employment when rhyme-pattern or stanza dictated, of the 'vague phrase,' the phrase which gave, to the idea conveyed, an odd and somewhat pleasing abstractness." Thus Robinson's fondness for using Latinate words to achieve a "larger and looser comprehensiveness."

Aiken goes on to say that in the early volumes this comprehensiveness was "often more apparent than real," that an "engaging magician" was performing his illusions for us. But with the *Man against the Sky* volume the "vague phrase" is "no longer specious but genuinely suggestive, and accurately indicative of a background left dim not because the author is only dimly aware of it, but because dimness serves to make it seem the more gigantic."

Although I would not draw the line so clearly between the pre-1910 poems, where the "vague phrase" is speciously employed, and the immediately post-1910 ones in which it is "genuinely suggestive," Aiken's perception is brilliantly right for purposes of getting at the life of Robinson's best lyrics. Consider the last stanza-and-a-half of "The Gift of God," a poem about a mother's unshakable belief in her son's high destiny, even though "others"—"we," "the town"—know he's a good deal more ordinary than she can see. Those others would "writhe and hesitate" if asked their opinion of him:

> While she, arranging for his days
> What centuries could not fulfill,

Transmutes him with her faith and praise,
And has him shining where she will.

Surely the magic in that word "transmutes" has something to
do with its un-ordinary weight; a baser metal has been turned
into shining gold through the uses of imagination, mother's
and poet's:

> She crowns him with her gratefulness
> And says again that life is good;
> And should the gift of God be less
> In him than in her motherhood,
> His fame, though vague, will not be small,
> As upward through her dream he fares,
> Half clouded with a crimson fall
> Of roses thrown on marble stairs.

"Both nuns and mothers worship images"—Yeats's phrase
from "Among School Children" comes to mind. Robinson's
way of making the son's fame both vague and large at once is
to use for his main verb the rather indeterminate "fares," then
to produce the stunning and also mysterious "crimson fall" of
those roses and those marble stairs. Here one can say, in
Aiken's phrase, that language is being used in genuinely
suggestive ways, as long as one doesn't have to specify closely
exactly what those ways are.

There is finally the widely anthologized "Eros Turannos,"
a poem taken seriously in a way that even admiring readers of
Robinson don't quite take "Luke Havergal" or "Miniver
Cheevy." The presumption is that it exhibits psychological,
even sociological penetration; and it is a poem for those who
see Robinson as having a deep and sensitive understanding of
the human heart. Winters called it one of the great short
poems in the language, claiming for it "the substance of a short
novel or of a tragic drama" and calling the writing (except for
the fifth stanza, in which a "we" speaks for the town which is
witness to the drama) beyond praise. The two middle stanzas
describe the "securing" of the traitorous man by the self-
deceiving woman in love with him:

> A sense of ocean and old trees
>   Envelops and allures him;
> Tradition, touching all he sees,
>   Beguiles and reassures him;
> And all her doubts of what he says
> Are dimmed with what she knows of days—
> Till even prejudice delays
>   And fades, and she secures him.
>
> The falling leaf inaugurates
>   The reign of her confusion;
> The pounding wave reverberates
>   The dirge of her illusion;
> And home, where passion lived and died,
> Becomes a place where she can hide,
> While all the town and harbor side
>   Vibrate with her seclusion.

Such handsome language for this "tragic drama," disposing
itself in such a rhythmically regular way (the heavy rhymes, the
audacity of rhyming "inaugurate" with "reverberate"!), the deft
and rare metrical substitution of that final "vibrate"—may
serve to conceal rather than more fully express the "human
content" presumed to lie behind it. Here and at other moments
in the poem, paraphrase feels hardly competent to translate the
richness into a correspondingly subtle kind of sense.

As with other Robinson poems there is the feeling that
everything has already happened, some place a long way back,
somewhere in myth or pre-history where one struggles with the
god and accepts the god's triumph:

> Though like waves breaking it may be,
> Or like a changed familiar tree,
> Or like a stairway to the sea
>   Where down the blind are driven.

Robinson is the least "dramatic" of modern poets, if drama
means a development in consciousness, a sense that the poem
is entertaining choices even as it proceeds to its outcome.
Instead the aim of "Eros Turannos" is to make the unknown
background seem dim, gigantic, intensely suggestive, an object
for us to wonder at, rather than penetrate or understand. It is
all as inevitable and unchangeable as the hapless woman's fate
in "The Poor Relation":

> With no illusion to assuage
> The lonely changelessness of dying.—
> Unsought, unthought-of, and unheard,
> She sits and watches like a bird,
> Safe in a comfortable cage
> From which there will be no more flying.

Robinson's individuality is not in question, but its nature
has not yet been fully defined, nor has it been in these pages.
But James Dickey's introduction to the Macmillan *Selected
Poems* (1965) comes so close to getting it right that it is
worthwhile trying to say how he nonetheless gets it a bit wrong.
His concluding account of Robinson's "new approach," which
Dickey sees as one of modern poetry's most remarkable
accomplishments, consists of "making of a refusal to pronounce definitively on his subjects a virtue that allows an
unparalleled fullness to his presentations, as well as endowing
them with some of the mysteriousness, futility, and proneness
to multiple interpretation that incidents and lives possess in the
actual world." What this account leaves out, and thereby in so
doing misstates Robinson's specialness, is the willfulness and
the cadence of the poems.

From Dickey's account one might intuit a thoughtful,
cautiously skeptical contemplator of experience, intent on not
bending it to suit his own temperamental inclinations. The
poems which issued from such an imagination would, on that
account, feel more truly open, more (to use the unlovely
Leavisian phrase) "exploratory-creative" than I take Robinson's
to be—either at their most typical or at their best. At the risk
of overstating the case in the other direction, I should call the
"speculation upon possibilities," which Dickey finds central to
the poems, less a real than an apparent phenomenon. Robinson's reticence, his solipsism even, are real enough gestures of
uncertainty, of how-can-we-say-for-sure-since-we-all-know-
so-little; yet the poems rhythms show no such uncertainty, no
haltingness of mind and impulse—quite the reverse. The
music carries us along, as if by magic.

Dickey goes on to call Robinson's poetry the kind of
communication that "tells the more the more it is not told."
Let us place the line in its context of his wonderful late sonnet
"The Sheaves," the note on which to take leave of Robinson:

> Where long the shadows of the wind had rolled,
> Green wheat was yielding to the change assigned;
> And as by some vast magic undivined
> The world was turning slowly into gold.
> Like nothing that was ever bought or sold
> It waited there, the body and the mind;
> And with a mighty meaning of a kind
> That tells the more the more it is not told.

The octet moves along so smoothly and inevitably that one
almost neglects to ask, what *is* being asserted here anyway? So
that Robinson can pay tribute to the "vast magic" he invites us
to notice, his gestures perform a beautiful hocus-pocus, tell us

what "it" is not—not economic tender, not to be divined by human words, telling us "the more" but not telling us more. The mysterious promise of the last two lines is what makes it memorable, quotable, seemingly full of rich insight, if only we don't question it too closely.

Where then does the poet turn?

> So in a land where all days are not fair,
> Fair days went on till on another day
> A thousand golden sheaves were lying there,
> Shining and still, but not for long to stay—
> As if a thousand girls with golden hair
> Might rise from where they slept and go away.

The extraordinary thing about these lines—the sestet of the poem—is how really unpredictable they are; one could not possibly have imagined *this* as the outcome of the poem, any more than one could have predicted the dash after "stay," then the final two lines thrown off "as if" they came by magic, by a sudden inspiration, on a charming whim. Frost alludes, in his introduction to *King Jasper*, to what he calls "the dazzle of all those golden girls" in "The Sheaves," and his language provides the right word for what the sonnet does. It dazzles by the purity of its concern, the pure poeticality of it, as if Robinson had no other motive in writing it than to write a poem. And although I wouldn't deny that "The Sheaves" is a very special poem even for Robinson to have written, it shares that purity with his poetry generally: telling the more the more it is not told, folding in upon itself rather than gazing out with love or insight or moral reproof on an "actual world." That "infolding" has been seen as a tragedy, an indication of the poet's warped nature or insufficient growth as a human being; it may have been that, but it was certainly the condition for his very considerable, very strange achievement in poetry.

THEODORE ROETHKE

1908–1963

Theodore Huebner Roethke was born on May 25, 1908, in Saginaw, Michigan, to Otto and Helen Huebner Roethke. His father died of cancer when he was fourteen years old. He was educated at the University of Michigan (B.A. and Phi Beta Kappa 1929, M.A. 1936) and did graduate work at Harvard University. From 1931 to 1935 he taught at Lafayette College; in 1935 he taught for three months at Michigan State College. He was hospitalized from November 1935 to January 1936 with his first mental breakdown; he would suffer them periodically for the rest of his life.

Roethke taught at Pennsylvania State College from 1936 through 1943; in 1941 he was rejected by the military because of his hospitalization for mental illness. His first book of poetry, *Open House*, was published in 1941. Over the next several years he established his reputation with a series of poems exploring the world of nature, plants, greenhouses, and swamps in lush, evocative language. From 1943 to 1946 he taught at Bennington College, returning to Pennsylvania State College in 1947. He was awarded a Guggenheim Fellowship in 1945. In September 1947 he began teaching at the University of Washington, where he remained for the rest of his life.

In 1948 Roethke published *The Lost Son and Other Poems*, considered one of his best works. In it Roethke explores the interior of the psyche, concerning himself particularly with chaos and mental disorder; the effect is dark and surreal. He was awarded a second Guggenheim Fellowship in 1950, and published *Praise to the End!* in 1951.

Roethke married his former student Beatrice O'Connell in 1953. That same year he published *The Waking: Poems 1933–1953*, for which he was awarded the Pulitzer Prize in 1954. *Words for the Wind: The Collected Verse of Theodore Roethke* was published in 1957 and won the National Book Award and the Bollingen Prize the next year. By this time Roethke was rivaled only by Robert Lowell among American poets in the eyes of many critics.

Roethke published two more books of poetry (*The Exorcism*, 1957, and *Sequence, Sometimes Metaphysical*, 1963) before his sudden death on August 1, 1963, in Seattle. One posthumous volume of original verse, *The Far Field*, was published in 1964; it won the National Book Award in 1965. Roethke also published a book of criticism (*On the Poet and His Craft: Selected Prose*, edited by Ralph J. Mills, Jr., 1965) and three books for children (*I Am! Says the Lamb*, 1961; *Party at the Zoo*, 1963; *Dirty Dinkey and Other Creatures: Poems for Children*, edited by Beatrice Roethke and Stephen Lushington, 1973). Roethke's *Collected Poems* appeared in 1966, and his *Selected Letters*, edited by Ralph J. Mills, Jr., was published in 1968.

STANLEY KUNITZ
"Roethke: Poet of Transformations"
New Republic, January 23, 1965, pp. 23–29

In the myth of Proteus we are told that at midday he rose from the flood and slept in the shadow of the rocks of the coast. Around him lay the monsters of the deep, whom he was charged with tending. He was famous for his gift of prophecy, but it was a painful art, which he was reluctant to employ. The only way anyone could compel him to foretell the future was by pouncing on him while he slept in the open. It was in order to escape the necessity of prophesying that he changed his shape, from lion to serpent to panther to swine to running water to fire to leafy tree—a series of transformations that corresponds with the seasons of the sacred king in his passage from birth to death. If he saw that his struggles were useless, he resumed his ordinary appearance, spoke the truth and plunged back into the sea.

A lifework that embodied the metamorphic principle was abruptly terminated on August 1, 1963, when Theodore Roethke died, in his fifty-fifth year, while swimming at Bainbridge Island, Washington. He was the first American bardic poet since Whitman who did not spill out in prolix and shapeless vulgarity, for he had cunning to match his daemonic energy and he had schooled himself so well in the formal disciplines that he could turn even his stammerings into art. If the transformations of his experience resist division into mineral, vegetable, and animal categories, it is because the levels are continually overlapped, intervolved, in the manifold tissue. Roethke's imagination is populated with shapeshifters, who turn into the protagonists of his poems. Most of these protagonists are aspects of the poet's own being, driven to know itself and yet appalled by the terrible necessity of self-knowledge; assuming every possible shape in order to find the self and to escape the finding; dreading above all the state of annihilation, the threat of non-being; and half-yearning at the last for the oblivion of eternity, the union of the whole spirit with the spirit of the whole universe.

Roethke's first book, *Open House* (1941), despite its technical resourcefulness in the deft probings for a style, provided only a few intimations of what was to develop into his characteristic idiom. The title poem, in its oracular end-stopping and its transparency of language, can serve as pro-logue to the entire work:

> My truths are all foreknown,
> This anguish self-revealed . . . .
>
> Myself is what I wear:
> I keep the spirit spare.

Perhaps the finest poem in this first volume is *Night Journey*, in which the poet, telling of a train ride back to his native Michigan, announces his life-long loyalty to what he never tired of describing, even if somewhat sardonically on occasion, as the American heartland. The poem opens:

> Now as the train bears west,
> Its rhythm rocks the earth . . .

—how important that verb of rocking is to become!—and it ends:

> I stay up half the night
> To see the land I love.

The middle of the poem is occupied by a quatrain that prefigures one of his typical patterns of response:

> Full on my neck I feel
> The straining at a curve;
> My muscles move with steel,
> I wake in every nerve.

Some thirty years later—he seemed never to forget an experience—in the first of his "Meditations of an Old Woman," the old woman being presumably his mother when she is not Roethke himself, he was to offer, through the medium of her voice recalling a bus ride through western country, a recapitulation of that same sensation: "taking the curves." His imagination was not conceptual but kinesthetic, stimulated by nerve-ends and muscles, and even in its wildest flights localizing the tension when the curve is taken. This is precisely what Gerard Manley Hopkins meant when, in one of his letters, he spoke of the "isolation of the hip area." The metamorphosis of the body begins in the isolation of the part.

Another poem in *Open House*, entitled "The Bat," concludes:

> For something is amiss or out of place
> When mice with wings can wear a human face.

It took time for Roethke to learn how full the world is of such apparitions . . . and worse!

The confirmation that he was in full possession of his art and of his vision came seven years later, with the publication of *The Lost Son* (1948), whose opening sequence of "green-house poems" recaptures a significant portion of his inheritance. Roethke was born, of Teutonic stock, in Saginaw, Michigan, in 1908. The world of his childhood was a world of spacious commercial greenhouses, the capital of his florist father's dominion. Greenhouse: "my symbol for the whole of life, a womb, a heaven-on-earth," was Roethke's revealing later gloss. In its moist fecundity, its rank sweats and enclosure, the greenhouse certainly suggests a womb, an inexhaustible mother. If it stands as well for a heaven-on-earth, it is a strange kind of heaven, with its scums and mildews and smuts, its lewd monkey-tail roots, its snaky shoots. The boy of the poems is both fascinated and repelled by the avidity of the life-principle, by the bulbs that break out of boxes "hunting for chinks in the dark." He himself endures the agony of birth, with "this urge, wrestle, resurrection of dry sticks, cut stems struggling to put down feet." "What saint," he asks, "strained so much, rose on such lopped limbs to a new life?" This transparent womb is a place of adventures, fears, temptations, where the orchids are "so many devouring infants!":

> They lean over the path,
> Adder-mouthed,
> Swaying close to the face,
> Coming out, soft and deceptive,
> Limp and damp, delicate as a young bird's tongue.

When he goes out to the swampland to gather moss for lining cemetery baskets, he learns of the sin committed *contra naturam*, the desecration against the whole scheme of life, as if he had "disturbed some rhythm, old and of vast importance, by pulling off flesh from the living planet"—his own flesh. And he encounters death in a thousand rotting faces—all of them his own—as at the mouldy hecatomb he contemplates death crowning death, in a dump of vegetation . . . "over the dying, the newly dead."

The poet's green, rich world of childhood was self-contained, complete in itself. Mother waited there: she was all flowering. When father entered, that principle of authority, he was announced by pipe-knock and the cry, "Ordnung! Ordnung!" So much wilderness! and all of it under glass, organized, controlled. For the rest of his life Roethke was to seek a house for his spirit that would be as green, as various, as ordered. And he was often to despair of finding it. In one of his last poems, "Otto," named after his father, he concludes:

> The long pipes knocked: it was the end of night.
> I'd stand upon my bed, a sleepless child
> Watching the waking of my father's world—
> O world so far way! O my lost world!

Roethke's passionate and near-microscopic scrutiny of the chemistry of growth extended beyond "the lives on a leaf" to the world of what he termed "the minimal," or "the lovely diminutives," the very least of creation, including "beetles in caves, newts, stone-deaf fishes, lice tethered to long limp subterranean weeds, squirmers in bogs, and bacterial creepers." These are creatures still wet with the waters of the beginning. At or below the threshold of the visible they correspond to that darting, multitudinous life of the mind under the floor of the rational, in the wet of the subconscious.

Roethke's immersion in these waters led to his most heroic enterprise, the sequence of interior monologues which he initiated with the title poem of *The Lost Son*, which he continued in *Praise to the End* (1951), and which he persisted up to the last in returning to, through a variety of modifications and developments. "Each poem," he once wrote, "is complete in itself; yet each in a sense is a stage in a kind of struggle out of the slime; part of a slow spiritual progress; an effort to be born, and later, to become something more." The method is associational rather than logical, with frequent time shifts in and out of childhood, in and out of primitive states of consciousness and even the synesthesia of infancy. Motifs are introduced as in music, with the themes often developing contrapuntally. Rhythmically he was after "the spring and rush of the child," he said . . . "and Gammer Gurton's concision: mütterkin's wisdom." There are throwbacks to the literature of the folk, to counting rhymes and play songs, to Mother Goose, to the songs and rants of Elizabethan and Jacobean literature, to the Old Testament, the visions of Blake and the rhapsodies of Christopher Smart. But the poems, original and incomparable, belong to the poet and not to his sources.

The protagonist, who recurrently undertakes the dark journey into his own underworld, is engaged in a quest for spiritual identity. The quest is simultaneously a flight, for he is being pursued by the man he has become, implacable, lost, soiled, confused. In order to find himself he must lose himself by reexperiencing all the stages of his growth, by reenacting all the transmutations of his being from seed-time to maturity. We must remember that it is the poet himself who plays all the parts. He is Proteus and all the forms of Proteus—flower, fish, reptile, amphibian, bird, dog, etc.—and he is the adversary who hides among the rocks to pounce on Proteus, never letting go his hold, while the old man of the sea writhes through his many shapes until, exhausted by the struggle, he consents to prophesy in the *claritas* of his found identity.

Curiously enough—for I am sure it was not a conscious application—Roethke recapitulated the distinctive elements of this Protean imagery in a prose commentary that appeared in 1950. "Some of these pieces," he wrote in *Mid-Century American Poets*, referring to his sequence of monologues, "Begin in the mire; as if man is no more than a shape writhing from the old rock." His annotation of a line of his from *Praise to the End*—"I've crawled from the mire, alert as a saint or a dog"—reads: "Except for the saint, everything else is dog, fish, minnow, bird, etc., and the euphoric ride resolves itself into a death-wish."

Roethke's explanation of his "cyclic" method of narration, a method that depends on periodic recessions of the movement instead of advances in a straight line, seems to me particularly noteworthy. "I believe," he wrote, "that to go forward as a spiritual man it is necessary first to go back. Any history of the psyche (or allegorical journey) is bound to be a succession of experiences, similar yet dissimilar. There is a perpetual slipping-back, then a going forward; but there is *some* 'progress'."

This comment can be linked with several others by Roethke that I have already quoted: references to "the struggle out of the slime," the beginning "in the mire." I think also of his unforgettably defiant affirmation: "In spite of all the muck and welter, the dark, the *dreck* of these poems, I count myself among the happy poets."

In combination these passages point straight to the door of Dr. Jung or to the door of Jung's disciple Maud Bodkin, whose *Archetypal Patterns in Poetry* was familiar to Roethke. In Jung's discussion of Progression and Regression as fundamental concepts of the libido-theory in his *Contributions to Analytical Psychology*, he describes progression as "the daily advance of the process of psychological adaptation," which at certain times fails. Then "the vital feeling" disappears; there is a damming-up of energy, of libido. At such times neurotic symptoms are observed, and repressed contents appear, of inferior and unadapted character. "Slime out of the depths," he calls such contents—but slime that contains not only "objectionable animal tendencies, but also germs of new possiblities of life." Before "a renewal of life" can come about, there must be an acceptance of the possibilities that lie in the unconscious contents of the mind "activated through regression . . . and disfigured by the slime of the deep."

This principle is reflected in the myth of "the night journey under the sea," as in the Book of Jonah, or in the voyage of The Ancient Mariner, and is related to dozens of myths, in the rebirth archetype, that tell of the descent of the hero into the underworld and of his eventual return back to the light. The monologues of Roethke follow the pattern of progression and regression and belong unmistakably to the rebirth archetype.

In the opening section of *The Lost Son*, for example, the hallucinated protagonist, regressing metamorphically, sinks down to an animistic level, begging from the sub-human some clue as to the meaning of his existence:

> At Woodlawn I heard the dead cry:
> I was lulled by the slamming of iron,
> A slow drip over stones,
> Toads brooding in wells.
> All the leaves stuck out their tongues;
> I shook the softening chalk of my bones,
> Saying,
> Snail, snail, glister me forward,
> Bird, soft-sigh me home.
> Worm, be with me.
> This is my hard time.

At the close of the same poem, which remains for me the finest of the monologues, the protagonist, turned human and adult again, is granted his moment of epiphany; but he is not ready yet to apprehend it wholly; he must wait:

> It was beginning winter,
> The light moved slowly over the frozen field,
> Over the dry seed-crowns,
> The beautiful surviving bones
> Swinging in the wind.
>
> Light traveled over the field;
> Stayed.
> The weeds stopped swinging.
> The mind moved, not alone,
> Through the clear air, in the silence.
>
>> Was it light?
>> Was it light within?
>> Was it light within light?
>> Stillness becoming alive,
>> Yet still?
>
> A lively understandable spirit
> Once entertained you.
> It will come again.
> Be still.
> Wait.

The love poems that followed early in the 1950's—Roethke was forty-four when he married—were a distinct departure from the painul excavations of the monologues and in some respects a return to the strict stanzaic forms of his earliest work. They were daring and buoyant, not only in their explicit sensuality, their "lewd music," but in the poet's open and arrogant usurpation of the Yeatsian beat and, to a degree, of the Yeatsian mantle:

> I take this cadence from a man named Yeats;
> I take it, and I give it back again. . . .

By this time Roethke had the authority, the self-assurance, indeed the euphoria—"I am most immoderately married"—to carry it off.

Even when he had been involved with the *dreck* of the monologues, he was able, in sudden ecstatic seizures of clarity, to proclaim "a condition of joy." Moreover, he had been delighted at the opportunity that the free and open form gave him to introduce juicy little bits of humor, mostly puns and mangled bawdry and indelicate innuendoes. He had also written some rather ferocious nonsense verse for children. Now he achieved something much more difficult and marvelous: a passionate love poetry that yet included the comic, as in *I Knew a Woman*, with its dazzling first stanza:

> I knew a woman, lovely in her bones,
> When small birds sighed, she would sigh back at
>   them;
> Ah, when she moved, she moved more ways than
>   one.
> The shapes a bright container can contain!
> Of her choice virtues only gods should speak,
> Or English poets who grew up on Greek
> (I'd have them sing in chorus, cheek to cheek).

Inevitably the beloved is a shapeshifter, like the poet himself. "Slow, slow as a fish she came." Or again, "She came toward me in the flowing air, a shape of change." "No mineral man," he praises her as dove, as lily, as rose, as leaf, even as "the oyster's weeping foot." And he asks himself, half fearfully: "Is she what I become? Is this my final Face?"

At the human level this tendency of his to become the other is an extension of that Negative Capability, as defined by Keats, which first manifested itself in the Roethke greenhouse. A man of this nature, said Keats, "is capable of being in uncertainties, mysteries, doubt, without any irritable reaching after fact and reason . . . he has no identity—he is continually in for and filling some other body." In "The Dying Man" Roethke assumes the character of the poet Yeats; in "Meditations of an Old Woman," he writes as though he were his mother; in several late poems he adopts the role and voice of his beloved.

The love poems gradually dissolve into the death poems. Could the flesh be transcended, as he had at first supposed, till passion burned with a spiritual light? Could his several selves perish in love's fire and be reborn as one? Could the dear and beautiful one lead him, as Dante taught, to the very footstool of God? In "The Dying Man" he proposes a dark answer: "All sensual love's but dancing on the grave." Roethke thought of himself as one with the dying Yeats: "I am that final thing, a man learning to sing."

The five-fold "Meditations of an Old Woman" that concludes Roethke's selective volume, *Words for the Wind* (1958) is almost wholly preoccupied with thoughts of death and with the search for God. He had started writing the sequence almost immediately after the death of his mother in 1955. Here he returns to the cyclic method of the earlier monologues. In the First Meditation the Old Woman introduces the theme of journeying. All journeys, she reflects, are the same, a movement forward after a few wavers, and then a slipping

backward, "backward in time." Once more we recognize the Jungian pattern of progression and regression embodied in the work. The journeys and the five meditations as a whole are conceived in a kind of rocking motion, and indeed the verb "to rock"—consistently one of the poet's key verbs of motion—figures prominently in the text. The rocking is from the cradle toward death:

> The body, delighting in thresholds,
> Rocks in and out of itself. . . .

An image of transformations. And toward the close:

> To try to become like God
> Is far from becoming God.
> O, but I seek and care!
> I rock in my own dark,
> Thinking, God has need of me.
> The dead love the unborn.

A few weeks before his death Roethke completed his arrangement of some fifty new poems, published last July under the title, *The Far Field*. The range and power of this posthumous volume, unquestionably one of the landmarks of the American imagination, have yet to be fully grasped or interpreted. Among its contents are two major sequences, *The North American Sequence*, consisting of six long meditations on the American landscape and on death . . . on dying into America, so to speak; and a group of twelve shorter, more formal lyrics, under the generic heading, *Sequence, Sometimes Metaphysical*, bearing witness to a state of spiritual crisis, the dance of the soul around the exhausted flesh and toward the divine fire.

"How to transcend this spiritual emptiness?" he cries in "The Longing," which opens the North American sequence. The self, retracing its transformations, seeks refuge in a lower order of being:

> And the spirit fails to move forward,
> But shrinks back into a half-life, less than itself,
> Falls back, a slug, a loose worm
> Ready for any crevice,
> An eyeless starer.

He longs "for the imperishable quiet at the heart of form."

In a sense he has completed his dark journey, but he has not yet found either his oblivion or his immortality. He yearns for the past which will also be future. The American earth calls to him, and he responds by struggling out of his lethargy: "I am coming!" he seems to be saying, "but wait a minute. I have something left to do. I belong to the wilderness. I will yet speak in tongues."

> I have left the body of the whale, but the mouth of
>   the night is still wide;
> On the Bullhead, in the Dakotas, where the eagles
>   eat well,
> In the country of few lakes, in the tall buffalo grass
>   at the base of the clay buttes,
> In the summer heat, I can smell the dead buffalo,
> The stench of their damp fur drying in the sun,
> The buffalo chips drying.
>
>> Old men should be explorers?
>> I'll be an Indian.
>> Ogallala?
>> Iroquoi.

That diminishing coda is a miracle of compression and connotation.

In "The Far Field," the fifth poem of the North American sequence and the title poem of the collection, Roethke speaks of his journeying, as his mother did in the earlier Meditations:

I dream of journeys repeatedly:
Of flying like a bat deep into a narrowing tunnel,
Of driving alone, without luggage, out a long pen-
    insula,
The road lined with snow-laden second growth,
A fine dry snow ticking the windshield,
Alternate snow and sleet, no oncoming traffic,
And no lights behind, in the blurred side-mirror,
The road changing from glazed tarface to a rubble of
    stone,
Ending at last in a hopeless sand-rut,
Where the car stalls,
Churning in a snowdrift
Until the headlights darken.

As always, in these soliloquies, the poet sinks through various levels of time and of existence. There was a field once where he found death in the shape of a rat, along with other creatures shot by the nightwatchman or mutilated by the mower; but he found life, too, in the spontaneous agitations of the birds, "a twittering restless cloud." And he tries to relive his selfhood back to its mindless source, so that he may be born again, meanwhile proclaiming his faith in the inexorable wheel of metamorphosis:

> I'll return again,
> As a snake or a raucous bird,
> Or, with luck, as a lion.

Sometimes the faith wavers. In "The Abyss," a poem outside the North American sequence, he inquires, "Do we move toward God, or merely another condition?" . . . "I rock between dark and dark."

An even deeper anguish saturates the verses of the *Sequence, Sometimes Metaphysical:*

> Dark, dark my light, and darker my desire.
> My soul, like some heat-maddened summer fly,
> Keeps buzzing at the sill. Which I is *I?*

But if the shapeshifter for a moment despairs of his identity, he still has strength and will enough to drag himself over the threshold of annihilation.

> A fallen man, I climb out of my fear.
> The mind enters itself, and God the mind,
> And one is One, free in the tearing wind.

I do not always believe in these ecstatic resolutions—they sometimes seem a cry of need rather than of revelation—but I am always moved by the presence of the need and by the desperation of the voice.

"Brooding on God, I may become a man," writes Roethke in "The Marrow," out of the same sequence—one of the great poems of the century, a poem at once dreadful and profound, electric and shuddering:

> Godhead above my God, are you there still?
> To sleep is all my life. In sleep's half-death,
> My body alters, altering the soul
> That once could melt the dark with its small breath.
> Lord, hear me out, and hear me out this day:
> From me to Thee's a long and terrible way.
>
> I was flung back from suffering and love
> When light divided on a storm-tossed tree;
> Yea, I have slain my will, and still I live:
> I would be near; I shut my eyes to see;
> I bleed my bones, their marrow to bestow
> Upon that God who knows what I would know.

Such furious intensity exacts a price. The selves of the poet could be fused only by the exertion of a tremendous pressure. If only he could be content to name the objects that he loved and not be driven to convert them into symbols—that painful ritual.

In "The Far Field," where he evokes his own valedictory image, Whitman is with him, and Prospero, and—in the shifting light—Proteus, the old man of the sea, fatigued by his changes:

> An old man with his feet before the fire,
> In robes of green, in garments of adieu.

The lines that follow have a touch of prophecy in them as the poet, renewed by the thought of death, leaving his skins behind him, moves out into the life-giving and obliterating waters:

> A man faced with his own immensity
> Wakes all the waves, all their loose wandering fire.
> The murmur of the absolute, the why
> Of being born fails on his naked ears.
> His spirit moves like monumental wind
> That gentles on a sunny blue plateau.
> He is the end of things, the final man.
>
> All finite things reveal infinitude:
> The mountain with its singular bright shade
> Like the blue shine on freshly frozen snow,
> The after-light upon ice-burdened pines;
> Odor of basswood on a mountain slope,
> A scent beloved of bees;
> Silence of water above a sunken tree:
> The pure serene of memory in one man,—
> A ripple widening from a single stone
> Winding around the waters of the world.

STEPHEN SPENDER

"Roethke: The Lost Son"

New Republic, August 27, 1966, pp. 23–25

Theodore Roethke was notoriously a poet of the ego: not the "egotistical sublime" of Wordsworth, but—one can write this today without appearing denigratory—the ego of the alluvial slime. The childhood center of his experience, the great greenhouse of his father's floral gardens, with its roses and orchids and mud and slugs, remained a point of reference for all his later experience. It was the authentic inner "I" one with outer "I" of nature. Roethke could have echoed Wordsworth:

> By day or star-light thus from my first dawn
> Of childhood didst thou intertwine for me
> The passions that built up our human soul.

For Wordsworth, the mountains, stars, clouds, rocks, storms and seasons: but for Roethke:

> I was privy to oily fungus and the algae of standing
>   waters;
> Honored, on my return, by the ancient fellowship of
>   rotten stems.
> I was pure as a worm on a leaf; I cherished the
>   mould's children.
> Beetles sweetened my breath.
> I slept like an insect.

Wordsworth was haunted by his childhood sense of being one with nature. Much of his adult life was spent trying to recapture feelings about the mountains and lakes so intense that later experiences seemed but shadows of them. However, it is a sensation rather than transubstantiation which confronts us with Wordsworth. He gives us impressions of rowing on the lake or climbing the mountains which we seem to feel with the muscles of our bodies. We enter into Wordsworth's poetry so thoroughly, just because he makes us know how it *feels* to be one with nature. He doesn't actually become a mountain or a cloud.

The peculiarity of Roethke is that when he writes about his greenhouse material, he seems, as poet, actually to become it. Or if not to become an insect or a flower, at least, like Alice, to have eaten of the mushroom which reduces him to the scale of the things in whose world he moves:

> The last time I nearly whispered myself away.
> I was far back, farther than anybody else.
> On the jackpine plains I hunted the bird nobody
>   knows;
> Fishing, I caught myself behind the ears.

The resemblance here is not so much to Wordsworth as to Wagner and to some of the more gnomish characters in *The Ring*. For as Nietzsche pointed out, Wagner's true genius lies not in his gigantism, but in his miniatures of the dust in the attic, the disquieting lives that go on in dark corners. Without there being any question of "influence," Roethke sometimes adopts the tone of the Nibelungs working in the deepest caverns of the earth, of Alberich, the dwarf. The wormy, mineral music of Alberich who turns into a serpent, and then into a frog is very close to Roethke. Who but Wagner could set this to music?—

> Pleasure on ground
> Has no sound,
> Easily maddens
> The uneasy man.
>
> Who, careless slips
> In coiling ooze
> Is trapped to the lips,
> Leaves more than shoes;
>
> Must pull off clothes
> To jerk like a frog
> On belly and nose
> From the sucking bog.

This is the world of Alberich: "*Krumm und grau / krieche Kroete!*"

Roethke's greenhouse poetry is not solipsist, because it is about a world in which the objective becomes the subjective. When we read these poems we are more aware of *things*— "The ferns had their ways and the pulsing rivers"—than of the poet's personality. It is the victory of the object over the subject which has made an unconditional surrender to the environment—Rimbaud's *on me pense*. Moreoever Roethke's wholly subjective approach becomes universal and has general applicability because it is, after all, our common mode of perception. Each one of us is an instrument of experience and perception, and the world, as objective experience, is the sum of the perceptions of a great many separate "I's." It is only when an "I" becomes self-reflecting, is aware of its own isolation, treats itself as unique reality, a special case, becomes self-expressive, that an outside spectator observes in all this signs of solipsism.

So paradoxically, it is when Roethke tries to break through his isolation into a life outside himself that we become aware of his compulsive self-obsession. When he is unquestionably imprisoned in his chameleon existence which takes on the coloration of his surroundings, he is the "I" who becomes "the other," of Rimbaud's "*je est un autre.*" But there inevitably is a stage when he becomes aware of the split between the "I" and "the other." Then it becomes a matter of life and death for him to bridge the gulf between insideness and outsideness. The means by which the gulf is to be bridged is, of course, love; and "the other" who can release him from his imprisonment in the self is a woman. When he has discovered his own true voice, Roethke's poetry divides into three distinct phases: the poetry of isolation; the poetry of bridging the gulf of self and not-self; and, thirdly, the poetry of more generally shared experience.

But Roethke never really does escape from his isolation. His poetry celebrates the will to do so, the impulse, the attempt, rather than the achievement. There are moments of triumph. These are exhilarating but always precarious. For this poet to sing "I love another!" means that he has discovered a moment's unison with another, after which he slumps back tragically into himself:

> I sing the wind around
> And hear myself return
> To nothingness, alone.
> The loneliest thing I know;
> Is my own mind at play.
> Is she all of light?
> I sniff the darkening air
> And listen to my own feet.
> A storm's increasing where
> The winds and waters meet.

His love poems have a peculiarly fleeting quality because they celebrate moments of loving, making love, achieved; but the emotion survives the moment not as fusion, but as a felt need. Love is "the dance" and loving is "singing," not just the poet singing, but the beloved joined in his song. It lasts as long as the song. Roethke is sharply different from Wallace Stevens in his failure to turn the emotions realized by his imagination in his poetry into the realities of everyday prose.

The poems of the second phase, in which he celebrates moments of escape into the world outside himself and into love, are extremely moving. They are completely modern in idiom and yet unlike other modern poetry, because most modern poets (Dylan Thomas is an exception), disagreeing with each other about other things, have yet for the most part agreed that poetry should be a weapon of the imagination which will enable them to fight against or come to terms with a world of prose reality. Eliot, Pound, Stevens, Auden, Marianne Moore—Cummings even—all argue in their poetry that worlds of the imagination are as real as the modern prose worlds of science and rationalism. The peculiar appeal of Roethke is that when he manages to transform his poetry from the Wagnerian *Wurm*, he becomes Don Quixote tilting against outside things which are really windmills.

In Don Quixote's mind outside things perform symbolic roles in the drama of inward fantasies. When Roethke writes poetry about his relations with the outside world, he often only rearranges the symbols derived from the garden and the greenhouse so that some of them play roles in a drama of outsideness and insideness, which nevertheless remains interior:

> Fish feed on fish, according to their need;
> My enemies renew me, and my blood
> Beats slower in my careless solitude.
> I bare a wound, and dare myself to bleed.
> I think a bird, and it begins to fly.
> By dying daily, I have come to be.
>
> All exultation is a dangerous thing.
> I see you, love, I see you in a dream;
> I hear a noise of bees, a trellis hum,
> And that slow humming rises into song.
> A breath is but a breath: I have the earth;
> I shall undo all dying by my death.

The idea—if I understand it—is that the poet, through allowing his isolated self to die, enters into that life which is the world outside him. Nevertheless this supposed outside world remains his own creation. Instead of the slug, the bird—but it is only in his imagination that it flies. The bees' humming becomes his song—but for them to become real he has to be singing, he has to invent their reality through the poetry. One dream symbol confronts another like Don Quixote fighting the windmills, but the dream hardly carries through into waking.

If any modern poet corresponds to Goethe's description of the poet as a "sleepwalker" (one keeps coming back, with Roethke, to German examples), it is Roethke. Goethe also suggested that it was dangerous for the sleepwalker to be made aware, through discussion of his poetry in periodicals, of his own development, which should remain unconscious. Reading Arnold Stein's collection of essays on Roethke's poetry (*Theodore Roethke: Essays on the Poetry*, 1965), I suspect that what I myself regard as the comparative failure of Roethke's last poems in the volume *The Far Field* was the result of the pressure of the surrounding contemporary critical atmosphere. In several of the essays in this volume, Roethke's problem is seen as that of achieving "maturity"; and although these were written since his death, he must surely during the latter part of his life have been conscious of the current critical view that his attitudes were immature.

His greenhouse poems, like the poetry of Dylan Thomas, are indeed immature. All the same "maturity" is, to the critics, one of those words directed towards producing a sophisticated kind of intellectual conformism. Whether the reader agrees with me about this, will depend on whether he thinks as I do that much of Roethke's later poetry is simply a skillful exercise in a manner derived from other modern poetry and adapted for the purposes of illustrating Roethke's own dilemmas:

> At the field's end, on the corner missed by the
>   mower,
> Where the turf drops off into a grass-hidden culvert,
> Haunt of the cat-bird, nesting-place of the field-
>   mouse,
> Not too far away from the ever-changing flower-
>   dump,
> Among the tin cans, tires, rusted pipes, broken
>   machinery,
> One learned of the eternal;
> And in the shrunken face of a dead rat, eaten by rain
>   and ground-beetles . . .

This is the Roethkeish greenhouse material adapted to an Eliotish idiom in the manner of *The Rock*. "I suffered for birds, for young rabbits caught in the mower," it goes on, and the "I" has ceased to be identical with the material; it has become the confessional "I" of the modern poet in trouble, waiting to be converted to a metaphysics which will provide him with a "structure" for his poetry, and which will be the product of a "mature" personality. Probably this development is a gain in maturity, but if maturity means loss of the poet's uniqueness, and his becoming top candidate in what is really a school of modern poetry paraphrasing theology, may not the sacrifice be too great? Many readers will disagree, and in doing so they will have the support of the most distinguished critics in Arnold Stein's collection of essays. But I think that Roethke's best poetry came out either of his early self-identification with an almost sub-human world, or his later inability to relate inner and outer worlds satisfactorily through exuberant moments of love-making. When he approaches the "mature" solution which we find in Eliot or Auden, he appears a lesser poet in their intellectual vein, because his genius lay in losing his way

and being able incomparably to express the sense of loss, rather than in finding it along the lines of his great contemporaries. For better or worse, together with Dylan Thomas, he is the lost child of modern poetry.

MICHAEL BENEDIKT
"The Completed Pattern"
Poetry, January 1967, pp. 262–66

Perhaps the thing one is most aware of in looking over Theodore Roethke's *Collected Poems* is the degree of risk courted in the work. Now, risk is not a quality which has been much valued in American poetry in the past quarter-century or so; and it seems to me worth looking at in and for itself. Of course, one might be writing of the very high quality of so many individual poems among this poet's *oeuvre*, but is there anyone who isn't aware of it by now? I should, in short, like to consider Roethke quantitatively, mostly.

Roethke's philosophy and technique were both of a kind seldom to be found in American verse in recent decades. From around the middle of this book and beyond, his view of things is totally that of a kind of mystic. He was really a particularly drastic kind of nature-mystic. He did not even need to be converted to this belief, moreover; from the very first, in such early poems as "The Auction" and "The Sale" he abolished the bric-a-brac of society, tacitly prescribing concentration on nature. In the very first book in this *Collected* he noted: "My truths are all foreknown." Roethke's beliefs did deepen and proliferate, however, first into the relatively ordinary connection with nature to be found in the magnificent early poems about his youth spent around his father's greenhouse (which might be described as the Vatican of Roethke's improvised religion); then into a still closer, and more daring association:

> In a dark wood I saw—
> I saw my several selves
> Come running from the leaves,
> Lewd, tiny, careless lives
> That scuttled under stones, . . .

At about the middle of this large volume nature becomes completely congruent with the lyric of Roethke's intimate thought; and, simultaneously, it occurs to him in force that it is the deepest nature of natural things to perish. "Mouth upon mouth, we sang/My lips pressed upon stone," Roethke once said. Now the intensity of this identification became vastly complicated by his increasing awareness of the imminence of death in all thing, both animate (through conventional expirations) and inanimate (through crumbling—it is symptomatic of Roethke's growing visionary inclination that he seems to have considered both forms as equally significant—as, indeed, according to the rules of atomic physics, they are). His ultimate conclusion was that, given all the foregoing, in the end death doesn't actually matter. "I know, as the dying know,/Eternity is now," he wrote in "The Dying Man." In a poem entitled, significantly, "The Tranced" (which is said to have been one of the poet's very last works) he added:

> Being, we came to be
> Part of eternity
> And what died with us was the will to die.

To have reached this conclusion is not so unconventional either poetically or otherwise ("Father, I'm far from home,/ And I have gone nowhere," he wrote in a gloomy mood in another late poem). What *is* impressive is that he asserted this syndrome of belief in a context of cogitation which actually supports it. Roethke's philosophy is remarkable not only because of its relative rarity among the beliefs of the best recent verse (has anyone noted that he had more than a provisional belief in reincarnation?), but this quality of credibility. When he wrote, also in "The Dying Man" that "I am that final thing,/A man learning to sing," one has an incomparable sense that this writer earned his education; that when in another of his final poems, "The Moment," he noted: "What else to say?/We end in joy," he very much deserved whatever dark laughter he may have had.

Roethke's extraordinary (again, from the viewpoint of most of the best contemporary verse) final philosophy is buttressed not only by a body of work which enabled him to maintain it convincingly, but by the remarkable *terms* of this philosophy: that is to say, by the appropriateness of his poetic technique. What seems to me to characterize the poems above all is a remarkable directness of technique. James Dickey once very eloquently noted, reviewing Roethke's poems, that "one feels guilty of an unjust act, of a dislocation of nature, in referring to them as 'literature' at all". Roethke's storehouse of imagery involved only a few items, which he returned to over and over again as his philosophy evolved, organizing and reorganizing: trees, plants, rocks, animals, a man, Eternity. Some of his best verse (free verse, usually) is of course quite simply descriptive of outward things. The greenhouse poems are justly celebrated, but throughout the work there are free-verse poems each dealing with some single sight or natural object: "Snake," "Siskins," "The Lizard," "The Meadow Mouse," and "The Pike" from his last books, for example. These poems have a power resulting from an ideal fusion of technique and object, so that keenness of observation is matched with phrasings whose proprieties perfectly capture the character of the wriggly-evasive things described. (The well-known "Elegy for Jane" is perhaps the most complex of what I call the descriptive poems, with its astonishing opening lines describing the dead girl with tendrils and pickerel; but it is typical in its strength.) In general, Roethke increasingly elevated his visionary sights, and in one of the last "descriptive" verses in the *Collected*, the relatively earth-bound felicities of technique are placed in the service of a purely visionary goal. *The Thing* thus goes so far as to describe the pursuit of a prey that neither the poet nor his audience can ever really focus on:

> Then the first bird
> Struck;
> Then another, another,
> Until there was nothing left,
> Not even feathers from so far away.

It seems to me that even Roethke's apparently most traditional verses—including such magnificent pieces as "In a Dark Time" and "I Knew a Woman"—are also best readable as direct versions of experience. As has been much remarked, Roethke was devoted, even over-devoted, to a mode of rhymed verse which seems alternately Yeatsian and metaphysical (the fine collection edited by Arnold Stein, *Theodore Roethke: Essays on the Poetry* is particularly excellent on this phase). Still, even here it seems to me that what Roethke was doing was not simply gulping down old modes, but filtering out the essence which he loved: the element of motion, which he associated with dancing, delight, and other reasons for living. It is not surprising that among the older poets he should, in "Four for Sir John Davies," have singled out this writer for special homage, since Davies was not only a near-metaphysical, but another man who appreciated the deeper mean-

ing of dance. And the role of dance in Yeats is, of course, central. In all, the rhymed poems seem to me to differ from the unrhymed poems in degree rather than in kind: while the latter are descriptive of the slow, uncurling motions of natural growth, the rhymed portray more acceleratedly kinetic happenings. Indeed, what could be further from mere metrical or stylistic *pastiche* than "I Knew a Woman":

> Love likes a gander, and adores a goose:
> Her full lips pursed, the errant note to seize;
> She played it quick, she played it light and loose;
> My eyes, they dazzled at her flowing knees;
> Her several parts could keep a pure repose,
> Or one hip quiver with a mobile nose
> (She moved in circles, and those circles moved).
>   . . .
> These old bones live to learn her wanton ways:
> (I measure time by how a body sways).

The deepest and most direct plunges of all occur in the multisectioned poems. They begin early, in the second book *The Lost Son* (1948—the work containing the great greenhouse cycle, also), and may be said to directly transcribe the most intimate motions of the "soul", to use a word of which this poet was boldly but, it seems to me, appropriately fond. The form of these poems is wayward in a fairly familiar way—one thinks at once of the debt to the Eliot *Quartets*, concluded just a few years before. What renders them original is their philosophy and—particularly in the earliest of the poems—their language. It is a combination of pre-verbal gibberish, nursery-rhyme remembrances, just possibly Automatic Writing (such lines as "A tongue without song/—Can still whistle in a jug" remind one of the Surrealist maxims composed by Breton and Eluard). Here Roethke's directness, his ability to risk with respect to his own most intimate self produces a "sound" new to any modern poetry:

> What's this? A dish for fat lips.
> Who says? A nameless stranger.
> Is he a bird or a tree? Not everyone can tell.
> Water recedes to the crying of spiders.
> An old scow bumps over black rocks.
> A cracked pod calls.

In his ability to meditate convincingly upon the mystical realities of natural existence, in seizing the unseen, Roethke has few parallels among poets in English.

SEAMUS HEANEY
"Canticles to the Earth"

Listener, August 22, 1968, pp. 245–46

A couple of years ago, an American poet who is better known as an academic critic told me that he and his generation had rejected irony and artfulness, and were trying to write poems that would not yield much to the suave investigations of the practical criticism seminar. And another poet present agreed, yes, he was now looking at English poetry to decide which areas seemed most in need of renovation, and then he was going to provide experiments that would enliven these sluggish, provincial backwaters. As poets, both seemed to be infected with wrong habits of mind. They had imbibed attitudes into their writing life which properly belong to the lecturer and the anthologist: a concern with generations, with shifting fashions of style, a belief that their role was complementary and responsible to a demonstrable literary situation.

For although at least one spirit of the age will probably be discernible in a poet's work, he should not turn his brain into a butterfly net in pursuit of it.

One thinks of Shakespeare's Poet (I can think of none better) and his right kind of self-consciousness:

> Our poesy is as a gum, which oozes
> From whence 'tis nourish'd: the fire i' the flint
> Shows not till it be struck; our gentle flame
> Provokes itself, and, like the current, flies
> Each bound it chafes.

It is such an awareness of the process, and such a trust in the possibility of his poetry, that a poet should attempt to preserve; and whatever else Roethke may have lacked, he did possess and nourish this trust in his own creative instincts. The spark is not struck from him by circumstances; his current flies continuously:

> Water's my will and my way,
> And the spirit runs, intermittently,
> In and out of the small waves,
> Runs with the intrepid shorebirds—
> How graceful the small before danger!

But the most remarkable thing about this watery spirit of his is that for all its motion, it never altogether finds its final bed and course. Through one half of the work, it is contained in the strict locks and levels of rhyme and stanzaic form; through the other, it rises and recedes in open forms like floods in broad meadows.

His first book has the quiet life of an old canal. 'Vernal Sentiment' would not be an unjust title for the whole collection. All the conflicting elements in Roethke's make-up are toned down and contained in well-behaved couplets and quatrains. The sense of fun is somewhat coy, the sense of natural forces somewhat explicit and the sense of form a bit monotonous. It is partly a case of the young man putting a hand across his daimon's mouth, for although the first poem calls,

> My secrets cry aloud.
> I have no need for tongue.
> My heart keeps open house,
> My doors are widely swung

we have to read the whole book to believe it. Indeed the life's work is neatly bracketed by the first and last lines of this collected volume. We move from 'My secrets cry aloud' to 'With that he hitched his pants and humped away,' and between the rhetoric and the rumbustiousness the real achievement is located.

That real achievement arrives from the boundaries of Roethke's experience: childhood and death are elements in which his best work lives. And love. He grew up in Michigan among his father's extensive greenhouses: 'They were to me, I realise now, both heaven and hell, a kind of tropics created in the savage climate of Michigan, where austere German-Americans turned their love of order and their terrifying efficiency into something truly beautiful. It was a universe, several worlds, which, even as a child, one worried about and struggled to keep alive.'

Growth, minute and multifarious life, became Roethke's theme. His second collection, *The Lost Son*, contained the famous greenhouse poems, a repossession of the childhood Eden. Now the free, nervous notation of natural process issues in a sense of unity with cosmic energies and quiet intimations of order and delight. They are acts of faith made in some state of grace:

> I can hear, underground, that sucking and sobbing,

> In my veins, in my bones I feel it,—
> The small waters seeping upward,
> The tight grains parting at last.
> When sprouts break out,
> Slippery as fish,
> I quail, lean to beginnings, sheath-wet.

Such celebration, however, was prelude to disturbance and desperation. Out of Eden the man must take his solitary way, and beyond the garden life is riotous; chaos replaces correspondence; consciousness thwarts communion, the light of the world will fade in the shadow of death. Until the final serenity and acceptance of all things in a dance of flux, which comes in the posthumous *The Far Field*, Roethke's work is driven in two opposite directions by his fall into manhood.

In the final poems of *The Lost Son* volume and all the work in *Praise to the End* there is an Apocalyptic straining towards unity. These are large, sectioned poems, ghosted by the rhythms of nursery rhyme. You feel that the archetypal properties are being manipulated a bit arbitrarily, that the abrupt syntax is for effect rather than effective and that in general the sense of fractured relations between the man and his physical and metaphysical elements is deliberately shrouded. These poems are more like constructs for the inarticulate than raids upon it. Yet despite the occasional echo of Dylan Thomas, they retain the authentic Roethke note, which is the note of energy and quest:

> Everything's closer. Is this a cage?
> The chill's gone from the moon.
> Only the woods are alive.
> I can't marry the dirt.

In direct contrast to these wandering tides of the spirit, there follows a series of tightly controlled and elaborately argued meditations and love poems. After the fidgety metres and fantastic flings of surrealism, he begins to contain his impulses to affirmation in a rapid, iambic line which owes much to Raleigh and Sir John Davies, even though in a moment of exuberance he declares:

> I take this cadence from a man named Yeats,
> I take it, and I give it back again.

The poems tend to have a strict shape and lively rhythm ('the shapes a bright container can contain!') and deal with the possibility of momentary order, harmony and illumination. Love and lyric are modes of staying the confusion and fencing off emptiness. Within the glass walls of the poem, something of the old paradisal harmony can be feigned:

> Dream of a woman, and a dream of death:
> The light air takes my being's breath away;
> I look on white, and it turns into gray—
> When will that creature give me back my breath?
> I live near the abyss. I hope to stay
> Until my eyes look at a brighter sun
> As the thick shade of the long night comes on.

There is a curious split in Roethke's work between the long Whitmanesque cataloguing poem, which works towards resolution by accumulating significant and related phenomena, and this other brisk, traditional type of artefact that dances to its own familiar music. Perhaps the explanation lies in Roethke's constant natural urge to praise, to maintain or recapture ecstasy.

I think the more relaxed and loaded form includes his best poems, all of which exhale something of a Franciscan love of every living thing, and at the same time invoke the notion of a divine unity working through them. They are canticles to the earth, if you like, written in a line that has exchanged its 'barbaric yawp' for a more civil note of benediction. When, on the other hand, he is not in full possession of his emotion, when tranquility is missing because in Roethke tranquility can only arrive through an act of praise, then he employs the artificer's resources of metre, stanza and rhyme to conduct himself and the poem towards a provisional statement. The stanzaic poems always sound as if they are attempting something. The best Roethke always gives the impression that the lines came ripe and easy as windfalls.

Ripeness is all in the latest work which appeared in this country two years after his death. In one of the poems he mentions 'that sweet man, John Clare', and one is reminded how both poets lived near the abyss but resolved extreme experience into something infinitely gentle. In the light of their last days, 'all's a scattering, a shining.' Their suffering breeds something larger than masochism. Roethke reflects when his field-mouse departs for the hazard of the fields:

> I think of the nestling fallen into the deep grass,
> The turtle gasping in the dusty rubble of the high-
>   way,
> The paralytic stunned in the tub, and the water
>   rising,—
> All things innocent, hapless, forsaken.

He is outside movements and generations, and his work is a true growth. He seems destined to grudging notice because he echoed the voices of other poets, or because people have grown afraid of the gentle note that was his own. But the *Collected Poems* are there, a true poet's testament:

> Pain wanders through my bones like a lost fire;
> What burns me now? Desire, desire, desire.

JAMES DICKEY
"The Greatest American Poet"
Atlantic, November 1968, pp. 53–58

Once there were three men in the living room of an apartment in Seattle. Two of them were present in body, watching each other with the wariness of new acquaintance, and the other was there by telephone. The two in Carolyn Kizer's apartment were Theodore Roethke and I, and the voice was Allan Seager in Michigan. All three had been drinking, I the most, Roethke the next most, and Seager, apparently, the least. After a long-distance joke about people I had never heard of, Roethke said, "Allan, I want you to meet a friend of mine. He's a great admirer of yours, by the way."

I picked up the phone and said, according to conviction and opportunity, "This is Charles Berry."

"This is *who?*"

"Your son, Amos. Charles Berry, the poet."

"The *hell* it is!"

"I thought you might like to know what happened to Charles after the end of the novel. In one way or the other, he became me. My name is James Dickey."

"Well, thanks for telling me. But I had other plans for Charles. Maybe even using him in another novel. I think he did finally become a poet. But not you."

"No, no; it's a joke."

"I had it figured. But it ain't funny."

"Sorry," I said. "I meant it as a kind of tribute, I guess."

"Well, thanks, I guess."

"Joke or not, I think your book *Amos Berry* is a great novel."

"I do too, but nobody else does. It's out of print, with the rest of my stuff."

"Listen," I said, trying to get into the phone, "I doubt if I'd've tried to be a poet if it weren't for Charles Berry. There was no call for poetry in my background, any more than there was in his. But he wanted to try, and he kept on with it. So I did, too."

"How about Amos? What did you think of him?"

"I like to think he's possible. My God! A middle-aged businessman trying to kick off all of industrial society! Get rid of the whole of Western civilization and go it on his own!"

"Yeah, but he failed."

"He failed, but it was a failure that mattered. And the scenes after the rebellious poet-son meets the rebellious father who's just killed his employer and gotten away with it—well, that's a *meeting!* And Amos turns out to be proud of his boy, who's doing this equally insane thing of writing poetry. Right?"

"Sure. Sure he's proud. Like many another, when the son has guts and does something strange and true to what he is. Say, is Ted Roethke still around there?"

"Yes. He's right here. Want to speak to him?"

"No; but he's another one. He's one of those sons. But his father didn't live long enough to know it."

That was my introduction to Allan Seager, a remarkable man and a writer whose works—*Equinox*, *The Inheritance*, *Amos Berry*, *Hilda Manning*, *The Old Man of the Mountain*, *The Death of Anger*, *A Frieze of Girls*—will, as Henry James said of his own, "kick off their tombstones" time after time, in our time and after. His last book and his only biography. *The Glass House*, is this life of Roethke, who is in my opinion the greatest poet this country had yet produced.

During his life and after his death in 1963, people interested in poetry heard a great many rumors about Roethke. Most of these had to do with his eccentricities, his periodic insanity, his drinking, his outbursts of violence, his unpredictability. He came to be seen as a self-destructive American genius somewhat in the pattern of Dylan Thomas. Roethke had a terrifying half-tragic, half-low-comedy life out of which he lifted, by the strangest and most unlikely means, and by endless labors and innumerable false starts, the poetry that all of us owe it to ourselves to know and cherish. If Beethoven said, "He who truly understands my music can never know unhappiness again," Roethke's best work says with equal authority, "He who truly opens himself to my poems will never again conceive his earthly life as worthless."

The Glass House is the record—no, the story, for Seager's novelistic talents give it that kind of compellingness—of how such poetry as Roethke's came to exist. It was written by a man who battled for his whole adult life against public indifference to novels and stories he knew were good, and fought to his last conscious hour to finish this book. Some time after meeting him by telephone, which was in the spring of 1963, I came to know him better, and two summers ago spent a week with him in Tecumseh, Michigan. Most of that time we talked about the biography and about Roethke, and went over the sections he had completed. From the first few words Seager read me, I could tell that this was no *mere* literary biography; there was too much of a sense of personal identification between author and subject to allow for mereness. Seager said to me, in substance, what he had written to a friend some time before this:

> Beatrice Roethke, the widow of Theodore Roethke, has asked me to write the authorized life of her husband. I was in college with him and knew him fairly intimately the rest of his life. It is a book I'd like to do. Quite aside from trying to evoke the character

that made the poetry, there are a good many things to say about the abrasion of the artist in America that he exemplifies. We were both born in Michigan, he in Saginaw, I in Adrian. We both came from the same social stratum. Much of his life I have acted out myself.

Though Seager did not witness the whole process of Roethke's development, not having known the poet in his childhood, he did see a great deal of it, and he told me that he had seen what happened to Roethke happen "in an evolutionary way." More than once he said, "Ted started out as a phony and became genuine, like Yeats." And, "I had no idea that he'd end up as fine a poet as he did. No one knew that in the early days, Ted least of all. We all knew he *wanted* to be a great poet or a great something, but to a lot of us that didn't seem enough. I could have told you, though, that his self-destructiveness would get worse. I could have told you that awful things were going to happen to him. He was headed that way; at times he seemed eager to speed up the process."

I saw Roethke only twice myself. I saw only a sad fat man who talked continually of joy, and although I liked him well enough for such a short acquaintance, came away from him each time with a distinct sense of relief. Like everyone else who knew him even faintly, I was pressed into service in the cause of his ego, which reeled and tottered pathetically at all hours and under all circumstances, and required not only props, but the *right* props. What did I think of Robert Lowell, Randall Jarrell, and "the Eastern literary gang"? What did I think of the "gutless Limey reviewers" in the *Times Literary Supplement?* I spent an afternoon with him trying to answer such questions, before giving a reading at the University of Washington. Carolyn Kizer, an old friend and former student of Roethke's, had given a party the day before the reading, and I was introduced to Roethke there. Though I had heard various things about him, ranging from the need to be honest with him to the absolute need *not* to be honest, I was hardly prepared for the way in which, as Southerners used to say, he "carried on." I was identified in his mind only as the man who had said (in the *Virginia Quarterly Review*, to be exact) that he was the greatest poet then writing in English. He kept getting another drink and bringing me one and starting the conversation over from that point, leading (more or less naturally for him, I soon discovered) into a detailed and meticulously quoted list of what other poets and critics had said about him. I got the impression that my name was added to those of Auden, Stanley Kunitz, Louise Bogan, and Rolfe Humphries not because I was in any way as distinguished in Roethke's mind as they were, but because I had provided him with a kind of *climactic* comment: something he needed that these others hadn't quite managed to say, at least in print. And later, when he introduced me at the reading, he began with the comment, and talked for eight or ten minutes about himself, occasionally mentioning me as though by afterthought. I did not resent this, though I found it curious, and I bring it up now only to call attention to qualities that must have astonished and confounded others besides myself.

Why should a poet of Roethke's stature conduct himself in this childish and embarrassing way? Why all this insistence on being the best, the acknowledged best, the *written-up* best? Wasn't the poetry itself enough? And why the really appalling pettiness about other writers, like Lowell, who were not poets to him but rivals merely? There was never a moment I was with Roethke when I was not conscious of something like this going on in his mind; never a moment when he did not have the look of a man fighting for his life in some way known only to him.

The strain was in the very air around him; his broad, babyish face had an expression of constant bewilderment and betrayal, a continuing agony of doubt. He seemed to cringe and brace himself at the same time. He would glare from the corners of his eyes and turn wordlessly away. Then he would enter into a long involved story about himself. "I used to spar with Steve Hamas," he would say. I remember trying to remember who Steve Hamas was, and by the time I had faintly conjured up an American heavyweight who was knocked out by Max Schmeling, Roethke was glaring at me anxiously. "What the hell's wrong?" he said. "You think I'm a damned liar?"

I did indeed, but until he asked me, I thought he was just rambling on in the way of a man who did not intend for others to take him seriously. He *seemed* serious enough, for he developed the stories at great length, as though he had told them, to others or to himself, a good many times before. Such a situation puts a stranger in rather a tough spot. If he suspects that the story is a lie, he must either pretend to go along with it, or hopefully enter a tacit conspiracy with the speaker in assuming that the whole thing is a joke, a put-on. Unfortunately I chose the latter, and I could not have done worse for either of us. He sank, or fell, rather, into a steep and bitter silence—we were driving around Seattle at the time—and there was no more said on that or any other subject until we reached his house on John Street. I must have been awfully slow to catch on to what he wanted of me, for in retrospect it seems quite clear that he wished me to help protect him from his sense of inadequacy, his dissatisfaction with what he was as a man.

My own disappointment, however, was not at all in the *fact* that Roethke lied, but in the obviousness and uncreativeness of the manner in which he did it. Lying of an inspired, habitual, inventive kind, given a personality, a form, and a rhythm, is mainly what poetry *is*, I have always believed. All art, as Picasso is reported to have said, is a lie that makes us see the truth. There are innumerable empirical "truths" in the world—billions a day, an hour, a minute—but only a few poems that surpass and transfigure them: only a few structures of words which do not so much tell the truth as *make* it. I would have found Roethke's lies a good deal more memorable if they had had some of the qualities of his best poems, and had not been simply the productions of the grown-up baby that he resembled physically. Since that time I have much regretted that Roethke did not write his prizefighting poems, his gangster poems and tycoon poems, committing his art to these as fully as he committed himself to them in conversation. This might have given his work the range and variety of subject matter that it so badly needed, particularly toward the end of his life, when he was beginning to repeat himself: they might have been the themes to make of him a poet of the stature of Yeats or Rilke.

Yet this is only speculation; his poems are as we have them, and many of them will be read as long as words retain the power to evoke a world and to relate the reader, through that world, to a more intense and meaningful version of his own. There is no poetry anywhere that is so valuably conscious of the human body as Roethke's; no poetry that can place the body in an *environment*—wind, seascape, greenhouse, forest, desert, mountainside, among animals or insects or stones—so vividly and evocatively, waking unheard of exchanges between the place and human responsiveness at its most creative. He more than any other is a poet of pure being. He is a great poet not because he tells you how it is with *him*—as, for example, the "confessional" poets endlessly do—but how it can be with you. When you read him, you realize with a great surge of astonishment and joy that, truly, you are not yet dead.

Roethke came to possess this ability slowly. *The Glass House* is like a long letter by a friend, telling how he came to have it. The friend's concern and occasional bewilderment about the subject are apparent, and also some of the impatience that Roethke's self-indulgent conduct often aroused even in those closest to him. But the main thrust of his life, his emergence from Saginaw, Michigan (of all places), into the heroic role of an artist working against the terrible odds of himself for a new vision, is always clear; clearer than it ever was to Roethke, who aspired to self-transcendence but continually despaired of attaining it.

Heroic Roethke certainly was; he struggled against more than most men are aware is possible. His guilt and panic never left him. No amount of praise could ever have been enough to reassure him or put down his sense of chagrin and bafflement over his relationship to his father, the florist Otto Roethke, who died early in Roethke's life and so placed himself beyond reconciliation. None of his lies—of being a nationally ranked tennis player, of having an "in" with the Detroit "Purple Gang," of having all kinds of high-powered business interests and hundred of women in love with him—would ever have shriven him completely, but these lures and ruses and deceptions did enable him to exist, though painfully, and to write; they were the paraphernalia of the wounded artist who cannot survive without them.

These things Seager deals with incisively and sympathetically. He is wonderful on the genesis of the poetry, and his accounts of Roethke's greatest breakthrough, the achievement of what Kenneth Burke calls his "greenhouse line," are moving indeed, and show in astonishing detail the extent to which Roethke lived his poems and identified his bodily existence with them in one animistic rite after another.

> On days when he was not teaching, he moped around Shingle Cottage alone, scribbling lines in his notebooks, sometimes, he told me, drinking a lot as a deliberate stimulus (later he came to see alcohol as a depressant and used to curb his manic states), popping out of his clothes, wandering around the cottage naked for a while, then dressing slowly, four or five times a day. There are some complex "birthday-suit" meanings here, the ritual of starting clean like a baby, casting one's skin like a snake, and then donning the skin again. It was not exhibitionism. No one saw. It was all a kind of magic.

He broke through to what had always been there; he discovered his childhood in a new way, and found the way to tell it, not "like it was" but as it might have been if it included all its own meanings, rhythms, and symbolic extensions. He found, in other words, the form for it; *his* form. Few writers are so obviously rooted (and in Roethke's case the word has special connotations because the poet has so magnificently put them there) in their childhood as Roethke, and Seager shows us in just what ways this was so: the authoritarian Prussian father and his specialized and exotic (especially in frozen, logged-out Saginaw) vocation of florist, the greenhouse, the "far field" behind it, the game park, the strange, irreducible life of stems and worms, the protection of fragile blooms by steam pipes, by eternal vigilance, and by getting "in there" with the plants and working with them as they not only required but seemed to want. Later there are the early efforts to write, the drinking, the first manic states, the terrible depressions, the marriage to Beatrice O'Connell (a former student of his at Bennington), the successive books, the prizes, the recognitions, the travels, the death at fifty-six.

I doubt very much if Roethke will ever have another

biography as good as this one. And yet something is wrong here, even so. One senses too much of an effort to mitigate certain traits of Roethke's, particularly in regard to his relations with women. It may be argued that a number of people's feelings and privacy are being spared, and that may be, as has been adjudged in other cases, reason enough to be reticent. And yet a whole—and very important—dimension of the subject has thereby been left out of account, and one cannot help believing that a writer of Seager's ability and fierce honesty would have found a way to deal with it if he had not been constrained. To his credit, however, he does his best to suggest what he cannot overtly say. For it is no good to assert, as some have done, that Roethke was a big lovable clumsy affectionate bear who just incidentally wrote wonderful poems. It is no good to insist that Seager show "the good times as well as the bad" in anything like equal proportions; these are not the proportions of the man's life. The driving force of him was agony, and to know him we must know all the forms it took. The names of people may be concealed; but the incidents we must know. It is far worse to leave these matters to rumor than to entrust them to a man of Seager's integrity.

Mrs. Roethke, in especial, must be blamed for this wavering of purpose, this evasiveness that was so far from Seager's nature as to seem to belong to someone else. It may be that she has come to regard herself as the sole repository of the "truth" of Roethke, which is understandable as a human—particularly a wifely—attitude, but is not pardonable in one who commissions a biography from a serious writer. Allan Seager was not a lesser man than Roethke, someone to be sacrificed to another writer's already overguarded reputation. As a human being he was altogether more admirable than his subject. He was a hard and devoted worker, and he believed deeply in this book; as he said, he had acted out much of it himself. If he hadn't spent the last years of his life on *The Glass House*, he might have been able to finish the big novel he had been working on for years. As it was—thanks again to Mrs. Roethke, who, in addition to other obstacles she placed in Seager's way, even refused him permission to quote her husband's poems—he died without knowing whether all the obstacles had been removed.

Certainly this is a dreadful misplacement of loyalty, for Roethke deserves the monument that this book could have been. He had, almost exclusively by his art, all but won out over his babydom, of which this constant overprotectiveness on the part of other people was the most pernicious part. He deserved to be treated, at last, as a man as well as a great poet. And it should be in the *exact* documentation of this triumph—this heroism—that we ought to see him stand forth with no excuses made, no whitewash needed. Seager had all the gifts: the devotion to his subject, the personal knowledge of it, the talent and the patience and the honesty, and everything but the time and the cooperation, and above all, the recognition of his own stature as an artist with a great personal stake in the enterprise. He died of lung cancer last May.

Since I was close to the book for some time, I am bound to be prejudiced; I am glad to be. Even allowing for prejudice, however, I can still say that this is the best biography of an American poet I have read since Philip Horton's *Hart Crane*, and that it is like no other. God knows what it would have been if Allan Seager had had his way, had been able to do the job he envisioned, even as he lay dying.

FREDERICK J. HOFFMAN
"Theodore Roethke: The Poetic Shape of Death"
Modern American Poetry: Essays in Criticism
ed. Jerome Mazzaro
1970, pp. 301–20

The poetry of Theodore Roethke describes four stages in the development of what he intended it to say. While this may not be a sensational truth, the intensity with which Roethke engages in each of the stages marks both it and him as exceptional. From the second volume (*The Lost Son*) on, Roethke made his verse his own, inscribed it with the signature of his inimitable temperament and fancy.

We might as well define these stages at the very beginning: they relate to a prenatal condition, to childhood, to the move toward maturity, and to the contemplation of the conditions and implications of death. Throughout, there is an overlapping of one upon the other, a spiral turning back, a reach for self-definition. More than normally, Roethke was overtaken by the fancies of childhood and by the fear of being forced out of that state, with no reliable surrogates for "papa" and "mama." The poems therefore abound in talk comparable to a semi-intelligible child's garble, a language in itself designed to induce security (because of its identification with a time when he *was* secure):

> Mips and ma the mooly moo,
> The likes of him is biting who,
> A cow's a care and who's a coo?—
> What footie does is final.
>
> My dearest dear my fairest fair,
> Your father tossed a cat in air,
> Though neither you nor I was there,—
> What footie does is final.
>
> Be large as an owl, be slick as a frog,
> Be good as a goose, be big as a dog,
> Be sleek as a heifer, be long as a hog,—
> What footie will do will be final.
>   ("Praise to the End!")

Roethke's poetry is one of the most exhaustive, vital, and vivid reports we have of a soul in the several agonies normally recorded in one human life. The intensity results from an absorption in a form of subliminal nature, a deep sense of the most elementary agonies attending the process and the necessity of living. But it has other causes as well. Roethke impressed both his friends and readers profoundly as a human being, almost overwhelmingly "present," in his person as in his poetry. When I saw him in the summer of 1957, I had been teaching a seminar at the University of Washington on the subject that led to the publication of *The Mortal No.* He told me then that he was much concerned with the mysteries and paradoxes of death, and that his new poetry reflected these concerns. It did just that; and the meditative poems that appeared in *Words for the Wind* and, recently, in *The Far Field* demonstrate this interest remarkably. Nowhere in modern American poetry are the metaphysically speculative and the naturally commonplace so well balanced, so reciprocal in effect.

I want especially to notice these two aspects of Roethke's verse: the "metaphysical fusion" I have spoken of and the effect upon it of the puzzle of death—not so much the expectation of it, but the exhausting contemplation of its curious nature and the struggle to define it in public terms.

Roethke was at the beginning so engrossed with the wonder of his origins—and of the origins of life—that his poetry described a spiral of flight, fear, and return; the place itself can be characterized as the condition of "underness," which exists "everywhere." In *Open House* (more formally written and imitative than his other work) there is little we may call characteristic of Roethke. Like most first volumes, it offers only clues as to his future direction, though it scarcely even serves for this purpose. Like a hundred others, the poem "Death Piece" states a general condition of insentience, without localizing it or investing it with emotional energy:

> Invention sleeps within a skull
> No longer quick with light,
> The hive that hummed in every cell
> Is now sealed honey-tight.
>
> His thought is tied, the curving prow
> Of motion moored to rock;
> And minutes burst upon a brow
> Insentient to shock.

Only with *The Lost Son* were his characteristic rhetorical gestures revealed. These have, of course, been much discussed: as a "peculiar balance of the natural and the artificial . . . ";[1] as describing the "agony of coming alike, the painful miracle of growth . . . ";[2] as a form of "Noh" monologue, in which, "wearing a mask painted with a fixed smile of pain, he visits a pond in a wood which is haunted by a nymph-like ghost, and performs a very slow and solemn pirouetting dance, . . . "[3]

Of course, the greenhouse provides the scene and source of all the poems in this volume and of many others. Roethke shows a remarkable awareness of the scene, as well as a sensitivity to its every conceivable affective meaning. He always reacts precisely and meaningfully to it, as a person deeply committed to it in memory and making it the basis of all meditations. The greenhouse has a peculiar usefulness as a microcosm of subhuman life. Within its vivid forms, a number of effects reside: the specially created climatic conditions, the *schwärmerei* of plant life awaiting the "knock" of attention and the flow of warmth which help their growth, and the artificially created "edenic" conditions which guarantee that freshness, beauty, and purity (the rose, the carnation) will survive.

Most of all, the image of "papa" dominates:

> That hump of a man bunching chrysanthemums
> Or pinching-back asters, or planting azaleas,
> Tamping and stamping dirt into pots,—
>   ("Old Florist")

As God, "papa" gives life and endows it with order, separating the good from the expendable nongood, "weeding" impurities from this floral Eden:

> Pipe-knock.
> Scurry of warm over small plants.
> Ordnung! ordnung!
> Papa is coming!
>
> > A fine haze moved off the leaves;
> > Frost melted on far panes;
> > The rose, the chrysanthemum turned
> >   toward the light.
> > Even the hushed forms, the bent
> >   yellowy weeds
> > Moved in a slow up-sway.
> >   ("The Return")

Roethke believed the "papa principle" to be indispensable to a forthgoing knowledge. Many of the poems in the volumes beginning with *The Lost Son* characteristically struggle to escape the "slime," the "loam," the level of prenatal existence; in short, they offer a portrayal of what Roethke called "an effort to be born, and later, to become something more."[4] Both being born and becoming "something more" are disturbed by the agonies of self-assertion and of separating the self from its prenatal associations. The language at this point is almost without abstraction, as indeed that of a small child is: full of long vowel sounds, one-syllabled words which label, questions for which there seems to be no answer. But the poems show a progression nevertheless. Roethke spoke of the need "first to go back," in order eventually to go forward ("Open Letter," p. 69). The poems move chiefly from dark (the "underness" that exists everywhere) to light: or, from the dark recesses of the almost entirely quiescent self, to the world where the light requires an activity of the mind, what he called "spirit" or "soul."

The basic natural origin is defined in terms of "Shoots dangled and drooped, / Lolling obscenely from mildewed crates"; "Even the dirt kept breathing a small breath." The leaf gives us a primary natural image of life; extended, it suggests the hand, and when the body dies, the hand has the appearance of a leaf deprived of its source of life. This deprivation resembles the kind of separation suffered by a leaf cut away from its tree, a flower taken from its sustaining soil. The title poem of *The Lost Son* describes the full experience of struggling to be—in this case, to be born, then to be, then simply once again to return to the being of the nearly born. The imagery describes the fear which accompanies the spiral movement; the agony of Part One is described in terms of a "going forth" in doubt and fear, like the birth of any organic being. The "under" side demonstrates its reality even more powerfully and persuasively than the outside.

> Where do the roots go?
>   Look down under the leaves.
> Who put the moss there?
>   These stones have been here too long.
> Who stunned the dirt into noise?
>   Ask the mole, he knows.
> I feel the slime of a wet nest.
> Beware Mother Mildew.
> Nibble again, fish nerves.
>
> ("The Pit")

But, along with these apparently simple queries, the poet suggests a growing awareness of the outer world. We stand "out there" when we look back upon the minimal life we have left. Ultimately, Roethke's protagonist (his "I," who comes very close to being himself) sees the natural world formally, as in the beginning of winter, when we so often acutely sense the quality of forms and surfaces, since the "underness" is quieted.

> Light traveled over the wide field;
> Stayed.
> The weeds stopped swinging.
> The mind moved, not alone,
> Through the clear air, in the silence.
>
> ("It was beginning winter.")

In time, this condition of silence will become symbolically contained, like and yet very different from the various stillnesses of T. S. Eliot's *Four Quartets*. Roethke's achievements of silence always indicate a move out of the noise, the thickness, the confusion of life (or a meaningful pause in it), while Eliot's seem forever to dominate life and to force it into a subsidiary and symbolic *ménage*.

These movements occur in much of Roethke's verse: the move outward ("Mother me out of here . . ."); the desire to return, for reinforcing sustenance, the occasional sense of quiet "at the centre" ("A rose sways least. / The redeemer comes a dark way."), and not always, but with increasing

frequency—a feeling of perfection, in which the noise of living lessens and one may contemplate the condition of life as a symbolically "free" condition:

> To know that light falls and fills, often without our
>   knowing,
> As an opaque vase fills to the brim from a quick
>   pouring,
> Fills and trembles at the edge yet does not flow over,
> Still holding and feeding the stem of the contained
>   flower.
>
> ("The Shape of the Fire")

The movement in Roethke's verse becomes more complicated, as the poetry itself becomes more meditative, more "metaphysically extended." It reaches out beyond the greenhouse world, but always with a sense of the need to return. *Praise to the End!* reminds us of the full cycle. Roethke's mind and sensibility were formed by the greenhouse experience, and most of his poems remind us of the poet's memories. He chose the title of his next book not so much to call our attention to Wordsworth's view of nature as to emphasize his own uniquely separate position. I cite enough lines from the 1805–1806 version of *The Prelude* to give some sense of the strange relationship:

>   . . . Praise to the end!
> Thanks likewise for the means! But I believe
> That Nature, oftentimes, when she would frame
> A favor'd Being, from his earliest dawn
> Of infancy doth open out the clouds,
> As at the touch of lightning, seeking him
> With gentlest visitation; not the less,
> Though haply aiming at the self-same end,
> Does it delight her sometimes to employ
> Severer interventions, ministry
> More palpable, and so she dealt with me.

The phrase which begins this quotation denotes a happy gratification over the sense of being that Wordsworth enjoys through the act of Nature upon his being; he is surprised that he should have "come through" so well, that the fears he suffered in the past should have anything to do with the making of "The calm existence that is mine when I / Am worthy of myself! . . . "[5] In one sense, Roethke's use of the phrase suggests a stage in his growth, though his sense of nature strikes us as far more "intimate," direct, and imagistic than Wordsworth's. The formalities of Roethke's verse and attitude, however, did increase with the publication of *Praise to the End!*[6] He was more and more drawn to a consideration of "last things," and the title phrase (as did Wordsworth's use of it) expressed surprise that nature should have permitted him to meditate about them seriously.

The verse bespeaks a genuine maturing. Beginning with *Praise*, Roethke followed the practice of combining selections from earlier volumes with new poems, to suggest the spiral or cyclic progression he had mentioned in his "Open Letter." But "progress" showed more obviously in the new poems, and the quality of memory changed. With the death of "papa" ("He was all whitey bones / And skin like paper"), a change occurred in the image of Godhood ("God's somewhere else"), which came more and more closely to resemble an independent self ("I'm somebody else now"). The responsibilities of the new self are seen everywhere. The echoes of childhood phrases slowly give way to the need of being—without regret—independently oneself. "There's no alas / Where I live" recalls the blessed simplicities of a childhood he finds it hard to give up. But the image of himself as "standing up" and alone ("When I stand, I'm almost a tree") appears more frequently than before. He defines himself in a new status through many devices:

> We'll be at the business of what might be
> Looking toward what we are. . . .
> I've played with the fishes
> Among the unwrinkling ferns
> In the wake of a ship of wind;
> But now the instant ages,
> And my thought hunts another body.
>
> ("Give Way, Ye Gates")

The other body offers both another meaning of self and another self. Roethke is involved both in his own maturing and in his finding another person, whose love will illuminate his own identity. His Dante must also know a Beatrice. He needs to take a long and fearsome journey to "somewhere else," but he is willing to assume the risks.

> Has the dark a door?
> I'm somewhere else,—
> I insist!
> I am.
>
> ("Sensibility! O La!")

"Praise to the End!" provides an especially revealing and significant statement of his new role, his "progress." The elements of nature (not Wordsworth's respected, capitalized Nature) remain, as do the childish sounds (moo–who–coo; frog–dog–hog); but the poet speaks mainly of the need to "separate": "I conclude! I conclude! / My dearest dust, I can't stay here." In his escape from the "under world" of the greenhouse, the poet retains the belief the natural world has given him. But he is also aware of the crisis of separation, the threat to childhood security:

> I have been somewhere else; I remember the sea-
> faced uncles.
> I hear, clearly, the heart of another singing,
> Lighter than bells,
> Softer than water.

The experience with nature now demands a transition to "somewhere else." "I can't crawl back through those veins, / I ache for another choice." Roethke calls to the small things of his past, to "sing" as symbols. Nature must become "A house for wisdom; a field for revelation." He has, in other words, found the need for other meanings, for ways of defining himself through others than "papa," in a world wider than Woodlawn.

The poet needs also to find another vocabulary, to reinforce the old one. The respect for life remains, but he approaches it obliquely, sometimes even with the aid of "literary" and "metaphysical" reflections. The famous sequence, "Four for Sir John Davies," refers to a sixteenth-century English poet, whose Spenserian poem, "Orchestra" (1596), attempts to present nature in a universal dance, or a solemn, orderly motion.[7] The importance of the sequence depends primarily upon its full commitment to sexual involvement. Roethke sees the sexual act as both a move away from the simplicities of childish "aloneness" and "an harmonious" recovery of life. The third step is now achieved. The poet sees love at the moment as not wearisome but rich in pleasure and delights. Moreover, we are aware of a "standing with"—a dancing with, a partnership. The "I" changes to "we" in this maneuver; the delights are not unmixed with doubt and wonder, but they seem to be a profitable means of sending the self toward that "somewhere else" that Roethke had earlier called "far away."

> Incomprehensible gaiety and dread
> Attended what we did. Behind, before,

> Lay all the lonely pastures of the dead;
> The spirit and the flesh cried out for more.
> We two, together, on a darkening day
> Took arms against our own obscurity.
>
> ("The Wraith")

Roethke uses a new vocabulary, even a newly formal verse pattern. The end pauses usually remain; but, the idea being more complex, the phrase which includes it enlarges. For at least a moment in his time, he pauses to speculate upon love, as later he will meditate upon dying, in the fashion of the modern "metaphysical poet," a John Crowe Ransom, probably more than an Allen Tate. Having chosen "desire" as a device for extending the range of self-definition, he must now define the word and overcome his doubts concerning its value. It is scarcely reassuring to know that "two" are more than "one" in the effort to shut out "our own obscurity," unless the "two" can become permanently a One in the economy of life. Beyond the dissolution of the two lies death; the danger of annihilation is already genuinely present, even in the most pleasant conditions. At least momentarily the union seems to hold:

> Did each become the other in that play?
> She laughed me out, and then she laughed me in;
> In the deep middle of ourselves we lay; . . .

The fourth poem of the sequence speaks even more confidently of the ministering effectiveness of love. Speaking of Dante's being blinded by the inner light of the Paradiso, Roethke defines it as the light of love, reducing it to love itself and to the verbal trickeries by which it is embellished and exalted. "All lovers live by longing, and endure: / Summon a vision and declare it pure."

The lovers "undid chaos to a curious sound"; the "I" of Roethke's world hopes now to give "thought" to "things," to work on the assumption that "We think by feeling . . .": that is, that we endow things, and acts, with ideal virtues by living and feeling them (or, by acting in a "necessary conjunction," in the spirit of Eliot's "East Coker").

Love assists in our fight to postpone death; it is also a testimony of Godhood. As a form of dying, love at least momentarily pushes the threat of dying out of mind. The protagonist concludes the *Waking* volume in a simple, calm assertion.

> Light takes the Tree; but who can tell us how?
> The lowly worm climbs up a winding stair;
> I wake to sleep, and take my waking slow.
>
> ("The Waking")

Love remains an important human gesture in *Words for the Wind*. The lover speaks again and again of the newly achieved confidence his love has given him. His cries are no longer prompted by fear, but by delight: ". . . I know / The root, the core of a cry." The title poem, from which this quotation comes, continues in a mood of frankly innocent confidence:

> I kiss her moving mouth,
> Her swart hilarious skin;
> She breaks my breath in half;
> She frolics like a beast;
> And I dance round and round,
> A fond and foolish man,
> And see and suffer myself
> In another being, at last.

The open sensuality remains a prominent element in the wit of "I Knew a Woman":

> She was the sickle; I, poor I, the rake,
> Coming behind her for her pretty sake
> (But what prodigious mowing we did make).

The thought of death is not precluded by the performance of love; it is only postponed, if even that. The sacrifice of the self to another yields much pleasure; but the Roethkean "I" eventually allows death to intrude: at first, by reconverting what was once a pure pleasure into a human gesture of dubious value. "The Sensualists" suggest a surfeit of love—in other words, the conclusion that it cannot always, entirely, put aside the thought of death. The lovers are, in fact, like Ransom's of "The Equilibrists," doomed to live in a prison of their love:

> "The bed itself begins to quake,
> I hate this sensual pen;
> My neck, if not my heart, will break
> If we do this again,"—
> Then each fell back, limp as a sack,
> Into the world of men.

With the apparent failure of love, the old questions return; only, now they seem more importunate, and the answers cannot be disguised in sentiment or in fantasy. Loving offers the last barrier to the thought of dying. The protagonist more than ever despairs of his power to define life and himself; he needs to do the first to prepare for death, the second in order personally to bear it. His thoughts return briefly to "papa"; his intellect inquires if "form" will help to limit himself. "Papa" had once been sufficient to pull the weeds from what the poet as God principle had wanted to survive. Now Roethke's "I" needs some formal way of saving himself from sensual chaos:

> I know I love, yet know now where I am;
> I paw the dark, the shifting midnight air.
> Will the self, lost, be found again? In form?
> I walk the night to keep my five wits warm.
> ("The Renewal")

Such a failure should now appear inevitable, a consequence of the physical circumstances of love. For, in the true "metaphysical" consensus of love, the individual dying was always associated with the final thrust of death, as in John Donne's "Canonization" ode. But in Roethke's poems the particulars of love are almost always linked to the past: to the warm, moist, subliminal world of the womb that sponsored all living and the "papa" who sustained it. He can only cry, "Father, I'm far from home, / And I have gone nowhere," and "I fear for my own joy." The failure is accompanied by the recurring imagery of the past and by the son's renewed fears. Father had been "Father of flowers"; but the son combines "several selves" which reflect at first "Lewd, tiny, careless lives / That scuttled under stones," and he eventually becomes "myself, alone."

He has finally to persuade himself of death. The poem "The Dying Man" is dedicated to Yeats, but actually the Roethke persona looks firmly at "Death's possibilities." Now, he sees dying as a continual becoming; this knowledge, of growth as a move toward mortality, is indispensable to the adjustment. The great poem of *Words*, "Meditations of an Old Woman," combines gracefully and skillfully the two vocabularies Roethke had developed, the "natural" and the "metaphysical." Once again, "The weeds hiss at the edge of the field"; but the old woman can no longer claim a superiority to the small natural particulars (when they do not frighten her, they bore her):

> I've become a strange piece of flesh,
> Nervous and cold, bird-furtive, whiskery,
> With a cheek soft as a hound's ear.

> What's left is light as a seed;
> I need an old crone's knowing.
> ("First Meditation")

This remarkable poem admits all types of encounter with mortality. The old woman, on the edge of death, has only her "meditations" to help her tolerate the expectation. She must, finally, learn to "sit still," in the spirit of Eliot's *Ash-Wednesday*, but without theological assurances. For, in her extremity, she must seek in the familiar details of nature the substitute for a god. "In such times," she says, thinking of the sights and smells and sounds of her past life, "lacking a god, / I am still happy." Yet she finds it difficult to speak of a soul, because in Roethke the soul must always somehow be activated; it cannot rest merely on a theological premise.

> The soul knows not what to believe,
> In its small folds, stirring sluggishly,
> In the least place of its life,
> A pulse beyond nothingness,
> A fearful ignorance. [8]
> ("What Can I Tell My Bones?")

In the end, the old woman lives only in dread of the rational view of death, and hopes that she may find some escape from its implications.

> I rock in my own dark,
> Thinking, God has need of me.
> The dead love the unborn.
> ("What Can I Tell My Bones?")

She expresses a sense of renewal in her final observations: as though nature will reclaim her in allowing others to be born, as though she were for a valiant moment "Anna Livia Plurabelle." Roethke is a poet who finds it unimaginable to rest with any large denial of life.

The Far Field demonstrates the extent to which Roethke had defined death to himself before the summer of 1963. The poems, or some of them, also testify to the agony of moving toward the threshold of death. I do not mean to say that the thought of death was constantly with him, but only that he suffered a type of "dark night" and that it was partly caused by his being unable to will a transcendence that he could also will to believe in. The "congress of stinks" of *The Lost Son* here becomes

> A kingdom of stinks and sighs,
> Fetor of cockroaches, dead fish, petroleum,
> Worse than castoreum of mink or weasels,
> Saliva dripping from warm microphones,
> Agony of crucifixion on barstools.
> ("The Longing")

There is reason to believe that Roethke suffered these agonies because (1) the world of "papa" no longer enlightened or assured him; and (2) he failed to secure consolation in the pleasures of what he called ". . . the imperishable quiet at the heart of form." But I also suspect that, occasionally at least, he saw—perhaps forced himself to see—the possibility of the flesh's assuming the role of the spirit. The image of water, which in *The Lost Son* was made equivalent to "Money money money," now more frequently takes on the conventional symbolic aspects of death and the soul:

> Water's my will, and my way,
> And the spirit runs, intermittently,
> In and out of the small waves,
> Runs with the intrepid shorebirds—
> How graceful the small before danger!
> ("Meditation at Oyster River")

However improvised this metaphor appears to be, it will certainly play an important role in the ultimate critical assessment of Roethke's work. With much of the evidence in, he appears to me to have alternated between the fear of death which his doubt of immortality forced upon him and the speculative pleasure in his own power of transcendence. I do not think this is an "aesthetic" power solely, or entirely, because much of the prospect of transcendence had to be willed; that is, his pleasure in the metaphors of transcendence undoubtedly was earned by a strong effort of the will.[9]

Ultimately, Roethke seems to have come back to a peculiarly American "stance," the Emersonian confidence in *seeing* the spirit in matter, also, in a sense, in *creating* matter (or forming it) through the power of the transcending will. Much more than Emerson's,[10] Roethke's mind was drenched in particulars. He had at the beginning to move away from them, in order to notice his own identity, to "be himself." The "papa" principle had eventually to yield to the search for adequate limits of self, simply because "papa" had died. Momentarily, he found a surrogate definition in the physical nature of love; when his confidence in this ceased, he was forced alternately to meditate upon the end of a temporal process and to will transcendence of it.

"In a Dark Time" illustrates the conditions persuasively. The "dark time" has several applications: to the darkness of "underness" which he found everywhere; to the darkness of despair that came to him when he found that he had alone both to define and to defend himself; and, of course, to the time of death, of what he calls "the deepening shade" and "the echoing wood." He conceives of himself as both creating (as in the poem) and living in the world of nature. Such a union of living and "making live" may surely be considered an act of voluntary creativity, in which the creator exists, surrounded by his creatures; the latter survive partly in his memory, but are refined in his having remembered them. As he has said in his "comment," the heron and the wren, the "beasts of the hill and serpents of the den," ought not to be thought of as either emblematic or strange, but rather as a part of his own experience. One may do too much by way of endowing Roethke as a "son of Blake," or of Yeats, or whomever.

The "madness" is a condition of the soul. One nurses his idiosyncrasies at his own peril, but there is nothing "mad" about his accommodation to the fact and the necessities of "the dark time." He is on the "edge" of meaning, looks out upon "that place among the rocks. . . ." Naturally, in consequence of the evidence we have already examined, he is assaulted by, not only a "congress of stinks," but "A steady storm of correspondences!" These are not unlike Baudelaire's "vivants piliers," which "Laissent parfois sortir de confuses paroles"; but Roethke does not want to be thought either "theoretical" or pompous about them. In fact, the analogical necessity is derived not from them in themselves, but from his need to stand apart from them and to strengthen both his facility of inference and his power of implication.

Ultimately, the issue becomes one of maneuvering within the circumstances of his mortality.

> A man goes far to find out what he is—
> Death of the self in a long, tearless night,
> All natural shapes blazing unnatural light.

The beautiful simplicity of these lines is convincing because they come at the end of a long career of defining self, a time during which the quest of the "I" has been dramatized brilliantly again and again. But the poet indicates not only a quest for "self-definition," despite the question, "Which I is

I?" He as much strives to escape the multiplicity of selves, the "storm of correspondences," as he does to steady himself for the prospect that *all* selves disintegrate, that death happens to all of them.

So, we have the brilliant final stanza, with its quzzicality of Emily Dickinson ("My soul, like some heat-maddened summer fly, / Keeps buzzing at the sill. . . ."), and its apparent Emersonian affirmation:

> A fallen man, I climb out of my fear.
> The mind enters itself, and God the mind,
> And one is One, free in the tearing wind.

As Roethke has said, these lines are far from the forced improvisation they have been accused of being:

> The moment before Nothingness, before near anni-hilation, the moment of supreme disgust is the worst: when change comes it is either total loss of con-sciousness—symbolical or literal death—or a quick break into another state, not necessarily serene, but frequently a bright blaze of consciousness that trans-lates itself into action.[11]

The "fallen man" is the self that has gone the long way toward deprivation; he recalls not only "the lost son" but the son of a dead father, and he must therefore find a way of making significant use of himself. He climbs "out of [his] fear," in the manner that we have watched so often in Roethke's books. He is that loathsome thing, the fly, what he has called "a disease-laden, heat-maddened fly—to me a more intolera-ble thing than a rat."[12] Surely no one will hesitate to grant him the choice. In any case, the fly is Emily Dickinson's only in *being* a fly; for her the insect is not loathsome because it serves as the *décor* of mortality.

If we grant Roethke the right to his first metaphors, we find it difficult not to permit him the concluding ones—despite the fact that these are more suddenly (or at least, more unexpectedly) grasped. The mind's entering itself seems to me to be Roethke's steady concern. Far from a solipsistic condition, or a madly egocentric one, what we have is the process of self-examination which all of us come to when we need to "stand aside," when we abandon the "papa principle" or it abandons us. We are less certain that God enters the mind. Roethke points out that God is not customarily supposed, by the "hot-gospelers," to enter the mind, but rather invades the heart.

In any case, the final line offers a neat possibility: if, after God enters the mind (not the heart or the liver, or even the soul), "one is One," then we may assume that the mind (with the help of God, perhaps) changes the "one" to the "One." To conceive of this change requires both creative ingenuity and daring. For the soul is "free in the tearing wind," and this freedom can scarcely be envied or ideally desired.

At least in terms of the evidence, Roethke has come the long way, to climb out of both his fear of chaos and his trust in easy and comfortable confidences, and to stand in the place of "papa," ministering not so much to the many as to the One he has himself created. Perhaps the idea strikes us as fanciful; but one can, I am sure, be too much handicapped by logical or even eschatological necessity, to see the neatness and convinc-ingness with which "In a Dark Time" stands as a genuine resolution of the mazes caused by life and the problems created by the expectation of death. Roethke's death, seen in the light of this *mort accomplie*, most properly sets the seal to his life, in terms of the imaginative brilliance and the moral courage which dominate and direct his poetry.

Notes

1. Kenneth Burke, "The Vegetal Radicalism of Theodore Roethke," *Sewanee Review*, LVI (Winter, 1950), 82.
2. Stanley Kunitz, "News of the Root," *Poetry*, LXXIII (January, 1949), 225.
3. Stephen Spender, "Words for the Wind," *New Republic*, CXLI (August 10, 1959), 22.
4. "Open Letter," in *Mid-Century American Poets*, ed. John Ciardi (New York, 1950), p. 68.
5. William Wordsworth, *The Prelude*, ed. Ernest de Selincourt and Helen Darbishire (Oxford, 1959), p. 22.
6. I do not mean that the verse became "classical." If anything, the use of the free line, controlled almost invariably by either end punctuation or caesural pause, increased; and the characteristic vigor remained much in evidence.
7. See Ralph Mills, *Theodore Roethke* (Minneapolis, 1963), pp. 31–35, for a discussion of this indebtedness.
8. Ultimately, in these "Meditations," Roethke arrives at the biblical phrase, "Do these bones live?" which Eliot made prominent in Part Two of "Ash-Wednesday." Roethke's woman is concerned not so much with the promise of resurrection which they originally suggested but rather with the old woman's power to speak *to* them. The title of this, the last section of the long poem, is "What Can I Tell My Bones?"
9. I should maintain this despite his statement that the last two lines of "In a Dark Time" were the product of pure inspiration. "This was a dictated poem," he said in 1961, "something given, scarcely mine at all. For about three days before its writing I felt disembodied, out of time; then the poem virtually wrote itself, on a day in summer, 1958." "The Poet and His Critics," ed. Anthony Ostroff, *New World Writing*, XIX (1961), 214.
10. Whom he might well have had in mind when he wrote "Prayer before Study":

   > A fool can play at being solemn
   > Revolving on his spinal column.
   >
   > Deliver me, O Lord, from all
   > Activity centripetal.

11. "The Poet and His Critics," pp. 217–218.
12. Ibid., p. 217.

RICHARD A. BLESSING
"Theodore Roethke: A Celebration"

Tulane Studies in English, 1972, pp. 169–80

Theodore Roethke was ever one to appreciate the process by which complaint becomes celebration, by which a tirade turns to kissing. He would have understood, I hope, my beginning a celebration of his poetry with a complaint—another man's complaint—against it. "We have," writes M. L. Rosenthal,

> no other modern American poet of comparable reputation who has absorbed so little of the concerns of his age into his nerve-ends, in whom there is so little reference direct or remote to the incredible experiences of the age—unless the damaged psyche out of which he spoke be taken as its very embodiment. But that was not quite enough. The confessional mode, reduced to this kind of self-recharging, becomes self-echoing as well and uses itself up after the first wild orgies of feeling. [1]

Rosenthal is no straw man, though I believe he is dead wrong here. There are, as always, straw men enough to be found. John Wain offers a comically conceived Soviet critic who denounces Roethke's failure to mention "the bread-lines, the war, the racial upheavals," [2] and I might offer a student or two who would venture to say that Roethke is not "relevant." But

Rosenthal is a good reader, and other good readers—some of them quite sympathetic to Roethke—have, in gentle ways, intimated that he does not give one "a sense of total participation in life," [3] or that he is "almost untouched by public happenings or by history." [4]

Nonetheless, I think it might be more accurate to say that few, if any, other modern American poets of comparable reputation have absorbed more wholly the concerns of our age into the nerve-ends, nor have more adequately represented in their art the incredible experiences of the age. If, as I believe, the essential experience of modern life is speed, movement, energy, whirl, a sense of unceasing and often violent motion, Roethke surely took it all into the nerve-endings, into the blood and pulse, into the rhythms of his giant body which became the rhythms of his poetry. "Live," he told his classes in verse writing, "out in your fingers." His fingers and their nerve-endings told him that his world was in motion, and he was wise enough to sense that the historical events that swirled around him were but varied forms of the same energy which drove him in his personal evolution as a man and an artist. In fact, I think the root metaphor in all of Roethke's work is the historical event, provided that one understands that any action with all of its context—its total sweep backward into the past and forward into the future—is an event in history. The teaching of a class, the death of a student, the journey out of the self, will serve as well to give a sense of the complexity and dynamism of life—of history—as will the battle of Gettysburg, the assassination of a president, a visit to China. The poet's task—and Roethke's genius—is to make his words become an event, to arrange them in such a way as to create in their reading the sweep and energy of the experience of our time.

Because Roethke was a teaching poet who labored lovingly to help his students discover the secrets of his craft and art, and because many of the notes from which he taught have been preserved, one may with some confidence theorize about what the poet tried to do in his poetry and how he went about doing it. Time and time again the jottings which became the classroom performance demonstrate the vocabulary of dynamism. The key words, repeated in varying forms and combinations, are "energy," "intensity," "speed," "flow." There are lists of devices for heightening intensity in a poem, for speeding the imagery, for creating energy in rhythm. There are aphorisms. "What is the most important element: energy." "Style: What is style but matter in motion?" "A poem means an extra, a surplus of energy." "The enemy of intensity: grandiloquence." [5] There are questions, apparently from students, and hastily scribbled answers:

Q. What do you want in the way of a rhythm, Mr. R.?

A. It's the nervousness, the tension, I think I value most. Blake's bounding line and old Willie's high imperial honking. [6]

Q. You speak of energy in rhythm. What are the factors that seem to enter into, or contribute to, this force?

A. They are so multiple that they constitute the whole art of writing; but I feel what comes to the aid are alliteration of initial sounds and a manipulation and a variation of interior sounds, (repetition of words) particularly vowels. The line—but the verbal forms particularly, particularly the "ing" participial form, impart, as would be expected, movement. *This may be because I see the world in motion*, but I don't think so. [7] [Italics added.]

There is also the testimony of Roethke's former students, for he seems to have been unforgettable in the classroom. One of the best of his pupils, David Wagoner, has told me that he remembers Roethke's saying, perhaps quoting someone else, that in poetry "motion is equal to emotion." Another, Oliver

Everette, writes that Roethke used to snarl, "You've got to have rhythm. If you want to dance naked in an open barndoor with a chalk stuck in your navel, I don't care! You've got to have rhythm. I don't care how you get it."[8] He also remembers that Roethke stressed "motion in poetry," telling the class that "Motion or action should be found in every line. The poetic mind sees things in motion."[9]

It seems to me that Roethke's problem as a classroom teacher was essentially the same problem with which he wrestled as a poet. Given that the poetic eye sees things in motion, given that energy is all, by what techniques does one transfer a sense of that motion and energy to the page or to another's ear? How does one "teach" energy? Not, I think, entirely by telling people to alliterate initial sounds and manipulate interior ones, though I do not wish to undervalue the importance of just such devices. A better clue, I believe, to Roethke's success as a teacher comes from the coed who once told him, "I don't understand a word you say, but I just watch your hands."[10] Or from Richard Hugo, now a fine poet in his own right, who says that he learned at least as much from Roethke's actions—from the boundless energy, what Hugo calls the "overstance," of the teaching performance—as he did from Roethke's words. In Roethke's classroom, apparently, the medium was, to an unusual degree, the message. How do you teach a beat? You don't. But many a student seems to have been surprised to find his foot tapping in time to Roethke's bear-like professorial dance.

"Talent talks," Roethke wrote in one of his notebooks. "Genius does." And Roethke was more than talented. Therefore, the critic who concerns himself primarily with what one of Roethke's poems "talks about," with a paraphrase of the "thinky-think," as Roethke called it, has only a part—and not the best part—of the poem. In his great poems Roethke's "meaning"—never mind the ostensible subject—is always a celebration of the energetic dance of being. To meet his own standards for genius he had to create a revelation of that dance for his audience, and he had to do it by means of his words. In short, he had to make the experience, not talk about it.

As Roethke himself suggested, the devices by which all this is accomplished are "multiple," surely too multiple to be discussed adequately in an article-length study. Nevertheless, a critical thesis ought to be followed by "pages of illustrations," and I have rather arbitrarily decided to illustrate this one by examining the techniques which present dynamism in a few of Roethke's elegies. Energy, the thrust and surge of life, is perhaps most clearly revealed by contrast, most felt when its way is blocked by obstacles or when its motion and sweep are set off against the perfect stillness of death. It is not surprising, then, that Roethke is often at his best in the elegiac mode. "Elegy for Jane, My Student, Thrown by a Horse," "Frau Bauman, Frau Schmidt, and Frau Schwartze," and the little piece called simply "Elegy" in *Words for the Wind* are some of his more successful attempts to represent the rhythm and pace of life.

Roethke's elegies always celebrate those who have been most active, those in whom energy has been most intensely present. I suppose he was naturally drawn to such people, and he seems to have identified the energy expressed by their bodies, the speed with which they moved and acted, with the creative energy that he prized above everything. The trick is to re-create that energy with words so that the bodily rhythms of the dead move again and breathe again and *are* again for so long as the poem is remembered. If the trick is brought off, the poet has, in a way, triumphed over death by creating a symbolic and immortal equivalent to the energetic rhythms of the human body.

The first stanza of the "Elegy for Jane" comes close to achieving just such a triumph:

> I remember the neckcurls, limp and damp as tendrils;
> And her quick look, a sidelong pickerel smile;
> And how, once startled into talk, the light syllables leaped for her,
> And she balanced in the delight of her thought,
> A wren, happy, tail into the wind,
> Her song trembling the twigs and small branches.
> The shade sang with her;
> The leaves, their whispers turned to kissing;
> And the mold sang in the bleached valley under the rose.[11]

The passage is a catalogue of memories expressed as images; it is a bombardment of the senses creating an experience greater than the sum of its parts, for the speed with which those parts are juxtaposed becomes an additional "meaning" given to the recollected portrait of the girl. Jane is a protean figure, evolving through shifting imagery from plant to fish to bird as Roethke's mind leaps from metaphorical association to association. She is clearly not idealized as a physical beauty. Few coeds would be pleased to have their neckcurls likened to tendrils and fewer still would appreciate having their quick sidelong glance bring to mind a "pickerel smile." It is not beauty, however, that Roethke is after here, but energy—the tendrils' thrust toward light, the violent rush of the pickerel. It is the sense of quickness, of startled leaping, of balancing, of motion so contagious that it causes all the world about to tremble in tune with the song Jane sings. There is much that appeals purely to the kinesthetic sense—a feeling of lightness and quickness, of rising and falling, of precarious balancing against the thrust of the wind.

There is an abundance of just that sort of "alliteration of initial sounds and manipulation of interior sounds" which Roethke suggested might contribute to the energy of a poetic rhythm. "Neckcurls" and "tendrils," "quick look" and "pickerel," "wren" and "wind," "startled" and "syllables," and "light" and "leaped" are among the more obvious examples of Roethke's continuous playing of sound against sound, of manipulation and variation of vowel and consonant. There is also the simple, almost primitive diction—a heavy preponderance of monosyllables, a careful avoidance of "grandiloquence." And there is, primarily in the choice and placement of verbs, the sense of the enormous activity of all things—of leaves that whisper and kiss, of mold and shade that sing.

The passage is primarily a hymn to the power of Jane's talking, to her ability to give the quickness of life to the "light syllables." She is the natural poet, her promise never to be fulfilled, and as such she serves as a kind of Edward King to Roethke's Milton. Just as Milton imaginatively gives King the power to move with his singing "The willows, and the hazel copses green," so Roethke imagines Jane's song to be answered by the shade and by the mold "in the bleached valleys under the rose." And, as in "Lycidas," the energy of the elegiac voice is the assurance that the power to make the light syllables leap is imperishable. Though he denies paternity, in one sense the poet *is* father to the Jane of the poem. His breath becomes the breath of her startled talking; his verbal energy becomes the rhythm to which her body sways.

One of Roethke's most effective devices for suggesting the flickering speed of life is that by which, as in a kind of double vision, he has Jane be both present and not present at the grave. "My sparrow, you are not here," he says, "Waiting like a fern, making a spiny shadow." The bird, the singer with tail into the wind, is not a creature to wait, to be still. Yet she is, at once, "My maimed darling," the Jane who goes to the earth, and "my skittery pigeon," the Jane whose bird-like energy endures in the memory and in the cadence of the poet.

Just as Jane is "not here" and very much "here," the poet is neither father nor lover and yet something of each. In many ways the poem is about a relationship with a student, a relationship which is fully disclosed by the word "love," a shocking four-letter word in this context. Neither the rights of love nor the rites of love allow for such a relationship. We honor the grief of fathers, sympathize with the grief of lovers, but there are no "rites" (surely the pun is deliberate) by which a male professor may speak the words of his love for his student Jane. Yet Roethke affirms and expresses his rights even as he denies that he has them. His role in the ceremonial mourning exists in motion of its own sort, flickering between the role of the father he was not and the role of the lover he was not, existing only in the nameless spaces gaping between those solid, respectable pillars in the house of grief.

"Frau Bauman, Frau Schmidt, and Frau Schwartze" (*CP* 44) manages to convey something of the same sense of an elusive, darting "reality," for the three ladies move so swiftly as to manage to be in two places at the same time, to be "Gone" and "still hover[ing]" simultaneously. The ladies, like Jane, have the power to transfer their energy creatively into the life around them, and it is that power which commends them to the memory and to the apotheosizing power of the imagination. The fraus are glimpsed through a flurry of active verbal forms—creaking, reaching, winding, straightening, tying, tucking, dipping up, sifting, sprinkling, shaking, standing, billowing, twinkling, flying, keeping, sewing, teasing, trellising, pinching, poking and plotting. Even nouns such as "Coils," "loops," "whorls," "nurses," "seed," "pipes," and others are potential verbs, suggesting that the names of greenhouse things are squirming with metaphorical action. The ladies are never still, for even when they stand astride the greenhouse pipes, their skirts billow and their hands twinkle "with wet." Their movement is always that of "picking up," and the movement of the poem, like the movement of the climbing roses, is upward from the earth toward the sun. So swiftly do the ladies scurry that the memory blurs fact into fiction, the historical ladies into the mythic. Flying "like witches," they become more and more enormous in their activity until at last they trellis the sun itself, giving support to that strange flower which is the life of our planet.

As the remembered ladies become apotheosized into mythic figures, Roethke images them to take on the fecund powers of earth mothers. They straddle the phallic pipes of the greenhouse, pipes belonging to Roethke's father, until their skirts billow "out wide like tents"—as if someone might live there. They have, we are told, the power to "tease out" the seed, to undo the lifeless "keeping" of the cold. And, finally, they give the poet himself a symbolic birth. Acting as midwives to themselves, they pick him up, pinch and poke him into shape, "Till I lay in their laps, laughing, / Weak as a whiffet." The ladies, trellisers of the sun, also trellis "the son," the boy fathered by the greenhouse owner.

Though the ladies are, as the first word of the poem insists, "Gone," they "still hover" in the air of the present. All of the verbs in the first stanza are, as one would expect in a remembrance, in the past tense. Nevertheless, Roethke refers to the fraus as "*These* nurses of nobody else" as if they were present, as if the memory had managed to recapture in part that which had been totally lost. And, of course, he says that "Now, when I'm alone and cold in my bed, / They still hover

over me, / These ancient leathery crones. . . . " The relationship between poet and crones is a highly dynamic one. On the one hand, the hovering mothers "still" have the power to give him life. He lies like a seed, cold and in his bed, and they breathe over him the breath of life, a snuff-laden blowing that lifts him from the keeping of the cold into a life that manifests itself in poetic blossoms. On the other hand, it is the poet who "keeps" the fraus alive, whose breath gives to the dead the power to move and be again. Their energy is entirely dependent upon his ability to intensity the language until their movement becomes tangible in empty air, becomes an event in the viscera of the reader. The poem itself takes its cadence from those German fraus, takes it and gives it back again.

As for the poet, he has, by the end of the poem, lost himself in two places at once. He is in his bed and the time is "Now," yet the crones who hover above him breathe "lightly over [him] in [his] first sleep," presumably that sleep from which one wakes at birth. They are the remembered gateway to the past, these witches capable of collapsing time so that the cold sleep of the adult is at one with the first sleep from which he wakened into life. They are the means by which Roethke demonstrates the sweep of the "Now" in which we always live; for through the fraus who were, through the fraus mythologized and through the fraus who remain as a felt presence, he has made a poetic representation of the living extension of the past into the ever-moving present.

The poem called "Elegy" is short enough to quote entirely:

> Should every creature be as I have been,
> There would be reason for essential sin;
> I have myself an inner weight of woe
> That God himself can scarcely bear.
>
> Each wills his death: I am convinced of that;
> You were too lonely for another fate.
> I have myself an inner weight of woe
> That Christ, securely bound, could bear.
>
> Thus I; and should these reasons fly apart,
> I know myself, my seasons, and I KNOW.
> I have myself one crumbling skin to show;
> God could believe: I am here to fear.
>
> What you survived I shall believe: the Heat,
> Scars, Tempests, Floods, the Motion of Man's Fate;
> I have myself and bear its weight of woe
> That God that God leans down His heart to hear.
>
> (CP 144)

"Elegy" is a poem that took several titles as Roethke worked it into its final shape. The piece was first called "Humility, Its Coarse Surprises Can," after the opening line, a line followed by "Undo the virtues of a carnal man." In that early form the poem was apparently intended as a tribute to an aunt, Julia Roethke. All of the pronouns referring to the dead person are feminine, and another draft, apparently of the same period, has as its subtitle "In Memoriam: Julia Roethke." Underneath her name Roethke had written and lightly crossed out "Dylan Thomas." In many drafts the poem is called "The Stumbling," and Roethke seems to have decided that it suited Thomas better than his aunt, after all. But in final form the poem is, wisely, I think, unassigned, and the neuter pronoun "you" replaces the limiting "he" or "she" which had referred to the dead person in the earlier versions. As it stand in *The Collected Poems*, "Elegy" celebrates the memory of everyman, all who have been begotten, born and died. [12]

It is a difficult poem, one easily misread. I believe Karl Malkoff, for one, misreads it in his study of Roethke. According to Malkoff, "Guilt is precisely the theme of 'Elegy'. . . . Indeed, the universe as man knows it is defined by the passage of the seasons, . . . by the passing out of existence of all life. Once this dissolution has occurred, man can no longer atone for his guilt; his 'essential sin,' his condemnation, is fact forever."[13] The poem does, indeed, open with an admission of heavy guilt, but such an admission demonstrates that sense of humility which may bring even a "carnal man" to salvation by the means of God's grace and with the help of His mercy. It is a poem, I think, that moves from near despair to comfort, from a weight of scarcely bearable woe to a weight that "God leans down His heart to hear."

The form of the poem supports this reading, for as Roethke manipulates his quatrains, they become highly dynamic, suggesting change and development rather than the static hopelessness of Malkoff's interpretation. "Elegy" has the soul of a villanelle; that is, the third and fourth lines of each quatrain act as refrain lines of a sort and give to the poem that satisfying effect of repetition that is the essential pleasure of, say, Thomas' "Do Not Go Gentle" or of Roethke's own "The Waking." With Roethke, however, refrain lines are always similar, but rarely the same. He manipulates such lines so that the reader is arrested by their continuous alteration as much as by their repetition. The ear is set up for an echo that never quite arrives; instead, the ear is teased by words that move about, altering meaning and value in every stanza.

Stanza one is an admission of the narrator's worthlessness, his sinful condition. If all creatures are like himself, he speculates, then the idea of original sin is rational enough. Indeed, his own sinful nature and the woe of the world he inhabits may well seem to make irrational any doctrine which does not begin by acknowledging some "essential sin" as explanation for the fallen nature of the world. Pondering such a creation and his sinful place in it, the poet skirts dangerously near despair, believing that his weight of sin and woe is such that "God himself can scarcely bear." Nonetheless, God "can" bear that weight, and the basis for future hope is established.

In the second stanza, Christ, God become man, takes upon Himself "the weight of woe," and does so "securely bound," as if with *both* hands tied behind His back. There is a possible pun here, in that Christ, bound on the cross, is bound for Heaven, and thus "securely bound" in a way that precariously bound man is not. In any case, God the Father, the harsh judge who tolerates with difficulty the foolishness of man, has taken on His more merciful aspect, the aspect of the saviour who offers Himself as a full, perfect and sufficient sacrifice for the sins of the world.

The third stanza marks a significant change in the attitude of the narrator, a change marked by a shift in rhyme scheme and the substitution of the word "fear" for the word "bear" that ended the first two stanzas. Essentially, the narrator turns from one kind of knowing to another, from the reasoned to the intuitive. He can bear his "inner weight of woe" because Christ could and did bear it; and should his carefully reasoned doctrine of essential sin fly apart, still he knows what he KNOWS. At the last, a man knows only what his experience tells him—and experience may tell him that he KNOWS some things beyond the need for "reasons." God could believe that the poet lives, is "here," for the purpose of being fearful. We do not ordinarily think of fear as a positive emotion, but in this case it seems to me that it is God Himself who is feared. And the fear of the Lord is the beginning of wisdom, a further step in humility for the spiritual stumbler toward grace. God is feared because of the narrator's awareness of his own sinfulness and of the enormous strain of such a weight upon the mercy of

God. He knows that he is a sinner in a crumbling skin and that Eternal Justice for such as he has been would be terrible indeed.

But if God can believe in the narrator's humility before Him, the narrator will believe in "the Motion of Man's Fate," in the human power to survive "the Heat, / Scars, Tempests, Floods." If it is the glory of God to show compassion to such woeful creatures as men, it is the glory of men to act creatively in the face of immense suffering, to survive the Tempests and sing (as Dylan Thomas sang) beneath a weight of woe. The poet who believes in the power of human survival and yet remains humble, fearing the Lord, possesses himself ("I have myself") and is capable of bearing the woe that is his portion of Man's Fate. And, for such a one, "That God that God leans down His Heart to hear." Because the narrator has moved from reasoning to KNOWing, because he has come to a contrite admission of his own fear, God has changed from the God who "scarcely" can bear (tolerate) human sinfulness to that God who bends compassionately toward man and listens, not with His judging mind, but with His merciful heart. It is a poem, like the other two elegies, about a dynamic relationship, in this case one in which man and God change as they interact with one another. Within the confines of a tight formal pattern, Roethke has managed to convey an impression of enormous motion and process, an impression heightened by shifting refrain lines, altered rhyme schemes, associative leaps that all but fracture syntax, and by changing the length of the final line, filling it out to five beats after closing the other quatrains with lines that were short a foot. If the poem works, and I think it does, it works because form and meaning are one, because Roethke's technical skill has been equal to the task of presenting process and change in his poem.

It would be foolish to suggest that these elegies represent an adequate sampling of Theodore Roethke's lifetime of poetry. Nonetheless, I think they do illustrate a few of his better techniques for presenting dynamism in a work of art. The propulsion, the forward thrust, of the free verse comes from the intensification of verbs, the frenetic lists of actions, the energetic rhythms, the associative leaps from image to image and the playing off of sound against sound, phrase against phrase. In the more formal piece, Roethke uses his modified repetition to underscore change and development, and he shifts rhyme scheme and line length to suggest shifts in mental or spiritual development. In all three poems the relationships between the poet and the dead or between the poet and God are highly dynamic ones, relationships which alter even as the poet speaks the words of his love. In these poems, as elsewhere in his work, Roethke manages to transfer the rhythm, the motion, of life from his pulse to the printed page. It is this energetic, dynamic quality which I find the essential characteristic of his craft and which makes his poetry worthy of celebration.

Notes

1. *The New Poets: American and British Poetry since World War II* (New York: Oxford Univ. Press, 1967), p. 118.
2. "The Monocle of My Sea-Faced Uncle," in *Thedore Roethke: Essays on the Poetry*, ed. Arnold Stein (Seattle: Univ. of Washington Press, 1965), p. 75.
3. Ibid, p. 76.
4. Ralph J. Mills, Jr. *Thedore Roethke* (Minneapolis: Univ. of Minnesota Press, 1967), p. 8.
5. These aphorisms, together with other material on how to intensify the "energy" in a piece of verse, were culled from box 65 of the University of Washington's collection of the manuscripts of

Theodore Roethke. I am grateful to Beatrice Roethke for permission to publish this previously unpublished material.

6. Theodore Roethke collection, box 28, folder 21 (previously unpublished).

7. Theodore Roethke collection, box 67, folder 2 (previously unpublished).

8. "Theodore Roethke: The Poet as Teacher," *West Coast Review*, 3 (1968), 6.

9. Ibid., pp. 6–7.

10. Theodore Roethke, *Straw for the Fire: From the Notebooks 1943–63*, selected and arranged by David Wagoner (Garden City: Doubleday, 1972), p. 261. Roethke concluded glumly, "Hardly a tribute to one's verbal powers."

11. *The Collected Poems of Theodore Roethke* (Garden City: Doubleday, 1966), p. 102. Subsequent page references to this edition will be given in the text and denoted as (*CP*).

12. Many drafts of this poem may be found in box 19, folder 25 of the Roethke collection. A complete version of "The Stumbling," dedicated to Julia Roethke, is included in a letter to John Crowe Ransom on pages 197–98 of the *Selected Letters of Theodore Roethke*, ed. Ralph J. Mills, Jr. (Seattle: Univ. of Washington Press, 1968).

13. *Theodore Roethke: An Introduction to the Poetry* (New York: Columbia Univ. Press, 1967), pp. 146–47.

DENIS DONOGHUE
"Theodore Roethke"
Connoisseurs of Chaos:
Ideas of Order in Modern American Poetry (1962)
1984, pp. 216–45

There is a poem called "Snake" in which Theodore Roethke describes a young snake turning and drawing away and then says:

> I felt my slow blood warm.
> I longed to be that thing,
> The pure, sensuous form.
> And I may be, some time. [1]

To aspire to a condition of purity higher than any available in the human world is a common urge. Poets often give this condition as a pure, sensuous form, nothing if not itself and nothing beyond itself. But it is strange, at first sight, that Roethke gives his parable in the image of a snake, because snakes tend to figure in his poems as emblems of the sinister. In "Where Knock Is Open Wide" one of the prayerful moments reads: "I'll be a bite. You be a wink. / Sing the snake to sleep." In "I Need, I Need" the term "snake-eyes" is enough to send its owner packing. And there is this, in "The Shape of the Fire":

> Up over a viaduct I came, to the snakes and sticks of
>   another winter,
> A two-legged dog hunting a new horizon of howls.

But this is at first sight, or at first thought, because Roethke, more than most poets, sought a sustaining order in the images of his chaos, and only those images would serve. If you offer a dove as answer to a snake, your answer is incomplete, an order not violent enough. Hence when the right time came, in "I'm Here," Roethke would find that a snake lifting its head is a fine sight, and a snail's music is a fine sound, and both are joys, credences of summer. As Roethke says in "The Longing," "The rose exceeds, the rose exceeds us all."

But he did not sentimentalize his chaos. He lived with it, and would gladly have rid himself of it if he could have done

so without an even greater loss, the loss of verifiable life. When he thought of his own rage, for instance, he often saw it as mere destructiveness. In one of his early poems he said: "Rage warps my clearest cry / To witless agony." And he often resorted to invective, satire, pseudonymous tirades, to cleanse himself of rage and hatred. In one of those tirades he said, "Behold, I'm a heart set free, for I have taken my hatred and eaten it." But "Death Piece" shows that to be released from rage is to be—quite simply—dead. And the price is too high. This is one of the reasons why Roethke found the last years of W. B. Yeats so rewarding, because Yeats made so much of his rage, in the *Last Poems*, *The Death of Cuchulain*, and *Purgatory*. In one of his own apocalyptic poems, "The Lost Son," Roethke says, "I want the old rage, the lash of primordial milk," as if to recall Yeats' cry, "Grant me an old man's frenzy." And in "Old Lady's Winter Words" he says: "If I were a young man, / I could roll in the dust of a fine rage . . . "; and in "The Sententious Man": "Some rages save us. Did I rage too long? / The spirit knows the flesh it must consume." Hence Roethke's quest for the saving rage. Call it—for it is this—a rage for order. He was sometimes tempted to seal himself against the rush of experience, and he reminds himself in "The Adamant" that the big things, such as truth, are sealed against thought; the true substance, the core, holds itself inviolate. And yet man is exposed, exposes himself. And, in a sense, rightly so. As Yeats says in the great "Dialogue of Self and Soul":

> I am content to live it all again
> And yet again, if it be life to pitch
> Into the frog-spawn of a blind man's ditch.

In "The Pure Fury" Roethke says, "I live near the abyss." What he means is the substance of his poetry. The abyss is partly the frog-spawn of a blind man's ditch, partly a ditch of his own contriving, partly the fate of being human in a hard time, partly the poet's weather. As discreetly as possible we can take it for granted, rehearsing it only to the extent of linking it with the abyss in other people. Better to think of it as the heart of each man's darkness. In "Her Becoming" Roethke speaks of it in one aspect:

> I know the cold fleshless kiss of contraries,
> The nerveless constriction of surfaces—
> Machines, machines, loveless, temporal;
> Mutilated souls in cold morgues of obligation.

And this becomes, in the "Fourth Meditation," "the dreary dance of opposites." (But so far it is common enough.)

It is still common enough when Roethke presents it through the ambiguities of body and soul. In "Epidermal Macabre" Roethke, like Yeats in *The Tower*, wishes the body away in favor of a spirit remorselessly sensual:

> And willingly would I dispense
> With false accouterments of sense,
> To sleep immodestly, a most
> Incarnadine and carnal ghost.

Or again, when the dance of opposites is less dreary, Roethke accepts with good grace the unwinding of body from soul:

> When opposites come suddenly in place,
> I teach my eyes to hear, my ears to see
> How body from spirit slowly does unwind
> Until we are pure spirit at the end.

Sometimes the body is "gristle." In "Praise to the End" Roethke says, "Skin's the least of me," and in the "First Meditation" it is the rind that "hates the life within." (Yeats' "dying animal" is clearly visible.) But there were other moments, as there were in Yeats. In "The Wraith" the body casts a spell, the flesh makes the spirit "visible," and in the "Fourth Meditation" "the husk lives on, ardent as a seed."

Mostly in Roethke the body seems good in itself, a primal energy. And when it is this it features the most distinctive connotations of the modern element: it is a good, but ill at ease with other goods. Above all, it does not guarantee an equable life in the natural world. More often than not in these poems man lives with a hostile nature, and lives as well as he can. In "I Need, I Need" intimations of waste, privation, and insecurity lead to this:

> The ground cried my name:
> Good-bye for being wrong.
> Love helps the sun.
> But not enough.

"I can't marry the dirt" is an even stronger version, in "Bring the Day," echoing Wallace Stevens' benign "marriage of flesh and air" while attaching to it now, as courageously as possible, the care note, "A swan needs a pond"; or, more elaborately in another poem, "A wretch needs his wretchedness." The aboriginal middle poems have similar cries on every page: "These wings are from the wrong nest"; "My sleep deceives me"; "Soothe me, great groans of underneath"; "Rock me to sleep, the weather's wrong"; "Few objects praise the Lord."

These are some of Roethke's intimations of chaos. They reach us as cries, laments, protests, intimations of loss. Most of Roethke's later poems are attempts to cope with these intimations by becoming—in Stevens' sense—their connoisseur. In "The Dance" Roethke speaks of a promise he has made to "sing and whistle romping with the bears"; and whether we take these as animals or constellations, the promise is the same and hard to keep. To bring it off at all, Roethke often plays in a child's garden, especially in poems like "O Lull Me, Lull Me," where he can have everything he wants by having it only in fancy. "Light fattens the rock," he sings, to prove that good children get treats. "When I say things fond, I hear singing," he reports, and we take his word for it; as we do again when we acknowledge, in a later poem, that "the right thing happens to the happy man." Perhaps it does. But when Roethke says, "I breathe into a dream,/And the ground cries . . . ," and again, "I could say hello to things;/I could talk to a snail," we think that he protests too much, and we know that his need is great. Roethke is never quite convincing in this note, or in the hey-nonny note of his neo-Elizabethan pastiche. Even when he dramatizes the situation in the "Meditations of an Old Woman" the answers come too easily. In two stanzas he has "the earth itself a tune," and this sounds like a poet's wishful dreaming. Roethke may have wanted the kind of tone that Stevens reached in his last poems, an autumnal calm that retains the rigor and the feeling but banishes the fretful note, the whine, the cry of pain. But Stevens earned this. And Yeats earned it too, in poems like "Beautiful Lofty Things." Roethke claimed it without really earning it. Here is a stanza from "Her Becoming":

> Ask all the mice who caper in the straw—
> I am benign in my own company.
> A shape without a shade, or almost none,
> I hum in pure vibration, like a saw.
> The grandeur of a crazy one alone!—
> By swoops of bird, by leaps of fish, I live.
> My shadow steadies in a shifting stream;
> I live in air; the long light is my home;
> I dare caress the stones, the field my friend;
> A light wind rises: I become the wind.

And here is Stevens, in a passage from "The Course of a Particular":

> The leaves cry. It is not a cry of divine attention,
> Nor the smoke-drift of puffed-out heroes, nor human cry.
> It is the cry of leaves that do not transcend themselves,
> In the absence of fantasia, without meaning more
> Than they are in the final finding of the air, in the thing
> Itself, until, at last, the cry concerns no one at all.

How can we compare these two passages except to say that Stevens speaks with the knowledge that there have been other days, other feelings, and the hope that there will be more of each, as various as before? Roethke speaks as if the old woman were now released from time and history and the obligations of each, released even from the memories that she has already invoked. There is too much fantasia in Roethke's lines, and this accounts for a certain slackness that fell upon him whenever he tried too hard to be serene. Stevens' poem is, in the full meaning of the word, mature; Roethke's is a little childish, second-childish. Stevens would affirm, when affirmation seemed just, but not before. Roethke longed to affirm, and when the affirmation would not come he sometimes—now and again—dressed himself in affirmative robes.

But only now and again. At his best he is one of the most scrupulous of poets. In "Four for Sir John Davies," for instance, the harmony between nature and man that Davies figures—the orchestra, the dance, the music of the spheres—is brought to bear upon the poem, critically and never naïvely or sentimentally. The divinely orchestrated universe of Davies' poem is more than a point of reference but far less than an escape route. For one thing, as Roethke says, "I need a place to sing, and dancing-room," and for another, there is no dancing master, and for a third, there isn't even at this stage a dancing partner. So he must do the best he can in his poverty. And if his blood leaps "with a wordless song," at least it leaps:

> But what I learned there, dancing all alone,
> Was not the joyless motion of a stone.

But even when the partner comes and they dance their joy, Roethke does not claim that this makes everything sweet or that nature and man will thereafter smile at each other. In the farthest reach of joy he says:

> We danced to shining; mocked before the black
> And shapeless night that made no answer back.

The sensual cry is what it is, and there are moments when it is or seems to be final, but man still lives in the element of antagonisms. In *Four Quartets* the "daunsynge" scene from Sir Thomas Elyot testifies to modes of being, handsome but archaic; it answers no present problem. Nor does Sir John Davies, who plays a similar role in Roethke's sequence. And even before that, in "The Return," man in the element of antagonisms feels and behaves like an animal in his self-infected lair, "With a stump of scraggy fang / Bared for a hunter's boot." And sometimes he turns upon himself in rage.

When Roethke thinks of man in this way, he often presents him in images of useless flurry. Like Saul Bellow's Dangling Man, he is clumsy, ungainly, an elephant in a pond. Roethke often thinks of him as a bat—by day, quiet, cousin to the mouse; at night, crazy, absurd, looping "in crazy figures." And when the human situation is extreme, Roethke thinks of man as a bat flying deep into a narrowing tunnel. Far from being a big, wide space, the world seems a darkening corridor. In "Bring the Day!" Roethke says, "Everything's closer. Is this a cage?" And if a shape cries from a cloud as it does in "The Exorcism," and calls to man's flesh, man is always somewhere else, "down long corridors." (Corridors, cages, tunnels, lairs—if these poems needed illustration, the painter is easily named: Francis Bacon, keeper of caged souls.)

In "Four for Sir John Davies" the lovers, Roethke says, "undid chaos to a curious sound," "curious" meaning careful as well as strange and exploratory. In this world to undo chaos is always a curious struggle, sometimes thought of as a release from constriction, a stretching in all directions, an escape from the cage. In "What Can I Tell My Bones?" Roethke says, "I recover my tenderness by long looking," and if tenderness is the proof of escape, long looking is one of the means. In *King Lear* it is to see feelingly. In some of Roethke's poems it is given as, quite simply, attention. In "Her Becoming" Roethke speaks of a "jauntier principle of order," but this is to dream. What he wants, in a world of cages and corridors, is to escape to an order, an order of which change and growth and decay are natural mutations and therefore acceptable. In many of the later poems it will be an order of religious feeling, for which the punning motto is, "God, give me a near."

The first step, the first note toward a possible order, is to relish what can be relished. Listening to "the sigh of what is," one attends, knowing, or at least believing, that "all finite things reveal infinitude." If things "flame into being," so much the better. "Dare I blaze like a tree?" Roethke asks at one point, like the flaming tree of Yeats' "Vacillation." And again Roethke says, "What I love is near at hand, / Always, in earth and air." This is fine, as far as it goes, but it is strange that Roethke is more responsive to intimations of being when they offer themselves in plants than in people; and here, of course, he differs radically from Yeats. In the first verion of "Cuttings" he is exhilarated when "the small cells bulge," when cuttings sprout into a new life, when bulbs hunt for light, when the vines in the forcing house pulse with the knocking pipes, when orchids draw in the warm air, when beetles, newts, and lice creep and wriggle. In "Slug" he rejoices in his kinship with bats, weasels, and worms. In "A Walk in Late Summer" being "delights in being, and in time." In the same poem Roethke delights in the "midnight eyes" of small things, and in several poems he relishes what Christopher Smart in *Jubilate Agno* calls "the language of flowers." Everywhere in Roethke there is consolation in the rudimentary when it is what it is, without fantasia. It is a good day when the spiders sail into summer. But Roethke is slow to give the same credences to man. Plants may be transplanted, and this is good, but what is exhilarating reproduction in insects and flowers is mere duplication in people. Girls in college are "duplicate gray standard faces"; in the same poem there is talk of "endless duplication of lives and objects." Man as a social being is assimilated to the machine; the good life is lived by plants. In the bacterial poems, weeds are featured as circumstance, the rush of things, often alien but often sustaining. "Weeds, weeds, how I love you," Roethke says in "The Shape of the Fire." In the "First Meditation," "On love's worst ugly day, / The weeds hiss at the edge of the field . . ." In "What Can I Tell My Bones?" "Weeds turn toward the wind weed-skeletons," presumably because "the dead love the unborn." But in "Praise to the End!" when the water's low and romping days are over, "the weeds exceed me."

There are two ways of taking this, and Roethke gives us both. Normally we invoke the rudimentary to criticize the complex: the lower organism rebukes the higher for falling short of itself as body rebukes the arrogance of vaunting mind or spirit. This works on the assumption that what is simple is more "natural" than what is complex, and that lower organ-

isms have the merit of such simplicity. Or, alternatively, one can imply that the most exalted objects of our human desire are already possessed, in silence and grace, by the lower organisms. Roethke often does this. In "The Advice," for instance, he says:

> A learned heathen told me this:
> Dwell in pure mind and Mind alone;
> What you brought back from the Abyss,
> The Slug was taught beneath his Stone.

This is so presumably because the slug had a teacher, perhaps the dancing master who has retired from the human romp. Roethke doesn't commit the sentimentality of implying, however, that all is sweetness and light in the bacterial world, and generally he avoids pushing his vegetal analogies too far. In his strongest poems the bacterial is featured as a return to fundamentals, a syntax of short phrases to represent the radical breaking-up that may lead to a new synthesis. In grammatical terms, we have broken the spine of our syntax by loading it with our own fetishes. So we must begin again as if we were learning a new language, speaking in short rudimentary phrases. Or, alternatively, we learn in simple words and phrases, hoping that eventually we may reach the light of valid sentences. In this spirit Roethke says, in a late poem, "God bless the roots!— Body and soul are one!" The roots, the sensory facts, are beneath or beyond doubt; in "The Longing" Roethke says, "I would believe my pain: and the eye quiet on the growing rose." Learning a new language in this way, we must divest ourselves at this first stage of all claims to coherence, synthesis, or unity. This is the secular equivalent of the "way of purgation" in "Four Quartets," and it serves a corresponding purpose, because here too humility is endless. If our humility is sufficient, if we attend to the roots, to beginnings, we may even be rewarded with a vision in which beginning and end are one, as in the poem "In Evening Air":

> Ye littles, lie more close!
> Make me, O Lord, a last, a simple thing
> Time cannot overwhelm.
> Once I transcended time:
> A bud broke to a rose,
>   And I rose from a last diminishing.

We can see how this goes in the first stanzas of "Where Knock Is Open Wide":

> A kitten can
> Bite with his feet;
> Papa and Mama
> Have more teeth.

We can take this as pure notation, the primitive vision linking things that to the complex adult eye seem incommensurate. But the adult eye is "wrong," and it must go to school again if it is ever to say, "I recover my tenderness by long looking." Roethke's lines are "intuitions of sensibility," the ground of our beseeching, acts of the mind at the very first stage, long before idea, generalization, or concept. And this is the only way to innocence—or so the poem suggests. Then he says in the second stanza:

> Sit and play
> Under the rocker
> Until the cows
> All have puppies.

Here the aimlessness of the kitten stands for the innocence of game and apprehension. The play is nonchalant, and it conquers time by the ease of its reception. Time is measured by the laws of growth and fruition, not by the clock. In this sense it is proper to say, as Roethke does in the next stanza:

His ears haven't time.
Sing me a sleep-song, please.
A real hurt is soft.

In Christopher Smart's *A Song to David* (the source of the title of the present poem[2]) stanza 77 includes the lines:

And in the seat to faith assigned
Where ask is have, where seek is find,
Where knock is open wide.

The cat's ears haven't time because they don't ask for it. If time is for men the destructive element, that is their funeral, and mostly their suicide. "Sing me a sleep-song, please" is a prayer to be released from time. "A real hurt is soft" is an attempt to render human pain as pure description, to eliminate self-pity. And the appropriate gloss is the second stanza of "The Lost Sun"—"Fished in an old wound, / The soft pond of repose"—to remind us that the primitive vision is at once harsh and antiseptic. (Roethke himself sometimes forgot this.) Hence these intuitions of rudimentary sensibility are exercises, akin to spiritual exercises, all the better if they are caustic, purgative, penitential. The exercises are never finished, because this is the way things are, but once they are well begun the soul can proceed; the energy released is the rage for a sustaining order.

The search for order begins easily enough in Roethke. Sometimes, as we have seen, it begins in celebration, relishing what there is to relish. Or again it may begin by sounding a warning note. The early poem "To My Sister" is a rush of admonition designed for survival and prudence. "Defer the vice of flesh," he tells her, but on the other hand, "Keep faith with present joys." Later, Roethke would seek and find value in intimations of change and growth, and then in love, normally sexual love. Many of the love poems are beautiful in an Elizabethan way, which is one of the best ways, and whether their delicacy is entirely Roethke's own or partly his way of acknowledging the delicacy of Sir Thomas Wyatt is neither here nor there. Some of the love poems are among Roethke's finest achievements. I would choose "The Renewal," "I Knew a Woman," "The Sensualists," "The Swan," "She," and "The Voice"—or this one, "Memory".

In the slow world of dream,
We breathe in unison.
The outside dies within,
And she knows all I am.

She turns, as if to go,
Half-bird, half-animal.
The wind dies on the hill.
Love's all. Love's all I know.

A doe drinks by a stream,
A doe and its fawn.
When I follow after them,
The grass changes to stone.

Love was clearly a principle of order in Roethke's poems, but it never established itself as a relation beyond the bedroom. It never became dialogue or *caritas*. Outside the bedroom Roethke became his own theme, the center of a universe deemed to exist largely because it had such a center. This does not mean that the entire university was mere grist to his mill; he is not one of the predatory poets. But on the other hand, he does not revel in the sheer humanity of the world. Indeed, his universe is distinctly underpopulated. Even Aunt Tilly entered it only when she died, thereby inciting an elegy. This is not to question Roethke's "sincerity"; poems are written for many reasons, one of which is the presence of poetic forms inviting attention. But to indicate the nature of Roethke's achievement it is necessary to mark the areas of his deepest response and to point to those areas that he acknowledged more sluggishly, if at all. I have already implied that he responded to the human modes of being only when a specific human relation touched him and he grasped it. He did not have that utter assent to other people, other lives, that marks the best poetry of William Carlos Williams or Richard Eberhart, the feeling that human life is just as miraculous as the growth of an orchid or the "excess" of a rose. Indeed, one might speculate along these lines: that Roethke's response to his father and mother and, in the love poems, to his wife was so vivid that it engrossed all other responses in the human world. It set up a monopoly. And therefore flowers and plants were closer to him than people.

Even when he acknowledged a natural order of things, Roethke invariably spoke of it as if it did not necessarily include the human order or as if its inclusion of that order were beside the point. The natural order of things included moss growing on rock, the transplanting of flowers, the cycle of mist, cloud, and rain, the tension of nest and grave, and it might even include what he calls, rather generally, "the wild disordered language of the natural heart." But the question of the distinctively human modes of life was always problematic. In Roethke's poems human life is endorsed when it manages to survive a storm, as in "Big Wind," where the greenhouse—Roethke's symbol for "the whole of life"—rides the storm and sails into the calm morning. There is also the old florist, standing all night watering the roses, and the single surviving tulip with its head swaggering over the dead blooms—and then Otto.

To survive, to live through the weeds—in Roethke's world you do this by taking appropriate security measures. Property is a good bet. In "Where Knock Is Open Wide" there is a passage that reads:

That was before. I fell! I fell!
The worm has moved away.
My tears are tired.

Nowhere is out. I saw the cold.
Went to visit the wind. Where the birds die.
How high is have?

The part we need is the last line, "How high is have?" This virtually identifies security with property. In several poems Roethke will pray for a close relation to God, and this will rate as security, but in the meantime every property in a material sense will help. And because he lived in our own society and sought order from the images of his chaos, security and property normally meant money. In "The Lost Son," for instance, there is this:

Good-bye, good-bye, old stones, the time-order is
     going,
I have married my hands to perpetual agitation,
I run, I run to the whistle of money.

        Money money money
        Water water water

And even if he wrote two or three poems to make fun of this, the fact remains: property and the fear of dispossession, money and the lack of it, were vivid terms in his human image. Property was money in one's purse, more reliable than most things—more reliable than reason, for instance.

In his search for a viable and live order Roethke used his mind for all it was worth, but he would not vote for reason. He did not believe that you could pit the rational powers against the weeks of circumstance and hope to win. When he spoke of reason it was invariably Stevens' "Reason's click-clack," a mechanical affair. In one poem Roethke says, "Reason? That dreary shed, that hutch for grubby schoolboys!" Indeed, reason normally appears in his poems, at least officially, as a constriction. Commenting on his poem "In a Dark Time," Roethke said that it was an attempt "to break through the barriers of rational experience."[3] The self, the daily world, reason, meant bondage; to come close to God you had to break through. These things were never the medium of one's encounter with God, always obstacles in its way. For such encounters you had to transcend reason; if you managed it, you touched that greater thing that is the "reason in madness" of *King Lear.* The good man takes the risk of darkness. If reason's click-clack is useless, there remains in man a primitive striving toward the light. Nature, seldom a friend to man, at least offers him a few saving analogies, one being that of darkness and light. Much of this is given in the last stanzas of "Unfold! Unfold!":

> Sing, sing, you symbols! All simple creatures,
> All small shapes, willow-shy,
> In the obscure haze, sing!
>
> A light song comes from the leaves.
> A slow sigh says yes. And light sighs;
> A low voice, summer-sad.
> Is it you, cold father? Father,
> For whom the minnows sang?
>
>> A house for wisdom; a field for revelation.
>> Speak to the stones, and the stars answer.
>> At first the visible obscures:
>> Go where light is.

To go where light is: the object is self-possession, sometimes featured as a relation to the world:

> I lose and find myself in the long water;
> I am gathered together once more;
> I embrace the world.

To be one's own man, to come upon "the true ease of myself," to possess oneself so fluently as to say, "Being, not doing, is my first joy"—these are definitive joys when "the light cries out, and I am there to hear." If it requires "the blast of dynamite" to effect such movements, well and good. At any cost Roethke must reach the finality in which, as he says in "Meditation at Oyster River," "the flesh takes on the pure poise of the spirit." (This is his version of Yeats' "Unity of Being.") Hence he admires the tendrils that do not need eyes to seek, the furred caterpillar that crawls down a string, anything that causes movement, gives release, breaks up constriction. In the natural world there is growth, the flow of water, the straining of buds toward the light. And in the poet's craft these move in harmony with the vivid cadence, fluency, Yeats' "tact of words," the leaping rhythm.

For the rest, Roethke's symbolism is common enough. The life-enhancing images are rain, rivers, flowers, seed, grain, birds, fish, veins. The danger signals are wind, storm, darkness, drought, shadow. And the great event is growth, in full light. "The Shape of the Fire" ends:

> To have the whole air!
> The light, the full sun
> Coming down on the flowerheads,
> The tendrils turning slowly,
> A slow snail-lifting, liquescent;
> To be by the rose
> Rising slowly out of its bed,
> Still as a child in its first loneliness;
> To see cyclamen veins become clearer in early
>   sunlight,
> And mist lifting out of the brown cattails;

> To stare into the after-light, the glitter left on the
>   lake's surface,
> When the sun has fallen behind a wooded island;
> To follow the drops sliding from a lifted oar,
> Held up, while the rower breathes, and the small
>   boat drifts quietly shoreward;
> To know that light falls and fills, often without our
>   knowing,
> As an opaque vase fills to the brim from a quick
>   pouring,
> Fills and trembles at the edge yet does not flow over,
> Still holding and feeding the stem of the contained
>   flower.

The flower, contained, securely held in a vase filled with water and light—with this image we are close to the core of Roethke's poetry, where all the analogies run together. The only missing element is what he often called "song," the ultimate in communication, and for that we need another poem, another occasion. One of his last poems, a love poem, ends:

> We met to leave again
> The time we broke from time;
> A cold air brought its rain,
> The singing of a stem.
> She sang a final song;
> Light listened when she sang.

If light listens, if light attends upon a human event, then the event is final. Kenneth Burke has pointed out that Roethke tends to link things, whenever there is a choice, by means of a word in the general vocabulary of communication. We need only add this, that when the relation is as close as a relation can be, the participants "sing," and there is singing everywhere, singing and listening. "The light cries out, and I am there to hear."

Pushed to their conclusion, or followed to their source, these analogies would run straight to the idea of God, or rather to the image of God. And taking such stock in the symbolism of creation and light, Roethke could hardly have avoided this dimension. Nor did he. One of his last and greatest poems is called "The Marrow":

> The wind from off the sea says nothing new.
> The mist above me sings with its small flies.
> From a burnt pine the sharp speech of a crow
> Tells me my drinking breeds a will to die.
> What's the worst portion in this mortal life?
> A pensive mistress, and a yelping wife.
>
> One white face shimmers brighter than the sun
> When contemplation dazzles all I see;
> One look too close can make my soul away.
> Brooding on God, I may become a man.
> Pain wanders through my bones like a lost fire;
> What burns me now? Desire, desire, desire.
>
> Godhead above my God, are you there still?
> To sleep is all my life. In sleep's half-death,
> My body alters, altering the soul
> That once could melt the dark with its small breath.
> Lord, hear me out, and hear me out this day:
> From me to Thee's a long and terrible way.
>
> I was flung back from suffering and love
> When light divided on a storm-tossed tree;
> Yea, I have slain my will, and still I live;
> I would be near; I shut my eyes to see;
> I bleed my bones, their marrow to bestow
> Upon that God who knows what I would know.[4]

The first stanza is all alienation—from nature and man and the self. The second is preparation for prayer, a relation with God as the light of light, source of the sun. The third is the prayer itself to the ground of all beseeching. In the fourth and last stanza the loss of selfhood is associated with the breakup of light on a storm-tossed tree, the emaciation of the human will; and then the last gesture—the voiding of the self, restitution, atonement (a characteristic sequence in late Roethke).

From the poems I have quoted, it might seem that Roethke was concerned with only one thing—himself. And this is true. But in his case it does not mean what it usually does. It does not mean that he is thrilled by his own emotions or that he spends much time in front of his mirror. The saving grace in Roethke, as in Whitman, is the assumption that he is a representative instance, no more if no less. When Roethke searches for value and meaning he assumes that this is interesting insofar as it is representative and not at all interesting when it ceases to be so. This is the source of Roethke's delicacy, as of Whitman's. When he says, in "I Need, I Need," "The Trouble is with No and Yes," or when he says, in "The Pure Fury," "Great Boehme rooted all in Yes and No," he advances this choice as a universal predicament rather than a proof of his own tender conscience. Again, in "The Waking" and other poems of similar intent, when he says, "I learn by going where I have to go," he is not claiming this as a uniquely sensitive perception; the line points to areas of feeling important because universal. And when he says, "Light takes the Tree; but who can tell us how?" the question is given with notable modesty, although indeed Roethke could have staked a higher claim for it, since it is the basis of several of his own religious poems. The motto for this delicacy in Roethke is a line from "The Sententious Man": "Each one's himself, yet each one's everyone." And there is the "Fourth Meditation" to prove that Roethke was never really in danger of solipsism.

With these qualifications, then, it is permissible to say that he was his own theme and to consider what this means in the poems—with this point in mind, however, that Whitman's equations were not available to Roethke. Roethke was not content to think of the self as the sum of its contents, even if he had Yeats to tell him that a mind is as rich as the images it contains. He would try to accumulate property, but only because he thought of property as a protective dike; behind the dike, one could live. But he never thought of this as having anything to do with the "nature" of the self. The self was problematic, but not a problem in addition. In one of his last and most beautiful poems, "In a Dark Time," he said:

> A man goes far to find out what he is—
> Death of the self in a long, tearless night,
> All natural shapes blazing unnatural light.
>
> Dark, dark my light, and darker my desire.
> My soul, like some heat-maddened summer fly,
> Keeps buzzing at the sill. Which I is *I*?[5]

That is still the question. In the early poems Roethke held to the common romantic idea of "the opposing self," the self defined by its grappling with the weeds of circumstance; hence, as Hopkins said, "Long Live the Weeds." Much later, Roethke was to consider this more strictly, notably in a poem like "The Exorcism," where he asks in a beguiling parenthesis, "(Father of flowers, who / Dares face the thing he is?)" And this question is joined to several bacterial images of man partaking uneasily of several worlds, beasts, serpents, the heron and the wren. In "Weed Puller" man is down in a fetor of weeds, "Crawling on all fours, / Alive, in a slippery grave."

Many of the middle poems feature a declared loss of self,

often given as division, absence. In "Where Knock Is Open Wide" Roethke says:

> I'm somebody else now.
> Don't tell my hands.
> Have I come to always? Not yet.
> One father is enough.
> Maybe God has a house.
> But not here.

There is a similar feeling in "Sensibility! O La!" and in "The Shimmer of Evil" perhaps the most explicit of all versions is, quite simply, "And I was only I"—which leads almost predictably but nonetheless beautifully to "There was no light; there was no light at all." The later poems tend to reflect upon the nature of the self by listing its demands; behind the love poems there is the assertion that "we live beyond / Our outer skin" even when the body sways to music. And much of this feeling culminates in the lovely "Fourth Meditation," which begins with many intuitions of sensibility and goes on to this:

> But a time comes when the vague life of the mouth
>   no longer suffices;
> The dead make more impossible demands from their
>   silence;
> The soul stands, lonely in its choice,
> Waiting, itself a slow thing,
> In the changing body.
>
>   The river moves, wrinkled by midges,
>   A light wind stirs in the pine needles.
>   The shape of a lark rises from a stone;
>   But there is no song.

This is a later version of the predicament, loss of self, which cries through the middle poems. In "The Lost Son" he says:

> Snail, snail, glister me forward,
> Bird, soft-sight me home.
> Worm, be with me.
> This is my hard time.

And a few lines later we read: "Voice, come out of the silence. / Say something." But there is no song in that "kingdom of bang and blab." In Roethke's poems song is proof that infinity clings to the finite. In "Old Lady's Winter Words" he says, "My dust longs for the invisible." What he wants is given in phrase, image, and rhythm: "the gradual embrace / of lichen around stones"; "Deep roots"; and, quite directly:

> Where is the knowledge that
> Could bring me to my God?

The only knowledge is reason in madness.

Thedore Roethke was a slow starter in poetry. He survived and grew and developed without attaching himself to schools or groups. He was never a boy wonder; he was never fashionable as the Beat poets were fashionable; most of the currents of easy feeling left him untouched, unmoved. He never set up shop as a left-wing poet or a right-wing poet or a Catholic poet or a New England poet or a Southern poet or a California poet. He never claimed privilege in any region of feeling. This was probably as good for his poetry as it was bad for his fame. He made his way by slow movements, nudgings of growth, like his own plants and flowers. But he grew, and his poems got better all the time—so much so, that his last poems were his greatest achievements, marvelously rich and humane.

Along the way he was helped by friends, often poets like Louise Bogan and Marianne Moore, but this is another story, not mine to tell. He was, however, helped also by other writers, earlier poets, and some of this story may be told, and the telling should disclose something of the poetry. Clearly, he was a careful, scrupulous poet. There are lines and phrases here and there that show that he was prone to infection, picking up things from lesser poets, like Dylan Thomas, and keeping them beyond the call of prudence. But the poets who really engaged him were those who offered him a challenge, a mode of feeling, perhaps, that he himself might not possess, or possessed without knowing that he did. The Elizabethan song-poets, and especially John Donne, challenged him in this way, and his own love poems reflect not only their own feeling but the strenuous competition of the Elizabethan masters. And then there were poets like Davies and Smart who disclosed certain modes of feeling and belief that were not so deeply a personal challenge but a measure of the time in which we live. And there were the great modern masters whom he could hardly have avoided hearing. He learned a lot from T. S. Eliot—mainly, I think, how to be expressive while holding most of his ammunition in reserve. And this often comes through the verse as a cadence, as in this passage from "I'm Here":

> At the stream's edge, trailing a vague finger;
> Flesh-awkward, half-alive,
> Fearful of high places, in love with horses;
> In love with stuffs, silks,
> Rubbing my nose in the wool of blankets;
> Bemused; pleased to be;
> Mindful of cries,
> The meaningful whisper,
> The wren, the catbird.

Consider the rhetoric of the short phrase, at once giving and taking; Eliot is a great master in these discriminations. Think of this passage in "East Coker":

> In the middle, not only in the middle of the way
> But all the way, in a dark wood, in a bramble,
> On the edge of a grimpen, where is no secure
>   foothold,
> And menaced by monsters, fancy lights,
> Risking enchantment.

Other cadences Roethke got from other poets—from Hopkins, notably, especially from "The Wreck of the Deutschland," which Roethke uses in the poem about the greenhouse in a storm, "Big Wind":

> But she rode it out,
> That old rose-house,
> She hove into the teeth of it,
> The core and pith of that ugly storm . . .

From Joyce Roethke learned one kind of language for the primitive, the rudimentary, the aboriginal, especially the Joyce of the *Portrait of the Artist as a Young Man*, bearing hard on the first chapter; and *Finnegans Wake* showed him one way of dealing with the unconscious. And there is Wallace Stevens. Roethke disapproved of Stevens' procedures in argumentative theory, but in fact he learned some fundamental lessons from Stevens. When he says, "I prefer the still joy," he is Stevens' pupil, conning a lesson he could well have done without. And I think he found in Stevens a justification of, if not an incitement to, his own propensity for the "pure moment." In one of his later poems he says, "O to be delivered from the rational into the realm of pure song." And if pure song is pure expression or pure communication, it is also close to Stevens' "hum of thoughts evaded in the mind." Stevens seems to me to be behind those poems in which Roethke longs for essence, for an essential "purity," or finds it in a still moment. He records it in a passage like this, for instance, from the "First Meditation":

> There are still times, morning and evening:
> The cerulean, high in the elm,

> Thin and insistent as a cicada,
> And the far phoebe, singing,
> The long plaintive notes floating down,
> Drifting through leaves, oak and maple,
> Or the whippoorwill, along the smoky ridges,
> A single bird calling and calling;
> A fume reminds me, drifting across wet gravel;
> A cold wind comes over stones;
> A flame, intense, visible,
> Plays over the dry pods,
> Runs fitfully along the stubble,
> Moves over the field,
> Without burning.
>   In such times, lacking a god,
>   I am still happy.

And Stevens is behind those poems in which Roethke presents the "single man" who contains everything:

> His spirit moves like monumental wind
> That gentles on a sunny blue plateau.
> He is the end of things, the final man.

When Whitman comes into the later poems, such as "Journey to the Interior," he shows Roethke how to deal with natural forms without hurting them, so that "the spirit of wrath becomes the spirit of blessing"; or how to give one thing after another without lining them up in symbolist rivalry, so that he can say "Beautiful my desire, and the place of my desire"; or how to preserve one's own integrity even when beset by "the terrible hunger for objects." But Whitman was a late consultant to Roethke. Much earlier, and toward the end of his poetic life, he attended upon Yeats' poems and contracted debts handsomely acknowledged in the "In Memoriam" and again in "The Dance." To Roethke—or so it seems from the poems—Yeats stood for the imperious note, concentration, magnificent rhetoric clashing against the bare notation, the dramatic play of self and soul.

> What's madness but nobility of soul
> At odds with circumstance? The day's on fire!
> I know the purity of pure despair,
> My shadow pinned against a sweating wall.
> That place among the rocks—is it a cave,
> Or winding path? The edge is what I have.

It peters out somewhat. Yeats would not have praised the last line. But the rest is very much in Yeats's shadow, particularly the Yeats of "Coole Park and Ballylee, 1931." The dramatic occasion; the landscape, moralized with a large showing; the poet, finding correspondences and emblems in herons, wrens, swans; nature with her tragic buskin on—these are the Yeatsian gestures. And, to take them a little further, Roethke knows that if he proposes to learn a high rhetoric he must do it in earnest. So he begins with the magisterially rhetorical question, then the short declaration, not yet intimate, "The day's on fire!" and only then the despair. And even now it is given as knowledge rather than romantic exposure, so that even the shadow, the other self, is presented as an object of contemplation before the poet acknowledges the feeling as his own in "a sweating wall."

One of the odd things in this list of relationships, however, is that it is quite possible to think of Roethke as one of the best modern poets without troubling about the fact that he was, after all, an American poet. When reading Stevens or Frost or Williams or Robert Lowell we are constantly aware that we are reading American poets; but this is not an insistent element in Roethke. Indeed, it is quite clear that he bears no special relation to either of the dominant traditions in American poetry—New England and the South. Temperamentally he is not too far away from such writers as Hawthorne, Melville, or James. Like them, in his quite different way, he was concerned with the wounded conscience, the private hazard. But while it is obviously proper in some sense to relate the poems of Robert Lowell to this tradition, it has little bearing on Roethke's work. And the tradition of the South can be ruled out. This suggests that the discussion of American literature in terms of these two traditions may by now have lost much of its force. To think of the New England tradition as scholastic, autocratic, and logical, and the Southern tradition as humanistic, Ciceronian, grammatical, and rhetorical is fine as far as it goes,[6] but its relevance clearly fades in regard to poets like Roethke. This may well be the point to emphasize, that Roethke and many of the poets of his generation took their food wherever they could find it. Yeats could well be more useful to them than, say, Hawthorne, because they saw their problems as being human, universal, in the first instance, and American problems only by application and inference. Roethke committed himself to his own life. He thought of it as a human event of some representative interest. And he set himself to work toward lucidity and order without turning himself into a case study entitled "The Still Complex Fate of Being an American." This is one aspect of Roethke's delicacy. Contemporary American poets, for the most part, are not going his way; they insist upon their complex fate and would not live without it. But Roethke's way of being an American is an eminently respectable way, and part of his achievement is that he makes it available to others.

"The Far Field"[7] is a distinguished example of this delicacy. It has four unequal sections. The first is a dream of journeys, journeys without maps, featuring imprisonment, attenuation of being, the self "flying like a bat deep into a narrowing tunnel" until there is nothing but darkness. It is life in a minor key, diminished thirds of being. The second stanza translates these into major terms, images of force, aggression, suffering, death, dead rats eaten by rain and ground beetles. But the poet, meditating upon these images, thinks of other images, of life, movement, freedom, everything he means by "song." And these natural configurations lead to thoughts of life as cycle, evolution and return, proliferations of being, the whole process of life, which the poet calls "infinity"; what Wallace Stevens in "The Bouquet" calls "the infinite of the actual perceived, / A freedom revealed, a realization touched, / The real made more acute by an unreal." In the third section the poet feels a corresponding change in himself, a moving forward, a quickening, and as he commits himself to earth and air he says, "I have come to a still, but not a deep center." Naturally it feels like a loss, another diminution of being, even if the sense of life-ordained process is strong. And this feeling leads straight into the fourth and last section:

The lost self changes,
Turning toward the sea,
A sea-shape turning around,—
An old man with his feet before the fire,
In robes of green, in garments of adieu.

A man faced with his own immensity
Wakes all the waves, all their loose wandering fire.
The murmur of the absolute, the why
Of being born fails on his naked ears.
His spirit moves like monumental wind

That gentles on a sunny blue plateau.
He is the end of things, the final man.

All finite things reveal infinitude:
The mountain with its singular bright shade
Like the blue shine on freshly frozen snow,
The after-light upon ice-burdened pines;
Odor of basswood on a mountain-slope,
A scent beloved of bees;
Silence of water above a sunken tree:
The pure serene of memory in one man,—
A ripple widening from a single stone
Winding around the waters of the world.

Roethke says: "The end of things, the final man"; Stevens asserts in "The Auroras of Autumn":

There is nothing until in a single man contained,
Nothing until this named thing nameless is
And is destroyed. He opens the door of his house
On flames. The scholar of one candle sees
An Arctic effulgence flaring on the frame
Of everything he is. And he feels afraid.

The difference is that Stevens identifies the man with his imagination, and his imagination with his vision—and insists upon doing so. And the imagination feeds upon as much reality as it can "see" and values only that; what it can't see won't hurt or help it. The scholar has only this one candle. Roethke's man is not a scholar at all, or if he is, he is an amateur, perhaps a mere teacher. His imagination is partly his memory, which offers hospitality to sights, sounds, and smells, and partly his conscience, and partly his feeling for modes of being that he cannot command, directions that he cannot chart. Hence his poems are the cries of their occasions, but rarely cries of triumph. This is what makes his later poems the noble things they are, stretchings of the spirit without fantasia or panache. "Which is the way?" they ask, and if they include God in their reply they do so with due deference, knowing that one can be "too glib about eternal things," too much "an intimate of air and all its songs."

Another way of putting it is that the poems, especially the middle poems, are cries of their occasions, sudden, isolated cries. The later poems turn cries into prayers, praying for a world order, a possible world harmony of which the cries are part, like voices in polyphony. The self in exposure is mono-tone; a sustaining society is polyphony; God is the Great Composer. The poet's ideal is the part song, music for several instruments, what the Elizabethans called "broken music." In "In Evening Air" Roethke says, "I'll make a broken music, or I'll die." In such poems as "The Marrow" and "In a Dark Time" he made a broken music at once personal and—in Stevens' sense—noble. And then, alas, he died.

Notes

1. Theodore Roethke, *Words for the Wind* (Bloomington: Indiana Univ. Press, 1961), p. 181.
2. I owe this to James S. Southworth.
3. Roethke, "The Poet and the Poem," *New World Writing*, No. 9 (Philadelphia: J. B. Lippincott, 1961), pp. 214–219.
4. Roethke, *The Far Field* (New York: Doubleday, 1964), pp. 89–90.
5. Ibid., p. 79.
6. See H. M. McLuhan, "Poe's Tradition," *Sewanee Review*, LII (1944), pp. 31ff.
7. *The Far Field*, pp. 25–28.

WILL ROGERS

1879–1935

Will Rogers was born on November 4, 1879, in Oologah, Indian Territory (now Oklahoma), and christened William Penn Adair Rogers; Indians were among his forebears. He attended boarding school in Missouri and later sold the family ranch to finance a trip around the world. He visited Africa, China, and Australia, performing in a Wild West show until his funds ran out. By 1905 he had reached New York, where he appeared in vaudeville shows at the Victoria Theater and developed the performing style that became his trademark: demonstrating difficult rope tricks while keeping up a humorous commentary on topics of current interest with the recurring line, "All I know is what I read in the newspapers." For many years he appeared in a succession of Broadway reviews, including the Ziegfeld Follies.

Between 1929 and 1935 Rogers acted in a number of films, including *David Harum* and *State Fair*, always playing a shrewd but slightly bumbling homespun American. For many years he contributed a syndicated column to the *New York Times* and other newspapers, and many of them were collected into books. These include *The Cowboy Philosopher on Prohibition* (1919), *The Cowboy Philosopher on the Peace Conference* (1919), *What We Laugh At* (1920), *The Illiterate Digest* (1924), *Letters of a Self-Made Diplomat to His President* (1927), *There's Not a Bathing Suit in Russia* (1927), and *Will Rogers' Political Follies* (1929).

Rogers, along with Wiley Post, the aviator, was killed in a plane crash near Point Barrow, Alaska, on August 15, 1935.

Will Rogers says: "All I know is what I read in the Papers." That isn't so. A lot of people read the papers. All some of them get is the names of buyers just come to town; sure tips on the horse races; what the dry goods stores are selling; what the stocks and bonds are doing, especially if the readers are trying to figure out how to do something about the trousers without sacrificing the vest; and perhaps a dip into the latest murder or divorce, just to keep up on the office conversation. Will Rogers is probably the only man in the country, outside of the political reporters, the politicians and the copy readers, who reads the political stories, and they only read their own stuff. He reads it all, and turns out nifties about it without raising his voice or pointing to himself with pride. ⟨. . .⟩

Rogers tries to put you off the track by speaking of himself in this fashion: "I am just an old country boy in a big town trying to get along." He pretends he does not know which knife and fork to eat his salad with at the big hotel banquets. He hesitates about the spelling of words of more than two syllables, so his readers and hearers won't think he is putting on the high tone. In the introduction he wrote himself (after failing to get Arthur Brisbane, Ring Lardner, Irvin S. Cobb, Ibáñez, Ilinor Glyn and other humorists to write it for him) he spoofs himself, before you can do it to him. He says of his own style: "His jugglery of correct words and perfect English sentences is magical, and his spelling is almost uncanny." Then when he gets off a wow like: "American people like to have you repent; then they are generous," you are to think that is just an accident. He didn't know he was doing it, and he has no idea what it means. He asks you to believe that "a comedian is not supposed to be serious nor to know much. As long as he is silly enough to get laughs, why, people let it go at that."

When Will Rogers comes on stage at the Follies, with his jaw full of chewing gum and his arms loaded with ropes, he makes you feel sorry for him. You know he is going to get tangled up in the ropes or lose a stroke of his gum. He stands there intent on getting a line of rope around each of the footlights, or that is how it looks from the other side. If he should miss one of the bulbs you know he would never get over it, and you sit forward in your seat, tearing off great strips of veneer with your fingernails. He begins talking in his Oklahoma drawl, and all the while he is chewing gum and playing with the ropes. You know you could do it better than he. When he begins to make the ropes writhe like snakes and strikes the bullseye again and again with his quaint, homely wit, you are as proud of him as if you had done it yourself. But those seemingly offhand remarks of his are neatly timed to coincide with some spectacular stunt with the ropes. It is not until afterward, when you try to tell it to some one who has not seen the Follies that you realize two things: he put it over in the only language and intonation possible, and he said something keen and penetrating and true. All in the name of gawky, innocent, country-jake, amateurishness.

This *Illiterate Digest* is goods off the same bolt. He is down in black and white where you can watch him closely and go back and see how he did it. He is just about as unsophisticated in doing his work as a Russian toe dancer, and one job is as intricate as the other. He gives the impression of being simply the cross-roads general merchandise store talkers of a continent rolled into one man. But the fact of the matter is that he knows just what he wants to do, just how he wants to do it, and he does it. He is an expert satirist masquerading as a helpless, inoffensive, ineffectual zany. Read what he says on the subject of the "Remodeled Chewing Gum Corporation":

> Gum is the only ingredient of our National life of which no one knows how or of what it is made. We know that Sawdust makes our Breakfast food. We know that Tomato Cans constitute Ford Bodies. We know that old Second-hand Newspapers make our 15-dollar Shoes. We know that Cotton makes our All-Wool suits. But no one knows yet what constitutes a mouthful of chewing gum.

Rogers is always for the man beneath. He puts a pin into the pompous and jeers at the self-righteous and the self-important. He is non-partisan in politics; you can name the administration, if you will let him crack jokes about it. Occasionally he drops his motley and lets loose with some Number One vitriol, as in his defense of the Prince of Wales against the cheap jokesmiths who never rode a horse in their lives, let alone had one fall under them. There are four or five pieces about the great oil scandals which appeared originally in *The New York Times*; they are not only among the best in the book but they rank high in American humorous literature. Rogers anticipated the popular reaction to the investigation, as expressed in the recent election, with uncanny foresight; he routed out and exposed a pharisaical stench in the horror of the liberals and made a burlesque of its farcical implications. His chapter on the grave problem of etiquette, or how to tell a butler, and when, is as good as Donald Ogden Stewart, and much less savage. The report of the Democratic National Convention is a classic of exaggeration, in the good old Artemus Ward–Mark Twain–Bill Nye tradition, but, like them, he works in a germ of hard, cold truth. "The World Tomorrow" is a selection of pithy, informing, moral paragraphs, after the fashion of a well-known and well-paid editorial writer; it is hilarious nonsense. But, as a matter of fact, it is hard to find one part of the book noticeably better than another part. It is all good.—JOHN CRAWFORD, "Will Rogers Knows More Than He Pretends," *NYTBR*, Dec. 14, 1924, p. 2

Mr. Will Rogers is a man of wisdom as well as wit. He flew from Berlin to Moscow, and sums up the present situation there very acutely in *There's Not a Bathing Suit in Russia*. He tells us of "a bird named Stalin, a great big two-fisted fighting egg from the Caucasus—a Borah of the Black Sea," and of the other notorieties in the "land of boots and blood," as he calls it. He is a fair critic, however, with few prejudices and a very shrewd sense not only of humour but of humanity. His final judgment seems to us as just as it is quaint: "Communism will never get anywhere till they get that basic idea of Propaganda out of their head and replace it with some work. If they plowed as much as they Propagandered, they would be richer than the Principality of Monaco. The trouble is they all got their theory's out of a book, instead of any of them ever going to work and practicing them. I read the same books these Birds learned from, and that's the books of that guy Marx. Why, he was like one of these efficiency experts. He could explain to you how you could save a million dollars, and he couldent save enough himself to eat on." The *Letters of a Self-Made Diplomat to His President* is as good or better. His description of our Parliament, our General Strike, and the bureaucratic "Sir" who kept him waiting for an hour in the Foreign Office strike the reader as thoroughly realistic, and are of distinct importance to those of us who would see ourselves as others see us, for Mr. Rogers is a representative albeit an exceptional American. His letters on Rome and on Signor Mussolini are both funny and wise. Of the Duce he says that many of his public utterances "sound like boasting, but are only meant for Home consumption." "You yourself, Mr. President," he slily adds, "know that you have to pull a lot of apple sauce on various occasions." Both these books combine entertainment and instruction and we thoroughly recommend them. —UNSIGNED, *Spec*, Sept. 3, 1927, p. 352

When, back in 1916, I wound up a New York holiday by going to see the Ziegfeld Follies in the big barn of the New Amsterdam Theatre and watched an actor in cowboy togs twirl a rope and heard him toss out some wisecracks (only I don't think the word had yet come in), it did not occur to me that I was listening to a durable contribution to American letters. Nor, I am sure, did it occur to the cowboy.

Will Rogers went on to write a column, and let us all be grateful for that, for while newspaper columns are, in their very nature, ephemeral, they are not nearly so much so as wisecracks across footlights. Since Will Rogers's column was widely syndicated, thousands of files of it are preserved all up and down the land. Of course, that does not make the stuff broadly accessible.

This book does. ⟨*The Autobiography of Will Rogers*⟩ is a compilation of simon-pure Rogersana, with the column which Will wrote from the end of 1922 to his death in Alaska in 1935 providing, happily, the bulk of the text. The result will be compared to Poor Richard, Puddn'head Wilson, Marcus Aurelius, and Samuel Pepys, and it can stand up under that comparison without having to produce a passport.

Here, for instance, is superb documentation of the boom and of the bust—primary historical source material of high authenticity and importance. Nothing will give the soul of Will Rogers greater delight, or make him chuckle with deeper satisfaction, than for him to turn to some authoritative elucidatory text, fifty or 500 years from now, and find "Rogers, *op. cit.*" peppered throughout the footnotes.

Today's reader is not so likely to chuckle. The Rogers scraps which we used to read twenty years ago with rueful grins now take on a tartness and a mordancy which were there all the while, but were hidden under the laugh. We Americans have always held to the principle of when-you-say-that-comma-smile—it is all right with us if our most sacred institutions are assaulted provided the attack is made in a spirit of good clean fun. Here it is not a case of the Rogers humor wearing off: rather has it mellowed into transparency and permitted us to look underneath. Thus:

> October 31, 1929: Sure must be a great consolation to the poor people who lost their stock in the late crash to know that it has fallen in the hands of Mr. Rockefeller, who will take care of it and see that it has a good home and never be allowed to wander around unprotected again.
>
> There is one rule that works in every calamity. Be it pestilence, war, or famine, the rich get richer and the poor get poorer. The poor even help arrange it. But it's just as I have been constantly telling you, "Don't gamble"; take all your savings and buy some good stock and hold it till it goes up, then sell it.
>
> If it don't go up, don't buy it.
>
> December 9: There is only one form of employment that I can think of but what has its bright spots and that's coal mining. There is generally an overproduction and they are out of work; if not that it's a strike. Then when they do go to work, the mine blows up. Then if none of these three things happen, they still have the worst job in the world.
>
> February 22, 1931: Here is what George Washington missed by not living to his 199th birthday. He would have seen our great political system of "equal rights to all and the privileges to none" working so smoothly that 7,000,000 are without a chance to earn their living; he would see 'em handing out rations in peace times—that would have reminded him of Valley Forge. In fact, we have reversed the old system; we all get fat in war times and thin during peace. I bet after seeing us he would sue us for calling him "father."
>
> March 13, 1935: Say, did you read about what Mr. Roosevelt said about those "Holding Companies"? A holding company is a thing where you hand an accomplice the goods while the policeman searches you.

If Will Rogers were alive today and said some of those things without smiling, some unsmiling committee would have him under the Capitol Hill klieglights as quick as you could say subpoena.

The purely factual autobiographical content of this titular autobiography is valuable in its own right. Will Rogers's father was one-eighth Cherokee Indian, his mother one-quarter. Will's public schooling stopped at the fourth grade, but he fourth-graded in so many different places that he got to know it by heart. On his own, he learned lariat-throwing. His father shipped him to school in Missouri to study for the ministry; the authorities took a large view of Will's yanking a stone goddess off her pedestal, but a narrower one of his unintentional roping of a professor. There was an interlude at a military school, but Will ran away from there. He took a job on a ranch, bummed his way to California and back, volunteered in steer-roping contests. He heard the Argentine was a great cattle country, traveled there by way of London, went broke, and took a job chaperoning cattle to South Africa. The Boer War was on; at its close Will joined Texas Jack's Wild West Show at Johannesburg—and a career had begun. It took him to New Zealand, Australia, and so to San Francisco. He had circum-navigated the globe on practically nothing. He joined Colonel Zack Mulhall's show, and in 1905 they performed in Madison Square Garden. (This was the Madison Square Garden on Madison Square.) He played Hammerstein's roof, and later Germany and England. In 1915 he joined Ziegfeld. That is about as far as the formal autobiography gets. In 1922 he started a weekly column, and 1926 a daily. He wrote pieces for *The Saturday Evening Post*; he was interviewed; he lectured. Out of it all comes this book. It is quite a book, by quite a man.—JOHN T. WINTERICH, "Simon-Pure Rogersana," *SR*, Oct. 15, 1949, pp. 19–20

Though we have not happened to run across one, we are willing to bet that shortly before 1915, some pundit was saying confidently that horse-sensible humor of the sort supplied by Poor Richard, Hosea Biglow, Major Jones, Josh Billings, Mark Twain, and hosts of others had been finally played out. But 1915 was the year when the most popular of all such comic dispensers of gumption rose to fame. He would be America's best known humorist for the next two decades.

This was an Oklahoma-born ex-cowboy, ex-Wild-West-show-lariat-twirler and ex-vaudeville-performer: Will Rogers. In 1915, Will became a star in Florenz Ziegfeld's *Midnight Frolic* by chewing gum, performing rope-tricks, and pausing now and then to drawl amusing comments on current events.

Anyone who had met up with the breed would soon see that, though he had unique charms, Rogers had all the brand marks. His outfit—battered broadbrim hat, bandana scarf, shirtsleeves and chaps—was that of a proletarian. "Grammar and I get along like a Russian and a bathtub," he boasted; and his store of words and frequently flawed spelling helped prove that he hadn't been besmirched by too much education. "Maybe ain't ain't so correct," he allowed, then he went on to state the time-hallowed American belief that book learning got you nowhere: "But I notice that lots of folks who ain't usin' ain't ain't eatin'." Will knew why he himself was doing better: "I've been eating pretty regular, and the reason I have been is because I stayed an old country boy." Will had chummy chats with Presidents reminiscent of those that old country boys Jack Downing and Artemus Ward said they had.

But because there was enough that was new about Will to keep him from seeming too old-hat, in time he was getting laughs from more of his countrymen than any humorist before him, including Mark Twain, had reached. He came from a recent frontier that Western novels, plays, and movies had

made glamorous: Will was the first great *cowboy* comedian to come along. That wasn't all he had going for him. More Americans than ever were there to be reached—and more media could reach them—than ever. Rogers got into all the acts that were available. He did his stuff on Broadway, not only in the *Frolics* but also in the *Follies*. He was booked into vaudeville circuits, movie-palace stage shows, and lecture halls. He was in movies—first silents, when his cracks were captions between segments, then talkies. The airwaves carried his shrewd comments. He wrote books, magazine articles and columns, the last for newspapers with forty million readers. News stories and newsreels told how in the Era of Beautiful Nonsense he turned Downing's and Ward's fancied encounters into actualities; he had real-life kidding sessions with Calvin Coolidge and his wife. He appeared by invitation before national conventions. So Rogers initiated impudent familiarities with White House denizens and leading politicians that professional wits would continue into the 1970's.—WALTER BLAIR, HAMLIN HILL, "Afterword" to *America's Humor*, 1978, pp. 521–23

NORRIS W. YATES
From "The Crackerbarrel Sage
in the West and South:
Will Rogers and Irvin S. Cobb"
The American Humorist
1964, pp. 113–18

As a frontispiece to the revised edition (1960) of his book, *Native American Humor*, Walter Blair has drawn a circle of nineteenth-century humorists seated around a potbellied stove, evidently swapping yarns. If Professor Blair had added one of George Ade's self-made men, and portraits of Abe Martin, Will Rogers, Irvin S. Cobb, and possibly E. W. Howe, O. O. McIntyre, Walt Mason, and Ellis Parker Butler, he might have emphasized a point made in the text and in his *Horse Sense in American Humor*, the point, namely, that the nineteenth-century hot-stove tradition in American humor continued unbroken into the twentieth. This tradition—associated, as seen, with rugged individualism in business, caution in politics, and stability in the home—reached a new high in popularity in Will Rogers. Not without certain modifications, however.

For one thing, Rogers gave a western tinge to the tradition. Some earlier humorists had written humor while living in the West—George Horatio Derby (John Phoenix) in California; Edgar Wilson (Bill) Nye and M. C. Barrow in Wyoming, for example—but no humorist had achieved a national reputation while presenting himself as a western character. Rogers, on the other hand, began early to bill himself as "the cowboy philosopher," and although he got his start in humor on the eastern vaudeville circuits, he came honestly by his lariat and his western saddle. His father, Clem Rogers, was one of the first—and last—of the cattle barons during the brief period of the open range and the trail drive. Will once remarked, "My father was one eighth Cherokee and my mother one fourth Cherokee, which I figure makes me about one eighth cigar-store Injun." Many times Rogers stressed that his people were the first Americans and had met, not sailed on, the *Mayflower*. He came from both the economic and the ethnic heart of the Old West.

Kin Hubbard once said that, "No feller ever ort t' get too

great t' register from th' little town where he lives." Rogers was born in a ranch house near Claremore, Oklahoma, and he always put down that town as his native place when he registered at hotels. His father was wealthy, but even in his teens Will preferred to make his way alone, and, after some country schooling and a two-year stay at Kemper Military Academy, he worked as a roughneck in the oil fields, punched cows in Texas and in Argentina, and traveled with a Wild West show in Africa, China, and Australia. As a result of the latter job, he began to appear on the stage as a trick roper. Probably by 1910 he was making wisecracks on current topics to pep up his act, and it was his homely verbal comedy as much as his rope tricks that got him a role with Ziegfeld's *Follies* in 1915.

Will's first two books, *The Cowboy Philosopher on the Peace Conference* (1919) and *The Cowboy Philosopher on Prohibition* (1919), were mostly collections of what he had said on the stage. In 1922, both the New York *Herald* and the McNaught Syndicate approached him with the notion that he should write a weekly humorous feature. He began for McNaught by imitating Mr. Dooley and presenting two quaint characters talking over the news, but he found he could not create characters—except for his own *persona*—nor write narrative. He tried putting his humor into epigrams and brief paragraphs, much as he had done orally, and his rise to popularity as a writer was shortly under way. Two years later he still had not quite learned that his natural media were the quip and the editorializing paragraph. When he added a daily feature he at first imitated the anecdotal style of Irvin S. Cobb, but he soon reverted to his natural methods. [1]

Both features were soon running in dozens of newspapers; it is said he eventually reached one hundred million readers a year. In addition to the daily paper, Rogers' humor reached the public through the stage, the lecture circuit, the movies, and the radio. When he was killed in a plane crash in 1935, Senate majority leader Joseph E. Robinson announced that Rogers was "Probably the most widely known citizen in the United States." [2]

Why did Rogers capture the public on a scale that probably surpassed even Mr. Dooley and Abe Martin? Blair has suggested that his cowboy origins helped. Through them he embodied a figure that people liked to feel was more representative of American life as a whole than was any farmer type; moreover (says Blair), he reached the public through more media than any other humorist had used. Other commentators have stressed that he was always just a little, but never too far, ahead of the main drifts of public opinion. Thus he was an early supporter of Wilson but quickly became cool to the League of Nations; he advocated "normalcy" before Harding—who might himself be called a crackerbox type—had unintentionally coined the word; he tried to sting the Hooverites into more action but became a traffic cop in blue jeans warning the Roosevelt cavalcade not to go too fast and too far.

It should be added that Rogers, at least in his role as a public man, was close kin to the mythical citizen on the make praised by William Graham Sumner, idealized by the Progressives, placed in a city tavern by Dunne, given wealth and a flighty family by Ade, and brought back to the village square by Hubbard. Behind the chaps and the lariat the public recognized the same familiar figure. Furthermore, Will knew how to impersonate—perhaps one should say, to *be*—several different varieties of this man. Thus, when he discussed prohibition, he appeared as a practical citizen who minded his own business and was skeptical of both the extreme wets and drys; in this role he appealed to millions who were sick of the whole issue. When he needled the public for its complacency during

the nineteen-twenties and called for moderate reforms that would reduce political immorality and help the farmer, he appeared more like the enlightened citizen the Progressives had postulated, and masses of readers who were disgusted with the corruption in high places but apathetic when it came to doing something about it responded sheepishly and joyously.

George Ade had advised that to get on, one should keep on being a country boy. Rogers strove consciously to perpetuate the image of a rube from the wide-open spaces seeking his fortune. He reproved Percy Hammond, drama critic for the New York *Herald Tribune*, with, "Percy, I am just an old country boy in a big town trying to get along. I have been eating Pretty regular, and the reason I have been is because I have stayed an old Country boy." (Hammond was from Cadiz, Ohio.) In reply to criticisms from Ed Sullivan, columnist on the New York *Daily News*, Rogers referred to "us country columnists." Like Kin Hubbard and O. O. McIntyre, Will often used his rural background to suggest the wise fool, especially with regard to literacy and letters. "Grammar and I get along like a Russian and a Bathtub," he said, and he made a point of never having got beyond McGuffey's Fourth Reader (which was not true). However, he also stated that his public was not "buying" grammar but ideas—and left unspoken the thought that possibly he had a few worth expressing, "fool" though he might be where language was concerned.

About formal literature: "Vergil must have been quite a fellow, but he didn't know enough to put his stuff in English like Shakespeare did, so you don't hear much of him any more, only in high school and roasting-ear colleges, where he is studied more and remembered less than any single person." When it came to pictorial art, Rogers was far behind Mark Twain, who in *Innocents Abroad* had admired a few paintings. From overseas, Rogers wrote in 1926, ". . . I don't care anything about Oil Paintings. Ever since I struck a dry hole near the old home ranch in Rogers County, Oklahoma I have hated oil, in the raw, and all its subsidiaries. You can even color it up, and it don't mean anything to me. I don't want to see a lot of old Pictures. . . . So when I tell you about Rome I just want you to picture it as it is, not as it is in the guidebooks, but as an ordinary hard-boiled American like you and I would see it." Rogers here flattered the Babbitts—"hard-boiled" Americans all—in language much like theirs. In 1934, when Diego Rivera was dismissed by Nelson Rockefeller for putting Lenin and other radical figures into his murals at Rockefeller Center, Rogers sided with the millionaires and with the conservatives in art, in contrast to E. B. White (a graduate of Cornell), who spoofed both sides in a poem on the controversy. When the common man was threatened with culture, Rogers, like Dunne, was often there to defend him.

In Rogers, the professional humorist and the man were unusually close. "All I know is what I read in the papers," was almost a literal truth, according to Mrs. Rogers. Will really had been a cowhand, and whenever he visited his old haunts in Oolagah and Claremore, he was received by the local ranchers and townspeople with an affection that gives a true ring to such statements as "I am mighty happy I am going home to my people, who know me as 'Willie, Uncle Clem Rogers' boy.'" On the other hand, the public image and private man did not match perfectly. Will's visits to Oklahoma after he became famous were brief, though fairly frequent. In addition, Lowell Thomas claimed that "The only pose in Will Rogers was the pretense that he was an ignorant and illiterate fellow," and P. J. O'Brien writes that "Underneath Will Rogers' mask of 'ignorance' was a well-mannered and cultured man with a shrewd, trained mind." Both Irvin S. Cobb and Homer Croy qualify the epitaph chosen by Will, "He joked about every prominent man in his time, but he never met a man he didn't like." Cobb says that although Will certainly liked most people, he could express his dislike of a few in salty language and the epitaph probably referred to prominent politicians only. Croy asserts that Rogers had two fist fights.[3]

Yet Rogers surely meant what he said when he told Max Eastman, "I don't like to make jokes that hurt anybody."[4] Even in unguarded moments he rarely made such jokes. His kindliness, and the verifiable nucleus of truth in his claim to be "just folks" render his personality and his *persona* closer to each other than those of any other humorist examined in this book ⟨*The American Humorist*⟩.

Notes

1. Homer Croy, *Our Will Rogers*, Duell, Sloan and Pearce (New York, 1953), pp. 173–179. Collections of Rogers' writings and sayings in book form include *The Cowboy Philosopher on Prohibition* (1919); *Rogers-isms, the Cowboy Philosopher on the Peace Conference* (1919); *What We Laugh At* (1920); *The Illiterate Digest* (1924); *Letters of a Self-Made Diplomat to His President* (1926); *There's Not a Bathing Suit in Russia* (1927); *Will Rogers' Political Follies* (1929); *Ether and Me* (1929); *Wit and Philosophy from the Radio Talks of America's Humorist, Will Rogers* (1930); Jack Lait (comp.), *Will Rogers, Wit and Wisdom* (1936); *The Autobiography of Will Rogers* (1949); *How We Elect Our Presidents* (1952); *Sanity Is Where You Find It* (1955). The last three compilations were made by Donald Day. Day has recently completed *Will Rogers: A Biography*, David McKay (New York, 1962) in which, among other new material, is recorded the fact that Will tried without much success to publish some of his jokes in *Life*.
2. P. J. O'Brien, *Will Rogers*, John C. Winston (Chicago and Philadelphia, 1935), p. 274.
3. Irvin S. Cobb, *Exit Laughing*, Bobbs-Merrill (Indianapolis and New York, 1941), pp. 406–407; Croy, *Our Will Rogers*, p. vii. Other major biographical sources include William Howard Payne and Jake G. Lyons (comps.), *Folks Say of Will Rogers*, Putnam (New York, 1936), and Betty Rogers, *Will Rogers, His Wife's Story*, Bobbs-Merrill (Indianapolis and New York, 1941).
4. Eastman, *Enjoyment of Laughter* (New York, 1937), p. 338.

JESSE BIER
From "Intercentury Humor"
The Rise and Fall of American Humor
1968, pp. 198–202

In this period, which includes the muckraking era, there is little surprise in tracing the strong careers of humorists like Bierce, Dunne, and Ade. The surprise is that the mild and rural Hubbard should be popular at all in a time of highly antithetic or ascendant urban comedy. Or that, later in this period and into the next, Will Rogers should rise to such bland heights of fame. This stubborn optimist, who "never met a man I didn't like," seemed subsequently unmoved by Al Capones in the Prohibition and Depression years and serenely unaware of imminent evil from Hitlerite gangsters overseas. But his incognizance was a result of his professionalizing himself as a native American, even to an indecent Cherokee pride. In so doing, he appears as the rural counterpart of O. Henry, sublimely and ruthlessly subduing his innate talent and clarity of mind. More and more, he became the occasionally irreverent critic but increasingly genial and harmless western type. Indeed, his reputation is established and even monumentalized in the larger than life sculpture of him at Colorado

Springs, that Rocky Mountain resort of the elderly and fond-hearted.

Both the success of Kin Hubbard and the phenomenon of Will Rogers can be explained, however, as the result of nostalgia in a period of accelerated urban growth. It was emphatically the time of the first growth of our cities, when the urban humorist and cosmopolitan satirist were superseding the crackerbox philosophers and all country types. Even O. Henry's citified stories are a clue to the change of taste and public. Bierce operates out of San Francisco (before disappearing over the Mexican border in complete renunciation of all American drab and drivel), heralding the great iconoclast who will by main force root himself in his city on the opposite coast, Baltimore's Mencken. Dunne's Dooley is the archetype of them all; Brackenridge's comic butt became a critical force to be reckoned with down the block. Even the deep-dyed Hoosier, George Ade, moves into the big city. Such profound demographic shifts, however, do not occur at once or without regret for the old crackerbox humor. During transition the public values the fading types, all the more as they become anachronized.

In the case of the Oklahoman, the substitution of the cowboy for the customary rural figure, coincident with early silent movie exploitation of the simple, wise, and mythic cowboy hero, presented an irresistible prototype. Rogers worked cannily at the individualism inhering in his character. To do him justice, he did in fact write and rewrite all his material, happy as a later columnist to get "one good gag a month." He did not lend himself to organization in the subsequent manner of most radio comics, who were actors primarily. He was still, and at least, his own comedian. And Hubbard acknowledged his supersedence: "the only time when having enough rope didn't end disastrously." True to their mutual last stand for the provincial, countrified type, Rogers would set himself explicitly against urban and industrial pressures and that symbol of New America, the Ford car, an image for standardization. All these Fords came like their drivers, with "the same parts, the same upholstery and the same noises." Sophisticated contemporary sociologists would have predicted the emergence of Rogers and succeeding variants of the type, (Hal Kinney, Andy Griffith, Herb Shriner), who diminish in number and force but run true to form. The disappointment we feel is that whatever was genuinely shrewd and sharp in Rogers turned almost wilfully antiseptic. The man who wrote, or culled from Thoreau, the definition of America as "a nation that flourished 1900–1942, conceived many odd inventions for getting somewhere, but could think of nothing to do when they got there" had a comic and satiric view which the limelight could only blind. At all events, that is what happened.

If it had not happened, he would have fit himself solidly into the main comedy of the period and not become a sentimental apologist. Bierce, for instance, had spared some of his time to attack pedantic pretensions. "EVERLASTING, adj. Lasting forever." And Dunne lets Dooley swing at what he thinks is a modish intellectualism. "I cud write pomes that'd make Shakespeare an' Mike Scanlan think they were wur-rkin' on a dredge . . . Life, says ye! There's no life in a book." Rogers was with them early, and his phraseology had just the little sting it needed for authenticity.

> "Shucks, I didn't know they was buyin' grammar now. . . . I had a notion it was thoughts and ideas. . . . I'm just an ignorant feller, without any education. . . . but I try to know what I'm talking about."

Later, his self-deprecation was to become much more insulated and rather harmless.

But his authentic irreverence was instant and sharp. If Dunne went after McKinley and even Theodore Roosevelt in national life, Rogers could follow suit. In his Downingesque association with great men he was introduced to President Coolidge and leaned forward to say, "I didn't catch the name." His endless gibes at Congress were traditional and more than a little safe, but he took his place with Dunne when he attacked Republicanism, a state of mind that had grown more than political. Still, there is no doubt that he had joy in the main thing as well as in the overtones. "Ohio claims they are due a President," he remarked on Harding's candidacy. "Look at the United States. They haven't had one since Lincoln." His literalism and comic momentum, like Groucho Marx's later, were most promising. "The nation is prosperous on the whole. But how much prosperity is there in a hole?"

But he moved away from the dangers of epitheticism and chose caution in generalized commentary. His punning could still serve comic pertinence—"The United States never lost a war or won a conference"—but he is carefully not hurting anybody. He might join the Anti-Bunk Party and oppose Prohibition, but he was already dropping the role of a Jack Downing and becoming the Uncle Tom of American humor. He accomplished the change-over mainly by indulging the self-mockery he had always been prone to but that no longer carried the outer criticism he had attached to it. His genuine pertinence and irreverence decreased.[1] He became lovable. The touches even of misogyny, relatively safe and expected by now, were dropped. Whenever he reverted to his role of prankster, it served the purposes of an almost exclusive insulation he was after. His use of an active alarm clock during his appearances on the stage and in the early days of radio was affected self-criticism; he was making secure fun of his garrulousness.

How far he had come from what he might have been in the contemporary mold and in the tradition of American humor is signaled by an illuminating contrast between him and Thoreau, whom he probably read at one time secretly in his dressing room. If he then took the author of *Walden* as a model for his definition of a feckless America, he later used him almost as an antitext. "I never met a man I didn't like" is practically the deliberated annulment of Thoreau's expression, "I have never yet met a man who was quite awake."

His complete recantation of antithetical humor and the comic criticism he had imaged in the Ford car is neatly symbolized for us is his later enthusiasm for American aviation, especially after Lindbergh's patriotic flight; he died in a fateful air crash with Wiley Post. But the man who perished then with the adventuring pilot was a man of such inveterate good will and optimistic faith that, it seems now, only the cruelest comic vengeance could have dashed him to earth. At that moment, in truth, we lost a potential American Firster instead of the anti-Bunkist. But we must avoid the mysticism of condemnation, which is as tempting as that of celebration, and merely summon up the first half of his career to counteract his decline and his sentimental enshrinement in Colorado. What is petrified for us there is only the apostate he was durably becoming in his last years, and not the humorist he had been. Thus his violent end remains saddening to two different groups of appreciators for entirely separate and opposed reasons.

Notes

1. He was less and less willing and able to observe in the old manner that we "shot [Mexicans] in the most cordial way possible," wanting "only their good will . . . and oil and coffee."

PHILIP ROTH

1933–

Philip Milton Roth was born March 19, 1933, in Newark, New Jersey, to Herman and Bess (née Finkel) Roth. He was educated at Rutgers University, Bucknell University (B.A., *magna cum laude*, 1954) and the University of Chicago (M.A. 1955). He enlisted in the U.S. Army in 1955, but was discharged in 1956 because of a back injury suffered in basic training. He was an instructor in English at the University of Chicago from 1956 to 1958; in addition, he has been a Writer-in-Residence at Princeton University and a Visiting Writer at the University of Iowa, the State University of New York at Stony Brook, and the University of Pennsylvania. In 1959 Roth married Margaret Martinson; they were separated in 1963, and Martinson died in an automobile accident in 1968. For many years he has lived with the actress Claire Bloom.

Roth published several short stories in the late fifties, most centered on Jewish concerns, particularly conflicts between modern and traditional Jewish culture. Some of them were collected in 1959 as *Goodbye, Columbus and Five Short Stories*, which won the National Book Award for Fiction in 1960. His first full-length novel, *Letting Go*, was published in 1962, followed by his second, *When She Was Good*, in 1967.

Roth's career took off in spectacular fashion in 1969 with the publication of *Portnoy's Complaint*, a sexually explicit and hilarious novel in which the narrator, Alexander Portnoy, confesses his life story to his psychiatrist. Roth was praised for his keen insights into modern American Jewish upbringing but criticized for the book's obscenity. Some critics even accused Roth of anti-Semitism in light of the overwhelmingly negative, guilt-drenched tone of the book. *Portnoy's Complaint* topped the best-seller lists and made Roth a household name.

None of Roth's novels subsequent to *Portnoy's Complaint* has matched its popularity, though many critics feel his work has continued to improve. Subsequent novels include *Our Gang*

(*Starring Tricky and His Friends*) (1971), a savage Swiftian attack on Richard Nixon that ends with Nixon campaigning against Satan for control of Hell; *The Breast* (1972), a Kafkaesque tale of a man transformed into a female breast; *The Great American Novel* (1973), a *tour de force* mixing a mythology of baseball with pastiches and parodies of famous works of fiction; and *My Life as a Man* (1974), marking a return to Roth's concerns with Jewish culture, also treated in *The Professor of Desire* (1977). His three most recent novels, *The Ghost Writer* (1979), *Zuckerman Unbound* (1981), and *The Anatomy Lesson* (1983), feature novelist Nathan Zuckerman, a semi-autobiographical character who contends with the vicissitudes of success. These have been collected into the trilogy *Zuckerman Bound* (1985), together with a novella-length epilogue, *The Prague Orgy*.

In addition to his fiction, Roth has published a book of criticism, *Reading Myself and Others* (1975). He was elected to the National Institute of Arts and Letters in 1970.

BARUCH HOCHMAN
From "Child and Man in Philip Roth"
Midstream, December 1967, pp. 68–72

Since the appearance of *Goodbye, Columbus* in 1959, Philip Roth has seemed to be one of those writers whose promise is perpetually in excess of fulfillment. That first collection of stories was the work of a writer who had a keen eye, a barbed pen, the knack of instant characterization—and a gift for pinpointing absurdity swiftly and with deadly accuracy. Their subject is the social and cultural conflict that arises in the experience of Jews as they make their way from the lower middle-class communities of the cities to the prosperous country-club civilization of the suburbs. In the title story, Neal Klugman works in a library and lives with his aunt in a small Newark apartment. He has an affair with Brenda Patimkin, whose father is a manufacturer of plumbing supplies and whose life is divided between the background this implies and the new-rich appurtenances of her family's existence in the well-to-do suburb of Short Hills outside Newark. World War II is the dividing line in this family's history: B.C. and A.D. line up on the two sides of Pearl Harbor, struggle going before and lush prosperity after.

Roth's wicked eye catches the absurdities and incongruities of this suburban life: the gargantuan athleticism of the Patimkins, with their vast quantities of sports equipment falling like fruit from the trees onto the lawn; their old regfrigerator in the basement, held over from humbler days in Newark, and now filled to overflowing with fruit; the conflict between Brenda and her mother over the question of cashmere from Bonwit's vs. lamb's wool from Orbach's; the callow sentimentality of Ron, Brenda's brother, with his passion for André Kostelanetz and for his alma mater's song, "Goodbye, Columbus." And above all there is the moral blindness of the Patimkins' relation to Neal: he is welcome to sleep in their house where he makes clandestine love with Brenda, but it is inconceivable to them that he form any serious liaison with her, since he is too poor and too socially backward.

Told in the first person from Neal's point of view, the story catches a young man in the throes of ambivalence about a life he both scorns and covets. It is, in its way, a brilliantly managed story, crackling with the tension of this ambivalence and galvanized by an authentic energy of observation and response. It moves briskly from sharp observation of manners and attitudes to what seems to be a crystallization of issues bearing on the moral life. This movement is above all what suggested that Roth might be a novelist in the making.

But the two novels he has published since that time—*Letting Go* in 1962 and *When She Was Good* in 1967—fall so far short of the promise of his volume of short stories that one is led to reconsider some of one's initial impressions. The tales were, after all, somewhat brittle and external, and seemed to

be sidestepping the issues they implicitly held up to question. Furthermore, they seem peculiarly out of balance. In these stories Roth identifies with the younger generation against its elders, the representatives of authority, and against the vestiges of a past with which their authority is linked. The young, to be sure, are also subject to scrutiny—as in "Eli the Fanatic" and "The Conversion of the Jews." But the animus is against their elders. "Epstein," both hilarious and unsavory, is a give-away in this regard, with its farcical doing-in of the sexual exploits and anxieties of those elders. More disconcerting is the fact that the force of Roth's criticism does not always seem to be justified by its objects, even when one tends to be in sympathy with the critical impulse. Why, one wonders, does the author lavish so much exasperation upon the vulgar prodigality of the Patimkins? Or upon the smug velleities of the rabbi in "The Conversion of the Jews," who tries to impose upon little Ozzie the tenets of a faith he cannot himself affirm? And is it unreasonable for middle-class parents to object to their young daughter's spending a weekend with the man they have just discovered to be her clandestine lover?

In retrospect, one has the feeling that the energy informing these stories is scarcely more than the energy of irritation, an irritation so great that it makes the exposure of inanity seem a meaningful moral act. For Roth does not really seem to be concerned with the substance of the values that he shows being eroded. It is not at all clear how Neal Klugman, who is so offended at the Patimkin's, stands for anything substantially different from what they stand for—setting aside the fact that he is poorer than they are, which he cannot help. His differences with them lie elsewhere than in the moral realm with which the story once seemed to be dealing. We are on the level of purely psychological motivations. But it is precisely on this level that "Goodbye, Columbus" and its companion stories become problematical: there is little in them to suggest how the characters came to feel as they did.

It was not until his two novels that Roth dealt with this problem, cutting underneath the surfaces of the questions that had initially engaged him. Indeed, Roth's novels, relinquishing the easy objects of contempt that had populated the *Goodbye, Columbus* stories, move ever further from that suburban Jewish scene in which his questions had first been posed. The novels focus upon the younger generation itself, and are far more concerned with probing their inner lives than with depicting the ironies of milieu. The technique, to be sure, remains "realistic," and there continues to be an interest in manners and in the revealing surfaces of human relations; but society as an issue recedes. We find ourselves almost wholly immersed in a close empathetic exploration of the experience of people on the threshold of life, involved in a struggle to forge their identities and find their place in a world without imperatives.

What we get in the novels is an elaborate and sometimes sensitive rendition of the inner problems of middle-class, post-adolescent youth in America. But there is an odd feeling of softness about them; they lack the intrusive force of the imperatives that normally come from society or the family, the very elements that ordinarily fill a novelistic world. In their place is simply a quagmire of feeling—or more precisely, of feelings: of need, of dependency, all manifestations of a world of infantile or adolescent muddle. Suddenly, the harsh, acerbic Roth of the early stories goes limp with empathy. Where once he attacked, now he attends. As a result the novels—even the almost too shapely *When She Was Good*—bog and sag. It is as though the old irascibility has gone underground, in the service of characters who lack the means of expressing it. The outcome is fiction that is static and often imprecise, and a wallowing sentimentality that masquerades as psychological interest.

Roth's two novels seem very different from each other, and both seem different from *Goodbye, Columbus*: yet they are closely akin to each other in their vital interests. The essential factor in all of them is Roth's close participation in the lives of people—most of them young—who are bursting with tamped fury and child-like frustration, but who haven't the faintest notion of what their troubles are about. Though we are asked to view them at a distance, we are so thoroughly implicated in their resentments that we finally become implicated in a child's-eye view of the world.

Significantly, the decisive events in both of the novels have to do with infants and with the displacement of adult needs and feelings onto them. In *Letting Go* one of these events occurs after Gabe Wallach—the financially independent son of a prosperous New York dentist—has arranged for his friends, Paul and Libbie Herz—a physically frail couple struggling under the burden of estrangement from their parents due to the difference in religion between them—to adopt an illegitimate child. The climax of this sequence comes when Gabe undertakes a wild drive across Chicago with the child, intending to force its real mother to consent to a legal adoption. In the wake of this experience, Gabe realizes that he has spent much of his life looking after others, engaged in perpetually unresolved relationships with people like Paul and Libbie, because he has not known how to look out for himself. He recoils from the tenuous quality of such relationships, decides he must "let go"—of Libbie, of Paul, of his father, of the entanglements of the past—and go off to make a life for himself.

This scene has followed closely upon a sequence in which we witness the half-conscious "accidental" killing of a small boy by his eight-year-old sister, both of them children of a divorced woman with whom Gabe has been having an affair. The incident is decisive in terminating Gabe's affair with the woman, and suggests the pathos of children caught up in the entanglements of modern marriage and divorce. It also serves, along with the episode of the drive through Chicago, to provide a watershed for a major current of feeling in the novel. We have been confronted throughout with the childish problems of the protagonists, with Libbie's incapacity to cope with almost any situation, with Paul's constant recoil from real feeling and contact, and with Gabe's struggles to keep away from the nagging demands of his pathetically dependent father. The entire novel has in fact pivoted on the unlovely feelings of childish castouts from unparadisical childhoods. As Gabe observes at one point, his life has been filled with the shuffling and reshuffling of parents; and it is in the emotional consequences of this history that we have been immersed.

There are touches in *Letting Go* that are reminiscent of the sharp, satirical eye of *Goodbye, Columbus*, such as the harshly etched renderings of the English Department at the University of Chicago; but most of the material upon which the novel focuses lacks clarity. The book abounds in "Freudian" material, but most of it doesn't jell. The odd thing about *Letting Go* is that everyone in it is perplexed most of the time, but the reader never clearly perceives what it is they are perplexed about. They are all very busy trying to be good, to do the right thing by others and by themselves, but they are perpetually sloshing in the agitated (if shallow) waters of selfhood. This contributes to the sense of childishness that pervades the novel. What the episodes involving children do is amplify and orchestrate all the uncomprehended and inarticulate feelings suffusing everyone's lives.

When She Was Good is a slicker novel than *Letting Go*, and is more boldly organized around its children. In it, Roth takes on a wholly new milieu—the American, Protestant Midwest. Lucy Nelson, the novel's main character, is the only daughter of a rather charming ne'er-do-well who had drifted since the Depression and had allowed himself and his family to live in his father-in-law's house, on the latter's charity. Lucy grows up with an overwhelming sense of the inadequacy of her elders—of the spinelessness of her mother, the endless wishy-washy forgivingness of her grandfather, and the wayward brutalities of her self-ingratiating father. She desperately wants her elders to be responsible and authoritative. When she is impregnated by her rather formless and childish young lover, she sets out to make of him the man and father she had always longed for but never known. In the end, her strident moralism drives him away.

This takes place only after she, believing that she has brought her husband around to a responsible approach to life, has conceived for a second time. Her confidence in regeneration has been further buttressed by her widowed mother's engagement to a pillar of the community. But her illusions collapse when her husband leaves her and her mother breaks the engagement. Bewildered by rage and guilt, she wanders about in a snowstorm until she freezes to death.

At the center of the issues in the novel is Lucy's rage at the fathers, her inability to come to grips with that rage, and the compulsions that follow from it. Lucy is insufferable but also pitiable. We see in her the formless resentments of an angry young woman, whose chief quality is an incapacity to find a viable perspective on her experience. As in *Letting Go*, we rattle around in the consciousness of people bewildered by their own adulthood, and by the relentless callowness bequeathed to them by inadequate childhoods. And again, so much of what we see here is from the vantage point of the victimized young: not only that of Lucy, but also, by the end of the novel, that of her son, and even ultimately, somehow, that of the unborn child who dies with her in the snow. Mingled with Roth's disapprobation of this unbearable woman is a deeper-lying sympathy, not only with Lucy, but with the whole endless and tragic chain of children, born and unborn, and child-adults, a succession of generations victimized by one another's blunderings. The "moral" of the story is that of *Letting Go*: that one must somehow let go of the entanglements of feelings imposed by the past, and that one can do so only by facing up to them. But the tragedy of the story is deeper than any "moral"; for Lucy is destroyed by the past she has tried to shed in her quest for respectability, but which lives on in the resentments and anxieties that are ineffaceably a part of her.

The novel has considerable faults—the people in it are limited and commonplace, and Roth's representation of them keeps somehow missing the mark, lapsing into stilted melodrama, full of exclamation points and cliché—but the fact remains that it is in touch with realities that are among the most vexing in our culture. However crudely rendered and uncritically viewed, a legitimate pathos is there in both novels: the pathos of an entire middle-class generation or generation-and-a-half whose culture is organized in such a way as to make it impossible for them to find an adequate perspective in which to view their lives and feelings. This is not merely a matter of a few individual psyches. It is the experience of a whole class today, who, like Gabe Wallach, are always adrift in the middle of their lives, pushed and pulled by childish resentments and by the certainty that, however smug they may be, they have not got what they want, and that they have a right to it—or who, like Lucy and her husband, are trapped prematurely in familial or professional situations which they do not begin to understand and with which they cannot possibly cope.

Whatever one's dissatisfactions with Roth as a writer, one must credit him with having provided some close and sympathetic accounts of various dimensions of the difficulty. Roth at least assumes responsibility for getting into the phenomenon and trying to render it and make sense of it. One suspects, as I have already suggested, that his failures so far have mainly to do with his excessive participation in the inchoate anger of his characters. This anger gave shape to his fiction in the early stories, even while it failed to explain or justify itself in the representation of its objects. In the novels, that active anger is in abeyance; he turns, so to speak, toward himself, and in so doing he loses perspective.

WILFRID SHEED
"The Good Word: Howe's Complaint"
New York Times Book Review, May 6, 1973, p. 2

"This is the novel the author always wanted to write, and we should now be glad he's gotten it over with and can get on with the ones he doesn't want to write." This kind of sentence has been going around a lot lately and is a menace to health. The particular example is plucked from my own past—probably one of the silliest sentences I ever committed. (Note especially the glib fatuity of "doesn't want to write," as if that insured a good book.)

It all comes under the chopped-liver heading: Reviewer's instructions to Author. In the bracing tones of a juvenile magistrate, we tell the shivering wretch out there to forget his nasty little mistake as quickly as possible and get on with the book we all know he can write. The mistake in question may have cost him his last pint of blood, his wife and his self-respect, and he may seriously doubt he has the strength for another assault. Never mind that: this sunken-cheeked ruin shall not be spared his pep-talk and his hearty slap on the butt from us.

Probably no one has received more such cumbersome advice than Philip Roth. Roth was cursed early with "promise," which Cyril Connolly once compared to the "medieval hangman who, having settled the noose, pushed his victim off the platform and jumped on his back." With the precocious promise of *Goodbye, Columbus*, Roth embarked on a career of disappointing people indefinitely.

Recently, the estimable Irving Howe put it all together in a kind of "Best of Philip Roth Advice" piece in *Commentary*. Being lectured by Howe is no joke. He not only argues mordantly—bites like a bulldog in fact—but with a note of grouchy integrity which suggests he isn't doing it for fun. You feel you must have done something very bad to have aroused this decent, serious man.

Much of what Howe says is just, not to say wearyingly intelligent. Yet it finally comes down to the kind of criticism a writer can only stare blankly at—the kind that doesn't speak to his real possibilities, but seems to be about somebody else altogether. For instance, Mr. Howe accuses Roth of dealing superficially with Jewish life, with not exploring, say, the real pathos of Mrs. Sophie Portnoy. But what would have happened to the book's manic drive, its unique tone, if he had done that? *Portnoy* would have been a more sensitive book under Howe's guidance but sensitive books are a dime a dozen. Roth tried a couple himself in *Letting Go* and *When She Was Good*, and Mr. Howe himself admits they were not very successful. Yet those are the very books he seems to want Roth to write again and again, never mind whether he does them well or not, simply because they are a superior kind of book.

Are funny books of any value at all? Howe uses the donnish phrase "amusing, but" a couple of times, which suggests that humor had better watch its step around him. It had, for openers, better tell us something about the human condition and all that great stuff. But unfortunately, much first-rate humor tells us nothing at all about the human condition, unless to lie about it, and is chronically superficial to boot: Mr. Portnoy's bowel movements, if humor they may be, may have a tragic explanation, but we don't want to hear it. Not in this book.

Humor also demands quick recognitions or stereotypes, than which nothing could be more superficial. Howe chides Roth for making Mrs. Patimkin (in *Goodbye*) a Hadassah lady, which he likens to writing about blacks in the watermelon patch. Well, admittedly Hadassah is a frowsy epithet by now—for which Roth may be partly to blame (when *Goodbye* first appeared, Howe found it "ferociously exact"; now he finds it full of comic hand-me-downs. Handed down by whom?). But the kind of nuanced Jewish satire Howe would presumably prefer would be lost outside the Jewish community. So too, a Catholic or Mason must stick to the known, if he wants to make a public joke. Does this mean that public jokes have to be, in Howe's word, vulgar? Of course. His definition of vulgar, "the impulse to submit the rich substance of human experience, sentiment [etc.] to a radically reductive levelling or simplification" takes in just about every joke I know.

But of course, as Howe rightly says, Roth comes on as something more than a comedian and cannot be granted full Woody Allen immunity. I agree. What I don't understand is why Howe can't see this as a real artistic problem for the author rather than a moral defect. Roth is a comedian as well as a novelist, and the novelist must make his fictions out of the clown's simplicities. Roth has tried evey way he knows to get his Panza and Quixote onto the same horse, but one of them usually falls off. Without his clown, as in *When She Was Good*, Roth doesn't quite make the weight. With Sancho up, as in *Portnoy*, the woeful knight slides gracefully off the horse's rump.

Howe accuses Roth of choosing an "audience" rather than "readers," and certainly his reputation as a baby tycoon suggests opportunism of a sort. Yet the striking thing about Roth's career is his vagrant choice of subjects, almost as though he were trying to shake off his audience. *The Breast*, for instance, reads like a most earnest attempt to shed any easy popularity he'd gained from *Portnoy*. Likewise, where another writer might have exploited the vein of *Goodbye, Columbus* unto 70 times Singer, he abruptly abandoned it, on the admirable Kipling principle that when you've mastered something, you should do something else. Perhaps he goes for the big money to insure against failure.

Portnoy itself might be taken for something of a hustle, except I'm told that the author had reason to believe it wouldn't be published at all. Perhaps for this reason he sold it piecemeal to magazines at no great profit, the book acquiring thereby its major defect, a lack of growth and development. Roth was obliged to set the table and trot out the characters again and again, with all their crotchets re-labeled, until they did begin to look like stock comic figures. Maybe a more saintly craftsman would have written over the cracks for book form, but it would have meant throwing out some great material, which is a lot to ask of a writer, and it might have damaged the delicate structure of the monologues. Critics should look to these technical problems before they reach for the moral ones.

Roth's one complete aberration was *Our Gang*, and I can't begin to explain it. It seems like the kind of snappy idea one might have at a party, which the great god Pan usually erases mercifully by morning. But it points up the problematic nature of Roth's gift: he is not precisely a satirist, nor exactly a pure humorist, just someone who has to keep on looking for things he can do.

People talk about talent as though it were some neutral substance that can be applied to anything. But talent is narrow and only functions with a very few subjects, which it is up to the writer to find. In this respect, Philip Roth's career is both honorable and adventurous. His new book *The Great American Novel* is reviewed elsewhere in this issue (I haven't seen the review), but it struck me as happy material for Roth. The opening depends too much on verbal virtuosity which, surprisingly, Roth hasn't got in great quantities. ("I am a plodder," said Scott Fitzgerald. For all his dazzle, Roth strikes me as a plodder too.) But the myth that follows, of a missing baseball league like Atlantis, gives scope to his galloping imagination, driven humor, cold heart. (His other heart, the warm one, just never works as well.) The delicate boy with the dirty mouth has found himself another Subject.

In the humor section of the same *Commentary*, Roth was accused of being anti-American, but this is like calling Dickens anti-English. There is no other frame of reference for Roth, no world outside America. It is his Universe, his Good and Evil. Howe says he lacks a culture, but we all lack one these days. That is his very material: the first generation to try winging it without a culture. And for it he can hardly pitch his voice in the sonorous tones of a major writer. An anxious wise guy, a quintessential punk with a fast, shallow mind is more like it. And don't think it doesn't take craft and hard work and real literary intelligence for Roth to achieve that effect.

Anyway, Howe would know better than to call Roth anti-American himself. What really saddens Howe is that Roth has lost Europe, a sadness we all share in our different modes, the Assimilation Blues. Like an immigrant father confiscating comic books, Howe dismisses the culture that the Roths have put together over here, out of old box-scores and radio shows and B movies, a barbarous culture perhaps but rich in legend and catch-phrase for the novelist to transmute if he can. The title *Great American Novel* is one more gag for the punk to throw at the elder. Can one make a great novel out of such flashing surfaces and carnival gee-gaws and neon strips? Who knows? As Tommy Dorsey once said to the serious conductor, after a gorgeous trombone tremolo, "It's the way we do it in Roseland."

STANLEY COOPERMAN
From "Philip Roth: 'Old Jacob's Eye' with a Squint"

Twentieth Century Literature, July 1973, pp. 203–9

In "Some Children of the Goddess," an essay on post-war American fiction, Norman Mailer remarked on the "religious preoccupation" of contemporary American novelists. Certainly a turning toward metaphysical problems—together with renewed identification with the racial or ethnic group—has been characteristic of contemporary writing. Philip Roth, however, despite his stature as "Jewish" novelist, in his recent work has been preoccupied with social rather than religious material. Unlike Malamud or Bellow, for whom the examination of religious symbol is essential to the novel even as social art, Roth (since *Letting Go*) has used religion almost solely in ironic terms. His attitude toward religion, in short, is that of the social realist rather than symbolist or moralist: he has come to use religion—and ethnic identification—as raw material for either parody or caricature.

The result, predictably, has been the increasing alienation of Roth from the tradition, the ethnic group, which has always provided the chief impetus for his best work. In a sense enjoying (or enduring) a self-imposed exile from the Jewish Diaspora, Roth is in exile from exile, and the result is a compounded alienation: a man at once outside the mainstream of American culture, and unable to come to terms with the culture, the tradition, which (quite without his permission) shaped his alienation in the first place.

If, as Ralph Ellison suggests, all Americans are perpetual immigrants, Philip Roth has become the perpetual emigrant—an emigrant, moreover, with no fixed destination, and no hope for one. Neither Jew nor "American," Roth wanders through a metaphysical comic nightmare in which moral value is reduced to mannerism and formal tradition to eccentricity—an eccentricity at best picturesque or exotic ("Roth writes Jewish novels for Gentiles"), and at worst graceless or hypocritical, a mouthing of obsolete incantation which has for its origin fear based upon ignorance.

The result is not simply the deliberate avoidance of tragic emotion, but rather its elimination. Neither mannerism, eccentricity, exoticism, nor ignorance are the stuff from which tragic heroes—or tragic victims—are born. It is difficult to escape the conviction that Roth's recent work, even (or especially) when most "real," is a process of surface mimicry: surface mannerism has come to define his aesthetic universe, and—to an unfortunate extent—his social or moral indignation as well.

"I am living in the middle of a Jewish joke!" says Alexander Portnoy, and since "joke" has no anchor in profound mortal risk (the historic origin of that peculiar blend of joy-and-suffering known as "Jewish humour"), Roth's laughter too often becomes thin-souled, a kind of simpering posture directed against human potential for significant pain or joy. This lack of significance shapes the essential *reductive* quality of Roth's work; in many of his short stories and novels, with the exception of *Letting Go*, whether writing of a Jewish milieu or (less convincingly) of a Gentile one, whether writing of sex, politics, marriage, religion, ambition, or motherhood, Roth reduces human beings to carnival snap-shots of themselves—sometimes comic, sometimes ugly, sometimes wistful, but always without that strength of existence, that awareness of moral truth which (even when attenuated) redeems our temporal grotesqueries into the possibility of significant human action.

Without such possibility, exact observation and a sense of incongruity may not, after all, be enough. A critic like Irving Howe, for example, while praising Roth's "malicious accuracy" in *Portnoy's Complaint*, insists that the book lacks "imaginative transformation." Realism itself, finally, unshaped by other than casebook significance, and existing on the literal level of observed mannerism, becomes merely another form of sentiment.

In a 1963 speech at Princeton, Bernard Malamud—the older Jewish novelist with whom Roth is most frequently compared—insisted that "fact," even the fact of the observed world, could achieve meaning only through the penetration of "reality" by imagination, the extension of "reality" into a moral universe of imaginatively perceived, analogic forms. For this reason, said Malamud, the job of the writer (especially the Jewish writer, for whom moral law has traditionally been palpable and real) is to portray "more than the merely realistic." That which he seeks in his own work, Malamud later added (in commenting upon *The Fixer*), is "the imaginative fact."

What makes Malamud's remarks particularly relevant here, is that they were a reply to an earlier attack by Roth in which the younger novelist accused Jewish writers in America of offering metaphysical escapism from the real problems of their time and place. Malamud's Jews, Roth had said in 1961 (writing for *Commentary*), were "only metaphors": that is, they were so overladen with burdens of "Myth" and "Universality," of "Truth," "Justice," and "Tradition," that the specific human condition of real men and women living out their actual lives, was subordinated or ignored as in some way unworthy of art.

Indeed, in *Letting Go* Roth steps directly into the well-cared for mouth of Gabe Wallach and voices an abiding distaste for "that great horde of young anagramists and manure-spreaders who . . . each year walk through classroom doors and lay siege to the minds of the young, revealing to them Zoroaster in Sam Clemens and the hidden phallus in the lives of our most timid lady poets." Metaphysical (or metaphorical) "significance," then, usually indicates febrile academic ambition or aesthetic flatulence: in either case it is to be avoided, like the delphic utterances of clergymen or sales personnel.

The attack is strong. It is necessary, however, to keep in mind that it is voiced by Gabe Wallach, who in *Letting Go* is a protagonist of complete moral no less than intellectual shallowness. Roth's own attitude, obviously, cannot be equated with Gabe's; despite his hard-headed public stance, Roth is uncertain of his own ground here, and the very fact that he uses someone like Gabe to voice the attack against "metaphor" is itself evidence of considerable ambiguity in his own thinking.

The public stance, however, certainly is clear enough. Even while teaching creative writing at Iowa, Roth showed considerable impatience with symbol-manufacturing (and symbol-hunting) among his students; "make it particular!" was his rallying-cry as a teacher, and his goal as a writer: if Malamud, like Saul Bellow, had used his protagonists as starting-points for abstract metaphysical questions (What is Jew? what is man? what is history?) Roth would concentrate on what Glen Meeter calls the "practical" problems of the novelist: that is, "what artistic sense can be made of the present world."

"All men are Jews," announced Bernard Malamud in his now celebrated formulation of universality in human suffering. While the intent is noble, the aesthetic result—for a writer

like Philip Roth—too easily becomes both unfocused and soggy. Roth is far more concerned, as Meeter points out, with demonstrating the less exalted but perhaps more pertinent fact that all Jews are men. In his recent work, then, Philip Roth attempts to embrace as his subject neither History nor Law, neither Time nor Eternity, but real men and women encased in their own skins, living out lives shaped by cultural particularity: their tragedies (if there is any tragic dimension to be found in the secularist, materialist culture of 20th Century America) may not be exalted, but it is their own.

The very absence of mythic allusion, the determined, frequently caustic, and always close observation of admittedly limited human beings for which Roth has been both praised and damned by his critics, may produce fiction at once uninspired and uninspiring, but (say Roth's defenders) it is the true fabric of American life. And Philip Roth, like the good tailor of fiction that he is, cuts this fabric to fit the actual bodies before him, no matter how grotesque or limited they might be.

There are no angels in Liberty Center, U.S.A.; nor in the suburbs, the army-camps, the middle-class urban ghettos. But there are men and women and children moving (or stumbling) through their own lives, often pursuing the illusion of Ideals or Mythologies, and just as often grotesquely victimized by the pursuit itself. Roy Brassart or Alexander Portnoy, Mary-Jane Reed or Eli Peck, Gentile or Jew, Roth's characters see before them Success, Freedom, Religious Truth, Revelation, Sexual Ecstasy; crippled either by too much sophistication or the lack of it, rebelling against moral law or searching for its manifestation, they run toward their particular golden mountain with their shoelaces tied together. The Promised Land for Philip Roth—and for the Americans of whom he writes—is still another "Jewish joke."

The "joke," however, has serious consequences, and in its examination of these consequences, Roth's work is both less ephemeral and less "particular" than many of his critics have supposed. Myth, after all, even when used as an instrument of parody, works toward the infusion of the particular with the universal. Despite his own disavowals, and despite the objective stance or posture of hip hard-boiledom with which the narrative voices in his work so often seek to protect themselves, action and event in Roth's books offers far more than a cinematic recording of literal surface.

In *Goodbye, Columbus* and *Letting Go*, in *When She Was Good* and *Portnoy's Complaint*, the reductive qualities of the actual lives before us are framed by an aura of moral law and religious faith. With the latter two books, however, Roth can affirm neither, even as possibility; comically distorted or pathetically attenuated, transformed into non-sequiturs by a culture in which both law and faith are rendered solely in terms of gesture or abstract (and therefore inoperable) verbalism, good and evil become but echoes of themselves: the parodies of, rather than exempla for, positive or negative moral force.

In *When She Was Good* and, most especially, in *Portnoy's Complaint*, parody is both the technique and substance of Roth's fiction, as it is of the work of a writer like Sinclair Lewis. Far more than Lewis, however, for whom mimetic surface— the act of ironic imitation—was its own reward, Roth is preoccupied with larger questions of moral possibility; and in this respect he is far closer to the lyric despair of F. Scott Fitzgerald than one would imagine from the enormously different textures of their work. For a basic theme of Fitzgerald, as it is of Roth, is the vision of a "Promised Land" reduced to what Fitzgerald, in *The Great Gatsby*, calls a "caterer's production."

Gatsby himself, in his pathetic attempt to realize spiritual values through material acquisition, is potentially a comic figure; just so is Alexander Portnoy, in his attempt to achieve freedom through orgasm, potentially a tragic one. Far more naive than Portnoy, hence far more "serious," Gatsby can indeed commit his life to the "Platonic conception" of what it ought to be. For Alexander Portnoy, however, not even this Crusade is possible: too aware (as Gatsby is not) of his own motivations, the hip adolescent posturing of his own appetites, Portnoy is left, finally, with no illusions at all. And if Gatsby gives up his life in a final, romantic, sacrificial gesture to protect "nothing," Alex Portnoy's flight toward freedom ends with a screeching session in a psychiatrist's office. In each case the punishment fits the criminal if not the crime.

The narrator of Fitzgerald's novel, Nick Carroway, returns from his own excursion into the fleshpots of New York with the admission that tolerance has "a limit." "Conduct may be founded on the hard rock or the wet marshes, but after a certain point I don't care what it's founded on." What he wants, says Nick, is a world that can be "at a sort of moral attention forever." Just as it is his need for moral conviction that makes it impossible for Fitzgerald's protagonist to function in a kaleidoscope of random appetite and distorted gesture, so too are Roth's protagonists defeated, destroyed, or absorbed by a moral universe that has turned into mush.

"If only they'd say no," reflects Lucy Nelson, in *When She Was Good*. "*NO LUCY, YOU CANNOT, NO LUCY WE FORBID IT*. But it seemed that none of them had the conviction any longer, or the endurance . . . " Neither conviction nor endurance: without these qualities moral action is irrelevant, and moral choice a non-sequitur. Law itself becomes debased into opportunism (as in "Defender of the Faith") or the sterile nagging of imposed form; Religion becomes the merest exoticism (as in "Eli the Fanatic") or a "caterer's production" of stuffed meat and overripe fruit; "love" becomes cannibalism (as in *Portnoy's Complaint*) and "responsibility" a death-sentence—as it is for Asher in *Letting Go*. There is no redemption from this, and no nobility of suffering either.

"Reserving judgment," says Nick Carroway in Fitzgerald's book, "is a matter of infinite hope." But Philip Roth persists in judging both his characters and his country with the clear, merciless, mocking, and (in Roth's case) unforgiving "old Jacob's eye"—that moral incisiveness which, remarks Cynthia Ozick in her brilliant essay on Jewish writing (*Congress Bi-Weekly*, 1971), has always been both the strength and burden of Jewish art.

In this respect Roth, no less than Elie Weisel, "bears witness" to a world of moral insanity; if—unlike Weisel—(whose Judaism has been invigorated rather than debilitated by the nightmares of our century) Roth reduces rather than ennobles, the reduction itself is inevitable when "judgment" springs not from coherent belief, but from its absence. Deliberately seeking, in *When She Was Good* and *Portnoy's Complaint*, to disassociate himself from those moral imperatives which would legitimize his attack on both American culture and Jewish-American culture, Roth's indignation occurs in a peculiar vacuum. "Old Jacob's eye" peers out from behind Madison Avenue horn-rims, and dissects or imitates what it cannot love.

If Roth attempts to avoid "spurning the real world" (the essence of his attack on Malamud and Bellow), neither can he avoid looking at it morally and symbolically. Despite his polemic assertions that America has enough surrealism without the novelist (Metaphysics? Read your daily newspaper!) there remains, in Roth's best work, almost in spite of his most

hard-headed intentions, that "talent for suffering," that anguished, self-lacerating moral judgment which is in essence Judaic—the incapacity to take up the objective posture of journalism. One might say of Roth's most successful fiction that, like Paul Herz in *Letting Go*, it is "afflicted with a deeper and deeper sense of consequence." And this consequence is metaphysical, moral, and historical.

"Real life" for Philip Roth, especially in *Letting Go*, is based upon moral judgment, and for this reason the book is a more powerful work—and a far more "Jewish" one—than the celebrated *Portnoy's Complaint*, in which moral choice is defined as neurosis, and moral anguish as discomfort. *Portnoy's Complaint*, indeed, despite its popularity (especially among non-Jewish readers), is a rather desperate attempt to escape from the charge of parochialism by means of stock character and hand-me-down psychiatric motivation. An extended shaggy-dog story, the novel represents an avoidance of precisely that moral substance which provides the chief impetus for Roth's best writing. Like Mailer's retreat into what Miss Ozick calls the "minor liturgical art" of journalism, *Portnoy* is an attempt to "be with it" by externalizing, through the reductive instrument of caricature, the moral universe itself. The book fails not because it is "too Jewish," but because it is not Jewish enough.

In 1964, speaking at the annual American-Israel dialogue at the Weizman Institute, Roth defiantly announced that "I am not a Jewish writer. I am a writer who is a Jew." In 1966 the critic Marvin Mudrick, writing in *University of Denver Quarterly*, predicted that Roth—like Malamud and Bellow—had "exhausted" the Jew-in-America as a subject for fiction; their future work, Professor Mudrick assured his readers, would henceforth be "American" and non-parochial.

Although Roth did follow the professor's blueprint with *When She Was Good*, his one excursion into WASP Americana, and although Bellow (in *Mosby's Memoirs*) produced some excellent short fiction using a non-Jewish milieu, since 1966 all three writers have returned to "Jewish material" for their novels. Judaism, in short, whether or not elevated into universal symbol, has continued to occupy the main creative centre for all three writers. So much for predictions.

And yet Professor Mudrick was not altogether wrong. For both Malamud and Bellow brilliantly fused "Jewish" material with the urgent problems of the decade: the problems of race, of violence, and of politics. Roth, on the other hand, with *Portnoy's Complaint*, returned to the family kitchen only to draw dirty pictures on its walls. If Malamud and Bellow still brought to bear on their age the moral and metaphysical judgments of "old Jacob's eye," Roth seemed determined to prove that he indeed was more (or less) than a mere "Jewish writer."

When She Was Good failed to arouse critical enthusiasm: the book was praised as a competent treatment of still another All-American bitch-heroine from Heartland, U.S.A. Even the ironies in the novel, its cold examination of destructive moralism and middle-class sterility, were familiar attacks upon traditional targets. Something was missing aside from Jews, most serious commentators agreed, and three years later Philip Roth—disinterring Wylie's attack on "Mom-ism"—unleashed the figure of Alexander Portnoy upon the literary clubs of America.

The result was instant best-sellerdom, a huge commercial success, and gobs of praise from reviewers (along with very mixed comments from the literary quarterlies). Never has masturbation paid off so well ("The Artist as Young Schmuck," sneered Harry Roskolenko in *Quadrant*). Roth outsold Malamud, outsold Bellow (Mailer was to leave the ring to talk about moon-men): and the effect, somehow, was an aesthetic anti-climax which for sheer pyrotechnic brilliance had few parallels in contemporary American literature.

Pyrotechnic brilliance: one thinks immediately of Joseph Heller, Grace Paley, Herb Gold, Bruce Jay Friedman, the young Saul Bellow—all of whom were notable for what Roth himself, in 1961 (not without a certain acerbity), described as the "boncy" prose rhythms of contemporary Jewish writing: that same rhythm which makes *Portnoy's Complaint* so attractive and fast-moving a book. Unlike the work of these, however, *Portnoy* skims along the surface of caricature, with Roth imposing borrowed psychoanalytic motivation in order to provide some dimension of consequence for what would otherwise be a series of grotesques. Where the stylized miming of these writers covered a moral concern no less deep than one finds in the work of a more overtly serious novelist like Edward Lewis Wallant, Roth's determination to avoid "Jewish metaphor" resulted merely in the substitution of the Oedipal abstraction for the ethnic one.

Like some critics who attempt to define Black literature as simply a variant of clinical neurosis (look: they are Just Like Us), Roth,—with *Portnoy's Complaint*—attempted to dissolve the Jewish preoccupation with *consequence* into a highly spiced stew of neurotic sexuality and "universal" casebook explanations. The attempt at universality fails. As Cynthia Ozick, herself a gifted fiction writer, remarks:

> Literature does not spring from the urge to Esperanto but from the tribe. When Carl Sandburg writes a poem "There is only one man, and his name is mankind," he is unwittingly calling for the end of culture. The annihilation of idiosyncrasy assures the annihilation of culture. It *is* possible to write "There is one ant, and its name is antkind"; anthood is praised thereby. The ants are blessed with the universal brotherhood of instinct. But they have no literature.

Portnoy's Complaint fails because the problems of moral judgment which are the focus of Roth's best work (and a central preoccupation of Jewish novelists)—the meaning of responsibility; the ancient fear of chaos; the relationship between tribe (Jew) and non-tribe (Gentile); the compulsive urge to teach and comment upon moral law; the ambiguities of love—these problems cannot be dismissed as a series of slick-magazine "repressions." "Ass is no panacea," says Uncle Asher, the decayed Bohemian, in *Letting Go:* good advice for art no less than for life.

BEN SIEGEL

From "The Myths of Summer:
Philip Roth's *The Great American Novel*"

Contemporary Literature, Spring 1976, pp. 171–77

Any careful discussion today of contemporary writing must point up the vigorous attempts by American novelists to reduce to fiction this nation's recent social confusions and anxieties. Their frenetic efforts help explain why in recent years the American novel has taken on a new or different look. For the "serious" works written since World War II resemble less and less those straightforward chronicles of national life that older Americans read as undergraduate and graduate students—those by, for example, Anderson, Lewis, Fitzgerald,

Dos Passos, Hemingway, Wolfe, Faulkner, and Steinbeck. Those novels (a few by Faulkner perhaps excepted), whatever their merits or demerits, were direct, *realistic* narratives of people whom a reader could recognize and accept or reject. The readers who wanted the ambiguous or even the "nonmeaning" could turn to poetry—to the poems of, among others, Pound, Eliot, and Stevens.

They need not do so today. Now, a reader may find as much of the complex and grotesque and irrational in fiction. For America's novelists, like those abroad, have found contemporary life here so baffling and unreal that they have felt the need to give freer and freer rein to their imaginations and rhetoric. Not surprisingly, therefore, these writers, in order to capture this society's present confusions, rely increasingly on fantasy and fable, on imaginative excess and adventurous form or technique; employing a style that tends to the "cool, farcical, zany, and slapstick," they concentrate on the thinness of line between dream and reality, fancy and fact, comedy and pathos. The imaginative and stylistic complexities confronting these writers, as Geoffrey Wolff points out, are formidable indeed. "The comic imagination," he writes, "seems to have been cornered by that American 'reality.' In a world in which so much is disordered, like an insane murderous joke, how do you recognize what is funny? How does the artist authenticate his invention?"[1]

One writer who tries repeatedly to recognize, reveal, and "authenticate" the ironic jokes underlying much of human motive and behavior is Philip Roth. Certainly no American novelist in recent years has challenged his readers' imagination, credulity, or patience more than he has. His concern that the American reality is outstripping, if not overwhelming, the American writer's creative powers[2] has caused him to move increasingly in his fiction from the realistic to the outlandish and fantastic. This shift has angered and embittered many readers who find his depictions of America's values, sex, and politics unduly negative and often vicious. "Roth is remarkably evenhanded," observes one reviewer, "he offends everybody and every imaginable group."[3]

Roth is clearly a writer about whom neutrality is difficult. But if uncompromising in his efforts to mirror modern life, he has not been reluctant to alter his style and subject matter. His first novels (*Goodbye, Columbus; Letting Go;* and *When She Was Good*), as well as his early short stories, were sharply etched segments of the American middle-class reality. These narratives, for all their individuality, belonged to American literature's normative or realistic tradition. They revealed Roth's strong wit and satiric bite, his sharp eye for the revealing gesture, and his keen ear for the accompanying inflection and nuance. In them Roth concerned himself primarily with what he has called (borrowing a Bruno Bettelheim phrase) "behavior in extreme situations." "Lucy Nelson, Gabe Wallach and Paul Herz, and Alex Portnoy are people," says Roth, "swept away . . . [by] their own righteousness or resentment . . . [and] living beyond their psychological and moral means."[4]

Many critics find Roth's embattled seekers disturbing and depressing. "Listening in on Roth," one of them comments, "has always been like listening in on the paranoia of the nation. . . ."[5] The collective critical reaction to Roth's work, not surprisingly, has been mixed. Indeed, the disappointing receptions accorded *Letting Go* and *When She Was Good,* plus his sense that reality repeatedly outstrips the creative imagination, seemingly brought Roth to a decision. For in *Portnoy's Complaint,* and then in "On the Air" and *Our Gang,* he imposed new demands on his own sensibilities and imagination—and on those of his readers. His prime mode of expression always has been laughter. "Roth's obsession," declares Geoffrey Wolff, "is with humor, with corrosive laughter as revenge against things as they are."[6] Wolff underscores what any careful reader should have discerned—that Roth's special humor has been growing more surrealistic and obsessive, as in each new fiction he tries not merely to surpass the daily news but to touch what is deeply private and dark in the modern psyche.

What should be understood, therefore, is that Roth, in *Portnoy's Complaint,* "On the Air," *Our Gang, The Breast,* and more recently in *The Great American Novel,* deviates sharply from the style and tone of his first three novels. He confesses that in both *Our Gang* and "On the Air" he relied heavily on distortion, exaggeration, and bad taste. In fact, the comedy in "On the Air," he insists, leans more to the "grotesque" and belongs "to the literary family of Paranoid Hallucinations—distant relatives would be Gogol's *Diary of a Madman* or *The Nose.*"[7] By contrast, he had tried in the earlier novels to reveal sensitive individuals at tether's end breaking down under their own inner and outer pressures. In his later fiction, however, he utilizes his "lesser, more eclectic skills" of parody and caricature. He indulges also what has been termed his "inclination to extend and complicate a situation rather than to plunge very deeply into it; his fondness for excess; his energy . . . [and] unflagging . . . imagination."[8] Employing these gifts as weapons, he aims at his society's most deeply embedded pieties and hypocrisies, enthusiasms and lunacies; his special targets are America's hyperpatriots and racists, her adolescent sexists and media vulgarians.

Nowhere does Roth exhibit more exuberantly his flair for biting, unleased comic extravaganza than in *The Great American Novel.*[9] Yet even here he strives again for a narrative in the classic American mode—at least one that deals with traditional values and lofty sentiments while laying bare their underlying greed and duplicity; what he wants, in other words, is to reveal some of the ways in which our myths and facts, our romantic fantasies and harsh realities, mingle in the national mind.[10] To this end, he focuses his comic vision on that most formidable and elusive chimera of them all: the Great American Novel. And to convey his sense of this quest's tenuous nature, he quotes for epigraph the assertion of Frank Norris that "the Great American Novel is not extinct like the Dodo, but mythical like the Hippogriff."[11] He then probes and parodies in his Hawthornian prologue the literary motives of Melville, Hawthorne, and Hemingway—with Hemingway even venomously parodying Melville. Roth's primary targets are not these novelists; he takes sharper aim at the American habit of ranking and labeling artists as we do athletes—a habit, admittedly, too often encouraged by the artists themselves.

But to provide theme and plot, imagery and lore, Roth draws upon another obsessive mix of memory, legend, and fantasy: baseball. Asked why he chose baseball, he replied, "Because whaling has already been used."[12] Roth is entitled to his small jokes. Still baseball—with its public pose of winning by fair play and sportsmanship—provides an obvious symbol of modern American life. It also proves a large and easy target; it enables Roth not only to belabor the self-inflating legends of macho and camaraderie upon which several sports-loving generations have been raised, but to expose the Boys of Summer for the dirty old men and dirty young men many of them have been all the time.

Roth avoids direct preaching in his fiction. He chooses instead to follow each new novel with an essay or interview arguing his lack of didactic, or even satiric, intent. He does not expect by his writing, he keeps insisting, to move men to cor-

rective action. His comedy is essentially not "satiric," he claims, nor is its "redeeming" value basically "social or cultural reform, or moral instruction." This is especially true, Roth asserts, of *The Great American Novel.* Here he allowed his comic invention, as he puts it, "to take complete charge" of his imagination, to "lead it where it may"; as a result, his narrative adheres to "its own comic logic," and this is the logic "of farce, of burlesque, of slapstick—rather than the logic or demands of a political satire, or of an individual 'integrated' psychology."[13] Thus the humorous thrust of this book he would have us believe, is a *"comic inventiveness"* devoid of political satire but one characterized instead by a "destructive, or lawless, playfulness" that is articulated for the sheer "fun of it." In fact, he dislikes the very word "satiric" because its "suggestion of cruel means employed for a higher purpose doesn't square with what I feel myself to be doing; it's too uplifting." A more precise term, he declares, would be "satyric," suggesting as it does "the sheer pleasure of exploring the anarchic and the unsocialized" (*RM,* p. 405).

Surprisingly enough, many critics, ignoring the obvious thrust and tone of his fiction, take him at his word.[14] They should not. Philip Roth is not only a satirist but a highly self-conscious and moralistic one. This becomes clear in his nonfiction as well. For even when denying in interviews and essays his satiric intent, he places himself in the comic tradition of savage moralists like Juvenal, Swift, and Kafka. More significantly, his novels and stories are essentially exposures of the disparity in American life between appearance and reality, between professed idealism or good will and an underlying self-seeking grossness or vulgarity. In short, Roth's fiction derives from the hypocrisy embodied in his society's maskings of its true behavior and urges by its moral, high-minded pretensions.

If some critics accept too readily Roth's disavowal of satiric purpose, many others misinterpret his literary motives and dismiss too quickly his social seriousness. John W. Aldridge, for example, finds in *The Great American Novel* no more than "a baffling mélange of hyperkinetic writing about the mythology of baseball."[15] To misread the book to this degree, Aldridge has to be misled or put off by Roth's irrepressible humor and wild imagination. Roth employs both qualities in a recent interview to suggest his own duality toward his work; he does so by acting as both interviewer and interviewee—and by both confessing and denying a "moral" component in his comedic method. Interviewer-Roth wryly chides novelist-Roth for disclaiming any satiric intent in his fiction. "But there is certainly satire in this novel," declares interviewer-Roth, referring to *The Great American Novel,* satire "directed, however playfully, at aspects of American popular mythology. The comedy may not be so free of polemical intent, or even of 'redeeming' social or moral value as you might like to think. And why would you want to think that anyway?" (*RM,* p. 405). Why, indeed? One reason apparently is that he thus can be a "responsible" and "serious" novelist and at the same time, as he later suggests, a "reckless" and "anarchic" humorist. And the latter guise is the one he much prefers his readers to see.

Yet whatever comic motives it embodies, *The Great American Novel* proves difficult to define. To label it merely a "baseball novel" hardly conveys Roth's purpose or range. To say, as does one reviewer, that the book deals with baseball's "power as heroic and pastoral myth," but that it is "savingly tempered" by Roth's grasp of "the awkward contradiction"[16] at the dream's center is to come closer. And if Roth has drawn upon that sport's lore and nostalgia, so have other novelists and essayists, songwriters and versifiers, and an occasional poet. What he has written, however, is an inventive, ironic, funny-sad "myth about myth-making"; in it he lays out and dissects the professed social verities and actual hypocrisies of the national mania that is professional baseball. Having much to say on winning and losing, on patriotism and paranoia, on bias and crudity, and on hypocrisy and greed, he fashions also a savage parable and parody not merely of the nation's social institutions and games but of the American dream of success—and of overweening literary ambition.

Notes

1. Geoffrey Wolff, "Beyond Portnoy," *Newsweek*, 3 Aug. 1970, p. 66.
2. See Philip Roth, "Writing American Fiction," *Commentary*, 31 (March 1961), 224–25.
3. Sheldon Frank, "Next Up: 'An Unbelievably Funny Novel,'" *National Observer*, 12 May 1973, p. 23.
4. Alan Lelchuk, "On *The Breast*: An Interview," *New York Review of Books*, 19 Oct. 1972, p. 26.
5. John Leonard, "Cheever to Roth to Malamud," *Atlantic*, 231 (June 1973), 115.
6. Wolff, p. 66.
7. Alan Lelchuk, "On Satirizing Presidents: An Interview with Philip Roth," *Atlantic*, 228 (Dec. 1971), 84.
8. Peter S. Prescott, "At the Old Ball Game," *Newsweek*, 14 May 1973, p. 125.
9. Philip Roth, *The Great American Novel* (New York: Holt, Rinehart and Winston, 1973). Parenthetical page references in the text, preceded by GAN, are to this edition.
10. See R. Z. Sheppard, "The Name of the Game," *Time*, 7 May 1973, p. 69; and Richard Gilman, "Ball Five," *Partisan Review*, 40, No. 3 (1973), 467.
11. Frank Norris, "The Great American Novelist," *The Responsibilities of the Novelist* (1903; rpt. Cambridge, Mass.: Walker-de Berry, Inc., 1962), p. 230.
12. Jack Meyers, "Letter from the Publisher," *Sports Illustrated*, 12 March 1973, p. 4.
13. Philip Roth, "Reading Myself," *Partisan Review*, 40, No. 3 (1973), 404–05. Subsequent references will be incorporated into the text with the abbreviation *RM*.
14. Describing "the problematic nature of Roth's gift," the generally acute Wilfrid Sheed agrees that "he is not precisely a satirist, nor exactly a pure humorist, just someone who has to keep looking for things he can do." See Wilfrid Sheed, "The Good Word: Howe's Complaint," *New York Times Book Review*, 6 May 1973, p. 2. See also Roth's comments on "the uses of satire," by others and himself, in Lelchuk, "On Satirizing Presidents," pp. 82–86, 88.
15. John W. Aldridge, "Literary Onanism," *Commentary*, 58 (Sept. 1974), 84.
16. Thomas R. Edwards, "*The Great American Novel*," *New York Times Book Review*, 6 May 1973, p. 27.

JOSEPH EPSTEIN
"What Does Philip Roth Want?"

Commentary, January 1984, pp. 62–67

There is, as the folks in the head trades might say, a lot of rage in Philip Roth. What, one wonders, is he so angry about? As a writer, he seems to have had a pretty good roll of the dice. His first book, the collection of stories entitled *Goodbye, Columbus*, published when he was twenty-six, was a very great critical success; in brilliance, his literary debut was second in modern America perhaps only to that of Delmore Schwartz. ("Unlike those of us who came howling into the world, blind and bare," wrote Saul Bellow in *Commentary*, "Mr. Roth appears with nails, hair, and teeth, speaking coherently. At twenty-six he is skillful, witty, and energetic and performs like a virtuoso.") After two further novels,

Letting Go (1962) and *When She Was Good* (1967), he wrote *Portnoy's Complaint* (1969), a *succès fou*, a tremendous hit both critically ("It's a marvelously entertaining book," wrote Theodore Solotaroff, "and one that mines a narrow but central vein more deeply than it has ever been done before"), and commercially (it was a bestseller of a kind that removes a writer permanently from the financial wars). One recalls the protagonist of Saul Bellow's *Henderson the Rain King*, regularly muttering, "I want! I want! I want!" Philip Roth, who at an early age had critical attention, wealth, and celebrity, continues to mutter, "It isn't enough. It isn't enough. It isn't enough."

What does Philip Roth want? For one thing, he wishes to be recognized as a great writer, the natural successor to Gogol and Chekhov and Kafka. He wishes also to have the right to strike out against the bourgeoisie—particularly the Jewish bourgeoisie—and to be adored for his acute perceptions of it. And he wishes to have appreciated what he takes to be the universal application of his own experience as it has been transformed by the imagination in his several novels. Recognition, adoration, appreciation—all this would be his if people would only understand what his work is really about. Or so he believes, and so he would have us believe. But thus far all too few people do understand. In fact, they don't seem to understand at all.

Not that Philip Roth, in his many interviews about his work, has neglected to enlighten them. The Roth *modus operandi* is to publish an interview around the time each of his new books appears, or shortly thereafter, and in these interviews meticulously explain what the book is about, what the influences behind it have been, and what its place is in the Roth canon. Sometimes other writers interview Roth; on occasion he interviews himself. In some cases—*Our Gang* (1971), *The Breast* (1972), *The Great American Novel* (1973)—the interviews are rather better than the novels. (Did you read the novel? No, but I saw the interview.) One thing is clear: Philip Roth is far and away the most generous critic we have of the writings of Philip Roth.

It may be useful to keep this in mind because when reading the novels of Philip Roth one discovers that he is not all that generous to anyone else. Make no mistake, he is an immensely talented writer. He is always very readable. He has a fine eye for the detail and texture of social scenery. He has a splendid ear and an accompanying gift of mimicry, which allows him to do the Jews in a thousand voices. He is famously funny, dangerously funny, as Mel Brooks once characterized the kind of humor that can cause strokes from laughter. He has a most solid literary education. Philip Roth has in fact everything but one thing: a generous spirit. Reading through his work, however, one begins to wonder if, in the case of a novelist, this one thing may not perhaps be the main thing.

Randall Jarrell once wittily defined a novel as "a prose narrative of some length that has something wrong with it," and there has certainly been no shortage of critics ready to declare various things wrong with Philip Roth's novels. Many a rabbi took to his pulpit to denounce the treatment of Jews in *Goodbye, Columbus*. *Letting Go* was in more than one quarter found sententious, Henry James on the graduate-school level, a point nicely caught in "Marjorie Morningstar Ph.D.," the title of John Gross's *New Statesman* review of the novel. Reviewing *When She Was Good* in *Commentary* (November 1967), Robert Alter noted of the characters in this, Roth's third book, that "Humanity is divided into those who are hateful and those who are merely contemptible. . . ." At the close of a review of Roth's slender novel *The Breast* (1972), Frederick

Crews offered a two-for-one critical sale, writing in a single sentence: "In a sense _The Breast_ is a more discouraging work than the straightforwardly vicious _Our Gang_ [Roth's 1971 travesty of Richard Nixon]."

Philip Roth, then, has taken his critical lumps. But the deepest and unkindest cut of all came from Irving Howe, who, in an essay in _Commentary_ entitled "Philip Roth Reconsidered" (December 1972), quite consummately eviscerated all Roth's work. Howe pointed out that Roth's "great need is for a stance of superiority," that one reason his stories "are unsatisfactory is that they come out of a thin personal culture," that "the cruelest thing anyone can do with _Portnoy's Complaint_ is to read it twice," that such literary narcissism as Roth has displayed throughout his career "is especially notable among minor artists, with whom it frequently takes the form of self-exemptive attacks on the shamefulness of humanity," and so on and on. When Howe is done, he has allowed that he thinks well of a single Roth short story, "Defender of the Faith."

I used the word eviscerate to describe this essay; its effect was as though Dr. Howe, working over the corpus of Roth's work, had removed all the patient's major organs, leaving only a small portion—that one short story—of the spleen. This essay, as we shall see, has left Philip Roth in the spiritual equivalent of intensive care for the more than a decade since it was written.

I have said that Philip Roth is always very readable, but I have recently learned that (as Howe pointed out) he is not very rereadable. Trial by rereading is a tough test for a novelist, and I am not sure exactly what it proves, except of course that it is obviously better to write books that can be reread with pleasure than not. (Ezra Pound once distinguished between journalism and literature by saying that literature could be read twice.) Roth, on a second reading, begins to seem smaller; one starts to notice glancing and low blows. In _Goodbye, Columbus_, for example, a cheap point is scored off Mrs. Patimkin, the mother of the family of rich and vulgar Jews who it is fair to say are the target of the novella, because she has never heard of Martin Buber. "Is he _reformed?_" she asks. The assumption here is that people who do not know the name of Martin Buber are swine, like people who listen to the recordings of Kostelanetz and Mantovani. The term for the thinking behind this assumption is intellectual snobbery, and of a fairly low order. In the novella Brenda Patimkin remarks to Neil Klugman, its protagonist, "Why do you always sound a little nasty to me!" This seems to be a good question.

Or, again, in rereading _When She Was Good_ I discovered myself feeling an unexpected rush of sympathy for that novel's main character, the moralizing and man-destroying Lucy Nelson. For all that Lucy Nelson is mean-spirited and endlessly judgmental, throughout the novel there is someone meaner and even more judgmental on her tail—her creator, the author. The novel is relentless, ending with Lucy Nelson's death in the cold, a chilling performance in every sense. Mighty is the wrath of the Lord; but the wrath of Roth, for those of his characters on whom he spews it—from the Patimkins to Lucy Nelson, to Jack and Sophie Portnoy, to assorted lady friends in various of the novels, to the critic Milton Appel in the recent _The Anatomy Lesson_—is not so easily borne either.

A highly self-conscious writer, the early Philip Roth no doubt felt the weight of his own crushing moralizing. True, in his first book he was moralizing against moralizing—yet it was still moralizing. Moral tunes were the ones he had been trained to dance to. "I was," Roth has written, "one of those

students of the 50's who came to books by way of a fairly good but rather priestly literary education, in which writing poems and novels was assumed to eclipse all else in what we called 'moral seriousness.'" The year before, in an interview with himself, he announced: "I imagined fiction to be something like a religious calling, and literature a kind of sacrament, a sense of things I have had reason to modify since." What may have caused Roth to modify his sense of moral earnestness was the unrelieved gloom in which it issued in such novels as _Letting Go_ and _When She Was Good_. Roth's early fiction was about what he construed to be the coercive forces in life—family, religion, culture. At some point he decided that among those coercive forces he had to add another: his own literary moral seriousness.

Near the end of the 1960's, that time of many liberations, Philip Roth achieved his own with the publication of _Portnoy's Complaint_. Toward the middle of _Goodbye, Columbus_ the hero notes: "I am not one to stick scalpels in myself"; henceforth, Roth's heroes will comport themselves as if taking acupuncture with scalpels. Of course, to blame the guilt of Alexander Portnoy, a guilt beginning in ceaseless masturbation, issuing in an adult case of raging sex fever, and closing in impotence—to blame this guilt on Portnoy's Jewish middle-class upbringing was certain to put Roth in solid with the Jewish friends he had already made through _Goodbye, Columbus_. Dwelling on masturbation, fellatio, cunnilingus, and other features of what H. L. Mencken once referred to as "non-Euclidean sex," the novel was deliberately in atrocious taste. It read rather like a more literate and extended Lenny Bruce skit. It was meant to cause the squeamish to squirm, the righteous to rave—and by and large succeeded in doing so. If Berkeley was what happened to the university during the 60's, Andy Warhol what happened to contemporary art, _Portnoy's Complaint_ was what happened to American Jewish fiction.

For Philip Roth, _Portnoy's Complaint_ was evidently, in one of the cant phrases of the day, a breakthrough. Suddenly, the sexual subject, with all its taboos shattered, was now fully his to command; suddenly, in his use of material and language, he was little boy blue. He had also developed a new tone, a detached intimacy such as a practiced analysand might adopt with his therapist. Psychoanalysts—variously called Spielvogel, Klinger, and other German names—will henceforth appear in Roth's novels, while Roth himself will come to view the psychoanalytic as an important mode of apprehending reality. Roth's explanation of the meaning of _Portnoy_ reflects this clearly enough, when he says, in yet another of his interviews, that the book "which was concerned with the comic side of the struggle between a hectoring superego and an ambitious id, seems now, in retrospect, to have realigned those forces as they act upon my imagination."

I myself prefer not to hear novelists using words like superego and id. Whatever aid they may bring to the suffering, however necessary they may be to the discourse of therapeutic workers, they are death on art, and on no art are they more deadly than fiction. Novelists do better to speak of morals and desire, of conscience and soul. The later Roth has, I believe, shed his true-believer views of psychoanalysis; in his most recent novel, _The Anatomy Lesson_, he seems to have shucked them off nearly altogether. But he has retained certain of the habits of the analysand—classically conceived, as they say down at the Institute—not the least of which is an unshakable belief in the importance of sex and an implacable confidence in the significance of one's own splendid self.

Although I have not taken an exact count, it strikes me that, along with John Updike and Norman Mailer, Philip Roth is a hot entry in the sweepstakes for the most fornication described within the pages of a single body of serious work. (Edmund Wilson once grouped a number of novelists of the 30's as "The Boys in the Back Room"; Updike, Mailer, Roth, and perhaps William Styron, all writers with a puerile interest in sex, might be thought of as The Men in the Boys' Room.) By now a practiced hand, Roth can describe sex as easily as Dickens could describe London, though the views Dickens offers are more interesting. Roth has mastered his technique to the point where he can advance his plots through dialogue while keeping his characters *in flagrante*. All this is by design. Roth has said that the direction his work has taken "since *Portnoy's Complaint* can in part be accounted for by my increased responsiveness to, and respect for, what is unsocialized in me."

Yet it isn't the sheer volume of sex in Roth's novels that is troubling; one feels, rather, that sex is one of the few subjects left to him, and that it has now begun to qualify as an uninteresting obsession. Like cityscapes to Bellow, so bedscapes to Roth; one senses he could do them in his sleep, and after a short while one wishes he would. I. B. Singer is a novelist quite as concerned with sex as Philip Roth, but, it seems to me, with a decisive difference. In Singer's fiction, the pleasures of sex mix with the terrors of guilt and sin, and somewhere off in the distance you feel perhaps God is watching. In a Roth novel, sex has to do with a writer paying respect to his "unsocialized side," and somewhere off in the distance you can hear a pen scratching.

You hear a pen scratching because, as a novelist, Philip Roth has lived for some while pretty close to the autobiographical bone. The relationship between fictional representation and autobiographical sources is endlessly complicated, and can usually only be properly understood by a literary biographer willing to spend decades with his subject. How much of Stendhal is in Julien Sorel, how much of Balzac in Lucien Chardon, how much of Tolstoy in Levin? The more contemporary the age, the more complex, and the more crucial, the question seems to grow. How much James Joyce in Stephen Dedalus, how much Proust in the Marcel of *Remembrance of Things Past*, how much of Kafka in Joseph K? The closer we get to our own day, the smaller the gap between the fictional and the autobiographical seems to be. A remark by E. R. Curtius goes a good way toward explaining the impetus behind this phenomenon. "Since Chateaubriand's *René*," Curtius writes, "literature has preferred to deal with the conflicts of the individual, the shipwreck of ideals, the disillusionment of the heart, the quarrel with society." All the items Curtius mentions, from the conflict within the individual to the quarrel with society, cry out to be dealt with directly, shorn of the mediating screen of fictional representation. And dealing directly with such things in fiction often means dealing with them in a highly autobiographical manner.

This is a touchy point for Philip Roth, who again and again has accused his critics and readers of confusing his life and his work. The confusion set in with a fine vengeance, he claims, with *Portnoy's Complaint*, when "a novel in the guise of a confession was received and judged by any number of readers as a confession in the guise of a novel." In an essay entitled "Portnoy's Fame—and Mine," Roth has told how, not long after the enormous success of *Portnoy's Complaint*, when Roth himself had become a gossip-column item, at one point romantically linked (I believe the phrase is) with Barbra Streisand, the rumor circulated that he had had a nervous breakdown—which, as he notes, given the original confusion between the author and the protagonist of *Portnoy's Com-*

plaint, makes a certain amount of sense, madness being the end preordained for onanists.

Time and again, in interviews and essays and now even in his fiction, Roth has gone on insisting that he is not, in his novels, writing about Philip Roth, except through the transmutations of art. "That writing is an act of imagination," says Nathan Zuckerman in *The Anatomy Lesson*, "seems to perplex and infuriate everyone." Roth has spoken of readers getting a "voyeuristic kick" from reading his autobiography into his books. I think "voyeuristic kick" is exactly the correct phrase, and my first response to it is that, if a writer doesn't wish to supply such kicks, perhaps he would do better not to undress before windows opening onto thoroughfares.

Yet one wonders if voyeuristic kicks are not precisely at the heart of Roth's recent novels (as well as those of other contemporary novelists). In an odd conjunction of circumstances, while novels seem to mean less and less to the way people live, at the same time a number of novelists have become celebrity figures: through television appearances, magazine interviews, gossip sheets. These novelists can hardly be unaware of their celebrity, however much they may say they do not like it, and they also ought to be aware that readers—and quite intelligent readers, too—will see the novelists' lives in their work, especially when the writer has taken so little trouble to disguise himself. If there is anyone in the world who believes that the hero of Saul Bellow's *The Dean's December* is anyone other than Saul Bellow, I should like to meet that person and have the opportunity to sell him some mining stock. If there is anyone who believes that young Stingo in *Sophie's Choice* is not the young William Styron, that person brings a freshness and an innocence to his reading that I believe borders on insanity. It is a cheap thrill but nonetheless one very much for the taking, this reading of gossip about famous novelists in—of all places—their own novels.

In short, it is the novelists who make this gossip, these voyeuristic kicks, possible in the first place. If they don't wish so to be read, the way out is through invention, imagination, fresh creation, greater subtlety. Another prospect, however, is simply to give way, to write about oneself almost straight-out, to cultivate the idiosyncratic vision, to plow away at one's own obsessions, becoming a bit of a crank, something of a crackpot, and risk being a minor writer indeed. Alas, I think this is the path that Philip Roth has set himself upon.

After *Portnoy's Complaint* Roth wrote two satires, the one about Nixon, *Our Gang*, and *The Great American Novel*, about baseball. Such works are known as *jeux d'esprits*; when they fail, as these two do for being excessively heavyhanded and insufficiently funny, they are also known as regrettable. There followed *The Breast* (1972), in which David Kepesh, a professor of English—surprising that Roth didn't make him a CUNY linguist—wakes up in a hospital to find himself turned into a breast. Kepesh feels that he got into this fix through reading fiction. He has been teaching Kafka and Gogol. "The books I've been teaching—they put the idea in my head." He asks: "Why this primitive identification with *the* object of infantile veneration?" Perhaps, he thinks, "Success itself! There is what I couldn't take—a happy life!" Other theories are tried out. Kepesh's psychoanalyst is consulted. To no avail. The reason David Kepesh has become a breast remains unknown both within the story and outside it. With *The Breast*, Philip Roth's problem has officially become identifying Philip Roth's problem.

At this point Roth's fictional works, like runny cooked vegetables on a plate, begin to bleed into one another. Three Roth protagonists come on the scene: Nathan Zuckerman,

Peter Tarnopol, and, not yet breastified, David Kepesh. A Chinese-box effect sets in. In *My Life as a Man* (1974) we are presented with a story written by Peter Tarnopol about the sexual adventures of the young Nathan Zuckerman; this Nathan Zuckerman will return as the author of a shocking bestseller about sexual liberation entitled *Carnovsky*, which sounds like nothing so much as *Portnoy's Complaint*. But back at *My Life as a Man*, Peter Tarnopol's editor asks him: "Is that what you're up to, or are you planning to write Zuckerman variations until you have constructed a kind of full-length fictional fugue?" By now, Philip Roth has written three books about this Nathan Zuckerman character. All that remains to complete the circle is for Peter Tarnopol to write a novel in which David Kepesh is teaching a year-long honors seminar on the novels of Philip Roth.

These characters have a number of qualities in common: they are bookish (two are writers, one a teacher of writing), Jewish, single, past or current analysands and hence mightily self-regarding, great prizers of their personal freedom (two have had disastrous first marriages, one, Nathan Zuckerman, has had three marriages about two of which not much is said), fearful of a great deal but above all of personal entrapment. Their characteristic condition is to feel put upon; their characteristic response is to whine and complain. Much of their time on the page is spent in the effort of self-analysis through which they hope to arrive at self-justification. Oh, yes, one other thing: for the above-mentioned reasons, none is in any way easy to sympathize with.

Reading these novels, one begins to sense with what pleasure a psychoanalyst must look forward to knocking off at the end of the day. It's a small world, that of the patient—it has, really, only one person of importance in it. So, too, with Roth's novels which feel so terribly underpopulated, confined, claustral. One admires their sentences, picks up on their jokes, notes the craft that went into their making, and finishes reading them with a slight headache and a sour taste in the mouth. One puts them down, finally, in not so different a condition, one assumes, from the psychoanalyst picking up his briefcase, sighing, and flicking off the light in the office; only, unlike the analyst, one has not been so well rewarded for the day's work.

Not that these novels are without brilliant passages and portraits. In the second section of *My Life as a Man*, the section entitled "Courting Disaster (or, Serious in the Fifties)," Nathan Zuckerman contracts a mistaken marriage for chiefly literary reasons. To escape his own cozy Jewish middle-class upbringing, to meet experience such as it is met in literature, he is drawn to a sad, broken woman, a perfect mismatch, chiefly because "she had suffered so much and because she was so brave." But this section of the novel, so beautifully done, is blown when, after many nightmarish years in the marriage, Zuckerman runs off to Italy with his very young stepdaughter. The appropriate reference is made to Nabokov. Roth and his characters have books on the brain, and not only great literature but criticism into the bargain. Zuckerman says of himself: "Where Emma Bovary had read too many romances of her period, it would seem that I had read too much of the criticism of mine."

In his later novels, Roth regularly measures himself against the great literary figures of the past, attempting to discover with whom among them he belongs. Peter Tarnopol is a great admirer of Flaubert, though at one point in *My Life as a Man* he notes: "I'll try a character like Henry Miller, or someone out-and-out bilious like Céline for my hero instead of Gustave Flaubert—and won't be such an Olympian writer as it

was my ambition to be back in the days when nothing called personal experience stood between me and aesthetic detachment." David Kepesh has a case on Kafka, and in *The Professor of Desire* pays a visit to the aged prostitute in Prague to whom Kafka was said to bring his custom. (No one ever said Philip Roth wasn't inventive.) In *The Anatomy Lesson* Nathan Zuckerman recalls his undergraduate experience of the magisterial, and majestic, presence of Thomas Mann lecturing on literature at the University of Chicago, and gauges how far his own artistic aspirations have fallen since that time. The way other people look to religion and philosophy, Roth and his heroes look to literature. "Literature got me into this," says Zuckerman in one of the sections of *My Life as a Man*, "and literature is gonna get me out." Thus far, it must be reported, it hasn't.

"Moral delinquency has its fascination for you," says Dr. Klinger, David Kepesh's analyst, and so it does for Philip Roth. In Roth's later novels, though, moral delinquency has almost exclusively meant sexual delinquency. Roth himself, in an interview published around the time of *The Breast*, formulated the moral war of his characters as "between the ethical and social yearnings and the implacable, singular lusts for the flesh and its pleasures." Yet in this particular war Philip Roth is in the embarrassing position of one of those Japanese soldiers holed up on a Pacific island, still polishing his boots and cleaning his rifle, who hasn't yet heard that the war between ethical and social yearnings and sexual appetite is long over. Ethical and social yearnings lost and sexual appetite promptly departed.

More and more of Roth's subject is falling away from him, like the hair on Nathan Zuckerman's head in *The Anatomy Lesson*. In *My Life as a Man* this same Zuckerman is said to have written a novel, filled with "moral indignation," entitled *A Jewish Father*. Roth himself, in such portraits as those of Mrs. Patimkin, Aunt Gladys, Sophie Portnoy, and others has been putting together a bitter volume that might be entitled *World of Our Mothers*. Now, however, that generation, in whose rage for order Roth read repression and perhaps unintended but nonetheless real malevolence, is old and dying and hardly any longer worth railing against. Even Roth appears to have recognized this, and some of the few touching moments in his later fiction—the scenes with David Kepesh's widowed father in *My Life as a Man*, memories of Nathan Zuckerman's mother in *Zuckerman Unbound* and *The Anatomy Lesson*—are tributes to the generation of his own parents.

When a writer has used up all other subjects within the realm of his experience, one subject remains—that of writing itself. Philip Roth's last three novels—the Zuckerman trilogy—are about precisely this subject. The first, *The Ghost Writer*, much of which takes place at the home of the ascetic writer E. I. Lonoff, is about the toll in loneliness and self-abnegation that the writing life exacts. Being a Roth novel, *The Ghost Writer* is not without its comic touches, or without its attempts to *épater les juifs*. In the latter category, the Zuckerman character imagines bringing home Anne Frank as his wife—the one sure way to please his parents, who are already aggrieved at what they construe to be his abetting of anti-Semitism by publishing stories about the seamier side of the family. Playing Anne Frank for laughs is Roth the bad boy at it again, attempting to make the Jews squirm. He cannot seem to help himself on this score. He can't leave it alone.

Zuckerman Unbound, the second Zuckerman novel, is about the wages paid for large-scale success in America, in this case paid out to Nathan Zuckerman for writing his shocking bestseller *Carnovsky*. The coin in which these wages are paid is that of the unwanted company of hustlers, intrusive idiotic publicity, and family misunderstanding. Here again one begins to feel many autobiographical teases. Did Roth's parents react to *Portnoy* as Zuckerman's did to *Carnovsky*? Does Roth feel the same petulance about publicity as Zuckerman? "Never trust the artist. Trust the tale," prounounced D. H. Lawrence. Yet the more it becomes apparent that there is little to choose between tale and teller, the more one ends up trusting neither. Part of the burden of *The Anatomy Lesson*, it seems to me, is that Roth may no longer trust either himself.

A long while ago Philip Roth removed the fig leaf; now, in *The Anatomy Lesson*, off—or nearly off—comes the mask. In this novel Nathan Zuckerman is suffering a great unexplained pain in his back and neck. So great is the pain that he cannot write. He can, though, while settled on his back upon a rubber mat on his living-room floor, carry on love affairs with four different women. But these affairs do not absorb him nearly so deeply as does an attack written on his work by a Jewish intellectual critic he once admired by the name of Milton Appel that appeared in the magazine *Inquiry*. Not many people will need to know this, but Milton Appel is another name for Irving Howe and *Inquiry* is intended to be *Commentary*. A few details have been shifted here and there, some with an almost pathetic indifference: Howe's essay on Roth appeared in *Commentary* in December 1972, Appel's on Zuckerman in March 1973. (What extraordinary transformations art can make!) I am sure a number of characters are invented, touches and twists are added, nothing is quite as it was in life, but at its center this is a *roman à clef*—one that is being used, through gross caricature and straight insult, to repay an old wound.

It is also a *roman* of clay. The only points of interest have to do with the sense it conveys that Philip Roth himself may feel he can go no further in this vein. He has written himself into a corner and up a wall. "There's nothing more wearying," Zuckerman tells a friend, "than having to go around pretending to be the author of one's own books—except pretending not to be." Elsewhere he remarks: "If you get out of yourself you can't be a writer because the personal ingredient is what gets you going, and if you hang on to the personal ingredient any longer you'll disappear right up your [orifice deleted]." And later he adds: "Chained to my dwarf drama till I die. Stories now about Milton Appel? Fiction about losing my hair? I can't face it." Neither, for much longer, I suspect, can we.

When, with *Portnoy's Complaint*, Philip Roth's career took its turn toward investigating the inner life, Roth must have thought he was on his way to becoming the Jewish Gogol, the American Kafka. But it has not worked out. Roth's fictional figures lack the requisite weight; they aren't clown-heroes out of Kafka or Gogol who have somehow been tricked by life, the butt of some towering cosmic joke. A character who is having love affairs with four women and wishes to get his own back at a literary critic—this is not, as Philip Roth the teacher of literature himself must know, exactly a figure of universal significance. No, it has not worked out. *Portnoy's Complaint* ended on the couch, with the psychiatrist remarking to Alex Portnoy, "Now vee may perhaps to begin. Yes?" *The Anatomy Lesson* ends with Nathan Zuckerman, determined to give up writing for a career in medicine, helping the interns in the hospital in which he himself is a patient. I should have preferred to see it, too, end in a psychoanalyst's office, with the analyst announcing to Portnoy-Tarnopol-Kepesh-Zuckerman-Roth: "Now, vee are concluded. Vee haf gone as far as vee can go. Yes?"

HELGE NORMANN NILSEN
"Rebellion against Jewishness: *Portnoy's Complaint*"

English Studies, December 1984, pp. 495–503

The Jewish-American fiction written after World War II naturally reflects the changes that occurred in American society and in the lives of the Jews as an ethnic group. Living conditions improved dramatically, and many Jews entered the middle class. The writers, like so many others, were better educated and began to merge into the mainstream of American life. At the same time they retained their commitment to humanistic values and their ancestral awareness of the tragedy of human existence. Thus the stage was set for the exploration of important conflicts between the Jewish sensibility and the agnostic consumer mentality of the larger society. J. D. Salinger's *The Catcher in the Rye* is a striking example of this clash, and there are also traces of it in Bellow's *Dangling Man* and Malamud's *The Assistant*. At the same time Jewish writers did not advocate any return to ethnic orthodoxy, being products of the modern age and regarding themselves as Americans, or humanists first and Jews second. Nevertheless, the basic conflict between their ethnic heritage and the wholly secularized environment emerges in various ways in much of the fiction that was produced. The early immigrants had embraced America, but for the writer of the fifties and sixties the situation had become more complex. No simple response or solution was possible any longer.

There had been uncertainties before the war, but there had also been valid alternatives. Jew or American, radical or moderate, these were some of the possibilities. But in the work of Nathanael West there is a tendency to discard all alternatives and embrace nihilism, and it is his voice that speaks most clearly for those who came after him. Philip Roth and Bellow may not be quite so bleak in their despair, but their work shows a rootlessness and scepticism which can be seen as the hallmark of contemporary Jewish-American prose fiction. For the first time, the effects of assimilation and Americanization are fully felt by writers of Jewish descent, and their Jewish heritage is perceived either as an impediment or a type of sensibility rather than any set of beliefs. *The Assistant* may be said to affirm Jewishness, but only in the vaguest of terms.

Portnoy's Complaint is thought of as a novel that is typical of the sixties, of a generation in rebellion against established values, but it has a curious resemblance to the immigrant school of Jewish-American fiction. Its hero rejects all things Jewish and struggles to become integrated into what he regards as a desirable, secular and liberal way of life. 'His is a late version of the old story of the newcomer struggling to become an American, bent on full assimilation, away from ghetto identity and towards American identity with its much wider horizons of possibility.'[1] However, the focus is different. The protagonists in immigrant fiction were caught up in a historical process of upward mobility that prevented them from concentrating too much on their individual psyches. In the case of Alexander Portnoy, Jewishness is above all a psychological burden that he labors to rid himself of. The intensity of his struggle is evidence of the power both of the tradition and the larger culture that is opposed to many of its mores and attitudes. Generally speaking there is much to be said for the view that Portnoy's battle against his heritage ends in a draw. It is a modern paradox that the hero cannot quite escape from a tradition that he no longer believes in and thus is doubly victimized.

Roth's novel has a great deal of psychological awareness built into it. The hero is prodigiously intelligent and well versed in his Freud and Marx, but his knowledge is of no help to him. Instead, he employs it as the instrument of an endless self-analysis that becomes an exercise in masochism. But on the theoretical level, at least, Portnoy's insight into his own predicament is remarkable: 'A disorder in which strongly-felt ethical and altruistic impulses are perpetually warring with extreme sexual longings, often of a perverse nature'. [2] This diagnosis can be applied to the entire Judeao-Christian tradition, not just the specific Jewish context. But because of their embattled situation the Jews have enforced the dictates of their religion and morality with greater severity than most of the surrounding world in order not to capitulate to it. The nearest parallel to their orthodoxy is found in Christian fundamentalist groups, among whose adherents the psychological dilemma of Portnoy may be as widespread as among the Jews themselves.

The novel consists of an uninterrupted monologue by the protagonist, with the psychoanalyst Dr. Spielvogel as silent audience. However, the principle of free association is discarded in favor of a coherent presentation by Portnoy of his conviction that his problems have been mainly caused by his background and his parents, especially his mother. Psychoanalysis becomes a vehicle for his attack on Jewish customs and values. The aim of analysis, to obtain emotional insight and experience catharsis, is largely subverted by a Portnoy who is bent on polemic and revenge rather than therapeutic breakthroughs. His portrait of his parents and the Jewish neighborhood is onesided, to put it mildly, and even if he is right in his criticism, his relentless attacks serve as an escape from himself and his own share in the continued existence of his problems.

One might question Alex's reliability as a narrator who is also a patient undergoing analysis, and it is clear that he is not wholly perceptive with regard to the nature of his condition. Also, he sees others largely in terms of his own needs and reactions. One cannot take everything he says at face value, but at the same time there is a persistent pattern of rejection in his reaction to the Jewish milieu. On the intellectual level, at least, he leaves no doubt as to his complete lack of enthusiasm for all the basic tenets of Judaism and the attitudes that go with them. There is a quality of sincerity in his abandonment of Jewish beliefs which seems to belong to a norm which is stronger, as it were, than the troubled hero himself, or remains unaffected by his problems. It may be here that Roth, as implied author, is perceived most clearly in the novel, whereas Alex, the narrator, generally suffers from a lack of distance between himself and much of his experience. This trait may weaken *Portnoy's Complaint* as a protest novel, but it makes the hero very convincing as a psychological portrait. Another indication of the author's distance from the narrator is Dr. Spielvogel's remark at the end of the book, where he suggests that Alex's treatment is yet to begin.

Alex's parents are close enough to the immigrant experience to cling to certain old world viewpoints, but they are also in a stage of transition, having moved into the suburbs and apparently also withdrawn themselves from Jewish religious activities. Portnoy senior has no higher education and seems to have only vague notions about the culture of his own race, yet he looks upon 'the saga' of the Jewish people with great reverence. But the atmosphere in the household is far from orthodox, and the Portnoys have been more strongly influenced by American values than they seem to be aware of. In fact, the greatest achievement they can think of is material success, and they persecute their son with demands that he fulfill their expectations and establish himself as a respectable citizen with a wife and family. They protest against his atheism, but they are not in any position to teach him Jewish cultural and religious values. The only active remnant of these are certain dietary bans on shellfish and hamburger meat which are ferociously upheld by Mrs. Portnoy. According to Harold Fisch, Alex's mother wants her son to marry and subject his children to 'the rituals of bar-mitzvah and marriage in an atmosphere of observance evacuated of any transcendent meaning'. [3]

Given such a background, the striving of Alex toward integration and secularization is a natural one, notwithstanding the horrified reactions of his parents. Seen in the larger context of the historical development from oppression in Europe to freedom in America, the entire Portnoy family have been moulded by the greater forces that have shaped the destiny of Jews in the United States. In Europe there was the misery of poverty, but the land of opportunity also exacts its price. It takes hard word to get ahead, and the family breadwinner has labored, 'in that ferocious and self-annihilating way in which so many Jewish men of his generation served their families'. (7) This is the trap that Alex wants to escape from, but he finds that he carries a burden of remorse and loneliness that may be the price that he will have to pay for his freedom.

Jake Portnoy is proud of his success as an insurance salesman and speaks with great respect of the Anglo-Saxon gentlemen who run the corporation that he works for. But he also feels their prejudice very keenly and is occasionally overcome with fury at these supercilious snobs. Similarly, Alex dreams of non-Jewish girls and wants to obliterate his ethnic background in order to become acceptable to them, although his sister Hanna warns him, arguing that he cannot escape his background. Being a Jew is an historical fact which the surrounding world will never allow to be forgotten. The argument is a time-honored one, but Alex refuses to accept it. He continues to protest and rebel, and it is hard to refute his indictment of the possessive and domineering ways of his mother. They were a source of torment for him when a child and have no doubt contributed to the formation of his present problems and anxieties.

Alex's main charge against his father is that he is weak and submissive and allows himself to be dominated both by his non-Jewish employers and his overpowering wife. He is a man who gives up any attempt at discovering and asserting his individuality and therefore becomes a negative example to his son. The elder Portnoy wants his son's love and to give him the same, but the latter cannot accept the premises: 'But what he had to offer I did not want—and what I wanted he did not have to offer'. (28) The father has gone too far in his acceptance of the rules laid down by the mother for Alex to be able to communicate with him. He is too much of a man of his generation, for whose members conventional success was of overwhelming importance, to be able to allow his son to develop in his own way. Moreover, he has a strong sense of his tradition as a Jew, although he cannot formulate his commitment very well, and thus feels impelled to see his son as one who will fulfill the father's ambitions and be a Jew of the kind that he himself would have wanted to be.

But the son turns against what he regards as the tyranny of the entire older generation of Jewish middle class citizens and singles out two prominent cases of parental oppression among them. His cousin Heschie had decided to marry a girl of Polish descent, but his father compelled him to relinquish her because she did not belong to the tribe. Soon after Heschie was killed in the Great War. This tragedy is eloquent testimony to the dark underside of the Jewish family feeling and sense of togetherness, that is, an intolerance and prejudice that are just as deplorable as anti-Semitism. The story of Ronald Nimkin, the obedient Jewish boy who commits suicide because of his parents' 'self-ishness and stupidity', is a pathetic one, though the question of who is responsible for the tragedy is not as clear here as in the case of Heschie. The causes of Ronald's death may be more complicated than Alex is ready to allow for, but then his whole approach to the Jewish milieu is that of the prosecutor rather than the impartial observer. But he no doubt has a valid point when he draws attention to the self-righteousness of the Jews and their imaginary moral superiority.

However, when looking back on his past, Alex is aware that there is another and more positive dimension that was also part of his childhood. There is never any doubt that the Portnoys loved their children, though Alex finds it easier to focus on certain happy moments with his father than recollecting similar ones with his mother. He does remember such episodes with his mother, too, and the pleasure associated with them is more poignant than anything else, but he had also been all too familiar with her threats of withdrawal of motherly love. But the story of how his father had taken Alex swimming one day in summer at the seashore is so full of tenderness that it seems almost incongruous amidst the welter of angry accusations that make up the major portion of the novel. Alex also asserts that he has many more such happy memories of his parents, and in that case the question inevitably arises why he concentrates so intensely on the negative influences of his early life. It seems unsatisfactory to argue that he does this because he is a social critic whose purpose is to expose the shortcomings of a certain environment. The enormous self-concern of Roth's protagonist is not easy to reconcile with the intentions of the literature of social protest because it diverts the attention from the problems in question to the person who is complaining about them. Even if his personality is considered relevant as evidence of what a narrowminded upbringing can lead to, a certain detachment is required when dealing with the narrator's own condition in order to convey successfully the idea that social criticism is the main concern of the novel.

Alex's relationships with women follow a pattern that is established in his battles with his mother. She uses a technique of alternately smothering him in love and threatening to cast him out of her life altogether, all in the name of giving him a good upbringing. In any case, this is how Alex remembers her behavior. He is extraordinarily sensitive and dependent on women's favors, but at the same time he is afraid of being trapped by them, thus losing his independence and even identity. His need for love is as strong as his desire for freedom from commitment, and the only 'solution' that seems possible for him as an adult is to lead a life of promiscuity. During his adolescence he indulges in frequent masturbation both as a means of satisfying his sex drive and of asserting his rebellious individuality in the face of the many taboos that the home and the entire environment impose upon him. At the deepest level, his sexual excesses may be regarded as part of his struggle to free himself of his identity as a Jew.

Alex is ambivalent in his feelings towards his parents, but not towards everything they stand for. He cannot forget the moments of love and bliss, but he is unequivocal in his rejection of their use of emotional blackmail and their sentimental and primitive attachment to Jewish customs and beliefs. Above all, Alex abandons the religion of his tribe, indeed, all religions, in favor of an atheism that is combined with a radical political commitment. He is also politically naive, with his belief that 'the rights of man' are realized in the Soviet Union, but he is sincere in his rationalism and atheism, and there is no sign that he ever recants from this position. His own experience supports his views, in that the Jews he has observed have accepted many of the secular standards of the surrounding society and uphold them with a zeal that is second to no other group. Alex is merciless, but also to the point, in his analysis of the function of religion. It is an 'opiate' for the ignorant masses, and the clergy, of any denomination, has an economic interest in maintaining the status quo. It is generally difficult to find any flaws in Alex's arguments against the intolerance, superstition and backwardness of the people of his parents' generation, and he is lucid and consistent in his criticism. His scepticism and rationalism are convincing and based on a keen understanding of human realities and motivations. But his maturity in this field is offset by his inability to utilize his insights in the area of his own emotional problems. Here he seems to be the victim of forces beyond his control, a helpless spectator to a conflict within him that he can analyze but not resolve.

No one can be more eloquent in his diagnosis of his condition than Alex himself. His is the conflict of Western culture, between duty and pleasure, conscience and transgression. But his goal, however difficult, is to rid himself of his own taboos and lead a life according to his own convictions. He wants to follow his own desire and enjoy it, but he has to admit that he is oppressed by 'shame and inhibition and fear'. Eileen Z. Cohen suggests that Alex is 'literal' and 'priggish in his expectations of perfection in himself'.[4] Every rebellious act is followed by guilt and remorse, no matter how much Alex hates his own inhibitions and knows that they have no rational foundation.

With regard to religion, dietary laws, tribal prejudices and materialistic obsessions, Alex has quite a good case against all of them, but this is not so clear in questions of sexual morality. His promiscuity may be an attempt to establish sexual freedom for himself, and even for others, but the project is utopian. People seem to need emotional security and stability also, even Alex, and besides, his many affairs cannot even provide him with a lasting sense of self-esteem. As far as sex is concerned, he is up against a deep-seated division within himself which is a major cause of his sufferings. He wants to be a swinger, a carefree hedonist, but his sexual and emotional egotism leads to disappointments and disillusion both for himself and his partners.

The women feel exploited by Portnoy, and with reason. He is an attractive man and quite successful in the social sense, but he has very little regard for the women's feelings if they fall in love with him and want to marry. He blames himself for having an overdeveloped superego in sexual matters, but he does not actually experience much remorse in connection with his various colorful sexual experiences, whether with his mistress, the Monkey, or prostitutes and other girls. Alex gives himself too much credit here, perhaps to cover up for an insensitivity and sheer coarseness in him which do not fit the image of himself that he wants to preserve. He experiences a fantasy of ending up in Hell for his sins and of being castigated for his lack of regard for others. He is told here in no uncertain terms that 'suffering mankind' means nothing to him and that the only feelings he has ever experienced have been located in his sexual organs. These charges have an unmistakable ring of truth about them. However, they are not expressed directly by Portnoy to himself, but by the Devil in the shape of Rabbi Warshaw, a character whom Alex regards as a pompous fraud. Thus he manages to take some of the edge off this self-criticism. Moreover, he skilfully draws the attention away from his own flaws by constantly finding fault with his partners, the Monkey in particular. He attacks Naomi, the Israeli girl, for criticizing him, but his own attitude to everyone he meets, including the women once he starts reacting to their personalities, is hypercritical, if not downright misanthropic.

The Monkey is unbalanced and sometimes even hysterical, but this must be seen in relation to her frustrated love for Alex. He is unable to respond to this feeling in her, and his behavior is almost entirely mechanical and sex-oriented. She justly accuses him of lack of feeling and involvement and stands out, in contrast to him, as a person who is alive and human in a broader sense than he is. According to Jesse Bier, 'He is even worse off, since some benighted *shiksas*, like the Monkey, try to fight back into human love or devotion, while the Portnoys of the modern world heartlessly run out on them'.[5] Alex is right in condemning the idiocies of his Jewish background, but in the process of liberating himself from it he has largely lost the warmth and ability to care for each other that the people of the tribe possessed.

Alex pursues non-Jewish girls as status symbols out of a sense of inferiority that derives partly from his minority origins. When he becomes acquainted with families and institutions different from his own, his reaction is highly ambivalent. He accepts an invitation to visit the family of his girlfriend Kay Campbell in Iowa, and he is impressed by their politeness and cool self-confidence. But his description of them is satirical, if anything, and during the Thanksgiving celebrations he has to admit to a feeling of homesickness. In spite of himself, Alex reacts like a Jew among Gentiles. He plans to marry Kay and jestingly suggests that she must then convert to Judaism, but when she refuses he becomes furious, much to his own surprise. But in fact he reacts in a fashion shared by many of his brethren to what he perceives as the haughty dismissal of the *goy*, or non-Jew, of his Jewish heritage, although these 'inherited reflexes of a pogrom-threatened enclave are inappropriate and self-defeating'.[6] He is fully aware of this and asks himself wonderingly: 'How could I be feeling a wound in a place where I was not even vulnerable?' (260-1).

Clearly, the liberation from Jewishness is a more complex process than Alex has reckoned with. His relationship with Kay also deteriorates when he begins to find her boring and predictable. Her placid demeanour is foreign to him, as he is used to the more tempestuous relations between people that he has witnessed in his own family. The Monkey does provide him with the sort of drama in question, but his own fear of commitment ultimately proves stronger than anything any woman can offer. Moreover, when he leaves a woman behind, he cannot help feeling gratified by the hurt that he inflicts on her. Beginning with his mother, he has developed an attitude of excessive dependence on female attentions and a consequent vulnerability towards women which is bound to stir resentment against them within him. Another complicating factor is that he mixes romance with social climbing in Gatsby-fashion; in his flight from Jewishness he falls in love with the background of the Sarah Maulsbys and Kay Campbells. The Monkey's main attraction is sexual, and she has a lower-class background, but her case parallels the others in that Alex establishes an object relationship to both categories of women. When Sarah refuses to perform fellation on him, he feels doubly wounded because he thinks her refusal is an expression of anti-Semitism. But when he looks

back on their affair, he demonstrates a keen insight into the reasons why he failed to love her: 'Intolerant of her frailties. Jealous of her accomplishments. Resentful of her family'. (271) However, when she finally gives in to his sexual demands, he does not really appreciate that this is her way of expressing her love for him. He registers and portrays vividly female suffering, but he does not take it quite seriously and detaches himself from it. He tries to excuse himself by regarding his behavior as a revenge upon the Wasps for their treatment of his father, but it seems obvious that he does this for motives of his own.

Alex complains to Dr. Spielvogel about the fatal flaws of the Jewish race: 'Please, who crippled us like this? Who made us so morbid and hysterical and weak?' (40) His identification of the problem here verges on a deterministic acceptance of the very stereotypes that he otherwise passionately rejects. In other words, he comes to surrendering not only to his Jewish weakness as a phase that can be overcome but as an ineradicable historical fact. It is at the point of this recognition that Arthur Levy in Ludwig Lewisohn's *The Island Within* goes the other way and embraces his heritage, whereas Portnoy balances on the sharp edge that divides his sense of hopelessness from his determination to transcend the limits that his background threatens to impose upon him. But he also reveals the influence of his birth in the contradiction between the self-contempt that he expresses and the pride he also feels as a Jew in his culture and its accomplishments, being secretly convinced that he is mentally superior to most non-Jews.

These and other examples suggest that Alex is endowed with a set of attitudes that define him as Jewish though he is wholly sincere in his rejection of the ancestral heritage. Quoting from Roth's novel, Seymour Siegel invokes Mordecai M. Kaplan's philosophy of Judaism as a 'civilization' and states that 'one may be identifiably Jewish even though denying the basic tenets of the faith'.[7] Alex himself is very much aware of this, but sees it as a curse rather than a potential for a positive development and sense of identity.

The firmness of Alex's assimilationist stand may be a reason for the vehement reactions against the novel demonstrated by a number of Jewish-American readers of the novel. Irving Howe recognizes the basic thrust of Roth's book when he argues that it is not anti-Semitic or an expression of a 'traditional Jewish self-hatred'. Howe argues that 'What the book speaks for is a yearning to undo the fate of birth', and this may be what Alex wants. But Howe proceeds from analysis of content to direct polemic when he goes on to say that this wish is a mere fantasy that any Jew worth his salt can only 'dally with' for a moment before rejecting it.[8] Such a dogmatic assertion that ethnicity equals fate is hardly in keeping with reality and is as much an admission of defeat as a recognition of the value of Jewish identity. Ruth Wisse aptly argues that *Portnoy's Complaint* 'presents the schlemiel condition as unbearable', rejecting a traditional Jewish way of turning pain into laughter and concentrating on revealing the pain to the fullest possible extent. But Wisse still shares the view expressed by Howe that assimilation is impossible and speaks of Alex's 'rather self-loving notion that we could be better if only we tried, the tired but persistent thesis of the little engine that could'.[9] It is no wonder that Alex is tired, given the magnitude of the task, but the novel does not support the idea that the objective is impossible. For all his outpourings about guilt and feeling hampered by his background, Alex's daily life seems to have virtually no 'Jewish' content at all. During his visit to Israel he dutifully sees all the sights and immerses himself in the atmosphere of the homeland of the Jews, but he has no sense of contact or identification with the land and its people. His trip rather seems to be his final and successful test of his own seriousness as an apostate. For him, Israel turns out to be a disappointment in the most vital sense when he discovers that he is impotent with one of its women.

Portnoy's position at the end is quite clear. He intends to leave Jewishness behind, although this does not mean that he wants to replace it with any new ideology or set of beliefs. Rather, he seeks to lead a life based on certain rational insights and values that he regards as having a much broader basis than any kind of tribal grouping. One may disagree with his generally liberal and left-oriented outlook, but there is no reason to deny that an individual, whether Jewish or not, can adhere to such views, even if someone like Portnoy will probably never be able to rid himself of his irrational reactions and sentiments. But he is ready to pay the price of assimilation more in full than the earlier generation who felt so greatly rewarded in the new homeland that the loss of ethnic traditions was softened in its impact. Moreover, at that stage in history those values were more intact, taken for granted and

perhaps carried along in an unconscious or unthinking manner even as a wholly new life was taking shape for the Jews in America.

Notes

1. Tony Tanner, *City of Words: American Fiction 1950–1970* (New York, 1971), p. 315.
2. *Portnoy's Complaint* (New York, 1969), p. vii. Subsequent citations are given page references in brackets.
3. 'Fathers, Mothers, Sons and Lovers: Jewish and Gentile Patterns in Literature', *Midstream* (March, 1972), 41.
4. 'Alex in Wonderland, or Portnoy's Complaint', *Twentieth Century Literature*, 17 (1971), 162.
5. 'In Defense of Roth', *Études Anglaises*, 26 (1973), 53.
6. Ruth Wisse, *The Schlemiel as Modern Hero* (Chicago, 1971), p. 119.
7. 'Mordecai M. Kaplan in Retrospect', *Commentary*, 74 (1982), 59.
8. *Jewish-American Literature: An Anthology of Fiction, Poetry, Autobiography, and Criticism*, ed. Abraham Chapman (New York, 1974), p. 66.
9. *Op. cit.*, p. 121.

JEROME ROTHENBERG

1931–

Jerome Dennis Rothenberg was born on December 11, 1931, in New York City, to Morris and Esther (née Lichtenstein) Rothenberg. He was educated at City College of New York (B.A., 1952) and the University of Michigan (M.A., 1953). He served in the U.S. Army in Germany from 1954 to 1955. Rothenberg has taught at a variety of institutions, including City College of New York, Mannes College of Music, the University of California at San Diego, the New School for Social Research, the University of Wisconsin at Milwaukee, San Diego State University, the University of California at Riverside, and the University of Oklahoma. He founded Hawk's Well Press, which he ran from 1958 to 1965, and edited *Poems from the Floating World* from 1960 to 1964; he co-edited *Some/Thing* from 1965 to 1969. From 1970 to 1976 he co-edited *Alcheringa: A First Magazine of Ethnopoetics*; since 1976 he has edited *New Wilderness Letter*. In addition, he has been a contributing editor to *Stony Brook*, *Change International*, *Dialectical Anthropology*, and *Sulfur*. He married Diane Brodatz in 1952; they have one child.

Rothenberg was associated, along with Robert Kelly, with the "deep image" movement of the late fifties, in which the poet subjected concrete details to the haphazard workings of the unconscious mind in an attempt to engender a powerful emotional response in the reader. His first book of poetry, *White Sun Black Sun* (1960), was praised by critics both for its compelling imagery and its musical qualities. Subsequent volumes of poetry, including *Sightings* (1964), *The Gorky Poems* (1966), and *Conversations* (1968), brought Rothenberg further critical praise, if little public attention.

In 1974 Rothenberg published the revised version of *Poland/1931* (it was initially published in 1969). It is an exploration of the Jewish experience and the beginning of Rothenberg's experiments with "ancestral poetry"; some critics consider it his most accomplished work. Rothenberg became a resident at the Allegheny Seneca Indian Reservation in 1972, staying there until 1974; the experience resulted in the various editions of *Seneca Journal* (published complete as *A Seneca Journal*, with Philip Sultz, 1978). Rothenberg has also been influenced by the Dadaists, particularly in *Abulafia's Circles* (1979), *Vienna Blood and Other Poems* (1980), and *That Dada Strain* (1983).

Rothenberg is a significant translator and anthologist, particularly of Native American traditional songs and verse. His anthologies are noted for unification of theme and for their demonstration of poetic qualities in areas not usually thought of as poetic; Rothenberg is dedicated to the expansion of the field of poetry to include all that is verbally and musically compelling. Among the most praised of his anthologies are *Technicians of the Sacred: A Range of Poetries from Africa, America, Asia, and Oceania* (1967, rev. 1985); *Shaking the Pumpkin: Traditional Poetry of the Indian North Americans* (1972); and the influential *America a Prophecy: A New Reading of American Poetry from Pre-Colombian Times to the Present* (with George Quasha, 1973).

Jerome Rothenberg is the first modern poet with the temerity to offer others like himself a guidebook for the ⟨. . .⟩ exploitation ⟨of primitive letters⟩. The jacket ⟨of *Technicians of the Sacred*⟩ summarizes his intent fairly enough:

> This volume presents a striking selection of primitive poetry from all over the world juxtaposed against examples of modern poetry in an attempt to show that primitive poetry has as profound a relation to modern poetry as primitive art to modern art, and that the life of modern man may be significantly colored in years to come by the consequences of this relationship.

The profundity of his failure cannot be apprehended by anyone not intimately conversant with the literature of primitive societies.

Malinowski said that myth to the primitive was not a story told but a reality lived. That is true not only for myth but for all his literature, all his art; where the whole of life is staying alive, every moment is a crisis of truth. What to us is the intellectual luxury of arts and letters is to the primitive a means of bonding himself to the security of the past, to protective gods and ancestors, to the land. His myth, the arts that depict it, and the ritual that renews his faith in it, all make it possible for him to live in a dangerous and unstable world. Doubt means death. On isolated Bentinck Island off the north coast of Australia three years ago a colleague of mine witnessed the power of living myth. In the easy wisdom of youth a young man disobeyed a taboo and entered a sacred cave whose myth threatened that a trespasser's stomach would eat itself. The young man died after being flown to the hospital at Darwin; muscle spasms had drawn his stomach in upon itself, where digestion destroyed it.

The same year on the edge of the Australian western desert a thousand miles to the southwest another Old Stone Age native turned doubt into a syncretion of Christ and the totemic ancestor Wati Kutjara. He wondered how saltbush and pearl shells could both come from the water, and resolved the mystery when he was taken aloft and saw his plane's shadow as a cross in the center of a circular rainbow. "I am the water of life," he murmured.

Between these places about the same time I recorded a "loving song" from a descendant of the Bard people, whom Dampier three centuries ago described so contemptuously that Swift created his Yahoos upon them. Translated, the song says, "I hold you like this, my sweetheart, because I am crying." When the most miserable people on earth can weep for a depth of love few of us have felt, there are patterns enough for any resourceless poet.

But Mr. Rothenberg is not honestly seeking new patterns. He outrageously distorts already questionable translations of primitive literature to facilitate specious analogies with the obscenities and idiocies published in the far-out journals. It is, he says, a "kind of distortion that can have a value in itself," leading to "random composition" that would have shocked Tzara, and distinguished by his one new contribution, the ultimate barbarism "&/or."

But many student practitioners of what is left of poetry will be taught from this book, and unwarned, they will confuse its labored contortions with brilliance. It will viscerally attract others, for what Rothenberg has perpetrated is the literary manifestation of what the Columbia rioters were "trying to tell us" when they defecated in President Kirk's office. Our civilization is strong enough to put up with educational and poetic anarchists, despite the exhaustion of its artistic patterns. But I say to Jerome Rothenberg what My Uncle Toby said to

the blowfly: this world is big enough for thee and me, but leave, sirrah, this despoliation of the earth's destroyed peoples. The few who remain deserve better of us.—JOHN GREENWAY, "Back to the Primitive," *At*, Feb. 1969, pp. 124–25

Technicians of the Sacred is an anthology in two sections. The first, some 350 pages in length, includes primitive and archaic texts grouped by theme or by geography; the second—the "Commentaries"—tries, in the editor's words "to fill-in the scene or to indicate a little of what the original poets would have expected their hearers to know." As a counterpoint to these "commentaries," the second section furnishes a generous variety of contemporary writing—poems, happenings—by Creeley, Breton, Neruda, Kaprow, Lorca, Wakoski, Gary Snyder, Ginsberg, Apollinaire, Gertrude Stein, Dick Higgins, Emmett Williams, LaMonte Young and Jackson MacLow, among others.

What is the function of this double thrust? The wealth of available primitive and archaic materials certainly suffices for an anthology of *any* size, unaccompanied by writings of another order. The editor seeks to emphasize the bonds and orders common to both ancient or primitive materials and the products of contemporary producers, whether folk rock, random poetry, jazz poetry, concrete poetry, picture poetry, "beast-language" poetry. Perhaps the most insistent problem in compiling such a collection involves the very definition of *poem*. This is a good time to approach the Sumerians or the Sioux: the republic of poetry is increasingly inclusive; such catholicity allows a contemporary collector—especially a formal experimenter like Rothenberg himself—great latitude in the discovery of *poems* within archaic or primitive matrices. Rothenberg takes for granted the metaphysical unity of primitive thought, its wholeness evident in the coalescence of dance, song, magic, rite. And that of course is the source of editorial headaches. How do you pick out individual, self-defined units, *poems*, from within a traditionalist context which makes no such extra-ritualistic separations? Rothenberg's concise—"primitive is complex"—and useful "pre-face" meets the problem head on:

> Like any collector, my approach to delimiting and recognizing what's a poem has been by analogy: in this case (beyond the obvious definition of poems as words-of-songs) to the work of modern poets. Since much of this work has been revolutionary & limit-smashing, the analogy in turn expands the range of what "we" can see as primitive poetry. It also shows some of the ways in which primitive poetry & thought are close to an impulse toward unity in our own time, of which the poets are forerunners.

There's no news in poetry as nonlogical dream, as noncausal image sequence, as nonlinear and random verbal adventure. What *is* new is the editor's encyclopedic stress on the ties that bind "us" and "them," a stress validated by Rothenberg's discernment and experience.

Poetry is hard put to retain significance and wide cultural status. This book is a monumental attempt to reclaim these attributes. We are in more trouble than the Britain of 1800, but our problems often bear similar markings. The destructive vise of the modern city has tightened. But with Wordsworth we also are victims of "the great national events which are daily taking place, and the increasing accumulation of men in cities, where the uniformity of their occupations produces a craving for extraordinary incident, which the rapid communication of intelligence hourly gratifies." In the welter of such noisy masscom irrelevancies, this book asks, what can we meaningfully salvage and depend upon?

No other anthology of which I am aware so adequately manifests what Rothenberg calls the "post-logical" phase of modern poetry; still within the context of Coleridgean organicism and Blakean prophecy, *Technicians of the Sacred* represents a modern attempt to nourish the sundered spirit. Throughout this book, overtly and inferentially, the editor insists upon what Cassirer found in the "primitive" ethos— "the consanguinity of all living things." And how does man reach out to this experience of a common being? Rothenberg answers:

> No people today is newly born. No people has sat in sloth for the thousands of years of its history. Measure everything by the Titan rocket & the transistor radio, & the world is full of primitive peoples. But once change the unit of value to the poem or the dance-event or the dream (all clearly artifactual situations) & it becomes apparent what all those people have been doing all those years with all that time on their hands.

The primitive and archaic materials in *Technicians of the Sacred* are comprehensive, involving vision, song, spell, exorcism, origin myth, naming sequence, mourning song, event, dream, animal tale—taken from such divergent cultures and areas as Australian Arnhelm Land, Tibet, Aztec, Sumeria, Andaman Islands, Fox, Egypt, Gabon Pygmy, India, African Bushman. And how about *that* time-trip as a counter to the coming Moon-voyage?

What makes so many of the anthologized entries available to the reader is the frequent high level of translation or adaptation. Done by poets or particularly sensitive ethnological writers, these versions commonly manifest a *poetic* relevance lacking in much of the primitive or archaic materials so far in general currency. The following magnificent adaptation, "To the God of Fire as a Horse," from the Indian Rig-Veda (ca. 1500 B.C.) will stand as instance; the adapter is Robert Kelly:

> Your eyes do not make mistakes.
> Your eyes have the sun's seeing.
> Your thought marches terribly in the night
> blazing with light & the fire
> breaks from your throat as you whinny in battle.
>
> This fire was born in a pleasant forest
> This fire lives in ecstasy somewhere in the night.
>
> His march is a dagger of fire
> His body is enormous
> His mouth opens & closes as he champs on the world
> He swings the axe-edge of his tongue
>   smelting & refining the raw wood he chops down.
>
> He gets ready to shoot & fits arrow to bowstring
> He hones his light to a fine edge on the steel
> He travels through night with rapid & various movements
> His thighs are rich with movement.
>   He is a bird that settles on a tree.

This collection of man's oldest and newest poem makings, enriched further by the mass and breadth of allusion, comment and interpretation in the "Commentaries" section, constitutes one of the significant aesthetic documents of the postwar period. Out of its almost infinite variety rises a deeply felt metaphysical monism whose ultimate claim to relevance involves the self-transcendent sense that "we" are "they." —ARMAND SCHWERNER, "The Poetry of Earth," *Nation*, July 28, 1969, pp. 86–87

Jerome Rothenberg, who has previously offered us anthologies of world poetry in his *Technicians of the Sacred* and of

American Indian poems in *Shaking the Pumpkin*, has dug among the ruins of our own century and discovered some fascinating artifacts of American avant-garde poetry that he offers as "A New Gathering," appropriately entitled *Revolution of the Word*. And a revolution it was, as even a cursory turning of pages makes evident: here are words gone mad, made into signboards and collages, turned sideways and upside down, "transformed utterly," in Yeats' words, until "a terrible beauty is born."

Significantly, the terms used to describe these revolutionary movements are better known in the world of painting than of poetry: futurism, surrealism, objectivism and, most familiar of all, expressionism. R. P. Blackmur in his *Anni Mirabiles 1921–1925* claimed that expressionistic art proposed "to undermine, to readjust, to put into fresh order the frames or forms in which me make the adventure of conduct tangible to our minds." Poetry, in other words, is both subversive and integrating. With the other arts, it is an adventure beyond the destructive and into the untried. One notes that the dates that round out Rothenberg's anthology include the two World Wars.

Here are familiar names: H.D., Carl Sandburg, T. S. Eliot, Ezra Pound, e.e. cummings, William Carlos Williams, Hart Crane, Marianne Moore, Gertrude Stein and Wallace Stevens. Rothenberg makes them look new and surprising again, with the shock readers must have felt when they picked up the *Dial, transition,* or the *Little Review*. Facsimile pages of Pound's *Vortex*, Duchamp's "The bride stripped bare by her bachelors, even" and the original format in which poems first appeared help create this impression of fresh discovery.

The main advantage of the anthology, however, comes with the reminder of less familiar names: Harry Crosby, Jackson MacLow, Walter Lowenfels, Marsden Hartley. Robert Duncan and Laura Riding (an American, after all) and the elder statesmen of the beatniks and hip poets, Kenneth Rexroth and Kenneth Patchem, stand in sharper focus than before. The whole poetic uprising announced by Allen Ginsberg's *Howl* appears as the continuation of a long-developing revolt. For, ironically, the avant-garde movement became the poetry of the status quo. Even the poet Donald Hall—no rebel he—could complain in 1962: "For thirty years an orthodoxy ruled American poetry. It derived from the authority of T. S. Eliot and the new critics; it exerted itself through the literary quarterlies and the universities." The poet of *The Waste Land*, the most revolutionary of poems, became the archetype of the literary establishment. How short our critical memories can be! Rothenberg does us all a favor by setting the record straight.—JAMES FINN COTTER, *Am*, June 21, 1975, pp. 486–88

There are few ventures better designed to restock a faltering imagination and rearrange the mind's furniture than a new intellectual field that crosses disciplinary boundaries. I am therefore grateful to poet Jerome Rothenberg for having invented this one by coining the term "ethnopoetics" (the poetics of "the others") in the late 1960s. We are dealing here (in *Symposium of the Whole*), then, with the cave of dreams, the brewing places of language (and thus self-consciousness), which shaped the cultural forms of "foreigners" such as Australian aborigines, Eskimo, Hopi Indians, the Zulu, and the Balinese among so many others—and what contemporary ethnologists and poets would make of them against the backdrop of the West's drift toward a monoculture. A monoculture which can only mean a terrible impoverishment of human horizons.

Anthologies do not usually qualify for inclusion in _Commonweal's_ book space, but gratitude for this one compels exception. The Rothenbergs have put together a selection of studies, essays, proposals, and polemics—Vico, Herder, and Blake juxtaposed with Marx, Rimbaud, Lévi-Strauss, and Charles Olson, Léopold Senghor, Mircea Eliade together with Antonin Artaud and Benjamin Lee Whorf among others—that ought to signal chaos; instead the friction generates intellectual sparks, a current of electricity. In many ways, this anthology is a sign of the resurgence of what could be Romanticism-come-of-age. Among other services, such a Romanticism would insist, as do many of the contributors here, that preserving the vast pool of the world's cultural diversity is no less imperative for us than saving endangered biological species. In neither case do we as yet know what use such prolific riches will have; what we do know well enough is that our current short-term pragmatism has the idiot cunning of Cyclops.

But ethnopoetics is not just proposing fun for romanticists or antiquarians. Its focus is really on the genre of performance—and that means ritual—and what that can reveal or make visible about what is actually going on beneath and behind our social and political dramas. As Victor Turner puts it,

> The mere fact that Westerners are now becoming aware of the potency of other traditions of thought and expressive culture is itself an act of "making visible" and at the same time an entering into reflexive relations with peoples, genders, classes; ethnicities, the sick, the marginal and the troubled, all of whom from beyond the pale or beneath our bureaucratic rationality insist that we are them. Their presence and their cultural product are "meta-commentaries" on our own lifeways—in which we are becoming increasingly disappointed as their lack of grace or blessing becomes more obvious.

How does one gain reflective distance from one's own culture, be in it but not of it? Well, one answer is through the perspective that comes through dwelling on the poetic forms, the myths, and rites of other cultures. In the current scene, moreover, such a cross-cultural perspective would seem essential to the kind of post-modern contemplative attitude we must have.

But there is more. Carnival, festival, sport, and theater represent the foci of a new generation of anthropologists who have thereby shifted attention from concepts such as structures, equilibrium, system, and regularity to concepts like process, indeterminacy, reflexivity, resilience, and the ritual performance that lets primal cultures know what their subconscious is up to. As I have said, the special focus here lies on performance and the kind of reflective awareness performance gives access to, one involving not just the head but the whole bodily and cultural organism. This new focus has brought ethnologists into fruitful alliance with poets, dramatic artists, and (potentially) liturgists—with all those, in fact, who recognize that ancient wisdom has much to tell us about the creation of sacred space and restoring the magic of the word. What is decidedly new in this conjunction is not just that poets are beginning to recover the ritual role of bards reciting an epic before the tribal or castle hearth, but that some academic anthropologists are dropping their scientific hiding places and getting into the act. It is not unusual these days to have an anthropologist conduct you on a shamanic "vision hunt." In short, to use Rothenberg's term, some of these heady experts are becoming "technicians of the sacred." They are not just

reminding us nostalgically of the sacred space and time our culture has supposedly lost, but devising ways of reanimating the wasteland.

Our culture, writes Victor Turner in an overview of ethnopoetics in these pages, stands at one of those betwixt and between times, the old frames collapsing, the new constellations nascent and taking shape in aesthetic fantasy rather than by the rule of law and ethics. The whole world, he says, can be viewed "as one vast initiatory seclusion camp." From this perspective, the East-West struggle looks like a battle between two cultural dinosaurs, each in its way blind to the birth-pangs of a new culture—whose mood is understandably subjunctive, full of "as ifs." At such a moment, poets—be they wordsmiths or scientists hypothesizing—resume their role as the "unacknowledged legislators of the race." Specifically, Turner would charge poet-performers with the task of picking up the pieces of that worldwide process through which the sacred body of tribal solidarity breaks into the competitive individual and myriad secular bodies. In the mode of ritual specialists, the possibility remains that they may reopen the secrets of another kind of membership, "in a 'risen body' of humankindness redeemed through 'mutual forgiveness of each vice' (Blake), forgiveness made possible through radical, existential reflexivity."

What, then, is this new confederacy of anthropologists and poets up to? Poet Robert Duncan calls it "a symposium of the whole." "In such a new 'totality,' all the old excluded orders must be included. The female, the proletariat, the foreign; the animal and the vegetative; the unconscious and the unknown; the criminal and the failure—all that has been outcast and vagabond must return to be admitted in the creation of what we consider we are."—DAVID TOOLAN, "Confederacy of Poets and Anthropologists," _Com_, Nov. 4, 1983, pp. 605–6

DIANE WAKOSKI
From "20th Century Music"

Parnassus: Poetry in Review, Fall–Winter 1972, pp. 143–47

Rothenberg is one of my favorite living poets. The work which recommends him to me, at this point in his career, is found in four sets of poems: _The Poland Poems; The Gorky Poems, The Seven Hells of Jigoku Zoshi,_ and _White Sun Black Sun._ By far the most interesting are the Poland poems, but Rothenberg's selected poems, _Poems for the Game of Silence,_ gives us a sample of not only his variety but also much of his best work, and I would recommend that every reader new to Rothenberg's work start with this book.

What makes me love Rothenberg's poetry? First, Rothenberg writes, as does Ginsberg, Lorca, or Whitman, to express a particular culture. Second, I like Rothenberg's subject matter and his narrative use of imagery (the imagery tells the story, often), and, third, the way his poems exist as sound objects. The expanded realization of "music" in poetry is the twentieth century's unique contribution to the history of poetry. That may sound naive to those who think of poets as bards, historically, and want to call poems songs and who think of poetry's music as the way one counts feet or beats in a line, or listens to phrasing. Reading Charles Olson's essays about breath, rhapsodizing about Auden's witty scansion, or if beaten at that, working on counting syllables, putting poetry with jazz groups—count, count, count. Counting has more to do with banking than with the music of poetry. Poetry is not a kind of music, and while it can be put into musical forms—

songs or operas—the music of twentieth century poetry, in its simplest terms, is what makes one want to hear a voice reading a poem out loud rather than wanting to look at or study it written on a page.

I almost never judge poetry by living poets any more unless I can hear it read aloud. Some fine poetry cannot successfully be read aloud; but frankly that poetry does not interest me. The poetry that comes to life when someone reads it out loud is the poetry that has come alive because of its music. Some poetry is hard to perform, like Paul Blackburn's or my own. Which doesn't mean that it's not written for performance.

Music in twentieth century poetry often takes the forms of long lines, dense concentrations of rhetorical patterns, lists of images, inserted dialogue, heavy concentration on narrative techniques, and an appearance on the page of prosiness. *The very opposite*, in fact, of what is traditionally referred to as the musical element of poetry. It is the difference between the dense sound of hard-rock music and the sparse sounds of 16th-century English court music. The man who says Ginsberg's *Howl* and *Kaddish* are sloppily written poems is simply listening for the music of another century. A confused man. Rothenberg's poetry is never as beautiful as when someone is reading aloud. At its best, this poetry maintains a thin narrative line, usually about a speaker who is observing the world of a particular culture, identifying with it, describing it. In "The Connoisseur of Jews," he says:

> she has their desire to be always in love
> always respectable
> as if prosperity were the name of a town
> or a house in the town
> & had no windows

And (In "The Wedding"):

> my mind is stuffed with tablecloths
> & with rings but my mind
> is dreaming of poland stuffed with poland
> brought in the imagination
> to a black wedding
> a naked bridegroom hovering above
> his naked bride mad poland
> how terrible thy jews at weddings
> thy synagogues with comphor smells & almonds

From "Soap II":

> The sugar at the bottom of his cup was brown and
>   hard
> Twice a month he had the hairs clipped from his
>   nose
> & thanked his barber
> (He had sold him shaving soap the day before)
> Selling soap to the pious
> Calling it *zeyf*
> Saying: *ah shtick zeyf*
> or saying: *ah shtickeleh zeyf* (dim.)
> Theirs was a business between friends
> & meant lying.
> But the tips of his fingers smelt good to him
> Women admired it.

Rothenberg's narratives most often create a landscape rather than tell a story. In *The Seven Hells of Jigoku Zoshi*, which contains some of his most beautiful imagery, he depicts traditional Japanese mythical punishments to the dead for sins committed in life to create Judeo-Christian incantation about right and wrong. Punishments and tortures are Dantean, but out of the pain, dirt, torture, and subjugation comes a particular pathos. It is the very spirit that Ginsberg finds in his

mother Naomi's ugly and pathetic attempts at sexuality as she ages and gets madder and madder and which Ginsberg, as the grieving son in *Kaddish*, flagellates himself with, finding almost sensual pleasure in relating the humanly ugly and still finding spiritual beauty. Both Ginsberg and Rothenberg use images, lists, and lists of images, to lift us out of the abasement of the narrative into the beauty of physical metaphor. For instance, in "The Wedding":

> how thy bells wrapped in their flowers toll
> how they do offer up their tongues to kiss the moon
> old moon old mother stuck in thy sky thyself
> an old bell with no tongue a lost udder
> o poland thy beer is ever made of rotting bread
> thy silks are linens merely thy tradesmen
> dance at weddings . . .
> o poland o sweet restless poland
> o poland of the saints unbuttoned poland repeating
> endlessly the triple names of mary

It is not a coincidence that Rothenberg has spent a major part of his career as a poet following a passion for the poetry of primitive cultures, all of which reflects cultural concerns and much of which reflects these concerns in religious form or formulae. The religious chant is never far from Rothenberg's voice. When he finds and reports anything, he has the odd gift (which would make him a terrible historian or anthropologist) of always sounding Jewish—whether his subject is the Senecas and their songs or Japanese mythology or his attempts at experimental poetry (e.g. *Sightings*). His poems are always Jewish. Beautifully, fully, deeply, poetically Jewish. *Poland, 1931* (the year Rothenberg was born in Brooklyn of Polish, Jewish parents) is a very long work in progress; it is the basic Rothenberg to me and my favorite of his works—the source book for all of his poetic energy. In "Portrait of a Jew Old Country Style," he says, "I deny autobiography," and yet what he is taking is the structure of his history as Jerome Rothenberg, Brooklyn, 1931, and writing a poetic history of Jews. In "The Connoisseur of Jews," he says:

> if there were locomotives to ride home on
> & no jews
> there would still be jews & locomotives
> just as there are jews & oranges
> & jews & Jars
> there would still be someone to write the jewish
>   poem
> others to write their mothers' names in lights—
> just as others, born angry,
> have the moon's face burnt onto their arms
> & dont complain

Poets in primitive societies had to summon a whole mythological culture to create an identity; so must Rothenberg. In "Esther K Comes to America 1931," Esther is his mother, his mother country, his wandering customs, his mystical origins, his exotic geography, and his self as a poet. In "Student's Testimony" Rothenberg returns to his favorite subject, or I should say, metaphor—demons. There is a pagan delight in his invocation of the ugly, the taboo, the sinful, the forbidden activities of his demon. This sensuality, which reminds me of an infant playing with shit and liking the texture, untroubled by the stink and the education that says shit is poisonous waste but liking the strong odor and the soft substance to squeeze in his hands, is something Rothenberg learned first from primitive poetries. Later it re-echoed in the poverty and persecution that invests so much of Jewish history with imagery and actuality that sanitary, hygenic-minded Americans find repugnant. But the forbidden is desireable. Thus, our romance with Dirt. Or poverty.

Read aloud, Rothenberg's poems make me feel I am in the presence of a deep rich imagination, and perhaps some real demon from the past. The sparse personal narrative keeps my mind on the poem. The sensuous use of language, as in "fish & Paradise," surprises me, makes me happy:

> Could there be ice. Could ice matter. Or be the
>   matter. Or be dead.
> I fish the moon
> & grow reluctant about corpses.

When I read Rothenberg, I become a Jew, a dreamer, an ancient demon, whatever he wants me to become—unquestioningly.

There are few poets I don't question. Rothenberg is one of them.

HELEN VENDLER

New York Times Book Review, December 30, 1973, pp. 7–8

If only the editors of ⟨*America a Prophesy: A New Reading of American Poetry from Pre-Columbian Times to the Present*⟩ wouldn't take themselves with such grisly seriousness, there would be no problem in reading or reviewing this collection at all: we could all forage in its fields, amusing ourselves with its good and bad poems alike. But the solemn editors insist on framing their collection with pretentious introductions and ponderous vocabulary, so as to take all the fun out of the reading.

Briefly put, you can be included in this anthology if you dig history, geography, anthropology or myth, mention the Mayans, invoke Tantric symbols, produce totems, write rites, propose riddles, imitate howls, commit a pictograph, recount dreams, follow almost any tradition of meditation, be a Shaker or a Mormon, preach the primitive or transcribe whale songs and you will be at home in these pages. Myth makes strange bedfellows, as a sample extract from the Table of Contents will show:

> WALT WHITMAN: Words (This is not a poem; it is
>   an excerpt, printed as a poem, from *An Amer-
>   ican Primer*)
> [PAPAGO]: From "Naming Events"
> GREGORY CORSO: Food
> [FLORENTINE CODEX]: Aztec Definitions
> COTTON MATHER: Stones (This isn't a poem
>   either, but an excerpt from some unnamed
>   piece of natural history)
> GERTRUDE STEIN: Chicken
> DANIEL SPOERRI/EMMETT WILLIAMS: Nail
> [ANONYMOUS]: Schizophrenic Definitions
> HARRY CROSBY: Short Introduction to the Word
> MARCEL DUCHAMP: *From* Notes and Projects for
>   the Large Glass
> GARY SNYDER: Wave
> BENJAMIN LEE WHORF: Movements from the
>   Punctual and Segmentative Aspects of Some
>   Hopi Verbs
> GEORGE BRECHT: Excerpts from Gloss for an
>   Unknown Language

Never mind, dear reader, that you never thought Marcel Duchamp belonged in an anthology of American Poetry, or that anonymous schizophrenics did either, or that Whorf would recognize himself so dignified. Once you get over your initial disbelief, it is lively enough reading, for a time. But lively for whom? Maybe for a jaded second-time-round reader: after you've done the grand tour, after you've seen the Forum and Chartres and the Alhambra and the Tower of London, why then you go on a series of successive more and more esoteric and yet homely tours. Perhaps, the first time, you go to Delphi and Stonehenge and Easter Island; the next time, you do the Mayan ruins and Angkor Wat; finally you get to village sites and maybe the arrowheads in your back yard, with a visit to a madhouse or a prison thrown in, as the 18th-century used to visit Bedlam and debtor's prison.

By this time you are affecting, or maybe even feeling, an entire weariness with those demanding monuments like cathedrals and palaces, with their eternal visionary dimensions. An unreconstructed pragmatism and playfulness arise; you want to see how people live and what they do. Even our most visionary poets have these moments—Wordsworth with the Leech-Gatherer, Rilke with the Acrobats. Fatigued with the view from Sinai, Pisgah or Olympus, the mind turns from the Apollonian to the Dionysian.

All this is nothing new at all (contrary to the editors' pretensions). A revolt against high culture is a stage in the life of many authors, and it is equally a stage in the life of many readers. Back to primitive roots we go—to runes, inscriptions, charms, riddles, spells, catalogues, invocations, rituals; to baby-talk, to nonsense rhymes, to madness, to syllable-chants; to myths and folk-tales and folk-songs; to the origins of language, to chronicles, inscriptions, ancestors and, we hope, the pristine unfallen vision of man, merely man, merely himself, before the corruptions of high culture.

From Rousseau to Pound, the history of Romantic primitivism shows a sturdy persistence, embracing everything from the "Lyrical Ballads" through Ruskin's fantastic etymologies, through Arnold's romanticizing of the wild Celts, through the worship of Homer, through Eliot's "shantih," through Fenollosa's orientalism and Pound's Anglo-Saxon and Provençal translations, through Cubist interest in primitive art, through the current fashionable patronizing of American Indian culture. For us all, there is probably no escaping that nostalgic glance to the fantasized primeval culture which, however, as Paul De Man remarks in respect to Rousseau, is itself only "a fictionally diachronic narrative or, if one prefers to call it so, an allegory," imposed on language to account for man's perpetual and irremediable distance from his world. In Whitman's words:

> There was never any more inception than there is
>   now,
> Nor any more youth or age than there is now,
> And will never be any more perfection than there is
>   now,
> Nor any more heaven or hell than there is now.

The romantic primitivism which seeks for a hidden knowledge, whether in the East or in the past or in the child, is thus doomed, entirely, to find itself mirrored, by its own principle of selection, in everything it chooses from the illimitable storehouse of history. Nothing is more "modern," alas, than to prize the primitive. That modern prizing, so clearly at work in this anthology, is a direct result of long acquaintance with the most sophisticated expressions of high culture: from Maeterlinck, Yeats goes to desert Arabs; from Keats, Williams goes to newspaper files in Paterson; from Blake, Ginsberg goes to Ray Charles. Fair enough. But this anthology is, at least in its paperback form, aimed at college students (one of its three epigraphs comes from Carlos Castaneda's Don

Juan, who recurs elsewhere in editorial matter) and gives them the cart without the horse.

American children no longer read any poetry to speak of in the schools: with Chaucer, Shakespeare, Milton, Wordsworth, Keats and Whitman not yet given to them, are they to read Pawnee Bear Songs and Dadaist experiments, aleatory "art" and Hoodoo chants? The smart "modernism" of this anthology (for all its obeisance to poetic "origins") leads to the total exclusion of Eliot, Auden, Frost, Aiken, Ransom, Lowell and Jarrell (the editors' own list). About these poets the editors had "little new to say in the present context," or, alternatively put, these authors "had been of slight importance in developing the structural side of the tradition of changes" (the anthology ends with a selection from the I Ching).

Of the "traditional" authors included there isn't much, and the principle of selection has been in no case to give the author's best or most representative work but rather any stray work with a myth or a dream or a vision in it. The "hidden aspects" of American poetry are clarified here, not by the best work of our best poets, but by poems of H.D., Zukofsky, Rexroth, Oppen, Fearing, Patchen, Olson, Duncan, etc., as well as by Harry Crosby, Eugene Jolas, Else von Freytag-Loringhoven, Marsden Hartley, Sherwood Anderson, Haniel Long and Lorine Neidecker, supplemented by poets who were "born elsewhere but did much of their mature work in America": Mina Loy, Max Ernst, Marcel Duchamp, Arturo Giovanitti, Sadakichi Hartmann, Anselm Hollo and Chögyam Trangpa (these lists too are the editors' own).

This is, then, a counter-anthology to the "received" anthologies, but it's not a convincing one. A perverse enjoyment attends its use; my favorite disinterment is Else von Freytag-Loringhoven (we have five poems of hers to one of Marianne Moore). Who would not find this poem a clue to the "hidden aspects" of American poetry, a key to its "prophecy," its "inner truth," its "rich history"?

> Ha—mine soul—I say "alas" and I say "alas" and "alas" and "alas"! because I am thine BODY! and this is mine flaming desire to-day: that he shall step into THEE through ME as it was in olden times and that we will play again that old WONDERFUL play of the "TWOTOGETHER"!—mine soul—if thus it will be—willst thou flare around him—about him—over him—hide him with shining curtain—hiss that song of savage joy—starry-eyes—willst thou heat—melt— make quiver—break down—dissolve—build up— SHAKE HIM—SHAKE HIM—SHAKE HIM—O mine starry-eyed soul? Heia! ja-hoho! hisses mine starry-eyed soul in her own language.

(Sylvia Plath is missing in this book, hissing Else standing for "the poetry of madness.")

The appeal of a relatively unselective history of literature is enormous to anyone with a taste for the freakish eddies of human culture; we all have dipped into gory 17th-century Moravian religious poems or awful American melodramas or elephantine epics, and the only reason, really, not to devote ourselves more to the frivolous pleasures of the bad is to have more time for the sublime pleasures of the great. It comes down to what we want ourselves and our students to experience—603 pages of what is, it must be admitted, part of the literary history of America, since most of what is here included was at least written down on the American continent—or 603 pages of American high art, such as it has been thought to be, from Anne Bradstreet (not in this company) to the major poets here excluded or very skimpily represented.

It could be argued that both are possible, but it is more likely in youth that one psychologically excludes the other, by Gresham's law. At least these editors were not able, or did not care, to put together an anthology which would be indeed a new total reading of American poetry (with Blake as its guru), perhaps emphasizing populist roots and branches more than other anthologies have done, but integrating such populism and primitivism with the work of our greatest poets.

The Random House blurb says that "European elements are only one strand of American civilization," and that is of course true: but to dismiss, as "European" in inspiration, our most accomplished poets is a new Philistinism. The impulse to know and to allude to past poetry (nowhere more evident than in primitive literature, incidentally, and so natural a habit in Eliot, Frost, Auden and Lowell, among others here excluded) is not "European," it is human. "Vision," "meditation," "the immediate energies of authentic speech" (qualities praised by the editors) all value the moment of particular, individual and perhaps irrational perception over sustained lyric writing with its intellectual burdens, its weight of abstract synthesizing consciousness and its wish to include, if only as penumbra, the rest of the world which the individual insight, in its first flash may forget.

Besides aboriginal and populist poetry, the editors add what they are pleased to call "metapoetry," including first, "diaries, letters, notebooks, novels, and scientific writing; second, nonverbal, visual, and ritual media, from Aztec murals, Mayan and Hopi glyphs, and Shaker 'emblem poems' to contemporary 'concrete poetry' and 'intermedia'; and third . . . free verse, imagism, dada, cubism, surrealism, objectivism, projective verse, change composition, etc." "But will they come when you do summon them?" we might say to the editors as they call up their isms. Or are we being too critical? Is not "the mythic plane of meaning" all we could desire? Are we not all solaced by whale songs?

"*Hypothesis:* the apparent resemblance between whales' songs and certain man-made structures (oral-tribal poetry; serial, electronic, and jazz music; etc.) may be a key to an interspecies poetics and psychic process." Do we not all need to be told by Don Juan how to see like a crow? Is it not our duty to wonder whether the Oraibi circles "could have been a sort of mapping of the internal sense of space-time" in a "way related both visually and functionally to Wilhelm Reich's sexual energy graphs?" If we meditate on a possible early visit by Irish monks to the Algonquins, can we not, reading of the Algonquin hanging of a dog on a cross-like structure, think, as the editors put it of "Christ as Coyote"?

Meanwhile, the hungry sheep look up and are not fed; the worthy bidden mouths of our greatest poets appear not at the feast; and lean and flashy songs are set, with no discrimination, cheek-by-jowl with poems by decent poets who have somehow slipped in under the editors' criteria. What becomes most clear, in the sponsoring of anthologies like this by reputable publishing houses, is that the hunger of the young for the greatest possible art is being terribly underestimated in the schools. What students hear in Ginsberg they would hear and appreciate in Blake, as Ginsberg himself has been the first to show them; what they discover in Hesse they would embrace in Rilke, if only they were taught him; what they sense in Dylan or Cohen is, if they only knew, waiting for them, to a degree that would satisfy them far more, in Keats. Their own concern for universal religious consciousness appears in Eliot, their yearning for brotherhood in Whitman, their interest in the land in Frost, their wish for wisdom literature in Dickinson.

Since esthetic response is at least in part culture-bound,

anthropology, though it can unearth primitive poetries, cannot ever make them so wholly ours as is poetry written in our own language and springing from our own culture, whether that of the folk or that of the educated. To know the world is no substitute, as Thoreau knew, for knowing one's own back yard. Perhaps we should have two concurrent courses in our schools—one with Samoan myths, Hopi chants, Eskimo drawings, Indian mantras and anything else the world-poetry advocates care to include; but let us keep, too, the intimacy, familiarity and love that our children can have only with the poetry, and the greatest poetry, of their mother-tongue. American poetry already forms a grand portion of poetry in English; it deserves better than this distortion of its history, a distortion its dead poets are helpless to protest.

MURIEL RUKEYSER

1913–1980

Muriel Rukeyser was born on December 15, 1913, in New York City, to Lawrence and Myra Lyons Rukeyser. She was educated at Ethical Culture School and Fieldston School from 1921 to 1930. From 1930 to 1932 she attended Vassar College, where she was on the staff of the *Student Review*. She also attended Columbia University summer school during 1931 and 1932, studying anthropology, psychology, and the short story. From 1933 to 1934 she attended the Roosevelt School of Aviation in New York City. She married painter Glynn Collins in 1945; the marriage was later annulled. She had a son in 1947. Rukeyser taught at Sarah Lawrence College in 1946, and again from 1956 to 1957. She was a Vice-President at the House of Photography in New York from 1946 to 1960, and President of the PEN American Center in 1975 and 1976.

Rukeyser was known both for her longevity (her career spans five decades) and for her outspoken political activism, which was frequently present in her poetry. She gained political awareness at an early age: she was arrested at the Scottsboro trials in 1933 (where she also contracted typhoid fever) and was present when civil war broke out in Spain in 1936. In more recent years she received attention for her trip to Hanoi in 1972 (with Denise Levertov and Jane Hart) and for her trip to South Korea on behalf of poet and political prisoner Kim Chi-Ha.

Her first book of poetry was *Theory of Flight*, published in 1935; she was also an Associate Editor at *New Theatre* magazine that year. She began to gain considerable attention with her next several books of poetry; *U.S. 1* (1938) was well received, and *A Turning Wind* (1939) won the Oscar Blumenthal Prize. Her next book, *The Soul and Body of John Brown* (1940), was the first recipient of the Harriet Monroe Poetry Award. Over the next several years she developed a distinct voice with such volumes as *Wake Island* (1942), *Beast in View* (1944), *The Green Wave* (1948), *Elegies* (1949), and *Orpheus* (1949). After her *Selected Poems* was published in 1951 it was seven years until the publication of her next book of poetry, *Body of Waking* (1958), during which time she was working on biographies, teaching, and writing an unpublished novel (with Helen Parkhurst).

Rukeyser resumed publishing poetry in earnest in the sixties, despite a stroke in 1964. *Waterlily Fire: Poems 1935–1962* (1962) won the Eunice Tietjens Memorial Prize. Further books include *The Outer Banks* (1967), *The Speed of Darkness* (1968), *29 Poems* (1970), *Breaking Open* (1973), and *The Gates* (1976). Throughout this period Rukeyser was admired for writing political poetry that was nonetheless personal and moving. She never reached a wide audience, but her admirers were enthusiastic, and her influence on modern poetry has been considerable. *The Collected Poems of Muriel Rukeyser* was issued in 1979.

During her career Rukeyser also published fiction (*The Orgy*, 1965), a play (*The Color of the Day*, 1961), translations of works by Octavio Paz and Gunnar Ekelöf, three books for children, biographies of Wendell Willkie and Willard Gibbs, and other nonfiction. She suffered her second stroke in 1977 and died on February 12, 1980.

This book ⟨*U.S. 1*⟩ is all to the good, three longish, subdivided poems and a group of lyrics relating almost without exception to the social revolution. There are moments in the book that are pretty dull, but that's bound to be the character of all good things if they are serious enough: when a devoted and determined person sets out to do a thing he isn't thinking first of being brilliant, he wants to get there even if he has to crawl— on his face. When he is able to—whenever he is able to—he gets up and runs.

Muriel Rukeyser doesn't know everything about writing— Lorca, Pound, Eluard—but she does show that she has a respect for some of the battles won for it in the recent past. So much so that her book is strong enough to stand up to critical attack.

In her first poem, "The Book of the Dead," her material, *not* her subject matter but her poetic material, is in part the notes of a congressional investigation, an x-ray report and the testimony of a physician under cross-examination. These she uses with something of the skill employed by Pound in the material of his *Cantos*. She knows how to use the *language* of an x-ray report or a stenographic record of a cross-examination. She knows, in other words, how to select and exhibit her material. She understands what words are for and how important it is not to twist them in order to make "poetry" of them.

This poem relates to big business and its "innocent" effects on the men it employs. If drills in silicate ore can work twice as fast dry as wet but, if dry, the dust they raise ultimately kills the men from a disease known as silicosis—then it still remains good business (if you can get away with it by bribery and other felonies of the sort) not to wet the drills. Inspired by her moral indignation Miss Rukeyser seizes upon the documentary facts of the cases in such a way as to make her points overwhelmingly convincing, so much so that a very real beauty results.

Miss Rukeyser's work is still very uneven. In some of her descriptions of natural loveliness in this poem and later she appears to forget that the beauty of a poem is not in what the poet sees but in what he makes of it. Plain statement is not quite enough in that case; nothing results but a piling up of words.

To me the best writing of the book aside from the use of the documentary evidence referred to above, is in the shorter poems of the second section. Here, because of the compactness, perhaps, the artist has been forced to select her words more carefully. The effect is satisfying. The third section, of the ship without a port, is an allegory too hastily written for my taste. The poet, possibly Hart Crane, is better handled than most of the other characters, but the effect of the whole is enlightening. I prefer the newspapers for that sort of thing. They at least have the correct date at the top. Nothing comes up clear to me; it seems insufficiently studied. The same for the fourth section, the removal of the group of foreign athletes from Barcelona for France at the outbreak of the fascist rebellion. Harder, sharper pictures are required. We see the man left behind on the dock, we get a glimpse of the Russian sailors, but we do not get them sharply enough to make their significance vocal; they are lost in a tangle of intervening words.

I hope Miss Rukeyser does not lose herself in her injudicious haste for a "cause," accepting, uncritically, what she does as satisfactory, her intentions being of the best. I hope she will stick it out the hardest way, a tough road, and invent! make the form that will embody her rare gifts of intelligence and passion for a social rebirth the chief object of her labors. Her passion will not be sacrificed, on the contrary it will be emphasized, by the success of such attention to technical detail. So will the revolution.—WILLIAM CARLOS WILLIAMS, "Muriel Rukeyser's *U.S. 1*" (1938), *Something to Say*, ed. James E. B. Breslin, 1985, pp. 89–91

These are the opening stanzas of an early poem by Miss Rukeyser:

> The drowning young man lifted his face from the
>   river
> to me, exhausted from calling for help and weeping;
> "My love!" I said; but he kissed me once for ever
> and returned to his privacy and secret keeping.
>
> His close face dripped with the attractive water,
> I stared in his eyes and saw there penalty,
> for the city moved in its struggle, loud about us,
> and the salt air blew down; but he would face the sea.

And one of her recent poems begins:

> Great Alexander sailing was from his true course
>   turned
> By a young wind from a cloud in Asia moving
> Like a most recognizable most silvery woman;
> Tall Alexander to the island came.
> The small breeze blew behind his turning head.
> He walked the foam of ripples into this scene.

Force, directness, affection for the separate word, tension, knowledge of cadence and syntax as components of meaning rather than vicissitudes of fabrication—there can be no doubt that Miss Rukeyser can write good poetry. But another side of her writing seems to me less effective, a mannerism enlarging as the years have gone by. I mean her way of doing without verbs:

> Eyes on the road at night, sides of a road like rhyme;
> the floor of the illumined shadow sea
> and shallows with their assembling flash and show
> of sight, root, holdfast, eyes of the brittle stars.
> And your eyes in the shadowy red room,
> scent of the forest entering, various time
> calling and the light of wood along the ceiling
> and over us birds calling and their circuit eyes.
> And in our bodies the eyes of the dead and the living
> giving us gifts at hand, the glitter of all their eyes.

One can see how this might happen; the search for immediacy, the hunger for experienced language that impelled the Imagists. But Miss Rukeyser's characteristic poem is busy, rather long, full of intellectual machinery, and I miss the motion-making words that would give it quickness. Instead the effect is like that of an impasto, colors heaped upon one another until the surface is thick and lightless.

There you have my like and dislike; and although I have known Miss Rukeyser's poems for a long time, I shall need to know them much longer still before I can decide whether or not they are, taken as a whole, really good. Possibly I will never decide. Must one stuff every book one reads into a category?

Anyway a reviewer ought not to presume to judge the poetic quality of a lifework in three pages. Something else about Miss Rukeyser is more suitable to my commentary; I mean her vigorous, brave, and I think nearly absolute honesty; this being—honesty—the nearest permissible approximation to an absolute of faith. Let us agree on what seems quite obvious to me: that a large part of lyric poetry is essentially prayer. Where does this leave the poet who cannot acknowledge a supernatural presence? You may go backward and forward in the anthologies of modern poetry and find this problem—a terrible problem—on almost every page. Ninety per cent of the poets are too lazy to deal with it, using such terms as "Lord" and "My God" with the implied reservation that they are fictions. Or they impute a fake divinity to great men, mountains, dead rodents, etc. But suppose you are absolutely honest; suppose, in the straits of your reason and experience, you must deny the existence of the supernatural but assert the existence of the ultranatural, those extreme susceptivities of consciousness which govern our spiritual and moral lives; and suppose you even raise ultranatural experience to a superpersonal level, the racial or the panhuman; do you then agree to call it by the name of God, do you stand up in church and say the *Credo* with your fingers crossed (as was lately recommended by a noted British humanist)? Miss Rukeyser does not; this is the quality of her honesty, and she recognizes that there is a point at which symbolism as a poetic technique turns into a substantial instrument of mendacity. I don't say she has solved the problem by any means. Consider it solely as a tactic of vocabulary: what terms shall the poet invent which can assume the richness and versatility of terms refined in centuries of Christian usage? Remember that even the most determined anti-Christians, from de Sade to Sartre, have argued in Christian terms. It would be mere obstinacy to ask Miss Rukeyser, or any single poet, to do a job which requires a sustained community of genius. Yet I know no other body of work in which the problem has been met more squarely; nor, generally speaking, any poetry which has brought more imagination and lyrical firmness to the task. Make no mistake, these poems are deeply felt; prayers, I should say quite desperate prayers, for the things which the poet needs but cannot command—peace and justice. For this reason they are intrinsically, connately a part of our ethical crisis, and as such ought to win the prior respect and endorsement of all of us, whatever esthetic considerations may arise later on. —HAYDEN CARRUTH,"The Closest Permissible Approximation," *Poetry*, Feb. 1963, pp. 358–60

Muriel Rukeyser has published a large body of work since her first collection, *Theory of Flight*, appeared when she was only twenty-one. It immediately marked her as an innovator, thoroughly American, Whitman-like in method and scope. Characteristic of her poetry, of which we now have a survey in *Waterlily Fire* (Poems 1935–1962), is the big canvas, the broad stroke, love of primary color and primary emotion. Her method is the opposite of the designer's, her vision is never small, seldom introverted. Her consciousness of *others* around her, of being but one member of a great writhing body of humanity surging out of the past, filling the present, groping passionately toward the future, is a generating force in her work. She celebrates science as much as nature or the restless human heart. Lines from an early poem like "The Gyroscope": "Power electric-clean, gravitating outward at all points, / moving in savage fire, fusing all durable stuff/but never itself being fused . . . " are echoed in Part II "The Island" of her final poem in this collection: "Hearing the sounds of building / the syllables of wrecking / A young girl watching / the man throwing red hot rivets / coals in a bucket of change. . . ." Another main fulcrum of her work is psychological, even mystical (but it never departs from a physical, in fact, a sexual base), an exploration of being and becoming and then of re-becoming, growing out of her interest in Eastern philosophy as well as Western primitivism.

Waterlily Fire contains selections from eight former books, and a group of new poems all written in 1962. *U.S. 1* (1938) offers a sensuous and environment-conscious catalogue of Southern working people and their lives, reported with the instantaneous honesty of her camera eye; people are realized with the same all-embracing empathy to which we thrill in Whitman. A *Turning Wind* (1939) includes a group of life-sized portraits of her personal heroes and "saints": Gibbs, Ryder, Chapman, Ann Burlak, Ives. Others of these, she says in a note, are yet to be written; they will include the lives of Kathe Kollwitz and Bessie Smith. There is a section of ten *Elegies* (1938–1945) "dedicated not to death but to war and love."

Beginning with "Rotten Lake" she reveals, in the intersticies of apocalyptic scenes of world battle, her own soul-struggle: "the chaos, the web of the heart, this bleeding knot . . ."; "ether dreams, surrounded beasts, the aftertoll of fear . . ."; until, in the spilling of agonies, the created poems become a catharsis: "Now green, now burning, I made a way for peace"—"clear water and order and an end to dreams." Although her proclivity is for the large spontaneous canvas, Miss Rukeyser is also master of the self-contained lyric, and it is good to have a choice of these, for instance from the volumes *Beast in View* (1944), *The Green Wave* (1947) and *Body of Waking* (1958). There are vivid poems that leave a single hypnotic impression on the mind, such as "Eyes of Night Time," "Salamander," "Haying Before Storm." Among the new poems, "For a Mexican Painter" is another such flawless lyric, wizardlike in its craft.

Miss Rukeyser's final section contains, as a crown piece, the striking "Waterlily Fire" in five parts, which is about the burning of Monet's *Waterlilies* in the Museum of Modern Art fire of 1958; it is also about the author's life on Manhattan Island, and (astonishingly) also about a nuclear war protest demonstration in City Hall Park in April, 1961. Like Whitman, she sings, "Born of this river and this rock island, I relate/the changes . . . Whatever can come to a city can come to this city." There rises before us, without its being stated, a prophetic vision of what may be destroyed by uncontrolled "Fire striking its word among us" and at the same time, what can be brought to birth, if men can be "touched, awakened . . . touched and turned one by one into flame": a blossoming—of peace, love, art.—MAY SWENSON, *Nation*, Feb. 23, 1963, pp. 164–65

The poems of Muriel Rukeyser are primordial and torrential. They pour out excitements of a large emotional force, taking in a great deal of life and giving out profound realizations of the significance of being. She has a natural force which for decades has built up monuments in words of the strong grasp on life of a strong mind.

There has always been a wide spectrum of poetic expression. We have the niceties of Marianne Moore, who allows little emotion but engages elegant subtleties of a sophisticated awareness. Another type shows the classic control, the order and restraint of the well-made poem in Housman's "To An Athlete Dying Young." A type of exaltation is found in Hopkins, who in "The Starlight Night" uses 11 exclamation points in its octave and five in the sestet.

Muriel Rukeyser for decades has consistently employed direct thrusts of strong emotion, a deep personal statement, in making her poems. It is not "confessional" poetry as we understand it in Anne Sexton, but massive awareness of large phases of existence. She has a remarkable variety of styles within her major style. She is artful and can be experimental. She belongs to the Whitman school of large confrontations and outpourings rather than to any school of the rigidly constructed poem.

Her new poems (in *The Speed of Darkness*) have splendors of passionate realization as had her earlier poems. They are about men, women, children, humanity, birth and death and struggle, man's lofty hopes, his endless losses, the continuous war which she feels is a hallmark of all who have lived as adults through the last three decades.

They are about the spirit, the ununderstandable spirit which is always trying to be understood. They are recognitions of man's inhumanity to man, and of his love, his devotion, the essential birth of new generations to assault and be assaulted by the old questions, despite the answers of the past.

Her own voice comes through all these poems, real and unmistakable. It is an open poetry, open-ended. It is not systematic except in the inchoate system and thrust of the passions throwing off poems in a continuum of poetic realization. She is not dogmatic, not prideful, not despairing despite knowledge of much death and hatred in our time, the continual wars, the children seen playing happily through the wars.

She is a realist, and celebrant of the spirit, rushes in where angels fear to tread as a matter of course, sees through hell to heaven. To her, hell and heaven are the world, our world as it is, seen through the Roman conquests, the wall of Jerusalem, the Spanish Civil War, whose scenes she revisits long after her passionate belief of the thirties ("Along my life and death backward toward that morning when all things fell open and I went into Spain."). There are many more poems on many subjects, short and long, which invite the reader to largeness of scope, tenderness, belief in life, honesty of perceptions, all the excellence of new work memorable and good.

Here is a short poem from the book; its title is "In Our Time":

> In our period, they say there is free speech.
> They say there is no penalty for poets.
> There is no penalty for writing poems.
> They say this. This is the penalty.
> —RICHARD EBERHART, "Personal Statement,"
> *NYTBR*, June 23, 1968, pp. 24–25

I. L. SALOMON
"From Union Square to Parnassus"

Poetry, April 1952, pp. 52–57

Any volume of selected verse by a contemporary has a mortuary air about it, needing only a committal service to attain the unread bookshelf. (*Selected Poems*) by Muriel Rukeyser will not be so readily disposed of, even if it is of unequal intensity and proportion. It is a selection made by the poet herself from all her previous volumes of verse. Perhaps Miss Rukeyser wants to save only the pieces and not the poems whole. Her habit of giving partial excerpts is an annoyance not easily overcome by even a sympathetic reviewer. Not that there aren't enough single poems given in their entirety, but the repeated use of dots, heavy and light, to indicate omission and a too frequent editorial "from" before a title hinder the continuity of the lengthier excerpts. It is apparent Miss Rukeyser had overwritten her long poems and, to correct the imbalance, excised lines and phrases. Either these particular poems were not entities in the round at original publication, or the several earlier publishers were uncritical and printed both the good and the uneven work. Despite the defect in present editorial judgment, this book is worthy of the modern reader's time.

Miss Rukeyser began her career in poetry as an avowed revolutionary, the darling of the literary Left, not the *avant-garde*. It is important to remember she assimilated the then current modernist techniques without originating innovations. Her first volume, *Theory of Flight* (1935), was an insurgent and dynamic book of verse. It began with a fearless acceptance of the problems of the thirties, and it revealed the great loneliness of the poet as modern, as one identified with the whole peoples of the world, needing them, yet not understood by them. The complex of emotions and ideas permeated by Marx resulted in a poetry that was affirmative of the good-will of the common people, Hitler having come to power and Republican Spain being the last bastion of a new democratic socialism. The domestic scene had witnessed the nadir of the Great Depression; the murder of Sacco and Vanzetti lay in the consciousness of the younger generation like a wound; the Scottsboro case had enlisted the mind and heart of the liberals in the country, including Felix Frankfurter, now one of the more conservative Supreme Court Justices; and Miss Rukeyser startled one part of the literary world with her first book. In the intervening years, the complex of emotions and ideas has shifted slowly, and the emphases in her final volumes are in part on natural primitivism in *The Green Wave* (1948) and on the mythopoetic in *Orpheus* (1949).

What gave Miss Rukeyser no small comfort was the congenial acceptance her first book received from critical authority. This, added to the passionate encouragement from the Left, strengthened her assurance that she was a writer for the masses. The result was *U.S. 1*, a title denoting the highway from Maine to Florida; what lay human and inhuman on both sides of the road is indicative of her fervent avowals. This temporizing with politics was responsible for a certain slackness in her writing and for a purposeful carelessness to add a devil-may-care tone to a poem. These are missing from the present volume, which has been cut fine. It must be understood that not all the poems included are, as a result of the excised passages, bowdlerizations.

The prestige that came to Miss Rukeyser early was not due to her sense of social outrage and her acceptance of the class struggle. She earned it by her technical competence, fused with a tense awareness that she was creating poems. In the larger plan, her extended poems are not entirely successful; the excisions attest to this. But critics, not partisan fomenters of a party line, recognized the vitality and warmth in her rhymed and unrhymed notation that not even her revolt against tradition, poetic and political, could waylay. That she preferred a loose structure in her elegiac strophes and in other poems in which she carried on a frontal attack in the name of the have-not poor is proof that, the themes aside, she was struggling with two of the perennial problems in poetry, language and form.

The instinctive control of form is one of the most difficult disciplines imposed upon the poet, who must be wary, particularly when the inclusion of news events of an era becomes one of his important devices. This is not to say *proper name x* or *headline y* must not be used in poetry, but the using must be resolved in the context, and it has been, by poets who speak in symbols and do not mistake those aspects of everyday living for imaginative reality. Instead of symbols, Miss Rukeyser substitutes highly charged feeling in language that has a fugal relationship to the themes of her particular compositions. She makes a union of opposites in such a phrase, as, "Not Sappho, Sacco." This is from "Poem out of Childhood," so cut from the original in *Theory of Flight* that to read it in this selection is to read a revaluated poem. In the later version, "These bandages of image wrap my head" refers inferentially and by only the wildest surmise to "a rush of triumphant violins answered me." In the original version, it refers to an accidental murder. Likewise, the "Not Sappho, Sacco" phrase followed a description of the poet of Lesbos; now it alludes more cogently to the academicians, "who manipulated and misused our youth." There are inescapable conclusions: Miss Rukeyser's sense of form is so elastic it can be subjected to the procrustean rack; her poems in the new setting are often elliptical; since the original sense no longer exists, the referents have been altered. This suggests that emotion adequate to one experience can be served anew; it implements a belief that Miss Rukeyser has not always met the exigencies of a poem as a mature artist. A disjunctive, if explosive, rhetoric obtains,—a penalty she cannot avoid.

And yet Miss Rukeyser is artist enough to integrate her lengthier selections, despite the interruptive ellipses. She merely needs time, and time as has been noted causes a shift in the complex of emotions and ideas. The elisions and various foci in the section entitled *Elegies* detract from the instantaneity of surprise and wonder. The individual passages show an acuity of observation, where the correspondences between form and matter are perfect; but the whole, rather than the parts, seems to be in a continuing process of being made. Miss Rukeyser subjected her work-in-progress to actual print. The startling line and the moving excerpt remain, but the completed harmony, the fusion of the imaginative act and the living fact, is wanting. It took ten years, Miss Rukeyser says in a note, to connect images and processes. There are ten elegies; the first five appeared in *A Turning Wind*. The first nine have been treated to a severe excision; only the last is reprinted without contextual change. They are replete with disparate, if concentrated, images of grief, grief for a wounded world and desire for survival, and faith in and vision for the immortal race, man. These elegiac strophes conclude in joyous affirmation:

> Or the expiation journey
> toward peace which is many wishes flaming to-
>   gether,
> fierce pure life, the many-living home.

Miss Rukeyser sees herself as a poet of outrage and possibility; this inference is drawn from *The Life of Poetry*, her book devoted to its meanings and dynamics. It is necessary, she says, that the twenty-fifth century know that we wrote trash. And she says further, our poems will have failed if our readers are not brought by them beyond the poems. Her first statement is a rationalization of the weakness in her social protest experimentations, now carefully expunged from this edition. There were good poets in the late thirties, Miss Rukeyser ought to remember, who were poets of outrage but did not succumb in their writing to the hypnotic hysteria of Union Square. In her second statement, she wants the poet—in Emerson's phrase—to open the eye of the intellect to see farther and better. To her, her poems were born in transition and may remain so. With a humility for the craft of poetry, she defines her own limit as an artist:

> What fire survive forever
> myself is for my time.

Her insights are valid not only in the extraordinary concluding poem, "Easter Eve," from which this quotation is taken, but also in her brief lyrics of childhood, her songs of loneliness, her love poems, and in her avowals as a poet for humankind. She has been a poet of rebellion, but the *Selected Poems* has lyrics of inordinate beauty and compassion. "Lift, wind, my exile from my eyes," she sings in a very brief lyric in which the impulse of breath and movement is perfectly achieved. In "A Certain Music" there are lines that are sensuous and restrained, as in, "Naked you walked through my body and I turned/to you with this far music you now withhold." And in "Madboy's Song" there is "Fly down, Death" with its iterative echo at just the right pauses in the poem.

Miss Rukeyser has endured an inward war with herself. The "expiation journey" in the *Elegies* becomes the theme for a philosophical poem in "Ajanta." She observes that the Buddhist painter-monks believe there is an analogy "in the sensation of space within ourselves . . . by which the world is known." This poem is complete and satisfying. It has an awareness of the intangibles of existence:

> So came I between heaven and my grave
> Past the serene smile of the voyeur, to
> This cave where the myth enters the heart again.

And the myth has. No, Miss Rukeyser has not sold her birthright for a mess of facts. What has saved her work from extinction is her maturing as a poet. She reaches out in the mythopoetic *Orpheus* towards pure poetry. Miss Rukeyser may deny this to be the unconscious fulfillment of the poet as seer. The *Orpheus* moves on planes she would have eschewed as ivory-tower when she first began. It is far from her first direction in *Theory of Flight*. It is written in free rhythms, the

images precise, without one careless word to mar a line. Yet, even in this, Miss Rukeyser has made slight changes, six in spacing and one in the alteration of a word. The advisability of shifting words or phrases for the exigency of space implies that the original rhythm did not matter, yet changing "tree of air" to "tree of nerves" is a felicitous enrichment.

The *Orpheus* in this edition suffers from the constricting pages. It is the kind of poem that breathes whole, and when it appeared under the imprint of The Centaur Press it had an aesthetic appearance that made it a delight to see and read. And it bears re-reading, for its dramatic theme, Orpheus murdered and dismembered by women, is enhanced by superb lyricism as he is reborn the god of poetry and song:

> The lyre is going up:
> the old lyre of Orpheus, . . .
>   Reaches the other stars.
> And these four strings now sing:
> Eurydice.

ROBERT COLES
"Muriel Rukeyser's *The Gates*"
American Poetry Review, May–June 1978, p. 15

Upon reading Muriel Rukeyser's latest volume of poems, upon going through *The Gates*, one feels silent, sad, instructed, grateful. No words of prose from a reviewer are needed to explain these poems; and to praise them is almost condescending. The woman who wrote them has been with us 20th century American readers almost a half a century: a gifted observer of this world; a person who can sing to us and make our duller, less responsive minds come more alive; and not least, someone who has proven it possible to be a sensible human being, a woman inclined to give, to extend herself toward others, and also a first-rate poet. We all struggle with the sin of pride; Muriel Rukeyser has been blessed with less narcissism than most of us—especially remarkable in such an introspective, sensitive, and self-aware person, who has for so long been committed to telling others what crosses her mind. She is saved from self-centeredness by a compassionate concern for others, all over the world, and by a wonderful capacity for self-mocking irony: "Anne Sexton the poet saying / ten days ago to that receptive friend, / the friend of the hand held camera: / 'Muriel is serene'. / Am I that in their sight?" And at another point: "I'd rather be Muriel / than be dead and be Ariel", an entire poem, and shorter than its title: "Not to be Printed / Not to be Said, / Not to be Thought".

Her poem "St. Roach" provides a beautiful lesson in the psychology and sociology of prejudice—worth dozens of social science articles or books. It is also an example of her capacity to distance herself from the self-serving demands of the ego. And as an additional bonus, we finally have a fitting rebuke to Kafka's *Metamorphosis*—Rukeyser's gentle, suggestive, wonderfully surprising moral lesson which, one suspects, would have prompted an appreciative smile in the Prague philosophical story-teller: "For that I never knew you, I only learned to dread you, / for that I never touched you, they told me you are filth, / they showed me by every action to despise your kind; / for that I saw my people making war on you, / I could not tell you apart, one from another, / for that in childhood I lived in places clear of you, / for that all the people I knew met you by / crushing you, stamping you to death, they poured boiling / water on you, they flushed you down, / for that I could not tell one from another / only that you were dark, fast on your feet, and slender. / Not like me."

She knows such a description is all too apt for other of God's creatures than the roach—especially so in this past decade of civil rights struggles and war in far off, "different" Vietnam. She reaches out for all that is part of this earth—for the distant past, even for inanimate matter in the present. In "Painters" she reminds us of the pre-historic men and women who etched animal forms on the walls of caves—an effort to make sense of things, a desire to represent, to show and tell. In "Artifact" she demonstrates an almost unnerving capacity for calm detachment. "When this hand is gone to earth, / this writing hand and the paper beneath it", she begins, and soon tells us what may be left, what may survive—tells us quietly, with no sense of triumph or satisfaction: an artifact—"This pen. Will it tell my? Will it tell our? / this thing made in bright metal by thousands unknown to me. . . ." She worries again, further on, about those who worked on assembly lines, men and women both, themselves rendered artifacts by the cold, manipulative, always profitable transactions of the entrepreneurs and those managerial lieutenants who keep the factories in fit shape: high output, high profits, just enough wages to keep things "moving".

She has a visionary side to her: "There were poems all over Broadway that morning. / Blowing across traffic. Against the legs." In her hands New York City becomes a series of brief images that remind one of James Agee's short film "In the Street". She has a nagging, important historical sense—a side of her that can jolt the reader. Simone Weil, who hated the Romans, saw them as early Fascists, would have loved "The Lost Romans"—a stunning reversal of coin, a reminder that we are all taught in school to think of Caesar and Cicero, of legions and battles and conquests: All Gaul is divided into three parts. Instead the poet asks us to think of other Romans: " . . . those young Romans / Who stood against the bitter imperial, their young / green life with its poems . . . " And the last line, a testimonial to a writer's broad-minded sense of kinship: "For we need you, sisters, far brothers, poems of our lost Rome."

A series of poems is subsumed under a larger thematic effort, titled "Gates", the book's title. "The poet is in solitary", she tells us in a prose prologue: "the expectation is that he will be tried and summarily executed . . . " Then another person is introduced, "an American woman [who] is sent to make an appeal for the poet's life." This person "stands in the mud and rain at the prison gates—also the gates of perception, the gates of the body." Again Muriel Rukeyser modestly places herself as an onlooker, a compassionate, aroused, decent person who is not quite the other poet whose "stinging work—like that of Burns or Brecht" has managed to get "under the skin of the highest officials". She is no Brecht, nor was meant to be. But she also shows her ideals through calls to brotherhood, sisterhood: "Through acts, through poems, / through our closenesses— / whatever links us in our variousness; / across worlds, love and poems and justices / wishing to be born."

Not that she blinks at the mean, ugly, corrupt, exploitative side of the world. In "New Friends" she makes clear her awareness of the terror many decent, morally honorable and outspoken individuals have to face, day after day. She is no friend to America's multinational corporations, but she is not deceived, either, by the repressive bureaucratic statism of Eastern Europe. The word "liberation", she tells us, has become a catch-all slogan, thrown around by anyone and everyone in the interest, often, of crooks, thieves, liars. But she is, again, not one for self-pity—or its larger, more ideological

version: social or political despair. She remembers the best messages of the Old and New Testaments. Her eye catches an infant, a "woman at vigil", a "woman seen as the fine tines of a pitchfork." She knows that if the "air fills with fear and the kinds of fear", there is also resistance: "Free our might free our lives free our poet." The "massacres" of this awful century haunt her: " . . . the butchered that across the fields of the world / lie screaming . . . " Still, there are friends, friends of the poet, friends of all that is decent and just in the world, friends who may be "unknown" to the poet, to all who suffer for their goodness and kindness and sensitivity, but who deserve recognition—hence a book titled "Gates", hence poems about the ordinary, the undramatic, hence a salute to those standing near the gates, no Brechts but comrades, indeed, and possessed of their own special, considerable, necessary virtue: Muriel Rukeyser, chief among them.

KENNETH REXROTH
"Foreword"
The Poetic Vision of Muriel Rukeyser
by Louise Kertesz
1980, pp. xi–xv

Muriel Rukeyser is the best poet of her exact generation. Kenneth Patchen, the only other claimant, spoke of himself as "born in one world and doomed to die in another." It was not a good time for poetry, because poetry was dominated by ideologies—and Left and Right—the so-called Proletarians and the self-styled Reactionary Generation. Today, if you return to these people you will be surprised at the flimsiness of their accomplishments. The Marxists do not sound like Mayakovsky or Neruda, and the Reactionary Generation most certainly do not sound like John Donne. Most of the Left broke with their political mentors and became so embittered that they stopped writing—like Herman Spector—or died young—like Sol Funaroff, or both—like Kenneth Fearing. Walter Lowenfels wasted years as a "functionary," but came back to vigorous poetic life in old age. Only Patchen, singularly intractable, and never a joiner, survived, and somewhat later the much unappreciated Thomas McGrath, who is still writing one of the best of the long poems of the period, *Letter to an Unknown Friend*. For all their emphasis on "form," poets of the Reactionary Generation simply didn't write well.

Vasari said of Tintoretto, "His was the most profound mind ever to lend itself to the art of painting." It is curious to read in this book the attacks on Muriel Rukeyser by what were, in fact, political opponents, for her lack of "depth." Purely as a thinker, she is certainly more profound than anyone else in her generation. It's just that her thoughts were not their thoughts. She is one of the most important writers of the Left of her time, and now with the death of Neruda and the ever-increasing sterility of Louis Aragon, she ranks very high indeed. Unlike the other writers of the Left, she never paid much, if any, attention to the corkscrew twists of the party line. So the critics of the Left alternately embraced and damned her. It is impossible to believe that she ever was a member of the Communist party; if she ever joined, she must have been quickly expelled. She does not have an ideology grafted into her head like these devices they attach to the brains of monkeys. She has a philosophy of life which comes out of her own flesh and bones. It is not a foreign body. So, likewise, this philosophy was totally unlike the superficial fadism of the *jeunesse dorée* of English Stately Home Weekend Soviets. She never gave it all up to enter the Anglican Church or edit a magazine for the CIA. Muriel Rukeyser is a traditionalist. But when everybody was running about talking about one tradition or another but doing nothing about it, her tradition was not recognized or was despised. Muriel Rukeyser is not a poet of Marxism, but a poet who has written directly about the tragedies of the working class. She is a poet of liberty, civil liberty, woman's liberty, and all the other liberties that so many people think they themselves just invented in the last ten years.

Today the only poet of the early twentieth century who wrote in the tradition of the fulfilled "American Dream" is Carl Sandburg. The intervening writers, especially the women, have been forgotten. Sandburg long ago succumbed to his Chicago police reporter sentimentality and the shallow patriotism, verging on jingoism. After all, poetry in the tradition of the "American Dream" must necessarily be tragic, because the community of love of Whitman and of all the communalist communities that flourished in his youth have not been realized. Muriel Rukeyser believes in the community of love, not because she is convinced that it is going to win, but because it is true, it is the right way for human beings to live. She has been accused of "optimism," and this in a country where the Left thinks the revolution is just around the corner and the rest of the population continuously invents new euphemisms for graveyards. (I think gravediggers [undertakers] now call themselves bereavement counselors.) In America you're either an optimist or a pessimist. Hardly anyone knows that "The world is a tragedy for those who feel, and a comedy for those who think." Muriel Rukeyser thinks and feels; and not only that, she seems to enjoy placing herself as an obstacle in the way of evil. Book after book has involved action—from personal investigation of the fate of miners doomed to die of silicosis in *U.S. 1*, to her fairly recent personal confrontation of a South Korean dictatorship in the case of a Catholic radical poet, Kim Chi-Ha, who had been condemned to death. Everywhere she went in Korea, she had only one message: "Free Kim Chi-Ha." They haven't freed him yet, but at least they commuted his sentence, and he undoubtedly owes his life to the worldwide agitation of the "nonpolitical" international writers organization PEN, which Muriel Rukeyser was representing. It takes guts, in middle age when most radicals have calmed down and embraced Zen or scientology or the *Reader's Digest*, to put yourself physically in the way of the Dictator Park, the KCIA, and the CIA, for a colleague on the other side of the world of whom few people had heard.

"*Revenons à nos moutons.*" What about Muriel's poetry? Her enemies have called it rhetorical, as though the "Ode to the Confederate Dead" was anything but rhetoric uncontaminated by intellect. She has a sonority as deep as her deep laughter, and it is this sense of the power over language that distinguishes her from the women who preceded her in her tradition, Lola Ridge, Evelyn Scott, Beatrice Ravenel, or men like James Oppenheim, or Wallace Gould. Except for Gould, they weren't anywhere near as good writers, and Lola Ridge can sometimes be embarrassing in her naïve exhortations.

Muriel Rukeyser does not embrace Zen, but she has more and more internalized her philosophy of life—but this in a special sense. It's one thing to be a suffragette, it's another thing to insist on being a woman, completely, in every sense of the word. All the years that Louise Bogan was poetry reviewer for the *New Yorker*, she carried on what can only be called a

malevolent vendetta with Muriel Rukeyser, which can only be accounted for by some unknown personal motivation. She was herself a militant feminist and "free woman," and much of her poetry is either a celebration of her womanhood or intensely, but cryptically erotic. In fact, she could be called a lesser and greatly more cooked Muriel Rukeyser. She never reviewed Muriel's books, but as each came out she took the opportunity to insert a few catty remarks in her column. Most extraordinary is the accusation that Muriel's poetry was devoid of human affection and sexual passion. One of her most anthologized poems derived from a famous love poem in the Chinese *Book of Songs*, "Effort at Speech Between Two People," beginning:

> Speak to me. Take my hand. What are you now?
> I will tell you all. I will conceal nothing.
> When I was three, a little child read a story about a
>   rabbit
> who died, in the story, and I crawled under a chair:
> a pink rabbit: it was my birthday, and a candle
> burnt a sore spot on my finger, and I was told to be
>   happy.

"Ajanta" is purportively a poem about the great painted caves in India, one of the high points of the world's art. When she wrote it, Muriel had never been to India, although, of course, she had seen the great portfolio of accurate reproductions. I have seen Ajanta, and I must say that the poem conveys, amongst other things, the feeling, the emotion, the very sensibility, of those long-gone Buddhist monks, that overwhelms you in the same way the poem does. "Ajanta" is an exploration with continuous discoveries of new meanings, of her own interior—in every sense. It is the interior of her mind as a human being, as a poet, and as a woman. It is the interior of her self as her own flesh. It is her womb. I am sure that she did not know, in those days, of the womb mandala of Tibetan and Japanese Shingon Buddhism, but in a sense that is what the poem is. We did not need Carl Jung to tell us that the mandalas of Buddhism and Hinduism are paradigms of the interior life, and that that life with its symbolic patterns is shared by all human beings to the extent that we all have the same physiology. After "Ajanta," in fact, she wrote a poem of introspection into her own womb where, to use Buddhist symbolism, Maitreya was seated in Peace. It is in nine parts, one for each month of pregnancy, and it is unique in the literature of feminine poetry.

Like Walt Whitman, as the horizons darkened and the community of love seemed to grow more distant, Muriel has sought ever deeper into her self for its meaning. She is far from being a member of that most profitable fraternity—a disillusioned radical. The message now is not, if it ever was, "All power to the people!" Kenneth Burke once turned to me as we were marching up Fifth Avenue chanting that slogan and said in his wispy way, "What do we mean by *all*? What do we mean by *power*? What do we mean by people? We don't even know what we mean by *to* or *the*." Power has fascinated Muriel since her first book, *Theory of Flight*. As is self-evident from her biography of Willard Gibbs, power has always meant to her not the power of Stalin or Mao that "comes out of the mouth of a gun." Power for her is the great dynamo within what used to be called the soul. Her later poems and her life have been devoted to research into the dynamics of that power, and as always, this has led her to actual physical confrontation with the mechanical power of despotism and exploitation. "Free Kim Chi-Ha!" she said to the Dictator Park, and nothing more.

JANE RULE

1931–

Jane Rule was born on March 28, 1931, in Plainfield, New Jersey. She was educated at Mills College, where she was elected to Phi Beta Kappa and received the B.A. in 1952. Rule taught English at Concord Academy in Massachusetts and then at the University of British Columbia in Vancouver. She has also worked as a typist, store clerk, teacher of handicapped children, and cashier in a gambling house to acquire background material for her writing.

Rule's first novel, *The Desert of the Heart*, was published in 1964. Her other novels include *Against the Season* (1971) and *The Young in One Another's Arms* (1977). Her short stories have appeared in numerous periodicals and have been widely anthologized; a collection, *Theme for Diverse Instruments*, appeared in 1975. A book of critical essays, *Lesbian Images*, was also published in 1975.

In addition to her writing and teaching, Rule is a civil liberties activist and visits the numerous children she had adopted in Europe under the Foster Parents' Plan.

JANE RULE

From an Interview by Geoff Hancock

Canadian Fiction Magazine, Volume 23 (1976), pp. 57–112

The following interview was taped on a Saturday afternoon and evening in October, 1976, at Jane Rule's home on Galiano Island, B.C. Though she was born in Plainfield, N.J. in 1931, Jane has lived in Vancouver over twenty years and recently moved to the island. To get to her house, one has to take the Gulf Island ferry from Tsawwassen, and our overnight visit was scheduled around the twice daily winter sailings. The Gulf Islands—Galiano, Mayne, Pender, Saltspring, and others—are, of course, British Columbia's heaven on earth, and even a weekend here convinces one books are somehow easier to write. The clear air is curiously Mediteranean, partly because the rainfall is less than a third that of Vancouver, some twenty miles across the Strait of Georgia, and partly because the peeling red bark of the arbutus trees gives the islands a mellow glow even on chilly days. A warm sun breaking through the autumn overcast, the smell of the sea, cormorants on the rocks in the harbour drying their wings like parodies of Imperial eagles, and Jane and Helen waiting at the dock convinced us we were arriving someplace special.

Jane and Helen's house is only a few miles away, their old Volvo moving smoothly along winding road and scruffy forest. The house is a Pan-Abode, with large smooth cedar timbers, and every wall is lined with paintings and drawings by their friends. A space above the view window contains a fine Hopi basket collection, an heirloom from Jane's grandmother and a reminder of the deserts of Arizona and Nevada where Jane and Helen holiday in winter. The stereo is massive and a space about the size of a large cupboard is filled with tapes of classical chamber music. Stereo speakers with central controls lead to every room, and no vulgarity here, the wires are well hidden. The house, like Jane and Helen, is gracious and classy, with the virtues of civility fairly bounding.

While Thea and Helen explored beach trails and the local cemetary (a offensive gravestone reads, "her marriage was her monument".) Jane and I retired to her well ordered and comfortable downstairs study. Besides the only xerox copier on Galiano—Jane has a crippling arthritic spine deterioration which forces her to wear a neck brace much of the time and excess typing is painful—the study has a wall of books, a great stone fireplace, two Judy Lodge paintings, a Scandanavian sofa, and a knockout view across the water. The three hour interview was interrupted only by Helen's delicious crab and artichoke salad and homemade wine.

Though she was very tired after a summer of houseguests and two previous interviews that week, Jane's answers were always direct. We raced the clock towards the end since Jane promised that as of midnight, this was the last interview she would ever do. ⟨. . .⟩

Hancock: Where did you go to school?

Rule: Dad worked for a national company. So I went to my first school in New Jersey, then to California, then to Illinois, then to Missouri, then back to California with short stretches in other places as well.

H: How did this affect you as a writer?

R: I think the moving around was very good in one sense. I learned very early that what a great many people thought of as 'values' were really 'manners' and that 'manners' shifted radically from community to community. When I was in California I was in a multi-racial school, but when I was in St. Louis I didn't go to school with blacks. Though there were a lot of black children in that world, they walked in the street and I walked on the sidewalk. In all kinds of less obvious ways the sense of how you behaved in somebody's house, what kind of language you used, what kind of *accent* you used, all seemed to the people who had always been there they way you always did it. For me, it was being a foreigner and figuring out what the rules of the game were. It forced me to evaluate details of living which were very useful by the time I started writing.

H: Did you have good teachers when you started writing?

R: When I started writing, yes. By this time I was in my early teens in private school. Before that I was in one enormous classroom after another. I didn't begin to read until I was about ten. Nobody knew it because I was very tall and I sat in the back row. I came into school about November and, if I didn't understand the book, the teacher felt it was because I hadn't read the first ten chapters because I hadn't been in school. I bluffed and stumbled and was so stupid I didn't understand why the boy across the aisle from me could read the board and I couldn't. I also didn't see anything that was going on. I didn't know that I needed glasses.

Until I came back from California at the age of twelve and went to private school. My teacher discovered not only that I couldn't read but that I had also skipped multiplication tables entirely. I didn't know what they were and I was trying to do long division. So I had a revelatory year, finding out that it wasn't magic: Math was perfectly understandable, the English language was locked up in the marks on the page. It was grand. ⟨. . .⟩

H: When did you begin writing fiction?

R: I suppose when I was around thirteen or fourteen. At that point I was much more interested in the sciences and I wanted to go into medicine. That was before I took chemistry which changed my life for the better. I was the kind of student who not only never did an experiment right, but got sponges stuck in the bottoms of test tubes. Just the housekeeping of chemistry was beyond me, never mind the experiment. I thought, if I fail chemistry in high school, I probably wouldn't do well in medicine. By that time I was also beginning to realize that, of course, medicine was not a science that dealt with people, but with parts of bodies. Though I didn't mind cutting up chickens and cleaning pigeons. It was not really a life's work.

I was already writing just for fun. When I was fifteen or sixteen, I decided I really wanted to write. ⟨. . .⟩

H: You've also travelled a good many places. England, Greece, the USA and now you're a Canadian citizen. Has that had an influence on your fiction? The variety of human types? That sort of thing?

R: Yes, certainly. And landscapes as well. Setting is very important to me. When I first began to write, I felt such a stranger in any environment I was in I didn't use settings at all. I didn't know the names of plants, or flowers, or streets. In school I never knew where the washroom was. So when I wrote, I wrote as if particular flowers, streets, rooms didn't exist. I think that *Desert of the Heart* was the first time I risked a landscape. I did an enormous amount of research for that. To be able to know the names of hills, roads. And I was what? In my late twenties. But I felt I had to deal with the landscape as a scholar would.

Read Virginia Woolf. Somebody wrote to her in high fury that she had a flower blooming in southern England that didn't bloom anywhere but Scotland. Virginia Woolf's answer was "it's my garden." I like that beautiful arrogance of somebody who owns a landscape, who is born to it, doesn't feel caught out or exposed as ignorant as a stranger or a foreigner. But I am still very careful to be accurate. I am still a stranger in landscapes.

As for types of people, I don't think in those ways. Though I realize I couldn't have made a Dina character as I did in *Against the Season* with a Greek character confidently unless I'd been to Greece. I felt as if I knew twenty times as much about the character as got into the book. Which is about the right balance. I feel freer to draw upon various cultural experiences from having been as many places as I have. ⟨. . .⟩

H: You have a very strong visual sense. Would you liked to have been a painter, a graphic artist, or a musician? Or maybe another way of putting this, how much do painting and music influence your prose?

R: Both very much. I have never been interested at all in being a painter or graphic artist. Nor seriously a musician. As a youngster I played clarinet in the school band, but nothing serious. I was raised in a musical family and I really use music, perhaps more than I use literature to teach myself what I want to do in my own style. I listen to a great deal of chamber music and I listen to the voices of the instruments. I don't think I pay a great deal of attention to transforming form from one art to the other. But the tonal controls, the balance of voices, and the relationships that instruments express together seem to me much closer to the way my characters, anyway, relate to each other. That's where I learn. And I think of the *timbre* of a character. I think of the range of a character. I think as you might of an instrument that a certain character can play a certain tonal part in a novel. A tuba cannot do certain kinds of things. A violin cannot do certain kinds of things. When I'm working to make a concert of characters, I listen to chamber music and think about relationships. It's something I do in every piece of work I do. There will be certain pieces of music I associate with certain books simply because the conflicts, the resolving harmonies, the movements and tonalities *belong* to the problems that are in the book. ⟨. . .⟩

I've always said that nine-tenths of the time I am functionally blind. I rarely notice a lot of detail unless I sit down and force myself to. I can take a walk and not see anything. I'm lost in what I'm thinking about. I can be riding in a car and not know where I am. I think a part of the importance of painting for me is to keep making me look. It's something I'm limited in so the art of painting becomes somebody else teaching me to see. Sometimes very reluctantly. The Bridget Riley retrospective in London. I didn't get over to it for six months because it's so terribly demanding an experience in thinking about light. Bridget Riley obviously does that by wandering around in the world. I really need to be broken out of my habit of obsessive concentration.

H: Do you not learn any of that from some contemporary writers?

R: I can't think of any writer who jars me awake in perception as I think of music and painting jarring me awake. It's not always a jar. Often it's a wonder. Often I feel interested, technically interested in other writers. I don't suppose it feels to me something I can't do for myself. I don't meant I don't learn from other writers. I certainly do. But it's a quieter, less conscious and self-conscious process.

H: Which writers then, classic or contemporary, have you learned from?

R: It's hard for me to know. I have never been a person with conscious models. Once I tried to have conscious models. I went through a phase where I thought I ought to learn from Gertrude Stein. And I suppose I have learned from Gertrude Stein. Probably the most influential period for me was 17th century English Literature, and that had to do with the long rhythmic control of prose. I don't suppose anybody reading my prose would think it sounds like a John Donne sermon. But that's where I learned how a sentence was made.

H: Which other writers do you value, not necessarily as influences?

R: William Butler Yeats, Shakespeare. The contemporary novelist I read with the most excitement is Patrick White because he's doing something with language that concerns me. That is, he doesn't lose any of the rich texture and imagery, yet at the same time he's using a lot of speech rhythms. And they're Australian. There's an extraordinary flavour. I was interested to hear he wanted to live in England—that was his spiritual home obviously. He felt much more comfortable there than in raw Australia. But he couldn't live outside the sound of his own language. I feel very much that way. The sound of the spoken language is very important to me. And he teaches me all sorts of ways to use it.

I also care enormously about (Harold) Pinter. Again, on the stage you are dealing with sound all the time. But what he's doing with language, what he's doing with silence, what he's doing with what is *not* said is something I'm interested in learning. ⟨. . .⟩

H: Let's talk about you: do you smoke or drink too much when you work?

R: I don't ever drink when I work and I smoke too much all the time.

H: Tea, coffee, drugs?

R: There's a rumour about me which is true. I drink Coca-Cola for breakfast.

H: Was there ever a moment when you were afraid of publishing your fiction? Fear of losing friends, family, job? Or to put it another way, as an art form the novel can be particularly dangerous because it demands such a total committment. The writer is sometimes pitted against the world in a confrontation that is more than aesthetic or intellectual. Has the novel ever been dangerous to you in that way?

R: I don't think of the artist as in an adversary position to his or her culture. That's alien to my whole sense of art as celebration. To think of the activity of writing the novel or the novel itself as a dangerous weapon is nothing that is in my consciousness at all. Nor do I think of myself as artist in relation to my culture as enemy adversary at all. Lover, more like. If there is a relationship at all and I'm not sure there is. Except perhaps my own relationship to my work while it's being done.

But back to the first part of the question. Have I ever been frightened of publishing? It's in some ways hard to look back and remember. I certainly must have been frightened because the kind of work I do was going to be a problem. I think I have been concerned to protect the people closest to me from having to take on anything that I had to take on. But there isn't anyway you can protect people close to you. So you simply have to learn to relinquish that responsibility because you can't do anything about it. ⟨. . .⟩

As far as worrying about losing a job. I have always, not only from writing, but in any other circumstances, wanted to feel that there never was a question of being worried about losing a job. I've always been a fairly good worker in whatever I've done, and I've always been able to do jobs. I mean, I have so many ghastly skills that there never would be a time that I would worry. If I needed a job, I could walk into a gambling casino and be a change girl. I'd sling hash. I'd be a clerk. I could do any number of things. I've never been afraid of work. If somebody would say, "Publish this book and you'll lose your job at the university," well, fair enough, if that's going to be the case. Life wouldn't be worth living if you lived in that kind of nervousness. ⟨. . .⟩

H: You have the deepest respect and concern for your characters. Where do they come from? And how do you get them beyond stereotypes?

R: When I'm conceiving a character it's a conglomerate, not just people I've known, but of experiences I've watched people deal with. I wouldn't do a portrait of someone I know. Occasionally there's a fictionalized portrait, but mostly it's a conglomerate. I'm not interested in creating a character and living with a character unless I am really interested in and respectful of the experience that's involved. I would be bored with creating characters I felt condescending to. You have to live with characters for a long time and I don't want to spend a great deal of time with people or ideas that I don't honour.

Now, I disagree violently with some of my characters. The most extreme example is the main character in *This Is Not for You.* Her vision is entirely opposed to my own. But she was an intelligent adversary. I tried not to be in a adversary position. Instead, I shut up my own sense and tried to get inside hers. It was a requirement, sometimes a tiring one. By the time I finished that book, I felt I had lockjaw because Kate is so *tight.* But it was worth it. It was an important requirement, an important concern. I don't think I'd ever want to write dealing

with concepts or people for whom I had no respect. There would be no point for me.

H: And in doing so, you can get away from the concept of women in motorcycle jackets?

R: It's not a concept that I've ever had. I think it's important to talk about the lesbian material in my books. It's certainly there, it's there very strongly and I suspect it will always be. I don't think of it, as I'm sure a great deal of my audience does, as a kind of special ghetto group in the world. I have never lived in a subculture, I have never felt excluded from the human family or job or social life. I feel as if the popular attitude toward lesbian experience does make cliches, does make ghettoes. Most of the homosexuals I know live in the ordinary community, working, having dinner parties, being themselves and being known. And yet there's the persistent sense that homosexuals are defined by their sexuality and excluded by their sexuality. I never have been, nor have numbers of my friends. The sense that homosexuality has to do with the bars downtown or motorcycles or costumes. There are a number of people who are homosexuals, who are heterosexuals, who like motorcycles and leather jackets. I would imagine if you lived in that world and knew those people, you would write about them as people, just as I write about people.

The sense, however, in society, is that special sexuality is totally defining and limiting. I'm not writing to try to prove that isn't so. I'm simply writing out of my sense of the world as I live in it. But there are so many misconceptions. One of the difficulties of my fiction is getting through to a sensibility that expects, first of all, it ought to be erotic because that's the only point in writing about people who are homosexual, and second, there is something morally depraved about it. Or, conversely, my fiction should connect readers with a whole sense of love, wonder and liberation.

I certainly don't write about love, wonder and liberation in any circumstance because we're all hedged around with requirements, bewilderments and questions. Many of the characters I write about are not homosexual. I think one of the most offensive things in my work for people who are defensive about it is that the people I write about who are homosexual, are not ghettoized, are not excluded, are not strange, peculiar, sick people. That's very scary. It's like saying, "These are human beings." And that's the one thing you mustn't say. You can say, "These are depraved, wild people," and everyone will buy the book. You can say, "These are the liberated people who are going to teach us how to live in zero population and why don't you all get on the band-wagon?" And that's perfectly acceptable. But when I say Rosemary and Dina live in a little city, or a big town and move about in a community with all different kinds of people, and have dinner with people and go to restaurants and buy property and worry about their own needs and concerns, then that's really scary. I don't know why. But I think that's where a lot of the distorted criticism comes from. ⟨. . .⟩

H: Would you comment on your attitude towards characters who keep relationships at a distance? Orphans, overseas foster children, adopted children are common motifs throughout your fiction.

R: What I'm interested in in relationships is suggested there. The novel has importantly dealt with families, with the structures of a small town where you really inherit your concerns and your cares. But most of us have moved into an urban world where we leave our families behind and where we leave the small town or farm values behind. We're left free to choose for ourselves. It is no longer important for any human being's survival that he or she marry; we're all free to marry or not, to have children or not. We have the mechanization to be able to do that. You can take away all of the requirements of human connection, of human interdependence, all the structures for it anyway.

What interests me is watching people detached from all those requirements, figuring out ways to build a human community that is satisfying and nourishing to them. I am often concerned with voluntary relationships, with the choice. Because I think that's where we are. I think it's a much more common experience.

We don't think of it as the common experience, but look about, particularly in urban worlds. How many people do we adopt as sister, as brother, as child, as friend, as surrogate-parent? How do we recreate the generations, not so close and demanding and genetically owing? We still want human community and we create it in all sorts of different ways.

For instance, in *Against the Season*, the only blood relationship is one with the dead. Amelia's sister is dead. All the other relationships are voluntary. There isn't one that is a simple requirement. You have to say, "No, I don't want to take care of my mother for the rest of my life. I want to be free. I don't want to be like my Daddy. I want to be free." All those characters have left that world behind. So how do they build a community of human care? The next book is about the same thing. That's what I'm interested in writing about. Voluntary human relationships. ⟨. . .⟩

H: And yet at the same time you do keep your character's relationships at that distance, they are reaching out for each other and in some cases they do touch, if only briefly. Yet these personal committments and permanent relationships don't seem to come easy to your characters. They have to fight for them, struggle for them.

Yet, I was quite impressed by the variety of relationships that you explored. I personally felt that *Against the Season* was one of the more perfect novels I've seen in revealing the number of relationships that are possible between characters and yet be all together in the social whole. I thought in a general way, it was something like the metaphor George Eliot used in *Middlemarch*, that society is a web in that you can't touch a single strand without disturbing all the others.

R: Yes, the sense of interrelationship is very important in that book. I think your sense that it's hard for all my characters to make any committments is true. That is also true of our contemporary society. We now can choose whether or not to make committments. The minute you introduce choice, where a woman doesn't *have* to marry to leave home and lead her own life, a man doesn't *have* to marry for him to have a economic unit that's viable for him to run the farm. Men and women don't have to *have* children, they don't *have* to take care of their parents—there's social security. We don't *have* to do anything.

The minute you take away that simply *expected* role in human relationships then stand with someone else, with other people and think—why, why are all of the questions of personal differences, of personal need which were minimal in a society that required relationship, why are these questions now our maximum concerns? No wonder, not only my characters, but people we all know, live together rather than marry, put off having children, maybe decide not to; move two thousand to five thousand miles away from their parents; lose track of their brothers and sisters. Why care? My characters are always asking, why care? Nine times out of ten there's a real answer. But it's a hard answer and it means a lot of voluntary risk. ⟨. . .⟩

H: One last question. Have you changed anybody's life with your fiction?

R: Mine.

MARILYN R. SCHUSTER
From "Strategies for Survival:
The Subtle Subversion of Jane Rule"
Feminist Studies, Fall 1981, pp. 431–47

Eroticism, camouflage, encoding, and fragmentation are a few of the strategies for survival to which lesbian writers have resorted in order to inscribe lesbianism in literary texts. [1] Monique Wittig has said that in literary terms, lesbianism "cannot even be described as taboo, for it has no real existence in the history of literature." [2] The little that has been called lesbian is distorted, false, borrowed, misnamed, and does not constitute a fictional tradition spoken through a lesbian voice and sensibility. The terms of literary language itself, forged as they have been in a male-dominated tradition, have obscured or obstructed that voice. ⟨. . .⟩

Just as Wittig's work represents a rupture with conventional discourse consistent with French feminist thought, Jane Rule's fiction effects a mining of convention from within in the tradition of Anglo-American feminism. Rule textures lesbian identity within the social and literary fabric of her novels. But her weaving in of lesbian images among the other strands of identity that constitute the integrity or her characters is as distinct from denial, subordination, or assimilation of lesbian identity as Wittig's more spectacular technique of rupture. Rule's implicit ideology is pragmatic. She assumes into her fictional universe the dominant social reality of North American, white, middle-class, Christian values and assumptions that fashioned her own formation. She does not blindly promote the norms generated by that cultural matrix, nor is she complacent about the privileges and deprivations that those norms protect and impose. Rather, she adopts a strategy of subtle subversion: social and literary conventions are put to the service of their own destruction. Rule has long been privately cherished among lesbian readers while being the object of sharp public rebuke by other lesbian feminists for not being political enough. [3] A close reading of her five novels and many short stories, though, uncovers a textual politics that illuminates the underside of social and literary conventions (imagery, language, genre, characterization, point of view), while opening into a transformed vision of society and literature. ⟨. . .⟩

As Rule's books shift away from American settings and toward Canada, they become increasingly concerned with the creation of community. At the same time, lesbianism as a theme occupies less narrative space, but remains an essential element of the text. In *Desert of the Heart* and *This is Not for You*, lesbianism is central because of the struggle for self imposed by social contexts governed wholly by the conventions of American middle-class white society. In *This Is Not for You*, fearful of ostracism, Kate internalizes her oppressor to speak the language of "respectable" American society. In *Desert of the Heart* hostile forces hover but are kept, momentarily, at bay. In *The Young in One Another's Arms*, the same forces have a more immediately disruptive effect on the community of survivors. Gradually there emerges in Rule's novels a middle ground between individual isolation and a faceless concept called society. The I/they polarity is modified by a communal "we." [4] In *Against the Season*, individuals take the power of defining their community back into their own hands. In *The Young in One Another's Arms*, the community is more mobile and fragile, but it is maintained against the threat of anonymous repressive policing by the state. The state, though

Canada, is shown to be in collusion with the Americans as they help to track down draft resisters. The presence of sheer unreasoning power is always lurking at the edges of Rule's fiction: an ominous warning that voluntary communities, however vital, are not immune to brute force.

The communities portrayed are *not* microcosms of the larger society, but voluntary groups analogous to the voluntary relationship[5] (as distinct from a relationship expected or required by family, law, social pressure) in *Desert of the Heart*. Difference is valued and jealously protected. The outcasts who form these communities evolve an unwritten social contract that protects their outcast status, rejecting blind, brutal conformity to a dominant norm. They are, in a sense, communities built on a lesbian model. Lesbian identity itself is not so much subsumed into the community as kept whole within it—one aspect of identity among others, not singled out as the defining characteristic or an angle of vision any more or less valid than others. If Wittig responds to ostracism and oppression by imagining islands of Amazons, Rule responds by creating neighborhoods within the city walls, so to speak, where differences are sorted out and kept intact in spite of the leveling machines of society.

Rule's latest novel, *Contract with the World*,[6] realizes in the manipulation of point of view the communal dynamic central to Rule's political and aesthetic vision. In an article she wrote in 1979, Rule talked about her preference for groups, for shared experience rather than autobiography or fantasy. She said: "The long tradition of fiction with a central character around whom all others must find their secondary place supports hierarchies I don't find interesting."[7] In *Contract with the World*, there are six central characters—three men and three women, artists and artisans—and the book is divided into six equal parts, each centered on a character. Vancouver, the setting, is also a sort of character as it is mapped by each character in a different way and in turn defines them. Each chapter is written not so much in a different voice, although there are strong variations in tone and language, as from a different angle of vision, under a different subjective light. In each chapter the reader perceives through a specific set of assumptions and feelings, through a distinct sensibility. Some of the sensibilities are more attractive than others, but Rule refuses to reduce even the most blustering heterosexist male to a dismissive stereotype. By drawing the reader into the heart of six different sensibilities and, in turn, by representing each of the characters as an object of the perception—and frequently the artistic arrangement—of the others, Rule forces sympathy in the strict sense of the word on the reader. Distance is collapsed so that the reader cannot facilely dismiss repugnant characters nor can one maintain undifferentiated sympathy. One has to contend with their reality and humanity.

Roxanne, the one politically conscious lesbian in the book, is a composer who records sounds throughout the city in order to create a sound map. Her *ars poetica* is a metaphor for the book and an expression of Rule's aesthetics and politics. She attempts in her house and in the city to record each distinctive sound—free from the values that manners or custom ascribe to them—fine tuning her recording to catch specificity of timbre. Then, maintaining the integrity of each sound, she is free to rearrange them in different patterns, listening to how they modulate, complement, clash in different combinations. It is a sort of hyperrealism: attentive, objective accuracy in the reproduction of the individual fragments and then the creation of an overall pattern that is a projection of the artist's subjectivity and vision. Further, the overall pattern is never fixed, it is in a state of constant change.

The importance of mobility, flexibility, and open-endedness in the book is stated first in the chapter titles, "Joseph Walking," "Alma Writing," and so forth. Each character is associated with a present participle, an ever-moving present. But more profoundly, there are throughout the book critiques of two kinds of rigidity that are shown to be interrelated. On the one hand, theories about art that attempt to define and confine creativity in fixed phrases are shown to be inadequate or ludicrous. Mike, a sculptor, preaches that art must be defined as rescuing form from usefulness, but his only really successful piece is rescued when it becomes useful: a toy for children to grow with. Similarly, fixed conventions concerning behavior, particularly gender stereotyping—again most clearly expressed through Mike—are shown to bear no real relationship to the reality he is trying to fix within their confines.

A profound distrust of ideological system, whatever its content, permeates this book and all of Rule's fiction and nonfiction. Allen, a homosexual photographer glibly indifferent to homophobia because of class privilege, is shocked into political consciousness after his lover commits suicide. But he arrives too quickly at a "personal is political" solution and avenges his lover's death by exposing homosexuals in high places. The tyranny of his eye-for-an-eye, exposure-for-exposure method is more elegant than the invasion of the police into the privacy of his life, but it is a tyrannical invasion of privacy nonetheless.

Whatever the scars this community inflicts on itself, the overall pattern of the book suggests that they are each other's only salvation in the face of mindless power imposed, again, by the forces of moral order in concert with the police. In the last chapter, written through Carlotta's justifiably paranoid sensibility, she sets up an exhibition on government money of portraits of her friends: the six protagonists. The show is in a small provincial town, the birthplace of Allen still smarting from public exposure as a homosexual and mourning his lover's death. The people viewing the show are transformed into an angry mob backed by the police as they throw red paint on the portraits and have all six subjects arrested. However the six view themselves and each other, the public views them with hostility and uncompromising rage.

Most of the six characters are riddled with class or gender bias of one sort or another, which is exposed in the book. Many cling to a set of conventions for (false) security. Rule does not create a utopian alternative purified of all traces of oppression. She takes carefully observed elements of reality and rearranges them into changing patterns in an effort to imagine beyond the confines of brute power which may in fact dominate ultimately anyway. The police helicopter hovers in *Desert of the Heart* and *The Young in One Another's Arms*, but here the community is literally carted away at the end. Against the simple-minded certainty of the mob, the community has only a tenacious uncertainty with which to defend itself. Within the police wagon, Carlotta observes her friends: "Carlotta pulled back away from that multiple embrace and discordant song, seeing them all . . . escaped from their destroyed portraits, survivors who had already grown far beyond her fixed ideas of them" (p. 339).

Rule refuses to force her fiction into a closed system. The only definitive closure in her books is imposed from the outside, the natural expression of a policed state. Open endings, ambivalence, and shifting meaning are valued over closure, single-mindedness, or fixed meanings that would replace one convention with another. It is precisely because she is wary of the laws that have sought to define and confine us that Rule urges the reader not to make laws in their place, but to be attentive to the changing, sometimes comic, sometimes tragic, patterns of our living.

The publication of *Contract with the World* last fall caused immediate furor in feminist and gay circles. Anticipating that lesbian feminists would be disappointed by the book's apparent failure to mirror correct politics, Rule devoted her column in *The Body Politic* to a defense of her fiction even before the book was released. "A good writer is not in the business of propaganda," she wrote, "because the nature of art is not to generalize but to reach the universal by way of the particular."[8] Barely a month later in the *Gay Community News*, Karla Jay wrote the review to which Rule had already responded, "many (probably most) lesbians are going to find the characters in this book not only politically incorrect, but distasteful as well."[9]

The heart of this debate is not a variant of the timeworn "art for art's sake" versus committed literature controversy. Rule, hardly apolitical, contributes regularly to feminist and gay liberationist publications and has frequently commented on the uneasy alliance between art and politics. But she is critical of simplistic or reductive approaches to art *or* politics by writers, readers, people allied by a common cause. To conceive of literature as a simple mirror for a political movement is to cheat both literature and politics. In an article for *Branching Out* in 1979, Rule defined the proper relationship between art and politics and the dangers of reversing the terms of that relationship: "Those movements which have shunned their writers or required them to follow the party line have got the literature they deserve."[10] Rule suggests here an important distinction between literature that is propagandistic and literature that is political. Propaganda reassures the group that commissions it. The burden is on the writer to interpret and illustrate a preexistent political text. In literature that is political the burden of interpretation is on the reader: to understand the workings of the text and to comprehend how the author's terms reach beyond the text.

Rule's fiction while being resolutely antipropagandistic is profoundly political in both social and literary terms. Like Wittig and other lesbian writers who understand the politics of sexuality and the politics of language, Rule is concerned not only with politics in the text, but also with the politics of the text. Unlike Wittig, however, her visionary community is not set apart, but placed squarely in the middle of the "powers that be." She is not a political or a literary separatist.

Notes

1. One need only think of Colette's demimondaines, Willa Cather's male protagonists, Gertrude Stein's elaborate codes, Violette Le Duc's self-punishment, Radclyffe Hall's costuming. Although these are important, cherished works, the strategies are fraught with danger. Adrienne Rich analyzes the process whereby "the unspoken—that which we are forbidden or dread to name and describe—becomes the unspeakable," in "The Transformation of Silence into Language and Action," in *Sinister Wisdom* 6 (Summer 1978): 17–25. It is one of four talks presented as a panel at the 1977 annual Modern Language Association convention. The other panelists, Mary Daly, Audre Lorde, and Judith McDaniel developed other aspects of the same problem. Rich's talk was revised and included in "Disloyal to Civilization: Feminism, Racism, Gynephobia," in *Lies, Secrets and Silence* (New York: W. W. Norton and Co., 1979).
2. Monique Wittig, Author's Note, *The Lesbian Body*, trans. David LeVay (New York: Avon Books, 1975), p. ix.
3. Bertha Harris, "Melancholia, and Why It Feels Good," *Sinister Wisdom* 9 (Spring 1979): 24–26; and Bonnie Zimmerman, "The New Tradition," *Sinister Wisdom* 1, no. 2 (Summer 1976): 34–41.
4. For an excellent discussion of the tensions between "I" and "we" in Rule's short stories, see Helen Sonthoff, "Celebration: Jane Rule's fiction," *Canadian Fiction Magazine* 23 (1976): 121–38. Sonthoff also analyzes Rule's fiction as a dynamic involving "convention and invention." The entire issue is devoted to Rule.
5. In a 1976 interview with Geoff Hancock in the issue of *Canadian Fiction Magazine* cited above (pp. 57–112), Rule talks about her concern with voluntary relationships free of the conventional requirements of human connection and her interest in "figuring out ways to build a human community that is satisfying and nurturing to them" (p. 96).
6. Jane Rule, *Contract with the World* (New York and London: Harcourt Brace Jovanovich, 1980). All references are to this edition, and page numbers will be supplied in parentheses in the text.
7. Jane Rule, "The Practice of Writing," *Canadian Women's Studies* 1, no. 3 (1970): 34–35.
8. Jane Rule, "Reflections," *The Body Politic*, no. 66 (September 1980): p. 17.
9. Karla Jay, "Debating the Rule," *Gay Community News*, 18 October 1980, p. 4 of Book Review Supplement.
10. Jane Rule, "Seventh Waves," *Branching Out* 6, no. 1 (1979): 16–17.

BARRY DEMPSTER
"Ferry of the Emotions"
Canadian Forum, January 1986, pp. 35–36

Inland Passage, Jane Rule's tenth published work, generously contains 21 short stories, making it a more sizeable collection than most. Expectations of variety are satisfied as the stories leap from 19-year-old brides to travelling salesmen to elderly famous writers awaiting death. Although voice and tone shift only slightly from story to story, Rule's style is neither as idiosyncratic as Margaret Atwood's nor as breezy as Leon Rooke's. Descriptions repeat themselves, settings are often blurry and endings sigh instead of bite. But Rule's characters, no matter their shared silences, their dim views, glow from the inside out: nightlights in a shadowy world. These are not eccentrics, however. None of her caricatures rely on weirdness to make them lovable. Rule's people are often lonely, occasionally lesbian, frequently at the end of their rope but most of all surprisingly normal, comprehensible. We recognize inside us all a child bride and something in the shape of death.

The first couple of stories, "Dulce" and "His Nor Hers," overflow Rule's hands, but as the book proceeds the stories improve in both focus and control. As if mimicking life itself, *Inland Passage* begins with more than it can handle and ends with clear priorities. What constitutes a real handful are Rule's attempts to analyze entire lives instead of recording only the most strategic heartbeats. Take "Dulce" for example: the character of the title is a woman who lives for and through the people in her life, yet is unable to recognize any one of their true selves. She is drawn first to Wilson C. Wilson, poet, iconoclast, rumoured homosexual, then to Lee Fair, poet, isolate, lesbian. Dulce's roles are the good listener, provider, mother, muse. But, of course, both poets leave her for their own complicated reasons and Dulce, unable to "learn from life," concludes by announcing her interest in "art rather than artists." It is an intriguing idea but details are sparse, all the major changes occuring off-page; time is evident only in words like "then" and "now." Dulce needs more space for awareness (as it is she seems blind instead of naive), more depth of recognition than one crowded story can provide.

Slowly, Rule's ability develops bigger hands and greater composure. For a short time, in stories like "The Real World," she surrenders to exaggeration in the place of focus: good hearts are super-good while the bad vibrations are so bad they almost cackle. It's in the George and Anna stories (five tales of a happily married couple and their two kids who were first introduced to us in *Theme for Diverse Instruments*) that Rule first fully demonstrates an ability to turn metaphor into truth and vice-versa. These stories dwell on one occurrence at a time (events concerning grandparents, pets, a Christmas holiday), yet create, through humour and compassion, a three-dimensional family that has both history and diversity.

At this point the stories grow middle-aged. The characters are tilting downwind. Divorce is common ground; either that or widowhood. Rule clearly cares for these women and men, but even more importantly, she gives the impression of being totally familiar with their lives. She is therefore able to concentrate on the present moment while educating us on the past with perfectly chosen memories, bits of dialogue, sudden parallels. There is no sense of clutter here, no claustrophobia. Through time and awareness, we all weave in and out of each other's lives.

"Slogans," the story of Jessica, a victim of cancer who is spending her remissions on "lovers, trips and swimming pools," proves that it is possible for the past to achieve balance. Dignity is the subject of "The End of Summer," where Judith

Thornburn, half-separated from her husband, ponders the nature of civility and sacrifice while helping to repair their country home's septic system; the metaphor of waste here is cleverly and quietly used. In "Blessed Are the Dead," Martin, a scholar on the nature of tragi-comedy, is abruptly faced with the death of an old friend, a true-blue scoundrel. Even for the experts, life is sometimes a devastating joke. Finally, Laura Thornstrum in "Power Failure" fights for independence after her house has burnt down. Should she move in with her children, become a burden, or should she rebuild despite her advanced years, her arthritis, her widowhood? No matter how close we come to death, the choice is still how best to live what life remains.

The inland passage of the title is not only a ship's route to Prince Rupert, but also a journey through another human being. No open waters, no salt breeze; instead, the closed quarters of a quiet life. Inwardly, privately, Jane Rule's characters are obsessed with one another, while outwardly even as innocent a question as "What are we going to do?" can send them dashing off in opposite directions. Much of life is lived only in the mind. Rule adds up the visible signs of such aloneness and finds—yes—divorce and death, prejudice and fear, but also a tough need for love and family, for reconciliation and time. As her stories mature, as her "handfuls" are dispersed and smoothed, *Inland Passage* becomes an important path, a place where some special people show us how, faultingly, they try best to manoeuvre their lives.

JOANNA RUSS

1937–

Joanna Russ was born on February 22, 1937, in New York City. She won a Westinghouse Science Prize as a teenager and was admitted to the prestigious Bronx High School of Science, but was unable to attend because of "family insanity," as she puts it. She attended Cornell University, where she studied writing under Vladimir Nabokov and graduated with high honors in 1957; she then did graduate work at the Yale School of Drama, receiving an M.F.A. in playwriting and dramatic literature in 1960. She has since taught at a variety of institutions, including the State University of New York at Binghamton, Cornell University, the University of Colorado at Boulder, and currently at the University of Washington. She has also been an instructor at various Clarion Science Fiction Writing Workshops.

Russ is known primarily as a science fiction writer. Her first story, "Nor Custom Stale," appeared in the *Magazine of Fantasy and Science Fiction* in 1959, and her short fiction continued to appear almost exclusively in that magazine for the next decade. In 1968 she published her first novel, *Picnic on Paradise*, the longest work in her cycle of SF and fantasy stories about a warrior named Alyx. In 1976 the novel and shorter works were collected in a single volume entitled *Alyx*; the cycle represents one of the genre's earliest extended treatments of an independent, competent female character.

Her second novel, *And Chaos Died* (1970), an ambitious rendering of telepathy from the inside, furthered her reputation as a prose stylist, but it was her third, *The Female Man* (1975), that firmly established her as one of the most important writers of modern SF. A controversial work both for its intricate structure and for its uncompromising feminist radicalism, it was the first of her books to receive significant attention outside SF, while inside the SF community critical discussion of it has continued to the present day.

Russ's next two novels were similarly controversial. *We Who Are about To . . .* (1977), reportedly written as a critique of survivalist ideology in SF, in particular as found in Marion Zimmer Bradley's *Darkover Landfall*, has been attacked for its unrelenting pessimism and praised as a brilliant meditation on death. *The Two of Them* (1978), a novel about the practical and ethical limitations on communication across wide culture gaps, has inspired equally vigorous critical debate.

Controversial though her novels have been, Russ's short fiction has received praise from critics throughout the SF field. A collection of her short stories did not, however, appear until 1983, when

JOANNA RUSS

WILL ROGERS

MURIEL RUKEYSER

PHILIP ROTH

J. D. Salinger

Carl Sandburg

Mari Sandoz

The Zanzibar Cat, containing the Nebula Award–winning "When It Changed" (1972), was released. Still, much of her short fiction remains uncollected. Her most recent science fiction book is the story cycle *Extra(ordinary) People* (1984), which includes the Hugo Award–winning novella "Souls."

Russ has also published two books of social and literary criticism (*How to Suppress Women's Writing*, 1983, and *Magic Mommas, Trembling Sisters, Puritans & Perverts*, 1985), a mainstream novel (*On Strike against God*, 1980), and a children's novel (*Kittatinny*, 1978). She has established herself as one of science fiction's most stringent and insightful critics, and a collection of her SF criticism is forthcoming. She has been married once and divorced, and currently lives in Seattle.

I very much admire the sense of speed that Russ often gives the reader, of eliminating intermediate steps and decisions. When you start one of her stories, it is not at all like an Ibsen play. You do not begin with the slow exposition, the first act with the maid dusting the parlor and telling the butler all about the curse of the family, which of course the butler knows as well as she does: "Today Per Lagersholm comes to visit his wife for the first time in forty-two years, so we must dust the entire house carefully, my Eric." "Why is it, Olga, that Per Lagersholm hasn't come to visit his wife in forty-two years, which must be about the day that they married, unless I am hideously mistaken." Joanna is not so kind to the slow reader. She has the habit of starting in medias res and in medias place. It's your job as the reader to work and try to figure out what's going on and where we are in earth or elsewhere, or far more importantly, what essentially is going on among all these articulate people.

It is a very jazzy style that she has in several of the short stories, a feeling of clever and controlled improvisation. I am in no wise suggesting that the stories are, in fact, improvisations; what I am trying to describe is a sense in them of much occurring and of bright people trying to understand what is happening and to enjoy it or control it or exploit it. I am thinking in particular of that short story "Nobody's Home." Nothing is explained and everything is given us. We find a large family taking in a new member who turns out to have the fatal character flaw for that time of not being exceptionally intelligent. In this story Russ has created a utopia of the bright. We shall not be lonely, we shall not be alone, we shall inherit the earth—not the lovers of power, not the big daddies with their nukes, not the controllers or the comptrollers, but the bright and the curious shall inherit the earth and create a society of multiple options and quick responses and large polymorphous perverse warm families in which art and child care and scientific curiosity and games are all intermingled.

She is seldom a self-indulgent writer, however, and thus sees even that society as one that fails some of its members through no fault of their own. What you finally carry away from these stories is a sense of possibilities, both negative and positive. Russ is one of our best novelists of ideas because she has all the traditional fictional virtues. She creates full-fleshed characters, full of quirks and odd memories and hot little sexual nodes that make them believable. She embodies her ideas in a fast-moving arc of action. Finally, she has effective emotional range, all the way from savage indignation to vaudeville routines, from the bleak to the lush, from extreme alienation to a warm and powerful projection of community. What Russ does not create is a world where love conquers all, certainly not her women. The push toward freedom, appetite, curiosity both intellectual and sensual, the desire to control and expand their own existence, figure far more importantly in the lives of her female characters than does traditional romance.—MARGE PIERCY, "Foreword" to *The Zanzibar Cat*, 1983, pp. xi–xii

SAMUEL R. DELANY
From "Alyx" (1975)
The Jewel-Hinged Jaw
1977, pp. 211–12, 223–30

I

In Joanna Russ's recently published novel *The Female Man* (Bantam Books, New York, 1975) a woman from an alternate future comes to live with a typical American family—father, mother, teenage daughter, in "Anytown, U.S.A." The encounter is shocking, traumatic, lives are changed, layers of social and psychological defenses are stripped, protesting, away.

In the last novella of the early series we call, after the name of its heroine, *Alyx*, a woman from an alternate future comes to live with a typical American family—father, mother, teenage daughter, somewhere in Green County during the summer of 1925 (the same summer that saw publication, in July, of fifteen-year-old Robert E. Howard's first story, "Spear and Fang," in *Weird Tales*). The encounter is so muted, so down-played, so low-key that, though this woman fights for the freedom of the Universe, chaperones the daughter to a dance, takes on an eccentric garage mechanic for a lover, commits murder, and makes love on the back porch, the suspicion lingers that perhaps, somehow, it is all a fantasy and not science fiction at all.

The last of the *Alyx* stories, "The Second Inquisition," may someday be called the end of "early Russ." There are plays and short stories from before then. But the major work till this time is certainly the series, here collected, that begins with "Bluestocking" (written 1963, published under the title "The Adventuress" in Damon Knight's *Orbit Two*, G. P. Putnam, New York, 1967), continues with "I Thought She Was Afeard Till She Stroked My Beard" (written 1963, published under the title "I Gave Her Sack and Sherry," also in *Orbit Two*), is furthered in "The Barbarian" (written 1965, published in *Orbit Three*, 1968), climaxes in the novel *Picnic in Paradise* (written during the winter of 1967/68, published under the title *Picnic on Paradise* by Ace Books, New York, 1968), and concludes with "The Second Inquisition" (written spring 1968, published in *Orbit Six*, 1970).

Were I asked for a single, subjective response to characterize these tales, I would call them "cold." I mean nothing so blatant as the fact that the novel, for instance, takes place on a world encased in ice. I mean an effect of language which, even as the words talk of high fervors, swordplay, or bone-staggering action, runs through the early March meadows of the mind like a morning freshet that, only hours before, was a ribbon of crackled ice, and whose edges still bear a lace of frost and whose current still carries frozen platelets to tick the collared grass-blades and clover stems jutting from it.

All the stories in the series are highly playful, though the playfulness in each is pitched at a different level. All are witty.

Most are deeply touching; but they touch and play with cold, cold fingers. ⟨. . .⟩

IV

The *Alyx* stories, as we have mentioned, *are* a series.

Practically every s-f writer has left us at least one. When one realizes that writers as different as Robert A. Heinlein and J. G. Ballard, Anne McCaffrey and Brian Aldiss have all written them; or that both Isaac Asimov's *Foundation* trilogy and Theodore Sturgeon's *More Than Human* are series stories put between sets of covers, one begins to suspect that perhaps the series is *the* basic form of the field.

The critical temptation with a series is to try to read successive installments as if they were chapters in some particularly loosely-constructed novel. Almost inevitably, though, they present us with signs that insist, despite other signs of a serial chronology, that, rather than successive chapters, they are really successive approximations of some ideal-but-never-to-be-achieved-or-else-overshot structuring of themes, settings, characters. One is tempted—especially when the syndrome is pronounced, as with Ballard's *Vermilion Sands* stories—to say that they are all rewrites of the same story, that all are different workings-out of a single, synchronous structure that persists, unchanged beneath various expressions. But the signs of a to-be-accepted fictive diachrony are also present . . .

Whether such ambiguously synchronic/diachronic structures are seen as rents in the otherwise coherent fictive field or truly rich contours in that same field where truly useful exploration may occur depends on our temperaments as readers, on what particularly we are looking for in our experience of a single author's multiple creative works.

The *Alyx* stories present us with a number of such fictive contours. Edarra of "Bluestocking," Iris of *Picnic on Paradise*, and the narrator of "The Second Inquisition" are by no means the "same character." They differ in age, temperament, cultural background, and general plot situation. Yet Alyx/Edarra, Alyx / Iris, and the "visitor" / narrator all organize our attention about a single problem: The problems a worldly woman has overseeing the maturation of a woman not so worldly.

Conflict between different cultural / historic moments yields another of these ambiguous parameters around which much of the reader's experience of the story ends up organized. In "The Barbarian," the conflict is ironic: The dials and lights of the fat man might as *well* be magic—or so all the signs of the sword-and-sorcery tale instruct us from beginning to end of the story. Yet it is precisely *because* Alyx recognizes them as the machines we know them to be (and, therefore, she knows their behavior is predictable) that the story exists. Philosophically, what this story is about is: Alyx knows the fat man is wrong (i.e., not God) because if he were right and the Universe were a mechanical product of his (specifically recognized as) machines (which he tries to pass off as magic), then the Universe would have to be deterministic. Alyx believes the Universe is indeterminate; probably this belief has something to do with the religious falling-away that precedes the first tale and that is, in a sense, the genesis of them all. Alyx knows the Universe is *over*determined, for that is what life on the margins of society teaches one. But she also knows—and this is the faith that traditionally comes to fill the absence left by the falling-away from any official dogma—that "overdetermined" is not the same as "determinate," no matter how much the evidence for one asks to be taken as evidence for the other. Thus her decisions: to save the governor's infant daughter—and kill the fat man.

In *Picnic on Paradise*, Alyx the barbarian is plucked by an offstage time-machine into the (a?) future and her barbaric talents are put at the service of a group of futuristic tourists who need someone to lead them across the ice of Paradise. The story (again) grows out of the conflict of cultures/histories: Alyx's "primitive" values against the "sophisticated" values of the tourists.

In the three stories that precede the novel, during her own epoch, Alyx's basic interest to us (most interestingly) is how much her general approach to life seems to be ahead of those around her. We have already mentioned her ability to recognize machines; and, in "I Thought She Was Afeared," her basic response to the carnage she has helped create on deck near the tale's end is: "'Why the devil,' she said with such sudden interest, 'don't the doctors cut up the bodies of dead people in schools to find out how they're put together?'"

That her black-bearded lover can offer no answer is, presumably, to be taken as an emblem of the many reasons that, in the next paragraph, she has left him. For all her good right arm, this is a much more modern consciousness than any that ever inhabited a Howard tale.

When Alyx arrives in the future, it is because of the practicality that underlies this (what can only be called, in the context of the landscape in which it occurs) intellectual whimsy—a very hard-headed attitude toward survival and destruction—that she is useful; that she is heroic.

In Russ's most recent novel, *We Who Are About To . . .* (Galaxy, 1975), in which a machine that translates voice into script allows us to read of the necessary extinction of yet another group of tourists stranded on yet another hostile world (but this time so much more subtly hostile!), this whimsicality has developed into (*not* been replaced by) a deep pessimism: Both the whimsicality and the pessimism express a rejection of transcendence as a socially (or logically) usable commodity— or what Jacques Derrida, our most incisive explicator of the relation between difference, deference, trace, and script, would call, approvingly, a denial of absolute presence.

But our concern is the series at hand.

The historical moments in conflict in the novella "The Second Inquisition" are that of a generation several ahead of the tourists' in *Picnic* and that of America in the summer of 1925. Over that gap passes the greatest violence—and the greatest compassion. I find it endlessly fascinating that this series,- which begins with three tales of sword-and-sorcery, should end with such a meticulous evocation of the extra-urban environment so close in feel to the one (Cross Plains, Texas) that the genre's inventor, with his *Conan* tales, tried to escape—an environment the nostalgia for which (if this is not to trivialize what was certainly Howard's real despair over his mother's imminent death) drove him to suicide in 1936.

V

⟨. . .⟩ The impetus among academics to define science fiction as a particular type of discourse, a particular sort of "word machine," that performs certain functions, literary and / or sociological, (e.g., the functions of "cognition and estrangement") rather than simply a group of themes and conventions, began in the middle sixties—at practically the same time that the s-f distinguishing itself as the most interesting then being written was busily appropriating for itself elements from other discourse modes outside the basic science-fiction battery: avant-garde fiction, poetry, journalism . . . That Russ's stories move from sword-and-sorcery to s-f and beyond puts them directly in the tradition of the s-f of its time that was so busily stepping over so many boundary lines. To put it in more high-flown, comp. lit. terms: In Russ's science fiction the privileges (i.e., the easy sureties) of one mode of discourse are subverted by employing signs from another mode—which cause us to reconstruct the discourse from one mode to the other: as soon as the story has fixed itself, by various signs, as sword-and-sorcery, new signs suddenly appear that cause us to take the whole thing apart in our head and put it back together again as s-f (this happens specifically in "The Barbarian"); or, as soon as we are settled with the idea that we are reading an s-f story, signs come along (as in "The Second Inquisition") that the story is psychological fantasy; and yet the moment we settle on this mode for our reading, other signs emerge that put us squarely back in s-f. These mental reconstructions do not represent confusion. They are organized so that they themselves become prime delights of the tale.

One set of such signs that the second reading of *Picnic on Paradise* clearly fixes is that every major incident in the novel is presaged by some passing thought, fear, or wish in Alyx's mind. If we were to read these presagements as strict s-f, they would send us off on what any sensible reader of the novel must agree is wild goose chases concerning clairvoyance or Alyx's possible strange mental powers that actually can effect the future. If, on the other hand, we were to read them as strict signs of psychological fantasy, then we would be thrown off on an equally wild chase about whether any of this was "really" happening: Perhaps, like the final illusion of Machine, it is *all* in Alyx's mind . . .

Of course these "presagements" are signs for neither one nor the other. They are not there for the second reading; they are there specifically for an ideal first, where the effect is to lend a rigorous, but subtle (yet nevertheless felt) psychological coherence to the book; their artful positioning *between* possible readings subverts the privileges of both modes and, by implication, posits a single field that, if not larger than both, is certainly larger than either.

That expansion is felt, by the sensitive reader, as a widening of the whole field.

Because of this and similar aesthetic rigors this very slender adventure novel was read by myself and a number of other writers as an incredibly liberating work for the s-f genre. It is a book which, after reading and rereading, has left me unable to think of writing quite so complacently as I had. And that is the highest compliment any writer can pay another.

MARILYN HACKER
From "Introduction"
The Female Man
1977, pp. xv–xxvii

*T*he Female Man* is (Russ's) third novel. In it, Janet Evason, a woman from Whileaway, a far future world technologically and ecologically superior to our own that is inhabited only by women, is transported to New York, 1969, in the course of her people's experiments in Probability Mechanics. She collects as companions Joanna, a woman of our time, and Jeannine Dadier, a woman from a parallel time-continuum (in which Hitler was thwarted, World War II never took place, and the Depression continues). After months as a goldfish-bowled celebrity/diplomat, she escapes notoriety and, with Jeannine and Joanna, takes up residence with a Typical American Small-Town Family. She is seduced by the brilliant teen-aged daughter. Just as Janet has collected Joanna and Jeannine, all

three of them are collected in turn by Jael Alice Reasoner, a woman from a different and more immediate future, in which the Sex War is a deadly shooting war. They learn about the similarity underlying their differences: they are genetically identical. They learn what effects their different and non-sequential worlds can have/have had on each other, and are offered the chance to act on this.

Russ has cited with approval a reader's description of the book's structure as "an inward-descending spiral."[1] Plot summary is difficult and eventually misleading. The novel is at least as much about each of the four protagonists in her own world, with her other "selves" and their worlds as resonating imaginative possibilities, as it is about their actual approach, meeting and interaction.

Russ began writing *The Female Man* in the spring of 1969, the year in which the "our-time" or "Joanna-time" episodes in the novel occur. It was completed in December 1971. 1969: Vietnam; Richard Nixon; My Lai; Kathleen Cleaver's green eyes, brown-gold Afro, and electric rhetoric; People's Park; Vietnam again; a 21-year-old Native American poet fasting in San Francisco's Grace Cathedral for a week in visceral protest at the killing and burning. (I was in San Francisco too, sharing an airy 8-room plant-filled flat with two gay men while doing theatrical productions and discussing poetry with others; effectively, I had no women friends.) 1969 had already seen published: Simone de Beauvoir's *The Second Sex* (1949); Betty Friedan's *The Feminine Mystique* (1963); Valerie Solanas' *The S.C.U.M. Manifesto* (1968); and Kate Millet's *Sexual Politics* (1969). ("Sex" was a ubiquitous word then; "woman" seems notably absent.) Not yet published: Shulamith Firestone's *The Dialectic of Sex* (1970); Germaine Greer's *The Female Eunuch* (1970); Phyllis Chesler's *Women and Madness* (1972); Judy Grahn's *A Woman Is Talking to Death* (1974); Jill Johnston's *Lesbian Nation* (1973); Piercy's *Small Changes*; Adrienne Rich's *Diving into the Wreck* (1973) and *Of Woman Born* (1976); anthologies unearthing and discovering women's poetry like *No More Masks* (1973) and *The World Split Open* (1974). Women's presses like Daughters Inc. and the Women's Press Collective were still unrealized ideas. The theoretical roots of feminism's second wave were dug in; we were only beginning to share the fruits. *The Female Man* is still in many ways a pre-feminist novel.

In January 1969, at Cornell University, where Joanna Russ was teaching English, there was a Feminist Intersession Colloquium: Kate Millett was there, along with Betty Friedan and others. Russ attended. She had also just recently read Ursula K. Le Guin's *The Left Hand of Darkness* (1969)

in which all the characters are humanoid hermaphrodites, and was wondering at the obduracy of the English language, in which everybody is "he" or "she" and "it" is reserved for typewriters. But how can one call a hermaphrodite "he," as Miss Le Guin does? I tried (in my head) changing all the masculine pronouns to feminine ones, and marvelled at the difference. . . . Weeks later the Daemon suddenly whispered "Katy drives like a maniac," and I found myself on Whileaway on a country road at night.[2]

That was the first sentence of "When It Changed," written in February 1969, first published in *Again Dangerous Visions* (1972), winner of the Nebula Award for Best Short Story in 1972. It is a first vision of Whileaway, and of Janet Evason, the first of *The Female Man*'s quaternity of protagonists.

Joanna, the third of the quaternity (in terms of her appearance in the novel), wrote the story's Afterword (I think she did, anyway) and began the four-way confrontation that is *The Female Man*. Joanna the novelistic-personage-to-be wrote:

> I also believe, like the villain of my story, that human beings are born with instincts (though fuzzy ones) and that being physically weaker than men and having babies makes a difference. But it makes less and less of a difference now. [3]

Joanna wrote:

> Resentment of the opposite sex . . . is something they (the Whileawayans) have yet to learn, thank God.
> Which is why I visit Whileaway—although I do not live there, because there are no men there [4]

And somebody asked, "Has anyone proposed the choice to you lately?" [5] Joanna Russ began to write the novel.

Between "When It Changed" and *The Female Man* quite a few things have happened. Notably the Earth-Whileaway balance of power has shifted. In "When It Changed" it is the Earth Men who invade Whileaway; the Whileawayans have no way to keep them out. *The Female Man* begins with Janet brought to Earth by Whileawayan probability mechanics—to an American 1969 without the ability to intrude on her world, or use it, as the Earth Man in "When It Changed" ominously hints, as a brood farm for the dwindling Earth genetic pool. (In *The Female Man* Janet also cheerfully explains to Jeannine why such an invasion would be well-nigh impossible. [6]) Here is Janet in "When It Changed," seeing male humans for the first time:

> They are bigger than we are. They are bigger and broader. Two were taller than me, and I am extremely tall, 1m, 80cm, in my bare feet. They are obviously of our species but *off*, indescribably off, and as my eyes could not and still cannot quite comprehend the lines of those alien bodies, I could not, then, bring myself to touch them. . . . He seemed to mean well, but I found myself shuddering back almost the length of the kitchen—and then I laughed apologetically—and then to set a good example (interstellar amity, I thought) did "shake hands" finally. A hard, hard hand. They are heavy as draft horses. Blurred, deep voices. [7]

And here is Janet in *The Female Man*, rather less impressed:

> What a strange woman; thick and thin, dried up, hefty in the back, with a grandmotherly moustache, a little one. How withered away one can be from a life of unremitting toil.
> *Aha! A man.*
> Shall I say my flesh crawled? Bad for vanity, but it did. This must be a man. I got off its desk. [8]

I had an initial impulse to see the novel as stacking the decks on the side of optimism, but in fact the story's speculation is at one greater remove: an all-female Good Society *and* a still male-dominated future Earth culture with the technology to invade it. The novel contrasts a fundamentally untransformed 1969 (somewhat schematized) with a Whileaway whose technological superiority is appropriate to its far-future setting, and two other continuing possible "thens".

"When It Changed" combines, in an expected way, two traditional science-fictional themes: the benign extraterrestrial civilization invaded, corrupted and / or destroyed by colonizing Earthlings, and the all-female or matriarchal culture reentered or redominated by (non-generic) Men. These last were, before, always a Bad Thing, of course: repressive, regimented, static, uncreative, modelled on the termite-colony or the boarding-school.

But the novel does something new: its four parallel worlds remain, essentially, parallel. They can instruct us, and each other, but the mechanics of any further macro-action are worked out after the final paragraph.

If "When It Changed" presages the destruction of a Utopia, *The Female Man* posits the Utopian possibility as an impetus to change in the present (a theme used again by Marge Piercy in *Woman at the Edge of Time*, a feminist SF novel not published as such). Russ began *The Female Man* because *her* Whileawayan component would not bow to tragic inevitability, would not be destroyed, and was not written out by a long shot. At first she brought Janet Evason "here," in part, she has said, [9] to reconcile her to a two-sexed world (where one sex, however, is Mankind, and the rest of us are—what? Extraterrestrials?). Janet, however, was not reconciled. She was *interested*—the way a doctoral candidate in anthropology is interested in her fieldwork among the Eskimos. And Joanna Russ became aware of Jeannine, and of the non-auctorial Joanna as participants in the proceedings, and of Jael. (Which of them had asked that inconvenient question?)

It is a truism that characters in novels are often manifestations of the novelist; literally, of course, they all are, however much they are "based" on Lytton Strachey or George Sand or the young man in the newspaper clipping on trial for shooting his mistress. [10] Most often, though auctorial sympathy and/or auctorial point of view, is vested in one subject/character/protagonist, with others cast as one sort of Object or another: antagonist, unattainable beloved, companion/chorus: Mary Crawford, Edmund Bertram and (to switch novels) Jane Bennet," for example. Sometimes they switch from one of those categories to another. If there is more than one point-of-view character (Dorothea and Lydgate in *Middlemarch*, Stephen Dedalus and Leopold Bloom in *Ulysses*, 1926), their intersection is either non-existent or, by definition, climactic. Virginia Woolf and Theodore Sturgeon are two novelists (among others) who have expanded the possibilities of multiple points of view.

Speculative fiction has provided the convention of two or more characters being distinct and yet nominally "the same"—one genotype in different time-continuums or historical periods, for example (explored to solipsistic vanishing point by Robert Heinlein in "All You Zombies," 1959). This *could* be taken as a metaphor for the aspect of internal dialogue implicit in fiction.

The Female Man more than admits to this aspect. It revels in it; it plays games with it; it thoroughly enjoys it. (No wonder the prevailing intellectual vice of Whileaway is solipsism!) There are four protagonists, completely different, equally "subject" and, at the same time, the same woman, changed—or parts of a gestalt. Their identity is not the punch-line or the "point"; *that* is their interplay, their actual and possible influence on each other, the vanishing point of their fusion. These things happen along with the novel, as the novel happens, in a way which conceivably surprised and delighted Russ as much as it does us. *The Female Man* reads like a fine contemporary poem, in that we readers have at least the illusion that the book was not plotted in advance to reach a foregone conclusion, with the points on the way charted and checked off—it invents itself as it goes along.

The Female Man shares with poetry, too, the use of verbal leitmotifs that weave among the four poles of consciousness and beyond: baby Janet's and baby Jeannine's first sentence, "See the Moon;" [12] and five-year-old Laura Rose's protest "I'm not a girl, I'm a genius!" echoed by seventeen-year-old Joanna 85 pages later. [13] (Aged eight, blazing with ego like an allergy, I pulled my knees and elbows into the eggshell and maroon

Eastburn Avenue upholstery and *knew* I would be . . . Michaelangelo, but more so; I had never heard the name of, for example, Artemisia Gentileschi—though her Esther at the Metropolitan Museum pleased my Baroque tastes.) (Laur is *not* Joanna, nor am I. . . .)

The J's identity is implicit in the verbal warp and woof; it is not made explicit until Jael, who has been only a voice-over or an undercurrent herself for the first seven of the novel's nine chapters, points it out. Our reaction is not "Oh, that explains it all." It is a reassessment of what these women are and what they might become, in terms of the possibilities that constrict or liberate them and of their new awareness of each other. No woman reading the book can entirely dissociate from herself the possibility or memory of being Jeannine, uncomfortable and downright painful as it is. But it is implied to us, perhaps for the first time, how Jeannine might (have) become someone else entirely, might become specifically Jael Alice Reasoner, the granddaughter of Causality, the trained assassin. A more conventional SF novel might have begun with Jeannine's assent to the Womanlanders using her world as a base, and ended with Jeannine the Victim becoming Jael the Avenger (and going elsewhen to recruit herself, ta-tum!)

But beyond these almost-bipolar two (because Jael lives for the Man in just as consuming a way as Jeannine does) is Janet, woman-identified by definition, and complete:

> whom we don't believe in and whom we deride but who is in secret our savior from utter despair. . . . the Might-be of our dreams, living as she does in a blessedness none of us will ever know, she is none-theless Everywoman. [14]

in whose behalf the delight and imaginative leaps and intellectual playfulness and sheer cussedness of one of the most agreeable (to a woman reader, anyway) Utopias extant were created.

Of course the J's are something else besides a variation on a chromosomal theme. They are four discrete women, but they are also, like figures in a medieval exemplum of the soul's life-journey, components of the whole of one even more complex woman:

> It's an attempt to get my head together—literally, in the novel, where there are at least four women with one head apiece, none of whom is a whole woman until they finally do get together . . . for Thanksgiving dinner. [15]

Russ has said that the four J's add up to the book's "Joanna," which is why there is so much less back- and foreground information about her than about the other three. (In fact, the information is *there*, but in throwaway lines rather than in the straight novelistic background fill-in given Jeannine, or the back-and-forth illumination—like a chapter out of *Medieval People* (Eileen Power, 1963)—of Janet *and* her world in the first section. Joanna is a thirty-five-year-old professor of English. She has a car. She was a precocious child. She had a husband. In a very different continuum, it is she who, considerably less self-assured than Janet, makes another break through Probability and makes love with Laura Rose.)

I think the four, Joanna included, add up to more: to the possibility of a woman whose wholeness and scope are indeed "speculative," a Joanna who acknowledges who she has been, who and where she is, and thus has knowledge and control of what she can become.

If the four are also one-in-four, what (besides very well-conceived science-fictional constructs) are their four worlds?

The worlds in *The Female Man* are not futures; they are here and now writ large. . . . A flat statement of it would be that Jeannine's world is the past (but still very much present); that Janet's world is a kind of ideal (into which I put all sorts of quirky things I happen to like, like public comic statuary); and that Jael's world is here-and-now carried to its logical extreme. Joanna keeps running from one to the other. Janet's world is the potential one, not Jael's. I've been asked why there are no men in Whileaway, and my only answer is that I tried but the Whileawayans wouldn't let me.

I can't imagine a two-sexed egalitarian society and I don't believe anyone else can, either. . . . Well, here you have the whole thing about SF. Where else could one even try out such visions? Yet in the end we will have to have models for the real thing, and I can find none yet, and that is why Whileaway is single-sexed. [16]

(Subsequent to *The Female Man*, at least three well-considered novelistic attempts at "a two-sexed egalitarian society" were made, fictions in which the elimination of sexual bias and prescribed gender roles are shown to have been intrinsic to a Good Society's formation: Ursula K. Le Guin's *The Dispossessed* (1974), Samuel R. Delany's *Triton* (1976), and Marge Piercy's *Woman on the Edge of Time* (1976). All three writers are, not surprisingly, acquainted and in correspondence with Russ, early readers of *The Female Man*. In my opinion, Le Guin's novel, whatever its intention, still *shows* a male-dominated and male-defined world (from which the male protagonist quickly travels to an openly sexist one). In *Triton*, the society's possibilities are revealed through the point of view of a closet sexist who can't take the pace. And in Piercy's novel, the Good Place's existence is posited as tentative: that future could wink out if someone Here and Now Doesn't Do Something Fast. It *is* hard to imagine, if you aren't imagining from a privileged-class point of view. [17]

If the center of *The Female Man* is an exchange among four women who are one woman (or, *a woman making herself up* in a way that does not imply Elizabeth Arden) who else is there? Many of the book's encounters involve characters who are personifications, in the manner of the figures in medieval tales. (In "What Can a Heroine Do," Russ cites Darko Suvin's suggestion of a resemblance between SF patterns and those of medieval literature, and elaborates on it. [18] Some of SF's best editors are medievalists!) Scenes in both Jael's world and Joanna's utilize these, not as lay-figures filling up the stage, but as the brightly or darkly costumed entities of a morality play—e.g., the party scene in Part Three, [19] whose verisimilitude I questioned until my job necessitated attending academic parties, and Jael's entire excursion into Manland with the other three J's, [20] culminating in murder.

Jeannine's world and Janet's, in contrast, are populated by multi-sided characters with names and implied histories. But there are two characters who exist on the same reality-level as the central J's, and who weave through the book in different permutations: Laura Rose and Cal.

Laur's presence in the book is too intricate and rich to have to elaborate. We see her in action, aspiration and repose: she has purpose, she has habits, she has gratuity which could also be called grace. We know her fantasies, her wardrobe, her mathematics, the texture of the nape of her neck.

We are certainly not given Cal with the same loving plenitude of detail. But he is pervasively present, too, and his presence gives the book one aspect of its depth. Cal is the man as victim, a male human being as much depleted by roles and their implications as Jeannine, his female counterpart. (He may not be as limited in his economic possibilities; although the positing of an attenuated Depression in his and Jeannine's world equalizes this somewhat as well.) His uncomprehension of Jeannine (we take her word for this) is matched by hers of him:

> Sometimes—*sometimes*—he likes to get *dressed up*. He gets into the drapes like a sarong and puts on all my necklaces around his neck, and stands there with the curtain rod for a spear. He wants to be an actor, you know. But I think there's something wrong with him. Is it what they call transvestism?
> JOANNA: No, Jeannine.[21]

She can't deal with his not (by her definition) Being A Man as much as she is obliged by him to Be A Woman.

There are in fact no actual scenes *with* Cal in the book—he is expected, remembered, talked about, telephoned, but not present. Yet he is "real" and not a lay-figure brought on to illustrate a point. A student in an SF seminar, when asked "What happens to Jeannine?" replied "She marries Cal." He was mostly adhering to easy expectations, but he was not *entirely* wrong-headed. There is the undercurrent of another reality in the book, where a different or composite "J" did marry Cal; perhaps the woman who later, not a Whileawayan, becomes Laura Rose's friend and lover.

Referring back to an earlier point: there are two possible figures that do *not* appear in *The Female Man*, either as full-scale characters or exemplary figures: a feminist and a Lesbian. Janet is *not* a Lesbian by any contemporary definition: her sexuality is, on her world, the norm, and indeed the only possible orientation. (If she had a preference for much younger, or much older, women, she would be a deviant from Whileaway's norm: this is the source of her mental anguish about her attraction to Laur.) And the novel's Joanna is not a feminist—yet. It is not an alternative that occurs to her; it is certainly not an alternative presented to her by anyone who *is*. That will, perhaps, be a result of her having become a Female Man, a self-transformation that happened in isolation. The next step will have to involve others.

The title of "When It Changed" implies the story's continuation: Whileaway *was* only For-A-While. The whole subtle or blatant nightmare of male domination will resume; perhaps a war will be fought, and lost, to stave it off. What happens at the end of *The Female Man* though? Everything. Nothing. Jeannine marries Cal. Jeannine does *not* marry Cal, and lets the Womanlanders use her world as a base of operations. Joanna and Jeannine visit Whileaway. Joanna becomes a feminist. Joanna becomes a Female Man. Janet goes back to Whileaway. Jael becomes Jeannine's mentor. Some of these things happen *in* the book, although strictly speaking they would happen after its conclusion. What happens after a line spirals to vanishing point? It spirals out again.

There are almost no completed internal or what I would call macro-actions in the book. (Completed external and specific ones there certainly are: a bone-crushing fight, a proposal of marriage, a story told to a grown-up by an eight-year-old, a trans-temporal teleportation, three-and-a-half sex scenes, a murder.) On the large scale, everything continues, and is explored through multiple probabilities. Thus the philosopher Dunyasha Bernadetteson (one of Russ' most engaging creations) can comment on the aim of Laura Rose's girlish yearnings ("Power!"),[22] although in the chronicle of Whileaway she died four hundred years before Janet Evason

visited Earth. Thus, though Joanna never visits Whileaway, she has a tale made up for and about her by a Whileawayan child; though she never visits Jeannine's world, she is stared at for her peculiar garments there on an interminable El ride.

The novel does not have the story's pessimistic conclusion, but it doesn't end with an optimistic conclusion, or a quick reconciliation of opposites, either. Its events reverberate in the reader's mind, setting off possibilities, just as the four protagonists reverberate in each other's. That is one of the reasons I have wanted to read *The Female Man* again and again; and I've found new focuses and new pleasures at each reading. Though I do not assume every new reader will automatically share the novel's premises, I think even those who do not will make discoveries, and ask new questions.

> In the end, *The Female Man* came over as possibly the only kind of propaganda there can be: either a celebration (to those who agree) or a construct which *forces* you through a certain cluster of experiences and states of mind. If you do not agree with the assumptions underlying the "portrait" of this experience, reading the book will be torture and it will make you very angry, but perhaps the only propaganda there can be for a forbidden feeling or belief or existence is simply to present it. . . .[23]

Notes

1. Joanna Russ, quoted in "Reflections on Science Fiction: An Interview with Joanna Russ," in *Quest, a feminist quarterly*, 2, i (Summer 1975), 45.
2. Joanna Russ, "Afterword" to "When It Changed," *Again, Dangerous Visions*, ed. Harlan Ellison (New York: Signet Books, 1972), p. 280–81.
3. Russ, "Afterword," p. 281.
4. Russ, "Afterword," p. 281.
5. *The Female Man* (New York: Bantam Books, 1975), p. 86.
6. *The Female Man*, p. 90–92.
7. "When It Changed," p. 273.
8. *The Female Man*, p. 22.
9. From personal communication between Russ and Hacker.
10. As are characters in Virginia Woolf's *The Waves* (1931), Honoré de Balzac's *Beatrice* (1840), and Stendahl's *Le Rouge et le noir* (1826).
11. In Jane Austen's *Mansfield Park* (1815) and *Pride and Prejudice* (1813), respectively.
12. *The Female Man*, p. 111.
13. *The Female Man*, p. 65 and p. 150.
14. *The Female Man*, p. 212–13.
15. Russ, quoted in *Quest* interview, p. 43.
16. Russ, quoted in *Quest* interview, pp. 46–47.
17. Thomas M. Disch's *334* (New York: Avon Books, 1974; Boston: Gregg Press, 1976) also depicts an egalitarian society, one in which hetero- and homosexuality are equally open and socially acceptable life choices. The society is by no means a utopia; in fact, it has many dystopian aspects—the fictional extensions of present-day overcrowding, wastefulness with natural resources, ubiquity and depersonalization of institutionalized social services—but, unlike some other novelists, Disch does not present sexual equality and freedom of sexual preference as illustrations of How Bad Things Are; they are among the society's redeeming features.
18. Russ, "What Can a Heroine Do, or Why Women Can't Write," in Susan K. Cornillon, ed., *Images of Women in Fiction: Feminist Perspectives* (Bowling Green, Ohio: Bowling Green University Popular Press, 1973), p. 18.
19. *The Female Man*, pp. 33–47.
20. *The Female Man*, pp. 165–84.
21. *The Female Man*, p. 85.
22. *The Female Man*, p. 68.
23. Russ, quoted in *Quest* interview, p. 43.

JEAN TOBIN
"Introduction"
We Who Are About To . . .
1978, pp. v–xxvi

One of two reasons for desert isolation in our common literature is, paradoxically, shipwreck. It's responsible for experiences like those (modelled on the real misfortunes of a Scottish sailor called Selkirk in 1704–9) of Daniel Defoe's classic survivor, the matter-of-fact hero of the *Strange Surprising Adventures of Robinson Crusoe* (1719). Others have since followed Crusoe and his man Friday's footprints, among them not only the members of Johann Wyss' *The Swiss Family Robinson* (1813), most familiar to children, but also the castaway crews and passengers of countless spaceships. Shipwreck or spaceship wreck, the scene remains the same. "The idyllic desert island," muses the unnamed narrator of Joanna Russ's fourth novel, *We Who Are About To . . .* ; "Odd how that started out 'deserted' and ended up 'desert.' Hence the conventional sand and palm trees" (p. 62). On this 11th day after being cast onto a "tagged" planet in the company of seven others, she continues by informing her vocoder, "No, 'desert' once meant only wild," then pauses, then bleakly adds, "That it is." She herself is aware of the familiar plot, and when all the others are dead, mocks it: "Had a fit of the giggles (Elaine On Desert Island—of which there are none on Earth that do not contain resort hotels—her 3-D viewer, her burning glass, her resourcefulness, ages eight to twelve.) . . . I didn't start a fire with my lighter, no need, though Elaine had a pocket lighter" (p. 105). The year is about 2040, and the literature—trash and otherwise—has increased.

The second common reason lends itself to no popular plot. Desert isolation in our literature, if not due to accident, is self-imposed. At times it is merely the misanthropic privacy of the recluse (the unnamed narrator once says she feels like the "Old Herb Lady who lives in the cave", p. 163). More often it is the solitude of the fasting hermit (ἐρῆμος, desert) or anchorite (ἀναχωρέω, to withdraw into solitude) seeking spiritual enlightenment. The prophet Elias and St. John the Baptist dwelt in the desert, and for 40 days Christ fasted there, but the idea of the anchorite life began with St. Antony, who entered the Egyptian desert at Pispir in 285 and moved on to wild Thebaid when Pispir filled up with followers. St. Paul of Thebes, who in fear of persecution fled into the desert earlier, and stayed in a splendid cave with a stream, eventually greeted Antony: "tell me, I pray thee, how fares the human race: if new roofs be risen in the ancient cities, whose empire is it that now sways the world . . ."[1] St. Ammon, the competitive Macarius of Alexandria, Hilarion of Palestine, St. Simeon the Stylite (who lived on a 30-foot pillar until he died about 459), and St. Basil were among the most notable of thousands who thereafter became ascetics in the desert. The Desert Fathers were a phenomenon particularly in the fourth century, and in Egypt, Palestine, and northern Syria, the desert became crowded: "In the valley of Nitria, as at Pispir, the monks dwelt in separate cells. . . . Very impressive must have been the sight of all the cells in tiers upon the sides of the valley and the sound of the chanting of Psalms proceeding from them morning and night."[2] Eventually the narrator of *We Who Are About To . . .* enjoys a similar concert when she contemplates the valley while sitting before her cave, complete with running water. She uses the conventional image when, having set about to deliberately starve herself to death, she tells the

vocoder, "Just realized: I am fasting like a Desert Father, so in a few days I'll have hallucinations anyway" (p. 108). Her choice of slow suicide has spiritual intent; early, she talked about the Northmen; who "used to say Deliver us from fire, plague, the fury of the Northmen, *and sudden death*. Those crazy people who took months to die. They had things to think about" (p. 27). A self-styled neo-Christian, she would give herself more time than those early Christians whose dying— like that of the gladiators who shouted, "Caesar, we who are about to die salute you!—was entertainment for both powerful and populace. She, like an honorable Roman, would practice *ars moriendi*, the art of dying.

Uncommonly, Joanna Russ uses both common reasons for desert isolation in the same book. This is daring. The thrusts of the two kinds of stories are opposed. They may even demand different styles of writing. On the desert island, for example, the emphasis is on practical survival. It may be an isle in the South Pacific or a planet seen, as noted science fiction critic, Robert Scholes describes Earth, to be "a speck-sized island of life in a vast cosmos of man-killing emptiness": this makes no difference.[3] Man's needs are primarily material, and much common sense and practical ingenuity go toward meeting them. Necessities and small comforts taken care of, possession increases, as survival becomes conquest. The plot goes, with few alterations, as accident, exploration, adaptation, colonization—the sort of activity the narrator sums up as "running into the brush yelling Colonize, Colonize, and all that" (p. 150).

Frequently values are found which would make leaving the island, whether south sea or spacial, faintly regrettable upon rescue. Usually the style of narration is objective, dry, matter-of-fact—a convenient style particularly for adventure stories and science fiction told in the first person. As Virginia Woolf points out when speaking of *Robinson Crusoe*, shortly into the narrative "we are swallowing monsters that we should have jibbed at if they had been offered us by an imaginative and flamboyant traveller. But anything that this sturdy middle-class man notices can be taken for a fact."[4] In contrast, in deliberately fasting in the desert, the emphasis is on spiritual enlightenment. Comforts and necessities alike are relinquished in hopes of intangible visions. The thrust here is toward progressively stripping down, down to a bareness, a total lack of possession. In giving up all material things, the seeker anticipates and prepares for death, in which one loses all. Thus he hopes for understanding, for grace, for God. The language needed here is not factual, but rather a language Woolf considered able to express the inexpressible, a poetic, even visionary language. Further, not only the vision, but the mind of the visionary must be shown.

In Russ's *We Who Are About To . . .* , interestingly, the narrator follows the fasting father pattern; the other seven survivors follow the colonizer pattern. They thus are in conflict. Discussing this matter further means briefly describing what happens: it seems fair to warn readers who prefer their plots pristine to turn now to the text—if they incautiously haven't already done so—to enjoy adventure before attending to further analysis and introduction.

Along colonizer-fasting father lines, the book effectively splits in half: the first part action, the second part reaction, or evaluation. In the first half, the narrator sardonically describes the first 12 days on the tagged planet, with "everybody running around cheerily into the Upper Paleolithic" (p. 20). Thus on day first, Valeria "Victrix" Graham and Victor Graham, a middleaged, unloving, formerly rich couple, venture outside the airlock to test the atmosphere: "Joy all around" (p. 18) is the narrator's laconic remark at their safe return. That night all go outside to find out where they are, but only confirm their castaway status: "there was almost nothing in the sky: a few bright stars near the zenith and halfway to the equatorial horizon a far, faint, dim blue. Island universes." (p. 19) Day two they plan to look for water; they find it on day four. By that time they've already held a meeting to discuss colonization, and have arranged a schedule of mating to best utilize the available gene pool. And so it continues, as they deal with practicalities, until day twelve, which finds them building a communal house. On that day, in this tale of survival and conquest, the man called Victor, ironically, is the first to die. About a week later, five others are murdered, and the seventh survivor commits suicide. That leaves the narrator.

In the second half of the book, as the narrator lengthens her fast, day by unnoted day, the narrative moves increasingly away from objective recounting of present events to subjective recall of past ones. Gradually she begins to clarify just what in the 21st century might have happened to a nice idealistic young woman, who once tried politics to create a new mundane world and neo-Christianity to create a new spiritual world, to make her capable of an act one ectoplasmic visitor terms "pocket genocide": "Probably the only person in history to depopulate a planet so easily" (p. 152). Ironically for a spiritual seeker, when finally she begins to hallucinate, rather than receiving the expected message that "God is love," she hears blunt words: "God hates you." (p. 153). Thus lacking assurance of boundless love from a God she doesn't believe in anyway, she tells the vocoder, "The neo-Christian theory of love is this: There is little of it. Use it where it's effective." (p. 159). At the very end, however, after she has reevaluated the people who came with her to the tagged planet and remembered the people who were most important to her years before, she is accorded grace of a kind. A musicologist on lecture tour, she recorded her major loss in the first vocoder entry: "O God, I miss my music." (p. 9). Now she records its return: "Bach from the hills and bushes and when I looked into the blazing blue sky, Handel. Very appropriate." (p. 163).

Although it is tempting to accept the narrator's early assessment of herself as one who wants merely "to get right in my soul before I die" (p. 75), the fact that she kills to achieve this end in itself makes her an atypical and untrustworthy "Desert Father." The fourth century ascetics were renowned for "their humility, their gentleness, their heart-breaking courtesy that was the seal of their sanctity . . . far beyond abstinence." Moreover, the narrator, although indeed set on suicide by starvation, is paradoxically as intent upon survival, in her own way, as any of the others. "Prisoners and political exiles write books," she says; "Would you write a book if you were alone on a desert island? Would you scratch in the sand?" (p. 34). Her vocoder diary, a solipsistic form that suits her well, is meant to ensure her continued presence in the universe. Occasionally she speculates despairingly about an eventual audience: "Nobody will find this any way or they'll have flippers so who cares" (p. 113). But she makes painstaking provisions for her vocoder and its printouts, eventually putting the latter in a metal box, and even preparing to die nearby as a precautionary measure: "And I have to be near the box or you won't find it. Whoever you are." (p. 169). The problem with any first person vocoder printout in diary form, however, is that we have only the narrator's view of reality, and further, that the day-by-day format allows no perspective on events other than the reader's. Thus we wonder if the narrator is reliable, particularly when none of her companions find her so. We wonder if she's twisting her account of events in order

to be judged more favorably in the future by her dear flippered readers. And who is she?

She's Nobody. In contrast to Robinson Crusoe, who is a sort of Everyman, representative of our human will to survive, the neo-Christian, unnamed narrator prefers to be regarded as Nobody. Unlike the trusted Robinson Crusoe, who in measured sentences begins his narrative at the beginning ("I was born in the year 1632, in the city of York, of a good family, though not of the country. . . .") the narrator permits herself to reveal some scattered but significant personal information only when she's greatly weakened by fasting. Even then, although she's very frail and hallucinating frequently, and although there's no real possibility of discovery until a routine check of tagged planets perhaps some 80 years in the future, she still stops to consider, and erase, incautious remarks. Much, certainly, she has not allowed even herself to remember. Thus, it's with some difficulty that one pieces together the story of Nobody's life.

The narrator's three references to childhood show her to have been an intelligent girl, with a precocious ability to cut through cultural cliches: "Send it to them," (p. 140) she said at seven, pushing her bowl of unshippable soup over to the adult who had reminded her of starving people. Briefly, she portrays herself as an inhibited, "very old-fashioned" adolescent, who increasingly wrapped herself up in intelligence. She neglects to tell anything about her early 20s, when presumably she finished college, but we learn that during the 2020s the world discovered hydrogen fusion, making a limited number of people rich and giving "a new lease on life" to capitalism by providing unlimited power. Sometime during her life Nobody watched her father die; some year during her life she worked in the "terminal counseling end" of a San Francisco hospital. Between the ages of 26 and 31, she experienced what seem to be the two most important events of her life. At 26, she joined a radical political group called the Populars, already a "travelling symposium" by that time, and spent the next year lecturing to university groups. Then, she records, "in some inexplicable way the tide turned against us (although the media had never picked us up) and one night I heard a sound from the audience . . . an ominous, slowly-rising roar . . . it occurred to me that they were after me—me, who had never harmed them!—and then I ran" (p. 115ff). Her decision to quit was "absolute, inflexible, and somehow automatic," (p. 123) and she never found out what happened to her friends. When she was 30 and attending graduate school, she fell deeply in love with a tuba-playing classmate, L. B. Hook. With her involvement, he founded neo-Christianity; the movement was ineffectual enough to be exploited by the press, and she left. The next 12 years seem to have been spent in self-hatred: "Foundations pay me to lecture on music and play tapes of it: that's why I travel. I'm a scrounge" (p. 12).

Even in greater detail, however, the pieced-together biography possible from vocoder printouts does not suffice to explain how the narrator developed certain skills. She is shown to be a capable orator, even though ineffectual on the tagged planet ("wrong rabble, wrong rouse"), and one knows she learned much while speaking for the Populars. She is shown to be knowledgeable about the "whole pharmacopoeia" she carries; her possession is explained by theft, her knowledge by the year in terminal counseling. But she also, like the government trainee, Nathalie, recognizes the pieces of a partially constructed "broom," a single-passenger hovercraft; Nathalie responds with a "glance of shock, of wild surmise— *are you one, too?*" (p. 15). Again, like only Nathalie, Nobody has access to crew records on passengers for what appears to be a commercial flight. She possesses a weapon designed for concealment; in contrast, rich Valeria and poor Cassie alike have no knowledge of guns, although probably Nathalie also conceals a weapon. Significantly, Nobody knows tricks of personal defense which Nathalie could be expected to know only if she'd been coming *from* government training. Moreover, Nobody hints at knowledge while speculating about "mirror-sister" Nathalie:

> I almost said to her once, aboard ship, 'Wait a few years, you won't be so eager.' But she was, desperate with her unbearable hatred of civilians, barely able to control herself until she could pass over into that other, real world.
> What would she have done if there'd been no accident? If she'd got there—and trained—and flunked?
> Become a music lecturer. Of course. (p. 133).

The very faint suspicion that Nobody betrayed her cause so fully as to train, even unsuccessfully, with the other side can neither be proven nor disproven, for needed information is deliberately withheld. Importantly, however, it does attest to the complexity of the character Joanna Russ has created. Russ encourages such careful speculation by providing mere indications of possible responses and motivations. For example, Nobody comments about her instantaneous decision to quit the Populars,

> I wasn't angry. I wasn't even afraid. I was, in fact, in some odd way, rather pleased with myself. I knew, of course, that the tide turning against us wasn't "inexplicable" but I didn't care as the others did; I only wondered how they did it, exactly. And who "they" were. And admired them. And thought I'd like to meet them, if I could, and find out what they were really up to. (p. 123).

Her next line, "Never will of course," is purposely ambiguous. In Nobody, Joanna Russ clearly has not created a heroine who can be dismissed in easy admiration.

Describing *We Who Are About To . . .* , Marilyn Hacker writes: "Baldly—it is a bald book—it is about failure and death."[5] Readers are accustomed to women who lose in literature, so when one encounters a woman like Nobody, who is smart, skilled, aggressive, and purposeful, one wants to believe she's a winner. For that reason, the extent of Nobody's failure and self-betrayal can more easily be seen and more fairly assessed by measuring her at length against another female former revolutionary who is about to die. In Ursula K. Le Guin's "The Day Before the Revolution," for example, Laia, renowned as Odo, regards herself as "a drooling old woman who had started a world revolution"; in *The Dispossessed* (1974), seven generations later, her writings are revered by the Odonions whose forebears left Urras to create on Anarres the anarchic utopian society she envisioned. Both women face their deaths with fortitude and humor; Laia has the advantage here of certitude: "To die was merely to go on in another direction." Both women, in facing their deaths, also regret not being in the center of history and of life. Laia, for example, feeling "really out of it," cannot share the excitement of coming revolution: "It's not easy, she said to herself in justification, laboriously climbing the stairs, to accept being out of it when you've been in it, in the center of it, for fifty years. Oh for God's love. Whining!"[6] Nobody places herself "on the periphery now . . . Outside the outside of the outside" and later she decides, "it's a bore, a dreadful bore, being outside history." In contrast to Laia, however, she wasn't inside very long: "I got arrested and was in jail overnight but I

certainly wasn't at the center of it" (p. 32). Long before she was cast onto the tagged planet, her placement outside history was a matter of choice:

> . . . they still thought they were *at the center.* You have to think that or die. Either you limit what you think about and who you think about (the commonest method) or you start raising a ruckus about being outside and wanting to get inside (then they try to kill you) or you say piously that God puts everybody on the inside (then they love you) or you become crazed in some way. Not insane but flawed . . .
> So I say Hey, if you're going to send mobs against me, I'll change what I say; I'll say God puts everybody on the inside . . . and I zipped like lightning back to the edge of the board. (p. 118).

Notably, Laia and Nobody often mean different things by "inside" and "at the center." Laia is speaking of revolutionary activity which will alter her world. Nobody often is talking about the existing power structure, which seems to be government but in actuality may be "big science," a technology which no longer has use for civilians. John Ude points out Nobody's hypocrisy on day six: "'Hear you were quite big in that power and planning stuff about fifteen years back.'" Lying perhaps even to herself, Nobody at that time replies: "'Then you heard wrong. I walked out one day and gave it all up. Hideously ineffectual.'" (p. 47). Late in her fast, she acknowledges the lie: "If the media ignored something as big as the Pops (and other such, as I found out later), it wasn't because we were dull; it's because we were dangerous" (p. 122).

In contrast to Laia, Nobody has betrayed her beliefs, her friends, her work, her life, her self, and feels betrayed by her love. Acknowledging herself to be someone who chose the third alternative, someone who says "God puts everybody on the inside," she clearly is also someone who has suffered the fourth alternative: she has become "not insane but flawed deep down somehow, like a badly-fired pot that breaks when you take it out of the kiln and the cold air hits it. Desperate." (p. 118). (With a touch of sardonic humor, Russ has even made Nobody a person who is easily chilled, and so remembers her many years of lecture touring as a period of continually running out of Interferogen and thus continually catching cold.) Continuing to measure her against the doughty old revolutionary, one discovers that Laia was willing to suffer for her beliefs, and Nobody was not. Nobody ran from danger as a Popular and kept on running. Unlike Laia, who spent fifteen years in jail, nine of them in the cell in Drio where she learned of the death of her husband among the Fourteen Hundred, Nobody was imprisoned one night. As a neo-Christian, she and three others were arrested in a city park and locked overnight in a carousel storage shed; she sums up the experience: "jail . . . that was a lark" (p. 116). Even endlessly in the cell in Drio, Laia knew what had happened to her friend and where they were, and on the morning of her death she still knows: "They had all used to be in jail. One laughed about it in those days, all the friends in all the jails. But they weren't even there, these days. They were in the prison cemeteries. Or in the common graves."[7] As a member of the Populars, Nobody, justifiably terrified when her large audience became angry mob, walked off the stage, then ran, and from cowardice or censorship—it's never made certain—completely lost contact: "Don't know what happened to my friends" (p. 126).

The two women also differ significantly in their response to the demands of work. While in the Fort in Drio, for example, Laia wrote *The Prison Letters* and the whole *Analogy*; she remembers that time with an old woman's toughness:

"How brave of you to go on, to work, to write, in prison, after such a defeat for the Movement, after your partner's death, people had used to say. Damn fools. What else had there been to do?"[8] Now, surrounded by young friends, visited by young admirers from around her world, Laia still works hard at the only work she can still do after suffering a stroke—her writing. In contrast, then and now, Nobody didn't go on. The shadow of John Ude reproves her timidity in giving up the Populars and becoming a neo-Christian: "God is easier than guns." Her own word for herself, put in ectoplasmic Alan's mouth, is "killer-coward." She tells the vocoder who is now her only friend that her politics had been "Communism and share-the-work." Early she envied technocrats and despised herself and the exiled passengers as "the new irrelevants: parasites, scum, proles, scroungers. People who do nothing real. . . . Stranded dinosaurs." (p. 13). In the first part of the book she oftens watches the other passengers dig the foundations of a communal house while, incapacitated by bad ankles, she plays cards with 12-year-old Lori.

Nobody's spiritual poverty can be seen clearly when placed against Laia's rich sense of fulfilment. On the day of her death, the old revolutionary has earned her knowledge of exactly who she was, who she is, and where she is now:

> She was the little girl with scabby knees, sitting on the doorstep staring down through the dirty golden haze of River Street in the heat of late summer, the six-year-old, the sixteen-year-old, the fierce, cross, dream-ridden girl, untouched, untouchable. She was herself. Indeed she had been the tireless worker and thinker, but a bloodclot in a vein had taken that woman away from her. Indeed she had been the lover, the swimmer in the midst of life, but Taviri, dying, had taken that woman away with him. There was nothing left, really, but the foundation. She had come home; she had never left home. "True voyage is return." Dust and mud and a doorstep in the slums.

Having dreamed that morning of Taviri, Laia reproves herself for a brief waking moment of sentimental weakness, but with full assurance still of shared love: "Of course she hadn't forgotten him. These things go without saying between husband and wife."[9] In contrast, the homeless woman who tersely describes herself as "myself. Which is nothing and nobody," hallucinates a similar visit from the man she deeply loved, and instead screams out her hurt and sense of betrayal: "You never loved me, never, you only pretended and then you fake things up because you know it wasn't like that and it's all just to destroy me!" (p. 152). Clearly, no one can condemn the disillusioned, despairing Nobody more than she does herself. As Marilyn Hacker points out, "The narrator . . . is . . . a failure in terms of her own life and beliefs: something which some readers, who see her as a sort of feminist avenging angel (she is none of those things) do not notice."[10]

Ironically, Nobody, an exile on an empty planet, is equally as identified with place as the revolutionary Laia, who sits on a dirty doorstep facing the open market called the Temeba and knows she has never left home. Gradually the desert planet becomes metaphor for the narrator. The desert is of the sort she thinks about, "Death Valley . . . in August," not a spring desert in full bloom. It is as sterile, barren, life-denying, death-dealing, as she is. People are hungry in the desert; it feeds no one. She herself, she finally admits, has been "unhumanly hungry and starved for years, as nasty as a starved rat" (p. 154). Her hunger, of course, is not merely physical.

Using the configuration of the neo-Christian quartered circle, shadow-Nathalie taunts her:

> When you were born, there was no real place for you, no one was fond of you, not really, . . . so you took the whole world on your back and put yourself in the center of it and said it's mine and said I'm going to get everything and I'm going to change everything. And when it didn't work you ran away, and when that didn't work you started starving yourself to death but slowly, slowly, with lectures you didn't like and friends you didn't know any more and when that didn't work you wanted to die . . . (p. 146ff).

Spiritually as dry as the empty desert, the narrator has denied the needs of others. Twelve years after being kept awake by baby sparrows screaming for food, she dreams of them again. She told L. B. at that time they couldn't be killed just because they were keeping her from sleeping: "You don't want to murder a whole bunch of helpless little cutey baby birds, now do you? . . . Elbee, have respect for the sanctity of life. . . . hey, Elbee, what would you do if it was people" (p. 156ff). Now, after killing her companions because they were keeping her from dying, she identifies the sparrows with "Nathalie, Alan, Val, & Co., all fledglings in a nest, all flopping about and squeeching like mad: oh feed, feed, feed! Agree! Agree! Agree!" (p. 159). During her fast, she can finally see the real despair of her companions, as L. B. reproves her: "You assumed, of course, that they ought to adapt to you; it never occurred to you that you ought to adapt to them. You simply didn't like them" (p. 151). Having destroyed her companions, the narrator fully deserves the emptiness of the desert planet. "Exiled to this place?" shadow-Nathalie tells her scornfully; "It was made for you; if it hadn't existed, you would have created it" (p. 146).

Long into her fast, the narrator thinks not only about the physical Death Valley, but also about the metaphysical valley of the shadow of death: "The people who walk in darkness, those who dwell in the land of the shadow of death," she explains, "they all do a lot of crying" (p. 165). Wondering about her own death, she recalls a night at the hospital after her friend Marilyn's daughter died and Marilyn herself was critically injured: the narrator saw a figure then "standing between two rooms, a lit one and a dark one, but they were both empty" (p. 167). The dark empty room is of course death, feared as much as the total loneliness of total darkness on the tagged planet under only the Smudge at night. The lighted empty room the narrator later associates with her own life: "Odd to look back . . . I don't suppose I did better with the room than most or worse or whatever. I mean if they make you rent it unfurnished, you see" (p. 168). She also associated it with her desert planet: "The splendid sun out there, lighting up the world. The lit room. The empty room" (p. 168). Eventually one sees that all the images of the narrator's life have the same components. They are flat bare illuminated places, empty of all others. Thus she tells her vocoder: "I had a dream full of echoes: I was standing alone on an empty stage, under one spotlight, singing with immense power and elan: When I'm calling you-hoo-hoo-hoo-hoo-hoo-hoo" (p. 106ff). The dream, of course, is transposed from memories, later recalled during the daytime: "I remember quite vividly standing on the platform and being able to see nothing but the light cage in the back of the hall, wondering if the bored looking person in it would turn the lights off me and on to the audience because if you do that, they can sometimes be diverted into smashing the lights, at least for a while" (p. 126). The elements of the desert experience are all contained within that single traumatic episode: flat emptiness, relentless light, loneliness, a desperate wish for true communication. In truth, she's never been able to run away from that moment: possibly it's determined her actions for years. All the world's a stage, but she's alone on that stage. She's now alone on an empty desert, on an empty planet, itself an island alone in empty space. She *is* her desert island. Student of the past up to the Baroque, even the name John Ude reminds her of John Donne, but as she shores up fragments against her ruins at the end of the vocoder printout, she omits his well-known words on death: "No man is an Iland, intire of it selfe; every man is a peece of the Continent, a part of the maine; if a Clod bee washed away by the Sea, Europe is the less, as well as if a Promontorie were, . . . any mans death diminishes me, because I am involved in Mankinde; And therefore never send to know for whom the bell tolls; It tolls for thee."[11] Nor does she quote the beginning of the song based on Donne's words:

No man is an island . . .
No man dies alone.

All this, however, has served to simplify a complex character, and Nobody will allow no one that intellectual comfort. "The crucial question about the feminism of a work," Joanna Russ stated, in an interview given to *Quest* at about the time portions of *We Who Are About To* . . . first appeared in *Galaxy Magazine*, "is not whether the women in it are strong and independent . . . but whether the assumptions underlying the entire narrative are feminist. . . . What's important is who wins and who loses . . . "[12] Clearly, in the second half of the novel, Nobody is shown to have been a failure in her past life. This is not automatic assurance the colonizers are winners, however. Some might argue Nobody ends up the winner by virtue of being the last left in the game; Nobody's crude killing at least makes the colonizers certain losers. Further, even putting that fact aside, no one could assert that on her desert planet Nobody presently represents simple, unmitigated failure. Her quick response to Donne's use of the generic, for example, would be, "heh heh that leaves me out . . . " Her first words stress the difference between our desert and desert island, and hers:

The Sahara is your back yard, so's the Pacific trench; die there and you won't be lonely. On Earth you are never more than 13,000 miles from anywhere . . .
We're nowhere.
We'll die alone. (p. 6).

Her situation is unique, she stubbornly insists. The standard responses won't do.

For this reason she's a valuable character in science fiction, where colonization is a cliché. "Survival's the name of the game," says Nathalie; "But for what?" the narrator thinks in response, and then realizes, "I had spoken out loud" (p. 75). The question endears her to the colonists even less than earlier remarks: "But *I* think that some kinds of survival are damned idiotic. Do you want your children to live in the Old Stone Age?" (p. 24). When John Ude states with unctuous certitude, "Civilization must be preserved," she sharply replies with cutting truth, "Civilization's doing fine . . . We just don't happen to be where it is" (p. 31). In other words, her role on the tagged planet, as she successfully seeks to meditate upon coming death, is much the same as her role had been on Earth, when earlier in life she briefly and unsuccessfully fought as a Popular activist: she questions accepted ways of doing things. "Don't push us," warns the professorial John Ude, "Don't you push us too much now" (p. 47). Nobody, however, is an intentionally very pushy woman.

"Often the treatment of women in sf is rationalized by setting the story on a far planet where the characters are colonists or are accidentally standard," Pamela Sargent observes in her introduction to *Women of Wonder*; ". . . Unfortunately, much of this type of science fiction assigns women to the traditional roles of bearing and caring for children and the home, on the grounds that are primary duty of the colonists is to procreate."[13] In *We Who Are About To . . .*, Nobody challenges precisely these assumptions. "If I've got to do it, you've got to do it," Nathalie tells her doggedly. "You . . . don't have to," (p. 59) the narrator manages to reply, but Nathalie is less intelligent than Nobody; she refuses to think the matter through and refuses to take the responsibility of choice. The narrator comments on this general escape from freedom, "I think everyone loves it here because their choices are all made for them; we were never very comfortable with our fate in our own hands, were we?" (p. 59). As Sargent notes, both colonists and the authors who create them too frequently treat colonization unimaginatively: "Our roles are, after all, often dictated by the surroundings in which we find ourselves. . . . it is surprising that the colonists do not experiment more with social structures and that reluctant women trapped in the constraints of certain roles are not treated more sympathetically." In footnote to this passage, Sargent calls on new SF to "show the conflict in a woman character between the role demanded by physical necessity and her desire to use her other abilities," and even to "resolve the problem" without "simply . . . having the woman find fulfillment as a mother."[14]

As if answering this request for more imaginative fiction, Nobody blasts the survivors with six minutes of valid objections when they make the stereotypical decision to colonize and multiply. When they go ahead anyway, establishing their mating schedules while still dependent upon a six months' supply of dried food, Nobody tells them bluntly: "Priorities backwards. First we have to poison Lori . . . I'm only trying to suggest that before we start any babies, we'd better start finding out what we can eat around here" (p. 55). The survivor's urgency in this matter can be justified only by the need to add Victor Graham's genes to the general pool before he dies; Sargent observes that "occasionally the colonists abandon monogamy, on the grounds that the full society will be healthier with as many different genetic combinations as possible," then goes on to point out, "This may be perfectly true, but it still leaves the women in the position of brood mares."[15] Thus Nobody, who first begins thinking of retreat during a confrontation over forced childbearing (thus faintly recalling the chastity of the Desert Fathers and the martyrdom of early Christian virgins and widows who would not marry), fiercely despises John Ude for treating his "walking womb" with a tenderness he would never have accorded the individual woman. Although as early as day two, Nobody talked of making careful preparation for death, her refusal to give up control over her own body is specifically what drives her into the desert. "They are going to force me to have babies," she tells hallucinated but accusing L. B.; "I was going to be tied to a tree and raped, for goodness sake" (p. 150). In both the first and second halves of the book, Nobody successfully maintains autonomy, and in addition to mocking stereotypes and challenging science fiction cliches, thus illustrates a problem in majority versus minority rights: Should society or the individual have control over the individual human body? The right to bear children or not (and to choose the time), the right to die or not (and given the eventual inevitability of death, to choose the time): the familiar issues seem two-fold, but have a single root.

"Social analysis or argument (as in Brecht, Ibsen, Shaw) is infinitely more difficult in narrative," states Joanna Russ, who received an MFA in playwriting and dramatic literature from Yale in 1960 and has seen her plays produced at Princeton and off-off-Broadway. [16] Born in February 1937, she grew up in the Bronx and eventually, despite the rigors of a 5:1 male-female quota system, was accepted at the Bronx High School of Science. She did not attend, she is often quoted as saying, "due to family insanity," but nonetheless she finished high school as one of the top ten Westinghouse Science Talent Search Winners. She decided she would "rather go on with poetry," laughed when people suggested she write science fiction, attended Cornell, and graduated in 1957 with high honors in English. In 1959, she published "Nor Custom Stale" in *The Magazine of Fantasy and Science Fiction*. During the next years, as Harlan Ellison tidily summarized when introducing her in *Again, Dangerous Visions* (1972), in addition to SF writing, Russ did "copy-editing, typing and copywriting for house organs, addressed cards for office temporaries, worked as a secretary to an irritable psychiatrist, and finally drifted into teaching." [17] The daughter of two teachers, she felt immediately at home in the classroom, and subsequently has taught at Queensborough Community College, Cornell, The State University of New York at Binghamton, The University of Colorado at Boulder, and The University of Washington in Seattle. Meanwhile she published *Picnic on Paradise* (1968), an Ace Science Fiction Special and Nebula Award nominee bitingly described by herself as "a magnificent and compelling novel . . . fraught with passion, peril, and all sorts of yum." [18] Her second novel, *And Chaos Died* (1970; Gregg Press edition, 1978), was similarly nominated for the Nebula Award; she won the Nebula Award for best short story with "When It Changed" (1972). In 1975, Russ published her major feminist novel, *The Female Man* (Gregg Press edition, 1977). *We Who Are About To . . .* (1977) is her fourth novel, and she has since published a fifth, *The Two of Them* (1978). A children's book, to be published by Daughters, Inc., has been serialized in *Sinister Wisdom*; in the third episode, "Kit Meets the Dragon," the fabulous beast confounds conventional expectations by being tender, awesome, and female: "She was gold all over, armored and barbed and ridged with gold, and Her great wings, membranous like a bat's wings, were folded back against Her spine." [19] Russ became a feminist late in the 1960s; in the 1975 *Quest* interview she explained: "I say 'feminism' as if it were a set of explicable beliefs, which in part it is, but there is also a kind a basic experience of which I was aware most of my life but which did not find political expression or a vocabulary until about seven years ago." [20] Increasingly, as Russ has continued to present what she calls the "dialectic of argument," the questions which have concerned her have been feminist issues.

In Russ's first novel, *Picnic on Paradise*, as in her fourth, *We Who Are About To . . .*, a small group of unrelated people find themselves alone on an alien and possibly hostile planet and attempt to survive. [21] Again the protagonist is an outsider to the group; again she feels superior and probably is. However, in *Picnic on Paradise*, Alyx takes charge of the group, ensures their survival, and wins both their admiration and affection. Alyx's former profession was "murderer," but in *Picnic on Paradise* the woman kills only in revenge for the death of the man she loved. Even the creation of such a mild heroine, relatively, caused Russ considerable anguish. Alyx appears at

"only just seventeen" in "I Thought She Was Afeard Till She Stroked My Beard," at 30 in "Adventuress," and at 34 or 5 in "The Barbarian," all now collected in *Alyx* (Gregg Press, 1976). In the stories, the feisty Tyrian heroine leaves her husband for dead, joins a blackbearded pirate but deserts him as dull, sails off with a red-haired teenager to encounter monsters and sailors, and—refusing to kill the governor's baby daughter—later kills the fat man who hired her and thereby magically cures "her man" of a murderous fever. In the summer of 1975, Russ described her creation of Alyx:

> Long before I became a feminist in any explicit way . . . I had turned from writing love stories about women in which women were losers, and adventure stories about men in which the men were winners, to writing adventure stories about a woman in which the woman won. It was one of the hardest things I ever did in my life. These are stories about a sword-and-sorcery heroine called Alyx, and before writing the first I spent about two weeks in front of my typewriter shaking . . .
>
> It was shifting my center of gravity from Him to Me and I think it's the most difficult thing an artist can do—a woman artist, that is. It's OK to write about artist-female with feet in the center of her own stage as long as she suffers a lot and is defeated and is wrong (the last is optional). But to win, and to express the anger that's in all of us, is a taboo almost as powerful as the taboo against being indifferent to The Man. [22]

Interestingly, there is more certain victory and less rage in *Picnic on Paradise* than in the much more difficult *We Who Are About To. . . .* The rage of Nobody fills Russ's fourth novel: "Perhaps I'm an addict," she tells the vocoder; "An anger addict" (p. 68).

Rage is the only feminist response Russ allows her women in *We Who Are About To. . . .* Usually, and most notably in *The Female Man*, her women form alliances. As both Samuel R. Delany and Marilyn Hacker have pointed out, her female protagonists most frequently oversee the education of younger or less experienced women; the specific relationship is common to "Adventuress," *Picnic on Paradise*, "The Second Inquisition," *The Female Man*, *The Two of Them*, and the forthcoming juvenile book about Kit. [23] In *We Who Are About To . . .*, however, although the older woman feels genuine tenderness for young Lori, responds to her desire to compose music, and kindly provides her with a favorable fortune, Nobody oversees only Lori's death. The women form no other feminist alliances either, although they have reason to unite, particularly after Alan has beaten up Nathalie and Nobody has been threatened with rape. The narrator tells her vocoder: "You must listen. You must understand that the patriarchy is coming back, has returned (in fact) in two days. By no design" (p. 34). The women are strong; generally they are tougher and smarter than the men, who in the first half of the book are close to stereotypes or counter-stereotypes. Alan, for example, is the beautiful dumb athlete; John Ude is the effete professor, complete with Pipe and Smile, of which, however, he is ironically aware. Victor sums up a life of focusing on appearance to attract and keep a powerful, wealthy mate in four words: "I can satisfy anybody" (p. 66). (The flat male characterizations, incidentally, belong to Nobody, not Russ; in the second half of the book, Nobody is more aware of the humanity of the three men and describes them, and everybody else, with greater subtlety.) Moreover, the women outnumber the men, particularly after the early death of Victor. Nobody and Nathalie are the quickest, strongest, and most resourceful; together they would be hard to beat. They are "mirror-sisters" and even briefly share a moment of unanimity while mocking Alan. Cassie seems to like Nobody, who definitely likes her. Possibilities for a feminist alliance are strongly there, and after Victor refuses to entertain his newly old and no-longer-wealthy wife, Mrs. Graham even "goes into the bungalow to make friends with Cassie," (p. 37) but the women don't trust one another, and older patterns prevail. Thus Mrs. Graham is still married to, although losing control over, Mr. Victor Graham. Lori Graham is "stuck on" Alan, who gains self-esteem from her adulation. Nathalie joins forces with John Ude the day after Alan's attack, and thus gains protection. Only Cassie and Nobody stay outside, and Cassie rejects Nobody's offer of companionship. Their alternative is suicide.

Whatever Nobody's noninvolvement in a feminist alliance, however, Russ clearly has found something for her heroine to do other than be "the protagonist of a Love Story," a task Russ described in "Why Women Can't Write" as "the one occupation of a female in literature, the one thing she can do, and by God she does it and does it and does it, over and over and over again. . . . As far as literature is concerned, heroines are still restricted to one vice, one virtue, and one occupation."[24] There are no love scenes in *We Who Are About To*. . . , except possibly Nobody's dream remembrances of talking about sparrows when in bed with L. B. and her delightful French dream only a few days later: "he said— peering at crotch level—'What is this?' and I 'What is that?' and we cried out together, 'Love!' and danced naked but very classically . . ." (p. 161). It's worth noting, however, that elsewhere, in other novels, Russ inventively breaks conventions when creating love scenes, for in "The Image of Women in Science Fiction," published in *Vertex* in 1974, Russ remarked that "the conventional idea that women are second-class people is a hard idea to shake; and while it is easy enough to show women doing men's work, or active in society, it is in the family scenes and the love scenes that one must look for the author's real freedom from our most destructive prejudices."[25]

One observes with interest that in *Picnic on Paradise*, Alyx falls in love with a silent man, Machine, who makes love to her only too well: "He began, as before, to kiss her . . . in short to do everything he had done before on the same schedule until it occurred to her that he was doing everything just as he had done it before and on the same schedule, until she tried to push him away, exclaiming angrily, feeling like a statuette or a picture, frightened and furious." (Later when they really love, Alyx is able to instruct Machine.) In *The Female Man*, Russ plays variations on this idea while at the same time writing a witty parody of passages fit for Kate Millett's *Sexual Politics* (1969). Jael makes love to Davy, a blond, blue-eyed, submissive, subservient, totally mindless, and thoroughly familiar beloved. Freshened by the reversal of sex roles, the absolute egoism of the typical love scene is too blatant to be borne, and it's a relief to discover Davy really is a machine. In *And Chaos Died*, Russ presents a homosexual protagonist who in a new world learns telepathy, telekinesis, teleportation, and love for Evne; as Hacker points out, homosexuality is relatively new to SF.[26] In "When It Changes," with only one sex on Whileaway, respectable marriages of course occur between women; one of the women, Janet, travels to Earth in *The Female Man*, and there makes love to Laura Rose while Jael hangs by one claw from the curtains and screeches her distress at this simultaneous violation of Earth's taboo against lovers of the same sex and Whileaway's taboo against lovers of differing ages. Later in the novel, a parallel scene showing Joanna

making love to Laur is drawn tenderly. In *The Two of Them*, Russ shows the love of two people of different sex, Irenee and Ernst, who seem at first to be equal.

In using SF to explore new roles and relationships for women, Russ moves beyond what she once called the "traditional assumptions which are nothing more than traditional strait jackets."[27] She stated in the 1975 *Quest* interview that "a feminist who goes to the novel rack (under 'sf') and picks at random is likely to be not only bored but genuinely insulted."[28] Nowhere is she herself more creative and more experimental than in *The Female Man*, already a major work of feminist science fiction, and a book passed around from hand to hand in much the same way as Doris Lessing's *The Golden Notebook* (1962) in the early '60s. Experimental in both form and content, the novel reminds one of *The Golden Notebook* in other ways too, for just as Lessing expressed Anna Wulf's fragmented inner state by creating a writer's block and having Anna put herself into four notebooks and several characters before at last bringing herself to unity in the golden notebook, so Russ splits her single character into four parts also: Jeannine, Joanna, Janet, Jael. Just as Lessing struggled against fragmentation in *The Golden Notebook*, so Russ described *The Female Man* as "an attempt to get my head together—literally, in the novel, where there are at least four women with one head apiece, none of whom is a whole woman until they finally do get together . . . for Thanksgiving dinner."[29] Earlier, Russ emphasized the experimental nature of the characters in *The Female Man*: "The women in it (except for Laur) are really part of one woman, and the two men (leaving out the spear-carriers) are the extremes of sexism as it impinges *on women's lives*."[30] In the use of one character who nonetheless is many, *The Female Man* also resembles Virginia Woolf's masterpiece, *The Waves* (1932). The great novelist and champion of women's right stated that in creating Bernard, Jinny, Rhoda, Louis, Susan, and Neville, she wished "that there should be many characters & only one."[31] *The Female Man*, like *The Waves* and *The Golden Notebook*, is highly experimental, for Russ, like Woolf and Lessing, had to find a form in which to say something which hadn't been said before. In it, as in *We Who Are About To* . . . , Russ widens the range of possibilities for women and for science fiction.

Notes

1. Jerome, *Vita S. Pauli*, in Helen Waddell, *The Desert Fathers* (Ann Arbor, Michigan: University of Michigan Press, 1957), p. 35.

2. Rev. Pierre Pourrat, *Christian Spirituality* (Westminster, Maryland: Newman Press, 1953), pp. 82–83.

3. Robert Scholes and Eric S. Rabkin, *Science Fiction: History, Science, Vision* (London: Oxford University Press, 1977), p. 117.

4. Virginia Woolf, *Collected Essays* (New York: Harcourt, Brace & World, 1967), Volume 1, p. 73.

5. Marilyn Hacker, "Science Fiction and Feminism: The Work of Joanna Russ," *Chrysalis*, Vol. 4, #1, 1978.

6. Ursula K. Le Guin, "The Day before the Revolution," in *More Women of Wonder*, ed. Pamela Sargent (New York: Vintage, 1976), pp. 285, 287, 284–5.

7. Ibid., p. 282.

8. Ibid., p. 286.

9. Ibid., pp. 299, 283.

10. Hacker, p. 77.

11. "XVII Meditation" from *Devotions upon Emergent Occasions* (1624), in *The Complete Poetry and Selected Prose of John Donne*, ed. Charles M. Coffin (New York: Modern Library, 1952), pp. 440–41.

12. "Reflections on Science Fiction: An Interview with Joanna Russ," *Quest*, II, 1 (Summer 1975), 44. *We Who Are About To* . . . was

published in *Galaxy Science Fiction Magazine*, XXXVII, 1–2 (Jan. and Feb. 1976), pp. 15–59 and 85–124.

13. Pamela Sargent, ed., *Women of Wonder* (New York: Vintage, 1974), p. xlvi.
14. Ibid., p. xlvii.
15. Ibid.
16. Russ, "Reflections," p. 43.
17. Harlan Ellison, ed., *Again, Dangerous Visions* (Garden City, New York: Doubleday, 1972), p. 232.
18. Joanna Russ, "Russ on Russ," *Epoch*, XVIII (1969), 239.
19. Joanna Russ, "Kit Meets the Dragon," *Sinister Wisdom* (Fall 1977), p. 9.
20. Russ, "Reflections," pp. 41–2.
21. This is again the starting point for Russ' second novel, *And Chaos Died*, in which Jai Vedh and the Captain find themselves temporarily alone on a silent planet after their ship explodes. Russ identifies this favorite pattern of "both science fiction and medieval tales" as "the journey of the soul from birth to death," and briefly describes it thus: "I find myself in a new world, not knowing who I am or where I came from. I must find these out, and also find out the rules of the world I inhabit." "Why Women Can't Write," in *Images of Women in Fiction*, ed. Susan Koppelman Cornillon (Bowling Green, Ohio: Bowling Green University Popular Press, 1972), pp. 18–19.
22. Russ, "Reflections," p. 42.
23. Samuel R. Delany, "Introduction," to Joanna Russ, *Alyx* (Boston: Gregg Press, 1976), pp. xvi–xviii; Marilyn Hacker, "Introduction," to Joanna Russ, *The Female Man* (Boston: Gregg Press, 1977), p. xv. in *Images of Women in Fiction*, p. 9.
24. Joanna Russ, "What Can a Heroine Do? or Why Women Can't Write," in *Images of Women in Fiction*, ed. Susan Koppelman Cornillon (Bowling Green, Ohio, 1972), p. 9.
25. Joanna Russ, "The Images of Women in Science Fiction," in *Images of Women in Fiction*, p. 72.
26. Hacker, p. 75.
27. Russ, "Image," p. 91.
28. Russ, "Reflections," p. 45.
29. Ibid., p. 43.
30. Ibid., p. 42.
31. Virginia Woolf, letter to John Lehmann dated 17 September (1931), in John Lehmann, *The Whispering Gallery* (New York: Longmans, Green, 1955), p. 171.

JOHN CLUTE

Foundation, January 1979, p. 103–5

It is another angry book. It is written as from anger, and it is clearly intended to anger its readers. Whether these readers are made angry at the book itself, or at the issues it raises with such edgy vigour, or both, seems not to concern Ms Russ, as perhaps it shouldn't. In this *The Two of Them* resembles *The Female Man* (1975), and in several ways is very much a pendant of that novel. The fundamental issues raised—centring around the punitive coercions women suffer in attempting to achieve and then sustain agenthood in the contemporary world—are certainly alike in nature, and are similarly put, in this case more enjoyably though with less bite. At the heart of each book's didactic strategy is an embittered (and for the sf reader looking for generic solaces deliberately embittering) disqualification ploy. In *The Female Man* it is hardly a ploy at all: it would take a pretty thick reader to understand the alternate sf universes presented in that book as being anything but translucent postulates laid down as exemplary surrounds for several theoretical versions of the central character who, like the protagonist of *The Two of Them*, is coeval with the author herself; the sf worlds of *The Female Man* are insultingly unreal, insultingly because our readerlike impulse to believe in

the toy worlds permitted us by our suspension of disbelief (however self-indulgent), is itself the petard she hoists us with: you think I'm telling you X; well I wouldn't tell you X if my life depended on it. In fact my life depends on my *not* allowing you to get away with hearing X from my lips. Your willingness to suspend disbelief so as to luxuriate in the telling of X is tantamount to complicity with the individious systemic violation of women in this world, whose roots are homologous with the engendering impulses behind traditional genre fiction, or X, baby. It tolls for thee. In *The Female Man* all of this is as nearly explicit as it needs to be (which is pretty), nor are the imagined worlds of that book anything but contemptuously transparent to the didactic motor, the anger. In *The Two of Them*, however, something hampers the sleight of hand of telling and not telling X.

Like the protagonist of the earlier book, Irene Waskiewicz of the current one grows up in the middle of the United States violently chafing at the edges—which she sees as designedly restrictive—of her life; she is violently unsure of how to achieve an adult "role" in mid-America which will not destroy her; she has a number of names she uses to describe various versions of herself, like Sklodowska (for when she's assuming anger), or Kopernik, or Lady Lovelace, or Irenee (all for differing states); and at the high peak of frustrated adolescence Ernst Neumann arrives at her parents' house, seemingly an old friend of her mother's, who seems to pass messages to him. Irene decides to leave home and to go with Neumann, and arrives at his hotel with her mind made up. They make love. More or less at this point, the long integrated flashback sequence which has narrated Irene's adolescence on Earth breaks off (never, significantly, to be resumed), so that we are not told anything of Neumanns role on Earth as a member of the great transtemporal organization whose function is seemingly to guide human cultures across the galaxy, presumably in the direction of civilization. Transtemporal agents seem to be permitted to extract the occasional native from his or her habitat, and to take him or her off adventuring; it is a sort of recruiting, and this is presumably what happens to Irene: eventually she becomes Neumann's partner. As his partner, she is the protagonist of the main action of the novel, action which begins it and which surrounds the flashback sequence.

The two of them are on the planet of Ka'abah, only inhabitable in claustrophobic caverns underground, where a neo-Arabic culture flourishes somewhat hectically. Women are of course kept in purdah, and those with any agent-like ambitions are likely to go quite insane. (The play between intergalactic agent and agenthood is very probably deliberate and central to the shape of *The Two of Them*.) On Ka'abah, Irene is violently enraged by what happens to women in general, and in particular what is about to happen to young Zubeydeh, daughter of the "Arab" she and Neumann have to deal with (though their business with him is left unexplained); Zubeydeh, adolescently ambitious as a poet, is about to be immolated into womanhood as Ka'abites see it. Irene forcefully objects, and opts to take Zubeydeh off-planet with her. Larger and more fierce than any Ka'abite, she browbeats Zubeydeh's father into signing the necessary papers, and gets her away successfully, on to the interstellar ship which, similarly claustrophobic to the planet itself, also constricts the action and deracinates it. On board ship, narrative tension (or, much the same thing, the assured forward thrust of "storytelling") soon becomes jerky, slackens and tugs in spasms, as though the book had a migraine. Irene finds she cannot any longer live with Ernst, despite his humanity and his lack of any avowedly sexist tendencies, though Irene does seem entirely capable of shaping his responses into a sexist mould. Unable to live with him, or to agree as to the rights and wrongs of her virtual abduction of Zubeydeh, she quarrels with him, and shoots him, perhaps dead, but at this point the novel becomes very much more transparent to the already intrusive voice of its implied author, who goes so far as to tell us that she has made up certain aspects of what she has so far narrated. And maybe all of it. Novel's close sees Irene and Zubeydeh back on Earth, playing the role of a divorcee with daughter in Albuquerque. The last images permit us to read the whole narration as an extended internal voyage on Irene's part, but with something perhaps stirring in the deep desert of her ravaged orgulous psyche, near the real Albuquerque.

As she is written, even at moments of generic action, Irene exhibits the pained subtle bitter complexity of many of the women whose lives in this world have been excruciated both by systemic bias and by their awareness of it. They have been *exposed*. To some men, they give off the frightening taste of the authentic human condition, without benefit of genre. And perhaps it is to point the lesson that Irene cannot ultimately inhabit genre, or protect herself through its buffering guidelines for conduct and self-definition, that Russ allows Irene's sf story on Ka'abah and amongst the stars to whinny off into a splitting grey morning headache in Albuquerque. Because destroy the novel she has certainly done. The story *fails*. It is not passed. Irene is too much for it. But Irene is also a failure. She has not been able to sustain herself, as Russ is also able to point out by flunking the story she's written. Somewhere in here somewhere reality has intruded. In recognizing this circumstance, Ms Russ may (or may not) be forgiven for failing to be sufficiently artful.

She gave me a headache. Perhaps I needed one.

MEREDITH TAX
From "Genre Benders"
Voice Literary Supplement, May 1985, pp. 8–9

Innocence is one of Joanna Russ's main attributes: the innocence of a baby or an Einstein, the ability to look at old things and see them new. Joanna Russ is a brilliant, moving, innovative writer and *Extra(ordinary) People* is her best yet. And when she is at her best, she has such an unequaled ability to show us what it would really feel like to be free of gender roles that she makes the current chic debate about sex/porn/violence/censorship seem unimaginative.

When she is not at her best, her writing can be flip or fall into pastiche, and her early books sometimes walked a knife edge between fiction and feminist polemic. This must be what got her the reputation for being difficult. She isn't hard to read, but she is demanding. She writes with feeling about uncomfortable and painful things, in a way quite remote from the field of boys' adventure tales, and can transfigure her subjects as few writers can. Partly because you have to be a grownup to do it.

Russ has two main subjects. The first is what she's known for: sex-gender differences, the way they are culturally determined and potentially mutable. She invented a planet called Whileaway, where the men all took sick and died from an unidentified virus that didn't harm the women. The women proceeded to reproduce by a kind of parthenogenesis; they formed marital relations, and built a civilization that lasted 300 years, a utopia in which all the available roles—auto mechanic, hero, poet—were filled by women, and all notions of what was feminine faded away. Then they were

discovered by a spaceship from Earth. I leave the rest to your imagination.

Russ worked that vein for some years, exploring the permutations of sex-role socialization. In *The Two of Them* Irene and her lover Ernst, agents of the Intergalactic Trans-Temporal Authority, are sent to the planet Ala-ed-deen, a Moslem world where the women are kept in purdah. Irene finds a brilliant, charming, doomed little girl, a girl like herself when young, and ends up rescuing her, taking her out of her own world into—what? Do the limitations imposed on humanness by gender end in space? Is there anywhere imaginable where a woman can be really free? Irene has a combination nervous breakdown/political rebellion trying to find out the answer.

Extra(ordinary) People gets astonishingly close to imagining such freedom. As always, Russ creates complex characters and writes, line by line, with as much natural feeling and eloquence as one could wish. The heroine of her first story, "Souls," which won the Hugo for best SF short story in 1983, is the Abbess Radegunde, head of a little nunnery in an English seacoast town. Some say she is a witch, some a saint. What is she really? Through the eyes of the narrator, a little boy she has saved, we see her change when the Vikings come to kill and rob, and we hear her earthy, pungent, mystical voice, which reminds me of Shaw's St. Joan.

> I determined to find a real, human lover, but when I raised my eyes from my fancies to the real, human men of Rome and unstopped my ears to listen to their talk, I realized that the thing was completely and eternally impossible. Oh, those younger sons with their skulking, jealous hatred of the rich, and the rich ones with their noses in the air because they thought themselves of such great consequence because of their silly money, and the timidity of the priests to their superiors, and their superiors' pride, and the artisans' hatred of the peasants, and the peasants being worked like animals from morning until night, and half the men I saw beating their wives and the other half out to cheat some poor girl of her money or her virginity or both—this was enough to put out any fire! And the women doing less harm only because they had less power to do harm, or so it seemed to me then. So I put all away, as one does with any disappointment. Men are not such bad folk when one stops expecting them to be gods, but they are not for me. If that state is chastity, then a weak stomach is temperance, I think.

The book is a tour de force in several ways. It is enormously playful in a literary sense, each tale being a parody of one or another form of popular literature, linked by a rather perfunctory frame tale that's like a joke on Erich von Daniken. There are loads of literary in-jokes and I don't get them all, but it doesn't matter. The sureness of her tone and her sense of fun carry one along.

And her imagination, which in "Bodies" takes us to a future where sexuality still exists but gender, in the sense of socially determined sex-appropriate ways of feeling and behaving, has long gone. Into this future world came two misfits from the past—James Bunch, a British transvestite, and the narrator, a wry Portland businesswoman of the 1970s. They are cloned by scientists who look for a specific EEG pattern ("The pattern is chronic misery"), then reach back and pinch a few cells, regrowing these people of our own day, with all their memories, in a world freer than their wildest dreams.

What will they make of such freedom? Can earth's miserable minority stand liberation?

Russ's second main theme, her central story in book after book, is this one: the orphan, crying unheard. It's the same story you find all over Hans Christian Andersen, Sherwood Anderson, Chekhov, Gorki, Dickens, Charlotte Brontë: the child whom no one understands, different from the rest, crushed by her environment, searching vainly for her own kind. It is William Blake's cry: "O, why was I born with a different Face? Why was I not born like this Envious Race?" It is the myth of the birth of the artist.

Russ's anger at human distortion and stupidity, at the way people are crushed between social stones, gives her writing energy; her compassion for the pain of these distorted, limited creatures lends her stories grace. But this is science fiction, with its elements of wild romance, so the orphan/artist can be rescued: Saved! Not just by enduring, or growing up and escaping, or by gaining wisdom through suffering, or becoming a revolutionary so that others will not suffer as she did. No, she can be really saved in time, before she dies of loneliness, by an angel, fairy godmother, alien come from whatever outer space to take her away and hold her and comfort her even in the most physical ways as well as through telepathic understanding. As the male/female/alien narrator in Russ's third tale, a parody of Victorian porn called "The Mystery of the Young Gentlemen," saves Maria-Dolores, the waif from the slums of Barcelona. How can anyone resist this? It's one of the central human

fantasies, the lonely child suffering trial by ordeal, then suddenly, miraculously, finding rescue, safety, warmth, food, and love that gives her a mother, friend, lover, and teacher all at once. Jane Eyre can have it all while there is still time, before she is deformed by bitterness.

No wonder they call it science fiction.

They could also call it literature. But some people in the trade object to that term. Commercial crossovers that bridge the gap between SF and best-sellerdom are fine. But Russ demands imaginative participation and emotional response from the reader. That sort of thing could get out of hand. Maybe that's why Larry Niven's books are still in print, while, of Joanna Russ's fiction, only *Extra(ordinary) People* and two books of short stories are available. Her best-known book, *The Female Man*, which sold well, has been out of print for nearly 10 years, as are her other novels (*And Chaos Died, Picnic on Paradise,* and *The Two of Them*). Two others, *Kittatinny* and *On Strike against God*, were published by a small press that has now folded.

I can't understand the book industry; half the time when publishers try to cut costs, they cut off a leg instead. Joanna Russ's work is one of the places fiction is going; they have to keep her in print to educate the future reading public. This woman is a major writer. But maybe that's the problem. Major writers aren't supposed to specialize in science fiction, any more than they're supposed to write historical novels or romances or westerns or detective stories.

J. R. SALAMANCA

1922–

Jack Richard Salamanca was born on December 10, 1922, in St. Petersburg, Florida, the son of a civil engineer and a writer, and grew up in Florida, Virginia, New York City, and Washington, D.C. He attended George Washington University and served as a radio-gunner in the Far Eastern theatre during World War II. After the war Salamanca moved to London, where he studied acting at the London School of Dramatic Art and the Royal Academy of Music, and worked as an actor before returning to the United States in the early 1950s.

Salamanca's first novel, *The Lost Country*, was published in 1958. His other novels include *Lilith* (1961), probably his best-known work; *A Sea Change* (1969); and *Embarkation* (1973). Married and the father of a son, Salamanca served for a time as writer-in-residence at the University of Connecticut. He is currently a professor of English at the University of Maryland, College Park.

When Hero Jim Blackstarr does any talking ⟨in *The Lost Country*⟩, he is all corn pone and hominy grits: "Look, Betty Lee, it i'n't goin' to be like this all the time. It won't be too long foah we kin git married . . ." But when Jim gets around to long thoughts about the landscape, Author Salamanca puts down these words about a summer storm: "It gets gray and cool and then the wind comes gusty from the mountains . . . and the tossing trees in the wind are like oceans with little silver fish slipping through the tops of the waves."

This odd contrast of styles has a crippling effect on Salamanca's torrential first novel, which carries Jim Blackstarr from his fourth to his 17th year in and around Charlottesville, Va. The book is drunk on nature, the round of the seasons, the beauty of women. Whatever lucky Jim wants in females he gets, whether it is Neighbor Betty Lee, whose "cool firm thighs were like two great silver carp," or Cousin Nory, whose thighs, "with their milk-white, melon-firm flesh, struck his mind with

ruinous astonishment," or Schoolteacher Irene, whose thighs are "like moist and mobile alabaster."

A sort of Thomas Wolfe cub, Author Salamanca, 34, has the Wolfeian flaws of logorrhea, overintensity and repetition. But he has some of the Wolfeian virtues as well: his characters—Christian and Uncle Rolfe and the rest—come thunderously alive; he can tumultuously evoke the rites of spring; he is equally sure in dealing with the frenzies of a crazed stallion or the moiling mind of an adolescent. What is needed is an editor.—Unsigned, "Wolfe Cub," *Time*, Nov. 3, 1958, p. 98

J. R. Salamanca's second novel is striking confirmation of the talent which aroused considerable excitement when his first novel, *The Lost Country*, appeared three years ago. Although narrower in scope and less resonant in style than his first novel, *Lilith* is a subtler continuation of the author's theme: gentle innocence journeying toward self-knowledge through cruelty and corruption, unguardedly embracing with flaring intensity the secret mysteries of human intimacy.

Told in the first person by Vincent Bruce from the safe distance of fifteen years and an uneasy peace with his now subdued nature, *Lilith* is the record of the relationship which shattered his tranquil image of his own value. After combat service in the Air Force, Vincent returns to his native Maryland village and to the grandparents who took him and his mother after their son had deserted them. Among those good old people whose love and strength of character provide the nest from which the fledgling male ventures forth to harsh encounters in the outside world, Vincent takes a job as an occupational therapist ("glorified attendant") in a private mental asylum whose presence in his placid home town had always engaged his boyhood curiosity. There he meets Lilith—rich, beautiful, intellectual, and demented—and with her, his innocence begins its journey through deceits, betrayals and cruelty, until the inevitable merging of charity and insanity releases corruption and violence in patient and keeper alike. The book, drawn from memory and from a journal Vincent kept at the time, becomes a sort of private therapy of his own through which he manages to maintain his hold on life.

Lilith demonstrates again Mr. Salamanca's rare sense of place, his sensuous, tender evocation of country people and country days, for it is within the setting he has known all his life, among the familiar and beloved hills and woods which nourished his boyhood, that Vincent becomes the victim of his own generosity and violates himself. It would be possible to view this book as it seems on the surface: a chilling exposure of the manipulation of the healthy by the demented (and vice versa). But *Lilith* is really something much rarer in contemporary fiction. As in *The Lost Country*, this gifted young novelist has taken the myths of masculine growing up—the hunger of the immature for involvement with the beautiful, the brilliant, and the unattainable—and woven them into a subtle canvas behind which dance the avid dreams of youth.

It is a tribute to J. R. Salamanca's great skill as a writer that both the surface of this novel—stylish in tone, precise in language, sure in evocation of place—and the unspoken knowledge which lies beneath it combine to produce a work of mature artistry.—HARDING LEMAY, "The Beautiful and Demented," *NYHT*, July 30, 1961, p. 9

In J. R. Salamanca's previous novels, *The Lost Country* and *Lilith*, the prose shuttles us back and forth between more or less straightforward exposition and a lyricism that yields interludes of phantasmagorical luxury. Offensive to literary puritans, a prose so often so highly charged not only makes Mr. Salamanca his own most interesting character but reminds us that, for some time now, enterprising fiction has been as much about words as about so-called characters. Now Mr. Salamanca offers a novel ⟨*A Sea Change*⟩ which, although less demonically bizarre than *Lilith*, reveals a good deal about the verbal monopoly a novelist has of his creatures, even to the extent of equipping a first-person narrator with two modes of expression: the one appropriate, the other hardly at all.

A Ph.D. employed by the Library of Congress, the narrator addresses us directly, even singling out one reader-type from another, and begs us to indulge him because his career as a chronicler "begins and ends with this single work." Simply, he has to work out why his wife, for whom he three years ago lost all desire, finally walked out. He even, in a vain effort to mend things, took her off to the French Riviera and there equipped her with a gigolo—since he had already enjoyed one fast fornication in Slagheap, Pa., and was enjoy-ing several sundrenched assignations with an English actress who as a girl tried to improve her bust with a toilet plunger. But the least dignified thing of all is that he, Michael, and she, Margaret, nickname each other Mickey; growing away from each other, they split internally, ruined by an endearment held in common.

Dismal as the situation is, it is funny as well. Mr. Salamanca saddles Michael with an idiom that turns erotic clinches into double clichés, though it improves toward the end as he achieves some degree of verbal competence. But the ridicule is the very thing that helps him cheat the stereotype: knowing his creator has framed him, we indulge him; and his hackneyed rhetoric wins him a sympathy we might have denied him if he'd put things well from the beginning. "Her eyes were dark with determination," he bemusedly records, "The frustration of the years had fulminated behind them and burned there in a kind of purple incandescence." The old pain is made new as he struggles to define it and bury it in the new medium.

Such are the games Mr. Salamanca plays with his creature, from time to time stepping up the humiliation by injecting luminously articulate sentences into Michael's dogged prose. The result is a kind of inconsistent schizophrenia: the infidelity motif becomes a pretext for a novelist's controlled experiment upon himself and his readers, testing his fidelity to his own style (and to that of Michael), until we come to relish his forbearances rather than deplore his intrusiveness.

The whole book—unless I'm on the wrong track altogether and Mr. Salamanca is just allowing himself some stale prose by proxy—is as nicely calculated and balanced as that. The spectacle of a literary inferior being increasingly invaded by his author is not only eerie; it's usefully contrapuntal too. Somehow, Salamanca at full rhetorical pressure—for example, on the glass figurine Margaret longs to own and which Michael buys for her to still his guilt, or on the sucking noises a yacht makes when the engine is cut in deep water, or on birdmen and two-legged donkeys at a fancy-dress party, or on Andrea the gigolo in wine-colored suede chukka boots and saffron-tufted Irish tweed—gains immeasurably by coming at us in between slabs of Michael's fustian.

Mr. Salamanca takes a sizable chance, aiming, I presume, to intensify our sense of the staleness of the formulas to which bewilderment and pain drive even the most articulate people. That his novel defies moldy old prejudices once thought to be rules (point of view, first-person or third-person narrator) and gets away with it, is the measure of Mr. Salamanca's prowess and mental flexibility. The mutability that is his theme is also his technique: not exactly a "new" novel (he's not that tricksy), but certainly not orthodox. His estranged couple might have come from Robbe-Grillet or Butor, resigned to mutual inscrutability amid the lustrous Riviera props that Michael infatuatedly lists and the sea-changes that recur but do not feel.

The ending is ludicrously congruous: just before chasing after Margaret on the next plane from Nice to the United States, Michael sends her a cable signed "Mickey" but inadvertently so words it that, when he arrives, he thinks it's from her. A giggle of disdain might be seemly here, but the novel as a whole exacts less superficial responses, and the malice of the presentation seems ultimately a defense against the helplessness of mere good will.—PAUL WEST, *NYTBR*, Dec. 21, 1969, p. 14

Goethe, who was fascinated with the image of the superior man long before Nietzsche gave him romantic and mystical trimmings and called him Zarathustra, believed that if we are strong-willed and know our goal people will step aside for us. In this novel ⟨ *Embarkation* ⟩ Joel Linthicum, the boat-builder as artist, would pass any test for the superior man, even a weight-lifting test (at a Maryland oyster roast he wins a wager by mounting on his back a frightened and struggling pony), and his older son Aaron compares him with the Elizabethans. Most Englishmen and Americans today would be intimidated if a Drake or a Raleigh came swaggering among them, sea salt in his beard and blood on his hands. Aaron, the narrator of *Embarkation*, admits he's intimidated and his growing up—one of the major themes of the novel—is a quiet struggle to crawl out from under the shadow of a man who belongs to a time when there were giants in the earth.

Though Salamanca gave the title character of his best-selling novel *Lilith* a rich fantasy life, he is no maker of fantasies himself. *Lilith* was based on a year's work in an asylum and its success was owing not only to its Gothic atmosphere but also to its finespun details and its author's power in identifying with the occupational therapist who served as narrator. In *Embarkation* Salamanca draws on his hobby of sailing and offers evidence that he has poked around alertly in the shops of independent boat-builders whose crafts-manship is becoming obsolete as corporate competition drives them into retirement. Salamanca dipped into his own experi-ences as well for the coloring of the London scenes in which Aaron studies acting and senses amid doubts that he might become an artist too if a distinctly lesser one than his father. An enchanted London closer to Dickens' and G. K. Chesterton's vision than to Gissing's is Aaron's London and he sees it as a city touched with greatness by centuries of memorable history and literature. Whether he is describing London or the odds-against struggle of the Linthicums with a gale off the Maryland coast, Salamanca writes with a lyricism that per-suaded a critic of his first novel, *The Lost Country*, to chide him as a Thomas Wolfe cub.

Salamanca differs from Wolfe, however, in ways impor-tant enough to indicate that he doesn't have to crawl out from under the shadow of *that* giant. Since *The Lost Country* he has been curbing a taste for verbiage and rhetoric and producing novels that have been *progressively* shorter. He is more inven-tive than Wolfe, never using nostalgia as an excuse for disguised and interminable autobiography. Most important, perhaps, he turns to mythology as Joyce and Faulkner and John Updike did before him but avoids the obtrusive parallels that become a wearisome trick in Updike's *The Centaur*. The Genesis story of Noah furnished Salamanca with hints for the primitive vigor and alternating scrupulousness and wayward-ness of Joel Linthicum. Having led a godly life before the flood, Noah slipped when he passed his 600th year and entered what psychologists would call a critical age. He planted a vineyard, drank too much wine, collapsed naked on the floor of his tent, and was observed in this shameless state by his youngest son Ham. As Ham was shocked by the sight of the patriarch in disarray; so Joel's older son and daughter are shocked when they find their father carousing with a mistress aboard one of his boats.

Sylvie, the daughter, thereupon turns to man-hating as if it were a full-time occupation. When she finally accepts a lover, he is none other than a gentle professor at the state university who would seem incapable of the sexual demands habitual to Joel Linthicum. Aaron, also finding his adolescent innocence behind him like the lost country of Jim Blackstarr, hero of Salamanca's first novel, tries for a healthy relationship with the opposite sex—and fails repeatedly. Disaster of a simpler kind strikes at the younger son Jamed, who suffers brain damage as a result of an accident his father might have prevented.

Jamed's retardation intensifies his father's love. For Joel Linthicum, despite his preoccupation with building the soundest and most beautiful boats in the world, surpasses other men in emotional warmth as he surpasses them in prodigality of talents. Perhaps the most astonishing of these talents is his gift for drawing rarest beauty and power from Shakespearean verse as he floats out to sea and shouts his favorite lines for the wind's benefit and his own. Here again he demonstrates that he belongs to another day and that his vulgarity, which he shares with the bearbaiting Elizabethans, doesn't cut him off from the pleasures of the esthete.

Joel Linthicum is not entirely credible—no semi-mythic hero could be—if measured by the standards of realistic fiction. Since he is larger than life, it is appropriate that his end should be as mysterious as the deaths of King Arthur and Frederick Barbarossa. Even though rumor has it that he was trapped in an Atlantic storm while testing one of his boats, his corpse never comes to light. Whatever his fate, we can be sure that he met it with courage and perhaps nose-thumbing for good measure. Linthicum is above all a contrast to the anti-heroes that have long dominated fiction and an answer—if one is wanted—to the despair of the '70s. His delight in living and eagerness to take risks limit him as a human being only in that they prevent him from understanding what the whimpering of the J. Alfred Prufrocks is all about.

The artist as a comic hero rather than a sensitive plant on Shelley's model is an uncommon theme and it is handled by Salamanca with romantic overtones that would jar if his lyricism weren't under delicate control. In moving from the Gothicism of *Lilith* and the overinsistent sexuality of *A Sea Change*, he has arrived at an artistic maturity that puts *Embarkation* first among his works.—JAMES WALT, "No Wolfe Cub," NR, Jan. 5, 1974, pp. 28–29

CHARLES BAXTER
"The Drowned Survivor:
The Fiction of J. R. Salamanca"

Critique, Volume 19, Number 1 (1977), pp. 75–86

Like Fowles, Salamanca is in neither the realistic nor the postmodern mode, though he has certain traits of both. If he must be pigeonholed at all, he would be more accurately placed in that line of twentieth-century novelists (including Djuna Barnes, Malcolm Lowry, Fitzgerald, and Fowles) who have perceived a loss of "presence" in consciousness and who have tried through various means to retrieve it, an effort that usually results in failure and disillusionment. The best cross-reference for these novelists is not, therefore, to other novelists but to the Romantic poets. Like them, these novelists tend to write about artists or artist-figures who cannot be satisfied with the abstractive process that converts all landscape into concept, or the subsequent play of comic (or nightmarish) self-reflection, which usually collapses under the weight of its own solipsism. Salamanca and Fowles, in particular, stand in opposition to these procedures by claiming for their art the *possibility* of momentary physical illumination, which is wholly self-justifying, no matter how much despair and de-struction it may leave behind. Such illumination, which would unite language to thought and object, is difficult to achieve (to say the least): it may be found only in the arms of an uncontrolled sexual urge, or in madness, or alcohol, or a mystery that defies labels altogether. When the moment of illumination is over, it may leave the survivor in a state of continuing mystery or with the death of desire. Fowles is the novelist of the former, Salamanca of the latter.

Such themes do not develop overnight, and they are not entirely in evidence in Salamanca's first novel, *The Lost Country*, a first novel in more ways than one. The story of the growth in rural Virginia of a young man, James Blackstarr, shares with other *Bildungsromanen* the necessity of naming and dramatizing the *first* of everything: Jim's first swim across a river, his first girl, first rifle, first fight, and since he is a budding writer, his first poems and stories. All these introductions are set in a narrative that reflects his innocence and eagerness *to see*: the book contains many paragraphs detailing his physical and spiritual education, whose sentences all begin "He loved. . . ." In the novel desire soaks every impulse, making both the act of the imagination and the act of physical love reciprocal. As Jim grows, he develops strength, honesty, manliness, and courage, in addition to his intelligence. Such novels are often called "torrential" and compared to Thomas Wolfe's; they live on, seemingly, only to embarrass their creators.

In one respect, though, *The Lost Country* initiates some themes that are to haunt Salamanca's later work, and they have to do with what happens to the objects of desire. Since these are mostly women, the relationship between a man and woman defines the self of both and further defines the nature of the social world in which they live (or are caught). If desire sets the self into motion in the world, the movement of desire then substantializes it. The individual may be poisoned by either an excess or a deficiency of desire, but without it the self cannot be defined at all. In *The Lost Country*, Jim Blackstarr (a name that portends schizophrenia, by the way [1]) has two girl friends who are his age, one "light" (Betty Lee Swanson) and one "dark" (Nory, his cousin). Nory is urban, dangerously temperamental, aloof, and fascinating. In the penultimate scene of the novel, Nory's father catches his daughter making love to Jim; in the subsequent uproar Jim leaves the town—ending the book, his youth, and the social bond that held him there.

These involvements are complicated, moreover, by a woman named Irene Carpenter, who is in succession Jim's grade-school teacher, his mentor in writing, and his mistress (the novel covers about fourteen years of his life). As a source of both erotic fascination and wisdom, she seems to represent the Jungian *anima*, the woman whose knowledge and wisdom is both potent and arcane. By introducing him to letters and mature sexuality, she acts as the guide into a new world of expression; unfortunately, her own desire for Jim grows so oppressive, and the circumstances of their affair so socially unacceptable, that she commits suicide, leaving Jim with a lifetime's worth of guilt (that she started as "mother" and ended as "lover" is unstated but obvious). She has made the worlds of "letters" and fantasy coterminous with the world of sexuality; sexual and oedipal guilt begin to spill into the world of "letters." By mixing the two up, Jim becomes incapable of writing *and* living in the world of plentitude—the lost country. Irene Carpenter will be reincarnated as Lilith in the next novel, but the problem will not be solved. Halfway through *The Lost Country*, Jim wonders whether "there was a true reality somewhere, apart from all those interpretations of it, which would never be available because the interpretations were all so inexact." [2] With Miss Carpenter he learns that there *is* such a reality, pre- or post-conscious, free of interpretation, but that its ecstasy does not permit any sort of ordinary life, and that the heightened sensitivity it induces leads very quickly to madness

or its adolescent-everyman surrogate, frenzy. *The Lost Country* shares, in part, the innocence of its protagonist, and what it assumes to be lost is the experience of what Geoffrey Hartman has called "unmediated vision." Even the novel's epigraph from Housman reinforces the note of regret.

In Salamanca's next novel, *Lilith*, the land of plentitude has been firmly reinstated in the center of eroticized subjectivity—the madhouse. The epigraph now is from Keats' "La Belle Dame sans Merci," a poem that sets the tone of ecstatic fear. The narrator is a young Army veteran named Vincent, who after enduring a "normal" childhood (though his father is absent and his mother turns out to be psychotic) and adolescence with his grandparents, and a "normal" initiation into the mysteries of war and death, returns to his hometown and goes to work in a private mental hospital. In the course of his work he meets and falls in love with a beautiful schizophrenic, Lilith. They begin an affair, but Lilith's desire is not limited to Vincent alone; with his professional position compromised, Vincent must accompany Lilith to several trysts with another, female, patient. As his jealousy grows, he begins himself to show signs of latent schizophrenia. The climax comes when Vincent tells another patient, Warren Evshevsky, who is in love with Lilith, that she despises Warren—an untruth that leads to Warren's suicide, plunges Lilith into irredeemable catatonia, and causes the narrator nightmarish and irresolvable guilt. To ransom himself, Vincent goes to work in his grandfather's restaurant and forces himself to accept all the middle-class values he once abhorred. On this note the novel ends.

The opposition between a wondrous subjectivity that cannot be sustained without psychic damage to all and a sober "realism" without intensity or meaning (but which is perpetual and unthreatening) is at the heart of much Romantic poetry—particularly Keats'—and tends to result, after illumination is past, in the feeling of derealization, of being in a spiritual no-man's land whose great bard is Matthew Arnold. The opposition set up in *Lilith* between numbed habit and ecstatic perception has no middle ground; in Arnold's words, it is "powerless to be born." Resignation to the "town" deadens the senses and leads to the teeth-grinding boredom of Vincent's ex-girl friend, Laura, who after a particularly unsuccessful marriage to a fatuous philistine begins to wither from the effect of her unlived life. Resignation to the world that Vincent is introduced to by Lilith leads to heightened perception—and, with it, jealousy, obsessional dread, and the abreactive fear of Keats' unlucky knight. Salamanca's Vincent *is* just such a knight, a fact underscored by his participation in a Maryland county fair's jousting tournament, complete with lances and hanging eyelets, in the novel's dramatic set piece whose sexual implications are not lost on anyone. Vincent's success in the tournament and the favorable impression it makes on Lilith win him her obsessional attention, including her stunning sexual force and an entry into her schizophrenic world. In winning Lilith, he cannot have it both ways: he cannot share Lilith's passion without becoming schizophrenic (in a first-person narrative that is literally harrowing). If desire is the yardstick for all meaning, then wishes lead to infatuation, to obsession and self-dispersal, and then to madness, the ultimate in both meaning and desire.

In the novel Salamanca has constructed a fictional version not only of "La Belle Dame sans Merci" but of "Ode to a Nightingale." The self travels to a realm where a different language takes over (Lilith has invented her own), where music fills the silences, and where the ego does not know where it is or where reality takes place—inside the head or outside in what others call "the world." If and when the ego comes back to itself, it thinks in dreams like this:

> The night that followed was full of terrible livid dreams, imposed upon the darkness out of which they rose like jewels lying on black velvet, and in which Warren's face appeared in a score of tormented images, sometimes drowned and bloated . . . In one . . . he appeared miraculously resurrected, in a robe of rotting and verminous sable, with a makeshift coronet of tinsel on his dark hair, clutching a broken, rusted sword in one hand and sitting in state beside Lilith at the end of a great narrow hall down which I advanced . . . while they beckoned to me, chuckling, with foolish, feverish gestures of their hands. It was just as I knelt before them to receive the touch of peerage on my shoulder that I awoke, shivering, in an icy ague of excitement, my hands pressed in homage to my breast.[3]

In *Lilith* the loss of ego-boundaries and the entry into the world of ecstasis is imaged through drowning. Lilith nearly manages to get her sensitive admirer, Warren, drowned at a picnic; in a late stage of his rapture, Vincent puts together an aquarium, then drowns a Lilith-doll in it; Lilith herself finally drowns in a Swiss lake, though her body is never found. Vincent is the only survivor who manages to resuscitate himself, after wishing that he might "lounge and drift in it all night, assuaged, dreaming water-dreams." After having drowned in Lilith's images and her world, he somehow survives. The man who has sunk—who has felt the confusion of realms within himself, his body atomized and dispersed like water into the landscape—ends by working in a restaurant to satisfy the hunger of others. He writes an account of his immersion, in the hopes of finding peace. In the profoundly bitter conclusion to the novel's final paragraph, he celebrates his return to the air and consequent loss of appetite:

> have I found the peace that I anticipated? I have come as close to it, I think, as I am ever likely to again. This is not to say that I confuse peace of so humble a degree with virtue or fulfillment, or that I believe my repentance to be perfect, for it can never be. And yet I exist; for along with many lesser virtues, I have lost the hunger for perfection. (381)

His confession represents the harried faith of the post-romantic who cannot live in his poetry and, therefore, writes prose; it is also emblematic of the fantasy lost within fiction. Like the word "forlorn" that tolls the poet back to himself, it returns the novelist from Lilith's world to the restaurant kitchen. It suggests, furthermore, that fictions like Lilith's (and Conchis' in *The Magus*) educate their victim/readers to learn that the "city of words" and the confusion of realms cannot be resolved to anyone's satisfaction. To hold up the fantasy is to live inside the book, an experience that lasts only as long as the book's pages are open.

If it were not for the luminous prose of the novel, the mesmerizing aestheticism might never get beyond the talking stage. If the style fails, the novel's preoccupations cannot even begin to convince, but Salamanca's prose manages in an uncanny way to combine both the ordinary and the bizarre; it is both ornate and flat, like a farmer telling fairy tales, as in the opening paragraph:

> I grew up in a small Southern town which was different from most other towns because it contained an insane asylum. At the time I was growing up there, however, I did not think of this as a distinction. As we had been aware of it from birth, it had for

us who lived there no aspect of novelty; it was simply one of the facts of our existence, and belonged . . . among those elemental institutions by which life is both sustained and interpreted. With the equanimity of a child I accepted the fact that there was madness everywhere, just as there was conflagration, illness, ignorance, and hunger. I can, indeed, remember being disconcerted, somewhere around the age of twelve, by the discovery that other towns did not have asylums, and engaging in much troubled speculation as to how the insane people of these communities were disposed of.

Note the innocence of the first phrase ("small Southern town") and the sinister tone of the last ("were disposed of"). Between these two voices the prose of *Lilith* oscillates.

In Salamanca's next novel, *A Sea Change*, the subject is again the loss of appetite, but the results are not so simple as those implied by the ending of *Lilith*. As the title suggests, boundary-loss and ec-stasis confront disillusion—and much of the novel is a working out of themes borrowed, somewhat tenuously, from *The Tempest*. At the heart of the dramatic situation is the question of what an individual is to do about or with the person he loves when his desire for her, quite simply, dies out. The sea change of the novel spans the passionate beginning of a relationship to its dismal mid-term (in which love heaps guilt upon itself) when needs are not being satisfied by desire. The result is a brilliant, sun-lit, and tremendously expressive novel whose central action involves terrible cruelty and self-deception.

As an undergraduate the narrator, Michael Pritchard, meets a woman named Margaret (they later, in tender moments of narcissism, call one another "Mickey"). After a literal whirlwind courtship, the greater part of which takes place on a friend's sailboat, they marry, despite Margaret's one deformity, a hand withered by polio. Thirteen years later, the couple is childless, and Michael's desire for his wife is gone; he is impotent. His job at the Library of Congress allows him to stay late and to hide from her. Finally, confronted, he proposes that they travel to southern France, in hopes that the sun, sand, and Mediterranean might revitalize their relation. At the end of the first part, Michael drifts into revery:

> We lie in silence for a while, lost in our respective fantasies. Mine are of water: shoreless expanses of ocean, pitching under blue, empty skies. I sink into these waters slowly, deeper and deeper into their bottomless chill depths, at last beyond all memory of the sun.[4]

In the second part, Michael and Margaret travel to St. Jean-Cap Ferrat, where they meet a troupe of actors preparing *The Tempest*, and several others, including a smarmy Italian "language tutor." Michael strikes up an affair with an actress named Gwynyth ("Gwynyth is Ariel"), and he engages the tutor's services (linguistic and sexual, the same as they were in *The Lost Country*) for his wife. Matters go on in this way for about as long as they can, until Margaret leaves both the scene and her husband, never to appear again. The novel ends somewhat as Lilith does, with the narrator putting together the story of the past as a therapeutic act of recovery and renunciation.

In a way, *A Sea Change* concerns a couple who have adapted too well to what they consider the objective world; in the process, they lose entirely their capacity for passion (which is mal-adaptive in the social world though not in the subjectivist one). Having done so, they can live publicly but not privately, where the loss of desire leaves no bond *but* language. In effect, Margaret is the opposite of Lilith: she kills passion for the sake of refinement and adaptability. It is no accident that, after meeting her, Michael becomes a librarian and that she is reprimanded by a wise old countess that her very civility has sucked out Michael's sense of self-promise. She has, the countess tells her, "disqualified him from the fields of revolution, of prophesy, of apostasy, and sin . . . It leaves him little to practice but husbandry—that nameless, that demoralizing thing" (181). If Lilith is the extreme, a kind of mad muse, then Margaret is the counter-norm, who does not perceive that some kind of public riot aids private happiness. Having adapted so well to the social world, Michael can satisfy her only through the social world's medium—money, paid to a gigolo. This act, provoked by misconceived pity (a crucial term), creates a shimmer of nightmare in the last section of the book that is as frightening in its sanity as *Lilith* is in its derangement. Michael, again, survives the drowning of his passion and pity, but he ends, like the narrator of *Lilith*, as a husk.

Lilith is a great examiner of hands; Margaret's hand (we are told near the start of the novel) is deformed, and Gwynyth's are ugly. That both novels concentrate obsessively on their characters' hands is to be expected in a world ruled by desire rather than (say) cognition. In Keats' poetry, particularly the last poems, the hand, not the face, is the agent of the self in the world. To express desire and to satisfy it requires in physical embodiment an act that only the hand can initially perform. In one of Keats' last poems, "This living hand," a hand emerges *from the poem* to grasp the reader. When desires are frustrated or inexpressible, the hands may, notoriously, go manic (Homer Simpson in *The Day of the Locust*) or express what has been repressed or sublimated out of language (Lady Macbeth's dreamhands). Margaret's damaged hand suggests that her entry into the world is muted, that her de-formity is not so much in thought as in intention. Beautiful hands, in this vision of interchange, process and embody desire; they direct it and receive it, just as grotesque hands in their eccentricity delineate a damming up of the self and its needs. They must be pitied, but since pity involves condescension, the mystery of desire must be absent.

Michael can have successful sexual affairs with women like Hildy Hunzinger, an art student he meets who possesses "mediterranean voluptuousness"; both she and Gwynyth have a certain coarseness that gives expression to both sexual and spiritual urges, and both are artists. They do not transform, as Margaret does, public virtues into private ones. In this gallery of souls pitted against the public and private worlds, one would expect some victims to go mad, but only one is mad: the narrator's mother, a lady of some refinement, alluded to early in the novel. She is a maniacal collector of antiques, the best of which are either broken or sent back by her husband. After years of such solitary concerns, she just gives up: "for after several years of seeing her treasures so tastelessly and arbitrarily disposed of, she managed, with a really unusual show of initiative, to contract pneumonia and die" (9).

With this background, Michael (like Vincent) runs the risk of finding another such woman—and in Margaret, in a less extreme form, he does. Her refinement makes the mystery of her character die out; nothing is left to possess. What happens is nobody's fault; each character is locked into one form or another of vindictive and deterministic personal history. Given such consequences, Mickey *cannot* possess Mickey; he cannot yearn toward what he already knows, owns, and *is*. All he can do is stare at the second stanza of Yeats' "The Lady's Second Song" that prays for the miracle:

He shall love my soul as though
Body were not all,
He shall love your body
Untroubled by the soul,
Love cram love's two divisions,
Yet keep his substance whole.
The Lord have mercy upon us.

Yet the miracle cannot occur, and at the end of the novel we are asked to wonder about the package that Margaret has sent him and which he has refused to open. What is inside does not matter; the package is a black box, both Michael's and Margaret's, which *cannot* be opened by either the reader or Michael himself. The box is a substitute for the mystery Margaret has lost. *Lilith* and *A Sea Change* illustrate, between them, the monstrosity of both desire that feeds on itself and the absence of desire, the illness of "romanticism" and "adjustment." The extraordinary popularity of *Lilith* simply indicates that more readers are enticed by the romance of romanticism than the horrors of adjustment; nonetheless, both novels answer one another.

Salamanca's most recent novel, *Embarkation* (1973),[5] concerning a passionate boat-builder father and his impotent children, seems to be a recasting of these same subjects, but since the narrator is not especially articulate, the novel cannot rise above the weight of its subject—weakness. Much of the novel focuses on the act of *selling out*: the father sets fire to his house to pay his bills, the son (an actor) does television commercials and loathes himself for it. Since the story is told by the passionless son, the father cannot be made to come alive. His shouting, drinking, and wenching seem so much cardboard noise, perhaps because Salamanca's narrative strategy compels him to tell the story of a passionate man through the voice of a zombie. The son has been crippled by his father's dominant personality; like Michael Pritchard, he is impotent. The father's suicide by drowning does not, however, help to cure his children. The effect of the entire novel is that of a man talking about emotions, rather than feeling them; the narrator's voice comes in a whisper—aware that he is damned, he cannot say why.

At the same time, however, the novel concerns possession, like *Lilith* and *A Sea Change*. Joel Linthicum, the dead father, possesses his son, Aaron, so completely that the son has no room left to grow; such a father can build beautiful boats, but he cannot nurture his offspring. The force of his personality prevents it, and they are all, one way or another, deformed or eccentric, radically imperfect creations. As in the previous novels, the crucial question involves who possesses language. In *Lilith*, Lilith owns a language and gives it to Vincent; in *A Sea Change*, Margaret learns a language from her paid tutor and lover and leaves her husband, stuck with the old language of their ruined marriage. In *Embarkation*, the father owns all the languages and teaches none to his children, who in a semi-articulate way must adopt the sounds of the marketplace. The father recites Shakespeare; the son, a failed actor, cannot. Since the son is also writing the book, the entire story is dispossessed of presence. In a curious way, *Embarkation* becomes an impossible novel, a story that cannot tell itself; it deconstructs its own life, and since it does not pretend to be an act of restitution or education for the narrator (as *Lilith* and *A Sea Change* are), what the past has to give the present is washed out of expression. All of Salamanca's novels look back at something dead; in *Embarkation* the deadness infects every word of telling.

When the self stops to consider what it is (what it has become), it may, in the first throes of dejection, put on whatever mask lies available. In Keats' early poetry the poet explains what a horror it is to face the self and to forget, for a moment, the "wonders" that surround it:

> There, when new wonders cease'd to float before,
> And thoughts of self came on; how crude and sore
> The journey homeward to habitual self!
> A mad-pursuing of the fog-born elf,
> Whose flitting lantern, through rude nettle-briar,
> Cheats us into a swamp, into a fire,
> Into the bosom of a hated thing.
>   (*Endymion*, Bk. II, ll. 274–280)

"The journey homeward to habitual self" is one that, in Salamanca as in Keats, few characters ever wish to take. The consciousness of consciousness is a hated thing, indeed, and for those few the *evasion of character* will be a lifetime project. In all of Salamanca's works, someone is trying to evade his or her character, a process which usually finds itself in the metaphor of the actor. The novels always have a crucial scene with actors: Jim Blackstarr exchanges glances with Irene Carpenter as he rehearses *A Midsummer Night's Dream*; Vincent rouses a catatonic patient by getting him to play a role in Joyce's *Exiles*; and in both *A Sea Change* and *Embarkation* the major figures are actors. The denial of the self, however, can take more extreme forms: Lilith's madness is partially the result of a refusal to confront the self (her own) that would commit incest. Her wild inventions and beautiful artistry delay but cannot eliminate the confrontation. When Michael cannot make love to Margaret, he paints her with lipstick and rouge, transforming her into "the tattooed lady" (he says) but actually putting her into disguise. He paints the body with which he cannot come to terms.

In this sense, the actor is a hero of sorts: in performing he allows the imagination to permeate his daily existence. When he evades his own character, he enters into a new world, no matter whether he recites memorized lines or acts in a role he himself has thought up. To keep the sense of potential alive, the actor becomes (for a moment) what he *can* be, always the instrument of his imagination or somebody else's. Only when a man is unable to perform (*A Sea Change*) or cannot get off the stage (*Lilith*) do we begin to see the hazards of both acting and the imagination. If he can do nothing but act or if he lives entirely in the world of the imagination, he is fated to live outside the given world, its laws, and his own character. He becomes, then, either schizophrenic or psychopathological.

To drown is to evade the self; to survive is to confront it again. The paradox of Salamanca's work is that his characters are most alive when they are drowning and most dead when they are "just living"—facing up to what they are and what fate has made them. In drowning, they go mad, are dispersed, or sink deep into their performances, their "acting." In surviving, they also die. At times the confrontation with the self—Lilith's facing up to the trauma of her incest—is so horrible that the self simply does not outlive the confrontation. Unlike Hawkes, whose works *begin* with the dreamworld of subjectivism and stay there, so that character can be evaded forever (the exception is *The Lime Twig*), Salamanca plunges his reader into a world where the self tries to establish its boundaries, loses them, and then faces up to the wreckage. To this extent his characters are cursed with ambition, to find a "presence" that disappears as soon as self-consciousness begins. They are defeated, both ways. As a consequence, Salamanca's work has little of the fancy and wit one associates with contemporary fiction. What it loses in wit it gains in emotional depth, in the risks it is willing to take.

Notes

1. R. D. Laing, *The Divided Self* (Baltimore: Penguin Books, 1965), p. 204. Laing discusses the common schizophrenic image of the "black sun" or the "occidental star."
2. J. R. Salamanca, *The Lost Country* (New York: Simon and Schuster, 1958), p. 312.
3. J. R. Salamanca, *Lilith* (New York: Simon and Schuster, 1961), p. 365–6. Subsequent references are to this edition.
4. J. R. Salamanca, *A Sea Change* (New York: Knopf, 1969), p. 167. Subsequent references are to this edition.
5. J. R. Salamanca, *Embarkation* (New York: Knopf, 1973).

J. D. SALINGER

1919–

Jerome David Salinger was born on January 1, 1919, in New York City. He was educated at Valley Forge Military Academy, where he edited *Cross Sabres*, graduating in 1936. He subsequently spent brief periods at New York University, Ursinus College, and Columbia University. From 1942 through 1946 he served in the 4th Infantry Division of the U. S. Army, achieving the rank of staff sergeant. He married Claire Douglas in 1955; they had two children before divorcing in 1967.

While at Columbia University, Salinger took a class in short-story writing from Whit Burnett, founding editor of *Story* magazine. Salinger subsequently sold his early fiction to *Story*, then quickly advanced to the higher-paying fiction magazines like the *Saturday Evening Post*, *Esquire*, and the *New Yorker*. Between 1941 and 1954 Salinger contributed some twenty stories to the "slicks."

The work Salinger wishes to be remembered for begins with the publication of "A Perfect Day for Bananafish," about the suicide of Seymour Glass; it is the touchstone for all the stories about the Glass family: those in *Nine Stories* (1953); *Franny and Zooey* (1961); "*Raise High the Roof Beam, Carpenters*" and "*Seymour—An Introduction*" (1963); and "Hapworth 16, 1924" (1965). The Glass family stories concern the efforts of flawed, well-meaning people to deal with the essential hypocrisy of the world, and are told from the viewpoints of various members of the Glass family. They range in tone from the kindness of Esmé in dealing with a psychologically shattered soldier in "For Esmé—with Love and Squalor" to the dark hopelessness of "Pretty Mouth and Green My Eyes."

Salinger's most famous work is *The Catcher in the Rye* (1951), one of the most popular novels of the latter half of the twentieth century. It tells the story of Holden Caulfield's struggle against hopelessness in a hypocritical world following his expulsion from prep school. Much of the book is cynical in tone, but Caulfield's despair is tempered with love for his sister and a vague sense of purpose in life. The book struck a powerful chord with the disenchanted yet idealistic youth of the fifties, and with an adult audience also conscious of repression and conformity. It has become a classic story of adolescence and continues to be read widely.

For a time in the fifties many considered Salinger the most accomplished writer of fiction in America. His reputation has declined somewhat since the mid-sixties, perhaps because he has published no new fiction since 1965. Certainly *The Catcher in the Rye* had continued to be influential, and the Glass stories remain a model of intricate story-cycle construction. His early uncollected stories were reprinted in an unauthorized edition (*The Complete Uncollected Stories of J. D. Salinger*, 2 vols.) in 1974. Since 1953 he has lived in seclusion in rural New Hampshire.

CHARLES CAGLE
"*The Catcher in the Rye* Revisited"
Midwest Quarterly, Autumn 1962, pp. 343–51

Little, it seems, remains to be said of the literary skyrocket of the fifties—J. D. Salinger's *The Catcher in the Rye*—except the inevitable: if critical attention be any criterion, it has succeeded in joining the ranks of the American classics. In which particular tradition it falls has become today as problematical as its very worth seemed when Virgilia Paterson, writing a review of the novel in the summer of 1951, warned that its inception would call for "a tempest of reactions." She was right—but now that Salinger has again spoken, the forces which marshalled in both praise and denunciation for *Catcher* have re-formed to descend on the fragile Glass family, leaving us relatively free to reconsider Holden Caulfield and his world. Viewed in a still youthful retrospect, the novel has assumed both a firmer critical position and a curiously prophetic shape as social literature.

It would be an endless difficulty to refute—or even discuss—the myriad views concerning *Catcher*. Five books of critical material on his fiction have already been published and, as with the article, the mountain grows. It is also pointless to examine the superficial levels of story and symbol. Like all American classics, *Catcher* can be interpreted on multi-levels. But it is, after all, a mere work of fiction—a story; in a mock-picaresque manner we are told about the adventures of one Holden Caulfield. And on a second level the book can be interpreted as a series of meaningful, tangible symbols: symbols meaningful within the context of the story only, woven into a fictional fabric which generates broader ideas only by an extension of character, atmosphere, and plot. All this, too, has been dealt with before, most notably by Carl F. Strauch in his "Kings in the Back Row: Meaning through Structure."

Concerning tradition, the book was early placed in any of several convenient categories—the individual in an Odyssean "quest" of self-identification; the saint isolated in the social milieu; the Innocent as whimsical, nasty, and sometimes prophetic social commentator; and the individual standing on the (psychological?) frontier of the new American dream (nightmare?). Each of these categories—and others more tenuous—has been treated at varying lengths by critics and all apparently with considerable justification.

Edwin Bowden, for example, makes a most convincing attempt to place *Catcher* in the fictional tradition of "frontier isolation"—along with Cooper's *Deerslayer*, Cather's *My Antonia* and (of course) Mark Twain's *Huckleberry Finn*. This tradition, Bowden says, forms merely a facet of the overall American theme of "human isolation . . . the loneliness of man separated from his fellow man"; but strikes, nevertheless, what is probably the most familiar chord in the psychical experience of Americans—the continual "myth of the flight of the hunter before dreaded civilization." Natty Bumppo, Huck Finn, the tragic Mr. Shimerda, and Holden Caulfield all face the deadly introspection of splenetic isolation. Holden's tragedy is, however, less poignant than Huck's, less sinister than Mr. Shimerda's. About Holden, Bowden writes:

> All he knows at the moment is that as he looks about him he sees only a world of 'phonies', of sham and pretense, or a world so devoted to selfish exclusiveness or shallow pleasures or degrading self-contentment, if not to more active cruelty, that a boy with self-respect and common decency and some feeling for the potentialities of the human being cannot be a part of it.

While this seems to indicate a sociological concern, Bowden's actual point is geographical rather than psychological, and it remains for other critics—such as Arthur Heisermann and James Miller—to get misfit Holden on the only mid-twentieth century escape raft still afloat: the psychiatrist's couch.

In this respect Messrs. Heisermann and Miller view Holden's real desire to move "outside society" as a traumatic confrontation—and a real calamity since geographically he has reached an impasse. In the ideal sense, Huck's Mississippi River merely empties into Cooper's placid Lake Glimmerglass; but Holden's imaginary forest is, from the beginning, cut off from any passage. It simply has ceased to exist in the same pragmatic way that social isolation has ceased to be functional. They write: "Huck Finn had the Mississippi and at the end of the Mississippi he had the wild west beyond Arkansas. The hero of *The Waste Land* had Shantih, the peace which passes human understanding. Bloom had Molly and his own ignorance; Dedalus had Paris and Zurich. But for Holden there is no place to go." Thus the geographical fact precipitates the psychological tragedy, bringing with it, presumably, the darker implications of social guilt in the collective, humanistic sense.

The only retreat open then to one so frustrated as Holden—so persecuted by his own exposed sensitivity—is sainthood; not canonization in the jazzed-up, disaffiliated sense of coffee-house rebel, but rather in the traditional role of Christian martyr—or perhaps as an adolescent and Westernized Bodhisattva. With such a platform the literary religionists speak out.

From Josephine Jacobsen's devout insistence that Salinger vibrates with the "human exchange of beatific signals" to Donald Barr's "theological conclusion" that Salinger's mystical sense does not reject life in the world but merely transforms it to "the terms of its essential godhead, and gives peace" we see laid the groundwork of what might be termed a critical obsession with the Salingersque dogma of Original Zen. But even that smacks too irreverently of the Kerouac brand of phony adultism for Dan Wakefield. He carefully lifts the moral framework of the "Salinger myth" (a myth he takes quite seriously) out of the tainted province of the Beats, whose "advertised search . . . has ended, at least literally, not with love but with heroin," and places him squarely in the upper regions—in fact, as the "only writer to emerge in America since the end of the Second World War who is writing on what has been the grandest theme of literature: the relationship of man to God, or lack of God." Granville Hicks, as a kind of visiting dignitary, seems pleased to add the benediction by declaring Holden simply "a seeker after truth."

After the religionists always come the politicians and the skeptics. In fact, as Henry Grunwald points out in his concise and often amusing introduction to *Salinger: A Critical and Personal Portrait*, the critics ride the whole "range of meaning" regarding Salinger and reach a zenith of particularity, from Hugh McClean's unintentional *bon mot* ("a terrifying picture of the conservative's plight today") to Angry Young Man Kenneth Tynan's public identification with Salinger's "society" ("Every fat woman on earth is Jesus Christ"). Grunwald himself, after brilliantly cataloging the various critical approaches, ends on the rather sisterly hope that "a few more celebrations" may be awarded us through the "delight" of more and more Salinger material.

Not all the critics, however, are delighted with even what Salinger we have. A leading skeptic, Leslie Fiedler, obliquely attacks the "latter day Pastoralism" of child-like innocence which is clearly the point of Holden's salvation for the religionists. In a brilliant but often dogmatic and always sensational essay on the cult of the child entitled "The Eye of Innocence," Fiedler places Holden in a Good-Bad-Boy category along with Huck Finn and Tom Sawyer, and then distrusts anyway the modern notion of moving the child from the periphery of art to the center of it. Peter J. Seng echoes the same conviction by calling Holden an "immature judge of life." And vitriolic Mary McCarthy, writing in *Harper's*, say *Catcher* is "based on a scheme of exclusiveness" with outsider Holden as "really an insider with the track all to himself."

The criticism grows even more violent with Maxwell Geismar and George Steiner. Geismar denounces the "dubious literary form" of *Catcher* in general, and the "sad little screwed-up hero" portrait of Holden in particular. Steiner, after tossing off his best invective against "the Salinger Industry" footnotes his grievances by noting "Salinger flatters the very ignorance and moral shallowness of his young readers,"—and, still unquiet, frowns on Salinger's "shoddy use" of a collegiate, and therefore watered-down, Zen.

Marius Bewley in his sweeping, critical book, *The Eccentric Design*, finds no room for mention of Salinger in relationship to form *or* tradition in the "classic" American novel. Of course, Salinger's proximity prevents his inclusion in any conservative critical appraisal of Tradition, but it is interesting to speculate on the criteria Bewley sets up by which to judge the "great American writers." For example, the influence of Fitzgerald and Lardner has often been cited in Salinger's work—even old Holden says, "I was crazy about *The Great Gatsby*"—and Bewley raises Fitzgerald to eminence as "one who fully deserves the company I put him in" (i.e., Cooper, Hawthorne, Melville, James). Bewley's identification of Fitzgerald as a "class" writer and his inclusion of Gatsby as a "mystic embodiment" in the tradition of Natty Bumppo, Huck

Finn, and Ishmael suggests the same critical ground which we have already seen prepared for Salinger. Stripped of romanticism, the mental and social affinity of John T. Unger, the hero of Fitzgerald's "The Diamond as Big as the Ritz" and member of "the most expensive and most exclusive boys' preparatory school in the world," is much closer to Pency Prep's failure (Holden) than to, say, Huck Finn. And Holden's "tragedy"—his inability to fathom the rationale of things—is a kind of extension of Jay Gatsby's tormented innocence.

Bewley merely holds a few writers responsible for contributing to "the new American experience" and declares they are "those who have been most seriously and intensely concerned with life." By *life* Bewley means "a distinctive quality and set of interests. . . . traditionally determined and conditioned by the deprivations and confinements of the American condition, and directed by a specific set of problems or tensions growing out of the historical circumstance of America's existence." He goes on to point out the catholicity of such writers as a group in the extraordinarily "non-sensuous" approach to their material and the fact that their best efforts have "been less of the senses than of the spirit, and less of the spirit than the mind." By non-sensuous Bewley obviously does not make a full bow to Puritanism and a lack of obscenity (he couldn't mean that and keep clear the socio-literary references to the Fitzgerald of the twenties): he does mean, however, that sensuous experience is used almost always "for the sake of making an abstract point." And it is precisely this "point" which a group of sympathetic critics—Kermode, Costello, Corbett, for example—make in regard to the language and sexual "situations" in *Catcher*.

The second qualification by which Bewley limits his selection of great writers is found in his definition of the term "tension." According to him, tensions are "merely so many channels by which we are able, however stumblingly, to reach the depth of meaning and the roots of creative impulse in these writers." In such realms, these writers "sometimes encountered problems that seemed insoluble, and which deflected them towards despair. . . . and nihilistic glooms. . . ." It is this inner struggle and personal search that is, at least currently, the fascinating aspect of the search for J. D. Salinger himself.

It is also and precisely this "nihilistic gloom" which pervades—literally haunts—the world of Holden Caulfield. Despite the early dismissal by Ernest Jones—who meandered into the Salinger criticism (*Catcher* is "predictable and boring") and out again in a 1951 review in *The Nation*—*Catcher* is not just "a mirror" held up to us all: it is a mirror of *mirrors*, mercilessly reflecting the multi-structures of a sick and frightened society based on "adjustments." And Salinger's art probes the neo-religious stirrings of a disoriented generation who must search for meaning in existence if only because they sense a personal guilt in *not* searching.

The serious artist, like Salinger, driven by Bewley's "tensions" and producing not solutions but *problems* of disorder, creates his world, his specific vision. Richard Chase, in *The American Novel and Its Tradition*, writes:

> Judging by our greatest novels, the American imagination, even when it wishes to assuage and reconcile the contradictions of life, has not been stirred by the possibility of catharsis or incarnation, by the tragic or Christian possibility. It has been stirred, rather, by the aesthetic possibilities of radical forms of alienation, contradiction, and disorder.

From the first awakening of the American novel the broadest sweep of intellectual interest has been not with the restating of common spiritual values, in the popular sense, but in at least two other directions. First, in a distrust in all values degraded by institutionalism; and second, in a quest for identity both within and without the social confines. The first direction was the legacy of politics, not art; when the primary artistic concern of the late eighteenth century American novelists seemed to be a degenerative elaboration of the French heroic romances subjected to a re-stylization of the English novel of manners, the nouveau American hero could be nothing but a paradox. He could exist only on the ether of a kind of "universal distrust"—a term which Dickens used to indicate the "one great blemish in the popular mind of America."

The foundation stones of this American and his distrust—this escape from his political and social nature into his "true" nature—were set down by the Age of the Enlightenment, particularly by the Social Contract of J. J. Rousseau. The right of society to govern man's behavior, according to Rousseau, did not come from nature but from institutions and conventions. It was to escape these conventions that man moved Westward with his mind and body, westward into the romance of the heart—Byron's "pathless woods"; and the adventure of the spirit—Governor Bradford's "more goodly country." It is toward the mythical, healing West that Salinger sends Holden Caulfield.

In *The Art of Fiction* Henry James points out the artist's "duty" to trace the actions of man in society; this is probably a more honest—more sensible—evaluation than Harry Levin's insistence that literature "is the cause of social effects." Fitzgerald, it should be argued, did not produce the Jazz Age—he was produced *by* it, and his literature merely subjectivizes a personal involvement. The influence of all art, at any rate, is entirely intellectual and limited to relatively minor cliques. We must accept and casually modify Auden's wonderful line to say, "Art makes nothing sociological happen."

Salinger's view of society, illustrated through the eyes of an immature but pure-at-heart adolescent simply raises the question of the fate of the individual who is impertinent with the closing-in walls of conformity. The sociologists have felt our pulse in such books as William H. Whyte's *The Organization Man*, David Reisman's *The Lonely Crowd*, and C. Wright Mills' *The Power Elite*. Out of the complexity of the human heart—bounded on one side by the willfulness to natural rebellion and on another by the desire to "belong" no matter what the consequences—the real struggle of our time is one of sociological adjustment. Emerson's dark thought on the "occult relations of scorpion and man" seems peculiarly ominous here. Cornered, man will destroy his soul rather than submit to a modification of his justice. If he is rescued by a society bent on adjusting him, scientifically, into a proper niche, then he is a frightening illustration of a world soon to come.

It is not merely sociological dogma to insist that the essence of *Catcher* is really the distilled and heady vibration of our own time, the same unquiet beating of restless feet which Fitzgerald heard thirty years ago when the world was caught between social change and economic disaster. The problem today is not merely an existential one, not merely one of all the sad young men ending in personal despair; it is a universal one—charged with the frightening neurosis of moral decay out of which there is little hope of survival for the sensitive American. *Catcher* is perhaps the one significant trumpet to sound our retreat into the next half-century.

ALFRED CHESTER
"Salinger: How to Love without Love"
Commentary, June 1963, pp. 467–74

Since I lived in outermost Paris during practically the whole of the 1950's, I was very late in learning of what seems to have been one of the chief American diversions during that decade: J. D. Salinger's Glass family. As matters appear to stand right now, I could, without stretching things too much, say that I didn't learn about the Glasses until they had not only ceased to be a diversion but had evidently ceased to be at all. First news of them reached me in a letter from a Jewish girl I'd known in New York, who, oddly, or not so oddly, enough, later married an Irish-American. Apropos of nothing I can especially remember, she asked: "Aren't you crazy for the Glass family? I am, especially for Seymour." It didn't occur to me that this had anything to do with Salinger—though I had some years earlier read "A Perfect Day for Bananafish"—and it was a year before I found out who the Glasses were.

I found out when I came to New York, where, needless to say, almost everyone was crazy for the Glass family and seemed to be on intimate terms with them. It made me feel very left out of things indeed, like the only man in town who hadn't been invited to a party. When I finally got around to crashing, I could hardly believe I'd come to the right place, for I never succeeded in finding those marvelous and celebrated people who'd been talked about so heatedly in living rooms and magazines. If "Franny," "Seymour," "Zooey," and "Raise High the Roof Beam, Carpenters" are really the right and only stories about the Glasses that appeared during the 50's, then the reason I couldn't find them is that they weren't there. They did not, in the simplest and more usual sense of the phrase, ever come alive, and I suspect that the reasons they did for so many readers were largely external. There was first of all the reservoir of love built by Salinger with *The Catcher in the Rye*; there was the very contemporary New York type family itself—Jewish and Irish and Central Park and middle class—given flattering depth with a lot of religious paraphernalia; there was the family chronicling (rather in the form of a writer's notes for a contemplated novel) that more and more pervaded each piece; and there was also the reader's confidence that, since the stories were beginning to read like serial installments, if lifelikeness didn't actually obtain among the Glasses, it would surely one day come—providing cancer, the atom bomb, or old age didn't get there first. Life would arrive soon or Soon. Salinger could be trusted. Who else, since the war, had created such a host of lifelike and memorable characters?

The genius or, if you will, ingenuity, of Salinger's earlier work lay not in his creation of individuals, but in his depiction of types. Nearly everyone in his stories and in his novel rang bells like mad. You could not have learned to know thyself better from reading his work, but you might have recognized some of your sillier traits, and you would definitely have recognized the people and the things around you in it. He was always putting his finger on just the right gesture, on the precise tone of voice, on the exact object or circumstance. And if one suspected that he was in scorn of the vanities and trivialities of the milieu he described, he made them nevertheless glamorous, or rather he did not subtract from metropolitan life any of its mythical and publicized glamor. From *The Catcher* one came away charmed by the very things that appalled Holden: the night-club, the theater, the pretentious sophisticates, the stupid office girls, the prep school, everything. It was all so precisely depicted that it gave one the pleasure of the miniature. You couldn't possibly be offended by it—even if you happened to be a stupid and pretentious night-club. *The Catcher* is, so far as I know, an unparalleled example of a writer's having the best of both worlds, of getting both God and Mammon to work for him wholeheartedly. (I'm not trying to diminish the value of *The Catcher* which—though both it and I have grown twelve years staler—is still one of the freshest novels this country has produced since the war.) The life in *The Catcher*, like the life in some of the *Nine Stories*—since whose appearance I have grown ten years staler, while they have grown a generation staler—springs from the swift, immediate, authentic response of the characters to the world around them. And the intense charm of the books came from the fact that his characters were responding to *our* world which also happened to be theirs. Their world will go as soon as our world goes (and then, of course, the charm will disappear, as it already has from Esmé, from Teddy, from most of them) because it was never transmuted; it was merely depicted. What once was the most moving scene in *The Catcher*—when Holden tries to explain his anguish over American civilization to the absurd girl he's with at Rockefeller Center—has now become flat and insufficient. The time for disgust over Cadillacs has passed and Holden's suffering does not seem interesting or real enough, enough *itself*, to make us separate it from its object, thereby turning the object into symbol and the suffering into our own. All his lament makes us want to do is prod him gently, wake him up, and say: nobody cares about Cadillacs any more.

That Salinger's feelings did not run very deep in his early work is ultimately why what he hated could charm us and why, when the object of his feelings was made trivial by time, so were his feelings. Of all Salinger's characters the one with the most staying power has proved to be Muriel Glass, Seymour the Suicide's wife in "A Perfect Day for Bananafish." It is still utterly delightful to see her polishing her nails and waving her hands around to dry the stuff, to listen to the inane things she says on the telephone, to watch her cross and uncross her legs, touch an ashtray, handle a cigarette, move the receiver. There is no doubt she never ceases to be a type, but it is Salinger's problem, not ours, if we cannot see so lively and physical a type as a good reason for Seymour's suicide. But Salinger, I suppose, wants us to think backward: if Seymour killed himself, he must have done it because—and the only because in the story is Muriel. So then we have to hate Muriel. It's rather like the traditional Hollywood technique of letting the audience know how to feel about a situation by showing how an on-the-scene observer reacts to it.

In "Bananafish," as in the Rockefeller Center scene from *The Catcher*, Salinger uses a device that he repeats elaborately and at great length in two of the Glass stories. It appears to be a simple contrasting: Seymour against Muriel, Holden against the girl, the individual against the type, intelligence against stupidity, real feeling against no feeling, what Salinger loves against what Salinger hates. The usual idea of contrast is to intensify white by putting it against black, and vice versa. But Salinger doesn't play the game quite straight in "Bananafish," for what he does is try to make us imagine white by putting void against black. As it happens, his trick backfires because the reader falls in love with Muriel the black, and Salinger is left holding an Act of Depth in search of a character. And Seymour? What is Seymour? Who is he? He is no one; he's just an idea.

So far as I know, no new story by Salinger appeared during the four years preceding 1955 when both "Franny" and "Raise High" were published in the *New Yorker*. I am convinced that those four silent years were spent by him on the road to Satori and in deepest spiritual anguish. How far along he got, and why he returned, seem like matters that shouldn't be speculated about in public; yet since he obtrudes himself and his own spiritual interests with ever-lessening embarrassment into the Glass pieces, and since it is impossible to understand his stories without gauging the status of Salinger's soul, I'll tell you what I have measured from his work. There is an often quoted Zen saying which goes something like this: "When you are unenlightened, mountains are mountains and rivers are rivers. When you are approaching Enlightenment, mountains are not mountains and rivers are not rivers. When you have attained Enlightenment, mountains are mountains and rivers are rivers." Well, I think Salinger got stuck about midway, where mountains and rivers aren't mountains and rivers. He went far enough along to undo himself and then stopped, or was stopped, cold, or perhaps hot, or perhaps, as he might put it, hot and cold. And he started talking. (If he sometimes talks as Americans often seem to talk when they are having at you from Satori Boulevard—whether they've been traveling via Zen, Gurdjieff, mescalin, LSD or whatever—as if he were a public relations made for the Godhead, it would nonetheless be diabolical, not to say asinine, to attack him for the product he represents rather than for his manner of pushing it.)

Why did he not go on? Because he couldn't, and you can often hear the wheels of his spirit spinning in the sand where they got caught. But qualities and textures, gestures and surfaces, the stuff of his early writings, were completely undone, peeled open; and Salinger fell to a level of feeling so deep, so complex, that his relationship to life no longer had any relevance to Cadillacs, nail polish, leg crossings, telephones, regional speech patterns, or American civilization. (With respect to the Zen quotation, one might also say: his relationship to life did not *as yet* have relevance to nail polish, etc.) But neither did it have relevance to Satori. Like Dante, he was chronologically *nel mezzo del camin'*, and like Dante he was in *la selva oscura*. Dante, of course, didn't talk about it for a long time; he waited, my ignorant memory tries to recollect, between ten and twenty years. But Salinger was impulsive, and he chose, or was driven, to speak not only of the sands in which he was still stuck but of the starting place, which no longer meant anything to him, and of the destination, which he could not even imagine. Not having arrived at his destination, he had not become the agent of prophetic statements (except insofar as he publicizes, through marvelous quotations, the statements of others), and among the resources of his humanity there had never been, as there had been for Dante, a great poetic imagination and an already formulated religious design to tell him what the second half of the road was like. Dante need have gotten no closer to Paradise than Salinger has to Satori for the *Comedy* to have found its way. Whatever the literal background of his honeymoons with Virgil and Beatrice, in his art *he* was leading *them*; he knew exactly where to go and what salvation looked like. The Church and his own medieval genius told him, and they told him in sensual, communicable images.

I would guess that Salinger's Glass stories are, or were intended to be, a religious allegory, with the seven Glass brothers and sisters representing the various stages toward Enlightenment, from Franny, the youngest, who is just entering the crisis, to Seymour, the oldest, who has made it, who is *there*, whose Bananafish suicide we are now told to see as his means of shooting himself out of this world—dying to life, as the expression goes—and into Satori. I would also guess that the allegory idea didn't come to Salinger until after "Franny" (which is the first, best, most tender of the later pieces), and that since it posits Seymour as the Enlightenment, the project was doomed from the start, for Seymour's enlightenment, which merits no capital "E," is a kind of cherry-flavored innocence, much inferior to Holden Caulfield's dream of catching children in the rye. Seymour is the captain of the God-ship lollipop.

For the form of "Franny," Salinger revisits "Bananafish" and Rockefeller Center. He sets up Franny and Lane Coutell as his White Queen and Black King, and it works beautifully. It works because, while Salinger thinks he is up to his old trick of materializing White by holding nothing up to Black, the emotion that is Franny is a real one, deeply felt. She *is* White. And what facility Salinger has lost in his dealings with the surfaces of things seems to be a gain, for it limits him, when talking of Franny the character (as opposed to Franny the Anguish), to flat unobtrusive descriptions:

> Franny saw [Lane's arm waving], and him, and waved extravagantly back. . . . She was wearing a sheared raccoon coat. . . . She threw her arms around him and kissed him. It was a station-platform kiss—spontaneous enough to begin with, but rather inhibited in the follow-through. . . . "Did you get my letter?" she asked, and added, almost in the same breath, "You look almost frozen, you poor man. Why didn't you wait inside?"

Just enough to get her on the page, to embody the emotion. The anguish of her crisis is all the rest of her, and it is so intense and so convincing that it doesn't matter a bit that she is appalled by virtually the same things that appalled Holden— the phonies and the activities of their world.

Even the Black King is improved by the depth of the new Salinger. It has been observed that Salinger is "unfair" in his treatment of Lane Coutell, that he trims from the boy everything that might reveal him as something more than a snob, a prig, a creature of fashion. This of course is a wicked way to write in our democratic and liberal present, but when that observation has been made, we can also observe that Salinger has never been able to do so wicked a thing before. His contempt for Lane comes through very clearly, as it never did with any of his early characters. Salinger ridicules him. He ridicules Lane not only for his vanity but for his humanity. He makes Lane's hunger ludicrous by having him gnaw at his meal while Franny is practically swooning with her suffering (and of course unable to touch the food on her plate); he makes Lane's love ludicrous by having him remember "that once, in a borrowed car, after kissing Franny for a half hour or so, he had kissed her coat lapel, as though it were a perfectly desirable, organic extension of the person itself." And because Salinger is honest and open—and without charm—in his hatred of Lane, his little game of setting his character up as a human being so that he can bowl him over with ridicule for being one makes Lane his single complete creation. At the end, having purged himself of his violent feelings, Salinger has a moment of tenderness toward Lane, gives up whipping him, and allows the boy to show himself as genuinely concerned and worried about Franny.

Heaven only knows what happened to Salinger during those months between "Franny" and "Raise High," a story that is fake from the word go. Salinger once again uses the "Bananafish" device of Black and White, but in a quite different way. There are a whole bunch of Blacks this time (pretentious guests from the bride's side at Seymour's wedding)

who take up all but a score or so of the hundred-odd pages; and the White is just a few pages of excerpts from Seymour's diary. (Seymour never appears; in fact he never ever makes an in-person appearance in these stories; and I think, if they continue, he never will; I think Buddy is his body, his worldly incarnation.) Shuttling between the Blacks and the White goes the narrator, Buddy the Body, second son of the Glasses, and though he is apparently very loyal to his older brother, he and Salinger make the mistake of printing verbatim the writings of Seymour the Soul. And what a mistake. All those "how sweets" and "so beautifuls" and "unbearably happys" and "overwhelmingly gratefuls" make a farce of Satori. Salinger has gotten out of his depth in his intentions and resorted to the fakest and most trivial kind of hagiography. Seymour is nothing but a mixture of cold blood and confectioner's sugar.

To compensate, Salinger makes his Blacks blacker than ever and more pretentious than ever. Seymour should look real by comparison, but he doesn't because the Blacks are stripped so entirely of virtues that they become merely grotesque, not Black. There is an unfortunate internal explosion as a result of all the shenanigans, and Salinger's malice, rather than the Blacks, becomes contrasted with Seymour. What is "human-size," however petty or vain, is beautiful to Seymour, but if Seymour is Salinger's conception of Enlightenment, then by his mistreatment of his characters, Salinger places himself in a pretty backward position. Another result of these problems is that Salinger becomes desperate in his style. Seeming not to know what to do next, he sets off in wild pursuit of himself, of the old Salinger. The voice under the prose begins to sound as if it belongs to Mann's Aschenbach, still dying his hair and powdering his face and chasing all over Venice for a glimpse of the boy. Since he can no longer reach the sensual world, Salinger must use a thousand abstract words to describe what once took ten concrete ones. For his lost charm, he substitutes archaisms, cutenesses, coynesses, leaden mannerisms. Listen to Buddy describing himself helping people into cars:

> I was not only twenty-three but a conspicuously re-tarded twenty-three. I remember loading people into cars without any degrees of competence whatever. On the contrary, I went about it with a certain disingen-uous, cadetlike semblance of single-mindedness, of adherence to duty. After a few minutes, in fact, I became all too aware that I was catering to the needs of a predominantly older, shorter, fleshier genera-tion, and my performance as an arm taker and door closer took on an even more thoroughly bogus puis-sance. I began to conduct myself like an exceptionally adroit, wholly engaging young giant with a cough.

Salinger also tries to get some feelings into the piece; there are none handily about, so he constructs them. Take a look at this Gigantic-Orchestration-of-Feelings-Appropriate-to-Great-Themes Charade that Buddy plays out after reading Seymour's diary while sitting on the edge of the bathtub:

> I remember closing the diary—actually, slamming it shut—after the word "happy." I then sat for several minutes with the diary under one arm, until I became conscious of a certain discomfort from hav-ing sat so long on the side of the bathtub. When I stood up, I found I was perspiring more profusely than I had all day, as though I had just got out of a tub, rather than just been sitting on the side of one. I went over to the laundry hamper, raised the lid, and, with an almost vicious wrist movement, literally threw Seymour's diary into some sheets and pillow-cases that were on the bottom of the hamper. Then,

for want of a better, more constructive idea, I went back and sat down on the side of the bathtub again. I stared for a minute or two at Boo Boo's message on the medicine-cabinet mirror, and then I left the bathroom, closing the door excessively hard after me, as though sheer force might lock up the place forever after.

Listen to all that Great Emotion banging like a broken piano in an old silent-movie house. What is Buddy's violent reaction all about? Is it his response to having read that sopping fraud, his older brother, whom he adores? He carries on as if Seymour were a sudden revelation to him, and yet he has known him intimately and spiritually all his life. Buddy is there to feel for us as in the Hollywood movies, so that we will know that Seymour's writings are Enormities, not Inanities. But Buddy himself isn't feeling a thing. How could he, when he is just a pile of cold words? And when Seymour is just a pile?

By the time he is done with "Raise High," Salinger is faced with a demented fraud playing Satori, a bunch of grotesques playing common humanity, and a clownish vacuum playing humanity, and a clownish vacuum playing himself. He can't look forward; he can't look backward; and he can't stay where he is because it is a loveless, unloving nowhere. What is he to do? Where is he to turn?

"Zooey," the longest of the four late pieces, was published in 1957, and though it appears to be a sequel to "Franny," it is actually a sequel to its more immediate predecessor. It is an attempt by Salinger to rescue, first of all, his own spiritual status by offering a Way of Love to the world, and a way, indeed, of loving those very same people he himself hates. It is also an attempt to rescue Seymour by making him the ultimate inventor of the Way. To avoid putting Seymour to any further tests, he keeps him out of the story. And to avoid putting the Way of Love to a test, Salinger keeps from the story anyone who might possibly upset him. Thus, not a Black in sight anywhere. Everyone is White—Franny, Zooey, and their mother—and they are all locked in the White Castle, the Glasses' Manhattan apartment. The action takes place a couple of days after "Franny," and Franny is home, but still in anguish. Her worried mother has a long dialogue with her sixth son Zooey while he takes a bath. She pleads with him to help Franny, and though he tries, he cannot. However, he is a television actor and he has a great plan up his sleeve which involves an elaborate interplay of identities, so cumbersome and complicated that you can't help tripping over a bunch of allegorical wires. (I don't know what it all means.) He goes to Seymour's and Buddy's old room and, using Seymour's telephone, which is on Buddy's desk, he calls Franny on the family telephone and, using Buddy's voice at first, but then later his own, and quoting Seymour, he cures Franny's anguish by telling her that everyone is Jesus Christ and therefore they all merit love even if they stink. (By this he means the Blacks, like Lane Coutell and the wedding guests in "Raise High" and everyone else in the world who isn't named Glass.) It is rather like the end of a Russian movie; the heartbroken girl unexpectedly hears a speech by a commissar and is made miraculously whole. Zooey-Buddy-Seymour's Christianity sounds very sweet, and Franny buys it, but of course it is just garbage. All Zooey is saying is that if you close your eyes and pretend that the Blacks are Whites, then you can love them, especially when they're not around, and especially when the particular "everyone" that Zooey is referring to is an imaginary fat lady that Seymour dreamed up to represent the non-Glasses.

Well, perhaps Salinger is fooling Franny and himself into feeling that Seymour, because he has provided the Way, is no fraud, and perhaps Salinger is enthralled by his spiritual status after having twisted out a syllogism that grants he loves the lower orders and yet permits him to avoid any soiling contact with them. However, that Salinger continues to loathe, has indeed increased his loathing of, things human is shown by the way he must sterilize the physical. When Zooey berates Franny for refusing Mama Glass's chicken soup, he berates her because she doesn't realize that it is "consecrated" chicken soup. And observe the way Salinger neutralizes Zooey's beauty; Buddy is the narrator, though he doesn't appear in the story:

> Close up, either full-face or in profile, he was surpassingly handsome, even spectacularly so. His eldest sister . . . has asked me to describe him as looking like "the blue-eyed Jewish-Irish Mohican scout who died in your arms at the roulette table at Monte Carlo." A more general and surely less parochial view was that he had just barely been saved from too-handsomeness, not to say gorgeousness, by virtue of one ear's protruding slightly more than the other. I myself hold a very different opinion from either of these. I submit that Zooey's face was close to being a wholly beautiful face. As such, it was of course vulnerable to the same variety of glibly undaunted and usually specious evaluations that any legitimate art object is.

Whatever flesh may have been on Zooey's surpassingly handsome face at the beginning of that description is thoroughly ripped off by the time we get to "holy" (spelled "wholly") beautiful. No, sir, you can't lust after our Zooey. And to make sure lust never even stirs in the reader, Salinger prefaces the face with this: "From the rear—particularly where his vertebrae were visible—he might almost have passed for one of those needy metropolitan children who are sent out every summer to endowed camps to be fattened and sunned." Where Zooey's body is submerged in the bath, water has a "dehydrating effect on him." Where his knees stick out, they are "dry islands." Body is so utterly negated in Zooey—as it is indeed in all the other Glasses—that when he characterizes Franny's statements that Lane Coutell is a nice boy as "just sex talking, buddy. I know that voice. Oh, do I know that voice!" the reader feels that if Zooey *does* know that voice, it must be from having heard it over the radio. (I imagine that Salinger's justification for unsexing the Glasses is that he wants to attribute to them, though they are adults, the same innocence that belonged to the children he used to write about.)

"Zooey" is nearly as bad a story as "Raise High." Salinger fails to gives his characters any degree of life, and he fails to give substance or reality to their whereabouts, despite the endless cataloguings of furniture and household items. Since most of the story is in dialogue, the characters must live through their voices. But their voices are never heard. Salinger individualizes and characterizes them with the dogtag method: Zooey is identifiable by mild oaths and the fact that he calls everyone "buddy"; Mrs. Glass is identifiable by oodles of italics; and Franny is identifiable by references to her crisis.

Any number of Salinger's readers—Alfred Kazin and John Updike among the most illustrious—have pointed out that he loves the Glasses too much and too exclusively. I think they are doing him the kindness of taking an attempt for an achievement, the protestation for the sentiment. Though he is trying very hard to act like it, I don't for a minute believe Salinger loves the Glasses. I think he probably hates them because they have never been willing to live off themselves, because he has had to construct them into pseudo-life, and thus they must represent for him the lifelessness of the idea he asks them to embody. I would guess the Glasses came into existence as postulates of the second half of the Satori road only after Salinger had despaired of getting beyond the first. To keep them alive may be for him some way of keeping the road open. Yet, they have walled up what is probably Salinger's only possible path to salvation: his art. Rebirth can come only after one gives up the idea of it; and paradoxically, Salinger's death-to-life can perhaps come only after he dies to death-to-life.

The marvel of "Seymour: An Introduction," which appeared in 1959, is that Salinger confronts himself. It is a chronicle of the confrontation between the writer and the saint, and he hardly bothers to pretend it is a fiction. How disingenuous it was of all those critics and reviewers to have spoken of the piece as though it were a story, and how heartless it was of them who had loved him so much to have rapped him on the knuckles because he, the emperor, was the first to point out that he was wearing no clothes, had in fact been naked for years. "Seymour" is a courageous act, a much more personal display than having photographs published or signing books in department stores or making public appearances. And having given himself totally to those who had been lusting after him ever since *The Catcher*, all they did was respond by crying, "Shame!"

Yes, of course, "Seymour" is mannered and self-conscious and boring, but so were the other Glass pieces—and they were in addition dishonest, except for "Franny"—even though Salinger managed to keep these things hidden from his readers, if not from himself. What he says in "Seymour" is that he cannot live without Seymour, that he cannot give up writing about Seymour even though he *cannot* write about Seymour, that there is no Seymour and he must construct him piece by piece, feature by feature. And in the process of saying so, all the literary pretensions and affectations and mannerisms are knitted into a hair-shirt which he is going to wear because that is the Way he has chosen for himself.

"Seymour" makes me think again of Aschenbach, this time in the confessional. Despite his makeup and dyed hair, he is confessing with all his heart and repenting with all his heart. His contrition is complete. Yet when he steps out of the church, where is he to go? All of the waters of Venice flow back to his love. All of Salinger's roads lead back to Seymour, or to silence, or to both.

DONALD P. COSTELLO
"Salinger and His Critics:
Autopsy of a Faded Romance"
Commonweal, October 25, 1963, pp. 132–35

As *"Raise High the Roof Beam, Carpenters"* and *"Seymour—An Introduction"* slips off the best-seller lists, the critics continue to snap at the heels of J. D. Salinger. The great disenchantment has set in among those whom Buddy Glass, the "alter-ego and collaborator" of J. D. Salinger, has called "camp followers of the arts." It is, I suppose, natural that the long-standing (since 1951) great love affair among Salinger, the public, and the critics could not continue at the same fever pitch of passion. The statistics of the love affair are phenomenal. Some two million copies of *The Catcher in the*

Rye have been sold in the United States alone; at last count the novel was required reading at 275 American colleges, enshrined not only in Bennett Cerf's Modern Library, but also in paperback editions by Signet and soon by Bantam. Recently a travelling critic has discovered that the book is a great commercial and critical success in Finland, Germany, France, Italy, Poland, Israel, Great Britain, Czechoslovakia, with many more translations now coming out. (How would " . . . all that David Copperfield kind of crap" sound in Czech?) Much more room is occupied on my bookshelf by collections of criticism of J. D. Salinger than by his collected works. Every time a Salinger story is published in *The New Yorker*, that issue of the magazine sells out in one day; and after the stories are clapped together into hard covers they have stayed on the best-seller lists for months upon months. Salinger himself has been canonized by a *Time* cover story, and by a *Life* feature, the whole point of which was that Mr. Luce's reporter couldn't get an interview.

But one look at the reviews of the latest of the Salinger hard-cover collections will show that the critics are beginning to jilt J. D. Salinger, no matter how faithful the public remains. I'm certainly not sure of all the *reasons* for the disenchantment of the last year or so. Perhaps it is partly because a critic finds it as much fun to destroy a reputation as to mold one. Perhaps it is also because such popularity as Salinger has enjoyed is taken as a sure sign of selling out. But I'm quite sure that the major reason is a misunderstanding of Salinger's attempt: he is simply not *trying* to be Ernest Hemingway. At any rate, for the past year, the cooling-off has been glacial.

Most critics are polite in their new disdain, some are sad, or merely tired. And then there is Mary McCarthy, thumbing her nose in a kind of bitchy pique. (She has seen to it that, lord knows, no reader would want to call *her* up.) In last year's *Harper's* article about Salinger's "closed circuit," Mary McCarthy asked, almost incidentally, "Who is to inherit the mantle of Papa Hemingway?" And with scorn she replied, "Who if not J. D. Salinger." She is, of course, right in spite of herself. Some years ago now Granville Hicks pointed out that for college generations of the fifties and the sixties, Salinger has had precisely the kind of importance that Hemingway had for the young people of the twenties. But it is, I think, precisely the difference between what Hemingway created in fiction and what Salinger is in the process of creating which is the key to the current critical assault on Salinger. To Miss McCarthy's Hemingway-fed generation, Salinger is a bad writer because he is the opposite of Hemingway.

Hemingway was the author of exile, the spokesman for a generation of expatriates. Withdrawal into self—to eat, to drink, to sleep with Catherine—was the answer for an age which saw man as so many ants on a log waiting to be roasted or steamed to death. In a world of Nada, a world which "kills the very good and the very gentle and the very brave impartially," a man could only—sad as it might be—face death bravely. So Hemingway invented a new manner—a style which for forty years has been the most influential style in literature. The Hemingway style, of course, mirrored the theme: withdrawn, cold, matter-of-fact, brisk, the person of the author totally uninvolved, dealing with surfaces and the senses: "In the late summer of that year we lived in a house in a village that looked across the river and the plain to the mountains. . . . After a while I went out and left the hospital and walked back to the hotel in the rain." Hemingway carried through the Joycean attempt (after Henry James and Joseph Conrad) to refine the story-teller "out of existence." This

Hemingway detachment was of course a pose, for no great author can be detached. Mary McCarthy is probably right in contending that "in Hemingway's work there was never anybody but Hemingway in a series of disguises." J. D. Salinger's purpose is exactly to *drop* the disguise, to bring the author, frankly and obtrusively and lovingly, back into the fiction. For J. D. Salinger is the opposite of Hemingway both in theme and in manner.

Hemingway's solution was Holden's disease—and Franny's, and probably Seymour's. Holden could not face a world of age, death, sickness, ugliness, sex and perversion, poverty, custom, and cant. He found phonies because that is all he looked for. And so he ran away, he withdrew. Franny, too, was "sick of pendants and conceited little tearer-downers," sick of "ego, ego, ego." Because she couldn't meet anybody she could respect, because "everything everybody does is so—I don't know—not wrong, or even mean, or even stupid necessarily. But just so tiny and meaningless and—sad-making," she, too, withdrew—into a false use of the mysticism of the Jesus Prayer. But Zooey, like Mr. Antolini, preaches a cure to this disease, a solution to the old problem of existence in an ugly world, a solution which is the opposite of withdrawal. The solution is not withdrawal or exile, but encounter. Mr. Antolini's message to Holden is to accept the world, to "live." Zooey's solution, in the "love story, pure and complicated" called "Zooey" (the solution which Franny discovers contains "all of what little or much wisdom there is in the world"), is also to *live*, not for self, but for others, out of love—even to eat Bessie's consecrated chicken soup. The Salinger solution is to live out of love for everyone, for "there isn't anyone out there who isn't Seymour's Fat Lady." There isn't anyone who isn't, that is, "Christ Himself. Christ Himself, buddy." Buddy Glass gives us the same solution as Zooey, at the end of "Seymour—An Introduction." He tells us that "there is no single thing I do that is more important than going into that awful Room 307," because "all we do our whole lives is go from one little piece of Holy Ground to the next."

It is, of course, dangerous to give answers in modern fiction. After the questioning of *The Catcher in the Rye*, Salinger has given some answers; and that doesn't set well with The Group, or with the *Partisan Review–Harper's* crowd. It is particularly dangerous if the answers, as Buddy Glass puts it, make any professional use of the word "God," except as a familiar, healthy American expletive. Salinger uses not only "God" but the love that dwells there. That's the trouble with the Glasses, says Mary McCarthy: "They are all good guys: they love each other and their parents and their cat and their gold-fish." John Updike complains that "Salinger seems to love his characters more than God loves them." And, indeed, at the beginning of "Seymour—An Introduction," the narrator admits—along with Kafka—that he writes of his characters "with steadfast love." I don't know how Updike *knows* how much God loves the Glasses; but he clearly doesn't like Salinger's loving them. Updike is certainly right: Salinger does love the Glasses, and asks us to love them. It is an accurate description, but a very bad complaint.

To preach his doctrine of loving encounter, of acceptance of the world as Holy Ground, rather than of withdrawal from Nada, Salinger has progressively developed a manner which *does* it, a manner which fits, and is therefore artistic, no matter how different it may be from Hemingway's artistic manner. To express an opposite theme, Salinger invents and develops an opposite style: personal, intimate, the narrator completely present, always in the mind of the reader in the person of the clever, self-conscious, idiosyncratic, even cute, Buddy Glass.

The germ of the purposeful, effective, developing Salinger style, which reaches its idiosyncratic peak in "Seymour—An Introduction," was noticeable even at the beginning, in *The Catcher in the Rye*. In 1953, a critic in *The Hudson Review* remarked: "Salinger has a quick ear and a fine talent . . . but to a certain extent he lacks detachment and disinterestedness. One has sometimes an oppressive and uncomfortable awareness of the author's nervous involvement in the hurt of his sensitive, witty, suicidal heroes." (Again, an accurate description, but a bad complaint.) And this new attached and interested style is, it seems, fast becoming as influential on the new generation as Hemingway's was on the old. Prophetically, The *Commonweal*'s review of *The Catcher in the Rye* remarked that Salinger's idiom and style were a "tour de force the American fiction writer will probably find himself increasingly doomed to attempt." Read any undergraduate short story these days and decide whether that was right.

Of all people aware of this new Salinger style, conscious of its difference from the detached Hemingway ideal of the past, none is more aware than Salinger himself. He admits everything that the critics could complain about in his style. In his dedication to *Franny and Zooey*, Salinger calls himself "hopelessly flamboyant," and in his introduction to "Zooey," Buddy Glass calls his style "excruciatingly personal." In "Seymour—An Introduction" Buddy tells us that he is "an ecstatically happy prose writer" who, therefore, "can't be moderate or temperate or brief." He tells us, indeed, that he "can't be detached." Buddy's very existence—as a *brother* to the family at hand—allows Salinger to increase his "nervous involvement." More and more Salinger has identified Buddy Glass with himself: on the dust jacket to *Franny and Zooey*, Salinger first calls Buddy Glass his "alter-ego and collaborator." In "Seymour—An Introduction" we learn that Buddy was born in 1919, the same year as J. D. Salinger; and Buddy describes his past books, which are clearly J. D. Salinger's past books; and even mentions the rumor that he spends "six months of the year in a Buddhist monastery and the other six in a mental institution." By the time of this most recent Salinger story, so successful has the informality and the Salinger-Buddy personal involvement become that Buddy writes, "It seems to me that this composition has never been in more danger than right now of taking on precisely the informality of underwear."

So personal a style will of course have "flaws" if one is expecting an opposite style. If the style is to communicate the love of a totally *involved* human being, it will not be neat or tidy or economical or cold or crisp: the letter in "Zooey," Buddy admits, was "virtually endless in length, over-written, teaching, repetitious, opinionated, remonstrative, condescending, embarrassing—and filled, to a surfeit, with affection." If the person writing is to be himself always present, is to be communicated as clever and self-conscious, the style will be rather obtrusively clever: "Cleverness," Seymour complains of Buddy's style, is his "permanent affliction," his "wooden leg." That is the cleverness we see throughout the later Salinger: obtrusive, certainly, but that's the point:

"If, with the right kind of luck, it comes off, it should be comparable in effect to a compulsory guided tour through the engine room, with myself, as guide, leading the way in an old one-piece Jantzen bathing suit. . . . She was wearing her usual at-home vesture—what her son Buddy (who was a writer, and consequently, as Kafka, no less, has told us, *not a nice man*) called her prenotification-of-death uniform. . . . Please accept from me this unpretentious bouquet of very early-blooming parentheses: (((( )))).″

Along with the self-conscious and involved style, what happens to the structure under this Salinger intent? It becomes not the conventional form of a short story, where we are aware that, chronologically, a story is being unfolded; nor is it a carefully constructed symbolic pattern. The form becomes instead personal, uneconomical, loose, spontaneous (and surprisingly delightful). "What I'm about to offer," Buddy tells us in "Zooey," "isn't really a short story at all but a sort of prose home movie." And in "Seymour—An Introduction" Buddy admits that he is "a narrator with extremely pressing personal needs." And that therefore: "I want to introduce, I want to describe, I want to distribute mementos, amulets, I want to break out my wallet and pass around snapshots, I want to follow my nose. In this mood, I don't dare go anywhere near the short-story form. It eats up fat little undetached writers like me whole."

The characters are affected, too, by the Salinger intent. Of the people in "Zooey," Buddy says, "Not one of the three, I might well add, showed any noticeably soaring talent for brevity of detail or compression of incident. A short-coming, I'm afraid, that will be carried over to this, the final, or shooting, version." We like the casually-revealed Salinger people for themselves, and—when we recognize in astonishing flashes thoughts we though were our own—we like them for ourselves which we see in them. It's marvelously *pleasant* to like Salinger characters—the simply pleasant is rare in modern fiction, perhaps rare enough to account for a good deal of Salinger's popularity. It's pleasant to like Salinger characters even when we are embarrassed by them, when, that is, we see that the joke is on us, as, for example, when Lane, in an affected blasé attitude, goes to meet Franny's train looking like "he has at least three lighted cigarettes in each hand." Everyone will have his own embarrassing moment of recognition in Salinger. Salinger's characters come alive astonishingly, "with a stunning and detailed air of presence," as Henry Anatole Grunwald has put it. And as we savor the people, we savor the present conversational moment which they are engaged in. We savor, in Salinger, what Seymour called "the main current of poetry that flows through things, all things," that which Salinger reveals to us through his style and structure and character. The *result* of the whole Salinger manner is a sense of leisure, delight in the moment, in the personality being revealed, in delightful witty people, delight in spontaneity, the delight we feel in even the long list of contents of the Glass' bathroom medicine cabinet.

"Salinger is a poet," Arthur Mizener has pointed out, "in the only sense that he himself would probably take seriously: he's a man with his own special insight into the meaning of experience." If Salinger's critics are abandoning him because it is becoming increasingly clear that he is not Ernest Hemingway, Salinger doesn't seem to mind. Buddy Glass does seem to know what he is doing, and where he is going. All the personal idiosyncracies of the Salinger manner are there because Salinger has chosen a personal, positive way to say a personal, positive thing, to express his own special insight into the meaning of experience. He knows he is moving along. "I think it's high time," Buddy tells us, "that all the elderly boy writers were asked to move along from the ballparks and the bull rings."

JONATHAN BAUMBACH
"The Saint as a Young Man:
The Catcher in the Rye by J. D. Salinger"
The Landscape of Nightmare
1965, pp. 55–67

There isn't anyone *anywhere* that isn't Seymour's Fat Lady. Don't you know that? . . . and don't you know—listen to me now—*don't you know who that Fat lady really is?* . . . Ah, buddy. Ah, buddy. It's Christ Himself. Christ Himself, buddy. (*Franny and Zooey*)

In reaction to its long period of over-repute, J. D. Salinger's first and only novel, *The Catcher in the Rye* (1951), has undergone in recent years a steady if overinsistent devaluation. The more it becomes academically respectable, the more it becomes fair game for those critics who are sworn to expose every manifestation of what seems to them a chronic disparity between appearance and reality. It is critical child's play to find fault with Salinger's novel. Anyone can see that the prose is mannered (which is the pejorative word for stylized); no one actually talks like its first-person hero Holden Caulfield. Moreover, we are told that Holden as poor little rich boy is too precocious and specialized an adolescent for his plight to have larger-than-prep-school significance. The novel is sentimental, it loads the deck for Holden and against the adult world; the small but corrupt group that Holden encounters is not a representative enough sampling to permit Salinger his inclusive judgments of the species. Holden's relation to his family is not explored; we meet his sister Phoebe, who is a younger version of himself, but his father never appears and his mother exists in the novel only as a voice from a dark room; and finally, what is Holden (or Salinger) protesting but the ineluctability of growing up, of having to assume the prerogatives and responsibilities of manhood?

I hope I have fairly entered all of the objections to the novel, because I think that despite them *The Catcher in the Rye* will endure. It will endure mainly because it has life and secondly because it is an original work full of insights into at least the particular truth of Holden's existence. Given the limited terms of its vision, Salinger's small book is almost perfectly achieved. It is, if such a distinction is meaningful, an important minor novel.

Like all of Salinger's fiction, *The Catcher in the Rye* is not only *about* innocence, it is actively *for* innocence, as if retaining one's childness were an existential possibility. The metaphor of the title—Holden's fantasy vision of standing in front of a cliff and protecting playing children from falling (Falling)—is, despite the impossibility of its realization, the only positive action affirmed in the novel. It is, in Salinger's Manichean universe of child angels and adult "phonies," the only moral alternative; otherwise all is corruption. And since to prevent the Fall is a spiritual as well as physical impossibility, Salinger's idealistic heroes are doomed to either suicide (Seymour) or insanity (Holden, Sergeant X) or mysticism (Franny); or to moral dissolution (Eloise, D. B., Mr. Antolini)—the way of the world. In Salinger's finely honed prose, at once idiomatically real and poetically stylized, we get the terms of Holden's ideal adult occupation.

Anyway, I kept picturing all these little kids playing some game in this big field of rye and all. Thousands of little kids, and nobody's around—nobody big, I mean—except me. And I'm standing on the edge of some crazy cliff. What I have to do,

I have to catch everybody if they start to go over the cliff—I mean if they're running and they don't look where they're going. I have to come out from somewhere and *catch* them. That's all I'd do all day. I'd just be the catcher in the rye and all. I know it's crazy, but that's the only thing I'd really like to be. [1]

Apparently Holden's wish is purely selfless. What he wants, in effect, is to be a saint—the protector and savior of innocence. But what he also wants—for he is still one of the running children himself—is that someone prevent *his* fall. This is his paradox; he must leave innocence to protect innocence. At sixteen he is ready to shed his innocence and move like Adam into the fallen adult world, but he resists because those who are no longer innocent seem to him foolish as well as corrupt. In a sense, then, he is looking for an exemplar, a wise and good father whose example will justify his own initiation into manhood. Before Holden can become a catcher in the rye, he must find another catcher in the rye to show him how it is done.

Immediately after Holden announces his "crazy" ambition to Phoebe, he calls up an old school teacher of his, a Mr. Antolini, who is both intelligent and kind—a potential catcher in the rye.

> He was the one that finally picked up that boy that jumped out of the window. . . . James Castle. Old Mr. Antolini felt his pulse and all, and then he took off his coat and put it over James Castle and carried him all the way to the infirmary. [p. 157]

Though Mr. Antolini is sympathetic because "he didn't even give a damn if his coat got all bloody," the incident is symbolic of the teacher's failure as a catcher in the rye. For all his good intentions, he was unable to catch James Castle or prevent his fall; he could only pick him up afterward when the boy was dead. The episode of the suicide is one of the looming shadows that darkens Holden's world, and Holden seeks out Antolini because he hopes that the gentle teacher—the substitute father—will "pick him up" before he is irrevocably fallen. Holden's real quest throughout the novel is for a spiritual father (an innocent adult). When he calls Antolini all the other fathers of his world have already failed him, including his real father, whose existence in the novel is represented solely by Phoebe's childish reiteration of "Daddy's going to kill you." The fathers in Salinger's child's-eye world do not catch falling boys, boys who have been thrown out of prep school, but "kill" them. Antolini, then, represents Holden's last chance to find a catcher-father. But Antolini's inability to save Holden has been prophesied in his failure to save James Castle; the episode of Castle's death narrated earlier in the novel provides an anticipatory parallel to Antolini's unwitting destruction of Holden.

The revelation that Antolini's kindness to Holden is motivated in part by a homosexual interest, though it comes as a shock to Holden, does not wholly surprise the reader. Many of the biographical details that Salinger has told us about him through Holden predicate this possibility. For example, that he has an older and unattractive wife whom he makes a great show of kissing in public is highly suggestive; yet the discovery itself, when Holden wakes to find Antolini sitting beside him and caressing his head, has considerable impact. We experience a kind of shock of recognition, the more intense for its having been anticipated. The scene has further power because Antolini is, for the most part, a good man, and his interest in Holden is genuine as well as perverted. His advice to Holden, which is offered as from father to son, is apparently well intentioned. Though for the most part his recommendations

are cleverly articulated platitudes, Antolini evinces a prophetic insight when he tells Holden, "'I have a feeling that you're riding for some kind of a terrible, terrible fall,'" though one suspects he is, at least in part, talking about himself. Ironically, Antolini becomes the agent of his "terrible, terrible fall" by violating Holden's image of him, by becoming a false father. Having lost his respect for Antolini as a man, Holden rejects him as authority; as far as Holden is concerned Antolini's example denies the import of his words. His disillusionment with Antolini, the man who had seemed to be the wise-good father, coming as the last and most intense in a long line of disillusionments, is the final straw. To Holden it is the equivalent of the loss of God. The world, devoid of good fathers (authorities), becomes for him a soul-destroying chaos in which his survival is possible only through withdrawal into childhood, into fantasy, into psychosis.

The action of the novel is compressed into two days in which Holden discovers through a series of disillusioning experiences that the adult world is unreclaimably corrupt. At the start of the novel we learn from Holden that he has flunked out of Pencey Prep for not applying himself; he has been resistant to what he considers foolish or "phony" authority. Like almost all of Salinger's protagonists, Holden is clearly superior to his surroundings; he functions by dint of his pure sight, his innocence and sensibility, as initiate in and conscience of the world of the novel. So, allowing for the exaggerations of innocence, we can generally accept Holden's value judgments of people and places as the judgments of the novel. For example, when Holden observes his seventy-year-old, grippe-ridden history teacher picking his nose: "He made out like he was only pinching it, but he was really getting the old thumb right in there. . . . I didn't *care*, except that it's pretty disgusting to watch somebody pick their nose" (p. 12), he is not being gratuitously malicious; he is being innocent. Whereas the adult observer, no matter how scrupulous, censors his irreverent or unpleasant responses because he is ashamed of them, the child tells all. In effect, Holden is passing what amounts to a moral judgment, although he is consciously doing no more than describing his reactions. Like Jane Austen, Salinger treats fools, especially pretentious ones, mercilessly. Though Spencer may be seventy-years-old and for that alone worthy of respect, he is nevertheless platitudinous and self-indulgent, interested less in Holden than in pontificating before a captive audience. In a world in which the child is the spiritual father of the man, old age represents not wisdom but spiritual blindness and physical corruption. Spencer is not only foolish and "phony" ("Life *is* a game, boy") but in his self-righteous way also actively malicious. Though Holden's is ostensibly a social visit, the old man badgers the boy about having failed history ("'I flunked you in history because you knew absolutely nothing.'"), and then insists on reading aloud Holden's inadequate exam. In this confrontation between Holden and Spencer, there is an ironic inversion of the traditional student-teacher, son-father relationship which extends throughout the novel and throughout Salinger's fictional world. While Spencer insensitively embarrasses the already wounded Holden, who has been irrevocably expelled from Pencey, out of a childish need for personal justification, the boy is in turn mature enough to be kind to his vulnerable antagonist. Holden accepts the full burden of responsibility for his scholastic failure so as to relieve the teacher of his sense of guilt ("I told him I would've done exactly the same thing if I'd been in his place"). In compassionately protecting his teacher's feelings, Holden is in a sense performing the role of wise father; he is here a kind of catcher in the rye for a clumsy old child.

Holden's compassion is extensive enough to include even those he dislikes, even those who have hurt him. As he tells Antolini later in the novel:

> You're wrong about that hating business. . . . What I may do, I may hate them for a *little* while, like this guy Stradlater I knew at Pencey, and this other boy, Robert Ackley. I hated *them* once in a while—I admit it—but it doesn't last too long, is what I mean. After a while, if I didn't see them, if they didn't come in the room . . . I sort of missed them. [pp. 168–69]

As Antolini and Spencer are too corrupt to notice, Holden is unable to cope with the world, not because he hates but because he loves and the world hates.

Spencer symbolizes (which is not to say that he does not also have a particular existence) all of the stupid and destructive teacher-fathers at Pencey Prep, which is in microcosm all schools—the world. In the short scene between Holden and Spencer, Salinger evokes a sense of Holden's entire "student" experience, in which flunking out is an act of moral will rather than a failure of application. Here as throughout the novel, the wise son resists the initiatory knowledge of the false ("phony") father and retains, at the price of dispossession, his innocence. As I mentioned before, Holden is not so much rebelling against all authority or even false authority as he is searching for a just father. That there are no good fathers in the world is its and Holden's tragedy. It is the tragedy of Salinger's cosmos that the loss of innocence is irremediable. Ejected from the fallow womb of the prep school, Holden goes out alone into the world of New York City in search of some kind of sustenance. His comic misadventures in the city, which lead to his ultimate disillusion and despair—after the Antolini episode Holden wants to withdraw from the world and become a deaf-mute—make up the central action of the novel.

Holden not only suffers as a victim from the effects of the evil in this world but *for* it as its conscience, so that his experiences are exemplary. In this sense, *The Catcher in the Rye* is a religious, or, to be more exact, spiritual novel. Holden is Prince Mishkin as a sophisticated New York adolescent, and like Mishkin, he experiences the guilt, the unhappiness, and the spiritual deformities of others more intensely than he does his own misfortunes. This is not to say that Holden is without faults; he is, on occasion, silly, irritating, thoughtless, irresponsible—he has the excesses of innocence. Yet he is, as nearly as possible, without sin. The most memorable love affair Holden has experienced has had its fruition in daily checker games with Jane Gallagher, an unhappy, sensitive girl who was his neighbor one summer. She has become the symbol to him of romantic love—that is, innocent love. When Holden discovers that his "sexy" roommate Stradlater has a date with her, he is concerned not only about the possible loss of Jane's innocence but about the loss of his dream of her, the loss of their combined checker-playing, love-innocence. Holden had one previous emotional breakdown at thirteen when his saint-brother Allie[2] died of leukemia. Allie's death is Holden's first recognition of the fact of evil—of what appears to be the gratuitous malevolence of the universe. Allie, who was, Holden tells us, more intelligent and nicer than anyone else, becomes for Holden a kind of saint-ideal. Therefore, Stradlater's rejection of an English theme on Allie's baseball glove that Holden has written for him, combined with his implication that he has "given Jane Gallagher the time," spiritually maims Holden; assails his only defense, his belief in the possibility of good in the world. ("I felt so lonesome, all of a sudden. I almost wished I was dead" [p. 46]).

It is in this state of near-suicidal despair that Holden leaves for New York. That Stradlater may have had sexual relations with Jane—the destruction of innocence is an act of irremediable evil in Holden's world—impels Holden's immediate flight from Pencey (not before he quixotically challenges the muscular Stradlater, who in turn bloodies his nose). At various times in New York Holden is on the verge of phoning Jane and twice he actually dials her number; that he is unable to reach her is symbolic of his loss of her innocence. The sexually experienced Stradlater, who is one of Holden's destructive fathers in the novel, has irreparably destroyed not so much Jane's innocence as Holden's idealized notion of her.[3]

In obliquely searching for good in the adult world, or at least something to mitigate his despair, Holden is continually confronted with the absence of good. On his arrival in the city, he is disturbed because his cab-driver is corrupt and unsociable and, worst of all, unable to answer one of his obsessive questions, which is where the ducks in Central Park go when the lake freezes over. What Holden really wants to know is whether there is a benevolent authority that takes care of ducks. If there is one for ducks, it sensibly follows that there may be one for people as well. Holden's quest for a wise and benevolent authority, then, is essentially a search for a God principle. However, none of the adults in Holden's world have any true answers for him. When he checks into a hotel room, he is depressed by the fact that the bellboy is an old man. As sensitized recorder of the moral vibrations of his world, Holden suffers the indignity of the aged bellhop's situation for him, as he had suffered for Spencer's guilt and Ackley's self-loathing. Yet, and this is part of his tragedy, he is an impotent saint—he is unable to redeem the fallen or prevent their fall.

Where the world of Holden's school was a muted purgatory, the world of his New York hotel is an insistent Hell. From his room with a view that looks into other hotel rooms, he sees a man dress himself in women's clothes and in another room a man and woman who squirt water at each other from their mouths; this is the "real" world with its respectable shade lifted. Holden is fascinated and, in a sense, seduced by its prurience. Having lost the sense of his innocence, he seeks sexual initiation as a means of redemption. That he is generally attracted to older women suggests that his quest for a woman is really a search for a mother whose love will provide a protection against the corrupt world as well as initiate him into it. Where the father-quest is a quest for wisdom and spirit (God), the mother-quest is not ultimately for sex but for love. They are, then, different manifestations, one intellectual, the other physical, of the same spiritual quest. Holden's search for sexual experience is, Salinger indicates, the only love alternative left him after his loss of Jane. Once the possibility of innocent love ceases to exist, sexual love seems the next best thing, a necessary compensation for the loss of the first. However, Holden is only mildly disappointed when he is unable to arrange a date with a reputedly promiscuous girl whose number he has inherited from a Princeton acquaintance. For all his avowed "sexiness," he is an innocent, and his innocence-impelled fear dampens his desire. Though the women he meets are by and large less disappointing than the men, they too fail Holden and intensify his despair. That they are not as good as he would like them to be seems to him *his* fault, *his* responsbility, *his* failure.

If Jane represents sacred love profaned, the prostitute who comes to Holden's room represents profane love unprofaned. Though he agrees to have her come to his room, he refuses to make love to her once she is there. The scene is a crucial one in defining Holden's nontraditional sainthood. Not on moral principle does Holden refuse the prostitute, but because the condition of her existence—she is about Holden's age and a kind of lost innocent—depresses him. When he hangs up her dress for her he imagines.

> her going in a store and buying it, and nobody in the store knowing she was a prostitute. The salesman probably just thought she was a regular girl when she bought it. It made me feel sad as hell. [p. 88]

Holden suffers the girl's sadness as if her degradation were also in some way his. He would save her if he could but she is far too fallen for any catcher in the rye. But as child-saint, Holden is quixotic. In not sleeping with her he means to protect her innocence, not his own; he is spiritually, and consequently physically, unable to be a party to her further degradation. The consequences are ironic. Holden as saint refuses to victimize the prostitute, but he, in turn, is victimized by the girl and her accomplice Maurice. Though Holden has paid the girl without using her, Maurice beats Holden and extorts five extra dollars from him. This episode is a more intense recapitulation of the Stradlater experience. In both cases Holden is punished for his innocence. If the hotel is a symbolic Hell, Maurice, as far as Holden is concerned, is its chief devil. In offering Holden the girl and then humiliating him for not accepting his expensive gift, Maurice is another of Holden's evil fathers.

Like so many heroes of contemporary fiction—Morris' Boyd, Ellison's Invisible Man, Malamud's Frank, Salinger's Seymour—Holden is, for all his good intentions, an impotent savior, a butter-fingered catcher in the rye. Because he can neither save his evil world nor live in it as it is, he retreats into fantasy, into childhood. I think the end of the novel has been generally misinterpreted because of a too literal reading of Holden's divulgence in the beginning that he is telling the story from some kind of rest home. Holden is always less insane than his world. The last scene, in which Holden, watching his kid sister Phoebe go around on a merry-go-round, sits in the pouring rain suffused with happiness, is not indicative of his crack-up, as has been assumed, but of his redemption. Whereas all of the adults in his world fail him, and he, in consequence, fails them, a ten-year-old girl, whom he protects as catcher in the rye, saves him—becomes his catcher. Love is the redemptive grace. Phoebe thus replaces Jane, whose loss had initiated Holden's despair, flight, and quest for experience as salvation. Holden's pure communion with Phoebe may be construed as a reversion to childhood innocence, but this, in Salinger's world, is the only way to redemption; there is no other good. Innocence is all. Love is innocence.

After his disillusionment with Antolini, who is, in effect, the most destructive of Holden's fathers because he is apparently the most benevolent, Holden suffers his emotional breakdown. His flight from Antolini's house, like his previous flights from school and from the hotel, is an attempt at escaping evil. The three are parallel experiences except that Holden is less sure of the justness of this third flight; he wonders if he has not misjudged his otherwise sympathetic teacher: " Maybe he *was* only patting my head just for the hell of it. The more I thought about it, though, the more depressed and screwed up I got" (p. 176). The ambivalence of his response racks him. If he has misjudged Antolini, Holden has not only wronged him but wronged himself; it is he, not Antolini, who has been guilty of corruption. Consequently, he suffers both for Antolini and himself. Holden's guilt-ridden despair manifests itself in nausea and in an intense sense of physical ill-being, as if he carried the whole awful corruption of the city inside him. Walking aimlessly through the city at

Christmastime, Holden experiences "the terrible, terrible fall" that Antolini had prophesied for him:

> Every time I came to the end of a block and stepped off the goddam curb, I had this feeling that I'd never get to the other side of the street. I thought I'd go down, down, down, and nobody'd ever see me again. Boy, did it scare me. . . . Everytime I'd get to the end of the block, I'd make believe I was talking to my brother, Allie. I'd say to him, "Allie, don't let me disappear. Allie, don't let me disappear. Please, Allie." And then when I reached the other side of the street without disappearing, I'd *thank* him. [p. 178]

Like Franny's prayer to Jesus in one of Salinger's later stories, Holden's prayer to Allie is not so much an act of anguish as an act of love, though it is in part both. Trapped in an interior hell, Holden seeks redemption, not by formal appeal to God or Jesus, who have in the Christmas season been falsified and commercialized, but by praying to his saint-brother, who in his goodness had God in him.

Unable to save himself or others, Holden decides to withdraw from the world, to become a deaf-mute and live by himself in an isolated cabin, to commit a symbolic suicide. It is an unrealizable fantasy but a death wish nevertheless. However, Holden's social conscious forces him out of spiritual retirement. When he discovers an obscenity scrawled on a wall in Phoebe's school, he rubs it out with his hand to protect the innocence of the children. He is for the moment a successful catcher in the rye. But then he discovers another such notice which has been imprinted with a knife, and then another. He realizes that he cannot possibly erase all the scribbled obscenities in the world, that he cannot catch all the children, that evil is ineradicable.

It is the final disillusionment, and dizzy with his terrible awareness, Holden insults Phoebe when she insists on running away with him. In his vision of despair, he sees Phoebe's irrevocable doom as well as his, and for a moment he hates her as he hates himself—as he hates the world. Once he has hurt her, however, he realizes the commitment that his love for her imposes on him; that is, if he is to palliate her pain, he must continue to live in the world. When she kisses him a few minutes later as a token of forgiveness and love, and as if in consequence it begins to rain, Holden, bathed by the rain, is purified—in a sense, redeemed. Like the narrator in "For Esmé—With Love and Squalor," Holden is redeemed by the love of an innocent girl. In both cases the protagonist is saved because he realizes that if there is any love at all in the world, even the love of a single child, Love exists.

On its surface, the last scene, with Holden drenched in Scott Fitzgerald's all-absolving rain,[4] is unashamedly sentimental. Certainly Salinger overstates the curative powers of children; innocence can be destructive as well as redemptive. Yet for all that, Salinger's view of the universe, in which all adults, even the most apparently decent, are corrupt and consequently destructive, is bleak and somewhat terrifying. If growing up in the real world is tragic, in Salinger's ideal world time must be stopped to prevent the loss of childhood, to salvage the remnants of our innocence. At one point in the novel Holden wishes that life were as changeless and as pure as the exhibitions under glass cases in the Museum of Natural History. This explains, in part, Holden's ecstasy in the rain at the close of the novel. In watching Phoebe go round and round on the carousel, in effect going nowhere, he sees her in the timeless continuum of art, on the verge of changing, yet unchanging, forever safe, forever loving, forever innocent.

Salinger's view of the world has obviously limited his

productiveness, also his range of concerns. In the last nine years he has published only four increasingly long, increasingly repetitive short stories, all treating some aspect of the mythic life and times of the Glass family, whose most talented member, Seymour, committed suicide in an early story called "A Perfect Day for Bananafish." But though Salinger may go on, as Hemingway did, mimicking himself, trying desperately to relocate his old youthful image in some narcissistic internal mirror, his achievement as a writer cannot be easily discounted. All his works, even the least successful of his stories, evince a stunning and, despite some stylistic debt to Fitzgerald and Lardner, original verbal talent. There is more real life in a small book like *The Catcher in the Rye* than in the combined pages of such a prolific and detailed chronicler of experience as John O'Hara. Like *The Great Gatsby*, which both Holden and Salinger admire, it is, as far as the human eye can see, a perfect novel; it is self-defining; that is, there seems to be an inevitability about its form. Although the craft of the book is unobtrusive, everything of consequence that happens in the novel has been anticipated by an earlier episode or reference. Each of Holden's disillusioning experiences is predicated by the preceding one. The rain that baptizes Holden at the end is, in symbol, the same rain that had fallen on Allie's gravestone, which had depressed Holden because the visitors' scurry for shelter had served only to emphasize Allie's immobility, his deadness. In praying to Allie, Holden implicitly accepts the fact of his brother's immortality, which his earlier response had denied. Through association, Salinger suggests that the purifying rain is a manifestation of Allie's blessed and blessing spirit. Like Phoebe's kiss, Allie's rain is an act of love.

The near perfection of *The Catcher in the Rye* is indicative of its limitation as well as its achievement. Salinger knows what he can do well and he does it, taking a few indulgences of risk, but no more. On the other hand, men of comparable talent like William Styron and Norman Mailer have continually overreached themselves, have written both more ambitious and more flawed books than Salinger's only novel. It would be easy to quote from Browning's "Andrea del Sarto" and to insist that great literature, like great painting, must always attempt more than it can do, but the problem is not so easily resolvable. As a case in point: it would be hard to convince me that a small masterpiece like *The Great Gatsby* is less important than *Look Homeward Angel*, or even Fitzgerald's own larger failure, *Tender Is the Night*. Selective comparisons, of course, are hardly generative of final principles. In any event, it seems to me that Styron's extravagant failure *Set This House on Fire*, for example, is somewhat more admirable if not more important than Salinger's cautious success. Holden, I suspect, would understand what I mean.

Notes

1. J. D. Salinger, *The Catcher in the Rye* (New York: New American Library, 1953), p. 156. All quotations are from this edition.
2. Holden's relation to Allie is, though less intense, the equivalent of Buddy's to Seymour in the several Glass family stories.
3. Another destructive father is Ackley, who refuses Holden solace after Holden has been morally and physically beaten by Stradlater. (The father concern is an intentional one on Salinger's part.) Both Ackley and Stradlater are two years old than Holden, and at one point Ackley reproves Holden's lack of respect, telling him, "'I am old enough to be your father.'"
4. It is the same symbolic rain that falls on Gatsby's coffin—at which Nick hears someone say, "'Blessed are the dead whom the rain falls on.'" I suspect that Salinger had the Fitzgerald passage in mind.

DAVID LODGE
"Family Romances"

Times Literary Supplement, June 13, 1975, p. 642

It is almost exactly ten years since *The New Yorker* published (on June 19, 1965) "Hapworth 16, 1924" by J. D. Salinger. That story, a further instalment in the saga of the Glass family which commenced back in 1948 with "A Perfect Day for Bananafish", itself broke a silence of six years following the publication of "Seymour: An Introduction" in June 1959. Since "Hapworth" Salinger has published nothing.

Ten years in literature is not as long as ten years in politics, but it is a long enough time in which to be forgotten, especially if your silence is total. Salinger's eremitic seclusion, his fanatical defence of his privacy, are of course well known— and while he was still publishing merely intensified public interest in him. Since he stopped publishing, however, his shunning of publicity has ceased to be noteworthy. To say he has been forgotten would not be quite accurate: his works are still in print and evidently sell steadily, especially *The Catcher in the Rye*, which seems assured of some kind of classic status. Rather, it is as if he had died. His name no longer sets off vibrations of expectancy and curiosity among readers of modern fiction. It seems to be generally assumed that his career is a closed chapter, belonging to the literary history of the 1950s: that his interesting and original talent fizzled out disappointingly in the 1960s and was swamped by a new wave of American fiction quite different in character.

A few months ago, however, Salinger broke his long silence and revealed that it may yet prove to be a pregnant one. In a telephone conversation with Lacey Fosburgh of the *New York Times* he stated that he was still writing busily, though not for publication. "There is a marvellous peace in not publishing", he said. "I love to write. But I write for myself and my own pleasure" (*New York Times*, November 3, 1974). What provoked this communiqué was the pirated publication in the United States of *The Complete Uncollected Short Stories of J. D. Salinger*, in two volumes.

These paperbacks, quite decently printed, though not very well proof-read and badly bound, were evidently hawked around the bookshops of San Francisco and other large cities by various young men all using the alias of Greenburg, and an estimated 25,000 sets have been sold at retail prices ranging from $3 to $5 a volume. At the time of the interview the pirates had not been traced, and Salinger was suing the bookshops.

It is, of course, deplorable that a writer's work should be reprinted against his will, quite apart from the financial robbery involved. With the exception of "Hapworth", all the uncollected stories are early work, and one understands Salinger's wish to let "them die a perfectly natural death". On the other hand, it is never possible to "unwrite" something that has once been published (perhaps this is why Salinger finds not publishing so peaceful), and all the pirated stories are available for inspection in large libraries.

Even the most immature of them have the uncanny, hypnotic readability that is the hallmark of his writing, while a few of them would not have disgraced *Nine Stories*. But perhaps the most interesting discovery to be made by investigating the uncollected stories is that from an early stage in his career Salinger was using the short story as a way of exploring a complex network of relationships between *families* of characters; and that although he is thought of as preeminently the literary voice of the post-Second World War younger generation, his earliest work (naturally enough when you recall that he was born in 1919) was written from a pre-war or wartime perspective.

Holden Caulfield, the teenage hero of *The Catcher in the Rye* (1951), was first referred to, though he did not actually appear, in a story called "Last Day of the Last Furlough" (1944) which is about two young soldiers on the eve of a wartime posting overseas: John F. "Babe" Gladwaller and his friend Vincent Caulfield, who

> has a kid brother in the Army who flunked out of a lot of schools. He talks about him a lot. Always pretending to pass him off as a nutty kid.

This brother is called Holden and is "missing".

Another story, a very good one called "This Sandwich Has No Mayonnaise" (1945), is told from the point of view of Vincent unsuccessfully trying to suppress his misery and anxiety about Holden's fate in the Pacific:

> Stop kidding around. Stop letting people think you're Missing. Stop wearing my robe to the beach. Stop taking the shots on my side of the court. Stop whistling. Sit up to the table.

Some of Vincent's reminiscences include his sister Phoebe Caulfield. In "The Stranger" (1945), Babe Gladwaller (who has a Holden-Phoebe relationship of his own with his kid sister Mattie) describes Vincent's death in action to the latter's ex-girlfriend, who says that Vincent "didn't believe anything from the time little Kenneth Caulfield died. His brother." Kenneth seems to be the first version of Holden Caulfield's deceased younger brother Allie, about whose baseball mitt Holden writes an essay assignment for the ungrateful Stradlater in *The Catcher in the Rye*. Allie, however, died on July 18, 1946, and the Holden of the novel is a *post*-war teenager.

Between these stories and *The Catcher in the Rye* came two directly about Holden, "I'm Crazy" (1945) and "Slight Rebellion off Madison" (1946), which were incorporated, greatly expanded, into the novel. There are no specific historical references in these stories, but it seems to me, given the dates of their original publication, that a pre-war setting was implied. Salinger's unwillingness to reprint any of the early stories about the Caulfields no doubt derives partly from a wish to conceal their various inconsistencies with *The Catcher in the Rye*.

In the stories I have mentioned one can see an embryonic family saga of the Glass type beginning to emerge; there are the same intense sibling relationships, the same quasi-religious pursuit by the central characters of integrity, purity and authenticity in ordinary living, the same struggle against alienation. Salinger, it seems, having changed his mind too often about the Caulfields, abandoned that family's history, and started afresh with the Glasses—beginning characteristically by killing off his main character, Seymour (in "Banana-fish"), and working outwards from that point, just as he had begun with Holden "missing". The question of period is settled by making Buddy Glass, the family scribe, the same age as Salinger himself. The formative years of Buddy and Seymour (two years his senior) are thus pre-war; but the size of the family means that the younger siblings, Zooey and Franny, can represent (as did Holden Mark II) the sensibility of post-war youth. The Caulfields, in fact, are not totally forgotten in the Glass saga. Buddy recalls in "Seymour":

> There used to be an exceptionally intelligent and likeable boy on the radio with S. and me—one Curtis Caulfield, who was eventually killed during one of the landings in the Pacific.

Buddy also alludes to the one novel he has published in terms which make it sound very like *The Catcher in the Rye*.

These teasing references, which deliberately entangle the myths of the Caulfields and the Glasses both with each other and with the historical J. D. Salinger, are typical of the writer's later work, where he is playing an elaborate game with his audience and with the conventions of his art. The name of the game is Assent. The more truth-telling, the more historical, the stories become in form (i. e., tending towards an apparently random, anecdotal structure, adopting an insistently personal, intimate, confessional tone, making elaborate play with letters, documents, and similar "evidence"), the less credible becomes the content (miraculous feats of learning, stigmata, prophetic glimpses, memories of previous incarnations etc). Purporting to tell us a "true" family history, and dropping heavy hints that he is the same person as J. D. Salinger, Buddy yet insists again and again on the autonomy of art and the irrelevance of biographical criticism. An extravagantly transcendental philosophy of life is put forward in terms of studied homeliness, wrapped around with elaborate qualifications, disclaimers, nods and winks, and mediated in a style that, for all its restless rhetorical activity, is strikingly lacking in any kind of "poetic" or symbolist resonances. With each successive story, Salinger has raised the stakes in the game of assent, and each time more and more readers have dropped out, unable to take the mysticism, the ESP, the God-knowingness at their face value. But what is it we are asked to believe in: the reality of these things, or the possibility of them? Clearly, since we are reading fiction, the latter; but it is easy to be confused by Salinger's method into thinking it is the former. To do so is to forfeit half the pleasure of reading him.

Unlikely as the comparison may seem at first glance, there is a certain similarity between the Salinger of "Zooey", "Raise High the Roof Beam, Carpenters" and "Seymour: An Introduction" and Sterne's *Tristram Shandy*, that eighteenth-century "prose home-movie". In both there is a delicate balance of sentiment and ironic self-consciousness, and a humorous running commentary on the activities of writing and reading. How Shandean, for instance, is Buddy's presentation to the reader, in "Seymour", of

> this unpretentious bouquet of very early-blooming parentheses: (((( )))). I suppose, most unflorally, I truly mean them to be taken, first off, as bow-legged—buckle-legged—omens of my state of mind and body at this writing.

One of the disappointments of "Hapworth" is that it lacks this teasing, cajoling relationship with the reader. Apart from a brief prologue and epilogue by Buddy, it consists of an inordinately long letter written by Seymour at the age of seven to his parents, from a summer camp. It is, needless to say, an extraordinarily precocious epistle, full of wise moralizing, advice, injunctions and prophecies, and concludes with a request for library books by Tolstoy, Cervantes, Dickens, George Eliot, Thackeray, Jane Austen, Bunyan, the Brontës, Victor Hugo, Balzac, Flaubert, Maupassant, Proust, and many others, each plea accompanied by a crisp if idiosyncratic critical appraisal of the author in question.

It is another, audacious, ploy in the game of assent; but although Salinger has skilfully fabricated a prose style that is just what you would expect from a prodigy like Seymour—preciously adult in syntax and diction, but not quite sure of its tone, and liable to sudden drops into childish vernacular—this is not quite enough to conceal the fact that Seymour is really a rather boring character (it is what others make of him that is interesting). Also, Seymour's somewhat fulsome enthusiasm for his younger brother's literary promise, unqualified by any ironic commentary from Buddy himself, is a little hard to take. Instead of the dialogue between writer and reader that animates the three preceding stories, we seem to be overhearing a self-congratulatory dialogue of the writer with himself. That is why, although it is good news that Salinger is still writing, one feels misgivings at the reported words, "I write just for myself and my own pleasure."

If "Hapworth" does not offer much cheer to faithful fans of Salinger, it no doubt brings a glow of righteous justification to those critics who detected a dangerous narcissism, or Pygmalionism, in the Glass stories as early as "Franny" and "Zooey". Yet it is a real question how far they contributed to the fulfilment of their own prophecies. Looking through H. A. Grunwald's useful collection of comment and criticism, *Salinger* (1962), it is clear that most critics turned against Salinger just when his work began to challenge customary modes of reading; while Salinger's dedication of his last volume, to "an amateur reader" if there is one "still left in the world", suggests a growing sense of desertion.

Whatever the reason, it seems a shame that so gifted a writer—probably the first since Hemingway to discover a wholly original mode of writing short stories—should have retreated into silent self-communing. No one, except a few cultural chauvinists and Mr Kingsley Amis giving his well-known impersonation of Evelyn Waugh, would seriously dispute the brilliance, the imaginative energy and daring of American fiction over the past ten or fifteen years. But there are moments (one might occur on reading page 235 of Pynchon's *Gravity's Rainbow* where the girl is defecating into the open mouth of Brigadier Pudding and you realize there are 500 pages still to go) when the reader may look back wistfully to the economy, the delicacy, the artful mimicry, the tenderly ironic domesticity, the goddam *ret*icence, if you want to know the truth, of vintage Salinger.

KERRY McSWEENEY
"Salinger Revisited"
Critical Quarterly, Spring 1978, pp. 61–68

For anyone who was a literate North-American adolescent during the 1950s, it is probably difficult, even after fifteen or twenty years, to go beyond a personal estimate and/or historical estimate of the fiction of J. D. Salinger and attempt a 'real' estimate. The task will be especially difficult for those who were in those days uncritical enthusiasts of *Nine Stories*, *The Catcher in the Rye* and the Glass stories; for a retrospective distaste and embarrassment over one's youthful intensities, idealisings and over-simplifications may well make for a prejudiced rereading.

The possibility of overreaction on my part may be indicated by a catalogue of the Salingeresque items—tokens of sensitivity, emblems of non-aggression, touchstones of self-lessness—that fell out of my copy of *Catcher* when I recently opened it for the first time in a decade and a half: (*a*) a transcript of a poem by the then Brother Antoninus, which begins

> Annul in me my manhood, Lord, and make
> Me women-sexed and weak,
> If by that total transformation
> I might know Thee more;

(*b*) another of a Bob Dylan song, which begins with

> I ain't looking to compete with you, beat or cheat or
>   mistreat you,
> Simplify you, classify you, deny, defy, or crucify
>   you,
> All I really want to do is, baby, be friends with you;

(*c*) a *Peanuts* cartoon, in which Linus, holding as ever his security blanket, declares to Charlie Brown that 'No problem is so big or so complicated that it can't be run away from'; and (*d*) a *New Yorker* cartoon of two men in dinner jackets, holding highball glasses and looking at a wall on which are mounted heads of a number of ferocious looking animals—except for the centrepiece: the enormous head of a benign, quietly smiling lion, whose post-prandial countenance echoes those of the men, one of whom is explaining that 'I was removing a thorn from its paw when I suddenly thought: "What a magnificent head".'

Still, one aspires to objectivity and disinterest, and there is little doubt that now is a good time for a retrospective assessment of Salinger. For one thing, Warren French may well be more than self-serving when he says in the preface to the newly revised edition of his *J. D. Salinger* that "former readers, alienated from Salinger during the activist 1960s, are now returning to his books with renewed interest and are commending them to their children and their students'. For another, the Salinger canon seems essentially complete. His last published work, the unreadable 'Hapworth 16, 1924', appeared in the *New Yorker* twelve years ago. This 'story' consisted of an interminable letter sent from summer camp to his parents by the then *seven*-year-old prodigy, poet, and saint, Seymour Glass. What can you say about a kid who describes his meals thus: 'While the food itself is not atrocious, it is cooked without a morsel of affection or inspiration, each string bean or simple carrot arriving on the camper's plate stripped of its tiny vegetal soul'? 'Hapworth 16, 1924' had given the impression that Salinger had become self-indulgent in his writing, and was withdrawing into a self-referential fantasy world. This seemed confirmed by the disheartening statement the author made in 1974 when he broke a public silence of more than twenty years to complain in a telephone interview with the *New York Times* about the publication of an unauthorised collection of his apprentice work: 'There is a marvellous peace in not publishing. It's peaceful. Still. Publishing is a terrible invasion of my privacy. I like to write. I love to write. But I write just for myself and my own pleasure.'

The first of his works that Salinger regarded as post-apprentice were among those included in his 1954 collection, *Nine Stories*. All these stories are set in the only world Salinger knows: that of upper middle class New York City. They contain an abundance of acute social notation: Salinger is particularly good at using the details of speech, dress and decor to register the nuances of social stratification and character type. The world of the stories is mimed by Salinger's characteristic prose: the mannered *New Yorker* style of coy hyperbole and sophisticated overstatement, the knowing tone, and the self-conscious, mandarin poise tempered by measured colloquialisms.

While Salinger clearly finds much that is wrong with the world he describes, unlike Flaubert or Joyce he does not reveal his disapproval through his style, which in fact tends to exemplify the values of that world. This important point was made by Frank Kermode in 1962: 'the really queer thing about this writer is that he carefully writes for an audience [a culture-acquisitive audience] he deplores.' To put the matter differently: while there is in *Nine Stories*, as in the rest of

Salinger, much excellent social observation, albeit of a very narrow part of the social spectrum, there is very little social vision because Salinger has no outside point of view to bring to bear on a world to which he can imagine no positive, post-puberty alternative and of which, *faute de mieux*, he remains a part. Philip Roth overstated the case in 1962, but one understands his exasperation: 'the problem of how to live *in* this world is by no means answered . . . The only advice we seem to get from Salinger is to be charming on the way to the loony bin.'

The dominant subject of *Nine Stories* is the opposition of the few (the sensitive, delicate and discerning, usually children or disturbed young men) and the many (the crass, insensitive and phony). The upshot of this opposition can be destructive: the first and last stories, 'A Perfect Day for Bananafish' and 'Teddy', end abruptly with the suicide of the representative of the few. But when two sensitive, non-aggressive souls can make contact, a more optimistic, even sentimental, conclusion becomes possible, as in 'De Daumier-Smith's Blue Period' and 'For Esmé—with Love and Squalor', for the latter of which, despite the narrator's Dostoyevskian rumblings, this quotation from *Silas Marner* would have made a perfect epigraph: 'In old days there were angels who came and took men by the hand and led them away from the city of destruction. We see no white-winged angels now. But yet men are led away from threatening destruction: a hand is put into theirs, which leads them gently towards a calm and bright land, so that they look no more backward; and the hand may be a little child's.'

Of course, some of the *Nine Stories* are better than others. One of the finest, 'Uncle Wiggily in Connecticut', has at its centre the quintessential Salinger theme of the true life which is absent. In 'Zooey', Franny Glass, on the brink of a breakdown, will say that the one person she wants to talk to is her dead brother Seymour; in *Catcher*, Holden Caulfield, when challenged to name just one person whom he really likes, will name his dead brother Allie. In 'Uncle Wiggily' two old friends, Mary Jane and Eloise, get together in the latter's suburban home for an afternoon of reminiscence, complaint and too much drink. As their conversation becomes intimate, Eloise begins to speak of the young man, a brother of Seymour Glass, who was different (the story's title alludes to one of his fey witticisms); who was in fact everything that her husband is not; whom she loved; and who was killed in an absurd accident during the war. The loss is nicely counterpointed by the relationship of Eloise's young daughter to her imaginary friend, Jimmy Jimmereeno. When Jimmy is run over, his place in the daughter's bed is taken by Mickey Mickeranno. But Eloise cannot make contact with her daughter—she even insists on making her sleep in the middle of the bed as a way of negating Mickey's existence—and for her there is nothing to fill the absence of Walt Glass except her maudlin insistence at the end of the story that she used to be a nice girl.

On the other hand, 'De Daumier-Smith's Blue Period', which has a similar theme, is a weak story. Its narrator is a sensitive young man stuck in a cheesy art correspondence school in Montreal, who becomes unilaterally involved through the mail with a nun in Toronto whose work shows promise but whose superiors unexpectedly require her to withdraw from the school. The nun, a variant of the Salingeresque child figure, is of course an embodiment of the absent true life for which the narrator yearns. The story's events take place when the narrator is nineteen; he is thirty-two when he recounts them (the same age, incidentally, as Salinger when he wrote the story, just as the narrator's initials are

identical with the author's). But the older narrator is indistinguishable from his younger self; there is no distancing, no perspective, no way of placing or grounding, the epiphany with which the story concludes. Gazing into the window of an orthopedic appliances shop, De Daumier-Smith suddenly has 'an extraordinary experience', a moment of vision which leaves 'twice blessed' the objects in the window and leads to the assertion that he can give up Sister Irma because 'Everybody is a nun. (*Tout le monde est une nonne*).' This climactic moment, a harbinger of the notorious ending of 'Zooey', where it is asserted that the Fat Lady is Christ, seems to me quite hollow and unearned, and, like the narrator, immature and callow. 'Twice blessed' is an empty poeticism borrowed (probably unconsciously) from Portia's speech in *The Merchant of Venice*. And 'Everybody is a nun' recalls the '*Tout est grâce*' at the end of Bernanos' great novel, *Journal d'un curé de campagne*, in a way that devastatingly points up the thinness, staginess, and merely notional quality of Salinger's scene.

One generalisation that could be made about these two stories involves the old chestnut about the relative difficulty in creating convincing fictional representations of unfallen as opposed to fallen, transcendent to quotidian, gain to loss, saint to sinner, selflessness to egotism. Salinger seems to be aware of this problem in that 'De Daumier-Smith's Blue Period' contains a degree of narrative self-consciousness (absent in 'Uncle Wiggily') which suggests uneasiness in the face of a difficult creative problem. For the same reason, narrative self-consciousness becomes more and more prominent in the four Glass family stories which began to appear in *The New Yorker* the year after the publication of *Nine Stories*.

One thing that can be said about all of the *Nine Stories* is that they are professional pieces of work, textbook examples of the short-story form. By the same token, despite a good deal of ingenuity, they are limited by the form's conventional boundaries. One senses Salinger's dissatisfaction with this, and sees him beginning to push beyond the boundaries in 'Franny'. As in the *Nine Stories*, the subject of this long short story is the opposition of the phony and the seeker after authenticity. Again, it is the phony—the splendid figure of Lane Coutell— that is better done. The presentation of Franny, an equally recognisable social type (a female Ivy Leaguer), is more fuzzy and uncertain. Particularly telling is the fact that Salinger can only convey a sense of Franny's spiritual yearnings by having her summarise the contents of a Russian religious work, cry a lot, and continually mumble the Jesus prayer.

In 'Raise High the Roof Beam, Carpenters', a novella-length short story (it is not a short novella), the same contrast is in some ways better handled. The members of the wedding-party diaspora who eventually gather in Buddy and Seymour Glass's apartment are the rather too exhaustively detailed equivalent of the Lane Coutell world. The contrasting figure is again a Glass sibling, this time Seymour, like Franny a quasi-mystic, a seeker after higher truth who is half drawn towards, half put off by sexual and emotional involvement (for Franny, Lane; for Seymour, Muriel).

It is in the contrast between Seymour and Franny that the superiority of 'Raise High the Roof Beam, Carpenters' lies. Seymour is a much stronger and more convincing representation of spirituality. The principal reason for this is that he never appears in the story. He is the true life whose absence is mediated by his loving brother Buddy, the narrator. Because Salinger does not present Seymour directly he can become an acceptable, almost palpable representative of the higher life. Even his metaphorical stigmata—'I have scars on my hands from touching certain people' (from a diary Buddy has found)—which seems particularly annoying to certain critics, seems to me a striking evocation of what George Eliot called 'a keen vision and feeling of all ordinary human life', which if we had them would be 'like hearing the grass grow and the squirrel's heart beat' and cause us to 'die of that roar which lies on the other side of silence'.

The two other Glass stories, 'Zooey' and 'Seymour: An Introduction', are both disappointing pieces of work, much shrunken from the dimensions they had for me in the late 1950s. Both, particularly the latter, represent an interesting technical development in Salinger's art, for in them he has broken away completely from the conventional short-story form. This has been mainly achieved through the increased self-consciousness of the author/narrator and his active involvement in the story he is trying to tell. As Philip Roth was perhaps the first to recognise, in these stories Salinger was concerned 'to place the figure of the writer directly in the reader's line of vision'. (More recently, in a piece in the 13 June 1975 _TLS_, David Lodge has suggestively discussed the 'elaborate game with his audience and with the conventions of his art' that the later Salinger is playing). For example, in 'Seymour: An Introduction' the subject of the story is as much the creative difficulties of Buddy Glass in presenting to the reader his saintly brother ('the one person who was always much, much too large to fit on ordinary typewriter paper') as it is Seymour himself. The spiritual theme (Seymour) and the epistemological/aesthetic theme (the apprehension and presentation of Seymour) become indistinguishable and are simultaneously held in the matrix of the writer-reader relationship.

It is from this technical point of view that 'Zooey' and 'Seymour: An Introduction' are most interesting. But this is not enough to save either story from its content. There is too much in the 44,000 words of 'Zooey' that is self-indulgent and inert; and the presentation and resolution of the religious problem is pitched in so shrill a key that one eventually comes to see that Salinger has taken Franny's rather run-of-the-mill collegiate identity crisis and tried to do much-too-much with it. And both the closing affirmation at the end of the 27,000 words of 'Seymour: An Introduction' ('all we do our whole lives is go from one little piece of Holy Ground to the next') and its climactic epiphany (the apparition of Seymour at 'the magic hour of the day' during a marble shooting game and his admonishing Buddy not to aim), though the latter once seemed to me the most incandescent moment in Salinger's canon, now seem too meagre and too much like cut-rate Zen to justify the expenditure of time and energy necessary to get to the end of the story.

The only work of Salinger's that has not shrunk with the passage of time is _The Catcher in the Rye_. The macro-subject of Salinger's only novel is that of all his fiction; as Carol and Richard Ohmann say in their provocative 'case study of capitalist criticism' of _Catcher_ in the autumn 1976 _Critical Inquiry_, the novel is 'among other things a serious critical mimesis of bourgeois life in the Eastern United States ca. 1950. The micro-subject is a crisis point in the adolescence of a sensitive and perceptive youth: Holden Caulfield is sixteen when the events in the novel take place; seventeen when he narrates them. The social notation is superb: the expensive prep school with its Ackleys and Stradlaters; the lobby of the Biltmore (the _in_ place for dates to meet); the Greenwich Village bar and the equally tony Wicker Bar uptown; the crowd in the theatre lobby at intermission; Mr and Mrs Antolini; the sad 'girls' from Seattle who are in the big city to have a good time; and so on.

Similarly, the macro-theme of _Catcher_ is that of the rest of Salinger; the almost Dickensian dichotomy between the lower world of the many and the innocent, constantly threatened world of the few: the dead Allie, who used to write poems all over his baseball mitt, and Jane Gallagher, who when playing checkers always kept her kings in the back row (both activities recall Seymour's admonition not to aim when shooting marbles); the two nuns who 'went around collecting dough in those beat-up old straw baskets'; and Phoebe, the wise child, for love of whom her exhausted brother is moved to tears on the novel's last page.

What is different in _Catcher_, and what must be considered the key to its success, is its method. Holden's first person narration _ipso facto_ removes from the novel any trace of _New Yorker_ preciosities. Everything is seen from Holden's point of view and reported in his pungent vernacular. The voice and the perceptions are wholly convincing and of sustained freshness. Indeed, the only comparatively flat scenes—on the train with Morrow's mother, in the restaurant with the nuns—are the two places in the novel where one feels that there is something derivative about Holden's characterisation and narration, that he is drawn more from _Huckleberry Finn_ than from life.

Holden's adolescent perspective, halfway between the childhood and adult worlds, fully a part of neither yet acutely sensitive to and observant of both, provides the perfect point of focus for _Catcher_. Holden is in a privileged though precarious position. A two- or three-year difference in his age, in either direction, would have made for an entirely different book. In his own image, to which the novel's title calls attention, Holden is 'on the edge of some crazy cliff', with little kids playing in a field of rye on one side of him, an abyss on the other. Like that of Nick Carraway, Fitzgerald's narrator in _The Great Gatsby_, Holden's bifocal vision allows him simultaneously to register both the phoniness and meretriciousness of the fallen world and the sense of wonder and tenderness, and the supernal _frissons_, of the innocent world. And since they are so well grounded (and thereby authenticated) in a particular person at a particular time of life, Holden's longings, needs and intimations of mystery never become sentimental or merely notional. Indeed they are the most resonant images in all of Salinger of the longing for the absent true life, as in Holden's haunting question of where the Central Park ducks go in the winter, his love for the dead brother, and for the live sister whom he wishes could, like things in the museum, always stay the way she now is and never have to grow up.

Near the end of _Catcher_ Holden reflects that there is no place where one is free from somebody sneaking up and writing 'Fuck you' right under your nose. Holden's erasures of this phrase recall the last page of _The Great Gatsby_ when Nick Carraway deletes an obscene word from Gatsby's steps before going down to the water's edge to begin meditation on the capacity for wonder and the longing for absent true life, which draws one ceaselessly back into the past. There are more similarities between Fitzgerald's and Salinger's novels (and between the two authors) than might at first meet the eye, and a brief concluding comparison of the two may be of help in making a stab at gauging the 'real' status of _Catcher_.

Both novels turn on the contrast of a fallen world of aggression, selfishness and phoniness and a tenuous higher world of (to use Fitzgerald's phrase) 'heightened sensitivity to the promises of life'. Both writers have been charged with having no real social vision to complement their acute social notation: what the Ohmanns say of Holden Caulfield may, _mutatis mutandis_, he said of his creator: 'for all his perceptiveness . . . he is an adolescent with limited understanding of what he perceives'. And Fitzgerald has of course been described as having been taken in by what he could see through. I believe that this remark is manifestly unfair to Fitzgerald at his best, and that there is much to ponder in his (admittedly oddly phrased) notebook comment that D. H. Lawrence was 'Essential[ly] pre-Marxian. Just as I am essentially Marxian.' There is real social insight in *Gatsby*, which offers a complex anatomy and moral evaluation of the world it describes. Because its bifocal vision is that of a discriminating adult, not that of an engagingly screwed-up teenager, the novel is able to offer a richer and more complex exploration both of the lower world and the higher world of threatened innocence and longing.

For these reasons, among others, *Gatsby* seems to me an appreciably greater novel than *Catcher*. But the difference is perhaps one of degree rather than of kind, and if one accepts

John Berryman's definition of a masterpiece (found in his excellent essay on *Gatsby* in *The Freedom of the Poet*)—

> a work of the literary imagination which is consistent, engaging, and dramatic, in exceptional degrees; which exhibits largely mastered a human subject of the first importance; and which seems in retrospect to illuminate the whole physical and spiritual situation of which it was, by the strange parturition of art, an accidental product. One easy test will be the rapidity with which, in the imagination of a good judge, other works of the period and kind will faint away under any suggested comparison with it.

—one may go on to say that both *The Great Gatsby* and *The Catcher in the Rye* belong on permanent display in the gallery of classic American fiction.

EDGAR SALTUS

1855–1921

Edgar Evertson Saltus was born on October 5, 1855, in New York City, a descendant of distinguished forebears who had settled there in the seventeenth and eighteenth centuries. He attended St. Paul's School and then studied briefly at Yale. Saltus spent several years abroad before earning a law degree at Columbia, but instead of practicing he devoted himself to writing. In 1884 he published a study of Balzac and in the following year *The Philosophy of Disenchantment*, a long essay on Schopenhauer and his school. *The Anatomy of Negation*, a study of anti-theist philosophies, appeared in 1886.

Saltus's first novel, *Mr. Incoul's Misadventures*, published in 1887, was the first in a series of more than a dozen popular works of fiction written by Saltus. Among his other works, all of them characterized by an exaggerated, sensational style and a tone of breathless excitement (Oscar Wilde was reported to have commented that "in the work of Edgar Saltus passion struggles with grammar on every page"), was *Imperial Purple* (1893), set in ancient Rome and said to have been a favorite book of President Harding. *Imperial Orgy* (1920) was a sensational account of czarist Russia. In addition, Saltus produced a number of popular nonfiction books anonymously for P. F. Collier & Son in the late 1890s, including *The Lovers of the World* and *The Great Battles of All Nations*.

Saltus was married three times. His last wife, Marie Giles, converted him to theosophy. He died on July 31, 1921, after a long illness, and is buried in Tarrytown, New York, in the same plot with Mrs. Saltus's dog Toto.

Personal

Did the author of *Imperial Purple* ever grant you an audience in recent years? The privilege, indeed, was extended to very few. It was easier for absolute strangers in whom the novelist had discovered some momentarily sympathetic trait to be admitted to his sanctum, somewhere near the river and upper Broadway, than for his oldtime friends of the days when Union Square was still a haunt of men of literary pursuits.

To attend Edgar Saltus's *salon solitaire* was a trifle awkward experience. It was weird and solemn. One felt a little foolish, shy and embarrassed, as one entered the spacious library, dimly lit and cluttered with books and *objets d'art*, Chinese hangings, Japanese screens, East Indian statuary. And there Edgar Saltus would sit on a sort of baldachined throne, much higher than the divans of his guests, dispense cigarettes ten inches long, read Chinese poetry and lecture, learnedly and enthusiastically, on the art ideals of the Far Orient. The "lady of his choice" (not necessarily the same one at each occasion) would bring him some treasured volume and he would declaim in a low musical voice by the hour. If you

wished to say something in praise, he would raise his hands imploringly, murmuring "no admiration, please", and thereupon continue. There was never much chance for conversation. It was a sort of monologue performance. Finally he would bow out his guests in his suavest and most polite manner. Saltus was always extremely courteous, and his gestures were like hieroglyphics made with his finger tips. In his dress he was neither loud nor eccentric, but rather up to date with the latest fashion, tailormade, immaculate. With his *boutonnière* and the traditional triangle of a silk handkerchief always visible, with white socks, gloves, stovepipe, and walking stick, he impressed one as a dandy of the MacAllister era. He was picturesque without being conspicuous. His face in later years had peculiarly deep lines about the nose and mouth, only partly hidden by a heavy brown moustache—the color no doubt was due to some generous process of rejuvenation, as the author was near sixty when I saw him last.

These extraordinary séances, given but to three or four or perchance only to one fortunate mortal at a time, had something soothing about them while one was in his presence, but afterward proved strangely irritating to a sensitive observer.

One asked himself, why has this man become a *recluse*, so exceptional and fastidious in his manners that it is impossible to live with him? There was a time when a fine metallic ring clung to his name and when he went about very much like the rest of us. But even in his Sorbonne days in Paris he was shy and reticent, had his own way of studying life and avoided new acquaintances. After his first marriage he disappeared entirely from public view, almost as completely as if he had been swallowed up by one of Ambrose Bierce's exterior ether spouts. His name became a mere memory. For a while he wrote for the *Journal*. Then came longer intervals of silence, and his style as a novelist deteriorated in an alarming degree. That the man who had written a *Philosophy of Disenchantment*, an *Anatomy of Negation*, and *The Truth about Tristrem Varick* should ever write *The Perfume of Eros*, *Daughters of the Rich*, and *The Paliser Case* is a tragedy in itself. No wonder that his later books attracted but little attention. He has no champions and his bibliography to this day is curiously limited. Only Percival Pollard, indefatigable in faint praise and hero worship, said a few kind words of appreciation. Also Van Vechten wrote quite amiably about the author of *Mary Magdalen* in his *Merry Go Round*, paragraphs that Arthur Symons apparently appreciated so much that he borrowed from them for use in one of his literary discussions.

In the 'eighties Saltus's style resembled that of Flaubert—at least we younger men thought so. Saltus was not quite so persistent and painstaking as a sentence builder, still he wrote with a rare fluency and colorful terseness. This marmorean splendor, alas, vanished soon; it became crumby and porous, and crumbled away into formless chunks. As with so many of our great artists, his temperament was against him, and he gradually lost all contact with contemporary art and life.

There are some plants so fragile that they shrivel up when touched by human hands. In a similar manner Saltus shunned actualities, life to him was too vulgar and insincere to be worth wooing, the frivolities of routine annoyed him, everything seemed to be out of harmony with his more intimate ideals. The author had a small independent income; this more than anything else came to his undoing. If an artist is poor he is forced to make the best of life. If he is rich he can assemble influences to further the success of his work. But if he has just enough to live comfortably, carefree materially, he will retire to commune with himself; and Saltus did retire. If such hermit natures have the real stuff in them, they will continue to produce—sometimes in a fanatic delirium like the painter A. P. Ryder—but otherwise indolence and indifference will mar and destroy even the finest talent. Saltus's resurrection could be brought about only through a reprint of his earlier work.

It was in the early 'nineties that I met Saltus at various occasions. He was then about thirty-four years old. He could be met at cafés and social functions, but generally only late in the day. I do not recall ever having seen him in anything but a dress suit. At that time Robert W. Chambers, "a promising genius", exploited the Bohemia of Washington Square, and W. D. Howells received the homage of us younger men at the Everett House. Saltus came most frequently to Edgar Fawcett's (I believe) Friday Evenings. It was quite a coterie that assembled there during the midnight hours. Among them were several writers of note, Francis Saltus, Edgar's brother, Stuart Merrill, George Pellew, Russel Sturgis, a translator of some of Maupassant's stories, and many others whose names I do not remember at this moment. But I must not forget one literary curiosity. He was the American safety valve in this æsthetic crowd, and astounded us by his stories of selling "Mr. Barnes"

"by the ton". What a contrast between these two men, one loud mouthed, purse proud, arrogant and commonplace, and the other one silent and languid like the prince of an Indian fairy tale. Saltus was rather slow of speech but fond of talking nevertheless, with a sort of subdued vehemence. There was something furtive, will o' the wisp like about his personality. At times he was strangely absentminded and self-absorbed, as if he took resource in hashish or some other drug to help him over the "dismal blanks of everyday existence".

One wintry day I saw him on Broadway accompanied by several cats, a curious spectacle which reminded me of the legend told of Gérard de Nerval leading a live lobster on a silk ribbon along the Parisian boulevards. Already in those days, not unlike the hero of Poe's story, Saltus was exaggeratedly fond of cats. In later life this fondness became almost a mania with him. Readers of his books will recall the lawyer in *The Paliser Case*, who never appears upon the scene without carrying a cat upon his shoulder. If by chance you talked to him about a cat and stopped for a moment in your story, he would urge you, "Go on, please!" and it is said of him, that he who was too aristocratic ever to go into a store to buy things for himself, would stop at the first butcher shop and purchase a piece of liver if he had just made an acquaintance with a stray cat in the street.

A strange ending to a literary career of promise.

I had expected more of Saltus than of anybody else of my contemporaries. I was doomed to disappointment. The author whose philosophy had been originally "to live without prejudice and principle" was losing his way mentally just in the opposite direction. There was more than one rift in his lute, but I shall always remember gratefully what a wonderful resonant instrument it was in the late 'eighties and early 'nineties, and what beautiful concertos he performed on it with the precision and grace of a real virtuoso.—SADAKICHI HARTMANN, "The Edgar Saltus I Knew," *Bkm*, Sept. 1923, pp. 17–19

General

Edgar Saltus owes much of his bizarre talent to his mixed origin, for he is of Dutch and American extraction; indeed, for much of what I might call his rather unholy genius. His pages exhale a kind of exotic and often abnormal perfume of colors, color of sensations, of heats, of crowded atmospheres. He gives his women baneful and baleful names, such as Stella Sixmouth, Shom Wyvell; these vampires and wicked creatures who ruin men's lives as cruelly as they ruin their own. His men have prodigious nerves, even more than his women; they commit all sorts of crimes, assassinations, poisonings, out of sheer malice and out of overexcited imaginations.

Of that most terrible of tragedies, the tragedy of a soul, he is for the most part utterly unconscious; and the very abracadabra of his art is in a sense—a curious enough and ultramodern sense—lifted from the Elizabethan dramatists. In them—as in many of his pages—a fine situation must have a murder in it, and some odious character removed by another more stealthy kind of obliteration. But, when he gives one a passing shudder, he leaves nothing behind it; yet in his perverted characters there can be found sensitiveness, hallucinations, obsessions; and some have that lassitude which is more than mere contempt. Some go solemnly on the path of blood, with no returning by a way so thronged with worse than memories. "No need for more crime," such men have cried, and for such reasons reaped the bitter harvest of tormenting dreams. Some have imagination that stands in the place of virtue; some, as in the case of Lady Macbeth, still keep the sensation of blood on their guilty hands.

Mary of Magdala (1891) is a vain attempt to do what Flaubert had done before Saltus in his *Hérodias*, and what Wilde has done after him in *Salome*, a drama that has a strange not easily defined fascination, which I can not dissociate from Beardsley's illustrations, in which what is icily perverse in the dialogue (it can not be designated drama) becomes in the ironical designs pictorial, a series of poses. To Wilde passion was a thing to talk about with elaborate and colored words. Salome is a doll, as many have imagined her, soulless, set in motion by some pitiless destiny, personified momentarily by her mother; Herod is a nodding mandarin in a Chinese grotesque.

In one page of Saltus's *Oscar Wilde: An Idler's Impressions* (1917) he evokes, with his cynical sense of the immense disproportion of things in this world and the next, the very innermost secret of Wilde. They dine in a restaurant in London and Wilde reads his MS. "Suddenly his eyes lifted, his mouth contracted, a spasm of pain—or was it dread?—had gripped him, a moment only. I had looked away. I looked again. Before me was a fat pauper, florid and over-dressed, who in the voice of an immortal, was reading the fantasies of the damned. In his hand was a manuscript, and we were supping on *Salome*."

Mr. Incoul's Misfortune seems to have its origin in some strange story of Poe's; for it gives one the sense of a monster, diabolical, inhuman, malevolent and merciless, who, after a mock marriage, abnormally sets himself to the devil's business of ruining his wife's lover's life, and of giving his wife a sudden death in three hideous forms: a drug to make her sleep, the gas turned on, and the door locked with "a nameless instrument."

The Truth about Tristrem Varick (1888) is based on social problems of the most unaccountable kind. It has something strangely convincing in both conception and execution; it has suspense, ugly enough and uglier crises; and that the unlucky Varick is supposed to be partially insane is part of the finely woven plot, which is concerned with strange and perilous incidents and accidents; and which is based on his passionate pursuit of the ravishing Viola Raritan; the pursuit, really, of the chimera of his imagination.

And among the hazards comes one, of an evil kind—such as I have often experienced in foreign cities—that, in turning down one street instead of the next, a man's existence, and not his only, may be thereby changed. To have stopped one's rival's lying mouth and his lying life at the same instant is to have done something original—it is done by a poisoned pin's point. Then, this Orestes having found no Electra to return his love, but finding her vile, he lets himself disappear out of life in an almost incredible fashion, leaving the woman who never loved him to say, "I will come to see him sentenced:" a sentence which writes her down a modern Clytemnestra.

What Saltus says of Gonfallon can almost be said of Saltus: "With a set of people that fancied themselves in possession of advanced views and were still in the Middle Ages, he achieved the impossible: he not only consoled, he flattered, he persuaded and fascinated as well." Saltus can not console, he can sometimes persuade; but he can flatter and fascinate his public, as with

A breeze of fame made manifest.

The novelist is the comedian of the pen: it is his duty to amuse, to entertain—or else to hold his peace: to one in his trade nothing imaginable comes amiss. It is not sin that appals him, but the consequences of sin; such as the fact that few sinners have ever turned into saints. In a word, he writes with his nerves.

Take, for instance, *A Transaction of Hearts* (1887), one of the queerest novels ever written and written with a kind of deliberate malice. Gonfallon, who becomes a bishop, falls passionately in love with an ardent and insolent girl who is his wife's sister; and before her beauty everything vanishes: virtue, genius, everything. "For a second that was an eternity he was conscious of her emollient mouth on his, her fingers inter-twined with his own. For that second he really lived—perhaps he really lived." One wonders why Saltus uses so many ugly phrases—a kind of decadent French fashion of transposing words; such as the one I have quoted, together with "Ruedelapaixia" (meant to describe a dress), "Rafflesia," "Mashed grasshoppers backed in saffron;" phrases chosen at random which are too frequently scattered in much too obvious a profusion over much too luxurious pages. I read somewhere that Oscar Wilde said to Amélie Rives: "In Edgar Saltus's work passion struggles with grammar on every page," which is certainly one of Wilde's finest paradoxes. I "cap this"—as Dowson often said to me in jest—with Léon Bloy's admirable phrase on Huysmans: "That he drags his images by the heels or the hair upside down the worm-eaten staircase of terrified syntax."

Imperial Purple (1906) shows the zenith of Saltus's talent, not in conceiving imaginary beings, but in giving modern conceptions of the most amazing creatures in the Roman Decadence, and in lyrical prose, which ought to have had for motto Victoria's stanza:—

Je suis l'Empire à la fin de la décadence,
Qui regarde passer les grands Barbares blancs,
En composant des acrostiches indolents,
D'un style d'or où la langueur du soleil danse.

Only Saltus is not Tacitus, in spite of having delved into his pages.—ARTHUR SYMONS, "Edgar Saltus," *Dramatis Personae*, 1923, pp. 263–68

Somewhere in that Never-Never Land of Lord Dunsany there is a dusty road that stretches from Here to There. Along this road there trudges a figure. From the fact that his clothes are ragged, that his shoes are split and that his face is a gray dead heaven in which are imbedded two big, black stars weltering in light you may infer that he is a Poet.

A Lady, with a nimbus and a wand, incorporates herself out o' th' air and walks besides the Superfluous Being. She is Fame. You may know that by the ironic grin in her eye.

They talk. And when Poet and Fame talk the fairies and the demons listen and the solid old earth becomes such a garden as one sees in the Kingdoms of the Pipe.

But the upshot of the fable is (and I am not telling the story strictly on the level) that Fame gives the Poet a rendez-vous—behind his tombstone one hundred years from date.

Saltus! Saltus! In what storied urn of memory reposed the word? In what sarcophagus of the past had I laid that verbal corpse? In what penetralia had I met the man with that name? At what Petronius feast of intellectuals had I clinked glasses with that being?

The bandalettes slipped from a hidden face and the blood came surging back into petrified arteries, and eyes that I thought sealed opened wide, and great jewels fell from them that sang in words and formed themselves into daggers called epigrams.

And Edgar Saltus rose out of his Pompeii. Well, as a matter of fact, he had only been summering in Oblivion.

There are three mysteries in American literature—the

appearance of Edgar Allan Poe, the disappearance of Ambrose Bierce and the burial alive of Edgar Saltus. It is fairly certain that the latter was pretty comfortable in his grave; and it is still more certain that he begemmed his coffin with prose poems scratched into the pine wood with worms—worms, which are the epigrams of the sod. Then, too, without doubt, he had his Théophile Gautier with him, his Baudelaire, and was fed from the amphoræ of those two angelic ghosts, Leconte de Lisle and Villiers de l'Isle-Adam.

Here is an American that knows his language, that knows the creative and mystical power of words, that knows the phrase that kills and the sentence that is winged. As exotic as Poe and Lafcadio Hearn, his books should be called Pomp and Purple.

A lyrical intellect, an implacable pessimist, a sublime snob, he stands aloof and alone in his work. His contempt and disdain of "merely human" things is beautiful. It is a gesture toward the Infinite.

This accounts for his unpopularity. He will have none of the mob. The sweat of everyday life to him is just sweat. The life of the poor is not a drama; it is a disease. The poor and the weary laden exist no more for him than they did for Emerson.

Whatever is not genius is dross. Whatever is beautiful is right. All life aspires to fiction. Humor is an attribute of God. Life itself is the conundrum of a Jester.

His books take apart the mechanism of the quick. When he wrote *The Philosophy of Disenchantment* he was crowned by some one as "the Prose Laureate of Pessimism." All is illusion in the worst of possible worlds—"so let us live in Paris." The characters in his novels of New York life move like hallucinated automatons. There is a hero in each book— Mephistopheles.

Saltus is so great that he is unpleasant. He is as unwholesome as truth. He sees so far that his brain cells must be made up of telescopes that gods in the Fourth Dimension use to study the humans in the Fifth Dimension. He is as uncanny as the thought of immortality. And above all his work hangs the irony of Brahma.

His *Tristrem Varick* is the greatest novel that ever came from the pen of an American—a fable, a philosophy and an enormous chunk of life. It is a tale of the pursuit of the Ideal by Man—and the end is a badly lighted room in the Tenderloin police station.

He is on intimate terms with the gods and pals with the predestined criminals of all time—from Cain to the Borgias. He plays hide and seek with Nero, Tiberius and the Kaiser—he wrote this in 1906 in a chapter on hyenas (the hyenas are Caligula, Attila, Tamerlane, Ivan the Terrible & Co.):

". . . The German Kaiser. Not long since somebody or other diagnosed in him the habitual criminal. We doubt that he is that. But we suspect that were it not for the press he would show more of the primitive man than he has thus far thought judicious."

But it is because of his style that he will live. He has said nothing new—because there is nothing new to be said. His brain is as old as Buddha's or that of the author of Ecclesiastes. His style is the measured tread of his wisdom. His sentences are cut from the jewelled heavens in which he lives. His words drip into the next paragraph and form pools of images. His crescendos flower in the art, and the flowers remain there, frozen gardens. One feels him moving behind the page like a pontiff behind a huge, swaying curtain. There is no creak, no noise, no jolt. He passes imperceptibly from Zeus to Brahma, from Brahma to Amon Râ like a sun-walker shod in ether.

The genius of Edgar Saltus is his masterly insincerity. He doesn't believe in himself, in the people he writes about, in the world he depicts, in you or me, or anything. He is a balancer, a juggler, a Houdini of phrases, a Gargantuan Capocomico who balances the Taj Mahal on his nose, the Alhambra and St. Peter's on his skull and tosses buddhas and bonzes, bibles and sultans in vast circles like eggs, precisely sure of never missing one, while the orchestra thunders a Valkyrean battle charge toward the Gates of Nowhere—an orchestra conducted by the Furies.

But only the profoundly sincere in spirit can enter the Kingdom of Insincerity. The Wildes, the Chestertons, the Hunekers, the Anatole Frances, the Shaws and the Renans are to the manner born. They may play battledore and shuttlecock with everything because they are everything—and nothing; they have the frivolous, ironic gayety of Nature, that emits swallows and earthquakes and bluebells and pests and lunatics and fairies and passes on with a sublime indifference.

Their imitators come along; then we see an elephant trying to play butterfly; Bottom doing Puck's tricks. Insincerity is the final sense of humor—it is the laughter of the nihilist from the chimney of the House of Life, where he plays with the tomcats, the stars and the blind bats of chance.

Neither Molière nor Balzac sat in the Academy. Edgar Saltus must remain our forty-first Immortal.—Benjamin De Casseres, "Edgar Saltus," *Forty Immortals*, 1926, pp. 88–93

Forty years ago Edgar Saltus was a shining star in the national literature, leading the way out of the Egyptian night of Victorian sentimentality. To-day he survives only as the favorite author of the late Warren Gamaliel Harding. I can recall, in the circle of Athene, no more complete collapse. Saltus plunged from the top of the world to the bottom of the sea. His books, of late, have been reissued, and his surviving third wife has printed a biography of him. But all his old following, save for a few romantic die-hards, has vanished.

The causes of the débâcle are certainly not hard to determine. They were set forth twenty-five years ago by that ingenious man, the late Percival Pollard, and you will find them in his book, *Their Day in Court*. Saltus was simply a bright young fellow who succumbed to his own cleverness. The gaudy glittering phrase enchanted him. He found early in life that he had a hand for shaping it; he found soon afterward that it had a high capacity for getting him notice. So he devoted himself to its concoction—and presently he was lost. His life after that was simply one long intoxication. He was drunk on words. Ideas gradually departed from him. Day and night, for years and years, he held his nozzle against the jug of nouns, adjectives, verbs, pronouns, prepositions and interjections. Some of his phrases, of course, were good ones. There were enough of that kind in *Imperial Purple*, for example, to fascinate the sainted Harding, a voluptuary in all the arts. But the rest quickly wore out—and with them Saltus himself wore out. He passed into the shadows, and was forgotten. When he died, a few years ago, all that remained of him was a vague name.

⟨. . .⟩ The man began life with everything in his favor. His family was well-to-do and of good social position in New York; he was sent to Eton and then to Heidelberg, and apparently made useful friends at both places; he plunged into writing at the precise moment when revolt against the New England Brahmins was rising; he attracted attention quickly, and was given a lavish welcome. No American author of 1885 was more talked about. When his first novel, *The Truth about Tristrem Varick*, came out in 1888 it made a genuine sensation. But the stick came down almost as fast as the rocket had gone up. His books set the nation agog for a short while, and were then quietly forgotten. He began as the hope of American letters, and ended as a writer of yellow-backs and a special correspondent for the Hearst papers. What ailed him was simply lack of solid substance. He could be clever, as cleverness was understood during the first Cleveland administration, but he lacked dignity, information, sense. His books of "philosophy" were feeble and superficial, his novels were only facile improvisations, full of satanic melodrama and wooden marionettes.

Of late I have been re-reading them—a sad job, surely, for when I was a schoolboy they were nine-day wonders, barred from all the libraries but devoured eagerly by every aspiring youth. Now their epigrams were dulled, and there is nothing else left. *The Anatomy of Negation* and *The Philosophy of Disenchantment* have been superseded by far better books; *The Truth about Tristrem Varick* reads like one of the shockers of Gertrude Atherton; *Mary Magdalen* is a dead shell; the essays and articles republished as *Uplands of Dream* are simply ninth-rate journalism. Of them all only *Imperial Purple* holds up. A certain fine glow is still in it; it has gusto if not profundity; Saltus's worst faults do not damage it appreciably. I find myself, indeed, agreeing thoroughly with the literary judgment of Dr. Harding. *Imperial Purple* remains Saltus's best book. It remains also, alas, his only good one!—H. L. MENCKEN, "Edgar Saltus," *Prejudices: Fifth Series*, 1926, pp. 277–82

CLAIRE SPRAGUE
"Afterword"
Edgar Saltus
1968, pp. 121–25

What it comes back to, in other words, is the intensity with which we live—and his intensity is recorded for us on every page of his work. (Henry James, "The Lesson of Balzac")

Like Henry James and other American contemporaries, Edgar Saltus had searched in his paradoxist way for "the human note in the huge American rattle of gold."[1] His point of view and his career support the thesis of many writers of the 1920's that post–Civil War America was inhospitable if not hostile to the artist. The nation's inhospitality did not mean Saltus could not find publishers, for the poison was subtler and more pervasive. It had to do with a point in time and a way of life which engendered, as Matthew Josephson believed, "the exotic, aborted, or estranged careers of American artists."[2] Josephson modified only a little the Van Wyck Brooks thesis that the American environment corrupts or corrodes artistic ability.

But Edgar Saltus is not in any obvious sense a victim of that environment. One critic commented, "Mr. Saltus came on the stage a little too late and very much too soon."[3] He may be right, for Saltus would more easily have found his place as a writer in pre–Civil War and post–World War I America. Within his own period, only the very best could produce at the high level of excellence that Saltus could recognize if not emulate.

Saltus was, with contemporaries like James Huneker, Vance Thompson, and Percival Pollard, at the very least, "a Service."[4] In his role as a cultural middleman, he brought to the newer and growing middle-class audience news of French and other European literatures and habits.[5] He helped to make American literary insularity impossible. The 1920's completed his job. He and his "decade of small things" anticipated other concerns and interests of the 1920's. His criticism of the American cultural environment included, for example, explicit use of the Puritan past as scapegoat and explicit awareness of the simplicities of the art-morality debates of the period. The Saltus who coined "Bourgeoisophobus" suggests some relationship with the Mencken who coined "booboisie." Both writers flourished when genius was more often equated with immorality than it is today. The existence of an avant-garde (now that it is dead, it is taken for granted) had its beginnings as an idea and as a fact in the American climate of opinion that included Saltus. This avant-garde insisted on craftsmanship and risked being called "esthetic" for that insistence.[6] The bare, early Saltus style, departing radically from classic nineteenth-century American prose style, is closer to twentieth-century practice. Saltus also looked eagerly to discoveries in psychology; he was particularly fascinated with pathology. Pathology might describe, if not explain, what happened to his deluded lovers. He saw the dust beneath the gilt and accepted in pessimism a thin explanation for frustration and reality. But pessimism allowed him to become an early subverter of "uplift."

His novels are transparent footnotes to pessimistic doctrine in which he tries to remind his confident contemporaries that "Happiness is a myth invented by Satan for our despair."[7] Although the novels are more ornamental than profoundly disenchanting, they are based on the discordance between idea and existence which erupts in disillusion and violence—a subject central to human experience that has had its special relevance in American literature. Saltus' interest in economics and politics, in the ecology of empire, and in the decay of the city was not accidental. He saw with Henry James that "nowhere else does pecuniary power so beat its wings in the void" as in the United States.[8] But he lacked major talent, adequate allies, and the audience (it could be small; it had to be supportive) to make his nibbling at materialism and provincialism sufficiently telling.

His was not merely a general disaffection for life; he was convinced of the special destructiveness of modern life. His ennui was not peculiar. It joins a long tradition of laments characteristic of the Romantic temperament for the loss of enthusiasm, of joy, of creative power. In his search for a credo, Saltus also joins other artists. He chose pessimism, theosophy, or elements of estheticism to supplant voids left by the failures of the dominant nineteenth-century systems of political and religious thought. His pessimism was more like stoicism or epicureanism than cynicism. He did not agree with Max Nordau, a preacher of dire decline before Spengler, that genius is morbid. For Saltus, not genius but pseudo-genius is morbid.[9]

Saltus managed to get his relatively sophisticated knowledge into the most unlikely places. In a New York *Journal* article on "An American Heiress's Melancholy Downfall," his introductory material is about Robert de Montesquiou, the original of Huysmans' Des Esseintes. Aware that de Montesquiou had, since his literary incarnation, been trying to live up to his fictional self, Saltus neatly and economically anatomizes the gentleman: "He was naif, yet depraved, with a pretty taste for paradox and a pertinacious desire to astound."[10] The severest Saltus critic might say the sentence anatomizes Saltus himself. He was, in a way, naif; for a man may have a knowledge of esoterica and still be naif. But he was not, as most 1890's figures were not, "depraved." And he knew and agreed with Aristotle that, although "art should always have a continual slight novelty . . . , a thing which startles or amazes is not art."[11]

When Saltus forgot, or could not follow, what he knew by

virtue of his limited endowments, his own work lapsed. The fine art of shocking was an art worth cultivating in his time. When that art became for the later Saltus a desperate effort to rescue himself from the commonplace, it was no longer fine but fake. Thrill overthrew truth; the shudder became melodrama. Perhaps by then what had happened to one of his characters had happened to him: he had gotten used to monsters and could not exorcise them—"In certain conditions the soul gets used to monsters. It makes itself at home with what it must."[12] At such a stage, it is impossible to turn the rage of disenchantment into enduring prose. That he reached this stage is only partly due to the pressures of his time and place.

Although Saltus is more the eclectic than the eccentric he has generally been made out to be, he cannot be rescued from complicity in the corruptions that he had the courage to see but not to resist. He had a real gift for popular entertainment and comic exaggeration, but left no enduring single work which shows the combination and maturation of these gifts. In fact, his reputation rests rather lopsidedly on his "purples," his diabolisms, and his clever style. It ought to rest a little more evenly: on several novels and on a number of his essays on society, manners, and trivia. Indeed, were the essay as popular as it once was, more readers would be enjoying Saltus. There is a residue of vision and conviction in Saltus left, even when posterity has completed her ruthless excisions from his work. More than the first-order writer, he reveals direct reactions to specific literary, cultural, and political issues of his era. For the social and intellectual historian, Saltus is, therefore, a prolific, highly coruscated and frequently sensitive register of the period.

Saltus might acknowledge the appropriateness of almost every epithet that has so far been ascribed to his era; it was "Mauve," "Brown," "Gilded," and "Innocent," but not "Confident" for him and for a number of his contemporaries. As a son of New York—from a family line that includes Van Dams, Hasbroucks, Howes, Reuters, and Roosevelts—and of a family history that sometimes analogues class, local, and national history in its movement from sea captains to merchants to iron ore producers to leisured dilettantes, he may tempt us to see in his career the death or attenuation of the Eastern Dutch-English literary ruling class. Saltus may finally represent the gifted aristocratic amateur now nearly extinct.

The American 1890's nourished no genius as the English 1890's nourished Yeats. This failure explains the essential discontinuity between the 1890's and the 1920's, between two generations that ought to have collaborated. Instead, the 1920's began again, with very little awareness than an earlier generation had begun its major battles. Within that earlier generation Saltus remains a first soldier. He was a frequently severe, brave, and witty critic of his own class and his own limitations. As his "mammoth menageries of money-getting" reminds us,

he could have mastered the rhetoric of comic exaggeration. But at crucial points his courage falters and he dissipates his comic gift to become only sporadically subversive in an era that required fiercer and deeper subversion.

His self-proffered conflict is suggestive; it speaks for so much in the Romantic and in the specifically American Romantic temperament: "I was born with a lot of vices that never put their nose to the window. I like wine and never drink—I would gamble perhaps but I don't know one card from another—I am a mystic at heart and believe in nothing. Debauchery attracts me and I live like a monk."[13] His remarks make a specialized addition to the literature of America's fear and fascination for experience. The self-portrait is very likely a literary creation, but even its imagined accuracy or its very conception show that longing and frustration which made the man and the era "almost" decadent. If achievement does come back, as Henry James felt, to "the intensity with which we live," then Saltus' intensity is recorded for us only fitfully and during the brief span of some ten years. His pilgrimage was not sufficiently passionate. It could not, like his grandfather's, make "a wilderness a paradise"; but it could and did make a small and interesting garden.

Notes

1. Henry James, *The American Scene* (New York, 1907, 1946), p. 114 in the 1946 edition.
2. Matthew Josephson, *Portrait of the Artist as American* (New York, 1930), p. 289.
3. Grant Overton, "Now about This Fellow Saltus," *Bookman*, LXI (August, 1925), 646.
4. Alfred Kazin, *On Native Grounds* (New York, 1942, 1956), p. 45.
5. As Harry Levin put it, the results of the period "may be counted in educated audiences, rather than achieved masterpieces." "The Discovery of Bohemia," *Literary History of the United States*, ed. Robert E. Spiller, et al. (New York, 1946, 1960), p. 1077.
6. William Gaunt reminds us that the *Penny Encyclopedia* of 1832 considers "esthetics" a German-derived term. For some time "esthetics" was to seem German property. See *The Aesthetic Adventure* (New York, 1945), p. 11.
7. *When Dreams Come True*, (New York, 1895), p. 84.
8. James, *The American Scene*, p. 159.
9. See "Our Note-book," *Collier's Weekly*, XVIII (October 29, 1896), 6.
10. Sunday, November 29, 1896, p. 29. The New York *Journal* may not have been so unlikely a location for allusions to Huysmans. Stephen Crane shared space in the October 25, 1896 issue with Saltus. His contribution was "The Tenderloin as It Really Is." These articles appeared during Hearst's ownership of the *Journal*. The first anniversary issue, Sunday, November 8, 1896, contained greetings from the paper's literary contributors, among them William Dean Howells and Julian Hawthorne as well as Saltus and Crane.
11. Notebook Three. Edgar Saltus Collection, Yale University.
12. *The Monster* (New York, 1912), p. 13.
13. Notebook Two. Edgar Saltus Collection, Yale University.

CARL SANDBURG

1878–1967

Carl August Sandburg was born January 6, 1878, in Galesburg, Illinois, to August and Clara Sandburg. He was educated at Lombard College from 1898 to 1902. In 1899 he served as a Private in the 6th Illinois Volunteers during the Spanish-American War. He married Lillian Steichen, the sister of photographer Edward Steichen, in 1908; they had three children, including the poet Helga Sandburg. He was active in socialist politics for many years, campaigning for presidential candidate Eugene V. Debs in 1908, acting as secretary for the socialist mayor of Milwaukee from 1910 through 1912, and writing pamphlets and articles for the Social Democratic Publishing Company and the *International Socialist Review*. He was also a journalist during much of his early career, working for *Lyceumite*, the Milwaukee *Journal*, the Milwaukee *Leader*, the Chicago *World*, *Day Book*, the Chicago *Daily News*, and *System: the Magazine of Business*, and wrote a syndicated column for the Chicago *Daily Times* from 1941 to the end of his life.

Sandburg's first book of poetry, *In Reckless Ecstasy*, was published in 1904. He received his first significant attention when Harriet Monroe published several of his poems in *Poetry* in 1914. His books *Chicago Poems* (1916) and *Cornhuskers* (1918) established him as one of America's leading poets. His rugged yet compassionate and graceful tone caught the fancy of the public better than any other poet of the time, with the possible exception of Robert Frost. Despite his occasional lapses of style, many critics felt that his concern for the common people combined with his confident, kindly, occasionally tragic voice made him the prototypical American poet. Such books as *Smoke and Steel* (1920), *Slabs of the Sunburnt West* (1922), *Good Morning, America* (1928), *The People, Yes* (1936), *Bronze Wood* (1941), and *Honey and Salt* (1963) kept Sandburg popular with both the critics and the public throughout his career; he was admired for his ability to make each book seem fresh and new while maintaining his distinctive, individual voice.

Besides his popularity as a poet, Sandburg is well known for his biography of Abraham Lincoln (*Abraham Lincoln: The Prairie Years*, 2 vols., 1926; and *Abraham Lincoln: the War Years*, 4 vols., 1939). Though it cannot be said to be a strictly accurate history, it is thoroughly researched and succeeds in communicating the personality of its subject. It was awarded the Pulitzer Prize for History in 1940.

Sandburg also wrote a novel (*Remembrance Rock*, 1948), several books for children, and other biographies. His autobiography, *Always the Young Strangers*, was published in 1953. He amassed an impressive array of awards during his long life, receiving honorary degrees from Northwestern University, Harvard University, Yale University, New York University, Wesleyan University, Lafayette College, Syracuse University, Dartmouth College, and the University of North Carolina, among others. In 1951 he was awarded the Pulitzer Prize for Poetry. He was designated Poet Laureate of Illinois in 1962, and was awarded the Order of the North Star by the King of Sweden in 1938. President Lyndon Johnson awarded him the Presidential Medal of Freedom in 1964.

Sandburg's *Complete Poems* appeared in 1950, with a revised edition in 1970. He died July 22, 1967, in Flat Rock, North Carolina.

Personal

At the age of six, as my fingers first found how to shape the alphabet, I decided to become a person of letters. At the age of ten I had scrawled letters on slates, on paper, on boxes and walls and I formed an ambition to become a sign-painter. At twenty I was an American soldier in Puerto Rico writing letters printed in the home town paper. At twenty-one I went to West Point, being a classmate of Douglas MacArthur and Ulysses S. Grant III—for two weeks—returning home after passing in spelling, geography, history, failing in arithmetic and grammar. At twenty-three I edited a college paper and wrote many a paragraph that after a lapse of fifty years still seems funny, the same applying to the college yearbook I edited the following year. Across several years I wrote many odd pieces—two slim books—not worth later reprint. In a six-year period came four books of poetry having a variety of faults, no other person more keenly aware of their accomplishments and shortcomings than myself. In the two books for children, in this period, are a few cornland tales that go on traveling, one about "The Two

Skyscrapers Who Decided to Have a Child." At fifty I had published a two-volume biography and *The American Songbag*, and there was puzzlement as to whether I was a poet, a biographer, a wandering troubadour with a guitar, a midwest Hans Christian Andersen, or a historian of current events whose newspaper reporting was gathered into a book *The Chicago Race Riots*. At fifty-one I wrote America's first biography of a photographer. At sixty-one came a four-volume biography, bringing doctoral degrees at Harvard, Yale, New York University, Wesleyan, Lafayette, Lincoln Memorial, Syracuse, Rollins, Dartmouth—Augustana and Uppsala at Stockholm. I am still studying verbs and the mystery of how they connect nouns. I am more suspicious of adjectives than at any other time in all my born days. I have forgotten the meaning of twenty or thirty of my poems written thirty or forty years ago. I still favor several simple poems published long ago which continue to have an appeal for simple people. I have written by different methods and in a wide miscellany of moods and have seldom been afraid to travel in lands and seas where I met fresh scenes and new songs. All my life I have been trying to learn to read, to see and hear, and to write. At sixty-five I began my first novel, and the five years lacking a month I took to finish it, I was still traveling, still a seeker. I should like to think that as I go on writing there will be sentences truly alive, with verbs quivering, with nouns giving color and echoes. It could be, in the grace of God, I shall live to be eighty-nine, as did Hokusai, and speaking my farewell to earthly scenes, I might paraphrase: "If God had let me live five years longer I should have been a writer."—CARL SANDBURG, "Notes for a Preface" (1950), *The Complete Poems of Carl Sandburg*, 1970, pp. xxx–xxxi

Carl Sandburg and I became acquainted some thirty years ago because of our common interest in two somewhat unrelated subjects: Abraham Lincoln and motion pictures. I was then a movie critic and Sandburg was writing *The Prairie Years*, that extraordinarily appropriate fusing of history and poetry which was the very essence of Lincoln himself.

Some years later I suddenly decided to try to become a playwright and inevitably got around to attempting a play called *Abe Lincoln in Illinois*. When this play was published in book form, Carl very graciously consented to write a foreword for it. In that same year, 1939, appeared *The War Years*, the completion of Sandburg's monumental work. I had the honor of reviewing this for the Sunday book section of *The New York Times*, and shortly thereafter Carl arrived in New York and telephoned me, saying, "Come down to the Harcourt, Brace office and we'll go for a walk." This was delivered not as an amiable, sociable suggestion but as a military command, and I could only reply, "Yes, sir."

It was late in the afternoon of a bitter, cold December day when we started walking northward from East Forty-fifth Street. Carl is a fast walker, and although I have a long stride, my breath is short, particularly when I am bucking a strong and frigid headwind. By the time we had reached about the middle of Central Park, somewhere around the Metropolitan Museum of Art, I began to wonder just how soon I should be compelled to break the news that I had had enough.

The walk had been conducted in almost total silence when I heard Carl start talking in his wonderful, measured tones, in which there was not the slightest evidence of breathlessness. I cannot presume to quote him directly. He was discussing the subject of life after death. I gathered that he had reached no firm conclusions about it but, for the sake of argument, he was prepared to concede that it exists. On that assumption, he said, let us suppose that the immortal spirit of Abraham Lincoln is hovering over the two of us as we walk through Central Park on this December evening. What does he think of the two of us?

I replied, feebly, "I know I should not be worrying about that if I were you."

He made no comment on that. We continued for awhile in silence and then I asked, "Still assuming that the immortal spirit of Abraham Lincoln is hovering over us, what do you think he would say to the proposition that you and I stop in someplace and have a drink?"

Several minutes passed while Carl Sandburg weighed this proposition. Finally he spoke—and now one could hear in his tones the resonance of thunder over the prairies: "I think he would approve."

So we repaired to 21 West Fifty-second Street and drank to the confusion of Adolf Hitler who was then embarked upon the conquest of the world.

The next time that I saw Carl was a year later when we were both in the White House working for the re-election of Franklin Delano Roosevelt.

Carl Sandburg is one of our great natural resources and I am proud to have walked with him, no matter how many years it may have taken off my life.—ROBERT SHERWOOD, "A Cold Walk with Carl," *A Tribute to Carl Sandburg at Seventy-five*, ed. Harry E. Pratt, 1953, pp. 327–28

Works

Before Carl Sandburg's thousand-page novel on American history, filled with his brooding religion of America, criticism is perhaps an impertinence. Thousands will read the book, and find in it solace and reassurance; of the innumerable recent efforts, this is the supreme and lengthiest celebration of the mystique of America, the most uninhibited, and the most naive. "They ought not to be forgotten," it croons, "the dead who held in their clenched hands that which became the heritage of us, the living."

Remembrance Rock is not really a novel; it is the chant of an antique Bard who fills out the beat with stereotypes and repetitions. Or rather, it is four novels for the price of one. There is at the beginning and the end a modern episode concerning the battle-fatigued grandson of a Supreme Court Justice, suffering from "concussion syndrome and a guilt complex." Just what he is guilty about is obscure, but he is invalided home from the Pacific crying that life is a fake: "The best men get the worst breaks and the worst men never get what's coming to them." His psychosis, vague as it seems, is that from which we all suffer. He comes back to his wife, and to a manuscript left by the recently deceased Justice; the body of the book is gradfather's re-creation of three episodes—the settlement of Plymouth, the Revolution, and the Civil War. By reliving these accounts, the shell-shocked veteran (and presumably the reader) is delivered from the nameless dread of self-condemnation.

Through the four episodes the same characters appear over and over. There is the girl with dancing feet, who is all woman—"a natural storm bird and a born homebody." In the seventeenth century she is Mary Windling—and then she is her daughter Remember. In the eighteenth she is Mim Wilming. In the nineteenth she is Mibs Wimbler—and, on V-J Day, she is Mimah. The young warrior, torn between his girl and his cause, distracted by her caprices but finding in her at last a helpmeet, is respectively Resolved Wayfare, Robert Winshore, Rodney Wayman, and finally grandson Raymond. The avuncular, presiding deity of interpretation always exhibits a face "half solemn and half comic," tells funny, folksy stories, and is variously Oliver Ball Windrow, Orton Wingate, Ordway Winshore, Omri Wonwold, and lastly Mr. Justice Orville Brand Windom. As the Justice (retired) he explains America to his fellow-Americans on a global radio hookup—and writes the tale of these girls in M, boys in R, and of his own previous incarnations.

Sandburg's point in these assonances is, as the Justice says, that if we go back over the centuries "we meet these same faces of men, women and children," all of whom "shared in the making of America." The runic device is his way of affirming his faith in continuity: "Their faces moved through shattering events and the heartbreak of war and revolution." There is suffering, endurance, passion and the war between the sexes; there is concussion and guilt, but also perpetual regeneration.

America, the moral appears to be, is agony. This chronic malady of the spirit is repeatedly expiated and purged in the starving time at Plymouth, in the snows of Valley Forge, in the Bloody Angle at Chancellorsville. But always out of purification emerges the new baby: "What you have heard from him was the cry of the Future," and "Their faces will rise to take the place of our faces which year by year they will see vanishing."

To the extent that we can credit the sincerity of the affirmation, we must respect the Bardic achievement. Sandburg's vision is a pantheistic confidence that though individuals disappear, "the earth stays and the transmission of energy." But he has elected to make this assertion as a historical novel. The romancer may quite properly—as Hervey Allen puts it—commit grand larceny on history, and no historian should complain. We do have a right to ask whether this is grand larceny or only petty forgery and counterfeiting. Page after page of *Remembrance Rock* is patently an uninspired paraphrase of history, wrapped in a turgid rhetoric, that descends to such small tricks as working whole segments of Bradford and Winthrop verbatim into the dialogue of unconvincing characters, or to printing a letter of Roger Williams and the Declaration of Independence as though they were free-verse lyrics by Carl Sandburg. The reiteration of his triangular drama is tedious. The effect is to show, unmistakably, some of the things a Bard falls short of—when he tries to contruct a novel out of no more intelligible or dramatic a comprehension of the past than his blind assurance that "Life goes on."

Quoting Henry James in conjunction with Sandburg is unfair. But when James heard Tennyson read aloud, the performance taught him what a bard might and might not be; with all the resonance of the chant, "the whole thing was yet still," and with all the long swing of motion, "it yet remained where it was." Curiously enough, Sandburg's book is utterly static. From Plymouth to Okinawa, the meaning of America is heaving, heartbreaking ordeal for the sake of the purification by ordeal. Or, if not just for the suffering, then for the cause of the motto which sustains Mibs through the Civil War: "Everyone is looking forward with eager and impatient expectation to that destined moment when America is to give the law to the rest of the world."

Those who believe that America is in fact the hope of the world may easily be the most distressed by such implications in what will certainly be an immensely popular book. But there is, I suspect, a simpler reading of it: the book's orientation is not toward any philosophical thesis whatsoever, but toward a Hollywood production. With its judicious mixture of sex, battle, and sentiment *Remembrance Rock* is a supercolossal script. When it goes before the cameras, three stars can play four roles in four different costumes. Either for length or for spectacle, it will make *Gone With the Wind* look like a one-reeler.

Whether wittingly or unwittingly, Carl Sandburg has written within the conventions of the panoramic film in technicolor. There is no more disheartening comment upon our era than to discover that at this point in his career the author of *Smoke and Steel* has lent himself to these maudlin devices.—PERRY MILLER, "Sandburg and the American Dream," *NYTBR*, Oct. 10, 1948, p. 1

It is hard for us now to recapture the spirit that animated us—or our fathers—in the second decade of this century, for there is a freshness about it, an enthusiasm, a youthfulness, almost an innocence, that we have lost. There had been two decades of criticism and protest and revolt; now a new generation was to be done with that and to go out on its own, break new paths, conquer new worlds. There was boldness and energy; there was originality and an eagerness to experiment; there was a deep humanitarianism and there was tenderness; there was a great deal of self-conscious Americanism.

It was an American Renaissance—it would "make the Italian Renaissance look like a tempest in a teapot," said Ezra Pound. It was a day when everything was New: the new woman, the new humanism, the new art, the new nationalism, the new freedom—even, with Robinson and Beard, the new history. It was the day of the Armory Show and of Stieglitz and of Frank Lloyd Wright. It was the day when Randolph Bourne and Van Wyck Brooks were hewing out a new literary criticism. It was the day of *The Masses* and *The New Republic* and the *Seven Arts* and the reborn *Dial* and—best of all perhaps—of *Poetry* magazine.

For above all it was the day of the new poetry, or so it seemed. "The fiddles are tuning up all over America," said William Butler Yeats; what he meant was that they were playing new tunes, many of them drawn from American folk music. For the fiddles had never stopped playing; it was merely that the tunes had come to be familiar and a bit tiresome. Whitman was not forgotten, but who were his successors? Emily Dickinson was unknown; Robinson was unacknowledged; William Vaughn Moody had turned to drama, and then died at the height of his powers. Who was there but Stoddard and Stedman, Aldrich and Gilder, Bliss Carman and Richard Hovey? And it was of these that Masters was to write his "Petit the Poet":

> Triolets, villanelles, rondels, rondeaus,
> Ballades by the score with the same old thought:
> The snows and the roses of yesterday are vanished
> And what is love but a rose that fades.

In 1912 the indomitable Harriet Monroe founded *Poetry* magazine, out in Chicago of all places, and the "new" poets came on with a rush. Within six years almost all of those who have since become our modern classics made their first appearance—or their first important appearance. Call the role of the newcomers: the "prairie poets," Masters and Lindsay and Sandburg; the imagists, Amy Lowell and Hilda Doolittle and Conrad Aiken; the lyricists, Edna Millay and Sara Teasdale and Elinor Wylie; the experimentalists, Ezra Pound and Archibald MacLeish and William Carlos Williams—these and a dozen others, including Stephen Bénet and Robert Frost. Not since New England's Golden Age had there been anything like it.

Of all those who appeared in *Poetry* magazine there was none whose poetry seemed more shocking, and was less so, than Carl Sandburg's. The March, 1914, issue of the magazine printed a tribute to Chicago:

> Hog Butcher of the World
> Tool Maker, Stacker of Wheat
> Player with Railroads and the Nation's
>   Freight Handler;
> Stormy, husky, brawling
> City of Big Shoulders.

To those who knew Whitman, or even Moody, it was not really either new or shocking. Yet Whitman was not yet wholly respectable, and the *Dial* entered a famous protest:

> The typographical arrangement for this jargon creates a suspicion that it is intended to be taken as some form of poetry, and the suspicion is confirmed by the fact that it stands in the forefront of the latest issues of a futile little periodical described as "a magazine of verse." . . . We think that such an effusion as the one now under consideration is nothing less than an impudent affront to the poetry-loving public.

There were more affronts ahead, and not from Sandburg alone, and in the end the *Dial* gave up and a new *Dial* was born. And now we read *Chicago Poems* much as we read the Bigelow Papers—with a sense of familiarity and affection. Now Sandburg has suffered the fate of most innovators: he has become respectable, he has become orthodox, he has become the very Dean of American poetry.

For almost all of that bright throng are gone now. Yet Sandburg remains a symbol, a monument, almost an institution. And he remains unchanged: the Sandburg of *The People, Yes* is the Sandburg of *Chicago Poems*: the technique is the same, and—more important—the philosophy. He has spilled out in many directions, to be sure. As he says in his preface, "there was puzzlement as to whether I was a poet, a biographer, a wandering troubadour with a guitar, a Midwest Hans Christian Andersen, or a historian of current events." There was good precedent for this catholicity, even in such revered figures as Longfellow and Whittier: what is important is that the change and development were quantitative rather than qualitative.

Sandburg has remained fundamentally the same—in his interests, his sympathies, his philosophy. None of our major poets is easier to understand, and this is not a criticism but a tribute. He is a democrat and an equalitarian; he is a humanitarian: he is a sociologist; he is an optimist and an idealist. He loves simple people and simple things, the things with which men and women work. He hates cruelty and insincerity and vulgarity and all those who climb on the shoulders of their fellow-men.

Above all, Sandburg is the poet of the plain people, of farmers and steel workers and coal miners, of the housewife and the stenographer, and the streetwalker, too; of children at play and at work; of hoboes and bums; of soldiers—the privates, not the officers; of Negroes as of whites; of immigrants as of natives—of *The People, Yes*. He quotes with approval some lines from Synge: "When men lose their poetic feeling for ordinary life, and cannot write poetry of ordinary things, their exalted poetry is likely to lose its strength of exaltation, in the way men cease to build beautiful churches when they have lost happiness in building shops." Sandburg has never lost his poetic feeling for ordinary life.—HENRY STEELE COMMAGER, "He Sings of America's Plain People," *NYTBR*, Nov. 19, 1950, pp. 1, 40

———

ALLAN NEVINS
From "Sandburg as Historian"
A Tribute to Carl Sandburg at Seventy-five
ed. Harry E. Pratt
1953, pp. 361–72

When Carl Sandburg's *Abraham Lincoln: The War Years*, that Gargantuan work of four stout volumes and two thousand five hundred pages, appeared in 1939, thirteen years had elapsed since the publication of his two-volume study of the prairie rail-splitter, storekeeper, lawyer, Congressman, debater, and Presidential candidate. Vague reports had stolen to the world of the task in progress at Harbert, Michigan—of the attic workroom, the shelves of books, the growing hillocks of notes and excerpts, the copyists tap-tapping downstairs, the biographer himself ceaselessly toiling through long spring and summer days at his cracker-box typewriter. Everyone who knew of Sandburg's rich, if unconventional, equipment for his task—his poetic insights, his mastery of human nature, his power of selecting the vital human details from a mass of arid

facts, his command of phrase and imagery, and above all his feeling for the mingled humor, pathos, shoddiness, and grandeur of democracy—expected a remarkable work. To history he brought just the faculty that the *London Spectator* had detected in Lincoln himself, "a mind at once singularly representative and singularly personal." No one, however, was prepared for the particular kind of masterwork that he laid before the country.

A book homely but beautiful, learned but simple, exhaustively detailed but panoramic, it occupied a niche all its own, unlike any other biography or history in the language. Its theme was the folk-hero of a great and terrible folk war; and its primary merit was that, with a subtle art masked by apparent artlessness, it rendered a convincing picture both of the Lincoln who belonged to the people, and of the people who belonged to Lincoln. In its pages Lincoln always held the center of the crowded stage, and yet the stage was always alive, moving, bright with color, and full of drama. Here were the gallant figures—Elmer Ellsworth, Edward Baker, Theodore Winthrop, all cut off so untimely by war; the strutters—Winfield Scott, "almost a parade by himself," John Pope, whose boasts turned to whines, Frémont, Ben Butler; the eccentric great—Stanton and his wild temper, Chase and his sleepless ambition, Sumner and his monumental vanity; the truly illustrious captains—Grant, Sherman, Thomas, Farragut; the figures of controversy—McClellan the cautious, Burnside the muddleheaded, Hooker the dissipated, Meade the tardy; the keen-eyed observers—Noah Brooks of the *Sacramento Union*, Orville Browning of a sharpsighted diary, Carpenter the watchful painter. Here above all was the multitude of plain people, who shook the President's hand at receptions, wrote him letters, and spent and fought for his cause. "Remember, Dick," Lincoln told Richard Oglesby, "to keep close to the people—they are always right and will mislead no one." In Sandburg's book he was shown always close to the people.

The greatness of Sandburg's achievement was instantly recognized. "When specialists have finished scraping, refining, dissenting, and adding," wrote Charles A. Beard, "I suspect that Mr. Sandburg's work will remain for long years to come a noble monument of American literature." The late Lloyd Lewis pierced in one sentence to the central merit of the biography. "A great American democrat has come at last to his most sympathetic, and, at the same time, his most searchingly detailed portrait at the hands of another great American democrat." A mighty summation, wrote Robert E. Sherwood. "It is so great a work that it will require great reading and great reflection before any true appreciation of its permanent value can be formed." Appearing just as the world plunged into its most terrible war, this study of our own bloodiest ordeal and our triumphant emergence was a stay to the spirits of countless readers from Pearl Harbor to Hiroshima.

Yet now that we have a dozen years' perspective on *The War Years*, and now that many of us have frequently re-read parts or all of it, our verdict upon the four volumes must be slightly different from that first given. All the initial critics were awed by the mass of detail in these million and a half words. "An indefatigable thoroughness characterizes his preparations and his pages," wrote Beard. Another critic spoke of Niagara. Still another wrote: "The technique is that of an attack in force; Sandburg masses his facts in regiments, marches them in and takes the field." Most of the early reviewers commented on the lack of system in the work. Compared with the formal, schematic organization of Nicolay and Hay, for example, it seemed at first glance disorderly. We can now see, I think, that a vigorous selective talent had been exercised upon the multitudinous facts, anecdotes, conversations, reports, documents, and other materials; that those chosen were relevant to a few central ideas. As Sandburg put it, "the teller does the best he can and picks out what to him is plain, moving, and important." We can also see that while seemingly unsystematic, the tremendous narrative (for it is all narrative) really has a careful underlying plan. It is a presentation of all that touched Lincoln immediately or remotely 1861–1865, set down chiefly as he saw or heard of it, and so arranged as to depict these years with the greatest possible verisimilitude. As the times were confused, a proper portraiture of the times has to contain confusion.

To Lincoln and the Northern people, the disorder, military, political, and social, must at times have seemed overwhelming. In that most poignant chapter entitled "Deep Shadows—Lincoln in Early '63," for example, the mass of detail mirrors the agonized jumble of the era all the better because we find commingled in it the abusive writings of Copperhead editors, the wartime activities of Frederick Douglass, the extravagance of New York parvenues, minstrel hall jokes, the story of arbitrary arrests, vignettes of Lincoln receiving Joseph Medill and helping a beggar, and a sketch of Washington as Walt Whitman saw it. A lack of sequence?—well, life lacks sequence. On a first reading the work seems to contain excursions and irrelevances that might be omitted; on a fifth reading we decide that nothing could be left out, for everything contributes to a realistic impression of the era. There is a place for Count Gurowski's bad manners and Tom Thumb's appearance in the White House no less than for Chase's resignation and the Gettysburg Address. In short, the book really has an interpretive principle which gives system to its rich promiscuity; and this principle is rooted in the vision of the poet.

We can see now, too, that Sandburg was happy in the moment when he took up his pen. Interest in Lincoln and the Civil War, far from being exhausted, was just rising in a new floodtide which is yet far from spent. At long last nearly all the material that was needed for a true picture of the era and its central hero was available. Forty years earlier, Ida Tarbell had opened a new era in the study of Lincoln by her realistic collection of materials on every side of the man, his weaknesses no less than his virtues, and by her thorough search for local and personal materials. Since that time a steady stream of histories, biographies, special studies, and memoirs had poured forth. The invaluable diary of Gideon Welles became available in 1911; the letters and diary of John Hay were revealed in part in 1908, in part in 1938; the two volumes of Orville H. Browning's diary were published in 1927 and 1933; and the diary of Edward Bates in 1930. The publication of Gilbert A. Tracy's *Uncollected Letters of Abraham Lincoln* took place in 1917 and that of Paul M. Angle's *New Letters and Papers of Lincoln* in 1930. Lives of lesser political figures, books on battles and military leaders, monographs on home politics and foreign affairs, had appeared in steady profusion from 1905 to 1935. So encyclopedic and sure a treatment as Sandburg gave us would not have been possible at an earlier date.

The most distinctive qualities of the Sandburg work are three: first, its pictorial vividness, a product of his graphic style, love of concrete detail, and ability to recreate scenes imaginatively in a few sentences; second, its human quality—its feeling for men and women, great and small, with all their frailties and heroisms; and third, the cumulative force of its detail in building up, step by step, an impression of the crowded,

discordant times, with problems rising in endless welter—and, by the same means, an impression of Lincoln learning to endure the storm, patiently developing his powers, and finally mastering all the adverse forces. These are the qualities of a great historian who is also a finished artist. In Beveridge's two volumes on the early career of Lincoln we had the enormous accumulation of detail—but his biography wanted vividness. Beveridge wrote a most instructive and satisfying book, which in its presentation of Lincoln the politician was almost revolutionary. It lacked, however, the engrossing gift for phrase and epithet shown by Sandburg on every page; the gift that hits off Greeley "with fishy eye and natural falsetto," that tells how guerrilla warfare in Tennessee "snarled and whanged," that puts Whitman's portrait in a phrase—"undersized, with graying whiskers, Quaker-blooded, soft-hearted, sentimental, a little crazy." And in no other American biography do we have the sympathy for humanity washed and unwashed that Sandburg constantly exhibits.

It is from the cumulative quality of the detail that readers get their comprehension of the intricate difficulties of the era, and of Lincoln's maturing greatness in wrestling with them. The book indulges in none of that hero-worship which so marred Nicolay and Hay's ten-volume panegyric. It frankly discloses Lincolns's want of organizing power, his uncouthness, his frequent mistakes of judgment, his bewilderment, his self-mistrust ("I sometimes think I am just an old fool," he told his son), his indecisions, his fits of gloom. But it also shows how steadfastly he strove against the problems that bethorned and quagmired his path, and which harried him to the melancholy verge of despair. It reveals the true magnitude of his labors from Sumter to Appomattox.

Out of Sandburg's 2,500 pages rises the picture of a people and a ruler caught in a terrible dilemma. Lincoln's central problem was that he had to captain a peace-loving democracy, its governmental machinery and political system totally unadapted to war purposes, in the most stubborn and costly conflict the world had known since Napoleon. Any terrible and prolonged war, if waged with real efficiency, demands an approach to a dictatorship. But neither Lincoln's soul, nor the nature of the republic, nor the temper of the American people, permitted a quasi-dictatorship; and, to carry the North to victory, a constant process of agonizing adjustment had to be made in every field. The country in 1861 was quite unorganized; by 1865 it was fully organized in some areas and half organized in others. But what a struggle to achieve that change, which laid the foundations of modern America! A leader less sagacious, less cautious, less gifted with the power to mold opinion and forge a national will that finally became like tempered steel would have involved himself and his country in disaster. "He is the best of us all," Seward wrote his wife—and Sandburg's pages explain just why.

⟨. . .⟩ it took Sandburg's mass of details, drawn from ten thousand sources, condensed, classified, and selected with an eye to the reproduction of all American life, to bring out the bewildering disorganization of the time, the soul-chilling uncertainty, and the searing agonies. In these 2,500 pages a distillation from a whole library, we have perhaps the best picture of a people in racked travail yet written by any pen. All facets of the popular temper are caught for us. The picture is not sombre—the people had too much vitality and exaltation for that; it is not bright—they had too much hardship and grief for *that*; it has the variegated tints of life itself. We see a people greedy and heroic, determined and slack, with plenty to weep over but with an unquenchable tendency to gossip, jest, and laugh. Sandburg's stage, with its thousands of defined faces, its endless incidents, its shifts of joy and sorrow, ease and strain, triumph and defeat, has a liveliness which we can match only in imaginative literature; it is the vitality of Whitman's catalogue poems, of Dickens and Balzac, almost of Shakespeare's world. Crowded streets, busy exchanges, smoking camps, roaring political conventions, the sobbing of women, the fever of speculators, the whispers of political plotters, the tramp of armies—all are here. In the end, the people proved dauntless.

But it is after all more biography than history; in this it differs from much of Beveridge and Freeman. The central figure is never lost to sight, as he frequently was in Nicolay and Hay. In essentials it is the familiar portrait that Sandburg redraws, the Lincoln of Carl Schurz, Miss Tarbell, and Lord Charnwood. But the eye is kindled to lustre, the features are quickened into a speaking image, the man is made to walk, gesture, and grow. Sandburg's biographical methods—the methods of an immense accretion of personal glimpses, stories, quoted speeches, revealing incidents, recorded acts—might not fit many great personages; it could hardly be applied to a reserved man, and would not do justice to a highly complicated and subtle person. But it does fit the genius and character of Lincoln, and is appropriate to the vast materials at hand. These materials are more abundant than if a Boswell had constantly followed Lincoln in the White House parlors and offices throughout his term. And endless array of keen-sighted men, pouring through his office, scrutinizing him whenever he went to camp or conference, treasured in their memories what he did and said; at first or second hand these memories went on paper; and we now possess an impression of Lincoln for almost every day of his administration. Sandburg's narrative is naturally less even and consistent than Boswell's, but it is almost as intimate, and is richer, more varied, and more multifariously interesting.

And who is this Lincoln as he emerges from the 2,500 pages? Basically the familiar Lincoln, as we have said; the Lincoln swift to spare and slow to smite, the Lincoln whom Stanton called the greatest leader of men ever born, the Lincoln whose noblest words are now a possession of all mankind. No striking changes of estimate occur here, such as Beveridge gave us in treating the younger Lincoln. But the biography is full of novel insights. Sandburg relishes the homely side of Lincoln, the rough-hewn Illinois speech. "Well, I have got that job husked out," he said after finishing a batch of papers; "chew and choke as much as possible," he telegraphed Grant when the armies were at grips. Sandburg sees the significance of the fact that Lincoln tipped his hat to officers, but doffed it to privates, and that at a White House reception he broke from the line to talk with bashful soldiers. He makes it plain that the gentle Lincoln could get very angry indeed; that on due provocation he could even swear. He dwells with real perception, too, on a fundamental perplexity of the war which sometimes baffled Lincoln:

> Nailed with facts of inevitable fate was his leadership. The gesture of stretching forth his hand and bestowing freedom on chattel slaves while attempting to enforce his will by the violence of the armies subjugating the masters of the slaves on their home soil, the act of trying to hold a just balance between the opposed currents of freedom and authority, raised up a riddle that gnawed in his thoughts.

It was sometimes impossible to walk the narrow line between liberty and coercion without deviation, to reconcile high and humane intentions with weapons of brutal power.

The final impression emphasizes three characteristics of Lincoln which sometimes clashed and jangled, sometimes interacted harmoniously: his magnanimity; his shrewdness or realism; and his attachment to compromise. Men who have Lincoln's generosity of spirit are rare, and men who can combine it with his hardheaded practical sagacity are rarer still. The diarist George Templeton Strong records the remark of his father-in-law S. B. Ruggles that one trifling consolation for Lincoln's assassination was that he could not pardon his murderer! But story after story, episode after episode, in Sandburg's book shows that while Lincoln was magnanimous indeed, he was also keen-witted and farsighted—quick to pierce to the motives of selfish men, expert in checking scoundrels, and sharp in his comprehension that what might appear the most generous course (an early emancipation of the slaves, for example) would sometimes really be damaging and ungenerous. The whole study of Lincoln's personality gains momentum, as the leader himself did. By the middle of the war he was expert, confident, and without arrogance convinced, as Donn Piatt observed, "of his own superiority" to his administration helpers; and by the middle of this book the reader quite appreciates his greatness. ⟨. . .⟩

"The tale is not idle," wrote Sandburg in the preface to his condensed "profile" of the Civil War, *Storm over the Land*, taken mainly from *The War Years*. He added that in another stormy era readers might perhaps "find shapes of great companions out of the past and possibly touches of instruction not to be used like broken eggs beyond mending." These words hold true of his four-volume work, which is likely to endure as long as his poetry. He will long be adjudged to have written one of the best of our biographies—and something more. For it is not merely a biography; it is a magnificent piece of history, a vital narrative of one of the most critical periods of the nation's life, and an epic story which for decades will hearten all believers in the virtues of democracy and the high potentialities of democratic leadership.

GAY WILSON ALLEN
"Carl Sandburg: Fire and Smoke"
South Atlantic Quarterly, Summer 1960, pp. 315–31

I

In 1950, at the age of seventy-two, Carl Sandburg published a collected edition of his poetry called *Complete Poems*. It was a heavy volume, running to nearly seven hundred large pages and spanning a generation of poetic output, from "Chicago," first published in Harriet Monroe's *Poetry* in March, 1914, to the great elegy on Franklin Roosevelt, "When Death Came April Twelve 1945." In his "Notes for a Preface" Sandburg wrote, "It could be, in the grace of God, I shall live to be eighty-nine, as did Hokusai, and speaking my farewell to earthly scenes, I might paraphrase: 'If God had let me live five years longer I should have been a writer.'"

Sandburg's most severe critics would probably grant that he is a "writer," even a gifted one, but whether he deserves to be called "poet" is still disputed. As he himself has stated:

> At fifty I had published a two-volume biography and *The American Songbag*, and there was puzzlement as to whether I was a poet, a biographer, a wandering troubadour with a guitar, a midwest Hans Christian Andersen, or a historian of current events whose newspaper reporting was gathered into a book *The Chicago Race Riots*. At fifty-one I wrote America's

first biography of a photographer. At sixty-one came a four-volume biography, bringing doctoral degrees at Harvard, Yale, New York University, Wesleyan, Lafayette, Lincoln Memorial, Syracuse, Rollins, Dartmouth—Augustana and Upsala at Stockholm. . . . At sixty-five I began my first novel, and the five years lacking a month I took to finish it, I was still traveling, still a seeker. [1]

The "puzzlement" experienced by critics thirty years ago becomes even more persistent now after Sandburg has completed his fourscore of years. To some extent this is the natural consequence of the shift in sensibility of both poets and critics during the past three decades, but it is also in part the result of the literary role that Sandburg chose for himself at the beginning of his career, as the reception of his *Complete Poems* demonstrated. It was widely and prominently reviewed, but reviewers betrayed by their words that they had not read the book; indeed, had hardly read Sandburg since the 1920's or 1930's, for the man they wrote about was the theatrical, self-conscious "Chicago poet" and the optimistic affirmer of *The People, Yes*. There was one exception; Louis D. Rubin, Jr., began his perceptive critique in the *Hopkins Review*:

> It seems to me that the critics who most dislike the poetry of Carl Sandburg do so for precisely the wrong reasons, and that those who praise Sandburg's work do so for equally mistaken reasons. What is bad in Sandburg is not his poetics, but his sentimentality. And when he is good, it is not because he sings of the common people, but because he has an extraordinarily fine gift of language and feeling for lyric imagery.

This is an admirably clear statement of the problem. And readers will either learn to distinguish the poetry from the propaganda and sentimentality or Sandburg's name will fade from the history of twentieth-century poetry. In old age he is still one of the most vivid personalities on the American scene, but his reputation has suffered in almost direct ratio to the rise of Eliot's and Pound's, both members of his own generation; and this is unfortunate, for he has written some poetry that deserves to live.

Sandburg's early role as the poet of Chicago and the sunburnt Midwest helped him gain quick recognition. What might now be called the "Midwest myth" was then in formation, and he found it both convenient and congenial. In part this myth was the final phase of American romantic nationalism. Emerson, in his history-making "American Scholar" address, called for literary independence from Europe; in the twentieth century a group of Midwestern writers adapted this threadbare doctrine to mean liberation from the cultural dominance of the Eastern United States. There were, of course, new experiences and environments in the region demanding newer literary techniques and a retesting of values and standards, and in the novel especially these needs were met with Realism and Naturalism which yielded stimulating and beneficial results.

Sandburg knew the Chicago described by Upton Sinclair in *The Jungle* and by Lincoln Steffens in *The Shame of the Cities*, and as a Socialist he sympathized with their exposures of economic and political corruption, but in his poetry he was often misled by a false, romantic logic, as in "Chicago":

> They tell me you are wicked and I believe them, for
>   I have seen your painted women under the gas
>   lamps luring the farm boys.
> And they tell me you are crooked and I answer: Yes,
>   it is true I have seen the gunman kill and go free
>   to kill again.

And they tell me you are brutal and my reply is: On
    the faces of women and children I have seen the
    marks of wanton hunger.
And having answered so I turn once more to those
    who sneer at this my city, and I give them back
    the sneer and say to them:
Come and show me another city with lifted head
    singing so proud to be alive and coarse and
    strong and cunning.
Flinging magnetic curses amid the toil of piling job
    on job, here is a tall bold slugger set vivid
    against the little soft cities. [2]

Here is the myth: other cities are "soft"; Chicago is brutal, wicked, and ugly, but to be young, strong, and proud is more important. In the first place, Chicago was not unique in its brutality or virility. For social and moral degradation, New York, Boston, or San Francisco could equal it, as Steffens had shown; and for business enterprise and physical expansion, Cleveland, Dallas, Seattle, and a dozen other cities were as dynamic. However, for the first three decades of the twentieth century the Midwest did produce more writers (notably, Anderson, Hart Crane, Dreiser, Fitzgerald, Hemingway, Masters, Lindsay, Frank Norris) than any other region of the United States, thus supporting the notion that the East was effete and that cultural vitality was shifting to mid-continent.

A more unfortunate influence on Sandburg's poetry than his acceptance of the Midwest myth was his own private myth, in which only the poor and oppressed have souls, integrity, the right to happiness, and the capability of enjoying life. There are only two classes in Sandburg's *Chicago Poems*, day laborers and "millionaires." He is contemptuous of the millionaire's "perfumed grief" when his daughter dies, but "I shall cry over the dead child of a stockyards hunky." Certainly a poet has a right to his sympathies, perhaps even a few prejudices—in which no poet could rival Pound. What is objectionable in Sandburg's attitudes and choice of subject in his early poems is his use of stereotypes and clichés. In "The Walking Man of Rodin" he finds "a regular high poem of legs" and praises the sculptor for leaving "off the head." This is one of Sandburg's worst stereotypes, leaving off the head, "The skull found always crumbling neighbor of the ankles." Consequently, in the 1930's, when proletarian sympathies were valued more than artistry or universal truth, Sandburg's reputation as a poet reached its highest point—though later surpassed by his fame as the biographer of Lincoln. In the 1950's, when social protest was less popular or even suspect, most serious critics simply ignored Sandburg. Perhaps, however, this is the most propitious time for a re-evaluation, for discovering exactly what as a poet he is or is not.

Sandburg is not, whatever else he may be, a thinker like Robinson or Eliot; not even a cracker-barrel philosopher like Frost. So far as he has a philosophy it is pluralistic, empirical, positivistic. He loves "facts," and has made a career of collecting them to be used in journalism, speeches, biography, a novel, and poetry. Yet he is in no sense a pedant; his facts (when they are facts and not prejudiced supposition) are alive and pertinent, and he is usually willing to let them speak for themselves. "What is instinct?" he asks in "Notes for a Preface" (and the title itself is characteristic). "What is thought? Where is the absolute line between the two. Nobody knows—as yet." He is still, he says, a "seeker." He might be called a pragmatic humanist. Certainly he is not a Naturalist, who believes that human nature is simply animal nature; or a supernaturalist, who has an equally low opinion of mankind. Among his new poems is a satire on a contemporary poet, probably Eliot, who believes that "The human race is its own Enemy Number One." There is no place for "original sin" in Sandburg's theology.

From first to last, Sandburg writes of man in the physical world, and he still regards the enemies of humanity as either social or political. Man's salvation, he thinks, is his instinctive yearning for a better world; in the practical sense: idealism, the "dream." At the end of World War II he wrote "The Long Shadow of Lincoln: A Litany," in which, remembering the "liberation" of Europe and the battles of the South Pacific, he advised his countrymen to

> Be sad, be kind, be cool,
> remembering, under God, a dreamdust
> hallowed in the ruts and gullies,
> solemn bones under the smooth blue sea,
> faces warblown in a falling rain. [1]

In this role as the conscience of his nation he has written some of his best poems, neither blatantly patriotic nor mawkishly sentimental. He plays this role, in fact, more gracefully than Whitman, whose best poems are usually his least self-consciously nationalistic.

II

Whitman is the older poet with whom Sandburg is most often compared, and there are superficial resemblances, in their humble origins, their anti-intellectual poses, their seeing beauty and nobility is common objects and simple people. It is true, too, that Sandburg greatly admires Whitman, and once wrote a preface for an edition of *Leaves of Grass*. Yet despite these affinities, the two poets are different in temperament, in sources of power, and especially in prosody.

Because most of Sandburg's poems are in "free verse" it has often been assumed that he has continued Whitman's verse techniques. Some of his long lines do resemble Whitman's, and achieve the same space empathy, which is one of their chief aesthetic functions. But the big difference is that Whitman composed by line units, making great use of parallelism (a "rhythm of thought"), with almost no enjambment. Sometimes he used true metrical patterns, but freely, organically. Yet regardless of metrics or their absence, his basic unit was the verse, or line—usually a complete predication:

> Houses and rooms are full of perfumes, the shelves
> are crowded with perfumes,
> I breathe the fragrance myself and know it and like it,
> The distillation would intoxicate me also, but I shall
> not let it.

This is not Sandburg's structure, or his music. Of course he was influenced by Whitman's freedom, but his versification is usually nearer the experiments of Arno Holz [3] in Germany and the French poets of the late nineteenth century, such as Jules Laforgue, Gustave Kahn, and Francis Vielé-Griffin, who gave currency to the term "vers libre."

These "free verse" experiments reached America in so many ways that it is impossible to trace specific influences on Sandburg. In his first volume of poems, *In Reckless Ecstasy*, privately published (1904) and wisely never reprinted, he still used conventional rhyme and meter, as in the trite "Pulse-Beats and Pen-Strokes":

> For the hovels shall pass and the shackles drop,
> The gods shall tumble and the systems fall;
> And the things they will make, with their loves at
> stake,
> Shall be the gladness of each and all.

At some period between 1904 and 1912 Sandburg adopted the newer phrasal prosody, in which neither number of syllables or counting of accents determined the pattern. The line might be a complete statement, as in "They tell me you are wicked . . ." quoted above, or it might be a single word:

> Bareheaded,
> Shoveling,
> Wrecking,
> Planning, etc. [2]

Here the arrangement is mainly typographical to emphasize thought, word, and even rhythm (a kind of grammatical rhyme). But in other poems that line division is by clause or sentence, in prose rhythms, often even without any striking or "poetic" imagery. One of many examples is "Happiness":

> I asked professors who teach the meaning of life to
> tell me what is happiness.
> And I went to famous executives who boss the work
> of thousands of men.
> They all shook their heads and gave me a smile as
> though I was trying to fool with them.
> And then one Sunday afternoon I wandered out
> along the Desplaines river
> And I saw a crowd of Hungarians under the trees
> with their women and children and a keg of beer
> and an accordion. [2]

This is essentially prose, but the terse, simple language does heighten the implied definition. It is a poem by Sandburg's own theory, which we should examine before further analysis.

He began, as the title of his first book plainly reveals, with the typical romantic concept that poetry is simply words arranged to evoke emotion. In his preface he agreed with Marie Corelli (from whom he derived his title) in her praise of "reckless ecstasies of language." In his own words, "There are depths of life that logic cannot sound. It takes feeling." Twenty-four years later, in *Good Morning, America*, he gives thirty-eight "Tentative (First Model) Definitions of Poetry." Here are some of them:

> 3. Poetry is the report of a nuance between two
>   moments, when people say, 'Listen!' and
>   'Did you see it?' 'Did you hear it? What was
>   it?'
> 10. Poetry is the journal of a sea animal living on
>   land, wanting to fly the air.
> 26. Poetry is a fresh morning spider-web telling a
>   story of moonlit hours of weaving and wait-
>   ing during a night.
> 34. Poetry is a phantom script telling how rainbows
>   are made and why they go away.
> 37. Poetry is a mystic, sensuous mathematics of fire,
>   smoke-stacks, waffles, pansies, people, and
>   purple sunsets. [1]

The basic concepts seem to be: poetry records an experience in which the poet has a momentary flash or insight or illumination of the meaning of life. Or it is the record of a brief intensity of feeling, capable of producing similar intensities in others. At times Sandburg perhaps also shares Poe's vain yearning for "supernal beauty": he speaks for himself when he calls the poet "a sea animal living on land, wanting to fly the air." All too frequently, too, his own poetry is a mixed "sensuous mathematics of fire, smoke-stacks, ⟨. . .⟩ and purple sunsets."

But many times it can still cause readers to listen, see, hear, and wonder; and curiously, this is precisely the highest function of poetry according to the theory of a poet quite unlike Sandburg—John Crowe Ransom, though he praises a kind of poetry, the "Metaphysical," which is not Sandburg's *forte*. The "conceit" or startling metaphor found in this type of poetry Ransom calls "miraculism." The poet makes a statement which in the realm of nature is impossible, [4] yet may convey the "truth" which the poet intended: "It suggests to us that the object [i.e., the poetic "object," which may be a sentiment or a conviction rather than a physical thing or state of being] is perceptually or physically remarkable, and we had better attend to it." Whether or not this is an adequate definition of "Metaphysical" poetry, with which we are not at present concerned, it works admirably for Sandburg, as in his imagistic fog that "comes / on little cat feet," or the "Stuff of the moon" in "Nocturne in a Deserted Brickyard," which

> Runs on the lapping sand
> Out to the longest shadows.
> Under the curving willows,
> And round the creep of the wave line,
> Fluxions of yellow and dusk on the waters
> Make a wide dreaming pansy of an old pond in the
>   night. [2]

Or in "Window";

> Night from a railroad car window
> Is a great, dark, soft thing
> Broken across with slashes of light. [2]

This is the whole poem: as crystal clear as Pound's imagistic "faces in the crowd; / Petals on a wet, black bough." And as enigmatic and evocative as a Japanese *haiku*.

Sandburg was never actively associated with Imagism, or any member of the group either in England or the United States, though of course he was contributing to *Poetry* at the same time that Miss Monroe was publishing Ezra Pound, T. S. Eliot, H.D., and Amy Lowell. Probably they had little to teach him; in fact, he might have taught them some imagistic tricks had they not been so doctrinaire and dogmatic. Nor did he, like John Gould Fletcher, make a special study of Japanese or Chinese poetry, yet he could write a brief poem, or a series of stanzas, in the *haiku* manner.

It is generally agreed that all Japanese poems are almost completely untranslatable, but this comparison may be indicated by a poem of Issa, one of the great masters of the *haiku*:

> Toshidama ya   futokoro no ko mo   tete wo shite

which R. H. Blyth in *Haiku* (Tokyo, 1952) renders:

> New Year's presents;
> The baby in the bosom also
> Holds out her tiny hands.

"Why on earth," Blyth asks, "should this be so affecting?" The answer, he says, is that, "In those small hands is seen the desires of Anthony and Cleopatra, the ambition of Napoleon." Although Sandburg demands less of his reader, a poem like "Haze" makes full use of the enigmatic metaphor or simile:

> I don't care who you are, man:
> I know a woman is looking for you
> and her soul is a corn-tassel kissing a south-west
>   wind. [1]

Sandburg's quoting Hokusai, mentioned in the first paragraph of this essay, does indicate some acquaintance with Japanese poets. He even wrote a poem on Hokusai's self-portrait, called "His Own Face Hidden":

> Hokusai's portrait of himself
> Tells what his hat was like
> And his arms and legs. The only faces

> Are a ruin and a mountain
> And two laughing farmers.
>   The smile of Hokusai
>   is under his hat. [1]

But regardless of sources and possible influences, these comparisons call attention to aspects of Sandburg's art that are often obscured by his banjo-strumming and preaching. What is frequently overlooked is not simply his delicacy, and his painting with a few deft strokes, like the Chinese or Japanese artist, but his oblique approach and (paradoxically) deeply etched implication. Consider "Washington Monument by Night":

> 1
> The stone goes straight.
> A lean swimmer dives into night sky,
> Into half-moon mist.
>   2
> Two trees are coal black.
> This is a great white ghost between.
> It is cool to look at.
> Strong men, strong women, come here.
>   3
> Eight years is a long time
> To be fighting all the time.
>   4
> The republic is a dream.
> Nothing happens unless first a dream. [1]

Strophes 5 and 6 describe more literally the wind and cold at Valley Forge, and 7 and 8 comment on the loneliness of fighting eight years, and that, "It takes a long time to forget an iron man." But the final strophe is wordless:

> 9
> . . .   .
> . . .   .

Here the unexpressed, eloquent in its silence, has the effect (though not the tone) of a haiku of Raizan (Blyth, II, 351):

> The cherry-flowers are blooming;
> I do not wish to die
>   But this illness . . .

Or Omitsura (Blyth, II, 361):

> The cherry flowers bloom;
> We gaze at them;
>   They fall, and. . . . . .

Sandburg's lines, of course, lack the Oriental emptiness. Stone endures, and the memory of men for "an iron man. . . ." There is a difference, but also a similarity. More ironic is the use of rhetorical questions and the silence of time in "Cool Tombs," one of Sandburg's finest and most original lyrics:

> When Abraham Lincoln was shoveled into the
>   tombs, he forgot the copperheads and the assas-
>   sin . . . in the dust, in the cool tombs.
> Pocahontas' body, lovely as a poplar, sweet as a red
>   haw in November or a pawpaw in May, did she
>   wonder? did she remember: . . . in the dust, in
>   the cool tombs.
> Take any streetful of people buying clothes and
>   groceries, cheering a hero or throwing confetti
>   and blowing tin horns . . . tell me if the lovers
>   are losers . . . tell me if any get more than the
>   lovers . . . in the dust . . . in the cool tombs. [5]

Regardless of how Sandburg acquired this approach to his subject, and his gift for selecting the pregnant image, we have here a basic technique—a basic structure as well as a kind of Zen sensibility. And these are characteristics of Sandburg's later poems as well as his earlier ones. In section 92 of *The People, Yes* we find these lines on some elusive aspects of nature:

> The breathing of the earth
> may be heard along with
> the music of the sea
> in their joined belongings.
> Consider the ears of a donkey
> and the varied languages entering them.
> Study the deep-sea squid
> and see how he does only what he has to,
> how the wild ducks of autumn
> come flying in a shifting overhead scroll,
> how rats earn a living and survive
> and pass on their tough germ plasms
> to children who can live where others die.
> Mink are spotlessly clean for special reasons.
> The face of a goat has profound contemplations.
> Only a fish can do the autobiography of a fish. [1]

Sandburg is not nostalgic over lost innocence, or bitter over his solipsism, or cynical because the ways of God are past his finding out. Even the elegiac note is seldom heard in his songs. He stands tiptoe with curiosity, boyish eagerness, and wonder. Above all he is the poet of wonder—seldom of awe, sometimes of bemusement—but he finds the riddle of man and the curious universe in which he lives an exhaustless subject for poetic contemplation, and he has developed methods for making his reader listen, see, hear, and wonder.

III

It is difficult for a poet to maintain a sense of form in free verse. Most poets who abandon rhyme and meter do so, like Whitman, under the influence of the "Organic Principle," which teaches that each subject, each attempt at poetic expression (or whatever motivates a poet in the act of creation), contains its own innate form and that the poem takes its own shape as the poet works with his material. In the words of Coleridge, "Nature, the prime genial artist, inexhaustible in diverse powers, is equally inexhaustible in forms;—each exterior is the physiognomy of the being within—its true image reflected and thrown out from the concave mirror. . . ."

This theory, however, did not lead Coleridge to use free verse, or Emerson either, who also accepted it. Even Pope, one of the most restricted prosodists of all English poets, believed and practiced the doctrine that "The sound must seem an echo of the sense." But by sound he meant something like onomatopoeia. His sense of form was conditioned by the heroic couplet. A poet who accepts the limitations of the couplet, blank verse, the Spenserian stanza, or the sonnet mould, still has a great deal of freedom. He can fill the container with whatever substance he finds more pleasing and appropriate, but he does have a container, with approximate—if not absolute—dimensions. The free-verse poet must weave his basket while he picks his apples, and this requires considerable legerdemain. Walt Whitman created a rhetorical pattern of his own which served for prosodic form, and he used it, with some variations, over and over again. Sometimes this form which he originated became as monotonous as the closed couplet, but often he succeeded in heaping his measure with choice fruit because he knew by practice how much it would hold.

Beginning with the *Chicago Poems* and continuing through to his latest compositions, Sandburg has always

created a new form—or at least format—for each poem, not counting the unconscious repetition of trivial mannerisms. He is, in fact, one of the most *formal* of all free-verse poets, with a greater sense of form than many poets who use rhyme and meter. His control of emotion and thought fluctuates, but his architectural instinct and judgment seldom desert him.

The famous "Chicago" poem has a clear, logical structure. [6] The introduction contains five short lines of brutal labels for the city—technically, synecdoches: "Hog Butcher . . . , / Tool Maker, Stacker of Wheat, ..." Then comes the logical development in seven long lines, which are banded and subdivided by parallelism, so perfectly balanced that they create a rhythmical pattern of their own: "They tell me . . . ," "Yes, it is true . . . ," but. . . . The poet flings back his answer with new similes, rising to another set of single-word attributes, displayed on the page as separate lines to balance the epithets of the opening lines of the poem: "Bare-headed, / Shouting, / Wrecking, / Planning," and,—with rising tempo,—"Building, breaking, rebuilding, . . ." (Both sense and rhythm are strengthened by placing "breaking" between "Building" and "rebuilding.") Then, more calmly, "Under the smoke . . . ," "Under the terrible burden . . . ," balanced by "Laughing . . . / Bragging . . . ," repeated with variations in the final line, which also completes the circle, returns to the epithets of the introduction, and makes a final logical application of them.

The very next poem in this early collection, "Sketch," has a decidedly different form and structure. Here syntactical and rhetorical patterns have very little to do with the line divisions, which are based on images. In his sketch the poet paints with words, but using words gives him the advantage of movement; his images are dynamic, and this enables one image to charge the contiguous image with its power.

> The shadows of the ships
> Rock on the crest
> In the low blue lustre
> Of the tardy and the soft inrolling tide.
>
> A long brown bar at the dip of the sky
> Puts an arm of sand in the span of salt.
> The lucid and endless wrinkles
> Draw in, lapse and withdraw.
> Wavelets crumble and white spent bubbles
> Wash on the floor of the beach.
>
> > Rocking on the crest
> > In the low blue lustre
> > And the shadows of the ships. [2]

The ships themselves are not seen, but their presence is felt in the undulating shadows and the rhythms of the waves,

> A long brown bar at the dip of the sky
> Puts an arm of sand in the span of salt.

The waves break, flow onto the beach, and ebb, in alternating pulsations but with variations in time of crest.

> The lucid and endless wrinkles
> Draw in, lapse and withdraw.
> Wavelets crumble and white spent bubbles
> Wash on the floor of the beach.

The emphasis on blue, brown, and white in the shimmering light gives the poem the form and color of a French impressionistic painting. The picture is complete without the last three lines, but the reiteration of the words and the composite images of the opening stanza (for the lines are spaced and function as a stanza) are typical of Sandburg's structure and demonstrate his sense of form.

In his "Notes for a Preface" Sandburg has classified the types of poetry under eight heads: "1. Chants. 2. Psalms. 3. Gnomics. 4. Contemplations. 5. Proverbs. 6. Epitaphs. 7. Litanies. 8. Incidents of intensely concentrated action or utterance." His own poems run this whole gamut, though some of these groups, especially four, seven, and eight, are too ambiguous to be of much help in studying his verse techniques. Yet in both the classification and his own practices we can see that the terse statement and the picturesque phrase appeal to him as "poetic." He himself offers an example from his novel, *Remembrance Rock*:

> He was a practical man
> who lived dreamless.
> Now he sleeps here
> as he lived—dreamless. [7]

Whitman, concentrating on the thought, would have written this as a couplet:

> He was a practical man who lived dreamless,
> Now he sleeps here as he lived—dreamless.

Sandburg's arrangement emphasizes not only the meaning of the words, but also the grammatical structure, the accentual pattern, and the fortuitous identical rhyme. The quatrain is almost a conventional stanza, composed of three-stressed lines rhyming *abcb*.

No schematic prosody or basic structural pattern can be educed from the study of Sandburg's *Complete Poems*. But he nevertheless has an intuitive sense of equivalence (balance and counterbalance); he likes a closed circuit in sound and sense. In his most ambitious effort to write a whole book on one theme (however general), *The People, Yes*, he made a compendium of folklore, vernacular observations, graphic descriptions of episodes and incidents in American life, and interspersed these with his epigrammatic comments. In appearance it is the most formless book he ever published; yet even in this loose composition his sense of form is apparent on every page. Section 87, for instance, begins in this way:

> The people learn, unlearn, learn,
> a builder, a wrecker, a builder again,
> a juggler of shifting puppets.
>   In so few eyeblinks
>   In transition lightning streaks,
> the people project midgets into giants,
> the people shrink titans into dwarfs.
>   Faiths blow on the winds
>   and become shibboleths
>   and deep growths
>   with man ready to die
> for a living word on the tongue,
> for a light alive in the bones,
> for dreams fluttering in the wrists. [1]

The end of this section, however, raises a serious question about Sandburg's diction:

> This free man is a rare bird and when you meet
>   him take a good look at him and try
>   to figure him out because
> Some day when the United States of the Earth
>   gets going and runs smooth and pretty
>   there will be more of him than we have
>   now. [1]

These mixtures of slang and colloquialism ("rare bird," "figure him out," "gets going," "runs . . . pretty," etc.) were deliberately chosen to represent the speech and thinking of common people, but the objections that Coleridge raised to

Wordsworth's similar theory of diction are still pertinent. Perhaps it might be argued that such usages in *The People, Yes* serve an aesthetic purpose that Sandburg probably did not consider: they serve to change pace and highlight by contrast the more dignified language that usually follows (as it does in the beginning of section 88). It is doubtful, however, that such contrasts sufficiently compensate for the loss of concentration, the diffusion of emotion, the general arousing of prosaic connotations. Yet it cannot be denied that Sandburg is light on his feet and constantly shifts his weight and stance. And it is on the most elevated plane that the book ends, with the identification of "the people" and cosmic laws:

> The people is a polychrome,
> a spectrum and a prism
> held in a moving monolith. . . . [1]

The People, Yes was written during the great economic depression, and when it appeared in 1936 many critics hailed it as a sociological document and political philosophy. Reading it today we can see that it was neither, and a poem should not be—better, cannot be. It is rather a psalm—or a series of psalms—written out of Sandburg's religion of humanity. This religion is less openly confessed today than it was a generation ago, and the change in religious fashions has affected Sandburg's poetic reputation. It is easy for a high church critic to rationalize his aesthetic objections to a poet who has not yet discovered original sin.

Carl Sandburg has traveled a long way on his poetic pilgrimage since the publication of "Chicago" in Miss Harriet Monroe's *Poetry* in 1914. He now lives in North Carolina and has not been a Midwest poet for a good many years, no more in mind than in body. He is more national than sectional, and less national than universal in his emotional and intellectual commitment. The "New Section" in *Complete Poems* contains several pieces that come near being his best, notably "The Fireborn are at Home in Fire," "The Long Shadow of Lincoln: A Litany," and "When Death Came April Twelve 1945." But these were first published in *Collier's*, the *Saturday Evening Post*, and *Woman's Home Companion*, respectively—magazines seldom read by the makers of critical opinion or the recorders of literary history; and even when collected in a book these poems appear not to have been read by most reviewers of *Complete Poems*, as remarked at the beginning of this essay.

The elegy for Franklin D. Roosevelt has the simplicity, depth of feeling, and strong conviction of the early Sandburg, but everything in it is under better control. The emotion does not become sentimental, the diction remains on a sufficiently high level, the imagery is in keeping with the solemnity of the occasion and its global significance for a world still at war, and the music is consistently the tolling bell and the resonant echo in the heart:

> Can a bell ring in the heart
> telling the time, telling a moment,
> telling off [*sic*] a stillness come,
> in the afternoon a stillness come
> and now never come morning?
> Can a bell ring in the heart
> in time with the tall headlines,
> the high fidelity transmitters,
> the somber consoles rolling sorrow,
> the choirs in ancient laments—chanting:
>   "Dreamer, sleep deep,
>   Toiler, sleep long,
>   Fighter, be rested now,
>   Commander, sweet good night." [1]

At the age of sixty-seven, when he published this elegy, Sandburg was still learning; but he need not pray, after he reaches eighty-nine, for God to spare him five more years so that he may become a writer. God made him a writer, and by his own efforts he has become a poet. How long he will be read only the future can decide, but certainly he is worthy of respect and deserves to be read—the kind of immortality dearest to every poet.

Notes

1. Carl Sandburg, *Complete Poems* (Harcourt, Brace and Company, 1950); quoted by permission.
2. Carl Sandburg, *Chicago Poems* (Henry Holt and Company, 1916); quoted by permission of Holt and Harcourt, Brace.
3. Note the opening lines of Holz's "Phantasus":

> Sieben Billionen Jahre vor meiner Geburt
> war ich
> eine Schwertlie.
>
> Meine suchenden Wurzeln
> saugten
> sich
> um einen Stern.

> Seven billion years before my birth
> I was
> a wild iris.
>
> My piercing roots
> imbedded
> themselves
> in a star.

The cosmic thought is nearer Whitman, but the spacing to assist—visually—the perception of the reader is more like Sandburg.

4. As an example he cites this stanza from Abraham Cowley:

> Oh take my Heart, and by that means you'll prove
> Within, too stor'd enough of love:
> Give me but yours, I'll by that change so thrive
> That Love in all my parts shall live,
> So powerful is this my change, it render can
> My outside Woman, and your inside Man.

5. Carl Sandburg, *Cornhuskers* (Henry Holt and Company, 1918); quoted by permission of Holt and Harcourt, Brace.
6. Both "form" and "structure" are subject to many connotations, though they are often used with similar denotation. As used here, "structure" applies to the various parts that fit together to create the whole poem, which is then said to have a "form."
7. Carl Sandburg, *Remembrance Rock* (Harcourt, Brace and Company, 1948); quoted by permission.

MARI SANDOZ

1896–1966

Mari Sandoz was born Marie Susette Sandoz on May 11, 1896, to Jules Ami and Mary Elizabeth (née Fehr) Sandoz, homesteaders in the Niobrara River region in rural Nebraska. Her childhood was difficult; she was expected from an early age to help run the farm and take care of the younger children. She received no formal education until the age of nine, at which point she spoke only Swiss German. She learned English rapidly, passed the county eighth grade and rural teacher's accreditation examinations in 1913, and began teaching at nearby elementary schools. In 1914 she married homesteader Wray Macumber; she filed for divorce in 1919, charging "extreme mental cruelty." Over the next several years she taught at various rural schools and worked at a number of newspapers, and wrote constantly in her spare time. In 1922 she gained entrance to the University of Nebraska, which she attended for the next three and a half years.

Sandoz achieved her first literary success when *Old Jules*, her biography of her father, won the Atlantic Nonfiction Prize in 1935 after fourteen rejections and revisions. It was extremely well received for its vivid evocation of her father's character and Nebraska frontier life, and was praised by Bernard De Voto and Stephen Vincent Benét, among others. *Old Jules* was the first in Sandoz's "Great Plains" series of nonfiction books about the American West. Others are *Crazy Horse: The Strange Man of the Oglalas* (1942); *Cheyenne Autumn* (1953); *The Buffalo Hunters: The Story of the Hide Men* (1954); *The Cattlemen: From the Rio Grande across the Far Marias* (1958); and *The Beaver Men: Spearheads of Empire* (1964). Her nonfiction is noted for her attention to detail and primary-source research, debunking of old myths, and championing of the cause of the American Indian.

Sandoz published her first novel, *Slogum House*, in 1937. It can be read as an allegory of political oppression, strongly influenced by Hitler's rise to power, and sets the tone for Sandoz's later fiction, which is usually didactic and often allegorical. Her fiction was more controversial than her nonfiction; she was still praised for her vivid characterization and detail, but some critics considered her stories excessively polemical. Particularly important among Sandoz's novels are *Capital City* (1939), *The Tom-Walker* (1947), and the novellas *Winter Thunder* (1954), *The Horsecatcher* (1957), and *The Story Catcher* (1963), the last of which won the 1963 Spur Award and the 1963 Levi Strauss Award for best novel on the West.

By the end of her life Sandoz was considered one of America's foremost Western historians. Her commitment to the American Indian is reflected in her Great Plains series and in her books *These Were the Sioux* (1961) and *The Battle of the Little Bighorn* (1966). Her short stories are collected in *Hostiles and Friendlies: Selected Short Writings of Mari Sandoz* (1959), and *Sandhill Sundays and Other Recollections* (1970). She died of bone cancer on March 10, 1966.

Old Jules is the biography of my father, Jules Ami Sandoz: I have also tried in a large sense to make it the biography of a community, the upper Niobrara country in western Nebraska.

The book grew out of a childhood and adolescence spent among the story-tellers of the frontier, for the frontier, whether by Turner's famous definiton or by any other, is a land of story-tellers, and in this respect remains frontier in nature until the last original settler is gone.

It grew, then, out of the long hours in the smoky old kitchen on the Running Water, the silent hours of listening behind the stove or in the wood box, when it was assumed that of course I was asleep in bed. So I—the Marie of the story—heard all the accounts of the hunts, the well accident, the fights with the cattlemen and the sheepmen; was given hints here and there of the tragic scarcity of women, when a man had to "marry anything that got off the train," as Old Jules often said; knew the drouths, the storms, and the wind and isolation. At school we heard other versions, partly through the natural cruelty of childhood, partly because a feud was on and we were actually outsiders in the school.

But the most impressive stories were those told me by Old Jules himself, perhaps on the top of Indian Hill, overlooking the spot where a man was hung under his leadership, and the scene of six years of lawing that drove his second wife into the insane asylum. Perhaps he limped through the orchard as he talked, with me close behind, my hands full of ducks or grouse or quail. Perhaps I followed among flowering cherry trees, carrying the plats to the orchard. Perhaps I drove the team on long trips while he smoked and talked of his own dreams and his joys and his disappointments. And always was I too frightened of him to voice either approval or surprise.

Although there was apparently no affection between us, my father somehow talked more sincerely to me, particularly when we went hunting, than was his custom. During these stories he never looked at me—almost as though he were talking to himself, without feeling any compunction to "throw in another grizzly." Perhaps it was because of my cringing cowardice from ridicule (I'm well over that now). He could be certain that I would not laugh.

Sometimes it seems that a quirk of fate has tied me to this father I feared so much, even into my maturity. The three crucial moments in his life after I could take part in our family life involved me as an unwilling participant: the snakebite, the near-killing of the Strasburgers and my near-ending with the same gun, and the final moment when he died.

Out of these events came the need to write this book, augmented by the one line my father wrote me in 1925, when I received honorable mention in the Harper Intercollegiate Short Story Contest, guarded by the name of Marie Macumber. He discovered my activities, sent me one line in his emphatic up-and-down strokes: "You know I consider writers and artists the maggots of society." The book became a duty the last day of his life, when he asked that I write of his struggles as a locator, a builder of communities, a bringer of fruit to the Panhandle.

Before I wrote one word of *Old Jules* I took notes on all references to the Panhandle in all the important papers of the state from 1880 to 1929, and more complete notes on every Panhandle or near-Panhandle paper from its establishment to the end. The gleanings fill three heavy notebooks. . . . Then of course I read all the frontier literature and history obtainable, with a study of frontier economics and politics. . . . In the archives of the Nebraska State Historical Society I went through the entire Ricker Collection, containing interviews with all the old-timers the late Judge Ricker of Chadron could

find in twenty years of diligent search. I exposed my mother to months of inquisitional inquiry and interviewed everyone available. Most valuable, however, were the 4000 letters and documents in the files—no, boxes—of Old Jules himself, a little mouldy from the leaky flat roof of our Kinkaid home, but generally intact. His habit of revising has saved many of his violent letters for me, in his own characteristically forceful push-and-pull penmanship.

As I read, the stories of my childhood came back to me with new significance. And as I arranged and rearranged the bits of information in what seemed the closest verisimilitude to life as those people lived it in the Running Water country, the duty became a privilege. Not one character, included or regretfully put aside, would I have one whit different: not my mother, who had the courage and the tenacity to live with this man so many years, or the Surbers, to whom many of us owe what joy we derive from music and from art; not Nell Sears; Jim the convict; the Peters'; Andy Brown, the yellah boy; the family that are the Schwartzes and that constituted the bit of glamour of our community; Tissot; Freese; Dr. Walter Reed, or Old Jules himself. These people have endured, and as I review them from the vantage point of twice knowledge my eyes mist. A gallant race, and I salute them.—MARI SANDOZ, "Foreword" to *Old Jules*, 1935, pp. vii–ix

In beginning a description of this masterly American book ⟨*Old Jules*⟩, so different from other studies of Western plains life, it is hard to know which of its many excellencies to mention first. Perhaps its basic quality is the unique relationship between the subject-matter and the author. As material for this record of her pioneer father and the Nebraska country where he lived, Mari Sandoz had, she tells us, a lifetime of listening to her father's talk, more than four thousand of his letters, hundreds of reminiscences from other old-timers, newspaper files, collections of historic documents, and her mother's memories, drawn out by endless questioning: a store-house of data which any historian would envy her. But her relation to these facts is by no means that of a mere historian. ⟨. . .⟩ For all the restraint and sobriety of her narrative, she seems to be telling the story as the Ancient Mariner told his, to exorcise its dread power over him.

It is startling to pick up a book which you take to be a historical study of the manner in which the plains around the upper Niobrara were settled, and find it taut with this troubling sense of reality. You do not read it as you read history, leaning back in your armchair, considering the presentation of facts. Almost at once your response to it becomes physical as well as mental. The shot in the saloon at Valentine cracks sharply in the room; the man with the Winchester rifle in the crook of his arms sits in ominous quiet across the table; grassy hills roll around you to the horizon; wedges of wild geese honk over your head; you reel back from the silencing blow on your mouth from Old Jules' long muscular hand; Indian riders, feathered and blanketed, are silhouetted against the sky; the kerosene lamp in your hand is shattered by the shot through the window; you eat fried potatoes out of the frying-pan in a grimly sordid hut; it snows, and "over it all, the brilliant sky pressed down and filled every gully, every crack and crevice in the snow with delicate harebell blue"; the room is full of the silver-beautiful voice of the young Bryan ringing with ardor for the empty phrases it is pouring out; you step wide to avoid the "dark nauseating splotches" of Old Jules' tobacco juice—this is not local history you are reading, this is real experience.

⟨. . .⟩ she can lay her hand on heaped up facts and make them come to ordered life. The troubled, tumultuous history of those Western plains, the long-drawn struggle between the farmer and the cattleman, the craze for settling on the land, almost as inexplicable to us now as the Dutch tulip craze, the mistakes in farming (and everything else) made by people to whom the new country was as unfamiliar as a new planet, the slow fading out of the Indians, the dismal flatness of the later acts of the drama—here is a passage of American history set before us with incomparable brilliance. If there were nothing else in the book it would be profitable and stirring reading.

Yet all this, too, is but the background. The foreground is wholly occupied by the full-length figure of Old Jules. There he stands, like the "Portrait of an Old Man" by Cranach. Every detail is put in with unsparing realism, his dirty, greasy clothes, the grimy toes on his bad foot protruding from the ragged overshoe, every deep wrinkle in his unshaven, unwashed face carved as though in wood. And from that dirty, lined face there looks out, again as in a Cranach portrait, a pair of formidably living eyes, keen, ruthless, mean yet bold, clear, vital, their arrogance absolutely untouched by poverty and defeat.

Here in Old Jules, himself, is the secret of the book's power. Perhaps because of the seldom found combination of literary skill, long and intimate knowledge of the subject, and intensity of feeling about it, the portrait his daughter has painted is very close to a masterpiece. ⟨. . .⟩

Yet, notable as the book is, what lifts it to the plane of real tragedy is something that is not in it at all, something that our own minds supply as we read—the knowledge brought to us by later research into the results of wind and drought on prairie land from which the protecting sod has been stripped, the knowledge that all this effort may have been in vain, worse than in vain, fatally wrong, that such country never should have been farmed, that the cattlemen were right, that Old Jules was wrong.—DOROTHY CANFIELD, "Old Jules," *BMCN*, Oct. 1935, pp. 2–4

Mention Custer's last fight, on the Little Big Horn, June 25, 1876, to any group of Americans and, unless some specialist in Western history happens to be present, the only Indian name that is likely to be spoken in connection with the tragic event will be that of Sitting Bull. It is commonly believed, even by some historians of distinction, that it was he who led the Sioux in the rubbing out of Long Hair and a third of the Seventh Cavalry in the twilight of the hoof-dust on the ridge above the Greasy Grass. The loudest shouting wins the empty ear; and Sitting Bull, the wily showman, was the most highly publicized of all our Western Indians. Truly there was greatness in him; not as the white man conceives him but as holy man and seer; and he was worthy of the fine biography that Stanley Vestal has given us.

But a greater man was there that day—great as a leader of fighting men, but above all by virtue of his spiritual qualities; a "god-intoxicated" man, as we would say, a dedicated man whose life was on a plane above self-seeking; a pious man in the fine old Vergilian sense of the term.

That man was Ta-Shunka-Witko, Crazy Horse of the Oglala Sioux; and it was he who turned the incipient panic of his people into an overwhelming will to victory that day. "Come on, Lakotas, it's a good day to die—a good day to die!"

According to many Indians who knew him, Crazy Horse was about 31 years old at this the high point of his career though some believe he was several years older; and he had but fifteen more moons to live in the deepening gloom of his disintegrating world. It was by no fluke of fortune that he had won his unique place of reverence and awe among his people—this "Strange Man of the Oglalas." His had been a

rich life, nobly lived; and now, for the first time, the complete story of that life, in so far as the details of such a life can be recaptured, has been told ⟨in *Crazy Horse: The Strange Man of the Oglalas*⟩. How admirably it has been told can be fully realized only by those who have had considerable experience in research among Indians.

Mari Sandoz was peculiarly well qualified for the difficult task that she assumed. "The home of my childhood," she reminds us, "was on the upper Niobrara River, the Running Water of the old-timers, at the edge of the region they called the Indian Country. It was close, or what seemed close in those open days, to the great Sioux reservations of South Dakota, to Fort Robinson and the Black Hills—the final places of refuge for many of the old buffalo-hunting Indians, the old traders, trappers and general frontiersmen who looked with contempt upon the coming of the barbed wire and the walking plow. Such men, with their heroic times all in the past, are often great story-tellers, and these my father, Old Jules, drew to him as a curl of smoke rising above a clump of trees would once have drawn them, or the smell of coffee boiling at sundown."

Through the tales that she heard, "like a painted strip of rawhide in a braided rope," ran the name of Crazy Horse; and one of the first ghost stories she remembers concerned the nightly walking of the chieftain's spirit on the guard-house path at Fort Robinson, Nebraska, where he was killed in September, 1877.

So it was with a rich background of sympathetic insight and understanding that Mari Sandoz undertook the telling of the story after exhaustive research, not only in the printed records, which are often wrong, but among the old "long-hairs" themselves, who had lived their part in the great man's saga.

To describe the work merely as a biography is to understate its value; for it is also the story of a heroic people in the evil days that came upon them with the westering white men, from the Fifties to the death of the hero. There is a surprising wealth of homely detail with which the daily life of the people is made real for the reader; and a skillful use of characteristic figure and idiom creates the illusion that the tale is growing directly out of an Indian consciousness.—JOHN G. NEIHARDT, "Crazy Horse, Who Led the Sioux at Custer's Last Fight," *NYTBR*, Dec. 20, 1942, p. 4

Of the subject of this book ⟨*Cheyenne Autumn*⟩ Struthers Burt wrote: "In all American history there is nothing finer than the loping march of the Cheyennes up from the Indian Territory and their subsequent incredible frozen flight. The march of Xenophon and his ten thousand was as nothing compared with it."

And this is no exaggeration.

After the Civil War a large body of Cheyennes were moved by the American Army from their own lands in the north to a reservation in the south in what was then Indian Territory. Another branch of the tribe, consisting of about a thousand men, women and children, under the leadership of Little Wolf, remained in the north, on their own land.

Things were moving very swiftly in the West at that time: settlers were coming in by the thousands, with the railroads following on their heels. Empire was roaring on toward the setting sun; the northern Cheyennes were in the way. In spite of their protests—and in spite of treaties—they were moved south, children, animals, possessions and all.

In the south the newcomers were not welcome. The southern Cheyennes, some of whose chiefs were now hand in glove with the white man, resented their presence. Game was scarce. Fall came and prospects of a hard winter. To top it all, there was the usual bungling in Washington.

Finally the northern Cheyennes could stand it no longer. In the fall of 1878 they set out—more than a thousand of them—for their own country fifteen hundred miles away across prairie, mountain, river and desert. Constantly harried by the United States Cavalry, cowboys, settlers, and Army scouts, they drove boldly, doggedly, relentlessly on, through freezing weather, blizzards and drought. Children were born on the way; old people died. Little by little the whole countryside was roused against them. They went on just the same.

This is the story of *Cheyenne Autumn*. And it's all there: the suffering, the cruelty, the hopelessness, the barbarity of both sides and the heroism. Here is the story of the chiefs involved. Of Little Wolf, "one of the Old Man Chiefs of the tribe, the bearer of the Sacred Chief's Bundle of the Northern Cheyennes, carrying with it the highest responsibility for the preservation of the people. He was also the tribe's fastest runner at 57, and soft-spoken but like a wounded grizzly in anger." Of Dull Knife, "also an Old Man Chief, and a famous soldier in his youth—who went to Washington with Little Wolf and the rest to ask for an agency, and, when nothing came, took his people north to the buffalo herds of the Crazy Horse Sioux."

Here, too, are memorable vignettes of death and destruction:

> The Cheyenne waited, packed in like antelope, the whitish windy sky standing over them, two eagles circling high, the soldiers charging. Howling Wolf looked over the frightened people stretching down the canyon out of sight, the horses with their heads down, too worn to shy from the bullets that hit among them, the people bowed too, the walkers dropped like resting bundles. So Howling Wolf sang his song of death:
>
> > It is a good day to die!
> > All the things of our life are here
> > All that are left of our people.
> > It is a good day to die!

Because of my bias in favor of all accounts and stories of the Old West, I hesitate to state categorically that this is a great book, but I have a deep suspicion that it is. And I say this in spite of the fact that the author annoys and irritates me with her wild partisanship in favor of the Cheyennes. The Indians are shown throughout as high-minded and well-intentioned— even when they are looting, killing, and burning. And, with few exceptions, the whites are shown as cowardly, drunken and generally repulsive and ridiculous. And yet this very understandable partisanship, particularly in a woman, is part of the strength of this Indian epic. Miss Sandoz, author of *Old Jules* and other books about the West, writes of the Cheyennes with deep insight, complete sympathy, and great knowledge.
—W. R. BURNETT, "The Frozen Flight of Little Wolf and His People," *NYTBR*, Nov. 22, 1953, p. 6

Here is a large statement but, I think, a true one: no one in our time wrote better than the late Mari Sandoz did, or with more authority and grace, about as many aspects of the Old West. She died early in 1966. A child of the Nebraska frontier, born about 1900, she made her name in 1935 with *Old Jules*, that stirring account of her homesteader father's tribulations and triumphs. She also knew intimately the world of the cattleman, the fur trader, the Indian, the buffalo hunter. *Old Jules Country* is a selection from seven of her books, together with a few random sketches, some of them previously unpublished in book form. She was not only a historian but, in style and feeling, a poet as well—as in a reconstruction of a Missouri River Indian village to which the early French beaver hunters came *(The Beaver Men)*, as in her life of a great Sioux chief *(Crazy Horse)*, as in her narrative of the agony and degradation of a Plains tribe whose mistreatment is a lasting disgrace to America *(Cheyenne Autumn)*, as in her descriptions of the dust and sweat of a cattle drive from Texas north to the railheads *(The Cattlemen)*. Specialists in Western American history could learn from her and doubtless did. Everyone, specialist or otherwise, could and did read her with the pleasure an artist evokes, with admiration for her love of the land that shaped her, her anger at its exploitation, her diligent but unsentimental reporting of a long gone time.
—JOHN K. HUTCHENS, "Old Jules Country," *BMCN*, July 1966, p. 11

At the recent White House swearing-in ceremony of the new Commissioner of Indian Affairs (the first Indian appointed to the position in almost one hundred years), a young Dakota (Sioux), who holds office in an international organization, handed to many of the persons invited to witness the occasion a printed card reading, "Custer died for your sins!" It brought some guarded chuckles by the whites, but also unsmiling nods of approval by many of the Indians, gathered there to represent tribal groups in every part of the country.

To both Indians and non-Indians, what happened at the Little Bighorn on June 25, 1876, is of enduring interest. But the two do not see it the same way. To the Indians—they who know and sing the sly song, written by Peter LaFarge: "With victories he was swimming / He killed children, dogs, and women / But the general he don't ride well anymore. / Crazy Horse sent out the Call / To Sitting Bull and Gall / And the general he don't ride well anymore"—the famous battle was not a massacre. It was a successful defense against an attack by the most contemptuous of all would-be exterminators of Indians trying to cling to their lands, ways of life and freedom. From that point of view, Custer the man lives on in the Indians' memories as the most vivid personification of all who have threatened—and still threaten—them and their lands.

The late Mari Sandoz, who was raised in the country of the Dakotas, understood those feelings and made clear their roots in her notable Indian biography, *Crazy Horse. The Battle of the Little Bighorn*, assigned to her by Hanson W. Baldwin as one of his Great Battles of History Series, was a perfect mating of subject and author. It was Miss Sandoz's final book, completed before her death last March, and it is probably the best account of the battle ever written.

No one knew both sides—all sides, considering the post-battle quarrels among the non-Indian survivors—better than she. This book takes no sides. It is a straightforward account of the battle, commencing with Custer's departure from the Yellowstone River three days before the conflict, and ending when the steamboat, the Far West, carried wounded cavalry survivors back to the Yellowstone a few days after the disaster. Although the book is written more from the white man's point of view than was the case in *Crazy Horse*, there is enough knowledgeable interrelation of the Indians' outlook and actions to give proper understanding to all that was transpiring.

There is really nothing new in the telling, save the quality of the telling itself, and this rises above all previous accounts. This is the author of *Old Jules*, bringing the same creative power and style to a great historic theme, enfolding in topdrawer literature what should have been there long ago. It is almost as if this were properly the climactic work of Miss Sandoz's career.

For the reader, there are no surprises in the story. But there is writing that takes us there: "The clouded night hung low and unbroken, the occasional flicker of lightning low in the northwest too far away to light even a silhouette of the rising hills called Wolf Mountain. Behind Custer the stinging alkali dust was riffled now and then by a light breeze that sprang up like a bird fleeing before a coyote. Then the little wind was gone, the temporary billowing of the dust cloud sensed more by the nostrils, even through a bandanna drawn up over the nose, than by the eye in the darkness. The horses within the troops still had trouble following each other; the van of the units was sometimes forced to halt and listen, hand cupped to the ear, to catch the direction of those ahead, perhaps guided by the signaling taps of a tin cup or a canteen against the saddle as the command felt its way."

There is sustained suspense, too, the skill of which becomes apparent in the account of Major Marcus Reno's long travail, usually anticlimactic to the recitals of the thunderous overrunning of Custer, but here lifted to a higher plateau with its own climax—the uneasy waiting for relief, and its arrival with the dumbfounding news of the finding of 197 bodies where Custer had disappeared.

Buffs may disagree with some of Miss Sandoz's interpretations and conclusions, but to the white man that is the basis of the continuing lure of the battle: no one but Indians knew exactly what happened to Custer, and no one will ever know for sure why Custer did what he did. Miss Sandoz makes no mention of something that old Indians had told her about, but of which she was unsure: that some of Custer's men had gotten down to the bank of the Little Bighorn, but had been driven back after a sharp fire-fight. Now, new evidence secured with metallic detectors (and as yet unpublicized) seems to confirm the Indians' story. On the other hand, the author is quite uninhibited in using the testimony of Arikara Indians concerning Custer's hope of winning a battle and being nominated for the Presidency to explain his motives that tragic June. Her Custer is deaf and brooding, riding in a trance, committed to an appointment.—ALVIN M. JOSEPHY, JR., "Soldiers and Indians," *NYTBR*, July 3, 1966, p. 6

In half a dozen books (*Old Jules, Slogum House*) about settlers, cowmen and sheepherders of the 1870s, Nebraska's Mari Sandoz, 61, has tilled her own neat field well enough to become one of the better sod sisters. Her latest novel ⟨*Son of the Gamblin' Man*⟩, despite its gamblin' title, is no card party. Her hero, John Jackson Cozad, was indeed a wily gentleman jackleg, but a green baize tabletop never confined his instinct for conquest. In 1872, when every faro den east of the Mississippi had barred its doors to his talent for bank breaking, Cozad made a down payment on 40,000 acres of Union Pacific land in Nebraska near the Platte River. A community there, he dreamed, would be his monument, and good farming families, lured from depression-strangled Ohio, would build it for him.

As Author Sandoz reconstructs the story from old diaries and memoirs. Cozad—man and town—prospered despite plagues of hungry insects, through dust storms and snow-storms, despite rampaging longhorn herds and quick-trigger cowprods. By 1882 he had harvested a fortune of $300,000, and raised two spunky sons. But black-tempered John Cozad was too powerful for his own good—and power tends to corrupt those who lack, as well as those who wield it. Settler jealousy festered into hatred. When Cozad, in patent self-defense,

gunned down a knife-flashing enemy, he had to skip town to avoid a lynching bee.

The town went on (it now bills itself as the alfalfa-growing center of the West), but John Cozad never was the same. He toyed furtively again with faro, failed as a resort owner in Atlantic City, N.J. When he died in New York in 1906, he had reached a century he did not understand. But he earned his monument. His younger son was Painter Robert Henri, a founder of New York's famed "Ashcan School" of realists; in a Manhattan gallery hangs Henri's stunning portrait of Gambler John Cozad, dark eyes brooding on a private empire whose sun had set.—UNSIGNED, "The Unspoken Drama," *Time*, May 2, 1960, pp. 99–100

HELEN WINTER STAUFFER
From "Introduction"
Mari Sandoz: Story Catcher of the Plains
1982, pp. 1–9

Mari Sandoz is recognized as a novelist, historian, and biographer, as well as an authority on the Indians of the Great Plains. Her work varies in quality, her novels usually considered least successful, and her histories, particularly her biographies, most trenchant. In the latter she has fused her skill as a writer, her mastery of historical research, and her empathy for her subjects to create works of unique and lasting value.

About some aspects of her writing Mari Sandoz had clear and precise theories; about others she was surprisingly vague. She seldom discussed biography as such, for example, in respect to either genre or technique; she seemed to assume it was something everybody knew about. ⟨. . .⟩ In her lectures, articles, and writing classes she concentrated on the writing of fiction; she seldom discussed nonfiction and biography hardly at all.

Mari seemed to make little conscious distinction between methods of writing fiction and those of writing nonfiction. She spoke of using the same techniques for biography and for fiction, except that in biography one must keep as close to the actual story, the actual people, and the actual times as possible. Her nonfiction written as narrative history used facts and was faithful to them, but she concentrated on specific events and characters to bring out the drama. Mari's interest, and the theme of all her books, was in the relationship of man and the land. "Why doesn't anyone who really understands the farmer's weaknesses, his strengths, his triumphs, and his problems—and appreciates the fierce affection that grows up in him for his not always friendly plot of soil—write of him?" she asked early in her career.[1] In particular, she spoke poetically about the country of the Running Water, the Niobrara River, which would never accept the intruder unless he gave himself wholly to it; not one, she said, who had ever been in that region could forget it. Her concern was not with the history of dates or wars, but with the history of man in his environment.

On her chosen landscape, the trans-Missouri basin, certain memorable men appeared from time to time, and it is their experiences she relates in her biographies and histories. Her subjects are significant because of their unique qualities as human beings, but also because in their individual lives they exhibit certain universal qualities. They respond and react to the force of events on the Great Plains, caught in a historical moment when one culture supersedes another.

Mari Sandoz also felt a strong need to preserve the past, seeing it as a guide to the future. Someday, she believed, man will learn that the same mistakes need not be made over and over, nor will each generation need to learn once more man's goodness, generosity, and courage. Her themes are the working of fate, the re-creation of the past, the importance of nature, the rhythm of life, the strength of evil as manifested in man's inhumanity to man, and, paradoxically, man's essential nobility. These themes shape her writing. Although Mari Sandoz left no written evidence of a consciously formulated philosophy of life, throughout her writing career her epic vision was remarkably consistent. She saw man romantically, larger than life, a creature who could occasionally display characteristics of grandeur. In her biographies, histories, and novellas, Mari Sandoz hoped to recreate the culture and virtues she found in the Plains societies of the past. Her feeling for the fine qualities of the Indian societies of the nineteenth century is evident in her recollection of He Dog, the aged Oglala Sioux chief, once famous companion of Crazy Horse, but in the years that she knew him blind and living in extreme poverty. Once he had stood with Crazy Horse and Sitting Bull and Gall against the power of the United States government, and she had no words to express her sorrow at his fate. It also "broke her heart" to see the young Indians of modern times forced to deny their individuality and heritage, trying to become like the whites so they could earn a decent living.[2] As early as 1932 she regretted the passing of the distinctiveness of communities: "The uniqueness of speech, the attitudes, and the very life of the isolated community are being endangered. The hinterland is trading its individuality for cheap imitations of that which is mediocre, the tawdry of our commercial centers."[3]

However, Mari Sandoz did not allow her sympathy for the cultures and the heroes of the past to stand in the way of what André Maurois has called the "indefatigable search for the truth." She worked constantly to correct false historical notions, as is attested by her frequent arguments with those who venerated such figures as Buffalo Bill Cody. Her quarrel was with history and biography that perpetuated the old, incorrect information. She combined her sympathy for her heroes with solid historical research, much of it in primary sources, some never used by other historians. One of her editors has written that her books are distinguished by "the poetry of structure and style, the combination of first-hand knowledge, absolute scholarship, and creative historical vision."[4]

It has been charged that western writers are too close to their material, that their personal involvement prevents objectivity. On the other hand, these writers have the inestimable advantage of writing from inside their subject, an asset that no outsider, no matter how skilled or sympathetic, can acquire. Although Mari Sandoz aimed for truth and objectivity, she could not, of course, achieve it completely, any more than can any other historian or biographer. Whatever her purpose in writing beyond simply presenting the facts, that purpose directed her use of the raw material. She recognized this when she acknowledged that every event in *Old Jules* could be authenticated but the interpretation of the action was hers, and that she tried to make the book artistically and philosophically as well as historically true. She agreed with those who believe that writing is both an ethical and aesthetic problem. ⟨. . .⟩

With the exception of John G. Neihardt, western writers seem not to have influenced Mari Sandoz directly. She seldom discussed them individually in her letters, and when she did, or when she reviewed their books, she judged them primarily on the basis of the amount of research undertaken and the accuracy of their historical re-creation. She approved or disapproved of authors according to how well they presented history, since she thought of herself as a historian. The writers she felt worthwhile were those who had a sense of responsibility to world society as well as to that of their own locale, who understood their obligation to see the present and future implications of their material wholly and clearly and who presented it as honestly as possible.[5] The trans-Missouri region was the one with which she had strong emotional ties and the one she knew best, but her writing was, she hoped, universal in scope.

As early as 1933, in speaking of *Old Jules*, she explained that instead of attempting to write a popular book she was trying to write one showing a way of life, bringing to the readers an experience they could get no other way, a book that would be good even fifty years later. Such books often deviated from the accepted standard for structure and treatment. As to her writing for the future, she stated that the twenty-first-century child would be so versed in psychology and so sensitive to human conflict that even the most elusive of present-day writers would seem obvious. She hoped in her writing not to escape the grasp of her contemporaries and not to be overly obvious to readers of future generations. Since she feared that none of her contemporaries understood her purpose and that very few in the past had been interested in what she thought important, she was forced to look to the future for understanding.[6] ⟨. . .⟩

By conventional literary standards, Mari Sandoz's nonfiction measures up well. Strongly affected by her sense of history, of time and of place, she wrote powerful and effective histories when working with protagonists whom she could identify with her own region. She mastered the art of recreating a man and his culture, emphasizing the moral issues involved when one culture destroys another, and illustrating her own romantic view that man has dignity and worth. She adhered closely to carefully researched information, and the strength of her artistic imagination lay in creating a verisimilitude of actual events, rather than in creating imaginary scenes. In her biographies particularly she succeeds in re-creating the living past. She accepted the artist's purpose: "The crude matter of life assumes significance from the shaping hand of the artist."[7]

The re-creation of early settler life abounds in Plains literature, but Mari Sandoz's *Old Jules* is so unusual it has few imitations. Her ability to fuse Jules's importance to the region with scenes from his domestic life, while involving herself, is rare. (The only biography I know that manages similar emotional material so unemotionally, achieving aesthetic distance, is Edmund Gosse's *Father and Son*, about life in the 1800s in England.) In 1935, *Old Jules* shocked people, not only because of the domestic scenes but because it showed the public a stark, unromantic view of the frontier. The strong language, the sometimes brutal realism, the frankness were all criticized vigorously, but they made the book powerful. The swearing no longer shocks contemporary readers, who are frequently confronted with pungent, and often pointless, profanity, but the realism and frankness are just as gripping now as they were then. The children cowering under the bed, Henriette's fright when a shot breaks the lamp in her hand, Uncle Emile shot down in front of his family by a hired gunman—these scenes as well as the descriptions of the prairie's beauty are still as effective as ever. The conflicts described best in *Old Jules*, *Crazy Horse*, and *Cheyenne Autumn* still hold significance, although the specific incidents are well in the past. The West is now tamed, and the Indians are, legally at least, freer to move about as they please, but the emotions engendered by those conflicts are universal. Mari's people experience love, hate, ambition, jealousy, sorrow, fear, satisfaction and joy. Some are caught by forces too large for them to control—by a government gigantic and relentless and sometimes apparently mindless. Some learn their fate is controlled by men too small for their responsibilities, too ignorant or too greedy to value human life. And some fight back. These things have been going on since long before the Greeks wrote of them, and we see them today. The theme of man and his fate is timeless. Mari Sandoz hoped to match her subject matter with her art. In these three books she succeeded.

Those books of her Great Plains series using an animal as the protagonist and humans as antagonists—*The Buffalo Hunters*, *The Cattlemen*, and *The Beaver Men*—have a less clear-cut focus, primarily because her efforts to cram a large amount of information into them make the works seem disjointed. Although the many minor characters, together with the vast amount of time and space involved, make these books less easily controlled by the author and sometimes a challenge to the reader's memory, they are stimulating, useful, and in most instances well written. Mari uses in these books the skills of the storytellers she heard and admired in her childhood to develop the many and disparate episodes making up the variegated thread of western history.

Mari Sandoz's prose, often lyrical and lovely, appears to be standing the test of time. Much of the timelessness is achieved through her use of images and symbols, the word-pictures by which she describes the geography of the Great Plains. Of special note is the language form she created for her narration of the Indian way of life. While other writers had stressed the Indian point of view, the language of the white author almost always interfered with the atmosphere of the Indian culture portrayed in the story. It is by means of her particular use of language in her Indian books that Mari Sandoz brings the reader to greater understanding and perhaps even identification with her Indian heroes.

It may be too soon to make serious critical judgments of Mari Sandoz's canon, but her work is impressive in both quantity and quality. John K. Hutchens says of it, "Here is a large statement but, I think, a true one: no one in our time wrote better than the late Mari Sandoz did, or with more authority and grace, about as many aspects of the Old West."[8]

Notes

1. Mari Sandoz, "Stay Home, Young Writer," MS for speech to Chi Delta Phi, 1937, later published in *Quill* 25 (June 1937).
2. Mari Sandoz to Elaine Goodale Eastman, 1 March 1944.
3. Mari Sandoz, "Midwestern Writers," *Prairie Schooner* 6, no. 1 (Winter 1932): 36.
4. Virginia Faulkner, review of *Old Jules Country*, *Western American Literature* 1, no. 3 (Fall 1966): 226.
5. Mari Sandoz to Robert Cumberland, 6 April 1945.
6. Mari Sandoz to Mamie Meredith, n.d. [1933?].
7. S. H. Butcher, translator and editor, *Aristotle's Theory of Poetry and Fine Art*, p. xli.
8. *Book-of-the-Month Club News*, July 1966, p. 11.

George Santayana

1863–1952

George Santayana was born in Madrid of Spanish parents on December 16, 1863, and came to the United States nine years later. He received his B.A. degree from Harvard in 1886 and taught philosophy at the university from 1889 until 1912, taking off a year during this period to study at Cambridge.

Santayana's first published philosophical work was *The Sense of Beauty* (1896), still considered important in the field of aesthetics. *The Life of Reason* (1905–06) was published in five volumes and shows the influence of Hegel; its recurrent theme is that reason results from the combining of instinct and ideation.

In 1912 Santayana left Harvard and returned to Europe, where he traveled extensively for many years. During this period he wrote *Scepticism and Animal Faith* (1923), which markes a turning point in his philosophy, formulating his scepticism. His new philosophical system was set forth in a major four-volume work, *Realms of Being* (*The Realm of Essence*, 1927; *The Realm of Matter*, 1930; *The Realm of Truth*, 1937; and *The Realm of Spirit*, 1940), in which he argues in a style praised for its elegance and clarity that the realm of matter is prior to the other realms of being. Santayana was the author of a number of other works on philosophy, religion, and literature, including *Interpretations of Poetry and Religion* (1900), *Three Philosophical Poets: Lucretius, Dante, Goethe* (1910); *Philosophical Opinions in America* (1918); *Character and Opinion in the United States* (1920); and *The Idea of Christ in the Gospels* (1946). Santayana also wrote three volumes of memoirs, collectively titled *Persons and Places* (1944–53).

In the realm of pure literature Santayana wrote one novel, *The Last Puritan* (1935), highly praised for its sympathetic yet penetrating portrayal of the New England temperament. Santayana also wrote several volumes of poetry, beginning with *Sonnets and Other Verses* (1894). His *Complete Poems* was edited in 1979 by William G. Holzberger.

At the beginning of World War II Santayana settled at a convent in Rome. He died there on September 26, 1952. Many volumes of his unpublished and uncollected writings have followed since his death.

Personal

You know Massachusetts Hall—as it was, not as it is. We sat on very long, rough benches, facing a small platform with a desk on it. The first time I saw Santayana, I saw a very dapper figure—carrying a bowler hat, gloves and cane.

He walks in almost unnoticed, seats himself at the desk while the usual classroom rustle and noises continue, hardly subsiding. Then he begins to talk.

There is something in the voice, and something in the way he doesn't look at you. He never looked at you. I found out later he was terribly nearsighted. There was a turn of the eye that made you think of religious pictures. I finally got to see him as a sort of Murillo madonna with a mustache—a stereotype.

Usually with lectures, even the best, there comes a time when you're bored. Students wriggle in their seats, move their hands, rustle their feet, make other noises. Not, however, these Freshmen in Philosophy 1-A. You listen and look, even if you don't agree. Three or four weeks after the course began, I couldn't contain myself any longer. The things that were said were challenging, and somewhat controverted things I'd learnt from my father; so I stepped up to the desk and asked Santayana some questions. The answers took us across the yard and over to Harvard Square. That peripatetic talk started a whole series. I wasn't living in Cambridge. When I was an undergraduate, the Yard was a place for buildings such as Massachusetts, Harvard or Seaver Halls, not a field of student life.

Coming back, this course was Philosophy 1-A, "History of Ancient Philosophy," and he used to alternate with George Herbert Palmer. When he got it the first term, Palmer would give Modern, and the following year Santayana would give Modern and Palmer would give Ancient. It would go on like that. This was 1902–03.

Santayana simply had an allure. It wasn't merely the voice; it was the way he addressed you. He talked pretty much as he wrote, and he wrote pretty much as he talked. Before I knew it, I was following him around. He had a noon course on Saturday, and he'd usually go to a football game, if there was a football game. It was across at Soldiers Field. I never had time to go to the game, but once he had a ticket for me, though I couldn't use it.

During my undergraduate years he was living on Brattle Street. It's an old house, now being used partly as a restaurant and partly as a place for the sale of I-don't-know-what—*objets d'art* supposedly. He had two rooms. Medici prints hung over the mantelpiece of the fireplace. And on his desk he had a couple of bowls filled with sand and in these bowls two long goose quills.

The goose quills fascinated me and absorbed my attention for a long time. I wondered what they meant. I discovered afterwards that they had been instruments of writing at Oxford when he was there, and he had carried them along; they had become a kind of antique in his house which he didn't use any more. He wrote with a pencil.

And one day I asked him why he'd kept the quills. He pulled them out and threw them in the fireplace. Apparently something had broken with the question.

I think I took about every course that Santayana gave while I was an undergraduate. And they involved the history of philosophy, Greek philosophy—Greek philosophy at Harvard was a wonderful, exciting thing. He was then preparing *The Life of Reason*; and the course out of which it grew was called the Philosophy of History. It was given afternoons in Harvard Hall; we went up a flight of stairs, the side stairs—still

standing. The platform was much higher than in Massachusetts Hall, and so he was raised very much above the audience. It was rare for a class to applaud at the end of a lecture, but usually once a week there would be a spontaneous outburst of applause.

He took my notes at the end of this two-term course; and as I had made side remarks and decorations, as well as recordings of what was said, I was a little disturbed; but they came back with pleasant comments. When I got through, I went to Princeton, and he went off also; the same two years that I was going to Princeton he was in Europe. And it was the first year, in 1904, that the first volume of *The Life of Reason* came out: *Reason in Common Sense*. The other volumes were produced soon after at intervals. He came back in 1906, and I, having been more or less kicked out of Princeton, came back too. Naturally I gravitated in his direction.

In the interval Emerson Hall had begun to function. (Emerson Hall was set up in 1903.) There he was in the modern classroom way down in front, waiting for students to come to talk to him. I somehow recognized the back, the posture, the character of the head; but when he turned around, there was a beard. A beaver. And the type of expression, the character and quality of the man were changed; there was something strange that didn't belong. He didn't carry that beard for more than half a term, but in the interval Denman Ross, who was a great master of science—though perhaps not of the art of painting—made a portrait of him with the beard, the derby, the gloves and the stick. I don't know what has become of that portrait. It may be hanging in Emerson Hall, alongside Mrs. Riebers's collocation of James, Palmer and Royce; but I am not sure. For a long time Ross kept it at home. He was doing it in some particular Spanish style, I think he said in the manner of Velasquez. It would be difficult to identify now, except that every time I think of that portrait there is something about the New England judgment of Santayana in it; and that judgment was not friendly. It was admiring but dubious; and he felt it very much.—HORACE M. KALLEN, *Dialogue on George Santayana*, eds. Corliss Lamont, Mary Redmer, 1959, pp. 10–15

General

It has become a commonplace to speak of Santayana as primarily a poet or to describe him by that term, not an unmixed compliment among academic philosophers, "philosopher poet." His earliest published work was a volume of poetry and his last writing was a poem of nobility and distinction. But when it is said that Santayana is first and foremost a poet, it is not generally meant simply that he wrote verse. Some of his early sonnets are permanent and beautiful, but he was perhaps correct in feeling that the English language became fully poetic only in the minds of those who had heard it "spoken in the nursery." His verse has about it even at its best the neo-classic rather than the classic touch. But where his prose is eloquent, as it so often is, it has the temper of poetry. It is rhythmic and imageful; it is at once musical and chiseled; its epithets open vistas and its suggestions set the imagination musing.

But there is something still more important and central meant by calling Santayana a poet. It may be argued, I think, and documented that his whole view of nature and life, his whole theory of essence and intuition, his entire conception of religion and society and science were colored and conditioned by his view of poetry and his general sense of awareness as a contemplation. Santayana regards knowledge as a beholding in which the immediate is the ultimate, the ultimate the immediate. The spectator beholds objects and events, persons and places, forms of government, ways of thought and of worship, myths and histories, as scenes, eternally and incorrigibly, indubitably what they are. Even in moral philosophy (which, he tells us in an autobiographical essay, is his chosen subject), his approach to human issues is that of a brooding imagination looking back upon history, and making judgments, in the last analysis aesthetic, on failures and successes in the life of reason. Even his general criterion is that of harmony; what matters about a civilization is the music it makes or fails to make to the attentive retrospective spirit.

The whole of Santayana's approach to philosophy is that of a musing, contemplative mind, for whom ideas are themes, events, occasions, even palpable things, essences, all images to be entertained, all forms to be looked upon.

"In philosophy itself," Santayana wrote in his introduction to *Three Philosophical Poets*, "investiation and reasoning are only preparatory and servile parts, means to an end. They terminate in insight, or what in the noblest sense of the word may be called *theory*, ϑεωρία,—a steady contemplation of all things in their order and worth. Such contemplation is imaginative. . . . A philosopher who attains it is, for the moment, a poet; and a poet who turns his practised and passionate imagination on the order of all things, or on anything in the light of the whole, is for the moment a philosopher."

Santayana, for all that his language intimates rather than defines, did not by any means neglect that reasoning which is for him the servile and preparatory part of philosophy. He is a shrewd critic of historical ideas and an apt dialectician in the unravelment of their intention. He took very seriously what he regarded as his orthodoxy of common sense. But it is as an imaginative poet of thought that he will live, one who had, who created, and who communicated persuasive vistas of nature and man and the vistas which man in his history developed. Knowledge itself is for him a perspective and religion is a story, full of moral suggestion and cosmic piety. Spirit is the flame generated by animal life, a flame that burns brightly in moments of ardor or insight, but that waxes and fades with the fortunes of the animal psyche which is its condition. The spiritual life, as described in *The Life of Reason*, is a life lived in the light of an envisaged ideal. In *The Realm of Spirit* it becomes something else, a clear and intense beholding of an essence raptly beheld. Such beholding is transient and precarious; essences are eternal but the psyche in which the spirit comes to focus, in which spirit briefly lodges, is mortal and vanishing, and even while the animal psyche lives, spirit does not always see clearly or burn brightly. Science itself is for Santayana an "intellectual landscape," and true immortality is not endless time, but an instant vision of timeless things.

What, perhaps, is most certain to live in Santayana is not his analysis, whose sharpness is often overlooked by those bemused by the melody and imagery he was too much of a poet ever quite to exile even from his most sober considerations. I suspect he will endure because his own philosophical writings so well exemplify his notion of what philosophy ultimately adds up to, contemplation by a spirit, liberated through intellectual discipline, looking out from the conditioned vantage ground of a mortal psyche at a given moment of time. Spirit is detached from prejudices and preoccupations and addressed with quiet ardor to whatever aspects the realm of the possible discloses to awareness, a beholding as direct as poetry, and as comprehensive and comprehending as wisdom.

Santayana's last writing shortly before his death was called "The Poet's Testament." It is the testament of a philosopher, too.

THE POET'S TESTAMENT

I give back to the earth what the earth gave,
All to the furrow, nothing to the grave.
The candle's out, the spirit's vigil spent;
Sight may not follow where the vision went.

I leave you but the sound of many a word
In mocking echoes haply overheard.
I sang to heaven. My exile made me free—
From world to world, from all worlds carried me.

Spared by the Furies, for the Fates were kind,
I paced the pillared cloisters of the mind;
All times my present, everywhere my place,
Nor fear, nor hope, nor envy saw my face.

Blow what winds would, the ancient truth was mine,
And friendship mellowed in the flush of wine,
And heavenly laughter, shaking from its wings
Atoms of light and tears for mortal things.

To trembling harmonies of field and cloud,
Of flesh and spirit, was my worship vowed.
Let form, let music, let the all-quickening air
Fulfill in beauty my imperfect prayer.
—IRWIN EDMAN, "Philosopher as Poet," *JP*, Jan. 21, 1954, pp. 62–64

In 1905, George Santayana wrote a letter to his colleague in the Department of Philosophy at Harvard, William James, in which, replying with some heat to James' recent criticisms of *The Life of Reason*, he broke out:

> You don't yet see my philosophy, nor my temper from the inside . . . it is not the past that seems to me affecting, entrancing or pitiful to lose. It is the ideal. It is that vision of perfection that we just catch, or for a moment embody in some work of art, or in some idealized reality: it is the concomitant inspiration of life, always various, always beautiful, hardly ever expressible in its fullness. And it is my adoration of this real and familiar good, this love often embraced but always elusive, that makes me detest the . . . myths by which people try to cancel the passing ideal, or to denaturalize it . . . much of the irritation which I may betray and which, I assure you, is much greater than I let it seem, comes of affection. It comes of exasperation at seeing the only things that are beautiful or worth having treated as if they were of no account. . .

This passage marks a high point in the life-long difficulty Santayana had with his fellow philosophers. He was explaining himself in his letters, making his position "clear," and surely what is most significant about the letters is not their expected brilliance and beauty, but that, despite the same brilliance and beauty, in his book, he was always having to write such letters in an effort to persuade the professionals that he was perfectly sound and consistent. ⟨. . .⟩

He described himself as a sceptic, an atheist, a naturalist, a Platonist—and was always careful to add that he was not "any of these things, taken alone." One could compile an interesting anthology of self-labeling from these letters—which make up ⟨. . .⟩ an apologia for his philosophy. "My nature," he once wrote, "compels me to believe in something . . . double-material nature with its animation on the one hand, and logical or mathematical forms on the other . . . so I embrace materialism on pragmatic grounds—and on transcendental grounds also."

The easiest way of explaining Santayana's comparative isolation in modern philosophy, the peculiarities and para-doxes of his position, is to remember that his heart was in his Spanish and Catholic tradition, though he had been brought up in Boston and trained at Harvard. Yet after he left Harvard (and America) in 1912—and how impatient he was to live in Europe—he was no more at home in Spain than he had been in England. If he finally settled in Italy, it was only, as he said, because Italy was such a stage setting that he could be alone there.

Santayana was not at home anywhere, as his constant wanderings show. And his life seems to me idle and tragic because he tried to frame into a technical system of philoso-phy, to sort out and then to bring together, what were essentially the "paradoxes" and complexities of a profoundly artistic person. He seems to me an extraordinary example of a man who, trained in philosophy, learned to philosophize with the best of them, but for whom the language of philosophy was not entirely necessary or entirely right. For this reason, despite his dazzling brilliance, he was always too conscious of himself philosophizing.

He did not find in philosophy his inescapable and necessary language—the trade by which, and by which alone, he saw the world. He used it as a skill which he could exercise superbly, which he exercised in terms that were professional and habitual, but which were not fundamental to him. For this reason he was concerned with locating his system, with clearing it up, rather than with making something that was crushingly necessary to him. Clarity of this kind is more formal than real. It is entirely verbal, for it is concerned with polishing and ordering one's ideas as something to put forward to the world rather than something one builds into the world. It is a home for one's own spirit, rather than a vision of what is.

Those who know Santayana's philosophy and his belief in essences can object that just the contrary was his intention, that it is precisely the Platonic, classical and trans-human side of philosophy that Santayana always maintained against the Subjectivists and Relativists of modern philosophy. But Santayana saw "truth" as something that effortlessly included man rather than as something that man discovered. He saw it, I feel, from a non-human perspective, since he pictured man as a spectator, as a connoisseur, rather than as someone who is in reality up to his ears and for whom philosophy represents the often desperate need to make sense of the world, to establish man in the world itself.

Santayana wrote one correspondent that his philosophy was not a romantic naturalism but "the hard, non-humanistic naturalism of the Ionian philosophers, of Democritus, Lucretius, and Spinoza." He wrote that he was "of course . . . never a Fascist in the sense of belonging to that Italian party . . . but considered, as it is for a naturalist, a product of the generative order of society, a nationalist or religious *institution* will probably have its good sides, and be better perhaps than the alternative that presents itself at some moment in some place."

He wrote a Catholic priest that he was a Catholic only to the census-taker, but that his philosophy was probably useful "in defending the moral, political and mystical doctrines of the Church. I think that all religious ideas are merely symbolical; but I think the same of the ideas of science and even of the senses: so that the way is cleared for faith, in deciding which set of symbols one will trust."

All these distinctions are really efforts to get hold of a vision that somehow sounds rhetorical or frivolous or naive in the technical language of philosophy. But Santayana was so verbal that his terms can often be replaced by each other, thus giving the smiling architect of the "system" the satisfaction of arranging something that in its bewildering subtlety and audacious joinings makes a work of art. What finally annuls the system is that these words were not entirely necessary to him.

One should feel about a philosopher, as about any other thinker, that no other medium would serve him equally well, that he has discovered his vision of things through the subject itself, and that the subject has become illuminated, as if to itself, through the individual work. In this sense, philosophy is always discovering what it really is through the work of philosophers, and the philosopher discovers not what he really thinks (or who "he" really is), but how the world itself really appears to him.

Santayana's effort to defend his individual vision against Protestant New England shows that he was trying to see his heritage and to defend it all. That is what a man must do, no doubt. But if Santayana tended to portray himself in this way, to emphasize the traditional and Spanish and Catholic ele-ments in his background, it was, finally, to do himself justice.

And this he more than did, for he was an artist. I just wonder how much greater he would have been with a language, an art, really his own. Perhaps we should be less conscious of him then, and more of what he had made, perhaps he would have been less angry about his lost "ideal"—"that vision of perfection that we just catch, or for a moment embody in some work of art, or in some idealized reality."—ALFRED KAZIN, "With a Love for the Passing Ideal," *NYTBR*, Nov. 13, 1955, pp. 6, 39

For my part, I was never able to take Santayana very seriously as a technical philosopher, although I thought that he served a useful function by bringing to bear, as a critic, points of view which are now uncommon. The American dress in which his writing appeared somewhat concealed the extremely reaction-ary character of his thinking. Not only did he, as a Spaniard, side politically with the Church in all its attempts to bolster up old traditions in that country, but, as a philosopher, he reverted in great measure to the scholasticism of the thirteenth century. He did not present this doctrine straightforwardly as neo-Thomists do; he insinuated it under various aliases, so that it was easy for a reader not to know where his opinions came from. It would not be fair to suggest that his views were completely those of medieval scholastics. He took rather more from Plato than St. Thomas did. But I think that he and St. Thomas, if they could have met, would have understood each other very well.

His two chief works in pure philosophy were *The Life of Reason*, published in 1905, and *Realms of Being*, published between 1927 and 1940. He deals with the life of reason under five headings: reason in common sense, in society, in religion, in art, and in science. I do not myself feel that this work is very likely to attract a reader to the sort of life which Santayana considers rational. It is too quiet, too much that of a mere spectator, too destitute of passion, which, though it may have to be controlled, seems, to me at least, an essential element in any life worth living. His *Realms of Being*, which was his last important philosophical work, deals successively with essence, matter, truth, and spirit. In this, as in his other philosophical books, he does not trouble to argue, and much of what he says, particularly as regards essence, ignores much work which most modern philosophers would consider relevant. He completely ignored modern logic, which has thrown much new light on the old problem of universals which occupied a very large part of the attention of the scholastics. Santayana's *Realm of*

Essence seems to presuppose, at any rate in some sense, the reality of universals. It would be rash to say that this doctrine is false, but it is characteristic of Santayana that he calmly assumes its truth without taking the trouble to offer any arguments in its favor.

Although most of his active life was spent as a professor of philosophy at Harvard, he was perhaps more important from a literary than from a philosophic point of view. His style, to my mind, is not quite what a style ought to be. Like his patent-leather boots, it is too smooth and polished. The impression one gets in reading him is that of floating down a smooth-flowing river, so broad that you can seldom see either bank; but, when from time to time a promontory comes into view, you are surprised that it is a new one, as you have been unconscious of movement. I find myself, in reading him, approving each sentence in an almost somnambulistic manner, but quite unable, after a few pages, to remember what it was all about.

Nevertheless, I owe him certain philosophical debts. When I was young, I agreed with G. E. Moore in believing in the objectivity of good and evil. Santayana's criticism, in a book called *Winds of Doctrine*, caused me to abandon this view, though I have never been able to be as bland and comfortable without it as he was.

He wrote a good deal of literary criticism, some of it excellent. There was a book called *Three Philosophical Poets* about Lucretius, Dante, and Goethe. He was rather hurt because I said that he was better about the two Italian poets than about the German one. His writing on Goethe seemed to me a *tour de force* in which his intellectual approval was continually at war with his temperamental disgust. I found the latter more interesting than the former, and wished he had given it free rein.

He had a considerable affection for England, and his *Soliloquies in England* is a book which any patriotic English person can read with pleasure. He wrote a novel in which my brother (for whom he had a considerable affection) appears as the villain. He wrote an autobiography in several parts, which is chiefly interesting as exhibiting the clash between his Spanish temperament and his Boston environment. He used to boast that his mother, as a widow in Boston, worried her New England friends by never being busy about anything; and, when they came on a deputation to ask her how she got through the time, she replied: "Well, I'll tell you. In summer I try to keep cool, and in winter I try to keep warm." Admiration for this answer prevented him from feeling at home in New England.

He wrote a great deal about American culture, of which he had no high opinion. He gave an address to the University of California called *The Genteel Tradition in American Philosophy*, the gist of which was to the effect that academic America is alien to the spirit of the country, which, he said, is vigorous but Philistine. It had seemed to me, in my wanderings through American universities, that they would be more in harmony with the spirit of the country if they were housed in skyscrapers and not in pseudo-Gothic buildings ranged round a campus. This was also Santayana's view. I felt, however, a certain difference. Santayana enjoyed being aloof and contemptuous, whereas I found this attitude, when forced upon me, extremely painful. Aloofness and facile contempt were his defects, and because of them, although he could be admired, he was a person whom it was difficult to love.

But it is only fair to counterbalance this judgment with his judgment of me. He says: "Even when Russell's insight is keenest, the very intensity of his vision concentrates it too much. The focus is microscopic; he sees one thing at a time with extraordinary clearness, or one strain in history or politics; and the vivid realization of that element blinds him to the rest." And he accuses me, oddly enough, of religious conservatism. I will leave the reader to form his own judgment on this matter.

Santayana never seems to have felt that his loyalty to the past, if he could have caused it to become general, would have produced a lifeless world in which no new good thing could grow up. If he had lived in the time of Galileo he would have pointed out the literary inferiority of Galileo to Lucretius. But Lucretius was setting forth a doctrine already several centuries old, and I doubt whether the works of Democritus and Epicurus which set forth the doctrine when it was new, were as aesthetically pleasing as the poem of Lucretius. But, perhaps fortunately for them, their works are lost and my opinion can be no more than a guess. What remains indubitable is that the new is never as mellow as the old, and that therefore the worship of mellowness is incompatible with new excellence. It is for this reason that Santayana's merits are literary rather than philosophical.—BERTRAND RUSSELL, "George Santayana," *Portraits from Memory and Other Essays*, 1956, pp. 94–98

Works

POETRY

⟨. . .⟩ what is extraordinary about Mr. Santayana is that in spite of his monastic life he is capable of writing poetry that is only in small part bloodless. In the preface to this new selection of his poems ⟨*Poems*, 1923⟩, he speaks of them as being "mental and thin" in texture; and as applied to his "Odes" and some of the "Various Poems" those adjectives are not inappropriate. At his least felicitous, Mr. Santayana is literary and somewhat otiose, but he is at his least felicitous in a surprisingly small proportion of the verses that he has reprinted. It would be nearer the truth to say that his best poetry has the sobriety of reflectiveness than to say it is "mental and thin." There is a sense in which all poetry is posthumous, and, as expression, comes after the stress of the emotion itself has died away: these poems of Mr. Santayana's have, more than most poetry, the quality of a record and even of a reminiscence, but that is in no marked degree a limitation.

The best of Mr. Santayana's work is the two series of sonnets, fifty in all, which stand at the beginning of this volume. Like all good poetry, they spring from the marriage of emotion with thought, and can not spring from either alone; yet he himself calls them his "philosophy in the making," and there is no injustice in interpreting them in that light. They are the utterance, then, of a kind of priestly Platonism, steeped in melancholy and regret; a Platonism into which the formulas of the schools have not entered and could not enter. Like every brooding spirit, Mr. Santayana is oppressed with the insufficiency of human wisdom, the inaccessibility of the ideal:

> Our knowledge is a torch of smoky pine
> That lights the pathway but one step ahead
> Across a void of mystery and dread.

He speaks of himself as "a homeless mind," and there is the stamp upon all these poems of an infinite spiritual forlornness, the nostalgia of a sensitive and other-worldly spirit.

If it were not for that other-worldliness as a background, there would be in his celebration of beauty and love something almost too insubstantial for poetry. To Mr. Santayana, beauty is not what it is for most poets, a thing to be sensuously enjoyed in itself, but an embodiment of the ideal, a "proof of heaven";

and it is not the ecstacy and turmoil of love that he sings, but its abstergent action, its power to set the soul free from the bondage of reality. As an aspiration towards perfection is the key to the thought of these poems, so a struggle for perfection shows itself in their formal finish: Mr. Santayana handles the sonnet with a precision which is as complete as is, on the whole, Blunt's negligence. He says himself that his sonnets lack perfect grace and naturalness because the English tongue is not, originally, his own: "its roots do not quite reach to my centre." Yet surely the shade by which these lines fail of the purest idiomatic quality, is an elusive and even unreal one:

> How liberal is beauty that, but seen,
> Makes rich the bosom of her silent lover!
> How excellent is truth, on which I lean!
> Yet my religion were a charmed despair,
> Did I not in thy perfect heart discover
> How beauty can be true and virtue fair.

That is the kind of lucidity and candour for which the word classic must be reserved, and the purity of his phrasing is sustained everywhere by the combined exactitude and flexibility of his structure; it is his constant success in keeping on that level that makes one wonder whether English verse has ever been written as excellently as Mr. Santayana has written it, by anyone else to whom the English language was not native.—NEWTON ARVIN, "Ex Libris," *Freeman*, March 28, 1923, p. 71

THE LAST PURITAN

⟨. . .⟩ Mr. Santayana's 'Memoir in the Form of a Novel' ⟨. . .⟩ is a philosophical-psychological-sociological analysis of Puritanism as seen in a diffident and somewhat unusually serious-minded young New Englander, Oliver Alden. Mr. Santayana can be sarcastic, but with a sense of propriety in the occasion; and realistically graphic, but with a due sense of neither wishing to obtrude nor be obvious, so that both forms of restraint suggest a distinguished and well-mannered book. Fraulein Irma, sailing for America, feels she may go down to history as the governess of a President, but suddenly feels that she had better go down to her cabin. Boats tied to a landing stage are like a bunch of bananas, but one is not asked to hold one's regard on them or on the genius of the author for making such a clever phrase. And when Nathaniel Alden holds out a "horizontal hand" at parting with his vivacious step-sister, one sees not the obtrusive hand but the horizontal mind of Mr. Alden. In fact, it is a weakness in *The Last Puritan*, though a deliberate technique, that realism is eschewed in order to get us down to the inner reality: so that the conversations are undramatic, and the commentary frequent and discursive and the ruminations of the characters more informative than credible.

Having said which one must say that *The Last Puritan* is, surely, one of the few modern books that will remain—whether as memoir or novel—grown, as it has, out of a personal intensity of feeling no less moving in the record, and possibly more effective for being at once tranquillised by thought and expressed with an urbanity salted by something very like disillusion. One may or may not see Oliver Alden, but how fully one realises him! His home where they discussed loftily too many opinions and people, and so emphasised his inherent Calvinist conscience, that awful Puritan conscience that was at the root of his tragedy ("not content merely to understand but eager to govern"), refusing to let him be equivocal about anything in a most equivocal world, and opposing always his diffidence that made him want like his

drug-taking father—Peter Alden is excellent—to be one of the birds in the echelon rather than the leader, or Mrs. Murphy's child in the lap rather than Mrs. Alden's child in the carriage. It is one of the few novels I know that is subjective without being self-engaged, and there is (what a relief!) no corroding self-pity. And if it is somewhat long and there is a good deal of philosophy it is the length of an interesting book and the philosophy of an interesting philosopher.—SEÁN O'FAOLÁIN, *Spec*, Nov. 1, 1935, p. 744

It is surely a choice piece of irony that *The Last Puritan*, the most nearly satisfactory analysis, in fiction, of the New England character, should have been written by a Catholic and a Latin. But perhaps, just the same, there is nothing surprising in it—perhaps Santayana's unique opportunity for a vision that should be at once detached and kindly, lay precisely in these accidents of difference. If the American has the advantage over the European that he can *become* European, the European has—and more often uses!—the same advantage over the American. During his years at Harvard, first as undergraduate and then as a professor of Philosophy, it is now obvious that Santayana "became" a New Englander, in the sense of realizing what it was to *be* one, more accurately and consciously than any other novelist of New England manners one can think of. James touched on this ground repeatedly, it is true, and saw it as itself a theme of the first importance, notably in some of the short stories: but he never got round to working it exhaustively. Santayana has worked it exhaustively—the thing is done, for good and all. *The Last Puritan* is as complete, in its way, as that New England autobiography of which it is the perfect companion-piece: *The Education of Henry Adams*.

Adams described New Englanders as "sane and steady men, well balanced, educated, and free from meanness or intrigue—men whom one liked to act with, and who, whether graduates or not, bore the stamp of Harvard College . . . as a rule, the New Englander's strength was his poise, which almost amounted to a defeat. He offered no more target for love than for hate; he attracted as little as he repelled; even as a machine, his motion seemed never accelerated." It is this sort of New Englander whom, with a miracle of tenderness, Santayana proceeds to destroy. His little twentieth-century Henry Adams, a bundle of inhibitions, an incarnated sense of duty, a skeptical awareness of which perhaps the first principle is an inherited fatigue, combined with that strangest of all paradoxes, a democratic sense of *noblesse oblige*—this unhappy creature serves only too admirably as the personification of the principles—or should we say obsessions—which Santayana so urbanely and cunningly attacked in his *Skepticism and Animal Faith*: the esurient negativism, the denial of life itself, implicit in any complete transcendentalism. It is as if he said, "This kind of self-destructive soul-searching and skepticism and conscientiousness can only grow in a moral atmosphere such as this, and from a thin soil like this." And it is as if he added, "It is a kind of uprooted refinement of which the inevitable ends are sterility and death." His Oliver Arden, born tired, child of a loveless and joyless marriage, austere, self-controlled, beautifully schooled and regimented, was doomed to remain a mere spectator in life, incapable of contact or immersion, incapable of animal faith. He might, and did, *will* a contact or immersion: but only to perceive at once, with tragic clearness, that this was by no means the same thing. "He conceived himself, on puritan grounds, that it was wrong to be a puritan. . . . Thought it his clear duty to give puritanism up, but couldn't." Once dedicated to the vision, there was somehow no surrendering it, no possiblity of finding any adequate substitute.

It may be objected that Santayana has a little unnecessarily loaded the dice against his tragic young man, made his inheritance, the congenital predicament, too complete. One hardly needs, in order to account for Oliver, the opium-fiend neurasthenic father, and perhaps the whole background is a shade overdrawn. But to this the answer is that Santayana has made the father, like every other character in the book, astonishingly and delightfully real. The process is leisurely, little or nothing happens, as in life itself things seldom seem to arrange themselves in scenes or dramatic actions; but if it is all placid and uneventful it is also everywhere vivid and rich and true. Unashamedly old-fashioned in its method, and in its quiet thoroughness, *The Last Puritan* makes the average contemporary novel, even the best, look two-dimensional by contrast. It has the solidity of a *Tom Jones* or *Clarissa Harlowe*, does for the New England scene, or a part of it, what those novels did for eighteenth-century England, and with the same air of easy classic completeness. Nor is it quite fair, either, to call it old-fashioned: for Santayana's employment of a kind of soliloquy-dialogue is an extremely interesting invention technically, and very skillfully done.

But the whole book is a delight, so richly packed with perceptions and wisdoms and humors, not to mention poetry, that it can be read and reread for its texture alone. It might be of himself that Santayana speaks when he says: "The odds and ends of learning stuck pleasantly in his mind, like the adventures of a Gil Blas or a Casanova; it was the little events, the glimpses of old life, like the cadences of old poetry, that had the savor of truth. Perhaps there were no great events: a great event was a name for our ignorance of the little events which composed it." Or again: "To him the little episodes painted in the corners were often the best of the picture: they revealed the true tastes of the artist and the unspoken parts of life." *The Last Puritan* is full of such intriguing corners—perhaps inevitably, since it is the work of the kindliest of living philosophers.—CONRAD AIKEN, "The New England Animal," NR, Feb. 5, 1936, p. 372

HAROLD STEARNS
"Distance Lends Enchantment"
Freeman, December 29, 1920, pp. 378–81

Intellectually speaking, M. Henri Bergson has never recovered from the quiet, merciless exposition of his philosophy which Professor Santayana included in a book of essays called *Winds of Doctrine*. The genuine terror before science of the author of *L'Evolution creatrice*, his horror of the mind as a kind of sorceror or witch, his "brilliant attempt to confuse the lessons of experience by refining upon its texture," his flattery of the irrational and impulsive temper of the times, his mystical verbalism—all are revealed by Professor Santayana with a critical perception, a subtle humour, and a stylistic charm that have been the envy, as they have been the despair, of more plodding and technical philosophers. For none have written before—and few perhaps will write again—of metaphysical problems with the worldly shrewdness, the rather Roman touch of austere detachment, the æsthetic graciousness, the verbal felicity, the non-technical aptness of phrase, in brief, with the distinction that has been Mr. Santayana's constant quality, even when he has discussed the more abstruse concepts of Mr. Bertrand Russell. Others, especially

James, have written with more vigour and human passion; many have contrived to adumbrate, as it were, more logical symphonies—the parts fitting in and woven together to an irresistible (and usually absurd) conclusion—more perfect systematic mosaics. But none, from a purely literary point of view, have come even to the point where comparisons are applicable.

In his most recent volume, *Character and Opinion in the United States*, Professor Santayana has written what one is inclined to believe will become the classic essays on William James and Josiah Royce. Not merely are the incisive critical perception and penetration as alertly in action here as in his essay on M. Bergson, but colouring and moulding the purely rationalistic considerations is a certain kindliness, the warmth and understanding of personal acquaintance and liking, which in all probability Professor Santayana could not have felt towards the French theorist, even if he had had the opportunity for academic intimacy. Thus Professor Santayana has here accomplished what biographical essayists usually aspire to and very rarely achieve—critical estimates that are, at the same time, most engaging and revealing personal portraits. As far as these two men are concerned, his title is apt: he gives us both their character and their opinions. But he does not do so separately or alternately; he gives them conjointly, in their subtle interaction and relationship, yet always—as might be expected of him—with more causative emphasis, so to speak, on their character and instinctive temperament than upon any of their theories. At all times would he be reluctant to attribute directive force to belief or mere cognition in itself; that would seem to him, I think, vanity or animal illusion.

Possibly Mr. Santayana's literary charm and persuasiveness, especially in this volume of essays and in *Winds of Doctrine* and in his more fugitive articles for the magazines, have been somewhat disarming to his lay critics. Certainly his failure to write systematic treatises (for in *The Life of Reason* he refused to be systematic), in the accepted manner of flat, pedagogical exposition, duly ticketed and paragraph-marked and underscored, has disconcerted the technical philosophers. At all events, the intrinsic substance of his own beliefs has been comparatively neglected. This is somewhat unfortunate, yet in a sense understandable. In the first place, *The Life of Reason* and *The Sense of Beauty* are, after all is said and done, glorious failures—they demanded that Mr. Santayana should play a role false to himself. He was expected by the professionals to be systematic and to employ the jargon of the schools. Temperamentally, Mr. Santayana was all incapable of living up to either of these expectations, a disability entirely creditable in itself. Nevertheless it alienated the philosophers from him; he hardly seemed to be playing their game according to the rules. On the other hand, the general reading public found the substance of these books to be much too strong as intellectual meat—and there was the further misfortune that his style is least attractive in these volumes. It suffers, I think, from his own inner conflict between the strong instinctive wish to be conversational and to write with the ease of a man of the world and the equally strong compulsion to be meticulous, orderly, and professional. He could hardly be both, and he did not succeed in being completely either.

The fact is, Mr. Santayana is much more the incomparable essayist than the precise dialectician. This is true even when he is most scrupulously logical—and that he always is. He is primarily a critic; he is at his stylistic best when he is most critical. Now the misfortune of critics, especially when they are as pungent and effective as Mr. Santayana, naturally is that their own beliefs and ideas are somewhat put in the shade.

When a writer is a cogent analyser of false notions, the reader somehow imputes to him correct notions, yet without stopping further to inquire what those notions consist of. Suddenly to be asked what the particular notions of the critic himself are, often proves embarrassing. Further, in Mr. Santayana's case it is a fact that it is extraordinarily difficult to pierce to the heart of his own beliefs. The writer of this review studied under him—how captivating and delightful were those witty, subtle lectures!— and has read with perhaps more than the layman's care many of his books. Yet, if I were asked offhand to describe his philosophy, I should feel rather presumptuous (as I most certainly would feel that I might be quite wrong) if I were to try to sum it up in one of the conventional words—materialist, naturalist, mechanist, pragmatist, or the like. Any word would need qualifying adjectives, and any phrase would need a certain aura of modifying sentences. No, the essence of his cluster of beliefs Mr. Santayana does not give us by direct exposition. It comes to us indirectly, by innuendo and suggestion. We have to search carefully through all the implications of the seemingly most innocent declaration. His ideas are a kind of emanation. They are a bias, but a consistent bias— which is perhaps the truest philosophy of all.

Yet it is important for one to try to understand that bias and direction of his thought in order to appreciate the setting and framework of the two books which are the crown of his work, *Winds of Doctrine* and the ⟨*Character and Opinion in the United States*⟩. No misunderstanding, for example, could well be more grotesque than that which attributes to him a liking for withdrawal from the world, a little desire to be *au-dessus de la mêlée*, although I have often heard this criticism made of him, even by his own students. To be sure, Mr. Santayana did not become an official Government propagandist, like M. Bergson, during the war, and in spite of his sympathies, seldom wrote on journalistically immediate issues. But this was due far less to superciliousness than to a basic sanity. Even the tumult of war could hardly shake his interest from things permanent and important to things transient and trivial. Far from being the charming skulker in his own intellectual tower of ivory, Mr. Santayana is the shrewdest and most worldly-wise of men. His whole bias, it seems to me, is distinctly for the instinctive beliefs of the common man rather than for the adroit fantasies of his so-called mental superiors. Certainly he never tires of exposing the trickeries of dialectics; and throughout *The Life of Reason* there are many cutting little gibes at the ease with which technicians fall into verbal mare's-nests of their own making. His constant battle against mere verbalism and the hypostasis of words was as keen and vigorous as any ever waged by the pragmatists or neo-realists.

With the common man, Mr. Santayana believes in the cardinal fact of nature; that it is a material fact, not to be washed away by idealism (and then restored by an act of God or by a generous integrating Principle of Rationality) or lost in the mists of solipsism, and that, further, the more nature is objectively studied and observed, the more it reveals a mechanistic order. Also with the common man, he believes in the cardinal fact of mind; that cogitation is a mental fact, to be observed and studied, in the same manner that the world of nature is observed and studied, that is to say, rationally. Whence would arise the conviction that animal illusion plays an unwonted part in the intellectual life of man, and the belief that irrationality of action is the common rule. But the rarity and comparative impotence of the life of reason would not detract from its desirability as a way of life nor from its value as a discipline. The difficulties inherent in it would not lead to its

romantic abandonment but rather to a humble sense of human limitation. At all events, one should be equally on one's guard from the crasser materialist, who reduces the life of reason to a mere cross-section of the objects of knowledge, and from the impulsive idealist, who reduces the order of nature to the shadowy categories of his own thought. I realize this has a suspiciously epiphenomenalistic sound—but is not the common man instinctively an epiphenomenalist?

Consider the implications of this passage:

> The so-called appearances, according to a perfected criticism of knowledge, are nothing private or internal; they are merely those portions of external objects which from time to time impress themselves on somebody's organs of sense and are responded to by his nervous system. Such is the doctrine of the new American realists, in whose devoted persons the logic of idealism has worked itself out and appropriately turned idealism itself into its opposite. Consciousness, they began by saying, is merely a stream of ideas; but then ideas are merely the parts of objects which happen to appear to a given person; but again, a person (for all you or he can discover) is nothing but his body and those parts of other objects which appear to him; and, finally, to appear, in any discoverable sense, can not be to have a ghostly sort of mental existence, but merely to be reacted upon by an animal body. Thus we come to the conclusion that objects alone exist, and that consciousness is a name for certain segments or groups of these objects.

This turns the tables on the realists very neatly; yet with characteristic insight and wit Mr. Santayana is not content to stop here. He is not interested solely in the technical side of the argument. He must show the human background, the temperamental compulsions. So he goes on:

> I think we may conjecture why this startling conclusion that consciousness does not exist, a conclusion suggested somewhat hurriedly by William James, has found a considerable echo in America, and why the system of Avenarius, which makes in the same direction, has been studied there sympathetically. To deny consciousness is to deny a prerequisite to the obvious, and to leave the obvious standing alone. That is a relief to an over-taxed and self-impeded generation; it seems a blessed simplification. It gets rid of the undemocratic notion that by being very reflective, circumspect, and subtle you might discover something that most people do not see. They can go on more merrily with their work if they believe that by being so subtle, circumspect, and reflective you would only discover a mare's-nest. The elimination of consciousness not only restores the obvious, but proves all parts of the obvious to be equally real. Not only colours, beauties, and passions, but all things formerly suspected of being creatures of thought, such as laws, relations, and abstract qualities, now become components of the existing object, since there is no longer any mental vehicle by which they might have been created and interposed. The young American is thus reassured; his joy in living and learning is no longer chilled by the contempt which idealism used to cast on nature for being imaginary and on science for being intellectual. All fictions and all abstractions are now declared to be parcels of the objective world; it will suffice to live on, to live forward, in order to see everything as it really is.

Really, could any criticism of the spirit of later American philosophy be more penetrating and luminous? For example, in a very able review of Professor John Dewey's most recent book, *Reconstruction in Philosophy*, the critic refers to how "in the sciences there is now scope for change and progress without ascertainable limit." This was exciting news, but I found myself asking what the progress was towards; what was the test of true growth? And sure enough, a little further on came this sentence: "The test of growth or discovery is more growth, more discovery." Growth without end, growth everlasting—yet somehow growth without meaning, just vegetative expansion. After all, growth must be with reference to some end—what humanistic meaning is to be derived from the statement that the end of growth is contained in the growth itself? One can not escape values and standards no matter how merrily one plunges into the whirl of experience; and how subtly Mr. Santayana has anticipated and explicated this development of American theory!

Consequently, we find our author bringing to his examination of American philosophers and of the intellectual temper of the country, not a system by which they can be measured in terms of truth and error, but rather a standard of values by which they can be appraised in terms of human desirability. The bias of this approach we might expect from previous writings: he will appraise them from a point of view fundamentally Greek, i.e., he will seek in their temperament and unguarded utterances for evidences that they are Protestant, romantic, rather capricious and amusingly wayward—in brief, somewhat barbarous. As a matter of fact, he will not have to search long or far for confirmations of this hypothesis. It is not difficult for Mr. Santayana to find in Josiah Royce, heir to the Calvinistic tradition, tortured by the sense of sin and evil in the world yet impelled by his own nature to take sides morally to the confusion of his logic (as in the case of the sinking of the *Lusitania*) which showed "all lives were parts of a single divine life in which all problems were solved and all evils justified,"— to find in this philosopher who, "although he was born in California . . . had never got used to the sunshine," a resemblance to "some great-hearted mediæval peasant visited by mystical promptings, whom the monks should have adopted and allowed to browse among their theological folios; a Duns Scotus, earnest and studious to a fault, not having the lightness of soul to despise these elaborate sophistries, yet minded to ferret out their secret for himself and walk by his inward light." Increase the number of your kettle-drums, tune up your brasses, and behold, you have Mr. H. L. Mencken exposing the *naïveté* of some confused but earnest yearner and author of a new religion living in Centreville, Ohio!

Equally sophisticated, much more beautiful in style, but with a greater respect and a more unfeigned admiration is Mr. Santayana's exquisite essay on James. Here, too, of course, he finds, for all its greatness, a mind essentially anarchistic, capricious, and romantic, a mystic in love with life. "He was comparable to Rousseau and to Walt Whitman; he expressed a generous and tender sensibility, rebelling against sophistication, and preferring daily sights and sounds, and a vague but indomitable faith in fortune, to any unsettled intellectual tradition calling itself science or philosophy." And finally, in his discussion of the academic environment at Harvard of the days of Royce and James—

> it represented faithfully the complex inspiration of the place and hour. As the university was a local Puritan college opening its windows to the scientific world, so at least the two most gifted of its philosophers were men of intense feeling, religious and romantic, but attentive to the facts of nature and the currents of worldly opinion; and each of them felt himself bound by two different responsibilities, that of describing things as they are, and that of finding them propitious to certain preconceived human desires.

In other words, the dice of thought were loaded.

Now, if such are Mr. Santayana's reservations respecting our two admittedly greatest thinkers since the Civil War, what must be his judgment on the *milieu* from which they sprang? What must he think of America?

On the whole, his answer to these questions is an extraordinarily kindly one. He prefers not to mention our intolerance, our hard regimentation, our paucity of deep feeling. He speaks even glowingly of our good-will (a genuine misunderstanding on his part, I believe) and our capacity for co-operation, albeit with a communal compulsion about it which seems to make him slightly shudder. But when he is most perceptive, he gives his generalizations amiably rather than scornfully. He can find our child-like pioneer optimism congruous with the nature of things in a still not fully filled-up land. Inevitably he finds us romantic, passionate, active, traditionless, crude. We are, in a word, children; and over and over again, even in his kindliest moments (for children have their natural charm), we can catch the accent of the sophisticated and cultivated man who finds himself homeless and alien:

> To be poor in order to be simple, to produce less in order that the product may be more choice and beautiful, and may leave us less burdened with unnecessary duties and useless possessions—that is an ideal not articulate in the American mind. . . . As self-trust may pass into self-sufficiency, so optimism, kindness and good-will may grow into a habit of doting on everything. To the good American many subjects are sacred: sex is sacred, women are sacred, children are sacred, business is sacred, America is sacred, Masonic lodges and college clubs are sacred. . . . The luckless American who is drawn to poetic subtlety, pious retreats, or gay passions, nevertheless has the categorical excellence of work, growth, enterprise, reform and prosperity dinned into his ears: every door is open in this direction and shut in the other. . . . Material restlessness was not yet ominous, the pressure of business enterprise was not yet out of scale with the old life or out of key with the old moral harmonies. A new type of American had not appeared—the untrained, pushing, cosmopolitan orphan, cock-sure in manner but none too sure in his morality, to whom the old Yankee, with his sour integrity, is almost a foreigner.

We must not forget—as the author never does—that Mr. Santayana left America in 1912, when we were still young, still in the national awkward-age. The American's views, he writes in one of the later chapters, "are not yet lengthened; his will is not yet broken or transformed. The present moment, however, in this, as in other things, may mark a great change in him; he is perhaps now reaching his majority, and all I say may hardly apply to-day, and may not at all apply tomorrow." Without intending to be sour or disgruntled, it is perhaps easier for us to see the author's reason for being so especially kindly (as he is, on the whole, in spite of the quiet irony revealed in these quotations). After all, distance lends enchantment, and Mr. Santayana does not have to come back to us. But the chief point is that the America of to-day is not the America of 1912; we have changed more in these last eight years than in the four decades before. Almost invariably we have changed for the worse; the war brought out our worse qualities and seems to have fixed them definitely. In 1912 it was possible and proper to hope that tares or more propitious seed might grow up in so generous a soil as ours; it was courteous of Mr. Santayana to suggest that the latter was the more likely to grow. In truth, however, only tares have grown up. When we think of 1912— with freedom of speech something of a reality, with no such unholy alliance between commerce and the university as that of to-day, with no thought of war or of its spiritual by-products, with belief in progress and international peace, with personal liberty assured, with intolerance impotent instead of dominant, with freedom of communication—it seems almost like a dream of an America that has gone. England, where Mr. Santayana has spent most of his time since leaving us, has perhaps suffered more in a material way than we have, but it has not had to bear such enormous spiritual casualties. In fact, we *have* grown up—but too rapidly; it has been a forced growth, bringing with it the twisted, distorted sides of our nature. In a sense, we had two paths to choose in 1912; to-day the choice has been made.

To be sure, it was not wholly of our own choosing, and Europe, along with the rest of the world, will regret the selection we have made. Our author was not altogether content or happy when he was living here in the old days. Would he be any less so if he came back to-day? Let us hope he can not be persuaded to do it. Perhaps, through the pathos of distance, there may remain some to write of us in a friendly spirit, remembering, before they were broken or scarred, our youth and our promise.

HENRY SEIDEL CANBY
"The Education of a Puritan"

Saturday Review of Literature, February 1, 1936, pp. 3–4, 12

Here at last after many months is a Book ⟨*The Last Puritan*⟩—a book worth attacking, worth defending, worth digesting, a book which may become a controversy in American literature, like *The Education of Henry Adams*, like *Moby-Dick*, to both of which it is subtly related by resemblance and contrast.

Santayana calls it "a memoir in the form of a novel." As a memoir, and it can be read that way, it is the record of a philosopher's thirty years of experience with youth and with America. Here is one of the subtlest minds of our time, a Latin of the Catholic tradition, an artist in English prose of the very first rank, perhaps the premier man-of-letters in English who is not a famous poet, not a dramatist at all, not till now a novelist. Here is a philosopher by profession who in his long career in the Protestant, and sometime Puritan, university of Harvard, emphasized no system but wrought intensely upon the picked minds of generation after generation of undergraduates. And here is the author of that slippery and difficult discourse in two volumes upon *Skepticism and Animal Faith*, and the wholly delightful *Soliloquies in England*, who now applies the philosophy of the first to his American experience, which was so much deeper and longer than his English sojourns. And indeed it will be a question in the minds of those who read this book as memoir, whether George Santayana is not more American than he himself realizes, whether, indeed, he is not one of those enlightened immigrants whose sympathetic criticism of the American way of life becomes part of our tradition, making it less English, less Protestant and Puritan, but not thereby less American.

The Last Puritan is "in the form of a novel." Nothing could be more surprising to those who think of Santayana as a speculative intellect above the turmoil of everyday life, nothing could be more natural if one remembers the great tradition of the novel in English. Since the eighteenth century it has been into the flexible narrative form of a long story—usually a biographical story—that writers in English have again and again unloaded their burden of a lifetime of philosophic observation. *Tom Jones* is furnished with a complete dialectics; *Tristram Shandy* is speculative to the point of fantasy; George Eliot's philosophical determinism has weighed down her novels below the level of contemporary interest; *The Ordeal of Richard Feverel* is in conception and execution a close parallel to *The Last Puritan*; and there is Hawthorne's skepticism, Melville's transcendentalism, Pater's estheticism, all seeking a medium in the long story. Nor should our current interests blind us to the fact that while the born story-tellers go on with sheer narrative, the thinkers and would-be thinkers of our day are using the novel to air theories of proletarian government or of socialist revolution, while the philosophy of behaviorism lies behind a hundred current novels which have no plot, no rounded characters, no significance except their faithful transcript of how twentieth century people behave when prodded by a novelist's pen. If an elderly philosopher takes to novel writing he is within his rights and proper expectation; the question is, does he succeed?

As a novel, *The Last Puritan* violates all the textbook rules but two. It has no plot, but only a biographical story, much interrupted. It has no dialogue as the modern understands dialogue, but only the gifted Mr. Santayana somewhat apologetically making situations articulate when the characters were too young or too reticent to say what they obscurely felt and would have liked to mean. Hence, with the exception of the Vicar's wife, who speaks her country dialect, all and sundry— the tongue-tied Oliver, hero of the story, the irrepressible Mario, light and liberated soul from the Catholic tradition, Lord Jim the un-Puritan sea captain, the grim matriarch, mother of Oliver, Peter, his father, lovely Rose the English Puritan girl, whose spirituality has been spilled out of a mind otherwise companioned with Oliver's—all speak in the dulcet and subtly varied English of Santayana, which is flexible, true to the situation, witty, and exquisite—and unrealistic to a degree which will make those perversely weary of excessive realism clap hands and reread. The arrogance, the insolence of a novelist who dares write a two-page soliloquy for a sixteen-year-old boy which is a model of intricate statement, saying at the end, this is what Oliver thought, although he could not express it! Neither could anyone else, except Santayana.

Nor has *The Last Puritan* a love story. "And how, my dear Vanny, how am I to manage the love scenes?" asks Santayana in the Prologue. And Mario, who has urged him to write the memoir of Oliver, replies, "Bah, there are love stories enough in the bookstalls for those who like them! This is to be a tale of sad life." There are, as a matter of fact, three love stories in the book, but two are absurd because Oliver's conception of love as a duty makes any love story absurd except on the old Testament model, and the third is abortive because Mario can make love but not take it. Nor has this novel a climax. Santayana's climax is the final and penetrating definition of a Puritan, a man who is "not content to understand but wishes to govern" in a world that will not be governed by one who seeks only the austerely best. Oliver is a bred-out perfectionist, too self-conscious to be simple, too conscience-stricken to be content with being inactively complex. Such characters have no climaxes.

But in two respects even the correspondence schools would have to admit that Mr. Santayana has satisfied the requirements of their courses in novel writing. There is drama in his book; not to be sure the kind of drama they specify, but spiritual drama tightened into effective scenes, the kind of drama which is incomparably the most satisfactory of all to a mature reader. And there are characters, real characters, with personality, significance, and that faculty of becoming frames of reference for one's own actual life which is the distinction of a real novelist or dramatist and his difference from behaviorists and autobiographers. Here I place Oliver's frightening mother, the perfect type of ten thousand rich American women, high-minded, dogmatic, spoiled, whose life has been made into a formula for being autocratic in a democracy. Santayana would have called her the last (and the worst) Protestant, if she had been the center of his book. And here I place Peter, the father, the Puritan relapsed into dilettanteism, reacting from duty into esthetics, humor, and drugs. And also Mario, and Uncle Nathaniel in whom nobody except Bostonians will believe, and Cousin Caleb, the Puritan abbot, old Salem gone metaphysical and more Catholic than the Pope, and the German governess Irma, the last sentimentalist. Lord Jim, Peter's captain, the perfect physical man without a soul or conscience, is too palpably a foil for Oliver; and there are other failures in character, for Santayana has no small talk in his narrative. If he weakens he has none of the tricks of the trade to save him. He will give you Eton complete in one chapter, but forget utterly in another that his people are in Williamstown or at the Harvard game in New Haven, and presumably are acting against a background, which he neglects to provide. And his characters are either magnificent because his philosophy suddenly becomes incarnate; or impossible because he invents a bad imitation of a man or woman to carry his thesis; or trivial like most of his young women, and best skipped. Oliver himself never quite comes to life, though his problems are dramatic. Rose is like an examination question in one of Mr. Santayana's courses. Now what, he asks his readers, do you suppose this young woman for whom I have written a poem and put it in the midst of my prose—what do you suppose she *means?*

Oliver's problem—that is the heart of this memoir-novel, which beats through every scene and mood and becomes articulate in Santayana's beautiful English. And here the story is important. It begins with his ancestors, Bostonians who hold their wealth as a sacred trust, but have begun to forget what they wanted to do with it. Oliver is the son of a rebel to tradition, of Peter who incredibly prefers the Irish of South Boston to Beacon Hill, takes to the Orient in order to escape conformity, but marries a healthy Puritan so that there shall be an heir to do something with the only religion left in this family, its determined grip upon its millions. And Oliver proves to be that rarity, the perfect inheritor, who, combining all the family traits, synthesizes an American line and brings together in one person the genes of all their bodies, and the acquired tendencies of all their social experience. Which means that he is a born athlete and democrat to whom the simple, strenuous equalitarianism of American comes as naturally as if he really believed himself only the equal of the boys at Great Falls public school: which means also that he is consistently Puritan, a spiritual aristocrat—"determined to remain . . . self-directed and inflexibly himself." And this attempt is his story, according to Santayana his "sad story." Actually it is the story of how his education, in school and out of it, was shattered upon his inflexible Puritan heart.

I doubt whether Santayana is more than half right about Oliver and America. It is easy for the Latin Catholic mind to disapprove of the man or the nation that is self-directed and inflexibly itself, although few Latin minds have disapproved with such sympathetic admiration. It is easy to show the futility of self-direction, each to show in the contemporary scene how Anglo-Saxon self-confidence has made a society which at the moment seems to please nobody and threatens to destroy itself by its own will-engendered energy. Santayana, like the very un-Catholic Hawthorne, is struck by the evident fact that as the Puritan race grows older and more secure in its place in the world, the finer spirits vibrate more and more to the agitations of conscience, and less and less to the rhythms of aggressive energy which made their name great. Then the self-direction by which they live lays a burden upon their wills which brings self-torture with it making a sad story. For Santayana's Puritans are not prigs or ascetics or sadists determined to make everyone good their way. They are men and women resolved first of all to govern themselves and to consent only to such life as seems to them best. They carry a burning coal of perfection at their heart. And so they fail, or at least Oliver fails, because he would triumph fastidiously or not at all.

I think also that there is a possible fallacy in Santayana's reasoning and in the biography of his Oliver which, though so personal and often so very human in its details, must be taken as a study of a soul. This golden son of wealth and culture has two handicaps for living, of which only the first is inevitable. From childhood his every action is inspired by duty to this inner fire of perfectionism. He plays football because of duty, makes love for duty, chooses his education by duty, gives freely of his energies for duty, but reserves always his inner self from everything and everyone. The sea and its freedoms tempt him; Jim, his first uninhibited friend, tempts him; Mario, who gives to God the responsibility for his pleasure-seeking nature, tempts him; but he is so little moved that he cannot conceive of love for his English Rose except as a means of making two Puritan souls, and little souls to follow, grow where one grew before. No one so constituted has a good time in life. Oliver's story was bound to be "sad."

But not necessarily tragic. Santayana has a great respect for what he would possibly call the animal faith of America, the simple, kindly, unreflective energy that makes this continent still a new world in comparison with the tight tenacity of England, the grasping caution of France, the excitable egoism of the Italians. And so had Oliver. His second handicap was that the Puritan perfectionism in him would not let him release his fastidiousness on this lower animal level. He could play that game and live in it, if only it would be made to mean enough to satisfy his exalted spirit. But he would not let his heart go either to a woman or to America.

And here I think that Mr. Santayana is a better novelist than social philosopher. He is thinking too much in terms of his selected Harvard experience. He knew his young Americans at the youthful peak of their intellectual intolerance. He knew America outside the college only as they knew it—a lovable country content with mediocrity. But surely it is by the wedding of such potential leadership as theirs and Oliver's with a hearty animal faith that civilizations are saved or made. And surely not all the Olivers will die discouraged and futile by accident in a war into which they have drifted because they could not summon will either to resist or to lead! As a novelist, Mr. Santayana can do what he pleases with his characters, and fortunately he has done so much with Oliver that even the end of this story is only proof that *The Last Puritan* must not be judged by the textbook canons of novel writing, but as a Book.

WILLIAM SAROYAN

1908–1981

William Saroyan was born in Fresno, California, on August 31, 1908, to Armenak and Takoohi Saroyan, Armenian immigrants. His father died when he was two years old; Saroyan and his siblings lived for the next five years in a Methodist orphanage in Oakland, California, while their mother worked as a domestic servant. Mother and children were reunited in Fresno in 1916. Saroyan left high school without a diploma in 1925, and went to work in an uncle's vineyards and offices. He had several jobs over the next few years, including a brief stint in the National Guard, before settling down as a local manager for Postal Telegraph in San Francisco in 1926. In 1928 the *Overland Monthly* bought his first article; he subsequently traveled to New York to seek his fortune, but returned home the next year and began another series of menial jobs.

In 1933 the Armenian magazine *Hairenik* published his poetry and his first short story, "The Broken Wheel," which was reprinted by Edward J. O'Brien in the 1934 *Best Short Stories* under the pseudonym Sirak Goyan, which he used on occasion early in his career. He made his reputation with "The Daring Young Man on the Flying Trapeze," published in *Story* in 1934, and the title story of his critically acclaimed collection published the same year. Further collections such as *Inhale and Exhale* (1936), *Little Children* (1937), *The Trouble with Tigers* (1938), *My Name Is Aram* (1940), and *The Assyrian and Other Stories* (1950) established Saroyan as one of the premier short-story writers of his generation.

In 1939 Saroyan turned to playwriting and directing; *My Heart's in the Highlands* and *The Time of Your Life* were immediate successes. *The Time of Your Life* won the Pulitzer Prize and the Critics Circle Award. Saroyan was an extremely prolific playwright of variable quality. Among his best-known plays are *The Beautiful People* (1941), *The Cave Dwellers* (1957), *The London Comedy* (1959), and *Settled Out of Court* (1959).

Saroyan led a somewhat troubled life; he periodically lost large sums of money gambling, and his marriage to Carol Marcus in 1942 was stormy, resulting in divorce in 1949, remarriage in 1951, and divorce again later the same year. He wrote extensively about his own life, in the autobiography *Here Comes There Goes You Know Who* (1962) and in several books of real and fictionalized memoirs, notably *The Bicycle Rider in Beverly Hills* (1952), *Boys and Girls Together* (1963), *Don't Go, But If You Must, Say Hello to Everybody* (1969), *Sons Come and Go, Mothers Hang in Forever* (1976), and *My Name Is Saroyan* (1983).

Saroyan was also noted for his work in Hollywood; a screenplay he wrote for MGM in 1942 was novelized to critical acclaim as *The Human Comedy* in 1943, but was never produced. Saroyan spent the last several years of his life as an American institution of sorts, writing largely about himself; his book *Obituaries* was nominated for an American Book Award in 1980. He died of cancer in Fresno on May 18, 1981.

Utilizing a spare quarter of an hour, Mr. Saroyan has written a not undiverting and by no means unnecessary demonstration of the fact that he was once even younger than he is now. *My Name is Aram* deals with the boyhood of a little shaver named Aram Garoghlanian, one of a numerous family. "As to whether or not," says Mr. Saroyan, "the writer himself is Aram Garoghlanian, the writer cannot very well say. He will, however, say that he is not, certainly *not* Aram Garoghlanian." Such coyness, pointing to a new and hitherto unsuspected reticence on Mr. Saroyan's part, need not be taken too seriously. It's a fair guess, with this or any other utterance by Mr. Saroyan, that he's talking about himself.

The method in this small book is no less familiar than the subject. Mr. Saroyan, as you all know, is the master of the guess-what's-coming school. His program is of the completely spontaneous and unrehearsed variety. Or, as he puts it, "If the truth is told, the writer, even as he wrote, was less writer than reader, and had as little idea as to what was coming next, for sure, as you are likely to have." Mr. Saroyan knows not what course others may take, but as for him, give him ad-liberty or give him death. *My Name Is Aram*, therefore, may be summarized as a series of extemporaneous remarks, some droll, some a touch dull, based on Mr. Saroyan's recollections

of his boyhood in and around Fresno, California, from 1915 to 1925.

All the Garoghlanians are eccentric and poetical, as you might guess, and their comments are in the now firmly established *Time of Your Life* tradition. Sometimes they are momentarily charming, these Garoghlanians, and sometimes momentarily wearying. In any case, their effect is momentary, as the effect of most extemporaneous remarks is apt to be. I happen to find wearying the anecdote about Cousin Mourad and the beautiful white horse; the one about the little Aram and his physical examination; the one about himself, his Cousin Arak, Miss Daffney, and the poem Arak wrote on the blackboard; the one about the circus; and the final anecdote, called "A Word to Scoffers." On the other hand, I find delightful Aram's adventures by letter with Lionel Strongfort; the story about his Cousin Dikran, the orator; the story of the Presbyterian choir singers, which is really funny rather than merely odd; and the one about Locomotive 38, the Ojibway Indian, which is the best piece of extemporaneousness in the book.

I regret that I cannot see in any of these sketches the "grown and many-colored artist, the genuine poet in prose, and spokesman for the youth of the world" that Mr.

Christopher Morley, for example, sees. They have the agreeable sentimentality that Mr. Saroyan's numerous opera have by now overfamiliarized us with, and at their best they are droll in a manner that is Mr. Saroyan's very own. The word "cute" is really the one I'm looking for; Mr. Saroyan is *cute*, cute as anything, and cuteness has its charm, no doubt. But all you have to do is stack this book up against *Tom Sawyer* or even *Penrod* or *The Story of a Bad Boy* to see that here is no masterpiece of boyhood. As for Mr. Saroyan's wisdom (life-is-so-lovely-and-queer-and-unexpected), I think I prefer my whimsy without frills, the way you get it in *Peter Pan*.

The illustrations, by Don Freeman, have their own ingratiating quality, but hardly seem to fit Mr. Saroyan's Armenians or to chime in with the wayward, non-literal Saroyan moods. Perhaps Mr. Saroyan should not be illustrated at all except in some highly volatile medium. Sky-writing? —CLIFTON FADIMAN, "William Saroyan's Songs of Innocence," *NY*, Dec. 28, 1940, pp. 61–62

In the past even the most fervent of Mr. Saroyan's admirers have had to admit that his greatest fault was a certain lack of self-discipline and form. He has now written his first novel, and it seems very little subject to this almost traditional criticism. *The Human Comedy* is a very moving book. It is a book you can read, and will want to read, in an evening, and when you have read it you will be the better for having read it. The story is typically Saroyan and depends upon devices which are not by any means original, but which are always effective when well handled. The principal device is the creation of a number of thoroughly good characters, good in a sense far exceeding the usual senses, good in a way that human nature never is good. Their every thought, action, word is kindly and wise and unselfish.

Of course, the trick is to do this without making them sugary or Pollyanna, and this is a trick which Mr. Saroyan mastered a long time ago. So we have the manager of a Postal Telegraph office; an old telegrapher; Mrs. Macauley, the widowed mother of all the Macauleys, who are really joint hero of the book. The effect produced is a strangely moral effect. (What philosophy there is is wacky, but it matters little.) You know perfectly well that people like this do not exist, that people never are so uniformly good. But somehow their doings and sayings do succeed in conveying that there is such a thing as natural goodness left in mankind, and that when we meet it we should value it and cherish it and recognize it for what it is.

Homer Macauley, the person we see the most of in the story, is a young messenger boy employed by the Postal Telegraph. His is a fine vantage point to observe what goes on in the small California city which is the locale of the novel. It is natural for a telegraph messenger to cross the paths of a great diversity of people and to be able to observe how they live and act. So by this perfectly simple device Mr. Saroyan gives form and structure to a novel covering the usual sprawling range of Saroyan characters. His secondary device is the Macauley family itself, with its son in the Army who gets killed and its daughter who becomes the girl of the soldier-son's buddy, with Mrs. Macauley and her youngest, the all-innocent Ulysses, and, of course, Homer himself. With these two unifying bonds, the book is knit firmly together, and one has the feeling, certainly unusual in Saroyan's work, that one would not like either to add or subtract a jot. It has been rumored that the text of the book was written after the forthcoming movie had been produced, which is very Saroyan indeed. But it makes one wonder whether other novelists might not benefit by trying the same system!

Perhaps the most striking thing about *The Human Comedy* is that it betrays none of the smart-aleck brashness which Saroyan seems to think is charming, and which he certainly has abused in his attempts to attract attention. That is clean gone, and we hope it never will return. Perhaps the realization that he was bound sooner or later to be inducted (it has since happened, and we have seen him in uniform eating Armenian grub at the Palace d'Orient on Lexington Avenue) into the Army and perhaps risk his life, has had a restraining effect. However this may be, *The Human Comedy* is the best Saroyan yet.—UNSIGNED, "Good Family," *Com*, Feb. 26, 1943, pp. 474–75

Mr. Saroyan's first novel, long awaited but never really expected, is almost exactly what one would have expected if one had really expected a novel out of Saroyan. Though it is a fairly short novel, it succeeds, like his stories and plays, in being discursive. It is profoundly romantic, deeply sentimental, indiscriminately compassionate, full of the curiosity of childhood and the naïveté which sometimes disturbingly approaches wisdom and sometimes only appears to. Mr. Saroyan himself would probably describe it as great, simple, cock-eyed and wonderful. Those of us who cannot, for lack of pin-point carbonation or other magic, always retain our effervescence must probably make some reservations.

Certainly *The Human Comedy* is simple. It records, without any particular regard to consecutiveness, incidents in the life of a town, Ithaca, Calif., and of a family, the Macauleys. The widow Macauley is a wise and wonderful mother. Bess Macauley is a pretty and young and wonderful girl. Homer Macauley, who gets a job as messenger at the Postal Telegraph office, is an intelligent and reliable and wonderful high school boy. Ulysses Macauley, his 4-year-old brother, is utterly fearless, incorrigibly curious and wonderful. Marcus Macauley, the oldest brother, whom the war ultimately kills, is brave and generous and understanding and wonderful, and plays the accordion. Other wonderful people are Spangler, the manager of the telegraph office; Grogan, the old sick, drunken, wise telegrapher, and Lionel Cabot, the neighborhood half-wit, "a great human being, faithful, generous and sweet-tempered."

The story, which concerns Homer Macauley's growing up to an understanding that everything is wonderful and worthy of love and compassion, and that even the death of his brother can neither interrupt nor impair the love which holds the family together, and that deep down all men are brothers and worthy of a brother's love, is a string of loosely connected incidents and anecdotes. Some of them, like the chapter in which the high school ancient history class wrangles and Homer Macauley delivers an oration on the nose, or the low-hurdle race after which some boys beat up the coach (almost the only non-wonderful person in the book), are neither credible nor amusing nor interesting. Others, like the capture of curious little Ulysses by a patented bear trap, come off better, and at least one, the lament of the melancholy grocer, Mr. Ara, over the vanity of human wishes, is quite simply wonderful.

Mr. Ara has spent most of the morning trying to satisfy the cravings of his sad little son with apples, oranges, candy, bananas. The heart's delight is in none of them. When a customer comes in wanting "cookies—raisins in" for a sick nephew, and both Mr. Ara's son and Mr. Ara's customer look hopefully to him to provide what he does not have. Mr. Ara is led to exclaim in despair, "*Is no cookies—raisins in.*" There never are cookies—raisins in. The heart's desire must remain unsatisfied. "Don't do this!" Mr. Ara shouts at his son. "Be happy! Be happy!"

That is what Mr. Saroyan is telling us all through this novel. Be happy! Be happy! I must confess that I like Mr. Ara's way of saying it better than Mr. Saroyan's. And though it seems almost unfair to appraise Mr. Saroyan on the basis of his ideas, or his Idea, and though he asks to be judged as a child, with a child's forgiveness and a child's wide-eyed innocence, still it is the philosophical underpinnings of Mr. Saroyan's writings which do not satisfy. He can be charming, he can be vastly amusing, he can be tender and innocent and even sometimes, as if by accident or inspiration, profound, but he can never be quite satisfying.

Mr. Saroyan is a complete romantic. His fancifulness, his ecstatic love and admiration for children and even half-wits, his enthusiasm, his delight, his wonder at everything and anything, his faith in the promptings of the heart over those of the head ("Trust your heart, which is a good one, to be right"), his conviction that good always drives out sickness and evil and that love conquers all, make him difficult to argue with. One can only disagree.

To understand all, Saroyan implies, is to forgive all, and to forgive all is to love all. No one is to blame for what he is, or even for what he does. We must take great care in judging and criticizing people unless we know how they got that way. That heresy has needed an inquisition for some time. Shall I, when I understand that the man who steals my rationed gasoline and ruins my daughter was spoiled by an indulgent mother, not merely forgive him but *love* him? Not in this world. I further think it intellectually dangerous and morally obfuscated to refer to half-wits as "great human beings." Both "great" and "human beings," being words, should mean something.

There are standards below which morality demands that human beings should not fall; there are scales of value and gradations of quality which the mind habituated to superlatives recks not of. Mr. Saroyan's is a mind habituated to superlatives; and though in theory he admits the presence of meanness and selfishness along with the native good in every man, in the practical job of building his characters he forgets that balancing set of impulses and creates a set of people who are almost monsters of goodness and naturalness and generosity and loving kindness. They say a good many sound and wise words, but their words ring hollow because they themselves are hardly credible.

If Spangler, Grogan, Mrs. Macauley, Homer and the rest were 70 per cent as decent and wonderful as they are in this novel, I would both believe and love them. But I cannot help feeling that the beauty and the goodness of the world, which Mr. Saroyan celebrates and in which I profoundly believe, are a more somber beauty and a less natural goodness than he implies. It is good to be alive, yes; it is better, unless one is a child, to be alive in the adult world with all its imperfections than in the fantasy world of a child where the imperfections are realized but not felt.—WALLACE STEGNER, "Saroyan's Wonderful People," *NYTBR*, Feb. 28, 1943, p. 7

———

Although he has always prided himself on his originality, William Saroyan's autobiography 〈*The Bicycle Rider in Beverly Hills*〉 follows the standard pattern of recollection for Americans who have made good, down to the lament for the lost boyhood and the questionably sincere confession of disenchantment with success. At 44, he is the perfect object of compassion with his Cadillac ("I have driven [it] more than 100,000 miles") and his "Spanish Mansion on North Rodeo in Beverly Hills," for which they soak him $445 a month: another wretch who spurned the blessings of failure and obscurity until it was too late, and now cries out in his anguish, "Enough of night, I want the light. Enough of culture's hours, I am a peasant. Enough of feasting, I want hunger. Enough of fat, I want muscle. . . ." He is so deeply moved by his own plight that he blurts out, between tears which could float a crocodile, that his poorest visitor in the recent past "was a writer who had just sold a story to a film producer for $50,000."

His writing has always been so full of junk, it is no wonder that his few good qualities have either been overlooked or deliberately ignored by most critics. These qualities, moreover, are of an unusual order, so that even if one is aware of their existence, he may well be at a loss what to make of them. With the provision that my remarks are not to be taken as a diagnosis of the writer but as a description of his work, I should say that Saroyan at his best turns out a peculiar literary version of schizophrenia. He writes of a world of strangers and loose ends in which there is no real human contact; it is a world in motion, but the laws of motion are suspended and none of the common patterns persists. Ordinary human feelings, such as hunger and loneliness—the two with which he is most often preoccupied—are presented in a minimum of setting, a social void, in which they are laid bare of the usual associations. The attention is concentrated on the isolated action or emotion, which is in turn distorted, blown out of its common proportions, by being projected out of context. The distinctions between dream and reality, imagination and fact are blurred, and the speeches and activities of his characters are a further acting-out of the schizophrenic's lonely phantasy-life, a charade in which the fixed meaning is contactlessness. At the same time, the distortion heightens the expressive effect, and what comes through, with a good deal of whimsical charm and insight, of Saroyan's "message"—that human beings are very much alone, and that there is in them and in the surrounding world a life-energy which renders every detail of existence precious—represents a preception which is frequently absent in the more crowded "realistic" view of the universe.

But "human kind cannot bear very much reality," and Saroyan can't stand even his own. He is in constant flight from it, dodging into any old corner, striking any odd pose to get away from his few moments of truthfulness and make perish the thought that he may have been serious. He acts very much like a man who has seen something that scared him, and yet wants the credit for what he has seen; and so he lays over his schizophrenic world a set of compulsions to restore it to commercial reality, and rattles his sentimentality, self-advertisement and saving vulgarity like a shaman working off a hex. This produces a remarkable result: with the exception of a few of the plays and short stories, nothing in his writing is nearly as noteworthy as the fact which has grown up around it—that he has converted charlatanism into a literary genre by discovering a way of both asserting and denying what he sees. No matter that he repudiates his own insight, reducing it in status to the fretwork on a cash register; it pays off. And it is a very neat trick, perhaps deserving its notoriety. One would think that the world of schizoprenia should lie out of reach of the success formula; and I can't help feeling as much a sense of surprise as of violation when I find its attenuated reality resting firmly in Saroyan's lunch hooks.—ISAAC ROSENFELD, "On One Built for Two," *NR*, Dec. 8, 1952, pp. 27–28

———

HARLAN HATCHER
"William Saroyan"

English Journal, March 1939, pp. 169–77

William Saroyan, the lively and vocal young Armenian-American from California, burst upon the literary scene in 1934 with such self-assertion that he could not be overlooked any longer. His short-story with the timely title, "The Daring Young Man on the Flying Trapeze," published by *Story* in January, 1934, won the O. Henry Memorial Award for the best short short-story of the year and was reprinted in the annual O. Henry collection with the observation that its author was "the most widely discussed discovery" of 1934. When the news came that the story had been accepted by the editors of *Story*, Saroyan deluged the magazine with his compositions, new and old, and before the year was over Random House had brought out a collection of twenty-six of these "stories" in a handsomely printed, odd-sized, book with the title *The Daring Young Man on the Flying Trapeze* stamped in black on a gold band. It became an immediate best seller, and the greatly unpublished writer of the Fresno vineyards was conspicuously in the public eye. He recorded this experience of becoming famous in a piece called "My Picture in the Paper."

Saroyan has kept himself in the spotlight almost continuously by his singular penchant for writing to the letter columns of the papers and magazines to protest criticisms of him by reviewers as his collections of stories keep coming from the press. Six volumes have already appeared in four years, magazines of all sorts are currently carrying his work, and there is no sign of the well going dry. That is to say, Saroyan has been before us long enough, and has accumulated a corpus of published work extensive enough, to warrant a critical examination and stock-taking. What is it all about?

First of all, it is chiefly about one William Saroyan, born in California of Armenian immigrants in 1908, how he has been growing up in the beautiful, mad, and tragic world before and after Hoover, what he has done and thought, and how it feels to be Mr. Saroyan inhaling and exhaling, meeting people, intoxicated with the awareness of his own separate ego in "the gay and melancholy flux," and fascinated by the fun of making comments on all that engages his restless attention by tapping away on the keys of a typewriter. His writing is intensely personal and contains a fairly complete autobiography, though it is important and only fair to remember that, since he usually employs the first person, even when writing of other characters, it is easy to mistake the created character for Saroyan himself.

Saroyan's own personality so completely dominates his writing, even when he tries to draw characters other than himself, that it becomes the first problem to be reckoned with. In the six collections published to date there are certain stories in which it is true that the author is excessively self-conscious, sometimes tricky, fond of posing, pleased with his own cleverness, and blatantly sardonic about the ways of the world which he observes with the beguiling naïveté of one who has just discovered it all for the first time in the history of the races of men. These particular qualities are offensive to many people—especially reviewers, who like to lecture him about them—and are responsible for the general opinion that has already taken hold of Saroyan's reputation and labeled him half-genius, half-phony. There are some grounds for this judgment, although they are easily exaggerated. In his percep-

tive, Whitman-like piece called "Myself upon the Earth," for example, included as the third story in his first collection, he wrote:

> I do not want to say the wrong thing. I do not want to be clever. I am horribly afraid of this. I have never been clever in life, and now that I have come to a labor even more magnificent than living itself I do not want to utter a single false word. For months I have been telling myself, "you must be humble. Above all things, you must be humble." I am determined not to lose my character.

That statement, of course, carries within it its own charming contradiction, and a humble Saroyan would not be William Saroyan whose writing we like. But, even assuming its truth, we turn to the facetious and boisterously clever preface to the collection and read:

> I immediately began to study all the classic rules, including Ring Lardner's, and in the end I discovered that the rules were wrong. . . . so I wrote some new rules.
>
> I wrote Number One when I was eleven and had just been sent home from the fourth grade for having talked out of turn and meant it.
>
> Do not pay any attention to the rules other people make, I wrote. They make them for their own protection, and to hell with them. (I was pretty sore that day.). . . .
>
> My third rule was: Learn to typewrite, so you can turn out stories as fast as Zane Grey.
>
> It is one of my best rules.

This side of Saroyan's personality, the simple explanation for which may be referred to the psychologists, is no doubt responsible also for the critical weakness which urges him to reprint some of his incredibly trivial pieces instead of allowing them to be generously forgotten in ephemeral magazine issues. But these irritations and mistakes of a boy suddenly famous in his mid-twenties, with his picture in the paper "along with a story about me and my writing," must not be permitted to obscure the fairly substantial number of rare and individual "stories" or the fresh young voice of this gifted writer.

Saroyan's first work was unique, perfectly timid (how important in our day!), and particularly refreshing. We had just come through the narrows of the depression in 1932–33. Each new sign of "recovery," however timorous, was publicized with rejoicing. The new and uninspired proletarian novels were flooding the market place. Then, at the beginning of 1934, Saroyan captured the newspaper headlines with his restrained and beautifully articulated story of the jobless young man who starved to death in a San Francisco rooming-house, with a single brightly polished penny on the table proclaiming "In God We Trust, Liberty, 1923," and some sheets of Y.M.C.A. paper on which he had begun to pen his "Application for Permission To Live." The story had utilized in an individual manner the new techniques for exploring the subconscious in sleep and wakefulness, it showed the tragic surrender of the young man crazed and sick with hunger, and it used the circus symbol of the flying trapeze, with exactly the right degree of irony, to enlarge the implications and to point the climax:

> *Through the air on the flying trapeze,* his mind hummed. Amusing it was, astoundingly funny. A trapeze to God, or to nothing, a flying trapeze to some sort of eternity; he prayed objectively for strength to make the flight with grace. . . . Then swiftly, neatly, with the grace of the young man on the trapeze, he was gone from his body. . . . The

earth circled away, and knowing that he did so, he turned his lost face to the empty sky and became dreamless, unalive, perfect.

In the more than two hundred Saroyan stories which have followed this beginning, few have reached the level of "The Daring Young Man," but many have used variants of the same theme. It is safe to say that nobody has spoken with greater poignancy and understanding of the dreams and sufferings of the impoverished young people in the 1930's than William Saroyan. He knows from firsthand personal experiences, as well as from observation, what it is like to be without the price of a date, a movie, a hamburger and coffee, or a week's rent of a dingy room. "You hear a lot of sad talk about all the young men who died in the Great War," he says in "Aspirin Is a Member of the N.R.A." "Well, what about this war? Is it less real because it destroys with less violence, with a more sustained pain?"

Some of Saroyan's best work is in this more serious vein. He writes about the dreams that disturb lonely young men in the furnished rooms. Sometimes it is poetry, random phrases remembered in dives and booking joints while they are "listening to the talk of another man, waiting for national recovery, *time to murder and create.*" Sometimes the depressed dreamer projects himself into the surroundings for which he longs and creates a house with a yard, trees, and flowers, a lovely girl at the door, and a fine job that will make a millionaire of him. For a brief moment it is all intensely real. In one especially good story with the title "1, 2, 3, 4, 5, 6, 7, 8," this longing for a sympathetic girl and romance gets itself identified with the haunting counterpoint of a cheap jazz record which he plays over and over on his phonograph. The eight swift chords beat on in his head with unaccountable persistence until they come to signify the approach of the same lonely desire of the girl at the other end of the teletype machine. Then, one sad day, the music and the girl, but not the longing, went away; so, also, in Saroyan restlessness, did the boy, "helplessly, weeping for this girl and the house, and sneering at myself for wanting more of life than there was in life to have." In another called "The Job," in the latest collection, *The Trouble with Tigers*, he writes of the bond of sentiment that unites through desperation two jobless and wandering boys, and of their code which compels the one who found a job to give support to his friend, and the more imperative code of self-respect which sends the friend on his way with the farewell, "All the luck in the world, kid, you'll need it."

All these stories make impressive reading. Though they tell of desperation and failure, they manage to keep to Saroyan's large thesis that "man has great dignity, do not imagine that he has not." They are well supported by another group, also in the serious vein, in which he writes about children and adolescence with a passionate closeness to experience that is almost as near as we can hope to get in words to the thing itself. He knows what it is like to sell papers on a street corner; to peddle oranges and curse poverty; to cut school for a day to wander about the country for no reason that he can explain to a schoolteacher; to lie in bed weeping for childhood's melancholy, far-off things; to smart under the vulgar personal remarks of grandmothers, uncles, and other relatives who notice his physical transitions; and the thousand and one impressions that make those early years so bewildering. In stories like "The World & the Theatre," "Resurrection of a Life," "Laura, Immortal," "The Oranges," in *Inhale & Exhale*; "And Man," in *The Daring Young Man*; several in the collection called *Little Children*; and the top-notch "The Man with His Heart in the Highlands" in *Three Times Three*,

Saroyan has made a genuine contribution to our short-story literature.

In still another group of stories that are more nearly personal essays, Saroyan has written of himself upon the earth and how he thinks and feels about it. Some of them are rather magnificent in the Emerson-Whitman manner, and some are only a little less impressive in the Byronic pose. These are the pieces that have excited most of the controversy among the reviewers. In them he tells himself about Man, Eternity, Death, Brotherhood, Literature, Love, Nothingness, the Great American Novel, and other large subjects. In "Myself upon the Earth" he says:

> The earth is vast. And with the earth all things are vast, the skyscraper and the blade of grass. . . . I am a story-teller, and I have but a single story—man. I want to tell this simple story in my own way, forgetting the rules of rhetoric, the tricks of composition. I have something to say and I do not wish to speak like Balzac.

In "The Tiger" he has his young author say:

> You see, when I write English I write Chinese, Japanese, Italian, French, and every other language. You see, I said, I am a writer. I write in every language, in English. . . . So far I have written only one word—God. . . . I wrote over two million false words before I achieved this one word.

He hopes to add two more words: *is* and *Love*. And in a characteristic and revealing passage in "A Cold Day" he reminds himself:

> Do not deceive. Do not make up lies for the sake of pleasing anyone. . . . Simply relate what is the great event of all history, of all time, the humble, artless truth of mere being. . . . The man you write of need not perform some heroic or monstrous deed in order to make your prose great. Let him do what he has always done, day in and day out, continuing to live. Let him walk and talk and think and sleep and dream and awaken and walk again and talk again and move and be alive. It is enough. There is nothing else to write about. You have never seen a short story in life. . . . Your own consciousness is the only form you need. Your own awareness is the only action you need.

This is a noble purpose with which no one could quarrel. But it is easier to announce the goal than to achieve it. It is not at all surprising that the author sometimes fails to arrive, or that he sometimes contents himself by staying at home entirely and talking about getting ready to commence to start. When he finds it hard to get going, he talks about his room, his typewriter, his cousin, his uncle, or Ezra Pound, or of his contempt for the phony and the trickster whom he can spot with uncommon accuracy in life or in the movies. That is, he is ill-content when he is not writing. When un-Saroyan authors would go into meditation to clarify and arrange their materials and wait for something to say, William Saroyan sits at his typewriter and writes about sitting at his typewriter without anything to say. When he runs down, he goes right on: "I don't feel like writing any more. How can anybody begin to mention everything." He ends "Myself upon the Earth" with these words:

> Day after day I had this longing, for my typewriter. This is the whole story. I don't suppose this is a very artful ending, but it is the ending just the same. The point is this: *day after day I longed for my typewriter.*

This morning I got it back. It is before me now and I am tapping at it, and this is what I have written.

In like manner, Saroyan, who is weak in invention but strong in perception, often does not construct his story; he merely blueprints it, puts up a scaffold, and contends that these appurtenances are more interesting than the finished structure. The people who stand for hours watching the steam shovels dipping dirt at Sixth Avenue and Forty-seventh Street will not be concerned with the smooth operation of the completed subway. William Saroyan is really too clever about it, even when he is good—as he usually is. His last collection, *The Trouble with Tigers*, has three of his good ones in this manner: "A Scenario for Karl Marx," "O.K. Baby, This Is the World," and "We Want a Touchdown." The second of these, incidentally, carries the Saroyan philosophy:

> The picture begins with this young doctor holding up a new-born baby by its legs and slapping life into it. The young doctor says, O.K. baby, this is the world, so inhale and exhale and be with us a while. They're not going to be kind to you out there because nobody was kind to them, but don't hate anybody. There's nobody to hate. You're going to be pushed around, and so forth and so on. That's the idea. He tells the baby how it is and what to expect and the story begins.

And in "We Want a Touchdown" he begins by telling his readers that he was, "by a great margin, the noisiest" writer that ever broke into print and then outlines a novel around one of those elaborate metaphors which he often uses so effectively, in this case the oval stadium, "holiest of all shapes," with the people looking *down* upon the field, the symbol of the world. "Sure, I said. If I were to concentrate on the theme I could do something great."

In this sentence Saroyan has offered a fair criticism of much of his writing. He plunges on headlong, trying to get the right word said about everything as he rushes by, and believing that, if you get that word said, everything is all right henceforth. He has tried to lunge at the human garden and grab the secrets of what grows there. Like other writers he has felt the barrier erected by words between perception and the report, and he has tried to tear through to greater immediacy. He therefore seldom takes time to construct a formal work, to tell an "artistic" story, or to follow the rules. He makes one story by throwing in crude, jagged-edged fragments of life on the wing, and then writes another to justify and explain his procedure and express his contempt for form. Some of his pieces are carried solely by their troubled impetuosity, as though he took seriously his own advice to a writer:

> Try to learn to breathe deeply, really to taste food when you eat, and when you sleep, really to sleep. Try as much as possible to be wholly alive, with all your might, and when you laugh, laugh like hell, and when you get angry, get good and angry. Try to be alive. You will be dead soon enough.

In fact, those words contain a summarizing truth about Saroyan. This sensitive but turbulent spirit who was kicked about in his youth by poverty and made to feel his separateness because he was Armenian; who writes with filial tenderness of his father, the unpublished writer and vine-grower of California, a man of great cultivation who had been a teacher of repute in his homeland but had fled it for political reasons and toiled as a janitor in New York to get money to bring the family to America; this young man, fulfilling in his own career toward acceptance and fame the ambition of his father, seems deter-

mined not to be embittered by experience and to let nothing escape until he can note it down in words. Inhale and exhale, and let the words fall into any shape they please, even if the result is sometimes, as Saroyan admits, some of "the worst prose ever written." His style, therefore, is like breathing and comes out now smooth and melodious, as some of the quoted examples show, and now in yells, in detached oaths and phrases from the street, and in the jerky rhythm of a man out of breath entirely. His sentence structure has been known to drive English teachers mad and to make Saroyan himself very happy. But there is always something behind the arrangements of the words. Here are two final examples of the unconnected, catalogue style in which he specializes, the first from "Woof Woof" and the second from "The Tiger" in *The Trouble with Tigers*:

> That's what money is. Forty-eight cents, forty-nine cents, woof woof, fifty cents, a cheap room in a decaying building on a main street, a hard bed containing eighty-five, eighty-six, woof woof, lice.
>
> After April came May and after New Orleans New York. Then June and the sea, Atlantic. Then Europe and the cities there, and I mean death, the tiger following each who lives, brother.

It must be obvious that with such a personality, interested in these materials, holding these views, and living in these dispersed times, one must reconcile one's self to accept what the author has to give and not complain too harshly because this tremendous talent is undisciplined and lacking in form and concentration. For his talent is genuine in its own genre, and his style, profane and raucous, impassioned and lyrical by turns, shows the beauty and the amorphousness that fits in with himself and the distracted discontinuity of his age.

MARY McCARTHY
"Saroyan, an Innocent on Broadway" (1940)
Sights and Spectacles
1956, pp. 46–52

William Saroyan has been in the writing business for eight years. He still retains his innocence. It is as valuable to him as an artist as virginity to Deanna Durbin. To keep it, he has, of course, had to follow a strict regimen—no late hours, no worries, and only a limited responsibility. That is, he has had to fight off Ideas, Movements, Sex, and Commercialism. Some of the benefits have been remarkable. He has stayed out of the literary rackets—the Hollywood racket, the New York cocktail-party racket, and the Stalinist racket, which became practically indistinguishable from both the others. What is more important, the well of inspiration, located somewhere in his early adolescence, has never run dry. He is still able to look at the world with the eyes of a sensitive newsboy, and to see it eternally brand-new and touched with wonder. The price is that the boundaries of this world are the boundaries of the newsboy's field of vision.

Saroyan is genuine, Saroyan is not mechanical, Saroyan is the real thing; he tells you this over and over again in the prefaces to his two plays. It is true. If you compare him with his contemporaries, Odets and Steinbeck, the purity of his work is blinding. Puerile and arrogant and sentimental as he may be, he is never cheap. Both Odets and Steinbeck are offering the public a counterfeit literature: Odets is giving an imitation of a lacerated Bronx boy named Odets who once wrote a play;

Steinbeck is giving an imitation of a serious novelist. Saroyan as a public figure does an impersonation of Saroyan, but as a writer he plays straight. Moreover, both Odets and Steinbeck suffer from a kind of auto-intoxication; they are continually plagiarizing themselves; and their frequent ascents into "fine writing" are punctuated with pauses for applause that are nearly audible. Now Saroyan, as I say, has created a public character for himself, and the chief attribute of this character is exhibitionism, but he has incorporated this character bolding into his work and let him play his role there. Vanity has become objectified and externalized; it has no need to ooze surreptitiously into the prose. Saroyan's writing remains fresh and crisp and never has the look of having been pawed over by the author. Furthermore, though Saroyan's work is all of a piece, and the same themes and symbols recur, you will rarely find a constellation of symbols repeating itself, you will rarely get the same effect warmed up for a second serving.

It may be that Saroyan's world of ice-cream cones and toys, of bicycles and bugles, and somersaults and shotguns, of hunger and of banquets that appear out of the air, of headlines that tell of distant disasters, of goodhearted grocers and lovable frauds, of drunk fairy princes and pinball games that pay, is naturally more at home in the theatre than in fiction. Or it may be that, his scope being necessarily as narrow as it is, he has exhausted the permutations of the short story and requires the challenge of a new medium. At any rate, he has written these two plays ⟨*My Heart's in the Highlands*, *The Time of Your Life*⟩; one caused a furore and the other is a hit.

My Heart's in the Highlands, produced by the Group Theatre on a geometric set, was the source of some distress to the New York critics, who had been getting acquainted with "fantasy" and "the poetic drama" through the agency of Maxwell Anderson. The meaning is in the title, "My heart's in the Highlands, my heart is not here, My heart's in the Highlands a-chasing the deer." It is a story of poor people and their hunger for poetry and music and theatre, which persists in the teeth of want, but can only be partly satisfied because society will not pay for these things. There are three principal characters: a poet and his son, and a fugitive from the Old People's Home, an ancient Shakespearean actor who plays the bugle. The critics talked about "experimental theatre" and "surrealism," but neither of these terms was quite satisfactory, even to the critics themselves. Actually, the play is half a pastoral and half a vaudeville. In *The Time of Your Life*, which was produced this year by Eddie Dowling on a realistic set, the pastoral element has dropped out, and what is left is almost pure vaudeville, a play that is closer to *Hellzapoppin* than to anything else in the theatre.

The action of this play takes place in a San Francisco waterfront saloon in the year 1939. Again there is a group of relatively simple people, a pure-hearted prostitute, a boy out of a job, a pinball enthusiast, a nice cop, a nice longshoreman, a Negro piano player, a hoofer, a mad old trapper, the proprietor of the saloon, a nurse, and a stiff young man who is desperately in love with her. All these characters seem to be trailing clouds of glory; they are beautiful and terrible just because they *are* people, Saroyan thinks. Each of them wants to do his own job, to do it tenderly, reverently, and joyfully, and to live at peace with his neighbors. Unfortunately, there are Frustrators at work, monstrous abstractions like Morality, and Labor and Capital, whose object is to flatten out these assertive individualists. The chief of these Frustrators is a Vice-Squad man named Blink, who stands for Morality, but Finance Capital is in the room in the shape of a gentleman slummer, and the voice of Labor can be heard outside in the waterfront strike.

But if this universe has its devil in Blick, it has its God in Joe, the character played by Eddie Dowling, a charming, indolent alcoholic, whose mysterious wealth is the life-blood of the joint. Buying champagne, buying newspapers, ordering drinks for the house, giving handouts to the Salvation Army, to the boy out of a job, to the unfortunate prostitute, he keeps the people of the play going, but, being detached from the life of action, he is powerless to save them from Blick. This is left for one of their own numbers, the old trapper (God the Son), who shoots the interfering moralist as calmly as if he did it every day, and regretfully throws his beautiful pearlhandled revolver into San Francisco Bay. When Joe sees that everything is straightened out, and that the two main characters are ready to start life on their own, he goes home, and the understanding is that he will not be back tomorrow.

There is no point in commenting on this intellectual structure, for it is not an intellectual structure at all, but a kind of finger-exercise in philosophy. Whenever it makes itself explicit, its juvenility is embarrassing; when it is allowed to lie somewhere behind the lines, it gives the play a certain strangeness, another dimension that is sensed but not seen. The real living elements of the play, however, owe nothing to philosophy; they stem straight from the Keith Circuit. Saroyan is still drawing on the street-life of his adolescence; it is inevitable, therefore, that his plays should belong to the theatre of that street-life, that is, to vaudeville. *The Time of Your Life* is full of vaudeville; indeed, almost every incident and character in it can be translated back into one of the old time acts. Kit Carson, the trapper, is W. C. Fields; the pinball machine that plays "America" and waves a flag when the jackpot is hit is out of Joe Cook; the toys Joe buys are a visual reminder of the juggling turn, and his money, deriving from nowhere and ostentatiously displayed, makes you think of the magic act; the young man who keeps telephoning his girl is the comic monologist; Harry the hoofer is Jimmy Durante; the boy out of a job is the stooge; and Joe (or God), as played by Eddie Dowling, who is himself an ex-hoofer, has that slim, weary, sardonic, city-slicker look that was the very essence of the vaudeville artist. Even the serious part of the play, the soul-searing drama involving Kitty, the beautiful prostitute, and the boy who wants to marry her, and Blick, takes you back to those short problem melodramas starring a passée actress that were occasionally interspersed with the regular acts. And *The Time of Your Life*, like an evening of vaudeville, is good when it engages the fancy and bad when it engages the feelings. *My Heart's in the Highlands* was a slightly different case. The sentiment there was a little cloying but not false. It proceeded from a different and more untainted source, the folk tale or pastoral that was also a part of Saroyan's Armenian-American boyhood.

Saroyan is in love with America, and very insistent about it. Just as a girl in his plays will be an ordinary girl and at the same time "the most beautiful girl in the world," because Saroyan is young and feeling good when he looks at her, so America is an ordinary place and at the same time "the most wonderful country in the world." This excessive, rather bumptious patriotism has created a certain amount of alarm; it has been suspected that Saroyan has joined the propagandists of the second crusade for democracy. The alarm is, I think, unjustified. Actually, the second statement is no more realistic than the first; it is not the literal fact but the state of mind that the reader is asked to believe in. And there is a kind of pathos about both statements that arises from the discrepancy that must exist between the thing described and the description of it. How far, in the second case, the pathos is intentional it is impossible to tell, but the contrasts in Saroyan's work show that he is at least partly aware of it.

In each of these plays there is a character that, more than the "gentle people" he talks so much about, represents the America he loves. This national type, exemplified by the bugler in *My Heart's in the Highlands* and by the trapper in *The Time of Your Life*, is an elderly boaster who is both a fraud and not a fraud, an impostor and a kind of saint. In *My Heart's in the Highlands* the bugler, with all his pretensions, is just a fugitive from the Old People's Home; yet, from the point of view of the people in the play, he is everything he purports to be, and more; he is the light-bringer. The same thing is true of the trapper in the second play, but the point is better made. Beginning with "Did you ever fall in love with a midget weighing thirty-nine pounds?" Kit Carson moves along through the plot telling one tall tale after another. At the end, after he has shot Blick offstage, he comes into the saloon and begins a narrative that sounds exactly like all the others: "Shot a man once. In San Francisco. In 1939, I think it was. In October. Fellow named Blick or Glick or something like that." This statement is a bombshell. It gives veracity to all the improbable stories that have preceded it, and at the same time the improbable stories cast a doubt on the veracity of this statement, which the audience nevertheless knows to be true. A boast becomes a form of modesty, and the braggart is maiden-shy.

This kind of character undoubtedly belongs to the tradition of American life and especially to the tradition of the West. It is Paul Bunyan and it is also the barker. But the tradition is dead now; it died when the frontier closed on the West Coast at some point in Saroyan's childhood. The type, if it exists at all outside of W. C. Fields, is now superannuated, for such anomalous human beings could only thrive under nomadic conditions of life. Today the barker has become an invisible radio announcer, and the genial, fraudulent, patent-medicine man has turned into a business house, with a public relations counsel. The America Saroyan loves is the old America, and the plays he weaves around it are not so much daring innovations as legends.

PHILIP RAHV

"William Saroyan: A Minority Report"

American Mercury, September 1943, pp. 371–77

I

When William Saroyan first began boosting his own "genius," it was taken for granted that this was but a passing phase in the career of a talented and spirited young writer. But Saroyan, persisting in his campaign, was knowingly or not acting on the principle that people are bound to believe you if you speak your piece loudly enough, and with sufficient frequency and self-confidence. Thus one noticed that a good many reviewers were beginning to support Saroyan's account of his own merits. And with the publication earlier this year of *The Human Comedy*, his first novel, it became altogether plain that most of them had finally been induced to abandon their previous reservations. Only a few hardy souls held out against the tide of enthusiasm that swept the book-pages. Clifton Fadiman, long out of patience with the Saroyan-cult, dismissed the latest opus by dubbing its author "the kiddies' Tolstoy." And though Fadiman is an influential critic, in this instance he was simply ignored by his colleagues.

It is some months after seeing the reviews that I read the novel. It seemed to me a puerile performance. Puerile not merely because it is a bad novel, but because of the glaring contradiction between its actual content and truly grandiose pretensions. For my part, I prefer a straight job of commercial writing to this compendium of pious sayings and pretty pictures of life as it is precisely *not* lived in a small California town or anywhere else. In most cases the commercial writer makes no bones about what he is up to. Saroyan, on the other hand, has been so oversold to the public that he can now pass himself off as a seer, a moralist, and a philosopher in a work which is in fact part and parcel of the escape-literature of our time.

There would be no point, of course, in taking Saroyan quite so seriously if it were not for the significance of his career as a symptom of the age we live in—as an object lesson in the atrophy of taste and decay of values to which the national literature has been exposed since the early 1930's. The fine level achieved by American writing in the past has virtually been forgotten. A new gentility now prevails, and those affected by it see nothing amiss in our creative life. The kind of sweetness and light shed by Saroyan, we are told, is exactly what we need to bolster our morale. But the truth is that fifteen or even ten years ago a novel like *The Human Comedy* would have made its author the laughingstock of the literary profession. Moreover, if Saroyan is at all the cagey fellow that I judge him to be, he is hardly the man to have produced such a novel except when it happens to suit current requirements.

The Human Comedy is composed according to the formula of "Ah, the wonder, the beauty, the poetry of it all!" made famous in Saroyan's plays. But the plays include scenes of pure vaudeville—some of it first-rate—which partly saves them from the unctuousness, the uplift, and sheer gush of this new work of fiction. Actually this work is a scenario in novel-form that technically as well as morally meets the specifications of the movie-trade. Which is not to say, however, that it is an ordinary Hollywood product. In a sense it is all the worse for being so much more ambitious. It is Hollywood in a playful mood yet gooey with love and spiritual yearnings—in other words, Hollywood camouflaged in the typical Saroyan manner. And this camouflage consists of a show of innocence and naïveté which is at bottom nothing more than the very latest form of commercial sophistication. People have been so frightened by the horrid events of recent years that they would like to be absolved of all responsibility, to see themselves as intrinsically innocent and naïve. The formula devised by Saroyan at once exploits and expresses this abject state of mind.

In a novel, as in any work of art, the form and content are so much of a piece that the quality of the one may be judged from the quality of the other. Now if *The Human Comedy* is examined from the formal angle, its pretensions can be seen through at a glance. This novel has the structure of a kindergarten primer; and its use of language is equally elementary. It is a use of language derived from the simplified prose-narrative of authors like Gertrude Stein, Anderson, and Hemingway. But Saroyan has further softened up this verbal technique; it goes slack in his hands because his purpose as a writer of fiction is so childishly simple as to eliminate any real need for a renewed effort in the handling of words.

But what about the characters of this novel? I would say that, properly speaking, there are none. The Macauley family, the telegraph operator Grogan, the office manager Spangler, the history teacher Miss Hicks—all of them, with the sole exception of the old-style villain, Byfield, are just so many versions of Saroyan in his corniest public rôle: that of the supremely devoted lover of mankind. All are impersonations of

Saroyan incessantly repeating that people are wonderful, life is wonderful, death is wonderful, war is wonderful and peace is wonderful—Saroyan saying "yes to all things"—Saroyan declaiming that evil is unreal and that only "the good endures forever."

Now it must take the fanciest kind of smugness to assert the unreality of evil in the midst of the most murderous war in history. But why deal at length with Saroyan's ideas? In so far as they are associated with Christian ideas, they belong to that innocuous and hence debased type of Christianity from which the tragic concept of evil had been removed. The rest is a mishmash of Whitmanesque pantheism, romantic rapture, and literary bohemianism thickly flavored with the famous Saroyan cuteness. No wonder the characters of *The Human Comedy* resolve their difficulties and tensions through sentimental dodges and are given to making long didactic speeches. The messenger boy, Homer Macauley, is an insufferably loquacious little saint, and if the child, Ulysses, comes off somewhat better it is mainly because he is too young to philosophize. This novel, ostensibly a picture of American boyhood, has more in common with Louisa Alcott's *Little Women* than with Mark Twain's *Huckleberry Finn*.

Saroyan's apologists will doubtless argue that I criticise him unfairly because his proper sphere is fantasy rather than realism. But literature is primarily concerned with the truth of human experience, and the writer of fantasies is no more exempt from searching out the truth than the writer of realistic fiction. Fantasy, like realism, is one technique among many. To the genuine artist it is but a means to an end—and the end is always the same.

II

To explain Saroyan's development one must go back to his first book, *The Daring Young Man on the Flying Trapeze*. It is still his best book, I think, dealing as it does not with the warmed-up abstractions of goodness and loving-kindness but with the very real theme of a starving young writer waiting for recognition and for "national recovery." The stories communicate feelings of loss and loneliness, and of defiance mixed with self-pity. Throughout the author strikes the note of bohemian dissidence—of the artist-hero who scorns social conventions and who likes nothing better than to exhibit his humor, his sensitive nature, and his integrity. But this "daring young man" is a familiar figure in modern fiction; you will find detailed accounts of him in all the languages of the Western world. One thought at the time that Saroyan was making too much of a fuss about him. Yet in retrospect one can see that it was an authentic portrait, set against an indigenous background, and fully conveying the subject's peculiar temperament, composed in equal measure of lyrical conceit and plain exasperation.

But the important thing about the "daring young man" as a type is what happens to him after he has broken through his isolation and come out into the world at large. What happened to Saroyan is that he became an enthusiast or, better still, an addict of his own success. The consequences are to be observed in the work he has published since *The Daring Young Man*. The writing in his first book is immensely superior to the writing in such later volumes as *Inhale and Exhale; Love, Here Is My Hat; Peace, It's Wonderful*, and *Aram*. The sharp speaking, the astringent taste of the early pieces is gone; what remains is the rhetoric and the cuteness. It is true that *Aram* contains some fine chapters; but in the greater part of it Saroyan is exploiting his Armenian background for its picturesqueness and so-called exotic humor. In reading the later

stories one generally feels that their author is not really composing them but ad-libbing from start to finish, that he is trading more and more on his reputation as a "character." The recreation of experience is replaced by mere talk about it—anecdotal and self-indulgent talk.

Saroyan seems incapable of grasping the crucial difference between the mere statement of a theme and its actual representation. This is why his prose is so markedly deficient in nearly all the primary elements of craft. And there is no craft without control. Above all, craft means the analysis and calculation of effects, the creative power of locating and mastering the endless difficulties of the medium. The old-time notion of art as pure inspiration and self-expression has long ago been discarded by the best modern thinking on the subject. In arguing the merits of his work, Saroyan has tried to revive this notion. He assumes that the charm of his spontaneity makes up for his lack of discipline. But spontaneity loses its charm when it becomes *chronic*, when there is literally no escape from it. Within a literary framework it sooner or later turns into a stratagem, a means of concealing the writer's inner passivity and tendency to easy accommodations.

III

In his plays Saroyan recovers his losses to some extent. This is particularly true of the shorter pieces. In some of the skits—*Hello Out There, Since Alexandre Dumas, The Great American Goof*—the lyrical strain in Saroyan and his talent for spoofing combine to form a kind of stylized vaudeville which has deep roots in urban folk-life and in the popular traditions of the theatre. The best of his shorter pieces, though, is the one act play *My Heart's in the Highlands*, where he succeeds in creating a scene and characters that truly objectify his formula of innocence.

But in his plays, as in his stories, Saroyan imitates himself *ad infinitum*. Having hit it off once in *My Heart's in the Highlands*, he has used the same dramatic scheme ever since. In the longer play this scheme invariably gets out of hand, spoiling the excellent fun of the vaudeville passages. The vaudeville is very good in *The Time of Your Life*, for example, especially in the Kit Carson episodes; but the stuff about the angelic streetwalker and the millennial person called Joe is pure corn. And as usual Saroyan goes too far in advancing his claims. Not content to let us enjoy his pastoral sentiments for what they are, he must needs try to persuade us that they contain deep ideas—a complete system of values, in fact.

Some of our drama critics have a good deal to answer for in building up Saroyan's reputation as a playwright "with ideas." Actually these ideas come to nothing more than the literary bohemianism or nihilism of *The Daring Young Man* minus its note of dissidence and exasperation. It is the initial Saroyan "ideology" rendered harmless and revamped in other ways to suit a more prosperous and respectable audience. The plot now deals not with a starving young man trying to push open the door to life but with lovable though somewhat erratic people who miraculously solve all problems simply by loafing and inviting their souls. This is the fairy-tale aspect of the Saroyan plays, and basically this is what accounts for their popular appeal.

Saroyan is so concerned with his own ego that now and then he cannot resist divulging the secret of his success. Each of his books contains at least one such revelation, suggesting that behind the formula of innocence there lurks an uncanny old-world cynicism, a cynicism so natural and so utterly taken for granted that it can well afford to manifest itself in a manner at once genial and sardonic.

Take, for instance, the last chapter in *Aram*, where the hero, leaving his large and ever so picturesque Armenian family, goes off to New York to make his fortune. On the way he stops over at Salt Lake City, and as he stands on a street-corner smoking a five-cent cigar and trying to get over his "young irreligious poise," he is accosted by a tall and melancholy-looking man who hands him a pamphlet entitled A *Word to Scoffers*. "Son, are you saved?" the tall man asks Aram. "I'm leaving town in fifteen minutes," Aram replies. Whereupon the man assures him that he once saved someone in four minutes. All he's got to do is to change his attitude.

That ought to be easy, I said.
    Easiest thing in the world, he said.
    I'm game, I said, I've got nothing to lose. How do I change my attitude?
    Well, said the religious man, you stop trying to figure things out and you believe.
    Believe, I said, believe *what*?
    Why, everything, he said. Everything you can think of, left, right, north, east, south, west, upstairs, downstairs and all around, inside out, visible and invisible, good and bad and neither and both. That's the little secret. . . .
    Is that all I have to do? I said.
    That's all, son, said the missionary.
    O.K., I said, I believe.
    Son, said the religious man, you're saved. You can go to New York now or anywhere else, and everything will be smooth and easy.

The closing paragraph of this chapter is equally interesting. Aram is now riding out from Salt Lake City and thinking over the lesson learned from the odd-looking missionary:

I thought I was kidding the old padre . . . getting back my vast book-knowledge and anti-religious poise, but I was sadly mistaken, because unwittingly I had been saved. In less than ten minutes after the bus left Salt Lake City I was believing everything, left and right, as the missionary had said, and it's been that way with me ever since.

I, for one, am disposed to take Aram's word for it. All spoofing aside, what else has his author been preaching all these years if not the doctrine of the old padre of Salt Lake City?

WILLIAM J. FISHER
"What Ever Happened to Saroyan?"

College English, March 1955, pp. 336–40, 385

In 1940, William Saroyan was a national legend. At the age of thirty-three, some seven years after his first story had been published, he was a phenomenally successful author and a familiar public personality, billed as "The Great Saroyan" in the feature article of a popular magazine. Over four hundred of his stories had been published, in nine collected volumes (*The Daring Young Man on the Flying Trapeze; Inhale and Exhale; Love, Here Is My Hat; My Name Is Aram*, etc.) and in just about every magazine in the country—from *Harper's* and the *Yale Review* to the *New Masses*, and from *Story* and the *New Yorker* to *Redbook* and *Esquire*. Three of his plays had been produced successfully on Broadway within a span of thirteen months, and he had turned down the Pulitzer prize awarded to one of them (*The Time of Your Life*). While columnists and reporters made flamboyant copy out of his egocentric idiosyn-

crasies, his bons mots were being repeated in salons and saloons from coast to coast.

Saroyan not only had gained material success and popular fame; he also had become a recognized, though controversial, literary figure. Some critics were acclaiming him as the Mark Twain of the twentieth century; at least as many were denouncing him as an exhibitionist, an escapist, a slick phony, a sentimental ass, a conceited and immature hack without talent or craft. Between these extremes, Edmund Wilson wrote qualifiedly in 1940 that "at their best, his soliloquies and stories recall the spontaneous songs of one of those instinctive composers who, with no technical knowledge of music, manage to finger out lovely melodies."

Today, Saroyan is still writing, still turning out a steady stream of plays, novels, stories, and radio and television scripts. But something has happened, somewhere along the way. For though Saroyan has his devotees, his fame and the quality of his work have fallen off sharply.

The story of William Saroyan's amazing success and rapid decline is, in microcosm, a history of American optimism. Saroyan rose in mid-Depression as a bard of the beautiful life, a restorer of faith in man's boundless capacities; he has declined as a troubled pseudo-philospher, forced to acknowledge man's limitations, yet uncomfortable in the climate of Evil. Indeed, he has come to dwell on Evil in order to deny its reality, reasserting, blatantly and defensively now, the American Dream of Unlimited Possibilities and Inevitable Progress. As a self-styled prophet of a native resurgence—believing in the virtue of self-reliant individualism, in the innate goodness of man and the rightness of his impulses—he has followed the tradition of American transcendentalism. (One critic has quite seriously called Saroyan the creator of "the new transcendentalism.") But it need hardly be said that Saroyan is no Emerson, either by temperament or by talent. The extent to which his later work has failed reflects, in one sense, the inadequacy of his equipment for the task he set himself. Yet it is also true that Saroyan is the representative American of the mid-twentieth-century, a man baffled at the failure of the Dream but unwilling to give it up; incapable of facing his dilemma frankly or of articulating it meaningfully.

When Saroyan's stories began appearing in the early 1930's, the literature of the day was somber with gloom or protest. And though Saroyan's fiction was also born of the Depression, often telling of desperate men, of writers dying in poverty, it nevertheless managed a dreamy affirmation. Politically and economically blind, Saroyan declared himself bent on a one-man crusade in behalf of the "lost imagination in America." In an era of group-consciousness, he was "trying to restore man to his natural dignity and gentleness." "I want to restore man to himself," he said. "I want to send him from the mob to his own body and mind. I want to lift him from the nightmare of history to the calm dream of his own soul."

This concept of restored individuality governed Saroyan's principal attitudes, his impulsive iconoclasm as well as his lyrical optimism. While Saroyan joined the protestants in damning the traditional villains—war, money, the success cult, standardization—he was really attacking the depersonalization which such forces had effected. He was just as much opposed to regimentation in protest literature as in everyday life. ("Everybody in America is organized except E. E. Cummings," he complained.) Writing about foreigners and exiles, the meek and isolated, "the despised and rejected," he celebrated the "kingdom within" each man. The artists in his stories preserved a crucial part of themselves; there was spiritual survival and triumph, let economics fall where it might. And in the glowing stories about men close to the earth of their vineyards, about glad children and fertile, generous women, Saroyan was affirming what he called the "poetry of life" and exalted with capital-letter stress: Love, Humor, Art, Imagination, Hope, Integrity.

In effect, Saroyan was restoring the perspective without which the writers of the thirties had often (for obvious reasons) reduced the individual potential to a materialism of physical survival. When a character in one of his plays insisted that food, lodging, and clothes were the only realities, another responded, "What you say is true. The things you've named are all precious—if you haven't got them. But if you have, or if you can get them, they aren't." However limiting Saroyan's simplifications might prove, they none the less contained important truths which had been lost sight of amidst the earnestness of agitation-propaganda. If Saroyan is given any place in future literary histories, he should be credited with helping to relax ideologically calcified attitudes.

Saroyan began writing plays in 1938. By 1942, he had completed six full-length plays and sixteen one-acters, and four of them (*My Heart's in the Highlands, The Time of Your Life, Love's Old Sweet Song, The Beautiful People*) had been produced on Broadway. Saroyan had become, for the moment, an important force in the American theatre—a symbol and an inspiration to playwrights, actors, and audiences. He had come to stand not only for personal freedom after the years of economic and emotional austerity, but also for freedom in style and form.

Whereas Saroyan's stories were often reminiscent of Mark Twain, Sherwood Anderson, or John Steinbeck, there was no recognizable literary tradition behind his playwriting. Rather, it was the showmanship and theatricality of the popular entertainers, made euphonious and articulate, that went into these early plays. "I take pride," Saroyan wrote, "in having sneaked into every theatre in my home town [Fresno, California] . . . ; into every circus that came to town; into the County Fairs; into the Summer stock company shows." He had developed a decided preference for vaudeville over Ibsen, Oscar Wilde, and the other "serious dramatists" because it was "easygoing, natural, and American."

Thus, his best works for the stage gave the impression of a jamboree which was springing to life spontaneously, right before one's eyes. The inhibitions of both stage people and audience were lifted by a mood of gentle intoxication (sometimes alcoholic, sometimes not). The impulse to play and sing and dance was given free rein without concern for plot or didactic point. In *The Time of Your Life*, a dancer, a boogie-woogie pianist, and a harmonica-player were casually introduced and as casually allowed to go through their paces. The children in the plays were instructed by the stage directions to enjoy themselves as children do—turn somersaults, whistle, stand on their heads, and the like.

Saroyan's element, indeed, was the flexible time of childhood; he was at his best when writing about dreams fulfilled and faith justified. He was a teller of joyful tales and tales of high sentiment, making a revel of life and lyricizing death, hardship, and villainy.

But not long after the peak of his success at the beginning of the forties, Saroyan's writing began to change. Concerned about the onesidedness of his outlook, he set out to *justify* his unadulterated hopefulness. Instead of the airy, uncontested supremacy of beauty and happiness, there were now, as Saroyan began to see things, misery and ugliness to contend with, imperfection to account for. At the same time that he took cognizance of the dark side of life, he began trying to *prove*

all for the best in the best of all possible worlds, with the result that his novels and plays became strange battlegrounds where belief struggled with skepticism. To retain his perfectionist version of man's life on earth, yet to get rid of the unpleasant realities he had come to acknowledge—this was Saroyan's new burden. Recently, in *The Bicycle Rider in Beverly Hills*, he has described his dilemma quite frankly, revealing the roots of an incurable, an implacable, optimism:

> Most of the time I felt that man was rightfully wonderful and dignified but had had these profound and powerful aspects of his nature driven out of him by something or other. Upon trying to understand what it was that had driven man away from himself I ran into grave difficulty. . . .
> I wanted him to be wonderful.
> I wanted his life—the minutes and years straight from birth to death—to be easy, joyous, loving, and intelligent.
> I wanted his death—or his end—to come as a benediction.
> I believed all this *could* happen, could be *made* to come to pass. [Saroyan's italics]

Among the earliest works to demonstrate that Saroyan was no longer able to dismiss "evil" casually or to proclaim "belief" summarily was his first novel, *The Human Comedy* (which Saroyan wrote originally as a motion picture in 1943). The protagonist was Saroyan's favorite character type—a young dreamer with untainted senses, a rich imagination, and warm sympathies. Instead of following the old blithe Saroyanesque line, however, the book became a study in doubt and faith, tracing prophetically the pattern of Saroyan's own career. The young hero, a Western Union messenger, is nearing the age of disenchantment and is especially vulnerable because he has been nourished on inflated ideals and has never been allowed to know adversity. His trust in the benevolence of the universe is consequently threatened when his personal idol, an older brother, goes off to war and faces death.

The outcome is abrupt and arbitrary, as Saroyan contrived to dissolve the conflict with a happy ending. The brother is killed in the war, and the boy is about to plunge into despair when, before mourning can get under way, a wounded buddy of the dead soldier—fortuitously an orphan without ties—appears on the scene and quite literally takes the brother's place in the household as if nothing had happened. Saroyan explained this miracle by inflating his idea of brotherliness into a concept of universal oneness which permits live men to be substituted for dead ones. Since "none of us is separate from any other," according to the logic of the novel, and since "each man is the whole world, to make over as he will," the stranger is able to become at once the son, brother, and lover that his friend had been. It is as simple as this because Saroyan is running the show. Death and disaster are ruled out of order, and the boy's illusions are protected.

But Saroyan was paying a high price for the preservation of unlimited possibilities. This novel had lost all but a modicum of the Saroyanesque buoyancy. In the course of thwarting misfortune, the author had to let the boy abandon his pranks and dreams to face the prospect of sorrow. Meanwhile, there was a moral point that had to be reinforced by sermons on virtue. Large doses of speculative talk adulterated the dreamy atmosphere. Always inclined toward sentimentality, Saroyan now landed with both feet deep in mush. By dwelling on the love and goodness he had previously taken with a skip and a holler, Saroyan was suffocating spontaneity.

In a recent radio interview on India's neutrality in

American-Soviet affairs, Henry Cassidy of N.B.C. asked Mme. Pandit whether one did not have to decide once and for all which side was *right* and which side was *wrong*. "Only an American could have asked that question," replied Mme. Pandit. The fact that this concept of the mutual exclusiveness of good and bad, right and wrong, beautiful and ugly has become an underlying assumption in Saroyan's struggle against disbelief is evidence of his "Americanism."

As Saroyan's success receded, a tart defiance began to sour his public personality. In an effort to defy financial backers who were now shying away from his plays because of weak scripts and uncertain box-office appeal, Saroyan, in the summer of 1942, embarked on an independent venture called "The Saroyan Theatre," devoted to the presentation on a repertory basis of the dramatic works of William Saroyan, with Saroyan as director, producer, and financial sponsor. The project closed six days after it opened, the impresario loudly blaming everybody connected with the production except himself. It was about this time that Saroyan wrote, "Listen to Saroyan. Ignore his critics. Spit in their eyes."

Within a few months after this debacle, Saroyan was drafted into the Army. After almost three years of resentful desk-service as a private, a period during which he did no writing—in protest against his being conscripted when he should have been serving humanity as a civilian writer—he recorded his angry sentiments in a diary (*The Adventures of William Saroyan*) and a novel (*The Adventures of Wesley Jackson*). The books were weighted down with aimless vitriol about the indignities of war and the Army; and in attempting to write seriously about statesmanship, propaganda, and international affairs, Saroyan exposed to full view his lack of intellectual discipline and integrative capacity.

Saroyan has perennially boasted an aesthetics of no-effort, denouncing "intellectualism" and contending that a man should write as a hen lays eggs—instinctively, without thought or planning. Confusing laziness with casualness and spontaneity, he has continued to oversimplify. Part of Saroyan's charm had been the way he had often, in his enthusiasm for everyday things and people, blurred but intensified the lines of his picture with superlatives: "The loveliest looking mess the girl had ever seen"; "nature at its proudest, dryest, loneliest, and loveliest"; "the crazy, absurd, magnificent agreement." But when, in his later work, he applied this indiscriminate approach to questions of morality and metaphysics, the effect became one of pretentiousness. With sweeping generalizations, he now implied that he was solving man's weightiest problems, yet without evidence of any careful or systematic consideration. He has his characters discuss matters like illusion-and-reality, the temporal flux, and immortality, and dismiss them—"resolved"—with a flick of a phrase, as offhandedly as they would formerly have bought a bag of jelly beans. The allegorical scheme he concocted for *Jim Dandy* was more ambitious than Thornton Wilder's in *The Skin of Our Teeth*. The assumption of Saroyan's play, as of Wilder's, was that "everybody in it had survived pestilence, famine, ignorance, injustice, inhumanity, torture, crime, and madness." But instead of a cohesive drama about man's survival through history by the skin of his teeth, Saroyan wrote an incoherent hodge-podge in which everything turns out just jim dandy, as if there had never been a serious threat at all.

When his one-act play *Across the Board on Tomorrow Morning* was published, Saroyan offered the following reassurance to anyone who might be puzzled by it: "This play isn't going to be the same for every person who sees it. Two times two is the same for everybody, but *one* never is, and you start

to understand everything when you start to understand one. One of everything. That's what art goes after. The whole. The works. One." Saroyan's efforts to provide clarification have often had this tendency to eliminate *all* distinctions, reducing meaning to some amorphous unit—if not to a cipher. In his yearning for a harmony, for an eradication of conflicts and contradictions, Saroyan is the heir of a tradition which, among Americans of a more reflective or mystical temperament, has included Jefferson's ideal of human perfectibility, Emerson's Oversoul, Whitman's multitudinous Self, Henry Adams' Lady of Chartres, and Waldo Frank's "Sense of the Whole."

In 1949, there appeared a volume of three full-length plays by William Saroyan, his major works for the theatre since the war. None of these plays—*Don't Go Away Mad*; *Sam Ego's House*; *A Decent Birth, a Happy Funeral*—has been given a Broadway production. Indeed so vaguely speculative are they that their author found it necessary to explain them in lengthy prefaces summarizing the plots and offering suggestions for deciphering the allegories. The pseudo-philosophical elements of Saroyan's writing had come more than ever to overshadow the vivid and the colorful.

Moreover, the preoccupation with death virtually excludes every other consideration, especially in *A Decent Birth, a Happy Funeral* and in *Don't Go Away Mad*. The action of the latter is set in a city hospital ward for cancer victims, and the characters are all "incurables," tortured by pain and by thoughts of their impending doom. While they clutch at prospects of the slightest delay, they brood over the crises and deaths of fellow inmates and talk endlessly about death, life, time, and the details of their physiological decadence. Yet even here, in these plays about death, Saroyan has conjured up endings of joy, for which he offers this revealing justification in the preface to *A Decent Birth* . . . :

> The tone of the play being reasonable rather than emotional, I felt justified in permitting the show-off not to have been killed, for he is the artist, and art goes on forever. I felt justified in not having the child die, or be sickly, or crippled. I know that a man who is said to be dead is more often than not dead. I know that mothers frequently die in childbirth, and that infants are frequently born dead, ill, or crippled. In short, I know exasperating, surprising, and terrible things do happen, but I chose not to make anything of this in this play.

To negate death has thus become for Saroyan the crucial test of man's free will and unlimited powers. Sometimes, instead of whisking it away by plot manipulations, he has tried to exorcise death by comic ritual, to be as airy about morbidity as he had been about little boys turning somersaults. (Many social analysts have noted the uneasy effort in America to euphemize death, glamorize it, sentimentalize it, and generally make it keep its distance.) He changed the title of his most dismal play from "The Incurables" to "Don't Go Away Mad." He tried to lighten an act-long funeral ceremony by having burlesque comedians conduct the service while they played with yo-yos and rubber balls and blew tin horns. And some years ago he hailed George Bernard Shaw as the first man "to make a complete monkey out of death and of the theory [*sic!*] of dying in general." But one of Saroyan's own characters declares that "Death begins with helplessness, and it's impossible to joke about." Perhaps Saroyan has begun to suspect that for him, "Death is a lousy idea from which there is no escape."

The latest novel by Saroyan is called *The Laughing Matter* (1953). Set in the California vineyards and dealing with a family of Armenian heritage, the book has on its opening pages an atmosphere of love and warmth which recalls the earliest and best Saroyan. When the boy and girl of the family are the book's concern, their enjoyment of life and their sensitivity to the world around them—the way they savor figs and grapes, drink in the warmth of the sun, wonder about the universe—are a delight. But before long, Saroyan is trying to handle adult problems and the tale bogs down. The children's mother has become pregnant through an adulterous relationship. The boy, confronted by the tragic situation which is rocking the security of his beautiful family, cries to the skies,

"What was the matter? What was it, always? Why couldn't anything be the way it *ought* to be? Why was everything always strange, mysterious, dangerous, delicate, likely to break to pieces suddenly?" For although his father has taught him the Armenian words, "It is right," and although everybody chants them over and over (one wise member of the family insists, meaning it, "Whatever you do is right. If you hate, it is. If you kill, it is."), nevertheless, everything goes wrong and there is death and disaster, and there is futility in the face of imperfection. And after it all, at the end of the book, still crying like an echo in the wilderness, is the repeated refrain, "It is right!"

DELMORE SCHWARTZ

1913–1966

Delmore Schwartz was born on December 8, 1913, in Brooklyn, New York. He was educated at the University of Wisconsin, New York University (B.A. in philosophy, 1935), and Harvard University. He married Gertrude Buckman in 1938, but they were divorced in 1944. In 1949 he married Elizabeth Pollet; they were divorced in 1957. He taught at Harvard University for several years, and then taught for brief periods at the Kenyon School of English, New York University, Indiana University, Princeton University, the University of Chicago, the University of California, and Syracuse University. From 1943 to 1955 he was an editor at *Partisan Review*. In addition, he served as a literary consultant to James Laughlin's New Directions Press in 1952 and 1953, and as poetry editor and film critic for the *New Republic* from 1955 to 1957.

Schwartz was not a prolific writer. He is primarily known as a poet, although he published only five volumes of poetry during his life. *In Dreams Begin Responsibilities* (1938), a collection which also included some prose, was the first; it was widely praised but read only by a small circle of intellectuals, a pattern that would persist for the remainder of his career. Subsequent books (*Shenandoah*, a verse play, 1941; *Genesis: Book One*, 1943; *Vaudeville for a Princess and Other Poems*, 1950; and *Summer Knowledge*, 1959) confirmed his reputation as a poet's poet, much admired in literary circles but virtually unknown to the general reading public.

Schwartz was an influential critic, associated with the *Partisan Review* circle. Much of his critical writing consists of general introductory overviews of various authors. He was also noted as a critic of other critics, publishing numerous insightful essays on T. S. Eliot, Yvor Winters, Lionel Trilling, and Edmund Wilson.

Although his output was small, Schwartz's influence has been considerable; writers as diverse as Saul Bellow and John Berryman have paid him tribute, and his reputation is probably greater now than it was during his lifetime. His *Selected Essays* appeared in 1970, and his *Letters* in 1984.

Delmore Schwartz led a troubled life. Plagued by insomnia, he eventually resorted to increasing amounts of alcohol and barbiturate in order to sleep; as a result, his life began to unravel just as he was starting to receive general recognition. Invited to President Kennedy's inauguration in 1961, he did not attend because he had moved so many times in that period that the mailed invitation failed to reach him until after the event. Schwartz was awarded the Bollingen Prize in Poetry for 1960; he was the youngest poet so honored up to that time.

Schwartz died under confused circumstances. Unexpectedly leaving his teaching post at Syracuse University in January 1966, he spent the next six months in Manhattan residential hotels and died in an ambulance en route to Roosevelt Hospital on July 11, 1966.

Personal

Your intelligence was so clear
In your first poems, like
Mozart in his music.
Yet it could not help you,
As you said,
When the old arguments,
The din around the family table,
Grew louder all about you—
The arguments we endlessly rehearse
When mind loses its own motion.

Then our jaws lock into the face
We had, on the words we said
Under our breath, to ourselves,
To our underselves, so fiercely deep
They were for years beyond hearing,
And now do all the talking.
—HARVEY SHAPIRO, "For Delmore Schwartz,"
  Poetry, June 1967, pp. 160–61

Works

Like Oedipus,
No one can go away from genesis,

WILLIAM SAROYAN

DELMORE SCHWARTZ

GEORGE SANTAYANA

ANNE SEXTON

ROBERT SERVICE

NTOZAKE SHANGE

KARL SHAPIRO

From parents, early crime, and character,
Guilty or innocent!

Five years ago Delmore Schwartz's first book, *In Dreams Begin Responsibilities*, was greeted with more critical acclaim than has come to any other American poet of his generation, the generation since Auden. As a result Schwartz was placed in the hardest position for a young writer to sustain in a spot-lighted age, a beginning poet with a reputation to live up to. When his short verse play, *Shenandoah*, seemed slight, it then became the fashion to declare that he had been overpraised and had not deserved his reputation in the first place. It is fortunate for both the poet and his readers that *Genesis* is a marked advance over all his previous work, and that it is impressive in a way that recent poetry has too seldom been—in the range of its subject-matter.

As he says in his preface, Schwartz aims to be "one more of the poets who seek to regain for Poetry the width of reference of prose without losing what the Symbolists discovered." He bears out this aim by presenting a whole phase of our cultural history, the image of American life that was formed for and by the immigrants of the end of the nineteenth century, who came from Central Europe to survive or endure in New York. Their intentions were not political; their American dream was that of greater wealth. The most strikingly drawn character in Schwartz's narrative, Hershey Green's father, becomes a terrifying embodiment of our naked lusts. Running away from Czarist Russia to join his older brother here, Jack Green soon gets his feet on the economic ladder. He climbs to being a successful dealer in real estate, and thus fulfills the intense feeling that he had brought with him from Europe, that "the ownership of land was the greatest material thing." His other passionate drive is for sensuality. His marriage with self-willed tactless Eva Newman is a succession of brutal scenes over his infidelities. ("Is not escape a major industry in North America?") At the time of the outbreak of the first World War, she is trying desperately to hold him by bearing him a son, and Jack Green feels proud and secure. Although the other lights may be going out in Europe, for him in America the radiance of making money surpassed them all in brilliance.

The form that Schwartz has devised for presenting his material is an alternating sequence of prose narrative and choric comment. The narrative consists of the compulsive reflections of sixteen year-old Hershey Green as he lies sleepless one night and rages through all that he knows of his history, from his own memory and from family report. The chorus, a shadowy group of the dead, give their minds to discuss and explain, since, in the detachment of death, their sole desire is for clarification through full knowledge. The advantages for the author in such a chorus are obvious: he can gain thereby great density of reference. But the dangers are equally patent. Such commentators can overinterpret, and can then prove merely a distraction from the forward-moving story. And although the poet cites Hardy among the modern witnesses for a chorus, the example of *The Dynasts* is different in two crucial respects. For one thing, Hardy's various groups, such as the Spirits of the Pities and the Spirits Ironic, are characterized by a dramatic point of view, whereas Schwartz's succession of voices have no clear identity and often lose themselves in mere fluidity. What is even more important, the form of the choruses seems frequently too relaxed for full effectiveness. To be sure, Schwartz has stated that he has "no wish to emulate Swinburne," but that he seeks rather to approximate the flat accents of ordinary speech. But one of the most living delights of art is the surprise of contrast, and, as an offset to the prose narrative, the reader's ear often longs for more of the resources of verse than Schwartz avails himself of, for more formal stanzaic patterns, and for at least an occasional tightening up by rhyme.

As it is, we are faced with the anomaly that the most lyrical passages of the book are expressed in prose. An exquisite moment occurs when Hershey, coming downstairs for his sixth Christmas and finding the bicycle for which he had longed, wheels it over to the window and comes face to face with an even more overpowering joy, the new snow, the deepest symbol to him always of the mystery of release. Schwartz's writing is masterly at such a juncture, and the chief reason why he can convey the warmth of breathless emotion is that he has disciplined his narrative as he has not disciplined his choruses, by stylizing his prose up to a tense rhythmical pattern. We have travelled a curious distance from the lesson that Eliot and Pound learned from Henry James, that poetry ought to be as well written as prose.

I may exaggerate this point, but the success of *Genesis* assuredly lies primarily in the accumulating richness of consciousness on the part of the growing boy. The narrative is thus a type of *Bildungsroman*, and is a further addition to what seems to have become about our most frequent modern genre since *Buddenbrooks* and *Swann's Way* and *A Portrait of the Artist as a Young Man*. But there is a peculiar freshness to Schwartz's contribution to the genre, a freshness that is owing to his most distinctive gift, irrespective of which medium he works in. He has a fine capacity for combining lyric immediacy with philosophical reflection, and can thus command both the particular and the general. His great flair for observing all the surfaces of Hershey's environment is not allowed to degenerate into the production of mere décor, for Schwartz holds tenaciously to the poet's high responsibility to intelligence. Thus the passage about the bicycle and the snow—and here the chorus serves Schwartz well—widens out into Aristotle's perception that motion "is being's deepest wish." It is the same case with Hershey's other discoveries. The street games of "Buttons" and "Picture Cards," in which he so delights, are seen as "drunk with contingency and private property, the deepest motives that surrounded the playing boys." The Katzenjammer Kids who bore and perplex Hershey "with their endless destruction" are discerned as "presenting the adult vision of childhood," the vision of the anarchy which adults "yearned for and could not have." The narrative sections on Hershey's first big league ball game and on his going to see Chaplin in *The Kid* become, through similar broad handling, memorable passages of moral history.

The first book of *Genesis* takes Hershey up through grade 4A in school, and thereby gives occasion for a passage on Lincoln, one of the most effectively unified of the choruses, which is underscored with the belief that

In fact, the North and South were losers both:
—Capitalismus won the Civil War.

The narrative comes to a violent climax when Eva Green and Hershey, out riding on a Sunday afternoon with friends, encounter Jack Green and his woman at a roadhouse:

Childhood was ended here! or innocence
—Henceforth suspicious of experience!

Hershey has already known for the first time what it is to be scorned as a Jew; and talking to a Catholic boy, he begins to have a sense of other mysteries. In continuing his story beyond this point, Schwartz will have to be on his guard to avoid becoming involved in Hershey's adolescent self-pity. A related problem for the form will be to devise some variation of the alternating narrative and chorus, which has already become monotonously expected by the end of this first book. But the deepening themes of Schwartz's thought give great promise for what lies ahead in Hershey Green's unfolding experience. For Schwartz's firm command of Marxist history has not prevented him from becoming aware of the renewed urgency of religious issues. And his profound belief that Europe is "the greatest thing in North America" should prove one of the important forces for the renewal of our culture in these days when we are continually threatened by a recrudescence of narrow nationalism.—F. O. MATTHIESSEN, "A New York Childhood," *PR*, May–June 1943, pp. 292–94

The unbelievable badness of these poems (*Vaudeville for a Princess*) is irrelevant to any criteria of technique. A more tortured "technique" might have masked it a bit, however. Mr. Schwartz has adopted a simpler and (fortunately or unfortunately, as you regard it) more transparent ruse. Having come on stage without his trousers, he has chosen to play Danny Kaye instead of Hamlet. Divers uncertainties of tone are extrapolated into frantic prose monologues that, alternating with the poems in Part I, are meant to suggest that a stylized systole and diastole is intended, that the maudlin self-abnegation of the verse is dramatically and delicately lighthearted: the clown's pathos, in fact.

This pathos is irrelevantly heightened by a sophisticated audience; the title, *Vaudeville for a Princess*, was suggested, we are told, "by Princess Elizabeth's admiration for Danny Kaye." Nudged toward the paradigm of royal enchantment, we readers can presumably take a hint.

Kaye's comedy is par excellence the charade of frenetic embarrassment; it is perhaps no accident that the seven very silly prose interludes read half like scripts for a Borscht-circuit monologuist and half like high-school imitations of Thurber (that prince of Mitty-ish sophisticates). That one of them, *Hamlet, or There Is Something Wrong with Everyone*, reminds us dimly of Laforgue's finest *Moralité* perhaps explains why the accompanying verse persistently recalls the gestures—but not the techniques—of "Prufock" and *Portrait of a Lady*:

> My clumsiness each time I try to dance,
> My mother's anger when I wore long pants.

These are the objective correlatives of the poetic real and earnest: Laforguian or Eliotic exacerbations without a trace of the appropriate irony. The poet feels terribly *inadequate*, that is his burden; he yearns for a time when "Goodness will not seem rare as bearded ladies" and invites us meanwhile to join him at his clowning, to

> play *cache-cache* or blind-man's buff
> And pin the tail on the abundant goat.

It is useless to ask why "abundant." We are beyond technical good and bad. Lyrics in which "foam" rhymes with "poem" ("One who hesitantly writes a poem"), rivers are (bitterly) "rotten", and Socrates, for no particular reason except perhaps a reminiscence of Antony, is "curly," bespeak not so much sheer incompetence (there was a Delmore Schwartz in earlier phases who was not spectacularly incompetent) as a reckless despair (corresponding to Mr. Kaye's frantic git-gat-gittle) in which the odd startling adjective is exploded because the princess' attention has been noted to wander.

The princess is ever so polite, but occasionally she yawns; that is the dramatic context of everything in the volume. Dagwood worrying less about nuclear annihilation than about being made to feel a fool by the plumber, his sword of Damocles simply a snub, typifies American social life whose context is a jungle of exacerbated nerve-endings that still awaits

its geographer. To afford a catharsis of beery self-distrust is the job of every popular entertainer from the crooner through Emily Post to the circus freak. It has seldom been attempted so directly, or with such disastrous evocation of the malaise it is supposed to anaesthetize, than in the present volume. Eddie Guest interposes a paternal assurance between his audience and his / its banality; Mr. Schwartz was neither sufficiently crooked to fake this (his one lightning rod, the clown disguise, inheres in title and arrangement merely) nor sufficiently wise to stop publishing until he felt stronger. Titles like "Passing beyond the Straits of Guilt and Doubt" and "After the Passion Which Made Me a Fool" illustrate his area of operations, and we notice in the final third a tendency to spin maudlin variations on the more plangent themes of *Finnegans Wake* ("When you said how you'd give me the keys to my heart"). Guilt, Doubt, and Embarrassment enclose the spectrum of passions:

> . . . the fears the adolescent knows,
> The panicky conceit, the precious pose,
> The stagefright and the footlights of the play.

This is from Part III, where the Princess has become Beloved as well as Audience. Again like Danny Kaye, Mr. Schwartz is *wooing* the audience. He wants to be loved; but "a long used poet such as I" can expect only jeers, that is his agony. "Darkling, I hardly know just what I mean," is his quasi-Prufrockian protest, but he knows well enough. He means that although

> Her candor and her gaze are marvelous,
> Marvelous shines her candor and her gaze,

still there isn't hope of rapprochement

> This news is meaningless. For she was born,
> Look, in some other world!—and you were not!

The distance between this posture vis-a-vis the loved one and a Renaissance serenity of unworthiness is measured by the incredible banalities the poet has maneuvered himself into thinking publishable.

It is in Part II, however, that we get the Real World:

> The roller-coaster soars and dives to fear.

> Hark, from the coiling track come screams like jazz,
> As if they jumped from brink of a burning house.

This pandemonium, our poet-analyst assures us, is attended by a great deal of Significance:

> Why do they hate their lives?
> Why do they wish to die?
> Believing in vicious lies,
> Afraid to remember and cry.

If only they would break down and blubber, then they would stop *hating* themselves and, presumably, ridiculing their poets! It could be so simple! Come, let's try to tell them! . . . so we get the five poems that commence "Dear Citizens" . . .

Mr. Schwartz has not, we are assured, adopted this vatic role without preparation. He has resolutely studied his craft (while walking the midnight streets, it seems) "cut off . . . from the normal pleasures of the citizen." Ah, that ascetic agony! He has in fact undergone exclusion from

> The party where the New Year popped and foamed,
> Opening like champagne or love's wet crush,
> The while I studied the long art which in
> America wins silence like a wall.

These rigors—who will doubt?—endow with pedagogic authority; to "the boys and girls" in his "ageing youth" he speaks "three words"

The true, the good, and the beautiful,
Shifting my tones as if I said to them
Candy, soda, fruits and flowers . . .

The tone for *Dear Citizens* is no less wistful but a little more hortatory:

—O Citizens, let us frankly confess
We know our lives are lived by lies.
And, Citizens, let us not be estranged.
Surely the wars will end, there will be peace.

But no one, it appears, confesses, and the crowd moves off. Us poets, Mr. Schwartz tells the world, have it tough:

These politicians have an easy time,
They can say anything, they have no shame . . .

Awed or indifferent, bemused or ill at ease,
We who are poets play the game which is
A deadly earnest searching of all hearts . . .

It's a pretty tense game, evidently, and lest we suppose that its occupational disease is imbecility, we are bidden to remember that "True recognition often is refused" (Columbus, Galileo) and that

We poets by the past and future used
Stare east and west distractedly at times.

And their distraction fits are at times embarrassingly lucid.
—Hugh Kenner, "Bearded Ladies and the Abundant Goat," *Poetry*, Oct. 1951, pp. 50–53

It is easy to say what has always been wrong with Delmore Schwartz's poetry. Briefly, he has rarely been able to sustain a whole poem at the level of its beginning. No one else but Auden in this century has so many wonderful first lines: "In the naked bed, in Plato's cave," "The beautiful American word, Sure," "A dog named Ego, the snowflakes as kisses," "The horns in the harbor booming, vaguely"—such beginnings, and with them a certain tone, a wrily humorous sense of tangled, painful complexities, are most memorable in Schwartz's writing. Unfortunately, it is hard to remember any larger movement into resolution in his pieces. A truly beautiful lyric poem will seem, in Hart Crane's phrase, an "inviolate curve," or else it will be an unfolding series of realizations that echo back and forth until what feels an ultimate resolution is reached.

And yet Schwartz has many moments of pure music to offer, and some moments in which he speaks in the accents of greatness, and he holds us even in his failures with the honesty and contemporaneity of his voice. The comparison may seem absurd, but I feel about many of his poems as I do about some of Shakespeare's sonnets that begin so grandly and then fall away by the roadside somewhere—they ride in triumph over their own incompleteness. Look at the first stanza of "Starlight like Intuition Pierced the Twelve":

The starlight's intuitions pierced the twelve,
The brittle night sky sparkled like a tune
Tinkled and tapped out on the xylophone.
Empty and vain, a glittering dune, the moon
Arose too big, and, in the mood which ruled,
Seemed like a useless beauty in a pit;
And then one said, after he carefully spat:
"No matter what we do, he looks at it."

This picture of the Apostles' dismay at what the life of Jesus has meant is altogether modern in its expression of what the poet calls elsewhere "the wound of consciousness." It hardly matters that the rest of the poem is a somewhat talkative expansion buoyed poetically only by its echoes of what has already been established in this stanza, just as it hardly matters what follows after Shakespeare's

Not marble, nor the gilded monuments
Of princes, shall outlive this powerful rhyme. . . .

Well, it does matter, but really less in Schwartz's case, I think. The rest of "Starlight like Intuition Pierced the Twelve" is *interesting* talk at least. Here, too, Schwartz resembles Auden, who influenced a whole generation of poets toward an artistically self-defeating but intellectually stimulating method of poetic structure. The method is to start with a single image or description or insight that is striking in itself and then to think about it and try to develop an attitude toward it. In the ideology-centered milieu of the thirties and early forties in which Schwartz grew up, a knowledgeable involvement with ideas until one felt tugged this way by Marx, that way by Freud, and hither-and-thither by the concitation of still other devils from Aristotle to Augustine to John Crowe Ransom seemed worth any five simple emotions. (See Auden's *The Orators* or, in this book ⟨*Summer Knowledge*⟩, Schwartz's "Coriolanus and His Mother.") This was not mere affectation, but the spiritual life of a generation drunk with the excitement of worlds of thought in conflict. And what Schwartz has to say involves us insinuatingly because we are still bound to that era. Greater poetry thrusts its premises on us without this kind of bond. Shakespeare's "They that have power to hurt, and will do none" *makes* us see life in terms of an alien aristocratic ideal. Schwartz's appeal is of a different order. It is something deeply familiar that he brings to the fore, something that weeps and snickers unworthily in the back alleys of modern hyperconsciousness. Thus, the buffoonery of his description of a newsreel: "Cartoons of Coming Shows Unseen Before" (unfortunately omitted from this volume)—

Churchill nudged Roosevelt. With handsome glee
Roosevelt winked! Upon life's peak they played
(Power is pleasure, thought anxious. Power is free!)

Or—a subtler buffoonery—the Chaplinesque manner in which, in "Prothalamion," the author reinterprets a famous figure of Dante's. So translated, the soul becomes an undignified, colloquially blurting ego:

"little soul, little flirting,
    little perverse one
        where are you off to now?
    little wan one, firm one
        little exposed one . . .
        and never make fun of me again."

It is perhaps inevitable that such a poet, whose very weaknesses betray the life-awareness of an age, should bring confession, aimless rhetoric and private gropings for mistily perceived meanings directly into his poetry. A poem like "Prothalamion," lacking the redeeming passionate art of a Robert Lowell, degenerates into autobiographical document:

I will forget the speech my mother made
In a restaurant, trapping my father there
At dinner with his whore. Her spoken rage
Struck down the child of seven years
With shame. . . .

Indeed, Schwartz constantly exploits his personal shames and guilts and the reader's natural sympathy with heartbroken children—

. . . I skated, afraid of policemen, five years old,
In the winter sunset, sorrowful and cold. . . .

Still, as I have tried to suggest, there is much more in his poems than unrelieved confessional or cosmic blarneying. It comes out best in the simplicity and concreteness with which he presents physical and psychological self-delineation, in a poem like "The Heavy Bear That Walks with Me" or "In the Naked Bed, in Plato's Cave." But it is present also in the confessionals and blarneyings, for if the poet is in love with his involvement in them he is at the same time forever trying to get at some hidden motive toward which they point. John Berry-man has caught this facet of Schwartz's poetic personality brilliantly in "At Chinese Checkers":

> Deep in the unfriendly city Delmore lies
> And cannot sleep, and cannot bring his mind
> And cannot bring those marvellous faculties
> To bear upon the day sunk down behind,
> The unsteady night, or the time to come. . . .

Most of what I have had to say about *Summer Knowledge* concerns the first half of the book, taken from the long out-of-print *In Dreams Begin Responsibilities* (1938). The second half, containing later work, lacks the general vibrancy and relevancy of that book, yet a sufficient number of the more recent poems show a suggestive turn toward a new directness and naturalness. The old sophistication is often sloughed off completely, and the poet attempts a translucent lyricism that occasionally soars in Shelleyan flight. Sometimes these poems accumulate a mounting charge of joy that erupts in a surging imagery of sky, sea and light; sometimes their mood is darker, or has a desolate "strangeness"—for instance, in "All of the Fruits Had Fallen." I do not make excuses for this section, but I have the impression from it that the poet has passed through a great spiritual change and is slowly finding his way in a new world. He has not yet discovered the right poetic idiom of that world, but it seems to have some continuity with such earlier work as "Far Rockaway," in which the vision is for a moment a similar one:

> The radiant soda of the seashore fashions
> Fun, foam, and freedom. The sea laves
> The shaven sand. And the light sways forward
> On the self-destroying waves. . . .
>   —M. L. ROSENTHAL, "Deep in the Unfriendly
>   City," *Nation*, June 11, 1960, pp. 515–16

I have written elsewhere about the tragedy of Delmore Schwartz, and I will write no more here, though it is so exemplary and so awful that I am tempted. I am sure all who knew him will go on thinking about him, if not writing about him, the rest of their lives. But no one needs a biography, because Schwartz's life is all there in his own writing. His *Selected Poems*, which he edited himself in 1958 and subtitled *Summer Knowledge*, is now re-issued as a paperback. To my mind it contains a great deal of bad poetry; yet never merely bad or merely uninteresting; Schwartz's genius is on every page, twisted, fouled, and set against itself. It is an excruciating record; redeemed (if that is the word) by perfect poems that rise here and there from the tangle, strong, lucid, eloquent, often rather old-fashioned, like wild roses in a bank of weeds.—HAYDEN CARRUTH, "Comment," *Poetry*, Sept. 1968, pp. 425–26

IRVING HOWE

"Delmore Schwartz—A Personal Appreciation"

New Republic, March 19, 1962, pp. 25–27

There are times when a reviewer ought to declare his bias plainly, and that is what I propose to do here. I cannot pretend to "objectivity" in writing about the work of Delmore Schwartz, for it has come to be a part of my experience, an imaginative incitement to that struggle for self-discovery by which one tries to remain alive. When I first came upon his poems and stories in the late thirties—those wry, depressed and insidiously clever evocations of the life of first and second generation Jews in New York—I felt a thrill of recognition. For not only did Schwartz's poems and stories reflect the qualities of that life with a comic intensity, they also helped one reach an emotional truce in relation to it. Sliding past the dangers of hate and sentimentalism which always beset writings on this subject, Schwartz's best work brought one to the very edge of the absurd, and there, almost as if ironic distance were a prerequisite for affection, one could find a certain half-peace in contemplating the world of one's youth.

At first glance a comedian of alienation, Schwartz also showed a gift for acceptance, a somewhat ambiguous recon-cilement with the demands and depletions of common expe-rience. Many writers have treated similar kinds of material, but even those, like Bellow and Malamud, whose fictions are more inclusive and substantial have not captured quite so keenly as has Schwartz the particular timbre, the tangled reverberations and complications of irony within irony, that once character-ized Jewish life in America. And what gave Schwartz's work its distinction was that he avoided the pieties of both fathers and sons, established community and estranged intellectuals; he worked his way past their fixed perspective, unfolding still another nuance of reflection by which to complicate and even undercut his own ironies. His poems and stories rested on what is for our time the most secure of foundations: the tempered humaneness of self-doubt.

To read him in the late thirties and early forties was part of one's education, and though I knew that some of his stories were much better than others, that "In Dreams Begin Respon-sibilities" was a masterpiece while "A Bitter Farce" was too soft and flat, the impulse to judgment was never very strong in me. For I felt involved with the emotional needs and resistances that had apparently led to the composition of these stories, so much so that I seldom ventured the discriminations one might make concerning the work of a stranger. I assumed that, whatever the proportion of success to failure, the body of Schwartz's writing was important, and there I think I was right; though after a time I found to my surprise that in certain tough-spirited sections of the country it had become fashion-able to sneer at Schwartz as a self-appointed spokesman for "New York alienation" and as a writer indulging his taste for self-pity.

The first of these complaints derived all too often from a narrow-spirited envy of the excitement people attribute to life in New York—and there *was* a time when that life beat with excitement. The second complaint was a piece of critical ineptitude, for while self-pity was one of Schwartz's recurrent themes and frequent temptations, he had the rare honesty to struggle with it out in the open and, thereby, in his best work to confront and transcend it. A good many other, less honest writers learn to mask their self-pity as heartiness or stoicism.

Nowhere else, to my knowledge, has the pathos and comic hopelessness of the conflict between immigrant families and intellectual sons been rendered so well as in Schwartz's early stories; nor has anyone else written so authoritatively, so very much from the "inside," about the later experience of those sons. Schwartz soon perfected, as does every original writer, a manner or style of his own: mockingly reflective, verbally awkward, full of ironic apothegms and burlesque sententiousness, wavering between self-comfort and self-attack, ready to take the risks of seeking through his narratives that fraction of wisdom which is all anyone can hope for these days. The tags and sayings that dot his early stories and poems— *America, America, a youthful author of promise, we carry our fathers on our backs, let your conscience be your bride, doesn't your father know what he is doing?*—these seemed like the joking emblems of the cultural predicaments shared by a whole generation.

In his stories Schwartz was seldom a mere fictional reporter or genre painter; he composed realistic fables with a minimum of emotional stress, in which the burden of meaning was carried by a twining narrative line, and in which the characters embodied possibilities of consciousness so troublesome that between their being and sense of being a guerrilla war was often in progress. Coming after the social fiction of the thirties, in which the author, panic-stricken by the claims of history, kept himself out of his fictions, Schwartz now put himself well to the forefront of his stories, appearing as the agent of reflexiveness, the voice of doubt, yearning and modulation.

In his lyrics, so deliberately awkward and anti-poetic—I sometimes felt that no one but a true New Yorker could appreciate the full comedy of their rhythms—one also found a poetry that spoke to the sense of prideful disenchantment felt by young people at the end of the thirties as they reckoned their legacy of intellectual trouble. In his limited way Schwartz was the poet of the historical moment quite as Auden was in England: two writers about as different as any two could be, yet each struggling, one with the courage of his chaos and the other with a yearning for new systems, to discover what could be made of "a diminishing thing." Schwartz taught his readers to accept the dignity of their self-consciousness.

In both stories and poems his tone was deflated, as if it were looking over its shoulder to see whether it was being followed by rhetoric. It seemed to be composed of several speech layers: the sing-song, slightly pompous intonations of Jewish immigrants educated in night-schools, the self-conscious affectionate mockery of that speech by American-born sons, its abstraction into the jargon of city intellectuals, and finally the whole body of this language flattened into a prose of uneasiness, an anti-rhetoric.

Schwartz's last book of stories, *The World Is a Wedding*, appeared in 1948. For some time both before and after its appearance he published very little, suffering apparently from that mid-journey crisis which comes upon all serious writers when they must choose between the safety of self-repetition and the threat of a new beginning. Though not quite so good as his earlier work, the stories collected in *Successful Love* show that he chose the path of risk. Just as his recent poems represent a new development—a somewhat forced venture into lyric rhapsody over the renewed possibilities of life—so his recent stories leave the thirties behind and turn toward the prosperous confusion of post-war America.

Schwartz has always displayed a keen sense of social incongruity—a sense of how submission to public roles transforms us into creatures of absurdity and self-mockery—and now, in turning to the paradoxes of recent American life, he has a fine occasion for releasing his gift. He has also shown a strong, if unstable and disturbing, awareness of the sheer foolishness of existence, the radical ineptitude of the human creature, such as occasionally reminds one a trifle of Dostoevsky's use of buffoonery in order to release aggressiveness toward characters and readers. The *persona* of buffoonery, which goes perfectly well with a high and sophisticated intelligence, brings with it obvious dangers and Schwartz does not always overcome them; but it allows him, as well, the

possibility of catching his audience off-guard, jabbing cleverly beneath its dignity, as if to remind us that we too are vain and weak and pompous.

Something new appears in his recent stories: a quizzical wonderment at the powers of the American innocent, the boy or girl born too late to know very much about the costs of history and, in the crazy-quilt world of mid-century America, supremely confident that he or she can reach success, goodness and fulfillment through a mere unfolding of personal charm. The theme of these stories might be described as the irrelevance and defeat of enlightenment: that enlightenment which cultivated persons now in their middle years fought so hard to acquire but which their children simply pass by, amiably indifferent to and even tolerant of their parents' earnest *gaucherie*.

"Successful Love," for example, is a story about a young American girl, child of nature and progress, who moves into rapid sexual experience and soon acquires an encyclopediac, nay, a paperback wisdom on the mysteries of sex. Her poor enlightened father is left gasping, "entirely lost in the terror and jungle of innocence." It is a story appropriate to the fifties, registering with sardonic good-humor the obsolescence of all persons able to remember as far back as Roosevelt's first or even second inauguration.

A similar theme is developed in "An American Fairy Tale," which records the odyssey of a bright young man eager to become a great composer but ending his career as a successful band leader, while his father, a retired businessman, becomes a celebrated painter of primitive abstractions. In an amusing reversal of roles, the father shouts to the son, "You have sold out to Tin Pan Alley. Why don't you be like Bela Bartok? Money is not everything . . . " And "for the first time in fifteen years" the son is silent: "He felt sure the world was coming to an end, or at least the world as he had known it."

The story which best captures the qualities of recent American life is "The Hartford Innocents." A college girl kidnaps a baby from her parents, noted liberals who have adopted the baby but have decided to turn it away upon being told it has a trace of Negro blood. Ferocious in her innocent determination to live by the proclaimed values of her parents, ready to defy college administration and probing senators who suspect a red plot, the girl brings an entire little world into a comic crisis; and the story ends with a very funny report by a member of the board of trustees in which all of Schwartz's gift for blending mimicry and reflection is put on display.

Some of the writing in *Successful Love* is drab and careless, for what is meant as a strategy of understatement has a way of slipping into mere flatness. In a few of the stories there is a sudden drop of energy at the end, and the action is left dangling and unresolved, as if Schwartz had become bored with his own inventions. But the book as a whole is the work of an important and gifted writer, whose voice is uniquely his own and through whose prose intelligence breaks like an irrepressible light.

ROBERT FLINT
"The Stories of Delmore Schwartz"
Commentary, April 1962, pp. 336–39

There is no doubt that Delmore Schwartz's first book of stories, *The World Is a Wedding*, was a considerable, though not popular, success. This may have surprised even the author, who was known in 1948, and may have wanted chiefly to be known, as a brilliant young poet. One can easily imagine Mr. Schwartz swept up by a reading of Turgenev or Chekhov or both and "trying his hand" in what seemed to him at the time a casual way at some social history *à la russe*, oblivious of the reigning vogue for symbols and mythological epiphanies, fairly careless of the unities, or the rule insisted upon by Frank O'Connor that a short story should encompass only one crisis or mood. But somehow a deeper necessity than merely hitting the average highbrow literary taste took hold of Schwartz, and he was faithful to a higher rule than any he flouted: namely, that an ounce of presentation is worth a pound of care; and drew what to my mind is the definitive portrait of the Jewish middle class in New York during the Depression.

How do I, knowing relatively little of this class at first hand, undertake such a verdict? Because these early stories still seem to me among the very best written anywhere at the time. They are acts of discovery and celebration such as no other group in the country at the time could have produced, and they have the great virtue of having been generated from the real, as against the ideological, preoccupations of their society, of aiming neither, like Salinger's stories, to fit the new life into the classical patterns of sentimental farce, nor, by gentle and subtle distortion, to revive lost folkish sentiments recovered from writers like Babel or Sholem Aleichem. This is New York Jewry, I venture to say, of an integrity and wholeness unmatched elsewhere in fiction, before the intellectual diaspora of the 40's began, before Leslie Fiedler began howling from Montana for an end to innocence or Karl Shapiro from Nebraska for an end to T. S. Eliot.

Marx and Freud are still good uncles in this book, not domineering schoolmarms. Alfred Kazin has written of the "sodden brilliance" of Jewish political dialectics in the New York of this era. By forgoing colloquial brilliance of the Salinger variety, Schwartz found a pace that avoided lapses into soddenness, either by omission or commission. The tempo of these stories matches their language; deliberate, careful, formal, gray to gray readers, tired to tired readers: tempo and language seem fourteen years later to have been exactly right, in the chronicle of a society discovering a new life along with a new language, a society moving with great circumspection in spite of its clannishness and intellectual assurance, a society that could not help sentimentalizing somewhat over what it took to be relics of an older and purer America and attempting to adopt them into its successful advance.

If it moved slowly, it also made the frontal attack on American mores that required a historian like Delmore Schwartz; to explain to itself and the world, for instance, that marriage in so fluid a society had become a career in itself at which people like the Baumanns in "America! America!" could excel when they excelled at little else, or that the majority of marriages in the United States cannot help seeming bizarre to friends of either party, so problematic has the institution become. Schwartz recorded the effect of business cycles on careers with impassive pity, or the incommensurability of talents and careers during a depression. That these crises have been "normalized" since the last war in no way lessens the relevance of Schwartz's history.

The histrionic richness of these stories is like that of Chekhov in his drama rather than his fiction, though where Chekhov is obliged to make his characters declare themselves fully, Schwartz does not scruple to provide the clues himself to his characters' endless misunderstandings. And this is because his mind moves towards a kind of *Weisheitsdichtung* that is impatient, under the circumstances, of an overly educated

literary subterfuge. In "New Year's Eve" Shenandoah Fish expresses the vision toward which the stories move: "Some other world, some world of goodness; some other life; some life where the nobility we admire is lived; some life in which those who have dedicated their being to the examination of consciousness live by the laws they face at every turn." In the last flare of naturalism which the early Schwartz celebrates, there is no retreat to Zen or the California Sierras or even to Durrell's Alexandria. His vision is measured against the lives of dentists, insurance agents, New York writers, teachers, and publishers; and if the colors tend to be dark, the composition is spacious and centripetal as the later fantasists rarely succeed in being. The humor is casual; the stories can equally well be read as serious or comic, according to the reader's temperament. Schwartz's master ironies are large enough to evoke any of a dozen conflicting emotions. The smaller ironies feed the larger; we are not surprised, for example, to learn, halfway through "The World Is a Wedding," that Rudyard Bell, hero and center of his circle, is a bully to his sister and perhaps a passive homosexual, or that Ruth Hart of "The Child Is the Meaning of This Life," the "powerful human being who lived through her devotion to her children" has, in fact, as she jokingly says at the end of the story, "the worst children in the world." These reverses follow the rhythm of the author's perception and are not intended to illustrate some borrowed thesis about Illusion and Reality, so dear to reviewers of fiction, but rather some very exact thesis about American urban society of the 30's, when intellectuals, however obliquely they came at it, had an especially vivid sense of the fate of their society. They knew it as tragic, hopeless, radically sick—the "place" of the party in "New Year's Eve" is the sense of "having-nowhere-better-to-go"—but they accepted it as a fate and not as a weapon in a cold war or as a springboard into exotic states of being.

To summarize the value of *The World Is a Wedding* is to say that the affection and interest it arouses, in this critic at least, require that it be treated in language no less formal than its own. Even the physical volume *is*, for me, New York, more than anything except some James, Wharton, and Hart Crane.

Schwartz's new collection, *Successful Love*, belongs very clearly to another era, the era for which Fiedler found a suitable epigraph in his title, *An End to Innocence*. None of these stories is concerned with Jewish life as such and thereby reflects the change that has weakened the emotional and intellectual ties of the community. One of the best, "The Hartford Innocents," is narrated in part by a Dewitt Howe, solemn officer of an unspecified charitable foundation, investigating the scandal that occurs in a fashionable progressive Eastern school when the forthright daughter of a liberal Protestant Midwestern clergyman decides to adopt a half-Negro child mysteriously left on her family's doorstep and raise it herself at school. This is about as far within continental limits as Schwartz could get from the atmosphere of *The World Is a Wedding*. He has, in fact, turned to writing the sort of fable that has become increasingly popular, stimulated perhaps by the example of Camus, Silone, and Moravia, and the desire to keep at least a rational, if not very physical, grip on reality. It is fascinating to see how he carries his fictional equipment almost intact into this new, windier territory.

"Successful Love," "Tales from the Vienna Woods," "The Gift," and "A Colossal Fortune" are gayer, snappier, more colloquial and cheerfully mundane than anything he has done before. They are the work of a self-confident author amusing himself with the fruit of much talk, experience, and casual reading. There is a tendency to construct characters out of variations on well-known figures: the hero of "An American Fairy Tale" strongly suggests Leonard Bernstein, and the father who becomes a "primitive abstractionist" on retirement from business suggests the senior Nemeroy (father of the poet Howard). But the peroration of this story leaves me at a loss:

> How beautiful this success story is, how good, how true! It is the equal of any fairy tale, it is full of purity, innocence and happiness. It is like a newborn child. It is as if one were to say, believe, and hope that America were going to be discovered again.

I *think* this may be a bitter irony, but am unwilling to wager that it is, so much more strongly are we asked to feel about these characters than we could possibly feel about their prototypes in life.

In any event, *something* is missing, and it is neither skill nor acuteness of perception nor humor. As counterpoint to the rational exfoliation of themes about a problem, Schwartz sounds an affecting new note of midnight lyricism:

> One for love, one for frustration, and one for desperation, brandy for hope and beer for nervousness, Martinis to eat and whiskey to sleep, one to be calm, two to be gay, one to be warm and a few to have something to say. A pint to make love and a case to get away from the guilt one cannot face after the great wild flower of the sunset has gone down and left one alone in the isolation and condemnation of the night, the darkness of fear amid electric light. One for the strength never to despair, one to be near the hope which is born of desperate fear, one to remember always that the greatest courage is born of the greatest danger, that courage is born of fear, one never to forget how hope is a way of being alive and living with the real people.

This sort of poetic prose, inextricably woven into the fabric of his earlier stories, detaches itself here and, so to speak, drops off at a bar for a drink by itself. Amidst the funny barroom banter or the solemn, formal brilliance of Dr. Manning's diagnosis of true charity in "The Hartford Innocents," one has no doubts of Schwartz's continuing skill. The missing element, I think, is simply a theme to match the theme or themes of *The World Is a Wedding*. I was uncomfortable when Leslie Fiedler discovered the dangers of innocence and am no less so now that Delmore Schwartz has discovered them. He seems too honest to be much convinced of anything but the theme's literary usefulness amidst the general vacancy, and this in turn does not seem quite enough.

> The infamy of innocence begins by concerting a valid legal postulate—that all human beings are *born* equal—into an ideal and an absolute which must be realized immediately; if it is not, we are all unconscionable scoundrels and hypocrites. . . . The attitudes and principles meant as theoretical limits of the structure of a democratic society had become not the boundary lines they were meant to be but the center of attention, consciousness and action. The Hartford girls, in their disregard for all but principle, acted as if human beings existed for the sake of having a democratic state, rather than the democratic state for the sake of the human beings inhabiting it.

This is eloquent and just, especially considering that it is a comment on what happens in Schwartz's own story where the girls act with an extraordinary degree of selfless idealism. But it comes at the end of a long demonstration of exactly what innocence can still achieve when joined to strong natural gifts. The very substance of the story, indeed, is little more than the

charm and power of innocence. The Negro baby that Candida Manning adopts might just as well, had the parents and school officials been less innocent, have been adopted by the proper agencies in the beginning.

It would be difficult to maintain that innocence is our chief danger. Schwartz does not attempt it. But the theme has a dismaying attraction today, because it permits the writer genially to patronize popular culture whose charms he both assimilates and ridicules, the dividing line between affection and ridicule becoming increasingly less visible to dull readers like myself. At the same time, he repudiates his doctrinaire past as partaking, at one remove perhaps, of the general climate of innocence. Whereas the innocence which made *The World Is a Wedding* possible—Schwartz's own in the 30's and 40's—gave its author a strong taste for the most general case within the strictest social limits, this new zeal in the exposure of innocence, however relieved by humor, cannot help bearing down on the special case, since to accuse a whole nation of innocence is to dissipate whatever point one may have had in mind. And this is a loss to fiction because there are many agencies more pressing than fiction for the airing of special cases. Inventive as Schwartz may be in concocting his fables, one cannot read them without suspecting that in about five minutes reality, aided by the press, TV, etc., will provide something better; that problem-posing, or according to the latest cant, Decision Making, has become so much the normal substance of life that fiction can only limp along behind. What we must have from fiction is life itself, and the life of an old language when it enters a new life in the world.

WILLIAM BARRETT
From "Delmore: A 30's Friendship and Beyond"
Commentary, September 1974, pp. 52–54

Now that he is dead the legend of the *poète maudit*—the doomed and sacrificial poet—has already claimed him. And before we submit to the distortions that current sentimentalities are likely to inject into this kind of legend, we had better attempt a cooler glimpse at the work he has left. It may, surprisingly enough, provide some strong imperatives to revise our stock notions of the alienation of poetry and the poet today.

Delmore had a beautiful lyrical talent, and so long as he continued able to write anything at all, this gift doesn't seem to have left him. It's too early to say what in our period, if anything, will be lasting; but my own judgment, perhaps partial, is that some of his lyrics will survive. But the great triumphs of modern poetry were nearly all in the lyric, and he wanted to help restore verse as a narrative medium. He admired Hardy's *Dynasts*, for example, before it became fashionable among some circles. But where Hardy had dealt with the fate of nations and empires, and the broad sweep of history, Delmore chose a very personal subject matter as the material for his own major narrative effort.

This work is *Genesis*, and in abstract the design of it does not look too unpromising. It's the story of the growing up of a Jewish boy (Delmore himself), of how his forebears came to this country, the strife of the parents and how it is inflicted as a trauma upon the boy. The narrative would be carried by the prose, but a rather cadenced and rhythmic prose that wouldn't be too glaring a contrast to its verse accompaniment. The latter would take the form of a poetic comment and explication of the narrative in the manner of a Greek chorus. Not bad as an idea, though the material is conventional: another version of the archetypal Making of an American. But the execution of the design fails badly. When I first read *Genesis* I was away from Delmore during the war, and I was disappointed by it as most of its readers were; but such was my faith in his powers that I imagined it a temporary stop and regrouping, the working-out of material that he had to get rid of, before he went on to the next stage. I have just reread it, with a greater effort at objectivity, and I am shocked at how bad it is. The subject matter is so intensely self-centered that it could have been better expressed lyrically, and so small in its actual narrative content that it might have been done in a short story. The verse is heavy and lumpy, lighted only occasionally by some lyrical gleams; the prose sections that carry the narrative are so drawn out that they become flat and monotonous. How could Delmore, so acutely perceptive as he then was, not have grasped one simple and central fact about this work: that it dragged and was dull? The only answer seems to be that he was so hypnotized by its personal subject matter—the history of his own childhood—that he became trapped in his narcissism and could not detach himself enough to judge the work as a piece of writing.

In fiction, he produced one perfect story, which—significantly enough—uses a kind of surrogate lyrical form to express his inveterate family material. Two other stories are notable, but not at the same level. For the rest, he falls off into the self-complacency of the raconteur retailing anecdotes. The flatness of style, originally deliberate, becomes monotonous because it is dodge—an evasion of the requirement that an author imaginatively project his characters before us. The raconteur assumes we all know the people he's gossiping about, and imagination in consequence becomes indolent.

He had great brilliance and potential, I believe, as a critic. His early pieces give very alert and sensitive readings of Hardy, Auden, Tate, and others. He was starting from Eliot as a base, but his young man's mind was swarming with ideas, and he was working toward a position and point of view of his own. But the patience and concentration needed for this were denied him—for a number of reasons, principally perhaps his own mental troubles. A few of his essays, as I knew personally, were produced under such stress that it's a wonder he could get them out as coherently as he did. Moreover, he tended to look on his own literary criticism as a *parergon*, an effort incidental to his main business of poetry. He once joked to me about the laboriousness with which Philip Rahv carved out his essays: "You've got to remember that English is still a foreign language for Philip." But Delmore's facility hasn't served him so well. Philip's essays stand up, rounded off and complete in their own terms; Delmore's provide us brilliant flashes.

When you add it all up, what have you? Certainly, not something at all negligible. To have written anything, however fragmentary, that lays claim to permanence is a higher achievement than to turn out something fully formed but glittering only for the moment. But just as certainly, a failure—and a failure all the more in relation to the power of the original gifts. It is that human failure that currently invokes the facile image of the *poète maudit*—the poet exiled and accursed by the tribe.

Delmore's case is thus assimilated to the suicides of Sylvia Plath and John Berryman (who, as it happens, dedicated his *Dream Songs* "to the sacred memory of Delmore Schwartz"). They are sacrificial victims—whether to the cruel Muse or to that usual scapegoat, Society, is not often clear. A. Alvarez, speaking of Sylvia Plath, actually says that her death was not suicide but murder—in this case, implying that she was slain by Poetry itself, a rather strange allegation of an abstraction's being an actual murderer. Dwight Macdonald attributes the cause to society, but in a peculiarly vague way. He compares Delmore's situation with Poe's a century earlier, and he cites an eloquent paragraph from Baudelaire about the solitude and isolation of Poe in 19th-century America. With all due respect to Macdonald, the comparison with Poe is downright foolish. Delmore had recognition, grants, sinecures; and in his last years he was given a position at a university when he was in a condition where anyone else would normally have been considered unemployable—the exception being made because of his eminence as a poet. In somewhat the same vein as Dwight Macdonald runs the blurb on the back of Delmore's *Selected Poems*, and its language is worth noting: "Delmore Schwartz acted out in his life . . . the alienation of the poet from our society." One has to ask just exactly what it would mean to "act out the alienation of the poet from society." I can only imagine a poet living alone and unknown, far from the center of things, whose manuscripts are discovered after his death. Delmore, however, had to be at the turbulent center of things, involved in a literary review where all the jangling wires of human intercourse got crossed, whereas the gentler "alienation" of a Wallace Stevens or William Carlos Williams might have benefited him and allowed him more time for his poetry. And he himself has already rejected these glib interpretations: in a lecture in 1956 when he delivered a blast against Allen Ginsberg and the Beat poets for their facile howl of alienation—an alienation which, as is quite inevitable in the course of modern society, had immediately become the *in* thing.

"I cultivate my hysteria," said Baudelaire, the spiritual father of the *poètes maudits*. It was a dangerous and a foolish thing to say. You don't cultivate your neurosis, it cultivates you—as the parasite cultivates and saps its parent host. With some significant modern artists neurosis has perhaps shaped their vision, but in doing so has also cramped and warped it. Baudelaire's own work suffered: the *nostalgie de la boue* makes the aspirations toward the spiritual life that much more unreal, distant and tenuous, and theatrical. When Tolstoy inveighs against Baudelaire, he is overemphatic as is his manner, but modern culture had better return to hearken to him. But however matters may lie in the perennial question of art and neurosis, the overwhelming lesson in Delmore's case is that the sickness impeded and ultimately destroyed the talent.

Macdonald does make a concession: "granting that . . . psychological difficulties were also important." In the post-Freud era this "granting" and "also" are really precious. The troubles of Delmore and Berryman (whom I knew for a while moderately well), and from my reading I would say Plath, were so obviously deep-seated in the personality that neither of those abstract specters, Society or Poetry, can be invoked as culprits. Berryman, when I knew him, was a meticulous enough person to have worked as a clerk or junior executive; he would have ended as an alcoholic nonetheless. And if Delmore had had another occupation, he would have had comparable difficulties to those he had.

One can construct the scenario of explanation for him that one wants. The materials for it are abundant and obvious enough. The violent split between father and mother; the father whom he admired as a hero and a pleasant companion, only to hear constantly vilified when he was back with his mother; and the constant closeness of his relation to the mother, who did everything she could to prolong his narcissism, exaggerate his ego with praise, and yet in her clever and poisonous way insinuate in the child, then the boy, and then the young man, that the love and trust of anybody was not to be believed.

But I offer no explanation. Before the human heart our explanations seem to fall short. Despite his absorption in Freud, Delmore would have liked the final word about himself to be spoken from the region that Dostoevsky inhabits. I simply report a conversation we had one afternoon in 1941 when I had come in from Providence to visit him over the weekend. Occasionally he liked to hear whatever I might be doing in class, partly to keep friendly tabs on me, partly to pick up something possibly for his own edification. I had been teaching Leibniz and somehow got into the problem of Predestination and Free Will. Students, however secular-minded they pretend to be, always go for this question, intrigued by its logical niceties. Egged on by them, and also out of my own curiosity, I had researched the question back through the medievals to the drastic passage in Paul, Romans IX, where he speaks of the Potter who, for reasons of His own, shapes some to be vessels of grace, and others to be "vessels of wrath." The last phrase caught Delmore's attention; he begged me to go on, and eventually flung himself passionately into the discussion. The point not to be forgotten—as well as the thorn in the side of all the philosophic commentators—is that these latter vessels retain their freedom throughout. They were created *to be* "vessels of wrath," but all along the way of that "to be" they conspire to make themselves such, their own will thus sealing their damnation. In their wrath they will themselves wrathfully; they cannot help willing in this way, but this "cannot help" is in turn the act of their own will affirming itself desperately and defiantly. The conversation evidently made a deep impression upon Delmore. When I came back next weekend he had written a sonnet about it, one of those prosaic ones he wrote from time to time both as an exercise in versification and to document some thought or experience he felt worth preserving for future use. "Yes," he said quietly, "I'm such a 'vessel of wrath.'" It was he who made the personal application; I hadn't even thought about that until he spoke.

I did see him and speak with him one last time, and I have kept this now to the end. It was in a Village restaurant. I'd come with some friends, husband and wife, passing through

from the Midwest, who had never been members of any New York circle. When we sat down, I saw Delmore across the room with a girl whom I didn't know. There came the ritual of the nod and the wave of the hand, but somehow this didn't seem enough now. Time had passed (this was 1961) and the memories of emotional violence had receded; I felt some more friendly or at least civilized gesture was called for. I went over to his table, said hello, and we talked rather pleasantly for a few minutes. He didn't bother to introduce the girl. When they had finished dinner and were on the way out, I invited him and the girl to sit down with us for a brandy. For a while he spoke quietly, and then there burst forth a Delmore I'd never seen or heard, not even in his most agitated moments. He started to rant and rave. I'd always been able to follow the acute zigs and zags of his talk without any effort, but this time I found him incoherent, and his voice raucous in a way I'd never heard it. He meant to be friendly, he wasn't ranting at me but *toward* me—toward me and against the world. Every so often the tones of our past friendship would emerge, waver haltingly for a moment, and then be quickly swallowed back into the wrathful and incoherent bellow. I did what I could by way of flattery and cajolery to make him feel better, but there was no moderating his torrent. The girl kept plucking his arm to leave, and at length he yielded.

Our waiter came running over: "I guess you'll want another brandy after that." Delmore's voice—yells, grunts, groans—had filled the place. Feeling shaken and drained, I gulped a double brandy; the effect was to relax me suddenly, and I burst into tears. I was embarrassing my friends, I knew, but they waited patiently for me to subside. At length the wife, a kindly but also matter-of-fact person, spoke out: "Don't take on so. There's nothing to be done. He's beyond salvaging." The voice of reason submitting to inexorable fact. There crossed my mind the ancient story of the father weeping for a dead child. A Stoic philosopher, passing by, tells the father: "Why do you weep? It is irrational. Your weeping will not bring him back to life." The father replies, "That is why I weep, because it cannot bring him back." I looked across the table at the open, clear, and uncomplicated face that had spoken, and thought: Yes, that is why I weep, because he cannot be salvaged.

DUNCAN CAMPBELL SCOTT

1862–1947

Duncan Campbell Scott was born in Ottawa, Ontario, on August 2, 1862, the son of a Methodist minister. He was educated in various towns in Canada where his father was sent to preach, and attended Stanstead College, Quebec. He then entered the Canadian civil service and served in the Department of Indian Affairs until his retirement in 1932.

During his career as a civil servant Scott also studied literature and music, and achieved a national reputation as a poet. His first volume of poetry, *The Magic House*, was published in 1893, and was followed over the years by seven additional volumes of original verse. An early collection of previously published poems, *Complete Poems*, appeared in 1926; *Selected Poems*, edited by E. K. Brown, was published posthumously in 1951. Scott was also the author of two volumes of short stories, *In the Village of Viger* (1896) and *The Witching of Elspie* (1923).

Scott, who was twice married, died at his home in Ottawa on December 19, 1947.

MELVIN H. DAGG
From "Scott and the Indians"

Humanities Research Bulletin, Fall 1972, pp. 5–9

If Scott's poetic attitude to the Indian is ever to be understood, ⟨. . .⟩ it is essential to look beyond his popular poems to such lines as the passage in "Lines in Memory of Edmund Morris," where Scott describes Morris marking the grave of the chief he had earlier painted:

> I can feel the wind on the prairie
> And see the bunch-grass wave,
> And the sunlights ripple and vary
> The hill with Crowfoot's grave,
> Where he "pitched off" for the last time
> In sight of the Blackfoot Crossing,
> Where in the sun for a pastime
> You marked the site of his tepee
> With a circle of stones. Old Napiw
> Gave you credit for that day. [1]

E. K. Brown is correct in stating that much of Scott's power in dealing with the Indian is achieved in "Lines in Memory of Edmund Morris." [2] That Brown chose to base his statement on the passage describing the death of Akoose probably results from a lack of the knowledge necessary to understand the lines I have here quoted, for Brown does not even acknowledge their existence. Although they achieve the same effect as the Akoose lines, their meaning is more intricately complex, and ultimately more revealing.

Like the Akoose passage, the Crowfoot lines function as a poem within a poem. Both passages are concerned with the deaths of Indian chiefs, Akoose, and here Crowfoot, within the larger thematic context of the whole poem, the death of Scott's friend, Edmund Morris. The implication is obvious. If the essence of Scott's Indian poetry is "a facile acceptance of the Indian 'nation's doom'," [3] ⟨. . .⟩ surely Scott would not have seen the death of Crowfoot and Akoose in the same context as the death of Edmund Morris, a man described by Brown as "an intimate of Scott's." [4]

Examining the "Crowfoot passage," one finds Morris, obviously in the presence of Scott, returning to the Blackfoot reserve after Crowfoot's death to mark "the site of his tepee/ With a circle of stones" [5]—two white men, unnoticed on the Albertan prairie, quietly creating a shrine of stones to an Indian they both revered. That is the scene. The significance is that through Morris, Scott, as a poet, has also created a small shrine to Crowfoot.

But the real significance of the "Crowfoot passage" cannot be appreciated without an understanding of the words "Old Napiw." [6] To the Blackfoot, to Crowfoot, and, significantly, to Scott and Morris, he is "Old Man," the creator of life, not in a Christian, but an Indian context:

> Old Man covered the plains with grass for the animals to feed on. He marked off a piece of ground, and in it he made to grow all kinds of roots and berries. He put all kinds of animals on the ground. . . .
> One day Old Man determined that he would make a woman and a child; so he formed them both—the woman and the child, her son—of clay. After he had moulded the clay in human shape, he said to the clay, "You must be people," and then he covered it up and left it, and went away. The next morning he went to the place and took the covering off, and saw that the clay shapes had changed a little.

The second morning there was still more change, and the third, still more. The fourth morning he went to the place, took the covering off, looked at the images, and told them to rise and walk; and they did so. They walked down to the river with their Maker, and then he told them that his name was *Napi*, Old Man. [7]

Thus, the lines "Old Napiw / Gave you credit for that day," [8] can be paraphrased as "the creation God of the Blackfoot would have approved of your actions." Once this is understood, the passage reveals layers of meaning. Firstly, Morris, and poetically, Scott, by encircling Crowfoot's tepee with stones, are raising Crowfoot to the same level as Old Man, Napi, himself—the same level of high regard in which Crowfoot is still held by Indian people today:

> Crowfoot of the Blackfoot nation was another great chief. People speak about him as if he were still alive today. [9]

Significantly, Napi, the creator, marked out his *being* in the precise manner in which Morris, and poetically, Scott, encircled Crowfoot's tepee, with stones:

> He made the Milk River and crossed it, and, being tired, went up on a little hill and lay down to rest. As he lay on his back, stretched out on the ground, with arms extended, he marked himself out with stones,—the shape of his body, head, legs, arms, and everything. There you can see those rocks today. [10]

Finally, in the larger elegiac context of the poem, Scott is giving Morris the blessing of an Indian, not a Christian God, thus, if not dispelling, at least qualifying Hirano's charge of "Christian moralizing." [11]

Now that the depth of Scott's understanding and sensitivity to the Indian has been established, I will closely re-examine two of his more familiar Indian poems in that light, poems which Hall and Hirano conveniently ignore, and traditional critics treat in a pedestrian manner.

Of its kind, a portrait of an Indian woman in youth and age, "Watkwenies" is, without exception, Scott's finest poem:

> VENGEANCE was once her nation's lore and law
> When the tired sentry stooped above the rill,
> Her long knife flashed, and hissed, and drank its fill;
> Dimly below her dripping wrist she saw,
> One wild hand, pale as death and weak as straw,
> Clutch at the ripple in the pool; while shrill
> Sprang through the dreaming hamlet on the hill,
> The war-cry of the triumphant Iroquois.
>
> Now clothed with many an ancient flap and fold,
> And wrinkled like an apple kept till May,
> She weighs the interest-money in her palm,
> And, when the Agent call her valiant name,
> Hears, like the war-whoops of her perished day,
> The lads playing snow-snake in the stinging cold. [12]

Here, within the tightness of the sonnet form, Scott succeeds where the narrative technique of "The Forsaken" fails. The poem moves from octave to sestet, from past to present, from triumph in youth, to inner triumph in old age, with the same sure swiftness as the flash of the woman's long knife. The slain "sentry" [13] of the octave becomes the Indian "Agent" [14] of the sestet; the hiss of her knife is heard again in the "snow-snake" [15] game of the boys; their playful yelling is an echo of her triumphant war-cry.

Moreover, the poem contains two brilliantly contrasted images. The first is the frightening sight of the dying sentry, mirrored in the pool, seen from behind by the woman who stabbed him in the back:

> Dimly below her dripping wrist she saw,
> One wild hand, pale as death and weak as straw,
> Clutch at the ripple in the pool; . . . [16]

Ironically, the second image belies the first, suggesting not a murderess, but a face of ageing innocence, a face "wrinkled like an apple kept 'till May."[17]

Finally, the poem is successful because, unlike "The Forsaken" and Scott's other "doomed figure" portraits, it presents the Indian triumphantly, both in the past and the present. She knows what is owed her, "she weighs it,"[18] it is only "the interest-money,"[19] and as head of Indian Affairs Scott also knew what was owing—the principal. Treaty money is merely interest, tokenism. Hirano was mistaken when he asserted that "there is no evidence that privately as a poet, he (Scott) took a completely different view from Scott the government official."[20]

"At Gull Lake, August 1810" appeared in the volume that culminated Scott's career as a poet, indeed, perhaps his finest volume, *The Green Cloister*. Similarly, "Gull Lake" itself is a culmination, and also a merging, of many of the themes contained in Scott's Indian poems. It should, for example, be read in close conjunction with "The Half-Breed Girl," though it surpasses it as a poem. Desmond Pacey dismisses it as "barely being saved from melodrama,"[21] preferring instead the subtle pounding of "Powassan's Drum," and what really is melodrama, "The Forsaken."

Scott begins his poem in the present, using the timeless images of nature, and the shifting patterns of the seasons, as a means of moving into the past, and the body of the poem, a narrative which took place a century ago:

> As of old the poplars shimmer
> As summer passes;
> Winter freezes the shallow lake to the core;
> Storm passes,
> Heat parches the sedges and grasses,
> Night comes with moon-glimmer,
> Dawn with the morning-star;
> All proceeds in the flow of Time
> As a hundred years ago. [22]

Thus the opening lines seem deceivingly simple. Yet before the narrative has even begun Scott has introduced its central symbol, and character, for they are one and the same. "Keejigo, star of the morning,"[23] as she is called in the narrative body of the poem. It is no coincidence, then, that in the opening stanza "Night comes with moon-glimmer / Dawn with the morning star."[24] For in order to understand this poem it is of absolute necessity to know that for prairie Indians the Gods of the sky, or as they called them, "the above people," were a holy triad consisting of Sun, Moon, and morning-star, in that order:

> The Sun is a man, the supreme chief of the world.
> The flat, circular earth in fact is his home, the floor
> of his lodge, and the over-arching sky is its covering.
> The moon, *Ko-komik-c-is*, night light, is the Sun's
> wife. The pair have had a number of children, all but
> one of whom were killed by pelicans. The survivor is
> the morning star, *A-pi-suahts*—early riser. [25]

Similarly, just as the central symbol of the poem, morning-star, is subtly introduced in the opening stanza, so too is the storm with which the narrative is climaxed.

Returning momentarily to the opening stanza, remembering that it is set in the present, the narrative in the past, it

can be seen that the holy triad is complete: Sun—"Heat parches the sedges and grasses;" Moon—"Night comes with moon-glimmer;" and Child of the Sun and Moon, morning-star—"Dawn with the morning star."[26] All three, Sun, Moon, and morning-star, are present and in unity.

But in the past, the narrative body of the poem, the child, morning-star, is separated from her heavenly or spiritual parents, Sun and Moon. Furthermore, her earthly parentage is mixed. She is the half-breed "daughter of Launay / the Normandy hunter / And Oshawan of the Saulteaux."[27] She is "troubled by fugitive visions,"[28] a line almost identical to that describing the dilemma of "The Half-Breed Girl,"—"shadows trouble her breast."[29] So that though morning-star is "third of the wives / Of Tabashaw Chief of the Saulteaux,"[30] she mistakenly seeks to free herself from her troubled, fugitive visions by enforcing the white blood already in her veins, by assimilating with a white man, by offering herself to the white trader, "Nairne of the Orkneys."[31] Before doing so, however, she prays to herself in "the beautiful speech of the Saulteaux,"[32] the final lines of which are here repeated:

> I am here my beloved,
> Heart's-blood on the feathers
> The foot caught in the trap.
>
> Take the flower in your hand,
> The wind in your nostrils;
> I am here my beloved;
> *Release the captive*
> *Heal the wound under the feathers.* [33]
> (italics mine, in the poem her entire prayer is off-set
> by italics)

The lines "Release the captive / Heal the wound under the feathers,"[34] are significant, for they at once reveal the motivating force behind morning-star's attempt to offer herself to the white trader, Nairne, while also stating, in striking imagery, Scott's attitude to her reasoning. "The wound under the feathers"[35] is an imagistic reference to her birth, the wound perpetuated by her white father, significantly, a hunter, upon her Indian mother, Oshawan. Again, then, morning-star feels that the wound can only be "healed" by reaffirming the white blood already within her.

But Sun and Moon, her heavenly parents, the Gods, do not approve. They are angry, and the utterance of her wish is immediately answered by

> A storm cloud marching
> Vast on the prairie,
> Scored with livid ropes of hail,
> Quick with nervous vines of lightning—[36]

Neither, of course, does Scott approve. Nothing could be a more explicit comment on "assimilation" than the image he has used to describe it—"the wound under the feathers."[37] Thus, though morning-star repeats her wish once more amidst the angry flashes of lightning and the roar of thunder,

> Her lips still moved to the words of her music
> "Release the captive,
> Heal the wound under the feathers, [38]

it is a wound, once perpetrated, that can never be healed, except in death. Tabashaw blinds her eyes, the old wives hurl her to her death:

> The old wives dragged her away
> And threw her over the bank
> Like a dead dog. [39]

Morning-star's wound can only be healed in death, and rebirth. The setting sun, her father, creates a rainbow. The wind unveils her mother, the moon, and morning-star rises to rejoin her holy parents, to complete the triad:

> The setting sun struck the retreating cloud
> With a rainbow, not an arc but a column
> Built with the glory of seven metals;
> Beyond in the purple deeps of the vortex
> Fell the quivering vines of the lightning.
> The wind withdrew the veil from the shrine of the
>   moon,
> She rose changing her dusky shade for the glow
> Of the prairie lily, till free of all blemish of colour
> She came to her zenith without a cloud or a star,
> A lovely perfection, snow-pure in the heaven of
>   midnight.
> After the beauty of terror the beauty of peace. [40]

Thus the poem is cyclical in nature. The holy triad, present in the opening stanza, but absent throughout the narrative, is once again complete. The parents have reclaimed their child, and in doing so, healed her wound. She is now "free of all blemish of colour."[41] Little wonder morning-star was, as the final stanza states, never found by her people. Only her mother, the moon, knows where she is. Scott's poem is a brilliant fusion of Indian religion and racial relationships.

Notes

 1. Duncan Campbell Scott, *Selected Poems* (Toronto: Ryerson Press, 1951), p. 92.
 2. E. K. Brown, *On Canadian Poetry* (Toronto: Ryerson Press, 1948), p. 133.
 3. Chipman Hall, "A Survey of the Indian's Role in English Canadian Literature to 1900" (diss., Dalhousie University, 1969), p. 60.
 4. E. K. Brown, *On Canadian Poetry*, p. 133.
 5. Duncan Campbell Scott, *Selected Poems*, p. 92.
 6. Ibid.
 7. George Bird Grinnell, *Blackfoot Lodge Tales* (Lincoln: University of Nebraska Press, 1962), pp. 137–138. Scott's phonology is rather unique. In his short story, "Charcoal," he transcribes "Motokiks" (Old Woman's secret society) as "Mow-to-kee". The point is *Napi* and *Napiw* are different transcriptions of the same word.
 8. Duncan Campbell Scott, *Selected Poems*, p. 92.
 9. Christine Daniels and Ron Christiansen, *Many Laws* (Metis Association of Alberta, 1970), p. 59.
10. George Bird Grinnell, *Blackfoot Lodge Tales*, p. 137.
11. Keiichi Hirano, "The Aborigine in Canadian Literature," *Canadian Literature*, No. 14 (Autumn, 1962), p. 47.
12. Duncan Campbell Scott, *Selected Poems*, p. 133.
13. Ibid.
14. Ibid.
15. Ibid.
16. Ibid.
17. Ibid.
18. Ibid.
19. Ibid.
20. Keiichi Hirano, p. 46.
21. Desmond Pacey, *Ten Canadian Poets* (Toronto: Ryerson Press, 1958), p. 160.
22. Duncan Campbell Scott, *Selected Poems*, p. 24.
23. Ibid., p. 25.
24. Ibid., p. 24.
25. George Bird Grinnell, *Blackfoot Lodge Tales*, p. 258. Also, J. W. Schultz, *The Sun Gods Children* (Boston: Houghton Mifflin Co., 1930).
26. Duncan Campbell Scott, *Selected Poems*, p. 24.
27. Ibid., p. 25.
28. Ibid.
29. Ibid., p. 62.
30. Ibid., p. 25.
31. Ibid.
32. Ibid., p. 26.
33. Ibid.
34. Ibid.
35. Ibid.
36. Ibid., p. 27.
37. Ibid., p. 26.
38. Ibid., p. 27.
39. Ibid.
40. Ibid., p. 28.
41. Ibid.

FRED COGSWELL
"No Heavenly Harmony:
A Reading of 'Powassan's Drum'"

Studies in Canadian Literature, Summer 1976, pp. 233–37

The notion of music and the musician as a force which upholds and sustains matter is enshrined in the Greek legends of Amphion and Orpheus. In English-poetry, it has found its most full expression in the lines from John Dryden's "A Song for St. Cecilia's Day":

> From harmony, from heavenly harmony
>   This universal frame began:
>   From harmony to harmony
> Through all the compass of the notes it ran,
> The diapason closing full in man.

Duncan Campbell Scott had been a musician before he had been a poet. As one, he must have known the feeling which every musician has when he plays, that of creative power, of building a harmonious universe of sound where had been silence before. It does not matter that the universe thus created passes with the creation and goes no further than the listening ears. Qualitatively, any creation is all creation while that creation is in progress.

It is easy therefore to imagine a cultured poet and musician, familiar with classical and English literature, turning to a musician and to music whenever it occurred to him to fashion a creation myth. Following the Greek tradition, Scott had used pastoral music in his great mythical poem of poetic creation, "The Piper of Arll." The Greek myth of musical creation and Dryden's Christian adaptation of it, however, were patently unsuitable for an apocalyptic vision of life. They posited a noble creator and a creation that was harmonious and good.

A man as sensitive and intelligent as Scott was could not be unaware, both as an official in the Department of Indian Affairs and a citizen of Canada in the twentieth century, that the harmony created by the musician, the poet, and the artist was of an order different from the details of daily life. By comparison, the latter were a flawed creation. When, therefore, he attempted an apocalyptic poem, dealing with his vision of these things, he found it necessary to posit a flawed creator. For this he found abundant precedent in the Indian legends of creative spirits, and in the personalities of the shamans or medicine men who preside as drummers at the rain dances and the ghost dances of Indian tribes and who "made magic" in a limited way among the daily affairs of Indian peoples. Indian demiurges were almost always less responsible and more malicious than the social goals which the Indians set for themselves. Indian medicine men, moreover, were chosen because their physical weaknesses and/or deformities unfitted them for the hunt. They wielded their magic powers with a certain malevolence toward more normal mortals. They were feared, not loved.

It is, then, both fitting and natural that Scott, in writing "Powassan's Drum," would have chosen for his flawed creator drumming into being a divided and doomed creation, an Indian medicine man, Powassan, a dwarf:

Wizened with fasting,
Fierce with thirst,
Making great medicine
In memory of hated things dead
Or in menace of hated things to come.

Powassan's creation is, of course, the artist's vision expressed in the

Throb-throb-throb-throb-throbbing
The sound of Powassan's Drum

and to Powassan, who creates it with closed eyes, and to the listener as well, the physical universe against which it is counterpointed "seems lost and shallow" in comparison. It is interpenetrated by the throbbing music of the drum as being is interpenetrated by the pulse of being. So close does this interpenetration come that the drumming, like the physical universe itself, is thought of as embracing all duration:

Has it gone on forever
As the pulse of being?
Will it last till the world's end
As the pulse of being?

As Powassan beats his drum continually and morning dawns and as day draws to twilight, the interpenetration is such that it seems to the listening animals, and to the poet describing the slow change of light, that the drumming is more than interpenetration, that Powassan's music is building the universe to one vast vision, an apocalyptic climax.

I shall quote the climax of the poem completely because in it can be found the keys to an understanding of the poem. It occurs immediately after the throbbing of Powassan's drum is categorized as "An infusion of bitter darkness" that "Stains the sweet water of twilight."

Then from the reeds stealing,
A shadow noiseless,
A canoe moves noiseless as sleep
Noiseless as the trance of deep sleep
And an Indian still as a statue
Molded out of deep sleep,
Sits modelled in full power,
Haughty in manful power,
Headless and impotent in power.
The canoe stealthy as death
Drifts to the throbbing of Powassan's Drum.
The Indian fixed like bronze
Trails his severed head
Through the dead water
Holding it by the hair.
Wound with sweet grass and tags of silver.
The face looks through the water
Up to its throne on the shoulders of power,
Unquenched eyes burning in the water,
Piercing beyond the shoulders of power
Up to the fingers of the storm cloud.

This passage presents so many implications all interlocked that it is difficult to sort them out and isolate them in one's mind. It is perhaps best, first of all, to consider it in relation to its immediate creator, the protagonist, Powassan. The Indian "modelled in full power/Haughty in manful power" is an embodiment of the physique which Powassan, the dwarf, longs to have but has not. He, therefore, out of malevolence has made

his otherwise perfect manly creation "Headless and impotent in power" while the canoe continues to drift as the throbbing of the drum whips up the storm which will overwhelm the symbol of Powassan's tribe's manhood. The vision, then, is both Powassan revenge on his own tribe for his physical inferiority and an assertion of his own superiority, through magic. As such, it is psychologically appropriate. The eyes in the severed head burn as Powassan's eyes had burned earlier in the poem.

There are larger implications, however, in this passage which Duncan Campbell Scott must have had in mind, so consistently are they worked out. The first consideration is, quite naturally when one considers the imagery of the poem, an ethnic one. Powassan's vision is, quite simply, the Indian considered as history. His physical shape (his body) is severed from his culture (his head), and he is unable to navigate his canoe (his power over his environment) through the "dead" water, and he therefore must perish in the first inevitable great storm. This pattern, however, is capable of amplification so long as certain salient facts are borne in mind. First and foremost is the consideration that "the head" is severed and trailed in the water and not in its rightful place "on the shoulders of power." In consequence the Indian cannot steer the canoe of his own volition. It either drifts on the river of life or is moved by some external harmony or disharmony. Whether the head symbolizes the human intellect and the body the human passions and desires, whether the head symbolizes leadership and the body the mass of the people (the body politic), whether the head symbolizes spiritual desires and the body material appetites, the implications are the same, and portentous for modern man: because man is not a unified whole, he is powerless of his own agency to direct the course of events which are leading to an inevitable catastrophe.

To me, the most interesting implication in this passage is what it reveals of Duncan Campbell Scott's insight into the nature and role of the artist in his own time. The head may be considered as the artist and the eyes as the artist's vision. Instead of being united with the body politic "on the shoulders of power" and able to steer according to his vision, the artist is trailed beside the boat and compelled to look through water toward its true throne. In an earlier passage, the world to the sound of the drum had "seemed full of water", an illusion created by the music of Powassan's hate. Water is not, therefore, a true medium of vision. It refracts and distorts what is seen through it. In consequence, the creative artist, although his eyes are "unquenched," sees not "the shoulders of power" but "beyond the shoulders of power/Up to the fingers of the storm-cloud." The eyes can see, but they overshoot their true home to a storm beyond. Artistic vision, then, severed from the rest of mankind and distorted by external passion, is both inaccurate and powerless to avert the violence which is the only answer that nature can give to the malevolent power expressed when hatred is unleashed.

Powassan's drumming is an orchestration of man's hates and fears working through history and building up to an apocalyptic vision of a divided mankind unable to act in the face of destruction:

The murdered shadow sinks in the water.
Uprises the storm
And crushes the dark world!
At the core of the rushing fury
Bursting hail, tangled lightning
Wind in a wild vortex
Lives the triumphant throb—throb—throb—throb
Throbbing of Powassan's Drum.

One final consideration illuminates what Duncan

Campbell Scott was expressing in "Powassan's Drum." That is his counterpointing of the movement of Nature against the conjuring vision of Powassan's drum. Here the creator of Nature is quite aptly symbolized by the sun—personified as an Indian of the opposite type from Powassan. Instead of skulking in his tent making magic, the sun is a brave who fishes his sky-ocean with admirable patience and self-control. Neither he nor the animals, nor the trees, nor the water, nor the sky can respond directly ("answer") the challenge of Powassan. There is nothing in the normal constructive pulse of Nature that can correspond to the malevolence drumming in the human will. But Nature has its cataclysmic other side, the destructive force of the storm, and the slow persistence of Powassan's drumming works a two-fold magic. On the one hand, it conjures up its

human vision of a headless Indian trailing his severed head by the side of a drifting canoe. On the other hand, through a gradual interpenetration with nature it builds up an impending storm that at the poem's conclusion sinks Powassan's own vision, "crushes the dark world," and overwhelms everything in a "Wild vortex" that "Lives in the triumphant throb—throb—throb—/throbbing of Powassan's Drum." Nature and Man are separate at the beginning of the poem. They are joined in destruction at its close. Nature will presumably survive, but when the "murdered shadow sinks in the water," man's hate-formed vision perishes in a greater storm. The implication is that this vision *is* mankind. "Powassan's Drum" is a superbly integrated apocalyptic poem, but what it expresses can bring no comfort to the human spirit.

EVELYN SCOTT

Elsie Dunn

1893–1963

Evelyn Scott was born Elsie Dunn in Clarksville, Tennessee, on January 17, 1893, and grew up in small towns in Tennessee and in New Orleans. Raised, she later claimed, as a conventional Southern belle, she was educated by private tutors and later attended Sophie Newcomb College and the Newcomb College of Art in New Orleans. At the age of twenty she eloped to Brazil with Frederick Wellman, the married dean of the School of Tropical and Preventative Medicine at Tulane University, and lived under extreme hardship for six years. At that time Wellman changed his name to Cyril Kay-Scott and Dunn adopted the name Evelyn Scott.

Evelyn and Cyril Kay-Scott returned to the United States in 1919 and settled in Greenwich Village as members of the bohemian artistic and literary set. Evelyn Scott, who had begun writing at the age of fourteen, published her first volume, a collection of poems (*Precipitations*), in 1920. Her first novel, the beginning of a trilogy that attacked conventional marriage and explored alternative domestic arrangements, was *The Narrow House*, published in 1921; it was followed by *Narcissus* (1922) and *The Golden Door* (1925). Over the next sixteen years Scott published eight more novels; *The Wave* (1929), a work of historical fiction with a Civil War setting, and *A Calendar of Sin* (1931), set in America prior to World War I, were singled out for praise by noted critics. Scott was also the author of several volumes of short stories, four books for children, and two volumes of autobiography: *Escapade* (1923), which describes her life in Brazil, and *Background in Tennessee* (1937), describing her youth and rebellion against the cultural and social milieu of the South.

For several years during the early 1920s Scott had a love affair with the painter Owen Merton, the father of Thomas Merton, following the death of his wife. She and Cyril Kay-Scott separated in the mid-1920s, and she later married John Metcalfe, a writer. Scott, who had a son, Creighton, by Cyril Kay-Scott, died in New York City on August 3, 1963.

Works

NOVELS

The Narrow House by Mrs. Evelyn Scott is absolutely in the mood of that little book of Huysmans, *A Vau-l'Eau*, which probably only a few of his admirers have had the curiosity to read. In that story of a lonely man's sordid and futile pursuit of decent comfort, there is the same insistence upon the drab, hideous dirtiness of genteel poverty. Mrs. Scott sees all the stains on the linen, all the dirt in the finger-nails; the filth in the street. The opening scene is dusty, shabby and dishevelled; the last describes a woman dabbling in the sink; and all through is a dreary litany of leaky gutters, buzzing flies, littered papers, and furtive, slinking, timorous, unhappy people. Beneath all

this belated realism runs the disjointed theme which shows that, though the author must be counted one with the most modern American novelists, she is yet but a curious echo of the naturalists of the 'eighties.

Like so many of her contemporaries, Mrs. Scott has come to the conclusion that, though Dr. Frank Crane's God may be in his heaven, all is not right with the world. The family, for one thing, is not what it seems to be in the works of Mrs. Gene Stratton-Porter. Within the narrow houses of domesticity there are foul and horrible things which sentimental romanticism succeeds in concealing with more or less success. Samuel Butler and the venerable Mr. Bernard Shaw, not to mention the distinguished author of *A Doll's House*, also suggested some years ago that family happiness covers a multitude of sins against the flesh and the spirit. Mrs. Scott insists rather effectively upon the former, but the spiritual tribulations of her characters are somewhat obscured in the fragmentarist style à la Joyce, which she employs. Nevertheless, this is a first novel of considerable interest, for it emphatically stresses the emancipation of the American novel from the conventions and traditions which have bound it hitherto. Both the form and the content are a defiant refusal to conform. In the main, the heretical novelists in this country have been contented with the challenge of the matter rather than of the manner of their writing. Mrs. Scott has attempted both challenges in a fashion which promises well for her future development.—ERNEST BOYD, "Progressing Backwards," *Freeman*, July 20, 1921, p. 453

Having read only those portions of Rupert Hughes which are pasted on the sides of newsstands, I can hardly venture to discuss him with authority. Yet, if I were to form a tentative judgement on those summaries and blurbs, I should say that Mr Hughes is an author who gives us something like a society drama, with characters, plot, and setting all more or less typical of some actual stratum, or condition, in society. In this I may be entirely unjust to Mr Hughes. But in revenge I am positive that it applies to Mrs Scott, who wrote *The Narrow House*, and who has now made that house gratifyingly less narrow in her new novel *Narcissus*.

But as Mrs Scott is quite plainly a much more complex writer than Mr Hughes, one feels at the start that the juxtaposition of the two names is false. To begin with, Mr Hughes would not write like this, which I take from *The Narrow House*:

> The room closed them like a coffin. Their life was their own. It did not flow in from the street.

No, that is not like Mr Hughes; it is like Mr Waldo Frank. There are other passages scattered through Mrs Scott's books which show the influence of *Ulysses*, a strain which it is safe to suppose has never defiled our great cinema novelist. However, Mrs Scott writes:

> "I'm suffering deeply, Julia. You are suffering. I see it. It is only the little person who doesn't suffer. Why do you resent me? Life is always making patterns. It has thrown us three—you and me, and your husband—into a design—a relationship to each other."

And although Mr Hughes would probably never have stepped so circumspectly around the word "triangle," it is safe to assume that the situation has occurred to him: Lawrence immersed in his chemical work; Dudley, a young artist, lover of Julia; Julia, the wife of Lawrence, beautiful and idle. But I have spoken of Mrs Scott's greater complexity; let us examine just how it affects her treatment of this vexing problem. First going back to *The Narrow House*.

The Narrow House was part of that astonishing post-war movement of anti-chauvinism among the intellectuals, a movement which attained its greatest expression in the sales of *Main Street* and the departure of Mr Harold Stearns for Europe. *The Narrow House*, then, was what might be termed "professionally depressing." Like most of 1921's record, it dipped back into Zola, being somewhat more circumspect and infinitely less powerful. It showed dull, broken lives, American lives which were so weary, so hateful, that even the American sun was discovered to shine with fatigue upon them.

In her second work Mrs Scott has cut away a great deal of this misery *praeter necessitatem*. The house is distinctly less narrow. The professional depression is for the most part lightened. Despite her public's approval of the patent gesture in *The Narrow House*, Mrs Scott seems to have developed a

distrust of it. But unfortunately, the resultant virtue is only a negative one; the author has gone through the excesses of *The Narrow House* to attain the neutralization of *Narcissus*.

At the same time she has attempted to graft upon her style elements of James Joyce and Waldo Frank. There is no objection to them as influences. There is no particular reason why writers should begin over again, when philosophers hand their apparatus from one to the other throughout the ages. Thus, my objection is neither to influences in general nor to these particular influences; but I do question the propriety of the influences as they appear in *Narcissus*.

For they produce a work which is peculiarly lacking in correlation. One feels this especially in the case of Waldo Frank, since his method is so specifically adapted to his own kind of writing. *Narcissus* is, as we have said, more or less of a society drama, wherein characters are presented for their objective reality, for their identity as people you see or shake hands with. But Waldo Frank's characters are meant to be like pebbles dropped into a pool: he tries to draw ever-widening circles around them. His plots are conceived in the same non-temporal, non-spatial tone. It is not to the point to attempt any judgements on this method at present. But it is to the point to insist that the method is as peculiarly adapted to one set of conditions as were dinosaurs or mastodons. Transferred, it is simply bones in a glass case.

Thus, the novel fluctuates between its strict localization and this lyrical drawing of the ever-widening circles. As a result the book has no consistent drive. Even the blurb is at a loss, for it heralds "A story of a group of people who are hindered by the relaxation of old standards of conduct and don't know what to do with their new freedom." There is, to be sure, one adolescent who enters and exits at intervals throughout the book, and who is undecided concerning his future. But even here the element of social transitions is only indirectly touched upon. (For which, by the way, let us be grateful.) I spoke of the opening triangle: Dudley, the artist; Julia, the wife; Lawrence, the husband. Actuated by a set of nuances which is not completely cogent—and the vagueness arises precisely because Mrs Scott always switches at such times from strict analysis of motives to Waldo Frank's type of lyrism—she tells Lawrence of their affair. He moves his bed into another room, and starts carrying his life from her bit by bit. She breaks off with Dudley—again by a set of elusive nuances—in the direction of a business man, and has an affair with him. After which she finally pierces Lawrence's steel on the last two pages, there is a reconciliation, and the book closes with:

> Unacknowledged, each kept for himself a pain which the other could not heal. Each pitied the other's illusion, and was steadied by it into gentleness.

Perhaps, in this fluctuation between the strict localizing of her characters and the drawing of lyrical circles, I have objected to the very thing which Mrs Scott was aiming for. But, if we are to have two poles of treatment, we must also have their polarity. It is not sufficient to juxtapose them without reconciliation. In the truest sense, significance is lost: the significance of some modus consistently and exclusively pursued.—KENNETH BURKE, "Enlarging the Narrow House," *Dial*, Sept. 1922, pp. 346–48

Historians and historical novelists of the conventional school have conspired to make us forget that wars happen to people as well as to governments. It has long been supposed that the best way to encompass artistically a great national event was to take a bird's-eye view of it; and, of course, from an altitude, a war would resolve itself into the movements of masses more or less controlled by the decisions of a few outstanding individuals and primarily actuated by some common ideal. That is the so-called heroic viewpoint.

For me, at least, the importance of Evelyn Scott's remarkable book ⟨*The Wave*⟩ lies in the fact that it is one of the few really formidable expressions in fiction of the anti-heroic viewpoint—or, if one may be permitted so lax a term, the modern viewpoint. It is not less sentimental than Barbusse or Remarque or Renn or Frey; but it seems to gain an added power and scope because it is so rigidly unautobiographical. Fine as is *All Quiet on the Western Front*, for example, one cannot help closing the book with the feeling that, after all, this is one man's war, fine-fibered and intelligent as that man may be. *The Wave* recounts no one man's war; it recounts the Civil War, whole and entire, by the one possible method: that of tracing its impact on several hundred individuals, from Abraham Lincoln down to a newsboy selling battle extras, from the Portuguese fop who has made a fortune in cotton speculation down to the Manchester factory hand who has been thrown out of work by the economic repercussions of a struggle three thousand miles away.

By the time these words appear, so much just praise will have been lavished on Mrs. Scott's obviously torrential creative power that it hardly seems worth while to make further comment. She has set in motion a veritable army of characters, each provided with a complete background, as if each were originally conceived as the central figure of a novel. Indeed, Mrs. Scott's insight into and curiosity about her own creations are so vital and enthusiastic that it is only with great difficulty that she avoids what must have loomed up as her major difficulty: that of so subordinating the tragedies and comedies of her individuals as to give the reader a continuous sense of the great national drama in which they played their parts. That we do achieve this sense, despite the fact that there is little further connection between the hundred or more sections of the book other than that of vague chronological sequence, is an astounding technical triumph for the author.

Criticism has been directed, and will continue to be directed, against the "formlessness" of the book. It is hardly necessary to point out that this formlessness is designed, that it is in itself a way, a valid and exciting way, of viewing the national cataclysm which was the Civil War. It is, more than that, the only way in which a thoroughly modern temperament *could* survey the war completely because only thus can the utter madness and senseless horror of strife be completely communicated. The indictments of a Remarque or a Frey are powerful enough; but they are individual indictments; they have a quality of isolation; and, more pertinently, the indignant emotions they arouse are rather simple ones which tend to disappear after the book is read. But the emotions aroused by *The Wave* are not the simple ones of horror and indignation at all, but something far more profound. The most blighting as well as the simplest thing one can say against war is that it brings wretchedness to millions of people—and in different ways. It is the multifariousness, the incoherent and unrelated multifariousness of the tragedies, that is the most dreadful thing about war. And of these multifarious, senseless, individual tragedies no one, before the appearance of *The Wave*, has given us more than a schematic picture. There is a certain nameless horror that comes with the reader's realization that the meanest Negro and General Robert E. Lee are both made sick to their very souls by the same event. As one reads on and on, passing from one social level to another, meeting soldiers, Negroes, generals, chaplains, old ladies, children, Polish immigrants, homeless Jews, bereft wives, deserters, politicians, one begins to lose sight of the fact that this is a war

between Confederates and Unionists, between two sharply demarcated economic and social ideologies. The "issues" of the war fade away, except in so far as they present themselves for our ironical survey; but the war as a tremendous *human* tragic event begins to engross us and finally to overwhelm us in its brutal variety and meaninglessness.

For myself, I find certain imperfections and disharmonies which are minor but perhaps worth pointing out. They are not the results of weakness but of an excess of strength. I could wish, for example, that Mrs. Scott's senses were not so keen and excitable, that she would refrain from packing every sentence with more visual and auditory metaphor than it will bear. Her style is so agonizingly alive that it occasionally becomes confusing. Similarly, she is so intent on avoiding a series of mere "snapshots" that (but very infrequently) she overloads her stories with biographical detail, as in the Kalicz episode. Finally, she may be charged once in a great while with selecting her stories too obviously in order to represent or typify some phase of the conflict. In so far as we recognize these episodes as "representative," they lose in emotional quality what they gain in mere pertinency.

But that Mrs. Scott's major conception has been fulfilled, cannot, I think, be denied; and only a carping critic would dare to disagree with Mr. Krutch's final judgment that here, if anywhere, the Civil War has received its most adequate treatment in fiction. There can be no doubt that *The Wave* is an outstanding achievement in recent American letters. —CLIFTON P. FADIMAN, "A Great National Drama," *Nation*, July 31, 1929, p. 119

With each succeeding novel, it becomes more and more apparent that Mrs. Scott uncovers a number of uneasy problems for the critic and reviewer. Unlike her peers—and here I would include Mrs. Wharton and Willa Cather—she has arrived at no final destination; she eludes those categories that we are so fond of making for the novelist, those neat distinctions by which we separate the writing of a novel from other activities in literature. I would say that from the very start of her career Mrs. Scott has been interested in something far beyond the formal limitations of her medium, and one might add that her growth in mastery over that medium is almost incidental. She has, I think, proved her ability as an artist in all varieties of the form that she has chosen: among her shorter pieces are those admirable novelettes in *Ideals*, and not content with these she turned to the larger canvases of *The Wave* and *The Calendar of Sin*. Falling between the novelettes and the longer studies are her first book *The Narrow House*, *Escapade*, *Migrations*, *Eva Gay*, and the present novel, *Breathe Upon These Slain*. I believe that this last is among the best of the dozen books that she has written, and listing a few facts about it will reveal, I think, its less obvious relationship to all the others.

In this last book there is a noticeable shift in environment; the scene is laid on the east coast of England and the central action of the novel is motivated by a series of events which took place forty years ago. The story is told by means of a special device: the narrator is living in a furnished house, and guided by family photographs hanging on the wall, reconstructs the history of the Courtneys who had made the house their home. It was one of those middle-class English families that wheeled slowly upward from moderate prosperity at the close of the last century to near wealth during the World War. This family represents, I think, the so-called "norm" established by middle-class society in England and America. Here we see the stuffy Victorian interior: heavy plush and satin clothed furniture and dead birds (given a dubious immortality by the skill of taxidermists) in life-like sleep under glass bells. Through locked doors and windows one hears the slow roaring of the sea. This near past, extending through the reigns of Victoria, Edward, and the present George, seems, because of its outmoded proximity, more distant than any other period in history. To go into the lives of the people is very like wandering among the ashes of old Rome, and though some may still survive in flesh, the world that gave them a confident excuse for being is now an edifice half destroyed by premature decay. It will be observed that even in Mrs. Scott's remarkable first novel, *The Narrow House*, the social structure that she revealed was on the point of ruin, and so again we see the signs of ruin here.

The photographs disclose the entire company of Courtneys. Philip and Fedelia, father and mother of the household; Bertram the son, Tilly who died young, Ethel, Meg, and Cora, the daughters. See again Philip, the successful man of business, portly, middle-aged, wistful, inarticulate, inept at home, brutal, arrogant, and by no means scrupulous in business hours. Fedelia, his wife, carries her domestic, blind, harsh virtues before her as one might hold a banner. She rules the house as Philip rules his office and her drive toward power, clearly shown, is as destructive as every human's reach toward earthy power becomes. Blindly, she maims her children. The weaker variations of Philip and Fedelia are the children, the highly sensitized Tilly, a family sacrifice, to become a symbol of childhood death for Courtneys, then Ethel, nervous, ecstatic, trapped in marriage to a commissioned naval officer, then shallow Cora, then ugly Meg doomed to neurotic spinsterhood, and last, ineffectual Bertram who was to be the family hero, fulfilling his destiny by death on the battlefield of the Somme. Ethel in trapped rebellion, and Bertram, closeted by an all-too-conscious despair, are the central figures in the latter sections of the novel. Ethel's sons are citizens of the new world, the material out of which fascists and communists are made, and their speeches are the means by which an epilogue is written.

So much for the particular range that Mrs. Scott has chosen for this latest novel, but on reading it one sees again the inner structure that was implied in *The Narrow House*. One may even go so far as to identify a similar cast of characters, but this detail is not important. It is the theme at the core of the two books that commands attention, a theme that reveals how human beings are trapped in their own toils, as inevitably, as fatally as Macbeth caught in the maze that surrounded his immediate ambitions. The story is an old one, and how then does Mrs. Scott make it significant to us and to our times? In *The Narrow House* a rapid insight into human motives guided her way. It was a violent book, written with such conviction, that admitting certain flaws, its publication promised the arrival of an important novelist. Here, I would say, Mrs. Scott's prose instrument lacked the flexibility required for her more subtle observations, for what she has to say will admit no facile means of speech and to drive her point home, a number of specific instances must be placed before her readers. For the most part, she has selected her examples from American life and revealed them in the light of melodrama. I know that I am oversimplifying her statement when I say that her people are trapped and thwarted by the demands of sex, of money, of a transitory position in society. One must read the novels as one reads poetry, to get the full impact of Mrs. Scott's argument. In this last book she no longer turns to a melodramatic statement of her thesis and the result is that of subdued lyricism, an elegy, if you will, of a society that is now about to die. The danger that Mrs. Scott sees in the new order is that mistaken confidence that human beings have in the victories of material power, that very power which breeds ambition and then frustrates its final gratification. Her warning to the younger communists is that they too may fall into the narrow house that holds the bones of their grandfathers, the Victorians who celebrated the hollow conquest of iron and of steel.

As I said at the beginning of this review, Mrs. Scott voices no final solution of the problems she presents to her critics. She, like the old philosopher who sought an honest man by carrying a lantern, is seeking for some ultimate expression of reality. Her novels represent the road she has traveled during the past twelve years. At this moment only a few, I think, will realize the full importance of that journey. From the evidence of this last book before me I doubt if Mrs. Scott will ever run to shelter; she will never relinquish, I think, her special power to observe the changing world. If I were looking for a parallel of this latest novel in modern literature I would be forced to reread Thomas Hardy and note again that courage to observe in human action the fatal end of earthly destiny.—HORACE GREGORY, "The Narrow House of Victorian England," *SR*, May 26, 1934, p. 709, 713

The intelligent artist is always concerned with his relation to society; but in an age when loyalties are confused or feverish poverty may tumble him into a self-consciousness that is deadening he wears his work, and all the attitudes that go into it, like Coleridge's albatross. He is not interested in society; he is merely afraid of losing or changing his place in it. His artistry may degenerate into elaborate, genteel shiftlessness; then he has not even a simple dignity. Sooner or later he feels himself branded by the name—or the disguise—of his art; he is unhealthily aware of his meager distinction. If he is a genuine artist, he is uncomfortable at something else; if he sticks it out, unrewarded and resentful, his perceptions are scattered. In time he may even confuse slick cynicism with the sense of tragedy, or jealousy with discrimination.

It is this situation—the bread-and-butter version of the artist problem—that has preoccupied Mrs. Scott. She uses it, of course, to mirror society, to ask questions about society: but the best ⟨*Bread and a Sword*⟩ is the technical adroitness with which she illuminates the tangled emotions of men and women under stress. As a social novel *Bread and a Sword* is a trifle crude; its information, like its commentary, is on a surprisingly low level. You never feel that her Alec Williams is asking himself "What must I do to be saved?" quite as fiercely as Mrs. Scott suggests that he does, nor that the characters know what they are talking about when they make political statements.

The value of *Bread and a Sword* lies in the supple rhythm of its narrative and in Mrs. Scott's device, somewhat reminiscent of the mechanical soliloquy in *Strange Interlude*, which enables her to present her characters on several planes of emotion and experience at once. It is in such sensitively written passages, marked by the insight and subtle grace of a poetic mind, that Mrs. Scott is at her best; and at her best she writes with a nimble intensity that makes a character quiver before our eyes. Yet one never sees the character whole; the emphasis is always on a moment or an appearance, on an instance of terror or disgust or exaltation; never on the part as evidence of the whole, on the design that would allow some projection to so many brilliant items.

One can explain this partly by the essential meagerness of the story. Mrs. Scott is writing what may properly be called a study: Alec and Kate Williams, figures in a narrative, are important to us chiefly because they are shown in so many different attitudes and against so many different objects. What matters is not where they are or what they are doing, but the response they make to this environment or that. The novel is thus a series of responses, with each calling up some memory of the past, joining that memory to some quick (and usually tortured) sensation about the present. There are fragments of personality, associations, moments of conflict; the mind struggles against its waywardness, against its antagonists; it tries to group emotions, to resolve conflict, and yet at the same time it is a flickering in time, a reflection of, and a guide to, activity.

Thus we meet Alec Kate Williams in Europe, and immediately the theme of their married existence—poverty and irritable struggle—makes itself felt, partly through their interminable quarrels, but more significantly in the furtive nostalgia that burdens each. Alec, a novelist, has been increasingly unsuccessful; Kate has given up her modest painting. With their two boys they are living from hand to mouth in Catalonia, sustained by the promise of a check from Alec's publishers. The check never comes, and painfully the Williamses make their way back to America, there to live on the bounty of Kate's parents.

In New Jersey the Hills turn out to be kindly but Philistine. More despondent than ever, unable to work, Alec learns that his publishers care little for his work, and are somewhat less than anxious to advance him money on works in which they have no confidence. Alec does not share his wife's radicalism—it is a little too inane for anybody's comfort; Mrs. Scott has Kate do everything but chirrup "comes the revolution." What love has remained to them is being eaten away by irritation. Finally they break away to work on a Pennsylvania farm.

There Alec finds that only his routine is different. At heart he remains an artist unable to practice his art, yet unable to relinquish it. Kate has drawn away from him to the extent of having an affair with a farmhand; ill from incessant overwork and worry, aged by the failure of their marriage, she finds that there is little left for her. When she is fatally stricken and taken to a hospital, Alec goes away again, this time to find stray work as a gardener and as an organist in a cheap theatre.

Finally Alec finds to his dismay that the wife of his current employer, exhilarated no end by finding an honest-to-goodness writer in her power, has fallen in love with him. Kate's death, it soon appears, has not liberated him; in a way, it has added further responsibilities. At this point the novel grows vague and repeats itself rather insistently; the conclusions about society which Mrs. Scott announces so elaborately in her preface are scarcely touched upon. At the end Alec finds himself at sea; both literally and figuratively farther away from home than ever. One anarchy, it is evident, has been succeeded by another.—ALFRED KAZIN, "Bread and a Sword and Some Other Recent Works of Fiction," *NYTBR*, April 18, 1937, p. 6

POETRY

One who would diagnose the ailments of minor contemporary poetry could find no better subject than *The Winter Alone*. Miss Scott's book is a typical example of the competent, frankly imitative verse, deriving from the Symbolists through Imagism, that is characteristic of our more conservative "advanced" periodicals. That is to say, it is serious, self-respecting verse, pitched half way between poetry and bathos; its technical deficiencies and its sententiousness prevent its ever rising to the one, while its earnestness and preoccupation with the "new" technic are usually enough to keep it from falling into the other. But it is called poetry, and is accepted as poetry, and one who is curious to account for the failure of most of the "poetry" of today will do well to examine this book. For the student of literary diseases, *The Winter Alone* is an unexcelled compendium of symptoms.

Miss Scott employs a "modern" technic. Not the most "modern," whose tendency (witness *transition*, *The Hound and Horn*, *The Criterion*; witness Eliot, Ransom, MacLeish) is toward conservatism, a modification of strict form; but the comfortably "modern," the *vers-libre* of the late Imagists. Unlike the Imagists, but in company with most contemporary writers in free-verse, Miss Scott doesn't seem to understand her own metrical technic very well. It is not that her lines give the effect of prose chopped up into verses of varying length: there is abundant rhythm; the trouble is rather that she is unable to stabilize the dominant rhythm of a poem, or to combine conflicting rhythms agreeably. Verse does not flow into verse. One thinks of water in a pan tilted now this way, now that. The lines falter, buck; or else break into a staggering see-saw trot. In such verses as these, for instance, there is none of the fine cadenced clash of rhythm upon rhythm that characterizes authentic *vers-libre*:

> From the apple-pink east,
> To the west, and the cloudy forests of the rain,
> Was ten centuries.
> From the circle scurfed with mist
> Where the sun,
> Looking at tomorrow,
> Saw its own reflection,
> Was another ten centuries.

The first three verses compose a fair cadence; but thereafter there is nothing, to me at least, but rhythmical chaos. The versification of this, and of the majority of these poems, is not so unpleasant as it is undistinguished.

Another Imagist trick is the violent image. Originally a seventeenth-century device—Doctor Johnson's *discordia concors*—Miss Lowell's group revived it as "the exact word." The inexpert soon converted this into a plea for license, of course, and the exact word became, more often than not, simply the extraordinary word. Verse abandoned the rhetoric of sonorous generalities (cf. Aldrich's "Enamoured architect of aery rhyme") for the no-less-rhetoric of startling "Truths" (cf. Cummings' "we were / two alert lice in the blond hair of nothing"). The error lies in believing that the *vis poetica* is resident in shock. The violent image, the wrenched metaphor, the *discordia concors*, are justifiable only when they arise integrally from the emotion, when they are the emotional intellectualization of experience, as in Webster's

There's a plumber laying pipe in my guts: it scalds—

or in Donne's use of alchemical symbology in "A Nocturnall upon S. Lucies Day." Now, whatever her intention, Miss Scott's poems impress me as pieces written for their detail. And the details is most often violent—a shock, an extraordinary "truth"—with the result that is sometimes irritating, sometimes amusing, but almost never truly poetic. Thus, the sky after sunset is "hell-pink and dappled," where the oxymoron "hell-pink," tastelessly flamboyant, nullifies the cliché "dappled;" or, the moon-lit sky is "fever green"—which is better than hell-pink, but far from good; or, straight from the junkyard of rhetoric:

> There are public mats of seaweed
> On the sea-wall's slime,

which says exactly nothing, says it selfconsciously, and stammers in the saying over an awkward syzygy in the second verse.

In fact, Miss Scott's greatest difficulties are with the manipulation of figures. Sometimes a good metaphor is destroyed and even made ridiculous by its successor:

> Blue moths that circle the moon,
> The soft stern eyes,

Reflecting bright pain
As sweet lakes reflect the brass of battle,

If the moths are circling the moon, are the eyes circling the face? and *do* moths reflect pain, or light, or anything else, as water is said to reflect in the very good second metaphor? Sometimes a simile is false. Thus, in a poem descriptive of a sow, Miss Scott forces the occasion to draw a comparison between the sow and Jesus:

As Jesus voluntarily did yield himself
That paltry man be saved,
The sow has unwittingly become a victim and a
lesson.

The immolation of the sow has not been mentioned in the preceding verses, and it is to be supposed that she was slaughtered in the usual way; but was her death "voluntary"? We are told that she died "unwittingly." But are *voluntarily* and *unwittingly* synonymous? Meditation convinces me that they are antithetical. And so the *as* is unjustifiable, and the comparison is no comparison at all, but merely a play of questionable taste. (Saint Thomas could write

Pie Pellicanee Jesu Domine
Me immundum munda tuo sanguine,

without offense, because the comparison of Jesus to a pelican, though sufficiently quaint, is not felt as a striving for cleverness; Miss Scott's sow-simile, however, though there is no reason on earth why Jesus should not be compared to a sow, is too consciously an attempt to shock the sensitive to be anything but rather cheap.) Or, if it is not a question of simile and metaphor, the diction itself is strained, awkward. Thus, the sow's magnificent "compendium" consists of "teats, thighs, ruddy belly." But what does *compendium* mean here? To go back to the root of the word, is it possible that Miss Scott might better have said *dependencies*? Again, we find "mothers who provide indulgence of a gustatory nature to their children, after Sunday School." I take it that this means that the children are given luncheon; but why does Miss Scott assume that bombastic humor, which is never funny, is any more successful as a poetic effect? Or, finally, there are ambiguities of structure,

violations of English usage, that can only destroy poetic force. So, the sow was "born naked to the world" (why *to*?), "where, due to some negligence I cannot understand, etc." (why *due to*? to what was the sow *due*? would it have been better to write *because of*?). Another instance is the ending of "The Splendid Sky," where a series of unattached ambiguous participial phrases subverts the entire meaning.

It is worth noting, also, that Miss Scott is very eager to convey a message, and that she is seldom content to allow her symbols to speak for themselves. She has a Duchess-like habit of appending morals, as she does, for instance, at the end of "Sow":

To be crucified,
Or buried in your flesh,
That others may pretend the universe is kindly—
It's the same thing!

(But it *isn't!*) Or "The Owl":

I shall suspect hereafter
That you are a poet:
Neither your friends, nor the sufferings of your
family,
Nor your victims,
Important to you,

which sounds like Dorothy Parker—a distressing thing to say about anyone.

The faults of this book are in part the faults of most of our poetry. There is a great deal of contemporary verse that is technically more expert than *The Winter Alone*; but the false brilliance, the simile that is no simile, the mixed metaphors, and the sententiousness—these are almost universal. We are too intent upon getting ourselves down on paper, too hurried, too careless of all the ramifications of our experience and thought. Our writing is too immediate. It is frequently moving, and the "revolutions" of the past twenty years have given us a great deal of superficial technic; but the worth is only an apparent worth, and there is no evidence yet that Eliot, MacLeish, Ransom, and Jeffers need tremble upon their thrones.—DUDLEY FITTS, "The Verse of Evelyn Scott," *Poetry*, Sept. 1930, pp. 338–43

ALAN SEEGER

1888–1916

Alan Seeger was born on June 22, 1888, in New York City. He lived for ten years on Staten Island, attending the Staten Island Academy, and later went to the Horace Mann School in Manhattan. When he was twelve his family moved to Mexico and young Seeger was sent to the Hackley School in Tarrytown, New York. He entered Harvard in 1906, where he was shy and reclusive, preferring to translate Dante and Ariosto; in his senior year he edited the *Harvard Monthly*. He lived in New York for several years after his graduation in 1910, then moved to Paris, where he lived and wrote in the Latin Quarter.

When the war began he enlisted in the Foreign Legion, where he immediately proved himself to be an intelligent and resourceful soldier. He served first on the Aisne and then went with his regiment to Champagne for the September 1915 offensive. On July 4, 1916, Seeger was wounded while serving with his company at Belloy-en-Santerre but remained at his post, cheering on his comrades; he was found dead the next morning in a shell hole. For his bravery he was awarded posthumously the Croix de Guerre and the Medaille Militaire.

Later in 1916 his *Collected Poems* were published, with an introduction by William Archer. His best-known poem, "I Have a Rendezvous with Death," has been widely anthologized and long associated with the generation of men who were killed in the war.

Personal

As a college student at Harvard, he describes himself as a devotee of learning for learning's sake. He shut himself off completely from the life of the University, scoffing at the ordinary pleasures of the undergraduate and feeling no need of comradeship. He led the life of a bookish anchorite. And then came the rude and sudden awakening. Like the young men of Balzac's novels, the first glimpse of the world left him *ébloui*. He was haunted by an image that destroyed immediately the peace of mind, the singleness of purpose, the power of concentration, so essential to the intellectual life. From the beginning he had been caught by the mediæval formula of the three categories, the lust for knowledge, the lust for feeling, the lust for power. And now, with the vision of the world's life cast up before him, the pursuit of knowledge is bereft of meaning and satisfaction, and he is caught by the full sweep of the lust for feeling. And so he ends his letter with this bit of advice to his correspondent:

> If ever you find yourself suddenly devoured by the divine passion, consult only your heart. Yield to your instincts. Possessed by the force which holds the stars in their orbits, you cannot err. For it is Nature that is asserting itself in you, and in Nature alone is truth. What though your abandonment to it bring deception and unhappiness. You have yet enriched your life with some particle of a beauty that can never fade.

For himself the opportunity of pressing the moment full with emotion came, not with love, but with the outbreak of war. The dedication to love alone, he says of himself, is good as far as it goes, but it goes only half way, and his aspiration was to "drink life to the lees." His interest in life was passion, his object to experience it in all rare and refined, in all intense and violent forms. The war having broken out, it was natural that he should have staked his life on learning what it alone would teach. And so he became a soldier. His motive was not hatred of the Germans; he was in fact an admirer of Teutonic institutions. Nor did the conflict possess for him any clear moral issue. "Peoples war," he says, "because strife is the law of nature and force the ultimate arbitrament among humanity no less than in the rest of the universe. He is on the side he is fighting for, not in the last analysis from ethical motives at all, but because destiny has set him in such a constellation." Being where he is, a man's part is to play the game boldly and honorably, as a cosmic gambler, so to speak, whose reward is in the intensity of the feelings aroused, no matter whether in the end he or death be the victor.

Let us admit that there is nothing mean or small in such a way of facing the issues of life and death, that it has the glow of youthful magnanimity; but is there not also in it something a little saddening? We speak not from the point of view of the pacifist; for the war is here, to be fought to its grim end. Our sadness, such as we feel, is rather a feeling of futility. Why was it that a youth of Seeger's keen intellectual interests should have suddenly found his pursuit of knowledge empty and meaningless? Why should so spirited a soul have left college with no central philosophy as an anchor against the winds of the world, with no sense of values save that which he drank in from the current Epicureanism? He thought, alas, he was pursuing glory and happiness; it is only too clear, to one who reads between the lines, that he was seeking escape from the terrible *ennui* of pleasure, and hoping to find in a soldier's obedience the healthful discipline of limitations which he had never learned at school. Of what avail is it to instruct a man in economics and government and biology and poetry and art and history, if he never learn the truth of his soul? Somehow we must get philosophy back into our schools or we are undone. Nor is there any avail in the trifling of pragmatism or the filth of Freudianism as these are taught in Seeger's college. There is a bitter truth for our philosophers themselves to learn before philosophy can be made again the centre of a truly humanistic education.—UNSIGNED, "Au Champ d'Honneur," *Nation*, June 28, 1917, pp. 758–59

Alan Seeger was conspicuous at Harvard. In thought, word, and deed he was different from his fellows. His appearance was striking. He made it more striking still. He was very tall, his hair was jet black, remarkably thick and straight, his eyes had a peculiar liquid look, and his face was a beautiful oval.

He lived in an atmosphere of mediæval romance, such as would have delighted Keats and Shelley. It was devotion to the past so poignant that one wondered how he could ever live in the modern work-a-day world.

One of his letters describes this period: "As you may remember, in the years when I was at college, I was a devotee of Learning for Learning's sake. . . . I led the life of an anchorite. At an age when the social instincts are usually most lively I came to understand the pleasures of solitude. My books were my friends. The opening to me of the shelves of the college library, a rare privilege, was like opening the gates of an earthly paradise. In those dark alleys I would spend afternoons entire, browsing among old folios, following lines of research that often had no connection with my courses, following them simply for the pleasure of the explorer discovering new countries. I never regret those years. They made their contribution. Their pleasures were tranquil and pure. Their desires were simple and all the means of satisfying them were at hand.

"But my hedonism, if such it may be called, was not superficial like that of so many, to whom the emotional means only the sexual. I was sublimely consistent. For seeing, in the macrocosm, all Nature revolve about the twin poles of Love and Strife, of attraction and repulsion, so no less in the microcosm of my individual being I saw the emotional life equally divided between those two cardinal principles. The dedication to Love alone, as Ovid prettily confesses his own in more than one elegy, is good as far as it goes, but it only goes half way, and my aspiration was to go all the gamut, to 'drink life to the lees.' My interest in life was passion, my object to experience it in all rare and refined, in all intense and violent forms."

Such a man could not exist successfully in the modern world. After graduation he stayed for a time in New York, and one of the legends about him at which we laughed immoderately was the story of his first love affair. In order to make a proper sacrifice for the young lady, he signalized the declaration of his love by giving up the precarious job on which he was absolutely dependent. The young lady could not appreciate this romantic type of sacrifice; poor Alan was rejected, and thrown on the town.

These gay rhymes describe him:

A timid footstep,—enter then the eager
KEATS-SHELLEY-SWINBURNE-MEDIAEVAL-SEEGER;
Poe's raven bang above Byronic brow,
And Dante's beak,—you have his picture now;
In fact he is, though feigning not to know it,
The popular conception of a poet.
Dreaming, his eyes are steadily alight
With splendours of a world beyond our sight;
He nothing knows of this material sphere,—

Unwilling seems, at times, to linger here;
Beauty is all his breath, his blood, he says,—
Beauty his shrine, and Love its priestesses.
Wildly he talks, with solemn, bell-like voice,
In words that might have been old Malory's choice.

A somewhat happier period of his life came when he went to Paris in 1913 and buried himself in that congenial city. It was his love for Paris—personified, of course, as a woman—which led him to enlist in the French Foreign Legion in the third week of the war. His sentimental and romantic nature here found its fulfilment. His reasons for enlisting he explained on several occasions: always in the simple terms of a lover fighting for his lady, or a son for his mother. And his tolerance for the German point of view was simple and instinctive.

But there was something else in the instinct which sent him to the front. "Peoples war because strife is the law of nature and force the ultimate arbitrament among humanity no less than in the rest of the universe," he wrote, describing the thoughts of a sentry. "He is on the side he is fighting for, not in the last analysis from ethical motives at all, but because destiny has set him in such a constellation." The sense of his responsibility is strong upon him. Playing a part in the life of nations he is taking part in the largest movement his planet allows him.

"He thrills with the sense of filling an appointed necessary place in the conflict of hosts, and facing the enemy's crest above which the Great Bear wheels upward to the zenith, he feels, with a sublimity of enthusiasm that he has never before known, a kind of companionship with the stars!

"This life agrees with me; there will be war for many years to come in Europe and I shall continue to be a soldier as long as there is war."

I do not suppose in all the armies there was such another paladin. The pure poetry in his makeup was never more evident than in this. He could even write: "Perhaps historic fatality has decreed that Germany shall come out of this struggle triumphant and that the German people shall dominate in the twentieth century as French, English, Spanish, and Italian have in preceding centuries. To me the matter of supreme importance is not to be on the winning side, but on the side where my sympathies lie. Feeling no greater dignity possible for a man than that of one who makes himself the instrument of Destiny in these tremendous moments, I naturally ranged myself on the side to which I owed the greatest obligation. But let it always be understood that I never took arms out of any hatred against Germany or the Germans, but purely out of love for France. The German contribution to civilization is too large, and German ideals too generally in accord with my own, to allow me to join in the chorus of hate against a people whom I frankly admire. It was only that the France, and especially the Paris, that I love should not cease to be the glory and the beauty that they are that I engaged."

That word "glory" is also typical. In his diary he sets down his dream of the triumphant French army entering an ancient city of northern France, and the climax is reached in a description of "the winged figure that her soldiers love to picture at the head of their victorious battalions—*la Gloire!*" I do not recall in any American recruiting poster, or appeal for war loans, or military communiqué, or speech in Congress, or note of President Wilson, one reference to "glory." To the American people the war was not glorious. To Alan Seeger it was.

He knew nothing and cared nothing for democracy. He instinctively revolted from its works. In a sonnet to Sidney he says:

I give myself some credit for the way
I have kept clean of what enslaves and lowers,
Shunned the ideals of our present day
And studied those that were esteemed in yours . . .
And lived in strict devotion all along
To my three idols—Love and Arms and Song.

In his published diary and letters there is never a sign of political emotion. The unique insulation of his poetic mind kept him in a curious degree "unspotted from the world." Unlike the other soldier-poets, he did not record disappointments, doubts, despairs, rages, horrors, self-abasements. In the midst of strife he was at peace.

On April 2, 1917, addressing the Congress of the United States, President Woodrow Wilson declared: "We shall fight for the things which we have always carried nearest our hearts—for democracy." Those ringing words would have found no echo in the dead heart of Alan Seeger. He was killed on July 4, 1916.

The manner of his death has been fittingly told. Two battalions of the Foreign Legion were to attack Belloy-en-Santerre. It was late afternoon. The companies forming the first wave were deployed in the plain, Alan Seeger's one of them. "How pale he was! His tall silhouette stood out on the green of the cornfield. He was the tallest man in his section. His head erect, and pride in his eye, I saw him running forward, with bayonet fixed." He fell mortally wounded, and his comrades swept by him.

They did not find his body until morning. Legend has it that his rifle was standing with bayonet fixed in the earth. The corpse was mother-naked. He had stripped off his clothes, with poetic ritualism, and went from the world as he came into it.

His citation reads in part: "*Jeune légionnaire, enthousiaste et énergique, aimant passionnément la France. . . . Glorieusement tombé le 4 juillet, 1916.*"—EDWARD EYRE HUNT, "Stelligeri: A Footnote on Democracy," *Essays in Memory of Barrett Wendell*, 1926, pp. 307–11

General

We are invited very often in these days of war to admire the work of a writer because he has chanced to meet death in battle or has laid down his life some other way in the service of his country. It is a little like being commanded to rank the pictures of some deaf and dumb artist as masterpieces because he is deaf and dumb. That fact may well add to the curious interest of the work; it may quite legitimately serve as an excuse for a philanthropist's purchasing the pictures in question; but it could never justify his presenting them to an art museum.

When an author suddenly grows into a romantic figure, the publisher's temptation to capitalize the fact is almost irresistible—and he cannot be expected even to try to resist it so long as the public continues content with such a standard for judging the value of literary work.

Sometimes the result is unusually unfortunate. The collected verse of Alan Seeger is a case in point. Seeger was a young American who had only just passed his twenty-eighth birthday when his division of the Foreign Legion was wiped out in a desperate charge on the German trenches at Belloy-en-Santerre. Such a death undeniably lends point and feeling to the following lines, which were written only a short while before:

But I've a rendezvous with Death
At midnight in some flaming town,
When Spring trips north again this year,

> And I to my pledged word am true,
> I shall not fail that rendezvous.

But the poem of which these are the closing lines (it rapidly is becoming well-known) would have a thrill in any case; and the habit of maudlinizing all criticism connected with the war makes it preferable to risk a lessening of this particular poem's sentimental interest for the sake of gaining a more discerning public judgment on contemporary verse in general.

As a matter of fact, a large part of the poems in this volume can reasonably well stand on their strictly literary merits. Some of the best of them have no connection with the war, no foreboding of tragic death, and the pointedly funereal black cover chosen by the publishers does not seem at all in keeping with Alan Seeger's usual spirit.

We like to think that if Rupert Brooke had lived he would have eliminated from his final volume some of the unnecessary gaucheries of expression, as well as some of the unworthy compositions which were rushed into print under the impulse of the sudden fame brought about by his death. The same thought occurs in the case of Alan Seeger. For example, there really doesn't seem any reason, either at the dictates of poetic diction or in the search for vigor of expression, for addressing America, in his last ode: "You have the guts and the grit I know." He might have realized the fact had he lived to revise his work.

It seems to have been Seeger's habit to view events taking place about him almost entirely subjectively. The moods of world capitals, the glories of nature, the ebb and flow of war across the greatest battle-fields of France—these he was interested in mainly as they happened to chime in or conflict with his own emotions. Toward the end of the book his use of the first person comes to seem almost too persistent. The sonnet addressed to Sidney is typical. It is, in part:

> I give myself some credit for the way
> I have kept clean of what enslaves and lowers,
> Shunned the ideals of the present day
> And studied those that were esteemed in yours;
> For, turning from the mob that buys Success
> By sacrificing all Life's better part,
> Down the free roads of human happiness
> I frolicked, poor of purse but light of heart,
> And lived in strict devotion all along
> To my three idols—Love and Arms and Song.

Not any supposed unfairness to other poets whose ways have not been the ways of war provokes this criticism of our habit of hero-worship—for the unfairness, if there be any, is all in the other direction, toward those thousands of other soldiers who have died for their country in foreign lands, with just as great good will and cheerfulness, unnamed and unnoticed. Measured by that scale those all are as great spirits as Brooke or Seeger. These are more; they are poets.—HAMILTON FISH ARMSTRONG, "The Boys of War," *Dial*, March 22, 1917, pp. 243–44

If Freud's theory of the artist is correct—that the artist is one in whom the pleasure principle of childhood never gives way to the reality principle of maturity—then we have a particularly typical artist, in this sense, in Alan Seeger. Alan Seeger was one of that large class who never see the world as it is, who always see it as they wish it to be. To a considerable extent that is true of all of us. We all remain children at least in part. The difference between the normal human being (if there is any) and the artist is merely quantitative; the artist, in addition to his power of speech, keeps more of the child's instinct for living in the imagination, for avoiding contact with the somewhat harsh—or, at any rate, indifferent—world of reality. There is, of course, another type of artist—the type to which Shakespeare, Euripides, Balzac, Turgenev and Meredith belong—which develops the pleasure principle and reality principle side by side, achieving the perfect balance which we call greatness. That type is rare and for the present does not concern us.

Alan Seeger belongs conspicuously to the former class. He was sensitive, retiring, idiosyncratic, lived very much if not exclusively in books during his youth, and developed the art of self-delusion to an extraordinary pitch. He cut himself off almost entirely from the real world of real (and, from his viewpoint, somewhat uninteresting) men and women, and equally so from any intellectual contact with it. An aesthetic attitude was all he believed in assuming toward the world which he was capable of perceiving, and in consequence he devoted his energies to the perfecting of himself as a sensorium. Thought, no doubt, seemed to him a thing essentially painful and to be avoided. The result of this characteristic in his poetry is precisely what we should expect. It is somewhat archaically romantic; mellifluous, always, in the effort to be sensuously decorative; a little self-consciously poetic. It is the kind of poetry which begins by omitting all words which seem to belong to prose; it divides speech into two classes, poetic and prosaic, and selects for its artificial purpose only the lovely (when taste is at its best) or the merely sensuous or pretty (when taste subsides a little). One gets, therefore, in reading Seeger's poems a mild and never intense pleasure. Vague sights and sounds, vague because somewhat cloudily seen and heard by the poet, flow past in pleasant rhythms. Nothing disturbs. All is as liquid and persuasive as drifting in a gondola. There are no ideas to take hold of, no emotions so intense as to shake one's repose. One has a drowsy impression of trees, flowers, ponds, clouds, blue sky, old walls, lutes; and youth in the foreground engaged in a faintly melancholy anguish of love. The tone of these poems, whether in the fragmentary and static narratives, or in the measured sonnets, seldom varies.

In short, Alan Seeger was a belated romantic poet—and a romantic poet without any peculiar originality. He had a keen ear, a flexible technique—but nothing new to say, and no new way of saying what had been said before. His verse, throughout, is a verse of close approximations; it is always mother-of-pearl, but seldom pearl.—CONRAD AIKEN, "Romantic Traditionalism: Alan Seeger," *Scepticisms*, 1919, pp. 133–35

T. STURGE MOORE
From "Alan Seeger"
Some Soldier Poets
1920, pp. 107–18

Love, arms and song, and a noble frankness that asserts, "My kingdom is of this world," characterise America's leading soldier poet, who fell in action on 4th July 1916.

Alan Seeger was born in New York in 1888, of old New England parentage. For ten years Staten Island, in the mouth of the harbour, was his home. Later the family settled at Mexico City, in the tropics, but 7400 feet above the sea. He entered Harvard in 1906 and came to Paris in 1912, and, when the war broke out, was among the first half-hundred of his countrymen to enlist in the Foreign Legion of France, and soon writes from the Front:

"I have always thirsted for this kind of thing, to be present where the pulsations are liveliest. Every minute here is worth weeks of ordinary experience. . . . This will spoil one for any other kind of life. . . . Death is nothing terrible after all. It may mean something even more wonderful than life. It cannot possibly mean anything worse to a good soldier. . . . Success in life means doing that thing than which nothing else conceivable seems more noble or satisfying or remunerative, and this enviable state I can truly say I enjoy, for had I the choice, I would be nowhere else in the world than where I am."

From him as from Grenfell this sentiment comes inevitably; and he was no soldier by profession, but, in so far as he had chosen any, a poet. At first sight they seem twin natures in ardour, in frankness, in courage, in devotion; only gradually can the spirit become reconciled to admitting an immense difference.

The temptation is to apply here the common English prejudice as to where the American fails. But this would be uncritical, for exceptional natures least conform to national foibles. Seeger contrasts with Grenfell as Byron with Shelley rather than as Yankee with Britisher. Only by crushing the grapes of his thought against a fine palate shall we be able to distinguish their flavour from very highly prized fruit. After a few pages his clarity, like that of Swinburne, confuses the reader, for if his virtue is not to hesitate, his fault is to let the thread sag in the hurry and volume of eloquence; and this great fluency and facility accompany a lack of delicate choicefulness. In vain you search for such precision in joy as inspired Ledwidge's happiest images, or for details that amount to revelations as did Thomas's best. All kinds of beauty are welcomed, but too indiscriminately. "You will say they are Persian attire; but let them be changed," is the instinctive comment of many resolute minds on encountering to-day that flaunting habit which ranges women and wine in a single category. Rakish nakedness offends their studied composure, and others may be surprised to find neither fatigue, hopelessness nor cynicism in the voice that proclaims:

> And in old times I should have prayed to her
> Whose haunt the groves of windy Cyprus were,
> To prosper me and crown with good success
> My will to make of you the rose-twined bowl
> From whose inebriating brim my soul
> Shall drink its last of earthly happiness.

This is from one of a series of sonnets written during leave from the Front. Another with the same object pursues:

> Enchanting girl, my faith is not a thing
> By futile prayers and vapid psalm-singing
> To vent in crowded nave and public pew.
> My creed is simple: that the world is fair,
> And beauty the best thing to worship there,
> And I confess it by adoring you.

And this world is defied as gallantly as the other:

> Let not propriety nor prejudice
> Nor the precepts of jealous age deny
> What Sense so incontestably affirms;
> Cling to the blessed moment and drink deep
> Of the sweet cup it tends, as there alone
> Were that which makes life worth the pain to live.

Nay, not even death, and what dreams may follow, can give him pause:

> Exiled afar from youth and happy love,
> If Death should ravish my fond spirit hence
> I have no doubt but, like a homing dove,
> It would return to its dear residence,

And through a thousand stars find out the road
Back into earthly flesh that was its loved abode.

Neither heaven nor the possibilities of time and space can offer anything better, a return to known delights is all that can be desired. The old have not infrequently gazed back with something of this feeling, and the illusions of perspective may excuse them; but that a young man should be so certain that he has seen the bottom of the cup of happiness, and that it could never be refilled with rarer liquors, suggests a near-sighted imagination. So masterful a conviction that no finer means than those you were born with could achieve more exquisite ends sets the mind pondering; and a plausible philosophy might maintain that youth's vivid apprehension of the worth of actual objects, persons and events was the source of all significance, the criterion by which everything else is really judged. Wordsworth could almost have subscribed to this belief; he expressed a very similar intuition though with a less truculent directness. In fact I think this comparison brings home to us a failure in the mood of Alan Seeger's ecstasy. We have all met these gifted young men who seem to tread above the heads of the crowd; perhaps most of us can recall something of how it feels inside them. The most coy have known the itch to swagger, the most staid have longed to shout from the house-top, and modesty itself has desired to stand forth naked and unashamed; so that a deep and widespread welcome greets these manifestations even among those who dare not avow their approval and whose lives would contradict them if they did. Wordsworth himself confessed that he had not written love poems because if he had done so they would have been too warm for publication.

> All true speech and large avowal
> Which the jealous soul concedes,
> All man's heart that brooks bestowal,
> All frank faith which passion breeds

are of the very essence of poetry, and will be cherished by every loyal nature. Propriety is forbidden to intervene when soul communes with soul, her sphere is downstairs in the world of half relations and approximate intercourse. But in proportion as you claim to go naked, you must keep near to the heart of things, and make the very truth your inseparable companion. Anything off-hand, anything insensitive or not quite alive offends these communicants, like the touch of a corpse. Humbleness like that of a child is born from this intensity. Any thought of the myriad eyes that overpeer a stage should be impossible; the world is forgotten when the spirit dances naked in the light to which joy entrusts it—tender joy for whom the damage of the pale green, ruby-eyed, lace-winged fly is a calamity to avert with tears and supplications. "Everything that lives is holy." If Seeger lives in his poetry, everything else passes like a ghost, like a reference only: his one imperious desire is to cast a personal spell upon us all. Will not something unmistakably itself arrest this fervid eloquence that deals in clouds and stars and all the commonplaces of poetry with such profusion! Were but the young women addressed, ever qualified by an adjective proper to some one girl! No, Alan Seeger is alone felt, with this delightful freshness, a presence, an inspiration!

> Sidney, in whom the hey-day of romance
> Came to its precious and most perfect flower,
> Whether you turneyed with victorious lance
> Or brought sweet roundelays to Stella's bower,
> I give myself some credit for the way
> I have kept clean of what enslaves and lowers,
> Shunned the ideals of our present day

And studied those that were esteemed in yours—
For, turning from the mob that buys Success
By sacrificing all Life's better part,
Down the free roads of human happiness
I frolicked, poor of purse but light of heart,
And lived in strict devotion all along
To my three idols—Love and Arms and Song.

"I could accuse myself of such things that it were better my mother had not borne me. . . . We are arrant knaves all"—in speaking thus was Hamlet so certainly mad as this sonnet implies? The worry and stress that "honesty of purpose and intellectual honesty" cost Grenfell are remembered with regret.

> I cannot rest
> While aught of beauty in any path untrod
> Swells into bloom and spreads sweet charms abroad
> Unworshipped of my love. I cannot see
> In Life's profusion and passionate brevity
> How hearts enamoured of life can strain too much
> In one long tension to hear, to see, to touch.

He is too eager, too arrogant, to await the visit of those wonders which steal unsought into consciousness. A "wise passiveness" was no mood of his. His ambition emulates Byron's, who hated to think himself a mere poet and itched for acted glory: thus Seeger, gazing beyond the war's end, cries:

> And the great cities of the world shall yet
> Be golden frames for me in which to set
> New masterpieces of more rare romance.

He fears no repetition of that defeat which yet enchanted the world with its misanthropy and cynicism, but strains after a vision fellow to that followed by the pilgrim lord from Harrow to Missolonghi. If in spite of failure this temperament achieved so much, what might it not succeed in? So active, so independent, so daring a nature has as many opportunities of acquiring wisdom as it has of refusing to bow its head under ruin. Though a soul consciously poses while loving, though when heroic it must be setting an example to half the world, this effrontery, largely inexperience, may betoken the very vigour that can grapple with the monster fact on the soul's behalf. Already he can philosophise his preoccupation with sexual passion.

> Oh Love whereof my boyhood was the dream
> My youth the beautiful novitiate,
> Life was so slight a thing and thou so great,
> How could I make thee less than all supreme!
> In thy sweet transports not alone I thought
> Mingled the twain that panted breast to breast,
> The sun and stars throbbed with them; they were
>   caught
> Into the pulse of Nature. . . .
> Doubt not that of a perfect sacrifice
> That soul partakes whose inspiration fills
> The spring-time and the depth of summer skies
> The rainbow and the clouds behind the hills,
> That excellence in earth and air and sea
> That makes things as they are the real divinity.

Yes, his brain keeps pace with his eloquence; but his soul? Hasty and crude and licensed to scorn the maimed and mauled by youth's ignorance of irreparable damage, he does not hesitate, on returning to the trenches, to offer his gallant comrades these ungenerous lines which were possibly not really aimed at the invalids he had met at Biarritz, but at those whom he could never forget, his equals in youth and strength, who then still lingered in the States.

> Apart sweet women (for whom heaven be blessed),
> Comrades, you cannot think how thin and blue
> Look the left-overs of mankind that rest,
> Now that the cream has been skimmed off in you.
>   . . . we turn disdainful backs
> On that poor world we scorn, yet die to shield,—
> That world of cowards, hypocrites and fools.

He has given himself for the freedom of all future souls, what right have we to question whether he gave his own conscience due reverence? Could we have divined *King Lear* from reading *Venus and Adonis*? That ready aptness of phrase which in my citations has delighted the reader is constantly achieved in his later poems, if only by four or six lines at a time. And though the inspired peaks rise tier behind tier above this plateau, you find few flowers more brilliant without climbing higher. Yet that failure in delicate choicefulness insistently prophesies woe, and was not so striking in Swinburne or more so in Byron at his years. *The Deserted Garden*, his longest poem, yielded as abundant opportunities as *Venus and Adonis* could, but no line like

> A lily prisoned in a gale of snow

takes the advantage. In spite of formlessness, how delightful the Keats of *Endymion* would have made this old Mexican garden, where the young Seeger dreams the meetings of bygone lovers. He, however, only maintains his obvious efficiency, and we are never "surprised with joy": in the end we are only surprised that he can keep it up, as we often have been when Swinburne was not first rate. Did the magnolia bud of this large soul lodge a canker? Yet, though we can only surmise what his full-blown splendour might have been, he was ever so slightly opening; his latest sonnets are not only the most manifold, but deeper and almost fragrant.

> Seeing you have not come with me, nor spent
> This day's suggestive beauty as we ought,
> I have gone forth alone and been content
> To make you mistress only of my thought.
> I am the field of undulating grass
> And you the gentle perfume of the Spring,
> And all my lyric being, when you pass,
> Is bowed and filled with sudden murmuring.
>
> For I have ever gone untied and free,
> The stars and my high thoughts for company;
> Wet with the salt spray and the mountain showers,
> I have had the sense of space and amplitude,
> And love in many places, silver-shoed,
> Has come and scattered all my path with flowers.

Four lines from two sonnets, six from a third, and you build up a new one richer and stronger than any of the three. For all these flashes are like the flap of a flame in a swirl of smoke; some pleasure in his own attitude, some self-assertion causes the momentary brilliance among the ever-flowing grey ghosts of scheduled ornament which make the bulk of a rhetorical style. But he has gentle, more promising moods.

> There have been times when I could storm and
>   plead,
> But you shall never hear me supplicate.
> These long months that have magnified my need
> Have made my asking less importunate;
> For now small favours seem to me so great
> That not the courteous lovers of old time
> Were more content to rule themselves and wait,
> Easing desire with discourse and sweet rhyme.

He even stands staring at the different tempers created in him by self-seeking and self-devotion.

Oh love of woman, you are known to be
A passion sent to plague the hearts of men;
For every one you bring felicity
Bringing rebuffs and wretchedness to ten.
I have been oft where human life sold cheap
And seen men's brains spilled out about their ears
And yet that never cost me any sleep;
I lived untroubled and I shed no tears.
Fools prate how war is an atrocious thing;
I always knew that nothing it implied
Equalled the agony and suffering
Of him who loves and loves unsatisfied.
War is a refuge to a heart like this;
Love only tells it what true torture is.

Playing his part with the best at the Front, he was by no means merely acting a *Message to America* in order to bring her into line. He really loved France and understood something of what she stands for in civilisation. He is compact with generosity which is none the less real for being self-appreciated.

O friends, in your fortunate present ease
(Yet faced by the self-same facts as these),
If you would see how a race can soar
That has no love, but no fear of war,
How each can turn from his private rôle
That all may act as a perfect whole,
How men can live up to the place they claim,
And a nation jealous of its good name,

Be true to its proud inheritance,
Oh, look over here and learn from France!

And he too seeks to think well of Death, and, having most fancied himself as a lover, thinks himself "half in love with" glorious Death.

⟨. . .⟩ His style takes no end of room; more time was demanded than love and arms could spare for it to grow as rare as it was large. Still, granted a more prolonged lease of pleasure-hunting, we might have had to deplore luxuriance tangled to perversity, no longer merely grown too fast for strength. To what extent war was a tonic to his extravagance remains uncertain, even after repeated readings of his later poems. Every young man has perforce many possible careers—unwritten books whose titles and contents we may dream of, though hands will never part their leaves, nor eyes peruse. Still there is some faint compensation for this in esteeming them at their highest possible value, though it but increase our sense of loss; for worth conceived is prophetic of that yet to be revealed by the ever-teeming future.

Look at him crowning himself, prematurely, as Shakespeare's hero prince did, yet, like him, conscious of deserving the "rigol" by innate capacity and determination. Both hands raise the empty hoop, then pause, for through it stars watch him, brilliant and remote. In black bronze he stands for ever returning their gaze—no work of Phidias, rather by some Scopas or Praxiteles, whose more indulgent rhythm induces a musical ripple throughout the war-hardened muscles of his twenty-eight years.

ROBERT W. SERVICE

1874–1958

Robert William Service was born in Preston, England, on January 16, 1874, and spent his youth in Glasgow, Scotland. After graduating from high school he worked briefly as a bank clerk, then emigrated to Canada, seeking adventure. For ten years he traveled up and down the Pacific Coast of Canada and the United States, working at various jobs and writing poetry. In 1905 he took a job as a teller with a Canadian bank and was sent first to a branch in Whitehorse and then to Dawson, in the Yukon. Here he began to write light, narrative poems about prospectors, trappers, and frontier taverns.

Service's first book of verse, *Songs of a Sourdough* (1907), was an enormous success and made him a wealthy man; it was later reprinted as *The Spell of the Yukon*. He left his bank job in 1909, the same year that he published a second volume of verse, *Ballads of a Cheechako*. *Rhymes of a Rolling Stone* followed in 1912. During World War I he went to the Balkans as a correspondent for the *Toronto Star*, then served as an ambulance driver and as an officer in the Canadian army.

After the war Service settled in France, returning to Canada for the duration of World War II. He published several more novels, additional verse, and two volumes of autobiography, *Ploughman of the Moon* (1945) and *Harper of Heaven* (1948), but none of his subsequent work achieved the popularity of his earlier, Yukon-inspired verse. His two most popular poems, "The Shooting of Dan McGrew" and "The Cremation of Sam McGee," have been enjoyed for several generations.

Robert Service died at his home in Lancieux, France, on September 11, 1958.

Is there an elocutionist that has not shrieked the tale of "A Madonna of the Streets" or a doughboy that has not heard (for the seventeenth time) "The Shooting of Dan McGrew"? . . . "The book *Songs of a Sourdough*, subsequently called *The Spell of the Yukon*" (I am now quoting the author's bird's-eye view of himself) "reached its seventh edition before the date of publication." . . . His "Rhymes of a Red Cross Man" had, as their text,

Have faith! Fight on! Amid the battle hell,
Love triumphs; Freedom beckons—all is well.

And, though no Judge Avery was on hand to nominate Service for the Hall of Fame, Witter Bynner, President of the Poetry Society, was roused to write, "It is what Kipling might have made of the War, had his genius been still young. . . . Excitement, pathos, terror and tenderness or humor and, in the end, imbuing this reader with a closer sense of life in the

Great War than any correspondent (*pace* Gibbs), novelist (such as Barbusse), or poet (*vide* Sassoon) has yet given." (The interjections are mine.) ⟨. . .⟩

The paper jacket of Robert W. Service's new collection, *Ballads of a Bohemian*, ⟨. . .⟩ has the figure of a man holding a pipe as its central motif. ⟨. . .⟩ In the smoke that drifts through the room, the figures of five smiling young ladies are seen, evidently visions of the smoker's bohemian past. They are grouped about a table in traditional attitudes of adoration and abandon; one is a dancer, one a model, one a midinette, the other two seem to be professional magazine-cover bohemians. So with the poems they epitomize. Temporarily abandoning the red-blood-and-guts style which he carried off so jauntily, turning away from his borrowings from Kipling, from "the lusts that lure us on, the hates that hound us", Service, thinly disguising himself as an obscure free lance in Montparnasse, gives us a series of seventy-five ballads and verses connected by shreds of prose. It is a gay, mad life he pictures—and such a startlingly original one! It is as faithful to life as Puccini's sugared opera, as Villonesque as Henry K. Hadley's correctly mincing *In Bohemia*. Here we have the Latin Quarter with its procession of libertine artists and dangerously beautiful models; its murderous *apache* lovers who forsake their haunts and lead honest lives as soon as their child is born; its half-sentimental, half-cynical *boulevardiers*; its sewing-girls who queen it in Moscow, Rome, and the Argentine and then come back to die in the gutters of Paris; its parade of absinthe-drinkers, dandies, grisettes, Philistines. . . . It is all so refreshingly novel! The treatment of these unusual themes is consistently individualized. The famous story of the tame flea (the one that escapes and, after a search of the guest of honor, is handed back to its owner who cries, "That isn't my Lucille!"), this story is told in the metre of Gilbert's "Yarn of the Nancy Bell":

> For you'll never know in that land of snow how
> lonesome a man can feel;
> So I made a fuss of the little cuss, and I christened it
> "Lucille".
> But the longest winter has its end, and the ice went
> out to sea,
> And I saw one day a ship in the bay, and there was
> the Nancy Lee.

"The Pencil Seller" (beginning, "A pencil, sir; a penny—won't you buy?") and others of the same parlor genre are told in the rich declamatory idiom of "The Face on the Bar-room Floor". And when he leaves the Parisian background, Service's adaptability grows even more varied. He can be as lyrical as Noyes imploring one to come down to Kew in lilac-time, in lilac-time, in lilac-time. Thus:

> Hurrah! I'm off to Finistere, to Finistere, to
> Finistere. . . .

He can play the "Danny Deever" Dead March in Kipling's own key:

> We're taking Marie Toro to her home in Pere-La-
> Chaise;
> We're taking Marie Toro to her last resting-place.

Eugene Field? Why not? The little toy soldier placed on a shelf by Little Boy Blue becomes:

> I'll put you away, little Teddy Bear,
> In the cupboard far from my sight;
> Maybe he'll come and he'll kiss you there,
> A wee white ghost in the night.

Naturally, Mr. Service, living in petulant Paris, lacks Edgar A. Guest's unflagging buoyancy. But he can also cheer his (according to the sales sheets) great army of readers by writing verses like "The Joy of Little Things", "The Contented Man", and "The Joy of Being Poor". Technically, Service is incalculably Guest's superior even though he tries to rhyme such ill-mated pairs as "lyric—hysteric" and "rondel—respond well". But it is his pæans of Paris that will win him the admiration of all those who found his other verses so restrained and true to life. This is the life!—here amid the tinkling patter of the Boul' Mich', the Café de la Paix, the imbibing of countless Pernods, the plashing of the Fontaine de Medicis, the ever-fascinating poet's garret—this is the life of the true bohemian! We recognize it at once, we who have read *The Parisienne*, who have seen a dozen ateliers in comic operas, we who find Merrick so much more effective than Murger. It is a rapidly growing gallery that Service is filling. Pictures of the Yukon, the War, the Red Cross, the Latin Quarter. It is almost time for the American laureate to rediscover his (and our) America.—LOUIS UNTERMEYER, "Our Living Laureates," *Bkm*, Jan. 1922, pp. 482–84

These two books of the works of this most popular poet, will, I am sure be enthusiastically welcomed by his many admirers. In the *Collected Poems* we have a treasure chest containing *The Spell of the Yukon, Ballads of the Cheechako, Rhymes of a Rolling Stone, Rhymes of a Red Cross Man, Ballads of a Bohemian* and the *Bar Room Ballads*. The easy style of Robert Service makes him a most readable poet. He described himself as a happy man, because his talent was in proportion to his ambition, and he was able to write the kind of verse that he liked to read. He wrote about everything he saw . . .

> The lonely sunsets flare forlorn
> Down valleys dreadly desolate;
> The lordly mountains sear in scorn
> As still as death as stern as fate.

So he describes the Yukon in 'The Land God Forgot'. He tells as vividly of the men and women who sort fame and fortune in its lonely wastes, where successes were few and failure usually meant death.

Many and varied were the characters who shared his Bohemian existence in Paris. Although he was by nature a solitary man, not given to making many friends, no one passed unnoticed. So that we may know who or what inspired each set of verses, during this time, they are linked by extracts from his diary, giving a complete picture of the hungry times, and the good times; and how the joy of his verses being accepted so often meant more than money to Robert Service.

With the outbreak of the 1914 war his whole world changed, but he continued to write to everyone he met, of the boys who marched gaily away to war full of Patriotic fervour, the hardened soldier who does his duty, and the women and children who love and fear for them. As an ambulance driver Robert Service served in the front line, and so we do not get the romantic death and glory view, but the full horror and futility of war. He writes. . . .

> And you yourself would mutter when
> You took the things that once were men
> And sped them through that zone of hate
> To where the dripping surgeons wait;
> And wonder too if in God's sight
> War ever, ever can be right.

His views in every aspect of life and death are presented to us to take or leave as we will; and all of them are assembled in this book to give us the whole picture of his life and times, an asset to any bookshelf.—CLARE MCCARTHY, "The Poetry of Robert Service," *CnR*, May 1979, pp. 276–77

STANLEY S. ATHERTON
"The Klondike Muse"

Canadian Literature, Winter 1971, pp. 67–72

The Klondike Trail of 1898, symbol of the last great gold rush in history, captured the imagination of a continent. By the time Robert Service reached the Yukon in 1904 as a teller for the Canadian Bank of Commerce, public interest in the area was widespread. Well before Service himself began to record his impressions, a "Klondike literature" was already rapidly accumulating from the numerous eye-witness reports, the travellers' accounts, and the books of advice to prospective gold-seekers. For the most part, however, these works emphasized factual events and situations, and only those that were specifically connected with the Gold Rush. While there was plenty of action recorded, little of a meditative or reflective nature could be found in such accounts. The way was open for a writer with talent enough to take advantage of the happy coincidence of event and location to mythologize the north.

Service, stimulated by the recent and contemporary events in his new surroundings, began to produce both poetry and fiction in an imaginative reconstruction of this world. What fame he has achieved continues to rest chiefly on the few volumes his eight years of residence in the Yukon yielded. These include *Songs of a Sourdough* (also published as *The Spell of the Yukon*) (1907), *Ballads of a Cheechako* (1909), *Rhymes of a Rolling Stone* (1912), and the novel, *The Trail of Ninety-Eight* (1910). This body of work, rarely examined critically, deserves attention as one of the earliest attempts in Canadian literary history to mythologize the environment.

In his early poetry Service used the subject matter of the Gold Rush as a point of departure for his comments on man's relationship to the land. In "The Spell of the Yukon", for example, the Gold Rush is dispensed with in the first stanza. From here the poet moves to a description of the physical environment, using the Klondike as a representative northern landscape. The third stanza, and the remaining six, catalogue the varying responses and attitudes the narrator takes towards the North.

A number of these reactions had been articulated a few years earlier by Hamlin Garland. In a *McClure's* article in 1897 he had termed the Yukon "a cruel and relentless land," and a "grim and terrible country." Service made these and similar reactions the subject matter for a number of his best-known poems. The untitled prefatory poem to *Song of a Sourdough* is characteristic.

> The lonely sunsets flare forlorn
>   Down valleys dreadly desolate:
> The lordly mountains soar in scorn,
>   As still as death, as stern as fate.
>
> The lonely sunsets flame and die;
>   The giant valleys gulp the night;
> The monster mountains scrape the sky,
>   Where eager stars are diamond-bright.
>
> So gaunt against the gibbous moon,
>   Piercing the silence velvet-piled,
> A lone wolf howls his ancient rune,
>   The fell arch-spirit of the Wild.
>
> O outcast land! O leper land!
>   Let the lone wolf-cry all express—
> The hate insensate of thy hand,
>   Thy heart's abysmal loneliness.

Here one finds a number of key concepts which recur with varying degrees of emphasis in the majority of the Klondike poems: a sense of loneliness, hints of the supernatural, hostile nature, an intense and meaningful silence, and a reminder of man's mortality.

Service is rarely content simply to describe the North. A number of his poems provide effective illustrations of the constant perils to human life in such a desolate area, perils which evoke a continual fear in man of the hostility implicit in the environment. He achieves his effects in various ways, often by utilizing the supernatural element found in indigenous Indian folklore. In "The Ballad of the Black Fox Skin", for instance, he recounts an Indian belief that a particular fox was invested with supernatural powers, and that any who attempted to do it harm would surely suffer. The sceptic who laughs at the superstition and kills the fox is later murdered, and the poem traces a trail of death marked out by all those who possess the cursed skin. By the corpse of the last possessor hoofprints are found, and the skin has mysteriously disappeared.

References such as this to specific supernatural occurrences are set against a wider background of mystery and other-worldliness which often characterizes the North for Service. The narrator of "The Ballad of the Northern Lights" views the aurora "as one bewitched" and describes its mystic beauty as "wild and weird and wan". In "The Ballad of Pious Pete" the presence of witches and frost-tyrants is recorded, adding a further dimension to the supernatural world, and relating it through the image of "cadaverous snows" to human mortality. The language of death abounds in the work, often coupled with Service's characteristic sardonic humour. This pre-occupation with morbidity may account partly for his poetry's continuing appeal. In an age when the threat of violent death is more than ever man's constant companion, the macabre humour of Service takes on a contemporary relevance. Intriguing examples of this "northern gothic" can be found in many of his better-known ballads. Besides those mentioned, they include "The Cremation of Sam McGee", "The Ballad of Blasphemous Bill", and "Clancy of the Mounted Police". In these ballads Service creates a nether world of terror in which men are driven mad or to their deaths. In "Clancy of the Mounted Police" the land terrifies and threatens: "Corpselike and stark was the land, with a quiet that crushed and awed, / And the stars of the weird Sub-arctic glimmered over its shroud." And in "The Ballad of the Black Fox Skin" the threat is personified in a frightening and archetypal fairy-tale situation: "The Valley's girth was dumb with mirth, the laughter of the wild; / The still sardonic laughter of an ogre o'er a child."

If Service had continued to react imaginatively to the North in this fashion, he might have created a valuable mythic vision. As it was, he became a magpie, randomly picking up physical or climatic characteristics of the North and using them as they suited his fancy at the time. The result is confusion, with one poem contradicting another; and it is this inconsistency that marks his failure to create a coherent Northern myth.

The point is easily illustrated by comparing "The Ballad of the Northern Lights" with the well-known "Call of the Wild". The silent North, a "land that listens", was described by Sir Gilbert Parker as a land where the silence led man to meditate on the divine power that created the universe, and which guided man in his worldly struggles. Service treats this theme in "The Ballad of the Northern Lights", where in a terrifying world "purged of sound" three half-demented men hope to gain brief respite from the elemental forces harrying them by meditating on the things they "ought to think". In the world of the poem, however, the North refuses to allow such meditation; two of the men die, and the third is driven mad.

The ambivalence of Service's responses is seen clearly when the reader moves to "The Call of the Wild", for in this poem the silent north is revealed as the repository of truth: "Have you known the Great White Silence, not a snow-gemmed twig a-quiver? / (Eternal truths that shame our soothing lies.) / . . . Have you seen God in His splendours, heard the text that nature renders? / (You'll never hear it in the family pew.)" Here Service says that only through intimate contact with the natural order can man come to a decision on the values he should use as a guide in life. The contrast with "The Ballad of the Northern Lights" is striking: in that poem the North is judge and executioner, resolutely condemning man to death for his weakness; here the north is teacher, benevolently aiding man to a more meaningful existence.

The conflicting attitudes toward the Canadian North which Service presents in his poetry are echoed in his novel of the Gold Rush, *The Trail of Ninety-Eight*. The novel is first of all a chronicle of a particular time and place, for, as the title indicates, it was the product of a specific historical event. Service, like Ballantyne and other writers on the North, found the subject matter for septentrional fiction in an event which had already stimulated widespread interest in the area. In one sense he was simply exploiting interest which the Gold Rush had created by producing a work of fiction to order, and one for which he could expect to find a favourable reception.

The Trail of Ninety-Eight dramatically retells the story of the struggles of men to reach the Klondike gold fields and their trials after arrival in Dawson. The hero, a romantic Scottish fortune hunter named Athol Meldrum, is introduced to the other characters on the steamer which carries him north to Skagway. Meldrum meets Berna Wilovich, the girl he eventually marries, and he comes into contact with the domineering and greedy Winklesteins, her guardians, and with Jack Locasto, the coarse brute who later intrigues with the Winklesteins to make Berna his mistress.

The terrible crossing of the mountains and the often tragic hardships of the trail from Skagway to Dawson are recounted in a series of illuminating instances which bring the trail to life in a manner reminiscent of Zola.

> It was an endless procession, in which every man was for himself. I can see them now, bent under their burdens, straining at their hand-sleighs, flogging their horses and oxen, their faces crimped and puckered with fatigue, the air acrid with their curses and heavy with their moans. Now a horse stumbles and slips into one of the sump-holes by the trail side. No one can pass, the army is arrested. Frenzied fingers unhitch the poor brute and drag it from the water. Men, frantic with rage, beat savagely at their beasts of burden to make up the precious lost time.

Service's peculiar sensibility required a complete fidelity to fact, yet at the same time he was striving to realize his world imaginatively. But the conventions of popular fiction demanded a dramatic contrast (and conflict) between a sterling hero and an unregenerate villain. So although Meldrum becomes thoroughly infected with the gold-fever on his arrival in Dawson, he is untouched by the easy virtue of a town where the "good old moralities don't apply". Aware of the mass appeal of exposure, Service made much of the immorality of those in positions of power. When Meldrum is cheated out of a claim he staked, for example, he makes a vehement denunciation of the official corruption which was widespread

at the time. While such passages help to make *The Trail of Ninety-Eight* valuable as a social record of the Canadian North seventy years ago, the plot is all too often unduly contrived to admit them.

The intrigues of the evil Locasto with the guardians of the virtuous Berna are melodramatically portrayed in a sequence of incidents which take place while the hero is out mining. Meldrum's return to find that Berna has been forced to become Locasto's mistress, and has since been leading the life of a dance-hall girl, results in his own fall into the world of sin and debauchery about him. At length he is rescued from his self-destroying debauch, and he and Berna live together in a love-sanctified union. The unexpected arrival of Garry, Meldrum's brother, complicates the idyllic existence of the couple. Shocked and disgusted by the common-law union, Garry attempts to seduce Berna to show his brother her true character. The attempt fails, and in a final climactic scene Meldrum and Berna (since quietly married) are caught together in a burning Dawson hotel with Garry and Locasto. Only the lovers escape the blaze.

Although it is obviously a contrived pot-boiler, *The Trail of Ninety-Eight* is nevertheless a significant contribution to literature about the Canadian North. It is one of the earliest attempts to make a myth of the north, to capture the spirit of the land and make it comprehensible. To do this, Service comes back again and again to the idea of the North as battlefield where man tests himself by contesting with the natural environment. While the idea of man and nature in conflict is conventional enough to be a cliché, Service might have used it freshly and effectively in the Northern setting. He failed to make it work, however, because he was unable to decide whether such a conflict brings out man's nobler or baser qualities. In a number of passages, of which the following evocation of the spirit of the Gold Trail is typical, the North clearly brings out the worst in man.

> The spirit of the Gold Trail, how shall I describe it? It was based on that primal instinct of self-preservation that underlies our thin veneer of humanity. It was rebellion, anarchy; it was ruthless, aggressive, primitive; it was the man of the stone age in modern garb waging his fierce, incessant warfare with the forces of nature. Spurred on by the fever of the gold-lust, goaded by the fear of losing in the race; maddened by the difficulties and obstacles of the way, men became demons of cruelty and aggression, ruthlessly thrusting down the weaker ones who thwarted their program.

Yet elsewhere, when the North is described as a new frontier, conflict with the environment calls forth nobler instincts. The challenge of untamed nature is met, the battle is joined until "overall . . . triumphed the dauntless spirit of the Pathfinder—the mighty Pioneer."

Similar contradictory reactions to the Northern landscape were noted in the poetry, and these are also evident in the novel. On the one hand, the North is repellent to man, its inhospitable nature an unwelcome reminder of his mortality.

> On all sides of the frozen lake over which they were travelling were hills covered with harsh pine, that pricked funereally up to the boulder-broken snows. Above that was a stormy and fantastic sea of mountains baring many a fierce peak-fang to the hollow heavens. The sky was a waxen grey, cold as a corpse-light. The snow was an immaculate shroud, unmarked by track of bird or beast. Death-sealed the

land lay in its silent vastitude, in its despairful desolation.

On the other hand it is alluring, a compelling presence which casts its spell on the human imagination: "Who has lived in the North will ever forget the charm, the witchery of those midnight skies. . . . Surely, long after all else is forgotten, will linger the memory of those mystic nights with all their haunting spell of weird, disconsolate solitude." But here, as in the poetry, Service seems incapable of bringing the conflicting views together to create a consistent and meaningful vision of man in the north. The reader leaves his work aware of contradiction rather than ambiguity.

In the Gold Rush and the Northern setting two elements for myth-making were ready to hand. The event and the land in which it happened combined to provide the first significant opportunity for mythologizing the north. Unfortunately for Canadian literature the talents of Service were inadequate to cope with the challenge, and the opportunity was lost.

ANNE SEXTON

1928–1974

Anne Sexton was born Anne Gray Harvey on November 9, 1928, in Newton, Massachusetts, to Ralph Churchill and Mary Gray Staples Harvey. She was educated at Garland Junior College from 1947 to 1948. She was a scholar at the Radcliffe Institute for Independent Study from 1961 to 1963, and taught at Boston University from 1970 to 1974. She also taught at Colgate University in 1972. She married Alfred M. Sexton in 1948; they had two daughters, and were divorced in 1974.

Anne Sexton came to Poetry through Robert Lowell's poetry workshops at Boston University, and was encouraged early in her career by Sylvia Plath, another workshop participant. She is associated with the confessional poets of the sixties (Plath, Lowell, John Berryman), but carved out a niche of her own with her vivid imagery and intense self-examination. She was hailed as a major poet almost immediately; her first two books (*To Bedlam and Part Way Back*, 1960, and *All My Pretty Ones*, 1962) earned her considerable critical admiration, although some critics were put off by her frank discussions of such subjects as menstruation and madness.

Sexton's subject matter was consistent throughout her career, but her tone and style varied considerably. Her early poetry, though often graphic, is hopeful and even joyful; her tone darkened considerably through the late sixties, and her style grew more spare, as evidenced by *Live or Die* (1966). It is considered her finest work by many, but criticized as bleak and self-indulgent by others. Her late work (notably *Transformations*, 1971; *The Book of Folly*, 1972; *The Death Notebooks*, 1974; and *The Awful Rowing toward God*, 1975) is riddled with despair and nightmare, but at the same time appears to resolve questions of Sexton's early poetry such as the nature of pain and the existence of God. This later poetry is her most controversial; her admirers acknowledge its inconsistency, but point to the power of many of the passages as evidence of a poet at the peak of her powers.

Sexton received an unusual amount of attention for such a short career; her poetry is widely read, if controversial, and even her detractors acknowledge her considerable influence. She was awarded the Pulitzer Prize in 1967 for *Live or Die*; her *Complete Poems* appeared in 1981. Sexton committed suicide on October 4, 1974.

Personal

Patricia Marx: I understand that you started writing poetry only in 1957. What made you begin at such a late date?

Anne Sexton: Well, it was actually personal experience, because I had had a nervous breakdown, and as I was recovering I started to write, and I got more and more serious about it, and I started out writing almost a poem a day. It was a kind of rebirth at twenty-nine.

P.M.: What do you think caused you to write poetry after a breakdown? What was the impetus?

A.S.: It's too strange. It's just a matter of coincidence. I think probably I'm an artist at heart, and I've found my own form, which I think is poetry. I was looking at educational television in Boston, and I. A. Richards was explaining the form of a sonnet, and I thought, "Well, so that's a sonnet." Although I had learned it in high school, I hadn't ever done anything about it. And so I thought, "I'll try that, too. I think maybe I could." So I sat down and wrote in the form of the sonnet. I was so pleased with myself that for about three months I wrote a sonnet every day. There are no sonnets in my book. They have since been discarded. But that's the way I started. ⟨. . .⟩

P.M.: There is a popular notion that creative genius is very close to insanity. Many of our major poets now, such as Robert Lowell and Theodore Roethke before he died, often had mental breakdowns. Do you feel there's truth in this notion?

A.S.: Well, their genius is more important than their disease. I think there are so many people who are mentally disturbed who are not writers, or artists, or painters or whatever, that I don't think genius and insanity grow in the same bed. I think the artist must have a heightened awareness. It is only seldom this sprouts from mental illness alone. However, there *is* this great feeling of heightened awareness that all artists must have.

P.M.: In your book, *All My Pretty Ones*, you quote this part of a letter written by Franz Kafka: "The books we need are the kind that act upon us like a misfortune, that make us suffer like the death of someone we love more than ourselves. . . . A book should serve as the axe for the frozen sea within us." Is this the purpose you want your poetry to serve?

A.S.: Absolutely. I feel it should do that. I think it should be a shock to the senses. It should almost hurt.

P.M.: Do you find that all poetry does this when you read it? Do you admire certain poetry more for doing this?

A.S.: No, not necessarily. I think it's just my little declaration to myself. I put it in the book to show the reader what I felt, but Kafka's work certainly works upon me as an axe upon a frozen sea. But I admire many poets, many writers who don't do this.

P.M.: I wonder if you would further explain that metaphor.

A.S.: I see it very literally as an axe, cutting right through a slab of ice. I think we go along very complacently and are brainwashed with all kinds of pablum, advertisements every minute, the sameness of supermarkets, everything—it's not only the modern world, even trees become trite—and we need something to shock us, to make us become more aware. It doesn't need to happen in such a shocking way, perhaps, as in my poetry. I think of the poetry of Elizabeth Bishop, which seems to have beautiful ordered clarity. Her fish hurts as much as Randall Jarrell's speaking people. They are two of my favorite poets. Their work shocks me into being more alive, and that's maybe what I mean. The poet doesn't have to use my method to have that happen to me. And Rilke, think of Rilke with his depth, his terrible pain!—

P.M.: Do you find that the writing of poetry achieves this for you as well as the reading of it?

A.S.: No, the writing actually puts things back in place. I mean, things are more chaotic, and if I can write a poem, I come into order again, and the world is again a little more sensible, and real. I'm more in touch with things. ⟨. . .⟩

P.M.: Is it a struggle or pleasure?

A.S.: Oh, it's a wonderful pleasure. It's a struggle, but there's great happiness in working. As anyone knows, if you're doing something that you love and you're struggling with it, there's happiness there, particularly if you can get it in the end. And I'm pretty stubborn. I need to keep after it, until I get it. Or I keep after it until I kill it.

P.M.: Do you discard many poems that you write?

A.S.: Well, now I think I prediscard them. I don't write them, which is one reason why I write less than I did in the beginning. I wrote a lot of unimportant poems, and now when I look at a poem, I always wonder why was this written. There should be a reason for it. It should do something to me. It should move me. I have some poems that have haunted me for four or five years, and they're unfinished and maybe they'll never be finished. I know they're not right, but it hurts not to write them. I have this great need somehow to keep that time of my life, that feeling. I want to imprison it in a poem, to keep it. It's almost in a way like keeping a scrapbook to make life mean something as it goes by, to rescue it from chaos—to make "now" last.

P.M.: In your first volume of poetry, *To Bedlam and Part Way Back*, you quote another passage from a letter, this time from Schopenhauer to Goethe, and it says, "It is the courage to make a clean breast of it in face of every question that makes the philosopher." I take it that you mean this courage also makes a poet.

A.S.: Yes, exactly. It's very hard to reveal yourself. Frankly, anything I say to you is useless and probably more deceiving than revealing. I tell so much truth in my poetry that I'm a fool if I say any more. To really get at the truth of something is the poem, not the poet.

P.M.: Do you find that you are more truthful in your poetry than you are to yourself?

A.S.: Yes, I think so. That's what I'm hunting for when I'm working away there in the poem. I'm hunting for the truth. It might be a kind of poetic truth, and not just a factual one, because behind everything that happens to you, every act, there is another truth, a secret life.—ANNE SEXTON, Interview by Patricia Marx, *HdR*, Winter 1965–66, pp. 560–65

Anne Sexton as I remember her on our first meeting in the late winter of 1957, tall, blue-eyed, stunningly slim, her carefully coifed dark hair decorated with flowers, her face skillfully made up, looked every inch the fashion model. And indeed she had briefly modeled for the Hart Agency in Boston. Earrings and bracelets, French perfume, high heels, matching lip and fingernail gloss bedecked her, all intimidating sophistications in the chalk-and-wet-overshoes atmosphere of the Boston Center for Adult Education, where we were enrolled in John Holmes's poetry workshop. Poetry—we were both ambitious beginners—and proximity—we lived in the same suburb—brought us together. As intimate friends and professional allies, we remained intensely committed to one another's writing and well-being to the day of her death in the fall of 1974.

The facts of Anne Sexton's troubled and chaotic life are well known; no other American poet in our time has cried aloud publicly so many private details. While the frankness of these revelations attracted many readers, especially women, who identified strongly with the female aspect of the poems, a number of poets and critics—for the most part, although not exclusively, male—took offense. For Louis Simpson, writing in *Harper's Magazine*, "Menstruation at Forty" was "the straw that broke this camel's back." And years before he wrote his best-selling novel, *Deliverance*, which centers on a graphic scene of homosexual rape, James Dickey, writing in the *New York Times Book Review*, excoriated the poems in *All My Pretty Ones*, saying "It would be hard to find a writer who dwells more insistently on the pathetic and disgusting aspects of bodily experience . . ." In a terse eulogy Robert Lowell declared, with considerable ambivalence it would seem, "For a book or two, she grew more powerful. Then writing was too easy or too hard for her. She became meager and exaggerated. Many of her most embarrassing poems would have been fascinating if someone had put them in quotes, as the presentation of some character, not the author." Sexton's work rapidly became a point of contention over which opposing factions dueled in print, at literary gatherings, and in the fastnesses of the college classroom.

And yet the ground for Sexton's confessional poems had been well prepared. In 1956, Allen Ginsberg's *Howl* had declaimed:

> I saw the best minds of my generation destroyed by
>   madness,
>   starving hysterical naked
>   . . . on the granite steps of
>   the madhouse with shaven heads and harlequin
>   speech of
>   suicide, demanding instantaneous lobotomy,
> and who were given instead the concrete void of
>   insulin metrasol
>   electricity hydrotherapy psychotherapy occupa-
>   tional therapy
>   pingpong & amnesia . . .

At the time Sexton began to work in the confessional mode, W. D. Snodgrass had already published his prize-winning collection, *Heart's Needle*, which included details of his divorce and custody struggle. Sylvia Plath and Robert Lowell were hammering out their own autobiographical accounts of alienation, despair, anomie, and madness. John Berryman, deceiving no one, charmingly protested in a prefatory note that the Henry of *The Dream Songs* "is essentially about an imaginary character (not the poet, not me) . . . who has suffered an irreversible loss and talks about himself sometimes in the first person, sometimes in the third, sometimes even in the second . . . " The use of *le moi* was being cultivated in fashionable literary journals everywhere. It seems curious that the major and by far most vitriolic expressions of outrage were reserved for Sexton.

Someone once said that we have art in order not to die of the truth, a dictum we might neatly apply to Sexton's perspectives. To Hayden Carruth, the poems "raise the never-solved problem of what literature really is, where you draw the line between art and documentary."

While Louise Bogan and Joyce Carol Oates for the most part appraise Sexton favorably, Mona Van Duyn finds Sexton's "delineation of femaleness so fanatical that it makes one wonder, even after many years of being one, what a woman is . . . " Muriel Rukeyser, who sees the issue as "survival, piece by piece of the body, step by step of poetic experience, and even more the life entire . . . ," finds much to praise, for instance singling out "In Celebration of My Uterus" as "one of the few poems in which a woman has come to the fact as symbol, the center after many years of silence and taboo."

Over and over in the critical literature dealing with the body of Sexton's work, we find these diametrical oppositions. The intimate details divulged in Sexton's poetry enchanted or repelled with equal passion. In addition to the strong feelings Anne's work aroused, there was the undeniable fact of her physical beauty. Her presence on the platform dazzled with its staginess, its props of water glass, cigarettes, and ashtray. She used pregnant pauses, husky whispers, pseudoshouts to calculated effect. A Sexton audience might hiss its displeasure or deliver a standing ovation. It did not doze off during a reading.

Anne basked in the attention she attracted, partly because it was antithetical to an earlier generation's view of the woman writer as "poetess," and partly because she was flattered by and enjoyed the adoration of her public. But behind the glamorously garbed woman lurked a terrified and homely child, cowed from the cradle onward, it seemed, by the indifference and cruelties of her world. Her parents, she was convinced, had not wanted her to be born. Her sisters, she alleged, competed against and won out over her. Her teachers, unable to rouse the slumbering intelligence from its hiding place, treated her with impatience and anger. Anne's counterphobic response to rejection and admonishment was always to defy, dare, press, contravene. Thus the frightened little girl became a flamboyant and provocative woman; the timid child who skulked in closets burst forth as an exhibitionist declaiming with her own rock group; the intensely private individual bared her liver to the eagle in public readings where almost invariably there was standing room only.

Born Anne Gray Harvey in 1928, she attended public school in Wellesley, Massachusetts, spent two years at Rogers Hall preparatory school, and then one year at Garland Junior College in Boston. A few months shy of her twentieth birthday, she eloped with Alfred Muller Sexton II (nicknamed Kayo), enrolled in a Hart Agency modeling course, and lived briefly in Baltimore and San Francisco while her husband served in the Navy. In 1953, she returned to Massachusetts, where Linda Gray Sexton was born.

The first breakdown, diagnosed as postpartum depression, occurred in 1954, the same year her beloved great-aunt Anna Ladd Dingley, the Nana of the poems, died. She took refuge in Westwood Lodge, a private neuropsychiatric hospital that was frequently to serve as her sanctuary when the voices that urged her to die reached an insistent pitch. Its director, Dr. Martha Brunner-Orne, figured in Anne's life as a benevolent but disciplinary mother, who would not permit this troubled daughter to kill herself.

Nevertheless, seven months after her second child, Joyce Ladd Sexton, was born in 1955, Anne suffered a second crisis and was hospitalized. The children were sent to live with her husband's parents; and while they were separated from her, she attempted suicide on her birthday, November 9, 1956. This was the first of several episodes, or at least the first that was openly acknowledged. Frequently, these attempts occurred around Anne's birthday, a time of year she came increasingly to dread. Dr. Martin Orne, Brunner-Orne's son, was the young psychiatrist at Glenside Hospital who attended Anne during this siege and treated her for the next seven years. After administering a series of diagnostic tests, he presented his patient with her scores, objective evidence that, despite the disapproving naysayers from her past, she was highly intelligent. Her associative gifts suggested that she ought to return to the writing of poetry, something she had shown a deft talent for during secondary school. It was at Orne's insistence that Anne enrolled in the Holmes workshop.

"You, Dr. Martin" came directly out of that experience, as did so many of the poems in her first collection, *To Bedlam and Part Way Back.* On a snowy Sunday afternoon early in 1957, she drove to my house to ask me to look at "something." Did she dare present it in class? Could it be called a poem? It was "Music Swims Back to Me," her first breakaway from adolescent lyrics in rhyming iambic pentameter.

Years later, when it seemed to her that all else in her life had failed—marriage, the succor of children, the grace of friendship, the promised land to which psychotherapy held the key—she turned to God, with a kind of stubborn absolutism that was missing from the Protestantism of her inheritance. The God she wanted was a sure thing, an Old Testament avenger admonishing his Chosen People, an authoritarian yet forgiving Father decked out in sacrament and ceremony. An elderly, sympathetic priest she called on—"accosted" might be a better word—patiently explained that he could not make her a Catholic by fiat, nor could he administer the sacrament (the last rites) she longed for. But in his native wisdom he said a saving thing to her, said the magic and simple words that kept her alive at least a year beyond her time and made *The Awful Rowing toward God* a possibility. "God is in your typewriter," he told her.

I cite these two examples to indicate the influence that figures of authority had over Anne's life in the most elemental sense; first the psychiatrist and then the priest put an imprimatur on poetry as salvation, as a worthy goal in itself. I am convinced that poetry kept Anne alive for the eighteen years of her creative endeavors. When everything else soured; when a succession of therapists deserted her for whatever good, poor, or personal reasons; when intimates lost interest or could not fulfill all the roles they were asked to play; when a series of catastrophes and physical illnesses assaulted her, the making of poems remained her one constant. To use her own metaphor, "out of used furniture [she made] a tree." Without this rich, rescuing obsession I feel certain she would have succeeded in committing suicide in response to one of the dozen impulses that beset her during the period between 1957 and 1974. ⟨. . .⟩

The stuff of Anne's life, mercilessly dissected, is here in the poems. Of all the confessional poets, none has had quite Sexton's "courage to make a clean breast of it." Nor has any displayed quite her brilliance, her verve, her headlong metaphoric leaps. As with any body of work, some of the later poems display only ragged, intermittent control, as compared to "The Double Image," "The Operation," and "Some Foreign Letters," to choose three arbitrary examples. The later work takes more chances, crosses more boundaries between the rational and the surreal; and time after time it evokes in the reader that sought-after shiver of recognition.

Women poets in particular owe a debt to Anne Sexton, who broke new ground, shattered taboos, and endured a barrage of attacks along the way because of the flamboyance of her subject matter, which, twenty years later, seems far less daring. She wrote openly about menstruation, abortion, masturbation, incest, adultery, and drug addiction at a time when the proprieties embraced none of these as proper topics for poetry. Today, the remonstrances seem almost quaint. Anne delineated the problematic position of women—the neurotic reality of the time—though she was not able to cope in her own life with the personal trouble it created. If it is true that she attracted the worshipful attention of a cult group pruriently interested in her suicidal impulses, her psychotic breakdowns, her frequent hospitalizations, it must equally be acknowledged that her very frankness succored many who clung to her poems as to the Holy Grail. Time will sort out the dross among these poems and burnish the gold. Anne Sexton has earned her place in the canon.—MAXINE KUMIN, "How It Was," *The Complete Poems*, 1981, pp. xix–xxiv, xxxiv

General

There are some areas of experience in modern life, Theodore Roethke has said, that simply cannot be rendered by either the formal lyric or straight prose. We must realize—and who could have enforced the realization upon us better than Roethke—that the writer in "freer forms" must have an even greater fidelity to his subject matter or his substance than the poet who has the support of form—of received form. He must be imaginatively "right," his rhythm must move as the mind moves, or he is lost. "On the simplest level, something must happen in this kind of poem." By which Roethke meant, I am certain, that it is not enough to report something happening in your life merely—it must be made to happen in your poem. You must begin somewhere, though, generally with your life, above all with your life when it seems to you to welter in a particular exemplary status. Such is Anne Sexton's case, and she has begun indeed with the report of her case:

> Oh! Honor and relish the facts!
> Do not think of the intense sensation
> I have as I tell you this
> but think only . . .

In fact, she has reported more than anyone else—anyone else who has set out to write poems—has ever cared or dared, and thereby she has gained, perhaps at the expense of her poetry, a kind of sacerdotal stature, the elevation of a priestess celebrating mysteries which are no less mysterious for having been conducted in all the hard glare of the marketplace and with all the explicitness mere print can afford.

Anne Sexton is the true Massachusetts heiress of little Pearl, who as the procession of Worthies passes by asks Hester Prynne if one man in it is the same minister who kissed her by the brook. "Hold thy peace, dear little Pearl," whispers her mother. "We must not always talk in the marketplace of what happens to us in the forest." Like the sibylline, often insufferable Pearl, Anne Sexton *does* speak of such things, and in such places, and it makes her, again like Pearl, both more and less

than a mere "person," something beyond a "character"; it makes her, rather, what we call a *figure*, the form of a tragic function. If you are wearing not only your heart on your sleeve, your liver on your lapel and the other organs affixed to various articles of your attire, but also a whole alphabet in scarlet on your breast, then your poetry must bear with losing the notion of *private parts* altogether and with gaining a certain publicity that has nothing to do with the personal. Further, if you regard, as Anne Sexton does, the poem as "a lie that tells the truth" (it was Cocteau who first spoke of himself this way), then you face the corresponding peril that the truth you tell will become a lie: "there is no translating that ocean," as Miss Sexton says. And it will become a lie because you have not taken enough care to "make something happen"—in short, to lie in the way poems must lie, by devising that imaginative rightness which Roethke located primarily in rhythm, but which has everything to do as well with the consecution of images, the shape language makes as it is deposited in the reader's mind, the transactions between beginnings and endings, the *devices*—no less—of art.

"Even one alone verse sometimes makes a perfect poem," Ben Jonson declared, and so much praise (it is the kind of praise that leaves out of the reckoning a great deal of waste, a great deal of botched work) it will be easy, and what is more it will be necessary, to give Anne Sexton; like the preposterous sprite whose "demon-offspring" impulses she resumes, this poet is likely, *at any moment*, to say those oracular, outrageous things we least can bear but most require:

> Fee-fi-fo-fum
> Now I'm borrowed
> Now I'm numb

It is when she speaks beyond the moment, speaks as it were consecutively that Anne Sexton finds herself in difficulties; if we are concerned with the poem as it grows from one verse to the next, enlarging itself by means of itself, like a growing pearl, the real one (Hawthorne's, for all he tells us, never grew up), then we must discover an Anne Sexton dead set, by her third book of poems, against any such process. Hers is the truth that cancels poetry, and her career as an artist an excruciating trajectory of self-destruction, so that it is by her failures in her own enterprise that she succeeds, and by her successes as an artist that she fails herself.—RICHARD HOWARD, "Anne Sexton: 'Some Tribal Female Who Is Known But Forbidden,'" *Alone with America*, 1969, pp. 442–44

Anne Sexton's poetry, unlike that of Lowell and Berryman, is strictly confined in its formal implications to the facts of neurosis, sickness and death. That is, these things are not given any other status or significance than their own actuality. Of course it might be argued that they *have* no other significance than in themselves. But, *in themselves*: things are not, if I may adapt Sartre, merely in-themselves, they are also *for-themselves*. That is, the act of writing poetry—the fact and decision of being-a-poet—is different in kind from the facts of being born, falling in love and dying. We might, at the risk of oversimplification, say that Anne Sexton's poetry is limited by and to its subject-matter. This would not be entirely true: she is, it is clear from the most cursory reading, an accomplished poet. The verse is at the opposite pole from mere effusion, self-expression (which might perhaps have been predicted from a facile reading of the account I have just offered). And yet her poetry fails consistently, I think, to go beyond its elected subject-matter: it tells us a lot about the way Anne Sexton feels about things, yet little about the way we might feel about them ourselves. The real paradox of poetry is that the more true to its own subject-matter (its subjectivity) it is, the more 'universal' it is. We touch here on a fundamental fact about poetry, and many fallacies abound in this territory. What Yeats attributed to the poetry of Wilfred Owen—a limitation to the passive suffering of war and the pity of war—I am myself attributing (some would say equally shamefully) to that of Anne Sexton. Yet there does seem to me all the difference in the world between the two cases: Owen experienced the 'tragic' dimension of things within a few months. What most men (Yeats was among them) experience in a middle age of slow adaptation, Owen experienced brutally in months, telescoped. Neither the sensibility nor the poetic technique of the man cracked under the pressure—the most inhuman, it could be argued, that civilized man has ever had to endure: Owen gave us—in 'Strange Meeting', 'The Offensive', 'Futility', 'Dulce et Decorum Est', and 'Exposure'—a handful of the indisputably great poems of the twentieth century. In Anne Sexton's accounts of attempted suicide, of madness, of a major operation, we are conscious of no attempt at 'transcending' the experience, no sense even that an unwelcome experience has come across the path of the poet (which is what we have, intensified to the last degree, in the war poems of Owen and Sassoon). Sexton cleaves to the humiliation, for instance, of being shaved, cleared out, objectified, handled, dehumanized and pitied in the course of preparation for an operation, almost as if it were her *karma*, waiting for her since her birth. 'The Operation' is true to the experiences, we feel: the verse moves well, the stanzas plumpen and narrow as they should. It is impossible to say that Sexton is 'enjoying' or relishing the things the poem reports as happening to her. She is manifestly sincere. Yet the alternatives are not merely those of enjoying the suffering or of being shocked by it. This would present us with a falsely clean dichotomy. Nowhere in the *Selected Poems* can we find evidence for the thesis that at some level Sexton was enjoying her suffering. And yet one misses altogether the note of deep shock, anger, bewilderment which informs the poems of Owen. And it seems to me reasonable to compare the equally intolerable situations. There is, I suggest, a level at which the intolerable and the real coalesce, and at which the ache of enduring the repulsive issues in a white joy of understanding. This light of illumination is akin to the crisis Pirandello described as lying at the heart of his drama. Although there is nothing false or willed about Anne Sexton's accounts of her sufferings, her poetry lacks the dimension of transcendence—what Eliot called 'surprise'. There is more than a suspicion that the experience of the operation or even the madhouse is, if not willed, at least acceded to: she accepts her sickness. It turns her into a 'shorn lamb', her bed becomes an 'aluminum crib'. She accepts being made a child, an object, a passive thing. In the same way she accepts her status as 'mad woman':

> we are the circle of the crazy ladies
> who sit in the lounge of the mental house
> and smile at the smiling woman . . .
> ('Ringing the Bells')

Is it that someone who experiences her madness like this cannot really *be* mad, and yet is determined to play mad, to accept the role that is like a solution? I hesitate before these facile-sounding generalizations, and yet again and again the verse makes me return to them:

> we stand in broken
> lines and wait while they unlock
> the door and count us at the frozen gate
> of dinner.
> ('You, Doctor Martin')

She speaks here with the voice of one of Solzhenitsyn's prisoners. Yet Solzhenitsyn's characters *are* prisoners, and their gates really *are* frozen: Solzhenitsyn's men would not be there if they were not held there. Thus there is a tension between the sense of freedom and the actual captivity. It is perhaps the feeling in Anne Sexton's writing that she would have nothing to offer if she were not 'mad' or 'depressed' that makes her poetry, though honest on the human level, at the deep level of art, inauthentic, flat, one-dimensional. For her, there is no world outside the madhouse, outside the neurosis: and thus the important tension of the Solzhenitsyn novel (the source of its interest for us) is absent. Her voice in these poems has a curious quality of dumb insolence, as if she were determined to play upon the sane man's uncertainty. She offers us almost too predictably the imagery of paranoia, of *Pierrot Lunaire*:

> It was the strangled cold of November
> even the stars were stopped in the sky
> and that moon too bright
> forking through the bars to stick me
> with a singing in the head.

It is as if she needs her visitors, the human company, in order to be able to reject them; alternatively, she needs real loneliness in order to be able to blame people.

Transformations was a logically irrational development for the author of *Selected Poems*. It seems on most levels a technical advance on the earlier work: the verse is free (sometimes to the point of being prose) yet economical; the fairy tales are well told, and there are many piercing insights. Each tale is given a vaguely Freudian rationale: 'Rapunzel' is about the love between the older and the younger woman, for instance; 'Snow White' about the sinister attractiveness of the Virgin; 'Cinderella' about economic wish-fulfilment; and so on. A characteristic feature (roughly parallel perhaps to the studied slanginess of the later Lowell) is the pillaging of the advertising and entertainment industries for imagery. The verse is clotted with Ace bandages and Bab-o and Coca Cola and Duz and Chuck Wagon dog food. We find Al Jolson, Houdini, Dior, the Boston Symphony—the whole gamut of mid-century America—giving a light, flip tone to the sardonic stance otherwise adopted. The witty commentary in fact often takes precedence over the sardonic rationale: these transformations are often enough mere doings-over of the tales, copy for a particularly elegant New York edition of Grimm to go along with a set of Charles Addams drawings. In this light it seems thoroughly characteristic of mid-century East Coast America: the clink of ice-cubes accompanies the disabused adult's bed-time stories.

And finally the spell enacted in the telling of the fairy tale fails to work. *The dream won't end.* In 'The Sleeping Beauty', which ends the selection, Grimm gives way finally to Dr Freud, fairy tale to sick joke:

> She married the prince
> and all went well
> except for the fear—
> the fear of sleep.
>
> Briar Rose
> was an insomniac.
> ('The Sleeping Beauty')

Sexton's Briar Rose had woken up, upon being kissed, with an all-American 'Daddy! Daddy!' And it is with her Daddy that Sexton's book ends:

> It's not the prince at all
> but my father
> drunkenly bent over my bed
> circling the abyss-like dark

my father thick upon me
like some sleeping jelly-fish.
('The Sleeping Beauty')

It is difficult to escape the conclusion that this rationale has been forced upon Sexton by psychoanalysis, that the world-view has been formed excessively by the peculiarly exasperating doctrines of Freud or of his American diluters. Anne Sexton still regards herself as a victim, and nothing but a victim. As a victim she expects to be humoured, but not to have to take responsibility for herself. She seems not to have succeeded in locating any centre of self. These are the fairy stories 'interpreted' according to psychoanalysis, not in order to illuminate or to deepen our understanding, but merely to convince us that they are all horrible, and where not horrible (as at the spell-breaking), phoney. It is the common tone of most literature over-exposed to psychoanalysis, from Salinger to Albee. Finally, one's sense of Anne Sexton's creative personality is not that it is too much itself to achieve transcendence, but on the contrary, too little.—GEOFFREY THURLEY, "The Poetry of Breakdown," *The American Moment: American Poetry in the Mid-Century*, 1977, pp. 86–90

ALICIA OSTRIKER

From "That Story: Anne Sexton
and Her Transformations"

American Poetry Review, July–August 1982, pp. 11–16

I

Anne Sexton is the easiest poet in the world to condescend to. Critics get in line for the pleasure of filing her under N for Narcissist and announcing that she lacks reticence. A recent example: "She indulges in self-revelation without stint, telling all in an *exposé* of her innermost workings that amounts to literary *seppuku*." The critic wonders whether "such messy preoccupations will remain to stain the linen of the culture for long or whether good taste bleaches out even the most stubborn stain eventually."[1]

In letters as in life, to expose a personal fragility is to invite attack. Cruelty and contempt follow vulnerability, just as respect follows snobbishness; it is a law of human nature. Having been on both sides of this reflex, I suspect that the sneer derives from fear—a fear of being stung into imaginative sympathy—and in Anne Sexton's case I suspect that the fear is threefold.

First of all, Sexton's material is heavily female and biological. She gives us full helpings of her breasts, her uterus, her menstruation, her abortion, her "tiny jail" of a vagina, her love life, her mother's and daughters' breasts, everyone's operations, the act of eating, the way her father's "serpent, that mocker, woke up and pressed against me like a great god" when she danced with him after much champagne at a wedding, even the trauma of her childhood enemas. Preoccupied with the flesh, she swings between experiencing it as sacred and fertile and experiencing it as filthy and defiled. This distinguishes her from Plath, for whom the body is mainly an emblem of pain and mutilation. But the distinction will not be an interesting one to the timid reader. Far more than Plath, Sexton challenges our residual certainties that the life of the body should be private and not public, and that women especially should be seen and not heard, except among each other, talking about their messy anatomies. We believe, I think, that civilization will fall if it is otherwise.

Second, Sexton is assertively emotional. A love junkie who

believes "touch" is "the kingdom and the kingdom come," she is driven by an unquenchable need for acceptance and caresses, and by bottomless guilt that she herself has been insufficiently loving to others. Simultaneously, the poetry presses intimately toward its audience. Feel what I feel, it says. Accept me, love me, love everything about me, my strength, my weakness. This of course is very much a feminine sort of demand, or rather it is a demand we discourage men from making explicitly (disguised versions are acceptable) and encourage women to make, with predictable results. Remember Marilyn Monroe? The egotistical sublime we tolerate; not the egotistical pathetic. The demand for love is narcissistic and childish. It is usually self-defeating, since most of us respond to another's need for love with aversion. Insofar as we manage (barely) to keep the upper lip stiff in our own lives, we judge neediness (in excess of our own) to be immoral. In the same way, wealth judges poverty and success perceives failure to be a consequence of low character. We understand that beggars and cripples exist, but do they have to put themselves where we can see them?

But what is most distressing about Sexton, I think, is her quality of unresignedness. She writes more fiercely than any poet in our time about physical and mental bliss and the holiness of the heart's affections. Her explorations of pathology are feverish attempts to "gnaw at the barrier" dividing us from each other and from the "weird abundance" of our creative capacities. She is sure not only that poetry saved her own life but that it can save others' lives. Many of her poems are gestures of rather pure human generosity. "To My Lover Returning to His Wife" and "December 12th" in *Love Poems* are two examples. Typically her work enacts a pitched battle between Thanatos and Eros, self-loathing and self-love, suicide and survival. This too is irritating. "The mass of men lead lives of quiet desperation," wrote Thoreau about a century ago, trying to twit them out of it. "We think of the key, each in his prison. Thinking of the key, each confirms a prison," wrote Eliot a half-century back, on the way to his conversion to Christianity. But consider how much of our literature, our high literature especially, and most especially our high poetry, confirms the prison. We are instructed perhaps in its interior decoration, but not encouraged to seek escape. John Fowles's Daniel Martin muses "how all through his writing life, he had avoided the happy ending, as if it were somehow in bad taste . . . offensive, in an intellectually privileged caste, to suggest publicly that anything might turn out well." If each in his cell believes himself locked up forever, the last thing he wants to hear from a neighboring cell is the noise of scratching, poundings, screamings for the jailer.

Antipathy to a writer like Sexton makes sense if we assume that poetry must somehow be decorous. Obviously a great deal of poetry, both great and trivial, is so. But I see no real reason why poetry should be limited to tasteful confirmations of my psychic *status quo ante*, or indeed why it should be limited in any way. Reticence and good taste are excellent things, but unscrewing the doors from their jambs is a good thing too. Our original sin as humanists is a tendency to forget that nothing human is alien to any of us. This means that the crazy suicidal lady is not to be condescended to by me. It also means that she is one of the inhabitants of my own proper attic, whom I deny at my peril. A poem does not have to be, yet may legitimately be, "an axe for the frozen sea" of sympathy and self-recognition "within us," provided only that its language be living and its form just.

This brings me to the vexed question of Anne Sexton's artistry, where I must say immediately and with regret that she is not a *fine* artist. At her best she is coarse. Musically her instrument is the kazoo. If Plath, say, is porcelain and Robert Lowell bronze, Sexton is brightly painted earthenware. Reading every book of hers but *Transformations*, I burn with the desire to edit. She repeats herself without noticing. Her early poems before she hits her stride tend to be too stiff, her late ones tend to be shapeless. Her phrasing is sometimes sentimental, her endings sometimes flat.

And yet the writing dazzles. Sexton's colloquial line, vigorous, flexible and earthy, is not only a standing rebuke to every sort of false dignity but a strategy for redeeming the common life. Her organic and domestic imagery captures species of phenomena for poetry that were never there before. Her metaphors, breathtaking as ski-jumps, direct attention both to the play of language and to the writer's intelligence—which is not the same as bookishness—and sheer capacity to describe. One does not rapidly exhaust the significance of a poem about the mad that says "what large children we are" and mentions the night nurse who "walks on two erasers," or a poem about a hospital stay concluding with the lines "and run along, Anne, and run along now , / my stomach stitched up like a football / for the game." Is one's body really a toy? To others; to the self? Consider a fantasy of dying that says, "I moved like a lobster, slower and slower," or a quick allegory of the poet's life in which Jonah, finding he cannot escape the whale, "cocked his head attentively / like a defendant at his own trial," or the simile of "tears falling down like mud," or the story of Eve giving birth to a rat "with its bellyful of dirt and its hair seven inches long" that she did not realize was ugly. It is writerliness and nothing else that enables Sexton to re-create the child-self more keenly than Roethke, to define inner demons more clearly than Lowell, and to evoke the complicated tensile strands of intimate relationships, which include physical need and revulsion, affection and fear, pride and guilt, resentment, jealousy and admiration, better than most novelists. As to the primitive style, anyone who thinks it is easier to write "raw" than "cooked" should try it.

Often Sexton's best poems in the early books are not the harrowing accounts of private trauma which understandably most gripped her first readers, but poems where self-knowledge makes possible the verbal crystallization of some larger piece of the human condition. "Housewife," a ten-line poem with four hairpin turns and a final two lines that are as important as the first two of "The Red Wheel Barrow" is a good example. It is this that brings me to my main subject. Though Sexton is always a strong poet of the subjective self, in the middle of her career her center of gravity shifted. Beginning with *Transformations*, which was a sort of poetic self-initiation, she set the uninhibited self to work interpreting prior, external, shared cultural traditions. ⟨. . .⟩ I believe that "confessional" or not, all these poems change the way we must look at our shared past. As their themes are increasingly ambitious, their conclusions are increasingly significant, culturally. Obviously they also change the way we must look at Sexton.

II

In the winter of 1969–70, with four volumes of intimately personal poems behind her, Anne Sexton embarked on a new sort of venture. The early work dealt with the poet's family, her struggles against madness, her loves, her terrors, her desires. "That narrow diary of my mind" was laid publicly bare both as a personal necessity and in the faith that to reveal rather than conceal one's private nightmares was to perform a poetic service. The orientation of her poetry was psychoanalytic, as befitted a poet who began writing as a form of therapy following mental breakdown, who enacted in her poems the analysand's

self-probing through examination of relationships with others, and who explained the vitality of her images by saying that "poetry, after all, milks the unconscious." Of all the poets subsequently labeled confessional or extremist—Snodgrass, Lowell, Berryman, Plath—she was the least reticent personally, and the most eager to have her poems "mean something else to someone else." Public popularity had spectacularly confirmed Sexton's convictions. For much of 1969 the poet immersed herself with the aid of a Guggenheim grant in the autobiographical drama *Mercy Street*, a work of extreme self-saturation which played for some weeks in the fall at the American Place Theater to mixed but respectful reviews. Up until this point, Sexton had not tried "to give you something else, something outside of myself."[2] Self was the center, self the perimeter, of her vision.

Concerning the new series of poems which retold sixteen fairy tales from the Brothers Grimm, neither the poet nor her publishers expressed great confidence. Houghton Mifflin wondered whether she should publish them at all, and wanted to consult an outside reader. Sexton was defensive and apologetic, worrying that "many of my former fans are going to be disappointed that these poems do not hover on the brink of insanity," and acknowledging that they were "a departure from my usual style . . . they lack the intensity and confessional force of my previous work." To persuade herself and her publishers that the work was good, she solicited an opinion from Stanley Kunitz. To boost it with the public, she arranged for an admiring preface by Kurt Vonnegut, Jr.

Transformations breaks the confined circle of a poetic mode Sexton had needed but outgrown, that of the purely personal. That folktales carry a heavy cultural burden has been understood since they were first collected. Mircea Eliade tells us they represent "an infinitely serious and responsible adventure" which he identifies with the universal ordeal of initiation, "passing by way of a symbolic death and resurrection from ignorance and immaturity to the spiritual age of the adult." Bruno Bettelheim believes they provide children with models for the mastery of psychological problems, teach them the necessity of struggle, and embody through fantasy "the process of healthy human development." We see these tales, in other words, as the expression of a social mandate favoring individual growth.

Sexton does not alter Grimm's plots. Her fidelity to the stories preserves what Eliade calls the "initiatory scenario," and this may partially explain why a poet who was perennially torn between remaining a child and assuming adulthood was attracted to these tales in the first place. Formally, the plot lines give her what she never had before: something nominally outside of her personal history to write about. What she does with this material is to seize it, crack it open, and *make* it personal. The result is at once a brilliant interpretation and a valid continuation of folktale tradition—and a piece of poetic subversion, whereby the "healthy" meanings we expect to enjoy are held up to icy scrutiny.

Syntax and diction in *Transformations* are conspicuously and brazenly twentieth-century American, stripped to the colloquial bone, in a mode probably generated for American poetry by Eliot's "Journey of the Magi." The technique brings us closer to the unsentimental pre-Christian origins of these stories, much as the language of Eliot's "Magi" intends not to deflate the significance of Christ's nativity but to force the reader to confront it more nakedly. But unlike Eliot (or Pound, or their imitators), far from being interested in the past for its own sake, Sexton makes the time of the tales our own. In her "Snow White":

> the virgin is a lovely number,
> cheeks fragile as cigarette paper,
> arms and legs made of Limoges,
> lips like Vin du Rhone,
> rolling her china-blue eyes
> open and shut.

This is the opening tale and sets the tone. Of the miller's daughter in "Rumpelstiltskin," threatened with extinction if she does not spin straw into gold, the narrator condoles, "Poor thing. / To die and never see Brooklyn." In "Cinderella" the heroine

> slept on the sooty hearth each night
> and walked around looking like Al Jolson.

The reader's initial response to these anachronisms may be one of delighted shock—Cinderella and Al Jolson, yes, of course, think of the parallels—it is like a blue volt leaping a gap. We need to remember that just such modernization and adaptation, making the tales locally meaningful, is what peasants and poets have done with traditional lore for millennia. The stories would never survive without it. But Sexton's telescoping of past and present is also a surface manifestation of a more profound interpretive activity.

The poet's effort to understand her stories on her own terms precipitates a transformed view of traditional social values, particularly those associated with feminine life patterns: love and marriage, beauty, family, and most radically, the idea of goodness and moral responsibility, all of which she slices through like butter. The fairy-tale ending of marriage, supposed to represent romantic and financial security ever after, becomes, ironically, "that story"—incredible in the first place, and, were it credible, pathetically dull:

> Cinderella and the prince
> lived, they say, happily ever after,
> like two dolls in a museum case
> never bothered by diapers or dust,
> never arguing over the timing of an egg,
> never telling the same story twice,
> never getting a middle-aged spread,
> their darling smiles pasted on for eternity.
> Regular Bobbsey Twins.
> That story.

Half of Sexton's tales end in marriage, and most of these marriages are seen as some form of either selfishness or captivity. Regarding the value of beauty, we learn in "Snow White" that an innocent virgin's unconscious beauty makes her a stupid doll, a commodity, while an experienced woman's conscious beauty makes her not only cruel but doomed. "Beauty is a simple passion, / But, oh my friends, in the end / you will dance the fire dance in iron shoes." Moreover, since "a woman *is* her mother," at the wedding celebration during which the stepmother gets tortured to death in those iron shoes, Snow White chillingly begins "referring to her mirror / as women do." Describing the sacred emotion of mother love, Sexton in "Rumplestiltskin" remarks with pure contempt:

> He was like most new babies
> as ugly as an artichoke
> but the queen thought him a pearl.
> She gave him her dumb lactation,
> delicate, trembling, hidden,
> warm, etc.

While none of the protagonists in Sexton's versions is described in terms of his or her virtue, which is Grimm's as it should be, pre-Disney and amoral, "evil" characters and deviant behavior commonly receive her sympathy. The witch

in "Hansel and Gretel" is cannibalistic and terrifying, as in the original, and her death is represented as poetic justice. But the poem's prologue has been a fantasia on the theme of a normally affectionate mother's desire to "eat up" her son, and the epilogue provocatively suggests that in a world governed by eating or being eaten, the witch in "the woe of the oven" has been a sacrifice "like something religious." Does Sexton mean that the witch is a Christ figure? Is this a reference to the subduing of the mother-goddess by a civilized daughter allied with the patriarchy? (Louise Gluck's "Gretzel in Darkness," by the way, raises similar questions.) In "Rapunzel," Sexton sees the witch as a lesbian in love with her imprisoned girl, and the poem stresses the emotional poignance of the older woman's loss, while perfunctorily dismissing the normality of the heterosexual lovers. "Rumplestiltskin" and other stories follow a similar pattern, prodding us toward identification with antagonist-loser instead of protagonist-winner.

By the same token a number of characters we have conventionally accepted as good are made repellent. In "The Maiden Without Hands," the king who weds the mutilated girl is motivated by "a desire to own the maiming / so that not one of us butchers / will come to him with crow-bars." So long as the queen is a cripple, the king will feel secure in his own wholeness. (This, by the way, is one of the few occasions when Sexton writes, albeit allegorically, about her own marriage. Asked in an interview whether she was not afraid of hurting others by her intimate revelations of family life, she explained that she wrote mainly about the dead who could not be hurt, and avoided saying painful things about the living.) In "The Twelve Dancing Princesses," which is transformed to an Eros-versus-Logos, or Pleasure-Principle-versus-Superego parable, Logos unfortunately wins, in the person of the clever young man who finds out where the irresponsible princesses do their dancing. His mean-minded success brings an end to their enjoyable night life. The shocking final poem, "Briar Rose" (Sleeping Beauty), eliminates the heroine's mother and makes the father not merely the possessive maintainer of his daughter's prepubescent purity—"He forced every male in the court to scour his tongue with Bab-O"—but its incestuous exploiter. Sleep in this poem brings "a voyage" into regressive infantilism. Wakened after her hundred-years' sleep, Briar Rose cries "Daddy! Daddy!" What she will see for the rest of her life when she wakens from the nightmares that plague her is

> another kind of prison.
> It's not the prince at all,
> but my father
> drunkenly bent over my bed,
> circling the abyss like a shark,
> my father thick upon me
> like some sleeping jellyfish.

Here and everywhere Sexton's interpretations discover and release elements already implicit in the stories. Over and over one thinks "of course." Were we to look at these poems as moral texts, we would have to see in them a demand for some transvaluation of social values.

But the appeal of the tales is primarily neither moral nor immoral. They are, as the central fact of magic in them partially indicates, rooted in and addressed to something less rational in our natures than the impulse toward social reform. Joseph Campbell makes the obvious point that folktale, like dream and myth, derives ultimately from the individual psyche, modified by the successions of cultures it travels through, and that its images are not simply relics of religious or superstitious periods in cultural history but projections of universal and primitive human desires and fears. It is proper, therefore, that Sexton's handling of these tales, while unconventionally personal and morally skeptical, is nevertheless designed to maintain, not reduce, their psychic impact. The poet does not rationalize or explain. She narrates, and with great swiftness and skill. She is funny, which makes sense since comedy is a major element in the traditional stories. She is intensely vivid. Her style excites, rather than soothes, the senses. Her imagery, to borrow a term from tabloids and horror movies, is sensational, full of food and feeding, sexuality, greed, and death—often fused, in a kind of synesthesia of appetites.

"Snow White," the first story in the volume, is sensationally and gratuitously oral. It tells us that the virgin is "unsoiled . . . white as a bonefish," and a few lines later that her stepmother "has been eaten, of course, by age." Where in Grimm the evil queen wants Snow White's heart merely as proof of her death, Sexton's stepmother expresses a cruder longing: "Bring me her heart . . . and I will salt it and eat it." Brought a boar's heart by the compassionate hunter, "The queen chewed it up like cube steak."

Proceeding with the story, Sexton embroiders. Snow White on entering the strange cottage eats "seven chicken livers" before sleeping, and then we meet what I and most of my students regard as the best single metaphor in the book, "the dwarfs, those little hot dogs." Revived after her first coma, the heroine is "as full of life as soda pop." When she bites the poison apple, the dwarfs "washed her with wine and rubbed her with butter," though to no avail; "She lay as still as a gold piece." The passive coin, recalling Plath's "I am your jewel, I am your valuable. The pure gold baby," parallels food in its appeal to greed.

Other poems similarly ply us with images of the tactile, the expensive, the devourable. The girl in "Rumplestiltskin" is "lovely as a grape." The dwarf commits suicide by tearing himself in two, "somewhat like a split broiler." Feeding and sexuality are cheerfully identified in the bawdy poem "The Little Peasant," tragically identified in "Rapunzel," where women in love "feed off each other." In "Little Red Riding Hood" and "Hansel and Gretel," Sexton again implies the interchangeability of feeding and being fed on, in dramas of death and rebirth.

Where the Grimm stories are violent, Sexton does not skimp on pain and gore, but describes with inventive detail:

> First your toes will smoke
> and then your heels will turn black
> and you will fry upward like a frog . . .

When Cinderella's sister cuts a toe off to fit the shoe, we see

> the blood pouring forth.
> That is the way with amputations.
> They don't just heal up like a wish.

and both sisters at Cinderella's wedding have their eyes pecked out, leaving "two hollow spots . . . like soup spoons." Well over half the tales include death or mutilation, and both in the individual poems and cumulatively, Sexton's images of killing and eating in *Transformations* seem not merely childish but infantile.

That, I think, is the point. The evocation of these desires and terrors reminds us of powers we can scarcely control even as adults, in our lives and in the world. We are reminded of the helpless ur-self whose whole world is touch and taste, who fantasizes omnipotence, who dreads annihilation in a thousand ways. And it is this self, we understand when reading *Transformations*, that generates fairy tales.

III

Although Sexton did not again write in the manner of *Transformations*, the volume marks a turning point. She had learned how to interpret the impersonal by the personal, the symbol belonging to a culture by experience belonging to the self. She had exercised for the first time a gift for iconoclasm regarding social and moral conventions. She had acquired, as her later work shows, a taste for the quasi-mythic narrative. Her final finished books, *The Book of Folly* (1972), *The Death Notebooks* (1974), and *The Awful Rowing toward God* (1974), return to a predominantly autobiographical mode. But they are bolder in language, formally more experimental, and readier to challenge convention than any of her earlier work. In them the poet increasingly sees herself not as merely a private person, certainly not as a psychoanalytic case study, but as the heroine in a spiritual quest. At the same time, the question of what it means to be feminine—not simply to the self but to the culture and within the religion created by that culture—deepens and darkens. In an early (1965) *Hudson Review* interview, Sexton says, "It's very hard to reveal yourself . . . I'm hunting for the truth . . . behind everything that happens to you, every act, there is another truth, a secret life." What the late books reveal is that behind the "live or die" struggle in Sexton's life was another struggle, which led her first to a re-envisioning of Christian myth, then to a re-imagining of God the Father. I am tempted to say that Sexton's final wrestling was between loving and loathing God, and that she lost because she knew too much.

The Book of Folly makes us think about gender in a way that moves a step past the deflating techniques of *Transformations*. It includes a group of *persona* pieces which enable the poet to imagine the violent personalities of one-legged man, assassin, wife beater—all of them castrated figures for whom woman is enemy, all of them evidently *animus*-figures for Sexton, as are "the ambition bird" in the finely sardonic and self-critical opening poem, and the destructive doppelganger in "The Other." In "The Red Shoes," a spinoff from *Transformations*, ambition is secretly and shamefully handed down from mother to daughter, is uncontrollable, and destroys them. "Anna Who Was Mad" and "The Hex" are secular salvation and damnation poems struggling with the poet's guilty fear that her ongoing life is responsible for the madness and death of the beloved aunt whose namesake she is. In "Mother and Daughter" Sexton's tone is glad and proud as she relinquishes "my booty, my spoils, my Mother & Co." and celebrates the daughter's growth to womanhood, but what womanhood means is:

> carrying keepsakes to the boys,
> carrying powders to the boys,
> carrying, my Linda, blood to
> the bloodletter.

There is a figure in the carpet here.[3] In all these poems self-sacrifice is the condition of self-acceptance, and to be feminine is to be either powerless or punished. The "Angels of the Love Affair" sonnet sequence, inspired by Rilke, challenges a set of elemental angels to know and exorcise what the poet knows of shame, defilement, paralysis, despair and solitude. In the one poem where the poet remembers herself taking a pleasurable initiative (stealing grandfather's forbidden raspberries), the angel is a punitive lady "of blizzards and blackouts." The three prose narratives in *The Book of Folly* still more clearly identify passive feminine roles (daughter, wife, erotic object) with victimization and self-victimization. The one figure who seems to escape passivity, the protagonist's adventurous friend Ruth in "The Letting Down of the Hair," finally finds Christ—and kills herself. Sexton does not tell us why. But the series of seven short poems entitled "The Jesus Papers" may explain.

Prior to *The Book of Folly*, in occasional poems dealing with Christ, Sexton had evidently identified with him as sufferer and public performer. "When I was Christ, I felt like Christ," she said of "In the Deep Museum." "My arms hurt, I desperately wanted to pull them in off the Cross. When I was taken down off the Cross, and buried alive, I sought solutions; I hoped they were Christian solutions." "That ragged Christ, that sufferer, performed the greatest act of confession." In "The Exorcists," an early poem about abortion, the title implies ironically that an aborted fetus is being cast out like a demon, but the poem's text, with its "I know you not" refrain, implies that on the contrary it is a Christ whom the speaker is betraying. Many of Sexton's letters depict an intense need for faith undermined by solid skepticism. "In case it's true, I tell my Catholic friend . . . in case it's true, I tell myself, and plead with it to be true after all. No matter what I write, I plead with it to be true!" (*Letters*, p. 125). [4] "God? spend half time wooing R. Catholics who will pray *for* you in case it's true. Spend other half knowing there is certainly no god. Spend fantasy time thinking that there is a life after death, because surely my parents, for instance, are not dead, they are, good god! just buried" (*Letters*, p. 235). "Oh, I really believe in God—it's Christ that boggles the mind" (*Letters*, p. 346). "Yes, it is time to think about Christ again. I keep putting it off. If he is the God man, I would feel a hell of a lot better. If there is a God . . . how do you explain him swallowing all those people up in Pakistan? Of course there's a God, but what kind of he?" (*Letters*, pp. 368–9). Sexton also experienced visions, of varied duration and of great physical urgency, of Christ, Mary, God, the martyred saints, the devil, in which "I feel that I can touch them almost . . . that they are part of me . . . I believed that I was talking to Mary, that her lips were upon my lips," she said in an interview. None of this data, however, explains the radical vision of "The Jesus Papers," which is a systematic and structured—if miniature—reinterpretation of Christian myth, as *Transformations* is of Grimm. The subject is of course far more audacious; indeed, only two other poets in English have attempted it, Milton in *Paradise Regained* and Blake in *The Everlasting Gospel*. Was Jesus a man? Very well then, let the poet imagine what manner of man. Let her begin, since much Christian iconography dwells on his infancy, by imagining what manner of infant, and take it from there. Allowing for the vast differences in scale, Sexton's Jesus is as disagreeable as Milton's in *Paradise Regained*—and perhaps as unintentionally so.

The opening poem, "Jesus Suckles," consists of three sections of dwindling length. As so often in Sexton we are in the mind of someone utterly dependent on love. The language at first is erotic-playful, rich, organic, unstructured—one of Sexton's catalogs in which the condition of happiness is expressed through images of fertility. There is a tone of amplified gratification, rather like that of "In Celebration of My Uterus," and for the same reason. It is the mental effect of physical bliss:

> Mary, your great
> white apples make me glad . . .
> I'm a jelly-baby and you're my wife.
> You're a rock and I the fringy algae.
> You're a lily and I'm the bee that gets inside . . .
> I'm a kid in a rowboat and you're the sea,
> the salt, you're every fish of importance.

But then:

> No. No.
> All lies.
> I am small
> and you hold me.
> You give me milk
> and we are the same
> and I am glad.
> No. No.
> All lies.
> I am a truck. I run everything.
> I own you.

First metaphor is killed, then the love, joy and sense of universal connection that generated the metaphor. We have a tidy drama of pleasure-principle succumbing to reality-principle, with both natural and super-natural implications. The poem reminds us that to a god, or a boy child, grateful love and helplessness are "all lies," and that reality—assuming the dualistic universe that Christianity does assume—means power, repugnance toward the flesh, and rejection of the mother. The relevant Biblical text attributes this moment of brutality to Jesus' adolescence: "Woman, what have I to do with thee?" Sexton merely pushes the time back. Blake's "To Tirzah" is a comparably cruel poem on the same text. The initial imagery implies that Mary is Mother Nature, or the pre-Christian goddesses who represent her divine fertility. Man and God are her privileged superiors and historical conquerors. The modern technological outcome of the split between Flesh and Logos which Christianity sacralizes is modestly accommodated by the synechdoche "truck." [5]

The succeeding poems trace what follows from the initial willed division of Jesus from Mary, boy child from mother, the will to control from the willingness to fondle and nurture. While the rest of the human and animal kingdom frolics and propagates, Jesus fasts. "His penis no longer arched with sorrow over Him"—the rainbow image recalling God's forgiving covenant with Noah and mankind—but "was sewn onto Him like a medal," an outrageous metaphor that not only disparages Jesus' celibacy but calls into question the Christian replacement of sexual love by *caritas*. Though he still desires Mary when asleep, he subdues his need, uses his penis as a chisel a la Rodin, and produces a Pieta so that they will be united in his death. *Civilization and Its Discontents* is the necessary gloss for this poem. For the next one *Justine* might do. When Jesus encounters the harlot Mary Magdalen being stoned ("Stones came at her like bees to candy / and sweet redheaded harlot that she was / she screamed out *I never, I never*"), he raises her up and efficiently heals her "terrible sickness" then and there by lancing with his thumbs her breasts, "those two boils of whoredom," until the milk runs out. Sexton's deadpan combination of Biblical and contemporary language here is typical:

> The harlot followed Jesus around like a puppy
> for He had raised her up.
> Now she forsook her fornications
> and became His pet.

In "Jesus Cooks" and "Jesus Summons Forth" we get the miracle of the loaves and fishes as a sleight of hand act and the raising of Lazarus by assembling his bones as if he were a model airplane kit. "Tenderness" appears in a single line and appears to be part of the instructions. As with the poems on Jesus' sexuality, the poet's wry self-projection is important here. The roles of food-provider and healer were Sexton's, as was the role of public performer for whom feeling was part of the act. In the bitterly comic "Jesus Dies," the crucifixion is like an ultimate Sexton poetry reading, where Jesus' self-revelation of his sore need for God—a "man-to-man thing" that is half-competitive, half-desperate—is mingled with furious irritation at his audience's sensation-seeking.

From crucifixion Sexton does not move on to resurrection, but drops back to another woman-poem. "Jesus Unborn," which turns out to be, like "Jesus Suckles," a judgment of the Virgin's role in Christianity. It is the moment before the Annunciation, and again the imagery is lushly natural. Mary sits among olive trees, feels lethargic as an animal, wants to settle down like a camel or doze like a dog:

> Instead a strange being leans over her
> and lifts her chin firmly
> and gazes at her with executioner's eyes.

So much for how many centuries of Mariolatry? How many centuries of sacred inconography? But in case Sexton has not made herself clear, she appends to "The Jesus Papers" a final poem entitled "The Author of the Jesus Papers Speaks," which defines the place not only of Mary but of all womankind in Western religion. It is a dream poem in three tiny episodes. First, Sexton milks a great cow, but instead of "the moon juice, the white mother," blood spurts "and covered me with shame." Several related readings are possible here: blood may be menstrual blood, shameful because taboo, sign of female pollutedness; or blood as sign that mothers surrender their own lives for others' lives, like beasts; or a reminder that all life leads to death. The cow might be Nature, or Mother-goddess, or Sexton's own mother who shamed and blamed her and whose "double image" she was. We have the beginnings of a rich female drama but there is no development, for at this point God speaks to Sexton and says "People say only good things about Christmas. If they want to say something bad, they whisper."

This is a change in tone as well as a non sequitur, it is funny, and it gives us a God who, like a boss or an earthly father, is half-uncomfortable with the way his governing role divides him from those he governs. God seems to be interrupting a mother-daughter interview, making a bid for attention—and sympathy—for his own concerns. But why should anyone say bad things about Christmas? Is God paranoid? Or guilty? Or, if this dream is taking place in the twentieth century, might we say that He doesn't know the half of it? In any case, Sexton's response is to go to the well and draw a baby out, which in her own drama means she moves from daughter-role to mother-role, and in God's terms means she produces the Christ. Judging by the poem's final seven lines, this is the submissive gesture God was looking for.

> Then God spoke to me and said:
> Here. Take this gingerbread lady
> and put her in your oven.
> When the cow gives blood
> and the Christ is born
> we must all eat sacrifices.
> We must all eat beautiful women.

Now the changed tone tells us that God has been, as it were, reassured and confirmed in His Godliness by Sexton's feminine compliance, much as a man tired and complaining after work will have his dignity renewed by a wife or daughter laying out a perfect dinner. This final speech is authoritative not only in the sense of issuing commands but in the sense of assuming verbal command over the poem's prior structure of symbols. Nature and femaleness (cow, moon, milk, blood), at first large and powerful, are reduced to domesticity and powerlessness. Dream-cow becomes cookie. "We" must at the advent of Christianity not *make* sacrifices but eat them, and God's pseudo-cosy "we" is the velvet glove of paternal imperative. The substitution of gingerbread lady for the bread that is Christ's body reminds us that the Christ-cult (and the Passover feast it builds on) takes its symbolism from earlier middle Eastern religion in which the object of primary worship was the fertile and nourishing mother. Perhaps it implies that the misogyny of the Church and its need to subordinate ("sacrifice") women derive ultimately from a forgotten time of usurpation and a dread lest the "cow" move again to the forefront of our dream.

As a comment on the "Jesus Papers" sequence, the epilogue is a recapitulation of the theme of divine male power and mortal female submission. But it also fixes the position of its author as one who is by no means protesting the images of herself and other women within Christianity. On the contrary, she complies, she obeys, in this final dream, just as Mary and the harlot comply within the sequence. For herself, and on behalf of all beautiful women, she accepts humiliation. We may even say, since after all the dream is her invention, that she requires it.

Notes

1. Rosemary Johnson, "The Woman of Private (But Published) Hungers." *Parnassus.* Fall/Winter 1979, p. 92.
2. The early volumes, all published by Houghton Mifflin, are *To Bedlam and Part Way Back* (1960), in which the apologia-poem "For John, Who Begs me Not to Enquire Further" appears; *All My Pretty Ones* (1962), *Live or Die* (1966), for which she received the Pulitzer Prize, and *Love Poems* (1969). The interviews I quote are in J. D. McClatchy, ed. *Anne Sexton: The Artist and Her Critics* (Bloomington, Indiana: Indiana University Press, 1978).
3. I mention this, I must confess, in specific irritation with W. H. Pritchard's authoritative pronouncement that "There is no figure in the poetry's carpet to worry about discovering—it's all smack on the surface," and that the late Sexton jettisoned "whatever modest technical accomplishment she possessed in favor of getting down the excitingly grotesque meanings" ("The Anne Sexton Show," *The Hudson Review.* Vol. XXXI, No. 2, Summer 1978, pp. 389, 391). He does not specify *what* meanings. But we do not see what we do not look for.
4. Sexton's letters are collected in *Anne Sexton: A Self-Portrait in Letters,* ed. Linda Grey Sexton and Lois Ames (Boston: Houghton Mifflin, 1977).
5. This image appears also in "Those Times . . ." of *Live or Die,* where Sexton writes of childhood humiliations inflicted by her mother and says "I did not know that my life, in the end, would run over my mother's like a truck." The distance between earlier and later poems makes a good index of Sexton's development. The earlier poem is private and familial; the later one locates the private scenario within a mythic context. The earlier poem is strictly autobiographical and describes the self as passive; in the later, "Jesus" becomes, among other things, a figure for active and aggressive (i.e., "male") elements in her character which she was reluctant to acknowledge while writing as a woman.

NTOZAKE SHANGE

Paulette Williams

1948–

Ntozake Shange was born Paulette Williams on October 18, 1948, in Trenton, New Jersey, the oldest child of a surgeon and a social worker. With her two younger brothers and sister she grew up in Trenton, at an air force base in upstate New York, and in St. Louis, Missouri. Her father painted and played percussion in addition to his duties as a physician, and she met many leading black figures in sports and the arts. She read widely as a child but began to rebel in her teens against the privilege of her life. A turning point occurred when she was bussed to an all-white school for the gifted in St. Louis; she was, she says, unprepared for the hostility and harassment of white students.

Paulette Williams went on to Barnard College, where she majored in American studies, specializing in Afro-American music and poetry. At Barnard she became active in the civil rights movement. After graduation in 1970 she went to the University of Southern California, teaching while earning a master's degree in American studies; the following year she changed her name, after consulting friends from the Xhosa tribe, who baptized her in the Pacific Ocean with her new African name. *Ntozake* means "she who comes with her own things"; *Shange* means "who walks like a lion."

Shange went on to teach in the women's studies program at Sonoma State College and began writing poetry intensively. Soon she was reading it at women's bars, accompanied by friends who were musicians and dancers. Out of these performances grew her first theatrical production, or "choreopoem," *For Colored Girls Who Have Considered Suicide/When the Rainbow Is Enuf*, a celebration of the survival and triumph of black women. Shange and her friend, choreographer Paula Moss, moved to New York City in the mid-1970s and first performed *For Colored Girls* in a jazz loft in Soho in July 1975. The show evolved through a series of highly successful Off-Broadway productions, then opened uptown at the Booth Theatre in the fall of 1976, the same year it was published in book form. Shange, who had been in the show's cast since its first performance, remained in the Broadway production for one month. *For Colored Girls* played on Broadway for two years, then was taken by touring companies to Canada, the Caribbean, and other cities in the United States.

Shange's second major work to be staged in New York was *A Photograph: A Study of Cruelty*, termed a "poemplay" by its author. The production, which explores the relationship between a black woman dancer and her talented but unsuccessful photographer lover, ran at the Public Theatre during the 1977–78 season but received mixed reviews. Shange did not appear in this play, having formed a three-woman ensemble called the Satin Sisters, who read their poetry against a background of jazz at the Public Theatre Cabaret.

Shange has written and performed in several theatrical pieces in New York in recent years, including *From Okra to Greens* (1978; published in 1984). Her adaptation of Bertolt Brecht's play *Mother Courage and Her Children* was presented at the Public Theatre in 1980. Her published books of verse include *Nappy Edges* (1978), *Sassafrass, Cypress and Indigo* (1982), and *A Daughter's Geography* (1983). *See No Evil: Prefaces, Essays and Accounts 1976–1983* appeared in 1984.

I hope a way may be devised to arrange a national tour to a presentation I recently saw at the Henry Street Settlement's New Federal Theatre (on Grand Street) in cooperation with Joseph Papp's Public Theatre: it was for me a signal event.

It is called *For Colored Girls Who Have Considered Suicide/When the Rainbow Is Enuf*. Its author, St. Louis-raised Ntozake Shange, is a young woman who appeared as one of its performers and is now an artist-in-residence of the New Jersey State Council on the Arts. She calls her piece a "choreopoem"—poems in verse and prose to be voiced singly, in pairs or in unison by four actresses and three women dancers, with occasional accompanying music. The women hail from various parts of the country.

Because the text is composed of a series of poems of decided literary worth, I first thought that the performance would have greater impact if they were recited so that no word was lost through movement. But as the evening went on (and on examining the script) I realized that my first impression was mistaken. The faces and bodies as well as the voices of the actresses give the occasion its special force. Much credit for the success of the event is also due to its director, Oz Scott, who saw the "play" in the material.

In a number of respects this work is unique. Its stress is on the experience of black women—their passionate outcry, as women, within the black community. There is no bad-mouthing the whites: feelings on that score are summed up in the humorously scornful lines addressed to a black man which begin: "ever since I realized there was someone callt a colored girl, a evil woman, a bitch or a nag, I been tryin' not to be that and leave bitterness in somebody elses cup. . . . I finally bein real no longer symmetrical and inervious to pain . . . so why don't we be white then and make everythin' dry and abstract wid no rhythm and no reelin' for sheer sensual pleasure. . . . " The woman who utters these words, like all the others, speaks not so much in apology or explanation of her black condition but in essential human protest against her black lover whose connection with her is the ordinary (white or black) callousness toward women. Thus she asserts "I've lost it / touch with reality / I know who's doin' it. . . . I should be unsure, if I'm still alive. . . . I survive on intimacy and to-morrow. . . . But bein' alive and bein' a woman and bein' colored is a metaphysical dilemma."

This gives only a pitifully partial notion of the pain and power, as well as the acrid wit—"so redundant in the modern world"—which much of the writing communicates. The thematic emphasis is constantly directed at the stupid crudity and downright brutality of their own men, which, whatever the causes, wound and very nearly destroy their women. These women have been driven to the very limits of their endurance (or "rainbow") and are desperately tired of hearing their men snivel that they're "sorry." Part of the joy in the performance lay in the ecstatic response of the women in the audience!

There is no black (or white) sentimentality here, no glamorizing of Harlem or any other ghetto existence; there is the eloquence of moral and sensory awareness couched in language powerful in common speech and a vocabulary both precise and soulfully felt.

I liked all the players, but one of them, Trazana Beverley—in her hilarious harangue against the man she has been wooing with no result, and in the most tragically violent story about her goon lover who kills their children—is so shattering in emotion and staggering in diction that I cried out to my neighbors in the seats around me, "That is how Shakespeare and Euripides should be acted!" A wonderful evening!—Harold Clurman, *Nation*, May 1, 1976, p. 542

Ntozake Shange's *Nappy Edges* is too long a book; there are far too many poems that borrow from and reflect upon popular culture without dramatizing the inner conflicts of many of Miss Shange's characters. But she is a highly literate writer, capable of expressing anger at the mistreatment of women by means of an artful reference to some popular song or a scene from a movie:

> i'm thinkin black & realizin
> colored
> cant stand no man to be callin me BABEE
> to my face /
> but if i hear some stylistics du-wah /
> donchu know i wanna give it away
> BABEEEEEEEEEE YOU MAKE ME FEEL SO
> BRAND NEW
>   ("lotsa body & cultural heritage/")
> she wd be still she wd pay
> like anybody else
> to get her hair fixed
> something like lena
> in stormy weather
>   ("an ol fashion lady")

Much of this collection, though, is more *tell* than *show*, references without sufficient characterization or depth to highlight the local color, apt cadence and immediacy of her desolation. Miss Shange's "Expiriese Girl Wanted" captures some of the drama, broken dreams and harsh realities of *Colored Girls*:

> everything you got / girl / is mine
> BLAM BLAM ya undastand
> sit down 'n shut up

> yeah, mama
> i like new york fine
> yeah, mama
> i gotta real nice job
> uh huh, in a restaurant
> real nice folks come there
> uh huh i get good tips
> everybody's been treatin me real nice
> & i'ma send for you 'n daddy
> soon as i get to know my way roun'
> 'n get usedta
> usedta . . .

Here the idiom is at once dramatic and restrained, but Miss Shange seldom offers insights as literate as those expressed in the epigraphs scattered through *Nappy Edges*, though one from Anaïs Nin—"all unfulfilled desires are imprisoned children"—is well chosen and brought to full life in the opening section of "closets":

> my grandpa waz a doughboy from carolina
> the other a garveyite from lakewood
> i got talked to abt the race & achievement
> bout color & propriety /
> nobody spoke to me about the moon
> daddy talked abt music & mama bout christians
> my sisters / we
> always talked & talked
> there waz never quiet
> trees were status symbols
> i've taken to fog /
> the moon still surprisin me
>   ("senses of heritage")

Miss Shange's poetic mode consists of sharp, intense vignettes with a minimum of commentary; when she ventures into longer poems the lines become slack and prosaic, her references too private to express her themes. And her analogy between jazz musicians and poets is weakened by their lack of a shared vocabulary and the different technical demands of their art. She would have profited from a more closely edited book.—Michael S. Harper, "Three Poets," *NYTBR*, Oct. 21, 1979, p. 22

Once you have heard Ntozake Shange read, it is impossible not to hear her voice in anything she writes. Her voice itself has a power few oral readers bring to their work. It's a rich and evocative ringing that lasts even longer than the images she describes. At a 1982 convention of the American Booksellers Association, Shange was a keynote speaker, along with Jimmy Carter and Calvin Trillin, all of whom talked about their books. Shange was the most impressive, not because of what she read but because of the way she was able to give emotional weight to her words through the wonderful timbre she projects. She began with the opening lines from her new novel, *Sassafrass, Cypress & Indigo*:

"Where there is a woman there is magic. If there is a moon falling from her mouth, she is a woman who knows her magic, who can share or not share her powers. A woman with a moon falling from her mouth, roses between her legs and tiaras of Spanish moss, this woman is a consort of the spirits."

The impression this paragraph gives is one of the remarkable openness and power of womanhood, perhaps because of all the o's in the sentences, perhaps because of the sharp imagery, perhaps because of the strong and clear way in which Shange, who is also a poet and playwright, is able to express herself.

The novel tells the stories of three sisters and their mother, black women in Charleston, South Carolina. Indigo is the youngest—a wildly imaginative patchwork child, attracted to velvets, ribbons, and dreams. She lives in a world surrounded by fifteen dolls. They go with her everywhere. She made them herself from socks stuffed with red beans, raw rice, bay leaves, and sawdust.

Cypress is the most fully developed character. Indeed, more than half the story is given over to her. She's a sensuous, wide-hipped dancer whose physicality is overwhelming, even to herself. She joins a gay women's dance collective called Azure Bosom, whose workplace was Ovary Studio in the Bowery. She falls in love with Idrina, another dancer, then follows that liaison with a more lasting one. Later Cypress joins Leroy, a successful jazz musician, and they decide to marry.

Sassafrass, the eldest, is a vague character. She lives with Mitch, a musician-junkie. Sassafrass weaves, joins the New Afrikans spirituality movement, leaves Mitch but comes back, gets pregnant, and has a baby named Ella Mae. Hilda Effania, the girl's mother, and Aunt Haydee the midwife help with the birth.

In the midst of the novel there are recipes for foods like Cypress's Sweetbread, Barbequed Lamb Manhattan, and Turkey Hash; prescriptions for life such as Numbers for Prosperity and Furthered Independence of the Race; suggested potents and brews to make, poems, and letters. *Sassafrass, Cypress & Indigo* is more like a pastiche, a collage of elements taken from a highly textured existence, than it is a novel. In fact, the strong sense the book gives is that the reader is not reading but seeing pictures, hearing voices, watching an unusual narrative presentation.

While the imagery is indeed potent, and much of the language is compelling, the narrative problems are great. In a way, it's as though Shange is asking us to see what the lives of those black women look like onstage, but not to participate vicariously in the lives: We don't become emotionally involved with the women because they are shown more as exotic bits and pieces than evolving, real people. She makes it possible for us to see them, but not to understand. Her writing is not explanatory: She doesn't tell us why Sassafrass, for instance, insists on staying with Mitch even though he is destructive, why she is compelled suddenly to lead a spiritual life, why she spends her life weaving. Nor does she explain why Cypress moves from women to men.

In separate stretches, in paragraphs here and there, Shange's writing overtakes any objections, and the power of her language is enough. Overall, though, the novel doesn't hold together. Even so, many of the fragments make the book worth reading.—ESTHER COHEN, "Three Sisters," *Prog*, Jan. 1983, p. 56

Ntozake Shange dedicates her latest book of poems ⟨*A Daughter's Geography*⟩ to her family, most especially to her daughter; and it opens with an epigraph consisting of a poem written by a woman in revolutionary Cuba. Both the dedication and the epigraph anticipate the major theme of the book, which is that Third-World peoples are united by long history and current oppression: that all of them are members of the same family with a common enemy. This theme is rendered by a voice more fierce than angry, more determined than defiant. It is a revolutionary volume, informed by a sensibility of struggle and hope.

The poems are divided into three groups. The first is a short prelude, striking the notes of remembrance, maternal protection, and yearning for revolution. It begins by evoking inspirational black figures—W. E. B. DuBois, Duke El-

lington, Paul Robeson—and this at a time when the black community was on the move, vibrant, filled with music, laughter, and love. By contrast, the present is a grim, empty place, where people are distracted by drugs and cheap thrills. They are without leaders or politics or vision. The present has lodged in the poet's throat—"i am choking to death"—as she catalogues the horrors that await her baby girl. She calls upon the spirits of strong men from a better time to live again. She longs to join "the souls of black folk" as she would to lay with a lover, for she needs the direction provided by common struggle in order that "a root of some healing spice might push up from my soils."

The uncompromising condemnation of racism and the call to revolutionary struggle are even stronger in the second section. This section opens and closes with a listing of countries victimized by imperialism, which are referred to as sons and daughters. Though divided by language, they are united in their struggle to overthrow "the same old men" and give birth to a new world. Shange's awareness of the connections between racism, imperialism, and sexism is evident as she mentions Chicago, Savannah, and Charleston in the same breath as San Juan, Luana, and Santiago. One poem is dedicated to the children murdered in Atlanta, where the disappearances are linked to lynching: "we black and poor and we just disappear / be gone." Another concerns a poet in the Sandinista revolution whose poems were burned by friends to protect him. Shange muses: "i must remember to remind my poet friends in America to keep matches in their houses." It is by no accident that the centerpiece of this group focusing on racism and imperialism, "Some Men," is about male dominance and brutalization of women. The same arrogance and chauvinism that have been highlighted in the poems about economic exploitation are here shown to be instrumental in the ways women are hurt by men: "he was a small man and cd handle only damaged goods." Women are not addressed directly as revolutionary fighters, but Shange is clearly sensitive to the fact that women are oppressed by many of the same forces as people of color.

The last section is more lyrical in tone and personal in subject matter, though Shange's political concerns are still evident. These are love poems in which Shange is at her best, combining humor, sassiness, sensuality, and street speech to produce images of passion: "spose the distance from yr collard to yr mustard is same as from the width of my field. . . . i gotta o.d. of greens / i'm sufferin so my pods are gleamin / ready to jump out the vertical / into the greens diagonal." There is extraordinary wit, spontaneity, and exuberance in these pieces as the poet searches for a suitable language for love speech: "sometimes you are angolan freedom songs / we take all confusions & reggae it / tosh marley & wailer / it we stroll in our own convers all-stars / in london & sao paulo / but what language is it big enough / to say yr name."

This volume delights, inspires, and enlightens. Shange's political astuteness, ear for the street, and earthiness are a rare combination and one to be savored.—MAUREEN HONEY, "A Sensibility of Struggle and Hope," *PSch*, Winter 1984, pp. 111–12

SANDRA HOLLIN FLOWERS
"Colored Girls: Textbook for the Eighties"

Black American Literature Forum, Summer 1981, pp. 51–54

There are as many ways of looking at Ntozake Shange's *For Colored Girls Who Have Considered Suicide/When the Rainbow Is Enuf* as there are hues in a rainbow. One can take it as an initiation piece, for instance, particularly with its heavily symbolic "Graduation Nite" and the girlhood perspectives of the mama's little baby / Sally Walker segment and in the voice of the eight-year-old narrator of "Toussaint." *Colored Girls* also might be seen as a black feminist statement in that it offers a black woman's perspective on issues made prominent by the women's movement. Still another approach is to view it as a literary coming-of-age of black womanhood in the form of a series of testimonies which, in Shange's words, "explore the realities of seven different kinds of women."[1] Indeed, the choreopoem is so rich that it lends itself to multiple interpretations which vary according to one's perspective and experiences.

I would suggest, however, that the least appropriate responses are those exemplified by reviewers who said that black men will find themselves portrayed in *Colored Girls* "as brutal con men and amorous double-dealers";[2] or that "The thematic emphasis is constantly directed at the stupid crudity and downright brutality of [black] men."[3] Comments such as these are particularly misleading because they appear in reviews which contain generous praise for *Colored Girls,* thus suggesting that it is the condemnation of black men, which gives the book its merit. Too, such comments have the effect of diminishing the work to nothing more than a diatribe against black men, when, quite the contrary, Shange demonstrates a compassionate vision of black men— compassionate because though the work is not without anger, it has a certain integrity which could not exist if the author lacked a perceptive understanding of the crisis between black men and women.

And there is definitely a crisis. Individually we have known this for some time, and lately black women as well as black men are showing growing concern about the steady deterioration of their relationships.[4] Black literature, however, has lagged somewhat behind. The works which usually comprise Afro-American literature curricula and become part of general reading materials, for instance, show the position of the black man in America; but generally we see the black woman only peripherally as the protagonist's lover, wife, mother, or in some other supporting (or detracting) role. Certainly black women can identify with the predicament of black men. Black women can identify, for example, with the problems articulated in Ellison's *Invisible Man* because they share the same predicaments. But for black women the predicament of the black male protagonist is compounded by concerns which affect them on yet another level. This, then, is what makes *Colored Girls* an important work which ranks with Ellison's *Invisible Man,* Wright's *Native Son,* and the handful of other black classics—it is an artistically successful female perspective on a long-standing issue among black people. If, however, black men fail to acknowledge the significance of *Colored Girls,* if they resent it or insist that is does not speak to their concerns or is not important because it deals with "women's issues," then the crisis is more severe than any thought it to be.

Colored Girls is certainly woman's art but it is also black art, or Third World art, as Shange probably would prefer to have it designated. Its language and dialect, its geography, its music, and the numerous allusions to Third World personalities make it an intensely cultural work. Much of these characteristics, however, are peculiar to Shange's upbringing, education, and experiences, with the result that the piece loses universality at points, as in the poem "Now I Love Somebody More Than" (pp. 11–13). But even here, black audiences are sure to know which lady loved gardenias: they will know the Flamingoes and Archie Shepp and Imamu. Then there is the poem "Sechita" (pp. 23–25) in which the dancer is linked to Nefertiti, hence to Africa and Olduvai Gorge, the "cradle of civilization"—all of which puts into perspective the cheapening of Sechita by the carnival audience. While "Sechita" speaks to the degradation of black womanhood, "Toussaint" (p. 25–30) speaks of the black woman's discovery of black pride. It also speaks, with subtle irony, of the black woman's awakening to the black man.

Even "Latent Rapists' " (pp. 17–21) and "Abortion Cycle #1" (pp. 22–23), which seem to deal exclusively with women's issues, are of political significance to black men. It is difficult to politicize rape among black women, for instance, because the feminist approach began with a strongly anti-male sentiment, whereas the black community is highly male-identified. Furthermore, blacks have their own historical perspective on rape—the thousands of black men who were lynched for "rape" of white women. The history of these persecutions, however, does not remove the black woman's need for a political consciousness about rape, such as the traditionally feminist one Shange articulates. By the same token, Shange has sensitively portrayed the trauma of abortion, a trauma which, to some extent, probably exists in every case, no matter how strongly a woman might advocate the right to choose abortion. Still, the black movement's rhetoric linking birth control to genocide cannot be lightly dismissed. These considerations ought to make clear the delicate balance between blackness and womanhood which Shange manages to strike in *Colored Girls.* Maintaining this balance is no easy task, and the black woman writer of some political consciousness is under tremendous pressure not to sacrifice issues of blackness to those of womanhood and vice versa.

As suggested, however, the primary focus of *Colored Girls* is on the quality of relationships between black women and their men. This focus dominates the last half of the work, beginning with "One" (pp. 31–35), in which loneliness is seen to be more powerful than sensuality. This loneliness-sensuality juxtaposition is an especially effective way of raising the issue of woman as a strictly sexual being rather than a person with the full range of human emotions and needs. Before we even know where the poem is headed, we have an instinctive understanding of why this woman "wanted to be unforgettable," why "she wanted to be a memory / a wound to every man / arragant [sic] enough to want her" (p. 32). Now in the prime of her sensuality and physical attractiveness, this woman is

> . . . the wrath
> of women in windows
> fingering shades / ol lace curtains
> camoflagin despair &
> stretchmarks.
>
> (p. 32)

At the end of the poem, though, we see that all along the woman has known that sensuality at its worst, which is what it has been reduced to in her case, is merely a surrogate for mutual caring and understanding. It is only a matter of time, she seems to know, until she will become one of those loveless women in the windows, camouflaging her own despair and stretch marks. And notice that Shange equates despair and stretch marks: they are one and the same in the game played by the woman in "One."

This, however, is but one kind of despair. A more overt kind is evident in "A Nite with Beau Willie Brown" (pp. 55–60), in which Shange skillfully weaves craft and theme in a poem about a young couple who have been lovers for nine years. As the narrative begins, Beau Willie and his woman Crystal are separated because Crystal, frightened by his erratic, brutal behavior toward her and their children, has gotten a court order barring Beau Willie from their apartment. Angry and indignant about Crystal's refusal to see him, Beau Willie forces his way into the apartment, coaxes the children to him and, dissatisfied with Crystal's response to his demands that she marry him, drops the children from the fifth story window.

The foregoing summary leaves out much that is revealed about Beau Willie during the narrative. He is, first of all, a Vietnam veteran experiencing a typical maladjustment upon coming back to the States. His situation is worsened by the fact that he is one of the thousands of black veterans who have their own horror stories of the front-line experience in Vietnam. Beau Willie is drug-dependent, shell-shocked, psychotic, disoriented, and paranoid.

> he'd see the spotlights in the alleyways downstairs movin in the air / cross his wall over his face / & get under the covers & wait for an all clear or till he cd hear traffic again. (p. 55)

Yet, "there waznt nothin wrong with him / he kept tellin crystal . . ." (p. 55). We can also deduce from the narrative that before he went to Vietnam, Beau had almost certainly been victimized by racism in the schools he attended—"he cdnt read wortha damn." When he returned home and tried to attend school on the GI Bill, "they kept right on puttin him in remedial classes . . . so beau cused the teachers of holdin him back & got himself a gypsy cab to drive . . ." (p. 56). His cab was always breaking down, though; he couldn't make much money, was robbed of what little he did make, and was frequently harassed by the police.

The pattern is obvious: Beau Willie Brown is the quintessential black man of his generation. By this, I do not mean, nor does Shange intend to imply, that Beau Willie Brown is all there is to black manhood. Conversely, I am not suggesting that the political realities embodied in Beau Willie justify his treatment of or his attitude toward Crystal. Instead, I believe that Shange's compassion for black men surfaces most noticeably in this poem and that her characterization of Beau Willie recognizes some of the external factors which influence relationships between black men and women. Twenty-five years ago, Beau Willie could have been a black Korean War veteran; thirty years ago, he might have been one of the black Tuskegee pilots who flew combat missions in World War II but were denied jobs as commercial airline pilots while their white counterparts were hired; sixty years ago he easily could have been one of World War I's black veterans who returned home to lynchings rather than heroes' welcomes.

This poem is purely political, although it has been misunderstood by critics.[5] Here, we are again talking about a question of perspective, specifically an artist's perspective which can transform a passing incident into a poem of far-reaching and chilling significance. On the writing of "A Nite with Beau Willie Brown," Shange, who was staying in a Harlem boarding house when she wrote the poem, says

It was hot. I was broke. I didn't have enough money for a subway token. I was miserable. The man in the next room was beating up his old lady. It went on for hours and hours. She was screaming. He was laughing. Everytime he hit her I would think, yeah, man, well that had already happened to me. So I sat down and wrote "Beau Willie." All my anger came out.[6]

One might assume that the anger is directed toward Beau Willie, the surrogate for the woman-beating neighbor, because of Shange's use of comic similes—"like he waz an ol frozen bundle of chicken . . ." (p. 55), or "beau sat straight up in the bed / wrapped up in the sheets lookin like john the baptist or a huge baby with stubble & nuts . . ." (p. 56). The comic elements, however, are so grotesque that Beau emerges as a tragic figure and it becomes apparent that Shange's anger is in response to the circumstances and impulses—whatever they are—which result in men brutalizing women. Consequently, while our sympathies might at first be entirely with Crystal, we ultimately come to understand that her pain is also Beau's and vice versa.

Finally, the significance of Beau Willie's and Crystal's children must not be overlooked. Their names—Naomi Kenya and Kwame Beau Willie—are important, for both contain elements of the African and the Western, the miscegenation which resulted in the Afro-American. Further, the girl and boy can be seen as nascent black womanhood and manhood. Literally and metaphorically, then, in dropping the children, Beau Willie is not only committing murder and—since they are his offspring—suicide; but he is also killing the hope of black manhood and womanhood.

Similarly, in "Pyramid" (pp. 39–42) three friends are pursued by one man. Two of them become involved with him but he rejects them both for yet another woman. If for no other reason than the fact that black women outnumber black men (by over 700,000, according to 1977 census data[7]), it is probable that most black women will be part of some kind of multiple love relationship, with or without their knowledge and cooperation. Shange's concept of a pyramid for portraying this circumstance offers a graphic illustration of how women function in such relationships. Like the women in this poem, clusters of women form a pyramid from which a man can select partners. The women's position on the pyramid shifts: they find themselves at the bottom occasionally, but they usually have some time at the top, as do the two friends in the poem. Seen in this way, as a simple reflection of reality, the man in Shange's "Pyramid" is not as heartless as the poem may suggest; he is merely exercising a prerogative which black women and circumstances have given him.

This particular pyramid, however, is made up of close friends, which makes the man's actions seem more callous. But theoretically, they are all sisters, therefore, whether or not they are friends with the other women in the pyramid, the man's playing them off against each other is potentially humiliating and painful for each, as the women in "Pyramid" find out. In theory, then, they should feel as much compassion for the discarded women in their own pyramids as they feel for the friends in Shange's poem when, at the end, the woman who was first rejected comforts her friend who has also been rejected:

> she held her head on her lap
> the lap of her sisters soakin up tears
> each understandin how much love stood between
>   them
> how much love between them
> love between them
> love like sisters.
>
> (p. 42)

But there is a great deal of ambivalence in these lines, just as there is in black women's relationships with each other. On the one hand, we might say that the sisterly love which previously existed between these women has been restored by the pain the man has given them. This interpretation would be in keeping with the upbeat ending of *Colored Girls* in which the women affirm themselves and each other. However, this idealistic interpretation is undermined by the incident of the rose. The first woman, in a mute gesture of love, leaves a rose by the man's pillow; she later finds this rose on her friend's desk. Betrayed by both her lover and her friend, it is no wonder that the poor woman is speechless as her friend tells her

> . . . i dont wanna hurt you
> but you know i need someone now
> & you know
> how wonderful he is.
>
> (p. 41)

One should note the irony and delicacy of language with which Shange has rendered the pain women inflict upon each other in the name of love. The love that stands between the two women is not necessarily love for one another, but their respective love for the man who has hurt them both. The "love between them," then, is a destructive presence which divides them. They cannot be like sisters again until they reexamine their priorities and find the true importance of themselves and of each other. This is precisely what they proceed to do in the following sequence of poems, those entitled "No More Love Poems."

Here, of course, Shange is being ironic, because what she calls "No More Love Poems" is actually love poetry of the most explicit and poignant kind. Each poem exposes the persona so completely that one understands that she is basically defenseless and vulnerable as far as love is concerned. More important, in being so open, each woman takes an awesome risk: If her lover has a misguided notion of manhood, his response to her admissions may be terribly painful for her because he will not be able to drop the poses his self-image requires and allow himself to be equally open and vulnerable with her. The pathos of this group of poems is probably most evident in "No More Love Poems #2." Here the lady in purple, who, piteously, used to "linger in non-english speakin arms so there waz no possibility of understandin" (p. 43) represents the epitome of the loveless love affair. Her inability to understand anything said by the person of the "non-english speakin arms" is symbolic of woman's attempts to understand man. He does not speak her language—which is to say that he is unable to express the kinds of feelings that she is capable of putting into words. At the same time, he lacks the ability to understand her and so she can never hope to make clear to him the things that are important to her.

While it may seem ridiculous that the lady in purple would deliberately involve herself with someone she knows cannot understand her, this is precisely what happens in every relationship in which communication is absent. In our naiveté, we might once have entered relationships under the assumption that we and our lovers would somehow *know* what each of us wanted and needed. That, after all, is supposed to be the nature of love: it does not lend itself to scrutiny and questioning and explication; it simply exists. In a less complex society or one in which love is of minimal importance to the success of a relationship, perhaps this is true. But here in the fragmented, abrasive universe of America, where intimate relationships are nearly the only outlet for expressing affection and caring; where the partnership or the family unit might be all to which one can really be said to belong; where, in short, one depends upon one's loved one for emotional sustenance—in such a climate, it becomes imperative for black women and men to articulate their needs and expectations of one another.

Black men and women have not communicated successfully. It might even be said that they have tried everything imaginable to avoid articulating their needs—extended families, promiscuity, no-strings-attached fatherhood, getting / staying high together, even the Black Power Movement in which black people were all sisters and brothers, which meant that everyone *naturally* had everyone else's welfare at heart and so there was no need to explain *anything*. Like the lady in purple, many black women find themselves saying, "i dont know any more tricks / i am really colored and really sad sometimes . . ." (p. 44).

Shange has given us an exquisite and very personal view of the politics of black womanhood and black male-female relationships. Too few black writers are doing that—perhaps because the truth is really as painful as that depicted in *Colored Girls*, and in telling it one opens oneself to charges of dividing the race and exposing blacks to ridicule by reinforcing stereotypes. That allegation has been levied against *Colored Girls*, which is unfortunate because the only thing of which Ntozake Shange is guilty is a sincere, eloquent rendering of what she has come to understand about black love relationships. Critics cannot afford to insist that black writers forgo expressing such visions simply because they are painful, embarrassing, or potentially divisive. If that is true, maybe it is because blacks have been so preoccupied with political and economic survival that they no longer know, if they ever did, how to confront their own responsibility for what happens between black men and women; in that case, blacks really *do* have a great need for *Colored Girls* and similar works.

"A Nite with Beau Willie Brown" seems particularly suitable for putting the problems of blacks into perspective. We know that there was a period in their relationship when Crystal wanted very much to be Beau Willie's wife. She was asking for a commitment, an affirmation of their relationship, which is precisely what the women in "Sorry," in "No More Love Poems," in "One"—in real life, in fact—are asking. Beau Willie, like the black men on whom he was modeled, had consistently told Crystal, "nothin doin." Finally, when Beau Willie wanted Crystal, needed her, in fact, to affirm himself, he found, but did not understand, that she had had to turn from him to ensure her own survival.

Notes

1. Ntozake Shange, *For Colored Girls Who Have Considered Suicide/ When the Rainbow Is Enuf* (New York: Macmillan Publishing Co., Inc., 1977), p. xii. All references are to this edition and are given parenthetically in the text.
2. T. E. Kalem, "He Done Her Wrong," rev. of *For Colored Girls Who Have Considered Suicide/When the Rainbow Is Enuf,* by Ntozake Shange, *Time,* 14 June 1976, p. 74.
3. Harold Clurman, rev. of *For Colored Girls Who Have Considered Suicide/When the Rainbow Is Enuf,* by Ntozake Shange, *The Nation,* 17 May 1976, p. 542.
4. What amounts to a small movement has developed in response to this crisis—college courses on the black family, a periodical called *Black Male/Female Relationships,* nationwide workshops and discussion groups, and numerous articles in journals. See Diane Weathers et al., "A New Black Struggle," *Newsweek,* 27 August 1979, pp. 58–60. Additionally, Alice Walker explores the black

male-female crisis in her novel *The Third Life of Copeland Grange* (New York: Harcourt Brace Jovanovich, 1970) and Michele Wallance analyzes the crisis in political perspective in *Black Macho and the Myth of the Superwoman* (New York: Dial Press, 1979).

5. Clurman, in describing Trazana Beverly's Broadway rendition of "A Nite with Beau Willie Brown," calls the poem a "tragically

violent story about her *goon lover*" (emphasis added). Kalem refers to the poem as "a crude tale of love and blood lust."

6. "Trying to Be Nice," rev. of *For Colored Girls Who Have Considered Suicide/When the Rainbow Is Enuf,* by Ntozake Shange, *Time,* 19 July 1976, pp. 44–45.

7. Weathers et al., p. 58.

KARL SHAPIRO

1913–

Karl Jay Shapiro was born on November 10, 1913, in Baltimore, Maryland. He was educated at the University of Virginia from 1932 to 1933, Johns Hopkins University from 1937 to 1939, and Pratt Library School in 1940. He served in the U.S. Army from 1941 to 1945. Shapiro has taught at various universities, including Johns Hopkins, Wisconsin, Loyola, California, Indiana, Nebraska, and Illinois. He edited *Poetry* from 1950 to 1956, the *Newberry Library Bulletin* from 1953 to 1955, and *Prairie Schooner* from 1956 to 1966. He was a consultant in poetry for the Library of Congress from 1946 to 1947. In 1945 he married Evalyn Katz, and they had three children before divorcing in 1967. He married Teri Kovach in 1967; she died in 1982.

Shapiro is an extremely versatile poet who has experimented with a number of themes and styles. His first book, *Poems,* was published in 1935, but significant attention first came in 1942 with the publication of *Person, Place, and Thing.* In 1944 he published *V-Letter and Other Poems,* a collection with war and social commentary as its focus and mostly written in traditional rhyming stanzas. It was awarded the Pulitzer Prize in 1945. He began to experiment with open verse forms in *Trial of a Poet and Other Poems* (1947). *Poems of a Jew* (1958) is an exploration of Shapiro's Jewish background and the search for identity.

In 1964 Shapiro published *The Bourgeois Poet,* composed entirely of prose poems on a wide variety of topics; it received mixed reviews. Shapiro returned to more traditional verse forms for his cycle of love poems, *White-Haired Lover* (1968), and the eclectic *Adult Bookstore* (1976). A volume of *Selected Poems* was published in 1968, and *Collected Poems 1940–1977* was issued in 1978. He won the Bollingen Poetry Prize in 1969. His most recent book of poems is *Love and War, Art and God* (1984).

Shapiro is also an influential critic, noted for his anti-intellectualism and his championing of such poets as Whitman, Williams, Jarrell, and Thomas over "culture poets" such as Eliot, Pound, Yeats, and Auden. Shapiro feels that modern poetry has been corrupted by the intellect at the expense of true experience and consciousness. He has written many books of criticism, the most significant of which are *In Defense of Ignorance* (1960) and *The Poetry Wreck: Selected Essays 1950–1970* (1975). He has also written a novel (*Edsel,* 1971) and two plays (*The Tenor,* 1957, and *The Soldier's Tale,* 1968).

If Karl Shapiro's *Essay on Rime* were an isolated phenomenon, one could dismiss it simply as an unfortunate misadventure of a gifted young poet in a didactic genre he of all poets should never have attempted. But it is not isolated, and has therefore to be examined as the child of the *Zeitgeist* that it is. Shapiro seems determined to be a straw in every fashionable wind: here is the new distrust of the dissident intellectual, of science, of the critic, of the difficulty of modern literature; and here too the misty wind of the vague new religiosity. Stating that his purpose is to "help solidify / The layman's confidence in a plainer art," Shapiro has written what amounts to an attack on all of modern literature: another manifesto in the anti-modernist movement of organized Philistia. And its public will have its book. Already saluted in an inexplicable review by F. O. Matthiessen in the *Times Book Review,* it now needs only one of Mr. J. Donald Adams' inimitable Sunday morning sermons to be properly launched on its career as a club over the heads of other writers, over modern poetry generally.

After charging blithely through the modern confusions in metre, rhythm, rhetoric and language, Shapiro prepares to plunge in the last section of his poem at a more terrifying

windmill: the whole intellectual situation of the modern writer. The reader, slightly winded from the previous demolitions, sits up again: here perhaps come the great deliverances, the resolving truths! After all, this section is labelled the modern "Confusion in Belief" (a confusion which arises, Shapiro thinks, fundamentally from the modern "failure in belief"), and shouldn't we expect that the man bold enough to pronounce the confusion and dissect the failure be able to restore order and successful functioning?

Shapiro attacks the modern poet for believing in, among other things, Psychoanalysis, Economics, Sociology, Freud, and Marx. Failure of belief! One would think this an excess, rather than a failure, in belief. But inconsistency is no hobgoblin to Shapiro's mind. The inconsistencies themselves would not matter so much if he were not dealing with a subject so large as the intellectual situation of modern man and showing himself at the same time incapable of ideas. It is not that Shapiro does not respond at all to ideas; he would not have been attracted otherwise into this intellectual jungle; there are good writers who are not touched at all by ideas, but Shapiro is not one of these. He is something much more impure: he responds to ideas, but he does not have them; what he has are half-ideas, vapors of ideas, approximations to ideas—to which inconsistency probably never struck him as particularly relevant, and perhaps isn't. Shapiro is attacking, of course, not a modern "failure in belief" generally, but, specifically, religious unbelief. What he is doing is to make use of one technique of confusion quite common among second-rate religious apologists—from whom he may unconsciously have picked it up: to speak of "Belief" and "Faith" in this vague and absolutely enveloping way so that our specific unbelief on one point is to be covertly saddled with the guilt of total skepticism. ⟨. . .⟩

Literature involves more than the individual writer's going off by himself to write; as an activity within and against society, it involves the perpetual struggle to keep standards alive, an audience from disintegrating, a certain kind of consciousness alive in a society inert or hostile to it. Shapiro's failure, in the last analysis, is that he does not see this social dimension of literature, or wants to escape it. A failure he shares with the tweedy professors of English, the Book of the Month Club businessmen, the nostalgic fantasists of Americana—all his fellow crusaders in the anti-modernist witchhunt. Hence his particular disdain for the critic (whose reason for existence is this struggle) as a purely gratuitous being. There may be too many critics now writing, as Shapiro repeatedly protests, but there are never enough to complete criticism's tasks—one of which is to remind the poet from time to time that poetic license does not extend to the world of ideas, that when the poet touches ideas, not everything goes.

Shapiro's whole poem breathes a pious aspiration towards a simpler state of literary being. When he urges poets to "the piety / Of simple craftsmen for their wood," he reveals his own wish that literature were as simple an occupation as woodturning or carpentry. If only one would chuck it all, go off by oneself to write poetry untroubled by the confusions of modern life! We may be touched by this aspiration towards simplicity, but we must point out the irresponsibility of turning one's back upon the difficulties of being a literary man in the modern world. The supreme irony is that the critical fraternity in which Shapiro may now have his pin as a full-fledged initiate should have applied the word "irresponsible" to the writers who have tried to face these difficulties.—WILLIAM BARRETT, "Pilgrim to Philistia," *PR*, Winter 1946, pp. 126–29

This is Mr. Shapiro's fourth volume of published poetry ⟨*Trial of a Poet*⟩, and in common with his previous volume, *Essay on Rime*, it shows him intensely preoccupied with the problem of how and what the poet should write. Considering that this problem is for him as yet unsolved, it seems a little tiresome that he should be so insistent that the solution should lie in writing like Karl Shapiro. Probably Shapiro would gain by dealing with his own problem as really his own and not every other poet's more than he gains by trying to make literary maps just at the time when his own difficulties are most obvious. Another danger for him lies in his own considerable mental power and energy which enable him to versify very effectively too many situations which are outside the one which is central to him in his present state of crisis.

Nevertheless, it is excellent that he should be in a critical and self-critical position: excellent not only for himself, but also for other poets, if and when he succeeds in getting out of the wood. In this review I shall try to indicate what I believe to be Mr. Shapiro's main strengths, weaknesses, true aims and false aims.

It is obvious that Mr. Shapiro has a considerable gift for projecting himself into dramatic situations, usually conceived in rather abstract terms. The first long poem in this volume, *Recapitulations*, is autobiographical self-dramatization. The Conscientious Objector, the Southerner, the Jew, the poet who is on trial in *Trial of a Poet*, with his entourage of the Priest, the Doctor, the Chorus who is the Public, indicate sufficiently Mr. Shapiro's capacity for inventing Masks.

However, Mr. Shapiro seems to have imposed on himself other disciplines which often rob these figures in their dramatic situations of those sensitive and personal turns of thought which are convincing. He is in full reaction against the personal, the sensitive, the peculiar, the idiosyncratic. He is determined to be metrically and intellectually respectable, as against the shoddiness of other contemporary poets whom he compares to crabs walking backwards in their retreat from our scientific hygienic age into superstition, magic and vicious eccentricity. The combination of these aims with self-dramatization results at times in the peculiar effect of a poetry written from a very personal point of view, which has been emptied of all personality. Thus in *Recapitulations*, which is an autobiographical confession, he succeeds in turning himself into a public situation, emptied of any emotion which would convince us that here we are confronted by a flesh and blood person:

> I raved like a scarlet banner,
> > Brave cloth of a single piece,
> I learned to despise all uncles,
> > All Congressmen, all police.
> I hated the coin of kindness,
> > Good deeds of the Octopus;
> It was evil to give to beggars
> > What beggars could give to us.
> O comrade of distant Russia,
> > How difficult for your kind
> To live in that even climate
> > Where no one may change his mind.

This is an intellectual predicament pretending to be a person, it bears no distinguishing note to strike the eye or ear with which one can really sympathize as with another human being.

A writer who passionately identifies himself with Faust, with the Jew, the Poet, etc., must have a personality somewhere, but reading some of these poems reminds one curiously of some work by Pirandello which might be called *Twenty Poems in Search of an Author*. The predicament of Mr. Shapiro seems to be that whilst he has a personality which violently wants to realize itself in poetry, he also has a set of rules, largely based on a critical reaction to his contemporaries, which prevents him from doing so. One searches for this real person and suddenly finds it in occasional lines such as:

> Within this square
> I am somewhere but difficult to find,
> As in a photograph of graduation
> Where youth predominates and looks alive.

or again, in the same poem, "Demobilization":

> Dimly it comes to me that this is home,
> This is my Maryland, these pines I know,
> This camp itself when budding green and raw
> I watched in agony of shame.

Indeed, I do not wish to give the impression that Mr. Shapiro does not succeed. At times he succeeds very finely as in "Demobilization." "Homecoming" is at least a partial success, although it suffers from overstatement which is not entirely convincing:

> My smile that would light up all darkness
> And ask forgiveness of the things that thrust
> Shame and all death on millions and on me.

Problems of overstatement such as the one that arises in these lines are important. For the problem here is one of truth. It is the problem not of the stanza and the metrical line but of the word. Not of the *mot juste* even but of the word which is faithful to the emotion felt which, in turn, is betrayed by any exaggeration. The fact is that smiles don't light up all darkness. However, if as well may be, the situation seems to require that the poet should invent such a smile, then he has to invent himself, he has to create his own poetic personality, he has to have the courage to be a monstrous egoist in his poetry, as Heine or D. H. Lawrence or Yeats were in theirs. You cannot eat your cake and have it even in poetry. You cannot substitute a violent, public and mechanical attitude for a vivid, convincing individual personality, through fear of lapsing into poetical incorrectitude. I could wish that Mr. Shapiro were a hundred times more the unabashed egoist in his poems. In a poem such as "In the Waxworks" where he gives us a glimpse of something monstrous in his own personality he is magnificent. In the *Trial of a Poet* he shows a power of organizing dramatic material and of expressing intellectual positions, but here again I find the situations mechanical.

Mr. Shapiro is a difficult poet to estimate, because whilst there are elements of technical accomplishment in his poetry which obviously command admiration, there are also elements of crudeness and insensitivity which make him vulnerable to a purist approach, and his very violence makes one uncertain of his power. Nevertheless he is a poet of rare intellectual strength, he has an exceptional power of being able to think of a poem as a single idea, and he has an interesting and perhaps passionate personality which his poetry at present partly conceals. If he were as preoccupied with the single word as he is with the stanza, he would gain enormously. At present he is too inclined to throw his words away on the wings of his stanzas. He is certainly one of the very few poets writing today whose development is an exciting subject for speculation. —STEPHEN SPENDER, "The Power and the Hazard," *Poetry*, March 1948, pp. 314–18

Karl Shapiro is an easterner, who has written for a long time now, with success, in an individual variant of one main period style of the late 1930's and early 1940's. Prosaic, candid, awkwardly careful to be just to the feeling desired, he, more than some poets his superior, evokes constant sympathy. His oddly titled new book, however, *Poems of a Jew*, is not new but a collection of poems from his selected volume *Poems 1940–1953*, as well as some omitted from it, and a few new ones, gathered with reference to his title—a thing upon which his strange Introduction throws, for me, little light. "These poems are not for poets," he begins, " . . . not religious poems . . . they present . . . the states of mind which in my case led to the writing of poems. . . . Being a Jew is the consciousness of being a Jew," et cetera. This is not the first time that Mr. Shapiro's prose has seemed to me more self-contradictory and obscure than his verse, and I would commend to the reader, instead of his Introduction, Isidore Epstein's admirable little Pelican book, *Judaism*. The poems are another matter. Omitting some of Shapiro's tough, vivid early work, this book gives a less satisfactory over-all view than the 1953 volume; but there is much pleasure to be had from it, and now and then thematic illumination *is* cast on a familiar piece, such as "Travelogue for Exiles," which I confess I had never thought of as Jewish. The particular poems are regularly better than the general:

"The First Time," for instance, is better than "The Synagogue" or "Israel," which should somehow have been better than its last stanza lets it be. Even the "Adam and Eve" suite, as he says himself in a note, is *not* symbolic. This contains his most open, finest work, I think, so far.

> And for the third time, in the third way, Eve:
> "The tree that rises from the middle part
> Of the garden," And almost tenderly, "Thou art
> The garden. *We.*" Then she was overcome,
> And Adam coldly, lest he should succumb
> To pity, standing at the edge of doom,
> Comforted her like one about to leave.

Surely this is remarkable, Dantesque; I have no feeling that his best work is yet written. One different point: the temptation to say beautiful things that may or may not be *true* seems hardly to have been experienced by this poet at all. It is something one would seldom recommend (Wallace Stevens is probably our most distinguished victim since Poe), but in so special and as it were muscle-bound a case . . . —JOHN BERRYMAN, "From the Middle and Senior Generations," *AS*, Summer 1959, pp. 386–88

Karl Shapiro has written an animated, corrupt, repetitious, illogical, necessary, and dangerous book (*In Defense of Ignorance*). He has written it in defense of ignorance, the indefensible—and in a shrill and ranting tone, which will offend all readers of good sense. At the same time, he has had the courage to throw into the open the whole plight of American poetry at the present time. Of course this plight is just what all poets and critics, even those whom Shapiro attacks most sharply, are worried about; but most of them have shied away from a serious public discussion of it because they have felt that such a discussion might jeopardize their own entrenched positions or, more commonly, because they have feared that it must lead to debilitating pessimism.

Shapiro for years has been chipping away at the critics. Usually in rather sedate language, to be sure, but his general position has been clear. Now he abandons his politeness, and in the heat of his argument (perhaps generated in part by the neglect his prose has suffered) he says many foolish things and often says them badly. But he at least does not disguise his animus or his convictions. The roots are exposed clearly in the early pages of the introductory essay. "Criticism," he writes, "is an attitude of mind, not simply a method of elucidation. It is what remains when literature itself has begun to expire. Criticism flourishes when literature has failed. . . ." And he goes on to say that modern criticism has substituted ideology for judgment, has elevated didactic poetry to a supreme position, has concentrated attention on meaning rather than on poetic value, and finally has itself supplanted poetry as the fashionable genre for young writers.

He sums up by proclaiming himself unashamedly an anti-intellectual, and assuredly that is the nub of the matter. "The intellectual," he writes disparagingly, "cannot experience anything without *thinking* about it." The italics are Shapiro's own, and indicate obviously to what camp his allegiance belongs, that is, to the peculiarly modern camp which believes that by mere force of feeling you can split asunder thought and experience, and then choose which of the two you prefer.

This split simply isn't possible. Thought and experience are inextricably bound together. Being bound together, neither can exist by itself, at least if we agree that we mean by experience something more than an instantaneously forgotten sensation; and therefore every poet since the beginning of time has necessarily been an intellectual according to Shapiro's definition. Take the American poets of the 20th-Century whom Shapiro condemns as intellectuals and whom other poetry-readers applaud as the authors of our most beautiful poems. Even in their old age these men are sensualists; at least so I have observed; and however much thinking they may do about their experience, they are always eager for the experience itself, sometimes to the point of disgrace. This doesn't mean just eating, drinking, etc., though the appetites are a large part of experience. ⟨. . .⟩

I have said that Shapiro's book is both necessary and dangerous. It is necessary because somebody had to say that the school of Eliot has, roughly speaking, become our Orthodoxy, an informal academy entrenched in our teaching and publishing apparatus. Much recent verse is dry, God knows, and anyone who has circulated among our academic scenes knows that many of the people who produce it are dry people, though this by no means applies to all. The dryness comes from the orthodoxy—that seems inescapable—and Shapiro has said this very well. But his book is dangerous because on the basis of this truth it appeals to the ignorant in behalf of a destructive and narrow program. By the ignorant I don't mean those who have done poorly in school, for many fine poets, including some of those attacked by Shapiro, have been bad scholars. I mean instead those who through laziness or impatience have not examined the workings of human consciousness. These are the people who will fail to understand that what we need is not poetry circumscribed by a stipulated kind of experience or written according to anyone's prescriptions, but poetry reconstituted upon the permanent foundations. Let us reassert an old principle. So far as art is concerned—and probably so far as life is concerned—the only and always valid thought is that which arises from and refers to genuine felt experience, whatever that experience may be. If once this is pounded into the heads of our young people, I guarantee the production of dry verse will fall off sharply. And perhaps at the same time we will be able to take (at last!) a dispassionate view of the poetry and criticism of our own bygone era.—HAYDEN CARRUTH "In Defense of Karl Shapiro," *NR*, June 20, 1960, pp. 19–20

Karl Shapiro's *The Bourgeois Poet*, which reads at times like a middle-aged *Howl*, must be read *in*, not *through*. As poetry, it is prose; as prose, it lacks continuity and characters, is more autobiography than anything else, though it really isn't autobiography. It is more the heart of Mr. Shapiro's journals, dateless and selected, evidently, from the evening paragraphs only, these written after the fifth highball or possibly a fifth, period. I do not mean to sound too flippant. I simply am not impressed, particularly so after *Trial of a Poet*, whose excellences make the present effort seem all the way downhill. I do not object to the form, since form is now anything the poet can manage. A man can do what he can do. I mean:

> Hymen's got a cold. Hymen, your nose is running.
> My love, you look like Beethoven, like you were hit
> by a truck.
> You look like a fucking skull.
> It's six o'clock, you're drunk, you speak Greek in
> your sleep, you snore like Henry the Ninth.
> Wake up and take the dimes off my eyes.

That's what I mean. If you're looking for a smile, all right; though the smile suffers a change when you remember a grown-up wrote this.—GEORGE SCARBROUGH, "One Flew East, One Flew West, One Flew Over the Cuckoo's Nest," *SwR*, Winter 1965, pp. 146–47

We have recently been given Karl Shapiro's *Collected Poems.*

His new book comes as a rather surprising addendum. Can seven years have passed since the Bourgeois Poet, in the anthology *Poet's Choice*, demanded, "Why must grown people listen to rhymes?" and confessed, "I feel ashamed when I write meter and rhyme, or dirty, as if I were wearing a dress." But now it appears that Eros and Hymen come only to parties more conventional than any the Beep in his exacerbations dreamed of:

> I swore to stab the sonnet with my pen,
> Squash the black widow in a grandstand play
> By gunning down the sonnet form—and then
> I heard you quote my schoolboy love Millay.
> I went to find out what she used to say
> About her tribulations and her men
> And loved her poetry though I now am gray
> And found out love of love poems once again.
> Now I'm the one that's stabbed—son of a bitch!
> With my own poisoned ballpoint pen of love
> And write in *sonnet* form to make my *pitch*,
> Words I no longer know the meaning of.
> If I could write one honest sentence now
> I'd say I love you but I don't know how.

The Beep is banished now, and Mr. Shapiro, who seems to thrive on such sea-change, appears before us as a White-Haired Lover. His thin book contains thirty-nine love poems, only roughly a sonnet sequence since a third are nonsonnets (these include a ballad, an epithalamium, various short lyrics, and one in unmetered, rhymeless strophes). In a year when John Berryman and Richard Eberhart have brought out the sonnets of their youthful affairs, Karl Shapiro has written a brand new set.

From Sir Philip Sidney to George Meredith and beyond, the sonnet sequence has seemed a form peculiarly apt for revealing in depth the psychology of love. Mr. Shapiro eschews all that, describing his courtship instead in tones that divigate between frank desire and amused detachment. This seems appropriate for a white-haired lover reliving a stage of his life he had thought bygone. The echoes in the verse are of Millay, Mrs. Browning, Rupert Brooke, and the epithalamium is titled "The Second Time Around."

No doubt *White-Haired Lover* will prove an interim book for Mr. Shapiro, a much more relaxed and unanguished kind of formal poetry than we have had from him. Its surprises are in the shifts of tone rather than in unsuspected depths of meaning, as in the more complex, earlier sequence, *Adam and Eve.* Mr. Shapiro's work is marked by radical changes in style, and the present book offers yet another stage in his alternation between constraints and self-determinations. Whatever comes next is bound to be different, but meanwhile we have these poems for an easy, enjoyable read.—DANIEL HOFFMAN, "Constraints and Self-Determinations," *Poetry*, Aug. 1969, pp. 336–38

KARL SHAPIRO
From an Interview by Andrea Gale Hammer
Prairie Schooner, Fall 1980, pp. 3, 12–19

"My own work is extra-familial," responds Karl Shapiro, when asked how he sees his poetry in relation to familial ties. "I am a great 'believer' in The Family in the conventional meaning of that term," he continues, "even in the political meaning. Also, I had and have a large close family, really a tribe. But I am not a close member of the tribe. On the contrary." Could it be, he says with characteristic indirection, that "poets have no family, as it were?" We schedule an interview to explore these remarks in depth. 〈. . .〉

Hammer: Let me try to approach the question of the poet and family from another direction. The other day, someone referred to you as a "child of Auden."

Shapiro: Almost all the people my age who were Americans starting to publish in the late thirties or early forties were what I call "Auden babies." The discovery of Auden was a great thing for American poets who were frequently referred to, me included, as neo-classical. When Auden began to write poems, not his very early poetry—that Anglo-Saxon, Skeltonic stuff—but poems that had frames almost like pictures, they had to do with a particular idea converted into imagery. But what got all of us about Auden was that he spoke a twentieth-century language better, it seemed to us, than any American poet did. It's almost impossible to be influenced by Frost, because he's too individualistic, too idiosyncratic. His idiom is so identified with him that you simply leave it alone. But Auden did one of the hardest things that poets always want to do, which is to be able to use "dead language," by which I mean sociological language—Auden was a great sociologist—and modern psychological terminology, without killing the poem.

Hammer: John Brinnin, who's of your generation, once wrote: "Like other young poets, I found that in order to save my poetic soul, I had to break the spell of the idiom Auden had invented." I wonder to what extent you feel "anxiety of influence," as Harold Bloom would have it.

Shapiro: Now Bloom, he's a nut.

Hammer: Yet, you've written this: "It is hard to imagine how the next true poet will escape all the masters lying in wait to receive him, but that is uniquely and eternally the problem of the young true poet."

Shapiro: [*Laughing.*] Did I say that? Why, it sounds like Bloom. I don't remember where that was from.

Hammer: It's from *Beyond Criticism*.

Shapiro: Well, I know one thing I was thinking of there. I believe very strongly that you learn to write poetry by imitation. You imitate those whose poetry you love. You want to be as good as they are; on the other hand, you don't want to be an imitator. The whole career of or development of the poet or any other artist is the process of assimilation simultaneous with the discovery of his own voice. This takes a very long time. I've even thought of it in terms of an exact number of years, like ten, because of what I notice about the process of breaking away from the masters. Bloom puts it in an adversary situation. I don't think it is that at all.

Hammer: You don't feel that the master poet becomes an unbearable burden for the young poet?

Shapiro: I don't think it's a question of rejection at all.

Hammer: Would Randall Jarrell agree with you?

Shapiro: Maybe Bloom would be right about him. Jarrell in the forties was writing a book in which he was going to destroy Auden. Some of it was published, but the book as a whole never was. Then he gave it up. Jarrell was *so* influenced by Auden, as we all were, that I think he really had it in his mind to kill him off. I think Berryman felt that same Auden influence, too, and it was years and years before Berryman found himself. He was always a good poet, but until he started to write those wild dream poems he was still under the influence of Auden.

Hammer: You're an admirer of Jarrell.

Shapiro: Yes, I'm a great fan of Jarrell. I knew him fairly well. I always felt he was a very—the Americans say "lonesome" person—he really was a loner, something of an orphan. Even though he was married and had stepchildren and lots of

friends, most of his relationships were intellectual and literary. His dependence on Robert Lowell was pathological. Lowell terrified everybody, and he was a bully. Jarrell, one of his main friends, debased himself in his relationship with Lowell. Still, I was crazy about Jarrell. He was a brilliant guy and very, very strange. He had a kind of child-like gentleness, which was extremely deceptive, because when he picked up a pen you had to run for your life.

Hammer: This dependence of Jarrell on Lowell and of you and others on Auden reminds me of another remark by John Brinnin, which paraphrases, perhaps simplifies, Bloom's point:

> The life of poetry, it seems to me, moves in a dynastic succession. Poets become the ancestors of other poets in a series that reflects a cast of mind and a disposition toward language as surely as facial features identify members of a family. Like most poets, I was first moved to write poetry as a way of recognizing and responding to poems I had discovered by myself and which struck me with as much wonder and excitement as I would have felt on finding buried treasure.[2]

Shapiro: Well, I would not disagree with what Brinnin said, although I would use different terminology.

Hammer: You wouldn't discuss, say, Auden's influence on you in familial terms at all, would you?

Shapiro: No, and I think maybe Brinnin can because he probably felt closer to Auden personally than I did or could. Brinnin wrote one of the first books about Dylan Thomas.

Hammer: Dylan Thomas in America.

Shapiro: That's right. He was responsible for Thomas's fame in this country. There was a period when all of my students in the forties and fifties imitated Thomas, and my job as teacher was to wean them away from him. They knew that themselves. They were overwhelmingly impressed by Thomas; in the same way, Thomas was so influenced by Yeats that he never really got him out of his style. Especially in the early poems. But my form of pedagogy in teaching and writing of poetry is to insist that you imitate. In order to be a poet or any other kind of artist you have got to have masters, and you've got to imitate them. You *do* imitate them, whether you like it or not. And you are smart enough to know that you're never going to be on your own until you have assimilated what they've taught you, and then you begin to express your own soul and to move away. [*Pauses.*] I guess that relationship between poets is familial in the sense that the masters are fathers.

Hammer: You downplay the sense of trauma involved in breaking away, in finding your own way. Why is that?

Shapiro: Well, I do that because I think the changeover is so gradual that you don't know it. It's certainly not as violent as puberty or adolescence; it's probably more like the transition from adolescence into maturity. Very subtle and gradual. I dislike that idea of the anxiety of influence, because it over-dramatizes.

Hammer: Your praise of Auden and criticism of Ginsberg, however, suggests a somewhat dramatic tension between generations of poets.

Shapiro: You know, if you've looked at some of my later criticism, that I dissociated myself from the poetry after Ginsberg that was close to propaganda or politics. I'm so opposed to the "politicizing" of poetry that it's a major point of reference with me. For that reason, there's a lot of poetry of people I admire very much, like Robert Bly, that I can't bring myself to like when it becomes cause-oriented.

Hammer: But Auden wrote politically-oriented poetry.

Shapiro: Certainly the generation that influenced me, like Spender, Isherwood, Koestler, Auden, and even Brecht, that whole group of both prose writers and poets, was very politically conscious. I'm discovering, though, in the case of Auden that even in his early so-called Marxist years his politics are suspect. He was never, I'm beginning to see, a convinced Marxist at all. He played the game for a while; he played it rather carefully, too.

Hammer: If you're saying that poetry is currently traveling the path Ginsberg blazed, you're also implying that the idiom you inherited from Auden is useless on such a journey. Are you suggesting that new poets refuse Auden's legacy of language? That the gap between generations is irreconcilable?

Shapiro: I think somewhere in the fifties there began to be a failure of poetry as a medium. Poetry as an art. It became an instrument for other purposes. Whatever the reasons, the quality of the writing had degenerated so badly that it had almost ceased to be poetry. And one thing I associate with that degeneration of art is the degeneration of education and taken-for-granted values of the past. I don't mean, necessarily, traditional values, but ordinary human values like honesty and peacefulness. Auden wrote some poems, one of them called "Doggerel by a Senior Citizen," in which he made the remark:

> Though I suspect the term is crap,
> If there *is* a Generation Gap,
> Who is to blame? Those, old and young,
> Who will not learn their Mother-Tongue.

Auden must have been very disturbed by the same kind of thing I am. The young poets no longer seem to be playing the game with language in the way they're supposed to play. If you're a poet, your primary interest has always got to be words and language.

Hammer: Eliot, too, said that the poet's first duty is to preserve the language inherited from the past and to allow its growth.

Shapiro: I agree with part of that; of course, I disagree with Eliot's reliance on the tradition. Eliot knew as well as anybody who ever wrote what that obligation of the poet is to his medium, which is his language. Everything is implicit in the language. In writing a review of *The English Auden*, I'm doing some of it in the first person because that's the only way I can express my involvement with Auden. I point out the critical crisis I had because of Auden's crisis, because he meant so much to me as a poet. I considered myself a kind of twentieth-century humanist. Certainly not an Anglican. When Auden had his religious conversion it was a great shock to people, as if he had died. Yet, to my delight I did not lose any of my admiration for what he was doing. Auden has written some of the great religious poetry in the English language. The *Horae Canonicae* is magnificent. Other poems, such as *For the Time Being*, are certainly as good as Eliot's and probably better in that genre.

Hammer: In one of his lines, Auden makes language into a kind of mother: "The poet is the father who begets the poem which the language bears."[3]

Shapiro: That's good. I would rather think of language as a mother, too. It's like the sea: immense and mysterious. It contains everything, all potentiality.

Hammer: Do you think that most poets feel estranged from the next generation of writers?

Shapiro: No, no. Not at all. I'm always looking for new poets and what I consider to be good poetry.

Hammer: Whom in particular, among the post-moderns, do you wholeheartedly back?

Shapiro: I've recently discovered a poet who's dead, a modern poet that I'd missed and who died at a very old age. He was a contemporary of William Carlos Williams. A guy named Charles Reznikoff. His books have been out of print for a long time, but he's first-rate. Well, he's not a young living poet, but he's a new poet, writing in that clean style of Williams in his early work. And I back a lot of the younger poets, but of course they wouldn't appear to be young, like May Swenson, for instance. She's not terribly well known, but I like her very much. I prefer her, in fact, to someone like Diane Wakoski. Now, there's a lot of Wakoski's poetry I admire, but on the whole I keep hearing that strident voice of "the cause," whatever "the cause" is. And some of Denise Levertov I like very much, but there again I recoil into my ivory tower with some of her political stuff that bores me so much. I always thought Anne Sexton was a very good poet, one who was self-made, whatever that means, although I think it's true that Sylvia Plath was more talented and probably wrote better poetry.

Hammer: Can you point to anybody writing now in whose work you can see your own influence?

Shapiro: Not anybody well known. I've had many students, a lot of whom have become poets and have published. I can sometimes detect devices having to do with imagery, or even a tone of voice.

Hammer: Jarrell once described your poems as "primitive."

Shapiro: Yes, I think putting the best construction on the term. I'm very fond of primitive in everything—except people. What he meant had to do with using primary colors. When I paint, I don't mix colors but use them just like they are in the tubes. But the other thing I pick up when I think someone has been influenced by me would be a certain tone or stance or attitude about occurrences. I'm fond of indirection and understatement. Somebody said to me recently that the little poem I wrote about T. S. Eliot, in *Collected Poems*, showed I had changed my feelings or views about him. I pointed out to her that there's one line or one word in there that contains the irony of the poem, and that's the word "mythic." "His mythic poetry that has stunned the world." I wasn't trying to do any put-down in that poem at all. I was trying to write a portrait of the most famous poet in the twentieth century getting ready to read his poems, by giving mostly a physical description and not saying anything else about it. This is what I mean by "indirection." For people to really get what I was trying to say in that poem, they'd have to know from other pieces I've written how I feel about Eliot and his influence.

Hammer: Can you assess your own contribution to a poetic tradition?

Shapiro: No, you never know. Maybe smarter writers can do that. From everything I've been able to pick up from other writers and poets, they never really know what effect they have nor where they stand. They're constantly surprised, as I am, by the reaction of critics to what they've written, whether the reaction is favorable or unfavorable. Writers are pretty much in the dark. In a way, that's how it should be. The creative person is something of a contemplative who is going to do his or her work, like Emily Dickinson, whether anyone sees it or not.

Notes

1. John Brinnin, *Poets on Poetry*, ed. Howard Nemerov (New York: Basic Books, Inc., 1966), p. 77.
2. Ibid, p. 72.
3. W. H. Auden is quoted by Elizabeth Drew, *Poetry* (New York: Dell Publishing Co., Inc., 1959), pp. 21–2.

IRWIN SHAW

1913–1984

Irwin Shaw was born on February 27, 1913, in New York City. He graduated from Brooklyn College in 1934 and immediately began his career as a writer. He first attracted critical attention with his acclaimed antiwar play, *Bury the Dead* (1936), and with his short stories, many of which first appeared in the *New Yorker*. His first collection of stories, *Sailor off the Bremen*, was published in 1939, and was followed by *Welcome to the City* (1942) and *Act of Faith* (1946). During this period Shaw served in the U.S. Army (1942–45) and published three more plays: *The Gentle People* (1939), *Sons and Soldiers* (1943), and *The Assassin* (1945). He received the 1944 O'Henry Memorial Award for his short story "Walking Wounded."

Shaw's first novel, *The Young Lions*, was published in 1948. The story of three soldiers who meet on a World War II battlefield, it became a best-seller, established Shaw as a writer of popular fiction, and was later made into a movie. Shaw went on to write other popular novels, including *Lucy Crown* (1956), *Two Weeks in Another Town* (1960), and *Rich Man, Poor Man* (1969); several of his later works were adapted for television. He also wrote screenplays and several travel books while he continued to produce short stories, later collected in a half-dozen volumes. One of his best-known tales is the title story of *Tip on a Dead Jockey*, published in 1957.

Shaw spent his later years in Klosters, Switzerland; he was married in 1939 and had one son. Shaw died suddenly of a heart attack in Davos, Switzerland, on May 16, 1984.

For twenty-two years the critics have been chiding Irwin Shaw over his failure to produce a novel that would justify the mighty reputation he earned as playwright and short-story writer in the Thirties and Forties. In reviewing his five previous novels they have accused him of structure that was too sprawling, social concepts that were oversimplified, characters that were superficially conceived, proceedings that were unlikely—in short, of writing slick, glib, showy fiction instead of the masterpiece of which he had seemed so capable.

Along with nearly everyone else, I was, and am, in awe of Irwin Shaw. In 1939 I saw his *Bury the Dead* produced alongside O'Neill's sea plays, and for me he was *the* Shaw. He is the kind of craftsman—sincere, knowledgeable, unassuming—that I am drawn to and want to see confirmed as one of our great writers. It is my agonizing duty to report that *Rich Man, Poor Man* does not redeem his long-standing promise.

Essentially it is the story of two brothers, Rudolph and Thomas Jordache, and their sister Gretchen. Although they are children of a brutal marriage and have all experienced a hardscrabble youth, their separate struggles for survival and fulfilment, which make up the fabric of *Rich Man, Poor Man*, are in sharp contrast.

Rudolph is the good one. Before he is out of his teens he is so diligent in the practice of self-denial, self-reliance, and industry that he has a running start on a half-page in *Who's Who*. Thomas is the reverse. He's a mean, pugnacious, foul-minded kid who gets his kicks from bullying the law-abiding citizens of Port Philip and spoiling their victory celebrations with a burning cross. Nor, when opportunity presents itself, is he above blackmail. He seems a sure bet for the penitentiary.

The beautiful Gretchen has capacity for both good and evil, but she's easily bored and succumbs early to temptation. She has been flirting with a black man, considering—not too seriously, yet considering—an affair with him, when she falls for her boss instead. He is Teddy Boylan, the wealthy *seigneur* of this part of the Hudson Valley, and the taste for luxury and the cultivated life she acquires from him starts Gretchen off through the primroses to Greenwich Village and Beverly Hills.

Presently Boylan is exercising a strong influence on Rudolph, too, pointing out to him the Horatio Algerish nature of the goals that led him through college and up the business and political ladders. In a less direct way, Boylan alters Thomas's life, launching him on a picaresque career as a prize fighter and vagrant who always ships out one jump ahead of the reckoning.

Ironically, only Thomas attains satisfaction in love, work, and happiness. Gretchen's life is blighted by casual relationships with men and the alienation of her child, while Rudolph's great tower of a career is shattered by the indiscretions of his desirable yet curiously corrupt wife, Jean. She has been contaminated by inherited wealth, as Boylan was, and thus spoils whatever she touches.

That's the theme of *Rich Man, Poor Man*. Gretchen states it when expressing her anger "at America because it produced men like Teddy Boylan and made life easy for men like Teddy Boylan," and again when accusing Rudolph: "You think you'd dress the way you do or be so interested in success and money and how to get there the fastest way possible without Teddy Boylan?" It's surprising that Mr. Shaw finds the familiar evil of easy money, wealth without sweat, to be the true corrupter of our bewildering times.

Does this sound too trivial an idea to form the basis of a family chronicle that covers two continents, three generations, and twenty-five years? Well, yes, it is. Does that account for the novel's fatal weakness, its arbitrariness and lack of conviction? No; it seems more symptom than cause. This notion of "Boylan's Way" as the worm in the Jordaches' apple is laid on, not part of their natures or motivations, and even Gretchen is unconvinced by it. Her remark is abandoned by both author and characters as they hurry on about their business.

But is it a clue, something to be taken at more than face value? Could it provide an answer to the essential question about *Rich Man, Poor Man*, the question why Irwin Shaw the novelist is so unwilling to reveal Irwin Shaw the man?

I keep thinking that within this book lies some such disclosure, that Mr. Shaw has left a message here, intentional or otherwise, about himself. Perhaps it is my eagerness to decipher it that enables me to read Gretchen's words as the confession of a writer who has bought, at too high a price, another man's vision—one that seemed alluringly fair and all-American at the time—when instead he might have fought, in Thomas Jordache fashion, for his own homelier one.

Oh, I admire the plotting, all that ingenuity in projection and fitting together, even when it doesn't work persuasively. I admire the bold strokes with which the author can sketch in a Thomas, eliciting fom his reader a full measure of fear, loathing, and fascination.

Irwin Shaw has a master's hand. But why doesn't he trust his heart? It would make the difference between believing and not believing his story. I suppose his heart has betrayed him at some time—and what a pity that is.—JOHN LEGGETT, *SR*, Oct. 17, 1970, pp. 34–36

If a writer deserves to be judged by his best work—and he does—then ⟨*Short Stories: Five Decades*⟩ is far and away the major book of Irwin Shaw's remarkable career.

Having said that, what have we said?

And why "remarkable?"

Taking them in inverse order: Had Shaw died 40 years ago, his obituaries—and he would have received them even then—would have mourned the passing of an unusually talented 25-year-old who was, at the time, a writer of social protest plays and sensitive *New Yorker* stories, a sort of Odets / Cheever gone to rest. If he died today, he would be bracketed with the brand-name novelists, the classy ones, maybe like Michener, maybe like Wouk.

He is, of course, none of the above.

What he is is this: a tale teller. There is narrative interest in everything the man puts down. Here is the first sentence of the first story in the book, "The Eighty Yard Run": "The pass was high and wide and he jumped for it, feeling it slap flatly against his hands, as he shook his hips to throw off the halfback who was diving at him."

And? We sit there reading. And then? Yes—go on, go on. Who is running and do they tackle him and when and *please continue.*

Coupled with the narrative gift is the ability to write with an ease and a clarity that only Fitzgerald had. There is never a wrong word, a phrase that makes you stop, reread, make sure you've gotten the sense right.

The following example of style is from "Tip on a Dead Jockey." The main character, Barber, has gone alone to a race track outside Paris on a chill and misty day.

> There was only one other spectator near him in the stand, a small, round man wearing an expensive-looking velours hat, and carrying a pair of binoculars and a rolled umbrella, like an Englishman. He smiled at Barber and nodded. As Barber smiled back politely, he realized that he had seen the man many times before, or his brother, or a half-dozen other men who looked like him, in restaurants and in bars and on the street, usually with tall girls who might have been lower-class mannequins or upper-class tarts.
>
> The man with the umbrella moved over to him along the damp concrete rows of seats. He had little, dapper feet, and a bright necktie, and he had a well-cared-for, international kind of face, with large, pretty dark eyes, fringed by thick black lashes. He had what Barber had come to call an import-export face. It was a face that was at the same time bland, cynical, self-assured, sensual, hopeless and daring, and its owner might be Turkish or Hungarian or Greek or he might have been born in Basra. It was a face you might see in Paris or Rome or Brussels or

Tangier, always in the best places, always doing business. It was a face, you felt somehow, that was occasionally of interest to the police.

What's unusual about the example is that it isn't unusual. There are passages like this literally in all of the 63 stories.

This is not to say that all of the stories work equally well or well at all. Sometimes he is too much on the side of the liberal angels. Sometimes he is simply too overtly manipulative and—because he writes with the already mentioned clarity—the manipulation is visible immediately. "The Inhabitants of Venus" shows both faults. It's about a Jew who accidentally sees, after the war, a German who left him to die before the holocaust began. The Jew decides, on the spot, to revenge himself and kill the German. He ultimately changes his mind because the German has lost a leg in the war.

The story is told with the standard skill, but in the end it's just too contrived. If a Faulkner had tried the piece, he would have obfuscated the telling to such an extent that we probably would not have noticed the manipulation.

But the vast majority of these pieces do work, and the dozen or so that work best—"Girls in Their Summer Dresses," "Sailor off the Bremen," "Main Currents of American Thought," "The Dry Rock," "Welcome to the City"—these are as fine as any stories written by anybody since Shaw entered the arena.

And if he is not held in higher esteem by the literary establishment it is because, for all his skill, he was not skillful enough to surmount the ultimate obstacle: popularity. Before the war, when no one was reading him, he was a critic's darling.

They never forgave him for *The Young Lions.*

Hemingway was able to get away with it. Salinger was able to get away with it. Capote may be herniating himself in an effort to get away with it.

Well I'm sorry and it's sad, but Hemingway just doesn't work well anymore. "The Short Happy Life of Francis Macomber" would make—and I mean this—a vintage skit for Saturday Night Live, with Chevy Chase as Macomber, Gilda Radner as his wife and John Belushi as the White Hunter. For those who may have forgotten, "Macomber" tells the story in which the crucial event is when a dilettante-type fellow runs away when this savage lion charges at him through the underbrush, and thereby proves himself to be nothing more nor less than a coward.

A coward? My God, who wouldn't run away?

It isn't that courage as a virtue is out of fashion that's ruined Hemingway. It's more that we've all passed our course in Kindergarten Freud now, and the glorification of lunatic courage, the my-chest-has-more-hair-than-your-chest kind, has been revealed to us all as simply sexual panic. And we just won't buy it anymore.

Irwin Shaw stays. He seems to be able to write about practically anything. Gangsters in Brooklyn and deputy sheriffs in New Mexico, rich people and poor, bartenders and barons, you name it. It's almost as if he's saying, "Here's a good one," and when he's finished and you've moved in closer, he says, "Here's another that's not so bad."

For his is a primitive skill possessed by very few sophisticated men; Maugham most recently. Do not look for symbolism in Irwin Shaw or Biblical puns. He is not interested in that. He wants only to get us safely through the terrors of the night. He asks only that we sit quietly in the cave, and build the fire high to frighten the wild animals outside.

And just listen . . .—WILLIAM GOLDMAN, "Rich and Poor, Bums and Barons," *NYTBR*, Nov. 12, 1978, pp. 3, 84–85

"The decline of Irwin Shaw" is a myth, and like all myths has its purpose. For while middlebrow taste has a strong stake in the standard American success story, highbrow taste has just as strong a commitment to its opposite—that the standard American success story is inevitably a story of moral corruption. (That this is to some degree the story Shaw himself tells in his novels only compounds the irony.)

Not that Shaw hasn't handed his critics enough weapons—several hundred thousand of his millions of words are indistinguishable from the computer printouts of Robbins, Wallace, Sheldon, and Susann. But the point is that, especially when re-read in light of *Bread upon the Waters*, his early novels, while full of promise, are hardly masterpieces of modern literature, and his later novels, while full of compromise, are hardly the epitome of drugstore trash. Put another way, his strengths and weaknesses have been there all along, in each and every novel.

Shaw's strengths as a novelist are those of another century—relentlessly fluid narrative, dramatically focused set pieces, and sharp, incisive dialogue—which help account for both his critical disfavor (the current canon stresses narrative fragmentation, inconclusive confrontation, and failed communication) and his commercial success (in the age of 90-minute electronic media, the public can turn only to the popular novel for sprawling saga). In short, Shaw is that most contemptible of contemporary writers—a believer in *stories*.

On the other hand, Shaw frequently suffers from the short-story writer's inability to form a coherent whole out of brilliant sequences. Furthermore, his work is too often cheapened by factitious glamour, shallow characterizations, and pompous attitudinizing, to say nothing of centerfold sex and gung-ho violence. Worst of all, the anti-rhetorical inheritance from Hemingway, laconically exposing the pious platitudes of the day, occasionally turns into a kind of sentimental cynicism.

But all the time, in every novel, sometimes embedded in the narrative structure itself, sometimes barely glimpsed through the smoke of post-coital cigarettes, we can now see that the key to his novels is moral choice. Yes, in Irwin Shaw's novels, one has to make moral choices even in Cannes! If one expects something more from the heir to Hemingway, one expects far less from the peer of Robbins.

In re-reading *The Young Lions*, for instance, published in 1948, one can see why many readers still regard it as his finest novel, but one can also find passages, scenes, and characters indistinguishable from those in novels regarded as his worst. What remains of enduring value, of course, are the demythologizing of the war (a sympathetic Nazi character; unflinching reminders of American anti-Semitism; a scorn for patriotic homilies); the shattering set pieces (the desert massacre of the English company; the white-maned preacher at Dover; Christian cutting the throat of the concentration camp commandant); and the unique Shaw voice ("She's the kind of girl who's always saying she doesn't like your shirts. Know that kind?"—what other writer has struck precisely that tone?).

But the same writer who could so brilliantly deromanticize ideology was also capable of romanticizing the glibbest cynicism. ("Same songs, same uniforms, same enemies, same defeats. Only new graves.") In fact, the lapses for which Shaw has been so severely castigated were there from the beginning: adolescent posing ("He loved the war because in no other way could a man be truly tested"); ponderous moralizing ("She was Roger's girl, and . . . it was inconceivable that he, Noah, could repay the generous acts of friendship even by the hidden duplicity of unspoken desire"); and preposterous "creative writing" ("Outside the room he heard the murmur of seven

million people walking through the streets and corridors of the city"). When we read prose like this, how can we talk of a subsequent "decline"? Yet for all its passages of brilliance and banality, we can now see that at the heart of the novel are the moral choices made by its three central characters.

While *The Young Lions* was forgiven for its lapses, *Rich Man, Poor Man* (1969) wasn't credited with its virtues. There's no need to dwell on its flaws—the papier-mâché characters, the paperback prose, the cheap macho irony. Instead, it must be acknowledged that Shaw's narrative drive remains unflagging, and that the novel contains far more incisive dialogue ("'There's nothing like a failing marriage,' she said, 'to bring out flights of rhetoric'"), concise characterization ("'They're nobody's friends,' Gretchen said. 'They're drinkers'"), and sharp insight ("He had old-fashioned manners and up-to-date hatreds") than any mere hack entertainer could hope to achieve in a lifetime. More to the point, all three of the novel's major characters struggle to become better people.

Re-read the other novels too, and discover neither Hemingway nor Robbins but the last of the tough old pros, halfway between the two. Behind *la dolce vita* of Rome's international film colony in *Two Weeks in Another Town* (1960) is the story of a man who looks back at the bright promise of his youth, and who attempts to salvage some decency and honor from the compromises and betrayals into which he fell. Or re-read *Evening in Byzantium* (1973), the story of a man attempting to retain his integrity in a tabloid world. Or still another example, *Beggerman, Thief* (1977), a story about the struggle, in short, to become a better man.

The story Irwin Shaw has told again and again, "the story of a man who looks back at the bright promise of his youth, and who attempts to salvage some decency and honor from the compromises and betrayals into which he fell"—this is also the story told of Irwin Shaw's career. Only his critics leave out the second half.—ROSS WETZSTEON, "The Conflict between Big Bucks and Good Books," *SR*, Aug. 1981, pp. 14–16

JOHN W. ALDRIDGE
From "Mailer, Burns, and Shaw: The Naked Zero"
After the Lost Generation
1951, pp. 146–56

The influence of *The New Yorker* magazine on the values and attitudes of this generation of writers will probably never be accurately estimated. Influences are usually clear only in their primary stages. As they are absorbed they tend to merge with originality, so that after a while it becomes impossible to tell whether a writer is seeing life in a particular way because his temperament requires him to see it that way or because outside influences have taught him to see it that way. But the *New Yorker* influence is a special thing, and when it is very strongly present in a writer's work, it has a way of taking over the work, cheating the writer out of his rightful ownership, and stamping it with that anonymous but universally familiar *New Yorker* label.

The code which *The New Yorker* teaches its writers is evident in everything they write—from the delicately thin little fantasies of Shirley Jackson that trail wispy spider webs of horror across the mind to the robustly thin little anecdotes of John O'Hara that echo farther and farther down the corridors of manful understatement until they refine themselves out of earshot. It is a code based on a fear of all emotion that cannot be expressed in the whisper of a nuance. It depends for its existence upon a view of the world as a vast cocktail party where the very best people say the most frightening things about themselves and one another in a language which the servants are not expected to understand, where the most tragic confession of personal ruin is at once diluted by the ironic titter in the speaker's voice. It is a world kept faintly amused by perpetual gossip about the cannibalism of sweet little girls in white, the madness of little boys beating dead dogs in vacant lots, the neurosis of lonely shop girls who fancy themselves pursued by daemon lovers or trapped in crumbling skyscrapers. It is a world where the most monstrous infidelities can be arranged and dismissed with the bored flicker of an eyelash and where all the impoverishment of modern man can be expressed in a single turn of phrase.

The writing that comes out of this world is distinguished by its overwhelming accuracy, its painful attention to detail. Produced out of a morbid fear of emotion, it loses itself in trivia so that it will not have to express emotion. It derives its power from a skillful arrangement of the endless unimportances which make up its parts—scraps of brittle dialogue, bits of carefully contrived scene and setting, little stifled orgasms of dramatic climax. But more than anything else, it is assured writing, rich with the wisdom of sour experience in the countless minor bars of many continents. Never is there a mischosen word, an inept phrase, a misplaced emphasis. It all has the slick perfection of freshly laid concrete, as if it had all been produced at the same moment by the same machine.

Irwin Shaw's *The Young Lions* might conceivably have appeared in a special issue of *The New Yorker* given over entirely to war fiction. Like John Hersey's *Hiroshima*, which it in no other way resembles, it has that special look of having been tailored to *New Yorker* specifications. Even the experience with which it deals appears to have been carefully arranged to happen by some *New Yorker* stooge who, one imagines, stood obligingly by ticking off climaxes with a stop watch while Shaw noted them down in his neat, bloodless prose. Everything about the book has an air of prefabrication and contrivance, of editorial rooms, expensive secretaries, and lunchtime martinis; and one finds it difficult to believe that Shaw went any farther for his material than the Algonquin and the *Times* morgue.

But the style is only the vehicle of other qualities that link the novel even more firmly to the *New Yorker* world. The dramatic value of many of the most important scenes is repeatedly crippled by that curious pulled punch which is the approved *New Yorker* method of dealing with emotion that might, if left alone, become strongly and genuinely serious. Where *The Naked and the Dead* at least had the strength of its emotional, if not its philosophical, conviction and managed to lift itself above failure by means of that strength, *The Young Lions* is as blandly and calculatedly subdued as Eustace Tilley himself.

This is most evident in the scenes devoted to New York life during the early years of the war. Like the people for whom *The New Yorker* seems to be specifically written, the people in these scenes have carefully cultivated the art of living perpetually with their spiritual guards up. They have developed a technique for dealing relaxedly with the constant tensions of their existence, for turning the world's irony upon themselves and defeating it with innuendo. On the most crucial occasions, they are never at a loss for the right word, the sleek phrase which will reduce the moment to manageable terms. Their conversation, whether it has to do with suicide, divorce, professional failure, or the advisability of having another drink,

is all conducted in the same key, as if all subjects had an equal value and deserved an equal indifference.

There is no suggestion here, as there is in the best of Hemingway's stories, of violently controlled passions: the language does not draw vitality from the implication that there is a hidden truth, immense and terrible, lying like a smoldering explosive just beneath the surface of the taut nerves and the monosyllables. These people are not members of a secret society, living by an unwritten code which preserves them from destruction. If they were, they would have a complexity worthy of our interest. They are simply sterile, meaningless shadows, talking mannequins, acting out the slick pantomime of life which Shaw has manufactured for them. They might be suitable as devices for satire, but there is no evidence that they are meant to be taken as satire. Shaw's method proclaims on every page his absolute commitment to their world. Its atmosphere seeps through the whole of his book until the method and the created world merge and become inseparable.

The contrivance that is clearly visible behind the architectural design of the novel is also part of this world. Like *Three Soldiers*, *The Young Lions* is built around the experience of three men, each of whom belongs to a different level of society and all of whom react in widely different ways to the impact of the war. But to compare the two books would be to give the genuine and the false an equal value; for Dos Passos' men, whatever else they may have been, at least had the breath of life in them, while Shaw's men, after they are through being all that Shaw wants them to be, have the breath of life crushed out of them. His Michael Whitacre, Noah Ackerman, and Christian Diestl, who epitomize, respectively, the quasi-liberal New York intellectual, the simple, persecuted, but ultimately valorous American Jew, and the bravely dedicated but ultimately defeated German soldier, are merely stereotypes. Their humanity is smothered again and again in the tight confinement of the roles they are intended to play, until, by the end of the novel, they are lost in a confusion of message and cheap rhetoric.

Shaw attempts to inject meaning into the vast panorama of experience which the novel encompasses through a system of carefully contrived parallels, near-parallels, and pseudo parallels which are apparently intended to flow back and forth through one another and give an effect of dramatic irony. Without them the novel would be, at best, merely three separate accounts of miscellaneous incidents occurring in several different countries over a number of years and variously affecting the lives of the three principal characters. At worst, it would simply be a chain of faintly related anecdotes or a series of second-rate short stories. Through the parallels Shaw manages to give the novel at least an appearance of unity, but when we look closely we discover that it is merely a unity of structure and not a unity of dramatic or symbolic meaning.

The parallels may be divided into two types, the primary and the secondary. The big primary parallel which brings together the main events of the novel and fixes them in an over-all design rests on what may only be described as the most improbable of coincidences. In the first chapter, Margaret Freemantle, an American girl on vacation in Austria in 1938, meets Christian Diestl, a young Austrian ski instructor who, although a Nazi, is still decent and humane. Later in the book, Margaret meets Michael Whitacre, a young and attractive Broadway director, and has a serious and extended affair with him. Still later, Whitacre, now in the Army, meets Noah Ackerman, whose story has been developed through the novel concurrently with Whitacre's and Diestl's. Then, in the closing chapter, Ackerman and Whitacre, having been separated, reunited, and brought through the last phases of the war together, are fired upon from ambush by Diestl, now a defeated and corrupt Nazi soldier with just enough strength left for one last act of resistance. His shot, of course, kills Ackerman, and it is left to Whitacre to bring the novel to a righteous end by tracking down Diestl and putting a bullet in his head. The horror which Margaret Freemantle glimpsed in Austria before the war and which Diestl then defended and later epitomized is thus loosed upon Ackerman (martyr to Nazi hate) and then revenged by Margaret's lover, Whitacre. All the principals are brought together on the stage in time for the grand finale.

The secondary parallels are even more interesting. It is particularly clever of Shaw to open the novel with three chapters devoted to the activities of the three main characters on the same day, New Year's Eve, 1937–38, in their widely separated worlds—Diestl in the Austrian Tyrol with Margaret Freemantle, Whitacre in New York, and Ackerman in California. It is also clever of Shaw to have Diestl, Margaret, and Whitacre attending New Year's parties while Ackerman sits in a cheap hotel room waiting for his father to die. But the cleverest stroke of all is Shaw's manipulation of the events which climax the two parties. While Margaret is fighting off a drunken Nazi who is attempting to rape her, a has-been playwright at Whitacre's party almost succeeds in committing suicide. Both incidents are apparently intended to illustrate the basic corruption and sickness which underlie the German and American cultures and to stand in ironic contrast to the drab but innately pure suffering of Ackerman as he waits by his father's bedside.

As the novel progresses, the three men are repeatedly set against one another, and each time the parallel is effected through a set of carefully planted and painfully obvious clues. Whitacre and Diestl are both prevented from rising to officer rank in their respective armies because of their prewar Communist affiliations. Ackerman cannot hope to be accepted even by the men in the enlisted ranks because he is a Jew. In the fourth chapter Diestl suffers a slight wound in the face while leading an armored unit triumphantly into Paris. In the fifth chapter, on the same day back in America, Whitacre suffers a similar wound when his enraged wife hurls a badminton racquet at him. But where Diestl's wound was a mark of the victory of his army, Whitacre's is a humiliating reminder of the defeat of his marriage. Immediately after each incident both men fall into a nostalgic conversation with a friend who has lived in Paris before the war, and both have direct contact with the French. But again Whitacre is the loser; for Diestl and his friend are enthusiastically welcomed by the prostitutes in a Paris brothel, while Whitacre and his friend are curtly dismissed by the two elderly French women who are present at the badminton party. In the seventh chapter Diestl, on a two-week leave in Berlin, enjoys a drunken orgy with his lieutenant's wife and her roommate. In the thirteenth chapter Ackerman and his wife enjoy an idyllic two-week honeymoon on Cape Cod. In the sixteenth chapter Diestl and Lieutenant Hardenburg leave their men to die defending an impossible position and retreat to fight again in another part of the front. In the eighteenth chapter Ackerman, after surviving a series of fist fights with the most powerful men in his company, deserts from the army and goes to New York to puzzle out his relations with the war. In the twenty-second chapter Whitacre, in London after a particularly severe German air raid, muses on the element of chance which makes the difference between life and death in war a matter of the slightest miscalculation of range in a frightened bombardier. In the twenty-fifth chapter Diestl, lying

wounded on the coast of France after a British strafing attack, ponders the same idea. In the twenty-sixth chapter Diestl, cut off from his unit during the Allied Invasion, bolsters the courage of his men with brandy. In the twenty-seventh chapter Whitacre, assigned to temporary duty in an army replacement camp, bolsters his own courage with gin.

The list could be infinitely extended—but to little purpose. It is true that the parallels bring certain minor ironies and paradoxes out into the open. They emphasize, for example, the familiar truth that corruption and fascism exist in all armies, that because of their common suffering, men fighting on opposite sides in a war often feel a closer kinship to one another, and often bear a closer resemblance to one another, than they do to their respective superiors. But the more thoroughly one examines them, the more one is convinced that the parallels do not yield up a significance that justifies the pains Shaw took with them; and one is forced to conclude that they are pointless embroidery intended either to give the novel an appearance of meaning which it does not in fact possess or to satisfy the reader's demand for complexity so well that he will be led to overlook the even more dubious devices Shaw uses to hammer his real message home. For there can certainly be no doubt that when we have been made aware of the parallels we are still no nearer to the sources of what the novel seems really to be saying.

To make his real point, then, Shaw resorts to other means; and foremost among these is distortion of the action itself in such a way that all the major events in the story are warped to fit the argument with which he wishes to convince us. His primary aim is to make a dramatic affirmation of faith in the struggle of the Jew for equality in the modern world. He wants to expose the corruptive evils of modern fascism in both America and Europe, and he wants particularly to show how the Jewish fight against fascism can end not only in Jewish victory but in victory for others who are inspired by the example of the Jew. Ackerman, Whitacre, and Diestl are the appointed instruments of his purpose, but, unfortunately, in acting out that purpose both Ackerman and Whitacre are reduced to implausibility as characters and, through a perverse irony, only Diestl manages to be convincing.

The single unavoidable truth of the events with which the novel is concerned is that war is a brutalizing and destructive experience. It is a truth that rises so inevitably out of the events—from those which transform the victorious German Army into an amorphous mass of frightened fugitives to those which turn the war careers of Ackerman and Whitacre into a nightmare struggle for survival—that the only possible consequence of them is disaster. Diestl is successful as a character because his development through the novel is the logical outcome of the events. As the events of the war turn the German advances into a series of accelerating retreats, he is changed into a defeated personality. He is brutalized and corrupted in strict accordance with the brutal and corrupt picture of war which Shaw presents.

But Ackerman and Whitacre, as the bearers of Shaw's affirmative message, pose an altogether different problem. Logically, they too should be defeated. They are victims of the same war, and Ackerman particularly is subjected to an incredible amount of punishment. But to have allowed them to be defeated, Shaw would have had to allow his point to be defeated. He was required, therefore, to twist them so that, logically or not, they would emerge from the war victorious. To do this, he had to treat the two men in such a way that they would take on character and meaning as the war destroyed character and meaning in the world around them. He had somehow to show them as changing from bad to good as the circumstances of their existence increasingly demanded a change from good to bad. Thus Ackerman is made to develop from the condition of meaninglessness and futility in which we find him at the death of his father through a series of triumphs to a condition of positive strength: he overcomes the deep racial prejudice of a Vermont farmer in order to marry his daughter; he fights the most powerful men in his company to assert his right to be treated in the army as a human being; he performs a magnificent act of heroism in battle out of sheer determination to prove himself; he becomes, in short, a living dynamo of Jewish fortitude. Whitacre is transformed from a soft, overcivilized intellectual, who has all the proper, liberal sentiments but who has never really believed in the war, into a serious and devoted soldier who ultimately takes positive action in the name of the war. These changes are effected through such a complete reversal of the impression the two men have previously made as characters that, by the end of the novel, they have left their humanity far behind and taken on the attributes of beatific emissaries.

The charge that Shaw had to go against the inner logic of his material in order to make his point is even more justified when we notice how forced and one-dimensional the concluding section of the novel seems. By now Shaw has put aside all pretense of credibility and concentrated his full energies on the final sermon which ties the novel into a nice neat package. The unit to which Ackerman and Whitacre belong arrives at a Nazi concentration camp a moment after the prisoners have rebelled against their guards and overthrown them. As order is being restored in the camp, one of the prisoners, a Jewish rabbi, approaches the American commander, Captain Green, and asks permission to conduct a Jewish religious service in the camp yard. Over the objections of an Albanian fascist who is conveniently present, Captain Green, who like Whitacre has up to now shown little sign of moral courage, replies as follows:

> "I am going to guarantee that you will hold your services in one hour in the square down there. I am also going to guarantee that there will be machine guns set on the roof of this building. And I will further guarantee that anybody who attempts to interfere with your services will be fired on by those machine guns." He turned to the Albanian. "And, finally, I guarantee," he said, "that if you ever try to come into this room again you will be locked up. That is all."

At this point it would seem that there could be nothing further left to do but bring up the music and flash on the coming attractions. But a few moments later, as Ackerman and Whitacre are walking on the road outside the camp, Ackerman strikes the final resounding chord. "The human beings are going to run the world!" he shouts. "The human beings! There's a lot of Captain Greens! He's not extraordinary! There're millions of them!" And it is of course at this instant, with the words still echoing in the sun-tipped treetops, that Diestl's shots ring out with a truly fiendish irony and Ackerman falls mortally wounded to the ground.

The indictment to which the *New Yorker* overtones and the manufactured parallels gave condemning testimony comes completely clear in these closing pages. What Mailer and Burns could not honestly affirm without distorting the inner truth of their material and, therefore, did not affirm, Shaw affirms through deliberate distortion and contrivance. The result is not a novel in the true sense but a piece of propaganda designed to give us not a man but a social problem, not an action drawn from life but a pseudo action drawn from Shaw's vast concern for the suffering of the Jewish race. The honesty and intensity of his concern is not our concern, nor is the social importance of the problem with which his book attempts to deal. Our concern must be with the honesty and intensity of his work in so far as it represents a literary achievement, and it is on these terms that his book is a failure.

It is to be hoped that the problems of race will eventually be treated successfully in a literary work of the first rank. If they are, they will be treated as human problems, and the dramatic situation through which they will be discovered will be a natural outgrowth of human emotions and not of forced polemics journalistically presented.[1]

Notes

1. Joyce's treatment of Leopold Bloom in *Ulysses* and Hemingway's treatment of Robert Cohn in *The Sun Also Rises* are, in my opinion, the most successful portraits of the Jew to be found in modern literature. Bloom and Cohn are convincing precisely because they are presented as human beings caught up in a concrete human dilemma and not merely as Jews reacting only when the forces of discrimination are in play.

WILFRID SHEED

1930–

Wilfrid Sheed was born on December 27, 1930, in London, the son of Frank Sheed and Maisie Ward, Roman Catholic publishers, writers, and activists. Maisie Ward was British, her husband Australian. Frank Sheed and Maisie Ward had established the avant-garde Catholic publishing house Sheed & Ward in London in 1926 and opened an American branch in New York City in 1933; Wilfrid and his older sister were thus raised for a time on both sides of the Atlantic. Young Sheed was educated at Downside Abbey in England and at schools in New Jersey and Pennsylvania.

An attack of polio at the age of fourteen prevented Sheed's further participation in athletics and turned his interest toward books, and he read widely in both English and American literature. He has described his resulting style as "Thurber . . . with a Wodehouse veneer." Sheed received a B.A. in history from Lincoln College, Oxford, in 1954 and a master's degree three years later. He then went to live with relatives in Australia for several years before settling in the United States to live and work.

Sheed became a free-lance journalist, writing for a number of periodicals, including *Life* and *The New York Times Magazine*. He worked as a movie critic for the Catholic magazine *Jubilee* (1959–61) and for *Esquire* (1967–69), and also wrote drama criticism for *Commonweal*. In the 1970s he wrote a column, "The Good Word," for *The New York Times Book Review*.

Sheed's first novel, *A Middle Class Education*, was published in 1960. It was followed by *The Hack* (1963) and *Square's Progress* (1965). Sheed's other novels include *Office Politics* (1966), *Max Jamison* (1970), *People Will Always Be Kind* (1973), and *Transatlantic Blues* (1978). Two long stories were published in a single volume, *The Blacking Factory and Pennsylvania Gothic*, in 1968. Sheed has also written biographies of Muhammad Ali, Clare Boothe Luce, and his parents. Other nonfiction works include collections of his reviews, columns, and essays.

Sheed, married and the father of three children, lives in Sag Harbor, Long Island.

A Middle Class Education, by Wilfrid Sheed, (is) a comedy with an academic background. England and America are inextricably intertwined in Mr. Sheed's biography, but as a writer he belongs squarely in the tradition of Kingsley Amis. His book centers on three middle-class Englishmen in their last year at Oxford, where they swill beer, make a great show of idleness, embroider the myths of their depravity, and regale themselves with stanchless facetiousness. Through them and around them, Mr. Sheed has painted a fine, ironic picture of the new Oxford created by the social revolution and of its new breed of undergraduates.

The first half of the novel is extremely funny. When the hero, John Chote, goes to New York on a fellowship and becomes involved with an American glamour girl, the author's form weakens, and his ending doesn't recapture the brio he displayed earlier. The trouble is that 425 pages is an awfully long stretch on which to sustain undergraduate comedy; pruned of a hundred pages, the novel might well have been an unqualified success. As it stands, the book shows comic gifts of a high order—a keen sense of the bogus and a derisive gaiety, backed by an ear for dialogue and a general command of language which are really first rate.—CHARLES ROLO, *At*, Feb. 1961, p. 112

Wilfrid Sheed writes wryly intelligent novels about frauds—men who are terribly "sane" in a dreadful way, men who back away from their feelings and flee sincerity like a plague, who take care that their self-confrontations are always partial and ironical. His first novel, *A Middle Class Education*, told the story of John Chote, one of those *déraciné*, up-from-the-lower-middle-class Englishmen who get into Oxford, major in glibness, and then don't quite know how gainfully to employ their expensively acquired snottiness. It was full of good needed observations; of Oxford undergraduates, for instance, he wrote: "Behind the dense smog of jesting they could be huskily modest in the best English tradition, and painstakingly unaccomplished." Mr. Sheed's honorable aspiration is to write in the tradition of the English novel of social comedy.

His new book, *The Hack*, recounts the nervous and moral breakdown of Bertram Flax, "a leading spiritual hack" who makes his suburban living writing "pious rubbish" for American Catholic journals with names like *The Tiny Messenger*. Bert is a pro: "He could look at the gray snow . . . and write about white snow; look at the jagged wastes and write about downy blankets. That was what professionalism meant." But as the Christmas season gets under way, everything starts to go wrong. He feels himself invaded by a cancerous boredom; his faith wobbles. Doubts erupt fitfully as blasphemies. The magazines he counts on to support his large family begin rejecting his stuff. On Christmas Day he finally collapses into a state of inertia and silence.

The first of the novel's ironies makes its appearance as the panicky journalist spills his "negative thoughts" in the confes-

sional: the priest advises him to look up a piece by Bert Flax. Next, the priest-editor of *The Passenger* rejects an article by this man who has made his living off the meretriciousness of American Catholic popular culture, and who has himself contributed fulsomely to that culture, on the grounds that the piece is insufficiently "sincere."

Now the ironies pelt down thick and fast. It turns out that Father Chubb, the apparently bovine editor who has printed Bert's "gush" for years, has all along despised him for his "grammar-school level" grasp of the faith and for his "simony." Bert's blasphemies send his old school pal Gilhouley, a Morningside Heights lapsed Catholic, back to the Church. Gilhouley's reconversion in turn infuriates Bert, speeding his disintegration. And finally, it is hinted that Bert's collapse will itself precipitate the conversion of his Protestant wife to a Catholicism far more honest than his own has ever been. As Mr. Sheed might say: ah there, Graham Greene!

The real central figure—the villain—of *The Hack* is popular American Catholicism at its dead-level commonest: smarmy, mindless, vulgar and hollow. Mr. Sheed loathes it, both morally (it is dishonest) and esthetically (it is ugly), as any intelligent, sensitive Catholic must. Unfortunately Mr. Sheed's angry clarity of conviction issues as fictional cloudiness. Too many of the characters' lines are too obviously his own. Too many intentions are blurry. What is Bert Flax's attitude toward his hack work? Sometimes it seems that, until his faith became shaky, he believed that his writing was quite decent, the expression of moments of genuine religious inspiration. This makes him a goodhearted dope. At other points it seems that Flax is a pretty acute fellow who has always judged his own prose accurately but has justified it pragmatically. It is hard to believe that a man who could write the following, could also have unself-critically churned out inanities for years:

"Propositions:

"(1) Intellect. All right, if you happen to be called St. Thomas. Otherwise, better leave it alone.

"(2) Emotion. Very, very bad. Untrustworthy—unless you happen to be somebody's dear old Irish grandmother, in which case your emotions are worth a hundred eminent theologians laid end to end.

"(3) Will. Very, very good. But wait a minute, not the way you think. Not Nietzschean will, not willful will, good heavens no. The will to submit is the ticket, to obey, to avoid bad movies . . ."

Again, take Flax's wife Betty. Now she is represented as having, at least for a while, thought her husband's writing quite good. Now she is shown as thinking herself inadequate to judge it. And now, in an improbable dialogue with a priest-editor, she is revealed as having known all along that Bert's work was "late Victorian junk."

What spoils *The Hack* is Mr. Sheed's insufficiently controlled desire to belabor the execrable. Look, he says, at this "good," "sane" man, Bert Flax: this pillar of the Church is a blasphemer of sacred things, he sullies the Church by making of God a four-cents-a-word commodity, he sullies his own emotions by pretending to more faith than he has. Mr. Sheed pounds away at that in American Catholicism which would accept shoddy work and thought because, falsely, the shoddy is believed to "do good." Bert Flax (lax, flaccid Catholicism) is pummeled altogether too much, by his wife, by Father Chubb, by the author. Toward the end, *The Hack* becomes more and more a sermon, with Mr. and Mrs. Flax, the mother-in-law, the priest, all helping deliver it. Like many crusaders in good cause, Mr. Sheed is loath to let others speak to any point but his own.

As noted before, Mr. Sheed is ambitious to join the ranks of those who carry on the great heritage of the English comic novel. Now that *The Hack* is off his chest, perhaps he will keep his characters on less tight a rein. Mr. Sheed is an eminently reasonable novelist, but a too-insistent reasonableness can be, in art, a hobbling caution. The writer can turn ventriloquist. Or too much can be assigned to overt comment and explanation. Huxley, Waugh, Amis, in their hilarious ways, Powell and Henry Green in quieter ways, all know how to release the magic, suddenly expanding bubble of pure comedy: the bubble bursts in a joyous explosion of the preposterous, the outrageous, the mad. Nothing fatigues like the "funny" book unless, at some point, the contraption soars.

Mr. Sheed has excellent equipment for the part he wishes to fill—intelligence, observation, wit. So one makes a quite unreasonable demand on him: please write us an unreasonably funny book.—WILLIAM ESTY, "The Decline and Fall of Bert Flax, Self-Deceiver," *Com*, Nov. 22, 1963, pp. 260–61

Wilfrid Sheed is a writer in transition, but he is not a writer fumbling for a new voice. The distinction is important. Mr. Sheed seems to know precisely where he is going and what he is doing. He has moved from the deliciously brittle satire of the opening chapters of *Office Politics* toward a fiction which, while the dazzle remains, has gained measurably in depth and subtlety. Some of this new depth can also be seen in his relatively recent novelettes, *Pennsylvania Gothic* and *The Blacking Factory*, though in the latter Mr. Sheed is guilty of uncharacteristic didacticism.

Max Jamison combines the world of *Office Politics* with the mood of *The Blacking Factory*, and draws together thematic elements of both. It is also Mr. Sheed's best book. It is funny, sad, tough, compassionate; its title character is realized in every nuance of personality; and the writing is splendid.

The world of *Max Jamison*, the New York literary world, is one Mr. Sheed himself moves through with epic virtuosity, yet he views it dispassionately as a tony warren in which you "consort only with delicate replicas of yourself." He probes through its facade of arrogant provincialism and exposes the insecurities and inadequacies beneath. Ultimately, as in *Office Politics*, the mood of the novel is dark.

Max Jamison is a literary lion, theater reviewer for the mass-circulation magazine *Now* and movie critic for the little magazine *Rearview*. He is fawned over by academics and suburban housewives, he beds nubile coeds and still-ripe divorcees. He is both self-aware (mocking the "slatternly metaphors" that creep into his *Now* reviews) and self-deceiving. He is a "son of a bitch in an imperfect world," a man for whom one can easily acquire an intense dislike. He treats people with random cruelty, forever holding them up to judgment and, invariably, scorn: "My husband," his wife observes during a period of separation, "was like a courtroom that was always in session." He is constantly performing,

sending hostesses swooning and grad students twittering in order to feed his ravenous ego. He bleats in self-pity over being removed from his young sons, yet when he sees them he cannot bend to them. He treats his women, his wife as well as his casual bedmates, with approximately the respect one accords toilets and other instruments of physical relief.

It is Mr. Sheed's achievement that Max Jamison is nonetheless a curiously admirable character for whom, in the end, one grieves. His pomposity is maddening, but in his insistence upon "standards" there is an old-fashioned deference to tradition which one must honor; he is a man of genuine if dubiously exercised integrity. For all his stiffness, his infuriating withdrawal from the turmoil and pain of life, he inspires sadness and sympathy. Nearing middle age, he is at that terrible moment in life when his failure dawns upon him— failure as husband, though his marriage survives for reasons having nothing to do with love, failure as a father, failure as *man*. He becomes obsessively defensive about his work for *Now* (in furious italics he cries out, "*It is brainless snobbery to think that working for a news magazine is automatically a sellout*") and his creative energies finally expire in a tired burst of self-pity.

Mr. Sheed explores his themes, mostly domestic, small and large at the same time, with skill and compassion. In his fiction the institution of family becomes a trap where, seeking protection, people find hurt. Parents hurt children, children hurt parents, parents hurt each other. Mr. Sheed understands the accommodations marriage demands and the pressures it builds up; one which stands out in *Max Jamison* is the aggressiveness of wives who make their husbands' careers their own: ". . . she had in her Midwestern bones this belief in motion. No matter how good it was where you were, you must keep going: . . . onward and upward, onward *was* upward, something new to tell people every season." Yet his impatience with pushy wives is tempered by his acknowledgment of the anguish to which indifferent and condescending husbands subject them. There are no villains in his work, merely people hurting and being hurt, trying to find an honorable way to get through life.

The focus of Mr. Sheed's work is narrow, concentrating on small worlds and delicate scenes. In some respects he is heir to the tradition of Marquand (Max Jamison and Allen Southby rather resemble each other), but he is moving that tradition into new and perhaps more complex patterns. Even at his darkest, he is a joy to read. His wit and perceptiveness are marvelous; he is a literary Buddy Rich, tossing off brilliant rimshots with offhand abandon. It is a measure of his achievement that we only rarely feel that the glitter is for its own sake.—JONATHAN YARDLEY, "Literary Lion," *NR*, May 23, 1970, pp. 27, 30

The chances are that it has already been said, and by Wilfrid Sheed himself. Whatever words you have found for his work he already has rejected, before moving on to words yet more apt. He turns your condescensions back on you before they have a chance to apply. He surrounds them with an irony that reveals what you left out. The condescensions of his essay "The Minor Novelist" are surrounded by the irony of his having written six "minor" novels himself: "At his best moments, he thinks of himself as the last of the old-fashioned craftsmen, turning out water clocks or filigreed sleeve garters." ⟨. . .⟩

At first glance the irony in Sheed's new novel ⟨*People Will Always Be Kind*⟩ seems to flow outward toward its author's life and toward recent public events. In the first part of the novel we read how Brian Casey—athletic, just past puberty—is stricken with polio. Thereafter, "Brian's legs were a wasteland where no life would stir again." In the second part we read an account by Sam Perkins, speech writer, Ivy-league smartie and civil-rights activist, of Senator Brian Casey's campaign for the Democratic party's Presidential nomination.

Sheed has already written how in his own athletic adolescence he was stricken with polio. And he has also written how he traveled with Eugene McCarthy making speeches during the Senator's campaign for the Democratic nomination. But Casey, Sheed and McCarthy are not alike, except in their Irishness, their "*Commonweal*-Catholicism," and their compulsive wittiness. Casey's character, background and career are different from Sheed's. Casey is not much like McCarthy either. For one thing, Casey is an interesting man. Nor does he sulk, or misquote Tacitus, or hanker after the esteem of poets. Clearly Sheed has used his own experiences as the material for the filligree, but the design is one devised for the occasion. And Brian Casey's character is precisely the church, so to speak, that we have to reconstruct from the very finely-rendered detail of the design. As it turns out, there is more to him than the mind's eye can see at any one time.

His unlucky parents, at any rate, see both more and less of him than is there. Their extraordinary love for him, combined with their ordinary human limitations, has a bad effect on his character and a worse effect on their own. His mother, "dripping love," encourages him to believe in a miracle cure and blackmails his father into pretending to believe in one too. Within one year the effect of this deception on the family makes his father a secret drinker who finds "becoming an extremely old man an excellent solution." Religious Aunt Bridget touts St. Jude, patron of lost causes—"not that your cause is lost, by any means. And here is St. Dismas, the good thief. He's always handy." Antireligious Aunt Portia touts Dr. Steinmetz, expert in the healing properties of leeches and elk sperm.

Casey's experiences with women are funny and sad too. He comes to associate sexually aroused women with spitting rage and cries of pain. His experience in general teaches him how to spit or cry for effect. It gives him a mind superconscious of its own activity but still incapable of preventing the deceptions and self-deceptions it hates itself for practicing. Campus politics at Columbia University teach him in what profession he can best deploy his rage, pain and deceptions to use friends and influence poeple: "There is no truth about politicians, only versions."

In the second half of the novel, set some twenty years later (that is, only yesterday), Sam Perkins tells us how he joins Brian Casey's political staff for a campaign that is much like McCarthy's up to the nominating convention and like McGovern's thereafter. Its jukes and reverses are a lesson in practical politics for Perkins and for us. Comapred to what the hardened old pros will do for patronage and compared to what young idealists like Perkins will do to advance their ideals, Casey's cynicism begins to look something like integrity. In the context of American politics, we gather, sincerity and truth only serve the purposes of self-indulgence and deceit. If there is a moral to be drawn from such paradoxes, Sheed, thank God, doesn't draw it.

Unless there is a moral in the fact that cynicism about all interests, including his own, allows Casey transcendent moments of disinterest, although he is cynical about that too. When the idealists on his staff want him to give a platform speech devious in behalf of principle, he is instead deviously principled—but to better effect than if he had been only principled (or only devious). He wins the nomination, with

admiration from the pros for his deviousness and from the idealists for his principles. His success only deepens his cynicism. Sheed's narration of all this is amazing for its savvy, verve, toughness and economy, for its avoidance of either maudlin pessimism or hard-headed gullibility.

It is also amazing for the tact with which it suggests, without debouching into a fictionalized autobiography or roman à clef, that Casey's polio is a type of the wound that drives people to seek mastery over their worlds by writing novels, say, or by seeking political office. "Was this same embittered cripple compensating with crazy power drives? Or was he a wise man matured with pain? You be the judge," says Casey. A proper judgment would include both alternatives or would suspend itself, along with the sentence.

Sam Perkins, an improper judge, chooses only one. His verdict on Casey is that "seeing people on his knees is all that he asks of life, the rest is spinach." But after Casey wins the nomination, he loses the election in part out of a will to defeat that nicely balances his will to mastery. Similarly, his desire to punish his family, his friends, his women, his God and the world, is nicely balanced by a desire to be punished by them— just because of his own desire to punish. Casey, as Perkins notes, "had a closetful of minds."

The detail-work in Sheed's account of the process by which Casey's contrary wills and many minds are formed is only one of this novel's pleasures. The inside dope on the dealing of politicians and on the sordid highs of campaigning gives the reader another pleasure—the kind that has always addicted readers to the novels of major as well as minor old-fashioned craftsmen. The prose, the pace, the humor are pleasures neither old-fashioned nor new-fangled, but simply unique to Sheed's writing. So is a certain quality of moral intelligence, one graced by an unflappable and chastened sanity, a charity precise and unsentimental.

Robert Graves, who has been called a minor poet for over 50 years now, once pointed out that the distinction between major and minor writers tells us less than the distinction between good and bad ones. *People Will Always Be Kind* is a very good novel by a very good novelist.—GEORGE STADE, *NYTBR*, April 8, 1973, pp. 1–2

Pendrid Chatworth, or, as he is renamed in real TV life, Monty Chatworth, is a bit of a devil. As a much-praised, triple-Emmy-award-winning spellbinder in both England and the U.S. he has had plenty of scope for working at the seven deadly sins. Not much Sloth, perhaps, but lots of Pride. He has made his name as the Thinking Man, Mr. Literacy, "the conscience of television," in that Frosty-Cavetty world of "one-inch foreheads where the two-inch forehead is king," and some of the time he is ashamed about it. So in the marvelous drunken opening chapter of this excellent novel ⟨*Transatlantic Blues*⟩ we meet him staggering about the first-class cabin of a New York-London jet clamoring for a confessor. Nobody wants the job so he turns on Father Sony, his tape-recorder. Most of the book, then, is a series of dramatized monologues, Chatworth in mid-life and mid-Atlantic, singing and recording his look-back blues.

Like his creator, Chatworth is the child of two cultures. He has left England at 12, during the War, for a Catholic prep school in New Jersey, returned to England at 16 to have an "education" quickly crammed into him, then back to the States for a year of Catholic college, and back again to Oxford for three years. Faced with postwar life in Old England he opts for America, becomes a West Coast disk-jockey, gets into TV, and is now in the jet-set big-time. His constant transatlantic jettings are a speeded-up version of what his nomad life has been since childhood.

This life has made him a permanent exile, given him full-time foreignness. And he has made his career of it by exploiting a sort of reverse chameleon effect; "the moment he stepped off the plane he became the country he had left." He is now a fully corrupt success; but there has been a "bloody apprenticeship," as a naive super-English schoolboy among hostile little Irish-Americans, a child gently terrorized into mimicry of his hosts, as a strident American adolescent awkwardly using his new talent amid the "aching, grinding flippancies" of the upper-class London young, and as a multi-voiced opportunist playing variations on each national role before an audience of bored Oxford undergraduates. A quick study, with a "passion for assimilation," he learns two languages and two cultures as fast and as superficially as he crams himself into Oxford. He becomes in fact a perfect candidate for a Transatlantic TV career, a career based on the deceptions of his voice. This voice business, with its compromises and velleities, is a symbolic as well as real version ("my voice is my confession") of all the other human deceptions and betrayals that lie heavily on his soul and are the main subject of his story.

Chatworth's voice, shrewd, sardonic, reductive—he is on to himself and on to everybody else—presents the Anglo-American scene, and particularly the Catholic scene, afresh. With that education, and stemming as he does from an upright father whose ancient family is stately-homed English Catholic and from an O'Grady mother who is sister under the skin to Catholic Dublin his viewpoint is sharply idiosyncratic. Class plays its usual murky role, and Chatworth's voice reaches new levels of satirical irony as he confronts and rings the changes on all the traps of American anglophilia and anglophobia, of English pro- and anti-Americanism. The voice gets sharper still as yet another excruciating Catholic struggle with sex is rehearsed. Cheerfuller comedy comes in his account of self-prostitution for the media. Chatsworth is too "vibrantly superficial" to engage in the trapped masochisms of a Mauriac or Greene protagonist; he is too buoyant for the sin of Despair. Yet the poles of his confession are self-hatred ("I satirize myself, a Catholic vice"), and self-esteem (once starved, but now well-fed by his audiences), and it becomes clear as his brilliant nervous gabble goes on that a more or less desperate search for a self is involved (as elsewhere in Sheed) with a real fear that once the onion is peeled away there will be nothing left.

For these are exercises in contrition as well as confession. Chatworth does not want psychiatrist couch stuff; sin is real. It is not only that, with his carefree TV specials on the world's trouble spots, he has publicly sinned against sincerity and authenticity. These true confessions provide a history of crushing private failures as well: failing his father and sister at crucial moments in their lives for example, or dishonestly wielding his thin Catholicism as a twisted weapon against his disturbingly honest lover (a brilliant chapter of dark comedy tells that story), and of course, failing himself, notably in relation to his father, who quietly dominates his conscience with his distant challenge of love. All these are failures of love, and a great success in this novel is the balanced way in which sympathies are involved; lover, wife, sister and father have their exploitative failings too.

But wit is the general solvent. Chatworth's ultimate ironic blasphemy, for instance, is to use his light Catholic training, his "spiritual insights" to get ahead in his TV shows, becoming a kind of public father confessor: "That was sort of like going

to confession" gushes a prominent actress, after one of his "probing" interviews. Wit is never set adrift from feeling, though. In the most poignant moments it still controls feeling. I think here of Kingsley Amis, who from the English end, in *I Want It Now* (about a TV personality) and in *One Fat Englishman* (about transatlantic encounters) has profitably explored somewhat similar territory. Amis also uses satirical wit to explore feeling. Yet (and there is a large issue here about secular and nonsecular habits of mind) at the crucial moment he is likely to lower the cruel sword and let sentiment in. Sheed never lets this happen. The insistent hardmouthed control ("When the M.C. called me a wit with a heart, I broke into that silly grin again and it wouldn't go away") only underlines the novel's seriousness of purpose.

The last chapters make the point. As he completes his tapes Chatworth knows that, at the height of his success, he is on the brink of decline; in twenty years time he will be "a trivia question; and then if I still haven't taken the hint and died, nothing at all." The novel ends in serious black comedy. On a sort of private secular retreat in New Jersey he plays all his tapes to a young ex-nun, a visiting journalist. Baring his soul to her he also bares his body and in a climactic passage, with Father Sony still working away, with his dead father (expert in primal scenes) there in spirit, and perhaps his quick-witted sister hinted at in Sister Veronica, a Mailer-ish procreation takes place. With whiffs of incense and incest wafting around Chatworth is reborn and reconciled. Or to use a more restrained Catholic formula, he has made a good confession. More than that, he has accepted the necessary penance of paternity and matrimony, absolution is at hand; he is in some sort of state of grace, "until" as his last words inexorably remind us, "the next time."—Bernard McCabe, "Bless Me, Father . . .," *Com*, April 14, 1978, pp. 248–49

SUSAN LARDNER
"Sheed's Tub"

New Yorker, November 30, 1968, pp. 234–42

Wilfrid Sheed is a resourceful and ubiquitous phrasemaker, who writes reviews of movies and books for magazines, and fiction in which he examines the increase in man's circumspection between youth and c. age thirty-eight. (By "fiction," an imposing term, I just mean his latest book, *The Blacking Factory & Pennsylvania Gothic*, published by Farrar, Straus & Giroux, and his next-to-latest, *Office Politics*—not three earlier novels, which I haven't read.) Both as critic and as novelist, Sheed works in the derogatory tradition of Samuel Butler and Diogenes the Cynic, with the difference that by now the world has grown accustomed to the scorn of its critics, having been browbeaten ever since Diogenes demonstrated his moral superiority to the Athenians by moving into a tub. Sheed's style matches the resilience of his public. His tone is genial rather than polemical or surly, and he attacks with clever phrases free of indignation or contempt. His pleasure with his own talent is always evident.

Office Politics, undoubtedly inspired by professional experience, is an accurate and entertaining representation of the parochialism that afflicts magazine office life, probably even at *Ramparts* and *Family Circle*. The subject is a struggle for power over a small magazine of liberal opinion called *The Outsider*, founded in passion but reduced to a stylized sop for twenty-one thousand senescent readers, who reflect a similar trend among the staff. The man with the power, whatever it's worth, is Gilbert Twining, imported to New York seven years back from England, where he ran *The Watchman*, the same kind of publication. Brian Fine and Fritz Tyler, uninspired typewriter liberals, and the business and advertising managers, Olga Marplate and Philo Sonnabend, slug it out while Twining lies in bed recovering from a heart attack suffered on a fund-raising trip to California. George Wren, a man who has lately abandoned a sellout job at C.B.S. for the chance to be an ill-paid *Outsider* editor, stands hesitantly at the edge of the battle, longing to find intellectual companionship and recover his youthful ideals. The others involved are Mrs. Wren and Mrs. Twining, Waldo Funk, the fusty drama critic, and Harriet Wadsworth, a financial backer of *Outsider*, who has her eye on Funk's job. The questions that are raised in the course of their quarrels pertain as much to their own seedy condition as to that of the magazine. Is *Outsider* really "a potentially valuable magazine," as Tyler suggests? Is it Twining's fault that the members of his staff feel limited and mediocre, that Tyler isn't the radical he used to be, that Brian Fine appears to be an inveterate hack? What is it that happens to fiery young men and crusading periodicals? Speaking around and through his characters with incessant irony, Sheed exposes them as victims of an intractable and unheroic obsession. He implies that, like most people, they don't have the energy to climb out of the rut or enough talent to make an escape worthwhile—not even Twining.

The story of the rebellion against Twining is mainly developed through facetious interior monologues in which the voices of Wren, Fine, and Tyler are distinguishable from Twining's only because they use faintly archaic Americanisms like "for Pete's sake," "shot to hell," "bushwa," "nut," "goofy," and "yeah, sure." As an Englishman, Twining naturally scores higher with "lads," "chaps," "bloody," "frightful," and "packing cases" (for "crates"). Sometimes the Yankees find themselves talking exactly like Twining, whose style is hard to separate from Sheed's.

Just as the issues of *Outsider* that the staff puts out during Twining's absence all become typical, the confrontations between characters that are provoked by turns in the plot become flights of uniform wit. Wren is posed as a man somewhat younger than his colleagues, and as an occasional poet and a man with a sense of humor, but his doubts about the proper attitude toward *Outsider* and Twining are too artfully expressed to break the surface of Sheed's prose. Wren's ambivalence is no more effective against the monotony than the fact that Twining is British or Olga Marplate rich or Harriet Wadsworth stupid or Philo Sonnabend a secret right-winger; his politics have as much to do with what happens as Wren's poetry, which isn't quoted. The sincerest speculation always comes to a witty dead end:

> [Twining] was frowning slightly over the layout dummy. Why he bothered to frown was hard to say, since the magazine looked exactly the same every time around. Was this the fault of Twining or was it an institutional problem? Could the magazine be reawakened by a kiss from a charming young editor?

The most interesting thing about the book is the opportunity it offers to judge the merits of particular conceits. I liked "two bottle-shaped men" and "snip short this skein of unraveling brain" better than "his slightly distended stomach recoiled from the hot water" or any of Twining's pithy generalizations about American character. How about "his face was zoned like a weather map, with angry depressions around the

eyes, c'mon fellows, at the mouth, indecision streaking the middle"? No. How about "little niggling things to trip him, slow him, send him sprawling over his deadline"? Maybe. "Polly Twining lay on one elbow, with her nightgown pouting around her thighs"? Definitely not.

The Blacking Factory and *Pennsylvania Gothic*, the components of Sheed's new book, are labelled "a short novel and a long story," but however a story and a novel are defined, it isn't a distinction worth making in this case. The two stories are nearly identical in form, each narrowly focussed on a tempestuous period during the adolescence of a more or less well-adjusted man in his late thirties. Both men are briefly portrayed—one in a prologue and the other in natural sequence. *The Blacking Factory*, the longer piece, is a more realistic version of a youthful crackup than *Pennsylvania Gothic*, which has a supernatural aspect, as the title indicates. Both stories are set in the forties—a fact that Sheed establishes with allusions to the war (II) and certain radio programs (Gabriel Heatter) rather than by manners of speaking or more intricate topical references. The characters, like the real-estate man cashing in on the "postwar boom" in *The Blacking Factory*, are not peculiar to that era.

The main character of *Pennsylvania Gothic* is Charles Trimble, who lives with his unhappy mother and father (a lawyer) in a gloomy house in a desolate suburb of Philadelphia. He falls prey, at the age of twelve, to fantasies of suicide and murder, which he shares in a mystical way with Miss Skinner, the old lady next door. Charlie is apparently freed from his nightmares when Miss Skinner dies, and he grows up to be a contented history professor with a psychoanalyst and a fiancée. Sheed raises the possibility that a nostalgic return by Charlie to the scene of his childhood might reopen the "crack in his brain," but he raises it skeptically, if I read him right.

In *The Blacking Factory*, James Bannister succumbs to his fantasy instead of losing or suppressing it, and his adult lot is more precarious. The story is a direct analogy with an anecdote Sheed uses to introduce both stories:

> When Charles Dickens was twelve years old, he was abruptly removed from school and put to work in a blacking factory. The effect of this episode was such that he mentioned it to no one for twenty years and only broke down when somebody recognized him from those days. . . . In his subsequent account, Dickens wrote: "I have no idea how long it lasted; whether for a year or much more or less." In fact, it lasted for less than six months.

Sheed's protagonist is suddenly dispatched, when he is fifteen, from New York to a British public school. He creates idyllic visions of America and England out of his longing to feel at home in one place or the other, and when both visions are shattered he breaks down completely. Grown up, he is shown to have become a militant patriot, broadcasting his mended American dream from his own radio stations in southern California, maybe about to enter politics. Sheed leaves him there, at a moment that ought to be the midpoint of a "long novel." *The Blacking Factory* is a more interesting story than the others, and Sheed tells it well by keeping it simple, although, like *Pennsylvania Gothic*, it could have been better told with a clearer difference between the narrator's choice of words and those of his less sophisticated hero.

The opening sentence of *Pennsylvania Gothic* contains the phrase "bad scene"—a nineteen-sixties formation apparently attributed to the inner thoughts of a 1941 boy. Later on in that train of thought, "jerky" and "lousy" occur, with greater chronological propriety, and yet "lousy" is part of a sentence in which Sheed's voice is obviously competing with Charlie's— an awkward effect: "The Walton debacle started off a chain of feeling lousy that lasted through the rest of the long day." And the metaphor is lousy. Notwithstanding Sheed's "mastery of the subtleties of the English language," advertised on the book jacket, he is not particularly careful in these two stories about the words he uses to express the feelings of his characters, and he frequently errs in favor of his native whimsey, as at the end of this speculative line: "He found himself for now just behind the headmaster, who was trudging up the slight incline to the dressing rooms and who looked unusually vulnerable in a pair of baggy tennis shorts. . . . A slingshot aimed at the left calf would produce the most endearing little dance." The habitual jocularity that led Sheed to pin a phrase like "most endearing little dance" on Jimmy Bannister must also account for his use, speaking for himself, of the word "eventuated"—the worst way of saying "took place"—not to mention circumlocutions like "a certain languor beyond the usual" and "the second bad condition came into effect," and the Sheedian adverb "squelchingly."

As a third-person narrator, Sheed is entitled to exaggerate the interior eloquence of Trimble and Bannister, but the license doesn't cover his practice of planting farfetched words and images in their heads. The odds are that an uprooted American teen-ager would not be struck by the resemblance between the layout of a cricket pitch and the appearance of stomachs recently operated on, or between his fellow-students and "a school of small bank managers," and it is hard to detect the special fitness of the Biblical echo in a comparison of sunburned shoulder blades with "pillars of fire."

Exerting his good-humored irony at every chance, Sheed dulls his point about the conventional ways in which Trimble and Bannister ultimately deal with their nightmares by disparaging their immediate anguish. Even in *Office Politics*, in which the facetious style is most appropriate, futility is so efficiently implied that the perfunctory plot loses its edge. Twice, in *Pennsylvania Gothic*, the association of images is so grotesque that it may be accidental. First, in an account of the death of Charlie's father:

> Mr. Trimble was technically a Catholic but had broken with the Church by killing himself. (By *drowning*, Charlie was relieved to hear.) Father Devlin came out from Philadelphia to explain the difficulties to Mrs. Trimble and she passed them on, in *watered* form, to Charlie.

Then, standing by Miss Skinner's deathbed holding a carving knife, struggling with the idea of stabbing her, Charlie is given this thought: "Her point about being dead in a few hours cut no mustard with him."

The most puzzling feature of Sheed's style, considering his treatment in both *Office Politics* and *The Blacking Factory* of Anglo-American differences from an American point of view, is a British accent—the result of his tendency to offer words as though he were holding them in a pair of tweezers. Maybe, like Bannister, whose faint British accent is a mystery to his California associates, Sheed is a man with a shameful un-American past.

SAM SHEPARD

1943–

Sam Shepard was born on November 5, 1943, in Fort Sheridan, Illinois, to Samuel Shepard Rogers and Jane Schook Rogers. The first twelve years of his life were spent at a number of different army bases; the family eventually settled in California in 1955. Shepard was active in theatre from an early age; in 1962 he joined the Bishop's Company Repertory Players and toured the country.

Shepard moved to New York in 1963, and his first plays, *Cowboys* and *The Rock Garden*, were produced the next year. He had five plays staged in 1965, setting the pace for his subsequent career; he is a prolific playwright. He began to receive a significant amount of attention in Off-Broadway theatre circles, and in 1967 two of his plays (*Melodrama Play* and *Forensic and the Navigators*) won Obie awards. Plays such as *The Unseen Hand* (1969) and *Operation Sidewinder* (1970) began to attract notice from mainstream critics as well. During this period Shepard began working in film, co-writing the script for Michelangelo Antonioni's *Zabriskie Point* and appearing in *Brand X* (both 1970).

Shepard, his wife O-Lan, and their son Jesse moved to London in 1971, and his plays began to be produced on the London stage; particularly notable are *The Tooth of Crime* (1972), *The Geography of a Horse Dreamer* (1974), and *Action* (1974). *The Tooth of Crime* and *Action* won their author two more Obie awards.

In 1974 Shepard and his family returned to the United States, settling in California, where they still live. His career has continued to build at an astonishing rate, both as a playwright and as an actor. *Curse of the Starving Class* (1977), *Buried Child* (1978), and *Fool for Love* (1983) all won Obie awards, *Fool for Love* winning four; *Buried Child* earned Shepard the Pulitzer Prize as well. He has appeared in several major films, and was nominated for an Academy Award in the Best Supporting Actor category for his performance as test pilot Chuck Yeager in *The Right Stuff* (1983). He also wrote the screenplay for Wim Wender's award-winning film *Paris, Texas* (1984). In addition to his published plays Shepard has written a book of poetry, *Hawk Moon* (1973); an account of a

Bob Dylan tour, *The Rolling Thunder Logbook* (1977); and a collection of prose, *Motel Chronicles* (1982).

Shepard's work is particularly noted for his vivid characterization and attention to detail; though he generally deals with such universal themes as love, loss, and emotional conflict, his work avoids the melodramatic. Few living playwrights have been as successful as Shepard at capturing the attention of the public and the critics.

I was riveted, troubled and in a way tormented by Sam Shepard's two new one-act plays, *Killer's Head* and *Action* (American Place Theatre). That is probably what Shepard wanted. As much as the play, the struggle within myself requires explanation.

In the very brief opening play, *Killer's Head*, a murderer about to be electrocuted speaks his inner thoughts. These consist of his persistent enthusiasm for race horses and motorcars. It is the drama (if it is drama) of nullity.

The second play, *Action*, contains plenty of that, but it is action without beginning or end, action without aim or reasoned meaning. It proceeds from nothing to nothingness. It begins in silence, with two hairless men and two slatternly women at a bare table sipping tea in slow draughts. After a while one of the men says, "I'm looking forward to my life. . . . I am looking forward to me." The rest is incoherence. He has not accumulated any experience from which he can make sense. He is null and void. He is capable only of sudden rages of impotent frustration in which he smashes the chairs he sits on until there are none left. In this vacuity the four people—in undefined space—"entertain" themselves by reading from a tattered book, but since they do not remember where they left off they cannot find the place to resume. Without utensils, they eat the last turkey available to them. They are at a dead end.

All is "symbol." In most traditional art, symbolic significance emerges from a context of action (or imagery) "imitating" or suggesting a continuity of recognizable behavior and phenomena in a real world. In these Shepard plays the symbols are only notations or abstractions. The context which they are presumed to denote is taken for granted. We are supposed to agree that our lives mean little: that they are hardly more than a series of spasms or jerks.

Thus, one of the women suddenly takes to nibbling and licking her arm, a sort of masturbation. In the absence of straight chairs, one of the men seats himself in a commodious but soiled armchair, which he enjoys and resolves never to leave. But he soon realizes that that is impossible. Then, when he tries to rise from his comfortable, but no longer tenable position, the armchair overturns and wedges him beneath it. In the end we see him crawling about under this carapace, like a turtle, while behind him the women are hanging their ragged things on a clothesline.

Many of these images are theatrically arresting. There are also several speeches that are poetically allusive. One of the men tells a story about a family of moths fascinated by a flame. Most of them avoid a close approach. One of them is bolder. "He embraced her [the flame] completely," the recital goes, "and his whole body became as red as fire. The leader of the moths who was watching from far off with the other moths saw that the flame and the moth appeared to be one. He turned to the other moths and said, 'He learned what he wanted to know but he was the only one who understands it.'" True knowledge is acquired only through union with what is outside ourselves—often powerfully consuming and sometimes lethal—in other words, through a "mystic" embrace.

There is a telling perception in this, but I wonder whether Shepard and those who write in his manner really have plunged into the "flame" and united themselves with it, or

whether, in this instance, the "flame" exists. I mean that, though it has become something of a convention to say that our lives are empty, one may doubt that such statements or inferences have been objectively validated through a close mingling with and participation in the substance of actual fact.

It is certainly true that most of us are bewildered, distraught and rendered miserable by the fraudulence and chaos of the moment, but something rich and real always remains which keeps us sentient and determined to find meaning and achieve values. What too often occurs in dramatic abstractions of the latest stripe is that, while much is alleged about "life," life itself is absent. And by life I here mean intimate contact with the sensory, social, historical, psychological, spiritual world, bodied forth so that a sense of concrete involvement has been experienced on all these levels. Life is a "mystery," but it is more or less always present for us: felt, touched, smelled, acted upon as it acts upon us. It makes for a consciousness of ourselves and of others—no matter how befuddled we may find ourselves.

I know only one incontrovertible truth: human beings wish to endure, to *live*. Were it not so humankind would have disappeared long ago. Though we suppose our age one of the most disheartening and painful—without sustained faith or moral stamina—I very much suspect that there has never been a halcyon day, a time when the world was free of widespread misery for the greatest number.

Yet withal there has been creation and even joy through our seemingly nonrational endeavor to make it all come out "right."

In most art nowadays, and in *avant-garde* theatre especially, there is an inclination to abstract from the already abstract. The tendency is generally a mode of escape without the courage, energy and passion of "the moth who merged with the flame." For myself, I am tired of the expression of futility; I am tired of tiredness. I am nauseated by the cry that all is nothingness. We act, we produce an infinity of splendors, we play, sing, we try to earn a living, we protect our children and we strive, as we should, for more and greater life!

None of this is said in condemnation of Shepard's new plays. He is an undoubtedly gifted person of considerable stage intuition; most of his plays are ironic protests against the common ache we now suffer. Even more, there is a buried religious strain in them. *Killer's Head* and *Action* once again sound the moan of devastation in our consciousness, but it worries me that in Shepard's myth making so much of the actual world is missing and so much generalization is pictured in minimal flashes.

In *Operation Sidewinder* and *The Tooth of Crime* Shepard was beginning to add certain realities to his symbols, fantasies and abstractions. I wish he would go further in that vein; otherwise he will remain congealed in the situation the artist in his *Melodrama Play* declared himself to be. "I was admired from coast to coast by the people dearest to me. . . . By the people of my generation. I was admired and cherished because . . . [my] song reflected accurately thoughts and feelings of our time and place. . . . But it was the only song I had. The only one. And I became stuck. . . . I got stuck somewhere in the middle."
—HAROLD CLURMAN, *Nation*, May 3, 1975, p. 542

Language can explode from the tiniest impulse. If I'm right inside the character in the moment, I can catch what he smells, sees, feels and touches. In a sudden flash, he opens his eyes, and the words follow. In these lightning-like eruptions words are not thought, they're felt. They cut through space and make perfect sense without having to hesitate for the "meaning."

From time to time I've practiced Jack Kerouac's discovery of jazz-sketching with words. Following the exact same principles as a musician does when he's jamming. After periods of this kind of practice, I begin to get the haunting sense that something in me writes but it's not necessarily me. At least it's not the "me" that takes credit for it. This identical experience happened to me once when I was playing drums with The Holy Modal Rounders, and it scared the shit out of me. Peter Stampfel, the fiddle player, explained it as being visited by the Holy Ghost, which sounded reasonable enough at the time.

What I'm trying to get at here is that the real quest of a writer is to penetrate into another world. A world behind the form. The contradiction is that as soon as that world opens up, I tend to run the other way. It's scary because I can't answer to it from what I know.

Now, here's the big rub—it's generally accepted in the scholarly world that a playwright deals with "*ideas.*" That idea in itself has been inherited by us as though it were originally written in granite from above and nobody, but nobody, better mess with it. The problem for me with this concept is that its adherents are almost always referring to ideas which speak only to the mind and leave out completely the body, the emotions and all the rest of it.

Myth speaks to everything at once, especially the emotions. By myth I mean a sense of mystery and not necessarily a traditional formula. A character for me is a composite of different mysteries. He's an unknown quantity. If he wasn't, it would be like coloring in the numbered spaces. I see an old man by a broken car in the middle of nowhere and those simple elements right away set up associations and yearnings to pursue what he's doing there.

The character of Crow in *Tooth of Crime* came from a yearning toward violence. A totally lethal human with no way or reason for tracing how he got that way. He just appeared. He spit words that became his weapons. He doesn't "mean" anything. He's simply following his most savage instincts. He speaks in an unheard-of tongue. He needed a victim, so I gave him one. He devoured him just like he was supposed to. When you're writing inside of a character like this, you aren't pausing every ten seconds to figure out what it all means. If you do, you lose the whole shot, because the character isn't going to hang around waiting for you. He's moving.

I write fast because that's the way it happens with me. Sometimes long stretches happen in between where I don't write for weeks. But when I start, I don't stop. Writing is born from a need. A deep burn. If there's no need, there's no writing.—SAM SHEPARD, "Language, Visualization and the Inner Library," *DrR*, Dec. 1977, pp. 55–56

ELIZABETH HARDWICK
From "Introduction"
La Turista by Sam Shepard

1968, pp. ix–xv

Nothing is harder to come by than a truly meaningful central image, one that opens out to possibility, encour-

ages invention. For some reason we must, aesthetically, be satisfied with the image, or situation, on the first plane of concreteness. Without that it is hard to give assent to the elaborations that will follow; in a sense you have to enter the structure the author gives you before you are willing to see what is inside. In this play the identity of the person—the tourist—and his affliction, that humbling diarrhea—"la turista"—are signified by a single word. This word and the two things it represents are the bare center of the play, the ruling image. The sickness is a sort of a joke—that kills.

Salem and Kent are literally tourists in Mexico in the first act. In the second, which in point of time takes place before the first, Kent is on another kind of journey—I won't say "trip"—in which American rhetoric is offered for his cure just as the blood of freshly killed chickens had been offered in "primitive" Mexico. Neither works.

Perhaps the characters are not profitably thought of as characters at all. They are actors, parodists. They slip from style to style; they carry a few props around with them as they change their roles; they "freeze" when they want to withdraw from the action on the stage. The essence of their being is energy, verbal energy. In the restless inventiveness of their parodies and tirades, a storm of feeling and experience blows across the stage. The parts are arias. In the last section of Act II Doc and Kent "sing" an extraordinary duet. These arias have to do with death. It is amazing the number of "deaths" that will fit the text: Vietnam, Santo Domingo, racial violence, dropouts, colonialism. ⟨. . .⟩

In *La Turista* there is a poignant meeting on some pure level of understanding of playwright, director and actor: the sort of unity that makes the Royal Shakespeare's production of *The Homecoming* so rare. Jacques Levy, the director, is a theatrical talent of unremitting inspiration. The actors are all first-rate, but in Sam Waterston the play has a young actor of such versatility and charm that one hardly knows how to express the degree of his talents. With this play, the promise of the lofts of off-off-Broadway, the dedication and independence, come to the most extraordinary fulfillment. You do not feel you are being given a package, assembled for a purpose, and in some ways this is disconcerting to the senses. The audience, accustomed to ensembles created as a calculation, may feel left out, slow to respond, trapped by a sluggish metabolism. In the long run, what is so beautiful is the graceful—in spite of the frenzied energy—concentration of the work as a whole, and for that, if one would take it in, the audience also has to work.

Sam Shepard, the author of *La Turista*, is twenty-three years old and even so he is not new to the theatre. He is not being "discovered" in this production. His plays have been off-off in the Cafe La Mama repertory; he has been at the Cherry Lane and will soon be in print. *La Turista* is his most ambitious play thus far but still it is in the same style and voice as *Chicago* and his other one-act plays. The scene opens on an electrifying set: a bright, bright formica yellow hotel room in Mexico. A young American couple—Salem and Kent—are sitting up in their twin beds. They are covered with a deep bronze suntan make-up and are holding their arms out stiffly. On the beach, as a part of their vacation, they have gotten a painful sunburn. They talk of first, second, and third—and *fourth* degree burns.

> Well, the epidermis is actually cooked, fried like a piece of meat over a charcoal fire. The molecular structure of the fatty tissue is partially destroyed by the sun rays and so the blood rushes to the surface to

repair the damage.
. . . It's just the blood rushing to the surface.

Mock scientific dialogue, inserted merely for itself, delivered in a cool, matter-of-fact way, but sharply, insistently, is characteristic of the writing. (Of course, the couple with their expensive, painful sunburns will bring to mind those other burns of our time.) The players hardly ever look at each other. There is a feeling of declamation, rather than of conversation or dialogue. And yet the monologues do not at all suggest that banality of Broadway—the "failure of communication"—but actually are quite the opposite. They are an extreme of communication. Kent, the young man, also has, in addition to his sunburn, "la turista," the intestinal distress that affects Americans when they visit poor countries like Mexico. At this point in the play, a young Mexican enters. He is one of the world's poor, with his American phrases ("I had to follow that cat around with a palm fan while he scored on all the native chicks")—he begs and yet he is intractable, unmanageable. He spits in the young American's face.

As the act progresses, Kent becomes very ill. Two wonderfully absurd witch doctors, Mexican style, are brought in, with live roosters, candles, voodoo and crucifixes. Kent dies, a sacrifice to "la turista"—his lack of resistance to the germs of the country he arrogantly patronizes with his presence. The second act has all the same elements as the first, but they are acted out in a Summit Hotel sort of room in America and the witch doctors are two circuit rider charlatans in Civil War dress. Here Kent dies of sleeping sickness, or perhaps he is on drugs; in any case he has an American disease this time—he doesn't like to be awake. His final monologue is a psychedelic tirade—and he jumps, in his pajamas, through the hotel wall, leaving the print of the outlines of his body in the wallpaper.

George Eliot said that she wrote all her novels out of the belief in "the orderly sequence by which the seed brings forth a crop of its kind." We all have a nostalgia and longing for this order because it has been the heart of European fiction and drama. Incident after incident, each growing out of the other, united in a chain of significant motivation, of cause and effect—moments of human destiny strung out like beads on a string. This is what we mean, perhaps, when we say we "understand" a work of literary art. Yet each decade brings us the conviction that this order is no longer present to the serious writer. It is most appealing to those writers who construct their works for some possibility of the marketplace. The episodic, the obscurely related, the collection of images, moods: connections in fiction and also in drama have become like those of poetry. Tone and style hold the work together, create whatever emotional effect it will have upon us. Out of episodes and images, characters and conflicts are made, but they are of a blurred and complex sort.

Formless images and meaningless happenings are peculiarly oppressive to the spirit, and the inanities of the experimental theatre could make a man commit suicide. Sam Shepard, on the other hand, possesses the most impressive literary talent and dramatic inventiveness. He is voluble, in love with long, passionate, intense monologues (both of the acts end in these spasms of speech) which almost petrify the audience. His play ends with sweating, breathless actors in a state of exhaustion. The characters put on a shawl and begin to declaim like an auctioneer at a slave mart, or a cowboy suit and fall into Texas harangues. They stop in the midst of jokes, for set pieces, some fixed action from childhood, perhaps influenced by the bit in Albee's *Zoo Story*. Despair and humor, each of a peculiarly expressive kind, are the elements out of

which the script of the play is made. The effect is very powerful and if it cannot be reduced to one or two themes it is still clearly about us and our lives. The diction, the acting, the direction, the ideas are completely American and it is our despair and humor Shepard gets onto the stage.

To return to the decision about the critics: it is a sacrificial act of the most serious sort. It means nothing less than, after a fixed short run, if one is lucky enough to have that, the play may suffer simple cessation for want of those and good and bad advertisements combed from the newspapers and television. Perhaps it is only young people, free of deforming ambitions, who would have the courage to submit to such a test. Or perhaps it is the strength of their art that allows them to wait for what will come or not come. There are worse things than silence.

CHARLES R. BACHMAN
"Defusion of Menace in the Plays of Sam Shepard"
Modern Drama, December 1976, pp. 405–15

For several years Sam Shepard has been acknowledged as the most talented and promising playwright to emerge from the Off-off Broadway movement. Now, more than a decade after his work was first performed, he is increasingly recognized as one of the more significant dramatists in the English-speaking world. Praised by Edward Albee and Elizabeth Hardwick,[1] he has been called "One of the three or four most gifted playwrights alive"[2] and "the most talented of his generation."[3] Catherine Hughes rightfully acknowledges that "there is no young American playwright who can match Shepard in his ability to employ language."[4] Ren Frutkin in an article in *Yale Theatre* asserts that "he has brought the word back into the theatre,"[5] and London director Kenneth Chubb believes that Shepard's "perspective on his material has a relevance and universality that earmarks great writers."[6] Granted the tendency of some reviewers to exaggerate in the enthusiasm of the moment, the body of positive opinion regarding Shepard's work is impressive. At least twenty-seven of his plays have been performed, not only in the United States and the United Kingdom,[7] but in Canada[8] and Australia[9] as well. At least twelve plays have been performed in London alone, where he has been living for the past four years.[10] Nineteen of his plays, as well as a book of poetry and prose, are in published form, and he has several screenplays to his credit.[11]

Shepard draws much of his material from popular culture sources such as B-grade westerns, sci-fi and horror films, popular folklore, country and rock music and murder-mysteries. In his best work he transforms the original stereotyped characters and situations into an imaginative, linguistically brilliant, quasi-surrealistic chemistry of text and stage presentation which is original and authentically his own. One source of the unique quality and tension of his dramas is his ambivalent attitude toward violence. The structure of his work reflects both an abhorrence for and fascination with it, and with the menace which may lead to it. This fascination is partly apparent in the "force of competitive virtuosity" noted by Frutkin in various pairs of Shepard characters, which in 1969 led that critic to observe that in Shepard's plays "the main dynamism . . . is not that of union—the dynamism of love—but of displacement—the dynamism of power."[12] At least until his last three published plays, however, such competition produces very little real menace or terrifying physical violence.

What Shepard's ambivalent attitude toward violence, menace and power does result in throughout his dramas is the following pattern of action: Menacing, potentially violent characters or forces are introduced, only to have the terror they create defused either by an avoidance of the threatened violence, or vitiation of its effect through audience alienation devices. In the dramas preceding *The Tooth of Crime* (1972),[13] this structure frequently involves characters who are self-indulgent, who often find their whims almost instantly gratified. Such a pattern is in contrast, for example, to that employed in Pinter's dramas, in which menace is almost never defused, but continues to build throughout the action, at times exploding into terrifying conflict.

Shepard's dramatic pattern, while never resulting in anything as sentimental as love or even union, bears some resemblance to the fictional patterns of Thomas Hardy, who, like Shepard, created in various novels all the ingredients for violent confrontation, then scrupulously avoided the potential conflict. Like Hardy's characters, those of Shepard ultimately turn out to be potential communers rather than potential conflicters.[14] Examples of this pattern throughout Shepard's work are the defusion of the threat posed by Bill, Howard and the offstage plane in *Icarus's Mother* (1965), Jim in *Red Cross* (1966), Doc and Boy in *La Turista* (1966), the Exterminators in *Forensic and the Navigators* (1967). Peter in *Melodrama Play* (1967), Geez in *Shaved Splits* (1969), the Young Man, Blood, and the Desert Tactical Troops in *Operation Sidewinder* (1970), Sycamore and The Kid in *The Unseen Hand* (1970), the Chindi and Ice in *The Holy Ghostly* (1970), the Beast in *Back Bog Beast Bait* (1971), and Yahoodi's threat to Captain Kidd in *Mad Dog Blues* (1971).

In *Melodrama Play* the defusion of menace occurs most obviously in regard to Peter, a huge henchman assigned to guard a rock star and his friends. After having shot the star's girlfriend in the head (significantly, this is not taken very seriously by the others) and knocked the star unconscious with his club, Peter sits the others on the couch and says: "I'd like to ask you both what you think of me as a person. Just frankly. Don't be afraid of hurting my feelings or anything like that. Just tell me what you think."[15] In spite of further head bashings and threats, this concern of Peter's, revealed also in two lengthy monologues, and the sudden resurrection and exit of the dead girl and one of the men, prevent Peter's poised club over the brother's head at the end of the play from being anything but comic or melodramatic—à propos of the title.

Forensic and the Navigators, a more satisfying drama, follows a similar pattern of defusion. The first menace is between Emmet and Forensic, two co-conspirators, who begin grappling over how to go about capturing a fortress (prison? mental institution?). Immediately a girl named Oolan enters, flipping a pancake, whereupon the fight ceases. The next source of terror is the two Exterminators who knock at the door. In spite of their being well-armed and *"huge men . . . dressed like California Highway patrolmen,"*[16] they speak with a harmless politeness which would do credit to a roach exterminator, become confused in their roles and susceptible to Oolan's charms, and end up as frightened of their home office as Emmet and Forensic were at their knock on the door. As at the end of *Melodrama Play*, a loud banging is heard on the door. Any remaining menace is the offstage and unknown source of the gas filling the auditorium. Terror from unknown sources is in fact almost the only kind which is ever very frightening in Shepard's work, and is the only type of terror he himself has specifically mentioned.[17]

In *Mad Dog Blues* the characters are engaged in one big,

comical self-gratification quest, led by Kosmo, a rock star, and his friend-envier, Yahoodi. In this work a character merely has to say he imagines Mae West or Marlene Dietrich, and she appears. A desire for buried treasure produces Captain Kidd, who has intuitive knowledge of its whereabouts. Until the fruitless interpersonal quest in the last section of the play, a character always has someone available to berate, talk or make love to, or somehow carry on with. The closest thing to menace in the drama occurs when Yahoodi threatens and shoots Captain Kidd. The latter does not remain dead, however, and the only thing denied the characters in this play is "roots," identity, fulfillment—though a short musical version of even that occurs in the linked-hand singing of "Home" at the end of the play.[18]

In *Cowboy Mouth* (1971), *The Tooth of Crime* (1972) and *Geography of a Horse Dreamer* (1974), Shepard utilizes to a much greater extent than before the methods of conventional dramatic realism such as believable characterization, psychological and emotional tension and crescendo of suspense. Concomitant with this development comes a virtual elimination of the brilliant, surrealistically grotesque monologues of his earlier work, and a more tightly-disciplined form. This affects his use of menace, which now becomes more seriously threatening than before, and approaches closer to actual physical conflict and violence.

In *Cowboy Mouth* a woman named Cavale ("mare") has kidnapped a half-resentful, half-fascinated Slim, hoping to turn him into a rock star. Like his earlier namesake in *Back Bog Beast Bait*, Slim loves to play the coyote (to Cavale's crow), but combines within himself some of the frustrations of both Kosmo and Yahoodi of *Mad Dog Blues*. Unlike the earlier Slim, however, he is young, and carries only faint traces of that perennial Shepardian character—the outlaw-hero of the American Southwest. This is, in fact, the first play since *Shaved Splits* which does not include such a figure. As in *Mad Dog Blues*, instant gratification patterns appear in the form of immediately-realized fantasies which may fuse with the concept of menace. Cavale wants red shoes, and, through the transformation technique of simply saying the word, she and Slim immediately imagine themselves downtown (or actually are downtown, depending upon one's interpretation) buying her shoes. When they want some lobster, they call the Lobster Man. Later, they want him back to play with. On both occasions, he enters looking like a giant lobster. Whatever hints of menace he carries with him onto the stage are quickly dissipated by his obvious harmlessness, reflected in his becoming the object of ridicule by Slim and Cavale. He is a comic-grotesque descendent of the Sidewinder, the Chindi in *The Holy Ghostly*, and the two-headed Beast in *Back Bog Beast Bait*. Like Cavale's stuffed crow, he is a stage version of Gerard de Nerval's pet—and just as peaceful. He plays a crucial role in the quest for a musical epiphany, which in this play is the most direct and sustained of any in Shepard's dramas. Johnny Ace, the first potential rock and roll "savior," had blown his brains out with a revolver in front of his audience. Slim, or someone else, will hopefully be the new one. Several of the numerous literary allusions in the play such as "rocking [sic] toward Bethlehem to be born"[19] relate to this hoped-for savior. Finally, the Lobster Man emerges from his shell as such a figure and points a revolver at his head. It fails to fire. End of play.

On the way to this final defusion of violence and terror, the major menace occurs between Slim and Cavale as they engage in cycles of aggression and amity with each other; and, for the first time in a play by Shepard, this involves some actual confrontation and conflict. At one point Cavale threatens Slim with her revolver. When he wards her off verbally, she accuses him of "wrecking" everything. At another time he *"starts tearing the place apart"* after calling her a "fucking cunt" (100). Yet no real violence comes to either of them. Its nearest approach is when Slim says, "Coyote he howl and howl and chomp down on that crow now. Tear into the crow now!" and *"jumps on CAVALE and tears into her. THEY roll around on the floor for awhile, then stop"* (103). Since this occurs within the context of the "coyote and crow game," it is not as menacing as it otherwise might be. Yet it is more menacing and believable than such situations in Shepard's earlier plays because, unlike earlier role-playing characters, Cavale and Slim are not mainly unaware enactors in a larger role-playing game which is the drama itself, but are themselves conscious and deliberate authors of several of their own interactive games. This is integral to their being more psychologically realistic than earlier Shepard characters, and permits the playwright to allow their outbursts of aggression to build more believably than before, and to explode at appropriate moments—but never into anything as direct as someone actually getting beaten or shot, as in the preceding eight plays.[20] *Cowboy Mouth* is more believably violent and aggressive than any previous Shepard play.

In *The Tooth of Crime* (1972), probably Shepard's best play to date[21] and his personal favorite,[22] the aggressive menace intensifies as the hoped-for rock and roll savior, the "beast rocking toward Bethlehem to be born," appears onstage in the form of the rock singer Crow. The name itself is not only one which recurred throughout *Cowboy Mouth*, but of course also recalls the controlling metaphor and titular anti-hero of Ted Hughes' magnificent series of poems. Whether or not Hughes was an actual influence, the searing image of "Crow"—as has been suggested numerous times—may well be an apt metaphor for our disillusioned time. Not coincidentally, it is the kind of image suggested by Mick Jagger of the Rolling Stones, and by Keith Richards, his co-writer for the group. In *Cowboy Mouth* Cavale felt that Mick Jagger was almost the rock and roll savior. In *The Tooth of Crime* Crow, upon entering the stage in the second act to challenge the older star, Hoss, in a battle of styles, is described as looking "just like Keith Richard."

As the play opens, Hoss, the aging Elvis Presley-style star, is sitting a bit uncomfortably on his throne. Aided by his advisor Becky, his Shepardian cowboy sidekick Cheyenne, and his stargazers and other miscellaneous retinue, he tries to "suss the scene"—to discover how close he is to really being at the top, and who the chief threats to his eminence might be. Though at a literal level Hoss's chief identity is in music, Shepard creates an effective build of biting menace by using the controlling metaphor of a Mafia-type battle over "turf." As Hoss discovers that some upstart has "knocked over Vegas"— up to now part of his "turf"—and he prepares to do battle with "skivs" (knives), it almost appears that the conflict is in fact not over popularity at all, but is of a more directly violent nature. Interwoven with the criminal turf metaphor is a masterful delineation of styles—which is what the conflict eventually comes down to. In spite of reassurances by Galactic Jack (Wolfman Jack) that "you is in, Jim. In like a stone winner" (14), and "You're number one with a bullet and you ain't even got the needle in the groove" (18), Hoss's unease remains. Like the style of "Gypsies" who threaten him by playing outside the charts and going immediately for the top-level kill, Hoss's style is not only defined by his music, but involves himself almost entirely: his cars, clothes and diction, his moves and gestures.

Somewhat arrogant in his self-esteem, he possesses a hip version of hubris before the fall, and embodies several of those traditional values which many of Shepard's self-indulgent, immediately gratified characters have tended thus far to reject: (1) Restraint and repression of fantasy gratification while young; he envies Crow that he "Lived out his fantasies" (71). (2) Patience, persistence, and desire for security; he tells Crow, "All my turf?! You know how long it's taken me to collect that ground? You know how many kills it's taken! I'm a fuckin' champion man [. . . .]. All my turf! That's all I've got" (64). After Hoss, defeated, ends his life, Cheyenne tells Crow, "He earned his style" (75).

Hoss is also troubled simply by his humanity. After his loss to Crow, the latter tells him, "Get mean. there's too much pity, man. Too much empathy" (66). Hoss yearns for a restored sense of personal identity, courage, non-vulnerability:

> Hoss: Now I'm outa control. I'm pulled and pushed
>   from one image to another. Nothin' takes a
>   solid form. Nothin' sure and final. Where do I
>   stand! Where the fuck do I stand!
> Crow: Alone, Leathers. [. . .] Too much searchin'. I
>   got no answers. Go beyond confidence. Beyond
>   loathing. . . . Keep away from fantasy. Shake
>   off the image. No pictures, just pure focus.
>   How does it feel? [. . .] Get down his animal.
>   [. . .] Keep him comin'. Pull him into ya'. Put
>   on his gestures. Wear him like a suit a' clothes.
> Hoss: Yeah. It *is* me. Just like I always wanted to be.
>   (65ff.)

Crow wins the match because he has sensed and articulated Hoss's vulnerability—a vulnerability he does not share because he has tightly disciplined himself into "pure focus," pure style, knife-like, sexual and super-cool down to his marrow, with no room for anything else. His style is all he is— and thus he has seemingly solved the age-old problems of security, repression, piety, justice and personal identity with which Hoss and Shepard have been burdened. The new savior is indeed enviable and/or pitiable, depending on one's mood and psychological set. He is certainly a Yeatsian "rough beast," with a hard edge much less cosmic yet, in its way, as pitiless as Hughes' Crow itself:

> Crow laughed.
> He bit the Worm. God's only son.
> Into two writhing halves.
> He stuffed into man the tail half
> With the wounded end hanging out.
>
> . . .
>
> Man awoke being dragged across the grass.
> Woman awoke to see him coming.
> Neither knew what had happened.
> God went on sleeping.
> Crow went on laughing.[23]

Hoss believes only at a conscious level that "Power. That's all there is." Crow knows it at gut-level as he *"cruises the stage with true contempt"* (41).

The only time in the three-round fight when Hoss begins to get to Crow occurs in Round Two, when he correctly shows him how little he knows—or wishes to acknowledge—of the origins of his style in Black soul music, including that of Little Brother Montgomery, King Oliver, Ma Rainey and Blind Lemon Jefferson. "You'd like a free ride on a Black Man's back," he tells Crow (59). That round, however, is called a draw, presumably because in the new order of things, a sense of historical indebtedness is irrelevant to "pure focus." Crow wins a TKO when he tells Hoss that in spite of trying to "Sound like a Dylan, sound like a Jagger," he "Can't get it together."

The Tooth of Crime utilizes to an even greater degree than *Cowboy Mouth* the traditional dramatic values of taut, disciplined structure, vivid and consistent characterization, and crescendo of suspense. In these it reflects both its major characters. Hoss may have been more self-restrained in not having lived out all his fantasies, but Crow is the more tightly disciplined of the two. The temptation arises to see the pattern of value conflict and its outcome in this drama as a fantasy of the playwright's reluctant yielding to what he feels is the necessity for a tighter discipline and control in his own work. Whether or not this is true, the tighter structure results in the almost complete disappearance of the casual movement patterns, instant gratifications and uninhibited, anti-hangup behaviors of characters in previous plays. For the first time, Shepard has brought onstage two potentially menacing characters, and placed them in open confrontation with each other. Temperamentally, they are nearer to Shepard's many cowboy heroes of the Southwest than to rock stars in previous plays.[24] Unlike their cowboy predecessors, however, they are not rendered harmless by being stereotyped, caricatured, or by immediately revealing cowardice and vulnerability. Even Hoss, the more vulnerable of the two, plays out the match, confident of victory. With the possible exception of a rather over-theatrical cheerleading scene during Round One (55) and Becky's famous auto-seduction scene (admittedly dramatic and comic in itself), the potential and actual conflict moves forward with an inevitability that is new in Shepard. As a result, this is his most menacing play.

The music adds to the menace. Shepard's plays contain many songs, and most of them serve to reinforce the movement and tone of the work in which they occur, sometimes adding touches of comedy or pathos, as in *Mad Dog Blues*. This is hardly surprising, since Shepard is a serious musician himself. But in *The Tooth of Crime*, Shepard's fourth play to contain rock musician characters,[25] music plays a more integral part than in any of his other works. The music in this play—written, along with the lyrics, by Shepard—not only helps to define and differentiate the styles of the two contenders; it is also strong enough, harmonically, melodically and rhythmically, to be consistent with and to reinforce the stylistic battle of the two opposing singers, though no songs are sung during the actual battle itself. In the hands of a strong-voiced rock singer, Crow's three songs especially have the potential of being menacingly chilling.[26]

The direct terror of even this confrontation, however, is eventually defused. Brechtian-style devices such as the auto-seduction scene and the presence and activity of cheerleaders and referee during the style battle reduce somewhat the immediate physical menace, though the audience is never quite sure that knives won't actually be used. The chief defusion occurs after Crow wins. Had he been as merciless as he is portrayed to that point, he would presumably have been less willing to teach Hoss his style. Yet their interaction after the battle is quite amiable. Shepard's impulse toward communion once more overrides the identifiable menace and potential violence in his drama. Hoss dies, not at the hands of Crow, but by committing suicide onstage. His recognition of an old-fashioned vulnerability and humanity in himself leads him to realize that suicide is the only authentic gesture he has left to make; and he makes it cleanly and dramatically, his back to the audience, with a revolver shot in the mouth. The suicidal ghost of de Nerval which had haunted the imagination

of Cavale in *Cowboy Mouth* but was unrealized as the pistol failed to fire, has here—for the first time in Shepard—entered the stage. Becky's immediate willingness to be part of Crow's entourage, and Cheyenne's refusal, are both believable and do not detract from the effect of Hoss's death. His final act forms the most appropriate finale to the agonized / comic search for authenticity, self, and community that has plagued Shepard's characters from the beginning. Yet Shepard never allows it to appear as an over-sentimental gesture. Crow's "A genius mark. I gotta hand it to ya'. It took ya long enough but you slid right home" (74), is the closest he comes.

The menace which remains at the end of *The Tooth of Crime* is of the same kind as ends most of Shepard's plays—the terror of the unknown that the playwright himself has spoken of. Here it is simultaneously two unknowns: at a superficial level, whatever unnamed singer will threaten, dethrone and destroy Crow, as he has destroyed Hoss; at a deeper level, the more terrifying and even vaguer menace of the exclusively stylistic value system represented by Crow himself, as he stands alone on stage, singing to a hauntingly relentless 6/8 beat and lament-style melody the words of "Rollin' Down":

> If I'm a fool then keep me blind
> I'd rather feel my way
> If I'm a tool for bigger game
> You better get down—you better get down and pray
> [. . .]
>
> (82)

Shepard's most recently published play, *Geography of a Horse Dreamer* (1974), is probably too derivative for its otherwise quite palpable menace to be very terrifying—in spite of the fact that the work involves perhaps Shepard's two most startling scenes of violence. Appropriately subtitled "A Mystery in Two Acts," this play is Shepard's closest attempt thus far at conventional realism. It combines a Runyonesque situation and a Raymond Chandler / Dashiell Hammett style with a touch of the one-sided western shoot-out at the end. Initially, the chief menace appears to be Fingers, whose syndicate keeps a Wyoming cowboy named Cody prisoner so that he can dream successful racehorse winners. The syndicate is displeased with Cody's slump, however. After conversation creates Fingers' menacing quality, he enters with an associate, the Doctor. Almost immediately, the terror aroused by Fingers is softened and finally shifted to the Doctor (who "looks like Sidney Greenstreet") as Fingers reveals a soft under-belly of sympathy and sensitivity. In the first of the two scenes of violence, the Doctor throws Fingers across the room and becomes steadily more menacing as he prepares to remove Cody's dreaming bone from his skull. Even this menace is defused, however, in the most violent ending Shepard has yet devised, Cody's two huge cowboy brothers enter with shotguns, cutting down Beaujo, Santee and the Doctor, but—with poetic justice—sparing Fingers.

There is no doubt that the initial impact of this scene, like that of the Doctor's violence toward Fingers, is startling. But whereas the impact of both these scenes suffers from the derivatively melodramatic quality of the play generally, the final scene is even less effective because, once the first split-second of total surprise is over, it conveys a completely deus ex machina quality—too sudden and unprepared to have been the outcome of suspense, but occurring in too serious a murder-mystery context to be defended as parodistic or deliberately comic.

The menace in this play is therefore not only defused, but also rendered clumsy. Unlike Shepard's best work—*Chicago*

(1965), *Forensic and the Navigators, Cowboy Mouth* and *The Tooth of Crime*—the characterization, dialogue and plot in *Geography of a Horse Dreamer* fail to develop beyond the stereotypes which were their sources. Fingers is the only character who begins to assume individuality and, significantly, his characterization is tightly integrated with the steady erosion of the menace he seems to represent. Equally significant for this essay is the fact that this drama contains no actual violent conflict: Cody cringes away from all threats, Fingers yields to the Doctor, who in turn has no chance against Cody's brothers. This action follows the pattern in all Shepard's dramas. It remains to be seen whether he will again utilize a conventionally realistic structure—but one that is less derivative—to do something he has not yet done: combine a crescendo of menace with its explosion in believably terrifying violence or violent conflict. Productions of his more recent plays suggest that he has moved in other directions for the present.[27]

Notes

1. Harold Clurman, *Nation*, 30 March 1970, 380.
2. Edith Oliver, *New Yorker*, 17 March 1973, 92.
3. Stanley Kauffmann, *New Republic*, 24 March 1973, 22.
4. Catherine Hughes, *America*, 31 March 1973, 290.
5. Ren Frutkin, "Sam Shepard: Paired Existence Meets the Monster," *Yale Theatre*, 2, No. 2 (Summer 1969), 22.
6. Kenneth Chubb, "Fruitful Difficulties of Directing Shepard," *Theatre Quarterly* (August, 1974), 17.
7. The best single source for performance statistics in the U.S. and U.K., synopses of the performed plays, and a bibliography on Shepard is C.W.E. Bigsby et. al., "Theatre Checklist No. 3 Sam Shepard," *Theatrefacts* (Aug.–Oct., 1974), 3–11.
8. Chubb, p. 17.
9. *The Tooth of Crime* opened at the Nimrod Theatre, Sydney, Jan., 1974, and *The Unseen Hand* at the Stables, Sydney, July, 1975.
10. This does not include the final scene of *Rock Garden*, which was performed in London as part of *Oh! Calcutta* in 1970.
11. See *Theatrefacts* checklist.
12. Frutkin, p. 24.
13. Years in parentheses refer to dates of first performances.
14. See Charles R. Bachman, "Communion and Conflict in Hardy and Hauptmann: A Contrast in Artistic Temperaments," *Revue des Langues Vivantes*, 35, 3 (Autumn 1969), 283–293.
15. *Five Plays by Sam Shepard* (Indianapolis, 1967), p. 157. Parenthetical page numbers refer to the edition of a drama cited in a footnote.
16. Sam Shepard, *The Unseen Hand and Other Plays* (Indianapolis, 1972), p. 57.
17. In discussing the experience which stimulated him to write *Icarus's Mother*, he commented, "And then you've got this emotional thing that goes a long way back, which creates a certain kind of chaos, a kind of terror, you don't know what the fuck's going on. . . . There's a vague kind of terror going on, the people not really knowing what is happening [. . .] "Metaphors, Mad Dogs and Old-Time Cowboys", Theatre Quarterly (August, 1974), 9.
18. Sam Shepard, *Mad Dog Blues and Other Plays* (New York, 1972), pp. 80–81.
19. *Mad Dog Blues and Other Plays*, p. 99.
20. These are *Melodrama Play, Cowboys #2, Forensic and the Navigators, The Holy Ghostly, The Unseen Hand, Operation Sidewinder, Shaved Splits* and *Mad Dog Blues*.
21. This opinion is shared by most reviews, which have been generally favorable to the script but unfavorable or mixed toward The Performance Group and Open Space productions. Some samples include: "Establishes him as a major theater figure" (Clurman, *New York Times*, 8 March 1973, 34); "Stunning in its sheer verbal dexterity" (Catherine Hughes, *America*, 31 March 1973, 290); "As chillingly old as a tribal rite" (T. E. Kalem, *Time* 27 Nov. 1972, 73); "Shepard's play picks up a fluid aural tradition and converts

it into a precise literary shape" (Irving Wardle, *The Times*, 4 Sept. 1974, 9).

The Royal Court production of June, 1974, in which much of the dialogue and most of the lyrics were evidently drowned out by high sound volume, received some unfavorable reviews. See *Guardian*, 6 June and *Sunday Times*, 9 June.
22. Michael White, "Underground Landscapes," interview with Shepard, *Guardian*, 20 Feb. 1974, 8.
23. Ted Hughes, "A Childish Prank," in *Crow* (New York, 1971), 7.
24. Southwestern figures include the two leads in *Cowboys #2* and *Forensic and the Navigators*, Pop in *The Holy Ghostly*, the Morphan brothers in *The Unseen Hand*, Mickey Free in *Operation Sidewinder*, Waco in *Mad Dog Blues*, and Slim and Shadow in *Back Bog Beast Bait*.
25. The others are *Melodrama Play, Mad Dog Blues* and *Cowboy Mouth*.
26. A judgment based upon my several years of experience as a professional musician. The actor-singers in the Performance Group production did not present the songs in the manner they deserve. Neither, evidently, did the Open Space or Royal Court productions. Shepard has said that he felt Lou Reed of the Velvet Underground would be right for the role of Crow (Chubb, p. 21).
27. See, for example, reviews of *Killer's Head* and *Action*, in *The Times*, 18 Sept. 1974, and *Nation*, 3 May 1975.

WILLIAM KLEB

From "Worse Than Being Homeless: *True West* and the Divided Self"

Theater, Fall–Winter 1980, pp. 67–71

True West seems to be Shepard's most realistic work to date: the dialogue is natural and colloquial; the characters, with the exception of Mom, psychologically motivated; the action, linear and causal. Despite certain structural strains, the play avoids the obvious surrealistic dislocations common in Shepard's earlier work, while his distinctive aria-like monologues are likewise virtually absent. Even the setting of *True West* seems intentionally mundane: in a manuscript "note," Shepard specifically warns against "grafting" a "concept" onto the set and insists that it be constructed realistically with no attempt to "distort its dimensions, shapes, objects or colors." In short, it is as if Shepard were stressing the reality of his play in the same way that the magazine *True West* used to certify on its cover that the tales contained inside were "non-fiction."

Reality is a slippery fish, as Shepard has demonstrated more than once, and such disclaimers usually arouse more doubts and questions than they allay. Indeed, even with its realistic skin *True West* has, from the beginning, a strange, obsessive, dream-like quality. The play opens at night, to the sound of crickets; Austin is illuminated by a small, kerosene lamp, while Lee's presence in Mom's small, dimly-lighted kitchen seems jarring, threatening, somehow irrational—he could almost be a figment of Austin's imagination, a nightmare. As the power struggle between the two brothers intensifies, this surrealistic undertone becomes stronger until, in the chaotic last scenes, it takes over the stage entirely. As the rational, self-controlled Austin crumbles, the realistic surface of the play itself seems to peel away, to disintegrate. Lee batters the typewriter, there's a fire on stage, Mom's counters fill up with toasters, the telephone is ripped off the wall, the kitchen drawers are emptied all over the floor. Finally Mom materializes at the door, an archetype and a parody, a kind of satiric *deus ex machina* without the will or power to restore order in her world—a mom without a country.

Of course, it is typical of Shepard to mix the real and the

surreal in his work. Unlike *The Curse of the Starving Class*, however, a play which it resembles in several ways, *True West* does not oscillate between fantasy and reality. Rather, the two levels co-exist: the one seems to displace the other even while the basic realistic framework of the play remains, more or less, intact. In other words, objective and subjective realities are not juxtaposed, they are superimposed; the "real" world is not simply challenged or questioned by "alternative levels of consciousness," it is suffused by them. (Shepard attempted this technique less successfully or subtly in both *Suicide in B^b* and *Buried Child*.) As a result, the reality of the play begins to vibrate with subjective energy and meaning: objects becomes symbols; characters, archetypes; actions, allegories.

This formal ambiguity is reflected on the level of signification. The conflict between Austin and Lee clearly has meaning beyond a study of sibling rivalry. Indeed, as Shepard describes them and as they appeared on stage at the Magic, the *reality* of their relationship is questionable: they couldn't look less alike; they seem to be, at the beginning at least, physical and psychological opposites. That is Shepard's point, of course. Although "brothers," Austin and Lee actually represent opposing styles, attitudes and values in Shepard's scheme. The most obvious reading of this opposition has to do with their major point of conflict—the film scripts that they each try to write. The creation of these scripts is a metaphor for the creative act; at issue is the nature of creativity.

Shepard's dialectic on this point is neither very original nor profound. Austin represents objectivity, self-control and self-discipline, form and order, the intellect, reason. Lee stands for subjectivity, anarchy, adventure, excess and exaggeration, intuition and imagination. Only when Austin abandons his professional project and pose and gets drunk is his repressed, imaginative side released. Then he creates the most inventive and startling (if unrealistic) image in the play, his toaster performance, and tells the play's most amusing and original tale, a story about his father's false teeth. Lee dramatizes the opposite lesson: without self-discipline and technique, he becomes frustrated, his creative energy turns violent and destructive. To sum up Shepard's point, Austin tells Lee, after the two have switched roles, that Kimmer "thinks we're the same person." Metaphorically, they are.

The relationship between order and invention is no news. What is interesting about Shepard's investigation is the manner in which it is resolved—or rather, the manner in which it is *not* resolved. Lee has the vision; Austin the skill and self-discipline. The latter, Shepard seems to be saying, must finally serve the former; even then this collaborative psychic process is a precarious one—a continual, nerve-racking battle. But in *True West*, the battle (work on the script) is abandoned. Mom appears and the work stops. And yet Austin has, apparently, relocated the imaginative root-force and is determined to return to its source—symbolically, his father's country, the desert. But, ironically, it is Lee, the Old Man's surrogate, who blocks his way. Then Mom leaves. Perhaps the struggle with Lee's script will begin again. Or perhaps Lee has, at last, lost control completely. The possibility has been there all along; as he says at one point early on: "What kinda people kill each other most . . . Family people. Brothers."

Moreover, throughout *True West*, the artistic impulse, the role of the artist, the idea of art itself seems dipped in a kind of corrosive contempt. Austin is too embarrassed even to refer to his project as a script, much less a work of art; he calls it "research." Lee, predictably, uses the words "art" and "artist" only with sarcasm and disdain. Art, for both, seems at best a not-very-acceptable or manly way to make money; as an activity, it definitely belongs in the kitchen. Shepard makes this connection obliquely at the end of his play. As Mom wanders through the wreckage, her plants dead, her grown sons squabbling about moving to the desert, somehow she is reminded that "Picasso's in town." Austin tells her that Picasso's dead. No, she says, he's visiting the local museum; she read about it in the newspaper. In short, Mom confuses Picasso's life with his art. To the characters in *True West*, it finally doesn't matter one way or the other: Austin lets the topic drop; Lee, naturally, has never heard of Picasso; Mom goes off to her motel. The artist is irrelevant; his work, a joke. And yet Picasso's name, in this absurd context, shines with another, more positive meaning: in the larger sense, Picasso *is* alive and his name becomes, in effect, a kind of emblem of artistic achievement and the integration of intellect and the imagination. Mom's startling *non sequitur* articulates Shepard's ambivalence on a thematic level.

A second theme in *True West* raises similar questions. It has to do with the nature of the American West. As his title implies, Shepard is asking what is the true, or real, West. Again the two brothers dramatize the metaphor, but, in a sense, they are simply stand-ins for Mom and the Old Man. The Old Man (and Lee) are clearly remnants of what Gary Snyder in *The Old Ways* calls the "first phase" of western "exploitation"—an "epic" or "heroic" period, at least in retrospect, characterized by images of manliness, vigor, mobility, unpredictability, rootlessness, humor and violence. It is a world that stands in direct opposition to the world of Mom (and Austin). These two represent the "new west"—the West of suburbs and freeways; toasters and color TVs; Cocker Spaniels and house plants; Safeway. Shepard's treatment of Mom and her world is harsh: he trashes her kitchen and kills her plants; his portrait of her is satiric. She may seem less vividly "the Terrible Mother" than Hailie in *Buried Child*, but her weird, iconographic presence seems just as threatening and life-denying. Moreover, like Ella, the mother in *The Curse of the Starving Class*, Mom is infected with what Shepard considers the most serious new-western sickness—alienation from the land. No wonder she seems flat, remote, lifeless, unreal. In fact, although at first this non-western landscape appears to be the most *real* world in *True West*—after all, the kitchen, its major symbol, is *really* there, in three dimensions on the stage—it becomes, ironically, a fantasy, a kind of mirage. Austin's metamorphosis makes him aware of this truth and increases his desperation to get to the desert. Initially, he insists that his world (and Mom's) is the only real or true one, and that he, not Lee, is really "in touch" with it: "I drive on the freeway every day! I swallow the smog! I watch the news in color! I shop in the Safeway!" But after this humiliation and transformation, he doesn't "recognize the place" anymore; it reminds him of the "'50s"; it lacks substance and has nothing for him now. A few moments later, Mom echoes Austin's words almost exactly: "I can't stay here," she says, wandering vaguely out of her kitchen. "This is worse than being homeless . . . I don't recognize this place."

On the other hand, Shepard's attitude toward the Old West does not seem, in the final analysis, much more favorable. Lee, its representative, may be the most vital and amusing character in *True West*, but he is also violent and devious, childish and totally self-absorbed; actually he envies Austin and even admits that he lives as he does only because he can't "make it" in Austin's world. And the Old Man seems, ultimately, nothing more than an eccentric drunk. Gary Snyder remarks that the "first phase" West was "in a sense psychologically occupied by boys without fathers and mothers, who are really free to get away with things for a while . . ." In fact, Lee and the Old Man are not adults, fathers, they are old boys (males to be sure). Creation is a kind of play and the artist (as Picasso demonstrated) must remain, in part at least, a child; if a sandbox is necessary to sustain the illusion, then into the sandbox. But in *True West*, Shepard's sandbox, the desert, seems just as immaterial, or unreal, as Mom's suburbs or Lee himself; the Old Man, after all, doesn't even appear on stage—he is a rumor, a ghost, a memory. In *Angel City*, Shepard uses film as a metaphor for the uneasy relationship between illusion and reality (surely an analogy that should be retired by now), and Lee's film script, predictably, makes Shepard's point about the Old West explicit. Lee insists that his is a "true story," yet it seems, in the telling, just another tall tale; it may have what Kimmer calls "the ring of truth" (i.e., archetypic resonance), but it also seems just as fake and contrived as Austin maintains. If it does say "something about the land," that land—that mythic western landscape—is becoming more and more remote, "a dead issue," as Austin puts it before his re-birth. In short, in *True West*, past and present both dissolve; Lee and Austin are left frozen, "stuck" between an empty dream and an insubstantial reality.

This condition is not an unfamiliar one in modern drama—Beckett bases his work on it as does Pinter, to whom *True West* owes a major debt (see Aston in *The Caretaker* and Lenny in *The Homecoming*, for instance). It reflects what R. D. Laing, in a book that seems remarkably apposite to Shepard's play, *The Divided Self*, calls a state of "primary ontological insecurity." In such a state, the individual lacks a firm, central sense of his own and other people's reality and identity; he doubts the permanence of things, the reliability and substantiality of natural processes, even the tangibility of others. As a result, Laing asserts, "there is a rent in his relation with the world," as well as a "disruption of his relation with himself; he does not experience himself as a complete person but rather as split in various ways, perhaps as a mind more or less tenuously linked to a body, or two or more selves and so on." For Laing, an existential psychiatrist, such a condition is "schizoid"; in extreme cases it can lead to psychotic schizophrenia. For Beckett and Pinter, existential writers, it reflects, quite simply, the psychic state of modern (western) man—homeless, anxious, irresolute, divided. Shepard apparently agrees. However, whereas *Waiting for Godot* or *The Caretaker* both seem to describe this state of mind, *True West* seems to take an *imprint* of it. And Shepard himself encourages such an immediate, even autobiographical reading of his play.

For example, it is well known that Shepard was raised on a small farm in Southern California, east of Los Angeles, and that his mother now lives in a suburb near Pasadena. Shepard's father remains publicly obscure, but it seems significant that the Old Man has points in common with the fathers in both of Shepard's semi-autobiographical plays, *The Curse of the Starving Class* and *Buried Child*—Weston (drunken, irresponsible, violent) and Tilden who has just returned from a mysterious, vagrant life in the Southwest. Further, like Austin (who, as played by Peter Coyote at the Magic, actually resembled Shepard physically), Shepard lives "up north" in a suburb of San Francisco with his wife and son; his literary and film successes (the Pulitzer Prize, starring roles in *Days of Heaven* and *Resurrection*) have presumably brought him securely into the upper-middle class, while he has in the past had several abortive, distasteful experiences as a fledgling screenwriter. Finally, Shepard has *no* brother. To those familiar with his life and legend, however, Lee is just as clearly based on Shepard himself as is Austin—he is Shepard's "cowboy mouth," his own self-dramatization (rock star, farmer, poet, yegg), the "bad

boy" Patti Smith glorifies in "Nine Random Years [7 + 2]." (Shepard even has two nominal identities; he was born Samuel Shepard Rogers II.) Thus, despite its objective reality, and its universal ambiguities and implications, *True West* may, in fact, be Shepard's most subjective, most personal play to date. Like the conflict at its core, the play seems locked in battle with itself; essentially an autodidactic writer, Shepard nevertheless imposes a strict, self-conscious structure on his work; again and again, unaccountably, he tries to pin down his symbols; when he does, they die. And yet the play itself continually rebels, breaks free, comes back to life.

ROBERT MAZZOCCO
"Heading for the Last Roundup"
New York Review of Books, May 9, 1985, pp. 21–27

I

When the plays of Sam Shepard began appearing in the Sixties at underground theaters like La Mama or the Caffe Cino he was often thought to be a surrealist dramatist. That's true enough of much of his atmospheric detail, early or late: *Angel City* and its phantasmal green slime, *Operation Sidewinder* and its serpentine computer. At the start of *Suicide in B^b* we discover, to quote from Shepard, that "the outline of a man's body sprawled out in an awkward position of death is painted in white" on the center of a darkened stage. And it's true that a dreamlike *mise en scène* inhabits most of his forty or so plays.

More likely, though, the boisterously prolific Shepard should be seen as an embattled realist, or an elusive one, with a highly picaresque view of the world, and a roguish sense of himself and of his characters in relation to that world. A number of these characters, whether buried in the "middle of nowhere" or ravaging among the graffiti of the metropolis, dote on the tall tale, are fascinated by the foxiness of old pretenders. Others are a kind of holy fool, drifters who are also questers, outlaws who are also poets. Even the most matter-of-fact are prey to orneriness. Mom, in *True West* (1980), in the Los Angeles of today, blithely informs her sons: "Picasso's in town. Isn't that incredible? . . . No, he's not dead. He's visiting the museum. I read it on the bus. We have to go down there and see him." Eventually in the unraveling of the tall tale calamity lurks, the horizon is electric with disaster, while for the holy fools paranoia is always possible, suitably guyed with touches of Shepard's humorous hyperbole: A funny thing happened to me on the way to Armageddon, as one of his characters might say.

Shepard's world, however idiosyncratic, is of course America. It is at once a "youth culture" America, full of hot rods and juke boxes, rap sessions and brand names (some of the characters are irreverently called Kent or Salem or Dodge), and a world always colored by the evocation of an American past—a highly selective one. For Shepard's is largely the America of Buffalo Bill and Andrew Jackson, but surely not that of Henry Adams or Henry James; the America of medicine shows and covered wagons, revivalist meetings and rodeos, but hardly of Debs or Sacco and Vanzetti or even of the robber barons of Wall Street. In short, a thoroughly demotic, folkloric America, the American past more or less as a Hollywood cliché—but an America, nonetheless, continually illuminated through the purview of the artist, the artist as tramp or seer.

If one is content to follow this hard-nosed, drug-induced, pop-flavored style, this perpetual retuning of old genres and old myths, one encounters, finally, a profuse and unique panorama of where we are now and where we have been. Because Shepard has written so much, because frequently his plays seem provisional reports whose vitality springs perhaps from a certain disgust with writing plays at all—Shepard likes to say that he took to writing so as "not to go off the deep end," that all along his real desire was to be a "rock-and-roll star"— it's extraordinarily difficult to write categorically about what goes on in his theater. But surely at the center of Shepard's America must stand his antipodean band of errant sons and ghostly fathers—his assortment of gangsters and gamblers, cowboys and farmers—variants either on the "child of nature" and "noble savage" or on the authority figure of the "old man," an abiding presence, home from the hills and now gone a bit daft. Shepard's women, themselves variants on mothers and whores, sisters or sweethearts, are, not surprisingly, dim in comparison to his macho pantheon, but they too have their moments.

Around these characters flourish the heady themes of the plays. In them, boyish adventures are both ardent and a disappointment, savaged usually with the threnody of despair. A fortune hunt in the harlequinade of *Mad Dog Blues* (1971) reveals nothing but two bags full of "millions of bottle caps." Memories of utopias rise and fall and leave not a trace behind: "What's a community?" Jeep, a disillusioned counterculturist, asks mockingly in *Action* (1975).

Much in Shepard is "invisible." Mice are everywhere in *4-H Club* (1965), but not one, apparently, is seen. Much is also "imaginary," particularly death, a recurrent motif. Bullets fly across the stage in *The Unseen Hand* (1969), but the actors, like the ogres of video games, are invulnerable to them. Carol, in *Red Cross* (1966), speaks eloquently, once, of her own death at the bottom of a ski slope. Language in the same play can be lethal, a trap for the unwary: a maid "drowns" while inattentively listening to instructions on how to swim. Or, conversely, language can be a means of staving off suffocation. "You gotta talk or you'll die," murmurs Tilden, the possessor of a terrible and barely discernible family secret in *Buried Child* (1978). Throughout, the grotesque vies with the perfunctory, the humdrum with the fabulous, panic is edged with a kind of cracker-barrel whimsy, and extraordinary behavior is *de rigueur*. In *Curse of the Starving Class* (1978), Wesley unzips his fly, takes out his pecker, and pees all over his sister's culinary demonstration charts lying at his feet.

Older dramatists, like Williams and Miller, had roots in a traditional literature, and their plays could suggest associations with the American theater or American fiction of the Twenties and Thirties. Albee, for all his postwar consciousness, can be similarly placed, even if he has roots in Salinger or Beckett (read "Pretty Mouth and Green My Eyes" for the genesis of *The Zoo Story's* conversational style, *Malone Dies* for the nucleus of Martha's hymn to her "son" in *Virginia Woolf*).

Only in Sam Shepard do we find in a playwright of equal importance a consequential break with the niceties of a literary past, and the triumph of a dramatic style largely improvisation, one related more and more to popular culture. Literary influences certainly exist, primarily those of Whitman and Kerouac, but these are less verbal than visual—Walt on the open road, Jack and Neal Cassady in their old jalopy—are part of the iconography of what Shepard calls the "car culture for the young." More important, these influences are always subject to greater ones: from music (rock and jazz), from art (Pollock or "happenings"), and above all from Hollywood and TV.

It's hardly surprising that in Shepard's *Motel Chronicles* (1982), a series of impressionistic reminiscences in verse and prose, one comes across "I keep praying / for a double bill / of *BAD DAY AT BLACK ROCK* / and / *VERA CRUZ*"— meaning a double bill of the films of the Fifties he'd seen in his adolescence. He seems to want, in fact, a double bill of the patriarchal and "buddy culture" aspects of these (and other) films—silver-haired Tracy saving the day at Black Rock, Cooper and Lancaster toughing things up at Vera Cruz—that have been so keenly enlivening his own folkloric landscapes. And if in his world a "new god" is sought, or a moment of "great expectation," the new god turns out to be, not unexpectedly, "a rock-and-roll Jesus with a cowboy mouth"— which, alas, sounds more like a description of Ronald Reagan, minus the rock-and-roll, than any invocation of a deity, new or old.

Much has been said of the deftness of Shepard's ear, his mastery of "living speech." The isolated monologues of his characters, those brilliant, scarifying arias for which he's justly famous, are in many cases the equivalent of the prose poem. One could make a little anthology of the best of these speeches and they would represent a good deal of what is most pertinent or piquant in his work. For these long monologues, when at full tilt, include the thematic hints of what's to come or heighten what's already been; they either point to an approaching storm or leave an eerie afterglow; contain, that is, both the emotional definition of the characters speaking and the design embodying these characters.

To take an elementary example, Stu, in *Cowboy #2* (1967), in an aria on peacocks and turtles and chickens in chicken coops, turns from the beauty of the peacocks to the awfulness of chickens expiring in "a pool of shit and piss and feathers and cluck"; then Chet, his buddy, starts another aria on breakfast cereals. Later, in a duet, they'll play at and "become" old men, old prospectors, fighting off imaginary Injuns on imaginary plains—and the underlying themes of guilelessness and death, youth and age, will subsequently evolve.

Yet these characters are rarely separable or memorable; they have none of the distinctiveness, the embroidery of portraiture of Blanche DuBois or Willy Loman. Not only do Stu and Chet frequently mimic each other or exchange identities with each other, but so also do Kosmo and Yahoodi in *Mad Dog Blues*, and Lee and Austin in *True West*; even in the incestuous coupling of *Fool for Love* (1983), May and Eddie, half-sister and half-brother, are virtually opposite sides of the same coin. These characters, as Elizabeth Hardwick has observed, are not so much characters as *actors*, members of some sort of revolving repertory company where the impresario is of course Shepard himself, Shepard exuberantly amplifying the possibilities of his own picaresque imagination or poetic roguery, Shepard delighting in the fact that the playwright is, as he says, "the only actor who gets to play all the roles."

In so celebrating the histrionic dexterity of the actor, Shepard is also insisting that we watch as well as listen, use our eyes no less than our ears. In his theater we encounter precipitate alterations of personality, or chimerical shifts in diction or mood or dress (disrobing or a bedraggled sumptuousness are common), and frequently accompanying the long monologues or interwoven among them, another character, on another part of the stage, might suddenly begin shadow boxing, or howl like a coyote, or slowly dance to a blues ballad, or sit in a heavy red armchair and maneuver it till it comes to resemble a "giant tortoise."

Admittedly, at times all this activity can be little more than an avant-garde burlesque of the "stage business" of yesteryear. At other times overall movement clearly falters:

Shepard either runs out of gas (the second half of *Angel City* is surely a letdown after the first) or has trouble getting started. But generally such choreography engages us as swiftly or effortlessly as possible; and even when the characters are seemingly doing nothing at all, lying about as if "dead," these moments are purely deceptive—at key points in the concluding sequences of *Melodrama Play* (1967) each of the "dead" will rise from the floor and exit, and the effect is startling.

A feeling for sound, a feeling for movement—these by themselves, however, might eventually pall, seem marginal or merely opaque. What's necessary, finally, is an energizing perspective, an element beyond the purely dramaturgical, a feeling for space, Here Shepard makes his larger, more personal and metaphorical claims, here his portrait of America, past and present, assumes consciousness, makes itself known. For whether one is watching a farmhouse, an office, a motel room, or a hideaway resort, whether a signal property on stage be a stuffed bird (*Cowboy Mouth*), a lasso (*Fool for Love*), or a blinking Christmas tree (*Action*), behind everything, incorporating everything, is Shepard's irrepressible sense of nomadic drift. He keeps propelling his characters from one circumstance to another, and out of this grows the general convulsiveness, the peculiar pathos encompassing the "buddy culture" and patriarchal components of his disparate texts.

First, then, the hoopla and zeal of the trail, paths open, forever beckoning toward more distant, more challenging vistas; later, inevitably, the solace and consolation of the hearth. Yet with Shepard neither the trail nor the hearth is ever completely satisfying in itself, though neither is possible without the other. Each, rather, is a part of an indefinable whole, the "whole" itself being similar to Shepard's definition of human behavior: "a fractured whole with bits of character flying off a central theme." If the family, either in union or disunion, is the emotional focal point of his world, then the central theme or symbol, the *fabula* of his theater, has to be that of the frontier.

Of course every part of America was once a frontier. Turner's diagram of the successive wave-after-wave peopling of the West is famous—the deerslayer to trek the unknown, the emigrants to settle and work it, the men of capital to market and control it, and once again Babylon arises in our midst, and once more the impulse to move still further on, to struggle toward yet another El Dorado mercilessly takes hold. This diagram (or its Hollywood version) is surely always buried deep somewhere in Shepard's imagination. "To not be fixed," he remarked in an interview, is his creed. "There's an incredible sense of dissatisfaction," he added, "when there is no danger." Danger, however, like violence has always been double-edged in American history. If a desire for a life free of the restrictions of civilization meant glorying in the wonders of a rugged individualism, it also meant a life in the wilderness full of conflict and mayhem. On the other hand, if the family shelters, the family also isolates and confines. And if rootedness allows for growth, rootedness also provokes restlessness. Quandaries develop. Irresistibly in Shepard, words like "compete" and "justification" come to the fore.

So one grows tired of one's travels—the position of Jeep in *Action*. And he asks his buddy, Shooter, to establish yet again one more reason for them to get up and go. "Some justification," he demands, "for me to find myself someplace else." Or, more drastically, one grows tired of being top dog, yet one cannot retire gracefully from the "game," one has to defend one's "rep"—the dilemma of Hoss in *The Tooth of Crime* (1972). "I wanna be a fuck-off again," Hoss says. "I don't wanna compete no more." And immediately we know that his

doom is sealed because fresher blood is already coming in off the trail to seek him out.

The Tooth of Crime, undoubtedly the quintessential Shepard play, is a dazzlingly corrosive work and one of the most original achievements in contemporary theater. It is also the play that best illustrates the various facets—at once highly eclectic and highly singular—of his genius. Though ostensibly a futuristic exposé, with sci-fi trimmings, of the sleaze of the recording industry—it was written in London after Shepard's meetings with members of the Who and the Stones—it is basically a rock fantasia on the new gun in town. Shepard's most bravura touches are here—woozy epithets, internal rhyme, musical syncopation, cockalorum and caricature, a knife thrower's dummy that spills real blood, as well as Shepard's prevailing belief that "language is a veil holding demons and angels which the other characters are always out of touch with." All these, despite some exasperating lapses, rise to a level of perfection that Shepard, I believe, has not matched since.

In *The Tooth of Crime* Hoss, a celebrated musician at the top of the charts, has an intemperate rival in the deadly Crow, a younger and sassier musician edging his way toward his place in the sun. Each is presented as a "killer," but each is also an "image maker" or a "marker." Neither can exist in union. "I'm a solo, man," Crow quips. "So are you . . . who'd be the leader?" Between them, as so often happens in Shepard, gunplay must become wordplay, the battle of the egos, who's got the muscle, whose self is the "real" self, being first and foremost a battle of "style." For Shepard, identity is bound up with one's style, and in his world both are fluid, and each necessarily comments on the other. The language of *The Tooth of Crime* is of course the language of the western, its argot, but only as a computer programmer or a devotee of *Billboard* or *Cashbox* might use it or fancy it. Here is Hoss encountering Crow for the first time, taking his measure, determined to daunt him with a demonstration of his own spiel, which Crow, got up to look like Keith Richard and exuding a "violent arrogance," will, since he plays harder ball, toss right back.

> Hoss: I musta' misfed my data somehow. I thought
> you were raw, unschooled. Ya' know? I mean,
> maybe the training's changed since my time.
> Look, I wanna just sound you for a while before
> we get down to the cut. O.K.? You don't know
> how lonely it's been. I can talk to Cheyenne but
> we mostly reminisce on old kills. Ya' know. I
> don't get new information. I'm starving for new
> food. Ya' know? That don't mean I won't be
> game to mark you when the time comes. I don't
> sleep standin' up. Ya' know what I mean? It's
> just that I wanna find out what's going on.
> None of us knows. I'm surrounded by boobs
> who're still playin' in the sixties. That's where I
> figured you were. Earlier. I figured you for
> Beach Boys in fact.

In this play—and in the best of the other plays written shortly after: *Suicide in B^b*, *Geography of a Horse Dreamer*, and, especially, *Seduced*—Shepard is examining, not so much in political or economic parallels as in those of domination and submission, the nature of power in America. Or, more precisely, the duplicitous nature of "success" and "failure," where it's implied that a failure of nerve and not that of a "life" is at the basis of both. For when a rattled Hoss, under pressure to advance even higher on the charts, to score yet another song hit or "kill," pauses to wonder, "Ain't there any farmers left, ranchers, cowboys, open space? Nobody just livin' their life,"

Becky, his girl, tells him: "That's old time boogie. The only way to be an individual is in the game." Hoss knows that in the world of the "game," where "there's a new star every week," he's not free, he's existing on borrowed time, stuck in an "image," "stuck in a mansion," awaiting his doppelgänger, another explosive kid "who's probably just like me. Just like I was then. A young blood. . . . I gotta roll him or he'll roll me."

The intricacy of the play—its multiple "codes" and "rules," approaching at times incoherence—can only be hinted at. In structure, however, *The Tooth of Crime* mirrors the strict pattern of crisis and catastrophe found in Shepard's earlier (and equally incantatory) *La Turista* (1967). The first act focuses on Hoss, caught up among his minions in all the cliché paraphernalia of being a "star," a "king," a "fucking industry." Hoss randomly meditates on his fame and his past, on his high school days or on his fear of "losin' direction." The act concludes fittingly in a soliloquy of "shifting voices," through which Hoss speaks both in his own voice and in that of his dead father, "old fishin' buddy," who advises, as always: "The road's what counts. Just look at the road. Don't worry about where it's goin'."

In the second and final act we arrive at the prolonged confrontation scene, Hoss and Crow in their virtuoso jousting match, a truly daring example of the interpolative velocity of Shepard's art. Against a suitably mercantile background of rock-and-roll and country-western, a skeletal set emphasizing Hoss's disputed Pharaonical "black throne," and amid all the absurdly terroristic jargon—"master" and "slave," "true," and "false"—of a Vegas casino, or a suggestion of same, Hoss and Crow will attempt to outperform or overcome each other, to symbolically attain or retain legendary frontier status. Yet however extravagantly drawn, neither is autonomous. And that is Shepard's point. Each is merely a combinative "pawn" in a "game," and the only way for either to win at the game is to keep reinventing the self, which means to keep proliferating one's "image," the "gypsy" or fatherless Crow being, in this respect, particularly factitious:

> Hoss: I just hope you never see yourself from the outside. Just a flash of what you're really like. A pitiful flash. . . .
> Crow: No chance, Leathers. The image is my survival kit.

The only way, in a counterfeit world, to win even if one loses, a world where they hierarchically "re-program the tapes," is ultimately to forfeit the one genuine article left— "losin' big" on a colossal scale. "A true gesture," as Hoss, the less dehumanized of the two, will explain, "that won't never cheat on itself 'cause it's the last of its kind. It can't be taught or copied or stolen or sold. It's mine. An original." At the end of the play, Hoss, bowing to the implacable style out of which he's sprung, will fire a bullet into his mouth and disappear in "one clean shot." Crow will indolently remark: "I gotta hand it to ya'. It took ya' long enough but you slid right home." The wheel of fashion will spin another turn, and Crow will have to await his own Crow, for the next shoot-out, the next "image" to supersede his own.

For Shepard, this is what the trail (or the "crime") has become: constant flux, which of course is its only permanence, a continual "rollin' down." "Keep me in my state a' grace," as Crow ironically prays in his victory song, which is also a funereal one, "Just keep me rollin' down." Here not even Hemingway's idea that "man is not made for defeat," that "a man can be destroyed but not defeated" is applicable. For inverting the Hemingway formula, Hoss is both defeated (by Crow) and destroyed (by himself).

The virulence of this nihilism is later compounded in the devastating portrait of the megalomaniacal billionaire, Henry Hackamore, the character supposedly modeled after Howard Hughes, in *Seduced*. Hackamore is kept alive through periodic injections of "genius blood," and exclaims: "I'm the demon they invented! Everything they ever aspired to. The nightmare of the nation! It's me . . . Only me!"

Such nihilism Shepard could only back away from. When he found his bearings again, it was in the late Seventies and early Eighties, in the four plays, generally referred to as his "family plays," where he turned from the game to the trap, from the trail back to the hearth, from warfare in a "buddy culture" to warfare among kith and kin. In these plays, *Curse of the Starving Class* and *Buried Child*, *True West* and *Fool for Love*, Shepard's old rambunctiousness, the tall tale and holy fool are still around, but chastened; the effect of all four is more or less like that of an elegiac vaudeville, which is true even of the knockabout sensual avidity of *Fool for Love*. Yet despite the engaging domestic detail or the mundane subject matter (sibling rivalry, financial plight, sexual infidelity), the sense of drift, of dispossession or disorientation, is paramount here as well.

In *Curse of the Starving Class*, Weston, desperate farmer, World War II vet, bumbling father, has trouble piecing together the patches of a bruised life, trouble, that is, grasping the point of the "whole." "The jumps," he says, "I couldn't figure out the jumps. From being born, to growing up, to droppin' bombs, to having kids, to hittin' bars, to this. . . . I kept looking for it out there somewhere. And all the time it was right inside this house . . . that's why you need a hard table once in a while . . . a good hard table to bring you back to life." Yet pitted against the tactile reality of Weston's past is always the slippery reality of the present: the "zombies" of Babylon at work once again. "Banks, car lots, investors," he muses. "The whole thing's geared to invisible money. You never hear the sound of change anymore. It's all plastic shuffling back and forth. It's all in everybody's heads."

In *Buried Child*, the title itself more than an echo of the thralldom of genealogy permeating the play, Vince, another of Shepard's irascible young drifters, who could just as easily be Weston's son Wesley, has an atavistic vision of himself in the windshield of his car on a furious all-night drive "clear to the Iowa border." As he studies his face in the glare of the windshield under a pelting rain, what he sees is not his own face but the face of a mummy, and beneath that the face of his father, and beneath that the face of his grandfather. Still here again pitted against Vince's atavistic vision lies a deeper one of genealogical dread and disgust. "You think just because people propagate they have to love their offspring?" Vince's grandfather asks Vince's girl, Shelly. "You never seen a bitch eat her puppies? Where are you from anyway?" And of course the "buried child" of the play's title is, in fact, a murdered child, the result, within the family, of some "unspeakable" or mysterious union between Tilden, Vince's father, and Tilden's mother.

II

The ineluctable pull toward "home," the last stop on the journey from which all journeys began; the nostalgia for a bloody denouement, as innocent as it is corrupt, for "one clean shot"; the perennial opposition of trail and hearth; above all, the kaleidoscopic vastness of America, a country growing more and more controlled and at the same time—as in the past so in the present—in danger of going completely out of control: these, now darkly etched, now lightly, now in a naturalist style, now an absurdist one, again and again define Shepard's world. But a question arises. Why has Shepard, so clearly a success for almost twenty years now, been so restlessly drawn to such paradoxes?

Shepard's father, an NCO, kept the family (Shepard, his mother, his two sisters) continually on the move from one army base to another, settling finally, during Shepard's adolescence, at a scrabbly avocado ranch in Duarte, California. The father, evidently a rover and an alcoholic, was fatally hit by a truck a year or so ago in Santa Fe, an accident that, as Shepard acknowledged in an interview in *American Film*, had more than likely been willed. This father, no matter how strong the disavowal of the autobiographical, surely connects with the protean figure of the "old man" of the plays. Shepard himself could be any of his young men, either the son searching for the lost father ("My heart was pounding," we hear Wesley say, recalling the "avocado blossoms" of his youth, "just from my dad coming back"), or, more deeply, given the Whitmanesque aura of Shepard's "buddy culture," the son searching for the brother he never had or, as in *True West*, the son in an ambiguous relationship with the brother he has.

In *Motel Chronicles*, where Shepard, for once, speaks directly about himself, we find, through the book's telegraphic scattered mementos, some warranty for the above: in glimpses of Shepard's mother carrying her child "in a brown Army blanket," the two pausing on a prairie in the Badlands, "at a place with huge white plaster dinosaurs" standing in a circle, the "lights shining up at them from the ground" (this and accompanying images are incorporated in the screenplay Shepard recently wrote for Wim Wenders, *Paris, Texas*); in glimpses of Shepard the teen-age dropout, stealing cars and IDs, working as actor or busboy.

Most telling of all are assorted glimpses of Shepard's "dad," particularly the scene where he pays his father a visit not too long before his death. The father is estranged from his wife and family, an anchorite in the "New Mexican dust," with his "prize" of an "original Al Jolson 78," his "collage" of "wall-to-wall magazine clippings . . . splattered with bacon grease," including one snap of "B-52 Bombers in Wing Formation." (Shepard's father participated in aerial missions over Italy, and it's amusing, or perhaps not so amusing, that his son, who grew up with a fear of flying, would later rise to Hollywood celebrity through portraying Chuck Yeager in *The Right Stuff*.) Shepard concludes his little litany with two clinching paragraphs:

> He spent all the food money I'd gave him on Bourbon. Filled the ice box with bottles. Had his hair cut short like a World War II fighter pilot. He gleamed every time he ran his hand across the bristles. Said they used to cut it short like that so their helmets would fit. Showed me how the shrapnel scars still showed on the nape of his neck.
>
> My Dad lives alone on the desert. He says he doesn't fit in with people.

Neither, as it turns out, does Travis, in *Paris, Texas*, a middle-aged drifter who has abandoned wife and child and has inexplicably spent four years wandering the "far distances" of Texas and Mexico, and now just as inexplicably reappears. Travis is surely the most impenetrable of all of Shepard's characters. In the same way that Shepard refuses to "interpret" his father, so it is with Travis. Nevertheless, the connection between them is obvious. Indeed, Harry Dean Stanton, the actor chosen to play Travis, bears, to judge by the photos in *Motel Chronicles*, an uncanny resemblance to Shepard's father.

Here too, Shepard's El Dorado motif crops up yet again,

for it is Travis's "calculation" that he had been "conceived" in the now forsaken eponymous town of Paris, when his parents had been in the throes of an idyllic love, later in married life to grow paranoid and thwarted, paralleling the fate of Travis in his own married life. His peregrinations, then, are his baffled means of recovering his origins or of reclaiming a presumably sanctified place. However, in this un-Freudian film, the diagnostic possibility of so curious a fancy is, typically, left undeveloped or unexplored.

Wim Wenders is the most American of the young directors of the "New German Cinema." Not only have Ford's *The Searchers*, Sturges's *Sullivan's Travels*, or Nicolas Ray's *They Live By Night* (probably the earliest sustained example of what we today call the "road movie") been models throughout his career, but even most of the "foreign" influences are, one might say, essentially American as well: Lang and Hitchcock, transplants in Hollywood from Germany or England. All of Wenders's best films deal with patterns of emotional dislocation set against an arresting geographical idiom. The characters, generally two young men, suffering crises of memory or of identity, keep moving from city to city, are always in flight (in the spectacular tracking shot at the Paris metro in *The American Friend*, Jonathan runs off from the scene of his crime, the video monitors reduplicating his checkered progress). Or at the end of a film, one may hope to complete in the future what one had sought to do at the beginning, and so the cycle resumes. Wenders shares a natural artistic affinity with Shepard and much from their association was to be expected.

Yet though *Paris, Texas* is the most interesting American film I've seen all year, it is finally not a success. The photography of Robby Müller, surpassing anything he and Wenders have previously done together, is exquisitely attuned to the film's tonal and visual rhythms, as is, for the most part, Shepard's dialogue, generally minimalist for the occasion. The trouble, however, lies with the tale: Travis unexpectedly surfaces out of nowhere, then magically brings together Jane, the lost wife, who's spent the last four years as a call girl at a Houston peep show, and Hunter, the lost son, who's spent the last four of the eight years of his life in the comfortable Los Angeles home of Travis's brother and his brother's wife. This tale, despite an air of verisimilitude, is nevertheless much too improbable or anecdotal to be real.

In perhaps the film's most striking sequence, we hear the amplified, if muffled, voice of a man, as we also watch Travis morosely traversing a windy overpass. The voice is apparently that of someone haranguing a crowd, or a political orator, but we discover, at the end of Travis's promenade, that it belongs to a derelict, a "crazy," shouting his malefic message to the air or to the indifferent roar of the traffic below. Travis pauses to pat the distraught fellow on the back, as if in complicity with the man's plight, then ambles on. It's a memorable moment, another of Shepard's apocalyptic tremors, but it does not open up the film. It merely encloses it further. Often the film might be the dream of Travis (particularly in view of Stanton's shuffling, somnambulist portrayal), Travis hallucinating the events of the film, or, more exactly, fabulating them, since the easy camaraderie later evinced between Travis and Hunter (or Shepard and his father) is surely more on the order of wish fulfillment than anything else.

Wenders, in an article in *Le Monde*, has suggested that he and Shepard had a larger dimension in mind, a distinctly Homeric one. But to imagine Travis as Ulysses, Jane as Penelope, Hunter as Telemachus—how, under the circumstances, would that be possible except in an ironic sense? With Jane's Penelope being the most ironic, or comic, of all: faithful

Penelope reduced to a kind of Circe and her importunate suitors to a collection of anonymous clients popping in off the streets of Houston for a cheap thrill. That Wenders and Shepard were obviously unaware of what fragile ground they treaded is confirmed, I believe, in the long and spiritless double monologue concluding the film. Here the idea of Travis as Ulysses, another wanderer and teller of tall tales, might have worked if Shepard had something to deliver. Alas, he has not. Nothing either Travis or Jane has to say is truly revelatory of their troublesome past; it is merely a *faux-naif* jumble about guilt and redemption, freedom and trust, the film evaporating finally in a folkloric mist, oddly reminiscent of *Enoch Arden*, mother and son, Jane and Hunter, reunited, and the noble and sacrificial Travis, his good deed accomplished, once more going off into the "far distances."

If we look back over the expanse of Shepard's work—the trash of human loneliness or human aggression, a feeling for "images that shine," as he says, "in the middle of junk" (the billboard culture of America serving him here) or for things that time and again are "blown away"—we can see in the jocose desolation or stoical amiability, in the interplay of ego and environment the unstinting vigor and originality of his vision. But also its limitations. Americans—that is, Americans en masse—have always celebrated their own ignorance. "The best place to hide something," Vachel Lindsay once wryly observed of the habits of his countrymen, "is in a book." And there's no doubt that Shepard, with his tall tales and holy fools, celebrates that national trait.

Superficially his general indictment of American materialism is similar to James's "interrogation of the past" as he gazes upon the industrial gloom of the New Jersey shore in *The American Scene*. But what a difference between Shepard and his lust for the old primordial thrill and the expatriate James and his manifold displacements, his "international theme" of "dispossessed princes and wandering heirs." Though one can find in Shepard any number of spiritual or ceremonial transformations (the mantic strain, the use of paradox and parable, being, I think, as present as the manic), one would be hard put to discover much in the way of cultural or intellectual emancipation. "Myth," as he puts it, "is a powerful medium," precisely "because it talks to the emotions and not the head."

Thus, again and again, what unites his heroes is the division of the spoils, the affirmation through negation: Jeep speaks of Whitman as "a passionate father bleeding for his country." Weston speaks of the family as "an animal thing." Hoss says of himself, "I couldn't take my life in my hands while I was alive but now I can take it in death." May tells Eddie that "anybody who doesn't half kill themselves falling off horses or jumping on steers" isn't a real "male" in his eyes. It's all vital and genuine, and wonderfully moving and sinister in an aboriginal way, and yet for all that a kind of shuck, a "game."

Of course, as we have seen, Shepard knows very well that it's a game, just as Hoss knows. "Genius," Hoss says, "is something outside the game. The game can't contain a true genius. It's too small." Shepard enlarges and elaborates upon what he knows, and damns, repeatedly, the computerized and depersonalized world that has arisen from the old patriarchy, the old macho assurances. Still, deep down, his heart goes out

to them, he remains in fealty to them, unwilling as he is to demystify or to confront these old myths and their dubious hold upon us or upon himself. Thus the splendor of his tapestries. Thus, too, the laceration of consciousness—"split," one of his favorite words—as we move from a raw and evergreen youthfulness traveling the "territory," constantly upping the ante, to the abrupt disgruntlement or dilapidation of age, and with very little else in between. Then comes the final severance, the final recoil, till one is left a ruminating shadow, as Shepard's father is left (or Cooper's Natty Bumppo at the end of *The Pioneers*), no longer able to "fit with people."

Shepard arrived on the scene at two crucial, if ephemeral, moments in recent American history, each of them bearing heavily upon his own development: during the late Fifties and early Sixties, the salutary aspects of mass culture drawn from such sources as rhythm and blues unexpectedly irradiated high culture, saving it from the academic solemnity or bourgeois conformity that had been stifling it; and the equally radical metamorphosis of the family (or the escape from the family) into a "generation of youth," what one used to call the "new sensibility" of the Sixties. These upheavals, of course, did not last, precisely because they had no real intellectual underpinnings to nourish or guide them; with the result that mass culture, with its assemblage of technocrats, taste makers, and "target audiences," is today far more of a corporate monolith than it's ever been.

From the Seventies to the present, we have been witnessing, with only the rarest of exceptions, and with much lap-dog palaver suggesting the contrary, an unprecedented acceleration of the banal or the bogusly sophisticated in American life and in popular culture—in the megabucks infantilism of the astral sagas of Lucas and Spielberg, in the cornball uplift of *On Golden Pond*, in Yahoo types like Indiana Jones, in the show-biz promotion of American fundamentalism and American politics (the evangelical President Reagan, when not chopping wood or pumping iron, deals in tall tales as if they were facts and figures; he calls his tall tales "anecdotes"), and, finally, in the emergence of a new generation of youth, dumber or shallower, perhaps, than any other generation of youth within memory. Adversary culture, traditionally the air hole of mainstream culture, is no longer a force; the heterogeneity of mass culture, such as it is, is dependent on what's left of the old liberation movements of the Sixties, on feminists, blacks, gays, or on the legacy of rock, as in the current "phenomena" of Harvey Fierstein, Eddie Murphy, or Prince.

Sam Shepard, only a few years out of his thirties, seems at a difficult point of an extraordinary career. Clearly he has been the dominant American playwright of his generation. And he has been more than that, for without him it is by no means certain that the contemporary American theater would have much of importance to speak of, the best of his colleagues, Lanford Wilson, David Mamet, or David Rabe, being in no sense his equals. He has already created a body of work distinctive enough for a lifetime. One may hope that he will not, like Travis at the end of *Paris, Texas*, disappear into more of the folklore of the "far distances," a folklore that has now become as emotionally threadbare as it is ideologically synthetic.

ROBERT E. SHERWOOD

1896–1955

Robert Emmet Sherwood was born on April 4, 1896, in New Rochelle, New York. He was educated at Milton Academy and at Harvard, where he wrote his first play, *A White Elephant*, for the Hasty Pudding Club. In 1917 he left Harvard to fight in World War I with the Canadian Black Guard, then returned to earn the B.A. from Harvard in 1918.

Sherwood served briefly as dramatic critic of *Vanity Fair*, then worked for *Life* magazine, where he began what is believed to be the first regular column of film criticism. Sherwood was editor of *Life* from 1924 to 1928, then became literary editor of *Scribner's Magazine*. By that time, however, his play *The Road to Rome* had had so successful a run that Sherwood could devote himself full time to playwrighting. Among his best-known plays are *Idiot's Delight* (1936), *Abe Lincoln in Illinois* (1939), and *There Shall Be No Night* (1940), which all won the Pulitzer Prize.

From the 1930s onward Sherwood worked extensively in film as screenwriter and producer. He won the Academy Award for the screenplay of *The Best Years of Our Lives* (1946), and he also adapted many of his own plays for the screen.

With the advent of World War II Sherwood entered the political arena. He had been president of the Dramatists' Guild from 1937 to 1940, but he then became a special assistant to the Secretary of War and later served in the Office of War Information and as assistant to the Secretary of the Navy. He formed part of the corps of speechwriters for Franklin D. Roosevelt, and his intimacy with the president led to the writing of his historical study, *Roosevelt and Hopkins* (1948), which won both the Pulitzer Prize in history and the Bancroft Prize for Distinguished Writing in American History.

Married twice, Sherwood was, upon his death on November 14, 1955, revered as both a literary and humanitarian figure.

EDITH J. R. ISAACS
From "Robert Sherwood: Man of the Hour"
Theatre Arts Monthly, January 1939, pp. 32–40

The outstanding fact about Sherwood's work is that while most of the other creative writers of his age and inclination have forgotten the war, by preference or because they could not live and write if they remembered it too steadily and too acutely, Sherwood seems never to have been able consciously or subconsciously to forget it. The terror and stupidity, the brutality and waste of those days and the disillusion that followed them remain constantly with him, in one way or another showing through everything of importance that he has written.

Sherwood's concentration on the idea that peace is better than war did not add to his craftsmanship. It seems for a considerable time to have interfered with it, to have gotten in the way of his plots and his characters, to have cramped a style that was neither sure enough nor sizeable enough to give his ideas range and form. Judging from the early plays, you would say that although the author admired the theatre as an effective medium, he did not respect it any too highly, and often took the theatre's easiest way, rather than its best way, to a given end. He learned very early how simple it was to get laughter and applause by certain theatrical tricks. He seemed to know instinctively how to pick a dramatic situation and the characters to enliven it. But he could not complete a plot or develop a character. So, to make his action progress he would often—unconsciously perhaps—shift his own ground, play up his guns and bombs and drums, and make puppets of his people.

Probably no dramatist who has had a success on the level of Sherwood's has ever written prefaces about the materials and the themes of his plays which show so clearly how far the plays themselves—all of the early ones down to *Reunion in Vienna*—are from his idea of what they were to be. If it is

making a case to fit a theory to say that Sherwood's war obsession was responsible for this hiatus between concept and realization, his own words support such a case.

The Road to Rome, Sherwood's first success, was presented by the Theatre Guild in 1927, with Philip Merivale and Jane Cowl in the leading parts. It is a play about Hannibal. You know that it is, because Sherwood says so himself in this paragraph of his preface:

'Hannibal is a unique figure in history—a sad, lonely and utterly baffling character. He was a brilliant soldier; his actual accomplishments prove that beyond all question. But of his qualities as a man, his habits, his beliefs, his philosophy, nothing definitely is known, nor ever will be known. With the exception of Archimedes, who was killed by the Romans in the siege of Syracuse, there was not one great mind in the world in Hannibal's time—no one who was qualified to appraise the true character of the conquering Carthaginian and to place it on file in the records of humanity. The student, however, is always at liberty to guess about Hannibal—and the play that is published herewith is the dramatization of a guess.'

And what Sherwood intended his play to indicate about the man, 'his habits, his beliefs, his philosophy', is here:

'He never accomplished his purpose; he saw the gates of Rome, but he did not shatter them. In the hour of his greatest victory, he turned from the goal toward which his father had pointed him, and marched away—to occupy a strange place in history as the triumphant leader of a lost cause.'

Such a man, such a soldier, such a masterful failure, is a fine protagonist for drama, and Hannibal's marching away from the walls of Rome, leaving behind him the fruits of his successful war, is a perfect measure of Sherwood's opinion of these despicable fruits, and, perhaps, Sherwood's comment on the Treaty of Versailles. But read the play, and there is little of all this in it, except the event of Hannibal's leaving, with a cause which translates its reason into a woman's whim.

Neither Hannibal nor Amytis, the Greek wife of the Roman dictator Fabius Maximus, who undertakes to conquer Hannibal by her feminine wiles, has any reality of character. Sherwood tried, in his use of historic material, to give the play the flavor of modernity by the use of colloquial language. But his people, though dressed in historic costume, were only clichés out of the modern theatre, speaking the language of Broadway. *The Road to Rome* is actable comedy, as its long and successful career shows, but it is essentially a false, rather than a theatrical, play.

After *The Road to Rome* came *The Love Nest*, an unsuccessful dramatization of a Ring Lardner story, and *The Queen's Husband*, an unimportant but again an actable comedy, and again with a lively and informing preface.

Sherwood's next serious play was *Waterloo Bridge* (1930). The preface to *Waterloo Bridge* is one of the best essays Sherwood has written. It is a picture of the war as reflected in London and as seen through a series of visits Sherwood paid to that city between the time—two years before the war—when he looked at it with the eyes of the usual American tourist, through November 1917, when he came back 'to the great, proud city' as a private soldier on leave, to the November day in 1918 when some of the patients from a war hospital, Sherwood among them, sneaked out through the barbed-wire fence, climbed on a Hammersmith bus, 'and rode into the insane bewilderment of London's celebration.' They passed a plowed field where some German prisoners were at work, and shouted at them, 'Hey, Heinie—the war's over!' But the Germans 'only grinned and waved amicably—not understanding, or not caring'.

A dramatist should be able to take the least corner of a situation and illumine it enough to make the whole surrounding luminous. Very often a human detail from a large canvas can touch the eye, the mind and the heart more deeply than the whole great canvas can. So there is no complaint when Sherwood chooses to show what the war was like—at the moment when Gotha bombers were hovering over London— through the fortunes of two Americans, a little chorus girl who would have been out of work except for a profession older than the chorus, and a young soldier from Syracuse who had joined the Canadian army because he just couldn't wait for America to get into the war. The only complaint with *Waterloo Bridge* is that even within the small theatrical strip he has chosen, Sherwood again fails to make use of the theatre's power of characterization and of illusion. The play has sentiment, a certain wistful sympathy, a picturesque realism in the early scenes, but little vitality.

Again there is an interlude for *This Is New York*, a banal and negligible melodrama with vigorous dialogue and a gangster–Park Avenue plot. In some ways, this was Sherwood's most disappointing play. With his talent for creating excitements on the stage, it seemed as if he should have been able to write effective melodrama. But melodrama, which looks so easy, is a tyrannical dramatic form requiring a secure style, and Sherwood still lacked a style in spite of his increasing fluency.

A turn in fortune came with *Reunion in Vienna*, the first play in which Sherwood showed an aptitude for developing a good theatre situation after he had created it. From this point on, you begin to see clearly in your mind's eye the people of whom he wrote, and although you do not always see them as people walking beside you in the world, they remain with you in the shape of the actors who took part in his plays. If they are not yet people of the real world, they are real people of the theatre world, and for certain kinds of plays, such as *Reunion in Vienna*, that is quite enough. The story of the comedy is

highly amusing. A leading and characteristically self-assured psychoanalyst is married to a beautiful woman who was for some years, before the expulsion of the Hapsburgs, the mistress of the wild but fascinating Archduke Rudolf Maximilian. The memory of Rudolf remains an active and disturbing presence in the household, and the doctor is convinced that one sight of her old lover, now a taxi-driver some place on the Riviera, is all that is needed to banish him from Elena's mind—and incidentally from his own. The opportunity arrives with a reunion of the old nobility, planned to celebrate a certain anniversary. Rudolf is to be there; the doctor urges Elena to go. Bright and somewhat bawdy comedy ensues, and the next morning the doctor, baffled but unbowed, graciously but firmly uses his influence to get Rudolf safely through the police lines at the border so that he may not be seen in Vienna again. The comedy has brisk action throughout, dialogue that is constantly lively and crisp, and enough undercurrent of mischief— suspected but unproved—to keep the interest challenged all the way. You can still hear Lynn Fontanne's voice as Elena turns a phrase; you can see Alfred Lunt's sharp gesture as the Archduke emphatically underscores a desire; you can follow Henry Travers' drawl as the doctor's old father calls out to his daughter-in-law, 'Elena, the Archduke Rudolf Maximilian von Hapsburg is calling on us and they're sending me to bed.'

Several years elapsed between *Reunion in Vienna* (1931) and Sherwood's next produced play (1935). During most of this time the earlier play continued to fill houses both in New York and in London as well as on the road. Critical opinion of Mr. Sherwood's work had settled down comfortably in the meantime with the decision that here was a writer of comedy, learning his craft a step at a time but steadily, sure to go on providing bright entertainment for his audiences. What Mr. Sherwood thought about the world, what he hoped might be done about it, what he intended to say in his plays, as indicated by his vivid and provocative prefaces, might well be forgotten in favor of what he so gaily accomplished.

Then, to disturb the critics' placidity, came *The Petrified Forest*, with one of the best first acts Sherwood has ever written, with a single speech that is quoted everywhere (and will be here) as indicating what the playwright thought of the trend of his own generation, and with a second act that rides full tilt into the most specious hokum with which the playwright has ever made a compromise. It is sincerely to be hoped that Mr. Sherwood regrets writing *The Petrified Forest* after *Reunion in Vienna*. It is all well enough to say that he intended to set the portrait of the man of action, the gangster-murderer Duke Mantee, against that of the intellectual man of inaction, Alan Squier, to show their equal futility. But conceding the dramatist's right to his choice of material and purpose, you must still ask, Did he do it?—to which the answer in this case is, No; and, Was it worth doing?—to which the answer is, Decidedly, no.

It may be the memory of Sherwood's technical success in this empty play, or of Leslie Howard's elegant and unimaginative performance that invariably arouses a certain harshness in regard to *The Petrified Forest*, or it may be just the fact that a man cannot, without paying the price of disappointment, write such a speech as this and throw it away:

> *Squier:* You see—the trouble with me is, I belong to a vanishing race. I'm one of the intellectuals.
> *Gabby:* That means you've got brains. I can see you have.
> *Squier:* Yes—brains without purpose. Noise without sound. Shape without substance. Have you ever read "The Hollow Men"? (*She shakes her*

head.) Don't. It's discouraging, because it's true. It refers to the intellectuals, who thought they'd conquered Nature. They dammed it up, and used its waters to irrigate the wastelands. They built streamlined monstrosities to penetrate its resistance. They wrapped it up in cellophane and sold it to drugstores. They were so certain they had it subdued. And now—do you realize what it is that is causing world chaos? . . . It's Nature hitting back. Not with the old weapons—floods, plagues, holocausts. We can neutralize them. She's fighting back with strange instruments called neuroses. She's deliberately afflicting mankind with the jitters. Nature is proving that she can't be beaten—not by the likes of us. She's taking the world away from the intellectuals and giving it back to the apes. . . .

There was only one Sherwood play produced in New York between *The Petrified Forest* and *Abe Lincoln in Illinois*, namely *Idiot's Delight*. Here again was war, not the war that Sherwood had lived through, but the one that looms ahead— an international, devastating war that is to bring the structure of the world tumbling down around our heads, as the winter resort hotel—the scene of the play—tumbles about the heads of the play's protagonists. Again Sherwood uses his favorite device of gathering together a group of people of various backgrounds and opinions so that he may fully exploit all facets of his theme. Again he uses the little people as his chorus, this time a group of blonde dancing girls who have lost their foot-hold in America and are trying to find one in the night-clubs of Europe. Again his people are only theatre portraits repainted after types well known in real life, but they have a theatre reality, they serve the play's needs and the author's argument. *Idiot's Delight* is successful melodrama, with a strong after-taste of ideas that are worth expressing.

It may be more than chance that gives *Idiot's Delight* a postscript instead of a preface. Of these paragraphs, which Sherwood wrote in March 1936, when 'the British Foreign Secretary, Mr. Eden' said that the current situation was 'dreadfully similar to 1914', we must make what we can today:

'Let me express here the conviction that those who shrug and say, "War is inevitable," are false prophets. . . . Of course, this delusion may still go on. If decent people will continue to be intoxicated by the synthetic spirit of patriotism, pumped into them by megalomaniac leaders . . . then war *is* inevitable. . . . But I don't believe this will be so. I believe that a sufficient number of people are aware of the persistent validity of the Sermon on the Mount, and they remember that, between 1914 and 1918, twelve million men died in violence to make safe for democracy the world which we see about us today. . . . The megalomaniac, to live, must inspire excitement, fear and awe. If, instead, he is greeted with calmness, courage and ridicule, he becomes a figure of supreme insignificance. A display of the three latter qualities by England, France, the Soviet Union and the United States will defeat Fascism in Germany, Italy and Japan, and remove the threat of war which is Fascism's last gesture of self-justification.

'By refusing to imitate the Fascists in their policies of heavily fortified isolation, their hysterical self-worship and psychopathic hatred of others, we may achieve the enjoyment of peaceful life on earth, rather than degraded death in the cellar.'

That was written more than two years ago. For almost ten times two years, Sherwood has been pondering the subject of his next play, the events which forced Abraham Lincoln into civil war, the character with which he approached the labor he abhorred. *Abe Lincoln in Illinois* says what all Sherwood's other serious plays and serious prefaces have tried to say, and says it so well and so convincingly that audiences rise to their feet to applaud it. Much of *Abe Lincoln* is in Lincoln's own words—his homely phrases, his anecdotes, his famous speeches; but the play is none the less Sherwood's creation. He has so immersed himself in Lincoln's style of simple, direct, rugged speech that you pass from Sherwood's words to Lincoln's with no sense of change. Every speech is in character as Sherwood has recreated Lincoln, and within that character a great man, a national hero with all of a nation's legend behind him, lives and moves as a man among men. To recreate such a figure out of history may seem an easier task than to mold a character out of a dramatist's own fresh clay. Indeed it is far harder, as the whole history of such endeavor shows. Great historic figures already live double lives, one of which is in the minds of their audience, and a dramatist who tries to put his own portrait of the man into words stands constantly at the edge of a precipice. Raymond Massey, who plays the part of Lincoln with a devotion to the character he represents almost equal to Sherwood's, and with a surprising personal likeness, deserves all the acclaim he has had for his performance. But you have only to read Sherwood's script before seeing the play to know that it is the dramatist who has given this Lincoln the spark of life.

Abe Lincoln in Illinois carries through three periods of Lincoln's life—in and about New Salem, Illinois, in the 1830's; in and about Springfield, Illinois, in the 1840's; the years 1858 to 1861 to the day when Lincoln, as President-Elect, parted with his neighbors at the railroad station to go on his honored and lonely way:

'Let us live to prove that we can cultivate the natural world that is about us, and the intellectual and moral world that is within us, so that we may secure an individual, social and political prosperity, whose course shall be forward, and which, while the earth endures, shall not pass away.'

Which is a good speech for a dramatist to end on, especially a dramatist who, years before, ended his preface to a very different play, *The Queen's Husband*, with this paragraph:

'The moon is not unattainable. Playwrights have reached for it in the past; they have even brought it down to earth, and pasted it on a back-drop. The moon is never more beautiful than when it is seen shining down on an insecure balcony, in a canvas Verona.'

JOHN GASSNER
From "Robert Emmet Sherwood"

Atlantic, January 1942, pp. 30–33

Like other men, ⟨Sherwood⟩ returned from the First World War with a changed outlook and some firm convictions. Brought up to believe that he was a 100 per cent American and a superior being, he discovered some wholesome facts about the community of man in the training camps, trenches, clinks, and hospitals. On one side of him during his convalescence lay an Australian who had been burned horribly by liquid fire; in the bed on the other side he found a South African Jew who was permanently paralyzed by a machine-gun bullet that had lodged in his spine. In addition to developing an intense aversion to war, he became 'internationally-minded,' was convinced that future wars could be avoided by the elimination of excessive nationalism, and was at first enthusiastic about the League of Nations. But his enthusiasm waned under the influence of the Wilson-haters. 'In 1920,' he has written, 'I confess with deep shame, my first vote as an American citizen was cast for Warren G. Harding. Thus, I did my bit in the great betrayal.' His position then was not inconsistent with hatred of war. This hatred he inserted into his plays, as did other fashionable writers of the twenties who vented their disillusionment with cynical vehemence but without much serious attention to the fundamental problem. In *The Road to Rome*, which was typical of his work in the twenties, he delivered himself of such passages as 'You say he is cruel. Is there any soldier who is otherwise?' and a jibe at womenfolk in war who 'sit at home and talk of the great sacrifices they are making.' But the cream of the story lay in fashionable digs at virtue and Babbittism, in gay indifference to national calamity, and in the jest of Hannibal overcome by a beautiful Roman woman and the respectable Fabius saddled with an illegitimate son. Characteristic was the debonair optimism which made Sherwood and his audience believe that a Hannibal could be cured of his lust for conquest by 'the human equation,' here represented by an evening of pleasant adultery.

Then came the stock-market crash of 1929; and the ensuing years of depression, climaxed by the rise of Hitler, rocked the foundations of the civilized world. The proletarian and near-proletarian writers reacted by adopting Marxist social optimism and activism. Sherwood responded, instead, with a philosophy of despair, harking back to 'The Hollow Men' and *The Waste Land* philosophy of T. S. Eliot. Believing profoundly in spiritual values and in the value of individuality, he could not accept either rationalistic science or collectivism as a solution. He set down their methods, in his preface to *Reunion in Vienna*, as a 'neutralization of nature' which led to a denial of individualism, maintaining that the disciples of both Galileo and Lenin 'are determined to exterminate it and can undoubtedly do so, with the aid of the disciples of Freud.'

He saw civilization and its intellectuals as hopelessly lost, deteriorated in their souls and helpless in the face of a world taken over by the uncivilized. The hero of *The Petrified Forest* (which Sherwood calls 'my first attempt to write a play about my own country in my own time') is a writer who frittered away his talent idling with a rich woman on the Riviera until, lacking something 'worth living for—and dying for,' he asks an obliging gangster to kill him. Self-pityingly he refers to his possessing 'brains without purpose,' and Sherwood, who could not supply him with one, fatalistically ascribed the result to Nature. Intellectual man, described as 'a vanishing race,' thought he had conquered Nature with science, and 'now there is only world-chaos.' 'It's Nature hitting back. Not with the old weapons—floods, plagues, holocausts. . . . She's fighting back with strange instruments called neuroses. She's deliberately afflicting mankind with the jitters. . . . She's taking the world away from the intellectuals and giving it back to the apes.'

Today, having found renewed strength of purpose, the author calls *The Petrified Forest* 'a negative, inconclusive sort of play,' but in 1932 its philosophy seemed to him sufficiently conclusive. He was too close to the hollow men and made them represent the whole intellectual world. The only comfort he could find—in *Acropolis*, which he had written just before—lay in the reflection that the world of the Periclean intellectuals did not after all die completely, since it lived in the memory of man. But here too the intellectuals—Phidias, Pericles, Socrates—were passively losing the world to the apes.

Sherwood's pessimism reached its climax in *Idiot's Delight*. Today he describes it as 'completely American in that it

represented a compound of blank pessimism and desperate optimism, of chaos and jazz.' If he intends this derogatorily, he is somewhat unfair to himself, since his fatalistic prediction of a second World War is justified by past and present fact. He also had a better case against the intellectual than before, when he showed the pacifistic labor leader Quillery succumbing to war hysteria and the internationally-minded scientist Waldersee returning to Germany to make poison gas instead of fighting cancer. If the play did not achieve any genuine clarification, this was because of shortcomings that its author shared with his generation. He made no strong effort to analyze causes, contenting himself with an incisive portrait of a munitions magnate and vague references to the fact that the war is 'everybody's fault' or the result of 'God-damned bad management'; and the negativism of the preceding plays still prevailed sufficiently to rule out any positive conclusions other than the hoofer's saltily stated faith that 'no matter how much the meek may be bulldozed or gypped, they will eventually inherit the earth'—which hardly helps the meek.

Something, however, happened to the pessimist at this time. He found his way back to the roots of American life and drew courage from them. His belief in the common man and in the spirit of American democracy became a white flame as he explored the life of Lincoln. It lighted his way not only to that notable play *Abe Lincoln in Illinois* but to a renewed faith in humanitarian striving and the brotherhood of man. Throughout the formative period of this faith, Sherwood had indeed begun to behave quite unlike his passive characters. In his particular craft, he began an active championship of American playwrights against producers in connection with contractual arrangements, became one of the leaders of the Dramatists' Guild, and in 1937 joined Elmer Rice, Maxwell Anderson, S. N. Behrman, and the late Sidney Howard in founding the Playwrights' Company with the object of putting on their plays independently. His interest also extended to bringing the professional theatre to all parts of the country, by means of an association for which he tried to raise $300,000.

In the larger world, Sherwood was at the same time actively concerned with social problems like slum clearance and municipal housing projects, and in politics he became an ardent New Dealer. The writing of *Abe Lincoln in Illinois* crystallized his growing realization that the intellectual could have both brains and a purpose. He was voicing his own convictions when he made Lincoln tell the townspeople who were seeing him off to Washington, 'Let us live to prove that we can cultivate the natural world that is about us, and the intellectual and moral world within us, so that we may secure an individual, social and political prosperity, whose course shall be forward, and which, while the earth endures, shall not pass away.'

A year after the play opened, that world was distinctly beginning to pass away, and Hitler's Germany began its triumphant march across Europe. Sherwood's new-won faith, however, stood him in good stead while others who had once been less pessimistic and passive than he despaired and stood idly by. He became aware that in his American chronicle he had told 'the story of a man of peace who had to face the issue of appeasement or war.' Sherwood went through the same doubts. 'It was,' he wrote, 'a bitter moment for me when I found myself on the same side as the Big Navy enthusiasts.'

In the hero of *There Shall Be No Night*, Dr. Valkonen, he retraced the stages of his own transformation, but he did not wait until he could find dramatic shape for his new convictions. He plunged into the battle as soon as he arrived at them, and after reconsidering his impulse to reënlist in the Canadian

Army, which would have relegated him to a desk job at his age, became one of the leaders of the 'Committee to Defend America by Aiding the Allies.' He wrote its historic advertisement, 'Stop Hitler Now,' on June 10, 1940, and paid the initial cost of $24,000 out of his own pocket. (He also sent part of his earnings to the Canadian Red Cross, and he gave $20,000 of his royalties from *There Shall Be No Night* to the Finnish Relief Fund.) With his pen he became the Committee's most formidable propagandist. When Charles Lindbergh's first radio speech called upon Americans to be 'as impersonal as a surgeon with his knife' with respect to the plight of Europe, Sherwood's scathing reply in *Time* branded the sentence an insult to the medical profession and rephrased it as signifying 'We must be as impersonal as the professional mourner, who doesn't lament the seriousness of the plague, or the number of fatalities, as long as it helps his own business.'

He became the leading advocate of Clarence Streit's 'Union Now' proposal at the time of Britain's darkest days, because, as he declared at the mass meeting at Mecca Temple, it would serve notice on Hitler 'that the power of the English-speaking world was too great for destruction by wanton bombing of British cities.' It was at this critical time, on August 30, 1940, while bombs were rocking London, that he also tried to hearten the English people with a speech over the Canadian Broadcasting Company in which he assured them that America stood by their side in their great trial. It was a bold move on the part of a private individual to promise American aid, and it was made more annoying to isolationists by his denunciation of Messrs. Ford and Lindbergh as machine worshipers who had succumbed to the 'degenerative influence of Hitlerism.' He became a close, if unofficial, associate of President Roosevelt, whom he admires greatly and supported for reëlection for a third term; he was slated to be Master of Ceremonies at the inauguration when he was stricken with the flu at the White House. Although no confirmation can be had from him, his frequent presence at the White House has been connected with the preparation of several presidential broadcasts, including the declaration of a state of emergency. In February 1941, there were even rumors of his being appointed ambassador to the Court of St. James's. This proved unfounded, but he did take a confidential flight to London from which he returned last October. When the draft bill was enacted he took temporary charge of the Committee on Education, Recreation and Community Service of the United States Army. He is now First Assistant to Colonel William Joseph Donovan, Coördinator of Information, occupying himself in a heavily guarded New York building with the important matter of short-wave broadcasting to Europe. He divides his time between his office and Washington.

He may be quietly completing a new play (he is always incommunicative about his playwriting), since he can write extremely rapidly. But there is enough in his diversified activities to occupy two men. The spirited hero of many a fracas since youth finds zest in his work. If he was once one of MacLeish's too severely taxed 'Irresponsibles,' there is no trace of it left today. He is also undoubtedly a happier man. Having emerged at last from the Slough of Despond, he is, like his Dr. Valkonen, convinced of the heroic possibilities in man's spirit and of the truth of the unknown Jewish mystic's assurance that 'there shall be no night there.'

WINIFRED L. DUSENBURY
From "The Lonely Hero"
The Theme of Loneliness in Modern American Drama
1960, pp. 181–85

Abe Lincoln in Robert Sherwood's play is driven by an inexorable fate as surely as is Oedipus. The gods will not be placated until Abe has fulfilled the function in life provided for him. With uncharacteristic callousness Abe, on the very day which was to have been their wedding day, refuses to marry Miss Mary Todd, because, as he says, "I don't want to be ridden and driven, upward and onward through life, with her whip lashing me, and her spurs digging into me!" But Billy Herndon, like a choric voice interpreting the speaker's motivation, claims

> You're only using her as a living sacrifice, offering her up, in the hope that you will thus gain forgiveness of the gods for your failure to do your own great duty! (II, vi)

Later, after the self-recognition scene, in which the hero comes to an understanding of his true destiny, Abe appeals to Mary to be his wife with the stoical avowal:

> The way I must go is the way you have always wanted me to go.
> *Mary:* And you will promise that never again will you falter, or turn to run away?
> *Abe:* I promise, Mary—if you will have me—I shall devote myself for the rest of my days to trying— to do what is right—as God gives me power to see what is right. (II, viii)

As the curtain falls upon Mary's protestations of love, Abe, holding her in a loose embrace, stares down at the carpet. The American predilection for the happy love affair has never altered the view that Abe's relationship with Mary was not a happy one for him personally. As Oedipus destroys himself to save his country, so Abe Lincoln renounces personal happiness to become the savior and uniter of his country.

If Abe seemed a lonely figure before his acceptance of his duty, how much more so he appears from that time on. Only in his love for Ann Rutledge had Abe ever found any true sense of belonging. Of her, he says:

> I used to think it was better to be alone. I was always most contented when I was alone. . . . And then— when I saw her, I knew there could be beauty and purity in people— . . . When I took hold of her hand and held it, all fear, all doubt went out of me. I believed in God. (I, iii)

After her death, he cries with frenzy, "I've got to die and be with her again, or I'll go crazy! I can't bear to think of her out there alone." With the death of the only person in the world who had ever given Abe a sense of happy relationship to others came an accentuation of what Nancy Green calls his hypochondria—"He listens too much to the whispers, that he heard in the forest where he grew up," she says. Even so, the loss of the one woman he had ever loved resulted perhaps in not such a lonely situation as that of attaching himself by marriage to one he did not love, especially since the admitted purpose of the attachment is to goad him on to greatness. Thus isolating himself from the few close friends he has had, Abe receives in return no affectionate communion with a wife. When, on the eve of his election to the presidency, he curses Mary—"Damn you! Damn you for taking every opportunity you can to make a public fool of me"—he gives vent to long years of resentment, not so much of her, as of the fate which has condemned him to greatness as well as to loneliness.

Mary is in the anomalous position in the play, as in the myth, of being honored by a grateful country for prodding Abe into the presidency while being disliked for her lack of understanding and inability to inspire him with love. Like Jonah, who tries to escape the duty God imposes upon him, Abe refuses at first to submit to Mary's whip; but, like Jonah, after he comes to a recognition of his fated course, Abe accepts with fortitude the obvious means provided to carry it through. Mary Todd thus becomes not so much a character in her own right as the *deus ex machina* of the drama. Since it is impossible for the hero to combine love with duty, Abe Lincoln could not have attained greatness if Ann Rutledge had lived to become his wife. It has been said that if a character like Abe Lincoln had not lived, it would have been necessary for Americans to create him.[1] Likewise, if Mary Todd had been beloved by Abe, it would have been necessary to alter the facts to make her, instead, his goad. The hero's is a lonely road. Mary Todd's function is not to alleviate, but to enhance, Abe's isolation. She accomplishes this purpose perfectly because her own selfish ambition is the motivation which makes her drive her husband to success. Abe recognizes that Mary's goading is not for the high, idealistic motive of his friend, Billy Herndon, that he save the Union and keep it free. But Billy does not succeed; therefore Abe is in the position of attaining greatness to satisfy a selfish woman's ambition. Before the entrance of Mary Todd, Abe says of the Civil War, "There seems to be one going on inside me all the time." How fierce the civil war within after Abe submits to Mary!

Robert Sherwood has subtitled his story of Abe Lincoln, "A Play in Twelve Scenes," apparently wishing to indicate that, in spite of the divisions into three acts, the continuity of the hero's life flows unbroken by dramatic technique. The playwright is, however, in agreement with the dictate of Maxwell Anderson[2] in making the recognition scene the climax of his play, with the preceding scenes all building toward this moment, and the following ones all dramatizing the hero's fulfillment of purpose. The scene in which Abe perceives his obligation to his people takes place on a moonlit night on the prairie near New Salem. Around a campfire, Abe is talking with an old friend, Seth Gale, who with his wife and sick child is traveling westward by covered wagon. The scene is as unpretentious as the hero. Seth's fears that the new country to which they are going will become slave country or else will secede from the Union are quieted by Abe's reassurance:

> You mustn't be scared, Seth. I know I'm a poor one
> to be telling you that—because I've been scared all
> my life. But—seeing you now—and thinking of the
> big thing you've set out to do—well, it's made me
> feel pretty small. It's made me feel that I've got to do
> something, too, to keep you and your kind in the
> United States of America. (II, vii)

After this Abe says a prayer for the sick child, and the short scene ends; but in the few moments of giving comfort to an old friend, Abe gets over being scared himself and sets out to devote his life to his country.

There might seem to be a certain grim humor in the fact that in the next scene, a few days later, Abe is seeking admittance to the parlor of Miss Mary Todd. But Americans do not laugh. Although Abe desires Mary no more than before, he has reached that resolve within himself which will enable him

to stand alone, to succeed in his mission in life, and to accept his isolation as inevitable. As Fishwick explains,

> The hero must turn within himself for the support
> and solution he needs. Then, like the boonbringer,
> he can return to the outside world and aid those in it.
> The hero is a man first of self-achieved submission
> and then of action. His path is like that represented
> in the rites of passage; separation, initiation, and
> return. This cycle is exemplified in the careers of
> Prometheus, Buddha, and Aeneas, as well as of
> many who have followed them.[3]

Abe's failure, up to the time of the scene on the prairie, ends with his initiation there into the true meaning of his life; and from that time on his path is a straightforward one of service to his fellow man. He is willing to sacrifice himself for the idea he envisions as surely as is Antigone for her brother's honor.

Lincoln's life follows most closely of all, perhaps, that of Christ, with its humble beginning, unpretentious rise, and martyr's death. Sherwood's drama covers only the middle span of Lincoln's life, but the audience's knowledge of his beginning and tragic conclusion adds weight to the significance of the action portrayed. Lincoln's "If I live," when asked if he would continue his law practice after serving as President, indicates his own premonition of his death; and his expression of his real sense of relief if he should fail to be elected President likewise arouses the sympathy of the audience for the beloved hero whose loneliness in his fated path is recognized. The whole drama, as well as the Lincoln myth, would seem to refute the opinion of Dixon Wecter that, to Americans, "the hero must be a man of good will and also a good neighbor, preferably something of a joiner. Of the solitudes and lonely isolations of a great man like Lincoln the public has little conception."[4] Of Lincoln's lonely isolations the public would seem to have a conception, and for them, a sympathy. Lincoln's fear that in a city as big as New Orleans the people would not be friendly causes his friend, Mentor, to accuse him of misanthropy, explaining to Abe that a misanthrope distrusts men and avoids their society. Lincoln himself claims that he likes people one by one, but not in crowds; but it is only Ann Rutledge who makes him feel closely akin to humanity. Nancy Green's exclamation, "Poor, lonely soul," as Lincoln grieves for Ann's death, expresses the reaction of the audience to this hero. Loneliness is intrinsic to the character of their idol. In E. P. Conkle's *Prologue to Glory* (1938) Lincoln, after the death of Ann Rutledge, walks out alone into the twilight and on toward Springfield as the final curtain falls. In Sherwood's play which covers a later period of Lincoln's life, as well as some of the same period, Lincoln still walks alone.

As a contrast to his treatment of America's hero, in *The Petrified Forest*, written three years earlier, Robert Sherwood does some satirizing of American hero worship within an exciting melodramatic plot. No less lonely than Lincoln, Alan Squier is the opposite to the President-hero in that he has no ideals to live by, no thought of service to his fellow man, and nothing but disillusionment about life in general. He expects to walk straight west to the Pacific Ocean and drown there. An intellectual, literally in the desert wasteland of Arizona, he is enchanted by a young girl who, while helping her family run an isolated filling station, hopes to travel to France where her mother lives. When the place is held up by the killer, Duke Mantee (a caricature of America's shooting heroes like Billy the Kid), Alan, having undergone the hero's rites of initiation through his spiritual transformation in loving Gabriele, and also being slightly drunk, persuades Duke Mantee to kill him, so that his insurance money may send the girl to Paris.

Fittingly enough, he will be buried like a hero, in the petrified forest. Had Sherwood's play about Abe Lincoln been as dramatically effective as this semisatirical portrayal of the lonely hero, it might well be the mainstay of little theaters through the years; episodic and constricted perhaps by the use of excerpts from Lincoln's own speeches, it does not attain dramatic heights. Thus far, however, no better play than Sherwood's has been written about Lincoln, but it is likely that in time a greater will be and that in it Lincoln's loneliness will be intrinsic to his character.

Notes

1. Marshall W. Fishwick, *American Heroes: Myth and Reality* (Washington, D.C.: Public Affairs Press, 1954), p. 15.
2. In a series of essays published under the title, *Off Broadway*, Maxwell Anderson insists that the one fundamental touchstone of every great tragedy is that it have a recognition scene, which, as Sherwood's does, should come at the end of the second act of a three-act play.
3. *American Heroes: Myth and Reality*, p. 8.
4. *The Hero in America* (New York: Charles Scribner's Sons, 1941), p. 485.

CHARLES SIMIC

1938–

Charles Simic was born in Belgrade, Yugoslavia, on May 9, 1938. He emigrated to the United States in 1954 and was naturalized in 1971. He was educated at the University of Chicago and New York University (B.A. 1967). He served in the U.S. Army from 1961 to 1963. He taught at California State College at Hayward from 1970 to 1973; since 1974 he has taught at the University of New Hampshire. He was an editorial assistant at *Aperture* magazine from 1966 to 1969. He married Helen Dubin in 1964; they have two children.

Simic published his first book of poems, *What the Grass Says*, in 1967. He quickly established himself among a new generation of Symbolists influenced by South American and European poetry, along with such poets as Mark Strand and W. S. Merwin. Simic's poetry emphasizes nightmarish surreal imagery combined with stark, simple language and disarming wit. He is particularly noted for his sense of irony and the absurd. Simic's most praised books of poetry include *Dismantling the Silence* (1971); *White* (1972, rev. 1980); *Return to a Place Lit by a Glass of Milk* (1974); *Charon's Cosmology* (1977); *School for Dark Thoughts* (1978); and *Austerities* (1982). His poems are collected in *Biography and a Lament: Poems 1961–1967* (1976) and *Weather Forecast for Utopia and Vicinity: Poems 1967–1982* (1983).

Simic is also a prolific translator of Yugoslavian poets, and has twice been given the PEN award for translation. In addition, he edited *Another Republic: 17 European and South American Writers* (1976) with Mark Strand. He was a receipient of a Guggenheim fellowship in 1972, and has twice been awarded fellowships by the National Endowment for the Arts. He received the American Academy Award in 1976 and the Harriet Monroe Poetry Award in 1980.

GEOFFREY THURLEY

From "Devices Among Words: Kinnell, Bly, Simic"
*The American Moment: American Poetry
in the Mid-Century*

1977, pp. 225–28

Simic seems to me a better poet than either Bly or Kinnell, yet his poetry's most distinctive quality (I hesitate to say straight out its strength) seems actually to be its most signal limitation. This is a brilliant fluency of invention that enables him to sustain a uniform texture through a whole poem and a whole collection of poems—*Dismantling the Silence*[1]—without its ever offering much substance for the mind to feed on. One would call it a natural metaphysics, except that the word suggests the essentially knotty poetry of the English seventeenth-century poets, and of their modern imitators, poetry which rewards the reader's intelligence with flight, and his diligence with release. The metaphysical conceit detonates in the mind at some depth from the surface, and the labour taken to unravel its complexities generates a light which is logically but mystically related to the substance of the figure chosen. In Charles Simic we have something totally different.

He was born in Yugoslavia and in a very material sense has remained a Slav rather than become an American. If we opened his book *Dismantling the Silence* at random, knowing nothing of the author but the verse offered, we could be forgiven for supposing it the work of some unimaginably brilliant translator, whose Balkan originals were blessedly free of the machine-age and of Americanization. For even the substance of his verse—its material referents—are European and rural rather than American and urban. Simic has 'taverns', 'fabled highwaymen', 'hermits', 'gallows', and so on. He speaks significantly at one stage of 'my migrant's bundle'. Otherwise, the world his poetry creates—or rather with its brilliant semantic evacuation *de-creates*—is that of central Europe—woods, ponds, peasant furniture (even the word 'table' has an archaic ring in Simic). We could say that he de-creates his world in an effort to forestall its non-existence: he makes mysterious the actual (America, now) and then de-materializes the mystery. So, his basic modus is the fairy-tale or *skazka*. There are faintly Audenesque allegories (in 'Explorers', especially), but in the main Simic practises his fabulous transmogrifications of the real after the fashion of the European poets he so often recalls—Juhasz, Kocbek and Popa. ⟨. . .⟩

Yet at the same time as the verse breathes like Rexroth's

the beneficence of the grass, it is strangely hellish, almost as if it is expecting at any moment to break into the black-and-white horror film to which it is the technicolor contrast. In poems like 'Marching', Simic writes as a European in a more than technical sense:

> Blood rose into my head shaking its little bells.
> In the valley the glow died in the udder of the cow.
> The trees ceased playing with their apples
> And the wind brought the sound of men marching.

An American poet cannot, of course, know such things, as the occasional efforts to imagine them (Stevens's 'Dry Loaf', for instance, or service poems like Eberhart's 'Fury of Aerial Bombardment') inform us. 'The worst is still to come,' Simic begins, in 'For the Victims':

> Then, at last, we'll get a true taste of ourselves.
> The ear will crawl back into the eye
> Like Jonah into his whale.

The modus is that of Bosch or Dali. Simic creates a world in which only emptiness finally exists: it is a world of silence, waiting for the unspeakable to happen, or subsisting in the limbo left afterwards:

> And always someone's missing
> and the light left for him in the window
> is now the oldest one on earth
> and still each day his shirt, bowl and spoon
> are washed by his mother and sister
> and the front door is unlocked just before nightfall
> because that's the time
> when the ones who have been gone so long
> like to return.
>
> ('Invention of the Invisible')

Except that no-one *is* going to return, ever. The 'place' that is invented (or that invents—the genitives are both subjective and objective) is hellish and beautiful at once, like the summer of 1939, emptied of adults, witnessed by children who register the menace without really being able to experience it:

> Two uniformed men
> stroll along the empty streets,
> solemn and slow
> they advance, stopping
> to look in shop-windows,
> into parked cars.
>
> One of them wears a brass whistle,
> the other hides a gun with a silencer.
> There's no-one left on the earth.
>
> (Simic, 'Invention of the Place')

The scene might be present-day midwest America; but it isn't. Or perhaps it is a limitation in Simic, here at least, that he doesn't make enough of the possible correlations: the past is re-imagined, it is not really seen in its relations with the present. He invents finally 'Nothing':

> I didn't notice
> while I wrote here
> that nothing remains of the world
> except my table and chair.
>
> ('Invention of Nothing')

The dimension of menace in Simic becomes metaphysics in itself, and if we compare his handling of certain motifs with that of Kinnell, for instance, we surely cannot doubt his superiority:

> And this chair will reveal itself
> As the exact shadow of someone
> Who stood here all this time
>
> (Simic, 'For the Victims')

The chair in the Kinnell poem ('The Supper after the Last') was merely waiting for a seducer: as Simic uses the image, it takes its place in an evocation of a world of political happening. Yet again, Simic finds in 'nothing' a strange beauty:

> Why am I so quiet then
> and so happy?
> (Simic, 'For the
> Victims')

Few things are so chilling as this happy peace resting on a surface tension of fear, and Simic's nothing is outlasted by 'the throat of an empty beer-bottle'. It seems strangely appropriate that this brilliant yet oddly vacuous volume should end with a *jeu d'esprit* on 'errata'.

Notes

1. (London 1971).

PETER SCHMIDT

From "*White*: Charles Simic's Thumbnail Epic"

Contemporary Literature, Fall 1982, pp. 528–42

> O how joys, dreads, convolutions, human shapes,
>   and all shapes, spring as from graves around me!
> O phantoms! you cover all the land and all the sea!
> O I cannot see in the dimness whether you smile or
>   frown upon me. . . .
> (Whitman, "Out of the Cradle Endlessly Rocking",
>   1867 version)

> A chaque être, plusieurs *autres* vies me semblaient
>   dues.
>
>   (Rimbaud, *Une Saison en Enfer*)

If each American generation must make its pact with Whitman, the particulars of that pact tell us much about what makes that generation distinct. Charles Simic is already recognized as one of the most important voices in the generation that came of age in the last decade. As it happens, one poem of his, a sequence of twenty-two lyrics called *White*, is a dramatic example of what sort of pact with Whitman Simic's generation is drawing up. Unfortunately, *White* is not so available or so well known as Simic's other work, for it has been published only by small presses. Simic first issued 1300 copies of it from New Rivers Press back in 1972, and two years ago he finished revising it and reissued it, in an even smaller edition, from Logbridge-Rhodes Press. He now dates the poem 1970–1980. After reading the work, it is easy to see why it has held Simic's imagination for a decade. Its drama, that of learning how to begin again, has always been at the heart of Simic's writing, and the lyrics in *White* provide a behind-the-scenes glimpse of many of Simic's most recognizable characters and settings as they might first emerge in his notebooks, before they are fully portrayed in the lyrics which make up the Braziller collections. It is Simic's private collection of beginnings, of summonings—the daily record of the battles he had confronting the white page. In it, he seeks to recover that ancient yet spontaneous voice which he, like the surrealists (the true last romantics), believes lies beneath the masks and ironies that we adopt in order to survive our history. *White* is also a distinguished attempt to solve a problem which many other poets of Simic's generation are now facing—the creation of a long poem out of a sequence of shorter ones. All poets who do that, particularly American ones, must face comparing their sequences to those by Whitman, and *White* is additionally interesting because, of all the poems Simic has written, it is the one in which he most determinedly confronts his American poetic origins.

White is composed of three parts. The first two are spoken by the poet and consist of ten ten-line lyrics each. The concluding section, two twenty-line poems, contains the reply of "White" to the poet and is entitled "What The White Had To Say." The "White" of the poem's title is a particular state of mind that the poet seeks to reach during the writing of each short poem, with the first two ten-part sections of *White* being the sum of these incantations. White is a *tabula rasa et alba*, a realm of pure possibility, new selves, new words, and new names, and may be said to be a modern version of the absolute expectancy of divine grace which was the desired climax of the meditative procedures employed by Catholic and Protestant poets in the Renaissance. "All that is near, / I no longer give it a name," the poet says in the second poem of *White*, and later adds, "There are words I need. / They are not near men."[1] Each poem is thus a summoning of the muse of strangeness and new selfhood; White is the only power who can help him shed his past selves and begin again. Instead of using a Ouija board, as James Merrill, another contemporary poet of meditation, has done, Simic places the "five ears" of his fingertips "Against the white page" (p. 12), listening for signs of the descent of his daemon-muse, the White who speaks at the poem's conclusion. During each ten-poem sequence, Simic uses all the strategies he possesses, from prayer and propitiation to temptation and trickery, to summon her. He puts on many masks, including those of an orphan child, a bridegroom, and a hermit scholar, and envisions White appearing in many forms, from bestial to celestial. ⟨. . .⟩

The closing passages of *White*, particularly Simic's reference to White as a "gaunt shadowy mother," may remind some readers of the "old crone" swathed in sweet garments who rocks the cradle in Whitman's "Out of the Cradle Endlessly Rocking" (1859). This relation of *White* to Walt Whitman is worth considering more closely. The music of Whitman's poem imitates first the mockingbird's lament for the loss of its mate and then the sinister susurrus of the sea, the "fierce old mother" incessantly moaning the word "death." Together, the songs of bird and sea cause the poet to understand for the first time that he will die. Soon after he overhears the bird pleading for its lost mate to appear against the background of the white breakers ("What is that little black thing I see there in the white?"), he himself is looking out to sea and beholding his own twin, a swimmer, and his "white arms out in the breakers." At first, the boy hopes that this figure's arms are "tirelessly tossing"; his vision is as much a wish-fulfillment as the mockingbird's. But by the poem's end he admits that the secret the sea has shown him is a "drowned" one. Intuitively, he understands that the swimmer could not survive: it was his childhood self struggling aginst the undertow of his new knowledge that he is not immortal. The adult poet, moreover, understands that the sea has nursed him on this bitter wisdom and given him his voice. It is as if the child's sudden experience of death compelled him to fill the void he felt with song—as if by pouring out words and music he could somehow will into being the vanished sense of wholeness he once knew:

> For I, that was a child, my tongue's use sleeping,
>   now I have heard you,
> Now in a moment I know what I am for, I awake,
>   . . .
> A thousand warbling echoes have started to life
>   within me . . .
>   . . .
> My own songs awaked from that hour. . . .

But if the experience of loss destroys the child's illusion that all is permanent (thus rendering him a spiritual orphan from the things of this world), paradoxically such experience also supports the child's new, more mature self. Images which first reminded the poet of his secure childhood (such as "Pour down your warmth, great sun! / While we bask we have two together, // Two together!") are by the end of the poem used to describe the experience of division, not wholeness. The poet's knowledge of death is a kind of grim but benevolent foster-parent, personified as an old crone "swathed in sweet garments" who bends her wrinkled face towards the child's, whispering in his ear, rocking his cradle, "pouring down" upon him her hoarse hissing, her bitter understanding that we are all orphans on this earth.

Simic's muse of Whiteness is also a half-benevolent, half-terrifying foster-mother, and his child-poet an orphan. The first and second parts of *White* have as their epigraph a line from "Out of the Cradle" which implies that the poet's songs, like those of Whitman's mockingbird, are inspired by loss: "What is that little black thing I see there in the white?" To make the connection between his poem and Whitman's even clearer, Simic in 1980 revised a central line in White's monologue from "I am the emptiness that tucks you in like a dove's nest" to "I am the emptiness that tucks you in like a mockingbird's nest."[2] In "Out of the Cradle" this nurturing figure modulated in the middle of the poem from the mockingbird to the sea-mother. Intuitively remembering this transformation, Simic has White in her monologues describe herself as both a mockingbird and an ocean: as a mockingbird she tucks the poet in at night, and as the sea she is the water "in which you are sinking." There are other parallels between "Out of the Cradle" and *White*. Both Whitman and Simic describe the death of the poet's earlier self, and both end their works with an ambiguous moment of rebirth. Whitman is "awaked" and sings of birth yet stares into what passes for a death's-head, the face of the old crone, while Simic "falls" asleep but finds a new self rising within him:

> Time slopes. We are falling head over heels
> At the speed of night. That milk tooth
> You left under the pillow, it's grinning.

Simic's milk tooth seems both sinister and heartening: it grins like a skull, suggesting the self which has died, but it also reminds us that a child's milk teeth are replaced by his adult ones, including his "wisdom" teeth.

Simic's reference to the "milk tooth" may also allude to other famous lines by Whitman about coming of age, the notorious section in "The Sleepers" in which he described a child's passage into adulthood by referring to teething:

> [I] am curious to know where my feet stand—and
>   what is this flooding me, childhood or man-
>   hood—and the hunber that crosses the bridge
>   between.
> The cloth laps a first sweet eating and drinking,
> Laps life-swelling yolks—laps ear of rose-corn, milky
>   and just ripened;
> The white teeth stay, and the boss tooth advances in
>   darkness. . . .
>
>   (1855 version)

The sudden changes of the body during the end of childhood are no less frightening to a child than the advancing stages of the mind's own transformations as one self yields to another. The boss tooth of the boy's manhood—his sexuality, his knowledge of evil and of death—ruthlessly expels his childhood self. This change is a prelude to the continual remaking of the self which is exemplified in "The Sleepers" and which Whitman wants the adult psyche to undergo each night during dreaming. Similarly, in *White* Simic uses references to drowning, falling, and teething to depict not just the passage from childhood to adulthood but also the passage he as an adult wants to make from one self to another.

Simic's *White* is also a meditation on another form of drowning and rebirth—the influence (literally, the in-flowing) of a previous writer's voice upon his own. Such a preoccupation with poetic predecessors is appropriate to *White*, for any poem about the poet's urge to be reborn must also be a poem about his origins. Simic seeks a new, "white," unknown voice to inhabit him, yet as his desire for such an event increases, so too does his knowledge of how thoroughly both his new and his old voices resound with those of his predecessors, particularly Whitman's. Indeed, like the child in "Out of the Cradle," he paradoxically comes of age and discovers his own voice only after he loses his illusions of wholeness and admits for the first time the terrifying insurge of an alien, foster-voice whose music is not his own. *White* is Simic's collection of strategies for summoning forth his muse. But when she appears, one of her masks is that of "White-man," Whitman.

Notes

1. Charles Simic, *White* (Durango, Colorado: Logbridge-Rhodes Press, 1980), pp. 4, 8. All other references to this edition will be cited in the text.

2. Simic's revisions also include changing selected lines, transposing a few lyrics, and cutting some others to replace them with new poems. In all cases in this essay except this one, I refer to Simic's 1980 version.

CHARLES SIMIC
From an Interview by Sherod Santos

Missouri Review, Number 3 (1984), pp. 61–73

Interviewer: Would you mind talking a little about the conditions in Yugoslavia just before you left?

Simic: I had what Jan Kott calls "a typical East European education." He means, Hitler and Stalin taught us the basics. When I was three years old the Germans bombed Belgrade. The house across the street was hit and destroyed. There was plenty more of that, as everybody knows. When the war ended I came in and said: "Now there won't be any more fun!" That gives you an idea what a jerk I was. The truth is, I did enjoy myself. From the summer of 1944 to mid-1945, I ran around the streets of Belgrade with other half-abandoned kids. You can just imagine the things we saw and the adventures we had. You see, my father was already abroad, my mother was working, the Russians were coming, the Germans were leaving. It was a three-ring circus.

I: I don't want to sound overly psychological, but there is in your work that peculiar element which blends so naturally horror and fun. Do you think it had its origin in those days?

S: Very probably. I'm the product of chance, the baby of ideologies, the orphan of History. Hitler and Stalin conspired to make me homeless. Well, then, is my situation tragic? No. There's been too much tragedy all around for anyone to feel like a Hamlet. More likely my situation is comic. It's "the amazement of the thinking spirit at itself" and its predicament—or so said Schlegel. One just has to laugh at the extent of our stupidity.

I: So what happened after 1945?

S: Well, from 1945 to 1948 it was just poverty. I remember being very, very hungry, and my mother crying because she had nothing to give me. Still later, it became clear to my mother that if I was ever going to become an American poet, we'd better get moving. That's Phil Levine's theory. Actually, my father was already in the U.S.A. working for the same telephone company he had worked for in Yugoslavia before the war. Anyway, we ended up in Chicago, and my father took me out one day to hear Coleman Hawkins. You could say the kid was hooked. Jazz made me both an American and a poet.

I: What was it about jazz that seemed to you so distinctly American.

S: I heard in it, experienced in it what it feels like to be sad or happy in America. Or more idiomatically: how to raise hell, or how to break someone's heart and make beautiful music in the process. I mean, it's fine to read the great lyric poets of the past, but one also has to know how the people in the language you're writing in sing.

I: Is there an identifiable influence jazz has made on your work? I'm wondering, for example, if you see surrealism in any way as a literary equivalent to jazz?

S: The poet is really not much different from that tenor player who gets up in a half-empty, smoke-filled dive at two in the morning to play the millionth rendition of "Body and Soul." Which is to say that one plays with the weight of all that tradition, but also to entertain the customers and to please oneself. One is both bound and free. One improvises but there are constraints, forms to obey. It's the same old thing which is always significantly different.

As for surrealism, I think there's more of it in the blues. The early stuff, especially. Most people know Bessie Smith and perhaps Robert Johnson, but there are many others. Incredible verbal invention. What one would call "jive," but also eroticism, the tragic sense of life. If the blues was French we'd be studying it at Yale. As it is, hardly anyone knows my heroes, people like Cripple Clarence Lofton, Frankie Jaxon, or Bessie Jackson, who also called herself Lucille Bogan. They are our Villons.

Anyway, blues taught me a number of things. How to tell a story quickly, economically. The value of gaps, ellipses, and most importantly, the virtues of simplicity and accessibility.

I: That erotic element, since you mention it, is an important part of your work as well; and now that I think about it, you use it in ways that are actually quite similar to the ways it's used in the blues. The last two stanzas of your poem "Breasts" is a good example:

> O my sweet, my wistful bagpipes.
> Look, everyone is asleep on the earth.
> Now, in the absolute immobility
> Of time, drawing the waist
> Of the one I love to mine,
>
> I will tip each breast
> Like a dark heavy grape
> Into the hive
> Of my drowsy mouth.

S: I don't know if I still care for the ending of that poem. "Wistful bagpipes" is awful. Also, the pace of these stanzas is awkward. The earlier ones are better, I think.

As for eroticism, isn't it synonymous with imagination? Eros as the cause of logos, and that sort of thing. The one lying in the dark and trying to visualize the loved one is at the mercy of both. . . . There's not much more that I can say. ⟨. . .⟩

I: Eliot once remarked that a poet's material is his own

language as it's actually spoken around him. That would seem to have been a much more complicated issue for a writer like yourself whose first language was not the language actually spoken around him.

S: I was never at any point capable of writing a poem in Serbian. By the time I started writing poetry in high school all my serious reading had been in English and American literature. So, it was inevitable. I read American poets and wanted to write like them. At that time, I didn't have the slightest idea of Serbian poetry.

I: What language do you dream in?

S: The language I dream and know best I speak with an accent.

I: About 1958 you moved from Chicago to New York. What was your life like there?

S: I worked during the day and went to school at night. I did just about every kind of work imaginable. I was a shirt salesman, a house painter, a payroll clerk, I had no thought of the future. No plans to be a professor or a poet. I mean, I wrote poetry, even published it, but that was it. That lasted twelve years. New York is, of course, a place that could have been imagined by Hieronymous Bosch. Rome must have been like that at the end of its days when all the barbarians got in. It's a city which either proves that the end of the world is near, or that human beings will survive no matter what. I always get that sense of hope when I watch those guys on street corners peddling stolen umbrellas, or some kind of idiotic wind-up toys. I love to breathe that air.

I: The more I read your work, the more I think of you as a poet of the city—in that particular way one thinks of poets like Baudelaire or Eliot or Auden or even Lowell—not so much in the landscape itself as in the way the city functions, both internally and externally, as a symbol of modernity.

S: When I close my eyes I go into cities. Others, I suppose, sail the ocean blue. The rat is my totem animal, the cockroach my wood thrush. My mother is calling my name out of a tenement window. She keeps calling and calling. My entire psychic life is there. ⟨. . .⟩

I: Okay, then let's talk for a moment about the act itself. Is it for you—as it was apparently for poets like Blake and Whitman—an ecstatic one?

S: Are you kidding me? My mother almost married a guy who used to compose his symphonies while sitting naked in an empty bathtub. I could've been his son. Anyway, that's not my style. Breton says "poetry is made in bed like love." I too have to be horizontal, and a bit lazy.

I: In your essay, "Some Thoughts about the Line," you say, "In the end, I'm always at the beginning. Silence—an endless mythical condition." Obviously you mean by silence something more than just that condition out of which poems grow.

S: I call silence what precedes language: the world and the sense of oneself existing. I always thought, if you will, that speaking is a bit like whistling in the dark. The universe, in my humble opinion, doesn't require me saying anything. When I'm attentive and silent I seem to be closer to the way things are. A number of my early poems are attempts to make that predicament into a myth of origins.

I: What is it then that makes you break that silence?

S: To speak as the translator of silence rather than its opposer. I think Thoreau said something like that, seeing language as but a minor ripple on the great pool of wordless silence, which, I agree, is our true environment. ⟨. . .⟩

I: I notice in reading reviews of your books that critics at times have a tendency to read your poems as parables. Is that the result of your working beyond the framework of realism?

S: I don't know. I don't write parables. If I say "rats in diapers" that's to be taken literally.

I: Then do you think of your poems as having a clearly communicative function, on rational or cognitive levels?

S: I don't know about "clearly communicative" and "cognitive," but the point of writing a poem, actually the need to do so, is to give, pass on, relate to someone something of value. I don't want to waste people's time. It matters to me (I mean, what goes on in the poem), and I want them to know about it. One can't always make it simple because many things are not simple, but it's worth trying.

I: You read a good deal of philosophy, and, I'm told, have a particular interest in Heidegger.

S: I always read philosophy. I suppose I'm a bit envious of that kind of disciplined thinking. Also, I am curious what human beings have been thinking for the last three thousand years about the nature of things. As for Heidegger, I admire the phenomenological impulse to reexamine the simplest, the long-taken-for-granted things. That's what a poet is supposed to do, too.

I: Is that the most important thing a poet is supposed to do?

S: No! You must have a pencil handy when the Muse barges in. My father told me that many poems came to him in his lifetime but just in those moments when he couldn't find anything to write with. Otherwise, it's pointless to say what a poem should do. Someone always comes along and does the opposite, and it's perfectly fine. What all good poetry has in common is the use of the imagination. Imagination, on the other hand, is like the universe of which only a small part has been explored.

ROBERT E. SHERWOOD

LOUIS SIMPSON

WILFRID SHEED

SAM SHEPARD

CLARK ASHTON SMITH

UPTON SINCLAIR

ISAAC BASHEVIS SINGER

W. D. SNODGRASS

LOUIS SIMPSON

1923–

Louis Aston Marantz Simpson was born in Kingston, Jamaica, on March 27, 1923, to Aston and Rosalind Marantz Simpson. He was educated at Columbia University (B.S. 1948, M.A. 1950, Ph.D. 1959). He served in the U.S. Army from 1943 to 1945, earning two Purple Hearts and the Bronze Star. He married Jeanne Claire Rogers in 1949; they had one child before divorcing in 1954. In 1955 he married Dorothy Roochvarg; they had two children, and were divorced in 1979. Simpson taught at Columbia University from 1955 to 1959, and at the University of California at Berkeley from 1959 to 1967; since 1967 he has been a Professor of English at the State University of New York at Stony Brook. He was an editor at Bobbs-Merrill from 1950 to 1955.

Simson published his first book of poetry (*The Arrivistes: Poems 1940–1949*) privately in 1949. It is traditional in form, and is largely concerned with Simpson's experiences during World War II. Simpson's next two books of poetry (*Good News of Death and Other Poems*, 1955, and *A Dream of Governors*, 1959) were similar to his first both in form and in subject matter. Some critics were impressed by the power of Simpson's imagery and the depth of his feeling; others saw him as conservative and repetitive.

At the End of the Open Road (1963) was a breakthrough for Simpson. In it he abandoned the rhyming and traditional metric forms he had relied on in favor of open forms; the result is liberating. The poems are surrealistic and image-centered, frequently nightmarish, and his subject matter has expanded to include a disturbing vision of modern America. The critical reaction was almost unanimously enthusaistic, and the volume won the Pulitzer Prize for Poetry in 1964.

Subsequent volumes (notably *Selected Poems*, 1966; *Adventures of the Letter I*, 1971; *Searching for the Ox*, 1976; *Caviare at the Funeral*, 1980) explore Simpson's past and cultural heritage in relation to America, his poetry, and his inner self; he has continued to experiment with open forms, and his poetry has taken on a mystical, spiritual quality, although it is still firmly grounded in image. His poetry has continued to be well received critically, although none of his subsequent books has been accorded the recognition given to *At the End of the Open Road*.

Simpson has also written a novel (*Riverside Drive*, 1962), several plays, and an autobiography (*Air with Armed Men*, 1972). His criticism is also highly regarded, particularly *Three on the Tower: The Lives and Works of Ezra Pound, T. S. Eliot, and William Carlos Williams* (1975) and *A Revolution in Taste: Studies of Dylan Thomas, Allen Ginsberg, Sylvia Plath, and Robert Lowell* (1979). Simpson currently lives in New York State.

A couple of years ago Louis Simpson anthologized in *New World Writing* some poems by his contemporaries, heading his selection "The Silent Generation." That title appears again above one of his own poems—"It was my generation / That put the Devil down / With great enthusiasm. / But now our occupation / Is gone. Our education / Is wasted on the town. / We lack enthusiasm." Among the results of the situation Mr. Simpson so deftly epitomizes has been an impoverishment of sensibility for poetry, as for other areas of life. A set of difficulties, doubtless long present, becomes intensified for the individual who would discover fecund relations with history, place, myth, time. Mr. Simpson's third book, *A Dream of Governors*, goes an impressively long way toward articulating such themes with an authoritative command of both subject and technique that seems to transcend these contemporary dilemmas. Something of his range is indicated by the division of his book into five sections. He modernizes myths to ironic advantage, and contrasts "My America" with "The Old World." A fourth group includes some of the best poems to have come out of the Second World War, and the fifth presents love poems effective alike in their delicacy and wry strength. From this catalogue of subjects one would scarcely guess the complexity with which he realizes each, nor the variety of modes and tones his verse commands. Even his exorcisms, his phantasmagoria, his ballad of a lunatic Nazi, are lucid in organization and language, while his rationally-developed poems, such as the neo-neoclassical "The Green Shepherd"

and "The Flight to Cytherea," are alive with surprises of perception and diction. I've space to quote but a stanza from two other poems, to suggest still further the ranges in Mr. Simpson's unified book. From "An American in the Thieves' Market":

> But I am an American, and bargain
> In the Thieves' Market, where the junk of culture
> Lies in the dust—clay shards, perhaps Etruscan,
>   And wedding rings . . .
> My father's ghost is ticking in a watch,
> My mother's, weeping in the antique bed,
> And, in a pile of swords, my cousin sheds
>   The tears of things.

And "The Lover's Ghost":

> "Did you not call?" she said,
> "Goodbye, then! For I go
> Where I am wanted."
> Till dawn I tossed in bed
> Wishing that I could know
> Who else she haunted.

Mr. Simpson is skillful beyond fluency, and seldom does he allow himself the too easy versification mere fluency invites, nor expose his influences. (Yeats seems vestigially present in a couple of poems—"And what's the aftermath? A murdered man, / A crying woman, and an empty dish. . . . ") In "The Runner" he turns from the short lyric to attempt a blank-verse redaction of the materials of *The Red Badge of Courage*. This thirty-page narrative poem is full of realistic observations that might have figured more potently in fiction; as it is, the texture of the verse is usually on its surface. There are fine touches of characterization and an unequivocal honesty in presentation but these virtues seem unassimilated into the verse. Perhaps the best part of the poem comes as the soldier, bivouacked in a rear area, stumbles into a trench dug in the first War. But Mr. Simpson makes more telling use of this conceit (or experience) in a short nightmare, "I Dreamed that in a City Dark as Paris," where he discovers that he *is* the alive statue of a World War One *poilu*:

> My confrere,
> In whose thick boots I stood, were you amazed
> To wander through my brain four decades later
> As I have wanderd in a dream through yours?
>
> The violence of waking life disrupts
> The order of our death. Strange dreams occur,
> For dreams are licensed as they never were.

A *Dream of Governors* belongs among the handful of durable books by younger poets in the past decade.—DANIEL G. HOFFMAN, "Between New Voice and Old Master," *SwR*, Autumn 1960, pp. 677–79

Louis Simpson is a poet whose first three volumes of verse I admire greatly. But in 1964 the Pulitzer committee awarded the poetry prize to Mr. Simpson's fourth book, *At the End of the Open Road*. It would be nice to think, as is so often claimed, that the award is for a poet's total work. *At the End of the Open Road* is less successful than Mr. Simpson's three earlier volumes. Furthermore, the twelve new pieces that conclude *Selected Poems* have not, for the most part, recaptured the earlier excellence.

There are very few of the early poems that are in free verse, while there are only three among the later that are not. Clearly Mr. Simpson, though writing in California, had boarded Brooklyn Ferry, which was capable of paddling all the way to the West Coast in any case. *At the End of the Open Road* is his acceptance of Walt Whitman's invitation from "The Song of the Open Road": "will you come travel with me." Literally the road stops at the Pacific Ocean. Figuratively the end of the road is the end of the promise of America, proclaimed so triumphantly by Whitman; it is also the end of the promise of life itself:

> Whitman was wrong about the People,
> But right about himself. The land is within.
> At the end of the open road we come to ourselves.
>
> Though mad Columbus follows the sun
> Into the sea, we cannot follow.
> We must remain, to serve the returning sun,
> And to set tables for death.
> For we are the colonists of Death—
> Not, as some think, of the English.
> ("Lines Written near San Francisco")

These lines are from the last poem in *At the End of the Open Road*; the pieces new to *Selected Poems* continue the theme. But Mr. Simpson's first three volumes are better. They convey the same themes more excitingly, more satisfyingly, and no little part of the earlier successes is an adherence to tight and demanding forms, which Mr. Simpson handles with great skill. The new freedoms he has allowed himself have not make it possible to do the old things better.

I know at last that the Pulitzer award was not for past work as well as present. It was bestowed for the more open and direct acknowledgment of the poet's master Whitman, which had always been there, but which in the earlier poems had been filtered through Hart Crane:

> Cathedral, vessel of the dead,
> O cast off these white anchors, Miserere,
> And spread your spinnakers Magnificat
> Laudemus to the horizon!
> ("American Preludes")

Mr. Simpson's review, in *Harper's*, of other new books of verse, complained that "There was a sense of form . . . that is absent from the works of many poets nowadays." And though Mr. Simpson has not yet abandoned form to the extent of Mr. Dickey or Miss Garrigue, one wonders why he has dissipated the strengths that firm poetic architecture gave his earlier work. For all his major themes—the faded promise of America and of life, the beginnings and ends of love—received happier framing in "Carentan O Carentan", "A Dream of Governors", "Hot Night on Water Street", "Summer Storm", "The Custom of the World", "The Green Shepherd", and "The Flight to Cytherea", all highly structured pieces from his first books.

One hopes that Mr. Simpson will return to a more formal utterance; one hopes that verse in English will recover strength, order, grace—its former sanity.—HARRY MORRIS, "A Formal View of the Poetry of Dickey, Garrigue, and Simpson," *SwR*, Spring 1969, pp. 324–25

I can't think of a poet other than Louis Simpson who says so well of life that there is nothing to be said for it. It is as if he believes poetry is the medium through which life's ironies are enabled to speak for themselves. Dead words, like dead stars, continue to send out reminders of their passing. It is no accident that Simpson in "To the Western World" provided the most striking image of the funeral which lies at the heart of the colonial man: 'The generations labour to possess / and grave by grave we civilize the ground'. The seance continues.

Oxen made an early appearance in his poems. In a poem of long ago they were pictured observing a couple whose passionate absorption broke with nature. 'The envious oxen in still rings would stand / Ruminating.' In the title poem of his new collection ⟨*Searching for the Ox*⟩, the ox is another beast entirely. 'Searching for the ox / I come upon a single hoofprint. / I find the ox and tame it, / and lead it home. In the next scene / the moon has risen, a cool light. / Both the ox and herdsman vanished.'

Simpson's bleak lyricism celebrates only what edges into his line of vision and even as he remarks on it he shows it to be fading:

> Beauty moves in the crowd up ahead
> on the avenue. There she is again—
> a flash of colour vanishing
> in the cool illusory air
> ("The Springs at Gadara")

Perhaps this helps to explain his fascination with place names and family names which made *Adventures of the Letter I*, a work of pure, brilliant invention, seem so realistic. Of that letter in which there is no trace of ego, the wealth of geographical information so helpfully tendered made the *Adventures of the Letter I* read like the A/Z. Place names have this great virtue: they speak up for themselves. While it is honourable, Simpson seems to feel, to put something in the place of nothing, it won't do to make too much of anything. To the paranoiac his paranoia, to the poet his poems. In "The Hour of Feeling" the disturbed woman appears to offer a glimpse of the real:

> She began to tremble. I can hear the sound
> her elbow made, rapping on the wood.

It was something to see and hear—
Not like the words that pass for life,
things you read about in the papers.

But on closer inspection the signs signify no more than themselves. Confronted by those with 'An unshakeable belief in their own importance,' he finds his lack of conviction strengthened. Obviously his own poetry cannot escape such a thorough-going scepticism:

Certainly, life would be a lot simpler.
You have to be mad, that's the catch.

As it is, I have no one to blame but myself.
I sit down to write . . .

An hour later the table is covered
with words
And then I start crossing them out.
                    ("The Sun and the Moon")

Simpson pads around the edges of his poems, apologetic at having been found on the scene at all, the illusionist who would guard against illusion. He is so fastidiously honest in showing up his own tricks that it amounts at times to a kind of offhandedness. So self-effacing, we wait for him to arrange his mirrors and vanish.—CHRISTOPHER HOPE, "Colonial Outposts," *Lon*, March 1977, pp. 83–84

⟨. . .⟩ *The Best Hour of the Night* proves that Louis Simpson's work and development, luckily for us, continues. Here the poet adds to his canon of poems about contemporary life by employing deft recombinations of, primarily, historical and mimetic impulses. In addition, he reminds us again that laughter can work in a poem and even be necessary. In "Physical Universe" a man comes downstairs at 5 A.M. and pours a cup of coffee. Finding his son's science text on the table, he begins to read. The text triggers a meditation on our civilization, on the fact that we find ourselves at-and-away-from home in it. The meditation comes full circle, back to the present day—"Tuesday, the day they pick up the garbage! / He leapt into action." This witty transition sets up the return to bed and one of the most tender moments I've seen in recent poetry.

Susan said, "Did you put out the garbage?"
But her eyes were closed.
She was sleeping, yet could speak in her sleep,
ask a question, even answer one.

. . .

He thought, perhaps she's an oracle,
speaking from the Collective Unconscious.
He said to her, "Do you agree with Darwin
that people and monkeys have a common ancestor?
Or should we stick to the Bible?"

She said, "Did you take out the garbage?"

How much tenderness, overcoming wit, is embedded in the woman's repeated question. In spite of the unpoetic focal point, in spite of the unpoetic character of what the characters say, the precariousness of love is illuminated.

Such moments abound in these poems, but nowhere do they appear with such regularity as in the long poem, "The Previous Tenant." In this tale the central character, sometimes detached, sometimes obsessed, pieces together the story of his predecessor. That fellow, a doctor, ruined his position by engaging in an ill-advised affair. Though he actually appears only once, in the poem's eighth section (to retrieve sullenly some of his belongings), we feel that we know him all too well by poem's end. And worse, we feel that we know the community's upstanding snobs who hounded him, too. Simpson's surgical social commentary is as devastating as ever. In Section

Seven, the narrator discovers a packet of the woman's letters to her lover behind a row of mystery novels and sits down to read them:

"If you have a new woman in your life
or you've gone back to your wife
I don't want to muck things up.
This is just a peacepipe, kid—
send me a smoke signal
if I'm getting in the way of anything.
Cheerio, Irene."

Then they picked up again where they'd left off.
They had been with each other
yesterday. She could still feel him inside her.
I was beginning to be afraid
for him. For her. For both of them.

Louis Simpson makes our collective fear beautiful, and helps us to believe that we can manage it.—ROBERT MCDOWELL, "Recombinative Poetry," *HdR*, Spring 1984, pp. 120–21

NORMAN FRIEDMAN
From "The Wesleyan Poets—II"

Chicago Review, 1966, pp. 66–72

Whatever Dickey's faults, he was from the beginning quite original and free of the dandified bric-a-brac of so many formal poets. Simpson's first book in the Wesleyan Series (which is actually his third book), A *Dream of Governors* (1959), is on the other hand a bit too self-consciously literary. His range of subjects and attitudes, however, is much broader than Dickey's, and the potentialities of his emotional intensity go much deeper. If he had farther to go because he began behind, he also goes farther because he has a more distant goal, and greater speed and staying power.

A *Dream of Governors* is divided into five sections, and each is provided with a helpful heading. The first is called "The Green Shepherd," which is the title of the first of its five poems. Immediately, we are in an elegant world of rhymed and metered stanzas, and consciously archaic diction, and in this world are two lovers ignoring the march of history around them as the ages pass. "I Dreamed That in a City Dark as Paris" is much less chi-chi, and presents the speaker imagining he is a French soldier in World War I, and that the French soldier is the speaker forty years later. "A Dream of Governors" brings us back to literature in a slightly mocking way by portraying a heroic knight who kills a dragon, wins the lady, becomes king, and then grows bored with the rest of his life. "Orpheus in the Underworld" is a moving poem about the loss of love, which shuttles effectively between Orpheus' loss and that of the speaker, but it is too artificial and mannered to convey fully the passion of the speaker's distress. And "The Flight to Cytherea" shows the speaker growing restless with his civilized life, infected by the "demon of decorum and despair," and dashing off in a half-whimsical way to have various adventures, until at last he finds contentment in his lady's eyes—which is a switch on the plot of "A Dream of Governors." These are poems, then, of war, love, and history, and if they are too stiffly brocaded, they are nevertheless based on a satisfying broad perspective.

The second section is called "My America," and it deals with the Europeans who came here ("To the Western World" and "Orpheus in America"), and what they made of it afterwards ("Hot Night on Water Street," "Landscape with Barns," "The Legend of Success," and "The Boarder"). It is in the latter, especially, that Simpson strikes an authentic, if somewhat sentimental note, working in his own way in the tradition of Masters and Sinclair Lewis. "Hot Night," for example, begins:

> A hot midsummer night on Water Street—
> The boys in jeans were combing their blond hair,
> Watching the girls go by on tired feet. . . .

And goes on to notice "Three hardware stores, a barbershop, a bar, / A movie playing Westerns"—and concludes:

> At the newsstand in the lobby, a cigar
> Was talkative: "Since I've been in this town
> I've seen one likely woman, and a car
> As she was crossing Main Street, knocked her down."
> I was a stranger here myself, I said,
> And bought the *New York Times*, and went to bed.

"The Boarder" is similarly effective, and I give it here entire (for Simpson is not cursed with Dickey's fatal prolixity):

> The time is after dinner. Cigarettes
>   Glow on the lawn;
> Glasses begin to tinkle; TV sets
>   Have been turned on.
>
> The moon is brimming like a glass of beer
>   Above the town,
> And love keeps her appointments—"Harry's here!"
>   "I'll be right down."
>
> But the pale stranger in the furnished room
>   Lies on his back
> Looking at paper roses, how they bloom,
>   And ceilings crack.

The third section is called "The Old World," and deals of course with Europe. The gratifying thing about these poems is that, just as Simpson keeps a consciousness of Europe awake as he writes about America, so too does he remember that he's an American when he writes about Europe. Certainly not, however, in any self-congratulatory way. In "Mediterranean," for example, he finds himself in a glittering scene, noticing the film-festival going on across the bay at Cannes, and hearing the television roar from the villas on the shore. The poem concludes wittily and pointedly:

> America, a female sage
> Remarked, is old. We were the first
> To enter on the modern age.
> So history has been reversed,
> And Europeans will discover
> Our follies when we give them over.
>
> And since this is the case in France,
> I have obtained a rubber boat.
> As the advantages advance
> I'll grow increasingly remote.
> The water laps around the bow.
> Goodbye. For I am leaving now.

The fourth section is called "The Runner," and deals with war. The first poem, after which this section has been named, is a narrative of over thirty pages which portrays the life of a messenger in the parachute and glider infantry during the Allied invasion of eastern Holland. It is easy reading and a mildly interesting tale, but I fail to see much point in it. In the "Old Soldier," a veteran dreams of danger. "The Bird" is a weird story about a Nazi concentration-camp officer. "The Silent Generation" and "Against the Age" depict the boredom and disillusionment of the returned servicemen after the war. And "Carentan O Carentan" tells, with an effective mockery of ballad-style, the story of a frightful ambush.

With the Love Poems of Part 5, Simpson goes literary again, although "Rough Winds Do Shake," "Summer Storm," and "The Custom of the World" are marvelously erotic.

All in all, *A Dream of Governors* has wit, sophistication, perceptiveness, intelligence, variety, and knowingness, but it comes perilously close to being a poetry of chic, avoiding at once the too-near of passion and the too-far of philosophy. The speaker of these poems is quizzical, good-natured, genial, charming, and satirical without bite, sexy without lust; he is never angry, or burning with desire, or impatient to understand, or anxious to interpret. He deals with myth, legend, fairy tale, and romance, and yet nothing seems deep, profound, or symbolic. He gives the impression of having had no trouble at all in slipping his feelings into well-worn sleeves; the poetry dominates, absorbs, and becomes a substitute for the feeling. It's as if the poet felt poems instead of emotions as he experienced life, and the transformation of experience into art took place almost before the emotion was felt.

At the End of the Open Road (1963), which won the Pulitzer Prize for 1964, is a different story entirely. Simpson has found the secret of releasing the meaning and power of his themes. The progress of a poem from the mundane to the eternal, from the outer to the inner, from fact to symbol, from situation to response, from the ordinary to the mysterious, from the rational to the subsconscious—this is no longer a matter of merely literary machinery but rather of a living shock. How to define and locate this urgency, which is crucial to the impact and intensity of a good poem? It is not simply that his stanzas, as is also the case with Dickey, are becoming more flexible and experimental: this in itself does not mean very much, and it does not in fact mean that much in Dickey's recent verse. What is more fundamental, it seems to me, is that greater stylistic flexibility should be the sign of growth in the character and thought of the speaker. Simpson is becoming more able to be a part of what he writes about, and to make what he writes about more a part of him. This is the opposite of Dickey's complacency, for it represents an openness to life in which the poet runs the risk of being affected and even altered by what he experiences. And change is a risk indeed, for one may find that he is not only no longer satisfied with his world but also no longer satisfied with himself. It is difficult to be an honest poet today and still remain an agreeable domestic man and model citizen. One may even go mad. But Simpson has so far managed to be distraught without becoming distracted, and his newer poems, instead of being somewhat over-elaborate, are now pulled taut so that they vibrate. It is the difference, which Dickey should learn, between drawing something out and packing it in. The emotions and ideas that were lacking in *A Dream of Governors* are present in *At the End of the Open Road*, and Simpson is surely on his way to becoming a major poet.

The book is divided into four sections, but only the first and third seem to form distinct groups. The first contains four poems about America, but the fourth section also contains three on the same subject. "In California" begins:

> Here I am, troubling the dream coast
> With my New York face,
> Bearing among the realtors
> And tennis-players my dark preoccupation.

Here is "In the Suburbs" entire:

> There's no way out.
> You were born to waste your life.
> You were born to this middleclass life

As others before you
Were born to walk in procession
To the temple, singing.

"The Redwoods" is a lovely poem, spoken by these great trees, and concluding:

O if there is a poet

let him come now! We stand at the Pacific
like great unmarried girls,

turning in our heads the stars and clouds,
considering whom to please.

"There Is" is spoken by an observer of the streets:

But I have no profession. Like a spy
I read the papers—Situations Wanted.
Surely there is a secret
which, if I knew it, would change everything!

Then there are the three poems at the end inspired by Whitman, who was invoked at the beginning in "In California." "Walt Whitman at Bear Mountain" says "The Open Road goes to the used-car lot." In "Pacific Ideas—A Letter to Walt Whitman," the speaker tells the spirit of the dead poet that the past insists upon repeating itself, and so cannot be cancelled out. And in "Lines Written near San Francisco," he realizes finally that:

Whitman was wrong about the People,
But right about himself. The land is within.
At the end of the open road we come to ourselves.

We have come a long way from the somewhat sentimental vision of "Hot Night on Water Street" and "The Boarder." America's emptiness now has a context and a cause, and the poet's satire now has bite and meaning.

Part III is a longish narrative called "The Marriage of Pocahontus," and, although it is very skilfully done, being told in the language of Capt. John Smith's *Generall Historie of Virginia, New England, and the Summer Isles*, I find no more point in it than I did in "The Runner."

Part II, however, opens with four delightful love poems which far transcend in passion, sensuality, and significance his earlier group of love poems. "Summer Morning," for example, tells of being with a girl in a hotel in a deserted section of New York where there were only small factories around, and it concludes:

Toys, hardware—whatever they made,
It's been worn out.
I'm fifteen years older myself—
Bad years and good.

So I have spoiled my chances.
For what? Sheer laziness,
The thrill of an assignation,
My life that I hold in secret.

And a few pages on, we meet this poem, which I quote in full:

In the morning light a line
Stretches forever. There my unlived life
Rises, and I resist,
Clinging to the steps of the throne.

Day lifts the darkness from the hills,
A bright blade cuts the reeds,
And my life, pitilessly demanding,
Rises forever in the morning light.

The book is full of these pleasures, poems which one feels compelled to read aloud to a friend. I must restrain myself now, however, and conclude with a brief consideration of two poems on poetry. The first is a cutting but good-natured satire on the early esthetic of T. E. Hulme and T. S. Eliot, and it is

preposterously entitled "New Lines for Cuscuscaraway and Mirza Murad Ali Beg." There is an epigraph from Hulme about "cheerful, dry and sophisticated" verse, and the poem opens with a vision of "Mr. Eliot leaning over a fence / Like a cheerful embalmer. . . . " And it concludes:

Let us be thoroughly dry.
Let us sing a new song unto the Lord,
A song of exclusion.
For it is not so much a matter of being chosen
As of not being excluded.
I will sing unto the Lord
In a voice that is cheerfully dry.

In a sense, his shift from the impersonal artifice of *A Dream of Governors* to the more personal and Whitmanesque passion of *At the End of the Open Road* is a shift away from Hulme and Eliot, and this poem is a not-too-serious laying of ghosts.

The second poem is called "American Poetry," and I quote it entire:

Whatever it is, it must have
A stomach that can digest
Rubber, coal, uranium, moons, poems.

Like the shark, it contains a shoe.
It must swim for miles through the desert
Uttering cries that are almost human.

Dickey's poems have digested moons, and Simpson's earlier poems digested poems. Simpson has now learned how to digest rubber, coal, and uranium, and is beginning his long swim through the desert.

C. B. COX
"The Poetry of Louis Simpson"
Critical Quarterly, Spring 1966, pp. 72–83

"Descriptions of poetry by men who are not poets are usually ridiculous, for they describe rational thought-processes." (Louis Simpson)

I

For the soldier in the last war a common experience was to be whisked off in a truck to an unknown destination, ordered to get out, to get back in again, in an apparently meaningless series of manoeuvres. This sequence is described in Louis Simpson's long narrative poem, 'The Runner',[1] as in 1944 the 101st Airborne Division of the U.S. Army moves into the Ardennes to counter a German attack. For Dodd, the main character, the journey seems dream-like, the occasional view of ravine, forest or black-clothed villagers like a glimpse into some fantasy world through which, against his will, he is forced to travel.

A feeling of being involved in historical processes which we only partly understand is typical of Simpson's work. His poems often convey a sense of hallucination, as if our everyday perceptions on our journey through time hide a reality that reason cannot fully comprehend. Dodd dreams that he hears voices of men who fought in the wars in the past; in another poem 'I Dreamed that in a City Dark as Paris' a modern soldier for a few moments inhabits the mind of a *poilu* in the 1914–18 War, watching with his eyes a dog-fight in the sky. As Simpson's imagination ranges over the history of the West, the many wars and the thousands killed, his characters appear to touch upon archetypal experiences which ordinarily we evade, but which are revealed by proximity to death. This hallucinatory quality provides one reason why he has written some of the best poems about World War II. Like Wilfred Owen, he presents the people and events of war not fixed by their particular backgrounds, but like shadows in some cosmic drama that involves all humanity.

'Carentan O Carentan' is perhaps his best war poem. The particular scene, vividly created as by "the shining green canal" the soldiers walk towards ambush, merges into the experience of all men as they pass through life towards death:

> Could you have seen us through a glass
> You would have said a walk
> Of farmers out to turn the grass,
> Each with his own hay-fork.

This shift of perspective, imposing a ghost-like pastoral scene on the menacing images of war, draws the everyday routine of the farmers into the context of death. The poem moves backwards and forwards in time, linking together the ambushed soldiers with the lovers who "in the old days" wandered hand in hand from Carentan. This changing perspective is also presented by the simple ballad form, which at first links the narrative to universal folk experience and the romantic associations evoked by the name 'Carentan'; but at the end a series of inappropriate images breaks down, almost with an excess of crudity, the illusions of magical romance:

> Lieutenant, what's my duty,
> My place in the platoon?
> He too's a sleeping beauty,
> Charmed by that strange tune.

II

'Carentan O Carentan' is typical of many Simpson poems in that it presents strikingly clear images which confuse and disturb. When his early work was reviewed in the American magazine *The Fifties*, he was accused of using the traditional forms of a previous age to assert modern revolutionary ideas, and the reviewer argued that the split between context and form was self-destructive. Simpson has often written in conventional rhythms and stanzas, and his name has been associated with the Academics in the battle against the Beats. Certainly his early books, *The Arrivistes* (1949), *Good News of Death and Other Poems* (1955) and *A Dream of Governors* (1959) include a fair number of poems in pedestrian style where the need to maintain patterns of rhyme and rhythm leads to clumsiness. But the successful poems, and these increase from volume to volume, often use traditional forms in highly novel and arresting ways. There are poems such as 'Song: "Rough Winds Do Shake the Darling Buds of May"', in which a parody of Elizabethan lyrical conventions associates them with an uncompromisingly physical account of sex. In 'The Bird' a child-like narrative in simple four-line rhymed stanzas is used for a story about the German gas-chambers. At the conclusion Heinrich, the simple-souled executioner, escapes from the Russians presumably by turning into a bird, still sadly singing his favourite song: "Ich wünscht', ich wäre ein Vöglein". The poem shifts in macabre and terrifying fashion from one area of experience to another—childish innocence, killing of Jews, nostalgia.

In Simpson's view, [2] the poets of Fifth Century Athens or Elizabethan England were closely associated with aristocratic communities, and so could relate their experiences to the conventional literary forms of their society. The poet used common forms to express thoughts which were acceptable to his fellow men. Since the end of the eighteenth century the artist has been in recoil from the middle class ethos of science and business and progress. Great modern poets are eccentrics,

"and in my opinion this must be so, for the modern world, with its pervasive materialism and wars, is by no means a happy place". These attitudes to history explain the repeated ironic contrasts in his work between traditional form and modern experience.

In his poetry satire of middle-class materialism is linked to rejection of the belief that there is an external world of objects, existing independently of our forms of description, which we can describe, if we are careful enough, just as it is, from an absolute standpoint. In his view poetry touches upon a reality beyond the compass of any trust in rationalism and 'hard facts'; it derives from the subconscious in a manner which must always remain incomprehensible: "Poetry is a mystery. No-one has ever been able to define it". In his poems the sudden shifts of tone and perspective reflect his belief that no single mode of apprehending reality can ever be fully satisfactory. In his later, more mature, work he introduces the 'deep image', which in itself contains a multiplicity of meanings, and which resists rational interpretation. In contrast to the early imagists, he does not forswear moral and intellectual comment, but weaves together imagery, irony and concept. His best poems refuse to limit themselves to obvious meanings, and in this way reflect the 'modern' belief that systems of harmony and order which explain every feature of the universe are no longer possible. In 'Tonight the Famous Psychiatrist' he mocks a successful American psychiatrist, enjoying his party of celebrities, but unable to cure his wife who thinks she still lives in Hungary. No explanation of human behaviour can ever be final. In his poems statement is followed by counter-statement, lyrical emotion by irony. Like Philip Larkin he mocks his own poses, refusing to settle in any one form of knowing:

> I have the poor man's nerve-tic, irony.
> I see through the illusions of the age!

Such conflicts between different ways of apprehension are strikingly illustrated in one of his best-known poems, 'My Father in the Night Commanding No'. This poem, as it examines parent-child relationships, proceeds by repeated reversals of tone, one form of knowing criticized implicitly by the next:

> My father in the night commanding No
> Has work to do. Smoke issues from his lips;
>   He reads in silence.
> The frogs are croaking and the streetlamps glow.

The first line, with its rhetorical flourish, recalls the child's response to absolute authority, to adult society with its strict positives and negatives; but the curious break at the end of the line disturbs its simple force. The father's command seems not to be an important moral pronouncement, for the verb "Has work to do" deflates him to an ordinary mortal ordering his child not to interrupt. "Smoke issues from his lips" recreates the strangeness of the father's world for the child, and the stanza ends with an evocative, magical landscape. In his 'Confessions of an American Poet', he contrasts his father, a lawyer with a passion for facts, with his exotic Polish mother, an emigrant who made a career in motion pictures. She had a passion for opera, and told him stories of Poland, in which snow was always falling and the wolves howling in the distance. In the second stanza of the poem his mother winds the gramophone, "The Bride of Lammermoor begins to shriek", or she reads a story of Thule, "at midnight when the mice are still". His father's life of practical reality is opposed by his mother's romanticism, but the word 'shriek' tips the scene over towards comedy. The poem proceeds by describing the poet's own romantic journeys to the great cities of Europe; he has even visited Thule itself. Eventually he finds himself a father in his turn.

> Here is my house. Under a red rose tree
> A child is swinging; another gravely plays.
>   They are not surprised
> That I am here; they were expecting me.

These lines, affirmative in tone, evoke the wonder of love and children, yet even here the narrator remains slightly bewildered by the enigmatic situations through which he moves. "And yet . . . And yet . . ." he continues, still unable completely to fathom the archetypal relationships between father and child, realism and romance. The poem ends inconclusively, with a series of questions, as the wind whispers an answer the children cannot hear:

> Father, why did you work? Why did you weep,
> Mother? Was the story so important?
>   "*Listen!*" the wind
> Said to the children, and they fell asleep.

The simple pattern of the four-line stanza is strictly adhered to, so that the uncertainties of the narrator are balanced by the lucidity of the form. Simpson is a brilliant verse technician. Here the end-stopped stanzas, with the first and fourth lines usually linked by very simple rhymes, provide brief striking images; such momentary flashes of illumination offer no total scheme of thought, only conflicting impressions.

The description of Nature in Simpson's poems, like those in his mother's stories, often seems appropriate for a tale of high romance: "The stars were large wtih rain", "rainpools glimmered in the moonlit fields", "wild is the wind". In 'The Troika' the narrator passes through archetypal romantic landscapes, as in a dream sequence: the greybeards playing chess, the moon looking down on the guardsmen in trenches "wind fluttering their rags", the nightmare when he loses his father's horses, the vision of the white bird which turns into a beautiful girl:

> Troika, troika! The snow moon
> whirls through the forest.

Such dream-like images, contributing to the hallucinatory quality of many poems, have a double effect. Their magic creates a sense of mystery, of imminent revelation, but at the same time they are slightly exaggerated, so noticeably archetypal we can never lose ourselves completely in their romantic evocations. Like Marvell, Simpson places moments of lyrical splendour in an ironic context:

> Ranching in Bolinas, that's the life,
> If you call cattle life.
> To sit on a veranda with a glass
> And see the sprinklers watering your land
> And hear the peaches dropping from the trees
> And hear the ocean in the redwood trees . . .

Here the contrast between the excess of Nature and the rancher sitting on his veranda, glass in hand, makes him appear comic. Simpson's imagination responds to hugeness in Nature, to expanses of sky or the antiquity and size of redwood forests in California. He has a wonderful lyric gift and has written many beautiful short poems—'The Boarder', 'Birch', 'Luminous Night'. But in the longer poems he usually retains a sense of ironic bewilderment, a refusal to delude himself that he has reached some final insight. Throughout his poems irony is in perpetual debate with romantic imagination. His poems move towards an understanding of man, but never underestimate his essential mystery:

> It seems that a man exists
> Only to say, Here I am in person.

These double attitudes are also reflected in the numerous poems he devotes to America, his adopted country. As epigraph to 'Walt Whitman at Bear Mountain', he quotes Ortega y Gasset: " . . . life which does not give the preference to any other life, of any previous period, which therefore prefers its own existence . . . " For him this is the life that America ought to represent, the dream of the pioneers who followed the open road to the West. In California, at the end of the trek, the cloud-wagons move on, "dreaming of a Pacific", but beneath the realtors have taken possession of the land; for the "Open Road goes to the used-car lot:" In 'Lines Written near San Francisco', he says;

> While we were waiting for the land
> They'd finished it—with gas drums
> On the hilltops, cheap housing in the valleys
> Where lives are mean and wretched.
> But the banks thrive and the realtors
> Rejoice—they have their America.

Always something of an alien, his criticisms reflect personal dissatisfaction because he can never completely associate his own cosmopolitan literary inheritance with the brash and expansive landscapes of America. For him the real search is not for new lands, but for one's true identity and the meaning of one's death:

> The land is within.
> At the end of the open road we come to ourselves.

Simpson's poems turn repeatedly to the significance of death. As poet he is like Orpheus, descending to the shades to bring back news of kingdoms beyond the range of normal understanding. In California, the "dream-coast", he troubles the realtors with his "dark preoccupation". His poem 'Orpheus in the Underworld' includes an eight-stanza straight-forward recreation of the story of Orpheus and Eurydice, but in other sections the figure of Orpheus merges with the poet himself, who by the Mediterranean once discovered in the dark night "the fearful sense Of mortal love". The sudden shifts from Orpheus to poet and back again make it difficult for the reader to locate himself in the poem. The journey into the shadows seems both a legendary event, which we can observe with cool detachment, and a concern of the present moment involving strong personal emotions. The legend of Orpheus thus becomes an archetypal experience, always waiting for the individual poet who must make his own way, to quote Lawrence, "among the splendour of torches of darkness".

In 'Good News of Death', a kind of mock pastoral, not very successful and not included in *Selected Poems*, Simpson contrasts Pagan and Christian attitudes to death. After the Agamemnon-Clytemnestra-Orestes cycle of murder and retribution comes Christ's good news of death. But one of the banished Furies insists that the turning wheel will eventually bring the Christian faith to its end:

> And the event will prove
> The truth is always so.

Truth is the fact of death, which men avoid by their 'dreams', by their 'yearning outwards', but acceptance of death releases a man to discover his true self. 'Lines Written near San Francisco' ends:

> Though mad Columbus follows the sun
> Into the sea, we cannot follow.
> We must remain, to serve the returning sun,
> And to set tables for death.
> For we are the Colonists of Death—
> Not, as some think, of the English.

And we are preparing thrones for him to sit,
Poems to read, and beds
In which it may please him to rest.

This is the land
The pioneers looked for, shading their eyes
Against the sun—a murmur of serious life.

III

It has sometimes been said that Simpson has considerable technical skill, but that he lacks a distinctive voice. His poems on America, for example, have been criticized as a kind of superior journalism. This seems to me quite untrue. The distinctive mark of a good Simpson poem is that the formal clarity, the self-controlled manipulation of language, build up total effects which, in their mingling of different accounts of reality, can both surprise and disturb. This is best seen by examining a complete poem, and so I quote the whole of 'Moving the Walls':

The Prince of Monaco
Was sick of English ladies.

The Prince had a yacht
And her name was *Hirondelle.*
She was cousin to the yacht of the Kaiser
And niece to the yacht of the Tsar.

And the Prince was interested in the sea—
That is, oceanography.
So he furnished the yacht with instruments
And with instruments of brass,
Burners and sinks and instruments
Of the most delicate glass.

There was also a whaleboat
And a whole crew of harpooners.
There was a helmet and suit of armor
For the wars of the ocean floor.

The *Hirondelle* trembled like a fern,
And the crew stood at attention,
And they piped the Captain aboard.

2

Cloud-sailed, the *Hirondelle*
Pursued the horizon.
At night she skimmed
The phosphorescent surges.

And now they are on the Pacific,
The bottomless sea.
And out of the deep they have drawn
The whale, Leviathan, with a hook.
They have captured the giant squid
That has ten arms, claws like a cat's, a beak like a
        parrot's,
And a large malevolent eye.

They stepped from the whaleboat onto shoals,
The crests of sunken mountains.
In nets they gathered
Plankton and weeds and crabs that looked astonished.

And there were nights, O Prince,
When you stretched your hands and feet
In the leaves of the pomegranate tree!

And all went into the log.
The various sea trophies
Were written down in the log.
The darkening sky, the storm,
And tranquil days—
All, all went into the log.

The Prince returned—a hero of sorts.
He returned to his former life,

To the lights of the Grand Hotel
And the Russian ladies with their eternal cigarettes.

Then he built a museum.
The wheel of the *Hirondelle* is there,
And also the laboratory, the strange heart of the ship
Uprooted, leaving red holes
In the deck that vanished in smoke.

Here are the trophies:
A walking stick made from the backbone of a shark;
Tortoiseshell combs, and fans of mother-of-pearl;
Corals that faded,
Losing the changing hues of sea and sky;
Sea shells under glass
That are as dull as buttons
Sewn on garments by girls who have faded.

The Philippine Islands are a box
And the smile of a lady in a mantilla.
A walrus stuffed with straw
Faces the diving helmet.
They remember Verdun and Passchendaele,
The mud-clouded wars of the ocean floor.

So all that oceanography, after all,
Was only a pawnshop.
For they brought home the tooth of the whale
And said, "Look!
It is only a doorstop, after all."

For Leviathan does not exist,
And the sea is no mystery.
For a shark is a walking stick.

And this we call the life of reason.

4

Idiots!
We too are all for reducing
The universe to human dimensions.
As if we could know what is human!

Just a few dippers of sea water
And a fair wind home . . .
Then surely we won't be destroyed.

A strange idea, if you consider
The dust of those settlements—
The parlors where no one lives;
The splinter that wounds the foot sole
On its way to the double bed;
And Leviathan over all,
The cloud shaped like a weasel or a whale,
Leviathan rising above the roof tops.

5

When men wanted the golden fleece
It was not wool they wanted.
They were the trophies that they sailed toward.

They were the sea and the wind
That hurled them over
Into the sea. They were the fishes
That stripped their thin bones. And they rose
In the night in new constellations.

They left no wreckage.
Nothing is floating on the surface.
For they yielded themselves
To the currents that moved from within.

They are mightily changed
In the corollas, the branched sea-heaven.

And you, my country,
These days your walls are moving,
These nights we are branching among the stars.
I say, but my mind is doubtful.

Are there any at sea?
If so, they have not whispered lately.

Bored with aristocratic society, the Prince of Monaco decides to amuse himself by exploring the unknown depths of the sea. The whole of the first section is delightfully ironic. Like the *Hirondelle*, the swallow, the Prince will only skim the surface. A dilettante, he treats Nature as a plaything, and is untouched by the hidden power of the sea, the great flood of archetypal experience. The tone of the narrator mimics the kind of childish wonder typical in stories of magic and adventure:

> There was also a whaleboat
> And a whole crew of harpooners.

"A whole crew"—how colossal an enterprise! This satire of aristocrats, indulging their fancies just before the outbreak of European war and Communist Revolution, is linked with ironic treatment of the pretence that reason and science can control and finally comprehend the universe. In the middle group of lines, the repetition of 'instruments' delicately mocks the Prince's determination to measure Nature scientifically. One line alone stands out from this slightly comic portrait— "the wars of the ocean floor". This hints at another form of reality whose importance will be revealed later in the poem.

In the second section the *Hirondelle* pursues the horizon, the unreachable limits of human apprehension, and skims over the phosphorescent magic of the seas. But soon the Prince's playing at exploration is contrasted with the mysteries of the bottomless sea; like the rationalist, he is trying to understand the unfathomable. Leviathan drawn with a 'hook' suggests ironically the inadequacy of his instruments. Again, the tone of the narrative, as in a child's adventure story, seems incongruous with the horrors of the deep—Leviathan, the monster that represents Satan, and the malevolent squid; even the crabs look "astonished", perhaps at the presumption of the sailors. Yet, against this comic background, the depths invite the travellers into a magical seascape, and the poem breaks out into lyrical exuberance:

> They stepped from the whaleboat onto shoals,
> The crests of sunken mountains
>
> . . .
>
> And there were nights, O Prince,
> When you stretched your hands and feet
> In the leaves of the pomegranate tree!

It is as if they step out of human limitations to become, for a brief space, involved with the mysteries of Nature. 'Onto' rather than 'into' shoals is highly evocative. They step not onto land but onto the sea itself—almost like Christ walking on the water. 'Shoals' suggest both low-lying waters and the abundance of fish, while "The crests of sunken mountains" associates them with magic undersea kingdoms. And so on some nights the Prince sensuously participates in the luxuriant beauty of Nature. These lines offer multiple suggestions, and are typical of Simpson's recent use of imagery. As in Marvell, moments of rich sensuousness and vision are presented in a tone of almost comic surprise. And so the section ends with irony, as everything is recorded precisely, superficially, in the log.

In section three the Prince, unchanged by his explorations, returns to his dull social round, and the wonders of the deep are translated into the knick-knackery of a museum. The life of reason reduces the underwater life to mundane, everyday articles. Yet the tearing out of "the strange heart of the ship" and the "red holes In the deck that vanished in smoke"

suggest that some explosive force has existed in the laboratory. Beneath the surface of pre-1914 aristocratic society waited the horror of Verdun and Passchendaele, the knowledge of evil and death which the Prince preferred to ignore.

In the fourth and fifth sections the narrator steps forward to provide a moral. Today we continue to evade the destructive element, to impose secure dimensions on the "mud-clouded wars of the ocean floor". The great epic heroes discovered themselves by their explorations, joined themselves to the hugeness of Nature. Perhaps America may repeat those epic journeys, moving the walls outwards, embracing the mysteries of the depths. But in the last stanza the poem turns round on itself:

> Are there any at sea?
> If so, they have not whispered lately.

The poem is set in a literary tradition, reminding us of the voyages of the Nautilus in Jules Verne's *Twenty Thousand Leagues under the Sea*, or of Captain Ahab's pursuit of Moby Dick. Throughout Simpson's poems we find echoes of other poets—Marvell, as we have seen, Auden or Eliot. In 'Moving the Walls' formal lucidity and the literary background provide a traditional means of control for the material. The experiences of the poem are set not in a rational framework but in this context of man's greatest imaginative responses to the enigma of the universe.

IV

In the 1950's, the debates between Movement and Maverick, Academic and Beat, were dangerous because both extremes limited the resources of poetry. Simpson finds no absolute value in any one form of communication, but uses both rational statement and evocative image to convey his personal sense of reality. In his most recent work his rhythms have become more free, less tied to iambic norms, and he makes increasing use of mysterious imagery whose total effect is beyond rational appraisal. The process reflects his own multiple response to life, what a *Times Literary Supplement* reviewer called "an anarchic personalism" which offers private revelations rather than large social, philosophical or religious schemes. In a recent poem, 'Things', an ironic 'I' debates with a man who has seen a vision. The visionary tells him that even household articles hold a mystery, and the 'I' replies:

> I said, "I have suspected
> The Mixmaster knows more than I do,
> The air conditioner is the better poet.
> My right front tire is as bald as Odysseus—
> How much it must have suffered!

The mock-epic tone, like that of Pope in *The Rape of the Lock*, works in two conflicting ways. It satirises the American worship of 'things', yet also evokes the fantastic wonder of modern inventions. So the poem ends when the 'I' acknowledges the mystery of objects, and asks for a kind of apprehension which unites the true functions of reason and imagination, irony and vision:

> Then, as things have a third substance
> Which is obscure to both our senses,
> Let there be a perpetual coming and going
> Between your house and mine".

Notes

1. Included in Louis Simpson's *Selected Poems*, Harcourt, Brace and World, 1965.
2. See his 'Confessions of an American Poet', *The New York Times Magazine*, May 2, 1965.

UPTON SINCLAIR

1878–1968

Upton Beall Sinclair, Jr., was born on September 20, 1878, in Baltimore, Maryland, to Upton Beall and Priscilla (née Harden) Sinclair. He attended City College of New York, graduating in 1897. He worked his way through four years of graduate school at Columbia University by writing pulp juvenile stories for the Street & Smith publishing firm, and jokes for the New York newspapers. Sinclair was active in socialist politics and social reform throughout his life, and social and economic concerns are of primary importance in his work. In 1900 he married Meta H. Fuller, and gave up writing pulp fiction. His early serious novels attracted little attention, and he and his wife lived in dire poverty for several years.

The Jungle (1906), Sinclair's exposé of the Chicago stockyards, catapulted him to fame and made him wealthy. Before turning his efforts to new books Sinclair wished to settle himself and his family in a cooperative colony. He founded Helicon Hall in 1907 and brought to the former boys' school near Englewood, New Jersey, an assortment of forty adults: intellectuals, New Thoughtists, socialists, single-taxers and two Yale dropouts (one of whom was Sinclair Lewis, who worked as a janitor). The social experiment came to a close when the building burned to the ground in 1908. Sinclair was divorced from Meta Fuller in 1913, and married Mary Craig Kimbrough the same year. He shocked the Socialist party when he resigned in 1917 owing to his disagreement with their anti-war policy; he later rejoined.

Sinclair was particularly productive during his early years, and produced several of his most important novels, including *The Money-Changers* (1908), *King Coal* (1917), *Oil!* (1927), and *Boston* (1928). Most of his fiction of the time is barely disguised polemic, with stereotypical characters who are nonetheless fervent and convincing.

Sinclair ran for governor of California in 1934 as a Democrat; he was narrowly defeated in a bitter campaign, with big business firmly on the side of his opponent. The experience was disillusioning, and Sinclair's late fiction is more bitter and cynical, although still accomplished. His major work in the latter part of his career was the ten-volume Lanny Budd series, published from 1940 to 1949. Mary Craig Sinclair died in 1961, and Sinclair married May Hard in 1962. He published his autobiography later the same year. Upton Sinclair is one of America's most popular writers overseas; his work has been translated into over fifty languages. He died on November 25, 1968.

Manassas, by Mr. Upton Sinclair, is a very different sort of book, having for its purpose not entertainment, but instruction and the revivifying of the intense emotions of the years preceding the war. It is only fair at the outset of our comment to give warning that it has a hero but no heroine. Although absolutely devoid of the love interest, which is not even hinted at in the course of these four hundred pages, it is one of the most thrillingly interesting books of its kind that we have ever read. We are not quite sure that it even has a hero, for the leading character, whose life is portrayed for us from childhood up, does not become a man of action until the very close, but is presented to us throughout as one in whose mind and feelings are reflected the interests and the passions of the period of anti-slavery agitation. The real drama of the book is the historical clash of the two civilizations, and individuals seem to be made use of only by way of incidental illustration. The hero, if we may so call him, is reared upon a Mississippi plantation which will eventually fall to him as an inheritance. When still a boy, he is taken to Boston, and there educated. He does not lose sympathy for his own people as a result of this removal, but his eyes are opened to the horrors of slavery, and he realizes that when the struggle comes it will be his duty to stand by the union. As the fundamental cause of that struggle slavery is emphasized, and rightly, as all-important. In the course of the narrative we are made acquainted with the workings of the Underground Railroad, the mobbing of abolitionists, the enforcement of the Fugitive Slave Law in Boston and elsewhere, and John Brown's mad enterprise at Harper's

Ferry. We are also given, although not taken to the scene, vivid accounts of the border warfare in Kansas, of the great slavery debates in the Senate, of the dastardly assault upon Sumner, and nearly every other matter affecting the slavery issue during the fifties. In fact, the reader, if he stops to think at all, must soon realize that what he is reading is not fiction at all, but a consecutive and almost documentary history of the period. It is history written with warmth and an eye for dramatic effect, to be sure, but it is nevertheless essentially history. It is the author's triumph that his readers are not likely to think very much about such things, so enthralling has he made his pages. It is only near the close that Sumter is fired upon, and the war begun. Then we get a few impressionist snap-shots of the excitement in both sections, a hurried account of the scenes of confusion in and about Washington, a glimpse of the new President as he seemed in those first days of trial to the men who had been too bewildered to take his true measure, and finally, the rout at Bull Run from the standpoint of the hero, a private in his first engagement. This battle episode suggests *The Red Badge of Courage*, only it seems to be better done. And here, having brought us just over the verge of actual conflict, the book ends—ends where most novels of the Civil War begin. It is a work deserving of very high praise. It does not treat its history as a spectacle simply, but has the rare quality of arousing our emotions almost to the pitch of those that made the war inevitable, and of enabling us of a later generation to feel the passion of those great past days when conscience counted for something in our politics, and when a worthy cause evoked our noblest national energies.—WILLIAM MORTON PAYNE, *Dial*, Jan. 1, 1905, pp. 15–16

The doctrine preached in this fat volume ⟨*The Goose-Step*⟩—to wit, that the American colleges and universities, with precious few exceptions, are run by stock-jobbers and manned by intellectual prostitutes—this doctrine will certain give no fillip of surprise to steady readers of my critical compositions. I have, in fact, maintained it steadily since the earliest dawn of the present marvelous century, and to the support of it I have brought forward an immense mass of glittering and irrefragable facts and a powerful stream of eloquence. Nor have I engaged in this moral enterprise *a cappella*. A great many other practitioners have devoted themselves to it with equal assiduity, including not a few reformed and conscience-stricken professors, and the net result of that united effort is that the old assumption of the pedagogue's *bona fides* is now in decay throughout the Republic. In whole departments of human knowledge he has become suspect, as it were, *ex officio*. I nominate, for example, the departments of history and of what is commonly called English language and literature. If a professor in the first field shows ordinary honesty, or, in the second field, ordinary sense, it is now regarded as a sort of marvel, and with sound reason. Barring a scant dozen extraordinary men, no American professor of history has written anything worth reading since the year 1917; nearly all the genuine history published in the United States since then has come from laymen, or from professors who have ceased to profess. And so in the domain of the national letters. The professors, with a few exceptions, mainly belated rice-converts, are unanimously and furiously consecrated to vain attacks upon the literature that is in being. Either, like the paleozoic Beers, of Yale, they refuse to read it and deny that it exists, or, like the patriotic Matthews, of Columbia, they seek to put it down by launching Ku Klux anathemas against it. The net result is that the professorial caste, as a whole, loses all its old dignity and influence. In universities large and small, East, West, North and South, the very sophomores rise in rebellion against the incompetence and imbecility of their preceptors, and in the newspapers the professor slides down gradually to the level of a chiropractor, a press-agent or a Congressman.

Thus there is nothing novel in the thesis of Dr. Sinclair's book, which deals, in brief, with the internal organization of the American universities, and their abject subjection to the Money Power, which is to say, to Chamber of Commerce and Rotary Club concepts of truth, liberty and honor. But there is something new, and very refreshing, in the manner of it, for the learned author, for the first time, manages to tell a long and dramatic story without intruding his private grievances into it. Sinclair's worst weakness, next to his vociferous appetite for Remedies that never cure, is his naïve and almost actorial vanity. As everyone knows, it botched *The Brass Check*. So much of that book was given over to a humorless account of his own combats with yellow journals—which, in the main, did nothing worse to him than laugh at him when he was foolish— that he left untold a great deal that might have been said, and with perfect justice and accuracy, about the venality and swinishness of American newspapers. In *The Profits of Religion* he wobbled almost as badly; the subject, no doubt, was much too vast for a single volume; the Methodists and Baptists alone, to say nothing of Holy Church, deserved a whole shelf. But in *The Goose-Step* he tells a straightforward story in a straightforward manner—simply, good-humoredly and convincingly. When he comes into the narrative himself, which is not often, he leaves off his customary martyr's chemise. There is no

complaining, no pathos, no mouthing of platitude; it is a plain record of plain facts, with names and dates—a plain record of truly appalling cowardice, disingenuousness, abjectness, and degradation. Out of it two brilliant figures emerge: first the typical American university president, a jenkins to wealth, an ignominious waiter in antechambers and puller of wires, a politician, a fraud and a cad; and secondly, the typical American professor, a puerile and pitiable slave.—H. L. MENCKEN, "The Grove of Academe" (1923), *Prejudices: Fifth Series*, 1926, pp. 133–36

Mr. Upton Sinclair, having supplied successively economic interpretations of American journalism, American religion and American education, has undertaken, in his new book *Mammonart: An Essay in Economic Interpretation*, to perform the same service for literature and art. "It is my intention," he writes, "to study these artists from a point of view so far as I know entirely new. . . . The book will present an interpretation of the arts from the point of view of the class struggle." One does not see how Mr. Sinclair, who has been intimately associated for so many years with radical ideas and literature, can imagine that this point of view is new. On the contrary, it has become so familiar that, as soon as we have learned what his book is about, we can predict almost exactly what we shall find in it—even though we may be unprepared for the extreme results in certain cases of the author's application of his point of view. Here, for example, is Mr. Sinclair's economic interpretation of *Kubla Khan*: "Note that every one of these images appeals to reactionary emotions, fear or sensuality. By sensuality the reason is dragged from its throne; while fear destroys all activity of the mind, causing abasement and submission. Moreover—and here is the point essential to our argument—almost every image in this poem turns out on examination to be a lie. There is no such place as Xanadu; and Kubla Khan has nothing to teach us but avoidance. His pleasures were bloody and infamous, and there was nothing 'stately' about his 'pleasure-dome.' There never was a river Alph, and the sacredness of any river is a fiction of a priestly caste, preying on the people. There are no 'caverns measureless to man'; while as for a 'sunless sea,' a few arc-lights would solve the problem. The 'woman wailing for her demon lover' is a savage's nightmare; while as for the 'Abyssinian maid,' she would have her teeth blackened and would stink of rancid palm oil. From the beginning to the end, the poem deals with things which are sensual, cruel and fatal to hope."

It would, however, be unjust to Mr. Sinclair to suggest that he does not appreciate *Kubla Khan*. It is true that he announces his intention of proving that "present-day technique is far and away superior to the technique of any art period preceding" and that he attempts to do so by comparing a sonnet of Milton's to one by Mr. Clement Wood to the disadvantage of the former. But, whatever Mr. Sinclair may say for the good of the socialist cause, he has a real appreciation of literature and this somewhat interferes with his indictment. In *The Brass Check*, his book on journalism, he set out to expose a field of which he had had little inside experience and for which he felt, in consequence, no sympathy; but he is dealing in *Mammonart* with the products of his own craft, and the result, from the doctrinaire point of view, is one of the least effective of his books.

Bernard Shaw, with his more rigorous mind, has made a similar revaluation of literature, but he carried it through more logically. He began by assigning all literary works to either one of two departments, according to whether these works were or were not designed to ameliorate social conditions; and he laid down the uncompromising principle that, artistic merits being equal, the second was inferior to the first. But Upton Sinclair has not based his discussion upon any such clear proposition— which at least keeps the artistic question distinct from the moral one. He has tried to write a treatise on art which should function as a socialist tract by asserting that "all art is propaganda" and then justifying this assertion by assuming that any work of art which implies a philosophy, a point of view or even a sensation or an impulse is a piece of propaganda in favor of it. Since no human work can exist that does not rest on some sort of assumptions on the part of the person who produced it, Mr. Sinclair can make out a case; but his book, as a socialist exposé, is by no means the bombshell he has promised. What he has written is an outline of literature (since he has little to say about the other arts) by an able pamphleteer with a real taste for books but some moral and political prejudices which do not seem to prevent his enjoying certain works that run counter to these prejudices but which at least make him protest that he shouldn't. As such an outline, *Mammonart*—at any rate, the latter part—is not at all bad. Mr. Sinclair's memory occasionally lets him down, as when, evidently confusing Paul of Tarsus with the fourth-century Saint Paulinus, he tells us that Saint Paul was "a renegade Roman gentleman and former official of the empire" and writes scathingly of Thackeray's sentimentalizing over the death of Major Pendennis under the impression that Major Pendennis died the death of Colonel Newcome. But, on the whole, he is quite well-informed as to history and literature and knows how to place the writers with whom he deals in relation to the life of their times. He is particularly interesting in his treatment of the American writers of the last generation. Mr. Sinclair is himself a survivor of the era of Frank Norris and Richard Harding Davis, and his account of this is probably unique in its combination of inside knowledge with unorthodox point of view. On Jack London, whom he knew well, he is especially illuminating. One has seen, in fact, a good many less readable and less intelligent literary histories than this of Upton Sinclair. Intending, in his role of political oracle, a devastating social criticism, what he has given us, in his character of literary man, is a book that stimulates one's interest in the arts of God and Mammon both.

What is vulnerable in *Mammonart* is the thinking of Upton Sinclair rather than his literary taste. If, for example, he had begun by reflecting what "Art for Art's sake" really means, he would not have felt obliged to denounce it from beginning to end of his book. "Art for Art's sake"—an excellent slogan— means simply that the artist has the right to practice his art with a view to the perfection of his own kind of product—that he should not be expected to meet the requirements of specialists of other kinds. If somebody, that is to say, is constructing from the phenomena of experience a satisfactory artistic system, it should not be demanded of him that he construct either a political or a moral system, and the critic should not take him to task if his pattern fails to match the patterns of other people's political and moral systems. The artist has his own technique for formulating his vision of truth, and he cannot be expected to worry about the constructions of other people who are working in different materials. Mr. Sinclair comes quite close to this point of view when he writes in connection with Strindberg: "Let the artist give us truth, and we can always find use for it." And I suppose he would not oppose a program of "Mathematics for Mathematics' sake." He speaks somewhere with admiration of the achievements of modern physics. Yet if mathematicians had not been permitted to indulge in "Mathematics for Mathematics' sake," these discoveries would have been impossible. When Karl Friedrich Gauss worked out his

fourth-dimensional coördinates, he was engaged in a speculation which not only was quite devoid of political or moral significance but did not even appear at the time to be susceptible of practical application. Yet it was precisely by the aid of these exercises in pure mathematics and of others in the same direction that Einstein arrived at his new discoveries; and it is in the light of Einstein's discoveries that Mr. Sinclair's physicists in California are conducting their researches into the structure of the atom. A work of pure literature of which Mr. Sinclair disapproves is Gautier's *Émaux et camées*. I take it that he would like to discourage the writing of any more such books. But how can he be sure that putting an end to writers of the type of Gautier might not mean inflicting on literary culture the same sort of injury that would have been inflicted on mathematical and physical culture if Gauss's experiments had been prevented? One of the first rules of civilization should be freedom for the artist and the scientist, and for every other kind of intellectual creator, to pursue his own researches and produce his own kind of work. If the Socialist Coöperative Commonwealth to which Mr. Sinclair looks forward is going to interfere with this, it is difficult to see how its culture will deserve to be considered superior to our own individualist one.—EDMUND WILSON, "Upton Sinclair's *Mammonart*" (1925), *The Shores of Light*, 1952, pp. 212–16

ROBERT CANTWELL
"Upton Sinclair"
After the Genteel Tradition, ed. Malcolm Cowley
1937, pp. 37–51

In terms of his professional career, Upton Sinclair is one of the oddest and most spectacular figures in American literary history. This pale and soft-voiced ascetic, with his near-sighted smile, his disarming candor and his strangely prim and dated pre-war air of good-fellowship and enthusiasm, has been involved, ever since he began to write, in knock-down and drag-out conflicts of such ferocity and ruthlessness they might well demoralize a dozen hardened captains of industry. When you look over his career as a whole it seems to have a lot in common with those old-fashioned serials in which the hero was at the point of being pushed over the cliff or shoved into a buzz-saw at the end of every chapter, only to be preserved for greater hazards and climaxes that, oddly enough, bore no relation to those he had just escaped. Few American public figures, let alone American inspirational novelists, have written so many books, delivered so many lectures, covered so much territory, advocated so many causes or composed so many letters to the editor, got mixed up in so many scandals, been so insulted, ridiculed, spied on, tricked and left holding the bag—few, in short, have jumped so nimbly from so many frying pans into so many fires, and none has ever managed to keep so sunny and buoyant while the flames were leaping around him.

So far as I can make out, about the only really calm period in Sinclair's career was that between the Eisenstein mess and the outbreak of his Epic campaign. Another time, back in 1910, there were a few relatively quiet months in a single-tax colony outside Philadelphia—during them Sinclair wrote an unpublished sequel to his "Love's Pilgrimage," was arrested for playing baseball on Sunday and fell in love with a famous suffragette, while his wife ran off with a young poet who celebrated the affair by writing a detailed account of his courtship. Aside from such pastoral interruptions, Sinclair's life has been one of incessant high-pressure executive activity, and what makes it appear fantastic and unreal is that Sinclair never seems to have been aware of this fact. In a way he belongs in the ranks of those good-hearted and unworldly eccentrics, of the type of Bronson Alcott, who have contributed so much to American culture—the starters of colonies and the believers in mental telepathy, the authors of prophetic works and the friends of cranks and faddists, the originators of diets and the apostles of nature therapy—but unlike them he has always been a man of action as well, plunging headlong into the teeming submoral atmosphere of American business and politics, with their everyday frame-ups and routine treacheries that, in business and political circles, are as completely taken for granted as the custom of shaking hands.

In his autobiography Sinclair pictures himself as a poet, a reformer, a prophet, a novelist, and writes about his naïveté with a humor and honesty that carry conviction; but the record emerges as more puzzling and interesting. He was born in Baltimore in 1878, into an old border-state family that had been split by the Civil War and that, a decade after Appomattox, had its prosperous enterprising branch, already adjusted to the commercial order of things, as well as its genteel and demoralized representatives of defeat. Sinclair was born into its poor branch; his father was a liquor salesman who became a drunkard. The boy's early memories were of his father's periodic drunkenness and remorse, of hunting for bedbugs in miserable hotel rooms, of dining with an aristocratic grandmother, in great style, on bread and dried herring; then of visiting rich relatives like Uncle Bland, founder of the United States Fidelity and Guaranty Company, or Grandfather Harden, treasurer of the Western Maryland Railway, who was recalled as a silent old man constantly carving unending quantities of chickens, turkeys, ducks and hams. At ten Sinclair enrolled in a tough New York East Side grammar school. At twelve he completed his course. At fourteen he entered City College and before he was graduated was making his living writing jokes for the newspapers and romances for pulp magazines. While he was a student at Columbia, before he was twenty, he was a full-fledged hack, with an income of $70 a week, two secretaries, and a weekly output of 56,000 words of patriotic drivel about the Spanish-American War.

He was intense, nervous, chaste, easily influenced, perplexed about religious problems and worried about sex, an amateur violinist who lectured his sweethearts about venereal diseases, went on fantastic bicycle rides of a hundred miles a day and suffered from blinding surges of unfocused emotion that he interpreted as symptoms of genius. At twenty-two he married and wrote his first serious novel. In the next four years he wrote three more, including the first volume of his unfinished Civil War trilogy, *Manassas*. His wife was separated from him by her parents after the birth of their son and rejoined him to live in poverty in a house in the woods outside Princeton—they were sick, humiliated, borrowing money and begging for subsidies, so harassed that once Sinclair, "grim and implacable," forced his wife to return a thirty-cent tablecloth she had purchased, and once he awakened at night to find her with a revolver in her hand, preparing to kill herself. They had no point of contact with their immediate environment. Sinclair had no faith in the poor farmers who were their neighbors; he felt sorry for them and he understood why they were poor and demoralized, but his essential attitude is expressed in his description of families containing "drunkards, degenerates, mental or physical defectives, semi-idiots, victims of tuberculosis or venereal diseases." Nor was there any companionship or strength or assistance to be drawn from

middle-class friends. The smooth intellectuals from Princeton who showed up, paying attention to his wife, evidently aroused in the novelist such animosity that when he came to create the most despicable character in his works he identified him only as a Princeton man. His inspiring associations were his Socialist friends and benefactors in New York City—such people as George Herron, a former clergyman who had married a rich woman, or Gaylord Wiltshire, a retired real-estate promoter of Los Angeles—wealthy radicals who were devoting their fortunes to the movement and who, as the sports and freaks in the mutations of capitalism, have figured more prominently in Sinclair's novels than any other native type.

At twenty-eight Sinclair was a national figure with *The Jungle*. He had a fortune of $30,000, had lunched with the President, turned down an offer of $300,000 to start a packing company, and had been defeated, by the votes of the poor farmers of whose weakness he was always so powerfully aware, as a Socialist candidate for Congress. At twenty-nine he had lost most of his money in Helicon Hall and was charged with having started the fire that destroyed it, in another newspaper sensation. Thereafter his life settled to its norm of battles and scandals, breaking out in Bermuda and on Mobile Bay, in New Jersey and in a physical-culture sanitarium at Battle Creek, Michigan; in California and on Long Island—struggles over the suppression of his books; imprisonment for picketing the Rockefellers after the Ludlow Massacre; polemics at the time of the split with the Socialists when he supported the entry of the United States into the War; the scandal of the Harry Kemp-Sinclair divorce case and the sensation of his remarriage, with the disinheriting of his wife by her wealthy and reactionary Mississippi family; all building up to the Eisenstein affair and to the Epic campaign, perhaps the single most significant development, in view of the forces supporting it and the way it was fought, in recent American political history. There was an almost perfect political symbolism in Sinclair's personal disputes. It was in the cards, given his Puritanism and his evangelical political fervor, that his household should be disrupted, not by the upholders of capitalism, but by some passing representative of bohemian irresponsibility—just as it was in the cards, in view of the inclusive, optimistic, uplift sort of socialism that Sinclair advocated, that he should first go to jail as the result of an absurd dispute with an anarchist.

Between battles and during them the books were written, usually aimed at some specific objective, filled with contradictions and repetitions and wretched writing, beginning well and ending badly, revealing a strong narrative power unfortunately devoted to telling the same stories again and again. Sinclair's works have scarcely been seriously criticized. Van Wyck Brooks's severe judgment was based on only three of his weakest novels, and Floyd Dell's biographical essay, while interesting for its facts, was written in a period when estheticism was dominant in American literature, and is primarily devoted to establishing the social value of Sinclair's books. There are times when, bogging down in their almost abandoned sentimentality, you feel sure they are nothing if they are not socially useful. To a generation of esthetes and sophisticates their shoddy writing served as the strongest possible reason for remaining in the ivory tower; and their stock situations, stock characters, stock jokes, the obvious collision between their earnest simplifications and the complexities of the post-war world, their lack of finish and their almost gushy hippity-hop humor, served to dramatize the difficulties in the way of creating a working-class literature or even of a literature that attempted to deal squarely with political issues. Sinclair became, and all the more strongly in view of the wide international circulation of his works, the prime example for reactionary critics of a creative writer whose sensitivity to people has been blunted by his political convictions and whose standards of taste have been sacrificed for the immediate necessities of his causes. At their worst his books were the products of a radical hack, and of no greater literary consequence than the Spanish War romances he turned out by the dozen in college—that they were sincere and unaffected, and that Sinclair had almost single-handedly uncovered a great unexplored area of American life, only deepened the problem.

Sinclair's novels abound in unconscious revelations of his indifference to his craft and his lack of regard for the memory of his readers. In the middle of *Mountain City* you stumble across the same situation found in *Oil!* except that in *Mountain City* it has almost nothing to do with the story, and the esthetic effect is about like that produced when the needle gets caught in a groove of a phonograph record. Then too, Sinclair's favorite jokes and his after-dinner illustrations of his various reforming messages keep turning up like old friends in volume after volume, until they wind up in his autobiography, where he tells where he first heard them. The plots of his novels are so devious as to call to mind those railroads that were laid out in the days of land grants and that circle all over the map to take in the power sites and the rich stands of timber—so Sinclair usually works his books around until he gets to some corruption high in the mountains of upper-class life, branching off to touch on how county officials are bribed and swinging far off his course again to introduce mental telepathy as well as the problem of a rich boy in love with a socialist lass. Many of these branch lines touch on rich natural dramatic resources, but Sinclair is usually too busy staking out the territory to exploit it carefully. Even at the end of *The Jungle*, which is his best and most deeply felt book, he went out of his way to bring in a manifesto he had once written and an advertisement for the newspaper that published the book; in the manuscript he had even reached out to Idaho to introduce the Big Bill Haywood frame-up, but he dropped it again as not having much connection.

But despite these lapses—and apart from the question of how influential they were in fortifying a whole generation of novelists in their political indifference—the picture of American society that emerges from Sinclair's books as a whole is in itself an achievement of a high order. Sinclair's moral strength has never let him escape an awareness of the degradation and humiliation that are the normal lot of the oppressed in *our* republic, and his honesty has never let him remain silent about them. The consciousness of writing primarily for a foreign audience—since *The Jungle* his books have circulated abroad more than at home, until he is probably the most widely read American writer—has given him a sensitivity to aspects of American life that his contemporaries have overlooked or scorned as too ephemeral to be dignified in prose. As a result he has recorded and explained a wide variety of native phenomena, ranging from the ramifications of prohibition to the development of religious revivals in southern California, and capturing those commonplace expressions of American culture that usually go unrecorded solely because they are commonplace. In the same way he preserved in his novels (where, in fact, they are usually lugged in by the heels) the jokes and gossip about the ways of millionaires and movie stars and politicians, the stories about Harding and Coolidge and Hearst, that it seems everyone knows too well to consider significant but that actually add up to an unconscious expression of the attitudes of ordinary citizens toward their heroes and rulers.

Indeed, it seems to me that Sinclair's major achievement lies in the preservation of such miscellaneous data rather than in his stylized and inflexible political studies. When he tells us how strikes are put down or sold out, or how public officials are corrupted, or how labor spies are planted, he is describing a formula, and with that his interest ceases and his imagination fails to give him anything new or fresh. But when he writes of such things as an automobile drive over the Ridge Route outside Los Angeles, in the days before the pavement was widened, then the musty details of road hogs and speed traps, of stopping to put on chains for rainy weather, summon up the already vanished mood of primitive motoring and make Sinclair a new type of unpretentious social historian. The memorable parts of his books lie in such details—the exact descriptions of how pigs were killed in the Chicago stockyards in 1906, the vivid account of the drilling of the wells in *Oil!* the picture of a Colorado mining town in *King Coal*—remaining when the hackneyed characterizations and the mechanical concept of how society is controlled have been forgotten.

Van Wyck Brooks's criticism of Sinclair's novels was that they create a mood of self-pity—that they invite a workman to feel sorry for himself rather than to develop his intelligence and study the world around him and the forms of action that are possible for him. The point is good, but it is not very relevant: Sinclair has scarcely attempted to interpret working-class life since *The Jungle*. His typical story is that of a rich young man who gets mixed up in the radical movement, and the drama lies in the dissolution of his ruling-class dogmas—the pattern of *King Coal*, *Roman Holiday* and *Oil!* His strongest and most original characterizations are middle-class types like Bunny's father in *Oil!* or the cranky old single-tax millionaire of *Mountain City*—people more or less akin to the George Herrons and Gaylord Wiltshires of his early days as a writer—while the miners around Hal in *King Coal*, or the oil workers around Bunny in *Oil!* or the rank and file of the coöperative movement in *Co-Op* serve primarily as background highlighting the situations of the aristocrats. For a decade after *The Jungle*, Sinclair's fiction dealt almost entirely with upper-class life—in *The Metropolis*, *The Moneychangers*, *Sylvia* and *Sylvia's Marriage*—and he did not return to working-class subjects and working-class characters until he wrote *King Coal* in 1917.

Their influence is more apparent in Sinclair's work than in the work of his less politically conscious contemporaries. In *Oil!* for example, Sinclair found it possible to write an exhaustive study of the industry, including a long and vivid description of how wells are drilled, without giving an account of what the oil workers themselves actually do. The limitation does not merely result in a general one-sidedness in his panorama—it accounts for a blurring of the technical descriptions and an elementary sort of vagueness in the prose. In *Roman Holiday* the same limitation is more strikingly dramatized—the young millionaire has come into direct conflict with the workers and has been responsible for the death of a working-class leader, whereupon the novel breaks in two, with its second section laid in ancient Rome and its ruling-class dilemma repeated in that antique setting.

Out of Sinclair's later works you get a definite impression that his attention is focused on the upper-class world that he usually describes with a mixture of heavy-handed satire and emotional appeals to reform itself. His imagination is filled with the intrigues and maneuvers and hypocrisies of capitalists—the exact fashion in which William Fox lost his fortune, the intricate detail behind the Teapot Dome scandal, the process by which an independent oil dealer challenges the monopolies, the limitless distortions and evasions of the newspapers, the inside stories of the Mellon distilleries in *Wet Parade*, or of Coolidge's actual behavior during the Boston police strike—almost as if he expected to find, within this mash of corruption and plotting, some secret key to the history of his time. But his exposés are never as enlightening as they promise to be, and his reiterated explanations of frame-ups and wire-pulling never really explain much.

All his works of this sort came to a climax in his account of the Epic campaign, when he was himself not only on the inside but at the very center, and so in a position to know at first hand the secrets of capitalist political control. And *I, Candidate for Governor and How I Got Licked* is a frank and conscientious record of those consequential weeks that tells everything except how Sinclair was defeated. It is filled with disclosures of what went on in hotel rooms and law offices and newspaper offices—what Westbrook Pegler said and what he wrote, what President Roosevelt promised Sinclair and how the promise was broken, what George Creel said and what William McAdoo said and what Giannini said and what James Farley said and what Fulton Oursler said—how some crafty lawyers tried to disfranchise the unemployed supporting Sinclair and the way the plot was discovered—how Sinclair's works were distorted and where Sinclair blundered—how the *Literary Digest* poll was rigged and how Sinclair received the news of his defeat—giving an interesting picture of a political campaign from the inside and a warning of what a genuinely popular reform move is up against. But it contains no disclosures of what went on in the ramshackle halls and the rented houses where the Epic movement grew, and no disclosures of what was going on in the minds of the masses who suddenly took political initiative out of the hands of professional politicians. Nor does it reveal what the anonymous thousands of volunteer workers said to each other as, in the space of a few months, they created a political party out of nothing, or what they said as they collected funds and held meetings and published newspapers and held together in spite of the sickening slanders in the press and the routine treacheries of the politicians— although their unstudied words might conceivably be more meaningful and interesting, as well as more deeply felt, than Roosevelt's unkept promises.

These paradoxes in Sinclair's writing and in his career are a measure of the difficulties in the task he set for himself. He is the first important American novelist to see in the struggle between capital and labor the driving force of modern industry; he has hammered away for a lifetime at the cruelties and injustices of exploitation as well as at the grossness and insensitivity of life among the exploiters, and his books, with all their unevenness and vacillations, have a simple literal honesty about them that makes the work of most of his contemporaries seem evasive and affected. He has done more than any other American novelist toward breaking the path for a full and realistic treatment of working-class life in fiction— the battles he has been engaged in, the enemies he has attracted and the silence and persecution with which his books have been met being his personal cost for that pioneering work. In his concern with the moral aspects of exploitation, his strong religious feeling, his indifference to Marxian theory, his reformism and his hope for a peaceful solution of the class struggle, he has been the outstanding literary representative of the Second International, in the way that a writer of the type of André Malraux—intense, defiant, scornful—promises now to become the voice in fiction of the hard-pressed and violent life of the Third.

ALFRED KAZIN
From "Progressivism: The Superman and the Muckrake"
On Native Grounds
1942, pp. 116–21

Today, when Upton Sinclair actually has been muckraking the Europe of Munich and Hitler in his recent novels with the same combative innocence that he once muckraked the Chicago stockyards, the mining and oil industries, the ways of Hollywood finance, and his own unsuccessful campaign for Governor of California in 1936, it is not difficult to see where he learned the reformer's and historian's passion that has carried him irrepressibly through four decades of American literature and conflict. If Sinclair lives to survive all the bright young novelists of today and to publish a thousand books (and he may yet), he will remain a touching and curious symbol of a certain old-fashioned idealism and quaint personal romanticism that have vanished from American writing forever. Something more than a "mere" writer and something less than a serious novelist, he must always seem one of the original missionaries of the modern spirit in America, one of the last ties we have with that halcyon day when Marxists still sounded like Methodists and a leading Socialist like Eugene V. Debs believed in "the spirit of love."

Sinclair burst into fame with the most powerful of all the muckraking novels, *The Jungle*, and he has been an irritant to American complacency ever since. His life, with its scandals and its headline excitements, its political excursions and alarums, its extraordinary purity and melodrama, is the story of a religious mission written, often in tabloid screamers, across the pages of contemporary history. As a novelist, he has suffered for his adventures, but it is doubtful if he would have been a novelist without them. The spirit of crusading idealism that gave Sinclair his chance inevitably made him a perennial crusader as well, and if his books and career have become hopelessly entangled in most people's minds, they have been entangled in his own from the day he leaped to invest his royalties from *The Jungle* in the single-tax colony of Helicon Hall. That confusion has always given his critics the opportunity to analyze his works by reciting the adventures of his life, and it is inevitable that they should. For what Sinclair had to give to modern American literature was not any leading ideas as such, but an energy of personal and intellectual revolt that broke barriers down wherever he passed. At a time when all the pioneer realists seemed to be aiming at their own liberation, Sinclair actually helped toward a liberation greater than his own by making a romantic epic out of the spirit of revolt. From the first he was less a writer than an example, a fresh current of air pouring through the stale rooms of the past. Impulsive and erratic as he may have been, often startlingly crude for all his intransigence, he yet represented in modern American literature what William Jennings Bryan represented in modern American politics—a provincialism that leaped ahead to militancy and came into leadership over all those who were too confused or too proud or too afraid to seize leadership and fight for it.

Sinclair's importance to the prewar literature is that he took his revolt seriously, he took himself seriously—how seriously we may guess from his statement that the three greatest influences on his thought were Jesus, Hamlet, and Shelley. A more ambitious writer as such would never have been able to indulge in so many heroics; but Sinclair seems to have felt from the first the kind of personal indignation against society which could be quickly channeled into a general criticism of society, and that capacity for indignation gave him his sense of mission. The impoverished son of a prominent Baltimore family, he thought of himself from his youth as a rebel against the disintegration of the South after the Civil War, and he was determined to recite the argosy of his early tribulations for all the world to hear. Even after forty years he wrote with special bitterness, in an autobiography otherwise distinguished only by its immense cheerfulness, of those early days when he had dined with his aristocratic grandmother in great state on dried herring and stale bread, of his father's shambling efforts to peddle the liquor that he drank more often than he sold, of the flight to New York, his life on the East Side, and the unhappy years when he worked his way through college as a hack writer of jokes and stories. In those first years Sinclair was a foreshadowing of the kind of titanic Weltschmerz which Thomas Wolfe was to personify all his life, and like Wolfe he became such a flood of words that he began to write romantic epics around himself. His subject was the young Upton Sinclair and his world young Upton Sinclair's enthusiasms. He had many enthusiasms—he was intermittently enthusiastic about chastity, for example—and in that early period before he turned to Socialism, he gave full vent to his insurgence in lyrical early books like *Springtime and Harvest* (later republished as *King Midas*) and *The Journal of Arthur Stirling*.

These books were Sinclair's *Sorrows of Werther*. Living in great poverty with his wife and young child, humiliated by his obscurity, he wrote out the story of his own struggles in *The Journal of Arthur Stirling*, the furious romantic confession of a starving young poet who was supposed to have taken his own life at twenty-two. When it was disclosed that the book was a "hoax" and that Sinclair himself was Stirling, the sensation was over; but the book was more authentic than anyone at the moment could possibly know. "The world which I see about me at the present moment," he wrote there in the character of Arthur Stirling, "the world of politics, of business, of society, seems to me a thing demoniac in its hideousness; a world gone mad with pride and selfish lust; a world of wild beasts writhing and grappling in a pit." Like the imaginary dead poet who had learned Greek while working on the horsecars and written a frenzied poetic drama, *The Captive*, at the point of death, Sinclair was full of grandiose projects, and when his early romantic novels failed he planned an ambitious epic trilogy of the Civil War that would record his family's failure and make him rich and famous. He took his family to a tent outside of Princeton, where he did the research for the first volume, *Manassas*, and supported himself by more hack work. But when even his historical novel, a work which he had written with all the furious energy that was to distinguish him afterwards, fell on a dead market, he found himself in the very situation that he had portrayed with such anguish in the story of Arthur Stirling, the epic of the romantic genius who had stormed the heights and failed.

The Jungle saved him. Tiring of romantic novels which no one would read, he had turned to the investigation of social conditions, and in his article on "Our Bourgeois Literature," in *Collier's*, 1904, he exclaimed significantly: "So long as we are without heart, so long as we are without conscience, so long as we are without even a mind—pray, in the name of heaven, why should anyone think it worthwhile to be troubled because we are without a literature?" Although he still thought of himself as a romantic rebel against "convention," he had come to identify his own painful gropings with the revolution-

ary forces in society, and when he received a chance to study conditions in the stockyards at Chicago, he found himself like St. Paul on the road to Damascus. Yet into the story of the immigrant couple, Jurgis and Ona, he poured all the disappointment of his own apprenticeship to life, all his humiliation and profound ambition. *The Jungle* attracted attention because it was obviously the most authentic and most powerful of the muckraking novels, but Sinclair wrote it as the great romantic document of struggle and hardship he had wanted to write all his life. In his own mind it was above all the story of the betrayal of youth by the America it had greeted so eagerly, and Sinclair recited with joyous savagery every last detail of its tribulations. The romantic indignation of the book gave it its fierce honesty, but the facts in it gave Sinclair his reputation, for he had suddenly given an unprecedented social importance to muckraking. The sales of meat dropped, the Germans cited the book as an argument for higher import duties on American meat, Sinclair became a leading exponent of the muckraking spirit to thousands in America and Europe, and met with the President. No one could doubt it, the evidence was overwhelming: Here in *The Jungle* was the great news story of a decade written out in letters of fire. Unwittingly or not, Sinclair had proved himself one of the great reporters of the Progressive era, and the world now began to look up to him as such.

Characteristically, however, Sinclair spent the small fortune he had received from the book on Helicon Hall, that latter-day Brook Farm for young rebels at which Sinclair Lewis is reported to have been so indifferent a janitor. In his own mind Upton Sinclair had become something more than a reporter; he was a crusader, and after joining with Jack London to found the Intercollegiate Socialist Society, a leading Socialist. "Really, Mr. Sinclair, you *must* keep your head," Theodore Roosevelt wrote to him when he insisted after the publication of *The Jungle* on immediate legislative action. But Sinclair would not wait. If society would not come to him, he would come to society and teach it by his books. With the same impulsive directness that he had converted Jurgis into a Socialist in the last awkward chapter of *The Jungle*, he jumped ahead to make himself a "social detective," a pamphleteer-novelist whose books would be a call to action. In *The Metropolis*, an attack on "the reign of gilt" which Phillips and Robert Herrick had already made familiar, Sinclair took the son of his Civil War hero in *Manassas*, Allan Montague, and made him a spectator of the glittering world of Wall Street finance. In *The Moneychangers* he depicted the panic of 1907; in *King Coal*, the Colorado strike; in *100%*, the activities of a labor spy. Yet he remained at the same time a busy exponent of the "new freedom" in morals, wrote the candid story of his own marriage in *Love's Pilgrimage*, "novelized" Brieux's famous shocker of the early nineteen-hundreds, *Damaged Goods*, and between pamphlets, fantasy plays, and famous anthologies like *The Cry for Justice* ("an anthology of the literature of social protest . . . selected from twenty-five languages covering a period of five thousand years") wrote stories of "the new woman" in *Sylvia* and *Sylvia's Marriage*.

Wherever it was that Sinclair had learned to write millions of words with the greatest of ease—probably in the days when he produced hundreds of potboilers—he now wrote them in an unceasing torrent on every subject that interested him. Like Bronson Alcott and William Jennings Bryan, he had an extraordinary garrulity, and his tireless and ubiquitous intelligence led him to expose the outrages of existence everywhere. He used his books for "social purposes" not because he had a self-conscious esthetic about "art and social purpose," but because his purposes actually were social. Few writers seemed to write less for the sake of literature, and no writer ever seemed to humiliate the vanity of literature so deeply by his many excursions around it. First things came first; the follies of capitalism, the dangers of drinking, the iniquities of wealthy newspapers and universities came first. "Why should anyone think it worthwhile to be troubled because we are without a literature?" His great talent, as everyone was quick to point out, was a talent for facts, a really prodigious capacity for social research; and as he continued to give America after the war the facts about labor in *Jimmie Higgins*, the petroleum industry in *Oil!*, the Sacco-Vanzetti case in *Boston*, Prohibition in *The Wet Parade*, it mattered less and less that he repeated himself endlessly, or that he could write on one page with great power, on another with astonishing self-indulgence and sentimental melodrama. He had become one of the great social historians of the modern era. Van Wyck Brooks might complain that "the only writers who can possibly aid in the liberation of humanity are those whose sole responsibility is to themselves as artists," but in a sense it was pointless to damn Sinclair as a "mere" propagandist. What would he have been without the motor power of his propaganda, his driving passion to convert the world to an understanding of the problems of labor, the virtues of the single tax, the promise of Socialism, the need of Prohibition, a credence in "mental radio," an appreciation of the sufferings of William Fox, the necessity of the "Epic" movement, and so much else? In a day when the insurgent spirit had become obsessed with the facts of contemporary society, and newspapermen could write their social novels in the city room, Sinclair proved himself one of the great contemporary reporters, a profound educative force. He was a hero in Europe, and one of the forces leading to the modern spirit in America; it seemed almost glory enough.

WALTER B. RIDEOUT
From "Realism and Revolution"
The Radical Novel in the United States, 1900–1954
1956, pp. 33–38

The Jungle is dedicated "To the Workingmen of America." Into it had gone Sinclair's heartsick discovery of the filth, disease, degradation, and helplessness of the packing workers' lives. But any muckraker could have put this much into a book; the fire of the novel came from Sinclair's whole passionate, rebellious past, from the insight into the pattern of capitalist oppression shown him by Socialist theory, and from the immediate extension into the characters' lives of his own and his wife's struggle against hunger, illness, and fear. It was the summation of his life and experience into a manifesto. The title of the book itself represented a feat of imaginative compression, for the world in which the Lithuanian immigrant Jurgis and his family find themselves is an Africa of unintelligibility, of suffering and terror, where the strong beasts devour the weak, who are dignified, if at all, only by their agony.

After their pathetically happy marriage, the descent of Jurgis and Ona into the social pit is steady. They are spiritually and, in the case of Ona, physically slaughtered, more slowly but quite as surely as the cattle in the packing plant. Disease spread by filthy working and living conditions attacks them, they endure cold in winter and clouds of flies in summer, bad food weakens their bodies, and seasonal layoffs leave them always facing starvation. When illness destroys Jurgis's great strength, he realizes that he has become a physical cast-off, one of the waste products of the plant, and must take the vilest job of all in the packing company's fertilizer plant. The forced seduction of his wife by her boss leads him to an assault on the man and thirty days in jail. Released without money, he returns to find his family evicted from their home and Ona dying in childbirth. After being laid off from a dangerous job in a steel plant, Jurgis becomes successively a tramp, the henchman of a crooked politician, a strikebreaker in the packing plant strike of 1904, and finally a bum. Having reached the bottom of the social pit, he wanders into a political meeting to keep warm and hears for the first time, though at first unaware that he is listening to a Socialist, an explanation of the capitalist jungle in which he has been hunted. The sudden realization of truth is as overwhelming to Jurgis as it had been to Jurgis's creator. He at once undertakes to learn more about Socialism, is given a job in a hotel owned by a Socialist, and is eventually taken to a meeting of radical intellectuals where he hears all the arguments for the Industrial Republic which Sinclair wants his readers to know. Jurgis throws himself into the political campaign of 1904, the one in which the Party actually made such astonishing gains, and the book concludes exultantly with a speech first given by Sinclair himself, proclaiming the coming victory of the Socialists, at which time Chicago will belong to the people.

The "conversion" pattern of *The Jungle* has been attacked as permitting too easy a dramatic solution; however, aside from the recognized fact that many conversions have occurred before and since Paul saw the light on the road to Damascus, it should be noted that in *The Jungle* Sinclair carefully prepares such an outcome by conducting Jurgis through all the circles of the workers' inferno and by attempting to show that no other savior except Socialism exists. Perhaps a more valid objection to the book is Sinclair's failure to realize his characters as "living" persons, a charge which, incidentally, may be brought against many nonconversion novels. Jurgis is admittedly a composite figure who was given a heaping share of the troubles of some twenty or thirty packing workers with whom Sinclair had talked, and the author's psychology of character is indeed a simple one. Although in the introductory wedding scene Jurgis and the other major characters are sharply sketched as they had appeared to the writer at an actual wedding feast in Packingtown, during the remainder of the book they gradually lose their individuality, becoming instead any group of immigrants destroyed by the Beef Trust. Yet parodoxically, the force and passion of the book are such that this group of lay figures with Jurgis at their head, these mere capacities for infinite suffering, finally do come to stand for the masses themselves, for all the faceless ones to whom things are done. Hardly individuals, they nevertheless collectively achieve symbolic status.

Sinclair's success in creating this jungle world emphasizes by contrast what is actually the book's key defect. Jurgis's conversion is probable enough, the Socialist explanation might well flash upon him with the blinding illumination of a religious experience; but practically from that point onward to the conclusion of his novel Sinclair turns from fiction to another kind of statement. Where the capitalist damnation, the destruction of the immigrants, has been proved almost upon the reader's pulses, the Socialist salvation, after its initial impact, is intellectualized. The reader cannot exist imaginatively in Jurgis's converted state even if willing, for Jurgis hardly exists himself. What it means to be a Socialist is given, not through the rich disorder of felt experience, but in such arbitrarily codified forms as political speeches, an essay on Party personalities, or the long conversation in monologues about the Coöperative Commonwealth which comprises most of the book's final chapter. *The Jungle* begins and lives as fiction; it ends as a political miscellany.

The fact that Jurgis's militant acceptance of Socialism is far less creatively realized than his previous victimization is indicative of how Sinclair's outraged moral idealism is attracted more to the pathos than the power of the poor, and suggests his real affinity for the mid-Victorian English reform novelists. More specifically, *The Jungle* is reminiscent of the work of the humanitarian Dickens, whose social protest had "thrilled" the young rebel. There are frequent resemblances between the two writers in narrative method, in presentation of character, in the tendency of both to intrude themselves with bubbling delight or horrified indignation into the scene described. Whole paragraphs on the wedding feast of Jurgis Rudkus and Ona recall, except for the Lithuanian, the manner of Dickens with the Cratchits' Christmas dinner, and Madame Haupt, fat, drunken, and filthy, might have been a midwife in Oliver Twist's London. Finally, the temper of Sinclair's protest is curiously like that of Dickens. Where the latter urges only the literal practice of Christianity as a remedy for the cruelties he describes, Sinclair, to be sure, demands the complete transformation of the existing order of things by the Socialist revolution; yet the revolution that the orator so apocalyptically envisages at the conclusion to *The Jungle* is to be accomplished by the ballot and not by the bullet. Sinclair's spirit is not one of blood and barricades, but of humanitarianism and brotherly love.

Both in life and in writings Sinclair has attempted, as did Dickens, to be the persuading intermediary between the contending classes. With admirable sweetness of temper, considering his lack of success, he has continued to argue that the owning class should perform a revolution by consent, that the capitalist should give up his profits and power in exchange for citizenship in an industrial democracy. But in the novels that he has so prodigally brought forth year after year since the publication of *The Jungle*, the lamb of his Christian spirit has rarely been able to lie down peacefully with the lion of his Marxian vocabulary. As a result, although Sinclair is the only one of the Socialist novelists who continued, and after a fashion continues, to write Socialist novels, his is the classic case among them for unresolved discrepancies between his fictional structure and the "message" that he is trying to convey. The formal flaw of *The Jungle* represents one such failure; other novels have others, and always the total effect of the fiction is weakened. *King Coal* (1917), to take only one of his better-known earlier novels, illustrates the point with a damning simplicity.

Like most of his fiction, *King Coal* is what Sinclair calls "a novel of contemporary life." This time Sinclair is exposing the conditions which led to the great Colorado coal strike of 1913–14. In a style reminiscent of his early hack-written boys' stories, he narrates the experiences of Hal Warner, a wealthy mine-owner's son, who has decided to work for a summer in a Colorado coal camp under an assumed name in order to supplement with practical experience what he is being taught at a college endowed by the chief mine operator of the state. What the coal camp teaches him is not the symmetry of classical economics, but the sprawling wretchedness of King Coal's prisoners and the brutal reality of the class struggle. North Valley turns out to be another Jungle, and the once-blithe college boy eventually leads a movement for honest weighing of the miners' output, gets a taste of class justice, and

then heads an unsuccessful strike against the coal company after a mine explosion has resulted from company carelessness.

Perhaps the squalid camp is most effectively described through the opening eyes of a representative of the owning class, although it is certainly absurd to express the strike almost completely in terms of the young man's adventures, which are of the very best Rover Boys variety. The author is also psychologically accurate in returning the enlightened Hal to his own class. But Hal goes back expressly to convert his class to the Truth, and here the discrepancy between fictional structure and political message gapes wide; for the young man, in spite of a rare opportunity which Sinclair affords him, has been unable to convert any of his wealthy friends during the course of the mine disaster and strike. The reader is left, not converted to Sinclair's implied solution, but rather, intensely aware of the disparity between the author's hopefulness of a "revolution by consent" and the hopelessness of the novel's events, which have demonstrated only the inevitable continuation of class warfare. The optimism of the book is simply irrelevant to the situation it describes.

Despite his artistic limitations, however, Upton Sinclair has built up over half a century a body of work which is a whole tradition in itself. The outstanding Socialist novelist of the first two decades, in the lonely twenties he almost *was* radical American literature. In the thirties the young Leftists, when they were not damning him as a "social fascist" in accordance with some current "Party line," admitted that his novels and tracts had been and still were instrumental in teaching them the facts of capitalist life. [1] But Sinclair's work, from *The Jungle* onward, had always pushed out from radical circles into the wide ranges of the whole reading public to inform them of the social and personal irresponsibility of capitalists, the disruption of the middle class, the struggle of labor to organize, and the martyrdom of radicals. In the forties his moderately Socialist tales of Lanny Budd and a stricken century sold to hundreds of thousands of American citizens, who found them the easiest way to learn what historical events had prepared the Second World War and were preparing the "Peace." If Sinclair has never been a great creative novelist (what is Lanny Budd beyond a mirror of history?), he has been something else of value—one of the great information centers in American literature. Few American novelists have done more to make their fellow citizens conscious of the society, all of it, in which they live.

Notes

1. For an example out of the late twenties, see Edward Newhouse, "Transition—1929," *New Masses*, V (July, 1929), 8: "Then the revelation . . . Upton Sinclair. Here was somebody who could offer an explanation to the perplexing chaos." Newhouse was subsequently to publish two "proletarian novels."

   It is worth noting that the influence of *The Jungle* on a number of our contemporary non-Communist labor leaders has been considerable. Walter Reuther includes it in a list of books "which most influenced me in my youth," as does Jacob S. Potofsky, president of the Amalgamated Clothing Workers, and "many of his colleagues." See Mark Starr, "American Labor and the Book," *The Saturday Review*, XXXVII (September 4, 1954), 10–11, 32–34.

HARVEY SWADOS
From "The World of Upton Sinclair"
Atlantic, December 1961, pp. 98–102

It must be nearly forty years now since Van Wyck Brooks blasted Upton Sinclair for coming to the writing of novels from the wrong set of preconceptions. And nothing that has happened in the world of fiction since then has served to weaken Brooks's case. It was his contention that it is folly, and the death of art, for the would-be novelist to think that he can write with full effectiveness about lumberjacks only by becoming one himself and living in the woods for years on end. Such misunderstanding of the author's role can only create one more bad lumberjack and one more bad novelist. The novelist must maintain a certain reserve, a certain distance from his characters in order to see them and know them most fully; otherwise he will inevitably collapse into the stammering sentimentalism of the overinvolved.

Unquestionably, subsequent developments in American fiction have in general sustained the Brooks thesis. The false identification of writer with class in the proletarian novel of the thirties, or of writer with uniform in the war novel of the forties, resulted largely in nothing more than flatulent overvaluing of human beings as types or models. Those novels which in turn have stood out from the ruck have been the products of writers whose primary devotion was not to their class or their credo but to their craft.

Besides, the more we examine a work like *The Jungle*, the more difficult it is to defend its specifically literary merits and the more it becomes obligatory for the commentator to make a pious listing of Sinclair's inadequacies and exaggerations. Very well. No one could deny that the style of the book is undistinguished at best. No one could deny that he drags out the agony and piles horror upon horror until we want to cry, Stop! Enough! No more! No one could deny that structurally it is a broken-backed book, with most of the intensity concentrated in the first two thirds, which is concerned with the struggle of the immigrants to sustain themselves in Packingtown, and most of the propaganda concentrated in the last third, during Jurgis Rudkus' conversion to socialism and after the dissolution of his family.

If what the reader wants is a fictional rendering of the psychological effect of prolonged association with the killing of helpless animals, then he should read the unforgettable story by Pierre Gascar, "The House of Blood." This tale, which deals with the life of a little boy apprenticed to a sadistic provincial French butcher, is to be found in Gascar's *Beasts and Men* and is in its own way definitive. If what the reader seeks is an allegorical revelation of some of the overtones of the endless parade of cattle to the abattoir, he must read James Agee's stunning story, "A Mother's Tale," which begins like a bedtime story, complete with talking beasts, and becomes a Christian parable as it grows to encompass a world of millions marching meekly to death camps.

Still, I should assert that there are certain human values which do not find complete expression in either of these stories and for which one must turn to a book like *The Jungle*. And so, as I would hope that the educated person would read all three, I must now say what it is about this book that does make us persist in reading it.

For me, it is the furious passion with which Upton Sinclair here apotheosizes the sweat and agony of an essential generation of Americans, an entire generation without which this country could not possibly have achieved what it has. If he

had done nothing more, Sinclair would have justified, as one way of functioning, the method not of immolation in the working class but of observation and creation which has gone so far out of fashion in recent years among Western novelists. We need not go through his complete works, so much of his enormous output being cranky or banal, to sustain such a statement about *The Jungle*, any more than we should feel compelled to justify all of Zola's immense output in order to come to a similar conclusion about *Germinal*. Both books were the products of men who proceeded, notebook in hand, to research a new territory and then retired to write, not in tranquillity but in the heat of anger and hope, about the price paid by countless thousands to build what is known as a civilization.

Zola's brutalized coal miners of northern France and Sinclair's immigrants of Chicago's Packingtown can nevermore be fully forgotten. They take their place in history as the cruelly used builders of the modern era, along with all the other untold millions who gave up their lives on the altar of production in the strange and terrible rites of the new industrial age.

This was not exactly what Sinclair had in mind. Judging from his own testimony, as well as from the internal evidence of the book itself, he (and many of his contemporaries, like Jack London) thought of *The Jungle* as a tract that would help win many converts to the ideas of socialism and to the growing Socialist Party. No doubt it did—at least the years following its serial publication in the mass-circulation Socialist weekly, *Appeal to Reason*, were the period of maximum growth and influence of American socialism—but over the generations the book's impact has been quite different. In fact, as a result of the disgust and outrage that swept not only this country but virtually the entire world, once it became clear that *The Jungle* was not simply the invention of an overheated mind, remedial reform legislation was enacted which did much to halt the revolutionary upsurge that Sinclair had been hoping to implement.

Indeed, when I came to reread *The Jungle* I found that I had forgotten quite completely the lengthy propagandist passages with which the last portion of the book is so replete, but that I had retained from boyhood an ineradicable memory of the wretchedness of the residents of Packingtown and of the horror of the industry in which they slaved. It is my impression that this is a common experience, and my guess is that no one who reads *The Jungle* will ever be able to erase from his memory its opening chapters.

No writer, not even the most ardent propagandist, can predict the consequences once he sets his pen to paper. If socialist agitation in the United States was to some degree blunted by the passage of such legislation as the Pure Food and Drug Act, in large part immediately inspired by the reaction of Theodore Roosevelt and others to *The Jungle*, the ultimate effect of this book on many thousands of minds cannot now be measured, nor will it ever be measurable.

It seems to me precisely now, as this country emerges from the mindless euphoria that has gripped it for at least a decade, that *The Jungle* must renew its hold on the imaginations of an entirely new generation of readers. For a time Americans of the vast middle range appeared hypnotized by the advertising mentality into believing not only that we "had it made," but that the American standard of living had been achieved at the cost of certain human expenditures which were at worst a trifle distressing and at best glamorous in a liberal patriotic kind of way. The sacrifice of millions of lives, of millions of proud and hopeful and bravely pioneering spirits, to the accumulation of capital, even though it took place within the memory of many Americans still alive and even though it continues in certain backward areas of American society, became something hardly to be believed, to be relegated to obscurity, to be mentioned, if at all, only jocularly, as with the abominable exploitation of women and children in factories, fields, and sweatshops.

But now we are entering a new time. We sense uneasily that we do not have it made, that with a war-economy prosperity have come new and staggering problems, and that there is a vast suffering world beyond our national boundaries, struggling in a variety of ways to accumulate capital and thus to move, as we have moved, up into the twentieth century. We sense, too, that throughout this world, no matter how the capital is accumulated and no matter whether it be in the Western sector, in the Communist zones, or in the burgeoning new nations of the formerly colonial areas, it is being done at a stupendous cost in human suffering. There is a close parallel between the payment in hunger, blood, and agony of the peoples of the underdeveloped world and that extracted from the immigrant builders of the American empire.

It is a parallel that we will neglect only at our own peril; it is one that should fill us with humility and compassion for all who must strain like beasts of the field to bring the world to the next epoch; it is one that *The Jungle* will help to sustain in the forefront of our consciousness, which is where it belongs. To the extent that it fulfills this function, this book now begins a new and vital existence as a force in the spiritual and social lives of a new and, it is to be hoped, a responsible generation of readers.

JON A. YODER

From "Upton Sinclair, Lanny, and the Liberals"

Modern Fiction Studies, Winter 1974–75, pp. 483–504

Lanny Budd, the American liberal, is a self-diagnosed schizophrenic. Seeing himself as caught between his own idealism and his own definition of realism, he sacrifices the first for the second, fully expecting his acute discomfort to be temporary and anticipating the American post-war return to normalcy—the state of affairs in which one's schizophrenia is not so bothersome. However, shortly after World War II, Lanny and the Liberals enlisted as Cold Warriors. Selling their ideals for a mess of containment, American progressives became staunch defenders of the status quo during decades demanding rapid social change—and all in the name of pragmatism.

II

Never the most subtle of writers, Sinclair made no effort to disguise the fact that in Lanny Budd he had created a type character. Many critics objected to this at the time,[1] but Sinclair (who had a gigantic, if genial, self-conceit) was undisturbed: "A type represents great numbers of persons and makes us aware of mass events. There are many novelists who are perfectly happy to portray individuals, and I leave it for them to do.[2] In his letters Sinclair stated simply his simple thesis:

> Of course every poet is free to write what he pleases, so is every human being; but the purpose of all writing is to communicate with other people, and if a poet writes in such a way as to make his commu-

nication difficult, it seems to me that the poet is demonstrably mistaken.[3]

In the world set up by Sinclair, Lanny becomes every idealistic American's dream come true. Posing as an art broker with fascist sympathies, Lanny moves in and out of circles of elite Europeans, gathering priceless information; he returns periodically to the United States in order to advise his grateful President, write Roosevelt's most important speeches, and serve generally in whatever superhuman capacity requested. Primarily, Sinclair used his character to preach liberal propaganda. To his Marxist European friend, Lanny says: "First, you have to give up the class struggle; forget it absolutely. There's only one enemy now, and that is Hitler. Churchill has to be your friend, no matter how little you like him."[4] Regarding the relationship between violence and social change, Lanny maintains that "these countries [England, France, United States] being 'democracies,' could bring about the changes peaceably. That was his way; he didn't want to hurt anybody, but to discuss ideas politely and let the best ideas win."[5] Only exaggerating the feelings many American liberals had for their President, Lanny sees F. D. Roosevelt as

> the large bundle of intelligence, kindness, and fun which was a gift of Providence to the people of the United States—a gift much better than they deserved, for they would never have chosen him if they had known in advance what he was going to do. Or so, at any rate, the worshipful Lanny thought.[6]

But the author of *The Jungle* had always been considered a propagandist. In order to understand the liberal mentality of the period, it is necessary to take note of a curious critical response to the Lanny Budd series. While realizing that Sinclair was not sounding quite like the socialist muckraker of old, some critics confused a modification of tone with something academic liberals were determined to find in themselves—a transcendence of ideology altogether. For instance, the reviewer for the New York *Times* concluded: "Mr. Sinclair has stepped out of the rather obvious role of a writer of moral tales with an old-line Socialist or new-line EPIC connotations. He has become a novelist. . . . "[7]

In other words, as Sinclair's propaganda began to sound increasingly like their own, these critics decided that he must no longer be propagandizing. He must have withdrawn from the fray, and, therefore, he could be used as evidence for the ideology of objective neutrality, an ideology proclaiming loftily that ideology itself was a bore. Witness Warren French:

> Perhaps the most striking evidence . . . that some kind of terminal had been reached was that the American writer whose name had been for three decades most conspicuously linked with the kind of social novel that he could fairly be said to have invented decided suddenly in 1939 to abandon his efforts to reform the world and to retreat into reminiscence. . . . Sensing . . . that an end was coming, Sinclair decided to withdraw from his characteristically active involvement in affairs and to look back over the era. . . . With almost uncanny aptitude, he chose for the first book of the sequence that was to win more readers than his crusading novels of the thirties a title that is a slogan for the period: World's End.[8]

French asks us to believe that a professional writer who produced one lengthy novel per year for ten successive years (and then has Lanny return in 1953 to correct some earlier statements about Stalin) "decided to withdraw from his characteristically active involvement in affairs." Was a man in his sixties with a semi-invalid wife who needed his constant care supposed to run for governor? No, what French *must* mean here is that Sinclair withdrew from the fray—that, although he continued to produce his annual book, he was no longer a crusader/propagandist.

This analysis of a changed Sinclair is deceptive because Sinclair's behavior in the Forties simply was not atypical for him. He supported the entry of the United States into World War I in precisely the same way as he supported his country during World War II and the Cold War. When his friends who felt compelled to stick by a Socialist Party analysis argued that American workers had no business helping British capitalists against their German counterparts, Sinclair withdrew from the party, contending that "the ability to think consists in the discovery of differences in things which appear alike. . . . It is fatally easy to say that all capitalist governments are alike, and that all must be opposed in the same way."[9] In short, being liberal meant for Sinclair being more nationalist than socialist whenever his nation was under attack.

Sinclair had always believed that a good liberal responds differently in periods of national emergency, a point he had made explicit in 1920: "*Except in time of war*, when a Nathan Hale may be a spy, spies are always necessarily drawn from the unwholesome and untrustworthy classes. A right-minded man refuses such a job."[10] Since it is impossible to read the Lanny Budd series without concluding that Sinclair intends Lanny to be a symbol of right-mindedness, the implication is clear. Lanny and his creator had gone to war.

True to his conviction that the goal of the artist is to get the audience to swallow the message, in a letter to Einstein he referred to his novels as "not just entertainment" but "sugar-coated history of our times with an attempt at interpretation."[11] And with his editor, he was even more candid: "What I am doing is giving the reader a great load of history and some propaganda, and I try to put in adventures as a sort of icing to the cake."[12] Far from the withdrawal French asserts, Sinclair's conscious goal was to "create a set of characters and carry my message in the story."[13] Far from abandoning his role as crusader in the Forties and Fifites, Sinclair merely modified his approach in order to help his country through a period of extreme stress.

This turn from critic to supporter, almost an automatic response by the American liberal when he sees the United States entering a period of emergency, has special implications after World War II because of basic changes in the nature of global conflict in a post-Nagasaki world. No longer able to drop liberal ideals "for the duration" with the intention of returning to the role of critic/reformer when things returned to normal, liberals such as Sinclair were caught flatfooted by the Cold War—by extreme stress becoming the normal and continuing condition to be endured by the American Way of Life.

So Sinclair is consistent; he never ceases doing battle for the liberal cause. However, during these years the cause itself changed rather appreciably, so that by 1952 Sinclair was still crusading, but he now found himself corresponding with the F.B.I.: "You will see from this that I am writing an Anti-Communist story. These 'Lanny Budd' books have been widely read, both in this country and abroad, and should be of great assistance in your work."[14] Of course, the Communist Party and the F.B.I. had both been in existence in 1942 as well as 1952, but liberalism—Sinclair's cause throughout the decades—had changed. To look closely at the Lanny Budd series is to see this change take place. Hopefully, it will make it possible to understand our own liberal mentality, the illiberal Cold War, and the failure of a generation to believe in itself.

III

It has been contended above that Lanny, as a typical liberal, is plagued by a schizoid perspective. This suggests that although he might function adequately in society under normal circumstances, he cannot cope with extreme and extended duress. To illustrate the failure of liberals as Cold Warriors, then, it is necessary to make explicit the tendencies which had been generally undisturbed beneath the surface of Lanny's behavior throughout the series.

There was one half of Lanny Budd—possibly a little more than half—which wanted to quarrel with an evil social order and to make sacrifices in the cause of truth-telling and justice; and there was another half, or near half, which liked to live in a well-appointed home, enjoy well-cooked food, be waited on, have a properly tuned piano—a long list of things which the world does not allot to its heroes, saints and martyrs.[15]

Lanny's job had brought him close to that state known to psychiatrists as schizophrenia; two minds living in the same body.[16]

With his role as a secret agent for Roosevelt constituting a living negation of the liberal ideal of seeing all sides of all issues while remaining free from dogmatic commitment, Lanny was simply unable to make his ideological theories come to life in his own particular case. He retained his stock in his conservative father's munitions company although his early version of liberalism concurrently saw these corporations as merchants of death.[17] In *Between Two Worlds*, he went so far as to come to his father's financial rescue when these merchants were being destroyed by the 1929 crash they had constructed.[18] It can, of course, be argued that nobody is capable of living up to his ideals; but in the case of the American liberal, continual capitulation to what appears to be the interest of the individual has added up to disaster on both personal and supranational scales.

For not only is Lanny unable to effect the sort of society he desires, but his constant sacrificing of principle for personal reasons eventually destroys his personality as effectively as it destroys those with whom he comes in contact. In *Dragon's Teeth*, a book for which Sinclair won the Pulitzer Prize, Lanny is willing to risk his own life to get a friend out of the hands of the Gestapo. Later in the series, when Trudi is captured by the Nazis, he is ready to risk everything—not to defeat Nazism (merely), but to free his wife. He is, of course, successful in his effort to defy Nazi security precautions, but with the prison successfully entered and the escape route working brilliantly, the person in the torture chamber turns out to be someone other than the expected loved one (who had been sent to her death in a German concentration camp). So Lanny leaves the victim behind, escaping with his fellow liberators in such a way that the Nazis never know what had been attempted. He rationalizes his decision in terms of the larger cause: "There wasn't a thing those three intruders could have done; to have carried the man out would have given the whole thing away and ruined the career of a presidential agent."[19]

Similarly, Lanny hides behind his own sexual conservatism to avoid taking the relatively small risk involved in saving the life of a German who literally meant nothing to him personally. Although he is a professional deceiver of Nazis, he rejects Rosika Diamant's suggestion that he marry her in Germany and thus help her avoid the fate reserved for beautiful Jewish women. Dismissing her suggestion, Lanny says: "I might do what you ask, but as it happens, I have a wife and baby in New York."[20] This despite the facts that the Nazis do not know of his marriage and (as depicted by Sinclair) they have tendencies toward leniency in their anti-Semitism when one of their own favorites casts a carnal eye on a Jewess— making them "honorary Aryans" for the duration of their desirability. Moreoover, Lanny's sexual code of honor is not really at stake since Rosika makes it perfectly clear to him that she is more interested in her own existence than in anything sexual, assuring him that she will get the "marriage" annulled as soon as she is outside Germany. So Lanny rejects her plan even though Sinclair writes that his response constitutes "what both of them knew was a death sentence."[21]

The implications of this go far beyond the importance of one character in a series of novels being unable to risk his larger cause unless he has a personal vested interest—in which case he does so vigorously. The point is that Sinclair cannot imagine his character acting in any other way even though he is aware of what this sort of selfishness does to the individual so concerned with himself. Depending on the degree of hostility one has toward this sort of liberal, one of the most touching or despicable scenes in the Lanny Budd novels involves Lanny's effort to reduce this incident to a joke—a gross effort at self-defensive humor which creates a taste of gall in the back of the mouth while a grin keeps trying to flash across the unhappy face:

> [Lanny] began to chuckle. "I have stayed too late, but you ought to hear the story of how I was tempted to commit bigamy. Perhaps you will give me permission for that! Or is it in Colonel Donovan's department?"
> He told the story of Rosika Diamant, which wasn't really funny but horribly tragic when you stopped to think. Roosevelt laughed first and then he frowned.[22]

It becomes increasingly clear that the liberal's concern for self runs at still deeper levels. For surely Sinclair is thinking of Lanny rather than Rosika when he uses the word "tragic." Surely it is the effect upon Lanny, his inability to do what he believes he ought to do, rather than the murder of Rosika that is intended to move us. So it is Lanny who must listen to what amounts to a message to the liberal mentality confronted with the 1940's and 1950's: "You are two men, and they are at war. Presently you will not know which you really are. Make up your mind, or it will go badly with you. I see a tragic fate in store for you."[23]

In this Sinclair was both perceptive and prophetic. He is important because he reflects tendencies present in the larger context of American liberalism, and this presentation of Lanny as a man who was tragically plagued by personal involvements mushrooms into the case of a Secretary of War who (like Lanny) got personally involved with the program of liberal administrations. Witness Dwight D. Eisenhower:

> We'd had a nice evening together at headquarters in Germany, nice dinner, everything was fine. Then Stimson got this cable saying the bomb had been dropped. . . . So then he told me they were going to drop it on the Japanese. Well, I listened, and I didn't volunteer anything because, after all, *my war was over* in Europe and it wasn't up to me. But I was getting more and more depressed just thinking about it. Then he asked for my opinion, so I told him I was against it on two counts. First, the Japanese were ready to surrender and it wasn't necessary to hit them with that awful thing. Second, I hated to see our country to be the first to use such a weapon. Well . . . the old gentleman got furious. And I can see how

he would. After all, *it had been his responsibility* to push for all the huge expenditure to develop the bomb. . . . Still, it was an awful problem.[24]

As uncomfortable as Lanny in feeling so bound by personal commitments, Stimson too decided that a joke might ease the pain:

> "I was a little fearful," Stimson told Truman, "that before we could get ready the Air Force might have Japan so thoroughly bombed out that the new weapon would not have a fair background to show its strength." To this the President "laughed and said he understood."[25]

V

⟨. . .⟩ Liberalism, Upton Sinclair, and Lanny Budd all became both dehumanized and ineffectual during the Cold War. Perhaps the saddest aspect of Sinclair's deterioration is his apparent unwillingness to realize what was happening to him as he was sucked into the mainstream current of American liberalism which was running swiftly downhill and to the right. In his letters, Sinclair tried to explain his apparent change of position by contending that while Russia had altered, he had remained ideologically consistent:

> In 1939 the deal between Stalin and Hitler put an end to my hopes forever. When Hitler made his attack upon Russia I, of course, agreed with Roosevelt and Churchill in accepting Russia as an ally. . . . But, as you doubtless know Roosevelt was disillusioned before his death, and I learned of his disillusionment. I realized then that Russia had become an imperialist nation. . . . Ever since that time I have been heartily supporting the Truman-Acheson policies, with the result that I am now in the eyes of the Russians a "Wall Street's Lackey. . . ." My position is exactly what it has always been; my formula is "the social ownership and democratic control of the instruments and means of production." I use the word "democratic" in the true American sense, and not in the fraudulent Russian sense.[26]

Actually, Sinclair tried to serve as Wall Street's lackey, but he was dismally ineffective. A man who had been remarkably open in his correspondence and fiction now had to learn to be specious, for Sinclair, whether he knew it or not, was producing a sort of propaganda differing from that which he had been publishing throughout his life, moving in lockstep with an American liberal mentality which had become reactionary. For example, having contended earlier that Communism was based on lies and thus bound to fail eventually, Sinclair became increasingly convinced that his earlier confidence in his own ideology was misplaced. In a letter to the American Civil Liberties Union, Sinclair wrote:

> I've been a Civil Liberties man all my life, but I have to admit that I am having great doubts at the present time of the wisdom in common sense of supporting the Communists in their right to destroy all civil liberties. Every day that I live I discover new evidence of their determination to destroy the civil liberties of all the rest of the world, and I am coming to the conclusion that we ought to take them at their word and abolish their civil liberties before they abolish ours.[27]

Sinclair seems unaware that this statement echoes the position which conservatives had asserted when he had been denied his civil liberties. For in the days when Sinclair had been on the side desiring changes, he had been jailed for reading the American Constitution at a time and place deemed subversive by the forces of the status quo. [28]

By the fall of 1952, the ambivalence expressed in the letter about Civil Liberties had dissipated: "It seems to me that people who repudiate moral law have no right to appeal to any moral law. It seems to me when they declare war on human society they come under the rule that all is fair in war." [29] And by 1955, a time when the aging Sinclair rarely made any public statements, his thinking had only grown more rigid along these cynical and illiberal lines:

> "I think that the Communists are cleverer than us, or at any rate more unscrupulous," Upton Sinclair, world-famed author and Monrovian resident, said today, in analyzing the troubled world condition . . . .
> "It's an unscrupulous world," he added dryly, "and our survival hinges on our realizing this fact." [30]

Liberalism cannot survive in an atmosphere where leading liberals equate cleverness with unscrupulousness, for the liberal ideal is to be effective in the world while retaining a humanistic outlook on life. What happened to Lanny in the last volume of the series demonstrates the dehumanization of the liberal individual who no longer believes in himself; and the failure of Sinclair with respect to this book gives clear indication of the ineffectuality of the liberal who begins to fight evil with evil. For the Lanny in Sinclair's final volume is a hard and cynical man, unaware that in his increasingly monomaniacal efforts to destroy communism, he has simply become an Ahab *sans grandeur*, a petty combatant for whom no holds are barred.

Early in the book, a Treasury agent is dismayed at Lanny's use of Fritz to spy on his own father—Lanny's boyhood friend, Kurt: "'Mr. Budd,' said the other gravely, 'the Nazis used children to report upon their parents, and the Reds are doing it now. But it is not our practice.'" [31] It soon became "our practice," however, as Lanny himself justifies a resort to totalitarian tactics in the name of the liberal cause. He receives an anonymous note informing him that Bess, his sister, is a Russian spy, a situation leading to the following conversation with his wife:

> "It is my plain duty to take it to the FBI."
> "Oh, Lanny, how dreadful! Could you bear to do it?"
> "Bess herself has given me the authority. You heard her say, 'The individual doesn't matter, only the cause matters.' You and I have a cause darling. Are we going to say it's less worthy than hers—that she can carry on secret war against us, and we have to lie down and take whatever comes to us? . . . No, the FBI are the people who know how to do this job, and it is the plain duty of every citizen to take them every scrap of information he may possess. To say that we must spare our own blood relatives is simply to yield to a superstition and in effect to deny our cause." [32]

Thus in order to support liberalism, one must accept the principle that the individual does not matter—a denial of the very basis of the liberal credo. Sinclair, who tends to make bald and explicit statements out of characteristics which more subtle liberals prefer to camouflage, received criticism from ideological colleagues who felt that liberalism should not present itself in quite so illiberal a way unless absolutely necessary. Witness Sidney Hook again, who rejoiced that Sinclair had rejoined his camp:

> My only criticism is that you *unnecessarily* make the

democrats adopt the kind of immoralism which characterized the Communist outlook. I do not think it is necessary to make Fritz, the *son* of Kirt [*sic*], or Hansi, the *husband* of Bess. Your critics will seize upon this to say that you approve tactics that the Stalinists and Nazis use. . . . I think that the use of children to denounce their parents . . . is also something we can forego. [33]

But Sinclair responded to this sort of complaint with the sort of logic which sent Jews to gas ovens:

> It is not merely a question of preserving one's own life, it is a question of preserving modern civilization with its ideals and its humanities. If Lanny has become hard it is because he has seen his ideals betrayed; he has been watching the process for thirty years, all his mature life. Anyhow that is the way I feel about it, and I chose these episodes deliberately for the purpose of saying so. [34]

Even at the height of McCarthyism, however, people were not listening to Sinclair's new song, demonstrating that the turncoat who has too long a record of advocating the other side is not likely to be trusted completely by those whom he later attempts to join. Perhaps this helps account for Sinclair's pathetic effort to develop a friendship with a man whose change of heart had received more publicity, Whittaker Chambers:

> I never doubted the truth about the case from the time I read your first statement. *It was only too easy for me to believe.* I followed the case in the newspapers and the magazines; then I read "Seeds of Treason," then your material in the *Saturday Evening Post* and now I have read the book straight through. It is a monument and it will convince millions of people and wake them up. [35]

In any case, Sinclair was unable to convince millions of Americans of the relevance of Lanny Budd's return. *World's End*, Sinclair's first effort of the series, eventually sold 23,669 copies within the United States; the next three volumes also sold approximately as well, but then sales climbed rapidly, reaching 86,000 with *Dragon Harvest*. However, a declining interest was reflected in lower sales for each successive novel in the last half of the series. But never was the decline so sharp as with *The Return of Lanny Budd*. For Sinclair's last gasp sold only 14,865 copies—about half the number sold of the novel immediately preceding it and far below the total with which he began the endeavor.[36]

Sales figures are subject to differing analyses, but an additional indication of the degradation of Sinclair is to be found in his correspondence. There the man began to beg help from men whom he had once vigorously opposed on principle. In a mimeographed appeal for support, Sinclair argued that organizations traditionally opposed to communism should not overlook the contribution of their new ally:

> This statement is being sent to individuals and organizations which may be interested in opposing the "cold war" in the field of letters. The project has to do with a novel, *The Return of Lanny Budd*, just published by Viking Press. . . . [The author] is thinking of small and backward lands in which the message of this book is . . . urgently needed: Turkey, Greece, Israel, Egypt, Iran, Siam; the native languages of India, and Chinese via Hong Kong. The Communists are working diligently in all these lands, and this book is a weapon against them. The author invites some public-service group to finance this

undertaking and he offers to donate the copyright. . . . Read the book, and see that it is a beacon light in a world threatened with darkness; a weapon in what William Blake calls "mental fight."[37]

Sinclair had often served as his own public relations manager, but the people to whom he now addressed himself represent a rather vivid contradiction of his claim that he had not changed his position. In *Dragon Harvest*, Sinclair had stated that Henry Ford

was, in all probability, the richest man in the world. . . . He had forbidden unions in his plants, and was fighting them by every means, not excluding criminal. But the New Deal was determined to break his will and force unions into all his plants. . . . As a result his plants swarmed with Nazis. . . . [38]

Despite this, and despite the fact that Sinclair's first jailing resulted from his too explicit labeling of John D. Rockfeller as a murderer of miners, their wives, and children,[39] Wall Street's would-be lackey offered himself and his new book to both the Ford and the Rockefeller foundations.[40]

Similarly, other organizations which Sinclair felt should welcome his aid were approached—and with similar results, as traditional conservatives hesitated to embrace an old liberal. A letter from Allen B. Willand, Director of the National Americanism Commission of the American Legion, informed Sinclair that nobody on the staff was familiar with his work, and thus Willand was unable to commit his organization to the sort of promotional campaign asked for by Sinclair.[41]

The Army chose to pass the book from department to department, with rejections which amounted to thanks, but no thanks: Wendell W. Fertig, Acting Chief of Psychological Warfare, approved of the ideological content of *The Return of Lanny Budd*, but he indicated that since his endeavors were limited to actual combat areas Sinclair would have to seek another agency.[42]

Allen Dulles reacted warmly to his advance copy of *Lanny's Return*: "I was particularly interested in the section dealing with Lanny's incarceration and the effort to extort a confession from him. You have made that unpleasant episode really live."[43] But this letter contains a hint that Sinclair may not have been able to deceive himself completely about his own new political stance. For what reason other than shame could have induced the world's most compulsive collector of everything relating to Upton Sinclair to have written in the corner of this particular letter an apparently overlooked injunction to destroy the document?

Given this scrawled bit of information, there is no way of knowing how many other letters were destined to elude the Lilly librarians altogether. But it was Sinclair himself who was destroyed by the Cold War—both as a believer in humane liberalism and as an effective propagandist. Not until his writing career had finally ended did American liberals begin to make tentative efforts to deal realistically with their own ideals by encouraging those manipulating the American experiment to grant the liberal hypothesis the dignity of trial under stress.

Notes

1. See Howard Mumford Jones, "The Continuing Story of Lanny Budd," *Saturday Review of Literature*, 28 (June 16, 1945). 10; and Granville Hicks, "The Survival of Upton Sinclair," *College English*, 4 (January 1943), 217.
2. Sinclair to Elizabeth Hughes, March 2, 1941, Sinclair MSS.
3. Sinclair to William Carlos Williams, October 16, 1951, Sinclair MSS. See also a letter to Jerry Bick, June 26, 1941, Sinclair MSS., in which he complains about the way Dos Passos "mixes up things in his long novels and makes them so hard to read."
4. Sinclair, *A World to Win* (New York: Viking Press, 1946), p. 12.
5. Sinclair, *Dragon's Teeth* (New York: Viking Press, 1942), p. 26. Sinclair, *One Clear Call* (New York: Viking Press, 1948), p. 17.
7. R. L. Duffus, "Upton Sinclair Carries On His Tale of Our Times," New York *Times*, March 23, 1941, Sec. VI, p. 4, col. 1.
8. *The Social Novel at the End of an Era* (Carbondale: Southern Illinois University Press, 1966), p. 15.
9. Sinclair, "Letter of Resignation," Chicago *Tribune*, July 22, 1917, Sec. VII, p. 5, col. 2. For discussion of Sinclair's attitude toward war see also Mary Craig Sinclair, *Southern Belle* (Phoenix: Sinclair Press, 1962), p. 236.
10. Sinclair, *100%, The Story of a Patriot* (Pasadena: Published by the Author, 1920), p. 320. [Emphasis added.]
11. Sinclair to Albert Einstein, October 31, 1941, Sinclair MSS.
12. Sinclair to B. W. Huebsch, October 2, 1943, Sinclair MSS.
13. Sinclair to Fay Rosen, June 23, 1944, Sinclair MSS.
14. Sinclair to Federal Bureau of Investigation, Los Angeles Office, June 9, 1952, Sinclair MSS.
15. Sinclair, *Dragon Harvest* (New York: Viking Press, 1945), p. 503.
16. Sinclair, *Presidental Agent* (New York: Viking Press, 1944), p. 533.
17. *Presidental Agent*, p. 547.
18. (New York: Viking Press, 1943), see especially pp. 823–837.
19. Sinclair, *Presidental Agent*, p. 533.
20. Sinclair, *Presidential Mission* (New York: Viking Press, 1947), p. 565.
21. *Presidential Mission*, p. 566.
22. *Presidential Mission*, p. 631.
23. *Presidential Mission*, p. 631.
24. "Ike on Ike," *Newsweek*, 62 (November 11, 1963), 108. [Emphasis added.]
25. Quoted by Gabriel Kolko, *The Politics of War* (New York: Random House, 1968), p. 540.
26. Sinclair to Deming Brown, March 10, 1952, Sinclair MSS.
27. Sinclair to P. M. Malin, April 25, 1952, Sinclair MSS.
28. See Sinclair's *Autobiography* (New York: Harcourt, Brace & World, 1962), pp. 228–231.
29. Sinclair to S. K. Ratcliffe, September 26, 1952, Sinclair MSS.
30. Monrovia *Daily News-Post*, February 9, 1955, p. 1, col. 2.
31. Sinclair, *The Return of Lanny Budd* (New York: Viking Press, 1953) p. 94.
32. *The Return of Lanny Budd*, p. 153.
33. Hook to Sinclair, October 9, 1952, Sinclair MSS. [Hook's emphasis.]
34. Sinclair to A. P. Biella, October 29, 1952, Sinclair MSS.
35. Sinclair to Chambers, July 10, 1952, Sinclair MSS. [Emphasis added.]
36. This information was graciously provided to me by Morton L. Levin, Vice President of Viking Press, Inc., in a letter dated March 10, 1970.
37. Two-page mimeographed statement, no date, in the Lilly Library.
38. P. 231.
39. See Sinclair's *Autobiography*.
40. See Sinclair MSS. of March 16 and March 17 and April 16, 1953 for rejections of Sinclair's proposition by the Rockefeller, Ford, and Carnegie Foundations respectively. See the letter from E. C. Talbot of February 27, 1953 for the hasty rejection by the Pew Foundation (Sun Oil Co.).
41. Willand to Sinclair, May 6, 1953, Sinclair MSS. See also the letter from L. C. Stevens, President of the American Committee for Liberation from Bolshevism, July 27, 1953, Sinclair MSS.
42. Wendell W. Fertig [Acting Chief of Psychological Warfare] to Sinclair, July 28, 1953, Sinclair MSS. See also the letter from J. Edgar Hoover of April 21, 1953, complaining that he had not yet received the promised gift copy.
43. Dulles to Sinclair, April 16, 1953, Sinclair MSS. Permission to quote from these letters is authorized in a letter to me from the estate of Allen W. Dulles dated March 16, 1973.

ISAAC BASHEVIS SINGER

1904–

Isaac Bashevis Singer was born on July 14, 1904, in Radzymin, Poland, to Pinchos-Mendel Singer and Bathsheva (née Zylberman) Singer. He emigrated to the United States in 1935, and was naturalized in 1943. He was educated at the Tachkemoni Rabbinical Seminary, Warsaw, from 1920 to 1922. He married Alma Haimann in 1940; they have one son. He was a proofreader and translator for *Literarishe Bleter* in Warsaw from 1923 to 1933, and has been a journalist for the *Jewish Daily Forward* in New York since 1935. He came from a literary family; his brother was the novelist Israel Joshua Singer and his sister the novelist Esther Kreitman.

Singer's earliest stories were written in Yiddish. Some were published anonymously in 1925; others followed in *Literarishe Bleter* ("Women") and *Warshawer Shriften* ("Grandchildren" and "The Village Gravedigger") in 1926 and 1927. He published his first novel, *Satan in Goray*, in 1934, and moved to Brooklyn the next year. He was distressed at the decay of Yiddish in the United States, and found himself unable to write Yiddish literature for the next seven years. He broke his dry spell in 1943 when *Satan in Goray* was reissued with five new stories.

In 1945 Singer began publishing his long family saga, *The Family Moskat*, serially in the *Jewish Daily Forward*; it was published in book form in 1950. Later that year *The Family Moskat* became Singer's first novel to be translated into English. Saul Bellow's translation of "Gimpel the Fool" in *Partisan Review* (1953) attracted critical attention, and Singer has since become widely regarded not only as the world's foremost Yiddish writer, but also as one of the major writers of the world in any language.

Satan in Goray was translated into English in 1955, and in 1957 *Gimpel the Fool and Other Stories* became Singer's first story collection to be published in English. Since then almost all of Singer's fiction has either been translated into English or written in English. His major novels include *The Magician of Lublin* (1960), *The Slave* (1962), *Shosha* (1978), *Reaches of Heaven* (1980), and the family epic *The Manor* (1967) and its sequel, *The Estate* (1969). His many story collections include the highly praised *The Spinoza of Market Street and Other Stories* (1961), *The Séance and Other Stories* (1968), *A Friend of Kafka and Other Stories* (1970), and *A Crown of Feathers and Other Stories* (1973). *Collected Stories* was published in 1982.

Singer has also written several books of memoirs, four plays, and more than a dozen books for children. His work is noted for its subtle philosophical themes masked with narrative drive and intensive detail; he is especially interested in conflicts between faith and skepticism and between the traditional and the progressive. He has won two National Book Awards, one for children's literature in 1970 and the other for fiction in 1974. He was awarded the Nobel Prize for Literature in 1978.

Isaac Bashevis Singer has lately become a figure in his own stories. He comes on as an embarrassed celebrity, awkwardly trying to fend off readers who regularly break in on him because they find him a link to their long suppressed Jewishness. The situation is inherently comic, problematical, unsettling to all parties concerned. For Singer's own "Jewishness" is unsentimental, occult, faithful in its own way to his rabbinical youth. But as in "The Admirer," the best of these stories ⟨*Passions and Other Stories*⟩, Singer's confused American fans breaking in on him tend to be even more confused about what they are looking for. They introduce complications that more than cancel out any pleasure their homage gives this Warsaw-born Yiddish writer who, after long struggles, acquired a wide American audience. Singer is amazed by his new readers. In some way, he feels himself to be their captive.

It is these "confusions" that give such characters their invincible craziness and thus their human interest. Singer writing about a wholly Jewish world recognizes in his "admirers" that to be Jewish is to be driven by forces that Jews understand no better than others do. The "mystery" of Jewish religion (and of Jewish persistence) may be especially a mystery to those who have suffered most for it.

In Singer's constant flow of stories about the multiple effects of the Holocaust, the victims of Hitler, just barely returned to life, are picturesquely crazed. In "Hanka," the story of an unreal lecture tour in Argentina, Singer hears from a woman who had been not so much hidden as buried by Poles during the war: "We all lived with death, and I want you to know that one can fall in love with death. Whoever has loved death cannot love anything else any more." Even the innocently vulgar American Jews in Miami Beach, as the next-best story, "Old Love," so conscious all day long of their new-found wealth, feel as naked as Job in the presence of their anxieties. Death calls them because their deepest attachments are to the dead. By contrast, the stories of old Poland show devout Jews as sleepwalkers, reiterating the daily vows and rituals of their religion, but able to do so only because they are cut off from a non-Jewish world. Soon this world will catch up with them and their descendants.

These descendants in America now come to Singer's door. In his pages they have discovered a world of tradition whose most exact beliefs are foreign to them. Singer, as he portrays this situation and himself, is both their *rebbe* and their victim. He seems to "know." What are we all about and what is the matter with us? Tell us!

But of course Singer is too foxy a storyteller to yield up his art to other people's nostalgia. Evidently he cannot stop writing about Jews and he cannot help writing so much, for what with Poland, New York, Miami Beach, Israel, there are stories within stories. Although some stories have the effect of anecdotes, (*Passions* is certainly an uneven collection), I never feel about this unstoppable writer that he repeats himself on purpose. Singer, like the ever-dwindling Yiddish audience for whom he writes directly in the *Jewish Daily Forward*, is endlessly fascinated by Jews, whose stories reach from the Bible to the 20th-century apocalypse. Singer portrays himself in these stories as a Jew also baffled by the convolutions of Jewish existence, and the exalted claims made for it. Jews are described as they are. In "Sabbath in Portugal," Singer arrives at a Lisbon hotel:

> The lobby was filled with compatriots from New York and Brooklyn. Their wives, with dyed hair and heavily made-up faces, smoked cigarettes, dealt cards, laughed and chattered all at once. Their daughters in mini-skirts formed their own circles. The men were studying the financial pages of the *International Herald Tribune*. Yes, these are my people, I said to myself. If the Messiah is to come, he will have to come because there are no others.

The problem with this book, nevertheless, is that Singer's naturally dry, matter-of-fact, laconic wit shines somewhat artificially in translation. The more anecdotal stories, which depend on the dramatic polarities of Yiddish speech, read as if the translations had been energized to cover up some unavoidable Yiddish intonation. Sentences startle and flip out at the reader with unbalanced effect. In "Hanka," we heard of a Polish-Jewish girl sold into prostitution in Argentina. "What could the girl do? They took her away on a ship and kept her in chains. She had already lost her innocence. She was sold into a brothel and had to do what she was told. Sooner or later she got a little worm in her blood, and with this she could not live long. After seven years of disgrace, her hair and teeth fell out, her nose rotted away, and the play was over. Since she was defiled, they buried her behind the fence. I remember my sister's asking 'Alive?'"

Singer consciously unsettles his reader, for his stories are all written within the compressiveness of magazine style. Unlike most short story writers today, who know not where to turn, Singer has an audience every week, and writes for this Yiddish audience, works on it, identifies with it. Only his great gifts enable him to elude it at times. Most Yiddish writers never do. But Singer's sly provocations of style are also an artistic necessity. There is so much material in Jewish lore, so much continuation into our day of the Jewish past, so much horror and unreality in the endless stories-within-stories of the Holocaust, that there is a too-enormous gallery of people to write about, a hall of mirrors to walk through. Singer's sentences have to speed through millennia of experience and human feeling:

> Those who stood at the threshold of death remain dead.
> I stood there, tense and miserable, and took a quick reckoning of man and his existence.
> The cockroaches in my apartment apparently knew that I was a vegetarian and that I felt no hatred for their species, which is a few hundred million years older than man and which will survive him.
> A cigar stuck out between his lips. His belly protruded like that of a woman in late pregnancy. He wore a navy blue jacket, green pants, brown shoes, a shirt with purple stripes, and a silk tie on which was painted the head of a lion.
> Each word, each sentence in that old (Hebrew) parchment was familiar to me with all its implications. I've studied the same laws in other volumes.

Senhor de Albeira asked, "Do you understand this?"
"I'm afraid I understand nothing else."
—ALFRED KAZIN, *NR*, Oct. 25, 1975, pp. 24–25

There are five hundred reasons why I began to write for children, but to save time I will mention only ten of them.

Number 1. Children read books, not reviews. They don't give a hoot about the critics.

Number 2. Children don't read to find their identity.

Number 3. They don't read to free themselves of guilt, to quench their thirst for rebellion, or to get rid of alienation.

Number 4. They have no use for psychology.

Number 5. They detest sociology.

Number 6. They don't try to understand Kafka or *Finnegans Wake*.

Number 7. They still believe in God, the family, angels, devils, witches, goblins, logic, clarity, punctuation, and other such obsolete stuff.

Number 8. They love interesting stories, not commentary, guides, or footnotes.

Number 9. When a book is boring, they yawn openly, without any shame or fear of authority.

Number 10. They don't expect their beloved writer to redeem humanity. Young as they are, they know that it is not in his power. Only the adults have such childish illusions.
—ISAAC BASHEVIS SINGER, "Why I Write for Children" (1978), *Nobel Lecture*, 1979, p. 21

IRVING HOWE
"Demonic Fiction of a Yiddish 'Modernist'"
Commentary, October 1960, pp. 350–53

Isaac Bashevis Singer is the only living Yiddish writer whose translated work has caught the imagination of the American literary public. Though his brilliant stories and novels are crowded with grotesque happenings, though they often seem to comprise an alien sub-world of imps, devils, whores, spirits in seizure, charlatans, and false messiahs, the contemporary reader—for whom the determination not to be shocked has become a point of honor—is likely to feel closer to Singer than to any, or most, of the other Yiddish writers. Offhand this may be surprising, for Singer's subjects are decidedly remote: in *Satan in Goray*, the orgiastic consequences of the false messianism of 17th-century East European Jews; in his book of stories *Gimpel the Fool*, a range of demonic, apocalyptic, and perversely sacred moments of *shtetl* life; and now in his new novel *The Magician of Lublin*, a portrait of a Jewish acrobat-magician-Don Juan in late 19th-century Poland who exhausts himself in sensuality and ends his life as a penitent ascetic. Yet one feels that, unlike many of the Yiddish writers who treat more familiar and up-to-date subjects, Singer commands a distinctively "modern" sensibility.

Now this is partly true—in the sense that Singer, though a master of Yiddish prose, has cut himself off from some of the traditional assumptions of Yiddish literature. But it is also not true—in the sense that any effort to assimilate Singer to literary "modernism" without registering how deeply involved he is with Jewish history and faith, is certain to distort the meanings of his work.

Those meanings, one might as well admit, are often enigmatic and hard to come by. It must be a common experience among Singer's readers to find a quick pleasure in the caustic surfaces of his prose, the nervous tokens of his virtuosity—for simply as a literary *performer* he has few peers among living writers—but then to acknowledge themselves baffled when they inquire into the point or purpose of his fictions. That these do have an insistent point and stringent purpose no one can doubt; Singer is too ruthlessly single-minded a writer to content himself with mere slices of representation or displays of the bizarre. His grotesquerie must be taken seriously, perhaps as a recoil from his perception of how ugly—how gratuitously ugly—human life can be. He is a writer completely absorbed by the demands of his vision, a vision gnomic and compulsive but with moments of high exaltation; so that while reading his stories one feels as if one were overhearing bits and snatches of a monologue, the impact of which is both notable and disturbing, but the meaning withheld.

Now these are precisely the qualities that the sophisticated reader, trained to docility before the exactions of "modernism," has come to applaud. Singer's stories work, or prey, upon the nerves. They leave one unsettled and anxious, the way a rationalist might feel if, walking at night in the woods, he suddenly found himself afraid of bats. Unlike most Yiddish fiction, Singer's stories neither round out the cycle of their intentions nor posit a coherent and ordered universe. They can be seen as paradigms of the arbitrariness, the grating injustice, at the heart of life. They offer instances of pointless suffering, dead-end exhaustion, inexplicable grace. And sometimes, as in Singer's masterpiece *Gimpel the Fool*, they turn about, refusing to rest with the familiar discomforts of the problematic, and drive toward a prospect of salvation on the other side of despair. But this prospect does not depend on any belief in the comeliness or lawfulness of the universe: whether or not God is there, surely He is no protector. Things happen, the probable bad and improbable good, both of them subject to the whim of the fortuitous—and the sacred fools, like Gimpel, learn to roll with the punch, finding the value of their life in a total passivity and openness to suffering.

It is hardly a secret that in the Yiddish literary world Singer is regarded with a certain suspicion or at least reserve. His powers of evocation, his resources as a stylist are acknowledged, yet many Yiddish literary people, including serious ones, seem to be uneasy about him. One reason is that "modernism"—which, as these people regard Singer, means a heavy stress upon sexuality, a concern for the irrational, expressionist distortions of character, and an apparent indifference to the more conventional aspects of Jewish life—has never won so strong a hold in Yiddish writing as it has in most Western literatures. For the Yiddish writers, "modernism" has often been a mere adornment of manner upon a subject inescapably traditional, or a means of intensifying a sense of estrangement from collective values to which they nevertheless remain bound.

The truly "modern" writer, however, is not quite trustworthy in his relation to his culture; he is a shifty character by choice and need, unable to settle into that representative solidity which would permit him to serve as a cultural "spoksman." And to the extent that Singer shares in the modernist outlook he will be regarded with distrust by Yiddish readers brought up on such "spokesmen" as Peretz, Abraham Reisen, and H. Leivick. There is, to be sure, no lack of admiration among Yiddish readers for Singer's work: anyone with half an ear must respond to the marvelously taut and subtle rhythms of his prose. Still, it is a qualified admiration. Singer's moral outlook, which seems to move equally toward the sensational and the ascetic, and his assumption that in fiction grotesquerie can be made to serve almost as a mode of

knowledge, are hardly traits calculated to put Yiddish readers at their ease.

I must confess that my first response to *The Magician of Lublin* was somewhat like the one I have been attributing here to Yiddish readers. The book is not quite so dazzling as *Satan in Goray*, but it does represent Singer at fairly close to his best, particularly in his gifts for evoking the textures of sensuous life and for driving straight to those moments of tension and inner division which reveal the souls of his characters. But while there is no difficulty in making out what happens in the book, there is a real question as to what it all signifies.

The Magician of Lublin centers on the figure of Yasha Mazur, a Jewish acrobat-magician who travels through the towns of Poland, giving performances and entangling himself with women. Like other figures in Singer's work, Yasha is "half Jew, half Gentile—neither Jew nor Gentile. He had worked out his own religion. There was a Creator, but He revealed Himself to no one, gave no indications of what was permitted or forbidden." The theme is recurrent in Singer: even the acknowledgment of God yields no moral assurance, and with or without Him men lose their way.

At the beginning, Yasha is seen during one of his rare visits home, basking in his prosperity and enjoying a good and faithful wife. But he is a restless creature, always driven to test his powers of performance and persuasion, to try out his gifts in still another place, with still another woman. These gifts constitute his curse, and his pleasure in observing his impact upon other people, his undoing.

Yasha moves on, leaving home, visiting his Gentile assistant, who is also a worshipful mistress, having a lively time with a Jewish whore, skirting the life of a gang of Jewish thieves, savoring an encounter with some Jewish white slavers, and finally ending in Warsaw with the biggest risk of his life: a scheme to run off, as he pretends to be unmarried, with a middle-class Gentile widow. This woman represents for him— the symbolism is clear but not insistent—the attractions of the outer cultivated world he had never been able to reach or conquer. Yasha undertakes a robbery to get money for his elopement, fails because of the residual power of his Jewish conscience, and then rapidly falls into flight, pain, collapse. "He had looked on the face of death and lechery and had seen that they were the same. . . . He had seen the hand of God. He had reached the end of the road." In an epilogue Yasha is seen at home again, now living as an ascetic who has locked himself in a hut behind his house, suffering cold, hunger, and sexual fantasies, worshipped by the credulous as a new miracle-worker, but still struggling to find his way to God.

From page to page the story, like anything Singer writes, is remarkably vivid. Everything springs to life, everything trembles with the breath of actuality. Yet, as one reads, one grows uneasy and begins to consider the kind of criticism to which Singer is sometimes subjected by Yiddish literary people. Why is this juicy description here, that sensual evocation there? Isn't there an indulgence in sensation for its own sake, a surrender to rather than a use of the grotesque? Does not Singer sometimes come close to the self-imitation which is the writer's greatest curse, that self-imitation which consists in falling back upon familiar devices and inflections?

It would be idle to say that these things never happen, yet once we bring to bear the perspectives of "modernism," it becomes a bit easier to grasp and thereby "justify" *The Magician of Lublin*. The very incongruity in the conception of a Jewish Don Juan has its obvious ironic appeal and significance—particularly a Jewish Don Juan with a record of success who fails at precisely the point where conventional Jewish wisdom would predict that he would: his encounter with Christian gentility. The ending of the novel also allows us to see that Singer is working out a complex pattern of suggestion, and not merely indulging in his repertoire of tricks. Yasha becomes a penitent, but so weak in body and faith that he cannot trust himself except under lock and key. Nothing is settled, nothing solved. At the end Yasha retains, embarrassingly, the charismatic powers he had enjoyed as a worldling: life is not so different even after the blessed revelation: the flesh continues to lust, the world remains full of temptations, and the fools who populate it still yearn for easy assuagements.

Between the epilogue and the bulk of the book there is, then, an ironic balance: each cancels out the implications of the other, so that finally, as at the beginning, what Singer offers are questions beyond answer. His particular power rests on this ability to hold such contrary elements as the miraculous and the skeptical, the moral and the exotic in a delicate tension. At times, his style seems almost *as if* it were the style of a man possessed, so thoroughly does he give himself to the subject; yet Singer also maintains a rigorous distance, one is always aware of the *conditional* nature of his involvement.

Having gone this far, we must now turn again. If Singer's work can be understood only on the assumption that in some crucial respects he is a "modernist" writer, one must add that in other ways he is profoundly related to the Jewish tradition. And if the Yiddish reader is inclined to slight the first side of his work, so the American reader is likely to underestimate the strength and persistence of the second.

Singer is related to the Jewish tradition not only in the obvious sense that he enjoys a close knowledge of the Jewish past. More importantly, he is one of the few Yiddish writers whose relation to the Jewish past does not depend on that body of attitudes and values we call Yiddishism. He writes *in* Yiddish, but is often quite apart from the Yiddish tradition. He is, so to say, a writer of the pre-Enlightenment and post-Enlightenment; he would be equally at home with a congregation of medieval Jews and a gathering of modern intellectuals, perhaps more so than at a meeting of the Yiddish PEN Club; he has a strong sense of the mystical and antique, but also a stern awareness of psychoanalytic disenchantment; he has evaded both the religious pieties and the humane rationalism of 19th-century East European Judaism. In his fiction Singer has "skipped over" the ideas of the historical epoch which gave birth to Yiddishism, for the truth is, I suppose, that Yiddish literature, in both its acceptance and denials, its writers of faith and its writers of skepticism, is thoroughly caught up with the Englightenment. Singer shares very little in the collective aspirations or the *Folkshtimmlichkeit* of the Yiddish masters; he does not celebrate *dos klaine menshele* as a paragon of sweetness and goodness; he is impatient with the sensual deprivations involved in the values of *Edelkeit*; and above all, he breaks away from a central assumption of both the 19th century and Yiddish literature, the assumption of *tachlis*, an immanent fate or end in human existence.

What remains? The Yiddish critic Shlomo Bickel has perceptively remarked that Singer's dominating principle is "anti-Prometheanism," a disbelief in the efficacy of defiance, striving, and pride, a doubt as to the sufficiency of knowledge or even wisdom. This seems true, but only if one remembers that in a good many of Singer's fictions, particularly in *The Magician of Lublin*, the central action does constitute a sort of Promethean ordeal or straining. Singer makes it abundantly clear that his characters have no choice: they must live out their hungers, their orgiastic yearnings and apocalyptic expectations. "Anti-Prometheanism" thus comes to rest upon a belief in the unavoidable recurrence of the Promethean urge— an urge which, in Singer's view of things, is reduced from ideal to obsession or, perhaps more accurately, makes it impossible to separate ideal from obsession.

In the end, what concerns Singer most of all is the possibilities for life that remain after the exhaustion of human effort, after failure and despair have come and gone. Singer watches his stricken figures from a certain distance, with enigmatic moral intent and no great outpouring of sympathy, almost as if to say that before their collapse neither judgment nor sympathy matters very much. Yet in all of his books the Promethean effort recurs, obsessional, churning with new energy and delusion. In the knowledge of its recurrence there may also lie hidden a kind of pity, for that too we would expect, and can learn to find, in the writer who created Gimpel.

SUSAN SONTAG
"Demons and Dreams"
Partisan Review, Summer 1962, pp. 460–63

The typical modern novel is "psychological" in that the world it presents is really a projection, a bodying forth of the self (or selves) whose analysis constitutes the subject of the novel. One feels the novelist does not really believe in the world in which he has ostensibly situated his characters, because we observe that his characters do not believe in it: the self-absorption of the characters in modern fiction devours both themselves and their world. The relations between self and world are variously but quite regularly defined as boredom, disgust, contempt, frustration, nostalgia. The world in such novels is not really "there" in the same sense that the characters are "there." Sometimes, as in the stories and novels of Kafka, the tales of Borges, and the newest French fiction, not even the characters are "there;" the arena of the novel has been preempted by the agony of disembodied emotional and intellectual struggles. The farthest reach of the post-classical novel in both its bias toward psychologizing and its verbal inventiveness is identical: it is an empty stage, an infinite enumeration, an indefinitely repeated gesture or cry. The purest form of the post-classical novel is the nightmare.

It is I think altogether to the credit of Isaac Bashevis Singer that his fiction provides modern taste with a generous ration of nightmare, in the form of demons, dreams, deformity, and disease—without sacrificing the centrality of plot or the substantiality of a world. In the age of post-classical fiction, Singer continues to practice the classical virtues. His rare gift for constructing inventive and compelling plots has been much remarked on by critics. What has not been sufficiently commended, however, is his extraordinary power of sensuous evocation. Every page of Singer's fiction is crowded with physical objects—phylacteries and prayer books, handkerchiefs and dogs, dunes and trees, chandeliers and fiddles, lemonade and knives, sleighs and garlic, beards and mice. These things are brought to life for the reader not by being described individually, but simply in their marvelous abundance and rightness of juxtaposition. They are neither accessories in a psychological drama, nor props to make credible a world. In most of his stories, objects are at the very center of the stage, actors in the dialectic between the material world and the spiritual forces, principally demonic, which invade it. There is no need for Singer to describe: objects are there, charged, over-charged, with the tension between their employment as instruments of righteousness and as vessels of demonry.

Singer does not face the typical problem of the modern writer—of having to improvise a milieu and make it credible to his readers, or of having to take a familiar (or potentially familiar) milieu and make it exotic to his readers. This is not because of anything inherently more plausible, or answerable to his readers' experience, in the world he presents; but simply because of the unfailing assurance and lack of apologetic distance with which he moves in it. It is an utterly bounded, though not a limited world: that of Eastern European, particularly Polish, Jewry, with its whole complex history from the seventeenth to the early twentieth century of Cabbalistic mysticism and magic, Cossack persecution and massacre, the Sabbatian heresy, Hassidism, and the translation under the pressure of the Enlightenment of the religious ideals of study and pious unworldliness into the secular ideal of the scholar-intellectual. On the face of this highly local and historically dense environment, Singer inscribes the universal conflicts of reason versus the flesh, and of creedal and ritual religion versus a free spirituality. Entirely absent from his work is any merely historical motive, the impulse to evoke this world and thereby to preserve it simply because it is both past and mercilessly destroyed. There is no nostalgia and no pathos, because there is no distance. Singer's fiction is intimate, meticulous, laconic, and unsentimental. At times he reminds one of Babel—except he is more spacious, less ambiguous and troubled in tone.

Singer's characters are typically beset by motives whose clarity and forcefulness confound the hesitations of our modern psychological sophistication. They are wholly conscious motives, that can be ranked on the traditional schedule of virtues and vices. Lust, envy, gluttony, pride, and avarice predominate among the vices; pity, simplicity, and humility among the virtues. (Singer's accounts of gluttony include some of the most stunning descriptions of the pleasures of eating since the *Iliad*.) He brilliantly executes this pre-modern account of motivation, which includes a self-understanding of character as a drama of contending supernatural forces. Of necessity, these are not characters in the modern, infinitely expandable, individual sense, but creatures of a vigorously collective psychology. Singer presents an image of Jewry not in terms of individuals struggling in an alien setting—the familiar image of the Jew from Shylock to Swann—but in terms of a rigorously bounded, sensuous community of physical things and almost palpable beliefs and avoidances. It is a world whose moving principle is appetite, whether the appetite for learning and salvation or for warm flesh and succulent foods and fine clothes and furnishings, and in this respect most deeply removed from the world of modern fiction, whose principal subject is the failure of appetite and passionate feeling.

In the treatment of his recurrent theme of the temptation of demonry, the strength of Singer's fiction lies in his exploration of the demonic not as a function of individual aberration but as the aberration of a community. The Jewry of which he writes is saturated with magical superstition, and convulsed by the inexplicable sorrows of persecution and the exaltations and hysterias of Messianic hope. It is an era magnetized by the mystery of transgression—enthralling as a subject of fiction and of great interest also as a crucial, but largely suppressed, chapter in Western religious history which reached its climax in the seventeenth century, the century in which Lurianic Cabbalism, with its indeterminate borderline between mysticism and magic, was the dominant spiritual influence throughout the Jewish Diaspora.

Usually in Singer's fiction, the devil has the last word, and his human characters do not survive the paradoxes of their

humanity. However, in Singer's latest novel, *The Slave*, as the author himself is reported to have said, for a change God has the last word. The novel is again set in Poland, over a period of twenty years following the Chmielnicki massacres, and traces the fortunes of a virtuous man both desperately encumbered and supremely graced by his own spiritual scruples, who struggles with physical bondage, prohibited love, the perverseness of oppression, and the coercions of his own oppressed community. Perhaps precisely because it is a study in goodness, *The Slave* differs from most of Singer's previous work in having a less hectic, less exotic atmosphere. The novel has a warmth, a wholesomeness which befits a work which dares to tell a passionate, exalted love story and to end with a large romantic gesture of reunion-in-death as tearfully satisfying and old-fashioned as the end of *Wuthering Heights*.

The demonic is more alien here, for the main representatives of superstition are the un-Christianized Polish peasants to whom the hero is sold as a slave, rather than the *shtetl* Jews. There is less dwelling on ethnic eccentricity, and more emphasis on the beauty and equanimity of nature. The tone also is more neutral, more classically "novelistic"—it is neither the chatty tone of the folk narrator of some of Singer's stories nor the ironic tone of the malicious spirit or demon who narrates others. The novel also has a greater inwardness of characterization, which follows on the fact that the two main characters are from the inception of the story separated off from their communities. The devout hero, Jacob, is twice alienated from the Jewish community from which he was torn by the Chmielnicki massacres: by solitude and the absence of his books during the period of his slavery, and by love for a Gentile woman, forbidden alike by Jewish and Polish law. The heroine, Wanda, is set apart from her brutish family and neighbors, first by her innate refinement and later by her love for Jacob, and then from the Jewish community in which she can live as Jacob's bride only by pretending to be mute. The novel recapitulates Singer's familiar themes—but at a certain remove, because the hero and heroine both transcend these conflicts. The way in which Jacob succumbs to but finally rejects the Sabbatian temptation, for instance, is only scantily described.

It cannot be denied that Singer has sacrificed a certain exotic intensity and sensuousness in the measured affirmations of *The Slave*. The sensuous charge of Singer's fiction does seem to have some inextricable connection with his vision of a universe in which the negative or demonic pole is the stronger. Let's assume, however, that the modern educated sensibility still has some appetite left for the climaxes of true love and noble death, alongside its appetite for the demonic and fantastic. This being the case, *The Slave* should not only renew our sense of the possibility of still writing good novels but also renew our capacities for emotional catharsis as distinct from the endless exacerbation of the emotions which most modern fiction provides.

PADDY CHAYEFSKY
"Of Dybbuks and Devilkins"
Reporter, April 22, 1965, pp. 40–43

This collection of sixteen short stories ⟨*Short Friday*⟩ is the first Isaac Bashevis Singer book I've read. I'm afraid I'm not properly up on my Peretz, Mendele Mocher S'forim, or even the more current Yiddish writers, and I have at best only a waving acquaintance with Sholom Aleichem, so I can't help out much in terms of genre criticism. But it doesn't matter really, for you can't put Singer safely away as a Yiddish writer. Nor can he be put away as a contemporary writer on Jewish themes after the manner of Bellow, Malamud, even Babel, even Kafka, who wrote in their national language rather than Yiddish and about Jews in a Gentile world not especially concerned with Jews—a world, in fact, whose Gentiles are quite as forsaken by God as the Jews and quite as dispersed and despairing. Singer doesn't write about those things at all. There is simply no non-Jewish world in his stories, not even in the one set in Brooklyn and the one set in Miami Beach. With those two exceptions, Singer's stories all take place in tiny Jewish villages in what seems to be the Polish countryside and in what should be taken as the late nineteenth century, perhaps early twentieth, a complete world centered on shabby little synagogues and gaberdined, bearded rabbis, pious matrons with shaven heads, ritual slaughterers and ritual bathhouses, a world separated from space by thick forests out of which occasionally tramps a muddy-booted peasant to buy tallow candles and buckwheat. These silent peasants are the only non-Jews who ever appear, and then only momentarily.

If, however, you think these tales are reminiscent or parochial, you are mistaken. Singer's stories are very immediate, and the net result of his parochialism is the very opposite of parochial. To Singer, the whole world is nineteenth-century Jewish Poland and just about everyone is a nineteenth-century Polish Jew. It is a world untroubled by the political upheavals of the moment, the revolutions, wars, and scientific discoveries. All that remains to be written about here are the people and their absolutes. The consequence of this is a simplicity of style and a natural elementariness. There is none of the cumbersome complexity of modern writing, no obsession with the externals of relationships, no fumbling about for profundity beneath the civilized sigh. In Singer's world, life and death, God and hell, reality and illusion are on the same level of observation as taking a bath or marketing for Friday-night dinner.

Singer's characters are all quite ordinary in their imperfections. They rage with lust and tremble with doubt. They steal, murder, cheat, are swept up by infatuation, are crushed down by gossip. They are homosexual, impotent; they are adulterers, apostates. They are vain, arrogant, ambitious, calculating, greedy, violent, selfish, occasionally tender, occasionally remorseful. They are, in short, exactly the sort of characters you expect to find in any modern book. However, all Singer's people are passionate in their imperfections. They reach the depths, and they achieve the heights. Singer, in point of fact, portrays characters very few authors have dared to deal with. The reader suddenly becomes aware halfway through the stories that the shy little sextons and lusty butchers' wives, muddling along through the familiar deceits of life, have become figures of the most profound passions—martyrs, ascetics, and murderers propelled by emotions so primeval, so savage, that Singer must exploit the supernatural to make them comprehensible.

Singer's demons, warlocks, succubi, trolls, cacodemons, lamias, dybbuks, and devilkins are as vivid and alive as his human characters. The fact is, Singer's dark spirits aren't even supernatural; you are never asked to accept anything as implausible as that. They can all be explained by the realistic conditions of the stories. In "Under the Knife," the hero is a habitual drunk, and the story is told through the device of his shadowy imaginings. In "The Fast," the main character is predisposed to hallucinations by his weakened physical state. In "Esther Kreindel the Second," the heroine is an over-

wrought girl motivated to her extraordinary impersonation—if you're tiresome enough to prefer that to a reincarnation—by the misery of her life. In those stories where the characters are themselves spirits and transmigratory souls, the author makes it clear in the very first sentence that he is being fanciful, and even these stories never degenerate into allegory but rather serve the purpose of social satire; they are the weakest stories in the lot. In any event, nothing ever happens in Singer's stories that wouldn't have happened without demons or any sort of supernatural agency.

Singer's demons serve a far more attractive purpose than the purpose of allegory. For one thing, they allow him to write a spare and swift prose made voluptuous by the strange sounds and sensual colors one expects from demons. Without ever pausing in his precise realism, Singer brings in all the suggestions of fetid and feral things, murks and miasmas that have always been the province of the romantic and decadent. But they are neither romantic nor decadent in these stories, nor is the author a demonologist or a symbolist. Singer is a relentless realist, far closer to Chekhov than to Hawthorne—to whom he has been compared, mainly for his preoccupation with the supernatural. He reads much more like Maupassant than Poe. He does not provoke terror in the reader as the supernatural writer does, but he makes the reader understand the terror or perhaps aspiration that people described as possessed must feel.

After "The Fast," one understands Saint Anthony in the desert or even Saint Joan as something more than a historical figure; one understands all ascetics or imbued persons who have seen an apparition or heard a voice. This is the seemingly amiable story of a wispy little man, never much of an eater, who, after he is abandoned by his wife and thus left untended and uncared for, pays even less attention to food, and even develops a pious distaste for it. Fasting becomes the proper order of things. But this turn to asceticism, so poignant and petty in this simple little man, who mortifies himself with backyard nettles and pebbles from the driveway, is unmotivated by any grand religiosity.

One Thursday night on the fifth day of a fast, as he lies stretched out on his bench, fitfully awake, fitfully dreaming, nightmare and reality follow in succeeding sentences:

> A huge frog opened its maw, ready to swallow him. The church-bell rang out. Itche Nokhum started up, trembling. Was there a fire or some other disaster? He waited for the bell to ring again. But there was only a distant, hollow echo. Itche Nokhum felt a need to urinate. He stood by the pail, but nothing came. He washed his hands, preparing to say the prayer proper for the occasion, but the urge returned. He felt a burning and a throbbing. His entrails contracted with cramps. A bitterness flooded his mouth, as on the verge of vomiting. "Shall I take a drink of water?" Itche Nokhum asked himself. He went to the stool, where a pitcher stood, half-filled with water for ritual hand-washing, and turned it over reluctantly. One of his socks became wet. "I'll not give in to him!" Itche Nokhum whispered. "Show a dog a finger and he'll snap up the whole hand . . ."

Then Itche Nokhum receives his first apparition, a succubus in the form of his ex-wife, Roise Genendel:

> Something began to stir in the dark by the door—a coiling wisp of vapor, airy and misty. . . . He tried to rise, but his legs were numb and heavy. The specter flowed toward him, dragging its tail of slime like a chick prematurely breaking out of the

shell. "The Primeval Substance!" something cried in Itche Nokhum. He recalled the Psalm: "Thine eyes did see my substance, yet being unperfect." He wanted to speak to the night-creature, but he was robbed of the power of speech. For a time he watched dumbly as she approached, half woman, half shapeless ooze, a monstrous fungus straining to break away from its root, a creature put together in haste. After a while, she began to melt away. Pieces dropped from her. The face dissolved, the hair scattered, the nose stretched out and became a snout, as in the manikins that people put on their window sills in winter to mock the frost. She spat out her tongue.

I include these extracts only to show how remorselessly real is Singer's supernaturalism. In the end, you can take it any way you like. Itche Nokhum was just a lonely little man, distressed to the point of hallucination by his abnegation, whose obsessive longing for his ex-wife induced this apparition. Or he was Saint Anthony in the desert. In either case, Saint Anthony comes out of it a comprehensible figure. I've read all sorts of accounts of the early eremites; Singer writes of the ascetic experience better than any. If you want to understand the deformed anguish of a genuine witch, you will find it in the story "Cunegunde." Reincarnation is treated with the graceful perception of a Willa Cather in "Esther Kreindel the Second," and the total depravity of lust turned to blood lust is to be found in "Blood," as memorable a story as I can remember.

I find depressing the current compulsion to decide not just whether a writer writes well or not or even whether he's an artist or not, but whether his work is durable or not. I have no idea of Singer's permanence or his stature; I don't think there's anyone around who can yet tell. I only know that he is a bold and skillful writer, a superb storyteller, unafraid of frightening emotion and with the ear and eye of a poet. And, as with that rye bread whose name I've forgotten for the moment, you don't have to be Jewish to enjoy him.

TED HUGHES
"The Genius of Isaac Bashevis Singer"
New York Review of Books, April 22, 1965, pp. 8–10

Isaac Bashevis Singer emigrated to the United States in 1935, which was the year of his first novel *Satan in Goray*. Since then, he has written more or less exclusively about the Jewish world of pre-war Poland, or more exactly—it's a relevant qualification—about the Hasidic world of pre-war Poland, into which he was born, the son of a rabbi, in 1904. So not only does he write in Yiddish, but his chosen subject is even further confined in place, and culture, and now to the past. Nevertheless, his work has been lucky with its translators, and he has to be considered among the really great living writers, on several counts.

He's produced three more novels, that have been translated, and three volumes of short stories. Looking over his novels in their chronological order (the stories are written in and among, but they belong with the novels) the first apparent thing is the enormous and one might say successful development of his vision. Vision seems to be the right word for what Singer is conveying. The most important fact about him, that determines the basic strategy by which he deals with his subject, is that his imagination is poetic, and tends toward

symbolic situations. Cool, analytical qualities are heavily present in everything he does, but organically subdued to a grasp that is finally visionary and redemptive. Without the genius, he might well have disintegrated as he evidently saw others disintegrate—between a nostalgic dream of ritual Hasidic piety on the one hand and cosmic dead-end despair on the other. But his creative demon (again, demon seems to be the right word) works deeper than either of these two extremes. It is what involves him so vehemently with both. It involves him with both because this demon is ultimately the voice of his nature, which requires at all costs satisfaction in life, full inheritance of its natural joy. It is what suffers the impossible problem; and dreams up the supernormal solution. It is what in most men stares dumbly through the bars. At bottom it is amoral, as interested in destruction as in creation, but being in Singer's case an intelligent spirit, it has gradually determined a calibration of degrees between good and evil, in discovering which activities embroil it in misery, pain, and emptiness, and conjure into itself cruel powers, and which ones concentrate it towards bliss, the fullest possession of its happiest energy. Singer's writings are the account of this demon's re-education through decades that have been—particularly for the Jews—a terrible school. They put the qeustion: "How shall man live most truly as a human being?" from the center of gravity of human nature, not from any temporary civic center or speculative metaphysic or far-out neurotic bewilderment. And out of the pain and wisdom of Jewish history and tradition they answer it. His work is not discursive, or even primarily documentary, but revelation—and we are forced to respect his findings because it so happens that he has the authority and power to force us to do so.

Up to 1945, this demon in Singer's work shows itself overpowered. *Satan in Goray* and *The Family Moskat* give the story of its defeat. In some way these two books belong together, though they are ten years apart. *Satan in Goray* seems to me his weakest book—important, and with a stunning finish, but for the most part confusingly organized. Perhaps we wouldn't notice this so much if we weren't comparing it with his later works, where the inspired rightness of his technical inventions are a study in themselves. *Satan in Goray* recounts the effects of the Sabbatai Zevi Messianic hysteria on a small Hasidic community in seventeenth-century Poland. Sabbatai Zevi's followers, who frequently appear in Singer's stories, effectually apotheosized the Evil One. They proclaimed salvation through a sort of ecstasy of sinning, as if there were something purifying in the sheer intensity with which they surrendered to the forbidden, to the supercharged otherworld of disruptive powers and supernaturals which the Law, in its wandering history, had collided with and put under and thereafter had to hold under—a terrific population accumulating under the Cabala and on the Holy Fringes of everything, several entire religions and erstwhile creators screwed down under dots, letters, and ritual gestures. This isn't altogether ancient history. Something of it has been dogmatized in modern psychology and avant-garde literature. One could argue that the whole of modern Western life is one vast scientifically programmed surrender to what was formerly unknown and forbidden, as if salvation lay that way. The Sabbatai Zevi psychic epidemic is an accurate metaphor for a cultural landslide that has destroyed all spiritual principles and dumped an entire age into a cynical materialism emptied of meaning. Which is why the sufferings of Netchele, the bride of the leader of the Sabbatai Zevi sect in Goray, in whose brain the general eruption of infernal license finally concentrates, belong to this century and not to the seventeenth. And why we can say her sufferings are perhaps an image of what Singer's own muse, representative of the Polish Jews, has undergone.

The key to Singer's works seems to be an experience of the collapse of the Hasidic way of life under the pressure of all that it had been developed to keep out. Something like this is a usual moral position among poets who come at some revolutionary moment, but who need to respect order. Singer comes at the moment when the profound, rich, intense Hasidic tradition, with the whole Jewish tradition behind it, debouches into the ideological chaos of the mid-twentieth century. Visited with all that the old Law excluded, such poets are burdened with the job of finding new Law. But when the hosts of liberated instinct and passion and intellectual adventure and powers of the air and revelations of physical truth are symbolized by Satan, as they must be for a Hasidic Jew, and the old, obsolete order is symbolized by the devotion and ritual that are a people's unique spiritual strength and sole means of survival, the position must be a perilous one to manage. We can trace the workings of the whole conflict much more definitely—though without the symbolic impact of *Satan in Goray*—in Singer's next book, *The Family Moskat*.

Coming ten years later, *The Family Moskat* is radically different in style from the earlier book, cast in panoramic Tolstoyan mould, 600 pages long, covering the fates of the rich, patriarchal Moskat's large family and—in suggested parallel—of a whole people, from the beginning of this century up to the first Nazi bombs on Warsaw. The protagonist is one Asa Heshel, a young, precociously freethinking but, to begin with, outwardly orthodox Hasidic Jew, the son of a provincial rabbi, who arrives in Warsaw seeking life and the divine truths. He becomes entangled with Moskat's family. Thereafter, it is the story of the moral disintegration of the Polish Jews.

It is a monumental, seethingly real picture of Warsaw Jewish life, without a mistimed paragraph. In this city, the Jews are under the millstone of the west, and their inner coherence is breaking up. In the process, typical mutations appear. But the main current of the book flows through two men, Asa Heshel and Abram. Abram is a volcanic enjoyer of life. The gentile pressures have stripped him of all but the last nods towards orthodoxy, but they haven't frightened his energy: he keeps his Hasidic wholeness and joy. Though he lives more or less entirely in sin in every direction, collapsing finally on a tart's bed and dying in his mistress's, he remains "a true Hasid" and "biologically a Jew." But it is all at a last gasp, it is all headlong into the new gentile age, into death, on the precarious foundations of a damaged, over-passionate heart. He is full-pressure Jewishness, making the leap, naively. He calls Asa Heshel, his protegé, a coward, and by superficial contrast Asa Heshel's behavior is cowardly all right. But Asa Heshel has recoiled. He has made the leap early, without dying bodily, into the wilderness of Darwin and the physicists, the ceaseless covert battleground of Western civilization, and he has recoiled. He has no illusion that life lies that way. Yet he has allowed the wind off it to deprive him of his traditional faith, the meaning of his life. And that first treachery to God spreads a faithlessness, a heartlessness, into all his actions and thoughts. His two marriages founder and struggle on in torture. His grand intellectual ambitions fritter out in sterility and cynicism. He regards all the possibilities of life with frozen distrust. For him, God has died, yet he can't love anything else. The creation is a heap of atoms, a sterile promontory battered by blind appetites. His deep suspicion and perhaps hatred of women is equalled by his cold, desperate lust for their bodies. The great projected work of his youth, "The Labora-

tory of Happiness," accompanies his pointless wanderings, decaying, finally lost. All the moral and intellectual consequences of his people's loss of faith, and their pursuit of the new, chaotic world, seem to have concentrated in his brain. Behind his coldness, he is suffering the death Netchele suffered, in *Satan in Goray*, possessed and out of her mind, and perhaps this is the connection between the two books.

Adele, his second wife, on the point of leaving him to escape to Israel from the first rumors of Hitler, finds the words for Asa Heshel: "He was one of those who must serve God or die. He had forsaken God and because of that he was dead— a living body with a dead soul." It is from this situation of Asa Heshel's that the general moral implications of Singer's vision radiate. Asa Heshel, after all, is not only a Hasidic Jew. He is a typical modern hero. Remembering that Singer writes in Yiddish, for a primarily Jewish public, we can still see that he writes out of such essential imagination that he raises Jewishness to a symbolic quality, and is no longer writing specifically about Jews but about man in relationship to God. And his various novels and stories—with a few exceptions among the stories—describe the various phases and episodes of this relationship, though in concrete Jewish terms. This is pretty near to saying that, in Singer, the Jew becomes the representative modern man of suffering, and of understanding, and exile from his Divine inheritance, which of course isn't altogether Singer's own invention.

Asa Heshel ends up, hurrying under the Nazi bombers with his latest woman, Jewish also, but a set Communist. He knows he has fallen the whole way. Communism is the ideological antithesis to the Holy Life, created by Jews living in defiance or denial of God, as Lucifer, fallen from praising in heaven, organized the abyss. In her company, Asa Heshel meets the philosopher, the bewildered genius, onetime hope of the gentilized Jewish intellectuals, who closes the book, among the falling bombs, with "The Messiah will come soon . . . Death is the Messiah. That's the real truth." This is the final logical point in Asa Heshel's progress, as death was the final point of Netchele's. The forsaking of God, the rejection of the life of Holy Disciplines, is a crime, as it turns out, without redemption, and, as history in this book seems to demonstrate, draws on itself the inevitable penalty: anonymous death— whether symbolic or actual hardly matters—in a meaningless wasteland of destruction and anguish.

Singer's vision arrived there, in despair in the absurd Universe, at a point where most comparable modern writers have remained, emotionally, despite their notable attempts to get beyond it. The Existential Choice, taken to its absolute limit of wholeheartedness, becomes inevitably a religion— because man is deeper and more complicated than merely rational controls can keep hold of. Then his beliefs, disciplines, and prohibitions have to be cultivated against the odds as in a world of poisons one chooses—sensibly after all—food that nourishes. Singer is at a point there, that is to say, where he has every sane and human reason to rebuild an appreciation of the Faith it was death for him to lose. So here again the Jewish Hasidic tradition takes on a Universal significance, as a paradigm of the truly effective Existential discipline, which perhaps it always has been. The core of the Jewish faith, unlike most larger persuasions, is one long perpetually-renewed back-to-the-wall Choice, one might say in this context, to affirm a mode of survival against tremendous odds. It has kept the Jewish heart in one piece through three thousand years of such oppressions and temptations as dissolved other peoples in a few decades. So it is not surprising if Singer, in his books, gravitates back towards it as a way out of the modern impasse, salvaging at the same time the life of spirit and all the great human virtues.

The Family Moskat is the matrix from which Singer's subsequent work grows. His next two novels, *The Magician of Lublin* and *The Slave* are like dreams out of Asa Heshel's remorse. The Magician, Yasha Mazur, fallen from the Faith, is a kind of Satan, the opportunist of his own inspired ingenuity. But, unlike Asa Heshel's, his belief has not wholly died, it has (merely) been buried. It recovers him from the pit, and in a bricked-up cell in his yard he becomes an ascetic, a famous Holy man. In this, he has not rejected the world. He has accepted the only life that does not lead to misery for himself and for everybody he knows. *The Slave* goes a great step further in the same direction. Jacob—a slave of Polish peasants in the seventeenth century—is brutishly treated. He is stalled among the beasts. He is threatened with constant death. Yet he keeps his faith. He falls in love with the peasant daughter of his master, converts her, and returns with her to live in a Jewish settlement. It is a story of heroic dedication: no disappointment or persecution or obstacle can shake him—as Asa Heshel was so easily shaken—from the chosen way, and he becomes, again, a kind of Saint.

In this book, one of Singer's deep themes comes right to the surface. Singer implies—and seems to build his novels instinctively around the fact—that there is an occult equivalence between a man's relationship to the women in his life and his relationship to his own soul—and so to God. Netchele, in *Satan in Goray*, seems to bear a relationship to Singer himself. Hadassah, Adele, Barbara, and Asa Heshel's mother, precisely define the stages of Asa Heshel's fall. Esther, Masha and Emilia define the three Yasha Mazurs, in *The Magician*. Wanda and Sarah, two names of one woman, correspond to Jacob creating his soul out of chaos, and Jacob and the Saint. These correspondences are subtle and revealing. On the mythical or symbolic plane, these women are always at the core of everything Singer is saying about his hero. And it's on this plane that we can best see what an achievement *The Slave* is, and perhaps why it comes to be such a burningly radiant, intensely beautiful book. Singer is answering his age like a prophet, though what he is saying may seem perverse and untimely. If the world is Gehenna, it is also the only "Laboratory of Happiness," and in *The Slave* Jacob and Sarah achieve a kind of Alchemical Marriage, a costly, precarious condition, but the only truly happy one. So what are we to understand? The dynamics of man's resistance to demoralization and confusion, the techniques of "creating" God and Holy Joy where there seemed to be only emptiness, never change, but they demand a man's whole devotion. And they can be abandoned in a day, whereon the world becomes, once more, Gehenna.

His stories fill out these guiding themes, or exploit situations suggested by them, in dozens of different ways, but they give freer play to his invention than the novels. At their best, they must be among the most entertaining pieces extant. Each is a unique exercise in tone, focus, style, form, as well as an unforgettable re-creation of characters and life. A comic note, a sort of savage enjoyment that scarcely appears in the novels, more or less prevails, though it is weirdly blended with pathos, simplicity, idyllic piety, horror. There is some connection here, in the actual intensity of the performance, and the impartial joy in the face of everything, with traditional Hasidic fervor. In substance, these stories recapitulate the ideas and materials of Jewish tradition. Intellectually their roots run into the high, conservative wisdom of the old Jewish sages. Yet it is only a slight thing that prevents many of them from being folk-tales, or even old wives' tales, narrated by a virtuoso. They all have the swift, living voice of the oral style. Some of them are very near a bare, point-blank, life-size poetry that hardly exists in English. "The Black Wedding," in the volume titled *The Spinoza of Market Street*, is a more alive, more ferocious piece of poetic imagination than any living poet I can think of would be likely to get near. Likewise "The Fast," and "Blood," in *Short Friday*. The stories often turn on almost occult insights—as the connection between blood-lust and sexual lust, in "Blood." It is his intimacy with this dimension of things that carry Singer beyond any easy comparision. Stories that are deadpan jokes, like "Jachid and Jechidah," or fantasies, like "Shiddah and Kuziba," are not only brilliantly done, but are also moral / theological fables of great force, and direct outriders of Singer's main preoccupations. No psychological terminology or current literary method has succeeded in rendering such a profound, unified and fully apprehended account of the Divine, the Infernal, and the suffering space of self-determination between, all so convincingly interconnected, and fascinatingly peopled. But it is in the plain, realistic tales, like "Under the Knife" in *Short Friday*, that we can isolate his decisive virtue: whatever region his writing inhabits, it is blazing with life and actuality. His powerful, wise, deep, full-face paragraphs make almost every other modern fiction seem by comparison labored, shallow, overloaded with alien and undigested junk, too fancy, fuddled, not quite squared up to life.

MAXIMILLIAN E. NOVAK
"Moral Grotesque and Decorative Grotesque in Singer's Fiction"
The Achievement of Isaac Bashevis Singer
ed. Marcia Allentuck
1969, pp. 44–63

In one section of the memoirs of his youth, *In My Father's Court*, Isaac Bashevis Singer mentions that during a period of isolation he spent his idle moments drawing "freakish humans and fantastic beasts." It was at that very time that he discovered his first true delight in literature—Dostoevsky's *Crime and Punishment*. The conjunction of these events might be casual, but they suggest something significant about his later writing. Of *Crime and Punishment* he wrote that it reminded him of the Cabbala, and his response to Dostoevsky's unique combination of psychological insight, eccentric characterization and a realism undercut by fantastic dreams are perfectly apparent in his longest novel, *The Family Moskat*; but with the exception of that novel and *The Manor*, Singer's novels and stories are haunted by a vivid literary rendering of those "freakish humans and fantastic beasts" he drew when he was a child. Though he is capable of creating a Poland with as much realism as Dostoevsky's Russia, he usually renders the psychological and moral nightmare that lies beneath the surface of the action and character in Dostoevsky's fiction in terms of human or demonic grotesques, more reminiscent of Hieronymus Bosch or Max Ernst than of the Russian novelist.

Though much has been written about the psychological effect of the grotesque in art and literature—the feeling of alienation caused by the combination of the terrifying and the ludicrous—few have discussed the particular techniques associated with the grotesque in fiction or attempted to see why a writer like Singer might be different from other writers we associate with the grotesque: Poe, Dickens, Kafka, and Mann. The very disparity of such a list might make one pause before trying to lump them together. To see what Singer does with his demonic world, it might be useful to take one of his less typical stories, a story called "Alone," set not in seventeenth-century Poland, where demons may be looked upon as part of the technique of historical realism, but in the present and at, of all places, Miami Beach. It might be thought that the "terrible grotesque," as Ruskin called that part of the form which involved a sense of spiritual horror, would hardly show its face in such a place, but Singer's Miami Beach is as haunted as his small Polish villages.

The narrator tells how the "Hidden Powers" or an "imp" must have heard his wish to be transported from the midst of the noisy hotel where he was staying to some hotel where he could be alone. Next morning the impossible happens: his luxurious hotel shuts down, and he yields to a certain miserliness to take an uncomfortable and ill-smelling room at $2.00 a day in a hotel presided over by a strange, hunchbacked Cuban girl. He lies in the sun, fantasizing over the possibility of a woman moving into the hotel and brooding over the eternal questions of God and existence. The isolation he sought suddenly becomes oppressing, and he decides to take a walk in a world which has become truly alien to him. The human beings around him assume the appearance of automatons while inanimate objects appear human. The coconuts seem to hang from the trees "like heavy testicles," the parrots scream with human voices, a recently caught fish testifies to the chthonic forces in the universe. With the coming of the hurricane everything seems to writhe with life, while he can only see himself in a "half-dissolved image" reflected in the mirror like the divided form in a cubist painting. At the height of the storm, the hunchbacked girl materializes first like a ghost, and then as some kind of monster: "I saw her sitting in the chair, a deformed creature in an overlarge nightgown, with a hunched back, disheveled hair, long hairy arms, and crooked legs, like a tubular monkey." Gradually she takes on the recognizable demonic form of vice. He had dreamed of himself as another Boas, of a Ruth coming to him, and instead found himself besieged by the "forces of darkness still in possession of their ancient powers":

> Something in me cried out: *Shaddai*, destroy Satan. Meanwhile, the thunder crashed, the seas roared and broke with watery laughter. The walls of my room turned scarlet. In the hellish glare the Cuban witch crouched low like an animal ready to seize its prey— mouth open, showing rotted teeth; matted hair, black on her arms and legs; and feet covered with carbuncles and bunions. Her nightgown had slipped down, and her wrinkled breasts sagged weightlessly. Only the snout and tail were missing.

Sensing that he is confronting the temptation of Lilith, the narrator refuses her advances, and the hurricane passes.

Most writers would not fail to have the morning light reveal the absurdity of the situation, and the narrator does awaken with a cold sore. But how are we to read the end which informs us that the woman was "a witch who had failed in her witchcraft, a silent partner of the demons surrounding me and of their cunning tricks"? There is much in this demon-haunted world of Singer which recalls Kafka; there is something of the same sense of detail, and surely the image of Ketev Mriri in "The Gentleman from Cracow" with his eye in his chest, his serpentine tail and revolving horn might remind one of Kafka's famous cockroach. But the fact is that the demonic in Kafka seems to open the abyss into the "estranged world" that

Wolfgang Kayser regarded as the key to the grotesque, while Singer's use of the grotesque confirms the reader in the sense of the reality of evil in the world. Indeed, in a larger sense, his demonic figures are symbols of the world and worldliness, and more often than not, Singer's treatment of the grotesque is put at the service of his moral vision. There are comic demons in Singer's stories but no moral ones, and this is why Singer's demons occasionally recall Bunyan rather than Poe, why he is often closer to the grotesque associated with Judaeo-Christian allegory than to the literary grotesque of nineteenth-century romanticism.

While there can be no question that Singer's techniques are literary in their origin and intent, what is perhaps most surprising is how thoroughly he has explored all facets of the grotesque. It is not surprising, however, that painters of the grotesque from Bosch to Grünwald, from Callot to Max Ernst, have chosen to paint a Temptation of St. Anthony. The painter of the grotesque selects the subject matter that will give him the best opportunity to display his talents and interests. As we shall see, there are times when Singer writes in the manner of such painters and appears to fit into Kayser's final definition of the grotesque as an "attempt to invoke and subdue the demonic aspects of the world," but at other times Singer can emphasize the ludicrous elements in the grotesque. There is little of John Ruskin's "noble grotesque" in the delightful autobiographical sketch, "Why the Geese Shrieked," in which a spiritual phenomenon accepted by Singer's father turns out to be amenable to the rationalistic explanations of his mother and reduced to the absurd and commonplace fact of wind making a noise as it rushes through the windpipes of some dead geese. In both this story and "Alone" there is a play with the demonic, but the one is comic and the other terrifying. Both are grotesque, but they are at opposite ends of the scale.

Probably the best example of Singer's pleasure in a purely decorative form of the grotesque is the story, "Cunegunde," which is little more than an exercise in that kind of horror which is usually associated with Hoffman and Poe and which has as its basic component the kind of pleasure in monsters, rats, snakes, and hairy plants that appears in such early forms of grotesque painting as Raphael's grotesque designs. The main character is a witch who appears in some of his other stories, and the tale exists almost entirely for its visual effects:

> Small and thick, she had a snout and eyes like a bull dog's, and a broad grisly chin. White hairs sprouted from the warts on her cheeks. The few strands of hair remaining on her head had twisted themselves into the semblance of a horn. Corns and bunions crowded her nailess toes. Cunegunde looked about her, sniffed the wind, frowned, "It's from the swamps," she murmured. "All pestilence and evil come from there."

Her mouth is "frog-like," she enjoys watching animals tortured, and she lives by devouring cats, dogs, and mice. She prays to devils and curses her enemies to death, and she, in turn, is finally beaten and stamped to death by a villager, dying surrounded by demons who rush at her with a "vengeful joy." It is a tribute to Singer's powers that he can transform such material into a powerful sketch. Singer's devils are a far cry from Dostoevsky's sophisticated, poor relation, Anatole France's witty companion or Shaw's bourgeois man of sensibility. They are real and vivid, even where their function is more or less to evoke horror for horror's sake.

Though the murder of Cunegunde seems to be little more than an added decoration, there are other stories that combine this kind of horror with the psychological terror achieved by tracing the thoughts of a murderer in the manner of Dostoevsky. The short story, "Under the Knife," takes us into the mind of the main character, Leib, as he plots his scheme to take revenge on his former wife, Rooshke. Here Singer has one of his rare exercises in the grotesque as Kayser's "play with the absurd." As Leib murders a whore in preparation for murdering Rooshke, he kills what seems to be an aged version of his former wife, and then, while being shaved by Rooshke's present husband, a barber, he learns that he has murdered the wrong woman, Rooshke's older sister. Within such a story, Singer heightens his effects with his customary use of caricature. The murderer has a missing eye, a pockmarked face, and a sunken mouth. The whore has only a few teeth left, and they are rusty and crooked; her eyes are yellow. The murdered sister is described as flabby and yellow-skinned with bulging eyes and false teeth. If, as Luckacs argues convincingly, Kafka creates a world of remarkable detail to make reality uncertain, Singer distorts the real world to suggest the evil nightmare that lies about us as an emanation of our fallen, sinful world. The Talmud would provide ample material to explain why Singer might want to create an image of the world which is at times horribly real and horribly ugly; what is important for our purposes are the skillful literary methods used to render that reality.

Singer never engages in the wildly comic distortions of reality that one finds in Gogol's "The Nose," with its remarkable ability to convince us of an absurd world in which noses may go about disguised as minor government officials. His approach is far more traditional, and for this reason Ruskin's rather old-fashioned approach to the grotesque is often more helpful than Kayser's psychological analysis. For Ruskin sees in what he calls the "noble grotesque" a full realization of sin and death, and this is almost always what Singer is about, whether in his supernatural or realistic stories. His rendering of such themes in his stories has sometimes been discussed in terms of the supernatural folk tale, and it is true that demons are often recognizable as those who appear in the traditional Chassidic tales. But the resemblance stops there. Singer's demons are described in such a way as to evoke the grotesque. The demon-haunted world evoked in those stories is narrated by demons, as in "The Last Demon," "The Unseen," "Zeidlus the Pope," "From the Diary of One Not Born," or "The Destruction of Kresheve." But it is not so much these occasionally comic demons with their geese-like feet or spider-like form that make Singer a writer of the grotesque so much as his ability to make them seem real through grotesque description. And once we acknowledge their reality, we become aware of the sense of sin inherent in the external world. Though one of Singer's holy men dies with the statement, "I want you to know that the material world has no substance," Singer will often fill that insubstantial world with demons. Often his characters have but to take one step in the direction of sin, a step allowed to man by the freedom of the will, to plunge into that nightmare world of grotesque evil, which finds its best artistic archetype in the free artistic play in the paintings of St. Anthony's temptation by Bosch and Callot.

In these paintings the figure of St. Anthony is barely to be seen, and by his inner concentration he is able to avoid giving attention to the monsters that surround him. Singer will often use such temptation themes, whether in a story set in the visitable past, like *The Magician of Lublin*, where the demonic is reduced to the symbolic by a realistic surface, or in a story like "The Mirror," where a demon is the narrator. A comparison between the two shows that the line between his realistic fiction and his tales of the supernatural is not at all so clear as

might at first be supposed. The demonic narrator of "The Mirror" tells how he tempts a beautiful and vain young wife in much the same way that Eve was tempted by the snake. The mirror, a rather familiar symbol in Singer's stories, is cracked, but the decoration of the frame, of "snakes, knobs, roses, and adders," is traditional grotesque ornament and prepares us for the entrance of the temptor. The demon catches her at the moment that she is admiring her breasts. He comes in a form similar to that in Dürer's engraving, *Knight, Death and Devil*: "there I was, black as tar, long as a shovel, with donkey's ears, a ram's horns, a frog's mouth, and a goat's beard. My eyes were all pupil." Zirel's reaction to his ugliness is not so much horror as amusement. The tone of the temptation is comic, and there is even something ludicrous about the little creatures who will devour her in Gehenna (hell), the worm and the mouse.

The demon convinces her with little difficulty that she will be happier living in Gehenna, and a few ritualistic transgressions lead her to a world of playful devils:

> Devils stood in a circle wiggling their tails. Two turtles were locked in embrace, and a male stone mounted a female stone. Shabriri and Bariri appeared. Shabriri had assumed the shape of a squire. He wore a pointed cap, a curved sword; he had the legs of a goose and a goat's beard. On his snout were glasses, and he spoke in a German dialect. Bariri was ape, parrot, rat, bat, all at once. . . . Zirel broke into lamentations. The sound roused Lilith from her sleep. She thrust aside Asmodeus' beard and put her head out of the cave, each of her hairs a curling snake. "What's wrong with the bitch?" she asked. "Why all the screaming?"
> "They're working on her."
> "Is that all? Add some salt."
> "And skim the fat."

The story ends with the demon's comment on the great fun that the demons have in torturing Zirel, and we withdraw from this scene of torture with the musings of the imp on the lack of promotion in Gehenna and on the eternal questions of the existence of God and a paradise.

Such a story may seem very different from *The Magician of Lublin*, which concerns a very real Europe just before the turn of the century, but it remains to be seen whether the grotesquerie of the real world is very different from Singer's vision of hell. The magician, Yasha Mazur, ends his life in the world by shutting himself off from that world in a closed cell. He finally comes to see that a "single step away from God plunged one into the deepest abyss." The moral is almost the reverse of what one finds in an existentialist novel like Camus' *The Stranger*; the hero flees from freedom and arrives at a spiritual state which is directly opposed to the atheistical freedom achieved by Camus' hero. Instead of creating a world alive with demons, Singer deliberately selects the world of the magician as illustrative of the grotesque in life. Yasha is surrounded by his animals, a non-human, chattering, whistling shrieking chorus, a living arabesque of snakes, peacocks, monkeys, and parrots. His helper is a Polish girl, who leaps to life in a few lines through Singer's capacity to create a grotesque character:

> She was in her late twenties but appeared younger; audiences thought her no more than eighteen. Slight, swarthy, flat-chested, barely skin-and-bones, it was hard to believe she was Elzbeta's child. Her eyes were grayish green, her nose snub, her lips full and pouting as if ready to be kissed, or like those of a child about to cry. Her neck was long and thin, her

hair ash-colored, the high cheekbones roseola-red. Her skin was pimply; at boarding school she had been nicknamed the Frog.

When her brother would threaten to harm Yasha, she would "rear back and hiss and spit like a cat at a dog." Indeed, her brother is described as having "nostrils wide as a bulldog's."

The relationship of this grotesque description to the demonic world of Singer is obvious enough, though its moral implications are not often so clearly delineated as they are in *The Magician of Lublin*, where the grotesque is almost invariably used to suggest a sense of evil—the evil inherent in the world and the evil inherent in freedom. Yasha is himself a figure capable of grotesque treatment; he is not only surrounded by grotesque humans and his menagerie, but he is also a magician, a person suspected of possessing supernatural powers. He can jump and dance on a tight rope, actions which Jennings maintains are most characteristic of the grotesque because they are "most calculated to call forth fear alongside amusement." One also thinks of Mann's grotesque and demonic Mario with his ability to control the will of his audience through hypnotism. For all *his* hypnotic power, Singer's Yasha is actually dependent upon and controlled by the people around him. And for all his seeming moral and intellectual emancipation, Yasha is torn by ethical doubts and actually believes that when his attempt at theft fails, he has been defeated by "a dybbuk, a satan."

After the death of Magda, who is carried off to the morgue like a dead chicken, Yasha confronts the real world in the grotesque figure of a giant, whom he sees in a cafe. Yasha himself is small, and the image of the giant's rotted teeth, pockmarked face and pimpled nose, of his eyes rolling in a kind of mad ecstasy, brings on a crisis of despair—a sense of nausea toward life and the world. Yasha reacts to this by destroying his freedom. From being a man in love with five women (one practically a child and another a prostitute), he becomes an ascetic. From being a man who dreamt of omnipotence, of flying and achieving wealth and fame, he becomes a recluse, whose fame is achieved, ironically enough, by withdrawing from the world he wished to conquer by his will.

The grotesque continues to function in Singer's fiction, then, whether the world he creates is overtly demonic or that of the realistic novel. One quality which the longer works permit, however, is a peculiar contrast between the beauty of nature and the grotesque world of human being and city. This satisfies the contrast between the normative and the monstrous that Santayana thought essential to grotesque art, but in *The Magician of Lublin* such a contrast has an essential moral function. As he rides along with Magda in his wagon, Yasha observes the beauty of the country in summer and is made to exclaim, "Oh, God Almighty, You are the magician, not I! . . . To bring out plants, flowers and colors from a bit of black soil." Though Yasha is brought to question any kind of spiritual significance in the operation of nature almost immediately after his exclamation, nature is always present to him as a reminder of the "Hidden Powers" that may lie behind appearances. In his cell at the end of the novel, he can only see that very essence of the grotesque, "death and lechery," in human nature, but in the world of snow flakes that fall on his window sill, in all of the physical nature, he finds the hand of God.

The narrative technique of *The Magician of Lublin* forces the reader to this conclusion. We see the world through Yasha, and through him we discover its meaning. The use of the grotesque buttresses the moral conclusions. Such a work is very different from Singer's most massive work so far, *The Family Moskat*, in which there is very little use of the

grotesque, and the distinction suggests that Singer only employs the grotesque when he wants particular effects. In *The Family Moskat* his emphasis is historical and external, the technique reminiscent of Tolstoy. The individual characters are seen as part of a larger pattern of change in the Jewish community of Poland from the beginning of the century to the Nazi invasion. Historical perspective is achieved by allowing brief flashes of insight into the minds of all the characters including anti-Semites. There is little comment on such momentary shifts in point of view and little to distinguish between the thoughts of the evil and those of Rabbi Dan as he regards the minds of those around him:

> This was the lower world, where Evil reigned. Where else would Satan build his fortress? . . . Even the Devil had his roots in the divine creation. The important thing was that man had free will. Every blemish would find its purification. Uncleanliness was in reality an illusion.

It is not at all clear that such thoughts represent any final solution. Singer is here attempting an objectivity reminiscent of the techniques of Flaubert or Chekhov.

There is much in *The Manor* that recalls the technique of *The Family Moskat*. Singer once more assumes a stance suggestive of a universal sympathy and sadness, but the attempt at objectivity is gone. *The Manor* uses historical change more as a metaphor than as a core of meaning. Historically the half-mad thief and murderer, the Polish aristocrat Lucian has his role in life with that of the pious, kindly Jew, Calman, but we are left without any question about where our sympathies should lie. And if Singer leaves us with a feeling like that at the end of *The Magician of Lublin*, that it may be possible for each man to create a small area in which he may achieve some kind of moral righteousness through self-enclosure, if we can see in Calman's "makeshift Synagogue" a mirror image of Yasha's cell, it is because in both works he has pictured the external world as ugly, demonic, and grotesque.

In *The Manor* Singer uses the grotesque in both scene and character. The servant, Getz, has "a nose shaped like a ram's horn"; Temerle has "round bird-like eyes"; Mrs. Frankel "was dark as a crow, had a beaked nose and black pouchy eyes rimmed with webs of wrinkles." Characters are quickly shaped into life by these animal grotesques or suddenly caricatured in their ugliness. Noses have warts and pimples; skin seems like swiss cheese. The death of the Rabbi of Marshinov is prolonged by a vision of Paradise followed by a sudden and horrible vision of Satan and his legions. Even in his novels of nineteenth-century Poland, then, the grotesque has become a kind of moral shorthand for describing a world gradually departing from an ancient ethical code.

But the fullest exploitation of the great themes of the grotesque—the demonic, the dance of death, the combination of the ludicrous and the terrible, strange contrasts of tall and short, youth and age, beauty and decay—may be found in his two novels of the seventeenth century, *The Slave* and, more particularly, *Satan in Goray*. Both occur in the period following the Chmelnicki massacre of 1648 and continue to the disastrous aftermath of the coming of the false messiah, Sabbatai Zvi, in 1666—a period of great suffering and disappointed expectation. In both novels Singer uses the grotesque to communicate his ethical preoccupations with the grotesque nature of evil and the possibility of finding some protection from this evil by a rigid conformity to the religious belief and virtue.

Taken into slavery after 1648, Jacob, the hero of *The Slave*, finds himself surrounded by the near-bestial peasantry:

These women were unclean, and had vermin in their clothes and elflocks in their hair; often their skins were covered with rashes and boils, they ate field rodents and the rotting carcasses of fowls. Some of them could scarcely speak Polish, grunted like animals, made signs with their hands, screamed and laughed madly. The village abounded in cripples, boys and girls with goiters, distended heads and disfiguring birth marks; there were also mutes, epileptics, freaks who had been born with six fingers on their hands or six toes on their feet.

Jacob's confrontation with nature in his labors among the mountains surrounding the village enables Singer to draw with even stronger lines than in *The Magician of Lublin* the contrast between the beauty of nature as an emanation of God and the grotesque humans who people the area. On the one hand we have descriptions of the sunrise that are worthy of Chekhov and which brings Jacob to believe that "God's wisdom was evident everywhere," and on the other the terrible facts of barbarism—the torture of Jewish children, rape, murder, and pillage. The only spiritual leader in the village is the decadent village priest, Dziobak, and Singer takes care of his moral state with a brief grotesque description: "He was a short, broad-shouldered man; he looked as if he had been sawed in half and glued and nailed together again. His eyes were green as gooseberries, his eyebrows dense as bushes. He had a thick nose with pimples and a receding chin."

Jacob eventually accompanies a howling mob of these grotesques in a kind of *Walpurgisnacht* revel during which he undergoes feelings similar to those of Coleridge's Ancient Mariner. He follows them, holding his nose against the smell of putrefaction, horrified by the sounds of horses, dogs, and donkeys emitted by the men, and wondering about their humanity. At first he finds some consolation in the belief that such a race can only be cured by complete extermination and that God was justified in destroying entire nations. But he shrinks from violence. He almost kills a "pock-marked fellow with a face like a turnip grater," and is horrified by his act. Then he sees a "monstrous square-headed girl with a goiter on her neck . . . hands, which were as long as a monkey's and as broad as a man's, their nails rotted away," a girl whose feet are full of boils and have a demonic goose-like quality, and he feels an overwhelming compassion. He realizes that his "mooncalf" actually understands the horror of her condition, and from his confidence that he had solved his dilemma about Moses's destruction of so many people, Jacob is once more turned back upon his prayers and his faith.

Though *Satan in Goray* treats the same time and many of the same problems as appear in *The Slave*, Singer takes the opportunity to treat the reaction of an entire Polish *shtetl* to the tempting freedoms offered by the followers of the false messiah, Sabbatai Zvi. Jacob also succumbs to the new ideas offered by the cult, but there is nothing surprising in Jacob's response to the liberalizing aspects of the sect. We know how he thinks, and we see the world through his eyes. In *Satan in Goray* the canvas is larger and the shifting point of view allows Singer a wider variety of psychological insights. The novel begins with a description of Goray after the great massacre. Dogs tear at the limbs of dismembered carcasses. The town is a spirtual and visual wilderness. Singer provides a brief historical synopsis of the rebuilding of the town under Rabbi Benish Ashkenazi to the year 1666, the great year of wonders in all of Europe, the year which many predicted would bring the end of the world and the judgment. The world which Singer conjures up for us is one in which the miraculous is part of everybody's expecta-

tions, though the use of the grotesque makes us suspicious about the final results. The first news of miracles is brought by a woman wrinkled "like a cabbage head" with a "ram's horn nose," and the leading member of the town defending Sabbatai Zvi as the true messiah is the crippled Mordecai Joseph, who dances with his crutch at the news.

But if the grotesque is used in association with the moral evil inherent in the new cult, the psychological heightening in dealing with life in Goray is of a kind that Singer usually reserves for favorite, Dostoevskian scenes of theft and violence. Rechele, the daughter of the man who used to be the town's richest citizen, may indeed be haunted by demons, but Singer describes with meticulous care the kind of psychological background that would make her capable not merely of believing in a demonic world but in being possessed by it. As a child she is persuaded by her grandmother that she is surrounded by demons and that the house is haunted. This lesson is reinforced by the outpouring of blood in the home of her uncle, Reb Aeydel Ber, a ritual slaughterer. Left alone in this house after the death of her grandmother, she sees or dreams of a nightmare world out of Hieronymus Bosch—a world in which the candle box may do a jig while the pots float about the room.

We can understand the psychological motivation which could produce visions in Rechele, but Singer gives concrete reality to these visions by his narrative method. The use of indirect discourse gives us Rechele's inner thoughts, while the third person narrative provides the illusion of objectivity. Sexually frustrated by her marriage to the impotent disciple of Sabbatai Zvi, Reb Itche Mates, Rechele begins to hear voices, and by a process long ago described by Swift in his *Tale of a Tub*, her suppressed sexuality finds an outlet in enthusiasm and prophecy. Her announcement that Reb Gedaliya is worthy "like Elijah, to behold the face of the Divine Presence" leads to the ritual slaughterer's entire domination of the town in the name of the new sect. He begins to reverse all the ethical teachings of the Talmud. He urges all the women to commit adultery, sleeps with Rechele, works cures by witchcraft, and finally plunges the entire town into evil. Singer takes the opportunity of some of his finest evocations of the demonic and the grotesque:

> A copper cross hung on his breast, under the fringed vest, and an image lay in his breast pocket. At night Lilith and her attendants Namah and Machlot visited him, and they consorted together. Sabbath eve, dressing in scarlet garments and a fez, like a Muslim he accompanied his disciples to the ruins of the old castle near Goray. There Samael presented himself to them, and they all prostrated themselves together before a clay image. Then they danced in a ring with torches in their hands. Rabbi Joseph de la Reina, the traitor, descended from Mount Seir to join them in the shape of a black dog. Afterward, as the legend went, they would enter the castle vaults and feast on flesh from the living—rending live fowl with their hands, and devouring the meat with the blood. When they had finished feasting, fathers would know their daughters, brothers their sisters, sons their mothers.

The plunge into freedom is invariably a plunge into the demonic. The passage builds dramatically from the traditional grotesquerie of the witch's sabbath to complete moral degradation.

And while Gedaliya leads the town into sin, Rechele's holy voices are gradually replaced by an image of the profane which takes concrete demonic form. Eventually she dreams that she is pursued and raped by the devil:

> A bearded figure pursued her, hairy and naked, wet and stinking, with long monkey hands and open maw. Catching her at last, he carried her as light as a feather (for she had all at once become weightless) and flew with her over dusk-filled streets and tall buildings, through a skyless space full of mounds, and pits, and pollution. At their back ran hosts of airy things, half-devil and half-man, pointing at them, pursuing them. The Thing swept her over steep rooftops, gutters, and chimneys, huge and mildewy; there was no escape. It was stifling and the Thing pressed her to him, leaned against her. The Thing was a male; he wanted to ravish her. He squeezed her breasts; he tried to force her legs apart with his bony knees. He spoke to her rapidly, hoarsely, breathing hard, imploring and demanding. . . . He threw her down and entered her. She cried a bitter cry, but there was no sound, and she started from sleep. With perfect clarity she saw that the dark house was crowded with evil things, insane beings running hither and thither, hopping as on hot coals, quivery and swaying, as though they were all kneading a great trough of dough.

The psychological power of terror implicit in waking from a nightmare to discover or believe for an instant that the dream is no dream at all is rendered brilliantly by Singer, but Rechele's experience is neither madness nor dream. Her vision has the feeling of concrete reality as well as a certain nightmarish, comic illogicality that makes it particularly grotesque. Rechele is frequently found to break into laughter.

Before the final chapter, Singer allows us to experience with Gedaliya the discovery of Rechele's possession, and we are not left to think that the blowing out of candles and the voice of Satan is merely a quirk of Rechele's tormented psyche. The treatment of the exorcism of the dybbuk, handled in terms of period demonology, confirms us in our belief that such a demon may indeed exist, though the fact that Reb Mordecai Joseph, who drove the holy Rabbi Benish out of Goray, is chosen as the hero of the "objective" account of the expulsion of the demon from the body of Rechele, may lead one to suspect a certain irony behind this report as it is seen within the total complex of events.

Satan in Goray is obviously so far superior to a story like "Cunegunde" that one might justly regard it of a different literary species. In the one, the grotesque takes on genuine moral significance, in the other it is little more than a kind of artistic play. But it is the impulse toward this particular kind of artistic decoration that lies behind some of Singer's finest efforts. A story like "Caricature" has no profound moral theme, but the grotesque portraits have a value of their own. Singer shows his protagonist, Dr. Margolis, looking with some distaste on his aging wife:

> She had grown smaller and smaller and puffier and puffier; her stomach stuck out like a Man's. Since she had practically no neck, her large square head just sat on her shoulders. Her nose was flat and her thick lips and jowls made him think of a bulldog. Her scalp showed through her hair. Worst of all she had begun to grow a beard, and though she had tried to cut, shave, singe off the hair, it had merely grown denser. The skin of her face was covered with roots from each of which sprouted a few prickly shoots of a nondescript color. Rouge peeled from the creases of

her face like plaster. Her eyes stared with a masculine severity.

This kind of sketch is what makes Singer such a magnificent writer of short stories, and it is within the short story that he exploits the full range of the grotesque: themes of disproportionate size ("Big and Little"), premature aging ("Esther Kreindel the Second" and "Three Tales"), confusion of sexes ("Yentl the Yeshiva Boy"). Sometimes Singer uses the grotesque for purely comic effect as in "Taibele and Her Demon," in which the teacher's helper, Alchonon, pretends to be a demon in order to have an affair with a widow, Taibele.

In his longer stories and novels, Singer has used the grotesque to express larger themes and given it a more significant function. Occasionally, this function is not very clear. In *The Slave*, for example, an old, crippled woman with a wart on her nose and hair on her chin proves to be completely saintly and teaches Jacob a lesson about the illusory nature of appearances. This is very different from the way the grotesque is used in *The Magician of Lublin*, but then Jacob is a man striving for an answer to his problems and often arriving at answers which are original and, perhaps, only suitable for himself. It should warn us that Singer is a novelist and short story writer, not a philosopher, and that the grotesque is a literary tool which he uses at his best, to lend significance to the world of his fiction and even in his slighter efforts, to provide a kind of excitement that few modern writers can match.

ISAAC BASHEVIS SINGER
Interview by Laurie Colwin

New York Times Book Review, July 23, 1978, pp. 1, 23–24

Q. Readers of all ages, nations, backgrounds and creeds read and love your books. Can you explain why you are so popular? What do you think are the elements that make it possible for everyone to appreciate what you write?

A. First of all, I don't think I'm so popular. All I would say is that, in the languages into which I am translated, there are people who are interested. A writer, like a woman, never knows why people like him or why people dislike him. We never know.

Q. Why don't you take a guess?

A. The guess is that there is always a kinship between souls. Souls are either close to one another or far from one another. There are people who, when they read me, they like what I say. And there's nothing else I can tell you. I wouldn't say Jewish people, because I'm translated into Japanese. The Japanese translate everything I write, immediately. They even publish me in English, with Japanese notes. And how could I explain why some Japanese in Yokohama will like to read what I write? Just as I would enjoy a Japanese writer, a Japanese man may enjoy a Yiddish writer.

Q. What sort of things would draw you to a Japanese writer?

A. I will tell you. I know nothing about the Japanese— really nothing . And, let's say, I read two Japanese books. I will say one is a good book and one is a bad book. How do I know, since I haven't lived in Japan? It seems that to enjoy a book you don't really have to go there and to know the land and the people, because human beings, although they are different, also have many things in common. And through this you get a notion which writer says the truth and which writer is fabricating.

How does it come that we read the Bible, which was written, parts of it, 3,000 years ago, and we understand the story of Joseph and the other stories? It seems that we are very much today basically as we were 3,000 years ago, and we are able to understand what another human being does.

I even suspect that if books are written on another planet somewhere in the universe, and if someone would make a translation, a reader would understand what is good and what is bad. But this is already too farfetched. Unless, one day, you would bring me a translation from the planet Mars, then we will see.

Q. You must have some notion of what you're doing that is this attractive. There must be some quality. You have been mentioned for a Nobel Prize.

A. Are you trying to convince me that I'm a big shot?

Q. You are a big shot. Now, tell me why you are.

A. I will tell you, Laurie: When I sit down to write a story, I'm not saying to myself I'm going to write a Jewish story. Just like when a Frenchman builds a house in France. He doesn't say he's going to build a French house. He's going to build a house for his wife and children, a convenient house. Since it's built in France, it comes out French.

When I sit down to write a story, I will write the kind of stories which I write. It's true that since I know the Jewish people best and since I know the Yiddish language best, so my heroes, the people of my stories, are always Jewish and speak Yiddish. I am at home with these people. But just the same, I'm not just writing about them because they speak Yiddish and are Jewish. I'm interested in the same things you are interested in and the Japanese are interested in: in love, and in treachery and in hopes and in disappointments.

Q. Do you ever feel that, like a photographer, you're preserving the last part of a vanished culture?

A. People tell me this, and while they tell me this I have a moment of feeling, yes, it is so. But I never sit down to write with this idea. I wouldn't be a writer if I would sit down to preserve the Yiddish language, or life in Poland, or make a better world or bring peace. I don't have all these illusions.

I know that my story will not do anything else but entertain a reader for half an hour. And this is enough for me. The word entertainment has become, lately, a very bad word. I call it the 13-letter word which writers are afraid to use, because the word entertainer means for them a cheap grade of writing. But it isn't so.

The great writers of the 19th century—Tolstoy and Dostoyevsky and Gogol and Dickens—were great entertainers. And Balzac. They wrote a novel or a story so that there was some suspense in it. When you began to read it, you wanted to know what would happen next. And they also published, some of them, their stories in magazines and in newspapers, where it was written, "It continues next week." And the reader had to be interested to read the continuation.

Q. A serial.

A. A serial, yes.

Q. You still do that in *The Forward*, don't you?

A. I still do it in *The Forward*, and I know whatever I write is immediately read, I would say, at least by 15,000 or 20,000 people, because we still have about 40,000 readers. And, since *The Forward* is a small newspaper, those who read it read everything in it, even the advertisements.

So I'm still connected with the reader. And these readers also don't read my story because they are Jewish, because Jewishness is not something new for them. They have been Jews all their life. They judge a writer from the point of view: Is he interesting or not interesting? Also, although some of them are ignorant people and primitive people, they know that a writer's not going to redeem the world, as some of the young writers think.

So, in other words, I'm before everything else a writer, not just Jewish, and I'm not doing it with some illusion that I'm going to do great things. I just feel that I have to tell a story.

I have said this a few times before, and I can repeat it: I need three conditions to write a story. One condition is I have to have a plot. I don't believe that you can write a story without a story—in other words, just sit down and write a slice of life hoping against hope that it will come out right. It happens once in a while, but most of the time if you don't have a plan there won't be a story.

The second condition is: I must have a desire to write the story—or a passion to write it. I must get up with an appetite to do this story.

And the third condition: I must have the illusion that I am the only one who can write such a story. Since I know the Yiddish writers, more or less, so I know what they could do and what I can do.

If I have these three conditions, I will sit down and do the work without worrying too much whether it is good for the Jews or bad for the Jews; whether it will redeem humanity immediately or whether it may take a few weeks until humanity is redeemed. I do the story, and I leave the rest to the reader, or to the critic—let them draw their own conclusions. Sometimes they find in it something.

Once I wrote a book called *The Magician of Lublin*. The hero repents at the end and hardens himself against the temptation of running after women. So once a psychoanalyst called me up, and he said: "I was delighted to see how you made your hero go back to his mother's womb." This had never occurred to me. But then I said to myself: He is just as good a reader as anybody else, and if he sees this it's just as good.

In other words, once you have written a story, it's not your private property anymore. And if someone wants to find in it sociological truths or psychological truths, he's entitled to do it. In my case, all I want is to write a story.

Q. How do you go about making up a plot? Do you know the steps your mind takes?

A. No, I'm not making up a plot. The plot comes to me.

Q. How does it come to you? Are you walking around the street? Are you sitting looking out the window?

A. No. No. No.

Q. Does it just come like a flash?

A. I would say: if something happens to me. And things happen—I'm alive, I am with people, I also have memory. I've had affairs in my life and women and all kinds of things. And I think about these things. Suddenly, I say, here is a story. In other words, I don't wake up in the morning and go out into the street to make a plot. This never happens.

Q. So, in other words, your mind is like a soup kettle. And you keep stirring it. And suddenly the ladle comes up and there's carrots and cabbage.

A. Listen, we are doing the same thing. We think about things. You think about what happened to you, and I think about what happened to me. All kinds of things. And suddenly here is a plot for a story.

Q. What kind of things do you like to read?

A. I love to read a story with real suspense. I mean, not that there should be only suspense—I don't read detective stories—but if it has a literary value and it has suspense. I often go back to the writers of the 19th century. I'm ashamed to tell you.

Q. Why?

A. Why should I read old books?

Q. Everybody does that. What interests you? Love? Treachery? Sex?

A. Yes. Love and sex more than anything else.

Q. Treachery is second?

A. If there's love, there is treachery. And then, also, crime interests me. When I was a boy of 12 years old *Crime and Punishment* came out in Yiddish, and I began to read it. A large book—in Yiddish it's twice as large as in English—and I was fascinated. I couldn't put it away. And I must tell you, a boy of 12 years there in Warsaw, I knew nothing of the world except what I studied in school, but I suddenly felt: Here is a great work. I remember that in one case, when Raskolnikov speaks to the district attorney, there is a moment when Raskolnikov gets up as if he would be about to leave and then he sits down immediately. And I said to myself, this is wonderful. As if he would say, "I'm finished with the whole business," and then the sitting down—it pleased me so much.

So, if a boy of 12 years, in Warsaw, who had no experience in life could understand, more or less, *Crime and Punishment*, there is really no reason why the Japanese and the Turks should not understand what you write or what I write. So, actually, the writer should never be afraid that he is not going to be understood. Those writers who are afraid of that really underestimate the reader. The reader is—I assume so—an intelligent person; he knows about life and love and crime and everything, just as much as I and in some cases much more than I. So, I really don't worry that if I'm going to be translated one day into Chinese that no one will understand what a Hassid is and what a rabbi is. They will understand it very well. If they have learned in the last few years how to build machine guns and airplanes, they will also understand what I have to say. What I worry about is if what I do is good enough to be translated or to be read, and I work accordingly.

Q. Do you think that having that stable *Forward* audience—and you're probably the last writer who has that kind of audience—makes a difference to a writer?

A. I think it has good sides and bad sides. The bad sides are that the writer sometimes is bound to repeat himself. Because since I write, so to say, from week to week and from day to day, I don't see the manuscript before my eyes, and sometimes I begin a novel without really knowing how it will end. So, I'm bound to repeat myself and to make mistakes.

The good sides are that you don't speak to the wall, you speak to a reader. My readers—since I write mostly about Warsaw and Poland—also come from Warsaw and Poland. They have lived there. Woe is to me if I make a mistake. I once made a mistake and said that the prayer for the dead was recited in the synagogue on the second day of Rosh ha-Shanah. It was a mistake because there is no such thing. It's every holiday, yes, but not on Rosh ha-Shanah. So I got hundreds of letters. The letter carrier couldn't believe what's going on here. And every letter began with the same thing: How could a man like you make such a mistake?

Also, now, if I would make a mistake about a street, I would get these letters. So, in other words, I cannot be a solipsist like some of these writers who really feel that no one exists except themselves. I know that the world . . . exists. It's not completely a dream. So this is a good thing.

Of course, whatever I write, there is always opposition if I write about sex. I remember that once I wrote a story—this is many years ago—and in the story there was a little bit of sex, and the sex was expressed in the words: " . . . and she did his will." That's all I said. So there came an angry letter from a man saying: "How do you dare to say such things? We have daughters, and these daughters read this sometimes."

But it's a good thing to have an audience before yourself, just like an actor who is playing and the audience is there.

Q. You once said that an army of Kafkas was killing literature. What do you mean by that?

A. Yes, yes, I will tell you. Avant-garde writers like Kafka and Joyce say to themselves: I don't care for the reader or for the critic or for anybody. I am going to say what I want. I have to please myself and nobody else.

I assume this is what they say. I wasn't there to listen to them, but this is more or less how they think. To me, Kafka was made of the material of genius. But just the same, he did things which a writer who writes for people, who has the audience before his eyes, would not do.

Let's say, if a writer imitates Tolstoy—and I think that Solzhenitsyn tries to write like Tolstoy—there is no misfortune, because, if he has talent and if he tries to write like Tolstoy and even if it doesn't come out 100 percent, it's still good. But if you try to imitate Kafka, Joyce, and you don't have their talent, it will come out completely bad. Because only a great talent can afford to say: I'm speaking only to myself.

Q. If you were a Ph.D. candidate and you had to do your thesis on Isaac Singer, what would your topic be?

A. I would do what all the students do. I would read the author's books and I would try to find what they call the central idea.

Q. What would the central idea be in the work of I. B. Singer?

A. I would say that the idea behind everything is that one should not belittle any emotion. The philosophers all belittled the emotions—especially a man like Spinoza, who considered all emotions as evil. I have convinced myself that everything that goes through our minds, no matter how trivial, no matter how silly, and no matter how terrible sometimes, is of some value. In other words, take away the emotions from a human being, and no matter how much logic he will have, he will be a vegetable. The emotions and man are the same. And I'm interested, especially, in the emotions that become passions.

Spinoza says in his *Ethics* that everything can become a passion, and I know that this is true. There is nothing that cannot become a passion. Especially if they are connected either with sex or with the supernatural—and I would say for me sex and the supernatural go very much together. I feel that the desire of one human being for another is not only a desire of the body but also of the soul. The two—a man and woman, or two men, or two women—when they embrace and they say they cannot live one without the other, and they fall one upon the other with a madness, that this is not just an act of the flesh, it's more than the flesh.

Q. So, in other words, your topic would be emotion and excess in the works of Isaac Bashevis Singer?

A. Yes, and if I would be the dean I would give you the Ph.D. right this minute.

LEON WIESELTIER
"The Revenge of I. B. Singer"

New York Review of Books, December 7, 1978, pp. 6–7

I must only imagine a door, a good old door, like the one in the kitchen of my childhood, with an iron handle and a bolt. There is no walled-in room that could not be opened by such a door, provided one were strong enough to suggest that such a door exists." These words evoke the stifled, timorous, obituary spirit of Isaac Bashevis Singer's new novel, *Shosha*. The words are not Singer's, however; they were written by Bruno Schulz, a writer he admires, in the doomed town of Drogobych, Poland, in 1937. By that time Singer, who, unlike Schulz, "did not have the privilege of going through the Hitler holocaust," was safe in Manhattan, trying to recapture in fiction the universe he had escaped. *Shosha* is another among these mordant retrievals.

It is a stunted novel about stunted lives. The saturnine Aaron Greidinger, a playwright, is chasing wisdom and girls in a Warsaw filled with despair. Hitler has taken hold of Germany and advances unopposed toward Poland. The revolution in Russia has deceived, too much blood has been spilled. Dreams of Palestine seem quixotic, and would anyway abolish the life from which the dreams sprang. And the Jews of Warsaw are genteel and indifferent to spiritual experiment. From all this Greidinger takes refuge in his work. He frequents the Writers' Club, where other Yiddish writers, the dauntless and the defeated, also ache for greatness, and wrestle with metaphysics over cognac, and with Trotsky's revolutionary promise over chess. At the Writer's Club the vexed Greidinger encounters Dr. Morris Feitelzohn, who wears English suits and is penniless, and who peddles Vaihinger and the Kabbala, Schopenhauer and the *rebbe* of Kotzk.

Greidinger—clearly Singer himself—is in the throes of a great and somewhat conventional revolt. He cannot locate God. Raised on the Talmud, he turns early to Spinoza. Spinoza will sponsor his worldliness, and even sanctify it. Worldliness for Greidinger means not politics—he has been forever disabused of the possibility of redemption—but only women. His cupidity is insatiable, virtually ideological. And so we are again treated to Singer's stable of randy Jewish women, and again to his customary musings on the spiritual rewards of sex. There is Celia, a melancholy older woman whose enlightened (and manifestly homosexual) husband invites Greidinger to find ecstasy in his wife's bed; Dora, a Communist with prodigious breasts; Tekin, the devoted rustic who cleans Greidinger's flat; and, most momentously, Betty, a lovely actress from America for whom Greidinger is commissioned to write a play. The play, about a woman rabbi and her Hasidic lovers, along with whores and fiddlers and dybbuks, eventually fails, but not before Greidinger seduces its leading lady.

All this Greidinger renounces to marry Shosha, whom he loved as a child. But Shosha—the only really intriguing figure in his story—has miraculously remained a child: she has "neither grown nor aged." She wears pigtails and eats candy and has never been with a man. And for this "sweet soul" Greidinger will not follow Betty to a haven in America. With Shosha, on the same Krochmalna Street where they both grew up, he chooses instead to await the ruin that impends for them all.

> I had made a decision and knew that I would keep it, but why I had made it was something I couldn't explain to myself or to anyone else. . . . This is precisely the case with those who commit suicide, I said to myself. They find a hook in the ceiling, fashion a noose, place a chair underneath and until the final second they don't know why they are doing it.

But it is not the imp of the perverse that has seized Greidinger. It is rather that in the chaste and unaccountably arrested Shosha he has come upon a way, in the eleventh hour, to thwart time. Shosha will restore for him the world she still inhabits—the world that still tolerated hope, in which the

search for truth had not yet degenerated into an ideological bazaar, in which there were no Nazis. Their union is mad, but it is Greidinger's sole avenue through despair, his only triumph. And Singer's as well: implausible Shosha is the genuinely affecting image of an immobility as delusive as it is fearless. Singer writes beautifully of the wedding night, tenderly mingling love with fatality:

> "Arele, I'm afraid."
> "I'm afraid too, but Hitler won't come tonight. Move over to me. So. . . . "
> "Oy, Arele, it is good to be with you. What will we do when the Nazis come?"
> "We will die."
> "Together?"
> "Yes, Shoshele."
> "The Messiah isn't coming?"
> "Not so quickly."
> "Arele, I just remembered a song."

Soon Hitler's troops are upon them. Greidinger and his frail bride leave Warsaw on foot for Bialystok. Shosha dies "on the way, like Mother Rachel." Greidinger makes it eventually to New York and at last achieves fame as a Yiddish writer of stories of the supernatural.

Singer the novelist has always seemed much less accomplished than Singer the writer of short stories. The novels have been shapeless, even slovenly, and *Shosha* is no exception. Not the stories, however. These are uncommonly vigorous and carefully fashioned. It is especially good, therefore, to have *Gimpel the Fool* back in print, because it contains Singer's best work, his boldest and liveliest inventions. And it belies at once his familiar disclaimer that he is only a storyteller. He is not. His tales are thick with speculation and prejudice, and both are damaging.

Singer's fiction sets out always from the experience of suffering. Theodicy is its plot. His people seek reasons for their pain, and—save for the somewhat inscrutable Rabbi Bainish of Komarov in "Joy"—they usually do not find them. What they find instead are ideas, a vast profusion of dangerous doctrines to do the work of the faith that has gone unrewarded. Singer's people are what they believe, or do not believe. They do not all, of course, possess the amazing resilience of Gimpel, who is so credulous he is sublime. Many turn dramatically to heresy, which they do not always quite understand.

There is, indeed, a great measure of human truth in the ordinariness of these adopted heterodoxies, in the poignant banality of Greidinger's grasp of Spinoza, in the awkwardness of Rabbi Bainish's inchoate nihilism. There is, unfortunately, also a certain philosophical insouciance about them. Singer plays too fast and too carelessly with his warring world views. There are too many imponderables, too much sheer, lingering mystery. All this obsessive heaven-storming comes to seem mannered, and even mischievous: it can seem as exercised by the slaughter of chickens as it is by the slaughter of Jews. What delights Singer most is the very spectacle of the struggle; he is sardonically amused by the inadequacy of his addled Jews' resources. He hobbles the devout and then laughs.

He discredits even their defections. For Singer's wronged believers demand not illumination so much as license. They yearn to sin. And it is in his rapt fascination with sin that Singer's sly modernism is disclosed. The sacrilegious practices of the Sabbatians and the abominations of the eighteenth-century false messiah Jacob Frank join here with the Satanism of Baudelaire and the criminality of Dostoevsky to produce a central vision of numinous vice; it is as if inspired depravity is the only religious expression that remains. And the most numinous vice, the outrage that will best engage the angry, hidden God, is fornication. "Wisdom extends no further than the first heaven," an apprentice devil advises the nubile Zirel in "The Mirror." "From there on everything is lust." Singer's eroticism is a matter of principle and it is vivid and inexhaustible. He revels in his voluptuaries in their caftans, taunting the Lord of the Universe in the fleshpots of Galicia.

Writing ardently in celebration of Singer years ago, the poet Ted Hughes—whose own bleak, nocturnal imagination was likely to be drawn to Singer's—observed that "Singer implies . . . that there is an occult equivalence between a man's relationship to the women in his life and his relationship to his own soul—and so to God." There is, to be sure, an ancient tradition of such an "occult equivalence" within Judaism. It is with that largely esoteric tradition, elaborated most extravagantly by the Kabbalists, that Singer often associates himself. "For me, religion and love, even sex, are attributes of the same substance, as they were for the Kabbalists of all generations." But his passion is not theirs; it is in truth a much more paltry and capricious passion than Hughes observed, for the simple reason that Singer seems to detest women. There is a shocking passage in one of his memoirs in which he admiringly recalls the impact on his thinking of Otto Weininger, the Austrian convert who wrote fanatically in praise of male superiority. And so, not surprisingly, the women in his narratives are always less than characters; they are only mere sites of iniquity—no more than creation's most savory forms of pork. It is not a mysticism of love that Singer expounds, but rather a kind of vulgar theological prurience. He has mistaken manhood for grace.

Misogyny is not all that confounds Singer's grand vision of salvation by sin. In *A Young Man in Search of Love*, a rather casual chronicle of the obstreperous desires of his youth, Singer alludes to "the great adventures inherent in Jewish history— the false Messiahs, the expulsions, the forcible conversions, the Emancipation, and the assimilations. . . ." Illusion, disorder, transgression, apostasy: in these are to be found the florid romances of Jewish experience. Not a word, however, of what was surely the most unlikely and daring Jewish adventure of all—the adventure of a life in *halakha*, of allegiance to the law in even the direst adversity, of individuals and communities fired by tradition's discipline and willing to remain steadfast unto death. Of those Jews who would seek release from the rabbinical way Singer writes with asperity, even scorn. He is not alive to their special strength. They appear in his works caricatured, as blind, bumbling, craven votaries of a bizarre and frozen culture. And it is this proud and bilious indifference to the character of piety that further vitiates Singer's thirst for its collapse. A comparison is instructive, and not far afield. *Yoshe Kalb*, by his brother I. J. Singer, is a novel also about the mutiny of the passions at the courts of the *rebbes*, but the elder Singer, who died in 1944, is throughout as attentive to the mentality of the orthodox as he is to that of the miscreants. Hence the strange authority, the almost eerie coolness of his account. Its author appears to have unburdened himself not only of faith, but also of its opposite.

Not so Isaac Bashevis Singer. His retrievals are, in the end, no solace at all, because he still chafes as he did on Krochmalna Street. He cannot forgive Jewish tradition its fetters, but neither can he entirely free himself of them. And he has taken an extraordinary vengeance in literature: a joyless, acid portrait of Jewish life surrendered to demons and doubt, a grotesque congeries of the uncanny and the perverse. Singer moves straight from the disappointments of reason to the raising of tables. His comedy is often brilliant, and just as often

cruel. And it agrees nicely with that facile infatuation with the demonic that currently prevails in American culture, not least among American Jews.

Singer's is certainly among the richest and most enchanting seditious talents in Jewish literature. "One must belong to a tradition," said Adorno, "to hate it properly." Singer still belongs and so his hatred is proper. His hatred is proper and so he still belongs. It is a supremely Jewish irony—as is the award of the Nobel Prize to a Yiddish writer most of whose audience no longer exists. It will be thrilling to hear Yiddish for the first time at Stockholm. And more saddening still, because it will be the last time.

HAROLD BLOOM
"Isaac Bashevis Singer's Jeremiad"
New York Times Book Review, September 25, 1983, pp. 3, 26–27

*T*he *Penitent* is a translation of a short novel called *Der Baal Tshuve* in Yiddish. Perhaps this title should have been translated as "The Master of Turning," which would have been more literal and also a proper tribute to its distinguished author, who is a master of metamorphoses. But perhaps this book, first published in 1974, ought not to have been translated at all. It is a very unplesant work, without any redeeming esthetic merit or humane quality. Singer's best book, retroactively worthy of the Nobel Prize he won in 1978, was his *Collected Stories*, published last year. *The Penitent*, a failed attempt at a Swiftian diatribe against the contemporary world, is his worst book, and yet it does expose limitations that are not Singer's alone, and so it sadly defines much that is uneasy and probably insoluble in the dilemmas of Jewish culture at this time.

Singer's strength in *The Collected Stories* is in a rare exuberance of narrative invention, rather than in the creation of character, but *The Penitent* has almost no story and invests itself in the character of its monologuist, Joseph Shapiro. Shapiro is introduced by what has become a prevalent formula in Singer's American stories: The famous writer is approached by an admiring reader, this time at the Western, or Wailing, Wall in Jerusalem: "The Almighty conducted business here on a twenty-four-hour basis." Shapiro is the master of penitence, having returned to orthodoxy after an archetypal Jewish wandering, from Poland in 1939 through Stalin's wartime Russia on to America, success in real estate, failure in marriage, disaster in a love affair, despair over all fashionable ideologies, and subsequent flight to vegetarianism and to Meah Shearim, the neighborhood of extreme orthodoxy in Jerusalem.

Unfortunately, the reader can develop no interest in Shapiro because the author develops none. Shapiro is only a voice: negative, intense, apprehensive, fascinated by lust yet filled with revulsion toward it. The voice is indistinguishable from Singer's own, and there is no way to read this book except as Singer's tirade. A tirade is in itself a perfectly respectable literary form; there are many splendid modern examples, ranging from the grand harangue of Shaw's mouthpiece, Don Juan, in *Man and Superman*, to the screeds of Nathanael West's surrogate, Shrike, in *Miss Lonelyhearts*. Singer is to be faulted not for his chosen genre but for his execution, his jeremiad has no surprises, no wit and little variety. Nevertheless, it does have force, though this force is hardly its own. It is a force internalized by many among us. Jew and gentile alike, and can be called the Moral Majoritarian hovering in each of us, however enlightened we pride ourselves on being.

Here is a typical passage from Shapiro's diatribes: "There's no such thing as morality without religion. If you don't serve one idol, you serve another. Of all the lies in the world, humanism is the biggest. Humanism doesn't serve one idol but all the idols. They were all humanists: Mussolini, Hitler, Stalin." The last of those sentences crosses over from extravagance into nonsense but is consonant with everything else asserted by Singer/Shapiro. Merely to list some of the moral reflections to which we are treated may suggest that this book is an involuntary satire upon itself. Denounced throughout are all women except those who are Orthodox Jewish; all "Jewish Reds" (rather widely defined); liberalism; the American judicial system; American newspapers; "acclaim of stupid books, dirty plays and films"; professors of history. To list more would be redundant. Sometimes, the uncanny effect is that Singer seems to be parodying come of Saul Below's minor characters.

Here is Singer/Shapiro in the kind of monologue that in Below would be deliberately satirical: "Believe me, a pure, decent woman can provide a man more physical satisfaction than all the refined whores in the world. When a man sleeps with a modern woman, he actually gets into bed with all her lovers. That's why there are so many homosexuals today, because modern man is sleeping spiritually with countless other men. He constantly wants to excel in sex because he knows that his partner is comparing him to the others. This is also the cause of impotence, from which so many suffer."

Even more parodistic are the musings in defense of creationism, worthy to be taken up by the Rev. Jerry Falwell (himself one of the demonstrations that reality in America surpasses the fictive inventiveness of a Thomas Pynchon): "Darwin and Karl Marx didn't reveal the secret of the world. Of all the theories about creation, the one expounded in Genesis is the most intelligent. All this talk about primordial mists or the Big Bang is a wild absurdity. If someone found a watch on an island and said it had been made by itself or that it developed through evolution, he would be considered a lunatic. But according to modern science, the universe evolved all on its own. Is the universe less complicated than a watch?"

Before one decides that Singer has simply become a Biblical literalist, one might remember that orthodox Judaism is now less a Biblical faith than it is the continuation of the particular interpretations that the rabbis have placed upon the Bible. Singer's spokesman, Shapiro, fitly prefers those interpretations to Scripture itself: "Lately, I have come to understand why pious Jews never believed, and still don't believe, in studying too much Scripture. The horror stories in the Scriptures somehow didn't befit the spirit of the Diaspora Jew. Rabbi Isaac Luria and Baal Shem Tov are closer and more understandable to him than Joshua, the son of Nun, and King David. Joshua and King David had to be justified and defended, but Rabbi Isaac Luria and Baal Shem Tov needed no defense whatsoever. . . . I'm not talking against the Scriptures, God forbid. The Scriptures are holy. But Jewishness has developed. All things start out raw, and ripen with time. When the apple is green, it doesn't have the same sweet taste as when it is ripe. The basement of a house is not as elegant as a drawing room."

Does "Jewishness" here mean Judaism? Singer's "Jewishness" can hardly be questioned, but is that the only aim of his spokesman's drive, of his repentant turning to become as Jewish a character as Singer is a Jewish writer? Isaac Luria, the 16th-century founder of a modern Kabbalah, and the Baal Shem Tov, 18th-century founder of Hasidism, and certainly the principal sages of the mystical and ecstatic strains in modern Jewish piety. But if one thinks of the Singer who wrote the major and famous stories, then even Luria and the Baal Shem Tov seems too normative and orthodox, too tame for the ethos of Singer's fictive world.

The Singer who matters most seems to be the complement to the late Gershom Scholem's massive studies in Jewish mysticism, messianic apostasy and Gnostic demonology. Against the Singer of those extraordinary tales, we perhaps now must set the strident moralizer of *The Penitent*. Ironically, Singer executes a very personal turn upon the patterns of messianic apostasy as charted by Scholem. The most remarkable of these messianic apostates was Sabbatai Zevi, who in the 17th century eventually converted to Mohammedanism. It is as though Singer is a Sabbatai Zevi who becomes not a Moslem but an orthodox bigot. Singer's most characteristic attributes as a writer—his sexual obsessions and demonic impulses—are thus reabsorbed into the most atavistic strains in contemporary Jewry.

Among the principal targets of Singer/Shapiro's diatribes one would expect to find psychoanalysis. Though there are some passing and glancing animadversions throughout, Singer shies away from a direct confrontation with Freud's critique of all religions, Judaism included. The doubly repressive force—of Singer's deliberate forgetfulness of both Freud and his own most intense impulses—becomes at once the rhetorical strength and the conceptual weakness of this book. The only amusing moment in *The Penitent* occurs on the flight to Israel, when Joseph Shapiro postpones his new life long enough to be frustrated by the difficulties of making love on a jetliner:

"It's hard to sin physically on an airplane. Passengers kept going to and from the rest rooms, the stewardesses weren't sleeping, the lights weren't completely extinguished, only dimmed. I felt some passion for this female, but I also felt revulsion. It's odd, but although modern woman is always ready to commit all kinds of abominations, nevertheless, she girds herself in such a thorough fashion that it's a struggle to get at her. The desire to appear slim is even stronger than the urge to sin. We fumbled around this way for many minutes."

Roused by what Freud would have called the "incitement premiums" of confined jet-space and well-girded woman, the unfortunate Shapiro is inspired to the very heights of his great argument on behalf of religious morality. Here the old Singer indeed breaks through, and for once the book's humor is not involuntary. But the new Singer then interposes himself, and the unintended hilarity returns:

"Suddenly a man walked by me. He wore a rabbinical hat, and a wide blond beard, long earlocks, and the front of his coat was open to display a ritual garment with fringes. . . . I realized at that moment that without earlocks and a ritual garment one cannot be a real Jew. A soldier who serves an emperor has to have a uniform, and this also applies to a soldier who serves the Almighty. Had I worn such an outfit that night, I wouldn't have been exposed to those temptations."

Singer / Shapiro is thus massively in agreement with Freud, though evidently he does not know it. Juxtapose a relevant passage from Freud's great book upon our discomfort in culture, *Civilization and its Discontents*: "Renunciation of gratification does not suffice here, for the wish persists and is not capable of being hidden from the super-ego. In spite of the renunciations made, feelings of guilt will be experienced. . . . A threatening external unhappiness—loss of love and punishment meted out by external authority—has been exchanged for a lasting inner unhappiness, the tension of a sense of guilt."

The Talmudic uniform becomes merely Singer/Shapiro's representation of his own admonishing super-ego, which thus appears in the disguise of what Freud called "the bodily ego," or the introjection by the self of an imaginary object. The novel's involuntary humor again displays itself to the reader who recalls the first mention of the young woman whose armor will so frustrate Joseph Shapiro's ardent gropings: "I sat down, and presently a young woman took the window seat. Aha! The Devil had prepared a temptation for me. It's characteristic of Satan that he never gets tired, never capitulates. One holy book says that even when a person is on his deathbed, Satan comes and tries to lure him into atheism and blasphemy. There is far greater knowledge of mankind in this statement than in all the ponderous volumes of all the Freudians, Jungians, Adlerians."

How has Singer come down to this? I do not think that we have here only another episode in the decline and fall of practically everybody. Singer, like the somewhat subtler though equally pungent Cynthia Ozick, is representative of what might be called Jewish literary neo-orthodoxy. This attitude condemns as anti-Judaism or idolatry every acknowledged rupture or felt discontinuity that exists between the tradition and contemporary Jewish intellectuals.

Yet it is the illumination of the ambivalences and the ambiguities of such rupture that may have made Freud and Kafka, somewhat unwillingly, the authentic representatives of Jewish culture in and for our time. Miss Ozick has praised Singer as a moralist who "tells us that it is natural to be good, and unholy to go astray." Perhaps that praise is merited by *The Penitent*. Had Singer written often thus, he would indeed be remembered as a master of neo-orthodoxy, but hardly as a master of the intricate turnings of stories.

A. J. M. SMITH

1902–1980

Arthur James Marshall Smith was born on November 8, 1902, in Montreal, Quebec. He was educated at McGill University, where he received his bachelor's and master's degrees, and at Edinburgh University, where he received a Ph.D. in English in 1931. As a young poet and student Smith helped establish Montreal as the center of Canadian poetry and was a co-founder of the *McGill Fortnightly Review* in 1925. After completing his schooling Smith taught at colleges in Indiana, Nebraska, and South Dakota before going to Michigan State University in 1936; he remained there as a professor in the English Department until his retirement in 1972.

While pursuing his academic career, Smith continued to write and publish poetry in a variety of periodicals in the United States and Canada. His first volume of poetry, *News of the Phoenix*, appeared in 1943. *The Worldly Muse* was published in 1951 and *A Sort of Ecstasy* in 1954. Smith's *Collected Poems* were published in 1962. He was also the editor of *The Book of Canadian Poetry* (1943; 1948; 1957), *Seven Centuries of Verse* (3rd ed., 1967), and *The Oxford Book of Canadian Verse* (1960). Smith edited and published several college anthologies of prose and poetry; was a contributor to a number of reference books, including *The Princeton Encyclopedia of Poetry and Poetics* and the *Encyclopaedia Britannica*; and co-authored *Exploring Poetry* with M. L. Rosenthal (1955). When Smith retired, Michigan State University established the A. J. M. Smith Award, an honor bestowed annually on the best volume of verse by a Canadian.

Smith died on November 21, 1980, in East Lansing, Michigan.

The good poems in this volume (*News of the Phoenix*) are distinguished by a disciplined expression of bitterness and by the biting implications that result from that control. They succeed in joining venial particulars to grand universals, communicating a sense of outrage through the pressure under which they are fused. The product is an unsentimental irony by which cherished ideas and things become weighted with an incongruous and effective pathos. Innocence becomes foolishness, the thinking reed becomes a listless straw. Man, as the Child, as Hamlet, or as Everyman, is caught in a world of anomalous mechanics; when he is most heartbroken he is most absurd. "Noctambule," perhaps, may serve as the best illustration of the method and content of these particular poems:

> Under the flag of this pneumatic moon,
> —Blown up to bursting, whitewashed white,
> And painted like the moon—the piracies of day
> Scuttle the crank hulk of witless night.
> The great black innocent Othello of a thing
> Is undone by the nice clean pockethandkerchief
> Of 6 a.m., and though the moon is only an old

> Wetwash snotrag—horsemeat for good rosbif—
> Perhaps to utilize substitutes is what
> The age has to teach us,
>   wherefor let the loud
> Unmeaning warcry of treacherous daytime
> Issue like whispers of love in the moonlight,
> —Poxy old cheat!
>   So mewed the lion,
> Until mouse roared once and after lashed
> His tail: shellshock came on again, his skin
> Twitched in the rancid margarine, his eye
> Like a lake isle in a florist's window:
> Reality at two removes, and mouse and moon
> Successful.

Beyond the three or four poems that achieve success in this expression, however, the reader finds a sort of rarefied grab-bag of unrealized, or conventional, poems which might be assigned easily to a place among the collected works of other poets, and which would rest there with an easy and marginal distinction. They are small poems reaching for large meanings and missing them, or attaining them in such a way that the informed reader is immediately reminded of their richer prototypes in Yeats or another and finds them obliterated by that memory. I am referring to such rhythmical parodies as the following stanza from "On Reading an Anthology of Popular Poetry":

> Is there no katharsis
> But "song" for this dull
> Pain, that every Saul of Tarsus
> Must pant himself into a Paul?

Smith employs a *décor* drawn from the Greek, the Christian, and the Romantic myths, but his inability to vitalize his images and his references in the terms of a contemporary conscience leaves him somewhat trapped in the clichés of each. He is, in turn, the Child in the dark wood, the musty Scholar among white sails, the god-ridden Christian amazed by Christ. Because the core of his vision is never established, these oracular masks, so to speak, serve to dislocate the impact of his whole expression rather than to provide it with dramatic variation or breadth.

It is my feeling that, rather than develop the implications of his various themes toward a creative negativism or a convincing belief, Smith evades the issues forced upon the modern conscience by escaping toward the large protecting certainty of Death.

> So for a moment, motionless, serene,
> Fixed between time and time, I aim and wait;
> Nothing remains for breath now but to waive
> His prior claim and let the barb fly clean
> Into the heart of what I know and hate—
> That central black, and ringed and targeted grave.

Though this preoccupation would seem, at times, to amount almost to psychological blocking, it would be ungenerous to deny the poet his right to the traditional emphasis. In these poems, however, the insight expressed remains so far from the cosmic rage of Yeats, or the mystic resignation of Eliot, that the result is a vernacular weariness barely evocative as personal vision, uninteresting or cliché as poetry. It is as though the weary imagination were consciously to conjure up baroque fancies, only to mock itself at failure to deny them or escape from them. Since the basic duality of this conflict has not been presented convincingly, at this point it is difficult for the reader to participate in the struggle. Though the drama seems real and the issues full of personal stress, the validity of the situation remains suspect. We get the effects of turmoil without a substantial knowledge of its causes. Consequently, our response is, at best, questioning, suspended. We must know more about the real keystones of this experience if we are to read the poems with satisfaction. We do not, as in the case of Yeats, possess a consciously constructed mythology to which we may refer, nor a record of poems which illustrate an expanding expression of central themes. For reference, we have only a number of incongruously pretty poems which bear no relation whatsoever to the closely reasoned, imaginatively fused elements of "Noctambule," and the disparity leaves us uneasy. It would seem that the poet must earn his mantle, otherwise it will fit only in places.—JOHN MALCOLM BRINNIN, "Views of the Favorite Mythologies," *Poetry*, Dec. 1944, pp. 157–60

A. J. M. Smith's influence on Canadian poetry has been an important one, primarily through his criticism and through his work as an editor and anthologist. His *Book of Canadian Poetry*, for example, first published in 1943, has gone through several editions. Smith's own poetic output has been relatively small in quantity. *Collected Poems* contains one hundred poems, some of which were previously published in various periodicals and others in Smith's two earlier volumes of poetry, *News of the Phoenix* (1943) and *A Sort of Ecstasy* (1954).

Collected Poems is divided into five parts, with certain discernible though not exclusive themes in each. Part two, for example, has eight poems, each concerned with some facet of nature, as "Tree", "The Creek", and the finely etched "The Lonely Land." Part four contains a number of Smith's ironically humourous and satiric poems, and part five poems that are chiefly concerned with death. This is the last part and ends with "Epitaph":

> Weep not on this quiet stone,
> I, embedded here
> Where sturdy roots divide the bone
> And tendrils split a hair,
> Bespeak you comfort of the grass
> That is embodied me,
> Which as I am, not as I was,
> Would choose to be.

So much for the body temporal. The cover design of *Collected Poems* is of a Phoenix, and a brief quotation from Santayana on the title page reads: "Every animal has his festive and ceremonial moments, when he poses or plumes himself and thinks; sometimes he even sings and flies aloft in a sort of ecstasy." The design and quotation could be misleading. At any rate, something appears to have misled the writer of the jacket advertisement, who states of the Phoenix, "the mythical bird dies only to rise from the fires, purified and strengthened. This image haunts the reader of A. J. M. Smith's *Collected Poems.*" This is to suggest a note of reassurance and hope, an ultimately optimistic view of man that is antithetical to the general tenor of Smith's poetry. In a world in which the heart is lonely and all must share the guilt of stupidity, selfishness, and complacency—in a world in which the politicians are bumblers and the common man becomes an exile in the universal plan, where the *pax mundi* may be a hydrogen holocaust, it is difficult to find anything purifying and strengthening. One may perhaps *sometimes* find ecstasy in momentary remembrances of childhood fostered by seasonal rebirth, as in "A Hyacinth for Edith", but the round of living in the present must inevitably return and there, as we are told in "Journey", man goes alone,

> The end unknown,
> On either hand a wall.

Ecstasy may also be sought in love and in the joy of the senses—the pursuit of the goat-god Pan—but a view of life nurtured by Christian doctors operates continually to deprive man of his character, to bind

> Him spiritless, whom Holiness designed
> To swell the vein with a secular flood
> In pure ferocious joy, efficient and good,
> Like a tiger's spring or the leap of the wind.

Perhaps, however, there is a sort of ecstasy in celebrating the God within, in asserting one's own creative power that would mould things closer to the heart's desire:

> Bring me my hammer! Bring my blade!
> I'll shape this world of stone
> Into the likeness of a heart
> Of flesh and blood and bone.
>
> I'll take it for my love, and I
> Will joy in it and sing
> How peace and loving-kindness are
> In many a stony thing,
> But not in hearts of flesh and blood

And not in living bone
That pride and chastity and scorn
Have withered into stone.

But if this is a new Jerusalem of the living spirit, it is not in a
green and pleasant land. It is to be had in a lonely Promethean
defiance rather than in fellowship with essence. And yet, as
man goes towards his end he may accept the premises of his
beginning, conclude

That all this energy and poise
Were but designed to cast
A richer flower from the earth
Surrounding its decay,
And like a child whose fretful mirth
Can find no constant play,
Bring one more transient form to birth
And fling the old away.

If the process goes on long enough it may be a kind of
becoming.

Though there are some light things in A. J. M. Smith's
poetry, most of his work requires careful reading. Even the
obviously humorous poems do not yield their full meaning
immediately, and allusions to Yeats, Coleridge, Vaughan, and
Blake, for example, command an attention that fuses the
experience of other poetry into new statement. Where some
poets might have written two or three poems with a redundancy of sound and a scattering of meaning, A. J. M. Smith
has preferred to polish individual expression. Though this may
occasionally lead to almost crypto-grammatic utterance, it
does not often do so. His poetry generally testifies to his pursuit
of the standards he would set for others,

. . . the worth of a hard thing done
Perfectly, as though without care.
—E. F. GUY, *Dal*, Autumn 1963, pp. 437–41

The next time I am trying to dissuade one of my students from
honouring in English Literature I will give him something to
read out of A. J. M. Smith's *New and Collected Poems*, for
Smith's work seems to typify what can happen to an art form
when it is dominated by an historically oriented academic
discipline. After reading this volume I have no doubt that
Smith knows exactly what he is doing, that his skill at playing
the versification game matches his long established reputation,
and that this kind of literary competence is of very little
consequence to me or the world in which I live.

For the most part Smith relies on the time-worn gimmicks
of traditional rhyme and regular metre, usually heavily iambic,
to give his pieces poetic unity and mark them as verse. In
keeping with this conventional approach he delights in figures
of speech, abstract and lofty diction, classical allusions,
inverted turns of phrase, generalized emotion, and occasionally gentlemanly wit. It is true that Smith has a certain
flexibility of form; his models range from the Seventeenth
Century Metaphysicals to Auden, Yeats and Eliot. The collection even contains a small section of imagistic nature poems
in free verse, and these I found relatively pleasant. However,
there is very little going on that is new or original. Everything
is a kind of pastiche:

Celestial strings might not surpass
Thy morning breezes in long grass;
The slow rain from the laden tree
Dropping from heaven, brought to thee
Sounds of purest harmony

Here Smith reproduces the flavour of Henry Vaughan, whom
he is celebrating. It is a clever exercise, but to what end? Even
Smith's themes are run-of-the-mill literary when one finally

chews through the reams of metaphor that dutifully obscure
them: a low-keyed concern with love, death, and creation,
spattered with smug erudition and polite unenthusiastic Christianity.

Perhaps the fact that I am not tuned in on A. J. M.'s wave
length colours my evaluation of these poems. I am ready to
admit that others are sometimes capable of enjoying what I find
inexorably dull, and I trust that persons with tastes differing
from my own will find this collection more to their liking. The
bad humour that it prompts in me personally stems, I believe,
from the conviction that a major poet should be capable of
doing a great deal more, of writing, for example, poems which
are direct and "unpoetic" enough to be somehow symptomatic
of human emotion. "Only the simplest words have meaning"
choruses Smith in a poem on the death of E. J. Pratt, yet
elsewhere in the collection he shows himself to be unconcerned with that kind of meaning. Perhaps truth is irrelevant in
contexts where Smith believes poetry should operate. It depends, I suppose, on what a person thinks poetry is, and what
he wants to do with it.—LIONEL KEARNS, "If There's Anything
I Hate It's Poetry," *CL*, Spring 1968, pp. 67–68

MILTON WILSON
"Second and Third Thoughts about Smith"

Canadian Literature, Winter 1963, pp. 11–17

I

According to T. S. Eliot, we learn to distrust the favourite
poets of our adolescence. To this custom he attributes
some of his uneasy feeling about Shelley. As an adolescent, I
couldn't have cared less about Shelley, but my favourite
Canadian poet was called Smith. I encountered him in that
invaluable anthology *New Provinces*, which, at the beginning
of the war, virtually *was* contemporary Canadian poetry to
someone who, like me, had only recently discovered that it
actually existed. But I don't attribute my second thoughts
about Smith mainly to premature exposure: I just started to
read his criticism.

I read it looking for the wrong things and distracted by the
Smith legend already growing up around his "difficult, lonely
music". Much of his terminology struck me as deriving from
an Eliot either misunderstood or vulgarized, and I attributed
an exaggerated importance to Smith's minor habits of speech.
Take "classical", for example, which is really more of a Smith
legend than a favourite Smith term, and which he generally
replaces with such supposed equivalents as "austere", "disciplined", "concise", etc. T. S. Eliot let us know in an unguarded moment that his critical ideals were classical, but he
never claimed that the term had much application to his own
poems, or to those of his leading contemporaries. Indeed, he
took pains to deny it. But Smith seemed to find the classical
role congenial and even possible, although he can hardly be
blamed for the extremes to which Pacey has taken him in it,
any more than for Collin's earlier attempt to turn him into a
"spiritual athlete" or desperate mystic. Certainly you don't
have to talk to Smith for long to realize that he relishes the
thought of being odd classical man out in a society of
romantics, and, from the jacket blurb of his *Collected Poems*,
we once again learn, presumably with the author's sanction,
that he knows how to be "austerely classic" in his own graceful
way. It's something of a let-down to discover how merely
Parnassian or decadent or imagistic his classicism can be.
Smith's less diffuse Medusa (in "For Healing") isn't that
different from Swinburne's, his Hellenic swallows from

H.D.'s, or even his Pan from Carman's. It is tempting (as I discovered in reviewing Smith's second collection of poems eight years ago) to resign this particular legend to the limbo of Auden's Oxford:

> And through the quads dogmatic words rang clear:
> "Good poetry is classic and austere."

More obtrusive and far less legendary in the Smith terminology is "metaphysical" and all the phrases that Eliot (himself the heir to a long line of nineteenth-century critical formulas, as Frank Kermode points out) has taught us to trail along behind it: the "disparate experience", "passion and thought" or "sense and intellect", "fused" into a "unified sensibility". It hardly seems to matter whether Smith is writing a jacket blurb on John Glassco, analyzing Ronald Hambledon's "Sockeye Salmon", improvising on Margaret Avison, addressing a conference of librarians on contemporary Canadian literature in general, reviewing *Towards the Last Spike*, or introducing Alfred Bailey's work by telling us how well his "learning" is "fused" with his "sensibility and feeling": the same formula automatically recurs. Indeed, it is so persistently and widely applied that in the end one balks at trying to understand what he means by Anne Wilkinson's "metaphysical romanticism" as much as by Wilfred Watson's "classical precision of form".

But how relevant are my second thoughts? Do unskillful classification and a perfunctory terminology really stand in the way of Smith's critical achievement? Not, I think, if we recognize where his real and remarkable virtues as a critic lie and refuse to demand what he has no intention of giving in the first place. Smith's key terms and classifications are useful only because, having provided something of the sort, he can then feel free to exercise his best talents elsewhere. The distinction between the natives and the cosmopolitans, on which Smith hung the organization of much of the first edition of A *Book of Canadian Poetry*, has in the latest edition been silently dropped, with no loss to the virtues of a difficult task finely carried out. He is lucky to have discovered, and been encouraged to take on, the rôle for which his critical skills best suit him. He seems born to be an anthologizer, not of familiar, well-stocked and well-combed fields, but of virgin territory; he is happily doomed to exercise his finely perceptive and carefully developed faculty of choice on the dubious, the unpromising, the untried and the provincial, and by his example to show his readers that such choice is both possible and necessary. Before Smith, Canadian anthologies were either uncritical appendages to national aspiration or simply of "the vacuum cleaner type" (as a reviewer has remarked of a recent example). Here are Smith's own words in 1939, when he was just starting to work on A *Book of Canadian Poetry*. "Discrimination has never been an essential part of a Canadian anthologist's equipment. Enthusiasm, industry, sympathy, yes; but taste, no." In the successive editions of the *Book* and in the more recent *Oxford Book of Canadian Verse*, he has given us a model of discrimination and scrupulous choice, which is salutary even for those whose preferences are very different from his. Smith offers no hard-won aesthetic principles, no freshly cleaned critical concepts, no brilliant arguments to inevitable conclusions; but one cannot read his Canadian anthologies (introduction and critical apparatus included) without responding to the firm, delicately sharpened, continuous pressures of a mind exercising its powers on materials which he finds half-alien and grudging in their Victorian beginnings, and perhaps equally alien, if a good deal richer, in their post-war ends, but which he manages somehow to coerce into satisfying the personal demands that he started with. I respond to the same process in his best essays and reviews, like the recent one on D. C. Scott in *Canadian Literature* and on Margaret Avison in the *Tamarack Review*. In reading the Scott essay, once I have repressed a few gestures of annoyance at the old surface habits (there is far too much invocation of that most delusive of standards, the "accurate image"), I can experience with great pleasure and profit his untwisting and discriminating and reweaving of the threads of Scott's sensibility, his finely selected anthology of quotations, and his convincing sympathy with a poetic mind whose qualities, I realize with something of a shock, are very like his own. He is equally discriminating on the diction and imagery of Margaret Avison, with whose centrifugal poetics and subordination of poem written to poem writing (she has almost no sense of authorial "natural piety"), he can have very little in common at all, although, of course, he manages to feel steady by invoking the "fusion" of "sensation and thought" in her "undissociated sensibility".

Smith, then, is a critic who stands or falls by purity of perception alone. He has a critical sense so fine (to adapt Eliot's famous remark on James) that it is incapable of being violated by an idea or even the lack of one. Far from being an intellectual critic, or (as he would no doubt prefer) a "unified" or "whole" one, he shows what can be done, and perhaps can only be done, by sharpening taste at the expense of its critical companions. But he shows this not only in writing criticism. As I read the *Collected Poems* which Oxford has just given us, I realize, as I never did before, just how all-of-a-piece, as well as how varied, Smith's work really is. "Metaphysical poetry and pure poetry are what I stand for," he has insisted. One may be justly dubious about his "metaphysical" qualities, but he is as pure a poet as he is a critic.

II

The hundred poems in this new collection come from thirty years of work. It contains every poem but one from *News of the Phoenix* (38) and *A Sort of Ecstasy* (22). The others (40) do include a few early, uncollected pieces, of which the longest and most interesting is "Three Phases of Punch", ninety per cent unchanged since its last appearance (as "Varia") in the *London Aphrodite* of April, 1929; but most of them, to the best of my knowledge, are the latest Smith. It is surely no longer necessary to waste time refuting the silliest of all the Smith legends: that his taste has stultified his invention and narrowed his range, that he has spent thirty years husbanding a minimum of creativity for a minimum of purposes. So I won't try to make a comprehensive survey of his long-sustained, inventive, and remarkably varied output, which is certainly equal in range to that of any Canadian poet of his generation. Instead, I would prefer simply to watch the Smith "purity" at work in a few characteristic places, concentrating on what he does to other poets (the tributes, parodies, pastiches and translations), where the continuity of his poetry and criticism is likely to be most apparent, and pursuing the argument into adjacent areas wherever it seems useful.

The tributes are inseparable from the parodies, the parodies from the pastiches, and the pastiches from the translations. There must be at least twenty poems which belong somewhere within this continuity of categories, beginning with the ode to Yeats and the praise of Jay Macpherson at one end, followed by the revisioning of Vaughan and the *reductio ad absurdum* of George Johnston, moving through the glazed, wooden hyacinth for Edith Sitwell, the variations on Anne Wilkinson and the love song in Tom Moore tempo, continuing with the souvenir of the twenties, the Jacobean prothalamium and the lyric to a Catullan Anthea, and reaching at last the Gautier and

Mallarmé translations at the other end. I cannot possibly think that Smith's translations are not as good English poems as the originals are French ones. In fact, what *could* be better than his version of "Brigadier"? And the high spirits of some of these pastiches are enough to convince even the most hidebound primitive that literature which claims to forswear precedent has no monopoly on vitality. What is more to my point, the process of discrimination and selection responsible for the anthologies and for the Scott and Avison essays can here be seen most clearly at work—in the lively redistorting mirror he provides for George Johnston, Tom Moore or Edith Sitwell, and in the more sober ecstasy that he filters through Anne Wilkinson or Henry Vaughan.

The Smith purity shows at its best in the admirable Vaughan poem, which is worth saving for the last. It works less convincingly on Yeats, as the somewhat faded intensities of the "Ode on the Death of W. B. Yeats" demonstrate. The obvious comparison is with Auden's "In Memory of W. B. Yeats". Smith shares some Auden mannerisms, particularly in the handling of epithets (see the third stanza), but the nature of his poem is very different. Auden's rich, diffuse, sectional elegy tries to include a great deal—intellectual, political, psychological, aesthetic—not only of Yeats but of the world in which Yeats died, and of course he ruminates and draws a moral or two. Smith's Yeats, however, is purified of almost everything except a few basic images. But, instead of distilling the essence of a great poet (as the Vaughan tribute does), the "Ode" succeeds only in reducing a great poet to the level of his own clichés.

> A wild swan spreads his fanatic wing.
> Ancestralled energy of blood and power
> Beats in his sinewy breast. . . .
> The swan leaps singing into the cold air . . .
> . . . crying
> To the tumultuous throng
> Of the sky his cold and passionate song.

Even if it were one of Yeats's most convincing poses that Smith has taken over, one could still detect something of the stock response at work here. In another Smith poem, "On Reading an Anthology of Popular Poetry", we are told how

> The old eternal frog
> In the throat that comes
> With the words *mother, sweetheart, dog*
> Excites and then numbs.

In reading early Smith, I feel the same way about the word *cold*.

Fortunately, the *Collected Poems* allows the reader to put Smith's more ascetic mannerisms in perspective. The poet may protest too much, he may risk succumbing to a formula, he may even seem to imagine that he can escape from a soft cliché by exchanging it for a hard one, but his talent is too rich to allow doctrinaire confinement. The angularities of "The Lonely Land" do have their important share in Smith's "sort of ecstasy", but his sensibility achieves its fullest release when the crisp, clear, cold, smooth, hard, pointed, austere, lonely, etc. (I choose my list of adjectives from "To Hold a Poem") is complemented by the shimmer and fluctuation, the flash and fade, which Smith has helped us to perceive in D. C. Scott. "The Fountain", "Nightfall" and (especially) "The Circle" are more fully characteristic of Smith than "Swift Current" or "In the Wilderness" or even "The Lonely Land" itself.

If the Smith brand of purity works better in the Vaughan poem than it did in the Yeats, it is perhaps because in the former so much potential impurity is held in willing suspension.

> Homesick? and yet your country Walks
> Were heaven'd for you. Such bright stalks
> Of grasses! such pure Green!

The gently puzzled and at first only half-comprehending tone in which Smith presents Vaughan's combination of homesickness for eternity with sensitiveness to the divinity of his place of exile (his peculiarly ungnostic gnosticism) is fully absorbed into a concentration and refinement of Vaughan's sensibility and idiom (Smith's extract of Vaughan—and a wonderful distillation it turns out to be), while the religious paradox

> (Yet thou art Homesick! to be gone
> From all this brave Distraction
> Wouldst seal thine ear, nail down thine eye; . . .
> Thou art content to beg a pall,
> Glad to be Nothing, to be all.)

seems in the end so transparent as almost to be purified of religious meaning. But what the Smith purification of Vaughan makes only half-apparent (Vaughan, after all, is a pretty special case) is unmistakable if one sets Smith beside "that preacher in a cloud from Paul's", his favourite Donne, from whom our basic concept of a metaphysical poet must necessarily come. Smith obviously lacks the sheer argumentativeness, the sequential pressure of intellectual give and take, the involvement in conceptual definition and differentiation which gives Donne so much of his flavour. What he possesses are such things as the intellectual high spirits of the superb "What Casey Jones Said to the Medium" or the forceful syntactic logic of poems like "The Archer", "To a Young Poet", "The Flesh Repudiates the Bone" and a good many others. I choose one short enough to quote.

> This flesh repudiates the bone
> With such dissolving force,
> In such a tumult to be gone,
> Such longing for divorce,
> As leaves the livid mind no choice
> But to conclude at last
> That all this energy and poise
> Were but designed to cast
> A richer flower from the earth
> Surrounding its decay,
> And like a child whose fretful mirth
> Can find no constant play,
> Bring one more transient form to birth
> And fling the old away.

If one must use the terminology of the sacred wood, then what Smith gives us is less like Eliot's required fusion of thought and emotion than like his "emotional equivalent of thought". And if one can't resist a seventeenth-century title, there's always "cavalier" ready for the taking. But the temptation had better be resisted. Having watched Smith refuse to be contained by his own formulas, I can hardly expect him to be contained by mine. "The plot against Proteus" can be left to other hands: "when you have him, call." In the meantime, the continuous liveliness of texture in these *Collected Poems* keep rousing my prejudices—for and against. My third thoughts about Smith are unlikely to be my last.

M. L. ROSENTHAL
"'Poor Innocent': The Poetry of A. J. M. Smith"

Modern Poetry Studies, Spring 1977, pp. 1–13

It has often struck me that A. J. M. Smith has something like perfect pitch in poetry. He has the ability to read a poem for the first time and, almost at once, catch its tones and associations. One might say that this was a critical rather than a creative gift, and, indeed, it is what makes his anthologies such triumphs of taste and makes conversations with him about poetry such interesting and delightful adventures. But the gift carries over into his poetry, most obviously in such a poem as "To Henry Vaughan," in which his mimetic empathy fills the lines with the light of a kindred sensibility aroused by his sheer love of Vaughan's phrasing.

More subtly, though, the empathy has to do with the nature of poetic process. It lies in Smith's feeling for the process—its traditions and its possibilities, the rich opportunities it provides for the convergence of creative energy with critical responsiveness. I am not speaking of an abstraction but of the way he writes his poems, the kind of play of form and private emotion that gives them their movement. Let me suggest an early instance, the half-light, half-serious poem called "Poor Innocent":

> It is a gentle natural (is it I?) who
> Visits timidly the big world of
> The heart, and stares a little while at love
> As at a plaited and ringleted paleblue
> Seascape, whence escapes a new, untrue,
> Refracted light, a shade or two above
> The infra fringe beyond which does he move
> He moves unsurely in an air askew.
>
> This pretty simpleton, myself or not,
> Squints at the filigree of wind and wave,
> Scanning the frothing for the Lord knows what—
> The foam-born rising, maybe, nude and swell,
> Or—*Back to your kennel, varlet! Fool, you rave!*
> *Unbind that seaweed, throw away that shell!*

One has to stop, and go back and notice, to see that this sweetly intense, self-ironic poem is a Petrarchan sonnet. Its lively surface-effects conceal the formal insistences of rhyme and turn and conclusion. The voice is witty and sophisticated, and yet the speaker *is* a "gentle natural"—an educated one, to be sure, skeptical about his own romantic vision and feelings and in all too great a hurry to tell himself to *come off it*. But he's still a "gentle natural" all the same. You can tell by the sheer fun he has looking at himself in the mirror of his supposedly deluded wonderment. Even the zest of his closing lines belies their claim to disillusionment. Aphrodite is truly being born again for him out there. He was right to go slangy with excitement just thinking how she would arrive: "the foam-born rising, maybe, nude and swell."

The sonnet-tradition, the Shakespearean phrase I have twice quoted, the effects in the octave slightly reminiscent of E. E. Cummings, the play on the Greek name of the goddess, the Romantic self-teasing at the end—these are all but details of the element in which the poet lives and breathes and in which his originality finds itself. Smith, an important force in modern Canadian poetry though still but little known in the United States, is an active esthetic intelligence whose life's work (like that of most other genuine poets of matured intelligence) refutes the very notion of an "anxiety of influence" that reduces the power of poetry to renew its energies because of the burden of its great past. Communion—

dialogue—with the past, and repossession of it in his own new, idiosyncratic way is the artist's enormous pleasure as he engages with everything that the present is. The epigraph from an essay by George Santayana printed in all four of Smith's books of poetry, and again at the close of his selected essays, describes this pleasure with wry elegance. Smith obviously took a great fancy to this way of putting things. It renders pomposity nil. "Every animal," writes Santayana, "has his festive and ceremonious moments, when he poses, or plumes himself, or thinks; sometimes he even sings and flies aloft in a sort of ecstasy." Here is the perfect creed for the gentle, sophisticated natural, whose joy in the creations of his predecessors and of his contemporaries could hardly diminish his own song.

Smith's poem "Ballade un peu banale" should be cited first of all, I think, if one wishes to understand why the Santayana quotation attracts him so strongly. The "Ballade" is an exquisitely bawdy embodiment of Santayana's idea. This is especially true, perhaps, of stanza 1 and stanzas 4–7:

> The bellow of good Master Bull
>   Astoundeth gentil Cow
> That standeth in the meadow cool
>   Where cuckoo singeth now . . .
> Bull boometh from the briary bush,
>   Advanceth, tail aloft—
> The meadow grass is long and lush,
>   The oozy turf is soft.
> He stampeth with his foremost foot,
>   His nostrils breathing bale;
> Uncouth, unhallowed is his suit;
>   The vestal turneth tail.
> He feinteth with his ivory horn,
>   Bites rump, bites flank, bites nape—
> Sweet Saviour of a Virgin born,
>   How shall this maid escape!
> He chaseth her to pasture wall;
>   She maketh stand, poor bird!
> He wields his tail like an iron flail.
>   Alas! he presseth hard!

We're listening to something like pure poetic engagement, the poet's happy engagement with this parody of sexual melodrama and with all the lovely paraphernalia of medieval lyric, of pastoral romance, and of earthy piety he can deploy in it. And then there is the simple sweetness of absurd erotic fantasy in which he indulges himself. This poem is in a cherished tradition, at once popular and learned, running twin risks of preciosity and vulgarity but certainly worth the effort. It goes back, obviously, to Rabelais and Chaucer and earlier. My favorite contemporary example beside this one, and exceedingly close to it in spirit, is the opening section of Basil Bunting's *Briggflatts*. There too we find a Master Bull in a state of pastoral arousal, although the hilarity is muted for the sake of a different kind of lyricism. Bunting's sequence as a whole has deeply serious, even depressed tones to contend with and develop. A whole world of personal and historical memory, the whole idiom of regional culture—the very grain of a people's self-regard—is being eroded. Moreover, the speaker feels something akin to all this in his own nature: a self-betrayal and a disloyalty to the simple folk and their ways that nourished his childhood and youth. If we viewed Smith's complete oeuvre as a unit, we would find in it analogous balancings of joy in the life-force and more depressive visions. But I do not want to touch on that side of things quite yet, except indirectly by pointing to another apparently frivolous poem or two. Take the memorably silly beginning of the one called "Political Intelligence."

> Nobody said Apples for nearly a minute—
> I thought I should die.
> Finally, though, the second sardine
> from the end, on the left,
> converted a try.
> (It brought down the house.
> The noise was terrific.
> I dropped my glass eye.)

This is unforgettable nonsense, especially the first two lines. One should, I know, hesitate to suggest that, nevertheless, it contains notes of the sinister and the disturbing and the seriously political, and that those notes lurk in the words "die" and "left" and in the phrases "brought down the house" and "glass eye." The next two stanzas, however, have strongly satiric and sombre tones that reinforce the suggestion:

> Meanwhile the P.M.
> managed to make himself heard.
> He looked sad
> but with characteristic aplomb said
> Keep calm there is no cause for alarm.
>
> Two soldiers' crutches
> crossed up a little bit of fluff
> from a lint bandage
> in the firing chamber of a 12-inch gun.
> People agreed not to notice.
> The band played a little louder.
> It was all very British.

But of those poems which can conceivably be called light or humorous, the one I most love is "Brigadier," translated from a French-Canadian song. The song is a dialogue between an egotistical general and his sardonically deferential sergeant, Pandore: variants on the Don Quixote-Sancho Panza pairing. Smith's English version beautifully juxtaposes the general's expansive, complacent romanticism (you *might* call it) and the sergeant's ironic detachment. The language of the one grows ever more fustian; the other's remains a reticent constant. In the two final stanzas, the teller of the tale takes over the general's style and echoes it mockingly, but Pandore's refrain has the last word. All our dreams, and all the mere literalness of whatever we experience, are implicit in the contrast. The poem is a music of opposing tones, joyous and melancholy and at the same time remarkably, ecstatically, impersonal.

> One Sunday morning soft and fine
> Two old campaigners let their nags meander;
> One was a Sergeant of the Line,
> The other a Brigade Commander.
> The general spoke with martial roar,
> 'Nice weather for this time of year!'
>   And 'Right you are,' replied Pandore,
>   'Right you are, my Brigadier.'
>
> 'A Guardsman's is a thankless calling,
> Protecting private property,
> In summer or when snows are falling,
> From malice, rape, or robbery;
> While the wife whom I adore
> Sleeps alone and knows no cheer.'
>   And 'Right you are,' replied Pandore,
>   'Right you are, my Brigadier.'
>
> 'I have gathered Glory's laurel
> With the rose of Venus twined—
> I am married, and a General;
> Yet, by Jesus, I've a mind
> To start like Jason for the golden shore

> And follow my Star—away from here!'
>   'Ah, right you are,' replied Pandore,
>   'Right you are, my Brigadier.'
>
> 'I remember the good days of my youth
> And the old songs that rang
> So cheerily. In that time, forsooth,
> I had a doting mistress, full of tang . . .
> But, ah! the heart—I know not wherefore—
> Loves to change its bill of fare.'
>   And 'Right you are,' replied Pandore,
>   'Right you are, my Brigadier!'
>
> Now Phoebus neared his journey's end;
> Our heroes' shadows fell behind:
> Yet still the Sergeant did attend,
> And still the General spoke his mind.
> 'Observe,' he said, 'how more and more
> Yon orb ensanguines all the sphere.'
>   And 'Right you are,' replied Pandore,
>   'Right you are, my Brigadier.'
>
> They rode in silence for a while:
> You only heard the measured tread
> Of muffled hoof beats, mile on mile—
> But when Aurora, rosy red,
> Unbarred her Eastern door,
> The faint refrain still charmed the ear,
>   As 'Right you are,' replied Pandore,
>   'Right you are, my Brigadier.'

The two characters, General and Sergeant, were a happy discovery for a poet at once full of luxurious dreams and all too ready to deflate them. In the Romantic-Classical debate, Smith tends to vote Classical on principle while his poems actually throw the balance of feeling and imagination a little the other way. Both his collected volumes, for instance, begin with the poem "Like an Old Proud King in a Parable." It starts out with Yeatsian flourishes although, as is usual in Smith's work, the discernible literary influences do not finally dominate the poem:

> A bitter king in anger to be gone
> From fawning courtier and doting queen
> Flung hollow spectre and gilt crown away,
> And breaking bound of all his counties green
> He made a meadow in the northern stone
> And breathed a palace of inviolable air
> To cage a heart that carolled like a swan,
> And slept alone, immaculate and gay,
> With only his pride for a paramour.

Thus the first stanza. It is followed by a single line set off by itself, in which the poet rejects the facile dream-notion that he is this king—some alienated Fergus ruling over the land of the imagination. "O who is that bitter king? It is not I." The poem should end just here. But what happens is that the speaker picks up the Yeatsian dream after all and indulges in the identification. The poet prays to be able to learn a proud, isolated art in spite of having (as in "Poor Innocent") placed himself abruptly in his own reality:

> And I will sing to the barren rock
> Your difficult, lonely music, heart,
> Like an old proud king in a parable.

But the second poem in both collected volumes, "Shadows There Are," is more deeply accurate. Modern classicism must be, not some bullying demand for superficially formal tightness or for demeaned and shrunken vision, but a hard pursuit of the implications of contemporary mentality and sensibility. The pursuit leads primarily to formal concentration, a pressing of the issues of realization beyond showing one has "interesting" sensitivities. That is, it involves a certain impersonality and distancing, just to get past the self-betrayal of the ego mirroring itself hungrily but falsely in passionate stereotypes. We can see the really serious classical poet at work in "Shadows There Are"—*and* the really serious romantic poet too, of course—

> Shadows there are, but shadows such as these
> Are shadows only in the mortal mind,
> Blown by the spirit, or the spirit's wind.
>
> Yet shadows I have seen, of me deemed deeper,
> That backed on nothing in the horrid air,
>
> And try as try, I cannot limn the form
> That some of them assume where I shall pass.
> They grow transparent, and as sharp, as glass.

The two three-line stanzas enclosing the light-rhyming couplet (and each containing another couplet, one with exact, the other with consonantal, rhyme) formally present us, as it were, with three distorted mirrors in their relationship of sound. They play with the idea of shadow and form in a way that suggests the mind's bafflement when confronting its own limitations. It is not far from a poem like this one to the death-obsessed pieces that have accumulated in Smith's successive volumes. Where I said "mind's bafflement," indeed, I should have said "self's bafflement," and perhaps have used the word "death" instead of "limitations." The ambiguity here is true to the lyric tradition. Smith reaches back to Elizabethan forerunners who flung a mood to the mercy of the language— to ravishing evocations, rhythms, echoes—and thereby discovered how a mood was a world of involvement and how the phrasing needed to evoke that world was, despite its quite possibly melancholy meaning, a sort of ecstasy in itself.

I suppose it's because he found in it an analogue to his own fascination with this paradox—our delight in finding the right language even for inescapable horror; the illusion of triumph over fatality this discovery brings us—that Smith translated Mallarmé's swan-poem that begins *"Le vierge, le vivace et le bel aujourd' hui."* His is the best rendering we have in English. It catches precisely the vision of romantic energy trapped within its own need for form (the *pressure* to be "classical") that Smith, as much as any modern writer in our language, shares with Mallarmé. The elusive glory of our dreams and desires, richly and tragically presented in the figure of the swan, is held ice-bound in language as "transparent, and as sharp, [to quote the poem we have just been looking at— "Shadows There Are"] as glass."

> The virginal, vivacious and beautiful today,
> Will it shatter for us with a drunken wing-blow
> This hard, forgotten lake haunted by frost's glow
> Where transparent glaciers of unknown flights stay!
>
> A swan of long ago remembers it is he,
> Magnificent, who without hope can yet forgive
> Himself not having sung a realm in which to live
> When sterile winter makes a splendour of ennui.
>
> His whole neck will shake off the white agony
> By space inflicted on the bird whose being denies
> All but earth's horror gripping his plumes like a vise.
>
> A Shade to this place by his pure brilliancy drawn,
> He's fixed in the icy dream of contumely
> That dresses the useless exile of the Swan.

The author of this translation and of a poem like "Shadows There Are" is unlikely to engage in proliferative rhetoric or witless exhibitionism to prove he has normal human feelings and a common touch. Naturally, he has both. His ordinary humanity is evident in his obvious preoccupation with love

and death and joy, and in his sense of the language. I realize that this proposition may not be self-evident to people who do not really believe that poetry is an art, or who disapprove of writing that does not, as they say, "let it all hang out," or who prefer their authors' commitments to be packaged in familiar slogans. Yet it should be clear that, loving wit and the evocative exploration of feeling as he does—and revealing them at every turn—Smith is inevitably an engaged poet in his own clear fashion. He does not know the answers any more than the rest of us do, but he knows the questions better than all but those other poets who, being his peers, can see what he is doing. I cite but one of the poems that best illustrate my point: "A Soldier's Ghost."

> How shall I speak
> To the regiment of young
> Whose throats break
> Saluting the god
> Descending onto the drumhead
> —Stalled
> Each in his proper stance
> Upholding the service?
> Bones
> Distilled in the frontier sand
> Fumble
> The natty chevron.
> Can a memberless ghost
> Tell?
> These lost
> Are so many brother bones.
> *The hieroglyph*
> *Of ash*
> *Concedes an anagram*
> *Of love.*

I prefer this poem to the ones by Smith that, if never blatant, yet spell out their fear of war and of the hypocrisy of governments more explicitly—or even to his other poem of comparable helpless compassion, "The Dead." "A Soldier's Ghost" asks for a message but has none to give save that the speaker knows no word to keep future generations from suffering the same betrayal (and he does not even call it betrayal) that he has experienced. The poem begins with his cry of inarticulateness; it ends with a delphic utterance of love expressed through an emblem of loss and perhaps of ultimate meaninglessness: "the hieroglyph of ash." The opening stanza might almost have come from the Greek Anthology; while the closing stanza, unpretentious yet transcendent, focuses the speaker's unmanageable emotion—not hysteria but just as real—in the words "hieroglyph" and "love." The poem's force derives from its rhythmic restraint of that emotion and from the beautifully modulated phrasing: the controlled intensity of the first stanza, the hard, technical literalness of the second, the deftly colloquial characterization of the third, the questioning of the fourth stanza that echoes that in the first two, and then the closing mystical half-assertion. The issue of youthful sacrifice in war has involved the whole emotional range of the speaking sensibility, rather than merely being the subject of rhetoric.

But now I should like to return for a moment to the frivolous Smith who so gaily and charmingly lets his imagination wander over meadowlands of erotic fancy, with such a mixture of classical and between-wars worldliness—or rather, would-be worldly playfulness. Take the poem "An Iliad for His Summer Sweetheart," with its epigraph from Pound's *Homage to Sextus Propertius*: "And if she play with me with her shirt off, / We shall construct many Iliads." It's hard to think of another contemporary who takes such innocent pleasure in innocent pleasure as Smith does, not to prove he has the usual male endowment or to suggest he's Don Juan redivivus but just out of glee that such things can be.

> I love to see my Amaryllis toss her shirt
>   Away and kick her panties off, and loll,
>   Languid and lazy, by the lily pool,
> While old Silenus leers and laughing Cupids squirt.
>
> My fancies swarm like bees about her golden head
>   And golden thighs, where love's best ore is found.
>   When she sinks softly to the sun-warmed ground
> We need no silken walls, no blinds, no feather bed.

To read this poem in the same volume as "A Soldier's Ghost" (*Poems New and Collected*) is to glimpse the connections of humane intelligence and human love that bind the various aspects of the poet's sensibility. For Smith is, in his own way, a libertarian, with a mind free to move beyond constraints of inhibition and gentility absolutely without notice. In some moods, it is true, he would like to see himself as a rigorously conservative intelligence—and why not? Ultimately, there's no contradiction there, just as there is none between his pleasantries about Amaryllis' panties and his frequent preoccupation with death. If, incidentally, he had written Pound's little poem "April," which presents a twin vision of death and delight, he would probably have changed the epigraph from "scattered limbs of the nymphs" (*nympharum disjecta membra*) to "scattered panties of the nymphs." Be that as it may, "April" speaks well for the kind of association that occurs in Smith's mind too:

> Three spirits came to me
> And drew me apart
> To where the olive boughs
> Lay stripped upon the ground:
> Pale carnage beneath bright mist.

It's the carnage, the presence of ever-ranging death, that absorbs his deepest poetic attention. It informs his strongest poems. You can see, in "What the Emanation of Casey Jones Said to the Medium," how it fuses all his characteristic tones and modes. Here is the ending:

> . . . the make-up of the mind
>
> Embellishes and protects,
> Draws beards between fabulous tits,
> Endorses the stranger's checks,
> Judges and always acquits.
>
> Turn inward to the brain:
> The signal stars are green,
> Unheard the ghost train
> Time, and Death can not be seen.

The comic title recalls, as the poem itself does more richly, the combination in the original folksong "Casey Jones" of rollicking colloquial speech and lively music with elegy. Smith picks up both the exuberance of the railroaders' lament and the grimmer note implicit in the mechanical power and speed of the engine and in the fatalistic symbolism of railroad tracks. The language of even the few lines I have quoted unites many levels of expression and consciousness—the speech of Amaryllis' lover, a metaphysical thinker's musings, a working stiff's lingo, and the imagination of a poet who thinks in metaphor at once original and popular: "The signal stars are green," "the ghost train."

Smith's combined life-exuberance, humanity, and death-obsession also produce some of his *noblest* effects of high lyrical evocation—for instance:

> A sigh of the inconsequential dead,
> A murmur in a drain,
> Lapping a severed head,
> Unlaurelled, unlamented, vain.

This is the ending of "What Is That Music High in the Air," whose title is a line in Eliot's *The Waste Land*. The tone, however, is Smith's own, something evolved by a process of contemplation and correction from the poem's ringing opening lines, whose mood was exalted but finally unacceptable:

> A voice from the heroic dead,
> Unfaltering and clear . . .

The nobility of his finest work has many aspects. I believe it can partly be accounted for by his high degree of empathic sensitization to the rhetoric of the most truly accomplished lyrical poetry generally. But his unabashedly human hatred of death is somehow another, and of necessity a more passionate, source. One rarely finds the position held with such thrilling clarity in poetry. The language is the pure, sustained, and subtle speech of a poet who sees his own nature as a relationship between his art and his fate. He commands the inevitable to happen in a manner that makes it seem subordinate to his own shaping will.

> Bend back thy bow, O Archer, till the string
> Is level with thine ear, thy body taut,
> Its nature art, thyself thy statue wrought
> Of marble blood, thy weapon the poised wing
> Of coiled and aquiline Fate. Then, loosening, fling
> The hissing arrow like a burning thought
> Into the empty sky that smokes as the hot
> Shaft plunges to the bullseye's quenching ring.
> So for a moment, motionless, serene,
> Fixed between time and time, I aim and wait;
> Nothing remains for breath now but to waive
> His prior claim and let the barb fly clean
> Into the heart of what I know and hate—
> That central black, the ringed and targeted grave.

That's giving our poor innocent, speaking for all the rest of us poor innocents, the very last word—or very nearly. The closest thing to it that I can think of readily is Cummings' "who's most afraid of death? thou," a poem much admired by Smith himself. But the prize for nobility and formal rigor must, in this instance, go to Smith's "The Archer."

CLARK ASHTON SMITH

1893–1961

Clark Ashton Smith was born on January 13, 1893, in Long Valley, California, to Fanny and Timeus Smith. He was educated privately, refusing a Guggenheim scholarship to the University of California at Berkeley. He married Carol Jones Dorman in 1954. Smith supported himself throughout his life by writing, supplemented by occasional short-term jobs such as fruit-picking and well-digging.

Smith sold his first stories to the *Black Cat* in 1910 at the age of seventeen, after which he abandoned fiction for more than fifteen years, concentrating on poetry. *The Star-Treader and Other Poems* (1912), published when Smith was nineteen, created a stir in California literary circles, and Smith was hailed as a "boy genius" akin to Keats, Shelley, and Swinburne. However, his later volumes of poetry—*Ebony and Crystal: Poems in Verse and Prose* (1922); *Sandalwood* (1925); *The Dark Chateau* (1951); *Spells and Philtres* (1958)—failed to attract much attention outside the fantasy and science fiction communities. His poetry includes translations from French, particularly of Baudelaire, and poems written in French and Spanish. His *Selected Poems* (1971) includes more than 500 of his poems, but much remains uncollected and unpublished.

Smith is primarily known as a fiction writer. His early influences include Edgar Allan Poe and William Beckford, and his stories are steeped in the fantastic and gruesome. Several notable tales, including "The City of the Singing Flame" (1931) and "The Monster of the Prophecy" (1932), effect a distinctive union between pure fantasy and science fiction. Smith wrote for the pulp magazines for several years, particularly *Weird Tales* and *Wonder Stories*; he was a correspondent and friend of H. P. Lovecraft during the 1920s and 1930s, and Lovecraft exerted a considerable influence upon Smith's later fiction. Smith's first important collection of stories, *Out of Space and Time* (1942), was published after he had largely abandoned fiction for poetry and his greatest love, painting and sculpture. Subsequent volumes of fiction were drawn mostly from Smith's stories for the pulps in the thirties, and established him as second only to Lovecraft in the field of horror and the supernatural. His major volumes of fiction include *Lost Worlds* (1944), *Genius Loci* (1948), *The Abominations of Yondo* (1960), *Tales of Science and Sorcery* (1965), and *Other Dimensions* (1970).

Smith suffered the first of a series of strokes in the early fifties, and they eventually led to his death on August 14, 1961.

Ignored by the literary establishment both during and after his lifetime, Smith early became a central figure in the fantasy fandom movement. Many of his volumes have been published by small or specialty presses. Smith himself published the slim *Double Shadow and Other Fantasies* (1933); the Futile Press issued *Nero and Other Poems* in 1937; while Smith's longtime friend and former literary executor Roy A. Squires has produced several limited editions of Smith's work, notably *The Hill of Dionysus* (1962). Smith's few essays were collected in *Planets and Dimensions* (1973), edited by Charles K. Wolfe, and his *Letters to H. P. Lovecraft* (1987) have been edited by Steve Behrends.

Personal

I had of course heard a great deal about Clark Ashton Smith, and seen many pictures of him, but none of this had prepared me adequately for the man himself. He is tall and slender but well-made, and has a much more striking and massive head than his pictures indicate. On the occasion of our visit he wore dark slacks with a light sport coat and of course his omnipresent beret; trivial, perhaps, to mention the man's clothes, but it seemed vaguely incongruous to find the man who had written the sort of thing he has, dressed like any college student. And even more incongruous was it to discover, with a touch of pleased surprise, that the man I had thought of as aged and vibrant with a knowledge not of this world was instead as youthful as any of us. Smith is extremely shy at first, but as he gradually comes to feel that he is among friends who will not ridicule his mode of life and thought, he unbends, and becomes one of the most gracious hosts and entertaining conversationalists I have ever known.

We spent the afternoon drinking wine, talking, and being shown Smith's collection. His books, a choice and varied lot, including many surpassingly beautiful illustrated editions, are very much worth examining, but the real stab came from the surprisingly large quantity of artwork, mostly the creation of Smith himself. His sculptures, using the small boulders picked up in his yard, are somewhat known to fantasy lovers, several of them having been shown on the dust jacket of *Lost Worlds* and in the illustrations in ⟨Lovecraft's⟩ *Marginalia*. There were far more of them, however, than I had imagined—at least a hundred.

But the high point of the afternoon came when Smith brought out a stack of original drawings and paintings at least two feet thick. Perhaps 25 or 30 of them were commercially published ones, including the originals of most of Smith's drawings from *Weird Tales*, and the Finlay original from "The Thing on the Doorstep". (This last, incidentally, is by far the best Finlay pen-and-ink I have ever seen. Made before Virgil started drawing to size, it measures something like two by three feet, and has a mellowed beauty encountered but rarely among magazine illustrations.) There were also several early Boks, including a couple of wonderful unpublished ones, and an unpublished Roy Hunt drawing of Tsathoggua.

Smith's own drawings and paintings, every one of them unpublished, made up the rest of the stack. Nothing of his that has been published gives any inkling of the man's stature as an artist. In technique, of course, he lacks a good deal, being entirely self-taught. But he more than makes up for it with subtle and bizarre ideas, by a surprisingly good sense of form and structure, and above all by his unconventional and often superlative use of color. Most of the paintings are done in showcard paint, or something very much like it; they tend to be garish, but yet there is a certain use of restraint that makes even the most unrestrained ones quite acceptable. Perhaps twenty show entities from the Cthulhu Mythos; the remainder are extraterrestrial landscapes, divided about equally between non-human architecture and alien plant life.

Of the conversation I no longer remember much. Unforgettable, though, was Smith's impressive recitation of a medieval formula to raise the Devil. The afternoon was just guttering away into twilight, leaving the room in a hazy half darkness; between the look in Smith's pale eyes, the overtones in his voice, and his powerful delivery, I must admit that the chills were really going to town playing hide-and-seek along my backbone. Materialist that I am, I was actually relieved when Smith paused and remarked that he wouldn't repeat the spell a third time, for fear it would work! Then he laughed and the spell broke. But the man has dramatic powers which I believe might have made him famous as an actor had he followed that art.

With the onset of darkness, we went into town for dinner, taking Smith to a Chinese restaurant he had recommended. Our entry took on the air of a triumphal procession when we encountered the Auburnites, nearly all of whom greeted Smith warmly by name. It was pleasant to see that he is so well thought of by his fellow townsman, a type of recognition not always given to creative artists.

Smith had a date at 8:00, so we left him downtown and headed the Weird Willys towards the Golden Gate. His parting sally was unforgettable. Aaron was riding high on a fresh fruit kick, and just as we were leaving he dashed into an open market and bought a large sack of grapes. Smith looked at him with an air of profound disbelief, turned to me and whispered, "That may be all right, but personally I prefer the finished product."—
Francis T. Laney, *Ah, Sweet Idiocy!*, 1948, pp. 27–29

General

> Bow down: I am the emperor of dreams;
> I crown me with the million-colored sun
> Of secret worlds incredible, and take
> Their trailing skies for vestment when I soar,
> Throned on the mounting zenith, and illume
> The spaceward-flown horizon infinite. . . .

So begins a *tour de force* in modern American poetry: the cosmic epic in blank verse called *The Hashish-Eater: or, The Apocalypse of Evil*, by Clark Ashton Smith. Those six lines alone reveal many of the beauties in Smith's verse—the vivid metaphor in the first line, the hoary archaism of the second, the picturesque compounds in the second and sixth, the *enjambement* at the third and fifth, and the mind-expanding effect of the whole to which Smith's colleague H. P. Lovecraft has given the term "cosmic." But who is this forgotten lyrist, this atheistic or pantheistic Milton who wrote haiku and translated Baudelaire? More importantly, why has American criticism failed to take notice of the prolific poet and fictioneer whose work was published both humbly and prestigiously during the first five decades of this century?

The first question is easier to answer than the second.

Clark Ashton Smith was born in Long Valley, California, on January 13, 1893, lived most of his life in Auburn, California, and died in Pacific Grove, California, on August 14, 1961. In that span of time Smith produced seven collections of poetry and five volumes of fiction, along with translations from French and Spanish and a handful of essays on poetry and imaginative fiction. He tells us that he began the writing of fiction at the age of eleven, the writing of poetry at thirteen. Under the guidance of fellow Californian George Sterling, who quickly recognized his poetic gifts, Smith flowered precociously and issued, at the age of nineteen, the epochal *Star-Treader and Other Poems* (San Francisco: A. M. Robertson, 1912). Smith was cast immediately into fame among higher literary circles, and no less a figure than Ambrose Bierce—two years before his disappearance whose mystery would equal anything that he, Smith, or Lovecraft ever wrote—praised the volume. Vachel Lindsay and George Bicknell were equally impressed.

Odes and Sonnets followed in 1918 from The Book Club of California, and *Ebony and Crystal: Poems in Verse and Prose* (the volume which, when showed to him by mutual friend Samuel Loveman, so impressed H. P. Lovecraft that he began corresponding with Smith) was published at Smith's own expense in 1922—an indication, perhaps, of his already declining popularity. About this time Smith began his correspondence with Benjamin De Casseres, the nature and content of whose prose seemed to be as unpopular as that of Smith's poetry. De Casseres lamented to Smith:

> Knopf has just rejected 6 of my books . . . ; they run
> when they see me coming. I'm the Black Mass. So
> are you. We are both among the Crucified; but we
> can get drunk as hell while we wait for the Archangel
> Lucifer to pull out the nails.

"We are both among the Crucified": no truer words were ever spoken about Smith and his compeers in fantastic literature. Smith is, indeed, only another in that long line of exoticists—beginning, perhaps, with Petronius, and moving on through Thomas Browne, William Beckford (whose fragmentary "Third Episode of Vathek" Smith completed), Edgar Allan Poe, Charles Baudelaire, Joris-Karl Huysmans, Edgar Saltus, Ambrose Bierce, Arthur Machen, and H. P. Lovecraft—to whom only the Latin dictum *pulchrum est paucorum hominum* ("Beauty is for the few") can apply. For it takes an effort to read Smith: a dictionary in hand (similar, perhaps, to the one which he read through as a boy), a receptiveness to visions of almost cloyingly exquisite beauty, soul-clutching horror, and awe-inspiring cosmism. Smith is the ultimate *kosmopolitēs*: his city is not merely the world, but the universe. More so than even the dizzying prose of Lovecraft, Smith's poetry captures the music of the spheres—the planets reeling on their axes, the sentient monsters that lurk behind suns, the hand that crushes supernovae as a jest or mistake. Smith frees us from the bondage of human limitations, and makes us understand the quintessential beauty of cosmism.

His prose is perhaps less effective than his poetry, although it is now the better known—largely because it was published in now celebrated pulp magazines (*Weird Tales, Wonder Stories*, et al.) and, later, in book form by August Derleth's and Donald Wandrei's firm of Arkham House, and can thus be revived in the wake of the Lovecraft renaissance of the present day. Smith's tales do indeed have undoubted power; and though his use of esoteric and rare words—brilliant in the concentrated form of poetry but less so in prose—gives his style a rather labored cast, his imaginative power has been rivaled by few. Like Lovecraft, L. Frank Baum, E. R. Eddison, Mervyn Peake, and J. R. R. Tolkien, Smith was a Demiurgos who created lands of exotic beauty and terror as a foil for the commonplaceness of twentieth-century America. Whole sagas were written not only around such sites as Atlantis and Hyperborea, but Averoigne (the mythical province in medieval France) and such realms at the edge of the cosmos as Xiccarph and the lost continent Zothique.

But Smith's stories—numbering more than a hundred and some of great length—are, in fact, less central to his work because they were produced not, as with his poetry, from pure and sincere inspiration but partly from need. The Depression hit Smith's family hard in 1929, and he began producing stories at a rate which floored his colleagues—particularly Lovecraft, whose own work was a model for Smith's. We are reminded of Dr. Johnson's writing the novel *Rasselas* in a week to pay for his mother's funeral. But in curious contrast to Johnson, Smith's fictional output ceased upon the death of his mother and father in 1935 and 1937, respectively—perhaps because these dismal events relieved the financial burden upon him. Then, too, the departure of Smith's associates in fantasy fiction, Robert E. Howard and H. P. Lovecraft—the former having died in 1936, the latter in 1937—may have had a hand in drying up Smith's inspiration. He wrote fiction only occasionally thereafter, despite the requests of many magazine publishers who clamored for his work to appease the growing legions of fantasy and science-fiction fans. He seems, however, to have been working on a novel-length work (now in a private collection) at the very end of his life. His poetic productions, however, never ceased; and he saw his work published not only in book form by Arkham House, but in such journals as *Poetry*, *The Saturday Review of Literature*, and other important periodicals.

And, yet, his rejections remained more numerous than his acceptances. Smith's work was antipodal to the trend of modern poetry, which was abandoning traditional form and meter. While Smith wrote some poetry in free verse, he regularly used the purest and strictest verse in English: blank verse, Italian sonnet form, quatrains, and even the heroic couplet. In addition, his subject matter—the horrific, the bizarre, the *outré*, mingled with touches of the erotic, with Graeco-Roman mythology, and with that *fin-de-siècle* brand of exquisiteness which made him a spiritual brother of Baudelaire—was not one to give him a great popular fame. But among a handful of aesthetes whose sensibilities went beyond the appreciation of Tennyson, Kipling, and Matthew Arnold, Clark Ashton Smith was a significant if solitary voice whose archaism of tone and uniqueness of subject proclaimed his liberation from the tiny world of American life and his adherence to the timeless beauties of the universe. *Pulchrum est paucorum hominum.*—S. T. JOSHI, MARC A. MICHAUD, "The Prose and Poetry of Clark Ashton Smith," *BB*, 1979, pp. 81–84

Works

POETRY

Kindly convey to young Smith of Auburn my felicitations on his admirable "Ode to the Aybss"—a large theme, treated with dignity and power. It has many striking passages—such, for example, as "The Romes of ruined spheres." I'm conscious of my sin against the rhetoricians in liking that, for it jolts the reader out of the Abyss and back to earth. Moreover, it is a metaphor which belittles, instead of dignifying. But I like it.

He is evidently a student of George Sterling, and being in the formative stage, cannot—why should he?—conceal the fact.—AMBROSE BIERCE, Letter to George Sterling (Aug. 8, 1911), *The Letters of Ambrose Bierce*, ed. Bertha Clark Pope, 1922, pp. 180–81

Who of us care to be present at the *accouchment* of the immortal? I believe that we so attend who are first to take this book in our hands. A bold assertion, truly, and one demonstrable only in years remote from these; and—dust wages no war with dust. But it is one of those things that I should most "like to come back and see."

Because he has lent himself the more innocently to the whispers of his subconscious daemon, and because he has set those murmurs to purer and harder crystal than we others, by so much the longer will the poems of Clark Ashton Smith endure. Here indeed is loot against the forays of moth and rust. Here we shall find none or little of the sentimental fat with which so much of our literature is larded. Rather shall one in Imagination's "mystic mid-region" see elfin rubies burn at his feet, witch-fires glow in the nearer cypresses, and feel upon his brow a wind from the unknown. The brave hunters of fly-specks on Art's cathedral windows will find little here for their trouble, and both the stupid and the over-sophisticated would best stare owlishly and pass by: here are neither kindergartens nor skyscrapers. But let him who is worthy by reason of his clear eye and unjaded heart wander across these borders of beauty and mystery and be glad.—GEORGE STERLING, "Preface" to *Ebony and Crystal*, 1922, p. ix

When I received from Clark Ashton Smith his *Ebony and Crystal* in 1923, I had not read far before I was conscious that I was in the presence of one of the rare company of the Brotherhood of the Unearthly Imagination.

He is brother-prince to Poe, Baudelaire, Shelley, Rimbaud, Laforgue, Leconte de Lisle, Keats, Chopin, Blake and El Greco.

Like Goya's skeleton, Clark Ashton Smith has written across the stars *Nada!—Nothing!* But he has written it with a finger dipped in the multi-colored fluid that flows only from the breast of Aphrodite—and the dark milk of Proserpina.

He is, in a manner, a far greater anomaly in America—hard-bitten, realistic America—than was Edgar Allan Poe. Poe lived in a time when America was still somewhat romantic, when the iron collar of industrialism and the ball-and-chain of machinery had not been fastened upon us, before the stench of "proletarian" literature had yet arisen from the privies of mental and spiritual sterility.

Ashton Smith hovers over the corpse of matter like a beautiful, ironic Chimera over a Sphinx that is silent because it has nothing but imbecility in its eyes and an eternal vacuity in its brain—the Sphinx of "modernity".

You will find nothing of today or yesterday or tomorrow in the four volumes of Ashton Smith's poetry. Nothing but beauty, immortal, speechless beauty, and the record of the dust of worlds and the decomposed illusions of man.

He is a sheer Nihilist, a devaluer of all values in the alembic of an "Olympian ecstasy" and "the darkness that is God".

He is a rebel and his lord is Lucifer, the fallen angel, the Morning Star that heralds the last day when space shall roll up like a carpet and time shrivel to a moveless, sterile point in the center of an omnipotent darkness.

There is no variation in the poems of Ashton Smith. His song is of the death of Maya, emergence from the Fiery Wheel and hypostatic union with Buddha in Nirvana.

Humor? Yes—vast and terrible. The humor of the

mocker, but a mocker whose head is crowned with thorns and from whose eyes flow tears of ice.

The Hashish-Eater, one of his longest poems, is a glut of beauty that leaves me breathless in one continuous reading. Here are magnificent words piled on words until the keyboard of sounds seems exhausted; vast visions that open, as always in the poetry of Ashton Smith, on perilous nightmares in super-terrestrial fairylands accursed—until we come upon those final lines of a black apocalypse:

> A huge white eyeless Face
> That fills the void and fills the universe,
> And bloats against the limbs of the world
> With lips of flame that open. . . .

I could quote endlessly from his poems—a useless task. They must be read, and read only by those who from birth have seen what he has seen, felt what he has felt, and *know what he knows.*

Here is a profound sincerity, a perfect artistry and a vision that comes only to the rare—and superfluous—sons of Asmodeus and Ashtoreth.

Like Baudelaire, Poe and Blake, he has seen profoundly into another world. In that world he is immortal, one of the Rishis that sit behind the suns and write the epitaph of all living things in the waveless sands of eternity.—BENJAMIN DE CASSERES, "Clark Ashton Smith: Emperor of Shadows" (1937), *Selected Poems*, 1971, pp. 3–4

SHORT STORIES

> A time-black tower against dim banks of cloud;
>   Around its base the pathless, pressing wood.
> Shadow and silence, moss and mould, enshroud
>   Grey, age-fell'd slabs that once as cromlechs stood.
> No fall of foot, no song of bird awakes
>   The lethal aisles of sempiternal night,
> Though oft with stir of wings the dense air shakes,
>   As in the tower there glows a pallid light.
>
> For here, apart, dwells one whose hands have wrought
>   Strange eidola that chill the world with fear;
> Whose graven runes in tones of dread have taught
>   What things beyond the star-gulfs lurk and leer.
> Dark Lord of Averoigne—whose windows stare
> On pits of dream no other gaze could bear!
>   —H. P. LOVECRAFT, "To Clark Ashton Smith,
>   Esq., upon His Phantastick Tales, Verses, Pic-
>   tures, and Sculptures" (1936), *Collected Po-*
>   *ems*, 1963, p. 92

In writing fantastic science tales, two themes have attracted me more than others, and have seemed to offer the amplest possibilities and the deepest stimulus to imagination: the interplanetary and the inter-dimensional themes. Among those of my stories that can be classed, more or less accurately, as science fiction, the majority have dealt either with worlds remote in space, or worlds hidden from human perception by their different vibratory rate or atomic composition.

I am glad that my tale of life on Venus, "World of Horror," found favour with many readers of *Tales of Wonder*. I hope to return presently to this type of story, which, though exploited by so many authors, is still rich in unsounded potentialities. Indeed, there are no limits to their development except those of the writer's imagination. Here, however, lies the difficulty, since it is impossible for one to conceive forms and conditions of life, matter and energy that are wholly diverse from all terrestrial states and forms.

And yet, when one considers the fantastic variations of life on this one tiny planet, there seems little reason to presuppose that life on other worlds will necessarily repeat, or even resemble, the types known to us. In future ages, when space-transit has become a reality, our wildest fictions may seem feeble and commonplace beside the fantasies of Nature itself that explorers will discover on alien globes.

Among my several inter-dimensional stories, I think "City of Singing Flame" is the best. I owe its inspiration to several camping sojourns amid the high Sierras, at a spot within easy walking distance of the Crater Ridge described by Angarth and Hastane. The Ridge is a wild eerie place, differing wholly in its geology and general aspect from the surrounding region, exactly as pictured in the story. It impressed my imagination profoundly, suggesting almost at first sight the contiguity of some unknown, invisible world to which it might afford the mundane approach and entrance. And, since I have never explored the whole of its area, I am not altogether sure that the worn, broken column-ends found by the story's narrators do not really exist somewhere among the curiously shaped and charactered stones that lie in such strange abundance there!

All fantasy apart, however, it seems to me that the theory of interlocking worlds is one that might be offered and defended. We know nothing of the ranges of vibration, the forms of matter and energy, that may lie beyond the testing of our most delicate instruments. Spheres and beings whose atomic structure removes them from all detection may float through or beside the Earth, no less oblivious of our existence than we of theirs. Transit between planes of space, though filled with obvious material difficulties, is at least more readily comprehensible than time-travelling.—CLARK ASHTON SMITH, "Planets and Dimensions" (1940), *Planets and Dimensions: Collected Essays of Clark Ashton Smith*, ed. Charles K. Wolfe, 1973, pp. 56–57

⟨*Lost Worlds*⟩ is the latest in a series of occult writings which Arkham House has been exhuming from the pages of *Weird Tales, Wonder Stories, Strange Tales* and *Astounding Stories*, to be enshrined in book form. This one, even more than its horrifying predecessors—the collected works of H. P. Lovecraft, Henry S. Whitehead and Donald Wandrei—deserves to be put on the shelf and admired; it cannot be read.

The object of all these tales is, of course, the creation of new worlds in which to house whatever of fantasy, horror or demonology the imagination can contrive. Mr. Smith deals with Atlantis, Hyperborea, Uzaldaroum, Mhu Thulan, Zothique, Xiccarph and other "Lost Worlds" dating before the "great Ice Age."

What is most fascinating about the present volume is the kind of obfuscatory prose which readers of *Weird Tales*, etc., are apparently willing to overcome for the sake of getting at whatever terror may lie at the end of the skull-dotted trail. For example:

> What loathly spawn of the primordial slime had come forth to confront us we did not pause to consider or conjecture. The monstrosity was too awful to permit of even a brief contemplation; also its intentions were too plainly hostile, and it gave evidence of anthropophagic inclinations, for it slithered toward us with an unbelievable speed and celerity of motion, opening as it came a toothless mouth of amazing capacity.

Another feature of this style is the use of two words in place of one: "consider or conjecture," "speed and celerity of motion." Why Mr. Smith failed to say a "mouth of amazing and astounding capacity" I don't know; perhaps he was in a hurry. Dealing as he does with primordial monsters and with death and decay, he often has occasion to speak of the smells accompanying such phenomena. For these he has developed a wonderful set of synonyms, such as "the unfamiliar fetor I have spoken of previously, which had now increased uncomfortably in strength." Or "Opening the sealed door, they were met by a charnel odor, and were gratified to perceive in the figure the unmistakable signs of decomposition."

I have no doubt that the pages of this book, which I have been turning over so admiringly, conceal a wealth of imagination. But I am reminded of an old Cummulmluthian proverb which can be roughly translated as, "He who would sing must beware of the lotus," or "Do not give opium to those you would teach." There is another proverb, dating from the Age of Steam, which comments simply, "The blood of Poe is running very thin."— MARJORIE FARBER, "Atlantis, Xiccarph," *NYTBR*, Nov. 19, 1944, p. 18

DONALD A. WANDREI
From "The Emperor of Dreams"

Overland Monthly, December 1926, pp. 380–81, 407–9

In 1912 there came from the press of A. M. Robertson, in San Francisco, a slender book of poems. Had that volume come from a well-known writer, it would have ranked him with the immortals. Had it come from a rising author, it would have spread his fame far and wide. It came from neither. It was little advertised, for it had no financial backing and the author had neither influential friends nor acquaintances among those who determine what the public may read. No attempt was made to popularize it. The book shortly passed from sight, almost unknown save to a few fortunate people who possessed copies. The book was, *The Star-Treader and Other Poems*; its author, Clark Ashton Smith, a young poet, not yet twenty, who had already dreamed and dared to dream as few men have in a lifetime. That book of poems is one of the great contributions to American literature. It contains some of our finest pure poetry, some of our best imaginative lyrics. A few of them would now be famous, had they been written by a Keats or Shelley, and a cause of laurels. The critics have ignored the volume. The literary pontiffs have passed it over. Today, not many persons know it, even by title. Yet the same critics decry the anaemic state of American letters, its lack of enduring works. A genius—in the true, not abused, sense—appears, his eyes on the other side of eternity, his poems of eternity, his work the kind that endures. He is unnoticed. He is given no encouragement. American poetry is still anaemic.

A thousand years hence, when the people of that distant time survey the accumulated mass of all literature, they will place high up on the roll of honor the name, Clark Ashton Smith; and looking backward, they will ask why the world of that age long ago did not appreciate him when it had him. Perhaps this is as it ought to be. The man of letters should be the possession of those who do appreciate him. It is not given to ordinary man to walk with the gods; nor, when it is so given, does he usually avail himself of the opportunity unless he is one of that group which is the justification of himself, the cornerstone of the arts, and the prophet of immortality.

A poet cannot live on visions, on dreams, on a prospect of future fame. He must live on something more material. And one can not write when it is necessary to earn a sustenance. Perhaps this was the reason that ten years elapsed before

another book appeared under the poet's name. Or perhaps it was the neglect, popular, which is of little importance, and critical, which may be of the greatest importance, given his first book. Or perhaps the dreamer lived in his own realm, indifferent to ephemeral external life, writing seldom and then mainly for his own pleasure. Or perhaps . . . One trembles at the thought. *Ebony and Crystal* was published by the author in 1922. Its fate is akin to that of *The Star-Treader*. Not many persons know it. Those who do regard it as worshippers a sanctum sanctorum, as connoisseurs a rare tapestry, as jewellers a priceless pearl.[1]

There is no place in contemporary prose and poetry for genius.

Was *Ebony and Crystal* worth the labor of ten years? It is a larger volume than the first and contains twice as many poems, one hundred and fourteen against fifty-five. Did eleven poems a year, and those not of unusual length, with one exception, justify the author a place among the front-rank poets? If fame is the criterion, no. If excellence, yes. *Ebony and Crystal* is the finest volume of pure poetry that has appeared in America since the opening of the twentieth century, perhaps the finest since the time of Edgar Allan Poe. Not until its publication did any of our poets approach him in imaginative power. *Ebony and Crystal* belongs on that shelf with Poe, Coleridge, Blake, Shelley, Baudelaire. In that group where each is coequally supreme, he may justly take his place.

Imagination is his god, beauty his ideal; his poems are an offering to both. He is the poet of the infinite, the envoy of eternity, the amanuensis of beauty. For even as beauty was deity to Keats and Shelley, so it is to him, and in its praise has he written. But he has not celebrated it as an abstract term or an aesthetic quality, but as a more tangible substance. He has constructed entire worlds of his own and filled them with creations of his own fancy. And his beauty has thus crossed the boundary between that which is mortal and that which is immortal, and has become the beauty of strange stars and distant lands, of jewels and cypresses and moons, of flaming suns and comets, of marble palaces, of fabled realms and wonders, of gods, and daemons, and sorcery. Time and Space have been his servants, the universe his domain; with the stars his steeds and the heavens his tramping ground, he has wandered in realms afar; and he has found there a wondrous beauty and a strange fear, the goal of his early dreams and the enchanted road to greater, all manner of things illusory and fantastical.

Some of his poems are like shadowed gold; some are like flame-encircled ebony; some are crystal-clear and pure; others are as unearthly starshine. One is coldly wrought in marble; another is curiously carved in jade; there are a few glittering diamonds; and there are many rubies and emeralds aflame, glowing with a secret fire. Here and there may be found a poppy-flower, an orchid from the hot-bed of Hell, the whisper of an eldritch wind, a breath from the burning sands of regions infernal. The wizard calls, and at his imperious summons come genie, witch, and daemon to open the portal to the haunted realms of faery; and their wonder is transmuted so that those who can open the door may listen to the murmuring waters of Acheron, or watch the passing of a phantom throng; and the fen-fires gleam; and the slow mists arise; and heavy perfumes, and poisons, and dank odors fill the air. A marble palace rises in the dusk, a treasure-house of gold, and ebony, and ivory; soft lutes play within; fair women, passionless and passionate, wander in the corridors; silks and tapestries adorn the walls, and fuming censers burn a rare incense. And fabulous demorgon and hippogriff guard the golden gateway to the hoarded wealth. The sky is black. But now and again white comets blaze, or suns of green, of crimson, of purple, flame across the firmament with silver moons. The sky is burning. Stars hurtle to destruction or waste away. All mysteries are uncurtained. One may watch a landscape of the moon, the seas of Saturn, the sunken fanes of old Atlantis, wars and wonders on some distant star.

There is no place in the poetry of Clark Ashton Smith for the conventional, the trite, the outworn. It is useless to search his work for offerings, to popular desire. Some authors pander to the public taste; their books may have a huge sale, but die with the author. Some writers have skill and ability but desire wealth or immediate fame; their work has not so great a popularity but endures longer. A very few have what is called "genius." They write primarily for themselves, or with a certain small group of people who know literature in mind. They are artists, word artists; and they fashion their prose or poetry with care and labor. They are seldom appreciated in their lifetime, and never have widespread popularity, but the highest minds of every age enjoy their work. These are ones who speak to us across the ages, who will speak across the ages to come. It is to this class that Clark Ashton Smith belongs. One will examine his poems in vain for the commonplaces that have so largely crept into our literature; and by so much as he has avoided ephemeral and written of immortal things, by so much the longer will his work endure.

II

The Star-Treader was his earliest volume, and it shows the effects of imagination in its first exuberance. Stars and suns and comets parade in all their majesty; Chaos, Infinity, and "the eldritch dark" are ever present; and the wonder, the inexplicable mystery of the Universe form the background of the book. It was then that the young poet wrote "The Song of a Comet;" it was then that he fashioned "The Song of the Stars;" and from his pen came "The Wind and the Moon." Of the fixed forms, the sonnet was his favorite, and nearly a third of the poems have its form. In most of them he strove to obtain single, dominant effects, to limn one unforgettable scene, as in "The Last Night," "The Medusa of the Skies," and "Averted Malefice." Occasionally, he was content with a single quatrain, or a pair, as "The Maze of Sleep" and "The Morning Pool." But he had a greater chance to display his power in the longer, more sustained poems, such as "Saturn," "The Star-Treader," and "The Masque of Forsaken Gods." They would have been accomplishments for a man of maturity, for one who had long written poetry, as the work of a youth they are remarkable achievements. The entire book has this note of maturity; it was a world-weary youth wise beyond his years who wrote these poems beautiful, fantastic, sometimes bitter and more than once inexpressibly terrible in their suggestion.

The Star-Treader was published in 1912. Not for ten years did another book come from the poet. What had he been doing those ten long years? Had the neglect of his first book compelled him to turn his mind into other channels? It is hard to say, but *Ebony and Crystal* is not a large volume for the work of ten years.

There is a great difference between the two, in imagery, in tone and subject, and in metrical skill. The first was, to some extent, experimental; the second, a fulfillment of the promise in the foreshadowing work. The craftsmanship of these later poems is wellnigh flawless; the volume is rich in perfectly planned, perfectly fashioned jewels. It is jewel-cutting that he was engaged in those ten years. Here may be found "such stuff as dreams are made of," and the dreams themselves; here the utterance of god and witch, the harmony

of the spheres, the strains of immortal music, the unveiling of an imagery unparalled. The beauty of these poems is intoxicating, for the poet who wrote them was haunted and intoxicated by loveliness immaculate and incarnate, by all beauty. And the poems are couched not in ordinary language, but in an English filled with curious and archaic forms, rare or obsolete words, unusual diction; and they have been given flowing rhythms and unforgettable melodies; and they move in measured intonation, and in cadence, and in musical sweep that are seldom found in poetry. They are whispers of the unearthly, rather than mortal work. They are enduring forms of unenduring dreams and ideals and desires. They are the unattainable, set in deathless words of gold. They are time-outlasting marble; they are lotus and poppy; they are fadeless amaranth and asphodel, pure, perfect shadows of the pure and perfect, eternal, aeonian. They are star-dust and star-shine, caught by a dreamer of the ages, fashioned in ebony and crystal. They are nectar and ambrosia, nepenthe, Lethean draughts to drown the world in forgetfulness and oblivion. They are the waters of paradise. ⟨. . .⟩

There is one long poem, however, that deserves special attention. It is *The Hashish-Eater*, containing many hundred lines of blank verse. But it is far different from what is usually called blank verse, from what one knows as ordinary iambic pentameter. This has always been a stately metre, capable of impressive effects; and in his hands, with the aid of his boundless imagination and descriptive powers, besides his technical skill, it has become the implement of a poem-colossus, gigantic in theme and treatment, told in a heavy, sonorous English that sweeps onward in measured roll with an ever-swelling rhythm from the imperial summons of the opening lines:

> Bow down: I am the emperor of dreams;
> I crown me with the million-colored sun
> Of secret worlds incredible, and take
> Their trailing skies for vestment, when I soar,
> Throned on the mounting zenith, and illume
> The spaceward-flown horizons infinite.

And at the very end of a volume which will one day be a prized literary heritage is the sombre and morbidly magnificent prose-poem, "The Shadows," a poem told with such care that no word is lost or wasted, and so well that it lingers in the memory as a sable fantasy enshrined, a rare perfume, darkly odorous and darkly poisonous, clinging to a bit of strangely shapen ebony.

III

In October, 1925, came the third of his published books, *Sandalwood*, a volume which, though slender, contains more poems than his first. After *Ebony and Crystal*, not much could be added to his laurels, but had that volume not existed, *Sandalwood* might have taken its place to a large extent. It is different from *Ebony and Crystal* in that the poems are less ambitious with regard to the depicting of strange, vast splendour, but more songlike, lyrical, and spontaneous, though the mastery of technique and the metrical skill displayed admit of neither spontaneity nor its attendant roughnesses. The poems may be divided into several classes, including nineteen translations from Baudelaire, and four songs from the uncompleted romantic drama, *The Fugitives*. And there is a poem of six stanzas, "We Shall Meet," told in an original or very rare but very beautiful verse form. But to one who has read the early work of Clark Ashton Smith, his later poems remain beyond praise. One may go into ecstasies at a vision of glory; but the greater glory surpasses description. And he who has sate on the ramparts of Heaven and Hell is mute before magnificence and pageantry that shame the speech.

No critic and no criticism can do justice to the work of this poet. There are some things which are beyond the reach of both, and in this rare group belongs the work of Clark Ashton Smith. For there are books so distinctive, so excellent, that they can not be compared with others of their class, by reason of their perfection. For them, there is no standard of judgment, and one can only admire what one is helpless to censure or to sanctify. To use homely language in estimating such work is to do it an injustice; and yet, superlatives are equally useless, for they have been so carelessly employed that nowadays they deprecate the work they are meant to extol.

Earlier in this essay, certain other poets of the romantic-imaginative group were mentioned. But Clark Ashton Smith can not be associated with any particular one. Each within that class was original, and by virtue of a similar originality, this modern poet deserves his rank. The great poets neither follow nor imitate; they create. And he has created, on a cosmic scale. The greatest indictment of contemporary verse is its lack of form, its deliberate exclusion of the most vital quality of a work of art, a quality which every book that aspires to greatness must have, above all else, if it is to endure. Substance—form; form—substance; of the two, form is by far the most important. And this element—including, as it does, diction, style, presentation, euphony, craftsmanship—is present in the poems of Clark Ashton Smith to such an extraordinary degree that, had

there been no substance, had he produced only rainbows and iridescent bubbles, he would still have deserved lasting attention. Indeed, the sole flaw in his poems is occasionally form in too great a degree. His gifts are so much beyond those of average poets, and his vocabulary is of such enormous content that the desired word is often an uncommon one. Yet even this lends a curious charm, a singularly effective atmosphere to the poem, at worst, it may only be considered what would be a god-send to the lamentably word-base verse of the Philistines. It is an example of his innate power of concentration, his ability to say best and to say beautifully the things that deserve to be clothed in costly raiment.

Just where the place of this emperor of dreams will ultimately be fixed in poetry can not, of course, be foretold, save that it should be very high. Nor can one prophesy the day he shall receive the recognition he has earned. It took the world forty years to appreciate Thomas Lovell Beddoes; it took longer for it to appreciate William Blake; Arthur O'Shaughnessy is still almost unknown; and few even of those occasional persons who have read *The Book of Jade* could tell the name of its author, Park Barnitz. And now, Clark Ashton Smith—

Notes

1. I have since been informed that the silence was due to the destruction of imperfect poems, and to ill-health. It is hard to believe this statement in a day when the least is treasured by those whose best is mediocre. But it explains the uniform excellence of his work, the lack of a single weak poem.

W. D. SNODGRASS

1926–

William De Witt Snodgrass was born on January 5, 1926, in Wilkinsburg, Pennsylvania, the son of an accountant and his wife. He served in the U.S. Navy at the end of World War II and was educated at Geneva College and at the University of Iowa, where he received an M.F.A. in poetry. He has taught at a number of universities, including Cornell, Rochester, Syracuse, and Delaware, and has been an active participant in poetry workshops and at writers' conferences.

Snodgrass published his first collection of poetry, *Heart's Needle*, in 1959; it won the Pulitzer Prize the following year and was also the recipient of Britain's Guinness Award in 1961. He has also written *After Experience* (1967) and *The Fuehrer Bunker* (1977), and translated, with Lore Segal, Christian Morgenstern's *Gallows Songs* (1967). A collection of critical essays, *In Radical Pursuit*, was published in 1975. Snodgrass has also translated Hungarian and Rumanian verse, and is a regular contributor of poetry and essays to a number of periodicals.

A member of the National Institute of Arts & Letters and a fellow of the Academy of American Poets, Snodgrass has received grants from the National Endowment for the Arts and the Guggenheim Foundation. He has been married several times, has three children, and lives in Erieville, New York.

UNSIGNED

"No Man Is a Battlefield"

Times Literary Supplement, January 2, 1969, p. 7

A poet in a country where anything can be turned in for a new one, W. D. Snodgrass stays loyal to his unpoetic surname, and the essential claim his poetry makes is that it is necessary to write beautifully in spite of circumstances. Reading his list of acknowledgments (in *After Experience*) (they have already been quoted by British reviewers, to whom names like the Corporation of Yaddo will always sound as if a homeward-

bound Dickens is contemptuously pronouncing them) and remembering earlier rewards and fellowships from the *Hudson Review*, the reader is more than mildly put off, as by the abstractly unimpressive rows of fruit salad on the chests of American generals. But the crucial point is that all this information is available: Snodgrass does not cover up. It is nowadays very difficult for an American poet of manifest talent to be put out of business by want or by neglect. Snodgrass does not pretend otherwise. Hemmed in by endpapers and wrappers proclaiming his jobs, honours and awards (naturally the foundation will bear your expenses), his poetry steers clear of the poet's condition, which is obviously in A1 shape, and concentrates on the personal condition, which seems to be in a fruitful state of permanent confusion.

If "confessional" poetry exists at all (and if it does, Snodgrass and Lowell are still the two best Americans writing it), its basic assumption is that the time-honoured separation of the private man and the public artist can now be closed: the pose is over, and all the masks can be put away. The trick is worked, when it works, not by lowering the universal to the level of personality, but by elevating the vicissitudes of private life to the level of the universal. Insofar as the poet succeeds in convincing the reader that his personal suffering has an impersonal resonance, his work will chime: insofar as he does not, it will grate. Snodgrass grated badly in passages like this from the title poem of his first book, *Heart's Needle*:

> In their smooth covering, white
> As quills to warm the resting bed
> Of birth or pain, spotless as pages spread
> For me to write.

Or this, from the same poem:

> Like nerves caught in a graph,
> the morning-glory vines
> frost has erased by half
> still crawl across their rigid twines.
> Like broken lines
> of verses I can't make.

Years later, in the work collected in *After Experience*, the same slate is scratched:

> Now I can earn a living
> By turning out elegant strophes.

The reader's first and sound reaction is that he does not want to hear this: just read the news, please. The reaction is sound because this new habit of calling attention to the practical business of putting words on paper is the trivialization of what for some centuries has correctly been regarded as a divine act, an act which no decent practitioner should regard as his own preserve. The effect is childish, even in a poet of Snodgrass's abilities: he is joined in this to those academically-environed hordes of giftless poets who utterly fail to realize that man is not the measure of art. But before we come to that general point, it can be put beyond doubt that Snodgrass is a poet capable of extraordinary effects. His acute, sparely employed (in fact under-indulged) metaphorical sense can put an era into an image:

> This moth caught in the room tonight
> Squirmed up, sniper-style, between
> The rusty edges of the screen;

Faster and neater than that you don't get: a whole background comes over in a flash. The well-known virtuoso effort "The Examination" (once "the Phi Beta Kappa ceremonial poem at Columbia University" save the mark), detailing the ghastly victimization of a generalized Otherness and recalling the eery dismemberment of angels in the film by Borowczik, has an exquisitely schooled timing in its local effects that creates for the reader a nightmare he cannot stop:

> Meantime, one of them has set blinders to the eyes,
> Inserted light packing beneath each of the ears
> And calked the nostrils in. One, with thin twine, ties
> The genitals off. With long wooden-handled shears,
> Another chops pinions out of the scarlet wings.

You can see how each line of the stanza infallibly brings something worse to life, and how, after the qualification "wooden-handled" has placed your own garden-shears in your hands, the jump across the gap to the next stanza tells you that the next thing is the worst of the lot. In an age of fake rough stuff turned out by those youngish poets who seem fascinated by greased hair and high boots this poem, and another called "A Flat One" about an old man dying, are evidence that Snodgrass is capable of genuine tragic power—a power that the fashionable preoccupation with violence tends to dissipate. And it is not accidental that in these two instances the viewpoint is impersonal: the crippling assumption that one man can be a world is not in evidence.

Of those poems referring to a life meant to sound like his own the best are those in which the experience has a general applicability to a time, to a culture. "What We Said", a gently singing reminiscence of estrangement, is a good example. When he tries extra hard to supply the specific detail which will give the sense of a particular life (this is really *me* talking) he tends to be in the first place flimsy ("Mementos I" fades right out beside Larkin's poem using the same properties, "Lines on a Young Lady's Photograph Album") and in the second place dishonourable, since the theme, reduced to the loss of happiness, seems to assume a *right* to happiness which for sound reasons has never been counted among an artist's legitimate expectations. Betraying themselves technically by a prevalence of shakily cantilevered rhymes (bringing the reader as near as he will ever get to groaning at poetry of this accomplishment), such poems demonstrate that a necessary consequence of abolishing the distinction of private life and public life is that ordinary privacy ceases to exist as a concept: characterized with a ruthless hand and unable to answer back, the true sufferers in "confessional" poetry are the poets' wives.

The contradiction inherent in "confessional" poetry which goes beyond its scope is damagingly evident in Snodgrass's attempt at a poem about Eichmann, "A Visitation". Technically very interesting, it creates an effect of jammed dialogue by interlacing two monologues, one by Eichmann, the other by the poet. (This exceedingly difficult trick of stereo voicing is used by Snodgrass elsewhere in "After Experience Taught Me . . ." and he may be said by now to hold the copyright on it.) But examined close to, the poem reveals itself to be dependent on all the usual weary banalities that would trace the phenomena of mass-murder to tendencies in the artist's own soul, provide the illusion of debate and flatter the pretensions of the liberal spirit towards a forgiving generosity. In view of this it is particularly unfortunate that the poem should carry as an epigraph a quotation from Hannah Arendt, who has certainly declared (in the very book from which Snodgrass quotes) that these events can be understood in the long run only by the poets, but who equally certainly, and as long ago as the appearance of her monumental *The Origins of Totalitarianism*, made her views known about those who thought "that inner experience could be given historical significance, that one's own self had become the battlefield of history".

"Confessional" poetry has taken a small, previously neglected field among all the possible fields of poetry and within that field pushed on to a new adventure. It becomes absurd when it usurps the impersonal fields with the language of the personal—when it fails to recognize its limitations. Eichmann's crimes, for example, were in the public realm; they are not to be traced to the sadistic impulse which is in all of us or to any other impulse which is in all of us: they can be understood only in history. When the poet pretends to contain, mirror or model history within his own suffering, his talent gives out for just as long as the folly lasts: the better he is, the worse the work he does; and even a first-rate talent like Snodgrass's produces the smoothly "distinguished" work which is the bane of our age and to which we do not normally expect a man of his powers to contribute.

WILLIAM HEYEN
From "Fishing the Swamp:
The Poetry of W. D. Snodgrass"
Modern American Poetry: Essays in Criticism
ed. Jerome Mazzaro
1970, pp. 352–61

In general, *Heart's Needle* is a poetry of experience, of present tense and present tension; *After Experience* (1968), as its ambiguous title implies, is at once a poetry of the poet's meditation on past happenings and a poetry of his determination to experience new ways of seeing, acting, and feeling. By the time of its appearance—though some of the poems date back to when Snodgrass was composing *Heart's Needle*—the poet has survived certain experiences and is out, after these, looking for others that will continue to make him feel alive. Snodgrass tells us again and again that one can exist only by living the passionate life, by freeing the soul, though this action itself will inevitably bring grief to those we love the most.

In *Heart's Needle* both the world men had some part in making and the natural world—the world of seasonal ebb and flow—dominate the poet-speaker. He is caught up in, and not a little stifled by, what seem to be inexorable cycles of existence. There are occasional pauses, moments of permanence, as in "The Operation" when "In my brandy bowl / Of sweet peas at the window, the crystal world / Is inverted, slow and gay." But there are no new directions. Monotonous patterns remind us only of the fact that we are moving closer to old age and death.

In "Ten Days Leave," the opening poem, the poet expects, returning home, that the war would have changed something:

> But no; it seems just like it seemed. His folks
> Pursue their lives like toy trains on a track.
> He can foresee each of his father's jokes
> Like words in some old movie that's come back.

And in the final section of "Heart's Needle," visiting the park with his daughter, the poet says that "our seasons bring us back once more / like merry-go-round horses," and he again fastens on the image of the train—"and the miniature painted train / wails on its oval track." Snodgrass' universe is oval and largely determined, but just as there may be room in Ishmael's woof-and-warp world for free choice, Snodgrass suggests that we can choose our fate. He tells his daughter: "Child, I have another wife, / another child. We try to choose our life" ("Heart's Needle," vi). And she, too, must still learn to choose the unavoidable.

The social protest and the uncomfortable feelings associated with the cyclic existence hinted at in "Ten Days Leave" are deepened in "Returned to Frisco, 1946." The speaker, one of those who had "scrambled like rabbits / Up hostile beaches," fears the land to which he is returning, "this land / Intent on luxuries and its old habits." The poem concludes:

> Off the port side, through haze, we could discern
> Alcatraz, lavender with flowers. Barred,
> The Golden Gate, fading away astern,
> Stood like the closed gate of your own backyard.

This is a brilliant stanza. Its ironic central images of prison and golden bridge become revelation, pierce the "haze" of the problem, posed by an earlier line, that we are "Free to choose just what they meant we should." We know from Nathaniel Hawthorne's *The Scarlet Letter* (1850) that our country's earliest immigrants had considered it a necessity to allot a portion of the soil for a prison. Here, then, is the American Dream. The Golden Gate stands barred from view and fades away astern. Alcatraz is lavender with flowers. Choice is always, perhaps, a matter of illusion. And the reality of the Dream: "Beyond, jagged stars / are glinting like jacks hurled / farther than eyes can gather" ("At the Park Dance").

Having lost his individuality during the war, having forgotten his name, the poet returns to what he calls "No Man's Land." In his "Home Town" he learns he is "no one here." To be a personality instead of a statistic, to have a name and to be able to sing it—these things are matters of life or living death. After, in "A Cardinal," cursing this bird for devouring an insect, the poet realizes he is being absurd. He hears the bird's indisputable song: "'I music out my name / and what I tell is who / in all the world I am.'" And he comes to realize that "Each trade has its way of speaking, / each bird its name to say." In "These Trees Stand . . ." he assures himself that "Snodgrass is walking through the universe." In "April Inventory" he tells us how, though "In thirty years I may not get / Younger, shrewder, or out of debt," he can afford the "costly seasons": "I taught myself to name my name." If, as in "A Cardinal," the noises of free enterprise are a "devil's Mass"; if, as in "The Campus on the Hill" (with its ironic echoes of E. A. Robinson's "The House on the Hill") and "April Inventory" even academia is shot through with twisted, nonhumanistic values; if the necessities to name his own name and beat out his own rhythms estrange him from others—he can still, as he writes in "Orpheus," be "Rich in the loss of all I sing."

Many of the lyrics in *Heart's Needle* are lasting achievements, but the title sequence of ten poems, one for each season over a period of two and a half years, is one that makes Snodgrass' volume as important as, perhaps, only a half dozen others during this century of American verse. The poet-father's voice here is unique: urgent but controlled, muted but passionate, unassuming but instructive. Snodgrass manages a poetry that moves from his own psychological problems to suggest what it feels like to be a man and to live in the mid-century world. The frequently reiterated charge that Snodgrass offends "aesthetic distance" is nonsense and is made by those who feel it necessary to group the poet with certain other flagrantly abusive autobiographical poets. We are likely to hear more talk about the women in Snodgrass' life and about his Iowa City background than we are about "Heart's Needle" as poetry.

The poet refuses, though he could so easily have fallen into sentimentality, to cry in his beer or look for the reader's shoulder. His verses are tightly rhymed and are rendered, with some variation, in accentual syllabics. Underneath the form is the recognition that there is to be no letting go, no backsliding into bathos. One of the stanzas that keep echoing in my mind is from Section IV, perhaps the tenderest and most passionate, and therefore the most aesthetically dangerous, of the sequence:

> No one can tell you why
> the season will not wait;
> the night I told you I
> must leave, you wept a fearful rate
> to stay up late.

The rhythmic poundings, the broken lines and full rhymes, make for an emotional music, but one with an edge of rage. These are the fourth, fifth, and sixth stanzas of the same poem:

> But the asters, too, are gray,
>   ghost-gray. Last night's cold
>   is sending on their way
> petunias and dwarf marigold,
>   hunched sick and old.
>
>   Like nerves caught in a graph,
>   the morning-glory vines
>   frost has erased by half
> still scrawl across their rigid twines.
>   Like broken lines
>
>   of verses I can't make.
>   In its unraveling loom
>   we find a flower to take,
> with some late buds that might still bloom,
>   back to your room.

What is apparent here is the speaker's self-control. His teeth, so to speak, are on edge with tenderness. The "twines" of "Heart's Needle" are rigid, and there is a dramatic irony that makes the sequence come alive. The poet is talking to himself and to us more than he is to his daughter. As he says to her in Section IX, "I write you only the bitter poems / that you can't read."

The title of the sequence comes from "The Frenzy of Suibne," an old Irish story. Even the epigraph adopted by Snodgrass suggests that what is to follow is to be no soulful, melancholy outpouring of grief: "'*Your daughter is dead*,' *said Loingsechan*. '*And an only daughter is the needle of the heart*,' *said Suibne*. '*Dead is your son who used to call you "Father*,"' *said Loingsechan*. '*Indeed*,' *said he*, '*that is the drop that brings a man to the ground*.'" The loss of an only daughter is, indeed, a needle in the heart, but it is the loss of a son that kills. And although the poet-father of the sequence finds that his daughter, separated from him because of his divorce, has changed, he concludes, addressing her, "And you are still my daughter."

The first section of the sequence consists of six quatrains, one sentence, a form that suggests that neither the enunciation of the conflicts begun when "I could not find / My peace in my will," nor the resolution of these conflicts is to be an easy matter. If the Korean War—in *Heart's Needle* war is as constant as the seasons—"fouled the snows" of Asia, his child's mind, "a landscape of new snow," is also likely to be marked by what he sees as his own "cold war." The speaker seems to realize that his passion, his heart's will, had to take him toward the "love I could not still," that his head's will had to lose. As he does in "The Operation," Snodgrass associates whiteness with innocence; his divorce, a peculiarly modern aspect of alienation, will be, for his daughter, a life's lesson, a movement toward experience.

The second poem, a parable for his daughter, concerns her garden, one she herself seems bent on destroying, and suggests that she, too, is a sprout that will come to full flower only when (and perhaps because) he will be away. The third poem, beginning "The child between them on the street / Comes to a puddle, lifts his feet / And hangs on their hands," continues the cold war theme. Here he wishes to assure his child that although he is "gone / As men must and let you be drawn / Off to appease another," he loves her: "Solomon himself might say / I am your real mother." This implies that to save his daughter he must be willing to give her up. Unfortunately, there is no wise king to decree that the two of them shall not be separated. For him the pain remains, and the rage: "what must not be seized / Clenches the empty fist."

With the fourth poem, four stanzas of which are quoted above, fall has arrived. Father and daughter walk among ghost-gray flowers and try to talk. As Donald T. Torchiana has written in *Poets in Progress* (1962), here the father's hopes "remain for his daughter's life in spite of the separation. These hopes also commingle with his fears for the halted scrawl of his own unfinished verses brought home to him by a glimpse of broken morning glories." The poem's final stanza portends grief for her and death for him, but unspoken here is also the realization that he must continue his writing:

> Night comes and the stiff dew.
> I'm told a friend's child cried
>   because a cricket, who
> had minstreled every night outside
>   her window died.

The fifth song of the sequence brings winter and a deadening of feeling. His daughter, growing strange to him, is happy and does not seem to mind "the squalls and storms / That are renewed long since"; he, at the same time, compares himself to a fox who "backtracks and sees the paw, / Gnawed off, he cannot feel; / Conceded to the jaw / Of toothed, blue steel." But April is the "cruellest" month. In the sixth poem "Easter has come around / Again." Memories are stirred by the spring thaw, and the father fears, because of a night he remembers when his daughter's "lungs caught and would not take the air," that she will not choose her own life. He is afraid that, letting her go as he let a pigeon go to its keeper, he has snarled her in a net. After a storm "torn limbs that could sap the tree" are hacked loose. "In the debris lay / starlings dead." The institutions of society, throughout *Heart's Needle*, are traps, prisons, tangles of branches. And destruction, perhaps, is the inevitable outcome of any attempt to live the individual life.

The push-pull of the poet's relationship with his daughter, his desire to turn her loose and, at the same time, to hold on to her, troubles him, and he weighs the destructiveness of this desire. In the seventh poem his heart's needle is seen as a force natural as gravity:

> Here in the scuffled dust
>   is our ground of play.
> I lift you on your swing and must
>   shove you away,
> see you return again,
>   drive you off, again, then
> stand quiet till you come.
>   You, though you climb
> higher, farther from me, longer,
>   will fall back to me stronger.

The left margin moves back and forth like a swing, and the sound-sense rhythms, as in the third and fourth lines above, attest to Snodgrass' metrical virtuosity.

In the eighth poem his daughter becomes the fox, visiting him over Halloween and not knowing what she has lost and what effect her relationship with her father has on her. He watches her sleeping. She grates her jaw, as cold war soldiers grind their jaws in the third poem, and he remarks: "Assuredly your father's crimes / are visited / on you." But it is as though, as his daughter breaks the "year's first crust of snow / off the runningboard to eat," she has accepted and chosen to live in the real world. No longer does she chew on "white, sweet clover." Her food is not to be stars cooked for dinner; rather, the meals that her "absentee bread-winner" father can prepare for her will be more earthy fare. And the father realizes that if he is to continue building "back from helplessness" she will have to visit him less often: "Indeed our sweet / foods leave us cavities."

Three months later and alone—although she is living less than a mile away it has been this long since he has seen his daughter—he visits a museum, the setting of the ninth and longest of the "Heart's Needle" sequence. The museum becomes for the poet a microcosm of the world and its passions, and this is also the darkest of the poem's movements; indeed, this is one of the darkest poems of our time. It is only in the museum that the evil and disease of the world is "arrested . . . in violent motion / like Napoleon's troops"; only here that stuffed animals "in their peaceable kingdoms freeze / to this still scene"; only here that "the malignancy man loathes / is held suspended." Outside the "world moves like a diseased heart / packed with ice and snow." The origin of the world's ills is traced back even to the "putty-colored children curled / in jars of alcohol." The poet doesn't know the answers. A return to the world, after the museum, is a return to the seasons, to cycles of both numbness and agony. The poem reads like a cynical and bitter suicide note. There is no such thing as a time that heals all wounds.

In the tenth and final poem, however, father and daughter are once more together. "The vicious winter finally yields"— not the winter of discontent, but the winter of absolute negation. It is as though the father, a prisoner of his passions, is determined to accept the bitter fruits of his life. His situation parallels that of the coons:

> If I loved you, they said, I'd leave
> and find my own affairs.
> Well, once again this April, we've
> come around to the bears;
> punished and cared for, behind bars,
> the coons on bread and water
> stretch thin black fingers after ours.
> And you are still my daughter.

At the end of the sequence the poet, still on bread and water, is in the same position he was in when he returned from "Frisco."

Heart's Needle remains a poetry without answers, but it is a poetry of total awareness. Inherent in its criticism of the way things are is the ability of the intelligence that informs its lyrics to accept this reality and to struggle against it at the same time. *Heart's Needle*, without caterwauling, free from what Ezra Pound calls "emotional slither," takes on dimensions of the tragic.

ROBERT PHILLIPS
From "W. D. Snodgrass and the Sad Hospital
of the World"
The Confessional Poets
1973, pp. 66–72

The Snodgrass of *Heart's Needle* was a taker of risks; too many of the purely personal poems in *After Experience* smack of the ingrown nail—everything growing inward, with too much consciousness of Self and Craft. The four new poet-daughter poems seem blurry, heavy carbons of the sharp originals. They were, perhaps, written at the time of the cycle and deliberately withheld from the book for that reason. And as if aware his situation is no longer so unique, his revelations no longer so revealing, in the second book Snodgrass coarsens his language as if that alone might still shock. Elegance has fled

from the poetry, the fine elegance of, say, "Winter Bouquet." When the poet passes a drive-in now, it must be described as one of the "hot pits where our teens / Finger fuck."

Not that Snodgrass need resort to gutter language to shock. The title poem, "After Experience," describing an act of self-defense so acutely painful no one can read it without a wince of the eye, a flop of the stomach, is ample evidence of his rhetorical powers. Aside from the purely personal and confessional poems with the manner, if not the power, of *Heart's Needle*, the poems in the second volume must be categorized in three other distinct groups. First come the more objective poems, including the supremely successful "A Flat One," which amplifies the hospital imagery of "The Operation" but makes the act of saving a life seem a selfish gesture and comments on modern life in a more devastating way than any other poem in recent American literature; "Lobsters in the Window," which imagistically re-creates the primordial life as it comments on mass conformity; and "The Platform Man," a poem in which guilt and mutilation fuse in a most beautifully placed and seemingly inevitable pun; as well as an uneven group of five poems attempting to reexperience particular paintings by Matisse, Vuillard, Manet, Monet, and Van Gogh. The last, a very fluid poem utilizing many quotations from the artist's letters, is the most successful of the group.

A third category is a generous selection of translations, fourteen in number, from Rilke, Bonnefoy, Rimbaud, and others. Though unqualified to comment on the linguistic veracity of these translations, we can say they are among the book's most moving poems. Snodgrass has managed to find in other languages poems which reflect his own plight—such as von Eichendorff's "On My Child's Death," that poet's loss by death paralleling Snodgrass's through divorce. In rendering these poems into the American idiom, Snodgrass has found a voice which at times seems more authentic than his own. As statements on grief, the translations are crucial to an understanding of Snodgrass and where the poet presently has arrived. (In the same year he published *After Experience* Snodgrass also published a quite different series of translations, the *Gallows Songs* of Christian Morgenstern, on which he collaborated with Lore Segal. This poet of fancy and lyricism, for whom "time and space are not realities," seems less suited to Snodgrass's personal vision than, say, Rilke and Rimbaud. To compare his translation of Morgenstern's "The Moonsheep" with that of E. M. Valk proves the point.)[1]

The fourth category is not a group at all, but a single poem, "The Examination," the only satire in the Snodgrassian canon. It is a dark allegory on the examining of Ph.D. candidates by university faculty members, perhaps the result of his own examination in literary history for the Ph.D. in English at Iowa. During the course of the poem's examination the victim is physically and spiritually dismembered. The penultimate stanza concludes, "Well, that's a beginning. The next time, they can split / His tongue and teach him to talk correctly, and give / Him opinions on fine books and choose clothing fit / For the integrated area where he'll live." The poem is an elaboration of the theme of Berryman's "Dream Song #8," in which officials of an institution tell the patient, "if you watch Us instead, / yet you may saved be. Yes," this after "They blew out his loves, his interests." Snodgrass's poem also stands comparison with Swinburne's "In Sepulcretis," in which a man is dismembered by those who "Spy, smirk, sniff, snap, snort, snivel, snarl and sneer." Swinburne's conclusion is, "This is fame." Snodgrass would probably disagree, and say, "This is life." Snodgrass's poem seems to have started a spate of such poetic allegories in our time, of which a late example is Erica Jong's "The Book," from her *Fruits & Vegetables* (1971), in which another examining committee decides "to repossess my typewriter, my legs / my Phi Beta Kappa key, one breast, / any children I may have, / & my expresso machine."

After Experience, like Anthony Hecht's second collection, *The Hard Hours*, bears testimony to the effort of a truly excellent poet to push a unique vision and practice beyond viability. Snodgrass's major achievements remain *Heart's Needle* and sections of the tougher *Remains*. But when in the second volume he does connect, as he does at least nine times in the hefty book, it is with poems which probably shall endure. "What We Said," "The Platform Man," "Leaving the Motel," "A Flat One," "Powwow"—and, for sheer singularity, "The Examination"—are all poetic events for which we should be grateful.

If *After Experience* seemed too varied a collection, the "Remains" poems of "S. S. Gardons" is a highly unified sequence. Just as a daughter lost through divorce was Snodgrass's subject for the ten poems of the "Heart's Needle" sequence, the loss of a sister by death provides the occasion for this new eight-poem cycle. The sequence begins with a poem on the poet's mother and ends with one addressed to his daughter. In between the quality of his experience is rendered with infinite detail. In all eight the pivotal experience is the sister's death, which occurs ironically enough on Independence Day. Only through death does the mousy sister achieve a kind of independence from sickness, a dull life, and a domineering mother.

The title, *Remains*, reverberates with meaning. On one level it refers to the bodily remains from which the spirit of the girl has departed, and on which the undertaker has undertaken an elaborate cosmetic job (in "Viewing the Body"). But "to remain" is also to be left behind, which is the case with the survivors of the dead girl. To remain is also not to be included or comprised, which is the situation of the poet himself, an alien in a small town which thrives on conformity and misfortune. Finally the title may be intended for the manuscript of the poems itself, which is blurbed by the publisher as the literary remains of "S. S. Gardons":

> This sequence of poems was collected by his friends after his disappearance on a hunting trip in the mountains. From the condition of his abandoned motorcycle, it was impossible to determine whether he suffered foul play, was attacked by animals, merely became confused and lost, or perhaps fell victim to amnesia. At present, the case is listed as unsolved. [2]

For the time being at least, Snodgrass has chosen to phase out his *nom de plume*.

Remains opens with portraits of Snodgrass's mother and father. The first is portrayed as one who "moves by habit, hungering and blind"; the second, one who exacts "no faith, no affection" and whose entire life has been a "programmed air of soft suspension" which he survives in, "cradled and sustained." To such a couple were born the poet and his sister, "The Mouse" of the poem by that title. Like the small mouse they once found outdoors, the sister—small and dull, yet ever so much more precious than the found creature—dies. Yet unlike the mouse, she is unmourned by the brother. As children they were taught to "be well-bred," not to cry over dead animals; so that when the genuine, human tragedy presents itself, the poet "wouldn't spare one tear." His upbringing bars the display of true emotion, an observation which holds true in relation to the writing of these poems themselves. William Heyen observes, "the potential for bathos is certainly

here, but the metrical control and hard rhymes, because the employment of conscious technique always implies the poet is attempting to control highly emotional matter by mind, stop the voice from breaking, stave off the purely melodramatic." [3] The brother/sister relationship here is reminiscent of that of Tom and Laura in Tennessee Williams's moving *The Glass Menagerie*, with the mousy sister especially resembling Laura.

The mouse analogy is carried into the next poem, "Viewing the Body," in which the girl's grey life is contrasted with the gaudiness of her death,

> Flowers like a gangster's funeral;
>   Eyeshadow like a whore.
> They all say isn't she beautiful.
>   She, who never wore
>
> Lipstick or such a dress.

Rather, "Gray as a mouse," she had crept about the dark halls of her mother's house. The shadow sister of the youthful hero of Housman's "To an Athlete Dying Young," this girl paradoxically achieves her only glory through dying. Yet it is a false victory, as all deaths must be, and the worldly trappings are grotesquely unsuitable as props for this girl's earthly departure. The red satin folds of the coffin are "obscene." The deadly circumstance and pomp seem a hideous parody of her life style.

Exactly one year after her death the poet and his wife are back in the parents' house, aware of the family's awareness of the anniversary. The girl's unworn party dress is still closeted, her stuffed animals still shelved. The poet senses that his young wife is unforgiven by the family for being alive—why her, and not the sister instead, the sister, whose deathday is ironically the wife's birthday? More metaphysical than most others of Snodgrass, this poem shifts into speculation on the kingdom of the dead, a wondering at where, "Into what ingrown nation has she gone / Among a people silent and withdrawn." Entering the still-mournful house after some Independence Day fireworks display, the poet realizes the full extent of his personal alienation: "No one would hear me, even if I spoke."

"Disposal," the next piece, is in many ways redundant. Though it carries forward the action of the cycle—the dead girl's personal effects are finally disposed of—it contributes little new to the appraisal of the girl. Her one party dress unworn, she lived in dresses sewn of canceled patterns and markdowns. The poet's preoccupation with the gaudy casket is again manifest; he compares her daily dress with the way she was laid out in death:

> . . . Spared of all need, all passion,
> Saved from loss, she lies boxed in satins
> Like a pair of party shoes
> That seemed never to find a taker.

The last two poems shift focus from the dead to the surviving. Out of morbid curiosity the poet makes his journey (another Snodgrassian journey!) home on the first "anniversary" of the girl's death, as we have seen, to find nothing changed. He has survived, the parents have survived, but his mother and father seem more like the living dead. That they do not even acknowledge the world about them is communicated symbolically by the two stone lions which guard their house entrance: ". . . someone has patched / Cement across their eyes." The poem carries other symbolic freight as well, including some cherries from a tree the parents still try to protect from neighborhood boys. Is it too much to suggest that these cherries are symbolic of the virginity they also tried, too successfully, to protect from neighboring males? The cherries which now rot in their lawn are one with the now-rotting virgin in her grave.

The final poem, "To a Child"—already mentioned in conjunction with the "Heart's Needle" cycle—is an inventory of past events, the cyclical nature of life, and its ironies. The child addressed is obviously the daughter of the earlier book, to which this poem might rightly be appended in some future edition. This is a bittersweet catalogue, like the earlier "April Inventory"; the poet concludes there is much for the living to learn from another's death, be it that of a sister or merely that of "the glow of rotten / Wood, the glimmering being that consumes / The flesh of a dead trout." The verse moves forward into a region of parasitic existences which suggest the lives of his parents. He urges his daughter, who has observed both his sister's death and her mother's pregnancy, to attain the possibility and the meaning of love. Without love we die. Yet—the final irony—"With love we kill each other." Love is for the poet the mistress without whom he cannot live, yet with whom he cannot live.

This last is a horrifying group of poems, less sentimental and more sensational than "Heart's Needle," which it echoes in part; compare the conclusion of the latter, "We have to try," with the line from the earlier, "We try to choose our life"; compare, "And you have been dead one year" with "And you are still my daughter." The tone, the rhythm, and the effect are the same. Which is why Snodgrass can never truly disguise these poems, no matter what name he appends to them. In each book he speaks in a voice of suffering and guilt of marginal characters and separations.

Notes

1. The Valk translation is readily available in *Modern European Poetry*, ed. Willis Barnstone (New York: Bantam Books, Inc., 1966).
2. "A Prefatory Note on the Author," unsigned preface to *Remains: Poems by S. S. Gardons* (Mt. Horeb, Wis.: Perishable Press, Ltd., 1969). All references are to this edition.
3. *Western Humanities Review*, 25, No. 3 (Summer 1971), 253.

GARY SNYDER

1930–

Gary Sherman Snyder was born on May 8, 1930, in San Francisco. He was educated at Reed College (B.A. in anthropology, 1951), Indiana University, and the University of California at Berkeley. He studied Buddhism in Japan for a number of years, completing his studies in 1968. He was a lecturer in English at the University of California at Berkeley from 1964 to 1965. He married Alison Gass in 1950, divorcing her in 1951. In 1960 he married noted poet Joanne Kyger; they were divorced in 1964. He married Masa Uehara in 1967; they have two children.

Snyder's first book of poetry, *Riprap*, was published in 1959. He was associated with the Beat movement early in his career, and was fictionalized as Japhy Ryder in Jack Kerouac's *The Dharma Bums* (1960). However, books such as *Riprap* and *Myths and Texts* (1960) soon established him as a poet with an individual voice. His early poetry is particularly concerned with nature and the conflict between modern and "primitive" society. Zen Buddhism has exerted a considerable influence on Snyder's work, particularly in his work-in-progress, *Mountains and Rivers without End* (various sections published as *Six Sections from Mountains and Rivers without End*, 1965; *The Blue Sky*, 1969; *Three Worlds, Three Realms, Six Roads*, 1966; *Regarding Wave*, 1969; and *The Fudo Trilogy*, 1970). His poetry has grown progressively more didactic: *Turtle Island* (1974), for example, includes a series of essays on ecology, one of Snyder's primary concerns. His work remains skillfully executed, and his most recent poetry—notably *Turtle Island*, *All in the Family* (1975), and *Axe Handles* (1983), as well as the uncompleted *Mountains and Rivers without End*— is generally considered among his best.

Snyder is an economical poet, utilizing simple language and primarily relying upon imagery. He is one of the most influential and widely read poets among the young; some critics attribute this to his simplicity and accuse him of superficiality. Others see his poetry as an important bridge between the critical establishment and the public, and feel there is more depth to his poetry than the surface would seem to indicate. In addition to his poetry, he has published criticism and edited, with Gutetsu Kanetsuki, *The Wooden Fish: Basic Sutras and Gathas of Rinzai Zen* (1961). He won the American Academy prize in 1966, and a Pulitzer Prize in 1975 for *Turtle Island*.

⟨. . .⟩ Snyder's verse is rather simple, usually honest, straightforward and (with exceptions) spare. There is nothing grandiose or egoistic about it. It is peculiarly impersonal, strong—in its quiet way—and reveals, again with some depressing exceptions, an unobtrusive, unaffected familiarity with oriental art. (There is little here of that wistful Midwestern club-woman who, having read some translated Haiku, and finding it "quaint", decides to write some.) And, though they do not attempt very much, at least three of these poems are fully convincing. One, which says briefly what Kerouac's *The*

Dharma Bums says at length, great length, is probably perfect. It is the first poem in the book and, like many of the others, is written in free verse. It is entitled "Mid-August at Sourdough Mountain Lookout":

> Down valley a smoke haze
> Three days heat, after five days rain
> Pitch glows on the fir-cones
> Across rocks and meadows
> Swarms of new flies.
>
> I cannot remember things I once read

A few friends, but they are in cities.
Drinking cold snow-water from a tin cup
Looking down for miles
Through high still air.

The poems which make up this book tend to begin either with a statement—quiet, considered, somewhat "apart" in tone—

The female is fertile, and discipline
(contra naturam) only
confuses her

or, with a description of some particular scene, a scene that involves, above all else, the poet's sense of vision. The poem, then, develops from this. An example (of the descriptive type) is a piece in three stanzas called "Tōji."

Men asleep in their underwear
Newspapers under their heads
Under the eaves of Tōji . . .

The second stanza, though it expands on the opening, is still based almost entirely on what has actually been *seen*. In this, and to some extent in "voice", the lines that follow are representative of a good deal of Snyder's work. Though they appeal, however, to but two senses, they are the most lavish in the book:

Peering through chickenwire grates
At dusty gold-leaf statues
A cynical curving round-belly
Cool Bodhisattva—maybe Avalokita—
Bisexual and tried it all, weight on
One leg, haloed in snake-hood gold
Shines through the shadow
An ancient hip smile
Tingling of India and Tibet.

The last two lines are two of several in *Riprap* that do not ring true. They seem unnecessarily easy and, as a result, even a bit phony. Apart from this, apart from its unevenness, the gravest fault with this book is its sameness: of tone, of "shape", of emotional range, or response. The poems are finally too much alike and, though they may work very well individually, lose something when seen together. The book *is* quite impressive, nonetheless. At times, though, it comes only too close to fulfilling one interpretation that can be made on the metaphor implied in the title. *Riprap* is defined as "a foundation or wall made of broken stones thrown together irregularly or loosely, as in water or on a soft bottom". Mr. Snyder's epigraph suggests something else, however, something truer of his book, and true, in a way, of the others as well:

a cobble of stone laid on steep slick rock
to make a trail for horses in the mountains.
—ROBERT S. SWARD, *Poetry*, July 1960, pp. 244–46

To a large group of devotional poems ⟨in *Turtle Island*⟩ which date back twenty years in some cases, in others which refer to attitudes and events of the most intimate proximity, Gary Snyder has added five prose texts, essays in solicitude and advocacy which afford a conscientious prospect of where we are and where he wants us to be, though the discrepancy registered between the two locales is so vast that the largely good-humored resonance of the poems attests to Snyder's forbearance, his enforced detachment. When the poet tells us, in his prose, "I wish to bring a voice from the wilderness, my constituency," he is not preaching to etiolate city-dwellers as a voice *in* the wilderness; there is, refreshingly, very little of the Jeremiad in Snyder's tone, very little of the howl in his timbre. In his poems, rather, the world becomes largely a matter of contours and traces to be guessed at, marveled over, left alone. And in prose Snyder seeks to recommend ways by which this listening life, this identity of observation merely, may be made easier—not only for himself (he does not particularly look for easy ways *there*: it is why we trust him), but for the rest of us, in suburb pent.

"At the root of where our civilization goes wrong," Snyder writes, in literally radical fashion, "is the mistaken belief that nature is something less than authentic, that nature is not as alive as man is, or as intelligent, that in a sense it is dead." One of the fashions, the senses in which nature is alive, poetically alive, for Snyder is its opacity, its resistance to being more than the signifier in what Hegel calls the prose of the world. That is why he can say "the poem was born elsewhere, and need not stay. Like the wild geese of the Arctic it heads home, far above the borders, where most things cannot cross." And the principal charm of *his* poems—transitory, elliptical, extraterritorial—will be, again and again, in the most unexpected contexts, that precipitate of experience without interpretation, the *salts* of an evaporated life, not raw (because not even conflated with the cooked, the processed) but rapt, "an offer", as he says, quite unconcerned with the taking, with our response:

the smell of bats.
the flavor of sandstone
grit on the tongue.

There will be nothing transcendent about such realia, vivid but never evoked, present because (merely!) perceived: there are no symbols in Snyder's poetry, no metaphors even, nothing ever stands for anything else: "There is no other life," he remarks with characteristic laconicism, though he is never wry, never sour. In fact, he is the master of a peculiar sweetness—peculiar in that it is not sentimental, not even consistent. A considerable poem like *The Bath* can celebrate with an exact exuberance the pleasures of bathing his two children and his wife as well, yet the "action" Snyder urges in a later (or earlier, for all I know) prose text is that we "try to correct traditional cultural attitudes that tend to force women into childbearing". Well, of course there is no forcing in the home-life thus exhibited, where it is not exposed, and perhaps that is the chill which these poems communicate—or what causes the chill. So accustomed are we, in the thirty centuries of our literature, to the notion that at *some* level, in *some* way, the poem is the product or the presumption of constraint, of conflict (even as the family is subject to social, to ritual pressures), that it is with a tighter breathing indeed, and zero at the bone, that we meet these narrow fellows:

Muddly slipping trail
wobbly twin pole bridges
gully throat
forks in

somebody clearing brush & growing tea
& out, turn here for home
along the Kamo River.
hold it close
give it all away.

The very punctuation—periods but no capitals, more often than not—(though when not, why not? one wonders, idly) is wonderfully in accord with Snyder's recuperation of a world not manhandled but merely, for once, inhabited by a humanity intended "to draw out strength from the realization that at the heart of things is some kind of serene and ecstatic process which is beyond qualities and beyond birth-and-death." The poems, then, being beyond qualities too in their endeavor to realize that process, to receive it, will not articulate an emotional shape we can recognize, they will not have a drama, they will be intransitive, and though we may thirst for more of a conclusion, more of an integral close than is afforded by Snyder's birds which

> . . . arc and loop & then
> their flight is done.
> they settle down.
> end of poem.

our thirst is to remain our thirst. We must be told that the poem ends. Such makings are neither found nor transformed things, neither inventions nor fictions—they are doings, actions, but not *to* anything else, not *for* or *from* or *upon*; without prepositions in their performance, such poems are evidences of what the poet calls "true affluence—not needing anything," and that is their sensational (though low-keyed) departure from most poems, from poetry: they do not need us.—RICHARD HOWARD, "Gary Snyder: 'To Hold Both History and Wilderness in Mind'" (1975), *Alone with America* (1969), 1980, pp. 575–77

RICHARD HOWARD
From "Gary Snyder: 'To Hold Both History and Wilderness in Mind'"
Alone with America (1969)
1980, pp. 562–75

Pertinently, on the title-page of his first publication, appearing in 1959, when he was not yet thirty, this poet defined the name assigned to the work gathered together there: *Riprap*—"a cobble of stone laid on steep slick rock to make a trail for horses in the mountains." Advisedly, I take the term "work" in its strong sense, for Snyder has provided a gloss on these substantial poems which deserves to stand as a determinative frame for any account of his undertaking: "The rhythms of my poems follow the rhythm of the physical work I'm doing at any given time . . . *Riprap* is really a class of poems I wrote under the influence of the geology of the Sierra Nevada and the daily trail-crew work of picking up and placing granite stones in tight cobble patterns on hard slab. Walking, climbing, placing with the hands." And in his second collection, *Myths and Texts*, completed by 1956 but published only in 1960, Snyder intensifies the notion until it becomes an emblem of the art in general: "Poetry a riprap on the slick rock of metaphysics."

The poems that follow this defensive recipe:

> ants and pebbles
> In the thin loam, each rock a word
> a creek-washed stone . . .
> all change, in thoughts,
> As well as things . . .

constitute a mill of process: autonomous voices seem to speak through the poet, grinding together the conflicting perceptions of reality that permit the poet, in a state of rapt self-communication, to utter rather than merely address:

> Pressure of sun on the rockslide
> Whirled me in dizzy hop-and-step descent,
> Pool of pebbles buzzed in a Juniper shadow,
> Tiny tongue of a this-year rattlesnake flicked,
> I leaped, laughing for a little boulder-color coil—
> Pounded by heat raced down the slabs to the creek
> Deep tumbling under arching walls and stuck
> Whole head and shoulders in the water:

> Stretched full on cobble—ears roaring
> Eyes open aching from the cold and faced a trout.

The point of riprap is to enable the traveller to ascend—to ascend on earth, not to slide back, nor to fly. The stone laid down has already been dressed by Pound, and by the famous formula of Dr. Williams: "no ideas but in things," yet it is his own work that Snyder is doing with it. Evidently he is as much in mortal fear as in mortal danger of vanishing with a screech into the Whitman Wind Tunnel, that celebrated American patent, and consequently clings to whatever will prop and counterweight his spirit, as by the work of hands:

> Lay down these words
> Before your mind like rocks.
> Placed solid, by hands
> In choice of place, set
> Before the body of the mind
> in space and time:
> Solidity of bark, leaf, or wall
> riprap of things

For all their oracular stance, then, turned away from the listener toward some inward audience, something in the self that may be convinced by all this substantiation, these poems are tough, sharp-edged, concentrated on the thing shown, "this moment one time true." Without Snyder's lifting a metrical foot, the plain facts are allowed, are obliged to comment on each other, and except for the reminder that it was the poet to whom they "happened," the facts are made to speak for themselves, as if they were their own occasion:

> We finished clearing the last
> Section of trail by noon,
> High on the ridge-side
> Two thousand feet above the creek—
> Reached the pass, went on
> Beyond the white pine groves,
> Granite shoulders, to a small
> Green meadow watered by the snow,
> Edged with Aspen . . .
> I spied
> A glitter, and found a flake
> Black volcanic glass—obsidian—
> By a flower. Hands and knees
> Pushing the Bear grass, thousands
> Of arrowhead leavings over a
> Hundred yards. Not one good
> Head, just razor flakes
> On a hill snowed all but summer,
> A land of fat summer deer,
> They came to camp. On their
> Own trails. I followed my own
> Trail here. Picked up the cold-drill,
> Pick, singlejack, and sack
> Of dynamite.
> Ten thousand years.

The tremendous impact of that last line, a concussion against the "things," the obsidian arrow-flakes which precede it, is a characteristic example of this poet's *ideas*. Once he has announced his occupational skills as logging, forestry, carpentry and seamanship, it is not surprising that Gary Snyder, who says that as a poet he holds "the most archaic values on earth," should have left this country where the forests have been stripped or burned off, where "the crews have departed," for the interior exile of Japanese monasteries and the rapturous life of a cosmic bum: "There is not much wilderness left to destroy, and the nature in the mind is being logged and burned off. The soil and human sensibilities may erode away forever, even without a great war." Thus this first little book can be read through as a circumstantial journal of alienation, a progressive engrossment by otherness:

> . . . a week and I go back
> Down 99, through towns, to San Francisco and
> Japan.
> All America south and east,
> Twenty-five years in it brought to a trip-stop
> Mind-point, where I turn
> Caught more on this land—rock tree and man,
> Awake, than ever before, yet ready to leave.

It is a departure from a world of fragments. The literature of process, as Northrop Frye has pointed out, being based on an irregular and unpredictable coincidence of patterns in experience, tends to seek the brief or even the partial utterance—to center itself in the lyrical:

> Raven
>   on a roost of furs
> No bird in a bird-book
>   black as the sun.

Lapidary as they are—and there is a visionary clarity about these twenty or so poems, "all the junk that goes with being human / drops away" and we are left with remarkable objects, revenant landscapes:

> One granite ridge
> A tree, would be enough
> Or even a rock, a small creek,
> A bark shred in a pool . . .

and lovely too—for this poet has the capacity for both planetary scope ("I will not cry Inhuman & think that makes us small and nature great . . .") and microscopic focus ("Granite: ingrained with torment of fire and weight, crystal and sediment linked hot") that satisfies Nabokov's famous requirement: "there is a point, arrived at by diminishing large things and enlarging small ones, that is intrinsically artistic"—and even heartbreaking:

> I cannot remember things I once read
> A few friends, but they are in cities.
> Drinking cold snow-water from a tin cup
> Looking down for miles
> Through high still air.

Yet these poems do not connect, they are discrete and for all their entanglement with *realia*, they are partial: that is the quality by which they are limited and compromised and finally determined. We remember that riprap, by a definition the poet does not provide, is also a kind of firework that when lighted makes a succession of sharp explosions and jumps.

Modesty, though, is its own reward as well as its own restriction. The imagery of a poetry is positive insofar as it names things that have a visible, tangible existence. *Riprap*, then, is a positive step taken in the mind's myth of itself. The dialectical step, cutting nature at the joints, as Plato said, is afforded and in part taken by *Myths and Texts*, a longer book, in which the texts are the world itself, the myths what the mind, that hearth of provisional faiths, puts together out of them. The work is divided into three long sections of some sixteen numbered parts each: "Logging," "Hunting" and "Burning." The decor of these poems is partly the American Northwest, partly Japan, and the rhythms are not so much those of work, of labor, as of contemplation—"long days of quiet in lookout cabins":

> Sourdough mountain called a fire in:
> Up Thunder Creek, high on a ridge.
> Hiked eighteen hours, finally found

> A snag and a hundred feet around on fire:
> All afternoon and into night
> Digging the fire line . . .
> Toward morning it rained.
> We slept in mud and ashes,
> Woke at dawn, the fire was out,
> The sky was clear, we saw
> The last glimmer of the morning star.

—and the songs and dances of Great Basin Indian tribes:

> Deer don't want to die for me.
>   I'll drink sea-water
> Sleep on beach pebbles in the rain
> Until the deer come down to die
>   in pity for my pain.

The very title of the book, again, is the clue to Snyder's conjugation of the possibilities—it refers to "the two sources of human knowledge, symbols and sense-impressions. I tried to make my life as a hobo and worker, the questions of history and philosophy in my head, and the glimpses of the roots of religion I'd seen through meditation, peyote, and 'secret frantic rituals' into one whole thing." The example of Pound, even more closely than before, is embraced and exalted, and into the narratives are woven a lot of quotations—from anthropological handbooks by Boas, Sapir and others, from John Muir (an extraordinary account, versified by Snyder, of nearly falling off Mount Ritter, of which the conclusion is relevant to the ethical impulse and the *ars poetica* Snyder has been urging:

> Life blazed
> Forth again with preternatural clearness.
> I seemed suddenly to become possessed
> Of a new sense. My trembling muscles
> Became firm again, every rift and flaw in
> The rock was seen as through a microscope.
> My limbs moved with a positiveness and precision
> With which I seemed to have
> Nothing at all to do.),

from the Buddhist texts (which for me are about as opaque, as purely decorative, as the Pound ideograms; they seem to be used as insurance for the poems, rather than to be taking the risk), even from the titles of paintings by Morris Graves, whose venue is very much a part of this poet's vocabulary (I am thinking of Graves' painting of a fish in the beak of a fierce bird of prey, eagle or osprey, between two streams represented in a highly symbolical manner, called "Each Time You Carry Me This Way." Snyder has a totemic boar emerging from the sea-depths, bearing "his treasure," the sacred being Prajapati on his tusks: "skewered body of the earth / Each time I carry you this way.").

The first section of the book, for all its syncretic references to St. Paul, Cybele, Buddha and the prophets of Israel, is the most secular. It is in part a complaint against "the ancient, meaningless / abstractions of the educated mind" which fails to perceive, to *sense* the very world it is destroying:

> Sea-foam washing the limpets and barnacles
> Rattling the gravel beach
> Salmon up creek, bear on the bank,
> Wild ducks over the mountains weaving
> In a long south flight, the land of
> Sea and fir tree with the pine-dry
> Sage-flat country to the east.

Laboring among "the rise and fall of rock and water," deploring as he wanders the "sense of journey in space that modern people have lost," the poet loops his steel cables around logs and watches the lumber industry die:

The groves are down
            cut down
Groves of Ahab, of Cybele
Pine trees, knobbed twigs
            thick cone and seed
            Cybele's tree this, sacred in groves
Pine of Seami, cedar of Haida
Cut down by the prophets of Israel
            the fairies of Athens
            the thugs of Rome
                both ancient and modern;
Cut down to make room for the suburbs
Bulldozed by Luther and Weyerhaeuser
Crosscut and chainsaw
            squareheads and finns
            high-lead and cat-skidding
Trees down
Creeks choked, trout killed, roads . . .

That is the outrage and the lyric measure of Pound, entirely possessed and transformed to new purposes. As James Dickey has said, "the music, drifting series of terse, observant statements, does fix Snyder's experiences and beliefs in such a fashion that they become available for us to live among and learn from." The "Logging" section concludes with an impassioned reproach to his kind by a poet who knows he must be ransomed by the messages of his senses:

Men who hire men to cut groves
Kill snakes, build cities, pave fields,
Believe in god, but can't
Believe their own senses
Let alone Gautama. Let them lie.

"Logging" has been part of the physical world, laborious, repetitive, and grounded in an apprehension of nature. The ritual of labor seems to be something of a voluntary effort to regain a vanished relation to the natural cycle. From it, the next sections take a great, a dialectical step—for the imagination works dialectically, separating what is desired from what is not, by higher organization determining what is wanted and what is not. In fact, the entire book has rather the structure suggested by Hanna Arendt in her division of the human condition into labor, work and action: "Logging" represents the first, with its repetitive, ritual motions in a physical world:

Each dawn is clear
Cold air bites the throat.
Thick frost on the pine bough
Leaps from the tree
            snapped by the diesel
Drifts and glitters in the
            horizontal sun.
In the frozen grass
            smoking boulders
            ground by steel tracks.
In the frozen grass
            wild horses stand
            beyond a row of pines.
The D8 tears through piss-fir,
Scrapes the seed-pine . . .

while "Hunting" suggests what Miss Arendt means by *work* —the making or doing which dramatizes the instrumental, symbolic qualities of life: irreversible, unique, meaningful. Hence the "shaman songs," the poems "for birds," "for bear," "for deer," and most significant, "the making of the horn spoon":

The head of the mountain goat is in the corner
            for the making of the horn spoon.

The black spoon. When fire's heat strikes it
            turn the head
Four days and hair pulls loose
            horn twists free.
Hand-adze, straightknife, notch the horn-base;
            rub with rough sandstone
Shave down smooth. Split two cedar sticks
            when water boils plunge the horn,
Tie mouth between sticks in the spoon shape
            rub with dried dogfish skin.
It will be black and smooth,
            a spoon.

And "Burning" is of course an adumbration of that stage of human action—the religious—by which life is illuminated for men individually and together, as the word religion itself suggests, beyond the laborer's ritual for survival and the craftsman's solitary joy—"Burning" has to do with the Buddha's fire sermon and with the burning of the great forests, "the hot seeds steaming underground, still alive." Here the sections are more nearly abstract:

The thin edge of nature rising fragile
And helpless with its love and sentient stone
And flesh, above dark drug-death dreams.
Clouds I cannot lose, we cannot leave.
We learn to love, horror accepted.

But here, as in the "Hunting" poems, there is a continual, resuscitating summons to the natural world, to its essentially foreign being:

One moves continually with the consciousness
Of that other, totally alien, non-human:
Humming inside like a taut drum,
Carefully avoiding any direct thought of it,
Attentive to the real-world flesh and stone.

At the end of "Burning" ("It's all falling or burning—rattle of boulders / steady dribbling of rocks down cliffs"), we leave the poet, still talking to himself, uncertain of everything but his upward movement, advancing through "a night of the long poem and the mined guitar" on the riprap of a reality perceived:

Walked all day through live oak and manzanita,
Scrabbling through dust dust down Tamalpais—
Thought of high mountains;
Looked on a sea of fog.
Two of us, carrying packs.

I do not mean to suggest, of course, that it is such an easy thing to achieve the stage of action, of religious reality—especially within the gestures of the quotidian, the demands of the insignificant untranscended, or that the poet has found his way to this sanctified state—"we fled and stumbled on the bright lit plain"—without let or hindrance. In the ten years since *Myths and Texts* was written, the poet has been living, mostly in Japan, in various stages of spiritual and economic vagrancy:

In the dark   white lanterns
            sending out rowboats, swinging
a thousand foot net
            five times down the length of the beach.
we help haul . . .
            a full-thighed young woman
            her dress tucked up in her pants tugs and curses
            an old man calling across the dark water sculling
                        . . .
they beach their boats
full of nets
their lamps bob over the dunes
we sleep in the sand
and our salt.

It is perhaps his very aspiration to an illuminated existence *within* what other men call reality that makes Snyder so poignantly aware of the waste, the devouring slough of human life, and in his later work there ceases to be anything so neat as a division between a poem of detritus and a poem of ecstasy, for merely the litany of constatation provides the poet with his ascent:

> . . . unfixed junk downstair—
> All emblems of the past—too close—
> 　　　heaped up in chilly dust and bare bulb glare
> of tables, wheelchairs, battered trunks and wheels
> & poets that boiled up coffee nineteen ten, *things*
> Swimming on their own and finally freed
> 　　　　　from human need. Or?
> 　　waiting a final flicker of desire
> To tote them out once more . . .

This is from a long poem Snyder has been promising for years, "a long poem I'm calling *Mountains and Rivers without End* after a sidewise Chinese scroll painting. It threatens to be like its title." In 1965 a pamphlet was published in San Francisco by the Four Seasons Foundation containing six sections from *Mountains and Rivers without End*, and there is every reason to expect more of this spiritual journalism in the future, for in these notations of "lost things—a universe of junk, all left alone" nothing begins or ends, all is an unremitting effort to rise through the compunctions of a rootless life to that heightened sense of Being where everything is divine. The six sections of the poem that have been published and the marginal poems attendent on its production suggest, within the dialectic of spiritual tug and material weight, a return to the necessary riprap or ballast to weight down the overwhelming Pursuits, all the more slippery as they are for being voiced, now, in the catechisms of Zen ("What is the way of non-activity? It is activity"). Thus in the fifth section, "The Market," there is a long, characteristic descant in the best Pound style on the worth of some change in the poet's pocket:

> 　　to market, the
> 　　　　　changes, how much
> 　　　　　is our change:
> Seventy-five feet hoed rows equals
> one hour explaining power steering
> equals two big crayfish =
> 　　　　　all the buttermilk you can drink
> = twelve pounds cauliflower
> = five cartons greek olives =
> hitch-hiking
> 　　　　from Ogden Utah to Burns Oregon
> = aspirin, iodine, and bandages
> = a lay in Naples = beef
> = lamp ribs =
> 　　　　long grain rice, eight pounds
> equals two kilograms soybeans . . .

The indications of equivalence are more than the articulation of a commercial undertaking that must, in these out-of-the-way places, do without common coin; here the equal signs are a token of spiritual indifference, or rather of spiritual equality, precisely: all things are worthy, Snyder is saying, and all things are blessed. Such lists (there was another great one in "Hunting" of "what food we lived on then": some forty-eight items from yucca flowers to turtles) are really a kind of religious mnemonics, an exercise recalling the self to the world that is its home, when its impulse—as classically in the American experience—is to transcend. We are reminded that Snyder is the true heir of that Thoreau who retired to Walden in order to discover the meaning of the word "property" and found it

meant only what was proper or essential to unbound human life. This self-exiled poet, like the one who withdrew from Concord, ballasts with what his senses tell him—as in another late poem, "Eight Sandbars on the Takano River," from which I quote but two beautifully phrased "bars":

> 　　gone wild
> 　　strawberry vine
> 　　each year more small
> 　　sour
> 　　mulched by pine
> 　　white peeled logs
> 　　toppled in sap
> 　　scalped branch
> 　　　　spring
> 　　　　　woods

—the radical assumptions of the soul, as in the greater, syncretic statement of "This Tokyo," in which the Buddhist mistrust of matter is earned, is justified by a milling, personal transaction with spirit; such statements require the strongest and most pervasive recuperation of the physical world, without which, as we know, existence is the "greatest impoverishment":

> 　　. . . We live
> On the meeting of sun and earth.
> We live—we live—and all our lives
> Have led to this, this city,
> Which is soon the world, this
> Hopelessness where love of man
> Or hate of man could matter
> None, love if you will or
> Contemplate or write or teach
> But know in your human marrow you
> Who read, that all you tread
> Is earthquake rot and matter mental
> Trembling freedom is a void,
> Peace war religion revolution
> Will not help.

No wonder the phenomenology of Snyder's landscape is so difficult to pin down! He is forever exchanging the trough of the wave for the crest, the mountain-top for the abyss, the world of cars and haircuts for the rocky desolation in which we are accustomed to find, reading the scroll inch by inch, a tiny, radiant sage under some tremendous crag—and that will be this odd American poet, our post-Hiroshima Lafcadio Hearn, who ends his latest excerpt from the endless poem-scroll of his life with this classic bit of spiritual geography, a human universal from Dante to Hiroshige:

> . . . We were at the bottom of the gorge.
> We started drifting up the canyon. "This is the
> way to the back country."

In 1966, the Fulcrum Press of London published, in a handsome and virtually inaccessible edition, Snyder's *Collected Poems* which reprint not only *Riprap* and *Myths and Texts* entire, but add the poet's two groups of translations, from Miyazawa Kenji (1896–1933) and, more impressively to my sense, from the T'ang master Han-Shan or "Cold Mountain." Snyder says the poems are "colloquial: rough and fresh," and he has had great success bringing them over into English, for indeed they echo and occasionally initiate his own project—as he says, Han-Shan became an Immortal "and you sometimes run on to him today in the skidrows, orchards, hobo jungles and logging camps of America":

> In my first thirty years of life
> I roamed hundreds and thousands of miles.

Walked by rivers through deep green grass
Entered cities of boiling red dust.
Tried drugs, but couldn't make Immortal;
Read books and wrote poems on history.
Today I'm back at Cold Mountain:
I'll sleep by the creek and purify my ears.

The translator has so evidently confounded his voice with the possibilities of his text that we cannot know whose impulse is being borrowed, whose lent; but the progress is certainly a logical one to the final section of the new book, the new poems gathered under the rubric already defined for us in the last quotation given from *Mountains and Rivers without End*, the unemphatic but suggestive label for all that is not here and now: *The Back Country*.

Thus Snyder has collected into four "books" of some dozen poems each all the "incidental" poems he has written outside the series. Explicitly, he says, "it is not necessary to think of a series," and indeed the word incidental goes far toward determining the category of these lyrics. All are under the sign of a quotation from Basho: "I, drawn like blown cloud, couldn't stop dreaming of roaming, roving the coast up and down . . . ," and the diffuse, rambling lines recount the incidents of a wondering vagrancy as

a hawk sails over the roof
a snake went under the floor
            how can hawks hunt in the rain?
I walk through the hallway:
the soul of a great-bellied cloud.

There is a different poignancy, an odd, rueful glance at an alternative convention in the several love poems here:

I might have gone to you
Hoping to win your love back.
You are still single.

I didn't.
I thought I must make it alone. I
Have done that . . .

as if it were impossible for the poet to admit the existence of Others in his rhapsody of concrete universals, though at least he knows *why* it is impossible and acknowledges the likelihood of failure, for he "may never now know / if I am a fool / or have done what my / karma demands." As for men in general, "all these crazed, hooked nations," Snyder claims to be merely an observer, exempt as he sinks into the detail of things ("spider gleams in his / new web / dew on the shingles, on the car, / on the mailbox—the mole, the onion, and the beetle / cease their wars") from the miniscule preoccupations of the humankind below:

I sit in the open window
& roll a smoke . . .

a soft continuous roar
comes out of the far valley
of the six-lane highway—thousands
and thousands of cars
driving men to work.

Watching the vapor-trails of two jets, the poet renounces all concern for the linear, the ongoing impulse of Being, for he is not only content but capsized by the perception of immediate pattern, the recurrent process that has swung him, rapt, in its endless commencements, "new rain / as we begin our life"; the terrible planes streak off toward "the day of criss-cross rockets / and white blossoming smoke of bomb" and Snyder, very much on the ground, aspires only—it is the supreme purpose—to sentience:

I stumble on the cobble rockpath,
      Passing through temples,
      Watching for two-leaf pine
   —spotting that design.

It is all there, the stumbling, the riprap, the sacred places and the participation in their significant pattern by "watching," "spotting." In fact, the entire venture is labelled and limited and then released by the over-all title Snyder gives his book of collected poems: "A Range of Poems." The mountainous suggestion of movement up and away, back of beyond, must not keep us from noting that there are *other* ranges, other registers and arrays of possibility which this poet has refused. Making it alone, he watches "the land drift north" and accounts for all that he sees while

plain men go into the ground . . .
plain men come out of the ground.

THOMAS PARKINSON
"The Theory and Practise of Gary Snyder"
Journal of Modern Literature, 1971–72, pp. 448–52

*E*arth House Hold* includes selections from Snyder's journals, as early as 1953, book reviews, notes on social and religious movements, and essays that define his sense of poetic mission. Although the initial impact of the book is miscellaneous, a sequence of prose unified only by his sensibility, that sensibility is so integral a cultural complex that the book has essential singleness of motive. If it does nothing else, it demonstrates in precept and example the base of his verse. Along with his most recent collection of poetry, *Regarding Wave*, it shows the continuity and development of his remarkable enterprise.

The world in *Earth House Hold* is the same world treated with the deepened intensity of poetry in *A Range of Poems* and *The Back Country*. The primary stress is on the forests of the western states and their seashore, Japan, India. In more ordered times China would play a large role. The interests are familiar: wilderness, work, poetry, Amerindian lore, Buddhism, political radicalism. They form a complex of concerns that mesh into an attractive whole. Snyder is no amateur in any of these areas. Some of the essays are review articles for professional anthropological journals. Some of them are the product of his disciplined proficiency in Oriental studies, both religious and linguistic, his life in Japanese Zen monasteries, his scholarly detailed knowledge of the several varieties of Buddhism. Underlying all these or rather interpenetrating them is his quest for the poetic measure that will release the major forms of experience in all their implication.

The random chronological form is misleading. The several segments of the book connect and culminate in the crystallizing form of the essay on "Poetry and the Primitive." The primitive and poetry—Snyder's meditations on the subject are revealing about his own work, but they also suggest certain speculations about current psychology. He cites Lévi-Strauss's analogy between the status of art and the status of a national park as permitted wilderness. The analogy fits, but it seems to me that in Snyder's arguments he tends to understress the basic difference: if one leaves alone and refuses to interfere with nature, it can regain (within limits) the status of wilderness. But leaving the human psyche alone does only that, leaves it without any reference except to the depleted and debilitating environment that has effectively denied psychic fullness.

Hence the primitive that Snyder admires can be attained only by disciplined exclusion and distortion, a gardening operation rather than a matter of drawing boundaries. A massive gardening operation is what we should call an enabling act that creates a national park or seashore or wilderness area.

The same process occurs in establishing the lines of a poem and of a poetic vision. The difficulty for current writers is that they are deluged with phenomena that are not accountable. This does not mean that the world is chaotic in any final sense, but that the disorders of mind and history have reached so great a volume that they menace any kind of order, natural, social, aesthetic, or personal. If one reads twenty or thirty books of new poetry a month (and that is only a sketchy survey) the most troubling thing is not the simplicity of much poetry but its messy repetitive complexity, its all unconscious reflecting of external and internal disorder. A purifying process is required previous to the poem. The process of stripping and cleansing is a personal undertaking as complex in its way as an enabling act of a legislature. It requires a sophistication that may eventually be left behind, and from such sophistication, such intellectual and imaginative exploration, true simplicity *may* emerge. Simplicity in the medieval sense: the elemental, irreducible.

If one takes Snyder's poetry as exemplary in this respect, one can also discriminate his work from that of many of his contemporaries. *Earth House Hold* is essentially the record of the intellectual and religious disciplines that underlay and preceded the poetry. Snyder is, however, not the purist that Yeats was, who wrote *A Vision* primarily to keep certain elements out of his poetry. He is not so inclusive as Robert Duncan, who attempts to take the reader through the process of poetic discovery. He is not so absorbed with his own inner tensions as Robert Lowell. There are poetic dimensions and vocabularies and obsessions that by will or temperament Snyder ignores or excludes.

Snyder is not an ideologue, but it is still true that among distinguished contemporary writers, he is one whose attitudes are his subjects. Insofar as the poetry involves struggle and tension—and it does so very infrequently—it is the struggle to create a mind purified of the lusts and greeds of history. This restoration of the primitive being would permit the inclusion of ritual that gives ratio to the ecstatic, the passionate, the physical. This is its positive direction, but in the prose and verse it is frequently defined as *non*: non-Western, non-Christian, non-white, non-capitalist, non-national, non-military, non-civilization. When the facility of negative definition is followed, these negations become prejudices growing from justified revulsion against the abominations of immediate life that can rightly be laid at the door of militarism, unbridled capitalist exploiting, debased Christianity, and white chauvinism. This is Snyder's main argument, in social terms, and his spiritual vocation is to offer measure that can be taken by the soul to create a world that "matters" and has texture and specific gravity and joy.

Underlying all this, as *Earth House Hold* bears witness, is a discipline of senses and of intelligence. The result in the realm of poetics is a theory curiously Miltonic (simple, sensuous, passionate) and even neo-classical. Without that discipline, the Snyder optique brings in a wave of stereotypes that are associated with romanticism, granted—Snyder mentions Rousseau approvingly—but there is something more rigorous at work. Ten years ago he wrote a note on the religious tendencies of the Beat movement. This note is excluded from *Earth House Hold*, probably on the ground that he has gone past that point. It seems worth recalling:

Discipline, aesthetics, and tradition. This was going on well before the beat generation got into print. It differs from the 'All is one' stance in that its practitioners settle on one traditional religion, try to absorb the feel of its art and history and carry out whatever ascesis is required. One could become an Aimu bear-dancer or a Yurok shaman as well as a Trappist monk, if he put himself to it.

In the preceding sections of the note, he cites "Quakers, Shinshu, Buddhism, Sufism" and Whitman as equivalents in spiritual power.

Now his attitudes seem more exclusive, to narrow on what has come to satisfy his needs, a limited religious and legendary matter, an almost stubborn closure. When he cites Lynn White's description of Christianity's role in creating the current ecological crisis, he does not mention White's description of the Franciscan alternative to the first chapter of Genesis. The *I Fiori* of St. Francis are close to Snyder's rendering of the "Record and life of the Ch'an Master Po-Chang Huai-Hai." Even St. Augustine's *City of God* advocates a custodial rather than exploitative relation between man and nature. Equal time for St. Francis? Hardly, and I don't expect Snyder to master Franciscan theology any more than he expects to master Zen. It may be ascribable to Snyder's maturing, but there is a drift toward orthodoxy in his thought, toward exclusion and limitation. The poetry then becomes subsidiary, only one of a set of instruments in a spiritual quest.

This is not only inevitable but in a serious sense right. Identity is limitation; to function, it is necessary to exclude. Snyder's distortions and omissions are no worse, are in fact considerably better, than the notorious selectivity of most modern artists. They grant his insights: the identification of the wilderness with the subconscious; the Oriental and European garden as product of guilty fear of threatening and at last destroyed nature; the proper stress on the interconnected mutual dependence of body, voice, and mind.

Revolutionary and counter-revolutionary minds produce neo-classical theories, the one projecting fixed values into an existent structure, the other creating an imagined and hence by definition fixed structure. Articulate modern neo-classicism from Hulme on has tended to be reactionary politically, and that blurs matters. When a poet is more concerned with what can be done through words than with the surface of his art, he tends toward the neo-classical, and that is where Snyder's poetry rests. Such a poetic action is in the most profound sense conservative; dependent upon a belief in some common sense of things that endures through fashion and historic changes. It does not imply the use of inherited forms but an obsession with traditional matter, so that the work of the poem is to vivify what would otherwise be lost.

To many people terms like neo-classicism and romanticism are pejorative or honorific. I intend them as descriptive, as a way of getting at the qualities of Snyder's verse, especially in *Regarding Wave*, and perhaps explaining problems that his verse raises.

One of the most annoying arguments against Snyder's verse is that it does not develop. This is part of the romantic prejudice, exacerbated by the rate of change in fad and fashion in the 20th century. Why should his poetry develop, other than in the sense that it comes to explore and include more life as he remains receptive to fresh perception? Limitation and exclusion are necessary parts of any poetic enterprise, and so long as Snyder's style answers to his vision of experience, then it would be frivolous of him to change for the sake of change. What should alter style is the revelation of subject matters that shatter the form hitherto adequate; or through the imposition of fresh technical demands by some other medium, like drama.

These poems in *Regarding Wave* provide no surprises because they impose no disturbing new subject matter and are contemplative presentative lyrics that make no fresh technical impositions. Snyder has become the most observed of all observers, and it doesn't seem to do much good. For one thing, it compels him to repeated publication, and if there is legitimate objection to *Regarding Wave* it comes from the fact that much of the material in the final sections of the book seems more appropriate to the notebook sections of *Earth House Hold*. Snyder's mind works at two distinct levels. One is fluent, wise, witty, meditative and hortatory; the other is measured, dramatic, definite (to avoid that cliché *concrete*) in design, formal, and contemplative. The second mode is the one that produces his best poetry; the first is essentially pre-poetic. When he is taken up, effectively carried by a subject, each poem gives momentum to the succeeding one. When he is accepting random notation, the poems are sketches toward a poetics, interesting but not any more interesting than the notes and explorations of *Earth House Hold*.

His choice of *Regarding Wave* for title is effectively explained in his essay on poetry and the primitive. The Muse is a woman, and the voice comes from a goddess. The Goddess Vāk is ". . . the lover of Brahma and his actual creative energy . . . the Divine in the aspect of wisdom and learning . . ."

> As Vāk is wife to Brahma ('wife' means 'wave' means 'vibrator' in Indo-European etymology) so the voice, in everyone, is a mirror of his own deepest self.

So the book is regarding—concerning, observing—this principle as manifest in Snyder's wife. At least the first three sections are.

And it is there that the book maintains its momentum, the poems blending to a steady harmony. These poems are classic in the best sense, as in "Not Leaving the House," presentation of a common moment that changes all being:

NOT LEAVING THE HOUSE

When Kai is born
I quit going out
Hang around the kitchen—make cornbread
Let nobody in.
Mail is flat.
   Masa lies on her side, Kai sighs,
   Non washes and sweeps
We sit and watch
   Masa nurse, and drink green tea.

Navajo turquoise beads over the bed
A peacock tail feather at the head
A badger pelt from Nagano-ken

For a mattress; under the sheet;
A pot of yogurt setting
Under the blankets, at his feet.
Masa, Kai,
And Non, our friend
In the green garden light reflected in
Not leaving the house.
From dawn til late at night
   making a new world of ourselves
   around this life.

Charm. In itself, the poem is full of charm and of magical charms, not least the child with such careful provisions. The child culminates the sequence—the final poem following it paraphrases freshly the relation between Vāk (voice) and Brahma, extending and rendering symbolic what was individual and domestic. And above all *common*.

In spite of the overtly contemporary poetics in *Regarding Wave*, Snyder stands to one side of the current poetic question. His appeal to a common sense of life has had a momentary echo in the conventions of the current young, who would certainly approve of what seems to be the quietism of this poem. It is all ok, organic, the helping friend, the nursing mother, the charms from Amerindia and Japan, the green garden light. A desirable life. The first thirty-five pages of *Regarding Wave* make that notation through the series of twenty-five poems that form the title section. Like his earlier *Myths and Texts*, *Regarding Wave* is an informing work exploring basic principles.

The remaining two sections, "Long Hair" and "Target Practice" are miscellaneous and relaxed. Snyder has made so attractive a complex of being—as opposed to an individual optique or style—that he finds himself compelled to publishing books that contain matter interesting enough but not working toward a cumulative effect. These two sections are notes of a witty intelligent man on experience. They lack the compressed intensity of art.

Earth House Hold and *Regarding Wave* certify Snyder's directions and involvements. His concern with the primitive is not romanticism but an effort to find basic common human elements, principles rather than subjects that he can undergo and explore. Sometimes he is concerned with keeping up a habit of perception, and the notation becomes relaxed and humorous and didactic. When he is in the grip of a major principle, something else occurs. He becomes the agent of a voice, that of common experience, and the personal and superficially exotic change to the general and present. In an age of multiple options he holds firmly to his vision of the classically humane. The superficial aspects are easy to imitate or ridicule, but what is fundamental has a life well beyond the particular.

SUSAN SONTAG

1933–

Susan Sontag was born on January 16, 1933, in New York City. She was educated at the University of California at Berkeley, the University of Chicago (B.A. 1951), Harvard University (M.A. 1955), and St. Anne's College, Oxford. She has taught at numerous institutions, including the University of Connecticut, Harvard University, City College of New York, Sarah Lawrence College, Columbia University, and Rutgers University. She was an editor at *Commentary* in 1959. She married Philip Rieff in 1950; they had one child before divorcing in 1957.

Sontag has published little fiction, but it has received considerable attention. Her first novel, *The Benefactor* (1963), concerns the uneasy relationship between dreams and reality. Inexplicable and unmotivated events occur throughout the book, recalling Sartre and Camus; the book received mixed reviews. Her second novel, *Death Kit* (1967), was even more ambiguous, concerning a man who is tormented by the question of whether he did or did not commit a murder. *Death Kit* was praised by some for its attention to concrete detail, but criticized by others for the remoteness of its characters. Both of Sontag's novels have a static quality associated with Robbe-Grillet and the French anti-novelists, and a driving concern with the processes of consciousness. Her short-story collection *I, etcetera* (1978) dealing with many of the same themes but in more compact form, was favorably received.

Sontag is also a prolific essayist, and is generally considered one of the most important and thought-provoking cultural critics of our time. Her first book of criticisms, *Against Interpretation and Other Essays* (1966), sparked considerable controversy, particularly in the title essay, in which Sontag argues for a sensual rather than an intellectual experience of art. The book also contains her well-known "Notes on 'Camp'" and "On Style." Her reputation continued to grow with *Styles of Radical Will* (1969), *On Photography* (1977), and *Illness as Metaphor* (1978). Her most recent collection of essays is *Under the Sign of Saturn* (1980). She has edited *Selected Writings of Artaud* (1976) and *A Barthes Reader* (1981).

Since the late sixties Sontag has concentrated on photography and the cinema as well as literature; she wrote and directed *Duet for Cannibals* (1970) and *Brother Carl* (1974), and directed the documentary *Promised Lands*. She considers cinema the "most alive, the most exciting, the most important of all art forms." She received an award from the American Academy of Arts and Letters in 1976, and the National Book Critics' Circle Award for Best Work of Criticism in 1977 for *On Photography*.

GORE VIDAL
"Miss Sontag's New Novel" (1967)
Reflections upon a Sinking Ship
1969, pp. 41–47

The beginning of a novel tends to reveal the author's ambition. The implicit or explicit obeisance he pays to previous works of literature is his way of "classing" himself, thereby showing interest in the matter. But as he proceeds, for better or worse his true voice is bound to be heard, if only because it is not possible to maintain for the length of a novel a voice pitched at a false level. Needless to say, the best and the worst novels are told in much the same tone from beginning to end, but they need not concern us here.

In the early pages of *Death Kit*, Susan Sontag betrays great ambition. Her principal literary sources are Nathalie Sarraute, Robbe-Grillet, Sartre, and Kafka, and she uses these writers in such a way that they must be regarded not so much as influences upon her prose as collaborators in the act of creation. Contemplating Nathalie Sarraute's *Portrait of a Man Unknown*, Sartre made much of Sarraute's "protoplasmic vision" of our interior universe: roll away the stone of the commonplace and we will find running discharges, slobberings, mucus; hesitant, amoeba-like movements. The Sarraute vocabulary is incomparably rich in suggesting the slow centrif-

ugal creeping of these viscous, live solutions. "Like a sort of gluey slaver, their thought filtered into him, sticking to him, lining his insides." This is a fair description of Sarraute's manner, which Miss Sontag has entirely appropriated.

The first few pages of *Death Kit* are rich with Sarrautesque phrases: "inert, fragile, sticky fabric of things," "the soft interconnected tissuelike days," "surfaces of people deformed and bloated with leaden and crammed with vile juices" (but Miss Sarraute would not have written "leaden" because a bloated person does not suggest metal; more to the point, "leaden" is not a soft, visceral word), "his jellied porous boss" (but isn't the particular horror of the true jelly its consistency of texture? a porous jelly is an anomaly). Fortunately, once past the book's opening, Miss Sontag abandons the viscous vision except for a brief reprise in mid-passage when we encounter, in quick succession, "affable gelatinous Jim Allen," "chicken looks like boiled mucus," "oozing prattling woman," "sticky strip of words." But later we are reminded of Miss Sarraute's addiction to words taken from the physical sciences. In "The Age of Suspicion" (an essay admired by Miss Sontag in her own collection of essays *Against Interpretation*), Miss Sarraute wrote that the reader "is immersed and held under the surface until the end, in a substance as anonymous as blood, a magma without name or contours." Enchanted by the word "magma," Miss Sontag describes *her* characters as being "All part of the same magma of sensation, in which pleasure and pain are one." But Miss Sarraute used the word precisely, while Miss Sontag seems not to have looked it up in the dictionary, trusting to her ear to get the meaning right, and failing.

The plot of *Death Kit* is elaborate. Aboard the Privateer (yes), a train from Manhattan to Buffalo, Diddy (a divorced man in his thirties who inhabits a life he does not possess) observes a blind girl and an older woman. He wonders who they are; he also meditates on the other occupants of the compartment (as in Proust). Then the train stalls in a tunnel. The lights go out. After what seems a long time, Diddy gets off the train. He makes his way in the dark to the front of the train, where he finds a workman removing a barrier. When the man does not respond to his questions, Diddy grows alarmed. Finally the man does speak; he appears to threaten Diddy, who kills him with a crowbar, a murder which is almost gratuitous, almost Gide. Diddy returns to the compartment to find the older woman asleep. He talks to the blind girl, whose name is Hester (*The Scarlet Letter?*). Then the train starts and he takes Hester to the washroom, where, excited by his murder (Mailer's *An American Dream*), he makes love to her. Later Hester tells him that he did not leave the compartment and so could not have killed the workman. But of course she is blind, while the older woman, her aunt, was asleep and so cannot bear witness. In any case, hallucination has begun, and we are embarked upon another of those novels whose contemporary source is Kafka. Do I wake or dream?

Diddy dreams a very great deal and his dreams are repeated at length. When awake, he attends business meetings of his company, whose trademark is a gilded dome, whose management is conservative, whose business is worldwide, whose prospects are bad . . . too much undercutting from the East (what can Miss Sontag *mean*?). He broods about the "murder" and moons about Hester, who is in a local clinic waiting for an operation to restore her sight. Diddy visits her; he loves her. But he is still obsessed by the murder. In the press he reads that a workman named Angelo Incarnadona (incarnated angel) was killed in the tunnel by the Privateer, which had not, apparently, stalled in the tunnel. Diddy's quest begins. Did he kill the angel? He talks to the widow, who tells him that the body was cremated; he is safe, there can never be an investigation. Meanwhile Hester's operation is a failure. But Diddy has decided to marry her. They return to Manhattan. He quits his job. They withdraw from the world, seldom leaving his apartment. Slowly he begins to fade, grows thinner, vaguer. Finally he (apparently) takes Hester with him to the tunnel in an effort to make her *see* what it was he did . . . or did he (Diddy)? In the tunnel they find a workman similar to the angel made flesh: again the man is at work removing a barrier. The scene more or less repeats the original, and once again Diddy separates the angel from its fleshly envelope with a crowbar. Then he makes love to Hester on the tunnel floor. But now we cease to see him from the outside. We enter his declining world, we become him as he walks naked through one subterranean room after another, among coffins and corpses heavy with dust, and in this last progress, simply written, Miss Sontag reveals herself as an artist with a most powerful ability to show us what it is she finally, truly sees.

The flash of talent at the book's end makes all the more annoying what precedes it. Miss Sontag is a didactic, naturalistic, Jewish-American writer who wants to be an entirely different sort of writer, not American but high European, not Jewish but ecumenical, not naturalistic in style but allusive, resonant, ambiguous. It is as an heiress to Joyce, Proust, and Kafka that she sees herself; her stand to be taken on foreign rather than on native ground. The tension between what she is and what she would like to be creates odd effects. She presents Diddy as a Gentile. But, to make a small point, middle-class American goyim do not address each other continually by name while, to make a larger point, Diddy's possession of a young brother who is a virtuoso musician seems better suited to a Clifford Odets drama than to one by Sherwood Anderson or William Faulkner. But Miss Sontag is nothing if not contemporary and perhaps she is reflecting the current fashion for Jewish writers to disguise Jewish characters as Gentiles, in much the same way that the homosexualists in our theater are supposed to write elaborate masquerades in which their own pathological relationships are depicted as heterosexual, thus traducing women and marriage. These playwrights have given us all many an anxious moment. Now the Jewish novelists are also indulging in travesty, with equally scandalous results.

As for style, Miss Sontag demonstrates a considerable gift for naturalistic prose, particularly in the later parts of the book when she abandons her sources and strikes out on her own. But she is not helped by the form in which she has cast her work. For no apparent reason, certain passages are indented on the page, while at maddeningly regular but seemingly random intervals she inserts the word "now" in parenthesis. If she intends these (now)s to create a sense of immediacy, of presentness, she fails. Also, though the story is told in the third person, on four occasions she shifts to the first person plural. It is a nice surprise, but one that we don't understand. Also, her well-known difficulties in writing English continue to make things hard for her. She is altogether too free with "sort ofs" and "kind ofs" and "reallys"; she often confuses number, and her ear, oddly enough, is better attuned to the cadences of the lower orders than to those of the educated. In the scenes between Diddy and the dead workman's widow, she writes not unlike Paddy Chayevsky at his best. She is, however, vulgar at moments when she means not to be, and on several occasions she refers to someone as "balding," betraying, if nothing else, her lovely goosey youth: those of us battered by decades of *Timestyle* refuse to use any word invented by that jocose and malicious publishing enterprise which has done so much to corrupt our Empire's taste, morals, and prose.

In a strange way, Miss Sontag has been undone as a novelist by the very thing that makes her unique and valuable among American writers: her vast reading in what English Departments refer to as comparative literature. As a literary broker, mediating between various contemporary literatures, she is awesome in her will to understand. This acquired culture sets her apart from the majority of American novelists (good and bad) who read almost nothing, if one is to admit as evidence the meager texture of their works and the idleness of their occasional commentaries. When American novelists do read, it is usually within the narrow limits of the American canon, a strange list of minor provincial writers grandiosely inflated into "world classics." Certainly few of our writers know anything of what is now being written in Europe, particularly in France. Yet for all the aridities and pretensions of the French "New Novelists," their work is the most interesting being done anywhere, and not to know what they are up to is not to know what the novel is currently capable of. As an essayist (and of course interpreter!) Miss Sontag has been, more than any other American, a link to European writing today. Not unnaturally, her reading has made her impatient with the unadventurous novels which our country's best-known (and often best) writers produce. She continues to yearn, as she recently wrote, for a novel "which people with serious and sophisticated [sic] taste in the other arts can take seriously," and she believes that such a work might be achieved "by a kind of total structuring" that is "analogous to music." This is all very vague, but at least she is radical in the right way; also her moral seriousness is considerably enhanced by a perfect absence of humor, that most devastating of gifts usually thrust at birth upon the writer in English. Unhindered by a sense of humor, she is able to travel fast in the highest country, unafraid of appearing absurd, and of course invulnerable to irony.

Unfortunately, Miss Sontag's intelligence is still greater than her talent. What she would do, she cannot do—or at least she has not done in *Death Kit*, a work not totally structured, not even kind of. Worse, the literary borrowings entirely obscure her own natural talent while the attitudes she strikes confuse and annoy, reminding one of Gide's weary complaint that there is nothing more unbearable than those writers who assume a tone and manner not their own. In the early part of *Death Kit*, Miss Sontag recklessly uses other writers in much the same way that certain tribes eat parts of their enemies in the hope that, magically, they may thus acquire the virtues and powers of the noble dead. No doubt the tribesmen do gain great psychological strength through their cannibalizing, but in literature only writers of the rank of Goethe and Eliot can feed promiscuously and brazenly upon the works of other men and gain strength. Yet the coda of Miss Sontag's novel suggests that once she has freed herself of literature, she will have the power to make it, and there are not many American writers one can say that of.

TONY TANNER
"Space Odyssey"

Partisan Review, Summer 1968, pp. 446–51

At one point in *Death Kit* Diddy, who is both the center and circumference of consciousness of the book, finds himself in an elevator inside the building which comprises the head-quarters of the firm he works for. The architecture of this building is marked by a particular eccentricity—a blue and gold dome. In Victorian times this dome was the top of a chapel, but the chapel has been cleared away and the space is now used for "research and technological development." So "the dome was (now) just a head missing a body, an idle, spiritually pretentious ornament atop a busy profane building. . . . The wrong head for this body." Diddy is drawn to the dome. "Diddy wishes the elevator could go straight up, into the dome. And nestle there." He would leave the elevator and then somehow shut all the others out of the dome. He thinks of possible ways: "any of these situations would do, as long as he can gain the dome by himself." Later on Diddy again thinks of that dome. "Diddy appreciated the fantasy the dome embodies." The dome is fairly obviously human consciousness, once religiously wedded to the actions of the body but now something of a functionless anachronism in this modern mechanical age. For the detached Diddy, this dome offers the ultimate refuge; and the novel concerns the fantasies that are possible, and only possible, in this retreat. This journey into interior space is made clear throughout, a journey undertaken because exterior space, and all that is contained in it, seems either alien or hostile to Diddy—"too agitated to entrust himself to the open spaces of the city streets, with their possibilities of haphazard, impersonal encounters." Even the various small man-made spaces he finds himself in—a railway carriage, a hotel room, a hospital ward, an elevator, a TV studio, etc.—are claustrophobic without being comforting: "however small the space Diddy means to

keep free for himself, it won't remain safe." The outside world is "running down"—another of those entropic nightmares common in contemporary American fiction. There is only one place left to go. "He will have to go further into himself, away from all coherent rational spaces." The route is signposted at regular intervals. "Diddy, inside himself. Which for Diddy, doesn't necessarily mean being in his body. In his mind, then?" There it is he wants to nestle, perchance to dream, perchance finally to find the release of dreamless sleep. Readers of this late review will not need much reminding of the narrative details of the novel—Diddy's abandoning of a train to explore a dark tunnel where he thinks he kills (or Didn't he?) a sinister workman on the tracks (who, I think, first saw the light of day in *Anna Karenina*); his deteriorating relationship with the blind girl Hester; the return to the tunnel to reenact his murder and their lovemaking; and Diddy's final exploration of the chambers of death to which the tunnel leads. In *The Benefactor* the narrator says "I am crawling through the tunnel of myself," and *Death Kit* is just such another long dark crawl. Again, there is much talk of a shell which Diddy dreams he throws from the train window. In the dream he leaves the train to look for it. At first he cannot find it, then he realizes that "It's because he's already inside it (now). The discarded shell, no longer small, is as vast and capacious as the tunnel. Tunnel and shell can substitute for each other, so Diddy can wander in either one he sees fit." Shortly before the end he feels like a sea creature rising "out of its shell" (I was reminded of Holmes's "Chambered Nautilus"), and in those fantastic rooms full of dead bodies through which he wanders, he sees "skulls like shells." Another phrase from *The Benefactor* seems apt here: it describes a woman "alone in the crammed shell of herself." As we watch Diddy crawling, or sinking, deeper and deeper into the dome/tunnel/shell, venturing less and less into the world, declining into lassitude, sickness and inertia, we may recall Miss Sontag's praise for "Beckett's delicate dramas of the withdrawn consciousness—pared down to essentials, cut off, often represented as physically immobilized." ("Didi" is, of course, the nickname of Vladimir in *Waiting for Godot*). Again from *The Benefactor*: "If I cannot be outside myself, I will be inside." (Since she seems to have read everything written this century, I wonder if Miss Sontag was influenced by Canetti's rather nightmarish book *Auto da fé*, with its programmatic schematization—"A Head without a World; Headless World; The World in the Head.")

From one point of view Miss Sontag's books are about how the head gets rid of the world. Whether this is diagnosed as something deplorable, or prescribed as something desirable, is left equivocal to say the least. But the energies of disburdenment—or the fatigues of relinquishment—are very evident in both her novels. The rather tiresome narrator of *The Benefactor* speaks of achieving individuality "through dissolution, unravelling, interment" (he is French, and given to cleverness); he too dreams of finding himself in ever smaller spaces, and his attitude is that "the advent of anything brings with it mainly the problem of its disburdenment." He aspires to "weightlessness"; he likes best "a well-cleared landscape"; and he intends "to live out to the fullest the meaning of privacy"—a privacy, surely, which few people would be tempted to disturb. Diddy, suffering a more recognizably American nausea, envies that continuous oblivion to the world (hence its negation) involved in blindness. "How fine that would be. Simply not to see. Garbage trucks, bums, neon signs, gutters, plastic toys, parking lots, unhappy children, Automats, old women on the benches of the traffic islands on upper Broadway." The problematics of vision are much to the fore in this novel and there is a lot of intricate and interesting play with eyes, lamps, torches, TV screens, microscopes, glasses and so on; and the alienating effect of being at once condemned to see but frightened to touch, is explored in a sensitive way which is particularly relevant for contemporary American fiction. But finally, Diddy discovers, or decides, that the "tunnel" is "essentially, unilluminable." Diddy abandons perception, just as he withdraws from communication; he loses weight as he loses world. His last words as he moves naked down the tunnel are "There is another world but it is inside this one." Soon he is among corpses. On the threshold he even arrives at a final formula. "Life = the world. Death = being completely inside one's own head." But this burst of clarity is, in a way, symptomatic of what I find unsatisfying about the novel, which from first to last is extremely formulaic. Miss Sontag would doubtless deplore and despise the fumbling "hermeneutics" of the preceding paragraphs, but it seems to me that her novel sets out to "mean" a very great deal. It is very much *about* "a hopeless, bumbling tourist in the somber labyrinth of his own consciousness." It contains many ideas concerning the problems of identity and relationships, but no people—only diagrams of dispositions, schemas of attitudes. It explores many interesting aspects of contemporary phenomenology and communications *media*, but at the level of theory. The idea behind the book is more interesting than the book itself, which is generalized to the point at which the novel starts to turn into something else. One example: when Diddy thinks about "the world. Which is partitioned off with walls, made of wood and brick and stone and cement; which is stocked with sharp pointed objects that cut the flesh; which is charged with dead looks and inhumane caresses that bruise the spirit." Certainly; but such summarizing deadens the novel which (it seems to me) thrives on specificity. We need the details of those sharp objects, the circumstances of those inhumane caresses. I am saying that Miss Sontag conveys little sense of *process*. She is capable of making all sorts of arresting clarifications concerning the torments of consciousness when it becomes disablingly aware of its separation from the general "otherness" of environment; but she cannot, or does not, dramatize, the engagement, the interpretation of consciousness and otherness which customarily provides the richness and energy of the novel. Her book is a long rumination—but it is a rumination without a view.

But if one complains that the novel is airless, viewless, unlocated and entirely adrift in time, Miss Sontag has one powerful rejoinder. Because, as one realizes by the last page (if one has not picked up the hints throughout the novel), the book is simply about the long moment of dying. There are, in truth, no external events—only the compressed fantasies of the last moments of Diddy's fading consciousness, a purely private narrative based on the transformed circumstances of his own suicide (e.g., the bad smell which occurs once or twice is the smell of his own vomit. At one point he has a series of bottles of red wine—blood transfusions?). In view of all this Miss Sontag might fairly say that such an account is perforce airless, viewless, etc., etc., because that suits the quality of the strange dreams thrown up by the final efflorescence of consciousness before it gives up the struggle and enters into that part of the dark tunnel from which there is no return. The repetition of the world "(now)" may be justified as serving to annul our habitual sense of chronological time, since in dreams there is no sense of temporal progression—only "now": "dreams taught me the secret of perpetual presentness," says the narrator of *The Benefactor*, and I need hardly remind any readers how preoccupied American writers have been, at least since Emerson, with "the strong present tense." This fictional device of revealing on the last page that the whole novel—with its

illusory externality—is the projection of a man's dying seconds has been used before by William Golding in his immensely powerful novel, *Pincher Martin*. I find that novel more compelling than *Death Kit* because it brings into focus one particular kind of man; it relates the actual appetites of his life to the fantasied stratagems of his death, and the last desperate motions and energies of this particular human consciousness are projected with a seamless force which Miss Sontag's more meditative and notional novel cannot emulate. To adopt two of her own chosen terms, her work is palpably "constructed" rather than "secreted."

In her own often brilliant criticism Miss Sontag says that a proper experience of art is "an experience of the qualities or forms of human consciousness." Art offers "the nourishment of consciousness": "the overcoming or transcending of the world in art is also a way of encountering the world," she says and, rightly in my opinion, she sees no limit to the number of different modes of encountering the world we can enjoy and be nourished by: "as the human will is capable of an indefinite number of stances, there are an indefinite number of possible styles for works of art." All this is admirably said, and is in the tradition of that great panegyrist of consciousness, William James: "We see that the mind is at every stage a theater of simultaneous possibilities. Consciousness consists in the comparison of these with each other, the selection of some, and the suppression of the rest by the reinforcing and inhibiting agency of attention. . . . The mind, in short, works on the data it receives very much as a sculptor works on his block of stone. . . . Other sculptors, other statues from the same stone! Other minds, other worlds from the same monotonous and inexpressive chaos [*The Principles of Psychology*]." To appreciate some of those "other worlds" which artists give us, is to expedite the exfoliation and energizing of our own consciousness. But Miss Sontag also says: "the work of art itself is also a vibrant, magical, and exemplary object which returns us to the world in some way more open and enriched." Again, I agree. But I couldn't find the "magic" in her novel. Let me give one example of what I think is part of the problem. If a novel is to have magic it has got to be in the words (or between them). Now in *Death Kit* there is evident a sort of revulsion against language itself. Words and talk in the book are variously described as "sticky as taffy or tough like over-chewed bubble gum"; "like cold greasy coffee"; "as physical and inexpressive as the mashed potatoes on Thursday night or the oatmeal for Monday, Wednesday, and Friday breakfasts"; words start to "thicken"; there is a "sticky strip of words," a "tray of words" and a general feeling for their unnourishing nastiness. This feeling is scarcely checked by the blank assertion—"Language is sacred." Sacred, perhaps, until people start to use it or speak it, when it becomes so much slop in the mouth. Now, it is entirely possible that Miss Sontag intended this effect very deliberately. Diddy's sense of the nasty taste of words may be a translation into the terms of fantasy of the brute fact that he is vomiting from, as it were, page 6 to page 312. This would be a rather clever effect (like Pincher Martin turning his aching tooth into a rock), but somehow this nausea of communication seems to infect the whole book, and the language as a whole is not really very "vibrant, magical"—or enriching. It *states*, rather than creates.

What I found most interesting and impressive about this book is its pursuit of some of the ultimate implications of that cultivation of "inner spaciousness" celebrated so splendidly by many of the great American writers. Make your mind like the dome of St. Peter's, says Melville, and his work indeed testifies to a veritable cathedral of consciousness. But more recent writers have revealed a sharp contraction in the dimensions of the architecture of consciousness. The hero of Walker Percy's *Last Gentleman*, for instance, (who lives mainly through his telescope), finds his ideal domicile in a small truck with a plexiglass roof, "mobile yet at home . . . in the world yet not of the world"; the isolated hero of William Gass's *In the Heart of the Heart of the Country* ("living at last in my eyes"), is cooped up in a very small house indeed; and now Susan Sontag's Diddy, (purveyor of microscopes), explores what happens when you withdraw into the furthest reaches of inner space. At one point (perhaps when he is making a bid for recovery), he thinks he will "try to view the world more generously. Not only as an arena of contamination, but also as a space to be continually reinvented and reexamined." But as often in American literature, the world is intractable, closing in like the walls on Poe's prisoner. Diddy "thinking . . . to etch his benign fantasy upon it. (Now) finds the world closing in on him, untransformed and unequivocally menacing." Under the circumstances it seems that the only way left is to draw further and further away from the world, into the shell and down the tunnel of self. And what Miss Sontag does show, and it makes her book an important and significant one, is that in the inmost center of the house of consciousness is to be found "the house of death." The "stately mansions" have given way to the morgue, and it is in the morgue, interestingly enough, that Miss Sontag's imagination shows most signs of life. I don't suppose she would approve of my finding a moral in her book, but I think there is one, and one of some moment for American writing of our day. Namely—what shall it profit a man if he shall gain his head, and lose the whole world?

JAY PARINI
From "Reading the Readers: Barthes and Sontag"
Hudson Review, Summer 1983, pp. 415–19

Sontag has done an able job of editing ⟨A Barthes Reader⟩, and her introduction is thoughtful, an elegiac retrospective, what in the eighteenth century would have been called an *éloge*—a commemoration of the illustrious dead. This introduction to Barthes forms the concluding essay in her own selection, A Susan Sontag Reader ⟨ed. Elizabeth Hardwick; New York: Farrar, Straus, Giroux, 1982⟩, which consists of essays and excerpts from her fiction. It is quite instructive to read the Barthes and Sontag *Readers* in tandem; the real thing looks even more real beside the imitation.

Sontag's ability to stay one step ahead of Continental Thinking has earned her high marks in the world of intellectual journalism. She is always a half-step ahead of the fashion, with a knack for saying the outrageous thing—*à la* Barthes—but without the impishness and controlled ambivalence of her master. Where Sontag is correct, she is often sophomoric; where she is wrong, she is irritating and, frequently, pretentious. Her style reflects this pompousness, as when she writes: "Spirituality = plans, terminologies, ideas of deportment aimed at resolving the painful structural contradictions inherent in the human situation, at the completion of human consciousness, at transcendence." Were her essays (and fiction) not bestrewn with such stuff, one would have to assume she was kidding.

Sontag is always dead serious, even when she is "being funny." Her first book was *The Benefactor* (1963), a novel about a young man called Hippolyte (move over, Racine!) who has strange dreams and then, for some reason, attempts to

duplicate them in his life. Says her hero: "I am surprised dreams are not outlawed. What a promise the dream is! How delightful! How private! And one needs no partner, one need not enlist the cooperation of anyone, female or male. Dreams are the onanism of the spirit." Perhaps this is meant to be funny. Sontag's *Reader* begins with eighty-five pages of this stiff, almost unreadable novel.

Five essays from *Against Interpretation* (1966) follow. They are written in a style reminiscent of Oscar Wilde and Barthes but with the suppleness of neither. "Against Interpretation," the title essay, argues that "all Western consciousness of and reflection upon art have remained within the confines staked out by the Greek theory of art as mimesis or representation." This is backed up by a sophomoric excursion into what Plato meant by mimesis. What is wrong here is that Sontag assumes a naive dichotomy of form and content, thus allowing herself (in the tradition of aestheticism) to champion form-as-style over content-as-message. She casts aspersions on all "reactionary" critics who stifle us with their boring "interpretations," pleading for "an erotics of art" in place of sterile academic hermeneutics. Her rhetoric is all fizz, without intellectual rigor or moral force.

Without any fear of inconsistency, she begins her essay "On Style" with this sentence: "It would be hard to find any respectable literary critic today who would care to be caught defending *as an idea* the old antithesis of style versus content." She goes on to say how they nevertheless assume a form and content division, anyway; they aim right for content like buzzards diving at a carcass. Again, she argues against "interpretation" along what might be called neo-Romantic lines, not unlike the Lawrence who said, in *Reflections on the Death of a Porcupine*, "Analysis presupposes a corpse." For Sontag, "'style' is art. And art is nothing more or less than various modes of stylized, dehumanized representation." Once more, she opts for style over content, although she does so with a contemporary flair, demanding self-sufficiency in the work of art. Her belief in the total absorption of content into the formal aspects of the work itself is her version of Romantic organicism, Russian formalism, and recent French poetics; but Sontag's refusal to acknowledge any mimetic qualities, which would be an admission of the world's ontological priority, leaves her on shaky ground. Her opinions are necessarily presented as aphorisms, in the form of "notes," since they do not add up to sustained arguments.

Sontag includes her famous "Notes on Camp," but she leaves out "On Culture and the New Sensibility," which was the most provocative piece in *Against Interpretation*. Perhaps she no longer wants to associate with the viewpoint represented there, where she wrote:

> One important consequence of the new sensibility (with its abandonment of the Matthew Arnold idea of culture) has already been alluded to—namely, that the distinction between "high" and "low" culture seems less and less meaningful. For such a distinction—inseparable from the Matthew Arnold apparatus—simply does not make sense for a creative community of artists and scientists engaged in programming sensations, uninterested in art as a species of moral journalism.

One can see why she would abandon this stance, which is blatantly anti-intellectual; nonetheless, her work retains this quality. Anti-intellectualism pervades the "Notes on Camp," for instance, with its celebration of Camp as "the sensibility of failed seriousness." Elitism surfaces (and does several pirouettes) in remarks like this one: "A pocket history of Camp might, of course, begin . . . with the mannerist artists like Pontormo, Rosso, and Carravaggio, or the extraordinarily theatrical paintings of Georges de La Tour, or euphuism (Lyly, etc.) in literature." So much for the Matthew Arnold idea of culture.

One has to wonder if Sontag is serious much of the time. Attempting on the one hand to abolish the distinctions between "high" and "low" art, she focuses repeatedly on works that might be called Camp Highbrow: Pierre Louÿs's *Trois Filles de leur mère*, George Bataille's *Histoire de l'oeil* and *Madame Edwards*, the *Mystica Theologia* of Dionysius the Aeropagite, and so forth. She uses the old trick of name-dropping to a ludicrous degree; unlike, say, George Steiner, whose excessive name-dropping at least suggests the resonating chamber of a deeply learned mind, Sontag does not call up the sense of connected worlds. The reader is asked to admire her range, which is all breadth and no depth, not enter into a process of thought with her.

From *I, etcetera* Sontag includes a curiosity called "Project for a Trip to China" (1972), which consists of notes jotted down in aphoristic fashion. A few examples:

I am going to China.

I will walk across the Lulu Bridge spanning the Sham Chun River between Hong Kong and China.

After having been in China for a while, I will walk across the Lulu Bridge spanning the Sham Chun River between China and Hong Kong.

Five variables:
Lulu Bridge
Sham Chun River
Hong Kong
China
peaked cloth caps

This is a Chaplinesque version of Keats's Egotistical Sublime. Sontag has made the not quite rare mistake of believing that since her most incidental thoughts are interesting to her, they must surely be interesting to readers. These jottings do, however, contain one morsel: "One certainty: China inspired the first lie I remember telling. Entering the first grade, I told my classmates that I was born in China. I think they were impressed." And this concluding remark: "Perhaps I will write the book about my trip to China before I go." Both point to continuing problems with Sontag as a writer: her desire to impress at whatever cost (including truthfulness), and her tendency to write about the world before she has taken time to understand it.

There is also another novel-excerpt, from *Death Kit* (1967), which concerns the feeble attempts of one "Diddy" to figure out whether or not he really did (*did he?* = Diddy) murder a workman in a train tunnel. Though very brief, the excerpt is unspeakably tedious—a thing no novelist can afford to be. The setting is entirely abstract, impalpable, idealized. Critical aphorisms (which sound like parodies of Barthes) jump out of the narrative to assert Sontag's presence: "Dying is overwork" or "The splendor of children is never, really, more than pathos." One marvels at Sontag's willingness to type out such a novel.

Her best work is certainly in the criticism, and one does find patches of brilliance, as in "The Image-World," taken from *On Photography* (1977), where she says:

The powers of photography have in effect de-Platonized our understanding of reality, making it less and less plausible to reflect upon our experience according to the distinction between images and things, between copies and originals. It suited Plato's derogatory attitude toward images to liken them to shadows—transitory, minimally informative, immaterial, impotent co-presences of the real things which cast them. But the force of photographic images comes from their being material realities in their own right, richly informative deposits left in the wake of whatever emitted them, potent means for turning the tables on reality—for turning *it* into a shadow.

This is cleverly said, but one wishes she did not feel compelled to go on and conclude that "if there can be a better way for the real world to include the one of images, it will require an ecology not only of real things but of images as well." The word *ecology* can afford only so much abuse.

Perhaps the main problem in Sontag is that she wants everything all ways: a "radical" stance (with the implicit choices involved) and the cool amoral impartiality of Wildean aestheticism. She wants to be a democrat, but she clings to Camp exclusiveness. She disdains critics who still separate content from style, then she does just that when it suits her argument. For instance, in "On Style" she defends the work of the Nazi filmmaker Leni Riefenstahl on the grounds that the "content has come to play a purely formal role." Style, she argues, is what counts in good filmmaking. Nine years later, in "Fascinating Fascism" (1974), she suddenly sees that content does occasionally matter, calling Riefenstahl's *Triumph of the Will* a "film whose very conception negates the possiblity of the filmmaker's having an aesthetic conception independent of propaganda." Called onto the carpet by an interviewer for this obvious breach of consistency (the interview is reprinted in the *Reader*), she replies:

The paragraph about Riefenstahl in "On Style" is correct—as far as it goes. It just doesn't go very far. While it is true that her films in some sense transcend the propaganda for which they are the vehicle, their specific qualities show how their aestheticizing conception is itself identical with a certain brand of propaganda.

This is called eating your cake and having it, too.

Both Sontag and Barthes argue from a position that cannot, finally, withstand excessive scrutiny. The aesthete can never resist putting key words in quotation marks, thus undermining the seriousness of any statement. Art is a form of play, but it is serious play—as is the play of children—what Auden called "a game of knowledge." Art depends upon what Wallace Stevens called "the necessary angel / of reality." If art is not a criticism of life, per se, as Matthew Arnold would have it, it is nonetheless an interpretation of it. Barthes, at his best, interprets the world-as-text, tacitly rendering judgments that can only be called moral. Sontag is just too dead-set against interpretation to read the world at all.

GILBERT SORRENTINO

1929–

Gilbert Sorrentino was born in Brooklyn, New York, on April 27, 1929. As a first-year student at Brooklyn College in 1950 he wrote his first piece of fiction, a story that later won an award offered by the college's literary magazine. Sorrentino's college career was interrupted from 1951 to 1953 while he served with the U.S. Army medical corps. During this time he sent some of his writing to William Carlos Williams and began a friendship with the poet that lasted until William's death in 1963. He returned to Brooklyn College in 1955 and helped found *Neon*, a literary magazine that included contributions from Williams, Ezra Pound, LeRoi Jones, and Charles Olson, among others. After leaving college in 1957 he wrote and published two minor works, *The Darkness Surrounds Us* (1960) and *Black and White* (1964). In the early 1960s he was associated with *Kulchur*, a magazine that brought together a diverse group of anti-Establishment writers, and he later worked as an editor at Grove Press (1965–1970).

Sorrentino's first important novel, *The Sky Changes*, appeared in 1966. A series of carefully structured episodes, the work established Sorrentino's distinctive style, which eschews a controlled narrative structure in favor of a synthesis of what the author calls "surfaces and flashes." This was followed by *Steelwork* (1970), a study of his old Brooklyn neighborhood, and *Imaginative Qualities of Actual Things* (1971), a satiric account of the avant-garde art community in New York during the 1960s. Of his later novels, *Mulligan Stew* (1979) has been singled out for praise as an extended comic synthesis of virtually everything Sorrentino had read or written during the previous twenty-five years; the work established him as a major comic writer. Sorrentino's most recent novel is *Crystal Vision* (1981). He has also published several volumes of poetry; his *Selected Poems: 1958–1980* was published in 1981. *Something Said* (1984) is a collection of essays on contemporary writers and literature.

Sorrentino, who is married and the father of one son, lives in New York City.

Gilbert Sorrentino ⟨. . .⟩ wrote an earlier, slighter, more tentative book ⟨*The Darkness Surrounds Us*, 1960⟩ before his new volume, and though *Black and White* is gratifyingly stronger than that book and contains many more completed poems (as opposed to notes for poems), nevertheless there is a continuity in this poet's entire effort, call it a generosity of vocation, which is not to be found in LeRoi Jones's work. Sorrentino is often, still, a self-acknowledged ephebus of Creeley, though his apprenticeship, in most of these poems, is over with—no longer writing "after Creeley," he might be said to be writing Creeley's poems before him. All of the work in this collection dates from '59 to '61, and affords a corollary proposition to his striking axiom in that first book:

> whatever will become
> of the lyric,
> that will become
> of the I.

The self these lyrics have created, then, is as centripetal as Jones's is explosive: Mr. Sorrentino prefers to bring the thorns of life into closer range, the better to examine and perhaps blunt them, rather than fling himself anywhere upon them. "The shape of the gesture, the form of it"—that is his preoccupation, and of course it permits him to accommodate the world far more accurately, more coherently than the other poet's deliquescence. Not fragments of the despairing self, but a consecution in observed phenomena: hence Sorrentino has a visionary response to nature:

> In Arizona: December
>
> Clouds crawling mountains
> the air is red
> with dust, the sky
>
> glitters with malice
> and pitiful
> rabbits

> are just able to keep
> their lives whole
> in this hell
>
> of tumbleweed
> and gasping green
> cactus and rock
>
> is the mountains
> and rock is the land
> and all grace
>
> is distorted there . . .

and a naturalistic one to personality:

> When I was younger
> I thought all stronger
>
> men were silent. I have always
> talked, too much, and hated
> it in myself. But what is speech
> but the release of strength
>
> that threatens to destroy us?
> What is speech but
> the incantation that can make
> men out of mud and mountains
>
> out of slime and nothingness? . . .

and his invention of selfhood has left, like so many worm-casts, a number of beautiful and original lyrics along the way: "The Memory," "Maytime"—probably the best single poem in the book—"Cards," "Fable, with Zodiac," "The Abstraction" and the long "Shapes of Winter," whose title, again, is indicative of this poet's concern.

Which is not to suggest that Sorrentino has an easy time of it: if there is a way in which he resembles Jones, it is in his struggle against an encroaching chaos and night, and in consequence all the edges of his world are tinged with doom or dread:

The calibrations
of these states are smudged so that I cannot tell
if they are fakes or actual precisions.

Anyway it all came out one color and one suit
as perfect as a flush, in spades. The night
drained through the hole the moon had made
and everything was clothed in gray.

He has, though, opposed the darkness, and his book is the reader's reward as well as his own. If he occasionally strikes one as solemn or humorless, that is the cost, surely, of making poems rather than jokes. The effort is not merely to endure, it is to complete.—RICHARD HOWARD, *Nation*, March 15, 1965, pp. 289–90

Every picture tells a story. So can pieces of music, sculpture, practically anything made by the imagination. But only fiction *must* tell a story, and be critically exhausted by an explication of its narrative facts. Of all the arts the novel alone is subjected to so close a comparison with the serial aspects of life, which is patently unfair. What's your story?

Gilbert Sorrentino's *Splendide-Hôtel* shows that the novel can transcend the story, that it may exist outside the world it pretends to deal with. Passing life, the easiest structure for fiction, can become a form so self-effacing that the sense of art may disappear entirely. So that a day in the life—or a slice of it—may not become the work itself, Sorrentino chooses a fully artificial structure, the twenty-six letters of the alphabet. Like baseball, his novel seeks play and virtuosity within defined limits: "The excellent pitcher mixes up his deliveries, all of which, however, travel sixty feet, six inches." And again like baseball, "it does not stand for anything else. It exists outside of metaphor and symbol" (Malamud, Coover, and Roth to the contrary). For Sorrentino it remains a "Shaped and polished artifact, a game of—nouns and verbs."

Although he has three other novels to his credit, Sorrentino remains best known as a poet, impressed and influenced by William Carlos Williams and, in our own day, Jack Spicer. "The poet is not an interpreter but a revealer," he has written of Spicer; things do not connect, they "correspond," and he shows in *Splendide-Hôtel* that "that miniscule flash, that occasion, has more value than the most staggering evasion by explanation of the real. Who will believe it?" Sorrentino's aesthetic is built around language itself, "divorced from the image" and disavowing objective connections as well as subjective, since he will not allow his egoism to impose a lie on what is "true chaos." Beware those who do. Motion exists to be frozen, time to be stopped. "One would almost think that in this peace there is some sort of truth."

The proper artist: through the employment of the imagination he lays bare the mundane. "The writer," we learn, "wishes to make this sense exact, or why bother? Precise registrations are beautiful, indeed. The popular novelist deals with feathery edges, one gets a 'tone.' One gets a 'feeling,'" but at worst it degenerates into a "story." "I know a writer," Sorrentino continues, "who wished his prose to be transparent so that only the growth of his story would be in evidence. What I mean by 'story' I leave up to you. Perhaps it is the story the unemployed auto worker tells his friend over red beer. The juke box is playing 'Your Cheating Heart,' another story. . . . The story ends with a quiet grace and one of the men gets up, spits phlegm on the floor, and plays Hank Williams again. They are totally unaware that they are in fashion." What these guys tell are real life stories, the kind that prompt reviewers to say the para-novelist "has created a character who can stand alongside Raskolnikov, Flem Snopes, and Yossarian. He lives,

he breathes, he walks off the pages!" Sorrentino keeps us on the pages, as a painter keeps us on the canvas, to have us sense "Movement of the line, its quantity, the shifting of the vowels, the A's breeding in decay." There are phrases that will change your life: by Lester Young, and by novelists like Gilbert Sorrentino.

Splendide-Hôtel will not retell in second-order terms a story about another reality. It is, as the author once wrote of Hubert Selby's work, something made—"it won't go away, a new thing has been made and placed in the world." Sorrentino's work stands for itself, and is also rich in the materials of life which will not allow themselves to be perverted into the mistruths of conventional "novelistic" signals, those instructions to the reader which lead to a presupposed meaning and thus obscure the writer's truth. Gilbert Sorrentino's fiction succeeds because its method controls its substance (instead of the other way around), which for all the forms of art is surprising only in the novel. A study not of things that happen but rather of how things happen to happen, his work avoids the bland business of para-historical recording and is instead representational of the imaginative qualities of actual things, of the totally artificial place where meanings reside.—JEROME KLINKOWITZ, "Gilbert Sorrentino's Super-Fiction," *CR*, 1974, pp. 86–88

Robert Duncan tells the story of a professor at Berkeley who began his lecture on Melville's *Moby-Dick* with the rather provocative announcement, "You've heard a lot about this novel's being symbolic of this and that, but to me it's nothing but a whopping *good* sea story . . . " Shyly, in part, I'd like to make the same pronouncement about Gilbert Sorrentino's novels, which begin, years ago, with *The Sky Changes*, the classic first novel of young love, its occasions, persons, and ultimate despairs. Knowing its author, I knew how specific in fact this book was to his life, and that moved me, rightly or wrongly. There is, for example, a Christmas Eve scene which I've never forgotten. It's a bleak night in a barren apartment. The kid's mother has gone out with one of a multiplicity of "uncles". Under the terrifying tree, if you can call such a meager collection of shedding sticks that, is the single small present, which, after some bemused consideration, the kid opens. It is a tin, mechanical, wind-up pig. And the kid's question, which echoes through all time and space for me, is, who would want it?

That pig comes back in the latest of Mr. Sorrentino's novels, *Aberration of Starlight*, although he's mentioned only in passing, simply an instance among many of the ex-father's sleazy presents as noted by the boy's mother—recalling that the pig had a little drum it beat when wound. So the question had been, who would want a little tin pig that beat a drum . . .

What briefly I'd like to emphasize is the moral disposition of Gilbert Sorrentino's writing, both prose and poetry—and the fact that an initial detailing of the world, as his first two novels, *The Sky Changes* and *Steelwork* introduce the persons and place significantly his own, emphasizes his explicit concern as to *why* the human world suffers so remarkably and so stupidly its persistent inabilities of judgement and perception. There are moments of intense anger, contempt, compassionately ironic sympathy, even a yearning disposition to save something, in Mr. Sorrentino's narratives. One can hardly *not* recognize how much this writer cares about the qualities of feeling and act in the human world he shares with others. *Imaginative Qualities of Actual Things* (the title itself a quotation from an equally moral writer, and a significant model for Mr. Sorrentino, William Carlos Williams) is an intensive judgement of the specific world of artists and writers of the New York Sixties, say, Max's Kansas City Before the Fall. It engages its various subjects most intentionally—real details from real lives—so that two thus, feeling themselves maliciously parodied, will not speak to him ever again, etc. But this is a risk the writer presumes to take, in this case with full responsibility. The necessity to make judgement, to define value, is *always* primary in this writer, no matter the formal means employed or the technical pattern.

In short, I feel Gilbert Sorrentino's continuing preoccupations as a writer have insistently to do with factors of relationship, really of the most usefully obvious kind (mother to son, husband to wife, friend to friend), and with the senses of place qualified as *a time*, that is, lived in and remembered. He will run a great many changes upon these possibilities— often wryly, nostalgically, with wit and a secure invention. *Splendide-Hôtel* is, in this way, not only a tour de force upon the possible categories of alphabetic 'order' and language but also a whimsical self-invention and recall including heroic "models". (Myself there, for example, in the reference to *Mr Blue*, I came upon much as an old photograph, and deeply enjoyed the permission.) We all make ourselves up, if that's the point. Mr. Sorrentino's competence in respect of his technical resources is part and parcel with his long time admiration of Louis Zukofsky's abilities as a poet—which, characteristically, he made most emphatically public in the NY *Times Book Review*. (Here one should check out *all* the critical writing he has done—for *Kulchur*, for example. Note that he *always* writes in the imagination of an *active* responsibility of anyone apropos the kind of world humans do make in which to live. He puts his values very unequivocally *out front*.)

Therefore one distraction for me, as reader and fellow writer, was to come upon this in the jacket blurb for *Aberration of Starlight*: ". . . stories that Mr. Sorrentino further enriches by using a variety of literary methods . . ."—which fact, somehow, is none of the publisher's *or* reader's business, dumb as that sounds. Or it was disappointing to find this same novel reviewed in the NY *Review of Books* from the same 'point of view'—Sorrentino's resources as stylist (as we used to say). But I've not read *Mulligan Stew*, the novel which brings his work this location—but I will, and have the gall to presume I can accurately anticipate the nature of its pleasures—which will be terrific. And so . . .

It's most interesting that some of the most impressive moral writing ever was done by prose writers capable of exceptional 'stylistic' invention. E.g., Melville, Sterne, Joyce, Céline, Lewis, et al. Feeling, even more than necessity, may well prove the crucial 'mother'. Gilbert Sorrentino may not approve his general life's company very simply, but he markedly and persistently cares, and in that feeling makes language the instrument of response and judgement it must, of necessity, be. If he has demonstrated a master's skill in *how* a novel may be put together these days, you can be certain that what has to get said is still his point. It's still a possible Christmas somewhere, and there are still kids—and tin pigs.—ROBERT CREELEY, "Xmas as in Merry," *RCF*, Spring 1981, pp. 157–58

JOSH RUBINS
From "Balancing Act"

New York Review of Books, December 18, 1980, pp. 63–64

In a Manhattan bookstore the other day, a knowing browser in suede picked up a copy of Gilbert Sorrentino's latest novel ⟨*Aberration of Starlight*⟩, turned it about in gingerly appraisal, and said to a friend: "I've heard that . . . this new book of his . . . , well, supposedly it . . . *tells a story*."

The tone of surprise was understandable. After all, over the past decade this non-storyteller has become perhaps the closest thing around to a hip, neighborhood "anti-novelist": Robbe-Grillet without tears, Barth without academic robes, an earthy anarchist who believes that anarchy begins at home. In *Steelwork* (1970) home was the Brooklyn streets, fifteen years of them crisscrossed by two or three dozen characters. True, the microscopic attention to that terrain's darkest corners may have owed more than a little to Hubert Selby, Jr.'s *Last Exit to Brooklyn*. But the grim playfulness and compulsive pattern-making—a street kid's nervy, shrewdly selective appropriation of the dada legacy—were Sorrentino's own. He cut up his Brooklyn episodes into tiny chapters, fastidiously tagged them with dates, then assembled them in a scrapbook without narrative: a snippet from 1945 followed by one from 1951, then '42 or '39 or '50. And the range of chapter-to-chapter styles included, along with the journalistic and the free-associative, what would become Sorrentino's specialty—the list. One hundred "facts" from pre-teen 1940 sexology. A list of thirty-five guys who hang out in Phil Yodel's corner store (as prepared and annotated by one Eddy Beshary).

Still, these joustings with form never subverted Sorrentino's essential nostalgia in *Steelwork*, and some readers could come to the end of it feeling satisfactions similar to those of much traditional storytelling. They could even, with a little enterprise and concentration, sort out the chronology, find a key character or two, and splice together a fair measure of linear development. But *Imaginative Qualities of Actual Things* (1971) was a different non-story. "There's no plot here to worry you," Sorrentino advised. He wasn't kidding. The game had switched from the Brooklyn streets to Manhattan lofts, and Sorrentino's scorn for the poses of marginal artistes (poets and sculptors especially) rolled out in disjointed scenes, scabrous footnotes, parodies, and lists.

Even so, no one was quite prepared for the monstrous fun of *Mulligan Stew* when it came along a few years later. The new target wasn't altogether surprising: this time the literary world, from eager-to-please novelists (avant-garde and otherwise) to venal, ignorant publishers to blathery critics. Now, however, Sorrentino was repudiating the novel's very premises, not only the virtues of narrative but also readability and coherence—by way of a manic, grandiloquently Joycean inventiveness which itself nearly became the subject of the book. Admittedly, after two works of fiction that tried hard to get along without a hero, *Mulligan Stew* had one: the disappointed writer Tony Lamont, going mad while struggling to make it big with a "new wave" murder mystery . . .

But the crazed writer's brainscape ultimately became just one of the dozens of conventions to be knocked down in this literary shooting gallery: there was never any doubt that it was Sorrentino's offstage rage and mischief, rather than Lamont's pathological condition, that generated the chaos of print piled up around the writer's desk. Chapters (in assorted, lampooned styles) from Lamont's hopeless manuscript. Pages from his notebooks and scrapbooks. The complaints and games and musings of Lamont's fictional characters—who demanded fiercely independent, non-Lamont lives of their own. Letters. A Jonsonian masque. Wretched erotic poems (sent to Lamont by Lorna Flambeaux). Parodies of reviews, interviews, publishers' catalogues, and footnoted academic discourse. Earnestly detailed answers to rhetorical questions. Lists, of course: imaginary authors and titles (sophomoric but irresistible); fifty phrases to be used in publisher's rejection letters; thirty-one ice cream flavors at "Kreemworks."

And, even before the title page: a presentation of the rejection letters (or convincing send-ups thereof) elicited by the *Mulligan Stew* manuscript; a fatuous, glowing mock-reader's-report from Grove Press (the book's actual publisher); and a letter from a lawyer at Hasard (Random) House—Grove's distributor—to explain why Hasard had chosen not to distribute the book, "nor to have anything to *do* with that work." That work, of course, did quite all right for itself, drawing unprecedented attention to Sorrentino's subversive comic genius.

So it's only to be expected that a new Gilbert Sorrentino novel is going to provoke skeptical whispers if it seems to have a "narrative"—one of the dirtiest words in the Lamont / Sorrentino world of "Sur-fiction . . . Ur-fiction, and Post-Modern fiction to boot." A veteran of *Mulligan Stew* might do a particular double-take, too, at the new book's title page: *Aberration of Starlight* is published by Random (Hasard) House. Is this the same Gilbert Sorrentino? Now that he's buried the novel (along with most of its critics), is he back to rob the grave?

One thing is unquestionable: whether or not Sorrentino intended to be telling a story in *Aberration of Starlight*, he definitely has one. And there's not a single poet or other literary sitting duck on the premises. No, this is close-up family drama, unmistakably autobiographical—the sort of material that many first novelists find themselves locked into. Moreover, the structure here is almost flagrantly shapely: conflicts and reversals and recognitions are neatly packed into a period of less than two days at a rural New Jersey boarding house in the summer of 1939. And there are only four low-budget vacationers in the Jersey foreground, all operating on approximately the same levels of reality. Marie Recco, an attractive but sexually timid divorcée. Her father-hungry, cross-eyed son Billy, age ten. Her derisive, possessive Poppa, John McGrath. Plus: a gentleman-caller-in-residence who will unleash Marie's fantasies, raise Billy's hopes, and yank McGrath's incestuous gnawings to the surface—rakish, possibly swinish Tom Thebus.

This certainly *could* be a story Sorrentino wants to tell us, and surely it would be a mistake to let his reputation for parody become an excuse to snicker at Marie and Billy and John McGrath. Nor should the fact that he makes use of the *Rashomon* device—the book is equally divided, with virtually to-the-line precision, into four angles on the same events—throw doubts on his sincerity; many a hack novelist would take the same tack. After all, the tiny clutch of episodes here—an invitation to a local dance, a half-consummated car-seat seduction, an ugly 1:30 AM father-daughter confrontation, a dribble of secondhand farewells—might not support novel-length exploration from any single point of view.

But Sorrentino goes far beyond what seems needed to bring out the psychological nuances in a sad, simple story. In fact, what Horace Rosette, the Grove Press reader in *Mulligan Stew*, would call Sorrentino's "Sur-Neo-fiction" design is far more conspicuous in *Aberration of Starlight* than in any other

of his novels. Those four exactly equal sections are further divided into groups of observation angles, a gauntlet (nearly identical for all four) of literary games: an opening by an omniscient narrator; two bits of documentary evidence (an actual letter, a precisely recorded swatch of conversation); a distancing, mock-clinical question-and-answer period; fantasies (a letter full of unmailable sentiments, aglow with period clichés, a rewritten past); and a working-back, through memories, to narrative neutrality.

Are we meant, then, to read this story as we do a chapter of Tony Lamont's manuscript in *Mulligan Stew*? Have these four people, their pigeon-hole-able imagery, and their case-history problems been set up—like Lamont's desperate lineup of literary conventions—so that Sorrentino's tough modern sensibility can come along and knock them all down? So you might conclude if you concentrated on the dialogue section in Marie's quadrant of the book. It's a conversation between Marie and a German widow, Helga (who has her eye on Marie's father), and Sorrentino annotates the women's platitude-ridden chat with smart-alecky footnotes full of multilingual allusions, weak puns, and arch asides.

This same terminally hip voice intrudes elsewhere, too—explicitly, in many of the queries and responses in the questionnaire sessions, and, implicitly, in the characters' cruelly cartooned fantasies, some of which (Marie's especially) have been embalmed in the stiffly goody-goody rhythms of 1930s radio domesticity and Hollywood happy endings. At other times, however, Sorrentino seems to be playing things just about as straight as he can. From page to page, in fact, it's almost as if he's giving his characters a good-cop/bad-cop third degree—kicking them around some, then helping them up and brushing them off, then back to the rough stuff. A Sorrentino aficionado might figure that the master is up to his old tricks, but on territory unworthy of his satiric powers. A less preconditioned reader might see a small but authentic situation being shredded and ornamented by a writer with a horror of his own sentimentality, with too great an investment in his stylistic tics. Just about anybody is going to be made uneasy.

Indeed, if it's a study of four people, *Aberration of Starlight* is no way to tell a story. Everything we learn about these four and their motives would register more effectively without the footnotes, the parodies, the put-downs, the blatant patterns—all the devices that often seem to push an already distanced treatment one step further away from flesh-and-blood, over into the frozen realm of the literary artifact where "story" is just one element in an inanimate design. *Steelwork*, for all its dislocations and grab-bag mannerisms, never made a move that might drain the life out of its people. *Aberration of Starlight*—as could have been expected, considering the books that followed *Steelwork*—makes dozens of such moves. It can most easily be read as an exercise in mummification.

I prefer to read it another way. Sorrentino *is* telling a story. But the story is about five people, not four, and one of them is a multilingual, smart-alecky, Manhattan writer named Gilbert Sorrentino who may or may not be Bill (Gilly?) Recco grown up. "Aberration of starlight," according to the encyclopedia entry provided as an epigraph here, is the distortion in an observer's perception of light from a star, a distortion caused by the observer's own velocity. If Sorrentino is the observer, his past is the star, and his own velocity—the distorting factor—is his unshakable perceptual baggage: the cynicism, the psycho-sexual sophistication, the intellectual superiority, the impulse toward dissection and derision. And all these qualities add up to the novel's fifth character, one whom Sorrentino-the-storyteller tries to regard as dispassionately as he does the other four.

Take that elaborately annotated conversation, for example. Anyone who's read *Mulligan Stew*—approximately 80 percent of which is unequivocally hilarious—knows that if Sorrentino wants to be funny, he can be funny. But the sniggering footnotes that try so hard to make fools of Marie and Helga are ostentatiously *un*-funny. The satiric strategy back-fires. Marie and Helga assume an odd sliver of dignity while, like any nightclub heckler whose insults come out of a safe, dark corner, the voice in those footnotes finds his smug remarks boomeranging. A bizarre effect—and it is the tip-off that the brittle, authorial persona that slithers through *Aberration of Starlight* is not altogether to be trusted, that Sorrentino is watching himself, with more than a little anguish and disdain, as he reflexively (defensively?) adopts characteristic postures—parodist, list-maker, designer, question-and-answer man—in order to deal with his most personal material.

Is this unnecessarily devious? Perhaps. But once Sorrentino lets us in on the divided nature of his literary games-playing, the cool devices take on surprising heat. "Give me the titles of some other poems that Marie had, in whole or in fragments, by heart," the tight-lipped interrogator suggests. The answer is a list, of course. When questions are asked about young Billy, too, the replies often come in paragraphs of listed sensations, memories, alternative interpretations. But unlike lists in previous books by Sorrentino, these can be hooked right up to the list-maker's pulse: his need to exert some control over swarms of emotionally charged details, to share his sense of the relentlessly accumulating data of life (and especially of child-hood). Feinting and ducking, punching and running, this complex fifth character—separate from "the author" in a way no straightforward memory-fiction narrator could ever be—finally emerges in tatters, just as much a victim of shackling circumstances and missed connections as the other four. (The book's last page quotes Brian O'Nolan's—Flann O'Brien's—"The meanest bloody thing in hell made this world.")

But if *Aberration of Starlight* does indeed tell a story of five characters, offering more of the traditional novelistic values—feeling, tension, atmosphere—than Sorrentino has allowed himself in years, it is also his most "experimental" fiction yet, in the sense that an experiment is something whose outcome you don't know in advance. After the bravura of *Mulligan Stew*, Sorrentino has retreated in order to go forward, and the high-risk/low-yield setup—something like Don Juan at the Junior Prom—is in itself strangely stirring: a writer determined to see if all the dazzling things he's learned how to do can't somehow be applied to a tiny, presumably unresolved patch of memory.

The hazards are tremendous. How much irony can you force onto a fragile situation without reducing it to powder? How much design can a story hold before it becomes a book about a design? From how many angles can you refract starlight and still remember what it looked like to begin with? *Aberration of Starlight* is fiction as balancing act, and it has to be said that the meeting of anti-novel and novel winds up more often flat on the ground than in mid-air. The attempt, however, is brave and fascinating, and, more than occasionally, insidiously affecting.

FRANK CIOFFI
"Gilbert Sorrentino's Science Fiction World"
Extrapolation, Summer 1981, pp. 140–45

Max Lerner and Edwin Mims, Jr., remark in their 1933 article, "Literature," that serious literature frequently models itself after popular, even primitive forms of art in an attempt to capture some of the vigor, sincerity, and immediacy that characterize productions of the "folk mind." "All these literary allegiances," they say, "to the folk mind, to the hero cult, to the primitive mode of life, to preoccupation with sex activity—spring in commmon from the continually felt need for the rebarbarization of a literature in which the experience represented is continually threatening to grow thin."[1] Though science fiction is not routinely barbaric, is is sometimes primitive, frequently preoccupied with heroes and sexuality. Most of all, though, it is vigorous and popular.

Gilbert Sorrentino's recent novel, *Mulligan Stew* (1979), is a good example of Lerner and Mims's "rebarbarization." The novel is a crazy quilt of popular culture, "sub-literary" genres, and unusual narrative voices. Its basic story of a novelist writing his most recent work is interlaced with all variety of playful, parodic, and fictive allusions. Eventually this motley produc-tion exemplifies Sorrentino's main concern: "Surfaces, I'm interested in surfaces," he remarked in a 1974 interview. "For me, life is right in front of you. Mysterious because it is not hidden. I'm interested in surfaces and flashes, episodes."[2] While many surface glints and flashes in *Mulligan Stew* spring from popular forms and suggest the "folk mind," many also spring from more sophisticated sources. The end product is more than a mere collection of superficialities: it is a metafiction that is more vital and accessible than much serious contem-porary fiction, and more mimetic than "popular" formulaic art.

The overall framework for *Mulligan Stew*, however, is a conventional one, revealed through letters which the main character, Antony Lamont, writes to his sister, a professor named Roche, a former lover, a young poetess, and other characters who are neither unbelievable nor fantastic. They make up the usual associations we see often portrayed in traditional narratives: family, friends, enemies, professional acquaintances, business associates, and the like. This is the "realistic" level of *Mulligan Stew*—the straightforward, poi-gnant story of a writer struggling to "find himself" both personally and artistically.

Mingled with this conventional dramatic situation are a number of other, less usual documents that surround Lamont's life, influencing it slightly or greatly. They exemplify Sorrentino's drawing upon popular, non-literary forms to make "art." Lists are used, as in Sorrentino's other novels, but to a much greater degree here. For example, there are five pages of book and magazine titles—*Cobbler, Rend My Shoe!* by Thom McCan; *The Male Lesbian* by K. Y. Geli; *Our Friend, the Cockroach*, by G. Blatta; *Nutcracker Sunday* by Gloria Shinem; *Say Yes to Love* by Molly Bloom; *Repairing Your Tree's Crotch* by Henry Thoreau; and so forth.[3] All of these titles recall, of course, jokes—some vulgar, some literary. There are, in addition, examples of evangelists' advertisements; writers' school brochures; capsule book reviews; a will; phrases from publishers' rejection letters (as well as a number of rejection letters in their entirety); pornographic poetry (some titles: "Hot Bodies," "The Sweat of Love," "Panting God," "The Slippery Flesh"); and a scientific article entitled "Recent Studies in Contravariant Behavior Processes in Complex Resolutions," lampooned in footnotes Lamont (or Sorrentino) appends. Even a masque called "Flawless Play Restored: The Masque of Fungo" is included. Sorrentino's "rebarbarization" is not only diverse but diachronic as well.

In addition to these often hilarious but sometimes self-indulgent parodies of commonly occurring cultural artifacts, the text and notebooks of Lamont's most recent novel, *Guinea Red*, are included. This novel within the novel is described by Sorrentino himself in the aforementioned interview as being "a terrible book, I mean a really rotten book, but one that has its moments" (p. 29). It starts as a curious kind of detective novel: "How absurd to find myself in this dilemma! It was I who made Ned Beaumont what he was, anyone can tell you that. Perhaps not 'anyone.' Why should I kill him? If I did" (p. 1). Later, however, the novel becomes mystical/pornographic/romantic, and the title changes to *Crocodile Tears*. The narrator falls in love with a character named Daisy Buchanan—a decidedly all-American girl—but is thwarted and humiliated by two voluptuous practitioners of the Black Arts named Corrie Corriendo and Berthe Delamode. All the action of the novel is actually flashback, antecedent to the scene described on page one.

Yet the most unusual instance of "rebarbarization" in *Mulligan Stew* is Sorrentino's use of a science fiction parallel world to show us another side of his novelist, Antony Lamont. *Guinea Red*'s main character, Martin Halpin, records his own thoughts and actions apart from those that Lamont creates for him. Halpin discusses his situation with Ned Beaumont, the other main character of *Guinea Red*—they are both very unhappy with their employer, Lamont—and then decides to explore the world they inhabit. Halpin describes the first road he walks down: "It was straight and totally anonymous, and the trees along it, for all I know of them, were all the same as far as I could tell—same shape, height, color, etc. They were trees in a kind of generic way, 'typical' trees. They looked amazingly like drawings. The sun was above and behind me and did not, throughout my walk, move. I cast no shadow" (p. 152). There are a number of significant features of this "other world": it is composed of characters who have appeared in any work of fiction, complete or incomplete, published or unpublished; it is itself a strangely nonrealistic landscape, a partially realized terrain; characters can take roles in works of several authors, though their careers are basically shaped by their first "employment." Many of the characters are unhappy, since they are essentially slaves to writers who force them into often unpleasant roles; particularly, Lamont's characters are vitriolic toward their creator (or employer) and claim he has ruined their lives. (One, for example, was cast as a heavy drinker in an early work of Lamont's and now "he was fit only for the parts of English rotters in novels set in Africa or India, where he would sit on verandas all day long, drinking whisky in khakis" [p. 153].)

This portrayal of another world interacting with the supposedly real one resembles that in much science fiction—it suggests the existence of a mythical plane (another dimension, time period, alternate or parallel world) which interacts with the depicted or implied actual world. But it is interesting to note that *Mulligan Stew* is only one of Sorrentino's works to employ this specific kind of rebarbarization. *The Sky Changes* (1966), *Steelwork* (1969), *Imaginative Qualities of Actual Things* (1971), and *Aberration of Starlight* (1980) all borrow styles and methods that spring from popular forms—lists, jokes, advertisements, sub-literary genres—but *Mulligan Stew* is the first to flesh out the science fiction parallel world. Indeed, this special kind of ploy is at the center of the novel, and in a way subsumes all the verbal pyrotechnics which

Sorrentino's other novels have displayed. In his 1974 interview, Sorrentino was asked to describe his work-in-progress, the novel that was to become *Mulligan Stew*:

> it's hard to describe. Certainly, it's comic. Have you ever read a book called *At Swim-Two-Birds* by Flann O'Brien? . . . Well, Flann O'Brien deals, partially, with characters in a novel living their own lives outside the novel. I think the idea came to me from reading *At Swim-Two-Birds* and what really delighted me is that Flann O'Brien makes it very clear in his book that a character can be used in more than one novel, as an employee. . . . And then another author can take him over and use him. . . . I've got characters from lots of writers in [the new novel in progress]. I tried it in *Imaginative Qualities* where I put Lolita in the book. That was *before* I read Flann O'Brien, oddly enough. (p. 29)

With *Mulligan Stew*, Sorrentino has found a metafiction/science fiction structure to coherently contain all the fragmented and often confusing pieces that usually comprise his work. What he calls "isolate flecks" can, in his most recent novel, work more than merely on their own individual energy. The lists he uses are not simply included as a clever change from the usual character-study, but as items that will show the reader facets of the world Halpin inhabits, and aspects of Lamont's character itself. The poems are not included merely as evidence that a certain character is a poor poet; as Lamont reads, analyzes, and dissembles about them to the author, his relationship to his own characters is prefigured. The "isolate flecks" of *Mulligan Stew* are part of the larger mosaic which concerns the process of making fiction.

While its component parts clearly connect *Mulligan Stew* to popular forms, the fact that it is finally a metafiction more explicitly links it with serious fiction. This kind of serious fiction eventually tapers off into science fiction. Sorrentino draws from three basic variants of the serious science fiction/metafiction novel: Pynchon's "realistic" fiction that seeks to uncover an informing—sometimes fictive, sometimes paranoid—structure beneath the commonsense phenomenal world (similar to much of the Strugatsky brothers' writing); Robbe-Grillet's novels that suggest there is no objective reality, only different versions of consciousness (much like the themes and concerns in the work of Stanislaw Lem); and finally the self-consciously metafictional Borgesian story that explicitly concerns writers and creators of fictions and posits an infinity of parallel universes (one science fiction variant of this would be Fredric Brown's *What Mad Universe*).

Mulligan Stew at once parodies and draws from all three of these metafiction/science fiction forms. As in *Gravity's Rainbow* and *The Crying of Lot 49*, an underlying and informing structure to reality is anatomized, a system whose workings are as arcane and byzantine as those of PISCES or "Achtung" or the Tristero. As in Robbe-Grillet, there are endlessly self-reflexive sections that in Flaubert's words (quoted by Albert Guerard) are "dependent on nothing external . . . held together by the strength of . . . style, just as the earth suspended in the void, depends on nothing external for support."[4] (I am thinking of Sorrentino's extended stylistic experiments such as the chapter written entirely in Shakespearean English.) Too, as in the metafiction of science fiction, there is a sense of infinite universes: "All possible combinations must exist," Fredric Brown writes. "Then somewhere *everything* must be true. I mean it would be impossible to write a fiction story—because no matter how wild it sounds, that very thing must be happening somewhere."[5]

What finally is so impressive about *Mulligan Stew* is that it achieves a convincing kind of mimesis while simultaneously showing that experience is not, ultimately, transcribable. The glimmers, glints, flashes, fragments, and episodes as well as the operative para-world very much mimic the sensory bombardment an average American citizen must endure every day, complete down to the evocation of the common feeling that there must be a comprehensible system underlying this at once complex and superficial congeries of events. But still, like the characters from Lamont's *Guinea Red/Crocodile Tears*, the characters and events of *Mulligan Stew* are—the structure constantly reminds us—only a highly selective, fictionalized offering. As Sorrentino himself remarks in *Imaginative Qualities of Actual Things*, "These people aren't real. I'm making them up as they go along, any section that threatens to flesh them out, and make them 'walk off the page,' will be excised. They should, rather, walk into the page, and break up, disappear: the subtlest tone or aroma (no cracks, please) is all that should be left of them."[6] Books like *Mulligan Stew*, to use Robert Scholes's words "reveal the nature of reality by their very failure to coincide with it."[7]

Mulligan Stew is, on one hand, serious fiction made more lively and interesting by its assumption of popular elements. On the other hand, it is a metafiction that parodies itself, presenting a metaphor for the fiction-writer's situation of never possibly knowing or being able to show all sides to his characters. On the third hand—this is acceptable since we are discussing science fiction here—it is a kind of fiction that has a faithfulness to phenomenal reality in a world in which we are bombarded with conceivabilities turning into actualities. But finally what *Mulligan Stew* most strongly attests to is that when fiction does not work under the burden of mimesis, it is freed

to do exciting things. Sorrentino ends his novel with a quotation about Cezanne that no doubt explains his own aesthetic approach: "He desired a synthesis that would allow him to *decorate* nature with the forms and colors that existed nowhere except in his own secret thought. Thus, his last painting nowhere shows forth nature's splendors, but instead, is a failure precipitated by his surrender to the pleasures of the imagination" (p. 446). Sorrentino's similar surrender is, ultimately, our gain.

Notes

1. Max Lerner and Edwin Mims, Jr., "Literature." *Encyclopedia of the Social Sciences* (New York: Macmillan, 1933), IX, 527. This citation was originally found in Philip Stevick, "Scheherazade Runs out of Plots, Goes on Talking; the King, Puzzled, Listens: An Essay on the New Fiction," *TriQuarterly*, No. 26, p. 356. Stevick found the reference to Lerner and Mims in Wellek and Warren's *Theory of Literature*. My preference for the original source over both Stevick and Wellek and Warren stems from the Lerner/Mims emphasis on the folk mind and the specifically non-literary, in addition to their implied extension of this folk mind into popular genres. Stevick and Wellek and Warren focus exclusively on popular art in their evaluations of "rebarbarization."
2. Barry Alpert, "Gilbert Sorrentino—An Interview," *Vort*, 2, No. 3 (1974), 10. Subsequent references will be inserted in the text.
3. Gilbert Sorrentino, *Mulligan Stew* (New York: Grove, 1979), pp. 31–35. Subsequent references will be inserted in the text.
4. Albert Guerard, "Notes on the Rhetoric of Anti-Realistic Fiction," *TriQuarterly*, No. 30 (1974), p. 8.
5. Fredric Brown, *What Mad Universe* (1949; rpt. New York: Bantam Books, 1978), p. 193.
6. Gilbert Sorrentino, *Imaginative Qualities of Actual Things* (New York: Pantheon Books, 1971), p. 27.
7. Robert Scholes, *Structural Fabulation* (Notre Dame, Indiana: Univ. of Notre Dame Press, 1975), p. 7.

JACK SPICER

1925–1965

Jack Spicer was born John Lester Spicer on January 30, 1925, in Hollywood, California. He was educated at the University of the Redlands and the University of California at Berkeley (B.A. 1947, M.A. 1950). He taught at the University of Minnesota from 1950 to 1952, the University of California at Berkeley from 1952 to 1953, the California School of Fine Arts from 1953 to 1955, and San Francisco State College in 1957. He was an assistant to David Reed on the Linguistic Geography project in Berkeley from 1957 to 1965. He co-founded the Six Gallery in San Francisco in 1953, founded the magazines *J.M.* and *Open Space*, and started White Rabbit Press in 1957.

Spicer published his first book of verse, *After Lorca*, in 1957. It was composed of original poetry, translations of the Spanish poet Frederico García Lorca, and an imagined correspondence between Spicer and Lorca. Further volumes such as *The Heads of the Town up to the Aether* (1962), *Lament for the Makers* (1962), *The Holy Grail* (1964), and *Language* (1965) elaborated upon Spicer's concerns with the problems of the poet communicating with both his audience and the poetic tradition, and his belief in the necessity of language to perceive true reality.

Spicer was very much a poet's poet; he was unfriendly to the academic literary establishment, and most of the attention he received in his lifetime came from fellow poets and little magazines. His books were particularly noted for their structural complexity; each individual poem is dependent upon the others in the series to be understood entirely. Spicer believed that the individual poetic voice was unimportant, and that the conscious mind interfered with the writing of true poetry; all his later poetry was composed by attempting to "empty himself" and let voices speak through him. For this reason, he refused to allow his work to be copyrighted, and his publishers occasionally had problems with unauthorized editions.

Spicer suffered from alcoholism and died early in his career, on August 17, 1965. Several books of previously uncollected poetry have been published since his death; his major work was printed in *The Collected Books of Jack Spicer* (1975), edited by Robin Blaser.

Susan Sontag

Gary Snyder

Wallace Stegner

Wilbur Daniel Steele

GERTRUDE STEIN

JOHN STEINBECK

WALLACE STEVENS

ROSS FIELD
From "Lowghost to Lowghost"

Parnassus: Poetry in Review, Spring–Summer 1976, pp. 5–9

Come to the end of his first book, and there's Jack Spicer himself handing you a last message as you leave, that "It was a game made out of summer and freedom and a need for poetry that would be more than the expression of my hatreds and desires. It was a game like Yeats' spooks or Blakes' sexless seraphim." And then, after one more poem's-worth of ado, you're out the door. This "game" that readers—and how many, in 1957, could there have been of the small-press first edition of *After Lorca?* a hundred? two?—held in their hands consisted of 34 poems, six letters addressed to Federico García Lorca beyond the grave, and a contemporary introduction by the same moldering Spaniard *in situ*. More like a joke. The poems were "translations"—the originals of some of which you could find and tag with your Lorca alongside, while others were half or more smudged away, and the rest no Lorca at all, pure Spicer. Through it all, meanwhile, back and forth, flowed tricky perfusions, flipped coins, compromised membranes: between Spanish and English, "real objects" and "the big lie of the personal," one dead poet and one live one. The letters were especially arresting, thick with the roots of a plain-spoken, strong, and cumulatively elegant aesthetic. A "game"—and here not only were the rules but also the Hall of Fame (Lorca, Yeats, Blake). Had it gone no further, had we been left only with this one strange book and not finally a total of twelve, *After Lorca* would have made for a spectacular artifact rather than an opus, a reputation. A twist of the poet's beloved lemon in our national drink—and we might have been forever intrigued but ultimately hazy about whether or not we wanted to play.

But there was an opus. Spicer's poems, in fact, got firmer, not slacker, as they went, and though wetting their lips there now and again, did not sit in precious pools or clever ones. How do we take them? We must decide.

Even in a self-conscious century, the fact of which we either embrace or avoid according to our (X-rayed) lights, no contemporary poet seems more art-occupied than Jack Spicer. Or more elusive. What he giveth in self-review he taketh away in a sort of holy thundering shyness that's more Jerome than Francis. What's more, self-consciousness leads also to sorrows, in particular loneliness—who else but me is looking?—and here also Spicer is no more fully satisfying: he's the poet's poet par excellence, no reference points except the very poem, yet he refuses to console us with homilies and buck-up, trade-union sermons. Wonderfully likable in his muscular, no-bullshit manner, and yet in a second he's gone, just as he originally intended. Is it, then, all worth it?

Yes. Spicer is something new and valuable, extremely so. He was the first poet to really *believe* the tradition that was being contemporaneously forged in American poetry in the 1950s. While others were busily crammed-mouth both with poems and announcements of the new in the making, Spicer was getting down to work, having accepted the clarion simply and at once. This is important to keep in mind. The hortatory, long-strided mode we indistinctly call the Black Mountain movement is eclipsed in subtlety by Spicer ten times over, but he is still of that widened-out mode. Clever, pithy, brilliant, daring as he may be, Spicer was set from the start upon the One Thing, larger-goaled even than Olson and his polis and culture-straddling. Spicer wanted no less than to clear the totals on poetry's machine, to introduce the proper multipliers

and dividers. Poem was all; and if so, what we made it from had to be more perdurable, of more lasting and truer clay than we ordinarily contributed. Spicer asked that it only be "objects," real things that the poet, totally subordinate, could "disclose . . . to make a poem that had no sound in it but the pointing of a finger." Ghosts, lemons, seagulls, rocks, diamonds, baseball, God, radio, dead letters: they are recurrently placed into the poems as *figuri*, as markers, as shims—but above all as absolute quiddities, made realer than real by a retrospective turn that Spicer would have both appreciated and half as much rued. Arguing for collage in poetry, in *After Lorca*, he says:

> But things decay, reason argues. Real things become garbage. The piece of lemon you shellac to the canvas begins to develop a mold, the newspaper tells of incredibly ancient events in forgotten slang, the boy becomes a grandfather. Yes, but the garbage of the real still reaches out into the current world making *its* objects, in turn, visible—lemon calls to lemon, newspaper to newspaper, boy to boy. As things decay, they bring their equivalents into being.

A luminous, bracing, finally naïve incantation. The equivalents, of course, never really do show; they knock on the door perhaps, but when the poet comes to answer they hide, and he has to fashion them himself in order not to stand dumb at the jamb. Spicer may always have known this—I would surely think he did—but not until the last works did he really give up hoping that the original garbage, set into the poem consciously, *dead-seriously*, would call up a metaphysical rhyme: an anti-poem, the "thing language" he wanted so hugely being neither an imagism or concretism but an anti-poetry. Spicer, finally, is an anti-poet.

This isn't, please, fashionable, jacket-copy monickering. All devotional poets are just that; their faith is in the things that are there, *out* there; whether or not those things deign to join their words is all accident. Spicer, by certain lamps, may look more trendily *meta-* than *anti-*, which may explain some of whatever audience he has, but not for long. The gradual, opus-long defeat of his own First Principle shows us this, and conversely shores up his triumph. Accidents, Thomistic *and* highway variety, are both exciting and sad, and for a poet who embraced a Yeatsian sort of "dictation" that directed him at times to purposely misspell, duplicate poems exactly, shackle not only the literary will but also the emotive one ("you're trying to write a poem on Vietnam and you write a poem about skating in Vermont"), Spicer maintains a balance that's astoundingly sure:

> It does not have to fit together. Like the pieces of a totally unfinished jigsaw puzzle my grandmother left in the bedroom when she died in the living room. The pieces of the poetry or of this love.
> . . . The intention that things do not fit together. As if my grandmother had chewed on the jigsaw puzzle before she died.

Absolute, brave, alert, star of his own game. Yet in the end he must hand himself over to a tremendous irony: that a poet who tried so hard to write personality-less poems brings forth one of the language's strongest personalities. That if his poems could never quite point the finger in that "infinitely small vocabulary" he hoped they could lead the way with, he himself did. The world is, alas, perfect, and the poet moves further away from it with each effort. To read these collected books is to watch a fine poet get finer but lose every gain. But the direction remains. It is a moving, exhilarating, and expanding journey.

FRANK SADLER
"The Frontier in Jack Spicer's 'Billy The Kid'"

Concerning Poetry, Fall 1976, pp. 15–21

> For the beginning is assuredly
> the end—since we know nothing, pure
> and simple, beyond
> our own complexities
> (William Carlos Williams)

This quotation from *Paterson* suggests one of the basic themes of Jack Spicer's poem "Billy The Kid"—that a poem is the working out of its possibilities. It implicitly suggests that the significance of a poem does not lie in its meaning, as that term is traditionally understood, but rather that the significance of the poem lies in its act of self-creation. This proposition rests on the assertion that a poem is a form of experience in which the moral dimension of life finds its expression in the act of creation, and in no other place. Thus the proper concern of the poet and, consequently, the poem is with poetry itself. And, if, as Williams apparently understood, "the beginning is assuredly / the end" and our knowledge of that "beginning" lies within the recognition of "our own complexities," then the poem becomes a search for the solution to the idea that creation itself may be endless. The exact expression of this concept is found in Spicer's poem "Psychoanalysis: An Elegy" in which the final line reads "I am thinking that a poem could go on forever."[1] The emphasis here is placed on the process of thought as a type of continuing or ongoing genesis for which the poem provides the mechanism by which the creative act may consummate itself. This act of the mind, of thinking itself, finds its expression in this "place" of the poem—"Billy The Kid."

The poem begins "Back where poetry is" in the complexities of the narrator's mind, for it is the mind of the narrator which orders and selects and makes subjective the world of the poem—the poem which we perceive. It is the background out of which all our acts are made known.

> The radio that told me about the death of Billy The
>   Kid
> (And the day, a hot summer day, with birds in the
>   sky)
> Let us fake out a frontier—a poem somebody could
>   hide in
> with a sheriff's posse after him—a thousand miles of
>   it if it is
> necessary for him to go a thousand miles—a poem
>   with no hard
> corners, no houses to get lost in, no underwebbing of
> customary magic, no New York Jew salesmen of
>   amethyst
> pajamas, only a place where Billy The Kid can hide
>   when he
> shoots people.

We are immediately within a mythic dimension in the mind of the poem's narrator. The subject of the poem is poetry itself, the creative act. The persona sits ostensibly in a room in which a radio announces that Billy is dead. The obvious incongruity between fact and time is obliterated, that is, the present with its various realities—the radio, the summer day, the birds, the absence of New York Jew salesmen, etc.,—is effaced in a type of space-time relativity in which the possibilities of the present exist in the working out of the alternatives of the past. The "frontier" with all its potentialities, both historical and imaginative, as a thing to be explored and mapped out,

is presented in terms of the poem, that is, not only in its physical existence as artifact but also in its descriptive process as a poem in which the frontier is a "poem somebody could hide in." Thus, in a sense, the poem becomes its own frontier, its own avant-garde, its own "house" without any "hard corners." The east—as suggested by "no New York Jew salesmen"—is contrasted against the west—the frontier, the sheriff's posse, etc. Further, the east becomes symbolic of tradition in art, of imposed order and form, whereas the west suggests openness and freedom from the intellectual traditions of past art with all its limitations and restrictions on style, structure, theme, and idea.

The poem presents a subjective world in which the reader is faced with the appearance of a rational and logical frame— the radio, the poem as artifact—but which, in the final analysis, is only appearance. The radio serves as a background out of which the world's events impinge upon the consciousness of the narrator. Further, the radio suggests the impersonal and mechanical, the closed world of fact, and is contrasted with the openness of the mind, of the poem, of the imagination. It also suggests that the poem, in a limited sense, will take the form of a news report. Finally, the emphasis in these opening lines is on "Let us fake out a frontier." The word "Let" permits us to escape from the confinement of the objective world, the radio, and permits us to lay out, to devise, the alternate routes we may take in coming to know the frontier, the poem, and consequently, the creative act.

The mythic dimension of the poem, of the death of "Billy The Kid," serves as a device by which the narrator erects a "death notice"—the poem itself, which becomes, in one sense, the gravestone of the historical figure, but which, at the same time, leaves the possibilities for creation open. As Eliot noted in "The Love Song of J. Alfred Prufrock," "There will be time, there will be time / To prepare a face to meet the faces that you meet; / There will be time to murder and create," and, in a sense, the narrator of the poem murders Billy in order to create. The frontier of the poem, of Billy mythically resurrected from the grave—regardless of whether he bears any resemblance to his day-to-day existence in real life—is presented through an imaginative rendering of historical fact in order to preserve the idea, the fiction, of a poem which works toward creating and defining itself—its background out of which the alternatives for continuing creation may take place. Clearly, then, "the beginning is assuredly / the end" and all that remains is to see how the poet works out the poem's ending.

With the second part of the first division of the poem the poet presents us with the possibilities, with the alternate routes, which he may take to render the past into a present that contains the solutions to the poem's complexities.

> Torture gardens and scenic railways. The radio
> That told me about the death of Billy The Kid
> the day a hot summer day. The roads dusty in the
> summer. The roads going somewhere. You can
>   almost see
> where they are going beyond the dark purple of the
>   horizon.
> Not even the birds know where they are going.
> The poem. In all that distance who could recog-
>   nize
>   his face.

The remaining parts of the poem each explore the alternate routes in turn but are quickly rejected as the persona of the poem comes to realize that the solution to the "roads going somewhere," to the direction of the poem, lies in the imaginative rendering of the possibilities of things. The narrator's search to try to "recognize his [Billy's] face" is an attempt to understand the face of creation, to come to terms with the enigma of the "haze," of the summer day and the meaning, to borrow from Marianne Moore's poem, of "all this fiddle." The thing that fixes, that defines, from within the world of the poem, the significance of the search is that very search itself. It is, as Spicer wrote, "You can almost / see where they [the roads] are going" but not quite, and the end of the road will not come until the final line of the poem has been written. Spicer, then, is aware that the success or failure of his poem lies in the way in which he works out the various alternatives that he has set up. And, it is these alternatives or possibilities which will determine and control the shape of the rest of the poem.

In the first part of the poem the emphasis on point-of-view is placed on information being directed toward the narrator by the radio—"The radio that told me . . . " But with the second part of the poem we move from the "me" of the first part—which establishes a type of controlling point-of-view or voice—to the internalization of that information. The radio acts as a device which links the world outside the room to the world within the room. This movement is paralleled by a shift in the perspective of the narrator from an auditory knowledge of the death of Billy to a visual knowledge of his death provided by the objects of the room itself. These objects in their own turn visually impinge their existence upon the consciousness of the narrator. Thus the movement of the poem, from external distances toward internal realities, parallels the movement of the first stanza in the same sense as the frontier, the horizon, continually recedes from the narrator's vision. All is movement and impression in the first part of the second stanza and the images of the room's objects are presented in a visual potential which furthers the suggestive possibilities of the radio's information. In short, we move from an auditory knowledge of the death of Billy to a visual knowledge of that death.

> A sprinkling of gold leafe looking like hell flowers
> A flat piece of wrapping paper, already wrinkled,
> > but wrinkled again by hand, smoothed into
> > > shape
> > by an electric iron
> A painting
> Which told me about the death of Billy The Kid.

The movement in these lines allows us to trace the actual movement of narrator's eyes as they fall upon objects in the room. Again, things have been framed and given the appearance of a rational and logical structure—a background out of which the narrator's acts may be made to stand out. This movement parallels the earlier contrast between the narrator's auditory knowledge of Billy's death and the visual perspective of the birds in the sky. But unlike the birds in the first part of the poem who do "Not . . . know where they are going" the implication is that the narrator does. With the second part of the second stanza of the poem we are ostensibly told what "heroes / really come by."

> Collage a binding together
> Of the real
> Which flat colors
> Tell us what heroes
> > really come by.
> No, it is not a collage. Hell flowers
> Fall from the hands of heroes
> > fall from all our hands flat
> As if we were not ever able quite to include them.

The idea here is that the narrator is not "ever able quite"

to capture the creative vision of Billy that is suggested by the objects of the room. Something is missing and incomplete in the reality presented to the narrator's conscious mind as he sees those objects and that something which is missing is nothing less, at this point, than recognition on the part of the narrator that the objects themselves are not the poem but simply the perceptual field which will make his acts significant. In the final lines of this second part the narrator moves into a consideration of the significance of the historical outlaw Billy and concludes that his life in the real world is unimportant.

> His gun
> > does not shoot real bullets
> > > his death
> Being done is unimportant.
> Being done
> In those flat colors
> Not a collage
> A binding together, a
> Memory.

In this poem we are dealing with a reflective intellectual consciousness which contains an empowered imagination. We are informed that Billy's existence is not dependent upon a "memory" of the past or a "binding together" of external objects—"a collage"—in the poem but with the imaginative rendering of the mind as it makes itself known in its exploration of the poem.

With the beginning of the third part of the poem the narrator makes the final leap from having things imposed upon his consciousness from outside to the complete and total internalization of the idea of "Billy" as a poem about poetry. Obviously there are other interesting questions raised by these first two parts—questions which deal with the theological implications of Billy as an Americanized Christ figure, the obvious Freudian sexuality of "shooting," etc., but these questions are too lengthy to handle here other than briefly mentioning them. With the beginning of the third part, then, the narrator who has simply been referred to as "me," "us," or "our" becomes the fictive "I" of the poem and refers to himself thereafter in the poem as "I" with the exception of a certain technical shift in point-of-view which deals with the identity of the narrator.

The creative process as developed in "Billy" and as exemplified by Charles Olson's remark that "FORM IS NEVER MORE THAN EXTENSION OF CONTENT" is the opposite of the so-called "confessional" school of poetry represented by Robert Lowell, Anne Sexton, John Berryman, and others.[2] Lowell's poetry is the expression of personal experience in which certain historical facts of his ancestry and background are dragged from the past and given objective and mythic weight in his poems. As such, Lowell's poems continually try to universalize the unique experience of one individual, where as Spicer's poem begins with a universal, a mythic figure which is already established in the American imagination, and makes it personal.

Thus in the first two stanzas of "Billy The Kid" we fluctuate between the world of external reality and the world of the imagination. Each swing inward moves us deeper and deeper into the life of the imagination until, in the third part, the narrator finds himself completely submerged in the creative process. With the opening lines of this stanza we are deep in the frontier with the narrator.

> There was nothing at the edge of the river
> But dry grass and cotton candy.
> "Alias," I said to him. "Alias,

Somebody there makes us want to drink the river
Somebody wants to thirst us."

It is within these lines and the ones which immediately
follow that a shift in the point-of-view of the poem occurs.
Theoretically we would expect the narrator of the first stanza,
who is informed by the radio of Billy's death, to become the
voice, the "I," who addresses himself to "Alias." And this view
is reinforced by the fact that we think of Billy in terms of the
possibilities that he used other names—aliases.

"Kid," he said, "No river
Wants to trap men. There ain't no malice in it. Try
To understand."

However, what does happen is that the "I" of these lines
becomes Billy speaking to someone else named "Alias." The
significance of this switch in the point-of-view of the poem is
such that the narrator has become his myth. This effacement
of the narrator and his replacement by Billy in this stanza,
however, is only temporary, for the stanza concludes

We stood there by that little river and Alias took
     off his shirt and I took off my shirt
I was never real. Alias was never real.
Or that big cotton tree or the ground.
Or the little river.

The fictive "I" which has become Billy admits that he
"was never real," and if he was never real and "Alias was never
real" the "they" must have been the narrator submerged within
his own consciousness. In one sense the act of removing the
shirts is a recognition by the narrator that in order to come to
an understanding of the heart of the creative process, of the life
of the imagination, he must rid himself of the "clothing" of
external objects, that is, he must "see" through and into his
own imagination. He must deny any significance for the
objects of *his* physical and external world. In so doing he
exposes the structure and pattern of the poem, since the life of
the imagination is his world—the poem. The narrator explains
in part four

What I mean is
I
Will tell you about the pain
It was a long pain
About as wide as a curtain
But long
As the great outdoors.
Stig-
          mata
Three bullet holes in the groin
One in the head
          dancing
Right below the left eyebrow
What I mean is I
Will tell you about his
Pain.

The pain which the narrator experiences is rightfully his
own but in order to come to the poem in its conclusion he
must tell of Billy's pain. He must, in essence, struggle with the
discipline of completing his act—the poem as it presents itself.
Thus the narrator is forced to explore the significance of Billy
before he can come to understand the meaning of his own
creative act.

The final stanza of the poem results in the unification of
the various themes in the poem with the narrator having
travelled the various routes presented at the beginning of the
poem as the possibilities of things, and in so doing the narrator

has looked back in time and become a reflective intellectual
consciousness.

Billy The Kid
I love you
Billy The Kid
I back anything you say
And there was the desert
And the mouth of the river
Billy The Kid
(In spite of your death notices)
There is honey in the groin
Billy.

With these final lines the perspective of the poem has
changed once again. The poem began in the present and
presented the possibilities of the past as alternatives that must
be worked out in order that the present may exist. The tense
changes from the present to the past—"And there was the
desert"—brings us to the understanding that the poem has set
up a mechanism by which it, the poem, "could go on forever."
Spicer's line "In spite of your death notices," which is given as
a type of aside, suggests that though the poem comes to its end
it contains the potential for endless growth, for endless creation. Thus the penultimate line "There is honey in the groin"
asserts the mythic vitality of the poem as a source for creation
itself.

Notes

1. Jack Spicer, "Psychoanalysis: An Elegy," *Evergreen Review*, I, No.
   2 (New York: Grove Press, Inc., 1957), pp. 56–57.
2. Charles Olson, "Projective Verse," *The New American Poetry*, ed.
   Donald M. Allen (New York: Grove Press, Inc., 1960), p. 387.

JAMES LIDDY

From "A Problem with Sparrows:
Spicer's Last Stance"

Boundary 2, Fall 1977, pp. 259–62

I arrived in San Francisco too late to see Jack Spicer but I
arrived in San Francisco to meet him. There are only a few
poets in a poet's life and you must be on time (a good poet's life
is a series of triumphs). Spicer though invisible was still around
in 1967, out in the fog amongst the quick and the singing. I
was introduced to his invisibility by three friends, Graham
Mackintosh, John Allen Ryan, and Robert Berg. George
Stanley took me over the ground more than once, "The
ground still squirming. The ground still not fixed as I thought
it would be. . . . " The "false ground" of a country he left, not
without reluctance and with ten books.

Graham confirmed my acquired lore from Dublin: what
poets talk about who have made it are their accountants and
when they haven't it's chairmen and editors. "Jack at a party
said what he wanted to say, and one cannot succeed that way."
The early sense of what I wanted to hear from Spicer: that he
was accused of being more interested in truth than in poetry.
He was obviously a person in a hurry with messages—
something godlike had happened. Younger, I yearned for such
an Orphic voice formulating out of nowhere, the animal-
remembering power, as barbarously yawping as the discoverer
of the country Spicer had to leave, Whitman. His critics at San
Francisco State who warned me against Spicer's North Beach
hominterm bleated like Thoreau when confronted with the
Calamus poems, "He does not celebrate love at all. It is as if
the beast spoke." Yet Spicer was more delicate with less of a

Victorian constitution, both as Ariel and Caliban (obviously Spicer was both), than the poet who heard the America he had invented singing. Spicer could not fulfill Whitman's self image-dream, "Merlin strong and wise and beautiful at 100 years old." Even if the dream was positioned not towards wisdom but magic; magic that without God comes too close to wisdom. "Rimbaud without wings."

Of his last book, posthumously published, it's not enough to agree with Blaser in "The Practice of Outside" (his commentary included in *The Collected Books of Jack Spicer*) that the writing is surreal or under the real. It is simply a message, stark and reductively absolute as, the life lived in the craft eclipsed, last statements or testaments are wont—a message, if it comes from anywhere, of ghost-voices from under the world. In all that fable of dictation theory that Spicer so elaborately goldleafed from Wordsworth and Yeats, the breathing of this already ghosting man (1964–65) into minimal staccato poetry! *Book of Magazine Verse* as gasps, as funeral sighs, substituting for rites (the repeated poem in the book beginning "Pieces of the past arising out of the rubble" must be reheard, for it is a rubric for a solemn dirge: vain rest, vain words for it), serves as the context for the death of the poet, the passing of King Cock, as it were on a dung hill, among the shadows of the future and the peculiar shapes of the past. And yet it says, Poetry is impersonal, one is not present as hero or victim even in death.

Book of Magazine Verse is divided into "books" with names of magazines that reflect a national or a Californian establishment. Some, if not most, are literary; others are radical-Catholic like *Ramparts*, and *The St. Louis Sporting News* is here for the irresistible baseball reference and the idea of "fixing." The poetics as poems thrust against the managers of each industry (including the poetry industry), the "Captains." *Poetry Chicago* and *The Nation* are corrupt corporations threatening both good poetry and promising young poetry. It is proper to ask why Robin Blaser, in editing *The Collected Books*, left out the dedication to *Book of Magazine Verse*, a mock acknowledgement of the rejection of the poems by editors Levertov and Rago. This seems as vital to me as the original cover—*The Collected Books* should have at the very least had the covers of each volume as illustrations—a take-off of the Pegasus drawing of *Poetry Chicago*. Spicer was a symbolist brother of Oscar Wilde, who said of his books, "I always begin with the cover." The merging of cover, paper, and poems was possible only with small non-commercial presses: a point Spicer must have wanted to make. The varying colors of each part in the first edition makes us remember Dorian Gray choosing different colors for his ten large paper editions of À *Rebours*: one to suit each mood. The paper of *Book of Magazine Verse* imitates the paper of the original publications. Newsprint for *The St. Louis Sporting News* and glossy paper for *Downbeat*, a jazz magazine. Aesthetic considerations mostly moved Spicer; the protest against selling out was, like the fluttering butterfly modes of Wilde and Firbank, an urge to preserve beauty in decay against the coming mass-produced apocalypse of coffee table books and paperbacks.

The manifesto of 35 poems (with one repeat) pushes towards extremes, past the author and beyond his targets but straight as an arrow towards the source of poetry, not just the "outside," where he knew it could no longer be a community but at least a flame. His bullshit quota full, a warrior for authenticity (real lives make good poems), Spicer had a virile, almost militaristic rage. His career seems a parade of warnings, this the final admonition: "No / One accepts this system better than poets. Their hurts healed for a few dollars." "These big trucks drive and in each one / There is a captain of poetry or

a captain of love or a captain of sex." "The road-captains, heartless and fast-moving. . . . " Simultaneous with the composition of these dire charges we have the tape of the Berkeley Poetry Festival talk and answer a month before his death. Here Olson is named as a big captain, the market is analysed for the young poet who wants to go there to sell out, and specifically *Poetry* is mentioned. We are told we cannot or shouldn't appear there because of whom our poems will have to rub shoulders with; when we are published in a magazine we become part of that community. It is as simple as being told to mind who our friends are—and, seeing the ersatz and low mimetic culture of published poetry now, we should take Spicer seriously. I do.

The first level theme then is the attack on the venality of being published in terms of politics not poetry. *Poetry* is what *U.S. News & World Report* would be to a devout Trotskyist. The spawning assaults, spurts of coherence fanning out to isolated statements of an absolute ideology, transvaluate the original privacy of the ideas. They also suggest exhaustion of his working methods.

We have assembled here, in ascending degree of traditionalism, in addition to the poet who protests the system and the bosses, two other central fortress positions: 1) the classic love poet in dying heat, and 2) the Christian believer a witness to transcendence and beguiled, as a preliminary, in "sweet Platonic spiritland." The main love poems are in the *Tish* and *Downbeat* sections. For the while I will just look at *Tish*, 2, where climate interacts with a love situation. The lover shivers at ten above freezing, becomes a bird flying through snow-clouds, nestles in the poet's palm. The lover becomes an Arctic snow goose "if there are such things" and finally a sparrow about to starve in snow, 30 below in the hand-holding of lover and poet. "A problem with sparrows." Spicer is wonderfully in the Roman tradition, the other is a *puer delicatus* of a male lover (add to this the folk belief of the lecherous nature of the birds, "The adulterous sparrows in the eaves"). As we are meant to, we go to the second "Lesbia" poem of Catullus, where his girl's sparrow is dead that "quem plus illa oculis suis amabat." The image of Lesbia caressing her bird in her hand is presented as her way of dampening down the flames of passion—a clear explanation in part of what is wrong in the *Tish* poem. Catullus and his world do not seem alien to Spicer, as they have not to other writer-lovers. For the designated heroes and victims (the poets of love), being in love constitutes a way of life, as Kenneth Quinn makes plain in his *The Catullan Revolution*. Love is a serious preoccupation for this kind of imagination, the *Praeceptor Amoris*. It is usual and traditional to engage in the pursuit of love with a young man; it is also usual and traditional that one's affairs stay at a frequent and casual level. It is this latter proposition that Spicer animadverts against. Passion is not quite sincerity, and what we have is the Christian reality (about the person) psychotically disturbing "the offered good." But when it is not offered, as in *Tish*, 3, conscience, having found a soul, is a consolation. But we know consolation is not for love. Belief without morals is what we Christian poets spread as merchandise. A problem with doves.

The final meaning of *Book of Magazine Verse* is that of a man at the end of his tether having to find a way out, and finding it in the Incarnation, the flesh on the poem of God. It is the melody of Job, past patience yet redemptive. There is no dark brewing lament like it. It is Osip Mandelstam's, "I drink the cold mountain air of Christianity." Mandelstam is a Christian poet of ultimates, one aware of Dante's rose in Paradise and Villon's "lyrical hermaphroditism." If only Spicer had been drinking on Russian Hill with Mandelstam, instead of the Celtic bore, Dylan Thomas, with no idea of history's cornucopia! Mandelstam's inspired essay on Villon contains a sentence which seems to sum up Jack's psychic nature: "By his very nature, a lyric poet is a bisexual creature, capable of an infinite number of fissions in the name of his inner dialogue."

Since Jesus is celibate, both man and woman on the cross, the poetry in this book is affirmative atonement material, with genitals appearing only to have access to the body. The soul is a sweet place, untouched yet untouchable. Ambiguities of vinegar and spear. Christsperm of "no love deserves the death it has."

JEAN STAFFORD

1915–1979

Jean Stafford was born on July 1, 1915, in Covina, California, the daughter of a writer and his wife. She received bachelor's and master's degrees from the University of Colorado and studied for a year at the University of Heidelberg (1936–37).

Stafford published her first novel, *Boston Adventure*, in 1944, and her second, *The Mountain Lion*, in 1947; both remain her best-known works. Over the years she contributed short stories to a variety of periodicals, including *The New Yorker*, *Vogue*, and *Harper's Bazaar*; many of them were later published in several collections. A selection of her stories was republished as *Collected Stories* in 1969; it was awarded a Pulitzer Prize in 1970. Stafford also wrote several other novels and children's books, and a nonfiction work, *A Mother in History* (1966), based on interviews with the mother of Lee Harvey Oswald.

Stafford was married to the poet Robert Lowell (1940–48) and a writer, Oliver Jensen (1950–53); both marriages ended in divorce. In 1959 she married the writer and critic A. J. Liebling, who died four years later. Stafford, who had been in failing health for several years, died on March 26, 1979, in White Plains, New York.

ELIZABETH JANEWAY
From "The Worlds of Jean Stafford"
Atlantic, March 1969, pp. 136–38

In a way Miss Stafford's themes are archaic as well as indigenous, for they are older than today, and they will be newer tomorrow. They are, however, re-examined very thoroughly. If Miss Stafford is still on the side of her Innocents Abroad, she does not take her stand there unequivocally. Innocence can be rather silly, can be adulterated with ignorance and lack of imagination. These qualities shadow the young girls who are the heroines of "Maggie Meriwether's Rich Experience" and "The Echo and the Nemesis," two of the first group of stories (in *The Collected Stories of Jean Stafford*). Reading them some years ago one felt a shock in them that has since been lost, and now one identifies less easily with the shocked heroine. It is a tribute to Miss Stafford's skill that the stories are not dated by this, but instead are changed and deepened. Our present doubts about American innocence, and our uneasy feeling that it contains the seeds of moral irresponsibility, existed already in these stories.

Another of Miss Stafford's strengths can be seen even in a rather slight story like "The Children's Game"—that is, her ability to tell us exactly what is happening and nevertheless to deepen the mystery of why her people behave as they do. A young American widow who has haunted the hotels of Europe like a ghost since her husband's sudden death finds herself returning to life by way of a friendly affair (or perhaps merely an idyllic friendship) with an English film director. In the course of a holiday trip together, they stop in a Flemish seaside town where there is a casino. The man reveals himself as an obsessive gambler, and the couple part. But it is not the gambling, or the man's still-existent though unhappy marriage,

which brings this about. He asks the heroine to try an evening at the tables, and she finds herself possessed by the same passion as her lover. The world around fades out. Nothing exists but the insane, lying, seductive promise to satisfy all one's yearnings which the roulette wheel offers: instant success! Having felt the strength of this morbid translation, the heroine leaves for home, for the lure of gambling is stronger than any love between this pair could be. We know what happened, but this brief present event is like a candle which lights up the caverns of past and future to show us glades of stone, flickering shadows, and further grottoes.

The Western stories, and most of those laid in New York too, fall into a different mood. The Innocents Abroad can go home again, but the children and young people caught in the provinces hate their homes and live there as despairing prisoners, aching to leave a world so small and mean it cramps the spirit. Again, this is an archaic American theme, a part (one might say) of the Matter of America, as Arthur and Gawain and Tristan belong to the Matter of Britain. Not only Mark Twain but Sherwood Anderson, Dreiser, and Willa Cather have dealt with it. Miss Stafford's story "In the Zoo" creates magnificently that emotion of waste, impotence, self-pity, self-contempt, and angry hopelessness that we refer to when we say "alienation" but that has never really been named. It haunts the Great Plains, and the slopes of the Rockies, as it haunted the thickets and the steppes of Chekhov's Russia. It is a way station on the road to paranoia. Even in happy later life, the children who breathed that atmosphere can suffer recurrences of distrust and despair, remembering their years of servitude to a foster-mother worse than Cinderella's. Indeed the "Gran" of "In the Zoo" is less a person than a local deity, mean as a Snopes but without Snopesian ambition, a Mrs. Grundy of the home, an injustice collector of genius. There are two of her in "The Liberation," and in other stories, like

"Bad Characters," "A Reading Problem," and "The Healthiest Girl in Town," one feels her unseen presence driving desperate children to look for refuge in the exhilarating, anarchic world of real outsiders instead of accepting the shabby community where Gran rules.

It is in the New England stories that one finds an alternative to Gran's world, and that is why they seem to me the most interesting. From the time she created Sonie Marburg of *Boston Adventure* twenty-five years ago Miss Stafford has regularly sent forth inquiring and ardent explorers of the one indisputable high culture which the United States has achieved. (The South produced no high art till it was far past its peak of power and reacting to other literatures.) What is it that we made there, in New England? Miss Stafford asks, and it is not a regional or a dated question, but an invitation to study the American identity through its quintessential social artifacts and, perhaps, to divine from these the American destiny.

Here come the outsiders, like Sonie Marburg and Rose Fabrizio in the story "The Bleeding Heart," drawn by a vision of order and of a civilization worthy of willing obedience. What fires must burn within to have produced the balanced and convoluted perfection without! Sonie sees Miss Pride as a replacement for her mad witch-mother. Rose imagines the handsome stranger she sees reading in the library as a foster-father. Then each penetrates the citadel. Rose finds madness and rot. Sonie's participation in the rites of civilization is not as priestess but as sacrificial victim. Of the creative fire that once burned, nothing remains but a spark like a maggot in the brain, or an incestuous flame that licks the last hickory logs on the hearth, which will blacken and die if they are separated.

And yet something was there, and something lingers, distorted and eccentric but incontestable. The best story in the book (no easy judgment on a collection containing "Bad Characters," "In the Zoo," and that marvelously controlled tale "The Interior Castle") is a Boston story, "Life Is No Abyss," which is published here for the first time. It is about eighty-year-old Isobel Carpenter, who has taken up residence in the poorhouse, to the horror of her rich relatives, and who refuses to leave. It is also about the nature of reality, and the value of confronting it, for reality is where Isobel dwells—or, rather, where she reigns—even though her motives for settling herself there are malice and spite. Cousin Will invested her fortune for her after her father, the Judge, died at the age of 103, invested it (says Isobel) "in banana plantations in Winnipeg," and immediately lost every penny. Horrified, Will invited her to share his home and his purse (and so did half a dozen others of the cousinage). A lesser woman might have done so, and spent her declining years in luxury and conscientious nagging. But Isobel is capable of the grand gesture. "Will put me in the poorhouse," she declared, and thither she departed.

There she has been for eighteen months on the day that pretty twenty-year-old Lily comes to call in place of poor Cousin Will, who has come down with bronchitis. Lily has been protected up to now from the sight of Isobel in the squalor of her surroundings, but she is warm-hearted and kind, and eager to help Will bear the burden which Isobel's revenge has thrust on him, for Lily too is penniless, orphaned by her parents' death in an accident, and dependent on Will's generosity. It is through her eyes that we see the three-bed ward which Isobel shares with mad, gentle Viola and a series of old women who arrive only to die. The food is awful. Isobel is clothed in a gruesome print uniform. Her arthritis is untreated. A radio plays incessantly, poor Viola croons, a disc jockey jokes. And here Isobel chooses to stay!

She is not crazy, for she judges her surroundings accurately and speaks her mind about them. She's neither lost her wit nor gained humility by living in conditions which only a saint could endure—and enduring them. Vicious-tongued, opinionated, unkind, Isobel is still alive and awake, for she has preserved the basic right of the individual, the right to choose. It may be a poor choice, Hobson's choice, but she is where she is by her own will and for her own continuing purpose, which is more than Lily can claim, or rich Cousin Augusta either, who is also calling to offer Isobel her hospitality. And whether she knows it or not—quite possibly she does not, but she may—there is a great deal to be said for her choice, for the poorhouse is where life is. After eighty years under the Judge's wing Isobel has found the gritty margin of experience where nerves react to real stimuli, where the senses transmit messages from outside, and the mind finds its vocation as an instrument of salvation. Whether or not Isobel will gain a reward for the sufferings she has chosen to endure, whether one can reach sainthood by way of fury and spite, *we* gain, reading the story of one who is neither an innocent nor yet corrupt.

I must not close without saying how moving these stories are, more austere than Miss Stafford's novels, but able at their best to reach as far and point as precisely. A particular grace is the dialogue. There is no one else writing today whose people speak more truly, and more surprisingly. This is something finer than "having an ear." It is the mark of a writer whose perceptions are so immediate and exact that she can use dialogue not just for color or plausibility or character drawing, but to embody and convey the very heart of her intentions.

M. M. LIEBERMAN
"The Collected Stories"
Sewanee Review, 1969, pp. 516–21

If one opens Jean Stafford's *Collected Stories* to, say, "The Lippia Lawn," which begins, "Although its roots are clever, the trailing arbutus at Deer Lick had been wrenched out by the hogs," he is promised the work of a kind of poet and this promise the other stories generally keep. It's the "clever", employed for all its worth, including *its* root sense that does it *almost* all; and this as it should be, if, as I suppose with a few other theorists, the short story is most like the lyric and its agent is neither plot nor character but diction. When the diction is felicitous and decorous, the tone and feeling will cradle characterization, enhance idea, and imply action which the novel must always dramatize—or fail. But this is not to say that the short story *is* a poem and here, too, is where some writers (and not a few critics) have gone wrong.

The short story is not quite a poem any more than it is quite a short novel boiled conveniently down to bite size. So it cannot, therefore, be done with sounds, sights, and symbols alone. Herbert Gold was right once when he contended that "the storyteller must have a story to tell, not merely some sweet prose to take out for a walk." And so was the editor who wrote to Katherine Anne Porter, "No plot, my dear, no story," although how he supposed that stricture applied to her I can imagine only in a way that does him no credit.

This "collection" (some of Miss Stafford's stories are not here), thirty strong, is grouped geographically under these headings: "The Innocents Abroad"; "The Bostonians" and "Other Manifestations of the American Scene"; "Cowboys and Indians" and "Magic Mountains"; and "Manhattan Island". This arrangement is, Miss Stafford in her prefatory note acknowledges, "arbitrary". In any case it is merely descriptive, and since she is not presuming to be critic of her own work, it is legitimate enough. As a practitioner here of evaluative criticism I would elect to see them as falling naturally into two rather than four groupings: real stories with sufficient verbal magic to compensate nicely for the absence of explicit causal-temporal logic essential only to the longer fictional forms; and alleged stories which no amount of verbal magic can rescue from a poverty of implied plot and other formal features. I found few of the latter in this book and even those got out of this pedant a grudging approval.

"The Captain's Gift" isn't, I think, a story, and neither, I suspect, is "Between the Porch and the Altar". Both seem to me programmatic tales calculated to make a fictional statement without ample fictional means. In the former, set in New York, in the years of World War II, "Mrs. Chester Ramsey, the widow of the general, has one of the very few private houses in the neighborhood." The neighborhood, a haven of nineteenth-century graciousness and gentility, now stinks of proletarian cooking, specifically Jewish, but Mrs. Ramsey will not move, despite the persistent urgings of her friends, who simply cannot understand her stubbornness, whereas Miss Stafford can. "She is an innocent child of seventy-five." She knows nothing of the quotidian world and scarcely knows that she doesn't know. "For example, if someone speaks of the mistakes of Versailles, she quite genuinely believes he refers to the way the flower beds are laid out in the palace gardens and she agrees warmly that they could have been ever so much nicer." Thus character is nicely laid out in a stroke. But a good part of the moral question is immediately introduced with the most tactful irony: "But one has no business being annoyed with her. Since there are so few years left to her (and since there is now no danger of our being bombed) it would be an unkind and playful sacrilege to destroy her illusion that the world is still good and beautiful and har-monious in all its parts. She need never know how barbarically civilization has been betrayed." For that matter, the question had been introduced earlier with the invocation of Versailles in all its implications. If civilization has been betrayed, as it surely has, wasn't it betrayed by someone? Isn't Mrs. Ramsey mon-strous in her innocence and hasn't she always been? Isn't that parenthetical clause an attribution of the height of moral ob-tuseness? Finally, if Mrs. Ramsey is to be left to die in peace, should the same be urged for Ramseyism? If this is Hell, should we not follow Vergil's example and eschew pity for the love of God? After all, Mrs. Ramsey is some kind of sinner if she can live among the Jews and not know the barbarous Europe of her time, with its own stink of cremated bodies. One can only admire the deftness with which the most weighty questions are asked in the most effortless narrative mode; fatuity and hypocrisy are so neatly balanced with intelligence and ethical sensibility that the reader is trapped into looking at himself almost before he sees the author's fictive truth. The hypocrisy is made the reader's; the intelligence, the author's. Only the author, how-ever, knows how it will all come out—that is, how the dance and the dancer will be distinguished; how Mrs. Ramsey with her Edwardian order, charm, and decency can be given her due human respect without sentimentality, for sentimentality in her milieu is now criminal.

It will all come out rather arbitrarily by means of an improbable grandson, Captain Arthur Cousins, a favorite of the old lady partly because he resembles her late husband. In the past he seemed to share her hothouse world, but now he is in the thick of Germany's wartime jungle. He writes to her regularly and recently he has told her that he is sending her "the best present that I have found for you yet". We do not see

Arthur in the round; none of his past is dramatized for us, nor is his relationship with anyone fleshed out. A fragment of his correspondence suggests a mind of whimsical conceits, and his mother has said that " . . . he is becoming more and more unrecognizable." He is improbable as a fictional character whose burden it is to outrage a morally ambiguous innocence and thereby resolve an ethically ambiguous dilemma. Some-one, somehow, would have to confront the old lady as she stands for a stunted moral imagination, since an ethical question is the work's theme; but in a fiction (the representa-tion of the motives of men, women, and children) that someone has to have a credible personal reason to be mean enough to take all the world's legitimate grievances out on one old lady:

> She delays no longer and snips the string. There in her lap lies a braid of golden hair. . . . It has been cut off cleanly at the nape of the neck. . . .
> She speaks aloud in the empty room. 'How unfriendly, Arthur!' she says, 'How unkind!' And as if there were a voice in the hair at her feet, she distinctly hears him saying, 'There's a war on, hadn't you heard?'

There is no reason to believe that, in the fictional world in which Miss Stafford has positioned Mrs. Ramsey and her grandson, either the latter could have said such a thing or the former could have imagined it. We have been treated to a serious subject and, in the figure of the hair, a fine image to bring it home. It has everything to do with Miss Stafford's fine moral sensibilities, but not enough, after all, to do with her characters. I repeat: in a short story the figurative resources of language, which can do it all in the lyric, can do only some of it.

The concept of innocence is treated rather differently and altogether successfully in "The Mountain Day", where it is realized simultaneously, not by fiat with the monstrous in human nature only, but amply in the possibility, in the young, of a consciousness of love, despite nature's indifference. The setting is Colorado, an altogether believable Eden for both the reader and the young college girl who experiences it as paradise and as paradise qualified by mortality. She thinks she will live forever because she thinks she loves a young man. In the end she learns that love is not a concern for another's opinion of one's self, but "it is wanting the beloved to be happy." In the hands of a lesser writer than Miss Stafford, such a configura-tion would in all likelihood have materialized as mass-circulation pap, not because the idea is false, but because baldly paraphrased it is as hollow as most abstractions. If love is a gift here, it can be a tyranny there. Who hasn't been unintentionally victimized by someone who wanted only one's happiness? But for the fictional moment, at least, the young protagonist's love for her "Rod" is real, not only because we have seen something of his suffering but because that about which he has suffered has been given a thorough fictional rendering. Rod has been pained into a sense of his own terrifying mortality and it is a pain which his fiancée has shared equally:

> Mary and Eileen could not have been in the water for more than a few hours, but in that time the hellbenders and the ravenous turtles had eaten their lovely faces and their work-swollen hands; no one, certainly no kinsman must see them.

The young lovers have been expelled from their Eden not for disobedience, but, worse, by accident. Everything in their bodies has been exhausted by the search for two young innocent

Irish servant girls who couldn't swim. All that is left to the couple is a guilty knowledge of their own past ignorance of the world, and its concomitant, their self-absorption. The fall, however, is fortunate; in the knowledge of a shared mortality is a knowledge of a common suffering and its fruit, love.

Stunned by the apparent violence and injustice of natural events, the grandmother, "as if she were alone, as if she were speaking to herself or to God, . . . murmured, 'I won't come here again with innocents.'" The play on the last word is just right. Fortunately the story does not depend on that kind of brilliance. Those "hellbenders and . . . ravenous turtles" were there all along, whereas in "The Captain's Gift" the golden braids were not.

In "The Maiden", a thoroughly effective effort to treat the familiar subject of how the people of Schiller and Beethoven could have become the nation of Hitler and Eichmann, we see that Miss Stafford can be about as satisfying a maker as we have around. What more can one ask of a writer of fiction than that she demonstrate again that poetry is more philosophical than history? A literary artist today is, perhaps, precisely one who can, in ten pages, turn the social scientists on their heads. Germany, we see, didn't become; it always was, given man's imperfect nature. Miss Stafford manages this in what one recognizes, finally, as her characteristic way to meaning. The macabre and the near-sublime are juxtaposed in such a manner and by such means as virtually to merge. The little gentle lawyer and his arcadian *fräulein* can now plan to marry because on this very day he has witnessed, in his professional capacity, the hideous execution of a wretch who stole a few pfennigs. In his formal attire, he is now a "full-fledged lawyer". At the ritual murder he experienced no disgust, only joy in his own living. His interlocutors are shocked at recognizing a *Totentanz*. But the tellingly awful is not the murder itself, nor the moral failure to recognize its significance. It is the fact, so perfectly rendered, of the lawyer's surpassingly decent marriage.

BLANCHE H. GELFANT

New Republic, May 10, 1975, pp. 22–25

Jean Stafford's novel *The Mountain Lion* (1947) tells of two children, brother and sister, growing up in America at a time more remote from us than the calendar conveys—an irrecoverable time, before World War II, when America still cherished innocence. As the novel opens Ralph is 10 and Molly eight. They are too young yet to have had the experience that dispels innocence. But in the four years their story spans, they are forced into growing up, a dangerous process, possibly deadly. For they must enter "a tunnel with no end," the dark tunnel of adolescence in which the child will be forever lost. In the shadows of this tunnel, where shamefully Ralph and Molly discover sin, their childhood expires—and with it, the dream of American possibilities that once we shared.

That was the dream of expansion, of growth and release, for which our symbol was the West. When early in the novel Ralph cries, "Golly *Moses*, I'd like to go out West," he fuses with a traditional figure of American history and literature— the roving young hero who leaves civilization behind, longing to escape its corruption, and sets out to find freedom in the territory ahead—Huck Finn's illusory place: the still untouched, uncontaminated, open spaces of the West. Summoned by their grandfather, a "half legendary" annual visitor from Colorado, a "sort of god of September"—who also

resembles an Indian and a "massive, slow-footed bear"—the children go West. They come upon the landscape of fable: of mountains, forests, glaciers, streams and pastures; of animals— coyotes, elk, deer, bighorn, beavers, cattle and horses; of rangy men and hunting rituals; of untold riches—an American landscape bathed in golden light. Here released from their mother's "sissy life," the children feel free to grow. Molly finds "an ideal glade" in the mountains where she writes poems and stories, collects ladybugs, and stalks wild animals with her Brownie. Ralph rides and hunts and becomes obsessed with a golden mountain lion, the last of its kind, which he alone must kill. One day he finds his lion, and for a precious fleeting moment, dream and reality coalesce. He shoots—and kills his sister Molly; and the burst of blood upon her forehead becomes the mark of inbred inescapable guilt in the American character. The letting of blood, with which the novel begins and ends, betrays the dream of innocence.

Why must Molly die? Why must brother and sister—so close they think and act and even bleed as one—fall into antagonistic roles that seem inevitable; and mutually destructive? Why must the male become a hunter, and the female, his prey? These questions strike me as crucial and implicatory— and too long overlooked. Raised here they can lead us to the reconsideration of a prophetic American novel we have in the past unjustly neglected; and to the reconsideration of an anachronistic American myth we may in the future finally disown.

Molly dies, I believe, in a sacrificial ceremony disguised in the novel as accident. Her death is demanded by the great masculine myth of the West—a symbolic place: where boys like Ralph become men; and girls like Molly become not only extraneous and intrusive, but actively threatening to the ritual of male initiation. For just as the West held the promise of innocence, so also it promised manhood. It defined the terms for manhood by its ritual, which, in the American novel, might be modified in its details, but never in its exclusion of women. The young hero going West was to leave all women behind. In the wilderness he was to join a male tribe of archetypal hunters. They were to designate a sacred spot of wilderness and a legendary animal, usually personified, as the place and object of the hunt. When the boy and animal met, in a mystically charged encounter, he achieved courage, skill and pride—and became a man. The greatest story in American fiction that enacts this myth—and its impossible strain in merging manhood and innocence—is William Faulkner's "The Bear." Ike McCaslin, the boy who hunts Old Ben in the wilderness of the South, casts his indelible shadow over Ralph, hunting "Goldilocks" the lion in the Colorado mountains (and more recently, over D. J. hunting Grizzer, old "Mr. Bear," in Norman Mailer's *Why Are We in Vietnam?*). Like Ike, Ralph has committed himself to a timeless ritual of initiation, and implicitly to the decision to break with Molly. For as a female she encumbers him in his obsessive stalking of the mountain lion, and of the masculinity that is for him the real trophy of the hunt. Her constant presence reminds him of a part of himself that he can no longer endure as he grows up, and indeed must kill: the feminine part of his nature.

Thus *The Mountain Lion* is a study in childhood ambivalence, in social intolerance. For American society does not tolerate ambivalent or shared sexual roles: it demands that the child growing up assume a clear-cut sexual identity. This demand destroys both Ralph and Molly as it turns them against each other, and involutes their love with hate. It destroys them because they are too much a part of each other to conform to the unequivocal roles of man and woman their society prescribes. Those who do conform—their twinkly older sisters, their Uncle Claude, their companion Winifred, tomboy turned coquette—are inane. As social satire *The Mountain Lion* is merciless and funny. Jean Stafford surveys the American scene, East and West, and finds everywhere that American characters are reduced to caricature. She presents familiar stereotypes—the fluttery, supercilious suburban mother; the tea-drinking, discreetly belching, chinless, platitudinous pastor; the red-necked, "gosh darn," weekend whooping cowhands; the wizened old wizardly black family cook; the grinning Oriental; the menacing Mexican gardener, a "bad man" singing "bad songs" in Spanish; the eccentric old-maid postmistress eating health foods and peering (hopefully?) under the bed. Tintypes all: flattened, glossy, gross figures. But they represent the adult world in which eventually the children must find their grown-up roles. As a comedy of manners *The Mountain Lion* is caustically funny. But as a social condemnation it is not funny at all. All our prejudices are here imprinted, both consciously and not. We must find the novel far more condemning than intended: for time, the sweeping course of events in recent American history, has reinforced the horror with which it ends. Time has shown that violence and the waste of young life are no accident. Ralph's dilemma is emblematic. If he is to grow up as a man acceptable to a society that polarizes men and women—if he is to resolve the deep-rooted and potentially life-enriching ambivalence within his nature—he must get rid of his sister.

Why must Molly die? So that Ralph can live up to a male image perpetuated by the myth of the West that makes violence and destruction the consummation of manhood. "Learning the ways of a man" out West, proving "his worth or manliness," Ralph inherits the legacy of confused moral values the ritual of initiation transmits. Killing, he learns, is an art. Through killing, as through art, one enters a timeless world of ritual and tradition, and one arrests time. So killing becomes also an act of love. For as one stops time he stops change: which means that whatever one loves remains fixed in form, within grasp, never to be lost in time but held forever in love. If this is the logic of madness, it nevertheless informs romantic literature, and Ralph becomes a romantic hero when he determines to kill the mountain lion, an animal whose beauty arouses his erotic fantasy, because he loves her: "Goldilocks . . . would be killed . . . out of his own love for her golden hide." Once she is dead he can possess her forever: "have her stuffed and keep her . . . all his life." With Molly also, killing becomes a confused expression of Ralph's love. He loves her for her "innocence," in which he seeks his own salvation: "Molly alone . . . did not urge him to corruption." But he finds innocence imperiled by time and change, which have already left him tainted. He wants her pure and inviolate, but if she grows up the knowledge of sex will be her sin. For in the minds of the children, molded by their fastidious mother— their father conveniently dead—sex and sin are synonymous. American puritanism asserts itself through Ralph's self-accusations of guilt over his sexual fantasies. The children's struggles to repudiate sex strike us now as old-fashioned and comic, but they turn out destructive. Their naive and strict attitude seems reinforced by Jean Stafford's rhetoric, which calls sex "sin," especially sex in women. Violence in men, however, is an earned virtue. As Ralph thrashes about trying to find both manhood and salvation—perennial priorities of the male hero in American fiction—he dooms his sister. Wedged between the cult of violence and the cult of virginity, Molly is crushed to death.

But Molly also collaborates in her death. A fascinating

aspect of the novel, I believe, is her willingness to accept death as an only alternative, and to elicit Ralph's unconscious support of her desire. In his profound sympathy with his sister, Ralph intuits her suicidal impulse. Much as he loves and needs her, he shares her wish; and when his initiation rite demands violence, he can with impunity comply with this wish because killing has become a sanctified act. Through ritualistic murder, he tries to save his sister, and, at the same time, by making her a scapegoat, to save himself. So both children are sacrificed, and the myth of the West—which separates men from boys, and boys from women—ultimately sustained. Seeing Ralph step into this myth and rigidly enact its ritual, we can no longer believe he kills Molly by chance: or without cultural sanction. We have become too sophisticated in our reading of the unconscious intentions of an individual, and of a society, to think that accident, even one so obviously contingent as Ralph's, strikes gratuitously, without motive or purpose—a freak occurrence. Within the novel Molly is portrayed as a freak, and chosen for her destiny.

Why does Molly *want* to die? She knows why, and says so. "I know I'm ugly. I know everyone hates me. I wish I were dead." We need not elaborate here on the price any American woman must pay for being ugly—for being *defined* as ugly, that is, by her culture. At the end of Katherine Anne Porter's famous novella "Old Mortality," an elderly maiden aunt reveals to the young heroine the persecution she has suffered because of her protruding teeth and receding chin: "All my life the whole family bedeviled me about my chin. My entire girlhood was spoiled by it. Can you imagine . . . people who call themselves civilized spoiling life for a young girl because she had one unlucky feature?" All of Molly's features are unlucky: height, "heavy eyebrows," dark skin, "prominent nose," lank black hair, weak eyes. In Ralph, her double, these features turn to advantage as he grows tall, dark and handsome, and, by a miracle reserved only for him, no longer needs eyeglasses. Molly's pretty older sisters, smugly on their way to marriage, serve as foil and reprimand to the quirky, awkward, critical, contentious little girl who strikes everyone as a "discord," being opposed to all "in temperament, in capacity, in propensities." These last are not Jean Stafford's words but Charlotte Brontë's describing Jane Eyre, another child misfit. Jane Eyre develops inner strength by becoming contemptuous of all those she could "never please" because she was not by nature a "sanguine, careless, exacting, handsome, romping child." Molly loses strength when she displaces her powerful and righteous feelings of contempt from others to herself. Her fatality lies in accepting the mean and ugly image that an unsympathetic world reflects to the child who is different. Hating herself, for the same reason others hate her—because she seems a freak—she wants to die. Though precocious, ambitious—she had wanted to be a writer—acutely critical and discerning, her talents go to waste. Her intelligence is labeled a "handicap." Only conventional beauty and simpering ways can save her, she thinks: "If only she had yellow hair, she thought, she would be an entirely different kind of person." But the image in the mirror does not reflect Shirley Temple. She hates the image so much that shortly before she dies she adds her own name to her diary's "list of unforgivables." Then she breaks down and cries: "and all the time she cried she watched herself in the mirror, getting uglier and uglier until she looked like an Airedale." In death she looks like "a monkey." Her limp body evokes the final pitiless judgment with which the book ends, the words of Magdalene, the tough old black cook whom Molly in her fantasies makes her mother; "Lord Jesus. The pore little old piece of white trash."

So the indictment of Molly is complete. It is, I believe, the novel's brilliant *tour de force* and leads to its inevitable climax. In her stories Jean Stafford shows the same brilliance when describing characters driven like Molly to internalize the social values they believe they have either rejected or transcended. Her prize story "In the Zoo" depicts two sisters recalling their childhood, not realizing, as we do with a shock, that they have grown up to be the kinds of women they despised. In "The End of a Career" a woman blessed with rare and exquisite beauty discovers she has been cursed. Because everyone valued her beauty she devoted her life to its care, only to discover at the end of her "career" that she had sacrificed her life to society's love of appearance. The young woman of "The Echo and the Nemesis" finds beauty and intellectual brilliance burdens too heavy for her to carry. So she splits her personality in two, bestowing beauty on one self, and brains on the other: a solution of insanity, painful and full of self-punishment of an almost diabolical kind. She eats herself into obesity—a fate worse than death for the American woman. In *The Mountain Lion* Ralph fears Molly is going "crazy." We certainly would declare her phobic about snakes and sex, and generally neurotic. We might declare her *driven* crazy; and find some of her neurotic ploys transparent and childishly endearing; funny; pesty and profoundly sad. Had she lived the sequel to her story might have been Sylvia Plath's *The Bell Jar*. But the point is she could not live. Given the rigidity of roles within her society, and her inability to play them, she could not grow up. She could only become more isolated, more unhappy, more eccentric. She tried. Even at the last, grown tall, her newest misfortune, she was still trying to cope by stooping and sidling through the schoolhalls like a crab.

Jean Stafford is a distinguished writer, winner of the Pulitzer prize in 1970. In 1947, when *The Mountain Lion* was published, critics praised it as a "beautifully modeled tale." Reconsidering it today, we may not be as impressed as the original readers by the perfection of its structure, too closed for our modern taste; or the polish of its wit and language, too stiff and glossy; or the manipulation of its Freudian symbols, too contrived. We may not be so unprepared for, nor so delighted with, its eruption of "sudden horror" at the end. We have seen the world erupt with so much horror that we hardly expect happy endings; we are more alert to symptoms of disorder. The symptoms are there on the first page when blood erupts from the children: simultaneous nosebleeds, the aftermath of a poisoning of their system not entirely cured, and probably not entirely curable. Their grandfather's blood—the grandfather from the East—also had been poisoned, and he died. Was something invidious being transmitted through the bloodstream of this typical American family, some poison flowing from one generation to the next, contaminating the children? In 1947 the reviewers did not see this strain in the novel: that it embodied a puritanical, even Calvinistic, view of life beneath its witty satire; that from the beginning, it had the children predestined to violence and horror. Every force in the novel pushed them toward this, and because they were good children and not rebellious, they did not resist. Ralph allowed himself to be alienated from his sister so that he could become a man without any "sissified" traits; a good boy, he was shocked by his incestuous fantasies, and bewildered by sex. To preserve his innocence he displaced his emotions by falling in love with a mountain lion to which he gave the endearing and childish name Goldilocks. Molly allowed herself to become alienated from herself and grew to hate herself when she should have hated the world that was driving her crazy. It would be nice to think that if the children were growing up today, they would

survive, perhaps even prevail. For while the intervening years have brought horror, they have also brought social changes that give children, boys and girls, more choices and more latitude in growing up. If *The Mountain Lion* makes us reconsider some of the ways children have been forced to grow up in America, then it should not remain out of print and neglected. In 1947 one reviewer hoped it would become "a modern classic." Apparently it has not. But if by classic we mean basic, typical and enduring, then upon reconsideration, perhaps that is what it is. For it embodies our basic prejudices and enduring myths, and it represents our typical consciousness as Americans. If by classic we mean high quality, *The Mountain Lion* fits that definition too.

JOYCE CAROL OATES
"The Interior Castle:
The Art of Jean Stafford's Short Fiction"
Shenandoah, Volume 30, Number 3 (1979), pp. 61–64

Certainly the stories are exquisitely wrought, sensitively imagined: like glass flowers, or arabesques, or the 'interior castle' of Pansy Vanneman's brain ("Not only the brain as the seat of consciousness, but the physical organ itself which she envisioned, romantically, now as a jewel, now as a flower, now as a light in a glass, now as an envelope of rosy vellum containing other envelopes, one within another, diminishing infinitely"). Dramatic tension is subdued, in a sense forced underground, so that while narrative conflict between individuals is rare, an extraordinary pressure is built up within the protagonists, who appear trapped inside their own heads, inside their lives (or the social roles their 'lives' have become), and despair of striking free. Intelligence and self-consciousness and even a measure of audacity are not quite enough to assure freedom, as the heroines of the late stories "Beatrice Trueblood's Story" and "The End of a Career" discover painfully; even "the liberation" of Polly Bay (in the story with that title) will strike the sympathetic reader as desperate, an adolescent's gesture. The finest of Jean Stafford's stories possess an eerily elegiac tone, though they are never morbid or self-pitying. "In the Zoo" tells a frightful tale, the narrator confesses that "my pain becomes intolerable," but the story concludes with an extravagant outburst of paranoia that manages to be comic as well as distressing; and poor Ramona/Martha Dunn of the early story "The Echo and the Nemesis", trapped within layers of fat, achieves a sort of grotesque triumph over the 'normal' and unimaginative Sue, who can only flee in terror the spirited (and insatiable) appetite Ramona represents. ("I am exceptionally ill," Ramona tells her friend, with as much pride as if she were saying, "I am exceptionally talented" or "I am exceptionally attractive.")

This is an art that curves inward toward the meditative, the reminiscent, given life not by bold gestures or strokes but by a patient accumulation of sharply-observed impressions: the wealth of a poet's eye, or a painter's. "The Lippia Lawn", for instance, is an exercise in recollection, so graphically presented as to allow the reader to share in the young woman's grasping, groping effort to isolate an image out of her past. The "friendless old bachelor" Mr. Oliphant, while an arresting character in himself, is far less real than the protagonist's thoughts—the 'interior castle' of her subjectivity. She half-listens to the old man's chatter as "the tenuous memory wove in and out of my thoughts, always tantalizingly just ahead of me. Like the butterfly whose yellow wings are camouflaged to look like sunlight, the flower I could not remember masquer-aded as arbutus. . . . Slowly, like a shadow, the past seeped back. A wise scout was reconnoitering for me and at last led me to a place where I never would have looked." In the deceptively tranquil, slow-moving "A Country Love Story" the young wife May eludes her husband Daniel—the tyranny of his almost reasonable madness—by imagining for herself a lover, a lover whose natural place is in an antique sleigh in the front yard of their home. The lover possesses a ghostly plausibility: " . . . there was a delicate pallor on his high, intelligent forehead and there was an invalid's langour in his whole attitude. He wore a white blazer and gray flannels and there was a yellow rosebud in his lapel. Young as he was, he did not, even so, seem to belong to her generation; rather, he seemed to be the reincar-nation of someone's uncle as he had been fifty years before." Escaping the oppressive authority of her cerebral husband, May drifts into a sinister, because more seductive and satisfying predicament; by the story's end she and Daniel have traded places. ("A Country Love Story" bears an interesting relation-ship to a very late story of Jean Stafford's "Lives of the Poets," published in 1978.)

One cannot quarrel with the prevailing critical assessment that finds Jean Stafford's art "poised," "highly reflective," "fastidious," "feminine." And certainly she worked within the dominant fictional mode or consciousness of her time—there are no experimental tales in the *Collected Stories* (which cover the years 1944–1969); no explorations beyond the Jamesian-Chekhovian-Joycean model in which most "literary" writers wrote during those years. (Joycean, that is, in terms of *Dubliners* alone.) Each story remains within the consciousness of an intelligent and highly sensitive observer who assembles details from the present and summons forth details from the past, usually with a graceful, urbane irony; each story moves toward an 'epiphany,' usually in the very last sentence. There is very little that remains mysterious in Stafford's stories, little that is perplexing or disturbing in terms of technique, struc-ture, or style. Some of the stories, it must be admitted, are marred by an arch, over-written self-consciousness, too elab-orate, too artificial, to have arisen naturally from the fable at hand (as in "I Love Someone," "Children Are Bored on Sunday," "The Captain's Gift"). Characters tend to resemble one another in speech and manners, and there is little distinction between men and women; occasionally the author offers clichés in place of careful observation—Beatrice Trueblood's neighborhood in New York City, for instance, is quickly assembled along the lines of a stage setting: there are rowdy street urchins, a bloody-faced "bum" on the sidewalk, brick facades of "odious mustardy brown."

When one considers the finest of the stories, however, one is impressed by the rigorous structure that underlies the "beautiful" prose. And there are of course sudden jarring images, sudden reversals, that brilliantly challenge the sensi-bility evoked by the fiction's near-constant authorial voice—which is, for the most part, reflective, obsessively analytical, compulsively self-conscious. Consider the brutal yet light-hearted—and charming!—Dr. Reinmuth of "The Maiden,"

offering as a dinnertable anecdote in post-war Heidelberg the story of how, invigorated by a guillotining he saw at the age of twenty-three, he rushed to propose to his presumably genteel German sweetheart. (Astonishing his fellow guests with his recollection of the guillotining Dr. Reinmuth says zestfully: "One, he was horizontal! Two, the blade descended! Three, the head was off the carcass and the blood shot out from the neck like a volcano, a geyser, the flame from an explosion. . . . I did not faint. You remember that this was a beautiful day in spring? And that I was a young man, all dressed up at seven in the morning? . . . I took the train to Furth and I called my sweetheart. . . . 'I know it's an unusual time of day to call, but I have something unusual to say. Will you marry me?'") Consider the vicious killing of Shannon, the monkey, by Gran's "watchdog" (and alter ego) Caesar of "In the Zoo"—and Caesar's protracted death-agonies when, next day, he is poisoned by Shannon's grieving owner. Less dramatic, per-haps, but no less cruel, is the haircut poor little Hannah must endure, as part of the ongoing duel of wife and husband in "Cops and Robbers," one of the most successful of the stories. The most startling image in all of Stafford's fiction is the 'perfectly cooked baby'—a black baby, of course—offered to the racist Sundstrom by a similarly racist friend in "A Modest Proposal": "It was charred on the outside, naturally, but I knew it was bound to be sweet and tender inside. So I took him home. . . . and told [Sundstrom] to come along for dinner. I heated the toddler up and put him on a platter and garnished him with parsley . . . and you never saw a tastier dish in your life. . . . And what do you think he did after all the trouble I'd gone to? Refused to eat any of it, the sentimentalist! And *he* called *me* a cannibal!" (It is one of the ironies of "A Modest Proposal" that the reader never learns whether the incident ever happened, or whether the speaker has been telling a tall tale to upset the Captain's guests.)

Subdued and analytical and beautifully-constructed sto-ries, then, in what might be called a 'conventional' fictional mode: but they are not to be too quickly grasped, too glibly assessed. The 'interior castle' of Stafford's art is one which will repay close scrutiny for its meanings open slowly outward, and each phrase, each word, is deliberately chosen. Consider, for instance, the terrifying yet rigorously controlled conclusion of Pansy Vanneman's parable-like story: "The knives ground and carved and curried and scoured the wounds they made; the scissors clipped hard gristle and the scalpels chipped off bone. It was as if a tangle of tiny nerves were being cut dexterously, one by one; the pain writhed spirally and came to her who was a pink bird and sat on the top of a cone. The pain was a pyramid made of diamond; it was an intense light; it was the hottest fire, the coldest chill, the highest peak, the fastest force, the furthest reach, the newest time. It possessed nothing of her but its one infinitesimal scene: beyond the screen as thin as gossamer, the brain trembled for its life. . . . " After the operation Pansy knows herself violated, her interior castle plundered; she is both healing, and doomed. She lies unmov-ing "as if in a hammock in a pause of bitterness. She closed her eyes, shutting herself up within her treasureless head."

WILLIAM STAFFORD

1914–

William Edgar Stafford was born on January 17, 1914, in Hutchinson, Kansas. He was educated at the University of Kansas (B.A. 1937, M.A. 1945), and the State University of Iowa (Ph.D. 1955). From 1948 to 1980 he taught at Lewis and Clark College in Portland, Oregon, and he has been a guest lecturer at Manchester College, San Jose State College, and elsewhere. In 1970 he served as poetry consultant for the Library of Congress.

Stafford's first book, *Down in My Heart* (1947), is an account of his experiences as a conscientious objector during World War II, but he is best known for his several volumes of poetry, beginning with *West of Your City* (1960) and continuing through *Traveling through the Dark* (1962; National Book Award), *The Rescued Year* (1966), *Allegiances* (1970), and *Going Places* (1973). Much of his poetry is gathered in *Stories That Could Be True: New and Selected Poems* (1977). Stafford has also written several textbooks on prose and poetry and a book of criticism, *Writing the Australian Crawl: Views on the Writer's Vocation* (1978). Stafford was the recipient of the American Academy and Institute of Arts and Letters Award in Literature in 1981, and has received honorary degrees from Ripon College, Linfield College, and Washington College.

Married to Dorothy Hope Franz and the father of four children, Stafford resides at Lake Oswego, Oregon.

WILLIAM HEYEN
From "William Stafford's Allegiances"
Modern Poetry Studies, 1970, pp. 307–11

Intentionally or not, several of the poems in William Stafford's *Allegiances* (1970) are parables of the poet in action, suggestions of where a Stafford poem comes from, how it gets its life, what its beliefs are, how it develops and turns in on itself as it moves out toward the reader's life. In "The Preacher at the Corner" Stafford—I sense less of a need in Stafford's later work to talk in terms of his masks—says:

> the way I found him is the way I like:
> to wander because I know the road,
> and find stray things, wherever they come from.

There's a lot going on here. Stafford believes in staying "loose in the harness," as Robert Frost phrased it, and we know that Frost didn't believe anyone should or even could play tennis with the net down. (This idea of the poet as athlete and the poem as an athletic performance goes a long way. When we see a Jerry West drive, we witness a combination of muscle memory and inspiration.) And Richard Wilbur has argued that the genie gets his power precisely because he is confined in a bottle. (Better lamp, the outer form plus the idea of light, lux, and the rubbing and wishing and ordering.) The compression principle. Piston and gas. Stafford, I think, would agree, but he'd say that if you dig in the corners of the old farms in the Midwest and West, excavate those mounds built up like the layers of Troy with decades of garbage, or maybe come across other dumps, overgrown, whose patrons are long since dead, you'll find the damndest bottles, all shapes and sizes, bitters and snakebite and patent medicine and mineral water bottles, some bent by the heat of old fires, but still unbroken, some stained by the earth or by their long tenure in the sun, some even fused together (for analogy's sake). The bottles are stray things but some of them may be as important as Keats's urn or Stevens' Tennessee jar, at once artifacts and mementos of our culture. And all sorts of smells, mildew and rot and the perfume of lingering traces of honeysuckle flow around in the air inside those bottles. The wind will sound like an owl as it

blows over the bottle's neck, or like no bird we have any name for.

Loose in the harness. Freedom within a form. You know those dog runs, a wire stretched between two trees where the leashed dog can get plenty of action. Or, the wind whipping a poplar just so far, to just so much of an arc, and no further, no more. After a while, says Stafford (no brag, just fact), you know the road because you've committed yourself to the integrity of the poem; you wouldn't dream of allowing it (if you can help it) to offend itself. At the same time, failures will prove you are human. But you will allow your poem to find the shape it wants, the shape it needs in order to say just what it has to say. You know the road, so it's all right to walk down the middle for a while, and then to scuffle up the dust and gravel at the edges, even to lean way out for some huckleberries ripening past the shoulders. Hell, even jump all the way off, but not for long because, and here's where the figure breaks down, this road can't get where it's going without you. After all, it's a road of words, and all the words we know can't exist all at once in any single utterance, and someone has to say the ones that want to be said and in the order they want to be heard. Stafford is fond of using what he calls "an organized form cavalierly treated." The room to follow impulse within outer strictness. The second line of Thomas Gray's *Elegy Written in a Country Churchyard*: "The lowing herd winds slowly o'er the lea." "Winds," the sense of a path, not necessarily the shortest, straightest line to the stable, but still a path within infinite possibilities of paths. The cattle of the imagination graze all over the place but, finally, the path winding homeward.

Stafford once told a group of us at dinner that he always has about fifty poems off in the mail. This kind of production has always been suspect to me, but Stafford is a natural. As James Dickey once said, Stafford turns out so much verse "not because he is glib and empty, but because he is a real poet, a born poet, and communicating in lines and images is not only the best way for him to get things said; it is the easiest." The thing is that Stafford is beginning to know and feel what a Stafford poem sounds like. There isn't that intense struggle for a voice, that hither and thither of angles and tones that cause us to label many a poet "promising." But Stafford doesn't just shoot from the hip and, to change the image from cowboy to circus, it's surprising how tight a tightrope so many of William Stafford's lines walk. The rope actually vibrates in the wind of the breath. Let me talk about this for a minute.

Certainly, sounds make meanings beyond the ability of criticism to get at them. Sound patterns give us the feeling of ritual, as John Crowe Ransom says somewhere, and the logical meanings of the sounds either are lost way back (as, I understand, is true of frequent passages in the Noh) or, perhaps, as the language changes, are just beginning to assert themselves, just becoming apparent in the clusters they make, the tints of feeling they give groups of related words. So, I can't say anything about the added meanings the sound control in a Stafford poem gives it any more than I can pinpoint the meaning of say, the repeated use of a hard g sound. But in an essay, "Finding the Language," Stafford describes his own faith in "certain reinforcing patterns of sound which the language, as if by chance, has taken up into itself. That is, all syllables tend to slide by inherent quality toward certain meanings, either because of varying demands on the throat in utterance, or because of relations among clusters of syllables which have become loaded with associated meanings, and so on." What I am trying to say here is that I cannot say anything specific about the added meanings the sound control in these ten lines (picked almost at random from ten poems in *Allegiances*) adds, but what is apparent and important is Stafford's need to ride range (back to the cowboy) on his choices and on the upwelling of the unconscious:

> according to any of us; but after the others
> the tone of his voice roamed, had more to find,
> he comprehends by fistfuls with both hands.
> One aims a single-shot and hears the muffled past
> the old saints, who battered their hearts,
> When winter strikes, that camp sinks
> alerting space by the way they wait
> In the yard I pray birds,
> teach me; for, somewhere inside, the clods are
> the world, wide, unbearably bright,

Stafford is a poet who allows the world's language to move in on him, nuances and suggestions, intimations; a poet who wants to keep himself ready for "those nudges of experience," as he calls them. And: "it's like fishing—the person who keeps his line wet catches a fish." But as the world does move in on him, he gathers it together, for his poem's sake, line by line, whole poem by whole poem. Notice the internal rhymes, the natural break at one sound and the locking-in of that sound at line's end, road's end. The art of successful repetition. Sort of a refrain. Lovely, really, the echoes in the lines, and the pacing (for there are in the end only two sounds, silence and non-silence), the pauses and then the poem going on. Resonance. The poem coming off the page, toward our bodies. Louis Zukofsky quoting Chapman's "the unspeakable good liquor there" and saying: "Obviously, the man who wrote that knew what it was to gargle something down his throat." Sounds connected with things and actions.

And I would think that Stafford, more than nine out of ten American poets, would *sound* like a poet to someone who couldn't understand English. The full rhymes are infrequent, pyrotechnics are at a minimum, but the lines are held together by a sort of unstudied point-counterpoint. It is apparent that they were said in a lot of different ways before just the right combination of sounds and silences declared themselves inseparable forever.

Well, anyway, I am an admirer of William Stafford's poetry. First, for the craft that does not call attention to itself—Stafford admits that he almost flaunts nonsophistication in his work—but which is always there, being necessary and important just by being there; second, though this is never distinct from the craft, for the downright power of what he has to say. Writing of "The Farm on the Great Plains" Stafford said: "plains, farm, home, winter, . . . these command my allegiance in a way that is beyond my power to analyze at the moment." Yes, and his world commands my allegiance. I am caught up in his sense of space and time and of the American Dream, his sense of loss, his sense of joy in the here and now, his feeling for the land and the seasons, his belief (manifested in the poems themselves) that the smallest events in our lives and the smallest feelings that travel our spines are miracles—a puff of air, an extension of muscle and memory as we reach out to turn on a light. In his best work I come away with a sense of myth, and of prophecy, that I had better not try to define here. In any case, there are four or five poems in *Allegiances* that do for me what Stafford wants them to: "I would not like to assert these poems; they would climb toward the reader without my proclaiming anything. But sometimes for every reader a poem would arrive: it would go out for him, and find his life." This is the dream of a real man, wanting his poems to be gifts, wanting, essentially, to leave the earth a little better place than it was when he began to draw breath.

ROGER DICKINSON-BROWN
From "The Wise, the Dull, the Bewildered: What Happens in William Stafford"
Modern Poetry Studies, Spring 1975, pp. 30–38

A friend once said to me that William Stafford's poems are "nice, but dull." My friend is a good artist, and she wasn't trying to be smug or clever. She knew the poems and had heard him read, and I am afraid she was partly right. Stafford's reputation is now growing beyond that even of the most important, "established" contemporary poets; but his is to some extent a cult reputation. Outside the cult many people still find his writing dull. To make things worse, the poems seem to have become duller as they have improved. Yet this dullness has not seemed to mar the poet's best work. Some of his early as well as his late poems are not only very good, but interesting and exciting as well. To show this I shall have to consider the dullness first: I don't want to speak only to advocates and friends. ⟨. . .⟩

The first and major cause of Stafford's dullness is a muting overexposure. The quantity of what he publishes is out of proportion to the really few things he has to say. Even allowing for the process of his development, the "complete" statement of what he has had to say could be contained in the space of any one of the approximately eighty-page volumes we get every four years or so. A restrained selection now, instead of restraint before, would be difficult, since what we have in the corpus of Stafford's writing is not eighty pages of good poems and a few hundred of dross, but rather hundreds of redundant poems, spread thin. Much of what is tiresome in Stafford is simply a matter of reading the same attitude and perception poem after poem. At its best, it is a good attitude, worth reading, but it is a simple one, profound but with few aspects. The release of the poems for publication should have been gauged accordingly. Further, in Stafford's poems detail does not figure very importantly either as subject or as ornament, nor even as illustration (not even, really, in the deer poem). Perhaps this means that he is a very serious poet, but the relatively minor importance of detail should have resulted in a small rather than a large number of poems. Stafford likes to write, and this is his prerogative; but the overabundant output has also become our problem. Already the excess has created a need for severe editing. Someone other than the poet will have to produce a "definitive" *Selected Poems*, or he will be buried in the clutter and culture he so eloquently observes. It would not be an unprecedented fate for a writer; we are all at the mercy of editors and anthologists. Yet even with this paring down, the problem of Stafford's "thinness" remains.

Another problem in the writing (is that) the dominating wisdom of his poems tends to deprive all human, and even wild, physical details—the grace of gesture, the motion of leaves—of any kind of significance—even of that hollow beauty embodied in Wallace Stevens' work. This is especially true in the later work, where details appear more rarely and where, by their own context, little can be made of them, even as items of pleasure. This deprives Stafford of one minor but prolific source of poetry. In the most successful poems, these details are replaced by a profound understanding of the limits of human nature. This understanding of man's limits is the subject of the conclusion of this essay. Nonetheless, in most of the late poems, a second source of interest is gone. Compare the remarkable lizard of the early "At the Bomb Testing Site" to these lines from "Witness," in the most recent *Someday, Maybe* (1973):

> On top of Fort Rock in the sun I spread
> these fingers to hold the world in the wind;
> along that cliff, in that old cave
> where men used to live, I grubbed in the dirt
> for those cool springs again.

The problem here is not abstraction; abstraction can cut deepest of all, and sometimes does in these late poems. The problem is that the style has become, through a peculiar philosophical process, concrete and vague.

A further cause of Stafford's dullness is prosodic. Along with an increasing number of contemporary writers, he uses what, alas, strikes me as a kind of genteel quasi-formalism: random rhyme and off-rhyme; lines that nearly scan to one system or another; groups of lines that look but don't act like stanzas. All of these are potential sources of extremely subtle and effective modulation, and sometimes that happens, as in these lines from one of the best poems in *Someday, Maybe*, "The Whole Story":

> When we shuddered and took into ourselves
> the cost of the way we had lived,
> I was a victim, touched by the blast.
> Death! I have death in me!
> No one will take me in from the cold.

This is a traditional accentual meter, the ancient beat of limericks and children's poems, folk poems, and art songs of the Middle Ages. Stafford almost never writes entirely in it, but he is often near it. Here a momentary traditional four-beat, three-beat line alteration is more or less sustained ("Christ that my love were in my arms / and I in my bed again"), but abandoned elsewhere in the poem. Line-lengths vary, the rhythm shifts in and out of meter, there is no rhyme. Except for this last characteristic, the poem is representative. Here, everything works very well, but the procedures more often yield different results: a certain smooth, uninteresting movement, as in these lines from "Hero" in the same volume:

> What if he came back, astounded
> to find his name so honored, schools
> named after him, a flame at his tomb,

his careless words cherished? How could
he ever face the people again, knowing
all he would know in that great clarity
of the other side? (His eyes flare into
the eyes of his wife. He searches his brothers'
drawn faces turned toward him suddenly still.)

This is not even graceful, much less perceptive: it is uneventful and banal.

The last source of dullness in Stafford's poety is especially difficult to define. Perhaps no one not already convinced will be persuaded that there is a complacency of tone throughout his poems that kills perception and what might be called perfectly true feeling. I suspect that this is "heresy," that Stafford is regarded, by those who like him, as an apostle of alert humility and radical wisdom. Sometimes I too see this, but more often I see a man seduced by his own habit of being very simple and very wise. Consider "Deerslayer's Campfire Talk" from *Allegiances*:

> Wherever I go they quote people
> who talk too much, the ones who
> do not care, just so they take the center
> and call the plans.

Or "Any Time" from the same volume:

> (Waves will quiet, wind lull; and in that
> instant I will have all the time in the world;
> something deeper than birthdays will tell me all I
> need.)

The complacency is often ghostly, but I believe it is almost always there. Only a thorough reading can really bring it out. It takes his edge away.

II

The best of William Stafford's poetry goes far beyond these limitations. The writing is abstract, distant, inhuman, almost inarticulate. Stafford's achievement is that he *is* here articulate. He has reached a profundity by pursuing a double path, and I must say that I have no sympathy for part of the pursuit. Everywhere he distrusts—in fact, he demeans—what is specifically human ("political" in Hannah Arendt's definition of the word), individually identified, mortal, not wild (therefore victimized in time, and transitory). This prejudice against social identities is most often neatly presupposed. For me, it is tiresome and annoying for being the cant of the last century or two. Take the views of "Composed, Composed" in *Someday, Maybe*, for example:

> The flat people in magazines hear
> the flat god of their tabletop say,
> "Let there be flat people," and
> there are ads and editorials.

Or there are Stafford's rather silly leaves in "The Little Lost Orphans" from the same volume:

> . . . every vein guides
> fate. I agree with all that happens
> at the end; right, right, right.
> No other guide but is
> leads onward. . . .

Hackneyed, comfortable, sentimental. And, again, in "The Eskimo National Anthem":

> Now while the boss talks or while an official
> tells me what to do, the bears at Talkeetna
> begin to dance, and the escaping files of
> birch trees make it away over the pass. . . .

The bears and the trees aren't bad, but the presentation in these poems of bosses and officials is slick and unexamined. God knows, officials, magazines, ads and editorials are imperfect, but all they get here is a place in a zealot's naive catalogue of evil: bosses and magazines are evil because they are bosses and magazines (This includes, presumably, the editors who choose Stafford's poems for publication in magazines). It is all very exasperating and silly.

It is important not to confuse this easy naïveté with something close to it, but deep and not familiar enough, though we have heard it in the poetry of Emily Dickinson and Robert Frost and some others. There is a subtle but real difference in what emerges as wisdom; human and social actions are not rendered foolish simply for being human or social, but they are depicted as terribly small and insignificant. Humanity is not demeaned, it is belittled, in a special modern way. "Now" from *Someday, Maybe* offers an example:

> . . . Fern arrives to
> batter the window. Every day gets lost
> in a stray sunset and little touches of air.
> Someone opens a door. It is this year.

This is something close to great art, not because it is new but because it is realized: the perception is important, difficult, and perfectly rendered. Detail illustrates and advances idea, is nowhere ornamental or superfluous. Exactly the right degree of particularity is achieved in every part, especially in the brilliant vagueness of "Someone opens a door. It is this year." The difference between this and the flat gods is huge.

If there are not as many aspects of this and other Stafford perceptions as there are poems, there are, nonetheless, different facets. Perhaps the most important of the facets in the most recent poems is what Stafford calls "now." Part of "now," as "The Earth" suggests, is simply *carpe diem* celebration, always worth a few lines:

> we come, we
> celebrate with our breath, we join on the curve
> of our street, never lost, the surge of the land
> all around us that always is ours,
> the beginning of the world and the end.

But "now" in poems like "The Moment" from the same volume becomes the best of Stafford: it becomes the poverty of all we have, tragic, the great distress. It becomes loss:

> Is it just you, Wind?
> Maybe. But it is Now;
> it is what happens, the moment,
> the stare of the moon, an
> opening birds call out of,
> anything true. We have it.
> That's what the rich old
> shepherd meant, pointing
> through the storm at
> the blowing past wind
> passing nothing:
> "Those who have gone
> and those who never existed,
> they don't have it."

Parts of this poem are perfectly focused, alive, and lonely. They realize what champions of Stafford's poetry wish readers to see in all the poems. Partly conventional, the perception and expression are not very new, but alertly realized and far away from the trite and the dull: clear, alive, alone—spoken, whatever Stafford's theories may be, not for people who have no names, but as "The Whole Story" affirms, out of a grown sense of what happens:

> . . . through the light on the hills
> I let children approach. In a pale straw slant

the sun angles down. Maybe the children will not see the victims, will somehow survive. The sun touches along and goes away, and while the stars come out the sky waits and wherever they look it is now and there is still time.

ROBERT COLES
"William Stafford's Long Walk"

American Poetry Review, July–August 1975, pp. 27–28

The United States of America is William Stafford's country; it is Richard Nixon's country, too, there is no doubt about that. Allen Ginsberg, from the Eastern seaboard, is right: there is plenty of greed, envy and murderous competitiveness abroad the land; but there are other sides to our people. The Nixons came from the mid-West, ended up near the Pacific, and soon enough confronted us with much of what we have become— and one has in mind not just the thirty-seventh President, but his two ever so adroit and vigorous brothers: no arrangement is too complex for them—and if there is any sanction needed, there is always that marvelous, smiling, dynamic Billy Graham around, who doubtless appeases any anxieties he has with the utterly compelling truth: a minister must not flinch from a sinner, and we are all sinners.

But William Stafford also comes from the mid-West, and he, too, found his way to the Pacific. And though his eyes are as sharp as Ginsberg's, and his ears as attentive, one meets quite another America in his poems. For ideologues the apparent contradiction is easily "resolved"—it is a matter of the superficial against the deep. Everything is rotten in the state of Denmark; or else, the nation is in fine shape, despite a few "problems"—and they, of course, are exaggerated for various reasons by various individuals. For Stafford, this is a land of compelling opposites, a nation which has indeed brutalized generations of Indians (toward whose habits, beliefs and customs he is drawn) but a nation which is blessed with a marvelously varied natural landscape, at once subtle, striking, awesome, and for him, impossible to overlook. And too, a nation whose people can be generous, kind, thoughtful; a nation of which his beloved parents and brother are citizens, and his son Kit, and the dying Bess, a librarian of tact and grace, and Althea, and the nameless girl whose boyfriend lied, and on and on. From those people, moments of whose lives Stafford evokes in his poems, one obtains a particular vision of America—not Whitman's lyrical urging, really, but not a voice of despair, either, and certainly no inclination to disgust or self-righteous condemnation.

Stafford is wonderously attentive to the land, sky, water and foliage of our mid-West and far-West. He presents us with territory many of his readers will, perhaps, know not at all: "At the border of October/where Montana meets Alberta/that white grass that worshipped wind/climbed from summer to the sky,/which began to change." He presents us with "the firred mountains of Oregon," the "hay towns beyond Salt Lake." He presents us with "cornfield farms," with "a town by the track in Colorado," with a "prairie town," and the prairie dogs he used to gaze at for long stretches. Born in Kansas, he "lived in Indiana once," we learn, and while there "put these hands into those lakes/of counties near Fort Wayne." He knows a tornado—knows it the way someone watching the weather map on the *Today* show over coffee in Boston or New York cannot: "first the soul of our house left, up the chimney/and part of the front window went outward—pursued/whatever tore at the chest." There are people, he knows, connected to the land he wants to bring before us, and in his own quiet, indirect, unauthoritative, yet telling manner he introduces them to us. In a few lines he can offer more than a shelf-full of sociological, anthropological and psychological studies (with their "worldviews," the "psycho-social" this or that of these or those):

> At the end of their ragged field
> a new field began:
> miles told the sunset that Kansas
> would hardly ever end,
> and that beyond the Cimarron crossing
> and after the row-crop land
> a lake would surprise the country
> and sag with a million birds.
>
> You couldn't analyze those people—
> a no-pattern had happened to them:
> their field opened and opened,
> level, and more, then forever,
> never crossed. Their world went everywhere.

So does his world it seems, in America at least—everywhere a lot of us tend to think of as nowhere. Who else brings us Elko, Nevada, or Sharon Springs, Kansas? More important, he has his very own way of bringing to bear nature on man, the willful and self-conscious one who threatens the planet with extinction. "At the Bomb Testing Site" goes like this:

> At noon in the desert a panting lizard waiting for
> history, its elbows tense, watching the curve of a
> particular road as if something might happen.
>
> It was looking for something farther off than people
> could see, an important scene
> acted in stone for little selves
> at the flute end of consequences.
>
> There was just a continent without much on it
> under a sky that never cared less.
> Ready for a change, the elbows waited
> The hands gripped hard on the desert.

History interests Stafford—the land's, our people's. He can't help noticing what people do, and leave behind, as they move about, fit into valleys, come close to rivers, trek the desert, accommodate themselves to mountains, to the seasons, to the ocean's final no: not a step beyond. The Indians, more than any other Americans, know and treasure the Western land, and of course, made a beginning of our history, long before "we" were here, so full of ourselves and so determined to bend history to our purposes. A section of *Someday, Maybe* is titled "Wind World," and contains poems which in one way or another address themselves to Indians, their experience on this continent, their way of looking at life. The poems turn out to be quite brief ("Indian Caves in the Dry Country": "These are some canyons/we might use again/sometime.") or only a little longer—"People of the South Wind" or "Origins." The latter offers a finely-wrought piece of Indian lore every bit worthy of what one hears Indian parents telling their children in the Southwest. No boasting and vainglory; no effort to prove one's superiority; no ethnic "pride"; but rather an almost casual effort to link one's ancestors with the concreteness of life's "everydayness," to draw upon a word both Kierkegaard and Heidegger have used in an attempt to fight off the demons of the abstract, so tempting to those two men, among others. "So long ago that we weren't people then," one is told, "our hands came upon this warm place on a rack/inside a high cave in the North, in the wilderness." A Hopi mother recently told me that when her children ask her about where they all came

from, she tells them: "It was too long ago for you or me or anyone to know. The stars know, though. They have watched, and they remember. They will not tell us, but that does not mean we have no history. In the world there is knowledge of us, even if we don't possess it." Such children may at first get restless: tell us more, make us more satisfied. So, she goes on: "There must have been a moment when a man and a woman stopped and began to dig into the earth. They spent the night nearby, and in the morning they felt the wind upon their skin, and heard the wind's message: stay. They did, and now we are here."

At times Stafford emphasizes the rootlessness of some Americans; he himself knows what it is to drive, drive, drive on Route 40, to enter and leave those towns, so many of them ghosts of their former selves, yet by no means dead and gone, simply holding on proudly and bravely for dear life. The sense of continuity, the faith in the ways of nature and at least a certain kind of man (themselves) which Indians unselfconsciously have as a psychological possession and as elements in their cultural tradition are not often to be taken for granted by the rest of us, even those Mr. Stafford knows, likes, is moved to portray. Somehow we have lost touch with the world around us and ourselves, and the two developments surely go together, at least in Stafford's gentle but tough vision of America. "It is the time for all the heroes to go home," he begins the poem whose title, "Allegiances," he has given to his most recent volume of poems. Then he adds one of his elliptical asides ("if they have any") and goes on: "time for all of us common ones/to locate ourselves by the real things/we live by." The rest of the poem goes like this—and it is not at all a long-winded pronouncement or a self-important philosophical credo, but simply a way of calling upon "heaven and earth," as those Palestinian nomads and prophets of several thousand years ago would put it:

> Far to the north, or indeed in any direction,
> strange mountains and creatures have always
>   lurked—
> elves, goblins, trolls, and spiders:—we
> encounter them in dread and wonder.
>
> But once we have tasted far streams, touched the
>   gold,
> found some limit beyond the waterfall,
> a season changes, and we come back, changed
> but safe, quiet, grateful.
>
> Suppose an insane wind holds all the hills
> while strange beliefs whine at the traveler's ears,
> we ordinary beings can cling to the earth and love
> where we are, sturdy for common things.

Stafford is just that, one of the "common ones," and he is indeed "sturdy for common things": "The writer's home he salvages from little pieces / along the roads, from distinctions he remembers, from what by chance he sees—his grabbed heritage; /and from people fading from his road, from history./ He reaches out far, being a desperate man; / he comprehends by fistfuls with both hands." Stafford will not let up; he will not be, he knows not how to be, immodest. In such a confessional poem there is no hidden agenda, that ironic self-congratulatory line or stanza that will serve to punch any literal-minded doubter in the nose and let him know that pity is not what the poem really wants, but rather, the kind of awe that may creep up, but eventually obtains complete control. No, the next lines establish Stafford's knowing, touching, lyrical voice as utterly and convincingly diffident and unassuming: "But what can bring in enough to save the tame/or be home for them who even with roofs are shelterless?" It is, he is telling us, for others to criticize, berate, condemn, "them," all those near and far away who are fellow citizens of this nation. He knows their sadness, the virtual hopelessness they must sense if not recognize, even as he knows how it has gone for Sitting Bull and his

descendents. And knowing, he still wants to sing—because as anyone who lives in a small town, however isolated, out West knows, you never can tell who will appear on the horizon, slowly work his way near, and reveal himself to have receptive ears and responsive eyes.

WILBUR DANIEL STEELE

1886–1970

Wilbur Daniel Steele was born on March 17, 1886, in Greensboro, North Carolina, the son of a minister and his wife. He was educated at the University of Denver, the Boston Museum of Fine Arts, the Académie Julian in Paris, and the Art Students League in New York City. He received a D.Litt. from the University of Denver in 1932.

Steele's first novel, *Storm*, was published in 1914, and a collection of short fiction, *Land's End*, appeared in 1918. Steele, who was an artist as well as an author, turned to writing full time in his mid-thirties after a story he wrote received an O. Henry Award in 1919. Over the years Steele published some two dozen short-story collections, novels, and plays (*Post Road*, written with his second wife, Norma Mitchell, was produced on Broadway in 1934), and contributed to numerous periodicals, including the *Atlantic Monthly*. *The Way to the Gold*, his last novel, was published in 1955.

Steele was married twice and had two sons. He died on May 26, 1970, in Essex, Connecticut.

"Best" is a provocative word. Select any one "best" story of Wilbur Daniel Steele's and a phalanx of others rises up to confute you. Even with the twenty-four titles included in the ⟨The Best Short Stories of Wilbur Daniel Steele⟩, even with the help—or would it be the hindrance?—of the author's own judgment on his work, there are still stories lacking which it would be welcome to find and some included for which this reader at least could have provided substitutes.

None the less, *The Best Short Stories of Wilbur Daniel Steele* is an admirable collection. "The Man Who Saw Through Heaven," "The Woman at Seven Brothers," "Footfalls," "Isles of Spice and Lilies," "The Dark Hour"—each of them not only allows for, but calls for, rereading. And if certain others, notably "Arab Stuff," are not to be found, it must be granted that selection from among Steele's stories presents a special difficulty. Present-day short story writers are, for the most part, short lived—short lived, that is, as story writers. Let an author achieve a moderate success with stories and he turns promptly to novels or the stage or Hollywood. Steele is the exception. As far back as 1924 Katharine Fuller Gerould, writing in *The Yale Review*, noted him as one of those few whose names on a magazine cover caused her always to stop and buy. She could have said the same thing twelve years earlier—as early as "White Horse Winter," to be exact—and twelve years later it would have been equally true.

But passing judgment on stories read one by one, as they appear in magazines, is one thing; meeting them in a volume is, as George III was fond of saying, quite another. It is a tribute to Steele's sustained excellence that the stories in this volume produce no sense of monotony. Read consecutively, however, certain common characteristics come to view which are perhaps best labeled "American." Story following story, the stories in this collection are as American as Des Moines, Iowa—and this though the locales presented may be half a world apart.

The contribution to this Americanism which it is easiest to lay a finger on is, of course, that of structure. Through most

of our literary history, the accepted definition of a short story has been that a story is a piece of writing within the length of which something happens, and happens with finality. This is by no means everybody's definition—witness "The Garden Party" and many of the titles in *Ivy Gripped the Steps*—but it has been, in the main, the American one. Not the presentation of a mood alone but also of the action that mood precipitates and of the resolution of that action. It is in the American tradition that the action shown should be of importance—a human relationship signally changed, a soul saved or lost. Why American practice runs in this channel, European practice so often in another, is anybody's guess, but the direction is clear. Irving, Hawthorne, Bret Harte, Henry James, Edith Wharton, Jack London—different as are their performances, they are at one as to what constitutes a story, and it is with these predecessors that Steele is found.

Steele was born in Greensboro, N. C. (O. Henry's birthplace as well; stories must grow on trees in Greensboro), went to college in Denver. Greensboro is 300 miles from salt water, Denver some thousands farther. It can hardly be charged to either place that the sea echoes like an organ accompaniment through these stories. And even apart from the sea (only it will not stay apart), the settings of the stories are romantic—Africa, Labrador, the Pacific islands, the fog-darkened New England ports. Romance, though, ends with the settings. The men who sail the ships, who tramp the exotic streets, are sharply realistic. That behind their prosaic actions they live inner lives more vivid to them than their outer ones makes them not less realistic but more so.

The men—not the women. Women play a small part in this collection. For the most part, they are seen through the veil of some man's illusion; or they are the mother-spirit, living for, or quite as often dying for, some male. Again, American? It is better to beg that question than to answer it, but it is safe to say that, with perhaps one exception, the stories having women as main figures are the least rereadable.

The foregoing paragraph suggests that Steele deals with his

women figures sentimentally. He does not—not often. The sentimentality lies in the thinking of his masculine creations. The relative lack of sentimentality in Steele's writing is, indeed, one of his chief virtues. Bret Harte's spiritual descendants, swarming as these are throughout the century whether under Saroyan's banner or under Caldwell's, can claim no cousinship with Steele. The destinies of his characters are decided oftener by the quality of their souls than by their environments. His detrimentals, though frequently provided with mental twists, are exhibited as detrimentals none the less, people irresponsible, cruel, devouring. His respectable characters ordinarily *are* respectable, which, except as usage has debased the word, means worthy of being respected.

No writer, though, escapes the impact of his time. Some of the effects upon Steele are evident in his interest in the disturbed mind and in the changing nature of that interest. It is a far cry, as any reader finds, from the overthrown minds displayed in his early stories—in "The Woman at Seven Brothers," for example—to the obscure obsessions dissected in the stories of the Thirties. Much as World War II broke up "shell shock," so Steele has fragmented "insanity." Hardly anybody in these later stories is clearly insane; hardly anybody is clearly sane. And with the same sureness and economy with which he sets a landscape before readers' eyes, so he makes believable the intricate aberrations of his characters.

And yet with it all—with substance, with powerful delineation, with a mastery over words which leaves phrase after phrase ringing in the mind—with all this, Steele is in the line of his great predecessors but yet not quite of that line. Humor is lacking, for one thing. Lacking, too, is that final magic which allows of making the imagined individual at once an individual and a symbol. The boy in "Isles of Spice and Lilies" is as convincing as is the hero of Conrad's "Youth"; he remains, though, that one boy and only that, never anywhere the echo of every boyhood.

But these two lacks being granted, the stories are still stories superbly told. Their appearance in one volume fittingly places Steele where Katharine Fullerton Gerould placed him twenty-two years ago—in the first rank of the American story tellers of his time.—EDITH RONALD MIRRIELEES, "The Best of Steele," *NYTBR,* July 14, 1946, pp. 5, 20

Mr. Steele is probably our greatest modern American writer of short stories. Other authors have written notable ones—Hemingway, Caldwell, Katherine Anne Porter—but none has so combined productivity with excellence.

Mr. Steele is an astonishing virtuoso. He can write with seemingly equal authority no matter what the scene or background, New England, the Southern mountains, the Middle West, Africa, or the South Pacific. His themes are widely various: psychology, madness, childhood, romantic adventure, murder, and melodrama. Completely realistic in detail, writing of weak and fallible persons and never of heroes, he yet delights in exotic material and ironic climaxes. So he might best be classified as half a realist, half a wonderful story-teller.

For it is stories he tells, not studies of mere mood and atmosphere. Things happen in a Steele story, dramatic things. Suspense, conflict, narrative pace, resolutions of psychological problems, and frequent tricky and flashy surprise endings insure engrossed attention from any reader. Mature, adroit, powerful, compelling in their power to evoke atmosphere, these stories are superb.—ORVILLE PRESCOTT, "Outstanding Novels," *YR,* Sept. 1946, pp. 191–92

BLANCHE COLTON WILLIAMS
From "Wilbur Daniel Steele"
Our Short Story Writers
1926, pp. 374–84

To the analyst, ⟨Steele's⟩ early stories reveal the author's inheritance; his own genius for depicting color, form, mood; and his skill in narrative structure. A strong theological flavor is manifest in the choice of certain of his characters, for example, Minister Malden, of "Ching, Ching"; in biblical references and allusions throughout a number of the stories, as in the title "For They Know Not What They Do,"[1] in fragments of church scenes and in echoes of the thunder rolling voice of the Puritan God. But this spirit is tempered and combined with the artist's love for vivid pictures, preferably pictures of the sea in storm. His sympathy with the unrest of nature has further witness in the title of his one novel (*Storm,* 1914). Since, however, our present concern is with his short stories, it need be remarked only that he has not succeeded, as yet, with the longer story, despite prognostications of certain critics, and that his characteristics are best exemplified in his briefer tales.

All the Urkey Island stories are told, logically, as if by "the Means boy" grown to manhood; for as they are of the past they seem to the author best unfolded by one still living and familiar to that past. Through this boy, then, Mr. Steele delights in recalling[2] the shouting of the Round Hill Bars, a shouting that filled the bowl of the invisible world and rumbled in tangled reverberations: "I could see the outer bar only as a white, distorted line athwart the gray, but the shoreward shallows were writhing, living things, gnawing at the sky with venomous teeth of spume. . . . " In this instance, also, is apparent that fine modulation or harmony whereby the real and the imagined perfectly merge. Says the narrator: "My mother used sometimes to sing a little Portuguese song to my brother Antone, the baby. It had a part which ran—

> The herd of the King's White Horses
> Comes up on the shore to graze . . . "

And so well has the author combined the boy's fancy of the ocean in frenzy as that of an animal gnawing with venomous teeth, the reader is hardly aware of the transition whereby the white horses of the bar pass into the splendid white steed that, washed ashore from the wreck, staggered up the face of the dune and stood against the sky. Further, the same tale illustrates the author's sense of structure. The salvation of the white horse would hardly be sufficient for a well rounded tale. With it, therefore, is inwoven the love story of the boy's sister, Agnes Means, and Jem Hodges, the owner of the white stallion. The narrative is not illustrative of Mr. Steele's procedure in composition; for though based on an actual occurrence, it stands alone in this regard. One other story may be excepted, in that the hero of "A Devil of a Fellow," Va Di, reflects a man of Mr. Steele's acquaintance.

Since in only these two instances has the author drawn upon life immediately, the conclusion is inevitable that he relies almost altogether upon imagination. Place or locale is the usual basis, but the evolution of the building process is confined to the celebrations of Mr. Steele. He says with too great modesty that this evolution is a matter of mechanics. He determines to write a story and gives himself up to meditation. The story comes. He cannot recall its genesis, save that he develops a mood from which the whole fabric seems to take shape. In former days this manner of creation would have been termed inspirational, a word of more exact application here than the word mechanical, but having always back of it—except in the assertions of literary mediocrity—hard work and knowledge of technique. If his method is in the least mechanical, it is because of the author's reliance upon mood, a mood which he from resolution or perhaps now with the ease of practice rigidly maintains. In 1920 I wrote in the Introduction to *O. Henry Memorial Prize Stories*, Volume I, "The tale predominantly of atmosphere, revealing, wherever found, the ability of the author to hold a dominant mood in which as in a calcium light characters and acts are colored, occurs so rarely as to challenge admiration when it does occur. 'For They Know Not What They Do' lures the reader into its exotic air and holds him, until he, too, is suffused, convinced." Stevenson practised this procedure, notably in *The Merry Men*, as he has told in one of his essays, nor is the work of Mr. Steele so reminiscent of any other author in this respect. Since he cannot recall following the example of the Scotch writer, however, Mr. Steele resembles him, out of doubt, only because of similar approach in workmanship.

Not Stevenson but Lafcadio Hearn is the writer for whose works Mr. Steele expresses enthusiasm. Between the author of *A Japanese Miscellany* and *Some Chinese Ghosts*, and the author of Provincetown and Urkey Island stories exists no obvious kinship, save in the apprehension and delicate use of the fanciful. Rather will "Down on Their Knees" and "A Devil of a Fellow" demand comparison with the fiction of Mr. Joseph C. Lincoln. Yet this challenge is met in a brief enumeration: Mr. Lincoln writes of another neighborhood in Cape Cod, both men relish the salt of locale and atmosphere, neither draws portraits—if they know it—of the living. Their styles are far apart. If Mr. Steele should ultimately settle upon a particular foreign soil and should emphasize his handling of the fantastic, he would afford reasons for the conclusion that he has, to a degree, profited by study of Hearn. His second period has inaugurated the possibility of such later deduction. As he was moved by the Portuguese of the Massachusetts coast, so he has reflected his visit to Bermuda in "At Two in the Bush," has written of "Both Judge and Jury" in the West Indies, has forecast a trip to the South Sea Islands in "The Shame Dance," and has interpreted to readers at home the Arab in Africa.

"The Shame Dance," titular story of his second collection, entertains by suggesting the origin of a dance popular toward the close of the second twentieth century decade. It illustrates, further, the grip in which Mr. Steele is held by the magnetizing influence of place, even from afar. It offers an etymology, interesting if not philologically correct, "Shame dance, Shem-dance, Shimmie dance."

Perhaps the war had something to do with Mr. Steele's change of locale as a setting, though admittedly he has "finished with Provincetown," to the extent of selling his home there. After the United States entered the conflict Mr. Steele, asked to write articles on the American Naval participation, visited the North Sea, Dunkirk, Brest, and North Ireland. The results he utilized in "Contact!" published in *Harper's*, September, 1919. This work excited provocation among critics who like to consider the question, "What, anyway, is a short story?" Three out of five declared that its finely imagined situation and its maintenance of the struggle placed it in the fiction class and that of the short story in particular. But the editors, when questioned, wrote: "It is a faithful portrayal of the work done by our destroyers and therefore falls under the category of 'articles.'" And the author: "I am not quite sure what to say. 'Contact!' was, in a sense, drawn from life, that is to say, it is made up of a number of impressions gained while

I was at sea with the U.S. destroyers off the coast of France. The characters are elaborations of real characters, and the 'contact' told of was such a one as I actually witnessed. Otherwise, the chronology of events, conversations, etc., were gathered from various sources and woven to the best of my ability so as to give a picture of the day's work of our convoying forces in the war."

No better instance can be adduced than this for showing the reorganizing habit of the fictionist by which the record of fact is imbued with the feeling and coloring of fancy.

"The Dark Hour," a conversation centered on the meaning of the struggle among the nations, was reprinted in O'Brien's anthology of 1918 as one of the best twenty stories of the year. Although it possesses literary merit, it is not a story; moreover, it displays its author in a philosophic rather than artistic state of mind. On his way home from France, Mr. Steele received news of the armistice. Its timeliness having departed, the rest of his war material was lost, temporarily at least, to the world.

In recent years, as has been indicated above, Mr. Steele has left far astern the curving peninsula of Cape Cod. Among the countries he has visited, and which have been summarized in preceding paragraphs, he has found North Africa fertile for his imagination. "Kairwan the Holy lay asleep, pent in its thick walls. The moon had sunk at midnight, but the chill light seemed scarcely to have diminished; only the limewashed city had become a marble city, and all the towers turned fabulous in the fierce dry needly rain of the stars that burn over the desert of mid-Tunisia." The story, "A Marriage in Kairwan," presents the crisis in the life of an Arabian lady who elects for herself her lover's standard of morality, a standard, as the outcome tragically reveals, one for his sex alone. The thread of the narrative may be a trifle thin, though somewhat strengthened by the terminal shock (nowise dulled because the reader is subtly prepared for it), and it runs through a warp and woof Orientally splendid, heavy as cloth of gold.

Akin to this story are "The Anglo-Saxon," "East and West," "He That Hideth His Secret," and "The Other Side of the South." Tales of Arabian nights and days, they have in common with his preceding stories the elements of the strange and fanciful. As in "The Woman at Seven Brothers" the ghost became for the author the best possible form of fairy tale, as in "Guiablesse" the jealousy of a ship for a woman constitutes the cause for conflict, so in "The Anglo-Saxon" the vision of the sands and the palm trees is the flotsam of memory by which the Anglo-Saxon recovers all his past.

"He That Hideth His Secret" brings together the Arabian and New York City, as "The Other Side of the South" performs a *tour de force* in a Civil War story. Over in Africa survives a blind one-time slave, whose story is told by the nephew leading him from place to place. It is the more diverting as a Steele story, in that the author has never revisited, in all his wanderings, the land of his birth; it apprehends the South of slavery through the author's interest in North Africa. A mighty compass, but he has fetched it round.

Although a tried device of the story-teller is that of creating a character who grasps the external world through fewer than the usual five senses, yet Mr. Steele has not emphasized the trick in "The Other Side of the South." He has done so in "Footfalls." Boaz Negro lived in one of those old Puritan sea-towns, which has become of late years an outpost of the Portuguese Islands. When in spite of blindness he relies on his ability to distinguish footfalls, he sets up suspense which is terminated only at the redemption of his son's name. Boaz's killing of the villain who had brought about the dishonor of that son is perhaps the best instance of surprise in all the narratives, if "For They Know Not What They Do" is excepted. The latter story presents a most poignant instance of sacrifice: a mother, lovely and virtuous, recognizes that the curse of insanity obsesses her son. He has discovered that his father and his father's father committed crimes, knowing not what they did. His own life seems doomed. To save him from himself the mother avers that her dead husband was not his father. Of course, he learns long after that she had lied gallantly; but, then, his mother, from whom he had withdrawn himself, was dead.

Ordinarily, surprise is a tool this author handles with not more than casual concern for its incisiveness. His management of a single vivid moment is frequently more compelling. For instance, in "A Man's a Fool," the narrator is rehearsing the struggle he and his brother Raphael endured with the *Flores*, and he has reached the point where the boom had broken Raphael's back: ". . . I get down beside my brother and I give him a kiss, and I see tears running down his face, and they was mine. And I says to him:

" 'Wait! You're all right, Raphael boy. You'll be all right and you ain't hurt bad. It's all right, Raphael boy. Only you wait here quiet a second while I heave over that anchor and I'll be back.'

"I give him another kiss on the cheek, and then I tumble up forward and heave that anchor over. It never take me no time. I was back like that. But yet what little sea there was had shift him a mite on the deck, and I see my brother was dead."

The passage is rescued from the sentimentality, which might otherwise be charged to it, by the previous long struggle between the two brothers over a woman. This is the resolution of the problem.

In 1922 Mr. Steele first came into extraordinary recognition when the O. Henry Memorial Committee awarded him a special prize for supremacy in story writing from the year 1919 to 1921, inclusive. They summed up his abilities as lying in an individual temperament that invests the real with the color of romance, in a sense of correct architecture, in the happy knowledge of unique situations, in the climactic development of struggle or complication, in the power to move the reader's emotions, and in a satisfactory dénouement. All these characteristics are manifest in tales marked by a distinctive style, a style dependent upon seizure and conveyance of atmosphere.

Notes

1. Awarded a prize of $250 by the O. Henry Memorial Award Committee as the second best story of the year, 1919. The late Edward J. Wheeler, Editor of *Current Opinion*, declared it "head and shoulders" above other short stories of that year.
2. "A White Horse Winter."

MARTIN BUCCO
"Conclusion"
Wilbur Daniel Steele
1972, pp. 158–64

Virtually unknown by students today and ignored by critics, Wilbur Daniel Steele nevertheless is an important transitional figure in the history of the American short story. Students of the genre, perhaps too ready to classify writers as pejoratively "old" or "new," have not explained (or explained away) the fact that from the mid-1910's to the early 1930's readers and teachers sensitive to the demands of the short story

regarded Steele as America's leading master of the form. Evidently, sympathizers for the "new" felt about him as did F. Scott Fitzgerald, who in 1938 advised a scholar against including the storyteller in a projected survey of contemporary literature: "Why Wilbur Daniel Steele, who left no mark whatever, invented nothing, created nothing except a habit of being an innocuous part of the O'Brien anthology?"[1] That Steele apparently had little influence on the direction of the "new story" does not mean that he neither invented nor created stories of literary merit and historical importance. To be sure, Steele's popularity, especially among the intelligent middle class, grew out of his own liberal but rigorously civilized formative years in Denver; but this fact in itself does not make for a pallid esthetic. Read singly or over, say, a dozen years, Steele's uniquely grim story doubtlessly oppress much less than they do when one systematically moves through seven collections—or even through this critical-analytical study.

Until he relinquished his hold on the short story, Steele gave full validity neither to the internal nor to the external world. As more and more "formless" case history and social documentation shaped the "life-like" stories in the little and the cultural magazines, influential critics and intellectuals consumed by burning issues rising out of front-page social, political, and economic contexts tended to regard as irrelevant Steele's well-wrought, atmospheric "fourth acts" of private paradox and specific irony. After fifteen years of daily toil (ones which terminated in the death of his charming, talented first wife), Steele found his mental and emotional resources sapped, his great potential gone. In describing the hero of "Footfalls," Steele prefigured his own loss: "Nothing in his life had been so hard to meet as this insidious drain of distrust in his own powers; this sense of a traitor within the walls."[2] With the help of his vibrant and able second wife, Steele resigned himself to change by turning first to the theater and then to the novel. In both ventures commercial failure followed commercial success—without benefit of critical success.

Today, many view Steele's innermost conviction of *life as struggle* as hopelessly Naturalistic—and *struggle as Godly* as hopelessly Romantic. But, unlike Anderson, Wolfe, Hemingway, among many others, Steele only infrequently projected literal autobiography into his fiction: "I seem," he once wrote, "to be pretty much the common or garden variety of person. . . . My main desire is to have the moon."[3] Unable to oblige readers who demanded restricted Realism and personal confession, Steele preferred to reshape what he saw and felt into something—a pictorial precept—that tried to be profoundly true rather than shockingly factual. He well realized that ideas have opposites and that he might be "at least half wrong about things"—but those who thought otherwise "also were half wrong."[4]

Unesthetically instructive in his attenuated or sprawling novels, Steele in his stories is nearly always appropriately moral. Time and again, he dramatized the tough-minded thesis that *experience* teaches us that: "Virtue leads as checkered a career as Vice, the Reputability often goes about in strange garments, that Good and Evil are sometimes only the way the penny turns, and that Life is forever getting her heroes and villains mixed."[5] Whether the fortunes of Steele's characters are good or bad, successful or unsuccessful, their outcomes grow from an unpredictable inevitability; and they usually stand in some heavy-handed ironic juxtaposition to their beginnings.

In comparing stories of the early 1920's with those of the early 1940's, Steele affirmed that vision is in the eyes, not in objects, and that roughly twenty years separates a writer's seeing from his telling. Steele wrote his own stories, he argued, out of a way of seeing the world of foreign concord and domestic activity at the turn of the century—when plot served the process of *doing* rather than of *feeling*, when stories exemplified pragmatic optimism: "U.S.A., of the Golden Age. . . . Life skipping pages in its eagerness to know, of anything, what came of it: the Happy Ending. And the happy ending was no mere catchpenny escape mechanism of those days. It was solid realism. It was such matter-of-fact in the faith of then, that most men discover gold mines on grubstakes and die wealthy, as it came to be in a later faith, that most men buy utilities on margin and live unhappily ever afterward."[6]

In the great Romantic tradition of Scott, Hawthorne, Stevenson, and Kipling, Steele tried to stir his readers' imaginations and to involve them in imaginary problems of individual morality by *heightening* empirical existence. Where a local-color Realist might do well to capture the literalness of, say, daily life in south Denver, the quasi-aristocratic, quasi-bohemian Anglo-Saxon from the Rockies ventured among the Portuguese of Cape Cod, the Negroes of the Caribbean, and the Semites of Algeria. Exotic novelty, though no more *externally* real than domestic familiarity, was for the incurable Romantic more real *internally*.

Educated contemporaries found in Steele not only escape from the everyday, but—more important—entrance into another place, another culture, another way of looking at life. Whether set at home or abroad, his stories embody a kind of unschematized history of certain values prevailing in America before and, to a lesser extent, following World War I. To such "Romantic" themes as suspected innocence, revenge and retribution, power of love or friendship, validity of premonition, and return from the "dead," Steele brought sinewy new twists; and through mystification he ironically clarified such "Realistic" ideas as heredity versus environment, law and conscience, divided self, quest for identity, and individual awakening. "Mystification is a good thing sometimes," Steele once wrote. "It gives the brain a fillip, stirs memory, puts the gears of imagination in mesh" ("Footfalls," 299).

Mimetically accurate—almost parodic—when necessary, Steele lured the reader from "normality" to an epistemological reality. In heightening the commonplace (Wordsworth's lyrical intent), Steele's "whole-cloth" mind also heightened coincidence to the point of "statistical" improbability—thus disturbing Aristotelians as well as champions of the "new" literary order. Apparently Steele's diplomatic silence contributed more to his desired effects (but less to his later reputation) than would even glancing references to hoary miracle or the hypothesis that events random to one set of laws might well be ordered to another. A world geared to expedient scientific determinism finds Steele's tacit but outmoded "chance" too "easy."

While transcending conventional stories, Steele did not abandon himself to the exhilarating freedom, even license, of the new informalism. Indeed, stories highly conscious, highly controlled, and highly unified are not incompatible with high art—even though older harmonies inevitably give way to newer ones. A master of Classical plot on the order of Sophoclean symmetry and a brilliant exploiter of inherent linguistic consecutiveness, Steele (like Poe) subordinated parts to the whole. Thus readers seeking a chain of "dramatic moments" sometimes find Steele's melodramas tedious.

Trained morally and esthetically to deplore loose ends, Steele perhaps too militantly forced chaos into order. In "Eternal Youth" he made a passing reference to the common ground of secular predestination and artistic design: "the last note strikes the key for the whole piece and pulls it together into something."[7] Steele's long search for ironic unities coincided, of course, with the kind of literary ending made fashionable by O. Henry's generation. Steele's analytical frame of mind and detective imagination (focused as it was on individual predicament and metaphysical puzzle—"*Who am I? What is happening?*) were eminently suited to problem-solving. Where Sherwood Anderson, in turn, achieved effect by simply raising problems, many young writers now achieve effect by dramatizing the difficulty or the impossibility of even doing so.

Today the device of literary problem-solving engenders nearly as much mirthful groaning as a non-Joycean pun. But far less meretricious than O. Henry's proverbial endings, Steele's "twists" generally offer a profounder response to dilemma. Momentarily, at least, the sense of completion liberates us from time and space. Through authoritative indirection and bold inference, Steele stages in silent print the eternal drama between appearance and reality. Formal surprise forces us to see what we missed seeing the first time.

To his literary formalism and to his psychological Romance Steele brought his early training in art. Unable to abide Hollywood, he early foresaw the possibilities in the film for combining pictorial with narrative art. His idiosyncratic application of "picture" to "word" is obvious. Like the Impressionists, Steele achieved his effects through suggestion. Like Corot, he favored *plein* settings: landscapes, seascapes, village streets, and figure studies. (Even sedentary Henry James saw Cape Cod as a delightful little triumph of Impressionism.) Like Courbet, Steel heightened "common" subjects. Like Morisot's brushwork, Steele's style is dense yet subtle. Like Manet's vignettes, Steele's scenes are bold. So conscious of impression was Steele that, as a young writer, he summoned up Stephen Crane's celebrated line in *The Red Badge of Courage* ("The sun was pasted in the sky like a red wafer") and reworked it in *Storm* to the point of parody: "The sun reclined on the skyline like a florid, rotten melon" (71).

When not eclipsed by formalism or by Impressionism, Steele's characters seem beautifully wedded to the baroque language of the whole story. The outcome of a character caught in the grip of circumstance is sometimes determined more by the quality of his soul than by the quality of his environment—enough to provide some readers with the sensation of antiquarianism. Usually, Steele's central character is a hero, heroine, villain, or vixen out of Romanticism curiously combined with an ambiguous victim, antihero or antiheroine, out of Realism. Steele's dramatis personae is wide, ranging from sophisticates who speak the "King's English" (or some other language), to the general American, to an assortment of primitives who speak the local patois. His onomatopoeically named individuals with their emblematic furniture curiously suggest such universal types as fatal female, pastoral innocent, hypocritical moralist, naïve minister, prodigal son, and revengeful husband. Even Steele's psychotics hover somewhere between the madman of Romance and the sick creature of Realism.

By boldly manipulating point of view and time, Steele created rare effects. As in Erckmann-Chatrian and in Conrad, many melodramatic actions in Steele cling to the point of view of the speaker, who may or may not be an eyewitness. This device contributes to Steele's double effect of illusion and reality. Simultaneously filtering reality and gaining esthetic distance, cross-sectioning incidents, shuttling back and forth in displaced time, Steele's first-person narrator is himself part of the story's total meaning. Although the narrator has no control over what is *happening*, his understanding of what finally has *happened* is a kind of Kantian construction on the chaos of the external world. What appears to be an almost Naturalistic objectivity serves to counterpoint the hysteria in the story proper. But even Steele's brand of hysteria seems a little outdated.

Since the end of World War II, only a few critics have commented about Steele. On the one hand, Ray West notes no "vigorous social attitudes"—only "brilliant surface glitter."[8] On the other hand, George K. Anderson sees "both beauty and cruelty . . . as well as a strangeness which is not freakish, a disquieting mood which is not merely shocking—and always an originality which expresses itself with firmness and courage."[9] In their *Great American Short Stories*, Wallace and Mary Stegner view Steele as a synthesis of James' "psychological curiosity," Crane's "bright impressionism," and the local colorists' "careful sense of place."[10] And the mother in Violet Weingarten's disturbing *Atlantic Monthly* story of 1966, entitled "The Man Who Saw Through Heaven," muses that America's youth has found none of that "triumphant" feeling of the hero of Steele's masterpiece.[11]

In spite of Poe's no doubt biased assertion that in prose the short story affords the fairest field for the exercise of the loftiest talent, literary history still discriminates against the "mere" story writer. To judge a "professional" writer like Steele, who gained a distinguished reputation from his bread-and-butter stories (but nothing *but* bread and butter from his plays and novels), requires an imaginative extension tantamount to a moral exercise. If our plethora of distinguished young writers is excluded, a list of America's finest short-story writers might include Washington Irving, Edgar Allen Poe, Nathaniel Hawthorne, Bret Harte, Sarah Orne Jewett, Stephen Crane, Henry James, O. Henry, Sherwood Anderson, Ring Lardner, William Saroyan, Ernest Hemingway, William Faulkner, Katherine Anne Porter, and Eudora Welty. If in his greatest work—*The Best Stories of Wilbur Daniel Steele* (1945)—Steele brought to and gave to the form of the short story less than some of those listed brought and gave—less creative imagination and invention, less purity of concentration, less rational control, less emotional response to life, a lower pitch of intelligence, and fewer linguistic resources—I fail to detect it.

Today Steele appears old-fashioned and reactionary, not because he lacks fantastic literary skill, but because fictional statements now in vogue are so different. Steele's imaginative realities and linguistic structures are made from words and from literary patterns that are not part of our current empirical reality. But, like Stevenson, O. Henry, and Kipling, Steele deserves to be "rediscovered"—if not in our time, then in another. If discriminating anthologists continue to reprint Steele's classic efforts, that time is sure to come. But if anthologists submit to the tyranny of the moment, then even John Updike and Bernard Malamud are in jeopardy.

The accolade once given to a fine story—to a Steele story—was "How extraordinary!" Then the accolade became "How true!" Writing for the Twenty-fifth Anniversary Edition of the 1943 *O. Henry Prize Stories*, Wilbur Daniel Steele recognized that, beyond question, the laudatory response "How true!" has made for a deeper, wider, more mature, more abundant literature. He added: "Just as it is beyond question that no story was, nor ever can be, truly extraordinary, without first and foremost being true."[12]

Notes

1. F. Scott Fitzgerald, letter to Dayton Kohler, March 4, 1938. Andrew Turnbull, ed., *The Letters of F. Scott Fitzgerald* (New York, 1963), p. 571.
2. "Footfalls," *Pictorial Review*, XXII (October, 1920), 291.
3. Stanley Kunitz and Howard Haycraft, eds., *Twentieth Century Authors* (New York, 1942), p. 1333.
4. Letter to sister Beulah, February 3, 1927. Wilbur Daniel Steele Papers, Stanford University Library.
5. *Storm* (New York, 1914), p. 113.
6. Herschel Brickell, ed., *O. Henry Memorial Prize Stories of 1943* (Garden City, N.Y., 1943), p. xxii.
7. "Eternal Youth," *Scribner's Magazine*, LXIII (April, 1918), 482.
8. Ray B. West, *The Short Story in America* (Chicago, 1956), p. 81.
9. George K. Anderson and Eda Lou Walton, *This Generation* (Chicago, 1949), p. 668.
10. Wallace and Mary Stegner, *Great American Short Stories* (New York, 1957), p. 22.
11. Violet Weingarten, "The Man Who Saw Through Heaven," *Atlantic Monthly*, CCXVIII (September, 1966), 105.
12. Brickell, ed., *O. Henry Memorial Prize Stories of 1943*, p. xxiii.

WALLACE STEGNER

1909–

Wallace Earle Stegner was born on February 18, 1909, in Lake Mills, Iowa, to George and Hilda Paulson Stegner. He was educated at the University of Utah (A.B. 1930), the University of Iowa (A.M. 1932, Ph.D. 1935), and the University of California at Berkeley. He married Mary Stuart Page in 1934; they have one child. He has taught at a number of institutions, including Augustana College, the University of Utah, the University of Wisconsin, Harvard University, and Stanford University. He was the West Coast editor for Houghton Mifflin from 1945 to 1953. He served as an assistant to the Secretary of the Interior in 1961, and as a member of the National Parks Advisory Board from 1962 to 1966. From 1966 to 1968 he edited *American West* magazine.

Stegner published his first novel, *Remembering Laughter*, in 1937. The first of his novels to receive significant attention was *On a Darkling Plain* (1940), about a young World War I veteran who isolates himself in the Canadian mountains because he feels the world has betrayed its promise. This disaffection with the modern world turns up frequently in Stegner's fiction, usually contrasted with "frontier virtues" such as courage and endurance. Subsequent novels established Stegner as one of the foremost writers dealing with the spirit of America, particularly to those who felt it was in decline. Especially well received were *The Big Rock Candy Mountain* (1943), *A Shooting Star*

(1961), *Angle of Repose* (1971), and *The Spectator Bird* (1976). Stegner's short stories, which concern many of the same themes, have been collected in *The Women on the Wall* (1950) and *The City of the Living* (1956).

Stegner is also a significant writer of American social history. Works such as *Mormon Country* (1942), *Wolf Willow: A History, a Story, and a Memory of the Last Plains Frontier* (1962), and *The Sound of Mountain Water: The Changing American West* (1969) place much of Stegner's fiction in historical context. His sense of the deteriorating human spirit and the decline of ambition, presented metaphorically in his fiction, is here expressed directly, and the result is in some ways more illuminating.

Stegner has always been critically appreciated, and as respect for his books has accumulated he has gradually come to be viewed as a major American author. He won the Pulitzer Prize in Fiction in 1972 for *Angle of Repose* and the National Book Award in 1977 for *The Spectator Bird*.

CHESTER E. EISINGER
from "Twenty Years of Wallace Stegner"
College English, December 1958, pp. 110–13

With the publication in 1956 of *The City of the Living*, a volume of short stories, Wallace Stegner rounded off the first twenty years of his writing career. Yet up to now no one has made an effort to evaluate his work or to place him. I should like to make a beginning by suggesting that Stegner, the author of nine volumes of fiction, is perhaps more important to contemporary literary history than he is to literature. Not that he isn't, especially in the short story, a writer of intrinsic interest. But he may with profit be regarded as a representative writer, in this Time of Hesitation, whose rejections and allegiances are characteristic of his time. He has rejected Marx, Darwin, and Freud—that is, radical social thought and deterministic science. In fact, he has rejected all extreme positions, both moral and social, for he finds them corrupted by cynicism and tyranny. He urges the discovery of some middle way of viewing man and his social experience in which the possibilities for good and evil will be reconciled and the possibilities for variety will be recognized. He thinks that the human will and morality are operative in our world. He is preoccupied with the problem of identity; he wants his characters to find out who they are.

No single writer of course can be representative of so fragmented an age as ours. What Stegner has accepted is very different from the contemporary cult of violence or the despair of nihilism; nor can it be said by any means that writers generally have declared Freud dead. But Stegner's withdrawal from politics and political ideology is representative, as the history of American letters since the outbreak of the second World War bears out, and this withdrawl has significant implications. Disenchantment with politics has led some older writers, like John Dos Passos and Granville Hicks, to dismiss all formulable and closed political philosophies. Others have made the nature of society a matter of indifference, accepting it as given. Some younger men, like Herman Wouk, have positively cuddled up to American society in either an uncritical or a calculated acceptance of it. No matter what their course, none of these writers has wanted to be alienated from his society.

Clearly the relationship between society and man has changed: whereas man in the fiction of the thirties rebelled against society and sought to alter its structure, he now makes society the *mise en scène* against which he tries to discover himself. Warren's *All the King's Men* and Trilling's *The Middle of the Journey* are distinguished examples of this use of society. In these novels, social and political considerations appear to be foremost, but the principal subject in each is the protagonist's quest for the self. The search for identity, in which the

individual becomes more important than the society in which he lives, may bear some relationship to the search for individual salvation which is a part of the current religious revival. It also explains, in part, the emphasis in recent fiction on childhood experience, where memory and sensitivity to the child's mind and emotions are the essential agents in the process of identification. Much modern fiction, then, tends to throw man back upon himself. From this strategy emerges a subjective interpretation of life experience concentrated upon the individual. Insofar as these generalizations describe modern American fiction, Stegner is a representative figure. And he is never more typical than when he affirms the goodness of life even though his characters know it is latent with horror.

It is perhaps too easy a formulation to say that Stegner has accepted a commitment to life. Yet it may be just as well to describe some of his early work in this broad, unsubtle way. His first novel, *Remembering Laughter* (1937), seems to me to be an attack upon the denial of life in dour Scotch Calvinism. Two sisters and a man, involved in an adulterous triangle, live out their lives yoked together by the demands of respectability. The chilled atmosphere of hatred and repressed emotion drives the man from the house and turns the two good and cheerful women into gloomy brooders. The reader might well anticipate from these conditions a tragic resolution such as we get in *Ethan Frome*, which in some respects seems to have been the model for this book. But Stegner does not move in obedience to the logic of the situation he has created. He seems impatient with his characters because they have forgotten laughter and have not adjusted to the irregularities of their lives. He permits the child of the adulterous union to run away from the problem, escaping, so to speak, into life. In this novel, Stegner's commitment to undefined life forces leads him, I think, to an evasion of moral and auctorial responsibility.

The Potter's House (1938) is a novelette in which Stegner manipulates a group of grotesque characters to make the point that we invite tragedy when the normal forces of nature are frustrated. Denied the proper expression of her motherhood, the potter's wife leaves him for a career of abandonment. Here Stegner permits nature to define life, and life becomes something we must accept.

Stegner's third novel, *On a Darkling Plain* (1940), makes the fullest statement to date of his characteristic position. It does so by examining the Thoreauvian case for solitary self-dependence and finding it wanting. The self-exiled protagonist of this book has decided that the world is a poisonous place, and the people in it are poisonous too. Yet despite the existence of flawed man in a flawed society, Stegner permits a sense of brotherhood and community to triumph. Somewhere between Thoreauvian romanticism and Swiftian misanthropy we must come to the somber realization that "Men are brothers by life lived, and are hurt for it." This is a line from Archibald MacLeish which stands as the epigraph for the novel.

The story concerns a young man, Edwin Vickers, who has been invalided out of the first World War with a conviction that men are cretins huddling together in a miasmatic society. He takes up a homestead in Saskatchewan where he can escape human idiocy and straighten out his own thoughts. He wants to discover who he is. He soon realizes that his independence is factitious and incomplete: in addition to living on a steady flow of money from indulgent parents, he must almost at once seek aid and comfort from his neighbors the Sundstroms, especially from their daughter Ina, to whom he looks for love. During the great flu epidemic of 1918 he must, in turn, help the Sundstroms. Vickers sees the disease as the physical manifestation of the spiritual meanness and illness of society, but he is reclaimed for humanity by a dedicated doctor and by participation in the suffering of the stricken community. Since Stegner does not make an honest case for self-sufficiency, his rejection of it is pretty much without force. The positive implications of the novel, if not convincing, are at least clear—and banal: man defines himself by accepting life among men.

In *Fire and Ice* (1941) we see again Stegner's fascination with the quest for identity and—is it still a youthful failure to master his materials?—his inability to pursue to the end the logic of his situations. In this novel about Communism on the campus, Paul Condon, the central figure, comes to the conclusion that economics will not solve his problem, for it will not bring him to a knowledge of himself. Yet Stegner throws away the opportunity that might lead Paul to self-analysis. A frustrated and envious student whose self-pity and rage find an outlet in the Young Communist League, Paul attempts the rape of a rich co-ed near the end of the book. He is put in jail. Out of the suffering and punishment that should attend his situation, Paul might well have come to some evaluation of himself. But he is made to suffer very little and he is punished hardly at all. Stegner has permitted his character once more to run away, since Paul is released from jail when the girl refuses to press charges against him. Instead of anguished appraisal from Paul, who never does come to self-knowledge, we get a superficial analysis from Stegner of the nature of campus radicalism.

In 1943 Stegner published *The Big Rock Candy Mountain*, a family novel in which Bruce Mason tries to find out who he is by coming to an understanding of his father, Bo. This novel is Stegner's most intensive study of the problem of identity; and in it he has also fully shaped his vision of the American West. Bruce decides at the close of the book that in the fashioning of a proper man it is necessary to have among one's predecessors a mother of gentleness and resilience and a father of energy and appetite for the new; then, after generations, the proper subtle blend of feminine and masculine will emerge. And he sees at the close of the book the delusive quality of the American Dream, especially as it is played out in the West, where the big rock candy mountain beckons always with unfulfilled and receding promise.

Bo Mason is victimized by the mountain much as Willy Loman falls before his version of the American myth. Bo, who is really the main character in the novel, is the frontiersman *manqué*, an anachronism in the America of the turn of the century. A virile, athletic, intelligent man of many manual skills, he might have stepped out of Whitman's hirsute pages. Perfectly competent to get over the obstacles raised by nature, he stumbles repeatedly at the obstacles society places in his way. Thus he seeks constantly for the main chance in the unexploited areas of the West, but time has caught him and passed him by. He is destroyed in a world he could not adapt

himself to. He follows a logical course of action for the frontier type frustrated: failing to find plenty of easy money in the legitimate activities of his society, he is forced outside the law—into bootlegging—to find the adventurous career suitable to his talents and the money commensurate with his appetite. In the end he is destroyed, for he is a child and a man; he is an undeveloped human being and an immature social animal, "and the further the nation goes the less room there is for that kind of man."

Stegner feels no nostalgia for the American society in which Bo fails. He does not regret the passing of the frontier or the decay of its myth, for he sees that the expansive air of the West has misled Bo, seeming always to promise more than it was prepared to deliver and making the promise of the future more important than the reality of the present. Moreover, the frontier ethos demanded that life adjust to a ruthlessly materialistic scale. Stegner's judgment here seems to me sound. Bruce survives his father, and indeed transcends him, because he understands reality whereas Bo has seen only illusion. Bruce's survival will be possible, not because he has a better society to live in (Stegner seems uninterested in this) but because he has a clearer vision than his father's.

He achieves this vision only after he is purged of his hatred for his father. Bo is crudely energetic, and Bruce is sensitive and easily bruised. The natural rebellion of the son against the father is intensified by Bo's destruction of the home, by his dependence upon his wife, by his moral cowardice, by the fact that he destroys his other son, Chet. All this fires a hatred and contempt in Bruce which are dissipated only when Bruce comes to an understanding of his father and himself. Then he sees that Bo was both good and bad, that in another environment he could have been a notable man. Out of hatred come pity and understanding and self-knowledge. Bruce has learned to see and, seeing, to accept.

BRUCE A. RONDA
"Themes of Past and Present in *Angle of Repose*"

Studies in American Fiction, Autumn 1982, pp. 217–26

"'I'm not writing a book of Western history,'" the narrator of Wallace Stegner's *Angle of Repose* tells his skeptical son, "'I'm writing about something else. A marriage, I guess.' . . . What really interests me is how two such unlike particles [his grandparents, the novel's protagonists] clung together, and under what strains, rolling downhill into their future until they reached the angle of repose where I knew them. That's where the interest is. That's where the meaning will be if I find any."[1] These lines from Stegner's 1971 Pulitzer Prize-winning novel contain three of the major issues that make it an important contribution to literature generated by the Western experience. Despite the disclaimer of the narrator, Lyman Ward, the novel *is* a part of Western history, or rather, of its reinterpretation. The role of women, the persistence of Eastern and Victorian cultural values, the place of investment, speculation, and industry—these are issues treated with increasing seriousness by historians of the West, and all are central to the novel. The marriage of the gifted New York artist, writer, and intellectual Susan Burling and the silent Western engineer Oliver Ward and the maintenance of their relationship suggest the strength of the Victorian configuration of the values of fidelity, duty, and self-sacrifice. *Angle of Repose* provides insights into the ways in which dominant

Victorian values lay at the core of much of the nineteenth-century Western experience and reveals how fiercely settlers clung to the conventions of manner, dress, and role, despite profound changes in environment. Finally, the "unlike particles" rolling from the past into the present of the narrator, a crippled historian who is Oliver and Susan's grandson, point to a concern with the relation of past and present. For Lyman Ward, the past, especially the Victorian past, is rich in authentic values, stable, predictable, while the present is shallow, violent, arbitrary, crippled. The invention and elaboration of such a past, the sense of loss and regret at its passing, the anxiety of living under the shade of such grandparental giants, the possibilities of recovering meaning from the past—all these comprise a third major theme the novel explores.

Stegner drew his nineteenth-century couple and their story from the life of Mary Anna Hallock, a successful New York illustrator who married the young mining engineer Arthur Foote in 1876. Stegner duplicated the Foote's sojourns at New Almaden, California, Leadville, Colorado, and the Idaho territory in his account of the Wards. Mary Foote tried to overcome her sense of personal loneliness and cultural isolation through a prolific correspondence with Richard Watson Gilder, editor of *Scribner's*, and his wife, Helena de Kaye Gilder, whom Stegner named Thomas and Augusta Hudson. Articles, short stories, illustrations, novels, and subsequent fame as an authentic voice of the West followed from this correspondence.[2]

Stegner has built this account into a narrative framework of a novel within a novel. The outer story deals with the grandson, Lyman Ward, who is obsessed with his grandparents' marriage and is seeking to account for its survival. Using letters, newspaper files, and journals, Lyman dictates his version of the past into a tape recorder, which is then transcribed by young Shelly Rasmussen. Shelly's naive openness and uninhibited sexuality form a central contrast with the reticence and privacy of Lyman's grandparents. Meanwhile, Lyman's son, Rodman, is attempting to persuade his father to forgo this exhausting project, confront the seriousness of his bone disease, and be admitted to a nursing home. Struggling for a sense of personal self-worth, convinced of the shallowness of the present, and driven to recover or invent the meaning of the past from the crippled present, Lyman presses on in his account of the Wards.

While Lyman's account ranges beyond the "evidence" he amasses, reconstructing major sections of dialogue and indeed imagining entire scenes, Stegner's novel as a whole is part of the recovery of a fuller Western history whose variety has not until recently been appreciated or documented. A Western novel with a woman as the central character certainly challenges the fictional orthodoxy that began with James Fenimore Cooper and may be seen in, among other novels, Owen Wister's *The Virginian* and Walter Tilburg Clark's *The Ox-Bow Incident*. The subordination or absence of women, the belief that the West was a man's world and a boy's adventure, are challenged here in the story of a woman whose career was compromised but not destroyed by the West, who saw family as but one source of fulfillment. In *Angle of Repose* Stegner dissents even from Willa Cather, who portrayed a strong and admirable female protagonist in *My Ántonia*, only to locate ultimate fulfillment in domestic bliss.

Although most Western communities had large and transient male populations, women made their presence felt quite quickly throughout the West as schoolteachers, missionaries, librarians, photographers, entrepreneurs, journalists, writers, and entertainers of various sorts. Recently, Julie Jeffrey has investigated the role of women in the West, and many of her observations find their fictional corroboration in Stegner's Susan Ward. Jeffrey stresses that the ideology of domesticity in the early nineteenth century stressed women's moral superiority and self-sacrificial domestic devotion. The preservation of the culture and its values depended on women's family-centeredness. Whether women assented to this role in society is difficult to determine; as Jeffrey says, "there was considerably more variety in the behavior of women than ideology would suggest."[3] Still, the ideology of domesticity was a shaping force on the lives of middle-class women, and emigration to the West posed serious challenges to the identity the ideology imparted. The journey likely involved a blurring of sex roles and threatened the stability and unity of the family. On the other hand, since women were seen as culture-bearers, they could participate in the creation of a new society in the West.

Jeffrey documents the considerable tension in the lives of many women emigrants between the desire to retain the conventions of Eastern life and the demands of traveling through and living in the primitive environment. She notes that "women coped with their sense of desolation by reproducing aspects of the world they had left behind. Thus, women arranged their wagons, writing in their journals of the little conveniences they had fixed . . . the rag carpet . . . the bedding, sleeping, and dressing arrangements." The desire to hold on to conventions of Eastern female life persisted after the new Western home was established. Women "tried to maintain the standards of domesticity and hospitality with which they had been familiar before emigration. . . . The interest in fashion and the attempts to dress in style were symbolic of the intention to remain feminine."[4]

Continuity with Eastern life is one of the most powerful themes in Stegner's novel and is a virtual obsession for Susan Ward. Real living goes on in the East, which contains all that is valuable in art, people, history. The West is meaningful to her only as she can spin a web that extends back East and in which she can catch whatever of valuable Eastern culture has wandered West. As Lyman Ward observes, "I am impressed with how much of my grandparents' life depended on continuities, contacts, connections, friendships, and blood relationships. Contrary to the myth, the West was not made entirely by pioneers who had thrown everything away but an ax and a gun" (p. 41).

Like her emigrant sisters, Susan Ward tries to recreate the East in her various homes. Again, Lyman Ward: "When frontier Historians theorize about the uprooted, the lawless, the purseless, and the socially cut-off who settled the West, they are not talking about people like my grandmother. . . . For that sort of pioneer, the West was not a new country being created, but an old one being reproduced" (p. 277). In the Wards' Leadville cabin, Susan comes closest to recreating the vibrant, stimulating world she had left behind: "In her single room whose usable space was hardly fifteen feet square there assembled every evening an extraordinary collection of education, culture, talent, eloquence, reputation, political power, and intellectual force" (p. 252).

Despite Susan Ward's fidelity to the East, despite her insistence that she came West "not to enjoy a new society but to endure it" (p. 81), she was very much like other emigrant women who in confronting the otherness of the West were transformed by it. Each of the Wards' moves, from California to Colorado to Idaho, marked a decline in their affection for each other, and "the birth of each child marked a decline in the security of their life. Now she would have her third child in a canyon cave, unattended, or attended by a rough-handed settler's wife. Meanwhile, her children ran daily through dangers that turned her cold even on that flaming hillside" (p. 408). Likewise, for the Western women Julie Jeffrey describes, the amenities of Eastern life gradually became a dream of the past. Frontier women did "men's" work, helping dig cellars, plowing, planting, as well as performing the conventional female domestic tasks. The frontier home became much more like the colonial center of economic and social activity and "not the quiet and cozy retreat that nineteenth-century culture envisioned."[5]

Angle of Repose also explores fictionally the ways in which the West was exploited by speculators, investors, and industrial combinations. This is of course no new story; many historians, including Ray Allen Billington and Frederick Merk, have depicted the exploitation of resources through mining and the theft of Western lands and resources through cartels and special legislation. More recently, Richard Bartlett has provided a panoramic view of far Western mining and industrialization, giving a particularly valuable account of hydraulic mining in California. Lawrence Goodwyn's history of the Farmers' Alliance and Populist revolts rounds out the picture that is also drawn in Stegner's novel: the same financial and industrial forces at work in the post-bellum East were at work in the West.[6] As Lyman Ward put it, "there are several dubious assumptions about the early West. One is that it was the home of intractable self-reliance amounting to anarchy, whereas in fact large parts of it were owned by Eastern and foreign capital and run by iron-fisted bosses" (p. 134).

Susan Ward's view of the mining town of New Almaden, California, as a pleasant orderly community is shattered when she descends into the mineshaft with her husband and the mine's manager, Kendall. "Under her feet as she walked in sunshine, under her stool and umbrella as she sat sketching, under the piazza as she rocked the baby in his cradle, creatures . . . were swinging picks, drilling holes, shoveling, pushing ore cars, sinking in cages to ever deeper levels, groping along black tunnels with the energy of ants. . . . It was as if she had suddenly discovered that the conduits of her blood teemed with tiny, busy, visible, vermin" (p. 139). These "creatures," "ants," "vermin" were kept in their place by methods that Eastern industrial workers would have recognized. Lyman Ward observes ironically,

> the West of my grandparents . . . is the early West, the last home of the freeborn American. It is all owned in Boston and Philadelphia and New York and London. The freeborn American who works for one of those corporations is lucky if he does not have a family, for then he has an added option: he can afford to quit if he feels like it. . . . Beyond question, once fired, you will be blacklisted (p. 154).

The Wards too are subject to financial forces beyond their control. After resigning in protest from New Almaden, Oliver works on a formula for cement, neglects to patent it, and watches it stolen and used by a corporation "for the making of bridges, piers, dams, highways, and all the works of Roman America that my grandfather's generation thought a part of Progress" (p. 192). Thus, although agriculture remained the basic endeavor for the masses of Western emigrants, industrial, engineering, and mining activities went on apace, and both farming and industry danced to a tune played east of the Mississippi.

One of the most striking features of *Angle of Repose* is the novel's celebration of the Victorian age and its values. The novel is a reminder that the major work of Western settlement went on during the reign of Victoria, and emigrants clung to the conventions and signs of their Eastern life with tenacity. Victorian perspectives on women, home, child-rearing, and sex, were all transferred to the West, although not without adaptation. Likewise, Victorian beliefs concerning conquest and self-conquest, ambition and exploitation, and the superiority of Anglo-Saxon culture were also transferred West.

The Victorian age in England and America encouraged certain personality traits, including earnestness, duty, self-denial, a worship of hard work, fidelity, and a kind of inner motivation or drive, an "inner-directedness,"[7] Oliver Ward certainly exemplifies these traits, especially earnestness and fidelity. During a sparkling conversation in their Leadville cabin with Helen Hunt Jackson, Clarence King, and others, Mrs. Jackson has been semi-seriously questioning King on the ethics of government-employed scientists, and Oliver insisted that King address this issue. Susan felt Oliver's seriousness was clumsy: "She saw he lacked some quality of elegance and ease, some fineness of perception, that these others had" (p. 259). Ironically, Oliver's earnest pursuit of the question is vindicated when King is later implicated in a misuse of his knowledge of natural resources.

Early in the novel, Lyman Ward describes the cultural milieu in which young Susan Burling moved. Susan writes in her reminiscences (which Lyman is using as a source for his "novel") that

> Osgood and Company had mysteriously invited her to Boston, and there surprised her with a dinner at which the whole Brahmin population of New England was present. Mr. Whittier was there. . . . Mr. Lowell paid her a flattering amount of attention. Mr. Holmes was very witty. Mr. Longfellow held her hand quite a long time and told her he was astonished that one so talented should be so young and charming. . . . Mr. Howells, the new editor of the *Atlantic*, praised her realism (p. 52).

As a close friend of Thomas Hudson and Augusta Drake, Susan happily explored the cultural wonders of New York. "In that Edith Wharton version of New York they ran around safe, platonic, and happy to galleries, theatres, and concerts" (p. 54).

Beyond description, Stegner's book praises and prefers Victorian values, portraying them as stronger, healthier, more mature than those of the present. Lyman's secretary, Shelly, manifests the contemporary fascination with sex, and she chides Ward for refusing to be more explicit about Susan and Oliver's sex life. "They were so puritan about their bodies in those days, it was bound to have screwed up their minds. Can you leave out anything that basic and still have a valid book? Modern readers might find a study of Victorian sex life interesting and funny" (p. 266). Lyman responds by pointing to his grandmother's portrait: " 'Look at her picture,' I said. 'What's in that face? Hypocrisy? Dishonesty? Prudery? Timidity? Or discipline, self-control, modesty? Modesty, there's a word 1970 can't even conceive' " (p. 269). Shelly's impatience with the traits of the Wards is shared by Lyman's son, Rodman, for whom "Victorian" means "quivering with sensibility and an inordinate respect for the genteel" (P. 68). To him, Lyman puts the central question of the novel, and in so doing identifies some of the traits he prizes: "What held [them] together for more than sixty years? Passion? Integrity? Culture? Convention? Inviolability of contract? Notions of possession?" (p. 212).

The central value explored and celebrated in this novel is surely fidelity. Oliver puts it this way: "I *believe* in trusting people, do you see? At least till they prove they can't be trusted. What kind of life is it when you can't?" (p. 497). Oliver's question carries added force because of the infidelity between Susan and his assistant Frank Sargent. The growing gap between Susan and Oliver over his repeated failures and the decline of the quality of their life are heightened as Susan succumbs emotionally to Frank's advances. During one of their trysts, the Wards' youngest child, Agnes, wanders into the nearby river and is drowned. Shortly thereafter, Frank commits suicide. Ollie, the Wards' oldest child and Lyman's father, had earlier witnessed "his mother and Frank Sargent walking close together with locked hands, coming down the trail with guilty distress written all over them" (p. 455) and is now permanently alienated from his mother. Despite these traumas and disasters, the Wards' marriage does not break up. Faithfulness despite the cooling of affection assumes an even greater place in the novel's hierarchy of values when it is contrasted with the relationship of Shelly Rasmussen and her lover Larry, whom Shelly describes as her husband for her parents' sake. For the honorable and self-controlled people in Ward's narrative, "inhibited from the casual promiscuity, adultery, and divorce that keep us so healthy" today, the consequences of illicit desire were platonic friendship, breakage of relationships, or emotional estrangement. Susan and Frank's is broken by suicide, Susan and Oliver's is strained but not broken.

In his celebration of Victorian reserve, duty, earnestness, and fidelity, Stegner has already indicated his preference for the past to the present. Lyman Ward's son, Rodman, a sociologist, typifies the casual and dismissive attitude toward the past that Lyman finds so maddening. "Rodman, like most sociologists, and most of his generation, was born without the sense of history. To him, it is only an aborted social science" (p. 15). With Saul Bellow's Moses Herzog, Lyman writes letters in his mind: "As a modern man and a one-legged man, I can tell you that the conditions are similar. We have been cut off, the past has been ended, and the family has broken up and the present is adrift in its wheelchair" (p. 17). Lyman says that "I believe in time" (p. 18) only to find that the passage of time has deposited him in a world that feels no vital connection to the past, that experiences itself as continually reborn. Lyman's hostility to this romantic and anti-historical view is most fully expressed in a scene in which Shelly brings him a manifesto announcing the rejection of "acquisitive society" and the establishment of a new community based and communal and natural values. Ward's reaction to this manifesto is most revealing of his belief not only in the past but more importantly in institutions, conventions, the rich denseness of organized cultural life: "I want to make a distinction between civilization and the wild life without confusing itself with it." As if to underline his anti-romantic view Ward attacks Thoreau for his rejectionist stance: "The civilization he was contemptuous of—that civilization of men who lived lives of quiet desperation—was stronger than he was, and maybe righter. . . . Civilizations grow by agreement and accommodations and accretions, not by repudiations" (p. 519).

It is no use, of course, to argue with Ward which century is better. He has himself provided enough evidence to swing the case either way. And the argument would be absurd in any case because, as Ward says, this is finally not Western history. It is Western mytho-history, the imagining of a better, deeper, more satisfying life lived in the American West. There are two ironies of the past celebrated in this novel. The first is that this mythic West is not that of individual enterprise in the new Eden but an extension westward of Victorian America. The second is that this very past which Ward spends his waning

energies to recover is in fact presented as irrecoverable: "The present is adrift in its wheelchair." The jumble of slogans, references, allusions, and quotations on the manifesto that Shelly brings suggests the shattering of any deep insight the study of the past might offer. The neoromantic present is only interested in dressing up in the clothes of the past, a point also made by Artur Sammler in Bellow's *Mr. Sammler's Planet*, another novel of the early 1970s decrying the excesses of romanticism.

After all of Ward's efforts at research and imagination, the book ends with the possibility only of a personal gesture. Oliver Ward could not bring himself to be reconciled with Susan, although he lived with her for fifty years after Agnes' death. Lyman wonders "if I am man enough to be a bigger man than my grandfather" (p. 569) and be reconciled with his wife, Ellen, who had deserted him after his surgery. The past that Ward has partly uncovered and partly invented can have no larger cultural significance because of the unbridgable gap between then and now. Thus, a third irony: Ward accuses Shelly's generation of having no historical consciousness, yet he creates a story so dominated by giants, so rich in cultural heroes and palpable with cultural depth, that both he and the reader have no choice but to feel awe, impotence, littleness, in comparison.

Of course Wallace Stegner may do as he pleases with his novel, freely imagining the story of Lyman Ward and *his* novel as well as imagining the details of Mary and Arthur Foote's lives. But Stegner has posed such a striking contrast between Victorian depth and modern superficiality and has, through Ward, made such pointed comments on the political and cultural protest of the late 1960s and early 1970s, that some interpretation of his interpretation is in order. Stegner's fictional hostility to the counter culture ignores the historical precedents for communalism and other challenges to conventional modes of living. Indeed, challenging the conventional and attempting to build new communities are integral to American cultural history. Stegner's romantic countercultural hippies are foils for the culturally rooted nineteenth-century Wards and are so stereotypically drawn as to reinforce rather effortlessly a Burkean political conclusion about the irrelevant nature of social and cultural protest. Stegner may think as he wishes about the protest of the last several decades, but his brilliant and complex novel is weakened because of his distortion of the recent past done to elevate the more distant past.

Angle of Repose is a powerful novel that is revisionist in several important respects. It insists on cultural continuity. It offers a strong woman as central character, a woman whose Victorian sensibilities do not smother her individuality or pride in her abilities. Yet, in Stegner's novel, the past, even the imagined past, is fixed and static; it does not impinge on the crippled present except in the life of Lyman Ward and then only to stand in judgment. Ultimately, Stegner's novel must join many other Western novels in celebrating a West in which giants walked the land, a West that is gone and irretrievable. The greatest irony is that, with a writer of such vision and a novel of such possibility, it did not have to be so.

Notes

1. Wallace Stegner, *Angle of Repose* (Garden City: Doubleday, 1971), p. 211. Page references will be to this edition of the novel and will hereafter be included in the body of the text.
2. Lee Ann Johnson has written an admirable biography of Stegner's model in *Mary Hallock Foote* (Boston: Twayne Publishers, 1980), although she does not treat the parallels between Stegner's novel

and Mary Foote in any detail. Other information may be found in Joan Swallow Reiter and Editors of Time-Life Books, *The Old West: The Women* (Alexandria: Time-Life Books, 1978), p. 104, and Thurman Wilkins, "Mary Anna Hallock Foote," *Notable American Women*, Edward T. James, et al., eds. (Cambridge: Belknap Press of Harvard Univ. Press, 1971), I, 643–45.

3. Julie Jeffrey, "Frontier Women," *The Trans-Mississippi West, 1840–1880* (New York: Hill and Wang, 1979), p. 10. Other useful treatments of women on the frontier include John Mack Faragher, *Women and Men on the Overland Trail* (New Haven: Yale Univ. Press, 1979), and John Unruh, *The Plains Across: The Overland Emigrants and the Trans-Mississippi West, 1840–1860* (Urbana: Univ. of Illinois Press, 1979).

4. Jeffrey, pp. 38, 73.

5. Jeffrey, p. 61.

6. Ray Allen Billington, *Westward Expansion*, fourth edition (New York: Harper and Row, 1956), Frederick Merk, *History of the Westward Movement* (New York: Alfred A. Knopf, 1978), which has an invaluable bibliography in "Further Reading"; Richard Bartlett, *The New Country: Social History of the American Frontier, 1776–1890* (New York: Oxford Univ. Press, 1978). Other book-length studies of the "industrial frontier" and the despoilment of the environment include Robert L. Kelley, *Gold versus Grain: The Hydraulic Mining Controversy in California's Sacramento Valley* (Glendale: A.H. Clarke Publishers, 1959, 1976); Hans

Huth, *Nature and the American* (Berkeley: Univ. of California Press, 1957); Roderick Nash, *Wilderness and the American Mind* (New Haven: Yale Univ. Press, 1967); and Rodman Paul, *California Gold* (Cambridge: Harvard Univ. Press, 1947).

7. "Victorianism in America" was the subject of a special issue of *American Quarterly* (27, No. 5 [December 1975]). Essays of special importance in assessing the persistence of Victorian characteristics and in thinking of Victorianism as an Anglo-American movement are Daniel Walker Howe, "American Victorianism as a Culture," Richard D. Brown, "Modernization: a Victorian Climax," David Hall, "The Victorian Connection," and D.H. Meyer, "American Intellectuals and the Victorian Crisis of Faith." The essays in this issue have been collected in Daniel Walker Howe, ed., *Victoria America* (Philadelphia: Univ. of Pennsylvania Press, 1976). Richard D. Brown, "Modernization and the Modern Personality in Early America, 1600–1865: A Sketch of a Synthesis," *Journal of Interdisciplinary History*, 2 (1972), 201–28, provides useful insights into Victorianism as the first "modern" period. Three older studies of Victorianism remain seminal sources of insight into the personal and social characteristics of the age: Walter Johnson Bate, *From Classic to Romantic* (Cambridge: Harvard Univ. Press, 1951), Jerome Buckley, *The Victorian Temper* (Cambridge: Harvard Univ. Press, 1951); and Walter Houghton, *The Victorian Frame of Mind* (New Haven: Yale Univ. Press, 1957).

GERTRUDE STEIN

1874–1946

Gertrude Stein was born on February 3, 1874, in Allegheny, Pennsylvania, to Daniel and Amelia (née Keyser) Stein. She spent her childhood in Vienna, Paris, and Oakland, California. Stein was educated at Radcliffe, where she studied under William James. Stein was particularly interested in psychology, and her first published work was an article, "Normal Motor Automatism," co-written with Leon Solomons and published in *Psychological Review* in 1896. She received a B.A. from Radcliffe in 1897 and began studying medicine at Johns Hopkins University, but left in 1902 without receiving her degree. In 1903 Stein moved to Paris with her brother Leo; she lived there the rest of her life, returning to America only once. She began collecting paintings in 1904, including early works by the then obscure Cézanne, Matisse, and Picasso. She was influenced by their aesthetic philosophies and styles, and in turn passed this influence on to a generation of younger writers. In 1907 she met Alice B. Toklas, with whom she lived from 1909 until her death.

Stein's first book, *Three Lives*, was published in 1909. Over the next four decades she wrote almost constantly, and produced scores of books, few of which were published within her lifetime. Her work was extremely controversial. Some critics hailed her stream-of-consciousness techniques as liberating and illuminating, clearing the way for a new, more open literature. Others saw her work as self-indulgent, deliberately obfuscatory, and intellectually dishonest, if not an outright fraud. Certainly Stein was one of the most influential writers of her time, and was at the center of a significant segment of the European artistic community; Sherwood Anderson and Ernest Hemingway were among those most directly in her debt. Her best-known works published in her lifetime are *Tender Buttons* (1914), *The Making of Americans* (1925), and *The Autobiography of Alice B. Toklas* (1932), the last of which was her only book to achieve wide popularity.

Gertrude Stein died on July 27, 1946. Since then her reputation has continued to grow; she is perhaps the writer most responsible for freeing prose from rigid narrative conventions, and her work has influenced subsequent generations of poets concerned with sound and the portrayal of consciousness. Much of her writing has been published since her death. Though she still has virulent detractors, she is recognized as one of the touchstones of twentieth-century literature.

One evening in the winter, some years ago, my brother came to my rooms in the city of Chicago bringing with him a book by Gertrude Stein. The book was called *Tender Buttons* and, just at that time, there was a good deal of fuss and fun being made over it in American newspapers. I had already read a book of Miss Stein's called *Three Lives* and had thought it

contained some of the best writing ever done by an American. I was curious about this new book.

My brother had been at some sort of a gathering of literary people on the evening before and someone had read aloud from Miss Stein's new book. The party had been a success. After a few lines the reader stopped and was greeted by loud shouts of laughter. It was generally agreed that the author had done a thing we Americans call "putting something across"—the meaning being that she had, by a strange freakish performance, managed to attract attention to herself, get herself discussed in the newspapers, become for a time a figure in our hurried, harried lives.

My brother, as it turned out, had not been satisfied with the explanation of Miss Stein's work then current in America, and so he bought *Tender Buttons* and brought it to me, and we sat for a time reading the strange sentences. "It gives words an oddly new intimate flavor and at the same time makes familiar words seem almost like strangers, doesn't it," he said. What my brother did, you see, was to set my mind going on the book, and then, leaving it on the table, he went away.

And now, after these years, and having sat with Miss Stein by her own fire in the rue de Fleurus in Paris I am asked to write something by way of an introduction to a new book she is about to issue.

As there is in America an impression of Miss Stein's personality, not at all true and rather foolishly romantic, I would like first of all to brush that aside. I had myself heard stories of a long dark room with a languid woman lying on a couch, smoking cigarettes, sipping absinthes perhaps and looking out upon the world with tired, disdainful eyes. Now and then she rolled her head slowly to one side and uttered a few words, taken down by a secretary who approached the couch with trembling eagerness to catch the falling pearls.

You will perhaps understand something of my own surprise and delight when, after having been fed up on such tales and rather Tom Sawyerishly hoping they might be true, I was taken to her to find instead of this languid impossibility a woman of striking vigor, a subtle and powerful mind, a discrimination in the arts such as I have found in no other American born man or woman, and a charmingly brilliant conversationalist.

"Surprise and delight" did I say? Well, you see, my feeling is something like this. Since Miss Stein's work was first brought to my attention I have been thinking of it as the most important pioneer work done in the field of letters in my time. The loud guffaws of the general that must inevitably follow the bringing forward of more of her work do not irritate me but I would like it if writers, and particularly young writers, would come to understand a little what she is trying to do and what she is in my opinion doing.

My thought in the matter is something like this—that every artist working with words as his medium, must at times be profoundly irritated by what seems the limitations of his medium. What things does he not wish to create with words! There is the mind of the reader before him and he would like to create in that reader's mind a whole new world of sensations, or rather one might better say he would like to call back into life all of the dead and sleeping senses.

There is a thing one might call "the extension of the province of his art" one wants to achieve. One works with words and one would like words that have a taste on the lips, that have a perfume to the nostrils, rattling words one can throw into a box and shake, making a sharp, jingling sound, words that, when seen on the printed page, have a distinct arresting effect upon the eye, words that when they jump out from under the pen one may feel with the fingers as one might caress the cheeks of his beloved.

And what I think is that these books of Gertrude Stein's do in a very real sense recreate life in words. ⟨. . .⟩

For me the work of Gertrude Stein consists in a rebuilding, an entire new recasting of life, in the city of words. Here is one artist who has been able to accept ridicule, who has even foregone the privilege of writing the great American novel, uplifting our English speaking stage, and wearing the bays of the great poets, to go live among the little housekeeping words, the swaggering bullying street-corner words, the honest working, money saving words, and all the other forgotten and neglected citizens of the sacred and half forgotten city.

Would it not be a lovely and charmingly ironic gesture of the gods if, in the end, the work of this artist were to prove the most lasting and important of all the word slingers of our generation!—SHERWOOD ANDERSON, "The Work of Gertrude Stein," *Geography and Plays*, 1922, pp. 5–8

Gertrude Stein in her younger days had liked to write all night and sleep all day. She also, it seems, ate copiously, drank wine, and smoked cigars. By the time I knew her, at fifty-two, she ate abstemiously; she neither drank nor smoked; and she was likely to wake, as people do in middle life, by nine. Her volume had been diminished too. Her appearance, nevertheless, on account of low stature (five feet, two), remained monumental, like that of some saint or sybil sculpted three-fourths life size. Her working powers also were intact, remained so, indeed, until her death at seventy-two.

Actually a whole domestic routine had been worked out for encouraging those powers to function daily. In the morning she would read, write letters, play with the dog, eventually bathe, dress, and have her lunch. In the afternoon she drove in the car, walked, window-shopped, spent a little money. She did nothing by arrangement till after four. At some point in her day she always wrote; and since she waited always for the moment when she would be full of readiness to write, what she wrote came out of fullness as an overflowing.

Year round, these routines varied little, except that in the country, if there were house guests, excursions by car might be a little longer, tea or lunch taken out instead of at home. When alone and not at work, Gertrude would walk, read, or meditate. She loved to walk; and she consumed books by the dozen, sent to her when away from home by the American Library in Paris. She read English and American history, memoirs, minor literature from the nineteenth century, and crime fiction, rarely modern art-writing, and never the commercial magazines. When people were around she would talk and listen, ask questions. She talked with anybody and everybody. When exchanging news and views with neighbors, concierges, policemen, shop people, garage men, hotel servants, she was thoroughly interested in them all. Gertrude not only liked people, she needed them. They were grist for her poetry, a relief from the solitudes of a mind essentially introspective.

Alice Toklas neither took life easy nor fraternized casually. She got up at six and cleaned the drawing room herself, because she did not wish things broken. (Porcelain and other fragile objects were her delight, just as pictures were Gertrude's; and she could imagine using violence toward a servant who might break one.) She liked being occupied, anyway, and did not need repose, ever content to serve Gertrude or be near her. She ran the house, ordered the meals, cooked on occasion, and typed out everything that got written into the blue copybooks that Gertrude had adopted from French school children. From 1927 or '28 she also worked petit point, matching in silk the colors and shades of designs made especially for her by Picasso. These tapestries were eventually applied to a pair of Louis XV small armchairs (*chauffeuses*) that Gertrude had bought for her. She was likely, any night, to go to bed by eleven, while Miss Stein would sit up late if there were someone to talk with.

Way back before World War I, in 1910 or so, in Granada Gertrude had experienced the delights of writing directly in the landscape. This does not mean just working out of doors; it means being surrounded by the thing one is writing about at the time one is writing about it. Later, in 1924, staying at Saint-Rémy in Provence, and sitting in fields beside the irrigation ditches, she found the same sound of running water as in Granada to soothe her while she wrote or while she simply sat, imbuing herself with the landscape's sight and sound. In the country around Belley, where she began to summer only a few years later, she wrote *Lucy Church Amiably* wholly to the sound of streams and waterfalls.

Bravig Imbs, an American poet and novelist who knew her in the late twenties, once came upon her doing this. The scene took place in a field, its enactors being Gertrude, Alice, and a cow. Alice, by means of a stick, would drive the cow around the field. Then, at a sign from Gertrude, the cow would be stopped; and Gertrude would write in her copybook. After a bit, she would pick up her folding stool and progress to another spot, whereupon Alice would again start the cow moving around the field till Gertrude signaled she was ready to write again. Though Alice now says that Gertrude drove the cow, she waiting in the car, the incident, whatever its choreography, reveals not only Gertrude's working intimacy with landscape but also the concentration of two friends on an act of composition by one of them that typifies and reveals their daily life for forty years. Alice had decided long before that "Gertrude was always right," that she was to have whatever she wanted when she wanted it, and that the way to keep herself always wanted was to keep Gertrude's writing always and forever unhindered, unopposed.

Gertrude's preoccupation with painting and painters was not shared by Alice except in so far as certain of Gertrude's painter friends touched her heart, and Picasso was almost the only one of these. Juan Gris was another, and Christian Bérard a very little bit. But Matisse I know she had not cared for, nor Braque. If it had not been for Gertrude, I doubt that Alice would ever have had much to do with the world of painting. She loved objects and furniture, practiced cooking and gardening, understood music. Of music, indeed, she had a long experience, having once, as a young girl, played a piano concerto in public. But painting was less absorbing to her than to Gertrude. ⟨. . .⟩

Her development had not been aided or arrested by public success, of which there had in fact been very little. The publication of *Three Lives* in 1909 she had subsidized herself, as she did in 1922 that of the miscellany *Geography and Plays*. *The Making of Americans*, published by McAlmon's Contact Editions in 1925, was her first book-size book to be issued without her paying for it; and she was over fifty. She had her first bookstore success at fifty-nine with the *Autobiography*. When she died in 1946, at seventy-two, she had been working till only a few months before without any diminution of power. Her study of technical problems never ceased; never had she felt obliged to fabricate an inspiration; and she never lost her ability to speak from the heart.

Gertrude lived by the heart, indeed; and domesticity was her theme. Not for her the matings and rematings that went on among the amazons. An early story from 1903, published after her death, *Things as They Are*, told of one such intrigue in post-Radcliffe days. But after 1907 her love life was serene, and it was Alice Toklas who made it so. Indeed, it was this tranquil life that offered to Gertrude a fertile soil of sentiment-security in which other friendships great and small could come to flower, wither away, be watered, cut off, or

preserved in a book. Her life was like that of a child, to whom danger can come only from the outside, never from home, and whose sole urgency is growth. It was also that of an adult who demanded all the rights of a man along with the privileges of a woman.

Just as Gertrude kept up friendships among the amazons, though she did not share their lives, she held certain Jews in attachment for their family-like warmth, though she felt no solidarity with Jewry. Tristan Tzara—French-language poet from Romania, Dada pioneer, early surrealist, and battler for the Communist party—she said was "like a cousin." Miss Etta and Dr. Claribel Cone, picture buyers and friends from Baltimore days, she handled almost as if they were her sisters. The sculptors Jo Davidson and Jacques Lipschitz, the painter Man Ray she accepted as though they had a second cousin's right to be part of her life. About men or goyim, even about her oldest man friend, Picasso, she could feel unsure; but a woman or a Jew she could size up quickly. She accepted without cavil, indeed, all the conditionings of her Jewish background. And if, as she would boast, she was "a bad Jew," she at least did not think of herself as Christian. Of heaven and salvation and all that she would say, "When a Jew dies he's dead." We used to talk a great deal, in fact, about our very different religious conditionings, the subject having come up through my remarking the frequency with which my Jewish friends would break with certain of theirs and then never make up. Gertrude's life had contained many people that she still spoke of (Mabel Dodge, for instance) but from whom she refused all communication. The Stettheimers' conversation was also full of references to people they had known well but did not wish to know any more. And I began to imagine this definitiveness about separations as possibly a Jewish trait. I was especially struck by Gertrude's rupture with her brother Leo, with whom she had lived for many years in intellectual and no doubt affectionate communion, but to whom she never spoke again after they had divided their pictures and furniture, taken up separate domiciles.

The explanation I offered for such independent behavior was that the Jewish religion, though it sets aside a day for private Atonement, offers no mechanics for forgiveness save for offenses against one's own patriarch, and even he is not obliged to pardon. When a Christian, on the other hand, knows he has done wrong to anyone, he is obliged in all honesty to attempt restitution; and the person he has wronged must thereupon forgive. So that if Jews seem readier to quarrel than to make up, that fact seems possibly to be the result of their having no confession-and-forgiveness formula, whereas Christians, who experience none of the embarrassment that Jews find in admitting misdeeds, arrange their lives, in consequence, with greater flexibility, though possibly, to a non-Christian view, with less dignity.

Gertrude liked this explanation, and for nearly twenty years it remained our convention. It was not till after her death that Alice said one day,

> You and Gertrude had it settled between you as to why Jews don't make up their quarrels, and I went along with you. But now I've found a better reason for it. Gertrude was right, of course, to believe that "when a Jew dies he's dead." And that's exactly why Jews don't need to make up. When we've had enough of someone we can get rid of him. You Christians can't, because you've got to spend eternity together.

—VIRGIL THOMSON, "A Portrait of Gertrude Stein," *Virgil Thomson*, 1966, pp. 169–80

I master pieces of it.
("Saints and
Singing")

Persuaded that she owed her conception to the death of another Stein child, Gertrude Stein regarded her very existence as precarious from the start; according to her accounts, her parents offered little security, for she represented herself as virtually motherless, while in her father she saw a model of blustering male injustice; so that she emerged into young womanhood anxious, mesmerized by the sexual mystery, and fantasizing incoherently of intimacies with men; but after long endeavoring to submerge her yearnings for closeness in the camaraderie of intellectual life, she responded with gratitude to the sensual overtures of more experienced women; and presently quit her censorious homeland in a cloud of defiance and guilt to take sanctuary with her already expatriated brother; who, although he served as her protector and brought her to the leading edge of modern art, withered her self-esteem with his neurotic condescension; so that, driven both to understand her unhappy condition and to be recognized as an independent human being, she martyred herself to extended exercises in the analysis of human character; which gradually turned inward to representations of her own consciousness, until, possessed of a reader whose devotion sanctioned her erratic perceptions, she began to record the pleasurable tensions of domesticity in her subjective shorthand; involuted experiments which were challenged by a war that initially panicked her into flight, then furnished her the opportunity of exerting a provincial leadership, which brought her out of the war with a new confidence; finding herself regarded now as a mentor of the literary avant-garde, she undertook to examine more carefully the bases of her art, at the same time defending herself against the first encroachments of time by cultivating serenity in the rural sun; until her memoirs transformed her into a celebrity, a role she accepted with enthusiasm, although at some cost to her inner stability; and as she sought to reconcile her public and private personalities, the pervasive social unrest surrounding her revived long-subdued anxieties, which the second world war confirmed by marooning her in an uneasy atmosphere of threat; over its long course, she managed to enlarge her fatalism to meet the dimensions of her despair, but although she endured until the liberation, like all conditions in her life, that happy event proved brief and perhaps even illusory, for she soon discovered herself fatally occupied by that implacable reality that she had dreaded all her life.

When assembled, so her story goes. She never told it directly, however, but offered it obscured, askew, incomplete, in pieces.

In pieces, because Gertrude Stein saw parts but no whole. Dedicated to discovering a comprehensive order in the bewildering tumult of her existence, she hoped for concord and often proclaimed its reign, as if assertion were sufficient to establish it. But what she perceived changed incessantly, tempting her with signs of apparent relationship, then mocking her with the unique and unexpected detail. All her attempts at classification failed. Abandoning received notions of objective exactitude, she sought consistency in the faithful registration of her verbal reactions to the immediate moment.

In pieces, then, because Gertrude Stein's prose echoed the cacophony of feelings, associations, and memories she distinguished in her mind. More than once she acknowledged her fear of suffering some irreparable split or lapse into incapacity. But her oblique and disconnected prose apparently saved her by furnishing an outlet for the tumbling, shifting

cargo of her consciousness. It provided the means by which she could express otherwise ineffable inner states. The verbal crazy-quilts she fashioned from her musings constituted her truest approximation of unity.

So, in pieces, because no term more accurately describes Gertrude Stein's unit of literary expression. Her compositions memorialize that daily half-hour when she gathered what came to mind and randomly, incidentally, shaped it into a prose that was part free association, part mechanical variation, part revelation only partially revealed. Her strength resides in those unpremeditated moments. Whatever else she may have been, she has proved herself master of the telling phrase, of the memorable and haunting assessment reached when the tide of her persistence carried her to a spontaneous height.—RICHARD BRIDGMAN, "Conclusion," *Gertrude Stein in Pieces*, 1970, pp. 346–47

THORNTON WILDER
From "Introduction"
Four in America
1947, pp. v–x, xxvii

Miss Gertrude Stein, answering a question about her line

A rose is a rose is a rose is a rose,

once said with characteristic vehemence:

"Now listen! I'm no fool. I know that in daily life we don't say 'is a . . . is a . . . is a . . .'"

She knew that she was a difficult and an idiosyncratic author. She pursued her aims, however, with such conviction and intensity that occasionally she forgot that the results could be difficult to others. At such times the achievements she had made in writing, in "telling what she knew" (her most frequent formulization of the aim of writing) had to her the character of self-evident beauty and clarity. A friend, to whom she showed recently completed examples of her poetry, was frequently driven to reply sadly: "But you forget that I don't understand examples of your extremer styles." To this she would reply with a mixture of bewilderment, distress, and exasperation:

"But what's the difficulty? Just read the words on the paper. They're in English. Just read them. Be simple and you'll understand these things."

Now let me quote the whole speech from which the opening remark in this introduction has been extracted. A student in her seminar at the University of Chicago had asked her for an "explanation" of the famous line. She leaned forward giving all of herself to the questioner in that unforgettable way which has endeared her to hundreds of students and to hundreds of soldiers in two wars, trenchant, humorous, but above all urgently concerned over the enlightenment of even the most obtuse questioner:

Now listen! Can't you see that when the language was new—as it was with Chaucer and Homer—the poet could use the name of a thing and the thing was really there? He could say "O moon," "O sea," "O love" and the moon and the sea and love were really there. And can't you see that after hundreds of years had gone by and thousands of poems had been written, he could call on those words and find that they were just wornout literary words? The excitingness of pure being had withdrawn from them; they were just rather stale literary words. Now the poet has to work in the excitingness of pure being; he has to get back that intensity into the language. We all know that it's hard to write poetry in a late age; and we know that you have to put some strangeness, something unexpected, into the structure of the sentence in order to bring back vitality to the noun. Now it's not enough to be bizarre; the strangeness in the sentence structure has to come from the poetic gift, too. That's why it's doubly hard to be a poet in a late age. Now you all have seen hundreds of poems about roses and you know in your bones that the rose is not there. All those songs that sopranos sing as encores about "I have a garden; oh, what a garden!" Now I don't want to put too much emphasis on that line, because it's just one line in a longer poem. But I notice that you all know it; you make fun of it, but you know it. Now listen! I'm no fool. I know that in daily life we don't go around saying "is a . . . is a . . . is a . . ." Yes, I'm no fool; but I think that in that line the rose is red for the first time in English poetry for a hundred years."

This book is full of that "strangeness which must come from the poetic gift" in order to restore intensity to images dusted over with accustomedness and routine. It is not required in poetry alone; for Miss Stein all intellectual activities—philosophical speculation, literary criticism, narration—had to be refreshed at the source.

There are certain of her idiosyncrasies which by this time should not require discussion—for example, her punctuation and her recourse to repetition. Readers who still baulk at these should not attempt to read this volume, for it contains idiosyncrasies far more taxing to conventional taste. The majority of readers ask of literature the kind of pleasure they have always received; they want "more of the same"; they accept idiosyncrasy in author and period only when it has been consecrated by a long-accumulated prestige, as in the cases of the earliest and the latest of Shakespeare's styles, and in the poetry of Donne, Gerard Manley Hopkins, or Emily Dickinson. They arrogate to themselves a superiority in condemning the novels of Kafka or of the later Joyce or the later Henry James, forgetting that they allow a no less astonishing individuality to Laurence Sterne and to Rabelais.

This work is for those who not only largely accord to others "another's way," but who rejoice in the diversity of minds and the tension of difference.

Miss Stein once said:

Every masterpiece came into the world with a measure of ugliness in it. That ugliness is the sign of the creator's struggle to say a new thing in a new way, for an artist can never repeat yesterday's success. And after every great creator there follows a second man who shows how it can be done easily. Picasso struggled and made his new thing and then Braque came along and showed how it could be done without pain. The Sistine Madonna of Raphael is all over the world, on grocers' calendars and on Christmas cards; everybody thinks it's an easy picture. It's our business as critics to stand in front of it and recover its ugliness.

This book is full of that kind of ugliness. It is perhaps not enough to say: "Be simple and you will understand these things"; but it is necessary to say: "Relax your predilection for the accustomed, the received, and be ready to accept an extreme example of idiosyncratic writing."

Distributed throughout Miss Stein's books and in the

Lectures in America can be found an account of her successive discoveries and aims as a writer. She did not admit that the word "experiments" be applied to them. "Artists do not experiment. Experiment is what scientists do; they initiate an operation of unknown factors in order to be instructed by its results. An artist puts down what he knows and at every moment it is what he knows at that moment. If he is trying things out to see how they go he is a bad artist." A brief recapitulation of the history of her aims will help us to understand her work.

She left Radcliffe College, with William James's warm endorsement, to study psychology at Johns Hopkins University. There, as a research problem, her professor gave her a study of automatic writing. For this work she called upon her fellow students—the number ran into the hundreds—to serve as experimental subjects. Her interest, however, took an unexpected turn; she became more absorbed in the subjects' varying approach to the experiments than in the experiments themselves. They entered the room with alarm, with docility, with bravado, with gravity, with scorn, or with indifference. This striking variation reawoke within her an interest which had obsessed her even in very early childhood—the conviction that a description could be made of all the types of human character and that these types could be related to two basic types (she called them independent-dependents and dependent-independents). She left the university and settling in Paris, applied herself to the problem. The result was the novel of one thousand pages, *The Making of Americans*, which is at once an account of a large family from the time of the grandparents' coming to this country from Europe and a description of "everyone who is, or has been, or will be." She then went on to give in *A Long Gay Book* an account of all possible relations of two persons. This book, however, broke down soon after it began. Miss Stein had been invaded by another compelling problem: how, in our time, do you describe anything? In the previous centuries writers had managed pretty well by assembling a number of adjectives and adjectival clauses side by side; the reader "obeyed" by furnishing images and concepts in his mind and the resultant "thing" in the reader's mind corresponded fairly well with that in the writer's. Miss Stein felt that that process did not work any more. Her painter friends were showing clearly that the corresponding method of "description" had broken down in painting and she was sure that it had broken down in writing.

In the first place, words were no longer precise; they were full of extraneous matter. They were full of "remembering"—and describing a thing in front of us, an "objective thing," is no time for remembering. Even vision (a particularly overcharged word), even sight, had been dulled by remembering. The painters of the preceding generation, the Impressionists, had shown that. Hitherto people had known that, close to, a whitewashed wall had no purple in it; at a distance it may have a great deal of purple, but many painters had not allowed themselves to see purple in a distant whitewashed wall because they remembered that close to it was uniformly white. The Impressionists had shown us the red in green trees; the Postimpressionists showed us that our entire sense of form, our very view of things, was all distorted and distorting and "educated" and adjusted by memory. Miss Stein felt that writing must accomplish a revolution whereby it could report things as they were in themselves before our minds had appropriated them and robbed them of their objectivity "in pure existing." To this end she went about her house describing the objects she found there in the series of short "poems" which make up the volume called *Tender Buttons*.

Here is one of these:

RED ROSES

A cool red rose and a pink cut pink, a collapse
and a sold hole, a little less hot.

Miss Stein had now entered upon a period of excited discovery, intense concentration, and enormous productivity. She went on to writing portraits of her friends and of places. She revived an old interest in drama and wrote scores of plays, many of which are themselves portraits of friends and of places. Two of her lectures in *Lectures in America* describe her aims in these kinds of work. She meditated long on the nature of narration and wrote the novel *Lucy Church Amiably*. This novel is a description of a landscape near Bilignin, her summer home in the south of France. Its subtitle and epigraph are: "A Novel of Romantic Beauty and Nature and which Looks Like an Engraving . . . '*and with a nod she turned her head toward the falling water. Amiably.*'"

Those who had the opportunity of seeing Miss Stein in the daily life of her home will never forget an impressive realization of her practice of meditating. She set aside a certain part of every day for it. In Bilignin she would sit in her rocking chair facing the valley she has described so often, holding one or the other of her dogs on her lap. Following the practice of a lifetime she would rigorously pursue some subject in thought, taking it up where she had left it on the previous day. Her conversation would reveal the current preoccupation: it would be the nature of "money," or "masterpieces," or "superstition," or "the Republican party." ⟨. . .⟩

And always with her great relish for human beings she was listening to people. She was listening with genial absorption to the matters in which they were involved. "Everybody's life is full of stories; your life is full of stories; my life is full of stories. They are very occupying, but they are not really interesting. What is interesting is the way everyone tells their stories"; and at the same time she was listening to the tellers' revelation of their "basic nature." "If you listen, really listen, you will hear people repeating themselves. You will hear their pleading nature or their attacking nature or their asserting nature. People who say that I repeat too much do not really listen; they cannot hear that every moment of life is full of repeating. There is only one repeating that is really dead and that is when a thing is taught." She even listened intently to dog nature. The often-ridiculed statement is literally true that it was from listening to her french poodle Basket lapping water that she discovered the distinction between prose and poetry.

It can easily be understood that the questions she was asking concerning personality and the nature of language and concerning "how you tell a thing" would inevitably lead to the formulization of a metaphysics. In fact, I think it can be said that the fundamental occupation of Miss Stein's life was not the work of art but the shaping of a theory of knowledge, a theory of time, and a theory of the passions. These theories finally converged on the master-question: what are the various ways in which creativity works in everyone? That is the subject of this book. It is a subject which she was to develop more specifically in a book which of all her works is most closely related to this one: *The Geographical History of America or the Relation of Human Nature to the Human Mind*. It led also to a reconsideration of all literature, reflected in the beautiful lecture, "What Are Master-pieces and Why Are There So Few of Them?" ⟨. . .⟩

The word "tears" occurs frequently in this book. What things in our human lot seem to have moved Miss Stein to tears? It was not the misfortunes of our human nature, though

she was a greatly sympathetic resource to her friends when their griefs were real. What moved her deeply was the struggle of the human mind in its work which is to know. It was of Henry James's mind (and the phrase applies as beautifully to those great heroines of his last novels who live not to assert themselves but to understand) that she says "he had no relief from any pang."

She said to me once: "Everyone when they are young has a little bit of genius, that is they really do listen. They can listen and talk at the same time. Then they grow a little older and many of them get tired and they listen less and less. But some, a very few continue to listen. And finally they get very old and they do not listen any more. That is very sad; let us not talk about that." This book is by an impassioned listener to life. Even up to her last years she listened to all comers, to "how their knowing came out of them." Hundreds of our soldiers, scoffing and incredulous but urged on by their companions, came up to Paris "to see the Eiffel Tower and Gertrude Stein." They called and found bent upon them those gay and challenging eyes and that attention that asked nothing less of them than their genius. Neither her company nor her books were for those who have grown tired of listening. It was an irony that she did her work in a world in which for many reasons and for many appalling reasons people have so tired.

NORMAN WEINSTEIN
From *"The Making of Americans:*
The Narrative Redefined"
Gertrude Stein and the Literature
of the Modern Consciousness
1970, pp. 28–45

The Making of Americans represents an attempt to create for the reader an aesthetic reality, substantial within itself, with an absolute minimum of references to the objective world. This hardly seems remarkable in itself. Certainly most mythological and fantasy literature shares a similar outlook. But what makes Gertrude Stein's book revolutionary is that it is the narrative of an actual family's progress in America over a span of generations. The subject matter is mundane, commonplace, middle-class, and frankly banal. Consider for a moment the task of writing a family chronicle with the following conditions imposed upon you as author: you must not put the family members in any definite temporal or spatial context; you must not maintain a sequential, logical time sequence of events; you must not consider any one event a family character experiences in his lifetime any more significant than any other event experienced by any other relative at any time. As well as these negative impositions, consider these positive injunctions: you must enumerate in your family chronicle every single person ever to come in contact with the household. You must record the lives of the family members from birth to death in all cases. You must clearly show the changes of mind that occur through the passages of generations as reflected in politics, art, sex, life style, religion, morality, and economics.

The conditions listed above are a summary of Gertrude Stein's concerns in *The Making of Americans*. The reasons behind these principles and their implications in this narrative we will now consider.

The Making of Americans is the "history" of two families: the Dehnings and the Herslands. Both families are traced back to their middle-class roots in Europe. I have put "history" in quotation marks because *The Making of Americans* is anything but family history as we are accustomed to view it in other literatures. In a novel that traces a family history through generations—Thomas Mann's *Buddenbrooks*, for instance—every effort is maintained by the author to literally trace the characteristics of the most contemporary generation discussed back to its ancestors. Phylogeny recapitulates ontogeny, and so we read through hundreds of pages of Mann's narrative writing until in the final chapters we are rewarded; all the seemingly irrelevant details of the family chronicle fall into a coherent pattern by the time the book's climax is reached.

Surely one of the pleasures of reading Proust's *Remembrance of Things Past* in its entirety is the sense of final cohesion that brings together the enormous weight of detail with which Proust so liberally decorates his narrative.

By contrast, one of the severe difficulties of even reading *The Making of Americans* in its entirety is the narrative discontinuities in a book that purports to be a "family history." For example the book opens with Gertrude Stein's reworking of a quote from Aristotle's ethics:

> Once an angry man dragged his father along the ground through his own orchard. "Stop!" cried the groaning old man at last, "Stop! I did not drag my father beyond this tree."
>
> It is hard living down the tempers we are born with. We all begin well, for in our youth there is nothing we are more intolerant of than our own sins writ large in others and we fight them fiercely in ourselves; but we grow old and we see that these sins our sins are of all sins the really harmless ones to own, nay that they give charm to any character. . . . [1]

This is Gertrude Stein speaking. And it is Gertrude Stein's omnipresent voice as narrator that resounds through the half million words of narrative. From the very start there is no ambiguity as to the nature of the narrator. She is perfectly in control of the thematic flow at all times. She is repetitious, for our particular storyteller is also a theorizing psychologist who believes the essence of the human personality is revealed in repetition:

> Repeating then is in every one, in every one their being and their feeling and their way of realizing everything and every one of them comes out in repeating. More and more then every one comes to be clear to some one. [2]

But the most striking characteristic of our narrator is her astonishing verbosity. Nearly a thousand pages of closely packed prose and a half million words are employed to depict the progress of the Dehning and Hersland families. Why this prolixity? Is the verbosity an outgrowth of the author's attempt to write the complete family chronicle of these families with every detail clear and intact?

Let us return to the plot of *The Making of Americans* a moment. After her prefacing paragraph stating the major didactic thread of the book (it is hard living down the tempers we are born with, etc.) Miss Stein proceeds to discuss the phenomena of being an American, a parent, a grandparent, a child. Not until the seventh page of the book is a specific family member, Henry Dehning, mentioned. Here is our introduction to him:

> Henry Dehning was a grown man and for his day a rich one when his father died away and left them. Truly he had made everything for himself very different; but it is not as a young man making himself

rich that we are now to feel him, he is for us an old grown man telling it all over to his children. [3]

We are told by the author "it is not as a young man that we are now to feel him." We receive the impression of the narrator as a master puppeteer controlling all the puppet's strings. This sense of narrator dominance is reinforced by the length of time that passes before a single, concrete personage is mentioned. This technique of cataloguing all the general human possibilities and then zooming in upon one specific family character occurs throughout the text. Consider this description prior to the introduction of Marsha Hersland:

> There are many that I know and I know it. They are many that I know and they know it. They are all of them themselves and they repeat it and I hear it. Always I listen to it. . . . They repeat themselves now and I listen to it. Every way that they do it now I hear it. [4]

I am insisting on this point because *The Making of Americans* gives the illusion of being a family history by opposing a few well-defined character descriptions against an illusionary backdrop of all those that have ever lived, are living, or will live. If we remember Miss Stein's notion of characterology the claim of all-inclusiveness appears less fantastic than at first sight.

Only a handful of characters from the Dehning and Hersland families are extensively described. Most of the attention is focused upon Julia Dehning, the oldest daughter of Henry Dehning, and on Alfred Hersland, the second of the three children of David Hersland. It could be argued that Julia and Alfred are the only characters in the book that emerge and are as successful artistically as the characters in *Three Lives*. The hundreds of other characters appear for brief moments, as their lives fleetingly come in contact with Julia and Alfred, and then disappear again. When a character has "spoken his part" he returns to that swelling, amorphous mass of "everyone" and "some ones" and "all those who are living ones" and "all those who are dead ones" that comprises the backdrop for the characters of the two families and their significant actions.

But if the central pivotal event of the book is the falling out of love of Julia Dehning and Alfred Hersland, why must we suffer through a thousand-page record of everyone and everything that occurred to them during their lives? Why must we be introduced to a regular who's who of nonentities in the form of Mary Waxworthing, the seamstress to the Hersland family, the two governesses before Madeline Wyman, and a host of others?

Gertrude Stein gives the raison d'être for such a technique in the lecture "Composition as Explanation."

> There is singularly nothing that makes a difference a difference in beginning and in the middle and in ending except that each generation has something different at which they are all looking. . . . There was [in making] a groping for using everything and there was a groping for a continuous present and there was an evitable beginning of beginning again and again. [5]

All of these ideas become translated into the following paragraph in *The Making of Americans*:

> Sometime there is a history of each one, of every one who ever has living in them and repeating in them and has their being coming out from them in their repeating that is always in all being. Sometime there is a history of everyone. [6]

The Making of Americans can be considered a "history of everyone who ever lived, is living and will live" because for

Gertrude Stein all persons can be fitted into her characterology. The roots for her characterology are found in *Three Lives*. Melanctha Herbert and Doctor Campbell were unable to love because of an essential discrepancy in the rhythm, the speed of their personalities. The same is true of Julia and Alfred, but in *The Making of Americans* the attempt is made to trace the roots of their discord all the way back—three generations back to European soil. The title "making of Americans" is meant to be taken literally. From the immigration of grandparents to the youngest American in the book, David Hersland, Jr., the aim is to show how the *American* consciousness is forged through the passage of generations. Such an encyclopedic task would be absurd from the start unless we grant some common pool of personality characteristics that exist as a constant from generation to generation. For Miss Stein these are the principles of the independent dependent and dependent independent personalities:

> There are always some then of the many millions of this first kind of them the independent dependent kind of them who never have it in them to have any such attacking in them. . . . Some of them have this in them as gentle pretty young innocence inside them. . . . In the second kind of them the dependent independent kind of them who have too all through their living servant girl nature in them, in this kind of them there are many there are many of them who have a scared timid submission in them with a resisting sometime somewhere in them. . . . [7]

Although the distinction between the two types always remains somehow vague, the following attributes can be classed under the two headings:

Independent Dependent:	*Dependent Independent:*
aggressive	meek
active	withdrawn, passive
independent in judgment	weak in judgment
buoyant, boisterous	shy, quiet
selfishness that can lead to sadism	selfishness that can lead to masochism, martyrdom
reckless	cautious

The left column totaled gives us a summary of Julia Dehning. The right column, of Alfred Hersland. And every single character in the book represents some combinations of elements in either the left- or right-hand columns. It is what is most heavily emphasized in each grouping that finally determines how a character will live his life. It sounds like Ben Jonson's old theory of "humors" revised by a student of Jamesian psychology. James insisted that the personality is a product of what one chooses to pay attention to in the consciousness stream. Gertrude Stein gives the objects in the consciousness field a weight, a quantifiable mass, and identifies the psychic self itself as a mixture of masses. She speaks of each character as having a "bottom nature" or psychological core and writes:

> There are some men and women having in them very much weakness as the bottom in them and *watery anxious feeling* and sometimes nervous anxious feeling in them and sometimes stubborn feeling in them. There are some that have *vague or vacant feeling in them* . . . [my italics]. [8]

Passions are quantified like Elizabethan humors, and what comprises a character is his peculiar balance at any point in time.

So what changes from generation to generation is not the type of psychological phenomenon but the distribution. What changes is not the fact that men perceive reality but what they choose to single out in their perception of reality. So we are dealing with a highly peculiar variety of family history in *The Making of Americans*. We are concerned with the gradualness of a change in viewing the objects of consciousness through a family's history. ⟨. . .⟩

One of the most persistent criticisms raised against *The Making of Americans* is its length. It drove Edmund Wilson to write: "I confess that I have not read the book all through and I do not know whether it is possible to do so," and compelled the critic B. L. Reid to proclaim:

> The complete *Making of Americans* is, I am convinced, unreadable for the normal mind. I have read every word of the shorter version (I think I have—it's hard to make sure), but I am not proud of the accomplishment, and I doubt that a score of people could be found to have done even that. [9]

It must be added that Mr. Reid finds most of Miss Stein "unreadable," and the quotation above was taken from his full-length critical assault on the mass of her creation. Nevertheless Mr. Reid has his point. *The Making of Americans* is not "for the normal mind" if by normalcy we imply conventional. The book assaults our notions of how any book should be organized, let alone stylistically accomplished.

Since there are no hierarchies of reality in Gertrude Stein's universe, not only will all people and objects have the same importance, but all time passages will be of equal significance. Hence absolutely no attempt is made to tell the events of a family history in linear, sequential time (A follows B follows). Time is, rather, seen in terms similar to Henri Bergson's psychological time. When events figure largest in determining character action they seem to exist in mammoth passages of time in spite of the fact that they occur in only a brief passage of ontological time. This tension between actual time and narrative, mental time is illustrated in a memory of Martha Hersland's childhood:

> . . . the one I am now beginning describing is Martha Hersland and this is a little story of the acting in her. . . . this one was a very little one then and she was running and she was in the street and it was a muddy one and she had an umbrella she was dragging and she was crying. "I will throw the umbrella in the mud," she was saying . . . "I will throw the umbrella in the mud," she was saying, . . . "I will throw the umbrella in the mud," and there was a desperate anger in her; "I have throwed the umbrella in the mud" burst from her, she had thrown the umbrella in the mud and that was the end of it for her. [10]

This marked deceleration in narrative time magnifies a seemingly trivial event several fold. Miss Stein wrote that her favorite novel was Richardson's *Clarissa Harlowe*, and it is perhaps from Richardson that Gertrude Stein learned the technique of occasionally decelerating time to emphasize select action. In any event, the actual act of throwing the umbrella that might have taken Martha five seconds at the most to accomplish is described as if hours or years had passed. The reason for decelerated time is twofold. First, each character reveals himself and his consciousness field by a concrete action that externalizes, brings to the forefront the nature of personal consciousness. This umbrella dumping of Martha is her quintessential response to frustration throughout her entire life. The child is the father of man. When several hundred pages later Martha's marriage to Philip Redfern collapses we can see reverberations from the childhood umbrella incident reverberating in the present. But the link is not a direct association through linear time. The novel is not organized to facilitate such recognizable links through time. In fact the contrary is true. The life events of the characters are so unsequentially arranged that hundreds of pages and thousands of paragraphs might intervene between events in any character's life.

Gertrude Stein maintains this temporal organization because this is her belief in how the human mind remembers and tells family histories. The endless digressions, asides, interminable lists of trivial personalities and banal objects and inconsequential events resemble nothing if not life as we live it daily in America. Daily family living for the middle class in America is Miss Stein's focal interest.

> I throw myself open to the public—I take a simple interest in the ordinary kind of families, histories. I believe in simple middle class monotonous tradition. [11]

And if the essence of middle-class living is revealed in monotony and repetition, the essence of American living is disembodiedness, dislocation, temporal discontinuity, unrootedness. ⟨. . .⟩

A second reason for decelerated time is related to Gertrude Stein's theory of human personality. From our reading of *Three Lives*, we singled out three characteristics of character consciousness that concerned Miss Stein: speed, density, and continuity. When Martha declares, "I will throw my umbrella, etc." she reveals something about the speed of her psychological processes. Not merely that she is slow in some simple-minded way (she is not "slow-minded" in the same way that Doctor Campbell is in *Three Lives*), but that passion is slowly, thoroughly emptied out of her in graduated steps. This gradualness of releasing passion is indicated in her speech patterns: "I will . . . I will . . . I have done."

For Gertrude Stein the "bottom nature" of every character is revealed in the nature of their repetitions. There is a direct correspondence between the rhythm of personality and the sentence rhythm. Every violation of conventional syntax, every word inversion, unqualified dangling clause, every repeated phrase or word is an indicant of consciousness. The changes in the field of consciousness from generation to generation are revealed both linguistically and syntactically. Julia Hersland does not speak like Henry Dehning, who in turn does not sound like his grandfather. It is not that the words they use in their daily discourse are different. The difference is not semantic. In *Three Lives* the two characters argue over the meaning of the words "regular living." The concern in *The Making of Americans* is with the organization of words (which for Miss Stein implies the movement of thought). She declares in her lecture "The Gradual Making of *The Making of Americans*":

> I began to get enormously interested in hearing how everybody said the same thing over and over again with infinite variations . . . until finally if you listened with great intensity you could hear it rise and fall and tell all that there was inside them, *not so much by the actual words* they said or the thoughts they had *but the movement* of their thoughts, endlessly the same and endlessly different [my italics]. [12]

Consider for a moment how a sentence says what it says. How does the sentence form carry semantic information?

The stock form in Standard American English is subject-verb-object. Our grammar, our conventional organization specifying how words might be related, insists upon the non-reversibility of the subject-object combination in many circumstances. A man climbs a building. A building can't climb a man and so on. Although we rarely consider grammar apart from daily language usage (i.e., a person lacks culture because he uses *ain't*) we might consider grammar as a system that determines how you report a temporal sequence of events.

If we limit our verbal reports of events to the subject-verb-object pattern alone, we find a discrepancy between our perceptual experiences and our verbal reports. To paraphrase William James: while I am typing a fly has flown through my window and my radiator has steamed over. If I am to keep within the limitations imposed by my grammatical model the only way I can convey my perceptual reality is to string together an infinitely long series of subject-verb-object units (this happened, and this, . . . and this). This is exactly what Gertrude Stein does throughout the first half of *The Making of Americans*. Conjunctions abound. But by the David Hersland section conventional syntax is violated entirely. What occurs between the rather conventionally organized (even if intensely overlong) sentences of the opening pages and the asyntactic patterns of the finale is the exhaustion of the conventionally organized sentence in its struggle to recreate consciousness states. Here is Gertrude Stein's own account of this struggle:

> When I was up against the difficulty of putting down the complete conception that I had of an individual, the complete rhythm of a personality that I had gradually acquired by listening seeing feeling and experience, I was faced by the trouble that I had acquired all this knowledge gradually but when I had it I had it completely at one time . . . And a great deal of *The Making of Americans* was a struggle to do this thing, to make a whole present out of something that took a great deal of time to find out. . . . [13]

Another way of stating the problem is this. The perceptual field is always going on. Because we are constantly receiving new knowledge from our senses every second we are always coming to know what we know. The sentence, the subject-verb-object matrix, cannot convey the gradualness of coming into the knowledge of an event. The possibility of revealing psychological process is limited. True, one can link an indefinite number of sentences together by conjunctions, but Miss Stein describes well what occurs:

> And my sentences grew longer and longer, my imaginary dependent clauses were constantly being dropped out, I struggled with relations between they them and then, I began with a relation between tenses that sometimes almost worked to do it. And I went on and on and then one day after I had written a thousand pages. . . . I just did not go on any more. [14]

A conventionally patterned sentence composed of X number of kernel sentences united by "ands" fails in communicating due to the limited range of human attention spans. By the fourth page of "and . . . and . . . and . . ." one simply forgets the initial point of the sentence. No better proof of this phenomenon can be found than in some of Miss Stein's sentences composed of twenty clauses, at least eighteen dangling. I would be surprised if she remembered to what even the two related clauses referred.

The escape from such a dilemma is simply to abandon conventional sentence patterns. This is exactly what Miss Stein did by the end of *The Making of Americans*.

Her eccentric punctuation, her play with verb tense, her clustering of present, active participles are all devices to achieve the illusion of continual presentness and going-on-ness. Consciousness is always "going on." Each character has it go on at a particular speed and density and continuity. But it is always moving. If writing is to accurately mirror the rhythm and directions of consciousness how can it do so?

In her lecture "Poetry and Grammar" Gertrude Stein writes:

> When I first began writing, I felt that writing should go on, I still do feel that it should go on but when I first began writing I was completely possessed by the necessity that writing should go on and if writing should go on what had colons and semi-colons to do with it, what had commas to do with it, what had periods to do with it what had small letters and capitals to do with it to do with writing going on which was at that time the most profound need I had in connection with writing. [15]

So in opposition to the conventionally patterned sentence Gertrude Stein developed her own personal organizations which are more capable of expressing the consciousness as she saw it. ⟨. . .⟩

The consequences of a nonhierarchical reality are finally revealed in the book's style as well as in its contents. If all people and objects and events are of equal significance, then all the words used to describe the consciousness of this reality are of equal significance. And if all words are of equal significance then the semantic weight of single words matters less than the plastic arrangement of words in terms of the whole flow. As we will examine in future chapters, this radical reconsideration of the role of words leads to Stein's total abandonment of them as discrete semantic carriers.

Suppose that individual words are no longer used to refer to singular realities but all words are subordinated to the flow in order to expose something about the consciousness flow itself. Once this device is put into practice the possibilities for word organization are nearly endless. The rigidity of word position in the English language is a product of our insistence that language communicate with optimum clarity semantically. We call *celery* a noun, which means that it can be positioned as object in the sentence: Mary eats celery. This positional qualification works quite effectively given the world of our social conventions. Certainly if I parroted Miss Stein and said to a friend: Celery her. Mary her celery. Her Mary celery! my academic career might end in institutional confinement.

But a book such as *The Making of Americans* compels us to question the efficacy of our conventional word organization in describing a non-Aristotelian, psychological, process-centered universe. If you grant Miss Stein's assumptions about personality and consciousness, her stylistic experimentation can be seen as an outgrowth of a writer's attempt to capture life by language, to capture the process of living by recreating English to make it a language more process-oriented.

I think that it is in the paintings of Cézanne that the closest analogy to what Gertrude Stein was attempting in literature can be found. What the French phenomenalist philosopher Merleau-Ponty says about Cézanne applies equally well to Gertrude Stein:

> His painting might seem a paradox: a quest for reality without the loss of sensation, without any other guide than nature in its immediacy, without delineating the contours, without framing the color by the drawing, without composing the perspective or the picture itself. This is what Bernard calls Cézanne's

suicide: to aim at reality and forbid oneself the means of attaining it. [16]

Substitute the word "consciousness" for "nature," "traditional novel form" for "contours," and "without subordinating consciousness flow to traditional sentence patterning" for "without framing the color by the drawing," and you have a sense of Gertrude Stein's achievement in *The Making of Americans*. I do not share the opinion that Cézanne's technique causes his artistic "suicide" anymore than I share Mr. Reid's opinion that *The Making of Americans* is "unreadable." I think both Cézanne and Stein compel us to drop our conventional assumptions regarding what a painting or novel is. As Cézanne paintings are meta-painting, critiques on painting itself (i.e., what is the purpose of applying color on a white canvas?) so Gertrude Stein's *The Making of Americans* is a meta-novel that makes us question not only the shape of the novel form itself but the nature of the medium, the linguistic "paint" that the writer applies to create a world.

Notes

1. Gertrude Stein, *The Making of Americans* (New York: Something Else Press, 1967), p. 3.
2. Gertrude Stein, *Lectures in America* (Boston: Beacon Press, 1959), p. 140.
3. *The Making of Americans*, p. 7.
4. Ibid., p. 303.
5. Gertrude Stein, *Selected Writings*, ed. Carl Van Vechten (New York: Random House, 1946), pp. 513, 518.
6. *The Making of Americans*, p. 190.
7. Ibid., p. 177.
8. Ibid., p. 456.
9. Michael Hoffman, *The Development of Abstractionism in the Writings of Gertrude Stein* (Philadelphia: University of Pennsylvania Press, 1965), p. 99.
10. *The Making of Americans*, p. 388.
11. Ibid., p. 34.
12. *Lectures in America*, p. 138.
13. Ibid., p. 147.
14. Ibid., p. 193.
15. Ibid., p. 217.
16. Maurice Marleau-Ponty, "Cézanne's Doubt," *Art and Literature*, 23, pp. 106–14.

LYNN Z. BLOOM
From "Gertrude Is Alice Is Everybody: Innovation and Point of View in Gertrude Stein's Autobiographies"

Twentieth Century Literature, Spring 1978, pp. 81–93

Gertrude Stein's major innovations as an autobiographer pertain to the creation of the alleged autobiography of another person to tell the story of the author's own life. Related to this are her variations on three major uses of point of view, to perform egotistical, interpretive, and objective functions within the autobiography.

Let us consider the autobiographical persona first.

> About six weeks ago Gertrude Stein said, it does not look to me as if you [Alice B. Toklas] were ever going to write that autobiography. You know what I am going to do. I am going to write it for you. I am going to write it as simply as Defoe did the autobiography of Robinson Crusoe. And she has and this is it. [1]

As an epilogue for *The Autobiography of Alice B. Toklas*, this passage, which illustrates a number of Gertrude Stein's innovations as an autobiographer, is *fitting* but *misleading*. Defoe, of course, created a fictitious character, Robinson Crusoe. Then, through Crusoe's alleged words, Defoe created and manipulated situations, language, and interpretations to suit his own authorial aims. For the purposes of the first volume of Gertrude Stein's own autobiography, *The Autobiography of Alice B. Toklas*, Alice B. Toklas is no more of an independently functioning person than is Robinson Crusoe.

This is true even though, unlike Robinson Crusoe, Alice Toklas not only read but typed the manuscript and provided occasional corrections, interpretations, and cancellations.[2] Among the most significant of her editings was her refusal to be made to proclaim enthusiasm for *The Making of Americans*: "She cancelled the italicized phrases in the following . . . : 'Mildred was very fond of Gertrude Stein and took a deep interest in the book's ending *and so did I*. It was over a thousand pages long and I was typewriting it *and I enjoyed every minute of it*.'"[3] Yet, to a large extent, Alice B. Toklas functions throughout the *Autobiography*, if not as the ventriloquist's dummy, then certainly as the ventriloquist's smart-ie, but as the ventriloquist's versatile tool nevertheless, skillfully performing a myriad of functions essential to the work's success.

Narration of one's own autobiography through the persona of the individual about whom the biography was supposedly written is, to the best of my knowledge of autobiographies in English, completely innovative and utterly unique. By the very nature of its form, autobiography-by-*Doppelgänger* veritably precludes repetition or imitation. The wit intrinsic in the initial endeavor becomes a joke progressively more stale with each repetition, guaranteed to annoy the readers of successive works, even though they are in the joke because they are cozily in league with the author, who has made the *real* subject of the autobiography unmistakable from the third page on.[4] Imagine the third volume of Stein's autobiography, *Wars I Have Seen*, rewritten as *Wars Alice B. Toklas Has Seen*! Once is genius; twice is gimmickry; thrice is boredom. The form itself is almost self-destructing.

Let us see why this is so, for the form has a number of advantages both literary and autobiographical which should surely have tempted imitators if the imitations were feasible.

In conventional autobiographies the form is usually quite commonplace—either a chronological or a topical presentation of its author's life. In these numerous instances, the reader's familiarity with the form breeds indifference or oblivion to it. As a result, he is much more likely to concentrate on the content and perhaps on the style.

Such cannot be the case when the form is so compellingly unique. It obliges attention, which is to Stein's advantage, for her skill and innovative craftsmanship warrant notice. The reader wonders what Gertrude will have Alice will have Gertrude say or do next; what Alice will reply; how Gertrude will react in this dialogue spoken by a monologist.

This unique form provides a persona—real or not (even though Toklas is, of course, a real person independent of the *Autobiography*)—to express the real Gertrude Stein's point of view. It allows the author much greater latitude of expression than she might have had if she'd been speaking in the first person, for she has two people speaking for one. Sutherland observes that Stein used

> as a sounding board her companion. . . . It has been said that the writing takes on very much Miss Toklas' conversational style, and while this is true the style is

still a variant of Miss Stein's conversational style, for she had about the same way with an anecdote or a sly observation in talking as Miss Toklas has. . . . it is part of the miracle of this little scheme of objectification that she could by way of imitating Miss Toklas put in writing something of her own beautiful conversation. So that, aside from making a real present of her past, she re-created a figure of herself, established an identity, a twin. . . .[5]

This ventriloquistic persona performs a number of functions which may be grouped into three major categories with several subtle variations on each: the egotistical, the interpretive, and the objective. These overlap and blend to produce a work far more interesting than one without such variety would be. One of the most important aspects of the *egotistical function* is to *disarm* or *distract* the reader from the egotism inherent in conventional autobiography. By consistently employing "Gertrude Stein" or "Miss Stein" when referring to the *Autobiography*'s real subject, and by using third-person pronouns less often than expected, *The Autobiography of Alice B. Toklas* escapes the egotism of the consistent first-person usage that is otherwise inevitable in conventional autobiography. This is an extraordinarily clever way to eliminate a plethora of *I*'s; "I" here refers to Alice B. Toklas and her persona uses it sparingly.

The forms of these references to Gertrude Stein serve an *honorific function* as well, for they give her dignity and authority that the plain, familiar "Gertrude" or the flippant "Gerty" would not sustain. Stein, through Toklas, thereby flouts the convention that has persisted in women's biographies throughout the centuries, of addressing women subjects by their first names, regardless of their age, rank, or social status.[6]

Yet paradoxically, removal of the first-person pronoun from the real subject of the autobiography permits Stein to be even more conspicuously egotistical than she might appear if she used the first person consistently. By putting references to herself in the third person instead of the first, Gertrude Stein as autobiographer gives herself the advantage of allowing Alice B. Toklas' persona to perform the *egotistical function* of referring to Gertrude Stein by her proper name many more times than are necessary for either clarity, emphasis, or stylistic grace. Characteristically, Stein has Toklas say:

> But to come back to Roché at Kathleen Bruce's studio. They all talked about one thing and another and Gertrude Stein happened to mention that they had just bought a picture from Sagot by a young spaniard named Picasso. Good good excellent, said Roché, he is a very interesting young fellow, I know him. Oh do you, said *Gertrude Stein*, well enough to take somebody to see him. Why certainly, said Roché. Very well, said *Gertrude Stein*, my brother I know is very anxious to make his acquaintance. And there and then the appointment was made and shortly after Roché and *Gertrude Stein*'s brother went to see Picasso.
>
> It was only a very short time after this that Picasso began the portrait of *Gertrude Stein*, now so widely known. . . . (p. 55)[7]

In all the italicized portions "she" or "her" could be substituted with no loss of meaning, but with considerably less emphasis on the name of the autobiographer. Thus the *self-advertising function* of the first person is omnipresent, but cleverly, with the appearance of being eliminated in favor of the third-person reference. Moreover, once Gertrude has been introduced (on p. 5), the other members of the Stein family are not mentioned anywhere in the autobiography by name, but only in their relation to the writer—"Gertrude Stein's older brother and his wife" (p. 5), "Gertrude Stein's mother" (p. 89). Thus her prominence is enhanced both within her family circle and throughout the autobiography.

Gertrude Stein's prominence within her own circle is augmented by a corollary manifestation of this technique, *the enhancement function of the selective inclusion of proper names*, not invented by Stein but certainly refined by her. When discussing habitués of her salon, or people to whom she gave literary advice or artistic encouragement, or other associates, Stein refers to the famous, the talented, and the notorious by name, and generally without identifying explanations. But except for a few close personal friends, she leaves anonymous most of the more innocuous persons. Since all are seen in relation to Gertrude Stein, rather than in relation to the autobiography's ostensible subject, and since Stein's name is, naturally, mentioned more frequently than the others, this technique has the repeated effect of making Gertrude Stein seem to be the focus of a coterie of luminaries. For the purposes of Stein's autobiographical books the relationships of various celebrities to one another are subordinate, however important they may actually have been, but perhaps this is the inevitable consequence of any autobiography.

The innovative device of a ventriloquizing persona of Alice B. Toklas in the *Autobiography* also performs a number of functions related to *interpreting* Gertrude Stein. A common aspect of this function is that of *reporter*. The persona of Alice can quote Gertrude Stein secondhand or refer (and defer) to Stein's opinions. This allows Stein-as-autobiographer much greater freedom and latitude of expression, with greater literary tact than she might have had if she had been speaking in the first person. For instance, Alice-as-reporter observes, "The young often when they have learnt all they can learn accuse her [Gertrude Stein] of an inordinate pride" (p. 94), and then quotes Stein indirectly:

> "She says yes of course. She realizes that in english literature in her time she is the only one. She has always known it and now she says it.
> She understands very well the basis of creation and therefore her advice and criticism is invaluable to all her friends. (p. 94)

This sort of self-congratulation, even if true, would appear insufferably egotistical if spoken directly by a first-person autobiographer, and as such would be likely to antagonize most readers, if it would not alienate them completely. So Stein's strategy is sound. *Alice-as-intermediary* softens the direct thrust, blunts the egotism, evades the hubris, and communicates her own appreciation of the rightness of Stein's opinion of herself. Judging from Toklas' own autobiography, *What Is Remembered*,[8] and from the critics referred to in this essay, this appreciation represents Alice B. Toklas' genuine attitude in real life and is not a posture Stein has forced her into for autobiographical purposes. *Alice-as-reinforcer* then supplements her own implied or stated judgments with the opinions of recognized masters, whose own confidence in Stein's judgments corroborates Toklas' views and validates those of Stein herself.

For example, immediately following "therefore her [Stein's] advice and criticism is invaluable to all her friends," *Alice-as-reinforcing-reporter* explains,

> How often have I heard Picasso say to her when she has said something about a picture of his and then

illustrated by something she was trying to do, racontez-moi cela. In other words tell me about it. These two even to-day have long solitary conversations. They sit in two little low chairs up in his apartment studio, knee to knee and Picasso says, expliquez-moi cela. And they explain to each other. They talk about everything, about pictures, about dogs, about death, about unhappiness. (p. 95)

Thus through such solidly specific details, the "little low chairs" in Picasso's studio, the intimate conversation about "everything"—dogs, death, unhappiness—Toklas' unobtrusive view (even though created or re-created by Stein) leavens Stein's manifest egotism and subtly aligns the reader with Toklas' own pleasant and pleasured perspective.

On other occasions, though less frequently, Alice functions more overtly as an *interpreter*: "Gertrude Stein was in those days a little bitter, all her unpublished manuscripts, and no hope of publication or serious recognition" (p. 241). Commonly, Alice's alleged interpretations are mingled more directly with Gertrude's. For instance, Alice begins: "Now as for herself she [Gertrude Stein] was not efficient, she was good humoured, she was democratic, one person was as good as another, and she knew what she wanted done." Then Gertrude, quoted by Alice, continues, "If you are like that she says, anybody will do anything for you. The important thing, she insists, is that you must have deep down as the deepest thing in you a sense of equality" (p. 215). Thus Stein the innovator transforms the monologue form of conventional autobiography into a pseudo-dialogue between Alice B. Toklas as pseudo-author and Gertrude Stein, real though covert author and real autobiographical subject. Again, because Alice illustrates her interpretations with such intimate, specific knowledge of her subject, the reader is likely to accept the perspective of Alice-as-interpreter as valid, even though he may suspect Gertrude of breathing rather heavily down Alice's neck at times.

Yet Alice's persona appears more independent-minded than the conventional yes-women. She occasionally interjects her own opinions: "I always say you cannot tell what a picture really is or what an object really is until you dust it every day and you cannot tell what a book is until you type it or proof-read it" (pp. 138–39). Despite Alice's self-assertiveness, I have searched the *Autobiography* in vain for instances where Alice-as-narrator contradicts Gertrude Stein or provides a corrective of her views, except in a jesting manner which is apparently not meant to be taken seriously, as in: "Gertrude Stein was born in Allegheny, Pennsylvania. As I am an ardent californian and as she spent her youth there I have often begged her to be born in California but she has always remained firmly born in Allegheny, Pennsylvania" (p. 85).

So, whether or not the correspondence of opinions is explicitly stated, the views of Alice-as-narrator, whether reporter, intermediary, reinforcer, or interpreter, would seem to be those of Gertrude Stein. But so insinuatingly does Alice manifest her point of view that it is almost impossible to react to Stein on terms other than those imputed to and imposed by the created Alice. So Stein, both through selecting and revealing the real Alice's real views and through creating the persona of Alice-as-narrator-of-Stein's autobiography, remains fully in control not only of her material but of her readers' reactions as well.

In imposing such control, Stein also imposes *objectivity*, the third major function of her autobiographical point of view. Gertrude Stein as autobiographer, of course, has absolute control not only over the literary image and personality of

Alice B. Toklas but over the persona and personality of herself that she chooses to present to the readers. This in itself, being germane to autobiography as a genre, is not particularly innovative, but Stein's apparent objectivity in that presentation is highly unusual and innovative in autobiography.

It is hard for the autobiographer to be objective in conventional autobiography, when the self is talking directly about the self. But Stein-the-writer has created both the ventriloquist, Alice Toklas, and Stein-the-puppet, who actually though subtly controls the ventriloquist. The continuous presence of two personages in action and interaction enables Stein to *appear* to present Gertrude Stein from the *outside*, rather than from the autobiographer's almost inevitable *inside*, perspective, for the reader sees her as she is allegedly seen by Toklas. "Sentences not only words but sentences and always sentences have been Gertrude Stein's life long passion" (p. 50) is much more external, impersonal than the conventional alternative, "I have always loved long sentences passionately." Likewise, secondhand fury is somewhat milder than firsthand wrath in such observations as: "Gertrude Stein used to get furious when the english all talked about german organisation. She used to insist that the germans had no organisation, they had method but no organisation" (pp. 187–88). As a result, Stein appears as solid and as foursquare as Jo Davidson's seated, washerwomanlike sculpture of her, and, like the sculpture, a human entity visible essentially from the outside.

That this objectivity is Stein's contrivance and not merely a recreation of Toklas' actual mode of expression is evident throughout Toklas' own autobiography. In *What Is Remembered* Toklas' own comments about Stein, though understated, are much more evocative than Stein's own, as is evident in Toklas' account of their first meeting.

> In the room were Mr. and Mrs. Stein and Gertrude Stein. It was Gertrude Stein who held my complete attention, as she did for all the many years I knew her until her death, and all these empty ones since then. She was a golden brown presence, burned by the Tuscan sun and with a golden glint in her warm brown hair. She was dressed in a warm brown corduroy suit. She wore a large round coral brooch and when she talked, very little, or laughed, a good deal, I thought her voice came from this brooch. It was unlike anyone else's voice—deep, full, velvety like a great contralto's, like two voices. She was large and heavy with delicate small hands and a beautifully modeled and unique head. [9]

Toklas' passage emanates the warmth she sees in Stein and feels for her—warm sights, warm sounds, the warm and dignifiedly uninhibited, moving reactions of an exposed personality who is not afraid to acknowledge the fullness of life with a beloved friend and the emptiness of life without her. In her own autobiography Toklas discloses, among other selves, a private, vulnerable self of the sort which Stein-as-autobiographer rarely reveals.

The advantages of Stein's autobiographical objectivity are numerous, despite some loss of warmth. Stein-as-autobiographer keeps control of her material—content, self-image(s), tone, mood—at all times, rather than self-indulgently letting it control her. Thus she is, and can be, nonsentimental, and devoid of maudlinity, self-pity, self-flagellation, false modesty, hypocrisy, and other demeaning, self-denigrating attitudes and images of self.

Her objectivity permits her to treat even the presumably painful with a certain detachment:

> Life in California came to its end when Gertrude Stein was about seventeen years old. The last few years had been lonesome ones and had been passed in an agony of adolescence. After the death of first her mother and then her father she . . . came to Baltimore and stayed with her mother's people. There she began to lose her lonesomeness. (p. 92).

Stein's dispassion avoids the self-pity that a conventional biographical point of view on unpleasant personal matters might encourage. And, for better or worse, it permits the reader to respond to the presentation of personal pain with an objectivity equal to the presenter's.

Stein's objectivity also avoids the confessional mode common to autobiography. She doesn't tell anything she doesn't want to, and because of Toklas as the intermediary persona, the reader doesn't *expect* Stein to be more revealing than she is. She leaves finances, personal conflicts (such as her estrangement from her brother Leo), and griefs vague, and never discusses her own sexuality, spinsterhood, or loves—except for dogs. The closest she comes to verging on the intimately sexual is a reference to a short first novel she had written during a gloomy, postadolescent period and then forgotten about until she accidentally discovered the manuscript some years later: "She was very bashful and hesitant about it, did not really want to read it. Louis Bromfield was at the house that evening and she handed him the manuscript and said to him, you read it" (p. 104). Yet she never reveals the novel's title or content, and does not discuss it again. Clarification of this enigma took nearly forty years, when Richard Bridgman, in *Gertrude Stein in Pieces*, identified the work as "Things as They Are," a tale written in 1903 of "three young women in passionate stalemate . . . based upon Gertrude Stein's frustrated romance with May Bookstaver, a Baltimore friend." [10]

Of course, one can raise the question of why Stein made even so oblique an allusion to a painful past. Evidently the *Autobiography* is full of numerous allusions meaningful to Stein and her immediate circle but inaccessible to the general public. [11] This may be yet another example of her "split-level" autobiographical technique of talking to two audiences, private and public, on two levels.

At other times Stein remains objective on personal matters by generalizing. She does not talk specifically about stresses with her own father, but instead, in *Everybody's Autobiography*, remarks of fathers in general: "Fathers are depressing. . . . Mothers may not be cheering but they are not as depressing as fathers." [12] She then shifts to the personal—not about her own father, but rather, remarking on Bennett Cerf and Thornton Wilder in father roles. After that she gives the generalities a political bite:

> There is too much fathering going on just now and there is no doubt about it fathers are depressing. Everybody nowadays is a father, there is father Mussolini and father Hitler and father Roosevelt and father Stalin and father Lewis and father Blum and father Franco is just commencing now and there are ever so many more ready to be one. [13]

Then Stein generalizes again: "Fathers are depressing." [14]

Stein's prevailing detachment and nonsentimentality permit her to treat herself and her milieu with considerable humor. Her somewhat self-indulgent laughter sets the tone for the readers' reaction as well. She can laugh at herself, as she does in recounting the anecdote when her servant drove Stein to profanity by pretending to have broken the writer's treasured black Renaissance plate—and thereby cured her hiccups, which was the maid's intention (pp. 106–07). Stein can also engage the reader in the laughter of rightness vindicated. She tells of a visit from the "very nice american young" (p. 83) vanity publisher's emissary concerning *Three Lives*, who said,

> slightly hesitant, the director of the Grafton Press is under the impression that perhaps your knowledge of English. [Here Stein lets the reader supply the devastating omission.] But I am an american, said Gertrude Stein indignantly. Yes yes I understand that perfectly now, he said, but perhaps you have not had much experience in writing. I suppose, said she laughing [as Stein's mood brightens, so does the reader's], you were under the impression that I was imperfectly educated. He blushed [we laugh], why no, he said, but you might not have had much experience in writing. (p. 84)

As both the humor and the tension build, Stein delivers her good-natured *coup de grâce*:

> Oh yes, she said, oh yes. Well it's alright. I will write to the director and you might as well tell him also that everything that is written in the manuscript is written with the intention of its being so written and all he has to do is print it and I will take the responsibility. The young man bowed himself out. (p. 84)

We appreciate the young man's polite discomfiture, but more particularly we appreciate Stein's astute awareness and defense of her talent. Thus Stein creates a prevailing mood of good humor and good-naturedness which enhances the *Autobiography's* zest and charm.

Moreover, by letting the reader in on the joke of the real authorship of the *Autobiography* right from the start, instead of publishing it anonymously or pseudonymously, Stein's strategy is to take the reader into league with her. Once she has him on her side as a participant in her joke, it's hard to turn against the perpetrator of it. Thus the reader is more inclined to accept Stein's image of herself (as seen by Toklas and by herself) as true than he might if he had the judgment of a bona fide intermediary biographer to question. Again Stein, through Toklas, controls the reader as well as her material.

If the subject's personality or psyche were suppressed, flattened, distorted, or falsified, some of the advantages of autobiography-by-indirection would be lost. But none of these occur in *The Autobiography of Alice B. Toklas*, in which both Gertrude Stein and Alice B. Toklas are very much alive and very well. All in all, the advantages of this innovative form are manifold, and as practiced by Stein it has no conspicuous disadvantages—except unrepeatability.

Another innovative aspect of *The Autobiography of Alice B. Toklas* is that, despite its intense focus on Gertrude Stein, a biographical portrait of the alleged autobiographical subject does emerge quite clearly. The work is a double portrait, of Stein and of Toklas. The *Autobiography* is further unusual in that Stein deliberately wrote it to emulate the oral speech mannerisms of another person—in choice of words, level of language, syntax, speech rhythms—rather than precisely her own, though the two are not incompatible.[15] Indeed, she succeeded very well, judging from Toklas' own style in *What Is Remembered* (see above), even allowing for the possibility that in the latter volume Toklas could have imitated Stein's imitation of herself. Stein always treats Toklas-as-narrator the way she evidently treated Toklas-as-intimate-lifelong-friend, with the respect that maintains Toklas' integrity and never makes her feeble or foolish, never jokes at Toklas' expense (unlike Boswell's sometimes silly sycophancy, with which

Toklas is occasionally wrongly compared). Thus Alice, like her biographical creator, is a vivid, witty, personable, tartly gracious presence in her own pseudo-autobiography, an enduring tribute to a friend and to a friendship, among other things.

Notes

1. Gertrude Stein, *The Autobiography of Alice B. Toklas* (New York: Harcourt, Brace, 1933), p. 310. All future references to this work appear in the text.
2. Richard Bridgman, *Gertrude Stein in Pieces* (New York: Oxford Univ. Press, 1970), pp. 212–13. After exploring the question of whether Toklas may have composed a preliminary autobiography, which might have influenced the *Autobiography's* striking departure from Stein's customary style, Bridgman states that "[t]he physical evidence indicates that *The Autobiography of Alice B. Toklas* was written by Gertrude Stein alone, with few hesitations or changes" (p. 212).
3. Ibid., pp. 212–13.
4. Donald Sutherland disagrees, claiming that "[t]he scheme of the second autobiography, *Everybody's Autobiography*, is an extension of the first. Having created her twin or reflection in the first autobiography and committed it to the public, she had to watch this second 'Gertrude Stein' get entirely away from her, as it was elaborated upon by the enormous publicity it received during her tour of America in 1934–35. So that now she could discover her past and present as reflected by 'everybody' just as before they had been reflected by Miss Toklas." *Gertrude Stein: A Biography of Her Work* (New Haven: Yale Univ. Press, 1951), p. 153. Since even in this view "everybody" speaks in the first person of Gertrude Stein herself in these later autobiographical works, I maintain that in them the advantages of the ventriloquized form of *The Autobiography of Alice B. Toklas* are absent (passim but see especially pp. 16–17).
5. Sutherland, pp. 148–49.
6. Men in biographies are much more often addressed by their last names and titles. A random sample reveals that in biographies of men, last names outnumber first four to one; in biographies of women, first names outnumber last nine to one. The exceptions are either feminist biographies or works written prior to the twentieth century, when modes of address were more formal anyway. Interestingly, biographies of women which call their subjects by their first names also tend to call the men in those works by their first names; the reverse is not often the case.
7. Emphasis mine.
8. Alice B. Toklas, *What Is Remembered* (New York: Holt, Rinehart and Winston, 1963).
9. Ibid., p. 23.
10. Bridgman, p. 40. In *Gertrude Stein: Her Life and Work* (New York: Harper, 1957), Elizabeth Sprigge treats the understated relationship in *Things as They Are* more delicately and ambiguously, claiming that Adele (Gertrude Stein's alias) was "using Helen as a subject for psychological experiment" and concludes, "Thus, through the pages of *Things as They Are* one watches Gertrude Stein developing from a raw girl to a mature young woman, and realizes that she had to break away from what she called 'the general American sisterhood'" (p. 49). Two years later John Malcolm Brinnin is equally discreet, referring only to "Gertrude Stein's ability to keep the forbidden subject muted" concerning "emotions . . . of a nature rarely hinted at in the literature of the time." *The Third Rose: Gertrude Stein and Her World* (Boston: Little, Brown, 1959), p. 46.
11. See Bridgman, p. 227.
12. Gertrude Stein, *Everybody's Autobiography* (New York: Random House, 1937), pp. 132–33.
13. Ibid., p. 133.
14. Ibid.
15. Sutherland, p. 148, quoting Carl Van Vechten, introduction to *Selected Writings* (New York: Random House, 1946), pp. xii–xiii.

JAMES E. BRESLIN
From "Gertrude Stein and
the Problems of Autobiography"
Georgia Review, Winter 1979, pp. 901–11

In many ways the autobiographical act is one at odds with, even a betrayal of, Gertrude Stein's aesthetic principles. Her essay "What Are Master-pieces and Why Are There So Few of Them" offers a concise statement of those principles: "The minute your memory functions while you are doing anything it may be very popular but actually it is dull," Stein warns; her desire to live and write in a continuous present thus turns her against the necessarily retrospective act of autobiography.[1] But Stein's opposition to the conventions of her genre runs even deeper than this, because her commitment to a continuous present forces her to reject the notion of identity altogether. "Identity is recognition," she writes: "I am I because my little dog knows me" (pp. 146–47). Identity, an artificial construction based on the perception of certain fixed traits that allow my little dog or anyone else to imagine that they know me, stresses repetition, which is, according to Stein, antithetical to creativity. Identity "destroys creation" (p. 147)—as does memory; both, carrying the past over into the present and structuring by repetition, are ways we have of familiarizing the strangeness, the mysterious being, of others. Masterpieces de-familiarize; they derive from "knowing that there is no identity and producing while identity is not" (p. 151). In part Stein is warning against self-imitation, and she quotes Picasso as saying that he is willing to be influenced by anyone but himself; but she is also stressing that to live in a continuous present, to *be* rather than to *repeat*, one must constantly break down identity. But can there be an *auto*-biography in which "there is no identity"? Or, to put the question somewhat differently: autobiographies are customarily *identified* as acts of *self*-representation, but Stein is challenged to refashion the form to show that she eludes or transcends the category of self or identity.

At the same time her belief in a continuous present sets Stein against the kind of narrative that we are accustomed (again) to find in auto-*bio*-graphy. "What is the use of being a boy if you are going to grow up to be a man?" she asks in "What Are Master-pieces" (p. 150). Like remembering and identifying, narrating—telling, say, the story of a girl becoming a woman—such narrating represents a linear sequence of time, not an ongoing present. In addition, remembering, identifying, and narrating all view things in relation to other things (e.g., girl in relation to woman), instead of viewing a thing as what Stein calls an "entity" (p. 149)—a thing existent in and for itself. A masterpiece, transcending linear time and recognizable identity, is itself an "entity," not, as Eliot had said, a revision of the literary tradition but an absolute act of creation. The fact that the early works of Cubism derive from such absolute acts of creation explains why, as we are told in *The Autobiography*, they are so strange, almost physically painful to look at—and yet must be looked at intently: the viewer must struggle to get beyond mere recognition, the comfortably familiar. But autobiographies are hardly absolute acts of creation; they are historical, referring to persons and events that clearly existed out there, in reality, prior to their representation in language. Finally, Stein holds that any concession to—or even consciousness of—an audience undermines creativity; as soon as a writer begins to think of him/herself in relation to an audience, he or she "writes what

the other person is to hear and so entity does not exist there are two present instead of one and so once again creation breaks down" (p. 148). But if we now find it problematic to think of even a lyric poem as autotelic, how can we imagine an autotelic autobiography? Can Stein create an autobiography without identity, memory, linear time? And if she did, could we bear to read it? In some ways *Everybody's Autobiography*, dealing with "what is happening" instead of what had happened, comes closer to these aims; but what makes *The Autobiography of Alice B. Toklas* so interesting is that it admits the conventions of memory, identity, chronological time—in order to fight against and ultimately to transcend their deadening effects.

When she was asked to write her autobiography, Stein replied, "Not possibly,"[2] and it is easier to imagine her writing an essay called "What Are Autobiographies and Why Are None of Them Masterpieces" than it is to imagine her writing her own autobiography. Of course, she did not write her own autobiography; she wrote *The Autobiography of Alice B. Toklas*. Or did she? Some writers have speculated that Alice B. Toklas wrote her own autobiography or at least substantial parts of it.[3] But perhaps the most important point about this debate is that it seems to have been generated not just by an extraliterary curiosity about the book's composition, but by an actual literary effect the book has on its readers—namely, the effect of raising questions about just whose book it is.

I will return to this issue; for the moment, assuming (as I have been) Stein to be the book's author, I want to suggest how she took up the formal challenge of autobiography by recalling a young man named Andrew Green, who appears briefly in the third chapter of *The Autobiography*. Andrew Green "hated everything modern." Once while staying at 27 rue de Fleurus for a month he covered "all the pictures with cashmere shawls"; he "could not bear" to look at the strange, frightening paintings. Significantly, "he had a prodigious *memory* and could recite all of Milton's *Paradise Lost* by heart" (my emphasis). "He adored as he said a simple centre and a continuous design." Green *has* an identity, so much so that his character can be fixed in a single, brief paragraph. Gertrude Stein does not have an identity; in attempting to represent her "self" she created in *The Autobiography of Alice B. Toklas* a book with an elusive center and a discontinuous design.

Even the title page of the current Vintage edition—*The Autobiography of Alice B. Toklas* BY Gertrude Stein—is enough to suggest that the center of the ensuing text may be difficult to locate. The original Harcourt edition made at the same point in a more subtle way: both the cover and the title page print only a title—*The Autobiography of Alice B. Toklas*—but no author's name is given. The frontispiece (facing the title page), however, is a Man Ray photograph which shows Stein in the right foreground, seated at a table, but with her back to the camera and in dark shadow; Alice B. Toklas stands in the left background, but she stands in light and framed by a doorway. The photograph, with its obscure foreground and distinct background, has no clear primary subject—like the book that follows; the seated Stein, however, is writing, and the possibility is raised that *she* may be the author of the book, an uncertainty not resolved for the reader of this edition until its final page—when "Toklas" tells us that Stein has in fact written *The Autobiography*. Moreover, the book's style blends the domestic particularity, whimsical humor, and ironic precision of Toklas with some of the leading features of Stein's writing—e.g., stylized repetition, digression, a language that continually points up its own artifice. The reader is not certain who it is he is listening to; nor is he meant to be. Richard

Bridgman has shown that "Stanzas in Meditation," written at the same time as *The Autobiography*, is at least partly about writing *The Autobiography*, and the poem strongly suggests that our uncertainties were an intended effect: "This is her autobiography one of two / But which it is no one . . . can know."[4]

But most readers are more like Andrew Green than Gertrude Stein; they don't like to dwell in uncertainties, and so most discussions of *The Autobiography* begin by assuming the character of Stein to be its easily identifiable center, and they proceed to discuss this character as if it were not mediated for the reader by a perspective that is to *some* degree external to it. Yet, even if we proceed along these lines, the character of Stein turns out to be an elusive and enigmatic "center." Stein, Toklas tells us, sought in her writing to give "the inside as seen from the outside" (p. 156); that is one reason she creates herself through the external perspective of Toklas. What she means by "the inside" can be clarified through *The Autobiography*'s account of Picasso's famous portrait of Stein; it was with this painting, we are told, that Picasso "passed from the Harlequin, the *charming* early italian period to the *intensive struggle* which was to end in cubism" (p. 54; my emphasis). Stein emphasizes the "intensive struggle" that went into the painting of the portrait itself. During the winter of 1907 Stein patiently posed for Picasso some eighty or ninety times, but then he abruptly "painted out the whole head." "I can't see you any longer when I look, he said irritably" (p. 53). At this point both Stein and Picasso left Paris for the summer, but the day he returned "Picasso sat down and out of his head painted the head in without having seen Gertrude Stein again." In the enigmatic sentence, "I can't see you any longer when I look," what is the referent of "you"? On the one hand, it is not the external, literal Stein, recognizable to her little dog or a realistic novelist. That is why, when Stein later cuts her hair short, Picasso, at first disturbed, can conclude that "all the same it is all there." He was not striving for a realistic mimesis, as Stein stresses in her account of Picasso's difficulties with what turned out to be the least realistic feature of the portrait, the face. On the other hand, Picasso was not trying to evoke the inner, subconscious depths of Stein, of the sort that might fascinate a psychological novelist; in fact, Toklas later claims that Stein had no subconscious (p. 79).

In the painting itself Stein's body is solid, massive, weighty, sculptured; the simple, severe lines of the eyebrows, nose and mouth, the slightly uneven eyes create a stylized, mask-like face. She inhabits an abstract space, her eyes conveying an almost fierce attentiveness, but she is calm, at rest, even serene. Picasso's Stein seems a regal, perhaps deific, figure, but the earth colors of her dress, blending with the tan background, modify the austerity of the face and the monumentality of the body to create warmth and to humanize Stein. The portrait is thus an instance of what Stein herself called "elemental abstraction" (p. 64); the "you" painted by Picasso is, therefore, not a personality, a recognizable identity, but an entity—Stein's being, awesome, serene, strange, mysterious yet human. Like Picasso's portrait, *The Autobiography* gives the inside by way of the outside; it plays down psychology and sticks to the surface, recording externals (objects, acts, dialogues) in a way that clearly manifests deliberate and idiosyncratic acts of selection and stylization. Such admitted artifice annoys many readers who, with simpler models of self and autobiography, demand a fuller intimacy and deeper psychology of their autobiographers. But Stein's stylization of the surface reveals the "you" that Picasso, having looked so long and intently, could no longer see when he

looked. *The Autobiography*, in short, gives us Gertrude Stein being.

⟨. . .⟩ Gertrude Stein can rest her head against a rock and stare at the Italian noonday sun; but like a masterpiece or the sun, Stein herself is hard to look at directly—another reason for the mediation of Toklas—and even Toklas approaches her, too, very slowly. Stein is first mentioned on page 5 where Toklas reports of their first meeting only that "I was impressed by the coral brooch she wore and her voice," and that "a bell within me rang" certifying that Stein was a genius. The reader expects the first meeting between the two women to be related with ample circumstantial and emotional detail; instead, only two rather oddly selected details are given, then a long leap is made to a perception of Stein's genius, though the playful tone makes it hard for us to be sure exactly how seriously we are to take this claim. The scene is deliberately simplified; circumstantial and psychological detail are eliminated—to foreground the powerful, strange presence of Stein and the intuitive powers of Toklas.

Stein is next glimpsed obliquely, through objects associated with her—again, as if her presence were too powerful to be looked at directly. Toklas remembers from her first visit to the atelier "a large table on which were horseshoe nails and pebbles and little pipe cigarette holders" which she later found "to be accumulations from the pockets of Picasso and Gertrude Stein" (p. 9). Without any clear associational values, these objects at once invite and frustrate psychological speculation, as the stylized surface of *The Autobiography* so often does; we are tempted to "identify" Stein but are shown that we can't. Resisting metaphorization, these simple objects nevertheless provide humanizing detail (like the earth colors of Picasso's portrait) before the mythologizing of Stein that follows just a few sentences later.

> The chairs in the room were also all italian renaissance, not very comfortable for short-legged people and one got the habit of sitting on one's legs. Miss Stein sat near the stove in a lovely high-backed one and she peacefully let her legs hang, which was a matter of habit, and when any one of the many visitors came to ask her a question she lifted herself up out of this chair and usually replied in french, not just now.

In this Gertrude Stein—sitting "peacefully" in a high, hard, uncomfortable chair, dispensing regal gestures of denial—the reader confronts a presence of profound, contemplative calm, a figure very like the one in Picasso's portrait. This first image points toward the Stein who, later, finds it restful to stare at the midday sun or at those disquieting paintings that Andrew Green covered with cashmere shawls; it also points toward the later mysterious, sibylline Stein who makes enigmatic pronouncements, who lives in a world of "hidden meanings" (p. 15) and who does not explain things to the reader or even to Toklas, leaving the adventure of discovery to us; it is this Stein who dismisses Pound as the "village explainer" (p. 200). But in this first representation of Stein, as throughout *The Autobiography*, the external perspective of Toklas, sticking to the observable surface, suggests the inside while leaving it mysterious. As a result, Stein is not created as a realistic, psychologically complex character; she is, rather, an abstraction, a deliberate simplification—a mythical figure whose peaceful self-sufficiency allows her to transcend external circumstances.

The *Autobiography* of Benjamin Franklin records the attempt to create an identity through acts of will; *The Education of Henry Adams* records the breakdown of a similar attempt and the dissolution of the very idea of identity. *The*

Autobiography of Alice B. Toklas takes the process one step further; the book shows us not someone striving to create a self, but someone who *exists* calmly in a world without any external orders. Again and again the book shows us Stein existing "peacefully" under circumstances that are often far more stressful than uncomfortable chairs. Even Picasso, the character closest to her equal, is "fussed" when he arrives late for a Stein dinner party; looks "sheepish" when he wrests his piece of bread back from Stein, who has accidentally picked it up; or becomes embarrassed when Stein mentions the possibility of his seeing Fernande after they have temporarily separated. Stein, on the other hand, seems to possess an inner stillness that allows her to respond to external pressures with serenity, sometimes even with good humor. When World War I starts while she is visiting London, Stein is concerned but not alarmed about the fate of her writings, all copies of which are back in Paris. Later, after her return to Paris, during an air raid, she calmly quiets an Alice B. Toklas who is so frightened her knees are literally knocking together; and in *The Autobiography*'s final chapter Stein enters the confused and diminished Paris of the postwar era with the same equanimity she had shown during the many crises of the war. Most impressive, however, is the cheerful confidence with which she meets the frugality, frequent disorder, and the public antagonism of the early years of her career. Stein remains steadfastly committed to her work, in spite of her difficulties in finding publication—and in spite of journalistic ridicule when her writing does appear. When *Three Lives* is privately printed, her publisher sends to 27 rue de Fleurus a young man, who questions her knowledge of English; Stein laughs—as she often does at moments when we expect her to be angry or embittered—and her response is contrasted with that of Matisse, two pages earlier, whose feelings are "frightfully" hurt by newspaper ridicule of his art school.

Yet the Stein of *The Autobiography* is by no means as easy to pin down as this discussion of her so far implies; rather, the book frustrates any attempt to fix Stein in a simply identity. In *Everybody's Autobiography* Stein admires paintings which move rather than being about movement and which seem to come out of the "prison" of their frames—as if the subject were alive, truly existing (*EA*, p. 312). Stein's own aesthetic theory, as we have seen, made her acutely aware that by attempting to incarnate her being in language in an autobiography, she was running the risk of merely fixing, of limiting and deadening, herself. But the pressures of autobiography, among them the pressure of language itself, constitute another set of external circumstances to which Stein calmly responds with a playful sense of adventure. The result is that *The Autobiography of Alice B. Toklas* presents a Gertrude Stein who keeps stepping out of the frame, as if she were alive, truly existing. The "psychology" of her character may be a simplified one, but a reader who tries to delineate this character in a careful way finds him/herself speaking in contradictions; and these very contradictions are what make the character of Stein remain mysterious, elusive—alive. ⟨. .. .⟩

Contradictions similarly proliferate when we examine the book's theories about and actual practice of writing. At times Stein speaks of her own work as if it were based on a very simple model of art as representation. Real life sources are given for characters in her fiction; Picasso's cubism is given a realistic basis in Spanish landscape and architecture (p. 90) and Stein speaks of art as the "exact reproduction of an inner or an outer reality" (p. 211). Yet in the same paragraph Stein asserts that "events" ought not to be "the material of poetry and prose"; her writing is often described as the making of sentences, as if it were more construction than representation; and she elsewhere affirms distortion and abstraction in art. Anyone who reads *The Autobiography* looking for a "key" to Stein's fictional works—and many do, as Stein knew they would—will be just as frustrated as the one who reads it looking for the "key" to Stein's private psychology. "Observation and construction make imagination," Stein says (p. 76), as if she were demystifying the imagination, making it a matter of perception and craft, but Stein, of course, *goes on*: "Observation and construction make imagination, that is granting the possession of imagination," and imagination and Stein herself remain playfully mystified. Oracular and witty, Stein is a sibylline presence, no village or even a Parisian explainer.

The oppositions in Stein's "theorizing" reappear in the writing of the book itself, which continually offers contradictory clues about what *kind* of book it is. Its anecdotal manner, its preoccupation with recognizable, real figures, its concern with "the heroic age of cubism" give it the quality of a memoir, as if it were presenting a true historical record. Yet it is *The Autobiography* OF *Alice B. Toklas*—BY Gertrude Stein: the book is marked at once as an autobiography and a fiction (since it is the autobiography of someone other than the author). An ingenuous sentence at the end tantalizes us in the same way: "I am going to write [the autobiography] for you," Stein tells Toklas. "I am going to write it as simply as Defoe did the autobiography of Robinson Crusoe" (p. 252). But how simply was that? Not even this sentence is very simple; it is one written by the (likely) actual author, Stein, imputed to the fictive author, Toklas, who is reporting something said by the character Stein to the character/author Toklas; the sentence, moreover, compares the autobiography of a fictional character (Robinson Crusoe) with that of a character who was real, at least until Stein started writing her autobiography for her. Throughout, *The Autobiography*'s whimsical, self-interrupting, repetitious, stylized prose marks it as a piece of admitted and self-conscious artifice. The book is an historical memoir; the book is a fictional construct.

Notes

1. "What Are Master-pieces and Why Are There So Few of Them," in *Writings and Lectures, 1911–1945*, ed. Patricia Meyerowitz (London: Owen, 1967), p. 150. Subsequent citations in the text are to this edition.
2. *The Autobiography of Alice B. Toklas* (London: Arrow Books, 1960), p. 251. Subsequent citations in the text are to this edition.
3. Richard Bridgman, *Gertrude Stein in Pieces* (New York: Oxford Univ. Press, 1970), pp. 209–17.
4. Bridgman, pp. 213–17.

MARY ALLEN
From "Gertrude Stein's Sense of Oneness"
Southwest Review, Winter 1981, pp. 1–6

Gertrude Stein's story "Many, Many Women" is riddled with the word *one*, which appears three thousand six hundred and sixty-three times. The phrases "she is one" and "she was one" occur hundreds of times. Frequently seeking a larger whole, Stein actually perceives oneness in the smallest unit—object, word, or person. Her belief that only matter broken into its most basic components exists in its integrity has everything to do with the fragmented effect of her writings. She shatters things that are commonly stuck together—related objects, words in familiar patterns, people bound to each other—so that the individual unit may flourish. Her new arrangements emphasize formerly unexposed characteristics of the individual parts rather than the creation of new entities. While Stein's critics observe that her work falls into pieces, what is not conceded is that a sense of wholeness comes after the shattering. Like other moderns she sees that things fall apart. But for her there is virtue in this condition. Stein tenderly breaks the world into pieces, and although she sometimes tries, she never puts it back together again.

Well in the American tradition of individualism, Stein does not hold to the convention that alienation and loneliness inevitably accompany that theme. The strong may earn a tough-minded pleasure in accepting the uniqueness and the aloneness that everyone inherits. The connections most desire, she sees, are too often based on destructive illusions. In combination, something is lost. Above everything, Stein values liberty, and her idea of freedom calls for the fresh view of a child who has not yet learned to put things together. His world is new, and it is pleasingly small. Excitement comes from seeing nearby things in original ways rather than in looking far for the exotic.

From William James Stein gained her invaluable lessons in perception. His experiments reveal that objects seen every day—an overcoat, a piece of paper, an orange—do not actually appear the same each time they are viewed, as one might imagine. Certainly the short-lived rose will not appear the same, seen three times or a hundred times. In the cubist painting Stein saw how common objects could be flattened onto an equal plane so that every detail is given value. Familiarity brings depth, especially when the item stands alone. Picasso shows one eye, not a pair of eyes. Stein came to believe that there is no such thing as repetition: there is *insistence*. Continued acquaintance is the way of getting to the "bottom being" of a thing; to understand a picture or an object, one must dust it every day.

As children perceive objects by quaint analogy, so Stein freshens monotonous vision. A James study shows how a child mistakes an egg for a potato because he is used to seeing the potato without the peel. In *Tender Buttons* Stein writes, "A shawl is a hat," as indeed it is to the child who sees a shawl used to cover the head. To allow one thing the function of another is to open the world not only to a poetic interpretation but to a fascinating realistic one, as the ingenious Don Quixote demonstrates when he turns a shaving basin over and creates a helmet. As a child does not limit the description of an object to the single conventional function assigned to it by the adult world, he may not separate the object from the emotions it evokes. Thus, buttons put into buttonholes by tender fingers are, then, tender buttons.

The marvelously playful *Tender Buttons* is a logic-defying work that has received a due amount of ridicule. But where it refuses analysis, it does not refuse pleasure, yielding the fun a child gets from poking at a world he would not expect to understand. A curious enjoyment can be derived from not "understanding" *Tender Buttons*, with its conscious attempt to dislodge logic. Critics continue, however, in their efforts to establish connections in this book of non sequiturs. In *Gertrude Stein in Pieces*, Richard Bridgman observes that objects share common qualities: a tiger skin and a coin are the same color. But when a common characteristic is located, with the suggestion of a true association, the essential differentness and impossibility of connection become even more noticeable. A coin and a tiger skin are so very *unlike*. *Tender Buttons* makes sly fun of the predilection of the highly trained, logical mind in its attempt to create meaningful wholes. The fresher child's approach is to accept the

individual object and to probe it for new significance. He plays with it. The art of play is the method of *Tender Buttons*, although the book is touched by a maternal tenderness for the strangely arranged "Objects," "Food," and "Rooms." Nothing in this small world, however, is grown up or dead. Things smash, but they are not destroyed. In fact, Stein had a particular weakness for breakable objects.

Gertrude loved to eat and was delighted by the French cuisine, with its adherence to every particular, as the familiar was made marvelous. As Bridgman notes, for Stein the "culinary mystery" is the "aesthetic one: . . . the whole can be sectioned and prepared, but never lost . . . obtaining, cooking, serving, slicing, eating, and digesting the outside world," even with images of ingestion and absorption as the food is transformed, cannot cause it to lose its integrity. Vegetables are chopped into marvelously small particles; celery is cut into extravagant curls. But all flavors and propensities remain. Even fluids, as Stein sees them, begin with tiny units that contain the essence: "a piece of coffee."

As each entity has its own essence, it also contains its own energy. The work of art itself is imbued with the potential to leap its boundaries—a picture to spring out of its frame. But as Stein attributes motion to matter, she produces this paradox: if wholeness is to be found only in the smallest unit, but that unit is endowed with the capacity for movement, the resultant motion appears to be a drive toward a greater wholeness. And yet, as the flow continues, without a limit, no sense of a greater wholeness can be achieved. With no frame for a picture and no end to the way an object may appear, there is no finality and no unity. The total effect in many of Stein's works, then, is that of a mass in movement going nowhere, in which the particle within it remains the most interesting aspect. The particles are not meant to connect, for to connect is to be finished, and in *Narration* Stein insists on the ultimacy of the continuous present: "anything really contained within itself has no beginning or middle or ending." She dislikes newspapers because they relate completed events. Her favorite reading matter is the detective story, for keeping up the suspense and *not* allowing events to connect until the end. Stein's own enormous energy resulted in her producing more than any major writer of our time, with six hundred titles, and one wonders if she kept on not because she always had new things to say but because she could not bear to stop.

As objects are imbued with movement, words are alive with potential meanings. Thus, the dictionary is at fault for completing a definition. Americans, Stein believes, make more ingenious use of their language than other people. In America, words have "a different feeling of moving . . . those same words that in the English were complete quietly or very slowly moving . . . began to detach themselves from the solidity of anything." As words are set off alone, they move and create. In this detachment, they exist. Stark words unfold new meanings to each reader, based on his perceptions and on the complex potential of the word itself. Far from being a symbolist, with the function of assigning a particular new meaning or meanings to an image, Stein avoids this *limitation* placed on a word. As conscious as she is of the vast possibilities for perception, she nevertheless refuses to get away from the thing itself.

It is misleading, then, that the first important critical notice of Stein appears in Edmund Wilson's study of the symbolist poets, *Axel's Castle*. He does acknowledge, however, that Stein "outdistanced any of the Symbolists in using words for pure purposes of suggestion—she has gone so far that she no longer even suggests." In his dissertation, "Gertrude Stein:

A Study of Her Theory and Practice," Harry Garvin proposes that Stein goes in a direction opposite to that of such a symbolist as Joyce, for example, with his addition of layers of intellectual meanings to a word. As Garvin says, Stein denudes them. This she does, even humorously removing a primary characteristic of a word to show that it may still possess its integrity, as in her description in *Everybody's Autobiography* of the Great Salt Lake: "after all it is a satisfaction to know that an ocean is interesting even if there is no water in it." Her refusal to bend to empirical logic is not only a source of humor but her method of paying respect to the untapped potential of matter. If an ocean may exist with no water in it, then it may also have other attributes not usually associated with it. Stein is not, then, the opposite of Joyce because she simplifies what he makes complex, but because she goes in an opposite direction to complexity.

Stein mistakenly believes that her more complex and longer forms will contain the emotion in writing that she desires: a sentence is merely a hope of a paragraph. But the Stein sentence is her great success, carrying the emotion and wit that her paragraphs never achieve. That Stein defines her sentence as a *hope* of a paragraph, however, suggests that the superiority of the longer form is only an ideal for her. She acknowledges that it is her little sentences that finally get under people's skins. Stein's theory of the equilibrium of the sentence, expressed in *Narration*, comes close to her general belief in the wholeness of the small unit: "the internal balance of sentences which are things that exist in and for itself [*sic*] does not have to have completion." She further contradicts her desire for length when she questions why a person cannot speak in pieces.

Stein's concept of the greatest integrity in the smallest unit applied to language would, of course, credit the word. Or perhaps the syllable. She participated in a memory experiment at Radcliffe which employed a technique of flashing unlike syllables on a screen in quick succession; words were literally chopped into pieces. She, too, splits words, *eat ting*, for example, with characteristic emphasis on the process of breaking matter apart.

In tearing words from their usual patterns, Stein often employs the poetic device of leaving space around a word to emphasize its shape and significance. She understandably separates *any one* and *some one*. In the "Food" section of *Tender Buttons*, items are arranged on the page under headings in the form of a shopping list: "EATING / SALAD / SAUCE / SALMON / ORANGE / ORANGE." Each item is importantly placed on its own line. It is essential. It is worth paying for. Shopping in Paris, too, meant going to many different shops. The *lack* of parallel value in this shopping-list arrangement is, however, the element of surprise. The eye naturally brings all the items into a position of balance—verb, prepared dishes, and single ingredients—so that they appear to be similar. But a second glance shows that they are not alike. And there is no new joining. Two different oranges remain aloof. Or is the same orange looked at twice?

In placing words together, Stein often does so to accentuate their separateness and the impossibility of their connecting. In "apple plum," without a connecting word, one fruit does not yield to the other; nor do they combine. Despite their similar coloring, the objects stand knobby and apart as they would in a still-life painting, the art form which most influenced the creation of *Tender Buttons*. In the section on "Rooms," the separate parts of the house are its important features, operating independently: "Act so that there is no use in a centre. A wide action is not a width." In "Objects," "a

closet does not connect under the bed." The same sense of separateness applies to the heavens: "star-light is a little light that is not always mentioned with the sun." Even light is a small spot, not a diffuse element.

Stein notes that the single word is rarely observed. As Carl Van Vechten relates in "A Stein Song," while having her hair cut she held her glasses close to her book, magnifying the words, and found that "reading word by word makes the writing that is not anything be something. . . . one at a time, oh one at a time is something oh yes definitely something." She believes that the only way to know a book is to type or proofread it. As the comprehensive (conventional) view is relinquished, a completely different, not necessarily inferior, method of knowing is substituted, one which is based not on connections but on familiarity with separate units. This is by no means an easy way to read, as anyone who has proofread knows. It is difficult *not* to seek the comprehensive idea, a process which may be a comfortable way of sliding over individual words. An emphasis on the single word, of course, has its obvious limits, and to suggest that the medium which by nature is based on relationships no longer make connections would be absurd. Any attempt to deal for long with single words inclines the reader at last to insist, to alter a phrase from Eliot, "I gotta use sentences when I talk to you."

In her continuous-present flow of language, Stein balks at punctuation for slowing down the process; she has a particular aversion to the comma. Admitting to the value of periods, however, she claims—with the charm of her illogic—that they are permissible because it is necessary to stop before starting again. The apostrophe hanging outside the plural possessive word distresses her, as it apparently violates the compactness of the word. But perhaps she simply does not like plurals. Because Stein considered nouns static, she ruled them out in favor of adjectives and verbs—although her belief that there are no repetitions and that each unit has its own energy would apparently preclude that possibility. She later modifies this view, however, admitting an affection for name words, as she so memorably demonstrates with her rose and her pigeons.

As familiarity with an object or a word enhances it, so continued listening to a person is a way to arrive at his bottom being. "More and more listening to repeating gives to me completed understanding," she writes in *The Making of Americans*. "Each one slowly comes to be a whole one to me." Stein's patient humanity reminds one of the gradual way in which Henry James reveals character. She takes to heart the message of the James brothers, that if one looks carefully enough at whatever is before him, there is no end to what he may see.

ELIZABETH FIFER

From "Rescued Readings: Characteristic Deformations in the Language of Gertrude Stein's Plays"

Texas Studies in Literature and Language, Winter 1982, pp. 394–402, 424–28

In her need to forge a private and expressive language, Stein's narrative techniques reflect an intense inner program of frightening and incongruous thoughts and feelings, often unacceptable to her. Especially in the collections of her plays, *Geography and Plays* (1924), *Operas and Plays* (1932), and *Last Operas and Plays* (1949), her texts are studded with inappropriate intrusions that appear to operate in areas beyond the author's volition. Disordered trains of thought[1] reveal inner equivocations and unresolved conflicts as well as those unexpected revelations that appear to surprise the author herself. The nature of her anticipated audience seems unsettled: at times she plainly fears they will disapprove or even punish her for her thought. At other times she treats them as confidants and even coconspirators.

Since Stein is of two minds about her audience, she addresses them in unpredictable ways. At times she seems to imagine a series of idiosyncratic auditors,[2] close and distant, approving and disapproving, understanding and misunderstanding her. Stein imagines both friends and enemies in her audience and alternately takes the part of each faction to dramatize their dilemma. "Can you be rowdier,"[3] she asks herself. Later in the play she replies:

> Yes I mean exactly that. I mean to be very exact. I
> mean to call you, I mean to come, I mean to be
> especially seen and very nearly established. I mean to
> cloud the rain and to articulate . . . very clearly . . .
> and to pronounce myself as aroused. Are you aroused
> by him or for them. (*OP, Saints and Singing*, p. 81)

Stein's audience always contains one who would question her purposes. Is she a lover or an exhibitionist? Is concealment needed to add piquancy? If Stein's words do not directly address her concerns, her indirections do help emphasize her position, her role as mediator between her attempt to "mean exactly" and her awareness of her potentially dangerous audience.

This writer-reader nexus is at the carefully formulated center of Stein's "difficult" style. Her evasive narrative strategies demand a language which can simultaneously be used to placate and to startle, to both say and unsay. The casual, disengaged, or unsympathetic reader is to be amused and misled, the sympathetic reader whispered to and courted, the two relationships maintained simultaneously. The effect of her efforts is both to compel and dispel her audience's attention. This essay charts the stylistic contortions and characteristic deformities in the language of Stein's plays and explores their strategies of concealment and revelation.

Stein's discourse is autobiographical, controlled and dominated by imagery arising from her inner life. Her insistence on absolute clarity and frankness must coexist with evasion, opposite speech, self-censorship, and other verbal arabesques, including denials and intrusions, disordered syntax, willful or irrational diction, constantly shifting referents, and other multiple "errors." Her excess of subjects and her free-recall method of invention mingles public and private realities, transporting both. Nonsense, disorder, contradiction, and fragmented logic both mask and mark her approach to "unacceptable" personal material.

I. Rescued Readings

Although Stein's writing often assumes a bantering tone, it speaks movingly of the anguish of being misunderstood, of needing a reader who will participate vigorously in the act of creating meaning. Caught in a web of words and struggling to be understood, Stein must use the very obfuscating language that created her previous difficulties. In a passage from *A Sweet Tail*, she admits her need for a reader to "rescue" her meaning: "Suppose a tremble, a ham, a little mouth told to wheeze more and a religion a reign . . . that makes a load registrar and passes best . . . gracious oh my cold under fur, under no rescued reading."[4] This monologue is in the conditional—"What if I were like that and no one understood?" Of course, Stein is like that. Her sexual and creative "tremble" is both emphasized and belittled by her use of the word "ham."[5] The "little

mouth," a reference to the vagina, is simultaneously the writer's mouth, "hamming it up"; and her text, told to "wheeze," is made purposefully difficult. Her lesbian love, "a religion a reign," is identifiable both by its serious and its "royal" nature.[6] The whole "load" of her sexuality must be interpreted by the reader, who either understands her garbled message by correcting it and passing it on, or who misunderstands and lets its truths "pass" unrecognized. This educational metaphor is explicit throughout Stein's difficult texts. Stein fears being unmasked, but she also fears going unrecognized. If she is not read clearly, she will become "cold," and her texts will betray their purpose.

The reader's task is rendered still more difficult by Stein's constant vacillations. Typically, she makes statements on either side of a logical equation and seesaws back and forth between them, emphasizing both their complementary and contradictory aspects. Also typically, she will avoid direct mention of her subject. Instead, she searches out a language calculated to conceal and reveal simultaneously: "If the message is sent and received and if the tunes have words then certainly there will be soon the centerpiece which has not been removed (*GP, Scenes. Actions and Disposition*, p. 113). Subjects must be approached with the greatest indirection. Only after examining the entire work will the observant reader find that the "tune" had "words" after all.

In the following passage, Stein can be seen carefully manipulating and overlaying her argument with sections of suggestive and distracting effects:

> Come in cubicle stern old wet places.
> Come in by the long excuse of more in
> place of . . . to cut a whole condition . . .
> all that can see the pen of pigs wide.
> All this man is a make of chins which
> is to be tall and most many women, in
> the directory that shows why the state
> which is absolutely with . . . plastering
> received with boast. All this in
> bedding.

> (*OP, Old and Old*, pp. 229–30)

Although the sexual nature of this passage is evident, its exact referents remain obscure. The language is twisted and reshaped, predictable syntax evaded and turned back in on itself. The "pen of pigs wide" is not only the sty of sexual shame but the author's pen that will ignore all expected decorum. English becomes a "foreign" tongue, impressive and melodious at times to be sure, but never fully grasped without an act of sympathetic interpretation.

Why does Stein use this difficult language? She herself gives us a partial answer in *A List* (*OP*, p. 94). "Change songs for safety . . . if they were . . . differently decided . . . delighted . . . accidentally relieved and repeatedly received and reservedly deceived." Stein must "change songs for safety." If she were "differently decided," if she were not a lesbian, perhaps she would write differently. Yet, in her trope of contradiction, her positive note is also clear. She claims to be "delighted" and "relieved" by both her writing and her life, indulging herself "repeatedly." She emphasizes two ideas: accident and deception (as opposed to intention) as keys to both her reception and her reserve.

II. Intrusions and Denials

Stein's coding strategy is a willed and intentional process, a carefully worn mask through which she artfully expresses her thoughts and feelings. But her intrusion "errors,"[7] uncensored areas of her discourse which intrude on prosaic statements and make them ambiguous, are far more frequent and far more puzzling. These intrusions seem to enter haphazardly into her texts, creating a randomized surface. It is as if parts of the message have actually appeared against her will or that Stein has no control over its development and logical direction.

Stein's basic technique for tolerating these intrusions is repeated complete denial. Stein seems almost smug as she describes an assumed historical identity, a figure called Byron, in the play of the same name, who "cannot be punished for the sins of commission and omission because partly and happily he earns nothing for any one."[8] "Happily he earns nothing," no punishment, and has thus effectively armored himself against the dangers and responsibilties of communication. For if Stein is ashamed of her message, then she must also be ashamed of her "system" of living (LO&P, *An Exercise in Analysis*, p. 125). Stein's personas, with all their verbal armor, are continually exposed and ever vulnerable: "I should not have mentioned it" (GP, *Mexico*, p. 328). So Stein is forced into thinking of different possibilities for "telling"—avoiding timidity, but admitting remorse, affirming the "telling" by separating it from its content. The anxiety about "telling" can be quelled by not hearing what is being said.

She will insist that she writes "a work of pure imagination in which no reminiscences intrude" (LO&P, *Paiseu*, p. 155). But in speaking of the imagination, Stein can make fine distinctions. What is "pure imagination?"

> Come up out of there is very well said when the instinct which has lead to the introduction of words and music not pictures and music, not pictures and words not pictures and music and words . . . not words when the instinct which has lead to the spread of rubbing has been shed then we will invite each one to sign himself Yours sincerely Herman G. Read and very quickly I include everything in that new name. (OP, *Objects Lie on a Table*, p. 107)

In the opening of this remarkable passage, Stein answers the reader who would have her "come up out of there"—out of her fears and prudishness, to reveal her secrets. The functional intrusion enters after the word "instinct," which, when repeated, seems to unleash the erotic mention of "spread," "rubbing," and "shed." By breaking through the barrier of "words . . . not words," the erotic language momentarily leads Stein to name herself "Herman" ("her-man"), referring to her marriage with Alice B. Toklas, in which Stein played the male role. The translation of this phrase can thus be achieved by reordering its elements. "Herman G. Read" becomes "read G (Gertrude), her man." Everything is included in that "new" name. But since the instinct referred to by "the spread of rubbing" (sexuality) will never be shed, Stein will never sign herself "sincerely" in this way. Clearly, Stein sometimes manages to have her imagination work both ways, pure and impure, at once.

Stein's intrusions usually occur when she is trying to rationalize the problem of sexuality. Just as she is telling us that she will not reveal herself or that it is probably better not to be associated with the idea of sexuality at all, Stein provocatively emphasizes the sexual content of her associations. In the following selection, for instance, the intrusions occur as physical descriptions of the earth, drawn from the vocabulary of mining: "It is as well to be without in their reverberation in the meantime ways which are in opening to their site do unexpectedly deliver it as in a tunnel and they attend the opening and the exit" (OP, *Madame Recamier*, p. 376). If, in the beginning, Stein seems to be begging the question of sexuality (using "reverberation" to refer to the

movement of orgasm), the very mention of this word causes the appearance of associated kinds of sexualized geological images such as the earthquake or the explosion that mining requires, in turn producing other metaphorically related words: "opening," "site," "deliver," "tunnel," "exit." These words intrude upon her originally framed denial to become a kind of contradictory approval of her original premise.

In the following example, flat denials again provoke a series of intrusions, as if Stein purposefully used an indirect method to prod her unconscious mind:

> There is no way of speaking English. What do you mean. I mean that anybody can begin and go on. And finish. It's easy enough and especially hard when there is a use. Why do you say exchange. I do not know what they say exchange. They say they believe in exchange. I often talk about nothing. What have I to say. I wish to speak to you what shall we do about water. The water is everywhere. Imagine me in bed. We were very careful to ask about it. Not for teeth. (GP, *He Said It*, p. 270)

The intrusions function to change the subject, coming up because for her "there is no way of speaking English," no way of telling the truth clearly, in a straightforward way. She will have to go "round about"— allowing the thought to catch her unaware, mid-sentence, and interrupt her.

These intrusions are sometimes present in the form of questions, which must be answered truthfully, as if they came from a real audience and she, as a writer, had a duty to address them. When repetition[9] plays a role in these intrusions, it propels her into greater and greater frankness. Intrusions in Stein's work can also appear as a series of free associations, with the original impetus coming from some key word which might appear neutral. Even seemingly noncommittal words like "it" and "thought" create these possibilities: "It was mostly thought out by records and moist houses, it was mostly thought out by moist houses that bedrooms should be heated" (OP, *Saints and Singing*, p. 73). Here again, even the concept of writing about "it" (the idea of sexuality) makes possible "moist houses" (the genitalia), "bedrooms," and "heat." These linked intrusions occur because she has meditated on the impermanence of records, which challenges her to have something to record. What is most important to the unconscious will eventually find expression, but the actuality of the author's reluctance remains.

Words may be produced inoffensively but still have the most telling effects as Stein alternately reveals and fights off their implications: "I do not wish to be married. I wish to be sure of marriage. I have selected my sisters. They do embroidery. I will not copy them. I am not so old . . . I do not pay attention. We do not pay attention to one another. I am in a way disappointed. I do believe in fish" (GP, *Do Let Us Go Away*, p. 223–34). What is striking in this passage, besides the inherently dramatic technique of interacting with an imagined audience, is her various considerations of the idea of marriage. Because marriage is such an important word, connoting the idea of her lesbian marriage with Alice B. Toklas as well as the conventional kinds of marriages she saw in the society around her, she couches her first mention of it in negative terms. Her very next sentence, "I wish to be sure of marriage," however, has positive connotations—being able to avoid loneliness and having a partner she has "selected." She modifies marriage with her first intrusion, "sisters," as she modifies "sisters" with a feminine activity, one she associates with Alice, "embroidery." Copying can be interpreted two ways: the author rejects the typical heterosexual mold and also distinguishes between the type of woman Alice is and the type of woman she, Gertrude, represents. This distinction of roles leads into an assertion of youthful vigor, but that revelation in turn triggers a disclaimer: I do not pay attention to what I write, and so you should not notice it either. The negative aspects of her sexuality and its positive elements (as in the fertility of a fish) remain precariously balanced. The fish imagery is remarkable in the sense that none of the preceding images prepares for it; it seems to well up from another more repressed source.

No matter how the speaker ornaments or disguises her communication, its strongest unconscious connotations usually prevail: "I do see what makes me thunder when the words are not repressed" (*OP, Re-read Another*, p. 127). Her word strings do embody meanings, however ambiguous, but the words themselves remain anomalous—without clear or expectable relation to one another. For Stein's words, as she observed, are "remarkable . . . in their resistance" (*LO&P, Paiseu*, p. 165).

Often the denial itself contains the essential "forbidden" material, but again it is surrounded by negative modifiers, as in "I am not a christian and I have no wife. Do be hot to-day" (*OP, Re-read Another*, p. 123). If we take the speaker to be the author, the first statement is true, the second is not, and the third discounts the second disclaimer. Such denials almost always arise from anxiety over punishment and the fear of discovery: "What I am afraid of is that they will just attract an awful bombardment on themselves in which they will have to be supported. Oh no they won't do that" (*GP, A Poem about Waldberg*, p. 166). The querulous side is comforted by the confident self, assuring her that no calamity awaits the speaker. The military metaphor, drawn from Stein's experience of World War I, indicates the destructive power she attributes to society and social norms. They are as capable of destroying the fortifications of her ego as bombs can destroy a city.

III. Self-Editing

Stein's structure of denial suggests that she both wants and does not want to know what she reveals. In her use of self-editing, she denies her real subject, avoids possible disapproval, and even cuts off discussion. In *Byron a Play* she speaks of excuses she has made for the lover, the ambiguous "him," and at the same time gives us a compendium of loving actions, the very ones her censor would have her hide. She stops speaking in this train of thought only after she has defined the steps in intimacy, inspired by her original attempt to shield the "him," her persona of lover. Stein fulfills the requirements of the perseverative mode by continuing to unfold her inner drama, carrying the speaker along after excuses that form a barrier between reader and author.

Important to note is that though constrained by her internal necessities of self-censorship, she never shows confidence that her denials will be believed and accepted. In *Lynn and the College de France* (*OP*, p. 269), she wishes to hide an event (one day) and "declares" her "reserve" and "denial." But those words are goads to more ambiguous statements, like "Infuse. Joining. To petition," even as she promises politeness will come from such "joinings." Even when she succeeds in preventing her messages from escaping, their very presence in her mind can waken her fears. She wants to deny "there is [an] example in this," tells herself to be "cautious" and "restrained" (*GP*, p. 294; even the title, *Not Slightly: A Play*, has negative connotations). In her role as editor-censor, denial itself forces her into admission. Every denial contains its antipode. The following passage is notable for its pairing of opposites, its divided structure:

> I please you as a dilatory victory . . . rub it . . . clean it . . . what are your passages. How often have you crossed the ocean . . . how very many are you willing to moisten rapid repetition with angular vibration. You are not angular, you do not vibrate nor do you caution men and women as to war and liberation . . . do divide beside . . . can you ring beside the use and air of elaboration and a vision. (*OP, Saints and Singing*, pp. 84–85)

This might be considered the "naive" mode of self-editing, the truth revealed and then quickly taken back, the extreme clarity of the many sexual words ("rub," "moisten," "rapid," "angular," "vibration") and her playful use of water ("ocean") to imply sex prompting a vigorous response from her internal censor, who exactingly replaces her positives and questions with negatives.

She continually warns us that her censor is awake and challenging her: "they are very careful. Of. Their memory . . . and their permission" (*OP, Lynn and the College de France*, p. 256). "This must not be put in a book. Why not. Because it mustn't. Yes Sir" (*GP, Bonne Année*, p. 302). The very existence of her words in print is threatening. She does not want to oblige the reader with easy admissions of guilt. She admits "it is never to be safe to see that" (*LO&P, Paiseu*, p. 158). She herself cannot be "seen," or interpreted by witnesses, or any who would remember what she wrote and implicate her. But "if writing is in little pieces . . . doors are not open" (*GP, France*, p. 27).

She wants to suggest "restraint and alarm and reserve and a mistake" (*OP, Old and Old*, p. 224), hoping the result will be "no witness signing" (*GP, Scenes. Actions and Disposition*, p. 109). Or she will mock her attempts at truthfulness through the use of rhyming mode, as in "it is useless to discover what they do in liking one another" (*OP, Madame Recamier*, p. 365). She recognizes that the reader may understand her subterfuge, but is determined to continue her self-imposed constraints: "pleasure . . . so agreeable so selected and so fairly denied" (*OP, They Weighed Weighed-Layed*, p. 238).

Self-editing takes many forms: it can balance, block, or modify a statement; it can take the form of a disclaimer that reveals the truth or of an admission that temporarily removes her social mask. Sometimes her editor has to be satisfied with bringing out a disclaimer secondarily, too late to hide what has been said but better than no disclaimer at all. The editing may be naive enough to make us suspect that it also serves Stein with a tool in her pursuit of total frankness; her difficult passages force the reader to search all the more diligently and deliberately for their partially revealed truths. ⟨. . .⟩

XV. Conclusion

For the most part, Stein's difficult texts simultaneously pursue two contradictory goals—to conceal the author's deepest feelings by drawing excessive attention to the surface of her text and to extend her experimental narrative technique to include as much personal information as possible. In pursuit of these goals, the torrents of Stein's words and images cluster around the obsessive foci of her attention. This pattern is not merely a case of Stein's verbal and conceptual structures being loose or freely formed. Her melodic sequences and rhetorical patterns do not grow out of a poetically sophisticated sense of the line or a logical argument but from vivid internal visions over which the author appears to have little or no control. Any stimulus or referent will serve her as a springboard for transformation. Her imagination leaps through inner space. But because this is a double leap—employing a simultaneously open and private methodology—Stein's difficult texts, especially her dramatic texts, appear at first to be nearly inexplicable. Her thought sequences seem broken or random; the construction of her sentences appears crude, primitive, or repetitive; her logic becomes questionable; her errors and narrative strategies seem designed to serve the express purpose of disguise or evasion.

Role ambiguity,[10] her diverse and inappropriate role identities, emphasized by her use of drama as an expressive mode, gives away to tone ambiguity,[11] her delight in the inappropriate tone or mood, her omissions, her silences. Stein all but completely effaces standard syntax and semantics in alterations, deformations, and transformations which appear to become a sort of glossomania, an obsessive attention to the surface of the text at the expense of all else. This overattention to purely musical and rhythmic suggestions—such as rhyme, alliteration, and rhythm—sacrifices semantics to phonetics, producing a "folie discordante verbale," a language functioning as an object in itself, quite apart from its identity as an instrument of communication. Her manipulation forces knowledgeable readers into a special relationship, one of "rescuing" her meaning, based on their willingness to persevere in the face of verbal anomalies and accumulating "errors" meant to distract unsympathetic readers and evade Stein's own internal censors:

> They may know. That. One is one.
> In made. To punish them. With one.
> It is. An anxious thing. To say . . .
> With which. They will. Please. Me.
> After all. It was not what. I had expected. It. Was
>   you.
> It was you. And. They. Will have pleasure.
> In that case.
> . . .
> They will be anxious. That they have. Seen me.
> (*OP, They Must Be Wedded to Their Wife*, p. 173)

Notes

1. Martin Harrow and Mel Prosen, "Intermingling and Disordered Logic as Influences on Schizophrenic 'Thought Disorders,' " *Archives of General Psychiatry*, 35 (Oct. 1978), 1213. "Disordered thinking," they write, "is believed by most clinicians and theorists to be the central or fundamental feature of schizophrenia." Psychiatrists often use the phrases "anomalous word strings" and "random thought trains" to characterize deviance in schizophrenic utterance. Stein was clearly not a schizophrenic and was entirely conscious of the experimental unorthodoxy of her style, including the deliberate deformations of, and departures from, conventional language. The psychoanalytic literature cited here and following is meant only to establish a useful vocabulary for describing Stein's "difficult texts."

2. Bertram D. Cohen, Gilead Nachmani, and Seymour Rosenberg ("Referent Communication Disturbances in Acute Schizophrenia," *Journal of Abnormal Psychology*, 83 [1974], 2) provide two models for communication in which "the speaker implicitly takes the role of listener in order to 'test' the adequacy of a sampled response before emitting (or rejecting) it. A self-editing function of this type is reminiscent of Sullivan's (1946) conception of the 'fantastic auditor' and Mead's (1934) conception of the 'generalized other.' . . . The function of this type of mechanism is to edit out utterances the speaker judges to be inappropriate . . . before they intrude into overt speech." Later they demonstrate how a schizophrenic's comparison and sampling procedure may deviate from that of a normal speaker (p. 3): "[The schizophrenic] samples from an idiosyncratic repertoire and bases his comparison stage judgements on correspondingly deviant associative strengths . . . if [he] tests his utterances . . . against idiosyncratic norms . . . his response will fail to communicate accurately."

3. Gertrude Stein, *Saints and Singing*, in her *Operas and Plays* (Paris: Plain Edition, 1932), p. 74 (hereafter cited as *OP*).

4. Gertrude Stein, *Geography and Plays* (1922; reprint ed. New York: Something Else Press, 1968), p. 67 (hereafter cited as *GP*).

5. Stein often free-associates from the idea of meat in its folkloric sexual sense.

6. Richard Bridgman (*Gertrude Stein in Pieces* [New York: Oxford University Press, 1970]) notes that Stein's dominant sexual role was often expressed by reference to herself as a great historic figure such as Caesar (see pp. 150–52).

7. Elaine Chaika ("A Linguist Looks at 'Schizophrenic Language,' " *Brain and Language*, 1 [July 1974], 272) discusses "intrusive word associations" as one of the characteristic features of schizophrenic thought, along with lack of coherence, redundancy, frequent punning, and rhyming. The same author also considers punning (pp. 264–65) as a kind of intrusion, "the deliberate assigning of the wrong semantic features for the context to a particular item in the lexicon." This is contrary to the views of Harrow and Prosen, who see schizophrenic intrusions as the " 'intermingling' of material into . . . verbalizations at a point . . . when it was inappropriate" (p. 1217).

8. Gertrude Stein, *Last Operas and Plays* (New York: Rinehart, 1949), p. 365 (hereafter cited as *LO&P*).

9. Brendan Maher, "The Language of Schizophrenia: A Review and Interpretation," *British Journal of Psychiatry*, 120 (1972), 8. "Frequent repetitions at smaller intervals is characteristic of schizophrenic subjects . . . repetition is evidence of excessive rigidity and need for security and should be interpreted as an anxiety-reducing symptom." Stein's repetition has attracted wide critical attention from, among others, Stein herself (*Lectures in America* [New York: Random House, 1935], pp. 166–67), Bridgman (in scattered sections throughout his text), Frederick J. Hoffman (*Gertrude Stein*, Pamphlets on American Writers no. 10 [Minneapolis: University of Minnesota Press, 1961], p. 20), Normal Weinstein (*Gertrude Stein and the Literature of Modern Consciousness* [New York: Ungar, 1970], p. 94), and Bruce Kawin (*Telling It Again and Again* [Ithaca: Cornell University Press, 1972], p. 17).

10. A lack of certainty about the speaker's own identity is reflected in possible multiple personalities. See Chaika's analysis of a schizophrenic speaker from the Kisker tapes ("Schizophrenic Language").

11. A lack of certainty on the part of the speaker is shown about the tone and mood to employ, as Chaika has said, "an inability to assess the social situation properly" (ibid., p. 274).

MARIANNE DeKOVEN
From *"Three Lives"*
A *Different Language:*
Gertrude Stein's Experimental Writing
1983, pp. 27–37

Gertrude Stein had written the story of Melanctha . . . which was the first definite step away from the nineteenth century and into the twentieth century in literature. (*The Autobiography of Alice B. Toklas*, 54)

Stein composed *Three Lives* while she stared at Cézanne's portrait of his wife and while she sat for Picasso's portrait of herself. It represents her first concerted break with conventional modes of writing. It is crucial to her experimental career, both as the source of her subsequent stylistic techniques and as a clue to the source of her rebellion against patriarchal linguistic structures.

Stein's break with literary convention in *Three Lives* is generally described as stylization of the prose surface in order to render directly the essence of a character's identity, which Stein calls the pulse of personality, and the critic Norman

Weinstein calls the unique "rhythm, density, continuity, speed, quantity" of consciousness.[1] Stein also manipulates the prose surface in *Three Lives* in order to render directly what she calls a "continuous present": a notion of time, derived from William James and akin to that of Henri Bergson, as a continuous process or succession of steadily shifting present moments rather than a linear progress or march from past through present to future. This stylization of the prose surface is seen by many critics as the beginning of Stein's progress toward an abstract, self-contained, plastic, autonomous literature, whose only concern is its articulation of formal features of language. As Richard Bridgman says, "While such examples [of dialogue from *Melanctha*] are still tied to the story, it is not difficult to see how they could easily lead to a preoccupation with the prose surface itself, at the expense of the imagined reality she was attempting to create."[2] Michael Hoffman makes a similar, even clearer statement:

> How does Stein move within just a few years from a stylized Jamesian realism to both a fragmented narrative structure and a ritualized style, and then, within less than a decade, turn to a use of language in which words cease to be purveyors of conventional meaning and become plastic counters to be manipulated purely in obedience to the artist's expressive will, just as painters manipulate nonsemantic line and color?[3]

Such judgments proceed from a concept of literary meaning borrowed from painting, where meaning must be either referential or abstract. Meaning in experimental writing need be neither: it often has no anterior, referential, thematic content, yet it has readable meaning—it is not abstract. Bridgman is certainly correct that Stein begins, with *Melanctha*, to abandon "the imagined reality she was attempting to create." But the "preoccupation with the prose surface" which leads her to do so is not, as Hoffman has it, a retreat from meaning into pure form. Rather it is the beginning of a shift from conventional, patriarchal to experimental, anti-patriarchal modes of articulating meaning.

The origins of this shift are clearest in the *overt* stylistic innovations of *Melanctha*, but they are also embedded in some of the more familiar modernist or impressionist features of all three novellas. Like a good deal of early modern fiction, *Three Lives* employs the device of obtuse or unrealiable narration.[4] Generally, obtuse narration is a function of subjectivity: the narrator's psychology and involvement in the story determine her or his version of it. By allowing for this subjective structuring, we are able simultaneously to chart the limits of the narrator's perception and to see beyond them (this process is often facilitated by multiple narration, as in Conrad's *Nostromo*, Woolf's *To the Lighthouse*, etc.). In *Three Lives*, the narration is "omniscient third," yet nonetheless obtuse: there is a discrepancy, sometimes to the point of contradiction, between the tone of the narrative voice and the content of the narrative. Some such discrepancy is, as we know, characteristic of fiction, where irony, understatement, or a conflict of conscious and unconscious creation so often generates a complex vision. But in *Three Lives*, the discrepancy is so extreme that the narrator seems at times entirely blind to the import of what she narrates.

While the narrative voice of *Three Lives* is consistently innocent, straightforward, mildly jolly, and approving, the content is often grotesque, sinister, ridiculous. The gulf between what the narrator tells us and what we see is most vivid in some of the brilliant brief portraits, such as this one of Mrs. Haydon, Lena's aunt:

> This aunt, who had brought Lena, four years before, to Bridgepoint, was a hard, ambitious, well meaning, german woman. . . . Mrs. Haydon was a short, stout, hard built, german woman. She always hit the ground very firmly and compactly as she walked. Mrs. Haydon was all a compact and well hardened mass, even to her face, reddish and darkened from its early blonde, with its hearty, shiny cheeks, and doubled chin well covered over with the uproll from her short, square neck.[5]

The avuncular simplicity, the cheerful straightforwardness of the narrator's tone, the words "well meaning" and "hearty," muffle the frightening, repulsive discord of the "hardened mass" and the "doubled chin well covered over with the uproll from her short, square neck." If we visualize Mrs. Haydon from this description, we see a monster, which is precisely what she becomes in the course of the story.

One of the best brief portraits is of Anna's half brother, the baker:

> Her half brother, the fat baker, was a queer kind of a man. He was a huge, unwieldy creature, all puffed out all over, and no longer able to walk much, with his enormous body and the big, swollen, bursted veins in his great legs. He did not try to walk much now. He sat around his place, leaning on his great thick stick, and watching his workmen at their work.
>
> On holidays, and sometimes of a Sunday, he went out in his bakery wagon. He went then to each customer he had and gave them each a large, sweet, raisined loaf of caky bread. At every house with many groans and gasps he would descend his heavy weight out of the wagon, his good featured, black haired, flat, good natured face shining with oily perspiration, with pride in labor and with generous kindness. Up each stoop he hobbled with the help of his big stick, and into the nearest chair in the kitchen or in the parlour, as the fashion of the house demanded, and there he sat and puffed, and then presented to the mistress or the cook the raisined german loaf his boy supplied him. (*Three Lives*, 48)

The incongruity in this portrait of the baker is summarized in the "good featured, black haired, flat, good natured face shining with oily perspiration, with pride in labor and with generous kindness." The negative "oily perspiration" is included casually, as if it conveyed the same message as the more positive "good features," "good nature," "pride in labor," and "generous kindness."

The narrative voice in *Three Lives* is not only straightforward, factual, reassuring; it is also childish, whimsical, consciously naive: the baker is "a queer kind of a man," "all puffed out all over," who "sits and puffs" in the kitchens of his customers. The diction and tone could be those of a children's story. This childish language heightens the discrepancy between narrative voice and content, here and elsewhere by means of its implied innocence concerning what seems a sexually charged disgust, and more generally in the novellas by masking the sophisticated complexity and somber implications of Stein's "imagined reality."

The three women's lives of the title all end in defeated, lonely death, a fact one would never surmise from the narrative tone. Anna, a generous, hardworking, stubborn, managing German immigrant (based on one of Stein's Baltimore servants), works herself to death for a series of selfish employers and friends who take all she offers, allow her to run their lives (the only repayment she exacts), then desert her when she has outlived her usefulness or when they are tired of her rigid control. She dies poor, of an unnamed disease, alone except for the one friend (Mrs. Drehten, the long-suffering, passive victim of poverty and a tyrannical husband) whose society represents no hope whatever of improving Anna's lot.

As "the good Anna" dies of her goodness, "the gentle Lena" dies of her gentleness. She is passive, dreamy, absent, slow-witted, out of touch with her feelings. She is forced into marriage by her aunt, the monstrous ("well meaning," "hearty") Mrs. Haydon, with the equally passive yet reluctant Herman Kreder. Herman comes into his own by triumphing over his fairytale witch of a mother—something his marriage has given him the strength to do—and his children give purpose and vitality to his life. Lena, unable to assert or even to know her will, steadily fades into near nonexistence, and dies giving birth to the fourth child.

Melanctha, who has no summarizing fatal female virtue, has a more complex death than Anna or Lena. Melanctha's story had been told before by Stein, in her first novel, originally entitled *Q.E.D.* (1903–5).[6] *Q.E.D.* is a straightforward account of Stein's first lesbian affair with May Bookstaver, whom she met while at Johns Hopkins Medical School. May was attached to a third woman whom she would not give up. The affair ended, in stalemate, with Stein's expatriation to Paris.[7] The triangle, origin of the title *Q.E.D.*, is absent in *Melanctha*, which focuses on the temperamental differences between Jeff Campbell, Stein's surrogate, and Melanctha, a transformation of May. Jeff's involvement with Melanctha— his painful growth and final disappointment—is the center of the story, but only one episode in Melanctha's life. Melanctha, an intelligent, reckless black woman, is a much more complicated heroine/victim than Anna or Lena (Stein calls her the "complex desiring Melanctha"). Where Anna is defeated simply by her goodness and Lena by her gentleness, Melanctha is defeated by what is emerging as the fatal flaw *par excellence* of heroines in women's fiction: a divided self.[8] At crucial times in her life, including the moment when she finally has the full and passionate love she needs from Jeff, she acts against her own best interests, destroying the relationships she has worked hard to build. "Melanctha Herbert was always seeking rest and quiet, and always she could only find new ways to be in trouble" (89). From Jeff she moves on to Jem Richards, an unreliable gambler, and to the shallow, selfish Rose Johnson. She loses Jem by pressing him when he's down, and finally she loses her last hope for safety, Rose Johnson, by being too kind to Rose's husband Sam. She dies of consumption, alone, in a sanatorium for the poor.

These plot summaries are accurate and yet misleading. The bitter implications, the powerful feminist morals of these stories (the "good" woman who dies of service to others, the "gentle" woman who dies in unwanted childbirth, the "complex, desiring" woman who dies of self-defeating complexity and unsatisfied desire) are concealed or overruled not only by the narrator's tone and diction but also by narrative emphasis and temporal structure. While Stein's uses of obtuse narration to distance language ironically from content and to avoid forcing on the reader any judgment of the story seem intentional (she was translating Flaubert's *Un Coeur simple* when she began *Three Lives*), her use of narrative tone and temporal structure as a defense against her own anger and despair appears unconscious. Throughout the novellas, Stein seems primarily interested in the comic manifestations of her heroines' psychologies, or in the inverse relation, among friends and lovers, between power and need, or in clashes resulting from the attraction of opposite temperaments. One has no

sense that Stein recognizes what is clear in each plot: the defeat of a woman by dominant personality traits which are culturally defined as female. The three deaths of this trilogy are achieved in quick closing sections, almost appended as afterthought or postscript (only *The Good Anna* is divided into parts; "Part III, The Death of the Good Anna" takes up six of the story's seventy-one pages; Melanctha dies in half a page, Lena in half a paragraph).

Our attention is also diverted from the thematic implications of the plots by the characteristically impressionist temporal structure of *Three Lives*. Impressionist narrative generally begins on the eve of an important event or time, without letting the reader know that it has any particular significance. The story then "flashes back" to the events or times in the protagonist's life which build to this crucial moment, constructing the whole picture through an accretion of episodes, until the reader has a full sense of the import of that initial moment. Both *The Good Anna* and *The Gentle Lena* begin during the short time of the heroine's happiness (in service to a congenial mistress) which just precedes the reversal of her fortunes; the greater part of each story is a flashback to the life that led to that pinnacle. *Melanctha* begins with the death of Rose Johnson's baby, an episode which, despite its casual cruelty, seems at first to have no negative implications for Melanctha. Since we do not know that these initial moments immediately precede the heroine's defeated death, each novella seems to be progressing not toward death but toward a happy, or at least promising time in the character's life. (Stein in fact holds out false hope for Melanctha in the beginning of her story: "Melanctha Herbert had not *yet* been really married" [85; italics added].) It is this structure which gives the deaths of the heroines the quality of afterthought or postscript, distracting us from their actual thematic centrality.

Temporal structure works against thematic structure on other levels within *Three Lives*. The morals of these three tales depend on linear causality: Anna can be said to die of her goodness only insofar as we can see her becoming worn out and sick *because* she works too hard, eats too little, gives all her money to her friends. But linear causality in *Three Lives* is counteracted or counterbalanced by two conflicting temporal models, one which Stein calls the "continuous present," and the other which we might call "spatial form," or simply stasis.[9] To the extent that the time of the narrative is a "continuous present," the chronological events in each heroine's life are not linked causally. Instead, they are seen as a process of continual change, where one condition or state of being persists for a time and then is either suddenly transformed or gradually shifted into a different (often opposite) condition. But whether change is sudden or gradual, it is part of the natural process of life and not dependent on the will of a character or the logic of other events in the narrative. Change is often sudden: "And so Jeff Campbell went on with this dull and sodden, heavy, quiet always in him, and he never seemed to be able to have any feeling. Only sometimes he shivered hot with shame when he remembered some things he once had been feeling. And then one day it all woke up, and was sharp in him" (*Melanctha*, 194).

For gradual change, which is most characteristic of the "continuous present," Stein uses the word "now":

> Jeff Campbell never asked Melanctha any more
> if she loved him. Now things were always getting
> worse between them. Now Jeff was always very silent
> with Melanctha. Now Jeff never wanted to be honest
> to her, and now Jeff never had much to say to her.
> Now when they were together, it was Melanctha

always did most of the talking. Now she often had other girls there with her. . . .

Every day it was getting harder for Jeff Campbell. It was as if now, when he had learned to really love Melanctha, she did not need any more to have him. Jeff began to know this very well inside him. . . .

Every day Melanctha Herbert was less and less near to him. She always was very pleasant in her talk and to be with him, but somehow now it never was any comfort to him.

Melanctha Herbert now always had a lot of friends around her. Jeff Campbell never wanted to be with them. Now Melanctha began to find it, she said it often to him, always harder to arrange to be alone now with him. (*Melanctha*, 188–189)

With each "now," the situation is slightly worse. Stein captures a process which takes place over a period of time without isolating a past time from the "continuous present" of the narrative.

Though the kinetic model of time (life as constant change) dominates the narrative structure, the static, anti-developmental temporal model is reflected in the circularity (minus death) of each novella, as well as in the internal structure of many vignettes. Lena sits in the park with the other servant girls, her friends, who always tease her. One day she is playing with a green paper accordion that her young charge has dropped. One of her friends, Mary, suddenly asks her what she has on her finger.

"Why, what is it, Mary, paint?" said Lena, putting her finger to her mouth to taste the dirt spot.

"That's awful poison Lena, don't you know?" said Mary, "that green paint that you just tasted."

Lena had sucked a good deal of the green paint from her finger. She stopped and looked hard at the finger. She did not know just how much Mary meant by what she said.

"Ain't it poison, Nellie, that green paint, that Lena sucked just now," said Mary. "Sure it is Lena, its real poison. I ain't foolin' this time anyhow."

Lena was a little troubled. She looked hard at her finger where the paint was, and she wondered if she had really sucked it.

It was still a little wet on the edges and she rubbed it off a long time on the inside of her dress, and in between she wondered and looked at the finger and thought, was it really poison that she had just tasted.

"Ain't it too bad, Nellie, Lena should have sucked that," Mary said. . . .

And so they all three sat with their little charges in the pleasant sunshine a long time. And Lena would often look at her finger and wonder if it was really poison that she had just tasted and then she would rub her finger on her dress a little harder. (*The Gentle Lena*, 241–42)

There is no climax, no denouement: just a simple, static event, with all the participants acting in characteristic ways. Crucially, development is replaced by repetition, as each character reveals her essence by repeating the actions (Mary's teasing, Lena's dumb, comic sucking, staring, and worrying) which Stein uses to identify or symbolize it.

As in much impressionist and modernist fiction, narrative tone and temporal structure are at odds in *Three Lives* with the thematic content deducible from close reading and a reconstruction of linear causality. The tone and emphasis are noncommittal, cheerful, naive, at most mildly mocking; the thematic content is bitter, angry, implying a sophisticated social-political awareness and judgment. Temporal structure is preponderantly either a "continuous present" or static, yet each novella plots a classic trajectory of rise and fall. Nothing better epitomizes the contradictions of *Three Lives* than its epigraph, a quotation from Jules Laforgue: "Donc je suis un malheureux et ce/n'est ni ma faute ni celle de la vie." These lines certainly belie the narrator's cheerful innocence, but they equally belie the conclusions we can draw with excellent justification from all three novellas that a cruel "life," at least, is very much to blame for the mistreatment and death of these women.

We need no longer speculate about the psychological reasons for Stein's diverting attention, both her own and the reader's, from her anger and sadness. Richard Bridgman and Catharine Stimpson have shown with great clarity that Stein simultaneously concealed and encoded in her literary work troublesome feelings about herself as a woman, about women's helplessness, and particularly about lesbianism, still very much considered by society a "pollutant," as Stimpson puts it, during most of Stein's life. [10] But Stein did not merely stifle or deny her anger, her sense that she did not fit and that the deficiency was not hers but rather that of the structure which excluded her. In effect, Stein's rebellion was channelled from content to linguistic structure itself. [11] A rebellion in language is much easier to ignore or misconstrue, but its attack, particularly in literature, penetrates far deeper, to the very structures which determine, within a particular culture, what can be thought.

Stein's anti-patriarchal rebellion was not conscious or intentional, as her denial of her own bitterness and anger in *Three Lives* suggests. But for her, as perhaps for Virginia Woolf, there is an extra dimension to the view of experimental writing as anti-patriarchal, because both writers defined themselves in opposition to the notions of women which patriarchy provides.

Stein's attitude toward her gender offers further material for speculation. ⟨. . .⟩ when this material becomes particularly relevant to Stein's writing, her female self-hatred was such that she was psychologically compelled to identify herself as a man in order to be a happy, sexually active person and a functioning writer. While she lived with her brother Leo, she was a frequently depressed, subservient sister; when Leo left and Alice Toklas moved in, she became a generally happy, very productive husband. This male identification did not shift until the late twenties, when there is evidence that Stein began to feel better about her female identity. Throughout her radically experimental period, therefore, she essentially thought of herself as a man (there is direct evidence of this identification in the notebooks, where Stein says "Pablo & Matisse have a maleness that belongs to genius. Moi aussi, perhaps"). [12] We might posit a speculative connection between this male identification, and the concomitant suppression of her female identity, with the shift of the rebellious impulse from thematic content to linguistic structure, where the subversive implications of the writing are at once more powerful and more abstruse.

In relying totally on language itself to effect the transformation of the world, Stein is also very squarely within what Richard Poirier has identified as the American literary tradition in which rebellious imaginers use style to create an alternative "world elsewhere." Writers in this tradition

resist within their pages the forces of environment that otherwise dominate the world. Their styles have an eccentricity of defiance . . . they [try] to create an environment of "freedom," though as writers their efforts must be wholly in language. American books are often written as if historical forces cannot possibly provide such an environment, as if history can give no life to "freedom," and as if only language can create the liberated place.[13]

Within *Three Lives*, narrative tone and temporal structure serve to detach the text from its (at least formally) more traditional elements of thematic content and causative sequence, but to no significantly greater extent than do the impressionist structures and obtuse or multiple narrations of many other early modern novels.[14] However, impressionist structure and obtuse narration have a different significance in this early work of Stein's than they have for Conrad or even Faulkner. For Stein, the detachment of writing from coherent thematic content is the beginning of leaving such content behind altogether, of attempting to create "the liberated place" entirely through language. In *Three Lives*, in addition to these impressionist forms, we begin to see some of the experimental stylistic techniques Stein will use to develop antipatriarchal modes of literary signification, independent of coherent, referential, unitary meaning, hierarchical order, and the dominant signified.

Notes

1. Weinstein, *Gertrude Stein and the Literature of Modern Consciousness* (New York: Frederick Ungar Publishing Co., 1970).
2. Bridgman, *Gertrude Stein in Pieces* (New York: Alfred A. Knopf, 1966), 57.
3. Michael Hoffman, *Gertrude Stein*, Twayne's United States Authors Series, ed. Sylvia E. Bowman (Boston: Twayne, 1976), 21.
4. Conrad's Marlow, Ford's Dowell, Faulkner's Quentin, Fitzgerald's Nick Carraway, etc.
5. Gertrude Stein, *Three Lives* (1909; rpt. New York: Random House, 1936), 242–243.
6. Gertrude Stein, *Q.E.D.*, in *Fernhurst, Q.E.D., and Other Early Writings* (New York: Liveright, 1971). The similarity between *Q.E.D.* and *Melanctha* has been demonstrated and discussed by Bridgman in *Gertrude Stein in Pieces* (52–54); Leon Katz, in his introduction to *Fernhurst, Q.E.D., and Other Early Writings* (ix–xx); and Catharine Stimpson in "The Mind, the Body and Gertrude Stein," *Critical Inquiry* 3 (1977), 499–502.
7. For a full account of this affair and of its fictionalization in *Q.E.D.*, see Katz's introduction to *Fernhurst, Q.E.D., and Other Early Writings*.
8. See particularly Elaine Showalter, *A Literature of Their Own* (Princeton: Princeton University Press, 1977), and Sandra M. Gilbert and Susan Gubar, *The Madwoman in the Attic* (New Haven: Yale University Press, 1979).
9. This term was invented by Joseph Frank in his famous essay "Spatial Form in Modern Literature," *Sewanee Review* (1945). See also Sharon Spencer, *Space, Time and Structure in the Modern Novel* (Chicago: Swallow Press, 1971), and Patricia Tobin, *Time and the Novel: The Genealogical Imperative* (Princeton: Princeton University Press, 1978).
10. Stimpson, "The Mind, the Body and Gertrude Stein," 493.
11. Stein mentions her rebellion, using the word "revolt," several times (p. 29 of the notebook numbered "2" by Professor Katz) in the notebooks; i.e., "Leon like me in ideas and revolt." (Leon is Leon Solomons, her close friend and coworker in William James's laboratory at Harvard, on whom the character of David Hersland in *The Making of Americans* is partly based.)
12. This remark appears in a late notebook: p. 21 of the notebook labeled "C" by Stein.
13. Richard Poirier, *A World Elsewhere* (New York: Oxford University Press, 1966), 5.
14. See Tobin, *Time and the Novel*.

JAYNE L. WALKER
From *"Tender Buttons:*
'The Music of the Present Tense'"
The Making of a Modernist: Gertrude Stein
from Three Lives *to* Tender Buttons
1984, pp. 127, 138–49

In *Tender Buttons* Stein channeled the flood of concrete particulars she first tapped in *G.M.P.* to create an artfully structured composition. Its three sections, "Objects," "Food," and "Rooms," form a provocative sequence. From the external objects we see and touch, the text moves inward to the substances we ingest and, in the final section, outward again to the spaces that surround us. *Tender Buttons* describes a female world (circa 1912) of domestic objects and rituals—a world of dresses and hats, tables and curtains, mealtimes and bedtimes, cleanliness and dirt. Although a few exotic items, including an elephant and a "white hunter," make momentary appearances, the iconography of domestic life dominates the text. Concrete nouns and adjectives name a wealth of homely particulars. But in its artful rearrangement of these details, the text models a world in which objects, foods, and rooms are liberated from their normal subordination to human routines and purposes. ⟨. . .⟩

While its concrete objects are animated with human qualities, *Tender Buttons* presents human beings simply as physical objects, equal to all the others named and arranged in these "still lifes": "and so between curves and outlines and real seasons and more out glasses and a perfectly unprecedented arrangement between old ladies and mild colds there is no satin wood shining" (473). Here, as in "A Feather" and many other pieces, spatial contiguity is the ordering principle of this "perfectly unprecedented arrangement," but "mild colds" and "real seasons" mingle with the "curves and outlines" of purely spatial configurations. Sometimes the human body is reduced to a set of synecdoches, as in "Colored Hats": "Colored hats are necessary to show that curls are worn by an addition of blank spaces, this makes the difference between single lines and broad stomachs" (473). Occasionally the discourse creates shocking juxtapositions of human bodies and inanimate objects, as in "Little sales ladies little sales ladies little saddles of mutton" (475). This equation of "little sales ladies" with pieces of meat strikingly illustrates how radically the order of *Tender Buttons* refuses to privilege human meanings and purposes. In her earlier works, Stein portrayed human beings in terms of essential character, abstracted from their concrete daily life in the physical world. The radical reversal in *Tender Buttons* suggests not so much a dehumanization as a new affirmation that human existence is intimately involved with the physicality of matter and of flesh. The physical world portrayed in *Tender Buttons* includes the most intimate realities of the female body. "A Petticoat" shows "a disgrace, an ink spot, a rosy charm" (471). And a "shallow hole rose on red, a shallow hole in and in this makes ale less," an obvious transmutation of Alice (474).

At a number of points, *Tender Buttons* ironically invokes the social rituals that mediate this human immersion in the world of matter. "A Time to Eat," is described as "A pleasant simple habitual and tyrannical and authorised and educated and resumed and articulate separation" (472). "A table means . . . a whole steadiness. . . . A table means necessary places" (474). In stark contrast to the "articulate separation" of the ritual of dining, "Food," the second section of the text, celebrates the mixtures of diverse elements that we actually consume: "A separation is not tightly in worsted and sauce, it is so kept well and sectionally. Put it in the stew" (486). Individual ingredients combine in stews and sauces. "It is not astonishing that bones mingle" (483). But in "Food," as in the rest of *Tender Buttons*, concrete nouns and adjectives mingle in more astonishing ways. "A cake, a real salve made of mutton and liquor, a specially retained rinsing and an established cork and blazing" transforms an ordinary dinner into an astonishingly unpalatable menu (483). Although the individual foods named are rather bland, the bill of fare includes such exotic items as a "buttered flower" and a "carpet steak"—delightful combinations that can exist only in the realm of language (484, 488).

Tender Buttons begins by describing individual objects in terms of others that are related by similarity or contiguity. As the text progresses, however, its discourse becomes a combinative play of purely linguistic possibilities. "What is" is challenged by what one can "suppose," and some of these suppositions are mind-stretching exercises in absurdity:

> Supposing a certain time selected is assured, suppose it is even necessary, suppose no other extract is permitted and no more handling is needed, suppose the rest of the message is mixed with a very long slender needle and even if it could be any black border, supposing all this altogether made a dress and *suppose it was actual*, suppose the mean way to state it was occasional, if you suppose this in August and even more melodiously, if you suppose this even in the necessary incident of there certainly being no middle in summer and winter, suppose this and an elegant settlement a very elegant settlement is more than of consequence, it is not final and sufficient and substituted. This which was so kindly a present was constant. (466–67; my emphasis)

Every clause in this series is a correctly formed utterance; in this sense, they are all equally possible according to the grammatical rules of sentence formation. And the power of concrete nouns and adjectives forces the reader momentarily to "suppose it was actual," to imagine a message as a material entity, mixed with a needle and made into a dress. At times, in the midst of these absurd and impossible variations, the discourse suddenly reminds the reader that the words that it has been treating as playthings name objects that have a physical presence outside the realm of language:

> Supposing there is a bone, there is a bone. Supposing there are bones. There are bones. When there are bones there is no supposing there are bones. There are bones and there is that consuming. (480)

The power of this discourse to threaten our habitual sense of the order of things depends on our recognition that the nouns it plays with name the objects that we see, touch, and eat.

Custom, "necessary places," would exclude this rich play of possibilities. The word "custom" recurs throughout *Tender Buttons* to invoke the habitual modes of order that it systematically defies. "Custom is in the centre," but the method of the text is to "[a]ct so that there is no use in a centre" (483, 498). The cubist painters' most subversive structural innovation was their absolute rejection of the time-honored convention of single-point perspective. Their paintings lack a privileged center; they provide no vantage point that allows the spectator's eye to resolve their iconography into familiar images of normalized human perception. The discourse of *Tender Buttons* "act[s] so that there is no use in a centre" in an analogous way. As it creates its mind-stretching combinations

of nouns and adjectives, it deliberately refrains from constituting a human subject that would invite the reader to normalize them in terms of a psychological or narrative context. It asks questions, gives commands, and articulates a set of theoretical premises. But the discourse systematically refuses to present an authorial I/eye to serve as its origin and to guarantee its truth. "The author of all that is in there behind the door," teasing the reader with deliberate absence (499).

By compelling the reader to confront this idea that it is a structure that lacks a center, *Tender Buttons* most aggressively asserts its modernity. [1] Unseating both the subject and Western logic as privileged centers and guarantors of truth, this text deliberately flaunts the unlimited freeplay of substitution that is possible within the structure of language. Stein clearly conceived of language as a system of internal differences: "I and y and a d and a letter makes a change" (LGB, 106). She was acutely aware of the laws that govern sentence formation and of the ways in which they limit the possibilities of signification. *Tender Buttons* systematically demonstrates the idea that Nietzsche insistently expounded: "There is a philosophical mythology concealed in language." [2] In "'Reason' in Philosophy," he declared, "I fear we are not getting rid of God because we still believe in grammar." [3] In *Tender Buttons*, the play of substitution and combination takes place within the grammatical rules of sentence formation; this is what makes the text so subversive. By exploiting these inherently rational structures to "cause connections" that defy the most fundamental principles of logic, this text reduces to absurdity the fundamental philosophical assumptions that shape our use of language.

By the time she wrote *Tender Buttons*, Stein was far more convinced than William James, her first mentor, of the radical incompatibility between the order of language and the "truth" of unmediated sensory experience. In "Funes el memorioso" Borges created a character whose perfect perception and memory of detail made him virtually incapable of thought: "To think is to forget differences, to generalize, to abstract. In the over-stocked world of Funes there were only details, contiguous details." [4] The intense particularity of Funes's perceptions made him reject as too general even Locke's impossible dream of a language in which each individual object had its own name. In *Tender Buttons*, to write is to "practice the sign that means that really means a necessary betrayal" (468). In *Two* Stein had rejected all forms of rational ordering as reductions of the plenitude of immediate experience. She wrote *Tender Buttons* with a full awareness that even the act of naming entails a "necessary betrayal" of this "reality."

If even concrete nouns are a "betrayal," syntax is far more problematic, because of its inherently rational structure. If Stein had intended only to inventory the diverse contents of the "stream of consciousness," she could have written simple lists or polysyndetic series of nouns and adjectives. She occasionally used this form in *Tender Buttons*. But in general the text does not model the "stream" that James described as the structure of consciousness. In *Ulysses* Molly Bloom's soliloquy flows, but *Tender Buttons* is broken into a series of discrete and discontinuous pieces, separated by titles. In a recent essay, Italo Calvino proclaims the contemporary model of consciousness as "quite simply the revenge and triumph of all that is discontinuous, divisible and combinatory over continuous flux with its entire range of inter-related nuances." [5] He uses game theory and mathematical models to define the particular contemporaneity of this structural conception, but it is clearly prefigured both in cubist collage and in *Tender Buttons*. In Stein's text, this structure is dictated by her analysis of the order of language, not by a Jamesian conception of the "stream of consciousness." Its sentences are systematically patterned to foreground the most fundamental logical operations of syntax. But the freeplay of substitution and combination that these grammatical structures contain defies their inherent logical order.

"To be" is the verb most frequently used to forge connections among nouns in *Tender Buttons*. [6] In its copulative functions, this verb forms propositions of identity and predicates attributes or properties. The discourse of *Tender Buttons* depends on these copulative functions of the verb to "cause connections," but the propositions of identity it asserts refuse to make sense in any conventional way: "The sudden spoon is the wound in the decision" (471); "A shawl is a hat and hurt and a red balloon and an under coat and a sizer a sizer of talks" (475). *Tender Buttons* contains a multitude of these propositions of identity that are logically absurd. This copulative function of the verb "to be" is fundamental to definitions. Beginning with its opening section, *Tender Buttons* demonstrates the problem of defining the uniqueness of any object in language. Frequent repetition of the phrase "what is" systematically foregrounds this problem, while the discourse continues to demonstrate its denial of the logical principle of identity in every copulative sentence it creates.

The word "use" also recurs again and again, often in the phrase "what is the use." This repetition frequently emphasizes that the names of objects in this text are liberated from their normal subordination to human use and freed to enter the combinative play of the discourse: "There is no use there is no use at all in smell, in taste, in teeth, in toast, in anything, there is no use at all and the respect is mutual" (479). "Rooms" contains a brilliant demonstration of the inherent difficulty of defining objects in terms of their use (502). It begins with a plausible definition of a cape: "A cape is a cover." But a complication immediately emerges: "a cape is not a cover in summer." If a cape is to be defined by its function, then what is it when the weather precludes its use? The issue is resolved facetiously: "a cape is a cover and the regulation is that there is no such weather." Summer must be banished from this closed system of definition. But another problem arises, and again the issue is use: "A cape is not always a cover, a cape is not a cover when there is another." Finally, the discourse ironically concedes that "there is some use in not mentioning changing," but the point of the demonstration is clear. Definitions based on use are inadequate. No definition can account for the actual circumstances of any particular object. Like the sign, the definition is a "necessary betrayal" of the rich diversity of the external world.

The principle of causality is also under siege in *Tender Buttons*. "To make" is second only to the verb "to be" in the frequency of its occurrence in the text. [7] In logical discourse, this verb asserts relationships of cause and effect. In *Tender Buttons*, "A curving example makes righteous finger-nails" (508). Human actions and emotions have startling physical effects: "sincerely graciously trembling, sincere in gracious eloping, all this makes a furnace and a blanket" (480). Frequent repetition of the words "why" and "because" also serves to foreground the principle of causality, while the sentences in which they appear reduce it to absurdity: "Why should ancient lambs be goats and young colts and never beef, why should they, they should because there is so much difference in age" (480). The question "Why?" often stands alone, unanswered and unanswerable. Some of these questions are provocative: "Why is there so much resignation in a package" (502). Some are absurd: "why is there no oyster

closer" (503). At one point this questioning turns back on itself: "Let us why, let us why weight, let us why winter chess, let us why why" (493). In "Rooms," the final section of *Tender Buttons*, the questions address the mysteries of man and nature: "why is there rain"; "Why is there so much useless suffering. Why is there" (502, 508). This persistent repetition of "why," in so many different contexts, acknowledges the perpetual human desire to assign causal explanations at the same time that it suggests the absence of any final cause that would arrest this incessant process of questioning.

The two other verbs that recur with a high degree of frequency in *Tender Buttons* are "to show" and "to mean." Like "to be" and "to make," they generally occur in lexical contexts that violate the logical processes of demonstration and interpretation:

> A white cup means a wedding. A wet cup means a vacation. A strong cup means an especial regulation. A single cup means a capital arrangement between the drawer and the place that is open. (484)
> The season gliding and the torn hangings receiving mending all this shows an example, it shows the force of sacrifice and likeness and disaster and a reason. (501)

The semantic content of these and many other similar sentences eludes the rational interpretive processes that the syntactical structures invoke. All the sentences in *Tender Buttons* serve as "examples" of the inherent logical order of language and the semantic incongruity it can be forced to contain. But the discourse also insists that "[a] sign is the specimen spoken" (483). The objects it names are "specimens"; they are not symbols. They resist interpretation, except as a parodic gesture: "The stamp that is not only torn but also fitting is not any symbol. It suggests nothing" (501).

Norman Weinstein has suggested that "[T]he sentence has lost its function in *Tender Buttons*, so its purpose is no longer purely informational. The sentence is used as an aesthetic construct rather than a logical, syntactical necessity." [8] The sentences in *Tender Buttons* are certainly not "purely informational." But Weinstein's comments fail to recognize how systematically this text patterns its language to undermine the "logical, syntactical necessity" of the sentence. Like Stein, the surrealists also used the sentence to bring logically unrelated nouns together into fortuitous unions. But as Lyotard has argued, their violations of sense do not seriously attack language as a system. [9] The tension that Stein's text creates between its deliberate semantic disorder and its relentless repetition of the fundamental grammatical structures of logical discourse systematically calls into question the order inherent in language. The motifs of containment and closure recur throughout *Tender Buttons*, and the sentence is presented as the ultimate closed structure: "A sentence of a vagueness that is violence is authority and a mission and stumbling and also certainly also a prison" (481). For Stein, as for Nietzsche, the inherent logic of the sentence is the "prison-house of language." Its authority delimits our thought. The method of this text is to expose the laws that govern this "prison" and to exploit their inherent force to consummate the most arbitrary and violent unions within its confines. Each of its sentences "is a spectacle, it is a binding accident" (468). No matter how "accidentally" its concrete nouns and adjectives are assembled, they are "bound" together by the conventional power of syntax.

At the end of each of the first two sections of *Tender Buttons*, the discourse uses another technique to subvert the imprisoning system of language. Meanings come undone as words are separated into clusters of phonemes: "bay labored," "be section," "sam in," "be where" (495, 493). "Easy" is transformed into "e c" (494). "Alice" becomes "eel us" and "ale less" (494, 474). The word "eating" generates the series "Eating he heat eating he heat it eating, he heat it heat eating. He heat eating" (494). In *A Long Gay Book* Stein wrote, "The doctrine which changed language was this, . . . it was the language segregating" (LGB, 109). This disintegration of words powerfully demonstrates the fact that language is a combinative system in which meaning is determined by internal differences. At the end of "Objects," this assault on the stability and coherence of words evokes suggestions of physical violence and sexual aggression:

> Aider, why aider why whow, whow stop touch, aider whow, aider stop the muncher, muncher munchers.
>   A jack in kill her, a jack in, makes a meadowed king, makes a to let. (TB, 476)

Near the end of "Food," the process of linguistic fragmentation culminates in a powerful aesthetic statement which, itself, immediately disintegrates into non-sense:

> real is, real is only, only excreate, only excreate a no since.
>   A no, a no since, a no since when, a no since when since, a no since when since a no since when since, a no since, a no since when since, a no since, a no, a no since a no since, a no since, a no since. (TB, 496)

Stein's pursuit of "reality" forced her to confront the irreconcilable difference between the order of language and the chaotic plenitude of immediate experience. As I emphasized earlier in this chapter, *Tender Buttons* claims that each of its "collections" of words "shows the disorder, . . . it shows more likeness than anything else." By the time she wrote this text, Stein's acute awareness of language as a "necessary betrayal," coupled with her continuing dedication to the "realism of the composition," had led her to conclude that, within language, "real is only, only excreate, only excreate a no since." Uniting the words creation and excretion, the verb "excreate" boldly asserts the inseparable connection between mind and matter. External to more conventional creativity, nonsense is the only viable model of the "real" that language can create.

Tender Buttons does not end with the kind of violent assaults on language that conlude the first two sections of the text. In "Rooms" the structures of words and sentences remain intact. The thematic interplay of separation and union continues to dominate the final portion of the text. But instead of culminating in disintegrative violence, "Rooms" builds to a final affirmation of harmonious union. Images of openness and spreading replace the boxes and other closed containers that dominate in "Objects," and the semantic field widens to encompass the world of nature as well as the man-made domestic interior. The natural world provides material for less problematic definitions—"Star-light, what is star-light, star-light is a little light that is not always mentioned with the sun, it is mentioned with the moon and the sun, it is mixed up with the rest of the time" (504)—perhaps because the question of "use" is irrelevant to something as distant as a star. Nature also suggests new metaphorical models for the creative process: "Nothing aiming is a flower. . . . Why is there more craving than there is in a mountain" (508). Restating its methods, the discourse reaffirms its power to create a purely poetic order: "centre no distractor, all order is in a measure" (506). Dance is used as another metaphor for the creative process: "Dance a

clean dream and an extravagant turn up" (508). Language playfully combines the ballerina's turn-out with the homely turnip. No object is too lowly to join in this measured dance of words. *Tender Buttons* begins with a closed container; it ends with expansive natural images: [10]

> The care with which the rain is wrong and the green is wrong and the white is wrong, the care with which there is a chair and plenty of breathing. The care with which there is incredible justice and likeness, all this make a magnificent asparagus, and also a fountain. (509)

By concluding with these images, *Tender Buttons* suggests an affinity between its artistic reordering of the familiar world and the fecund, replete harmony of nature that transcends the conceptual orders imposed by man. The poetic order it creates never claims to represent objective truth: "Claiming nothing, not claiming anything, not a claim in everything, collecting claiming, all this makes a harmony, it even makes a succession" (480). It asserts no facts; it does not solicit the reader's belief in the particular "harmonies" it creates. *Tender Buttons* is a playful text, a text to play with. What it offers is not truth but a joyous transgression of rationality, an imaginative liberation from our habitual sense of "reality": "all the pliable succession of surrendering makes an ingenious joy" (484). But the reader who surrenders to the lure of this playful and subversive discourse is challenged to reevaluate his customary idea of the order of "reality" and forced to recognize the extent to which it is shaped by the order of language.

In *Tender Buttons*, Stein joyfully embraced what she later identified as the "reality of the twentieth century . . . a time when everything cracks, where everything is destroyed, everything isolates itself" (P, 49). Later in her career she asserted that the "creator of the new composition in the arts is an outlaw until he is a classic," until the time when the "modern composition having become past is classified and the description of it is classical" (SW, 514). From our vantage point, we can readily situate *Tender Buttons* within the historical poetics of modernism. In Yeats's "Second Coming," "[t]hings fall apart; the center cannot hold." In *The Waste Land*, a "heap of broken images" is presented as the sum of human knowledge. Fragmentation and the loss of a center have become part of our "classical description" of the themes and structural principles of literary modernism. But Stein remained an "outlaw" long after writers like Yeats and Eliot were enshrined as "classics." The playful, domesticated disorder of *Tender Buttons* is strikingly different from the apocalyptic "rough beast" presaged by Yeats's vision of chaos or the spiritual aridity of Eliot's "waste land." In *Tender Buttons* the absence of a center is presented not as a loss but as a liberation that allows limitless invention of new, purely poetic orders.

Stein's earlier texts trace the arduous resistance that preceded this affirmation of the "reality of the twentieth century," which shaped all of her work after 1912. It is because her confrontation with this "reality" entailed such a radical critique of language that she still remains something of an "outlaw" in the Anglo-American literary tradition. In the texts that preceded *Tender Buttons*, she manipulated the material resources of language to embody her goal of "completed understanding." By the time she wrote *Tender Buttons*, she had left behind this pursuit of total knowledge in and through language and, with it, all nostalgic longing for this ideal. No longer conceived as an instrument for embodying external truth, language became her playground. Years later, she recalled the initial ecstasy of this liberation:

I found myself plunged into a vortex of words, burning words, cleansing words, liberating words, feeling words, and the words were all ours, and it was enough that we held them in our hands to play with them; whatever you can play with is yours, and this was the beginning of knowing. [11]

This statement highlights the fundamental seriousness of Stein's most playful texts. They are all based on the premise that knowledge must begin with a knowledge of language. Rigorously investigating its laws and testing its limits, Stein's texts continue to challenge their readers to a new awareness of the system of language as both the necessary instrument and the inevitable "prison" of thought.

Notes

1. Jacques Derrida has identified this kind of "decentering," which rejects the notion of any certain presence that exists outside of structure, as characteristic of the modern era. He associates this "rupture" with the "moment . . . when language invaded the universal problematic, . . . when, in the absence of a center or an origin, everything became discourse . . . that is to say everything became a system in which the central signified, the originary or transcendental signified, is never absolutely present outside a system of differences. The absence of the transcendental signified infinitely extends the field and the play of signification" ("La Structure, le signe, et le jeu dans le discours des sciences humaines," in *L'Ecriture et la différence* [Paris: Seuil, 1967], pp. 409–11).

2. From *The Wanderer and His Shadow* (1880), quoted in Friedrich Nietzsche, *Twilight of the Idols and the Anti-Christ*, trans. R. J. Hollingdale (London: Penguin Books, 1968), p. 191.

3. *Twilight of the Idols*, p. 38.

4. "Sospecho, sin embargo, que no era muy capaz de pensar. Pensar es olvidar diferencias, es generalizar, abstraer. En el abarrotado mundo de Funes no había sino detalles, casi immediatos" (Jorge Luis Borges, *Ficciones* [Buenos Aires: Emecé Editores, 1956], p. 126).

5. Italo Calvino, "Notes toward a Definition of the Narrative Form as a Combinative Process," trans. Bruce Merry, *Twentieth Century Studies* 3 (May 1970): 95.

Neil Schmitz's essay "Gertrude Stein as Post-Modernist" (*Journal of Modern Literature* 3, 5 [July 1974]: 1203–18) is the only previous treatment of *Tender Buttons* to address the "core of its linguistic pact" (p. 1204). Correctly rejecting Brinnin's and Hoffman's analogies between Stein's work and cubist painting, Schmitz too readily dismisses the paintings themselves in his argument that *Tender Buttons* is a *post*-modernist work, unrelated to the aesthetics of cubism. As my comparative references in this chapter and elsewhere indicate, I see more continuity than rupture between the "modernism" of Stein and Picasso and both "post-modernist" literature and "post-structuralist" literary theory.

6. In *Gertrude Stein: A Biography of Her Work* (New Haven: Yale University Press, 1951), Donald Sutherland noted that Stein's "constant use of *is* or *makes* as the main verb is a simple sum or equation" (p. 95).

7. It seems important to emphasize the pervasiveness of the verbs I discuss in this section. A rough count indicates that "to make" occurs 95 times in the text; "to show," 93 times; "to mean," 59 times. Forms of the verb "to be" appear 382 times. "To have" is the only other frequent verb (60). Miscellaneous verbs total only 377.

8. Weinstein, *Gertrude Stein and the Literature of the Modern Consciousness* (New York: Frederick Ungar, 1970), p. 64.

9. "No attack on language as a system, only violations within the utterance. And at least in the case of Breton, the violations are exclusively semantic [*Pas d'atteinte à langue, seulement des dérogations de parole. Et chez Breton au moins, exclusivement semantique*]" (Lyotard, *Discours, figure*, p. 325; cf. p. 289). For Breton, the "light of the image" is the essential power of surrealist writing, and the most forceful images are those that represent the highest degree of arbitrariness in the "two realities" they bring together (*Manifestes du surréalisme*, pp. 50–51).

10. Allegra Stewart first noted this, in *Gertrude Stein and the Present* (Cambridge, MA: Harvard University Press, 1967), p. 132.

11. "American Language and Literature" (1944), manuscript #548 in YCAL.

JOHN STEINBECK

1902–1968

John Ernst Steinbeck was born on February 27, 1902, in Salinas, California, to John Ernst and Olive Hamilton Steinbeck. He attended Stanford University, where he took courses in science, becoming interested in marine biology. He later formed a close friendship with noted marine biologist Edward F. Ricketts, who for many years was Steinbeck's mentor and critic. Their expedition to the Galapagos Islands was the basis for *The Sea of Cortez* (1941), and Ricketts appears as a character in several other works. In 1930 Steinbeck married Carol Henning; they were divorced in 1942, and in 1943 he married Gwyndolen Conger. The couple had two sons before their divorce in 1948. In 1950 Steinbeck married Elaine Scott.

Steinbeck's first novel, *Cup of Gold* (1929), went largely unnoticed, as did his next two, *The Pastures of Heaven* (1932) and *To a God Unknown* (1933), although *The Pastures of Heaven* later received greater critical attention. His first significant recognition came with the publication of *Tortilla Flat* (1935), and then with the play and novel *Of Mice and Men* (1937). Steinbeck was praised for his accomplishments as a writer in the American idiom, and the play *Of Mice and Men* won the New York Drama Critics' Circle Award. *The Grapes of Wrath*, published in 1939, made Steinbeck famous. This epic of dispossessed Oklahoma sharecroppers in search of a promised land in California was extremely topical, and also crystallized themes that remained prominent in Steinbeck's writing thereafter: concern for the working classes, the preying of men upon one another, and sentimental attachments to land and community. The book won the Pulitzer Prize for fiction in 1940 and was made into an acclaimed motion picture.

Steinbeck's later work, including *Cannery Row* (1944), *The Pearl* (1947), *The Wayward Bus* (1947), *East of Eden* (1952), *Sweet Thursday* (1954), *The Winter of Our Discontent* (1961), and *The Short Reign of Pippin IV* (1957), have been criticized for inconsistent quality and structural awkwardness, and simultaneously praised for their realistic, compassionate stories and powerful characterizations. In 1962 Steinbeck published *Travels with Charley*, a journalistic account of his journey across America with his dog; that year he was awarded the Nobel Prize for literature. Steinbeck died on December 20, 1968, in New York City.

EDMUND WILSON
From "The Boys in the Back Room" (1941)
Classics and Commercials
1950, pp. 35–45

V. *John Steinbeck*

John Steinbeck is also a native Californian, and he has occupied himself more with the life of the State than any of these other writers. His exploration in his novels of the region of the Salinas Valley has been more tenacious and searching than anything else of the kind in our recent fiction, with the exception of Faulkner's exhaustive study of the State of Mississippi.

And what has Mr. Steinbeck found in this country he knows so well? I believe that his virtuosity in a purely technical way has tended to obscure his themes. He has published eight volumes of fiction, which represent a variety of forms and which have thereby produced an illusion of having been written from a variety of points of view. *Tortilla Flat* was a comic idyl, with the simplification almost of a folk tale; *In Dubious Battle* was a strike novel, centering around Communist organizers and following a fairly conventional pattern; *Of Mice and Men* was a compact little drama, contrived with almost too much cleverness, and a parable which criticized humanity from a non-political point of view; *The Long Valley* was a series of short stories, dealing mostly with animals, in which poetic symbols were presented in realistic settings and built up with concrete detail; *The Grapes of Wrath* was a propaganda novel, full of preachments and sociological interludes, and developed on the scale of an epic. Thus attention has been diverted from the content of Mr. Steinbeck's work by the fact that when his curtain goes up, he always puts on a different kind of show.

Yet there is in Mr. Steinbeck's fiction a substratum which remains constant and which gives it a certain weight. What is constant in Mr. Steinbeck is his preoccupation with biology. He is a biologist in the literal sense that he interests himself in biological research. The biological laboratory in the short story called *The Snake* is obviously something which he knows at first hand and for which he has a strong special feeling; and it is one of the peculiarities of his vocabulary that it runs to biological terms. But the laboratory described in *The Snake*, the tight little building above the water, where the scientist feeds white rats to rattlesnakes and fertilizes starfish ova, is also one of the key images of his fiction. It is the symbol of Mr. Steinbeck's tendency to present human life in animal terms.

Mr. Steinbeck almost always in his fiction is dealing either with the lower animals or with humans so rudimentary that they are almost on the animal level; and the relations between animals and people are as intimate as those in the zoöphile fiction of David Garnett and D. H. Lawrence. The idiot in *The Pastures of Heaven*, who is called Little Frog and Coyote, shows his kinship with the animal world by continually making pictures of birds and beasts. In *Tortilla Flat*, there is the Pirate, who lives in a kennel with his dogs and has practically forgotten human companionship. In *In Dubious*

Battle, there is another character whose personality is confused with that of his dogs. In *The Grapes of Wrath*, the journey of the Joads is figured at the beginning by the progress of a turtle, and is accompanied and parodied all the way by animals, insects and birds. When the expropriated sharecroppers in shelter, to another wretched victim of famine and flood, on the point of death from starvation. To what end should ponies and Oakies continue to live on the earth? "And I wouldn' pray for a ol' fella that's dead," the preacher goes on to say. "He's awright. He got a job to do, but it's all laid out for 'im an' there's on'y one way to do it. But us, we got a job to do, an' they's a thousan' ways, an' we don' know which one to take. An' if I was to pray, it'd be for the folks that don't know which way to turn."

This preacher who has lost his religion does find a way to turn: he becomes a labor agitator; and this theme has already been dealt with more fully in the earlier novel, *In Dubious Battle*. But what differentiates Mr. Steinbeck's picture of a labor movement with radical leadership from most treatments of such subjects of its period is again the biological point of view. The strike leaders, here, are Communists, as they are in many labor novels, but *In Dubious Battle* is not really based on the formulas of Communist ideology. The kind of character produced by the Communist movement and the Communist strategy in strikes (of the Communism of the day before yesterday) is *described* by Mr. Steinbeck, and it is described with a certain amount of admiration; yet the party member of *In Dubious Battle* does not talk like a Marxist of even the Stalinist revision. The cruelty of these revolutionists, though they are working for a noble ideal and must immolate themselves in the struggle, is not palliated by the author any more than the cruelty of the half-witted Lennie; and we are made to feel all through the book that, impressive though the characters may be, they are presented primarily as examples of how life in our age behaves. There is developed in the course of the story—especially by a fellow-traveller doctor who seems to come closer than the Communist to expressing Mr. Steinbeck's own ideas—a whole philosophy of "group-man" as an "animal."

> "It might be like this, Mac: When group-man wants to move, he makes a standard. 'God wills that we recapture the Holy Land'; or he says 'We fight to make the world safe for democracy'; or he says, 'We will wipe out social injustice with communism.' But the group doesn't care about the Holy Land, or Democracy, or Communism. Maybe the group simply wants to move, to fight, and uses these words simply to reassure the brains of individual men. . . . "
> "How," asks Mac, "do you account for people like me, directing things, moving things? That puts your group-man out."
> "You might be an effect as well as a cause, Mac. You might be an expression of group-man, a cell endowed with a special function, like an eye cell, drawing your force from group-man, and at the same time directing him, like an eye. Your eye both takes orders from and gives orders to your brain."
> "This isn't practical," objects Mac. "What's all

this kind of talk got to do with hungry men, with lay-offs and unemployment?"

"It might have a great deal to do with them. It isn't a very long time since tetanus and lockjaw were not connected. There are still primitives in the world who don't know children are the result of intercourse. Yes, it might be worth while to know more about group-man, to know his nature, his ends, his desires. They're not the same as ours. The pleasure we get in scratching an itch causes death to a great number of cells. Maybe group-man gets pleasure when individual men are wiped out in a way."

Later, when the mob of striking fruit-pickers begins to get out of hand, the Communists themselves begin to think of them in these infra-human terms:

"They're down there now. God, Mac, you ought to of seen them. It was like all of them disappeared, and it was just one big animal, going down the road. Just all one animal." . . .

"The *animal* don't want the barricade. I don't know what it wants. Trouble is, guys that study people always think it's men, and it isn't men. It's a different kind of animal. It's as different from men as dogs are. Jim, it's swell when we can use it, but we don't know enough. When it gets started it might do anything."

So the old pioneer of "The Leader of the People" describes a westward migration which he himself once led as "a whole bunch of people made into one big crawling beast. . . . Every man wanted something for himself, but the big beast that was all of them wanted only westering."

This tendency on Steinbeck's part to animalize humanity is evidently one of the causes of his relative unsuccess at creating individual humans. The *paisanos* of *Tortilla Flat* are not really quite human beings: they are cunning little living dolls that amuse us as we might be amused by pet guinea-pigs, squirrels or rabbits. They are presented through a special convention which is calculated to keep them cut off from any kinship with the author or the reader. In *The Grapes of Wrath*, on the other hand, Mr. Steinbeck has summoned all his resources to make the reader feel his human relationship with the family of dispossessed farmers; yet the result of this, too, is not quite real. The characters of *The Grapes of Wrath* are animated and put through their paces rather than brought to life; they are like excellent character actors giving very conscientious performances in a fairly well-written play. Their dialect is well managed, but they always sound a little stagy; and, in spite of Mr. Steinbeck's efforts to make them figure as heroic human symbols, one cannot help feeling that these Okies, too, do not exist for him quite seriously as people. It is as if human sentiments and speeches had been assigned to a flock of lemmings on their way to throw themselves into the sea. One remembers the short story called "Johnny Bear." Johnny Bear is another of Steinbeck's idiots: he has exactly the physique of a bear and seems in almost every way subhuman; but he is endowed with an uncanny gift for reproducing with perfect mimicry the conversations he overhears, though he understands nothing of their human meaning.

It is illuminating to look back from *The Grapes of Wrath* to one of the earliest of Steinbeck's novels, *To a God Unknown*. In this book he is dealing frankly with the destructive and reproductive forces as the cardinal principles of nature. In one passage, the hero is described by one of the other characters as never having "known a person": "You aren't aware of persons, Joseph, only people. You can't see units,

Joseph, only the whole." He finds himself, almost unconsciously and in contravention of Christianity, practising a primitive nature cult, to which, in time of terrible drought, he sacrifices first his wife, then himself, as blood offerings to bring the rain. This story, though absurd, has a certain interest, and it evidently represents, on the part of Steinbeck just turned thirty, an honorably sincere attempt to find expression for his view of the world and his conception of the powers that move it. When you husk away the mawkish verbiage from the people of his later novels, you get down to a similar conception of a humanity not of "units" but lumped in a "whole," to a vision equally grim in its cycles of extinction and renewal.

Not, however, that John Steinbeck's picture of human beings as lemmings, as grass that is left to die, does not have its striking validity for the period in which we are living. In our time, Shakespeare's angry ape, dressed in his little brief authority, seems to make of all the rest of mankind angry apes or cowering rodents. The one thing that was imagined with intensity in Aldous Huxley's novel, *After Many a Summer Dies the Swan*, was the eighteenth-century exploiter of the slave-trade degenerating into a fetal anthropoid. Many parts of the world are today being flooded with migrants like the Joads, deprived of the dignity of a human society, forbidden the dignity of human work, and made to flee from their houses like prairie-dogs driven before a prairie fire. Aldous Huxley has a good deal to say, as our American "Humanists" did, about a fundamental moral difference which he believes he is able to discern between a human and an animal level, and the importance of distinguishing between them; and, like the Humanists, he has been frightened back into one of those synthetic cults which do duty for our evaporated religions. The doctor of *In Dubious Battle* is made, on the contrary, to deprecate even such elements of religion as have entered into the labor cause at the same time that he takes no stock in the utopianism of the Marxists. When he is depressed by the barbarity of the conflict and is reminded by the neophyte Jim that he "ought to think only of the end: out of all this struggle a good thing is going to grow," he answers that in his "little experience the end is never very different in its nature from the means . . . It seems to me that man has engaged in a blind and fearful struggle out of a past he can't remember, into a future he can't foresee nor understand. And man has met and defeated every obstacle, every enemy except one. He cannot win over himself. How mankind hates itself." "We don't hate ourselves," says Jim. "We hate the invested capital that keeps us down." "The other side is made of men, Jim, men like you. Man hates himself. Psychologists say a man's self-love is balanced neatly with self-hate. Mankind must be the same. We fight ourselves and we can only win by killing man."

The philosophy of Mr. Steinbeck is obviously not satisfactory in either its earlier or its later form. He has nothing to oppose to this vision of man's hating and destroying himself except an irreducible faith in life; and the very tracts he writes for the underdog let us see through to the biological realism which is his natural habit of mind. Yet I prefer his approach to the animal-man to the mysticism of Mr. Huxley; and I believe that we shall be more likely to find out something of value for the control and ennoblement of life by studying human behavior in this spirit than through the code of self-contemplation that seems to grow so rootlessly and palely in the decay of scientific tradition which this latest of the Huxleys represents.

For the rest, Mr. Steinbeck is equipped with resources of observation and invention which are exceptional and sometimes astonishing, and with color which is all his own but which does not, for some reason, possess what is called magic.

It is hard to feel that any of his books, so far, is really first-rate. He has provided a panorama of California farm-life and California landscape which is unique in our literature; and there are passages in some ways so brilliant that we are troubled at being forced to recognize that there is something artistically bad about them. Who has ever caught so well such a West Coast scene as that in *To a God Unknown* in which we visit the exalted old man, with the burros, who has built his hut high on the cliff so that he can look down on the straight pillars of the redwoods and off at the sea far below, and know that he is the last man in the western world to see the sun go down? What is wrong here is the animal sacrifice which the old man performs at this moment and which reminds us of the ever-present paradox of the mixture of seriousness and trashiness in the writing of Mr. Steinbeck. I am not sure that *Tortilla Flat*, by reason of the very limitations imposed by its folk-tale convention, is not artistically his most successful work.

Yet there remains behind the journalism, the theatricalism and the tricks of his other books a mind which does seem first-rate in its unpanicky scrutiny of life.

STANLEY ALEXANDER
"The Conflict of Form in *Tortilla Flat*"
American Literature, March 1968, pp. 58–66

Critical study of Steinbeck's fiction has been inhibited by the hostile, imprecise use of "primitivism" as a piece of critical invective. More unfortunate than this circumstance, however, critics who are sympathetic to Steinbeck have been constrained to deny that his imagination is in any way formed by primitivistic ideas. [1] Peter Lisca, for example, mentions primitivism only in his introduction, where he successfully arraigns the shortcomings of some thirty years of criticism which followed the direction taken in Edmund Wilson's offhand early essay, [2] and in the chapter on *Tortilla Flat*, the one work of Steinbeck's which Lisca finds it necessary to defend against charges of primitivistic idealism. [3] In this defense Lisca quotes from Mark Schorer's essay, "Technique as Discovery," in support of his contention that *Tortilla Flat* is exploratory and satirical rather than primitivistic: "As for the resources of language, these, somehow, we almost never think of as part of the technique of fiction—language as used to create a certain texture and tone which in themselves state and define themes and meanings." He applies Schorer's statement as follows:

This function of language is very crucial in *Tortilla Flat*, and it is the failure to perceive the fact that has resulted in that book's being hailed by critics as expressing Steinbeck's ideal of a primitivistic humanity and society, and by the reading public as presenting a quaint and curious picture of the dispossessed. That neither of these was intended by Steinbeck is clear not only from the carefully sustained language of the book and the special Foreword he wrote for the Modern Library edition, but from the tenor of his next four books—*In Dubious Battle, Of Mice and Men, The Grapes of Wrath*, and especially, *The Forgotten Village*. In none of these is the "natural" state of man seen as ideal; nor are poor diet and filth considered quaint or superior to more civilized standards of living. . . . in *Tortilla Flat* he wished to "explore the strong but different philosophic-moral systems" of these *paisanos*. [4]

The inadequacies of this widely accepted view are many. In the first place, Schorer's idea that the tone and texture of language in fiction can "define themes and meanings" can be used quite as well to argue that there is idealization of the *paisanos'* social lowness and quaintness and simplicity, and hence that there is a significant measure of primitivism and pastoralism in *Tortilla Flat*. Second, the meanings imparted by tone and texture in *Tortilla Flat* are enormously complicated by the parodistic mock-heroic form of the novel. For Steinbeck, as also for Anderson, Hemingway, and Faulkner, relatively primitive humanity is where you find it, and it was particularly convenient to Steinbeck in the California *paisanos*. Third, it seems an age late to correct Lisca's too easy dependence on the doctrine of artistic intention. Steinbeck has indeed denied that he meant to give a "quaint and curious picture of the dispossessed." I shall return to the mode and implications of this denial later. It is enough to say at this point that by his denial Steinbeck has, in effect, imputed to his readers the motives that he finds so objectionable. In this essay I hope to show that this confusion has to do with conflict between the novel's mock-heroic form and Steinbeck's affinity for pastoral. [5]

Steinbeck is, despite his dabblings in biological science and philosophy, a romantic artist; his gambits into transcendental mysticism and his own doctrine of non-teleological thought should warn us against expecting an absolute thematic or formal unity among his works in their entirety or between any two. On the other hand, the single quality of his works which most strongly suggests unity of purpose and theme is his glorification of relatively primitive humanity. Lisca's progressive-humanist righteousness in Steinbeck's behalf is sometimes obtuse; of course, Steinbeck does not hold "poor diet and filth" as being "quaint or superior to more civilized standards of living." But one powerful implication of the novel is, certainly, that nutrition and sanitation, the touchstones of scientific progressivism, are not the absolute boons the twentieth century considers them. More important, the novel bears the implication that outside Tortilla Flat, down in Monterey proper, "getting and spending" have laid waste the innate and spontaneously expressed qualities which define humanity and which make life worth living. This, it seems to me, is a major part of the burden of meaning carried by "tone and texture" in *Tortilla Flat*. Before the full measure can be taken of the importance of tone and texture in *Tortilla Flat*, we must understand the form which Steinbeck's language was fitted to.

Form constitutes a major problem with regard to Steinbeck's fiction for the reason that he is, although novel and "creative"—romantic—perhaps the most derivative and technically conventional of recent American writers. His derivativeness is most remarkable in the category of narrative form; biblical narrative provides him with the paradisal form which emphasizes locale and a related exodus form which features removal, journey or search, and discovery as thematic concomitants. Steinbeck is exceptionally inventive in his use of traditional form, however, and this inventiveness is nowhere more remarkable than in *Tortilla Flat*, where, incongruously, primitive-pastoral feeling is conveyed by means of a variety of mock-heroic, nominally and originally a form designed to satirize the social classes pushing up from below. In its very gradually progressive episodic form, its approximation of the Round Table in arrangement of characters, and, above all, its playful mimicry of heraldic language, this novel is a descendant of *The Dunciad* and *M'Fingal*.

Mock-heroic ostensibly treats *as if they were heroic* individuals who, by virtue of their character and their class, everyone knows *cannot possibly be heroic*. Now pastoral does virtually the same thing, but in sentimental fashion, without the historical and heraldic paraphernalia, and for different purposes. Whereas, for purposes of ridicule, mock-heroic imputes conventionally admirable heroic traits to persons, groups or classes who do not possess them, pastoral literature, for the sake of social unity and mystical naturalism, treats peasant or lower-class people sentimentally, as being naturally good, wise, and happy. That is to say, mock-heroic gains its peculiar satirical effect by violating a literary convention which has strong social connections or, as Kenneth Burke might put it, by incongruously rearranging an established ratio between act and actor. Before the democratic-romantic revolution in social dramatism, heroism in literature was a noble or at least an aristocratic attribute; lower-class characters of drama and narrative might aspire to courage or "heart," but heroism implied the whole man and his ancestry as well. Mock-heroic, furthermore, comes into prominence with the Augustans and can be seen as a commentary on the same social movements which had produced the Tory-Whig rivalry in politics. Mock-heroic is a product of genteel self-awareness, of the nagging awareness that history does not cover the same ground twice (that there was scarcely anything left in genteel life which conformed to heroic ideals), and a product, more immediately, of the social pressures originating from below in the commercial and yeoman classes. What comes under attack in mock-heroic, however, is not the failing genteel social order or the magical, nature-nourished pastoral (peasant) class, but the usurping middle class. Mock-heroic, then, commits comic aggressions against an emergent powerful middle class which disturbs the beneficent relationship between nobility and peasantry.

Joseph Fontenrose, the author of a recent book on Steinbeck,[6] draws out in some detail the parallelism between *Tortilla Flat* and Malory's *Morte Darthur*, points out the presence of both picaresque and social satire in the novel, and discusses most intelligently the essentially biological substructure of the book. Fontenrose is, however, the too-willing victim of his primary interest—myth criticism. Hence he is led to argue that:

> . . . the term "mock-heroic" seems misleading if applied to *Tortilla Flat*. Steinbeck is too fond of both paisanos and Arthurian legend to be guilty of belittling either. *Tortilla Flat* both illuminates the Dark Ages and dignifies the paisanos. We are again confronted with an antithesis: the actual lives of men who enjoy fighting, live on others' labor, and shun work are opposed to the legendary lives of men whose mode of life was much the same. If anything, the paisanos are more amusing and less dangerous than the knights. The sort of thing that they do is the stuff that legends are made of. . . .[7]

One can agree with almost everything in this passage and yet feel that it constitutes a misconception of the kind of book, in its combination of tradition and imagination, *Tortilla Flat* is. For example, Fontenrose correctly points out that the *paisanos* are "more amusing and less dangerous than the knights," but he indicates no awareness of the implications of this disparity when literary convention is considered. Perhaps he is correct to argue, as I understand him, that Steinbeck intends naturalistically to "debunk" the Arthurian legends by superimposing them on the most incongruous material, but he seems to me to see the thing in reverse. This juxtaposition of nobility and lowness is a form of literary joking that comes under the heading of "mock-heroic" and, as such, does not so much analyze the heraldic legendry as comically impute an incongruous nobility to Danny and his friends. There is literary parody here, but here is also a mixture of two incipiently antagonistic kinds of form and tone, mock-heroic and pastoral.

It seems plain to me also that critics have missed an important part of the meaning of *Tortilla Flat* when they have taken Danny and his friends as being exclusively the actual *paisanos* of Steinbeck's sympathetic and affectionate experience. There is justice in the frequently uttered complaint that Danny and Pilon and Pablo and Jesus Maria Corcoran and the others are not "real people" or "living characters," that they are merely picturesque, animalistic mannikins which are subject to Steinbeck's too-easy manipulation. But this criticism often is based, like Lisca's defense of *Tortilla Flat*, on a rather narrow, progressivist preference for ethical realism. This preference tends to withhold approval from any except what Northrop Frye calls the "low mimetic" in fiction and to reward only "social realism." Thus Maxwell Geismar in *Writers in Crisis*:

> The more mature author of *The Grapes of Wrath* might, indeed, have found a few disturbing factors in the life of *Tortilla Flat*. Isn't our Danny, in sober truth, being exploited somewhat? . . . In all this sexual activity which marks the paisano life, what is the proportion of social disease. . . . whenever, indeed, there is opportunity in *Tortilla Flat* for more serious social appraisal, Steinbeck avoids reflection by the use of an intellectual conceit. Just as he might have deepened his book by the illumination of the positive human values in the paisano society, as compared with our own, he again ignores the more realistic significance of the paisano existence. His folk epic becomes rather too strongly a fantasy.[8]

This kind of trained incapacity strikes one as ludicrous now, but Geismar brings us closer to insight than more recent critics like Lisca and Fontenrose. Geismar recognizes at once that the novel "avoids reflection by the use of an intellectual conceit." That is, the novel's broadest symbolic and social effect was to take pressure off its ethically bedeviled middle-class readers, to let them view the poor and dispossessed once again as pastoral creatures in a timeless order of things. The Arthurian legendry on which it is framed and the language in which it is presented militate against a narrowly political type of symbolic action, but *Tortilla Flat* has a politics—a very complacent politics, indeed—which allows its readers to feel blamelessly sentimental and innocently primitive.

What William Empson says of *The Beggar's Opera* applies very neatly to Steinbeck's novel:

> Some queer forces often at work in literature can be seen there unusually clearly; its casualness and inclusiveness allow it to collect into it things that had been floating in tradition. It is both mock-heroic and mock-pastoral, but these take Heroic and Pastoral for granted; they must be used as conventions and so as ways of feeling if they are even to be denied. It would be as reasonable to say that human nature is exalted as that it is debased by this process. . . . But pastoral usually works like that; it describes the lives of "simple" low people to an audience of refined wealthy people, so as to make them think first "this is true about everyone" and then "this is especially true about us."[9]

In particular these ideas are useful for understanding the marked disparity between Steinbeck's conception of his novel and that of the reviewers and readers, and as well, between Lisca's reading of the novel as objective, mildly satirical fiction and my reading of it as a mixture of mock-heroic and mock-pastoral which, although it does not perhaps "take primitive values for granted," yet conveys these values in significant measure.

Steinbeck's purported intentions and his reiterated "fondness" for the Monterey *paisanos* are substantial and irreducible facts, but they are facts of a different order from the fact constituted by the book *Tortilla Flat*. These extraliterary facts may well prove misleading if they are imported into a critical consideration of the book itself because the book seems to convey something more than Steinbeck's fondness for the *paisanos*. There is a kind of disjunction between Steinbeck's sympathetic intentions with regard to these characters and the symbolic action which is produced in the book. [10] *Tortilla Flat* produces a certain uneasiness, just as Hemingway's Spanish stories do, especially in respect to such peasants as those in *For Whom the Bell Tolls*. The artfully concealed (or unconscious) but unconcealable condescension of the original pastoral artifice shows through in Hemingway to a truly objectionable extent and the more so when the Hemingway protagonist is present to provide the once edifying social juxtaposition. How is it that *Tortilla Flat* offends, then, when there is no representative of the exploitative middle-class (not even a new aristocrat such as Doc in *Cannery Row*) by which the *paisanos'* lowliness is to be measured? I think it is because of the mock-heroic form; an identifiably genteel-aristocratic viewpoint is so strongly projected that no such actual presence is required among the personnel of the novel. This is, of course, nothing new; Wordsworth's genteel presence effectively provided the exalted persona required as the other half of the pastoral formula of social harmony, and Gray's presence quite redeemed the already vanished personalities of the lowly dead in the country churchyard. The thing to notice here is that the narrative point of view is enormously superior to its subjects, the *paisanos*, so much so, in fact, that it can maintain indefinitely the elaborate conceit of Arthurian identification.

The justice of this analysis is, I think, borne out by the rather too righteous distress of Steinbeck's angry Foreword to the Modern Library edition of *Tortilla Flat*—written in 1937, two years after original publication and after the book had put his career on a new footing; the Foreword's burden is that the *paisanos'* stories were not written because they were quaint and thus fit to be re-told for superior readers.

> I wrote these stories because they were true stories and because I liked them. But literary slummers have taken people up with vulgarity of duchesses who are amused and sorry for a peasantry. These stories are out, and I cannot recall them. But I shall never again subject to the vulgar touch of the decent these good people of laughter and kindness, of honest lusts and direct eyes, of courtesy beyond politeness. If I have done them harm by telling a few of their stories, I am sorry. It will never happen again. [11]

That the easy vicarious pastoralism of many of the reviews had aroused Steinbeck to this temper—this alone seems to me not an adequate explanation. It seems probable that the sentimental and superior attitudes of readers and reviewers led Steinbeck to make a discovery about himself, the discovery that his romantically naturalistic view of the *paisanos* was more complicated than he had known and that his primitivistic, underdog, democratic, working-class sympathies were at least moderately alloyed with other feelings. On the other hand, one doubts that Steinbeck was ever aware that his ethical conflicts were parallel with the novel's mock-heroic and pastoral literary conventions.

That Steinbeck remained unaware of the exact nature of his embarrassment and anger seems to me certain, else how could he have included as the dramatized argument of the Foreword the sweetish, child-cultish story of his school-friend the *piojo*, who was "a nice, kind, brown little boy," an orphan who is kept by his sister, the "hoor-lady." The hoor-lady is a good woman and despite Steinbeck's long subjection to decency he still cannot think of her as "(that nastiest of words) a prostitute, nor of *piojo's* many uncles, jolly men who sometimes give us nickels, as her clients." [12]

This locution, "can't think of her as . . . a prostitute," is of the very essence of that literary pastoralism which avoids seeing the life below as "it actually is," limited and deprived and sometimes brutal, and substitutes for objective vision a highly conventionalized sentimental image of "natural" freedom and happiness. It is this pastoral feeling which in the Tortilla Flat *paisanos* as much as in the beggars and thieves of *The Beggar's Opera* celebrates a kind of primitive "cult of Independence," as Empson calls it. Tone and texture render the *paisanos* the equals (and in the Arthurian context, the superiors) of us respectable middle-class folk. They appeal ambiguously to our pastoralist need to feel superior even while we sentimentally praise the limited life and to our primitivist conviction that the simple, independent man who acts on his libidinal impulse is truly better off. This literary ambiguity is untoward and unfortunate, but it truly represents some ethical ambiguities which few in our society have yet been able to resolve.

Notes

1. As I use the term, primitivism refers to a broad range of ideas and values, a consistent feature of which is their antithetical relation to the norms of modern culture, society, and psychology. The primitivist in literature tends to find value in the historical and cultural past, or at some point rather low on the social scale, or in the instinct-related, "basic" emotion. An engaging but unconvincing different opinion is given by Kingsley Widmer in "The Primitivistic Aesthetic: D. H. Lawrence," *Journal of Aesthetics and Art Criticism*, XVII, 344–353 (March, 1959). Widmer makes a distinction between primitivism as a fairly consistent rationale and what he calls "the *primitivistic*," the recent use of the primitive as ethically burdened but essentially aesthetic literary artifact and symbol. I do not agree, holding rather that the relatively primitive material in Lawrence, Faulkner, Hemingway, and Steinbeck is weighted more heavily on its ethical, "antimodern" side.

2. Peter Lisca, *The Wide World of John Steinbeck* (New Brunswick, N. J., 1958), pp. 6–9. Wilson's essay is reprinted in *Classics and Commercials* (New York, 1950).

3. Lisca, pp. 88–89.

4. Ibid., pp. 81–82.

5. William Empson, *Some Versions of Pastoral* (New York, 1960). Empson defines pastoral literature in ways that are suggestive and illuminating to students of American literature. Large spans and particular strains of our literature become more understandable from the viewpoint he demonstrates (although he scarcely mentions an American writer). Particularly useful is his notion that the pastoral's essential form consists in bringing together socially high and socially low characters in the same scene. In this way, the pastoral is able to share in the best motives of both heroic and folk literatures. The same is true, still, of Romantic and American writing where the more or less exalted character has, perhaps for egalitarian reasons, retreated behind the author's own sensibility. And now tone is as important as form. Describing the pastoral formula which lies behind the convention of the wise fool in *As You Like It*, Empson could as well be writing of *Tortilla Flat* or *Cannery Row* (or Willa Cather's story "Neighbor Rossicky," or Faulkner's *Go Down, Moses* or Hemingway's Spanish stories): he says that under this convention "The simple man becomes a clumsy fool who yet has better 'sense' than his betters and can say things more fundamentally true; he is 'in contact with nature,'

which the complex man needs to be . . . he is in contact with the mysterious forces of our own nature, so that the clown has the wit of the Unconscious; he can speak the truth because he has nothing to lose" (p. 14).

6. Joseph Fontenrose, *John Steinbeck: An Introduction and Interpretation* (New York, 1963).

7. Ibid., p. 40.

8. Maxwell Geismar, *Writers in Crisis* (New York, 1958).

9. Empson, pp. 185–186.

10. For an early argument somewhat along these lines, see Joseph Warren Beach, "John Steinbeck, Journeyman Artist," reprinted in *Steinbeck and His Critics: A Record of Twenty-five Years,* ed. E. W. Tedlock, Jr., and C. V. Wicker (Albuquerque, 1957), pp. 80–91. Steinbeck's fondness for the *paisanos* seems to Beach a fondness for the underdog, in whom "the primary human impulses are less overlaid with disguise, and stand out in stark simplicity. But this last, observe, is an artistic reason, a literary reason. The likings of an artist are always open to suspicion; and we have to distinguish between his liking for people themselves and his liking for his subject." My argument is that frequently Steinbeck has not been able (or seen fit) to make such a distinction.

11. John Steinbeck, *Tortilla Flat,* Modern Library edition (New York, 1937), Foreword.

12. Ibid., p. 11.

PETER LISCA

"The Dynamics of Community in
The Grapes of Wrath" (1970)
From Irving to Steinbeck:
Studies of American Literature
in Honor of Harry R. Warfel
eds. Motley Deakin and Peter Lisca
1972, pp. 127–40

The Grapes of Wrath, more than Steinbeck's other novels, remains viable not just in drugstore racks of Bantam paperbacks or in college survey courses but in the world of great literature, because in that novel he created a community whose experience, although rooted firmly in the particulars of the American Depression, continues to have relevance. Certainly one aspect of that community experience which contributes to its viability is its dimension of social change. It is not coincidence that in the last decade, full of violent social action in so many aspects of American life, we have found ourselves turning with new interest toward the 1930s, recognizing there an immediate political and emotional relevance. *The Grapes of Wrath* moves not only along Route 66, east to west, like some delayed Wagon Wheels adventure, but along the unmapped roads of social change, from an old concept of community based on sociological conditions breaking up under an economic upheaval, to a new and very different sense of community formulating itself gradually on the new social realities.

Various facets of the old community concept are solidly developed in the first quarter of the book. The novel opens with a panoramic description of the land itself, impoverished, turning to dust and quite literally blowing away. It can no longer sustain its people in the old way, one small plot for each family, and it is lost to the banks and holding companies—impersonal, absentee landlords—which can utilize the land with a margin of profit by the ruthless mechanical exploitation of large tracts. But for the old community the land was something more than a quick-money crop or columns of profit and loss in a financial ledger, more even than the actual physical sustenance of potatoes, carrots, melons, pigs and chickens. Nor is it fear of the unknown that keeps the community attached to the now useless land. For these are a people with pioneer blood in their veins. The old community is further tied to the land by memories of family history. It is Muley who speaks this most convincingly:

> I'm just wanderin' aroun' like a damn ol' graveyard ghos'. . . . I been goin' aroun' the places where stuff happened. Like there's a place over by our forty; in a gulley there's a bush. Fust time I ever laid with a girl was there. Me fourteen an' stampin' an' jerkin' an' snortin' like a buck deer, randy as a billygoat. So I went there an' I laid down on the groun', an' I seen it all happen again. An' there's the place down by the barn where Pa got gored to death by a bull. An' his blood is right in that groun', right now. . . . An' I put my han' on that groun' where my own Pa's blood is part of it. . . . An' I seen my Pa with a hole through his ches', an' I felt him shiver up against me like he done. . . . An' me a little kid settin' there. . . . An' I went into the room where Joe was born. Bed wasn't there, but it was the room. An' all them things is true, an' they're right in the place they happened. Joe came to life right there.

Muley rambles, but his selection is not arbitrary—copulation, birth, death. And these are not just vague memories or abstractions. In the presence of the actual bush, the actual barnyard, the same room, this essential past is relived in the present. Muley asks, "What'd they take when they tractored the folks off the lan'? What'd they get so their 'margin a profit' was safe? They got Pa dyin' on the groun', an' Joe yellin' his first breath, an' me jerkin' like a billygoat under a bush in the night. What'd they get? God knows the lan' ain't no good. . . . They jus' chopped folks in two. Place where folks live is them folks."

Here Muley speaks not only for himself, but for an entire community, the people in whose deserted houses at night he can still sense the "parties an' dancin'," the "meetin's an' shoutin' glory. They was weddin's, all in them houses." So strong is his attachment that he chooses to stay with the land and its empty houses rather than move away with the rest of his family. Grandpa Joad, too, despite his eagerness at the beginning, was not able to leave the land and had to be given an overdose of pain-killer and carried off. When he dies, just before crossing the Oklahoma border, Casy assures the folks that "Grampa didn't die tonight. He died the minute you took 'im off the place. . . . Oh, he was breathin', but he was dead. He was that place, an' he knowed it. . . . He's jus' stayin' with the lan'. He couldn't leave it." This is amplified to the level of community experience in one of the interchapters, when the choric voices intone: "This land, this red land is us; and the flood years and the dust years and the drought years are us."

As the land itself and its houses are imbued with a traditional experience, so are the farm tools, horses, wagons, the household goods whose value cannot be measured in money: the beaded headband for the bay gelding, "'Member how he lifted his feet when he trotted?" And the little girl who liked to plait red ribbons in his mane. "This book. My father had it. . . . Pilgrim's Progress. Used to read it. . . . This china dog . . . Aunt Sadie brought it from the Saint Louis fair. See? Wrote right on it." It is a community experience which is imaginatively voiced to the buyers of these goods: "You are not buying only junk, you're buying junked lives. . . . How can we live without our lives? How will we know it's us without our past?"

In addition to the identity invested in the land, the houses and personal possessions, all of which must be left behind, the community is also defined in terms of social customs and mores. That it is patriarchal, for example, is clear from the deference of the women to male decision and authority. When the decision is made to include Casy in the group, Ma Joad is consulted about whether there would be food enough and space, but once that decision is made, Casy, who "knew the government of families," takes his place among the planning men. "Indeed, his position was eminent, for Uncle John moved sideways, leaving space between Pa and himself for the preacher. Casy squatted down like the others, facing Grampa enthroned on the running board. Ma went to the house again." It does not matter that Grampa is senile and utterly useless. Formally, his titular headship must be acknowledged, and, at this point in the novel, Ma must leave men to men's business. Again, when the family is seating itself in their truck, ready to leave, Uncle John would have liked his pregnant niece, Rosasharn, instead of himself, to sit up front in the comfortable seat next to the driver. But he knows "this was impossible, because she was young and a woman." The traditional distinction in social role is also evident in Ma's embarrassment at Casy's offer to salt down the pork. "I can do it," he says; "there's other stuff for you to do." Ma "stopped her work then and inspected him oddly, as though he suggested a curious thing. . . . 'It's women's work,' she said finally." The preacher's reply is significant of many changes to come in the community's sense of identity and the individual's sense of his total role: "It's all work," he replies. "They's too much of it to split it up to men's or women's work."

It is fitting that this break from domestic traditions should be announced by Casy, who is the first person from his community whom Tom meets on the way home from prison, and who announces at that meeting that he, the preacher, the spiritual source and authority of that community, has already abandoned the old dispensation and is seeking a new and better one. And after hearing his short, two-sentence, unorthodox testament of belief in an oversoul, a human spirit "ever'body's a part of," Tom says, "You can't hold no church with idears like that. People would drive you out of the country with idears like that. Jumpin' an' yellin'. That's what folks like. Makes you feel swell. When Granma got to talkin' in tongues, you couldn't tie her down. She could knock over a full-growed deacon with her fist." Later in the novel other details of this old-time religion are given, such as the mass total immersions; Pa, full of the spirit, jumping over a high bush and breaking his leg; and Casy going to lie in the grass with young girls of his congregation whose religious fervor he had excited. But Casy is through with all that now, and these particular aspects of community, like those inherent in the land, the houses and personal goods, the domestic codes—all must be left behind.

This is not to say, however, that the sense and need of community is lost or has been destroyed. Steinbeck presents this sense and need on several levels from the biological to the mythical and religious. The novel's first interchapter is that masterful description of the turtle crossing the road, surviving both natural hazards and the attempts of man to frustrate its efforts. The turtle is clearly a symbol of the unthinking yet persistent life force. "Nobody can't keep a turtle though," says Casy. "They work at it and work at it, and at last one day they get out and away they go. . . . " The fact that this turtle has been going southwest, that Tom picks it up as a present to the family, and that it continues southwest when released, clearly identifies this turtle and its symbolic attributes with the Joads and the migrants. In them too, there exists the instinct for

survival and the necessity for movement which form, on the most elemental level, the basis of community.

The last interchapter of the novel's first part (before the Joads actually start their trip) also presents a biological argument. The abandoned houses are only temporarily without life. Soon they are part of a whole new ecology.

When the folks first left, and the evening of the first day came, the hunting cats slouched in from the fields and mewed on the porch. And when no one came out, the cats crept through the open doors and walked mewing through the empty rooms. And then they went back to the fields and were wild cats from then on, hunting gophers and field mice, and sleeping in ditches in the daytime. When the night came, the bats, which had stopped at the doors for fear of light, swooped into the houses and sailed about through the empty rooms, and in a little while they stayed in dark room corners during the day, folded their wings high, and hung headdown among the rafters, and the smell of their droppings was in the empty houses.

And the mice moved in and stored weed seeds in corners, in boxes, in the backs of drawers in the kitchens. And weasels came in to hunt the mice, and the brown owls flew shrieking in and out again.

Now there came a little shower. The weeds sprang up in front of the doorstep, where they had not been allowed, and grass grew up through the porch boards. . . . The wild cats crept in from the fields at night, but did not mew at the doorstep any more. They moved like shadows of a cloud across the moon, into the rooms to hunt the mice.

This life force, which manifests itself in getting the turtle across the road and in creating a new biological community around the abandoned houses, lies also in the nature of man. And because man can abstract and conceptualize, that force is present in him not only in his instinct for physical survival, but also as projected in his gregariousness and social constructs. Thus, despite the fact that the anonymous truck driver in chapter two, a not particularly likable person, is forbidden to carry riders, and may lose his very valuable job for doing so, it is his need for human contact as well as his need of being a "good guy" that prompts him to give Tom Joad a ride: "Fella says once that truck skinners eats all the time. . . . Sure they stop, but it ain't to eat. They ain't hardly ever hungry. They're just goddamn sick of goin'—get sick of it. Joints is the only place you can pull up, an' when you stop you got to buy somepin' so you can sling the bull with the broad behind the counter."

Even Tom Joad, who comes into the novel aggressively independent, not only recollects how a fellow inmate at prison who had been paroled came back to prison because it made him feel "lonesome out there," but admits to the same desire for human community in himself. "'The guy's right too,' he said. 'Las' night, thinkin' where I'm gonna sleep, I got scared. An' I got thinkin' about my bunk, an' I wonder what the stir-bug I got for a cell mate is doin'. Me an' some guys had a strang band goin'. Good one. Guy said we ought to go on the radio. An' this mornin' I didn't know what time to get up. Jus' laid there waitin' for the bell to go off.'" Casy understands this need of man for community. When he tells Tom, "They's an army of us without no harness. . . . All along I seen it. . . . Everplace we stopped I seen it. Folks hungry for sidemeat, an' when they get it they ain't fed," he is saying in his own words that man cannot live by bread alone, that it takes more than a full stomach to make man happy. In one of the interchapters the choric voice defines in communal terms this "harness" which man needs:

> The last clear definite function of man—muscles aching to work, minds aching to create beyond the single need—this is man. To build a wall, to build a house, a dam, and in the wall and house and dam to put something of Manself [note he does not say *him*self], and to Manself take back something of the wall, the house, the dam. . . . For man, unlike any other thing organic or inorganic in the universe, grows beyond his work, walks up the stairs of his accomplishments. . . . Fear the time when Manself will not suffer and die for a concept, for this one quality is the foundation of Manself, and this one quality is man, distinctive in the universe.

It is this inherent feeling of "Manself," to use Steinbeck's term, which forges the link of community, making out of all the scattered, lonely individuals a huge and irresistible "WE."

Further, in *The Grapes of Wrath* these seemingly inherent biological drives toward community are supported and given authority through a continuum of historical and religious reference. The Joads trace their ancestry back to the colonization of the new world: "We're Joads," says Ma. "We don't look up to nobody. Grampa's grampa, he fit in the Revolution." Looking into the terrible desert which they are about to cross, Al exclaims, "Jesus, what a place. How'd you like to walk across her?" "People done it," says Tom. "Lots a people done it; an' if they could, we could." "Lots must a died," says Al. "Well," replies Tom, "we ain't come out exactly clean." As she consoles Tom for the necessity of suffering insults meekly (when they are stopped by vigilantes at the roadblock), Ma Joad repeats again this sense of being supported by participation in a historical community: "You got to have patience. Why, Tom—us people will go on living when all them people is gone. Why, we're the people—we go on." And one of these phrases, "We're the people," strikes echoes answered in Psalm 95: "For He is our God; and we are the people of his pasture, and the sheep of his hand," thus giving the Joads community with the "chosen people."

The details which further this association are so numerous and have been pointed out by scholars so frequently as to need little discussion here. Briefly, the twelve Joads are the twelve tribes of Judea; they suffer oppression in Oklahoma (Egypt) under the banks (Pharaohs); undertake an exodus; and arrive in California (Canaan, the land of milk and honey) to be received with hostility by the native peoples. The novel's title, through "The Battle Hymn of the Republic," alludes to Deuteronomy, Jeremiah, and Revelation, as for example "And the angel thrust in his sickle into the earth, and gathered the vine of the earth, and cast it into the great winepress of the wrath of God." In some of the interchapters the strong echoes of the King James Old Testament poetically identify the evils of the present with those decried and lamented by the Prophets:

> Burn coffee for fuel in the ships. Burn corn to keep warm, it makes a hot fire. Dump potatoes in the river and place guards along the banks to keep the hungry people from fishing them out. Slaughter the pigs and bury them, and let the putrescence drip down into the earth.
> There is a crime here that goes beyond denunciation. There is a sorrow here that weeping cannot symbolize. There is a failure here that topples all our success. The fertile earth, the straight tree rows, the sturdy trunks, and the ripe fruit. And children dying

of pellagra must die because a profit cannot be taken from an orange.

As the numerous allusions and parallels to the Old Testament establish a historical community between the oppressed migrants and the Israelites, the even more numerous allusions and parallels to the New Testament establish a religious community in Christianity. Again, the evidence is so extensive and has been so thoroughly analyzed elsewhere that little discussion is needed here. The most important of these elements is the itinerant preacher, who has lately left off preaching. Beginning with his initials, J.C.; his rebellion against the old religion; his time of meditation in the wilderness; his announcement of the new religion; his taking on his head the sins of others; to his persecution and death crying out, "You don' know what you're doin'"; Jim Casy is clearly a modern Christ figure. The new messiah arrives in a rich context of traditional Christian symbology, and his message, like that of Christ, is one that considerably broadens man's sense of spiritual community.

It rejects theological notions of sin ("There ain't no sin and there ain't no virtue. There's just stuff people do."); it defines the religious impulse as human love ("What's this call, this sperit? . . . It's love."); and it identifies the Holy Spirit as all men, the human spirit ("Maybe all men got one big soul ever'body's a part of."). Later in the novel, Casy becomes bolder and extends this community beyond man—"All that lives is holy"—and finally embraces even the inorganic world—"There was the hills, an' there was me, an' we wasn't separate no more. We was one thing. An' that one thing was holy." His disciple, Tom Joad, repeats Casy's notion of an Oversoul, and immediately quotes from Ecclesiastes to further support the notion of community: "Two are better than one, because they have a good reward for their labor. For if they fall, the one will lif' up his fellow, but woe to him that is alone when he falleth, for he hath not another to help him up." When his mother expresses fear that they may kill him, he replies, "Then it don' matter. Then I'll be ever'where—wherever you look. Wherever there's a fight so hungry people can eat, I'll be there. . . . I'll be in the way kids laugh when they're hungry an' they know supper's ready." As another said before him, "Behold, I am always with you."

These forces for community which Steinbeck presents in the novel—biological, social, historical, religious—are impressive for their strength and variety, manifesting themselves in a range from the physical functions of unthinking organisms to the efflux of divine spirit. But in *The Grapes of Wrath* we do not see the realization of utopian community, for there are anticommunity forces as well; and these, too, are strong and manifest themselves in a wide range. Even the religious impulse, which in Casy and Tom is a positive force, can be a negative one, a perversion of its real purpose. Thus Uncle John's sense of personal sin isolates him from his fellowman and drives him to debauchery and a further sense of sin and isolation. Religion is seen as an isolating force also in the fanatic Mrs. Sandry, who frightens Rosasharn with her descriptions of the horrible penalties God visits on pregnant women who see plays, or does "clutch-an-hug dancin'," seeing *these* as the causes of miscarriage and malformation, rather than disease and malnutrition, as Satan, in the guise of the camp manager, claims. The greatest practical realization of community in the novel is the government camp at Weedpatch, especially the dance. Despite the strong forces against them the people foil attempts to instigate a fight which will give the corrupt police the power to break up the camp. It is important, therefore, that during the dance the religious fanatics are seen as separate: "In front of their tents the Jesus-lovers sat and watched, their faces hard and contemptuous. They did not speak to one another, they watched for sin, and their faces condemned the whole proceeding."

Back at the other end of the scale, we see anticommunity forces at work also on the biological level of sheer survival. It is not greed or hatred or even ignorance that makes Willy drive one of the destroying tractors: "I got two little kids," he says. "I got a wife an' my wife's mother. Them people got to eat. Fust an' on'y thing I got to think about is my own folks." But Muley notes what is behind the bluster: "Seems like he's shamed, so he gets mad." Mr. Thomas, the owner of a small orchard who is pressured by the Farmers Association to lower his wages, is also doing what he is ashamed of in order to survive, and he too speaks "irritably" and becomes gruff. Near the end of the novel, Ma Joad sees through the glib gibes of the pathetic little clerk in the expensive company store: "Doin' a dirty thing like this. Shames ya, don't it? Got to act flip, huh?" Whether or not the used-car salesmen overcharging for their jalopies also feel shame we do not learn. But clearly these people, as well as many others in the novel, are working against community because of the need for individual survival. Perhaps that is one of the significances of those calm little descriptions of predatory activity in nature which are found throughout the novel. Immediately preceding the car salesmen, for example, we have this: "gradually the skittering life of the ground, of holes and burrows, of the brush, began again; the gophers moved, and the rabbits crept to green things, the mice scampered over clods, and the winged hunters moved soundlessly overhead."

Sometimes the instinct of mere survival shades into selfishness and greed, as when the large owners squeeze out the little people and pay far lower wages than they can afford. It is interesting of Steinbeck's method that selfishness as an anticommunity drive, absolutely apart from any necessity for survival, receives its barest treatment in an episode involving the Joads themselves, the children. At the government camp, Ruthie breaks into a peaceful, established croquet game, unwilling to wait her turn. Insisting, "I wanta play now," she wrestles a mallet from a player. The actions of the other children are interesting. Under the guidance of the supervisor, they simply abandon the game to her, refusing community so to speak, leaving her alone and ridiculous on the court until she runs away in tears.

A third anticommunity force is the result of still another step beyond mere survival—the creation of a system, a machine, a monster, which seems to have a life of its own. Steinbeck presents it in a hypothetical choric dialogue:

We're sorry. It's not us. It's the monster. The bank isn't like a man.
Yes, but the bank is only made of men.
No, you're wrong there—quite wrong there. The bank is something else than men. It happens that every man in the bank hates what the bank does, and yet the bank does it. The bank is something more than men, I tell you. It's the monster. Men made it, but they can't control it.

But a monster need not be a bank. It may be "an owner with fifty-thousand acres," or it may be the entire economic structure itself which works against community: "Men who can graft the trees and make the seed fertile and big can find no way to let the hungry people eat their produce. Men who have created new fruits in the world cannot create a system whereby their fruits may be eaten . . . the works of the roots of the vines, of the trees must be destroyed to keep up the price. . . . And

coroners must fill in the certificates—died of malnutrition—because the food must rot, must be forced to rot."

In the light of certain cliches about the social message in Steinbeck's supposedly "revolutionary" novel, it is interesting that these concepts of the "monster" and of a backward religion are only two of several anticommunity forces, and that the rest lie not in social structures but in man's own nature or individuality, as with the forces toward survival and selfishness discussed above and the forces of suspicion and ignorance. It is distrust that makes the transport company place a "No Riders" sign on the windshield of its trucks. It is a suspiciousness learned in jail that makes Tom, before his conversion, say for the second time, "I'm just puttin' one foot in front a the other," and again in a few pages, "I ruther jus' lay one foot down in front a the other." He doesn't trust people enough to extend himself. So deeply engrained is this suspicion that even at the government camp he is immediately suspicious of the "committee" which he is told will visit them tomorrow, and Pa Joad is openly hostile toward the camp manager's visit, although both occasions are friendly and helpful. Casy tells the story of the organizer who got a union started to help the workers: "An' know what? Them very folks he been tryin' to help tossed him out. Wouldn' have nothin' to do with 'im. Scared they'd get saw in his company. Says, 'Git out. You're a danger on us.'"

Along with suspicion and distrust is ignorance. There is the simple ignorance of the hired tractor driver who perhaps lives twenty miles away in town and needs not come back to his tractor for weeks or months:

And this is easy and efficient. So easy that the wonder goes out of work, so efficient that the wonder goes out of land and the working of it, and with the wonder the deep understanding and the relation. And in the tractor man there grows the contempt that comes only to a stranger who has little understanding and no relation. For nitrates are not the land, not phosphates; and the length of fiber in the cotton is not the land. Carbon is not a man, nor salt nor water nor calcium. He is all of these, but he is much more, much more; and the land is so much more than its analysis. The man who is more than his chemistry, walking on the earth, turning his plow point for a stone, dropping his handles to slide over an outcropping, kneeling in the earth to eat his lunch; that man who is more than his elements knows the land that is more than its analysis. But the machine man driving a dead tractor on land that he does not know and love, understands only chemistry; and he is contemptuous of the land and of himself. When the corrugated iron doors are shut, he goes home, and his home is not the land.

A more complex aspect of ignorance as a force against community appears in the interchapters, most clearly in that chapter wherein migrants are forced to sell their household goods to profiteers who take advantage of their need in order to pay very little for honest goods, and who are addressed by the choric voice: "you're buying bitterness. Buying a plow to plow your own children under, buying the arms and spirits that might have saved you. Five dollars, not four. I can't haul them back—Well, take 'em for four. But I warn you, you're buying what will plow your own children under. And you won't see. You can't see. . . . But watch it, mister. There's a premium goes with this pile of junk and the bay horses—so beautiful—a packet of bitterness to grow in your house and to flower some day. We could have saved you, but you cut us down, and soon you will be cut down and there'll be none of us to save you." Perhaps no other passage in the novel carries so convincingly this great truth of human community, that no man is an island, that what you do unto the least of these you do unto me. The tenor of all these forces of ignorance against community is, of course, in Casy's dying words, an echo of Christ's own words—"You don't know what you're doin'."

Because it is not theological or sociological determinism, but ignorance breeding selfishness and distrust, that is so largely responsible for the forces against community, it follows that the establishment of the new community will come out of true knowledge, out of which in turn will come love and sharing. It is Casy, the spiritual leader, who first abandons the old ways and becomes a seeker for new truth. When he first appears he has already abandoned his conventional notions of sin, hellfire, and the salvation of individual souls for the doctrine of universal love and the transcendental Oversoul. He asks to go along with the Joads because he wants to learn more: "I'm gonna work in the fiel's, in the green fiel's, an' I'm gonna try to learn. Gonna learn why the folks walks in the grass, gonna hear 'em talk, gonna hear 'em sing. Gonna listen to kids eatin' mush. Gonna hear husban' an' wife poundin' the mattress in the night. Gonna eat with 'em an' learn." What he finally learns, in jail after giving himself up to save Tom and Floyd, is that man's spiritual unity must express itself in a social unity, which is why he becomes an organizer. The grace which he reluctantly gives over his first breakfast with the Joads is already groping in this direction: "I got to thinkin' how we was holy when we was one thing, an' mankin' was holy when it was one thing. An' it on'y got unholy when one mis'able little fella got the bit in his teeth an' run off his own way, kickin' an' draggin' an' fightin'. Fella like that bust the holiness. But when they're all workin' together, not one fella for another fella, but one fella kind of harnessed to the whole shebang—that's right, that's holy."

It is this growing knowledge of the necessity of sharing with strangers far beyond the usual circle of family and friends that becomes the most powerful force for establishing the new community. The novel's action opens with a series of acts of sharing. The truck driver shares a ride, Tom offers to share his whiskey with him and does share it with Casy. Muley not only shares his rabbits, but makes the first statement of this new principle: "'I ain't got no choice of the matter.' He stopped on the ungracious sound of his words. 'That ain't like I mean it. That ain't. I mean'—he stumbled—'what I mean, if a fella's got somepin' to eat an' another fella's hungry—why, the first fella ain't got no choice. I mean, s'pose I pick up my rabbits an' go off somewheres an' eat 'em. See?'" To this is added Mrs. Wilson's answer to Ma Joad's thanks for help: "People needs— to help." Just a few pages later Ma Joad, in replying to Mrs. Wilson's thanks for help, gives the concept a further turn: "you can't let help go unwanted." It is significant that the first example of spontaneous sharing with strangers on the journey is a symbolic merging of two families: Grampa's death in the Wilson's tent, his burial in one of the Wilson's blankets with a page torn from the Wilson's bible, and Ma Joad's promise to care for Mrs. Wilson. As Pa Joad expresses it later, "We almost got a kin bond." And Ma Joad, who starts off with a ferocious defense of her family against all comers—"All we got is the fambly"—four hundred pages later says, "Use' ta be the fambly was fust. It ain't so now. It's anybody. Worse off we get, the more we got to do." Her progress is charted by the numerous occasions for sharing which are described in the novel—their past, their knowledge, their food and hunger, gasoline, transportation, shelter, work, talent, joy and sorrow.

The narrative is saturated with the particulars of this sharing, and it is in the choric voice of the interchapter: "And because they were lonely and perplexed . . . they huddled together; they talked together; they shared their lives, their food, and the things they hoped for in the new country. . . . In the evening twenty families became one family, the children were the children of all. The loss of home became one loss, and the golden time in the west was one dream." It is this sharing that creates the unity, the change from "I" to "We," the new sense of community through which the people survive. And those who do not share, who continue selfish and distrustful, "the companies, the banks worked at their own doom and they did not know it."

The more one reads *The Grapes of Wrath*, the more thoroughly one knows the many ramifications of its informing theme, the more perfect and moving seems the novel's ending. Here, in this one real and symbolic act everything is brought together. Rosasharn gives her milk out of biological necessity to do so; she feeds not her own baby but an old man, a stranger. The Rose of Sharon, Christ, offers his body in communion. Biology, sociology, history, and religion become one expression of the community of mankind.

HOWARD LEVANT
From "Preface"
The Novels of John Steinbeck: A Critical Study
1974, pp. 1–9

A sad parallel to the popularity of John Steinbeck is the consensus among critics: Steinbeck is a flawed artist. No one denies Steinbeck's brilliance—in the handling of individual scenes, the creation of memorable characters, and above all in the possession of a superb and varied colloquial style. But there is an absence of some essential quality, noticeable before 1940, and pronounced—often disastrously pronounced—after 1940.

That something is missing is not in question, but what is missing has never quite been defined.

My belief is that Steinbeck has an abundance of every gift and craft the novelist can have—except an intelligent and coherent sense of what structure is and can do. I have written this book to consider in depth the structural adequacy of Steinbeck's longer fiction. For this purpose, I accept the rather precise definitions of both structure and materials offered by Austin Warren and René Wellek:

> It would be better [in view of the difficulties in the use of such terms as form and content for literary analysis] to rechristen all of the aesthetically indifferent elements "materials," while the manner in which they acquire aesthetic efficacy may be styled "structure." This distinction is by no means a simple renaming of the old pair, content and form. It cuts right across the old boundary lines. "Materials" include elements formerly considered part of the content, and parts formerly considered formal. "Structure" as a concept includes both content and form so far as they are organized for aesthetic purposes. [1]

As a gloss on this definition, consider the established distinction "with respect to structure . . . between two overlapping but recognizable types of fiction—the panoramic (or epic) and the dramatic (scenic or well-made)." [2]

These definitions summarize a widely accepted perspective in critical theory; that perspective illuminates the essential reason for Steinbeck's inability in most of his novels, especially over a range of novels, to reach the highest eminence. Particularly, he has a continuing difficulty in fusing a structure and specific materials into a harmonious unity.

Steinbeck was very much aware of this problem, as evidenced in private letters and notes, in his published criticism, and in the novels themselves. It is not too much to say that for Steinbeck the significantly conscious effort in writing a novel was located precisely in attempts to work out a relationship between structure and materials. Not many writers—not even Henry James—have been as self-conscious or as puzzled as Steinbeck in facing this aspect of the art of narrative. It follows that Steinbeck is not benefited markedly by his striking if occasional success in handling the relationship between structure and materials, for each try tends to be a new effort within a consistent range. Most obviously, certain identifiable technical stiuations recur in Steinbeck's longer fiction.

A Steinbeck novel tends to have either a panoramic or a dramatic structure. Steinbeck works at the extremes; he rarely combines panoramic and dramatic structures. Usually a panoramic structure in a Steinbeck novel is a series of episodes that are related to each other by little more than chronology. A dramatic structure in a Steinbeck novel is more tightly organized: Events and characters are bound neatly into firm relationships by a brief or highly selective time sequence and often by a moral or philosophic motif. Steinbeck uses a fairly relaxed style with a panoramic structure; his dramatic structure has a tenser, more patterned style. A typical defect in a Steinbeck novel is that its structure—whatever its type—is developed for its own sake, independent of the materials, to the extent that structure and materials tend to pull apart. This defect is evident in a majority of Steinbeck's novels, but it is especially evident when Steinbeck relies on allegorical elements or an allegorical scheme to shore up or stiffen either type of structure. On the other hand, a Steinbeck novel is most successful when its structure is fused harmoniously with the greatest possible variety of materials. This success is rare, but it is nearly absolute when it does occur. Finally, in such novels Steinbeck mingles panoramic and dramatic structures in developing the materials.

Repeatedly Steinbeck uses a number of formal devices to intensify the ordinary effect of a structure or, more frequently, to achieve the external appearance of an operative form by means of technique when an organic structure is not inherent in particular materials. The proliferation of such devices is a measure of Steinbeck's interest in form. I note the most common:

1. the frame,
2. the repetition or the leading use of names or significant initials,
3. interchapters or general statements of intention within the novel,
4. moral fables woven into the novel,
5. paired characters that suggest moral opposites,
6. split (not double or duplicate) heroes who suggest some basic human division, as between mind and body,
7. certain thematic motifs that become allegorical abstractions when they are not realized personal, social, or moral facts: the juxtaposition of life and death, love and hate, the people and impersonal instruments of power, or the ideal good life in contrast to reality.

At best, these devices serve to intensify the effect of a structure that is developing well, but they cannot save a structure that fails to develop properly for other reasons. Hence, they are distinctly secondary aids to order.

Certain broad stylistic effects appear on occasion to help in providing a novel with an adequate structure by establishing a tone or frame of reference. Extreme examples include argot, which is used in a number of novels, and the "universal language" in *Burning Bright*. Like the formal devices just listed—and for the same reason—these stylistic effects are secondary aids to an orderly development of a Steinbeck novel.

Steinbeck worked out a general theory of value in 1940 in *Sea of Cortez*; the theory has exact relevance to the peculiarly exaggerated extension of panoramic structure that appears in many of the late novels. Steinbeck gives his theory two names, "non-teleological" and "is" thinking. Merely for convenience, I shall refer consistently to the theory as "is" thinking. I quote, then, from the "Easter Sunday sermon" in *Sea of Cortez*:

> Non-teleological thinking concerns itself primarily not with what should be, or could be, or might be, but rather with what actually "is"—attempting at most to answer the already sufficiently difficult questions *what* or *how*, instead of *why*. [3]

Steinbeck lists several practical examples which suggest that cause–effect relationships are too simplified to be true in experience, that "the truest reason for anything's being so is that it *is*," and that the various genuine reasons for anything "could include everything." [4] The effect of the theory on structure is that any presumed need for artful design in the novel is no longer valid for Steinbeck. The theory implies that characters and events have an order and a rationale as they appear in the objective world; that art cannot improve on this order and rationale; that hence the only function of the artist is to report accurately whatever he sees in the natural world. This subordination of art to observation results in an exaggeratedly objective realism, an almost wholly undirected panoramic narrative. Steinbeck's last five or six novels exemplify the resulting narrative freedom—or chaos. For example, in the later novels the narrative reach can be epic, or it can be reduced to a series of "true" observations or episodes that are sometimes incoherently free of working thematic relationships. In these novels the reader can be told that certain events have certain meanings within an allegorical system, which forces a conflict between the loose method of narration and the close meaning that is imposed on the narrative. All of these elements are full grown in *East of Eden*. Significantly, they are present also in Steinbeck's earliest fiction, although much less at an extreme. The literary application of "is" thinking exaggerates several tendencies that are deeply rooted in Steinbeck's art. The critic's problem, therefore, is to trace and perhaps to explain a development rather than to study a new departure. In short, the career proceeds in a more orderly way than a first glance might suggest, for what may seem to be new starts are deeply rooted in Steinbeck's concern to achieve a harmony between structure and materials.

I propose that to study the novels from this viewpoint can permit a judicious, friendly judgment of each novel in the context of a greater appreciation of a shape to Steinbeck's long career. The unpleasant fact is that too often Steinbeck's work has been viewed piecemeal, even when the critical intention has been to achieve a rounded view. As the main result, Steinbeck's "place" among American writers has continued to be less secure—since less defined—than any of the major novelists of his age. Notoriously, a seesaw of defense or attack in particular instances is the striking characteristic of much Steinbeck criticism. I am not, to be sure, the first or the only Steinbeckian to attempt a rounded evaluation or to think that such evaluation is preferable to self-contained divisions into pro or con. I can but hope that my viewpoint has its claimed efficacy in the candid judgment of the ideal or Johnsonian reader. ⟨. . .⟩

Steinbeck begins with a developed sense of the artful in fiction. He does not write a disguised autobiography two or three times over. From the beginning, he searches for ways to achieve an ordered harmony in his art. He finds two distinct kinds of structure—panoramic and dramatic—to order his materials. Each of the first two novels is a fairly pure example of each structure. A number of aesthetic problems emerge, but Steinbeck does not solve them. Indeed, he is never able to work clear of these problems except partially and (as it were) by accident when circumstances minimize or resolve them. The combination of panoramic and dramatic structures is most evident in *In Dubious Battle* and to a somewhat lesser extent in *The Grapes of Wrath*. Steinbeck reaches his peak as an artist in these two novels. Meanwhile, various events and pressures lead to a simplified approach to structure, as in the three play-novelettes, and the results are unfortunate. At about the same time, "is" thinking offers a promising lead. Following such different novels as *Cannery Row* and *The Pearl* and the rather pure allegory, *The Wayward Bus* (all indebted to "is" thinking, for better or worse), Steinbeck settles on an extreme panoramic structure in *East of Eden* and the novels that follow. Frequently, in his final years, Steinbeck turned to journalism. In this work, as in all his work, an interest in technique was directed toward a harmony of structure and materials.

This sketch reveals a complexity which forbids any simple reduction of Steinbeck's career. He is serious and talented. His extremely uneven career calls for a particularly careful evaluation of his work; it precludes any simplistic dismissal.

Still, beyond the pattern of a constant search for an elusive harmony between structure and materials, it does appear that Steinbeck tends to move away from narrative order over the range of his longer fiction. Steinbeck worked largely by instinct, but he felt a strong need to work from a plan.[5] Often, in practice, he deviated widely and disastrously from a cogent plan that implied the achievement of a harmony between structure and materials; the result could be a novel consisting of a visible structure and visible materials that are not resolved in each other. On rare occasions, when a structure is "given," so to speak (in the sense that *The Pearl* is a natural parable), Steinbeck reverses his movement away from order. Whether total or partial, this reversal is momentary at best, but it occurs more than once. Hence, Steinbeck's career proceeds in a series of zigzags, not in a straight line, and he does not "grow" as better or more fortunate writers do by applying the lessons of imperfect work to the present. There is a slow but definite movement—much accelerated in his last years—away from order.

This situation creates a number of problems for the analytical critic of Steinbeck's longer fiction. First, the critic must be especially careful and insightful in matching criteria that are inevitably blunt (however closely terms are defined) with the actual complexities in Steinbeck's career. There is the critic's temptation to presume false similarities between novels. In fact, in its order, each novel presents a somewhat different approach, and often enough a radically different approach, to the achievement of a harmony between structure and materials. The author's search is fairly constant; the particular approaches and circumstances are not. Frequently, even apparent connections between different novels are quite misleading. Group-man occurs in several novels but the meaning of the concept shifts; the character named "Doc" recurs but changes strikingly from novel to novel; even a reuse of materials, such as class war, biological studies, or *paisano* life, does not ensure a thematic similarity between two novels. Yet the uncommonly irregular career does not permit the uncomplicated judgment that Steinbeck merely changed his mind. Certainly there is a pattern in Steinbeck's work, but it is not simple: It is Steinbeck's constant but changing search for a harmony between structure and materials. That search, in its dual directions, justifies the welter of technical devices and the differing materials and clarifies Steinbeck's tendency to move away from order in the latest novels. The one direction suggests efforts to achieve harmony externally, through new devices or materials; the other suggests despair of achieving a harmony. It is true that, at his best, when structure and materials most fully cohere, Steinbeck has produced some of the more distinguished literature of our time, in spite of the equal truth that much of his longer fiction contains enough imperfection to have removed a less gifted writer from critical attention. ⟨. . .⟩

A second critical difficulty relates to Steinbeck's tendency to proceed with fresh starts—there are notable exceptions—once it is clear that a certain technique or materials lead away from or do not lead directly toward a harmony between structure and materials. But the vital and constant factor is Steinbeck's continuing efforts to achieve, or at least to define, a fictive harmony.

A third consideration is that panoramic and dramatic structures occur separately or in combination in novel after novel; a specific novel under discussion may be quite different from its neighbors, depending on what kind of structure is predominant and on how adequately it functions.

Fourth, because Steinbeck tends to compose by parts, not by the whole (with some notable exceptions), and can permit himself considerable freedom of invention once the general form of the novel is established, the critic may be faced with a novel in which excellent episodes do not connect fully with other episodes or advance on otherwise strong development. In either circumstance, critical analysis is correspondingly complicated.

Finally, at times the longer fiction has been viewed rather exclusively in terms of the ideas it expresses. For example, group-man may be considered an ideological concept. No one denies the relevance of that consideration, but an analytical viewpoint must emphasize the dramatic function of the concept in its fictive context, whereas a purely ideological approach lifts out the concept, free of the novel, into a life of its own. The main point is that an analysis of Steinbeck's art necessitates a transfer from the criticism of ideas to the criticism of aesthetic values. ⟨. . .⟩

The most sympathetic judgment cannot always be favorable if it is to be honest, not to say rational. Simple and exclusive praise is not synonymous with the exercise of critical judgment. Yet, on the testimony of a devotion of twenty years to the work of John Steinbeck, I can say that my delight and respect have increased, not withered, and my contemplation of a great artist with great flaws has been an immeasurable reward of the spirit, measured against the ruin of the years.

Notes

1. René Wellek and Austin Warren, *Theory of Literature* (New York: Harcourt, Brace & Co., 1949), p. 141.
2. *Dictionary of World Literature*, ed. Joseph T. Shipley (New York: The Philosophical Library, 1943), p. 408.

3. John Steinbeck and Edward F. Ricketts, *Sea of Cortez* (New York: The Viking Press, Inc., 1941), p. 135.
4. Ibid., p. 148.
5. Lewis Gannett, "Introduction: John Steinbeck's Way of Writing," *The Viking Portable Steinbeck* (New York: The Viking Press, Inc., 1946), pp. vii–xxvii; Peter Lisca, *The Wide World of John Steinbeck* (New Brunswick: Rutgers University Press, 1958), pp. 39–40, 56–57, 73–79, 112, 133–34, 146–47, 184–86, 219, 231–32, 262.

PETER LISCA
From "*Sea of Cortez, Travels with Charley,* and Other Nonfiction"
John Steinbeck: Nature and Myth
1978, pp. 213–34

The nonfiction which Steinbeck has written varies widely in quality and subject matter. Furthermore, these variations correspond generally to the fluctuations of his fiction. His articles on migrant labor ("Dubious Battle in California," "The Harvest Gypsies" series, and two other pieces) have in common with *In Dubious Battle* and *The Grapes of Wrath* a high level of accomplishment as well as their materials. They remain the best of his short nonfiction.

Of the longer works, *Sea of Cortez* (1941) is in itself the most interesting, and the most valuable for its discussion of some important ideas embodied in Steinbeck's fiction. It was written in collaboration with Edward F. Ricketts, with whom he had undertaken a research trip into the Gulf of California. The trip had been conceived late in 1939 when Steinbeck, who had recently become a partner in Ricketts' Pacific Biological Laboratories, accompanied Ricketts on a specimen collecting expedition to the coast north of San Francisco. It was also in that year that Ricketts, who had left the University of Chicago without a degree after three years, published, in collaboration with Jack Calvin, *Between Pacific Tides*, a handbook of marine life along the Pacific shores of the United States. This book, innovative and advanced in its methods, has remained a standard in its field, continuously in print through several editions. It's somewhat technical and very functional Introduction was written by Steinbeck.

Had Steinbeck been merely a writer and Ricketts merely a scientist, it is doubtful that such a strong relationship would have developed between them. The figure of Doc in *Cannery Row*, although lacking certain important characteristics (curiously not supplied in Steinbeck's "About Ed Ricketts" written six years later) is an acceptable beginning for an understanding of Ricketts' character. To appreciate the extent of Ricketts' collaborative role in *Sea of Cortez*, however, it is necessary to know not only of his scientific work, such as *Between Pacific Tides* and numerous unpublished studies, but also that his literary, musical, and philosophical sophistication went far beyond the simplicities of his fictional portrait. He was a friend and correspondent of some impressive figures such as Joseph Campbell and Henry Miller, as well as familiar with the colony of bohemian intellectuals with whom Steinbeck consorted. Philosophically, he can be described, in part, as a "naturalistic mystic"—one whose feeling of kinship with the cosmic whole, whose sense of awe, is achieved through the facts of science and the truths of nature, rather than through the inward contemplation typical of traditional mysticism. To a large extent this is also true of Steinbeck. Both men, however, reinforced the naturalistic sources of their mysticism with selective reading in philosophy, religion, and psychology.

Ostensibly, *Sea of Cortez* is a day-by-day account of a six-week specimen-collecting trip to the Gulf of California in March and April of 1940, preceded by an account of the motivations and preparations for such an undertaking. What makes this book of fascinating interest, however, are the numerous passages of informal speculation, some quite extended, to which the events of the journey give rise. It is divided into two major parts, the "Narrative" and the "Phyletic Catalogue," but it must not be assumed that Steinbeck, the writer, did the former and Ricketts, the scientist, did the latter. Both men repeatedly resisted such identification. "It is a true compilation [sic] in every sense of the word," wrote Ricketts; and Steinbeck replied to his editor's plan to credit the authors separately, that he found the suggestion "outrageous" and that he "forbid" it because the book was "the product of the work and thinking of both of us." Later, in his sketch "About Ed Ricketts," Steinbeck described the continuous game of "speculative metaphysics" in which he and his friend engaged, saying that they worked so closely together that he did not know in some cases who had started a particular line of speculation; "the end thought was the product of both minds." Yet, although one can accept this statement for the purpose of comparing the ideas in *Sea of Cortez* to Steinbeck's fiction in a general way, an examination of the book's history of composition suggests certain refinements.

From further statements by both men and from an examination of the manuscripts, it is clear that Steinbeck did the actual writing of the narrative portion, but that most of the text derives closely from a forty-six page, single-spaced, typed transcription of a journal of the expedition kept by Ricketts. Steinbeck had this in hand while writing; he himself had not kept a journal. As Ricketts put it, with admiration, "He takes my words and gives them a little twist, and puts in some of his own beauty of concept and expression and the whole thing is so lovely you can't stand it." Sometimes, however, Steinbeck follows Ricketts almost verbatim for extended passages. This is not to say that Steinbeck merely revised the journal; but the bulk of raw material derives directly from it. Furthermore, the book's most significant chapter, the Easter Sunday "sermon" (March 24), incorporates, with a few merely grammatical and syntactical changes, a twenty-page unpublished essay by Ricketts called "Non-teleological Thinking." In addition, the Ricketts journal itself contains numerous passages paraphrased from other of his unpublished essays.

Steinbeck's hand is much more importantly evident in the larger shaping of the book. Essentially, Steinbeck took a collection of field notes and random thoughts and gave them an aesthetic form which expressively embodies their import. "The design of a book," wrote Steinbeck on the first page, "is the pattern of a reality controlled and shaped by the mind of the writer." This simple statement gives a clue to the book's place alongside Thoreau's *Walden* and Hemingway's *Green Hills of Africa* as imaginative reconstructions of experience rather than mere journalistic recordings. Not least important in this shaping is what of Ricketts' material and personal recollections Steinbeck *left out*. For example, although his wife, Carol, was on the trip and appears in Ricketts' journal, she is not mentioned in the narrative; and omitted completely is any account of the return trip from the Gulf to Monterey. These and other details had no part in Steinbeck's careful design. Conversely, where Ricketts begins his journal as they pass Point Sur, leaving Monterey, Steinbeck precedes this with four chapters concerning the genesis of the trip and its preparations. These four chapters not only create the proper expectations but, with the material omitted at the end and some internal telescoping, serve to stretch out the actual chronology so that the important "sermon" on nonteleological thinking which is the book's philosophical center comes on Easter Sunday, exactly in the book's center although only one fourth of the collecting stations have been covered by that time.

Steinbeck emphasizes the circularity of his departure-arrival-departure pattern by certain accents. The voyage begins as the *Western Flyer* leaves the sheltered waters of Monterey Bay and enters the open sea. The boat is greeted by a flock of pelicans and a sea lion who looks like the old man of the sea himself; aboard ship, "the forward guy-wire of our mast began to sing under the wind, a deep and yet penetrating tone." The voyage ends as they leave the Gulf of California, at which time "a crazy literary thing happened. As we came opposite the Point there was one great clap of thunder, and immediately we hit the great swells of the Pacific and the wind freshened against us. The water took on a gray tone." And the last words in the book: "The big guy-wire, from bow to mast took up its vibration like the low pipe on a tremendous organ. It sang its deep note into the wind." These accents mark the limits of a mythic voyage, in quest of new knowledge, to an unknown sea.

Within this frame the book is shaped by the free flow of varied observations, incidents and speculations, and the inflexibilities of time and tide. Steinbeck's discourse on steering in chapter five, at the beginning of the voyage, becomes an image of their quest—"the working out of the ideal [a compass point] into the real [a destination]" and of "the relationship between inward and outward, microcosm to macrocosm." As they move along the shores of the Gulf between high and low tides, picking up specimens, comparing, examining, so the book's thought moves along the shores of human society, picking up specimens of thought and deed, comparing, examining. The little intertidal societies and the human society become manifestations of common principles, so that finally "all things are one thing and that one thing is all things—plankton, a shimmering phosphorescence on the sea and the spinning planets and an expanding universe, all bound together by the elastic string of time."

To give all the philosophical sources of this and other speculations, where possible to detail further the distinct contributions to the book of each collaborator, and to draw the correspondences between certain passages of *Sea of Cortez* and Steinbeck's other works is a task far beyond the limits of this book. Only some suggestions can be made. The clearest philosophical influences on *Sea of Cortez* are, appropriately, those of naturalist and evolutionary philosophers: W. C. Allee, with whom Ricketts had studied at Chicago and whose book, *Animal Aggregations*, contains parallels to Steinbeck's "group-man" concept; William Emerson Ritter (*The Natural History of Our Conduct*), zoologist at Berkeley, whose organismal conception of the universe is extensively paraphrased in *Sea of Cortez*, as in the passage quoted above; Jan Smuts (*Holism and Evolution*); Robert Briffault (*The Making of Humanity*); and, especially, John Elof Boodin (A *Realistic Universe, Cosmic Evolution* and *The Social Mind*), whose maxim—"the laws of thought are the laws of things"—appears at least twice in Steinbeck's work. There is documentary evidence that Steinbeck and Ricketts were familiar with all of these philosophers. From these central figures the circle of influence widens to the more conventional figures of Western and Eastern philosophy. The influence of Jung's psychology is everywhere present.

Although both collaborators shared holistic and organismal views of life and the universe (that every part is related to every other as in one super organism), they were sometimes divided in their thinking about society and its problems. It can be said, generally, that the laissez-faire tendency of the nonteleological thinking essay (chapter 14) and some other passages in the book are more Ricketts than Steinbeck. It was he who tended to oppose primitivism to "the virus of civilization." Thus *Sea of Cortez* does not indicate a change in Steinbeck's attitude from the active, engaged role which Steinbeck had played in the 1930's. In fact, upon returning from the Gulf of California, and before completing his work on the narrative, he went to Mexico to write and work upon a documentary film *(The Forgotten Village)*, encouraging backward Indian villages to accept medical aid.

Significantly, Ricketts, who visited Steinbeck on location, disagreed with his friend's notions of progress and went so far as to write his own script which he said was "motivated oppositely" to that of Steinbeck. Although Steinbeck had written *Tortilla Flat* in praise of indolence, and was soon to write *Cannery Row*, rejecting the Western values of materialism and activism, these are both, in a sense, escapist novels. They are fictive versions of the free speculation which he liked to carry on with Ed Ricketts.

Concerning the relationship of *Sea of Cortez* to Steinbeck's other works, it can be said that there is hardly an idea in the novels preceding *East of Eden* which is not found in this journal. Compare the relationship of group-man concepts as elucidated in *In Dubious Battle* and *The Grapes of Wrath* to the observation on the characteristics of school fish in *Sea of Cortez*; the description of La Paz as a "colonial animal" in *The Pearl* and the social dynamics of Monterey in *Tortilla Flat* and *Cannery Row* to the colonial pelagic tunicates in *Sea of Cortez*; the Jungian race memory in *To a God Unknown* and *The Winter of Our Discontent* to the passage on the vestigial gill slits of the human foetus in *Sea of Cortez*; the holistic and organismic views of life in *To a God Unknown* and *The Grapes of Wrath* to the passage on the merging of species in *Sea of Cortez*; the adaptations to a changing environment of the migrants in *The Grapes of Wrath* and the adaptations of species to a changing ecology in *Sea of Cortez*. Even, within limits, compare the doctrine of nonteleological thinking to certain aspects of *In Dubious Battle* and *The Grapes of Wrath* which seem to accept the social situation as part of a vastly complex "field" of forces making the assignment of blame or specific cause rather pointless. The relationship of "good," "bad," and survival values is discussed not only in *Cannery Row*, but in *Sea of Cortez* also. The theory of leadership in *In Dubious Battle* and *The Grapes of Wrath* receives its authority from biological observations in *Sea of Cortez*. Even Steinbeck's life-long suspicion and finally hatred of Communism finds its biological analogues in the "overornamentation" of species preceding their extinction, and the necessary elimination of the unusually swift and strong and intelligent, as well as the slow and weak, in schools of fish or herds of animals or flocks of birds.

But although *Sea of Cortez* can be read with great profit for understanding the relationship between Ricketts and Steinbeck and a fuller knowledge of the intellectual backgrounds of Steinbeck's fiction, it is above all a very entertaining book, full of gusto for all forms of life, and reverence for the known and unknowable universe. ⟨. . .⟩

The only work of more than passing interest in Steinbeck's last phase is *Travels with Charley: In Search of America* (1962). Upon his return from England late in 1959, Steinbeck realized that for some time now he had been observing the changes in his own country "only from books and newspapers," that he had "not felt the country for twenty years," and hence "was writing of something I did not know about." So, shortly after Labor Day 1960, he set out to see the country by way of a pick-up truck specially equipped for comfortable camping. This he named *Rocinante,* and accompanied by a Sancho Panza in the form of Charley, his poodle, set forth not unlike Don Quixote himself. He returned home before Christmas, having been in thirty-four states and having covered ten thousand miles in a counterclockwise circle which took him from Long Island to Maine, across the northern states and down the coast to his familiar California scenes, returning across the southern states.

Ironically, there is very little in the 245 pages of *Travels with Charley* that Steinbeck could not have written without ever leaving New York. For he had not really lost touch with his country, but had purposefully insulated himself from a reality with which he felt increasingly uncomfortable, in which he could no longer immerse himself. Yet he could not altogether turn his back, either. He was motivated by a Whitmanesque compulsion to identify with and speak for the whole country. That this compulsion would be frustrated is suggested in the very first incident of his journey, the encounter with a submarine crewman anxious for duty on an atomic vessel, confident he would get used to staying under for three months at a time. "It's his world, not mine anymore," thinks Steinbeck. "It's his world now. Perhaps he understands things I will never learn." Only a quarter along the way, he is overcome with doubts about the value of his effort: "I came with the wish to learn what America is like. And I wasn't sure I was learning anything. I found I was talking aloud to Charley." It is this sense of alienation that persists throughout his comments upon the people and scenes he visited, persists in spite of occasional strident attempts to celebrate "the other things I know are there" but of which he can gather only scattered intimations. By the time he reaches the halfway point he has already lost even the illusion of "discovering America." He notes that his "impressionable gelatin plate was getting muddled" and determines "to inspect two more sections and call it a day—Texas and a sampling of the Deep South." Ten pages later he admits what he has "concealed" from himself—

that he has been driving himself, pounding out the miles because he is "no longer hearing or seeing," that he has passed his "limit of taking in," that he is "helpless to assimilate anymore." The returning half of his trip is covered in just sixty pages. At the end of the book, he admits again that his journey was over before he returned home.

Perhaps it was over even before he left, for in addition to his alienation he took with him all the baggage of the third-rate journalist who sees only the stereotype and the cliché. We are never presented with the way it really was, but rather with manipulated "set-ups," experiences and conversations upon which he can lecture Charley or us about one of his two favorite topics—how Americans are all different and yet unique and homogeneous, or how everything seems to be going to hell but it isn't really.

Travels with Charley should have had as its subtitle not "In Search of America," but, after Thomas Wolfe, "You Can't Go Home Again." Steinbeck's real search—like that of Don Quixote—is not for present reality but for an idealized past. This search approaches its climax in Johnny Garcia's bar in Monterey, Steinbeck's old home ground. He not only resists Johnny's plea that nothing essential has changed, actually quoting the title of Wolfe's novel, but also insists that with the past "the greatest part of what we were is dead," and the new reality "perhaps good" is "nothing we can know." Speaking of Ed Ricketts, Joe Portagee, Flora Wood, and others now dead, Steinbeck insists that it is not these dear companions who are the true ghosts: "We're the ghosts." In the next scene, the climax of his search for America, Steinbeck goes to Fremont's Peak, a spot familiar to his youth and from which he can survey the entire world of his childhood, his "Long Valley": "I printed it once more on my eyes, south, west, and north, and then we hurried away from the permanent and changeless past. . . ." Just sixty pages later, he is back in New York, having discovered what he already knew, that he was caught between two Americas, one dead and the other a stranger.

GEORGE STERLING

1869–1926

George Sterling was born on December 1, 1869, in Sag Harbor, Long Island, the oldest son of a physician and his wife. When he was in high school his father became a Roman Catholic, and the entire family followed him into the Church, although George's conversion was apparently in name only. However, he was sent to a Catholic college, St. Charles, in Maryland. He did not graduate; neither did he become a priest, despite his father's wishes. Because he seemed unable to settle into any line of work, he was sent in 1890 to Oakland, California, to work in an uncle's real estate office as a clerk; he remained there, unhappily, for fifteen years. The only bright spots in his life during much of this period were his friendships with Ambrose Bierce and Jack London, who encouraged his writing.

In 1905 a gift from his aunt enabled Sterling to buy land in Carmel, build a house, and devote his life to poetry. His first volume, *The Testimony of the Suns,* had been published in 1903 and was widely praised. This and most of his subsequent work were published in San Francisco, and he became a famous poet throughout the West while remaining virtually unknown in the East. Sterling wrote more than a dozen additional volumes of poetry, including *A Wine of Wizardry* (1907), *The House of Orchids* (1911), *Yosemite* (1916), *Sails and Mirage* (1921), and *Strange Waters* (1926). He was also the author of five plays. His *Selected Poems* was published in 1923, and a posthumous volume of verse, *After Sunset,* appeared in 1939.

In San Francisco Sterling was considered "a classic bohemian," and was a well-known and much-loved figure in the artistic community. He married in 1896 but his wife left him in 1912 because of his many extra-marital affairs and committed suicide the following year. Depressed by his struggle with alcoholism and his failing literary powers, Sterling also took his own life, swallowing poison at Bohemian Grove, on the Russian River north of San Francisco, on November 17, 1926.

Whatever length of days may be accorded to this magazine ⟨*Cosmopolitan*⟩, it is not likely to do anything more notable in literature than it accomplishes in this issue by publication of Mr. George Sterling's poem, A *Wine of Wizardry*. Doubtless the full significance of this event will not be immediately apprehended by more than a select few, for understanding of poetry has at no time been a very general endowment of our countrymen. After a not inconsiderable acquaintance with American men of letters and men of affairs I find myself unable to name a dozen of whom I should be willing to affirm their possession of this precious gift—for a gift it indubitably is; and of these not all would, in my judgment, be able to discern the light of genius in a poem not authenticated by a name already famous, or credentialed by a general assent. It is not commonly permitted to even the luckiest of poets to "set the Thames on fire" with his first match; and I venture to add that the Hudson is less combustible than the Thames. Anybody can see, or can think that he sees, what has been pointed out, but original discovery is another matter. Carlyle, indeed, has noted that the first impression of a work of genius is disagreeable— which is unfortunate for its author if he is unknown, for upon editors and publishers a first impression is usually all that he is permitted to make.

From the discouraging operation of these uncongenial conditions Mr. Sterling is not exempt, as the biography of this poem would show; yet Mr. Sterling is not altogether unknown. His book, *The Testimony of the Suns and Other Poems*, published in 1903, brought him recognition in the literary Nazareth beyond the Rocky Mountains, whose passes are so vigilantly guarded by cismontane criticism. Indeed, some sense of the might and majesty of the book's title poem succeeded in crossing the dead-line while watch-worn sentinels slept "at their insuperable posts." Of that work I have the temerity to think that in both subject and art it nicks the rock as high as anything of the generation of Tennyson, and a good deal higher than anything of the generation of Kipling; and this despite its absolute destitution of what contemporary taste insists on having—the "human interest." Naturally, a dramatist of the heavens, who takes the suns for his characters, the deeps of space for his stage, and eternity for his "historic period," does not "look into his heart and write" emotionally; but there is room in literature for more than emotion. In the "other poems" of the book the lower need is supplied without extravagance and with no admixture of sentimentality. But what we are here concerned with is A *Wine of Wizardry*.

In this remarkable poem the author proves his allegiance to the fundamental faith of the greatest of those "who claim the holy Muse as mate"—a faith which he has himself "confessed" thus:

> Remiss the ministry they bear
> Who serve her with divided heart;
> She stands reluctant to impart
> Her strength to purpose, end, or care.

Here, as in all his work, we shall look in vain for the "practical," the "helpful." The verses serve no cause, tell no story, point no moral. Their author has no "purpose, end, or care" other than the writing of poetry. His work is as devoid of motive as is the song of a skylark—it is merely poetry. No one knows what poetry is, but to the enlightened few who know what is poetry it is a rare and deep delight to find it in the form of virgin gold. "Gold," says the miner "vext with odious subtlety" of the mineralogist with his theories of deposit—"gold is where you find it." It is no less precious whether you have crushed it from the rock, or washed it from the gravel, but some of us care to be spared the labor of reduction, or sluicing. Mr. Sterling's reader needs no outfit of mill and pan.

I am not of those who deem it a service to letters to "encourage" mediocrity—that is one of the many ways to starve genius. From the amiable judgment of the "friendly critic" with his heart in his head, otherwise unoccupied, and the *laudator literarum* who finds every month, or every week—according to his employment by magazine or newspaper—more great books than I have had the luck to find in a half-century, I dissent. My notion is that an age which produces a half-dozen good writers and twenty books worth reading is a memorable age. I think, too, that contemporary criticism is of small service, and popular acclaim of none at all, in enabling us to know who are the good authors and which the good books. Naturally, then, I am not overtrustful of my own judgment, nor hot in hope of its acceptance. Yet I steadfastly believe and hardily affirm that George Sterling is a very great poet—incomparably the greatest that we have on this side of the Atlantic. And of this particular poem I hold that not in a lifetime has our literature had any new thing of equal length containing so much poetry and so little else. It is as full of light and color and fire as any of the "ardent gems" that burn and sparkle in its lines. It has all the imagination of *Comus* and all the fancy of *The Faerie Queene*. If Leigh Hunt should return to earth to part and catalogue these two precious qualities he would find them in so confusing abundance and so inextricably interlaced that he would fly in despair from the impossible task. ⟨. . .⟩

One of a poet's most authenticating credentials may be found in his epithets. In them is the supreme ordeal to which he must come and from which is no appeal. The epithets of the versifier, the mere metrician, are either contained in their substantives or add nothing that is worth while to the meaning; those of the true poet are instinct with novel and felicitous significances. They personify, ennoble, exalt, spiritualize, endow with thought and feeling, touch to action like the spear of Ithuriel. The prosaic mind can no more evolve such than ditch-water in a champagne-glass can sparkle and effervesce, or cold iron give off coruscations when hammered. Have the patience to consider a few of Mr. Sterling's epithets ⟨. . .⟩:

"Purpled" realm; "striving" billows; "wattled" monsters; "timid" sapphires of the snow; "lit" wastes; a "stainèd" twilight of the South; "tiny" twilight in the jacinth, and "wintry" orb of the moonstone; "winy" agate and "banded" onyx; "lustrous" rivers; "glowering" pyres of the burning-ghaut, and so forth.

Do such words come by taking thought? Do they come ever to the made poet?—to the "poet of the day"—poet by resolution of a "committee on literary exercises"? Fancy the poor pretender, conscious of his pretense and sternly determined to conceal it, laboring with a brave confusion of legs and a copious excretion of honest sweat to evolve felicities like these!—AMBROSE BIERCE, "A Poet and His Poem" (1907), *Collected Works*, Vol. 10, 1911, pp. 177–86

The Pacific states are loyal to their own artists to a degree which other sections of this vast nation might well emulate. Because, in spite of the manifest danger of provincialism, art, like charity, should begin at home; indeed, must begin at home if it is not to be a wanderer on the face of the earth, seeking forlornly an alien audience.

So it was a satisfaction to discover, everywhere along "The Coast," a devotion to Mr. George Sterling which was not alone enthusiasm for his poetry, but also pride in him as a personality and a possession. As California loves Keith and certain later painters because they were—and are—faithful interpreters of her beauty, so she rewards this poet for his love of her.

One can forgive her if she seems to overrate him. I own to my surprise on hearing one enthusiast call him "the greatest poet since Dante," and on finding him the only living poet whose words were inscribed—along with Confucius and Firdausi, with Shakespeare and Goethe—on the triumphal arches of the Panama-Pacific Exposition. I rubbed my eyes—had I been blind and deaf? In 1909 and 1911 I had read *A Wine of Wizardry* and *The House of Orchids* without discovering a poet of the first order. Manifestly, I must re-read these books, and add the poet's first volume, *The Testimony of the Suns*, and his latest, *Beyond the Breakers*. All of which I have done.

Now, if I can not quite rise to the Californian estimate, at least I find in Mr. Sterling a gift, a poetic impulse, which might have carried him much further than it has as yet. His first long poem, *The Testimony of the Suns*, does indeed make one feel the sidereal march, make one shiver before the immensity and shining glory of the universe—this in spite of shameless rhetoric which often threatens to engulf the theme beyond redemption, and in spite of the whole second part, an unhappy afterthought. Already the young poet's brilliant but too facile craftsmanship was tempted by the worst excesses of the Tennysonian tradition: he never *thinks*—he *deems*; he does not *ask*, but *crave*; he is *fain* for this and that; he deals in *emperies* and *auguries* and *antiphons*, in *causal throes* and *lethal voids*—in many other things of tinsel and fustian, the frippery of a by-gone fashion. ⟨. . .⟩

The truth is, this sort of pomposity has died the death. If the imagists have done nothing else, they have punctured the gas bag—English poetry will be henceforth more compact and stern—"as simple as prose," perhaps. Against the Victorian excesses we might quote the rhetorical advice of Tennyson's *Ancient Sage* in favor of another kind of temperance:

> Nor care
> To vex the noon with fiery gems, or fold
> Thy presence in the silk of sumptuous looms;
> Nor roll thy viands on a luscious tongue,
> Nor drown thyself, like flies, in honeyed wine.

When Mr. Sterling learns to avoid the "luscious tongue" and the "honeyed wine," he may become the poet he was meant to be.—HARRIET MONROE, "The Poetry of George Sterling," *Poetry*, March 1916, pp. 307–11

Always to me, as to others, he was a very gentle and faithful friend, and the kindest of mentors. Perhaps we did not always agree in matters of literary taste; but it is good to remember that our occasional arguments or differences of opinion were never in the least acrimonious. Indeed, how could they have been?—one might quarrel with others, but never with him: which, perhaps, is not the poorest tribute that I can pay to George Sterling. . . . But words are doubly inadequate, when one tries to speak of such a friend; and the best must abide in silence.

Turning today the pages of his many volumes, I, like others who knew him, find it difficult to read them in a mood of dispassionate or abstract criticism. But I am not sure that poetry should ever be read or criticized in a perfectly dispassionate mood. A poem is not a philosophic or scientific thesis, or a problem in Euclid, and the essential "magic" is more than likely to elude one who approaches it, as too many do, in a spirit of cold-blooded logic. After all, poetry is properly understood only by those who love it.

Sterling, I remember, considered *The Testimony of the Suns* his greatest poem. Bierce said of it, that, "written in French and published in Paris, it would have stirred the very stones of the street." In this poem, there are lines that evoke the silence of infinitude, verses in which one hears the crash of gliding planets, verses that are clarion-calls in the immemorial war of suns and systems, and others that are like the cadences of some sidereal requiem, chanted by the seraphim over a world that is "stone and night." One may quote from any page:

> How dread thy reign, O Silence, there!
>   A little, and the deeps are dumb—
>   Lo, thine eternal feet are come
> Where trod the thunders of Altair!"
>
> Crave ye a truce, O suns supreme?
>   What Order shall ye deign to hark,
>   Enormous shuttles of the dark,
> That weave the everlasting dream?"

In the same volume with *The Testimony of the Suns* is a blank verse poem, "Music," in which the muse Terpsichore was hymned as never before or since:

> Her voice we have a little, but her face
> Is not of our imagining nor time.

Also, there is the gorgeous lyric "To Imagination," and many chryselephantine sonnets, among which "Reincarnation," "War," and "The Haunting" are perhaps the most perfect.

As I have already hinted, I feel a peculiar partiality for *A Wine of Wizardry*, the most colorful, exotic, and, in places, macabre, of Sterling's poems. (This, however, is not tantamount to saying that I consider it necessarily his most important achievement.) Few things in literature are more serviceable as a test for determining whether people feel the verbal magic of poetry—or whether they merely comprehend and admire the thought, or philosophic content. It is not a poem for the literal-minded, for those lovers of the essential prose of existence who edit and read our *Saturday Reviews* and *Literary Digests*. In one of the very last letters that he wrote me, Sterling said that no one took the poem seriously any more, "excepting cranks and mental hermits." It is not "vital" poetry, he said, as "vital" is used by our self-elected high-brows (which probably, means that it is lacking in "sex-kick," or throws no light on the labor problem and the increase of moronism). I was unable to agree with him. Personally, I find it impossible to take the "vital" school with any degree of seriousness, and see it only as a phase of materialism and didacticism. The proponents of the utile and the informative should stick to prose—which, to be frank, is all that they achieve, as a rule. Before leaving *A Wine of Wizardry*, I wish, for my own pleasure, to quote a favorite passage:

> Within, lurk orbs that graven monsters clasp;
> Red-embered rubies smoulder in the gloom,
> Betrayed by lamps that nurse a sullen flame,
> And livid roots writhe in the marble's grasp,
> As moaning airs invoke the conquered rust
> Of lordly helms made equal in the dust.
> Without, where baleful cypresses make rich

The bleeding sun's phantasmagoric gules,
Are fungus-tapers of the twilight witch,
Seen by the bat above unfathomed pools,
And tiger-lilies known to silent ghouls,
Whose king hath digged a sombre carcanet
And necklaces with fevered opals set.

No, A *Wine of Wizardry* is not "vital verse." Thank God for *that*, as Benjamin De Casseres would say.

Notable, also, in Sterling's second volume, is the lovely "Tasso to Leonora" and "A Dream of Fear." His third volume, *A House of Orchids*, is compact of poetry; and, if I were to name my favorites, it would be equivalent to quoting almost the entire index. However, the dramatic poem, *Lilith*, is, I believe, the production by which he will be most widely known. One must go back to Swinburne and Shelley to find its equal as a lyric drama. The tragedy and poetry of life are in this strange allegory, and the hero, Tancred, is the mystic analogue of all men. Here, in the conception of Lilith, the eternal and ineluctable Temptress, Sterling verges upon that incommensurable poet, Charles Baudelaire. In scene after scene, one hears the fugue of good and evil, of pleasure and pain, set to chords that are almost Wagnerian. Upon the sordid reality of our fate there falls, time after time, a light that seems to pass through lucent and iridescent gems; and vibrant echoes and reverberant voices cry in smitten music from the profound of environing mystery.

One might go on, to praise and quote indefinitely; but, in a sense, all that I can write or could write seems futile, now that Sterling is "one with that multitude to whom the eternal Night hath said 'I am.'" Anyway, his was not, as Flecker's,

The song of a man who was dead
Ere any had heard of his song.

From the beginning, he had the appreciation and worship of poetry lovers, if not of the crowd or of the critical moguls and pontiffs.

Of his death—a great bereavement to me, as to other friends—I feel that there is really little that need be said. I know that he must have had motives that he felt to be ample and sufficient, and this is enough for me. I am totally incapable of understanding the smug criticism that I have read or heard on occasion. To me, the popular attitude concerning suicide is merely one more proof of the degeneracy and pusillanimity of the modern world: in a more enlightened age, felo-de-se will be honored again, as it was among the ancients.—CLARK ASHTON SMITH, "George Sterling—An Appreciation" (1927), *Planets and Dimensions: Collected Essays of Clark Ashton Smith*, ed. Charles K. Wolfe, 1973, pp. 5–8

UPTON SINCLAIR
"My Friend George Sterling"

Bookman (New York), September 1927, pp. 30–32

I write here of the dearest friend I ever had among men. Since he is gone, there seems a large hole in the world.

It was Jack London who gave him to me, some twenty-five years ago, sending me a book of poems, *The Testimony of the Suns*, by George Sterling. In the fly-leaf he wrote, "I have a friend, the dearest in the world". Since friendship is a thing without limits, I also took possession of this poet. We corresponded for some seven or eight years, and then I went to California to visit him, and stayed several months at Carmel. A year or two later the fates played a strange prank upon us—

he lost his heart to the woman who not long after became my wife.

How much of that strange story will it be decent for me to tell? It is hard for me to judge, because what the world calls "tact" is not my strong point; I cannot ask my wife, because she is ill, and since our friend's dreadful death I do not mention him. Some day the story will be known, because he wrote her a hundred or so of sonnets, the most beautiful in the world. For sixteen years his attitude never changed: her marriage made no difference—when he came to visit us, he would follow her about with his eyes, and sit and murmur her name as if under a spell; our friends would look at us and smile, but George never cared what they thought.

When he first met her, and was bringing her a sonnet every day, they were walking on Riverside Drive one afternoon, and I chanced to come along. She was working on a book, and I, with my customary reformer's impulse, remarked, "You have been overworking; you are worn out". She answered, "This poet has just been telling me that I look like a star in alabaster". "Well, I think you look like a skull," I said, and went on, leaving the poet grinding his teeth in fury. "Some day I am going to kill that man!" he exclaimed; and his companion replied, "That is the first man that ever told me the truth in my life. I am going to marry him!"

She did so; and for a while there appeared a certain element of acerbity in the criticisms which George would pen upon the margins of my manuscripts. But tenderness and patience were the least contribution I could make to our friendship; so I would laugh, and presently George would grow remorseful, and tell me that maybe I was half right after all.

There were two men in him, and a strange duel forever going on in his soul. In his literary youth he had fallen under the spell of Ambrose Bierce, a great writer, a bitter black cynic, and a cruel, domineering old bigot. He stamped inerasably upon George's sensitive mind the heartless art-for-art's-sake formula, the notion of a poet as a superior being, aloof from the problems of men, and writing for the chosen few. On the other hand, George was a chum of Jack London and others of the young "reds", and became a Socialist and remained one to the end. Bierce quarreled with him on this account, and broke with him, as he did with everyone else. But in art the Bierce influence remained dominant, and George Sterling would write about the interstellar spaces and the writhing of oily waters in San Francisco harbor, and the white crests of the surf on Point Lobos, and the loves of ancient immoral queens.

After which he would go about the streets of New York on a winter night, and come back without his overcoat, because he had given it to some poor wretch on the bread-line; he would be shivering, not with cold, but with horror and grief, and would break all the art-for-art's-sake rules, and pour out some lines of passionate indignation, which he refused to consider poetry, but which I assured him would outlive his fancy stuff.

At the time of our "mourning pickets" on Broadway, during the Colorado coal strike of 1914, George was in New York, and his "Star in Alabaster" was walking up and down eight hours a day amid a mob of staring idlers, her husband in jail and only a few "wobblies" and Jewish "reds" from the East Side to keep her company. George appeared and offered her his arm. "Go away," she said; "this is no job for a poet!" But of course he would not go; he stuck by her side for two weeks, and up at the Lamb's Club, where he was staying, the art-snobs and wealthy loafers "joshed" him mercilessly—some even insulted him, and there was a fight or two. During these excitements George wandered down to the Battery, and looking out over the bay he wrote that shining poem, "To the Statute of Liberty":

> Oh! is it bale-fire in thy brazen hand—
> The traitor-light set on betraying coasts
> To lure to doom the mariner? . . .

You will find that in my anthology, *The Cry for Justice*. Also his song about Babylon, which really is New York, and San Francisco too:

> In Babylon, high Babylon,
>   What gear is bought and sold?
> All merchandise beneath the sun
>   That bartered is for gold;
> Amber and oils from far beyond
>   The desert and the fen,
> And wines whereof our throats are fond—
>   Yea! and the souls of men!
>
> In Babylon, grey Babylon,
>   What goods are sold and bought?
> Vesture of linen subtly spun,
>   And cups from agate wrought;
> Raiment of many-colored silk
>   For some fair denizen,
> And ivory more white than milk—
>   Yea! and the souls of men! . . .

Also I mention his tribute to the Episcopal church—and others—quoted in "The Profits of Religion":

> Within the House of Mammon his priesthood stands
>   alert
> By mysteries attended, by dusk and splendors girt,
> Knowing, for faiths departed, his own shall still
>   endure,
> And they be found his chosen, untroubled, solemn,
>   sure.
>
> Within the House of Mammon the golden altar lifts
> Where dragon-lamps are shrouded as costly incense
>   drifts—
> A dust of old ideals, now fragrant from the coals,
> To tell of hopes long-ended, to tell the death of souls.

After George's death my friend Mencken asked me to write about Sterling without mentioning alcohol. The first time I visited George I was to be the orator at a dinner of the Ruskin Club in Oakland, and George was to read a poem. We met at the Bohemian Club in San Francisco, and George drank a couple of cocktails on an empty stomach, and we set out. On the ferry-boat I had difficulty in understanding his conversation; and finally the painful realization dawned over me that the great poet was drunk. My own father had been a drinking man, and several of my relatives in the South, so I was no stranger to the spectacle; but this was the first time I had ever seen an intellectual man in that condition; and the next day I wrote George a note, saying it was too painful, and I was not going to stay at Carmel. He came running over to my house, and with tears in his eyes vowed that he would never touch another drop while I was in California. Sometimes I have wished I might have stayed the rest of my life; it might be that is the greatest service I could have rendered to the future.

From that day on I never saw George with any sign of drink on him. He visited us at Croton, and went over the huge manuscript of *The Cry for Justice*, and chopped down some dead chestnut trees and cut them up for our fireplace. He was an athlete, and beautiful to look at—a face like Dante's, grave and yet tender, and a tall, active body. We have a snapshot of him in bathing-trunks, standing upon the rocks of Point Lobos

with an abalone hook in his hand, and nothing more graceful was ever planned by a Greek sculptor.

George went back to San Francisco and lived at the Bohemian Club, where some admirer had bequeathed him a room for life. It is a place of satyrs, and the worst environment that could have been imagined under the circumstances. George had begun his drinking with Jack London and Ambrose Bierce, and then it was all gaiety and youth, the chanting of George's "Abalone Song", and the "grove play", and the Bohemian "jinks". But later on in life it becomes something different. Others may sing the romance and the charm of San Francisco; to me it is a plague-city, where all the lovely spirits drink poison—first Nora May French, and then Carrie Sterling, and then Jack London, and then my best of friends.

George had more admirers than any other man I ever knew, and he gave himself to them without limit. When they were drinking, he could not sit apart; and so tragedy closed upon him. He would come to visit us in Pasadena, and always then he was "on the wagon" and never going to drink again, but we could see his loneliness, and his despair—not about himself, for he was too proud to voice that, but for mankind, and for the universe. It may seem a strange statement, that a poet could be killed by the nebular hypothesis; but Mary Craig Sinclair declares that is what happened to George Sterling. I believe the leaders of science now reject the nebular hypothesis, and have a new one; but meantime, they had fixed firmly in George's mind the idea that the universe is running down like a clock, that in some millions of years the earth will be cold, and in some hundreds of millions of years the sun will be cold, and so what difference does it make what we poor insects do? You will find that at the beginning, in *The Testimony of the Suns*, and at the end in the drama, *Truth*. It is what one might call applied atheism.

Once, Mary Craig Sinclair tells me, George offered never to drink again, if she would ask him not to. But her notion of fair play did not permit her to do this. What could she give him in return? The cares of her own life were too many; she had a husband who refused to be afraid of his enemies, and so she had to be afraid for two, and there were long periods when she could not even answer George's letters. He stayed in San Francisco, and now and then he would say he was coming to see us, and when he did not come, we would know why.

Mencken was coming to visit George, and just before his coming George was drunk. He was fifty-six years old, and there was no longer any fun about it, but an agony of pain and humiliation; and so he took cyanide of potassium, as he had many times threatened to do. To me it is something so cruel that I would not talk about it, were it not for the next generation of poets and writers, who are parroting the art-for-art's-sake devilment, and dancing to hell with John Bootleg.

Consider my friend Mencken. The death of this beautiful and noble and generous-souled poet has taught him nothing whatsoever; he writes the same cheerfully flippant letters in celebration of the American saloon. "Liquor was George's only consolation in life, and the reason he quit was because he could no longer get the kick out of it." I say that more poisonous nonsense than this was never penned by an intellectual man. How many pleasures there are which do not pall with age, and do not destroy their devotees! The pleasures of knowledge, for example—of gaining it, and helping to spread it. The pleasures of sport; I play tennis, and it is just as much fun to me at forty-eight as it was at fourteen. The pleasures of music; I play the violin, after a fashion, and my friend

Mencken plays it better, I hope—and does he find that every year he has to play more violently in order to bear it, and that after playing he suffers agonies of sickness, remorse and dread? I say for shame upon an intellectual man who cannot make such distinctions; for shame upon a teacher of youth who has no care whether he sets their feet upon the road to wisdom and happiness, or to misery and suicide!

STANTON A. COBLENTZ
"George Sterling: Western Phenomenon"

Arizona Quarterly, Spring 1957, pp. 54–60

I have often remembered the pungent statement of William Alexander Percy, made many years ago in his introduction to the selected poems of Arthur O'Shaughnessy: "Even the most beautiful things perish if the opportunity for reading or seeing or hearing them is not offered the vexed and hurrying children of men."

This remark comes back to mind in connection with George Sterling, at one time a legend on the Pacific Coast, its most celebrated poet, and almost its recognized embodiment of *The Bard*. Turbulent and varied waters have flowed beneath the bridges of the world since that day in the Twenties when Sterling was found dead in his room in the Bohemian Club in San Francisco, under circumstances suggestive of suicide. But unhappily, amid the commotions and confusions of decades, which have brought us new idols and dreams, many of the old dreams and idols have been obliterated or forgotten; and among them the name of the once-famed California poet has receded into the mists.

He himself would have taken this eclipse of his renown philosophically. I recall how, smiling at me out of his long, lean aesthete's face across the luncheon table at the Bohemian Club, he confessed his modest hope: "I feel that, if a hundred years from now a few of my poems are remembered and loved, I will not have written in vain." More than a third of the specified century has already passed, and unquestionably there are readers who still do remember and love Sterling's poems. But it is my own view, on a re-perusal of his work, that the number of his admirers should be many times greater, and that his name should still be revered a century and much more than a century hence.

Let me begin by pointing out that, from the superficial point of view, Sterling does not reflect the poetic inclinations of our day. His is the grand manner, and at times the grandiloquent style; his is the cosmic perspective, which is not content merely with noting the convolutions of the *I* in man, but looks upon our species against the background of the worlds and ages, with a judgment that at times may seem impassive and pitiless, but that can be vibrant and resplendent. Such is the case in his sequence, *Sonnets by the Night Sea*, beginning with the memorable lines

> Surely the dome of unremembered nights
> Was heavy with those stars!

and proceeding through other striking lines,

> The wind of night is like an ocean's ghost,

and

> Swung as a pendulum from life to sleep,
> From sleep to life, from Timelessness to Time,

while the philosophy of the whole is summarized in this suggestive sestet:

> Yea! and the Deep is troubled! In this heart
> Are voices of a far and shadowy Sea,
>   Above whose wastes no lamp of earth
>   shall gleam.
> Farewells are spoken and the ships depart
> For that horizon and its mystery
>   Whose stars tell not if life, or death,
>   is dream

The same sense of greatness, of wonder, of mystery, and of magnificence is to be found in other poems: in the three sonnets on *Ocean Sunsets*, in the *Sonnets on the Night Skies*, and notably in the long philosophical poem in the *In Memoriam* stanza, *The Testimony of the Suns*. Although Sterling lived before the day of that incredible expansion of astronomical knowledge which resolved the spiral nebulae into galaxies estimated to contain as many as a hundred billion suns each, he consulted the less staggering astronomical knowledge of his own day in order to draw conclusions that later scientific findings (if his premises be correct) would only reinforce. Though I, as a reader, must confess to noting a certain majestic coldness in the lines, and though I hold that the philosophical conclusions are as questionable as those of much other fine poetry (for example, the celebrated *Rubaiyat*), I believe that the poem is unique in several respects, and deserving of continued attention. In ways not shared by any other poem I can recall, it is distinctively an utterance of the modern age—an utterance that could have come from the lips of no man in any former era. It is the exclamation of one seduced and overawed, and at the same time baffled and appalled and stung to irony and despair by the observations of a science that has seemingly left man overshadowed and diminished. Unlike the ancients, who could view the stars as the message books of the Immortals, Sterling looks upon the constellations with the grimness of one who sees in them the arenas of prodigious blind battling forces, constantly retreating and as constantly renewed amid immensities in which man is but the mote of a moment:

> Ever the star, unstable, frames
>   Her transitory throne of fire,
>   But in thy sight how soon expire.
> How soon recur, the inviolate flames!
>
> What silence rules the ghostly hours
>   That guard the close of human sleep!
>   Aldebaran crowns the western deep;
> Belted with suns Orion row'rs,
>
> And greaved with light of worlds destroyed,
>   And girt with firmamental gloom,
>   Abides his far, portended doom
> And menace of the warring void.

Bleak as is the underlying concept—for Sterling believes in the overlordship of vast, impersonal law and time and death, and contends that an eternal future cannot reveal the secret that an eternal past has not unbared—the poet succeeds in drawing consolation even from the spectacle of the immense impassiveness of the universe, and shares in the art of many another writer in conjuring poetry out of despair. A lyrical mood permeates lines such as these:

> My sleep was like a summer sky
>   That held the music of a lark:
>   I waken to the voiceless dark
> And life's more silent mystery.
>
> Night with her fleeting hours, how brief
>   To watch beyond her vault sublime
>   The gyrant systems meting Time,
> That holds the timelessness of grief!

How pure the light their legions shed!
How calm above the crumbling tomb
Of race and epoch passed to gloom
No ray can pierce nor mortal tread!

For the taste of many a present-day reader, content with mental fare in capsule form, *The Testimony of the Suns* with its several hundred lines may be altogether too long. But this disadvantage, if it be a disadvantage, hardly applies to various other offerings of George Sterling.

Sometimes he writes with a brevity, a directness and immediacy of communication that have none of the statuesque quality of his longer work, but that go directly to the reader's heart. Such is "Willy Pitcher," in which a timeless emotion is expressed in the simplest of language. The first two stanzas follow:

He is forgotten now,
And humble dust these thirty years and more
He whose young eyes and beautiful wide brow
My thoughts alone restore.

Dead, and his kindred dead!
And none remembers in that quiet place,
The slender form, the brown and faunlike head,
The wildly wistful face.

An emotional element, linked to a grace and delicacy of expression suggestive of one of the lyrical masters, is to be found in the exquisite "Dirge" from *Lilith*:

O lay her gently where the lark is nesting
And wingéd things are glad.
Tears end, and now begins the time of resting
For her whose heart was sad.

Give roses, but a fairer bloom is taken.
Strew lilies—she was one,
Gone in her silence to a place forsaken
By roses and the sun.

Deep is her slumber at the last of sorrow,
Of twilight and the rain.
Her eyes have closed forever on tomorrow
And on tomorrow's pain.

The same lyricism, mixed with a wistful and curiously mystical ingredient that may come as a surprise in a man who can write with Sterling's convinced agnosticism, permeates certain other poems, such as "In Autumn," in which the author is sad for

. . . a country not of time and space,
Some fair and irrecoverable place
I roamed ere birth and cannot now recall.

After expressing the feeling that "I have lost that which I never had," the poet stands perplexed by that unaccountable melancholy which we have all felt at times:

And voices of the wind alone transmute
The music that I lost so long ago.
I stand irresolute,
Lonely for some one I shall never know.

After the somewhat dreamy nostalgia of these lines, one turns with something of a shock to work in which Sterling criticizes the material world. Exercising the poet's timeless right to strike out against the evils of society, he permits himself now and then a social commentary, though one in which poetry predominates over criticism, in accordance with his view that the function of poetry is not so much to say new things as to phrase old things memorably. Accordingly, he does not disdain time-honored images, as in the case of "In the Market-Place," which is much more of a song than a social document, though its underlying thought may be divined from this typical stanza:

In Babylon, dark Babylon,
Who take the wage of shame?
The scribe and singer, one by one,
That toil for gold and fame.

They grovel to their masters' mood;
The blood upon the pen
Assigns their souls to servitude—
Yea! and the souls of men!

A similar mood and a similar grace of expression mark "The Common Cult," and again the poet uses a worn symbol to drive home his point:

Up to the House of Mammon, from dawn to sister dawn,
Called by remembered voices the sons of men are drawn;
By noon the dust flies skyward, by night the torches flare,
On veining roads that mingle . . . and you and I are there.
The ebony House of Mammon goes up against the sky;
The north wind and the south wind before its portals die.
Its towers go near to Heaven, its vaults go nearer Hell,
And all are fat with favor to some who serve them well.

But it may be urged that this is not typical of Sterling. He is at his characteristic best not when limiting his observations to the external world, but when the subjective and objective are mingled, with the former tending to predominate. It is then that he gives us work marked peculiarly with his own personality, thoughtful and wistful, wrapped in dreams and splendors, and with a pessimism which, like that of Omar Khayyam or of the second James Thomson, can be magnificent even when at its bleakest. A good example (to go beyond the excerpts quoted earlier in this paper) is the first of the two sonnets, *"Omnia Exeunt in Mysterium"*:

The stranger in my gates—lo! that am I,
And what my land of birth I do not know,
Nor yet the hidden land to which I go.
One may be lord of many ere he die,
And tell of many sorrows in one sigh,
But know himself he shall not, nor his woe,
Not to what sea the tears of wisdom flow,
Nor why one star is taken from the sky.

An urging is upon him evermore,
And tho he bide, his soul is wanderer,
Scanning the shadows with a sense of haste
Where fade the tracks of all who went before—
A dim and solitary traveller
On ways that end in evening and the waste.

Various objections may be listed against Sterling's work. Sometimes, the reader may contend, it is a little too frigid, too remote, too marmoreal; sometimes, like the nineteenth-century verse from which it derives, it is more prolix than its substance would seem to warrant; occasionally its pomp of expression may approach pomposity. The language, again, is marked with poeticisms, with forms of expression now regarded as archaic, even if not so considered when Sterling wrote (though let us, before judging these superficials too harshly, not forget that our own most advanced writers, beneath the wheel of changing conventions, may be considered hopelessly out of date, if not ridiculously old-fashioned, before this century closes).

But whatever one may conclude as to the above, I hold to my conviction that Sterling has not only produced a considerable body of work which deserves to be perpetuated, but himself represents a tradition that should be but has not been preserved. For he was one of the last visible embodiments of that phenomenon, known to the world for centuries, but now apparently extinct as the passenger pigeon: the *full-time poet*, the man for whom poetry is both vocation and avocation, the man who lives poetry almost as a Beethoven, a Haydn, or a Mozart lived music. Nourished and groomed as a poet by no less a character than Ambrose Bierce, accepted in San Francisco as a poet and devoting his working time there and in Carmel to nothing but the propagation of poetry, he was in many ways more truly a poet laureate than many crowned with that name by parliaments or legislatures. Though poets will continue to write, nothing short of a revolution within society seems likely to bring Sterling's kind back again. And that is why, remembering him, we cannot keep from remembering also his lines, whose very obsolescence of expression but reinforces their yearning mood:

> In vain, in vain
> We labor that thou stay,
> Beauty who wast, and shall not be again!

WALLACE STEVENS

1879–1955

Wallace Stevens was born on October 2, 1879, in Reading, Pennsylvania, to Garrett Barckalow Stevens and Mary Catherine (née Zeller) Stevens. He was educated at Harvard University and New York University Law School, and was admitted to the New York bar in 1904. He was a reporter for the New York *Herald Tribune* from 1900 to 1901, and practiced law in New York from 1904 to 1916. In 1916 he joined the Hartford Accident and Indemnity Company in Connecticut, where he was a vice-president from 1934 to 1955. He married Elsie V. Kachel in 1909; they had one daughter.

His first poetry (apart from undergraduate work at Harvard) was published in *Poetry* and *Trend* in 1914. His poetry appeared regularly in magazines for the next several years, including the well-known "Peter Quince at the Clavier" (1915) and *The Comedian as the Letter C* (1922; originally titled *From the Journal of Crispin*) but his first book, *Harmonium*, was not published until 1923. It sold fewer than a hundred copies, but was praised by Marianne Moore, among others.

Business concerns prevented him from writing from 1924 to 1929. In 1930 he began publishing poetry again, and in 1931 a second edition of *Harmonium* appeared, dropping three poems and adding fourteen. His second book, *Ideas of Order*, was published in 1935 to generally positive reviews, although Stanley Burnshaw accused Stevens of social indifference. Stevens responded to Burnshaw with *Owl's Clover* (1935).

Stevens was by this time considered a major poet, and subsequent volumes added to his reputation. Among the most significant were *The Man with the Blue Guitar and Other Poems* (1937), *Parts of a World* (1942), *Transport to Summer* (1947), and *The Auroras of Autumn* (1950). Stevens won the Bollingen Prize for 1949, the National Book Award in 1951 for *The Auroras of Autumn*, and the Pulitzer Prize and a second National Book Award in 1955 for his *Collected Poems* (1954).

By the time of his death on August 2, 1955, Wallace Stevens was regarded as one of America's most important poets. Stevens also wrote three plays (two of which are contained in *Opus Posthumous*, 1957, edited by Samuel French Morse), and some criticism, most of which is included in *The Relations between Poetry and Painting* (1951) and *The Necessary Angel: Essays on Reality and the Imagination* (1951). His *Letters* (edited by his daughter Holly Stevens) were issued in 1966.

R. P. BLACKMUR
"Examples of Wallace Stevens" (1931)
Language as Gesture
1952, pp. 221–49

The most striking if not the most important thing about Mr. Stevens' verse is its vocabulary—the collection of words, many of them uncommon in English poetry, which on a superficial reading seems characteristic of the poems. An air of preciousness bathes the mind of the casual reader when he finds such words as fubbed, girandoles, curlicues, catarrhs, gobbet, diaphanes, clopping, minuscule, pipping, pannicles, carked, ructive, rapey, cantilene, buffo, fiscs, phylactery, princox, and funest. And such phrases as "thrum with a proud douceur," or "A pool of pink, clippered with lillies scudding the bright chromes," hastily read, merely increase the feeling of preciousness. Hence Mr. Stevens has a bad reputation among those who dislike the finicky, and a high one, unfortunately, among those who value the ornamental sounds of words but who see no purpose in developing sound from sense.

Both classes of reader are wrong. Not a word listed above is used preciously; not one was chosen as an elegant substitute for a plain term; each, in its context, was a word definitely meant. The important thing about Mr. Stevens' vocabulary is not the apparent oddity of certain words, but the uses to which he puts those words with others. It is the way that Mr. Stevens combines kinds of words, unusual in a single context, to reveal the substance he had in mind, which is of real interest to the reader.

Good poets gain their excellence by writing an existing language *as if* it were their own invention; and as a rule success in the effect of originality is best secured by fidelity, in an extreme sense, to the individual words as they appear in the dictionary. If a poet knows precisely what his words represent, what he writes is much more likely to seem new and strange—and even difficult to understand—than if he uses his words ignorantly and at random. That is because when each word has definite character the combinations cannot avoid uniqueness. Even if a text is wholly quotation, the condition of quotation itself qualifies the text and makes it so far unique. Thus a quotation made from Marvell by Eliot has a force slightly different from what it had when Marvell wrote it. Though the combination of words is unique it is read, if the reader knows his words either by usage or dictionary, with a shock like that of recognition. The recognition is not limited, however, to what was already known in the words; there is a perception of something previously unknown, something new which is a result of the combination of the words, something which is literally an access of knowledge. Upon the poet's skill in combining words as much as upon his private feelings, depends the importance or the value of the knowledge.

In some notes on the language of E. E. Cummings I tried to show how that poet, by relying on his private feelings and using words as if their meanings were spontaneous with use, succeeded mainly in turning his words into empty shells. With very likely no better inspiration in the life around him, Mr. Stevens, by combining the insides of those words he found fit to his feelings, has turned his words into knowledge. Both Mr. Stevens and Cummings issue an ambiguity—as any good poet does; but the ambiguity of Cummings is that of the absence of known content, the ambiguity of a phantom which no words could give being; while Mr. Stevens' ambiguity is that of a substance so dense with being, that it resists paraphrase and can be truly perceived only in the form of words in which it was given. It is the difference between poetry which depends on the poet and poetry which depends on itself. Reading Cummings you either guess or supply the substance yourself. Reading Mr. Stevens you have only to know the meanings of the words and to submit to the conditions of the poem. There is a precision in such ambiguity all the more precise because it clings so closely to the stuff of the poem that separated it means nothing.

Take what would seem to be the least common word in the whole of *Harmonium*[1]—funest (page 74, line 6). The word means sad or calamitous or mournful and is derived from a French word meaning fatal, melancholy, baneful, and has to do with death and funerals. It comes ultimately from the Latin *funus* for funeral. Small dictionaries do not stock it. The poem in which it appears is called "Of the Manner of Addressing Clouds," which begins as follows:

> Gloomy grammarians in golden gowns,
> Meekly you keep the mortal rendezvous,
> Eliciting the still sustaining pomps
> Of speech which are like music so profound
> They seem an exaltation without sound.
> Funest philosophers and ponderers,
> Their evocations are the speech of clouds.
> So speech of your processionals returns
> In the casual evocations of your tread
> Across the stale, mysterious seasons. . . .

The sentence in which funest occurs is almost a parenthesis. It *seems* the statement of something thought of by the way, suggested by the clouds, which had better be said at once before it is forgotten. In such a casual, disarming way, resembling the way of understatement, Mr. Stevens often introduces the most important elements in his poems. The oddity of the word having led us to look it up we find that, once used, funest is better than any of its synonyms. It is the essence of the funeral in its sadness, not its sadness alone, that makes it the right word: the clouds are going to their death, as not only philosophers but less indoctrinated ponderers know; so what they say, what they evoke, in pondering, has that much in common with the clouds. Suddenly we realize that the effect of funest philosophers is due to the larger context of the lines preceding, and at the same time we become aware that the statement about their evocations is central to the poem and illuminates it. The word pomps, above, means ceremony and comes from a Greek word meaning procession, often, by association, a funeral, as in the phrase funeral pomps. So the pomps of the clouds suggest the funeral in funest.

The whole thing increases in ambiguity the more it is analyzed, but if the poem is read over after analysis, it will be seen that *in the poem* the language is perfectly precise. In its own words it is clear, and becomes vague in analysis only because the analysis is not the poem. We use analysis properly in order to discard it and return that much better equipped to the poem.

The use of such a word as funest suggests more abstract considerations, apart from the present instance. The question is whether or not and how much the poet is stretching his words when they are made to carry as much weight as funest carries above. Any use of a word stretches it slightly, because any use selects from among many meanings the right one, and then modifies that in the context. Beyond this necessary stretching, words cannot perhaps be stretched without coming to nullity—as the popular stretching of awful, grand, swell, has more or less nullified the original senses of those words. If Mr. Stevens stretches his words slightly, as a live poet should and must, it is in such a way as to make them seem more precisely themselves than ever. The context is so delicately illuminated, or adumbrated, that the word must be looked up, or at least thought carefully about, before the precision can be seen. This is the precision of the expert pun, and every word, to a degree, carries with it in any given sense the puns of all its senses.

But it may be a rule that only the common words of a language, words with several, even groups of meanings, can be stretched the small amount that is possible. The reader must have room for his research; and the more complex words are usually plays upon common words, and limited in their play. In the instance above the word funest is not so much itself stretched by its association with philosophers as the word philosophers—a common word with many senses—stretches funest. That is, because Mr. Stevens has used the word funest, it cannot easily be detached and used by others. The point is subtle. The meaning so doubles upon itself that it can be understood only in context. It is the context that is stretched by the insertion of the word funest; and it is that stretch, by its ambiguity, that adds to our knowledge.

A use of words almost directly contrary to that just discussed may be seen in a very different sort of poem—"The Ordinary Women" (page 13). I quote the first stanza to give the tone:

> Then from their poverty they rose.
> From dry catarrhs, and to guitars

They flitted
Through the palace walls.

Then skipping a stanza, we have this, for atmosphere:

The lacquered loges huddled there
Mumbled zay-zay and a-zay, a-zay.
The moonlight
Fubbed the girandoles.

The loges huddled probably because it was dark or because they didn't like the ordinary women, and mumbled perhaps because of the moonlight, perhaps because of the catarrhs, or even to keep key to the guitars. Moonlight, for Mr. Stevens, is mental, fictive, related to the imagination and meaning of things; naturally it fubbed the girandoles (which is equivalent to cheated the chandeliers, was stronger than the artificial light, if any) . . . Perhaps and probably but no doubt something else. I am at loss, and quite happy there, to know anything literally about this poem. Internally, inside its own words, I know it quite well by simple perusal. The charm of the rhymes is enough to carry it over any stile. The strange phrase, "Fubbed the girandoles," has another charm, like that of the rhyme, and as inexplicable: the approach of language, through the magic of elegance, to nonsense. That the phrase is not nonsense, that on inspection it retrieves itself to sense, is its inner virtue. Somewhere between the realms of ornamental sound and representative statement, the words pause and balance, dissolve and resolve. This is the mood of Euphues, and presents a poem with fine parts controlled internally by little surds of feeling that save both the poem and its parts from preciousness. The ambiguity of this sort of writing consists in the double importance of both sound and sense where neither has direct connection with the other but where neither can stand alone. It is as if Mr. Stevens wrote two poems at once with the real poem somewhere between, unwritten but vivid.

A poem which exemplifies not the approach merely but actual entrance into nonsense is "Disillusionment of Ten O'Clock" (page 88). This poem begins by saying that houses are haunted by white nightgowns, not nightgowns of various other colors, and ends with these lines:

People are not going
To dream of baboons and periwinkles.
Only, here and there, an old sailor,
Drunk and asleep in his boots,
Catches tigers
In red weather.

The language is simple and declarative. There is no doubt about the words or the separate statements. Every part of the poem makes literal sense. Yet the combination makes a nonsense, and a nonsense much more convincing than the separate sensible statements. The statement about catching tigers in red weather coming after the white nightgowns and baboons and periwinkles, has a persuasive force out of all relation to the sense of the words. Literally, there is nothing alarming in the statement, and nothing ambiguous, but by so putting the statement that it appears as nonsense, infinite possibilities are made terrifying and plain. The shock and virtue of nonsense is this: it compels us to scrutinize the words in such a way that we see the enormous ambiguity in the substance of every phrase, every image, every word. The simpler the words are the more impressive and certain is the ambiguity. Half our sleeping knowledge is in nonsense; and when put in a poem it wakes.

The edge between sense and nonsense is shadow thin, and in all our deepest convictions we hover in the shadow, uncertain whether we know what our words mean, neverthe-

less bound by the conviction to say them. I quote the second half of "The Death of a Soldier" (page 129):

Death is absolute and without memorial,
As in a season of autumn,
When the wind stops,
When the wind stops and, over the heavens,
The clouds go, nevertheless,
In their direction.

To gloss such a poem is almost impertinent, but I wish to observe that in the passage just quoted, which is the important half of the poem, there is an abstract statement, "Death is absolute and without memorial," followed by the notation of a natural phenomenon. The connection between the two is not a matter of course; it is syntactical, poetic, human. The point is, by combining the two, Mr. Stevens has given his abstract statement a concrete, sensual force; he has turned a conviction, an idea, into a feeling which did not exist, even in his own mind, until he had put it down in words. The feeling is not exactly in the words, it is because of them. As in the body sensations are definite but momentary, while feelings are ambiguous (with reference to sensations) but lasting; so in this poem the words are definite but instant, while the feelings they raise are ambiguous (with reference to the words) and have importance. Used in this way, words, like sensations, are blind facts which put together produce a feeling no part of which was in the data. We cannot say, abstractly, in words, any better what we know, yet the knowledge has become positive and the conviction behind it indestructible, because it has been put into words. That is one business of poetry, to use words to give quality and feeling to the precious abstract notions, and so doing to put them beyond words and beyond the sense of words.

A similar result from a different mode of the use of words may be noticed in such a poem as "The Emperor of Ice-Cream" (page 85):

Call the roller of big cigars,
The muscular one, and bid him whip
In kitchen cups concupiscent curds.
Let the wenches dawdle in such dress
As they are used to wear, and let the boys
Bring flowers in last month's newspapers.
Let be be finale of seem.
The only emperor is the emperor of ice-cream.

Take from the dresser of deal,
Lacking the three glass knobs, that sheet
On which she embroidered fantails once
And spread it so as to cover her face.
If her horny feet protrude, they come
To show how cold she is, and dumb.
Let the lamp affix its beam.
The only emperor is the emperor of ice-cream.

The poem might be called Directions for a Funeral, with Two Epitaphs. We have a corpse laid out in the bedroom and we have people in the kitchen. The corpse is dead; then let the boys bring flowers in last month's (who would use today's?) newspapers. The corpse is dead; but let the wenches wear their everyday clothes—or is it the clothes they are used to wear at funerals? The conjunction of a muscular man whipping desirable desserts in the kitchen and the corpse protruding horny feet, gains its effect because of its oddity—not of fact, but of expression: the light frivolous words and rapid meters. Once made the conjunction is irretrievable and in its own measure exact. Two ideas or images about death—the living and the dead—have been associated, and are now permanently fused. If the mind is a rag-bag, pull out two rags and sew them together. If the materials were contradictory, the very contradiction, made permanent, becomes a kind of unison. By associating ambiguities found in nature in a poem we reach a clarity, a kind of transfiguration even, whereby we learn *what* the ambiguity was.

The point is, that the oddity of association would not have its effect without the couplets which conclude each stanza with the pungency of good epitaphs. Without the couplets the association would sink from wit to low humor or simple description. What, then, do the couplets mean? Either, or both, of two things. In the more obvious sense, "Let be be finale of seem," in the first stanza, means, take whatever seems to be, as really being; and in the second stanza, "Let the lamp affix its beam," means let it be plain that this woman is dead, that these things, impossibly ambiguous as they may be, are as they are. In this case, "The only emperor is the emperor of ice-cream," implies in both stanzas that the only power worth heeding is the power of the moment, of what is passing, of the flux. [2]

The less obvious sense of the couplets is more difficult to set down because, in all its difference, it rises out of the first sense, and while contradicting and supplanting, yet guarantees it. The connotation is, perhaps, that ice-cream and what it represents is the only power *heeded*, not the only power there is to heed. The irony recoils on itself: what seems *shall* finally be; the lamp *shall* affix its beam. The only emperor is the emperor of ice-cream. The king is dead; long live the king.

The virtue of the poem is that it discusses and settles these matters without mentioning them. The wit of the couplets does the work.

Allied to the method of this poem is the method of much of *Le Monocle de Mon Oncle*. The light word is used with a more serious effect than the familiar, heavy words commonly chosen in poems about the nature of love. I take these lines from the first stanza (page 16):

> The sea of spuming thought foists up again
> The radiant bubble that she was. And then
> A deep up-pouring from some saltier well
> Within me, bursts its watery syllable.

The words foist and bubble are in origin and have remained in usage both light. One comes from a word meaning to palm false dice, and the other is derived by imitation from a gesture of the mouth. Whether the history of the words was present in Mr. Stevens' mind when he chose them is immaterial; the pristine flavor is still active by tradition and is what gives the rare taste to the lines quoted. By employing them in connection with a sea of spuming thought and the notion of radiance whatever vulgarity was in the two words is purged. They gain force while they lend their own lightness to the context; and I think it is the lightness of these words that permits and conditions the second sentence in the quotation, by making the contrast between the foisted bubble and the bursting syllable possible.

Stanza IV of the same poem (pages 17–18) has a serious trope in which apples and skulls, love and death, are closely associated in subtle and vivid language. An apple, Mr. Stevens says, is as good as any skull to read because, like the skull, it finally rots away in the ground. The stanza ends with these lines:

> But it excels in this, that as the fruit
> Of love, it is a book too mad to read
> Before one merely reads to pass the time.

The light elegance and conversational tone give the stanza the cumulative force of understatement, and make it seem to carry

a susurrus of irony between the lines. The word excels has a good deal to do with the success of the passage; superficially a syntactical word as much as anything else, actually, by its literal sense it saves the lines from possible triviality.

We have been considering poems where the light tone increases the gravity of the substance, and where an atmosphere of wit and elegance assures poignancy of meaning. It is only a step or so further to that use of language where tone and atmosphere are very nearly equivalent to substance and meaning themselves. "Sea Surface Full of Clouds" (page 132) has many lines and several images in its five sections which contribute by their own force to the sense of the poem, but it would be very difficult to attach special importance to any one of them. The burden of the poem is the color and tone of the whole. It is as near a tone-poem, in the musical sense, as language can come. The sense of single lines cannot profitably be abstracted from the context, and literal analysis does nothing but hinder understanding. We may say, if we like, that Mr. Stevens found himself in ecstasy—that he stood aside from himself emotionally—before the spectacle of endlessly varied appearances of California seas off Tehuantepec; and that he has tried to equal the complexity of what he saw in the technical intricacy of his poem. But that is all we can say. Neither the material of the poem nor what we get out of it is by nature susceptible of direct treatment in words. It might at first seem more a painter's subject than a poet's, because its interest is more obviously visual and formal than mental. Such an assumption would lead to apt criticism if Mr. Stevens had tried, in his words, to present a series of seascapes with a visual atmosphere to each picture. His intention was quite different and germane to poetry; he wanted to present the tone, in the mind, of five different aspects of the sea. The strictly visual form is in the background, merely indicated by the words; it is what the visual form gave off after it had been felt in the mind that concerned him. Only by the precise interweaving of association and suggestion, by the development of a delicate verbal pattern, could he secure the overtones that possessed him. A looser form would have captured nothing.

The choice of certain elements in the poem may seem arbitrary, but it is an arbitrariness without reference to their rightness and wrongness. That is, any choice would have been equally arbitrary, and, esthetically, equally right. In the second stanza of each section, for example, one is reminded of different kinds of chocolate and different shades of green, thus: rosy chocolate and paradisal green; chop-house chocolate and sham-like green; porcelain chocolate and uncertain green; musky chocolate and too-fluent green; Chinese chocolate and motley green. And each section gives us umbrellas variously gilt, sham, pied, frail, and large. The ocean is successively a machine which is perplexed, tense, tranced, dry, and obese. The ocean produces sea-blooms from the clouds, mortal massives of the blooms of water, silver petals of white blooms, figures of the clouds like blooms, and, finally, a wind of green blooms. These items, and many more, repeated and modified, at once impervious to and merging each in the other, make up the words of the poem. Directly they do nothing but rouse the small sensations and smaller feelings of atmosphere and tone. The poem itself, what it means, is somewhere in the background; we know it through the tone. The motley hue we see is crisped to "clearing opalescence."

> Then the sea
> And heaven rolled as one and from the two
> Came fresh transfigurings of freshest blue.

Here we have words used as a tone of feeling to secure the

discursive evanescence of appearances; words bringing the senses into the mind which they created; the establishment of interior experience by the construction of its tone in words. In "Tattoo" (page 108), we have the opposite effect, where the mind is intensified in a simple visual image. The tone existed beforehand, so to speak, in the nature of the subject.

> The light is like a spider.
> It crawls over the water.
> It crawls over the edges of the snow.
> It crawls under your eyelids
> And spreads its webs there—
> Its two webs.
>
> The webs of your eyes
> Are fastened
> To the flesh and bones of you
> As to rafters or grass.
>
> There are filaments of your eyes
> On the surface of the water
> And in the edges of the snow.

The problem of language here hardly existed: the words make the simplest of statements, and the poet had only to avoid dramatizing what was already drama in itself, the sensation of the eyes in contact with what they looked at. By attempting *not* to set up a tone the tone of truth is secured for statements literally false. Fairy tales and Mother Goose use the same language. Because there is no point where the statements stop being true, they leap the gap unnoticed between literal truth and imaginative truth. It is worth observing that the strong sensual quality of the poem is defined without the use of a single sensual word; and it is that ambiguity between the words and their subject which makes the poem valuable.

There is nothing which has been said so far about Mr. Stevens' uses of language which might not have been said, with different examples, of any good poet equally varied and equally erudite[3]—by which I mean intensely careful of effects. We have been dealing with words primarily, and words are not limited either to an author or a subject. Hence they form unique data and are to be understood and commented on by themselves. You can hardly more compare two poets' use of a word than you can compare, profitably, trees to cyclones. Synonyms are accidental, superficial, and never genuine. Comparison begins to be possible at the level of the more complicated tropes than may occur in single words.

Let us compare then, for the sake of distinguishing the kinds of import, certain tropes taken from Ezra Pound, T. S. Eliot, and Mr. Stevens.

From Mr. Pound—the first and third from the *Cantos* and the second from *Hugh Selwyn Mauberley*:

> In the gloom, the gold gathers the light against it.
>
> Tawn foreshores
> Washed in the cobalt of oblivion.
>
> A catalogue, his jewels of conversation.

From T. S. Eliot—one from "Prufrock," one from *The Waste Land*, and one from *Ash-Wednesday*:

> I should have been a pair of ragged claws
> Scuttling across the floors of silent seas.
>
> The awful daring of a moment's surrender
> Which an age of prudence can never retract.
>
> Struggling with the devil of the stairs who wears
> The deceitful face of hope and of despair.

The unequaled versatility of Ezra Pound (Eliot in a dedication addresses him as *Il miglior fabbro*) prevents assurance that the three lines quoted from him are typical of all his

work. At least they are characteristic of his later verse, and the kind of feeling they exhibit may be taken as Pound's own. Something like their effect may be expected in reading a good deal of his work.

The first thing to be noticed is that the first two tropes are visual images—not physical observation, but something to be seen in the mind's eye; and that as the images are so seen their meaning is exhausted. The third trope while not directly visual acts as if it were. What differentiates all three from physical observation is in each case the non-visual associations of a single-word—*gathers*, which in the active voice has an air of intention; *oblivion*, which has the purely mental sense of forgetfulness; and, less obviously, *conversation*, in the third trope, which while it helps *jewels* to give the line a visual quality it does not literally possess, also acts to condense in the line a great many non-visual associations.

The lines quoted from T. S. Eliot are none of them in intention visual; they deal with a totally different realm of experience—the realm in which the mind dramatizes, at a given moment, its feelings toward a whole aspect of life. The emotion with which these lines charge the reader's mind is a quality of emotion which has so surmounted the senses as to require no longer the support of direct contact with them. Abstract words have reached the intensity of thought and feeling where the senses have been condensed into abstraction. The first distich is an impossible statement which in its context is terrifying. The language has sensual elements but as such they mean nothing: it is the act of abstract dramatization which counts. In the second and third distichs words such as *surrender* and *prudence*, *hope* and *despair*, assume, by their dramatization, a definite sensual force.

Both Eliot and Pound condense; their best verse is weighted—Pound's with sensual experience primarily, and Eliot's with beliefs. Where the mind's life is concerned the senses produce images, and beliefs produce dramatic cries. The condensation is important.

Mr. Stevens' tropes, in his best work and where he is most characteristic, are neither visual like Pound nor dramatic like Eliot. The scope and reach of his verse are no less but are different. His visual images never condense the matter of his poems; they either accent or elaborate it. His dramatic statements, likewise, tend rather to give another, perhaps more final, form to what has already been put in different language.

The best evidence of these differences is the fact that it is almost impossible to quote anything short of a stanza from Mr. Stevens without essential injustice to the meaning. His kind of condensation, too, is very different in character and degree from Eliot and Pound. Little details are left in the verse to show what it is he has condensed. And occasionally, in order to make the details fit into the poem, what has once been condensed is again elaborated. It is this habit of slight re-elaboration which gives the firm textural quality to the verse.

Another way of contrasting Mr. Stevens' kind of condensation with those of Eliot and Pound will emerge if we remember Mr. Stevens' *intentional* ambiguity. Any observation, as between the observer and what is observed, is the notation of an ambiguity. To Mr. Stevens the sky, "the basal slate," "the universal hue," which surrounds us and is always upon us is the great ambiguity. Mr. Stevens associates two or more such observations so as to accent their ambiguities. But what is ambiguous in the association is not the same as in the things associated; it is something new, and it has the air of something condensed. This is the quality that makes his poems grow, rise in the mud like a tide. The poems cannot be exhausted, because the words that make them, intentionally ambiguous at their crucial points, are themselves inexhaustible. Eliot obtains many of his effects by the sharpness of surprise, Pound his by visual definition; they tend to exhaust their words in the individual use, and they are successful because they know when to stop, they know when sharpness and definition lay most hold on their subjects, they know the maximal limit of their kinds of condensation. Mr. Stevens is just as precise in his kind; he brings ambiguity to the point of sharpness, of reality, without destroying, but rather preserving, clarified, the ambiguity. It is a difference in subject matter, and a difference in accent. Mr. Stevens makes you aware of how much is *already* condensed in any word.

The first stanza of *Sunday Morning* may be quoted (page 89). It should be remembered that the title is an integral part of the poem, directly affecting the meaning of many lines and generally controlling the atmosphere of the whole.

> Complacencies of the peignoir, and late
> Coffee and oranges in a sunny chair,
> And the green freedom of a cockatoo
> Upon a rug mingle to dissipate
> The holy hush of ancient sacrifice.
> She dreams a little, and she feels the dark
> Encroachment of that old catastrophe,
> As a calm darkens among water-lights.
> The pungent oranges and bright, green wings
> Seem things in some procession of the dead,
> Winding across wide water, without sound.
> The day is like wide water, without sound,
> Stilled for the passing of her dreaming feet
> Over the seas, to silent Palestine,
> Dominion of the blood and sepulchre.

A great deal of ground is covered in these fifteen lines, and the more the slow ease and conversational elegance of the verse are observed, the more wonder it seems that so much could have been indicated without strain. Visually, we have a woman enjoying her Sunday morning breakfast in a sunny room with a green rug. The image is secured, however, not as in Pound's image about the gold gathering the light against it, in directly visual terms, but by the almost casual combination of visual images with such phrases as "*complacencies* of the peignoir," and "the green *freedom* of the cockatoo," where the italicized words are abstract in essence but rendered concrete in combination. More important, the purpose of the images is to show how they dissipate the "holy hush of ancient sacrifice," how the natural comfort of the body is aware but mostly unheeding that Sunday is the Lord's day and that it commemorates the crucifixion.

From her half-awareness she feels the more keenly the "old catastrophe" merging in the surroundings, subtly, but deeply, changing them as a "calm darkens among water-lights." The feeling is dark in her mind, darkens, changing the whole day. The oranges and the rug and the day all have the quality of "wide water, without sound," and all her thoughts, so loaded, turn on the crucifixion.

The transit of the body's feeling from attitude to attitude is managed in the medium of three water images. These images do not replace the "complacencies of the peignoir," nor change them; they act as a kind of junction between them and the Christian feeling traditionally proper to the day. By the time the stanza is over the water images have embodied both feelings. In their own way they make a condensation by appearing in company with and showing what was already condensed.

If this stanza is compared with the tropes quoted from Pound, the principal difference will perhaps seem that while

Pound's lines define their own meaning and may stand alone, Mr. Stevens' various images are separately incomplete and, on the other hand, taken together, have a kind of completeness to which Pound's lines may not pretend: everything to which they refer is present. Pound's images exist without syntax, Mr. Stevens' depend on it. Pound's images are formally simple, Mr. Stevens' complex. The one contains a mystery, and the other, comparatively, expounds a mystery.

While it would be possible to find analogues to Eliot's tropes in the stanzas of *Sunday Morning*, it will be more profitable to examine something more germane in spirit. Search is difficult and choice uncertain, for Mr. Stevens is not a dramatic poet. Instead of dramatizing his feelings, he takes as fatal the drama that he sees and puts it down either in its least dramatic, most meditative form, or makes of it a simple statement. Let us then frankly take as pure a meditation as may be found, "The Snow Man" (page 12), where, again, the title is integrally part of the poem:

> One must have a mind of winter
> To regard the frost and the boughs
> Of the pine-trees crusted with snow;
>
> And have been cold a long time
> To behold the junipers shagged with ice,
> The spruces rough in the distant glitter
>
> Of the January sun; and not to think
> Of any misery in the sound of the wind,
> In the sound of a few leaves,
>
> Which is the sound of the land
> Full of the same wind
> That is blowing in the same bare place
>
> For the listener, who listens in the snow,
> And, nothing himself, beholds
> Nothing that is not there and the nothing that is.

The last three lines are as near as Mr. Stevens comes to the peculiar dramatic emotion which characterizes the three tropes quoted from Eliot. Again, as in the passage compared to Pound's images, the effect of the last three lines depends entirely on what preceded them. The emotion is built up from chosen fragments and is then stated in its simplest form. The statement has the force of emotional language but it remains a statement—a modest declaration of circumstance. The abstract word *nothing*, three times repeated, is not in effect abstract at all; it is synonymous with the data about the winter landscape which went before. The part which is not synonymous is the emotion: the overtone of the word, and the burden of the poem. Eliot's lines,

> The awful daring of a moment's surrender
> Which an age of prudence can never retract,

like Pound's lines, for different reasons, stand apart and on their own feet. The two poets work in contrary modes. Eliot places a number of things side by side. The relation is seldom syntactical or logical, but is usually internal and sometimes, so far as the reader is concerned, fatal and accidental. He works in violent contrasts and produces as much by prestidigitation as possible. There was no reason in the rest of "Prufrock" why the lines about the pair of ragged claws should have appeared where they did and no reason, perhaps, why they should have appeared at all; but once they appeared they became for the reader irretrievable, complete in themselves, and completing the structure of the poem.

That is the method of a dramatic poet, who molds wholes out of parts themselves autonomous. Mr. Stevens, not a dramatic poet, seizes his wholes only in imagination; in his poems the parts are already connected. Eliot usually moves from point to point or between two termini. Mr. Stevens as a rule ends where he began; only when he is through, his beginning has become a chosen end. The differences may be exaggerated but in their essence is a true contrast.

If a digression may be permitted, I think it may be shown that the different types of obscurity found in the three poets are only different aspects of their modes of writing. In Pound's verse, aside from words in languages the reader does not know, most of the hard knots are tied round combinations of classical and historical references. A passage in one of the Cantos, for example, works up at the same time the adventures of a Provençal poet and the events in one of Ovid's *Metamorphoses*. If the reader is acquainted with the details of both stories, he can appreciate the criticism in Pound's combination. Otherwise he will remain confused: he will be impervious to the plain facts of the verse.

Eliot's poems furnish examples of a different kind of reference to and use of history and past literature. The reader must be familiar with the ideas and the beliefs and systems of feeling to which Eliot alludes or from which he borrows, rather than to the facts alone. Eliot does not restrict himself to criticism; he digests what he takes; but the reader must know what it is that has been digested before he can appreciate the result. The Holy Grail material in *The Waste Land* is an instance: like Tiresias, this material is a dramatic element in the poem.

Mr. Stevens' difficulties to the normal reader present themselves in the shape of seemingly impenetrable words or phrases which no wedge of knowledge brought from outside the body of Mr. Stevens' own poetry can help much to split. The wedge, if any, is in the words themselves, either in the instance alone or in relation to analogous instances in the same or other poems in the book. Two examples should suffice.

In *Sunday Morning*, there is in the seventh stanza (page 93) a reference to the sun, to which men shall chant their devotion—

> Not as a god, but as a god might be,
> Naked among them, like a savage source.
> Their chant shall be a chant of paradise,
> Out of their blood, returning to the sky; . . .

Depending upon the reader this will or will not be obscure. But in any case, the full weight of the lines is not felt until the conviction of the poet that the sun is origin and ending for all life is shared by the reader. That is why the god might be naked among them. It takes only reading of the stanza, the poem, and other poems where the fertility of the sun is celebrated, to make the notion sure. The only bit of outside information that might help is the fact that in an earlier version this stanza concluded the poem.—In short, generally, you need only the dictionary and familiarity with the poem in question to clear up a good part of Mr. Stevens' obscurities.

The second example is taken from "The Man Whose Pharynx Was Bad" (page 128):

> Perhaps, if winter once could penetrate
> Through all its purples to the final slate.

Here, to obtain the full meaning, we have only to consult the sixth stanza of *Le Monocle de Mon Oncle* (page 18):

> If men at forty will be painting lakes
> The ephemeral blues must merge for them in one,
> The basic slate, the universal hue.
> There is a substance in us that prevails.

Mr. Stevens has a notion often intimated that the sky is the only permanent background for thought and knowledge; he would see things against the sky as a Christian would see them

against the cross. The blue of the sky is the prevailing substance of the sky, and to Mr. Stevens it seems only necessary to look at the sky to share and be shared in its blueness.

If I have selected fairly types of obscurity from these poets, it should be clear that whereas the obscurities of Eliot and Pound are intrinsic difficulties of the poems, to which the reader must come well armed with specific sorts of external knowledge and belief, the obscurities of Mr. Stevens clarify themselves to the intelligence alone. Mode and value are different—not more or less valuable, but different. And all result from the concentrated language which is the medium of poetry. The three poets load their words with the maximum content; naturally, the poems remain obscure until the reader takes out what the poet puts in. What still remains will be the essential impenetrability of words, the bottomlessness of knowledge. To these the reader, like the poet, must submit.

Returning, this time without reference to Pound and Eliot, among the varieties of Mr. Stevens' tropes we find some worth notice which comparison will not help. In *Le Monocle de Mon Oncle*, the ninth stanza (page 20), has nothing logically to do with the poem; it neither develops the subject nor limits it, but is rather a rhetorical interlude set in the poem's midst. Yet it is necessary to the poem, because its rhetoric, boldly announced as such, expresses the feeling of the poet toward his poem, and that feeling, once expressed, becomes incorporated in the poem.

> In verses wild with motion, full of din,
> Loudened by cries, by clashes, quick and sure
> As the deadly thought of men accomplishing
> Their curious fates in war, come, celebrate
> The faith of forty, ward of Cupido.
> Most venerable heart, the lustiest conceit
> Is not too lusty for your broadening.
> I quiz all sounds, all thoughts, all everything
> For the music and manner of the paladins
> To make oblation fit. Where shall I find
> Bravura adequate to this great hymn?

It is one of the advantages of a non-dramatic, meditative style, that pure rhetoric may be introduced into a poem without injuring its substance. The structure of the poem is, so to speak, a structure of loose ends, spliced only verbally, joined only by the sequence in which they appear. What might be fustian ornament in a dramatic poem, in a meditative poem casts a feeling far from fustian over the whole, and the slighter the relation of the rhetorical interlude to the substance of the whole, the more genuine is the feeling cast. The rhetoric does the same thing that the action does in a dramatic poem, or the events in a narrative poem; it produces an apparent medium in which the real substance may be borne.

Such rhetoric is not reserved to set interludes; it often occurs in lines not essentially rhetorical at all. Sometimes it gives life to a serious passage and cannot be separated without fatal injury to the poem. Then it is the trick without which the poem would fall flat entirely. Two poems occur where the rhetoric is the vital trope—"A High-Toned Old Christian Woman" (page 79), and "Bantams in Pine-Woods" (page 101), which I quote entire:

> Chieftain Iffucan of Azcan in caftan
> Of tan with henna hackles, halt!
> Damned universal cock, as if the sun
> Was blackamoor to bear your blazing tail.
> Fat! Fat! Fat! I am the personal.
> Your world is you. I am my world.

You ten-foot poet among inchlings. Fat!
Begone! An inchling bristles in these pines,
Bristles, and points their Appalachian tangs,
And fears not portly Azcan nor his hoos.

The first and last distichs are gauds of rhetoric; nevertheless
they give not only the tone but the substance to the poem. If
the reader is deceived by the rhetoric and believes the poem is
no more than a verbal plaything, he ought not to read poetry
except as a plaything. With a different object, Mr. Stevens'
rhetoric is as ferociously comic as the rhetoric in Marlowe's *Jew
of Malta*, and as serious. The ability to handle rhetoric so as to
reach the same sort of intense condensation that is secured in
bare, non-rhetorical language is very rare, and since what
rhetoric can condense is very valuable it ought to receive the
same degree of attention as any other use of language. Mr.
Stevens' successful attempts in this direction are what make
him technically most interesting. Simple language, dealing
obviously with surds, draws emotion out of feelings; rhetorical
language, dealing rather, or apparently, with inflections,
employed with the same seriousness, creates a surface *equivalent* to an emotion by its approximately complete escape from
the purely communicative function of language. [4]

We have seen in a number of examples that Mr. Stevens
uses language in several different ways, either separately or in
combination; and I have tried to imply that his success is due
largely to his double adherence to words and experience as
existing apart from his private sensibility. His great labor has
been to allow the reality of what he felt personally to pass into
the superior impersonal reality of words. Such a transformation
amounts to an access of knowledge, as it raises to a condition
where it may be rehearsed and understood in permanent form
that body of emotional and sensational experience which in its
natural condition makes life a torment and confusion.

With the technical data partly in hand, it ought now to be
possible to fill out the picture, touch upon the knowledge itself,
in Mr. Stevens' longest and most important poem, *The
Comedian as the Letter C*. Everywhere characteristic of Mr.
Stevens' style and interests, it has the merit of difficulty—
difficulty which when solved rewards the reader beyond his
hopes of clarity.

Generally speaking the poem deals with the sensations
and images, notions and emotions, ideas and meditations,
sensual adventures and introspective journeyings of a protagonist called Crispin. More precisely, the poem expounds the
shifting of a man's mind between sensual experience and its
imaginative interpretation, the struggle, in that mind, of the
imagination for sole supremacy and the final slump or ascent
where the mind contents itself with interpreting pain and
common things. In short, we have a meditation, with instances, of man's struggle with nature. The first line makes the
theme explicit: "Nota: man is the intelligence of his soil, the
sovereign ghost." Later, the theme is continued in reverse
form: "His soil is man's intelligence." Later still, the soil is
qualified as suzerain, which means sovereign over a semi-
independent or internally autonomous state; and finally, at the
end of the poem, the sovereignty is still further reduced when
it turns out that the imagination can make nothing better of the
world (here called a turnip), than the same insoluble lump it
was in the beginning.

The poem is in six parts of about four pages each. A
summary may replace pertinent discussion and at the same
time preclude extraneous discussion. In Part I, called "The
World without Imagination," Crispin, who previously had
cultivated a small garden with his intelligence, finds himself at

sea, "a skinny sailor peering in the sea-glass." At first at loss and
"washed away by magnitude," Crispin, "merest minuscule in
the gales," at last finds the sea a vocable thing,

But with a speech belched out of hoary darks
Noway resembling his, a visible thing,
And excepting negligible Triton, free
From the unavoidable shadow of himself
That elsewhere lay around him.

The sea "was no help before reality," only "one vast subjugating final tone," before which Crispin was made new. Con-
comitantly, with and because of his vision of the sea, "The
drenching of stale lives no more fell down."

Part II is called "Concerning the Thunder-Storms of
Yucatan," and there, in Yucatan, Crispin, a man made vivid
by the sea, found his apprehensions enlarged and felt the need
to fill his senses. He sees and hears all there is before him, and
writes fables for himself

Of an aesthetic tough, diverse, untamed,
Incredible to prudes, the mint of dirt,
Green barbarism turning paradigm.

The sea had liberated his senses, and he discovers an earth like
"A jostling festival of seeds grown fat, too juicily opulent," and
a "new reality in parrot-squawks." His education is interrupted
when a wind "more terrible than the revenge of music on
bassoons," brings on a tropical thunderstorm. Crispin, "this
connoisseur of elemental fate," identifies himself with the
storm, finding himself free, which he was before, and "more
than free, elate, intent, profound and studious" of a new self:

the thunder, lapsing in its clap,
Let down gigantic quavers of its voice,
For Crispin to vociferate again.

With such freedom taken from the sea and such power
found in the storm, Crispin is ready for the world of the
imagination. Naturally, then, the third part of the poem,
called "Approaching Carolina," is a chapter in the book of
moonlight, and Crispin "a faggot in the lunar fire." Moonlight
is imagination, a reflection or interpretation of the sun, which
is the source of life. It is also, curiously, this moonlight, North
America, and specifically one of the Carolinas. And the
Carolinas, to Crispin, seemed north; even the spring seemed
arctic. He meditates on the poems he has denied himself
because they gave less than "the relentless contact he desired."
Perhaps the moon would establish the necessary liaison between himself and his environment. But perhaps not. It
seemed

Illusive, faint, more mist than moon, perverse,
Wrong as a divagation to Peking. . . .
Moonlight was an evasion, or, if not,
A minor meeting, facile, delicate.

So he considers, and teeters back and forth, between the sun
and moon. For the moment he decides against the moon and
imagination in favor of the sun and his senses. The senses,
instanced by the smell of things at the river wharf where his
vessel docks, "round his rude aesthetic out" and teach him
"how much of what he saw he never saw at all."

He gripped more closely the essential prose
As being, in a world so falsified,
The one integrity for him, the one
Discovery still possible to make,
To which all poems were incident, unless
That prose should wear a poem's guise at last.

In short, Crispin conceives that if the experience of the
senses is but well enough known, the knowledge takes the form
of imagination after all. So we find as the first line of the fourth

part, called "The Idea of a Colony," "Nota: his soil is man's intelligence," which reverses the original statement that man is the intelligence of his soil. With the new distinction illuminating his mind, Crispin plans a colony, and asks himself whether the purpose of his pilgrimage is not

> to drive away
> The shadow of his fellows from the skies,
> And, from their stale intelligence released,
> To make a new intelligence prevail?

The rest of the fourth part is a long series of synonymous tropes stating instances of the new intelligence. In a torment of fastidious thought, Crispin writes a prolegomena for his colony. Everything should be understood for what it is and should follow the urge of its given character. The spirit of things should remain spirit and play as it will.

> The man in Georgia waking among pines
> Should be pine-spokesman. The responsive man,
> Planting his pristine cores in Florida,
> Should prick thereof, not on the psaltery,
> But on the banjo's categorical gut.

And as for Crispin's attitude toward nature, "the melon should have apposite ritual" and the peach its incantation. These "commingled souvenirs and prophecies"—all images of freedom and the satisfaction of instinct—compose Crispin's idea of a colony. He banishes the masquerade of thought and expunges dreams; the ideal takes no form from these. Crispin will be content to "let the rabbit run, the cock declaim."

In Part V, which is "A Nice Shady Home," Crispin dwells in the land, contented and a hermit, continuing his observations with diminished curiosity. His discovery that his colony has fallen short of his plan and that he is content to have it fall short, content to build a cabin,

> who once planned
> Loquacious columns by the ructive sea,

leads him to ask whether he should not become a philosopher instead of a colonizer.

> Should he lay by the personal and make
> Of his own fate an instance of all fate?

The question is rhetorical, but before it can answer itself, Crispin, sapped by the quotidian, sapped by the sun, has no energy for questions, and is content to realize, that for all the sun takes

> it gives a humped return
> Exchequering from piebald fiscs unkeyed.

Part VI, called "And Daughters with Curls," explains the implications of the last quoted lines. The sun, and all the new intelligence which it enriched, mulcted the man Crispin, and in return gave him four daughters, four questioners and four sure answers. He has been brought back to social nature, has gone to seed. The connoisseur of elemental fate has become himself an instance of all fate. He does not know whether the return was "Anabasis or slump, ascent or chute." His cabin—that is the existing symbol of his colony—seems now a phylactery, a sacred relic or amulet he might wear in memorial to his idea, in which his daughters shall grow up, bidders and biders for the ecstasies of the world, to repeat his pilgrimage, and come, no doubt, in their own cabins, to the same end.

Then Crispin invents his doctrine and clothes it in the fable about the turnip:

> The world, a turnip once so readily plucked,
> Sacked up and carried overseas, daubed out
> Of its ancient purple, pruned to the fertile main,
> And sown again by the stiffest realist,

> Came reproduced in purple, family font,
> The same insoluble lump. The fatalist
> Stepped in and dropped the chuckling down his craw,
> Without grace or grumble.

But suppose the anecdote was false, and Crispin a profitless philosopher,

> Glozing his life with after-shining flicks,
> Illuminating, from a fancy gorged
> By apparition, plain and common things,
> Sequestering the fluster from the year,
> Making gulped potions from obstreperous drops,
> And so distorting, proving what he proves
> Is nothing, what can all this matter since
> The relation comes, benignly, to its end.
> So may the relation of each man be clipped.

The legend or subject of the poem and the mythology it develops are hardly new nor are the instances, intellectually considered, very striking. But both the clear depth of conception and the extraordinary luxuriance of rhetoric and image in which it is expressed, should be at least suggested in the summary here furnished. Mr. Stevens had a poem with an abstract subject—man as an instance of fate, and a concrete experience—the sensual confusion in which the man is waylaid; and to combine them he had to devise a form suitable to his own peculiar talent. The simple statement—of which he is a master—could not be prolonged to meet the dimensions of his subject. To the dramatic style his talents were unsuitable, and if by chance he used it, it would prevent both the meditative mood and the accent of intellectual wit which he needed to make the subject his own. The form he used is as much his own and as adequate, as the form of *Paradise Lost* is Milton's or the form of *The Waste Land* is Eliot's. And as Milton's form filled the sensibility of one aspect of his age, Mr. Stevens' form fits part of the sensibility—a part which Eliot or Pound or Yeats do little to touch—of our own age.

I do not know a name for the form. It is largely the form of rhetoric, language used for its own sake, persuasively to the extreme. But it has, for rhetoric, an extraordinary content of concrete experience. Mr. Stevens is a genuine poet in that he attempts constantly to transform what is felt with the senses and what is thought in the mind—if we can still distinguish the two—into that realm of being, which we call poetry, where what is thought is felt and what is felt has the strict point of thought. And I call his mode of achieving that transformation rhetorical because it is not lyric or dramatic or epic, because it does not transcend its substance, but is a reflection upon a hard surface, a shining mirror of rhetoric.

In its nature depending so much on tone and atmosphere, accenting precise management of ambiguities, and dealing with the subtler inflections of simple feelings, the elements of the form cannot be tracked down and put in order. Perhaps the title of the whole poem, *The Comedian as the Letter* C, is as good an example as any where several of the elements can be found together. The letter C is, of course, Crispin, and he is called a letter because he is small (he is referred to as "merest minuscule," which means small letter, in the first part of the poem) and because, though small, like a letter he stands for something—his colony, cabin, and children—as a comedian. He is a comedian because he deals finally with the quotidian (the old distinction of comedy and tragedy was between everyday and heroic subject matter), gorged with apparition, illuminating plain and common things. But what he deals with is not comic; the comedy, in that sense, is restricted to his perception and does not touch the things perceived or himself. The comedy is the accent, the play of the words. He is at various times a realist, a clown, a philosopher, a colonizer, a father, a faggot in the lunar fire, and so on. In sum, and any sum is hypothetical, he may be a comedian in both senses, but separately never. He is the hypothesis of comedy. He is a piece of rhetoric—a persona in words—exemplifying all these characters, and summing, or masking, in his persuasive style, the essential prose he read. He is the poem's guise that the prose wears at last.

Such is the title of the poem, and such is the poem itself. Mr. Stevens has created a surface, a texture, a rhetoric in which his feelings and thoughts are preserved in what amounts to a new sensibility. The contrast between his subjects—the apprehension of all the sensual aspects of nature as instances of fate,—and the form in which the subjects are expressed is what makes his poetry valuable. Nature becomes nothing but words and to a poet words are everything.

Notes

1. The references are to the new edition of *Harmonium*, New York: Alfred A. Knopf, 1931. This differs from the first edition in that three poems have been cut out and fourteen added.
2. Mr. Stevens wrote me that his daughter put a superlative value on ice-cream. Up daughters!
3. See *Words and Idioms*, by Logan Pearsall Smith, Boston: Houghton Mifflin, 1926, page 121. "One of the great defects of our critical vocabulary is the lack of a neutral, non-derogatory name for these great artificers, these artists who derive their inspiration more from the formal than the emotional aspects of their art, and who are more interested in the masterly control of their material, than in the expression of their own feelings, or the prophetic aspects of their calling." Mr. Smith then suggests the use of the words erudite and erudition and gives as reason their derivation "from *erudire* (E 'out of,' and *rudis*, 'rude,' 'rough' or 'raw'), a verb meaning in classical Latin to bring out of the rough, to form by means of art, to polish, to instruct." Mr. Stevens is such an *erudite*; though he is often more, when he deals with emotional matters as if they were matters for *erudition*.
4. There is a point at which rhetorical language resumes its communicative function. In the second of "Six Significant Landscapes" (page 98), we have this image:

> A pool shines
> Like a bracelet
> Shaken at a dance,

which is a result of the startling associations induced by an ornamental, social, rhetorical style in dealing with nature. The image perhaps needs its context to assure its quality.

YVOR WINTERS
From "Wallace Stevens
or the Hedonist's Progress" (1943)
On Modern Poets
1959, pp. 11–34

Though Wallace Stevens has published almost nothing in the way of criticism, he has nevertheless been very clear in stating his theories of life and of literature, and he may justifiably be treated, I believe, in a series of essays on literary theorists.[1]

His fundamental ideas are stated in *Sunday Morning*, an early poem, and in some ways his greatest. The poem consists of eight stanzas in blank verse, each containing fifteen lines, and it presents a clear and fairly coherent argument.

The first stanza sets the stage and identifies the protago-nist. We are given a woman, at home on a Sunday morning, meditating on the meaning of death. The second stanza asks the question which provides the subject of the poem; it asks what divinity this woman may be thought to possess as a recompense for her ultimate surrender to death; and having asked the question, it replies that her divinity, which must live within herself, consists wholly in her emotions—not in her understanding of the emotions, but in the emotions as a good in themselves. This answer is not quite the orthodox romantic answer, which would offer us in the emotions either a true guide to virtue or a more or less mystical experience leading to some kind of union with some kind of deity. Any philosophy which offers the cultivation of the emotions as an end in itself, I suppose, is a kind of hedonism. In any event, that is the kind of philosophy which we find here.

The third stanza, by means of the allegory of Jove and his human loves, through his union with whom he crossed the heavenly strain upon the human, implies that man has a capacity which may at least figuratively be termed divine; the stanza is a subordinate commentary on the one preceding, and does not really advance the argument.

In the fourth stanza, however, the argument moves forward. The protagonist objects to the concept which has been offered her; she states that the beauties of this life are transient and that she longs to believe in a Paradise beyond them. The remainder of the stanza, and the greater part of it, is the poet's reply: in a passage of great rhetorical power, he denies the possibility of Paradise, at the same time that he communicates through the feeling of his language a deep nostalgic longing to accept the ideas which he is rejecting. In the first two lines of the fifth stanza, the woman repeats her objection, and the poet then replies with an explanation of the function of death: it is our awareness of the imminence of death which heightens our emotions and sharpens our perceptions; our knowledge of life's transience stimulates our perception of life's beauty.

In the sixth stanza the poet considers an hypothetical paradise, and, since he can imagine it only in terms of a projection of the good life as the hedonist understands the good life, he deduces that paradise would become tedious and insipid: we have in this stanza the first sharp vision of the ennui which is to obsess the later work of the poet and which is ultimately to wreck his talent, an ennui arising from the fact that emotion is not a good in itself, but that if cultivated for itself alone is merely a pleasant diversion so long as the novelty of a given experience endures, at most as long as new experiences can give us the illusion of novel excitement, and then becomes a disease of the spirit, a state of indifferency in which there is neither novelty nor significance.

The seventh stanza presents a vision of a future race of men engaged in a religious ritual, the generating principle of which is their joy in the world as it is given them and their sense of brotherhood as "men that perish." The stanza contains suggestions of a pantheism which goes beyond the bounds of a strict hedonism, but they are merely suggestions and they appear nowhere else. The eighth and last stanza begins by denying the immortality of Jesus, and, by implication, of man; and it places the protagonist finally and irretrievably on a small but beautiful planet, floating like a tropical island in boundless space, "in an old chaos of the sun."

This summary, even as summaries go, is extremely skeletalized. It has been my intention, here, merely to isolate the hedonistic theme for future consideration; the theme is not thus isolated in the poem, but is complicated by its interconnections with other human problems from which not even a hedonist can escape. Whatever the defects of the hedonistic

But he is bent on discovering not the reality of his own nature, but rather the reality of his native country. Man is no longer, as in the first line of the first part, the intelligence of his soil; but the soil, as we note in the first line of the next and fourth section, is man's intelligence. These statements do not have the philosophical lucidity which would delight the present simple paraphraser, but they seem to mean, in their relationship to this poem, that Crispin has been turned away first from the attempt to study himself directly, and second from the attempt to indulge in exotic experiences, and that he has been turned instead to the attempt to master his native environment—to master it, that is, for the purposes of poetry. The nature of this last procedure I do not pretend to understand, and since the words which I have just used are my own and are not quoted from Stevens, it is possible that my confusion is of my own contriving. But in general, I should say that Stevens appears to have slipped here into the Whitmanian form of a romantic error common enough in our literature, but current especially in Stevens' generation and espoused in particular by Stevens' friend W. C. Williams: the fallacy that the poet achieves salvation by being, in some way, intensely of and expressive of his country. A common variant of this notion is the idea that the poet should bear the same relationship to his time, and in fact the two versions are perhaps most commonly combined, as they are in Williams. Felt with sufficient intensity, they become indistinguishable, as in Crane or even in Whitman, from pantheism, and go quite beyond the bounds of hedonism; but the notions in question represent merely a casual subject for meditation in Stevens, a subject which he considers because he is confused but which involves a spiritual quality, a capacity for naively whole-hearted enthusiasm, which is quite foreign to his nature. The ideas are the attempt to justify a kind of extroversion: the poet, cut off from human nature, which is his proper subject matter, seeks to find a subject in the description, or, as the saying goes, in the expression, of what is round about him. In practice, this results mainly, as in Williams, in a heavy use of the native landscape, sometimes as legitimate symbolism or background, sometimes as the subject of mere description, sometimes as false symbolism:[6] in the first of these three instances, the poet is actually intent on doing something not adequately explained by his theory; in the second he is doing something relatively easy and unimportant; and in the third he is writing badly. Crispin seeks, then, an understanding not of himself but of his native landscape, and his native landscape is a temperate one, which does not offer the flamboyant and succulent excitements of Yucatan:

> The spring came there in clinking pannicles
> Of half-dissolving frost, the summer came,
> If ever, whisked and wet, not ripening,
> Before the winter's vacancy returned.

This landscape is the one which appears in "The Man Whose Pharynx Was Bad," and which Stevens there uses to symbolize his own frustration. But Crispin, having returned from Yucatan, hopes now to achieve the beatific pleasure reserved for the successful hedonist, not by extravagance of experience, but by honesty and accuracy of experience: by honesty and accuracy, however, so far as we can judge from the poem, merely in describing the scenery which surrounds him, as if, perhaps, there were some ulterior virtue in this process which cannot quite be defined in words. The fourth section of the poem is really an elaboration upon the central ideas of the third, and it scarcely calls for comment at present. In the fifth and sixth parts, Crispin's concentration upon the normal world

about him results in his marrying and begetting daughters; and finding that the facts which he had set out to describe with such exemplary honesty are more engrossing than the description of them, he abandons his art, in order, as very young people are sometimes heard to say, to live. This is not surprising, for the honest description which Crispin set out to achieve is in itself a moral experience, though of a very limited kind: honest description renders the feeling appropriate to purely sensory experience, and is hence a kind of judgment of that experience. But if Crispin had realized this, he would have realized the whole moral basis of art, and would have proceeded to more complex subjects; not realizing this, he lost interest in his simplified art, and found the art even in this simplified form to be the last element of confusion remaining in his experience: to achieve intelligent objectivity, Crispin is forced to abandon his description and merely enjoy the subject matter of his description in the most naked possible of conditions:

> He first, as realist, admitted that
> Whoever hunts a matinal continent
> May, after all, stop short before a plum
> And be content and still be realist.
> The words of things entangle and confuse.
> The plum survives its poems . . .
>   . . . it survives in its own form,
> Beyond these changes, good fat guzzly fruit.

We have now the complete argument, I believe, which leads to Crispin's renunciation. The passage in which the renunciation takes place, however, is interesting for another reason; for the quality of the rhetoric employed at this particular juncture helps us profoundly to understand Stevens himself. The passage follows closely upon the lines just quoted and will be found about half-way through the fifth section:

> Was he to bray this in profoundest brass
> Arointing his dreams with fugal requiems?
> Was he to company vastest things defunct
> With a blubber of tom-toms harrowing the sky?
> Scrawl a tragedian's testament? Prolong
> His active force in an inactive dirge,
> Which, let the tall musicians call and call,
> Should merely call him dead? Pronounce amen
> Through choirs infolded to the outmost clouds?
> Because he built a cabin who once planned
> Loquacious columns by the ructive sea?
> Because he turned to salad beds again?

What I wish the reader to note is this: that the passage describes Crispin's taking leave of his art, and describes also his refusal to use art in the process of leave-taking, because the art is, after all, futile and contemptible. Yet for Stevens himself the entire poem is a kind of tentative leave-taking; he has not the courage to act as his hero acts and be done with it, so he practices the art which he cannot justify and describes it in terms of contempt. Furthermore, the chief instrument of irony in this passage, and throughout the poem, and indeed throughout much of the rest of Stevens, is a curious variant on the self-ridicule, the romantic irony, with which we are familiar from Byron through Laforgue and his modern disciples;[7] the instrument is self-parody, a parody occasionally subtle, often clumsy, of the refined and immutable style of Stevens at his best. To estimate at least a part of the tragedy represented by Stevens' career, the reader can scarcely do better than compare the lines quoted above with the last section of the much earlier *Sunday Morning*:

> She hears upon that water without sound,
> A voice that cries, "The tomb in Palestine
> Is not the porch of spirits lingering.

It is the grave of Jesus where he lay."
We live in an old chaos of the sun,
Or old dependency of day and night,
Or island solitude, unsponsored, free,
Of that wide water, inescapable.
Deer walk upon our mountains, and the quail
Whistle about us their spontaneous cries;
Sweet berries ripen in the wilderness;
And, in the isolation of the sky,
At evening, casual flocks of pigeons make
Ambiguous undulations as they sink,
Downward to darkness, on extended wings.

Since the poet, having arrived at the predicament to which we have traced him, however, is not to abandon his art, there remains only the possibility that he seek variety of experience in the increasingly perverse and strange; that he seek it, moreover, with no feeling of respect toward the art which serves as his only instrument and medium. In the poem entitled "The Revolutionists Stop for Orangeade," we are given the theory of this type of poetry:

Hang a feather by your eye,
Nod and look a little sly.
This must be the vent of pity,
Deeper than a truer ditty
Of the real that wrenches,
Of the quick that's wry.

And from this point onward there remains little but the sly look and a perverse ingenuity in confusing the statement of essentially simple themes. *The Man with the Blue Guitar*,[8] for example, which is one of his most recent performances, is merely a jingling restatement of the old theme of the severance between the rational understanding and the poetic imagination. But the statement is never quite clear; and since the theme, though unsound, is far from difficult to understand, one is inclined to suspect that the lack of clarity is the result of a deliberate choice, a choice motivated, perhaps, by the hope that some note more moving than the poet has a right to expect may be struck from the obscurity. And if one does not always encounter such willful semiobscurity in the later poems, one much too commonly encounters the kind of laborious foolishness to be found in the following poem, entitled "The Mechanical Optimist," published in *New Directions* for 1936:

A lady dying of diabetes
Listened to the radio,
Catching the lesser dithyrambs.
So heaven collects its bleating lambs.

Her useless bracelets fondly fluttered,
Paddling the melodic swirls,
The idea of God no longer sputtered
At the roots of her indifferent curls.

The idea of the Alps grew large,
Not yet, however, a thing to die in.
It seemed serener just to die,
To float off on the floweriest barge,

Accompanied by the exegesis
Of familiar things in a cheerful voice,
Like the night before Christmas and all the carols.
Dying lady, rejoice, rejoice!

The generating mood is one of ennui; the style represents an effort, half bored and half desperate, to achieve originality; the victim of the irony is very small game, and scarcely worthy of the artillery of the author of *Sunday Morning*; the point of view is adolescent. The author of *Sunday Morning* and of *Le Monocle de Mon Oncle*, the heir of Milton and of Jonson, is endeavoring, in his old age, to épater les bourgeois. The poem

is the work of a man who twenty or twenty-five years earlier was one of the great poets of the English language.

This is the outline, I believe, of the sequence of ideas and states of mind which have debased the greatest American poetic talent of the twentieth century. The sequence is offered merely as a species of logical sequence; it is only imperfectly chronological. Stevens was a hedonist from the beginning, and the entire complex of ideas and feelings which I have recounted are to be found in his work from the beginning. But although it is possible to find some of his most willful nonsense—"Earthy Anecdote," let us say, or "Metaphors of a Magnifico"—among his earlier poems, it is likewise true that all of his great poetry is early. *Sunday Morning* is one of the earliest compositions; "The Snow Man," *Le Monocle de Mon Oncle*, "On the Manner of Addressing Clouds," "Of Heaven Considered as a Tomb," "The Death of the Soldier," "Domination of Black" are all of the next few years. All of these poems were written and first published before 1923, the date of the first edition of *Harmonium*; and if there is a later poem as good I do not know it or cannot appreciate it. There are other poems, more or less early, less perfect or of smaller scope but still of considerable beauty, such as "Peter Quince at the Clavier" or "Cortège for Rosenbloom," and such poems as these one may find equalled occasionally, though very rarely, at a later date; but these two surpass anything by the author which I have read in the past decade.

Some of the virtues of *Sunday Morning* I have indicated in very general terms, but one cannot turn from the poem that may be the greatest American work of our century without considering briefly some of its more haunting beauties, if it be only as an act of piety.

I have already quoted the final stanza of the poem, and its beauty should be obvious; yet as removed from its context, the stanza loses much of its complexity. The "water without sound," the "wide water inescapable," is not only an image representing infinite space; it is an image, established in the first stanza, representing a state of mind, a kind of bright and empty beatitude, over which the thought of death may darken suddenly and without warning:

She dreams a little, and she feels the dark
Encroachment of that old catastrophe,
As a calm darkens among water-lights.

The language has the greatest possible dignity and subtlety, combined with perfect precision. The imminence of absolute tragedy is felt and recorded, but the integrity of the feeling mind is maintained. The mind perceives, as by a kind of metaphysical sense, the approach of invading impersonality; yet knowing the invasion to be inevitable and its own identity, while that identity lasts, the only source of any good whatever, maintains that identity in its full calm and clarity, that nothing may be sacrificed without need. This combination of calm and terror, in dealing with this particular theme, will be found in only one other poet in English, in Shakespeare as one finds him in a few of the more metaphysical sonnets.[9] The calm clarity of tone enables the poet to deal with a variety of kinds of feeling which would be impossible were the terror emphasized for a moment at any point, were the complete and controlled unity of the experiencing mind for a moment disordered by its own perceptions. The same poem, for example, is able to contain the following lines, of a sweetness and of an illusory simplicity which again are scarcely less than Shakespearean:

She says, "I am content when wakened birds,
Before they fly, test the reality

Of misty fields, by their sweet questionings;
But when the birds are gone, and their warm fields
Return no more, where, then, is paradise?"

And out of this passage proceeds the great lament for the lost myths, which I have already mentioned. This passage and others similar, though beautiful in themselves, are a preparation for the descriptive lines in the last stanza, and when we finally come to those lines, they are weighted with meaning and feeling accumulated from all that has gone before. It is difficult for this reason to quote from the poem for the purpose of illustrating its beauty. ⟨. . .⟩

Le Monocle de Mon Oncle, a work produced a few years later than *Sunday Morning*, endeavors to treat the subject of love in hedonistic terms and confesses ironically to encountering more than one difficulty. The poem is often obscure, and, perhaps because one cannot easily follow it, appears far less a unit than *Sunday Morning*; it contains extraordinary writing, however. The second stanza may fairly illustrate what I have said:

A red bird flies across the golden floor.
It is a red bird that seeks out his choir
Among the choirs of wind and wet and wing.
A torrent will fall from him when he finds.
Shall I uncrumple this much-crumpled thing?
I am a man of fortune greeting heirs;
For it has come that thus I greet the spring.
These choirs of welcome choir for me farewell.
No spring can follow past meridian.
Yet you persist with anecdotal bliss
To make believe a starry connaissance.

The first four lines are incomprehensible, except as description, and the claim of the fifth line is unjustified; the remainder of the stanza, however, displays a combination of bitterness, irony, and imperturbable elegance not unworthy of Ben Jonson.

"On the Manner of Addressing Clouds" deals essentially with the same subject as the passage in which Crispin contemplates the plum, but deals with it in a different mood; that is, the poet sees much the same relationship between his art and his subject as does Crispin, but since he sees himself alone in the "old chaos of the sun," "that drifting waste," amid the "mute bare splendors of the sun and moon," he is glad to retain his art as a mitigation of his solitude: what kind of mitigation he does not venture to say, but the mere fact of mitigation suffices him. The opening lines of this poem display a faint suggestion of Stevens' self-parody in one of its most frequent forms, an excess of alliteration which renders the style perversely finical. If one will compare these lines to the opening of *The Comedian as the Letter C*, he may readily see how rapidly the method can degenerate into very crude comedy. "Of Heaven Considered as a Tomb" is a vision of death as extinction. These two poems deal with the evaluation of the central theme of *Sunday Morning*, with the irremediable tragedy, and they are free from all in that poem which invites question as well as much that provides richness and variety. The style of both has a cold concentration, related to this purity of motive, which almost surpasses, for me, the beauty of the longer poem. "The Snow Man" and "The Death of the Soldier" deal respectively with life and with death in a universe which is impersonal and devoid of any comfort except that which one may derive from the contemplation of the mute bare splendors. They have great power, but probably less than the other short poems which I have just mentioned, perhaps because of the metrical form. [10]

There appears to be in the best of the early poems, as I have said, a traditional seriousness of attitude and a traditional rhetoric cognate with that attitude and precisely expressive of it. This traditional element in the early work enables Stevens' talent to function at its highest power; but it is not only unjustified and unsupported by Stevens' explicit philosophy, it is at odds with that philosophy. And the conflict between the traditional element and the element encouraged by the philosophy results little by little in the destruction of the traditional element and the degradation of the poet's style. It is extremely important that we understand Stevens for more reasons than one; he has written great poems, and we should know them and know why they are great; and we should know what is bad, and why it is bad, so that we may separate the bad from the good and the more surely preserve the good. But beyond this, he gives us, I believe, the most perfect laboratory of hedonism to be found in literature. He is not like those occasional poets of the Renaissance who appear in some measure to be influenced by a pagan philosophy, but who in reality take it up as a literary diversion at the same time that they are beneath the surface immovably Christian. Stevens is released from all the restraints of Christianity, and is encouraged by all the modern orthodoxy of Romanticism: his hedonism is so fused with Romanticism as to be merely an elegant variation on that somewhat inelegant System of Thoughtlessness. His ideas have remained essentially unchanged for more than a quarter of a century, and on the whole they have been very clearly expressed, so that there is no real occasion to be in doubt as to their nature; and he began as a great poet, so that when we examine the effect of those ideas upon his work, we are examining something of very great importance.

Notes

1. All poems mentioned in this essay, unless otherwise identified, are to be found in the second edition of *Harmonium*, by Wallace Stevens, published by Alfred A. Knopf, New York, 1931. The book is small, indexed, and well known, and page references seem unnecessary.
2. From "The Poetic Principle," p. 12 of Vol. I of the three volumes of criticism in Poe's works, the edition of Stedman and Woodberry. Quoted and elucidated in my essay on Poe, in *In Defense of Reason*.
3. "Dionysus in Dismay," by Stanley P. Chase, in *Humanism and America*, edited by Norman Foerster, Farrar and Rinehart, New York, 1930, p. 211.
4. "Wallace Stevens and Other Poets," by Howard Baker, *The Southern Review*, Vol. I, Number 2, Autumn 1935, p. 376.
5. Op. cit., Vol. III, p. 107.
6. This whole topic is discussed at length in the essay entitled "The Experimental School in American Poetry" (the section on pseudo-reference) in my volume *In Defense of Reason*.
7. This entire subject is discussed in the latter part of my second essay in *In Defense of Reason*, already mentioned.
8. *The Man with the Blue Guitar*, by Wallace Stevens, Alfred A. Knopf, N.Y., 1937.
9. I have discussed this attitude of Shakespeare and some of its historical background in *Poetry: A Magazine of Verse* for February, March, and April, 1939; and have analyzed the 77th sonnet with this attitude in mind on p. 49 of the issue for April.
10. The scansion of free verse and the influence of the meter on the total poetic result may be found discussed at great length on pp. 103 to 150 of *In Defense of Reason*. The scansion of "The Snow Man" is there marked. That of "The Death of the Soldier" is similar in principle, but simpler in form.

RANDALL JARRELL
"Reflections on Wallace Stevens"
Poetry and the Age
1953, pp. 133–48

Let me begin with a quotation from Stendhal: "'What I find completely lacking in all these people,' thought Lucien, 'is the unexpected. . . .' He was reduced to philosophizing." In my quotation Lucien stands for Stevens, "these people" for America and Business, "the unexpected" for Culture, the exotic, the past, the Earth-minus-America; "philosophizing" stands for, alas! philosophizing. . . . But before Stevens was reduced to it, he drew the unexpected from a hundred springs. There has never been a travel poster like *Harmonium*: how many of its readers must have sold what they had, given the money to steamship agents, and gone to spend the rest of their lives in Lhasa. Yet there was nothing really unusual in what Stevens felt. To have reached, in 1900, in the United States, the age of twenty-one, or fifteen, or twelve—as Stevens and Pound and Eliot did—this was so hard a thing for poets, went so thoroughly against the grain, that they emigrated as soon as they could, or stayed home and wrote poems in which foreignness, pastness, is itself a final good. "But how absurd!" a part of anyone protests. "Didn't they realize that, to a poet, New York City means just as much as Troy and Jerusalem and all the rest of those *immensely overpaid accounts* that Whitman begged the Muse, *install'd amid the kitchenware*, to cross out?" They didn't realize it; if one realizes it, one is not a poet. The accounts have been overpaid too many years for people ever to stop paying; to keep on paying them is to be human. To be willing to give up Life for the last local slice of it, for all those Sears Roebuck catalogues which, as businessmen and generals say, would be the most effective propaganda we could possibly drop on the Russians—this is a blinded chauvinism, a provincialism in space and time, which is even worse than that vulgar exoticism which disregards both what we have kept and what we are unique in possessing, which gives up *Moby-Dick* for the Journals of André Gide. Our most disastrous lacks—delicacy, awe, order, natural magnificence and piety, "the exquisite errors of time," and the rest; everything that is neither bought, sold, nor imagined on Sunset Boulevard or in Times Square; everything the absence of which made Lorca think Hell a city very like New York—these things were the necessities of Stevens' spirit. Some of his poems set about supplying these lacks—from other times and places, from the underlying order of things, from the imagination; other poems look with mockery and despair at the time and place that cannot supply them, that do not even desire to supply them; other poems reason or seem to reason about their loss, about their nature, about their improbable restoration. His poetry is obsessed with lack, a lack at last almost taken for granted, that he himself automatically supplies; if sometimes he has restored by imagination or abstraction or re-creation, at other times he has restored by collection, almost as J. P. Morgan did—Stevens likes something, buys it (at the expense of a little spirit), and ships it home in a poem. The feeling of being a leisured, cultivated, and sympathetic tourist (in a time-machine, sometimes) is essential to much of his work; most of his contact with values is at the distance of knowledge and regret—an aesthetician's or an archaeologist's contact with a painting, not a painter's.

Many of Stevens' readers have resented his—so to speak—spending his time collecting old porcelain: "if old things are

what you want," they felt, "why don't you collect old Fords or Locomobiles or Stutz Bearcats, or old Mother Bloors, right here at home?" But, for an odd reason, people have never resented the cruel truths or half-truths he told them about the United States. Once upon a time Richard Dehmel's poems, accused of obscenity, were acquitted on the grounds that they were incomprehensible—and almost exactly this happened to Stevens' home-truths. Yet they were plain, sometimes. Looking at General Jackson confronting the "mockers, the mickey mockers," Stevens decided what the "American Sublime" is: the sublime "comes down / To the spirit itself, / The spirit and space, / The empty spirit / In vacant space." Something like this is true, perhaps, always and everywhere; yet it is a hard truth for your world to have reduced you to: it is no wonder the poem ends, "What wine does one drink? / What bread does one eat?" And in "The Common Life" the church steeple is a "black line beside a white line," not different in any way from "the stack of the electric plant"; in the "flat air," the "morbid light," a man is "a result, a demonstration"; the men "have no shadows / And the women only one side." We live "no longer on the ancient cake of seed, / The almond and deep fruit. . . . We feast on human heads"; the table is a mirror and the diners eat reflections of themselves. "The steeples are empty and so are the people," he says in "Loneliness in Jersey City"; the poem is full of a despairing frivolity, as Stevens looks from Room 2903 out over that particular countryside which, I think, God once sent angels to destroy, but which the angels thought worse than anything they could do to it. And "In Oklahoma, / Bonnie and Josie, / Dressed in calico, / Danced around a stump. / They cried, / 'Ohoyaho, / Ohoo' . . . / Celebrating the marriage / Of flesh and air." Without what's superfluous, the excess of the spirit, man is a poor, bare, forked animal. In "Country Words" the poet sits under the willows of exile, and sings "like a cuckoo clock" to Belshazzar, that "putrid rock, / putrid pillar of a putrid people"; he sings "an old rebellious song, / An edge of song that never clears." But if it should clear, if the cloud that hangs over his heart and mind should lift, it would be because Belshazzar heard and understood:

> What is it that my feeling seeks?
> I know from all the things it touched
> And left beside and left behind.
> It wants the diamond pivot bright.
> It wants Belshazzar reading right
> The luminous pages on his knee,
> Of being, more than birth and death.
> It wants words virile with his breath.

If this intellectual is "isolated," it is not because he wants to be. . . . But Stevens' most despairing, amusing, and exactly realized complaint is "Disillusionment of Ten O'Clock":

> The houses are haunted
> By white nightgowns.
> None are green,
> Or purple with green rings,
> Or green with yellow rings,
> Or yellow with blue rings.
> None of them are strange,
> With socks of lace
> And beaded ceintures.
> People are not going
> To dream of baboons and periwinkles.
> Only, here and there, an old sailor,
> Drunk and asleep in his boots,
> Catches tigers
> In red weather.

Any schoolboy (of the superior Macaulayish breed) more or less feels what this poem means, but it is interesting to look at one or two details. Why *ten o'clock?* They have all gone to bed early, like good sensible machines; and the houses' ghosts, now, are only nightgowns, the plain white nightgowns of the Common Man, Economic Man, Rational Man—pure commonplace, no longer either individual or strange or traditional; and the dreams are as ordinary as the nightgowns. Here and there a drunken and disreputable *old sailor* still lives in the original reality (he dosen't dream of catching, he *catches*): *sailor* to bring in old-fashioned Europe, old-fashioned Asia, the old-fashioned ocean; *old* to bring in the past, to make him a dying survival. What indictment of the Present has ever compared, for flat finality, with "People are not going / To dream of baboons and periwinkles"? Yet isn't this poem ordinarily considered a rather nonsensical and Learish poem?

It is not until later that Stevens writes much about what America has in common with the rest of the world; then he splits everything differently, and contrasts with the past of America and of the world their present. In *Harmonium* he still loves America best when he can think of it as wilderness, naturalness, pure potentiality (he treats with especial sympathy Negroes, Mexican Indians, and anybody else he can consider wild); and it is this feeling that is behind the conclusion of *Sunday Morning*:

> She hears, upon that water without sound,
> A voice that cries, "The tomb in Palestine
> Is not the porch of spirits lingering.
> It is the grave of Jesus, where he lay."
> We live in an old chaos of the sun,
> Or old dependency of day and night,
> Or island solitude, unsponsored, free,
> Of that wide water, inescapable.
> Deer walk upon our mountains, and the quail
> Whistle about us their spontaneous cries;
> Sweet berries ripen in the wilderness;
> And, in the isolation of the sky,
> At evening, casual flocks of pigeons make
> Ambiguous undulations as they sink
> Downward to darkness, on extended wings.

Here—in the last purity and refinement of the grand style, as perfect, in its calm transparency, as the best of Wordsworth—is the last wilderness, come upon so late in the history of mankind that it is no longer seen as the creation of God, but as the Nature out of which we evolve; man without myth, without God, without anything but the universe which has produced him, is given an extraordinarily pure and touching grandeur in these lines—lines as beautiful, perhaps, as any in American poetry. Yet Stevens himself nearly equals them in two or three parts of *Esthétique du Mal*, the best of his later poems; there are in *Harmonium* six or eight of the most beautiful poems an American has written; and a book like *Parts of a World* is delightful as a whole, even though it contains no single poem that can compare with the best in *Harmonium*. But *Auroras of Autumn*, Stevens' last book, is a rather different affair. One sees in it the distinction, intelligence, and easy virtuosity of a master—but it would take more than these to bring to life so abstract, so monotonous, so overwhelmingly *characteristic* a book. Poems like these are, always, the product of a long process of evolution; in Stevens' case the process has been particularly interesting.

The habit of philosophizing in poetry—or of seeming to philosophize, of using a philosophical tone, images, constructions, of having quasi-philosophical daydreams—has been unfortunate for Stevens. Poetry is a bad medium for philosophy. Everything in the philosophical poem has to satisfy irreconcilable requirements: for instance, the last demand that we should make of philosophy (that it be interesting) is the first we make of a poem; the philosophical poet has an elevated and methodical, but forlorn and absurd air as he works away at his flying tank, his sewing-machine that also plays the piano. (One thinks of Richard Wilbur's graceful "Tom Swift has vanished too, / Who worked at none but wit's expense, / Putting dirigibles together, / Out in the yard, in the quiet weather, / Whistling behind Tom Sawyer's fence.") When the first thing that Stevens can find to say of the Supreme Fiction is that "it must be *abstract*," the reader protests, "Why, even Hegel called it a *concrete* universal"; the poet's medium, words, is abstract to begin with, and it is only his unique organization of the words that forces the poem, generalizations and all, over into the concreteness and singularity that it exists for. But Stevens has the weakness—a terrible one for a poet, a steadily increasing one in Stevens—of thinking of particulars as primarily illustrations of general truths, or else as aesthetic, abstracted objects, simply there to be contemplated; he often treats things or lives so that they seem no more than generalizations of an unprecedentedly low order. But surely a poet *has* to treat the concrete as primary, as something far more than an instance, a hue to be sensed, a member of a laudable category—for him it is always the generalization whose life is derived, whose authority is delegated. Goethe said, quite as if he were talking about Stevens: "It makes a great difference whether the poet seeks the particular in relation to the universal or contemplates the universal in the particular . . . [In the first case] the particular functions as an example, as an instance of the universal; but the second indeed represents the very nature of poetry. He who grasps this particular as living essence also encompasses the universal."

As a poet Stevens has every gift but the dramatic. It is the lack of immediate contact with lives that hurts his poetry more than anything else, that has made it easier and easier for him to abstract, to philosophize, to treat the living dog that wags its tail and bites you as the "canoid patch" of the epistemologist analyzing that great problem, the world; as the "cylindrical arrangement of brown and white" of the aesthetician analyzing that great painting, the world. Stevens knows better, often for poems at a time:

> At dawn,
> The paratroopers fall and as they fall
> They mow the lawn. A vessel sinks in waves
> Of people, as big bell-billows from its bell
> Bell-bellow in the village steeple. Violets,
> Great tufts, spring up from buried houses
> Of poor, dishonest people, for whom the steeple,
> Long since, rang out farewell, farewell, farewell.

This is a map with people living on it. Yet it is fatally easy for the scale to become too small, the distance too great, and us poor, dishonest people no more than data to be manipulated.

As one reads Stevens' later poetry one keeps thinking that he needs to be possessed by subjects, to be shaken out of himself, to have his subject individualize his poem; one remembers longingly how much more individuation there was in *Harmonium*—when you're young you try to be methodical and philosophical, but reality keeps breaking in. The best of *Harmonium* exists at a level that it is hard to rise above; and Stevens has had only faintly and intermittently the dramatic insight, the capacity to be obsessed by lives, actions, subject-matter, the chameleon's shameless interest in everything but itself, that could have broken up the habit and order and general sobering matter-of-factness of age. Often, nowadays, he seems disastrously set in his own ways, a fossil imprisoned in the rock of himself—the best marble but, still, marble.

All his *tunk-a-tunks*, his *hoo-goo-boos*—those mannered, manufactured, individual, uninteresting little sound-inventions —how typical they are of the lecture-style of the English philosopher, who makes grunts or odd noises, uses homely illustrations, and quotes day in and day out from *Alice*, in order to give what he says some appearance of that raw reality it so plainly and essentially lacks. These "tootings at the wedding of the soul" are fun for the tooter, but get as dreary for the reader as do all the foreign words—a few of these are brilliant, a few more pleasant, and the rest a disaster: "one cannot help deploring his too extensive acquaintance with the foreign languages," as Henry James said, of Walt Whitman, to Edith Wharton.

Stevens is never more philosophical, abstract, rational, than when telling us to put our faith in nothing but immediate sensations, perceptions, aesthetic particulars; for this is only a generalization offered for assent, and where in the ordinary late poem are the real particulars of the world—the people, the acts, the lives—for us to put our faith in? And when Stevens makes a myth to hold together aesthetic particulars and generalizations, it is as if one were revisited by the younger Saint-Simon, Comte, and that actress who played Reason to Robespierre's approving glare; Stevens' myths spring not from the soil but from the clouds, the arranged, scrubbed, reasoning clouds in someone's head. He is too rational and composedly fanciful a being to make up a myth—one could as easily imagine his starting a cult in Los Angeles. When one reads most eighteenth-century writing one is aware of some man of good sense and good taste and good will at the bottom of everything and everybody; but in Stevens—who is always swinging between baroque and rococo, and reminds one of the eighteenth century in dozens of ways—this being at the bottom of everything is cultivated and appreciative and rational out of all reason: the Old Adam in everybody turns out to be not Robinson Crusoe but Bernard Berenson.

Metastasio began as an improviser and ended as a poet; as one reads the average poem in *Auroras of Autumn* one feels that the opposite has been happening to Stevens. A poem begins, revealingly: "An exercise in viewing the world. / On the motive! But one looks at the sea / As one improvises, on the piano." And not the sea only. One reads a book like this with odd mixed pleasure, not as if one were reading poems but as if one were reading some *Travel-Diary of an Aesthetician*, who works more for pleasure than for truth, puts in entries regularly, and gives one continual pleasure in incidentals, in good phrases, interesting ideas, delicate perceptions, but who hardly tries to subordinate his Method to the requirements of any particular situation or material. The individual poems are less and less differentiated; the process is always more evident than what is being processed; everything is so familiarly contrived by will and habit and rule of thumb (for improvisation, as Virgil Thomson says, "among all the compositional techniques is the one most servile to rules of thumb") that it does not seem to matter exactly which being is undergoing these immemorial metamorphoses. Stevens' passagework, often, is so usual that we can't believe past the form to the matter: what truth could survive these pastry-cook's, spun-sugar, parallel qualifications?

> It was like sudden time in a world without time,
> This world, this place, the street in which I was,
> Without time: as that which is not has not time,
> Is not, or is of what there was, is full. . . .

And on the shelf below:

> It was nowhere else, it was there and because
> It was nowhere else, its place had to be supposed,
> Itself had to be supposed, a thing supposed
> In a place supposed, a thing that reached
> In a place that he reached. . . .

It is G. E. Moore at the spinet. And it looks worst of all when one compares it with a passage from that classic of our prose, that generalizer from an Age of Reason, that hapless victim of Poetic Diction, that—but let me quote:

> As Hags hold Sabbaths, less for joy than spite,
> So these their merry, miserable Night;
> Still round and round the Ghosts of Beauty glide,
> And haunt the places where their Honor died.
> See how the World its Veterans rewards!
> A Youth of Frolics, an old Age of Cards;
> Fair to no purpose, artful to no end,
> Young without Lovers, old without a Friend;
> A Fop their Passion, but their Prize a Sot;
> Alive, ridiculous, and dead, forgot!

The immediacy and precision and particularity, the live touch of things, the beauty that exists in precarious perfection in so many poems in *Harmonium*—

>   the beauty
> Of the moonlight
> Falling there,
> Falling
> As sleep falls
> In the innocent air—

this, at last, is lost in rhetoric, in elaboration and artifice and contrivance, in an absolutely ecumenical Method of seeing and thinking and expressing, in *craftsmanship*: why has no loving soul ever given Stevens a copy of that *Principles of Art* in which Collingwood argues at length—many people might say *proves*—that art is not a craft at all? (I hardly dare to quote one great poet's even more sweeping "But I deny that poetry is an art.") In *Auroras of Autumn* one sees almost everything through a shining fog, a habitualness not just of style but of machinery, perception, anything: the green spectacles show us a world of green spectacles; and the reader, staring out into this Eden, thinks timidly: "But it's all so *monotonous*." When Marx said that he wasn't a Marxist he meant, I suppose, that he himself was not one of his own followers, could not be taken in by the prolongation and simplification of his own beliefs that a disciple would make and believe; and there is nothing a successful artist needs to pray so much as: "Lord, don't let me keep on believing *only this*; let me have the courage of something besides my own convictions; let me escape at last from the maze of myself, from the hardening quicksilver womb of my own characteristicalness."

I have felt as free as posterity to talk in this way of Stevens' weaknesses, of this later mold in which he has cast himself, since he seems to me—and seems to my readers, I am sure— one of the true poets of our century, someone whom the world will keep on reading just as it keeps on listening to Vivaldi or Scarlatti, looking at Tiepolo or Poussin. His best poems are the poetry of a man fully human—of someone sympathetic, magnanimous, both brightly and deeply intelligent; the poems see, feel, and think with equal success; they treat with mastery that part of existence which allows of mastery, and experience the rest of it with awe or sadness or delight. Minds of this quality of genius, of this breadth and delicacy of understanding, are a link between us and the past, since they are, for us, the past made living; and they are our surest link with the future, since they are the part of us which the future will know.

As one feels the elevation and sweep and disinterestedness, the thoughtful truthfulness of the best sections of a poem like *Esthétique du Mal*, one is grateful for, overawed by, this poetry that knows so well the size and age of the world; that reminds us, as we sit in chairs produced from the furniture exhibitions of the Museum of Modern Art, of that immemorial order or disorder upon which our present scheme of things is a monomolecular film; that counsels us—as Santayana wrote of Spinoza—"to say to those little gnostics, to those circumnavigators of being: *I do not believe you; God is great.*" Many of the poems look greyly out at "the immense detritus of a world / That is completely waste, that moves from waste / To waste, out of the hopeless waste of the past / Into a hopeful waste to come"; but more of the poems see the unspoilable delights, the inexhaustible interests of existence—when you have finished reading Stevens' best poems you remember once more that man is not only the jest and riddle of the world, but the glory.

Some of my readers may feel about all this, "But how can you reconcile what you say with the fact that *Auroras of Autumn* is not a good book? Shouldn't the Mature poet be producing late masterpieces even better than the early ones?" (They might ask the same thing about *The Cocktail Party*.) All such questions show how necessary it is to think of the poet as somebody who has prepared himself to be visited by a daemon, as a sort of accident-prone worker to whom poems happen—for otherwise we *expect* him to go on writing good poems, better poems, and this is the one thing you cannot expect even of good poets, much less of anybody else. Good painters in their sixties may produce good pictures as regularly as an orchard produces apples; but Planck is a great scientist because he made one discovery as a young man—and I can remember reading in a mathematician's memoirs a sentence composedly recognizing the fact that, since the writer was now past forty, he was unlikely ever again to do any important creative work in mathematics. A man who is a good poet at forty *may* turn out to be a good poet at sixty; but he is more likely to have stopped writing poems, to be doing exercises in his own manner, or to have reverted to whatever commonplaces were popular when he was young. A good poet is someone who manages, in a lifetime of standing out in thunderstorms, to be struck by lightning five or six times; a dozen or two dozen times and he is great.

RICHARD ELLMANN
"Wallace Stevens' Ice-Cream"
Kenyon Review, Winter 1957, pp. 89–105

In contemplating the poetry written by executives of large insurance companies, it is hard not to be curious about their treatment of the great fact of death upon which their ample livelihood depends. Lugubrious as the subject is, it offers a way into the obliquities of Wallace Stevens. Death appears importunately several times in Stevens' first volume, *Harmonium*, and less frequently thereafter, but a better beginning is his early play, *Three Travellers Watch a Sunrise*, because in it the principal bit of stage property is a corpse. It is the corpse of a dead lover, murdered by his girl's father; and the question in the play is how the three Chinese travellers, who have come out to watch the sunrise and not to look at corpses, will take the discovery of the body. It soon becomes apparent that they do not mind it a bit; they sympathize with the grief-stricken girl, but the corpse itself they treat as one more matter to be included in their surveal of the scene. The sun, they say, will shine on the corpse as on another new thing:

> Red is not only
> The color of blood.
> Or [indicating the body.]
> Of a man's eyes,
> Or [Pointedly.]
> Of a girl's.
> And as the red of the sun
> Is one thing to me
> And one thing to another,
> So it is the green of one tree
> And the green of another.
> Without which it would all be black.
> Sunrise is multiplied,
> Like the earth on which it shines,
> By the eyes that open on it,
> Even dead eyes,
> As red is multiplied by the leaves of trees.

They have no horror of death and no fear of it; but rather they take it as part of some larger order which they have long since learned to accept as essential. The green of life, and the red of grief or death, are both preferable to blackness. The sun shines not indifferently but intimately upon death as upon life. A corpse contributes to the variety of the landscape. Probably Stevens put this point of view, which is his own, into the mouths of three Chinese, because it seemed to him vaguely oriental. But his setting is not China but eastern Pennsylvania, his Chinese are Chinese Americans, and we would be wrong to follow his equivocal hint in assuming that he advocates that the west accept the acceptance of the east.

If we look at his poems about death, we will find that he has decisive personal views about it. The early poems are even a little truculent. In "The Death of a Soldier," he tells us that the soldier "does not become a three-days personage, / Imposing his separation, / Calling for pomp," and in "Cortège for Rosenbloom," a more difficult poem, he defends the view of death which he has labeled Chinese by challenging its opposite, by challenging, that is, the notion that death is something apart and isolated. The ceremony of conventional mourning, its stilted decorum, its withdrawal of the dead man from the natural world, its figmental afterlife, are all satirized here. *Que faites vous dans ce galère*, what are *you* doing in this mortician's heaven? the poet seems to be asking "the wry Rosenbloom" whose body is so absurdly apotheosized. The name of Rosenbloom suggests both an ordinary man and someone who springs like a flower out of nature and should not be separated from it.

> Now, the wry Rosenbloom is dead
> And his finical carriers tread,
> On a hundred legs, the tread
> Of the dead.
> Rosenbloom is dead.

The finical mourners are made buglike.

> They carry the wizened one
> Of the color of horn
> To the sullen hill,
> Treading a tread
> In unison for the dead.

(Horn is death's color in Stevens' verse.)

> Rosenbloom is dead.
> The tread of the carriers does not halt
> On the hill, but turns
> Up the sky.
> They are bearing his body into the sky.

The next stanza makes quite clear what the poet thinks of this extraordinary ascent from the *ground*, from the solidity of the real, towards the nothingness and nebulousness:

> It is the infants of misanthropes
> And the infants of nothingness
> That tread
> The wooden ascents
> Of the ascending of the dead.

The mourners are infants because their concepts of man are undeveloped and founded on a dislike of man's real nature; hence they love their extra-human illusions.

> It is turbans they wear
> And boots of fur
> As they tread the boards
> In a region of frost,
> Viewing the frost;

These are the tripsters of mourning; here they come with their conventional accoutrements, viewing death as an isolated, frigid country.

> To a chirr of gongs
> And a chitter of cries
> And the heavy thrum
> Of the endless tread
> That they tread;

again they are insect-like, ant-like, their absurd noises adding to their general absurdity.

> To a jangle of doom
> And a jumble of words
> Of the intense poem
> Of the strictest prose
> Of Rosenbloom.
>
> And they bury him there,
> Body and soul,
> In a place in the sky.
> The lamentable tread!
> Rosenbloom is dead.

The real nature of man, Stevens is suggesting to us, is comprehended only in terms of an adult, human culture; Rosenbloom himself is an intense poem, is strictest prose, and prose and poetry are set against infants and insects. No wonder the mourners jumble the essence of Rosenbloom. This cortège, then, in the simplest terms, is the wrong way to conduct a funeral. What is the right way? "The Emperor of Ice-Cream" is the right way. Here the poet is hortatory, not descriptive, and his tone is buoyant and defiant. It defies the mourners of Rosenbloom, who would like to treat this corpse with the usual ceremony, but the poet will have none of their services. Instead he summons the living, and, to emphasize his point, he makes clear that everyone living is welcome, and especially those who proceed by nature with scant ceremony; this time the season is summer, as favored in Stevens' verse as winter is disfavored.

> Call the roller of big cigars,
> The muscular one, and bid him whip
> In kitchen cups concupiscent curds.
> Let the wenches dawdle in such dress
> As they are used to wear, and let the boys
> Bring flowers in last month's newspapers.
> Let be be finale of seem.
> The only emperor is the emperor of ice-cream.
>
> Take from the dresser of deal,
> Lacking the three glass knobs, that sheet
> On which she embroidered fantails once
> And spread it so as to cover her face.

> If her horny feet protrude, they come
> To show how cold she is, and dumb.
> Let the lamp affix its beam.
> The only emperor is the emperor of ice-cream.

The way to treat death is to wear ordinary clothes, not turbans or boots of fur. It is to whip up some ice cream in the kitchen, not to be finical; it is to spread flowers, not to toll the bell or ululate. Death, as we learned from the Chinese, is not horrible. The horny feet may protrude, and if they do, it is just as well. Do not call the embalmers. "Let be be finale of seem"—that is, away with the panoply of empty conventional mourning and empty conventional myths of death and after-life. Let us accept being, which like the sun's rays comprehends death with life.

The last battlement before us is the line, "The only emperor is the emperor of ice-cream." There are two going interpretations of this line, one that the emperor is life, the other that he is death. When Stevens was informed of this difference of critical opinion, he said, in effect, "So much the better!" and refused to judge between them. If we take the emperor to be life, and the poet's whole sympathy to be with the living, then why does the poem deal so precisely and deliberately with the corpse in the second stanza? Why not push it out of the way instead of displaying it? And can a wake, even an ice-cream wake, be completely detached from death? On the other hand, if the emperor is to be identified with death, why bring in the cigar-rolling, ice-cream-mixing muscular man? Is concupiscence desirable at funerals?

I think we may reach a little nearer if we remember that the characteristics of ice cream are that it is tasty, transitory, and cold. Life may be tasty and perishable, but it is not cold. Death may be cold but scarcely transitory, unless we assume that Stevens believes in an afterlife, which he doesn't, or tasty, unless we assume he has a death-wish, which he doesn't. Whoever the emperor is, he is realer than the run-of-the-mill emperors, the kaisers and Erlkönige, and his domain seems to include both life and death. The coldness of ice-cream suggests the corpse, as its sweetness suggests life's concupiscence. Stevens has said that his only daughter had a superlative liking for ice-cream, and is reported to have said also that she asked him to write a poem about it. Whether she did or not, there is a child-like quality about the poem—its absence of taboo, its complete, simultaneous, unruffled acceptance of conventional contraries—party food and horny feet. The child examines both without distaste. Both are included in the imperial domain. Ice-cream then is death and life.

But we must not think of death and life as a dual monarchy loosely joined by an indifferent ruler. The emperor is more than his ice-cream empire; he is the force that inspires and makes it one. Here again I call Stevens for my rather uncommunicative witness. He commented of the poem that it contained something of the essential gaudiness of poetry; this gaudiness must affect our estimate of the emperor. It is the more appropriate when we remember that in the poem "Metaphor as Degeneration," Stevens asserts that *being* includes death and the imagination. My candidate for the emperor of ice-cream, then, is the force of being, understood as including life, death, and the imagination which plays in this poem so gustily upon both. The emperor creates ice-cream, expresses himself through death and life, conceives of them as a unity, and is immanent in both of them.

If the volume *Harmonium* has an integrating theme, it is this deliberate acceptance of death with life. Stevens will have none of heaven or immortality; these fictions, always of questionable value, are worn through. In both *Sunday Morn-*

ing and *Le Monocle de Mon Oncle* Stevens endeavors to show just what place death has in being. The first is an argument with a woman who, on Sunday morning, is prompted to think of Christ's sacrificial death and of the heaven which Christ opened to man by dying for him. The poet asks, "Why should she give her bounty to the dead?" and calls to her mind the beauty of the landscape. But when she continues to long for some imperishable bliss as contrasted with the cyclical, seasonal landscape, he advises her:

> Death is the mother of beauty; hence from her,
> Alone, shall come fulfilment to our dreams
> And our desires. Although she strews the leaves
> Of sure obliteration on our paths,
> The path sick sorrow took, the many paths
> Where triumph rang its brassy phrase, or love
> Whispered a little out of tenderness,
> She makes the willow shiver in the sun
> For maidens who were wont to sit and gaze
> Upon the grass, relinquished to their feet.
> She causes boys to pile new plums and pears
> On disregarded plate. The maidens taste
> And stray impassioned in the littering leaves.

The threat of something contrary to love, of obliteration, is what gives love its force. If there were no door there would be no room, but we are interested in the room, not the door. Then the poet mocks heaven and its attempt to abstract life from being and leave death behind:

> Is there no change of death in paradise?
> Does ripe fruit never fall? Or do the boughs
> Hang always heavy in that perfect sky,
> Unchanging, yet so like our perishing earth,
> With rivers like our own that seek for seas
> They never find, the same receding shores
> That never touch with inarticulate pang?
> Why set the pear upon those river-banks
> Or spice the shores with odors of the plum?
> Alas, that they should wear our colors there,
> The silken weavings of our afternoons,
> And pick the strings of our insipid lutes!
> Death is the mother of beauty, mystical,
> Within whose burning bosom we devise
> Our earthly mothers waiting, sleeplessly.

It is in the context of death that we see our earthly mothers of beauty—our loves, who are waiting sleeplessly because, like the heroine, they are anxious with the problem of perishability.

> Supple and turbulent, a ring of men
> Shall chant in orgy on a summer morn
> Their boisterous devotion to the sun,
> Not as a god, but as a god might be,
> Naked among them, like a savage source.
> Their chant shall be a chant of paradise,
> Out of their blood, returning to the sky;
> And in their chant shall enter, voice by voice,
> The windy lake wherein their lord delights,
> The trees, like serafin, and echoing hills,
> That choir among themselves long afterward.
> They shall know well the heavenly fellowship
> Of men that perish and of summer morn.
> And whence they came and whither they shall go
> The dew upon their feet shall manifest.

Here, in more mellifluous phrases, are the same elements as in "The Emperor of Ice-Cream"; the men are supple, in the other poem muscular; here they are turbulent, boisterous, in orgy, there they are eaters of concupiscent curds. The sun to which they chant cannot be taken only as the power which creates life, for Stevens emphasizes that the singers are men who perish like dew; it has to be also the power that moves in death. Let us say tentatively that it is what Dylan Thomas calls the force that through the green fuse drives the flower and blasts the roots of trees. Here we not only accept being, we worship it. And because life is such a good thing, death, upon which it depends, must be a good thing too. But death is only a small part of being; instead of speaking of life and death as if they were equals, we might speak of a god whose death is no more than a cue for his instant rebirth.

Stevens returns to the problem of death in another fine poem in *Harmonium, Le Monocle de Mon Oncle*. It is characteristic of this poet, who wrote English as if it were French (just as Carlyle wrote English as if it were German), that he puts his most serious thoughts into a courtly dialogue between a man and a woman. The poem begins in a wilfully pretentious style:

> "Mother of heaven, regina of the clouds,
> O sceptre of the sun, crown of the moon,
> There is not nothing, no, no, never nothing,
> Like the clashed edges of two words that kill."

The first two lines, which echo the litany, are pseudo-religious, in violent contrast with the next two. The lethal quality of two words is itself illustrated by the jarring double negatives of the third line. But there is more to the third line than that. It has been suggested that this is just one of Stevens' playful linguistic tricks, but the real reason will become clear as we proceed:

> And so I mocked her in magnificent measure.
> Or was it that I mocked myself alone?
> I wish that I might be a thinking stone.
> The sea of spuming thought foists up again
> The radiant bubble that she was. And then
> A deep up-pouring from some saltier well
> Within me, bursts its watery syllable.
>
> A red bird flies across the golden floor.
> It is a red bird that seeks out his choir
> Among the choirs of wind and wet and wing.
> A torrent will fall from him when he finds.
> Shall I uncrumple this much-crumpled thing?
> I am a man of fortune greeting heirs;
> For it has come that thus I greet the Spring.
> These choirs of welcome choir for me farewell.
> No Spring can follow past meridian.
> Yet you persist with anecdotal bliss
> To make believe a starry *connaissance*.
>
> Is it for nothing, then, that old Chinese
> Sat titivating by their mountain pools
> Or in the Yangtse studied out their beards?
> I shall not play the flat historic scale.
> You know how Utamaro's beauties sought
> The end of love in their all-speaking braids.
> You know the mountainous coiffures of Bath.
> Alas! Have all the barbers lived in vain
> That not one curl in Nature has survived?
> Why, without pity on these studious ghosts,
> Do you come dripping in your hair from sleep?

The repetition of *nothing* in the third stanza makes clear that the word nothing is one which he has borrowed from her and therefore repeated so mockingly in the first stanza. We have to imagine the dialogue as beginning before the poem starts, when the woman, having left her bed with her hair in disarray, says to the poet that now that she is middle-aged there is *nothing* left for her but old age and death and after that, she hopes, heaven—that starry *connaissance* for lovers once young. The problem of the poem then is to win her over to accepting death and denying an afterlife. The speaker begins by associating himself with her feeling of age and regret, but ends by insisting that we should concern ourselves, even in old age, with life rather than with death.

> This luscious and impeccable fruit of life
> Falls, it appears, of its own weight to earth.
> When you were Eve, its acrid juice was sweet,
> Untasted, in its heavenly, orchard air—

So long as we remain immortal in Eden, we long for life, and pluck its apple even if death comes with it:

> An apple serves as well as any skull
> To be the book in which to read a round,
> And is as excellent, in that it is composed
> Of what, like skulls, comes rotting back to ground.

The poet then offers a series of parabolic instances, the first of which proves that

> The honey of heaven may or may not come,
> But that of earth both comes and goes at once,

for this honey, like ice-cream, is vested in perishability. He next establishes that life and love continue even though individuals depart, and finally demonstrates that life, which has offered strong passions to the young, offers to the aged the power to value its ephemeral, perishing moments.

In his later poetry Stevens continues his efforts to make death subordinate to life. His attitude does not alter, but his emphasis in later poems falls less on rebuking others for erroneous ideas of death than on attempting to portray his own idea. He endeavors to find a picture of death which will not terrify us and will not separate it from life. Some of these treatments of death, such as *The Owl in the Sarcophagus*, where he finds death to be made up of three modern mythological personages—peace, sleep, and memory; "The Airman's Death," where the airman sinks into a profound emptiness which yet is somehow made close and a part of us; and "Burghers of Petty Death," where actual death seems a little thing beside the feeling of death that sometimes pervades the mind, are not so seductive as his early arguments. In *Esthétique du Mal*, Stevens tries in the seventh section to come to grips with the problem entirely in pictorial form, and this poem is more winning. Like "Cortège for Rosenbloom," it begins by anchoring the hero in nature like a rose:

> How red the rose that is the soldier's wound,
> The wounds of many soldiers, the wounds of all
> The soldiers that have fallen, red in blood,
> The soldier of time grown deathless in great size.
>
> A mountain in which no ease is ever found,
> Unless indifference to deeper death
> Is ease, stands in the dark, a shadows' hill,
> And there the soldier of time has deathless rest.
>
> Concentric circles of shadows, motionless
> Of their own part, yet moving on the wind,
> Form mystical convolutions in the sleep
> Of time's red soldier deathless on his bed.
>
> The shadows of his fellows ring him round
> In the high night, the summer breathes for them
> Its fragrance, a heavy somnolence, and for him,
> For the soldier of time, it breathes a summer sleep,
>
> In which his wound is good because life was.
> No part of him was ever part of death.
> A woman smoothes her forehead with her hand
> And the soldier of time lies calm beneath that stroke.

This death is deathless in the sense that it is close to nature, close to life, close to the community of men living and men dead. It has nothing to do with the great looming abstraction of capitalized Death. The woman smoothing her hair might seem altogether detached from the soldier, but the soldier has never left the living and her gesture is a part of his being. This conception begins with the physical nearness of living and dead, but implies a metaphysical bond as well.

In Stevens' later verse there are many suggestions that death is what we make of it. "Madame la Fleurie" is a poem about a man who read horror into nature, and instead of seeing her as a lady with flowers conceived of her as a bearded queen, wicked in her dead light. He died in this falsification, and the result is that there are no bluejays for him to remember, now that he is dead; he is not like the soldier whose death is merely an extension, in a different tempo, of his life.

I suggested earlier that to Stevens the sun is the primal force which, as in Dylan Thomas, creates and destroys. I think we should correct this now to indicate that the destructive force is much less important for Stevens than for Thomas, that they are nearly opposites. For in Thomas, who sees the body as a shroud, and life as either a rapturous ignorance of death or a knowing horror of it, the main revelation is that death pervades life, while in Stevens it is that life pervades death. In Thomas the glory of life is stolen from death. Stevens' vision, for it is almost that, is of living and unliving—a term which seems closer to his ideas than dead—men joined together in admiration, whether vocal or mute, of being. Being is the great poem, and all our lesser poems only approximate its intensity and power.

The sun is this primal force of being, reflected alike by living and unliving, by people and by things. Our dualisms disguise their single origin. It can be called God or the Imagination ("Final Soliloquy of the Interior Paramour") though these terms are also only metaphors for what is ultimately a mystery to be worshipped rather than fathomed. The beauty that the sun creates antedates human life; long before we came on the earth the sun was covering the rock of reality with leaves, but once arrived here, we too participate in it. The sun is the Ulysses to which we and the world are the faithful Penelope. Its force is constant, and anchors in repetition all the changes which occur in the world, as the everchanging gleams of sunshine stem always from the same burning source. It is bodiless, unreal in that sense, yet it fills bodies with light and inspirits them. "It is the ever-never-changing-same," Stevens writes in "Adult Epigram," and elsewhere he says it is the will to change which underlies all changes. We are, he writes in "An Ordinary Evening in New Haven," in a permanence composed of impermanence.

Many of Stevens' poems can be read as accounts of the interaction of imagination and reality, but they have a theme which underlies that. "Peter Quince at the Clavier," for instance, seems to be about an Abt Vogler building up a mountain of music from a few hints in experience, but the theme which was, I think, even more important to Stevens, is summarized in the lines,

> The body dies, the body's beauty lives.
> So gardens die, in their green going
> A wave interminably flowing.

The wave is a frequent metaphor for the force elsewhere saluted as the sun. As Stevens says in one of his essays, "A wave is a force and not the water of which it is composed, which is never the same." Sometimes he epitomizes this force as a river called Swatara, or simply as an unnamed river in Connecticut that flows nowhere like the sea; sometimes it is a changing giant (*Things of August*), sometimes a bodiless serpent ("St. John and the Back-Ache," *The Auroras of Autumn*). But the force can also be found in a creature like the blackbird in "Thirteen Ways of Looking at a Blackbird," a poem which we would be well advised to read not as a declaration that there are thirteen ways of looking at a blackbird but that there is a blackbird behind all these impressions. I do not think it has been remarked that Stephens is unsympathetic to only one of the thirteen ways, Number 11, in which the protagonist is not "I" but "He."

> He rode over Connecticut
> In a glass coach.
> Once, a fear pierced him,
> In that he mistook
> The shadow of his equipage
> For blackbirds.

The error of the man in the glass coach—and glass is almost always a bar to sight in Stevens' poems—is that he sees the blackbird merely as death; the further proof of his error is that he has *not* seen the blackbird, has seen only his own dark mind, the shadow of his equipage. And so, like the man in "Madame la Fleurie," he abstracts the blackbird from nature and sees only fear in it.

Most of Stevens' poems are based upon images which somehow participate in this primal force of being, and it is the existence of the force in them that he is concerned to demonstrate. The sense of "The Worms at Heaven's Gate" is almost destroyed by its isolation in anthologies, where it seems to mean that the sardonic worms are handing up bits of a corpse with ironic comments on their deterioration. For Stevens the beauty does continue, it survives corruption, and the worms, not sardonic at all, can only talk of beauty, not of death.

In the individual person, the self, as Stevens says in "The Planet on the Table," is the sun. This self should be dominated by the imagination, a solar light within the mind. In expressing our imagination we express the force of being. But in the individual man the light may be deflected. The imagination may look not upon the rest of being, but only upon itself; so, like Chieftain Iffucan, it may disparage the world of nature, or, like the other bantam in pine woods, solipsistically fail to recognize that we are all parts of a common world and bound together by the shared light of the sun. The danger of such narcissism is that it leads to empty hallucinations, such as that denial of being which is heaven, that denial of beauty which is modern religion, that denial of the imagination which is reason, that denial of life which is nostalgia. The trouble with all these is that they are petrifying, they produce bad statues instead of men, the creative fire is thwarted in them. The imagination should queen it over the mind, with reason as her obsequious butler and memory as her underpaid maid-of-all-work. But she must always see the teeming earth, not the empty sky, as her domain. If she doesn't, the world becomes fixed and inert instead of malleable and suffusable. The imagination is constantly re-shaping and reforming reality; it is not the poet's exclusive preserve—everyone has it—but the poet uses it more steadily and powerfully and with more recognition of its value. It is the imagination, like the sun, which keeps the world from being black. Memory and reason can aid instead of impeding it, by confirming the imagination's felt bond with all existence.

We can see why Stevens' poetry is so different from that of Eliot. Although Stevens occasionally takes note of our age as a leaden time, this is not at all a principal theme. In no sense does Stevens sigh for lost beliefs; rather he is elated that old hallucinations are over now so that the imagination can get a

fresh start. They have prevented us from living in the physical world, and the great poverty for man is not to live there. The major man—Stevens' modest version of the superman—is the man who brings most sunlight to most rock, most imagination to most reality, and is closest to the primal force.

Although there is an obvious similarity between Stevens and Yeats in that they both worship in the church of the imagination, Stevens conceives of the primal force as existing independent of man and prior to him, while Yeats often suggests that it begins with man and is altogether human. In Stevens the imagination is impersonal and anonymous; it reminds us of Ortega y Gasset's contention that much modern art is dehumanized; but for Yeats the imagination works always through proper names. I find, more brashly, a second imperfect parallel in Stevens and his fellow-American, the muscular one, Ernest Hemingway. When we think of Hemingway's stories about death, and particularly of "The Snows of Kilimanjaro," what strikes us is that the rather ignoble hero is given in the end a noble hero's death, and for a moment we may be baffled and ask why this man who has made such a mess of his talents and of his marriages should be treated by his creator so well. It is because, with all his defects, he has remained true to his eye; the great virtue in Hemingway is not to live the good life, but to see, as the great virtue in Stevens is to imagine. Even if the hero of "The Snows" has not done anything else, he has seen, and so mastered reality. In Wallace Stevens, the soldier, wounded also by life, is also saved by what he has found in it. Death, in both Stevens and Hemingway, comes beneficently to those who have expressed the primal force of vision, who have lived in the sun.

Most of Stevens' poetry is an essay in the intricacies of contentment, the mind and nature conspiring to render more lovely and awesome the force of being. There are sensual poems about plums, and philosophical poems about the mind's embrace of the plum, and a few, but only a few, poems about plumlessness, a state which depends upon plums for recognition. Stevens objects to those poets who make their pleas to the night-bird, who dwell upon discontent. His interest in grief, anger, and other unpleasant emotions is cursory. He does not evade tragedy, but he does not regard it as very important. An atmosphere of elation pervades his work as he surveys the marvels of the world; he insures us against death by assigning it so minor and integral a place in being. He is too fascinated by the endless procession of beauties to pay much mind to the retirements of particular individuals. He confronts us with a table of fragrancies and succulencies, solemnly reminds us that all of these, like us, are islanded between the nothingness that precedes form and the rot that ends it, and then urges us to fall to.

NORTHROP FRYE
"The Realistic Oriole: A Study of Wallace Stevens"
Hudson Review, Autumn 1957, pp. 353–70

Wallace Stevens was a poet for whom the theory and the practice of poetry were inseparable.[1] His poetic vision is informed by a metaphysic; his metaphysic is informed by a theory of knowledge; his theory of knowledge is informed by a poetic vision. He says of one of his long meditative poems that it displays the theory of poetry as the life of poetry (486), and in the introduction to his critical essays that by the theory of poetry he means "poetry itself, the naked poem" (N.A. viii). He thus stands in contrast to the dualistic approach of Eliot, who so often speaks of poetry as though it were an emotional and sensational soul looking for a "correlative" skeleton of thought to be provided by a philosopher, a Cartesian ghost trying to find a machine that will fit. No poet of any status—certainly not Eliot himself—has ever "taken over" someone else's structure of thought, and the dualistic fallacy can only beget more fallacies. Stevens is of particular interest and value to the critical theorist because he sees so clearly that the only ideas the poet can deal with are those directly involved with, and implied by, his own writing: that, in short, "Poetry is the subject of the poem" (176).

It has been established in criticism ever since Aristotle that histories are direct verbal imitations of action, and that anything in literature with a story in it is a secondary imitation of an action. This means, not that the story is at two removes from reality, but that its actions are representative and typical rather than specific. For some reason it has not been nearly so well understood that discursive writing is not thinking, but a direct verbal imitation of thought; that any poem with an idea in it is a secondary imitation of thought, and hence deals with representative or typical thought: that is, with forms of thought rather than specific propositions. Poetry is concerned with the ambiguities, the unconscious diagrams, the metaphors and the images out of which actual ideas grow. Poet and painter alike operate in "the flux Between the thing as idea and the idea as thing" (295). Stevens is an admirable poet in whom to study the processes of poetic thought at work, and such processes are part of what he means by the phrase "supreme fiction" which enters the title of his longest poem. The poet, he says, "gives to life the supreme fictions without which we are unable to conceive of it" (N.A. 31), and fictions imitate ideas as well as events.

Any discussion of poetry has to begin with the field or area that it works in, the field described by Aristotle as nature. Stevens calls it "reality," by which he means, not simply the external physical world, but "things as they are," the existential process that includes ordinary human life on the level of absorption in routine activity. Human intelligence can resist routine by arresting it in an act of consciousness, but the normal tendency of routine is to work against consciousness. The revolution of consciousness against routine is the starting-point of all mental activity, and the centre of mental activity is imagination, the power of transforming "reality" into aware-ness of reality. Man can have no freedom except what begins in his own awareness of his condition. Naturally historical periods differ greatly in the amount of pressure put on free consciousness by the compulsions of ordinary life. In our own day this pressure has reached an almost intolerable degree that threatens to destroy freedom altogether and reduce human life to a level of totally preoccupied compulsion, like the life of an animal. One symptom of this is the popular demand that the artist should express in his work a sense of social obligation. The artist's primary obedience however is not to reality but to the "violence from within" (N.A. 36) of the imagination that resists and arrests it. The minimum basis of the imagination, so to speak, is ironic realism, the act of simply becoming aware of the surrounding pressures of "things as they are". This devel-ops the sense of alienation which is the immediate result of the imposing of consciousness on reality:

> From this the poem springs: that we live in a place
> That is not our own and, much more, not ourselves.
> (383)

The "act of the mind" (240) in which imagination begins, then, is an arresting of a flow of perceptions without and of

impressions within. In that arrest there is born the principle of form or order: the inner violence of the imagination is a "rage for order" (130). It produces the "jar in Tennessee" (76), the object which not only is form in itself, but creates form out of all its surroundings. Stevens follows Coleridge in distinguish-ing the transforming of experience by the imagination from the re-arranging of it by the "fancy," and ranks the former higher (ignoring, if he knew it, T. E. Hulme's clever pseudo-critical reversal of the two). The imagination contains reason and emotion, but the imagination keeps form concrete and partic-ular, whereas emotion and reason are more apt to seek the vague and the general respectively.

There are two forms of mental activity that Stevens regards as unpoetic. One is the breaking down of a world of discrete objects into an amorphous and invisible substratum, a search for a "pediment of appearance" (361), a slate-colored world of substance (15, 96) which destroys all form and particularity, symbolized by the bodiless serpent introduced in *The Auroras of Autumn* (411), "form gulping after formlessness". This error is typically an error of reason. The other error is the breaking down of the individual mind in an attempt to make it a medium for some kind of universal or pantheistic mind. This is typically an error of emotion, and one that Stevens in his essays calls "romantic," which is a little confusing when his own poetry is so centrally in the Romantic tradition. What he means by it is the preference of the invisible to the visible which impels a poet to develop a false rhetoric intended to be the voice, not of himself, but of some invisible super-bard within him (N.A. 61). In "Jumbo" (269), Stevens points out that such false rhetoric comes, not from the annihilation of the ego, but from the ego itself, from "Narcissus, prince Of the secondary men". Such an attitude produces the "nigger mystic" (195, 265), a phrase which naturally has nothing to do with Negroes, but refers to the kind of intellectual absolute that has been compared to a night in which all cows are black, a world clearly no improvement on "reality," which is also one color (N.A. 26).

A third mode of mental activity, which is poetic but not Stevens' kind of poetry, is the attempt to suggest or evoke universals of mind or substance, to work at the threshold of consciousness and produce what Stevens calls "marginal" poetry and associates with Valéry (N.A. 115). Whatever its merit, such poetry for him is in contrast with "central" poetry based on the concrete and particular act of mental experience. Stevens speaks of the imagination as moving from the hieratic to the credible (N.A. 58), and marginal poetry, like the structures of reason and the surrenderings of emotion, seeks a "hierophant Omega" (469) or ultimate mystery. There is a strong tendency, a kind of intellectual death-wish, to conceive of order in terms of finality, as something that keeps receding from experience until experience stops, when it becomes the mirage of an "after-life" on which all hierophants, whether poets or priests, depend. But for the imagination "Reality is the beginning not the end" (469), "The imperfect is our paradise" (194), and the only order worth having is the "violent order" produced by the explosion of imaginative energy which is also a "great disorder" (215).

This central view of poetry is for Stevens based on the straight Aristotelian principle that if art is not quite nature, at least it grows naturally out of nature. He dislikes the term "imitation," but only because he thinks it means the naive copying of an external world: in its proper Aristotelian sense of creating a form of which nature is the content, Stevens' poetry is as imitative as Pope's. Art then is not so much nature methodized as nature realized, a unity of being and knowing, existence and consciousness, achieved out of the flow of time and the fixity of space. In content it is reality and we are "Participants of its being" (463); in form it is an art which "speaks the feeling" for "things as they are" (424). All through Stevens' poetry we find the symbol of the alphabet or syllable, the imaginative key to reality which, by bringing reality into consciousness, heightens the sense of both, "A nature that is created in what it says" (490).

However, the imagination does bring something to reality which is not there in the first place, hence the imagination contains an element of the "unreal" which the imaginative form incorporates. This unreal is connected with the fact that conscious experience is liberated experience. The unreal, "The fabulous and its intrinsic verse" (31), is the sense of exhilaration and splendor in art, the "radiant and productive" atmosphere which it both creates and breathes, the sense of the virile and the heroic implied by the term "creative" itself, "the way of thinking by which we project the idea of God into the idea of man" (N.A. 150). All art has this essential elegance or nobility, including ironic realism, but the nobility is an attribute of art, not its goal: one attains it by not trying for it, as though it were definable or extrinsic. Although art is in one sense an escape from reality (i.e., in the sense in which it is an escape *of* reality), and although art is a heightening of consciousness, it is not enough for art simply to give one a vision of a better world. Art is practical, not speculative; imaginative, not fantastic; it transforms experience, and does not merely interrupt it. The unreal in imaginative perception is most simply described as the sense that if something is not there it at least ought to be there. But this feeling in art is anything but wistful: it has created the tone of all the civilizations of history. Thus the "central" poet, by working outwards from a beginning instead of onwards toward an end, helps to achieve the only genuine kind of progress. As Stevens says, in a passage which explains the ambivalence of the term "mystic" in his work: "The adherents of the central are also mystics to begin with. But all their desire and all their ambition is to press away from mysticism toward that ultimate good sense which we term civilization" (N.A. 116).

Such ultimate good sense depends on preserving a balance between objective reality and the subjective unreal element in the imagination. Exaggerating the latter gives us the false heroics that produce the aggressive symbols of warfare and the cult of "men suited to public ferns" (276). Exaggerating the former gives us the weariness of mind that bores the "fretful concubine" (211) in her splendid surroundings. Within art itself there has been a corresponding alternation of emphasis. In some ages, or with some poets, the emphasis is on the imaginative heightening of reality by visions of a Yeatsian "noble rider"

> On his gold horse striding, like a conjured beast,
> Miraculous in its panache and swish.
>
> (426)

At other times the emphasis is ironic, thrown on the minimum role of the imagination as the simple and subjective observer of reality, not withdrawn from it, but detached enough to feel that the power of transforming it has passed by. These two emphases, the green and the red as Stevens calls them (340), appear in Stevens' own poetry as the summer vision and the autumn vision respectively.

The summer vision of life is the *gaya scienza* (248), the "Lebensweisheitspielerei" (504), in which things are perceived in their essential radiance when "the world is larger" (514). This summer vision extends all over the *Harmonium* poems, with their glowing still lifes and gorgeous landscapes of Florida and the Caribbean coasts. Its dominating image is the sun, "that brave man" (138), the hero of nature who lives in heaven but transforms the earth from his mountain-top (65), "the strong man vaguely seen" (204). As "we are men of sun" (137), our creative life is his, hence the feeling of alienation from nature in which consciousness begins is really inspired by exactly the opposite feeling. "I am what is around me" (86), the poet says; the jar in Tennessee expresses the form in Tennessee as well as in itself, and one feels increasingly that "The soul . . . is composed Of the external world" (51) in the sense that in the imagination we have "The inhuman making choice of a human self" (N.A. 89), a subhuman world coming to a point of imaginative light in a focus of individuality and consciousness. Such a point of imaginative light is a human counterpart of the sun. The poet absorbs the reality he contemplates "as the Angevine Absorbs Anjou" (224), just as the sun's light, by giving itself and taking nothing, absorbs the world in itself. The echo to the great trumpet-call of "Let there be light" is "All things in the sun are sun" (104).

There are two aspects of the summer vision, which might be called, in Marvellian language, the visions of the golden lamp and of the green night. The latter is the more contemplative vision of the student in the tradition of Milton's penseroso poet, Shelley's Athanase, and Yeats's old man in the tower. In this vision the sun is replaced by the moon (33 ff.), or, more frequently, the evening star (25), the human counterpart of which is the student's candle (51, 523). Its personified form, corresponding to the sun, is often female, an "archaic" (223) or "green queen" (339), the "desired" (505) one who eventually becomes an "interior paramour" (524) or Jungian anima (cf. 321), the motionless spinning Penelope (520) to whom every voyager returns, the eternal Eve (271) or naked bride (395) of the relaxed imagination. Here we are, of course, in danger of the death-wish vision, of reading a blank book. Some of the irony of this is in "Phosphor Reading by his Own Light" (267), as well as in "The Reader" (146). The bride of such a narcist vision is the sinister "Madame La Fleurie" (507). But in its genuine form such contemplation is the source of major imagination (387–8), and hence Stevens, like Yeats, has his tower-mountain of vision or "Palaz of Hoon" (65; cf. 121), where sun and poet come into alignment:

> It is the natural tower of all the world,
> The point of survey, green's green apogee,
> But a tower more precious than the view beyond,
> A point of survey squatting like a throne,
> Axis of everything.
>
> (373)

From this point of survey we are lifted above the "cat" symbol of life absorbed in being without consciousness, and the "rabbit" who is "king of the ghosts" and is absorbed in consciousness without being (209, 223).

The autumnal vision begins in the poet's own situation. To perceive "reality" as dingy or unattractive is itself an imaginative act ("The Plain Sense of Things," 502), but an ironic act, an irony deepened by the fact that other modes of perception are equally possible, the oriole being as realistic as the crow (154), and there can be no question of accepting only one as true. It is a curious tendency in human nature to believe in disillusionment: that is, to think we are nearest the truth when we have established as much falsehood as possible. This is the vision of "Mrs. Alfred Uruguay" (248), who approaches her mountain of contemplation the wrong way round, starting at the bottom instead of the top. (Her name is apparently based on an association with "Montevideo.") The root of the reductive tendency, at least in poetry, is perhaps the transience of the emotional mood which is the framework of the lyric. In *Harmonium* the various elaborations of vision are seen as projected from a residual ego, a comedian (27 ff.) or clown (Peter Quince is the leader of a group of clowns), who by himself has only the vision of the *"esprit bâtard"* (102), the juggler in motley who is also a magician and whose efforts are "conjurations." When we add the clown's conjurations to the clown we get "man the abstraction, the comic sun" (156): the term "abstraction" will meet us again.

This *esprit bâtard* or dimmed vision of greater maturity, *un monocle d'un oncle*, so to speak, comes into the foreground after the "Credences of Summer" (372) and the *Things of August* (489) have passed by. In September the web of the imagination's pupa is woven (208); in November the moon lights up only the death of the god (107); at the onset of winter the auroras of a vanished heroism flicker over the sky, while in the foreground stand the scarecrows or hollow men of the present (293, 513).

To this vision belong the bitter "Man on the Dump" (201), the ironic *Esthétique du Mal* (313), with its urbane treatment of the religio-literary clichés, such as "The death of Satan was a tragedy For the imagination," which are the stock in trade of lesser poets, and the difficult and painfully written war poems. It is more typical of Stevens, of course, to emphasize the reality which is present in the imaginative heightening of misery, the drudge's dream of "The Ordinary Women" (10) which none the less reminds us that "Imagination is the will of things" (84). The true form of the autumnal vision is not the irony which robs man of his dignity, but the tragedy which confers it ("In a Bad Time," 426).

At the end of autumn come the terrors of winter, the sense of a world disintegrating into chaos which we feel socially when we see the annihilation wars of our time, and individually when we face the fact of death in others or for ourselves. We have spoken of Stevens' dislike of projecting the religious imagination into a world remote in space and time. The woman in *Sunday Morning* (66) stays home from church and meditates on religion surrounded by the brilliant oranges and greens of the summer vision, and in "A High-Toned Old Christian Woman" (59) it is suggested that the poet, seeking an increase rather than a diminishing of life, gets closer to a genuinely religious sense than morality with its taboos and denials. For Stevens all real religion is concerned with a renewal of earth rather than with a surrender to heaven. He even says "the great poems of heaven and hell have been written and the great poem of the earth remains to be written" (N.A. 142). It is part of his own ambition to compose hymns "Happy rather than holy but happy-high" (185) which will "take the place Of empty heavens" (167), and he looks forward to a world in which "all men are priests" (254). As this last phrase shows, he has no interest in turning to some cellophane-wrapped version of neo-paganism. He sees, like Yeats, that the poet is a "Connoisseur of Chaos" (215) aware that "Poetry is a Destructive Force" (192), and Stevens' imagery, for all its luxuriance and good humor, is full of menace. From the "firecat" of the opening page of the *Collected Poems*, through the screaming peacocks of "Domination of Black" (8), the buzzard of "The Jack-Rabbit" (50; cf. 318), the butcher of "A Weak Mind in the Mountains" (212), the bodiless serpent of *The Auroras of Autumn* (411) and the bloody lion of "Puella Parvula" (456), we are aware that a simple song of *carpe diem* is not enough.

In the later poems there is a growing preoccupation with death, as, not the end of life or an introduction to something

unconnected with life, but as itself a part of life and giving to life itself an extra dimension. This view is very close to Rilke, especially the Rilke of the Orpheus sonnets, which are, like Stevens' poetry in general, "a constant sacrament of praise" (92). "What a ghastly situation it would be," Stevens remarks, "if the world of the dead was actually different from the world of the living" (N. A. 76), and in several poems, especially the remarkable *Owl in the Sarcophagus* (431), there are references to carrying on the memories or "souvenirs" of the past into a world which is not so much future as timeless, a world of recognition or "rendezvous" (524), and which lies in the opposite direction from the world of dreams:

> There is a monotonous babbling in our dreams
> That makes them our dependent heirs, the heirs
> Of dreamers buried in our sleep, and not
> The oncoming fantasies of better birth.
>
> (39)

In the poems of the winter vision the solar hero and the green queen become increasingly identified with the father and mother of a Freudian imago (439). The father and mother in turn expand into a continuous life throughout time of which we form our unitary realizations. The father, "the bearded peer" (494), extends back to the primordial sea (501), the mother to the original maternity of nature, the "Lady Lowzen" of "Oak Leaves are Hands" (272). In *The Owl in the Sarcophagus* these figures are personified as sleep and memory. The ambivalence of the female figure is expressed by the contrast between the "regina of the clouds" in *Le Monocle de Mon Oncle* (13) and the "Sister and mother and diviner love" of "To the One of Fictive Music" (87). The poet determined to show that "being Includes death and the imagination" (444) must go through the same world as the "nigger mystic," for a "nigger cemetery" (150) lies in front of him too, just as the sunrise of the early play, *Three Travellers Watch a Sunrise*, is heralded by a hanged man. The search for death through life which is a part of such recreation leads to a final confronting of the self and the rock (N.A. viii), the identification of consciousness and reality in which the living soul is identified with its tombstone which is equally its body (528). In this final triumph of vision over death the death-symbols are turned into symbols of life. The author of the Apocalypse prophesies to his "back-ache" (which is partly the *Weltschmerz* of the past) that the venom of the bodiless serpent will be one with its wisdom (437). The "black river" of death, Swatara (428), becomes "The River of Rivers in Connecticut" (533), a river *this* side of the Styx which "flows nowhere, like a sea" because it is in a world in which there is no more sea.

If we listen carefully to the voice of "the auroral creature musing in the mind" (263), the auroras of autumn will become, not the after-images of remembrance, but the *Morgenrot* of a new recognition. As the cycle turns through death to a new life, we meet images of spring, the central one being some modification of Venus rising from the sea: the "paltry nude" of the poem of that name (5); "Infanta Marina" (7); Susanna lying in "A wave, interminably flowing" (92); "Celle qui fût Heaulmiette" (438) reborn from the mother and father of the winter vision, the mother having the "vague severed arms" of the maternal Venus of Milo. This reborn girl is the Jungian anima or interior paramour spoken of before, the "Golden Woman in a Silver Mirror" (460). She is also associated with the bird of Venus, "The Dove in the Belly" (366; cf. 357 and "Song of Fixed Accord," 519). It is also a bird's cry, but one outside the poet, which heralds "A new knowledge of reality" in the last line of the *Collected Poems*.

The spring vision often has its origin in the commonplace, or in the kind of innocent gaudiness that marks exuberant life. Of the spring images in "Celle qui fût Heaulmiette" the author remarks affectionately, "Another American vulgarity"; the "paltry nude" is a gilded ship's prow, and the "emperor of ice-cream" presides over funeral obsequies in a shabby household (64). "It is the invasion of humanity That counts," remarks a character in *Three Travellers Watch a Sunrise*. "Only the rich remember the past," the poet says (225) and even in "Final Soliloquy of the Interior Paramour" (524) there is still a parenthetical association of new vision with a poverty which has nothing to lose.

In "Peter Quince at the Clavier" beauty is called "The fitful tracing of a portal." Portal to what? The word itself seems to mean something to Stevens (N.A. 60, 155), and in the obviously very personal conclusion of *The Rock* it is replaced by "gate" (528). Perhaps Stevens, like Blake, has so far only given us the end of a golden string, and after traversing the circle of natural images we have still to seek the centre.

The normal unit of poetic expression is the metaphor, and Stevens was well aware of the importance of metaphor, as is evident from the many poems which use the word in title or text. His conception of metaphor is regrettably unclear, though clearer in the poetry than in the essays. He speaks of the creative process as beginning in the perception of "resemblance," adding that metamorphosis might be a better word (N.A. 72). By resemblance he does not mean naive or associative resemblance, of the type that calls a flower a bleeding heart, but the repetitions of color and pattern in nature which become the elements of formal design in art. He goes on to develop this conception of resemblance into a conception of "analogy" which, beginning in straight allegory, ends in the perception that "poetry becomes and is a transcendent analogue composed of the particulars of reality" (N.A. 130). But nowhere in his essays does he suggest that metaphor is anything more than likeness or parallelism. "There is always an analogy between nature and the imagination, and possibly poetry is merely the strange rhetoric of that parallel" (N.A. 118).

Clearly, if poetry is "merely" this, the use of metaphor could only accentuate what Stevens' poetry tries to annihilate, the sense of a contrast or great gulf fixed between subject and object, consciousness and existence. And in fact we often find metaphor used pejoratively in the poems as a form of avoiding direct contact with reality. The motive for metaphor, we are told, is the shrinking from immediate experience (288). Stevens appears to mean by such metaphor, however, simile or comparison, "the intricate evasions of as" (486; cf. "Add This to Rhetoric," 198). And metaphor is actually nothing of the kind. In its literal grammatical form metaphor is a statement of identity: this is that, A is B. And Stevens has a very strong sense of the crucial importance of poetic identification, "where as and is are one" (476), as it is only there that one finds "The poem of pure reality, untouched By trope or deviation" (471). Occasionally it occurs to him that metaphor might be used in a less pejorative sense. He speaks of "The metaphor that murders metaphor" (N.A. 84), implying that a better kind of metaphor can get murdered, and "Metaphor as Degeneration" (444) ends in a query how metaphor can really be degeneration when it is part of the process of seeing death as a part of life.

When metaphor says that one thing "is" another thing, or that a man, a woman and a blackbird are one (93), things are being identified *with* other things. In logical identity there is only identification *as*. If I say that the Queen of England "is" Elizabeth II, I have not identified one person with another, but one person as herself. Poetry also has this type of identifica-

tion, for in poetic metaphor things are identified with each other, yet each is identified as itself, and retains that identity. When a man, a woman and a blackbird are said to be one, each remains what it is, and the identification heightens the distinctive form of each. Such a metaphor is necessarily illogical (or anti-logical, as in "A violent disorder is an order") and hence poetic metaphors are opposed to likeness or similarity. A perception that a man, a woman and a blackbird were in some respects alike would be logical, but would not make much of a poem. Unfortunately in prose speech we often use the word identical to mean very similar, as in the phrase "identical twins," and this use makes it difficult to express the idea of poetic identity in a prose essay. But if twins were really identical they would be the same person, and hence could be different in form, like a man and the same man as a boy of seven. A world of total simile, where everything was like everything else, would be a world of total monotony; a world of total metaphor, where everything is identified as itself and with everything else, would be a world where subject and object, reality and mental organization of reality, are one. Such a world of total metaphor is the formal cause of poetry. Stevens makes it clear that the poet seeks the particular and discrete image: many of the poems in *Parts of a World*, such as "On the Road Home" (203), express what the title of the book expresses, the uniqueness of every act of vision. Yet it is through the particular and discrete that we reach the unity of imagination, which respects individuality, in contrast to the logical unity of the generalizing reason, which destroys it. The false unity of the dominating mind is what Stevens condemns in "The Bagatelles the Madrigals" (213), and in the third part of "The Pure Good of Theory" (331–2), where we find again a pejorative use of the term metaphor.

When a thing is identified as itself, it becomes an individual of a class or total form: when we identify a brown and green mass as a tree we provide a class name for it. This is the relating of species to genera which Aristotle spoke of as one of the central aspects of metaphor. The distinctively poetic use of such metaphor is the identifying of an individual with its class, where a tree becomes Wordsworth's "tree of many one," or a man becomes mankind. Poets ordinarily do not, like some philosophers, replace individual objects with their total forms; they do not, like allegorists, represent total forms by individuals. They see individual and class as metaphorically identical: in other words they work with *myths*, many of whom are human figures in whom the individual has been identified with its universal or total form.

Such myths, "archaic forms, giants Of sense, evoking one thing in many men" (494) play a large role in Stevens' imagery. For some reason he speaks of the myth as "abstract." "The Ultimate Poem is Abstract" (429; cf. 270, 223 and elsewhere), and the first requirement of the "supreme fiction" is that it must be abstract (380), though as far as dictionary meanings are concerned one would expect rather to hear that it must be concrete. By abstract Stevens apparently means artificial in its proper sense, something constructed rather than generalized. In such a passage as this we can see the myth forming out of "repetitions" as the individual soldier becomes the unknown soldier, and the unknown soldier the Adonis or continuously martyred god:

How red the rose that is the soldier's wound,
The wounds of many soldiers, the wounds of all
The soldiers that have fallen, red in blood,
The soldier of time grown deathless in great size.
(318)

Just as there is false metaphor, so there is false myth.

There is in particular the perverted myth of the average or "root-man" (262), described more expressively as "the total man of glubbal glub" (301). Whenever we have the root-man we have, by compensation, "The super-man friseured, possessing and possessed" (262), which is the perversion of the idea of *Übermenschlichkeit* (98) into the Carlylean great man or military hero. Wars are in their imaginative aspect a "gigantomachia" (289) of competing aggressive myths. The war-myth or hero of death is the great enemy of the imagination: he cannot be directly fought except by another war-myth; he can only be contained in a greater and more genuine form of the same myth (280, section xv). The genuine form of the war-hero is the "major man" (334; 387–8) who, in *The Owl in the Sarcophagus*, is personified as peace (434), the direct opposite of the war-hero, and the third of the figures in "the mythology of modern death" which, along with sleep and memory, conquer death for life.

We thus arrive at the conception of a universal or "central man" (250), who may be identified with any man, such as a fisherman listening to wood-doves:

> The fisherman might be the single man
> In whose breast, the dove, alighting, would grow
> still.
>
> (357)

This passage, which combines the myth of the central man with the anima myth of the "dove in the belly" (366), is from a poem with the painfully exact title, "Thinking of a Relation between the Images of Metaphors." The central man is often symbolized by glass or transparency, as in "Asides on the Oboe" (250) and in "Prologues to What Is Possible" (515). If there is a central man, there is also a central mind (298) of which the poet feels peculiarly a part. Similarly there is a "central poem" (441) identical with the world, and finally a "general being or human universe" (378), of which all imaginative work forms part:

> That's it. The lover writes, the believer hears,
> The poet mumbles and the painter sees,
> Each one, his fated eccentricity,
> As a part, but part, but tenacious particle,
> Of the skeleton of the ether, the total
> Of letters, prophecies, perceptions, clods
> Of color, the giant of nothingness, each one
> And the giant ever changing, living in change.
>
> (443)

In "Sketch of the Ultimate Politician" (335) we get a glimpse of this human universe as an infinite City of Man.

To sum up: the imaginative act breaks down the separation between subject and object, the perceiver shut up in "the enclosures of hypothesis" (516) like an embryo in a "naked egg" (173) or glass shell (297), and a perceived world similarly imprisoned in the remoteness of its "irreducible X" (N.A. 83), which is also an egg (490). Separation is then replaced by the direct, primitive identification which Stevens ought to have called metaphor and which, not having a word for it, he calls "description" (339) in one of his definitive poems, a term to which he elsewhere adds "apotheosis" (378) and "transformation" (514; cf. N.A. 49), which come nearer to what he really means. The maxim that art should conceal art is based on the sense that in the greatest art we have no sense of manipulating, posing or dominating over nature, but rather of emancipating it. "One confides in what has no Concealed creator" (296), the poet says, and again:

> There might be, too, a change immenser than
> A poet's metaphors in which being would

> Come true, a point in the fire of music where
> Dazzle yields to a clarity and we observe,
> And observing is completing and we are content,
> In a world that shrinks to an immediate whole,
> That we do not need to understand, complete
> Without secret arrangements of it in the mind.
>
> (341)

The theoretical postulate of Stevens' poetry is a world of total metaphor, where the poet's vision may be identified with anything it visualizes. For such poetry the most accurate word is apocalyptic, a poetry of "revelation" (344) in which all objects and experiences are united with a total mind. Such poetry gives us:

> . . . the book of reconciliation,
> Book of a concept only possible
> In description, canon central in itself,
> The thesis of the plentifullest John.
>
> (345)

Apocalypse, however, is one of the two great narrative myths that expand "reality," with its categories of time and space, into an infinite and eternal world. A myth of total man recovering a total world is hardly possible without a corresponding myth of a Fall, or some account of what is wrong with our present perspective. Stevens' version of the Fall is similar to that of the "Orphic poet" at the end of Emerson's *Nature*:

> Why, then, inquire
> Who has divided the world, what entrepreneur?
> No man. The self, the chrysalis of all men
> Became divided in the leisure of blue day
> And more, in branchings after day. One part
> Held fast tenaciously in common earth
> And one from central earth to central sky
> And in moonlit extensions of them in the mind
> Searched out such majesty as it could find.
>
> (468–9)

Such poetry sounds religious, and in fact does have the infinite perspective of religion, for the limits of the imagination are the conceivable, not the real, and it extends over death as well as life. In the imagination the categories of "reality," space and time, are reversed into form and creation respectively, for art is "Description without Place" (339) standing at the centre of "ideal time" (N.A. 88), and its poetry is "even older than the ancient world" (N.A. 145). Religion seems to have a monopoly of talking about infinite and eternal worlds, and poetry that uses such conceptions seems to be inspired by a specifically religious interest. But the more we study poetry, the more we realize that the dogmatic limiting of the poet's imagination to human and subhuman nature that we find, for instance, in Hardy and Housman, is not normal to poetry but a technical *tour de force*. It is the normal language of poetic imagination itself that is heard when Yeats says that man has invented death; when Eliot reaches the still point of the turning world; when Rilke speaks of the poet's perspective as that of an angel containing all time and space, blind and looking into himself; when Stevens finds his home in "The place of meta-men and para-things" (448). Such language may or may not go with a religious commitment: in itself it is simply poetry speaking as poetry must when it gets to a certain pitch of metaphorical concentration. Stevens says that his motive is neither "to console Nor sanctify, but plainly to propound" (389).

In *Harmonium*, published in the Scott Fitzgerald decade, Stevens moves in a highly sensuous atmosphere of fine pictures, good food, exquisite taste and luxury cruises. In the later poems, though the writing is as studiously oblique as ever, the sensuousness has largely disappeared, and the reader accustomed only to *Harmonium* may feel that Stevens' inspiration has failed him, or that he is attracted by themes outside his capacity, or that the impact of war and other ironies of the autumnal vision has shut him up in an uncommunicative didacticism. Such a view of Stevens is of course superficial, but the critical issue it raises is a genuine one.

In the criticism of drama there is a phase in which the term "theatrical" becomes pejorative, when one tries to distinguish genuine dramatic imagination from the conventional clichés of dramatic rhetoric. Of course eventually this pejorative use has to disappear, because Shakespeare and Aeschylus are quite as theatrical as Cecil de Mille. Similarly, one also goes through a stage, though a shorter one, in which the term "poetic" may acquire a slightly pejorative cast, as when one may decide, several hundred pages deep in Swinburne, that Swinburne can sometimes be a poetic bore. Eventually one realizes that the "poetic" quality comes from allusiveness, the incorporating into the texture of echoes, cadences, names and thoughts derived from the author's previous literary experience. Swinburne is poetic in a poor sense when he is being a parasite on the literary tradition; Eliot is poetic in a better sense when, in his own phrase, he steals rather than imitates. The "poetic" normally expresses itself as what one might loosely call word-magic or incantation, charm in its original sense of spell, as it reinforces the "act of the mind" in poetry with the dream-like reverberations, echoes and enlarged significances of the memory and the unconscious. We suggested at the beginning that Eliot lacks what Stevens has, the sense of an autonomous poetic theory as an inseparable part of poetic practice. On the other hand Eliot has pre-eminently the sense of a creative tradition, and this sense is partly what makes his poetry so uniquely penetrating, so easy to memorize unconsciously.

In Stevens there is a good deal of incantation and imitative harmony; but the deliberately "magical" poems, such as "The Idea of Order at Key West," "To the One of Fictive Music," and the later "Song of Fixed Accord" have the special function of expressing a stasis or harmony between imagination and reality, and hence have something of a conscious rhetorical exercise about them. In "The Idea of Order at Key West" the sense of carefully controlled artifice enters the theme as well. In other poems where the texture is dryer and harder, the schemata on which "word-magic" depends are reduced to a minimum. The rhymes, for instance, when they occur, are usually sharp barking assonances, parody-rhymes (e.g., "The Swedish cart to be part of the heart," 369), and the metres, like the curious blank *terza rima* used so often, are almost parody-metres. A quality that is not far from being anti-"poetic" seems to emerge.

Just as the "poetic" is derived mainly from the reverberations of tradition, so it is clear that the anti-"poetic" quality in Stevens is the result of his determination to make it new, in Pound's phrase, to achieve in each poem a unique expression and force his reader to make a correspondingly unique act of apprehension. This is a part of what he means by "abstract" as a quality of the "supreme fiction." It was Whitman who urged American writers to lay less emphasis on tradition, thereby starting another tradition of his own, and it is significant that Whitman is one of the very few traditional poets Stevens refers to, though he has little in common with him technically. It is partly his sense of a poem as belonging to experiment rather than tradition, separated from the stream of time with its conventional echoes, that gives Stevens' poetry its marked

affinity with pictures, an affinity shown also in the curiously formalized symmetry of the longer poems. *Notes toward a Supreme Fiction*, for instance, has three parts of ten sections each, each section with seven tercets, and similarly rectangular distributions of material are found in other poems.

When we meet a poet who has so much rhetorical skill, and yet lays so much emphasis on novelty and freshness of approach, the skill acquires a quality of courage: a courage that is without compromise in a world full of cheap rhetoric, yet uses none of the ready-made mixes of rhetoric in a world full of compromise. Stevens was one of the most courageous poets of our time, and his conception of the poem as "the heroic effort to live expressed As victory" (446) was unyielding from the beginning. Courage implies persistence, and persistence in a distinctive strain often develops its complementary opposite as well, as with Blake's fool who by persisting in his folly became wise. It was persistence that transformed the tropical lushness of *Harmonium* into the austere clairvoyance of *The Rock*, the luxurious demon into the necessary angel, and so rounded out a vision of major scope and intensity. As a result Stevens became, unlike many others who may have started off with equal abilities, not one of our expendable rhetoricians, but one of our small handful of essential poets.

Notes

1. All references to Stevens' poetry are accompanied by the page number in *The Collected Poems of Wallace Stevens*, New York, 1954, and all references to his critical essays by the page number in *The Necessary Angel*, New York, 1951, preceded by the letters N.A. I am sorry if this procedure makes the article typographically less attractive, but the proper place for such references, the margin, has disappeared from modern layout.

A. ALVAREZ
"Wallace Stevens: Platonic Poetry"
The Shaping Spirit
1958, pp. 124–39

I love work. It fascinates me. I can sit and look at it
for hours. (Jerome K. Jerome, *Three Men in a Boat*)

There has been some distinguished disagreement about the relative excellence of Wallace Stevens's poems and disagreement again about where exactly the excellence lies. But there is no doubt that excellence of a kind he had. The mere fact that Stevens was still writing in America somehow helped preserve the tone and standards for the rest. His assurance was an implicit judgment on uneasy and slipshod writing. Eliot apart, Stevens is the most perfectly finished poet America has turned out. And this is a great deal in an age in which so much poetic talent has been short-circuited. Pound, Crane, Robert Lowell—to keep only to American writers—have all produced, in their different ways, first-class verse. Yet all are more important in a handful of poems than in their total *œuvre*. On the other hand, Stevens's achievement is very much the sum of all his poems. Although I don't much believe in what Marianne Moore called "the interacting veins of life between his early and late poems", his best poems are extraordinarily at one with his pedestrian efforts. Stevens worked his talent to its full. He might very easily have been a worse poet. It is hard to see that he could have been any better. His standard is that of accomplishment. And it is very high.

Stevens published his first book of poems in middle age— he was 44—his second big volume thirteen years later. The subsequent books appeared more frequently, but still rarely enough. When his verse first came out in bulk, that is, it was already fully formed. Indeed, most of his best known work is in that first volume, *Harmonium*. For myself, I agree with Marius Bewley: *Transport to Summer* contains poems at least as good as any in the earlier book and it has far fewer irritations of style. But though Stevens's poetry changed a little, it hardly matured. There is a new clarity to the later verse; that rather wilful ruffling of the surface has gone and it is easier to see down to the depths that are there. But maturity is a continual deepening and broadening of experience, a continually growing power of expression. Stevens's maturity is something he started with; it is a fact of middle age more than anything attained. He is intelligent and serious and mostly worth-while; but he has none of that self-renewing freshness of, say, Lawrence. Early on, Stevens seems to have discovered the theme of his poetry; he played variations on it throughout the rest of his work. Lawrence's gift was to remain continually available to experience. He lacked preconceptions where Stevens relied on them.

I have invoked Lawrence simply because of that word "maturity". Otherwise they touch at no point. If Stevens owes anything to a modern poet, it is to Eliot. He is one of the few important poets whose language was influenced by Eliot's own practice instead of by the earlier authors Eliot made fashionable. Yet whatever similarities there are—and they are few—Stevens and Eliot start from opposite directions. Eliot's poetic world is withdrawn and of a great composed formal perfection. But the stuff of it which undergoes this perfecting is the painful and changing stuff of living. Stevens's world is one of luminous and distinct images which earn their place not as they approximate to something he has gone through but as they justify ideas. The tension and pressure of Stevens's verse is all in the ideas.

He is, in fact, at a level of considerable subtlety, something of a philosophical poet; his poetry comes to rest in the clarity of abstractions rather than of experience. This section, for example, from *The Man with the Blue Guitar*:

> Slowly the ivy on the stones
> Becomes the stones. Women become
>
> The cities, children become the fields
> And men in waves become the sea.
>
> It is the chord that falsifies.
> The sea returns upon the men,
>
> The fields entrap the children, brick
> Is a weed and all the flies are caught,
>
> Wingless and withered, but living alive.
> The discord merely magnifies.
>
> Deeper within the belly's dark
> Of time, time grows upon the rock.

I take it he means that the harmonies the imagination imposes—the conflicting sounds resolved in the chords of the blue guitar—are a false and blurred reality. Time perverts them all destructively and inevitably. Beneath our fictions the true and unchanging identification of things is buried, dark and threatening. Something of this order seems to be intended. What matters is that the objects he arranges in the verse resolve themselves into ideas. I'm not at all sure that the doom that hangs over it all is anything more personal than the impossibility of knowledge and the futility of art. In contrast:

> There was a man of double deed
> Sowed his garden full of seed.
> When the seed began to grow
> Twas like a garden full of snow.
> When the snow began to melt
> Twas like a ship without a belt.

> When the ship began to sail
> Twas like a bird without a tail.
> When the bird began to fly
> Twas like an eagle in the sky.
> When the sky began to roar
> Twas like a lion at the door.
> When the door began to crack
> Twas like a stick across my back.
> When my back began to smart
> Twas like a penknife in my heart.
> When my heart began to bleed
> Twas death and death and death indeed.

This is from *The Oxford Dictionary of Nursery Rhymes*. No doubt it is a good deal less polished and more wasteful than Stevens's poem. The casting around is done with less grace. But both pieces have a muffled ominousness to them; and the nursery rhyme has considerably more power. The difference is that the things are not fitted to ideas. They generate terror of themselves by a sort of perverse dream-logic. And the terror is a matter of the sharpest sensation. It is the helpless passive terror of dream suffering. The poem works to a climax of painfulness. Its logic is personal inevitability.

It seems to me that for all his care and precision Stevens never achieved this kind of inevitability. The images that bear the weight of so much of his verse seem to arrive there in a somewhat arbitrary manner.

> If there is a man white as marble
> Sits in a wood, in the greenest part,
> Brooding sounds of the images of death,
>
> So there is a man in black space
> Sits in nothing we know,
> Brooding sounds of river noises;
>
> And these images, these reverberations,
> And others, make certain how being
> Includes death and imagination. . . .
>   ("Metaphor as Degeneration")

To me, this sounds less like a poet's imagery than those eternal hypothetical tigers and rhinoceroses of the philosophers. They are chosen because they are, if nothing else, clear; there is no sense of their having chosen themselves. The logical paraphernalia that encloses them seems more important than the images themselves. In a way, Stevens was the only poet ever to take Imagism seriously. That is, he took it to its conclusion. The bulk of Imagist poetry was a more or less high-minded game played out in the consciously pregnant silences around the images. It needed an audience to be shocked into exclaiming: "How can you say so little?" and a poet who, with some satisfaction, could turn the question back on the asker: "How can you *see* so little?" But Stevens, not content with the occasionally wise passiveness the pure Imagist might, with luck, attain, made his poetry out of the problems with which those silences teemed.

What exactly the problems were has been gone over in detail a number of times. The reader had best go to the essays by R. P. Blackmur in *Language as Gesture* and by Marius Bewley in *The Complex Fate*. I will only try to give my interpretation of the theme briefly so that I can move on. It is almost a denial of Imagism, as though by practising the style Stevens had arrived at its contradiction. It is a poetry of irritation. He seems to be continually baffled by the impossibility of describing anything at all with finality. A motion of the wrist, the slightest variation in light or in the mood of the observer, and the object is utterly different. The impossible endlessness of observation, then, is Stevens's creative premiss. Almost any of his ambitious poems will have this theme hidden away in it somewhere; to give just three examples of three quite distinct manners: "Metaphors of a Magnifico", "Sea Surface Full of Clouds" and *The Man with the Blue Guitar*. Perhaps the studied manner in which he has varied his rhetoric is an attempt to evolve an instrument flexible enough to cope with his subject. I will return to this. The acceptance of limitation, however, is only a beginning. The better the verse, the more strenuously he works towards something more positive. Things as they are are at their best a little frustrating, at their worst deadening and negative. But there is, he discovers, a moment at which they come truly alive: the moment at which they are caught in all their subtlety by the imagination. Then they take to themselves meaning. And this is not a projection of the poet's self. It is a moment of purity when what is grasped is neither the commotion at the surface of the thing observed nor the commotion inside the observer. It is something that sparks between them: an essential imaginative life. As a procedure it sounds almost unexceptionable, so long as it remains a demand for rigorous disinterestedness. It doesn't.

> You must become an ignorant man again
> And see the sun again with an ignorant eye
> And see it clearly in the idea of it.
>
> Never suppose an inventing mind as source
> Of this idea nor for that mind compose
> A voluminous master folded in his fire.
>
> How clean the sun when seen in its idea,
> Washed in the remotest cleanliness of a heaven
> That has expelled us and our images . . .
> (*Notes toward a Supreme Fiction*, I)

Stevens at his best—and this has all the superb conviction of his best—is not merely acting on poetic principle, on something that will give him the best practical results; he is involved in a tense logical process which takes him from the purity of the description to the idea of the thing described. He has come out on the far side of Imagism into its opposite, the Platonic world of Ideas.

Of course, there is no clear-cut ontology in Stevens's poetry, no world of meaning that has its separate existence aside from the poetry, like the "meaning" of Spenser's allegory—whatever that is. Stevens's style is too rooted in images for generalizations ever to get away in it on their own. But his preoccupations take him off into a realm where his poetry must get along on a rarified diet. It is a question of what the poet feels strongly about. And Stevens has great feeling for two things: for the truth that lurks below the changing surface of appearances, and for the mode by which this is perceived, the imagination. Certainly, the truth Stevens's imagination seizes upon is kept supple and varied by its dealings with images; but its method of dealing with them is more questionable. In his Princeton lecture he was quite firm about the business of the poet:

> . . . although he himself has witnessed, during the long period of his life, a general transition to reality, his own measure as a poet, in spite of all the passions of all the lovers of truth, is the measure of his power to abstract himself, and to withdraw with him, into his abstraction, the reality on which the lovers of truth insist. He must be able to abstract himself, and also to abstract reality, which he does by placing it in his imagination.

I am suspicious of such high-mindedness. But the extraordinary thing is the pertinacity with which Stevens stuck to his beliefs. A poet's penchant for theory as often as not makes little difference to his best poems; Coleridge's, for instance. But in Stevens's work it is all important; not only are his poems again

and again about themselves, about the imagination, about the validity of metaphor, and so on; underneath all his work is an abiding *belief* in abstraction. His poetic method is controlled by an abstracting principle. Unless you are willing to treat his imagery only as a set of toy bricks, carefully made and elegantly arranged, you find yourself forced away continually into a spare, abstract world. For example, a large number of his poems have the titles of paintings—"Woman Looking at a Vase of Flowers", or "The Well Dressed Man with a Beard"—yet the titles are on a mere nodding acquaintance with what follows. It is often as though he had left out the opening stanzas from his poems. The reason is that for Stevens a scene, an object, is only a starting-point for a voyage into abstraction. His method is the exact reverse of the slogan William Carlos Williams uses in his epic *Paterson*: instead of Williams' axiom, "No ideas but in things", Stevens has "No things but in ideas". The ideas are interpretative of the images; they are not rigid and separate generalizations. His "Examination of the Hero in Time of War", for instance, has nothing whatever to do with the concept of the hero, but everything to do with the modes by which we, the observers, apprehend the hero. It seems as though Stevens was never happy unless he could have all the images and figures with which his verse abounds tidied away into a framework of decent abstraction. His poetry is analytical—away from the detail towards the related ideas. I am convinced that his favourite word is "it". He is, anyway, the great poet of the third person. However much he may conceive of the imagination as an instrument of profound insight, he uses it to arrive at the type of coherence that a philosopher is more usually intent on. Stevens's, in fact, is the reverse of the usual method of poetry which starts out with the fullness of the experience, worries away at the hidden motives, and leaves the abstractions to take care of themselves. Perhaps it is this insistence on reasons and his relative indifference to motives that gives that air of arbitrariness to much of Stevens's imagery. For his images don't have to define; they are instead the source of definitions.

Stevens is a philosophical poet only in a specifically modern manner: he believes in the need for coherence and perhaps would like to arrive at some sort of finality, if it were not that he hardly trusts even philosophy itself. It is as though he had read the subject at Oxford. So he ties his deductions to observation, and proceeds steadily, minutely, without any justifiable spurts from generalizations and with few conclusions large enough to notice. Instead, he seems intent on making the best of a bad philosophical world. His air is at times foreboding, almost grim, as though only he really knew quite how bad things are, and how important are the least clearings of sense he can make. There is a certain hopeless poignancy in his persistence in the hunt for what he feels all along to be ultimately elusive.

However many and obscure the regions into which he follows his quarry, he is always stalking the same creature: imaginative coherence. And he always ends with the same painful sense of what might have been. It is this that, for me, makes many of his long poems almost unreadable: they are difficult, very difficult, but below the trouble is a certain steady repetition; you work down to what he is saying on *this* topic only to find that it is much the same as he has always said about everything else. It is like a number of very elaborate dwellings carved into the same cliff-face. Everything he has to say is in his two masterpieces, *Sunday Morning* and *Notes toward a Supreme Fiction*. The first is his profoundest statement of disbelief in anything beyond what is now; the other is his final tribute to the imagination, the power which justifies and dignifies his disbelief. This last catching together of all the themes in his work shows how deeply he feels them, how important the abstractions are for him. This is not always apparent elsewhere. Often his abstractions can rouse him to no more than stylistic device; and then the repetition is not solely in the theme:

> Inescapable romance, inescapable choice
> Of dreams, disillusion as the last illusion,
> Reality as a thing seen by the mind,
>
> Not that which is but that which is apprehended,
> A mirror, a lake of reflections in a room,
> A glassy ocean lying at the door,
>
> A great town hanging pendent in a shade,
> An enormous nation happy in a style,
> Everything as unreal as real can be,
>
> In the inexquisite eye . . .
> *(An Ordinary Evening in New Haven*, V)

The air is logical, but the effect is of a number of rough drafts for one statement, as though the randomness were trying to lose itself in multiplication. There is a point with Stevens, and he reaches it often, at which profundity becomes blurred with rhetoric.

His rhetoric is at times a distraction from what he is saying, at others it is the whole tale. Stevens's fatal Cleopatra was undoubtedly the turn of phrase. I find it difficult to know quite how to take his encrusted style. Certainly, in much of the earlier verse there is a large element of game; but the dandyism continues where game is seemingly not in question:

> If men at forty will be painting lakes
> The ephemeral blues must merge for them in one,
> The basic slate, the universal hue.
> There is a substance in us that prevails.
> But in our amours amorists discern
> Such fluctuations that their scrivening
> Is breathless to attend each quirky turn.
> *(Le Monocle de Mon Oncle*, VI)

The rhetoric seems to build up a motion of its own, not quite that of the poem's start. I feel Stevens had not decided whether to be compelling, ironical, or merely whimsical. And yet his extraordinary rhythmical control, that sense of perfect balance and strictness without ever using, or needing, rhymes, is an assurance at least that the hesitation is not in the craftsmanship. It is a matter, I think, of the medium itself. Throughout his work, and particularly in *Harmonium*, Stevens seems to me to be writing in a language that does not quite belong to him. It has something of the quality of the latinized English of the seventeenth-century scholars; it is done with skill, precision and devotion, but the writer is never quite able to get the sound of older, foreign voices out of his own. Often it is something more tenuous and a good deal more subtle than rhetoric:

> If her horny feet protrude, they come
> To show how cold she is, and dumb.
> ("The Emperor of Ice-Cream")

It is a beautiful and solemn cadence. But behind it somewhere, and I am not sure how far behind, is the echo of another poet. I can be no more precise than that. Since I first read the poem a long time ago, I have been trying to remember what it reminds me of. But without success. R. P. Blackmur suggested that Stevens's early rhetoric has affinities with Marlowe. It seems to me much closer to that of Sir Thomas Browne: quiet and intelligent, concerned only with one or two problems which come up again and again, beautifully embellished in a language full of the echoes of earlier stylists.

Stevens's style, of course, is in no way imitative; but it is something contrived. Often there is a disparity between his elaborate furnishings and the rather stringent bareness of the ideas. And even in those poems where meaning and style go most together he still moves, and is moved, by indirections:

> Above the forest of the parakeets,
> A parakeet of parakeets prevails,
> A pip of life amid a mort of tails.
> (The rudiments of tropics are around,
> Aloe of ivory, pear of rusty rind.)
> His lids are white because his eyes are blind.
>
> He is not paradise of parakeets,
> Of his gold ether, golden alguazil,
> Except because he broods there and is still.
> ("The Bird with the Coppery, Keen Claws")

For all the incisive delicacy and wit, there is some sort of deliberate redundance in the writing. He proceeds like a fashionable hostess at someone else's party; at each step he pauses for an elaborate gesture: "Aloe of ivory, pear of rusty rind", "Of his gold ether, golden alguazil". No doubt part of the wit lies in the exotic style; here the grandiose exaggeration is very much to the point. But often the gestures claim all of your attention—the over-rated "Bantams in Pine-Woods", for example—and then the poems hardly exist below the level of style.

The poems that have received too little attention are a number of far quieter ones, in which the style is subdued into clarity, and the lack of surface commotion leaves the metrical perfection to speak for itself. I am thinking of pieces like "The Snow Man", "The Curtains in the House of the Metaphysician", "Gubbinal", "Two at Norfolk", "Restatement of Romance", "Château Gallant", "Less and Less Human, O Savage Spirit", "The House Was Quiet and the World Was Calm", "The Beginning". There are a large number of these—poems of the order of Robert Frost's best, "Never Again Would Bird-Song Be the Same"—and they show how very accomplished Stevens was. It was the consistency of his output that somehow, as I said at the start, seemed to preserve the standards of good writing. And yet the absence in these poems both of the dominant themes and the hard surface of stylistic device makes me feel that Stevens did not set very much store by them. They seem to have happened a little to one side of his main creative effort. Yet the qualities he set most by—sustained precision of movement and sustained richness of style—which at other times puff his poetry up, as though with ambition, in these poems relax into a slighter and more personal perfection.

Perhaps the word "ambition" is the key to all the hesitations I have about Stevens's poetry. He is content to let these smaller poems go with personal statements. But his bigger themes are entangled with his theory of abstraction and a purity of perception which has only disdainful truck with the personal world. In the poems in which Stevens more or less succeeds with his ideal—there are many of them, and they are beautiful and original—the writing has an extraordinary lucidity; it was not for nothing that his ideal of perfection, as Mr. Bewley pointed out, was in the word "transparency". But when he failed to attain this perfection, he was left only with the means to it: a principle of continuous abstraction and a certain elegance of expression. Left hanging in the air without personal support, these seem sometimes a little pathetic, sometimes trivial.

Stevens was too intelligent and too gifted to be content with small subjects. His grand purpose was serious, lucid and difficult. Twice he achieved it, in *Sunday Morning* and *Notes* toward a Supreme Fiction, and these are great poems; a number of times he got very near it, in, for example, *Le Monocle de Mon Oncle*, "Peter Quince at the Clavier", "The Idea of Order at Key West"; he also wrote a number of excellent and much slighter poems. But in his ambitious failures—*An Ordinary Evening in New Haven*, for example, or *The Comedian as the Letter C*—he leaves you only with the precision and elaboration of method and ideas. Personally, I don't share his enthusiasm for these. And so I find the poems dull. It may be a little late to begin to quibble with words, but there is one hair that needs to be split: at some time while Stevens was discovering what he had to say about the world, he became muddled in the distinction between poetic *intellect* and poetic *intelligence*, The first he always has—hence the rigour and tight-lipped skill of his verse. The other, like most other poets, he can only fully achieve from time to time.

HELEN VENDLER
"Fugal Requiems"
On Extended Wings
1969, pp. 38–64

Was he to bray this in profoundest brass
Anointing his dreams with fugal requiems?

Commentaries on *The Comedian as the Letter C* (1923)[1] have in general ended with its ending, seeing what happens in the poem as the equivalent of what happens in its fable. But this poem speaks one language in its narrative plot, another in the success or failure of its rhetoric. As Lawrence said about earlier American writers, we must not trust the artist, but the tale. Nevertheless, behind the poet stands the man, who may be engaged in an effort to believe what the poet in him cannot enact. A separation of these strands of saying can lessen certain kinds of unease that anyone reading this first of Stevens' long poems must feel.

The plot of the *Comedian* is an epic one—the grand voyage and the return home. The ironic treatment of the voyager, critics have been quick to say, makes this poem a mock epic,[2] and the genre, asserted in the title, is comedy. But Stevens' more accurate readers, notably R. P. Blackmur,[3] have seen that no matter how slyly and briskly the poem moves, its subject is serious and skirts the tragic, and that in spite of its mock-heroic mode the poem conveys some sort of heroism, at least in its first cantos. All paraphrases unite in rendering the poem, in spite of its self-minimizing shrugs, as a testament, a reflection of the odyssey of one modern poet. Such summaries do not match the tone of the poem as we have it, and conclude in paying homage to the "seriousness" of its intent while honoring the surface of the poem, if at all, as the sparkling but almost irrelevant iridescence over the serious "topic."

The Comedian as the Letter C is fantastic in its language, and belongs, in the spectrum of poetic effort, at the end where we find anagrams, schemes, acrostics, figure poems, double sestinas, and so on—the poetry of ingenuity, the poetry with overt verbal designs on its readers. At least, that is our first impression. Then we notice a strange ebb and flow to that fantasy of language so that together with the obvious simplicity of the plot we have occasional corresponding simplicities of speech, lulls in the erratic gothic harmonies of the words. These simplicities are of several kinds, just as the coruscations are; together they bound the stylistic extremes of the poem and frame its rhetorical architecture.

Since all language in a poem is deliberate language, even simplicities, especially in strategic locations, have their wit. One form of simplicity that the *Comedian* and later poems depend on is the epigram, where the concepts may not be simple, but the rhetoric is:

> Man is the intelligence of his soil . . .
> His soil is man's intelligence.

These are punctuations in the poem, where it finds momentary pause. So are the titles of the cantos, deliberately laconic or banal—"The Idea of a Colony," "A Nice Shady Home"—which seem all the plainer when we reflect on the vagaries of entitling that Stevens allows himself in the *Collected Poems*. Equally plain is the final optative of the *Comedian*, which stands as Crispin's epitaph: "So may the relation of each man be clipped." Nothing of this prosaic sort occurs in Stevens' serious Romantic models, those voyages of nineteenth-century heroes in narrative verse. Around these dryly-put themes Stevens clusters his variations.

Stevens' range, beyond this primary level, makes simple definition awkward. He joins "high" syntax—an imposing parade of appositions, for instance—with mixed high and low diction in his first description of Crispin: "Socrates of snails, lutanist of fleas, imperative haw of hum."[4] The high syntax and some of the diction of royal address persist, but are diminished in their sphere of operation by Crispin's Lilliputian domestic range. If incongruity between high and low is the basis for the self-irony in such passages, there is no such incongruity in some other equally ironic appositions:

> An eye most apt in
> > gelatines
> > and jupes,
> > [and] berries of villages,
> a barber's eye,
> an eye
> > of land,
> > of simple salad beds,
> > of honest quilts,
> the eye of Crispin.

The earlier appositive epithets had pointed to Crispin's exaltation of himself as "principium and lex." But these later ones point to his simultaneous defensive diminution of self into the *honnête homme, l'homme moyen sensuel*. The protesting rusticity in "simple" and "honest" comes from Crispin's intimidation by the sea; what results is a scared claim for the decent reliable God-fearing land inhabitant. These simplicities are Crispin's two forms of romanticizing the self, and whether he sees himself as an exalted personage ruling a minute kingdom or, plaintively, as just an ordinary man like everyone else, these delusions have their appropriate forms of speech. The exalted personage talks in theological and philosophical terms, the *honnête homme* in ostentatiously *villageois* language.

Although the *Comedian* is written in the third person, there is no consistent speaking voice. Some readers have seen the speaker as an older Crispin ironically retelling his past voyage, but the narrator can be placed equally well at a further remove, as a third voice which modulates into both of the voices of Crispin, high and low. Crispin in fact is dead, and the third voice claims no temporal continuity with him at all, however much it may be true that all three are Stevens. The third voice speaks the "neutral" lines: "Crispin was washed away by magnitude." And this grave third voice, expressing itself often without irony, gives the poem its claim to high seriousness on life and fate. When it becomes fussily scholastic, a didactic voice retelling an exemplary voyage, we are given the mock hagiographer or anatomist. The "Nota" and "Sed quaeritur" of the opening are *its* mode of irony, [5] as it goes on with scholarly detachment to preach or to expound, via the life of its safely entombed exemplum, the anecdote of Crispin, of which the *sentence* is *De te fabula.* Pseudo-scholarly interest in a historical precedent is the governing ironic mode of the whole: we are given Crispin as zoological sample ideally preserved, as an exemplary allegorical model to be followed, as anything but a taxing living creature. And the inclusive irony is that even the scientific examination of an instructive case is vitiated:

> What can all this matter since
> The relation comes, benignly, to its end?
>
> (vi)

The only resolution is a temporal ending, not the moral resolution that the scholar-voice had intended, and the whole elaborate house of cards topples to the ground.

The sea and sky that wash Crispin away have, too, a double stylistic self, just as he has: a self of immense simplicity and a self of decorative variety. The poem attempts to appreciate both the strict austerity of "one vast subjugating final tone" and the "gaudy gusty panoply . . . caparison of wind and cloud." As always, Stevens wants reality both as monad and as plenitude, as the impenetrable rock-face and as Madame La Fleurie. What he desires is not necessarily what he perceives, and the double vision of reality shared by the narrator and by Crispin is the source of some confusion.

For a voyager, Crispin, like his prototype in *Alastor,* is remarkably passive. Things happen to him—first the sea, then a thunderstorm, then a family. These passages are the most explicit in the poem as the narrator speaks of undeniable physical happenings:

> Crispin was washed away by magnitude.
> The whole of life that still remained in him
> Dwindled to one sound strumming in his ear,
> Ubiquitous concussion, slap and sigh,
> Polyphony beyond his baton's thrust.
>
> (i)
>
> The white cabildo darkened, the façade,
> As sullen as the sky, was swallowed up
> In swift, successive shadows, dolefully.
> The rumbling broadened as it fell.
>
> (ii)
>
> And so it came, his cabin shuffled up,
> His trees were planted, his duenna brought
> Her prismy blonde and clapped her in his hands . . .
> The chits came for his jigging, bluet-eyed.
>
> (v)

We may take this as swift and unequivocal narration, where the flickers of comedy are overcome by the general march of ceremonious narrative. But where the sea and sky are elemental fate, the daughters are human fate, and are not consequently either purely simple or purely decorative, as the sky and sea, in this poem, are free to be. The idiom of the last canto of the *Comedian,* in describing the daughters, becomes the most forced in the poem: except for the opening definitions of Crispin, there are no excesses of elaboration to equal the density of the picture of Crispin's cabin as he returns to social nature:

> The return to social nature, once begun,
> Anabasis or slump, ascent or chute,
> Involved him in midwifery so dense
> His cabin counted as phylactery,
> Then place of vexing palankeens, then haunt
> Of children nibbling at the sugared void,

> Infants yet eminently old, then dome
> And halidom for the unbraided femes,
> Green crammers of the green fruits of the world.
>
> (vi)

The cabin, in a word, is not a place where anyone would want to live, or could live without being buried alive. The revulsion from the proliferation of life, subliminally ever present throughout Stevens, is nowhere clearer than in this account of Crispin's daughters, especially in what they have done to Crispin's cabin—deprived it of style, finally, with all those palankeens and fruit-crammings.

In the enumeration of the daughters, Stevens becomes more schematic than ever before or since, first announcing them in language that is a parody of an invocation to the Muse (vi, 1–8)[6] and then counting them, over and over: they are counted in their coming, counted in their growing, and counted, finally, in their being—an equivocal abacus, since the daughters, though insistently four, are scarcely differentiable[7] except for the one who becomes a queerly inane lady poet, "gaping at the orioles . . . a pearly poetess, peaked for rhapsody." The first two marry successively the same husband, who is presumably Cupid, "the full-pinioned one." The second sister has a chance because the first was inept:

> The second sister dallying was shy
> To fetch the one full-pinioned one himself
> Out of her botches, hot embosomer.
>
> (vi)

The sexual flinching underlying the ostentatious lustiness of the last epithet resembles the revulsion from the flesh which dictates the gobbet-like description of the fourth baby, compounded of

> Mere blusteriness that gewgaws jollified
> All din and gobble, blasphemously pink.
>
> (vi)

That daughter becomes tolerable only when she is the residual inhabitant, single, of the cabin, "pent now, a digit curious." Crispin, as we know him, is allegorized in his environment, and the moral explicitly drawn from marriage and the engendering of these overwhelming daughters is that this fertility and multiplication is a benign end, inundating the stage with new dramatis personae:

> Four daughters in a world too intricate
> In the beginning, four blithe instruments
> Of differing struts, four voices several
> In couch, four more personae, intimate
> As buffo, yet divers, four mirrors blue
> That should be silver, four accustomed seeds
> Hinting incredible hues, four selfsame lights
> That spread chromatics in hilarious dark,
> Four questioners and four sure answerers.
>
> (vi)

This insistent summary of the daughters' effect, altogether milder than the din and gobble and nibbling children, excludes the more embarrassing of its own antecedents, especially the extinction of Crispin's self which necessarily precedes his marriage and family. That extinction of self offered him two choices in the way of song, and he considers the first at length: it is to sing fugal requiems, chant dirges, and wear mourning. He rejects that option in the *Comedian,* but the falling-off in poetry which comes when he decides for a posthumous family life makes us doubt the wisdom of the fatalist choice. As Stevens was to say in his last extended poem, he had an instinct for earth as well as an instinct for heaven, but in his earlier years he seems to have been mistaken about what parts of the earth he had an instinct for. He felt obliged to pretend an instinct for the fertility of earth, when his true instinct was for its austerities and its dilapidations. Pursuing the *ignis fatuus* of luxuriance, he came to grief, not only in the poetry of the daughters but in other parts of the *Comedian* as well, where in convulsions of diction violence is done to language by archaism, slang, and affectation all jumbled together.

Stevens' active repugnance in the presence of the sensual and social daughters is matched only by his response to the tropics in the poem. His exposure begins with the melodic and archaic vocabulary of celestial vision:

> The fabulous and its intrinsic verse
> Came like two spirits parleying, adorned
> In radiance from the Atlantic coign.

And then, revulsion:

> But they came parleying of such an earth,
> So thick with sides and jagged lops of green . . .
> So streaked with yellow, blue and green and red
> In beak and bud and fruity gobbet-skins,
> That earth was like a jostling festival
> Of seeds grown fat, too juicily opulent,
> Expanding in the gold's maternal warmth.
>
> (ii)

This travesty of Porphyro's table offers a pulpy vocabulary of overripeness that we find elsewhere in Stevens:

> Our bloom is gone. We are the fruit thereof.
> Two golden gourds distended on our vines,
> Into the autumn weather, splashed with frost,
> Distorted by hale fatness, turned grotesque.
> We hang like warty squashes, streaked and rayed,
> The laughing sky will see the two of us
> Washed into rinds by rotting winter rains.
>
> (16)

When he acknowledges his own choking on the lush and opulent fruit of life, Stevens criticizes his incapacity—"Man proved a gobbet in my mincing world" (17)—but he cannot deny his reaction. He spits out gobbets, he draws back from the fat and fruity, in language as in experience. His verse describing "hale fatness" (a condition which he perceives as distention, distortion, grotesquerie) issues from the fastidious shudder of the involuntary ascetic.[8]

Stevens repudiates fertility in favor of discreet fineness; his gift above all others was to see, both comically and tragically, that "fluttering things have so distinct a shade." This capacity for the fluctuating engages us by virtuoso turns in "Sea Surface Full of Clouds" and by equivocal thresholds of expression in "To an Old Philosopher in Rome," where the physical and the spiritual are not placed in a mutually annihilatory relation, as they are in the *Comedian.* Stevens' best verse trembles always at halfway points, at the point of metamorphosis, when day is becoming darkness, when winter is becoming spring, when the rock is becoming the ivy, when a shadowy myth takes form before dissolving, when the revolving *mundo* hesitates in a pause. It is a poetry of the transitional moment, of the not-quite-here and the not-yet-gone, and is expressed, as Randall Jarrell finely said, in a dialectical movement: "In Stevens the unlikely tenderness of this movement—the one, the not-quite-that, the other, the not-exactly-the-other, the real one, the real other—is like the tenderness of the sculptor or draftsman, whose hand makes but looks as if it caressed."[9] Neither the unbodied nor the embodied engages Stevens for long; he is engrossed in "a voyaging up and down, between two elements," and the emphasis should be on the "between." Stevens is not a poet of antinomies, but a poet of the midworld between them, a world not of infinite Miltonic dimensions but

of limited space. Stevens cannot go "on spredden wings" through "deep space" (404) like his angels and Canons for more than a moment, any more than he can range with natural flexibility through the earth, at least not without abnormal strains on his language.

Stevens' predicament, though is has been sometimes voiced, and by Stevens too, as a predicament of the modern agnostic, seems rather the result of a wintry temperament, as Stevens' saw when he wrote, "Life is an affair of people not of places. But for me life is an affair of places and that is the trouble" (*OP*, 158). The lively things of this world—human, animal, vegetable—do not touch him as they did Keats or Wordsworth; he cannot become a sparrow or a stoat; he is not transfixed by a girl, a gibbet, and a beacon; the minutiae of the scene pass by unobserved; the natural cast of his eyes is upward, and the only phenomenon to which he is passionately attached is the weather. Natural forms, even when they are drawn from particular Pennsylvania or Connecticut landscapes, are generalized, abstracted, made almost anonymous in his poetry.

The entire absence of immersed attention to the details of the natural scene is nowhere more striking than in Stevens' divergence from his Romantic forebears, even when he is echoing them. The famous and beautiful ending of *Sunday Morning* derives, as everyone has noticed, from Keats's more famous and more beautiful final description of autumn:

> While barred clouds bloom the soft-dying day,
>   And touch the stubble-plains with rosy hue;
> Then in a wailful choir the small gnats mourn
>   Among the river swallows, borne aloft
>   Or sinking as the light wind lives or dies;
> And full-grown lambs loud bleat from hilly bourn;
>   Hedge-crickets sing; and now with treble soft
>   The red-breast whistles from a garden-croft;
>   And gathering swallows twitter in the skies.

In Stevens, this becomes:

> Deer walk upon our mountains, and the quail
> Whistle about us their spontaneous cries;
> Sweet berries ripen in the wilderness;
> And, in the isolation of the sky,
> At evening, casual flocks of pigeons make
> Ambiguous undulations as they sink
> Downward to darkness, on extended wings.
>
> (viii)

Both passages seem to be generalized scenes, but in Keats the implication of a present event (this is happening *now*, not this is what happens on autumn days), perceptible in the use of "while" in lieu of the more usual "when," is made unequivocal as the poem focuses, with full pathos, in the mind of a single observer with a vantage point in space to which the sounds are referred: the red-breast whistles not in, but from, the garden croft; the lambs bleat from the hilly bourn. Keats's observer is also located at a single and particular moment in time—"And *now* with treble soft / The red-breast whistles." Although Autumn has been gently deified in the previous stanzas, the mythology is equally gently discarded, and Ceres is reabsorbed in the minimal natural sounds, "the concretions which must, in the end, speak for themselves."[10]

Though Stevens, like Keats, mentions natural objects, they are allegorical instances of the abstract formulation earlier in the poem:

> We live in an old chaos of the sun,
> Or old dependency of day and night,
> Or island solitude, unsponsored, free,
> Of that wide water, inescapable.
>
> (viii)

Stevens' deer represent solitude, the spontaneous quail are unsponsored, the berries mature in the "free" wilderness, and the casual (also unsponsored) isolated (or islanded) pigeons make ambiguous undulations (close to chaos) as they sink (in dependency) downward to darkness (from day to night) on wings extended wide, hovering over that wide water. The scene, in short, is being used largely as an instance of a thesis, not surrendered to in and for itself.

Like Stevens, Crispin has only two choices in respect to the natural world: to be repelled by it, or to abstract it and make it scan. When Crispin "humbles himself" to the turnip, it has to be by a deliberate quelling of his natural fastidiousness, and with a *nostalgie de la boue* he hunts down all the "arrant stinks" that might help him "round his rude aesthetic out." There seems no middle ground in the *Comedian*—we have either the memorial gesturings of Triton or else resinous rankness, with the daughters, a simple perpetuation of self, no real poetic solution. The veritable small, the everyday, the sparrow at the window or the quarrel in the street—these, for all Crispin's pretensions to family life, are absent, and so is the visionary. Crispin's dilemma is not a universal one, as some readers of Stevens assume: it is only a dilemma for Stevens' very special vantage point in the person of Crispin, the vantage point of the man for whom the senses do not provide transcendent moments, who is repelled as the provocations of the senses reach excess, who is almost indifferent by temperament to any world except an arranged or speculative one—and who nevertheless "knows" that this world is all there is, that this is the unique item of ecstasy.

To embrace the quotidian is Stevens' "answer" in the *Comedian*, but it is not his only, nor his most characteristic answer, since in other poems he chooses to emphasize the world as a construction of the imagination, to reject or at least to surpass the mediations and satisfactions of the senses. Stevens' self seems to have presented him with a world excessively interior, in which the senses, with the exception of the eye, are atrophied or impoverished, and he writes about the world he has, putting in active terms, as a voyage, what is in fact involuntary. When the attempt at a transformation of reality fails, as it does with Crispin, when he is faced with the same insoluble lump only disastrously multiplied, he is embittered. Stevens certainly cannot write lovingly about a collection of raw turnips, though he conveys their appalling rawness by din and gobble; nor can he truly transform them, though he tries to cast the mantle of the transformed over what he feels as the deformed by calling the multiplied turnips "four questioners and four sure answerers."

Though Stevens writes superbly about the frail tentatives of reality—the single croak, the scrawny cry, the pre-history of February—when he is faced with the gross heterogeneity of the world he recoils. His preferred view of totality is not the heterogeneous but a great One—the Celestial Sun—which is, needless to say, still far away. When, on the other hand, Stevens exposes his dislike for that multiple reality which makes a dump of the world, the voice becomes unhampered, though self-critical; as soon as he tries to see the dump as fertile and prolific, the revulsion shows. He can ask finely of the present uncoiffed image,

> Why, without pity for these studious ghosts,
> Do you come dripping in your hair from sleep?
>
> (14)

But when he tries to describe natural curls, as he does with the four daughters, he is balked, since he does not naturally perceive the world as an inrush of curls and riches—that inrush is the springlike song of the nightingale that he can never hear, bound as he is to an autumn refrain in this long "autumn compendium."

What can Stevens mean, then, when he talks of the "affluence" (532) of this planet? Certainly not the heterogeneity of the physical. The end of *Esthétique du Mal* suggests one answer, the one that Stevens will finally adopt after forsaking the false direction of the *Comedian*:

> And out of what one sees and hears and out
> Of what one feels, who could have thought to make
> So many selves, so many sensuous worlds,
> As if the air, the mid-day air, was swarming
> With the metaphysical changes that occur,
> Merely in living as and where we live.
>
> (326)

Stevens' affluence is in that glass which catches the mannerism of nature and makes it into the mannerism of a spirit, "a glass aswarm with things going as far as they can" (510), "the swarming activities of the formulae of statement" (488), rather than in the false familial swarm of the daughters. The physical world will become, for Stevens, a minor *point d'appui* on which the immense structures of the imagination are erected, and his style, at the end, will be mercifully freed from those reproductive gestures toward jaunty fertility which so clog the texture of the *Comedian*.

The Comedian as the Letter C, like many of the poems in *Harmonium*, is an exercise in stressed physicality and stressed tropicality. Brilliant as it is, *Harmonium* gives sometimes the impression of a strained Dionysian *tripudium*, the classic instances being "Life Is Motion" and "Ploughing on Sunday." We recall that even *Sunday Morning*, in its original printing of stanzas chosen by Harriet Monroe but arranged by Stevens, ended with a prophetic vision of men chanting in orgy their boisterous devotion to the sun.[11] Stevens' resolute attempts to make himself into a ribald poet of boisterous devotion to the gaudy, the gusty, and the burly are a direct consequence of a depressing irony in respect to the self he was born with and an equally depressing delusion about the extent to which that self could be changed. These ribaldries take two stylistic forms in *Harmonium*—the willed and artificial primitivism of poems like "Earthy Anecdote," "Ploughing on Sunday," and so on, and the verbal mimetic reproduction, persistent only in the *Comedian*, of the actual density of the physical world. Neither is destined to become Stevens' persistent mode. Stevens as ironist never fades entirely (even in *The Rock*, Mr. Homburg is one of his *personae*), but the corrosive deflations of the *Comedian* are nowhere else so relentless.

The lines in the *Comedian* that are most continuous with *The Auroras of Autumn* or *The Rock* are the description of the divested Triton and the equally divested Crispin, as we see them unforcedly present:

> Triton incomplicate with that
> Which made him Triton, nothing left of him,
> Except in faint, memorial gesturings,
> That were like arms and shoulders in the waves,
> Here, something in the rise and fall of wind
> That seemed hallucinating horn, and here,
> A sunken voice, both of remembering
> And of forgetfulness, in alternate strain.
>
> (i)

> The salt hung on his spirit like a frost,
> The dead brine melted in him like a dew
> Of winter, until nothing of himself

Remained, except some starker, barer self
In a starker, barer, world.

(i)

The glimpse of Triton, the invisible voice, the hallucination in
surfaces, the voice of suggestion ("nothing except . . . like . . .
seemed . . . both, and") are all ways leading to the language of
the older Stevens affirming that reality may be "a shade that
traverses/ A dust, a force that traverses a shade" (480). And the
bareness of the surviving Crispin will lead to a later question:

Shall we be found hanging in the trees next spring?
Of what disaster is this the imminence;
Bare limbs, bare trees and a wind as sharp as salt?

(419)

Or we might choose, out of the *Comedian*, as central to the
"continuous" Stevens, the picture not of the myth divested but
of the world endowed, the plum hazily and beautifully
bloomed by its poems:

The plum survives its poems. It may hang
In the sunshine placidly, colored by ground
Obliquities of those who pass beneath,
Harlequined and mazily dewed and mauved
In bloom.

(v)

This is Stevens at his adorning best, happy in the reflections
cast by the mind on the world. But as soon as he attempts the
gross *Ding an sich*, the old shudder returns:

. . . Mazily dewed and mauved
In bloom. Yet it survives in its own form,
Beyond these changes, good, fat, guzzly fruit.

(v)

Stevens' Guzzla Gracile, his appetite for both the dewed and
the guzzly, chokes on its own avidity. We learn to trust the
Stevens of obliquities and appearances, the Stevens of "like,"
"as," and "seem," the Stevens of phenomena in all their
shimmers of investiture and raggedness. But the Stevens of
guzzling, rankness, and bluster disappoints and is false, except
when he is engaged in such charming self-parodies as "Bantams in Pine-Woods."

The true tale of Crispin, then, is a tale of false attempts
and real regrets, which presumes intellectually on its felt
satisfactions, asserting an ironic benignity it cannot render
without revulsion, refusing to acknowledge an asceticism it
cannot hide. The veiled autobiography, the semi-ironic confessional, is the form Stevens elected for his first long poem,
but never took up again, no doubt because the narrative
progress was deeply uncongenial to his mind, which moved
always in eddies, never in dramatic sequence. Stevens' tendency, as he says in *An Ordinary Evening in New Haven*, is to
branch, to proliferate, to multiply, not to come to an end.
Crispin's voyages and plans are, after all, rhetorical variations
on a single theme, the mutual accommodation of the self and
the world, and in the nature of things any "end" to such a
theme must be falsely concocted, as Stevens came to realize in
his ever more tentative resolutions.

It is odd, and can probably be explained only in terms of
such Romantic models as *Alastor*, that Stevens should have
attempted a quasi-narrative at all, especially since he had
already found an apt form in the "magnificent measure" of
Sunday Morning (1915) and *Le Monocle de Mon Oncle*
(1917).[12] Together with the *Comedian*, these poems show us
what Stevens was capable of, and show his somewhat intractable extremes. The relative proportions of elegy, gusto, and
irony are still uncertain in *Harmonium*. No later long poem
will ever be so purely archaic and nostalgic at once as *Sunday*

Morning, and no single one will ever muster the heavy irony of
the *Comedian*, an irony which can only be understood as a
flight from the mournfulness of his "noble accents and lucid
inescapable rhythms" as they appear in his poem of the
Götterdämmerung, Sunday Morning. "To see the gods dispelled in mid-air and dissolve like clouds is one of the great
human experiences. It is not as if they had gone over the
horizon to disappear for a time; nor as if they had been
overcome by other gods of greater power and profounder
knowledge. It is simply that they came to nothing. Since we
have always shared all things with them and have always had a
part of their strength and, certainly, all of their knowledge, we
shared likewise this experience of annihilation. It was their
annihilation, not ours, and yet it left us feeling that in a
measure, we, too, had been annihilated" (OP, 206–207). So it
is his own annihilation as well as that of the gods that Stevens
mourns in this "poem of long celestial death." Stevens has no
Nietzschean brio, and his prophecies of a new divinity are
wistfully and even disbelievingly made. At their least exalted,
they spring from self-pity:

The sky will be much friendlier then than now . . .
Not this dividing and indifferent blue.

(iii)

At their most delusory, the prophecies spring from an anachronistic primitivism masked as prediction:

Supple and turbulent, a ring of men
Shall chant in orgy on a summer morn
Their boisterous devotion to the sun.

(vii)

At their best, the stanzas of *Sunday Morning* are always
elegiac, even in passion:

The maidens taste
And stray impassioned in the littering leaves.

(v)

The apparently non-elegiac phrases of the poem are inevitably
embedded in an autumnal text, as the bough of summer is
reduced to the winter branch, and as elations are surrounded
by sadder motions of the soul:

Divinity must live within herself:
Passions of rain, or moods in falling snow;
Grievings in loneliness, or unsubdued
Elations when the forest blooms; gusty
Emotions on wet roads on autumn nights;
All pleasures and all pains, remembering
The bough of summer and the winter branch.
These are the measures destined for her soul.

(ii)

These gravities of resignation belong to the preceptor who
speaks the poem, and whose grieving measured tones correct
the woman's protestations:

"But in contentment I still feel
The need of some imperishable bliss."

She cries this need, and is answered by a voice of disembodied
and ghostly wisdom:

Death is the mother of beauty, hence from her
Alone, shall come fulfillment to our dreams.

(v)

For this older voice, all sorrow, triumph, and love are infinitely
distanced in some remote and remembered pathos of the past,
re-enacted now in equal pathos by the young, unaware of death:

Although she strews the leaves
Of sure obliteration on our paths,
The path sick sorrow took, the many paths

Where triumph rang its brassy phrase, or love
Whispered a little out of tenderness,
She makes the willow shiver in the sun
For maidens who were wont to sit and gaze
Upon the grass, relinquished to their feet.
She causes boys to pile new plums and pears
On disregarded plate. The maidens taste
And stray impassioned in the littering leaves.

(v)

It is a voice from the sepulcher that speaks these lines, one who has himself long since relinquished the taste of that early autumnal fruit.

The exquisite cadences of *Sunday Morning* are in fact corpse-like, existing around the woman's desires in a waxy perfection of resignation. Some remnant of the last claims made on life exist in the person of the woman, the pre-sepulchral self of the poet, but he has given up all active engagement and deals in bleak and funeral finalities. In the most oracular of them, he becomes a voice out of the air:

> The tomb in Palestine
> Is not the porch of spirits lingering,
> It is the grave of Jesus, where he lay.

Nevertheless, there is no suicidal thrust to the poem. The poet decides to prolong his posthumous life, to bide his time in the twilight of the gods, to live, perhaps, in a suspended animation. The close of the poem reflects his suspension as it broadens to as reluctant a construction as a sentence can have, pause by pause:

> And,
>   in the isolation of the sky,
>   at evening,
>   casual flocks of pigeons make ambiguous
>   undulations
>   as they sink,
>   downward to darkness,
>   on extended wings.

The final clause floats in its own equilibrium, knowing its inevitable direction, but not hastening the drift, just as the noting eye sees the undulations but deliberately, phrase by phrase, waits to locate them in time and space before giving them a name. [13]

The brisk ironic resignation of Crispin and the elegiac resignation of *Sunday Morning* both testify to throes which must have preceded their final stances. The memorial to these throes is a poem more radically imperfect, perhaps, than the *Comedian*, and more stylistically impure than the serener *Sunday Morning*, but indispensable as the clue to them both, the poem in which Stevens represses nothing, neither his sadness as he does in the *Comedian* nor his irony as he does in *Sunday Morning*. Grotesque as it sometimes becomes, *Le Monocle de Mon Oncle* comes nearer to encompassing, however awkwardly, the whole of Stevens. Here the skeleton is still alive, still pursuing the origin and course of love, not yet resigned, not yet posthumous, not yet wise. [14] The poem sees a dreadful paralysis on the horizon, but has not yet succumbed to it.

We witness in the poem the death-in-life—summed up in the death of love—of a young man turning old. The lover turns into a monocled avuncular sage:

> When amorists grow bald, then amours shrink
> Into the compass and curriculum
> Of introspective exiles, lecturing.

(vi)

We are to follow this shrinking of the soul as Stevens begins to turn into the final dwarf of himself, but not without watching the anguished and unwilling struggle of the last vanquished adolescent energies of love and faith, now exhausted in a depleted marriage. A sardonic pity and antagonism separate the conscious poet from his self-deceiving wife: [15]

> And so I mocked her in magnificent measure.
> Or was it that I mocked myself alone?
> I wish that I might be a thinking stone.
> The sea of spuming thought foists up again
> The radiant bubble that she was. And then
> A deep up-pouring from some saltier well
> Within me, burst its watery syllable.

(i)

On the poignant, Stevens superimposes the mordant, taking the model readist to hand for grim wit, Hamlet in the graveyard, and in that borrowed voice scrutinizing his own elegiac forms. The Ananke of the last poems appears here as the Newtonian apple of disillusion, falling inevitably and necessarily "of its own weight":

> The luscious and impeccable fruit of life
> Falls, it appears, of its own weight to earth.
> When you were Eve, its acrid juice was sweet,
> Untasted, in its heavenly, orchard air.
> An apple serves as well as any skull
> To be the book in which to read a round,
> And is as excellent, in that it is composed
> Of what, like skulls, comes rotting back to ground.

(iv)

But this heavy grotesquerie, though Stevens is clearly driven to it as an antidote to his fugal requiems, goes too far into the anatomy of decay, and forms too pat and "metaphysical" a parallel between apple and skull.

The other and more physical antidote is a grossly cynical counterpoint to the harmonies of love, as a frog booms "from his very belly / Odious chords" of sex, insisting on the ruthless necessity of sex even while the poet recognizes its insufficiency. The dubiousness of blaming the entire melancholy of forty on an absence of desire is antithetical to Stevens' taste for finding all the contexts of a given whole, but simple rage prevails against elegiac feeling for one stanza:

> If sex were all, then every trembling hand
> Could make us squeak, like dolls, the wished-for
>   words.
> But note the unconscionable treachery of fate,
> That makes us weep, laugh, grunt and groan, and
>   shout
> Doleful heroics, pinching gestures forth
> From madness or delight, without regard
> To that first, foremost law. Anguishing hour!
> Last night, we sat beside a pool of pink,
> Clippered with lilies scudding the bright chromes,
> Keen to the point of starlight, while a frog
> Boomed from his very belly odious chords.

(xi)

Though the violence here is not typical of Stevens, the argument is conducted in his manner as he puts two untenable hypotheses: if sex were all, if love were enough. The tyranny of the body is unsparingly voiced: sex is not all, but it is the first, foremost law, and everything else must follow on it. The early theatrical gestures of romantic love, made when Eve's apple was as yet untasted, disappear forever when the essential sexual instinct is found to be absent. Eve, like the pool, is still pink, bright, chromatic, lilied, starry like her *connaissance*, but she and her Adam lack what even the odious frogs possess by nature.

It is not often that Stevens will try the ultimate in determinism—that men's gestures, determined by fate, are absurd and puppetlike, and deserve a puppet language; more usually, he will prefer the stoic defense, but that too requires an assent to a virtual death. He seems to escape that death in one mysterious stanza of *Le Monocle*, where a parable adopts a stoic stance but saves itself by a myth of uncertain reference. Stevens begins by disavowing rapturous memories of inspiration and the effeminate poetry they produce:

> The fops of fancy in their poems leave
> Memorabilia of the mystic spouts,
> Spontaneously watering their gritty soils.
> I am a yeoman, as such fellows go.
> I know no magic trees, no balmy boughs,
> No silver-ruddy, gold-vermilion fruits.
> (x)

This is the stance that will be taken up in the *Comedian*, a dismissal of rhapsodies in favor of yeoman plainness, in itself a stoic choice. But Stevens cannot rest in pure self-sufficiency; he may dismiss mystic inspiration, but he retains a source of unending nourishment:

> But, after all, I know a tree that bears
> A semblance to the thing I have in mind.
> It stands gigantic, with a certain tip
> To which all birds come sometime in their time.
> But when they go that tip still tips the tree.
> (x)

This is yeoman language to suit a yeoman mystique, but the magic tree in the second half of the poem seems only another version of the dismissed magic trees in the first half. The parable is more intelligible rewritten in *Esthétique du Mal*, vi (318), in the serious but charming image of the mutual sustenance of sun and bird. This kind of plain parable offers a middle ground between the personal and the abstract, always with a slight overlay of fairy-tale pleasure, subduing private tone to public manner but without the blankness of public generalization. Nevertheless, Stevens is no staunch peasant, and the stoicism of yeomanry is no true solution to his melancholy.

There are other possible defenses against requiems, and *Le Monocle* tries two with great success. One is wry history, as the poet realizes the recurrent cycles of success and failure, which Stevens represents by the ceaseless decorative efforts of coiffeurs. Against their strategies he sets the obdurate return of hair to its uncoiffed state:

> Is it for nothing, then, that old Chinese
> Sat tittivating by their mountain pools
> Or in the Yangtse studied out their beards?
> I shall not play the flat historic scale.
> You know how Utamaro's beauties sought
> The end of love in their all-speaking braids.
> You know the mountainous coiffures of Bath.
> Alas! Have all the barbers lived in vain
> That not one curl in nature has survived?
> Why, without pity on these studious ghosts,
> Do you come dripping in your hair from sleep?
> (iii)

This stanza forecasts the relation of subject and style in the *Comedian*—exaggeration and comedy in the surface of language, with tittivating Chinese, barbers, and Bath coiffures like mountains, but not a shred of comedy in the emotion undergone. This manner, found in shorter poems too, succeeds as one tone among many, but the veil in the *Comedian* will become tedious in its discrepancy with matter or, as Joseph Riddel has put it, in the conflict between language and

meaning.[16] Stevens' truer defense against elegy is to see the decline into the nonchromatic as offering a new and haunting color to be explored:

> If men at forty will be painting lakes
> The ephemeral blues must merge for them in one,
> The basic slate, the universal hue.

Riddel has very truly called this "the most prophetic stanza in early Stevens," just as he rightly praised *Le Monocle* for "an emotional variety which is rare throughout [Stevens'] canon."[17] Stevens chooses to abandon both the star of Venus and the odious frogs for a new intermediate area of life, the "little kin" of fireflies and crickets, descended, no doubt, from Keats's gnats:

> In the high west there burns a furious star.
> It is for fiery boys that star was set
> And for sweet-smelling virgins close to them.
> The measure of the intensity of love
> Is measure, also, of the verve of earth.
> For me, the firefly's quick, electric stroke
> Ticks tediously the time of one more year.
> And you? Remember how the crickets came
> Out of their mother grass, like little kin,
> In the pale nights, when your first imagery
> Found inklings of your bond to all that dust.
> (v)

These are the "fluttering things," Venus' doves turned to pigeons, the light of Venus diminished to fireflies, that have nevertheless "so distinct a shade."

In spite of these felicities, *Le Monocle de Mon Oncle* remains both uncertain and derivative, uncertain in its wild variations of mood and self-regard, derivative in its blank verse. These choiring verses are to give way to the sparer art of the wasted figure propounding blank final music; and the ravishing but inherited harmonies of *Sunday Morning*, so composed to console and sanctify, will yield to a wish for a sparer rhetoric, meant "plainly to propound." As for *The Comedian as the Letter C*, its torrential expansions will be mercilessly contracted, and its central personage totally expunged, as Stevens undertakes his next long poem, *Like Decorations in a Nigger Cemetery*.

Notes

1. The following conventions will be observed. Numbers in parentheses refer to pages in the *Collected Poems* (New York, 1955), except in the case of *Owl's Clover*, where they refer to pages in *Opus Posthumous*. Other parenthetical numbers are preceded by one of the following: *OP*: *Opus Posthumous*, ed. Samuel French Morse (New York, 1957); *NA*: *The Necessary Angel* (New York, 1951); *L*: *Letters*, ed. Holly Stevens (New York, 1966). Names of long poems, separately treated, have been italicized. Numbers of cantos or sections of long poems are in lowercase Roman numerals. Dates given in parentheses after first mention of long poems are dates of first publication or of first reading.

    The Comedian as the Letter C was composed at the end of 1921, submitted in an early form for the Blindman prize under the title "From the Journal of Crispin" (*L*, 224 and 224n), and first published in *Harmonium*, 1923.

2. Cf. Daniel Fuchs, *The Comic Spirit of Wallace Stevens* (Durham, N.C., 1963), p. 32 and chapter 2 passim.

3. R. P. Blackmur, "Examples of Wallace Stevens," reprinted in *The Achievement of Wallace Stevens*, pp. 52–80. See especially p. 80: "What he deals with is not comic; the comedy, in that sense, is restricted to his perception and does not touch the things perceived or himself." Stevens himself (*L*, 778) wrote that his translator should "try to reproduce the every-day plainness of the central figure and the plush, so to speak, of his stage," recognizing, implicitly at least, the limitations of his comedy noted by

Blackmur. The disproportion between Crispin and his much elaborated environment may be attributed to a passivity like that which Roman Jakobson noted in Pasternak, "a tendency," as Victor Erlich says in paraphrase of Jakobson, "to substitute the 'action' for the 'actor' and the 'setting' for the 'action,' to resolve the image of the hero into . . . a series of objectified states of mind or of surrounding objects." Erlich, *Russian Formalism* (The Hague, 1955), p. 177, quoting Roman Jakobson, "Randbemerkungen zur Prosa des Dichters Pasternak," *Slavische Rundschau,* 7 (1935): 357–374. Erlich also remarks (p. 211) that in some poems, action is the pretext for what Shklovskii called the "unfolding of the verbal material," and this seems particularly true of a pseudo-narrative like the *Comedian.*

4. I have been reminded by Marie Borroff of the similarity of this description of Crispin to Berowne's description of Cupid in *Love's Labour's Lost* (III, i, 176ff).

5. Reappearing, for instance, in the "ecce" of *The Man with the Blue Guitar* (182).

6. See *Owl's Clover,* the beginning of canto ii and the conclusion of canto vii, for similar invocations of the Muse.

7. The attempts to match the daughters with the seasons, the points of the compass, or any other quaternary group seem vitiated by the lack of specific detail in Stevens' description. He had no children of his own when he wrote the poem, though he had been married since 1909.

8. Herbert J. Stern, in *Wallace Stevens* (Ann Arbor, 1966), says, after quoting the quite horrible lines describing tropical blossoms, that "Stevens shared with Freud the conviction that temporal happiness is attainable only through a release from sensual and sexual repression." But the tropical plants represent no joyous enfranchising of the sexual: they are

> Fibrous and dangling down,
> Oozing cantankerous gum
> Out of their purple maws,
> Darting out of their purple craws
> Their musky and tingling tongues.

Stevens may share, intellectually, Freud's conviction, but he is not, in Arnold's terms, at ease in Zion.

9. "The Collected Poems of Wallace Stevens," reprinted in *The Achievement of Wallace Stevens,* p. 185.

10. This is the formulation of a former student at Swarthmore, Geoffrey Joseph.

11. The poem says that the men will chant, but this is a signal case in which the rhetoric of the stanza, which is prophetic, is belied by the tone, which is nostalgic.

12. *Sunday Morning* was first published, in a five-stanza version, in *Poetry,* 7 (November 1915): 81–83, with the stanzas chosen by Harriet Monroe but arranged by Stevens in the order i, viii, iv, v, vii. *Le Monocle de Mon Oncle* was first published in *Others,* 5 (December 1918): 9–12. Both were republished in *Harmonium* (1923), *Sunday Morning* of course in its full eight stanzas.

13. The movement in the close of the ode *To Autumn* is entirely different. Stevens begins with mountains and ends with a motion downward to darkness, while Keats begins with the barred clouds and ends also in the panorama of the sky. Stevens' broadest clause is his last, while Keats's is the first, on the gnats. Stevens' passage consists of three equal items and a fourth, syntactically parallel but much enlarged; Keats's five items are given 3, 1, $1/2$, $1^{1/2}$, and 1 lines respectively, a subtler distribution entirely than Stevens'.

14. The fact that *Sunday Morning* precedes *Le Monocle de Mon Oncle* does not change the psychological relation between them, since the states involved are bound to alternate with each other.

15. While it is quite true that the Eve to Stevens' Adam has resemblances to the interior paramour (she has "imagery" in stanza v, for example), the persistent reference seems to be to a woman, once Eve, now turned, like the poet, into a grotesque autumnal fruit: "We hang like warty squashes, streaked and rayed." For the pool of stanza xi, see *L,* 144.

16. Joseph N. Riddel, *The Clairvoyant Eye* (Baton Rouge, 1965), p. 96. He adds that Crispin's voyage "is never seen in true focus," but he founds the difficulty in Stevens' "devotion to the physical world" (93), which I think was largely nonexistent. Stevens' *wish* to be devoted to the physical world was of course real.

17. Ibid., pp. 91, 90.

HAROLD BLOOM
From *"The Rock* and Final Lyrics"
Wallace Stevens: The Poems of Our Climate
1977, pp. 338–51

Stevens' last phase (1950–55) was his best. No single poem written after he turned seventy has the scope and ambition of his three masterpieces, *Notes, The Auroras, An Ordinary Evening.* But *The Rock,* the elegy "To an Old Philosopher in Rome," and some twenty-five shorter poems have an uncanny intensity and originality that surpass nearly all his previous work at middle length or shorter.

As at a Theatre (1950) can be taken as the inauguration of the final phase. The images are all familiar denizens of Stevens' theatre of mind: green and blue, the "primitive," "reality," the candle of being. The stance is different, however, and the poet's vision asserts its conscious change. For the sunlight is "another sunlight," and the yearning is for "the artifice of a new reality," a "time to come," though all this is heavily qualified by a customary sequence of "likes." What might be is "the candle of another being," a self-meditating image in a wholly transcendental world, a world without walls. All this is "as at a theatre," yet the azure world-beyond (outre-terre) disclosed is important not for the content of fulfilled desire, or "universe without life's limp and lack, / Philosophers' end," but for the only difference Stevens now seems compelled to recognize. The mind, which could never be satisfied, never, just for once requires a sense of having fulfilled itself. This impatience is so much against the wisdom that Stevens has spent a lifetime acquiring that his reader is warned of another crisis, to which *The Rock* is addressed, together with its triad of related lyrics of 1950: A *Discovery of Thought,* "The Course of a Particular," and "Final Soliloquy of the Interior Paramour."

Of all Stevens' poems, none opens so bleakly as "Seventy Years Later," the first section of *The Rock.* The poet is seventy years old, and so the "later" in the title evidently means "since birth." Seventy years after our birth, we have touched a moment in consciousness that makes having lived at all, let alone being alive now, seem an illusion. "Illusion" always had been a hurtful word for Stevens and had meant (as it does here) an error in the perception of reality. *Extracts* had identified being "naked of any illusion" with being "in poverty," but *An Ordinary Evening,* IV, mocked its poet's "last plainness of a man who has fought / Against illusion and was," a fight dismissed in the next canto as "inescapable romance, inescapable choice / Of dreams, disillusion as the last illusion." Stevens' challenge to himself now is to call life an illusion without indulging in another romance of disillusion. His precursors, as always when he is in crisis, come out of his American tradition. Emerson's motto to his powerful essay "Illusions" could be the epigraph to *The Rock:*

> Flow, flow the waves hated,
> Accursed, adored,
> The waves of mutation;
> No anchorage is.
> Sleep is not, death is not;
> Who seem to die live.
> House you were born in,

Friends of your springtime,
Old man and young maid,
Day's toil and its guerdon,
They are all vanishing,
Fleeing to fables,
Cannot be moored.

Though there are echoes of "Illusions," and of other essays in *The Conduct of Life*, throughout Stevens' last phase, the precursor text in Emerson for *The Rock* is the essay "Experience," as J. Hillis Miller has shown. The sequence of "Experience" is like that of *The Rock*; it begins with a first third that proclaims a series of illusions, so intense that Emerson is driven to the ironic assertion: "Nothing is left us now but death. We look to that with a grim satisfaction, saying, There at least is reality that will not dodge us." Stevens lacks even that grim satisfaction in the opening tercets of *The Rock*:

It is an illusion that we were ever alive,
Lived in the houses of mothers, arranged ourselves
By our own motions in a freedom of air.

Regard the freedom of seventy years ago.
It is no longer air. The houses still stand,
Though they are rigid in rigid emptiness.

In his vision of the mother's house in *The Auroras of Autumn*, III, Stevens had been driven to the image of two-dimensionality: "Upstairs / The windows will be lighted, not the rooms," an image made more powerful because the lighting is being done by the aurora borealis. The house reduced from three dimensions to just two has its parallels in the reduced mementoes and memories of the mother: "The necklace is a carving not a kiss. / The soft hands are a motion not a touch. / The house will crumble." In the first of *Three Academic Pieces*, written in 1947 just before *The Auroras of Autumn*, Stevens had a stronger sense of the link between memory and resemblance: "Apparently objects of sentiment most easily prove the existence of this kind of resemblance: something in a locket. . . . One may find intimations of immortality in an object on the mantelpiece; and these intimations are as real in the mind in which they occur as the mantelpiece itself."[1]

One way of understanding the opening of *The Rock* is to see it as the last of three phases in the decay of Stevens' version of the Wordsworthian intimations or visionary gleam, in which the first phase is a reality in the mind as the mind perceives resemblances, and the second is when "the necklace is a carving not a kiss." Regarding (not beholding) his origins, the poet sees his memories as having suffered a loss of air, until

Even our shadows, their shadows, no longer remain.
The lives these lived in the mind are at an end.
They never were . . .

It is not that memory is dying but that memory is no longer *felt*. Precisely what Wordsworth feared most has happened to Stevens. And if memory has no vitality, then Stevens was not and is not a poet:

The sounds of the guitar
Were not and are not. Absurd. The words spoken
Were not and are not. It is not to be believed.

Stevens' tone was never more uncanny. As I read this, "The sounds of the guitar / Were not and are not" is flat, almost toneless, but the following "Absurd" is a shocked, disbelieving, anguished whisper. Again, "The words spoken / Were not and are not," though a touch harsher, returns to relative tonelessness, but then an even more hushed, bewildered, quasi-protesting urgency is heard in "It is not to be believed." What follows is an even greater anguish, as the one great romantic

memory of the poet's life is rehearsed as though it too was not and is not:

The meeting at noon at the edge of the field seems
    like
An invention, an embrace between one desperate
    clod
And another in a fantastic consciousness,
In a queer assertion of humanity.

Again Stevens returns to a vision of *The Auroras of Autumn*, but in an ironical substitution for the tenderness of the earlier account:

The rendezvous, when she came alone,
By her coming became a freedom of the two,
An isolation which only the two could share.

Regarding that freedom of forty-six years ago, Stevens again must think: "It is no longer air." Yet his language is more positive in its implications: "invention," "fantastic consciousness," "queer assertion of humanity" all convey the humanizing struggle to imagine love, to speak words of the world that might become the life of the world. It is important to notice that there is no full stop after "it is not to be believed" until Stevens reaches close to the end of "Seventy Years Later" with "In a birth of sight." From "The meeting at noon" until "a birth of sight" is a continuity, in which the meeting at last engenders the birth. Where does the upward movement begin that allows Stevens to begin a sense of "being alive, an incessant being alive"? This upward turn can be located, retrospectively but precisely, when we re-enter the poem just where we left it:

A theorem proposed between the two—
Two figures in a nature of the sun,
In the sun's design of its own happiness,

As if nothingness contained a métier,
A vital assumption, an impermanence
In its permanent cold, an illusion so desired.

From clods to mathematical figures is only an abstract upward turn, but "figures" is revealed to mean "tropes" as well as "persons" or "forms," images of the sun's cosmos, but even more of its "design of its own happiness," and with "design" the poem has changed. Where there is design, there can be métier, vital assumptions, and a movement from mere illusion to desired illusion. Stevens' qualifications are, as always, intense, yet they do not withdraw the assertion of the change that desire makes, the effect of an illusion so desired:

That the green leaves came and covered the high
    rock
That the lilacs came and bloomed, like a blindness
    cleaned,
Exclaiming bright sight, as it was satisfied,

In a birth of sight. The blooming and the musk
Were being alive, an incessant being alive,
A particular of being, that gross universe.

The fictions of the leaves, the rock, and the lilacs are synecdoches or tropes of Power, not ironies or tropes of Fate like the undesired illusions of the first sixteen lines of the poem. When we reach the dash at the end of line sixteen, "A theorem proposed between the two—" we touch the disjunction between the *illusio* of Stevens' opening swerve away from origins and the synecdoche that antithetically restitutes or completes the poet's initial dearth of meaning. Between the proposed theorem and the sun's nature a crossing or crisis of interpretation takes place, very subtly between "two" and "two," that is, between clods and figures, things and words.

This is the most rarefied of all Stevens' Crossings of Election, strongly and affirmatively answering the question "Am I still a poet, or was I truly a poet?"

Of the three synecdochal fictions, that of the leaves is Shelleyan and Whitmanian, the lilacs wholly Whitmanian, and the high rock uniquely Stevens' own, the most original of his major tropes. To catalog the whole course of this particular in Stevens would occupy too much space; I give here only what seem to me the main phases of its development in his work. The sole appearance of the image in *Harmonium* is very tentative, at the close of the odd allegory "The Bird with the Coppery, Keen Claws," of which the final revision was to be the great death-poem, *Of Mere Being*. The "parakeet of parakeets" ends the early poem by continuing to flare "in the sun-pallor of his rock," which is evidently mere nature or things-as-they-are. Far more remarkable is the sudden emergence of the image of the rock in *How to Live. What to Do*[2] in *Ideas of Order*, where "this rock" is a great height, "beyond all trees," participating in the heroic isolation of the human as beaten upon by a cold wind of solitude. In *The Man with the Blue Guitar*, XI, "time grows upon the rock," which appears to have widened so as to be all of the earth. When the rock returns, in the more positive *Blue Guitar*, XXVI, it is the world as shore, "whether sound or form / Or light, the relic of farewells, / Rock, of valedictory echoings." This is the metaphysical rock that recurs in Stevens' later poetry, at once land, sea, air, and sound, and always a little beyond common experience. In *This as Including That*,[3] the rock is wholly internalized, for the first time: "It is true that you live on this rock / And in it. It is wholly you." "Two Versions of the Same Poem," in *Transport to Summer*, presents the sea as "insolid rock" and the earth as a rock against which "the human ocean beats." We have seen the culmination of the image in *Credences of Summer*, VI, where the rock explicitly is made equal to, but not the same as, the Christian emblem of the truth, and where it is identified with the visible and the audible of summer.

This aspect of the rock is summed up in *The Auroras of Autumn*, VI, where the terrestrial cosmos is seen in one Sublime vision:

> It is a theatre floating through the clouds,
> Itself a cloud, although of misted rock
> And mountains running like water, wave on wave,
> Through waves of light.

The painful and eloquent poem "Imago," also in *The Auroras of Autumn* volume, extends this image into the February expectation of a return of warmth:

> Something returning from a deeper quarter,
> A glacier running through delirium,
> Making this heavy rock a place,
> Which is not of our lives composed . . .

This progression toward the poem *The Rock* ends in *An Ordinary Evening*, XV, where "the shadow of bare rock, Becomes the rock of autumn, glittering, / Ponderable source of each imponderable." How are we to interpret the image's anteriority in Stevens, when we encounter it as "the high rock" toward the end of the first section of *The Rock*? Stevens' own interpretation comes in the "Introduction" to *The Necessary Angel* (1951), where he quotes himself as saying, "[Poetry] is an illumination of a surface, the movement of a self in the rock" (viii). Further on in the book (48–49), Stevens quotes Henri Focillon (*The Life of Forms in Art*) as saying of Piranesi's *Prisons*: "Twenty years later, Piranesi returned to these etchings, and on taking them up again, he poured into them

shadow after shadow, until one might say that he excavated this astonishing darkness not from the brazen plates, but from the living rock of some subterranean world."

Shall we say of Stevens' rock that at last it is both self *and* other, me *and* not-me, mind *and* sky, imagination *and* reality? That would make it his image-of-images, a composite trope for his repression or internalization of poetic tradition. Of course, that makes it also too large and self-contradictory a trope, which is the particular fault of section III, "Forms of the Rock in a Night-Hymn." There the rock is alpha and omega, final reduction and final reimagining, the way up and the way down, and too much else besides. As we begin reading section II, "The Poem as Icon," we can say, provisionally, that the rock is the given, the most barren of all first ideas, life as it is, which has been covered with green leaves and lilacs by the "illusion so desired" of the poet's love for his wife.

Why the poem as *icon?* The word "icon" does not appear anywhere else in Stevens' poetry, so that we have no clues as to what precise shade of meaning it had for him. "The fiction of the leaves is the icon / Of the poem, the figuration of blessedness, / And the icon is the man." Are these two icons the same, so that the poet himself is only a fiction of the leaves? "These leaves are the poem, the icon and the man," the text goes on to say, and section II ends by proclaiming, "His words are both the icon and the man." The Shelleyan fiction of the leaves here is largely displaced by the Whitmanian one, though Whitman's fiction owed much to Shelley's. Yet Whitman's fiction, more than Shelley's, aptly can be called poem, icon, and man. "Icon" does not offer a varied choice of meanings. Essentially there are only three (and these tend to merge rather easily): a representation or image, a symbol or synecdoche, and a sacred picture of a sacred person in the Eastern Orthodox church. Stevens' "icon" seems to be a precise synonym for synecdoche as a trope of Power and restitution, and by calling fiction, poem, figuration, self, man, and word, each and all of them, tropes, Stevens follows Emerson and Whitman; he does not deconstruct or undermine his American precursors. Probably he is remembering the derivation of "icon" from the Greek *eikon*, "likeness," but he wishes also to appropriate for his poem some of the spiritual force of the Christian synecdoche, so as to give a kind of sacredness to the poem, as Whitman triumphantly had done before him.

What does Stevens mean by "cure" in "The Poem as Icon"?

> It is not enough to cover the rock with leaves.
> We must be cured of it by a cure of the ground
> Or a cure of ourselves, that is equal to a cure
> Of the ground, a cure beyond forgetfulness.

J. Hillis Miller has written the fullest commentary yet ventured on *The Rock*, and the notion of "cure" is central to his reading:

> The cure of the ground would be a caring for the ground, a securing of it, making it solid, as one cures a fiberglass hull by drying it carefully. At the same time the cure of the ground must be an effacing of it, making it vanish as a medicine cures a man of a disease by taking it away, making him sound again, or as an infatuated man is cured of a dangerous illusion. "Cure" comes from Latin *cura*, care, as in "curate" or "a cure of souls." The word "scour" . . . has the same root. A cure of the ground would scour it clean, revealing the bedrock beneath. . . . The cure of the ground proposed in the poem is the poem itself. The poem is an icon, at once a "copy of the sun" and a figure of the ground, though the relation of sun and ground remains to be established. The

icon (image, figure, resemblance) at once creates the ground, names it "properly," reveals it, and covers it over.

Following Derrida, Miller's comments depend upon the assumption that, as he phrases it, "The vocabulary of a poet is not a gathering or a closed system, but a dispersal, a scattering." To which I would both assent and disagree; a poet's vocabulary is not a closed system, but it is not just a dissemination. It is both a breaking apart and a restituting, and Stevens' "cure" is each, a scouring clean of the ground and a healing of it, but not I think a securing of it, which Miller admits as one of his meanings. A cure of the rock is a cure of one's own reductiveness and, with it, freedom to have a larger idea of what it is to be wholly human. But a cure of the rock is not possible, since that means curing either nature, "the ground," or the self, and neither is going to be cured beyond the possibility of perpetual repression:

And yet the leaves, if they broke into bud,
If they broke into bloom, if they bore fruit,
And if we ate the incipient colorings
Of their fresh culls might be a cure of the ground.

"Culls" means having been picked out rather than having been rejected. "Incipient" is a strong word for Stevens. On it he centers the meaning of "July Mountain," one of his very last poems:[4]

We live in a constellation
Of patches and of pitches,
Not in a single world,
In things said well in music,
On the piano, and in speech,
As in a page of poetry—
Thinkers without final thoughts
In an always incipient cosmos,
The way, when we climb a mountain,
Vermont throws itself together.

Stevens might have called this "Anecdote of the Jar Retold," except that he dispensed with the jar and relied instead on the idea of the poem, always freshly beginning, to firm up Vermont even as the perspectivizing jar had firmed up slovenly Tennessee. In *The Rock*, insofar as we are poets or "thinkers without final thoughts," our ingestion of the perpetual fresh possibilities of our own tropes might do for us what Keats did for himself in the induction to *The Fall of Hyperion*. The cure of the ground took him back into Eden and then to the shrine of poetry. Steven hints at as great a transformation:

The fiction of the leaves is the icon

Of the poem, the figuration of blessedness,
And the icon is the man. The pearled chaplet of spring,
The magnum wreath of summer, time's autumn snood,

Its copy of the sun, these cover the rock.
These leaves are the poem, the icon and the man.
These are a cure of the ground and of ourselves,

In the predicate that there is nothing else.

What matters here is the absence of winter, or the uncovered rock, true ground of our being. So much comes together in these lines that, for the reader of Stevens, they are indeed inexhaustible, whether to analysis or to meditation. They are the prelude to a final Crossing of Solipsism that intervenes between their climactic "nothing else" and the subsequent passage of ecstasy that begins "They bud and bloom and bear their fruit without change." The fiction of the leaves is now Stevens' fiction, as well as that of the precursors Shelley and Whitman, and the story it figures is its poet's own blessedness, his new freedom from winter or: "the icon is the man." Spring, summer, and autumn adorn the rock of reality even as a woman is adorned, the principle being the Platonic one of copying the sun as source of all images. "These leaves" finally take on the emphasis the phrase has when Whitman applies it to his own poems, and so "these leaves" means "the whole of *Harmonium*," which lends the peculiarly American *ethos* to this enterprise of the Native Strain: "In the predicate that there is nothing else," a line whose grim dignity is at once Emersonian and Nietzschean.

That predicate, which might be phrased as "all is trope," is a negative moment of freedom, the freedom of crossing into meaningfulness, which is the Romantic predicate proper. When the crossing has been accomplished, Stevens is able to grant himself a chant of the Sublime, of a quiet glory unmatched elsewhere in his work:

They bud and bloom and bear their fruit without change.
They are more than leaves that cover the barren rock.

They bud the whitest eye, the pallidest sprout,
New senses in the engenderings of sense,
The desire to be at the end of distances,
The body quickened and the mind in root.
They bloom as a man loves, as he lives in love.
They bear their fruit so that the year is known,

As if its understanding was brown skin,
The honey in its pulp, the final found,
The plenty of the year and of the world.

If they *are* more than leaves, then they are no longer language, and the leaves have ceased to be tropes or poems and have become magic or mysticism, a Will-to-Power over nature rather than over the anteriority of poetic imagery. Stevens literalizes his own images in an overtly fine desperation that itself is another version of the American Sublime. But this belated version, by necessity, fiercely represses not only the history of the fiction of the leaves but Stevens' own psychic history of doubting or denying his own Transcendentalism. For once he seems willing to risk becoming the rabbit masquerading as king of the ghosts, a consciousness asserting that it holds "the plenty of the year and of the world." So thoroughly has he trained us, his readers, that we are made to be both uneasy and exalted by this denial of all reductiveness, this sudden representation of what it might mean "to be at the end of distances." When we reach "so that the year is known, / As if its understanding was brown skin," we are rightly moved, and the erotic force of this trope of *pathos* seems as fully earned as the parallel moments in Whitman's dark sublimities. This "final found" is of touch, or touch taken up into the mind, and contrasts significantly with "the final finding of the ear" in "The Course of a Particular," a poem composed very soon after *The Rock*.

Perhaps Stevens should have ended "The Poem as Icon" with "The plenty of the year and of the world," but he risked an even more self-assertive exaltation:

In this plenty, the poem makes meanings of the rock,
Of such mixed motion and such imagery
That its barrenness becomes a thousand things

And so exists no more. This is the cure
Of leaves and of the ground and of ourselves.
His words are both the icon and the man.

In gesture, in imaginative *stance*, these seem to me the most Whitmanian lines in Stevens, the lines asserting the largest claims for poetry and for the poet. "Mixed motion" is the truly difficult trope here, reminding us how vital the image of motion is for Stevens. Verses, waves, thought, music, women, wind and weather, time, and indeed all things are in rapid, Paterian flux and motion throughout Stevens' poetry, and the word "motion" is for him an honorific term. Perhaps the key line is from the late *Looking Across the Fields and Watching the Birds Fly:* "A moving part of a motion, a discovery"; or else the prayer to the affirming father in *The Auroras of Autumn,* the father who is "of motion the ever-brightening origin." "Mixed motion" is the true cure "of the ground and of ourselves," but what is this motion if it is not the movement, tropological and topological, of substitutions, of crossings that generate meaningfulness in poems?

The Rock's forward motion, as poem, ends there, but Stevens added, as reflective coda, "Forms of the Rock in a Night-Hymn," which may be the lasting glory of the whole poem and is an authentic rival to the majestic closing strophes of Whitman's *Lilacs* elegy. Stevens hardly could hymn the night without invoking Whitman, whose visions had established the difference of the American night, a night wider, more fragrant, more vivid and promising, and finally more mothering in its erotic deathliness than even the nights of southern European tradition.

Yet Stevens' night-hymn begins most deceptively with a parodistic language of metaphysical description, which modulates from the rock's identity with "the gray particular of man's life" through the rock as "the stern particular of the air" on to the evening redness of decay and "evil dreams." But a different movement begins with "The difficult rightness of half-risen day," as Stevens reminds himself of his love for that daily moment of crossing when "there are no shadows in our sun." By the time Stevens has modulated to a final perspective upon the rock, we come to see that the poet is at a Transcendental degree of a Crossing of Identification, a massive, Whitmanian acceptance or coming to terms with the necessity of his own dying:

> It is the rock where tranquil must adduce
> Its tranquil self, the main of things, the mind,
>
> The starting point of the human and the end,
> That in which space itself is contained, the gate
> To the enclosure, day, the things illumined
>
> By day, night and that which night illumines,
> Night and its midnight-minting fragrances,
> Night's hymn of the rock, as in a vivid sleep.

"I fled forth to the hiding receiving night that talks not," Whitman gratefully sang, after he had learned to walk "as with companions, and as holding the hands of companions," these being the knowledge of death and the thought of death. In "A Clear Midnight" (a short poem that Stevens quoted, as we have seen), midnight is the hour of the soul's full emergence into the theme it loves best: "Night, sleep, death and the stars." What the night (and its equivalents) meant to Whitman, the rock finally now means to Stevens, the refuge that the end creates, the hiding and receiving hypostasis to which one might flee. The self cites its own tranquility as means of proof, at the rock, where by apposition the mind and the external realm are brought together as a dialectical alpha and omega. In the closing lines, Stevens makes a Transcendental lunge beyond, to a larger hypostasis, containing space and day and night, and something more than those, something illumined and minted by fragrances: "Night's hymn of the rock, as in a vivid sleep." A vivid sleep that is also a hymn suggests the world of dream, but here a dream of what is to come, or what Keats might have

called a dream of reality. Wherever these last tropes abandon us, what matters is how remarkably far we have come from "It is an illusion that we were ever alive." Perhaps no other single poem by Stevens travels so far, in so brief a compass.

Notes

1. *The Necessary Angel* (New York, 1951), p. 75.
2. *Collected Poems* (New York, 1955), p. 125.
3. *Opus Posthumous* (New York, 1957), p. 88.
4. *Opus Posthumous,* pp. 114–15.

WILLIAM H. PRITCHARD
From "Poet of the Academy"
Southern Review, October 1979, pp. 851–76

Stevens was born nine years before Pound, thirteen before Eliot, yet in the story of modern poetry his place seems to be after them. It is not that his work is explicitly a response, as in part Hart Crane's was, to challenges and principles set or affirmed by the revolutionary expatriates with their commitment to tradition, their piety toward the "Mind of Europe," and their patronizing condescension to most native American poets. Stevens regarded Eliot as a negative force and seems to have avoided Pound's work quite successfully, although my guess is that he never considered his poetry as primarily a response to theirs. But if we look at the course of American poetic reputations over the years since Eliot's death in 1965, it is clear that Stevens and William Carlos Williams have each been put forth as the two American poets who make claim to a centrality, a local identity, a human expressiveness more inspiriting than either Pound's or Eliot's.

For example, one remembers hearing in the late 1960s that Williams was "in" and that college students were responding to the freedoms of his verse and the democratic warmth of his sympathies, in contrast to Eliot, the chilly anti-lifer whose stock was diminishing in value. Williams seems to have been rediscovered after his death in 1963; but quite the opposite occurred with Eliot—it was as if people were relieved at last to put down the poems they had spent so many hours in explicating. That possibility, and the rhetoric of "liberation" heard so often in those years, may have been responsible for whatever shift in relative valuing took place. The Williams boom was relatively short-lived. But the rise of Stevens to a commanding position as *the* modern American poet has been more gradual and is likely to prove more lasting, at least insofar as academic critics call the turn. For it is evident that some of the best or most influential critics of poetry at this time—Helen Vendler, Denis Donoghue, Frank Kermode, and especially the Yale triumvirate of Harold Bloom, Geoffrey Hartman, and Hillis Miller—concur in a quite exalted estimate of Stevens' contribution and of his place in the hierarchy of American poetic tradition: he is the legitimate successor to Emerson and Whitman, and he presides (so at least Bloom would argue) over the most important American verse written today.

I call this an exalted estimate because it maintains itself by accepting Stevens' uses of language as in the main brilliant, richly and imaginatively satisfying. Although these critics don't agree on which is his best long poem—it may be *Notes toward a Supreme Fiction* or *The Auroras of Autumn* or *Esthétique du Mal* (it will *not* be *Sunday Morning*)—they do not question the overall authority and splendor of them, seeking rather to interpret more fully the meanings as they emerge. It seems to be agreed that these meanings are significant, and that Stevens' concern generally with the imagination and reality, with the "fiction" of the poem in its many guises, is to be taken with some reverence as perhaps the most dignified and worthy of modern poetic concerns. It may also be observed, as an indication of this reverence, that critics of Stevens often write sentences about the poem under question by quoting (or merely incorporating) lines and phrases from other Stevens poems, as if to insist upon (I will now employ the same technique) the omnipresent "total grandeur of a total edifice."

It is all a bit like going to church, but presumably much more exhilarating and free-breathing than going to church with T. S. Eliot. But as there were always those who refused to worship Eliot's poems, so there have been early and later dissenters from the canonization of Stevens. Yvor Winters, writing in the 1940s, judged that this poet's hedonistic philosophy was the cause of his downfall and deterioration after the early masterpieces in *Harmonium*. A few years later Randall Jarrell lamented Stevens in the guise of philosopher ("G. E. Moore at the spinet") and the resultant aridities found particularly in *The Auroras of Autumn*. More recently, the author of one of the best appreciations of *Sunday Morning*, J. V. Cunningham, wrote an essay for the purpose, he said, of rescuing Stevens from "himself and his friends." In aggressively polemical terms, Cunningham made the following charge:

> The situation is this: there are over twelve thousand lines of poetry, almost four hundred separate titles, and much of this is junk, and most is repetitious. There is furthermore, an immense body of commentary which is, with some notable exceptions, scandalously wrong, irrelevant, and confusing, much of it consisting of centos of phrases from the poetry.

He compared the reader of Stevens to one of Emily Dickinson; each will have "gotten his hands inextricably involved in the taffy—oversaturated, bewildered, unable to tell the good from the bad, snatching at this poem and that, this passage and that, to save something from the confusion." Cunningham's conviction is that, like Dickinson, Stevens was an amateur with "a homemade machine for the endless production of poems," written again and ever again, to convince himself he was a poet.

I should like to promote the rescue of Stevens from his more uncritical disciples and interpreters by specifying further than Cunningham does the undeniable pleasures of those poems which stand out from the "junk" and are not just repetitions of ones written earlier. But there is no way to read Stevens repeatedly over numbers of years without getting yourself thoroughly, if not inextricably, involved in the taffy. He became involved in it himself, as is testified to by his long letters to exegetes who queried him about this line or that stanza from various poems. Unlike most poets, at least in our century, he was willing to go on at great length, making modest and sensible paraphrases which nevertheless induce weariness in us if we try to read them through; he must have thought that his own poetry presented a challenge to the rational intelligence sufficient to justify these explanatory labors in its behalf. Going further, and to make my own bias clear: I propose that no other modern poet, not even Pound in the *Cantos*, can be as exasperating an acquaintance, as trying of our patience. Stevens, not the moon, is the "Arabian" of *Notes toward a Supreme Fiction*, with his damned hoobla-hoobla-hoobla-how." And yet he can also make us feel, as at the end of this section in the poem, that "life's nonsense pierces us with strange relation." ⟨. . .⟩

"After all, what is there odd about being a lawyer and being or doing something else at the same time?" Stevens wrote Harvey Breit in 1942, by way of turning down Breit's request for an interview. He had joined the New York office of the Hartford Accident and Indemnity Co. back in 1916, moved to Hartford soon after, and was appointed vice-president of the company in 1934. *Harmonium* was published in 1923; his daughter Holly was born the next year, and she tells us in her edition of her father's letters that whatever the causes were— the "failure" of *Harmonium* in commercial terms (Stevens says at one point that he netted $6.70 in profits), the presence of a young child in the house, much time spent in listening to classical music or in gardening, the pressures of his job—that Stevens wrote little poetry for eight or so years at a time when (between the ages of forty-four and fifty-two) one might have expected the reverse. His accession to the vice-presidency of the firm in 1934 may be taken as the point when his creative energies had begun to move back into poetry. Holly Stevens suggests that he wanted at all costs to avoid being taken as an "oddity," and thus passed over, by his business colleagues. Years later, in the course of a letter to one of his correspondents about Ceylon, a place he had become strongly interested in imagining, he confided that "I try to draw a definite line between poetry and business," and that he didn't want his Hartford friends to know about his poetry because "once they know they never think of you as anything but a poet and, after all, one is inevitably much more complicated than that."

One might turn the statement around and consider it from a poetry reader's rather than the Hartford colleague's point of view. Stevens didn't want his poetry friends to know anything about insurance and how the money was made; otherwise they might think of him, with sentimental patronization or a tinge of contempt, as an American businessman with a hobby. "One is inevitably much more complicated than that": one doesn't want to be understood as either an aesthete or a robust philistine, though one sees the attractions of both modes of behavior when sufficiently regulated. Why should the left hand know what the right hand was doing? Here we are drawn toward the center of Stevens' immense stubbornness, his insistence on going his own way, caring intensely about only what he cared about. So there is most decidedly no point in pretending that we can appreciate the poems more truly if we dose ourselves up with the life; a life that, through the letters, we get only glimpses of, though they are sometimes rich glimpses.

Hannah Arendt quotes Gilson's remark about how if a philosopher should try to write his autobiography he would find that insofar as he was a philosopher he had no life. This observation takes on special point in relation to Stevens when he is compared to a poet such as Yeats. The occasional nature of so many of Yeats's poems, the clear connections between his response to public and private events, in letters or essays, and his responses to them in poems, give us the illusion that both life and work are comprehensible, open for inspection by the rational intellect, no matter how many "irrational" materials they make use of. There is no such security with Stevens; the "definite line between poetry and business" he succeeded in drawing makes both his activities the more inscrutable. Whatever he did at the office of Hartford Accident and Indemnity Co. we imagine to have been thoroughly self-contained, ceasing at 5 P.M.; while after hours (in 1942, an important moment in his poetic career) he wrote in about two months his most ambitious, and possibly most successful, attempt to demonstrate how poetry can help us to live our lives.

With the literary historian's penchant for dividing careers

into Early, Middle, and Late, we are tempted to call *Notes toward a Supreme Fiction* the prime example of Middle Stevens—with *Harmonium* representing the earlier work and the poems from the 1950s, beginning in *Collected Poems* with *The Rock*, representing the late. But in fact over half of the collected poems were composed within the last thirteen years of Stevens' life, from 1942 to his death in 1955, and *Notes* is the fully mature expression of a man of sixty-three, not really "middle" anything. I want with particular respect to this poem, but with implications for Stevens' other poems as well, to express both my admiration for it—my delight in its rhetoric, its "sound"—and also my bafflement at it, my uncertainty that it is a "great poem." But I must do so in what is a dangerously foreshortened way, dealing only with a couple of representative sections.

We are especially fortunate to have the fine commentaries of Helen Vendler and Harold Bloom to help in finding our way about in it. Vendler's account is characteristically subtle, comprehensive, and assured; for her the "flawless energy" of *Notes* feels both "liberated and restrained":

> Stevens' willingness to abate the claims of imagina-
> tion invigorates the verse; the will that had, for so
> many years, strained toward an aspiring apotheosis is
> deflected now into an exhilaration of manner and a
> lightening of mood in all directions. Stevens is freed
> into equilibrium: released from protesting too much,
> he can vest himself in easier language and motion.

The triadic stanza which he settled on for this poem (and for succeeding ones like *The Auroras of Autumn* and *An Ordinary Evening in New Haven*), with seven unrhymed triads to a section and ten sections making up each of its three parts, is perfect for providing him with the room to expand, yet pull himself up after twenty-one lines and modulate into a different key. Vendler also finds the poem memorable for its array of personifications and fables, saying (rather strangely to my eyes) that the poem immortalizes not "mythical objects"—as in the earlier long poem *Owl's Clover*—but objects that are "quotidian, recognizable, accessible, or at least naturalized." She then provides a list of the significant figures of *Notes*: "the Arabian, the Ephebe, the MacCullough, The Man in the Old Coat, the President, General du Puy, the Planter, Nanzia Nunzio, the Blue Woman, the Lasting Visage, the Captain and Bawda, Canon Aspirin and his Sister, the Angel, The Fat Girl."

Readers familiar with the poem will of course recognize these "figures," or at least most of them, but listing them as Vendler does has rather the opposite effect from convincing me that they represent accessible and recognizable parts of the world. They indicate rather, in summary form, the exotic nature of Stevens' art, in this poem as elsewhere, and the fanciful character—the "belle design of foppish line"—his expression aspires to. Whereas Vendler and Bloom treat these figures either as (in Vendler's case) diverse inventions to be welcomed for their plenitude, or (in Bloom's case) phenomena to be interpreted, I suggest that neither interpretation nor acceptance is an adequate response to the oddities of which *Notes* is full. For this poet of sound and rhetoric, with such a cast of characters as named above by Vendler, not only "resists the intelligence almost successfully"—as Stevens said a poem must do—but teases, overwhelms, wearies, and exhausts us with his fanciful excess. It may be that I am merely confessing to insufficient appetite for certain kinds of poetic extravagance, and my only answer to that charge is to ask whether other readers have felt any of the same discomfort, at least have responded in a more divided way than with either an enthu-

siastic yea-saying to whatever piece of invention or "figure" the poem brings before them, or with an eager plunge into the activity of interpretation.

A comparison of a "fanciful" episode or passage with one which, in Wordsworth's sense, seems more truly imaginative will help distinguish Stevens' highest and finest style from his more idiosyncratic and potentially trivial one. In the second part of *Notes*, titled "It Must Change," we confront various sorts of permanences which, like the artificial paradise imagined in stanza VI of *Sunday Morning* ("Is there no change of death in paradise? Does ripe fruit never fall? Or do the boughs / Hang always heavy in that perfect sky . . . "), do not satisfy the imagination because they do not change. In "Notes" such unchanging beings are represented by the statue of General du Puy which "rested immobile," or by the birds repeating "Ké-ké" ("a single text, granite monotony") or, most wittily, the "President's" ordaining "the bee to be immortal." In section II Stevens moves from his able mockery of this delusive activity into an elevated lyrical utterance which shows itself eager to believe that change is good, is life, is the mother of beauty and fullness:

> Why, then, when in golden fury
> Spring vanishes the scraps of winter, why
> Should there be a question of returning or
> Of death in memory's dream? Is spring a sleep?
>
> This warmth is for lovers at last accomplishing
> Their love, this beginning, not resuming, this
> Booming and booming of the new-come bee.

Here is Stevens' art at its subtlest and noblest, the conceited play on "bee" being an occasion for something more than clever winks and nods, the verse rising to celebrate spring and the lovers. It is poetry which feels extremely witty, also natural and inevitable.

After the section about General du Puy, an instance of how "nothing had happened because nothing had changed," Stevens sets himself in section IV to show something happening, something changing:

> Two things of opposite natures seem to depend
> On one another, as a man depends
> On a woman, day on night, the imagined
>
> On the real. This is the origin of change.
> Winter and spring, cold copulars, embrace
> And forth the particulars of rapture come.
>
> Music falls on the silence like a sense,
> A passion that we feel, not understand.
> Morning and afternoon are clasped together
>
> And North and South are an intrinsic couple
> And sun and rain a plural, like two lovers
> That walk away as one in the greenest body.
>
> In solitude the trumpets of solitude
> Are not of another solitude resounding;
> A little string speaks for a crowd of voices.
>
> The partaker partakes of that which changes him.
> The child that touches takes a character from the
>   thing,
> The body, it touches. The captain and his men
>
> Are one and the sailor and the sea are one.
> Follow after, O my companion, my fellow, my self,
> Sister and solace, brother and delight.

Aside from the fifth triad, with its rather obscure reference to the "little string," this is language and syntax of the greatest dignity and clarity; and except for the witty play on "copulars," which feels solemn in import, the diction doesn't call attention to itself. Like that of the passage quoted above about the coming of spring, it seems as inevitable as is the gradual building of example of "copulars" embracing until, in the last two triads, examples come thick and fast: from partaker, to child, to the captain and the sailor. At which point the voice addresses us, and with "O my companion" invites us into the partaking by a particular rapture which is the real vindication for this attempt to imagine a "supreme fiction." It is Stevens' most authentic gesture of communion, akin to the sacramental "Drink this in remembrance of me," and celebrating, not the blood of our Lord Jesus Christ but rather, as in *Sunday Morning*, "the heavenly fellowship of men that perish and of summer morn." If such a passage can exist only because it is surrounded and set off by others, less intensely passionate in their directness, then so be it.

But consider now the section from "It Must Change" which follows: the fable of the planter, which Harold Bloom calls "one of the triumphs of *Notes*, the summation of major Stevens," and with which Helen Vendler begins her discussion of the poem, singling it out for the "tact" of its "negative praise"—the way it avoids too positive enthusiasms and elegiac overstatements:

On a blue island in a sky-wide water
The wild orange trees continued to bloom and to
    bear,
Long after the planter's death. A few limes re-
    mained,
Where his house had fallen, three scraggy trees
    weighted
With garbled green. These were the planters tur-
    quoise
And his orange blotches, these were his zero green,
A green baked greener in the greenest sun.
These were his beaches, his sea-myrtles in
White sand, his patter of the long sea-slushes.

There was an island beyond him on which rested,
An island to the South, on which rested like
A mountain, a pineapple pungent as Cuban sum-
    mer.

And là-bas, là-bas, the cool bananas grew,
Hung heavily on the great banana tree,
Which pierces clouds and bends on half the world.

He thought often of the land from which he came,
How that whole country was a melon, pink
If seen rightly and yet a possible red.

An unaffected man in a negative light
Could not have borne his labor nor have died
Sighing that he should leave the banjo's twang.

It is this sort of poetry that, I would maintain, separates the deepest admirers of Stevens from lesser ones like myself. Always ready to gloss his poems at the request of inquiring correspondents, Stevens was willing to call the planter a symbol of change, more specifically "the laborious human who lives in illusions and who, after all the great illusions have left him, still clings to one that pierces him." He also confessed to a great fondness for this canto. Bloom proceeds to identify the planter with Stevens, as equally men who could be "pierced"—in the language of the poem, were not "unaffected"—and he also finds here that Stevens is "very moved," that his rhetoric persuades us to be "immensely moved," and that in fact, rather than being a symbol of change, the planter vindicates the claim of *Le Monocle de Mon Oncle* that "there is a substance in us that prevails."

It is certainly a Stevens passage par excellence; fabulous, full of sensuous objects and colors, blue and orange and pink

and red, but especially green: "garbled green" and "zero green" and "a green baked greener in the greenest sun," with much alliterative transmuting of objects into sound-effects—"garbled green" and "sea-slushes," "pungent pineapples," melons, and above all the cool bananas growing "là-bas, là-bas." It is great fun to read aloud, particularly at the climactic invocation of those bananas. It is charming. But that it is by any stretch of the imagination great poetry, and that Stevens can be regarded with reverence when he composes in such a style—and he does so very frequently in *Notes* and throughout his work—seems to me unthinkable except in the writings of critics who have ceased to think critically and have delivered themselves wholly into the poet's hands, becoming fans rather than discriminators. If this sounds pompous, too much like a high-toned, old, ungrateful critic, I hope to have shown some gratitude; I find the passage, like much of the *Notes*, engaging and lively. But I do not believe great poetry can be made out of such materials, out of the color wheel, a few fruits, and the mystical repetition of a French word which can be rolled on the palate and mixed with bananas. It is poetry of the fancy, foppish and extravagant in a not very complicated sense; nor is, to mention the final line, the "banjo's twang" in any way an adequate image to call up the elegiac depths which in Bloom's commentary, for example, planter, poet and reader all climb into together and are supposedly moved.

So that however "flawless" the energy of *Notes* may be (I refer to Vendler's words), there are reasons for taking the poetry with a grain of salt, for asking whether it ever falls into archness, an all-too-fancy fancifulness, a let's-pretend license to imagine anything and the more whimsical the better. If it does, and if Stevens' poetry at its best—here and elsewhere— does not, then the distinction should not be obscured or obliterated in the interests of making him the poet of inevitable profundity.

In contrast to this claim, Hugh Kenner's account of Stevens in *A Homemade World* must appear to Stevensians as a trivializing and devaluing one, and my own sympathy for it puts these remarks in danger of being similarly misunderstood. At least it should be pointed out that in picking up, as I have done, the cue about "nonsense" most fully developed in Blackmur's early essay, Kenner's and my own accounts attempt to emphasize the great stylistic originality and individuality of Stevens' use of language—"the sound of its words"—at the same time as they are unable to take the style with full seriousness as an instrument for illuminating and understanding a real world of people and objects—of the "nature" that in their different ways Hardy and Frost and Yeats and Pound and eventually Eliot put us in touch with. Speaking of Mallarmé's and other French poets' discovery of Poe, Kenner says wittily that "they thought, so to speak, that they were reading Wallace Stevens," and claims that Stevens, not Poe, deserves the honor of being a constructor of supreme fictions independent of existing things: "His word-wizardry is what Poe's was thought to be: a kind of poetry, in the English language, which some very subtle and passionate Frenchmen intuited."

One of the many pleasures in reading Stevens' letters from his late age is to watch the way he constructs elegant supreme fictions, independent of existing things even of the most tempting and elemental sort. Here is a lovely instance of such constructing, beginning with one of his trips to New York to buy wine or food and to look at pictures:

When I was in New York on Saturday I bought a lot
of fruit in the place in 58th Street. One likes to look
at fruit as well as to eat it and that is precisely the

right spot to find fruit to look at. Then, too, I bought a chocolate cake because it was Saturday and Saturday and cakes are part of the same thing. In any case, last evening Holly and Peter [his grandson] dropped in and as the top of the cake had some sugar on it: a couple of roses, sprays and leaves, we put Peter in a chair and placed the cake in front of him and let him go to it to see what he would do. He had it all over the place. But he liked it and it was a good way to get rid of it because I am afraid that cakes, too, ought merely to be looked at.

This is more than the necessary prudence to be observed in eating habits when the subject is approaching seventy. More positively, the interest is in looking; in looking-on and providing the opportunity for readers to be onlookers also, through the frame of a supreme fiction. The fine last line from a late poem, "Prologues to What Is Possible," speaks of "the way a look or a touch reveals its unexpected magnitudes." More likely, for Stevens, it would be a look rather than a touch; you can only have a vision of "good, fat guzzly fruit" if you refrain from eating it—or so Stevens' way has it. This is the magician's way, the user of language who conjures up a scene in poems just as he put the cake in front of his grandson and deployed word-wizardry about it.

Kenner has had the temerity to suggest that we reconsider the seriousness with which we take Stevens's work:

> So many scrupulously arrested gestures, so laborious an honesty, such a pother of fine shades and nuanced distinctions; yet that forty years' work revolves about nothing more profound than bafflement with a speechless externality which poets can no longer pretend is animate. This fact invalidates no Stevens poem, only the terms on which some of the poems ask us to take them.

Surely the main terms on which Stevens' critics have taken him over the past twenty years or so have been extremely solemn ones: philosophical with a modern Continental twist, or Emersonianly Romantic. The last poems in particular have been seen as effecting some final reconciliation between imagination and reality, and it may be that Stevens himself had such an aspiration in their regard. Yet what makes them—many of them—so splendid, and arguably the best ones he ever wrote, is their preoccupation with (in Kenner's derogatory phrase) "nothing more profound" than how to respond, as a man and poet of seventy years, to the "speechless externality" which is no longer animate.

In the severely limited context of poems considered here, *Sunday Morning* was an early response to speechless externality which proposed an ingenious fiction—"Death is the mother of beauty"—as a way of imaginatively animating a world without God. And so, it is with a personal and terrifying edge that "Madame La Fleurie" welcomes the man to his final home:

> Weight him down, O side-stars, with the great weightings of the end.
> Seal him there. He looked in a glass of the earth and thought he lived in it.
> Now, he brings all that he saw into the earth, to the waiting parent.
> His crisp knowledge is devoured by her, beneath a dew.

"Madame La Fleurie" undoes poetry, turns back upon the poet the speech he had so gloriously contrived in so many poems, as in its final four lines:

> The thick strings stutter the finial gutturals.

> He does not lie there remembering the blue-jay, say the jay.
> His grief is that his mother should feed on him, himself and what he saw,
> In that distant chamber, a bearded queen, wicked in her dead light.

Bloom reminds us that the "jay" comes in here by way of *The Man with the Blue Guitar* who at the end of that poem would teach us to play "the imagined pine, the imagined jay"; the "gutturals" recall a poem at the very beginning of *Harmonium*—"The Plot against the Giant" in which the nymph of poetry would "whisper heavenly labials in a world of gutturals," thereby undoing the giant of reality. But most fearful is the mother, no longer the mother of beauty, and of a different sort than could have been devised in *Sunday Morning* when the vision of "our earthly mothers waiting, sleeplessly" was immediately followed by a ring of supple and turbulent men, chanting their faith in the goodness of mortality. In "Madame La Fleurie" these no longer so supreme fictions are replaced by a darker one which could pass for truth.

The impulse bears a resemblance to Yeats's attempt in his *Last Poems* to move beyond the metaphors (supreme fictions) or "circus animals" of his early poems which have now deserted him. So, Yeats tells us in the poem of that name, now that his metaphorical "ladder" is gone, "I must lie down where all the ladders start: / In the foul rag-and-bone shop of the heart." But in evoking the heart this incorrigible metaphormaker can't just call it a "heart"; it becomes an exciting, sinister rag-and-bone shop of a one. Likewise in Stevens' poem, the "bearded queen, wicked in her dead light" is at least as aggressive an invention as to "say the jay" or to announce that "death is the mother of beauty." Stevens confronts this paradoxical energy of the human imagination as it confronts blankness, absence, death, and formulates it most succinctly in "The Plain Sense of Things," where the lesson learned is that "the absence of imagination had itself to be imagined."

A year short of his seventieth birthday he suddenly confessed in a letter that "what I want more than anything else in music, painting and poetry, in life and in belief is the thrill that I experienced once in all the things that no longer thrill me at all." What is most human about the final *Rock* section from the *Collected Poems* are moments in which the poems become infused with an analogous thrill: the way in "To an Old Philosopher in Rome," a poem about Santayana in old age (and about Stevens), the philosopher's room becomes "the threshold of heaven" and a source of happiness:

> The bed, the books, the chair, the moving nuns,
> The candle as it evades the sight, these are
> The sources of happiness in the shape of Rome . . .
> A light on the candle tearing against the wick
> To join a hovering excellence . . .

or the way the "flick" of "Prologues to What Is Possible" becomes, in the concluding list of possibles, a moving response to the pressure of reality:

> A flick which added to what was real and its vocabulary,
> The way some first thing coming into Northern trees
> Adds to them the whole vocabulary of the South,
> The way the earliest single light in the evening sky, in spring,
> Creates a fresh universe out of nothingness by adding itself,
> The way a look or a touch reveals its unexpected magnitudes.

or, in "The World as Meditation," Penelope's continuing effort to imagine Ulysses' return, to compose "two in a deep-founded sheltering, friend and dear friend," finds in the very act of composing that

> It was Ulysses and it was not. Yet they had met,
> Friend and dear friend and a planet's encourage-
>   ment.
> The barbarous strength within her would never fail.

These poems exhibit the fullest, most ample and leisured response, to that "bafflement" Stevens had expressed early on, very beautifully, in "Anatomy of Monotony," a poem which appeared in the revised *Harmonium* and which explored the way human beings are one with the speechless externality— "Our nature is her nature"—yet not one and the same in that we will die and know that we will die. The poem concludes

> So be it. Yet the spaciousness and light
> In which the body walks and is deceived,
> Falls from that fatal and that barer sky,
> And this the spirit sees and is aggrieved.

The great difference between the last work and *Harmonium* is that Stevens has conceived of so many ways to extend the "So be it" into poems which neither console in facile ways, nor divert us through fancy and "nonsense." It is not only Penelope and Ulysses who "meet," but the reader and Stevens, "in a queer assertion of humanity" as a line from *The Rock* has it.

Stevens lived into his seventy-sixth year and the letters from his seventies are in their muted, sometimes bleak, but often humorous way, as interesting as the New York ones written fifty years before. He had by now developed ways of coming to terms with nearly everything; such as for example a member of the Yale faculty who had given a Sunday night talk over the radio, in December of 1953, about the religious significance of Christmas: "When I feel sore about Christmas cards and someone gets on the air and talks about the Incarnation and its practical value for all of us, I clap my hands and stamp my feet and say Bravo, Bravo! Perhaps that only goes to show how queer you become if you remain in New England long enough." He could never live in New England long enough, where "everything is normal beyond belief. My neighbors are returning from cruises. This morning I rode in town with a man burned the darkest brown. Personally I like *not* to go on cruises. There is a specific ease that comes from the office, going to bed and getting up early, which equals the relaxation of cruises. Good-luck and bon voyage! I shall follow you in my mind as you experience Spain anew," he writes to the departing Barbara Church, putting her and himself in their places. It is impossible to overestimate the importance of going to "the office" and its attendant routines in producing the specific ease in which the late poems bloomed; while the privilege of following someone in the mind, rather than traveling along with them in reality, is essential Stevens.

Knopf published the *Collected Poems* at the end of 1954 when he was seventy-five, to much respectful acclaim and the National Book Award. Stevens allowed as how he "intended to stay 75 for some years after that"; but time would not relent. His wife had the first of many strokes in January of the new year, then in April he went into the hospital for an exploratory operation that revealed an inoperable cancer which he was not told about. Two months later he returned to the office, "coming in at 10.00 and leaving at 1.30 and doing very little in the meantime except seeing people who want to know how I feel." This was in July, the Hartford heat "appalling," the

upstairs of his house "like an oven." He wrote to Samuel French Morse that "there is no chance, I think, of any new poems," that most of the time he felt drowsy and limp, and ended his letter with a particularly poignant statement:

> Call me up when you return to Hartford. I have not been to the Canoe Club now for a long time and believe that even a single Martini would be a disaster. The most I might be able to do would be to go and sit on the porch and drink lemonade and I should be glad to do that one of these days because I always loved the porch over there. But I know nothing of the lemonade.

One thinks again of the letter to Witter Bynner from many years before, and it is sad for what has perforce replaced the cool drink, the Panatella, the orchestra playing somewhere nearby, the crowd at a distance. Still, that last straight-faced sentence about the uncertain status of Canoe Club lemonade has the imaginative "flick" which just makes the difference. The next month he was dead.

Near the very end of *Collected Poems* stands one which to my knowledge is neglected by commentators and stands nowhere near the top of anybody's list of favorite Stevens poems. It is near the top of mine, however, and is a good poem to close with because of the extremely satisfying way it closes itself yet leaves open the sense of possibility he so warmed to and cherished. It is about subjectivity and objectiveness, about what to do with the mind's "bafflement with a speechless externality which poets can no longer pretend to animate," and about how, it turns out, poets exist to show us the way in which it is animate after all:

> The one moonlight, in the simple-colored night,
> Like a plain poet revolving in his mind
> The sameness of his various universe,
> Shines on the mere objectiveness of things.
>
> It is as if being was to be observed,
> As if, among the possible purposes
> Of what one sees, the purpose that comes first,
> The surface, is the purpose to be seen,
>
> The property of the moon, what it evokes.
> It is to disclose the essential presence, say,
> Of a mountain, expanded and elevated almost
> Into a sense, an object the less; or else
>
> To disclose in the figure waiting on the road
> An object the more, an undetermined form
> Between the slouchings of a gunman and a lover,
> A gesture in the dark, a fear one feels
>
> In the great vistas of night air, that takes this form,
> In the arbors that are as if of Saturn-star.
> So, then, this warm, wide, weatherless quietude
> Is active with a power, an inherent life,
>
> In spite of the mere objectiveness of things,
> Like a cloud-cap in the corner of a looking-glass,
> A change of color in the plain poet's mind,
> Night and silence disturbed by an interior sound,
>
> The one moonlight, the various universe, intended
> So much just to be seen—a purpose, empty
> Perhaps, absurd perhaps, but at least a purpose,
> Certain and ever more fresh. Ah! Certain, for
>   sure . . .

It was not his habit to end poems with ellipses or to use "Ah" in their final line. Their presence here in "Note on Moonlight" is an especially happy indication of the interior sound of his imagination, profound enough to last us for a lifetime.

ADDITIONAL READING

E. J. PRATT

Brown, E. K. "E. J. Pratt." In *On Canadian Poetry*. Toronto: Ryerson Press, 1943, pp. 132–52.

Clever, Glenn, ed. *The E. J. Pratt Symposium*. Ottawa: University of Ottawa Press, 1976.

Frye, Northrop. *The Bush Garden: Essays on the Canadian Imagination*. Toronto: House of Anansi Press, 1971, pp. 181–97.

Gingell, Susan. *E. J. Pratt on His Life and Poetry*. Toronto: University of Toronto Press, 1983.

Smith, A. J. M. *Some Poems of E. J. Pratt: Aspects of Imagery and Theme*. Western Bay, Newfoundland: St. John's Memorial University, 1969.

REYNOLDS PRICE

Barnes, David R. "The Names and Faces of Reynolds Price." *Kentucky Review* 2 (1968): 76–91.

Eichelberger, Clayton L. "Reynolds Price: 'A Banner in Defeat.'" *Journal of Popular Culture* 1 (1968): 410–17.

Kaufman, Wallace. "A Conversation with Reynolds Price." *Shenandoah* 17 (1966): 3–25.

Shepherd, Allen. "Love (and Marriage) in *A Long and Happy Life*." *Twentieth Century Literature* 17 (1971): 29–35.

Solotaroff, Theodore. "The Reynolds Price Who Outgrew the Southern Pastoral." *Saturday Review*, 26 September 1970, pp. 27–29, 46.

Vauthier, Simone. "The 'Circle in the Forest': Fictional Space in Reynolds Price's *A Long and Happy Life*." *Mississippi Quarterly* 28 (1975): 123–46.

FREDERIC PROKOSCH

Carpenter, Richard C. "The Novels of Frederic Prokosch." *College English* 18 (1956–57): 261–67.

Kohler, Dayton. "Frederic Prokosch." *English Journal* 32 (1943): 413–19.

Loveman, Amy. "Prokosch . . . " *Saturday Review of Literature*, 16 August 1941, p. 7.

Origo, Iris. "Found in a Basket." *New York Times Book Review*, 14 January 1968, pp. 5, 38.

Prokosch, Frederic. "Credo of a Writer." *Writer* 58 (1945): 167.

Squires, Radcliffe. *Frederic Prokosch*. New York: Twayne, 1964.

Strauss, Harold. "A Strange and Haunting Tale Set in Central Asia." *New York Times Book Review*, 29 August 1937, p. 3.

AL PURDY

Atwood, Margaret. "Love is Ambiguous . . . Sex Is a Bully." *Canadian Literature* No. 49 (Summer 1971): 71–75.

Bowering, George. *Al Purdy*. Toronto: Copp Clark, 1970.

Bukowski, Charles, and Al Purdy. *The Bukowski/Purdy Letters 1964–1974*. Ed. Seamus Cooney. Santa Barbara: Paget Press, 1983.

Doyle, Mike. "Proteus at Robin Lake." *Canadian Literature* No. 61 (Summer 1974): 7–23.

Geddes, Gary. "A. W. Purdy: An Interview." *Canadian Literature* No. 15 (Winter 1963): 66–72.

Lye, John. "The Road to Ameliasburg." *Dalhousie Review* 57 (1977–78): 242–53.

Marshall, Tom. "Space and Ancestors: Al Purdy." In *Harsh and Lovely Land*. Vancouver: University of British Columbia Press, 1979, pp. 89–98.

Woodcock, George. "On the Poetry of Al Purdy." In Purdy's *Selected Poems*. Toronto: McClelland & Stewart, 1972.

JAMES PURDY

Adams, Stephen D. *James Purdy*. London: Vision Press, 1976.

Baldanza, Frank. "Playing House for Keeps with James Purdy." *Contemporary Literature* 11 (1970): 488–510.

Burris, Shirley W. "The Emergency in Purdy's 'Daddy Wolf.'" *Renascence* 20 (1967): 94–98, 103.

Chupack, Henry. *James Purdy*. Boston: Twayne, 1975.

Kennard, Jean P. "James Purdy: Fidelity to Failure." In *Number and Nightmare: Forms of Fantasy in Contemporary Fiction*. Hamden, CT: Archon Books, 1975, pp. 82–100.

Pease, Donald. "False Starts and Wounded Allegories in the Abandoned House of Fiction of James Purdy." *Twentieth Century Literature* 28 (1982): 335–49.

Schott, Webster. "James Purdy: American Dreams." *Nation*, 23 March 1964, pp. 300–302.

Schwarzchild, Bettina. *The Not-Right House: Essays on James Purdy*. Columbia: University of Missouri Press, 1968.

Sitwell, Edith. Review of *Children Is All*. *New York Herald Tribune Books*, 18 November 1962, p. 6.

THOMAS PYNCHON

Cooper, Peter L. *Signs and Symptoms: Thomas Pynchon and the Contemporary World*. Berkeley: University of California Press, 1983.

Cowart, David. *Thomas Pynchon: The Art of Illusion*. Carbondale: Southern Illinois University Press, 1980.

Critique 18, No. 3 (1977). Special Thomas Pynchon issue.

Hite, Molly. *Ideas of Order in the Novels of Thomas Pynchon*. Columbus: Ohio State University Press, 1983.

Levine, George, and David Leverenz, eds. *Mindful Pleasures; Essays on Thomas Pynchon*. Boston: Little, Brown, 1976.

Mendelson, Edward. *Pynchon: A Collection of Critical Essays*. Englewood Cliffs, NJ: Prentice-Hall, 1978.

Pearce, Richard, ed. *Critical Articles on Thomas Pynchon*. Boston: G. K. Hall, 1981.

Schaub, Thomas H. *Pynchon: The Voice of Ambiguity*. Urbana: University of Illinois Press, 1981.

Scotto, Robert M. *Three Contemporary Novelists: An Annotated Bibliography of Works by and about John Hawkes, Joseph Heller, and Thomas Pynchon*. New York: Garland, 1977.

Siegel, Mark. *Creative Paranoia in* Gravity's Rainbow. Port Washington, NY: Kennikat Press, 1978.

Slade, Joseph. *Thomas Pynchon*. New York: Warner Books, 1974.

Stark, John O. *Pynchon's Fictions: Thomas Pynchon and the Literature of Information*. Athens: Ohio University Press, 1980.

Twentieth Century Literature 21, No. 2 (1975). Special Thomas Pynchon issue.

AYN RAND

Donegan, Patricia. "A Point of View." *Commonweal*, 8 November 1957, pp. 155–56.

Hicks, Granville. "A Parable of Buried Talents." *New York Times Book Review*, 13 October 1957, pp. 13–14.

Kobler, John. "The Curious Cult of Ayn Rand." *Saturday Evening Post*, 11 November 1961, pp. 98–101.

McGann, Kevin. "Ayn Rand in the Stockyard of the Spirit." In *The Modern American Novel and the Movies*, ed. Gerald Peary and Roger Shatzkin. New York: Frederick Ungar, 1978, pp. 325–35.

Sayre, Nora. "The Cult of Ayn Rand." *New Statesman*, 11 March 1966, p. 332.

JOHN CROWE RANSOM

Buffington, Robert. *The Equilibrist: A Study of John Crowe Ransom's Poems, 1916–1963*. Nashville: Vanderbilt University Press, 1967.

Jarrell, Randall. "John Ransom's Poetry." *Sewanee Review* 58 (1948): 378–90.

Koch, Vivienne. "The Achievement of John Crowe Ransom." *Sewanee Review* 58 (1950): 227–61.

Magner, James E., Jr. *John Crowe Ransom: Critical Principles and Preoccupations*. The Hague: Mouton, 1971.

Stewart, John L. *John Crowe Ransom*. Minneapolis: University of Minnesota Press, 1962.

Warren, Robert Penn. "John Crowe Ransom: A Study in Irony." *Virginia Quarterly Review* 11 (1935): 93–112.

Young, Thomas Daniel. *Gentleman in a Dustcoat: A Biography of John Crowe Ransom*. Baton Rouge: Louisiana State University Press, 1976.

———. *John Crowe Ransom: An Annotated Bibliography*. New York: Garland, 1982.

MARJORIE KINNAN RAWLINGS

Bellman, Samuel I. *Marjorie Kinnan Rawlings*. Boston: Twayne, 1974.

———. "Marjorie Kinnan Rawlings' Existentialist Nightmare *The Yearling*." *Costerus* 9 (1973): 9–18.

Bigelow, Gordon E. *Frontier Eden: The Literary Career of Marjorie Kinnan Rawlings*. Gainesville: The University of Florida Press, 1966.

Cech, John. "Marjorie Kinnan Rawlings' *The Secret River*: A Fairytale, a Place, a Life." *Southern Studies* 19 (1980): 29–38.

JOHN RECHY

Giles, James. "Religious Alienation and 'Homosexual Consciousness' in *City of Night* and *Go Tell It on the Mountain*." *College English* 36 (1974): 369–80.

Rechy, John. Interview by James Giles and Wanda Giles. *Chicago Review* 25 (1973): 19–31.

ISHMAEL REED

Bush, Ronald E. "Werewolf of the Wild West: On a Novel by Ishmael Reed." *Black World* 23 (January 1974): 51–52, 64–66.

Crouch, Stanley. "The HooDoo Wrath of Ishmael Reed." *Village Voice*, 22 January 1979, p. 75.

Fabre, Michel. "Postmodernist Rhetoric in Ishmael Reed's *Yellow-Back Radio Broke-Down*." In *The Afro-American Novel since 1960*, ed. Peter Bruck and Wolfgang Karrer. Amsterdam: B. R. Grüner, 1982, pp. 167–88.

Ford, Nick Aaron. "A Note on Ishmael Reed: Revisionary Novelist." *Studies in the Novel* 3 (1971): 216–18.

Hicks, Jack. "A One-Man Heathen Horde." *Nation*, 11 March 1978, p. 277.

Schmitz, Neil. "Neo-HooDoo: The Experimental Fiction of Ishmael Reed." *Twentieth Century Literature* 20 (1974): 126–40.

Settle, Elizabeth A., and Thomas A. Settle. *Ishmael Reed: A Primary and Secondary Bibliography*. Boston: G. K. Hall, 1982.

KENNETH REXROTH

Ciardi, John. "One for Rexroth." In *In Fact*. New Brunswick, NJ: Rutgers University Press, 1962, p. 54.

Foster, Richard. "With Great Passion, a Kind of Person." *Hudson Review* 13 (1960): 149–54.

Lipton, Lawrence. "Notes toward an Understanding of Kenneth Rexroth with Special Attention to 'The Homestead Called Damascus.'" *Quarterly Review of Literature* 9, No. 2 (1957): 37–46.

———. "The Poetry of Kenneth Rexroth." *Poetry* 90 (1957): 168–80.

Podhoretz, Norman. "A Howl of Protest in San Francisco." *New Republic*, 16 September 1957, p. 20.

Stock, Robert. "The Hazards of Art." *Nation*, 24 March 1969, p. 378.

Unterecker, John. "Calling the Heart to Order." *New York Times Book Review*, 23 July 1967, p. 8.

Williams, William Carlos. "Two New Books by Kenneth Rexroth." *Poetry* 90 (1957): 180–90.

ELMER RICE

Durham, Frank. *Elmer Rice*. New York: Twayne, 1970.

Hogan, Robert Goode. *The Independence of Elmer Rice*. Carbondale: Southern Illinois University Press, 1965.

Levin, Meyer. "Elmer Rice." *Theater Arts* 16 (1932): 54–62.

ADRIENNE RICH

Boyers, Robert. "On Adrienne Rich: Intelligence and Will." *Salmagundi* 22/23 (1973): 133–48.

Cooper, Jane Roberta, ed. *Reading Adrienne Rich: Reviews and Re-Visions, 1951–81*. Ann Arbor: University of Michigan Press, 1984.

Diaz-Diocaretz, Myriam. *The Transforming Power of Language: The Poetry of Adrienne Rich*. Utrecht: HES, 1984.

Feit Diehl, Joanne. "'Cartographies of Silence': Rich's *Common Language* and the Woman Poet." *Feminist Studies* 6 (1980): 530–46.

Friedman, Susan Stafford. "'I Go Where I Love': An Intertextual Study of H.D. and Adrienne Rich." *Signs* 9 (1983): 228–45.

Gelpi, Albert, and Barbara Charlesworth Gelpi. *Adrienne Rich's Poetry*. New York: W. W. Norton, 1975.

Gould, Jean. "Adrienne Rich." In *Modern American Woman Poets*. New York: Dodd, Mead, 1984, pp. 210–37.

Kalstone, David. "Adrienne Rich: Face to Face." In *Five Temperaments*. New York: Oxford University Press, 1977, pp. 129–69.

Mariani, Dacia. "On *Of Woman Born*," tr. Mary Jane Cicarello. *Signs* 4 (1979): 687–94.

Martin, Wendy. "Adrienne Rich: 'A Woman with a Certain Mission.'" In *An American Triptych: Anne Bradstreet, Emily Dickinson, Adrienne Rich*. Chapel Hill: University of North Carolina Press, 1984, pp. 167–234.

Morris, Adelaide. "'Saving the Skein': The Structure of *Diving into the Wreck*." *Contemporary Poetry* 3 (1978): 43–61.

Rich, Adrienne. "Blood, Bread and Poetry: The Location of the Poet." *Massachusetts Review* 24 (1983): 521–40.

Slowik, Mary. "The Friction of the Mind: The Early Poetry of Adrienne Rich." *Massachusetts Review* 25 (1984): 142–60.

Speigelman, Willard. "*Voice of the Survivor*: The Poetry of Adrienne Rich." *Southeast Review* 6 (1975): 370–88.

MORDECAI RICHLER

Davidson, Arnold E. *Mordecai Richler*. New York: Frederick Ungar, 1983.

Dooley, D. J. "Mordecai Richler and Duddy Kravitz: A Moral Apprenticeship?" In *Moral Vision in the Canadian Novel*. Toronto: Clark, Irwin, 1979, pp. 93–107.

McSweeney, Kerry. "Revaluing Mordecai Richler." *Studies in Canadian Literature* No. 4 (1979): 120–31.

Moss, John. "Strange Bedfellows: Atwood and Richler." In *Sex and Violence in the Canadian Novel: The Ancestral Present*. Toronto: McClelland & Stewart, 1977, pp. 123–46.

Sheps, G. David, ed. *Mordecai Richler*. Toronto: McGraw-Hill Ryerson, 1971.

CONRAD RICHTER

Barnes, Robert J. *Conrad Richter*. Austin, TX: Steck-Vaughn, 1968.

Flanagan, John T. "Conrad Richter: Romancer of the Southwest." *Southwest Review* 43 (1958): 189–96.

Gaston, Edwin W., Jr. *Conrad Richter*. New York: Twayne, 1965.

LaHood, Marvin J. *Conrad Richter's America*. The Hague: Mouton, 1975.

———. "Richter's Early America." *University Review* 30 (1964): 311–16.

Meldrum, Barbara. "Conrad Richter's Southwestern Ladies." In *Women, Women Writers, and the West*, ed. L. L. Lee and Merrill Lewis. Troy, NY: Whitston, 1979, pp. 119–29.

LAURA RIDING

Adams, Barbara. "Laura Riding's Poems: A Double Ripeness." *Modern Poetry Studies* 11 (1982): 189–95.

Auster, Paul. "The Return of Laura Riding." *New York Review of Books*, 7 August 1975, pp. 36–38.

Clark, Alan. "The One Story: Laura (Riding) Jackson, *The Telling*, and Before." *Stand* 15 (1973): 32–37.

[Davie, Donald.] "An Ambition Beyond Poetry." *Times Literary Supplement*, 9 February 1973, pp. 151–52.

Fuller, Roy. "The White Goddess." *Review* 23 (September–November 1970): 3–9.

Raiziss, Sonia. "An Appreciation." *Chelsea* 12 (September 1962): 28–31.

Symons, Julian. "Out of Time and into Poetry." *Times Literary Supplement*, 18 July 1980, pp. 795–96.

Wexler, Joyce Piell. *Laura Riding: A Bibliography*. New York: Garland, 1981.

ELIZABETH MADOX ROBERTS

Campbell, Harry Modean, and Ruel E. Foster. *Elizabeth Madox Roberts, American Novelist*. Norman: University of Oklahoma Press, 1956.

Genovese, Kathryn. "Time, Nature and Character in Elizabeth Madox Roberts's *The Time of Man*." *Adena* 1 (1976): 33–39.

McDowell, Frederick P. W. *Elizabeth Madox Roberts*. New York: Twayne, 1963.

EDWIN ARLINGTON ROBINSON

Barnard, Ellsworth. *Edwin Arlington Robinson: A Critical Study*. New York: Macmillan, 1952.

———, ed. *Edwin Arlington Robinson: Centenary Essays*. Athens: University of Georgia Press, 1969.

Brown, Rollo Walter. *Next Door to a Poet*. New York: D. Appleton-Century, 1937.

Cary, Richard. *Early Reception of Edwin Arlington Robinson: The First Twenty Years*. Waterville, ME: Colby College Press, 1974.

Coxe, Louis. *Edwin Arlington Robinson: The Life of Poetry*. New York: Pegasus, 1969.

Franchere, Hoyt C. *Edwin Arlington Robinson*. New York: Twayne, 1968.

Fussell, Edwin S. *Edwin Arlington Robinson: The Literary Background of a Traditional Poet*. Berkeley: University of California Press, 1954.

Hagedorn, Hermann. *Edwin Arlington Robinson: A Biography*. New York: Macmillan, 1938.

Hogan, Charles Beecher. *A Bibliography of Edwin Arlington Robinson*. New Haven: Yale University Press, 1936.

Joyner, Nancy. *Edwin Arlington Robinson: A Reference Guide*. New York: Garland, 1978.

Neff, Emery. *Edwin Arlington Robinson*. New York: William Sloane Associates, 1948.

Redman, Ben Ray. *Edwin Arlington Robinson*. New York: Robert M. McBride, 1926.

Robinson, W. R. *Edwin Arlington Robinson: A Poetry of the Act*. Cleveland: Press of Western Reserve University, 1967.

Smith, Chard Powers. *Where the Light Falls: A Portrait of Edwin Arlington Robinson*. New York: Macmillan, 1965.

THEODORE ROETHKE

Blessing, Richard A. "Theodore Roethke's Sometimes Metaphysical Motion." *Texas Studies in Literature and Language* 14 (1973): 731–49.

Bowers, Neal. *Theodore Roethke: The Journey from I to Otherwise*. Columbia: University of Missouri Press, 1982.

Burke, Kenneth. "The Vegetal Radicalism of Theodore Roethke." *Sewanee Review* 58 (1950): 68–108.

Eberhart, Richard. "On Theodore Roethke's Poetry." *Southern Review* 1 (1965): 612–20.

McClatchy, J. D. "Sweating Light from a Stone: Identifying Theodore Roethke." *Modern Poetry Studies* 3 (1972): 1–24.

McMichael, James. "The Poetry of Theodore Roethke." *Southern Review* 5 (1969): 4–25.

Mazzaro, Jerome. "Theodore Roethke and the Failures of Language." *Modern Poetry Studies* 1 (1970): 73–96.

Meredith, William. "A Steady Stream of Correspondences: Theodore Roethke's Long Journey out of the Self." *Shenandoah* 16 (1964): 41–54.

Parini, Jay. *Theodore Roethke: An American Romantic*. Amherst: University of Massachusetts Press, 1979.

Seager, Allan. *The Glass House: The Life of Theodore Roethke*. New York: McGraw-Hill, 1968.

Sullivan, Rosemary. *Theodore Roethke: The Garden Master*. Seattle: University of Washington Press, 1975.

Williams, Harry. *"The Edge Is What I Have": Theodore Roethke and After*. Lewisburg, PA: Bucknell University Press, 1977.

WILL ROGERS

Brown, William R. *Imagemaker: Will Rogers and the American Dream*. Columbia: University of Missouri Press, 1970.

Clark, Blue. "The Literary Will Rogers." *Chronicles of Oklahoma* 57 (1979): 385–94.

Gibson, Arrell Morgan. *Will Rogers: A Centennial Tribute*. Oklahoma City: Oklahoma Historical Society, 1979.

Ketchum, Richard M. *Will Rogers: His Life and Times*. New York: American Heritage, 1973.

Tyson, Carl N. "'I'm Off to Coolidge's Follies': Will Rogers and the Presidential Nominations, 1924–1932." *Chronicles of Oklahoma* 54 (1976): 192–98.

Unsigned. "Will Rogers Takes to the Air." *New York Times Book Review*, 26 June 1927, p. 11.

PHILIP ROTH

Bettleheim, Bruno. "Portnoy Psychoanalyzed." *Midstream* 15 (June–July 1969): 3–10.

Deer, Irving, and Harriet Deer. "Philip Roth and the Crisis in American Fiction." *Minnesota Review* 6 (1966): 353–60.

Donaldson, Scott. "Philip Roth: The Meanings of *Letting Go*." *Contemporary Literature* 11 (1970): 21–35.

Friedman, Alan Warren. "The Jew's Complaint in Recent American Fiction: Beyond Exodus and Still in the Wilderness." *Southern Review* 8 (1972): 41–59.

Howe, Irving. "Philip Roth Reconsidered." *Commentary* 54 (December 1972): 69–77.

Israel, Charles M. "The Fractured Hero of Roth's *Goodbye, Columbus*." *Critique* 16, No. 2 (1974): 5–11.

Lee, Hermione. *Philip Roth*. London: Methuen, 1982.

McDaniel, John N. *The Fiction of Philip Roth*. Haddonfield, NJ: Haddonfield House, 1974.

Monaghan, David. "*The Great American Novel* and *My Life as a Man*: An Assessment of Philip Roth's Achievement." *International Fiction Review* 2 (1975): 113–20.

Podhoretz, Norman. "Laureate of the New Class." *Commentary* 54 (December 1972), 4, 7.

Quart, Barbara Koenig. "The Rapacity of One Nearly Buried Alive." *Massachusetts Review* 24 (1983): 590–608.

Raban, Jonathan. "The New Philip Roth." *Novel* 2 (1969): 153–63.

Sabiston, Elizabeth. "A New Fable for Critics: Philip Roth's *The Breast*." *International Fiction Review* 2 (1975): 27–34.

Schechner, Mark. "Philip Roth." *Partisan Review* 41 (1974): 410–27.

Wolff, Geoffrey. "Beyond Portnoy." *Newsweek*, 3 August 1970, pp. 66–67.

JEROME ROTHENBERG

Power, Kevin. "*Poland/1931*: Pack Up Your Troubles in Your Troubles in Your Old Kit Bag and Smile, Smile, Smile, from Diaspora to Galut." *Boundary 2* 3 (1975): 683–705.

Rothenberg, Jerome. "The Thwarting of Ends: An Interview." In *Prefaces and Other Writings*. New York: New Directions, 1981, pp. 219–24.

MURIEL RUKEYSER

Adkins, Joan F. "The Esthetics of Science: Muriel Rukeyser's 'Waterlily Fire.'" *Contemporary Poetry* 1, No. 2 (1973): 23–27.

Barber, David S. "Finding Her Voice: Muriel Rukeyser's Poetic Development." *Modern Poetry Studies* 11 (1982): 127–38.

Terris, Virginia R. "Muriel Rukeyser: A Retrospective." *American Poetry Review* 3 (May–June 1974): 10–15.

JANE RULE

Hay, Linda MacKinley. "Dying to be Born." *Canadian Forum* 52 (1972): 59.

Niemi, Judith. "Jane Rule and the Reviewers." *Margins* 8 (1975): 34–37.

Rule, Jane. *Lesbian Images*. Garden City, NY: Doubleday, 1975.

Sonthoff, Helen. "Celebration: Jane Rule's Fiction." *Canadian Fiction Magazine* 23 (1976): 121–38.

Zimmerman, Bonnie. "Beyond Coming Out: New Lesbian Novels." *Ms.*, June 1985, pp. 65–66.

JOANNA RUSS

Delany, Samuel R. "Russ." In *Starboard Wine*. Elizabethtown, NY: Dragon Press, 1984, pp. 101–28.

DuPlessis, Rachel Blau. "The Feminist Apologues of Lessing, Piercy, and Russ." *Frontiers* 4 (Spring 1979): 1–8.

Feeley, Gregory. Review of *The Adventures of Alyx* and *The Zanzibar Cat*. *Foundation* No. 30 (March 1984): 72–74.

Silverberg, Robert. "Introduction" to *And Chaos Died*. Boston: Gregg Press, 1978, pp. v–xi.

Spector, Judith A. "Dr. Jekyll and Mrs. Hyde: Gender-Related Conflict in the Science Fiction of Joanna Russ." *Extrapolation* 24 (1983): 370–79.

J. R. SALAMANCA

Maclean, Alisdair. Review of *Embarkation*. *Times Literary Supplement*, 22 November 1974, p. 1308.

Weeks, Edward. Review of *A Sea Change*. *Atlantic* 225 (February 1970): 118–19.

Unsigned. Review of *A Sea Change*. *New Yorker*, 15 November 1969, pp. 236–38.

J. D. SALINGER

Alsen, Eberhard. *Salinger's Glass Stories as a Composite Novel*. Troy, N.Y.: Whitson, 1983.

Bryan, James. "The Psychological Structure of *The Catcher in the Rye*." *PMLA* 89 (1974): 1065–74.

Burke, Brother Fidelian. "Salinger's 'Esmé': Some Matters of Balance." *Modern Fiction Studies* 12 (1966): 341–47.

Cotter, James Finn. "Religious Symbols in Salinger's Shorter Fiction." *Studies in Short Fiction* 15 (1978): 121–32.

Davison, Richard Allan. "Salinger Criticism and 'The Laughing Man': A Case of Arrested Development." *Studies in Short Fiction* 18 (1981): 1–15.

Edwards, Duane. "Holden Caulfield: 'Don't Ever Tell Anybody Anything.'" *ELH* 44 (1977): 556–67.

Goldstein, Bernice and Sanford Goldstein. "Ego and 'Hapworth 16, 1924.'" *Renascence* 24 (1972): 159–67.

Grunwald, Henry Anatole, ed. *Salinger: A Critical and Personal Portrait*. New York: Harper, 1962.

Hamilton, Kenneth. "J. D. Salinger's Happy Family." *Queen's Quarterly* 71 (1964): 176–87.

Kinny, Arthur F. "J. D. Salinger and the Search for Love." *Texas Studies in Literature and Language* 5 (1963–64): 111–26.

Metcalf, Frank. "The Suicide of Salinger's Seymour Glass." *Studies in Short Fiction* 9 (1972): 243–46.

Mizener, Arthur. "Defining 'the Good American.'" *Listener*, 16 August 1962, pp. 241–42.

Ohmann, Carol, and Richard Ohmann. "Reviewers, Critics, and *The Catcher in the Rye*." *Critical Inquiry* 3 (1976): 15–37.

Rosen, Gerald. "A Retrospective Look at *The Catcher in the Rye*." *American Quarterly* 29 (1977): 547–62.

Trowbridge, Clinton W. "The Symbolic Structure of *The Catcher in the Rye*." *Sewanee Review* 54 (1966): 681–93.

EDGAR SALTUS

Colles, Ramsey. "A Publicist: Edgar Saltus." *Westminster Review* 162 (1904): 464–74.

McKintrick, Eric. "Edgar Saltus of the Obsolete." *American Quarterly* 3 (1951): 22–35.

Madigan, Michael John. "The Saltus Family." Ph.D. diss.: University of Michigan, 1973.

Peckham, Morse. "Edgar Saltus and the Heroic Decadence." *Tulane Studies in English* 23 (1978): 61–69.

Saltus, Marie. *Edgar Saltus the Man*. Chicago: Pascal Covici, 1925.

Van Doren, Carl. "The Roving Critic." *Nation*, 11 January 1922, p. 45.

Van Vechten, Carl. "Edgar Saltus." In *Excavations: A Book of Advocacies*. New York: Alfred A. Knopf, 1926.

CARL SANDBURG

Durnell, Hazel. *The America of Carl Sandburg*. Washington, DC: University Press of Washington, D.C., 1965.

Golden, Harry. *Carl Sandburg*. Cleveland: World Publishing Co., 1961.

Krim, Seymour. "A Voice of America." *Commonweal*, 17 July 1955, pp. 283–84.

Sherwood, Robert E. "The Lincoln of Carl Sandburg." *New York Times Book Review*, 3 December 1939, pp. 1, 14.

Trilling, Diana. "Fiction in Review." *Nation*, 30 October 1948, pp. 500–501.

Van Doren, Mark. "Carl Sandburg." *Nation*, 31 October 1928, pp. 456–57.

Williams, William Carlos. "Carl Sandburg's Complete Poems." *Poetry* 78 (1951): 345–51.

MARI SANDOZ

Lowe, David. "A Meeting with Mari Sandoz." *Prairie Schooner* 42 (1968): 21–26.

Nicoll, Bruce H. "Mari Sandoz: Nebraska Loner." *American West* 2 (1965): 32–36.

Switzer, Dorothy Nott. "Mari Sandoz's Lincoln Years." *Prairie Schooner* 45 (1971): 107–15.

GEORGE SANTAYANA

Ames, Van Meter. *Proust and Santayana: The Aesthetic Way of Life*. Chicago: Willett, Clark, 1937.

Arnett, Willard E. *Santayana and the Sense of Beauty*. Bloomington: Indiana University Press, 1955.

Baker, Carlos. "The Philosopher as Critic." *Saturday Review*, 8 December 1956, pp. 19–20.

Bridges, Robert. "George Santayana." *Dial* 69 (1920): 534–35.

Cory, Daniel. *Santayana: The Later Years*. New York: George Brazilier, 1963.

Hughson, Lois. *Thresholds of Reality: George Santayana and Modernist Poetics*. Port Washington, NY: Kennikat Press, 1977.

Phelps, William Lyon. "Harvard of the Nineties to America of Today." *New York Times Book Review*, 22 August 1920, pp. 8–9.

Priestley, J. B. "Mr. George Santayana." In *Figures in Modern Literature*. London: John Lane/The Bodley Head, 1924, pp. 165–87.

Singer, Irving. *Santayana's Aesthetics: A Critical Introduction*. Cambridge, MA: Harvard University Press, 1957.

Sprigge, Timothy L. S. *Santayana: An Examination of His Philosophy*. London: Routledge & Kegan Paul, 1974.

WILLIAM SAROYAN

Balakian, Nona. "So Many Saroyans." *New Republic*, 7 August 1950, pp. 19–20.

Burgum, Edwin Berry. "The Lonesome Young Man on the Flying Trapeze." In *The Novel and the World's Dilemma*. New York: Oxford University Press, 1947, pp. 260–71.

Fadiman, Clifton. "Novels, Novels, Novels." *New Yorker*, 27 February 1943, p. 63.

Gassner, John. "Saroyan: *The Time of Your Life*." In *The Theatre in Our Time*. New York: Crown, 1954.

Lee, Lawrence, and Barry Gifford. *Saroyan: A Biography*. New York: Harper & Row, 1984.

Remenyi, Joseph. "William Saroyan: A Portrait." *College English* 6 (1944): 92–99.

Rhoads, Kenneth W. "Joe as Christ-Type in Saroyan's *The Time of Your Life*." *Essays in Literature* 3 (1976): 227–43.

Schulberg, Budd. "William Saroyan: Ease and Unease on the Flying Trapeze." In *The Four Seasons of Success*. Garden City, NY: Doubleday, 1972.

Wilson, Edmund. "William Saroyan and His Darling Old Providence." In *Classics and Commercials*. New York: Farrar, Straus & Giroux, 1950, pp. 327–30.

DELMORE SCHWARTZ

Atlas, James. *Delmore Schwartz: The Life of an American Poet*. New York: Farrar, Straus, & Giroux, 1977.

Blackmur, R. P. "Commentary by Ghosts." *Kenyon Review* 5 (1943): 467–71.

Halio, Jay L. "Delmore Schwartz's Felt Abstractions." *Southern Review* 1 (1965): 802–19.

Leibowitz, Herbert. Review of *The Selected Essays of Delmore Schwartz*. *New York Times Book Review*, 17 January 1971, pp. 3, 33.

Lowell, Robert. "To Delmore Schwartz." In *Life Studies*. New York: Farrar, Straus & Cudahy, 1959, pp. 53–54.

Macdonald, Dwight. "Delmore Schwartz (1913–1966)." *New York Review of Books*, 8 September 1966, pp. 14–16.

Politzer, Heinz. "The Two Worlds of Delmore Schwartz: Lucifer in Brooklyn." *Commentary* 10 (1950): 561–68.

Rahv, Philip. "Delmore Schwartz: The Paradox of Precocity." *New York Review of Books*, 20 May 1971, pp. 19–22.

Valenti, Lila Lee. "The Apprenticeship of Delmore Schwartz." *Twentieth Century Literature* 20 (1974): 201–16.

DUNCAN CAMPBELL SCOTT

Dragland, Stanley, ed. *Duncan Campbell Scott: A Book of Criticism*. Ottawa: Tecumseh Press, 1974.

Lynch, Gerald. "An Endless Flow: D. C. Scott's Indian Poems." *Studies in Canadian Literature* 7 (1982): 27–54.

Stich, K. P., ed. *The Duncan Campbell Scott Symposium*. Ottawa: University of Ottawa Press, 1980.

Waterston, Elizabeth. "The Missing Face: Five Short Stories of Duncan Campbell Scott." *Studies in Canadian Literature* 1 (1976): 223–29.

EVELYN SCOTT

Fadiman, Clifton. "Eros in America." *Nation*, 11 November 1931, pp. 521–22.

Hutchinson, Percy. Review of *The Wave*. *New York Times Book Review*, 30 June 1929, pp. 1, 19.

Lewis, Sinclair. Review of *The Narrow House*. *New York Times Book Review*, 13 March 1921, p. 18.

Lovett, Robert Morss. Review of *Escapade*. *New Republic*, 22 August 1923, pp. 363–64.

Nevins, Allan. "Cape-Smith's First Book." *Saturday Review of Literature*, 29 June 1929, p. 1142.

Parsons, Alice Beal. "The Saint and Love." *Nation*, 8 July 1925, p. 76.

ALAN SEEGER

Archer, William. "Introduction" to *Poems* by Alan Seeger. New York: Scribner's, 1916, pp. ix–xlvi.

Bryant, Arthur. "Two American Poets of the Twentieth Century." In *The American Ideal*. London: Longmans, 1936, pp. 234–51.

Kinne, B. I. "Emotionalism and War." *Dial*, 13 September 1917, pp. 206–7.

Werstein, Irving. *Sound No Trumpet: The Life and Death of Alan Seeger*. New York: Thomas W. Crowell, 1967.

ROBERT W. SERVICE

Bucco, Martin. "Folk Poetry of Robert W. Service." *Alaska Review* 2 (Fall 1965): 16–26.

Hirsch, Edward. "A Structural Analysis of Robert Service's Yukon Ballads." *Southern Folklore Quarterly* 40 (1976): 125–40.

Klinck, Carl F. *Robert Service: A Biography*. New York: Dodd, Mead, 1976.

Whatley, W. A. "Kipling Influence in the Verse of Robert Service." *Texas Review* 6 (July 1921): 299–308.

ANNE SEXTON

George, Diana Hume. "Anne Sexton's Suicide Poems." *Journal of Popular Culture* 18 (Fall 1984): 17–31.

Gould, Jean. "Anne Sexton—Maxine Kumin." In *Modern American Women Poets*. New York: Dodd, Mead, 1984, pp. 151–75.

Johnson, Rosemary. "The Woman of Private (But Published) Hungers." *Parnassus* 8 (Fall–Winter 1979): 92–107.

McClatchy, J. D., ed. *Anne Sexton: The Artist and Her Critics*. Bloomington: Indiana University Press, 1978.

Markey, Janice. *A New Tradition?: The Poetry of Sylvia Plath, Anne Sexton, and Adrienne Rich*. New York: P. Lang, 1985.

Middlebrook, Diane Wood. "Housewife into Poet: The Apprenticeship of Anne Sexton." *New England Quarterly* 56 (1983): 483–503.

Northouse, Cameron, and Thomas P. Walsh. *Sylvia Plath and Anne Sexton: A Reference Guide*. Boston: G. K. Hall, 1974.

Ostriker, Alicia. "'What Are Patterns For?': Anger and Polarization in Women's Poetry." *Feminist Studies* 10 (1984): 485–503.

Sexton, Anne. *No Evil Star: Selected Essays, Interviews, and Prose*. Edited by Steven E. Colburn. Ann Arbor: University of Michigan Press, 1985.

Sexton, Linda Gray, and Lois Ames, eds. *Anne Sexton: A Self-Portrait in Letters*. Boston: Houghton Mifflin, 1977.

Shurr, William H. "Anne Sexton's *Love Poems*: The Genre and the Differences." *Modern Poetry Studies* 10 (1980): 58–68.

NTOZAKE SHANGE

Blackwell, Henry. "An Interview with Ntozake Shange." *Black American Literature Forum* 13 (1979): 134–38.

Latour, Martine. "Ntozake Shange: Driven Poet/Playwright." *Mademoiselle*, September 1976, pp. 182, 226.

Peters, Erskine. "Some Tragic Propensities of Ourselves: The Occasion of Ntozake Shange's *For Colored Girls Who Have Considered Suicide/When the Rainbow Is Enuf*." *Journal of Ethnic Studies* 6 (1978): 79–85.

Staples, Robert. "The Myth of Black Macho: A Response to Angry Black Feminists." *Black Scholar* 10 (March–April 1979): 24–32.

Vallely, Jean. "Trying to Be Nice." *Time*, 19 July 1976, pp. 44–45.

Unsigned. "Ntozake Shange." *New Yorker*, 2 August 1976, pp. 17–19.

KARL SHAPIRO

Cowley, Malcolm. "A Lively and Deadly Wit." *Poetry* 61 (1943): 620–22.

Fitts, Dudley. "Mr. Shapiro's Ars Poetica." *Poetry* 68 (1946): 39–44.

Jackson, Richard. "Signing the Syllables: The Poetry of Karl Shapiro." *South Carolina Review* 14 (Fall 1981): 109–20.

Kazin, Alfred. "The Poet against the English Department." *Reporter*, 9 June 1960, pp. 44–47.

Kohler, Dayton. "Karl Shapiro: Poet in Uniform." *College English* 7 (1946): 243–49.

Malkoff, Karl. "The Self in the Modern World: Karl Shapiro's Jewish Poems." In *Contemporary American-Jewish Literature*, ed. Irving Malin. Bloomington: Indiana University Press, 1973, pp. 213–28.

Richman, Robert. "Alchemy or Poetry." *Sewanee Review* 54 (1946): 684–90.

IRWIN SHAW

Eisinger, Chester E. "Irwin Shaw: The Popular Ideas of the Old Liberalism." In *Fiction of the Forties*. Chicago: University of Chicago Press, 1963, pp. 106–13.

Evans, Bergen. "Irwin Shaw." *English Journal* 50 (1951): 485–91.

Fiedler, Leslie A. "Irwin Shaw: Adultery, the Last Politics." *Commentary* 22 (1956): 71–74.

Giles, James R. *Irwin Shaw*. Boston: Twayne, 1983.

Kazin, Alfred. "Introduction" to *Short Stories: Five Decades*. New York: Delacorte Press, 1984, pp. xiii–xix.

Peden, William. "Best of Irwin Shaw." *Saturday Review*, 18 November 1950, pp. 27–28.

Trilling, Lionel. "Some Are Gentle, Some Are Not." *Saturday Review*, 9 June 1951, pp. 8–9.

WILFRID SHEED

Balliett, Whitney. "The Way It Really Was." *New Yorker*, 21 December 1963, pp. 94–95.

Connell, Evan S., Jr. "Sinister Embraces." *New York Times Book Review*, 8 September 1968, pp. 4–5.

Hughes, Riley. Review of *A Middle Class Education*. *Catholic World* 192 (1960–61): 309.

Lodge, David. Review of *Max Jamison*. *Commonweal*, 8 May 1970, p. 197.

Mo, Timothy. "Sick Fantasy." *New Statesman*, 18 January 1974, p. 86.

Moynahan, Julian. "Anglo-American Attitudes." *New York Times Book Review*, 15 January 1978, pp. 1, 19.

SAM SHEPARD

Auerbach, Doris. *Sam Shepard, Arthur Kopit, and the Off-Broadway Theater*. Boston: Twayne, 1982.

Chubb, Kenneth. "Fruitful Difficulties of Directing Sam Shepard." *Theatre Quarterly*, August 1974, pp. 17–25.

Falk, Florence. "The Role of Performance in Sam Shepard's Plays." *Theatre Journal* 33 (1981): 182–98.

Gilman, Richard. "Introduction" to *Seven Plays* by Sam Shepard. New York: Bantam, 1981, pp. i–xxv.

Oumano, Ellen. *Sam Shepard: The Life and Work of an American Dreamer*. New York: St. Martin's Press, 1986.

Wetzsteon, Ross. "Introduction" to *Fool for Love and Other Plays* by Sam Shepard. New York: Bantam, 1984, pp. 1–15.

ROBERT E. SHERWOOD

Behrman, S. N. "Old Monotonous." *New Yorker*, 1 June 1940, pp. 33–40; 8 June 1940, pp. 24–31.

Brown, John Mason. *The Ordeal of a Playwright: Robert E. Sherwood and the Challenge of War*. Edited by Norman Cousins. New York: Harper & Row, 1970.

_____. *The Worlds of Robert E. Sherwood: Mirror to His Times 1896–1939.* New York: Harper & Row, 1965.

Gould, Jean. "Robert Sherwood." In *Modern American Playwrights.* New York: Dodd, Mead, 1966, pp. 99–117.

Meserve, Walter J. *Robert E. Sherwood: Reluctant Moralist.* New York: Pegasus, 1970.

Shuman, R. Baird. *Robert E. Sherwood.* New York: Twayne, 1964.

CHARLES SIMIC

Jackson, Richard. "Charles Simic and Mark Strand: The Presence of Absence." *Contemporary Poetry* 21 (Winter 1980): 136–45.

Mitgutsch, Waltraud. "Metaphysical Gaps and Negation in the Poetry of W. S. Merwin, Mark Strand, and Charles Simic." In *On Poets and Poetry.* Salzburg: Institut für Anglistik & Amerikanistik, 1980, pp. 3–30.

Seluzicki, Charles. "Charles Simic: A Bibliographical Checklist." *American Book Collector* 3, No. 4 (1981): 34–39.

Simic, Charles. "The Partial Explanation." In *Fifty Contemporary Poets*, ed. Alberta T. Turner. New York: David McKay, 1977, pp. 278–81.

_____. *The Uncertain Certainty: Interviews, Essays, and Notes on Poetry.* Ann Arbor: University of Michigan Press, 1985.

Vendler, Helen. "Ten Poets." In *Part of Nature, Part of Us: Modern American Poets.* Cambridge, MA: Harvard University Press, 1980, pp. 357–59.

LOUIS SIMPSON

Bly, Robert [as "Crunk"]. "The Work of Louis Simpson." *Fifties* No. 1 (1958): 22–25.

Gray, Yohma. "The Poetry of Louis Simpson." *Tri-Quarterly* 5 (Spring 1963): 33–39.

Hymes, Dell. "Louis Simpson's 'The Deserted Boy.'" *Poetics* 5 (June 1976): 119–55.

Lensing, George S., and Ronald Moran. "Louis Simpson." In *Four Poets and the Emotive Imagination: Robert Bly, James Wright, Louis Simpson, and William Stafford.* Baton Rouge: Louisiana State University Press, 1976, pp. 133–75.

Locke, Duane. "New Directions in Poetry: The Work of Louis Simpson." *dust* 1 (Fall 1964): 67–69.

Moran, Ronald. *Louis Simpson.* New York: Twayne, 1972.

UPTON SINCLAIR

Becker, George J. "Upton Sinclair: Quixote in a Flivver." *College English* 21 (1959): 133–40.

Blinderman, Abraham, ed. *Critics on Upton Sinclair.* Coral Gables: University of Miami Press, 1975.

Bloodworth, William A., Jr. *Upton Sinclair.* Boston: Twayne, 1977.

Dell, Floyd. *Upton Sinclair: A Study in Social Protest.* New York: George H. Doran, 1927.

Harris, Leon. *Upton Sinclair: American Rebel.* New York: Crowell, 1975.

Sinclair, Upton. *The Autobiography of Upton Sinclair.* New York: Harcourt, 1962.

Taylor, Alva W. "Sacco-Vanzetti Fictionalized." *Christian Century* 46 (1929): 359–60.

Yoder, Jon A. *Upton Sinclair.* New York: Frederick Ungar, 1975.

ISAAC BASHEVIS SINGER

Alexander, Edward. *Isaac Bashevis Singer.* Boston: Twayne, 1980.

Bucher, Irving H. *Isaac Bashevis Singer and the Eternal Past.* New York: New York University Press, 1969.

Fixler, Michael. "The Redeemers: Themes in the Fiction of Isaac Bashevis Singer." *Kenyon Review* 26 (1964): 371–86.

Jacobson, Dan. "The Problem of Isaac Bashevis Singer." *Commentary* 39 (February 1965): 48–52.

Malin, Irving. *Critical Views of Isaac Bashevis Singer.* New York: New York University Press, 1969.

Miller, David Neal. *Fear of Fiction: Narrative Strategies in the Works of Isaac Bashevis Singer.* Albany: State University of New York Press, 1985.

Rosenblatt, Paul, and Gene Koppel. *A Certain Bridge: Isaac Bashevis Singer on Literature and Life.* Tucson: University of Arizona Press, 1971.

Siegel, Ben. *Isaac Bashevis Singer.* Minneapolis: University of Minnesota Press, 1969.

Singer, Isaac Bashevis. *Love and Exile.* Garden City, NY: Doubleday, 1984.

_____, and Richard Burgin. *Conversations with Isaac Bashevis Singer.* Garden City, NY: Doubleday, 1985.

A. J. M. SMITH

Darling, Michael. "The Myth of Smith." *Essays on Canadian Writing* 20 (1981): 68–76.

Djwa, Sandra A. "A. J. M. Smith: Of Metaphysics and Dry Bones." *Studies in Canadian Literature* 3 (1978): 17–34.

Edel, Leon. "The Worldly Muse of A. J. M. Smith." *University of Toronto Quarterly* 47 (1978): 200–213.

Ferns, John. *A. J. M. Smith.* Boston: Twayne, 1979.

Mandel, Eli. "Masks of Criticism: A. J. M. Smith as Anthologist." *Canadian Poetry* No. 4 (Spring–Summer 1979): 17–28.

Warkentin, Germaine. "Criticism and the Whole Man." *Canadian Literature* No. 64 (Spring 1975): 83–91.

CLARK ASHTON SMITH

Behrends, Steve. "The Song of the Necromancer: 'Loss' in Clark Ashton Smith's Fiction." *Studies in Weird Fiction* 1 (1986): 3–13.

Chalker, Jack L., ed. *In Memoriam: Clark Ashton Smith.* Baltimore: Anthem, 1963.

Fryer, Donald Sidney. *Emperor of Dreams: A Clark Ashton Smith Bibliography.* West Kingston, RI: Donald M. Grant, 1978.

_____. *The Last of the Great Romantic Poets.* Albuquerque, NM: Silver Scarab Press, 1973.

Nyctalops No. 7 (August 1972). Special Clark Ashton Smith issue.

Rickard, Dennis. *The Fantastic Art of Clark Ashton Smith.* Baltimore: Mirage Press, 1973.

W. D. SNODGRASS

Carroll, Paul. "The Thoreau Complex amid the Solid Scholars." In *The Poem in Its Skin.* New York: Follett, 1968, pp. 174–87.

Dillon, David. "Toward Passionate Utterance: An Interview with W. D. Snodgrass." *Southwest Review* 60 (1975): 278–90.

Farrelly, David. "Heart's Fling: The Poetry of W. D. Snodgrass." *Perspective* 13 (1964): 185–99.

Gaston, David L. *W. D. Snodgrass.* Boston: Twayne, 1978.

_____. "W. D. Snodgrass and *The Führer Bunker*: An Interview." *Papers on Language and Literature* 13 (1977): 295–311, 401–12.

McClatchy, J. D. "W. D. Snodgrass: The Mild, Reflective Art." *Massachusetts Review* 16 (1975): 281–314.

Mazzaro, Jerome. "The Public Intimacy of W. D. Snodgrass." *Salmagundi* No. 19 (Spring 1972): 96–111.

White, William. *W. D. Snodgrass: A Bibliography.* Detroit: Wayne State University Library, 1960.

GARY SNYDER

Altieri, Charles. "Gary Snyder's *Turtle Island:* The Problem of Reconciling the Roles of Seer and Prophet." *Boundary 2* 4 (1976): 761–77.

Bly, Robert. "The Work of Gary Snyder." *Sixties,* Spring 1962, pp. 25–42.

Gitzen, Julian. "Gary Snyder and the Poetry of Compassion." *Critical Quarterly* 15 (1973): 341–57.

Kern, Robert. "Clearing the Ground: Gary Snyder and the Modernist Imperative." *Criticism* 19 (1977): 158–77.

McLean, William Scott, ed. *The Real Work: Interviews and Talks, 1964–1979.* New York: New Directions, 1980.

Molesworth, Charles. *Gary Snyder's Vision: Poetry and the Real Work.* Columbia: University of Missouri Press, 1983.

Rothberg, Abraham. "A Passage to More Than India: The Poetry of Gary Snyder." *Southwest Review* 61 (1976): 26–38.

SUSAN SONTAG

Bellamy, Joe David. "Susan Sontag." In *The New Fiction.* Urbana: University of Illinois Press, 1974, pp. 113–29.

Gass, William H. "A Different Kind of Art." *New York Times Book Review,* 18 December 1977, pp. 7, 30–31.

Gilman, Richard. "Susan Sontag and the Question of the New." *New Republic,* 3 May 1969, pp. 23–28.

Koch, Stephen. "On Susan Sontag." *TriQuarterly* 7 (Fall 1966): 153–60.

Nairn, Tom. "The New Sensibility." *New Statesman,* 24 March 1967, pp. 408–9.

Solotaroff, Theodore. "Interpreting Susan Sontag." In *The Red Hot Vacuum.* New York: Atheneum, 1970, pp. 261–68.

Wain, John. "Song of Myself, 1963." *New Republic,* 21 September 1963, pp. 26–30.

GILBERT SORRENTINO

Bruns, Gerald L. "A Short Defense of Plagiary." *Review of Contemporary Fiction* 1 (1981): 96–103.

Sorrentino, Gilbert. Interview by Dennis Barone. *Partisan Review* 48 (1981): 236–46.

Unsigned. Review of *Spendide-Hotel. Antioch Review* 34 (1975): 244–45.

JACK SPICER

Boundary 2 6 (Fall 1977). Special Jack Spicer issue.

Elman, Richard. Review of *The Collected Books of Jack Spicer. New York Times Book Review,* 23 November 1975, pp. 26, 28.

Finkelstein, Norman M. "Jack Spicer's Ghosts and the Gnosis of History." *Boundary 2* 9 (Winter 1981): 81–100.

Trimbur, John. Review of *One Night Stand and Other Poems. Western American Literature* 16 (1981): 226–27.

Vernon, John. "A Gathering of Poets." *Western Humanities Review* 30 (1976): 265–76.

JEAN STAFFORD

Avila, Wanda. *Jean Stafford: A Comprehensive Bibliography.* New York: Garland, 1983.

Burns, Stuart L. "Counterpoint in Jean Stafford's *The Mountain Lion." Critique* 9, No. 2 (1967): 20–32.

Hicks, Granville. "Mother of the Accursed." *Saturday Review,* 5 March 1966, pp. 33–34.

Leary, William G. "Through Caverns Measureless to Man: Jean Stafford's 'The Interior Castle.'" *Shenandoah* 34, No. 4 (1984): 79–95.

Mann, Jeanette W. "Toward New Archetypal Forms: *Boston Adventure." Studies in the Novel* 8 (1976): 291–303.

Trilling, Diana. "A New Talent." *Nation,* 30 September 1944, p. 383.

Walsh, Mary Ellen Williams. "The Young Girl in the West: Disenchantment in Jean Stafford's Short Fiction." In *Women and Western American Literature,* ed. Helen Winter Stauffer and Susan J. Rosowski. Troy, NY: Whitston, 1982, pp. 230–43.

WILLIAM STAFFORD

Bunge, Nancy. "William Stafford: An Interview." *American Poetry Review* 10 (November–December 1981): 8–11.

Holden, Jonathan. *To Mark the Turn: A Reading of William Stafford's Poetry.* Lawrence: University Press of Kansas, 1976.

Lauber, John. "World's Guest—William Stafford." *Iowa Review* 5, No. 2 (1974): 88–89.

Lensing, George S. "William Stafford, Mythmaker." *Modern Poetry Studies* 6 (1975): 1–17.

Singh, Kirpal. "The Quiet Breath: An Essay on the Poetry of William Stafford." *Literary Criterion* 14, No. 4 (1979): 70–77.

WILBUR DANIEL STEELE

Elser, Frank B. "Oh, Yes . . . Wilbur Daniel Steele." *Bookman* (New York) 62 (February 1926): 691–94.

Finn, Judith Ann. "A Critical Study of the Novels of Wilbur Daniel Steele." Ph.D. diss.: Texas A & M University, 1974.

Graham, Gladys. "I Corinthians VIII:13." *Saturday Review of Literature,* 10 March 1928, p. 666.

Walker, Warren S. "'Never Anything That Fades . . .': Steele's Eleusinian Mysteries." *Studies in Short Fiction* 17 (1980): 127–32.

WALLACE STEGNER

Abrahams, William. "The Real Thing." *Atlantic* 227 (April 1971): 96–97.

Canzoneri, Robert. "Wallace Stegner: Trial by Existence." *Southern Review* 9 (1973): 796–827.

Hudson, Lois Phillips. "*The Big Rock Candy Mountain:* No Roots—and No Frontier." *South Dakota Review* 9 (1971): 3–13.

Lewis, Merrill, and Lorene Lewis. *Wallace Stegner.* Boise: Boise State College, 1972.

Robinson, Forrest G. "Wallace Stegner's Family Saga: From *The Big Rock Candy Mountain* to *Recapitulation." Western American Literature* 17 (1982): 101–16.

White, Robin and Ed McClanahan. "An Interview with Wallace Stegner." *Per/Se* 3 (Fall 1968): 28–34.

GERTRUDE STEIN

Brinnin, John Malcolm. *The Third Rose: Gertrude Stein and Her World.* Boston: Little, Brown, 1959.

Dubnick, Randa. *The Structure of Obscurity: Gertrude Stein, Language, and Cubism.* Urbana: University of Illinois Press, 1984.

Hobhouse, Janet. *Everybody Who Was Anybody: A Biography of Gertrude Stein.* New York: Putnam's, 1975.

Hume, Beverly. "Prolonged Banality: Time and Stein's *Three Lives." Notes on Modern American Literature* 8 (Autumn 1984): Item 13.

Moore, Marianne. "The Spare American Emotion." *Dial* 80 (1926): 153–56.

Neuman, S. C. *Gertrude Stein: Autobiography and the Problem of Narration.* Victoria, BC: University of Victoria Press, 1979.

Rogers, W. G. *Gertrude Stein Is Gertrude Stein Is Gertrude Stein: Her Life and Work.* New York: Thomas Y. Crowell, 1973.

Simon, Linda, ed. *Gertrude Stein: A Composite Portrait.* New York: Avon Books, 1974.

Stein, Gertrude. *A Primer for the Gradual Understanding of Gertrude Stein.* Edited by Robert Bartlett Haas. Los Angeles: Black Sparrow Press, 1971.

Steiner, Wendy. *Exact Resemblance to Exact Resemblance: The Literary Portraiture of Gertrude Stein.* New Haven: Yale University Press, 1978.

Stewart, Allegra. *Gertrude Stein and the Present.* Cambridge, MA: Harvard University Press, 1967.

Stimpson, Catharine R. "Gertrice/Altrude: Stein, Toklas, and the Paradox of the Happy Marriage." In *Mothering the Mind: Twelve Studies of Writers and Their Silent Partners,* ed. Ruth Perry and Martine Watson Brownley. New York: Holmes & Meier, 1984, pp. 123–39.

Toklas, Alice B. *What Is Remembered.* New York: Holt, Rinehart & Winston, 1963.

White, Ray Lewis. *Gertrude Stein and Alice B. Toklas: A Reference Guide.* Boston: G. K. Hall, 1984.

JOHN STEINBECK

Donoghue, Agnes McNeill. *A Casebook on* The Grapes of Wrath. New York: Thomas Y. Crowell, 1968.

Fontenrose, Joseph. *John Steinbeck: An Introduction and Interpretation.* New York: Holt, Rinehart & Winston, 1963.

French, Warren. *John Steinbeck.* New York: Twayne, 1961.

Hayashi, Tetsumaro. "Steinbeck's Women in *The Grapes of Wrath*: A New Perspective." *Kyushu American Literature* 18 (October 1977): 1–4.

Jones, Lawrence William. *John Steinbeck as Fabulist.* Muncie, IN: John Steinbeck Society of America, 1973.

Lisca, Peter. *The Wide World of John Steinbeck.* New Brunswick, NJ: Rutgers University Press, 1958.

_____, ed. The Grapes of Wrath: *Text and Criticism.* New York: Viking, 1972.

Marks, Lester Jay. *Thematic Design in the Novels of John Steinbeck.* The Hague: Mouton, 1969.

Moore, Harry T. *The Novels of John Steinbeck: A First Critical Study.* Chicago: Normandie House, 1939.

Pratt, John Clark. *John Steinbeck: A Critical Essay.* Grand Rapids, MI: William B. Eerdmans, 1970.

Tedlock, E. W., Jr., and C. V. Wicker, ed. *Steinbeck and His Critics: A Record of Twenty-five Years.* Albuquerque: University of New Mexico Press, 1957.

Watt, F. W. *John Steinbeck.* Edinburgh: Oliver and Boyd, 1962.

Yano, Shigeharu. "*The Grapes of Wrath*: The Symbol of Eternity." *Reitaku University Quarterly* 23 (July 1977): 35–37.

GEORGE STERLING

Benediktsson, Thomas E. *George Sterling.* Boston: Twayne, 1980.

Bennett, Raine Edward. "Don Passe." *Literary Review* 15 (1971–72): 133–47.

de Ford, Miriam Allen. "Laureate of Bohemia: George Sterling." In *They Were San Franciscans.* Caldwell, ID: Caxton Printers, 1941, pp. 295–321.

Fryer, Donald Sidney. "Hesperian Laureate: George Sterling, 1889–1926." *Romantist* 1 (1977): 11–27.

Longton, Ray C. *Three Writers of the Far West: A Reference Guide.* Boston: G. K. Hall, 1980.

Noel, Joseph. *Footloose in Arcadia: A Personal Record of Jack London, George Sterling, Ambrose Bierce.* New York: Carrick & Svens, 1940.

Stevenson, Lionel. "George Sterling's Place in Modern Poetry." *University of California Chronicle* 31 (1929): 404–21.

WALLACE STEVENS

Ackerman, R. D. "Believing in a Fiction: Wallace Stevens at the Limits of Phenomenology." *Philosophy and Literature* 3 (1979): 79–90.

Baird, James. *The Dome and the Rock: Structure in the Poetry of Wallace Stevens.* Baltimore: Johns Hopkins Press, 1968.

Brown, Merle E. *Wallace Stevens: The Poem as Act.* Detroit: Wayne State University Press, 1970.

Buttel, Robert. *Wallace Stevens: The Making of* Harmonium. Princeton: Princeton University Press, 1967.

Cook, Eleanor. "Wallace Stevens: *The Comedian as the Letter C.*" *American Literature* 49 (1977): 192–205.

DeMaria, Robert, Jr. "'The Thinker as Reader': The Figure of the Reader in the Writing of Wallace Stevens." *Genre* 12 (1979): 243–68.

Doggett, Frank. *Stevens' Poetry of Thought.* Baltimore: Johns Hopkins Press, 1966.

Enck, John J. *Wallace Stevens: Images and Judgments.* Carbondale: Southern Illinois University Press, 1964.

Fuchs, Daniel. *The Comic Spirit of Wallace Stevens.* Durham: Duke University Press, 1963.

Heringman, Bernard. "Wallace Stevens: The Use of Poetry." *ELH* 16 (1949): 325–36.

Kessler, Edward. *Images of Wallace Stevens.* New Brunswick: Rutgers University Press, 1972.

Litz, A. Walton. *Introspective Voyager: The Poetic Development of Wallace Stevens.* New York: Oxford University Press, 1972.

Martz, Louis L. "Wallace Stevens: The World as Meditation." *Yale Review* 47 (1957–58): 517–36.

Morse, Samuel French. "The Native Element." *Kenyon Review* 20 (1958): 446–65.

O'Connor, William Van. *The Shaping Spirit: A Study of Wallace Stevens.* Chicago: Henry Regnery, 1950.

Patke, Rajeev S. *The Long Poems of Wallace Stevens.* Cambridge: Cambridge University Press, 1985.

Pearce, Roy Harvey. "The Poet as Person." *Yale Review* 41 (1952): 421–40.

Richardson, Joan. *Wallace Stevens: The Early Years, 1879–1923.* New York: Morrow, 1986.

Simons, Hi. "*The Comedian as the Letter C*: Its Sense and Its Significance." *Southern Review* 5 (1939–40): 453–68.

Stallknecht, Newton P. "Absence in Reality: A Study in the Epistemology of *The Blue Guitar.*" *Kenyon Review* 21 (1959): 545–62.

Sypher, Wylie. "Connoisseur in Chaos: Wallace Stevens." *Partisan Review* 13 (1946): 83–94.

Watts, Harold H. "Wallace Stevens and the Rock of Summer." *Kenyon Review* 14 (1952): 122–40.

Woodman, Leonora. "'A Giant on the Horizon': Wallace Stevens and the 'Idea of Man.'" *Texas Studies in Literature and Language* 15 (1974): 759–86.

ACKNOWLEDGMENTS

Mark Abley. "Oh God, oh Montreal," *Times Literary Supplement*, December 21, 1984, copyright © 1984 by Times Newspapers Ltd.

J. Donald Adams. "Speaking of Books," *New York Times Book Review*, May 20, 1951, copyright © 1951 by New York Times Co. Reprinted with permission of the publisher.

Conrad Aiken. "The New England Animal," *New Republic*, February 5, 1936, copyright © 1936 by The New Republic, Inc. Review of *My Heart and My Flesh, New York Evening Post*, November 12, 1927, copyright © 1927 by New York Evening Post. "Romantic Traditionalism: Alan Seeger," *Scepticisms*, copyright © 1919 by Alfred A. Knopf, Inc. Reprinted with permission of Brandt & Brandt, Inc.

John Aldridge. "Mailer, Burns and Shaw: The Naked Zero," *After the Lost Generation*, copyright © 1951 by John Aldridge. Reprinted with permission of the author.

Gay Wilson Allen. "Carl Sandburg: Fire and Smoke," *South Atlantic Quarterly*, Summer 1960, copyright © 1960 by Duke University Press. Reprinted with permission of the publisher.

Mary Allen. "Gertrude Stein's Sense of Oneness," *Southwest Review*, Winter 1981, copyright © 1981 by Southern Methodist University. Reprinted with permission of the publisher.

Stanley S. Atherton. "The Klondike Muse," *Canadian Literature*, Winter 1971, copyright © 1971.

Charles R. Bachman. "Defusion of Menace in the Plays of Sam Shepard," *Modern Drama*, December 1976, copyright © 1976 by University of Toronto Graduate Center for Study of Drama. Reprinted with permission of the publisher.

William Barrett. "Delmore: A 30's Friendship and Beyond," *Commentary*, September 1974, copyright © 1974 by American Jewish Committee. Reprinted with permission of the author and publisher. "Pilgrim to Philistia," *Partisan Review*, Winter 1946, copyright © 1946.

Jonathan Baumbach. "The Saint as a Young Man: *The Catcher in the Rye*," *The Landscape of Nightmare*, copyright © 1965 by New York University Press. Reprinted with permission of the publisher.

Charles Baxter. "The Drowned Survivor: The Fiction of J. R. Salamanca," *Critique*, 1977, copyright © 1977 by James Dean Young.

Fredericka Beatty. "Edwin Arlington Robinson as I Knew Him," *South Atlantic Quarterly*, April 1944, copyright © 1944, 1972 by Duke University Press. Reprinted with permission of the publisher.

Michael Benedikt. "The Completed Pattern," *Poetry*, January 1967, copyright © 1967 by Modern Poetry Association. Reprinted with permission of author and publisher.

Jesse Bier. "Intercentury Humor," *The Rise and Fall of American Humor*, copyright © 1968 by Jesse Bier.

Richard A. Blessing. "Theodore Roethke: A Celebration," *Tulane Studies in English*, 1972, copyright © 1972 by Tulane University.

Harold Bloom. "Isaac B. Singer's Jeremiad," *New York Times Book Review*, September 25, 1983, copyright © 1983 by New York Times Co. Reprinted with permission of the publisher.

Lynn Z. Bloom. "Gertrude Stein Is Alice Everybody: Innovation and Point of View in Gertrude Stein's Autobiographies," *Twentieth Century Literature*, Spring 1978, copyright © 1978 by Hofstra University Press. Reprinted with permission of the publisher.

Barbara Branden. "Prologue," *The Passion of Ayn Rand*, copyright © 1986 by Barbara Branden.

James E. Breslin. "Gertrude Stein and the Problems of Autobiography," *Georgia Review*, Winter 1979, copyright © 1979 by University of Georgia. Reprinted with permission of the publisher.

Richard Bridgman. "Conclusion," *Gertrude Stein in Pieces*, copyright © 1970 by Richard Bridgman.

Cleanth Brooks. "The Doric Delicacy," *Sewanee Review*, July–September 1948, copyright © 1948 by University of the South. Reprinted with permission of the publisher.

Ronald Bryden. "Northern Light," *New York Times Book Review*, June 3, 1984, copyright © 1984 by New York Times Co. Reprinted with permission of the publisher.

Martin Bucco. "Conclusion," *Wilbur Daniel Steele*, copyright © 1972 by Twayne Publishers, Inc. Reprinted with permission of G. K. Hall & Co.

Pearl S. Buck. "People and Scenes of Modern Asia," *Saturday Review of Literature*, November 16, 1935, copyright © 1935. Reprinted with permission of Saturday Review, Inc.

Peter Buitenhuis. "E. J. Pratt," *The Canadian Imagination*, copyright © 1977 by Peter Buitenhuis. Reprinted with permission of the author.

W. R. Burnett. "The Frozen Flight of Little Wolf and His People," *New York Times Book Review*, November 22, 1953, copyright © 1953 by New York Times Co. Reprinted with permission of the publisher.

Charles Cagle. "*The Catcher in the Rye* Revisited," *Midwest Quarterly*, Autumn 1962, copyright © 1962 by *Midwest Quarterly*. Reprinted with permission of the publisher.

Edward Cain. "Ayn Rand as Theorist," *They'd Rather Be Right: Youth and the Conservative Movement*, copyright © 1963 by Edward Cain. Reprinted with permission of Macmillan Publishing Co.

Henry Seidel Canby. "The Education of a Puritan," *Saturday Review of Literature*, February 1, 1936, copyright © 1936 by Saturday Review, Inc. Reprinted with permission of the publisher.

Dorothy Canfield. "Old Jules," *Book-of-the-Month Club News*, October 1935, copyright © 1935 by Book-of-the-Month Club.

Robert Cantwell. "Upton Sinclair," *After the Genteel Tradition: American Writers since 1910*, ed. Malcolm Cowley, copyright © 1937 by Malcolm Cowley. Reprinted with permission of Malcolm Cowley.

Hayden Carruth. "The Closest Permissible Approximation," *Poetry*, February 1963, copyright © 1963 by Modern Poetry Association. Reprinted with permission of the publisher and author. "In Defense of Karl Shapiro," *New Republic*, June 20, 1960, copyright © 1960 by Harrison-Blaine. Reprinted with permission of New Republic, Inc.

Alfred Chester. "Salinger: How to Love without Love," *Commentary*, June 1963, copyright © 1963 by the American Jewish Committee.

Carol P. Christ. "Homesick for a Woman, for Ourselves: Adrienne Rich," *Diving Deep and Surfacing: Women Writers on Spiritual Quest*, copyright © 1980 by Carol P. Christ. Reprinted with permission of the Beacon Press.

Daniela M. Ciani. "Kenneth Rexroth: Poet of Nature and Culture," *For Rexroth*, ed. Geoffrey Gardner, copyright © 1980 by The Ark.

Harold Clurman. "Theatre," *Nation*, May 1, 1976, copyright © 1976 by Nation, Inc. Reprinted with permission of the publisher. Review of *Killer's Head* and *Action*, *Nation*, May 3, 1975, copyright © 1975 by Nation, Inc. Reprinted with permission of the publisher.

John Clute. Review of *The Two of Them, Foundation*, January 1979, copyright © 1979 by Science Fiction Foundation. Reprinted with permission of the author and publisher.

Stanton A. Coblentz. "George Sterling: Western Phenomenon," *Arizona Quarterly*, Spring 1957, copyright © 1957 by *Arizona Quarterly*. Reprinted with permission of the publisher and author.

Ofelia Cohn-Sfectu. "The Privilege of Finding an Opening in the Past: Al Purdy and the Tree of Experience," *Queen's Quarterly*, Summer 1976, copyright © 1976.

Robert Coles. "Muriel Rukeyser's *The Gates*," *American Poetry Review*, May–June 1978, copyright © 1978 by American Poetry Review. "William Stafford's Long Walk," *American Poetry Review*, July–August 1975, copyright © 1975 by World Poetry, Inc. Reprinted with permission of the author and publisher.

Henry Steele Commager. "He Sings of America's Plain People," *New York Times Book Review*, November 19, 1950, copyright © 1950 by New York Times Co. Reprinted with permission of the publisher.

Donald P. Costello. "Salinger and His Critics: Autopsy of a Faded Romance," *Commonweal*, October 25, 1963, copyright © 1963 by Commonweal Publishing Co., Inc. Reprinted with permission of the publisher.

James Finn Cotter. Review of *Revolution of the Word*, *America*, June 21, 1975, copyright © 1975 by America Press. Reprinted with permission of the publisher.

C. B. Cox. "The Poetry of Louis Simpson," *Critical Quarterly*, Spring 1966, copyright © 1966. Reprinted with permission of the author.

John Crawford. "Will Rogers Knows More Than He Pretends," *New York Times Book Review*, December 14, 1924, copyright © 1924 by New York Times Co. Reprinted with permission of the publisher.

David Daiches. "A Preface to James Purdy's *Malcolm*," *Antioch Review*, Spring 1962, copyright © 1962 by The Antioch Review.

Robert Murray Davis. "Parody, Paranoia, and the Dead End of Language in *The Crying of Lot 49*," *Genre*, December 1972, copyright © 1972 by the Editors of *Genre*.

Benjamin De Casseres. "Clark Ashton Smith: Emperor of Shadows," *Selected Poems* by Clark Ashton Smith, copyright © 1971 by Mrs. Clark Ashton Smith.

Marianne DeKoven. "*Three Lives*," *A Different Language: Gertrude Stein's Experimental Writing*, copyright © 1983 by the Board of Regents of the University of Wisconsin System. Reprinted with permission of the publisher.

Samuel R. Delany. "Alyx," *The Jewel-Hinged Jaw*, copyright © 1977 by Samuel R. Delany.

Barry Dempster. "Ferry of the Emotions," *Canadian Forum*, January 1986, copyright © 1986. Reprinted with permission of the publisher.

James Dickey. "The Greatest American Poet," *Atlantic*, November 1968, copyright © 1968 by The Atlantic Monthly Co.

Roger Dickinson-Brown. "The Wise, the Dull, the Bewildered: What Happens in William Stafford," *Modern Poetry Studies*, Spring 1975, copyright © 1975 by Jerome Mazzaro.

Sandra Djwa. "The Problem Hero: *Brébeuf and His Brethren*," *E. J. Pratt: The Evolutionary Vision*, copyright © 1974 by Sandra Djwa.

Denis Donoghue. "Edwin Arlington Robinson, J. V. Cunningham, Robert Lowell," "Theodore Roethke," *Connoisseurs of Chaos, Ideas of Order in Modern American Poetry*, copyright © 1962 by Denis Donoghue.

Robert Drake. "Coming of Age in North Carolina," *Southern Review*, Winter 1967, copyright © 1967 by Louisiana State University. Reprinted with permission of the author and publisher.

Winifred Dusenbury. "The Lonely Hero," *The Theme of Loneliness in Modern American Drama*, copyright © 1960 by University of Florida Board of Commissioners. Reprinted with permission of the publisher.

Richard Eberhart. "Personal Statement," *New York Times Book Review*, June 23, 1968, copyright © 1968 by New York Times Co. Reprinted with permission of the publisher.

Clifford D. Edwards. "Conclusion," *Conrad Richter's Ohio Trilogy*, copyright © 1970 by Mouton Publishers. Reprinted with permission of the publisher.

Chester E. Eisinger. "Twenty Years of Wallace Stegner," *College English*, December 1958, copyright © 1958 by The National Council of Teachers of English.

Joseph Epstein. "What Does Philip Roth Want?," *Commentary*, January 1984, copyright © 1984 by American Jewish Committee. Reprinted with permission of Georges Borchardt, Inc.

William Esty. "The Decline and Fall of Bert Flax, Self-Deceiver," *Commonweal*, November 22, 1963, copyright © 1963 by Commonweal Publishing Co., Inc. Reprinted with permission of the publisher.

Clifton P. Fadiman. "A Great National Drama," *Nation*, July 31, 1929, copyright © 1929. Reprinted with permission of the publisher. "William Saroyan's Songs of Innocence," *New Yorker*, December 28, 1940, copyright © 1940 by F. R. Publishing Corp. Reprinted with permission of Lescher & Lescher.

Marjorie Farber. "Atlantis, Xiccarph," *New York Times Book Review*, November 19, 1944, copyright © 1944 by New York Times Co. Reprinted with permission of the publisher.

Otis Ferguson. "They Still Tell Stories," *New Republic*, May 20, 1940, copyright © 1940 by The New Republic.

Ross Field. "Lowghost to Lowghost," *Parnassus: Poetry in Review*, Spring–Summer 1976, copyright © 1976 by Poetry in Review Foundation. Reprinted with permission of the publisher.

Elizabeth Fifer. "Rescued Readings: Characteristic Deformations in the Language of Gertrude Stein's Plays," *Texas Studies in Literature and Language*, Winter 1982, copyright © 1982 by the University of Texas Press.

William J. Fisher. "What Ever Happened to Saroyan?," *College English*, March 1955, copyright © 1954, 1955 by the National Council of Teachers of English.

Dudley Fitts. "The Verse of Evelyn Scott," *Poetry*, September 1930, copyright © 1930 by Modern Poetry Association. Reprinted with permission of the author and publisher.

William Fitzgerald. "Twenty Years of Hard Labor," *Poetry*, Nov. 1940, copyright © 1940 by Modern Poetry Association. Reprinted with permission of the publisher.

Robert Flint. "The Stories of Delmore Schwartz," *Commentary*, April 1962, copyright © 1962 by American Jewish Committee. Reprinted with permission of the author and publisher.

Sandra Hollin Flowers. "Colored Girls: Textbook for the Eighties," *Black American Literature Forum*, Summer 1981, copyright © 1981 by Indiana State University. Reprinted with permission of *Black American Literature Forum*.

Richard Foster. "The Voice of a Poet: Kenneth Rexroth," *Minnesota Review*, Spring 1962, copyright © 1962 by The Minnesota Review.

Douglas Fowler. "Pynchon as Gothicist," *A Reader's Guide to Gravity's Rainbow*, copyright © 1980 by *Ardis*. Reprinted with permission of the publisher.

Anne Hobson Freeman. "Penetrating a Small Patch of the Surface of Earth," *Virginia Quarterly Review*, Autumn 1975, copyright © 1975 by *Virginia Quarterly Review*. Reprinted with permission of the publisher.

Norman Friedman. "The Wesleyan Poets—II," *Chicago Review*, copyright © 1966 by *Chicago Review*. Reprinted with permission of the publisher.

John Gassner. "Robert Emmet Sherwood," *Atlantic*, January 1942, copyright © 1942.

Blanche H. Gelfant. "No Title," *New Republic*, May 10, 1975, copyright © 1975 by The New Republic, Inc. Reprinted with permission of the publisher.

Richard Gilman. "John Rechy," *The Confusion of Realms*, copyright © 1963 by Richard Gilman. Reprinted with permission of the publisher.

Max Gissen. "Back to Earth," *New Republic*, April 6, 1942, copyright © 1942 by The New Republic.

William Goldman. "Rich and Poor, Bums and Barons," *New York Times Book Review*, November 12, 1978, copyright © 1978 by New York Times Co. Reprinted with permission of the publisher.

Philip Gordon. "The Extroflective Hero: A Look at Ayn Rand," *Journal of Popular Culture*, Spring 1977, copyright © 1977 by Ray B. Browne. Reprinted with permission of the publisher.

Graham Greene. "Fiction," *Spectator*, October 20, 1939, copyright © 1939. Reprinted with permission of Laurence Pollinger, Ltd.

John Greenway. "Back to the Primitive," *Atlantic*, February 1969, copyright © 1969 by Atlantic Monthly.

Horace Gregory. "The Narrow House of Victorian England," *Saturday Review*, May 26, 1934, copyright © 1934. Reprinted with permission of *Saturday Review*.

Marilyn Hacker. "Introduction" to *The Female Man* by Joanna Russ, copyright © 1977 by G. K. Hall & Co.

Elizabeth Hardwick. "Introduction" to *La Turista* by Sam Shepard, copyright © 1968 by Sam Shepard.

Michael S. Harper. "Three Poets," *New York Times Book Review*, October 21, 1979, copyright © 1979 by New York Times Co. Reprinted with permission of the publisher.

Harlan Hatcher. "William Saroyan," *English Journal*, March 1939, copyright © 1939 by University of Chicago Press. Reprinted with permission of the publisher.

H. R. Hays. "The Expatriate Consciousness," *Poetry*, May 1939, copyright © 1939 by Modern Poetry Association. Reprinted with permission of the author and publisher.

Seamus Heaney. "Canticles to the Earth," *Listener*, August 22, 1968, copyright © 1968 by British Broadcasting Corporation. Reprinted with permission of the author and Faber & Faber, Ltd.

Roger B. Henkle. "The Morning and the Evening Funnies: Comedy in *Gravity's Rainbow*," *Approaches to* Gravity's Rainbow, ed. Charles Clerc, copyright © 1983 by the Ohio State University Press. Reprinted with permission of the publisher.

William Heyen. "William Stafford's Allegiances," *Modern Poetry Studies*, 1970, copyright ©1970 by Jerome Mazzaro.

Baruch Hochman. "Child and Man in Philip Roth," *Midstream*, December 1967, copyright © 1967 by Theodore Herzl Foundation. Reprinted with permission of the publisher.

Daniel G. Hoffman. "Between New Voice and Old Master," *Sewanee Review*, Autumn 1960, copyright © 1960 by University of the South. Reprinted with permission of the publisher.

Stanton Hoffman. "The Cities of Night: John Rechy's *City of Night* and the American Literature of Homosexuality," *Chicago Review*, 1964, copyright © 1964 by *Chicago Review*. Reprinted with permission of the publisher.

Maureen Honey. "A Sensibility of Struggle and Hope," *Prairie Schooner*, Winter 1984, copyright © 1984 by University of Nebraska Press. Reprinted with permission of the publisher.

Christopher Hope. "Colonial Outposts," *London Magazine*, March 1977, copyright © 1977 by *London Magazine*. Reprinted with permission of the publisher.

Richard Howard. "Anne Sexton: 'Some Tribal Female Who Is Known but Forbidden,'" *Alone with America*, copyright © 1969.

Irving Howe. "Delmore Schwartz—A Personal Appreciation," *New Republic*, March 19, 1962, copyright © 1962 by Harrison-Blaine. Reprinted with permission of The New Republic, Inc. "Demonic Fiction of a Yiddish 'Modernist,'" *Commentary*, October 1960, copyright © 1960 by American Jewish Committee. Reprinted with permission of the publisher.

Ted Hughes. "The Genius of Isaac Bashevis Singer," *New York Review of Books*, April 22, 1965, copyright © 1965 by The New York Review.

Edward Eyre Hunt. "Stelligeri: A Footnote on Democracy," *Essays in Memory of Barrett Wendell*, copyright © 1926 by the President and Fellows of Harvard College. Reprinted with permission of the publisher.

John K. Hutchens. "Old Jules Country," *Book-of-the-Month Club News*, July 1966, copyright © 1966 by Book-of-the-Month Club.

Elizabeth Janeway. "The Worlds of Jean Stafford," *Atlantic*, March 1969, copyright © 1969 by The Atlantic Monthly Co.

Alvin M. Josephy, Jr. "Soldiers and Indians," *New York Times Book Review*, July 3, 1966, copyright © 1966 by New York Times Co. Reprinted with permission of the publisher.

S. T. Joshi and Marc Michaud. "The Prose and Poetry of Clark Ashton Smith," *Books at Brown*, 1979, copyright © 1979 by Brown University. Reprinted with permission of the publisher.

Horace M. Kallen. *Dialogue on George Santayana*, eds. Corliss Lamont and Mary Redmer, copyright © 1959 by Horizon Press, Inc.

Alfred Kazin. "*Bread and Sword* and Some Other Recent Works of Fiction," *New York Times Book Review*, April 18, 1937, copyright © 1937 by New York Times Co. Reprinted with permission of the publisher. "Father Rexroth and the Beats," *Reporter*, March 3, 1960, copyright © 1960. Review of *Passions and Other Stories*, *New Republic*, October 25, 1975, copyright © 1975 by New Republic, Inc. Reprinted with permission of the publisher. "With a Love for the Passing Ideal," *New York Times Book Review*, November 13, 1955, copyright © 1955 by New York Times Co. Reprinted with permission of the publisher.

Hugh Kenner. "Bearded Ladies and the Abundant Goat," *Poetry*, October 1951, copyright © 1951 by Modern Poetry Association.

Frank Kermode. "The Use of the Codes," *Approach to Poetics*, ed. Seymour Chatman, copyright © 1973 by Columbia University Press. Reprinted with permission of the publisher.

Michael Kirkham. "Laura Riding's Poems," *Cambridge Quarterly*, Spring 1971, copyright © 1971 by the Editors.

Julia M. Klein. Review of *Mourners Below*, by James Purdy, *New Republic*, July 18, 1981, copyright © 1981 by The New Republic, Inc. Reprinted with permission of the publisher.

Jerome Klinkowitz. "Ishmael Reed's Multicultural Aesthetic," *Literary Subversions: New American Fiction and the Practice of Criticism*, copyright © 1985 by The Board of Trustees, Southern Illinois University.

Dayton Kohler. "Conrad Richter: Early Americana," *College English*, February 1947, copyright © 1947.

Leonard Kriegel. "Rexroth: Citizen of Bohemia," *Nation*, June 6, 1966, copyright © 1966 by Nation, Inc. Reprinted with permission of the publisher.

Joseph Wood Krutch. "The Drama of Social Criticism," *The American Dream since 1918*, copyright © 1939 by Random House, Inc.

Maxine Kumin. "How It Was," *The Complete Poems*, copyright © 1981 by Maxine Kumin. Reprinted with permission of Houghton Mifflin.

Stanley Kunitz. "Roethke: Poet of Transformations," *New Republic*, January 23, 1965, copyright © 1965 by Harrison-Blaine. Reprinted with permission of The New Republic, Inc.

Marvin J. LaHood. "*The Light in the Forest*: History as Fiction," *English Journal*, March 1966, copyright © 1966 by The National Council of Teachers of English. "Richter's Pennsylvania Trilogy," *Susquehanna University Studies*, June 1968, copyright © 1968.

Susan Lardner. "Sheed's Tub," *New Yorker*, November 30, 1968, copyright © 1968 by New Yorker Magazine, Inc. Reprinted with permission of the publisher.

Dennis Lee. "Running and Dwelling: Homage to Al Purdy," *Saturday Night*, July 1972, copyright © 1972.

John Leggett. Review of *Rich Man, Poor Man* by Irwin Shaw, *Saturday Review*, October 17, 1970, copyright © 1970 by Saturday Review, Inc. Reprinted with permission of the publisher.

Harding Lemay. "The Beautiful and Demented," *New York Herald Tribune*, July 30, 1961, copyright © 1961 by The New York Herald Tribune.

Allan Lewis. "The Tired Deans—Elmer Rice and S. N. Behrman," *American Plays and Playwrights of the Contemporary Theatre*, copyright © 1965 by Allan Lewis. Reprinted with permission of Crown Publishing Co.

R. W. B. Lewis. "Our Jaws are Sagging after Our Bout with Existence," *New York Times Book Review*, October 9, 1960, copyright © 1960 by New York Times Co. Reprinted with permission of the publisher.

James Liddy. "A Problem with Sparrows: Spicer's Last Stance," *Boundary 2*, Fall 1977, copyright © 1977 by Department of English at SUNY: Binghamton, New York. Reprinted with permission of the publisher.

M. M. Lieberman. "*The Collected Stories*," *Sewanee Review*, Summer 1969, copyright © 1969 by University of the South. Reprinted with permission of the publisher.

David Lodge. "Family Romances," *Times Literary Supplement*, June 13, 1975, copyright © 1975 by Times Newspapers Ltd. "To-ing and Fro-ing," *Times Literary Supplement*, September 26, 1980, copyright © 1980 by Times Newspapers Ltd.

Robert Morss Lovett. Review of *The Time of Man*, *New Republic*, September 8, 1926, copyright © 1926 by The New Republic.

Alfred MacAdam. "Pynchon as Satirist," *Yale Review*, June 1978, copyright © 1978 by Yale University. Reprinted with permission of the publisher.

Bernice McCabe. "Bless Me, Father . . . ," *Commonweal*, April 14, 1978, copyright © 1978 by Commonweal Publishing Co., Inc. Reprinted with permission of the publisher.

Clare McCarthy. "The Poetry of Robert Service," *Contemporary Review*, May 1979, copyright © 1979 by Contemporary Review Co. Reprinted with permission of the publisher.

Mary McCarthy. "The Latest Shudder," *Nation*, September 18, 1937, copyright © 1937 by Nation, Inc. Reprinted with permission of the publisher. "Saroyan, an Innocent on Broadway," *Sights and Spectacles*, copyright © 1940 by Mary McCarthy. Reprinted with permission of the author.

Nathaniel Mackey. "Ishmael Reed and the Black Aesthetic," *CLA*

Journal, March 1978, copyright © 1978 by the College Language Association. Reprinted with permission of the publisher.

Archibald MacLeish. "On Rereading Robinson," *Colby Library Quarterly*, March 1969, copyright © 1969. Reprinted with permission of *Colby College Quarterly*.

Kerry McSweeney. "Salinger Revisited," *Critical Quarterly*, Spring 1978, copyright © 1978 by Manchester University Press. Reprinted with permission of the publisher.

F. O. Matthiessen. "A New York Childhood," *Partisan Review*, May–June 1943, copyright © 1943 by Partisan Review, Inc. Reprinted with permission of the publisher.

Robert Mazzocco. "Heading for the Last Roundup," *New York Review of Books*, May 9, 1985, copyright © 1985 by The New York Review of Books.

John A. Meixner. "The All-Purpose Quest," *Kenyon Review*, Autumn 1963, copyright © 1963 by Kenyon College. Reprinted with permission of the publisher.

H. L. Mencken. "Edgar Saltus," "The Grove of Academe," *Prejudices: Fifth Series*, copyright © 1926 by Alfred A. Knopf, Inc. Reprinted with permission of the publisher.

Perry Miller. "Sandburg and the American Dream," *New York Times Book Review*, October 10, 1948, copyright © 1948 by New York Times Co. Reprinted with permission of the publisher.

Edith Mirrielees. "The Best of Steele," *New York Times Book Review*, July 14, 1946, copyright © 1946 by New York Times Co. Reprinted with permission of the publisher.

T. Sturge Moore. "Alan Seeger," *Some Soldier Poets*, copyright © 1920.

Adelaide Morris. "Imitations and Identities: Adrienne Rich's *A Change of World*," *Modern Poetry Studies*, 1981, copyright © 1981 by Media Study, Inc.

Harry Morris. "A Formal View of the Poetry of Dickey, Garrigue and Simpson," *Sewanee Review*, Spring 1969, copyright © 1969 by University of the South. Reprinted with permission of the publisher.

Samuel French Morse. "Spectre over Europe," *Poetry*, November 1938, copyright © 1938–39 by Modern Poetry Association. Reprinted with permission of the author and publisher.

Eric Mottram. "Introduction" to *The Rexroth Reader*, copyright © 1972 by Jonathan Cape, Ltd. Reprinted with permission of the publisher.

Robert Nadeau. "Thomas Pynchon," *Readings from the New Book of Nature*, copyright © 1981 by University of Massachusetts Press. Reprinted with permission of the publisher.

John G. Neihardt. "Crazy Horse, Who Led the Sioux at Custer's Last Fight," *New York Times Book Review*, December 20, 1942, copyright © 1942 by New York Times Co. Reprinted with permission of the publisher.

Helge Normann Nilsen. "Rebellion against Jewishness: *Portnoy's Complaint*," *English Studies*, December 1984, copyright © 1984 by Swets & Zeitlinger. Reprinted with permission of the publisher.

Maximillian E. Novak. "Moral Grotesque and Decorative Grotesque in Singer's Fiction," *The Achievement of Isaac Bashevis Singer*, ed. Maria Allentuck, copyright © 1969 by Southern Illinois University Press.

Joyce Carol Oates. "The Interior Castle: The Art of Jean Stafford's Short Fiction," *Shenandoah*, 1979, copyright © 1979 by *Shenandoah*. Reprinted with permission of the publisher.

Raymond M. Olderman. "The Illusion and the Possibility of Conspiracy," *Beyond the Waste Land: A Study of the American Novel in the Nineteen-Sixties*, copyright © 1972 by Yale University Press. Reprinted with permission of the publisher.

Alicia Ostriker. "That Story: Anne Sexton and Her Transformations," *American Poetry Review*, July–August 1982, copyright © 1982. "Her Cargo: Adrienne Rich and the Common Language," *American Poetry Review*, July–August 1979, copyright © 1979 by American Poetry Review.

Anthony F. R. Palmieri. "Conclusion," *Elmer Rice: A Playwright's Vision of America*, copyright © 1980 by Associated University Presses, Inc.

Robert Phillips. "W. D. Snodgrass and the Sad Hospital of the World," *The Confessional Poets*, copyright © 1973 by Southern Illinois University Press.

Marge Piercy. "Foreword" to *The Zanzibar Cat* by Joanna Russ, copyright © 1983 by Joanna Russ.

William M. Plater. "In Which Various Things Come Together," *The Grim Phoenix: Reconstructing Thomas Pynchon*, copyright © 1978 by William M. Plater. Reprinted with permission of Indiana University Press.

Reynolds Price. "The Writer and His Tradition," *The Writer and His Tradition: Festival Proceedings*, ed. Robert Drake, copyright © 1969 by University of Tennessee. Reprinted with permission of the publisher.

William H. Pritchard. "Edwin Arlington Robinson: The Prince of Heartaches," *American Scholar*, Winter 1978–79, copyright © 1979 by the United Chapters of Phi Beta Kappa. Reprinted with permission of the publisher.

Victor J. Ramraj. "Diminishing Satire: A Study of V. S. Naipaul and Mordecai Richler," *Awakened Conscience: Studies in Commonwealth Literature*, ed. C. D. Narasimhaiah, copyright © 1978 by C. D. Narasimhaiah.

Philip Blair Rice. "A World Between Two Wars," *Nation*, October 3, 1936, copyright © 1936 by Nation, Inc. Reprinted with permission of the publisher.

Adrienne Rich. "When We Dead Awaken: Writing as Re-Vision," *College English*, October 1972, copyright © 1972 by The National Council of Teachers of English.

Walter B. Rideout. "Realism and Revolution," *The Radical Novel in the United States, 1900–1954*, copyright © 1956 by the President and Fellows of Harvard College. Reprinted with permission of the publisher.

Bruce A. Ronda. "Themes of Past and Present in *Angle of Repose*," *Studies in American Fiction*, Autumn 1982, copyright © 1982 by Northeastern University. Reprinted with permission of the publisher.

Isaac Rosenfeld. "On One Built for Two," *New Republic*, December 8, 1952, copyright © 1952 by Westbury Publications, Inc.

M. L. Rosenthal. "Deep in the Unfriendly City," *Nation*, June 11, 1960, copyright © 1960 by Nation, Inc. Reprinted with permission of the publisher.

Earl H. Rovit. "Introduction" to *Herald to Chaos*, copyright © 1960 by University of Kentucky Press. Reprinted with permission of the publisher.

Jane Rule. "An Interview with Jane Rule," *Canadian Fiction Magazine*, 1976, copyright © 1977 by The Canadian Fiction Magazine.

Bertrand Russell. "George Santayana," *Portraits from Memory and Other Essays*, copyright © 1952, 1957 by Simon & Schuster. Reprinted with permission of Allen & Unwin, Ltd.

Frank Sadler. "The Frontier in Jack Spicer's 'Billy The Kid,'" *Concerning Poetry*, Fall 1976, copyright © 1982 by Western Washington University. Reprinted with permission of the publisher.

Roger Sale. "What Went Wrong," *New York Review of Books*, October 21, 1971, copyright © 1971 by The New York Review of Books.

I. L. Salomon. "From Union Square to Parnassus," *Poetry*, April 1952, copyright © 1952 by Modern Poetry Association. Reprinted with permission of the author and publisher.

Mari Sandoz. "Foreword" to *Old Jules*, copyright © 1935 by Mari Sandoz.

Sherod Santos. "An Interview with Charles Simic," *Missouri Review*, 1984, copyright © 1984 by University of Missouri Press. Reprinted with permission of the publisher.

Ben Satterfield. "John Rechy's Tormented World," *Southwest Review*, Winter 1982, copyright © 1982 by Southern Methodist University. Reprinted with permission of the author and publisher.

Peter Schmidt. "*Whtie*: Charles Simic's Thumbnail Epic," *Contemporary Literature*, Fall 1982, copyright © 1982 by the Regents of the University of Wisconsin System. Reprinted with permission of the publisher.

Neil Schmitz. "Describing the Demon: The Appeal of Thomas Pynchon," *Partisan Review*, 1975, copyright © 1975 by Partisan Review, Inc. Reprinted with permission of the publisher. "Down Home with Ishmael Reed: Chattanooga," *Modern Poetry Studies*, Autumn 1974, copyright © 1974 by Jerome Mazzaro.

Delmore Schwartz. "Instructed of Much Mortality: A Note on the Poetry of John Crowe Ransom," *Sewanee Review*, Summer 1946, copyright © 1946 by University of the South. Reprinted with permission of the publisher.

Armand Schwerner. "The Poetry of Earth," *Nation*, July 28, 1969, copyright © 1969 by Nation, Inc. Reprinted with permission of the publisher.

Winfield Townley Scott. "The Zephyrs of Death," *New Republic*, November 17, 1962, copyright © 1962 by Harrison-Blaine. Reprinted with permission of The New Republic, Inc.

Harvey Shapiro. "For Delmore Schwartz," *Poetry*, June 1967, copyright © 1967 by Modern Poetry Association. Reprinted with permission of the publisher and author.

Karl Shapiro. "Poetry and Family: An Interview with Karl Shapiro," *Prairie Schooner*, Fall 1980, copyright © 1980 by University of Nebraska Press. Reprinted with permission of the publisher.

Wilfrid Sheed. "The Good World: Howe's Complaint," *New York Times Book Review*, May 6, 1973, copyright © 1973 by New York Times Co. Reprinted with permission of the publisher.

Allen Shepherd. "Notes on Nature in the Fiction of Reynolds Price," *Critique*, 1973, copyright © 1973 by Critique.

Earl Shorris. "The Worldly Palimpsest of Thomas Pynchon," *Harper's*, June 1973, copyright © 1973 by The Minneapolis Star and Tribune Co., Inc.

Ben Siegel. "The Myths of Summer: Philip Roth's *The Great American Novel*, Spring 1976, copyright © 1976 by the Board of Regents of the University of Wisconsin System. Reprinted with permission of the publisher.

Isaac Bashevis Singer. "Interview with Laurie Colwin," *New York Times Book Review*, July 23, 1978, copyright © 1978 by New York Times Co. Reprinted with permission of the publisher. "Why I Write for Children," *Nobel Lecture*, copyright © 1978.

Henry Sloss. "Price's Reliques," *Shenandoah*, Spring 1971, copyright © 1971 by *Shenandoah*. Reprinted with permission of the publisher.

William James Smith. *"The Missolonghi Manuscript,"* *Commonweal*, April 12, 1968, copyright © 1968 by Commonweal Publishing Co., Inc. Reprinted with permission of the publisher.

Susan Sontag. "Demons and Dreams," *Partisan Review*, Summer 1962, copyright © 1962 by Partisan Review. "Laughter in the Dark," *New York Times Book Review*, October 25, 1964, copyright © 1964 by New York Times Co. Reprinted with permission of the publisher.

Stephen Spender. "The Power and the Hazard," *Poetry*, March 1978, copyright © 1948 by Modern Poetry Association. Reprinted with permission of the author and publisher. "Roethke: The Lost Son," *New Republic*, August 27, 1966, copyright © 1966 by Harrison-Blaine. Reprinted with permission of The New Republic, Inc.

Claire Sprague. "Afterword," *Edgar Saltus*, copyright © 1968 by Twayne Publishers, Inc. Reprinted with permission of G. K. Hall & Co.

George Stade. "People Will Always Be Kind," *New York Times Book Review*, April 8, 1973, copyright © 1973 by New York Times Co. Reprinted with permission of the publisher.

Helen Winter Stauffer. "Introduction" to *Mari Sandoz: Story Catcher of the Plains*, copyright © 1982 by University of Nebraska Press. Reprinted with permission of the publisher.

Wallace Stegner. "Saroyan's Wonderful People," *New York Times Book Review*, February 28, 1943, copyright © 1943 by New York Times Co. Reprinted with permission of the publisher.

Richard G. Stern. "Lost in Geography," *New York Times Book Review*, October 30, 1960, copyright © 1960 by New York Times Co. Reprinted with permission of the publisher.

Walter Sullivan. "Gifts, Prophecies, and Prestidigitations: Fictional Frameworks, Fictional Modes," *Sewanee Review*, Winter 1985, copyright © 1977 by University of the South. Reprinted with permission of the publisher.

Harvey Swados. "The World of Upton Sinclair," *Atlantic*, December 1961, copyright © 1961 by The Atlantic Monthly Co.

May Swenson. Review of *Waterlily Fire: Poems 1935–1962*, *Nation*, Feb. 23, 1963, copyright © 1963 by Nation, Inc. Reprinted with permission of the publisher.

Arthur Symons. "Edgar Saltus," *Dramatis Personae*, copyright © 1923 by Bobbs-Merrill Co.

Warren Tallman. "Need for Laughter," *Canadian Literature*, Spring 1973, copyright © 1973 by Canadian Literature.

Tony Tanner. "Early Short Fiction," *Thomas Pynchon*, copyright © 1982 by Tony Tanner. "Space Odyssey," *Partisan Review*, Summer 1968, copyright © 1968 by Partisan Review.

Meredith Tax. "Genre Bender," *Voice Literary Supplement*, May 1985, copyright © 1985 by Village Voice, Inc. Reprinted with permission of the author and publisher.

Lawrance Thompson. "Introduction" to *Tilbury Town: Selected Poems of Edwin Arlington Robinson*, copyright © 1953 by the Macmillan Co. Reprinted with permission of the publisher.

Virgil Thomson. "A Portrait of Gertrude Stein," *Virgil Thomson*, copyright © 1966 by Virgil Thomson. Reprinted with permission of Random House/Alfred A. Knopf, Inc., and George Weidenfeld & Nicolson.

Geoffrey Thurley. "Devices Among Words: Kinnell, Bly, Simic," "The Poetry of Breakdown," *The American Moment: American Poetry in the Mid-Century*, copyright © 1977 by Geoffrey Thurley. Reprinted with permission of St. Martin's Press and Jonathan Cape, Ltd.

Judith Thurman. "Forgeries of Ourselves," *Nation*, November 30, 1974, copyright © 1974 by Nation, Inc. Reprinted with permission of the publisher.

Jean Tobin. "Introduction" to *We Who Are About To . . .* by Joanna Russ, copyright © 1978 by Jean Tobin.

David Toolan. "Confederacy of Poets and Anthropologists," *Commonweal*, November 4, 1983, copyright © 1983 by Commonweal Publishing Co., Inc. Reprinted with permission of the publisher.

Dorothy Van Doren. Review of *Not by Strange Gods*, *Nation*, June 28, 1941, copyright © 1941 by Nation, Inc. Reprinted with permission of the publisher.

Helen Vendler. "America as Prophecy," *New York Times Book Review*, December 30, 1973, copyright © 1974 by New York Times Co. Reprinted with permission of the publisher.

Gore Vidal. "Disaster and Flight," *New York Times Book Review*, March 22, 1953, copyright © 1953 by New York Times Co. Reprinted with permission of the publisher. "Miss Sontag's New Novel," *Reflections upon a Sinking Ship*, copyright © 1967 by Gore Vidal, 1969 by Little, Brown. Reprinted with permission of the publisher. "Two Immoralists," *Esquire*, July 1961, copyright © 1961 by Esquire.

Diane Wakoski. "20th Century Music," *parnassus: Poetry in Review*, Fall–Winter 1972, copyright © 1972 by Poetry in Review Foundation. Reprinted with permission of the publisher.

Jayne Walker. *"Tender Buttons: 'The Music of the Present Tense,'"* *The Making of a Modernist: Gertrude Stein from Three Lives to Tender Buttons*, copyright © 1976, 1984 by Jayne L. Walker. Reprinted with permission of the University of Massachusetts.

James Walt. "No Wolfe Cub," *New Republic*, January 5, 1974, copyright © 1974 by The New Republic, Inc. Reprinted with permission of the publisher.

Robert Penn Warren. "Life Is from Within," *Saturday Review*, March 2, 1963, copyright © 1963 by Saturday Review, Inc. Reprinted with permission of the publisher. "Notes on the Poetry of John Crowe Ransom at His Eighteenth Birthday," *Kenyon Review*, 1968, copyright © 1968 by Kenyon College. Reprinted with permission of the publisher and author.

Gerard Weales. "No Face and No Exit: The Fiction of James Purdy and J. P. Donleavy," *Contemporary American Novelists*, ed. Harry T. Moore, copyright © 1964 by Southern Illinois University Press.

Norman Weinstein. "The Making of Americans: the Narrative Redefined," *Gertrude Stein and the Literature of the Modern Consciousness*, copyright © 1970 by Frederick Ungar Publishing Co. Reprinted with permission of the publisher.

Paul West. Review of *A Sea Change*, *New York Times Book Review*, December 21, 1969, copyright © 1969 by New York Times Co. Reprinted with permission of the publisher.

Ross Wetzsteon. "The Conflict between Big Bucks and Good Books," *Saturday Review*, August 1981, copyright © 1981 by Saturday

Review Magazine Corporation. Reprinted with permission of the publisher.

Joyce Piell Wexler. "Poems of Passionate Intelligence," *Laura Riding's Pursuit of Truth*, copyright © 1979 by Joyce Wexler. Reprinted with permission of Ohio University Press.

Leon Wieseltier. "The Revenge of I. B. Singer," *New York Review of Books*, December 7, 1978, copyright © 1978 by The New York Review.

Thorton Wilder. "Introduction" to *Four in America* by Gertrude Stein, copyright © 1947 by Alice B. Toklas. Reprinted with permission of Yale University Press.

John H. Wildman. "Beyond Classification—Some Notes on Distinction," *Southern Review*, January 1973, copyright © 1973 by Louisiana State University. Reprinted with permission of the publisher and author.

Blanche Colton Williams. "Wilbur Daniel Steele," *Our Short Story Writers*, copyright © 1926.

Miller Williams. "What Grey Man Is This? Irony," *The Poetry of John Crowe Ransom*, copyright © 1972 by Miller Williams. Reprinted with permission of Rutgers University Press.

William Carlos Williams. "Muriel Rukeyser's *U.S. 1*," *Something to Say: William Carlos Williams on Younger Poets*, ed. James E. B. Breslin, copyright © 1985 by William Eric Williams and Paul H. Williams. "Verse with a Jolt to It," *New York Times Book Review*, January 28, 1951, copyright © 1951 by New York Times Co. Reprinted with permission of the publisher.

Edmund Wilson. "Upton Sinclair's *Mammonart*," *The Shores of Light*, copyright © 1952 by Edmund Wilson.

John T. Winterrich. "Simon-Pure Rogersana," *Saturday Review*, October 15, 1949, copyright © 1949 by Saturday Review, Inc. Reprinted with permission of the publisher.

Yvor Winters. "Conclusion," *Edwin Arlington Robinson*, copyright © 1946 by New Directions.

Frances Woodward. *Atlantic Monthly* June 1938, copyright © 1938 by Atlantic Monthly Co.

Jonathan Yardley. "Literary Lion," *New Republic*, May 23, 1970, copyright © 1970 by Harrison-Blaine. Reprinted with permission of The New Republic, Inc.

Norris W. Yates. "The Crackerbarrel Sage in the West and South: Will Rogers and Irvin S. Cobb," *The American Humorist*, copyright © 1964 by Iowa State University Press. Reprinted with permission of the publisher.

Jon A. Yoder. "Upton Sinclair, Lanny and the Liberals," *Modern Fiction Studies*, Winter 1974–75, copyright © 1974 by Purdue Research Foundation. Reprinted with permission of the publisher.

Lamar York. "Marjorie Kinnan Rawlings's Rivers," *Southern Literary Journal*, Spring 1977, copyright © 1977 by Department of English at the University of North Carolina. Reprinted with permission of the publisher.

Stark Young. "Street Scene," *Immortal Shadows: A Book of Dramatic Criticism*, copyright © 1948 by Charles Scribner's Sons.

Unsigned. "Au Champ d'Honeur," *Nation* June 28, 1917, copyright © 1917. Reprinted with permission of the publisher. "Good Family," *Commonweal*, February 26, 1943, copyright © 1943 by Commonweal Publishing Co., Inc. Reprinted with permission of the publisher. "No Man Is a Battlefield," *Times Literary Supplement*, January 2, 1969, copyright © 1969 by Times Newspapers, Ltd. "The Unspoken Drama," *Time*, May 2, 1960, copyright © 1960 by Time, Inc. Reprinted with permission of the publisher. "Wolfe Cub," *Time*, November 3, 1958, copyright © 1958 by Time, Inc. Reprinted with permission of the publisher.